Creation, Life and Beauty,

undone by death and wrongdoing,

regained by God's surprising victory,

AS TOLD IN THE BOOKS OF

THE HOLY BIBLE

NEW INTERNATIONAL VERSION®

ZONDERVAN®

Published by Zondervan, *Grand Rapids, Michigan*
www.zondervan.com

Printed in the United States of America.

17 18 19 20 21 22 23 /DPM/ 13 12 11 10 09 08 07 06 05 04 03 02

A portion of the purchase price of your NIV® Bible is provided to Biblica so together we support the mission of *Transforming lives through God's Word.*

Biblica provides God's Word to people through translation, publishing and Bible engagement in Africa, Asia Pacific, Europe, Latin America, Middle East, and North America. Through its worldwide reach, Biblica engages people with God's Word so that their lives are transformed through a relationship with Jesus Christ.

THE DRAMA OF THE BIBLE IN SIX ACTS

The Bible is a collection of letters, poems, stories, visions, prophetic oracles, wisdom and other kinds of writing. The first step to good Bible reading and understanding is to engage these collected works as the different kinds of writing that they are, and to read them as whole books. We encourage you to read big, to not merely take in little fragments of the Bible. The introductions at the start of each book will help you to do this.

But it is also important not to view the Bible as a gathering of unrelated writings. Overall, the Bible is a narrative. These books come together to tell God's true story and his plan to set the world right again. This story of the Bible falls naturally into six key major acts, which are briefly summarized below.

But even more precisely, we can say the story of the Bible is a drama. The key to a drama is that it has to be acted out, performed, lived. It can't remain as only words on a page. A drama is an activated story. The Bible was written so we could enter into its story. It is meant to be lived.

> "I had always felt life first as a story: and if there is a story, there is a story-teller."
>
> G.K. Chesterton

All of us, without exception, live our lives as a drama. We are on stage every single day. What will we say? What will we do? According to which story will we live? If we are not answering these questions with the biblical script, we will follow another. We can't avoid living by someone's stage instructions, even if merely our own.

This is why another key to engaging the Bible well is to recognize that its story has not ended. God's saving action continues. We are all invited to take up our own roles in this ongoing story of redemption and new creation. So, welcome to the drama of the Bible. Welcome to the story of how God intends to renew your life, and the life of the world. God himself is calling you to engage with his word.

Act 1: GOD'S INTENTION

The drama begins (in the first pages of the book of Genesis) with God already on the stage creating a world. He makes a man and a woman, Adam and Eve, and places them in the Garden of Eden to work it and take care of it. The earth is created to be their home. God's intention is for humanity to be in close, trusting relationship with him and in harmony with the rest of creation that surrounds them.

In a startling passage, the Bible tells us that human beings are God's image-bearers, created to share in the task of bringing God's wise and beneficial rule to the rest of the world. Male and female together, we are significant, decision-making, world-shaping beings. This is our vocation, our purpose as defined in the biblical story.

An equally remarkable part of Act 1 is the description of God as coming into the garden to be with the first human beings. Not only is the earth the God-intended place for humanity, God himself comes to make the beautiful new creation his home as well.

God then gives his own assessment of the whole creation: *God saw all that he had made, and it was very good.* Act 1 reveals God's original desire for the world. It shows us that life itself is a gift from the Creator. It tells us what we were made for and provides the setting for all the action that follows.

Act 2: EXILE

Tension and conflict are introduced to the story when Adam and Eve decide to go their own way and seek their own wisdom. They listen to the deceptive voice of God's enemy, Satan, and doubt God's trustworthiness. They decide to live apart from the word that God himself has given them. They decide to be a law to themselves.

The disobedience of Adam and Eve—the introduction of sin into our world—is presented in the Bible as having devastating consequences. Humans were created for healthy, life-giving relationship: with God, with each other, and with the rest of creation. But now humanity must live with the fracturing of all these relations and with the resulting shame, brokenness, pain, loneliness—and death.

Heaven and earth—God's realm and our realm—were intended to be united. God's desire from the beginning was clearly to live with us in the world he made. But now God is hidden. Now it is possible to be in our world and not know him, not experience his presence, not follow his ways, not live in gratitude.

As a result of this rebellion, the first exile in the story takes place. The humans are driven away from God's presence. Their offspring throughout history will seek to find their way back to the source of life. They will devise any number of philosophies and religions, trying to make sense of a fallen, yet haunting world. But death now stalks them, and they will find that they cannot escape it. Having attempted to live apart from God and his good word, humans will find they have neither God nor life.

New questions arise in the drama: Can the curse on creation be overcome and the relationship between God and humanity restored? Can heaven and earth be reunited? Or did God's enemy effectively end the plan and subvert the story?

Act 3: CALLING ISRAEL TO A MISSION

We see the direction of God's redemptive plan when he calls Abraham, promising to make him into a great nation. God narrows his focus and concentrates on one group of people. But the ultimate goal remains the same: to bless all the peoples on earth and remove the curse from creation.

When Abraham's descendants are enslaved in Egypt, a central pattern in the story is set: God hears their cries for help and comes to set them free. God makes a covenant with this new nation of Israel at Mt. Sinai. Israel is called by God to be a light to the nations, showing the world what it means to follow God's ways for living. If they will do this, he will bless them in their new land and will come to live with them.

However, God also warns them that if they are not faithful to the covenant, he will send them away, just as he did with Adam and Eve. In spite of God's repeated warnings through his prophets, Israel seems determined to break the covenant. So God abandons the holy temple—the sign of his presence with his people—and it is smashed by pagan invaders. Israel's capital city Jerusalem is sacked and burned.

Abraham's descendants, chosen to reverse the failure of Adam, have now apparently also failed. The problem this poses in the biblical story is profound. Israel, sent as the divine answer to Adam's fall, cannot escape Adam's sin. God, however, remains committed to his people and his plan, so he sows the seed of a different outcome. He promises to send a new king, a descendant of Israel's great King David, who will lead the nation back to its destiny. The very prophets who warned Israel of the dire consequences of its wrongdoing also pledge that the good news of God's victory will be heard in Israel once again.

Act 3 ends tragically, with God apparently absent and the pagan nations ruling over Israel. But the hope of a promise remains. There is one true God. He has chosen Israel. He will return to his people to live with them again. He will bring justice, peace and healing to Israel, and then to the world. He will do this in a final and climactic way. God will send his anointed one—the Messiah. He has given his word on this.

Act 4: THE SURPRISING VICTORY OF JESUS

"He is the god made manifest . . . the universal savior of human life." These words referring to Caesar Augustus (found in a Roman inscription from 4 BC in Ephesus) proclaim the gospel of the Roman Empire. This version of the good news announces that Caesar is the lord who brings peace and prosperity to the world.

Into this empire a son of David is born, and he announces the gospel of God's kingdom. Jesus of Nazareth brings the good news of the coming of God's reign. He begins to show what God's new creation looks like. He announces the end of Israel's exile and the forgiveness of sins. He heals the sick and raises the dead. He overcomes the dark spiritual powers. He welcomes sinners and those considered unclean. Jesus renews the nation, rebuilding the twelve tribes of Israel around himself in a symbolic way.

But the established religious leaders are threatened by Jesus and his kingdom, so they have him brought before the Roman governor. During the very week that the Jews were remembering and celebrating Passover—God's ancient rescue of his people from slavery in Egypt—the Romans nail Jesus to a cross and kill him as a false king.

But the Bible claims that this defeat is actually God's greatest victory. How? Jesus willingly gives up his life as a sacrifice on behalf of the nation, on behalf of the world. Jesus takes onto himself the full force of evil and empties it of its power. In this surprising way, Jesus fights and wins Israel's ultimate battle. The real enemy was never Rome, but the spiritual powers that lie behind Rome and every other kingdom whose weapon is death. Through his blood Jesus pays the price and reconciles everything in heaven and on earth to God.

God then publicly declares this victory by reversing Jesus' death sentence and raising him back to life. The resurrection of Israel's king shows that the great enemies of God's creation—sin and death—really have been defeated. The resurrection is the great sign that the new creation has begun.

Jesus is the fulfillment of Israel's story and a new start for the entire human race. Death came through the first man, Adam. The resurrection of the dead comes through the new man, Jesus. God's original intention is being reclaimed.

Act 5: THE RENEWED PEOPLE OF GOD

If the key victory has already been secured, why is there an Act 5? The answer is that God wants the victory of Jesus to spread to all the nations of the world. The risen Jesus says to his disciples, *"Peace be with you! As the Father has sent me, I am sending you."* So this new act in the drama tells the story of how the earliest followers of Jesus began to spread the good news of God's reign.

According to the New Testament, all those who belong to Israel's Messiah are children of Abraham, heirs of both the ancient promises and the ancient mission. The task of bringing blessing to the peoples of the world has been given again to Abraham's family. Their mission is to live out the liberating message of the good news of God's kingdom.

God is gathering people from all around the world and forming them into assemblies of Jesus-followers—his church. Together they are God's new temple, the place where his Spirit lives. They are the community of those who have pledged their allegiance to Jesus as the true Lord of the world. They have crossed from death into new life, through the power of God's Spirit. They demonstrate God's love across the usual boundaries of race, class, tribe and nation.

Forgiveness of sins and reconciliation with God can now be announced to all. Following in the steps of Jesus, his followers proclaim this gospel in both word and deed. The power of this new, God-given life breaking into the world is meant to be shown by the real-world actions of the Christian community. But the message also has a warning. When the Messiah returns, he will come as the rightful judge of the world.

The Bible is the story of the central struggle weaving its way through the history of the world. And now the story arrives at our own time, enveloping us in its drama.

So the challenge of a decision confronts us. What will we do? How will we fit into this story? What role will we play? God is inviting us to be a part of his mission of re-creation—of bringing restoration, justice and forgiveness. We are to join in the task of making things new, to be a living sign of what is to come when the drama is complete.

Act 6: GOD COMES HOME

God's future has come into our world through the work of Jesus the Messiah. But for now, the present evil age also continues. Brokenness, wrongdoing, sickness and even death remain. We live in the time of the overlap of the ages, the time of in-between. The final Act is coming, but it has not yet arrived.

We live in the time of invitation, when the call of the gospel goes out to every creature. Of course, many still live as though God doesn't exist. They do not acknowledge the rule of the Messiah. But the day is coming when Jesus will return to earth and the reign of God will become an uncontested reality throughout the world.

God's presence will be fully and openly with us once again, as it was at the beginning of the drama. God's plan of redemption will reach its goal. The creation will experience its own Exodus, finding freedom from its bondage to decay. Pain and tears, regret and shame, suffering and death will be no more.

When the day of resurrection arrives God's people will find that their hope has been realized. The dynamic force of an indestructible life will course through their bodies. Empowered by the Spirit, and unhindered by sin and death, we will pursue our original vocation as a renewed humanity. We will be culture makers, under God but over the world. Having been remade in the image of Christ, we will share in bringing his wise, caring rule to the earth.

At the center of it all will be God himself. He will return and make his home with us, this time in a new heavens and a new earth. We, along with the rest of creation, will worship him perfectly and fulfill our true calling. God will be all in all, and the whole world will be full of his glory.

WHAT NOW?

The preceding overview of the drama of the Bible is meant to give you a framework so you can begin to read the books that make up the story. The summary we've provided is merely an invitation for you to engage the sacred books themselves.

Many people today follow the practice of reading only small, fragmentary snippets of the Bible—verses—and often in isolation from the books of which they are a part. This does not lead to good Bible understanding. We encourage you instead to take in whole books, the way their authors wrote them. This is really the only way to gain deep insight to the Scriptures.

Go deep and read big.

The more you immerse yourself in the script of this drama, the better you will be able to find your own place in the story. The following page, called *Living the Script*, will help you with practical next steps for taking up your role in the Bible's drama of renewal.

LIVING
THE SCRIPT

From the beginning God made it clear that he intends for us to be significant players in his drama. No doubt, it is first and foremost God's story. But we can't passively sit back and just watch what happens. At every stage he invites humans to participate with him.

Here are three key steps to finding your place in the drama:

1. IMMERSE YOURSELF IN THE BIBLE

If we are unfamiliar with the text of the drama itself, there's no chance of living our parts well. Only when we read both deeply and widely in the Bible, marinating in it and letting it soak into our lives, will we be prepared to effectively take up our roles. The more we read the Bible, the better readers we will become. Rather than skimming the surface, we will become skilled at interpreting and practicing what we read.

2. COMMIT TO FOLLOW JESUS

We've all taken part in the brokenness and wrongdoing that came into the story in Act 2. The victory of Jesus in Act 4 now offers us the opportunity to have our lives turned around. Our sins can be forgiven. We can become part of God's story of new creation.

Turn away from your wrongdoing. God has acted through the death and resurrection of the Messiah to deal decisively with evil—in your life and in the life of the world. His death was a sacrifice, and his resurrection a new beginning. Acknowledge that Jesus is the rightful ruler of the world, and commit to follow him and join with God's people.

3. LIVE YOUR PART

Followers of Jesus are gospel players in local communities living out the biblical drama together. But we do not have an exact script for our lines and actions in the drama today. Our history has not yet been written. And we can't just repeat lines from earlier acts in the drama. So what do we do?

We read the Bible to understand what God has already done, especially through Jesus the Messiah, and to know how we carry this story forward. *The Bible helps us answer the key question about everything we say and do: Is this an appropriate and fitting way to live out the story of Jesus today?* This is how we put the Scriptures into action. Life's choices can be messy, but God has given us his word and promised us his Spirit to guide us on the way. You are God's artwork, created to do good works. May your life be a gift of beauty back to him.

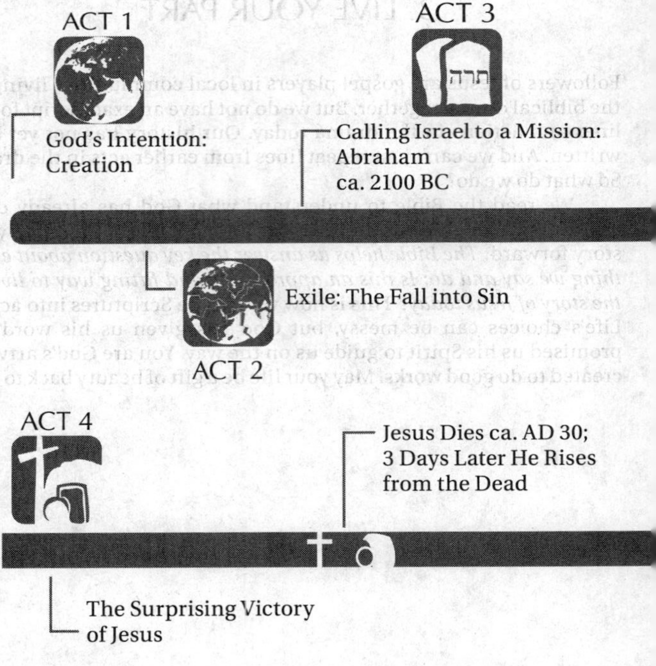

WORLD EVENTS

Pyramids built, 2500's BC
Hinduism gains influence in India, 1100's BC
Buddhism founded in India, 500's BC
Alexander the Great begins rule, 336 BC
China begins construction on The Great Wall, 214 BC
Rise of the Roman Empire, 27 BC

THE DRAMA OF THE BIBLE:
A Visual Chronology

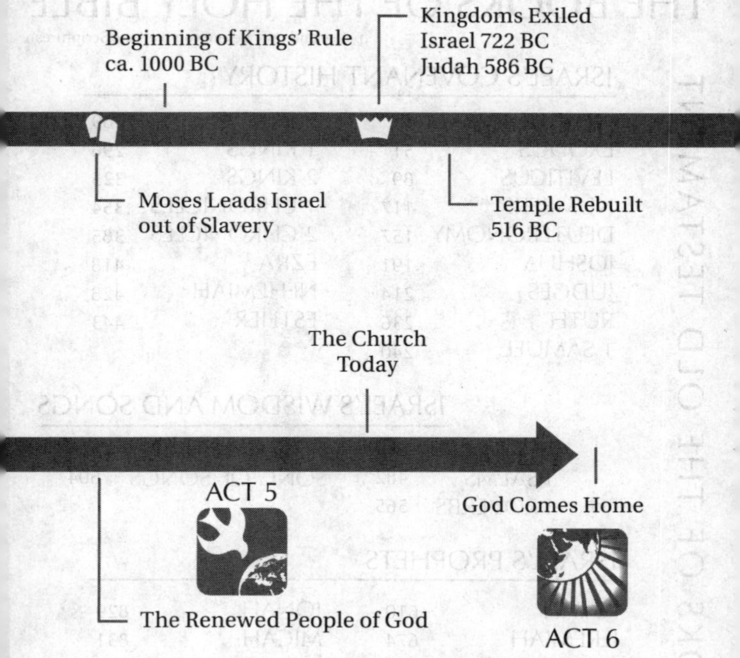

IN THE FRONT...

A GUIDE TO THE BOOKS OF THE HOLY BIBLE

(pause and pray before you read the Scriptures)

THE BOOKS OF THE OLD TESTAMENT

ISRAEL'S COVENANT HISTORY

ISRAEL'S WISDOM AND SONGS

ISRAEL'S PROPHETS

THE BOOKS OF THE NEW TESTAMENT

STORIES ABOUT JESUS

LETTERS FROM PAUL

Messages on STAYING FAITHFUL

WISDOM TEACHINGS

LETTERS from other leaders

AN APOCALYPSE

AT THE BACK...

The story of
GOD'S CREATION OF THE WORLD,
its fall from his intention,
AND THE CALLING OF ABRAHAM
AND HIS DESCENDANTS
–THE PEOPLE OF ISRAEL–
to be God's instrument
FOR BRINGING BLESSING
TO ALL PEOPLES ON EARTH,

PRESENTED
IN THE BOOKS OF THE

OLD TESTAMENT

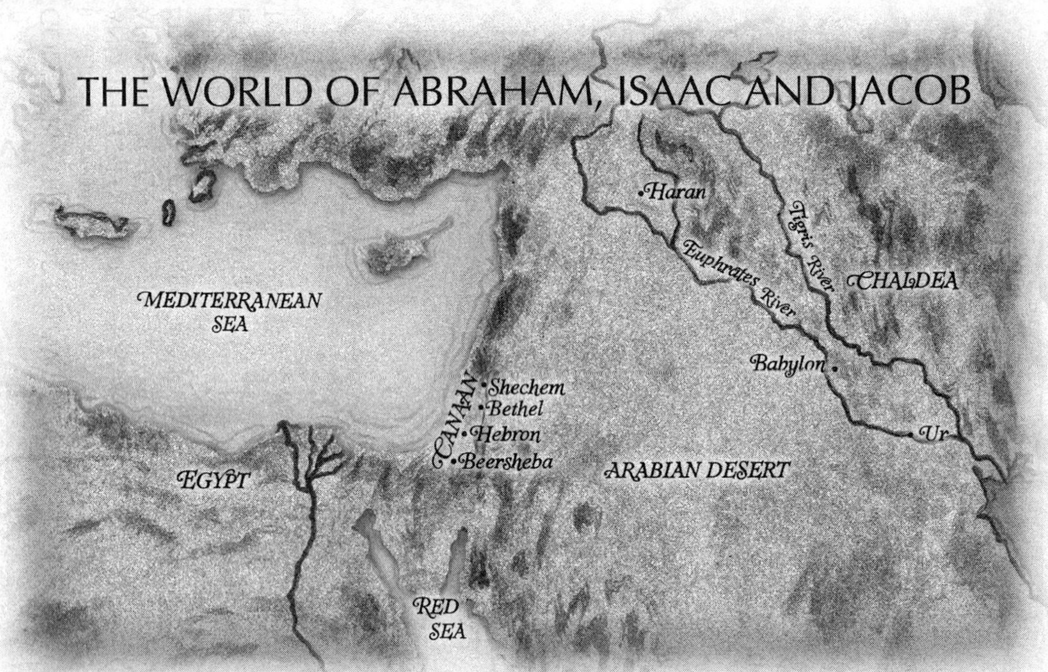
THE WORLD OF ABRAHAM, ISAAC AND JACOB
Haran
Tigris River
Euphrates River
CHALDEA
MEDITERRANEAN SEA
Babylon
Shechem
Bethel
Hebron
Beersheba
CANAAN
Ur
EGYPT
ARABIAN DESERT
RED SEA

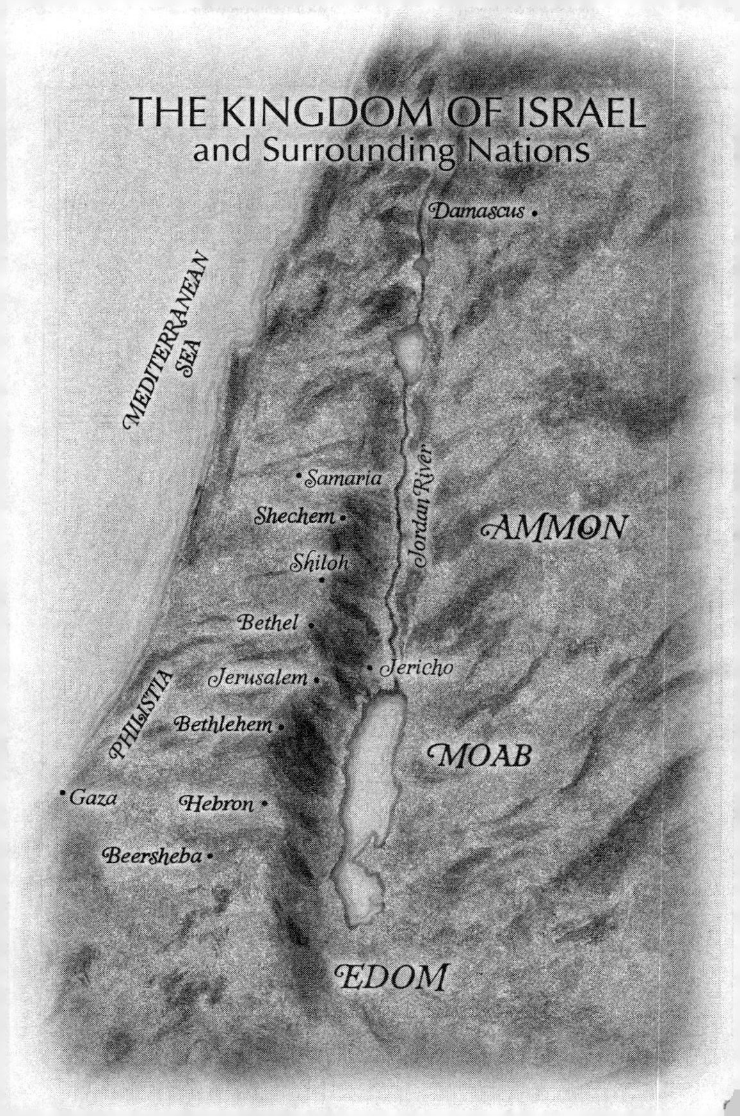
THE KINGDOM OF ISRAEL
and Surrounding Nations
Damascus
MEDITERRANEAN SEA
Samaria
Jordan River
Shechem
AMMON
Shiloh
Bethel
Jericho
PHILISTIA
Jerusalem
Bethlehem
MOAB
Gaza
Hebron
Beersheba
EDOM

David Thomason 2010

GENESIS

Genesis and the other "books of Moses" (Exodus, Leviticus, Numbers and Deuteronomy) introduce the continuous story of Israel running through the first quarter of the Bible. Genesis is traditionally attributed to Moses, the one who led the people of Israel out of Egypt.

Genesis explains how one nation comes to have a special role in God's plan for all of humanity. Early on, the order and harmony of God's good creation are overwhelmed by the destructive consequences of human rebellion and pride. The violence, injustice and suffering that follow lead God to condemn and restrain human wickedness through the judgment of the great flood. God then makes a covenant with Abraham and his descendants, providing an ongoing framework for the story. The family of Abraham—Israel—will be God's chosen means to bring the nations back to himself. Genesis closes with Abraham's descendants having grown into a league of large tribes, but they are not in the land God has promised them. So the story leads naturally into the books that follow.

The book is divided into twelve parts by eleven repetitions of the phrase *this is the account of.* Each section is about the life and family of the person named. These are woven together to document the story of human history and the beginning of God's plan to restore humanity and their place in his world through Israel.

---

1 In the beginning God created
the heavens and the earth. 2 Now
the earth was formless and empty,
darkness was over the surface of the
deep, and the Spirit of God was hovering over the waters.

3 And God said, "Let there be light," and
there was light. 4 God saw that the
light was good, and he separated the
light from the darkness. 5 God called
the light "day," and the darkness he
called "night." And there was evening, and there was morning—the
first day.

6 And God said, "Let there be a vault between the waters to separate water
from water." 7 So God made the vault
and separated the water under the
vault from the water above it. And it
was so. 8 God called the vault "sky."
And there was evening, and there
was morning—the second day.

9 And God said, "Let the water under
the sky be gathered to one place,
and let dry ground appear." And it
was so. 10 God called the dry ground
"land," and the gathered waters he
called "seas." And God saw that it
was good.

11 Then God said, "Let the land
produce vegetation: seed-bearing
plants and trees on the land that
bear fruit with seed in it, according
to their various kinds." And it was
so. 12 The land produced vegetation:
plants bearing seed according to
their kinds and trees bearing fruit
with seed in it according to their
kinds. And God saw that it was good.
13 And there was evening, and there
was morning—the third day.

14 And God said, "Let there be lights in
the vault of the sky to separate the
day from the night, and let them
serve as signs to mark sacred times,
and days and years, 15 and let them
be lights in the vault of the sky to
give light on the earth." And it was
so. 16 God made two great lights—
the greater light to govern the day
and the lesser light to govern the
night. He also made the stars. 17 God
set them in the vault of the sky to
give light on the earth, 18 to govern
the day and the night, and to separate light from darkness. And God
saw that it was good. 19 And there
was evening, and there was morning—the fourth day.

20 And God said, "Let the water teem
with living creatures, and let birds
fly above the earth across the vault
of the sky." 21 So God created the
great creatures of the sea and every
living thing with which the water
teems and that moves about in it,
according to their kinds, and every
winged bird according to its kind.
And God saw that it was good. 22 God
blessed them and said, "Be fruitful

and increase in number and fill the
water in the seas, and let the birds
increase on the earth." 23And there
was evening, and there was morning—the fifth day.
24And God said, "Let the land produce
living creatures according to their
kinds: the livestock, the creatures
that move along the ground, and
the wild animals, each according
to its kind." And it was so. 25God
made the wild animals according to
their kinds, the livestock according
to their kinds, and all the creatures
that move along the ground according to their kinds. And God saw that
it was good.
26Then God said, "Let us make
mankind in our image, in our likeness, so that they may rule over
the fish in the sea and the birds
in the sky, over the livestock and
all the wild animals,[a] and over all
the creatures that move along the
ground."

27So God created mankind in his own
image,
in the image of God he created
them;
male and female he created them.

28God blessed them and said to
them, "Be fruitful and increase in
number; fill the earth and subdue
it. Rule over the fish in the sea and
the birds in the sky and over every
living creature that moves on the
ground."
29Then God said, "I give you every seed-bearing plant on the face
of the whole earth and every tree
that has fruit with seed in it. They
will be yours for food. 30And to all
the beasts of the earth and all the
birds in the sky and all the creatures
that move along the ground—everything that has the breath of life
in it—I give every green plant for
food." And it was so.
31God saw all that he had made,
and it was very good. And there was
evening, and there was morning—
the sixth day.

2 Thus the heavens and the earth
were completed in all their vast array.
2By the seventh day God had finished
the work he had been doing; so on
the seventh day he rested from all
his work. 3Then God blessed the
seventh day and made it holy, because on it he rested from all the
work of creating that he had done.

4This is the account of the heavens
and the earth when they were created,
when the LORD God made the earth and
the heavens.
5Now no shrub had yet appeared on
the earth[b] and no plant had yet sprung
up, for the LORD God had not sent rain
on the earth and there was no one to
work the ground, 6but streams[c] came
up from the earth and watered the whole
surface of the ground. 7Then the LORD
God formed a man[d] from the dust of the
ground and breathed into his nostrils
the breath of life, and the man became
a living being.
8Now the LORD God had planted a garden in the east, in Eden; and there he put
the man he had formed. 9The LORD God
made all kinds of trees grow out of the
ground—trees that were pleasing to the
eye and good for food. In the middle of
the garden were the tree of life and the
tree of the knowledge of good and evil.
10A river watering the garden flowed
from Eden; from there it was separated into four headwaters. 11The name of
the first is the Pishon; it winds through
the entire land of Havilah, where there
is gold. 12(The gold of that land is good;
aromatic resin[e] and onyx are also there.)
13The name of the second river is the Gihon; it winds through the entire land
of Cush.[f] 14The name of the third river
is the Tigris; it runs along the east side
of Ashur. And the fourth river is the Euphrates.
15The LORD God took the man and put
him in the Garden of Eden to work it and
take care of it. 16And the LORD God commanded the man, "You are free to eat
from any tree in the garden; 17but you

[a] *26* Probable reading of the original Hebrew text (see Syriac); Masoretic Text *the earth* [b] *5* Or *land;* also in verse 6 [c] *6* Or *mist* [d] *7* The Hebrew for *man (adam)* sounds like and may be related to the Hebrew for *ground (adamah);* it is also the name *Adam* (see verse 20). [e] *12* Or *good; pearls* [f] *13* Possibly southeast Mesopotamia

must not eat from the tree of the knowledge of good and evil, for when you eat
from it you will certainly die."
18 The LORD God said, "It is not good
for the man to be alone. I will make a
helper suitable for him."
19 Now the LORD God had formed out
of the ground all the wild animals and
all the birds in the sky. He brought them
to the man to see what he would name
them; and whatever the man called each
living creature, that was its name. 20 So
the man gave names to all the livestock,
the birds in the sky and all the wild animals.

But for Adam[a] no suitable helper was
found. 21 So the LORD God caused the
man to fall into a deep sleep; and while
he was sleeping, he took one of the man's
ribs[b] and then closed up the place with
flesh. 22 Then the LORD God made a
woman from the rib[c] he had taken out
of the man, and he brought her to the
man.
23 The man said,

"This is now bone of my bones
 and flesh of my flesh;
she shall be called 'woman,'
 for she was taken out of man."

24 That is why a man leaves his father
and mother and is united to his wife, and
they become one flesh.
25 Adam and his wife were both naked,
and they felt no shame.

3 Now the serpent was more crafty than
any of the wild animals the LORD God
had made. He said to the woman, "Did
God really say, 'You must not eat from
any tree in the garden'?"
2 The woman said to the serpent, "We
may eat fruit from the trees in the garden, 3 but God did say, 'You must not eat
fruit from the tree that is in the middle
of the garden, and you must not touch it,
or you will die.' "
4 "You will not certainly die," the serpent said to the woman. 5 "For God
knows that when you eat from it your
eyes will be opened, and you will be like
God, knowing good and evil."
6 When the woman saw that the fruit of
the tree was good for food and pleasing
to the eye, and also desirable for gaining
wisdom, she took some and ate it. She
also gave some to her husband, who was
with her, and he ate it. 7 Then the eyes of
both of them were opened, and they realized they were naked; so they sewed
fig leaves together and made coverings
for themselves.
8 Then the man and his wife heard the
sound of the LORD God as he was walking
in the garden in the cool of the day, and
they hid from the LORD God among the
trees of the garden. 9 But the LORD God
called to the man, "Where are you?"
10 He answered, "I heard you in the
garden, and I was afraid because I was
naked; so I hid."
11 And he said, "Who told you that you
were naked? Have you eaten from the
tree that I commanded you not to eat
from?"
12 The man said, "The woman you put
here with me—she gave me some fruit
from the tree, and I ate it."
13 Then the LORD God said to the woman, "What is this you have done?"

The woman said, "The serpent deceived me, and I ate."
14 So the LORD God said to the serpent,
"Because you have done this,

"Cursed are you above all livestock
 and all wild animals!
You will crawl on your belly
 and you will eat dust
 all the days of your life.
15 And I will put enmity
 between you and the woman,
 and between your offspring[d] and hers;
he will crush[e] your head,
 and you will strike his heel."

16 To the woman he said,

"I will make your pains in childbearing very severe;
 with painful labor you will give birth to children.
Your desire will be for your husband,
 and he will rule over you."

17 To Adam he said, "Because you listened to your wife and ate fruit from the
tree about which I commanded you,
'You must not eat from it,'

"Cursed is the ground because of you;
 through painful toil you will eat food from it

[a] 20 Or *the man* [b] 21 Or *took part of the man's side* [c] 22 Or *part* [d] 15 Or *seed* [e] 15 Or *strike*

all the days of your life.
18 It will produce thorns and thistles for
you,
and you will eat the plants of the
field.
19 By the sweat of your brow
you will eat your food
until you return to the ground,
since from it you were taken;
for dust you are
and to dust you will return."

20 Adam[a] named his wife Eve,[b] because she would become the mother of
all the living.
21 The LORD God made garments of
skin for Adam and his wife and clothed
them. 22 And the LORD God said, "The
man has now become like one of us,
knowing good and evil. He must not be
allowed to reach out his hand and take
also from the tree of life and eat, and live
forever." 23 So the LORD God banished
him from the Garden of Eden to work the
ground from which he had been taken.
24 After he drove the man out, he placed
on the east side[c] of the Garden of Eden
cherubim and a flaming sword flashing
back and forth to guard the way to the
tree of life.

4 Adam[a] made love to his wife Eve, and
she became pregnant and gave birth
to Cain.[d] She said, "With the help of the
LORD I have brought forth[e] a man." 2 Later she gave birth to his brother Abel.
Now Abel kept flocks, and Cain worked
the soil. 3 In the course of time Cain
brought some of the fruits of the soil as
an offering to the LORD. 4 And Abel also
brought an offering—fat portions from
some of the firstborn of his flock. The
LORD looked with favor on Abel and his
offering, 5 but on Cain and his offering
he did not look with favor. So Cain was
very angry, and his face was downcast.
6 Then the LORD said to Cain, "Why
are you angry? Why is your face downcast? 7 If you do what is right, will you not
be accepted? But if you do not do what
is right, sin is crouching at your door; it
desires to have you, but you must rule
over it."
8 Now Cain said to his brother Abel,
"Let's go out to the field."[f] While they
were in the field, Cain attacked his
brother Abel and killed him.
9 Then the LORD said to Cain, "Where
is your brother Abel?"
"I don't know," he replied. "Am I my
brother's keeper?"
10 The LORD said, "What have you
done? Listen! Your brother's blood cries
out to me from the ground. 11 Now you
are under a curse and driven from the
ground, which opened its mouth to receive your brother's blood from your
hand. 12 When you work the ground,
it will no longer yield its crops for you.
You will be a restless wanderer on the
earth."
13 Cain said to the LORD, "My punishment is more than I can bear. 14 Today
you are driving me from the land, and I
will be hidden from your presence; I will
be a restless wanderer on the earth, and
whoever finds me will kill me."
15 But the LORD said to him, "Not so[g];
anyone who kills Cain will suffer vengeance seven times over." Then the
LORD put a mark on Cain so that no one
who found him would kill him. 16 So Cain
went out from the LORD's presence and
lived in the land of Nod,[h] east of Eden.
17 Cain made love to his wife, and
she became pregnant and gave birth to
Enoch. Cain was then building a city,
and he named it after his son Enoch.
18 To Enoch was born Irad, and Irad was
the father of Mehujael, and Mehujael
was the father of Methushael, and Methushael was the father of Lamech.
19 Lamech married two women, one
named Adah and the other Zillah.
20 Adah gave birth to Jabal; he was the father of those who live in tents and raise
livestock. 21 His brother's name was Ju-
bal; he was the father of all who play
stringed instruments and pipes. 22 Zillah
also had a son, Tubal-Cain, who forged
all kinds of tools out of[i] bronze and iron.
Tubal-Cain's sister was Naamah.
23 Lamech said to his wives,
"Adah and Zillah, listen to me;
wives of Lamech, hear my words.
I have killed a man for wounding me,

[a] *20,1* Or *The man* [b] *20* *Eve* probably means *living.* [c] *24* Or *placed in front* [d] *1* *Cain* sounds like the Hebrew for *brought forth* or *acquired.* [e] *1* Or *have acquired* [f] *8* Samaritan Pentateuch, Septuagint, Vulgate and Syriac; Masoretic Text does not have *"Let's go out to the field."* [g] *15* Septuagint, Vulgate and Syriac; Hebrew *Very well* [h] *16* *Nod* means *wandering* (see verses 12 and 14). [i] *22* Or *who instructed all who work in*

a young man for injuring me.
24 If Cain is avenged seven times,
then Lamech seventy-seven times."

25 Adam made love to his wife again, and she gave birth to a son and named him Seth,[a] saying, "God has granted me another child in place of Abel, since Cain killed him." 26 Seth also had a son, and he named him Enosh.

At that time people began to call on[b] the name of the LORD.

5 This is the written account of Adam's family line.

When God created mankind, he made them in the likeness of God. 2 He created them male and female and blessed them. And he named them "Mankind"[c] when they were created.

3 When Adam had lived 130 years, he had a son in his own likeness, in his own image; and he named him Seth. 4 After Seth was born, Adam lived 800 years and had other sons and daughters. 5 Altogether, Adam lived a total of 930 years, and then he died.

6 When Seth had lived 105 years, he became the father[d] of Enosh. 7 After he became the father of Enosh, Seth lived 807 years and had other sons and daughters. 8 Altogether, Seth lived a total of 912 years, and then he died.

9 When Enosh had lived 90 years, he became the father of Kenan. 10 After he became the father of Kenan, Enosh lived 815 years and had other sons and daughters. 11 Altogether, Enosh lived a total of 905 years, and then he died.

12 When Kenan had lived 70 years, he became the father of Mahalalel. 13 After he became the father of Mahalalel, Kenan lived 840 years and had other sons and daughters. 14 Altogether, Kenan lived a total of 910 years, and then he died.

15 When Mahalalel had lived 65 years, he became the father of Jared. 16 After he became the father of Jared, Mahalalel lived 830 years and had other sons and daughters. 17 Altogether, Mahalalel lived a total of 895 years, and then he died.

18 When Jared had lived 162 years, he became the father of Enoch. 19 After he became the father of Enoch, Jared lived 800 years and had other sons and daughters. 20 Altogether, Jared lived a total of 962 years, and then he died.

21 When Enoch had lived 65 years, he became the father of Methuselah. 22 After he became the father of Methuselah, Enoch walked faithfully with God 300 years and had other sons and daughters. 23 Altogether, Enoch lived a total of 365 years. 24 Enoch walked faithfully with God; then he was no more, because God took him away.

25 When Methuselah had lived 187 years, he became the father of Lamech. 26 After he became the father of Lamech, Methuselah lived 782 years and had other sons and daughters. 27 Altogether, Methuselah lived a total of 969 years, and then he died.

28 When Lamech had lived 182 years, he had a son. 29 He named him Noah[e] and said, "He will comfort us in the labor and painful toil of our hands caused by the ground the LORD has cursed." 30 After Noah was born, Lamech lived 595 years and had other sons and daughters. 31 Altogether, Lamech lived a total of 777 years, and then he died.

32 After Noah was 500 years old, he became the father of Shem, Ham and Japheth.

6 When human beings began to increase in number on the earth and daughters were born to them, 2 the sons of God saw that the daughters of humans were beautiful, and they married any of them they chose. 3 Then the LORD said, "My Spirit will not contend with[f] humans forever, for they are mortal[g]; their days will be a hundred and twenty years."

4 The Nephilim were on the earth in those days—and also afterward—when the sons of God went to the daughters of humans and had children by them. They were the heroes of old, men of renown.

5 The LORD saw how great the wickedness of the human race had become on the earth, and that every inclination of the thoughts of the human heart was only evil all the time. 6 The LORD regretted that he had made human beings

[a] 25 *Seth* probably means *granted.* [b] 26 Or *to proclaim* [c] 2 Hebrew *adam* [d] 6 *Father* may mean *ancestor*; also in verses 7-26. [e] 29 *Noah* sounds like the Hebrew for *comfort.* [f] 3 Or *My spirit will not remain in* [g] 3 Or *corrupt*

on the earth, and his heart was deeply
troubled. 7So the LORD said, "I will wipe
from the face of the earth the human
race I have created — and with them the
animals, the birds and the creatures that
move along the ground — for I regret that
I have made them." 8But Noah found favor in the eyes of the LORD.

9This is the account of Noah and his
family.

Noah was a righteous man, blameless
among the people of his time, and he
walked faithfully with God. 10Noah had
three sons: Shem, Ham and Japheth.
11Now the earth was corrupt in God's
sight and was full of violence. 12God
saw how corrupt the earth had become,
for all the people on earth had corrupted their ways. 13So God said to Noah,
"I am going to put an end to all people, for the earth is filled with violence
because of them. I am surely going to
destroy both them and the earth. 14So
make yourself an ark of cypress[a] wood;
make rooms in it and coat it with pitch
inside and out. 15This is how you are
to build it: The ark is to be three hundred cubits long, fifty cubits wide and
thirty cubits high.[b] 16Make a roof for
it, leaving below the roof an opening
one cubit[c] high all around.[d] Put a door
in the side of the ark and make lower,
middle and upper decks. 17I am going
to bring floodwaters on the earth to destroy all life under the heavens, every
creature that has the breath of life in it.
Everything on earth will perish. 18But
I will establish my covenant with you,
and you will enter the ark — you and
your sons and your wife and your sons'
wives with you. 19You are to bring into
the ark two of all living creatures, male
and female, to keep them alive with
you. 20Two of every kind of bird, of every kind of animal and of every kind of
creature that moves along the ground
will come to you to be kept alive. 21You
are to take every kind of food that is to
be eaten and store it away as food for
you and for them."
22Noah did everything just as God
commanded him.

7 The LORD then said to Noah, "Go into
the ark, you and your whole family,
because I have found you righteous in
this generation. 2Take with you seven
pairs of every kind of clean animal, a
male and its mate, and one pair of every kind of unclean animal, a male and
its mate, 3and also seven pairs of every
kind of bird, male and female, to keep
their various kinds alive throughout the
earth. 4Seven days from now I will send
rain on the earth for forty days and forty nights, and I will wipe from the face
of the earth every living creature I have
made."
5And Noah did all that the LORD commanded him.
6Noah was six hundred years old when
the floodwaters came on the earth. 7And
Noah and his sons and his wife and his
sons' wives entered the ark to escape the
waters of the flood. 8Pairs of clean and
unclean animals, of birds and of all creatures that move along the ground, 9male
and female, came to Noah and entered
the ark, as God had commanded Noah.
10And after the seven days the floodwaters came on the earth.
11In the six hundredth year of Noah's
life, on the seventeenth day of the second month — on that day all the springs
of the great deep burst forth, and the
floodgates of the heavens were opened.
12And rain fell on the earth forty days
and forty nights.
13On that very day Noah and his sons,
Shem, Ham and Japheth, together with
his wife and the wives of his three sons,
entered the ark. 14They had with them
every wild animal according to its kind,
all livestock according to their kinds,
every creature that moves along the
ground according to its kind and every
bird according to its kind, everything
with wings. 15Pairs of all creatures that
have the breath of life in them came to
Noah and entered the ark. 16The animals
going in were male and female of every
living thing, as God had commanded
Noah. Then the LORD shut him in.
17For forty days the flood kept coming
on the earth, and as the waters increased
they lifted the ark high above the earth.
18The waters rose and increased greatly

[a] *14* The meaning of the Hebrew for this word is uncertain. [b] *15* That is, about 450 feet long, 75 feet wide and 45 feet high or about 135 meters long, 23 meters wide and 14 meters high [c] *16* That is, about 18 inches or about 45 centimeters [d] *16* The meaning of the Hebrew for this clause is uncertain.

on the earth, and the ark floated on the
surface of the water. 19They rose greatly on the earth, and all the high mountains under the entire heavens were
covered. 20The waters rose and covered
the mountains to a depth of more than
fifteen cubits.[a,b] 21Every living thing
that moved on land perished—birds,
livestock, wild animals, all the creatures that swarm over the earth, and
all mankind. 22Everything on dry land
that had the breath of life in its nostrils
died. 23Every living thing on the face of
the earth was wiped out; people and animals and the creatures that move along
the ground and the birds were wiped
from the earth. Only Noah was left, and
those with him in the ark.

24The waters flooded the earth for a
hundred and fifty days.

8 But God remembered Noah and all
the wild animals and the livestock
that were with him in the ark, and he
sent a wind over the earth, and the waters receded. 2Now the springs of the
deep and the floodgates of the heavens had been closed, and the rain had
stopped falling from the sky. 3The water receded steadily from the earth. At
the end of the hundred and fifty days
the water had gone down, 4and on the
seventeenth day of the seventh month
the ark came to rest on the mountains
of Ararat. 5The waters continued to re-
cede until the tenth month, and on the
first day of the tenth month the tops of
the mountains became visible.

6After forty days Noah opened a window he had made in the ark 7and sent
out a raven, and it kept flying back and
forth until the water had dried up from
the earth. 8Then he sent out a dove to
see if the water had receded from the
surface of the ground. 9But the dove
could find nowhere to perch because
there was water over all the surface of
the earth; so it returned to Noah in the
ark. He reached out his hand and took
the dove and brought it back to himself
in the ark. 10He waited seven more days
and again sent out the dove from the ark.
11When the dove returned to him in the
evening, there in its beak was a freshly
plucked olive leaf! Then Noah knew that
the water had receded from the earth.
12He waited seven more days and sent
the dove out again, but this time it did
not return to him.

13By the first day of the first month of
Noah's six hundred and first year, the
water had dried up from the earth. Noah
then removed the covering from the ark
and saw that the surface of the ground
was dry. 14By the twenty-seventh day of
the second month the earth was completely dry.

15Then God said to Noah, 16"Come
out of the ark, you and your wife and
your sons and their wives. 17Bring out
every kind of living creature that is with
you—the birds, the animals, and all the
creatures that move along the ground—
so they can multiply on the earth and be
fruitful and increase in number on it."

18So Noah came out, together with his
sons and his wife and his sons' wives.
19All the animals and all the creatures
that move along the ground and all
the birds—everything that moves on
land—came out of the ark, one kind after another.

20Then Noah built an altar to the LORD
and, taking some of all the clean animals
and clean birds, he sacrificed burnt offerings on it. 21The LORD smelled the
pleasing aroma and said in his heart:
"Never again will I curse the ground because of humans, even though[c] every inclination of the human heart is evil from
childhood. And never again will I destroy all living creatures, as I have done.

22 "As long as the earth endures,
seedtime and harvest,
cold and heat,
summer and winter,
day and night
will never cease."

9 Then God blessed Noah and his sons,
saying to them, "Be fruitful and increase in number and fill the earth. 2The
fear and dread of you will fall on all the
beasts of the earth, and on all the birds
in the sky, on every creature that moves
along the ground, and on all the fish in
the sea; they are given into your hands.
3Everything that lives and moves about
will be food for you. Just as I gave you the
green plants, I now give you everything.

4"But you must not eat meat that has

[a] 20 That is, about 23 feet or about 6.8 meters [b] 20 Or *rose more than fifteen cubits, and the mountains were covered* [c] 21 Or *humans, for*

its lifeblood still in it. 5And for your lifeblood I will surely demand an accounting. I will demand an accounting from
every animal. And from each human being, too, I will demand an accounting for
the life of another human being.

6"Whoever sheds human blood,
by humans shall their blood be
shed;
for in the image of God
has God made mankind.

7As for you, be fruitful and increase in
number; multiply on the earth and increase upon it."

8Then God said to Noah and to his sons
with him: 9"I now establish my covenant
with you and with your descendants after you 10and with every living creature
that was with you — the birds, the livestock and all the wild animals, all those
that came out of the ark with you — every
living creature on earth. 11I establish my
covenant with you: Never again will all
life be destroyed by the waters of a flood;
never again will there be a flood to destroy the earth."

12And God said, "This is the sign of the
covenant I am making between me and
you and every living creature with you, a
covenant for all generations to come: 13I
have set my rainbow in the clouds, and it
will be the sign of the covenant between
me and the earth. 14Whenever I bring
clouds over the earth and the rainbow
appears in the clouds, 15I will remember
my covenant between me and you and
all living creatures of every kind. Never
again will the waters become a flood to
destroy all life. 16Whenever the rainbow appears in the clouds, I will see it
and remember the everlasting covenant
between God and all living creatures of
every kind on the earth."

17So God said to Noah, "This is the
sign of the covenant I have established
between me and all life on the earth."

18The sons of Noah who came out of
the ark were Shem, Ham and Japheth.
(Ham was the father of Canaan.) 19These
were the three sons of Noah, and from
them came the people who were scattered over the whole earth.

20Noah, a man of the soil, proceeded[a]
to plant a vineyard. 21When he drank
some of its wine, he became drunk and
lay uncovered inside his tent. 22Ham,
the father of Canaan, saw his father naked and told his two brothers outside.
23But Shem and Japheth took a garment
and laid it across their shoulders; then
they walked in backward and covered
their father's naked body. Their faces
were turned the other way so that they
would not see their father naked.

24When Noah awoke from his wine
and found out what his youngest son had
done to him, 25he said,

"Cursed be Canaan!
The lowest of slaves
will he be to his brothers."

26He also said,

"Praise be to the LORD, the God of
Shem!
May Canaan be the slave of Shem.
27May God extend Japheth's[b] territory;
may Japheth live in the tents of
Shem,
and may Canaan be the slave of
Japheth."

28After the flood Noah lived 350 years.
29Noah lived a total of 950 years, and
then he died.

10 This is the account of Shem, Ham
and Japheth, Noah's sons, who
themselves had sons after the flood.

2The sons[c] of Japheth:
Gomer, Magog, Madai, Javan, Tubal, Meshek and Tiras.
3The sons of Gomer:
Ashkenaz, Riphath and Togarmah.
4The sons of Javan:
Elishah, Tarshish, the Kittites and
the Rodanites.[d] 5(From these the
maritime peoples spread out into
their territories by their clans
within their nations, each with its
own language.)

6The sons of Ham:
Cush, Egypt, Put and Canaan.
7The sons of Cush:

[a] 20 Or *soil, was the first* [b] 27 *Japheth* sounds like the Hebrew for *extend.* [c] 2 *Sons* may mean *descendants* or *successors* or *nations*; also in verses 3, 4, 6, 7, 20-23, 29 and 31. [d] 4 Some manuscripts of the Masoretic Text and Samaritan Pentateuch (see also Septuagint and 1 Chron. 1:7); most manuscripts of the Masoretic Text *Dodanites*

Seba, Havilah, Sabtah, Raamah
and Sabteka.
The sons of Raamah:
Sheba and Dedan.

8 Cush was the father[a] of Nimrod, who
became a mighty warrior on the earth.
9 He was a mighty hunter before the
LORD; that is why it is said, "Like Nimrod, a mighty hunter before the LORD."
10 The first centers of his kingdom were
Babylon, Uruk, Akkad and Kalneh, in[b]
Shinar.[c] 11 From that land he went to
Assyria, where he built Nineveh, Rehoboth Ir,[d] Calah 12 and Resen, which is
between Nineveh and Calah—which is
the great city.

13 Egypt was the father of
the Ludites, Anamites, Lehabites,
Naphtuhites, 14 Pathrusites, Kasluhites (from whom the Philistines came) and Caphtorites.
15 Canaan was the father of
Sidon his firstborn,[e] and of the
Hittites, 16 Jebusites, Amorites,
Girgashites, 17 Hivites, Arkites, Sinites, 18 Arvadites, Zemarites and
Hamathites.

Later the Canaanite clans scattered
19 and the borders of Canaan reached
from Sidon toward Gerar as far as Gaza,
and then toward Sodom, Gomorrah, Admah and Zeboyim, as far as Lasha.
20 These are the sons of Ham by their
clans and languages, in their territories
and nations.

21 Sons were also born to Shem, whose
older brother was[f] Japheth; Shem was
the ancestor of all the sons of Eber.

22 The sons of Shem:
Elam, Ashur, Arphaxad, Lud and
Aram.
23 The sons of Aram:
Uz, Hul, Gether and Meshek.[g]
24 Arphaxad was the father of[h] Shelah,
and Shelah the father of Eber.
25 Two sons were born to Eber:
One was named Peleg,[i] because in
his time the earth was divided; his
brother was named Joktan.
26 Joktan was the father of
Almodad, Sheleph, Hazarmaveth,
Jerah, 27 Hadoram, Uzal, Diklah,
28 Obal, Abimael, Sheba, 29 Ophir,
Havilah and Jobab. All these were
sons of Joktan.

30 The region where they lived stretched
from Mesha toward Sephar, in the eastern hill country.
31 These are the sons of Shem by their
clans and languages, in their territories
and nations.
32 These are the clans of Noah's sons,
according to their lines of descent,
within their nations. From these the
nations spread out over the earth after
the flood.

11 Now the whole world had one language and a common speech. 2 As
people moved eastward,[j] they found a
plain in Shinar[c] and settled there.
3 They said to each other, "Come, let's
make bricks and bake them thoroughly."
They used brick instead of stone, and tar
for mortar. 4 Then they said, "Come, let
us build ourselves a city, with a tower
that reaches to the heavens, so that we
may make a name for ourselves; otherwise we will be scattered over the face of
the whole earth."
5 But the LORD came down to see
the city and the tower the people were
building. 6 The LORD said, "If as one
people speaking the same language they
have begun to do this, then nothing they
plan to do will be impossible for them.
7 Come, let us go down and confuse their
language so they will not understand
each other."
8 So the LORD scattered them from
there over all the earth, and they
stopped building the city. 9 That is why
it was called Babel[k]—because there
the LORD confused the language of the
whole world. From there the LORD scattered them over the face of the whole
earth.

10 This is the account of Shem's family line.

[a] *8 Father* may mean *ancestor* or *predecessor* or *founder*; also in verses 13, 15, 24 and 26. [b] *10* Or *Uruk and Akkad—all of them in* [c] *10,2* That is, Babylonia [d] *11* Or *Nineveh with its city squares* [e] *15* Or *of the Sidonians, the foremost* [f] *21* Or *Shem, the older brother of* [g] *23* See Septuagint and 1 Chron. 1:17; Hebrew *Mash.* [h] *24* Hebrew; Septuagint *father of Cainan, and Cainan was the father of* [i] *25 Peleg* means *division.* [j] *2* Or *from the east;* or *in the east* [k] *9* That is, Babylon; *Babel* sounds like the Hebrew for *confused.*

Two years after the flood, when Shem
was 100 years old, he became the father[a]
of Arphaxad. 11 And after he became the
father of Arphaxad, Shem lived 500 years
and had other sons and daughters.

12 When Arphaxad had lived 35 years,
he became the father of Shelah. 13 And
after he became the father of Shelah,
Arphaxad lived 403 years and had other
sons and daughters.[b]

14 When Shelah had lived 30 years, he
became the father of Eber. 15 And after
he became the father of Eber, Shelah
lived 403 years and had other sons and
daughters.

16 When Eber had lived 34 years, he
became the father of Peleg. 17 And after he became the father of Peleg, Eber
lived 430 years and had other sons and
daughters.

18 When Peleg had lived 30 years, he
became the father of Reu. 19 And after
he became the father of Reu, Peleg lived
209 years and had other sons and daughters.

20 When Reu had lived 32 years, he
became the father of Serug. 21 And after he became the father of Serug, Reu
lived 207 years and had other sons and
daughters.

22 When Serug had lived 30 years, he
became the father of Nahor. 23 And after he became the father of Nahor, Serug
lived 200 years and had other sons and
daughters.

24 When Nahor had lived 29 years, he
became the father of Terah. 25 And after
he became the father of Terah, Nahor
lived 119 years and had other sons and
daughters.

26 After Terah had lived 70 years, he
became the father of Abram, Nahor and
Haran.

27 This is the account of Terah's family line.

Terah became the father of Abram,
Nahor and Haran. And Haran became
the father of Lot. 28 While his father Terah was still alive, Haran died in Ur of
the Chaldeans, in the land of his birth.
29 Abram and Nahor both married. The
name of Abram's wife was Sarai, and the
name of Nahor's wife was Milkah; she
was the daughter of Haran, the father
of both Milkah and Iskah. 30 Now Sarai
was childless because she was not able
to conceive.

31 Terah took his son Abram, his grandson Lot son of Haran, and his daughter-
in-law Sarai, the wife of his son Abram,
and together they set out from Ur of the
Chaldeans to go to Canaan. But when
they came to Harran, they settled there.

32 Terah lived 205 years, and he died
in Harran.

12 The LORD had said to Abram, "Go
from your country, your people and
your father's household to the land I will
show you.

2 "I will make you into a great nation,
and I will bless you;
I will make your name great,
and you will be a blessing.[c]
3 I will bless those who bless you,
and whoever curses you I will
curse;
and all peoples on earth
will be blessed through you."[d]

4 So Abram went, as the LORD had told
him; and Lot went with him. Abram
was seventy-five years old when he set
out from Harran. 5 He took his wife Sarai, his nephew Lot, all the possessions
they had accumulated and the people
they had acquired in Harran, and they
set out for the land of Canaan, and they
arrived there.

6 Abram traveled through the land as
far as the site of the great tree of Moreh
at Shechem. At that time the Canaanites
were in the land. 7 The LORD appeared
to Abram and said, "To your offspring[e]
I will give this land." So he built an altar there to the LORD, who had appeared
to him.

8 From there he went on toward the
hills east of Bethel and pitched his tent,
with Bethel on the west and Ai on the
east. There he built an altar to the LORD
and called on the name of the LORD.

[a] *10 Father* may mean *ancestor*; also in verses 11-25. [b] *12,13* Hebrew; Septuagint (see also Luke 3:35, 36 and note at Gen. 10:24) *35 years, he became the father of Cainan. 13 And after he became the father of Cainan, Arphaxad lived 430 years and had other sons and daughters, and then he died. When Cainan had lived 130 years, he became the father of Shelah. And after he became the father of Shelah, Cainan lived 330 years and had other sons and daughters* [c] *2* Or *be seen as blessed* [d] *3* Or *earth / will use your name in blessings* (see 48:20) [e] *7* Or *seed*

9 Then Abram set out and continued toward the Negev.

10 Now there was a famine in the land, and Abram went down to Egypt to live there for a while because the famine was severe. 11 As he was about to enter Egypt, he said to his wife Sarai, "I know what a beautiful woman you are. 12 When the Egyptians see you, they will say, 'This is his wife.' Then they will kill me but will let you live. 13 Say you are my sister, so that I will be treated well for your sake and my life will be spared because of you."

14 When Abram came to Egypt, the Egyptians saw that Sarai was a very beautiful woman. 15 And when Pharaoh's officials saw her, they praised her to Pharaoh, and she was taken into his palace. 16 He treated Abram well for her sake, and Abram acquired sheep and cattle, male and female donkeys, male and female servants, and camels.

17 But the LORD inflicted serious diseases on Pharaoh and his household because of Abram's wife Sarai. 18 So Pharaoh summoned Abram. "What have you done to me?" he said. "Why didn't you tell me she was your wife? 19 Why did you say, 'She is my sister,' so that I took her to be my wife? Now then, here is your wife. Take her and go!" 20 Then Pharaoh gave orders about Abram to his men, and they sent him on his way, with his wife and everything he had.

13 So Abram went up from Egypt to the Negev, with his wife and everything he had, and Lot went with him. 2 Abram had become very wealthy in livestock and in silver and gold.

3 From the Negev he went from place to place until he came to Bethel, to the place between Bethel and Ai where his tent had been earlier 4 and where he had first built an altar. There Abram called on the name of the LORD.

5 Now Lot, who was moving about with Abram, also had flocks and herds and tents. 6 But the land could not support them while they stayed together, for their possessions were so great that they were not able to stay together. 7 And quarreling arose between Abram's herders and Lot's. The Canaanites and Perizzites were also living in the land at that time.

8 So Abram said to Lot, "Let's not have any quarreling between you and me, or between your herders and mine, for we are close relatives. 9 Is not the whole land before you? Let's part company. If you go to the left, I'll go to the right; if you go to the right, I'll go to the left."

10 Lot looked around and saw that the whole plain of the Jordan toward Zoar was well watered, like the garden of the LORD, like the land of Egypt. (This was before the LORD destroyed Sodom and Gomorrah.) 11 So Lot chose for himself the whole plain of the Jordan and set out toward the east. The two men parted company: 12 Abram lived in the land of Canaan, while Lot lived among the cities of the plain and pitched his tents near Sodom. 13 Now the people of Sodom were wicked and were sinning greatly against the LORD.

14 The LORD said to Abram after Lot had parted from him, "Look around from where you are, to the north and south, to the east and west. 15 All the land that you see I will give to you and your offspring[a] forever. 16 I will make your offspring like the dust of the earth, so that if anyone could count the dust, then your offspring could be counted. 17 Go, walk through the length and breadth of the land, for I am giving it to you."

18 So Abram went to live near the great trees of Mamre at Hebron, where he pitched his tents. There he built an altar to the LORD.

14 At the time when Amraphel was king of Shinar,[b] Arioch king of Ellasar, Kedorlaomer king of Elam and Tidal king of Goyim, 2 these kings went to war against Bera king of Sodom, Birsha king of Gomorrah, Shinab king of Admah, Shemeber king of Zeboyim, and the king of Bela (that is, Zoar). 3 All these latter kings joined forces in the Valley of Siddim (that is, the Dead Sea Valley). 4 For twelve years they had been subject to Kedorlaomer, but in the thirteenth year they rebelled.

5 In the fourteenth year, Kedorlaomer and the kings allied with him went out and defeated the Rephaites in Ashteroth Karnaim, the Zuzites in Ham, the Emites in Shaveh Kiriathaim 6 and the Horites in the hill country of Seir, as far

[a] *15* Or *seed*; also in verse 16 [b] *1* That is, Babylonia; also in verse 9

as El Paran near the desert. 7 Then they
turned back and went to En Mishpat
(that is, Kadesh), and they conquered
the whole territory of the Amalekites, as
well as the Amorites who were living in
Hazezon Tamar.
8 Then the king of Sodom, the king of
Gomorrah, the king of Admah, the king
of Zeboyim and the king of Bela (that is,
Zoar) marched out and drew up their battle lines in the Valley of Siddim 9 against
Kedorlaomer king of Elam, Tidal king of
Goyim, Amraphel king of Shinar and Arioch king of Ellasar — four kings against
five. 10 Now the Valley of Siddim was full
of tar pits, and when the kings of Sodom
and Gomorrah fled, some of the men fell
into them and the rest fled to the hills.
11 The four kings seized all the goods of
Sodom and Gomorrah and all their food;
then they went away. 12 They also carried
off Abram's nephew Lot and his possessions, since he was living in Sodom.
13 A man who had escaped came and
reported this to Abram the Hebrew. Now
Abram was living near the great trees of
Mamre the Amorite, a brother[a] of Eshkol and Aner, all of whom were allied
with Abram. 14 When Abram heard that
his relative had been taken captive, he
called out the 318 trained men born in
his household and went in pursuit as far
as Dan. 15 During the night Abram divided his men to attack them and he routed
them, pursuing them as far as Hobah,
north of Damascus. 16 He recovered all
the goods and brought back his relative
Lot and his possessions, together with
the women and the other people.
17 After Abram returned from defeating Kedorlaomer and the kings allied
with him, the king of Sodom came out to
meet him in the Valley of Shaveh (that is,
the King's Valley).
18 Then Melchizedek king of Salem brought out bread and wine. He
was priest of God Most High, 19 and he
blessed Abram, saying,

"Blessed be Abram by God Most
High,
Creator of heaven and earth.
20 And praise be to God Most High,
who delivered your enemies into
your hand."

Then Abram gave him a tenth of everything.
21 The king of Sodom said to Abram,
"Give me the people and keep the goods
for yourself."
22 But Abram said to the king of Sodom, "With raised hand I have sworn an
oath to the LORD, God Most High, Creator of heaven and earth, 23 that I will
accept nothing belonging to you, not
even a thread or the strap of a sandal, so
that you will never be able to say, 'I made
Abram rich.' 24 I will accept nothing but
what my men have eaten and the share
that belongs to the men who went with
me — to Aner, Eshkol and Mamre. Let
them have their share."
15 After this, the word of the LORD
came to Abram in a vision:

"Do not be afraid, Abram.
I am your shield,[b]
your very great reward.[c]"

2 But Abram said, "Sovereign LORD,
what can you give me since I remain
childless and the one who will inherit[d]
my estate is Eliezer of Damascus?" 3 And
Abram said, "You have given me no children; so a servant in my household will
be my heir."
4 Then the word of the LORD came to
him: "This man will not be your heir, but
a son who is your own flesh and blood
will be your heir." 5 He took him outside
and said, "Look up at the sky and count
the stars — if indeed you can count
them." Then he said to him, "So shall
your offspring[e] be."
6 Abram believed the LORD, and he
credited it to him as righteousness.
7 He also said to him, "I am the LORD,
who brought you out of Ur of the Chaldeans to give you this land to take possession of it."
8 But Abram said, "Sovereign LORD,
how can I know that I will gain possession of it?"
9 So the LORD said to him, "Bring me
a heifer, a goat and a ram, each three
years old, along with a dove and a young
pigeon."
10 Abram brought all these to him, cut
them in two and arranged the halves opposite each other; the birds, however, he
did not cut in half. 11 Then birds of prey

[a] *13* Or *a relative;* or *an ally* [b] *1* Or *sovereign* [c] *1* Or *shield; / your reward will be very great*
[d] *2* The meaning of the Hebrew for this phrase is uncertain. [e] *5* Or *seed*

came down on the carcasses, but Abram
drove them away.
12As the sun was setting, Abram fell
into a deep sleep, and a thick and dreadful darkness came over him. 13Then the
LORD said to him, "Know for certain that
for four hundred years your descendants
will be strangers in a country not their
own and that they will be enslaved and
mistreated there. 14But I will punish
the nation they serve as slaves, and afterward they will come out with great
possessions. 15You, however, will go to
your ancestors in peace and be buried
at a good old age. 16In the fourth generation your descendants will come back
here, for the sin of the Amorites has not
yet reached its full measure."
17When the sun had set and darkness
had fallen, a smoking firepot with a blazing torch appeared and passed between
the pieces. 18On that day the LORD made
a covenant with Abram and said, "To
your descendants I give this land, from
the Wadi[a] of Egypt to the great river, the
Euphrates— 19the land of the Kenites,
Kenizzites, Kadmonites, 20Hittites, Perizzites, Rephaites, 21Amorites, Canaanites, Girgashites and Jebusites."

16 Now Sarai, Abram's wife, had borne
him no children. But she had an
Egyptian slave named Hagar; 2so she
said to Abram, "The LORD has kept me
from having children. Go, sleep with
my slave; perhaps I can build a family
through her."
Abram agreed to what Sarai said. 3So
after Abram had been living in Canaan
ten years, Sarai his wife took her Egyptian slave Hagar and gave her to her
husband to be his wife. 4He slept with
Hagar, and she conceived.
When she knew she was pregnant, she
began to despise her mistress. 5Then
Sarai said to Abram, "You are responsible for the wrong I am suffering. I put
my slave in your arms, and now that
she knows she is pregnant, she despises me. May the LORD judge between you
and me."
6"Your slave is in your hands," Abram
said. "Do with her whatever you think
best." Then Sarai mistreated Hagar; so
she fled from her.
7The angel of the LORD found Hagar
near a spring in the desert; it was the
spring that is beside the road to Shur.
8And he said, "Hagar, slave of Sarai,
where have you come from, and where
are you going?"
"I'm running away from my mistress
Sarai," she answered.
9Then the angel of the LORD told her,
"Go back to your mistress and submit to
her." 10The angel added, "I will increase
your descendants so much that they will
be too numerous to count."
11The angel of the LORD also said to
her:

"You are now pregnant
and you will give birth to a son.
You shall name him Ishmael,[b]
for the LORD has heard of your
misery.
12He will be a wild donkey of a man;
his hand will be against everyone
and everyone's hand against him,
and he will live in hostility
toward[c] all his brothers."

13She gave this name to the LORD who
spoke to her: "You are the God who sees
me," for she said, "I have now seen[d] the
One who sees me." 14That is why the
well was called Beer Lahai Roi[e]; it is still
there, between Kadesh and Bered.
15So Hagar bore Abram a son, and
Abram gave the name Ishmael to the son
she had borne. 16Abram was eighty-six
years old when Hagar bore him Ishmael.

17 When Abram was ninety-nine years
old, the LORD appeared to him and
said, "I am God Almighty[f]; walk before
me faithfully and be blameless. 2Then
I will make my covenant between me
and you and will greatly increase your
numbers."
3Abram fell facedown, and God said
to him, 4"As for me, this is my covenant
with you: You will be the father of many
nations. 5No longer will you be called
Abram[g]; your name will be Abraham,[h]
for I have made you a father of many nations. 6I will make you very fruitful; I will
make nations of you, and kings will come
from you. 7I will establish my covenant
as an everlasting covenant between me

[a] 18 Or *river* [b] 11 *Ishmael* means *God hears.* [c] 12 Or *live to the east / of* [d] 13 Or *seen the back of*
[e] 14 *Beer Lahai Roi* means *well of the Living One who sees me.* [f] 1 Hebrew *El-Shaddai* [g] 5 *Abram* means
exalted father. [h] 5 *Abraham* probably means *father of many.*

and you and your descendants after you
for the generations to come, to be your
God and the God of your descendants
after you. 8The whole land of Canaan,
where you now reside as a foreigner, I
will give as an everlasting possession to
you and your descendants after you; and
I will be their God."
9Then God said to Abraham, "As for
you, you must keep my covenant, you
and your descendants after you for the
generations to come. 10This is my covenant with you and your descendants
after you, the covenant you are to keep:
Every male among you shall be circumcised. 11You are to undergo circumcision, and it will be the sign of the covenant between me and you. 12For the
generations to come every male among
you who is eight days old must be circumcised, including those born in your
household or bought with money from a
foreigner—those who are not your offspring. 13Whether born in your household or bought with your money, they
must be circumcised. My covenant in
your flesh is to be an everlasting covenant. 14Any uncircumcised male, who
has not been circumcised in the flesh,
will be cut off from his people; he has
broken my covenant."
15God also said to Abraham, "As for
Sarai your wife, you are no longer to call
her Sarai; her name will be Sarah. 16I
will bless her and will surely give you a
son by her. I will bless her so that she will
be the mother of nations; kings of peoples will come from her."
17Abraham fell facedown; he laughed
and said to himself, "Will a son be born
to a man a hundred years old? Will Sarah
bear a child at the age of ninety?" 18And
Abraham said to God, "If only Ishmael
might live under your blessing!"
19Then God said, "Yes, but your wife
Sarah will bear you a son, and you will
call him Isaac.[a] I will establish my covenant with him as an everlasting covenant for his descendants after him.
20And as for Ishmael, I have heard you:
I will surely bless him; I will make him
fruitful and will greatly increase his
numbers. He will be the father of twelve
rulers, and I will make him into a great
nation. 21But my covenant I will establish with Isaac, whom Sarah will bear to
you by this time next year." 22When he
had finished speaking with Abraham,
God went up from him.
23On that very day Abraham took his
son Ishmael and all those born in his
household or bought with his money, every male in his household, and circumcised them, as God told him. 24Abraham
was ninety-nine years old when he was
circumcised, 25and his son Ishmael
was thirteen; 26Abraham and his son
Ishmael were both circumcised on that
very day. 27And every male in Abraham's
household, including those born in his
household or bought from a foreigner,
was circumcised with him.
18 The LORD appeared to Abraham
near the great trees of Mamre while
he was sitting at the entrance to his tent
in the heat of the day. 2Abraham looked
up and saw three men standing nearby.
When he saw them, he hurried from the
entrance of his tent to meet them and
bowed low to the ground.
3He said, "If I have found favor in your
eyes, my lord,[b] do not pass your servant
by. 4Let a little water be brought, and
then you may all wash your feet and rest
under this tree. 5Let me get you something to eat, so you can be refreshed and
then go on your way—now that you have
come to your servant."
"Very well," they answered, "do as you
say."
6So Abraham hurried into the tent to
Sarah. "Quick," he said, "get three seahs[c] of the finest flour and knead it and
bake some bread."
7Then he ran to the herd and selected a choice, tender calf and gave it to a
servant, who hurried to prepare it. 8He
then brought some curds and milk and
the calf that had been prepared, and set
these before them. While they ate, he
stood near them under a tree.
9"Where is your wife Sarah?" they
asked him.
"There, in the tent," he said.
10Then one of them said, "I will surely
return to you about this time next year,
and Sarah your wife will have a son."
Now Sarah was listening at the entrance to the tent, which was behind
him. 11Abraham and Sarah were already

[a] *19 Isaac* means *he laughs.* [b] *3* Or *eyes, Lord* [c] *6* That is, probably about 36 pounds or about 16 kilograms

very old, and Sarah was past the age of
childbearing. 12So Sarah laughed to herself as she thought, "After I am worn out
and my lord is old, will I now have this
pleasure?"
13Then the LORD said to Abraham,
"Why did Sarah laugh and say, 'Will I
really have a child, now that I am old?'
14Is anything too hard for the LORD? I
will return to you at the appointed time
next year, and Sarah will have a son."
15Sarah was afraid, so she lied and
said, "I did not laugh."
But he said, "Yes, you did laugh."
16When the men got up to leave, they
looked down toward Sodom, and Abraham walked along with them to see
them on their way. 17Then the LORD
said, "Shall I hide from Abraham what
I am about to do? 18Abraham will surely become a great and powerful nation,
and all nations on earth will be blessed
through him.[a] 19For I have chosen him,
so that he will direct his children and
his household after him to keep the way
of the LORD by doing what is right and
just, so that the LORD will bring about for
Abraham what he has promised him."
20Then the LORD said, "The outcry
against Sodom and Gomorrah is so great
and their sin so grievous 21that I will go
down and see if what they have done is
as bad as the outcry that has reached me.
If not, I will know."
22The men turned away and went toward Sodom, but Abraham remained
standing before the LORD.[b] 23Then
Abraham approached him and said:
"Will you sweep away the righteous
with the wicked? 24What if there are fifty righteous people in the city? Will you
really sweep it away and not spare[c] the
place for the sake of the fifty righteous
people in it? 25Far be it from you to do
such a thing—to kill the righteous with
the wicked, treating the righteous and
the wicked alike. Far be it from you! Will
not the Judge of all the earth do right?"
26The LORD said, "If I find fifty righteous people in the city of Sodom, I will
spare the whole place for their sake."
27Then Abraham spoke up again:
"Now that I have been so bold as to
speak to the Lord, though I am nothing
but dust and ashes, 28what if the number of the righteous is five less than fifty?
Will you destroy the whole city for lack of
five people?"
"If I find forty-five there," he said, "I
will not destroy it."
29Once again he spoke to him, "What
if only forty are found there?"
He said, "For the sake of forty, I will
not do it."
30Then he said, "May the Lord not be
angry, but let me speak. What if only
thirty can be found there?"
He answered, "I will not do it if I find
thirty there."
31Abraham said, "Now that I have been
so bold as to speak to the Lord, what if
only twenty can be found there?"
He said, "For the sake of twenty, I will
not destroy it."
32Then he said, "May the Lord not be
angry, but let me speak just once more.
What if only ten can be found there?"
He answered, "For the sake of ten, I
will not destroy it."
33When the LORD had finished speaking with Abraham, he left, and Abraham
returned home.

19 The two angels arrived at Sodom
in the evening, and Lot was sitting
in the gateway of the city. When he saw
them, he got up to meet them and bowed
down with his face to the ground. 2"My
lords," he said, "please turn aside to your
servant's house. You can wash your feet
and spend the night and then go on your
way early in the morning."
"No," they answered, "we will spend
the night in the square."
3But he insisted so strongly that they
did go with him and entered his house.
He prepared a meal for them, baking
bread without yeast, and they ate. 4Be-
fore they had gone to bed, all the men
from every part of the city of Sodom—
both young and old—surrounded the
house. 5They called to Lot, "Where are
the men who came to you tonight? Bring
them out to us so that we can have sex
with them."
6Lot went outside to meet them and
shut the door behind him 7and said,
"No, my friends. Don't do this wicked thing. 8Look, I have two daughters
who have never slept with a man. Let
me bring them out to you, and you can

[a] *18* Or *will use his name in blessings* (see 48:20)
[b] *22* Masoretic Text; an ancient Hebrew scribal tradition *but the LORD remained standing before Abraham*
[c] *24* Or *forgive*; also in verse 26

do what you like with them. But don't do anything to these men, for they have come under the protection of my roof."

9 "Get out of our way," they replied. "This fellow came here as a foreigner, and now he wants to play the judge! We'll treat you worse than them." They kept bringing pressure on Lot and moved forward to break down the door.

10 But the men inside reached out and pulled Lot back into the house and shut the door. 11 Then they struck the men who were at the door of the house, young and old, with blindness so that they could not find the door.

12 The two men said to Lot, "Do you have anyone else here—sons-in-law, sons or daughters, or anyone else in the city who belongs to you? Get them out of here, 13 because we are going to destroy this place. The outcry to the LORD against its people is so great that he has sent us to destroy it."

14 So Lot went out and spoke to his sons-in-law, who were pledged to marry[a] his daughters. He said, "Hurry and get out of this place, because the LORD is about to destroy the city!" But his sons-in-law thought he was joking.

15 With the coming of dawn, the angels urged Lot, saying, "Hurry! Take your wife and your two daughters who are here, or you will be swept away when the city is punished."

16 When he hesitated, the men grasped his hand and the hands of his wife and of his two daughters and led them safely out of the city, for the LORD was merciful to them. 17 As soon as they had brought them out, one of them said, "Flee for your lives! Don't look back, and don't stop anywhere in the plain! Flee to the mountains or you will be swept away!"

18 But Lot said to them, "No, my lords,[b] please! 19 Your[c] servant has found favor in your[c] eyes, and you[c] have shown great kindness to me in sparing my life. But I can't flee to the mountains; this disaster will overtake me, and I'll die. 20 Look, here is a town near enough to run to, and it is small. Let me flee to it—it is very small, isn't it? Then my life will be spared."

21 He said to him, "Very well, I will grant this request too; I will not overthrow the town you speak of. 22 But flee there quickly, because I cannot do anything until you reach it." (That is why the town was called Zoar.[d])

23 By the time Lot reached Zoar, the sun had risen over the land. 24 Then the LORD rained down burning sulfur on Sodom and Gomorrah—from the LORD out of the heavens. 25 Thus he overthrew those cities and the entire plain, destroying all those living in the cities—and also the vegetation in the land. 26 But Lot's wife looked back, and she became a pillar of salt.

27 Early the next morning Abraham got up and returned to the place where he had stood before the LORD. 28 He looked down toward Sodom and Gomorrah, toward all the land of the plain, and he saw dense smoke rising from the land, like smoke from a furnace.

29 So when God destroyed the cities of the plain, he remembered Abraham, and he brought Lot out of the catastrophe that overthrew the cities where Lot had lived.

30 Lot and his two daughters left Zoar and settled in the mountains, for he was afraid to stay in Zoar. He and his two daughters lived in a cave. 31 One day the older daughter said to the younger, "Our father is old, and there is no man around here to give us children—as is the custom all over the earth. 32 Let's get our father to drink wine and then sleep with him and preserve our family line through our father."

33 That night they got their father to drink wine, and the older daughter went in and slept with him. He was not aware of it when she lay down or when she got up.

34 The next day the older daughter said to the younger, "Last night I slept with my father. Let's get him to drink wine again tonight, and you go in and sleep with him so we can preserve our family line through our father." 35 So they got their father to drink wine that night also, and the younger daughter went in and slept with him. Again he was not aware of it when she lay down or when she got up.

36 So both of Lot's daughters became pregnant by their father. 37 The older

[a] *14* Or *were married to* [b] *18* Or *No, Lord*; or *No, my lord* [c] *19* The Hebrew is singular. [d] *22* *Zoar* means *small*.

daughter had a son, and she named him Moab[a]; he is the father of the Moabites of today. 38The younger daughter also had a son, and she named him Ben-Ammi[b]; he is the father of the Ammonites[c] of today.

20 Now Abraham moved on from there into the region of the Negev and lived between Kadesh and Shur. For a while he stayed in Gerar, 2and there Abraham said of his wife Sarah, "She is my sister." Then Abimelek king of Gerar sent for Sarah and took her.

3But God came to Abimelek in a dream one night and said to him, "You are as good as dead because of the woman you have taken; she is a married woman."

4Now Abimelek had not gone near her, so he said, "Lord, will you destroy an innocent nation? 5Did he not say to me, 'She is my sister,' and didn't she also say, 'He is my brother'? I have done this with a clear conscience and clean hands."

6Then God said to him in the dream, "Yes, I know you did this with a clear conscience, and so I have kept you from sinning against me. That is why I did not let you touch her. 7Now return the man's wife, for he is a prophet, and he will pray for you and you will live. But if you do not return her, you may be sure that you and all who belong to you will die."

8Early the next morning Abimelek summoned all his officials, and when he told them all that had happened, they were very much afraid. 9Then Abimelek called Abraham in and said, "What have you done to us? How have I wronged you that you have brought such great guilt upon me and my kingdom? You have done things to me that should never be done." 10And Abimelek asked Abraham, "What was your reason for doing this?"

11Abraham replied, "I said to myself, 'There is surely no fear of God in this place, and they will kill me because of my wife.' 12Besides, she really is my sister, the daughter of my father though not of my mother; and she became my wife. 13And when God had me wander from my father's household, I said to her, 'This is how you can show your love to me: Everywhere we go, say of me, "He is my brother."'"

14Then Abimelek brought sheep and cattle and male and female slaves and gave them to Abraham, and he returned Sarah his wife to him. 15And Abimelek said, "My land is before you; live wherever you like."

16To Sarah he said, "I am giving your brother a thousand shekels[d] of silver. This is to cover the offense against you before all who are with you; you are completely vindicated."

17Then Abraham prayed to God, and God healed Abimelek, his wife and his female slaves so they could have children again, 18for the LORD had kept all the women in Abimelek's household from conceiving because of Abraham's wife Sarah.

21 Now the LORD was gracious to Sarah as he had said, and the LORD did for Sarah what he had promised. 2Sarah became pregnant and bore a son to Abraham in his old age, at the very time God had promised him. 3Abraham gave the name Isaac[e] to the son Sarah bore him. 4When his son Isaac was eight days old, Abraham circumcised him, as God commanded him. 5Abraham was a hundred years old when his son Isaac was born to him.

6Sarah said, "God has brought me laughter, and everyone who hears about this will laugh with me." 7And she added, "Who would have said to Abraham that Sarah would nurse children? Yet I have borne him a son in his old age."

8The child grew and was weaned, and on the day Isaac was weaned Abraham held a great feast. 9But Sarah saw that the son whom Hagar the Egyptian had borne to Abraham was mocking, 10and she said to Abraham, "Get rid of that slave woman and her son, for that woman's son will never share in the inheritance with my son Isaac."

11The matter distressed Abraham greatly because it concerned his son. 12But God said to him, "Do not be so distressed about the boy and your slave woman. Listen to whatever Sarah tells you, because it is through Isaac that your offspring[f] will be reckoned. 13I will make the son of the slave into a nation also, because he is your offspring."

[a] *37* *Moab* sounds like the Hebrew for *from father.* [b] *38* *Ben-Ammi* means *son of my father's people.* [c] *38* Hebrew *Bene-Ammon* [d] *16* That is, about 25 pounds or about 12 kilograms [e] *3* *Isaac* means *he laughs.* [f] *12* Or *seed*

14Early the next morning Abraham
took some food and a skin of water and
gave them to Hagar. He set them on her
shoulders and then sent her off with the
boy. She went on her way and wandered
in the Desert of Beersheba.
15When the water in the skin was gone,
she put the boy under one of the bushes.
16Then she went off and sat down about
a bowshot away, for she thought, "I cannot watch the boy die." And as she sat
there, she[a] began to sob.
17God heard the boy crying, and the
angel of God called to Hagar from heav-
en and said to her, "What is the matter,
Hagar? Do not be afraid; God has heard
the boy crying as he lies there. 18Lift the
boy up and take him by the hand, for I
will make him into a great nation."
19Then God opened her eyes and she
saw a well of water. So she went and
filled the skin with water and gave the
boy a drink.
20God was with the boy as he grew up.
He lived in the desert and became an archer. 21While he was living in the Desert
of Paran, his mother got a wife for him
from Egypt.
22At that time Abimelek and Phicol the
commander of his forces said to Abraham, "God is with you in everything you
do. 23Now swear to me here before God
that you will not deal falsely with me or
my children or my descendants. Show to
me and the country where you now reside as a foreigner the same kindness I
have shown to you."
24Abraham said, "I swear it."
25Then Abraham complained to
Abimelek about a well of water that
Abimelek's servants had seized. 26But
Abimelek said, "I don't know who has
done this. You did not tell me, and I
heard about it only today."
27So Abraham brought sheep and cattle and gave them to Abimelek, and the
two men made a treaty. 28Abraham set
apart seven ewe lambs from the flock,
29and Abimelek asked Abraham, "What
is the meaning of these seven ewe lambs
you have set apart by themselves?"
30He replied, "Accept these seven
lambs from my hand as a witness that I
dug this well."
31So that place was called Beersheba,[b] because the two men swore an oath
there.
32After the treaty had been made at
Beersheba, Abimelek and Phicol the
commander of his forces returned to
the land of the Philistines. 33Abraham
planted a tamarisk tree in Beersheba,
and there he called on the name of the
LORD, the Eternal God. 34And Abraham
stayed in the land of the Philistines for
a long time.

22 Some time later God tested Abraham. He said to him, "Abraham!"
"Here I am," he replied.
2Then God said, "Take your son, your
only son, whom you love—Isaac—and
go to the region of Moriah. Sacrifice him
there as a burnt offering on a mountain I
will show you."
3Early the next morning Abraham
got up and loaded his donkey. He took
with him two of his servants and his son
Isaac. When he had cut enough wood
for the burnt offering, he set out for the
place God had told him about. 4On the
third day Abraham looked up and saw
the place in the distance. 5He said to
his servants, "Stay here with the donkey
while I and the boy go over there. We will
worship and then we will come back to
you."
6Abraham took the wood for the burnt
offering and placed it on his son Isaac,
and he himself carried the fire and the
knife. As the two of them went on together, 7Isaac spoke up and said to his father
Abraham, "Father?"
"Yes, my son?" Abraham replied.
"The fire and wood are here," Isaac
said, "but where is the lamb for the burnt
offering?"
8Abraham answered, "God himself
will provide the lamb for the burnt offering, my son." And the two of them went
on together.
9When they reached the place God
had told him about, Abraham built an
altar there and arranged the wood on
it. He bound his son Isaac and laid him
on the altar, on top of the wood. 10Then
he reached out his hand and took the
knife to slay his son. 11But the angel of
the LORD called out to him from heaven,
"Abraham! Abraham!"
"Here I am," he replied.

a 16 Hebrew; Septuagint *the child* b 31 *Beersheba* can mean *well of seven* and *well of the oath.*

12“Do not lay a hand on the boy,” he
said. “Do not do anything to him. Now
I know that you fear God, because you
have not withheld from me your son,
your only son.”
13Abraham looked up and there in
a thicket he saw a ram[a] caught by its
horns. He went over and took the ram
and sacrificed it as a burnt offering instead of his son. 14So Abraham called
that place The LORD Will Provide. And
to this day it is said, “On the mountain of
the LORD it will be provided.”
15The angel of the LORD called to
Abraham from heaven a second time
16and said, “I swear by myself, declares
the LORD, that because you have done
this and have not withheld your son,
your only son, 17I will surely bless you
and make your descendants as numerous as the stars in the sky and as the
sand on the seashore. Your descendants
will take possession of the cities of their
enemies, 18and through your offspring[b]
all nations on earth will be blessed,[c] because you have obeyed me.”
19Then Abraham returned to his servants, and they set off together for Beersheba. And Abraham stayed in Beersheba.
20Some time later Abraham was told,
“Milkah is also a mother; she has borne
sons to your brother Nahor: 21Uz the
firstborn, Buz his brother, Kemuel (the
father of Aram), 22Kesed, Hazo, Pildash,
Jidlaph and Bethuel.” 23Bethuel became
the father of Rebekah. Milkah bore these
eight sons to Abraham’s brother Nahor.
24His concubine, whose name was Reu-
mah, also had sons: Tebah, Gaham, Ta-
hash and Maakah.

23 Sarah lived to be a hundred and
twenty-seven years old. 2She died
at Kiriath Arba (that is, Hebron) in the
land of Canaan, and Abraham went to
mourn for Sarah and to weep over her.
3Then Abraham rose from beside his
dead wife and spoke to the Hittites.[d]
He said, 4“I am a foreigner and stranger
among you. Sell me some property for a
burial site here so I can bury my dead.”
5The Hittites replied to Abraham,
6“Sir, listen to us. You are a mighty
prince among us. Bury your dead in the
choicest of our tombs. None of us will
refuse you his tomb for burying your
dead.”
7Then Abraham rose and bowed down
before the people of the land, the Hittites. 8He said to them, “If you are willing to let me bury my dead, then listen
to me and intercede with Ephron son of
Zohar on my behalf 9so he will sell me
the cave of Machpelah, which belongs to
him and is at the end of his field. Ask him
to sell it to me for the full price as a burial
site among you.”
10Ephron the Hittite was sitting among
his people and he replied to Abraham in
the hearing of all the Hittites who had
come to the gate of his city. 11“No, my
lord,” he said. “Listen to me; I give[e] you
the field, and I give[e] you the cave that is
in it. I give[e] it to you in the presence of
my people. Bury your dead.”
12Again Abraham bowed down before
the people of the land 13and he said to
Ephron in their hearing, “Listen to me, if
you will. I will pay the price of the field.
Accept it from me so I can bury my dead
there.”
14Ephron answered Abraham, 15“Listen to me, my lord; the land is worth four
hundred shekels[f] of silver, but what is
that between you and me? Bury your
dead.”
16Abraham agreed to Ephron’s terms
and weighed out for him the price he
had named in the hearing of the Hittites: four hundred shekels of silver, according to the weight current among the
merchants.
17So Ephron’s field in Machpelah near
Mamre — both the field and the cave in
it, and all the trees within the borders
of the field — was deeded 18to Abraham as his property in the presence of
all the Hittites who had come to the gate
of the city. 19Afterward Abraham buried his wife Sarah in the cave in the field
of Machpelah near Mamre (which is at
Hebron) in the land of Canaan. 20So the
field and the cave in it were deeded to
Abraham by the Hittites as a burial site.

24 Abraham was now very old, and
the LORD had blessed him in every

[a] *13* Many manuscripts of the Masoretic Text, Samaritan Pentateuch, Septuagint and Syriac; most manuscripts of the Masoretic Text *a ram behind him* [b] *18* Or *seed* [c] *18* Or *and all nations on earth will use the name of your offspring in blessings* (see 48:20) [d] *3* Or *the descendants of Heth*; also in verses 5, 7, 10, 16, 18 and 20 [e] *11* Or *sell* [f] *15* That is, about 10 pounds or about 4.6 kilograms

way. 2He said to the senior servant in his
household, the one in charge of all that
he had, "Put your hand under my thigh.
3I want you to swear by the LORD, the
God of heaven and the God of earth, that
you will not get a wife for my son from
the daughters of the Canaanites, among
whom I am living, 4but will go to my
country and my own relatives and get a
wife for my son Isaac."
5The servant asked him, "What if
the woman is unwilling to come back
with me to this land? Shall I then take
your son back to the country you came
from?"
6"Make sure that you do not take my
son back there," Abraham said. 7"The
LORD, the God of heaven, who brought
me out of my father's household and my
native land and who spoke to me and
promised me on oath, saying, 'To your
offspring[a] I will give this land'—he will
send his angel before you so that you can
get a wife for my son from there. 8If the
woman is unwilling to come back with
you, then you will be released from this
oath of mine. Only do not take my son
back there." 9So the servant put his hand
under the thigh of his master Abraham
and swore an oath to him concerning
this matter.
10Then the servant left, taking with
him ten of his master's camels loaded
with all kinds of good things from his
master. He set out for Aram Naharaim[b]
and made his way to the town of Nahor.
11He had the camels kneel down near
the well outside the town; it was toward
evening, the time the women go out to
draw water.
12Then he prayed, "LORD, God of my
master Abraham, make me successful
today, and show kindness to my master
Abraham. 13See, I am standing beside
this spring, and the daughters of the
townspeople are coming out to draw water. 14May it be that when I say to a young
woman, 'Please let down your jar that I
may have a drink,' and she says, 'Drink,
and I'll water your camels too'—let her
be the one you have chosen for your servant Isaac. By this I will know that you
have shown kindness to my master."
15Before he had finished praying,
Rebekah came out with her jar on her
shoulder. She was the daughter of Bethuel son of Milkah, who was the wife of
Abraham's brother Nahor. 16The woman was very beautiful, a virgin; no man
had ever slept with her. She went down
to the spring, filled her jar and came up
again.
17The servant hurried to meet her and
said, "Please give me a little water from
your jar."
18"Drink, my lord," she said, and
quickly lowered the jar to her hands and
gave him a drink.
19After she had given him a drink,
she said, "I'll draw water for your camels too, until they have had enough to
drink." 20So she quickly emptied her jar
into the trough, ran back to the well to
draw more water, and drew enough for
all his camels. 21Without saying a word,
the man watched her closely to learn
whether or not the LORD had made his
journey successful.
22When the camels had finished
drinking, the man took out a gold nose
ring weighing a beka[c] and two gold
bracelets weighing ten shekels.[d] 23Then
he asked, "Whose daughter are you?
Please tell me, is there room in your father's house for us to spend the night?"
24She answered him, "I am the daughter of Bethuel, the son that Milkah bore
to Nahor." 25And she added, "We have
plenty of straw and fodder, as well as
room for you to spend the night."
26Then the man bowed down and
worshiped the LORD, 27saying, "Praise
be to the LORD, the God of my master
Abraham, who has not abandoned his
kindness and faithfulness to my master. As for me, the LORD has led me on
the journey to the house of my master's
relatives."
28The young woman ran and told her
mother's household about these things.
29Now Rebekah had a brother named
Laban, and he hurried out to the man at
the spring. 30As soon as he had seen the
nose ring, and the bracelets on his sister's arms, and had heard Rebekah tell
what the man said to her, he went out to
the man and found him standing by the
camels near the spring. 31"Come, you
who are blessed by the LORD," he said.
"Why are you standing out here? I have

[a] *7* Or *seed* [b] *10* That is, Northwest Mesopotamia
[d] *22* That is, about 4 ounces or about 115 grams
[c] *22* That is, about 1/5 ounce or about 5.7 grams

a skillful hunter, a man of the open
country, while Jacob was content to stay
at home among the tents. 28 Isaac, who
had a taste for wild game, loved Esau,
but Rebekah loved Jacob.
29 Once when Jacob was cooking
some stew, Esau came in from the open
country, famished. 30 He said to Jacob,
"Quick, let me have some of that red
stew! I'm famished!" (That is why he was
also called Edom.[a])
31 Jacob replied, "First sell me your
birthright."
32 "Look, I am about to die," Esau said.
"What good is the birthright to me?"
33 But Jacob said, "Swear to me first."
So he swore an oath to him, selling his
birthright to Jacob.
34 Then Jacob gave Esau some bread
and some lentil stew. He ate and drank,
and then got up and left.
So Esau despised his birthright.

26 Now there was a famine in the
land — besides the previous famine in Abraham's time — and Isaac went
to Abimelek king of the Philistines in
Gerar. 2 The LORD appeared to Isaac
and said, "Do not go down to Egypt;
live in the land where I tell you to live.
3 Stay in this land for a while, and I will
be with you and will bless you. For to
you and your descendants I will give
all these lands and will confirm the
oath I swore to your father Abraham.
4 I will make your descendants as numerous as the stars in the sky and will
give them all these lands, and through
your offspring[b] all nations on earth will
be blessed,[c] 5 because Abraham obeyed
me and did everything I required of
him, keeping my commands, my decrees and my instructions." 6 So Isaac
stayed in Gerar.
7 When the men of that place asked
him about his wife, he said, "She is my
sister," because he was afraid to say,
"She is my wife." He thought, "The men
of this place might kill me on account of
Rebekah, because she is beautiful."
8 When Isaac had been there a long
time, Abimelek king of the Philistines
looked down from a window and saw
Isaac caressing his wife Rebekah. 9 So
Abimelek summoned Isaac and said,
"She is really your wife! Why did you say,
'She is my sister'?"
Isaac answered him, "Because I
thought I might lose my life on account
of her."
10 Then Abimelek said, "What is this
you have done to us? One of the men
might well have slept with your wife, and
you would have brought guilt upon us."
11 So Abimelek gave orders to all the
people: "Anyone who harms this man or
his wife shall surely be put to death."
12 Isaac planted crops in that land and
the same year reaped a hundredfold, because the LORD blessed him. 13 The man
became rich, and his wealth continued
to grow until he became very wealthy.
14 He had so many flocks and herds and
servants that the Philistines envied him.
15 So all the wells that his father's servants had dug in the time of his father
Abraham, the Philistines stopped up,
filling them with earth.
16 Then Abimelek said to Isaac, "Move
away from us; you have become too
powerful for us."
17 So Isaac moved away from there and
encamped in the Valley of Gerar, where
he settled. 18 Isaac reopened the wells
that had been dug in the time of his father Abraham, which the Philistines had
stopped up after Abraham died, and he
gave them the same names his father
had given them.
19 Isaac's servants dug in the valley and
discovered a well of fresh water there.
20 But the herders of Gerar quarreled
with those of Isaac and said, "The water is ours." So he named the well Esek,[d]
because they disputed with him. 21 Then
they dug another well, but they quarreled over that one also; so he named it
Sitnah.[e] 22 He moved on from there and
dug another well, and no one quarreled
over it. He named it Rehoboth,[f] saying,
"Now the LORD has given us room and
we will flourish in the land."
23 From there he went up to Beersheba.
24 That night the LORD appeared to him
and said, "I am the God of your father
Abraham. Do not be afraid, for I am with
you; I will bless you and will increase the
number of your descendants for the sake
of my servant Abraham."

[a] 30 *Edom* means *red.* [b] 4 Or *seed* [c] 4 Or *and all nations on earth will use the name of your offspring in blessings* (see 48:20) [d] 20 *Esek* means *dispute.* [e] 21 *Sitnah* means *opposition.* [f] 22 *Rehoboth* means *room.*

25Isaac built an altar there and called
on the name of the LORD. There he
pitched his tent, and there his servants
dug a well.
26Meanwhile, Abimelek had come to
him from Gerar, with Ahuzzath his personal adviser and Phicol the commander of his forces. 27Isaac asked them,
"Why have you come to me, since you
were hostile to me and sent me away?"
28They answered, "We saw clearly
that the LORD was with you; so we said,
'There ought to be a sworn agreement
between us'—between us and you. Let
us make a treaty with you 29that you will
do us no harm, just as we did not harm
you but always treated you well and sent
you away peacefully. And now you are
blessed by the LORD."
30Isaac then made a feast for them,
and they ate and drank. 31Early the next
morning the men swore an oath to each
other. Then Isaac sent them on their way,
and they went away peacefully.
32That day Isaac's servants came and
told him about the well they had dug.
They said, "We've found water!" 33He
called it Shibah,[a] and to this day the
name of the town has been Beersheba.[b]
34When Esau was forty years old, he
married Judith daughter of Beeri the
Hittite, and also Basemath daughter of
Elon the Hittite. 35They were a source of
grief to Isaac and Rebekah.

27 When Isaac was old and his eyes
were so weak that he could no longer see, he called for Esau his older son
and said to him, "My son."
"Here I am," he answered.
2Isaac said, "I am now an old man and
don't know the day of my death. 3Now
then, get your equipment—your quiver
and bow—and go out to the open country to hunt some wild game for me. 4Pre-
pare me the kind of tasty food I like and
bring it to me to eat, so that I may give
you my blessing before I die."
5Now Rebekah was listening as Isaac
spoke to his son Esau. When Esau left
for the open country to hunt game and
bring it back, 6Rebekah said to her son
Jacob, "Look, I overheard your father say
to your brother Esau, 7'Bring me some
game and prepare me some tasty food
to eat, so that I may give you my blessing in the presence of the LORD before I
die.' 8Now, my son, listen carefully and
do what I tell you: 9Go out to the flock
and bring me two choice young goats, so
I can prepare some tasty food for your father, just the way he likes it. 10Then take
it to your father to eat, so that he may
give you his blessing before he dies."
11Jacob said to Rebekah his mother,
"But my brother Esau is a hairy man
while I have smooth skin. 12What if my
father touches me? I would appear to be
tricking him and would bring down a
curse on myself rather than a blessing."
13His mother said to him, "My son, let
the curse fall on me. Just do what I say;
go and get them for me."
14So he went and got them and brought
them to his mother, and she prepared
some tasty food, just the way his father
liked it. 15Then Rebekah took the best
clothes of Esau her older son, which
she had in the house, and put them on
her younger son Jacob. 16She also covered his hands and the smooth part of
his neck with the goatskins. 17Then she
handed to her son Jacob the tasty food
and the bread she had made.
18He went to his father and said, "My
father."
"Yes, my son," he answered. "Who
is it?"
19Jacob said to his father, "I am Esau
your firstborn. I have done as you told
me. Please sit up and eat some of my
game, so that you may give me your
blessing."
20Isaac asked his son, "How did you
find it so quickly, my son?"
"The LORD your God gave me success,"
he replied.
21Then Isaac said to Jacob, "Come
near so I can touch you, my son, to know
whether you really are my son Esau or
not."
22Jacob went close to his father Isaac,
who touched him and said, "The voice
is the voice of Jacob, but the hands are
the hands of Esau." 23He did not recognize him, for his hands were hairy like
those of his brother Esau; so he proceeded to bless him. 24"Are you really my son
Esau?" he asked.
"I am," he replied.
25Then he said, "My son, bring me

[a] 33 *Shibah* can mean *oath* or *seven*. [b] 33 *Beersheba* can mean *well of the oath* and *well of seven*.

some of your game to eat, so that I may
give you my blessing."
Jacob brought it to him and he ate; and
he brought some wine and he drank.
26 Then his father Isaac said to him,
"Come here, my son, and kiss me."
27 So he went to him and kissed him.
When Isaac caught the smell of his
clothes, he blessed him and said,

"Ah, the smell of my son
 is like the smell of a field
 that the LORD has blessed.
28 May God give you heaven's dew
 and earth's richness —
 an abundance of grain and new
 wine.
29 May nations serve you
 and peoples bow down to you.
Be lord over your brothers,
 and may the sons of your mother
 bow down to you.
May those who curse you be cursed
 and those who bless you be
 blessed."

30 After Isaac finished blessing him,
and Jacob had scarcely left his father's
presence, his brother Esau came in from
hunting. 31 He too prepared some tasty
food and brought it to his father. Then
he said to him, "My father, please sit up
and eat some of my game, so that you
may give me your blessing."
32 His father Isaac asked him, "Who
are you?"
"I am your son," he answered, "your
firstborn, Esau."
33 Isaac trembled violently and said,
"Who was it, then, that hunted game and
brought it to me? I ate it just before you
came and I blessed him — and indeed he
will be blessed!"
34 When Esau heard his father's words,
he burst out with a loud and bitter cry
and said to his father, "Bless me — me
too, my father!"
35 But he said, "Your brother came deceitfully and took your blessing."
36 Esau said, "Isn't he rightly named Jacob[a]? This is the second time he has tak-
en advantage of me: He took my birthright, and now he's taken my blessing!"
Then he asked, "Haven't you reserved
any blessing for me?"
37 Isaac answered Esau, "I have made
him lord over you and have made all his
relatives his servants, and I have sustained him with grain and new wine. So
what can I possibly do for you, my son?"
38 Esau said to his father, "Do you have
only one blessing, my father? Bless me
too, my father!" Then Esau wept aloud.
39 His father Isaac answered him,

"Your dwelling will be
 away from the earth's richness,
 away from the dew of heaven
 above.
40 You will live by the sword
 and you will serve your brother.
But when you grow restless,
 you will throw his yoke
 from off your neck."

41 Esau held a grudge against Jacob because of the blessing his father had giv-
en him. He said to himself, "The days of
mourning for my father are near; then I
will kill my brother Jacob."
42 When Rebekah was told what her
older son Esau had said, she sent for
her younger son Jacob and said to him,
"Your brother Esau is planning to avenge
himself by killing you. 43 Now then, my
son, do what I say: Flee at once to my
brother Laban in Harran. 44 Stay with
him for a while until your brother's fury
subsides. 45 When your brother is no longer angry with you and forgets what you
did to him, I'll send word for you to come
back from there. Why should I lose both
of you in one day?"
46 Then Rebekah said to Isaac, "I'm
disgusted with living because of these
Hittite women. If Jacob takes a wife from
among the women of this land, from Hittite women like these, my life will not be
worth living."

28 So Isaac called for Jacob and
blessed him. Then he commanded
him: "Do not marry a Canaanite woman. 2 Go at once to Paddan Aram,[b] to the
house of your mother's father Bethuel. Take a wife for yourself there, from
among the daughters of Laban, your
mother's brother. 3 May God Almighty[c]
bless you and make you fruitful and increase your numbers until you become
a community of peoples. 4 May he give
you and your descendants the blessing
given to Abraham, so that you may take

[a] 36 *Jacob* means *he grasps the heel*, a Hebrew idiom for *he takes advantage of* or *he deceives*. [b] 2 That is, Northwest Mesopotamia; also in verses 5, 6 and 7 [c] 3 Hebrew *El-Shaddai*

possession of the land where you now
reside as a foreigner, the land God gave
to Abraham." 5Then Isaac sent Jacob on
his way, and he went to Paddan Aram, to
Laban son of Bethuel the Aramean, the
brother of Rebekah, who was the mother
of Jacob and Esau.

6Now Esau learned that Isaac had
blessed Jacob and had sent him to Paddan Aram to take a wife from there, and
that when he blessed him he commanded him, "Do not marry a Canaanite
woman," 7and that Jacob had obeyed
his father and mother and had gone to
Paddan Aram. 8Esau then realized how
displeasing the Canaanite women were
to his father Isaac; 9so he went to Ishmael and married Mahalath, the sister of
Nebaioth and daughter of Ishmael son
of Abraham, in addition to the wives he
already had.

10Jacob left Beersheba and set out for
Harran. 11When he reached a certain
place, he stopped for the night because
the sun had set. Taking one of the stones
there, he put it under his head and lay
down to sleep. 12He had a dream in
which he saw a stairway resting on the
earth, with its top reaching to heaven,
and the angels of God were ascending
and descending on it. 13There above it[a]
stood the LORD, and he said: "I am the
LORD, the God of your father Abraham
and the God of Isaac. I will give you and
your descendants the land on which you
are lying. 14Your descendants will be
like the dust of the earth, and you will
spread out to the west and to the east, to
the north and to the south. All peoples
on earth will be blessed through you and
your offspring.[b] 15I am with you and will
watch over you wherever you go, and I
will bring you back to this land. I will not
leave you until I have done what I have
promised you."

16When Jacob awoke from his sleep,
he thought, "Surely the LORD is in this
place, and I was not aware of it." 17He
was afraid and said, "How awesome is
this place! This is none other than the
house of God; this is the gate of heaven."

18Early the next morning Jacob took
the stone he had placed under his head
and set it up as a pillar and poured oil on
top of it. 19He called that place Bethel,[c]
though the city used to be called Luz.

20Then Jacob made a vow, saying, "If
God will be with me and will watch over
me on this journey I am taking and will
give me food to eat and clothes to wear
21so that I return safely to my father's
household, then the LORD[d] will be my
God 22and[e] this stone that I have set
up as a pillar will be God's house, and
of all that you give me I will give you a
tenth."

29 Then Jacob continued on his journey and came to the land of the eastern peoples. 2There he saw a well in the
open country, with three flocks of sheep
lying near it because the flocks were watered from that well. The stone over the
mouth of the well was large. 3When all
the flocks were gathered there, the shepherds would roll the stone away from the
well's mouth and water the sheep. Then
they would return the stone to its place
over the mouth of the well.

4Jacob asked the shepherds, "My
brothers, where are you from?"

"We're from Harran," they replied.

5He said to them, "Do you know Laban, Nahor's grandson?"

"Yes, we know him," they answered.

6Then Jacob asked them, "Is he well?"

"Yes, he is," they said, "and here comes
his daughter Rachel with the sheep."

7"Look," he said, "the sun is still high;
it is not time for the flocks to be gathered. Water the sheep and take them
back to pasture."

8"We can't," they replied, "until all the
flocks are gathered and the stone has
been rolled away from the mouth of the
well. Then we will water the sheep."

9While he was still talking with them,
Rachel came with her father's sheep, for
she was a shepherd. 10When Jacob saw
Rachel daughter of his uncle Laban,
and Laban's sheep, he went over and
rolled the stone away from the mouth of
the well and watered his uncle's sheep.
11Then Jacob kissed Rachel and began
to weep aloud. 12He had told Rachel
that he was a relative of her father and
a son of Rebekah. So she ran and told
her father.

[a] 13 Or *There beside him* [b] 14 Or *will use your name and the name of your offspring in blessings* (see 48:20) [c] 19 *Bethel* means *house of God.* [d] 20,21 Or *Since God . . . father's household, the LORD* [e] 21,22 Or *household, and the LORD will be my God, 22then*

13 As soon as Laban heard the news about Jacob, his sister's son, he hurried to meet him. He embraced him and kissed him and brought him to his home, and there Jacob told him all these things. 14 Then Laban said to him, "You are my own flesh and blood."

After Jacob had stayed with him for a whole month, 15 Laban said to him, "Just because you are a relative of mine, should you work for me for nothing? Tell me what your wages should be."

16 Now Laban had two daughters; the name of the older was Leah, and the name of the younger was Rachel. 17 Leah had weak[a] eyes, but Rachel had a lovely figure and was beautiful. 18 Jacob was in love with Rachel and said, "I'll work for you seven years in return for your younger daughter Rachel."

19 Laban said, "It's better that I give her to you than to some other man. Stay here with me." 20 So Jacob served seven years to get Rachel, but they seemed like only a few days to him because of his love for her.

21 Then Jacob said to Laban, "Give me my wife. My time is completed, and I want to make love to her."

22 So Laban brought together all the people of the place and gave a feast. 23 But when evening came, he took his daughter Leah and brought her to Jacob, and Jacob made love to her. 24 And Laban gave his servant Zilpah to his daughter as her attendant.

25 When morning came, there was Leah! So Jacob said to Laban, "What is this you have done to me? I served you for Rachel, didn't I? Why have you deceived me?"

26 Laban replied, "It is not our custom here to give the younger daughter in marriage before the older one. 27 Finish this daughter's bridal week; then we will give you the younger one also, in return for another seven years of work."

28 And Jacob did so. He finished the week with Leah, and then Laban gave him his daughter Rachel to be his wife. 29 Laban gave his servant Bilhah to his daughter Rachel as her attendant. 30 Jacob made love to Rachel also, and his love for Rachel was greater than his love for Leah. And he worked for Laban another seven years.

31 When the LORD saw that Leah was not loved, he enabled her to conceive, but Rachel remained childless. 32 Leah became pregnant and gave birth to a son. She named him Reuben,[b] for she said, "It is because the LORD has seen my misery. Surely my husband will love me now."

33 She conceived again, and when she gave birth to a son she said, "Because the LORD heard that I am not loved, he gave me this one too." So she named him Simeon.[c]

34 Again she conceived, and when she gave birth to a son she said, "Now at last my husband will become attached to me, because I have borne him three sons." So he was named Levi.[d]

35 She conceived again, and when she gave birth to a son she said, "This time I will praise the LORD." So she named him Judah.[e] Then she stopped having children.

30 When Rachel saw that she was not bearing Jacob any children, she became jealous of her sister. So she said to Jacob, "Give me children, or I'll die!"

2 Jacob became angry with her and said, "Am I in the place of God, who has kept you from having children?"

3 Then she said, "Here is Bilhah, my servant. Sleep with her so that she can bear children for me and I too can build a family through her."

4 So she gave him her servant Bilhah as a wife. Jacob slept with her, 5 and she became pregnant and bore him a son. 6 Then Rachel said, "God has vindicated me; he has listened to my plea and given me a son." Because of this she named him Dan.[f]

7 Rachel's servant Bilhah conceived again and bore Jacob a second son. 8 Then Rachel said, "I have had a great struggle with my sister, and I have won." So she named him Naphtali.[g]

9 When Leah saw that she had stopped having children, she took her servant Zilpah and gave her to Jacob as a wife. 10 Leah's servant Zilpah bore Jacob a son.

[a] 17 Or *delicate* [b] 32 *Reuben* sounds like the Hebrew for *he has seen my misery*; the name means *see, a son.* [c] 33 *Simeon* probably means *one who hears.* [d] 34 *Levi* sounds like and may be derived from the Hebrew for *attached.* [e] 35 *Judah* sounds like and may be derived from the Hebrew for *praise.* [f] 6 *Dan* here means *he has vindicated.* [g] 8 *Naphtali* means *my struggle.*

11 Then Leah said, "What good fortune!"[a]
So she named him Gad.[b]
12 Leah's servant Zilpah bore Jacob
a second son. 13 Then Leah said, "How
happy I am! The women will call me
happy." So she named him Asher.[c]
14 During wheat harvest, Reuben
went out into the fields and found some
mandrake plants, which he brought to
his mother Leah. Rachel said to Leah,
"Please give me some of your son's mandrakes."
15 But she said to her, "Wasn't it enough
that you took away my husband? Will
you take my son's mandrakes too?"
"Very well," Rachel said, "he can sleep
with you tonight in return for your son's
mandrakes."
16 So when Jacob came in from the
fields that evening, Leah went out to
meet him. "You must sleep with me,"
she said. "I have hired you with my son's
mandrakes." So he slept with her that
night.
17 God listened to Leah, and she became pregnant and bore Jacob a fifth
son. 18 Then Leah said, "God has rewarded me for giving my servant to my husband." So she named him Issachar.[d]
19 Leah conceived again and bore Jacob a sixth son. 20 Then Leah said, "God
has presented me with a precious gift.
This time my husband will treat me
with honor, because I have borne him
six sons." So she named him Zebulun.[e]
21 Some time later she gave birth to a
daughter and named her Dinah.
22 Then God remembered Rachel; he
listened to her and enabled her to conceive. 23 She became pregnant and gave
birth to a son and said, "God has taken
away my disgrace." 24 She named him
Joseph,[f] and said, "May the LORD add to
me another son."
25 After Rachel gave birth to Joseph, Jacob said to Laban, "Send me on my way
so I can go back to my own homeland.
26 Give me my wives and children, for
whom I have served you, and I will be on
my way. You know how much work I've
done for you."
27 But Laban said to him, "If I have
found favor in your eyes, please stay.
I have learned by divination that the
LORD has blessed me because of you."
28 He added, "Name your wages, and I
will pay them."
29 Jacob said to him, "You know how I
have worked for you and how your livestock has fared under my care. 30 The little you had before I came has increased
greatly, and the LORD has blessed you
wherever I have been. But now, when
may I do something for my own household?"
31 "What shall I give you?" he asked.
"Don't give me anything," Jacob replied. "But if you will do this one thing
for me, I will go on tending your flocks
and watching over them: 32 Let me go
through all your flocks today and remove from them every speckled or spotted sheep, every dark-colored lamb and
every spotted or speckled goat. They will
be my wages. 33 And my honesty will testify for me in the future, whenever you
check on the wages you have paid me.
Any goat in my possession that is not
speckled or spotted, or any lamb that
is not dark-colored, will be considered
stolen."
34 "Agreed," said Laban. "Let it be as
you have said." 35 That same day he removed all the male goats that were
streaked or spotted, and all the speckled or spotted female goats (all that had
white on them) and all the dark-colored
lambs, and he placed them in the care
of his sons. 36 Then he put a three-day
journey between himself and Jacob,
while Jacob continued to tend the rest of
Laban's flocks.
37 Jacob, however, took fresh-cut
branches from poplar, almond and plane
trees and made white stripes on them by
peeling the bark and exposing the white
inner wood of the branches. 38 Then he
placed the peeled branches in all the
watering troughs, so that they would be
directly in front of the flocks when they
came to drink. When the flocks were in
heat and came to drink, 39 they mated
in front of the branches. And they bore
young that were streaked or speckled
or spotted. 40 Jacob set apart the young
of the flock by themselves, but made the
rest face the streaked and dark-colored
animals that belonged to Laban. Thus

[a] *11* Or *"A troop is coming!"* [b] *11* *Gad* can mean *good fortune* or *a troop.* [c] *13* *Asher* means *happy.* [d] *18* *Issachar* sounds like the Hebrew for *reward.* [e] *20* *Zebulun* probably means *honor.* [f] *24* *Joseph* means *may he add.*

he made separate flocks for himself and did not put them with Laban's animals. 41 Whenever the stronger females were in heat, Jacob would place the branches in the troughs in front of the animals so they would mate near the branches, 42 but if the animals were weak, he would not place them there. So the weak animals went to Laban and the strong ones to Jacob. 43 In this way the man grew exceedingly prosperous and came to own large flocks, and female and male servants, and camels and donkeys.

31 Jacob heard that Laban's sons were saying, "Jacob has taken everything our father owned and has gained all this wealth from what belonged to our father." 2 And Jacob noticed that Laban's attitude toward him was not what it had been.

3 Then the LORD said to Jacob, "Go back to the land of your fathers and to your relatives, and I will be with you."

4 So Jacob sent word to Rachel and Leah to come out to the fields where his flocks were. 5 He said to them, "I see that your father's attitude toward me is not what it was before, but the God of my father has been with me. 6 You know that I've worked for your father with all my strength, 7 yet your father has cheated me by changing my wages ten times. However, God has not allowed him to harm me. 8 If he said, 'The speckled ones will be your wages,' then all the flocks gave birth to speckled young; and if he said, 'The streaked ones will be your wages,' then all the flocks bore streaked young. 9 So God has taken away your father's livestock and has given them to me.

10 "In breeding season I once had a dream in which I looked up and saw that the male goats mating with the flock were streaked, speckled or spotted. 11 The angel of God said to me in the dream, 'Jacob.' I answered, 'Here I am.' 12 And he said, 'Look up and see that all the male goats mating with the flock are streaked, speckled or spotted, for I have seen all that Laban has been doing to you. 13 I am the God of Bethel, where you anointed a pillar and where you made a vow to me. Now leave this land at once and go back to your native land.'"

14 Then Rachel and Leah replied, "Do we still have any share in the inheritance of our father's estate? 15 Does he not regard us as foreigners? Not only has he sold us, but he has used up what was paid for us. 16 Surely all the wealth that God took away from our father belongs to us and our children. So do whatever God has told you."

17 Then Jacob put his children and his wives on camels, 18 and he drove all his livestock ahead of him, along with all the goods he had accumulated in Paddan Aram,[a] to go to his father Isaac in the land of Canaan.

19 When Laban had gone to shear his sheep, Rachel stole her father's household gods. 20 Moreover, Jacob deceived Laban the Aramean by not telling him he was running away. 21 So he fled with all he had, crossed the Euphrates River, and headed for the hill country of Gilead.

22 On the third day Laban was told that Jacob had fled. 23 Taking his relatives with him, he pursued Jacob for seven days and caught up with him in the hill country of Gilead. 24 Then God came to Laban the Aramean in a dream at night and said to him, "Be careful not to say anything to Jacob, either good or bad."

25 Jacob had pitched his tent in the hill country of Gilead when Laban overtook him, and Laban and his relatives camped there too. 26 Then Laban said to Jacob, "What have you done? You've deceived me, and you've carried off my daughters like captives in war. 27 Why did you run off secretly and deceive me? Why didn't you tell me, so I could send you away with joy and singing to the music of timbrels and harps? 28 You didn't even let me kiss my grandchildren and my daughters goodbye. You have done a foolish thing. 29 I have the power to harm you; but last night the God of your father said to me, 'Be careful not to say anything to Jacob, either good or bad.' 30 Now you have gone off because you longed to return to your father's household. But why did you steal my gods?"

31 Jacob answered Laban, "I was afraid, because I thought you would take your daughters away from me by force. 32 But if you find anyone who has your gods, that person shall not live. In the

[a] *18* That is, Northwest Mesopotamia

presence of our relatives, see for yourself whether there is anything of yours here with me; and if so, take it." Now Jacob did not know that Rachel had stolen the gods.
33So Laban went into Jacob's tent and
into Leah's tent and into the tent of the two female servants, but he found nothing. After he came out of Leah's tent, he
entered Rachel's tent. 34Now Rachel had
taken the household gods and put them inside her camel's saddle and was sitting on them. Laban searched through everything in the tent but found nothing.
35Rachel said to her father, "Don't be
angry, my lord, that I cannot stand up in your presence; I'm having my period." So he searched but could not find the household gods.
36Jacob was angry and took Laban to
task. "What is my crime?" he asked Laban. "How have I wronged you that you
hunt me down? 37Now that you have
searched through all my goods, what have you found that belongs to your household? Put it here in front of your relatives and mine, and let them judge between the two of us.
38"I have been with you for twenty
years now. Your sheep and goats have not miscarried, nor have I eaten rams
from your flocks. 39I did not bring you
animals torn by wild beasts; I bore the loss myself. And you demanded payment from me for whatever was stolen
by day or night. 40This was my situation:
The heat consumed me in the daytime and the cold at night, and sleep fled
from my eyes. 41It was like this for the
twenty years I was in your household. I worked for you fourteen years for your two daughters and six years for your flocks, and you changed my wages ten
times. 42If the God of my father, the God
of Abraham and the Fear of Isaac, had not been with me, you would surely have sent me away empty-handed. But God has seen my hardship and the toil of my hands, and last night he rebuked you."
43Laban answered Jacob, "The women
are my daughters, the children are my children, and the flocks are my flocks. All you see is mine. Yet what can I do today about these daughters of mine, or about the children they have borne?
44Come now, let's make a covenant, you
and I, and let it serve as a witness between us."
45So Jacob took a stone and set it up as
a pillar. 46He said to his relatives, "Gather some stones." So they took stones and piled them in a heap, and they ate there
by the heap. 47Laban called it Jegar Sahadutha, and Jacob called it Galeed.[a]
48Laban said, "This heap is a witness
between you and me today." That is
why it was called Galeed. 49It was also
called Mizpah,[b] because he said, "May the LORD keep watch between you and me when we are away from each other.
50If you mistreat my daughters or if you
take any wives besides my daughters, even though no one is with us, remember that God is a witness between you and me."
51Laban also said to Jacob, "Here is
this heap, and here is this pillar I have
set up between you and me. 52This heap
is a witness, and this pillar is a witness, that I will not go past this heap to your side to harm you and that you will not go past this heap and pillar to my side
to harm me. 53May the God of Abraham
and the God of Nahor, the God of their father, judge between us."
So Jacob took an oath in the name of
the Fear of his father Isaac. 54He offered
a sacrifice there in the hill country and invited his relatives to a meal. After they had eaten, they spent the night there.
55Early the next morning Laban kissed
his grandchildren and his daughters and blessed them. Then he left and returned home.[c]

32[d] Jacob also went on his way, and
the angels of God met him. 2When
Jacob saw them, he said, "This is the camp of God!" So he named that place Mahanaim.[e]
3Jacob sent messengers ahead of him
to his brother Esau in the land of Seir,
the country of Edom. 4He instructed
them: "This is what you are to say to my lord Esau: 'Your servant Jacob says, I have been staying with Laban and have
remained there till now. 5I have cattle
and donkeys, sheep and goats, male and female servants. Now I am sending this

[a] 47 The Aramaic *Jegar Sahadutha* and the Hebrew *Galeed* both mean *witness heap.* [b] 49 *Mizpah* means *watchtower.* [c] 55 In Hebrew texts this verse (31:55) is numbered 32:1. [d] In Hebrew texts 32:1-32 is numbered 32:2-33. [e] 2 *Mahanaim* means *two camps.*

message to my lord, that I may find favor
in your eyes.'"
6When the messengers returned to Jacob, they said, "We went to your brother
Esau, and now he is coming to meet you,
and four hundred men are with him."
7In great fear and distress Jacob divided the people who were with him into
two groups,[a] and the flocks and herds
and camels as well. 8He thought, "If
Esau comes and attacks one group,[b] the
group[b] that is left may escape."
9Then Jacob prayed, "O God of my father Abraham, God of my father Isaac,
LORD, you who said to me, 'Go back to
your country and your relatives, and I
will make you prosper,' 10I am unworthy
of all the kindness and faithfulness you
have shown your servant. I had only my
staff when I crossed this Jordan, but now
I have become two camps. 11Save me, I
pray, from the hand of my brother Esau,
for I am afraid he will come and attack
me, and also the mothers with their children. 12But you have said, 'I will surely
make you prosper and will make your
descendants like the sand of the sea,
which cannot be counted.'"
13He spent the night there, and from
what he had with him he selected a gift
for his brother Esau: 14two hundred female goats and twenty male goats, two
hundred ewes and twenty rams, 15thir-
ty female camels with their young, forty
cows and ten bulls, and twenty female
donkeys and ten male donkeys. 16He
put them in the care of his servants, each
herd by itself, and said to his servants,
"Go ahead of me, and keep some space
between the herds."
17He instructed the one in the lead:
"When my brother Esau meets you and
asks, 'Who do you belong to, and where
are you going, and who owns all these
animals in front of you?' 18then you are
to say, 'They belong to your servant Jacob. They are a gift sent to my lord Esau,
and he is coming behind us.'"
19He also instructed the second, the
third and all the others who followed the
herds: "You are to say the same thing to
Esau when you meet him. 20And be sure
to say, 'Your servant Jacob is coming behind us.'" For he thought, "I will pacify
him with these gifts I am sending on
ahead; later, when I see him, perhaps he
will receive me." 21So Jacob's gifts went
on ahead of him, but he himself spent
the night in the camp.
22That night Jacob got up and took his
two wives, his two female servants and
his eleven sons and crossed the ford of
the Jabbok. 23After he had sent them
across the stream, he sent over all his
possessions. 24So Jacob was left alone,
and a man wrestled with him till daybreak. 25When the man saw that he
could not overpower him, he touched
the socket of Jacob's hip so that his hip
was wrenched as he wrestled with the
man. 26Then the man said, "Let me go,
for it is daybreak."
But Jacob replied, "I will not let you go
unless you bless me."
27The man asked him, "What is your
name?"
"Jacob," he answered.
28Then the man said, "Your name will
no longer be Jacob, but Israel,[c] because
you have struggled with God and with
humans and have overcome."
29Jacob said, "Please tell me your
name."
But he replied, "Why do you ask my
name?" Then he blessed him there.
30So Jacob called the place Peniel,[d]
saying, "It is because I saw God face to
face, and yet my life was spared."
31The sun rose above him as he passed
Peniel,[e] and he was limping because of
his hip. 32Therefore to this day the Israelites do not eat the tendon attached to
the socket of the hip, because the socket
of Jacob's hip was touched near the tendon.

33 Jacob looked up and there was
Esau, coming with his four hundred men; so he divided the children
among Leah, Rachel and the two female
servants. 2He put the female servants
and their children in front, Leah and her
children next, and Rachel and Joseph in
the rear. 3He himself went on ahead and
bowed down to the ground seven times
as he approached his brother.
4But Esau ran to meet Jacob and embraced him; he threw his arms around
his neck and kissed him. And they wept.
5Then Esau looked up and saw the wom-

[a] 7 Or *camps* [b] 8 Or *camp* [c] 28 *Israel* probably means *he struggles with God.* [d] 30 *Peniel* means *face of God.* [e] 31 Hebrew *Penuel,* a variant of *Peniel*

en and children. "Who are these with
you?" he asked.

Jacob answered, "They are the children God has graciously given your servant."

6Then the female servants and their
children approached and bowed down.
7Next, Leah and her children came and
bowed down. Last of all came Joseph
and Rachel, and they too bowed down.

8Esau asked, "What's the meaning of
all these flocks and herds I met?"

"To find favor in your eyes, my lord,"
he said.

9But Esau said, "I already have plenty, my brother. Keep what you have for
yourself."

10"No, please!" said Jacob. "If I have
found favor in your eyes, accept this gift
from me. For to see your face is like seeing the face of God, now that you have
received me favorably. 11Please accept
the present that was brought to you, for
God has been gracious to me and I have
all I need." And because Jacob insisted,
Esau accepted it.

12Then Esau said, "Let us be on our
way; I'll accompany you."

13But Jacob said to him, "My lord
knows that the children are tender and
that I must care for the ewes and cows
that are nursing their young. If they are
driven hard just one day, all the animals
will die. 14So let my lord go on ahead of
his servant, while I move along slowly at
the pace of the flocks and herds before
me and the pace of the children, until I
come to my lord in Seir."

15Esau said, "Then let me leave some
of my men with you."

"But why do that?" Jacob asked. "Just
let me find favor in the eyes of my lord."

16So that day Esau started on his way
back to Seir. 17Jacob, however, went
to Sukkoth, where he built a place for
himself and made shelters for his livestock. That is why the place is called
Sukkoth.[a]

18After Jacob came from Paddan
Aram,[b] he arrived safely at the city of
Shechem in Canaan and camped within
sight of the city. 19For a hundred pieces of silver,[c] he bought from the sons of
Hamor, the father of Shechem, the plot
of ground where he pitched his tent.
20There he set up an altar and called it
El Elohe Israel.[d]

34 Now Dinah, the daughter Leah had
borne to Jacob, went out to visit the
women of the land. 2When Shechem son
of Hamor the Hivite, the ruler of that
area, saw her, he took her and raped her.
3His heart was drawn to Dinah daughter
of Jacob; he loved the young woman and
spoke tenderly to her. 4And Shechem
said to his father Hamor, "Get me this
girl as my wife."

5When Jacob heard that his daughter
Dinah had been defiled, his sons were
in the fields with his livestock; so he did
nothing about it until they came home.

6Then Shechem's father Hamor went
out to talk with Jacob. 7Meanwhile, Jacob's sons had come in from the fields as
soon as they heard what had happened.
They were shocked and furious, because
Shechem had done an outrageous thing
in[e] Israel by sleeping with Jacob's daughter — a thing that should not be done.

8But Hamor said to them, "My son
Shechem has his heart set on your
daughter. Please give her to him as his
wife. 9Intermarry with us; give us your
daughters and take our daughters for
yourselves. 10You can settle among us;
the land is open to you. Live in it, trade[f]
in it, and acquire property in it."

11Then Shechem said to Dinah's father
and brothers, "Let me find favor in your
eyes, and I will give you whatever you
ask. 12Make the price for the bride and
the gift I am to bring as great as you like,
and I'll pay whatever you ask me. Only
give me the young woman as my wife."

13Because their sister Dinah had been
defiled, Jacob's sons replied deceitfully
as they spoke to Shechem and his father
Hamor. 14They said to them, "We can't
do such a thing; we can't give our sister
to a man who is not circumcised. That
would be a disgrace to us. 15We will enter into an agreement with you on one
condition only: that you become like us
by circumcising all your males. 16Then
we will give you our daughters and take
your daughters for ourselves. We'll settle among you and become one people
with you. 17But if you will not agree to

[a] *17 Sukkoth* means *shelters.* [b] *18* That is, Northwest Mesopotamia [c] *19* Hebrew *hundred kesitahs;* a kesitah was a unit of money of unknown weight and value. [d] *20 El Elohe Israel* can mean *El is the God of Israel* or *mighty is the God of Israel.* [e] *7* Or *against* [f] *10* Or *move about freely;* also in verse 21

be circumcised, we'll take our sister and go."

18Their proposal seemed good to Hamor and his son Shechem. 19The young man, who was the most honored of all his father's family, lost no time in doing what they said, because he was delighted with Jacob's daughter. 20So Hamor and his son Shechem went to the gate of their city to speak to the men of their city. 21"These men are friendly toward us," they said. "Let them live in our land and trade in it; the land has plenty of room for them. We can marry their daughters and they can marry ours. 22But the men will agree to live with us as one people only on the condition that our males be circumcised, as they themselves are. 23Won't their livestock, their property and all their other animals become ours? So let us agree to their terms, and they will settle among us."

24All the men who went out of the city gate agreed with Hamor and his son Shechem, and every male in the city was circumcised.

25Three days later, while all of them were still in pain, two of Jacob's sons, Simeon and Levi, Dinah's brothers, took their swords and attacked the unsuspecting city, killing every male. 26They put Hamor and his son Shechem to the sword and took Dinah from Shechem's house and left. 27The sons of Jacob came upon the dead bodies and looted the city where[a] their sister had been defiled. 28They seized their flocks and herds and donkeys and everything else of theirs in the city and out in the fields. 29They carried off all their wealth and all their women and children, taking as plunder everything in the houses.

30Then Jacob said to Simeon and Levi, "You have brought trouble on me by making me obnoxious to the Canaanites and Perizzites, the people living in this land. We are few in number, and if they join forces against me and attack me, I and my household will be destroyed."

31But they replied, "Should he have treated our sister like a prostitute?"

35 Then God said to Jacob, "Go up to Bethel and settle there, and build an altar there to God, who appeared to you when you were fleeing from your brother Esau."

2So Jacob said to his household and to all who were with him, "Get rid of the foreign gods you have with you, and purify yourselves and change your clothes. 3Then come, let us go up to Bethel, where I will build an altar to God, who answered me in the day of my distress and who has been with me wherever I have gone." 4So they gave Jacob all the foreign gods they had and the rings in their ears, and Jacob buried them under the oak at Shechem. 5Then they set out, and the terror of God fell on the towns all around them so that no one pursued them.

6Jacob and all the people with him came to Luz (that is, Bethel) in the land of Canaan. 7There he built an altar, and he called the place El Bethel,[b] because it was there that God revealed himself to him when he was fleeing from his brother.

8Now Deborah, Rebekah's nurse, died and was buried under the oak outside Bethel. So it was named Allon Bakuth.[c]

9After Jacob returned from Paddan Aram,[d] God appeared to him again and blessed him. 10God said to him, "Your name is Jacob,[e] but you will no longer be called Jacob; your name will be Israel.[f]" So he named him Israel.

11And God said to him, "I am God Almighty[g]; be fruitful and increase in number. A nation and a community of nations will come from you, and kings will be among your descendants. 12The land I gave to Abraham and Isaac I also give to you, and I will give this land to your descendants after you." 13Then God went up from him at the place where he had talked with him.

14Jacob set up a stone pillar at the place where God had talked with him, and he poured out a drink offering on it; he also poured oil on it. 15Jacob called the place where God had talked with him Bethel.[h]

16Then they moved on from Bethel. While they were still some distance from Ephrath, Rachel began to give

[a] 27 Or *because* [b] 7 *El Bethel* means *God of Bethel.* [c] 8 *Allon Bakuth* means *oak of weeping.* [d] 9 That is, Northwest Mesopotamia; also in verse 26 [e] 10 *Jacob* means *he grasps the heel,* a Hebrew idiom for *he deceives.* [f] 10 *Israel* probably means *he struggles with God.* [g] 11 Hebrew *El-Shaddai* [h] 15 *Bethel* means *house of God.*

birth and had great difficulty. 17And as
she was having great difficulty in childbirth, the midwife said to her, "Don't despair, for you have another son." 18As
she breathed her last—for she was dying—she named her son Ben-Oni.[a] But
his father named him Benjamin.[b]
19So Rachel died and was buried on
the way to Ephrath (that is, Bethlehem).
20Over her tomb Jacob set up a pillar,
and to this day that pillar marks Rachel's tomb.
21Israel moved on again and pitched
his tent beyond Migdal Eder. 22While
Israel was living in that region, Reuben went in and slept with his father's concubine Bilhah, and Israel heard of it.

Jacob had twelve sons:
23The sons of Leah:
Reuben the firstborn of Jacob,
Simeon, Levi, Judah, Issachar and
Zebulun.
24The sons of Rachel:
Joseph and Benjamin.
25The sons of Rachel's servant Bilhah:
Dan and Naphtali.
26The sons of Leah's servant Zilpah:
Gad and Asher.
These were the sons of Jacob, who were born to him in Paddan Aram.

27Jacob came home to his father Isaac
in Mamre, near Kiriath Arba (that is, Hebron), where Abraham and Isaac
had stayed. 28Isaac lived a hundred and
eighty years. 29Then he breathed his last
and died and was gathered to his people, old and full of years. And his sons Esau and Jacob buried him.

36
This is the account of the family line of Esau (that is, Edom).

2Esau took his wives from the women of Canaan: Adah daughter of Elon the Hittite, and Oholibamah daughter of Anah and granddaughter of Zibeon the Hivite— 3also
Basemath daughter of Ishmael and sister of Nebaioth.
4Adah bore Eliphaz to Esau, Basemath bore Reuel, 5and Oholibamah
bore Jeush, Jalam and Korah. These were the sons of Esau, who were born to him in Canaan.

6Esau took his wives and sons and daughters and all the members of his household, as well as his livestock and all his other animals and all the goods he had acquired in Canaan, and moved to a land some distance from his brother Jacob. 7Their
possessions were too great for them to remain together; the land where they were staying could not support them both because of their livestock. 8So Esau (that is, Edom) set-
tled in the hill country of Seir.

9This is the account of the family line of Esau the father of the Edomites in the hill country of Seir.

10These are the names of Esau's sons:
Eliphaz, the son of Esau's wife Adah, and Reuel, the son of Esau's wife Basemath.
11The sons of Eliphaz:
Teman, Omar, Zepho, Gatam and Kenaz.
12Esau's son Eliphaz also had a concubine named Timna, who bore him Amalek. These were grandsons of Esau's wife Adah.
13The sons of Reuel:
Nahath, Zerah, Shammah and Mizzah. These were grandsons of Esau's wife Basemath.
14The sons of Esau's wife Oholibamah daughter of Anah and granddaughter of Zibeon, whom she bore to Esau:
Jeush, Jalam and Korah.

15These were the chiefs among Esau's descendants:
The sons of Eliphaz the firstborn of Esau:
Chiefs Teman, Omar, Zepho, Kenaz, 16Korah,[c] Gatam and Amalek. These were the chiefs descended from Eliphaz in Edom; they were grandsons of Adah.
17The sons of Esau's son Reuel:
Chiefs Nahath, Zerah, Shammah and Mizzah. These were the chiefs descended from Reuel in Edom; they were grandsons of Esau's wife Basemath.
18The sons of Esau's wife Oholibamah:

[a] *18 Ben-Oni* means *son of my trouble.* [b] *18 Benjamin* means *son of my right hand.* [c] *16* Masoretic Text; Samaritan Pentateuch (also verse 11 and 1 Chron. 1:36) does not have *Korah.*

Chiefs Jeush, Jalam and Korah. These were the chiefs descended from Esau's wife Oholibamah daughter of Anah.

19 These were the sons of Esau (that is, Edom), and these were their chiefs.

20 These were the sons of Seir the Horite, who were living in the region:

Lotan, Shobal, Zibeon, Anah,
21 Dishon, Ezer and Dishan. These sons of Seir in Edom were Horite chiefs.

22 The sons of Lotan:
Hori and Homam.[a] Timna was Lotan's sister.

23 The sons of Shobal:
Alvan, Manahath, Ebal, Shepho and Onam.

24 The sons of Zibeon:
Aiah and Anah. This is the Anah who discovered the hot springs[b] in the desert while he was grazing the donkeys of his father Zibeon.

25 The children of Anah:
Dishon and Oholibamah daughter of Anah.

26 The sons of Dishon[c]:
Hemdan, Eshban, Ithran and Keran.

27 The sons of Ezer:
Bilhan, Zaavan and Akan.

28 The sons of Dishan:
Uz and Aran.

29 These were the Horite chiefs:
Lotan, Shobal, Zibeon, Anah,
30 Dishon, Ezer and Dishan. These were the Horite chiefs, according to their divisions, in the land of Seir.

31 These were the kings who reigned in Edom before any Israelite king reigned:

32 Bela son of Beor became king of Edom. His city was named Dinhabah.

33 When Bela died, Jobab son of Zerah from Bozrah succeeded him as king.

34 When Jobab died, Husham from the land of the Temanites succeeded him as king.

35 When Husham died, Hadad son of Bedad, who defeated Midian in the country of Moab, succeeded him as king. His city was named Avith.

36 When Hadad died, Samlah from Masrekah succeeded him as king.

37 When Samlah died, Shaul from Rehoboth on the river succeeded him as king.

38 When Shaul died, Baal-Hanan son of Akbor succeeded him as king.

39 When Baal-Hanan son of Akbor died, Hadad[d] succeeded him as king. His city was named Pau, and his wife's name was Mehetabel daughter of Matred, the daughter of Me-Zahab.

40 These were the chiefs descended from Esau, by name, according to their clans and regions:

Timna, Alvah, Jetheth, 41 Oholibamah, Elah, Pinon, 42 Kenaz, Teman, Mibzar, 43 Magdiel and Iram. These were the chiefs of Edom, according to their settlements in the land they occupied.

This is the family line of Esau, the father of the Edomites.

37 Jacob lived in the land where his father had stayed, the land of Canaan.

2 This is the account of Jacob's family line.

Joseph, a young man of seventeen, was tending the flocks with his brothers, the sons of Bilhah and the sons of Zilpah, his father's wives, and he brought their father a bad report about them.

3 Now Israel loved Joseph more than any of his other sons, because he had been born to him in his old age; and he made an ornate[e] robe for him.
4 When his brothers saw that their father loved him more than any of them, they hated him and could not speak a kind word to him.

5 Joseph had a dream, and when he told it to his brothers, they hated him all the more.
6 He said to them, "Listen to this

[a] *22* Hebrew *Hemam,* a variant of *Homam* (see 1 Chron. 1:39) [b] *24* Vulgate; Syriac *discovered water;* the meaning of the Hebrew for this word is uncertain. [c] *26* Hebrew *Dishan,* a variant of *Dishon* [d] *39* Many manuscripts of the Masoretic Text, Samaritan Pentateuch and Syriac (see also 1 Chron. 1:50); most manuscripts of the Masoretic Text *Hadar* [e] *3* The meaning of the Hebrew for this word is uncertain; also in verses 23 and 32.

dream I had: 7We were binding sheaves
of grain out in the field when suddenly
my sheaf rose and stood upright, while
your sheaves gathered around mine and
bowed down to it."
8His brothers said to him, "Do you
intend to reign over us? Will you actually rule us?" And they hated him all the
more because of his dream and what he
had said.
9Then he had another dream, and he
told it to his brothers. "Listen," he said,
"I had another dream, and this time the
sun and moon and eleven stars were
bowing down to me."
10When he told his father as well as
his brothers, his father rebuked him
and said, "What is this dream you had?
Will your mother and I and your brothers actually come and bow down to the
ground before you?" 11His brothers were
jealous of him, but his father kept the
matter in mind.
12Now his brothers had gone to graze
their father's flocks near Shechem, 13and
Israel said to Joseph, "As you know, your
brothers are grazing the flocks near Shechem. Come, I am going to send you to
them."
"Very well," he replied.
14So he said to him, "Go and see if
all is well with your brothers and with
the flocks, and bring word back to me."
Then he sent him off from the Valley of
Hebron.
When Joseph arrived at Shechem, 15a
man found him wandering around in
the fields and asked him, "What are you
looking for?"
16He replied, "I'm looking for my
brothers. Can you tell me where they are
grazing their flocks?"
17"They have moved on from here,"
the man answered. "I heard them say,
'Let's go to Dothan.'"
So Joseph went after his brothers and
found them near Dothan. 18But they
saw him in the distance, and before he
reached them, they plotted to kill him.
19"Here comes that dreamer!" they
said to each other. 20"Come now, let's
kill him and throw him into one of these
cisterns and say that a ferocious animal devoured him. Then we'll see what
comes of his dreams."
21When Reuben heard this, he tried
to rescue him from their hands. "Let's
not take his life," he said. 22"Don't shed
any blood. Throw him into this cistern
here in the wilderness, but don't lay a
hand on him." Reuben said this to rescue him from them and take him back
to his father.
23So when Joseph came to his brothers, they stripped him of his robe—the
ornate robe he was wearing— 24and
they took him and threw him into the
cistern. The cistern was empty; there
was no water in it.
25As they sat down to eat their meal,
they looked up and saw a caravan of
Ishmaelites coming from Gilead. Their
camels were loaded with spices, balm
and myrrh, and they were on their way
to take them down to Egypt.
26Judah said to his brothers, "What
will we gain if we kill our brother and
cover up his blood? 27Come, let's sell
him to the Ishmaelites and not lay our
hands on him; after all, he is our brother, our own flesh and blood." His brothers agreed.
28So when the Midianite merchants
came by, his brothers pulled Joseph up
out of the cistern and sold him for twenty
shekels[a] of silver to the Ishmaelites, who
took him to Egypt.
29When Reuben returned to the cistern and saw that Joseph was not there,
he tore his clothes. 30He went back to his
brothers and said, "The boy isn't there!
Where can I turn now?"
31Then they got Joseph's robe, slaughtered a goat and dipped the robe in the
blood. 32They took the ornate robe back
to their father and said, "We found this.
Examine it to see whether it is your son's
robe."
33He recognized it and said, "It is my
son's robe! Some ferocious animal has
devoured him. Joseph has surely been
torn to pieces."
34Then Jacob tore his clothes, put
on sackcloth and mourned for his son
many days. 35All his sons and daughters
came to comfort him, but he refused to
be comforted. "No," he said, "I will continue to mourn until I join my son in the
grave." So his father wept for him.
36Meanwhile, the Midianites[b] sold Jo-

[a] *28* That is, about 8 ounces or about 230 grams [b] *36* Samaritan Pentateuch, Septuagint, Vulgate and Syriac (see also verse 28); Masoretic Text *Medanites*

seph in Egypt to Potiphar, one of Pharaoh's officials, the captain of the guard.

38 At that time, Judah left his brothers and went down to stay with a man of Adullam named Hirah. 2There Judah met the daughter of a Canaanite man named Shua. He married her and made love to her; 3she became pregnant and gave birth to a son, who was named Er. 4She conceived again and gave birth to a son and named him Onan. 5She gave birth to still another son and named him Shelah. It was at Kezib that she gave birth to him.

6Judah got a wife for Er, his firstborn, and her name was Tamar. 7But Er, Judah's firstborn, was wicked in the LORD's sight; so the LORD put him to death.

8Then Judah said to Onan, "Sleep with your brother's wife and fulfill your duty to her as a brother-in-law to raise up offspring for your brother." 9But Onan knew that the child would not be his; so whenever he slept with his brother's wife, he spilled his semen on the ground to keep from providing offspring for his brother. 10What he did was wicked in the LORD's sight; so the LORD put him to death also.

11Judah then said to his daughter-in-law Tamar, "Live as a widow in your father's household until my son Shelah grows up." For he thought, "He may die too, just like his brothers." So Tamar went to live in her father's household.

12After a long time Judah's wife, the daughter of Shua, died. When Judah had recovered from his grief, he went up to Timnah, to the men who were shearing his sheep, and his friend Hirah the Adullamite went with him.

13When Tamar was told, "Your father-in-law is on his way to Timnah to shear his sheep," 14she took off her widow's clothes, covered herself with a veil to disguise herself, and then sat down at the entrance to Enaim, which is on the road to Timnah. For she saw that, though Shelah had now grown up, she had not been given to him as his wife.

15When Judah saw her, he thought she was a prostitute, for she had covered her face. 16Not realizing that she was his daughter-in-law, he went over to her by the roadside and said, "Come now, let me sleep with you."

"And what will you give me to sleep with you?" she asked.

17"I'll send you a young goat from my flock," he said.

"Will you give me something as a pledge until you send it?" she asked.

18He said, "What pledge should I give you?"

"Your seal and its cord, and the staff in your hand," she answered. So he gave them to her and slept with her, and she became pregnant by him. 19After she left, she took off her veil and put on her widow's clothes again.

20Meanwhile Judah sent the young goat by his friend the Adullamite in order to get his pledge back from the woman, but he did not find her. 21He asked the men who lived there, "Where is the shrine prostitute who was beside the road at Enaim?"

"There hasn't been any shrine prostitute here," they said.

22So he went back to Judah and said, "I didn't find her. Besides, the men who lived there said, 'There hasn't been any shrine prostitute here.' "

23Then Judah said, "Let her keep what she has, or we will become a laughingstock. After all, I did send her this young goat, but you didn't find her."

24About three months later Judah was told, "Your daughter-in-law Tamar is guilty of prostitution, and as a result she is now pregnant."

Judah said, "Bring her out and have her burned to death!"

25As she was being brought out, she sent a message to her father-in-law. "I am pregnant by the man who owns these," she said. And she added, "See if you recognize whose seal and cord and staff these are."

26Judah recognized them and said, "She is more righteous than I, since I wouldn't give her to my son Shelah." And he did not sleep with her again.

27When the time came for her to give birth, there were twin boys in her womb. 28As she was giving birth, one of them put out his hand; so the midwife took a scarlet thread and tied it on his wrist and said, "This one came out first." 29But when he drew back his hand, his brother came out, and she said, "So this is how you have broken out!" And he was

named Perez.[a] 30 Then his brother, who
had the scarlet thread on his wrist, came
out. And he was named Zerah.[b]

39 Now Joseph had been taken down
to Egypt. Potiphar, an Egyptian
who was one of Pharaoh's officials, the
captain of the guard, bought him from
the Ishmaelites who had taken him
there.

2 The LORD was with Joseph so that he
prospered, and he lived in the house of
his Egyptian master. 3 When his master saw that the LORD was with him and
that the LORD gave him success in everything he did, 4 Joseph found favor in
his eyes and became his attendant. Potiphar put him in charge of his household,
and he entrusted to his care everything
he owned. 5 From the time he put him in
charge of his household and of all that he
owned, the LORD blessed the household
of the Egyptian because of Joseph. The
blessing of the LORD was on everything
Potiphar had, both in the house and in
the field. 6 So Potiphar left everything
he had in Joseph's care; with Joseph in
charge, he did not concern himself with
anything except the food he ate.

Now Joseph was well-built and handsome, 7 and after a while his master's
wife took notice of Joseph and said,
"Come to bed with me!"

8 But he refused. "With me in charge,"
he told her, "my master does not concern
himself with anything in the house; everything he owns he has entrusted to
my care. 9 No one is greater in this house
than I am. My master has withheld nothing from me except you, because you
are his wife. How then could I do such
a wicked thing and sin against God?"
10 And though she spoke to Joseph day
after day, he refused to go to bed with
her or even be with her.

11 One day he went into the house to
attend to his duties, and none of the
household servants was inside. 12 She
caught him by his cloak and said, "Come
to bed with me!" But he left his cloak in
her hand and ran out of the house.

13 When she saw that he had left his
cloak in her hand and had run out of
the house, 14 she called her household
servants. "Look," she said to them, "this
Hebrew has been brought to us to make
sport of us! He came in here to sleep with
me, but I screamed. 15 When he heard me
scream for help, he left his cloak beside
me and ran out of the house."

16 She kept his cloak beside her until
his master came home. 17 Then she told
him this story: "That Hebrew slave you
brought us came to me to make sport of
me. 18 But as soon as I screamed for help,
he left his cloak beside me and ran out
of the house."

19 When his master heard the story his
wife told him, saying, "This is how your
slave treated me," he burned with anger. 20 Joseph's master took him and put
him in prison, the place where the king's
prisoners were confined.

But while Joseph was there in the prison, 21 the LORD was with him; he showed
him kindness and granted him favor in
the eyes of the prison warden. 22 So the
warden put Joseph in charge of all those
held in the prison, and he was made responsible for all that was done there.
23 The warden paid no attention to anything under Joseph's care, because the
LORD was with Joseph and gave him
success in whatever he did.

40 Some time later, the cupbearer
and the baker of the king of Egypt
offended their master, the king of Egypt.
2 Pharaoh was angry with his two officials, the chief cupbearer and the chief
baker, 3 and put them in custody in the
house of the captain of the guard, in the
same prison where Joseph was confined.
4 The captain of the guard assigned them
to Joseph, and he attended them.

After they had been in custody for
some time, 5 each of the two men — the
cupbearer and the baker of the king of
Egypt, who were being held in prison —
had a dream the same night, and each
dream had a meaning of its own.

6 When Joseph came to them the next
morning, he saw that they were dejected. 7 So he asked Pharaoh's officials who
were in custody with him in his master's
house, "Why do you look so sad today?"

8 "We both had dreams," they answered, "but there is no one to interpret
them."

Then Joseph said to them, "Do not
interpretations belong to God? Tell me
your dreams."

[a] 29 *Perez* means *breaking out.* [b] 30 *Zerah* can mean *scarlet* or *brightness.*

9So the chief cupbearer told Joseph his dream. He said to him, "In my dream I saw a vine in front of me, 10and on the vine were three branches. As soon as it budded, it blossomed, and its clusters ripened into grapes. 11Pharaoh's cup was in my hand, and I took the grapes, squeezed them into Pharaoh's cup and put the cup in his hand."

12"This is what it means," Joseph said to him. "The three branches are three days. 13Within three days Pharaoh will lift up your head and restore you to your position, and you will put Pharaoh's cup in his hand, just as you used to do when you were his cupbearer. 14But when all goes well with you, remember me and show me kindness; mention me to Pharaoh and get me out of this prison. 15I was forcibly carried off from the land of the Hebrews, and even here I have done nothing to deserve being put in a dungeon."

16When the chief baker saw that Joseph had given a favorable interpretation, he said to Joseph, "I too had a dream: On my head were three baskets of bread.[a] 17In the top basket were all kinds of baked goods for Pharaoh, but the birds were eating them out of the basket on my head."

18"This is what it means," Joseph said. "The three baskets are three days. 19Within three days Pharaoh will lift off your head and impale your body on a pole. And the birds will eat away your flesh."

20Now the third day was Pharaoh's birthday, and he gave a feast for all his officials. He lifted up the heads of the chief cupbearer and the chief baker in the presence of his officials: 21He restored the chief cupbearer to his position, so that he once again put the cup into Pharaoh's hand — 22but he impaled the chief baker, just as Joseph had said to them in his interpretation.

23The chief cupbearer, however, did not remember Joseph; he forgot him.

41 When two full years had passed, Pharaoh had a dream: He was standing by the Nile, 2when out of the river there came up seven cows, sleek and fat, and they grazed among the reeds. 3After them, seven other cows, ugly and gaunt, came up out of the Nile and stood beside those on the riverbank. 4And the cows that were ugly and gaunt ate up the seven sleek, fat cows. Then Pharaoh woke up.

5He fell asleep again and had a second dream: Seven heads of grain, healthy and good, were growing on a single stalk. 6After them, seven other heads of grain sprouted — thin and scorched by the east wind. 7The thin heads of grain swallowed up the seven healthy, full heads. Then Pharaoh woke up; it had been a dream.

8In the morning his mind was troubled, so he sent for all the magicians and wise men of Egypt. Pharaoh told them his dreams, but no one could interpret them for him.

9Then the chief cupbearer said to Pharaoh, "Today I am reminded of my shortcomings. 10Pharaoh was once angry with his servants, and he imprisoned me and the chief baker in the house of the captain of the guard. 11Each of us had a dream the same night, and each dream had a meaning of its own. 12Now a young Hebrew was there with us, a servant of the captain of the guard. We told him our dreams, and he interpreted them for us, giving each man the interpretation of his dream. 13And things turned out exactly as he interpreted them to us: I was restored to my position, and the other man was impaled."

14So Pharaoh sent for Joseph, and he was quickly brought from the dungeon. When he had shaved and changed his clothes, he came before Pharaoh.

15Pharaoh said to Joseph, "I had a dream, and no one can interpret it. But I have heard it said of you that when you hear a dream you can interpret it."

16"I cannot do it," Joseph replied to Pharaoh, "but God will give Pharaoh the answer he desires."

17Then Pharaoh said to Joseph, "In my dream I was standing on the bank of the Nile, 18when out of the river there came up seven cows, fat and sleek, and they grazed among the reeds. 19After them, seven other cows came up — scrawny and very ugly and lean. I had never seen such ugly cows in all the land of Egypt. 20The lean, ugly cows ate up the seven

a 16 Or *three wicker baskets*

fat cows that came up first. 21 But even after they ate them, no one could tell that they had done so; they looked just as ugly as before. Then I woke up.

22 "In my dream I saw seven heads of grain, full and good, growing on a single stalk. 23 After them, seven other heads sprouted—withered and thin and scorched by the east wind. 24 The thin heads of grain swallowed up the seven good heads. I told this to the magicians, but none of them could explain it to me."

25 Then Joseph said to Pharaoh, "The dreams of Pharaoh are one and the same. God has revealed to Pharaoh what he is about to do. 26 The seven good cows are seven years, and the seven good heads of grain are seven years; it is one and the same dream. 27 The seven lean, ugly cows that came up afterward are seven years, and so are the seven worthless heads of grain scorched by the east wind: They are seven years of famine.

28 "It is just as I said to Pharaoh: God has shown Pharaoh what he is about to do. 29 Seven years of great abundance are coming throughout the land of Egypt, 30 but seven years of famine will follow them. Then all the abundance in Egypt will be forgotten, and the famine will ravage the land. 31 The abundance in the land will not be remembered, because the famine that follows it will be so severe. 32 The reason the dream was given to Pharaoh in two forms is that the matter has been firmly decided by God, and God will do it soon.

33 "And now let Pharaoh look for a discerning and wise man and put him in charge of the land of Egypt. 34 Let Pharaoh appoint commissioners over the land to take a fifth of the harvest of Egypt during the seven years of abundance. 35 They should collect all the food of these good years that are coming and store up the grain under the authority of Pharaoh, to be kept in the cities for food. 36 This food should be held in reserve for the country, to be used during the seven years of famine that will come upon Egypt, so that the country may not be ruined by the famine."

37 The plan seemed good to Pharaoh and to all his officials. 38 So Pharaoh asked them, "Can we find anyone like this man, one in whom is the spirit of God[a]?"

39 Then Pharaoh said to Joseph, "Since God has made all this known to you, there is no one so discerning and wise as you. 40 You shall be in charge of my palace, and all my people are to submit to your orders. Only with respect to the throne will I be greater than you."

41 So Pharaoh said to Joseph, "I hereby put you in charge of the whole land of Egypt." 42 Then Pharaoh took his signet ring from his finger and put it on Joseph's finger. He dressed him in robes of fine linen and put a gold chain around his neck. 43 He had him ride in a chariot as his second-in-command,[b] and people shouted before him, "Make way[c]!" Thus he put him in charge of the whole land of Egypt.

44 Then Pharaoh said to Joseph, "I am Pharaoh, but without your word no one will lift hand or foot in all Egypt." 45 Pharaoh gave Joseph the name Zaphenath-Paneah and gave him Asenath daughter of Potiphera, priest of On,[d] to be his wife. And Joseph went throughout the land of Egypt.

46 Joseph was thirty years old when he entered the service of Pharaoh king of Egypt. And Joseph went out from Pharaoh's presence and traveled throughout Egypt. 47 During the seven years of abundance the land produced plentifully. 48 Joseph collected all the food produced in those seven years of abundance in Egypt and stored it in the cities. In each city he put the food grown in the fields surrounding it. 49 Joseph stored up huge quantities of grain, like the sand of the sea; it was so much that he stopped keeping records because it was beyond measure.

50 Before the years of famine came, two sons were born to Joseph by Asenath daughter of Potiphera, priest of On. 51 Joseph named his firstborn Manasseh[e] and said, "It is because God has made me forget all my trouble and all my father's household." 52 The second son he named Ephraim[f] and said, "It is because God has made me fruitful in the land of my suffering."

[a] 38 Or *of the gods* [b] 43 Or *in the chariot of his second-in-command*; or *in his second chariot* [c] 43 Or *Bow down* [d] 45 That is, Heliopolis; also in verse 50 [e] 51 *Manasseh* sounds like and may be derived from the Hebrew for *forget.* [f] 52 *Ephraim* sounds like the Hebrew for *twice fruitful.*

53 The seven years of abundance in
Egypt came to an end, 54 and the seven
years of famine began, just as Joseph
had said. There was famine in all the
other lands, but in the whole land of
Egypt there was food. 55 When all Egypt
began to feel the famine, the people
cried to Pharaoh for food. Then Pharaoh
told all the Egyptians, "Go to Joseph and
do what he tells you."

56 When the famine had spread over
the whole country, Joseph opened all
the storehouses and sold grain to the
Egyptians, for the famine was severe
throughout Egypt. 57 And all the world
came to Egypt to buy grain from Joseph,
because the famine was severe everywhere.

42 When Jacob learned that there was
grain in Egypt, he said to his sons,
"Why do you just keep looking at each
other?" 2 He continued, "I have heard
that there is grain in Egypt. Go down
there and buy some for us, so that we
may live and not die."

3 Then ten of Joseph's brothers went
down to buy grain from Egypt. 4 But Jacob did not send Benjamin, Joseph's
brother, with the others, because he was
afraid that harm might come to him. 5 So
Israel's sons were among those who went
to buy grain, for there was famine in the
land of Canaan also.

6 Now Joseph was the governor of the
land, the person who sold grain to all
its people. So when Joseph's brothers
arrived, they bowed down to him with
their faces to the ground. 7 As soon as
Joseph saw his brothers, he recognized
them, but he pretended to be a stranger
and spoke harshly to them. "Where do
you come from?" he asked.

"From the land of Canaan," they replied, "to buy food."

8 Although Joseph recognized his
brothers, they did not recognize him.
9 Then he remembered his dreams about
them and said to them, "You are spies!
You have come to see where our land is
unprotected."

10 "No, my lord," they answered. "Your
servants have come to buy food. 11 We
are all the sons of one man. Your servants are honest men, not spies."

12 "No!" he said to them. "You have
come to see where our land is unprotected."

13 But they replied, "Your servants
were twelve brothers, the sons of one
man, who lives in the land of Canaan.
The youngest is now with our father, and
one is no more."

14 Joseph said to them, "It is just as I
told you: You are spies! 15 And this is how
you will be tested: As surely as Pharaoh
lives, you will not leave this place unless your youngest brother comes here.
16 Send one of your number to get your
brother; the rest of you will be kept in
prison, so that your words may be tested
to see if you are telling the truth. If you
are not, then as surely as Pharaoh lives,
you are spies!" 17 And he put them all in
custody for three days.

18 On the third day, Joseph said to
them, "Do this and you will live, for I
fear God: 19 If you are honest men, let
one of your brothers stay here in prison,
while the rest of you go and take grain
back for your starving households. 20 But
you must bring your youngest brother to
me, so that your words may be verified
and that you may not die." This they proceeded to do.

21 They said to one another, "Surely
we are being punished because of our
brother. We saw how distressed he was
when he pleaded with us for his life, but
we would not listen; that's why this distress has come on us."

22 Reuben replied, "Didn't I tell you not
to sin against the boy? But you wouldn't
listen! Now we must give an accounting
for his blood." 23 They did not realize that
Joseph could understand them, since he
was using an interpreter.

24 He turned away from them and began to weep, but then came back and
spoke to them again. He had Simeon
taken from them and bound before their
eyes.

25 Joseph gave orders to fill their bags
with grain, to put each man's silver back
in his sack, and to give them provisions
for their journey. After this was done for
them, 26 they loaded their grain on their
donkeys and left.

27 At the place where they stopped for
the night one of them opened his sack to
get feed for his donkey, and he saw his
silver in the mouth of his sack. 28 "My
silver has been returned," he said to his
brothers. "Here it is in my sack."

Their hearts sank and they turned to

each other trembling and said, "What is
this that God has done to us?"
29When they came to their father Jacob in the land of Canaan, they told him
all that had happened to them. They
said, 30"The man who is lord over the
land spoke harshly to us and treated us
as though we were spying on the land.
31But we said to him, 'We are honest
men; we are not spies. 32We were twelve
brothers, sons of one father. One is no
more, and the youngest is now with our
father in Canaan.'
33"Then the man who is lord over the
land said to us, 'This is how I will know
whether you are honest men: Leave one
of your brothers here with me, and take
food for your starving households and
go. 34But bring your youngest brother to
me so I will know that you are not spies
but honest men. Then I will give your
brother back to you, and you can trade[a]
in the land.'"
35As they were emptying their sacks,
there in each man's sack was his pouch
of silver! When they and their father saw
the money pouches, they were frightened. 36Their father Jacob said to them,
"You have deprived me of my children.
Joseph is no more and Simeon is no
more, and now you want to take Benjamin. Everything is against me!"
37Then Reuben said to his father, "You
may put both of my sons to death if I do
not bring him back to you. Entrust him
to my care, and I will bring him back."
38But Jacob said, "My son will not go
down there with you; his brother is dead
and he is the only one left. If harm comes
to him on the journey you are taking,
you will bring my gray head down to the
grave in sorrow."

43 Now the famine was still severe in
the land. 2So when they had eat-
en all the grain they had brought from
Egypt, their father said to them, "Go
back and buy us a little more food."
3But Judah said to him, "The man
warned us solemnly, 'You will not see
my face again unless your brother is
with you.' 4If you will send our brother along with us, we will go down and
buy food for you. 5But if you will not
send him, we will not go down, because
the man said to us, 'You will not see my
face again unless your brother is with
you.'"
6Israel asked, "Why did you bring this
trouble on me by telling the man you had
another brother?"
7They replied, "The man questioned
us closely about ourselves and our family. 'Is your father still living?' he asked
us. 'Do you have another brother?' We
simply answered his questions. How
were we to know he would say, 'Bring
your brother down here'?"
8Then Judah said to Israel his father,
"Send the boy along with me and we will
go at once, so that we and you and our
children may live and not die. 9I myself
will guarantee his safety; you can hold
me personally responsible for him. If I
do not bring him back to you and set him
here before you, I will bear the blame before you all my life. 10As it is, if we had
not delayed, we could have gone and returned twice."
11Then their father Israel said to them,
"If it must be, then do this: Put some of
the best products of the land in your
bags and take them down to the man as
a gift—a little balm and a little honey,
some spices and myrrh, some pistachio
nuts and almonds. 12Take double the
amount of silver with you, for you must
return the silver that was put back into
the mouths of your sacks. Perhaps it was
a mistake. 13Take your brother also and
go back to the man at once. 14And may
God Almighty[b] grant you mercy before
the man so that he will let your other
brother and Benjamin come back with
you. As for me, if I am bereaved, I am
bereaved."
15So the men took the gifts and double the amount of silver, and Benjamin
also. They hurried down to Egypt and
presented themselves to Joseph. 16When
Joseph saw Benjamin with them, he said
to the steward of his house, "Take these
men to my house, slaughter an animal
and prepare a meal; they are to eat with
me at noon."
17The man did as Joseph told him and
took the men to Joseph's house. 18Now
the men were frightened when they
were taken to his house. They thought,
"We were brought here because of the
silver that was put back into our sacks

[a] 34 Or *move about freely* [b] 14 Hebrew *El-Shaddai*

the first time. He wants to attack us and
overpower us and seize us as slaves and
take our donkeys."
19 So they went up to Joseph's steward
and spoke to him at the entrance to the
house. 20 "We beg your pardon, our lord,"
they said, "we came down here the first
time to buy food. 21 But at the place where
we stopped for the night we opened our
sacks and each of us found his silver—
the exact weight—in the mouth of his
sack. So we have brought it back with us.
22 We have also brought additional silver
with us to buy food. We don't know who
put our silver in our sacks."
23 "It's all right," he said. "Don't be
afraid. Your God, the God of your father,
has given you treasure in your sacks; I
received your silver." Then he brought
Simeon out to them.
24 The steward took the men into Joseph's house, gave them water to wash
their feet and provided fodder for their
donkeys. 25 They prepared their gifts for
Joseph's arrival at noon, because they
had heard that they were to eat there.
26 When Joseph came home, they presented to him the gifts they had brought
into the house, and they bowed down
before him to the ground. 27 He asked
them how they were, and then he said,
"How is your aged father you told me
about? Is he still living?"
28 They replied, "Your servant our father is still alive and well." And they
bowed down, prostrating themselves
before him.
29 As he looked about and saw his
brother Benjamin, his own mother's son,
he asked, "Is this your youngest brother, the one you told me about?" And he
said, "God be gracious to you, my son."
30 Deeply moved at the sight of his brother, Joseph hurried out and looked for a
place to weep. He went into his private
room and wept there.
31 After he had washed his face, he
came out and, controlling himself, said,
"Serve the food."
32 They served him by himself, the
brothers by themselves, and the Egyptians who ate with him by themselves,
because Egyptians could not eat with
Hebrews, for that is detestable to Egyptians. 33 The men had been seated before him in the order of their ages, from
the firstborn to the youngest; and they
looked at each other in astonishment.
34 When portions were served to them
from Joseph's table, Benjamin's portion was five times as much as anyone
else's. So they feasted and drank freely
with him.

44 Now Joseph gave these instructions to the steward of his house:
"Fill the men's sacks with as much food
as they can carry, and put each man's silver in the mouth of his sack. 2 Then put
my cup, the silver one, in the mouth of
the youngest one's sack, along with the
silver for his grain." And he did as Joseph said.
3 As morning dawned, the men were
sent on their way with their donkeys.
4 They had not gone far from the city
when Joseph said to his steward, "Go
after those men at once, and when you
catch up with them, say to them, 'Why
have you repaid good with evil? 5 Isn't
this the cup my master drinks from and
also uses for divination? This is a wicked
thing you have done.'"
6 When he caught up with them, he repeated these words to them. 7 But they
said to him, "Why does my lord say such
things? Far be it from your servants to
do anything like that! 8 We even brought
back to you from the land of Canaan the
silver we found inside the mouths of our
sacks. So why would we steal silver or
gold from your master's house? 9 If any
of your servants is found to have it, he
will die; and the rest of us will become
my lord's slaves."
10 "Very well, then," he said, "let it be as
you say. Whoever is found to have it will
become my slave; the rest of you will be
free from blame."
11 Each of them quickly lowered his
sack to the ground and opened it. 12 Then
the steward proceeded to search, beginning with the oldest and ending with
the youngest. And the cup was found
in Benjamin's sack. 13 At this, they tore
their clothes. Then they all loaded their
donkeys and returned to the city.
14 Joseph was still in the house when
Judah and his brothers came in, and
they threw themselves to the ground before him. 15 Joseph said to them, "What
is this you have done? Don't you know
that a man like me can find things out
by divination?"
16 "What can we say to my lord?" Judah

replied. "What can we say? How can we
prove our innocence? God has uncovered your servants' guilt. We are now my
lord's slaves — we ourselves and the one
who was found to have the cup."
17 But Joseph said, "Far be it from me
to do such a thing! Only the man who
was found to have the cup will become
my slave. The rest of you, go back to your
father in peace."
18 Then Judah went up to him and
said: "Pardon your servant, my lord, let
me speak a word to my lord. Do not be
angry with your servant, though you
are equal to Pharaoh himself. 19 My lord
asked his servants, 'Do you have a father or a brother?' 20 And we answered,
'We have an aged father, and there is a
young son born to him in his old age. His
brother is dead, and he is the only one
of his mother's sons left, and his father
loves him.'
21 "Then you said to your servants,
'Bring him down to me so I can see him
for myself.' 22 And we said to my lord,
'The boy cannot leave his father; if he
leaves him, his father will die.' 23 But you
told your servants, 'Unless your youngest brother comes down with you, you
will not see my face again.' 24 When we
went back to your servant my father, we
told him what my lord had said.
25 "Then our father said, 'Go back and
buy a little more food.' 26 But we said, 'We
cannot go down. Only if our youngest
brother is with us will we go. We cannot
see the man's face unless our youngest
brother is with us.'
27 "Your servant my father said to us,
'You know that my wife bore me two
sons. 28 One of them went away from me,
and I said, "He has surely been torn to
pieces." And I have not seen him since.
29 If you take this one from me too and
harm comes to him, you will bring my
gray head down to the grave in misery.'
30 "So now, if the boy is not with us
when I go back to your servant my father,
and if my father, whose life is closely
bound up with the boy's life, 31 sees that
the boy isn't there, he will die. Your servants will bring the gray head of our father down to the grave in sorrow. 32 Your
servant guaranteed the boy's safety to
my father. I said, 'If I do not bring him
back to you, I will bear the blame before
you, my father, all my life!'
33 "Now then, please let your servant
remain here as my lord's slave in place
of the boy, and let the boy return with his
brothers. 34 How can I go back to my father if the boy is not with me? No! Do not
let me see the misery that would come
on my father."

45 Then Joseph could no longer control himself before all his attendants, and he cried out, "Have everyone
leave my presence!" So there was no
one with Joseph when he made himself
known to his brothers. 2 And he wept so
loudly that the Egyptians heard him, and
Pharaoh's household heard about it.
3 Joseph said to his brothers, "I am Joseph! Is my father still living?" But his
brothers were not able to answer him,
because they were terrified at his presence.
4 Then Joseph said to his brothers,
"Come close to me." When they had done
so, he said, "I am your brother Joseph,
the one you sold into Egypt! 5 And now,
do not be distressed and do not be angry
with yourselves for selling me here, because it was to save lives that God sent
me ahead of you. 6 For two years now
there has been famine in the land, and
for the next five years there will be no
plowing and reaping. 7 But God sent me
ahead of you to preserve for you a remnant on earth and to save your lives by a
great deliverance.[a]
8 "So then, it was not you who sent me
here, but God. He made me father to
Pharaoh, lord of his entire household
and ruler of all Egypt. 9 Now hurry back
to my father and say to him, 'This is what
your son Joseph says: God has made me
lord of all Egypt. Come down to me;
don't delay. 10 You shall live in the region
of Goshen and be near me — you, your
children and grandchildren, your flocks
and herds, and all you have. 11 I will provide for you there, because five years of
famine are still to come. Otherwise you
and your household and all who belong
to you will become destitute.'
12 "You can see for yourselves, and so
can my brother Benjamin, that it is really
I who am speaking to you. 13 Tell my father
about all the honor accorded me in Egypt

[a] 7 Or *save you as a great band of survivors*

and about everything you have seen. And
bring my father down here quickly."
14 Then he threw his arms around his
brother Benjamin and wept, and Benjamin embraced him, weeping. 15 And
he kissed all his brothers and wept over
them. Afterward his brothers talked
with him.

16 When the news reached Pharaoh's
palace that Joseph's brothers had come,
Pharaoh and all his officials were pleased.
17 Pharaoh said to Joseph, "Tell your
brothers, 'Do this: Load your animals and
return to the land of Canaan, 18 and bring
your father and your families back to me.
I will give you the best of the land of Egypt
and you can enjoy the fat of the land.'

19 "You are also directed to tell them,
'Do this: Take some carts from Egypt
for your children and your wives, and
get your father and come. 20 Never mind
about your belongings, because the best
of all Egypt will be yours.'"

21 So the sons of Israel did this. Joseph
gave them carts, as Pharaoh had commanded, and he also gave them provisions for their journey. 22 To each of
them he gave new clothing, but to Benjamin he gave three hundred shekels[a] of
silver and five sets of clothes. 23 And this
is what he sent to his father: ten donkeys
loaded with the best things of Egypt, and
ten female donkeys loaded with grain
and bread and other provisions for his
journey. 24 Then he sent his brothers
away, and as they were leaving he said
to them, "Don't quarrel on the way!"

25 So they went up out of Egypt and
came to their father Jacob in the land of
Canaan. 26 They told him, "Joseph is still
alive! In fact, he is ruler of all Egypt."
Jacob was stunned; he did not believe
them. 27 But when they told him everything Joseph had said to them, and when
he saw the carts Joseph had sent to carry
him back, the spirit of their father Jacob
revived. 28 And Israel said, "I'm convinced! My son Joseph is still alive. I will
go and see him before I die."

46 So Israel set out with all that was
his, and when he reached Beershe-
ba, he offered sacrifices to the God of his
father Isaac.
2 And God spoke to Israel in a vision at
night and said, "Jacob! Jacob!"

"Here I am," he replied.

3 "I am God, the God of your father,"
he said. "Do not be afraid to go down to
Egypt, for I will make you into a great nation there. 4 I will go down to Egypt with
you, and I will surely bring you back
again. And Joseph's own hand will close
your eyes."

5 Then Jacob left Beersheba, and Israel's sons took their father Jacob and their
children and their wives in the carts
that Pharaoh had sent to transport him.
6 So Jacob and all his offspring went to
Egypt, taking with them their livestock
and the possessions they had acquired
in Canaan. 7 Jacob brought with him to
Egypt his sons and grandsons and his
daughters and granddaughters — all his
offspring.

8 These are the names of the sons of
Israel (Jacob and his descendants) who
went to Egypt:

Reuben the firstborn of Jacob.
9 The sons of Reuben:
Hanok, Pallu, Hezron and Karmi.
10 The sons of Simeon:
Jemuel, Jamin, Ohad, Jakin, Zohar
and Shaul the son of a Canaanite
woman.
11 The sons of Levi:
Gershon, Kohath and Merari.
12 The sons of Judah:
Er, Onan, Shelah, Perez and Zerah
(but Er and Onan had died in the
land of Canaan).
The sons of Perez:
Hezron and Hamul.
13 The sons of Issachar:
Tola, Puah,[b] Jashub[c] and Shimron.
14 The sons of Zebulun:
Sered, Elon and Jahleel.

15 These were the sons Leah bore to
Jacob in Paddan Aram,[d] besides his
daughter Dinah. These sons and daughters of his were thirty-three in all.

16 The sons of Gad:
Zephon,[e] Haggi, Shuni, Ezbon,
Eri, Arodi and Areli.

[a] *22* That is, about 7 1/2 pounds or about 3.5 kilograms [b] *13* Samaritan Pentateuch and Syriac (see also 1 Chron. 7:1); Masoretic Text *Puvah* [c] *13* Samaritan Pentateuch and some Septuagint manuscripts (see also Num. 26:24 and 1 Chron. 7:1); Masoretic Text *Iob* [d] *15* That is, Northwest Mesopotamia
[e] *16* Samaritan Pentateuch and Septuagint (see also Num. 26:15); Masoretic Text *Ziphion*

17 The sons of Asher:
Imnah, Ishvah, Ishvi and Beriah.
Their sister was Serah.
The sons of Beriah:
Heber and Malkiel.
18 These were the children born to Ja-
cob by Zilpah, whom Laban had given to
his daughter Leah — sixteen in all.

19 The sons of Jacob's wife Rachel:
Joseph and Benjamin. 20 In Egypt,
Manasseh and Ephraim were born
to Joseph by Asenath daughter of
Potiphera, priest of On.[a]
21 The sons of Benjamin:
Bela, Beker, Ashbel, Gera, Naaman, Ehi, Rosh, Muppim, Huppim
and Ard.
22 These were the sons of Rachel who
were born to Jacob — fourteen in all.

23 The son of Dan:
Hushim.
24 The sons of Naphtali:
Jahziel, Guni, Jezer and Shillem.
25 These were the sons born to Jacob
by Bilhah, whom Laban had given to his
daughter Rachel — seven in all.

26 All those who went to Egypt with Jacob — those who were his direct descendants, not counting his sons' wives —
numbered sixty-six persons. 27 With the
two sons[b] who had been born to Joseph
in Egypt, the members of Jacob's family, which went to Egypt, were seventy[c]
in all.

28 Now Jacob sent Judah ahead of him
to Joseph to get directions to Goshen.
When they arrived in the region of Goshen, 29 Joseph had his chariot made
ready and went to Goshen to meet his
father Israel. As soon as Joseph appeared
before him, he threw his arms around
his father[d] and wept for a long time.
30 Israel said to Joseph, "Now I am
ready to die, since I have seen for myself
that you are still alive."
31 Then Joseph said to his brothers
and to his father's household, "I will go
up and speak to Pharaoh and will say
to him, 'My brothers and my father's
household, who were living in the land
of Canaan, have come to me. 32 The men
are shepherds; they tend livestock, and
they have brought along their flocks and
herds and everything they own.' 33 When
Pharaoh calls you in and asks, 'What is
your occupation?' 34 you should answer,
'Your servants have tended livestock
from our boyhood on, just as our fathers
did.' Then you will be allowed to settle in
the region of Goshen, for all shepherds
are detestable to the Egyptians."

47 Joseph went and told Pharaoh,
"My father and brothers, with their
flocks and herds and everything they
own, have come from the land of Canaan and are now in Goshen." 2 He chose
five of his brothers and presented them
before Pharaoh.
3 Pharaoh asked the brothers, "What is
your occupation?"
"Your servants are shepherds," they
replied to Pharaoh, "just as our fathers
were." 4 They also said to him, "We have
come to live here for a while, because
the famine is severe in Canaan and
your servants' flocks have no pasture.
So now, please let your servants settle
in Goshen."
5 Pharaoh said to Joseph, "Your father
and your brothers have come to you,
6 and the land of Egypt is before you; settle your father and your brothers in the
best part of the land. Let them live in
Goshen. And if you know of any among
them with special ability, put them in
charge of my own livestock."
7 Then Joseph brought his father Jacob
in and presented him before Pharaoh.
After Jacob blessed[e] Pharaoh, 8 Pharaoh
asked him, "How old are you?"
9 And Jacob said to Pharaoh, "The
years of my pilgrimage are a hundred
and thirty. My years have been few and
difficult, and they do not equal the years
of the pilgrimage of my fathers." 10 Then
Jacob blessed[f] Pharaoh and went out
from his presence.
11 So Joseph settled his father and his
brothers in Egypt and gave them property in the best part of the land, the district of Rameses, as Pharaoh directed.
12 Joseph also provided his father and
his brothers and all his father's household with food, according to the number
of their children.
13 There was no food, however, in the

[a] *20* That is, Heliopolis [b] *27* Hebrew; Septuagint *the nine children* [c] *27* Hebrew (see also Exodus 1:5 and note); Septuagint (see also Acts 7:14) *seventy-five* [d] *29* Hebrew *around him* [e] *7* Or *greeted*
[f] *10* Or *said farewell to*

whole region because the famine was
severe; both Egypt and Canaan wasted
away because of the famine. 14 Joseph
collected all the money that was to be
found in Egypt and Canaan in payment
for the grain they were buying, and he
brought it to Pharaoh's palace. 15 When
the money of the people of Egypt and Canaan was gone, all Egypt came to Joseph
and said, "Give us food. Why should we
die before your eyes? Our money is all
gone."

16 "Then bring your livestock," said
Joseph. "I will sell you food in exchange
for your livestock, since your money is
gone." 17 So they brought their livestock
to Joseph, and he gave them food in exchange for their horses, their sheep
and goats, their cattle and donkeys.
And he brought them through that
year with food in exchange for all their
livestock.

18 When that year was over, they came
to him the following year and said, "We
cannot hide from our lord the fact that
since our money is gone and our livestock belongs to you, there is nothing
left for our lord except our bodies and
our land. 19 Why should we perish before
your eyes — we and our land as well? Buy
us and our land in exchange for food,
and we with our land will be in bondage
to Pharaoh. Give us seed so that we may
live and not die, and that the land may
not become desolate."

20 So Joseph bought all the land in
Egypt for Pharaoh. The Egyptians, one
and all, sold their fields, because the
famine was too severe for them. The
land became Pharaoh's, 21 and Joseph reduced the people to servitude,[a] from one
end of Egypt to the other. 22 However, he
did not buy the land of the priests, because they received a regular allotment
from Pharaoh and had food enough from
the allotment Pharaoh gave them. That
is why they did not sell their land.

23 Joseph said to the people, "Now that
I have bought you and your land today
for Pharaoh, here is seed for you so you
can plant the ground. 24 But when the
crop comes in, give a fifth of it to Pharaoh. The other four-fifths you may keep
as seed for the fields and as food for
yourselves and your households and
your children."

25 "You have saved our lives," they said.
"May we find favor in the eyes of our lord;
we will be in bondage to Pharaoh."

26 So Joseph established it as a law concerning land in Egypt — still in force today — that a fifth of the produce belongs
to Pharaoh. It was only the land of the
priests that did not become Pharaoh's.

27 Now the Israelites settled in Egypt
in the region of Goshen. They acquired
property there and were fruitful and increased greatly in number.

28 Jacob lived in Egypt seventeen years,
and the years of his life were a hundred
and forty-seven. 29 When the time drew
near for Israel to die, he called for his son
Joseph and said to him, "If I have found
favor in your eyes, put your hand under
my thigh and promise that you will show
me kindness and faithfulness. Do not
bury me in Egypt, 30 but when I rest with
my fathers, carry me out of Egypt and
bury me where they are buried."

"I will do as you say," he said.

31 "Swear to me," he said. Then Joseph
swore to him, and Israel worshiped as he
leaned on the top of his staff.[b]

48 Some time later Joseph was told,
"Your father is ill." So he took his
two sons Manasseh and Ephraim along
with him. 2 When Jacob was told, "Your
son Joseph has come to you," Israel rallied his strength and sat up on the bed.

3 Jacob said to Joseph, "God Almighty[c]
appeared to me at Luz in the land of Canaan, and there he blessed me 4 and said
to me, 'I am going to make you fruitful
and increase your numbers. I will make
you a community of peoples, and I will
give this land as an everlasting possession to your descendants after you.'

5 "Now then, your two sons born to you
in Egypt before I came to you here will
be reckoned as mine; Ephraim and Manasseh will be mine, just as Reuben and
Simeon are mine. 6 Any children born to
you after them will be yours; in the territory they inherit they will be reckoned
under the names of their brothers. 7 As I
was returning from Paddan,[d] to my sorrow Rachel died in the land of Canaan
while we were still on the way, a little

[a] *21* Samaritan Pentateuch and Septuagint (see also Vulgate); Masoretic Text *and he moved the people into the cities* [b] *31* Or *Israel bowed down at the head of his bed* [c] *3* Hebrew *El-Shaddai* [d] *7* That is, Northwest Mesopotamia

distance from Ephrath. So I buried her there beside the road to Ephrath" (that is, Bethlehem).

8 When Israel saw the sons of Joseph, he asked, "Who are these?"

9 "They are the sons God has given me here," Joseph said to his father.

Then Israel said, "Bring them to me so I may bless them."

10 Now Israel's eyes were failing because of old age, and he could hardly see. So Joseph brought his sons close to him, and his father kissed them and embraced them.

11 Israel said to Joseph, "I never expected to see your face again, and now God has allowed me to see your children too."

12 Then Joseph removed them from Israel's knees and bowed down with his
face to the ground. 13 And Joseph took
both of them, Ephraim on his right toward Israel's left hand and Manasseh on his left toward Israel's right hand, and
brought them close to him. 14 But Israel reached out his right hand and put it on Ephraim's head, though he was the younger, and crossing his arms, he put his left hand on Manasseh's head, even though Manasseh was the firstborn.

15 Then he blessed Joseph and said,

"May the God before whom my
fathers
Abraham and Isaac walked
faithfully,
the God who has been my shepherd
all my life to this day,
16 the Angel who has delivered me from
all harm
— may he bless these boys.
May they be called by my name
and the names of my fathers
Abraham and Isaac,
and may they increase greatly
on the earth."

17 When Joseph saw his father placing his right hand on Ephraim's head he was displeased; so he took hold of his father's hand to move it from Ephraim's head to
Manasseh's head. 18 Joseph said to him, "No, my father, this one is the firstborn; put your right hand on his head."

19 But his father refused and said, "I know, my son, I know. He too will become a people, and he too will become great. Nevertheless, his younger brother will be greater than he, and his descendants will become a group of nations."
20 He blessed them that day and said,

"In your[a] name will Israel pronounce
this blessing:
'May God make you like Ephraim
and Manasseh.' "

So he put Ephraim ahead of Manasseh.

21 Then Israel said to Joseph, "I am about to die, but God will be with you[b] and take you[b] back to the land of your[b]
fathers. 22 And to you I give one more ridge of land[c] than to your brothers, the ridge I took from the Amorites with my sword and my bow."

49 Then Jacob called for his sons and said: "Gather around so I can tell you what will happen to you in days to come.

2 "Assemble and listen, sons of Jacob;
listen to your father Israel.

3 "Reuben, you are my firstborn,
my might, the first sign of my
strength,
excelling in honor, excelling in
power.
4 Turbulent as the waters, you will no
longer excel,
for you went up onto your father's
bed,
onto my couch and defiled it.

5 "Simeon and Levi are brothers—
their swords[d] are weapons of
violence.
6 Let me not enter their council,
let me not join their assembly,
for they have killed men in their
anger
and hamstrung oxen as they
pleased.
7 Cursed be their anger, so fierce,
and their fury, so cruel!
I will scatter them in Jacob
and disperse them in Israel.

8 "Judah,[e] your brothers will praise
you;
your hand will be on the neck of
your enemies;

[a] *20* The Hebrew is singular. [b] *21* The Hebrew is plural. [c] *22* The Hebrew for *ridge of land* is identical with the place name Shechem. [d] *5* The meaning of the Hebrew for this word is uncertain. [e] *8* *Judah* sounds like and may be derived from the Hebrew for *praise.*

your father's sons will bow down to
you.
9 You are a lion's cub, Judah;
you return from the prey, my son.
Like a lion he crouches and lies down,
like a lioness — who dares to rouse
him?
10 The scepter will not depart from
Judah,
nor the ruler's staff from between
his feet,[a]
until he to whom it belongs[b] shall
come
and the obedience of the nations
shall be his.
11 He will tether his donkey to a vine,
his colt to the choicest branch;
he will wash his garments in wine,
his robes in the blood of grapes.
12 His eyes will be darker than wine,
his teeth whiter than milk.[c]

13 "Zebulun will live by the seashore
and become a haven for ships;
his border will extend toward
Sidon.

14 "Issachar is a rawboned[d] donkey
lying down among the sheep pens.[e]
15 When he sees how good is his resting
place
and how pleasant is his land,
he will bend his shoulder to the
burden
and submit to forced labor.

16 "Dan[f] will provide justice for his
people
as one of the tribes of Israel.
17 Dan will be a snake by the roadside,
a viper along the path,
that bites the horse's heels
so that its rider tumbles backward.
18 "I look for your deliverance, LORD.

19 "Gad[g] will be attacked by a band of
raiders,
but he will attack them at their
heels.

20 "Asher's food will be rich;
he will provide delicacies fit for a
king.

21 "Naphtali is a doe set free
that bears beautiful fawns.[h]

22 "Joseph is a fruitful vine,
a fruitful vine near a spring,
whose branches climb over a wall.[i]
23 With bitterness archers attacked him;
they shot at him with hostility.
24 But his bow remained steady,
his strong arms stayed[j] limber,
because of the hand of the Mighty
One of Jacob,
because of the Shepherd, the Rock
of Israel,
25 because of your father's God, who
helps you,
because of the Almighty,[k] who
blesses you
with blessings of the skies above,
blessings of the deep springs below,
blessings of the breast and womb.
26 Your father's blessings are greater
than the blessings of the ancient
mountains,
than[l] the bounty of the age-old hills.
Let all these rest on the head of
Joseph,
on the brow of the prince among[m]
his brothers.

27 "Benjamin is a ravenous wolf;
in the morning he devours the prey,
in the evening he divides the
plunder."

28 All these are the twelve tribes of Israel, and this is what their father said to
them when he blessed them, giving each
the blessing appropriate to him.
29 Then he gave them these instructions: "I am about to be gathered to my
people. Bury me with my fathers in the
cave in the field of Ephron the Hittite,
30 the cave in the field of Machpelah,
near Mamre in Canaan, which Abraham bought along with the field as a
burial place from Ephron the Hittite.
31 There Abraham and his wife Sarah
were buried, there Isaac and his wife
Rebekah were buried, and there I buried
Leah. 32 The field and the cave in it were
bought from the Hittites.[n]"

[a] 10 Or *from his descendants* [b] 10 Or *to whom tribute belongs*; the meaning of the Hebrew for this phrase is uncertain. [c] 12 Or *will be dull from wine, / his teeth white from milk* [d] 14 Or *strong* [e] 14 Or *the campfires*; or *the saddlebags* [f] 16 *Dan* here means *he provides justice.* [g] 19 *Gad* sounds like the Hebrew for *attack* and also for *band of raiders.* [h] 21 Or *free; / he utters beautiful words* [i] 22 Or *Joseph is a wild colt, / a wild colt near a spring, / a wild donkey on a terraced hill* [j] 23,24 Or *archers will attack . . . will shoot . . . will remain . . . will stay* [k] 25 Hebrew *Shaddai* [l] 26 Or *of my progenitors, / as great as* [m] 26 Or *of the one separated from* [n] 32 Or *the descendants of Heth*

33 When Jacob had finished giving instructions to his sons, he drew his feet up into the bed, breathed his last and was gathered to his people.

50 Joseph threw himself on his father and wept over him and kissed him. 2 Then Joseph directed the physicians in his service to embalm his father Israel. So the physicians embalmed him, 3 taking a full forty days, for that was the time required for embalming. And the Egyptians mourned for him seventy days.

4 When the days of mourning had passed, Joseph said to Pharaoh's court, "If I have found favor in your eyes, speak to Pharaoh for me. Tell him, 5 'My father made me swear an oath and said, "I am about to die; bury me in the tomb I dug for myself in the land of Canaan." Now let me go up and bury my father; then I will return.' "

6 Pharaoh said, "Go up and bury your father, as he made you swear to do."

7 So Joseph went up to bury his father. All Pharaoh's officials accompanied him—the dignitaries of his court and all the dignitaries of Egypt— 8 besides all the members of Joseph's household and his brothers and those belonging to his father's household. Only their children and their flocks and herds were left in Goshen. 9 Chariots and horsemen[a] also went up with him. It was a very large company.

10 When they reached the threshing floor of Atad, near the Jordan, they lamented loudly and bitterly; and there Joseph observed a seven-day period of mourning for his father. 11 When the Canaanites who lived there saw the mourning at the threshing floor of Atad, they said, "The Egyptians are holding a solemn ceremony of mourning." That is why that place near the Jordan is called Abel Mizraim.[b]

12 So Jacob's sons did as he had commanded them: 13 They carried him to the land of Canaan and buried him in the cave in the field of Machpelah, near Mamre, which Abraham had bought along with the field as a burial place from Ephron the Hittite. 14 After burying his father, Joseph returned to Egypt, together with his brothers and all the others who had gone with him to bury his father.

15 When Joseph's brothers saw that their father was dead, they said, "What if Joseph holds a grudge against us and pays us back for all the wrongs we did to him?" 16 So they sent word to Joseph, saying, "Your father left these instructions before he died: 17 'This is what you are to say to Joseph: I ask you to forgive your brothers the sins and the wrongs they committed in treating you so badly.' Now please forgive the sins of the servants of the God of your father." When their message came to him, Joseph wept.

18 His brothers then came and threw themselves down before him. "We are your slaves," they said.

19 But Joseph said to them, "Don't be afraid. Am I in the place of God? 20 You intended to harm me, but God intended it for good to accomplish what is now being done, the saving of many lives. 21 So then, don't be afraid. I will provide for you and your children." And he reassured them and spoke kindly to them.

22 Joseph stayed in Egypt, along with all his father's family. He lived a hundred and ten years 23 and saw the third generation of Ephraim's children. Also the children of Makir son of Manasseh were placed at birth on Joseph's knees.[c]

24 Then Joseph said to his brothers, "I am about to die. But God will surely come to your aid and take you up out of this land to the land he promised on oath to Abraham, Isaac and Jacob." 25 And Joseph made the Israelites swear an oath and said, "God will surely come to your aid, and then you must carry my bones up from this place."

26 So Joseph died at the age of a hundred and ten. And after they embalmed him, he was placed in a coffin in Egypt.

[a] 9 Or *charioteers* [b] *11 Abel Mizraim* means *mourning of the Egyptians.* [c] *23* That is, were counted as his

EXODUS

The books of Exodus, Leviticus and Numbers continue the story of how God formed the nation of Israel to play a special role in his plans for the whole world. When the Israelites were enslaved in Egypt, God came to them and worked powerfully through Moses to deliver them. At Mount Sinai, God revealed his laws to Moses, including the Ten Commandments, and confirmed his covenant with the young nation. Israel built a "tabernacle," or "tent of meeting," so that God could live among them. The people then traveled through the wilderness to the land of Canaan.

The boundaries between the books of Exodus, Leviticus and Numbers are not sharply drawn. The key structure throughout the books relates to the various places the Israelites stopped on their journey. Each location is noted, and the events at each one are described. The key location is Mount Sinai; the second half of Exodus, all of Leviticus, and the beginning of Numbers describe what took place there. Leviticus specifically contains the laws and regulations the LORD gave to Israel. Numbers reports how the people were organized into a fighting force and moved toward the promised land.

Numbers reaches back across Leviticus and Exodus and repeats the phrase that structures Genesis: *This is the account of the family of Aaron and Moses* (p. 119). Appropriately, we hear this phrase for the twelfth time as the twelve tribes are being organized into a nation. Near the end of Numbers the prophet Balaam says to Israel, *May those who bless you be blessed and those who curse you be cursed.* This recalls God's promise to Abraham in Genesis, *I will bless those who bless you, and whoever curses you I will curse.* These references show that together these books tell a single story of the beginning of God's redemptive work in the world.

---

1 These are the names of the sons of
Israel who went to Egypt with Jacob,
each with his family: 2Reuben, Simeon,
Levi and Judah; 3Issachar, Zebulun and
Benjamin; 4Dan and Naphtali; Gad and
Asher. 5The descendants of Jacob numbered seventy[a] in all; Joseph was already
in Egypt.
6Now Joseph and all his brothers and
all that generation died, 7but the Israelites were exceedingly fruitful; they multiplied greatly, increased in numbers
and became so numerous that the land
was filled with them.
8Then a new king, to whom Joseph
meant nothing, came to power in Egypt.
9"Look," he said to his people, "the Israelites have become far too numerous for
us. 10Come, we must deal shrewdly with
them or they will become even more numerous and, if war breaks out, will join
our enemies, fight against us and leave
the country."
11So they put slave masters over them
to oppress them with forced labor, and
they built Pithom and Rameses as store
cities for Pharaoh. 12But the more they
were oppressed, the more they multiplied and spread; so the Egyptians came
to dread the Israelites 13and worked them
ruthlessly. 14They made their lives bitter
with harsh labor in brick and mortar and
with all kinds of work in the fields; in all
their harsh labor the Egyptians worked
them ruthlessly.
15The king of Egypt said to the Hebrew
midwives, whose names were Shiph-
rah and Puah, 16"When you are helping
the Hebrew women during childbirth
on the delivery stool, if you see that the
baby is a boy, kill him; but if it is a girl,
let her live." 17The midwives, however,
feared God and did not do what the king
of Egypt had told them to do; they let the
boys live. 18Then the king of Egypt summoned the midwives and asked them,
"Why have you done this? Why have you
let the boys live?"
19The midwives answered Pharaoh,
"Hebrew women are not like Egyptian
women; they are vigorous and give birth
before the midwives arrive."
20So God was kind to the midwives
and the people increased and became
even more numerous. 21And because

[a] 5 Masoretic Text (see also Gen. 46:27); Dead Sea Scrolls and Septuagint (see also Acts 7:14 and note at Gen. 46:27) *seventy-five*

the midwives feared God, he gave them families of their own.

22 Then Pharaoh gave this order to all his people: "Every Hebrew boy that is born you must throw into the Nile, but let every girl live."

2 Now a man of the tribe of Levi married a Levite woman, 2 and she became pregnant and gave birth to a son. When she saw that he was a fine child, she hid him for three months. 3 But when she could hide him no longer, she got a papyrus basket[a] for him and coated it with tar and pitch. Then she placed the child in it and put it among the reeds along the bank of the Nile. 4 His sister stood at a distance to see what would happen to him.

5 Then Pharaoh's daughter went down to the Nile to bathe, and her attendants were walking along the riverbank. She saw the basket among the reeds and sent her female slave to get it. 6 She opened it and saw the baby. He was crying, and she felt sorry for him. "This is one of the Hebrew babies," she said.

7 Then his sister asked Pharaoh's daughter, "Shall I go and get one of the Hebrew women to nurse the baby for you?"

8 "Yes, go," she answered. So the girl went and got the baby's mother. 9 Pharaoh's daughter said to her, "Take this baby and nurse him for me, and I will pay you." So the woman took the baby and nursed him. 10 When the child grew older, she took him to Pharaoh's daughter and he became her son. She named him Moses,[b] saying, "I drew him out of the water."

11 One day, after Moses had grown up, he went out to where his own people were and watched them at their hard labor. He saw an Egyptian beating a Hebrew, one of his own people. 12 Looking this way and that and seeing no one, he killed the Egyptian and hid him in the sand. 13 The next day he went out and saw two Hebrews fighting. He asked the one in the wrong, "Why are you hitting your fellow Hebrew?"

14 The man said, "Who made you ruler and judge over us? Are you thinking of killing me as you killed the Egyptian?" Then Moses was afraid and thought, "What I did must have become known."

15 When Pharaoh heard of this, he tried to kill Moses, but Moses fled from Pharaoh and went to live in Midian, where he sat down by a well. 16 Now a priest of Midian had seven daughters, and they came to draw water and fill the troughs to water their father's flock. 17 Some shepherds came along and drove them away, but Moses got up and came to their rescue and watered their flock.

18 When the girls returned to Reuel their father, he asked them, "Why have you returned so early today?"

19 They answered, "An Egyptian rescued us from the shepherds. He even drew water for us and watered the flock."

20 "And where is he?" Reuel asked his daughters. "Why did you leave him? Invite him to have something to eat."

21 Moses agreed to stay with the man, who gave his daughter Zipporah to Moses in marriage. 22 Zipporah gave birth to a son, and Moses named him Gershom,[c] saying, "I have become a foreigner in a foreign land."

23 During that long period, the king of Egypt died. The Israelites groaned in their slavery and cried out, and their cry for help because of their slavery went up to God. 24 God heard their groaning and he remembered his covenant with Abraham, with Isaac and with Jacob. 25 So God looked on the Israelites and was concerned about them.

3 Now Moses was tending the flock of Jethro his father-in-law, the priest of Midian, and he led the flock to the far side of the wilderness and came to Horeb, the mountain of God. 2 There the angel of the LORD appeared to him in flames of fire from within a bush. Moses saw that though the bush was on fire it did not burn up. 3 So Moses thought, "I will go over and see this strange sight — why the bush does not burn up."

4 When the LORD saw that he had gone over to look, God called to him from within the bush, "Moses! Moses!"

And Moses said, "Here I am."

5 "Do not come any closer," God said. "Take off your sandals, for the place where you are standing is holy ground."

[a] 3 The Hebrew can also mean *ark*, as in Gen. 6:14. [b] *10 Moses* sounds like the Hebrew for *draw out*.
[c] *22 Gershom* sounds like the Hebrew for *a foreigner there*.

6 Then he said, "I am the God of your father,[a] the God of Abraham, the God of
Isaac and the God of Jacob." At this, Moses hid his face, because he was afraid to
look at God.
7 The LORD said, "I have indeed seen
the misery of my people in Egypt. I have
heard them crying out because of their
slave drivers, and I am concerned about
their suffering. 8 So I have come down to
rescue them from the hand of the Egyptians and to bring them up out of that
land into a good and spacious land, a
land flowing with milk and honey—the
home of the Canaanites, Hittites, Amorites, Perizzites, Hivites and Jebusites.
9 And now the cry of the Israelites has
reached me, and I have seen the way the
Egyptians are oppressing them. 10 So
now, go. I am sending you to Pharaoh
to bring my people the Israelites out of
Egypt."
11 But Moses said to God, "Who am I
that I should go to Pharaoh and bring the
Israelites out of Egypt?"
12 And God said, "I will be with you.
And this will be the sign to you that it
is I who have sent you: When you have
brought the people out of Egypt, you[b]
will worship God on this mountain."
13 Moses said to God, "Suppose I go to
the Israelites and say to them, 'The God
of your fathers has sent me to you,' and
they ask me, 'What is his name?' Then
what shall I tell them?"
14 God said to Moses, "I AM WHO I AM.[c]
This is what you are to say to the Israelites: 'I AM has sent me to you.'"
15 God also said to Moses, "Say to the
Israelites, 'The LORD,[d] the God of your
fathers—the God of Abraham, the God
of Isaac and the God of Jacob—has sent
me to you.'

"This is my name forever,
the name you shall call me
from generation to generation.

16 "Go, assemble the elders of Israel and
say to them, 'The LORD, the God of your
fathers—the God of Abraham, Isaac and
Jacob—appeared to me and said: I have
watched over you and have seen what
has been done to you in Egypt. 17 And I
have promised to bring you up out of
your misery in Egypt into the land of
the Canaanites, Hittites, Amorites, Perizzites, Hivites and Jebusites—a land
flowing with milk and honey.'
18 "The elders of Israel will listen to
you. Then you and the elders are to go
to the king of Egypt and say to him, 'The
LORD, the God of the Hebrews, has met
with us. Let us take a three-day journey
into the wilderness to offer sacrifices to
the LORD our God.' 19 But I know that the
king of Egypt will not let you go unless
a mighty hand compels him. 20 So I will
stretch out my hand and strike the Egyptians with all the wonders that I will perform among them. After that, he will let
you go.
21 "And I will make the Egyptians favorably disposed toward this people,
so that when you leave you will not go
empty-handed. 22 Every woman is to ask
her neighbor and any woman living in
her house for articles of silver and gold
and for clothing, which you will put on
your sons and daughters. And so you will
plunder the Egyptians."

4 Moses answered, "What if they do not
believe me or listen to me and say,
'The LORD did not appear to you'?"
2 Then the LORD said to him, "What is
that in your hand?"
"A staff," he replied.
3 The LORD said, "Throw it on the
ground."
Moses threw it on the ground and it became a snake, and he ran from it. 4 Then
the LORD said to him, "Reach out your
hand and take it by the tail." So Moses
reached out and took hold of the snake
and it turned back into a staff in his
hand. 5 "This," said the LORD, "is so that
they may believe that the LORD, the God
of their fathers—the God of Abraham,
the God of Isaac and the God of Jacob—
has appeared to you."
6 Then the LORD said, "Put your hand
inside your cloak." So Moses put his
hand into his cloak, and when he took
it out, the skin was leprous[e]—it had become as white as snow.
7 "Now put it back into your cloak," he
said. So Moses put his hand back into his
cloak, and when he took it out, it was restored, like the rest of his flesh.

[a] 6 Masoretic Text; Samaritan Pentateuch (see Acts 7:32) *fathers* [b] 12 The Hebrew is plural. [c] 14 Or *I WILL BE WHAT I WILL BE* [d] 15 The Hebrew for *LORD* sounds like and may be related to the Hebrew for *I AM* in verse 14. [e] 6 The Hebrew word for *leprous* was used for various diseases affecting the skin.

8Then the LORD said, "If they do not
believe you or pay attention to the first
sign, they may believe the second. 9But if
they do not believe these two signs or listen to you, take some water from the Nile
and pour it on the dry ground. The water you take from the river will become
blood on the ground."
10Moses said to the LORD, "Pardon
your servant, Lord. I have never been eloquent, neither in the past nor since you
have spoken to your servant. I am slow of
speech and tongue."
11The LORD said to him, "Who gave human beings their mouths? Who makes
them deaf or mute? Who gives them
sight or makes them blind? Is it not I, the
LORD? 12Now go; I will help you speak
and will teach you what to say."
13But Moses said, "Pardon your servant, Lord. Please send someone else."
14Then the LORD's anger burned
against Moses and he said, "What about
your brother, Aaron the Levite? I know
he can speak well. He is already on his
way to meet you, and he will be glad to
see you. 15You shall speak to him and put
words in his mouth; I will help both of
you speak and will teach you what to do.
16He will speak to the people for you, and
it will be as if he were your mouth and as
if you were God to him. 17But take this
staff in your hand so you can perform
the signs with it."
18Then Moses went back to Jethro his
father-in-law and said to him, "Let me return to my own people in Egypt to see if
any of them are still alive."
Jethro said, "Go, and I wish you well."
19Now the LORD had said to Moses in
Midian, "Go back to Egypt, for all those
who wanted to kill you are dead." 20So
Moses took his wife and sons, put them
on a donkey and started back to Egypt.
And he took the staff of God in his hand.
21The LORD said to Moses, "When you
return to Egypt, see that you perform before Pharaoh all the wonders I have giv-
en you the power to do. But I will harden
his heart so that he will not let the people
go. 22Then say to Pharaoh, 'This is what
the LORD says: Israel is my firstborn son,
23and I told you, "Let my son go, so he
may worship me." But you refused to let
him go; so I will kill your firstborn son.' "
24At a lodging place on the way, the
LORD met Moses[a] and was about to kill
him. 25But Zipporah took a flint knife,
cut off her son's foreskin and touched
Moses' feet with it.[b] "Surely you are a
bridegroom of blood to me," she said.
26So the LORD let him alone. (At that time
she said "bridegroom of blood," referring
to circumcision.)
27The LORD said to Aaron, "Go into
the wilderness to meet Moses." So he
met Moses at the mountain of God and
kissed him. 28Then Moses told Aaron everything the LORD had sent him to say,
and also about all the signs he had commanded him to perform.
29Moses and Aaron brought together all the elders of the Israelites, 30and
Aaron told them everything the LORD
had said to Moses. He also performed
the signs before the people, 31and they
believed. And when they heard that the
LORD was concerned about them and
had seen their misery, they bowed down
and worshiped.

5 Afterward Moses and Aaron went to
Pharaoh and said, "This is what the
LORD, the God of Israel, says: 'Let my
people go, so that they may hold a festival to me in the wilderness.' "
2Pharaoh said, "Who is the LORD, that
I should obey him and let Israel go? I do
not know the LORD and I will not let Israel go."
3Then they said, "The God of the Hebrews has met with us. Now let us take
a three-day journey into the wilderness
to offer sacrifices to the LORD our God,
or he may strike us with plagues or with
the sword."
4But the king of Egypt said, "Moses
and Aaron, why are you taking the people away from their labor? Get back to
your work!" 5Then Pharaoh said, "Look,
the people of the land are now numerous, and you are stopping them from
working."
6That same day Pharaoh gave this order to the slave drivers and overseers in
charge of the people: 7"You are no longer
to supply the people with straw for making bricks; let them go and gather their
own straw. 8But require them to make
the same number of bricks as before;
don't reduce the quota. They are lazy;

[a] 24 Hebrew *him* [b] 25 The meaning of the Hebrew for this clause is uncertain.

that is why they are crying out, 'Let us go
and sacrifice to our God.' [9]Make the work
harder for the people so that they keep
working and pay no attention to lies."

[10]Then the slave drivers and the overseers went out and said to the people,
"This is what Pharaoh says: 'I will not
give you any more straw. [11]Go and get
your own straw wherever you can find it,
but your work will not be reduced at all.'"
[12]So the people scattered all over Egypt
to gather stubble to use for straw. [13]The
slave drivers kept pressing them, saying,
"Complete the work required of you for
each day, just as when you had straw."
[14]And Pharaoh's slave drivers beat the
Israelite overseers they had appointed,
demanding, "Why haven't you met your
quota of bricks yesterday or today, as before?"

[15]Then the Israelite overseers went
and appealed to Pharaoh: "Why have you
treated your servants this way? [16]Your
servants are given no straw, yet we are
told, 'Make bricks!' Your servants are being beaten, but the fault is with your own
people."

[17]Pharaoh said, "Lazy, that's what you
are — lazy! That is why you keep saying,
'Let us go and sacrifice to the LORD.'
[18]Now get to work. You will not be given
any straw, yet you must produce your full
quota of bricks."

[19]The Israelite overseers realized they
were in trouble when they were told, "You
are not to reduce the number of bricks
required of you for each day." [20]When
they left Pharaoh, they found Moses and
Aaron waiting to meet them, [21]and they
said, "May the LORD look on you and
judge you! You have made us obnoxious
to Pharaoh and his officials and have put
a sword in their hand to kill us."

[22]Moses returned to the LORD and
said, "Why, Lord, why have you brought
trouble on this people? Is this why you
sent me? [23]Ever since I went to Pharaoh
to speak in your name, he has brought
trouble on this people, and you have not
rescued your people at all."

6 Then the LORD said to Moses, "Now
you will see what I will do to Pharaoh:
Because of my mighty hand he will let
them go; because of my mighty hand he
will drive them out of his country."

[2]God also said to Moses, "I am the
LORD. [3]I appeared to Abraham, to Isaac
and to Jacob as God Almighty,[a] but by my
name the LORD[b] I did not make myself
fully known to them. [4]I also established
my covenant with them to give them
the land of Canaan, where they resided
as foreigners. [5]Moreover, I have heard
the groaning of the Israelites, whom the
Egyptians are enslaving, and I have remembered my covenant.

[6]"Therefore, say to the Israelites: 'I am
the LORD, and I will bring you out from
under the yoke of the Egyptians. I will
free you from being slaves to them, and
I will redeem you with an outstretched
arm and with mighty acts of judgment.
[7]I will take you as my own people, and
I will be your God. Then you will know
that I am the LORD your God, who
brought you out from under the yoke of
the Egyptians. [8]And I will bring you to
the land I swore with uplifted hand to
give to Abraham, to Isaac and to Jacob.
I will give it to you as a possession. I am
the LORD.'"

[9]Moses reported this to the Israelites,
but they did not listen to him because of
their discouragement and harsh labor.

[10]Then the LORD said to Moses, [11]"Go,
tell Pharaoh king of Egypt to let the Israelites go out of his country."

[12]But Moses said to the LORD, "If the Israelites will not listen to me, why would
Pharaoh listen to me, since I speak with
faltering lips[c]?"

[13]Now the LORD spoke to Moses and
Aaron about the Israelites and Pharaoh
king of Egypt, and he commanded them
to bring the Israelites out of Egypt.

[14]These were the heads of their families[d]:

The sons of Reuben the firstborn
son of Israel were Hanok and Pallu,
Hezron and Karmi. These were the
clans of Reuben.

[15]The sons of Simeon were Jemuel,
Jamin, Ohad, Jakin, Zohar and Sha-
ul the son of a Canaanite woman.
These were the clans of Simeon.

[16]These were the names of the
sons of Levi according to their records: Gershon, Kohath and Merari.
Levi lived 137 years.

[a] *3* Hebrew *El-Shaddai* [b] *3* See note at 3:15. [c] *12* Hebrew *I am uncircumcised of lips*; also in verse 30
[d] *14* The Hebrew for *families* here and in verse 25 refers to units larger than clans.

17The sons of Gershon, by clans, were Libni and Shimei.

18The sons of Kohath were Amram, Izhar, Hebron and Uzziel. Kohath lived 133 years.

19The sons of Merari were Mahli and Mushi.

These were the clans of Levi according to their records.

20Amram married his father's sister Jochebed, who bore him Aaron and Moses. Amram lived 137 years.

21The sons of Izhar were Korah, Nepheg and Zikri.

22The sons of Uzziel were Mishael, Elzaphan and Sithri.

23Aaron married Elisheba, daughter of Amminadab and sister of Nahshon, and she bore him Nadab and Abihu, Eleazar and Ithamar.

24The sons of Korah were Assir, Elkanah and Abiasaph. These were the Korahite clans.

25Eleazar son of Aaron married one of the daughters of Putiel, and she bore him Phinehas.

These were the heads of the Levite families, clan by clan.

26It was this Aaron and Moses to whom
the LORD said, "Bring the Israelites out
of Egypt by their divisions." 27They were
the ones who spoke to Pharaoh king of
Egypt about bringing the Israelites out
of Egypt—this same Moses and Aaron.
28Now when the LORD spoke to Moses in Egypt, 29he said to him, "I am the
LORD. Tell Pharaoh king of Egypt everything I tell you."
30But Moses said to the LORD, "Since
I speak with faltering lips, why would
Pharaoh listen to me?"

7 Then the LORD said to Moses, "See, I
have made you like God to Pharaoh,
and your brother Aaron will be your
prophet. 2You are to say everything I
command you, and your brother Aaron is
to tell Pharaoh to let the Israelites go out
of his country. 3But I will harden Pharaoh's heart, and though I multiply my
signs and wonders in Egypt, 4he will not
listen to you. Then I will lay my hand on
Egypt and with mighty acts of judgment
I will bring out my divisions, my people
the Israelites. 5And the Egyptians will
know that I am the LORD when I stretch
out my hand against Egypt and bring the
Israelites out of it."
6Moses and Aaron did just as the LORD
commanded them. 7Moses was eighty
years old and Aaron eighty-three when
they spoke to Pharaoh.
8The LORD said to Moses and Aaron,
9"When Pharaoh says to you, 'Perform
a miracle,' then say to Aaron, 'Take your
staff and throw it down before Pharaoh,'
and it will become a snake."
10So Moses and Aaron went to Pharaoh and did just as the LORD commanded. Aaron threw his staff down in front of
Pharaoh and his officials, and it became
a snake. 11Pharaoh then summoned wise
men and sorcerers, and the Egyptian
magicians also did the same things by
their secret arts: 12Each one threw down
his staff and it became a snake. But Aaron's staff swallowed up their staffs. 13Yet
Pharaoh's heart became hard and he
would not listen to them, just as the LORD
had said.
14Then the LORD said to Moses, "Pharaoh's heart is unyielding; he refuses to
let the people go. 15Go to Pharaoh in
the morning as he goes out to the river.
Confront him on the bank of the Nile,
and take in your hand the staff that was
changed into a snake. 16Then say to him,
'The LORD, the God of the Hebrews, has
sent me to say to you: Let my people go,
so that they may worship me in the wilderness. But until now you have not listened. 17This is what the LORD says: By
this you will know that I am the LORD:
With the staff that is in my hand I will
strike the water of the Nile, and it will
be changed into blood. 18The fish in the
Nile will die, and the river will stink; the
Egyptians will not be able to drink its
water.'"
19The LORD said to Moses, "Tell Aaron, 'Take your staff and stretch out your
hand over the waters of Egypt—over
the streams and canals, over the ponds
and all the reservoirs—and they will
turn to blood.' Blood will be everywhere
in Egypt, even in vessels[a] of wood and
stone."
20Moses and Aaron did just as the
LORD had commanded. He raised his
staff in the presence of Pharaoh and

[a] *19* Or *even on their idols*

his officials and struck the water of the
Nile, and all the water was changed into
blood. 21 The fish in the Nile died, and the
river smelled so bad that the Egyptians
could not drink its water. Blood was everywhere in Egypt.
22 But the Egyptian magicians did the
same things by their secret arts, and
Pharaoh's heart became hard; he would
not listen to Moses and Aaron, just as the
LORD had said. 23 Instead, he turned and
went into his palace, and did not take
even this to heart. 24 And all the Egyptians dug along the Nile to get drinking
water, because they could not drink the
water of the river.
25 Seven days passed after the LORD
8[a] struck the Nile. 1 Then the LORD said
to Moses, "Go to Pharaoh and say to
him, 'This is what the LORD says: Let my
people go, so that they may worship me.
2 If you refuse to let them go, I will send
a plague of frogs on your whole country.
3 The Nile will teem with frogs. They will
come up into your palace and your bedroom and onto your bed, into the houses
of your officials and on your people, and
into your ovens and kneading troughs.
4 The frogs will come up on you and your
people and all your officials.' "
5 Then the LORD said to Moses, "Tell
Aaron, 'Stretch out your hand with your
staff over the streams and canals and
ponds, and make frogs come up on the
land of Egypt.' "
6 So Aaron stretched out his hand over
the waters of Egypt, and the frogs came
up and covered the land. 7 But the magicians did the same things by their secret
arts; they also made frogs come up on the
land of Egypt.
8 Pharaoh summoned Moses and Aaron and said, "Pray to the LORD to take the
frogs away from me and my people, and I
will let your people go to offer sacrifices
to the LORD."
9 Moses said to Pharaoh, "I leave to you
the honor of setting the time for me to
pray for you and your officials and your
people that you and your houses may be
rid of the frogs, except for those that remain in the Nile."
10 "Tomorrow," Pharaoh said.
Moses replied, "It will be as you say, so
that you may know there is no one like
the LORD our God. 11 The frogs will leave
you and your houses, your officials and
your people; they will remain only in the
Nile."
12 After Moses and Aaron left Pharaoh,
Moses cried out to the LORD about the
frogs he had brought on Pharaoh. 13 And
the LORD did what Moses asked. The
frogs died in the houses, in the courtyards and in the fields. 14 They were piled
into heaps, and the land reeked of them.
15 But when Pharaoh saw that there was
relief, he hardened his heart and would
not listen to Moses and Aaron, just as the
LORD had said.
16 Then the LORD said to Moses, "Tell
Aaron, 'Stretch out your staff and strike
the dust of the ground,' and throughout
the land of Egypt the dust will become
gnats." 17 They did this, and when Aaron stretched out his hand with the staff
and struck the dust of the ground, gnats
came on people and animals. All the
dust throughout the land of Egypt became gnats. 18 But when the magicians
tried to produce gnats by their secret
arts, they could not.
Since the gnats were on people and
animals everywhere, 19 the magicians
said to Pharaoh, "This is the finger of
God." But Pharaoh's heart was hard and
he would not listen, just as the LORD had
said.
20 Then the LORD said to Moses, "Get
up early in the morning and confront
Pharaoh as he goes to the river and say
to him, 'This is what the LORD says: Let
my people go, so that they may worship
me. 21 If you do not let my people go, I will
send swarms of flies on you and your officials, on your people and into your
houses. The houses of the Egyptians will
be full of flies; even the ground will be
covered with them.
22 " 'But on that day I will deal differently with the land of Goshen, where
my people live; no swarms of flies will
be there, so that you will know that I,
the LORD, am in this land. 23 I will make
a distinction[b] between my people and
your people. This sign will occur tomorrow.' "
24 And the LORD did this. Dense
swarms of flies poured into Pharaoh's
palace and into the houses of his offi-

[a] In Hebrew texts 8:1-4 is numbered 7:26-29, and 8:5-32 is numbered 8:1-28. [b] 23 Septuagint and Vulgate; Hebrew *will put a deliverance*

cials; throughout Egypt the land was ruined by the flies.

25 Then Pharaoh summoned Moses and Aaron and said, "Go, sacrifice to your God here in the land."

26 But Moses said, "That would not be right. The sacrifices we offer the LORD our God would be detestable to the Egyptians. And if we offer sacrifices that are detestable in their eyes, will they not stone us?
27 We must take a three-day journey into the wilderness to offer sacrifices to the LORD our God, as he commands us."

28 Pharaoh said, "I will let you go to offer sacrifices to the LORD your God in the wilderness, but you must not go very far. Now pray for me."

29 Moses answered, "As soon as I leave you, I will pray to the LORD, and tomorrow the flies will leave Pharaoh and his officials and his people. Only let Pharaoh be sure that he does not act deceitfully again by not letting the people go to offer sacrifices to the LORD."

30 Then Moses left Pharaoh and prayed
to the LORD,
31 and the LORD did what Moses asked. The flies left Pharaoh and his officials and his people; not a fly remained.
32 But this time also Pharaoh hardened his heart and would not let the people go.

9 Then the LORD said to Moses, "Go to Pharaoh and say to him, 'This is what the LORD, the God of the Hebrews, says: "Let my people go, so that they may worship me."
2 If you refuse to let them go and continue to hold them back,
3 the hand of the LORD will bring a terrible plague on your livestock in the field—on your horses, donkeys and camels and on your cattle, sheep and goats.
4 But the LORD will make a distinction between the livestock of Israel and that of Egypt, so that no animal belonging to the Israelites will die.'"

5 The LORD set a time and said, "Tomorrow the LORD will do this in the land."
6 And the next day the LORD did it: All the livestock of the Egyptians died, but not one animal belonging to the Israelites died.
7 Pharaoh investigated and found that not even one of the animals of the Israelites had died. Yet his heart was unyielding and he would not let the people go.

8 Then the LORD said to Moses and Aaron, "Take handfuls of soot from a furnace and have Moses toss it into the air in the presence of Pharaoh.
9 It will become fine dust over the whole land of Egypt, and festering boils will break out on people and animals throughout the land."

10 So they took soot from a furnace and stood before Pharaoh. Moses tossed it into the air, and festering boils broke out on people and animals.
11 The magicians could not stand before Moses because of the boils that were on them and on all the Egyptians.
12 But the LORD hardened Pharaoh's heart and he would not listen to Moses and Aaron, just as the LORD had said to Moses.

13 Then the LORD said to Moses, "Get up early in the morning, confront Pharaoh and say to him, 'This is what the LORD, the God of the Hebrews, says: Let my people go, so that they may worship me,
14 or this time I will send the full force of my plagues against you and against your officials and your people, so you may know that there is no one like me in all the earth.
15 For by now I could have stretched out my hand and struck you and your people with a plague that would have wiped you off the earth.
16 But I have raised you up[a] for this very purpose, that I might show you my power and that my name might be proclaimed in all the earth.
17 You still set yourself against my people and will not let them go.
18 Therefore, at this time tomorrow I will send the worst hailstorm that has ever fallen on Egypt, from the day it was founded till now.
19 Give an order now to bring your livestock and everything you have in the field to a place of shelter, because the hail will fall on every person and animal that has not been brought in and is still out in the field, and they will die.'"

20 Those officials of Pharaoh who feared the word of the LORD hurried to bring their slaves and their livestock inside.
21 But those who ignored the word of the LORD left their slaves and livestock in the field.

22 Then the LORD said to Moses, "Stretch out your hand toward the sky so that hail will fall all over Egypt—on people and animals and on everything

[a] 16 Or *have spared you*

growing in the fields of Egypt." 23When
Moses stretched out his staff toward the
sky, the LORD sent thunder and hail, and
lightning flashed down to the ground.
So the LORD rained hail on the land of
Egypt; 24hail fell and lightning flashed
back and forth. It was the worst storm
in all the land of Egypt since it had become a nation. 25Throughout Egypt hail
struck everything in the fields—both
people and animals; it beat down everything growing in the fields and stripped
every tree. 26The only place it did not hail
was the land of Goshen, where the Israelites were.

27Then Pharaoh summoned Moses
and Aaron. "This time I have sinned," he
said to them. "The LORD is in the right,
and I and my people are in the wrong.
28Pray to the LORD, for we have had
enough thunder and hail. I will let you
go; you don't have to stay any longer."

29Moses replied, "When I have gone
out of the city, I will spread out my hands
in prayer to the LORD. The thunder will
stop and there will be no more hail,
so you may know that the earth is the
LORD's. 30But I know that you and your
officials still do not fear the LORD God."

31(The flax and barley were destroyed,
since the barley had headed and the flax
was in bloom. 32The wheat and spelt,
however, were not destroyed, because
they ripen later.)

33Then Moses left Pharaoh and went
out of the city. He spread out his hands
toward the LORD; the thunder and hail
stopped, and the rain no longer poured
down on the land. 34When Pharaoh saw
that the rain and hail and thunder had
stopped, he sinned again: He and his officials hardened their hearts. 35So Pharaoh's heart was hard and he would not
let the Israelites go, just as the LORD had
said through Moses.

10 Then the LORD said to Moses, "Go
to Pharaoh, for I have hardened his
heart and the hearts of his officials so
that I may perform these signs of mine
among them 2that you may tell your
children and grandchildren how I dealt
harshly with the Egyptians and how I
performed my signs among them, and
that you may know that I am the LORD."

3So Moses and Aaron went to Pharaoh
and said to him, "This is what the LORD,
the God of the Hebrews, says: 'How long
will you refuse to humble yourself before
me? Let my people go, so that they may
worship me. 4If you refuse to let them
go, I will bring locusts into your country tomorrow. 5They will cover the face
of the ground so that it cannot be seen.
They will devour what little you have left
after the hail, including every tree that
is growing in your fields. 6They will fill
your houses and those of all your officials and all the Egyptians—something
neither your parents nor your ancestors
have ever seen from the day they settled in this land till now.'" Then Moses
turned and left Pharaoh.

7Pharaoh's officials said to him, "How
long will this man be a snare to us? Let
the people go, so that they may worship
the LORD their God. Do you not yet realize that Egypt is ruined?"

8Then Moses and Aaron were brought
back to Pharaoh. "Go, worship the LORD
your God," he said. "But tell me who will
be going."

9Moses answered, "We will go with
our young and our old, with our sons
and our daughters, and with our flocks
and herds, because we are to celebrate a
festival to the LORD."

10Pharaoh said, "The LORD be with
you—if I let you go, along with your
women and children! Clearly you are
bent on evil.[a] 11No! Have only the men go
and worship the LORD, since that's what
you have been asking for." Then Moses
and Aaron were driven out of Pharaoh's
presence.

12And the LORD said to Moses, "Stretch
out your hand over Egypt so that locusts
swarm over the land and devour everything growing in the fields, everything
left by the hail."

13So Moses stretched out his staff over
Egypt, and the LORD made an east wind
blow across the land all that day and all
that night. By morning the wind had
brought the locusts; 14they invaded all
Egypt and settled down in every area
of the country in great numbers. Never before had there been such a plague
of locusts, nor will there ever be again.
15They covered all the ground until it
was black. They devoured all that was

[a] 10 Or *Be careful, trouble is in store for you!*

left after the hail—everything growing
in the fields and the fruit on the trees.
Nothing green remained on tree or plant
in all the land of Egypt.
16 Pharaoh quickly summoned Moses and Aaron and said, "I have sinned
against the LORD your God and against
you. 17 Now forgive my sin once more and
pray to the LORD your God to take this
deadly plague away from me."
18 Moses then left Pharaoh and prayed
to the LORD. 19 And the LORD changed the
wind to a very strong west wind, which
caught up the locusts and carried them
into the Red Sea.[a] Not a locust was left
anywhere in Egypt. 20 But the LORD hardened Pharaoh's heart, and he would not
let the Israelites go.
21 Then the LORD said to Moses,
"Stretch out your hand toward the sky
so that darkness spreads over Egypt—
darkness that can be felt." 22 So Moses
stretched out his hand toward the sky,
and total darkness covered all Egypt for
three days. 23 No one could see anyone
else or move about for three days. Yet
all the Israelites had light in the places
where they lived.
24 Then Pharaoh summoned Moses
and said, "Go, worship the LORD. Even
your women and children may go with
you; only leave your flocks and herds
behind."
25 But Moses said, "You must allow us
to have sacrifices and burnt offerings to
present to the LORD our God. 26 Our livestock too must go with us; not a hoof is
to be left behind. We have to use some of
them in worshiping the LORD our God,
and until we get there we will not know
what we are to use to worship the LORD."
27 But the LORD hardened Pharaoh's
heart, and he was not willing to let them
go. 28 Pharaoh said to Moses, "Get out of
my sight! Make sure you do not appear
before me again! The day you see my face
you will die."
29 "Just as you say," Moses replied. "I
will never appear before you again."
11 Now the LORD had said to Moses, "I
will bring one more plague on Pharaoh and on Egypt. After that, he will let
you go from here, and when he does, he
will drive you out completely. 2 Tell the
people that men and women alike are to
ask their neighbors for articles of silver
and gold." 3 (The LORD made the Egyptians favorably disposed toward the
people, and Moses himself was highly
regarded in Egypt by Pharaoh's officials
and by the people.)
4 So Moses said, "This is what the LORD
says: 'About midnight I will go throughout Egypt. 5 Every firstborn son in Egypt
will die, from the firstborn son of Pharaoh, who sits on the throne, to the firstborn son of the female slave, who is at
her hand mill, and all the firstborn of the
cattle as well. 6 There will be loud wailing throughout Egypt—worse than there
has ever been or ever will be again. 7 But
among the Israelites not a dog will bark
at any person or animal.' Then you will
know that the LORD makes a distinction
between Egypt and Israel. 8 All these officials of yours will come to me, bowing
down before me and saying, 'Go, you and
all the people who follow you!' After that
I will leave." Then Moses, hot with anger,
left Pharaoh.
9 The LORD had said to Moses, "Pharaoh will refuse to listen to you—so that
my wonders may be multiplied in Egypt."
10 Moses and Aaron performed all these
wonders before Pharaoh, but the LORD
hardened Pharaoh's heart, and he would
not let the Israelites go out of his country.
12 The LORD said to Moses and Aaron in Egypt, 2 "This month is to be
for you the first month, the first month
of your year. 3 Tell the whole community of Israel that on the tenth day of this
month each man is to take a lamb[b] for his
family, one for each household. 4 If any
household is too small for a whole lamb,
they must share one with their nearest
neighbor, having taken into account the
number of people there are. You are to
determine the amount of lamb needed
in accordance with what each person
will eat. 5 The animals you choose must
be year-old males without defect, and
you may take them from the sheep or
the goats. 6 Take care of them until the
fourteenth day of the month, when all
the members of the community of Israel
must slaughter them at twilight. 7 Then
they are to take some of the blood and
put it on the sides and tops of the door-

[a] 19 Or *the Sea of Reeds* [b] 3 The Hebrew word can mean *lamb* or *kid*; also in verse 4.

frames of the houses where they eat the lambs. 8 That same night they are to eat the meat roasted over the fire, along with bitter herbs, and bread made without yeast. 9 Do not eat the meat raw or boiled in water, but roast it over a fire—with the head, legs and internal organs. 10 Do not leave any of it till morning; if some is left till morning, you must burn it. 11 This is how you are to eat it: with your cloak tucked into your belt, your sandals on your feet and your staff in your hand. Eat it in haste; it is the LORD's Passover.

12 "On that same night I will pass through Egypt and strike down every firstborn of both people and animals, and I will bring judgment on all the gods of Egypt. I am the LORD. 13 The blood will be a sign for you on the houses where you are, and when I see the blood, I will pass over you. No destructive plague will touch you when I strike Egypt.

14 "This is a day you are to commemorate; for the generations to come you shall celebrate it as a festival to the LORD—a lasting ordinance. 15 For seven days you are to eat bread made without yeast. On the first day remove the yeast from your houses, for whoever eats anything with yeast in it from the first day through the seventh must be cut off from Israel. 16 On the first day hold a sacred assembly, and another one on the seventh day. Do no work at all on these days, except to prepare food for everyone to eat; that is all you may do.

17 "Celebrate the Festival of Unleavened Bread, because it was on this very day that I brought your divisions out of Egypt. Celebrate this day as a lasting ordinance for the generations to come. 18 In the first month you are to eat bread made without yeast, from the evening of the fourteenth day until the evening of the twenty-first day. 19 For seven days no yeast is to be found in your houses. And anyone, whether foreigner or native-born, who eats anything with yeast in it must be cut off from the community of Israel. 20 Eat nothing made with yeast. Wherever you live, you must eat unleavened bread."

21 Then Moses summoned all the elders of Israel and said to them, "Go at once and select the animals for your families and slaughter the Passover lamb. 22 Take a bunch of hyssop, dip it into the blood in the basin and put some of the blood on the top and on both sides of the doorframe. None of you shall go out of the door of your house until morning. 23 When the LORD goes through the land to strike down the Egyptians, he will see the blood on the top and sides of the doorframe and will pass over that doorway, and he will not permit the destroyer to enter your houses and strike you down.

24 "Obey these instructions as a lasting ordinance for you and your descendants. 25 When you enter the land that the LORD will give you as he promised, observe this ceremony. 26 And when your children ask you, 'What does this ceremony mean to you?' 27 then tell them, 'It is the Passover sacrifice to the LORD, who passed over the houses of the Israelites in Egypt and spared our homes when he struck down the Egyptians.'" Then the people bowed down and worshiped. 28 The Israelites did just what the LORD commanded Moses and Aaron.

29 At midnight the LORD struck down all the firstborn in Egypt, from the firstborn of Pharaoh, who sat on the throne, to the firstborn of the prisoner, who was in the dungeon, and the firstborn of all the livestock as well. 30 Pharaoh and all his officials and all the Egyptians got up during the night, and there was loud wailing in Egypt, for there was not a house without someone dead.

31 During the night Pharaoh summoned Moses and Aaron and said, "Up! Leave my people, you and the Israelites! Go, worship the LORD as you have requested. 32 Take your flocks and herds, as you have said, and go. And also bless me."

33 The Egyptians urged the people to hurry and leave the country. "For otherwise," they said, "we will all die!" 34 So the people took their dough before the yeast was added, and carried it on their shoulders in kneading troughs wrapped in clothing. 35 The Israelites did as Moses instructed and asked the Egyptians for articles of silver and gold and for clothing. 36 The LORD had made the Egyptians favorably disposed toward the people, and they gave them what they asked for; so they plundered the Egyptians.

37 The Israelites journeyed from Rameses to Sukkoth. There were about six

hundred thousand men on foot, besides women and children. 38 Many other people went up with them, and also large droves of livestock, both flocks and herds. 39 With the dough the Israelites had brought from Egypt, they baked loaves of unleavened bread. The dough was without yeast because they had been driven out of Egypt and did not have time to prepare food for themselves.

40 Now the length of time the Israelite people lived in Egypt[a] was 430 years. 41 At the end of the 430 years, to the very day, all the LORD's divisions left Egypt. 42 Because the LORD kept vigil that night to bring them out of Egypt, on this night all the Israelites are to keep vigil to honor the LORD for the generations to come.

43 The LORD said to Moses and Aaron, "These are the regulations for the Passover meal:

"No foreigner may eat it. 44 Any slave you have bought may eat it after you have circumcised him, 45 but a temporary resident or a hired worker may not eat it.

46 "It must be eaten inside the house; take none of the meat outside the house. Do not break any of the bones. 47 The whole community of Israel must celebrate it.

48 "A foreigner residing among you who wants to celebrate the LORD's Passover must have all the males in his household circumcised; then he may take part like one born in the land. No uncircumcised male may eat it. 49 The same law applies both to the native-born and to the foreigner residing among you."

50 All the Israelites did just what the LORD had commanded Moses and Aaron. 51 And on that very day the LORD brought the Israelites out of Egypt by their divisions.

13 The LORD said to Moses, 2 "Consecrate to me every firstborn male. The first offspring of every womb among the Israelites belongs to me, whether human or animal."

3 Then Moses said to the people, "Commemorate this day, the day you came out of Egypt, out of the land of slavery, because the LORD brought you out of it with a mighty hand. Eat nothing containing yeast. 4 Today, in the month of Aviv, you are leaving. 5 When the LORD brings you into the land of the Canaanites, Hittites, Amorites, Hivites and Jebusites—the land he swore to your ancestors to give you, a land flowing with milk and honey—you are to observe this ceremony in this month: 6 For seven days eat bread made without yeast and on the seventh day hold a festival to the LORD. 7 Eat unleavened bread during those seven days; nothing with yeast in it is to be seen among you, nor shall any yeast be seen anywhere within your borders. 8 On that day tell your son, 'I do this because of what the LORD did for me when I came out of Egypt.' 9 This observance will be for you like a sign on your hand and a reminder on your forehead that this law of the LORD is to be on your lips. For the LORD brought you out of Egypt with his mighty hand. 10 You must keep this ordinance at the appointed time year after year.

11 "After the LORD brings you into the land of the Canaanites and gives it to you, as he promised on oath to you and your ancestors, 12 you are to give over to the LORD the first offspring of every womb. All the firstborn males of your livestock belong to the LORD. 13 Redeem with a lamb every firstborn donkey, but if you do not redeem it, break its neck. Redeem every firstborn among your sons.

14 "In days to come, when your son asks you, 'What does this mean?' say to him, 'With a mighty hand the LORD brought us out of Egypt, out of the land of slavery. 15 When Pharaoh stubbornly refused to let us go, the LORD killed the firstborn of both people and animals in Egypt. This is why I sacrifice to the LORD the first male offspring of every womb and redeem each of my firstborn sons.' 16 And it will be like a sign on your hand and a symbol on your forehead that the LORD brought us out of Egypt with his mighty hand."

17 When Pharaoh let the people go, God did not lead them on the road through the Philistine country, though that was shorter. For God said, "If they face war, they might change their minds and return to Egypt." 18 So God led the people around by the desert road toward the Red Sea.[b] The Israelites went up out of Egypt ready for battle.

[a] *40* Masoretic Text; Samaritan Pentateuch and Septuagint *Egypt and Canaan* [b] *18* Or *the Sea of Reeds*

19 Moses took the bones of Joseph with
him because Joseph had made the Israelites swear an oath. He had said, "God
will surely come to your aid, and then
you must carry my bones up with you
from this place."[a]

20 After leaving Sukkoth they camped
at Etham on the edge of the desert. 21 By
day the LORD went ahead of them in a
pillar of cloud to guide them on their
way and by night in a pillar of fire to give
them light, so that they could travel by
day or night. 22 Neither the pillar of cloud
by day nor the pillar of fire by night left
its place in front of the people.

14 Then the LORD said to Moses, 2 "Tell
the Israelites to turn back and encamp near Pi Hahiroth, between Migdol and the sea. They are to encamp by
the sea, directly opposite Baal Zephon.
3 Pharaoh will think, 'The Israelites are
wandering around the land in confusion, hemmed in by the desert.' 4 And I
will harden Pharaoh's heart, and he will
pursue them. But I will gain glory for myself through Pharaoh and all his army,
and the Egyptians will know that I am
the LORD." So the Israelites did this.

5 When the king of Egypt was told that
the people had fled, Pharaoh and his officials changed their minds about them
and said, "What have we done? We have
let the Israelites go and have lost their
services!" 6 So he had his chariot made
ready and took his army with him. 7 He
took six hundred of the best chariots,
along with all the other chariots of Egypt,
with officers over all of them. 8 The LORD
hardened the heart of Pharaoh king of
Egypt, so that he pursued the Israelites,
who were marching out boldly. 9 The
Egyptians—all Pharaoh's horses and
chariots, horsemen[b] and troops—pursued the Israelites and overtook them
as they camped by the sea near Pi Hahiroth, opposite Baal Zephon.

10 As Pharaoh approached, the Israelites looked up, and there were the
Egyptians, marching after them. They
were terrified and cried out to the LORD.
11 They said to Moses, "Was it because
there were no graves in Egypt that you
brought us to the desert to die? What
have you done to us by bringing us out
of Egypt? 12 Didn't we say to you in Egypt,
'Leave us alone; let us serve the Egyptians'? It would have been better for us
to serve the Egyptians than to die in the
desert!"

13 Moses answered the people, "Do
not be afraid. Stand firm and you will
see the deliverance the LORD will bring
you today. The Egyptians you see today
you will never see again. 14 The LORD will
fight for you; you need only to be still."

15 Then the LORD said to Moses, "Why
are you crying out to me? Tell the Israelites to move on. 16 Raise your staff and
stretch out your hand over the sea to divide the water so that the Israelites can
go through the sea on dry ground. 17 I
will harden the hearts of the Egyptians
so that they will go in after them. And I
will gain glory through Pharaoh and all
his army, through his chariots and his
horsemen. 18 The Egyptians will know
that I am the LORD when I gain glory
through Pharaoh, his chariots and his
horsemen."

19 Then the angel of God, who had been
traveling in front of Israel's army, withdrew and went behind them. The pillar
of cloud also moved from in front and
stood behind them, 20 coming between
the armies of Egypt and Israel. Throughout the night the cloud brought darkness
to the one side and light to the other side;
so neither went near the other all night
long.

21 Then Moses stretched out his hand
over the sea, and all that night the LORD
drove the sea back with a strong east
wind and turned it into dry land. The
waters were divided, 22 and the Israelites went through the sea on dry ground,
with a wall of water on their right and on
their left.

23 The Egyptians pursued them, and all
Pharaoh's horses and chariots and horsemen followed them into the sea. 24 During the last watch of the night the LORD
looked down from the pillar of fire and
cloud at the Egyptian army and threw it
into confusion. 25 He jammed[c] the wheels
of their chariots so that they had difficulty driving. And the Egyptians said, "Let's
get away from the Israelites! The LORD is
fighting for them against Egypt."

[a] *19* See Gen. 50:25. [b] *9* Or *charioteers*; also in verses 17, 18, 23, 26 and 28 [c] *25* See Samaritan Pentateuch, Septuagint and Syriac; Masoretic Text *removed*

26 Then the LORD said to Moses,
"Stretch out your hand over the sea so
that the waters may flow back over the
Egyptians and their chariots and horsemen." 27 Moses stretched out his hand
over the sea, and at daybreak the sea
went back to its place. The Egyptians
were fleeing toward[a] it, and the LORD
swept them into the sea. 28 The water
flowed back and covered the chariots
and horsemen — the entire army of Pharaoh that had followed the Israelites into
the sea. Not one of them survived.
29 But the Israelites went through the
sea on dry ground, with a wall of water
on their right and on their left. 30 That
day the LORD saved Israel from the
hands of the Egyptians, and Israel saw
the Egyptians lying dead on the shore.
31 And when the Israelites saw the mighty
hand of the LORD displayed against the
Egyptians, the people feared the LORD
and put their trust in him and in Moses
his servant.

15 Then Moses and the Israelites sang
this song to the LORD:

"I will sing to the LORD,
for he is highly exalted.
Both horse and driver
he has hurled into the sea.

2 "The LORD is my strength and my
defense[b];
he has become my salvation.
He is my God, and I will praise him,
my father's God, and I will exalt
him.
3 The LORD is a warrior;
the LORD is his name.
4 Pharaoh's chariots and his army
he has hurled into the sea.
The best of Pharaoh's officers
are drowned in the Red Sea.[c]
5 The deep waters have covered them;
they sank to the depths like a stone.
6 Your right hand, LORD,
was majestic in power.
Your right hand, LORD,
shattered the enemy.

7 "In the greatness of your majesty
you threw down those who opposed
you.
You unleashed your burning anger;
it consumed them like stubble.
8 By the blast of your nostrils
the waters piled up.
The surging waters stood up like a
wall;
the deep waters congealed in the
heart of the sea.
9 The enemy boasted,
'I will pursue, I will overtake them.
I will divide the spoils;
I will gorge myself on them.
I will draw my sword
and my hand will destroy them.'
10 But you blew with your breath,
and the sea covered them.
They sank like lead
in the mighty waters.
11 Who among the gods
is like you, LORD?
Who is like you —
majestic in holiness,
awesome in glory,
working wonders?

12 "You stretch out your right hand,
and the earth swallows your
enemies.
13 In your unfailing love you will lead
the people you have redeemed.
In your strength you will guide them
to your holy dwelling.
14 The nations will hear and tremble;
anguish will grip the people of
Philistia.
15 The chiefs of Edom will be terrified,
the leaders of Moab will be seized
with trembling,
the people[d] of Canaan will melt away;
16 terror and dread will fall on them.
By the power of your arm
they will be as still as a stone —
until your people pass by, LORD,
until the people you bought[e]
pass by.
17 You will bring them in and plant them
on the mountain of your
inheritance —
the place, LORD, you made for your
dwelling,
the sanctuary, Lord, your hands
established.

18 "The LORD reigns
for ever and ever."

19 When Pharaoh's horses, chariots and
horsemen[f] went into the sea, the LORD

[a] 27 Or *from* [b] 2 Or *song* [c] 4 Or *the Sea of Reeds*; also in verse 22 [d] 15 Or *rulers* [e] 16 Or *created*
[f] 19 Or *charioteers*

brought the waters of the sea back over
them, but the Israelites walked through
the sea on dry ground. 20Then Miriam
the prophet, Aaron's sister, took a timbrel
in her hand, and all the women followed
her, with timbrels and dancing. 21Miri-
am sang to them:

"Sing to the LORD,
for he is highly exalted.
Both horse and driver
he has hurled into the sea."

22Then Moses led Israel from the Red
Sea and they went into the Desert of Shur.
For three days they traveled in the desert without finding water. 23When they
came to Marah, they could not drink its
water because it was bitter. (That is why
the place is called Marah.[a]) 24So the
people grumbled against Moses, saying,
"What are we to drink?"

25Then Moses cried out to the LORD,
and the LORD showed him a piece of
wood. He threw it into the water, and the
water became fit to drink.

There the LORD issued a ruling and
instruction for them and put them to
the test. 26He said, "If you listen carefully to the LORD your God and do what is
right in his eyes, if you pay attention to
his commands and keep all his decrees,
I will not bring on you any of the diseases
I brought on the Egyptians, for I am the
LORD, who heals you."

27Then they came to Elim, where there
were twelve springs and seventy palm
trees, and they camped there near the
water.

16 The whole Israelite community
set out from Elim and came to the
Desert of Sin, which is between Elim and
Sinai, on the fifteenth day of the second
month after they had come out of Egypt.
2In the desert the whole community
grumbled against Moses and Aaron.
3The Israelites said to them, "If only we
had died by the LORD's hand in Egypt!
There we sat around pots of meat and
ate all the food we wanted, but you have
brought us out into this desert to starve
this entire assembly to death."

4Then the LORD said to Moses, "I will
rain down bread from heaven for you.
The people are to go out each day and
gather enough for that day. In this way I
will test them and see whether they will
follow my instructions. 5On the sixth
day they are to prepare what they bring
in, and that is to be twice as much as they
gather on the other days."

6So Moses and Aaron said to all the Israelites, "In the evening you will know
that it was the LORD who brought you out
of Egypt, 7and in the morning you will
see the glory of the LORD, because he
has heard your grumbling against him.
Who are we, that you should grumble
against us?" 8Moses also said, "You will
know that it was the LORD when he gives
you meat to eat in the evening and all the
bread you want in the morning, because
he has heard your grumbling against
him. Who are we? You are not grumbling
against us, but against the LORD."

9Then Moses told Aaron, "Say to the
entire Israelite community, 'Come before the LORD, for he has heard your
grumbling.'"

10While Aaron was speaking to the
whole Israelite community, they looked
toward the desert, and there was the glory of the LORD appearing in the cloud.

11The LORD said to Moses, 12"I have
heard the grumbling of the Israelites.
Tell them, 'At twilight you will eat meat,
and in the morning you will be filled with
bread. Then you will know that I am the
LORD your God.'"

13That evening quail came and covered the camp, and in the morning there
was a layer of dew around the camp.
14When the dew was gone, thin flakes
like frost on the ground appeared on the
desert floor. 15When the Israelites saw it,
they said to each other, "What is it?" For
they did not know what it was.

Moses said to them, "It is the bread the
LORD has given you to eat. 16This is what
the LORD has commanded: 'Everyone is
to gather as much as they need. Take an
omer[b] for each person you have in your
tent.'"

17The Israelites did as they were told;
some gathered much, some little. 18And
when they measured it by the omer, the
one who gathered much did not have
too much, and the one who gathered lit-

[a] 23 *Marah* means *bitter*. [b] 16 That is, possibly about 3 pounds or about 1.4 kilograms; also in verses 18, 32, 33 and 36

tle did not have too little. Everyone had
gathered just as much as they needed.
19 Then Moses said to them, "No one is
to keep any of it until morning."
20 However, some of them paid no attention to Moses; they kept part of it until
morning, but it was full of maggots and
began to smell. So Moses was angry with
them.
21 Each morning everyone gathered as
much as they needed, and when the sun
grew hot, it melted away. 22 On the sixth
day, they gathered twice as much — two
omers[a] for each person — and the leaders of the community came and reported
this to Moses. 23 He said to them, "This is
what the LORD commanded: 'Tomorrow
is to be a day of sabbath rest, a holy sabbath to the LORD. So bake what you want
to bake and boil what you want to boil.
Save whatever is left and keep it until
morning.'"
24 So they saved it until morning, as
Moses commanded, and it did not stink
or get maggots in it. 25 "Eat it today," Moses said, "because today is a sabbath to
the LORD. You will not find any of it on
the ground today. 26 Six days you are to
gather it, but on the seventh day, the Sabbath, there will not be any."
27 Nevertheless, some of the people
went out on the seventh day to gather it,
but they found none. 28 Then the LORD
said to Moses, "How long will you[b] refuse
to keep my commands and my instructions? 29 Bear in mind that the LORD has
given you the Sabbath; that is why on the
sixth day he gives you bread for two days.
Everyone is to stay where they are on the
seventh day; no one is to go out." 30 So the
people rested on the seventh day.
31 The people of Israel called the bread
manna.[c] It was white like coriander seed
and tasted like wafers made with honey.
32 Moses said, "This is what the LORD has
commanded: 'Take an omer of manna
and keep it for the generations to come,
so they can see the bread I gave you to eat
in the wilderness when I brought you out
of Egypt.'"
33 So Moses said to Aaron, "Take a jar
and put an omer of manna in it. Then
place it before the LORD to be kept for the
generations to come."
34 As the LORD commanded Moses,
Aaron put the manna with the tablets of
the covenant law, so that it might be preserved. 35 The Israelites ate manna forty years, until they came to a land that
was settled; they ate manna until they
reached the border of Canaan.
36 (An omer is one-tenth of an ephah.)

17 The whole Israelite community set
out from the Desert of Sin, traveling
from place to place as the LORD commanded. They camped at Rephidim,
but there was no water for the people to
drink. 2 So they quarreled with Moses
and said, "Give us water to drink."
Moses replied, "Why do you quarrel
with me? Why do you put the LORD to
the test?"
3 But the people were thirsty for water
there, and they grumbled against Moses.
They said, "Why did you bring us up out
of Egypt to make us and our children and
livestock die of thirst?"
4 Then Moses cried out to the LORD,
"What am I to do with these people? They
are almost ready to stone me."
5 The LORD answered Moses, "Go out in
front of the people. Take with you some
of the elders of Israel and take in your
hand the staff with which you struck
the Nile, and go. 6 I will stand there before you by the rock at Horeb. Strike the
rock, and water will come out of it for the
people to drink." So Moses did this in
the sight of the elders of Israel. 7 And he
called the place Massah[d] and Meribah[e]
because the Israelites quarreled and because they tested the LORD saying, "Is
the LORD among us or not?"
8 The Amalekites came and attacked
the Israelites at Rephidim. 9 Moses said
to Joshua, "Choose some of our men and
go out to fight the Amalekites. Tomorrow I will stand on top of the hill with the
staff of God in my hands."
10 So Joshua fought the Amalekites as
Moses had ordered, and Moses, Aaron
and Hur went to the top of the hill. 11 As
long as Moses held up his hands, the Israelites were winning, but whenever he
lowered his hands, the Amalekites were
winning. 12 When Moses' hands grew
tired, they took a stone and put it under

[a] *22* That is, possibly about 6 pounds or about 2.8 kilograms [b] *28* The Hebrew is plural. [c] *31* *Manna* sounds like the Hebrew for *What is it?* (see verse 15). [d] *7* *Massah* means *testing.* [e] *7* *Meribah* means *quarreling.*

him and he sat on it. Aaron and Hur held
his hands up — one on one side, one on
the other — so that his hands remained
steady till sunset. 13 So Joshua overcame
the Amalekite army with the sword.

14 Then the LORD said to Moses, "Write
this on a scroll as something to be remembered and make sure that Joshua
hears it, because I will completely blot
out the name of Amalek from under
heaven."

15 Moses built an altar and called it The
LORD is my Banner. 16 He said, "Because
hands were lifted up against[a] the throne
of the LORD,[b] the LORD will be at war
against the Amalekites from generation
to generation."

18 Now Jethro, the priest of Midian and
father-in-law of Moses, heard of everything God had done for Moses and for
his people Israel, and how the LORD had
brought Israel out of Egypt.

2 After Moses had sent away his wife
Zipporah, his father-in-law Jethro received her 3 and her two sons. One son
was named Gershom,[c] for Moses said,
"I have become a foreigner in a foreign
land"; 4 and the other was named Eliezer,[d] for he said, "My father's God was
my helper; he saved me from the sword
of Pharaoh."

5 Jethro, Moses' father-in-law, together
with Moses' sons and wife, came to him
in the wilderness, where he was camped
near the mountain of God. 6 Jethro had
sent word to him, "I, your father-in-law
Jethro, am coming to you with your wife
and her two sons."

7 So Moses went out to meet his father-
in-law and bowed down and kissed him.
They greeted each other and then went
into the tent. 8 Moses told his father-in-
law about everything the LORD had done
to Pharaoh and the Egyptians for Israel's
sake and about all the hardships they
had met along the way and how the LORD
had saved them.

9 Jethro was delighted to hear about all
the good things the LORD had done for
Israel in rescuing them from the hand
of the Egyptians. 10 He said, "Praise be
to the LORD, who rescued you from the
hand of the Egyptians and of Pharaoh,
and who rescued the people from the
hand of the Egyptians. 11 Now I know that
the LORD is greater than all other gods,
for he did this to those who had treated
Israel arrogantly." 12 Then Jethro, Moses'
father-in-law, brought a burnt offering
and other sacrifices to God, and Aaron
came with all the elders of Israel to eat
a meal with Moses' father-in-law in the
presence of God.

13 The next day Moses took his seat to
serve as judge for the people, and they
stood around him from morning till evening. 14 When his father-in-law saw all
that Moses was doing for the people, he
said, "What is this you are doing for the
people? Why do you alone sit as judge,
while all these people stand around you
from morning till evening?"

15 Moses answered him, "Because the
people come to me to seek God's will.
16 Whenever they have a dispute, it is
brought to me, and I decide between the
parties and inform them of God's decrees
and instructions."

17 Moses' father-in-law replied, "What
you are doing is not good. 18 You and
these people who come to you will
only wear yourselves out. The work is
too heavy for you; you cannot handle it
alone. 19 Listen now to me and I will give
you some advice, and may God be with
you. You must be the people's representative before God and bring their disputes to him. 20 Teach them his decrees
and instructions, and show them the way
they are to live and how they are to behave. 21 But select capable men from all
the people — men who fear God, trustworthy men who hate dishonest gain —
and appoint them as officials over thousands, hundreds, fifties and tens. 22 Have
them serve as judges for the people at all
times, but have them bring every difficult case to you; the simple cases they
can decide themselves. That will make
your load lighter, because they will share
it with you. 23 If you do this and God so
commands, you will be able to stand the
strain, and all these people will go home
satisfied."

24 Moses listened to his father-in-law
and did everything he said. 25 He chose
capable men from all Israel and made
them leaders of the people, officials over
thousands, hundreds, fifties and tens.
26 They served as judges for the peo-

[a] *16* Or *to* [b] *16* The meaning of the Hebrew for this clause is uncertain. [c] *3* *Gershom* sounds like the Hebrew for *a foreigner there.* [d] *4* *Eliezer* means *my God is helper.*

ple at all times. The difficult cases they
brought to Moses, but the simple ones
they decided themselves.
27 Then Moses sent his father-in-law on
his way, and Jethro returned to his own
country.

19 On the first day of the third month
after the Israelites left Egypt—on
that very day—they came to the Desert
of Sinai. 2 After they set out from Rephidim, they entered the Desert of Sinai,
and Israel camped there in the desert in
front of the mountain.
3 Then Moses went up to God, and the
LORD called to him from the mountain
and said, "This is what you are to say to
the descendants of Jacob and what you
are to tell the people of Israel: 4 'You yourselves have seen what I did to Egypt, and
how I carried you on eagles' wings and
brought you to myself. 5 Now if you obey
me fully and keep my covenant, then out
of all nations you will be my treasured
possession. Although the whole earth is
mine, 6 you[a] will be for me a kingdom of
priests and a holy nation.' These are the
words you are to speak to the Israelites."
7 So Moses went back and summoned
the elders of the people and set before
them all the words the LORD had commanded him to speak. 8 The people all
responded together, "We will do everything the LORD has said." So Moses
brought their answer back to the LORD.
9 The LORD said to Moses, "I am going to come to you in a dense cloud, so
that the people will hear me speaking
with you and will always put their trust
in you." Then Moses told the LORD what
the people had said.
10 And the LORD said to Moses, "Go to
the people and consecrate them today
and tomorrow. Have them wash their
clothes 11 and be ready by the third day,
because on that day the LORD will come
down on Mount Sinai in the sight of all
the people. 12 Put limits for the people
around the mountain and tell them, 'Be
careful that you do not approach the
mountain or touch the foot of it. Whoever touches the mountain is to be put
to death. 13 They are to be stoned or shot
with arrows; not a hand is to be laid on
them. No person or animal shall be permitted to live.' Only when the ram's horn
sounds a long blast may they approach
the mountain."
14 After Moses had gone down the
mountain to the people, he consecrated them, and they washed their clothes.
15 Then he said to the people, "Prepare
yourselves for the third day. Abstain
from sexual relations."
16 On the morning of the third day
there was thunder and lightning, with
a thick cloud over the mountain, and a
very loud trumpet blast. Everyone in the
camp trembled. 17 Then Moses led the
people out of the camp to meet with God,
and they stood at the foot of the mountain. 18 Mount Sinai was covered with
smoke, because the LORD descended on
it in fire. The smoke billowed up from it
like smoke from a furnace, and the whole
mountain[b] trembled violently. 19 As the
sound of the trumpet grew louder and
louder, Moses spoke and the voice of God
answered him.[c]
20 The LORD descended to the top of
Mount Sinai and called Moses to the
top of the mountain. So Moses went up
21 and the LORD said to him, "Go down
and warn the people so they do not force
their way through to see the LORD and
many of them perish. 22 Even the priests,
who approach the LORD, must consecrate themselves, or the LORD will break
out against them."
23 Moses said to the LORD, "The people
cannot come up Mount Sinai, because you
yourself warned us, 'Put limits around the
mountain and set it apart as holy.'"
24 The LORD replied, "Go down and
bring Aaron up with you. But the priests
and the people must not force their way
through to come up to the LORD, or he
will break out against them."
25 So Moses went down to the people
and told them.

20 And God spoke all these words:

2 "I am the LORD your God, who
brought you out of Egypt, out of
the land of slavery.
3 "You shall have no other gods before[d] me.

[a] 5,6 Or *possession, for the whole earth is mine.* 6 *You* [b] 18 Most Hebrew manuscripts; a few Hebrew manuscripts and Septuagint *and all the people* [c] 19 Or *and God answered him with thunder* [d] 3 Or *besides*

4 "You shall not make for yourself an
image in the form of anything
in heaven above or on the earth
beneath or in the waters below.
5 You shall not bow down to
them or worship them; for I, the
LORD your God, am a jealous
God, punishing the children for
the sin of the parents to the third
and fourth generation of those
who hate me, 6 but showing love
to a thousand generations of
those who love me and keep my
commandments.
7 "You shall not misuse the name of
the LORD your God, for the LORD
will not hold anyone guiltless
who misuses his name.
8 "Remember the Sabbath day by
keeping it holy. 9 Six days you
shall labor and do all your work,
10 but the seventh day is a sabbath to the LORD your God. On
it you shall not do any work, neither you, nor your son or daughter, nor your male or female servant, nor your animals, nor any
foreigner residing in your towns.
11 For in six days the LORD made
the heavens and the earth, the
sea, and all that is in them, but
he rested on the seventh day.
Therefore the LORD blessed the
Sabbath day and made it holy.
12 "Honor your father and your mother,
so that you may live long in the
land the LORD your God is giving
you.
13 "You shall not murder.
14 "You shall not commit adultery.
15 "You shall not steal.
16 "You shall not give false testimony
against your neighbor.
17 "You shall not covet your neighbor's
house. You shall not covet your
neighbor's wife, or his male or
female servant, his ox or donkey,
or anything that belongs to your
neighbor."

18 When the people saw the thunder
and lightning and heard the trumpet and
saw the mountain in smoke, they trembled with fear. They stayed at a distance
19 and said to Moses, "Speak to us yourself and we will listen. But do not have
God speak to us or we will die."

20 Moses said to the people, "Do not be
afraid. God has come to test you, so that
the fear of God will be with you to keep
you from sinning."

21 The people remained at a distance,
while Moses approached the thick darkness where God was.

22 Then the LORD said to Moses, "Tell
the Israelites this: 'You have seen for
yourselves that I have spoken to you
from heaven: 23 Do not make any gods to
be alongside me; do not make for yourselves gods of silver or gods of gold.

24 " 'Make an altar of earth for me and
sacrifice on it your burnt offerings and
fellowship offerings, your sheep and
goats and your cattle. Wherever I cause
my name to be honored, I will come to
you and bless you. 25 If you make an altar of stones for me, do not build it with
dressed stones, for you will defile it if you
use a tool on it. 26 And do not go up to my
altar on steps, or your private parts may
be exposed.'

21 "These are the laws you are to set
before them:

2 "If you buy a Hebrew servant, he is
to serve you for six years. But in the seventh year, he shall go free, without paying anything. 3 If he comes alone, he is to
go free alone; but if he has a wife when
he comes, she is to go with him. 4 If his
master gives him a wife and she bears
him sons or daughters, the woman and
her children shall belong to her master,
and only the man shall go free.

5 "But if the servant declares, 'I love my
master and my wife and children and
do not want to go free,' 6 then his master must take him before the judges.[a] He
shall take him to the door or the doorpost and pierce his ear with an awl. Then
he will be his servant for life.

7 "If a man sells his daughter as a servant, she is not to go free as male servants do. 8 If she does not please the
master who has selected her for himself,[b]
he must let her be redeemed. He has no
right to sell her to foreigners, because
he has broken faith with her. 9 If he selects her for his son, he must grant her
the rights of a daughter. 10 If he marries

[a] 6 Or *before God* [b] 8 Or *master so that he does not choose her*

another woman, he must not deprive the
first one of her food, clothing and marital
rights. 11 If he does not provide her with
these three things, she is to go free, without any payment of money.
12 “Anyone who strikes a person with a
fatal blow is to be put to death. 13 However, if it is not done intentionally, but God
lets it happen, they are to flee to a place
I will designate. 14 But if anyone schemes
and kills someone deliberately, that person is to be taken from my altar and put
to death.
15 “Anyone who attacks[a] their father or
mother is to be put to death.
16 “Anyone who kidnaps someone is to
be put to death, whether the victim has
been sold or is still in the kidnapper's
possession.
17 “Anyone who curses their father or
mother is to be put to death.
18 “If people quarrel and one person
hits another with a stone or with their
fist[b] and the victim does not die but is
confined to bed, 19 the one who struck
the blow will not be held liable if the other can get up and walk around outside
with a staff; however, the guilty party
must pay the injured person for any loss
of time and see that the victim is completely healed.
20 “Anyone who beats their male or female slave with a rod must be punished
if the slave dies as a direct result, 21 but
they are not to be punished if the slave
recovers after a day or two, since the
slave is their property.
22 “If people are fighting and hit a
pregnant woman and she gives birth
prematurely[c] but there is no serious injury, the offender must be fined whatever the woman's husband demands and
the court allows. 23 But if there is serious
injury, you are to take life for life, 24 eye
for eye, tooth for tooth, hand for hand,
foot for foot, 25 burn for burn, wound for
wound, bruise for bruise.
26 “An owner who hits a male or female
slave in the eye and destroys it must let
the slave go free to compensate for the
eye. 27 And an owner who knocks out the
tooth of a male or female slave must let
the slave go free to compensate for the
tooth.
28 “If a bull gores a man or woman to
death, the bull is to be stoned to death,
and its meat must not be eaten. But the
owner of the bull will not be held responsible. 29 If, however, the bull has had the
habit of goring and the owner has been
warned but has not kept it penned up
and it kills a man or woman, the bull is
to be stoned and its owner also is to be
put to death. 30 However, if payment is
demanded, the owner may redeem his
life by the payment of whatever is demanded. 31 This law also applies if the
bull gores a son or daughter. 32 If the bull
gores a male or female slave, the owner
must pay thirty shekels[d] of silver to the
master of the slave, and the bull is to be
stoned to death.
33 “If anyone uncovers a pit or digs one
and fails to cover it and an ox or a donkey
falls into it, 34 the one who opened the pit
must pay the owner for the loss and take
the dead animal in exchange.
35 “If anyone's bull injures someone
else's bull and it dies, the two parties
are to sell the live one and divide both
the money and the dead animal equally. 36 However, if it was known that the
bull had the habit of goring, yet the owner did not keep it penned up, the owner
must pay, animal for animal, and take
the dead animal in exchange.

22[e] “Whoever steals an ox or a sheep
and slaughters it or sells it must
pay back five head of cattle for the ox and
four sheep for the sheep.
2 “If a thief is caught breaking in at
night and is struck a fatal blow, the defender is not guilty of bloodshed; 3 but if
it happens after sunrise, the defender is
guilty of bloodshed.
“Anyone who steals must certainly
make restitution, but if they have nothing, they must be sold to pay for their
theft. 4 If the stolen animal is found alive
in their possession — whether ox or donkey or sheep — they must pay back double.
5 “If anyone grazes their livestock in a
field or vineyard and lets them stray and
they graze in someone else's field, the
offender must make restitution from the
best of their own field or vineyard.
6 “If a fire breaks out and spreads into
thornbushes so that it burns shocks of
grain or standing grain or the whole

[a] *15* Or *kills* [b] *18* Or *with a tool* [c] *22* Or *she has a miscarriage* [d] *32* That is, about 12 ounces or about 345 grams [e] In Hebrew texts 22:1 is numbered 21:37, and 22:2-31 is numbered 22:1-30.

field, the one who started the fire must
make restitution.
7 "If anyone gives a neighbor silver or
goods for safekeeping and they are stolen from the neighbor's house, the thief,
if caught, must pay back double. 8 But if
the thief is not found, the owner of the
house must appear before the judges,
and they must[a] determine whether the
owner of the house has laid hands on the
other person's property. 9 In all cases of
illegal possession of an ox, a donkey, a
sheep, a garment, or any other lost property about which somebody says, 'This
is mine,' both parties are to bring their
cases before the judges.[b] The one whom
the judges declare[c] guilty must pay back
double to the other.
10 "If anyone gives a donkey, an ox,
a sheep or any other animal to their
neighbor for safekeeping and it dies or
is injured or is taken away while no one
is looking, 11 the issue between them will
be settled by the taking of an oath before
the LORD that the neighbor did not lay
hands on the other person's property.
The owner is to accept this, and no restitution is required. 12 But if the animal
was stolen from the neighbor, restitution must be made to the owner. 13 If it
was torn to pieces by a wild animal, the
neighbor shall bring in the remains as
evidence and shall not be required to pay
for the torn animal.
14 "If anyone borrows an animal from
their neighbor and it is injured or dies
while the owner is not present, they must
make restitution. 15 But if the owner is
with the animal, the borrower will not
have to pay. If the animal was hired, the
money paid for the hire covers the loss.
16 "If a man seduces a virgin who is not
pledged to be married and sleeps with
her, he must pay the bride-price, and she
shall be his wife. 17 If her father absolutely refuses to give her to him, he must still
pay the bride-price for virgins.
18 "Do not allow a sorceress to live.
19 "Anyone who has sexual relations
with an animal is to be put to death.
20 "Whoever sacrifices to any god other
than the LORD must be destroyed.[d]
21 "Do not mistreat or oppress a foreigner, for you were foreigners in Egypt.
22 "Do not take advantage of the widow or the fatherless. 23 If you do and they
cry out to me, I will certainly hear their
cry. 24 My anger will be aroused, and I
will kill you with the sword; your wives
will become widows and your children
fatherless.
25 "If you lend money to one of my people among you who is needy, do not treat
it like a business deal; charge no interest.
26 If you take your neighbor's cloak as a
pledge, return it by sunset, 27 because
that cloak is the only covering your
neighbor has. What else can they sleep
in? When they cry out to me, I will hear,
for I am compassionate.
28 "Do not blaspheme God[e] or curse the
ruler of your people.
29 "Do not hold back offerings from
your granaries or your vats.[f]
"You must give me the firstborn of your
sons. 30 Do the same with your cattle and
your sheep. Let them stay with their
mothers for seven days, but give them to
me on the eighth day.
31 "You are to be my holy people. So
do not eat the meat of an animal torn by
wild beasts; throw it to the dogs.

23 "Do not spread false reports. Do not
help a guilty person by being a malicious witness.
2 "Do not follow the crowd in doing
wrong. When you give testimony in a
lawsuit, do not pervert justice by siding
with the crowd, 3 and do not show favoritism to a poor person in a lawsuit.
4 "If you come across your enemy's ox
or donkey wandering off, be sure to return it. 5 If you see the donkey of someone who hates you fallen down under its
load, do not leave it there; be sure you
help them with it.
6 "Do not deny justice to your poor people in their lawsuits. 7 Have nothing to do
with a false charge and do not put an innocent or honest person to death, for I
will not acquit the guilty.
8 "Do not accept a bribe, for a bribe
blinds those who see and twists the
words of the innocent.
9 "Do not oppress a foreigner; you yourselves know how it feels to be foreigners,
because you were foreigners in Egypt.
10 "For six years you are to sow your

[a] 8 Or *before God, and he will* [b] 9 Or *before God* [c] 9 Or *whom God declares* [d] 20 The Hebrew term refers to the irrevocable giving over of things or persons to the LORD, often by totally destroying them.
[e] 28 Or *Do not revile the judges* [f] 29 The meaning of the Hebrew for this phrase is uncertain.

fields and harvest the crops, 11but during the seventh year let the land lie
unplowed and unused. Then the poor
among your people may get food from
it, and the wild animals may eat what is
left. Do the same with your vineyard and
your olive grove.
12"Six days do your work, but on the
seventh day do not work, so that your ox
and your donkey may rest, and so that
the slave born in your household and
the foreigner living among you may be
refreshed.
13"Be careful to do everything I have
said to you. Do not invoke the names of
other gods; do not let them be heard on
your lips.
14"Three times a year you are to celebrate a festival to me.
15"Celebrate the Festival of Unleavened Bread; for seven days eat bread
made without yeast, as I commanded
you. Do this at the appointed time in
the month of Aviv, for in that month you
came out of Egypt.
"No one is to appear before me empty-handed.
16"Celebrate the Festival of Harvest
with the firstfruits of the crops you sow
in your field.
"Celebrate the Festival of Ingathering
at the end of the year, when you gather in
your crops from the field.
17"Three times a year all the men are to
appear before the Sovereign LORD.
18"Do not offer the blood of a sacrifice
to me along with anything containing
yeast.
"The fat of my festival offerings must
not be kept until morning.
19"Bring the best of the firstfruits of
your soil to the house of the LORD your
God.
"Do not cook a young goat in its mother's milk.
20"See, I am sending an angel ahead
of you to guard you along the way and to
bring you to the place I have prepared.
21Pay attention to him and listen to
what he says. Do not rebel against him;
he will not forgive your rebellion, since
my Name is in him. 22If you listen carefully to what he says and do all that I say,
I will be an enemy to your enemies and
will oppose those who oppose you. 23My
angel will go ahead of you and bring you
into the land of the Amorites, Hittites,
Perizzites, Canaanites, Hivites and Jebusites, and I will wipe them out. 24Do
not bow down before their gods or worship them or follow their practices. You
must demolish them and break their
sacred stones to pieces. 25Worship the
LORD your God, and his blessing will be
on your food and water. I will take away
sickness from among you, 26and none
will miscarry or be barren in your land. I
will give you a full life span.
27"I will send my terror ahead of you
and throw into confusion every nation
you encounter. I will make all your enemies turn their backs and run. 28I will
send the hornet ahead of you to drive the
Hivites, Canaanites and Hittites out of
your way. 29But I will not drive them out
in a single year, because the land would
become desolate and the wild animals
too numerous for you. 30Little by little I
will drive them out before you, until you
have increased enough to take possession of the land.
31"I will establish your borders from
the Red Sea[a] to the Mediterranean Sea,[b]
and from the desert to the Euphrates River. I will give into your hands the people
who live in the land, and you will drive
them out before you. 32Do not make a
covenant with them or with their gods.
33Do not let them live in your land or they
will cause you to sin against me, because
the worship of their gods will certainly
be a snare to you."

24 Then the LORD said to Moses,
"Come up to the LORD, you and
Aaron, Nadab and Abihu, and seventy
of the elders of Israel. You are to worship at a distance, 2but Moses alone is
to approach the LORD; the others must
not come near. And the people may not
come up with him."
3When Moses went and told the people all the LORD's words and laws, they
responded with one voice, "Everything
the LORD has said we will do." 4Moses
then wrote down everything the LORD
had said.
He got up early the next morning and
built an altar at the foot of the mountain
and set up twelve stone pillars representing the twelve tribes of Israel. 5Then

[a] 31 Or *the Sea of Reeds* [b] 31 Hebrew *to the Sea of the Philistines*

he sent young Israelite men, and they
offered burnt offerings and sacrificed
young bulls as fellowship offerings to
the LORD. 6Moses took half of the blood
and put it in bowls, and the other half he
splashed against the altar. 7Then he took
the Book of the Covenant and read it to
the people. They responded, "We will do
everything the LORD has said; we will
obey."

8Moses then took the blood, sprinkled
it on the people and said, "This is the
blood of the covenant that the LORD has
made with you in accordance with all
these words."

9Moses and Aaron, Nadab and Abihu, and the seventy elders of Israel went
up 10and saw the God of Israel. Under
his feet was something like a pavement
made of lapis lazuli, as bright blue as
the sky. 11But God did not raise his hand
against these leaders of the Israelites;
they saw God, and they ate and drank.

12The LORD said to Moses, "Come up to
me on the mountain and stay here, and I
will give you the tablets of stone with the
law and commandments I have written
for their instruction."

13Then Moses set out with Joshua his
aide, and Moses went up on the mountain of God. 14He said to the elders, "Wait
here for us until we come back to you.
Aaron and Hur are with you, and anyone
involved in a dispute can go to them."

15When Moses went up on the mountain, the cloud covered it, 16and the glory
of the LORD settled on Mount Sinai. For
six days the cloud covered the mountain,
and on the seventh day the LORD called
to Moses from within the cloud. 17To the
Israelites the glory of the LORD looked
like a consuming fire on top of the mountain. 18Then Moses entered the cloud as
he went on up the mountain. And he
stayed on the mountain forty days and
forty nights.

25 The LORD said to Moses, 2"Tell the
Israelites to bring me an offering.
You are to receive the offering for me
from everyone whose heart prompts
them to give. 3These are the offerings
you are to receive from them: gold, silver and bronze; 4blue, purple and scarlet yarn and fine linen; goat hair; 5ram
skins dyed red and another type of durable leather[a]; acacia wood; 6olive oil
for the light; spices for the anointing oil
and for the fragrant incense; 7and onyx
stones and other gems to be mounted on
the ephod and breastpiece.

8"Then have them make a sanctuary
for me, and I will dwell among them.
9Make this tabernacle and all its furnishings exactly like the pattern I will
show you.

10"Have them make an ark[b] of acacia
wood — two and a half cubits long, a cubit and a half wide, and a cubit and a half
high.[c] 11Overlay it with pure gold, both
inside and out, and make a gold molding around it. 12Cast four gold rings for
it and fasten them to its four feet, with
two rings on one side and two rings on
the other. 13Then make poles of acacia
wood and overlay them with gold. 14In-
sert the poles into the rings on the sides
of the ark to carry it. 15The poles are to
remain in the rings of this ark; they are
not to be removed. 16Then put in the ark
the tablets of the covenant law, which I
will give you.

17"Make an atonement cover of pure
gold — two and a half cubits long and a
cubit and a half wide. 18And make two
cherubim out of hammered gold at the
ends of the cover. 19Make one cherub on
one end and the second cherub on the
other; make the cherubim of one piece
with the cover, at the two ends. 20The
cherubim are to have their wings spread
upward, overshadowing the cover with
them. The cherubim are to face each
other, looking toward the cover. 21Place
the cover on top of the ark and put in the
ark the tablets of the covenant law that
I will give you. 22There, above the cover
between the two cherubim that are over
the ark of the covenant law, I will meet
with you and give you all my commands
for the Israelites.

23"Make a table of acacia wood — two
cubits long, a cubit wide and a cubit
and a half high.[d] 24Overlay it with pure
gold and make a gold molding around
it. 25Also make around it a rim a handbreadth[e] wide and put a gold molding on

[a] *5* Possibly the hides of large aquatic mammals [b] *10* That is, a chest [c] *10* That is, about 3 3/4 feet long and 2 1/4 feet wide and high or about 1.1 meters long and 68 centimeters wide and high; similarly in verse 17 [d] *23* That is, about 3 feet long, 1 1/2 feet wide and 2 1/4 feet high or about 90 centimeters long, 45 centimeters wide and 68 centimeters high [e] *25* That is, about 3 inches or about 7.5 centimeters

the rim. 26 Make four gold rings for the table and fasten them to the four corners,
where the four legs are. 27 The rings are to
be close to the rim to hold the poles used
in carrying the table. 28 Make the poles
of acacia wood, overlay them with gold
and carry the table with them. 29 And
make its plates and dishes of pure gold,
as well as its pitchers and bowls for the
pouring out of offerings. 30 Put the bread
of the Presence on this table to be before
me at all times.

31 "Make a lampstand of pure gold.
Hammer out its base and shaft, and
make its flowerlike cups, buds and
blossoms of one piece with them. 32 Six
branches are to extend from the sides of
the lampstand—three on one side and
three on the other. 33 Three cups shaped
like almond flowers with buds and blossoms are to be on one branch, three on
the next branch, and the same for all
six branches extending from the lampstand. 34 And on the lampstand there are
to be four cups shaped like almond flowers with buds and blossoms. 35 One bud
shall be under the first pair of branches
extending from the lampstand, a second
bud under the second pair, and a third
bud under the third pair—six branches in all. 36 The buds and branches shall
all be of one piece with the lampstand,
hammered out of pure gold.

37 "Then make its seven lamps and set
them up on it so that they light the space
in front of it. 38 Its wick trimmers and
trays are to be of pure gold. 39 A talent[a] of
pure gold is to be used for the lampstand
and all these accessories. 40 See that you
make them according to the pattern
shown you on the mountain.

26 "Make the tabernacle with ten
curtains of finely twisted linen
and blue, purple and scarlet yarn, with
cherubim woven into them by a skilled
worker. 2 All the curtains are to be the
same size—twenty-eight cubits long
and four cubits wide.[b] 3 Join five of the
curtains together, and do the same with
the other five. 4 Make loops of blue material along the edge of the end curtain
in one set, and do the same with the end
curtain in the other set. 5 Make fifty loops
on one curtain and fifty loops on the end
curtain of the other set, with the loops
opposite each other. 6 Then make fifty
gold clasps and use them to fasten the
curtains together so that the tabernacle
is a unit.

7 "Make curtains of goat hair for the
tent over the tabernacle—eleven altogether. 8 All eleven curtains are to be the
same size—thirty cubits long and four
cubits wide.[c] 9 Join five of the curtains
together into one set and the other six
into another set. Fold the sixth curtain
double at the front of the tent. 10 Make
fifty loops along the edge of the end curtain in one set and also along the edge of
the end curtain in the other set. 11 Then
make fifty bronze clasps and put them
in the loops to fasten the tent together as
a unit. 12 As for the additional length of
the tent curtains, the half curtain that is
left over is to hang down at the rear of the
tabernacle. 13 The tent curtains will be a
cubit[d] longer on both sides; what is left
will hang over the sides of the tabernacle so as to cover it. 14 Make for the tent
a covering of ram skins dyed red, and
over that a covering of the other durable
leather.[e]

15 "Make upright frames of acacia wood
for the tabernacle. 16 Each frame is to be
ten cubits long and a cubit and a half
wide,[f] 17 with two projections set parallel
to each other. Make all the frames of the
tabernacle in this way. 18 Make twenty
frames for the south side of the tabernacle 19 and make forty silver bases to go
under them—two bases for each frame,
one under each projection. 20 For the other side, the north side of the tabernacle,
make twenty frames 21 and forty silver
bases—two under each frame. 22 Make
six frames for the far end, that is, the
west end of the tabernacle, 23 and make
two frames for the corners at the far end.
24 At these two corners they must be double from the bottom all the way to the top
and fitted into a single ring; both shall be
like that. 25 So there will be eight frames
and sixteen silver bases—two under
each frame.

[a] *39* That is, about 75 pounds or about 34 kilograms [b] *2* That is, about 42 feet long and 6 feet wide or about 13 meters long and 1.8 meters wide [c] *8* That is, about 45 feet long and 6 feet wide or about 13.5 meters long and 1.8 meters wide [d] *13* That is, about 18 inches or about 45 centimeters [e] *14* Possibly the hides of large aquatic mammals (see 25:5) [f] *16* That is, about 15 feet long and 2 1/4 feet wide or about 4.5 meters long and 68 centimeters wide

26 “Also make crossbars of acacia wood:
five for the frames on one side of the tabernacle, 27 five for those on the other side,
and five for the frames on the west, at the
far end of the tabernacle. 28 The center
crossbar is to extend from end to end at
the middle of the frames. 29 Overlay the
frames with gold and make gold rings
to hold the crossbars. Also overlay the
crossbars with gold.
30 “Set up the tabernacle according to
the plan shown you on the mountain.
31 “Make a curtain of blue, purple and
scarlet yarn and finely twisted linen,
with cherubim woven into it by a skilled
worker. 32 Hang it with gold hooks on
four posts of acacia wood overlaid with
gold and standing on four silver bases.
33 Hang the curtain from the clasps and
place the ark of the covenant law behind
the curtain. The curtain will separate
the Holy Place from the Most Holy Place.
34 Put the atonement cover on the ark of
the covenant law in the Most Holy Place.
35 Place the table outside the curtain on
the north side of the tabernacle and put
the lampstand opposite it on the south
side.
36 “For the entrance to the tent make a
curtain of blue, purple and scarlet yarn
and finely twisted linen — the work of an
embroiderer. 37 Make gold hooks for this
curtain and five posts of acacia wood
overlaid with gold. And cast five bronze
bases for them.

27 “Build an altar of acacia wood,
three cubits[a] high; it is to be square,
five cubits long and five cubits wide.[b]
2 Make a horn at each of the four corners,
so that the horns and the altar are of one
piece, and overlay the altar with bronze.
3 Make all its utensils of bronze — its pots
to remove the ashes, and its shovels,
sprinkling bowls, meat forks and firepans. 4 Make a grating for it, a bronze
network, and make a bronze ring at each
of the four corners of the network. 5 Put
it under the ledge of the altar so that it
is halfway up the altar. 6 Make poles of
acacia wood for the altar and overlay
them with bronze. 7 The poles are to be
inserted into the rings so they will be on
two sides of the altar when it is carried.
8 Make the altar hollow, out of boards. It
is to be made just as you were shown on
the mountain.
9 “Make a courtyard for the tabernacle. The south side shall be a hundred
cubits[c] long and is to have curtains of
finely twisted linen, 10 with twenty posts
and twenty bronze bases and with silver hooks and bands on the posts. 11 The
north side shall also be a hundred cubits
long and is to have curtains, with twenty
posts and twenty bronze bases and with
silver hooks and bands on the posts.
12 “The west end of the courtyard shall
be fifty cubits[d] wide and have curtains,
with ten posts and ten bases. 13 On the
east end, toward the sunrise, the courtyard shall also be fifty cubits wide.
14 Curtains fifteen cubits[e] long are to be
on one side of the entrance, with three
posts and three bases, 15 and curtains
fifteen cubits long are to be on the other
side, with three posts and three bases.
16 “For the entrance to the courtyard,
provide a curtain twenty cubits[f] long, of
blue, purple and scarlet yarn and finely
twisted linen — the work of an embroiderer — with four posts and four bases.
17 All the posts around the courtyard
are to have silver bands and hooks, and
bronze bases. 18 The courtyard shall be
a hundred cubits long and fifty cubits
wide,[g] with curtains of finely twisted
linen five cubits[h] high, and with bronze
bases. 19 All the other articles used in the
service of the tabernacle, whatever their
function, including all the tent pegs for
it and those for the courtyard, are to be
of bronze.
20 “Command the Israelites to bring
you clear oil of pressed olives for the light
so that the lamps may be kept burning.
21 In the tent of meeting, outside the curtain that shields the ark of the covenant
law, Aaron and his sons are to keep the
lamps burning before the LORD from
evening till morning. This is to be a lasting ordinance among the Israelites for
the generations to come.

28 “Have Aaron your brother brought
to you from among the Israelites,

[a] *1* That is, about 4 1/2 feet or about 1.4 meters [b] *1* That is, about 7 1/2 feet or about 2.3 meters long and wide [c] *9* That is, about 150 feet or about 45 meters; also in verse 11 [d] *12* That is, about 75 feet or about 23 meters; also in verse 13 [e] *14* That is, about 23 feet or about 6.8 meters; also in verse 15 [f] *16* That is, about 30 feet or about 9 meters [g] *18* That is, about 150 feet long and 75 feet wide or about 45 meters long and 23 meters wide [h] *18* That is, about 7 1/2 feet or about 2.3 meters

along with his sons Nadab and Abihu,
Eleazar and Ithamar, so they may serve
me as priests. 2 Make sacred garments for
your brother Aaron to give him dignity
and honor. 3 Tell all the skilled workers to
whom I have given wisdom in such matters that they are to make garments for
Aaron, for his consecration, so he may
serve me as priest. 4 These are the garments they are to make: a breastpiece,
an ephod, a robe, a woven tunic, a turban and a sash. They are to make these
sacred garments for your brother Aaron
and his sons, so they may serve me as
priests. 5 Have them use gold, and blue,
purple and scarlet yarn, and fine linen.

6 "Make the ephod of gold, and of blue,
purple and scarlet yarn, and of finely twisted linen—the work of skilled
hands. 7 It is to have two shoulder pieces
attached to two of its corners, so it can
be fastened. 8 Its skillfully woven waistband is to be like it—of one piece with
the ephod and made with gold, and with
blue, purple and scarlet yarn, and with
finely twisted linen.

9 "Take two onyx stones and engrave
on them the names of the sons of Israel
10 in the order of their birth—six names
on one stone and the remaining six on
the other. 11 Engrave the names of the
sons of Israel on the two stones the way a
gem cutter engraves a seal. Then mount
the stones in gold filigree settings 12 and
fasten them on the shoulder pieces of the
ephod as memorial stones for the sons of
Israel. Aaron is to bear the names on his
shoulders as a memorial before the LORD.
13 Make gold filigree settings 14 and two
braided chains of pure gold, like a rope,
and attach the chains to the settings.

15 "Fashion a breastpiece for making
decisions—the work of skilled hands.
Make it like the ephod: of gold, and of
blue, purple and scarlet yarn, and of
finely twisted linen. 16 It is to be square—
a span[a] long and a span wide—and folded double. 17 Then mount four rows of
precious stones on it. The first row shall
be carnelian, chrysolite and beryl; 18 the
second row shall be turquoise, lapis lazuli and emerald; 19 the third row shall
be jacinth, agate and amethyst; 20 the
fourth row shall be topaz, onyx and jasper.[b] Mount them in gold filigree settings. 21 There are to be twelve stones,
one for each of the names of the sons of
Israel, each engraved like a seal with the
name of one of the twelve tribes.

22 "For the breastpiece make braided
chains of pure gold, like a rope. 23 Make
two gold rings for it and fasten them to
two corners of the breastpiece. 24 Fasten
the two gold chains to the rings at the
corners of the breastpiece, 25 and the other ends of the chains to the two settings,
attaching them to the shoulder pieces of
the ephod at the front. 26 Make two gold
rings and attach them to the other two
corners of the breastpiece on the inside
edge next to the ephod. 27 Make two more
gold rings and attach them to the bottom
of the shoulder pieces on the front of the
ephod, close to the seam just above the
waistband of the ephod. 28 The rings of
the breastpiece are to be tied to the rings
of the ephod with blue cord, connecting
it to the waistband, so that the breastpiece will not swing out from the ephod.

29 "Whenever Aaron enters the Holy
Place, he will bear the names of the sons
of Israel over his heart on the breastpiece
of decision as a continuing memorial before the LORD. 30 Also put the Urim and
the Thummim in the breastpiece, so
they may be over Aaron's heart whenever he enters the presence of the LORD.
Thus Aaron will always bear the means
of making decisions for the Israelites
over his heart before the LORD.

31 "Make the robe of the ephod entirely of blue cloth, 32 with an opening for
the head in its center. There shall be a
woven edge like a collar[c] around this
opening, so that it will not tear. 33 Make
pomegranates of blue, purple and scarlet yarn around the hem of the robe, with
gold bells between them. 34 The gold
bells and the pomegranates are to alternate around the hem of the robe. 35 Aaron must wear it when he ministers. The
sound of the bells will be heard when he
enters the Holy Place before the LORD
and when he comes out, so that he will
not die.

36 "Make a plate of pure gold and engrave on it as on a seal: HOLY TO THE
LORD. 37 Fasten a blue cord to it to attach
it to the turban; it is to be on the front of
the turban. 38 It will be on Aaron's fore-

[a] *16* That is, about 9 inches or about 23 centimeters [b] *20* The precise identification of some of these precious stones is uncertain. [c] *32* The meaning of the Hebrew for this word is uncertain.

head, and he will bear the guilt involved
in the sacred gifts the Israelites consecrate, whatever their gifts may be. It will
be on Aaron's forehead continually so
that they will be acceptable to the LORD.
39 "Weave the tunic of fine linen and
make the turban of fine linen. The sash is
to be the work of an embroiderer. 40 Make
tunics, sashes and caps for Aaron's sons
to give them dignity and honor. 41 After
you put these clothes on your brother
Aaron and his sons, anoint and ordain
them. Consecrate them so they may
serve me as priests.

42 "Make linen undergarments as a
covering for the body, reaching from the
waist to the thigh. 43 Aaron and his sons
must wear them whenever they enter the
tent of meeting or approach the altar to
minister in the Holy Place, so that they
will not incur guilt and die.

"This is to be a lasting ordinance for
Aaron and his descendants.

29 "This is what you are to do to consecrate them, so they may serve
me as priests: Take a young bull and two
rams without defect. 2 And from the finest wheat flour make round loaves without yeast, thick loaves without yeast and
with olive oil mixed in, and thin loaves
without yeast and brushed with olive oil.
3 Put them in a basket and present them
along with the bull and the two rams.
4 Then bring Aaron and his sons to the
entrance to the tent of meeting and wash
them with water. 5 Take the garments
and dress Aaron with the tunic, the robe
of the ephod, the ephod itself and the
breastpiece. Fasten the ephod on him
by its skillfully woven waistband. 6 Put
the turban on his head and attach the
sacred emblem to the turban. 7 Take the
anointing oil and anoint him by pouring
it on his head. 8 Bring his sons and dress
them in tunics 9 and fasten caps on them.
Then tie sashes on Aaron and his sons.[a]
The priesthood is theirs by a lasting ordinance.

"Then you shall ordain Aaron and his
sons.

10 "Bring the bull to the front of the tent
of meeting, and Aaron and his sons shall
lay their hands on its head. 11 Slaughter it
in the LORD's presence at the entrance to
the tent of meeting. 12 Take some of the
bull's blood and put it on the horns of the
altar with your finger, and pour out the
rest of it at the base of the altar. 13 Then
take all the fat on the internal organs, the
long lobe of the liver, and both kidneys
with the fat on them, and burn them on
the altar. 14 But burn the bull's flesh and
its hide and its intestines outside the
camp. It is a sin offering.[b]

15 "Take one of the rams, and Aaron
and his sons shall lay their hands on its
head. 16 Slaughter it and take the blood
and splash it against the sides of the altar. 17 Cut the ram into pieces and wash
the internal organs and the legs, putting
them with the head and the other pieces.
18 Then burn the entire ram on the altar.
It is a burnt offering to the LORD, a pleasing aroma, a food offering presented to
the LORD.

19 "Take the other ram, and Aaron and
his sons shall lay their hands on its head.
20 Slaughter it, take some of its blood and
put it on the lobes of the right ears of Aaron and his sons, on the thumbs of their
right hands, and on the big toes of their
right feet. Then splash blood against the
sides of the altar. 21 And take some blood
from the altar and some of the anointing oil and sprinkle it on Aaron and his
garments and on his sons and their garments. Then he and his sons and their
garments will be consecrated.

22 "Take from this ram the fat, the fat
tail, the fat on the internal organs, the
long lobe of the liver, both kidneys with
the fat on them, and the right thigh. (This
is the ram for the ordination.) 23 From
the basket of bread made without yeast,
which is before the LORD, take one round
loaf, one thick loaf with olive oil mixed
in, and one thin loaf. 24 Put all these in
the hands of Aaron and his sons and
have them wave them before the LORD as
a wave offering. 25 Then take them from
their hands and burn them on the altar
along with the burnt offering for a pleasing aroma to the LORD, a food offering
presented to the LORD. 26 After you take
the breast of the ram for Aaron's ordination, wave it before the LORD as a wave
offering, and it will be your share.

27 "Consecrate those parts of the ordination ram that belong to Aaron and
his sons: the breast that was waved and

[a] 9 Hebrew; Septuagint *on them* [b] 14 Or *purification offering*; also in verse 36

the thigh that was presented. 28 This is
always to be the perpetual share from
the Israelites for Aaron and his sons. It
is the contribution the Israelites are to
make to the LORD from their fellowship
offerings.
29 "Aaron's sacred garments will belong to his descendants so that they
can be anointed and ordained in them.
30 The son who succeeds him as priest
and comes to the tent of meeting to minister in the Holy Place is to wear them
seven days.
31 "Take the ram for the ordination and
cook the meat in a sacred place. 32 At the
entrance to the tent of meeting, Aaron
and his sons are to eat the meat of the
ram and the bread that is in the basket. 33 They are to eat these offerings by
which atonement was made for their ordination and consecration. But no one
else may eat them, because they are sacred. 34 And if any of the meat of the ordination ram or any bread is left over till
morning, burn it up. It must not be eaten,
because it is sacred.
35 "Do for Aaron and his sons everything I have commanded you, taking
seven days to ordain them. 36 Sacrifice
a bull each day as a sin offering to make
atonement. Purify the altar by making
atonement for it, and anoint it to consecrate it. 37 For seven days make atonement for the altar and consecrate it. Then
the altar will be most holy, and whatever
touches it will be holy.
38 "This is what you are to offer on
the altar regularly each day: two lambs
a year old. 39 Offer one in the morning
and the other at twilight. 40 With the first
lamb offer a tenth of an ephah[a] of the finest flour mixed with a quarter of a hin[b] of
oil from pressed olives, and a quarter of
a hin of wine as a drink offering. 41 Sacrifice the other lamb at twilight with the
same grain offering and its drink offering
as in the morning — a pleasing aroma, a
food offering presented to the LORD.
42 "For the generations to come this
burnt offering is to be made regularly at
the entrance to the tent of meeting, before the LORD. There I will meet you and
speak to you; 43 there also I will meet with
the Israelites, and the place will be consecrated by my glory.
44 "So I will consecrate the tent of
meeting and the altar and will consecrate Aaron and his sons to serve me as
priests. 45 Then I will dwell among the
Israelites and be their God. 46 They will
know that I am the LORD their God, who
brought them out of Egypt so that I might
dwell among them. I am the LORD their
God.

30 "Make an altar of acacia wood for
burning incense. 2 It is to be square,
a cubit long and a cubit wide, and two cubits high[c] — its horns of one piece with it.
3 Overlay the top and all the sides and the
horns with pure gold, and make a gold
molding around it. 4 Make two gold rings
for the altar below the molding — two on
each of the opposite sides — to hold the
poles used to carry it. 5 Make the poles of
acacia wood and overlay them with gold.
6 Put the altar in front of the curtain that
shields the ark of the covenant law — before the atonement cover that is over the
tablets of the covenant law — where I will
meet with you.
7 "Aaron must burn fragrant incense on
the altar every morning when he tends
the lamps. 8 He must burn incense again
when he lights the lamps at twilight so
incense will burn regularly before the
LORD for the generations to come. 9 Do
not offer on this altar any other incense
or any burnt offering or grain offering,
and do not pour a drink offering on it.
10 Once a year Aaron shall make atonement on its horns. This annual atonement must be made with the blood of the
atoning sin offering[d] for the generations
to come. It is most holy to the LORD."
11 Then the LORD said to Moses,
12 "When you take a census of the Israelites to count them, each one must pay
the LORD a ransom for his life at the time
he is counted. Then no plague will come
on them when you number them. 13 Each
one who crosses over to those already
counted is to give a half shekel,[e] according to the sanctuary shekel, which
weighs twenty gerahs. This half shekel is
an offering to the LORD. 14 All who cross
over, those twenty years old or more, are

[a] *40* That is, probably about 3 1/2 pounds or about 1.6 kilograms [b] *40* That is, probably about 1 quart or about 1 liter [c] *2* That is, about 1 1/2 feet long and wide and 3 feet high or about 45 centimeters long and wide and 90 centimeters high [d] *10* Or *purification offering* [e] *13* That is, about 1/5 ounce or about 5.8 grams; also in verse 15

to give an offering to the LORD. 15 The rich are not to give more than a half shekel and the poor are not to give less when you make the offering to the LORD to atone for your lives. 16 Receive the atonement money from the Israelites and use it for the service of the tent of meeting. It will be a memorial for the Israelites before the LORD, making atonement for your lives."

17 Then the LORD said to Moses, 18 "Make a bronze basin, with its bronze stand, for washing. Place it between the tent of meeting and the altar, and put water in it. 19 Aaron and his sons are to wash their hands and feet with water from it. 20 Whenever they enter the tent of meeting, they shall wash with water so that they will not die. Also, when they approach the altar to minister by presenting a food offering to the LORD, 21 they shall wash their hands and feet so that they will not die. This is to be a lasting ordinance for Aaron and his descendants for the generations to come."

22 Then the LORD said to Moses, 23 "Take the following fine spices: 500 shekels[a] of liquid myrrh, half as much (that is, 250 shekels) of fragrant cinnamon, 250 shekels[b] of fragrant calamus, 24 500 shekels of cassia—all according to the sanctuary shekel—and a hin[c] of olive oil. 25 Make these into a sacred anointing oil, a fragrant blend, the work of a perfumer. It will be the sacred anointing oil. 26 Then use it to anoint the tent of meeting, the ark of the covenant law, 27 the table and all its articles, the lampstand and its accessories, the altar of incense, 28 the altar of burnt offering and all its utensils, and the basin with its stand. 29 You shall consecrate them so they will be most holy, and whatever touches them will be holy.

30 "Anoint Aaron and his sons and consecrate them so they may serve me as priests. 31 Say to the Israelites, 'This is to be my sacred anointing oil for the generations to come. 32 Do not pour it on anyone else's body and do not make any other oil using the same formula. It is sacred, and you are to consider it sacred. 33 Whoever makes perfume like it and puts it on anyone other than a priest must be cut off from their people.'"

34 Then the LORD said to Moses, "Take fragrant spices—gum resin, onycha and galbanum—and pure frankincense, all in equal amounts, 35 and make a fragrant blend of incense, the work of a perfumer. It is to be salted and pure and sacred. 36 Grind some of it to powder and place it in front of the ark of the covenant law in the tent of meeting, where I will meet with you. It shall be most holy to you. 37 Do not make any incense with this formula for yourselves; consider it holy to the LORD. 38 Whoever makes incense like it to enjoy its fragrance must be cut off from their people."

31 Then the LORD said to Moses, 2 "See, I have chosen Bezalel son of Uri, the son of Hur, of the tribe of Judah, 3 and I have filled him with the Spirit of God, with wisdom, with understanding, with knowledge and with all kinds of skills—4 to make artistic designs for work in gold, silver and bronze, 5 to cut and set stones, to work in wood, and to engage in all kinds of crafts. 6 Moreover, I have appointed Oholiab son of Ahisamak, of the tribe of Dan, to help him. Also I have given ability to all the skilled workers to make everything I have commanded you: 7 the tent of meeting, the ark of the covenant law with the atonement cover on it, and all the other furnishings of the tent—8 the table and its articles, the pure gold lampstand and all its accessories, the altar of incense, 9 the altar of burnt offering and all its utensils, the basin with its stand—10 and also the woven garments, both the sacred garments for Aaron the priest and the garments for his sons when they serve as priests, 11 and the anointing oil and fragrant incense for the Holy Place. They are to make them just as I commanded you."

12 Then the LORD said to Moses, 13 "Say to the Israelites, 'You must observe my Sabbaths. This will be a sign between me and you for the generations to come, so you may know that I am the LORD, who makes you holy.

14 "'Observe the Sabbath, because it is holy to you. Anyone who desecrates it is to be put to death; those who do any work on that day must be cut off from their people. 15 For six days work is to be done, but the seventh day is a day of sabbath rest, holy to the LORD. Whoever does any work on the Sabbath day is to be put to death.

[a] *23* That is, about 12 1/2 pounds or about 5.8 kilograms; also in verse 24 [b] *23* That is, about 6 1/4 pounds or about 2.9 kilograms [c] *24* That is, probably about 1 gallon or about 3.8 liters

16The Israelites are to observe the Sabbath, celebrating it for the generations
to come as a lasting covenant. 17It will
be a sign between me and the Israelites
forever, for in six days the LORD made the
heavens and the earth, and on the seventh day he rested and was refreshed.'"
18When the LORD finished speaking
to Moses on Mount Sinai, he gave him
the two tablets of the covenant law, the
tablets of stone inscribed by the finger
of God.

32 When the people saw that Moses
was so long in coming down from
the mountain, they gathered around Aaron and said, "Come, make us gods[a] who
will go before us. As for this fellow Moses
who brought us up out of Egypt, we don't
know what has happened to him."
2Aaron answered them, "Take off the
gold earrings that your wives, your sons
and your daughters are wearing, and
bring them to me." 3So all the people
took off their earrings and brought them
to Aaron. 4He took what they handed him
and made it into an idol cast in the shape
of a calf, fashioning it with a tool. Then
they said, "These are your gods,[b] Israel,
who brought you up out of Egypt."
5When Aaron saw this, he built an altar in front of the calf and announced,
"Tomorrow there will be a festival to the
LORD." 6So the next day the people rose
early and sacrificed burnt offerings and
presented fellowship offerings. Afterward they sat down to eat and drink and
got up to indulge in revelry.
7Then the LORD said to Moses, "Go
down, because your people, whom you
brought up out of Egypt, have become
corrupt. 8They have been quick to turn
away from what I commanded them and
have made themselves an idol cast in the
shape of a calf. They have bowed down
to it and sacrificed to it and have said,
'These are your gods, Israel, who brought
you up out of Egypt.'
9"I have seen these people," the LORD
said to Moses, "and they are a stiff-necked
people. 10Now leave me alone so that my
anger may burn against them and that I
may destroy them. Then I will make you
into a great nation."
11But Moses sought the favor of the
LORD his God. "LORD," he said, "why
should your anger burn against your
people, whom you brought out of Egypt
with great power and a mighty hand?
12Why should the Egyptians say, 'It was
with evil intent that he brought them
out, to kill them in the mountains and
to wipe them off the face of the earth'?
Turn from your fierce anger; relent and
do not bring disaster on your people.
13Remember your servants Abraham,
Isaac and Israel, to whom you swore by
your own self: 'I will make your descendants as numerous as the stars in the sky
and I will give your descendants all this
land I promised them, and it will be their
inheritance forever.'" 14Then the LORD
relented and did not bring on his people
the disaster he had threatened.
15Moses turned and went down the
mountain with the two tablets of the
covenant law in his hands. They were
inscribed on both sides, front and back.
16The tablets were the work of God; the
writing was the writing of God, engraved
on the tablets.
17When Joshua heard the noise of
the people shouting, he said to Moses,
"There is the sound of war in the camp."
18Moses replied:

"It is not the sound of victory,
it is not the sound of defeat;
it is the sound of singing that I hear."

19When Moses approached the camp
and saw the calf and the dancing, his anger burned and he threw the tablets out
of his hands, breaking them to pieces at
the foot of the mountain. 20And he took
the calf the people had made and burned
it in the fire; then he ground it to powder,
scattered it on the water and made the Israelites drink it.
21He said to Aaron, "What did these
people do to you, that you led them into
such great sin?"
22"Do not be angry, my lord," Aaron answered. "You know how prone these people are to evil. 23They said to me, 'Make
us gods who will go before us. As for this
fellow Moses who brought us up out of
Egypt, we don't know what has happened
to him.' 24So I told them, 'Whoever has
any gold jewelry, take it off.' Then they
gave me the gold, and I threw it into the
fire, and out came this calf!"

[a] *1* Or *a god*; also in verses 23 and 31 [b] *4* Or *This is your god*; also in verse 8

25 Moses saw that the people were running wild and that Aaron had let them
get out of control and so become a laughingstock to their enemies. 26 So he stood
at the entrance to the camp and said,
"Whoever is for the LORD, come to me."
And all the Levites rallied to him.
27 Then he said to them, "This is what
the LORD, the God of Israel, says: 'Each
man strap a sword to his side. Go back
and forth through the camp from one
end to the other, each killing his brother and friend and neighbor.' " 28 The Levites did as Moses commanded, and that
day about three thousand of the people
died. 29 Then Moses said, "You have been
set apart to the LORD today, for you were
against your own sons and brothers, and
he has blessed you this day."
30 The next day Moses said to the people, "You have committed a great sin. But
now I will go up to the LORD; perhaps I
can make atonement for your sin."
31 So Moses went back to the LORD and
said, "Oh, what a great sin these people
have committed! They have made themselves gods of gold. 32 But now, please
forgive their sin — but if not, then blot me
out of the book you have written."
33 The LORD replied to Moses, "Whoever has sinned against me I will blot out
of my book. 34 Now go, lead the people to
the place I spoke of, and my angel will
go before you. However, when the time
comes for me to punish, I will punish
them for their sin."
35 And the LORD struck the people with
a plague because of what they did with
the calf Aaron had made.
33 Then the LORD said to Moses, "Leave
this place, you and the people you
brought up out of Egypt, and go up to
the land I promised on oath to Abraham,
Isaac and Jacob, saying, 'I will give it to
your descendants.' 2 I will send an angel
before you and drive out the Canaanites,
Amorites, Hittites, Perizzites, Hivites and
Jebusites. 3 Go up to the land flowing with
milk and honey. But I will not go with you,
because you are a stiff-necked people and
I might destroy you on the way."
4 When the people heard these dis-
tressing words, they began to mourn
and no one put on any ornaments. 5 For
the LORD had said to Moses, "Tell the Israelites, 'You are a stiff-necked people. If
I were to go with you even for a moment,
I might destroy you. Now take off your
ornaments and I will decide what to do
with you.' " 6 So the Israelites stripped off
their ornaments at Mount Horeb.
7 Now Moses used to take a tent and
pitch it outside the camp some distance
away, calling it the "tent of meeting."
Anyone inquiring of the LORD would go
to the tent of meeting outside the camp.
8 And whenever Moses went out to the
tent, all the people rose and stood at the
entrances to their tents, watching Moses until he entered the tent. 9 As Moses
went into the tent, the pillar of cloud
would come down and stay at the entrance, while the LORD spoke with Moses. 10 Whenever the people saw the pillar
of cloud standing at the entrance to the
tent, they all stood and worshiped, each
at the entrance to their tent. 11 The LORD
would speak to Moses face to face, as one
speaks to a friend. Then Moses would
return to the camp, but his young aide
Joshua son of Nun did not leave the tent.
12 Moses said to the LORD, "You have
been telling me, 'Lead these people,' but
you have not let me know whom you will
send with me. You have said, 'I know you
by name and you have found favor with
me.' 13 If you are pleased with me, teach
me your ways so I may know you and
continue to find favor with you. Remember that this nation is your people."
14 The LORD replied, "My Presence will
go with you, and I will give you rest."
15 Then Moses said to him, "If your
Presence does not go with us, do not
send us up from here. 16 How will anyone
know that you are pleased with me and
with your people unless you go with us?
What else will distinguish me and your
people from all the other people on the
face of the earth?"
17 And the LORD said to Moses, "I will
do the very thing you have asked, because I am pleased with you and I know
you by name."
18 Then Moses said, "Now show me
your glory."
19 And the LORD said, "I will cause all
my goodness to pass in front of you, and I
will proclaim my name, the LORD, in your
presence. I will have mercy on whom I
will have mercy, and I will have compassion on whom I will have compassion.
20 But," he said, "you cannot see my face,
for no one may see me and live."

21 Then the LORD said, "There is a place
near me where you may stand on a rock.
22 When my glory passes by, I will put you
in a cleft in the rock and cover you with
my hand until I have passed by. 23 Then I
will remove my hand and you will see my
back; but my face must not be seen."

34 The LORD said to Moses, "Chisel
out two stone tablets like the first
ones, and I will write on them the words
that were on the first tablets, which you
broke. 2 Be ready in the morning, and
then come up on Mount Sinai. Present
yourself to me there on top of the mountain. 3 No one is to come with you or be
seen anywhere on the mountain; not
even the flocks and herds may graze in
front of the mountain."

4 So Moses chiseled out two stone tablets
like the first ones and went up Mount Sinai early in the morning, as the LORD had
commanded him; and he carried the two
stone tablets in his hands. 5 Then the LORD
came down in the cloud and stood there
with him and proclaimed his name, the
LORD. 6 And he passed in front of Moses,
proclaiming, "The LORD, the LORD, the
compassionate and gracious God, slow
to anger, abounding in love and faithfulness, 7 maintaining love to thousands,
and forgiving wickedness, rebellion and
sin. Yet he does not leave the guilty unpunished; he punishes the children and
their children for the sin of the parents to
the third and fourth generation."

8 Moses bowed to the ground at once
and worshiped. 9 "Lord," he said, "if I
have found favor in your eyes, then let
the Lord go with us. Although this is a
stiff-necked people, forgive our wickedness and our sin, and take us as your
inheritance."

10 Then the LORD said: "I am making a
covenant with you. Before all your people I will do wonders never before done
in any nation in all the world. The people
you live among will see how awesome is
the work that I, the LORD, will do for you.
11 Obey what I command you today. I will
drive out before you the Amorites, Canaanites, Hittites, Perizzites, Hivites and
Jebusites. 12 Be careful not to make a treaty with those who live in the land where
you are going, or they will be a snare
among you. 13 Break down their altars,
smash their sacred stones and cut down
their Asherah poles.[a] 14 Do not worship
any other god, for the LORD, whose name
is Jealous, is a jealous God.

15 "Be careful not to make a treaty with
those who live in the land; for when they
prostitute themselves to their gods and
sacrifice to them, they will invite you and
you will eat their sacrifices. 16 And when
you choose some of their daughters as
wives for your sons and those daughters
prostitute themselves to their gods, they
will lead your sons to do the same.

17 "Do not make any idols.

18 "Celebrate the Festival of Unleavened Bread. For seven days eat bread
made without yeast, as I commanded
you. Do this at the appointed time in
the month of Aviv, for in that month you
came out of Egypt.

19 "The first offspring of every womb
belongs to me, including all the firstborn males of your livestock, whether
from herd or flock. 20 Redeem the firstborn donkey with a lamb, but if you do
not redeem it, break its neck. Redeem all
your firstborn sons.

"No one is to appear before me empty-handed.

21 "Six days you shall labor, but on the
seventh day you shall rest; even during
the plowing season and harvest you
must rest.

22 "Celebrate the Festival of Weeks with
the firstfruits of the wheat harvest, and
the Festival of Ingathering at the turn of
the year.[b] 23 Three times a year all your
men are to appear before the Sovereign
LORD, the God of Israel. 24 I will drive out
nations before you and enlarge your territory, and no one will covet your land
when you go up three times each year to
appear before the LORD your God.

25 "Do not offer the blood of a sacrifice
to me along with anything containing
yeast, and do not let any of the sacrifice
from the Passover Festival remain until
morning.

26 "Bring the best of the firstfruits of your
soil to the house of the LORD your God.

"Do not cook a young goat in its mother's milk."

27 Then the LORD said to Moses, "Write
down these words, for in accordance with
these words I have made a covenant with

[a] *13* That is, wooden symbols of the goddess Asherah

[b] *22* That is, in the autumn

you and with Israel." [28]Moses was there
with the LORD forty days and forty nights
without eating bread or drinking water.
And he wrote on the tablets the words of
the covenant—the Ten Commandments.
[29]When Moses came down from Mount
Sinai with the two tablets of the covenant
law in his hands, he was not aware that
his face was radiant because he had spoken with the LORD. [30]When Aaron and all
the Israelites saw Moses, his face was radiant, and they were afraid to come near
him. [31]But Moses called to them; so Aaron and all the leaders of the community
came back to him, and he spoke to them.
[32]Afterward all the Israelites came near
him, and he gave them all the commands
the LORD had given him on Mount Sinai.
[33]When Moses finished speaking to
them, he put a veil over his face. [34]But
whenever he entered the LORD's presence to speak with him, he removed
the veil until he came out. And when he
came out and told the Israelites what he
had been commanded, [35]they saw that
his face was radiant. Then Moses would
put the veil back over his face until he
went in to speak with the LORD.

35 Moses assembled the whole Israelite community and said to them,
"These are the things the LORD has commanded you to do: [2]For six days, work is
to be done, but the seventh day shall be
your holy day, a day of sabbath rest to the
LORD. Whoever does any work on it is to
be put to death. [3]Do not light a fire in any
of your dwellings on the Sabbath day."
[4]Moses said to the whole Israelite
community, "This is what the LORD has
commanded: [5]From what you have, take
an offering for the LORD. Everyone who is
willing is to bring to the LORD an offering
of gold, silver and bronze; [6]blue, purple
and scarlet yarn and fine linen; goat hair;
[7]ram skins dyed red and another type of
durable leather[a]; acacia wood; [8]olive oil
for the light; spices for the anointing oil
and for the fragrant incense; [9]and onyx
stones and other gems to be mounted on
the ephod and breastpiece.
[10]"All who are skilled among you are
to come and make everything the LORD
has commanded: [11]the tabernacle with
its tent and its covering, clasps, frames,
crossbars, posts and bases; [12]the ark
with its poles and the atonement cover
and the curtain that shields it; [13]the table with its poles and all its articles and
the bread of the Presence; [14]the lampstand that is for light with its accessories,
lamps and oil for the light; [15]the altar of
incense with its poles, the anointing oil
and the fragrant incense; the curtain
for the doorway at the entrance to the
tabernacle; [16]the altar of burnt offering
with its bronze grating, its poles and all
its utensils; the bronze basin with its
stand; [17]the curtains of the courtyard
with its posts and bases, and the curtain
for the entrance to the courtyard; [18]the
tent pegs for the tabernacle and for the
courtyard, and their ropes; [19]the woven
garments worn for ministering in the
sanctuary—both the sacred garments
for Aaron the priest and the garments for
his sons when they serve as priests."
[20]Then the whole Israelite community
withdrew from Moses' presence, [21]and
everyone who was willing and whose
heart moved them came and brought
an offering to the LORD for the work on
the tent of meeting, for all its service,
and for the sacred garments. [22]All who
were willing, men and women alike,
came and brought gold jewelry of all
kinds: brooches, earrings, rings and ornaments. They all presented their gold as
a wave offering to the LORD. [23]Everyone
who had blue, purple or scarlet yarn or
fine linen, or goat hair, ram skins dyed
red or the other durable leather brought
them. [24]Those presenting an offering of
silver or bronze brought it as an offering to the LORD, and everyone who had
acacia wood for any part of the work
brought it. [25]Every skilled woman spun
with her hands and brought what she
had spun—blue, purple or scarlet yarn
or fine linen. [26]And all the women who
were willing and had the skill spun the
goat hair. [27]The leaders brought onyx
stones and other gems to be mounted
on the ephod and breastpiece. [28]They
also brought spices and olive oil for the
light and for the anointing oil and for the
fragrant incense. [29]All the Israelite men
and women who were willing brought
to the LORD freewill offerings for all the
work the LORD through Moses had commanded them to do.

[a] *7* Possibly the hides of large aquatic mammals; also in verse 23

[30]Then Moses said to the Israelites,
"See, the LORD has chosen Bezalel son of
Uri, the son of Hur, of the tribe of Judah,
[31]and he has filled him with the Spirit
of God, with wisdom, with understanding, with knowledge and with all kinds
of skills— [32]to make artistic designs
for work in gold, silver and bronze, [33]to
cut and set stones, to work in wood and
to engage in all kinds of artistic crafts.
[34]And he has given both him and Oholiab son of Ahisamak, of the tribe of Dan,
the ability to teach others. [35]He has filled
them with skill to do all kinds of work as
engravers, designers, embroiderers in
blue, purple and scarlet yarn and fine
linen, and weavers—all of them skilled
36 workers and designers. [1]So Bezalel,
Oholiab and every skilled person to
whom the LORD has given skill and ability to know how to carry out all the work of
constructing the sanctuary are to do the
work just as the LORD has commanded."

[2]Then Moses summoned Bezalel and
Oholiab and every skilled person to
whom the LORD had given ability and
who was willing to come and do the
work. [3]They received from Moses all the
offerings the Israelites had brought to
carry out the work of constructing the
sanctuary. And the people continued to
bring freewill offerings morning after
morning. [4]So all the skilled workers who
were doing all the work on the sanctuary left what they were doing [5]and said
to Moses, "The people are bringing more
than enough for doing the work the LORD
commanded to be done."

[6]Then Moses gave an order and they
sent this word throughout the camp: "No
man or woman is to make anything else
as an offering for the sanctuary." And so
the people were restrained from bringing
more, [7]because what they already had
was more than enough to do all the work.

[8]All those who were skilled among the
workers made the tabernacle with ten
curtains of finely twisted linen and blue,
purple and scarlet yarn, with cherubim
woven into them by expert hands. [9]All
the curtains were the same size—twenty-eight cubits long and four cubits wide.[a]
[10]They joined five of the curtains together and did the same with the other five.
[11]Then they made loops of blue material
along the edge of the end curtain in one
set, and the same was done with the end
curtain in the other set. [12]They also made
fifty loops on one curtain and fifty loops
on the end curtain of the other set, with
the loops opposite each other. [13]Then
they made fifty gold clasps and used them
to fasten the two sets of curtains together
so that the tabernacle was a unit.

[14]They made curtains of goat hair for
the tent over the tabernacle—eleven altogether. [15]All eleven curtains were the
same size—thirty cubits long and four
cubits wide.[b] [16]They joined five of the
curtains into one set and the other six into
another set. [17]Then they made fifty loops
along the edge of the end curtain in one set
and also along the edge of the end curtain
in the other set. [18]They made fifty bronze
clasps to fasten the tent together as a unit.
[19]Then they made for the tent a covering
of ram skins dyed red, and over that a covering of the other durable leather.[c]

[20]They made upright frames of acacia
wood for the tabernacle. [21]Each frame
was ten cubits long and a cubit and a half
wide,[d] [22]with two projections set parallel
to each other. They made all the frames of
the tabernacle in this way. [23]They made
twenty frames for the south side of the tabernacle [24]and made forty silver bases to go
under them—two bases for each frame,
one under each projection. [25]For the other side, the north side of the tabernacle,
they made twenty frames [26]and forty silver bases—two under each frame. [27]They
made six frames for the far end, that is,
the west end of the tabernacle, [28]and two
frames were made for the corners of the
tabernacle at the far end. [29]At these two
corners the frames were double from the
bottom all the way to the top and fitted
into a single ring; both were made alike.
[30]So there were eight frames and sixteen
silver bases—two under each frame.

[31]They also made crossbars of acacia
wood: five for the frames on one side of
the tabernacle, [32]five for those on the
other side, and five for the frames on
the west, at the far end of the tabernacle.
[33]They made the center crossbar so that

[a] *9* That is, about 42 feet long and 6 feet wide or about 13 meters long and 1.8 meters wide [b] *15* That is, about 45 feet long and 6 feet wide or about 14 meters long and 1.8 meters wide [c] *19* Possibly the hides of large aquatic mammals (see 35:7) [d] *21* That is, about 15 feet long and 2 1/4 feet wide or about 4.5 meters long and 68 centimeters wide

it extended from end to end at the middle
of the frames. 34 They overlaid the frames
with gold and made gold rings to hold the
crossbars. They also overlaid the crossbars with gold.
35 They made the curtain of blue, purple and scarlet yarn and finely twisted
linen, with cherubim woven into it by a
skilled worker. 36 They made four posts of
acacia wood for it and overlaid them with
gold. They made gold hooks for them and
cast their four silver bases. 37 For the entrance to the tent they made a curtain of
blue, purple and scarlet yarn and finely
twisted linen—the work of an embroiderer; 38 and they made five posts with
hooks for them. They overlaid the tops of
the posts and their bands with gold and
made their five bases of bronze.
37 Bezalel made the ark of acacia
wood—two and a half cubits long,
a cubit and a half wide, and a cubit and a
half high.[a] 2 He overlaid it with pure gold,
both inside and out, and made a gold
molding around it. 3 He cast four gold
rings for it and fastened them to its four
feet, with two rings on one side and two
rings on the other. 4 Then he made poles
of acacia wood and overlaid them with
gold. 5 And he inserted the poles into the
rings on the sides of the ark to carry it.
6 He made the atonement cover of pure
gold—two and a half cubits long and a
cubit and a half wide. 7 Then he made two
cherubim out of hammered gold at the
ends of the cover. 8 He made one cherub on one end and the second cherub on
the other; at the two ends he made them
of one piece with the cover. 9 The cherubim had their wings spread upward,
overshadowing the cover with them.
The cherubim faced each other, looking
toward the cover.
10 They[b] made the table of acacia
wood—two cubits long, a cubit wide
and a cubit and a half high.[c] 11 Then they
overlaid it with pure gold and made a gold
molding around it. 12 They also made
around it a rim a handbreadth[d] wide and
put a gold molding on the rim. 13 They
cast four gold rings for the table and fastened them to the four corners, where the
four legs were. 14 The rings were put close
to the rim to hold the poles used in carrying the table. 15 The poles for carrying the
table were made of acacia wood and were
overlaid with gold. 16 And they made from
pure gold the articles for the table—its
plates and dishes and bowls and its pitchers for the pouring out of drink offerings.
17 They made the lampstand of pure
gold. They hammered out its base and
shaft, and made its flowerlike cups, buds
and blossoms of one piece with them.
18 Six branches extended from the sides
of the lampstand—three on one side and
three on the other. 19 Three cups shaped
like almond flowers with buds and blossoms were on one branch, three on the
next branch and the same for all six
branches extending from the lampstand.
20 And on the lampstand were four cups
shaped like almond flowers with buds
and blossoms. 21 One bud was under the
first pair of branches extending from the
lampstand, a second bud under the second pair, and a third bud under the third
pair—six branches in all. 22 The buds and
the branches were all of one piece with the
lampstand, hammered out of pure gold.
23 They made its seven lamps, as well as
its wick trimmers and trays, of pure gold.
24 They made the lampstand and all its accessories from one talent[e] of pure gold.
25 They made the altar of incense out of
acacia wood. It was square, a cubit long
and a cubit wide and two cubits high[f]—
its horns of one piece with it. 26 They overlaid the top and all the sides and the horns
with pure gold, and made a gold molding
around it. 27 They made two gold rings
below the molding—two on each of the
opposite sides—to hold the poles used to
carry it. 28 They made the poles of acacia
wood and overlaid them with gold.
29 They also made the sacred anointing
oil and the pure, fragrant incense—the
work of a perfumer.
38 They[g] built the altar of burnt offering of acacia wood, three cubits[h]
high; it was square, five cubits long and
five cubits wide.[i] 2 They made a horn

[a] *1* That is, about 3 1/4 feet long and 2 1/4 feet wide and high or about 1.1 meters long and 68 centimeters wide and high; similarly in verse 6 [b] *10* Or *He*; also in verses 11-29 [c] *10* That is, about 3 feet long, 1 1/2 feet wide and 2 1/4 feet high or about 90 centimeters long, 45 centimeters wide and 68 centimeters high [d] *12* That is, about 3 inches or about 7.5 centimeters [e] *24* That is, about 75 pounds or about 34 kilograms [f] *25* That is, about 1 1/2 feet long and wide and 3 feet high or about 45 centimeters long and wide and 90 centimeters high [g] *1* Or *He*; also in verses 2-9 [h] *1* That is, about 4 1/2 feet or about 1.4 meters [i] *1* That is, about 7 1/2 feet or about 2.3 meters long and wide

at each of the four corners, so that the
horns and the altar were of one piece,
and they overlaid the altar with bronze.
3 They made all its utensils of bronze —
its pots, shovels, sprinkling bowls, meat
forks and firepans. 4 They made a grating
for the altar, a bronze network, to be under its ledge, halfway up the altar. 5 They
cast bronze rings to hold the poles for the
four corners of the bronze grating. 6 They
made the poles of acacia wood and overlaid them with bronze. 7 They inserted
the poles into the rings so they would be
on the sides of the altar for carrying it.
They made it hollow, out of boards.

8 They made the bronze basin and its
bronze stand from the mirrors of the
women who served at the entrance to
the tent of meeting.

9 Next they made the courtyard. The
south side was a hundred cubits[a] long
and had curtains of finely twisted linen,
10 with twenty posts and twenty bronze
bases, and with silver hooks and bands
on the posts. 11 The north side was also
a hundred cubits long and had twenty
posts and twenty bronze bases, with silver hooks and bands on the posts.

12 The west end was fifty cubits[b] wide
and had curtains, with ten posts and
ten bases, with silver hooks and bands
on the posts. 13 The east end, toward
the sunrise, was also fifty cubits wide.
14 Curtains fifteen cubits[c] long were
on one side of the entrance, with three
posts and three bases, 15 and curtains
fifteen cubits long were on the other side
of the entrance to the courtyard, with
three posts and three bases. 16 All the
curtains around the courtyard were of
finely twisted linen. 17 The bases for the
posts were bronze. The hooks and bands
on the posts were silver, and their tops
were overlaid with silver; so all the posts
of the courtyard had silver bands.

18 The curtain for the entrance to the
courtyard was made of blue, purple and
scarlet yarn and finely twisted linen —
the work of an embroiderer. It was twenty cubits[d] long and, like the curtains of
the courtyard, five cubits[e] high, 19 with
four posts and four bronze bases. Their
hooks and bands were silver, and their
tops were overlaid with silver. 20 All the
tent pegs of the tabernacle and of the
surrounding courtyard were bronze.

21 These are the amounts of the ma-
terials used for the tabernacle, the tabernacle of the covenant law, which were
recorded at Moses' command by the Levites under the direction of Ithamar son
of Aaron, the priest. 22 (Bezalel son of Uri,
the son of Hur, of the tribe of Judah, made
everything the LORD commanded Moses;
23 with him was Oholiab son of Ahisamak,
of the tribe of Dan — an engraver and de-
signer, and an embroiderer in blue, purple and scarlet yarn and fine linen.) 24 The
total amount of the gold from the wave
offering used for all the work on the sanctuary was 29 talents and 730 shekels,[f] according to the sanctuary shekel.

25 The silver obtained from those of
the community who were counted in
the census was 100 talents[g] and 1,775
shekels,[h] according to the sanctuary
shekel — 26 one beka per person, that is,
half a shekel,[i] according to the sanctuary
shekel, from everyone who had crossed
over to those counted, twenty years old
or more, a total of 603,550 men. 27 The
100 talents of silver were used to cast the
bases for the sanctuary and for the curtain — 100 bases from the 100 talents,
one talent for each base. 28 They used
the 1,775 shekels to make the hooks for
the posts, to overlay the tops of the posts,
and to make their bands.

29 The bronze from the wave offering
was 70 talents and 2,400 shekels.[j] 30 They
used it to make the bases for the entrance
to the tent of meeting, the bronze altar
with its bronze grating and all its utensils, 31 the bases for the surrounding
courtyard and those for its entrance and
all the tent pegs for the tabernacle and
those for the surrounding courtyard.

39 From the blue, purple and scarlet
yarn they made woven garments for
ministering in the sanctuary. They also
made sacred garments for Aaron, as the
LORD commanded Moses.

[a] *9* That is, about 150 feet or about 45 meters [b] *12* That is, about 75 feet or about 23 meters [c] *14* That is, about 22 feet or about 6.8 meters [d] *18* That is, about 30 feet or about 9 meters [e] *18* That is, about 7 1/2 feet or about 2.3 meters [f] *24* The weight of the gold was a little over a ton or about 1 metric ton. [g] *25* That is, about 3 3/4 tons or about 3.4 metric tons; also in verse 27 [h] *25* That is, about 44 pounds or about 20 kilograms; also in verse 28 [i] *26* That is, about 1/5 ounce or about 5.7 grams [j] *29* The weight of the bronze was about 2 1/2 tons or about 2.4 metric tons.

2They[a] made the ephod of gold, and of
blue, purple and scarlet yarn, and of finely twisted linen. 3They hammered out
thin sheets of gold and cut strands to be
worked into the blue, purple and scarlet
yarn and fine linen — the work of skilled
hands. 4They made shoulder pieces for
the ephod, which were attached to two
of its corners, so it could be fastened. 5Its
skillfully woven waistband was like it —
of one piece with the ephod and made
with gold, and with blue, purple and
scarlet yarn, and with finely twisted lin-
en, as the LORD commanded Moses.

6They mounted the onyx stones in gold
filigree settings and engraved them like
a seal with the names of the sons of Israel. 7Then they fastened them on the
shoulder pieces of the ephod as memorial stones for the sons of Israel, as the
LORD commanded Moses.

8They fashioned the breastpiece — the
work of a skilled craftsman. They made it
like the ephod: of gold, and of blue, purple and scarlet yarn, and of finely twisted
linen. 9It was square — a span[b] long and
a span wide — and folded double. 10Then
they mounted four rows of precious
stones on it. The first row was carnelian,
chrysolite and beryl; 11the second row
was turquoise, lapis lazuli and emerald;
12the third row was jacinth, agate and
amethyst; 13the fourth row was topaz,
onyx and jasper.[c] They were mounted in
gold filigree settings. 14There were twelve
stones, one for each of the names of the
sons of Israel, each engraved like a seal
with the name of one of the twelve tribes.

15For the breastpiece they made braided chains of pure gold, like a rope. 16They
made two gold filigree settings and two
gold rings, and fastened the rings to two
of the corners of the breastpiece. 17They
fastened the two gold chains to the rings
at the corners of the breastpiece, 18and
the other ends of the chains to the two
settings, attaching them to the shoulder
pieces of the ephod at the front. 19They
made two gold rings and attached them
to the other two corners of the breastpiece on the inside edge next to the
ephod. 20Then they made two more gold
rings and attached them to the bottom
of the shoulder pieces on the front of the
ephod, close to the seam just above the
waistband of the ephod. 21They tied the
rings of the breastpiece to the rings of
the ephod with blue cord, connecting it
to the waistband so that the breastpiece
would not swing out from the ephod — as
the LORD commanded Moses.

22They made the robe of the ephod entirely of blue cloth — the work of a weaver — 23with an opening in the center of
the robe like the opening of a collar,[d] and
a band around this opening, so that it
would not tear. 24They made pomegranates of blue, purple and scarlet yarn and
finely twisted linen around the hem of
the robe. 25And they made bells of pure
gold and attached them around the hem
between the pomegranates. 26The bells
and pomegranates alternated around
the hem of the robe to be worn for ministering, as the LORD commanded Moses.

27For Aaron and his sons, they made
tunics of fine linen — the work of a weaver — 28and the turban of fine linen, the
linen caps and the undergarments of finely twisted linen. 29The sash was made of
finely twisted linen and blue, purple and
scarlet yarn — the work of an embroiderer — as the LORD commanded Moses.

30They made the plate, the sacred emblem, out of pure gold and engraved on it,
like an inscription on a seal: HOLY TO THE
LORD. 31Then they fastened a blue cord
to it to attach it to the turban, as the LORD
commanded Moses.

32So all the work on the tabernacle, the
tent of meeting, was completed. The Israelites did everything just as the LORD
commanded Moses. 33Then they brought
the tabernacle to Moses: the tent and all its
furnishings, its clasps, frames, crossbars,
posts and bases; 34the covering of ram
skins dyed red and the covering of another durable leather[e] and the shielding curtain; 35the ark of the covenant law with
its poles and the atonement cover; 36the
table with all its articles and the bread of
the Presence; 37the pure gold lampstand
with its row of lamps and all its accessories, and the olive oil for the light; 38the
gold altar, the anointing oil, the fragrant
incense, and the curtain for the entrance
to the tent; 39the bronze altar with its
bronze grating, its poles and all its uten-

[a] *2* Or *He*; also in verses 7, 8 and 22 [b] *9* That is, about 9 inches or about 23 centimeters [c] *13* The precise identification of some of these precious stones is uncertain. [d] *23* The meaning of the Hebrew for this word is uncertain. [e] *34* Possibly the hides of large aquatic mammals

sils; the basin with its stand; 40the curtains of the courtyard with its posts and
bases, and the curtain for the entrance to
the courtyard; the ropes and tent pegs for
the courtyard; all the furnishings for the
tabernacle, the tent of meeting; 41and the
woven garments worn for ministering in
the sanctuary, both the sacred garments
for Aaron the priest and the garments for
his sons when serving as priests.

42The Israelites had done all the work
just as the LORD had commanded Moses. 43Moses inspected the work and saw
that they had done it just as the LORD had
commanded. So Moses blessed them.

40 Then the LORD said to Moses: 2"Set
up the tabernacle, the tent of meeting, on the first day of the first month.
3Place the ark of the covenant law in
it and shield the ark with the curtain.
4Bring in the table and set out what belongs on it. Then bring in the lampstand
and set up its lamps. 5Place the gold altar
of incense in front of the ark of the covenant law and put the curtain at the entrance to the tabernacle.

6"Place the altar of burnt offering in
front of the entrance to the tabernacle,
the tent of meeting; 7place the basin between the tent of meeting and the altar
and put water in it. 8Set up the courtyard
around it and put the curtain at the entrance to the courtyard.

9"Take the anointing oil and anoint the
tabernacle and everything in it; consecrate it and all its furnishings, and it will
be holy. 10Then anoint the altar of burnt
offering and all its utensils; consecrate the
altar, and it will be most holy. 11Anoint the
basin and its stand and consecrate them.

12"Bring Aaron and his sons to the entrance to the tent of meeting and wash
them with water. 13Then dress Aaron in
the sacred garments, anoint him and consecrate him so he may serve me as priest.
14Bring his sons and dress them in tunics.
15Anoint them just as you anointed their
father, so they may serve me as priests.
Their anointing will be to a priesthood
that will continue throughout their generations." 16Moses did everything just as
the LORD commanded him.

17So the tabernacle was set up on the
first day of the first month in the second
year. 18When Moses set up the tabernacle, he put the bases in place, erected the
frames, inserted the crossbars and set up
the posts. 19Then he spread the tent over
the tabernacle and put the covering over
the tent, as the LORD commanded him.

20He took the tablets of the covenant
law and placed them in the ark, attached
the poles to the ark and put the atonement
cover over it. 21Then he brought the ark
into the tabernacle and hung the shielding
curtain and shielded the ark of the covenant law, as the LORD commanded him.

22Moses placed the table in the tent of
meeting on the north side of the tabernacle outside the curtain 23and set out the
bread on it before the LORD, as the LORD
commanded him.

24He placed the lampstand in the tent
of meeting opposite the table on the
south side of the tabernacle 25and set up
the lamps before the LORD, as the LORD
commanded him.

26Moses placed the gold altar in the
tent of meeting in front of the curtain
27and burned fragrant incense on it, as
the LORD commanded him.

28Then he put up the curtain at the entrance to the tabernacle. 29He set the altar of burnt offering near the entrance to
the tabernacle, the tent of meeting, and
offered on it burnt offerings and grain offerings, as the LORD commanded him.

30He placed the basin between the
tent of meeting and the altar and put
water in it for washing, 31and Moses and
Aaron and his sons used it to wash their
hands and feet. 32They washed whenever they entered the tent of meeting or
approached the altar, as the LORD commanded Moses.

33Then Moses set up the courtyard
around the tabernacle and altar and put
up the curtain at the entrance to the courtyard. And so Moses finished the work.

34Then the cloud covered the tent of
meeting, and the glory of the LORD filled
the tabernacle. 35Moses could not enter
the tent of meeting because the cloud
had settled on it, and the glory of the
LORD filled the tabernacle.

36In all the travels of the Israelites,
whenever the cloud lifted from above
the tabernacle, they would set out; 37but
if the cloud did not lift, they did not set
out—until the day it lifted. 38So the
cloud of the LORD was over the tabernacle by day, and fire was in the cloud by
night, in the sight of all the Israelites during all their travels.

LEVITICUS

See the Invitation to Exodus, Leviticus and Numbers on p. 51.

1 The LORD called to Moses and spoke
to him from the tent of meeting. He
said, 2 "Speak to the Israelites and say to
them: 'When anyone among you brings
an offering to the LORD, bring as your offering an animal from either the herd or
the flock.
3 " 'If the offering is a burnt offering
from the herd, you are to offer a male
without defect. You must present it at the
entrance to the tent of meeting so that it
will be acceptable to the LORD. 4 You are
to lay your hand on the head of the burnt
offering, and it will be accepted on your
behalf to make atonement for you. 5 You
are to slaughter the young bull before the
LORD, and then Aaron's sons the priests
shall bring the blood and splash it against
the sides of the altar at the entrance to
the tent of meeting. 6 You are to skin the
burnt offering and cut it into pieces. 7 The
sons of Aaron the priest are to put fire on
the altar and arrange wood on the fire.
8 Then Aaron's sons the priests shall arrange the pieces, including the head and
the fat, on the wood that is burning on
the altar. 9 You are to wash the internal
organs and the legs with water, and the
priest is to burn all of it on the altar. It is a
burnt offering, a food offering, an aroma
pleasing to the LORD.
10 " 'If the offering is a burnt offering
from the flock, from either the sheep or
the goats, you are to offer a male without defect. 11 You are to slaughter it at
the north side of the altar before the
LORD, and Aaron's sons the priests shall
splash its blood against the sides of the
altar. 12 You are to cut it into pieces, and
the priest shall arrange them, including
the head and the fat, on the wood that is
burning on the altar. 13 You are to wash
the internal organs and the legs with water, and the priest is to bring all of them
and burn them on the altar. It is a burnt
offering, a food offering, an aroma pleasing to the LORD.
14 " 'If the offering to the LORD is a burnt
offering of birds, you are to offer a dove or
a young pigeon. 15 The priest shall bring it
to the altar, wring off the head and burn
it on the altar; its blood shall be drained
out on the side of the altar. 16 He is to
remove the crop and the feathers[a] and
throw them down east of the altar where
the ashes are. 17 He shall tear it open by
the wings, not dividing it completely,
and then the priest shall burn it on the
wood that is burning on the altar. It is a
burnt offering, a food offering, an aroma
pleasing to the LORD.

2 " 'When anyone brings a grain offering to the LORD, their offering is to be
of the finest flour. They are to pour olive oil on it, put incense on it 2 and take
it to Aaron's sons the priests. The priest
shall take a handful of the flour and oil,
together with all the incense, and burn
this as a memorial[b] portion on the altar,
a food offering, an aroma pleasing to the
LORD. 3 The rest of the grain offering belongs to Aaron and his sons; it is a most
holy part of the food offerings presented
to the LORD.
4 " 'If you bring a grain offering baked in
an oven, it is to consist of the finest flour:
either thick loaves made without yeast
and with olive oil mixed in or thin loaves
made without yeast and brushed with olive oil. 5 If your grain offering is prepared
on a griddle, it is to be made of the finest
flour mixed with oil, and without yeast.
6 Crumble it and pour oil on it; it is a grain
offering. 7 If your grain offering is cooked
in a pan, it is to be made of the finest flour
and some olive oil. 8 Bring the grain offering made of these things to the LORD;
present it to the priest, who shall take it
to the altar. 9 He shall take out the memorial portion from the grain offering and
burn it on the altar as a food offering, an
aroma pleasing to the LORD. 10 The rest of
the grain offering belongs to Aaron and
his sons; it is a most holy part of the food
offerings presented to the LORD.
11 " 'Every grain offering you bring to
the LORD must be made without yeast,
for you are not to burn any yeast or honey

[a] *16* Or *crop with its contents*; the meaning of the Hebrew for this word is uncertain. [b] *2* Or *representative*; also in verses 9 and 16

in a food offering presented to the LORD.
12You may bring them to the LORD as an
offering of the firstfruits, but they are not
to be offered on the altar as a pleasing
aroma. 13Season all your grain offerings
with salt. Do not leave the salt of the covenant of your God out of your grain offerings; add salt to all your offerings.
14" 'If you bring a grain offering of firstfruits to the LORD, offer crushed heads of
new grain roasted in the fire. 15Put oil
and incense on it; it is a grain offering.
16The priest shall burn the memorial
portion of the crushed grain and the oil,
together with all the incense, as a food
offering presented to the LORD.

3 " 'If your offering is a fellowship offering, and you offer an animal from
the herd, whether male or female, you
are to present before the LORD an animal without defect. 2You are to lay your
hand on the head of your offering and
slaughter it at the entrance to the tent of
meeting. Then Aaron's sons the priests
shall splash the blood against the sides
of the altar. 3From the fellowship offering you are to bring a food offering to the
LORD: the internal organs and all the fat
that is connected to them, 4both kidneys
with the fat on them near the loins, and
the long lobe of the liver, which you will
remove with the kidneys. 5Then Aaron's
sons are to burn it on the altar on top of
the burnt offering that is lying on the
burning wood; it is a food offering, an
aroma pleasing to the LORD.
6" 'If you offer an animal from the flock
as a fellowship offering to the LORD, you
are to offer a male or female without defect. 7If you offer a lamb, you are to present it before the LORD, 8lay your hand
on its head and slaughter it in front of the
tent of meeting. Then Aaron's sons shall
splash its blood against the sides of the
altar. 9From the fellowship offering you
are to bring a food offering to the LORD:
its fat, the entire fat tail cut off close to
the backbone, the internal organs and
all the fat that is connected to them,
10both kidneys with the fat on them near
the loins, and the long lobe of the liver,
which you will remove with the kidneys.
11The priest shall burn them on the altar
as a food offering presented to the LORD.
12" 'If your offering is a goat, you are
to present it before the LORD, 13lay your
hand on its head and slaughter it in front
of the tent of meeting. Then Aaron's sons
shall splash its blood against the sides of
the altar. 14From what you offer you are
to present this food offering to the LORD:
the internal organs and all the fat that
is connected to them, 15both kidneys
with the fat on them near the loins, and
the long lobe of the liver, which you will
remove with the kidneys. 16The priest
shall burn them on the altar as a food
offering, a pleasing aroma. All the fat is
the LORD's.
17" 'This is a lasting ordinance for the
generations to come, wherever you live:
You must not eat any fat or any blood.' "

4 The LORD said to Moses, 2"Say to the
Israelites: 'When anyone sins unintentionally and does what is forbidden
in any of the LORD's commands—

3" 'If the anointed priest sins, bringing
guilt on the people, he must bring to the
LORD a young bull without defect as a sin
offering[a] for the sin he has committed.
4He is to present the bull at the entrance
to the tent of meeting before the LORD.
He is to lay his hand on its head and
slaughter it there before the LORD. 5Then
the anointed priest shall take some of the
bull's blood and carry it into the tent of
meeting. 6He is to dip his finger into the
blood and sprinkle some of it seven times
before the LORD, in front of the curtain
of the sanctuary. 7The priest shall then
put some of the blood on the horns of the
altar of fragrant incense that is before the
LORD in the tent of meeting. The rest of
the bull's blood he shall pour out at the
base of the altar of burnt offering at the
entrance to the tent of meeting. 8He shall
remove all the fat from the bull of the sin
offering—all the fat that is connected to
the internal organs, 9both kidneys with
the fat on them near the loins, and the
long lobe of the liver, which he will remove with the kidneys— 10just as the fat
is removed from the ox[b] sacrificed as a
fellowship offering. Then the priest shall
burn them on the altar of burnt offering.
11But the hide of the bull and all its flesh,
as well as the head and legs, the internal
organs and the intestines— 12that is, all
the rest of the bull—he must take outside

[a] *3* Or *purification offering*; here and throughout this chapter [b] *10* The Hebrew word can refer to either male or female.

the camp to a place ceremonially clean,
where the ashes are thrown, and burn it
there in a wood fire on the ash heap.

13 “‘If the whole Israelite community
sins unintentionally and does what is forbidden in any of the LORD's commands,
even though the community is unaware
of the matter, when they realize their
guilt 14 and the sin they committed becomes known, the assembly must bring
a young bull as a sin offering and present
it before the tent of meeting. 15 The elders
of the community are to lay their hands
on the bull's head before the LORD, and
the bull shall be slaughtered before the
LORD. 16 Then the anointed priest is to
take some of the bull's blood into the tent
of meeting. 17 He shall dip his finger into
the blood and sprinkle it before the LORD
seven times in front of the curtain. 18 He
is to put some of the blood on the horns
of the altar that is before the LORD in the
tent of meeting. The rest of the blood he
shall pour out at the base of the altar of
burnt offering at the entrance to the tent
of meeting. 19 He shall remove all the fat
from it and burn it on the altar, 20 and do
with this bull just as he did with the bull
for the sin offering. In this way the priest
will make atonement for the community,
and they will be forgiven. 21 Then he shall
take the bull outside the camp and burn
it as he burned the first bull. This is the
sin offering for the community.

22 “‘When a leader sins unintentionally and does what is forbidden in any
of the commands of the LORD his God,
when he realizes his guilt 23 and the sin
he has committed becomes known, he
must bring as his offering a male goat
without defect. 24 He is to lay his hand
on the goat's head and slaughter it at the
place where the burnt offering is slaughtered before the LORD. It is a sin offering.
25 Then the priest shall take some of the
blood of the sin offering with his finger
and put it on the horns of the altar of
burnt offering and pour out the rest of
the blood at the base of the altar. 26 He
shall burn all the fat on the altar as he
burned the fat of the fellowship offering.
In this way the priest will make atonement for the leader's sin, and he will be
forgiven.

27 “‘If any member of the community sins unintentionally and does what
is forbidden in any of the LORD's commands, when they realize their guilt
28 and the sin they have committed becomes known, they must bring as their
offering for the sin they committed a
female goat without defect. 29 They are
to lay their hand on the head of the sin
offering and slaughter it at the place of
the burnt offering. 30 Then the priest is
to take some of the blood with his finger and put it on the horns of the altar
of burnt offering and pour out the rest of
the blood at the base of the altar. 31 They
shall remove all the fat, just as the fat is
removed from the fellowship offering,
and the priest shall burn it on the altar
as an aroma pleasing to the LORD. In this
way the priest will make atonement for
them, and they will be forgiven.

32 “‘If someone brings a lamb as their
sin offering, they are to bring a female
without defect. 33 They are to lay their
hand on its head and slaughter it for a
sin offering at the place where the burnt
offering is slaughtered. 34 Then the priest
shall take some of the blood of the sin offering with his finger and put it on the
horns of the altar of burnt offering and
pour out the rest of the blood at the base
of the altar. 35 They shall remove all the
fat, just as the fat is removed from the
lamb of the fellowship offering, and the
priest shall burn it on the altar on top of
the food offerings presented to the LORD.
In this way the priest will make atonement for them for the sin they have committed, and they will be forgiven.

5 “‘If anyone sins because they do not
speak up when they hear a public
charge to testify regarding something
they have seen or learned about, they
will be held responsible.

2 “‘If anyone becomes aware that they
are guilty—if they unwittingly touch
anything ceremonially unclean (whether the carcass of an unclean animal, wild
or domestic, or of any unclean creature
that moves along the ground) and they
are unaware that they have become unclean, but then they come to realize their
guilt; 3 or if they touch human uncleanness (anything that would make them
unclean) even though they are unaware
of it, but then they learn of it and realize
their guilt; 4 or if anyone thoughtlessly
takes an oath to do anything, whether
good or evil (in any matter one might

carelessly swear about) even though they are unaware of it, but then they learn of it and realize their guilt— 5when anyone becomes aware that they are guilty in any of these matters, they must confess in what way they have sinned. 6As a penalty for the sin they have committed, they must bring to the LORD a female lamb or goat from the flock as a sin offering[a]; and the priest shall make atonement for them for their sin.

7"'Anyone who cannot afford a lamb is to bring two doves or two young pigeons to the LORD as a penalty for their sin—one for a sin offering and the other for a burnt offering. 8They are to bring them to the priest, who shall first offer the one for the sin offering. He is to wring its head from its neck, not dividing it completely, 9and is to splash some of the blood of the sin offering against the side of the altar; the rest of the blood must be drained out at the base of the altar. It is a sin offering. 10The priest shall then offer the other as a burnt offering in the prescribed way and make atonement for them for the sin they have committed, and they will be forgiven.

11"'If, however, they cannot afford two doves or two young pigeons, they are to bring as an offering for their sin a tenth of an ephah[b] of the finest flour for a sin offering. They must not put olive oil or incense on it, because it is a sin offering. 12They are to bring it to the priest, who shall take a handful of it as a memorial[c] portion and burn it on the altar on top of the food offerings presented to the LORD. It is a sin offering. 13In this way the priest will make atonement for them for any of these sins they have committed, and they will be forgiven. The rest of the offering will belong to the priest, as in the case of the grain offering.'"

14The LORD said to Moses: 15"When anyone is unfaithful to the LORD by sinning unintentionally in regard to any of the LORD's holy things, they are to bring to the LORD as a penalty a ram from the flock, one without defect and of the proper value in silver, according to the sanctuary shekel.[d] It is a guilt offering. 16They must make restitution for what they have failed to do in regard to the holy things, pay an additional penalty of a fifth of its value and give it all to the priest. The priest will make atonement for them with the ram as a guilt offering, and they will be forgiven.

17"If anyone sins and does what is forbidden in any of the LORD's commands, even though they do not know it, they are guilty and will be held responsible. 18They are to bring to the priest as a guilt offering a ram from the flock, one without defect and of the proper value. In this way the priest will make atonement for them for the wrong they have committed unintentionally, and they will be forgiven. 19It is a guilt offering; they have been guilty of[e] wrongdoing against the LORD."

6[f] The LORD said to Moses: 2"If anyone sins and is unfaithful to the LORD by deceiving a neighbor about something entrusted to them or left in their care or about something stolen, or if they cheat their neighbor, 3or if they find lost property and lie about it, or if they swear falsely about any such sin that people may commit— 4when they sin in any of these ways and realize their guilt, they must return what they have stolen or taken by extortion, or what was entrusted to them, or the lost property they found, 5or whatever it was they swore falsely about. They must make restitution in full, add a fifth of the value to it and give it all to the owner on the day they present their guilt offering. 6And as a penalty they must bring to the priest, that is, to the LORD, their guilt offering, a ram from the flock, one without defect and of the proper value. 7In this way the priest will make atonement for them before the LORD, and they will be forgiven for any of the things they did that made them guilty."

8The LORD said to Moses: 9"Give Aaron and his sons this command: 'These are the regulations for the burnt offering: The burnt offering is to remain on the altar hearth throughout the night, till morning, and the fire must be kept burning on the altar. 10The priest shall then put on his linen clothes, with linen un-

[a] *6* Or *purification offering*; here and throughout this chapter [b] *11* That is, probably about 3 1/2 pounds or about 1.6 kilograms [c] *12* Or *representative* [d] *15* That is, about 2/5 ounce or about 12 grams [e] *19* Or *offering; atonement has been made for their* [f] In Hebrew texts 6:1-7 is numbered 5:20-26, and 6:8-30 is numbered 6:1-23.

dergarments next to his body, and shall
remove the ashes of the burnt offering
that the fire has consumed on the altar
and place them beside the altar. 11Then
he is to take off these clothes and put
on others, and carry the ashes outside
the camp to a place that is ceremonially clean. 12The fire on the altar must be
kept burning; it must not go out. Every
morning the priest is to add firewood and
arrange the burnt offering on the fire and
burn the fat of the fellowship offerings on
it. 13The fire must be kept burning on the
altar continuously; it must not go out.

14" 'These are the regulations for the
grain offering: Aaron's sons are to bring
it before the LORD, in front of the altar.
15The priest is to take a handful of the
finest flour and some olive oil, together
with all the incense on the grain offering, and burn the memorial[a] portion
on the altar as an aroma pleasing to the
LORD. 16Aaron and his sons shall eat
the rest of it, but it is to be eaten without
yeast in the sanctuary area; they are to
eat it in the courtyard of the tent of meeting. 17It must not be baked with yeast; I
have given it as their share of the food
offerings presented to me. Like the sin
offering[b] and the guilt offering, it is most
holy. 18Any male descendant of Aaron
may eat it. For all generations to come it
is his perpetual share of the food offerings presented to the LORD. Whatever
touches them will become holy.[c] ' "

19The LORD also said to Moses, 20"This
is the offering Aaron and his sons are
to bring to the LORD on the day he[d] is
anointed: a tenth of an ephah[e] of the finest flour as a regular grain offering, half
of it in the morning and half in the evening. 21It must be prepared with oil on a
griddle; bring it well-mixed and present
the grain offering broken[f] in pieces as an
aroma pleasing to the LORD. 22The son
who is to succeed him as anointed priest
shall prepare it. It is the LORD's perpetual share and is to be burned completely.
23Every grain offering of a priest shall be
burned completely; it must not be eat-
en."

24The LORD said to Moses, 25"Say to
Aaron and his sons: 'These are the regulations for the sin offering: The sin offering is to be slaughtered before the LORD
in the place the burnt offering is slaughtered; it is most holy. 26The priest who
offers it shall eat it; it is to be eaten in the
sanctuary area, in the courtyard of the
tent of meeting. 27Whatever touches any
of the flesh will become holy, and if any
of the blood is spattered on a garment,
you must wash it in the sanctuary area.
28The clay pot the meat is cooked in must
be broken; but if it is cooked in a bronze
pot, the pot is to be scoured and rinsed
with water. 29Any male in a priest's family may eat it; it is most holy. 30But any sin
offering whose blood is brought into the
tent of meeting to make atonement in the
Holy Place must not be eaten; it must be
burned up.

7 " 'These are the regulations for the
guilt offering, which is most holy:
2The guilt offering is to be slaughtered
in the place where the burnt offering
is slaughtered, and its blood is to be
splashed against the sides of the altar.
3All its fat shall be offered: the fat tail
and the fat that covers the internal organs, 4both kidneys with the fat on them
near the loins, and the long lobe of the
liver, which is to be removed with the
kidneys. 5The priest shall burn them on
the altar as a food offering presented to
the LORD. It is a guilt offering. 6Any male
in a priest's family may eat it, but it must
be eaten in the sanctuary area; it is most
holy.

7" 'The same law applies to both the sin
offering[g] and the guilt offering: They belong to the priest who makes atonement
with them. 8The priest who offers a burnt
offering for anyone may keep its hide for
himself. 9Every grain offering baked in
an oven or cooked in a pan or on a griddle
belongs to the priest who offers it, 10and
every grain offering, whether mixed with
olive oil or dry, belongs equally to all the
sons of Aaron.

11" 'These are the regulations for the
fellowship offering anyone may present
to the LORD:

12" 'If they offer it as an expression of
thankfulness, then along with this thank
offering they are to offer thick loaves

[a] *15* Or *representative* [b] *17* Or *purification offering*; also in verses 25 and 30 [c] *18* Or *Whoever touches them must be holy*; similarly in verse 27 [d] *20* Or *each* [e] *20* That is, probably about 3 1/2 pounds or about 1.6 kilograms [f] *21* The meaning of the Hebrew for this word is uncertain. [g] *7* Or *purification offering*; also in verse 37

made without yeast and with olive oil
mixed in, thin loaves made without yeast
and brushed with oil, and thick loaves of
the finest flour well-kneaded and with
oil mixed in. 13Along with their fellowship offering of thanksgiving they are
to present an offering with thick loaves
of bread made with yeast. 14They are to
bring one of each kind as an offering, a
contribution to the LORD; it belongs to
the priest who splashes the blood of the
fellowship offering against the altar.
15The meat of their fellowship offering of
thanksgiving must be eaten on the day it
is offered; they must leave none of it till
morning.

16" 'If, however, their offering is the result of a vow or is a freewill offering, the
sacrifice shall be eaten on the day they
offer it, but anything left over may be
eaten on the next day. 17Any meat of the
sacrifice left over till the third day must
be burned up. 18If any meat of the fellowship offering is eaten on the third day, the
one who offered it will not be accepted. It
will not be reckoned to their credit, for it
has become impure; the person who eats
any of it will be held responsible.

19" 'Meat that touches anything ceremonially unclean must not be eaten; it
must be burned up. As for other meat,
anyone ceremonially clean may eat
it. 20But if anyone who is unclean eats
any meat of the fellowship offering belonging to the LORD, they must be cut
off from their people. 21Anyone who
touches something unclean—whether
human uncleanness or an unclean animal or any unclean creature that moves
along the ground[a]—and then eats any of
the meat of the fellowship offering belonging to the LORD must be cut off from
their people.' "

22The LORD said to Moses, 23"Say to
the Israelites: 'Do not eat any of the fat of
cattle, sheep or goats. 24The fat of an animal found dead or torn by wild animals
may be used for any other purpose, but
you must not eat it. 25Anyone who eats
the fat of an animal from which a food
offering may be[b] presented to the LORD
must be cut off from their people. 26And
wherever you live, you must not eat the
blood of any bird or animal. 27Anyone
who eats blood must be cut off from their
people.' "

28The LORD said to Moses, 29"Say to the
Israelites: 'Anyone who brings a fellowship offering to the LORD is to bring part
of it as their sacrifice to the LORD. 30With
their own hands they are to present the
food offering to the LORD; they are to
bring the fat, together with the breast,
and wave the breast before the LORD as a
wave offering. 31The priest shall burn the
fat on the altar, but the breast belongs to
Aaron and his sons. 32You are to give the
right thigh of your fellowship offerings
to the priest as a contribution. 33The son
of Aaron who offers the blood and the
fat of the fellowship offering shall have
the right thigh as his share. 34From the
fellowship offerings of the Israelites, I
have taken the breast that is waved and
the thigh that is presented and have giv-
en them to Aaron the priest and his sons
as their perpetual share from the Israelites.' "

35This is the portion of the food offerings presented to the LORD that were allotted to Aaron and his sons on the day
they were presented to serve the LORD as
priests. 36On the day they were anointed,
the LORD commanded that the Israelites
give this to them as their perpetual share
for the generations to come.

37These, then, are the regulations for
the burnt offering, the grain offering,
the sin offering, the guilt offering, the
ordination offering and the fellowship
offering, 38which the LORD gave Moses
at Mount Sinai in the Desert of Sinai on
the day he commanded the Israelites to
bring their offerings to the LORD.

8 The LORD said to Moses, 2"Bring
Aaron and his sons, their garments,
the anointing oil, the bull for the sin
offering,[c] the two rams and the basket
containing bread made without yeast,
3and gather the entire assembly at the
entrance to the tent of meeting." 4Moses
did as the LORD commanded him, and
the assembly gathered at the entrance to
the tent of meeting.

5Moses said to the assembly, "This is
what the LORD has commanded to be
done." 6Then Moses brought Aaron and
his sons forward and washed them with

[a] *21* A few Hebrew manuscripts, Samaritan Pentateuch, Syriac and Targum (see 5:2); most Hebrew manuscripts *any unclean, detestable thing* [b] *25* Or *offering is* [c] *2* Or *purification offering*; also in verse 14

water. 7He put the tunic on Aaron, tied the sash around him, clothed him with the robe and put the ephod on him. He also fastened the ephod with a decorative waistband, which he tied around him. 8He placed the breastpiece on him and put the Urim and Thummim in the breastpiece. 9Then he placed the turban on Aaron's head and set the gold plate, the sacred emblem, on the front of it, as the LORD commanded Moses.

10Then Moses took the anointing oil and anointed the tabernacle and everything in it, and so consecrated them. 11He sprinkled some of the oil on the altar seven times, anointing the altar and all its utensils and the basin with its stand, to consecrate them. 12He poured some of the anointing oil on Aaron's head and anointed him to consecrate him. 13Then he brought Aaron's sons forward, put tunics on them, tied sashes around them and fastened caps on them, as the LORD commanded Moses.

14He then presented the bull for the sin offering, and Aaron and his sons laid their hands on its head. 15Moses slaughtered the bull and took some of the blood, and with his finger he put it on all the horns of the altar to purify the altar. He poured out the rest of the blood at the base of the altar. So he consecrated it to make atonement for it. 16Moses also took all the fat around the internal organs, the long lobe of the liver, and both kidneys and their fat, and burned it on the altar. 17But the bull with its hide and its flesh and its intestines he burned up outside the camp, as the LORD commanded Moses.

18He then presented the ram for the burnt offering, and Aaron and his sons laid their hands on its head. 19Then Moses slaughtered the ram and splashed the blood against the sides of the altar. 20He cut the ram into pieces and burned the head, the pieces and the fat. 21He washed the internal organs and the legs with water and burned the whole ram on the altar. It was a burnt offering, a pleasing aroma, a food offering presented to the LORD, as the LORD commanded Moses.

22He then presented the other ram, the ram for the ordination, and Aaron and his sons laid their hands on its head. 23Moses slaughtered the ram and took some of its blood and put it on the lobe of Aaron's right ear, on the thumb of his right hand and on the big toe of his right foot. 24Moses also brought Aaron's sons forward and put some of the blood on the lobes of their right ears, on the thumbs of their right hands and on the big toes of their right feet. Then he splashed blood against the sides of the altar. 25After that, he took the fat, the fat tail, all the fat around the internal organs, the long lobe of the liver, both kidneys and their fat and the right thigh. 26And from the basket of bread made without yeast, which was before the LORD, he took one thick loaf, one thick loaf with olive oil mixed in, and one thin loaf, and he put these on the fat portions and on the right thigh. 27He put all these in the hands of Aaron and his sons, and they waved them before the LORD as a wave offering. 28Then Moses took them from their hands and burned them on the altar on top of the burnt offering as an ordination offering, a pleasing aroma, a food offering presented to the LORD. 29Moses also took the breast, which was his share of the ordination ram, and waved it before the LORD as a wave offering, as the LORD commanded Moses.

30Then Moses took some of the anointing oil and some of the blood from the altar and sprinkled them on Aaron and his garments and on his sons and their garments. So he consecrated Aaron and his garments and his sons and their garments.

31Moses then said to Aaron and his sons, "Cook the meat at the entrance to the tent of meeting and eat it there with the bread from the basket of ordination offerings, as I was commanded: 'Aaron and his sons are to eat it.' 32Then burn up the rest of the meat and the bread. 33Do not leave the entrance to the tent of meeting for seven days, until the days of your ordination are completed, for your ordination will last seven days. 34What has been done today was commanded by the LORD to make atonement for you. 35You must stay at the entrance to the tent of meeting day and night for seven days and do what the LORD requires, so you will not die; for that is what I have been commanded."

36So Aaron and his sons did everything the LORD commanded through Moses.

9 On the eighth day Moses summoned
Aaron and his sons and the elders of
Israel. 2He said to Aaron, "Take a bull
calf for your sin offering[a] and a ram for
your burnt offering, both without defect, and present them before the LORD.
3Then say to the Israelites: 'Take a male
goat for a sin offering, a calf and a lamb—
both a year old and without defect—for a
burnt offering, 4and an ox[b] and a ram for
a fellowship offering to sacrifice before
the LORD, together with a grain offering
mixed with olive oil. For today the LORD
will appear to you.' "
5They took the things Moses commanded to the front of the tent of meeting, and the entire assembly came near
and stood before the LORD. 6Then Moses
said, "This is what the LORD has commanded you to do, so that the glory of
the LORD may appear to you."
7Moses said to Aaron, "Come to the
altar and sacrifice your sin offering and
your burnt offering and make atonement
for yourself and the people; sacrifice the
offering that is for the people and make
atonement for them, as the LORD has
commanded."
8So Aaron came to the altar and
slaughtered the calf as a sin offering for
himself. 9His sons brought the blood to
him, and he dipped his finger into the
blood and put it on the horns of the altar; the rest of the blood he poured out
at the base of the altar. 10On the altar he
burned the fat, the kidneys and the long
lobe of the liver from the sin offering,
as the LORD commanded Moses; 11the
flesh and the hide he burned up outside
the camp.
12Then he slaughtered the burnt offering. His sons handed him the blood,
and he splashed it against the sides of
the altar. 13They handed him the burnt
offering piece by piece, including the
head, and he burned them on the altar.
14He washed the internal organs and the
legs and burned them on top of the burnt
offering on the altar.
15Aaron then brought the offering that
was for the people. He took the goat for
the people's sin offering and slaughtered
it and offered it for a sin offering as he did
with the first one.
16He brought the burnt offering and
offered it in the prescribed way. 17He also
brought the grain offering, took a handful of it and burned it on the altar in addition to the morning's burnt offering.
18He slaughtered the ox and the ram
as the fellowship offering for the people.
His sons handed him the blood, and he
splashed it against the sides of the altar. 19But the fat portions of the ox and
the ram—the fat tail, the layer of fat, the
kidneys and the long lobe of the liver—
20these they laid on the breasts, and then
Aaron burned the fat on the altar. 21Aar-
on waved the breasts and the right thigh
before the LORD as a wave offering, as
Moses commanded.
22Then Aaron lifted his hands toward
the people and blessed them. And having sacrificed the sin offering, the burnt
offering and the fellowship offering, he
stepped down.
23Moses and Aaron then went into the
tent of meeting. When they came out,
they blessed the people; and the glory
of the LORD appeared to all the people.
24Fire came out from the presence of the
LORD and consumed the burnt offering
and the fat portions on the altar. And
when all the people saw it, they shouted
for joy and fell facedown.

10 Aaron's sons Nadab and Abihu took
their censers, put fire in them and
added incense; and they offered unauthorized fire before the LORD, contrary
to his command. 2So fire came out from
the presence of the LORD and consumed
them, and they died before the LORD.
3Moses then said to Aaron, "This is what
the LORD spoke of when he said:

" 'Among those who approach me
I will be proved holy;
in the sight of all the people
I will be honored.' "

Aaron remained silent.
4Moses summoned Mishael and Elzaphan, sons of Aaron's uncle Uzziel, and
said to them, "Come here; carry your
cousins outside the camp, away from the
front of the sanctuary." 5So they came
and carried them, still in their tunics,
outside the camp, as Moses ordered.
6Then Moses said to Aaron and his
sons Eleazar and Ithamar, "Do not let
your hair become unkempt[c] and do not

[a] 2 Or *purification offering*; here and throughout this chapter
[b] 4 The Hebrew word can refer to either male or female; also in verses 18 and 19.
[c] 6 Or *Do not uncover your heads*

tear your clothes, or you will die and the
LORD will be angry with the whole community. But your relatives, all the Israelites, may mourn for those the LORD has
destroyed by fire. 7 Do not leave the entrance to the tent of meeting or you will
die, because the LORD's anointing oil is
on you." So they did as Moses said.
8 Then the LORD said to Aaron, 9 "You
and your sons are not to drink wine or
other fermented drink whenever you go
into the tent of meeting, or you will die.
This is a lasting ordinance for the generations to come, 10 so that you can distinguish between the holy and the common, between the unclean and the clean,
11 and so you can teach the Israelites all
the decrees the LORD has given them
through Moses."
12 Moses said to Aaron and his remaining sons, Eleazar and Ithamar, "Take the
grain offering left over from the food offerings prepared without yeast and presented to the LORD and eat it beside the
altar, for it is most holy. 13 Eat it in the
sanctuary area, because it is your share
and your sons' share of the food offerings
presented to the LORD; for so I have been
commanded. 14 But you and your sons
and your daughters may eat the breast
that was waved and the thigh that was
presented. Eat them in a ceremonially
clean place; they have been given to you
and your children as your share of the
Israelites' fellowship offerings. 15 The
thigh that was presented and the breast
that was waved must be brought with the
fat portions of the food offerings, to be
waved before the LORD as a wave offering. This will be the perpetual share for
you and your children, as the LORD has
commanded."
16 When Moses inquired about the goat
of the sin offering[a] and found that it had
been burned up, he was angry with Eleazar and Ithamar, Aaron's remaining
sons, and asked, 17 "Why didn't you eat
the sin offering in the sanctuary area? It
is most holy; it was given to you to take
away the guilt of the community by making atonement for them before the LORD.
18 Since its blood was not taken into the
Holy Place, you should have eaten the
goat in the sanctuary area, as I commanded."
19 Aaron replied to Moses, "Today they
sacrificed their sin offering and their
burnt offering before the LORD, but
such things as this have happened to
me. Would the LORD have been pleased
if I had eaten the sin offering today?"
20 When Moses heard this, he was satisfied.

11 The LORD said to Moses and Aaron, 2 "Say to the Israelites: 'Of all
the animals that live on land, these are
the ones you may eat: 3 You may eat any
animal that has a divided hoof and that
chews the cud.
4 "'There are some that only chew the
cud or only have a divided hoof, but you
must not eat them. The camel, though
it chews the cud, does not have a divided hoof; it is ceremonially unclean for
you. 5 The hyrax, though it chews the
cud, does not have a divided hoof; it is
unclean for you. 6 The rabbit, though it
chews the cud, does not have a divided
hoof; it is unclean for you. 7 And the pig,
though it has a divided hoof, does not
chew the cud; it is unclean for you. 8 You
must not eat their meat or touch their
carcasses; they are unclean for you.
9 "'Of all the creatures living in the
water of the seas and the streams
you may eat any that have fins and
scales. 10 But all creatures in the seas
or streams that do not have fins and
scales — whether among all the swarm-
ing things or among all the other living
creatures in the water — you are to regard as unclean. 11 And since you are to
regard them as unclean, you must not
eat their meat; you must regard their
carcasses as unclean. 12 Anything living in the water that does not have fins
and scales is to be regarded as unclean
by you.
13 "'These are the birds you are to regard as unclean and not eat because
they are unclean: the eagle,[b] the vulture, the black vulture, 14 the red kite,
any kind of black kite, 15 any kind of raven, 16 the horned owl, the screech owl,
the gull, any kind of hawk, 17 the little
owl, the cormorant, the great owl, 18 the
white owl, the desert owl, the osprey,
19 the stork, any kind of heron, the hoopoe and the bat.
20 "'All flying insects that walk on all

[a] *16* Or *purification offering*; also in verses 17 and 19
[b] *13* The precise identification of some of the birds, insects and animals in this chapter is uncertain.

fours are to be regarded as unclean by
you. 21There are, however, some flying
insects that walk on all fours that you
may eat: those that have jointed legs
for hopping on the ground. 22Of these
you may eat any kind of locust, katydid,
cricket or grasshopper. 23But all other
flying insects that have four legs you are
to regard as unclean.
24"'You will make yourselves unclean
by these; whoever touches their carcasses will be unclean till evening. 25Who-
ever picks up one of their carcasses must
wash their clothes, and they will be unclean till evening.
26"'Every animal that does not have a
divided hoof or that does not chew the
cud is unclean for you; whoever touches the carcass of any of them will be unclean. 27Of all the animals that walk on
all fours, those that walk on their paws
are unclean for you; whoever touches
their carcasses will be unclean till evening. 28Anyone who picks up their carcasses must wash their clothes, and they
will be unclean till evening. These animals are unclean for you.
29"'Of the animals that move along
the ground, these are unclean for you:
the weasel, the rat, any kind of great lizard, 30the gecko, the monitor lizard, the
wall lizard, the skink and the chame-
leon. 31Of all those that move along the
ground, these are unclean for you. Whoever touches them when they are dead
will be unclean till evening. 32When
one of them dies and falls on something,
that article, whatever its use, will be unclean, whether it is made of wood, cloth,
hide or sackcloth. Put it in water; it will
be unclean till evening, and then it will
be clean. 33If one of them falls into a clay
pot, everything in it will be unclean, and
you must break the pot. 34Any food you
are allowed to eat that has come into
contact with water from any such pot
is unclean, and any liquid that is drunk
from such a pot is unclean. 35Anything
that one of their carcasses falls on becomes unclean; an oven or cooking pot
must be broken up. They are unclean,
and you are to regard them as unclean.
36A spring, however, or a cistern for collecting water remains clean, but anyone
who touches one of these carcasses is
unclean. 37If a carcass falls on any seeds
that are to be planted, they remain clean.
38But if water has been put on the seed
and a carcass falls on it, it is unclean for
you.
39"'If an animal that you are allowed
to eat dies, anyone who touches its carcass will be unclean till evening. 40Any-
one who eats some of its carcass must
wash their clothes, and they will be unclean till evening. Anyone who picks up
the carcass must wash their clothes, and
they will be unclean till evening.
41"'Every creature that moves along
the ground is to be regarded as unclean;
it is not to be eaten. 42You are not to
eat any creature that moves along the
ground, whether it moves on its belly
or walks on all fours or on many feet; it
is unclean. 43Do not defile yourselves
by any of these creatures. Do not make
yourselves unclean by means of them
or be made unclean by them. 44I am the
LORD your God; consecrate yourselves
and be holy, because I am holy. Do not
make yourselves unclean by any creature that moves along the ground. 45I
am the LORD, who brought you up out of
Egypt to be your God; therefore be holy,
because I am holy.
46"'These are the regulations concerning animals, birds, every living thing that
moves about in the water and every creature that moves along the ground. 47You
must distinguish between the unclean
and the clean, between living creatures
that may be eaten and those that may not
be eaten.'"

12 The LORD said to Moses, 2"Say to
the Israelites: 'A woman who becomes pregnant and gives birth to a
son will be ceremonially unclean for
seven days, just as she is unclean during her monthly period. 3On the eighth
day the boy is to be circumcised. 4Then
the woman must wait thirty-three days
to be purified from her bleeding. She
must not touch anything sacred or go to
the sanctuary until the days of her purification are over. 5If she gives birth to a
daughter, for two weeks the woman will
be unclean, as during her period. Then
she must wait sixty-six days to be purified from her bleeding.
6"'When the days of her purification for
a son or daughter are over, she is to bring
to the priest at the entrance to the tent of
meeting a year-old lamb for a burnt offering and a young pigeon or a dove for a

sin offering.[a] 7 He shall offer them before
the LORD to make atonement for her, and
then she will be ceremonially clean from
her flow of blood.
"'These are the regulations for the
woman who gives birth to a boy or a girl.
8 But if she cannot afford a lamb, she is
to bring two doves or two young pigeons,
one for a burnt offering and the other for
a sin offering. In this way the priest will
make atonement for her, and she will be
clean.'"

13 The LORD said to Moses and Aaron,
2 "When anyone has a swelling or a
rash or a shiny spot on their skin that may
be a defiling skin disease,[b] they must be
brought to Aaron the priest or to one of
his sons[c] who is a priest. 3 The priest is
to examine the sore on the skin, and if
the hair in the sore has turned white and
the sore appears to be more than skin
deep, it is a defiling skin disease. When
the priest examines that person, he shall
pronounce them ceremonially unclean.
4 If the shiny spot on the skin is white but
does not appear to be more than skin
deep and the hair in it has not turned
white, the priest is to isolate the affected
person for seven days. 5 On the seventh
day the priest is to examine them, and if
he sees that the sore is unchanged and
has not spread in the skin, he is to isolate them for another seven days. 6 On
the seventh day the priest is to examine
them again, and if the sore has faded and
has not spread in the skin, the priest shall
pronounce them clean; it is only a rash.
They must wash their clothes, and they
will be clean. 7 But if the rash does spread
in their skin after they have shown themselves to the priest to be pronounced
clean, they must appear before the priest
again. 8 The priest is to examine that
person, and if the rash has spread in the
skin, he shall pronounce them unclean;
it is a defiling skin disease.
9 "When anyone has a defiling skin
disease, they must be brought to the
priest. 10 The priest is to examine them,
and if there is a white swelling in the
skin that has turned the hair white and
if there is raw flesh in the swelling, 11 it
is a chronic skin disease and the priest
shall pronounce them unclean. He is not
to isolate them, because they are already
unclean.
12 "If the disease breaks out all over
their skin and, so far as the priest can
see, it covers all the skin of the affected
person from head to foot, 13 the priest
is to examine them, and if the disease
has covered their whole body, he shall
pronounce them clean. Since it has all
turned white, they are clean. 14 But whenever raw flesh appears on them, they
will be unclean. 15 When the priest sees
the raw flesh, he shall pronounce them
unclean. The raw flesh is unclean; they
have a defiling disease. 16 If the raw flesh
changes and turns white, they must go
to the priest. 17 The priest is to examine
them, and if the sores have turned white,
the priest shall pronounce the affected
person clean; then they will be clean.
18 "When someone has a boil on their
skin and it heals, 19 and in the place where
the boil was, a white swelling or reddish-
white spot appears, they must present
themselves to the priest. 20 The priest is
to examine it, and if it appears to be more
than skin deep and the hair in it has
turned white, the priest shall pronounce
that person unclean. It is a defiling skin
disease that has broken out where the
boil was. 21 But if, when the priest examines it, there is no white hair in it and it is
not more than skin deep and has faded,
then the priest is to isolate them for seven
days. 22 If it is spreading in the skin, the
priest shall pronounce them unclean; it
is a defiling disease. 23 But if the spot is
unchanged and has not spread, it is only
a scar from the boil, and the priest shall
pronounce them clean.
24 "When someone has a burn on their
skin and a reddish-white or white spot
appears in the raw flesh of the burn,
25 the priest is to examine the spot, and
if the hair in it has turned white, and it
appears to be more than skin deep, it is
a defiling disease that has broken out
in the burn. The priest shall pronounce
them unclean; it is a defiling skin disease. 26 But if the priest examines it and
there is no white hair in the spot and if
it is not more than skin deep and has
faded, then the priest is to isolate them
for seven days. 27 On the seventh day the

[a] *6* Or *purification offering*; also in verse 8 [b] *2* The Hebrew word for *defiling skin disease*, traditionally translated "leprosy," was used for various diseases affecting the skin; here and throughout verses 3-46.
[c] *2* Or *descendants*

priest is to examine that person, and if it
is spreading in the skin, the priest shall
pronounce them unclean; it is a defiling skin disease. 28If, however, the spot
is unchanged and has not spread in the
skin but has faded, it is a swelling from
the burn, and the priest shall pronounce
them clean; it is only a scar from the
burn.

29"If a man or woman has a sore on
their head or chin, 30the priest is to examine the sore, and if it appears to be
more than skin deep and the hair in it
is yellow and thin, the priest shall pronounce them unclean; it is a defiling
skin disease on the head or chin. 31But
if, when the priest examines the sore, it
does not seem to be more than skin deep
and there is no black hair in it, then the
priest is to isolate the affected person
for seven days. 32On the seventh day the
priest is to examine the sore, and if it has
not spread and there is no yellow hair in
it and it does not appear to be more than
skin deep, 33then the man or woman
must shave themselves, except for the
affected area, and the priest is to keep
them isolated another seven days. 34On
the seventh day the priest is to examine
the sore, and if it has not spread in the
skin and appears to be no more than skin
deep, the priest shall pronounce them
clean. They must wash their clothes,
and they will be clean. 35But if the sore
does spread in the skin after they are
pronounced clean, 36the priest is to examine them, and if he finds that the sore
has spread in the skin, he does not need
to look for yellow hair; they are unclean.
37If, however, the sore is unchanged so
far as the priest can see, and if black hair
has grown in it, the affected person is
healed. They are clean, and the priest
shall pronounce them clean.

38"When a man or woman has white
spots on the skin, 39the priest is to examine them, and if the spots are dull white,
it is a harmless rash that has broken out
on the skin; they are clean.

40"A man who has lost his hair and is
bald is clean. 41If he has lost his hair from
the front of his scalp and has a bald forehead, he is clean. 42But if he has a reddish-white sore on his bald head or forehead, it is a defiling disease breaking out
on his head or forehead. 43The priest is
to examine him, and if the swollen sore
on his head or forehead is reddish-white
like a defiling skin disease, 44the man is
diseased and is unclean. The priest shall
pronounce him unclean because of the
sore on his head.

45"Anyone with such a defiling disease
must wear torn clothes, let their hair be
unkempt,[a] cover the lower part of their
face and cry out, 'Unclean! Unclean!'
46As long as they have the disease they
remain unclean. They must live alone;
they must live outside the camp.

47"As for any fabric that is spoiled with
a defiling mold—any woolen or linen
clothing, 48any woven or knitted material of linen or wool, any leather or anything made of leather— 49if the affected
area in the fabric, the leather, the woven
or knitted material, or any leather article, is greenish or reddish, it is a defiling
mold and must be shown to the priest.
50The priest is to examine the affected area and isolate the article for seven
days. 51On the seventh day he is to examine it, and if the mold has spread in the
fabric, the woven or knitted material, or
the leather, whatever its use, it is a persistent defiling mold; the article is unclean.
52He must burn the fabric, the woven or
knitted material of wool or linen, or any
leather article that has been spoiled; because the defiling mold is persistent, the
article must be burned.

53"But if, when the priest examines it,
the mold has not spread in the fabric, the
woven or knitted material, or the leather
article, 54he shall order that the spoiled
article be washed. Then he is to isolate it
for another seven days. 55After the article has been washed, the priest is to examine it again, and if the mold has not
changed its appearance, even though
it has not spread, it is unclean. Burn it,
no matter which side of the fabric has
been spoiled. 56If, when the priest examines it, the mold has faded after the
article has been washed, he is to tear the
spoiled part out of the fabric, the leather,
or the woven or knitted material. 57But
if it reappears in the fabric, in the woven
or knitted material, or in the leather article, it is a spreading mold; whatever has
the mold must be burned. 58Any fabric,

[a] 45 Or *clothes, uncover their head*

woven or knitted material, or any leather
article that has been washed and is rid of
the mold, must be washed again. Then it
will be clean."
59These are the regulations concerning defiling molds in woolen or linen
clothing, woven or knitted material, or
any leather article, for pronouncing them
clean or unclean.

14 The LORD said to Moses, 2"These
are the regulations for any diseased
person at the time of their ceremonial
cleansing, when they are brought to the
priest: 3The priest is to go outside the
camp and examine them. If they have
been healed of their defiling skin disease,[a] 4the priest shall order that two live
clean birds and some cedar wood, scarlet yarn and hyssop be brought for the
person to be cleansed. 5Then the priest
shall order that one of the birds be killed
over fresh water in a clay pot. 6He is then
to take the live bird and dip it, together
with the cedar wood, the scarlet yarn
and the hyssop, into the blood of the bird
that was killed over the fresh water. 7Sev-
en times he shall sprinkle the one to be
cleansed of the defiling disease, and then
pronounce them clean. After that, he is to
release the live bird in the open fields.
8"The person to be cleansed must
wash their clothes, shave off all their hair
and bathe with water; then they will be
ceremonially clean. After this they may
come into the camp, but they must stay
outside their tent for seven days. 9On the
seventh day they must shave off all their
hair; they must shave their head, their
beard, their eyebrows and the rest of
their hair. They must wash their clothes
and bathe themselves with water, and
they will be clean.
10"On the eighth day they must bring
two male lambs and one ewe lamb a
year old, each without defect, along with
three-tenths of an ephah[b] of the finest
flour mixed with olive oil for a grain offering, and one log[c] of oil. 11The priest
who pronounces them clean shall present both the one to be cleansed and
their offerings before the LORD at the entrance to the tent of meeting.
12"Then the priest is to take one of the
male lambs and offer it as a guilt offering,
along with the log of oil; he shall wave
them before the LORD as a wave offering.
13He is to slaughter the lamb in the sanctuary area where the sin offering[d] and
the burnt offering are slaughtered. Like
the sin offering, the guilt offering belongs to the priest; it is most holy. 14The
priest is to take some of the blood of the
guilt offering and put it on the lobe of
the right ear of the one to be cleansed,
on the thumb of their right hand and on
the big toe of their right foot. 15The priest
shall then take some of the log of oil, pour
it in the palm of his own left hand, 16dip
his right forefinger into the oil in his
palm, and with his finger sprinkle some
of it before the LORD seven times. 17The
priest is to put some of the oil remaining
in his palm on the lobe of the right ear
of the one to be cleansed, on the thumb
of their right hand and on the big toe of
their right foot, on top of the blood of the
guilt offering. 18The rest of the oil in his
palm the priest shall put on the head of
the one to be cleansed and make atonement for them before the LORD.
19"Then the priest is to sacrifice the
sin offering and make atonement for the
one to be cleansed from their uncleanness. After that, the priest shall slaughter
the burnt offering 20and offer it on the altar, together with the grain offering, and
make atonement for them, and they will
be clean.
21"If, however, they are poor and cannot afford these, they must take one male
lamb as a guilt offering to be waved to
make atonement for them, together with
a tenth of an ephah[e] of the finest flour
mixed with olive oil for a grain offering,
a log of oil, 22and two doves or two young
pigeons, such as they can afford, one for
a sin offering and the other for a burnt
offering.
23"On the eighth day they must bring
them for their cleansing to the priest
at the entrance to the tent of meeting,
before the LORD. 24The priest is to take
the lamb for the guilt offering, together
with the log of oil, and wave them before

[a] *3* The Hebrew word for *defiling skin disease*, traditionally translated "leprosy," was used for various diseases affecting the skin; also in verses 7, 32, 54 and 57. [b] *10* That is, probably about 11 pounds or about 5 kilograms [c] *10* That is, about 1/3 quart or about 0.3 liter; also in verses 12, 15, 21 and 24 [d] *13* Or *purification offering*; also in verses 19, 22 and 31 [e] *21* That is, probably about 3 1/2 pounds or about 1.6 kilograms

the LORD as a wave offering. 25He shall
slaughter the lamb for the guilt offering
and take some of its blood and put it on
the lobe of the right ear of the one to be
cleansed, on the thumb of their right
hand and on the big toe of their right foot.
26The priest is to pour some of the oil into
the palm of his own left hand, 27and with
his right forefinger sprinkle some of the
oil from his palm seven times before the
LORD. 28Some of the oil in his palm he
is to put on the same places he put the
blood of the guilt offering—on the lobe
of the right ear of the one to be cleansed,
on the thumb of their right hand and on
the big toe of their right foot. 29The rest
of the oil in his palm the priest shall put
on the head of the one to be cleansed,
to make atonement for them before the
LORD. 30Then he shall sacrifice the doves
or the young pigeons, such as the person
can afford, 31one as a sin offering and the
other as a burnt offering, together with
the grain offering. In this way the priest
will make atonement before the LORD on
behalf of the one to be cleansed."

32These are the regulations for anyone
who has a defiling skin disease and who
cannot afford the regular offerings for
their cleansing.

33The LORD said to Moses and Aaron,
34"When you enter the land of Canaan,
which I am giving you as your possession,
and I put a spreading mold in a house in
that land, 35the owner of the house must
go and tell the priest, 'I have seen something that looks like a defiling mold in
my house.' 36The priest is to order the
house to be emptied before he goes in
to examine the mold, so that nothing in
the house will be pronounced unclean.
After this the priest is to go in and inspect the house. 37He is to examine the
mold on the walls, and if it has greenish
or reddish depressions that appear to
be deeper than the surface of the wall,
38the priest shall go out the doorway of
the house and close it up for seven days.
39On the seventh day the priest shall return to inspect the house. If the mold has
spread on the walls, 40he is to order that
the contaminated stones be torn out and
thrown into an unclean place outside
the town. 41He must have all the inside
walls of the house scraped and the material that is scraped off dumped into an
unclean place outside the town. 42Then
they are to take other stones to replace
these and take new clay and plaster the
house.

43"If the defiling mold reappears in
the house after the stones have been
torn out and the house scraped and plastered, 44the priest is to go and examine it
and, if the mold has spread in the house,
it is a persistent defiling mold; the house
is unclean. 45It must be torn down—its
stones, timbers and all the plaster—and
taken out of the town to an unclean
place.

46"Anyone who goes into the house
while it is closed up will be unclean till
evening. 47Anyone who sleeps or eats in
the house must wash their clothes.

48"But if the priest comes to examine
it and the mold has not spread after the
house has been plastered, he shall pronounce the house clean, because the defiling mold is gone. 49To purify the house
he is to take two birds and some cedar
wood, scarlet yarn and hyssop. 50He
shall kill one of the birds over fresh water in a clay pot. 51Then he is to take the
cedar wood, the hyssop, the scarlet yarn
and the live bird, dip them into the blood
of the dead bird and the fresh water, and
sprinkle the house seven times. 52He
shall purify the house with the bird's
blood, the fresh water, the live bird, the
cedar wood, the hyssop and the scarlet
yarn. 53Then he is to release the live bird
in the open fields outside the town. In
this way he will make atonement for the
house, and it will be clean."

54These are the regulations for any defiling skin disease, for a sore, 55for defiling molds in fabric or in a house, 56and
for a swelling, a rash or a shiny spot, 57to
determine when something is clean or
unclean.

These are the regulations for defiling
skin diseases and defiling molds.

15 The LORD said to Moses and Aaron,
2"Speak to the Israelites and say to
them: 'When any man has an unusual bodily discharge, such a discharge is
unclean. 3Whether it continues flowing
from his body or is blocked, it will make
him unclean. This is how his discharge
will bring about uncleanness:

4"'Any bed the man with a discharge
lies on will be unclean, and anything
he sits on will be unclean. 5Anyone who
touches his bed must wash their clothes

and bathe with water, and they will be
unclean till evening. 6Whoever sits on
anything that the man with a discharge
sat on must wash their clothes and bathe
with water, and they will be unclean till
evening.
7"'Whoever touches the man who has
a discharge must wash their clothes and
bathe with water, and they will be unclean till evening.
8"'If the man with the discharge spits
on anyone who is clean, they must wash
their clothes and bathe with water, and
they will be unclean till evening.
9"'Everything the man sits on when
riding will be unclean, 10and whoever
touches any of the things that were under
him will be unclean till evening; whoever picks up those things must wash their
clothes and bathe with water, and they
will be unclean till evening.
11"'Anyone the man with a discharge
touches without rinsing his hands with
water must wash their clothes and bathe
with water, and they will be unclean till
evening.
12"'A clay pot that the man touches
must be broken, and any wooden article
is to be rinsed with water.
13"'When a man is cleansed from his
discharge, he is to count off seven days
for his ceremonial cleansing; he must
wash his clothes and bathe himself with
fresh water, and he will be clean. 14On
the eighth day he must take two doves or
two young pigeons and come before the
LORD to the entrance to the tent of meeting and give them to the priest. 15The
priest is to sacrifice them, the one for a
sin offering[a] and the other for a burnt
offering. In this way he will make atonement before the LORD for the man because of his discharge.
16"'When a man has an emission of semen, he must bathe his whole body with
water, and he will be unclean till evening.
17Any clothing or leather that has semen
on it must be washed with water, and it
will be unclean till evening. 18When a
man has sexual relations with a woman
and there is an emission of semen, both
of them must bathe with water, and they
will be unclean till evening.
19"'When a woman has her regular
flow of blood, the impurity of her monthly period will last seven days, and anyone
who touches her will be unclean till evening.
20"'Anything she lies on during her period will be unclean, and anything she
sits on will be unclean. 21Anyone who
touches her bed will be unclean; they
must wash their clothes and bathe with
water, and they will be unclean till evening. 22Anyone who touches anything
she sits on will be unclean; they must
wash their clothes and bathe with water, and they will be unclean till evening.
23Whether it is the bed or anything she
was sitting on, when anyone touches it,
they will be unclean till evening.
24"'If a man has sexual relations with
her and her monthly flow touches him,
he will be unclean for seven days; any
bed he lies on will be unclean.
25"'When a woman has a discharge of
blood for many days at a time other than
her monthly period or has a discharge
that continues beyond her period, she
will be unclean as long as she has the
discharge, just as in the days of her period. 26Any bed she lies on while her discharge continues will be unclean, as is
her bed during her monthly period, and
anything she sits on will be unclean, as
during her period. 27Anyone who touches them will be unclean; they must wash
their clothes and bathe with water, and
they will be unclean till evening.
28"'When she is cleansed from her discharge, she must count off seven days,
and after that she will be ceremonially
clean. 29On the eighth day she must take
two doves or two young pigeons and
bring them to the priest at the entrance
to the tent of meeting. 30The priest is to
sacrifice one for a sin offering and the
other for a burnt offering. In this way
he will make atonement for her before
the LORD for the uncleanness of her discharge.
31"'You must keep the Israelites separate from things that make them unclean,
so they will not die in their uncleanness
for defiling my dwelling place,[b] which is
among them.'"
32These are the regulations for a man
with a discharge, for anyone made unclean by an emission of semen, 33for a
woman in her monthly period, for a man

[a] *15* Or *purification offering;* also in verse 30 [b] *31* Or *my tabernacle*

or a woman with a discharge, and for a
man who has sexual relations with a
woman who is ceremonially unclean.

16 The LORD spoke to Moses after the
death of the two sons of Aaron who
died when they approached the LORD.
2The LORD said to Moses: "Tell your
brother Aaron that he is not to come
whenever he chooses into the Most Holy
Place behind the curtain in front of the
atonement cover on the ark, or else he
will die. For I will appear in the cloud
over the atonement cover.

3"This is how Aaron is to enter the
Most Holy Place: He must first bring a
young bull for a sin offering[a] and a ram
for a burnt offering. 4He is to put on the
sacred linen tunic, with linen undergarments next to his body; he is to tie the lin-
en sash around him and put on the linen
turban. These are sacred garments; so he
must bathe himself with water before he
puts them on. 5From the Israelite community he is to take two male goats for
a sin offering and a ram for a burnt offering.

6"Aaron is to offer the bull for his own
sin offering to make atonement for himself and his household. 7Then he is to
take the two goats and present them before the LORD at the entrance to the tent
of meeting. 8He is to cast lots for the two
goats — one lot for the LORD and the other for the scapegoat.[b] 9Aaron shall bring
the goat whose lot falls to the LORD and
sacrifice it for a sin offering. 10But the
goat chosen by lot as the scapegoat shall
be presented alive before the LORD to be
used for making atonement by sending it
into the wilderness as a scapegoat.

11"Aaron shall bring the bull for his
own sin offering to make atonement for
himself and his household, and he is to
slaughter the bull for his own sin offering. 12He is to take a censer full of burning coals from the altar before the LORD
and two handfuls of finely ground fragrant incense and take them behind the
curtain. 13He is to put the incense on the
fire before the LORD, and the smoke of
the incense will conceal the atonement
cover above the tablets of the covenant
law, so that he will not die. 14He is to take
some of the bull's blood and with his finger sprinkle it on the front of the atonement cover; then he shall sprinkle some
of it with his finger seven times before
the atonement cover.

15"He shall then slaughter the goat for
the sin offering for the people and take
its blood behind the curtain and do with
it as he did with the bull's blood: He shall
sprinkle it on the atonement cover and
in front of it. 16In this way he will make
atonement for the Most Holy Place because of the uncleanness and rebellion
of the Israelites, whatever their sins have
been. He is to do the same for the tent of
meeting, which is among them in the
midst of their uncleanness. 17No one
is to be in the tent of meeting from the
time Aaron goes in to make atonement in
the Most Holy Place until he comes out,
having made atonement for himself, his
household and the whole community of
Israel.

18"Then he shall come out to the altar
that is before the LORD and make atonement for it. He shall take some of the
bull's blood and some of the goat's blood
and put it on all the horns of the altar.
19He shall sprinkle some of the blood on
it with his finger seven times to cleanse
it and to consecrate it from the uncleanness of the Israelites.

20"When Aaron has finished making
atonement for the Most Holy Place, the
tent of meeting and the altar, he shall
bring forward the live goat. 21He is to lay
both hands on the head of the live goat
and confess over it all the wickedness
and rebellion of the Israelites — all their
sins — and put them on the goat's head.
He shall send the goat away into the wilderness in the care of someone appointed
for the task. 22The goat will carry on itself
all their sins to a remote place; and the
man shall release it in the wilderness.

23"Then Aaron is to go into the tent of
meeting and take off the linen garments
he put on before he entered the Most
Holy Place, and he is to leave them there.
24He shall bathe himself with water in
the sanctuary area and put on his regular
garments. Then he shall come out and
sacrifice the burnt offering for himself
and the burnt offering for the people, to
make atonement for himself and for the
people. 25He shall also burn the fat of the
sin offering on the altar.

[a] 3 Or *purification offering*; here and throughout this chapter word is uncertain; also in verses 10 and 26.

[b] 8 The meaning of the Hebrew for this

26 “The man who releases the goat as
a scapegoat must wash his clothes and
bathe himself with water; afterward he
may come into the camp. 27 The bull and
the goat for the sin offerings, whose blood
was brought into the Most Holy Place to
make atonement, must be taken outside
the camp; their hides, flesh and intestines are to be burned up. 28 The man
who burns them must wash his clothes
and bathe himself with water; afterward
he may come into the camp.
29 “This is to be a lasting ordinance
for you: On the tenth day of the seventh
month you must deny yourselves[a] and
not do any work—whether native-born
or a foreigner residing among you—
30 because on this day atonement will be
made for you, to cleanse you. Then, before the LORD, you will be clean from all
your sins. 31 It is a day of sabbath rest, and
you must deny yourselves; it is a lasting
ordinance. 32 The priest who is anointed and ordained to succeed his father as
high priest is to make atonement. He is to
put on the sacred linen garments 33 and
make atonement for the Most Holy Place,
for the tent of meeting and the altar, and
for the priests and all the members of the
community.
34 “This is to be a lasting ordinance for
you: Atonement is to be made once a year
for all the sins of the Israelites.”
And it was done, as the LORD commanded Moses.

17 The LORD said to Moses, 2 “Speak
to Aaron and his sons and to all the
Israelites and say to them: ‘This is what
the LORD has commanded: 3 Any Israelite who sacrifices an ox,[b] a lamb or a
goat in the camp or outside of it 4 instead
of bringing it to the entrance to the tent
of meeting to present it as an offering
to the LORD in front of the tabernacle
of the LORD—that person shall be considered guilty of bloodshed; they have
shed blood and must be cut off from
their people. 5 This is so the Israelites
will bring to the LORD the sacrifices they
are now making in the open fields. They
must bring them to the priest, that is, to
the LORD, at the entrance to the tent of
meeting and sacrifice them as fellowship offerings. 6 The priest is to splash
the blood against the altar of the LORD at
the entrance to the tent of meeting and
burn the fat as an aroma pleasing to the
LORD. 7 They must no longer offer any of
their sacrifices to the goat idols[c] to whom
they prostitute themselves. This is to be
a lasting ordinance for them and for the
generations to come.’
8 “Say to them: ‘Any Israelite or any foreigner residing among them who offers
a burnt offering or sacrifice 9 and does
not bring it to the entrance to the tent of
meeting to sacrifice it to the LORD must
be cut off from the people of Israel.
10 “ ‘I will set my face against any Israelite or any foreigner residing among them
who eats blood, and I will cut them off
from the people. 11 For the life of a creature is in the blood, and I have given it
to you to make atonement for yourselves
on the altar; it is the blood that makes
atonement for one’s life.[d] 12 Therefore I
say to the Israelites, “None of you may
eat blood, nor may any foreigner residing among you eat blood.”
13 “ ‘Any Israelite or any foreigner residing among you who hunts any animal or
bird that may be eaten must drain out the
blood and cover it with earth, 14 because
the life of every creature is its blood. That
is why I have said to the Israelites, “You
must not eat the blood of any creature,
because the life of every creature is its
blood; anyone who eats it must be cut
off.”
15 “ ‘Anyone, whether native-born or
foreigner, who eats anything found dead
or torn by wild animals must wash their
clothes and bathe with water, and they
will be ceremonially unclean till evening; then they will be clean. 16 But if
they do not wash their clothes and bathe
themselves, they will be held responsible.’ ”

18 The LORD said to Moses, 2 “Speak
to the Israelites and say to them: ‘I
am the LORD your God. 3 You must not
do as they do in Egypt, where you used
to live, and you must not do as they do in
the land of Canaan, where I am bringing
you. Do not follow their practices. 4 You
must obey my laws and be careful to follow my decrees. I am the LORD your God.
5 Keep my decrees and laws, for the person who obeys them will live by them. I
am the LORD.

[a] 29 Or *must fast*; also in verse 31 [b] 3 The Hebrew word can refer to either male or female. [c] 7 Or *the demons* [d] 11 Or *atonement by the life in the blood*

6“ ‘No one is to approach any close relative to have sexual relations. I am the LORD.

7“ ‘Do not dishonor your father by having sexual relations with your mother. She is your mother; do not have relations with her.

8“ ‘Do not have sexual relations with your father’s wife; that would dishonor your father.

9“ ‘Do not have sexual relations with your sister, either your father’s daughter or your mother’s daughter, whether she was born in the same home or elsewhere.

10“ ‘Do not have sexual relations with your son’s daughter or your daughter’s daughter; that would dishonor you.

11“ ‘Do not have sexual relations with the daughter of your father’s wife, born to your father; she is your sister.

12“ ‘Do not have sexual relations with your father’s sister; she is your father’s close relative.

13“ ‘Do not have sexual relations with your mother’s sister, because she is your mother’s close relative.

14“ ‘Do not dishonor your father’s brother by approaching his wife to have sexual relations; she is your aunt.

15“ ‘Do not have sexual relations with your daughter-in-law. She is your son’s wife; do not have relations with her.

16“ ‘Do not have sexual relations with your brother’s wife; that would dishonor your brother.

17“ ‘Do not have sexual relations with both a woman and her daughter. Do not have sexual relations with either her son’s daughter or her daughter’s daughter; they are her close relatives. That is wickedness.

18“ ‘Do not take your wife’s sister as a rival wife and have sexual relations with her while your wife is living.

19“ ‘Do not approach a woman to have sexual relations during the uncleanness of her monthly period.

20“ ‘Do not have sexual relations with your neighbor’s wife and defile yourself with her.

21“ ‘Do not give any of your children to be sacrificed to Molek, for you must not profane the name of your God. I am the LORD.

22“ ‘Do not have sexual relations with a man as one does with a woman; that is detestable.

23“ ‘Do not have sexual relations with an animal and defile yourself with it. A woman must not present herself to an animal to have sexual relations with it; that is a perversion.

24“ ‘Do not defile yourselves in any of
these ways, because this is how the nations that I am going to drive out before
you became defiled. 25Even the land was
defiled; so I punished it for its sin, and
the land vomited out its inhabitants.
26But you must keep my decrees and my
laws. The native-born and the foreigners
residing among you must not do any of
these detestable things, 27for all these
things were done by the people who
lived in the land before you, and the land
became defiled. 28And if you defile the
land, it will vomit you out as it vomited
out the nations that were before you.

29“ ‘Everyone who does any of these
detestable things—such persons must
be cut off from their people. 30Keep my
requirements and do not follow any of
the detestable customs that were practiced before you came and do not defile
yourselves with them. I am the LORD
your God.’ ”

19 The LORD said to Moses, 2“Speak
to the entire assembly of Israel and
say to them: ‘Be holy because I, the LORD
your God, am holy.

3“ ‘Each of you must respect your mother and father, and you must observe my Sabbaths. I am the LORD your God.

4“ ‘Do not turn to idols or make metal gods for yourselves. I am the LORD your God.

5“ ‘When you sacrifice a fellowship offering to the LORD, sacrifice it in such a
way that it will be accepted on your behalf. 6It shall be eaten on the day you sacrifice it or on the next day; anything left
over until the third day must be burned
up. 7If any of it is eaten on the third day,
it is impure and will not be accepted.
8Whoever eats it will be held responsible because they have desecrated what
is holy to the LORD; they must be cut off
from their people.

9“ ‘When you reap the harvest of your
land, do not reap to the very edges of
your field or gather the gleanings of your
harvest. 10Do not go over your vineyard
a second time or pick up the grapes that
have fallen. Leave them for the poor and
the foreigner. I am the LORD your God.

11“ ‘Do not steal.
“ ‘Do not lie.
“ ‘Do not deceive one another.
12“ ‘Do not swear falsely by my name
and so profane the name of your God. I
am the LORD.
13“ ‘Do not defraud or rob your neighbor.
“ ‘Do not hold back the wages of a hired
worker overnight.
14“ ‘Do not curse the deaf or put a stumbling block in front of the blind, but fear
your God. I am the LORD.
15“ ‘Do not pervert justice; do not show
partiality to the poor or favoritism to the
great, but judge your neighbor fairly.
16“ ‘Do not go about spreading slander
among your people.
“ ‘Do not do anything that endangers
your neighbor’s life. I am the LORD.
17“ ‘Do not hate a fellow Israelite in
your heart. Rebuke your neighbor frank-
ly so you will not share in their guilt.
18“ ‘Do not seek revenge or bear a
grudge against anyone among your people, but love your neighbor as yourself. I
am the LORD.
19“ ‘Keep my decrees.
“ ‘Do not mate different kinds of animals.
“ ‘Do not plant your field with two
kinds of seed.
“ ‘Do not wear clothing woven of two
kinds of material.
20“ ‘If a man sleeps with a female slave
who is promised to another man but
who has not been ransomed or given
her freedom, there must be due punishment.[a] Yet they are not to be put to
death, because she had not been freed.
21The man, however, must bring a ram
to the entrance to the tent of meeting for
a guilt offering to the LORD. 22With the
ram of the guilt offering the priest is to
make atonement for him before the LORD
for the sin he has committed, and his sin
will be forgiven.
23“ ‘When you enter the land and plant
any kind of fruit tree, regard its fruit as
forbidden.[b] For three years you are to
consider it forbidden[b]; it must not be
eaten. 24In the fourth year all its fruit
will be holy, an offering of praise to the
LORD. 25But in the fifth year you may eat
its fruit. In this way your harvest will be
increased. I am the LORD your God.
26“ ‘Do not eat any meat with the blood
still in it.
“ ‘Do not practice divination or seek
omens.
27“ ‘Do not cut the hair at the sides of
your head or clip off the edges of your
beard.
28“ ‘Do not cut your bodies for the dead
or put tattoo marks on yourselves. I am
the LORD.
29“ ‘Do not degrade your daughter by
making her a prostitute, or the land will
turn to prostitution and be filled with
wickedness.
30“ ‘Observe my Sabbaths and have
reverence for my sanctuary. I am the
LORD.
31“ ‘Do not turn to mediums or seek out
spiritists, for you will be defiled by them.
I am the LORD your God.
32“ ‘Stand up in the presence of the
aged, show respect for the elderly and
revere your God. I am the LORD.
33“ ‘When a foreigner resides among
you in your land, do not mistreat them.
34The foreigner residing among you must
be treated as your native-born. Love
them as yourself, for you were foreigners
in Egypt. I am the LORD your God.
35“ ‘Do not use dishonest standards
when measuring length, weight or
quantity. 36Use honest scales and honest
weights, an honest ephah[c] and an honest hin.[d] I am the LORD your God, who
brought you out of Egypt.
37“ ‘Keep all my decrees and all my
laws and follow them. I am the LORD.’ ”

20 The LORD said to Moses, 2“Say to
the Israelites: ‘Any Israelite or any
foreigner residing in Israel who sacrifices any of his children to Molek is to be
put to death. The members of the community are to stone him. 3I myself will
set my face against him and will cut him
off from his people; for by sacrificing
his children to Molek, he has defiled my
sanctuary and profaned my holy name.
4If the members of the community close
their eyes when that man sacrifices one
of his children to Molek and if they fail
to put him to death, 5I myself will set my
face against him and his family and will

[a] 20 Or *be an inquiry* [b] 23 Hebrew *uncircumcised* [c] 36 An ephah was a dry measure having the capacity of about 3/5 of a bushel or about 22 liters. [d] 36 A hin was a liquid measure having the capacity of about 1 gallon or about 3.8 liters.

cut them off from their people together with all who follow him in prostituting themselves to Molek.

6 "'I will set my face against anyone who turns to mediums and spiritists to prostitute themselves by following them, and I will cut them off from their people.

7 "'Consecrate yourselves and be holy, because I am the LORD your God. 8 Keep my decrees and follow them. I am the LORD, who makes you holy.

9 "'Anyone who curses their father or mother is to be put to death. Because they have cursed their father or mother, their blood will be on their own head.

10 "'If a man commits adultery with another man's wife—with the wife of his neighbor—both the adulterer and the adulteress are to be put to death.

11 "'If a man has sexual relations with his father's wife, he has dishonored his father. Both the man and the woman are to be put to death; their blood will be on their own heads.

12 "'If a man has sexual relations with his daughter-in-law, both of them are to be put to death. What they have done is a perversion; their blood will be on their own heads.

13 "'If a man has sexual relations with a man as one does with a woman, both of them have done what is detestable. They are to be put to death; their blood will be on their own heads.

14 "'If a man marries both a woman and her mother, it is wicked. Both he and they must be burned in the fire, so that no wickedness will be among you.

15 "'If a man has sexual relations with an animal, he is to be put to death, and you must kill the animal.

16 "'If a woman approaches an animal to have sexual relations with it, kill both the woman and the animal. They are to be put to death; their blood will be on their own heads.

17 "'If a man marries his sister, the daughter of either his father or his mother, and they have sexual relations, it is a disgrace. They are to be publicly removed from their people. He has dishonored his sister and will be held responsible.

18 "'If a man has sexual relations with a woman during her monthly period, he has exposed the source of her flow, and she has also uncovered it. Both of them are to be cut off from their people.

19 "'Do not have sexual relations with the sister of either your mother or your father, for that would dishonor a close relative; both of you would be held responsible.

20 "'If a man has sexual relations with his aunt, he has dishonored his uncle. They will be held responsible; they will die childless.

21 "'If a man marries his brother's wife, it is an act of impurity; he has dishonored his brother. They will be childless.

22 "'Keep all my decrees and laws and follow them, so that the land where I am bringing you to live may not vomit
you out. 23 You must not live according
to the customs of the nations I am going to drive out before you. Because they did
all these things, I abhorred them. 24 But I
said to you, "You will possess their land; I will give it to you as an inheritance, a land flowing with milk and honey." I am the LORD your God, who has set you apart from the nations.

25 "'You must therefore make a distinction between clean and unclean animals and between unclean and clean birds. Do not defile yourselves by any animal or bird or anything that moves along the ground—those that I have set apart as
unclean for you. 26 You are to be holy to
me because I, the LORD, am holy, and I have set you apart from the nations to be my own.

27 "'A man or woman who is a medium or spiritist among you must be put to death. You are to stone them; their blood will be on their own heads.'"

21 The LORD said to Moses, "Speak to the priests, the sons of Aaron, and say to them: 'A priest must not make himself ceremonially unclean for any
of his people who die, 2 except for a close
relative, such as his mother or father,
his son or daughter, his brother, 3 or an
unmarried sister who is dependent on him since she has no husband—for her
he may make himself unclean. 4 He must
not make himself unclean for people related to him by marriage,[a] and so defile himself.

5 "'Priests must not shave their heads or shave off the edges of their beards

[a] 4 Or *unclean as a leader among his people*

or cut their bodies. 6They must be holy
to their God and must not profane the
name of their God. Because they present
the food offerings to the LORD, the food
of their God, they are to be holy.
7" 'They must not marry women defiled by prostitution or divorced from
their husbands, because priests are holy
to their God. 8Regard them as holy, because they offer up the food of your God.
Consider them holy, because I the LORD
am holy — I who make you holy.
9" 'If a priest's daughter defiles herself
by becoming a prostitute, she disgraces her father; she must be burned in the
fire.
10" 'The high priest, the one among his
brothers who has had the anointing oil
poured on his head and who has been
ordained to wear the priestly garments,
must not let his hair become unkempt[a]
or tear his clothes. 11He must not enter a
place where there is a dead body. He must
not make himself unclean, even for his
father or mother, 12nor leave the sanctuary of his God or desecrate it, because he
has been dedicated by the anointing oil
of his God. I am the LORD.
13" 'The woman he marries must be a
virgin. 14He must not marry a widow, a
divorced woman, or a woman defiled by
prostitution, but only a virgin from his
own people, 15so that he will not defile
his offspring among his people. I am the
LORD, who makes him holy.' "
16The LORD said to Moses, 17"Say to
Aaron: 'For the generations to come
none of your descendants who has a defect may come near to offer the food of
his God. 18No man who has any defect
may come near: no man who is blind
or lame, disfigured or deformed; 19no
man with a crippled foot or hand, 20or
who is a hunchback or a dwarf, or who
has any eye defect, or who has festering
or running sores or damaged testicles.
21No descendant of Aaron the priest
who has any defect is to come near to
present the food offerings to the LORD.
He has a defect; he must not come near
to offer the food of his God. 22He may eat
the most holy food of his God, as well as
the holy food; 23yet because of his defect, he must not go near the curtain or
approach the altar, and so desecrate my
sanctuary. I am the LORD, who makes
them holy.' "
24So Moses told this to Aaron and his
sons and to all the Israelites.

22 The LORD said to Moses, 2"Tell Aaron and his sons to treat with respect
the sacred offerings the Israelites consecrate to me, so they will not profane my
holy name. I am the LORD.
3"Say to them: 'For the generations to
come, if any of your descendants is ceremonially unclean and yet comes near the
sacred offerings that the Israelites consecrate to the LORD, that person must be
cut off from my presence. I am the LORD.
4" 'If a descendant of Aaron has a defiling skin disease[b] or a bodily discharge,
he may not eat the sacred offerings until
he is cleansed. He will also be unclean if
he touches something defiled by a corpse
or by anyone who has an emission of semen, 5or if he touches any crawling thing
that makes him unclean, or any person
who makes him unclean, whatever the
uncleanness may be. 6The one who
touches any such thing will be unclean
till evening. He must not eat any of the
sacred offerings unless he has bathed
himself with water. 7When the sun goes
down, he will be clean, and after that he
may eat the sacred offerings, for they
are his food. 8He must not eat anything
found dead or torn by wild animals, and
so become unclean through it. I am the
LORD.
9" 'The priests are to perform my service in such a way that they do not become guilty and die for treating it with
contempt. I am the LORD, who makes
them holy.
10" 'No one outside a priest's family may eat the sacred offering, nor may
the guest of a priest or his hired worker
eat it. 11But if a priest buys a slave with
money, or if slaves are born in his household, they may eat his food. 12If a priest's
daughter marries anyone other than a
priest, she may not eat any of the sacred
contributions. 13But if a priest's daughter becomes a widow or is divorced, yet
has no children, and she returns to live
in her father's household as in her youth,
she may eat her father's food. No unauthorized person, however, may eat it.
14" 'Anyone who eats a sacred offering

[a] 10 Or *not uncover his head* [b] 4 The Hebrew word for *defiling skin disease*, traditionally translated "leprosy," was used for various diseases affecting the skin.

by mistake must make restitution to the
priest for the offering and add a fifth of
the value to it. 15 The priests must not desecrate the sacred offerings the Israelites
present to the LORD 16 by allowing them
to eat the sacred offerings and so bring
upon them guilt requiring payment. I am
the LORD, who makes them holy.'"
17 The LORD said to Moses, 18 "Speak
to Aaron and his sons and to all the
Israelites and say to them: 'If any of
you—whether an Israelite or a foreigner residing in Israel—presents a gift
for a burnt offering to the LORD, either
to fulfill a vow or as a freewill offering,
19 you must present a male without defect
from the cattle, sheep or goats in order
that it may be accepted on your behalf.
20 Do not bring anything with a defect,
because it will not be accepted on your
behalf. 21 When anyone brings from the
herd or flock a fellowship offering to the
LORD to fulfill a special vow or as a freewill offering, it must be without defect or
blemish to be acceptable. 22 Do not offer
to the LORD the blind, the injured or the
maimed, or anything with warts or festering or running sores. Do not place any
of these on the altar as a food offering
presented to the LORD. 23 You may, however, present as a freewill offering an ox[a]
or a sheep that is deformed or stunted,
but it will not be accepted in fulfillment
of a vow. 24 You must not offer to the LORD
an animal whose testicles are bruised,
crushed, torn or cut. You must not do
this in your own land, 25 and you must
not accept such animals from the hand
of a foreigner and offer them as the food
of your God. They will not be accepted on
your behalf, because they are deformed
and have defects.'"
26 The LORD said to Moses, 27 "When a
calf, a lamb or a goat is born, it is to remain with its mother for seven days.
From the eighth day on, it will be acceptable as a food offering presented to
the LORD. 28 Do not slaughter a cow or a
sheep and its young on the same day.
29 "When you sacrifice a thank offering
to the LORD, sacrifice it in such a way that
it will be accepted on your behalf. 30 It
must be eaten that same day; leave none
of it till morning. I am the LORD.
31 "Keep my commands and follow
them. I am the LORD. 32 Do not profane
my holy name, for I must be acknowledged as holy by the Israelites. I am the
LORD, who made you holy 33 and who
brought you out of Egypt to be your God.
I am the LORD."

23 The LORD said to Moses, 2 "Speak
to the Israelites and say to them:
'These are my appointed festivals, the
appointed festivals of the LORD, which
you are to proclaim as sacred assemblies.
3 "'There are six days when you may
work, but the seventh day is a day of sabbath rest, a day of sacred assembly. You
are not to do any work; wherever you live,
it is a sabbath to the LORD.
4 "'These are the LORD's appointed
festivals, the sacred assemblies you are
to proclaim at their appointed times:
5 The LORD's Passover begins at twilight
on the fourteenth day of the first month.
6 On the fifteenth day of that month the
LORD's Festival of Unleavened Bread begins; for seven days you must eat bread
made without yeast. 7 On the first day
hold a sacred assembly and do no regular work. 8 For seven days present a food
offering to the LORD. And on the seventh
day hold a sacred assembly and do no
regular work.'"
9 The LORD said to Moses, 10 "Speak to
the Israelites and say to them: 'When
you enter the land I am going to give
you and you reap its harvest, bring to
the priest a sheaf of the first grain you
harvest. 11 He is to wave the sheaf before
the LORD so it will be accepted on your
behalf; the priest is to wave it on the day
after the Sabbath. 12 On the day you wave
the sheaf, you must sacrifice as a burnt
offering to the LORD a lamb a year old
without defect, 13 together with its grain
offering of two-tenths of an ephah[b] of the
finest flour mixed with olive oil—a food
offering presented to the LORD, a pleasing aroma—and its drink offering of a
quarter of a hin[c] of wine. 14 You must not
eat any bread, or roasted or new grain,
until the very day you bring this offering
to your God. This is to be a lasting ordinance for the generations to come, wherever you live.
15 "'From the day after the Sabbath,
the day you brought the sheaf of the

[a] *23* The Hebrew word can refer to either male or female. [b] *13* That is, probably about 7 pounds or about 3.2 kilograms; also in verse 17 [c] *13* That is, about 1 quart or about 1 liter

wave offering, count off seven full weeks.
16 Count off fifty days up to the day after
the seventh Sabbath, and then present an
offering of new grain to the LORD. 17 From
wherever you live, bring two loaves made
of two-tenths of an ephah of the finest
flour, baked with yeast, as a wave offering of firstfruits to the LORD. 18 Present
with this bread seven male lambs, each
a year old and without defect, one young
bull and two rams. They will be a burnt
offering to the LORD, together with their
grain offerings and drink offerings — a
food offering, an aroma pleasing to the
LORD. 19 Then sacrifice one male goat
for a sin offering[a] and two lambs, each a
year old, for a fellowship offering. 20 The
priest is to wave the two lambs before the
LORD as a wave offering, together with
the bread of the firstfruits. They are a sacred offering to the LORD for the priest.
21 On that same day you are to proclaim a
sacred assembly and do no regular work.
This is to be a lasting ordinance for the
generations to come, wherever you live.

22 " 'When you reap the harvest of your
land, do not reap to the very edges of
your field or gather the gleanings of your
harvest. Leave them for the poor and for
the foreigner residing among you. I am
the LORD your God.' "

23 The LORD said to Moses, 24 "Say to the
Israelites: 'On the first day of the seventh
month you are to have a day of sabbath
rest, a sacred assembly commemorat-
ed with trumpet blasts. 25 Do no regular
work, but present a food offering to the
LORD.' "

26 The LORD said to Moses, 27 "The
tenth day of this seventh month is the
Day of Atonement. Hold a sacred assembly and deny yourselves,[b] and present a
food offering to the LORD. 28 Do not do
any work on that day, because it is the
Day of Atonement, when atonement is
made for you before the LORD your God.
29 Those who do not deny themselves on
that day must be cut off from their people. 30 I will destroy from among their
people anyone who does any work on
that day. 31 You shall do no work at all.
This is to be a lasting ordinance for the
generations to come, wherever you live.
32 It is a day of sabbath rest for you, and
you must deny yourselves. From the evening of the ninth day of the month until
the following evening you are to observe
your sabbath."

33 The LORD said to Moses, 34 "Say to
the Israelites: 'On the fifteenth day of
the seventh month the LORD's Festival of
Tabernacles begins, and it lasts for seven
days. 35 The first day is a sacred assembly; do no regular work. 36 For seven days
present food offerings to the LORD, and
on the eighth day hold a sacred assembly
and present a food offering to the LORD.
It is the closing special assembly; do no
regular work.

37 (" 'These are the LORD's appointed
festivals, which you are to proclaim as
sacred assemblies for bringing food offerings to the LORD — the burnt offerings
and grain offerings, sacrifices and drink
offerings required for each day. 38 These
offerings are in addition to those for the
LORD's Sabbaths and[c] in addition to your
gifts and whatever you have vowed and
all the freewill offerings you give to the
LORD.)

39 " 'So beginning with the fifteenth
day of the seventh month, after you have
gathered the crops of the land, celebrate
the festival to the LORD for seven days;
the first day is a day of sabbath rest, and
the eighth day also is a day of sabbath
rest. 40 On the first day you are to take
branches from luxuriant trees — from
palms, willows and other leafy trees —
and rejoice before the LORD your God for
seven days. 41 Celebrate this as a festival
to the LORD for seven days each year.
This is to be a lasting ordinance for the
generations to come; celebrate it in the
seventh month. 42 Live in temporary
shelters for seven days: All native-born
Israelites are to live in such shelters 43 so
your descendants will know that I had
the Israelites live in temporary shelters
when I brought them out of Egypt. I am
the LORD your God.' "

44 So Moses announced to the Israelites
the appointed festivals of the LORD.

24 The LORD said to Moses, 2 "Command the Israelites to bring you
clear oil of pressed olives for the light
so that the lamps may be kept burning continually. 3 Outside the curtain
that shields the ark of the covenant law
in the tent of meeting, Aaron is to tend

[a] 19 Or *purification offering* [b] 27 Or *and fast*; similarly in verses 29 and 32 [c] 38 Or *These festivals are in addition to the LORD's Sabbaths, and these offerings are*

the lamps before the LORD from evening till morning, continually. This is
to be a lasting ordinance for the generations to come. 4The lamps on the pure
gold lampstand before the LORD must be
tended continually.
5"Take the finest flour and bake twelve
loaves of bread, using two-tenths of an
ephah[a] for each loaf. 6Arrange them in
two stacks, six in each stack, on the table
of pure gold before the LORD. 7By each
stack put some pure incense as a memorial[b] portion to represent the bread
and to be a food offering presented to
the LORD. 8This bread is to be set out before the LORD regularly, Sabbath after
Sabbath, on behalf of the Israelites, as
a lasting covenant. 9It belongs to Aaron
and his sons, who are to eat it in the sanctuary area, because it is a most holy part
of their perpetual share of the food offerings presented to the LORD."
10Now the son of an Israelite mother
and an Egyptian father went out among
the Israelites, and a fight broke out in
the camp between him and an Israelite.
11The son of the Israelite woman blasphemed the Name with a curse; so they
brought him to Moses. (His mother's
name was Shelomith, the daughter of
Dibri the Danite.) 12They put him in custody until the will of the LORD should be
made clear to them.
13Then the LORD said to Moses: 14"Take
the blasphemer outside the camp. All
those who heard him are to lay their
hands on his head, and the entire assembly is to stone him. 15Say to the Israelites: 'Anyone who curses their God will
be held responsible; 16anyone who blasphemes the name of the LORD is to be put
to death. The entire assembly must stone
them. Whether foreigner or native-born,
when they blaspheme the Name they are
to be put to death.
17"'Anyone who takes the life of a human being is to be put to death. 18Any-
one who takes the life of someone's animal must make restitution — life for life.
19Anyone who injures their neighbor is
to be injured in the same manner: 20frac-
ture for fracture, eye for eye, tooth for
tooth. The one who has inflicted the injury must suffer the same injury. 21Whoev-
er kills an animal must make restitution,
but whoever kills a human being is to be
put to death. 22You are to have the same
law for the foreigner and the native-born.
I am the LORD your God.'"
23Then Moses spoke to the Israelites,
and they took the blasphemer outside
the camp and stoned him. The Israelites
did as the LORD commanded Moses.

25 The LORD said to Moses at Mount
Sinai, 2"Speak to the Israelites and
say to them: 'When you enter the land I
am going to give you, the land itself must
observe a sabbath to the LORD. 3For six
years sow your fields, and for six years
prune your vineyards and gather their
crops. 4But in the seventh year the land is
to have a year of sabbath rest, a sabbath
to the LORD. Do not sow your fields or
prune your vineyards. 5Do not reap what
grows of itself or harvest the grapes of
your untended vines. The land is to have
a year of rest. 6Whatever the land yields
during the sabbath year will be food for
you — for yourself, your male and female
servants, and the hired worker and temporary resident who live among you, 7as
well as for your livestock and the wild
animals in your land. Whatever the land
produces may be eaten.
8"'Count off seven sabbath years —
seven times seven years — so that the
seven sabbath years amount to a period
of forty-nine years. 9Then have the trumpet sounded everywhere on the tenth
day of the seventh month; on the Day of
Atonement sound the trumpet throughout your land. 10Consecrate the fiftieth
year and proclaim liberty throughout
the land to all its inhabitants. It shall be
a jubilee for you; each of you is to return
to your family property and to your own
clan. 11The fiftieth year shall be a jubilee for you; do not sow and do not reap
what grows of itself or harvest the untended vines. 12For it is a jubilee and is
to be holy for you; eat only what is taken
directly from the fields.
13"'In this Year of Jubilee everyone is
to return to their own property.
14"'If you sell land to any of your own
people or buy land from them, do not
take advantage of each other. 15You are
to buy from your own people on the basis
of the number of years since the Jubilee.
And they are to sell to you on the basis

[a] 5 That is, probably about 7 pounds or about 3.2 kilograms [b] 7 Or *representative*

of the number of years left for harvesting crops. 16When the years are many,
you are to increase the price, and when
the years are few, you are to decrease the
price, because what is really being sold
to you is the number of crops. 17Do not
take advantage of each other, but fear
your God. I am the LORD your God.

18"'Follow my decrees and be careful
to obey my laws, and you will live safely in the land. 19Then the land will yield
its fruit, and you will eat your fill and live
there in safety. 20You may ask, "What
will we eat in the seventh year if we do
not plant or harvest our crops?" 21I will
send you such a blessing in the sixth
year that the land will yield enough for
three years. 22While you plant during
the eighth year, you will eat from the old
crop and will continue to eat from it until
the harvest of the ninth year comes in.

23"'The land must not be sold permanently, because the land is mine and
you reside in my land as foreigners and
strangers. 24Throughout the land that
you hold as a possession, you must provide for the redemption of the land.

25"'If one of your fellow Israelites becomes poor and sells some of their property, their nearest relative is to come and
redeem what they have sold. 26If, however, there is no one to redeem it for them
but later on they prosper and acquire
sufficient means to redeem it themselves, 27they are to determine the value
for the years since they sold it and refund
the balance to the one to whom they sold
it; they can then go back to their own
property. 28But if they do not acquire the
means to repay, what was sold will remain in the possession of the buyer until
the Year of Jubilee. It will be returned in
the Jubilee, and they can then go back to
their property.

29"'Anyone who sells a house in a
walled city retains the right of redemption a full year after its sale. During that
time the seller may redeem it. 30If it is not
redeemed before a full year has passed,
the house in the walled city shall belong
permanently to the buyer and the buyer's descendants. It is not to be returned
in the Jubilee. 31But houses in villages
without walls around them are to be considered as belonging to the open country. They can be redeemed, and they are
to be returned in the Jubilee.

32"'The Levites always have the right
to redeem their houses in the Levitical towns, which they possess. 33So the
property of the Levites is redeemable—
that is, a house sold in any town they
hold—and is to be returned in the Jubilee, because the houses in the towns of
the Levites are their property among the
Israelites. 34But the pastureland belonging to their towns must not be sold; it is
their permanent possession.

35"'If any of your fellow Israelites become poor and are unable to support
themselves among you, help them as you
would a foreigner and stranger, so they
can continue to live among you. 36Do not
take interest or any profit from them, but
fear your God, so that they may continue
to live among you. 37You must not lend
them money at interest or sell them food
at a profit. 38I am the LORD your God,
who brought you out of Egypt to give you
the land of Canaan and to be your God.

39"'If any of your fellow Israelites become poor and sell themselves to you,
do not make them work as slaves. 40They
are to be treated as hired workers or
temporary residents among you; they
are to work for you until the Year of Jubilee. 41Then they and their children are
to be released, and they will go back to
their own clans and to the property of
their ancestors. 42Because the Israelites
are my servants, whom I brought out of
Egypt, they must not be sold as slaves.
43Do not rule over them ruthlessly, but
fear your God.

44"'Your male and female slaves are
to come from the nations around you;
from them you may buy slaves. 45You
may also buy some of the temporary residents living among you and members
of their clans born in your country, and
they will become your property. 46You
can bequeath them to your children as
inherited property and can make them
slaves for life, but you must not rule over
your fellow Israelites ruthlessly.

47"'If a foreigner residing among you
becomes rich and any of your fellow
Israelites become poor and sell themselves to the foreigner or to a member
of the foreigner's clan, 48they retain the
right of redemption after they have sold
themselves. One of their relatives may
redeem them: 49An uncle or a cousin or
any blood relative in their clan may re-

deem them. Or if they prosper, they may
redeem themselves. 50They and their
buyer are to count the time from the year
they sold themselves up to the Year of Jubilee. The price for their release is to be
based on the rate paid to a hired worker
for that number of years. 51If many years
remain, they must pay for their redemption a larger share of the price paid for
them. 52If only a few years remain until
the Year of Jubilee, they are to compute
that and pay for their redemption accordingly. 53They are to be treated as workers
hired from year to year; you must see to
it that those to whom they owe service do
not rule over them ruthlessly.

54" 'Even if someone is not redeemed
in any of these ways, they and their children are to be released in the Year of Jubilee, 55for the Israelites belong to me as
servants. They are my servants, whom I
brought out of Egypt. I am the LORD your
God.

26 " 'Do not make idols or set up an
image or a sacred stone for yourselves, and do not place a carved stone
in your land to bow down before it. I am
the LORD your God.

2" 'Observe my Sabbaths and have reverence for my sanctuary. I am the LORD.

3" 'If you follow my decrees and are
careful to obey my commands, 4I will
send you rain in its season, and the
ground will yield its crops and the trees
their fruit. 5Your threshing will continue
until grape harvest and the grape harvest
will continue until planting, and you will
eat all the food you want and live in safety in your land.

6" 'I will grant peace in the land, and
you will lie down and no one will make
you afraid. I will remove wild beasts
from the land, and the sword will not
pass through your country. 7You will
pursue your enemies, and they will fall
by the sword before you. 8Five of you will
chase a hundred, and a hundred of you
will chase ten thousand, and your enemies will fall by the sword before you.

9" 'I will look on you with favor and
make you fruitful and increase your
numbers, and I will keep my covenant
with you. 10You will still be eating last
year's harvest when you will have to
move it out to make room for the new.
11I will put my dwelling place[a] among
you, and I will not abhor you. 12I will
walk among you and be your God, and
you will be my people. 13I am the LORD
your God, who brought you out of Egypt
so that you would no longer be slaves to
the Egyptians; I broke the bars of your
yoke and enabled you to walk with heads
held high.

14" 'But if you will not listen to me and
carry out all these commands, 15and if
you reject my decrees and abhor my laws
and fail to carry out all my commands
and so violate my covenant, 16then I will
do this to you: I will bring on you sudden terror, wasting diseases and fever
that will destroy your sight and sap your
strength. You will plant seed in vain, because your enemies will eat it. 17I will
set my face against you so that you will
be defeated by your enemies; those who
hate you will rule over you, and you will
flee even when no one is pursuing you.

18" 'If after all this you will not listen to
me, I will punish you for your sins sev-
en times over. 19I will break down your
stubborn pride and make the sky above
you like iron and the ground beneath you
like bronze. 20Your strength will be spent
in vain, because your soil will not yield
its crops, nor will the trees of your land
yield their fruit.

21" 'If you remain hostile toward me
and refuse to listen to me, I will multiply
your afflictions seven times over, as your
sins deserve. 22I will send wild animals
against you, and they will rob you of your
children, destroy your cattle and make
you so few in number that your roads
will be deserted.

23" 'If in spite of these things you do
not accept my correction but continue
to be hostile toward me, 24I myself will
be hostile toward you and will afflict you
for your sins seven times over. 25And
I will bring the sword on you to avenge
the breaking of the covenant. When you
withdraw into your cities, I will send a
plague among you, and you will be given
into enemy hands. 26When I cut off your
supply of bread, ten women will be able
to bake your bread in one oven, and they
will dole out the bread by weight. You
will eat, but you will not be satisfied.

27" 'If in spite of this you still do not

[a] *11* Or *my tabernacle*

listen to me but continue to be hostile toward me, 28 then in my anger I will be hostile toward you, and I myself will punish you for your sins seven times over. 29 You will eat the flesh of your sons and the flesh of your daughters. 30 I will destroy your high places, cut down your incense altars and pile your dead bodies[a] on the lifeless forms of your idols, and I will abhor you. 31 I will turn your cities into ruins and lay waste your sanctuaries, and I will take no delight in the pleasing aroma of your offerings. 32 I myself will lay waste the land, so that your enemies who live there will be appalled. 33 I will scatter you among the nations and will draw out my sword and pursue you. Your land will be laid waste, and your cities will lie in ruins. 34 Then the land will enjoy its sabbath years all the time that it lies desolate and you are in the country of your enemies; then the land will rest and enjoy its sabbaths. 35 All the time that it lies desolate, the land will have the rest it did not have during the sabbaths you lived in it.

36 " 'As for those of you who are left, I will make their hearts so fearful in the lands of their enemies that the sound of a windblown leaf will put them to flight. They will run as though fleeing from the sword, and they will fall, even though no one is pursuing them. 37 They will stumble over one another as though fleeing from the sword, even though no one is pursuing them. So you will not be able to stand before your enemies. 38 You will perish among the nations; the land of your enemies will devour you. 39 Those of you who are left will waste away in the lands of their enemies because of their sins; also because of their ancestors' sins they will waste away.

40 " 'But if they will confess their sins and the sins of their ancestors — their unfaithfulness and their hostility toward me, 41 which made me hostile toward them so that I sent them into the land of their enemies — then when their uncircumcised hearts are humbled and they pay for their sin, 42 I will remember my covenant with Jacob and my covenant with Isaac and my covenant with Abraham, and I will remember the land. 43 For the land will be deserted by them and will enjoy its sabbaths while it lies desolate without them. They will pay for their sins because they rejected my laws and abhorred my decrees. 44 Yet in spite of this, when they are in the land of their enemies, I will not reject them or abhor them so as to destroy them completely, breaking my covenant with them. I am the LORD their God. 45 But for their sake I will remember the covenant with their ancestors whom I brought out of Egypt in the sight of the nations to be their God. I am the LORD.' "

46 These are the decrees, the laws and the regulations that the LORD established at Mount Sinai between himself and the Israelites through Moses.

27 The LORD said to Moses, 2 "Speak to the Israelites and say to them: 'If anyone makes a special vow to dedicate a person to the LORD by giving the equivalent value, 3 set the value of a male between the ages of twenty and sixty at fifty shekels[b] of silver, according to the sanctuary shekel[c]; 4 for a female, set her value at thirty shekels[d]; 5 for a person between the ages of five and twenty, set the value of a male at twenty shekels[e] and of a female at ten shekels[f]; 6 for a person between one month and five years, set the value of a male at five shekels[g] of silver and that of a female at three shekels[h] of silver; 7 for a person sixty years old or more, set the value of a male at fifteen shekels[i] and of a female at ten shekels. 8 If anyone making the vow is too poor to pay the specified amount, the person being dedicated is to be presented to the priest, who will set the value according to what the one making the vow can afford.

9 " 'If what they vowed is an animal that is acceptable as an offering to the LORD, such an animal given to the LORD becomes holy. 10 They must not exchange it or substitute a good one for a bad one, or a bad one for a good one; if they should substitute one animal for another, both it and the substitute become holy. 11 If what they vowed is a ceremonially unclean

[a] *30* Or *your funeral offerings* [b] *3* That is, about 1 1/4 pounds or about 575 grams; also in verse 16
[c] *3* That is, about 2/5 ounce or about 12 grams; also in verse 25 [d] *4* That is, about 12 ounces or about 345 grams [e] *5* That is, about 8 ounces or about 230 grams [f] *5* That is, about 4 ounces or about 115 grams; also in verse 7 [g] *6* That is, about 2 ounces or about 58 grams [h] *6* That is, about 1 1/4 ounces or about 35 grams [i] *7* That is, about 6 ounces or about 175 grams

animal—one that is not acceptable as
an offering to the LORD—the animal
must be presented to the priest, 12who
will judge its quality as good or bad.
Whatever value the priest then sets, that
is what it will be. 13If the owner wishes to
redeem the animal, a fifth must be added
to its value.

14" 'If anyone dedicates their house as
something holy to the LORD, the priest
will judge its quality as good or bad.
Whatever value the priest then sets, so
it will remain. 15If the one who dedicates their house wishes to redeem it,
they must add a fifth to its value, and the
house will again become theirs.

16" 'If anyone dedicates to the LORD
part of their family land, its value is to
be set according to the amount of seed
required for it—fifty shekels of silver to
a homer[a] of barley seed. 17If they dedicate a field during the Year of Jubilee, the
value that has been set remains. 18But if
they dedicate a field after the Jubilee, the
priest will determine the value according to the number of years that remain
until the next Year of Jubilee, and its set
value will be reduced. 19If the one who
dedicates the field wishes to redeem it,
they must add a fifth to its value, and the
field will again become theirs. 20If, however, they do not redeem the field, or if
they have sold it to someone else, it can
never be redeemed. 21When the field is
released in the Jubilee, it will become
holy, like a field devoted to the LORD; it
will become priestly property.

22" 'If anyone dedicates to the LORD a
field they have bought, which is not part
of their family land, 23the priest will determine its value up to the Year of Jubilee,
and the owner must pay its value on that
day as something holy to the LORD. 24In
the Year of Jubilee the field will revert to
the person from whom it was bought, the
one whose land it was. 25Every value is to
be set according to the sanctuary shekel,
twenty gerahs to the shekel.

26" 'No one, however, may dedicate the
firstborn of an animal, since the firstborn
already belongs to the LORD; whether an
ox[b] or a sheep, it is the LORD's. 27If it is
one of the unclean animals, it may be
bought back at its set value, adding a fifth
of the value to it. If it is not redeemed, it is
to be sold at its set value.

28" 'But nothing that a person owns and
devotes[c] to the LORD—whether a human
being or an animal or family land—may
be sold or redeemed; everything so devoted is most holy to the LORD.

29" 'No person devoted to destruction[d]
may be ransomed; they are to be put to
death.

30" 'A tithe of everything from the land,
whether grain from the soil or fruit from
the trees, belongs to the LORD; it is holy
to the LORD. 31Whoever would redeem
any of their tithe must add a fifth of the
value to it. 32Every tithe of the herd and
flock—every tenth animal that passes
under the shepherd's rod—will be holy
to the LORD. 33No one may pick out the
good from the bad or make any substitution. If anyone does make a substitution,
both the animal and its substitute become holy and cannot be redeemed.' "

34These are the commands the LORD
gave Moses at Mount Sinai for the Israelites.

[a] *16* That is, probably about 300 pounds or about 135 kilograms [b] *26* The Hebrew word can refer to either male or female. [c] *28* The Hebrew term refers to the irrevocable giving over of things or persons to the LORD. [d] *29* The Hebrew term refers to the irrevocable giving over of things or persons to the LORD, often by totally destroying them.

NUMBERS

See the Invitation to Exodus, Leviticus and Numbers on p. 51.

1 The LORD spoke to Moses in the tent
of meeting in the Desert of Sinai on
the first day of the second month of the
second year after the Israelites came out
of Egypt. He said: 2 “Take a census of the
whole Israelite community by their clans
and families, listing every man by name,
one by one. 3 You and Aaron are to count
according to their divisions all the men
in Israel who are twenty years old or
more and able to serve in the army. 4 One
man from each tribe, each of them the
head of his family, is to help you. 5 These
are the names of the men who are to assist you:

from Reuben, Elizur son of Shedeur;
6 from Simeon, Shelumiel son of Zurishaddai;
7 from Judah, Nahshon son of Amminadab;
8 from Issachar, Nethanel son of Zuar;
9 from Zebulun, Eliab son of Helon;
10 from the sons of Joseph:
from Ephraim, Elishama son of
Ammihud;
from Manasseh, Gamaliel son of
Pedahzur;
11 from Benjamin, Abidan son of Gideoni;
12 from Dan, Ahiezer son of Ammishaddai;
13 from Asher, Pagiel son of Okran;
14 from Gad, Eliasaph son of Deuel;
15 from Naphtali, Ahira son of Enan.”

16 These were the men appointed from
the community, the leaders of their ancestral tribes. They were the heads of the
clans of Israel.

17 Moses and Aaron took these men
whose names had been specified, 18 and
they called the whole community together on the first day of the second month.
The people registered their ancestry by
their clans and families, and the men
twenty years old or more were listed by
name, one by one, 19 as the LORD commanded Moses. And so he counted them
in the Desert of Sinai:

20 From the descendants of Reuben the
firstborn son of Israel:
All the men twenty years old or
more who were able to serve in
the army were listed by name, one
by one, according to the records
of their clans and families. 21 The
number from the tribe of Reuben
was 46,500.

22 From the descendants of Simeon:
All the men twenty years old or
more who were able to serve in
the army were counted and listed
by name, one by one, according to
the records of their clans and families. 23 The number from the tribe
of Simeon was 59,300.

24 From the descendants of Gad:
All the men twenty years old or
more who were able to serve in the
army were listed by name, according to the records of their clans
and families. 25 The number from
the tribe of Gad was 45,650.

26 From the descendants of Judah:
All the men twenty years old or
more who were able to serve in the
army were listed by name, according to the records of their clans
and families. 27 The number from
the tribe of Judah was 74,600.

28 From the descendants of Issachar:
All the men twenty years old or
more who were able to serve in the
army were listed by name, according to the records of their clans
and families. 29 The number from
the tribe of Issachar was 54,400.

30 From the descendants of Zebulun:
All the men twenty years old or
more who were able to serve in the
army were listed by name, according to the records of their clans
and families. 31 The number from
the tribe of Zebulun was 57,400.

32 From the sons of Joseph:
From the descendants of Ephraim:
All the men twenty years old or
more who were able to serve in the
army were listed by name, according to the records of their clans
and families. 33 The number from
the tribe of Ephraim was 40,500.

34 From the descendants of Manasseh:
All the men twenty years old or
more who were able to serve in the
army were listed by name, according to the records of their clans
and families. 35 The number from
the tribe of Manasseh was 32,200.

36 From the descendants of Benjamin:
All the men twenty years old or
more who were able to serve in the
army were listed by name, according to the records of their clans
and families. 37 The number from
the tribe of Benjamin was 35,400.

38 From the descendants of Dan:
All the men twenty years old or
more who were able to serve in the
army were listed by name, according to the records of their clans
and families. 39 The number from
the tribe of Dan was 62,700.

40 From the descendants of Asher:
All the men twenty years old or
more who were able to serve in the
army were listed by name, according to the records of their clans
and families. 41 The number from
the tribe of Asher was 41,500.

42 From the descendants of Naphtali:
All the men twenty years old or
more who were able to serve in the
army were listed by name, according to the records of their clans
and families. 43 The number from
the tribe of Naphtali was 53,400.

44 These were the men counted by Moses
and Aaron and the twelve leaders of Israel, each one representing his family. 45 All
the Israelites twenty years old or more
who were able to serve in Israel's army
were counted according to their families.
46 The total number was 603,550.

47 The ancestral tribe of the Levites,
however, was not counted along with
the others. 48 The LORD had said to Moses: 49 "You must not count the tribe of
Levi or include them in the census of the
other Israelites. 50 Instead, appoint the
Levites to be in charge of the tabernacle
of the covenant law — over all its furnishings and everything belonging to it. They
are to carry the tabernacle and all its furnishings; they are to take care of it and
encamp around it. 51 Whenever the tabernacle is to move, the Levites are to take
it down, and whenever the tabernacle is
to be set up, the Levites shall do it. Anyone else who approaches it is to be put to
death. 52 The Israelites are to set up their
tents by divisions, each of them in their
own camp under their standard. 53 The
Levites, however, are to set up their tents
around the tabernacle of the covenant
law so that my wrath will not fall on the
Israelite community. The Levites are to
be responsible for the care of the tabernacle of the covenant law."

54 The Israelites did all this just as the
LORD commanded Moses.

2 The LORD said to Moses and Aaron:
2 "The Israelites are to camp around
the tent of meeting some distance from
it, each of them under their standard and
holding the banners of their family."

3 On the east, toward the sunrise,
the divisions of the camp of Judah
are to encamp under their standard.
The leader of the people of Judah is
Nahshon son of Amminadab. 4 His
division numbers 74,600.

5 The tribe of Issachar will camp
next to them. The leader of the people of Issachar is Nethanel son of
Zuar. 6 His division numbers 54,400.

7 The tribe of Zebulun will be next.
The leader of the people of Zebulun
is Eliab son of Helon. 8 His division
numbers 57,400.

9 All the men assigned to the camp
of Judah, according to their divisions, number 186,400. They will set
out first.

10 On the south will be the divisions
of the camp of Reuben under their
standard. The leader of the people
of Reuben is Elizur son of Shedeur.
11 His division numbers 46,500.

12 The tribe of Simeon will camp
next to them. The leader of the people of Simeon is Shelumiel son of
Zurishaddai. 13 His division numbers 59,300.

14 The tribe of Gad will be next. The
leader of the people of Gad is Eliasaph son of Deuel.[a] 15 His division
numbers 45,650.

[a] *14* Many manuscripts of the Masoretic Text, Samaritan Pentateuch and Vulgate (see also 1:14); most manuscripts of the Masoretic Text *Reuel*

16 All the men assigned to the
camp of Reuben, according to their
divisions, number 151,450. They will
set out second.

17 Then the tent of meeting and the
camp of the Levites will set out in
the middle of the camps. They will
set out in the same order as they encamp, each in their own place under
their standard.

18 On the west will be the divisions
of the camp of Ephraim under their
standard. The leader of the people of
Ephraim is Elishama son of Ammihud. 19 His division numbers 40,500.
20 The tribe of Manasseh will be
next to them. The leader of the people of Manasseh is Gamaliel son of
Pedahzur. 21 His division numbers
32,200.
22 The tribe of Benjamin will be
next. The leader of the people of
Benjamin is Abidan son of Gideoni.
23 His division numbers 35,400.
24 All the men assigned to the
camp of Ephraim, according to their
divisions, number 108,100. They will
set out third.

25 On the north will be the divisions of the camp of Dan under their
standard. The leader of the people of
Dan is Ahiezer son of Ammishaddai.
26 His division numbers 62,700.
27 The tribe of Asher will camp next
to them. The leader of the people of
Asher is Pagiel son of Okran. 28 His
division numbers 41,500.
29 The tribe of Naphtali will be
next. The leader of the people of
Naphtali is Ahira son of Enan. 30 His
division numbers 53,400.
31 All the men assigned to the camp
of Dan number 157,600. They will set
out last, under their standards.

32 These are the Israelites, counted according to their families. All
the men in the camps, by their divisions, number 603,550. 33 The Levites, however, were not counted
along with the other Israelites, as the
LORD commanded Moses.

34 So the Israelites did everything the
LORD commanded Moses; that is the way
they encamped under their standards,
and that is the way they set out, each of
them with their clan and family.

3 This is the account of the family of
Aaron and Moses at the time the LORD
spoke to Moses at Mount Sinai.
2 The names of the sons of Aaron were
Nadab the firstborn and Abihu, Eleazar
and Ithamar. 3 Those were the names of
Aaron's sons, the anointed priests, who
were ordained to serve as priests. 4 Nadab and Abihu, however, died before the
LORD when they made an offering with
unauthorized fire before him in the Desert of Sinai. They had no sons, so Eleazar
and Ithamar served as priests during the
lifetime of their father Aaron.
5 The LORD said to Moses, 6 "Bring the
tribe of Levi and present them to Aaron the priest to assist him. 7 They are to
perform duties for him and for the whole
community at the tent of meeting by doing the work of the tabernacle. 8 They are
to take care of all the furnishings of the
tent of meeting, fulfilling the obligations
of the Israelites by doing the work of the
tabernacle. 9 Give the Levites to Aaron
and his sons; they are the Israelites who
are to be given wholly to him.[a] 10 Appoint
Aaron and his sons to serve as priests;
anyone else who approaches the sanctuary is to be put to death."
11 The LORD also said to Moses, 12 "I
have taken the Levites from among the
Israelites in place of the first male offspring of every Israelite woman. The
Levites are mine, 13 for all the firstborn
are mine. When I struck down all the
firstborn in Egypt, I set apart for myself
every firstborn in Israel, whether human
or animal. They are to be mine. I am the
LORD."
14 The LORD said to Moses in the Desert of Sinai, 15 "Count the Levites by their
families and clans. Count every male a
month old or more." 16 So Moses counted
them, as he was commanded by the word
of the LORD.
17 These were the names of the sons of
Levi:
Gershon, Kohath and Merari.
18 These were the names of the Gershonite clans:

[a] 9 Most manuscripts of the Masoretic Text; some manuscripts of the Masoretic Text, Samaritan Pentateuch and Septuagint (see also 8:16); *to me*

Libni and Shimei.
19 The Kohathite clans:
Amram, Izhar, Hebron and Uzziel.
20 The Merarite clans:
Mahli and Mushi.
These were the Levite clans, according
to their families.

21 To Gershon belonged the clans of the
Libnites and Shimeites; these were the
Gershonite clans. 22 The number of all
the males a month old or more who were
counted was 7,500. 23 The Gershonite
clans were to camp on the west, behind
the tabernacle. 24 The leader of the families of the Gershonites was Eliasaph son
of Lael. 25 At the tent of meeting the Gershonites were responsible for the care of
the tabernacle and tent, its coverings,
the curtain at the entrance to the tent of
meeting, 26 the curtains of the courtyard,
the curtain at the entrance to the courtyard surrounding the tabernacle and
altar, and the ropes—and everything
related to their use.

27 To Kohath belonged the clans of the
Amramites, Izharites, Hebronites and
Uzzielites; these were the Kohathite
clans. 28 The number of all the males a
month old or more was 8,600.[a] The Kohathites were responsible for the care
of the sanctuary. 29 The Kohathite clans
were to camp on the south side of the
tabernacle. 30 The leader of the families
of the Kohathite clans was Elizaphan son
of Uzziel. 31 They were responsible for the
care of the ark, the table, the lampstand,
the altars, the articles of the sanctuary
used in ministering, the curtain, and everything related to their use. 32 The chief
leader of the Levites was Eleazar son of
Aaron, the priest. He was appointed over
those who were responsible for the care
of the sanctuary.

33 To Merari belonged the clans of the
Mahlites and the Mushites; these were
the Merarite clans. 34 The number of all
the males a month old or more who were
counted was 6,200. 35 The leader of the
families of the Merarite clans was Zuriel
son of Abihail; they were to camp on the
north side of the tabernacle. 36 The Merarites were appointed to take care of the
frames of the tabernacle, its crossbars,
posts, bases, all its equipment, and everything related to their use, 37 as well as
the posts of the surrounding courtyard
with their bases, tent pegs and ropes.

38 Moses and Aaron and his sons were
to camp to the east of the tabernacle, toward the sunrise, in front of the tent of
meeting. They were responsible for the
care of the sanctuary on behalf of the
Israelites. Anyone else who approached
the sanctuary was to be put to death.

39 The total number of Levites counted
at the LORD's command by Moses and
Aaron according to their clans, including every male a month old or more, was
22,000.

40 The LORD said to Moses, "Count all
the firstborn Israelite males who are
a month old or more and make a list of
their names. 41 Take the Levites for me in
place of all the firstborn of the Israelites,
and the livestock of the Levites in place
of all the firstborn of the livestock of the
Israelites. I am the LORD."
42 So Moses counted all the firstborn
of the Israelites, as the LORD commanded him. 43 The total number of firstborn
males a month old or more, listed by
name, was 22,273.
44 The LORD also said to Moses, 45 "Take
the Levites in place of all the firstborn of
Israel, and the livestock of the Levites in
place of their livestock. The Levites are
to be mine. I am the LORD. 46 To redeem
the 273 firstborn Israelites who exceed
the number of the Levites, 47 collect five
shekels[b] for each one, according to the
sanctuary shekel, which weighs twenty gerahs. 48 Give the money for the redemption of the additional Israelites to
Aaron and his sons."
49 So Moses collected the redemption money from those who exceeded
the number redeemed by the Levites.
50 From the firstborn of the Israelites he
collected silver weighing 1,365 shekels,[c]
according to the sanctuary shekel. 51 Moses gave the redemption money to Aaron
and his sons, as he was commanded by
the word of the LORD.

[a] *28* Hebrew; some Septuagint manuscripts *8,300*
[b] *47* That is, about 2 ounces or about 58 grams
[c] *50* That is, about 35 pounds or about 16 kilograms

4 The LORD said to Moses and Aaron: 2“Take a census of the Kohathite branch of the Levites by their clans and families. 3Count all the men from thirty to fifty years of age who come to serve in the work at the tent of meeting.

4“This is the work of the Kohathites at the tent of meeting: the care of the most holy things. 5When the camp is to move, Aaron and his sons are to go in and take down the shielding curtain and put it over the ark of the covenant law. 6Then they are to cover the curtain with a durable leather,[a] spread a cloth of solid blue over that and put the poles in place.

7“Over the table of the Presence they are to spread a blue cloth and put on it the plates, dishes and bowls, and the jars for drink offerings; the bread that is continually there is to remain on it. 8They are to spread a scarlet cloth over them, cover that with the durable leather and put the poles in place.

9“They are to take a blue cloth and cover the lampstand that is for light, together with its lamps, its wick trimmers and trays, and all its jars for the olive oil used to supply it. 10Then they are to wrap it and all its accessories in a covering of the durable leather and put it on a carrying frame.

11“Over the gold altar they are to spread a blue cloth and cover that with the durable leather and put the poles in place.

12“They are to take all the articles used for ministering in the sanctuary, wrap them in a blue cloth, cover that with the durable leather and put them on a carrying frame.

13“They are to remove the ashes from the bronze altar and spread a purple cloth over it. 14Then they are to place on it all the utensils used for ministering at the altar, including the firepans, meat forks, shovels and sprinkling bowls. Over it they are to spread a covering of the durable leather and put the poles in place.

15“After Aaron and his sons have finished covering the holy furnishings and all the holy articles, and when the camp is ready to move, only then are the Kohathites to come and do the carrying. But they must not touch the holy things or they will die. The Kohathites are to carry those things that are in the tent of meeting.

16“Eleazar son of Aaron, the priest, is to have charge of the oil for the light, the fragrant incense, the regular grain offering and the anointing oil. He is to be in charge of the entire tabernacle and everything in it, including its holy furnishings and articles.”

17The LORD said to Moses and Aaron, 18“See that the Kohathite tribal clans are not destroyed from among the Levites. 19So that they may live and not die when they come near the most holy things, do this for them: Aaron and his sons are to go into the sanctuary and assign to each man his work and what he is to carry. 20But the Kohathites must not go in to look at the holy things, even for a moment, or they will die.”

21The LORD said to Moses, 22“Take a census also of the Gershonites by their families and clans. 23Count all the men from thirty to fifty years of age who come to serve in the work at the tent of meeting.

24“This is the service of the Gershonite clans in their carrying and their other work: 25They are to carry the curtains of the tabernacle, that is, the tent of meeting, its covering and its outer covering of durable leather, the curtains for the entrance to the tent of meeting, 26the curtains of the courtyard surrounding the tabernacle and altar, the curtain for the entrance to the courtyard, the ropes and all the equipment used in the service of the tent. The Gershonites are to do all that needs to be done with these things. 27All their service, whether carrying or doing other work, is to be done under the direction of Aaron and his sons. You shall assign to them as their responsibility all they are to carry. 28This is the service of the Gershonite clans at the tent of meeting. Their duties are to be under the direction of Ithamar son of Aaron, the priest.

29“Count the Merarites by their clans and families. 30Count all the men from thirty to fifty years of age who come to serve in the work at the tent of meeting. 31As part of all their service at the tent, they are to carry the frames of the tabernacle, its crossbars, posts and bases, 32as well as the posts of the surrounding courtyard with their bases, tent pegs, ropes, all their equipment and every-

[a] 6 Possibly the hides of large aquatic mammals; also in verses 8, 10, 11, 12, 14 and 25

thing related to their use. Assign to each
man the specific things he is to carry.
33This is the service of the Merarite clans
as they work at the tent of meeting under
the direction of Ithamar son of Aaron,
the priest."
34Moses, Aaron and the leaders of the
community counted the Kohathites by
their clans and families. 35All the men
from thirty to fifty years of age who
came to serve in the work at the tent of
meeting, 36counted by clans, were 2,750.
37This was the total of all those in the
Kohathite clans who served at the tent
of meeting. Moses and Aaron counted
them according to the LORD's command
through Moses.
38The Gershonites were counted by
their clans and families. 39All the men
from thirty to fifty years of age who came
to serve in the work at the tent of meeting, 40counted by their clans and families, were 2,630. 41This was the total of
those in the Gershonite clans who served
at the tent of meeting. Moses and Aaron
counted them according to the LORD's
command.
42The Merarites were counted by their
clans and families. 43All the men from
thirty to fifty years of age who came to
serve in the work at the tent of meeting,
44counted by their clans, were 3,200.
45This was the total of those in the Merarite clans. Moses and Aaron counted
them according to the LORD's command
through Moses.
46So Moses, Aaron and the leaders of
Israel counted all the Levites by their
clans and families. 47All the men from
thirty to fifty years of age who came to
do the work of serving and carrying the
tent of meeting 48numbered 8,580. 49At
the LORD's command through Moses,
each was assigned his work and told
what to carry.

Thus they were counted, as the LORD
commanded Moses.

5 The LORD said to Moses, 2"Command
the Israelites to send away from the
camp anyone who has a defiling skin disease[a] or a discharge of any kind, or who is
ceremonially unclean because of a dead
body. 3Send away male and female alike;
send them outside the camp so they
will not defile their camp, where I dwell
among them." 4The Israelites did so; they
sent them outside the camp. They did just
as the LORD had instructed Moses.
5The LORD said to Moses, 6"Say to
the Israelites: 'Any man or woman who
wrongs another in any way[b] and so is
unfaithful to the LORD is guilty 7and
must confess the sin they have committed. They must make full restitution for
the wrong they have done, add a fifth of
the value to it and give it all to the person
they have wronged. 8But if that person
has no close relative to whom restitution
can be made for the wrong, the restitution belongs to the LORD and must be
given to the priest, along with the ram
with which atonement is made for the
wrongdoer. 9All the sacred contributions
the Israelites bring to a priest will belong
to him. 10Sacred things belong to their
owners, but what they give to the priest
will belong to the priest.'"
11Then the LORD said to Moses,
12"Speak to the Israelites and say to them:
'If a man's wife goes astray and is unfaithful to him 13so that another man has sexual relations with her, and this is hidden
from her husband and her impurity is un-
detected (since there is no witness against
her and she has not been caught in the
act), 14and if feelings of jealousy come
over her husband and he suspects his
wife and she is impure—or if he is jealous
and suspects her even though she is not
impure— 15then he is to take his wife to
the priest. He must also take an offering
of a tenth of an ephah[c] of barley flour on
her behalf. He must not pour olive oil on
it or put incense on it, because it is a grain
offering for jealousy, a reminder-offering
to draw attention to wrongdoing.
16"'The priest shall bring her and have
her stand before the LORD. 17Then he shall
take some holy water in a clay jar and put
some dust from the tabernacle floor into
the water. 18After the priest has had the
woman stand before the LORD, he shall
loosen her hair and place in her hands
the reminder-offering, the grain offering
for jealousy, while he himself holds the
bitter water that brings a curse. 19Then
the priest shall put the woman under
oath and say to her, "If no other man has

[a] 2 The Hebrew word for *defiling skin disease,* traditionally translated "leprosy," was used for various diseases affecting the skin. [b] 6 Or *woman who commits any wrong common to mankind* [c] 15 That is, probably about 3 1/2 pounds or about 1.6 kilograms

had sexual relations with you and you have not gone astray and become impure while married to your husband, may this bitter water that brings a curse not harm you. 20But if you have gone astray while married to your husband and you have made yourself impure by having sexual relations with a man other than your husband"— 21here the priest is to put the woman under this curse—"may the LORD cause you to become a curse[a] among your people when he makes your womb miscarry and your abdomen swell. 22May this water that brings a curse enter your body so that your abdomen swells or your womb miscarries."

"'Then the woman is to say, "Amen. So be it."

23"'The priest is to write these curses on a scroll and then wash them off into the bitter water. 24He shall make the woman drink the bitter water that brings a curse, and this water that brings a curse and causes bitter suffering will enter her. 25The priest is to take from her hands the grain offering for jealousy, wave it before the LORD and bring it to the altar. 26The priest is then to take a handful of the grain offering as a memorial[b] offering and burn it on the altar; after that, he is to have the woman drink the water. 27If she has made herself impure and been unfaithful to her husband, this will be the result: When she is made to drink the water that brings a curse and causes bitter suffering, it will enter her, her abdomen will swell and her womb will miscarry, and she will become a curse. 28If, however, the woman has not made herself impure, but is clean, she will be cleared of guilt and will be able to have children.

29"'This, then, is the law of jealousy when a woman goes astray and makes herself impure while married to her husband, 30or when feelings of jealousy come over a man because he suspects his wife. The priest is to have her stand before the LORD and is to apply this entire law to her. 31The husband will be innocent of any wrongdoing, but the woman will bear the consequences of her sin.'"

6 The LORD said to Moses, 2"Speak to the Israelites and say to them: 'If a man or woman wants to make a special vow, a vow of dedication to the LORD as a Nazirite, 3they must abstain from wine and other fermented drink and must not drink vinegar made from wine or other fermented drink. They must not drink grape juice or eat grapes or raisins. 4As long as they remain under their Nazirite vow, they must not eat anything that comes from the grapevine, not even the seeds or skins.

5"'During the entire period of their Nazirite vow, no razor may be used on their head. They must be holy until the period of their dedication to the LORD is over; they must let their hair grow long.

6"'Throughout the period of their dedication to the LORD, the Nazirite must not go near a dead body. 7Even if their own father or mother or brother or sister dies, they must not make themselves ceremonially unclean on account of them, because the symbol of their dedication to God is on their head. 8Throughout the period of their dedication, they are consecrated to the LORD.

9"'If someone dies suddenly in the Nazirite's presence, thus defiling the hair that symbolizes their dedication, they must shave their head on the seventh day—the day of their cleansing. 10Then on the eighth day they must bring two doves or two young pigeons to the priest at the entrance to the tent of meeting. 11The priest is to offer one as a sin offering[c] and the other as a burnt offering to make atonement for the Nazirite because they sinned by being in the presence of the dead body. That same day they are to consecrate their head again. 12They must rededicate themselves to the LORD for the same period of dedication and must bring a year-old male lamb as a guilt offering. The previous days do not count, because they became defiled during their period of dedication.

13"'Now this is the law of the Nazirite when the period of their dedication is over. They are to be brought to the entrance to the tent of meeting. 14There they are to present their offerings to the LORD: a year-old male lamb without defect for a burnt offering, a year-old ewe lamb without defect for a sin offering, a ram without defect for a fellowship offering, 15together with their grain offerings and drink offerings, and a basket

[a] *21* That is, may he cause your name to be used in cursing (see Jer. 29:22); or, may others see that you are cursed; similarly in verse 27. [b] *26* Or *representative* [c] *11* Or *purification offering*; also in verses 14 and 16

of bread made with the finest flour and
without yeast—thick loaves with olive
oil mixed in, and thin loaves brushed
with olive oil.
16 " 'The priest is to present all these before the LORD and make the sin offering
and the burnt offering. 17 He is to present
the basket of unleavened bread and is to
sacrifice the ram as a fellowship offering
to the LORD, together with its grain offering and drink offering.
18 " 'Then at the entrance to the tent of
meeting, the Nazirite must shave off the
hair that symbolizes their dedication.
They are to take the hair and put it in the
fire that is under the sacrifice of the fellowship offering.
19 " 'After the Nazirite has shaved off
the hair that symbolizes their dedication, the priest is to place in their hands a
boiled shoulder of the ram, and one thick
loaf and one thin loaf from the basket,
both made without yeast. 20 The priest
shall then wave these before the LORD as
a wave offering; they are holy and belong
to the priest, together with the breast
that was waved and the thigh that was
presented. After that, the Nazirite may
drink wine.
21 " 'This is the law of the Nazirite who
vows offerings to the LORD in accordance
with their dedication, in addition to
whatever else they can afford. They must
fulfill the vows they have made, according to the law of the Nazirite.' "
22 The LORD said to Moses, 23 "Tell Aaron and his sons, 'This is how you are to
bless the Israelites. Say to them:

24 " ' "The LORD bless you
and keep you;
25 the LORD make his face shine on you
and be gracious to you;
26 the LORD turn his face toward you
and give you peace." '

27 "So they will put my name on the Israelites, and I will bless them."

7 When Moses finished setting up the
tabernacle, he anointed and consecrated it and all its furnishings. He also
anointed and consecrated the altar and
all its utensils. 2 Then the leaders of Israel, the heads of families who were the
tribal leaders in charge of those who were
counted, made offerings. 3 They brought
as their gifts before the LORD six covered
carts and twelve oxen—an ox from each
leader and a cart from every two. These
they presented before the tabernacle.
4 The LORD said to Moses, 5 "Accept
these from them, that they may be used
in the work at the tent of meeting. Give
them to the Levites as each man's work
requires."
6 So Moses took the carts and oxen and
gave them to the Levites. 7 He gave two
carts and four oxen to the Gershonites,
as their work required, 8 and he gave four
carts and eight oxen to the Merarites, as
their work required. They were all under
the direction of Ithamar son of Aaron,
the priest. 9 But Moses did not give any
to the Kohathites, because they were to
carry on their shoulders the holy things,
for which they were responsible.
10 When the altar was anointed, the
leaders brought their offerings for its
dedication and presented them before
the altar. 11 For the LORD had said to Moses, "Each day one leader is to bring his
offering for the dedication of the altar."

12 The one who brought his offering on
the first day was Nahshon son of Amminadab of the tribe of Judah.
13 His offering was one silver plate
weighing a hundred and thirty shekels[a] and one silver sprinkling bowl
weighing seventy shekels,[b] both
according to the sanctuary shekel, each filled with the finest flour
mixed with olive oil as a grain offering; 14 one gold dish weighing ten
shekels,[c] filled with incense; 15 one
young bull, one ram and one male
lamb a year old for a burnt offering;
16 one male goat for a sin offering[d];
17 and two oxen, five rams, five male
goats and five male lambs a year old
to be sacrificed as a fellowship offering. This was the offering of Nahshon son of Amminadab.

18 On the second day Nethanel son of
Zuar, the leader of Issachar, brought his
offering.
19 The offering he brought was one
silver plate weighing a hundred and
thirty shekels and one silver sprin-

[a] *13* That is, about 3 1/4 pounds or about 1.5 kilograms; also elsewhere in this chapter [b] *13* That is, about 1 3/4 pounds or about 800 grams; also elsewhere in this chapter [c] *14* That is, about 4 ounces or about 115 grams; also elsewhere in this chapter [d] *16* Or *purification offering*; also elsewhere in this chapter

kling bowl weighing seventy shekels, both according to the sanctuary
shekel, each filled with the finest
flour mixed with olive oil as a grain
offering; [20]one gold dish weighing ten shekels, filled with incense;
[21]one young bull, one ram and one
male lamb a year old for a burnt offering; [22]one male goat for a sin offering; [23]and two oxen, five rams,
five male goats and five male lambs
a year old to be sacrificed as a fellowship offering. This was the offering
of Nethanel son of Zuar.

[24]On the third day, Eliab son of Helon,
the leader of the people of Zebulun,
brought his offering.
[25]His offering was one silver plate
weighing a hundred and thirty shekels and one silver sprinkling bowl
weighing seventy shekels, both according to the sanctuary shekel, each
filled with the finest flour mixed with
olive oil as a grain offering; [26]one
gold dish weighing ten shekels, filled
with incense; [27]one young bull, one
ram and one male lamb a year old for
a burnt offering; [28]one male goat for
a sin offering; [29]and two oxen, five
rams, five male goats and five male
lambs a year old to be sacrificed as a
fellowship offering. This was the offering of Eliab son of Helon.

[30]On the fourth day Elizur son of Shedeur, the leader of the people of Reuben,
brought his offering.
[31]His offering was one silver plate
weighing a hundred and thirty
shekels and one silver sprinkling
bowl weighing seventy shekels, both
according to the sanctuary shekel, each filled with the finest flour
mixed with olive oil as a grain offering; [32]one gold dish weighing ten
shekels, filled with incense; [33]one
young bull, one ram and one male
lamb a year old for a burnt offering;
[34]one male goat for a sin offering;
[35]and two oxen, five rams, five male
goats and five male lambs a year old
to be sacrificed as a fellowship offering. This was the offering of Elizur
son of Shedeur.

[36]On the fifth day Shelumiel son of Zurishaddai, the leader of the people of Simeon, brought his offering.
[37]His offering was one silver plate
weighing a hundred and thirty
shekels and one silver sprinkling
bowl weighing seventy shekels, both
according to the sanctuary shekel, each filled with the finest flour
mixed with olive oil as a grain offering; [38]one gold dish weighing ten
shekels, filled with incense; [39]one
young bull, one ram and one male
lamb a year old for a burnt offering;
[40]one male goat for a sin offering;
[41]and two oxen, five rams, five male
goats and five male lambs a year old
to be sacrificed as a fellowship offering. This was the offering of Shelumiel son of Zurishaddai.

[42]On the sixth day Eliasaph son of Deuel,
the leader of the people of Gad, brought
his offering.
[43]His offering was one silver plate
weighing a hundred and thirty shekels and one silver sprinkling bowl
weighing seventy shekels, both according to the sanctuary shekel, each
filled with the finest flour mixed with
olive oil as a grain offering; [44]one
gold dish weighing ten shekels, filled
with incense; [45]one young bull, one
ram and one male lamb a year old for
a burnt offering; [46]one male goat for
a sin offering; [47]and two oxen, five
rams, five male goats and five male
lambs a year old to be sacrificed as a
fellowship offering. This was the offering of Eliasaph son of Deuel.

[48]On the seventh day Elishama son of
Ammihud, the leader of the people of
Ephraim, brought his offering.
[49]His offering was one silver plate
weighing a hundred and thirty
shekels and one silver sprinkling
bowl weighing seventy shekels, both
according to the sanctuary shekel, each filled with the finest flour
mixed with olive oil as a grain offering; [50]one gold dish weighing ten
shekels, filled with incense; [51]one
young bull, one ram and one male
lamb a year old for a burnt offering;
[52]one male goat for a sin offering;
[53]and two oxen, five rams, five male
goats and five male lambs a year old
to be sacrificed as a fellowship offering. This was the offering of Elishama son of Ammihud.

54On the eighth day Gamaliel son of Pedahzur, the leader of the people of Manasseh, brought his offering.
55His offering was one silver plate
weighing a hundred and thirty
shekels and one silver sprinkling
bowl weighing seventy shekels, both
according to the sanctuary shekel, each filled with the finest flour
mixed with olive oil as a grain offering; 56one gold dish weighing ten
shekels, filled with incense; 57one
young bull, one ram and one male
lamb a year old for a burnt offering;
58one male goat for a sin offering;
59and two oxen, five rams, five male
goats and five male lambs a year old
to be sacrificed as a fellowship offering. This was the offering of Gamaliel son of Pedahzur.

60On the ninth day Abidan son of Gideoni, the leader of the people of Benjamin,
brought his offering.
61His offering was one silver plate
weighing a hundred and thirty shekels and one silver sprinkling bowl
weighing seventy shekels, both according to the sanctuary shekel, each
filled with the finest flour mixed with
olive oil as a grain offering; 62one
gold dish weighing ten shekels, filled
with incense; 63one young bull, one
ram and one male lamb a year old for
a burnt offering; 64one male goat for
a sin offering; 65and two oxen, five
rams, five male goats and five male
lambs a year old to be sacrificed as a
fellowship offering. This was the offering of Abidan son of Gideoni.

66On the tenth day Ahiezer son of Ammishaddai, the leader of the people of Dan,
brought his offering.
67His offering was one silver plate
weighing a hundred and thirty
shekels and one silver sprinkling
bowl weighing seventy shekels, both
according to the sanctuary shekel, each filled with the finest flour
mixed with olive oil as a grain offering; 68one gold dish weighing ten
shekels, filled with incense; 69one
young bull, one ram and one male
lamb a year old for a burnt offering;
70one male goat for a sin offering;
71and two oxen, five rams, five male
goats and five male lambs a year old
to be sacrificed as a fellowship offering. This was the offering of Ahiezer
son of Ammishaddai.

72On the eleventh day Pagiel son of Okran, the leader of the people of Asher,
brought his offering.
73His offering was one silver plate
weighing a hundred and thirty shekels and one silver sprinkling bowl
weighing seventy shekels, both according to the sanctuary shekel, each
filled with the finest flour mixed with
olive oil as a grain offering; 74one
gold dish weighing ten shekels, filled
with incense; 75one young bull, one
ram and one male lamb a year old for
a burnt offering; 76one male goat for
a sin offering; 77and two oxen, five
rams, five male goats and five male
lambs a year old to be sacrificed as a
fellowship offering. This was the offering of Pagiel son of Okran.

78On the twelfth day Ahira son of Enan,
the leader of the people of Naphtali,
brought his offering.
79His offering was one silver plate
weighing a hundred and thirty
shekels and one silver sprinkling
bowl weighing seventy shekels, both
according to the sanctuary shekel, each filled with the finest flour
mixed with olive oil as a grain offering; 80one gold dish weighing ten
shekels, filled with incense; 81one
young bull, one ram and one male
lamb a year old for a burnt offering;
82one male goat for a sin offering;
83and two oxen, five rams, five male
goats and five male lambs a year old
to be sacrificed as a fellowship offering. This was the offering of Ahira
son of Enan.

84These were the offerings of the Israelite leaders for the dedication of the
altar when it was anointed: twelve silver
plates, twelve silver sprinkling bowls
and twelve gold dishes. 85Each silver
plate weighed a hundred and thirty
shekels, and each sprinkling bowl seventy shekels. Altogether, the silver dishes weighed two thousand four hundred
shekels,[a] according to the sanctuary

[a] 85 That is, about 60 pounds or about 28 kilograms

shekel. 86 The twelve gold dishes filled
with incense weighed ten shekels each,
according to the sanctuary shekel. Altogether, the gold dishes weighed a hundred and twenty shekels.[a] 87 The total
number of animals for the burnt offering
came to twelve young bulls, twelve rams
and twelve male lambs a year old, together with their grain offering. Twelve
male goats were used for the sin offering.
88 The total number of animals for the
sacrifice of the fellowship offering came
to twenty-four oxen, sixty rams, sixty
male goats and sixty male lambs a year
old. These were the offerings for the dedication of the altar after it was anointed.
89 When Moses entered the tent of
meeting to speak with the LORD, he heard
the voice speaking to him from between
the two cherubim above the atonement
cover on the ark of the covenant law. In
this way the LORD spoke to him.

8 The LORD said to Moses, 2 "Speak to
Aaron and say to him, 'When you set
up the lamps, see that all seven light up
the area in front of the lampstand.' "
3 Aaron did so; he set up the lamps so
that they faced forward on the lampstand, just as the LORD commanded
Moses. 4 This is how the lampstand was
made: It was made of hammered gold—
from its base to its blossoms. The lampstand was made exactly like the pattern
the LORD had shown Moses.
5 The LORD said to Moses: 6 "Take the
Levites from among all the Israelites and
make them ceremonially clean. 7 To purify them, do this: Sprinkle the water of
cleansing on them; then have them shave
their whole bodies and wash their clothes.
And so they will purify themselves. 8 Have
them take a young bull with its grain offering of the finest flour mixed with olive
oil; then you are to take a second young
bull for a sin offering.[b] 9 Bring the Levites
to the front of the tent of meeting and assemble the whole Israelite community.
10 You are to bring the Levites before the
LORD, and the Israelites are to lay their
hands on them. 11 Aaron is to present the
Levites before the LORD as a wave offering from the Israelites, so that they may
be ready to do the work of the LORD.
12 "Then the Levites are to lay their
hands on the heads of the bulls, using
one for a sin offering to the LORD and the
other for a burnt offering, to make atonement for the Levites. 13 Have the Levites
stand in front of Aaron and his sons and
then present them as a wave offering to
the LORD. 14 In this way you are to set the
Levites apart from the other Israelites,
and the Levites will be mine.
15 "After you have purified the Levites
and presented them as a wave offering,
they are to come to do their work at the
tent of meeting. 16 They are the Israelites
who are to be given wholly to me. I have
taken them as my own in place of the
firstborn, the first male offspring from
every Israelite woman. 17 Every firstborn
male in Israel, whether human or animal, is mine. When I struck down all the
firstborn in Egypt, I set them apart for
myself. 18 And I have taken the Levites
in place of all the firstborn sons in Israel. 19 From among all the Israelites, I have
given the Levites as gifts to Aaron and his
sons to do the work at the tent of meeting
on behalf of the Israelites and to make
atonement for them so that no plague
will strike the Israelites when they go
near the sanctuary."
20 Moses, Aaron and the whole Israelite community did with the Levites just
as the LORD commanded Moses. 21 The
Levites purified themselves and washed
their clothes. Then Aaron presented
them as a wave offering before the LORD
and made atonement for them to purify them. 22 After that, the Levites came
to do their work at the tent of meeting
under the supervision of Aaron and his
sons. They did with the Levites just as the
LORD commanded Moses.
23 The LORD said to Moses, 24 "This
applies to the Levites: Men twenty-five
years old or more shall come to take part
in the work at the tent of meeting, 25 but
at the age of fifty, they must retire from
their regular service and work no longer.
26 They may assist their brothers in performing their duties at the tent of meeting, but they themselves must not do the
work. This, then, is how you are to assign
the responsibilities of the Levites."

9 The LORD spoke to Moses in the Desert of Sinai in the first month of the
second year after they came out of Egypt.
He said, 2 "Have the Israelites celebrate

[a] *86* That is, about 3 pounds or about 1.4 kilograms [b] *8* Or *purification offering*; also in verse 12

the Passover at the appointed time. 3Cel-
ebrate it at the appointed time, at twilight
on the fourteenth day of this month, in
accordance with all its rules and regulations."
4So Moses told the Israelites to celebrate the Passover, 5and they did so
in the Desert of Sinai at twilight on the
fourteenth day of the first month. The Israelites did everything just as the LORD
commanded Moses.
6But some of them could not celebrate
the Passover on that day because they
were ceremonially unclean on account
of a dead body. So they came to Moses
and Aaron that same day 7and said to
Moses, "We have become unclean because of a dead body, but why should
we be kept from presenting the LORD's
offering with the other Israelites at the
appointed time?"
8Moses answered them, "Wait until I
find out what the LORD commands concerning you."
9Then the LORD said to Moses, 10"Tell
the Israelites: 'When any of you or your
descendants are unclean because of a
dead body or are away on a journey, they
are still to celebrate the LORD's Passover, 11but they are to do it on the fourteenth day of the second month at twilight. They are to eat the lamb, together
with unleavened bread and bitter herbs.
12They must not leave any of it till morning or break any of its bones. When they
celebrate the Passover, they must follow
all the regulations. 13But if anyone who
is ceremonially clean and not on a journey fails to celebrate the Passover, they
must be cut off from their people for not
presenting the LORD's offering at the appointed time. They will bear the consequences of their sin.
14" 'A foreigner residing among you is
also to celebrate the LORD's Passover in
accordance with its rules and regulations. You must have the same regulations for both the foreigner and the native-born.' "
15On the day the tabernacle, the tent of
the covenant law, was set up, the cloud
covered it. From evening till morning the
cloud above the tabernacle looked like
fire. 16That is how it continued to be; the
cloud covered it, and at night it looked
like fire. 17Whenever the cloud lifted
from above the tent, the Israelites set out;
wherever the cloud settled, the Israelites
encamped. 18At the LORD's command the
Israelites set out, and at his command
they encamped. As long as the cloud
stayed over the tabernacle, they remained
in camp. 19When the cloud remained over
the tabernacle a long time, the Israelites
obeyed the LORD's order and did not set
out. 20Sometimes the cloud was over the
tabernacle only a few days; at the LORD's
command they would encamp, and then
at his command they would set out.
21Sometimes the cloud stayed only from
evening till morning, and when it lifted
in the morning, they set out. Whether
by day or by night, whenever the cloud
lifted, they set out. 22Whether the cloud
stayed over the tabernacle for two days or
a month or a year, the Israelites would remain in camp and not set out; but when
it lifted, they would set out. 23At the
LORD's command they encamped, and at
the LORD's command they set out. They
obeyed the LORD's order, in accordance
with his command through Moses.

10 The LORD said to Moses: 2"Make
two trumpets of hammered silver,
and use them for calling the community together and for having the camps set
out. 3When both are sounded, the whole
community is to assemble before you at
the entrance to the tent of meeting. 4If
only one is sounded, the leaders—the
heads of the clans of Israel—are to assemble before you. 5When a trumpet
blast is sounded, the tribes camping on
the east are to set out. 6At the sounding
of a second blast, the camps on the south
are to set out. The blast will be the signal
for setting out. 7To gather the assembly,
blow the trumpets, but not with the signal for setting out.
8"The sons of Aaron, the priests, are to
blow the trumpets. This is to be a lasting
ordinance for you and the generations
to come. 9When you go into battle in
your own land against an enemy who
is oppressing you, sound a blast on the
trumpets. Then you will be remembered
by the LORD your God and rescued from
your enemies. 10Also at your times of rejoicing—your appointed festivals and
New Moon feasts—you are to sound the
trumpets over your burnt offerings and
fellowship offerings, and they will be a
memorial for you before your God. I am
the LORD your God."

11 On the twentieth day of the second month of the second year, the cloud lifted from above the tabernacle of the covenant law. 12 Then the Israelites set out from the Desert of Sinai and traveled from place to place until the cloud came to rest in the Desert of Paran. 13 They set out, this first time, at the LORD's command through Moses.

14 The divisions of the camp of Judah went first, under their standard. Nahshon son of Amminadab was in command. 15 Nethanel son of Zuar was over the division of the tribe of Issachar, 16 and Eliab son of Helon was over the division of the tribe of Zebulun. 17 Then the tabernacle was taken down, and the Gershonites and Merarites, who carried it, set out.

18 The divisions of the camp of Reuben went next, under their standard. Elizur son of Shedeur was in command. 19 Shelumiel son of Zurishaddai was over the division of the tribe of Simeon, 20 and Eliasaph son of Deuel was over the division of the tribe of Gad. 21 Then the Kohathites set out, carrying the holy things. The tabernacle was to be set up before they arrived.

22 The divisions of the camp of Ephraim went next, under their standard. Elishama son of Ammihud was in command. 23 Gamaliel son of Pedahzur was over the division of the tribe of Manasseh, 24 and Abidan son of Gideoni was over the division of the tribe of Benjamin.

25 Finally, as the rear guard for all the units, the divisions of the camp of Dan set out under their standard. Ahiezer son of Ammishaddai was in command. 26 Pagiel son of Okran was over the division of the tribe of Asher, 27 and Ahira son of Enan was over the division of the tribe of Naphtali. 28 This was the order of march for the Israelite divisions as they set out.

29 Now Moses said to Hobab son of Reuel the Midianite, Moses' father-in-law, "We are setting out for the place about which the LORD said, 'I will give it to you.' Come with us and we will treat you well, for the LORD has promised good things to Israel."

30 He answered, "No, I will not go; I am going back to my own land and my own people."

31 But Moses said, "Please do not leave us. You know where we should camp in the wilderness, and you can be our eyes. 32 If you come with us, we will share with you whatever good things the LORD gives us."

33 So they set out from the mountain of the LORD and traveled for three days. The ark of the covenant of the LORD went before them during those three days to find them a place to rest. 34 The cloud of the LORD was over them by day when they set out from the camp.

35 Whenever the ark set out, Moses said,

"Rise up, LORD!
May your enemies be scattered;
may your foes flee before you."

36 Whenever it came to rest, he said,

"Return, LORD,
to the countless thousands of
Israel."

11 Now the people complained about their hardships in the hearing of the LORD, and when he heard them his anger was aroused. Then fire from the LORD burned among them and consumed some of the outskirts of the camp. 2 When the people cried out to Moses, he prayed to the LORD and the fire died down. 3 So that place was called Taberah,[a] because fire from the LORD had burned among them.

4 The rabble with them began to crave other food, and again the Israelites started wailing and said, "If only we had meat to eat! 5 We remember the fish we ate in Egypt at no cost—also the cucumbers, melons, leeks, onions and garlic. 6 But now we have lost our appetite; we never see anything but this manna!"

7 The manna was like coriander seed and looked like resin. 8 The people went around gathering it, and then ground it in a hand mill or crushed it in a mortar. They cooked it in a pot or made it into loaves. And it tasted like something made with olive oil. 9 When the dew settled on the camp at night, the manna also came down.

10 Moses heard the people of every family wailing at the entrance to their tents. The LORD became exceedingly angry,

[a] 3 *Taberah* means *burning.*

and Moses was troubled. [11]He asked the LORD, "Why have you brought this trouble on your servant? What have I done to displease you that you put the burden of all these people on me? [12]Did I conceive all these people? Did I give them birth? Why do you tell me to carry them in my arms, as a nurse carries an infant, to the land you promised on oath to their ancestors? [13]Where can I get meat for all these people? They keep wailing to me, 'Give us meat to eat!' [14]I cannot carry all these people by myself; the burden is too heavy for me. [15]If this is how you are going to treat me, please go ahead and kill me — if I have found favor in your eyes — and do not let me face my own ruin."

[16]The LORD said to Moses: "Bring me seventy of Israel's elders who are known to you as leaders and officials among the people. Have them come to the tent of meeting, that they may stand there with you. [17]I will come down and speak with you there, and I will take some of the power of the Spirit that is on you and put it on them. They will share the burden of the people with you so that you will not have to carry it alone.

[18]"Tell the people: 'Consecrate yourselves in preparation for tomorrow, when you will eat meat. The LORD heard you when you wailed, "If only we had meat to eat! We were better off in Egypt!" Now the LORD will give you meat, and you will eat it. [19]You will not eat it for just one day, or two days, or five, ten or twenty days, [20]but for a whole month — until it comes out of your nostrils and you loathe it — because you have rejected the LORD, who is among you, and have wailed before him, saying, "Why did we ever leave Egypt?"'"

[21]But Moses said, "Here I am among six hundred thousand men on foot, and you say, 'I will give them meat to eat for a whole month!' [22]Would they have enough if flocks and herds were slaughtered for them? Would they have enough if all the fish in the sea were caught for them?"

[23]The LORD answered Moses, "Is the LORD's arm too short? Now you will see whether or not what I say will come true for you."

[24]So Moses went out and told the people what the LORD had said. He brought together seventy of their elders and had them stand around the tent. [25]Then the LORD came down in the cloud and spoke with him, and he took some of the power of the Spirit that was on him and put it on the seventy elders. When the Spirit rested on them, they prophesied — but did not do so again.

[26]However, two men, whose names were Eldad and Medad, had remained in the camp. They were listed among the elders, but did not go out to the tent. Yet the Spirit also rested on them, and they prophesied in the camp. [27]A young man ran and told Moses, "Eldad and Medad are prophesying in the camp."

[28]Joshua son of Nun, who had been Moses' aide since youth, spoke up and said, "Moses, my lord, stop them!"

[29]But Moses replied, "Are you jealous for my sake? I wish that all the LORD's people were prophets and that the LORD would put his Spirit on them!" [30]Then Moses and the elders of Israel returned to the camp.

[31]Now a wind went out from the LORD and drove quail in from the sea. It scattered them up to two cubits[a] deep all around the camp, as far as a day's walk in any direction. [32]All that day and night and all the next day the people went out and gathered quail. No one gathered less than ten homers.[b] Then they spread them out all around the camp. [33]But while the meat was still between their teeth and before it could be consumed, the anger of the LORD burned against the people, and he struck them with a severe plague. [34]Therefore the place was named Kibroth Hattaavah,[c] because there they buried the people who had craved other food.

[35]From Kibroth Hattaavah the people traveled to Hazeroth and stayed there.

12 Miriam and Aaron began to talk against Moses because of his Cushite wife, for he had married a Cushite. [2]"Has the LORD spoken only through Moses?" they asked. "Hasn't he also spoken through us?" And the LORD heard this.

[3](Now Moses was a very humble man, more humble than anyone else on the face of the earth.)

[a] *31* That is, about 3 feet or about 90 centimeters [b] *32* That is, possibly about 1 3/4 tons or about 1.6 metric tons [c] *34* *Kibroth Hattaavah* means *graves of craving.*

4 At once the LORD said to Moses, Aaron and Miriam, "Come out to the tent of
meeting, all three of you." So the three
of them went out. 5 Then the LORD came
down in a pillar of cloud; he stood at the
entrance to the tent and summoned Aaron and Miriam. When the two of them
stepped forward, 6 he said, "Listen to my
words:

"When there is a prophet among you,
  I, the LORD, reveal myself to them in visions,
  I speak to them in dreams.
7 But this is not true of my servant Moses;
  he is faithful in all my house.
8 With him I speak face to face,
  clearly and not in riddles;
  he sees the form of the LORD.
Why then were you not afraid
  to speak against my servant Moses?"

9 The anger of the LORD burned against
them, and he left them.
10 When the cloud lifted from above
the tent, Miriam's skin was leprous[a]—it
became as white as snow. Aaron turned
toward her and saw that she had a defiling skin disease, 11 and he said to Moses,
"Please, my lord, I ask you not to hold
against us the sin we have so foolish-
ly committed. 12 Do not let her be like a
stillborn infant coming from its mother's
womb with its flesh half eaten away."
13 So Moses cried out to the LORD,
"Please, God, heal her!"
14 The LORD replied to Moses, "If her
father had spit in her face, would she not
have been in disgrace for seven days?
Confine her outside the camp for seven
days; after that she can be brought back."
15 So Miriam was confined outside the
camp for seven days, and the people did
not move on till she was brought back.

16 After that, the people left Hazeroth
and encamped in the Desert of Paran.

13 The LORD said to Moses, 2 "Send
some men to explore the land of Canaan, which I am giving to the Israelites.
From each ancestral tribe send one of its
leaders."
3 So at the LORD's command Moses
sent them out from the Desert of Paran.
All of them were leaders of the Israelites.
4 These are their names:

from the tribe of Reuben, Shammua son of Zakkur;
5 from the tribe of Simeon, Shaphat son of Hori;
6 from the tribe of Judah, Caleb son of Jephunneh;
7 from the tribe of Issachar, Igal son of Joseph;
8 from the tribe of Ephraim, Hoshea son of Nun;
9 from the tribe of Benjamin, Palti son of Raphu;
10 from the tribe of Zebulun, Gaddiel son of Sodi;
11 from the tribe of Manasseh (a tribe of Joseph), Gaddi son of Susi;
12 from the tribe of Dan, Ammiel son of Gemalli;
13 from the tribe of Asher, Sethur son of Michael;
14 from the tribe of Naphtali, Nahbi son of Vophsi;
15 from the tribe of Gad, Geuel son of Maki.

16 These are the names of the men Moses
sent to explore the land. (Moses gave Hoshea son of Nun the name Joshua.)
17 When Moses sent them to explore
Canaan, he said, "Go up through the Negev and on into the hill country. 18 See
what the land is like and whether the
people who live there are strong or weak,
few or many. 19 What kind of land do they
live in? Is it good or bad? What kind of
towns do they live in? Are they unwalled
or fortified? 20 How is the soil? Is it fertile
or poor? Are there trees in it or not? Do
your best to bring back some of the fruit
of the land." (It was the season for the
first ripe grapes.)
21 So they went up and explored the
land from the Desert of Zin as far as Rehob, toward Lebo Hamath. 22 They went
up through the Negev and came to Hebron, where Ahiman, Sheshai and Talmai, the descendants of Anak, lived. (Hebron had been built seven years before
Zoan in Egypt.) 23 When they reached the
Valley of Eshkol,[b] they cut off a branch
bearing a single cluster of grapes. Two of
them carried it on a pole between them,
along with some pomegranates and figs.

[a] *10* The Hebrew for *leprous* was used for various diseases affecting the skin. [b] *23* *Eshkol* means *cluster*; also in verse 24.

24That place was called the Valley of Eshkol because of the cluster of grapes the
Israelites cut off there. 25At the end of
forty days they returned from exploring
the land.

26They came back to Moses and Aaron and the whole Israelite community
at Kadesh in the Desert of Paran. There
they reported to them and to the whole
assembly and showed them the fruit
of the land. 27They gave Moses this account: "We went into the land to which
you sent us, and it does flow with milk
and honey! Here is its fruit. 28But the
people who live there are powerful, and
the cities are fortified and very large. We
even saw descendants of Anak there.
29The Amalekites live in the Negev; the
Hittites, Jebusites and Amorites live in
the hill country; and the Canaanites live
near the sea and along the Jordan."

30Then Caleb silenced the people before Moses and said, "We should go up
and take possession of the land, for we
can certainly do it."

31But the men who had gone up with
him said, "We can't attack those people;
they are stronger than we are." 32And
they spread among the Israelites a bad
report about the land they had explored.
They said, "The land we explored devours those living in it. All the people we
saw there are of great size. 33We saw the
Nephilim there (the descendants of Anak
come from the Nephilim). We seemed
like grasshoppers in our own eyes, and
we looked the same to them."

14 That night all the members of the
community raised their voices and
wept aloud. 2All the Israelites grumbled against Moses and Aaron, and the
whole assembly said to them, "If only we
had died in Egypt! Or in this wilderness!
3Why is the LORD bringing us to this
land only to let us fall by the sword? Our
wives and children will be taken as plunder. Wouldn't it be better for us to go back
to Egypt?" 4And they said to each other,
"We should choose a leader and go back
to Egypt."

5Then Moses and Aaron fell facedown
in front of the whole Israelite assembly gathered there. 6Joshua son of Nun
and Caleb son of Jephunneh, who were
among those who had explored the land,
tore their clothes 7and said to the entire
Israelite assembly, "The land we passed
through and explored is exceedingly
good. 8If the LORD is pleased with us, he
will lead us into that land, a land flowing
with milk and honey, and will give it to
us. 9Only do not rebel against the LORD.
And do not be afraid of the people of
the land, because we will devour them.
Their protection is gone, but the LORD is
with us. Do not be afraid of them."

10But the whole assembly talked about
stoning them. Then the glory of the LORD
appeared at the tent of meeting to all the
Israelites. 11The LORD said to Moses,
"How long will these people treat me
with contempt? How long will they refuse to believe in me, in spite of all the
signs I have performed among them? 12I
will strike them down with a plague and
destroy them, but I will make you into a
nation greater and stronger than they."

13Moses said to the LORD, "Then the
Egyptians will hear about it! By your
power you brought these people up from
among them. 14And they will tell the inhabitants of this land about it. They have
already heard that you, LORD, are with
these people and that you, LORD, have
been seen face to face, that your cloud
stays over them, and that you go before
them in a pillar of cloud by day and a pillar of fire by night. 15If you put all these
people to death, leaving none alive,
the nations who have heard this report
about you will say, 16'The LORD was not
able to bring these people into the land
he promised them on oath, so he slaughtered them in the wilderness.'

17"Now may the Lord's strength be displayed, just as you have declared: 18'The
LORD is slow to anger, abounding in love
and forgiving sin and rebellion. Yet he
does not leave the guilty unpunished; he
punishes the children for the sin of the
parents to the third and fourth generation.' 19In accordance with your great
love, forgive the sin of these people, just
as you have pardoned them from the
time they left Egypt until now."

20The LORD replied, "I have forgiven
them, as you asked. 21Nevertheless, as
surely as I live and as surely as the glory of the LORD fills the whole earth, 22not
one of those who saw my glory and the
signs I performed in Egypt and in the
wilderness but who disobeyed me and
tested me ten times — 23not one of them
will ever see the land I promised on

oath to their ancestors. No one who has
treated me with contempt will ever see
it. 24 But because my servant Caleb has
a different spirit and follows me wholeheartedly, I will bring him into the land
he went to, and his descendants will inherit it. 25 Since the Amalekites and the
Canaanites are living in the valleys, turn
back tomorrow and set out toward the
desert along the route to the Red Sea.[a]"
26 The LORD said to Moses and Aaron:
27 "How long will this wicked community grumble against me? I have heard
the complaints of these grumbling Israelites. 28 So tell them, 'As surely as I
live, declares the LORD, I will do to you
the very thing I heard you say: 29 In this
wilderness your bodies will fall—every
one of you twenty years old or more who
was counted in the census and who has
grumbled against me. 30 Not one of you
will enter the land I swore with uplifted
hand to make your home, except Caleb son of Jephunneh and Joshua son of
Nun. 31 As for your children that you said
would be taken as plunder, I will bring
them in to enjoy the land you have rejected. 32 But as for you, your bodies will fall
in this wilderness. 33 Your children will
be shepherds here for forty years, suffering for your unfaithfulness, until the
last of your bodies lies in the wilderness.
34 For forty years—one year for each of
the forty days you explored the land—
you will suffer for your sins and know
what it is like to have me against you.' 35 I,
the LORD, have spoken, and I will surely do these things to this whole wicked
community, which has banded together
against me. They will meet their end in
this wilderness; here they will die."
36 So the men Moses had sent to explore the land, who returned and made
the whole community grumble against
him by spreading a bad report about it—
37 these men who were responsible for
spreading the bad report about the land
were struck down and died of a plague
before the LORD. 38 Of the men who went
to explore the land, only Joshua son of
Nun and Caleb son of Jephunneh survived.
39 When Moses reported this to all the
Israelites, they mourned bitterly. 40 Early the next morning they set out for the
highest point in the hill country, saying, "Now we are ready to go up to the
land the LORD promised. Surely we have
sinned!"
41 But Moses said, "Why are you dis-
obeying the LORD's command? This will
not succeed! 42 Do not go up, because the
LORD is not with you. You will be defeated by your enemies, 43 for the Amalekites
and the Canaanites will face you there.
Because you have turned away from the
LORD, he will not be with you and you
will fall by the sword."
44 Nevertheless, in their presumption
they went up toward the highest point
in the hill country, though neither Moses nor the ark of the LORD's covenant
moved from the camp. 45 Then the Amalekites and the Canaanites who lived
in that hill country came down and attacked them and beat them down all the
way to Hormah.
15 The LORD said to Moses, 2 "Speak to
the Israelites and say to them: 'After
you enter the land I am giving you as a
home 3 and you present to the LORD food
offerings from the herd or the flock, as an
aroma pleasing to the LORD—whether
burnt offerings or sacrifices, for special
vows or freewill offerings or festival offerings— 4 then the person who brings
an offering shall present to the LORD a
grain offering of a tenth of an ephah[b] of
the finest flour mixed with a quarter of a
hin[c] of olive oil. 5 With each lamb for the
burnt offering or the sacrifice, prepare
a quarter of a hin of wine as a drink offering.
6 " 'With a ram prepare a grain offering
of two-tenths of an ephah[d] of the finest
flour mixed with a third of a hin[e] of olive oil, 7 and a third of a hin of wine as a
drink offering. Offer it as an aroma pleasing to the LORD.
8 " 'When you prepare a young bull as
a burnt offering or sacrifice, for a special
vow or a fellowship offering to the LORD,
9 bring with the bull a grain offering of
three-tenths of an ephah[f] of the finest
flour mixed with half a hin[g] of olive oil,
10 and also bring half a hin of wine as a

[a] 25 Or *the Sea of Reeds* [b] 4 That is, probably about 3 1/2 pounds or about 1.6 kilograms [c] 4 That is, about 1 quart or about 1 liter; also in verse 5 [d] 6 That is, probably about 7 pounds or about 3.2 kilograms [e] 6 That is, about 1 1/3 quarts or about 1.3 liters; also in verse 7 [f] 9 That is, probably about 11 pounds or about 5 kilograms [g] 9 That is, about 2 quarts or about 1.9 liters; also in verse 10

drink offering. This will be a food offering, an aroma pleasing to the LORD.
11 Each bull or ram, each lamb or young
goat, is to be prepared in this manner.
12 Do this for each one, for as many as
you prepare.
13 " 'Everyone who is native-born must
do these things in this way when they
present a food offering as an aroma
pleasing to the LORD. 14 For the generations to come, whenever a foreigner or
anyone else living among you presents
a food offering as an aroma pleasing to
the LORD, they must do exactly as you
do. 15 The community is to have the
same rules for you and for the foreigner
residing among you; this is a lasting ordinance for the generations to come. You
and the foreigner shall be the same before the LORD: 16 The same laws and regulations will apply both to you and to the
foreigner residing among you.' "
17 The LORD said to Moses, 18 "Speak to
the Israelites and say to them: 'When you
enter the land to which I am taking you
19 and you eat the food of the land, present a portion as an offering to the LORD.
20 Present a loaf from the first of your
ground meal and present it as an offering
from the threshing floor. 21 Throughout
the generations to come you are to give
this offering to the LORD from the first of
your ground meal.
22 " 'Now if you as a community unintentionally fail to keep any of these commands the LORD gave Moses— 23 any of
the LORD's commands to you through
him, from the day the LORD gave them
and continuing through the generations
to come— 24 and if this is done unintentionally without the community being
aware of it, then the whole community is
to offer a young bull for a burnt offering as
an aroma pleasing to the LORD, along with
its prescribed grain offering and drink offering, and a male goat for a sin offering.[a]
25 The priest is to make atonement for the
whole Israelite community, and they will
be forgiven, for it was not intentional and
they have presented to the LORD for their
wrong a food offering and a sin offering.
26 The whole Israelite community and the
foreigners residing among them will be
forgiven, because all the people were involved in the unintentional wrong.
27 " 'But if just one person sins unintentionally, that person must bring a year-
old female goat for a sin offering. 28 The
priest is to make atonement before the
LORD for the one who erred by sinning
unintentionally, and when atonement
has been made, that person will be forgiven. 29 One and the same law applies
to everyone who sins unintentionally,
whether a native-born Israelite or a foreigner residing among you.
30 " 'But anyone who sins defiantly,
whether native-born or foreigner, blasphemes the LORD and must be cut off
from the people of Israel. 31 Because they
have despised the LORD's word and broken his commands, they must surely be
cut off; their guilt remains on them.' "
32 While the Israelites were in the wilderness, a man was found gathering
wood on the Sabbath day. 33 Those who
found him gathering wood brought him
to Moses and Aaron and the whole assembly, 34 and they kept him in custody,
because it was not clear what should be
done to him. 35 Then the LORD said to
Moses, "The man must die. The whole
assembly must stone him outside the
camp." 36 So the assembly took him outside the camp and stoned him to death,
as the LORD commanded Moses.
37 The LORD said to Moses, 38 "Speak to
the Israelites and say to them: 'Throughout the generations to come you are to
make tassels on the corners of your garments, with a blue cord on each tassel.
39 You will have these tassels to look at
and so you will remember all the commands of the LORD, that you may obey
them and not prostitute yourselves
by chasing after the lusts of your own
hearts and eyes. 40 Then you will remember to obey all my commands and will
be consecrated to your God. 41 I am the
LORD your God, who brought you out of
Egypt to be your God. I am the LORD your
God.' "

16 Korah son of Izhar, the son of Kohath, the son of Levi, and certain
Reubenites—Dathan and Abiram, sons
of Eliab, and On son of Peleth—became
insolent[b] 2 and rose up against Moses.
With them were 250 Israelite men, well-
known community leaders who had
been appointed members of the council.

[a] 24 Or *purification offering*; also in verses 25 and 27
[b] 1 Or *Peleth—took men*

3 They came as a group to oppose Moses
and Aaron and said to them, "You have
gone too far! The whole community is
holy, every one of them, and the LORD
is with them. Why then do you set yourselves above the LORD's assembly?"
4 When Moses heard this, he fell facedown. 5 Then he said to Korah and all
his followers: "In the morning the LORD
will show who belongs to him and who
is holy, and he will have that person
come near him. The man he chooses he
will cause to come near him. 6 You, Korah, and all your followers are to do this:
Take censers 7 and tomorrow put burning coals and incense in them before the
LORD. The man the LORD chooses will
be the one who is holy. You Levites have
gone too far!"
8 Moses also said to Korah, "Now listen,
you Levites! 9 Isn't it enough for you that
the God of Israel has separated you from
the rest of the Israelite community and
brought you near himself to do the work
at the LORD's tabernacle and to stand
before the community and minister to
them? 10 He has brought you and all your
fellow Levites near himself, but now you
are trying to get the priesthood too. 11 It
is against the LORD that you and all your
followers have banded together. Who is
Aaron that you should grumble against
him?"
12 Then Moses summoned Dathan
and Abiram, the sons of Eliab. But they
said, "We will not come! 13 Isn't it enough
that you have brought us up out of a land
flowing with milk and honey to kill us in
the wilderness? And now you also want
to lord it over us! 14 Moreover, you haven't
brought us into a land flowing with milk
and honey or given us an inheritance
of fields and vineyards. Do you want to
treat these men like slaves[a]? No, we will
not come!"
15 Then Moses became very angry and
said to the LORD, "Do not accept their
offering. I have not taken so much as a
donkey from them, nor have I wronged
any of them."
16 Moses said to Korah, "You and all
your followers are to appear before the
LORD tomorrow—you and they and
Aaron. 17 Each man is to take his censer
and put incense in it—250 censers in
all—and present it before the LORD. You
and Aaron are to present your censers
also." 18 So each of them took his censer, put burning coals and incense in it,
and stood with Moses and Aaron at the
entrance to the tent of meeting. 19 When
Korah had gathered all his followers in
opposition to them at the entrance to
the tent of meeting, the glory of the LORD
appeared to the entire assembly. 20 The
LORD said to Moses and Aaron, 21 "Separate yourselves from this assembly so I
can put an end to them at once."
22 But Moses and Aaron fell facedown
and cried out, "O God, the God who gives
breath to all living things, will you be angry with the entire assembly when only
one man sins?"
23 Then the LORD said to Moses, 24 "Say
to the assembly, 'Move away from the
tents of Korah, Dathan and Abiram.'"
25 Moses got up and went to Dathan and
Abiram, and the elders of Israel followed
him. 26 He warned the assembly, "Move
back from the tents of these wicked men!
Do not touch anything belonging to
them, or you will be swept away because
of all their sins." 27 So they moved away
from the tents of Korah, Dathan and
Abiram. Dathan and Abiram had come
out and were standing with their wives,
children and little ones at the entrances
to their tents.
28 Then Moses said, "This is how you
will know that the LORD has sent me to
do all these things and that it was not my
idea: 29 If these men die a natural death
and suffer the fate of all mankind, then
the LORD has not sent me. 30 But if the
LORD brings about something totally
new, and the earth opens its mouth and
swallows them, with everything that belongs to them, and they go down alive
into the realm of the dead, then you will
know that these men have treated the
LORD with contempt."
31 As soon as he finished saying all this,
the ground under them split apart 32 and
the earth opened its mouth and swallowed them and their households, and
all those associated with Korah, together with their possessions. 33 They went
down alive into the realm of the dead,
with everything they owned; the earth
closed over them, and they perished

[a] *14* Or *to deceive these men*; Hebrew *Will you gouge out the eyes of these men*

and were gone from the community.
34 At their cries, all the Israelites around
them fled, shouting, "The earth is going
to swallow us too!"
35 And fire came out from the LORD and
consumed the 250 men who were offering the incense.
36 The LORD said to Moses, 37 "Tell Eleazar son of Aaron, the priest, to remove the
censers from the charred remains and
scatter the coals some distance away, for
the censers are holy— 38 the censers of
the men who sinned at the cost of their
lives. Hammer the censers into sheets to
overlay the altar, for they were presented
before the LORD and have become holy.
Let them be a sign to the Israelites."
39 So Eleazar the priest collected the
bronze censers brought by those who
had been burned to death, and he had
them hammered out to overlay the altar, 40 as the LORD directed him through
Moses. This was to remind the Israelites
that no one except a descendant of Aaron should come to burn incense before
the LORD, or he would become like Korah
and his followers.
41 The next day the whole Israelite
community grumbled against Moses
and Aaron. "You have killed the LORD's
people," they said.
42 But when the assembly gathered
in opposition to Moses and Aaron and
turned toward the tent of meeting, suddenly the cloud covered it and the glory of the LORD appeared. 43 Then Moses
and Aaron went to the front of the tent of
meeting, 44 and the LORD said to Moses,
45 "Get away from this assembly so I can
put an end to them at once." And they fell
facedown.
46 Then Moses said to Aaron, "Take
your censer and put incense in it, along
with burning coals from the altar, and
hurry to the assembly to make atonement for them. Wrath has come out from
the LORD; the plague has started." 47 So
Aaron did as Moses said, and ran into
the midst of the assembly. The plague
had already started among the people,
but Aaron offered the incense and made
atonement for them. 48 He stood between
the living and the dead, and the plague
stopped. 49 But 14,700 people died from
the plague, in addition to those who
had died because of Korah. 50 Then Aaron returned to Moses at the entrance to
the tent of meeting, for the plague had
stopped.[a]
17[b] The LORD said to Moses, 2 "Speak to
the Israelites and get twelve staffs
from them, one from the leader of each
of their ancestral tribes. Write the name
of each man on his staff. 3 On the staff of
Levi write Aaron's name, for there must
be one staff for the head of each ancestral
tribe. 4 Place them in the tent of meeting
in front of the ark of the covenant law,
where I meet with you. 5 The staff belonging to the man I choose will sprout, and
I will rid myself of this constant grumbling against you by the Israelites."
6 So Moses spoke to the Israelites, and
their leaders gave him twelve staffs, one
for the leader of each of their ancestral
tribes, and Aaron's staff was among
them. 7 Moses placed the staffs before the
LORD in the tent of the covenant law.
8 The next day Moses entered the tent
and saw that Aaron's staff, which represented the tribe of Levi, had not only
sprouted but had budded, blossomed
and produced almonds. 9 Then Moses
brought out all the staffs from the LORD's
presence to all the Israelites. They looked
at them, and each of the leaders took his
own staff.
10 The LORD said to Moses, "Put back
Aaron's staff in front of the ark of the
covenant law, to be kept as a sign to the
rebellious. This will put an end to their
grumbling against me, so that they will
not die." 11 Moses did just as the LORD
commanded him.
12 The Israelites said to Moses, "We will
die! We are lost, we are all lost! 13 Anyone
who even comes near the tabernacle of
the LORD will die. Are we all going to
die?"
18 The LORD said to Aaron, "You, your
sons and your family are to bear
the responsibility for offenses connected with the sanctuary, and you and your
sons alone are to bear the responsibility
for offenses connected with the priesthood. 2 Bring your fellow Levites from
your ancestral tribe to join you and assist you when you and your sons minister before the tent of the covenant law.
3 They are to be responsible to you and

[a] *50* In Hebrew texts 16:36-50 is numbered 17:1-15. [b] In Hebrew texts 17:1-13 is numbered 17:16-28.

are to perform all the duties of the tent,
but they must not go near the furnishings of the sanctuary or the altar. Otherwise both they and you will die. 4 They
are to join you and be responsible for the
care of the tent of meeting — all the work
at the tent — and no one else may come
near where you are.
5 "You are to be responsible for the care
of the sanctuary and the altar, so that my
wrath will not fall on the Israelites again.
6 I myself have selected your fellow Levites from among the Israelites as a gift
to you, dedicated to the LORD to do the
work at the tent of meeting. 7 But only
you and your sons may serve as priests in
connection with everything at the altar
and inside the curtain. I am giving you
the service of the priesthood as a gift.
Anyone else who comes near the sanctuary is to be put to death."
8 Then the LORD said to Aaron, "I myself have put you in charge of the offerings presented to me; all the holy offerings the Israelites give me I give to you
and your sons as your portion, your perpetual share. 9 You are to have the part of
the most holy offerings that is kept from
the fire. From all the gifts they bring me
as most holy offerings, whether grain or
sin[a] or guilt offerings, that part belongs
to you and your sons. 10 Eat it as something most holy; every male shall eat it.
You must regard it as holy.
11 "This also is yours: whatever is set
aside from the gifts of all the wave offerings of the Israelites. I give this to you and
your sons and daughters as your perpetual share. Everyone in your household
who is ceremonially clean may eat it.
12 "I give you all the finest olive oil and
all the finest new wine and grain they
give the LORD as the firstfruits of their
harvest. 13 All the land's firstfruits that
they bring to the LORD will be yours. Everyone in your household who is ceremonially clean may eat it.
14 "Everything in Israel that is devoted[b]
to the LORD is yours. 15 The first offspring
of every womb, both human and animal,
that is offered to the LORD is yours. But
you must redeem every firstborn son and
every firstborn male of unclean animals.
16 When they are a month old, you must
redeem them at the redemption price set
at five shekels[c] of silver, according to the
sanctuary shekel, which weighs twenty
gerahs.
17 "But you must not redeem the firstborn of a cow, a sheep or a goat; they are
holy. Splash their blood against the altar and burn their fat as a food offering,
an aroma pleasing to the LORD. 18 Their
meat is to be yours, just as the breast of
the wave offering and the right thigh are
yours. 19 Whatever is set aside from the
holy offerings the Israelites present to
the LORD I give to you and your sons and
daughters as your perpetual share. It is
an everlasting covenant of salt before the
LORD for both you and your offspring."
20 The LORD said to Aaron, "You will
have no inheritance in their land, nor
will you have any share among them;
I am your share and your inheritance
among the Israelites.
21 "I give to the Levites all the tithes in
Israel as their inheritance in return for
the work they do while serving at the tent
of meeting. 22 From now on the Israelites
must not go near the tent of meeting, or
they will bear the consequences of their
sin and will die. 23 It is the Levites who
are to do the work at the tent of meeting
and bear the responsibility for any offenses they commit against it. This is a
lasting ordinance for the generations to
come. They will receive no inheritance
among the Israelites. 24 Instead, I give to
the Levites as their inheritance the tithes
that the Israelites present as an offering
to the LORD. That is why I said concerning them: 'They will have no inheritance
among the Israelites.' "
25 The LORD said to Moses, 26 "Speak to
the Levites and say to them: 'When you
receive from the Israelites the tithe I give
you as your inheritance, you must present a tenth of that tithe as the LORD's offering. 27 Your offering will be reckoned
to you as grain from the threshing floor
or juice from the winepress. 28 In this
way you also will present an offering to
the LORD from all the tithes you receive
from the Israelites. From these tithes
you must give the LORD's portion to Aaron the priest. 29 You must present as the
LORD's portion the best and holiest part
of everything given to you.'
30 "Say to the Levites: 'When you pre-

[a] 9 Or *purification* [b] 14 The Hebrew term refers to the irrevocable giving over of things or persons to the LORD. [c] 16 That is, about 2 ounces or about 58 grams

sent the best part, it will be reckoned to you as the product of the threshing floor or the winepress. 31 You and your households may eat the rest of it anywhere, for it is your wages for your work at the tent of meeting. 32 By presenting the best part of it you will not be guilty in this matter; then you will not defile the holy offerings of the Israelites, and you will not die.' "

19 The LORD said to Moses and Aaron: 2 "This is a requirement of the law that the LORD has commanded: Tell the Israelites to bring you a red heifer without defect or blemish and that has never been under a yoke. 3 Give it to Eleazar the priest; it is to be taken outside the camp and slaughtered in his presence. 4 Then Eleazar the priest is to take some of its blood on his finger and sprinkle it seven times toward the front of the tent of meeting. 5 While he watches, the heifer is to be burned — its hide, flesh, blood and intestines. 6 The priest is to take some cedar wood, hyssop and scarlet wool and throw them onto the burning heifer. 7 After that, the priest must wash his clothes and bathe himself with water. He may then come into the camp, but he will be ceremonially unclean till evening. 8 The man who burns it must also wash his clothes and bathe with water, and he too will be unclean till evening.

9 "A man who is clean shall gather up the ashes of the heifer and put them in a ceremonially clean place outside the camp. They are to be kept by the Israelite community for use in the water of cleansing; it is for purification from sin. 10 The man who gathers up the ashes of the heifer must also wash his clothes, and he too will be unclean till evening. This will be a lasting ordinance both for the Israelites and for the foreigners residing among them.

11 "Whoever touches a human corpse will be unclean for seven days. 12 They must purify themselves with the water on the third day and on the seventh day; then they will be clean. But if they do not purify themselves on the third and seventh days, they will not be clean. 13 If they fail to purify themselves after touching a human corpse, they defile the LORD's tabernacle. They must be cut off from Israel. Because the water of cleansing has not been sprinkled on them, they are unclean; their uncleanness remains on them.

14 "This is the law that applies when a person dies in a tent: Anyone who enters the tent and anyone who is in it will be unclean for seven days, 15 and every open container without a lid fastened on it will be unclean.

16 "Anyone out in the open who touches someone who has been killed with a sword or someone who has died a natural death, or anyone who touches a human bone or a grave, will be unclean for seven days.

17 "For the unclean person, put some ashes from the burned purification offering into a jar and pour fresh water over them. 18 Then a man who is ceremonially clean is to take some hyssop, dip it in the water and sprinkle the tent and all the furnishings and the people who were there. He must also sprinkle anyone who has touched a human bone or a grave or anyone who has been killed or anyone who has died a natural death. 19 The man who is clean is to sprinkle those who are unclean on the third and seventh days, and on the seventh day he is to purify them. Those who are being cleansed must wash their clothes and bathe with water, and that evening they will be clean. 20 But if those who are unclean do not purify themselves, they must be cut off from the community, because they have defiled the sanctuary of the LORD. The water of cleansing has not been sprinkled on them, and they are unclean. 21 This is a lasting ordinance for them.

"The man who sprinkles the water of cleansing must also wash his clothes, and anyone who touches the water of cleansing will be unclean till evening. 22 Anything that an unclean person touches becomes unclean, and anyone who touches it becomes unclean till evening."

20 In the first month the whole Israelite community arrived at the Desert of Zin, and they stayed at Kadesh. There Miriam died and was buried.

2 Now there was no water for the community, and the people gathered in opposition to Moses and Aaron. 3 They quarreled with Moses and said, "If only we had died when our brothers fell dead

before the LORD! [4]Why did you bring the LORD's community into this wilderness, that we and our livestock should die here? [5]Why did you bring us up out of Egypt to this terrible place? It has no grain or figs, grapevines or pomegranates. And there is no water to drink!"

[6]Moses and Aaron went from the assembly to the entrance to the tent of meeting and fell facedown, and the glory of the LORD appeared to them. [7]The LORD said to Moses, [8]"Take the staff, and you and your brother Aaron gather the assembly together. Speak to that rock before their eyes and it will pour out its water. You will bring water out of the rock for the community so they and their livestock can drink."

[9]So Moses took the staff from the LORD's presence, just as he commanded him. [10]He and Aaron gathered the assembly together in front of the rock and Moses said to them, "Listen, you rebels, must we bring you water out of this rock?" [11]Then Moses raised his arm and struck the rock twice with his staff. Water gushed out, and the community and their livestock drank.

[12]But the LORD said to Moses and Aaron, "Because you did not trust in me enough to honor me as holy in the sight of the Israelites, you will not bring this community into the land I give them."

[13]These were the waters of Meribah,[a] where the Israelites quarreled with the LORD and where he was proved holy among them.

[14]Moses sent messengers from Kadesh to the king of Edom, saying:

"This is what your brother Israel says: You know about all the hardships that have come on us. [15]Our ancestors went down into Egypt, and we lived there many years. The Egyptians mistreated us and our ancestors, [16]but when we cried out to the LORD, he heard our cry and sent an angel and brought us out of Egypt.

"Now we are here at Kadesh, a town on the edge of your territory. [17]Please let us pass through your country. We will not go through any field or vineyard, or drink water from any well. We will travel along the King's Highway and not turn to the right or to the left until we have passed through your territory."

[18]But Edom answered:

"You may not pass through here; if you try, we will march out and attack you with the sword."

[19]The Israelites replied:

"We will go along the main road, and if we or our livestock drink any of your water, we will pay for it. We only want to pass through on foot—nothing else."

[20]Again they answered:

"You may not pass through."

Then Edom came out against them with a large and powerful army. [21]Since Edom refused to let them go through their territory, Israel turned away from them.

[22]The whole Israelite community set out from Kadesh and came to Mount Hor. [23]At Mount Hor, near the border of Edom, the LORD said to Moses and Aaron, [24]"Aaron will be gathered to his people. He will not enter the land I give the Israelites, because both of you rebelled against my command at the waters of Meribah. [25]Get Aaron and his son Eleazar and take them up Mount Hor. [26]Remove Aaron's garments and put them on his son Eleazar, for Aaron will be gathered to his people; he will die there."

[27]Moses did as the LORD commanded: They went up Mount Hor in the sight of the whole community. [28]Moses removed Aaron's garments and put them on his son Eleazar. And Aaron died there on top of the mountain. Then Moses and Eleazar came down from the mountain, [29]and when the whole community learned that Aaron had died, all the Israelites mourned for him thirty days.

21 When the Canaanite king of Arad, who lived in the Negev, heard that Israel was coming along the road to Atharim, he attacked the Israelites and captured some of them. [2]Then Israel made this vow to the LORD: "If you will deliver these people into our hands, we will

[a] *13 Meribah* means *quarreling.*

totally destroy[a] their cities." 3The LORD
listened to Israel's plea and gave the Canaanites over to them. They completely
destroyed them and their towns; so the
place was named Hormah.[b]

4They traveled from Mount Hor along
the route to the Red Sea,[c] to go around
Edom. But the people grew impatient on
the way; 5they spoke against God and
against Moses, and said, "Why have you
brought us up out of Egypt to die in the
wilderness? There is no bread! There is
no water! And we detest this miserable
food!"
6Then the LORD sent venomous snakes
among them; they bit the people and
many Israelites died. 7The people came
to Moses and said, "We sinned when we
spoke against the LORD and against you.
Pray that the LORD will take the snakes
away from us." So Moses prayed for the
people.
8The LORD said to Moses, "Make a
snake and put it up on a pole; anyone
who is bitten can look at it and live." 9So
Moses made a bronze snake and put it
up on a pole. Then when anyone was bitten by a snake and looked at the bronze
snake, they lived.

10The Israelites moved on and camped
at Oboth. 11Then they set out from Oboth
and camped in Iye Abarim, in the wilderness that faces Moab toward the sunrise.
12From there they moved on and camped
in the Zered Valley. 13They set out from
there and camped alongside the Arnon,
which is in the wilderness extending into
Amorite territory. The Arnon is the border of Moab, between Moab and the Amorites. 14That is why the Book of the Wars
of the LORD says:

"... Zahab[d] in Suphah and the
ravines,
the Arnon 15and[e] the slopes of the
ravines
that lead to the settlement of Ar
and lie along the border of Moab."

16From there they continued on to Beer,
the well where the LORD said to Moses,
"Gather the people together and I will
give them water."
17Then Israel sang this song:

"Spring up, O well!
Sing about it,
18about the well that the princes dug,
that the nobles of the people sank—
the nobles with scepters and staffs."

Then they went from the wilderness to
Mattanah, 19from Mattanah to Nahaliel,
from Nahaliel to Bamoth, 20and from Bamoth to the valley in Moab where the top
of Pisgah overlooks the wasteland.

21Israel sent messengers to say to Sihon king of the Amorites:

22"Let us pass through your country. We will not turn aside into any
field or vineyard, or drink water
from any well. We will travel along
the King's Highway until we have
passed through your territory."

23But Sihon would not let Israel pass
through his territory. He mustered his
entire army and marched out into the
wilderness against Israel. When he
reached Jahaz, he fought with Israel.
24Israel, however, put him to the sword
and took over his land from the Arnon
to the Jabbok, but only as far as the Ammonites, because their border was fortified. 25Israel captured all the cities of the
Amorites and occupied them, including
Heshbon and all its surrounding settlements. 26Heshbon was the city of Sihon
king of the Amorites, who had fought
against the former king of Moab and had
taken from him all his land as far as the
Arnon.
27That is why the poets say:

"Come to Heshbon and let it be
rebuilt;
let Sihon's city be restored.
28"Fire went out from Heshbon,
a blaze from the city of Sihon.
It consumed Ar of Moab,
the citizens of Arnon's heights.
29Woe to you, Moab!
You are destroyed, people of
Chemosh!

[a] 2 The Hebrew term refers to the irrevocable giving over of things or persons to the LORD, often by totally destroying them; also in verse 3. [b] 3 *Hormah* means *destruction.* [c] 4 Or *the Sea of Reeds* [d] 14 Septuagint; Hebrew *Waheb* [e] 14,15 Or *"I have been given from Suphah and the ravines / of the Arnon 15to*

He has given up his sons as fugitives
and his daughters as captives
to Sihon king of the Amorites.

30 "But we have overthrown them;
Heshbon's dominion has been
destroyed all the way to Dibon.
We have demolished them as far as
Nophah,
which extends to Medeba."

31 So Israel settled in the land of the
Amorites.
32 After Moses had sent spies to Jazer,
the Israelites captured its surrounding
settlements and drove out the Amorites
who were there. 33 Then they turned and
went up along the road toward Bashan,
and Og king of Bashan and his whole
army marched out to meet them in battle at Edrei.
34 The LORD said to Moses, "Do not be
afraid of him, for I have delivered him
into your hands, along with his whole
army and his land. Do to him what you
did to Sihon king of the Amorites, who
reigned in Heshbon."
35 So they struck him down, together
with his sons and his whole army, leaving them no survivors. And they took
possession of his land.

22 Then the Israelites traveled to the
plains of Moab and camped along
the Jordan across from Jericho.
2 Now Balak son of Zippor saw all that
Israel had done to the Amorites, 3 and
Moab was terrified because there were
so many people. Indeed, Moab was filled
with dread because of the Israelites.
4 The Moabites said to the elders of
Midian, "This horde is going to lick up
everything around us, as an ox licks up
the grass of the field."
So Balak son of Zippor, who was king
of Moab at that time, 5 sent messengers to
summon Balaam son of Beor, who was at
Pethor, near the Euphrates River, in his
native land. Balak said:

"A people has come out of Egypt;
they cover the face of the land and
have settled next to me. 6 Now come
and put a curse on these people, because they are too powerful for me.
Perhaps then I will be able to defeat
them and drive them out of the land.
For I know that whoever you bless is
blessed, and whoever yo urse is
cursed."

7 The elders of Moab and M
taking with them the fee for div
When they came to Balaam, th
him what Balak had said.
8 "Spend the night here," Balaan
to them, "and I will report back to
with the answer the LORD gives me.
the Moabite officials stayed with him.
9 God came to Balaam and asked, "Who
are these men with you?"
10 Balaam said to God, "Balak son of
Zippor, king of Moab, sent me this message: 11 'A people that has come out of
Egypt covers the face of the land. Now
come and put a curse on them for me.
Perhaps then I will be able to fight them
and drive them away.'"
12 But God said to Balaam, "Do not go
with them. You must not put a curse on
those people, because they are blessed."
13 The next morning Balaam got up and
said to Balak's officials, "Go back to your
own country, for the LORD has refused to
let me go with you."
14 So the Moabite officials returned to
Balak and said, "Balaam refused to come
with us."
15 Then Balak sent other officials, more
numerous and more distinguished than
the first. 16 They came to Balaam and
said:

"This is what Balak son of Zippor says: Do not let anything keep
you from coming to me, 17 because I
will reward you handsomely and do
whatever you say. Come and put a
curse on these people for me."

18 But Balaam answered them, "Even if
Balak gave me all the silver and gold in
his palace, I could not do anything great
or small to go beyond the command of
the LORD my God. 19 Now spend the night
here so that I can find out what else the
LORD will tell me."
20 That night God came to Balaam and
said, "Since these men have come to
summon you, go with them, but do only
what I tell you."
21 Balaam got up in the morning, saddled his donkey and went with the Moabite officials. 22 But God was very angry
when he went, and the angel of the LORD
stood in the road to oppose him. Balaam was riding on his donkey, and his

its were with him. 23When the
two saw the angel of the LORD stand-
do e road with a drawn sword in his
it turned off the road into a field.
am beat it to get it back on the road.
24Then the angel of the LORD stood in a
arrow path through the vineyards, with
alls on both sides. 25When the donkey
saw the angel of the LORD, it pressed
close to the wall, crushing Balaam's foot
against it. So he beat the donkey again.
26Then the angel of the LORD moved on
ahead and stood in a narrow place where
there was no room to turn, either to the
right or to the left. 27When the donkey
saw the angel of the LORD, it lay down under Balaam, and he was angry and beat it
with his staff. 28Then the LORD opened
the donkey's mouth, and it said to Balaam, "What have I done to you to make
you beat me these three times?"
29Balaam answered the donkey, "You
have made a fool of me! If only I had a
sword in my hand, I would kill you right
now."
30The donkey said to Balaam, "Am I
not your own donkey, which you have always ridden, to this day? Have I been in
the habit of doing this to you?"
"No," he said.
31Then the LORD opened Balaam's
eyes, and he saw the angel of the LORD
standing in the road with his sword
drawn. So he bowed low and fell facedown.
32The angel of the LORD asked him,
"Why have you beaten your donkey these
three times? I have come here to oppose
you because your path is a reckless one
before me.[a] 33The donkey saw me and
turned away from me these three times.
If it had not turned away, I would certainly have killed you by now, but I would
have spared it."
34Balaam said to the angel of the LORD,
"I have sinned. I did not realize you were
standing in the road to oppose me. Now
if you are displeased, I will go back."
35The angel of the LORD said to Balaam, "Go with the men, but speak only
what I tell you." So Balaam went with Balak's officials.
36When Balak heard that Balaam was
coming, he went out to meet him at the
Moabite town on the Arnon border, at the
edge of his territory. 37Balak said to Balaam, "Did I not send you an urgent summons? Why didn't you come to me? Am I
really not able to reward you?"
38"Well, I have come to you now," Balaam replied. "But I can't say whatever I
please. I must speak only what God puts
in my mouth."
39Then Balaam went with Balak to
Kiriath Huzoth. 40Balak sacrificed cattle
and sheep, and gave some to Balaam and
the officials who were with him. 41The
next morning Balak took Balaam up to
Bamoth Baal, and from there he could
see the outskirts of the Israelite camp.

23 Balaam said, "Build me seven altars
here, and prepare seven bulls and
seven rams for me." 2Balak did as Balaam said, and the two of them offered a
bull and a ram on each altar.
3Then Balaam said to Balak, "Stay here
beside your offering while I go aside. Perhaps the LORD will come to meet with me.
Whatever he reveals to me I will tell you."
Then he went off to a barren height.
4God met with him, and Balaam said, "I
have prepared seven altars, and on each
altar I have offered a bull and a ram."
5The LORD put a word in Balaam's
mouth and said, "Go back to Balak and
give him this word."
6So he went back to him and found him
standing beside his offering, with all the
Moabite officials. 7Then Balaam spoke
his message:

"Balak brought me from Aram,
the king of Moab from the eastern
mountains.
'Come,' he said, 'curse Jacob for me;
come, denounce Israel.'
8How can I curse
those whom God has not cursed?
How can I denounce
those whom the LORD has not
denounced?
9From the rocky peaks I see them,
from the heights I view them.
I see a people who live apart
and do not consider themselves one
of the nations.
10Who can count the dust of Jacob
or number even a fourth of Israel?
Let me die the death of the righteous,
and may my final end be like
theirs!"

[a] 32 The meaning of the Hebrew for this clause is uncertain.

11 Balak said to Balaam, "What have
you done to me? I brought you to curse
my enemies, but you have done nothing
but bless them!"

12 He answered, "Must I not speak what
the LORD puts in my mouth?"

13 Then Balak said to him, "Come with
me to another place where you can see
them; you will not see them all but only
the outskirts of their camp. And from
there, curse them for me." 14 So he took
him to the field of Zophim on the top of
Pisgah, and there he built seven altars
and offered a bull and a ram on each altar.

15 Balaam said to Balak, "Stay here beside your offering while I meet with him
over there."

16 The LORD met with Balaam and put a
word in his mouth and said, "Go back to
Balak and give him this word."

17 So he went to him and found him
standing beside his offering, with the
Moabite officials. Balak asked him,
"What did the LORD say?"

18 Then he spoke his message:

"Arise, Balak, and listen;
hear me, son of Zippor.
19 God is not human, that he should lie,
not a human being, that he should
change his mind.
Does he speak and then not act?
Does he promise and not fulfill?
20 I have received a command to bless;
he has blessed, and I cannot
change it.

21 "No misfortune is seen in Jacob,
no misery observed[a] in Israel.
The LORD their God is with them;
the shout of the King is among
them.
22 God brought them out of Egypt;
they have the strength of a wild ox.
23 There is no divination against[b]
Jacob,
no evil omens against[b] Israel.
It will now be said of Jacob
and of Israel, 'See what God has
done!'
24 The people rise like a lioness;
they rouse themselves like a lion
that does not rest till it devours its
prey
and drinks the blood of its victims."

25 Then Balak said to Balaam, "Neither
curse them at all nor bless them at all!"

26 Balaam answered, "Did I not tell you
I must do whatever the LORD says?"

27 Then Balak said to Balaam, "Come,
let me take you to another place. Perhaps
it will please God to let you curse them
for me from there." 28 And Balak took Balaam to the top of Peor, overlooking the
wasteland.

29 Balaam said, "Build me seven altars
here, and prepare seven bulls and sev-
en rams for me." 30 Balak did as Balaam
had said, and offered a bull and a ram on
each altar.

24 Now when Balaam saw that it
pleased the LORD to bless Israel,
he did not resort to divination as at other times, but turned his face toward the
wilderness. 2 When Balaam looked out
and saw Israel encamped tribe by tribe,
the Spirit of God came on him 3 and he
spoke his message:

"The prophecy of Balaam son of Beor,
the prophecy of one whose eye sees
clearly,
4 the prophecy of one who hears the
words of God,
who sees a vision from the
Almighty,[c]
who falls prostrate, and whose eyes
are opened:

5 "How beautiful are your tents, Jacob,
your dwelling places, Israel!

6 "Like valleys they spread out,
like gardens beside a river,
like aloes planted by the LORD,
like cedars beside the waters.
7 Water will flow from their buckets;
their seed will have abundant
water.

"Their king will be greater than
Agag;
their kingdom will be exalted.

8 "God brought them out of Egypt;
they have the strength of a wild ox.
They devour hostile nations
and break their bones in pieces;
with their arrows they pierce them.
9 Like a lion they crouch and lie down,
like a lioness — who dares to rouse
them?

[a] 21 Or *He has not looked on Jacob's offenses / or on the wrongs found* [b] 23 Or *in* [c] 4 Hebrew *Shaddai*; also in verse 16

"May those who bless you be blessed
and those who curse you be
cursed!"

10 Then Balak's anger burned against
Balaam. He struck his hands together
and said to him, "I summoned you to
curse my enemies, but you have blessed
them these three times. 11 Now leave at
once and go home! I said I would reward
you handsomely, but the LORD has kept
you from being rewarded."
12 Balaam answered Balak, "Did I not
tell the messengers you sent me, 13 'Even
if Balak gave me all the silver and gold
in his palace, I could not do anything of
my own accord, good or bad, to go beyond the command of the LORD—and
I must say only what the LORD says'?
14 Now I am going back to my people,
but come, let me warn you of what this
people will do to your people in days to
come."
15 Then he spoke his message:

"The prophecy of Balaam son of Beor,
the prophecy of one whose eye sees
clearly,
16 the prophecy of one who hears the
words of God,
who has knowledge from the Most
High,
who sees a vision from the Almighty,
who falls prostrate, and whose eyes
are opened:
17 "I see him, but not now;
I behold him, but not near.
A star will come out of Jacob;
a scepter will rise out of Israel.
He will crush the foreheads of Moab,
the skulls[a] of[b] all the people of
Sheth.[c]
18 Edom will be conquered;
Seir, his enemy, will be conquered,
but Israel will grow strong.
19 A ruler will come out of Jacob
and destroy the survivors of the
city."

20 Then Balaam saw Amalek and spoke
his message:

"Amalek was first among the nations,
but their end will be utter
destruction."

21 Then he saw the Kenites and spoke
his message:

"Your dwelling place is secure,
your nest is set in a rock;
22 yet you Kenites will be destroyed
when Ashur takes you captive."

23 Then he spoke his message:

"Alas! Who can live when God does
this?[d]
24 Ships will come from the shores of
Cyprus;
they will subdue Ashur and Eber,
but they too will come to ruin."

25 Then Balaam got up and returned
home, and Balak went his own way.

25 While Israel was staying in Shittim,
the men began to indulge in sexual immorality with Moabite women,
2 who invited them to the sacrifices to
their gods. The people ate the sacrificial
meal and bowed down before these gods.
3 So Israel yoked themselves to the Baal
of Peor. And the LORD's anger burned
against them.
4 The LORD said to Moses, "Take all the
leaders of these people, kill them and
expose them in broad daylight before
the LORD, so that the LORD's fierce anger
may turn away from Israel."
5 So Moses said to Israel's judges, "Each
of you must put to death those of your
people who have yoked themselves to
the Baal of Peor."
6 Then an Israelite man brought into
the camp a Midianite woman right before the eyes of Moses and the whole
assembly of Israel while they were weeping at the entrance to the tent of meeting. 7 When Phinehas son of Eleazar, the
son of Aaron, the priest, saw this, he left
the assembly, took a spear in his hand
8 and followed the Israelite into the tent.
He drove the spear into both of them,
right through the Israelite man and into
the woman's stomach. Then the plague
against the Israelites was stopped; 9 but
those who died in the plague numbered
24,000.
10 The LORD said to Moses, 11 "Phinehas son of Eleazar, the son of Aaron, the
priest, has turned my anger away from
the Israelites. Since he was as zealous for

[a] *17* Samaritan Pentateuch (see also Jer. 48:45); the meaning of the word in the Masoretic Text is uncertain.
[b] *17* Or possibly *Moab, / batter* [c] *17* Or *all the noisy boasters* [d] *23* Masoretic Text; with a different word division of the Hebrew *The people from the islands will gather from the north.*

my honor among them as I am, I did not
put an end to them in my zeal. 12 Therefore tell him I am making my covenant
of peace with him. 13 He and his descendants will have a covenant of a lasting
priesthood, because he was zealous for
the honor of his God and made atonement for the Israelites."

14 The name of the Israelite who was
killed with the Midianite woman was
Zimri son of Salu, the leader of a Sime-
onite family. 15 And the name of the Midianite woman who was put to death was
Kozbi daughter of Zur, a tribal chief of a
Midianite family.

16 The LORD said to Moses, 17 "Treat the
Midianites as enemies and kill them.
18 They treated you as enemies when they
deceived you in the Peor incident involving their sister Kozbi, the daughter of a
Midianite leader, the woman who was
killed when the plague came as a result
of that incident."

26 After the plague the LORD said to
Moses and Eleazar son of Aaron,
the priest, 2 "Take a census of the whole
Israelite community by families—all
those twenty years old or more who are
able to serve in the army of Israel." 3 So on
the plains of Moab by the Jordan across
from Jericho, Moses and Eleazar the
priest spoke with them and said, 4 "Take
a census of the men twenty years old or
more, as the LORD commanded Moses."

These were the Israelites who came out of Egypt:

5 The descendants of Reuben, the firstborn son of Israel, were:
through Hanok, the Hanokite clan;
through Pallu, the Palluite clan;
6 through Hezron, the Hezronite clan;
through Karmi, the Karmite clan.
7 These were the clans of Reuben; those
numbered were 43,730.

8 The son of Pallu was Eliab, 9 and the
sons of Eliab were Nemuel, Dathan and
Abiram. The same Dathan and Abiram
were the community officials who rebelled against Moses and Aaron and
were among Korah's followers when they
rebelled against the LORD. 10 The earth
opened its mouth and swallowed them
along with Korah, whose followers died
when the fire devoured the 250 men. And
they served as a warning sign. 11 The line
of Korah, however, did not die out.

12 The descendants of Simeon by their
clans were:
through Nemuel, the Nemuelite clan;
through Jamin, the Jaminite clan;
through Jakin, the Jakinite clan;
13 through Zerah, the Zerahite clan;
through Shaul, the Shaulite clan.
14 These were the clans of Simeon; those
numbered were 22,200.

15 The descendants of Gad by their clans
were:
through Zephon, the Zephonite clan;
through Haggi, the Haggite clan;
through Shuni, the Shunite clan;
16 through Ozni, the Oznite clan;
through Eri, the Erite clan;
17 through Arodi,[a] the Arodite clan;
through Areli, the Arelite clan.
18 These were the clans of Gad; those
numbered were 40,500.

19 Er and Onan were sons of Judah, but
they died in Canaan.
20 The descendants of Judah by their
clans were:
through Shelah, the Shelanite clan;
through Perez, the Perezite clan;
through Zerah, the Zerahite clan.
21 The descendants of Perez were:
through Hezron, the Hezronite clan;
through Hamul, the Hamulite clan.
22 These were the clans of Judah; those
numbered were 76,500.

23 The descendants of Issachar by their
clans were:
through Tola, the Tolaite clan;
through Puah, the Puite[b] clan;
24 through Jashub, the Jashubite clan;
through Shimron, the Shimronite clan.
25 These were the clans of Issachar; those
numbered were 64,300.

26 The descendants of Zebulun by their
clans were:
through Sered, the Seredite clan;
through Elon, the Elonite clan;

[a] *17* Samaritan Pentateuch and Syriac (see also Gen. 46:16); Masoretic Text *Arod* [b] *23* Samaritan Pentateuch, Septuagint, Vulgate and Syriac (see also 1 Chron. 7:1); Masoretic Text *through Puvah, the Punite*

through Jahleel, the Jahleelite clan.
27 These were the clans of Zebulun; those numbered were 60,500.

28 The descendants of Joseph by their clans through Manasseh and Ephraim were:

29 The descendants of Manasseh:
through Makir, the Makirite clan (Makir was the father of Gilead);
through Gilead, the Gileadite clan.
30 These were the descendants of Gilead:
through Iezer, the Iezerite clan;
through Helek, the Helekite clan;
31 through Asriel, the Asrielite clan;
through Shechem, the Shechemite clan;
32 through Shemida, the Shemidaite clan;
through Hepher, the Hepherite clan.
33 (Zelophehad son of Hepher had no sons; he had only daughters, whose names were Mahlah, Noah, Hoglah, Milkah and Tirzah.)
34 These were the clans of Manasseh; those numbered were 52,700.

35 These were the descendants of Ephraim by their clans:
through Shuthelah, the Shuthelahite clan;
through Beker, the Bekerite clan;
through Tahan, the Tahanite clan.
36 These were the descendants of Shuthelah:
through Eran, the Eranite clan.
37 These were the clans of Ephraim; those numbered were 32,500.

These were the descendants of Joseph by their clans.

38 The descendants of Benjamin by their clans were:
through Bela, the Belaite clan;
through Ashbel, the Ashbelite clan;
through Ahiram, the Ahiramite clan;
39 through Shupham,[a] the Shuphamite clan;
through Hupham, the Huphamite clan.
40 The descendants of Bela through Ard and Naaman were:
through Ard,[b] the Ardite clan;
through Naaman, the Naamite clan.
41 These were the clans of Benjamin; those numbered were 45,600.

42 These were the descendants of Dan by their clans:
through Shuham, the Shuhamite clan.
These were the clans of Dan: 43 All of them were Shuhamite clans; and those numbered were 64,400.

44 The descendants of Asher by their clans were:
through Imnah, the Imnite clan;
through Ishvi, the Ishvite clan;
through Beriah, the Beriite clan;
45 and through the descendants of Beriah:
through Heber, the Heberite clan;
through Malkiel, the Malkielite clan.
46 (Asher had a daughter named Serah.)
47 These were the clans of Asher; those numbered were 53,400.

48 The descendants of Naphtali by their clans were:
through Jahzeel, the Jahzeelite clan;
through Guni, the Gunite clan;
49 through Jezer, the Jezerite clan;
through Shillem, the Shillemite clan.
50 These were the clans of Naphtali; those numbered were 45,400.

51 The total number of the men of Israel was 601,730.

52 The LORD said to Moses, 53 "The land is to be allotted to them as an inheritance based on the number of names.
54 To a larger group give a larger inheritance, and to a smaller group a smaller one; each is to receive its inheritance according to the number of those listed.
55 Be sure that the land is distributed by lot. What each group inherits will be according to the names for its ancestral tribe.
56 Each inheritance is to be distributed by lot among the larger and smaller groups."

[a] *39* A few manuscripts of the Masoretic Text, Samaritan Pentateuch, Vulgate and Syriac (see also Septuagint); most manuscripts of the Masoretic Text *Shephupham* [b] *40* Samaritan Pentateuch and Vulgate (see also Septuagint); Masoretic Text does not have *through Ard*.

57 These were the Levites who were
counted by their clans:
through Gershon, the Gershonite
clan;
through Kohath, the Kohathite
clan;
through Merari, the Merarite clan.
58 These also were Levite clans:
the Libnite clan,
the Hebronite clan,
the Mahlite clan,
the Mushite clan,
the Korahite clan.
(Kohath was the forefather of Amram; 59 the name of Amram's wife
was Jochebed, a descendant of
Levi, who was born to the Levites[a]
in Egypt. To Amram she bore Aaron, Moses and their sister Miriam.
60 Aaron was the father of Nadab and
Abihu, Eleazar and Ithamar. 61 But
Nadab and Abihu died when they
made an offering before the LORD
with unauthorized fire.)

62 All the male Levites a month old or
more numbered 23,000. They were not
counted along with the other Israelites
because they received no inheritance
among them.

63 These are the ones counted by Moses and Eleazar the priest when they
counted the Israelites on the plains of
Moab by the Jordan across from Jericho. 64 Not one of them was among those
counted by Moses and Aaron the priest
when they counted the Israelites in the
Desert of Sinai. 65 For the LORD had told
those Israelites they would surely die in
the wilderness, and not one of them was
left except Caleb son of Jephunneh and
Joshua son of Nun.

27 The daughters of Zelophehad son of
Hepher, the son of Gilead, the son
of Makir, the son of Manasseh, belonged
to the clans of Manasseh son of Joseph.
The names of the daughters were Mahlah, Noah, Hoglah, Milkah and Tirzah.
They came forward 2 and stood before
Moses, Eleazar the priest, the leaders
and the whole assembly at the entrance
to the tent of meeting and said, 3 "Our father died in the wilderness. He was not
among Korah's followers, who banded
together against the LORD, but he died
for his own sin and left no sons. 4 Why
should our father's name disappear from
his clan because he had no son? Give us
property among our father's relatives."

5 So Moses brought their case before
the LORD, 6 and the LORD said to him,
7 "What Zelophehad's daughters are saying is right. You must certainly give them
property as an inheritance among their
father's relatives and give their father's
inheritance to them.

8 "Say to the Israelites, 'If a man dies
and leaves no son, give his inheritance
to his daughter. 9 If he has no daughter,
give his inheritance to his brothers. 10 If
he has no brothers, give his inheritance
to his father's brothers. 11 If his father had
no brothers, give his inheritance to the
nearest relative in his clan, that he may
possess it. This is to have the force of law
for the Israelites, as the LORD commanded Moses.' "

12 Then the LORD said to Moses, "Go up
this mountain in the Abarim Range and
see the land I have given the Israelites.
13 After you have seen it, you too will be
gathered to your people, as your brother Aaron was, 14 for when the community rebelled at the waters in the Desert of
Zin, both of you disobeyed my command
to honor me as holy before their eyes."
(These were the waters of Meribah Kadesh, in the Desert of Zin.)

15 Moses said to the LORD, 16 "May the
LORD, the God who gives breath to all
living things, appoint someone over this
community 17 to go out and come in before them, one who will lead them out
and bring them in, so the LORD's people
will not be like sheep without a shepherd."

18 So the LORD said to Moses, "Take
Joshua son of Nun, a man in whom is the
spirit of leadership,[b] and lay your hand
on him. 19 Have him stand before Eleazar the priest and the entire assembly
and commission him in their presence.
20 Give him some of your authority so
the whole Israelite community will obey
him. 21 He is to stand before Eleazar the
priest, who will obtain decisions for him
by inquiring of the Urim before the LORD.
At his command he and the entire community of the Israelites will go out, and at
his command they will come in."

[a] 59 Or *Jochebed, a daughter of Levi, who was born to Levi* [b] 18 Or *the Spirit*

22Moses did as the LORD commanded
him. He took Joshua and had him stand
before Eleazar the priest and the whole
assembly. 23Then he laid his hands on
him and commissioned him, as the LORD
instructed through Moses.

28 The LORD said to Moses, 2"Give this
command to the Israelites and say
to them: 'Make sure that you present to
me at the appointed time my food offerings, as an aroma pleasing to me.' 3Say to
them: 'This is the food offering you are
to present to the LORD: two lambs a year
old without defect, as a regular burnt offering each day. 4Offer one lamb in the
morning and the other at twilight, 5to-
gether with a grain offering of a tenth of
an ephah[a] of the finest flour mixed with
a quarter of a hin[b] of oil from pressed olives. 6This is the regular burnt offering
instituted at Mount Sinai as a pleasing
aroma, a food offering presented to the
LORD. 7The accompanying drink offering is to be a quarter of a hin of fermented drink with each lamb. Pour out the
drink offering to the LORD at the sanctuary. 8Offer the second lamb at twilight,
along with the same kind of grain offering and drink offering that you offer in
the morning. This is a food offering, an
aroma pleasing to the LORD.

9"'On the Sabbath day, make an offering of two lambs a year old without
defect, together with its drink offering
and a grain offering of two-tenths of an
ephah[c] of the finest flour mixed with
olive oil. 10This is the burnt offering for
every Sabbath, in addition to the regular
burnt offering and its drink offering.

11"'On the first of every month, present to the LORD a burnt offering of two
young bulls, one ram and seven male
lambs a year old, all without defect.
12With each bull there is to be a grain
offering of three-tenths of an ephah[d] of
the finest flour mixed with oil; with the
ram, a grain offering of two-tenths of
an ephah of the finest flour mixed with
oil; 13and with each lamb, a grain offering of a tenth of an ephah of the finest
flour mixed with oil. This is for a burnt
offering, a pleasing aroma, a food offering presented to the LORD. 14With each
bull there is to be a drink offering of half
a hin[e] of wine; with the ram, a third of a
hin[f]; and with each lamb, a quarter of a
hin. This is the monthly burnt offering
to be made at each new moon during the
year. 15Besides the regular burnt offering
with its drink offering, one male goat is
to be presented to the LORD as a sin offering.[g]

16"'On the fourteenth day of the first
month the LORD's Passover is to be held.
17On the fifteenth day of this month
there is to be a festival; for seven days
eat bread made without yeast. 18On the
first day hold a sacred assembly and do
no regular work. 19Present to the LORD
a food offering consisting of a burnt offering of two young bulls, one ram and
seven male lambs a year old, all without
defect. 20With each bull offer a grain offering of three-tenths of an ephah of the
finest flour mixed with oil; with the ram,
two-tenths; 21and with each of the sev-
en lambs, one-tenth. 22Include one male
goat as a sin offering to make atonement
for you. 23Offer these in addition to the
regular morning burnt offering. 24In
this way present the food offering every
day for seven days as an aroma pleasing
to the LORD; it is to be offered in addition to the regular burnt offering and
its drink offering. 25On the seventh day
hold a sacred assembly and do no regular work.

26"'On the day of firstfruits, when you
present to the LORD an offering of new
grain during the Festival of Weeks, hold
a sacred assembly and do no regular
work. 27Present a burnt offering of two
young bulls, one ram and seven male
lambs a year old as an aroma pleasing
to the LORD. 28With each bull there is
to be a grain offering of three-tenths of
an ephah of the finest flour mixed with
oil; with the ram, two-tenths; 29and with
each of the seven lambs, one-tenth. 30In-
clude one male goat to make atonement
for you. 31Offer these together with their
drink offerings, in addition to the regular
burnt offering and its grain offering. Be
sure the animals are without defect.

[a] *5* That is, probably about 3 1/2 pounds or about 1.6 kilograms; also in verses 13, 21 and 29 [b] *5* That is, about 1 quart or about 1 liter; also in verses 7 and 14 [c] *9* That is, probably about 7 pounds or about 3.2 kilograms; also in verses 12, 20 and 28 [d] *12* That is, probably about 11 pounds or about 5 kilograms; also in verses 20 and 28 [e] *14* That is, about 2 quarts or about 1.9 liters [f] *14* That is, about 1 1/3 quarts or about 1.3 liters [g] *15* Or *purification offering*; also in verse 22

29 "'On the first day of the seventh
month hold a sacred assembly and
do no regular work. It is a day for you to
sound the trumpets. 2As an aroma pleasing to the LORD, offer a burnt offering of
one young bull, one ram and seven male
lambs a year old, all without defect.
3With the bull offer a grain offering of
three-tenths of an ephah[a] of the finest
flour mixed with olive oil; with the ram,
two-tenths[b]; 4and with each of the sev-
en lambs, one-tenth.[c] 5Include one male
goat as a sin offering[d] to make atonement
for you. 6These are in addition to the
monthly and daily burnt offerings with
their grain offerings and drink offerings
as specified. They are food offerings presented to the LORD, a pleasing aroma.

7"'On the tenth day of this seventh
month hold a sacred assembly. You must
deny yourselves[e] and do no work. 8Pre-
sent as an aroma pleasing to the LORD a
burnt offering of one young bull, one ram
and seven male lambs a year old, all without defect. 9With the bull offer a grain offering of three-tenths of an ephah of the
finest flour mixed with oil; with the ram,
two-tenths; 10and with each of the sev-
en lambs, one-tenth. 11Include one male
goat as a sin offering, in addition to the
sin offering for atonement and the regular burnt offering with its grain offering,
and their drink offerings.

12"'On the fifteenth day of the seventh
month, hold a sacred assembly and do
no regular work. Celebrate a festival to
the LORD for seven days. 13Present as an
aroma pleasing to the LORD a food offering consisting of a burnt offering of thirteen young bulls, two rams and fourteen
male lambs a year old, all without defect. 14With each of the thirteen bulls offer a grain offering of three-tenths of an
ephah of the finest flour mixed with oil;
with each of the two rams, two-tenths;
15and with each of the fourteen lambs,
one-tenth. 16Include one male goat as a
sin offering, in addition to the regular
burnt offering with its grain offering and
drink offering.

17"'On the second day offer twelve
young bulls, two rams and fourteen
male lambs a year old, all without defect.
18With the bulls, rams and lambs, offer
their grain offerings and drink offerings
according to the number specified. 19In-
clude one male goat as a sin offering, in
addition to the regular burnt offering
with its grain offering, and their drink
offerings.

20"'On the third day offer eleven bulls,
two rams and fourteen male lambs a
year old, all without defect. 21With the
bulls, rams and lambs, offer their grain
offerings and drink offerings according
to the number specified. 22Include one
male goat as a sin offering, in addition to
the regular burnt offering with its grain
offering and drink offering.

23"'On the fourth day offer ten bulls,
two rams and fourteen male lambs a
year old, all without defect. 24With the
bulls, rams and lambs, offer their grain
offerings and drink offerings according
to the number specified. 25Include one
male goat as a sin offering, in addition to
the regular burnt offering with its grain
offering and drink offering.

26"'On the fifth day offer nine bulls,
two rams and fourteen male lambs a
year old, all without defect. 27With the
bulls, rams and lambs, offer their grain
offerings and drink offerings according
to the number specified. 28Include one
male goat as a sin offering, in addition to
the regular burnt offering with its grain
offering and drink offering.

29"'On the sixth day offer eight bulls,
two rams and fourteen male lambs a
year old, all without defect. 30With the
bulls, rams and lambs, offer their grain
offerings and drink offerings according
to the number specified. 31Include one
male goat as a sin offering, in addition to
the regular burnt offering with its grain
offering and drink offering.

32"'On the seventh day offer seven
bulls, two rams and fourteen male lambs
a year old, all without defect. 33With the
bulls, rams and lambs, offer their grain
offerings and drink offerings according
to the number specified. 34Include one
male goat as a sin offering, in addition to
the regular burnt offering with its grain
offering and drink offering.

35"'On the eighth day hold a clos-

[a] 3 That is, probably about 11 pounds or about 5 kilograms; also in verses 9 and 14 [b] 3 That is, probably about 7 pounds or about 3.2 kilograms; also in verses 9 and 14 [c] 4 That is, probably about 3 1/2 pounds or about 1.6 kilograms; also in verses 10 and 15 [d] 5 Or *purification offering*; also elsewhere in this chapter [e] 7 Or *must fast*

ing special assembly and do no regular
work. 36Present as an aroma pleasing to
the LORD a food offering consisting of a
burnt offering of one bull, one ram and
seven male lambs a year old, all without
defect. 37With the bull, the ram and the
lambs, offer their grain offerings and
drink offerings according to the number specified. 38Include one male goat as
a sin offering, in addition to the regular
burnt offering with its grain offering and
drink offering.

39"'In addition to what you vow and
your freewill offerings, offer these to the
LORD at your appointed festivals: your
burnt offerings, grain offerings, drink
offerings and fellowship offerings.'"

40Moses told the Israelites all that the
LORD commanded him.[a]

30[b] Moses said to the heads of the
tribes of Israel: "This is what the
LORD commands: 2When a man makes
a vow to the LORD or takes an oath to ob-
ligate himself by a pledge, he must not
break his word but must do everything
he said.

3"When a young woman still living in
her father's household makes a vow to
the LORD or obligates herself by a pledge
4and her father hears about her vow or
pledge but says nothing to her, then all
her vows and every pledge by which she
obligated herself will stand. 5But if her
father forbids her when he hears about
it, none of her vows or the pledges by
which she obligated herself will stand;
the LORD will release her because her father has forbidden her.

6"If she marries after she makes a vow
or after her lips utter a rash promise by
which she obligates herself 7and her
husband hears about it but says nothing
to her, then her vows or the pledges by
which she obligated herself will stand.
8But if her husband forbids her when
he hears about it, he nullifies the vow
that obligates her or the rash promise
by which she obligates herself, and the
LORD will release her.

9"Any vow or obligation taken by a
widow or divorced woman will be binding on her.

10"If a woman living with her husband
makes a vow or obligates herself by a
pledge under oath 11and her husband
hears about it but says nothing to her and
does not forbid her, then all her vows or
the pledges by which she obligated herself will stand. 12But if her husband nullifies them when he hears about them,
then none of the vows or pledges that
came from her lips will stand. Her husband has nullified them, and the LORD
will release her. 13Her husband may confirm or nullify any vow she makes or any
sworn pledge to deny herself.[c] 14But if
her husband says nothing to her about it
from day to day, then he confirms all her
vows or the pledges binding on her. He
confirms them by saying nothing to her
when he hears about them. 15If, however, he nullifies them some time after he
hears about them, then he must bear the
consequences of her wrongdoing."

16These are the regulations the LORD
gave Moses concerning relationships between a man and his wife, and between a
father and his young daughter still living
at home.

31 The LORD said to Moses, 2"Take
vengeance on the Midianites for the
Israelites. After that, you will be gathered
to your people."

3So Moses said to the people, "Arm
some of your men to go to war against
the Midianites so that they may carry out
the LORD's vengeance on them. 4Send
into battle a thousand men from each of
the tribes of Israel." 5So twelve thousand
men armed for battle, a thousand from
each tribe, were supplied from the clans
of Israel. 6Moses sent them into battle,
a thousand from each tribe, along with
Phinehas son of Eleazar, the priest, who
took with him articles from the sanctuary and the trumpets for signaling.

7They fought against Midian, as the
LORD commanded Moses, and killed
every man. 8Among their victims were
Evi, Rekem, Zur, Hur and Reba—the
five kings of Midian. They also killed Balaam son of Beor with the sword. 9The
Israelites captured the Midianite wom-
en and children and took all the Midianite herds, flocks and goods as plunder. 10They burned all the towns where
the Midianites had settled, as well as all
their camps. 11They took all the plunder
and spoils, including the people and animals, 12and brought the captives, spoils

[a] *40* In Hebrew texts this verse (29:40) is numbered 30:1. [b] In Hebrew texts 30:1-16 is numbered 30:2-17.
[c] *13* Or *to fast*

and plunder to Moses and Eleazar the priest and the Israelite assembly at their camp on the plains of Moab, by the Jordan across from Jericho.

13 Moses, Eleazar the priest and all the leaders of the community went to meet them outside the camp. 14 Moses was angry with the officers of the army—the commanders of thousands and commanders of hundreds—who returned from the battle.

15 "Have you allowed all the women to live?" he asked them. 16 "They were the ones who followed Balaam's advice and enticed the Israelites to be unfaithful to the LORD in the Peor incident, so that a plague struck the LORD's people. 17 Now kill all the boys. And kill every woman who has slept with a man, 18 but save for yourselves every girl who has never slept with a man.

19 "Anyone who has killed someone or touched someone who was killed must stay outside the camp seven days. On the third and seventh days you must purify yourselves and your captives. 20 Purify every garment as well as everything made of leather, goat hair or wood."

21 Then Eleazar the priest said to the soldiers who had gone into battle, "This is what is required by the law that the LORD gave Moses: 22 Gold, silver, bronze, iron, tin, lead 23 and anything else that can withstand fire must be put through the fire, and then it will be clean. But it must also be purified with the water of cleansing. And whatever cannot withstand fire must be put through that water. 24 On the seventh day wash your clothes and you will be clean. Then you may come into the camp."

25 The LORD said to Moses, 26 "You and Eleazar the priest and the family heads of the community are to count all the people and animals that were captured. 27 Divide the spoils equally between the soldiers who took part in the battle and the rest of the community. 28 From the soldiers who fought in the battle, set apart as tribute for the LORD one out of every five hundred, whether people, cattle, donkeys or sheep. 29 Take this tribute from their half share and give it to Eleazar the priest as the LORD's part. 30 From the Israelites' half, select one out of every fifty, whether people, cattle, donkeys, sheep or other animals. Give them to the Levites, who are responsible for the care of the LORD's tabernacle." 31 So Moses and Eleazar the priest did as the LORD commanded Moses.

32 The plunder remaining from the spoils that the soldiers took was 675,000 sheep, 33 72,000 cattle, 34 61,000 donkeys 35 and 32,000 women who had never slept with a man.

36 The half share of those who fought in the battle was:

337,500 sheep, 37 of which the tribute for the LORD was 675;
38 36,000 cattle, of which the tribute for the LORD was 72;
39 30,500 donkeys, of which the tribute for the LORD was 61;
40 16,000 people, of whom the tribute for the LORD was 32.

41 Moses gave the tribute to Eleazar the priest as the LORD's part, as the LORD commanded Moses.

42 The half belonging to the Israelites, which Moses set apart from that of the fighting men— 43 the community's half—was 337,500 sheep, 44 36,000 cattle, 45 30,500 donkeys 46 and 16,000 people. 47 From the Israelites' half, Moses selected one out of every fifty people and animals, as the LORD commanded him, and gave them to the Levites, who were responsible for the care of the LORD's tabernacle.

48 Then the officers who were over the units of the army—the commanders of thousands and commanders of hundreds—went to Moses 49 and said to him, "Your servants have counted the soldiers under our command, and not one is missing. 50 So we have brought as an offering to the LORD the gold articles each of us acquired—armlets, bracelets, signet rings, earrings and necklaces—to make atonement for ourselves before the LORD."

51 Moses and Eleazar the priest accepted from them the gold—all the crafted articles. 52 All the gold from the commanders of thousands and commanders of hundreds that Moses and Eleazar presented as a gift to the LORD weighed 16,750 shekels.[a] 53 Each soldier had tak-

[a] *52* That is, about 420 pounds or about 190 kilograms

en plunder for himself. 54 Moses and Eleazar the priest accepted the gold from
the commanders of thousands and commanders of hundreds and brought it into
the tent of meeting as a memorial for the
Israelites before the LORD.

32 The Reubenites and Gadites, who
had very large herds and flocks, saw
that the lands of Jazer and Gilead were
suitable for livestock. 2 So they came to
Moses and Eleazar the priest and to the
leaders of the community, and said, 3 "Ataroth, Dibon, Jazer, Nimrah, Heshbon,
Elealeh, Sebam, Nebo and Beon— 4 the
land the LORD subdued before the people of Israel—are suitable for livestock,
and your servants have livestock. 5 If we
have found favor in your eyes," they said,
"let this land be given to your servants as
our possession. Do not make us cross the
Jordan."

6 Moses said to the Gadites and Reubenites, "Should your fellow Israelites
go to war while you sit here? 7 Why do
you discourage the Israelites from crossing over into the land the LORD has giv-
en them? 8 This is what your fathers did
when I sent them from Kadesh Barnea to
look over the land. 9 After they went up to
the Valley of Eshkol and viewed the land,
they discouraged the Israelites from entering the land the LORD had given them.
10 The LORD's anger was aroused that day
and he swore this oath: 11 'Because they
have not followed me wholeheartedly,
not one of those who were twenty years
old or more when they came up out of
Egypt will see the land I promised on
oath to Abraham, Isaac and Jacob—
12 not one except Caleb son of Jephunneh
the Kenizzite and Joshua son of Nun, for
they followed the LORD wholeheartedly.'
13 The LORD's anger burned against Israel
and he made them wander in the wilderness forty years, until the whole generation of those who had done evil in his
sight was gone.

14 "And here you are, a brood of sinners,
standing in the place of your fathers and
making the LORD even more angry with
Israel. 15 If you turn away from following
him, he will again leave all this people in
the wilderness, and you will be the cause
of their destruction."

16 Then they came up to him and said,
"We would like to build pens here for our
livestock and cities for our women and
children. 17 But we will arm ourselves for
battle[a] and go ahead of the Israelites until we have brought them to their place.
Meanwhile our women and children will
live in fortified cities, for protection from
the inhabitants of the land. 18 We will not
return to our homes until each of the Israelites has received their inheritance.
19 We will not receive any inheritance
with them on the other side of the Jordan,
because our inheritance has come to us
on the east side of the Jordan."

20 Then Moses said to them, "If you
will do this—if you will arm yourselves
before the LORD for battle 21 and if all of
you who are armed cross over the Jordan
before the LORD until he has driven his
enemies out before him— 22 then when
the land is subdued before the LORD, you
may return and be free from your obligation to the LORD and to Israel. And this
land will be your possession before the
LORD.

23 "But if you fail to do this, you will be
sinning against the LORD; and you may
be sure that your sin will find you out.
24 Build cities for your women and children, and pens for your flocks, but do
what you have promised."

25 The Gadites and Reubenites said
to Moses, "We your servants will do as
our lord commands. 26 Our children and
wives, our flocks and herds will remain
here in the cities of Gilead. 27 But your
servants, every man who is armed for
battle, will cross over to fight before the
LORD, just as our lord says."

28 Then Moses gave orders about them
to Eleazar the priest and Joshua son of
Nun and to the family heads of the Israelite tribes. 29 He said to them, "If the Gadites and Reubenites, every man armed
for battle, cross over the Jordan with you
before the LORD, then when the land is
subdued before you, you must give them
the land of Gilead as their possession.
30 But if they do not cross over with you
armed, they must accept their possession with you in Canaan."

31 The Gadites and Reubenites answered, "Your servants will do what the
LORD has said. 32 We will cross over before the LORD into Canaan armed, but

[a] *17* Septuagint; Hebrew *will be quick to arm ourselves*

the property we inherit will be on this
side of the Jordan."
33 Then Moses gave to the Gadites, the
Reubenites and the half-tribe of Manasseh son of Joseph the kingdom of Sihon
king of the Amorites and the kingdom of
Og king of Bashan — the whole land with
its cities and the territory around them.
34 The Gadites built up Dibon, Ataroth, Aroer, 35 Atroth Shophan, Jazer,
Jogbehah, 36 Beth Nimrah and Beth Haran as fortified cities, and built pens for
their flocks. 37 And the Reubenites rebuilt Heshbon, Elealeh and Kiriathaim,
38 as well as Nebo and Baal Meon (these
names were changed) and Sibmah. They
gave names to the cities they rebuilt.
39 The descendants of Makir son of Manasseh went to Gilead, captured it and
drove out the Amorites who were there.
40 So Moses gave Gilead to the Makirites,
the descendants of Manasseh, and they
settled there. 41 Jair, a descendant of Manasseh, captured their settlements and
called them Havvoth Jair.[a] 42 And Nobah
captured Kenath and its surrounding
settlements and called it Nobah after
himself.

33 Here are the stages in the journey of
the Israelites when they came out of
Egypt by divisions under the leadership
of Moses and Aaron. 2 At the LORD's command Moses recorded the stages in their
journey. This is their journey by stages:

3 The Israelites set out from Rameses on the fifteenth day of the first
month, the day after the Passover.
They marched out defiantly in full
view of all the Egyptians, 4 who were
burying all their firstborn, whom the
LORD had struck down among them;
for the LORD had brought judgment
on their gods.
5 The Israelites left Rameses and
camped at Sukkoth.
6 They left Sukkoth and camped at
Etham, on the edge of the desert.
7 They left Etham, turned back to
Pi Hahiroth, to the east of Baal Zephon, and camped near Migdol.
8 They left Pi Hahiroth[b] and passed
through the sea into the desert, and
when they had traveled for three
days in the Desert of Etham, they
camped at Marah.
9 They left Marah and went to Elim,
where there were twelve springs
and seventy palm trees, and they
camped there.
10 They left Elim and camped by
the Red Sea.[c]
11 They left the Red Sea and
camped in the Desert of Sin.
12 They left the Desert of Sin and
camped at Dophkah.
13 They left Dophkah and camped
at Alush.
14 They left Alush and camped at
Rephidim, where there was no water
for the people to drink.
15 They left Rephidim and camped
in the Desert of Sinai.
16 They left the Desert of Sinai and
camped at Kibroth Hattaavah.
17 They left Kibroth Hattaavah and
camped at Hazeroth.
18 They left Hazeroth and camped
at Rithmah.
19 They left Rithmah and camped
at Rimmon Perez.
20 They left Rimmon Perez and
camped at Libnah.
21 They left Libnah and camped at
Rissah.
22 They left Rissah and camped at
Kehelathah.
23 They left Kehelathah and
camped at Mount Shepher.
24 They left Mount Shepher and
camped at Haradah.
25 They left Haradah and camped
at Makheloth.
26 They left Makheloth and camped
at Tahath.
27 They left Tahath and camped at
Terah.
28 They left Terah and camped at
Mithkah.
29 They left Mithkah and camped
at Hashmonah.
30 They left Hashmonah and
camped at Moseroth.
31 They left Moseroth and camped
at Bene Jaakan.
32 They left Bene Jaakan and
camped at Hor Haggidgad.

[a] 41 Or *them the settlements of Jair* [b] 8 Many manuscripts of the Masoretic Text, Samaritan Pentateuch and Vulgate; most manuscripts of the Masoretic Text *left from before Hahiroth* [c] 10 Or *the Sea of Reeds*; also in verse 11

33 They left Hor Haggidgad and
camped at Jotbathah.
34 They left Jotbathah and camped
at Abronah.
35 They left Abronah and camped
at Ezion Geber.
36 They left Ezion Geber and
camped at Kadesh, in the Desert of
Zin.
37 They left Kadesh and camped at
Mount Hor, on the border of Edom.
38 At the LORD's command Aaron the
priest went up Mount Hor, where
he died on the first day of the fifth
month of the fortieth year after the
Israelites came out of Egypt. 39 Aaron was a hundred and twenty-three
years old when he died on Mount
Hor.
40 The Canaanite king of Arad, who
lived in the Negev of Canaan, heard
that the Israelites were coming.
41 They left Mount Hor and camped
at Zalmonah.
42 They left Zalmonah and camped
at Punon.
43 They left Punon and camped at
Oboth.
44 They left Oboth and camped at
Iye Abarim, on the border of Moab.
45 They left Iye Abarim and camped
at Dibon Gad.
46 They left Dibon Gad and camped
at Almon Diblathaim.
47 They left Almon Diblathaim and
camped in the mountains of Abarim, near Nebo.
48 They left the mountains of Abarim and camped on the plains of
Moab by the Jordan across from Jericho. 49 There on the plains of Moab
they camped along the Jordan from
Beth Jeshimoth to Abel Shittim.

50 On the plains of Moab by the Jordan
across from Jericho the LORD said to Moses, 51 "Speak to the Israelites and say to
them: 'When you cross the Jordan into
Canaan, 52 drive out all the inhabitants
of the land before you. Destroy all their
carved images and their cast idols, and
demolish all their high places. 53 Take
possession of the land and settle in it,
for I have given you the land to possess.
54 Distribute the land by lot, according to
your clans. To a larger group give a larger inheritance, and to a smaller group a
smaller one. Whatever falls to them by
lot will be theirs. Distribute it according
to your ancestral tribes.
55 " 'But if you do not drive out the inhabitants of the land, those you allow to
remain will become barbs in your eyes
and thorns in your sides. They will give
you trouble in the land where you will
live. 56 And then I will do to you what I
plan to do to them.' "

34 The LORD said to Moses, 2 "Command the Israelites and say to
them: 'When you enter Canaan, the land
that will be allotted to you as an inheritance is to have these boundaries:

3 " 'Your southern side will include
some of the Desert of Zin along the border of Edom. Your southern boundary
will start in the east from the southern
end of the Dead Sea, 4 cross south of
Scorpion Pass, continue on to Zin and
go south of Kadesh Barnea. Then it will
go to Hazar Addar and over to Azmon,
5 where it will turn, join the Wadi of Egypt
and end at the Mediterranean Sea.
6 " 'Your western boundary will be the
coast of the Mediterranean Sea. This will
be your boundary on the west.
7 " 'For your northern boundary, run
a line from the Mediterranean Sea to
Mount Hor 8 and from Mount Hor to Lebo
Hamath. Then the boundary will go to
Zedad, 9 continue to Ziphron and end at
Hazar Enan. This will be your boundary
on the north.
10 " 'For your eastern boundary, run a
line from Hazar Enan to Shepham. 11 The
boundary will go down from Shepham to
Riblah on the east side of Ain and continue along the slopes east of the Sea of
Galilee.[a] 12 Then the boundary will go
down along the Jordan and end at the
Dead Sea.
" 'This will be your land, with its
boundaries on every side.' "
13 Moses commanded the Israelites:
"Assign this land by lot as an inheritance.
The LORD has ordered that it be given to
the nine and a half tribes, 14 because the
families of the tribe of Reuben, the tribe
of Gad and the half-tribe of Manasseh
have received their inheritance. 15 These
two and a half tribes have received their

[a] 11 Hebrew *Kinnereth*

inheritance east of the Jordan across
from Jericho, toward the sunrise."

16 The LORD said to Moses, 17 "These
are the names of the men who are to assign the land for you as an inheritance:
Eleazar the priest and Joshua son of Nun.
18 And appoint one leader from each tribe
to help assign the land. 19 These are their
names:

Caleb son of Jephunneh,
from the tribe of Judah;
20 Shemuel son of Ammihud,
from the tribe of Simeon;
21 Elidad son of Kislon,
from the tribe of Benjamin;
22 Bukki son of Jogli,
the leader from the tribe of Dan;
23 Hanniel son of Ephod,
the leader from the tribe of Manasseh son of Joseph;
24 Kemuel son of Shiphtan,
the leader from the tribe of Ephraim son of Joseph;
25 Elizaphan son of Parnak,
the leader from the tribe of Zebulun;
26 Paltiel son of Azzan,
the leader from the tribe of Issachar;
27 Ahihud son of Shelomi,
the leader from the tribe of Asher;
28 Pedahel son of Ammihud,
the leader from the tribe of Naphtali."

29 These are the men the LORD commanded to assign the inheritance to the
Israelites in the land of Canaan.

35 On the plains of Moab by the Jordan
across from Jericho, the LORD said
to Moses, 2 "Command the Israelites to
give the Levites towns to live in from the
inheritance the Israelites will possess.
And give them pasturelands around the
towns. 3 Then they will have towns to live
in and pasturelands for the cattle they
own and all their other animals.

4 "The pasturelands around the towns
that you give the Levites will extend a
thousand cubits[a] from the town wall.
5 Outside the town, measure two thousand cubits[b] on the east side, two thousand on the south side, two thousand
on the west and two thousand on the
north, with the town in the center. They
will have this area as pastureland for the
towns.

6 "Six of the towns you give the Levites
will be cities of refuge, to which a person
who has killed someone may flee. In addition, give them forty-two other towns.
7 In all you must give the Levites forty-
eight towns, together with their pasturelands. 8 The towns you give the Levites
from the land the Israelites possess are
to be given in proportion to the inheritance of each tribe: Take many towns
from a tribe that has many, but few from
one that has few."

9 Then the LORD said to Moses: 10 "Speak
to the Israelites and say to them: 'When
you cross the Jordan into Canaan, 11 select some towns to be your cities of refuge, to which a person who has killed
someone accidentally may flee. 12 They
will be places of refuge from the avenger, so that anyone accused of murder
may not die before they stand trial before the assembly. 13 These six towns you
give will be your cities of refuge. 14 Give
three on this side of the Jordan and three
in Canaan as cities of refuge. 15 These six
towns will be a place of refuge for Israelites and for foreigners residing among
them, so that anyone who has killed another accidentally can flee there.

16 "'If anyone strikes someone a fatal
blow with an iron object, that person is
a murderer; the murderer is to be put to
death. 17 Or if anyone is holding a stone
and strikes someone a fatal blow with it,
that person is a murderer; the murderer is to be put to death. 18 Or if anyone
is holding a wooden object and strikes
someone a fatal blow with it, that person
is a murderer; the murderer is to be put
to death. 19 The avenger of blood shall put
the murderer to death; when the avenger
comes upon the murderer, the avenger
shall put the murderer to death. 20 If anyone with malice aforethought shoves
another or throws something at them
intentionally so that they die 21 or if out
of enmity one person hits another with
their fist so that the other dies, that person is to be put to death; that person is a
murderer. The avenger of blood shall put
the murderer to death when they meet.

22 "'But if without enmity someone
suddenly pushes another or throws

[a] 4 That is, about 1,500 feet or about 450 meters
[b] 5 That is, about 3,000 feet or about 900 meters

something at them unintentionally [23]or,
without seeing them, drops on them a
stone heavy enough to kill them, and
they die, then since that other person
was not an enemy and no harm was intended, [24]the assembly must judge between the accused and the avenger of
blood according to these regulations.
[25]The assembly must protect the one
accused of murder from the avenger of
blood and send the accused back to the
city of refuge to which they fled. The accused must stay there until the death of
the high priest, who was anointed with
the holy oil.

[26]" 'But if the accused ever goes outside
the limits of the city of refuge to which
they fled [27]and the avenger of blood
finds them outside the city, the avenger
of blood may kill the accused without being guilty of murder. [28]The accused must
stay in the city of refuge until the death
of the high priest; only after the death of
the high priest may they return to their
own property.

[29]" 'This is to have the force of law for
you throughout the generations to come,
wherever you live.

[30]" 'Anyone who kills a person is to be
put to death as a murderer only on the
testimony of witnesses. But no one is to
be put to death on the testimony of only
one witness.

[31]" 'Do not accept a ransom for the life
of a murderer, who deserves to die. They
are to be put to death.

[32]" 'Do not accept a ransom for anyone
who has fled to a city of refuge and so allow them to go back and live on their own
land before the death of the high priest.

[33]" 'Do not pollute the land where you
are. Bloodshed pollutes the land, and
atonement cannot be made for the land
on which blood has been shed, except by
the blood of the one who shed it. [34]Do not
defile the land where you live and where
I dwell, for I, the LORD, dwell among the
Israelites.' "

36 The family heads of the clan of Gilead son of Makir, the son of Manasseh, who were from the clans of the
descendants of Joseph, came and spoke
before Moses and the leaders, the heads
of the Israelite families. [2]They said,
"When the LORD commanded my lord to
give the land as an inheritance to the Israelites by lot, he ordered you to give the
inheritance of our brother Zelophehad to
his daughters. [3]Now suppose they marry men from other Israelite tribes; then
their inheritance will be taken from our
ancestral inheritance and added to that
of the tribe they marry into. And so part
of the inheritance allotted to us will be
taken away. [4]When the Year of Jubilee for
the Israelites comes, their inheritance
will be added to that of the tribe into
which they marry, and their property
will be taken from the tribal inheritance
of our ancestors."

[5]Then at the LORD's command Moses
gave this order to the Israelites: "What
the tribe of the descendants of Joseph
is saying is right. [6]This is what the LORD
commands for Zelophehad's daughters:
They may marry anyone they please as
long as they marry within their father's
tribal clan. [7]No inheritance in Israel is to
pass from one tribe to another, for every
Israelite shall keep the tribal inheritance
of their ancestors. [8]Every daughter who
inherits land in any Israelite tribe must
marry someone in her father's tribal
clan, so that every Israelite will possess
the inheritance of their ancestors. [9]No
inheritance may pass from one tribe to
another, for each Israelite tribe is to keep
the land it inherits."

[10]So Zelophehad's daughters did as
the LORD commanded Moses. [11]Zelo-
phehad's daughters — Mahlah, Tirzah,
Hoglah, Milkah and Noah — married
their cousins on their father's side.
[12]They married within the clans of the
descendants of Manasseh son of Joseph,
and their inheritance remained in their
father's tribe and clan.

[13]These are the commands and regulations the LORD gave through Moses to
the Israelites on the plains of Moab by
the Jordan across from Jericho.

DEUTERONOMY

The book of Deuteronomy records the great speech Moses gives just before his death. He addresses the generation of Israelites who grew up in the wilderness just as they are preparing to enter the land of Canaan. God wants this promised land to show what renewed life under God's blessing looks like. The book presents the covenant in a form commonly used by rulers of the time to make treaties with those they ruled over. The standard form of these treaties included five elements:

: The great ruler is identified by name and title.
: The history and mighty acts of the great ruler are told.
: The allegiance and specific duties expected of the ruler's servants are spelled out.
: Blessings for keeping the treaty and curses for breaking it are listed.
: Provisions for continuing the covenant with future generations are laid out.

Deuteronomy follows this pattern very closely. Moses is identified as the representative of the Great King—the God of Israel—whose mighty acts for his people are recalled. Moses reminds them to give exclusive allegiance to their king and lists their duties. He then calls on the people to join in a sacred oath to ratify the covenant. After naming a successor and climbing a mountain to look out over the land, Moses dies. The people of Israel stand on the edge of their inheritance, the promise of a new creation before them.

---

1 These are the words Moses spoke to
all Israel in the wilderness east of the
Jordan — that is, in the Arabah — opposite Suph, between Paran and Tophel,
Laban, Hazeroth and Dizahab. 2(It takes
eleven days to go from Horeb to Kadesh
Barnea by the Mount Seir road.)
3In the fortieth year, on the first day of
the eleventh month, Moses proclaimed to
the Israelites all that the LORD had commanded him concerning them. 4This
was after he had defeated Sihon king of
the Amorites, who reigned in Heshbon,
and at Edrei had defeated Og king of Bashan, who reigned in Ashtaroth.

5East of the Jordan in the territory of
Moab, Moses began to expound this law,
saying:
6The LORD our God said to us at Horeb, "You have stayed long enough at this
mountain. 7Break camp and advance into
the hill country of the Amorites; go to all
the neighboring peoples in the Arabah,
in the mountains, in the western foothills, in the Negev and along the coast, to
the land of the Canaanites and to Lebanon, as far as the great river, the Euphrates. 8See, I have given you this land. Go in
and take possession of the land the LORD
swore he would give to your fathers — to
Abraham, Isaac and Jacob — and to their
descendants after them."
9At that time I said to you, "You are
too heavy a burden for me to carry
alone. 10The LORD your God has increased your numbers so that today you
are as numerous as the stars in the sky.
11May the LORD, the God of your ancestors, increase you a thousand times and
bless you as he has promised! 12But how
can I bear your problems and your burdens and your disputes all by myself?
13Choose some wise, understanding and
respected men from each of your tribes,
and I will set them over you."
14You answered me, "What you propose to do is good."
15So I took the leading men of your
tribes, wise and respected men, and
appointed them to have authority over
you — as commanders of thousands, of
hundreds, of fifties and of tens and as
tribal officials. 16And I charged your
judges at that time, "Hear the disputes
between your people and judge fairly,
whether the case is between two Israelites or between an Israelite and a foreigner residing among you. 17Do not
show partiality in judging; hear both
small and great alike. Do not be afraid
of anyone, for judgment belongs to God.
Bring me any case too hard for you, and I
will hear it." 18And at that time I told you
everything you were to do.
19Then, as the LORD our God commanded us, we set out from Horeb and

went toward the hill country of the Amorites through all that vast and dreadful wilderness that you have seen, and so we reached Kadesh Barnea. 20Then I said to you, "You have reached the hill country of the Amorites, which the LORD our God is giving us. 21See, the LORD your God has given you the land. Go up and take possession of it as the LORD, the God of your ancestors, told you. Do not be afraid; do not be discouraged."

22Then all of you came to me and said, "Let us send men ahead to spy out the land for us and bring back a report about the route we are to take and the towns we will come to."

23The idea seemed good to me; so I selected twelve of you, one man from each tribe. 24They left and went up into the hill country, and came to the Valley of Eshkol and explored it. 25Taking with them some of the fruit of the land, they brought it down to us and reported, "It is a good land that the LORD our God is giving us."

26But you were unwilling to go up; you rebelled against the command of the LORD your God. 27You grumbled in your tents and said, "The LORD hates us; so he brought us out of Egypt to deliver us into the hands of the Amorites to destroy us. 28Where can we go? Our brothers have made our hearts melt in fear. They say, 'The people are stronger and taller than we are; the cities are large, with walls up to the sky. We even saw the Anakites there.'"

29Then I said to you, "Do not be terrified; do not be afraid of them. 30The LORD your God, who is going before you, will fight for you, as he did for you in Egypt, before your very eyes, 31and in the wilderness. There you saw how the LORD your God carried you, as a father carries his son, all the way you went until you reached this place."

32In spite of this, you did not trust in the LORD your God, 33who went ahead of you on your journey, in fire by night and in a cloud by day, to search out places for you to camp and to show you the way you should go.

34When the LORD heard what you said, he was angry and solemnly swore: 35"No one from this evil generation shall see the good land I swore to give your ancestors, 36except Caleb son of Jephunneh. He will see it, and I will give him and his descendants the land he set his feet on, because he followed the LORD wholeheartedly."

37Because of you the LORD became angry with me also and said, "You shall not enter it, either. 38But your assistant, Joshua son of Nun, will enter it. Encourage him, because he will lead Israel to inherit it. 39And the little ones that you said would be taken captive, your children who do not yet know good from bad — they will enter the land. I will give it to them and they will take possession of it. 40But as for you, turn around and set out toward the desert along the route to the Red Sea.[a]"

41Then you replied, "We have sinned against the LORD. We will go up and fight, as the LORD our God commanded us." So every one of you put on his weapons, thinking it easy to go up into the hill country.

42But the LORD said to me, "Tell them, 'Do not go up and fight, because I will not be with you. You will be defeated by your enemies.'"

43So I told you, but you would not listen. You rebelled against the LORD's command and in your arrogance you marched up into the hill country. 44The Amorites who lived in those hills came out against you; they chased you like a swarm of bees and beat you down from Seir all the way to Hormah. 45You came back and wept before the LORD, but he paid no attention to your weeping and turned a deaf ear to you. 46And so you stayed in Kadesh many days — all the time you spent there.

2 Then we turned back and set out toward the wilderness along the route to the Red Sea,[a] as the LORD had directed me. For a long time we made our way around the hill country of Seir.

2Then the LORD said to me, 3"You have made your way around this hill country long enough; now turn north. 4Give the people these orders: 'You are about to pass through the territory of your relatives the descendants of Esau, who live in Seir. They will be afraid of you, but be very careful. 5Do not provoke them

[a] 40,1 Or *the Sea of Reeds*

to war, for I will not give you any of their land, not even enough to put your foot on. I have given Esau the hill country of Seir as his own. 6 You are to pay them in silver for the food you eat and the water you drink.'"

7 The LORD your God has blessed you in all the work of your hands. He has watched over your journey through this vast wilderness. These forty years the LORD your God has been with you, and you have not lacked anything.

8 So we went on past our relatives the descendants of Esau, who live in Seir. We turned from the Arabah road, which comes up from Elath and Ezion Geber, and traveled along the desert road of Moab.

9 Then the LORD said to me, "Do not harass the Moabites or provoke them to war, for I will not give you any part of their land. I have given Ar to the descendants of Lot as a possession."

10 (The Emites used to live there—a people strong and numerous, and as tall as the Anakites. 11 Like the Anakites, they too were considered Rephaites, but the Moabites called them Emites. 12 Horites used to live in Seir, but the descendants of Esau drove them out. They destroyed the Horites from before them and settled in their place, just as Israel did in the land the LORD gave them as their possession.)

13 And the LORD said, "Now get up and cross the Zered Valley." So we crossed the valley.

14 Thirty-eight years passed from the time we left Kadesh Barnea until we crossed the Zered Valley. By then, that entire generation of fighting men had perished from the camp, as the LORD had sworn to them. 15 The LORD's hand was against them until he had completely eliminated them from the camp.

16 Now when the last of these fighting men among the people had died, 17 the LORD said to me, 18 "Today you are to pass by the region of Moab at Ar. 19 When you come to the Ammonites, do not harass them or provoke them to war, for I will not give you possession of any land belonging to the Ammonites. I have given it as a possession to the descendants of Lot."

20 (That too was considered a land of the Rephaites, who used to live there; but the Ammonites called them Zamzummites. 21 They were a people strong and numerous, and as tall as the Anakites. The LORD destroyed them from before the Ammonites, who drove them out and settled in their place. 22 The LORD had done the same for the descendants of Esau, who lived in Seir, when he destroyed the Horites from before them. They drove them out and have lived in their place to this day. 23 And as for the Avvites who lived in villages as far as Gaza, the Caphtorites coming out from Caphtor[a] destroyed them and settled in their place.)

24 "Set out now and cross the Arnon Gorge. See, I have given into your hand Sihon the Amorite, king of Heshbon, and his country. Begin to take possession of it and engage him in battle. 25 This very day I will begin to put the terror and fear of you on all the nations under heaven. They will hear reports of you and will tremble and be in anguish because of you."

26 From the Desert of Kedemoth I sent messengers to Sihon king of Heshbon offering peace and saying, 27 "Let us pass through your country. We will stay on the main road; we will not turn aside to the right or to the left. 28 Sell us food to eat and water to drink for their price in silver. Only let us pass through on foot— 29 as the descendants of Esau, who live in Seir, and the Moabites, who live in Ar, did for us—until we cross the Jordan into the land the LORD our God is giving us." 30 But Sihon king of Heshbon refused to let us pass through. For the LORD your God had made his spirit stubborn and his heart obstinate in order to give him into your hands, as he has now done.

31 The LORD said to me, "See, I have begun to deliver Sihon and his country over to you. Now begin to conquer and possess his land."

32 When Sihon and all his army came out to meet us in battle at Jahaz, 33 the LORD our God delivered him over to us and we struck him down, together with his sons and his whole army. 34 At that time we took all his towns and com-

[a] *23* That is, Crete

pletely destroyed[a] them — men, women
and children. We left no survivors. 35But
the livestock and the plunder from the
towns we had captured we carried off
for ourselves. 36From Aroer on the rim of
the Arnon Gorge, and from the town in
the gorge, even as far as Gilead, not one
town was too strong for us. The LORD our
God gave us all of them. 37But in accordance with the command of the LORD
our God, you did not encroach on any of
the land of the Ammonites, neither the
land along the course of the Jabbok nor
that around the towns in the hills.

3 Next we turned and went up along the
road toward Bashan, and Og king of
Bashan with his whole army marched
out to meet us in battle at Edrei. 2The
LORD said to me, "Do not be afraid of
him, for I have delivered him into your
hands, along with his whole army and
his land. Do to him what you did to Sihon king of the Amorites, who reigned
in Heshbon."

3So the LORD our God also gave into
our hands Og king of Bashan and all his
army. We struck them down, leaving no
survivors. 4At that time we took all his
cities. There was not one of the sixty cities that we did not take from them — the
whole region of Argob, Og's kingdom
in Bashan. 5All these cities were fortified with high walls and with gates and
bars, and there were also a great many
unwalled villages. 6We completely destroyed[a] them, as we had done with Sihon king of Heshbon, destroying[a] every
city — men, women and children. 7But
all the livestock and the plunder from
their cities we carried off for ourselves.

8So at that time we took from these
two kings of the Amorites the territory east of the Jordan, from the Arnon
Gorge as far as Mount Hermon. 9(Hermon is called Sirion by the Sidonians;
the Amorites call it Senir.) 10We took all
the towns on the plateau, and all Gilead, and all Bashan as far as Salekah and
Edrei, towns of Og's kingdom in Bashan.
11(Og king of Bashan was the last of the
Rephaites. His bed was decorated with
iron and was more than nine cubits long
and four cubits wide.[b] It is still in Rabbah of the Ammonites.)

12Of the land that we took over at
that time, I gave the Reubenites and
the Gadites the territory north of Aroer
by the Arnon Gorge, including half the
hill country of Gilead, together with its
towns. 13The rest of Gilead and also all
of Bashan, the kingdom of Og, I gave
to the half-tribe of Manasseh. (The
whole region of Argob in Bashan used
to be known as a land of the Rephaites.
14Jair, a descendant of Manasseh, took
the whole region of Argob as far as the
border of the Geshurites and the Maaka-
thites; it was named after him, so that to
this day Bashan is called Havvoth Jair.[c])
15And I gave Gilead to Makir. 16But to the
Reubenites and the Gadites I gave the
territory extending from Gilead down to
the Arnon Gorge (the middle of the gorge
being the border) and out to the Jabbok
River, which is the border of the Ammonites. 17Its western border was the
Jordan in the Arabah, from Kinnereth to
the Sea of the Arabah (that is, the Dead
Sea), below the slopes of Pisgah.

18I commanded you at that time: "The
LORD your God has given you this land
to take possession of it. But all your
able-bodied men, armed for battle, must
cross over ahead of the other Israelites.
19However, your wives, your children
and your livestock (I know you have
much livestock) may stay in the towns
I have given you, 20until the LORD gives
rest to your fellow Israelites as he has to
you, and they too have taken over the
land that the LORD your God is giving
them across the Jordan. After that, each
of you may go back to the possession I
have given you."

21At that time I commanded Joshua: "You have seen with your own eyes
all that the LORD your God has done to
these two kings. The LORD will do the
same to all the kingdoms over there
where you are going. 22Do not be afraid
of them; the LORD your God himself will
fight for you."

23At that time I pleaded with the LORD:
24"Sovereign LORD, you have begun to
show to your servant your greatness and
your strong hand. For what god is there
in heaven or on earth who can do the
deeds and mighty works you do? 25Let

[a] *34,6* The Hebrew term refers to the irrevocable giving over of things or persons to the LORD, often by totally destroying them. [b] *11* That is, about 14 feet long and 6 feet wide or about 4 meters long and 1.8 meters wide [c] *14* Or *called the settlements of Jair*

me go over and see the good land beyond the Jordan — that fine hill country
and Lebanon."
26But because of you the LORD was angry with me and would not listen to me.
"That is enough," the LORD said. "Do not
speak to me anymore about this matter.
27Go up to the top of Pisgah and look
west and north and south and east. Look
at the land with your own eyes, since you
are not going to cross this Jordan. 28But
commission Joshua, and encourage and
strengthen him, for he will lead this
people across and will cause them to inherit the land that you will see." 29So we
stayed in the valley near Beth Peor.

4 Now, Israel, hear the decrees and
laws I am about to teach you. Follow
them so that you may live and may go
in and take possession of the land the
LORD, the God of your ancestors, is giving you. 2Do not add to what I command
you and do not subtract from it, but keep
the commands of the LORD your God
that I give you.
3You saw with your own eyes what the
LORD did at Baal Peor. The LORD your
God destroyed from among you everyone who followed the Baal of Peor, 4but
all of you who held fast to the LORD your
God are still alive today.
5See, I have taught you decrees and
laws as the LORD my God commanded
me, so that you may follow them in the
land you are entering to take possession
of it. 6Observe them carefully, for this
will show your wisdom and understanding to the nations, who will hear about
all these decrees and say, "Surely this
great nation is a wise and understanding
people." 7What other nation is so great
as to have their gods near them the way
the LORD our God is near us whenever
we pray to him? 8And what other nation
is so great as to have such righteous decrees and laws as this body of laws I am
setting before you today?
9Only be careful, and watch yourselves closely so that you do not forget
the things your eyes have seen or let
them fade from your heart as long as you
live. Teach them to your children and
to their children after them. 10Remem-
ber the day you stood before the LORD
your God at Horeb, when he said to me,
"Assemble the people before me to hear
my words so that they may learn to revere me as long as they live in the land
and may teach them to their children."
11You came near and stood at the foot of
the mountain while it blazed with fire to
the very heavens, with black clouds and
deep darkness. 12Then the LORD spoke
to you out of the fire. You heard the
sound of words but saw no form; there
was only a voice. 13He declared to you
his covenant, the Ten Commandments,
which he commanded you to follow
and then wrote them on two stone tablets. 14And the LORD directed me at that
time to teach you the decrees and laws
you are to follow in the land that you are
crossing the Jordan to possess.
15You saw no form of any kind the
day the LORD spoke to you at Horeb out
of the fire. Therefore watch yourselves
very carefully, 16so that you do not become corrupt and make for yourselves
an idol, an image of any shape, whether formed like a man or a woman, 17or
like any animal on earth or any bird that
flies in the air, 18or like any creature that
moves along the ground or any fish in
the waters below. 19And when you look
up to the sky and see the sun, the moon
and the stars — all the heavenly array —
do not be enticed into bowing down to
them and worshiping things the LORD
your God has apportioned to all the nations under heaven. 20But as for you, the
LORD took you and brought you out of
the iron-smelting furnace, out of Egypt,
to be the people of his inheritance, as
you now are.
21The LORD was angry with me because of you, and he solemnly swore
that I would not cross the Jordan and
enter the good land the LORD your God
is giving you as your inheritance. 22I will
die in this land; I will not cross the Jordan; but you are about to cross over and
take possession of that good land. 23Be
careful not to forget the covenant of the
LORD your God that he made with you;
do not make for yourselves an idol in the
form of anything the LORD your God has
forbidden. 24For the LORD your God is a
consuming fire, a jealous God.
25After you have had children and
grandchildren and have lived in the
land a long time — if you then become
corrupt and make any kind of idol, doing evil in the eyes of the LORD your God

and arousing his anger, 26I call the heavens and the earth as witnesses against you this day that you will quickly perish from the land that you are crossing the Jordan to possess. You will not live there long but will certainly be destroyed. 27The LORD will scatter you among the peoples, and only a few of you will survive among the nations to which the LORD will drive you. 28There you will worship man-made gods of wood and stone, which cannot see or hear or eat or smell. 29But if from there you seek the LORD your God, you will find him if you seek him with all your heart and with all your soul. 30When you are in distress and all these things have happened to you, then in later days you will return to the LORD your God and obey him. 31For the LORD your God is a merciful God; he will not abandon or destroy you or forget the covenant with your ancestors, which he confirmed to them by oath.

32Ask now about the former days, long before your time, from the day God created human beings on the earth; ask from one end of the heavens to the other. Has anything so great as this ever happened, or has anything like it ever been heard of? 33Has any other people heard the voice of God[a] speaking out of fire, as you have, and lived? 34Has any god ever tried to take for himself one nation out of another nation, by testings, by signs and wonders, by war, by a mighty hand and an outstretched arm, or by great and awesome deeds, like all the things the LORD your God did for you in Egypt before your very eyes?

35You were shown these things so that you might know that the LORD is God; besides him there is no other. 36From heaven he made you hear his voice to discipline you. On earth he showed you his great fire, and you heard his words from out of the fire. 37Because he loved your ancestors and chose their descendants after them, he brought you out of Egypt by his Presence and his great strength, 38to drive out before you nations greater and stronger than you and to bring you into their land to give it to you for your inheritance, as it is today.

39Acknowledge and take to heart this day that the LORD is God in heaven above and on the earth below. There is no other. 40Keep his decrees and commands, which I am giving you today, so that it may go well with you and your children after you and that you may live long in the land the LORD your God gives you for all time.

41Then Moses set aside three cities east of the Jordan, 42to which anyone who had killed a person could flee if they had unintentionally killed a neighbor without malice aforethought. They could flee into one of these cities and save their life. 43The cities were these: Bezer in the wilderness plateau, for the Reubenites; Ramoth in Gilead, for the Gadites; and Golan in Bashan, for the Manassites.

44This is the law Moses set before the Israelites. 45These are the stipulations, decrees and laws Moses gave them when they came out of Egypt 46and were in the valley near Beth Peor east of the Jordan, in the land of Sihon king of the Amorites, who reigned in Heshbon and was defeated by Moses and the Israelites as they came out of Egypt. 47They took possession of his land and the land of Og king of Bashan, the two Amorite kings east of the Jordan. 48This land extended from Aroer on the rim of the Arnon Gorge to Mount Sirion[b] (that is, Hermon), 49and included all the Arabah east of the Jordan, as far as the Dead Sea,[c] below the slopes of Pisgah.

5 Moses summoned all Israel and said: Hear, Israel, the decrees and laws I declare in your hearing today. Learn them and be sure to follow them. 2The LORD our God made a covenant with us at Horeb. 3It was not with our ancestors[d] that the LORD made this covenant, but with us, with all of us who are alive here today. 4The LORD spoke to you face to face out of the fire on the mountain. 5(At that time I stood between the LORD and you to declare to you the word of the LORD, because you were afraid of the fire and did not go up the mountain.) And he said:

> 6"I am the LORD your God, who
> brought you out of Egypt, out of
> the land of slavery.
>
> 7"You shall have no other gods before[e] me.

[a] *33* Or *of a god* [b] *48* Syriac (see also 3:9); Hebrew *Siyon* [c] *49* Hebrew *the Sea of the Arabah*
[d] *3* Or *not only with our parents* [e] *7* Or *besides*

8 "You shall not make for yourself an
image in the form of anything
in heaven above or on the earth
beneath or in the waters below. 9 You shall not bow down
to them or worship them; for I,
the LORD your God, am a jealous
God, punishing the children
for the sin of the parents to the
third and fourth generation of
those who hate me, 10 but showing love to a thousand generations of those who love me and
keep my commandments.
11 "You shall not misuse the name of
the LORD your God, for the LORD
will not hold anyone guiltless
who misuses his name.
12 "Observe the Sabbath day by keeping it holy, as the LORD your God
has commanded you. 13 Six days
you shall labor and do all your
work, 14 but the seventh day is a
sabbath to the LORD your God.
On it you shall not do any work,
neither you, nor your son or
daughter, nor your male or female servant, nor your ox, your
donkey or any of your animals,
nor any foreigner residing in
your towns, so that your male
and female servants may rest,
as you do. 15 Remember that
you were slaves in Egypt and
that the LORD your God brought
you out of there with a mighty
hand and an outstretched arm.
Therefore the LORD your God
has commanded you to observe
the Sabbath day.
16 "Honor your father and your mother, as the LORD your God has
commanded you, so that you
may live long and that it may
go well with you in the land the
LORD your God is giving you.
17 "You shall not murder.
18 "You shall not commit adultery.
19 "You shall not steal.
20 "You shall not give false testimony
against your neighbor.
21 "You shall not covet your neighbor's
wife. You shall not set your desire on your neighbor's house or
land, his male or female servant,
his ox or donkey, or anything
that belongs to your neighbor."

22 These are the commandments the
LORD proclaimed in a loud voice to your
whole assembly there on the mountain
from out of the fire, the cloud and the
deep darkness; and he added nothing
more. Then he wrote them on two stone
tablets and gave them to me.

23 When you heard the voice out of
the darkness, while the mountain was
ablaze with fire, all the leaders of your
tribes and your elders came to me. 24 And
you said, "The LORD our God has shown
us his glory and his majesty, and we have
heard his voice from the fire. Today we
have seen that a person can live even if
God speaks with them. 25 But now, why
should we die? This great fire will consume us, and we will die if we hear the
voice of the LORD our God any longer.
26 For what mortal has ever heard the
voice of the living God speaking out of
fire, as we have, and survived? 27 Go near
and listen to all that the LORD our God
says. Then tell us whatever the LORD our
God tells you. We will listen and obey."

28 The LORD heard you when you spoke
to me, and the LORD said to me, "I have
heard what this people said to you. Everything they said was good. 29 Oh, that
their hearts would be inclined to fear me
and keep all my commands always, so
that it might go well with them and their
children forever!

30 "Go, tell them to return to their tents.
31 But you stay here with me so that I may
give you all the commands, decrees and
laws you are to teach them to follow in
the land I am giving them to possess."

32 So be careful to do what the LORD
your God has commanded you; do not
turn aside to the right or to the left.
33 Walk in obedience to all that the LORD
your God has commanded you, so that
you may live and prosper and prolong
your days in the land that you will possess.

6 These are the commands, decrees
and laws the LORD your God directed me to teach you to observe in the
land that you are crossing the Jordan
to possess, 2 so that you, your children
and their children after them may fear
the LORD your God as long as you live by
keeping all his decrees and commands
that I give you, and so that you may enjoy
long life. 3 Hear, Israel, and be careful to
obey so that it may go well with you and

that you may increase greatly in a land
flowing with milk and honey, just as the
LORD, the God of your ancestors, promised you.
4 Hear, O Israel: The LORD our God,
the LORD is one.[a] 5 Love the LORD your
God with all your heart and with all your
soul and with all your strength. 6 These
commandments that I give you today
are to be on your hearts. 7 Impress them
on your children. Talk about them when
you sit at home and when you walk along
the road, when you lie down and when
you get up. 8 Tie them as symbols on your
hands and bind them on your foreheads.
9 Write them on the doorframes of your
houses and on your gates.
10 When the LORD your God brings
you into the land he swore to your fathers, to Abraham, Isaac and Jacob, to
give you—a land with large, flourishing
cities you did not build, 11 houses filled
with all kinds of good things you did
not provide, wells you did not dig, and
vineyards and olive groves you did not
plant—then when you eat and are satisfied, 12 be careful that you do not forget
the LORD, who brought you out of Egypt,
out of the land of slavery.
13 Fear the LORD your God, serve him
only and take your oaths in his name.
14 Do not follow other gods, the gods of
the peoples around you; 15 for the LORD
your God, who is among you, is a jealous God and his anger will burn against
you, and he will destroy you from the
face of the land. 16 Do not put the LORD
your God to the test as you did at Massah. 17 Be sure to keep the commands of
the LORD your God and the stipulations
and decrees he has given you. 18 Do what
is right and good in the LORD's sight,
so that it may go well with you and you
may go in and take over the good land
the LORD promised on oath to your ancestors, 19 thrusting out all your enemies
before you, as the LORD said.
20 In the future, when your son asks
you, "What is the meaning of the stipulations, decrees and laws the LORD our
God has commanded you?" 21 tell him:
"We were slaves of Pharaoh in Egypt, but
the LORD brought us out of Egypt with a
mighty hand. 22 Before our eyes the LORD
sent signs and wonders—great and terrible—on Egypt and Pharaoh and his
whole household. 23 But he brought us out
from there to bring us in and give us the
land he promised on oath to our ancestors. 24 The LORD commanded us to obey
all these decrees and to fear the LORD our
God, so that we might always prosper and
be kept alive, as is the case today. 25 And if
we are careful to obey all this law before
the LORD our God, as he has commanded
us, that will be our righteousness."

7 When the LORD your God brings you
into the land you are entering to possess and drives out before you many
nations—the Hittites, Girgashites, Amorites, Canaanites, Perizzites, Hivites
and Jebusites, seven nations larger and
stronger than you— 2 and when the
LORD your God has delivered them over
to you and you have defeated them, then
you must destroy them totally.[b] Make
no treaty with them, and show them no
mercy. 3 Do not intermarry with them.
Do not give your daughters to their sons
or take their daughters for your sons,
4 for they will turn your children away
from following me to serve other gods,
and the LORD's anger will burn against
you and will quickly destroy you. 5 This is
what you are to do to them: Break down
their altars, smash their sacred stones,
cut down their Asherah poles[c] and burn
their idols in the fire. 6 For you are a people holy to the LORD your God. The LORD
your God has chosen you out of all the
peoples on the face of the earth to be his
people, his treasured possession.
7 The LORD did not set his affection on
you and choose you because you were
more numerous than other peoples, for
you were the fewest of all peoples. 8 But
it was because the LORD loved you and
kept the oath he swore to your ancestors
that he brought you out with a mighty
hand and redeemed you from the land of
slavery, from the power of Pharaoh king
of Egypt. 9 Know therefore that the LORD
your God is God; he is the faithful God,
keeping his covenant of love to a thousand generations of those who love him
and keep his commandments. 10 But

[a] *4* Or *The LORD our God is one LORD*; or *The LORD is our God, the LORD is one*; or *The LORD is our God, the LORD alone* [b] *2* The Hebrew term refers to the irrevocable giving over of things or persons to the LORD, often by totally destroying them; also in verse 26. [c] *5* That is, wooden symbols of the goddess Asherah; here and elsewhere in Deuteronomy

those who hate him he will repay to
their face by destruction;
he will not be slow to repay to their
face those who hate him.

11 Therefore, take care to follow the commands, decrees and laws I give you today.
12 If you pay attention to these laws
and are careful to follow them, then the
LORD your God will keep his covenant of
love with you, as he swore to your ancestors. 13 He will love you and bless you and
increase your numbers. He will bless
the fruit of your womb, the crops of your
land—your grain, new wine and olive
oil—the calves of your herds and the
lambs of your flocks in the land he swore
to your ancestors to give you. 14 You will
be blessed more than any other people; none of your men or women will be
childless, nor will any of your livestock
be without young. 15 The LORD will keep
you free from every disease. He will not
inflict on you the horrible diseases you
knew in Egypt, but he will inflict them
on all who hate you. 16 You must destroy
all the peoples the LORD your God gives
over to you. Do not look on them with
pity and do not serve their gods, for that
will be a snare to you.
17 You may say to yourselves, "These
nations are stronger than we are. How
can we drive them out?" 18 But do not be
afraid of them; remember well what the
LORD your God did to Pharaoh and to
all Egypt. 19 You saw with your own eyes
the great trials, the signs and wonders,
the mighty hand and outstretched arm,
with which the LORD your God brought
you out. The LORD your God will do the
same to all the peoples you now fear.
20 Moreover, the LORD your God will
send the hornet among them until even
the survivors who hide from you have
perished. 21 Do not be terrified by them,
for the LORD your God, who is among
you, is a great and awesome God. 22 The
LORD your God will drive out those nations before you, little by little. You will
not be allowed to eliminate them all at
once, or the wild animals will multiply
around you. 23 But the LORD your God
will deliver them over to you, throwing
them into great confusion until they are
destroyed. 24 He will give their kings into
your hand, and you will wipe out their
names from under heaven. No one will
be able to stand up against you; you will
destroy them. 25 The images of their gods
you are to burn in the fire. Do not covet the silver and gold on them, and do
not take it for yourselves, or you will be
ensnared by it, for it is detestable to the
LORD your God. 26 Do not bring a detestable thing into your house or you, like it,
will be set apart for destruction. Regard
it as vile and utterly detest it, for it is set
apart for destruction.

8 Be careful to follow every command I
am giving you today, so that you may
live and increase and may enter and possess the land the LORD promised on oath
to your ancestors. 2 Remember how the
LORD your God led you all the way in the
wilderness these forty years, to humble
and test you in order to know what was
in your heart, whether or not you would
keep his commands. 3 He humbled you,
causing you to hunger and then feeding
you with manna, which neither you nor
your ancestors had known, to teach you
that man does not live on bread alone
but on every word that comes from the
mouth of the LORD. 4 Your clothes did not
wear out and your feet did not swell during these forty years. 5 Know then in your
heart that as a man disciplines his son,
so the LORD your God disciplines you.
6 Observe the commands of the LORD
your God, walking in obedience to him
and revering him. 7 For the LORD your
God is bringing you into a good land—
a land with brooks, streams, and deep
springs gushing out into the valleys and
hills; 8 a land with wheat and barley,
vines and fig trees, pomegranates, olive
oil and honey; 9 a land where bread will
not be scarce and you will lack nothing;
a land where the rocks are iron and you
can dig copper out of the hills.
10 When you have eaten and are satisfied, praise the LORD your God for the
good land he has given you. 11 Be careful that you do not forget the LORD your
God, failing to observe his commands,
his laws and his decrees that I am giving
you this day. 12 Otherwise, when you eat
and are satisfied, when you build fine
houses and settle down, 13 and when
your herds and flocks grow large and
your silver and gold increase and all you
have is multiplied, 14 then your heart will
become proud and you will forget the
LORD your God, who brought you out of

Egypt, out of the land of slavery. 15He led
you through the vast and dreadful wilderness, that thirsty and waterless land,
with its venomous snakes and scorpions.
He brought you water out of hard rock.
16He gave you manna to eat in the wilderness, something your ancestors had
never known, to humble and test you so
that in the end it might go well with you.
17You may say to yourself, "My power
and the strength of my hands have produced this wealth for me." 18But remember the LORD your God, for it is he who
gives you the ability to produce wealth,
and so confirms his covenant, which he
swore to your ancestors, as it is today.

19If you ever forget the LORD your God
and follow other gods and worship and
bow down to them, I testify against you
today that you will surely be destroyed.
20Like the nations the LORD destroyed
before you, so you will be destroyed for
not obeying the LORD your God.

9 Hear, Israel: You are now about to
cross the Jordan to go in and dispossess nations greater and stronger than
you, with large cities that have walls up
to the sky. 2The people are strong and
tall—Anakites! You know about them
and have heard it said: "Who can stand
up against the Anakites?" 3But be assured today that the LORD your God is
the one who goes across ahead of you
like a devouring fire. He will destroy
them; he will subdue them before you.
And you will drive them out and annihilate them quickly, as the LORD has
promised you.

4After the LORD your God has driven
them out before you, do not say to yourself, "The LORD has brought me here to
take possession of this land because of
my righteousness." No, it is on account
of the wickedness of these nations that
the LORD is going to drive them out before you. 5It is not because of your righteousness or your integrity that you
are going in to take possession of their
land; but on account of the wickedness
of these nations, the LORD your God
will drive them out before you, to accomplish what he swore to your fathers,
to Abraham, Isaac and Jacob. 6Under-
stand, then, that it is not because of your
righteousness that the LORD your God is
giving you this good land to possess, for
you are a stiff-necked people.

7Remember this and never forget how
you aroused the anger of the LORD your
God in the wilderness. From the day you
left Egypt until you arrived here, you
have been rebellious against the LORD.
8At Horeb you aroused the LORD's wrath
so that he was angry enough to destroy
you. 9When I went up on the mountain
to receive the tablets of stone, the tablets
of the covenant that the LORD had made
with you, I stayed on the mountain forty days and forty nights; I ate no bread
and drank no water. 10The LORD gave me
two stone tablets inscribed by the finger
of God. On them were all the commandments the LORD proclaimed to you on
the mountain out of the fire, on the day
of the assembly.

11At the end of the forty days and forty
nights, the LORD gave me the two stone
tablets, the tablets of the covenant.
12Then the LORD told me, "Go down
from here at once, because your people
whom you brought out of Egypt have become corrupt. They have turned away
quickly from what I commanded them
and have made an idol for themselves."

13And the LORD said to me, "I have seen
this people, and they are a stiff-necked
people indeed! 14Let me alone, so that
I may destroy them and blot out their
name from under heaven. And I will
make you into a nation stronger and
more numerous than they."

15So I turned and went down from the
mountain while it was ablaze with fire.
And the two tablets of the covenant were
in my hands. 16When I looked, I saw that
you had sinned against the LORD your
God; you had made for yourselves an
idol cast in the shape of a calf. You had
turned aside quickly from the way that
the LORD had commanded you. 17So I
took the two tablets and threw them out
of my hands, breaking them to pieces
before your eyes.

18Then once again I fell prostrate
before the LORD for forty days and forty nights; I ate no bread and drank no
water, because of all the sin you had
committed, doing what was evil in the
LORD's sight and so arousing his anger.
19I feared the anger and wrath of the
LORD, for he was angry enough with
you to destroy you. But again the LORD
listened to me. 20And the LORD was angry enough with Aaron to destroy him,

but at that time I prayed for Aaron too.
21 Also I took that sinful thing of yours,
the calf you had made, and burned it in
the fire. Then I crushed it and ground it
to powder as fine as dust and threw the
dust into a stream that flowed down the
mountain.

22 You also made the LORD angry at
Taberah, at Massah and at Kibroth Hattaavah.

23 And when the LORD sent you out
from Kadesh Barnea, he said, "Go up and
take possession of the land I have given
you." But you rebelled against the command of the LORD your God. You did not
trust him or obey him. 24 You have been
rebellious against the LORD ever since I
have known you.

25 I lay prostrate before the LORD those
forty days and forty nights because the
LORD had said he would destroy you. 26 I
prayed to the LORD and said, "Sovereign
LORD, do not destroy your people, your
own inheritance that you redeemed by
your great power and brought out of
Egypt with a mighty hand. 27 Remember
your servants Abraham, Isaac and Jacob. Overlook the stubbornness of this
people, their wickedness and their sin.
28 Otherwise, the country from which
you brought us will say, 'Because the
LORD was not able to take them into the
land he had promised them, and because he hated them, he brought them
out to put them to death in the wilderness.' 29 But they are your people, your
inheritance that you brought out by
your great power and your outstretched
arm."

10 At that time the LORD said to me,
"Chisel out two stone tablets like
the first ones and come up to me on the
mountain. Also make a wooden ark.[a]
2 I will write on the tablets the words
that were on the first tablets, which you
broke. Then you are to put them in the
ark."

3 So I made the ark out of acacia wood
and chiseled out two stone tablets like
the first ones, and I went up on the
mountain with the two tablets in my
hands. 4 The LORD wrote on these tablets what he had written before, the Ten
Commandments he had proclaimed to
you on the mountain, out of the fire, on
the day of the assembly. And the LORD
gave them to me. 5 Then I came back
down the mountain and put the tablets
in the ark I had made, as the LORD commanded me, and they are there now.

6 (The Israelites traveled from the
wells of Bene Jaakan to Moserah. There
Aaron died and was buried, and Eleazar
his son succeeded him as priest. 7 From
there they traveled to Gudgodah and
on to Jotbathah, a land with streams of
water. 8 At that time the LORD set apart
the tribe of Levi to carry the ark of the
covenant of the LORD, to stand before
the LORD to minister and to pronounce
blessings in his name, as they still do
today. 9 That is why the Levites have no
share or inheritance among their fellow
Israelites; the LORD is their inheritance,
as the LORD your God told them.)

10 Now I had stayed on the mountain
forty days and forty nights, as I did the
first time, and the LORD listened to me
at this time also. It was not his will to destroy you. 11 "Go," the LORD said to me,
"and lead the people on their way, so that
they may enter and possess the land I
swore to their ancestors to give them."

12 And now, Israel, what does the LORD
your God ask of you but to fear the LORD
your God, to walk in obedience to him,
to love him, to serve the LORD your God
with all your heart and with all your
soul, 13 and to observe the LORD's commands and decrees that I am giving you
today for your own good?

14 To the LORD your God belong the
heavens, even the highest heavens, the
earth and everything in it. 15 Yet the
LORD set his affection on your ancestors
and loved them, and he chose you, their
descendants, above all the nations—as
it is today. 16 Circumcise your hearts,
therefore, and do not be stiff-necked any
longer. 17 For the LORD your God is God
of gods and Lord of lords, the great God,
mighty and awesome, who shows no partiality and accepts no bribes. 18 He defends the cause of the fatherless and the
widow, and loves the foreigner residing
among you, giving them food and clothing. 19 And you are to love those who are
foreigners, for you yourselves were foreigners in Egypt. 20 Fear the LORD your
God and serve him. Hold fast to him and

[a] *1* That is, a chest

take your oaths in his name. [21]He is the
one you praise; he is your God, who performed for you those great and awesome
wonders you saw with your own eyes.
[22]Your ancestors who went down into
Egypt were seventy in all, and now the
LORD your God has made you as numerous as the stars in the sky.

11 Love the LORD your God and keep
his requirements, his decrees, his
laws and his commands always. [2]Re-
member today that your children were
not the ones who saw and experienced
the discipline of the LORD your God:
his majesty, his mighty hand, his outstretched arm; [3]the signs he performed
and the things he did in the heart of
Egypt, both to Pharaoh king of Egypt
and to his whole country; [4]what he did
to the Egyptian army, to its horses and
chariots, how he overwhelmed them
with the waters of the Red Sea[a] as they
were pursuing you, and how the LORD
brought lasting ruin on them. [5]It was not
your children who saw what he did for
you in the wilderness until you arrived
at this place, [6]and what he did to Dathan
and Abiram, sons of Eliab the Reubenite,
when the earth opened its mouth right
in the middle of all Israel and swallowed them up with their households,
their tents and every living thing that
belonged to them. [7]But it was your own
eyes that saw all these great things the
LORD has done.

[8]Observe therefore all the commands
I am giving you today, so that you may
have the strength to go in and take over
the land that you are crossing the Jordan to possess, [9]and so that you may
live long in the land the LORD swore to
your ancestors to give to them and their
descendants, a land flowing with milk
and honey. [10]The land you are entering
to take over is not like the land of Egypt,
from which you have come, where you
planted your seed and irrigated it by
foot as in a vegetable garden. [11]But the
land you are crossing the Jordan to take
possession of is a land of mountains and
valleys that drinks rain from heaven. [12]It
is a land the LORD your God cares for; the
eyes of the LORD your God are continually on it from the beginning of the year
to its end.

[13]So if you faithfully obey the commands I am giving you today—to love
the LORD your God and to serve him with
all your heart and with all your soul—
[14]then I will send rain on your land in its
season, both autumn and spring rains,
so that you may gather in your grain,
new wine and olive oil. [15]I will provide
grass in the fields for your cattle, and you
will eat and be satisfied.

[16]Be careful, or you will be enticed to
turn away and worship other gods and
bow down to them. [17]Then the LORD's
anger will burn against you, and he will
shut up the heavens so that it will not
rain and the ground will yield no produce, and you will soon perish from the
good land the LORD is giving you. [18]Fix
these words of mine in your hearts and
minds; tie them as symbols on your
hands and bind them on your foreheads.
[19]Teach them to your children, talking
about them when you sit at home and
when you walk along the road, when you
lie down and when you get up. [20]Write
them on the doorframes of your houses
and on your gates, [21]so that your days
and the days of your children may be
many in the land the LORD swore to give
your ancestors, as many as the days that
the heavens are above the earth.

[22]If you carefully observe all these
commands I am giving you to follow—
to love the LORD your God, to walk in
obedience to him and to hold fast to
him— [23]then the LORD will drive out all
these nations before you, and you will
dispossess nations larger and stronger
than you. [24]Every place where you set
your foot will be yours: Your territory
will extend from the desert to Lebanon, and from the Euphrates River to
the Mediterranean Sea. [25]No one will
be able to stand against you. The LORD
your God, as he promised you, will put
the terror and fear of you on the whole
land, wherever you go.

[26]See, I am setting before you today
a blessing and a curse— [27]the blessing
if you obey the commands of the LORD
your God that I am giving you today;
[28]the curse if you disobey the commands of the LORD your God and turn
from the way that I command you today
by following other gods, which you have

[a] 4 Or *the Sea of Reeds*

not known. 29When the LORD your God
has brought you into the land you are
entering to possess, you are to proclaim
on Mount Gerizim the blessings, and on
Mount Ebal the curses. 30As you know,
these mountains are across the Jordan,
westward, toward the setting sun, near
the great trees of Moreh, in the territory
of those Canaanites living in the Arabah
in the vicinity of Gilgal. 31You are about
to cross the Jordan to enter and take possession of the land the LORD your God is
giving you. When you have taken it over
and are living there, 32be sure that you
obey all the decrees and laws I am setting before you today.

12 These are the decrees and laws you
must be careful to follow in the land
that the LORD, the God of your ancestors,
has given you to possess — as long as you
live in the land. 2Destroy completely all
the places on the high mountains, on
the hills and under every spreading tree,
where the nations you are dispossessing
worship their gods. 3Break down their
altars, smash their sacred stones and
burn their Asherah poles in the fire; cut
down the idols of their gods and wipe out
their names from those places.

4You must not worship the LORD
your God in their way. 5But you are to
seek the place the LORD your God will
choose from among all your tribes to
put his Name there for his dwelling.
To that place you must go; 6there bring
your burnt offerings and sacrifices,
your tithes and special gifts, what you
have vowed to give and your freewill offerings, and the firstborn of your herds
and flocks. 7There, in the presence
of the LORD your God, you and your
families shall eat and shall rejoice in
everything you have put your hand to,
because the LORD your God has blessed
you.

8You are not to do as we do here today,
everyone doing as they see fit, 9since you
have not yet reached the resting place
and the inheritance the LORD your God
is giving you. 10But you will cross the Jordan and settle in the land the LORD your
God is giving you as an inheritance, and
he will give you rest from all your enemies around you so that you will live
in safety. 11Then to the place the LORD
your God will choose as a dwelling for
his Name — there you are to bring everything I command you: your burnt offerings and sacrifices, your tithes and special gifts, and all the choice possessions
you have vowed to the LORD. 12And there
rejoice before the LORD your God — you,
your sons and daughters, your male and
female servants, and the Levites from
your towns who have no allotment or
inheritance of their own. 13Be careful not to sacrifice your burnt offerings
anywhere you please. 14Offer them only
at the place the LORD will choose in one
of your tribes, and there observe everything I command you.

15Nevertheless, you may slaughter
your animals in any of your towns and
eat as much of the meat as you want, as if
it were gazelle or deer, according to the
blessing the LORD your God gives you.
Both the ceremonially unclean and the
clean may eat it. 16But you must not eat
the blood; pour it out on the ground like
water. 17You must not eat in your own
towns the tithe of your grain and new
wine and olive oil, or the firstborn of
your herds and flocks, or whatever you
have vowed to give, or your freewill offerings or special gifts. 18Instead, you are
to eat them in the presence of the LORD
your God at the place the LORD your God
will choose — you, your sons and daughters, your male and female servants, and
the Levites from your towns — and you
are to rejoice before the LORD your God
in everything you put your hand to. 19Be
careful not to neglect the Levites as long
as you live in your land.

20When the LORD your God has enlarged your territory as he promised
you, and you crave meat and say, "I
would like some meat," then you may eat
as much of it as you want. 21If the place
where the LORD your God chooses to put
his Name is too far away from you, you
may slaughter animals from the herds
and flocks the LORD has given you, as I
have commanded you, and in your own
towns you may eat as much of them as
you want. 22Eat them as you would gazelle or deer. Both the ceremonially unclean and the clean may eat. 23But be
sure you do not eat the blood, because
the blood is the life, and you must not eat
the life with the meat. 24You must not eat
the blood; pour it out on the ground like
water. 25Do not eat it, so that it may go
well with you and your children after

you, because you will be doing what is
right in the eyes of the LORD.
26But take your consecrated things
and whatever you have vowed to give,
and go to the place the LORD will choose.
27Present your burnt offerings on the altar of the LORD your God, both the meat
and the blood. The blood of your sacrifices must be poured beside the altar of
the LORD your God, but you may eat the
meat. 28Be careful to obey all these regulations I am giving you, so that it may
always go well with you and your children after you, because you will be doing
what is good and right in the eyes of the
LORD your God.
29The LORD your God will cut off before you the nations you are about to
invade and dispossess. But when you
have driven them out and settled in
their land, 30and after they have been
destroyed before you, be careful not to
be ensnared by inquiring about their
gods, saying, "How do these nations
serve their gods? We will do the same."
31You must not worship the LORD your
God in their way, because in worshiping
their gods, they do all kinds of detestable
things the LORD hates. They even burn
their sons and daughters in the fire as
sacrifices to their gods.
32See that you do all I command you;
do not add to it or take away from it.[a]
13[b] If a prophet, or one who foretells
by dreams, appears among you
and announces to you a sign or wonder, 2and if the sign or wonder spoken of
takes place, and the prophet says, "Let
us follow other gods" (gods you have
not known) "and let us worship them,"
3you must not listen to the words of that
prophet or dreamer. The LORD your God
is testing you to find out whether you
love him with all your heart and with all
your soul. 4It is the LORD your God you
must follow, and him you must revere.
Keep his commands and obey him; serve
him and hold fast to him. 5That prophet
or dreamer must be put to death for inciting rebellion against the LORD your
God, who brought you out of Egypt and
redeemed you from the land of slavery.
That prophet or dreamer tried to turn
you from the way the LORD your God
commanded you to follow. You must
purge the evil from among you.
6If your very own brother, or your
son or daughter, or the wife you love,
or your closest friend secretly entices you, saying, "Let us go and worship
other gods" (gods that neither you nor
your ancestors have known, 7gods of
the peoples around you, whether near
or far, from one end of the land to the
other), 8do not yield to them or listen to
them. Show them no pity. Do not spare
them or shield them. 9You must certainly put them to death. Your hand must be
the first in putting them to death, and
then the hands of all the people. 10Stone
them to death, because they tried to turn
you away from the LORD your God, who
brought you out of Egypt, out of the land
of slavery. 11Then all Israel will hear and
be afraid, and no one among you will do
such an evil thing again.
12If you hear it said about one of the
towns the LORD your God is giving you
to live in 13that troublemakers have aris-
en among you and have led the people of
their town astray, saying, "Let us go and
worship other gods" (gods you have not
known), 14then you must inquire, probe
and investigate it thoroughly. And if it is
true and it has been proved that this detestable thing has been done among you,
15you must certainly put to the sword all
who live in that town. You must destroy it
completely,[c] both its people and its livestock. 16You are to gather all the plunder
of the town into the middle of the public
square and completely burn the town
and all its plunder as a whole burnt offering to the LORD your God. That town
is to remain a ruin forever, never to be
rebuilt, 17and none of the condemned
things[c] are to be found in your hands.
Then the LORD will turn from his fierce
anger, will show you mercy, and will
have compassion on you. He will increase your numbers, as he promised on
oath to your ancestors — 18because you
obey the LORD your God by keeping all
his commands that I am giving you today and doing what is right in his eyes.
14 You are the children of the LORD
your God. Do not cut yourselves
or shave the front of your heads for the

[a] *32* In Hebrew texts this verse (12:32) is numbered 13:1. [b] In Hebrew texts 13:1-18 is numbered 13:2-19.
[c] *15,17* The Hebrew term refers to the irrevocable giving over of things or persons to the LORD, often by totally destroying them.

dead, 2for you are a people holy to the
LORD your God. Out of all the peoples on
the face of the earth, the LORD has chosen you to be his treasured possession.
3Do not eat any detestable thing.
4These are the animals you may eat:
the ox, the sheep, the goat, 5the deer,
the gazelle, the roe deer, the wild goat,
the ibex, the antelope and the mountain sheep.[a] 6You may eat any animal
that has a divided hoof and that chews
the cud. 7However, of those that chew
the cud or that have a divided hoof you
may not eat the camel, the rabbit or the
hyrax. Although they chew the cud, they
do not have a divided hoof; they are ceremonially unclean for you. 8The pig is
also unclean; although it has a divided
hoof, it does not chew the cud. You are
not to eat their meat or touch their carcasses.
9Of all the creatures living in the water, you may eat any that has fins and
scales. 10But anything that does not
have fins and scales you may not eat; for
you it is unclean.
11You may eat any clean bird. 12But
these you may not eat: the eagle, the vulture, the black vulture, 13the red kite, the
black kite, any kind of falcon, 14any kind
of raven, 15the horned owl, the screech
owl, the gull, any kind of hawk, 16the
little owl, the great owl, the white owl,
17the desert owl, the osprey, the cormorant, 18the stork, any kind of heron, the
hoopoe and the bat.
19All flying insects are unclean to you;
do not eat them. 20But any winged creature that is clean you may eat.
21Do not eat anything you find already
dead. You may give it to the foreigner residing in any of your towns, and they
may eat it, or you may sell it to any other
foreigner. But you are a people holy to
the LORD your God.
Do not cook a young goat in its mother's milk.
22Be sure to set aside a tenth of all that
your fields produce each year. 23Eat the
tithe of your grain, new wine and olive oil, and the firstborn of your herds
and flocks in the presence of the LORD
your God at the place he will choose
as a dwelling for his Name, so that you
may learn to revere the LORD your God
always. 24But if that place is too distant
and you have been blessed by the LORD
your God and cannot carry your tithe
(because the place where the LORD will
choose to put his Name is so far away),
25then exchange your tithe for silver,
and take the silver with you and go to the
place the LORD your God will choose.
26Use the silver to buy whatever you like:
cattle, sheep, wine or other fermented
drink, or anything you wish. Then you
and your household shall eat there in
the presence of the LORD your God and
rejoice. 27And do not neglect the Levites
living in your towns, for they have no allotment or inheritance of their own.
28At the end of every three years, bring
all the tithes of that year's produce and
store it in your towns, 29so that the Levites (who have no allotment or inheritance of their own) and the foreigners,
the fatherless and the widows who live
in your towns may come and eat and
be satisfied, and so that the LORD your
God may bless you in all the work of your
hands.
15 At the end of every seven years you
must cancel debts. 2This is how it is
to be done: Every creditor shall cancel
any loan they have made to a fellow Israelite. They shall not require payment
from anyone among their own people,
because the LORD's time for canceling
debts has been proclaimed. 3You may
require payment from a foreigner, but
you must cancel any debt your fellow Israelite owes you. 4However, there need
be no poor people among you, for in the
land the LORD your God is giving you
to possess as your inheritance, he will
richly bless you, 5if only you fully obey
the LORD your God and are careful to
follow all these commands I am giving
you today. 6For the LORD your God will
bless you as he has promised, and you
will lend to many nations but will borrow from none. You will rule over many
nations but none will rule over you.
7If anyone is poor among your fellow
Israelites in any of the towns of the land
the LORD your God is giving you, do not
be hardhearted or tightfisted toward
them. 8Rather, be openhanded and
freely lend them whatever they need.
9Be careful not to harbor this wicked

[a] 5 The precise identification of some of the birds and animals in this chapter is uncertain.

thought: "The seventh year, the year
for canceling debts, is near," so that you
do not show ill will toward the needy
among your fellow Israelites and give
them nothing. They may then appeal to
the LORD against you, and you will be
found guilty of sin. 10 Give generously
to them and do so without a grudging
heart; then because of this the LORD
your God will bless you in all your work
and in everything you put your hand to.
11 There will always be poor people in
the land. Therefore I command you to
be openhanded toward your fellow Israelites who are poor and needy in your
land.

12 If any of your people—Hebrew men
or women—sell themselves to you and
serve you six years, in the seventh year
you must let them go free. 13 And when
you release them, do not send them
away empty-handed. 14 Supply them lib-
erally from your flock, your threshing
floor and your winepress. Give to them
as the LORD your God has blessed you.
15 Remember that you were slaves in
Egypt and the LORD your God redeemed
you. That is why I give you this command today.

16 But if your servant says to you, "I
do not want to leave you," because he
loves you and your family and is well off
with you, 17 then take an awl and push it
through his earlobe into the door, and
he will become your servant for life. Do
the same for your female servant.

18 Do not consider it a hardship to set
your servant free, because their service
to you these six years has been worth
twice as much as that of a hired hand.
And the LORD your God will bless you in
everything you do.

19 Set apart for the LORD your God
every firstborn male of your herds and
flocks. Do not put the firstborn of your
cows to work, and do not shear the firstborn of your sheep. 20 Each year you
and your family are to eat them in the
presence of the LORD your God at the
place he will choose. 21 If an animal has
a defect, is lame or blind, or has any serious flaw, you must not sacrifice it to
the LORD your God. 22 You are to eat it in
your own towns. Both the ceremonially
unclean and the clean may eat it, as if it
were gazelle or deer. 23 But you must not
eat the blood; pour it out on the ground
like water.

16 Observe the month of Aviv and celebrate the Passover of the LORD
your God, because in the month of Aviv
he brought you out of Egypt by night.
2 Sacrifice as the Passover to the LORD
your God an animal from your flock or
herd at the place the LORD will choose
as a dwelling for his Name. 3 Do not eat it
with bread made with yeast, but for sev-
en days eat unleavened bread, the bread
of affliction, because you left Egypt in
haste—so that all the days of your life
you may remember the time of your
departure from Egypt. 4 Let no yeast be
found in your possession in all your land
for seven days. Do not let any of the meat
you sacrifice on the evening of the first
day remain until morning.

5 You must not sacrifice the Passover
in any town the LORD your God gives you
6 except in the place he will choose as a
dwelling for his Name. There you must
sacrifice the Passover in the evening,
when the sun goes down, on the anni-
versary[a] of your departure from Egypt.
7 Roast it and eat it at the place the LORD
your God will choose. Then in the morning return to your tents. 8 For six days eat
unleavened bread and on the seventh
day hold an assembly to the LORD your
God and do no work.

9 Count off seven weeks from the time
you begin to put the sickle to the standing grain. 10 Then celebrate the Festival
of Weeks to the LORD your God by giving
a freewill offering in proportion to the
blessings the LORD your God has giv-
en you. 11 And rejoice before the LORD
your God at the place he will choose as a
dwelling for his Name—you, your sons
and daughters, your male and female
servants, the Levites in your towns, and
the foreigners, the fatherless and the
widows living among you. 12 Remember
that you were slaves in Egypt, and follow
carefully these decrees.

13 Celebrate the Festival of Tabernacles for seven days after you have gathered the produce of your threshing floor
and your winepress. 14 Be joyful at your
festival—you, your sons and daughters,
your male and female servants, and the

[a] 6 Or *down, at the time of day*

Levites, the foreigners, the fatherless
and the widows who live in your towns.
15 For seven days celebrate the festival to
the LORD your God at the place the LORD
will choose. For the LORD your God will
bless you in all your harvest and in all
the work of your hands, and your joy will
be complete.
16 Three times a year all your men
must appear before the LORD your God
at the place he will choose: at the Festival of Unleavened Bread, the Festival of
Weeks and the Festival of Tabernacles.
No one should appear before the LORD
empty-handed: 17 Each of you must bring
a gift in proportion to the way the LORD
your God has blessed you.
18 Appoint judges and officials for
each of your tribes in every town the
LORD your God is giving you, and they
shall judge the people fairly. 19 Do not
pervert justice or show partiality. Do
not accept a bribe, for a bribe blinds the
eyes of the wise and twists the words
of the innocent. 20 Follow justice and
justice alone, so that you may live and
possess the land the LORD your God is
giving you.
21 Do not set up any wooden Asherah
pole beside the altar you build to the
LORD your God, 22 and do not erect a sacred stone, for these the LORD your God
hates.

17 Do not sacrifice to the LORD your
God an ox or a sheep that has any
defect or flaw in it, for that would be detestable to him.
2 If a man or woman living among you
in one of the towns the LORD gives you is
found doing evil in the eyes of the LORD
your God in violation of his covenant,
3 and contrary to my command has worshiped other gods, bowing down to them
or to the sun or the moon or the stars in
the sky, 4 and this has been brought to
your attention, then you must investigate it thoroughly. If it is true and it has
been proved that this detestable thing
has been done in Israel, 5 take the man
or woman who has done this evil deed
to your city gate and stone that person
to death. 6 On the testimony of two or
three witnesses a person is to be put to
death, but no one is to be put to death on
the testimony of only one witness. 7 The
hands of the witnesses must be the first
in putting that person to death, and then
the hands of all the people. You must
purge the evil from among you.
8 If cases come before your courts that
are too difficult for you to judge—whether bloodshed, lawsuits or assaults—take
them to the place the LORD your God will
choose. 9 Go to the Levitical priests and
to the judge who is in office at that time.
Inquire of them and they will give you
the verdict. 10 You must act according to
the decisions they give you at the place
the LORD will choose. Be careful to do
everything they instruct you to do. 11 Act
according to whatever they teach you
and the decisions they give you. Do not
turn aside from what they tell you, to the
right or to the left. 12 Anyone who shows
contempt for the judge or for the priest
who stands ministering there to the
LORD your God is to be put to death. You
must purge the evil from Israel. 13 All the
people will hear and be afraid, and will
not be contemptuous again.
14 When you enter the land the LORD
your God is giving you and have taken
possession of it and settled in it, and
you say, "Let us set a king over us like all
the nations around us," 15 be sure to appoint over you a king the LORD your God
chooses. He must be from among your
fellow Israelites. Do not place a foreigner over you, one who is not an Israelite.
16 The king, moreover, must not acquire
great numbers of horses for himself or
make the people return to Egypt to get
more of them, for the LORD has told you,
"You are not to go back that way again."
17 He must not take many wives, or his
heart will be led astray. He must not ac-
cumulate large amounts of silver and
gold.
18 When he takes the throne of his
kingdom, he is to write for himself on a
scroll a copy of this law, taken from that
of the Levitical priests. 19 It is to be with
him, and he is to read it all the days of
his life so that he may learn to revere
the LORD his God and follow carefully
all the words of this law and these decrees 20 and not consider himself better
than his fellow Israelites and turn from
the law to the right or to the left. Then
he and his descendants will reign a long
time over his kingdom in Israel.

18 The Levitical priests—indeed, the
whole tribe of Levi—are to have
no allotment or inheritance with Isra-

el. They shall live on the food offerings
presented to the LORD, for that is their
inheritance. 2They shall have no inheritance among their fellow Israelites; the
LORD is their inheritance, as he promised them.
3This is the share due the priests
from the people who sacrifice a bull or a
sheep: the shoulder, the internal organs
and the meat from the head. 4You are to
give them the firstfruits of your grain,
new wine and olive oil, and the first wool
from the shearing of your sheep, 5for the
LORD your God has chosen them and
their descendants out of all your tribes
to stand and minister in the LORD's
name always.
6If a Levite moves from one of your
towns anywhere in Israel where he is
living, and comes in all earnestness to
the place the LORD will choose, 7he may
minister in the name of the LORD his
God like all his fellow Levites who serve
there in the presence of the LORD. 8He is
to share equally in their benefits, even
though he has received money from the
sale of family possessions.
9When you enter the land the LORD
your God is giving you, do not learn to
imitate the detestable ways of the nations there. 10Let no one be found among
you who sacrifices their son or daughter
in the fire, who practices divination or
sorcery, interprets omens, engages in
witchcraft, 11or casts spells, or who is a
medium or spiritist or who consults the
dead. 12Anyone who does these things is
detestable to the LORD; because of these
same detestable practices the LORD your
God will drive out those nations before
you. 13You must be blameless before the
LORD your God.
14The nations you will dispossess listen to those who practice sorcery or divination. But as for you, the LORD your
God has not permitted you to do so.
15The LORD your God will raise up for
you a prophet like me from among you,
from your fellow Israelites. You must listen to him. 16For this is what you asked
of the LORD your God at Horeb on the
day of the assembly when you said, "Let
us not hear the voice of the LORD our
God nor see this great fire anymore, or
we will die."
17The LORD said to me: "What they
say is good. 18I will raise up for them a
prophet like you from among their fellow Israelites, and I will put my words in
his mouth. He will tell them everything
I command him. 19I myself will call to
account anyone who does not listen to
my words that the prophet speaks in my
name. 20But a prophet who presumes to
speak in my name anything I have not
commanded, or a prophet who speaks
in the name of other gods, is to be put
to death."
21You may say to yourselves, "How can
we know when a message has not been
spoken by the LORD?" 22If what a prophet proclaims in the name of the LORD
does not take place or come true, that is a
message the LORD has not spoken. That
prophet has spoken presumptuously, so
do not be alarmed.

19 When the LORD your God has destroyed the nations whose land he
is giving you, and when you have driven
them out and settled in their towns and
houses, 2then set aside for yourselves
three cities in the land the LORD your
God is giving you to possess. 3Deter-
mine the distances involved and divide
into three parts the land the LORD your
God is giving you as an inheritance, so
that a person who kills someone may
flee for refuge to one of these cities.
4This is the rule concerning anyone
who kills a person and flees there for
safety—anyone who kills a neighbor
unintentionally, without malice aforethought. 5For instance, a man may go
into the forest with his neighbor to cut
wood, and as he swings his ax to fell
a tree, the head may fly off and hit his
neighbor and kill him. That man may
flee to one of these cities and save his
life. 6Otherwise, the avenger of blood
might pursue him in a rage, overtake
him if the distance is too great, and kill
him even though he is not deserving of
death, since he did it to his neighbor
without malice aforethought. 7This is
why I command you to set aside for yourselves three cities.
8If the LORD your God enlarges your
territory, as he promised on oath to your
ancestors, and gives you the whole land
he promised them, 9because you carefully follow all these laws I command
you today—to love the LORD your God
and to walk always in obedience to
him—then you are to set aside three

more cities. 10 Do this so that innocent
blood will not be shed in your land,
which the LORD your God is giving you
as your inheritance, and so that you will
not be guilty of bloodshed.
11 But if out of hate someone lies in
wait, assaults and kills a neighbor, and
then flees to one of these cities, 12 the
killer shall be sent for by the town elders, be brought back from the city, and
be handed over to the avenger of blood
to die. 13 Show no pity. You must purge
from Israel the guilt of shedding innocent blood, so that it may go well with
you.
14 Do not move your neighbor's boundary stone set up by your predecessors in
the inheritance you receive in the land
the LORD your God is giving you to possess.
15 One witness is not enough to convict
anyone accused of any crime or offense
they may have committed. A matter
must be established by the testimony of
two or three witnesses.
16 If a malicious witness takes the
stand to accuse someone of a crime,
17 the two people involved in the dispute
must stand in the presence of the LORD
before the priests and the judges who are
in office at the time. 18 The judges must
make a thorough investigation, and if
the witness proves to be a liar, giving
false testimony against a fellow Israelite, 19 then do to the false witness as that
witness intended to do to the other party. You must purge the evil from among
you. 20 The rest of the people will hear of
this and be afraid, and never again will
such an evil thing be done among you.
21 Show no pity: life for life, eye for eye,
tooth for tooth, hand for hand, foot for
foot.

20 When you go to war against your
enemies and see horses and chariots and an army greater than yours, do
not be afraid of them, because the LORD
your God, who brought you up out of
Egypt, will be with you. 2 When you are
about to go into battle, the priest shall
come forward and address the army.
3 He shall say: "Hear, Israel: Today you
are going into battle against your enemies. Do not be fainthearted or afraid;
do not panic or be terrified by them. 4 For
the LORD your God is the one who goes
with you to fight for you against your enemies to give you victory."
5 The officers shall say to the army:
"Has anyone built a new house and not
yet begun to live in it? Let him go home,
or he may die in battle and someone
else may begin to live in it. 6 Has anyone
planted a vineyard and not begun to enjoy it? Let him go home, or he may die in
battle and someone else enjoy it. 7 Has
anyone become pledged to a woman and
not married her? Let him go home, or he
may die in battle and someone else marry her." 8 Then the officers shall add, "Is
anyone afraid or fainthearted? Let him
go home so that his fellow soldiers will
not become disheartened too." 9 When
the officers have finished speaking to
the army, they shall appoint commanders over it.
10 When you march up to attack a city,
make its people an offer of peace. 11 If
they accept and open their gates, all the
people in it shall be subject to forced labor and shall work for you. 12 If they refuse to make peace and they engage you
in battle, lay siege to that city. 13 When
the LORD your God delivers it into your
hand, put to the sword all the men in it.
14 As for the women, the children, the
livestock and everything else in the
city, you may take these as plunder for
yourselves. And you may use the plunder the LORD your God gives you from
your enemies. 15 This is how you are to
treat all the cities that are at a distance
from you and do not belong to the nations nearby.
16 However, in the cities of the nations
the LORD your God is giving you as an
inheritance, do not leave alive anything
that breathes. 17 Completely destroy[a]
them—the Hittites, Amorites, Canaanites, Perizzites, Hivites and Jebusites—
as the LORD your God has commanded
you. 18 Otherwise, they will teach you to
follow all the detestable things they do
in worshiping their gods, and you will
sin against the LORD your God.
19 When you lay siege to a city for a long
time, fighting against it to capture it, do
not destroy its trees by putting an ax to
them, because you can eat their fruit. Do
not cut them down. Are the trees people,

[a] *17* The Hebrew term refers to the irrevocable giving over of things or persons to the LORD, often by totally destroying them.

that you should besiege them?[a] 20 However, you may cut down trees that you
know are not fruit trees and use them
to build siege works until the city at war
with you falls.

21 If someone is found slain, lying in
a field in the land the LORD your
God is giving you to possess, and it is not
known who the killer was, 2 your elders
and judges shall go out and measure the
distance from the body to the neighboring towns. 3 Then the elders of the town
nearest the body shall take a heifer that
has never been worked and has never
worn a yoke 4 and lead it down to a valley
that has not been plowed or planted and
where there is a flowing stream. There in
the valley they are to break the heifer's
neck. 5 The Levitical priests shall step
forward, for the LORD your God has chosen them to minister and to pronounce
blessings in the name of the LORD and to
decide all cases of dispute and assault.
6 Then all the elders of the town nearest
the body shall wash their hands over the
heifer whose neck was broken in the valley, 7 and they shall declare: "Our hands
did not shed this blood, nor did our eyes
see it done. 8 Accept this atonement for
your people Israel, whom you have redeemed, LORD, and do not hold your
people guilty of the blood of an innocent person." Then the bloodshed will
be atoned for, 9 and you will have purged
from yourselves the guilt of shedding innocent blood, since you have done what
is right in the eyes of the LORD.

10 When you go to war against your
enemies and the LORD your God delivers them into your hands and you take
captives, 11 if you notice among the captives a beautiful woman and are attracted to her, you may take her as your wife.
12 Bring her into your home and have
her shave her head, trim her nails 13 and
put aside the clothes she was wearing
when captured. After she has lived in
your house and mourned her father and
mother for a full month, then you may go
to her and be her husband and she shall
be your wife. 14 If you are not pleased
with her, let her go wherever she wishes. You must not sell her or treat her as a
slave, since you have dishonored her.

15 If a man has two wives, and he loves
one but not the other, and both bear him
sons but the firstborn is the son of the
wife he does not love, 16 when he wills
his property to his sons, he must not
give the rights of the firstborn to the son
of the wife he loves in preference to his
actual firstborn, the son of the wife he
does not love. 17 He must acknowledge
the son of his unloved wife as the firstborn by giving him a double share of all
he has. That son is the first sign of his father's strength. The right of the firstborn
belongs to him.

18 If someone has a stubborn and rebellious son who does not obey his father and mother and will not listen to
them when they discipline him, 19 his
father and mother shall take hold of him
and bring him to the elders at the gate of
his town. 20 They shall say to the elders,
"This son of ours is stubborn and rebellious. He will not obey us. He is a glutton
and a drunkard." 21 Then all the men of
his town are to stone him to death. You
must purge the evil from among you. All
Israel will hear of it and be afraid.

22 If someone guilty of a capital offense
is put to death and their body is exposed
on a pole, 23 you must not leave the body
hanging on the pole overnight. Be sure
to bury it that same day, because anyone who is hung on a pole is under God's
curse. You must not desecrate the land
the LORD your God is giving you as an
inheritance.

22 If you see your fellow Israelite's ox
or sheep straying, do not ignore it
but be sure to take it back to its owner. 2 If
they do not live near you or if you do not
know who owns it, take it home with you
and keep it until they come looking for
it. Then give it back. 3 Do the same if you
find their donkey or cloak or anything
else they have lost. Do not ignore it.

4 If you see your fellow Israelite's donkey or ox fallen on the road, do not ignore
it. Help the owner get it to its feet.

5 A woman must not wear men's clothing, nor a man wear women's clothing,
for the LORD your God detests anyone
who does this.

6 If you come across a bird's nest beside the road, either in a tree or on the
ground, and the mother is sitting on the
young or on the eggs, do not take the

[a] 19 Or *down to use in the siege, for the fruit trees are for the benefit of people.*

mother with the young. 7 You may take
the young, but be sure to let the mother
go, so that it may go well with you and
you may have a long life.
8 When you build a new house, make
a parapet around your roof so that you
may not bring the guilt of bloodshed on
your house if someone falls from the
roof.
9 Do not plant two kinds of seed in your
vineyard; if you do, not only the crops
you plant but also the fruit of the vineyard will be defiled.[a]
10 Do not plow with an ox and a donkey
yoked together.
11 Do not wear clothes of wool and lin-
en woven together.
12 Make tassels on the four corners of
the cloak you wear.
13 If a man takes a wife and, after sleeping with her, dislikes her 14 and slanders
her and gives her a bad name, saying,
"I married this woman, but when I approached her, I did not find proof of her
virginity," 15 then the young woman's father and mother shall bring to the town
elders at the gate proof that she was a
virgin. 16 Her father will say to the elders,
"I gave my daughter in marriage to this
man, but he dislikes her. 17 Now he has
slandered her and said, 'I did not find
your daughter to be a virgin.' But here
is the proof of my daughter's virginity."
Then her parents shall display the cloth
before the elders of the town, 18 and the
elders shall take the man and punish
him. 19 They shall fine him a hundred
shekels[b] of silver and give them to the
young woman's father, because this man
has given an Israelite virgin a bad name.
She shall continue to be his wife; he must
not divorce her as long as he lives.
20 If, however, the charge is true and no
proof of the young woman's virginity can
be found, 21 she shall be brought to the
door of her father's house and there the
men of her town shall stone her to death.
She has done an outrageous thing in Israel by being promiscuous while still in
her father's house. You must purge the
evil from among you.
22 If a man is found sleeping with another man's wife, both the man who
slept with her and the woman must die.
You must purge the evil from Israel.
23 If a man happens to meet in a town
a virgin pledged to be married and he
sleeps with her, 24 you shall take both of
them to the gate of that town and stone
them to death—the young woman because she was in a town and did not
scream for help, and the man because he
violated another man's wife. You must
purge the evil from among you.
25 But if out in the country a man happens to meet a young woman pledged to
be married and rapes her, only the man
who has done this shall die. 26 Do nothing to the woman; she has committed
no sin deserving death. This case is like
that of someone who attacks and murders a neighbor, 27 for the man found the
young woman out in the country, and
though the betrothed woman screamed,
there was no one to rescue her.
28 If a man happens to meet a virgin
who is not pledged to be married and
rapes her and they are discovered, 29 he
shall pay her father fifty shekels[c] of silver. He must marry the young woman,
for he has violated her. He can never divorce her as long as he lives.
30 A man is not to marry his father's
wife; he must not dishonor his father's
bed.[d]

23[e] No one who has been emasculat-
ed by crushing or cutting may enter the assembly of the LORD.
2 No one born of a forbidden marriage[f]
nor any of their descendants may enter
the assembly of the LORD, not even in the
tenth generation.
3 No Ammonite or Moabite or any of
their descendants may enter the assembly of the LORD, not even in the tenth
generation. 4 For they did not come to
meet you with bread and water on your
way when you came out of Egypt, and
they hired Balaam son of Beor from Pethor in Aram Naharaim[g] to pronounce a
curse on you. 5 However, the LORD your
God would not listen to Balaam but
turned the curse into a blessing for you,
because the LORD your God loves you.
6 Do not seek a treaty of friendship with
them as long as you live.

[a] 9 Or *be forfeited to the sanctuary* [b] *19* That is, about 2 1/2 pounds or about 1.2 kilograms [c] *29* That is, about 1 1/4 pounds or about 575 grams [d] *30* In Hebrew texts this verse (22:30) is numbered 23:1. [e] In Hebrew texts 23:1-25 is numbered 23:2-26. [f] *2* Or *one of illegitimate birth* [g] *4* That is, Northwest Mesopotamia

7 Do not despise an Edomite, for the Edomites are related to you. Do not despise an Egyptian, because you resided as foreigners in their country. 8 The third generation of children born to them may enter the assembly of the LORD.

9 When you are encamped against your enemies, keep away from everything impure. 10 If one of your men is unclean because of a nocturnal emission, he is to go outside the camp and stay there. 11 But as evening approaches he is to wash himself, and at sunset he may return to the camp.

12 Designate a place outside the camp where you can go to relieve yourself. 13 As part of your equipment have something to dig with, and when you relieve yourself, dig a hole and cover up your excrement. 14 For the LORD your God moves about in your camp to protect you and to deliver your enemies to you. Your camp must be holy, so that he will not see among you anything indecent and turn away from you.

15 If a slave has taken refuge with you, do not hand them over to their master. 16 Let them live among you wherever they like and in whatever town they choose. Do not oppress them.

17 No Israelite man or woman is to become a shrine prostitute. 18 You must not bring the earnings of a female prostitute or of a male prostitute[a] into the house of the LORD your God to pay any vow, because the LORD your God detests them both.

19 Do not charge a fellow Israelite interest, whether on money or food or anything else that may earn interest. 20 You may charge a foreigner interest, but not a fellow Israelite, so that the LORD your God may bless you in everything you put your hand to in the land you are entering to possess.

21 If you make a vow to the LORD your God, do not be slow to pay it, for the LORD your God will certainly demand it of you and you will be guilty of sin. 22 But if you refrain from making a vow, you will not be guilty. 23 Whatever your lips utter you must be sure to do, because you made your vow freely to the LORD your God with your own mouth.

24 If you enter your neighbor's vineyard, you may eat all the grapes you want, but do not put any in your basket. 25 If you enter your neighbor's grainfield, you may pick kernels with your hands, but you must not put a sickle to their standing grain.

24 If a man marries a woman who becomes displeasing to him because he finds something indecent about her, and he writes her a certificate of divorce, gives it to her and sends her from his house, 2 and if after she leaves his house she becomes the wife of another man, 3 and her second husband dislikes her and writes her a certificate of divorce, gives it to her and sends her from his house, or if he dies, 4 then her first husband, who divorced her, is not allowed to marry her again after she has been defiled. That would be detestable in the eyes of the LORD. Do not bring sin upon the land the LORD your God is giving you as an inheritance.

5 If a man has recently married, he must not be sent to war or have any other duty laid on him. For one year he is to be free to stay at home and bring happiness to the wife he has married.

6 Do not take a pair of millstones — not even the upper one — as security for a debt, because that would be taking a person's livelihood as security.

7 If someone is caught kidnapping a fellow Israelite and treating or selling them as a slave, the kidnapper must die. You must purge the evil from among you.

8 In cases of defiling skin diseases,[b] be very careful to do exactly as the Levitical priests instruct you. You must follow carefully what I have commanded them. 9 Remember what the LORD your God did to Miriam along the way after you came out of Egypt.

10 When you make a loan of any kind to your neighbor, do not go into their house to get what is offered to you as a pledge. 11 Stay outside and let the neighbor to whom you are making the loan bring the pledge out to you. 12 If the neighbor is poor, do not go to sleep with their pledge in your possession. 13 Return their cloak by sunset so that your neighbor may sleep in it. Then they will thank you, and

[a] *18* Hebrew *of a dog* [b] *8* The Hebrew word for *defiling skin diseases*, traditionally translated "leprosy," was used for various diseases affecting the skin.

it will be regarded as a righteous act in
the sight of the LORD your God.
14 Do not take advantage of a hired
worker who is poor and needy, whether that worker is a fellow Israelite or a
foreigner residing in one of your towns.
15 Pay them their wages each day before
sunset, because they are poor and are
counting on it. Otherwise they may cry
to the LORD against you, and you will be
guilty of sin.
16 Parents are not to be put to death for
their children, nor children put to death
for their parents; each will die for their
own sin.
17 Do not deprive the foreigner or the
fatherless of justice, or take the cloak of
the widow as a pledge. 18 Remember that
you were slaves in Egypt and the LORD
your God redeemed you from there. That
is why I command you to do this.
19 When you are harvesting in your
field and you overlook a sheaf, do not go
back to get it. Leave it for the foreigner,
the fatherless and the widow, so that the
LORD your God may bless you in all the
work of your hands. 20 When you beat
the olives from your trees, do not go over
the branches a second time. Leave what
remains for the foreigner, the fatherless
and the widow. 21 When you harvest the
grapes in your vineyard, do not go over
the vines again. Leave what remains for
the foreigner, the fatherless and the widow. 22 Remember that you were slaves in
Egypt. That is why I command you to do
this.
25 When people have a dispute, they
are to take it to court and the judges will decide the case, acquitting the
innocent and condemning the guilty.
2 If the guilty person deserves to be beat-
en, the judge shall make them lie down
and have them flogged in his presence
with the number of lashes the crime deserves, 3 but the judge must not impose
more than forty lashes. If the guilty party is flogged more than that, your fellow
Israelite will be degraded in your eyes.
4 Do not muzzle an ox while it is treading out the grain.
5 If brothers are living together and
one of them dies without a son, his widow must not marry outside the family.
Her husband's brother shall take her
and marry her and fulfill the duty of
a brother-in-law to her. 6 The first son
she bears shall carry on the name of the
dead brother so that his name will not be
blotted out from Israel.
7 However, if a man does not want to
marry his brother's wife, she shall go to
the elders at the town gate and say, "My
husband's brother refuses to carry on his
brother's name in Israel. He will not fulfill the duty of a brother-in-law to me."
8 Then the elders of his town shall summon him and talk to him. If he persists
in saying, "I do not want to marry her,"
9 his brother's widow shall go up to him
in the presence of the elders, take off one
of his sandals, spit in his face and say,
"This is what is done to the man who will
not build up his brother's family line."
10 That man's line shall be known in Israel as The Family of the Unsandaled.
11 If two men are fighting and the wife
of one of them comes to rescue her husband from his assailant, and she reaches
out and seizes him by his private parts,
12 you shall cut off her hand. Show her
no pity.
13 Do not have two differing weights
in your bag — one heavy, one light. 14 Do
not have two differing measures in your
house — one large, one small. 15 You
must have accurate and honest weights
and measures, so that you may live long
in the land the LORD your God is giving
you. 16 For the LORD your God detests
anyone who does these things, anyone
who deals dishonestly.
17 Remember what the Amalekites did
to you along the way when you came out
of Egypt. 18 When you were weary and
worn out, they met you on your journey
and attacked all who were lagging behind; they had no fear of God. 19 When
the LORD your God gives you rest from
all the enemies around you in the land
he is giving you to possess as an inheritance, you shall blot out the name of Amalek from under heaven. Do not forget!
26 When you have entered the land
the LORD your God is giving you
as an inheritance and have taken possession of it and settled in it, 2 take some
of the firstfruits of all that you produce
from the soil of the land the LORD your
God is giving you and put them in a basket. Then go to the place the LORD your
God will choose as a dwelling for his
Name 3 and say to the priest in office at
the time, "I declare today to the LORD

your God that I have come to the land
the LORD swore to our ancestors to give
us." 4The priest shall take the basket
from your hands and set it down in front
of the altar of the LORD your God. 5Then
you shall declare before the LORD your
God: "My father was a wandering Aramean, and he went down into Egypt with
a few people and lived there and became
a great nation, powerful and numerous.
6But the Egyptians mistreated us and
made us suffer, subjecting us to harsh
labor. 7Then we cried out to the LORD,
the God of our ancestors, and the LORD
heard our voice and saw our misery, toil
and oppression. 8So the LORD brought us
out of Egypt with a mighty hand and an
outstretched arm, with great terror and
with signs and wonders. 9He brought
us to this place and gave us this land, a
land flowing with milk and honey; 10and
now I bring the firstfruits of the soil that
you, LORD, have given me." Place the
basket before the LORD your God and
bow down before him. 11Then you and
the Levites and the foreigners residing
among you shall rejoice in all the good
things the LORD your God has given to
you and your household.

12When you have finished setting
aside a tenth of all your produce in the
third year, the year of the tithe, you shall
give it to the Levite, the foreigner, the
fatherless and the widow, so that they
may eat in your towns and be satisfied.
13Then say to the LORD your God: "I have
removed from my house the sacred portion and have given it to the Levite, the
foreigner, the fatherless and the widow,
according to all you commanded. I have
not turned aside from your commands
nor have I forgotten any of them. 14I
have not eaten any of the sacred portion
while I was in mourning, nor have I removed any of it while I was unclean, nor
have I offered any of it to the dead. I have
obeyed the LORD my God; I have done
everything you commanded me. 15Look
down from heaven, your holy dwelling
place, and bless your people Israel and
the land you have given us as you promised on oath to our ancestors, a land
flowing with milk and honey."

16The LORD your God commands you
this day to follow these decrees and laws;
carefully observe them with all your
heart and with all your soul. 17You have
declared this day that the LORD is your
God and that you will walk in obedience
to him, that you will keep his decrees,
commands and laws — that you will listen to him. 18And the LORD has declared
this day that you are his people, his treasured possession as he promised, and
that you are to keep all his commands.
19He has declared that he will set you in
praise, fame and honor high above all
the nations he has made and that you
will be a people holy to the LORD your
God, as he promised.

27 Moses and the elders of Israel commanded the people: "Keep all these
commands that I give you today. 2When
you have crossed the Jordan into the
land the LORD your God is giving you,
set up some large stones and coat them
with plaster. 3Write on them all the
words of this law when you have crossed
over to enter the land the LORD your
God is giving you, a land flowing with
milk and honey, just as the LORD, the
God of your ancestors, promised you.
4And when you have crossed the Jordan, set up these stones on Mount Ebal,
as I command you today, and coat them
with plaster. 5Build there an altar to the
LORD your God, an altar of stones. Do
not use any iron tool on them. 6Build the
altar of the LORD your God with field-
stones and offer burnt offerings on it to
the LORD your God. 7Sacrifice fellowship offerings there, eating them and rejoicing in the presence of the LORD your
God. 8And you shall write very clearly all
the words of this law on these stones you
have set up."

9Then Moses and the Levitical priests
said to all Israel, "Be silent, Israel, and
listen! You have now become the people
of the LORD your God. 10Obey the LORD
your God and follow his commands and
decrees that I give you today."

11On the same day Moses commanded
the people:

12When you have crossed the Jordan,
these tribes shall stand on Mount Gerizim to bless the people: Simeon, Levi,
Judah, Issachar, Joseph and Benjamin.
13And these tribes shall stand on Mount
Ebal to pronounce curses: Reuben, Gad,
Asher, Zebulun, Dan and Naphtali.

14The Levites shall recite to all the
people of Israel in a loud voice:

15 "Cursed is anyone who makes
an idol—a thing detestable to the
LORD, the work of skilled hands—
and sets it up in secret."

Then all the people shall
say, "Amen!"

16 "Cursed is anyone who dishonors their father or mother."

Then all the people shall
say, "Amen!"

17 "Cursed is anyone who moves
their neighbor's boundary stone."

Then all the people shall
say, "Amen!"

18 "Cursed is anyone who leads the
blind astray on the road."

Then all the people shall
say, "Amen!"

19 "Cursed is anyone who withholds justice from the foreigner, the
fatherless or the widow."

Then all the people shall
say, "Amen!"

20 "Cursed is anyone who sleeps
with his father's wife, for he dishonors his father's bed."

Then all the people shall
say, "Amen!"

21 "Cursed is anyone who has sexual relations with any animal."

Then all the people shall
say, "Amen!"

22 "Cursed is anyone who sleeps
with his sister, the daughter of his
father or the daughter of his mother."

Then all the people shall
say, "Amen!"

23 "Cursed is anyone who sleeps
with his mother-in-law."

Then all the people shall
say, "Amen!"

24 "Cursed is anyone who kills
their neighbor secretly."

Then all the people shall
say, "Amen!"

25 "Cursed is anyone who accepts
a bribe to kill an innocent person."

Then all the people shall
say, "Amen!"

26 "Cursed is anyone who does not
uphold the words of this law by carrying them out."

Then all the people shall
say, "Amen!"

28 If you fully obey the LORD your God
and carefully follow all his commands I give you today, the LORD your
God will set you high above all the nations on earth. 2 All these blessings will
come on you and accompany you if you
obey the LORD your God:

3 You will be blessed in the city
and blessed in the country.
4 The fruit of your womb will be
blessed, and the crops of your land
and the young of your livestock—
the calves of your herds and the
lambs of your flocks.
5 Your basket and your kneading
trough will be blessed.
6 You will be blessed when you
come in and blessed when you go
out.

7 The LORD will grant that the enemies
who rise up against you will be defeated
before you. They will come at you from
one direction but flee from you in seven.
8 The LORD will send a blessing on your
barns and on everything you put your
hand to. The LORD your God will bless
you in the land he is giving you.
9 The LORD will establish you as his
holy people, as he promised you on oath,
if you keep the commands of the LORD
your God and walk in obedience to him.
10 Then all the peoples on earth will see
that you are called by the name of the
LORD, and they will fear you. 11 The LORD
will grant you abundant prosperity—in
the fruit of your womb, the young of your
livestock and the crops of your ground—
in the land he swore to your ancestors to
give you.
12 The LORD will open the heavens, the
storehouse of his bounty, to send rain
on your land in season and to bless all
the work of your hands. You will lend to
many nations but will borrow from none.
13 The LORD will make you the head, not
the tail. If you pay attention to the commands of the LORD your God that I give
you this day and carefully follow them,
you will always be at the top, never at the
bottom. 14 Do not turn aside from any of
the commands I give you today, to the
right or to the left, following other gods
and serving them.

15 However, if you do not obey the LORD
your God and do not carefully follow all
his commands and decrees I am giving
you today, all these curses will come on
you and overtake you:

16You will be cursed in the city
and cursed in the country.
17Your basket and your kneading
trough will be cursed.
18The fruit of your womb will be
cursed, and the crops of your land,
and the calves of your herds and the
lambs of your flocks.
19You will be cursed when you
come in and cursed when you go
out.

20The LORD will send on you curses,
confusion and rebuke in everything you
put your hand to, until you are destroyed
and come to sudden ruin because of the
evil you have done in forsaking him.[a]
21The LORD will plague you with diseases until he has destroyed you from the
land you are entering to possess. 22The
LORD will strike you with wasting disease, with fever and inflammation, with
scorching heat and drought, with blight
and mildew, which will plague you until you perish. 23The sky over your head
will be bronze, the ground beneath you
iron. 24The LORD will turn the rain of
your country into dust and powder; it
will come down from the skies until you
are destroyed.
25The LORD will cause you to be defeated before your enemies. You will
come at them from one direction but flee
from them in seven, and you will become
a thing of horror to all the kingdoms on
earth. 26Your carcasses will be food for
all the birds and the wild animals, and
there will be no one to frighten them
away. 27The LORD will afflict you with
the boils of Egypt and with tumors, festering sores and the itch, from which you
cannot be cured. 28The LORD will afflict
you with madness, blindness and confusion of mind. 29At midday you will grope
about like a blind person in the dark. You
will be unsuccessful in everything you
do; day after day you will be oppressed
and robbed, with no one to rescue you.
30You will be pledged to be married to
a woman, but another will take her and
rape her. You will build a house, but you
will not live in it. You will plant a vineyard, but you will not even begin to enjoy its fruit. 31Your ox will be slaughtered
before your eyes, but you will eat none
of it. Your donkey will be forcibly taken
from you and will not be returned. Your
sheep will be given to your enemies, and
no one will rescue them. 32Your sons
and daughters will be given to another
nation, and you will wear out your eyes
watching for them day after day, powerless to lift a hand. 33A people that you do
not know will eat what your land and labor produce, and you will have nothing
but cruel oppression all your days. 34The
sights you see will drive you mad. 35The
LORD will afflict your knees and legs
with painful boils that cannot be cured,
spreading from the soles of your feet to
the top of your head.
36The LORD will drive you and the king
you set over you to a nation unknown to
you or your ancestors. There you will
worship other gods, gods of wood and
stone. 37You will become a thing of horror, a byword and an object of ridicule
among all the peoples where the LORD
will drive you.
38You will sow much seed in the field
but you will harvest little, because locusts will devour it. 39You will plant
vineyards and cultivate them but you
will not drink the wine or gather the
grapes, because worms will eat them.
40You will have olive trees throughout
your country but you will not use the oil,
because the olives will drop off. 41You
will have sons and daughters but you
will not keep them, because they will go
into captivity. 42Swarms of locusts will
take over all your trees and the crops of
your land.
43The foreigners who reside among
you will rise above you higher and higher, but you will sink lower and lower.
44They will lend to you, but you will not
lend to them. They will be the head, but
you will be the tail.
45All these curses will come on you.
They will pursue you and overtake you
until you are destroyed, because you did
not obey the LORD your God and observe
the commands and decrees he gave you.
46They will be a sign and a wonder to you
and your descendants forever. 47Because
you did not serve the LORD your God joyfully and gladly in the time of prosperity,
48therefore in hunger and thirst, in nakedness and dire poverty, you will serve
the enemies the LORD sends against you.

[a] 20 Hebrew *me*

He will put an iron yoke on your neck
until he has destroyed you.
49 The LORD will bring a nation against
you from far away, from the ends of the
earth, like an eagle swooping down,
a nation whose language you will not
understand, 50 a fierce-looking nation
without respect for the old or pity for
the young. 51 They will devour the young
of your livestock and the crops of your
land until you are destroyed. They will
leave you no grain, new wine or olive oil,
nor any calves of your herds or lambs of
your flocks until you are ruined. 52 They
will lay siege to all the cities throughout
your land until the high fortified walls in
which you trust fall down. They will besiege all the cities throughout the land
the LORD your God is giving you.
53 Because of the suffering that your
enemy will inflict on you during the
siege, you will eat the fruit of the womb,
the flesh of the sons and daughters the
LORD your God has given you. 54 Even
the most gentle and sensitive man
among you will have no compassion on
his own brother or the wife he loves or
his surviving children, 55 and he will not
give to one of them any of the flesh of his
children that he is eating. It will be all he
has left because of the suffering your enemy will inflict on you during the siege
of all your cities. 56 The most gentle and
sensitive woman among you—so sensitive and gentle that she would not venture to touch the ground with the sole
of her foot—will begrudge the husband
she loves and her own son or daughter
57 the afterbirth from her womb and the
children she bears. For in her dire need
she intends to eat them secretly because
of the suffering your enemy will inflict
on you during the siege of your cities.
58 If you do not carefully follow all the
words of this law, which are written in
this book, and do not revere this glorious and awesome name—the LORD
your God— 59 the LORD will send fearful
plagues on you and your descendants,
harsh and prolonged disasters, and severe and lingering illnesses. 60 He will
bring on you all the diseases of Egypt
that you dreaded, and they will cling to
you. 61 The LORD will also bring on you
every kind of sickness and disaster not
recorded in this Book of the Law, until
you are destroyed. 62 You who were as
numerous as the stars in the sky will be
left but few in number, because you did
not obey the LORD your God. 63 Just as it
pleased the LORD to make you prosper
and increase in number, so it will please
him to ruin and destroy you. You will be
uprooted from the land you are entering
to possess.
64 Then the LORD will scatter you
among all nations, from one end of the
earth to the other. There you will worship other gods—gods of wood and
stone, which neither you nor your ancestors have known. 65 Among those nations you will find no repose, no resting
place for the sole of your foot. There the
LORD will give you an anxious mind,
eyes weary with longing, and a despairing heart. 66 You will live in constant
suspense, filled with dread both night
and day, never sure of your life. 67 In the
morning you will say, "If only it were evening!" and in the evening, "If only it were
morning!"—because of the terror that
will fill your hearts and the sights that
your eyes will see. 68 The LORD will send
you back in ships to Egypt on a journey I
said you should never make again. There
you will offer yourselves for sale to your
enemies as male and female slaves, but
no one will buy you.

29 [a] These are the terms of the covenant the LORD commanded Mo-
ses to make with the Israelites in Moab,
in addition to the covenant he had made
with them at Horeb.
2 Moses summoned all the Israelites
and said to them:

Your eyes have seen all that the LORD
did in Egypt to Pharaoh, to all his officials and to all his land. 3 With your own
eyes you saw those great trials, those
signs and great wonders. 4 But to this
day the LORD has not given you a mind
that understands or eyes that see or ears
that hear. 5 Yet the LORD says, "During
the forty years that I led you through the
wilderness, your clothes did not wear
out, nor did the sandals on your feet.
6 You ate no bread and drank no wine or
other fermented drink. I did this so that
you might know that I am the LORD your
God."

[a] In Hebrew texts 29:1 is numbered 28:69, and 29:2-29 is numbered 29:1-28.

7When you reached this place, Sihon
king of Heshbon and Og king of Bashan
came out to fight against us, but we defeated them. 8We took their land and
gave it as an inheritance to the Reubenites, the Gadites and the half-tribe of
Manasseh.
9Carefully follow the terms of this
covenant, so that you may prosper in everything you do. 10All of you are standing today in the presence of the LORD
your God—your leaders and chief men,
your elders and officials, and all the
other men of Israel, 11together with your
children and your wives, and the foreigners living in your camps who chop
your wood and carry your water. 12You
are standing here in order to enter into
a covenant with the LORD your God, a
covenant the LORD is making with you
this day and sealing with an oath, 13to
confirm you this day as his people, that
he may be your God as he promised you
and as he swore to your fathers, Abraham, Isaac and Jacob. 14I am making
this covenant, with its oath, not only
with you 15who are standing here with
us today in the presence of the LORD our
God but also with those who are not here
today.
16You yourselves know how we lived
in Egypt and how we passed through
the countries on the way here. 17You
saw among them their detestable images and idols of wood and stone, of silver
and gold. 18Make sure there is no man or
woman, clan or tribe among you today
whose heart turns away from the LORD
our God to go and worship the gods of
those nations; make sure there is no
root among you that produces such bitter poison.
19When such a person hears the words
of this oath and they invoke a blessing
on themselves, thinking, "I will be safe,
even though I persist in going my own
way," they will bring disaster on the watered land as well as the dry. 20The LORD
will never be willing to forgive them; his
wrath and zeal will burn against them.
All the curses written in this book will
fall on them, and the LORD will blot out
their names from under heaven. 21The
LORD will single them out from all the
tribes of Israel for disaster, according to
all the curses of the covenant written in
this Book of the Law.
22Your children who follow you in later generations and foreigners who come
from distant lands will see the calamities that have fallen on the land and
the diseases with which the LORD has
afflicted it. 23The whole land will be a
burning waste of salt and sulfur—nothing planted, nothing sprouting, no vegetation growing on it. It will be like the
destruction of Sodom and Gomorrah,
Admah and Zeboyim, which the LORD
overthrew in fierce anger. 24All the nations will ask: "Why has the LORD done
this to this land? Why this fierce, burning anger?"
25And the answer will be: "It is because
this people abandoned the covenant of
the LORD, the God of their ancestors, the
covenant he made with them when he
brought them out of Egypt. 26They went
off and worshiped other gods and bowed
down to them, gods they did not know,
gods he had not given them. 27There-
fore the LORD's anger burned against
this land, so that he brought on it all the
curses written in this book. 28In furious
anger and in great wrath the LORD uprooted them from their land and thrust
them into another land, as it is now."
29The secret things belong to the LORD
our God, but the things revealed belong
to us and to our children forever, that we
may follow all the words of this law.

30 When all these blessings and curses I have set before you come on you
and you take them to heart wherever the
LORD your God disperses you among the
nations, 2and when you and your children return to the LORD your God and
obey him with all your heart and with
all your soul according to everything
I command you today, 3then the LORD
your God will restore your fortunes[a]
and have compassion on you and gather you again from all the nations where
he scattered you. 4Even if you have been
banished to the most distant land under
the heavens, from there the LORD your
God will gather you and bring you back.
5He will bring you to the land that belonged to your ancestors, and you will
take possession of it. He will make you
more prosperous and numerous than

a 3 Or *will bring you back from captivity*

your ancestors. 6The LORD your God will
circumcise your hearts and the hearts
of your descendants, so that you may
love him with all your heart and with
all your soul, and live. 7The LORD your
God will put all these curses on your enemies who hate and persecute you. 8You
will again obey the LORD and follow all
his commands I am giving you today.
9Then the LORD your God will make you
most prosperous in all the work of your
hands and in the fruit of your womb, the
young of your livestock and the crops of
your land. The LORD will again delight
in you and make you prosperous, just as
he delighted in your ancestors, 10if you
obey the LORD your God and keep his
commands and decrees that are written
in this Book of the Law and turn to the
LORD your God with all your heart and
with all your soul.

11Now what I am commanding you today is not too difficult for you or beyond
your reach. 12It is not up in heaven, so
that you have to ask, "Who will ascend
into heaven to get it and proclaim it to
us so we may obey it?" 13Nor is it beyond
the sea, so that you have to ask, "Who
will cross the sea to get it and proclaim it
to us so we may obey it?" 14No, the word
is very near you; it is in your mouth and
in your heart so you may obey it.

15See, I set before you today life and
prosperity, death and destruction. 16For
I command you today to love the LORD
your God, to walk in obedience to him,
and to keep his commands, decrees and
laws; then you will live and increase, and
the LORD your God will bless you in the
land you are entering to possess.

17But if your heart turns away and you
are not obedient, and if you are drawn
away to bow down to other gods and
worship them, 18I declare to you this
day that you will certainly be destroyed.
You will not live long in the land you are
crossing the Jordan to enter and possess.

19This day I call the heavens and the
earth as witnesses against you that I
have set before you life and death, blessings and curses. Now choose life, so that
you and your children may live 20and
that you may love the LORD your God,
listen to his voice, and hold fast to him.
For the LORD is your life, and he will give
you many years in the land he swore to
give to your fathers, Abraham, Isaac and
Jacob.

31 Then Moses went out and spoke
these words to all Israel: 2"I am now
a hundred and twenty years old and I am
no longer able to lead you. The LORD has
said to me, 'You shall not cross the Jordan.' 3The LORD your God himself will
cross over ahead of you. He will destroy
these nations before you, and you will
take possession of their land. Joshua also
will cross over ahead of you, as the LORD
said. 4And the LORD will do to them
what he did to Sihon and Og, the kings of
the Amorites, whom he destroyed along
with their land. 5The LORD will deliver
them to you, and you must do to them all
that I have commanded you. 6Be strong
and courageous. Do not be afraid or terrified because of them, for the LORD your
God goes with you; he will never leave
you nor forsake you."

7Then Moses summoned Joshua and
said to him in the presence of all Israel, "Be strong and courageous, for you
must go with this people into the land
that the LORD swore to their ancestors
to give them, and you must divide it
among them as their inheritance. 8The
LORD himself goes before you and will
be with you; he will never leave you nor
forsake you. Do not be afraid; do not be
discouraged."

9So Moses wrote down this law and
gave it to the Levitical priests, who carried the ark of the covenant of the LORD,
and to all the elders of Israel. 10Then Moses commanded them: "At the end of every seven years, in the year for canceling
debts, during the Festival of Tabernacles,
11when all Israel comes to appear before
the LORD your God at the place he will
choose, you shall read this law before
them in their hearing. 12Assemble the
people — men, women and children, and
the foreigners residing in your towns —
so they can listen and learn to fear the
LORD your God and follow carefully all
the words of this law. 13Their children,
who do not know this law, must hear it
and learn to fear the LORD your God as
long as you live in the land you are crossing the Jordan to possess."

14The LORD said to Moses, "Now the
day of your death is near. Call Joshua
and present yourselves at the tent of

meeting, where I will commission him."
So Moses and Joshua came and presented themselves at the tent of meeting.
15 Then the LORD appeared at the tent
in a pillar of cloud, and the cloud stood
over the entrance to the tent. 16 And the
LORD said to Moses: "You are going to
rest with your ancestors, and these people will soon prostitute themselves to
the foreign gods of the land they are entering. They will forsake me and break
the covenant I made with them. 17 And in
that day I will become angry with them
and forsake them; I will hide my face
from them, and they will be destroyed.
Many disasters and calamities will come
on them, and in that day they will ask,
'Have not these disasters come on us
because our God is not with us?' 18 And
I will certainly hide my face in that day
because of all their wickedness in turning to other gods.
19 "Now write down this song and
teach it to the Israelites and have them
sing it, so that it may be a witness for me
against them. 20 When I have brought
them into the land flowing with milk
and honey, the land I promised on oath
to their ancestors, and when they eat
their fill and thrive, they will turn to other gods and worship them, rejecting me
and breaking my covenant. 21 And when
many disasters and calamities come on
them, this song will testify against them,
because it will not be forgotten by their
descendants. I know what they are disposed to do, even before I bring them
into the land I promised them on oath."
22 So Moses wrote down this song that
day and taught it to the Israelites.
23 The LORD gave this command to
Joshua son of Nun: "Be strong and courageous, for you will bring the Israelites
into the land I promised them on oath,
and I myself will be with you."
24 After Moses finished writing in a
book the words of this law from beginning to end, 25 he gave this command to
the Levites who carried the ark of the
covenant of the LORD: 26 "Take this Book
of the Law and place it beside the ark
of the covenant of the LORD your God.
There it will remain as a witness against
you. 27 For I know how rebellious and
stiff-necked you are. If you have been rebellious against the LORD while I am still
alive and with you, how much more will
you rebel after I die! 28 Assemble before
me all the elders of your tribes and all
your officials, so that I can speak these
words in their hearing and call the heavens and the earth to testify against them.
29 For I know that after my death you are
sure to become utterly corrupt and to
turn from the way I have commanded
you. In days to come, disaster will fall
on you because you will do evil in the
sight of the LORD and arouse his anger
by what your hands have made."
30 And Moses recited the words of this
song from beginning to end in the hearing of the whole assembly of Israel:

32 Listen, you heavens, and I will speak;
hear, you earth, the words of my mouth.
2 Let my teaching fall like rain
and my words descend like dew,
like showers on new grass,
like abundant rain on tender plants.

3 I will proclaim the name of the LORD.
Oh, praise the greatness of our God!
4 He is the Rock, his works are perfect,
and all his ways are just.
A faithful God who does no wrong,
upright and just is he.

5 They are corrupt and not his children;
to their shame they are a warped and crooked generation.
6 Is this the way you repay the LORD,
you foolish and unwise people?
Is he not your Father, your Creator,[a]
who made you and formed you?

7 Remember the days of old;
consider the generations long past.
Ask your father and he will tell you,
your elders, and they will explain to you.
8 When the Most High gave the nations their inheritance,
when he divided all mankind,
he set up boundaries for the peoples
according to the number of the sons of Israel.[b]
9 For the LORD's portion is his people,
Jacob his allotted inheritance.

[a] 6 Or *Father, who bought you* [b] 8 Masoretic Text; Dead Sea Scrolls (see also Septuagint) *sons of God*

7 And this he said about Judah:

"Hear, LORD, the cry of Judah;
bring him to his people.
With his own hands he defends his
cause.
Oh, be his help against his foes!"

8 About Levi he said:

"Your Thummim and Urim belong
to your faithful servant.
You tested him at Massah;
you contended with him at the
waters of Meribah.
9 He said of his father and mother,
'I have no regard for them.'
He did not recognize his brothers
or acknowledge his own children,
but he watched over your word
and guarded your covenant.
10 He teaches your precepts to Jacob
and your law to Israel.
He offers incense before you
and whole burnt offerings on your
altar.
11 Bless all his skills, LORD,
and be pleased with the work of his
hands.
Strike down those who rise against
him,
his foes till they rise no more."

12 About Benjamin he said:

"Let the beloved of the LORD rest
secure in him,
for he shields him all day long,
and the one the LORD loves rests
between his shoulders."

13 About Joseph he said:

"May the LORD bless his land
with the precious dew from heaven
above
and with the deep waters that lie
below;
14 with the best the sun brings forth
and the finest the moon can yield;
15 with the choicest gifts of the ancient
mountains
and the fruitfulness of the
everlasting hills;
16 with the best gifts of the earth and its
fullness
and the favor of him who dwelt in
the burning bush.
Let all these rest on the head of
Joseph,
on the brow of the prince among[a]
his brothers.
17 In majesty he is like a firstborn bull;
his horns are the horns of a wild ox.
With them he will gore the nations,
even those at the ends of the earth.
Such are the ten thousands of
Ephraim;
such are the thousands of
Manasseh."

18 About Zebulun he said:

"Rejoice, Zebulun, in your going out,
and you, Issachar, in your tents.
19 They will summon peoples to the
mountain
and there offer the sacrifices of the
righteous;
they will feast on the abundance of
the seas,
on the treasures hidden in the
sand."

20 About Gad he said:

"Blessed is he who enlarges Gad's
domain!
Gad lives there like a lion,
tearing at arm or head.
21 He chose the best land for himself;
the leader's portion was kept for
him.
When the heads of the people
assembled,
he carried out the LORD's righteous
will,
and his judgments concerning
Israel."

22 About Dan he said:

"Dan is a lion's cub,
springing out of Bashan."

23 About Naphtali he said:

"Naphtali is abounding with the favor
of the LORD
and is full of his blessing;
he will inherit southward to the
lake."

24 About Asher he said:

"Most blessed of sons is Asher;
let him be favored by his brothers,
and let him bathe his feet in oil.

[a] 16 Or *of the one separated from*

25 The bolts of your gates will be iron
and bronze,
and your strength will equal your
days.

26 "There is no one like the God of
Jeshurun,
who rides across the heavens to
help you
and on the clouds in his majesty.
27 The eternal God is your refuge,
and underneath are the everlasting
arms.
He will drive out your enemies before
you,
saying, 'Destroy them!'
28 So Israel will live in safety;
Jacob will dwell[a] secure
in a land of grain and new wine,
where the heavens drop dew.
29 Blessed are you, Israel!
Who is like you,
a people saved by the LORD?
He is your shield and helper
and your glorious sword.
Your enemies will cower before you,
and you will tread on their heights."

34 Then Moses climbed Mount Nebo
from the plains of Moab to the top
of Pisgah, across from Jericho. There
the LORD showed him the whole land—
from Gilead to Dan, 2 all of Naphtali, the
territory of Ephraim and Manasseh, all
the land of Judah as far as the Mediterranean Sea, 3 the Negev and the whole region from the Valley of Jericho, the City
of Palms, as far as Zoar. 4 Then the LORD
said to him, "This is the land I promised
on oath to Abraham, Isaac and Jacob
when I said, 'I will give it to your descendants.' I have let you see it with your
eyes, but you will not cross over into it."
5 And Moses the servant of the LORD
died there in Moab, as the LORD had
said. 6 He buried him[b] in Moab, in the
valley opposite Beth Peor, but to this day
no one knows where his grave is. 7 Moses was a hundred and twenty years old
when he died, yet his eyes were not weak
nor his strength gone. 8 The Israelites
grieved for Moses in the plains of Moab
thirty days, until the time of weeping
and mourning was over.
9 Now Joshua son of Nun was filled
with the spirit[c] of wisdom because Moses had laid his hands on him. So the Israelites listened to him and did what the
LORD had commanded Moses.
10 Since then, no prophet has risen in
Israel like Moses, whom the LORD knew
face to face, 11 who did all those signs
and wonders the LORD sent him to do
in Egypt—to Pharaoh and to all his officials and to his whole land. 12 For no one
has ever shown the mighty power or performed the awesome deeds that Moses
did in the sight of all Israel.

[a] 28 Septuagint; Hebrew *Jacob's spring is* [b] 6 Or *He was buried* [c] 9 Or *Spirit*

JOSHUA

The books of Joshua and Judges tell the story of the early years of Israel as a nation. They describe how the Israelites conquer and occupy the land of Canaan, and then struggle to live up to their covenant with God. The Bible's drama here moves to an important new stage—God's people are in God's land. Yet it becomes clear that the road to reconciliation between God and humanity will not be easy.

The story describes the preparations and battles of Israel's invasion, as well as how the land was divided among the tribes. Since pockets of resistance remained, Joshua in his final speech urges each tribe to take full possession of its territory. Next he leads the people to renew their commitment to the covenant relationship with God.

Judges then relates the troubling cycle of Israel's repeated covenant breaking, falling under the rule of other nations, and then crying out to God for help. God responds by raising up "judges" to fight for them and save them. But the relief is temporary as Israel falls back into wrongdoing once again. ("Judges" are both military leaders and legal authorities.)

Just as Israel was made up of twelve tribes, so the book tells of twelve judges. But as the people persist in going their own way, we see that they have rejected their true Judge and Ruler. As the anarchy and atrocities increase, Israel's need for a king becomes more evident. By the end the questions are urgent: Can Israel fulfill its destiny and calling to be God's light to the nations? Who can rule Israel to help it find its proper role in the drama?

---

1 After the death of Moses the servant
of the LORD, the LORD said to Joshua son of Nun, Moses' aide: 2"Moses my
servant is dead. Now then, you and all
these people, get ready to cross the Jordan River into the land I am about to give
to them—to the Israelites. 3I will give
you every place where you set your foot,
as I promised Moses. 4Your territory will
extend from the desert to Lebanon, and
from the great river, the Euphrates—all
the Hittite country—to the Mediterranean Sea in the west. 5No one will be able
to stand against you all the days of your
life. As I was with Moses, so I will be with
you; I will never leave you nor forsake you.
6Be strong and courageous, because you
will lead these people to inherit the land I
swore to their ancestors to give them.
7"Be strong and very courageous. Be
careful to obey all the law my servant
Moses gave you; do not turn from it to the
right or to the left, that you may be successful wherever you go. 8Keep this Book
of the Law always on your lips; meditate
on it day and night, so that you may be
careful to do everything written in it.
Then you will be prosperous and successful. 9Have I not commanded you? Be
strong and courageous. Do not be afraid;
do not be discouraged, for the LORD your
God will be with you wherever you go."
10So Joshua ordered the officers of the
people: 11"Go through the camp and tell
the people, 'Get your provisions ready.
Three days from now you will cross the
Jordan here to go in and take possession
of the land the LORD your God is giving
you for your own.'"
12But to the Reubenites, the Gadites
and the half-tribe of Manasseh, Joshua
said, 13"Remember the command that
Moses the servant of the LORD gave you
after he said, 'The LORD your God will
give you rest by giving you this land.'
14Your wives, your children and your
livestock may stay in the land that Moses
gave you east of the Jordan, but all your
fighting men, ready for battle, must cross
over ahead of your fellow Israelites. You
are to help them 15until the LORD gives
them rest, as he has done for you, and until they too have taken possession of the
land the LORD your God is giving them.
After that, you may go back and occupy
your own land, which Moses the servant
of the LORD gave you east of the Jordan
toward the sunrise."
16Then they answered Joshua, "Whatever you have commanded us we will
do, and wherever you send us we will go.
17Just as we fully obeyed Moses, so we
will obey you. Only may the LORD your
God be with you as he was with Moses.
18Whoever rebels against your word and
does not obey it, whatever you may command them, will be put to death. Only be
strong and courageous!"

2 Then Joshua son of Nun secretly sent
two spies from Shittim. "Go, look over
the land," he said, "especially Jericho."
So they went and entered the house of
a prostitute named Rahab and stayed
there.
2 The king of Jericho was told, "Look,
some of the Israelites have come here
tonight to spy out the land." 3 So the king
of Jericho sent this message to Rahab:
"Bring out the men who came to you and
entered your house, because they have
come to spy out the whole land."
4 But the woman had taken the two men
and hidden them. She said, "Yes, the men
came to me, but I did not know where
they had come from. 5 At dusk, when it
was time to close the city gate, they left.
I don't know which way they went. Go after them quickly. You may catch up with
them." 6 (But she had taken them up to the
roof and hidden them under the stalks of
flax she had laid out on the roof.) 7 So the
men set out in pursuit of the spies on the
road that leads to the fords of the Jordan,
and as soon as the pursuers had gone out,
the gate was shut.
8 Before the spies lay down for the
night, she went up on the roof 9 and said
to them, "I know that the LORD has giv-
en you this land and that a great fear of
you has fallen on us, so that all who live in
this country are melting in fear because
of you. 10 We have heard how the LORD
dried up the water of the Red Sea[a] for you
when you came out of Egypt, and what
you did to Sihon and Og, the two kings
of the Amorites east of the Jordan, whom
you completely destroyed.[b] 11 When we
heard of it, our hearts melted in fear and
everyone's courage failed because of you,
for the LORD your God is God in heaven
above and on the earth below.
12 "Now then, please swear to me by the
LORD that you will show kindness to my
family, because I have shown kindness to
you. Give me a sure sign 13 that you will
spare the lives of my father and mother,
my brothers and sisters, and all who belong to them — and that you will save us
from death."
14 "Our lives for your lives!" the men assured her. "If you don't tell what we are
doing, we will treat you kindly and faithfully when the LORD gives us the land."
15 So she let them down by a rope
through the window, for the house she
lived in was part of the city wall. 16 She
said to them, "Go to the hills so the pursuers will not find you. Hide yourselves
there three days until they return, and
then go on your way."
17 Now the men had said to her, "This
oath you made us swear will not be
binding on us 18 unless, when we enter
the land, you have tied this scarlet cord
in the window through which you let us
down, and unless you have brought your
father and mother, your brothers and
all your family into your house. 19 If any
of them go outside your house into the
street, their blood will be on their own
heads; we will not be responsible. As for
those who are in the house with you, their
blood will be on our head if a hand is laid
on them. 20 But if you tell what we are doing, we will be released from the oath you
made us swear."
21 "Agreed," she replied. "Let it be as
you say."
So she sent them away, and they departed. And she tied the scarlet cord in
the window.
22 When they left, they went into the
hills and stayed there three days, until
the pursuers had searched all along the
road and returned without finding them.
23 Then the two men started back. They
went down out of the hills, forded the
river and came to Joshua son of Nun and
told him everything that had happened
to them. 24 They said to Joshua, "The
LORD has surely given the whole land into
our hands; all the people are melting in
fear because of us."

3 Early in the morning Joshua and all
the Israelites set out from Shittim and
went to the Jordan, where they camped
before crossing over. 2 After three days
the officers went throughout the camp,
3 giving orders to the people: "When you
see the ark of the covenant of the LORD
your God, and the Levitical priests carrying it, you are to move out from your positions and follow it. 4 Then you will know
which way to go, since you have never
been this way before. But keep a distance
of about two thousand cubits[c] between
you and the ark; do not go near it."
5 Joshua told the people, "Consecrate

[a] 10 Or *the Sea of Reeds* [b] 10 The Hebrew term refers to the irrevocable giving over of things or persons to the LORD, often by totally destroying them. [c] 4 That is, about 3,000 feet or about 900 meters

yourselves, for tomorrow the LORD will
do amazing things among you."
6 Joshua said to the priests, "Take up
the ark of the covenant and pass on ahead
of the people." So they took it up and went
ahead of them.
7 And the LORD said to Joshua, "Today
I will begin to exalt you in the eyes of all
Israel, so they may know that I am with
you as I was with Moses. 8 Tell the priests
who carry the ark of the covenant: 'When
you reach the edge of the Jordan's waters,
go and stand in the river.'"
9 Joshua said to the Israelites, "Come
here and listen to the words of the LORD
your God. 10 This is how you will know
that the living God is among you and that
he will certainly drive out before you the
Canaanites, Hittites, Hivites, Perizzites,
Girgashites, Amorites and Jebusites.
11 See, the ark of the covenant of the Lord
of all the earth will go into the Jordan
ahead of you. 12 Now then, choose twelve
men from the tribes of Israel, one from
each tribe. 13 And as soon as the priests
who carry the ark of the LORD — the Lord
of all the earth — set foot in the Jordan,
its waters flowing downstream will be
cut off and stand up in a heap."
14 So when the people broke camp to
cross the Jordan, the priests carrying the
ark of the covenant went ahead of them.
15 Now the Jordan is at flood stage all during harvest. Yet as soon as the priests who
carried the ark reached the Jordan and
their feet touched the water's edge, 16 the
water from upstream stopped flowing. It
piled up in a heap a great distance away,
at a town called Adam in the vicinity of
Zarethan, while the water flowing down
to the Sea of the Arabah (that is, the Dead
Sea) was completely cut off. So the people crossed over opposite Jericho. 17 The
priests who carried the ark of the covenant
of the LORD stopped in the middle of the
Jordan and stood on dry ground, while all
Israel passed by until the whole nation had
completed the crossing on dry ground.

4 When the whole nation had finished
crossing the Jordan, the LORD said
to Joshua, 2 "Choose twelve men from
among the people, one from each tribe,
3 and tell them to take up twelve stones
from the middle of the Jordan, from right
where the priests are standing, and carry
them over with you and put them down at
the place where you stay tonight."
4 So Joshua called together the twelve
men he had appointed from the Israelites,
one from each tribe, 5 and said to them,
"Go over before the ark of the LORD your
God into the middle of the Jordan. Each
of you is to take up a stone on his shoulder, according to the number of the tribes
of the Israelites, 6 to serve as a sign among
you. In the future, when your children
ask you, 'What do these stones mean?'
7 tell them that the flow of the Jordan was
cut off before the ark of the covenant of
the LORD. When it crossed the Jordan, the
waters of the Jordan were cut off. These
stones are to be a memorial to the people
of Israel forever."
8 So the Israelites did as Joshua commanded them. They took twelve stones
from the middle of the Jordan, according to the number of the tribes of the
Israelites, as the LORD had told Joshua;
and they carried them over with them to
their camp, where they put them down.
9 Joshua set up the twelve stones that had
been[a] in the middle of the Jordan at the
spot where the priests who carried the
ark of the covenant had stood. And they
are there to this day.
10 Now the priests who carried the ark
remained standing in the middle of the
Jordan until everything the LORD had
commanded Joshua was done by the people, just as Moses had directed Joshua.
The people hurried over, 11 and as soon
as all of them had crossed, the ark of the
LORD and the priests came to the other side while the people watched. 12 The
men of Reuben, Gad and the half-tribe of
Manasseh crossed over, ready for battle,
in front of the Israelites, as Moses had
directed them. 13 About forty thousand
armed for battle crossed over before the
LORD to the plains of Jericho for war.
14 That day the LORD exalted Joshua in
the sight of all Israel; and they stood in
awe of him all the days of his life, just as
they had stood in awe of Moses.
15 Then the LORD said to Joshua,
16 "Command the priests carrying the
ark of the covenant law to come up out of
the Jordan."
17 So Joshua commanded the priests,
"Come up out of the Jordan."

[a] 9 Or *Joshua also set up twelve stones*

18And the priests came up out of the
river carrying the ark of the covenant of
the LORD. No sooner had they set their
feet on the dry ground than the waters
of the Jordan returned to their place and
ran at flood stage as before.
19On the tenth day of the first month
the people went up from the Jordan and
camped at Gilgal on the eastern border of
Jericho. 20And Joshua set up at Gilgal the
twelve stones they had taken out of the
Jordan. 21He said to the Israelites, "In the
future when your descendants ask their
parents, 'What do these stones mean?'
22tell them, 'Israel crossed the Jordan
on dry ground.' 23For the LORD your God
dried up the Jordan before you until you
had crossed over. The LORD your God did
to the Jordan what he had done to the Red
Sea[a] when he dried it up before us until
we had crossed over. 24He did this so that
all the peoples of the earth might know
that the hand of the LORD is powerful and
so that you might always fear the LORD
your God."

5 Now when all the Amorite kings west
of the Jordan and all the Canaanite
kings along the coast heard how the LORD
had dried up the Jordan before the Israelites until they[b] had crossed over, their
hearts melted in fear and they no longer
had the courage to face the Israelites.
2At that time the LORD said to Joshua,
"Make flint knives and circumcise the
Israelites again." 3So Joshua made flint
knives and circumcised the Israelites at
Gibeath Haaraloth.[c]
4Now this is why he did so: All those
who came out of Egypt—all the men of
military age—died in the wilderness
on the way after leaving Egypt. 5All the
people that came out had been circumcised, but all the people born in the wilderness during the journey from Egypt
had not. 6The Israelites had moved about
in the wilderness forty years until all
the men who were of military age when
they left Egypt had died, since they had
not obeyed the LORD. For the LORD had
sworn to them that they would not see
the land he had solemnly promised their
ancestors to give us, a land flowing with
milk and honey. 7So he raised up their
sons in their place, and these were the
ones Joshua circumcised. They were still
uncircumcised because they had not
been circumcised on the way. 8And after
the whole nation had been circumcised,
they remained where they were in camp
until they were healed.
9Then the LORD said to Joshua, "Today
I have rolled away the reproach of Egypt
from you." So the place has been called
Gilgal[d] to this day.
10On the evening of the fourteenth day
of the month, while camped at Gilgal on
the plains of Jericho, the Israelites celebrated the Passover. 11The day after the
Passover, that very day, they ate some
of the produce of the land: unleavened
bread and roasted grain. 12The manna
stopped the day after[e] they ate this food
from the land; there was no longer any
manna for the Israelites, but that year
they ate the produce of Canaan.
13Now when Joshua was near Jericho,
he looked up and saw a man standing in
front of him with a drawn sword in his
hand. Joshua went up to him and asked,
"Are you for us or for our enemies?"
14"Neither," he replied, "but as commander of the army of the LORD I have
now come." Then Joshua fell facedown to
the ground in reverence, and asked him,
"What message does my Lord[f] have for
his servant?"
15The commander of the LORD's army
replied, "Take off your sandals, for the
place where you are standing is holy."
And Joshua did so.

6 Now the gates of Jericho were securely barred because of the Israelites. No
one went out and no one came in.
2Then the LORD said to Joshua, "See, I
have delivered Jericho into your hands,
along with its king and its fighting men.
3March around the city once with all the
armed men. Do this for six days. 4Have
seven priests carry trumpets of rams'
horns in front of the ark. On the seventh
day, march around the city seven times,
with the priests blowing the trumpets.
5When you hear them sound a long blast
on the trumpets, have the whole army
give a loud shout; then the wall of the city
will collapse and the army will go up, everyone straight in."
6So Joshua son of Nun called the priests
and said to them, "Take up the ark of the
covenant of the LORD and have seven

[a] 23 Or *the Sea of Reeds* [b] *1* Another textual tradition *we* [c] *3 Gibeath Haaraloth* means *the hill of foreskins.* [d] *9 Gilgal* sounds like the Hebrew for *roll* [e] *12* Or *the day* [f] *14* Or *lord*

priests carry trumpets in front of it." 7 And
he ordered the army, "Advance! March
around the city, with an armed guard going ahead of the ark of the LORD."
8 When Joshua had spoken to the people, the seven priests carrying the seven
trumpets before the LORD went forward,
blowing their trumpets, and the ark of
the LORD's covenant followed them.
9 The armed guard marched ahead of the
priests who blew the trumpets, and the
rear guard followed the ark. All this time
the trumpets were sounding. 10 But Joshua had commanded the army, "Do not
give a war cry, do not raise your voices,
do not say a word until the day I tell you to
shout. Then shout!" 11 So he had the ark of
the LORD carried around the city, circling
it once. Then the army returned to camp
and spent the night there.
12 Joshua got up early the next morning and the priests took up the ark of
the LORD. 13 The seven priests carrying the seven trumpets went forward,
marching before the ark of the LORD and
blowing the trumpets. The armed men
went ahead of them and the rear guard
followed the ark of the LORD, while the
trumpets kept sounding. 14 So on the second day they marched around the city
once and returned to the camp. They did
this for six days.
15 On the seventh day, they got up at
daybreak and marched around the city
seven times in the same manner, except
that on that day they circled the city sev-
en times. 16 The seventh time around,
when the priests sounded the trumpet
blast, Joshua commanded the army,
"Shout! For the LORD has given you the
city! 17 The city and all that is in it are to
be devoted[a] to the LORD. Only Rahab the
prostitute and all who are with her in her
house shall be spared, because she hid
the spies we sent. 18 But keep away from
the devoted things, so that you will not
bring about your own destruction by taking any of them. Otherwise you will make
the camp of Israel liable to destruction
and bring trouble on it. 19 All the silver
and gold and the articles of bronze and
iron are sacred to the LORD and must go
into his treasury."
20 When the trumpets sounded, the
army shouted, and at the sound of the
trumpet, when the men gave a loud
shout, the wall collapsed; so everyone
charged straight in, and they took the
city. 21 They devoted the city to the LORD
and destroyed with the sword every living thing in it — men and women, young
and old, cattle, sheep and donkeys.
22 Joshua said to the two men who had
spied out the land, "Go into the prostitute's house and bring her out and all who
belong to her, in accordance with your
oath to her." 23 So the young men who had
done the spying went in and brought out
Rahab, her father and mother, her brothers and sisters and all who belonged to
her. They brought out her entire family
and put them in a place outside the camp
of Israel.
24 Then they burned the whole city
and everything in it, but they put the silver and gold and the articles of bronze
and iron into the treasury of the LORD's
house. 25 But Joshua spared Rahab the
prostitute, with her family and all who
belonged to her, because she hid the men
Joshua had sent as spies to Jericho — and
she lives among the Israelites to this day.
26 At that time Joshua pronounced this
solemn oath: "Cursed before the LORD is
the one who undertakes to rebuild this
city, Jericho:

"At the cost of his firstborn son
  he will lay its foundations;
at the cost of his youngest
  he will set up its gates."

27 So the LORD was with Joshua, and his
fame spread throughout the land.
7 But the Israelites were unfaithful in
regard to the devoted things[b]; Achan
son of Karmi, the son of Zimri,[c] the son
of Zerah, of the tribe of Judah, took some
of them. So the LORD's anger burned
against Israel.
2 Now Joshua sent men from Jericho to
Ai, which is near Beth Aven to the east of
Bethel, and told them, "Go up and spy
out the region." So the men went up and
spied out Ai.
3 When they returned to Joshua, they
said, "Not all the army will have to go up

[a] *17* The Hebrew term refers to the irrevocable giving over of things or persons to the LORD, often by totally destroying them; also in verses 18 and 21. [b] *1* The Hebrew term refers to the irrevocable giving over of things or persons to the LORD, often by totally destroying them; also in verses 11, 12, 13 and 15.
[c] *1* See Septuagint and 1 Chron. 2:6; Hebrew *Zabdi*; also in verses 17 and 18.

against Ai. Send two or three thousand
men to take it and do not weary the whole
army, for only a few people live there." 4So
about three thousand went up; but they
were routed by the men of Ai, 5who killed
about thirty-six of them. They chased the
Israelites from the city gate as far as the
stone quarries and struck them down on
the slopes. At this the hearts of the people
melted in fear and became like water.

6Then Joshua tore his clothes and fell
facedown to the ground before the ark
of the LORD, remaining there till evening. The elders of Israel did the same,
and sprinkled dust on their heads. 7And
Joshua said, "Alas, Sovereign LORD, why
did you ever bring this people across the
Jordan to deliver us into the hands of the
Amorites to destroy us? If only we had
been content to stay on the other side of
the Jordan! 8Pardon your servant, Lord.
What can I say, now that Israel has been
routed by its enemies? 9The Canaanites
and the other people of the country will
hear about this and they will surround
us and wipe out our name from the earth.
What then will you do for your own great
name?"

10The LORD said to Joshua, "Stand up!
What are you doing down on your face?
11Israel has sinned; they have violated
my covenant, which I commanded them
to keep. They have taken some of the devoted things; they have stolen, they have
lied, they have put them with their own
possessions. 12That is why the Israelites
cannot stand against their enemies; they
turn their backs and run because they
have been made liable to destruction. I
will not be with you anymore unless you
destroy whatever among you is devoted
to destruction.

13"Go, consecrate the people. Tell
them, 'Consecrate yourselves in preparation for tomorrow; for this is what the
LORD, the God of Israel, says: There are
devoted things among you, Israel. You
cannot stand against your enemies until
you remove them.

14" 'In the morning, present yourselves
tribe by tribe. The tribe the LORD chooses shall come forward clan by clan; the
clan the LORD chooses shall come forward family by family; and the family the
LORD chooses shall come forward man
by man. 15Whoever is caught with the
devoted things shall be destroyed by fire,
along with all that belongs to him. He has
violated the covenant of the LORD and
has done an outrageous thing in Israel!' "

16Early the next morning Joshua had
Israel come forward by tribes, and Judah was chosen. 17The clans of Judah
came forward, and the Zerahites were
chosen. He had the clan of the Zerahites
come forward by families, and Zimri was
chosen. 18Joshua had his family come
forward man by man, and Achan son of
Karmi, the son of Zimri, the son of Zerah,
of the tribe of Judah, was chosen.

19Then Joshua said to Achan, "My son,
give glory to the LORD, the God of Israel,
and honor him. Tell me what you have
done; do not hide it from me."

20Achan replied, "It is true! I have
sinned against the LORD, the God of Israel. This is what I have done: 21When I
saw in the plunder a beautiful robe from
Babylonia,[a] two hundred shekels[b] of silver and a bar of gold weighing fifty shekels,[c] I coveted them and took them. They
are hidden in the ground inside my tent,
with the silver underneath."

22So Joshua sent messengers, and they
ran to the tent, and there it was, hidden
in his tent, with the silver underneath.
23They took the things from the tent,
brought them to Joshua and all the Israelites and spread them out before the
LORD.

24Then Joshua, together with all Israel,
took Achan son of Zerah, the silver, the
robe, the gold bar, his sons and daughters, his cattle, donkeys and sheep, his
tent and all that he had, to the Valley of
Achor. 25Joshua said, "Why have you
brought this trouble on us? The LORD will
bring trouble on you today."

Then all Israel stoned him, and after
they had stoned the rest, they burned
them. 26Over Achan they heaped up a
large pile of rocks, which remains to this
day. Then the LORD turned from his fierce
anger. Therefore that place has been
called the Valley of Achor[d] ever since.

8 Then the LORD said to Joshua, "Do not
be afraid; do not be discouraged. Take
the whole army with you, and go up and
attack Ai. For I have delivered into your
hands the king of Ai, his people, his city

[a] *21* Hebrew *Shinar* [b] *21* That is, about 5 pounds or about 2.3 kilograms [c] *21* That is, about 1 1/4 pounds or about 575 grams [d] *26* *Achor* means *trouble.*

and his land. 2 You shall do to Ai and its king as you did to Jericho and its king, except that you may carry off their plunder and livestock for yourselves. Set an ambush behind the city."

3 So Joshua and the whole army moved out to attack Ai. He chose thirty thousand of his best fighting men and sent them out at night 4 with these orders: "Listen carefully. You are to set an ambush behind the city. Don't go very far from it. All of you be on the alert. 5 I and all those with me will advance on the city, and when the men come out against us, as they did before, we will flee from them. 6 They will pursue us until we have lured them away from the city, for they will say, 'They are running away from us as they did before.' So when we flee from them, 7 you are to rise up from ambush and take the city. The LORD your God will give it into your hand. 8 When you have taken the city, set it on fire. Do what the LORD has commanded. See to it; you have my orders."

9 Then Joshua sent them off, and they went to the place of ambush and lay in wait between Bethel and Ai, to the west of Ai—but Joshua spent that night with the people.

10 Early the next morning Joshua mustered his army, and he and the leaders of Israel marched before them to Ai. 11 The entire force that was with him marched up and approached the city and arrived in front of it. They set up camp north of Ai, with the valley between them and the city. 12 Joshua had taken about five thousand men and set them in ambush between Bethel and Ai, to the west of the city. 13 So the soldiers took up their positions—with the main camp to the north of the city and the ambush to the west of it. That night Joshua went into the valley.

14 When the king of Ai saw this, he and all the men of the city hurried out early in the morning to meet Israel in battle at a certain place overlooking the Arabah. But he did not know that an ambush had been set against him behind the city. 15 Joshua and all Israel let themselves be driven back before them, and they fled toward the wilderness. 16 All the men of Ai were called to pursue them, and they pursued Joshua and were lured away from the city. 17 Not a man remained in Ai or Bethel who did not go after Israel. They left the city open and went in pursuit of Israel.

18 Then the LORD said to Joshua, "Hold out toward Ai the javelin that is in your hand, for into your hand I will deliver the city." So Joshua held out toward the city the javelin that was in his hand. 19 As soon as he did this, the men in the ambush rose quickly from their position and rushed forward. They entered the city and captured it and quickly set it on fire.

20 The men of Ai looked back and saw the smoke of the city rising up into the sky, but they had no chance to escape in any direction; the Israelites who had been fleeing toward the wilderness had turned back against their pursuers. 21 For when Joshua and all Israel saw that the ambush had taken the city and that smoke was going up from it, they turned around and attacked the men of Ai. 22 Those in the ambush also came out of the city against them, so that they were caught in the middle, with Israelites on both sides. Israel cut them down, leaving them neither survivors nor fugitives. 23 But they took the king of Ai alive and brought him to Joshua.

24 When Israel had finished killing all the men of Ai in the fields and in the wilderness where they had chased them, and when every one of them had been put to the sword, all the Israelites returned to Ai and killed those who were in it. 25 Twelve thousand men and women fell that day—all the people of Ai. 26 For Joshua did not draw back the hand that held out his javelin until he had destroyed[a] all who lived in Ai. 27 But Israel did carry off for themselves the livestock and plunder of this city, as the LORD had instructed Joshua.

28 So Joshua burned Ai[b] and made it a permanent heap of ruins, a desolate place to this day. 29 He impaled the body of the king of Ai on a pole and left it there until evening. At sunset, Joshua ordered them to take the body from the pole and throw it down at the entrance of the city gate. And they raised a large pile of rocks over it, which remains to this day.

30 Then Joshua built on Mount Ebal an altar to the LORD, the God of Israel, 31 as Moses the servant of the LORD had commanded the Israelites. He built it accord-

[a] *26* The Hebrew term refers to the irrevocable giving over of things or persons to the LORD, often by totally destroying them. [b] *28* *Ai* means *the ruin*.

ing to what is written in the Book of the
Law of Moses—an altar of uncut stones,
on which no iron tool had been used. On
it they offered to the LORD burnt offerings and sacrificed fellowship offerings.
32There, in the presence of the Israelites,
Joshua wrote on stones a copy of the law
of Moses. 33All the Israelites, with their
elders, officials and judges, were standing on both sides of the ark of the covenant of the LORD, facing the Levitical
priests who carried it. Both the foreigners
living among them and the native-born
were there. Half of the people stood in
front of Mount Gerizim and half of them
in front of Mount Ebal, as Moses the servant of the LORD had formerly commanded when he gave instructions to bless the
people of Israel.

34Afterward, Joshua read all the words
of the law—the blessings and the curses—just as it is written in the Book of the
Law. 35There was not a word of all that
Moses had commanded that Joshua did
not read to the whole assembly of Israel,
including the women and children, and
the foreigners who lived among them.

9 Now when all the kings west of the Jordan heard about these things—the
kings in the hill country, in the western
foothills, and along the entire coast of the
Mediterranean Sea as far as Lebanon (the
kings of the Hittites, Amorites, Canaanites, Perizzites, Hivites and Jebusites)—
2they came together to wage war against
Joshua and Israel.

3However, when the people of Gibeon
heard what Joshua had done to Jericho
and Ai, 4they resorted to a ruse: They
went as a delegation whose donkeys were
loaded[a] with worn-out sacks and old
wineskins, cracked and mended. 5They
put worn and patched sandals on their
feet and wore old clothes. All the bread
of their food supply was dry and moldy.
6Then they went to Joshua in the camp at
Gilgal and said to him and the Israelites,
"We have come from a distant country;
make a treaty with us."

7The Israelites said to the Hivites, "But
perhaps you live near us, so how can we
make a treaty with you?"

8"We are your servants," they said to
Joshua.

But Joshua asked, "Who are you and
where do you come from?"

9They answered: "Your servants have
come from a very distant country because of the fame of the LORD your God.
For we have heard reports of him: all that
he did in Egypt, 10and all that he did to
the two kings of the Amorites east of the
Jordan—Sihon king of Heshbon, and
Og king of Bashan, who reigned in Ashtaroth. 11And our elders and all those
living in our country said to us, 'Take
provisions for your journey; go and meet
them and say to them, "We are your servants; make a treaty with us."' 12This
bread of ours was warm when we packed
it at home on the day we left to come to
you. But now see how dry and moldy it is.
13And these wineskins that we filled were
new, but see how cracked they are. And
our clothes and sandals are worn out by
the very long journey."

14The Israelites sampled their provisions but did not inquire of the LORD.
15Then Joshua made a treaty of peace
with them to let them live, and the leaders of the assembly ratified it by oath.

16Three days after they made the treaty
with the Gibeonites, the Israelites heard
that they were neighbors, living near
them. 17So the Israelites set out and on
the third day came to their cities: Gibeon,
Kephirah, Beeroth and Kiriath Jearim.
18But the Israelites did not attack them,
because the leaders of the assembly had
sworn an oath to them by the LORD, the
God of Israel.

The whole assembly grumbled against
the leaders, 19but all the leaders answered, "We have given them our oath
by the LORD, the God of Israel, and we
cannot touch them now. 20This is what
we will do to them: We will let them live,
so that God's wrath will not fall on us for
breaking the oath we swore to them."
21They continued, "Let them live, but let
them be woodcutters and water carriers
in the service of the whole assembly." So
the leaders' promise to them was kept.

22Then Joshua summoned the Gibeonites and said, "Why did you deceive us
by saying, 'We live a long way from you,'
while actually you live near us? 23You are
now under a curse: You will never be re-

[a] *4* Most Hebrew manuscripts; some Hebrew manuscripts, Vulgate and Syriac (see also Septuagint) *They prepared provisions and loaded their donkeys*

leased from service as woodcutters and
water carriers for the house of my God."
24They answered Joshua, "Your servants were clearly told how the LORD
your God had commanded his servant
Moses to give you the whole land and to
wipe out all its inhabitants from before
you. So we feared for our lives because
of you, and that is why we did this. 25We
are now in your hands. Do to us whatever
seems good and right to you."
26So Joshua saved them from the Israelites, and they did not kill them. 27That
day he made the Gibeonites woodcutters
and water carriers for the assembly, to
provide for the needs of the altar of the
LORD at the place the LORD would choose.
And that is what they are to this day.

10 Now Adoni-Zedek king of Jerusalem heard that Joshua had taken Ai
and totally destroyed[a] it, doing to Ai and
its king as he had done to Jericho and its
king, and that the people of Gibeon had
made a treaty of peace with Israel and
had become their allies. 2He and his people were very much alarmed at this, because Gibeon was an important city, like
one of the royal cities; it was larger than
Ai, and all its men were good fighters. 3So
Adoni-Zedek king of Jerusalem appealed
to Hoham king of Hebron, Piram king of
Jarmuth, Japhia king of Lachish and Debir king of Eglon. 4"Come up and help me
attack Gibeon," he said, "because it has
made peace with Joshua and the Israelites."
5Then the five kings of the Amorites —
the kings of Jerusalem, Hebron, Jarmuth,
Lachish and Eglon — joined forces. They
moved up with all their troops and took
up positions against Gibeon and attacked it.
6The Gibeonites then sent word to
Joshua in the camp at Gilgal: "Do not
abandon your servants. Come up to us
quickly and save us! Help us, because all
the Amorite kings from the hill country
have joined forces against us."
7So Joshua marched up from Gilgal
with his entire army, including all the
best fighting men. 8The LORD said to
Joshua, "Do not be afraid of them; I have
given them into your hand. Not one of
them will be able to withstand you."
9After an all-night march from Gilgal, Joshua took them by surprise. 10The
LORD threw them into confusion before
Israel, so Joshua and the Israelites defeated them completely at Gibeon. Israel
pursued them along the road going up to
Beth Horon and cut them down all the
way to Azekah and Makkedah. 11As they
fled before Israel on the road down from
Beth Horon to Azekah, the LORD hurled
large hailstones down on them, and more
of them died from the hail than were
killed by the swords of the Israelites.
12On the day the LORD gave the Amorites over to Israel, Joshua said to the
LORD in the presence of Israel:

"Sun, stand still over Gibeon,
  and you, moon, over the Valley of
    Aijalon."
13So the sun stood still,
  and the moon stopped,
  till the nation avenged itself on[b] its
    enemies,

as it is written in the Book of Jashar.
The sun stopped in the middle of the
sky and delayed going down about a full
day. 14There has never been a day like it
before or since, a day when the LORD listened to a human being. Surely the LORD
was fighting for Israel!
15Then Joshua returned with all Israel
to the camp at Gilgal.
16Now the five kings had fled and hidden in the cave at Makkedah. 17When
Joshua was told that the five kings had
been found hiding in the cave at Makkedah, 18he said, "Roll large rocks up to the
mouth of the cave, and post some men
there to guard it. 19But don't stop; pursue
your enemies! Attack them from the rear
and don't let them reach their cities, for
the LORD your God has given them into
your hand."
20So Joshua and the Israelites defeated them completely, but a few survivors
managed to reach their fortified cities.
21The whole army then returned safely to
Joshua in the camp at Makkedah, and no
one uttered a word against the Israelites.
22Joshua said, "Open the mouth of
the cave and bring those five kings out
to me." 23So they brought the five kings
out of the cave — the kings of Jerusalem,
Hebron, Jarmuth, Lachish and Eglon.
24When they had brought these kings to

[a] *1* The Hebrew term refers to the irrevocable giving over of things or persons to the LORD, often by totally destroying them; also in verses 28, 35, 37, 39 and 40. [b] *13* Or *nation triumphed over*

Joshua, he summoned all the men of Israel and said to the army commanders who
had come with him, "Come here and put
your feet on the necks of these kings." So
they came forward and placed their feet
on their necks.
25 Joshua said to them, "Do not be
afraid; do not be discouraged. Be strong
and courageous. This is what the LORD
will do to all the enemies you are going
to fight." 26 Then Joshua put the kings to
death and exposed their bodies on five
poles, and they were left hanging on the
poles until evening.
27 At sunset Joshua gave the order and
they took them down from the poles and
threw them into the cave where they had
been hiding. At the mouth of the cave
they placed large rocks, which are there
to this day.
28 That day Joshua took Makkedah.
He put the city and its king to the sword
and totally destroyed everyone in it. He
left no survivors. And he did to the king
of Makkedah as he had done to the king
of Jericho.
29 Then Joshua and all Israel with him
moved on from Makkedah to Libnah and
attacked it. 30 The LORD also gave that
city and its king into Israel's hand. The
city and everyone in it Joshua put to the
sword. He left no survivors there. And he
did to its king as he had done to the king
of Jericho.
31 Then Joshua and all Israel with him
moved on from Libnah to Lachish; he
took up positions against it and attacked
it. 32 The LORD gave Lachish into Israel's
hands, and Joshua took it on the second
day. The city and everyone in it he put to
the sword, just as he had done to Libnah.
33 Meanwhile, Horam king of Gezer had
come up to help Lachish, but Joshua defeated him and his army—until no survivors were left.
34 Then Joshua and all Israel with him
moved on from Lachish to Eglon; they
took up positions against it and attacked
it. 35 They captured it that same day and
put it to the sword and totally destroyed
everyone in it, just as they had done to
Lachish.
36 Then Joshua and all Israel with him
went up from Eglon to Hebron and attacked it. 37 They took the city and put it
to the sword, together with its king, its
villages and everyone in it. They left no
survivors. Just as at Eglon, they totally destroyed it and everyone in it.
38 Then Joshua and all Israel with
him turned around and attacked Debir.
39 They took the city, its king and its villages, and put them to the sword. Everyone in it they totally destroyed. They left
no survivors. They did to Debir and its
king as they had done to Libnah and its
king and to Hebron.
40 So Joshua subdued the whole region,
including the hill country, the Negev,
the western foothills and the mountain
slopes, together with all their kings. He
left no survivors. He totally destroyed all
who breathed, just as the LORD, the God
of Israel, had commanded. 41 Joshua subdued them from Kadesh Barnea to Gaza
and from the whole region of Goshen to
Gibeon. 42 All these kings and their lands
Joshua conquered in one campaign, because the LORD, the God of Israel, fought
for Israel.
43 Then Joshua returned with all Israel
to the camp at Gilgal.

11 When Jabin king of Hazor heard of
this, he sent word to Jobab king of
Madon, to the kings of Shimron and Akshaph, 2 and to the northern kings who
were in the mountains, in the Arabah
south of Kinnereth, in the western foothills and in Naphoth Dor on the west;
3 to the Canaanites in the east and west;
to the Amorites, Hittites, Perizzites and
Jebusites in the hill country; and to the
Hivites below Hermon in the region of
Mizpah. 4 They came out with all their
troops and a large number of horses and
chariots—a huge army, as numerous as
the sand on the seashore. 5 All these kings
joined forces and made camp together at
the Waters of Merom to fight against Israel.
6 The LORD said to Joshua, "Do not be
afraid of them, because by this time tomorrow I will hand all of them, slain, over
to Israel. You are to hamstring their horses and burn their chariots."
7 So Joshua and his whole army came
against them suddenly at the Waters
of Merom and attacked them, 8 and the
LORD gave them into the hand of Israel.
They defeated them and pursued them
all the way to Greater Sidon, to Misrephoth Maim, and to the Valley of Mizpah
on the east, until no survivors were left.
9 Joshua did to them as the LORD had di-

rected: He hamstrung their horses and burned their chariots.

10 At that time Joshua turned back and captured Hazor and put its king to the sword. (Hazor had been the head of all these kingdoms.) 11 Everyone in it they put to the sword. They totally destroyed[a] them, not sparing anyone that breathed, and he burned Hazor itself.

12 Joshua took all these royal cities and their kings and put them to the sword. He totally destroyed them, as Moses the servant of the LORD had commanded. 13 Yet Israel did not burn any of the cities built on their mounds—except Hazor, which Joshua burned. 14 The Israelites carried off for themselves all the plunder and livestock of these cities, but all the people they put to the sword until they completely destroyed them, not sparing anyone that breathed. 15 As the LORD commanded his servant Moses, so Moses commanded Joshua, and Joshua did it; he left nothing undone of all that the LORD commanded Moses.

16 So Joshua took this entire land: the hill country, all the Negev, the whole region of Goshen, the western foothills, the Arabah and the mountains of Israel with their foothills, 17 from Mount Halak, which rises toward Seir, to Baal Gad in the Valley of Lebanon below Mount Hermon. He captured all their kings and put them to death. 18 Joshua waged war against all these kings for a long time. 19 Except for the Hivites living in Gibeon, not one city made a treaty of peace with the Israelites, who took them all in battle. 20 For it was the LORD himself who hardened their hearts to wage war against Israel, so that he might destroy them totally, exterminating them without mercy, as the LORD had commanded Moses.

21 At that time Joshua went and destroyed the Anakites from the hill country: from Hebron, Debir and Anab, from all the hill country of Judah, and from all the hill country of Israel. Joshua totally destroyed them and their towns. 22 No Anakites were left in Israelite territory; only in Gaza, Gath and Ashdod did any survive.

23 So Joshua took the entire land, just as the LORD had directed Moses, and he gave it as an inheritance to Israel according to their tribal divisions. Then the land had rest from war.

12 These are the kings of the land whom the Israelites had defeated and whose territory they took over east of the Jordan, from the Arnon Gorge to Mount Hermon, including all the eastern side of the Arabah:

2 Sihon king of the Amorites, who reigned in Heshbon.
He ruled from Aroer on the rim of the Arnon Gorge—from the middle of the gorge—to the Jabbok River, which is the border of the Ammonites. This included half of Gilead. 3 He also ruled over the eastern Arabah from the Sea of Galilee[b] to the Sea of the Arabah (that is, the Dead Sea), to Beth Jeshimoth, and then southward below the slopes of Pisgah.

4 And the territory of Og king of Bashan, one of the last of the Rephaites, who reigned in Ashtaroth and Edrei.
5 He ruled over Mount Hermon, Salekah, all of Bashan to the border of the people of Geshur and Maakah, and half of Gilead to the border of Sihon king of Heshbon.

6 Moses, the servant of the LORD, and the Israelites conquered them. And Moses the servant of the LORD gave their land to the Reubenites, the Gadites and the half-tribe of Manasseh to be their possession.

7 Here is a list of the kings of the land that Joshua and the Israelites conquered on the west side of the Jordan, from Baal Gad in the Valley of Lebanon to Mount Halak, which rises toward Seir. Joshua gave their lands as an inheritance to the tribes of Israel according to their tribal divisions. 8 The lands included the hill country, the western foothills, the Arabah, the mountain slopes, the wilderness and the Negev. These were the lands of the Hittites, Amorites, Canaanites, Perizzites, Hivites and Jebusites. These were the kings:

9 the king of Jericho	one
the king of Ai (near Bethel)	one
10 the king of Jerusalem	one

[a] *11* The Hebrew term refers to the irrevocable giving over of things or persons to the LORD, often by totally destroying them; also in verses 12, 20 and 21. [b] *3* Hebrew *Kinnereth*

the king of Hebron one
11 the king of Jarmuth one
the king of Lachish one
12 the king of Eglon one
the king of Gezer one
13 the king of Debir one
the king of Geder one
14 the king of Hormah one
the king of Arad one
15 the king of Libnah one
the king of Adullam one
16 the king of Makkedah one
the king of Bethel one
17 the king of Tappuah one
the king of Hepher one
18 the king of Aphek one
the king of Lasharon one
19 the king of Madon one
the king of Hazor one
20 the king of Shimron Meron one
the king of Akshaph one
21 the king of Taanach one
the king of Megiddo one
22 the king of Kedesh one
the king of Jokneam in
Carmel one
23 the king of Dor
(in Naphoth Dor) one
the king of Goyim in Gilgal one
24 the king of Tirzah one
thirty-one kings in all.

13 When Joshua had grown old, the
LORD said to him, "You are now very
old, and there are still very large areas of
land to be taken over.

2 "This is the land that remains: all
the regions of the Philistines and
Geshurites, 3 from the Shihor River
on the east of Egypt to the territory
of Ekron on the north, all of it counted as Canaanite though held by the
five Philistine rulers in Gaza, Ashdod, Ashkelon, Gath and Ekron; the
territory of the Avvites 4 on the south;
all the land of the Canaanites, from
Arah of the Sidonians as far as Aphek
and the border of the Amorites; 5 the
area of Byblos; and all Lebanon to
the east, from Baal Gad below Mount
Hermon to Lebo Hamath.

6 "As for all the inhabitants of the mountain regions from Lebanon to Misrephoth
Maim, that is, all the Sidonians, I myself
will drive them out before the Israelites.
Be sure to allocate this land to Israel for
an inheritance, as I have instructed you,
7 and divide it as an inheritance among
the nine tribes and half of the tribe of
Manasseh."

8 The other half of Manasseh,[a] the Reubenites and the Gadites had received the
inheritance that Moses had given them
east of the Jordan, as he, the servant of
the LORD, had assigned it to them.

9 It extended from Aroer on the rim of
the Arnon Gorge, and from the town
in the middle of the gorge, and included the whole plateau of Medeba
as far as Dibon, 10 and all the towns
of Sihon king of the Amorites, who
ruled in Heshbon, out to the border
of the Ammonites. 11 It also included Gilead, the territory of the people
of Geshur and Maakah, all of Mount
Hermon and all Bashan as far as Salekah — 12 that is, the whole kingdom
of Og in Bashan, who had reigned in
Ashtaroth and Edrei. (He was the last
of the Rephaites.) Moses had defeated them and taken over their land.
13 But the Israelites did not drive out
the people of Geshur and Maakah, so
they continue to live among the Israelites to this day.

14 But to the tribe of Levi he gave no inheritance, since the food offerings presented to the LORD, the God of Israel, are
their inheritance, as he promised them.

15 This is what Moses had given to the
tribe of Reuben, according to its clans:

16 The territory from Aroer on the
rim of the Arnon Gorge, and from
the town in the middle of the gorge,
and the whole plateau past Medeba
17 to Heshbon and all its towns on
the plateau, including Dibon, Bamoth Baal, Beth Baal Meon, 18 Jahaz,
Kedemoth, Mephaath, 19 Kiriathaim,
Sibmah, Zereth Shahar on the hill in
the valley, 20 Beth Peor, the slopes of
Pisgah, and Beth Jeshimoth — 21 all
the towns on the plateau and the
entire realm of Sihon king of the
Amorites, who ruled at Heshbon.
Moses had defeated him and the
Midianite chiefs, Evi, Rekem, Zur,

[a] 8 Hebrew *With it* (that is, with the other half of Manasseh)

Hur and Reba—princes allied with Sihon—who lived in that country. 22 In addition to those slain in battle, the Israelites had put to the sword Balaam son of Beor, who practiced divination. 23 The boundary of the Reubenites was the bank of the Jordan. These towns and their villages were the inheritance of the Reubenites, according to their clans.

24 This is what Moses had given to the tribe of Gad, according to its clans:

25 The territory of Jazer, all the towns of Gilead and half the Ammonite country as far as Aroer, near Rabbah; 26 and from Heshbon to Ramath Mizpah and Betonim, and from Mahanaim to the territory of Debir; 27 and in the valley, Beth Haram, Beth Nimrah, Sukkoth and Zaphon with the rest of the realm of Sihon king of Heshbon (the east side of the Jordan, the territory up to the end of the Sea of Galilee[a]). 28 These towns and their villages were the inheritance of the Gadites, according to their clans.

29 This is what Moses had given to the half-tribe of Manasseh, that is, to half the family of the descendants of Manasseh, according to its clans:

30 The territory extending from Mahanaim and including all of Bashan, the entire realm of Og king of Bashan—all the settlements of Jair in Bashan, sixty towns, 31 half of Gilead, and Ashtaroth and Edrei (the royal cities of Og in Bashan). This was for the descendants of Makir son of Manasseh—for half of the sons of Makir, according to their clans.

32 This is the inheritance Moses had given when he was in the plains of Moab across the Jordan east of Jericho. 33 But to the tribe of Levi, Moses had given no inheritance; the LORD, the God of Israel, is their inheritance, as he promised them.

14 Now these are the areas the Israelites received as an inheritance in the land of Canaan, which Eleazar the priest, Joshua son of Nun and the heads of the tribal clans of Israel allotted to them. 2 Their inheritances were assigned by lot to the nine and a half tribes, as the LORD had commanded through Moses. 3 Moses had granted the two and a half tribes their inheritance east of the Jordan but had not granted the Levites an inheritance among the rest, 4 for Joseph's descendants had become two tribes—Manasseh and Ephraim. The Levites received no share of the land but only towns to live in, with pasturelands for their flocks and herds. 5 So the Israelites divided the land, just as the LORD had commanded Moses.

6 Now the people of Judah approached Joshua at Gilgal, and Caleb son of Jephunneh the Kenizzite said to him, "You know what the LORD said to Moses the man of God at Kadesh Barnea about you and me. 7 I was forty years old when Moses the servant of the LORD sent me from Kadesh Barnea to explore the land. And I brought him back a report according to my convictions, 8 but my fellow Israelites who went up with me made the hearts of the people melt in fear. I, however, followed the LORD my God wholeheartedly. 9 So on that day Moses swore to me, 'The land on which your feet have walked will be your inheritance and that of your children forever, because you have followed the LORD my God wholeheartedly.'[b]

10 "Now then, just as the LORD promised, he has kept me alive for forty-five years since the time he said this to Moses, while Israel moved about in the wilderness. So here I am today, eighty-five years old! 11 I am still as strong today as the day Moses sent me out; I'm just as vigorous to go out to battle now as I was then. 12 Now give me this hill country that the LORD promised me that day. You yourself heard then that the Anakites were there and their cities were large and fortified, but, the LORD helping me, I will drive them out just as he said."

13 Then Joshua blessed Caleb son of Jephunneh and gave him Hebron as his inheritance. 14 So Hebron has belonged to Caleb son of Jephunneh the Kenizzite ever since, because he followed the LORD, the God of Israel, wholeheartedly. 15 (Hebron used to be called Kiriath Arba after Arba, who was the greatest man among the Anakites.)

Then the land had rest from war.

[a] 27 Hebrew *Kinnereth* [b] 9 Deut. 1:36

15 The allotment for the tribe of Judah, according to its clans, extended down to the territory of Edom, to the Desert of Zin in the extreme south.

2 Their southern boundary started from the bay at the southern end of the Dead Sea,
3 crossed south of Scorpion Pass, continued on to Zin and went over to the south of Kadesh Barnea. Then it ran past Hezron up to Addar and curved around to Karka.
4 It then passed along to Azmon and joined the Wadi of Egypt, ending at the Mediterranean Sea. This is their[a] southern boundary.

5 The eastern boundary is the Dead Sea as far as the mouth of the Jordan.

The northern boundary started from the bay of the sea at the mouth of the Jordan,
6 went up to Beth Hoglah and continued north of Beth Arabah to the Stone of Bohan son of Reuben.
7 The boundary then went up to Debir from the Valley of Achor and turned north to Gilgal, which faces the Pass of Adummim south of the gorge. It continued along to the waters of En Shemesh and came out at En Rogel.
8 Then it ran up the Valley of Ben Hinnom along the southern slope of the Jebusite city (that is, Jerusalem). From there it climbed to the top of the hill west of the Hinnom Valley at the northern end of the Valley of Rephaim.
9 From the hilltop the boundary headed toward the spring of the waters of Nephtoah, came out at the towns of Mount Ephron and went down toward Baalah (that is, Kiriath Jearim).
10 Then it curved westward from Baalah to Mount Seir, ran along the northern slope of Mount Jearim (that is, Kesalon), continued down to Beth Shemesh and crossed to Timnah.
11 It went to the northern slope of Ekron, turned toward Shikkeron, passed along to Mount Baalah and reached Jabneel. The boundary ended at the sea.

12 The western boundary is the coastline of the Mediterranean Sea.

These are the boundaries around the people of Judah by their clans.

13 In accordance with the LORD's command to him, Joshua gave to Caleb son of Jephunneh a portion in Judah — Kiriath Arba, that is, Hebron. (Arba was the forefather of Anak.)
14 From Hebron Caleb drove out the three Anakites — Sheshai, Ahiman and Talmai, the sons of Anak.
15 From there he marched against the people living in Debir (formerly called Kiriath Sepher).
16 And Caleb said, "I will give my daughter Aksah in marriage to the man who attacks and captures Kiriath Sepher."
17 Othniel son of Kenaz, Caleb's brother, took it; so Caleb gave his daughter Aksah to him in marriage.

18 One day when she came to Othniel, she urged him[b] to ask her father for a field. When she got off her donkey, Caleb asked her, "What can I do for you?"

19 She replied, "Do me a special favor. Since you have given me land in the Negev, give me also springs of water." So Caleb gave her the upper and lower springs.

20 This is the inheritance of the tribe of Judah, according to its clans:

21 The southernmost towns of the tribe of Judah in the Negev toward the boundary of Edom were:

Kabzeel, Eder, Jagur,
22 Kinah, Dimonah, Adadah,
23 Kedesh, Hazor, Ithnan,
24 Ziph, Telem, Bealoth,
25 Hazor Hadattah, Kerioth Hezron (that is, Hazor),
26 Amam, Shema, Moladah,
27 Hazar Gaddah, Heshmon, Beth Pelet,
28 Hazar Shual, Beersheba, Biziothiah,
29 Baalah, Iyim, Ezem,
30 Eltolad, Kesil, Hormah,
31 Ziklag, Madmannah, Sansannah,
32 Lebaoth, Shilhim, Ain and Rimmon — a total of twenty-nine towns and their villages.

33 In the western foothills:

Eshtaol, Zorah, Ashnah,
34 Zanoah, En Gannim, Tappuah, Enam,
35 Jarmuth, Adullam, Sokoh, Azekah,
36 Shaaraim, Adithaim and Gederah (or Gederothaim)[c] — fourteen towns and their villages.

37 Zenan, Hadashah, Migdal Gad,
38 Dilean, Mizpah, Joktheel,
39 Lachish, Bozkath, Eglon,
40 Kabbon, Lahmas, Kitlish,
41 Gederoth, Beth

[a] 4 Septuagint; Hebrew *your* [b] 18 Hebrew and some Septuagint manuscripts; other Septuagint manuscripts (see also note at Judges 1:14) *Othniel, he urged her* [c] 36 Or *Gederah and Gederothaim*

Dagon, Naamah and Makkedah—sixteen towns and their villages.

42 Libnah, Ether, Ashan, 43 Iphtah, Ashnah, Nezib, 44 Keilah, Akzib and Mareshah—nine towns and their villages.

45 Ekron, with its surrounding settlements and villages; 46 west of Ekron, all that were in the vicinity of Ashdod, together with their villages; 47 Ashdod, its surrounding settlements and villages; and Gaza, its settlements and villages, as far as the Wadi of Egypt and the coastline of the Mediterranean Sea.

48 In the hill country:

Shamir, Jattir, Sokoh, 49 Dannah, Kiriath Sannah (that is, Debir), 50 Anab, Eshtemoh, Anim, 51 Goshen, Holon and Giloh—eleven towns and their villages.

52 Arab, Dumah, Eshan, 53 Janim, Beth Tappuah, Aphekah, 54 Humtah, Kiriath Arba (that is, Hebron) and Zior—nine towns and their villages.

55 Maon, Carmel, Ziph, Juttah, 56 Jezreel, Jokdeam, Zanoah, 57 Kain, Gibeah and Timnah—ten towns and their villages.

58 Halhul, Beth Zur, Gedor, 59 Maarath, Beth Anoth and Eltekon—six towns and their villages.[a]

60 Kiriath Baal (that is, Kiriath Jearim) and Rabbah—two towns and their villages.

61 In the wilderness:

Beth Arabah, Middin, Sekakah, 62 Nibshan, the City of Salt and En Gedi—six towns and their villages.

63 Judah could not dislodge the Jebusites, who were living in Jerusalem; to this day the Jebusites live there with the people of Judah.

16 The allotment for Joseph began at the Jordan, east of the springs of Jericho, and went up from there through the desert into the hill country of Bethel. 2 It went on from Bethel (that is, Luz),[b] crossed over to the territory of the Arkites in Ataroth, 3 descended westward to the territory of the Japhletites as far as the region of Lower Beth Horon and on to Gezer, ending at the Mediterranean Sea. 4 So Manasseh and Ephraim, the descendants of Joseph, received their inheritance.

5 This was the territory of Ephraim, according to its clans:

The boundary of their inheritance went from Ataroth Addar in the east to Upper Beth Horon 6 and continued to the Mediterranean Sea. From Mikmethath on the north it curved eastward to Taanath Shiloh, passing by it to Janoah on the east. 7 Then it went down from Janoah to Ataroth and Naarah, touched Jericho and came out at the Jordan. 8 From Tappuah the border went west to the Kanah Ravine and ended at the Mediterranean Sea. This was the inheritance of the tribe of the Ephraimites, according to its clans. 9 It also included all the towns and their villages that were set aside for the Ephraimites within the inheritance of the Manassites.

10 They did not dislodge the Canaanites living in Gezer; to this day the Canaanites live among the people of Ephraim but are required to do forced labor.

17 This was the allotment for the tribe of Manasseh as Joseph's firstborn, that is, for Makir, Manasseh's firstborn. Makir was the ancestor of the Gileadites, who had received Gilead and Bashan because the Makirites were great soldiers. 2 So this allotment was for the rest of the people of Manasseh—the clans of Abiezer, Helek, Asriel, Shechem, Hepher and Shemida. These are the other male descendants of Manasseh son of Joseph by their clans.

3 Now Zelophehad son of Hepher, the son of Gilead, the son of Makir, the son of Manasseh, had no sons but only daughters, whose names were Mahlah, Noah, Hoglah, Milkah and Tirzah. 4 They went to Eleazar the priest, Joshua son of Nun, and the leaders and said, "The LORD commanded Moses to give us an inheritance among our relatives." So Joshua gave them an inheritance along with the brothers of their father, according to the LORD's command. 5 Manasseh's share consisted of ten tracts of land be-

[a] 59 The Septuagint adds another district of eleven towns, including Tekoa and Ephrathah (Bethlehem).
[b] 2 Septuagint; Hebrew *Bethel to Luz*

sides Gilead and Bashan east of the Jordan, 6because the daughters of the tribe
of Manasseh received an inheritance
among the sons. The land of Gilead belonged to the rest of the descendants of
Manasseh.

7The territory of Manasseh extended from Asher to Mikmethath
east of Shechem. The boundary ran
southward from there to include the
people living at En Tappuah. 8(Manasseh had the land of Tappuah, but
Tappuah itself, on the boundary of
Manasseh, belonged to the Ephraimites.) 9Then the boundary continued
south to the Kanah Ravine. There
were towns belonging to Ephraim
lying among the towns of Manasseh,
but the boundary of Manasseh was
the northern side of the ravine and
ended at the Mediterranean Sea.
10On the south the land belonged to
Ephraim, on the north to Manasseh.
The territory of Manasseh reached
the Mediterranean Sea and bordered
Asher on the north and Issachar on
the east.

11Within Issachar and Asher, Manasseh also had Beth Shan, Ibleam
and the people of Dor, Endor, Taanach and Megiddo, together with
their surrounding settlements (the
third in the list is Naphoth[a]).
12Yet the Manassites were not able to
occupy these towns, for the Canaanites
were determined to live in that region.
13However, when the Israelites grew
stronger, they subjected the Canaanites
to forced labor but did not drive them out
completely.

14The people of Joseph said to Joshua,
"Why have you given us only one allotment and one portion for an inheritance?
We are a numerous people, and the LORD
has blessed us abundantly."

15"If you are so numerous," Joshua answered, "and if the hill country of Ephraim is too small for you, go up into the
forest and clear land for yourselves there
in the land of the Perizzites and Rephaites."

16The people of Joseph replied, "The
hill country is not enough for us, and all
the Canaanites who live in the plain have
chariots fitted with iron, both those in
Beth Shan and its settlements and those
in the Valley of Jezreel."

17But Joshua said to the tribes of Joseph—to Ephraim and Manasseh—"You
are numerous and very powerful. You
will have not only one allotment 18but the
forested hill country as well. Clear it, and
its farthest limits will be yours; though
the Canaanites have chariots fitted with
iron and though they are strong, you can
drive them out."

18 The whole assembly of the Israelites
gathered at Shiloh and set up the
tent of meeting there. The country was
brought under their control, 2but there
were still seven Israelite tribes who had
not yet received their inheritance.

3So Joshua said to the Israelites: "How
long will you wait before you begin to
take possession of the land that the LORD,
the God of your ancestors, has given you?
4Appoint three men from each tribe. I
will send them out to make a survey of
the land and to write a description of
it, according to the inheritance of each.
Then they will return to me. 5You are to
divide the land into seven parts. Judah
is to remain in its territory on the south
and the tribes of Joseph in their territory
on the north. 6After you have written de-
scriptions of the seven parts of the land,
bring them here to me and I will cast lots
for you in the presence of the LORD our
God. 7The Levites, however, do not get a
portion among you, because the priestly
service of the LORD is their inheritance.
And Gad, Reuben and the half-tribe of
Manasseh have already received their
inheritance on the east side of the Jordan. Moses the servant of the LORD gave
it to them."

8As the men started on their way to map
out the land, Joshua instructed them, "Go
and make a survey of the land and write a
description of it. Then return to me, and I
will cast lots for you here at Shiloh in the
presence of the LORD." 9So the men left
and went through the land. They wrote
its description on a scroll, town by town,
in seven parts, and returned to Joshua in
the camp at Shiloh. 10Joshua then cast
lots for them in Shiloh in the presence of
the LORD, and there he distributed the
land to the Israelites according to their
tribal divisions.

[a] *11* That is, Naphoth Dor

11 The first lot came up for the tribe of
Benjamin according to its clans. Their
allotted territory lay between the tribes
of Judah and Joseph:

12 On the north side their boundary began at the Jordan, passed the
northern slope of Jericho and headed west into the hill country, coming
out at the wilderness of Beth Aven.
13 From there it crossed to the south
slope of Luz (that is, Bethel) and went
down to Ataroth Addar on the hill
south of Lower Beth Horon.

14 From the hill facing Beth Horon
on the south the boundary turned
south along the western side and
came out at Kiriath Baal (that is, Kiriath Jearim), a town of the people of
Judah. This was the western side.

15 The southern side began at the
outskirts of Kiriath Jearim on the
west, and the boundary came out
at the spring of the waters of Nephtoah. 16 The boundary went down to
the foot of the hill facing the Valley
of Ben Hinnom, north of the Valley
of Rephaim. It continued down the
Hinnom Valley along the southern
slope of the Jebusite city and so to En
Rogel. 17 It then curved north, went to
En Shemesh, continued to Geliloth,
which faces the Pass of Adummim,
and ran down to the Stone of Bohan
son of Reuben. 18 It continued to the
northern slope of Beth Arabah[a] and
on down into the Arabah. 19 It then
went to the northern slope of Beth
Hoglah and came out at the northern
bay of the Dead Sea, at the mouth of
the Jordan in the south. This was the
southern boundary.

20 The Jordan formed the boundary
on the eastern side.

These were the boundaries that marked
out the inheritance of the clans of Benjamin on all sides.

21 The tribe of Benjamin, according to its
clans, had the following towns:

Jericho, Beth Hoglah, Emek Keziz,
22 Beth Arabah, Zemaraim, Bethel,
23 Avvim, Parah, Ophrah, 24 Kephar
Ammoni, Ophni and Geba—twelve
towns and their villages.

25 Gibeon, Ramah, Beeroth, 26 Mizpah, Kephirah, Mozah, 27 Rekem,
Irpeel, Taralah, 28 Zelah, Haeleph,
the Jebusite city (that is, Jerusalem),
Gibeah and Kiriath—fourteen towns
and their villages.

This was the inheritance of Benjamin for
its clans.

19 The second lot came out for the tribe
of Simeon according to its clans.
Their inheritance lay within the territory
of Judah. 2 It included:

Beersheba (or Sheba),[b] Moladah,
3 Hazar Shual, Balah, Ezem, 4 Eltolad,
Bethul, Hormah, 5 Ziklag, Beth Markaboth, Hazar Susah, 6 Beth Lebaoth
and Sharuhen—thirteen towns and
their villages;

7 Ain, Rimmon, Ether and Ashan—
four towns and their villages— 8 and
all the villages around these towns
as far as Baalath Beer (Ramah in the
Negev).

This was the inheritance of the tribe of
the Simeonites, according to its clans.
9 The inheritance of the Simeonites was
taken from the share of Judah, because
Judah's portion was more than they needed. So the Simeonites received their inheritance within the territory of Judah.

10 The third lot came up for Zebulun according to its clans:

The boundary of their inheritance
went as far as Sarid. 11 Going west
it ran to Maralah, touched Dabbe-
sheth, and extended to the ravine
near Jokneam. 12 It turned east from
Sarid toward the sunrise to the territory of Kisloth Tabor and went on to
Daberath and up to Japhia. 13 Then it
continued eastward to Gath Hepher
and Eth Kazin; it came out at Rimmon
and turned toward Neah. 14 There the
boundary went around on the north
to Hannathon and ended at the Valley of Iphtah El. 15 Included were
Kattath, Nahalal, Shimron, Idalah
and Bethlehem. There were twelve
towns and their villages.

16 These towns and their villages were the
inheritance of Zebulun, according to its
clans.

17 The fourth lot came out for Issachar
according to its clans. 18 Their territory
included:

Jezreel, Kesulloth, Shunem, 19 Haph-

[a] *18* Septuagint; Hebrew *slope facing the Arabah* [b] *2* Or *Beersheba, Sheba*; 1 Chron. 4:28 does not have *Sheba.*

araim, Shion, Anaharath, 20 Rabbith,
Kishion, Ebez, 21 Remeth, En Gannim,
En Haddah and Beth Pazzez. 22 The
boundary touched Tabor, Shahazu-
mah and Beth Shemesh, and ended at
the Jordan. There were sixteen towns
and their villages.
23 These towns and their villages were
the inheritance of the tribe of Issachar,
according to its clans.

24 The fifth lot came out for the tribe of
Asher according to its clans. 25 Their territory included:
Helkath, Hali, Beten, Akshaph,
26 Allammelek, Amad and Mishal.
On the west the boundary touched
Carmel and Shihor Libnath. 27 It
then turned east toward Beth Dagon, touched Zebulun and the Valley of Iphtah El, and went north to
Beth Emek and Neiel, passing Kabul
on the left. 28 It went to Abdon,[a] Rehob, Hammon and Kanah, as far as
Greater Sidon. 29 The boundary then
turned back toward Ramah and went
to the fortified city of Tyre, turned
toward Hosah and came out at the
Mediterranean Sea in the region of
Akzib, 30 Ummah, Aphek and Rehob.
There were twenty-two towns and
their villages.
31 These towns and their villages were the
inheritance of the tribe of Asher, according to its clans.

32 The sixth lot came out for Naphtali according to its clans:
33 Their boundary went from He-
leph and the large tree in Zaanannim, passing Adami Nekeb and Jabneel to Lakkum and ending at the
Jordan. 34 The boundary ran west
through Aznoth Tabor and came out
at Hukkok. It touched Zebulun on
the south, Asher on the west and the
Jordan[b] on the east. 35 The fortified
towns were Ziddim, Zer, Hammath,
Rakkath, Kinnereth, 36 Adamah, Ramah, Hazor, 37 Kedesh, Edrei, En Hazor, 38 Iron, Migdal El, Horem, Beth
Anath and Beth Shemesh. There were
nineteen towns and their villages.
39 These towns and their villages were
the inheritance of the tribe of Naphtali,
according to its clans.

40 The seventh lot came out for the tribe of
Dan according to its clans. 41 The territory of their inheritance included:
Zorah, Eshtaol, Ir Shemesh, 42 Sha-
alabbin, Aijalon, Ithlah, 43 Elon, Timnah, Ekron, 44 Eltekeh, Gibbethon,
Baalath, 45 Jehud, Bene Berak, Gath
Rimmon, 46 Me Jarkon and Rakkon,
with the area facing Joppa.
47 (When the territory of the Danites
was lost to them, they went up and attacked Leshem, took it, put it to the sword
and occupied it. They settled in Leshem
and named it Dan after their ancestor.)
48 These towns and their villages were the
inheritance of the tribe of Dan, according
to its clans.

49 When they had finished dividing the
land into its allotted portions, the Israelites gave Joshua son of Nun an inheritance among them, 50 as the LORD had
commanded. They gave him the town
he asked for — Timnath Serah[c] in the hill
country of Ephraim. And he built up the
town and settled there.
51 These are the territories that Eleazar the priest, Joshua son of Nun and
the heads of the tribal clans of Israel assigned by lot at Shiloh in the presence of
the LORD at the entrance to the tent of
meeting. And so they finished dividing
the land.

20 Then the LORD said to Joshua: 2 "Tell
the Israelites to designate the cities
of refuge, as I instructed you through Moses, 3 so that anyone who kills a person
accidentally and unintentionally may
flee there and find protection from the
avenger of blood. 4 When they flee to one
of these cities, they are to stand in the entrance of the city gate and state their case
before the elders of that city. Then the
elders are to admit the fugitive into their
city and provide a place to live among
them. 5 If the avenger of blood comes in
pursuit, the elders must not surrender the
fugitive, because the fugitive killed their
neighbor unintentionally and without
malice aforethought. 6 They are to stay in
that city until they have stood trial before
the assembly and until the death of the
high priest who is serving at that time.
Then they may go back to their own home
in the town from which they fled."

[a] *28* Some Hebrew manuscripts (see also 21:30); most Hebrew manuscripts *Ebron* [b] *34* Septuagint; Hebrew *west, and Judah, the Jordan,* [c] *50* Also known as *Timnath Heres* (see Judges 2:9)

7So they set apart Kedesh in Galilee in
the hill country of Naphtali, Shechem in
the hill country of Ephraim, and Kiriath
Arba (that is, Hebron) in the hill country
of Judah. 8East of the Jordan (on the other
side from Jericho) they designated Bezer
in the wilderness on the plateau in the
tribe of Reuben, Ramoth in Gilead in the
tribe of Gad, and Golan in Bashan in
the tribe of Manasseh. 9Any of the Israelites or any foreigner residing among
them who killed someone accidentally
could flee to these designated cities and
not be killed by the avenger of blood prior
to standing trial before the assembly.

21 Now the family heads of the Levites
approached Eleazar the priest, Joshua son of Nun, and the heads of the other
tribal families of Israel 2at Shiloh in Canaan and said to them, "The LORD commanded through Moses that you give us
towns to live in, with pasturelands for
our livestock." 3So, as the LORD had commanded, the Israelites gave the Levites
the following towns and pasturelands
out of their own inheritance:

4The first lot came out for the Kohathites, according to their clans. The Levites who were descendants of Aaron the
priest were allotted thirteen towns from
the tribes of Judah, Simeon and Benjamin. 5The rest of Kohath's descendants
were allotted ten towns from the clans
of the tribes of Ephraim, Dan and half of
Manasseh.

6The descendants of Gershon were
allotted thirteen towns from the clans
of the tribes of Issachar, Asher, Naphtali and the half-tribe of Manasseh in Bashan.

7The descendants of Merari, according
to their clans, received twelve towns from
the tribes of Reuben, Gad and Zebulun.

8So the Israelites allotted to the Levites
these towns and their pasturelands, as
the LORD had commanded through Moses.

9From the tribes of Judah and Simeon they allotted the following towns by
name 10(these towns were assigned to the
descendants of Aaron who were from the
Kohathite clans of the Levites, because
the first lot fell to them):

11They gave them Kiriath Arba
(that is, Hebron), with its surrounding pastureland, in the hill country
of Judah. (Arba was the forefather
of Anak.) 12But the fields and villages around the city they had given to
Caleb son of Jephunneh as his possession.

13So to the descendants of Aaron
the priest they gave Hebron (a city
of refuge for one accused of murder),
Libnah, 14Jattir, Eshtemoa, 15Holon,
Debir, 16Ain, Juttah and Beth Shemesh, together with their pasturelands — nine towns from these two
tribes.

17And from the tribe of Benjamin
they gave them Gibeon, Geba, 18Ana-
thoth and Almon, together with their
pasturelands — four towns.

19The total number of towns for the
priests, the descendants of Aaron, came
to thirteen, together with their pasturelands.

20The rest of the Kohathite clans of the
Levites were allotted towns from the
tribe of Ephraim:

21In the hill country of Ephraim
they were given Shechem (a city of
refuge for one accused of murder)
and Gezer, 22Kibzaim and Beth Horon, together with their pasturelands — four towns.

23Also from the tribe of Dan they
received Eltekeh, Gibbethon, 24Aija-
lon and Gath Rimmon, together with
their pasturelands — four towns.

25From half the tribe of Manasseh they received Taanach and Gath
Rimmon, together with their pasturelands — two towns.

26All these ten towns and their pasturelands were given to the rest of the Kohathite clans.

27The Levite clans of the Gershonites
were given:

from the half-tribe of Manasseh,
Golan in Bashan (a city of refuge for
one accused of murder) and Be Esh-
terah, together with their pasturelands — two towns;

28from the tribe of Issachar,
Kishion, Daberath, 29Jarmuth and
En Gannim, together with their pas-
turelands — four towns;

30from the tribe of Asher,
Mishal, Abdon, 31Helkath and Rehob, together with their pasturelands — four towns;

32from the tribe of Naphtali,

Kedesh in Galilee (a city of refuge for
one accused of murder), Hammoth
Dor and Kartan, together with their
pasturelands—three towns.
33The total number of towns of the Gershonite clans came to thirteen, together
with their pasturelands.

34The Merarite clans (the rest of the Levites) were given:
from the tribe of Zebulun,
Jokneam, Kartah, 35Dimnah and
Nahalal, together with their pasturelands—four towns;
36from the tribe of Reuben,
Bezer, Jahaz, 37Kedemoth and Mephaath, together with their pasturelands—four towns;
38from the tribe of Gad,
Ramoth in Gilead (a city of refuge for
one accused of murder), Mahanaim,
39Heshbon and Jazer, together with
their pasturelands—four towns in
all.
40The total number of towns allotted to
the Merarite clans, who were the rest of
the Levites, came to twelve.
41The towns of the Levites in the territory held by the Israelites were forty-eight
in all, together with their pasturelands.
42Each of these towns had pasturelands
surrounding it; this was true for all these
towns.

43So the LORD gave Israel all the land
he had sworn to give their ancestors,
and they took possession of it and settled there. 44The LORD gave them rest on
every side, just as he had sworn to their
ancestors. Not one of their enemies with-
stood them; the LORD gave all their enemies into their hands. 45Not one of all the
LORD's good promises to Israel failed; every one was fulfilled.

22 Then Joshua summoned the Reubenites, the Gadites and the half-
tribe of Manasseh 2and said to them,
"You have done all that Moses the servant
of the LORD commanded, and you have
obeyed me in everything I commanded. 3For a long time now—to this very
day—you have not deserted your fellow
Israelites but have carried out the mission the LORD your God gave you. 4Now
that the LORD your God has given them
rest as he promised, return to your homes
in the land that Moses the servant of the
LORD gave you on the other side of the
Jordan. 5But be very careful to keep the
commandment and the law that Moses
the servant of the LORD gave you: to love
the LORD your God, to walk in obedience
to him, to keep his commands, to hold
fast to him and to serve him with all your
heart and with all your soul."
6Then Joshua blessed them and sent
them away, and they went to their homes.
7(To the half-tribe of Manasseh Moses
had given land in Bashan, and to the
other half of the tribe Joshua gave land
on the west side of the Jordan along with
their fellow Israelites.) When Joshua sent
them home, he blessed them, 8saying,
"Return to your homes with your great
wealth—with large herds of livestock,
with silver, gold, bronze and iron, and a
great quantity of clothing—and divide
the plunder from your enemies with your
fellow Israelites."
9So the Reubenites, the Gadites and the
half-tribe of Manasseh left the Israelites
at Shiloh in Canaan to return to Gilead,
their own land, which they had acquired
in accordance with the command of the
LORD through Moses.
10When they came to Geliloth near the
Jordan in the land of Canaan, the Reubenites, the Gadites and the half-tribe of
Manasseh built an imposing altar there
by the Jordan. 11And when the Israelites
heard that they had built the altar on the
border of Canaan at Geliloth near the Jordan on the Israelite side, 12the whole assembly of Israel gathered at Shiloh to go
to war against them.
13So the Israelites sent Phinehas son
of Eleazar, the priest, to the land of Gilead—to Reuben, Gad and the half-tribe
of Manasseh. 14With him they sent ten of
the chief men, one from each of the tribes
of Israel, each the head of a family division among the Israelite clans.
15When they went to Gilead—to Reuben, Gad and the half-tribe of Manasseh—they said to them: 16"The whole
assembly of the LORD says: 'How could
you break faith with the God of Israel like
this? How could you turn away from the
LORD and build yourselves an altar in rebellion against him now? 17Was not the
sin of Peor enough for us? Up to this very
day we have not cleansed ourselves from
that sin, even though a plague fell on the
community of the LORD! 18And are you
now turning away from the LORD?

"'If you rebel against the LORD today, tomorrow he will be angry with the
whole community of Israel. 19If the land
you possess is defiled, come over to the
LORD's land, where the LORD's tabernacle
stands, and share the land with us. But do
not rebel against the LORD or against us
by building an altar for yourselves, other than the altar of the LORD our God.
20When Achan son of Zerah was unfaithful in regard to the devoted things,[a] did
not wrath come on the whole community of Israel? He was not the only one who
died for his sin.'"

21Then Reuben, Gad and the half-tribe
of Manasseh replied to the heads of the
clans of Israel: 22"The Mighty One, God,
the LORD! The Mighty One, God, the
LORD! He knows! And let Israel know! If
this has been in rebellion or disobedience to the LORD, do not spare us this day.
23If we have built our own altar to turn
away from the LORD and to offer burnt
offerings and grain offerings, or to sacrifice fellowship offerings on it, may the
LORD himself call us to account.

24"No! We did it for fear that some day
your descendants might say to ours,
'What do you have to do with the LORD,
the God of Israel? 25The LORD has made
the Jordan a boundary between us and
you—you Reubenites and Gadites! You
have no share in the LORD.' So your descendants might cause ours to stop fearing the LORD.

26"That is why we said, 'Let us get
ready and build an altar—but not for
burnt offerings or sacrifices.' 27On the
contrary, it is to be a witness between
us and you and the generations that follow, that we will worship the LORD at his
sanctuary with our burnt offerings, sacrifices and fellowship offerings. Then in
the future your descendants will not be
able to say to ours, 'You have no share in
the LORD.'

28"And we said, 'If they ever say this to
us, or to our descendants, we will answer:
Look at the replica of the LORD's altar,
which our ancestors built, not for burnt
offerings and sacrifices, but as a witness
between us and you.'

29"Far be it from us to rebel against
the LORD and turn away from him today
by building an altar for burnt offerings,
grain offerings and sacrifices, other than
the altar of the LORD our God that stands
before his tabernacle."

30When Phinehas the priest and the
leaders of the community—the heads of
the clans of the Israelites—heard what
Reuben, Gad and Manasseh had to say,
they were pleased. 31And Phinehas son
of Eleazar, the priest, said to Reuben,
Gad and Manasseh, "Today we know that
the LORD is with us, because you have not
been unfaithful to the LORD in this matter. Now you have rescued the Israelites
from the LORD's hand."

32Then Phinehas son of Eleazar, the
priest, and the leaders returned to Canaan from their meeting with the Reubenites and Gadites in Gilead and reported to the Israelites. 33They were glad
to hear the report and praised God. And
they talked no more about going to war
against them to devastate the country
where the Reubenites and the Gadites
lived.

34And the Reubenites and the Gadites
gave the altar this name: A Witness Between Us—that the LORD is God.

23 After a long time had passed and the
LORD had given Israel rest from all
their enemies around them, Joshua, by
then a very old man, 2summoned all Israel—their elders, leaders, judges and officials—and said to them: "I am very old.
3You yourselves have seen everything the
LORD your God has done to all these nations for your sake; it was the LORD your
God who fought for you. 4Remember how
I have allotted as an inheritance for your
tribes all the land of the nations that remain—the nations I conquered—between the Jordan and the Mediterranean
Sea in the west. 5The LORD your God
himself will push them out for your sake.
He will drive them out before you, and
you will take possession of their land, as
the LORD your God promised you.

6"Be very strong; be careful to obey all
that is written in the Book of the Law of
Moses, without turning aside to the right
or to the left. 7Do not associate with these
nations that remain among you; do not
invoke the names of their gods or swear
by them. You must not serve them or bow
down to them. 8But you are to hold fast

[a] *20* The Hebrew term refers to the irrevocable giving over of things or persons to the LORD, often by totally destroying them.

to the LORD your God, as you have until
now.
9 "The LORD has driven out before you
great and powerful nations; to this day
no one has been able to withstand you.
10 One of you routs a thousand, because
the LORD your God fights for you, just as
he promised. 11 So be very careful to love
the LORD your God.
12 "But if you turn away and ally yourselves with the survivors of these nations
that remain among you and if you intermarry with them and associate with
them, 13 then you may be sure that the
LORD your God will no longer drive out
these nations before you. Instead, they
will become snares and traps for you,
whips on your backs and thorns in your
eyes, until you perish from this good
land, which the LORD your God has giv-
en you.
14 "Now I am about to go the way of all
the earth. You know with all your heart
and soul that not one of all the good
promises the LORD your God gave you
has failed. Every promise has been fulfilled; not one has failed. 15 But just as
all the good things the LORD your God
has promised you have come to you, so
he will bring on you all the evil things
he has threatened, until the LORD your
God has destroyed you from this good
land he has given you. 16 If you violate the
covenant of the LORD your God, which he
commanded you, and go and serve other
gods and bow down to them, the LORD's
anger will burn against you, and you will
quickly perish from the good land he has
given you."

24 Then Joshua assembled all the tribes
of Israel at Shechem. He summoned
the elders, leaders, judges and officials
of Israel, and they presented themselves
before God.
2 Joshua said to all the people, "This is
what the LORD, the God of Israel, says:
'Long ago your ancestors, including Terah the father of Abraham and Nahor,
lived beyond the Euphrates River and
worshiped other gods. 3 But I took your father Abraham from the land beyond the
Euphrates and led him throughout Canaan and gave him many descendants.
I gave him Isaac, 4 and to Isaac I gave Jacob and Esau. I assigned the hill country
of Seir to Esau, but Jacob and his family
went down to Egypt.
5 "'Then I sent Moses and Aaron, and
I afflicted the Egyptians by what I did
there, and I brought you out. 6 When I
brought your people out of Egypt, you
came to the sea, and the Egyptians pursued them with chariots and horsemen[a]
as far as the Red Sea.[b] 7 But they cried
to the LORD for help, and he put darkness between you and the Egyptians; he
brought the sea over them and covered
them. You saw with your own eyes what
I did to the Egyptians. Then you lived in
the wilderness for a long time.
8 "'I brought you to the land of the Amorites who lived east of the Jordan. They
fought against you, but I gave them into
your hands. I destroyed them from before you, and you took possession of their
land. 9 When Balak son of Zippor, the
king of Moab, prepared to fight against
Israel, he sent for Balaam son of Beor to
put a curse on you. 10 But I would not listen to Balaam, so he blessed you again
and again, and I delivered you out of his
hand.
11 "'Then you crossed the Jordan and
came to Jericho. The citizens of Jericho
fought against you, as did also the Amorites, Perizzites, Canaanites, Hittites,
Girgashites, Hivites and Jebusites, but I
gave them into your hands. 12 I sent the
hornet ahead of you, which drove them
out before you—also the two Amorite
kings. You did not do it with your own
sword and bow. 13 So I gave you a land on
which you did not toil and cities you did
not build; and you live in them and eat
from vineyards and olive groves that you
did not plant.'
14 "Now fear the LORD and serve him
with all faithfulness. Throw away the
gods your ancestors worshiped beyond
the Euphrates River and in Egypt, and
serve the LORD. 15 But if serving the LORD
seems undesirable to you, then choose for
yourselves this day whom you will serve,
whether the gods your ancestors served
beyond the Euphrates, or the gods of the
Amorites, in whose land you are living.
But as for me and my household, we will
serve the LORD."
16 Then the people answered, "Far be it
from us to forsake the LORD to serve other

[a] 6 Or *charioteers* [b] 6 Or *the Sea of Reeds*

gods! 17 It was the LORD our God himself
who brought us and our parents up out of
Egypt, from that land of slavery, and performed those great signs before our eyes.
He protected us on our entire journey and
among all the nations through which we
traveled. 18 And the LORD drove out before us all the nations, including the Amorites, who lived in the land. We too will
serve the LORD, because he is our God."

19 Joshua said to the people, "You are
not able to serve the LORD. He is a holy
God; he is a jealous God. He will not forgive your rebellion and your sins. 20 If
you forsake the LORD and serve foreign
gods, he will turn and bring disaster on
you and make an end of you, after he has
been good to you."

21 But the people said to Joshua, "No!
We will serve the LORD."

22 Then Joshua said, "You are witnesses
against yourselves that you have chosen
to serve the LORD."

"Yes, we are witnesses," they replied.

23 "Now then," said Joshua, "throw
away the foreign gods that are among
you and yield your hearts to the LORD,
the God of Israel."

24 And the people said to Joshua, "We
will serve the LORD our God and obey
him."

25 On that day Joshua made a covenant
for the people, and there at Shechem he
reaffirmed for them decrees and laws.
26 And Joshua recorded these things in
the Book of the Law of God. Then he took
a large stone and set it up there under the
oak near the holy place of the LORD.

27 "See!" he said to all the people. "This
stone will be a witness against us. It has
heard all the words the LORD has said to
us. It will be a witness against you if you
are untrue to your God."

28 Then Joshua dismissed the people,
each to their own inheritance.

29 After these things, Joshua son of
Nun, the servant of the LORD, died at
the age of a hundred and ten. 30 And they
buried him in the land of his inheritance,
at Timnath Serah[a] in the hill country of
Ephraim, north of Mount Gaash.

31 Israel served the LORD throughout the
lifetime of Joshua and of the elders who
outlived him and who had experienced
everything the LORD had done for Israel.

32 And Joseph's bones, which the Israelites had brought up from Egypt, were
buried at Shechem in the tract of land
that Jacob bought for a hundred pieces of
silver[b] from the sons of Hamor, the father
of Shechem. This became the inheritance
of Joseph's descendants.

33 And Eleazar son of Aaron died and
was buried at Gibeah, which had been
allotted to his son Phinehas in the hill
country of Ephraim.

[a] 30 Also known as *Timnath Heres* (see Judges 2:9)
[b] 32 Hebrew *hundred kesitahs*; a kesitah was a unit of money of unknown weight and value.

JUDGES

See the Invitation to Joshua and Judges on p. 191.

1 After the death of Joshua, the Israelites asked the LORD, "Who of us is to
go up first to fight against the Canaanites?"
2The LORD answered, "Judah shall
go up; I have given the land into their
hands."
3The men of Judah then said to the
Simeonites their fellow Israelites, "Come
up with us into the territory allotted to
us, to fight against the Canaanites. We in
turn will go with you into yours." So the
Simeonites went with them.
4When Judah attacked, the LORD gave
the Canaanites and Perizzites into their
hands, and they struck down ten thousand men at Bezek. 5It was there that they
found Adoni-Bezek and fought against
him, putting to rout the Canaanites and
Perizzites. 6Adoni-Bezek fled, but they
chased him and caught him, and cut off
his thumbs and big toes.
7Then Adoni-Bezek said, "Seventy
kings with their thumbs and big toes cut
off have picked up scraps under my table.
Now God has paid me back for what I did
to them." They brought him to Jerusalem,
and he died there.
8The men of Judah attacked Jerusalem
also and took it. They put the city to the
sword and set it on fire.
9After that, Judah went down to fight
against the Canaanites living in the
hill country, the Negev and the western
foothills. 10They advanced against the
Canaanites living in Hebron (formerly
called Kiriath Arba) and defeated Sheshai, Ahiman and Talmai. 11From there
they advanced against the people living
in Debir (formerly called Kiriath Sepher).
12And Caleb said, "I will give my daughter Aksah in marriage to the man who
attacks and captures Kiriath Sepher."
13Othniel son of Kenaz, Caleb's younger
brother, took it; so Caleb gave his daughter Aksah to him in marriage.
14One day when she came to Othni-
el, she urged him[a] to ask her father for a
field. When she got off her donkey, Caleb
asked her, "What can I do for you?"
15She replied, "Do me a special favor. Since you have given me land in the
Negev, give me also springs of water."
So Caleb gave her the upper and lower
springs.
16The descendants of Moses' father-in-
law, the Kenite, went up from the City of
Palms[b] with the people of Judah to live
among the inhabitants of the Desert of
Judah in the Negev near Arad.
17Then the men of Judah went with the
Simeonites their fellow Israelites and
attacked the Canaanites living in Ze-
phath, and they totally destroyed[c] the
city. Therefore it was called Hormah.[d]
18Judah also took[e] Gaza, Ashkelon and
Ekron — each city with its territory.
19The LORD was with the men of Judah.
They took possession of the hill country,
but they were unable to drive the people from the plains, because they had
chariots fitted with iron. 20As Moses had
promised, Hebron was given to Caleb,
who drove from it the three sons of Anak.
21The Benjamites, however, did not drive
out the Jebusites, who were living in Jerusalem; to this day the Jebusites live there
with the Benjamites.
22Now the tribes of Joseph attacked
Bethel, and the LORD was with them.
23When they sent men to spy out Bethel (formerly called Luz), 24the spies saw
a man coming out of the city and they
said to him, "Show us how to get into the
city and we will see that you are treated
well." 25So he showed them, and they put
the city to the sword but spared the man
and his whole family. 26He then went to
the land of the Hittites, where he built a
city and called it Luz, which is its name
to this day.
27But Manasseh did not drive out the
people of Beth Shan or Taanach or Dor or
Ibleam or Megiddo and their surrounding settlements, for the Canaanites were
determined to live in that land. 28When
Israel became strong, they pressed the

[a] *14* Hebrew; Septuagint and Vulgate *Othniel, he urged her* [b] *16* That is, Jericho [c] *17* The Hebrew term refers to the irrevocable giving over of things or persons to the LORD, often by totally destroying them. [d] *17* *Hormah* means *destruction.* [e] *18* Hebrew; Septuagint *Judah did not take*

Canaanites into forced labor but never drove them out completely. 29 Nor did Ephraim drive out the Canaanites living in Gezer, but the Canaanites continued to live there among them. 30 Neither did Zebulun drive out the Canaanites living in Kitron or Nahalol, so these Canaanites lived among them, but Zebulun did subject them to forced labor. 31 Nor did Asher drive out those living in Akko or Sidon or Ahlab or Akzib or Helbah or Aphek or Rehob. 32 The Asherites lived among the Canaanite inhabitants of the land because they did not drive them out. 33 Neither did Naphtali drive out those living in Beth Shemesh or Beth Anath; but the Naphtalites too lived among the Canaanite inhabitants of the land, and those living in Beth Shemesh and Beth Anath became forced laborers for them. 34 The Amorites confined the Danites to the hill country, not allowing them to come down into the plain. 35 And the Amorites were determined also to hold out in Mount Heres, Aijalon and Shaalbim, but when the power of the tribes of Joseph increased, they too were pressed into forced labor. 36 The boundary of the Amorites was from Scorpion Pass to Sela and beyond.

2 The angel of the LORD went up from Gilgal to Bokim and said, "I brought you up out of Egypt and led you into the land I swore to give to your ancestors. I said, 'I will never break my covenant with you, 2 and you shall not make a covenant with the people of this land, but you shall break down their altars.' Yet you have disobeyed me. Why have you done this? 3 And I have also said, 'I will not drive them out before you; they will become traps for you, and their gods will become snares to you.' "

4 When the angel of the LORD had spoken these things to all the Israelites, the people wept aloud, 5 and they called that place Bokim.[a] There they offered sacrifices to the LORD.

6 After Joshua had dismissed the Israelites, they went to take possession of the land, each to their own inheritance. 7 The people served the LORD throughout the lifetime of Joshua and of the elders who outlived him and who had seen all the great things the LORD had done for Israel.

8 Joshua son of Nun, the servant of the LORD, died at the age of a hundred and ten. 9 And they buried him in the land of his inheritance, at Timnath Heres[b] in the hill country of Ephraim, north of Mount Gaash.

10 After that whole generation had been gathered to their ancestors, another generation grew up who knew neither the LORD nor what he had done for Israel. 11 Then the Israelites did evil in the eyes of the LORD and served the Baals. 12 They forsook the LORD, the God of their ancestors, who had brought them out of Egypt. They followed and worshiped various gods of the peoples around them. They aroused the LORD's anger 13 because they forsook him and served Baal and the Ashtoreths. 14 In his anger against Israel the LORD gave them into the hands of raiders who plundered them. He sold them into the hands of their enemies all around, whom they were no longer able to resist. 15 Whenever Israel went out to fight, the hand of the LORD was against them to defeat them, just as he had sworn to them. They were in great distress.

16 Then the LORD raised up judges,[c] who saved them out of the hands of these raiders. 17 Yet they would not listen to their judges but prostituted themselves to other gods and worshiped them. They quickly turned from the ways of their ancestors, who had been obedient to the LORD's commands. 18 Whenever the LORD raised up a judge for them, he was with the judge and saved them out of the hands of their enemies as long as the judge lived; for the LORD relented because of their groaning under those who oppressed and afflicted them. 19 But when the judge died, the people returned to ways even more corrupt than those of their ancestors, following other gods and serving and worshiping them. They refused to give up their evil practices and stubborn ways.

20 Therefore the LORD was very angry with Israel and said, "Because this nation has violated the covenant I ordained for their ancestors and has not listened to me, 21 I will no longer drive out before them any of the nations Joshua left when

[a] 5 *Bokim* means *weepers.* [b] 9 Also known as *Timnath Serah* (see Joshua 19:50 and 24:30)
[c] *16* Or *leaders*; similarly in verses 17-19

he died. 22I will use them to test Israel
and see whether they will keep the way
of the LORD and walk in it as their ancestors did." 23The LORD had allowed those
nations to remain; he did not drive them
out at once by giving them into the hands
of Joshua.

3 These are the nations the LORD left to
test all those Israelites who had not
experienced any of the wars in Canaan
2(he did this only to teach warfare to the
descendants of the Israelites who had
not had previous battle experience): 3the
five rulers of the Philistines, all the Canaanites, the Sidonians, and the Hivites
living in the Lebanon mountains from
Mount Baal Hermon to Lebo Hamath.
4They were left to test the Israelites to
see whether they would obey the LORD's
commands, which he had given their ancestors through Moses.

5The Israelites lived among the Canaanites, Hittites, Amorites, Perizzites,
Hivites and Jebusites. 6They took their
daughters in marriage and gave their
own daughters to their sons, and served
their gods.

7The Israelites did evil in the eyes of
the LORD; they forgot the LORD their God
and served the Baals and the Asherahs.
8The anger of the LORD burned against
Israel so that he sold them into the hands
of Cushan-Rishathaim king of Aram Naharaim,[a] to whom the Israelites were subject for eight years. 9But when they cried
out to the LORD, he raised up for them a
deliverer, Othniel son of Kenaz, Caleb's
younger brother, who saved them. 10The
Spirit of the LORD came on him, so that
he became Israel's judge[b] and went to
war. The LORD gave Cushan-Rishathaim
king of Aram into the hands of Othniel,
who overpowered him. 11So the land had
peace for forty years, until Othniel son of
Kenaz died.

12Again the Israelites did evil in the
eyes of the LORD, and because they did
this evil the LORD gave Eglon king of
Moab power over Israel. 13Getting the
Ammonites and Amalekites to join him,
Eglon came and attacked Israel, and they
took possession of the City of Palms.[c]
14The Israelites were subject to Eglon
king of Moab for eighteen years.

15Again the Israelites cried out to the
LORD, and he gave them a deliverer—
Ehud, a left-handed man, the son of Gera
the Benjamite. The Israelites sent him
with tribute to Eglon king of Moab. 16Now
Ehud had made a double-edged sword
about a cubit[d] long, which he strapped
to his right thigh under his clothing.
17He presented the tribute to Eglon king
of Moab, who was a very fat man. 18After
Ehud had presented the tribute, he sent
on their way those who had carried it.
19But on reaching the stone images near
Gilgal he himself went back to Eglon and
said, "Your Majesty, I have a secret message for you."

The king said to his attendants, "Leave
us!" And they all left.

20Ehud then approached him while he
was sitting alone in the upper room of his
palace[e] and said, "I have a message from
God for you." As the king rose from his
seat, 21Ehud reached with his left hand,
drew the sword from his right thigh and
plunged it into the king's belly. 22Even
the handle sank in after the blade, and
his bowels discharged. Ehud did not pull
the sword out, and the fat closed in over
it. 23Then Ehud went out to the porch[f]; he
shut the doors of the upper room behind
him and locked them.

24After he had gone, the servants came
and found the doors of the upper room
locked. They said, "He must be relieving
himself in the inner room of the palace."
25They waited to the point of embarrass-
ment, but when he did not open the doors
of the room, they took a key and unlocked
them. There they saw their lord fallen to
the floor, dead.

26While they waited, Ehud got away.
He passed by the stone images and escaped to Seirah. 27When he arrived there,
he blew a trumpet in the hill country of
Ephraim, and the Israelites went down
with him from the hills, with him leading them.

28"Follow me," he ordered, "for the
LORD has given Moab, your enemy, into
your hands." So they followed him down
and took possession of the fords of the
Jordan that led to Moab; they allowed
no one to cross over. 29At that time they
struck down about ten thousand Moab-

[a] *8* That is, Northwest Mesopotamia [b] *10* Or *leader* [c] *13* That is, Jericho [d] *16* That is, about 18 inches or about 45 centimeters [e] *20* The meaning of the Hebrew for this word is uncertain; also in verse 24.
[f] *23* The meaning of the Hebrew for this word is uncertain.

ites, all vigorous and strong; not one escaped. 30 That day Moab was made subject to Israel, and the land had peace for
eighty years.
31 After Ehud came Shamgar son of
Anath, who struck down six hundred
Philistines with an oxgoad. He too saved
Israel.

4 Again the Israelites did evil in the
eyes of the LORD, now that Ehud
was dead. 2 So the LORD sold them into
the hands of Jabin king of Canaan, who
reigned in Hazor. Sisera, the commander of his army, was based in Harosheth
Haggoyim. 3 Because he had nine hundred chariots fitted with iron and had
cruelly oppressed the Israelites for
twenty years, they cried to the LORD for
help.
4 Now Deborah, a prophet, the wife of
Lappidoth, was leading[a] Israel at that
time. 5 She held court under the Palm of
Deborah between Ramah and Bethel in
the hill country of Ephraim, and the Israelites went up to her to have their disputes decided. 6 She sent for Barak son of
Abinoam from Kedesh in Naphtali and
said to him, "The LORD, the God of Israel, commands you: 'Go, take with you ten
thousand men of Naphtali and Zebulun
and lead them up to Mount Tabor. 7 I will
lead Sisera, the commander of Jabin's
army, with his chariots and his troops to
the Kishon River and give him into your
hands.'"
8 Barak said to her, "If you go with me,
I will go; but if you don't go with me, I
won't go."
9 "Certainly I will go with you," said
Deborah. "But because of the course you
are taking, the honor will not be yours,
for the LORD will deliver Sisera into the
hands of a woman." So Deborah went
with Barak to Kedesh. 10 There Barak
summoned Zebulun and Naphtali, and
ten thousand men went up under his
command. Deborah also went up with
him.
11 Now Heber the Kenite had left the
other Kenites, the descendants of Hobab,
Moses' brother-in-law,[b] and pitched his
tent by the great tree in Zaanannim near
Kedesh.
12 When they told Sisera that Barak
son of Abinoam had gone up to Mount
Tabor, 13 Sisera summoned from Harosheth Haggoyim to the Kishon River all
his men and his nine hundred chariots
fitted with iron.
14 Then Deborah said to Barak, "Go!
This is the day the LORD has given Sisera into your hands. Has not the LORD
gone ahead of you?" So Barak went down
Mount Tabor, with ten thousand men
following him. 15 At Barak's advance, the
LORD routed Sisera and all his chariots
and army by the sword, and Sisera got
down from his chariot and fled on foot.
16 Barak pursued the chariots and
army as far as Harosheth Haggoyim, and
all Sisera's troops fell by the sword; not a
man was left. 17 Sisera, meanwhile, fled
on foot to the tent of Jael, the wife of Heber the Kenite, because there was an alliance between Jabin king of Hazor and the
family of Heber the Kenite.
18 Jael went out to meet Sisera and said
to him, "Come, my lord, come right in.
Don't be afraid." So he entered her tent,
and she covered him with a blanket.
19 "I'm thirsty," he said. "Please give me
some water." She opened a skin of milk,
gave him a drink, and covered him up.
20 "Stand in the doorway of the tent," he
told her. "If someone comes by and asks
you, 'Is anyone in there?' say 'No.'"
21 But Jael, Heber's wife, picked up a
tent peg and a hammer and went quietly
to him while he lay fast asleep, exhausted. She drove the peg through his temple
into the ground, and he died.
22 Just then Barak came by in pursuit of Sisera, and Jael went out to meet
him. "Come," she said, "I will show you
the man you're looking for." So he went
in with her, and there lay Sisera with the
tent peg through his temple—dead.
23 On that day God subdued Jabin king
of Canaan before the Israelites. 24 And the
hand of the Israelites pressed harder and
harder against Jabin king of Canaan until
they destroyed him.

5 On that day Deborah and Barak son of
Abinoam sang this song:

2 "When the princes in Israel take the
lead,
when the people willingly offer
themselves—
praise the LORD!

[a] 4 Traditionally *judging* [b] 11 Or *father-in-law*

3 "Hear this, you kings! Listen, you
rulers!
I, even I, will sing to[a] the LORD;
I will praise the LORD, the God of
Israel, in song.

4 "When you, LORD, went out from
Seir,
when you marched from the land of
Edom,
the earth shook, the heavens poured,
the clouds poured down water.
5 The mountains quaked before the
LORD, the One of Sinai,
before the LORD, the God of Israel.

6 "In the days of Shamgar son of Anath,
in the days of Jael, the highways
were abandoned;
travelers took to winding paths.
7 Villagers in Israel would not fight;
they held back until I, Deborah,
arose,
until I arose, a mother in Israel.
8 God chose new leaders
when war came to the city gates,
but not a shield or spear was seen
among forty thousand in Israel.
9 My heart is with Israel's princes,
with the willing volunteers among
the people.
Praise the LORD!

10 "You who ride on white donkeys,
sitting on your saddle blankets,
and you who walk along the road,
consider 11 the voice of the singers[b] at
the watering places.
They recite the victories of the
LORD,
the victories of his villagers in Israel.

"Then the people of the LORD
went down to the city gates.
12 'Wake up, wake up, Deborah!
Wake up, wake up, break out in
song!
Arise, Barak!
Take captive your captives, son of
Abinoam.'

13 "The remnant of the nobles came
down;
the people of the LORD came down
to me against the mighty.
14 Some came from Ephraim, whose
roots were in Amalek;
Benjamin was with the people who
followed you.
From Makir captains came down,
from Zebulun those who bear a
commander's[b] staff.
15 The princes of Issachar were with
Deborah;
yes, Issachar was with Barak,
sent under his command into the
valley.
In the districts of Reuben
there was much searching of heart.
16 Why did you stay among the sheep
pens[c]
to hear the whistling for the flocks?
In the districts of Reuben
there was much searching of heart.
17 Gilead stayed beyond the Jordan.
And Dan, why did he linger by the
ships?
Asher remained on the coast
and stayed in his coves.
18 The people of Zebulun risked their
very lives;
so did Naphtali on the terraced
fields.

19 "Kings came, they fought,
the kings of Canaan fought.
At Taanach, by the waters of
Megiddo,
they took no plunder of silver.
20 From the heavens the stars fought,
from their courses they fought
against Sisera.
21 The river Kishon swept them away,
the age-old river, the river Kishon.
March on, my soul; be strong!
22 Then thundered the horses' hooves—
galloping, galloping go his mighty
steeds.
23 'Curse Meroz,' said the angel of the
LORD.
'Curse its people bitterly,
because they did not come to help the
LORD,
to help the LORD against the
mighty.'

24 "Most blessed of women be Jael,
the wife of Heber the Kenite,
most blessed of tent-dwelling
women.
25 He asked for water, and she gave him
milk;

[a] *3* Or *of* [b] *11,14* The meaning of the Hebrew for this word is uncertain. [c] *16* Or *the campfires*; or *the saddlebags*

in a bowl fit for nobles she brought
him curdled milk.
26 Her hand reached for the tent peg,
her right hand for the workman's
hammer.
She struck Sisera, she crushed his
head,
she shattered and pierced his
temple.
27 At her feet he sank,
he fell; there he lay.
At her feet he sank, he fell;
where he sank, there he fell — dead.

28 "Through the window peered Sisera's
mother;
behind the lattice she cried out,
'Why is his chariot so long in coming?
Why is the clatter of his chariots
delayed?'
29 The wisest of her ladies answer her;
indeed, she keeps saying to herself,
30 'Are they not finding and dividing the
spoils:
a woman or two for each man,
colorful garments as plunder for
Sisera,
colorful garments embroidered,
highly embroidered garments for my
neck —
all this as plunder?'

31 "So may all your enemies perish,
LORD!
But may all who love you be like the
sun
when it rises in its strength."

Then the land had peace forty years.

6 The Israelites did evil in the eyes of
the LORD, and for seven years he gave
them into the hands of the Midianites.
2 Because the power of Midian was so oppressive, the Israelites prepared shelters
for themselves in mountain clefts, caves
and strongholds. 3 Whenever the Israelites planted their crops, the Midianites,
Amalekites and other eastern peoples invaded the country. 4 They camped on the
land and ruined the crops all the way to
Gaza and did not spare a living thing for
Israel, neither sheep nor cattle nor donkeys. 5 They came up with their livestock
and their tents like swarms of locusts. It
was impossible to count them or their
camels; they invaded the land to ravage
it. 6 Midian so impoverished the Israelites
that they cried out to the LORD for help.
7 When the Israelites cried out to the
LORD because of Midian, 8 he sent them
a prophet, who said, "This is what the
LORD, the God of Israel, says: I brought
you up out of Egypt, out of the land of
slavery. 9 I rescued you from the hand of
the Egyptians. And I delivered you from
the hand of all your oppressors; I drove
them out before you and gave you their
land. 10 I said to you, 'I am the LORD your
God; do not worship the gods of the Amorites, in whose land you live.' But you
have not listened to me."
11 The angel of the LORD came and sat
down under the oak in Ophrah that belonged to Joash the Abiezrite, where his
son Gideon was threshing wheat in a
winepress to keep it from the Midianites.
12 When the angel of the LORD appeared
to Gideon, he said, "The LORD is with you,
mighty warrior."
13 "Pardon me, my lord," Gideon replied, "but if the LORD is with us, why has
all this happened to us? Where are all his
wonders that our ancestors told us about
when they said, 'Did not the LORD bring
us up out of Egypt?' But now the LORD has
abandoned us and given us into the hand
of Midian."
14 The LORD turned to him and said,
"Go in the strength you have and save Israel out of Midian's hand. Am I not sending you?"
15 "Pardon me, my lord," Gideon replied, "but how can I save Israel? My clan
is the weakest in Manasseh, and I am the
least in my family."
16 The LORD answered, "I will be with
you, and you will strike down all the Midianites, leaving none alive."
17 Gideon replied, "If now I have found
favor in your eyes, give me a sign that it is
really you talking to me. 18 Please do not
go away until I come back and bring my
offering and set it before you."
And the LORD said, "I will wait until
you return."
19 Gideon went inside, prepared a
young goat, and from an ephah[a] of flour
he made bread without yeast. Putting the
meat in a basket and its broth in a pot, he
brought them out and offered them to
him under the oak.

[a] *19* That is, probably about 36 pounds or about 16 kilograms

20The angel of God said to him, "Take
the meat and the unleavened bread,
place them on this rock, and pour out
the broth." And Gideon did so. 21Then
the angel of the LORD touched the meat
and the unleavened bread with the tip of
the staff that was in his hand. Fire flared
from the rock, consuming the meat and
the bread. And the angel of the LORD disappeared. 22When Gideon realized that it
was the angel of the LORD, he exclaimed,
"Alas, Sovereign LORD! I have seen the
angel of the LORD face to face!"
23But the LORD said to him, "Peace! Do
not be afraid. You are not going to die."
24So Gideon built an altar to the LORD
there and called it The LORD Is Peace. To
this day it stands in Ophrah of the Abiezrites.
25That same night the LORD said to
him, "Take the second bull from your father's herd, the one seven years old.[a] Tear
down your father's altar to Baal and cut
down the Asherah pole[b] beside it. 26Then
build a proper kind of[c] altar to the LORD
your God on the top of this height. Using
the wood of the Asherah pole that you cut
down, offer the second[d] bull as a burnt
offering."
27So Gideon took ten of his servants
and did as the LORD told him. But because he was afraid of his family and the
townspeople, he did it at night rather
than in the daytime.
28In the morning when the people of
the town got up, there was Baal's altar,
demolished, with the Asherah pole beside it cut down and the second bull sacrificed on the newly built altar!
29They asked each other, "Who did
this?"
When they carefully investigated, they
were told, "Gideon son of Joash did it."
30The people of the town demanded
of Joash, "Bring out your son. He must
die, because he has broken down Baal's
altar and cut down the Asherah pole beside it."
31But Joash replied to the hostile crowd
around him, "Are you going to plead Baal's cause? Are you trying to save him?
Whoever fights for him shall be put to
death by morning! If Baal really is a god,
he can defend himself when someone
breaks down his altar." 32So because
Gideon broke down Baal's altar, they gave
him the name Jerub-Baal[e] that day, saying, "Let Baal contend with him."
33Now all the Midianites, Amalekites
and other eastern peoples joined forces
and crossed over the Jordan and camped
in the Valley of Jezreel. 34Then the Spirit of the LORD came on Gideon, and he
blew a trumpet, summoning the Abiezrites to follow him. 35He sent messengers
throughout Manasseh, calling them to
arms, and also into Asher, Zebulun and
Naphtali, so that they too went up to meet
them.
36Gideon said to God, "If you will save
Israel by my hand as you have promised— 37look, I will place a wool fleece
on the threshing floor. If there is dew
only on the fleece and all the ground is
dry, then I will know that you will save
Israel by my hand, as you said." 38And
that is what happened. Gideon rose early
the next day; he squeezed the fleece and
wrung out the dew—a bowlful of water.
39Then Gideon said to God, "Do not
be angry with me. Let me make just one
more request. Allow me one more test
with the fleece, but this time make the
fleece dry and let the ground be covered
with dew." 40That night God did so. Only
the fleece was dry; all the ground was
covered with dew.

7 Early in the morning, Jerub-Baal (that
is, Gideon) and all his men camped at
the spring of Harod. The camp of Midian
was north of them in the valley near the
hill of Moreh. 2The LORD said to Gideon,
"You have too many men. I cannot deliver
Midian into their hands, or Israel would
boast against me, 'My own strength has
saved me.' 3Now announce to the army,
'Anyone who trembles with fear may
turn back and leave Mount Gilead.'" So
twenty-two thousand men left, while ten
thousand remained.
4But the LORD said to Gideon, "There
are still too many men. Take them down
to the water, and I will thin them out for
you there. If I say, 'This one shall go with
you,' he shall go; but if I say, 'This one
shall not go with you,' he shall not go."
5So Gideon took the men down to the
water. There the LORD told him, "Sepa-

[a] 25 Or *Take a full-grown, mature bull from your father's herd* [b] 25 That is, a wooden symbol of the goddess Asherah; also in verses 26, 28 and 30 [c] 26 Or *build with layers of stone an* [d] 26 Or *full-grown*; also in verse 28 [e] 32 *Jerub-Baal* probably means *let Baal contend.*

rate those who lap the water with their
tongues as a dog laps from those who
kneel down to drink." 6Three hundred of
them drank from cupped hands, lapping
like dogs. All the rest got down on their
knees to drink.
7The LORD said to Gideon, "With the
three hundred men that lapped I will
save you and give the Midianites into
your hands. Let all the others go home."
8So Gideon sent the rest of the Israelites
home but kept the three hundred, who
took over the provisions and trumpets of
the others.
Now the camp of Midian lay below
him in the valley. 9During that night the
LORD said to Gideon, "Get up, go down
against the camp, because I am going
to give it into your hands. 10If you are
afraid to attack, go down to the camp
with your servant Purah 11and listen to
what they are saying. Afterward, you will
be encouraged to attack the camp." So he
and Purah his servant went down to the
outposts of the camp. 12The Midianites,
the Amalekites and all the other eastern
peoples had settled in the valley, thick as
locusts. Their camels could no more be
counted than the sand on the seashore.
13Gideon arrived just as a man was telling a friend his dream. "I had a dream,"
he was saying. "A round loaf of barley
bread came tumbling into the Midianite
camp. It struck the tent with such force
that the tent overturned and collapsed."
14His friend responded, "This can be
nothing other than the sword of Gideon
son of Joash, the Israelite. God has given
the Midianites and the whole camp into
his hands."
15When Gideon heard the dream and
its interpretation, he bowed down and
worshiped. He returned to the camp of
Israel and called out, "Get up! The LORD
has given the Midianite camp into your
hands." 16Dividing the three hundred
men into three companies, he placed
trumpets and empty jars in the hands of
all of them, with torches inside.
17"Watch me," he told them. "Follow
my lead. When I get to the edge of the
camp, do exactly as I do. 18When I and all
who are with me blow our trumpets, then
from all around the camp blow yours and
shout, 'For the LORD and for Gideon.'"
19Gideon and the hundred men with
him reached the edge of the camp at the
beginning of the middle watch, just after
they had changed the guard. They blew
their trumpets and broke the jars that
were in their hands. 20The three companies blew the trumpets and smashed
the jars. Grasping the torches in their left
hands and holding in their right hands
the trumpets they were to blow, they
shouted, "A sword for the LORD and for
Gideon!" 21While each man held his position around the camp, all the Midianites
ran, crying out as they fled.
22When the three hundred trumpets
sounded, the LORD caused the men
throughout the camp to turn on each
other with their swords. The army fled to
Beth Shittah toward Zererah as far as the
border of Abel Meholah near Tabbath.
23Israelites from Naphtali, Asher and
all Manasseh were called out, and they
pursued the Midianites. 24Gideon sent
messengers throughout the hill country
of Ephraim, saying, "Come down against
the Midianites and seize the waters of
the Jordan ahead of them as far as Beth
Barah."
So all the men of Ephraim were called
out and they seized the waters of the Jordan as far as Beth Barah. 25They also captured two of the Midianite leaders, Oreb
and Zeeb. They killed Oreb at the rock
of Oreb, and Zeeb at the winepress of
Zeeb. They pursued the Midianites and
brought the heads of Oreb and Zeeb to
Gideon, who was by the Jordan.

8 Now the Ephraimites asked Gideon,
"Why have you treated us like this?
Why didn't you call us when you went to
fight Midian?" And they challenged him
vigorously.
2But he answered them, "What have I
accomplished compared to you? Aren't
the gleanings of Ephraim's grapes better
than the full grape harvest of Abiezer?
3God gave Oreb and Zeeb, the Midianite
leaders, into your hands. What was I able
to do compared to you?" At this, their resentment against him subsided.
4Gideon and his three hundred men,
exhausted yet keeping up the pursuit,
came to the Jordan and crossed it. 5He
said to the men of Sukkoth, "Give my
troops some bread; they are worn out,
and I am still pursuing Zebah and Zalmunna, the kings of Midian."
6But the officials of Sukkoth said, "Do
you already have the hands of Zebah

and Zalmunna in your possession? Why
should we give bread to your troops?"
7 Then Gideon replied, "Just for that,
when the LORD has given Zebah and
Zalmunna into my hand, I will tear your
flesh with desert thorns and briers."
8 From there he went up to Peniel[a] and
made the same request of them, but they
answered as the men of Sukkoth had.
9 So he said to the men of Peniel, "When
I return in triumph, I will tear down this
tower."
10 Now Zebah and Zalmunna were in
Karkor with a force of about fifteen thousand men, all that were left of the armies
of the eastern peoples; a hundred and
twenty thousand swordsmen had fallen.
11 Gideon went up by the route of the nomads east of Nobah and Jogbehah and attacked the unsuspecting army. 12 Zebah
and Zalmunna, the two kings of Midian,
fled, but he pursued them and captured
them, routing their entire army.
13 Gideon son of Joash then returned
from the battle by the Pass of Heres. 14 He
caught a young man of Sukkoth and questioned him, and the young man wrote
down for him the names of the seventy-
seven officials of Sukkoth, the elders of
the town. 15 Then Gideon came and said
to the men of Sukkoth, "Here are Zebah
and Zalmunna, about whom you taunted
me by saying, 'Do you already have the
hands of Zebah and Zalmunna in your
possession? Why should we give bread
to your exhausted men?'" 16 He took the
elders of the town and taught the men of
Sukkoth a lesson by punishing them with
desert thorns and briers. 17 He also pulled
down the tower of Peniel and killed the
men of the town.
18 Then he asked Zebah and Zalmunna, "What kind of men did you kill at Tabor?"

"Men like you," they answered, "each
one with the bearing of a prince."
19 Gideon replied, "Those were my
brothers, the sons of my own mother.
As surely as the LORD lives, if you had
spared their lives, I would not kill you."
20 Turning to Jether, his oldest son, he
said, "Kill them!" But Jether did not draw
his sword, because he was only a boy and
was afraid.
21 Zebah and Zalmunna said, "Come,
do it yourself. 'As is the man, so is his
strength.'" So Gideon stepped forward
and killed them, and took the ornaments
off their camels' necks.
22 The Israelites said to Gideon, "Rule
over us—you, your son and your grandson—because you have saved us from
the hand of Midian."
23 But Gideon told them, "I will not rule
over you, nor will my son rule over you.
The LORD will rule over you." 24 And he
said, "I do have one request, that each of
you give me an earring from your share
of the plunder." (It was the custom of the
Ishmaelites to wear gold earrings.)
25 They answered, "We'll be glad to give
them." So they spread out a garment, and
each of them threw a ring from his plunder onto it. 26 The weight of the gold rings
he asked for came to seventeen hundred
shekels,[b] not counting the ornaments,
the pendants and the purple garments
worn by the kings of Midian or the chains
that were on their camels' necks. 27 Gideon made the gold into an ephod, which
he placed in Ophrah, his town. All Israel
prostituted themselves by worshiping it
there, and it became a snare to Gideon
and his family.
28 Thus Midian was subdued before the
Israelites and did not raise its head again.
During Gideon's lifetime, the land had
peace forty years.
29 Jerub-Baal son of Joash went back
home to live. 30 He had seventy sons of
his own, for he had many wives. 31 His
concubine, who lived in Shechem, also
bore him a son, whom he named Abimelek. 32 Gideon son of Joash died at a good
old age and was buried in the tomb of his
father Joash in Ophrah of the Abiezrites.
33 No sooner had Gideon died than the
Israelites again prostituted themselves
to the Baals. They set up Baal-Berith as
their god 34 and did not remember the
LORD their God, who had rescued them
from the hands of all their enemies on
every side. 35 They also failed to show any
loyalty to the family of Jerub-Baal (that is,
Gideon) in spite of all the good things he
had done for them.

9 Abimelek son of Jerub-Baal went to
his mother's brothers in Shechem and
said to them and to all his mother's clan,
2 "Ask all the citizens of Shechem, 'Which

[a] *8* Hebrew *Penuel,* a variant of *Peniel;* also in verses 9 and 17 [b] *26* That is, about 43 pounds or about 20 kilograms

is better for you: to have all seventy of Jerub-Baal's sons rule over you, or just one
man?' Remember, I am your flesh and
blood."
3When the brothers repeated all this
to the citizens of Shechem, they were inclined to follow Abimelek, for they said,
"He is related to us." 4They gave him seventy shekels[a] of silver from the temple of
Baal-Berith, and Abimelek used it to hire
reckless scoundrels, who became his followers. 5He went to his father's home in
Ophrah and on one stone murdered his
seventy brothers, the sons of Jerub-Baal.
But Jotham, the youngest son of Jerub-
Baal, escaped by hiding. 6Then all the
citizens of Shechem and Beth Millo gathered beside the great tree at the pillar in
Shechem to crown Abimelek king.
7When Jotham was told about this, he
climbed up on the top of Mount Gerizim
and shouted to them, "Listen to me, citizens of Shechem, so that God may listen
to you. 8One day the trees went out to
anoint a king for themselves. They said
to the olive tree, 'Be our king.'
9"But the olive tree answered, 'Should
I give up my oil, by which both gods and
humans are honored, to hold sway over
the trees?'
10"Next, the trees said to the fig tree,
'Come and be our king.'
11"But the fig tree replied, 'Should I
give up my fruit, so good and sweet, to
hold sway over the trees?'
12"Then the trees said to the vine,
'Come and be our king.'
13"But the vine answered, 'Should I give
up my wine, which cheers both gods and
humans, to hold sway over the trees?'
14"Finally all the trees said to the
thornbush, 'Come and be our king.'
15"The thornbush said to the trees, 'If
you really want to anoint me king over
you, come and take refuge in my shade;
but if not, then let fire come out of the
thornbush and consume the cedars of
Lebanon!'
16"Have you acted honorably and in
good faith by making Abimelek king?
Have you been fair to Jerub-Baal and
his family? Have you treated him as he
deserves? 17Remember that my father
fought for you and risked his life to rescue you from the hand of Midian. 18But
today you have revolted against my father's family. You have murdered his
seventy sons on a single stone and have
made Abimelek, the son of his female
slave, king over the citizens of Shechem
because he is related to you. 19So have
you acted honorably and in good faith toward Jerub-Baal and his family today? If
you have, may Abimelek be your joy, and
may you be his, too! 20But if you have not,
let fire come out from Abimelek and consume you, the citizens of Shechem and
Beth Millo, and let fire come out from
you, the citizens of Shechem and Beth
Millo, and consume Abimelek!"
21Then Jotham fled, escaping to Beer,
and he lived there because he was afraid
of his brother Abimelek.
22After Abimelek had governed Israel
three years, 23God stirred up animos-
ity between Abimelek and the citizens
of Shechem so that they acted treacherously against Abimelek. 24God did this in
order that the crime against Jerub-Baal's
seventy sons, the shedding of their blood,
might be avenged on their brother Abimelek and on the citizens of Shechem, who
had helped him murder his brothers. 25In
opposition to him these citizens of Shechem set men on the hilltops to ambush
and rob everyone who passed by, and this
was reported to Abimelek.
26Now Gaal son of Ebed moved with
his clan into Shechem, and its citizens
put their confidence in him. 27After
they had gone out into the fields and
gathered the grapes and trodden them,
they held a festival in the temple of their
god. While they were eating and drinking, they cursed Abimelek. 28Then Gaal
son of Ebed said, "Who is Abimelek, and
why should we Shechemites be subject to
him? Isn't he Jerub-Baal's son, and isn't
Zebul his deputy? Serve the family of
Hamor, Shechem's father! Why should
we serve Abimelek? 29If only this people
were under my command! Then I would
get rid of him. I would say to Abimelek,
'Call out your whole army!' "[b]
30When Zebul the governor of the city
heard what Gaal son of Ebed said, he was
very angry. 31Under cover he sent messengers to Abimelek, saying, "Gaal son of
Ebed and his clan have come to Shechem
and are stirring up the city against you.

[a] *4* That is, about 1 3/4 pounds or about 800 grams [b] *29* Septuagint; Hebrew *him." Then he said to Abimelek, "Call out your whole army!"*

32Now then, during the night you and
your men should come and lie in wait in
the fields. 33In the morning at sunrise,
advance against the city. When Gaal and
his men come out against you, seize the
opportunity to attack them."
34So Abimelek and all his troops set out
by night and took up concealed positions
near Shechem in four companies. 35Now
Gaal son of Ebed had gone out and was
standing at the entrance of the city gate
just as Abimelek and his troops came out
from their hiding place.
36When Gaal saw them, he said to Zebul, "Look, people are coming down from
the tops of the mountains!"
Zebul replied, "You mistake the shadows of the mountains for men."
37But Gaal spoke up again: "Look, people are coming down from the central
hill,[a] and a company is coming from the
direction of the diviners' tree."
38Then Zebul said to him, "Where is
your big talk now, you who said, 'Who
is Abimelek that we should be subject to
him?' Aren't these the men you ridiculed?
Go out and fight them!"
39So Gaal led out[b] the citizens of Shechem and fought Abimelek. 40Abimelek
chased him all the way to the entrance
of the gate, and many were killed as they
fled. 41Then Abimelek stayed in Arumah,
and Zebul drove Gaal and his clan out of
Shechem.
42The next day the people of Shechem
went out to the fields, and this was reported to Abimelek. 43So he took his
men, divided them into three companies
and set an ambush in the fields. When he
saw the people coming out of the city, he
rose to attack them. 44Abimelek and the
companies with him rushed forward to a
position at the entrance of the city gate.
Then two companies attacked those in
the fields and struck them down. 45All
that day Abimelek pressed his attack
against the city until he had captured it
and killed its people. Then he destroyed
the city and scattered salt over it.
46On hearing this, the citizens in the
tower of Shechem went into the stronghold of the temple of El-Berith. 47When
Abimelek heard that they had assembled there, 48he and all his men went up
Mount Zalmon. He took an ax and cut
off some branches, which he lifted to his
shoulders. He ordered the men with him,
"Quick! Do what you have seen me do!"
49So all the men cut branches and followed Abimelek. They piled them against
the stronghold and set it on fire with the
people still inside. So all the people in the
tower of Shechem, about a thousand men
and women, also died.
50Next Abimelek went to Thebez and
besieged it and captured it. 51Inside
the city, however, was a strong tower, to
which all the men and women—all the
people of the city—had fled. They had
locked themselves in and climbed up
on the tower roof. 52Abimelek went to
the tower and attacked it. But as he approached the entrance to the tower to set
it on fire, 53a woman dropped an upper
millstone on his head and cracked his
skull.
54Hurriedly he called to his armor-
bearer, "Draw your sword and kill me, so
that they can't say, 'A woman killed him.'"
So his servant ran him through, and
he died. 55When the Israelites saw that
Abimelek was dead, they went home.
56Thus God repaid the wickedness that
Abimelek had done to his father by murdering his seventy brothers. 57God also
made the people of Shechem pay for all
their wickedness. The curse of Jotham
son of Jerub-Baal came on them.

10 After the time of Abimelek, a man
of Issachar named Tola son of Puah,
the son of Dodo, rose to save Israel. He
lived in Shamir, in the hill country of
Ephraim. 2He led[c] Israel twenty-three
years; then he died, and was buried in
Shamir.
3He was followed by Jair of Gilead,
who led Israel twenty-two years. 4He had
thirty sons, who rode thirty donkeys.
They controlled thirty towns in Gilead,
which to this day are called Havvoth
Jair.[d] 5When Jair died, he was buried in
Kamon.
6Again the Israelites did evil in the eyes
of the LORD. They served the Baals and
the Ashtoreths, and the gods of Aram, the
gods of Sidon, the gods of Moab, the gods
of the Ammonites and the gods of the
Philistines. And because the Israelites
forsook the LORD and no longer served
him, 7he became angry with them. He

[a] 37 The Hebrew for this phrase means *the navel of the earth.* [b] 39 Or *Gaal went out in the sight of*
[c] 2 Traditionally *judged;* also in verse 3 [d] 4 Or *called the settlements of Jair*

sold them into the hands of the Philistines and the Ammonites, 8 who that year
shattered and crushed them. For eighteen
years they oppressed all the Israelites on
the east side of the Jordan in Gilead, the
land of the Amorites. 9 The Ammonites
also crossed the Jordan to fight against
Judah, Benjamin and Ephraim; Israel
was in great distress. 10 Then the Israelites cried out to the LORD, "We have
sinned against you, forsaking our God
and serving the Baals."

11 The LORD replied, "When the Egyptians, the Amorites, the Ammonites, the
Philistines, 12 the Sidonians, the Amalekites and the Maonites[a] oppressed you and
you cried to me for help, did I not save you
from their hands? 13 But you have forsak-
en me and served other gods, so I will no
longer save you. 14 Go and cry out to the
gods you have chosen. Let them save you
when you are in trouble!"

15 But the Israelites said to the LORD,
"We have sinned. Do with us whatever
you think best, but please rescue us now."
16 Then they got rid of the foreign gods
among them and served the LORD. And
he could bear Israel's misery no longer.

17 When the Ammonites were called to
arms and camped in Gilead, the Israelites assembled and camped at Mizpah.
18 The leaders of the people of Gilead said
to each other, "Whoever will take the lead
in attacking the Ammonites will be head
over all who live in Gilead."

11 Jephthah the Gileadite was a mighty
warrior. His father was Gilead; his
mother was a prostitute. 2 Gilead's wife
also bore him sons, and when they were
grown up, they drove Jephthah away.
"You are not going to get any inheritance
in our family," they said, "because you
are the son of another woman." 3 So Jephthah fled from his brothers and settled in
the land of Tob, where a gang of scoundrels gathered around him and followed
him.

4 Some time later, when the Ammonites were fighting against Israel, 5 the elders of Gilead went to get Jephthah from
the land of Tob. 6 "Come," they said, "be
our commander, so we can fight the Ammonites."

7 Jephthah said to them, "Didn't you
hate me and drive me from my father's
house? Why do you come to me now,
when you're in trouble?"

8 The elders of Gilead said to him, "Nevertheless, we are turning to you now;
come with us to fight the Ammonites,
and you will be head over all of us who
live in Gilead."

9 Jephthah answered, "Suppose you
take me back to fight the Ammonites and
the LORD gives them to me — will I really
be your head?"

10 The elders of Gilead replied, "The
LORD is our witness; we will certainly do
as you say." 11 So Jephthah went with the
elders of Gilead, and the people made
him head and commander over them.
And he repeated all his words before the
LORD in Mizpah.

12 Then Jephthah sent messengers to
the Ammonite king with the question:
"What do you have against me that you
have attacked my country?"

13 The king of the Ammonites answered
Jephthah's messengers, "When Israel
came up out of Egypt, they took away my
land from the Arnon to the Jabbok, all
the way to the Jordan. Now give it back
peaceably."

14 Jephthah sent back messengers to the
Ammonite king, 15 saying:

> "This is what Jephthah says: Israel
> did not take the land of Moab or the
> land of the Ammonites. 16 But when
> they came up out of Egypt, Israel
> went through the wilderness to the
> Red Sea[b] and on to Kadesh. 17 Then
> Israel sent messengers to the king of
> Edom, saying, 'Give us permission
> to go through your country,' but the
> king of Edom would not listen. They
> sent also to the king of Moab, and he
> refused. So Israel stayed at Kadesh.
>
> 18 "Next they traveled through
> the wilderness, skirted the lands of
> Edom and Moab, passed along the
> eastern side of the country of Moab,
> and camped on the other side of the
> Arnon. They did not enter the terri-
> tory of Moab, for the Arnon was its
> border.
>
> 19 "Then Israel sent messengers
> to Sihon king of the Amorites, who
> ruled in Heshbon, and said to him,
> 'Let us pass through your country
> to our own place.' 20 Sihon, however,

[a] *12* Hebrew; some Septuagint manuscripts *Midianites*
[b] *16* Or *the Sea of Reeds*

did not trust Israel[a] to pass through
his territory. He mustered all his
troops and encamped at Jahaz and
fought with Israel.
21 "Then the LORD, the God of Israel, gave Sihon and his whole army
into Israel's hands, and they defeated
them. Israel took over all the land of
the Amorites who lived in that country, 22 capturing all of it from the Arnon to the Jabbok and from the desert to the Jordan.
23 "Now since the LORD, the God of
Israel, has driven the Amorites out
before his people Israel, what right
have you to take it over? 24 Will you
not take what your god Chemosh
gives you? Likewise, whatever the
LORD our God has given us, we will
possess. 25 Are you any better than
Balak son of Zippor, king of Moab?
Did he ever quarrel with Israel or
fight with them? 26 For three hundred years Israel occupied Heshbon,
Aroer, the surrounding settlements
and all the towns along the Arnon.
Why didn't you retake them during
that time? 27 I have not wronged you,
but you are doing me wrong by waging war against me. Let the LORD, the
Judge, decide the dispute this day
between the Israelites and the Ammonites."

28 The king of Ammon, however, paid no
attention to the message Jephthah sent
him.
29 Then the Spirit of the LORD came on
Jephthah. He crossed Gilead and Manasseh, passed through Mizpah of Gilead,
and from there he advanced against the
Ammonites. 30 And Jephthah made a vow
to the LORD: "If you give the Ammonites
into my hands, 31 whatever comes out of
the door of my house to meet me when I
return in triumph from the Ammonites
will be the LORD's, and I will sacrifice it
as a burnt offering."
32 Then Jephthah went over to fight the
Ammonites, and the LORD gave them into
his hands. 33 He devastated twenty towns
from Aroer to the vicinity of Minnith, as
far as Abel Keramim. Thus Israel subdued Ammon.
34 When Jephthah returned to his home
in Mizpah, who should come out to meet
him but his daughter, dancing to the
sound of timbrels! She was an only child.
Except for her he had neither son nor
daughter. 35 When he saw her, he tore his
clothes and cried, "Oh no, my daughter!
You have brought me down and I am devastated. I have made a vow to the LORD
that I cannot break."
36 "My father," she replied, "you have
given your word to the LORD. Do to me
just as you promised, now that the LORD
has avenged you of your enemies, the
Ammonites. 37 But grant me this one request," she said. "Give me two months to
roam the hills and weep with my friends,
because I will never marry."
38 "You may go," he said. And he let her
go for two months. She and her friends
went into the hills and wept because
she would never marry. 39 After the two
months, she returned to her father, and
he did to her as he had vowed. And she
was a virgin.

From this comes the Israelite tradition
40 that each year the young women of Israel go out for four days to commemorate
the daughter of Jephthah the Gileadite.

12 The Ephraimite forces were called
out, and they crossed over to Zaphon. They said to Jephthah, "Why did
you go to fight the Ammonites without
calling us to go with you? We're going to
burn down your house over your head."
2 Jephthah answered, "I and my people
were engaged in a great struggle with the
Ammonites, and although I called, you
didn't save me out of their hands. 3 When
I saw that you wouldn't help, I took my
life in my hands and crossed over to fight
the Ammonites, and the LORD gave me
the victory over them. Now why have you
come up today to fight me?"
4 Jephthah then called together the
men of Gilead and fought against Ephraim. The Gileadites struck them down because the Ephraimites had said, "You Gileadites are renegades from Ephraim and
Manasseh." 5 The Gileadites captured
the fords of the Jordan leading to Ephraim, and whenever a survivor of Ephraim
said, "Let me cross over," the men of Gilead asked him, "Are you an Ephraimite?"
If he replied, "No," 6 they said, "All right,
say 'Shibboleth.'" If he said, "Sibbo-
leth," because he could not pronounce

[a] 20 Or *however, would not make an agreement for Israel*

went to visit his wife. He said, "I'm going
to my wife's room." But her father would
not let him go in.
2 "I was so sure you hated her," he said,
"that I gave her to your companion. Isn't
her younger sister more attractive? Take
her instead."
3 Samson said to them, "This time I have
a right to get even with the Philistines; I
will really harm them." 4 So he went out
and caught three hundred foxes and tied
them tail to tail in pairs. He then fastened
a torch to every pair of tails, 5 lit the torches and let the foxes loose in the standing
grain of the Philistines. He burned up the
shocks and standing grain, together with
the vineyards and olive groves.
6 When the Philistines asked, "Who did
this?" they were told, "Samson, the Tim-
nite's son-in-law, because his wife was
given to his companion."
So the Philistines went up and burned
her and her father to death. 7 Samson
said to them, "Since you've acted like
this, I swear that I won't stop until I get
my revenge on you." 8 He attacked them
viciously and slaughtered many of them.
Then he went down and stayed in a cave
in the rock of Etam.
9 The Philistines went up and camped
in Judah, spreading out near Lehi. 10 The
people of Judah asked, "Why have you
come to fight us?"
"We have come to take Samson prisoner," they answered, "to do to him as he
did to us."
11 Then three thousand men from Judah went down to the cave in the rock of
Etam and said to Samson, "Don't you realize that the Philistines are rulers over
us? What have you done to us?"
He answered, "I merely did to them
what they did to me."
12 They said to him, "We've come to tie
you up and hand you over to the Philistines."
Samson said, "Swear to me that you
won't kill me yourselves."
13 "Agreed," they answered. "We will
only tie you up and hand you over to
them. We will not kill you." So they bound
him with two new ropes and led him up
from the rock. 14 As he approached Lehi,
the Philistines came toward him shouting. The Spirit of the LORD came powerfully upon him. The ropes on his arms
became like charred flax, and the bind-
ings dropped from his hands. 15 Finding
a fresh jawbone of a donkey, he grabbed it
and struck down a thousand men.
16 Then Samson said,

"With a donkey's jawbone
  I have made donkeys of them.[a]
With a donkey's jawbone
  I have killed a thousand men."

17 When he finished speaking, he threw
away the jawbone; and the place was
called Ramath Lehi.[b]
18 Because he was very thirsty, he cried
out to the LORD, "You have given your
servant this great victory. Must I now
die of thirst and fall into the hands of the
uncircumcised?" 19 Then God opened
up the hollow place in Lehi, and water
came out of it. When Samson drank, his
strength returned and he revived. So the
spring was called En Hakkore,[c] and it is
still there in Lehi.
20 Samson led[d] Israel for twenty years
in the days of the Philistines.

16 One day Samson went to Gaza,
where he saw a prostitute. He went
in to spend the night with her. 2 The people of Gaza were told, "Samson is here!"
So they surrounded the place and lay
in wait for him all night at the city gate.
They made no move during the night,
saying, "At dawn we'll kill him."
3 But Samson lay there only until the
middle of the night. Then he got up and
took hold of the doors of the city gate, together with the two posts, and tore them
loose, bar and all. He lifted them to his
shoulders and carried them to the top of
the hill that faces Hebron.
4 Some time later, he fell in love with
a woman in the Valley of Sorek whose
name was Delilah. 5 The rulers of the Philistines went to her and said, "See if you
can lure him into showing you the secret of his great strength and how we can
overpower him so we may tie him up and
subdue him. Each one of us will give you
eleven hundred shekels[e] of silver."
6 So Delilah said to Samson, "Tell me
the secret of your great strength and how
you can be tied up and subdued."

[a] 16 Or *made a heap or two*; the Hebrew for *donkey* sounds like the Hebrew for *heap*. [b] *17 Ramath Lehi* means *jawbone hill*. [c] *19 En Hakkore* means *caller's spring*. [d] *20* Traditionally *judged* [e] *5* That is, about 28 pounds or about 13 kilograms

7Samson answered her, "If anyone
ties me with seven fresh bowstrings that
have not been dried, I'll become as weak
as any other man."
8Then the rulers of the Philistines
brought her seven fresh bowstrings that
had not been dried, and she tied him with
them. 9With men hidden in the room, she
called to him, "Samson, the Philistines
are upon you!" But he snapped the bowstrings as easily as a piece of string snaps
when it comes close to a flame. So the secret of his strength was not discovered.
10Then Delilah said to Samson, "You
have made a fool of me; you lied to me.
Come now, tell me how you can be tied."
11He said, "If anyone ties me securely with new ropes that have never been
used, I'll become as weak as any other
man."
12So Delilah took new ropes and tied
him with them. Then, with men hidden
in the room, she called to him, "Samson, the Philistines are upon you!" But he
snapped the ropes off his arms as if they
were threads.
13Delilah then said to Samson, "All this
time you have been making a fool of me
and lying to me. Tell me how you can be
tied."

He replied, "If you weave the seven
braids of my head into the fabric on the
loom and tighten it with the pin, I'll become as weak as any other man." So while
he was sleeping, Delilah took the seven
braids of his head, wove them into the
fabric 14and[a] tightened it with the pin.

Again she called to him, "Samson, the
Philistines are upon you!" He awoke from
his sleep and pulled up the pin and the
loom, with the fabric.
15Then she said to him, "How can you
say, 'I love you,' when you won't confide
in me? This is the third time you have
made a fool of me and haven't told me
the secret of your great strength." 16With
such nagging she prodded him day after
day until he was sick to death of it.
17So he told her everything. "No razor
has ever been used on my head," he said,
"because I have been a Nazirite dedicated to God from my mother's womb. If my
head were shaved, my strength would
leave me, and I would become as weak as
any other man."
18When Delilah saw that he had told
her everything, she sent word to the rulers of the Philistines, "Come back once
more; he has told me everything." So the
rulers of the Philistines returned with the
silver in their hands. 19After putting him
to sleep on her lap, she called for someone to shave off the seven braids of his
hair, and so began to subdue him.[b] And
his strength left him.
20Then she called, "Samson, the Philistines are upon you!"

He awoke from his sleep and thought,
"I'll go out as before and shake myself
free." But he did not know that the LORD
had left him.
21Then the Philistines seized him,
gouged out his eyes and took him down
to Gaza. Binding him with bronze shackles, they set him to grinding grain in the
prison. 22But the hair on his head began
to grow again after it had been shaved.
23Now the rulers of the Philistines assembled to offer a great sacrifice to Dagon their god and to celebrate, saying,
"Our god has delivered Samson, our enemy, into our hands."
24When the people saw him, they
praised their god, saying,

"Our god has delivered our enemy
into our hands,
the one who laid waste our land
and multiplied our slain."

25While they were in high spirits, they
shouted, "Bring out Samson to entertain
us." So they called Samson out of the prison, and he performed for them.

When they stood him among the pillars, 26Samson said to the servant who
held his hand, "Put me where I can feel
the pillars that support the temple, so
that I may lean against them." 27Now the
temple was crowded with men and wom-
en; all the rulers of the Philistines were
there, and on the roof were about three
thousand men and women watching
Samson perform. 28Then Samson prayed
to the LORD, "Sovereign LORD, remember
me. Please, God, strengthen me just once
more, and let me with one blow get revenge on the Philistines for my two eyes."
29Then Samson reached toward the two
central pillars on which the temple stood.
Bracing himself against them, his right

[a] *13,14* Some Septuagint manuscripts; Hebrew *replied, "I can if you weave the seven braids of my head into the fabric on the loom." 14So she* [b] *19* Hebrew; some Septuagint manuscripts *and he began to weaken*

hand on the one and his left hand on the
other, 30Samson said, "Let me die with
the Philistines!" Then he pushed with all
his might, and down came the temple on
the rulers and all the people in it. Thus
he killed many more when he died than
while he lived.
31Then his brothers and his father's
whole family went down to get him.
They brought him back and buried him
between Zorah and Eshtaol in the tomb
of Manoah his father. He had led[a] Israel
twenty years.

17 Now a man named Micah from the
hill country of Ephraim 2said to his
mother, "The eleven hundred shekels[b] of
silver that were taken from you and about
which I heard you utter a curse—I have
that silver with me; I took it."
Then his mother said, "The LORD bless
you, my son!"
3When he returned the eleven hundred
shekels of silver to his mother, she said,
"I solemnly consecrate my silver to the
LORD for my son to make an image overlaid with silver. I will give it back to you."
4So after he returned the silver to his
mother, she took two hundred shekels[c]
of silver and gave them to a silversmith,
who used them to make the idol. And it
was put in Micah's house.
5Now this man Micah had a shrine,
and he made an ephod and some household gods and installed one of his sons
as his priest. 6In those days Israel had no
king; everyone did as they saw fit.
7A young Levite from Bethlehem in
Judah, who had been living within the
clan of Judah, 8left that town in search of
some other place to stay. On his way[d] he
came to Micah's house in the hill country
of Ephraim.
9Micah asked him, "Where are you
from?"
"I'm a Levite from Bethlehem in Judah," he said, "and I'm looking for a place
to stay."
10Then Micah said to him, "Live with
me and be my father and priest, and I'll
give you ten shekels[e] of silver a year, your
clothes and your food." 11So the Levite
agreed to live with him, and the young
man became like one of his sons to him.
12Then Micah installed the Levite, and
the young man became his priest and
lived in his house. 13And Micah said,
"Now I know that the LORD will be good
to me, since this Levite has become my
priest."

18 In those days Israel had no king.
And in those days the tribe of the
Danites was seeking a place of their own
where they might settle, because they had
not yet come into an inheritance among
the tribes of Israel. 2So the Danites sent
five of their leading men from Zorah and
Eshtaol to spy out the land and explore it.
These men represented all the Danites.
They told them, "Go, explore the land."
So they entered the hill country of
Ephraim and came to the house of Micah, where they spent the night. 3When
they were near Micah's house, they recognized the voice of the young Levite;
so they turned in there and asked him,
"Who brought you here? What are you
doing in this place? Why are you here?"
4He told them what Micah had done for
him, and said, "He has hired me and I am
his priest."
5Then they said to him, "Please inquire
of God to learn whether our journey will
be successful."
6The priest answered them, "Go in
peace. Your journey has the LORD's approval."
7So the five men left and came to Laish,
where they saw that the people were living in safety, like the Sidonians, at peace
and secure. And since their land lacked
nothing, they were prosperous.[f] Also,
they lived a long way from the Sidonians and had no relationship with anyone
else.[g]
8When they returned to Zorah and
Eshtaol, their fellow Danites asked them,
"How did you find things?"
9They answered, "Come on, let's attack
them! We have seen the land, and it is very
good. Aren't you going to do something?
Don't hesitate to go there and take it over.
10When you get there, you will find an
unsuspecting people and a spacious land
that God has put into your hands, a land
that lacks nothing whatever."

[a] *31* Traditionally *judged* [b] *2* That is, about 28 pounds or about 13 kilograms [c] *4* That is, about 5 pounds or about 2.3 kilograms [d] *8* Or *To carry on his profession* [e] *10* That is, about 4 ounces or about 115 grams [f] *7* The meaning of the Hebrew for this clause is uncertain. [g] *7* Hebrew; some Septuagint manuscripts *with the Arameans*

11 Then six hundred men of the Danites,
armed for battle, set out from Zorah and
Eshtaol. 12 On their way they set up camp
near Kiriath Jearim in Judah. This is why
the place west of Kiriath Jearim is called
Mahaneh Dan[a] to this day. 13 From there
they went on to the hill country of Ephraim and came to Micah's house.

14 Then the five men who had spied
out the land of Laish said to their fellow
Danites, "Do you know that one of these
houses has an ephod, some household
gods and an image overlaid with silver?
Now you know what to do." 15 So they
turned in there and went to the house
of the young Levite at Micah's place and
greeted him. 16 The six hundred Danites,
armed for battle, stood at the entrance of
the gate. 17 The five men who had spied
out the land went inside and took the
idol, the ephod and the household gods
while the priest and the six hundred
armed men stood at the entrance of the
gate.

18 When the five men went into Micah's
house and took the idol, the ephod and
the household gods, the priest said to
them, "What are you doing?"

19 They answered him, "Be quiet! Don't
say a word. Come with us, and be our
father and priest. Isn't it better that you
serve a tribe and clan in Israel as priest
rather than just one man's household?"
20 The priest was very pleased. He took
the ephod, the household gods and the
idol and went along with the people.
21 Putting their little children, their livestock and their possessions in front of
them, they turned away and left.

22 When they had gone some distance
from Micah's house, the men who lived
near Micah were called together and
overtook the Danites. 23 As they shouted
after them, the Danites turned and said
to Micah, "What's the matter with you
that you called out your men to fight?"

24 He replied, "You took the gods I made,
and my priest, and went away. What else
do I have? How can you ask, 'What's the
matter with you?' "

25 The Danites answered, "Don't argue with us, or some of the men may get
angry and attack you, and you and your
family will lose your lives." 26 So the Danites went their way, and Micah, seeing
that they were too strong for him, turned
around and went back home.

27 Then they took what Micah had
made, and his priest, and went on to Laish, against a people at peace and secure.
They attacked them with the sword and
burned down their city. 28 There was no
one to rescue them because they lived a
long way from Sidon and had no relationship with anyone else. The city was in a
valley near Beth Rehob.

The Danites rebuilt the city and settled
there. 29 They named it Dan after their
ancestor Dan, who was born to Israel—
though the city used to be called Laish.
30 There the Danites set up for themselves
the idol, and Jonathan son of Gershom,
the son of Moses,[b] and his sons were
priests for the tribe of Dan until the time
of the captivity of the land. 31 They continued to use the idol Micah had made, all
the time the house of God was in Shiloh.

19 In those days Israel had no king.
Now a Levite who lived in a remote
area in the hill country of Ephraim took
a concubine from Bethlehem in Judah.
2 But she was unfaithful to him. She left
him and went back to her parents' home
in Bethlehem, Judah. After she had been
there four months, 3 her husband went
to her to persuade her to return. He had
with him his servant and two donkeys.
She took him into her parents' home, and
when her father saw him, he gladly welcomed him. 4 His father-in-law, the woman's father, prevailed on him to stay; so
he remained with him three days, eating
and drinking, and sleeping there.

5 On the fourth day they got up early
and he prepared to leave, but the woman's father said to his son-in-law, "Refresh yourself with something to eat; then
you can go." 6 So the two of them sat down
to eat and drink together. Afterward the
woman's father said, "Please stay tonight
and enjoy yourself." 7 And when the man
got up to go, his father-in-law persuaded
him, so he stayed there that night. 8 On
the morning of the fifth day, when he rose
to go, the woman's father said, "Refresh
yourself. Wait till afternoon!" So the two
of them ate together.

9 Then when the man, with his concubine and his servant, got up to leave, his
father-in-law, the woman's father, said,

[a] 12 *Mahaneh Dan* means *Dan's camp.* [b] 30 Many Hebrew manuscripts, some Septuagint manuscripts and Vulgate; many other Hebrew manuscripts and some other Septuagint manuscripts *Manasseh*

"Now look, it's almost evening. Spend
the night here; the day is nearly over.
Stay and enjoy yourself. Early tomorrow
morning you can get up and be on your
way home." 10But, unwilling to stay another night, the man left and went toward
Jebus (that is, Jerusalem), with his two
saddled donkeys and his concubine.

11When they were near Jebus and the
day was almost gone, the servant said to
his master, "Come, let's stop at this city of
the Jebusites and spend the night."

12His master replied, "No. We won't go
into any city whose people are not Israelites. We will go on to Gibeah." 13He added, "Come, let's try to reach Gibeah or Ramah and spend the night in one of those
places." 14So they went on, and the sun
set as they neared Gibeah in Benjamin.
15There they stopped to spend the night.
They went and sat in the city square, but
no one took them in for the night.

16That evening an old man from the
hill country of Ephraim, who was living
in Gibeah (the inhabitants of the place
were Benjamites), came in from his work
in the fields. 17When he looked and saw
the traveler in the city square, the old
man asked, "Where are you going? Where
did you come from?"

18He answered, "We are on our way
from Bethlehem in Judah to a remote
area in the hill country of Ephraim where
I live. I have been to Bethlehem in Judah
and now I am going to the house of the
LORD.[a] No one has taken me in for the
night. 19We have both straw and fodder
for our donkeys and bread and wine for
ourselves your servants—me, the woman and the young man with us. We don't
need anything."

20"You are welcome at my house," the
old man said. "Let me supply whatever you need. Only don't spend the night
in the square." 21So he took him into his
house and fed his donkeys. After they had
washed their feet, they had something to
eat and drink.

22While they were enjoying themselves, some of the wicked men of the city
surrounded the house. Pounding on the
door, they shouted to the old man who
owned the house, "Bring out the man
who came to your house so we can have
sex with him."

23The owner of the house went outside
and said to them, "No, my friends, don't
be so vile. Since this man is my guest,
don't do this outrageous thing. 24Look,
here is my virgin daughter, and his concubine. I will bring them out to you now,
and you can use them and do to them
whatever you wish. But as for this man,
don't do such an outrageous thing."

25But the men would not listen to him.
So the man took his concubine and sent
her outside to them, and they raped her
and abused her throughout the night,
and at dawn they let her go. 26At daybreak
the woman went back to the house where
her master was staying, fell down at the
door and lay there until daylight.

27When her master got up in the morning and opened the door of the house and
stepped out to continue on his way, there
lay his concubine, fallen in the doorway of the house, with her hands on the
threshold. 28He said to her, "Get up; let's
go." But there was no answer. Then the
man put her on his donkey and set out
for home.

29When he reached home, he took a
knife and cut up his concubine, limb by
limb, into twelve parts and sent them into
all the areas of Israel. 30Everyone who
saw it was saying to one another, "Such
a thing has never been seen or done, not
since the day the Israelites came up out
of Egypt. Just imagine! We must do something! So speak up!"

20 Then all Israel from Dan to Beersheba and from the land of Gilead came
together as one and assembled before the
LORD in Mizpah. 2The leaders of all the
people of the tribes of Israel took their
places in the assembly of God's people,
four hundred thousand men armed with
swords. 3(The Benjamites heard that the
Israelites had gone up to Mizpah.) Then
the Israelites said, "Tell us how this awful
thing happened."

4So the Levite, the husband of the murdered woman, said, "I and my concubine
came to Gibeah in Benjamin to spend the
night. 5During the night the men of Gibeah came after me and surrounded the
house, intending to kill me. They raped
my concubine, and she died. 6I took my
concubine, cut her into pieces and sent
one piece to each region of Israel's inheri-

[a] *18* Hebrew, Vulgate, Syriac and Targum; Septuagint *going home*

tance, because they committed this lewd
and outrageous act in Israel. 7Now, all
you Israelites, speak up and tell me what
you have decided to do."
8All the men rose up together as one,
saying, "None of us will go home. No, not
one of us will return to his house. 9But
now this is what we'll do to Gibeah: We'll
go up against it in the order decided by
casting lots. 10We'll take ten men out of
every hundred from all the tribes of Israel, and a hundred from a thousand, and
a thousand from ten thousand, to get
provisions for the army. Then, when the
army arrives at Gibeah[a] in Benjamin, it
can give them what they deserve for this
outrageous act done in Israel." 11So all
the Israelites got together and united as
one against the city.
12The tribes of Israel sent messengers
throughout the tribe of Benjamin, saying, "What about this awful crime that
was committed among you? 13Now turn
those wicked men of Gibeah over to us so
that we may put them to death and purge
the evil from Israel."
But the Benjamites would not listen
to their fellow Israelites. 14From their
towns they came together at Gibeah to
fight against the Israelites. 15At once the
Benjamites mobilized twenty-six thousand swordsmen from their towns, in addition to seven hundred able young men
from those living in Gibeah. 16Among all
these soldiers there were seven hundred
select troops who were left-handed, each
of whom could sling a stone at a hair and
not miss.
17Israel, apart from Benjamin, mustered four hundred thousand swordsmen, all of them fit for battle.
18The Israelites went up to Bethel[b] and
inquired of God. They said, "Who of us is
to go up first to fight against the Benjamites?"
The LORD replied, "Judah shall go
first."
19The next morning the Israelites got
up and pitched camp near Gibeah. 20The
Israelites went out to fight the Benjamites
and took up battle positions against them
at Gibeah. 21The Benjamites came out of
Gibeah and cut down twenty-two thousand Israelites on the battlefield that
day. 22But the Israelites encouraged one
another and again took up their positions
where they had stationed themselves the
first day. 23The Israelites went up and
wept before the LORD until evening, and
they inquired of the LORD. They said,
"Shall we go up again to fight against the
Benjamites, our fellow Israelites?"
The LORD answered, "Go up against
them."
24Then the Israelites drew near to Benjamin the second day. 25This time, when
the Benjamites came out from Gibeah
to oppose them, they cut down another
eighteen thousand Israelites, all of them
armed with swords.
26Then all the Israelites, the whole
army, went up to Bethel, and there they
sat weeping before the LORD. They fasted that day until evening and presented
burnt offerings and fellowship offerings
to the LORD. 27And the Israelites inquired
of the LORD. (In those days the ark of the
covenant of God was there, 28with Phinehas son of Eleazar, the son of Aaron,
ministering before it.) They asked, "Shall
we go up again to fight against the Benjamites, our fellow Israelites, or not?"
The LORD responded, "Go, for tomorrow I will give them into your hands."
29Then Israel set an ambush around
Gibeah. 30They went up against the Benjamites on the third day and took up positions against Gibeah as they had done before. 31The Benjamites came out to meet
them and were drawn away from the city.
They began to inflict casualties on the
Israelites as before, so that about thirty men fell in the open field and on the
roads — the one leading to Bethel and the
other to Gibeah. 32While the Benjamites
were saying, "We are defeating them as
before," the Israelites were saying, "Let's
retreat and draw them away from the city
to the roads."
33All the men of Israel moved from
their places and took up positions at
Baal Tamar, and the Israelite ambush
charged out of its place on the west[c] of
Gibeah.[d] 34Then ten thousand of Israel's
able young men made a frontal attack on
Gibeah. The fighting was so heavy that
the Benjamites did not realize how near
disaster was. 35The LORD defeated Ben-

[a] *10* One Hebrew manuscript; most Hebrew manuscripts *Geba,* a variant of *Gibeah* [b] *18* Or *to the house of God*; also in verse 26 [c] *33* Some Septuagint manuscripts and Vulgate; the meaning of the Hebrew for this word is uncertain. [d] *33* Hebrew *Geba,* a variant of *Gibeah*

jamin before Israel, and on that day the
Israelites struck down 25,100 Benjamites,
all armed with swords. 36Then the Benjamites saw that they were beaten.

Now the men of Israel had given way
before Benjamin, because they relied on
the ambush they had set near Gibeah.
37Those who had been in ambush made
a sudden dash into Gibeah, spread out
and put the whole city to the sword. 38The
Israelites had arranged with the ambush
that they should send up a great cloud of
smoke from the city, 39and then the Israelites would counterattack.

The Benjamites had begun to inflict
casualties on the Israelites (about thirty),
and they said, "We are defeating them as
in the first battle." 40But when the column of smoke began to rise from the city,
the Benjamites turned and saw the whole
city going up in smoke. 41Then the Israelites counterattacked, and the Benjamites
were terrified, because they realized that
disaster had come on them. 42So they fled
before the Israelites in the direction of the
wilderness, but they could not escape the
battle. And the Israelites who came out of
the towns cut them down there. 43They
surrounded the Benjamites, chased them
and easily[a] overran them in the vicinity
of Gibeah on the east. 44Eighteen thousand Benjamites fell, all of them valiant
fighters. 45As they turned and fled toward
the wilderness to the rock of Rimmon, the
Israelites cut down five thousand men
along the roads. They kept pressing after the Benjamites as far as Gidom and
struck down two thousand more.

46On that day twenty-five thousand
Benjamite swordsmen fell, all of them
valiant fighters. 47But six hundred of
them turned and fled into the wilderness
to the rock of Rimmon, where they stayed
four months. 48The men of Israel went
back to Benjamin and put all the towns
to the sword, including the animals and
everything else they found. All the towns
they came across they set on fire.

21 The men of Israel had taken an oath
at Mizpah: "Not one of us will give
his daughter in marriage to a Benjamite."

2The people went to Bethel,[b] where
they sat before God until evening, raising
their voices and weeping bitterly. 3"LORD,
God of Israel," they cried, "why has this
happened to Israel? Why should one tribe
be missing from Israel today?"

4Early the next day the people built an
altar and presented burnt offerings and
fellowship offerings.

5Then the Israelites asked, "Who from
all the tribes of Israel has failed to assemble before the LORD?" For they had taken
a solemn oath that anyone who failed to
assemble before the LORD at Mizpah was
to be put to death.

6Now the Israelites grieved for the tribe
of Benjamin, their fellow Israelites. "Today one tribe is cut off from Israel," they
said. 7"How can we provide wives for
those who are left, since we have taken an
oath by the LORD not to give them any of
our daughters in marriage?" 8Then they
asked, "Which one of the tribes of Israel failed to assemble before the LORD at
Mizpah?" They discovered that no one
from Jabesh Gilead had come to the camp
for the assembly. 9For when they counted the people, they found that none of the
people of Jabesh Gilead were there.

10So the assembly sent twelve thousand fighting men with instructions to
go to Jabesh Gilead and put to the sword
those living there, including the women
and children. 11"This is what you are to
do," they said. "Kill every male and every woman who is not a virgin." 12They
found among the people living in Jabesh
Gilead four hundred young women who
had never slept with a man, and they took
them to the camp at Shiloh in Canaan.

13Then the whole assembly sent an offer of peace to the Benjamites at the rock
of Rimmon. 14So the Benjamites returned
at that time and were given the women of
Jabesh Gilead who had been spared. But
there were not enough for all of them.

15The people grieved for Benjamin,
because the LORD had made a gap in the
tribes of Israel. 16And the elders of the
assembly said, "With the women of Benjamin destroyed, how shall we provide
wives for the men who are left? 17The
Benjamite survivors must have heirs,"
they said, "so that a tribe of Israel will not
be wiped out. 18We can't give them our
daughters as wives, since we Israelites
have taken this oath: 'Cursed be anyone
who gives a wife to a Benjamite.' 19But
look, there is the annual festival of the

[a] *43* The meaning of the Hebrew for this word is uncertain. [b] *2* Or *to the house of God*

LORD in Shiloh, which lies north of Bethel, east of the road that goes from Bethel to Shechem, and south of Lebonah."
20So they instructed the Benjamites,
saying, "Go and hide in the vineyards
21and watch. When the young women of
Shiloh come out to join in the dancing, rush from the vineyards and each of you seize one of them to be your wife. Then return to the land of Benjamin.
22When their fathers or brothers complain to us, we will say to them, 'Do us the favor of helping them, because we did not get wives for them during the war. You will not be guilty of breaking your oath because you did not give your daughters to them.'"
23So that is what the Benjamites did. While the young women were dancing, each man caught one and carried her off to be his wife. Then they returned to their inheritance and rebuilt the towns and settled in them.
24At that time the Israelites left that place and went home to their tribes and clans, each to his own inheritance.
25In those days Israel had no king; everyone did as they saw fit.

RUTH

The short book of Ruth is a bridge between the two major parts of Israel's covenant history. The first part (Genesis–Judges) focuses on how Abraham's descendants became a nation and on the covenant God made with Israel. The second part (Samuel–Kings) tells the story of the nation's kings and the covenant God made with David as the head of Israel's royal line. Ruth helps the transition by opening in the days of the judges and ending with the genealogy of David.

The book appears to have been written to defend David's right to be king. He was the great-grandson of a Moabite named Ruth. Because the people of Moab didn't help the Israelites when they came out of Egypt, the law didn't permit any descendant of a Moabite to join Israel, down to the tenth generation. If they couldn't even join the community, how could one of them serve as king?

The book sets up a drama or stage play in ten scenes. Each scene features a short introduction and then dialogue between the characters. The book ends with a ten-generation genealogy leading up to David. So the form of the book mirrors its purpose, which is to show that genuine faith was present in a woman from a nation whose descendants were normally excluded for ten generations.

The book also shows how God's purposes are accomplished in the world. God's good laws (allowing the poor to collect grain in the fields), his providence over events, and the personal kindness of people all combine to help the story find a redemptive conclusion.

---

1 In the days when the judges ruled,[a]
there was a famine in the land. So a man from Bethlehem in Judah, together with his wife and two sons, went to live for a while in the country of Moab.
2The man's name was Elimelek, his wife's name was Naomi, and the names of his two sons were Mahlon and Kilion. They were Ephrathites from Bethlehem, Judah. And they went to Moab and lived there.
3Now Elimelek, Naomi's husband, died, and she was left with her two sons.
4They married Moabite women, one named Orpah and the other Ruth. After they had lived there about ten years,
5both Mahlon and Kilion also died, and Naomi was left without her two sons and her husband.
6When Naomi heard in Moab that the LORD had come to the aid of his people by providing food for them, she and her daughters-in-law prepared to return

[a] *1* Traditionally *judged*

home from there. 7With her two daughters-in-law she left the place where she
had been living and set out on the road
that would take them back to the land of
Judah.
8Then Naomi said to her two daughters-in-law, "Go back, each of you, to your
mother's home. May the LORD show you
kindness, as you have shown kindness to
your dead husbands and to me. 9May the
LORD grant that each of you will find rest
in the home of another husband."
Then she kissed them goodbye and
they wept aloud 10and said to her, "We
will go back with you to your people."
11But Naomi said, "Return home, my
daughters. Why would you come with
me? Am I going to have any more sons,
who could become your husbands? 12Re-
turn home, my daughters; I am too old to
have another husband. Even if I thought
there was still hope for me — even if I had
a husband tonight and then gave birth to
sons — 13would you wait until they grew
up? Would you remain unmarried for
them? No, my daughters. It is more bitter
for me than for you, because the LORD's
hand has turned against me!"
14At this they wept aloud again. Then
Orpah kissed her mother-in-law goodbye, but Ruth clung to her.
15"Look," said Naomi, "your sister-in-
law is going back to her people and her
gods. Go back with her."
16But Ruth replied, "Don't urge me to
leave you or to turn back from you. Where
you go I will go, and where you stay I will
stay. Your people will be my people and
your God my God. 17Where you die I will
die, and there I will be buried. May the
LORD deal with me, be it ever so severely, if even death separates you and me."
18When Naomi realized that Ruth was
determined to go with her, she stopped
urging her.
19So the two women went on until
they came to Bethlehem. When they arrived in Bethlehem, the whole town was
stirred because of them, and the women
exclaimed, "Can this be Naomi?"
20"Don't call me Naomi,[a]" she told
them. "Call me Mara,[b] because the Almighty[c] has made my life very bitter. 21I
went away full, but the LORD has brought
me back empty. Why call me Naomi? The
LORD has afflicted[d] me; the Almighty has
brought misfortune upon me."
22So Naomi returned from Moab accompanied by Ruth the Moabite, her
daughter-in-law, arriving in Bethlehem
as the barley harvest was beginning.
2 Now Naomi had a relative on her husband's side, a man of standing from the
clan of Elimelek, whose name was Boaz.
2And Ruth the Moabite said to Naomi,
"Let me go to the fields and pick up the
leftover grain behind anyone in whose
eyes I find favor."
Naomi said to her, "Go ahead, my
daughter." 3So she went out, entered a
field and began to glean behind the harvesters. As it turned out, she was working in a field belonging to Boaz, who was
from the clan of Elimelek.
4Just then Boaz arrived from Bethlehem and greeted the harvesters, "The
LORD be with you!"
"The LORD bless you!" they answered.
5Boaz asked the overseer of his harvesters, "Who does that young woman
belong to?"
6The overseer replied, "She is the Moabite who came back from Moab with Naomi. 7She said, 'Please let me glean and
gather among the sheaves behind the
harvesters.' She came into the field and
has remained here from morning till now,
except for a short rest in the shelter."
8So Boaz said to Ruth, "My daughter,
listen to me. Don't go and glean in another field and don't go away from here. Stay
here with the women who work for me.
9Watch the field where the men are harvesting, and follow along after the wom-
en. I have told the men not to lay a hand
on you. And whenever you are thirsty, go
and get a drink from the water jars the
men have filled."
10At this, she bowed down with her face
to the ground. She asked him, "Why have
I found such favor in your eyes that you
notice me — a foreigner?"
11Boaz replied, "I've been told all about
what you have done for your mother-in-
law since the death of your husband —
how you left your father and mother and
your homeland and came to live with a
people you did not know before. 12May
the LORD repay you for what you have
done. May you be richly rewarded by

[a] 20 *Naomi* means *pleasant.* [b] 20 *Mara* means *bitter.* [c] 20 Hebrew *Shaddai*; also in verse 21
[d] 21 Or *has testified against*

the LORD, the God of Israel, under whose
wings you have come to take refuge."
13 "May I continue to find favor in your
eyes, my lord," she said. "You have put me
at ease by speaking kindly to your servant — though I do not have the standing
of one of your servants."
14 At mealtime Boaz said to her, "Come
over here. Have some bread and dip it in
the wine vinegar."
When she sat down with the harvesters, he offered her some roasted grain.
She ate all she wanted and had some left
over. 15 As she got up to glean, Boaz gave
orders to his men, "Let her gather among
the sheaves and don't reprimand her.
16 Even pull out some stalks for her from
the bundles and leave them for her to pick
up, and don't rebuke her."
17 So Ruth gleaned in the field until evening. Then she threshed the barley she
had gathered, and it amounted to about
an ephah.[a] 18 She carried it back to town,
and her mother-in-law saw how much
she had gathered. Ruth also brought out
and gave her what she had left over after
she had eaten enough.
19 Her mother-in-law asked her, "Where
did you glean today? Where did you
work? Blessed be the man who took notice of you!"
Then Ruth told her mother-in-law
about the one at whose place she had
been working. "The name of the man I
worked with today is Boaz," she said.
20 "The LORD bless him!" Naomi said to
her daughter-in-law. "He has not stopped
showing his kindness to the living and
the dead." She added, "That man is our
close relative; he is one of our guardian-
redeemers.[b]"
21 Then Ruth the Moabite said, "He even
said to me, 'Stay with my workers until
they finish harvesting all my grain.'"
22 Naomi said to Ruth her daughter-in-
law, "It will be good for you, my daughter, to go with the women who work for
him, because in someone else's field you
might be harmed."
23 So Ruth stayed close to the women of
Boaz to glean until the barley and wheat
harvests were finished. And she lived
with her mother-in-law.

3 One day Ruth's mother-in-law Naomi
said to her, "My daughter, I must find a
home[c] for you, where you will be well provided for. 2 Now Boaz, with whose women
you have worked, is a relative of ours. Tonight he will be winnowing barley on the
threshing floor. 3 Wash, put on perfume,
and get dressed in your best clothes.
Then go down to the threshing floor, but
don't let him know you are there until he
has finished eating and drinking. 4 When
he lies down, note the place where he is
lying. Then go and uncover his feet and
lie down. He will tell you what to do."
5 "I will do whatever you say," Ruth answered. 6 So she went down to the threshing floor and did everything her mother-
in-law told her to do.
7 When Boaz had finished eating and
drinking and was in good spirits, he went
over to lie down at the far end of the grain
pile. Ruth approached quietly, uncovered
his feet and lay down. 8 In the middle of
the night something startled the man; he
turned — and there was a woman lying at
his feet!
9 "Who are you?" he asked.
"I am your servant Ruth," she said.
"Spread the corner of your garment over
me, since you are a guardian-redeemer[d]
of our family."
10 "The LORD bless you, my daughter,"
he replied. "This kindness is greater than
that which you showed earlier: You have
not run after the younger men, whether
rich or poor. 11 And now, my daughter,
don't be afraid. I will do for you all you
ask. All the people of my town know that
you are a woman of noble character. 12 Although it is true that I am a guardian-redeemer of our family, there is another
who is more closely related than I. 13 Stay
here for the night, and in the morning if
he wants to do his duty as your guardian-
redeemer, good; let him redeem you. But
if he is not willing, as surely as the LORD
lives I will do it. Lie here until morning."
14 So she lay at his feet until morning, but
got up before anyone could be recognized;
and he said, "No one must know that a
woman came to the threshing floor."
15 He also said, "Bring me the shawl
you are wearing and hold it out." When

[a] *17* That is, probably about 30 pounds or about 13 kilograms [b] *20* The Hebrew word for *guardian-redeemer* is a legal term for one who has the obligation to redeem a relative in serious difficulty (see Lev. 25:25-55).
[c] *1* Hebrew *find rest* (see 1:9) [d] *9* The Hebrew word for *guardian-redeemer* is a legal term for one who has the obligation to redeem a relative in serious difficulty (see Lev. 25:25-55); also in verses 12 and 13.

she did so, he poured into it six measures
of barley and placed the bundle on her.
Then he[a] went back to town.
16 When Ruth came to her mother-in-
law, Naomi asked, "How did it go, my
daughter?"
Then she told her everything Boaz
had done for her 17 and added, "He gave
me these six measures of barley, saying,
'Don't go back to your mother-in-law
empty-handed.'"
18 Then Naomi said, "Wait, my daughter, until you find out what happens. For
the man will not rest until the matter is
settled today."

4 Meanwhile Boaz went up to the town
gate and sat down there just as the
guardian-redeemer[b] he had mentioned
came along. Boaz said, "Come over here,
my friend, and sit down." So he went over
and sat down.
2 Boaz took ten of the elders of the town
and said, "Sit here," and they did so. 3 Then
he said to the guardian-redeemer, "Naomi, who has come back from Moab, is
selling the piece of land that belonged to
our relative Elimelek. 4 I thought I should
bring the matter to your attention and
suggest that you buy it in the presence of
these seated here and in the presence of
the elders of my people. If you will redeem
it, do so. But if you[c] will not, tell me, so I
will know. For no one has the right to do it
except you, and I am next in line."
"I will redeem it," he said.
5 Then Boaz said, "On the day you buy
the land from Naomi, you also acquire
Ruth the Moabite, the[d] dead man's widow, in order to maintain the name of the
dead with his property."
6 At this, the guardian-redeemer said,
"Then I cannot redeem it because I might
endanger my own estate. You redeem it
yourself. I cannot do it."
7 (Now in earlier times in Israel, for
the redemption and transfer of property to become final, one party took off his
sandal and gave it to the other. This was
the method of legalizing transactions in
Israel.)
8 So the guardian-redeemer said to
Boaz, "Buy it yourself." And he removed
his sandal.
9 Then Boaz announced to the elders
and all the people, "Today you are witnesses that I have bought from Naomi
all the property of Elimelek, Kilion and
Mahlon. 10 I have also acquired Ruth the
Moabite, Mahlon's widow, as my wife, in
order to maintain the name of the dead
with his property, so that his name will
not disappear from among his family or
from his hometown. Today you are witnesses!"
11 Then the elders and all the people at
the gate said, "We are witnesses. May the
LORD make the woman who is coming
into your home like Rachel and Leah, who
together built up the family of Israel. May
you have standing in Ephrathah and be
famous in Bethlehem. 12 Through the offspring the LORD gives you by this young
woman, may your family be like that of
Perez, whom Tamar bore to Judah."
13 So Boaz took Ruth and she became
his wife. When he made love to her, the
LORD enabled her to conceive, and she
gave birth to a son. 14 The women said
to Naomi: "Praise be to the LORD, who
this day has not left you without a guardian-redeemer. May he become famous
throughout Israel! 15 He will renew your
life and sustain you in your old age. For
your daughter-in-law, who loves you and
who is better to you than seven sons, has
given him birth."
16 Then Naomi took the child in her
arms and cared for him. 17 The women
living there said, "Naomi has a son!" And
they named him Obed. He was the father
of Jesse, the father of David.

18 This, then, is the family line of Perez:

Perez was the father of Hezron,
19 Hezron the father of Ram,
Ram the father of Amminadab,
20 Amminadab the father of Nahshon,
Nahshon the father of Salmon,[e]
21 Salmon the father of Boaz,
Boaz the father of Obed,
22 Obed the father of Jesse,
and Jesse the father of David.

[a] *15* Most Hebrew manuscripts; many Hebrew manuscripts, Vulgate and Syriac *she* [b] *1* The Hebrew word for *guardian-redeemer* is a legal term for one who has the obligation to redeem a relative in serious difficulty (see Lev. 25:25-55); also in verses 3, 6, 8 and 14. [c] *4* Many Hebrew manuscripts, Septuagint, Vulgate and Syriac; most Hebrew manuscripts *he* [d] *5* Vulgate and Syriac; Hebrew (see also Septuagint) *Naomi and from Ruth the Moabite, you acquire the* [e] *20* A few Hebrew manuscripts, some Septuagint manuscripts and Vulgate (see also verse 21 and Septuagint of 1 Chron. 2:11); most Hebrew manuscripts *Salma*

1 SAMUEL

The books commonly known as 1 & 2 Samuel and 1 & 2 Kings are really one long book. (They were separated due to the length of ancient scrolls.) Beginning with Samuel, the last of the judges, this book describes what happened in the days of the kings who ruled first the whole nation, and then the divided kingdoms of Israel and Judah. The reigns of Saul and David are described in detail. The repeating structure within the book tells how old a king was when he came to the throne, where and for how long he ruled, and something about his character and the notable events of his reign. (Some traditions call this book the "Book of Reigns.")

Beneath this pattern of historical succession, however, another rhythm can be discerned. Saul, the first king, does not follow God faithfully, and God announces he will seek a man after his own heart to rule Israel. God finds this person in David. He puts him on the throne, promising that his descendants will always rule Israel if they continue to serve him. Unfortunately, the kings after David are not committed to following God's way. Many of them abandon God and lead the people to do the same, although a few of them call the people back to obedience. Using David's wholehearted dedication to the LORD as its standard, the book of Samuel-Kings traces the tragic wavering of the people's devotion to God. Their covenant failure leads to the nation first being divided and then later conquered by the powerful empires to the east.

The "Book of Reigns" is therefore a tragic closing of the whole covenant history that began in Genesis. Just as the first humans were exiled from God's garden, now Israel is sent out of the "new Eden" God intended in the promised land. Land and temple have been lost in the darkness of judgment, and only a flickering light remains. The deeper purpose of God for Israel—to bring blessing and restoration to the nations—seems to have been frustrated. But hope remains alive in God's promise to bring a descendant of David back to the throne.

---

1 There was a certain man from Ramathaim, a Zuphite[a] from the hill country of Ephraim, whose name was Elkanah
son of Jeroham, the son of Elihu, the son
of Tohu, the son of Zuph, an Ephraimite.
2 He had two wives; one was called Hannah and the other Peninnah. Peninnah
had children, but Hannah had none.
3 Year after year this man went up from
his town to worship and sacrifice to the
LORD Almighty at Shiloh, where Hophni
and Phinehas, the two sons of Eli, were
priests of the LORD. 4 Whenever the day
came for Elkanah to sacrifice, he would
give portions of the meat to his wife Peninnah and to all her sons and daughters.
5 But to Hannah he gave a double portion
because he loved her, and the LORD had
closed her womb. 6 Because the LORD
had closed Hannah's womb, her rival
kept provoking her in order to irritate
her. 7 This went on year after year. Whenever Hannah went up to the house of the
LORD, her rival provoked her till she wept
and would not eat. 8 Her husband Elkanah would say to her, "Hannah, why are
you weeping? Why don't you eat? Why are
you downhearted? Don't I mean more to
you than ten sons?"
9 Once when they had finished eating
and drinking in Shiloh, Hannah stood up.
Now Eli the priest was sitting on his chair
by the doorpost of the LORD's house. 10 In
her deep anguish Hannah prayed to the
LORD, weeping bitterly. 11 And she made
a vow, saying, "LORD Almighty, if you will
only look on your servant's misery and remember me, and not forget your servant
but give her a son, then I will give him to
the LORD for all the days of his life, and no
razor will ever be used on his head."
12 As she kept on praying to the LORD,
Eli observed her mouth. 13 Hannah was
praying in her heart, and her lips were
moving but her voice was not heard. Eli
thought she was drunk 14 and said to her,
"How long are you going to stay drunk?
Put away your wine."
15 "Not so, my lord," Hannah replied,
"I am a woman who is deeply troubled.
I have not been drinking wine or beer;
I was pouring out my soul to the LORD.
16 Do not take your servant for a wicked

[a] *1* See Septuagint and 1 Chron. 6:26-27,33-35; or *from Ramathaim Zuphim.*

woman; I have been praying here out of
my great anguish and grief."
17 Eli answered, "Go in peace, and may
the God of Israel grant you what you have
asked of him."
18 She said, "May your servant find favor in your eyes." Then she went her way
and ate something, and her face was no
longer downcast.
19 Early the next morning they arose
and worshiped before the LORD and then
went back to their home at Ramah. Elkanah made love to his wife Hannah, and
the LORD remembered her. 20 So in the
course of time Hannah became pregnant
and gave birth to a son. She named him
Samuel,[a] saying, "Because I asked the
LORD for him."
21 When her husband Elkanah went up
with all his family to offer the annual sacrifice to the LORD and to fulfill his vow,
22 Hannah did not go. She said to her husband, "After the boy is weaned, I will take
him and present him before the LORD,
and he will live there always."[b]
23 "Do what seems best to you," her
husband Elkanah told her. "Stay here
until you have weaned him; only may
the LORD make good his[c] word." So the
woman stayed at home and nursed her
son until she had weaned him.
24 After he was weaned, she took the
boy with her, young as he was, along with
a three-year-old bull,[d] an ephah[e] of flour
and a skin of wine, and brought him to
the house of the LORD at Shiloh. 25 When
the bull had been sacrificed, they brought
the boy to Eli, 26 and she said to him, "Pardon me, my lord. As surely as you live, I
am the woman who stood here beside
you praying to the LORD. 27 I prayed for
this child, and the LORD has granted me
what I asked of him. 28 So now I give him
to the LORD. For his whole life he will
be given over to the LORD." And he worshiped the LORD there.

2 Then Hannah prayed and said:

"My heart rejoices in the LORD;
in the LORD my horn[f] is lifted high.
My mouth boasts over my enemies,
for I delight in your deliverance.
2 "There is no one holy like the LORD;
there is no one besides you;
there is no Rock like our God.

3 "Do not keep talking so proudly
or let your mouth speak such
arrogance,
for the LORD is a God who knows,
and by him deeds are weighed.

4 "The bows of the warriors are broken,
but those who stumbled are armed
with strength.
5 Those who were full hire themselves
out for food,
but those who were hungry are
hungry no more.
She who was barren has borne seven
children,
but she who has had many sons
pines away.

6 "The LORD brings death and makes
alive;
he brings down to the grave and
raises up.
7 The LORD sends poverty and wealth;
he humbles and he exalts.
8 He raises the poor from the dust
and lifts the needy from the ash heap;
he seats them with princes
and has them inherit a throne of
honor.

"For the foundations of the earth are
the LORD's;
on them he has set the world.
9 He will guard the feet of his faithful
servants,
but the wicked will be silenced in
the place of darkness.

"It is not by strength that one prevails;
10 those who oppose the LORD will be
broken.
The Most High will thunder from
heaven;
the LORD will judge the ends of the
earth.

"He will give strength to his king
and exalt the horn of his anointed."

11 Then Elkanah went home to Ramah,
but the boy ministered before the LORD
under Eli the priest.

[a] 20 *Samuel* sounds like the Hebrew for *heard by God.* [b] 22 Masoretic Text; Dead Sea Scrolls *always. I have dedicated him as a Nazirite—all the days of his life."* [c] 23 Masoretic Text; Dead Sea Scrolls, Septuagint and Syriac *your* [d] 24 Dead Sea Scrolls, Septuagint and Syriac; Masoretic Text *with three bulls* [e] 24 That is, probably about 36 pounds or about 16 kilograms [f] 1 *Horn* here symbolizes strength; also in verse 10.

12 Eli's sons were scoundrels; they had
no regard for the LORD. 13 Now it was
the practice of the priests that, whenever any of the people offered a sacrifice,
the priest's servant would come with a
three-pronged fork in his hand while
the meat was being boiled 14 and would
plunge the fork into the pan or kettle or
caldron or pot. Whatever the fork brought
up the priest would take for himself. This
is how they treated all the Israelites who
came to Shiloh. 15 But even before the fat
was burned, the priest's servant would
come and say to the person who was sacrificing, "Give the priest some meat to
roast; he won't accept boiled meat from
you, but only raw."
16 If the person said to him, "Let the fat
be burned first, and then take whatever
you want," the servant would answer,
"No, hand it over now; if you don't, I'll
take it by force."
17 This sin of the young men was very
great in the LORD's sight, for they[a] were
treating the LORD's offering with contempt.
18 But Samuel was ministering before
the LORD—a boy wearing a linen ephod.
19 Each year his mother made him a little
robe and took it to him when she went
up with her husband to offer the annual
sacrifice. 20 Eli would bless Elkanah and
his wife, saying, "May the LORD give you
children by this woman to take the place
of the one she prayed for and gave to[b] the
LORD." Then they would go home. 21 And
the LORD was gracious to Hannah; she
gave birth to three sons and two daughters. Meanwhile, the boy Samuel grew up
in the presence of the LORD.
22 Now Eli, who was very old, heard
about everything his sons were doing
to all Israel and how they slept with the
women who served at the entrance to
the tent of meeting. 23 So he said to them,
"Why do you do such things? I hear from
all the people about these wicked deeds
of yours. 24 No, my sons; the report I hear
spreading among the LORD's people is not
good. 25 If one person sins against another, God[c] may mediate for the offender; but
if anyone sins against the LORD, who will
intercede for them?" His sons, however,
did not listen to their father's rebuke, for it
was the LORD's will to put them to death.
26 And the boy Samuel continued to
grow in stature and in favor with the
LORD and with people.
27 Now a man of God came to Eli and
said to him, "This is what the LORD says:
'Did I not clearly reveal myself to your ancestor's family when they were in Egypt
under Pharaoh? 28 I chose your ancestor out of all the tribes of Israel to be my
priest, to go up to my altar, to burn incense, and to wear an ephod in my presence. I also gave your ancestor's family
all the food offerings presented by the
Israelites. 29 Why do you[d] scorn my sacrifice and offering that I prescribed for my
dwelling? Why do you honor your sons
more than me by fattening yourselves on
the choice parts of every offering made by
my people Israel?'
30 "Therefore the LORD, the God of Israel, declares: 'I promised that members
of your family would minister before me
forever.' But now the LORD declares: 'Far
be it from me! Those who honor me I will
honor, but those who despise me will be
disdained. 31 The time is coming when
I will cut short your strength and the
strength of your priestly house, so that no
one in it will reach old age, 32 and you will
see distress in my dwelling. Although
good will be done to Israel, no one in your
family line will ever reach old age. 33 Every one of you that I do not cut off from
serving at my altar I will spare only to
destroy your sight and sap your strength,
and all your descendants will die in the
prime of life.
34 "'And what happens to your two
sons, Hophni and Phinehas, will be a sign
to you—they will both die on the same
day. 35 I will raise up for myself a faithful
priest, who will do according to what is
in my heart and mind. I will firmly establish his priestly house, and they will
minister before my anointed one always.
36 Then everyone left in your family line
will come and bow down before him for
a piece of silver and a loaf of bread and
plead, "Appoint me to some priestly office
so I can have food to eat."'"

3 The boy Samuel ministered before
the LORD under Eli. In those days the
word of the LORD was rare; there were not
many visions.
2 One night Eli, whose eyes were be-

[a] *17* Dead Sea Scrolls and Septuagint; Masoretic Text *people* [b] *20* Dead Sea Scrolls; Masoretic Text *and asked from* [c] *25* Or *the judges* [d] *29* The Hebrew is plural.

coming so weak that he could barely
see, was lying down in his usual place.
3 The lamp of God had not yet gone out,
and Samuel was lying down in the house
of the LORD, where the ark of God was.
4 Then the LORD called Samuel.

Samuel answered, "Here I am." 5 And
he ran to Eli and said, "Here I am; you
called me."

But Eli said, "I did not call; go back and
lie down." So he went and lay down.

6 Again the LORD called, "Samuel!" And
Samuel got up and went to Eli and said,
"Here I am; you called me."

"My son," Eli said, "I did not call; go
back and lie down."

7 Now Samuel did not yet know the
LORD: The word of the LORD had not yet
been revealed to him.

8 A third time the LORD called, "Samuel!" And Samuel got up and went to Eli
and said, "Here I am; you called me."

Then Eli realized that the LORD was
calling the boy. 9 So Eli told Samuel, "Go
and lie down, and if he calls you, say,
'Speak, LORD, for your servant is listening.'" So Samuel went and lay down in
his place.

10 The LORD came and stood there,
calling as at the other times, "Samuel!
Samuel!"

Then Samuel said, "Speak, for your servant is listening."

11 And the LORD said to Samuel: "See, I
am about to do something in Israel that
will make the ears of everyone who hears
about it tingle. 12 At that time I will carry
out against Eli everything I spoke against
his family—from beginning to end. 13 For
I told him that I would judge his family
forever because of the sin he knew about;
his sons blasphemed God,[a] and he failed
to restrain them. 14 Therefore I swore to
the house of Eli, 'The guilt of Eli's house
will never be atoned for by sacrifice or offering.'"

15 Samuel lay down until morning and
then opened the doors of the house of the
LORD. He was afraid to tell Eli the vision,
16 but Eli called him and said, "Samuel,
my son."

Samuel answered, "Here I am."

17 "What was it he said to you?" Eli
asked. "Do not hide it from me. May God
deal with you, be it ever so severely, if
you hide from me anything he told you."
18 So Samuel told him everything, hiding
nothing from him. Then Eli said, "He is
the LORD; let him do what is good in his
eyes."

19 The LORD was with Samuel as he
grew up, and he let none of Samuel's
words fall to the ground. 20 And all Israel
from Dan to Beersheba recognized that
Samuel was attested as a prophet of the
LORD. 21 The LORD continued to appear at
Shiloh, and there he revealed himself to
Samuel through his word.

4 And Samuel's word came to all Israel.
Now the Israelites went out to fight
against the Philistines. The Israelites
camped at Ebenezer, and the Philistines
at Aphek. 2 The Philistines deployed their
forces to meet Israel, and as the battle
spread, Israel was defeated by the Philistines, who killed about four thousand of
them on the battlefield. 3 When the soldiers returned to camp, the elders of Israel asked, "Why did the LORD bring defeat
on us today before the Philistines? Let us
bring the ark of the LORD's covenant from
Shiloh, so that he may go with us and save
us from the hand of our enemies."

4 So the people sent men to Shiloh, and
they brought back the ark of the covenant
of the LORD Almighty, who is enthroned
between the cherubim. And Eli's two
sons, Hophni and Phinehas, were there
with the ark of the covenant of God.

5 When the ark of the LORD's covenant
came into the camp, all Israel raised
such a great shout that the ground shook.
6 Hearing the uproar, the Philistines
asked, "What's all this shouting in the
Hebrew camp?"

When they learned that the ark of the
LORD had come into the camp, 7 the Philistines were afraid. "A god has[b] come
into the camp," they said. "Oh no! Nothing like this has happened before. 8 We're
doomed! Who will deliver us from the
hand of these mighty gods? They are the
gods who struck the Egyptians with all
kinds of plagues in the wilderness. 9 Be
strong, Philistines! Be men, or you will
be subject to the Hebrews, as they have
been to you. Be men, and fight!"

10 So the Philistines fought, and the Israelites were defeated and every man fled
to his tent. The slaughter was very great;

[a] *13* An ancient Hebrew scribal tradition (see also Septuagint); Masoretic Text *sons made themselves contemptible* [b] *7* Or *"Gods have* (see Septuagint)

Israel lost thirty thousand foot soldiers.
11 The ark of God was captured, and Eli's
two sons, Hophni and Phinehas, died.
12 That same day a Benjamite ran from
the battle line and went to Shiloh with
his clothes torn and dust on his head.
13 When he arrived, there was Eli sitting on his chair by the side of the road,
watching, because his heart feared for
the ark of God. When the man entered
the town and told what had happened,
the whole town sent up a cry.
14 Eli heard the outcry and asked, "What
is the meaning of this uproar?"
The man hurried over to Eli, 15 who was
ninety-eight years old and whose eyes
had failed so that he could not see. 16 He
told Eli, "I have just come from the battle
line; I fled from it this very day."
Eli asked, "What happened, my son?"
17 The man who brought the news replied, "Israel fled before the Philistines,
and the army has suffered heavy losses.
Also your two sons, Hophni and Phinehas, are dead, and the ark of God has
been captured."
18 When he mentioned the ark of God,
Eli fell backward off his chair by the side
of the gate. His neck was broken and he
died, for he was an old man, and he was
heavy. He had led[a] Israel forty years.
19 His daughter-in-law, the wife of Phinehas, was pregnant and near the time of
delivery. When she heard the news that
the ark of God had been captured and
that her father-in-law and her husband
were dead, she went into labor and gave
birth, but was overcome by her labor
pains. 20 As she was dying, the women
attending her said, "Don't despair; you
have given birth to a son." But she did not
respond or pay any attention.
21 She named the boy Ichabod,[b] saying,
"The Glory has departed from Israel" —
because of the capture of the ark of God
and the deaths of her father-in-law and
her husband. 22 She said, "The Glory has
departed from Israel, for the ark of God
has been captured."
5 After the Philistines had captured the
ark of God, they took it from Ebenezer to Ashdod. 2 Then they carried the
ark into Dagon's temple and set it beside
Dagon. 3 When the people of Ashdod rose
early the next day, there was Dagon, fall-
en on his face on the ground before the
ark of the LORD! They took Dagon and put
him back in his place. 4 But the following morning when they rose, there was
Dagon, fallen on his face on the ground
before the ark of the LORD! His head and
hands had been broken off and were lying on the threshold; only his body remained. 5 That is why to this day neither
the priests of Dagon nor any others who
enter Dagon's temple at Ashdod step on
the threshold.
6 The LORD's hand was heavy on the
people of Ashdod and its vicinity; he
brought devastation on them and afflicted them with tumors.[c] 7 When the people
of Ashdod saw what was happening, they
said, "The ark of the god of Israel must
not stay here with us, because his hand is
heavy on us and on Dagon our god." 8 So
they called together all the rulers of the
Philistines and asked them, "What shall
we do with the ark of the god of Israel?"
They answered, "Have the ark of the
god of Israel moved to Gath." So they
moved the ark of the God of Israel.
9 But after they had moved it, the LORD's
hand was against that city, throwing it
into a great panic. He afflicted the people of the city, both young and old, with
an outbreak of tumors.[d] 10 So they sent
the ark of God to Ekron.
As the ark of God was entering Ekron,
the people of Ekron cried out, "They
have brought the ark of the god of Israel
around to us to kill us and our people."
11 So they called together all the rulers of
the Philistines and said, "Send the ark of
the god of Israel away; let it go back to its
own place, or it[e] will kill us and our people." For death had filled the city with
panic; God's hand was very heavy on it.
12 Those who did not die were afflicted
with tumors, and the outcry of the city
went up to heaven.
6 When the ark of the LORD had been
in Philistine territory seven months,
2 the Philistines called for the priests and
the diviners and said, "What shall we do
with the ark of the LORD? Tell us how we
should send it back to its place."
3 They answered, "If you return the ark
of the god of Israel, do not send it back

[a] *18* Traditionally *judged* [b] *21* *Ichabod* means *no glory.* [c] *6* Hebrew; Septuagint and Vulgate *tumors. And rats appeared in their land, and there was death and destruction throughout the city* [d] *9* Or *with tumors in the groin* (see Septuagint) [e] *11* Or *he*

to him without a gift; by all means send
a guilt offering to him. Then you will be
healed, and you will know why his hand
has not been lifted from you."
4The Philistines asked, "What guilt offering should we send to him?"
They replied, "Five gold tumors and
five gold rats, according to the number of
the Philistine rulers, because the same
plague has struck both you and your rulers. 5Make models of the tumors and of
the rats that are destroying the country,
and give glory to Israel's god. Perhaps he
will lift his hand from you and your gods
and your land. 6Why do you harden your
hearts as the Egyptians and Pharaoh
did? When Israel's god dealt harshly with
them, did they not send the Israelites out
so they could go on their way?
7"Now then, get a new cart ready, with
two cows that have calved and have never been yoked. Hitch the cows to the cart,
but take their calves away and pen them
up. 8Take the ark of the LORD and put it on
the cart, and in a chest beside it put the
gold objects you are sending back to him
as a guilt offering. Send it on its way, 9but
keep watching it. If it goes up to its own
territory, toward Beth Shemesh, then the
LORD has brought this great disaster on
us. But if it does not, then we will know
that it was not his hand that struck us but
that it happened to us by chance."
10So they did this. They took two such
cows and hitched them to the cart and
penned up their calves. 11They placed
the ark of the LORD on the cart and along
with it the chest containing the gold rats
and the models of the tumors. 12Then the
cows went straight up toward Beth Shemesh, keeping on the road and lowing all
the way; they did not turn to the right or
to the left. The rulers of the Philistines
followed them as far as the border of Beth
Shemesh.
13Now the people of Beth Shemesh
were harvesting their wheat in the valley, and when they looked up and saw the
ark, they rejoiced at the sight. 14The cart
came to the field of Joshua of Beth Shemesh, and there it stopped beside a large
rock. The people chopped up the wood
of the cart and sacrificed the cows as a
burnt offering to the LORD. 15The Levites
took down the ark of the LORD, together
with the chest containing the gold objects, and placed them on the large rock.
On that day the people of Beth Shemesh
offered burnt offerings and made sacrifices to the LORD. 16The five rulers of the
Philistines saw all this and then returned
that same day to Ekron.
17These are the gold tumors the Philistines sent as a guilt offering to the
LORD—one each for Ashdod, Gaza, Ashkelon, Gath and Ekron. 18And the number of the gold rats was according to the
number of Philistine towns belonging to
the five rulers—the fortified towns with
their country villages. The large rock on
which the Levites set the ark of the LORD
is a witness to this day in the field of Joshua of Beth Shemesh.
19But God struck down some of the
inhabitants of Beth Shemesh, putting
seventy[a] of them to death because they
looked into the ark of the LORD. The people mourned because of the heavy blow
the LORD had dealt them. 20And the people of Beth Shemesh asked, "Who can
stand in the presence of the LORD, this
holy God? To whom will the ark go up
from here?"
21Then they sent messengers to the
people of Kiriath Jearim, saying, "The
Philistines have returned the ark of the
LORD. Come down and take it up to your
7 town." 1So the men of Kiriath Jearim
came and took up the ark of the LORD.
They brought it to Abinadab's house on
the hill and consecrated Eleazar his son
to guard the ark of the LORD. 2The ark remained at Kiriath Jearim a long time—
twenty years in all.
Then all the people of Israel turned
back to the LORD. 3So Samuel said to all
the Israelites, "If you are returning to the
LORD with all your hearts, then rid yourselves of the foreign gods and the Ashtoreths and commit yourselves to the LORD
and serve him only, and he will deliver
you out of the hand of the Philistines."
4So the Israelites put away their Baals
and Ashtoreths, and served the LORD
only.
5Then Samuel said, "Assemble all Israel at Mizpah, and I will intercede with
the LORD for you." 6When they had assembled at Mizpah, they drew water and
poured it out before the LORD. On that

[a] *19* A few Hebrew manuscripts; most Hebrew manuscripts and Septuagint *50,070*

day they fasted and there they confessed,
"We have sinned against the LORD." Now
Samuel was serving as leader[a] of Israel at
Mizpah.
7 When the Philistines heard that Israel had assembled at Mizpah, the rulers of
the Philistines came up to attack them.
When the Israelites heard of it, they were
afraid because of the Philistines. 8 They
said to Samuel, "Do not stop crying out to
the LORD our God for us, that he may rescue us from the hand of the Philistines."
9 Then Samuel took a suckling lamb and
sacrificed it as a whole burnt offering to
the LORD. He cried out to the LORD on
Israel's behalf, and the LORD answered
him.
10 While Samuel was sacrificing the
burnt offering, the Philistines drew near
to engage Israel in battle. But that day
the LORD thundered with loud thunder
against the Philistines and threw them
into such a panic that they were routed
before the Israelites. 11 The men of Israel rushed out of Mizpah and pursued the
Philistines, slaughtering them along the
way to a point below Beth Kar.
12 Then Samuel took a stone and set it
up between Mizpah and Shen. He named
it Ebenezer,[b] saying, "Thus far the LORD
has helped us."
13 So the Philistines were subdued and
they stopped invading Israel's territory.
Throughout Samuel's lifetime, the hand
of the LORD was against the Philistines.
14 The towns from Ekron to Gath that the
Philistines had captured from Israel were
restored to Israel, and Israel delivered the
neighboring territory from the hands of
the Philistines. And there was peace between Israel and the Amorites.
15 Samuel continued as Israel's leader
all the days of his life. 16 From year to year
he went on a circuit from Bethel to Gilgal to Mizpah, judging Israel in all those
places. 17 But he always went back to Ramah, where his home was, and there he
also held court for Israel. And he built an
altar there to the LORD.
8 When Samuel grew old, he appointed his sons as Israel's leaders.[c] 2 The
name of his firstborn was Joel and the
name of his second was Abijah, and they
served at Beersheba. 3 But his sons did not
follow his ways. They turned aside after
dishonest gain and accepted bribes and
perverted justice.
4 So all the elders of Israel gathered together and came to Samuel at Ramah.
5 They said to him, "You are old, and your
sons do not follow your ways; now appoint a king to lead[d] us, such as all the
other nations have."
6 But when they said, "Give us a king to
lead us," this displeased Samuel; so he
prayed to the LORD. 7 And the LORD told
him: "Listen to all that the people are
saying to you; it is not you they have rejected, but they have rejected me as their
king. 8 As they have done from the day I
brought them up out of Egypt until this
day, forsaking me and serving other gods,
so they are doing to you. 9 Now listen to
them; but warn them solemnly and let
them know what the king who will reign
over them will claim as his rights."
10 Samuel told all the words of the LORD
to the people who were asking him for
a king. 11 He said, "This is what the king
who will reign over you will claim as his
rights: He will take your sons and make
them serve with his chariots and horses,
and they will run in front of his chariots.
12 Some he will assign to be commanders
of thousands and commanders of fifties, and others to plow his ground and
reap his harvest, and still others to make
weapons of war and equipment for his
chariots. 13 He will take your daughters
to be perfumers and cooks and bakers.
14 He will take the best of your fields and
vineyards and olive groves and give them
to his attendants. 15 He will take a tenth of
your grain and of your vintage and give
it to his officials and attendants. 16 Your
male and female servants and the best
of your cattle[e] and donkeys he will take
for his own use. 17 He will take a tenth of
your flocks, and you yourselves will become his slaves. 18 When that day comes,
you will cry out for relief from the king
you have chosen, but the LORD will not
answer you in that day."
19 But the people refused to listen to
Samuel. "No!" they said. "We want a king
over us. 20 Then we will be like all the other nations, with a king to lead us and to go
out before us and fight our battles."
21 When Samuel heard all that the people said, he repeated it before the LORD.

[a] *6* Traditionally *judge*; also in verse 15 [b] *12* *Ebenezer* means *stone of help.* [c] *1* Traditionally *judges*
[d] *5* Traditionally *judge*; also in verses 6 and 20 [e] *16* Septuagint; Hebrew *young men*

22 The LORD answered, “Listen to them
and give them a king.”
Then Samuel said to the Israelites, “Everyone go back to your own town.”

9 There was a Benjamite, a man of
standing, whose name was Kish son
of Abiel, the son of Zeror, the son of Be-
korath, the son of Aphiah of Benjamin.
2 Kish had a son named Saul, as handsome a young man as could be found
anywhere in Israel, and he was a head
taller than anyone else.
3 Now the donkeys belonging to Saul’s
father Kish were lost, and Kish said to
his son Saul, “Take one of the servants
with you and go and look for the donkeys.” 4 So he passed through the hill
country of Ephraim and through the
area around Shalisha, but they did not
find them. They went on into the district of Shaalim, but the donkeys were
not there. Then he passed through the
territory of Benjamin, but they did not
find them.
5 When they reached the district of
Zuph, Saul said to the servant who was
with him, “Come, let’s go back, or my father will stop thinking about the donkeys
and start worrying about us.”
6 But the servant replied, “Look, in this
town there is a man of God; he is highly
respected, and everything he says comes
true. Let’s go there now. Perhaps he will
tell us what way to take.”
7 Saul said to his servant, “If we go, what
can we give the man? The food in our
sacks is gone. We have no gift to take to
the man of God. What do we have?”
8 The servant answered him again.
“Look,” he said, “I have a quarter of a
shekel[a] of silver. I will give it to the man
of God so that he will tell us what way to
take.” 9 (Formerly in Israel, if someone
went to inquire of God, they would say,
“Come, let us go to the seer,” because
the prophet of today used to be called a
seer.)
10 “Good,” Saul said to his servant.
“Come, let’s go.” So they set out for the
town where the man of God was.
11 As they were going up the hill to the
town, they met some young women coming out to draw water, and they asked
them, “Is the seer here?”
12 “He is,” they answered. “He’s ahead
of you. Hurry now; he has just come to
our town today, for the people have a
sacrifice at the high place. 13 As soon as
you enter the town, you will find him before he goes up to the high place to eat.
The people will not begin eating until he
comes, because he must bless the sacrifice; afterward, those who are invited
will eat. Go up now; you should find him
about this time.”
14 They went up to the town, and as
they were entering it, there was Samuel,
coming toward them on his way up to the
high place.
15 Now the day before Saul came,
the LORD had revealed this to Samuel:
16 “About this time tomorrow I will send
you a man from the land of Benjamin.
Anoint him ruler over my people Israel;
he will deliver them from the hand of the
Philistines. I have looked on my people,
for their cry has reached me.”
17 When Samuel caught sight of Saul,
the LORD said to him, “This is the man
I spoke to you about; he will govern my
people.”
18 Saul approached Samuel in the gateway and asked, “Would you please tell me
where the seer’s house is?”
19 “I am the seer,” Samuel replied. “Go
up ahead of me to the high place, for today you are to eat with me, and in the
morning I will send you on your way and
will tell you all that is in your heart. 20 As
for the donkeys you lost three days ago,
do not worry about them; they have been
found. And to whom is all the desire of Israel turned, if not to you and your whole
family line?”
21 Saul answered, “But am I not a Benjamite, from the smallest tribe of Israel,
and is not my clan the least of all the clans
of the tribe of Benjamin? Why do you say
such a thing to me?”
22 Then Samuel brought Saul and his
servant into the hall and seated them
at the head of those who were invited—
about thirty in number. 23 Samuel said to
the cook, “Bring the piece of meat I gave
you, the one I told you to lay aside.”
24 So the cook took up the thigh with
what was on it and set it in front of Saul.
Samuel said, “Here is what has been kept
for you. Eat, because it was set aside for
you for this occasion from the time I said,

[a] *8* That is, about 1/10 ounce or about 3 grams

'I have invited guests.'" And Saul dined
with Samuel that day.
25After they came down from the high
place to the town, Samuel talked with
Saul on the roof of his house. 26They rose
about daybreak, and Samuel called to
Saul on the roof, "Get ready, and I will
send you on your way." When Saul got
ready, he and Samuel went outside together. 27As they were going down to the
edge of the town, Samuel said to Saul,
"Tell the servant to go on ahead of us"—
and the servant did so—"but you stay
here for a while, so that I may give you a
message from God."
10 Then Samuel took a flask of olive
oil and poured it on Saul's head and
kissed him, saying, "Has not the LORD
anointed you ruler over his inheritance?[a]
2When you leave me today, you will meet
two men near Rachel's tomb, at Zelzah on
the border of Benjamin. They will say to
you, 'The donkeys you set out to look for
have been found. And now your father
has stopped thinking about them and is
worried about you. He is asking, "What
shall I do about my son?"'
3"Then you will go on from there until
you reach the great tree of Tabor. Three
men going up to worship God at Bethel
will meet you there. One will be carrying
three young goats, another three loaves
of bread, and another a skin of wine.
4They will greet you and offer you two
loaves of bread, which you will accept
from them.
5"After that you will go to Gibeah of
God, where there is a Philistine outpost.
As you approach the town, you will meet
a procession of prophets coming down
from the high place with lyres, timbrels,
pipes and harps being played before
them, and they will be prophesying. 6The
Spirit of the LORD will come powerfully
upon you, and you will prophesy with
them; and you will be changed into a different person. 7Once these signs are fulfilled, do whatever your hand finds to do,
for God is with you.
8"Go down ahead of me to Gilgal. I
will surely come down to you to sacrifice
burnt offerings and fellowship offerings,
but you must wait seven days until I come
to you and tell you what you are to do."
9As Saul turned to leave Samuel, God
changed Saul's heart, and all these signs
were fulfilled that day. 10When he and
his servant arrived at Gibeah, a procession of prophets met him; the Spirit of
God came powerfully upon him, and he
joined in their prophesying. 11When all
those who had formerly known him saw
him prophesying with the prophets, they
asked each other, "What is this that has
happened to the son of Kish? Is Saul also
among the prophets?"
12A man who lived there answered,
"And who is their father?" So it became
a saying: "Is Saul also among the prophets?" 13After Saul stopped prophesying,
he went to the high place.
14Now Saul's uncle asked him and his
servant, "Where have you been?"
"Looking for the donkeys," he said.
"But when we saw they were not to be
found, we went to Samuel."
15Saul's uncle said, "Tell me what Samuel said to you."
16Saul replied, "He assured us that the
donkeys had been found." But he did not
tell his uncle what Samuel had said about
the kingship.
17Samuel summoned the people of Israel to the LORD at Mizpah 18and said to
them, "This is what the LORD, the God
of Israel, says: 'I brought Israel up out of
Egypt, and I delivered you from the power of Egypt and all the kingdoms that oppressed you.' 19But you have now rejected
your God, who saves you out of all your
disasters and calamities. And you have
said, 'No, appoint a king over us.' So now
present yourselves before the LORD by
your tribes and clans."
20When Samuel had all Israel come forward by tribes, the tribe of Benjamin was
taken by lot. 21Then he brought forward
the tribe of Benjamin, clan by clan, and
Matri's clan was taken. Finally Saul son of
Kish was taken. But when they looked for
him, he was not to be found. 22So they inquired further of the LORD, "Has the man
come here yet?"
And the LORD said, "Yes, he has hidden
himself among the supplies."
23They ran and brought him out, and as
he stood among the people he was a head
taller than any of the others. 24Samuel

[a] *1* Hebrew; Septuagint and Vulgate *over his people Israel? You will reign over the LORD's people and save them from the power of their enemies round about. And this will be a sign to you that the LORD has anointed you ruler over his inheritance:*

said to all the people, "Do you see the man the LORD has chosen? There is no one like him among all the people."

Then the people shouted, "Long live the king!"

25 Samuel explained to the people the rights and duties of kingship. He wrote them down on a scroll and deposited it before the LORD. Then Samuel dismissed the people to go to their own homes.

26 Saul also went to his home in Gibeah, accompanied by valiant men whose hearts God had touched. 27 But some scoundrels said, "How can this fellow save us?" They despised him and brought him no gifts. But Saul kept silent.

11 Nahash[a] the Ammonite went up and besieged Jabesh Gilead. And all the men of Jabesh said to him, "Make a treaty with us, and we will be subject to you."

2 But Nahash the Ammonite replied, "I will make a treaty with you only on the condition that I gouge out the right eye of every one of you and so bring disgrace on all Israel."

3 The elders of Jabesh said to him, "Give us seven days so we can send messengers throughout Israel; if no one comes to rescue us, we will surrender to you."

4 When the messengers came to Gibeah of Saul and reported these terms to the people, they all wept aloud. 5 Just then Saul was returning from the fields, behind his oxen, and he asked, "What is wrong with everyone? Why are they weeping?" Then they repeated to him what the men of Jabesh had said.

6 When Saul heard their words, the Spirit of God came powerfully upon him, and he burned with anger. 7 He took a pair of oxen, cut them into pieces, and sent the pieces by messengers throughout Israel, proclaiming, "This is what will be done to the oxen of anyone who does not follow Saul and Samuel." Then the terror of the LORD fell on the people, and they came out together as one. 8 When Saul mustered them at Bezek, the men of Israel numbered three hundred thousand and those of Judah thirty thousand.

9 They told the messengers who had come, "Say to the men of Jabesh Gilead, 'By the time the sun is hot tomorrow, you will be rescued.'" When the messengers went and reported this to the men of Jabesh, they were elated. 10 They said to the Ammonites, "Tomorrow we will surrender to you, and you can do to us whatever you like."

11 The next day Saul separated his men into three divisions; during the last watch of the night they broke into the camp of the Ammonites and slaughtered them until the heat of the day. Those who survived were scattered, so that no two of them were left together.

12 The people then said to Samuel, "Who was it that asked, 'Shall Saul reign over us?' Turn these men over to us so that we may put them to death."

13 But Saul said, "No one will be put to death today, for this day the LORD has rescued Israel."

14 Then Samuel said to the people, "Come, let us go to Gilgal and there renew the kingship." 15 So all the people went to Gilgal and made Saul king in the presence of the LORD. There they sacrificed fellowship offerings before the LORD, and Saul and all the Israelites held a great celebration.

12 Samuel said to all Israel, "I have listened to everything you said to me and have set a king over you. 2 Now you have a king as your leader. As for me, I am old and gray, and my sons are here with you. I have been your leader from my youth until this day. 3 Here I stand. Testify against me in the presence of the LORD and his anointed. Whose ox have I taken? Whose donkey have I taken? Whom have I cheated? Whom have I oppressed? From whose hand have I accepted a bribe to make me shut my eyes? If I have done any of these things, I will make it right."

4 "You have not cheated or oppressed us," they replied. "You have not taken anything from anyone's hand."

5 Samuel said to them, "The LORD is witness against you, and also his anointed is witness this day, that you have not found anything in my hand."

"He is witness," they said.

6 Then Samuel said to the people, "It is the LORD who appointed Moses and Aaron and brought your ancestors up out of

[a] *1* Masoretic Text; Dead Sea Scrolls *gifts. Now Nahash king of the Ammonites oppressed the Gadites and Reubenites severely. He gouged out all their right eyes and struck terror and dread in Israel. Not a man remained among the Israelites beyond the Jordan whose right eye was not gouged out by Nahash king of the Ammonites, except that seven thousand men fled from the Ammonites and entered Jabesh Gilead. About a month later,* [1]*Nahash*

Egypt. 7Now then, stand here, because I
am going to confront you with evidence
before the LORD as to all the righteous
acts performed by the LORD for you and
your ancestors.
8"After Jacob entered Egypt, they cried
to the LORD for help, and the LORD sent
Moses and Aaron, who brought your ancestors out of Egypt and settled them in
this place.
9"But they forgot the LORD their God;
so he sold them into the hand of Sisera,
the commander of the army of Hazor,
and into the hands of the Philistines and
the king of Moab, who fought against
them. 10They cried out to the LORD and
said, 'We have sinned; we have forsaken
the LORD and served the Baals and the
Ashtoreths. But now deliver us from the
hands of our enemies, and we will serve
you.' 11Then the LORD sent Jerub-Baal,[a]
Barak,[b] Jephthah and Samuel,[c] and he
delivered you from the hands of your enemies all around you, so that you lived in
safety.
12"But when you saw that Nahash king
of the Ammonites was moving against
you, you said to me, 'No, we want a king
to rule over us'—even though the LORD
your God was your king. 13Now here is
the king you have chosen, the one you
asked for; see, the LORD has set a king
over you. 14If you fear the LORD and serve
and obey him and do not rebel against his
commands, and if both you and the king
who reigns over you follow the LORD your
God—good! 15But if you do not obey the
LORD, and if you rebel against his commands, his hand will be against you, as it
was against your ancestors.
16"Now then, stand still and see this
great thing the LORD is about to do before
your eyes! 17Is it not wheat harvest now?
I will call on the LORD to send thunder
and rain. And you will realize what an
evil thing you did in the eyes of the LORD
when you asked for a king."
18Then Samuel called on the LORD, and
that same day the LORD sent thunder and
rain. So all the people stood in awe of the
LORD and of Samuel.
19The people all said to Samuel, "Pray
to the LORD your God for your servants
so that we will not die, for we have added to all our other sins the evil of asking
for a king."
20"Do not be afraid," Samuel replied.
"You have done all this evil; yet do not
turn away from the LORD, but serve the
LORD with all your heart. 21Do not turn
away after useless idols. They can do you
no good, nor can they rescue you, because they are useless. 22For the sake of
his great name the LORD will not reject
his people, because the LORD was pleased
to make you his own. 23As for me, far be
it from me that I should sin against the
LORD by failing to pray for you. And I will
teach you the way that is good and right.
24But be sure to fear the LORD and serve
him faithfully with all your heart; consider what great things he has done for you.
25Yet if you persist in doing evil, both you
and your king will perish."

13 Saul was thirty[d] years old when he
became king, and he reigned over
Israel forty-[e] two years.
2Saul chose three thousand men from
Israel; two thousand were with him at
Mikmash and in the hill country of Bethel, and a thousand were with Jonathan at
Gibeah in Benjamin. The rest of the men
he sent back to their homes.
3Jonathan attacked the Philistine outpost at Geba, and the Philistines heard
about it. Then Saul had the trumpet
blown throughout the land and said,
"Let the Hebrews hear!" 4So all Israel
heard the news: "Saul has attacked the
Philistine outpost, and now Israel has
become obnoxious to the Philistines."
And the people were summoned to join
Saul at Gilgal.
5The Philistines assembled to fight Israel, with three thousand[f] chariots, six
thousand charioteers, and soldiers as numerous as the sand on the seashore. They
went up and camped at Mikmash, east of
Beth Aven. 6When the Israelites saw that
their situation was critical and that their
army was hard pressed, they hid in caves
and thickets, among the rocks, and in
pits and cisterns. 7Some Hebrews even
crossed the Jordan to the land of Gad and
Gilead.

[a] *11* Also called *Gideon* [b] *11* Some Septuagint manuscripts and Syriac; Hebrew *Bedan* [c] *11* Hebrew; some Septuagint manuscripts and Syriac *Samson* [d] *1* A few late manuscripts of the Septuagint; Hebrew does not have *thirty*. [e] *1* Probable reading of the original Hebrew text (see Acts 13:21); Masoretic Text does not have *forty-*. [f] *5* Some Septuagint manuscripts and Syriac; Hebrew *thirty thousand*

Saul remained at Gilgal, and all the
troops with him were quaking with fear.
8He waited seven days, the time set by
Samuel; but Samuel did not come to Gilgal, and Saul's men began to scatter. 9So
he said, "Bring me the burnt offering and
the fellowship offerings." And Saul offered up the burnt offering. 10Just as he
finished making the offering, Samuel arrived, and Saul went out to greet him.
11"What have you done?" asked Samuel.

Saul replied, "When I saw that the men
were scattering, and that you did not
come at the set time, and that the Philistines were assembling at Mikmash, 12I
thought, 'Now the Philistines will come
down against me at Gilgal, and I have not
sought the LORD's favor.' So I felt compelled to offer the burnt offering."

13"You have done a foolish thing,"
Samuel said. "You have not kept the command the LORD your God gave you; if you
had, he would have established your
kingdom over Israel for all time. 14But
now your kingdom will not endure; the
LORD has sought out a man after his own
heart and appointed him ruler of his people, because you have not kept the LORD's
command."

15Then Samuel left Gilgal[a] and went up
to Gibeah in Benjamin, and Saul counted
the men who were with him. They numbered about six hundred.

16Saul and his son Jonathan and the
men with them were staying in Gibeah[b] in Benjamin, while the Philistines
camped at Mikmash. 17Raiding parties
went out from the Philistine camp in
three detachments. One turned toward
Ophrah in the vicinity of Shual, 18another
toward Beth Horon, and the third toward
the borderland overlooking the Valley of
Zeboyim facing the wilderness.

19Not a blacksmith could be found
in the whole land of Israel, because the
Philistines had said, "Otherwise the Hebrews will make swords or spears!" 20So
all Israel went down to the Philistines to
have their plow points, mattocks, axes
and sickles[c] sharpened. 21The price was
two-thirds of a shekel[d] for sharpening
plow points and mattocks, and a third of
a shekel[e] for sharpening forks and axes
and for repointing goads.

22So on the day of the battle not a soldier with Saul and Jonathan had a sword
or spear in his hand; only Saul and his
son Jonathan had them.

23Now a detachment of Philistines had
gone out to the pass at Mikmash.

14 1One day Jonathan son of Saul said
to his young armor-bearer, "Come, let's
go over to the Philistine outpost on the
other side." But he did not tell his father.

2Saul was staying on the outskirts of
Gibeah under a pomegranate tree in Migron. With him were about six hundred
men, 3among whom was Ahijah, who was
wearing an ephod. He was a son of Ichabod's brother Ahitub son of Phinehas, the
son of Eli, the LORD's priest in Shiloh. No
one was aware that Jonathan had left.

4On each side of the pass that Jonathan
intended to cross to reach the Philistine
outpost was a cliff; one was called Bozez
and the other Seneh. 5One cliff stood to
the north toward Mikmash, the other to
the south toward Geba.

6Jonathan said to his young armor-
bearer, "Come, let's go over to the outpost
of those uncircumcised men. Perhaps the
LORD will act in our behalf. Nothing can
hinder the LORD from saving, whether by
many or by few."

7"Do all that you have in mind," his
armor-bearer said. "Go ahead; I am with
you heart and soul."

8Jonathan said, "Come on, then; we
will cross over toward them and let them
see us. 9If they say to us, 'Wait there until we come to you,' we will stay where we
are and not go up to them. 10But if they
say, 'Come up to us,' we will climb up, because that will be our sign that the LORD
has given them into our hands."

11So both of them showed themselves
to the Philistine outpost. "Look!" said
the Philistines. "The Hebrews are crawling out of the holes they were hiding in."
12The men of the outpost shouted to Jonathan and his armor-bearer, "Come up to
us and we'll teach you a lesson."

So Jonathan said to his armor-bearer,
"Climb up after me; the LORD has given
them into the hand of Israel."

[a] 15 Hebrew; Septuagint *Gilgal and went his way; the rest of the people went after Saul to meet the army, and they went out of Gilgal* [b] 16 Two Hebrew manuscripts; most Hebrew manuscripts *Geba,* a variant of *Gibeah* [c] 20 Septuagint; Hebrew *plow points* [d] 21 That is, about 1/4 ounce or about 8 grams [e] 21 That is, about 1/8 ounce or about 4 grams

13Jonathan climbed up, using his
hands and feet, with his armor-bearer right behind him. The Philistines fell
before Jonathan, and his armor-bearer
followed and killed behind him. 14In that
first attack Jonathan and his armor-bearer killed some twenty men in an area of
about half an acre.
15Then panic struck the whole army—
those in the camp and field, and those in
the outposts and raiding parties—and
the ground shook. It was a panic sent by
God.[a]
16Saul's lookouts at Gibeah in Benjamin saw the army melting away in all
directions. 17Then Saul said to the men
who were with him, "Muster the forces
and see who has left us." When they did, it
was Jonathan and his armor-bearer who
were not there.
18Saul said to Ahijah, "Bring the ark of
God." (At that time it was with the Israelites.)[b] 19While Saul was talking to the
priest, the tumult in the Philistine camp
increased more and more. So Saul said to
the priest, "Withdraw your hand."
20Then Saul and all his men assembled
and went to the battle. They found the
Philistines in total confusion, striking
each other with their swords. 21Those
Hebrews who had previously been with
the Philistines and had gone up with
them to their camp went over to the Israelites who were with Saul and Jonathan.
22When all the Israelites who had hidden in the hill country of Ephraim heard
that the Philistines were on the run, they
joined the battle in hot pursuit. 23So on
that day the LORD saved Israel, and the
battle moved on beyond Beth Aven.
24Now the Israelites were in distress
that day, because Saul had bound the people under an oath, saying, "Cursed be anyone who eats food before evening comes,
before I have avenged myself on my enemies!" So none of the troops tasted food.
25The entire army entered the woods,
and there was honey on the ground.
26When they went into the woods, they
saw the honey oozing out; yet no one
put his hand to his mouth, because they
feared the oath. 27But Jonathan had not
heard that his father had bound the people with the oath, so he reached out the
end of the staff that was in his hand and
dipped it into the honeycomb. He raised
his hand to his mouth, and his eyes
brightened.[c] 28Then one of the soldiers
told him, "Your father bound the army
under a strict oath, saying, 'Cursed be
anyone who eats food today!' That is why
the men are faint."
29Jonathan said, "My father has made
trouble for the country. See how my eyes
brightened when I tasted a little of this
honey. 30How much better it would have
been if the men had eaten today some of
the plunder they took from their enemies.
Would not the slaughter of the Philistines
have been even greater?"
31That day, after the Israelites had
struck down the Philistines from Mikmash to Aijalon, they were exhausted.
32They pounced on the plunder and, taking sheep, cattle and calves, they butchered them on the ground and ate them,
together with the blood. 33Then someone
said to Saul, "Look, the men are sinning
against the LORD by eating meat that has
blood in it."

"You have broken faith," he said. "Roll
a large stone over here at once." 34Then
he said, "Go out among the men and tell
them, 'Each of you bring me your cattle
and sheep, and slaughter them here and
eat them. Do not sin against the LORD by
eating meat with blood still in it.'"

So everyone brought his ox that night
and slaughtered it there. 35Then Saul
built an altar to the LORD; it was the first
time he had done this.
36Saul said, "Let us go down and pursue the Philistines by night and plunder
them till dawn, and let us not leave one
of them alive."

"Do whatever seems best to you," they
replied.

But the priest said, "Let us inquire of
God here."
37So Saul asked God, "Shall I go down
and pursue the Philistines? Will you give
them into Israel's hand?" But God did not
answer him that day.
38Saul therefore said, "Come here, all
you who are leaders of the army, and let
us find out what sin has been committed
today. 39As surely as the LORD who rescues Israel lives, even if the guilt lies with
my son Jonathan, he must die." But not
one of them said a word.

[a] 15 Or *a terrible panic* [b] 18 Hebrew; Septuagint *"Bring the ephod." (At that time he wore the ephod before the Israelites.)* [c] 27 Or *his strength was renewed*; similarly in verse 29

40 Saul then said to all the Israelites,
"You stand over there; I and Jonathan my
son will stand over here."
"Do what seems best to you," they replied.
41 Then Saul prayed to the LORD, the
God of Israel, "Why have you not answered your servant today? If the fault is
in me or my son Jonathan, respond with
Urim, but if the men of Israel are at fault,[a]
respond with Thummim." Jonathan and
Saul were taken by lot, and the men were
cleared. 42 Saul said, "Cast the lot between me and Jonathan my son." And
Jonathan was taken.
43 Then Saul said to Jonathan, "Tell me
what you have done."
So Jonathan told him, "I tasted a little
honey with the end of my staff. And now
I must die!"
44 Saul said, "May God deal with me, be
it ever so severely, if you do not die, Jonathan."
45 But the men said to Saul, "Should Jonathan die—he who has brought about this
great deliverance in Israel? Never! As surely as the LORD lives, not a hair of his head
will fall to the ground, for he did this today
with God's help." So the men rescued Jonathan, and he was not put to death.
46 Then Saul stopped pursuing the Philistines, and they withdrew to their own
land.
47 After Saul had assumed rule over Israel, he fought against their enemies on
every side: Moab, the Ammonites, Edom,
the kings[b] of Zobah, and the Philistines.
Wherever he turned, he inflicted punishment on them.[c] 48 He fought valiantly
and defeated the Amalekites, delivering
Israel from the hands of those who had
plundered them.
49 Saul's sons were Jonathan, Ishvi
and Malki-Shua. The name of his older daughter was Merab, and that of the
younger was Michal. 50 His wife's name
was Ahinoam daughter of Ahimaaz. The
name of the commander of Saul's army
was Abner son of Ner, and Ner was Saul's
uncle. 51 Saul's father Kish and Abner's father Ner were sons of Abiel.
52 All the days of Saul there was bitter
war with the Philistines, and whenever
Saul saw a mighty or brave man, he took
him into his service.

15 Samuel said to Saul, "I am the one
the LORD sent to anoint you king
over his people Israel; so listen now to
the message from the LORD. 2 This is
what the LORD Almighty says: 'I will
punish the Amalekites for what they did
to Israel when they waylaid them as they
came up from Egypt. 3 Now go, attack the
Amalekites and totally destroy[d] all that
belongs to them. Do not spare them; put
to death men and women, children and
infants, cattle and sheep, camels and
donkeys.'"
4 So Saul summoned the men and mustered them at Telaim—two hundred
thousand foot soldiers and ten thousand
from Judah. 5 Saul went to the city of Amalek and set an ambush in the ravine.
6 Then he said to the Kenites, "Go away,
leave the Amalekites so that I do not destroy you along with them; for you showed
kindness to all the Israelites when they
came up out of Egypt." So the Kenites
moved away from the Amalekites.
7 Then Saul attacked the Amalekites
all the way from Havilah to Shur, near
the eastern border of Egypt. 8 He took
Agag king of the Amalekites alive, and all
his people he totally destroyed with the
sword. 9 But Saul and the army spared
Agag and the best of the sheep and cattle,
the fat calves[e] and lambs—everything
that was good. These they were unwilling to destroy completely, but everything
that was despised and weak they totally
destroyed.
10 Then the word of the LORD came to
Samuel: 11 "I regret that I have made Saul
king, because he has turned away from
me and has not carried out my instructions." Samuel was angry, and he cried
out to the LORD all that night.
12 Early in the morning Samuel got up
and went to meet Saul, but he was told,
"Saul has gone to Carmel. There he has
set up a monument in his own honor and
has turned and gone on down to Gilgal."
13 When Samuel reached him, Saul
said, "The LORD bless you! I have carried
out the LORD's instructions."
14 But Samuel said, "What then is this

[a] *41* Septuagint; Hebrew does not have *"Why . . . at fault.* [b] *47* Masoretic Text; Dead Sea Scrolls and Septuagint *king* [c] *47* Hebrew; Septuagint *he was victorious* [d] *3* The Hebrew term refers to the irrevocable giving over of things or persons to the LORD, often by totally destroying them; also in verses 8, 9, 15, 18, 20 and 21. [e] *9* Or *the grown bulls*; the meaning of the Hebrew for this phrase is uncertain.

bleating of sheep in my ears? What is this
lowing of cattle that I hear?"
15Saul answered, "The soldiers brought
them from the Amalekites; they spared
the best of the sheep and cattle to sacrifice to the LORD your God, but we totally
destroyed the rest."
16"Enough!" Samuel said to Saul. "Let
me tell you what the LORD said to me last
night."
"Tell me," Saul replied.
17Samuel said, "Although you were
once small in your own eyes, did you not
become the head of the tribes of Israel?
The LORD anointed you king over Israel.
18And he sent you on a mission, saying,
'Go and completely destroy those wicked people, the Amalekites; wage war
against them until you have wiped them
out.' 19Why did you not obey the LORD?
Why did you pounce on the plunder and
do evil in the eyes of the LORD?"
20"But I did obey the LORD," Saul said.
"I went on the mission the LORD assigned
me. I completely destroyed the Amalekites and brought back Agag their king.
21The soldiers took sheep and cattle from
the plunder, the best of what was devoted
to God, in order to sacrifice them to the
LORD your God at Gilgal."
22But Samuel replied:

"Does the LORD delight in burnt
offerings and sacrifices
as much as in obeying the LORD?
To obey is better than sacrifice,
and to heed is better than the fat of
rams.
23For rebellion is like the sin of
divination,
and arrogance like the evil of
idolatry.
Because you have rejected the word of
the LORD,
he has rejected you as king."

24Then Saul said to Samuel, "I have
sinned. I violated the LORD's command
and your instructions. I was afraid of the
men and so I gave in to them. 25Now I beg
you, forgive my sin and come back with
me, so that I may worship the LORD."
26But Samuel said to him, "I will not
go back with you. You have rejected the
word of the LORD, and the LORD has rejected you as king over Israel!"
27As Samuel turned to leave, Saul
caught hold of the hem of his robe, and
it tore. 28Samuel said to him, "The LORD
has torn the kingdom of Israel from you
today and has given it to one of your
neighbors — to one better than you. 29He
who is the Glory of Israel does not lie or
change his mind; for he is not a human
being, that he should change his mind."
30Saul replied, "I have sinned. But
please honor me before the elders of my
people and before Israel; come back with
me, so that I may worship the LORD your
God." 31So Samuel went back with Saul,
and Saul worshiped the LORD.
32Then Samuel said, "Bring me Agag
king of the Amalekites."
Agag came to him in chains.[a] And he
thought, "Surely the bitterness of death
is past."
33But Samuel said,

"As your sword has made women
childless,
so will your mother be childless
among women."

And Samuel put Agag to death before the
LORD at Gilgal.
34Then Samuel left for Ramah, but
Saul went up to his home in Gibeah of
Saul. 35Until the day Samuel died, he did
not go to see Saul again, though Samuel
mourned for him. And the LORD regretted that he had made Saul king over Israel.
16 The LORD said to Samuel, "How long
will you mourn for Saul, since I have
rejected him as king over Israel? Fill your
horn with oil and be on your way; I am
sending you to Jesse of Bethlehem. I have
chosen one of his sons to be king."
2But Samuel said, "How can I go? If
Saul hears about it, he will kill me."
The LORD said, "Take a heifer with you
and say, 'I have come to sacrifice to the
LORD.' 3Invite Jesse to the sacrifice, and
I will show you what to do. You are to
anoint for me the one I indicate."
4Samuel did what the LORD said. When
he arrived at Bethlehem, the elders of the
town trembled when they met him. They
asked, "Do you come in peace?"
5Samuel replied, "Yes, in peace; I have
come to sacrifice to the LORD. Consecrate
yourselves and come to the sacrifice with

[a] 32 The meaning of the Hebrew for this phrase is uncertain.

me." Then he consecrated Jesse and his
sons and invited them to the sacrifice.
6 When they arrived, Samuel saw Eliab
and thought, "Surely the LORD's anointed
stands here before the LORD."
7 But the LORD said to Samuel, "Do not
consider his appearance or his height, for
I have rejected him. The LORD does not
look at the things people look at. People
look at the outward appearance, but the
LORD looks at the heart."
8 Then Jesse called Abinadab and had
him pass in front of Samuel. But Samuel
said, "The LORD has not chosen this one
either." 9 Jesse then had Shammah pass
by, but Samuel said, "Nor has the LORD
chosen this one." 10 Jesse had seven of his
sons pass before Samuel, but Samuel said
to him, "The LORD has not chosen these."
11 So he asked Jesse, "Are these all the
sons you have?"
"There is still the youngest," Jesse answered.
"He is tending the sheep."
Samuel said, "Send for him; we will not
sit down until he arrives."
12 So he sent for him and had him
brought in. He was glowing with health
and had a fine appearance and handsome features.
Then the LORD said, "Rise and anoint
him; this is the one."
13 So Samuel took the horn of oil and
anointed him in the presence of his
brothers, and from that day on the Spirit
of the LORD came powerfully upon David.
Samuel then went to Ramah.
14 Now the Spirit of the LORD had departed
from Saul, and an evil[a] spirit from
the LORD tormented him.
15 Saul's attendants said to him, "See,
an evil spirit from God is tormenting
you. 16 Let our lord command his servants
here to search for someone who can play
the lyre. He will play when the evil spirit
from God comes on you, and you will
feel better."
17 So Saul said to his attendants, "Find
someone who plays well and bring him
to me."
18 One of the servants answered, "I
have seen a son of Jesse of Bethlehem
who knows how to play the lyre. He is a
brave man and a warrior. He speaks well
and is a fine-looking man. And the LORD
is with him."
19 Then Saul sent messengers to Jesse
and said, "Send me your son David, who
is with the sheep." 20 So Jesse took a donkey
loaded with bread, a skin of wine and
a young goat and sent them with his son
David to Saul.
21 David came to Saul and entered his
service. Saul liked him very much, and
David became one of his armor-bearers.
22 Then Saul sent word to Jesse, saying,
"Allow David to remain in my service, for
I am pleased with him."
23 Whenever the spirit from God came
on Saul, David would take up his lyre
and play. Then relief would come to Saul;
he would feel better, and the evil spirit
would leave him.

17 Now the Philistines gathered their
forces for war and assembled at Sokoh
in Judah. They pitched camp at Ephes
Dammim, between Sokoh and Azekah.
2 Saul and the Israelites assembled and
camped in the Valley of Elah and drew
up their battle line to meet the Philistines.
3 The Philistines occupied one hill
and the Israelites another, with the valley
between them.
4 A champion named Goliath, who
was from Gath, came out of the Philistine
camp. His height was six cubits and
a span.[b] 5 He had a bronze helmet on his
head and wore a coat of scale armor of
bronze weighing five thousand shekels[c];
6 on his legs he wore bronze greaves, and a
bronze javelin was slung on his back. 7 His
spear shaft was like a weaver's rod, and its
iron point weighed six hundred shekels.[d]
His shield bearer went ahead of him.
8 Goliath stood and shouted to the
ranks of Israel, "Why do you come out
and line up for battle? Am I not a Philistine,
and are you not the servants of Saul?
Choose a man and have him come down
to me. 9 If he is able to fight and kill me, we
will become your subjects; but if I overcome
him and kill him, you will become
our subjects and serve us." 10 Then the
Philistine said, "This day I defy the armies
of Israel! Give me a man and let us
fight each other." 11 On hearing the Philistine's
words, Saul and all the Israelites
were dismayed and terrified.
12 Now David was the son of an Ephrathite
named Jesse, who was from Bethlehem
in Judah. Jesse had eight sons, and

[a] 14 Or *and a harmful*; similarly in verses 15, 16 and 23
[c] 5 That is, about 125 pounds or about 58 kilograms
[b] 4 That is, about 9 feet 9 inches or about 3 meters
[d] 7 That is, about 15 pounds or about 6.9 kilograms

in Saul's time he was very old. [13]Jesse's
three oldest sons had followed Saul to
the war: The firstborn was Eliab; the second, Abinadab; and the third, Shammah.
[14]David was the youngest. The three oldest followed Saul, [15]but David went back
and forth from Saul to tend his father's
sheep at Bethlehem.

[16]For forty days the Philistine came
forward every morning and evening and
took his stand.

[17]Now Jesse said to his son David,
"Take this ephah[a] of roasted grain and
these ten loaves of bread for your brothers and hurry to their camp. [18]Take along
these ten cheeses to the commander of
their unit. See how your brothers are and
bring back some assurance[b] from them.
[19]They are with Saul and all the men
of Israel in the Valley of Elah, fighting
against the Philistines."

[20]Early in the morning David left the
flock in the care of a shepherd, loaded
up and set out, as Jesse had directed. He
reached the camp as the army was going
out to its battle positions, shouting the
war cry. [21]Israel and the Philistines were
drawing up their lines facing each other.
[22]David left his things with the keeper of
supplies, ran to the battle lines and asked
his brothers how they were. [23]As he was
talking with them, Goliath, the Philistine
champion from Gath, stepped out from
his lines and shouted his usual defiance,
and David heard it. [24]Whenever the Israelites saw the man, they all fled from him
in great fear.

[25]Now the Israelites had been saying,
"Do you see how this man keeps coming out? He comes out to defy Israel. The
king will give great wealth to the man
who kills him. He will also give him his
daughter in marriage and will exempt his
family from taxes in Israel."

[26]David asked the men standing near
him, "What will be done for the man who
kills this Philistine and removes this disgrace from Israel? Who is this uncircumcised Philistine that he should defy the
armies of the living God?"

[27]They repeated to him what they had
been saying and told him, "This is what
will be done for the man who kills him."

[28]When Eliab, David's oldest brother, heard him speaking with the men,
he burned with anger at him and asked,
"Why have you come down here? And
with whom did you leave those few sheep
in the wilderness? I know how conceited
you are and how wicked your heart is; you
came down only to watch the battle."

[29]"Now what have I done?" said David.
"Can't I even speak?" [30]He then turned
away to someone else and brought up the
same matter, and the men answered him
as before. [31]What David said was overheard and reported to Saul, and Saul sent
for him.

[32]David said to Saul, "Let no one lose
heart on account of this Philistine; your
servant will go and fight him."

[33]Saul replied, "You are not able to go
out against this Philistine and fight him;
you are only a young man, and he has
been a warrior from his youth."

[34]But David said to Saul, "Your servant has been keeping his father's sheep.
When a lion or a bear came and carried
off a sheep from the flock, [35]I went after
it, struck it and rescued the sheep from its
mouth. When it turned on me, I seized it
by its hair, struck it and killed it. [36]Your
servant has killed both the lion and the
bear; this uncircumcised Philistine will
be like one of them, because he has defied the armies of the living God. [37]The
LORD who rescued me from the paw of
the lion and the paw of the bear will rescue me from the hand of this Philistine."

Saul said to David, "Go, and the LORD
be with you."

[38]Then Saul dressed David in his own
tunic. He put a coat of armor on him and
a bronze helmet on his head. [39]David
fastened on his sword over the tunic and
tried walking around, because he was not
used to them.

"I cannot go in these," he said to Saul,
"because I am not used to them." So he
took them off. [40]Then he took his staff in
his hand, chose five smooth stones from
the stream, put them in the pouch of his
shepherd's bag and, with his sling in his
hand, approached the Philistine.

[41]Meanwhile, the Philistine, with his
shield bearer in front of him, kept coming
closer to David. [42]He looked David over
and saw that he was little more than a
boy, glowing with health and handsome,
and he despised him. [43]He said to David,

[a] *17* That is, probably about 36 pounds or about 16 kilograms [b] *18* Or *some token*; or *some pledge of spoils*

"Am I a dog, that you come at me with
sticks?" And the Philistine cursed David
by his gods. 44 "Come here," he said, "and
I'll give your flesh to the birds and the
wild animals!"
45 David said to the Philistine, "You
come against me with sword and spear
and javelin, but I come against you in the
name of the LORD Almighty, the God of
the armies of Israel, whom you have defied. 46 This day the LORD will deliver you
into my hands, and I'll strike you down
and cut off your head. This very day I will
give the carcasses of the Philistine army
to the birds and the wild animals, and
the whole world will know that there is
a God in Israel. 47 All those gathered here
will know that it is not by sword or spear
that the LORD saves; for the battle is the
LORD's, and he will give all of you into
our hands."
48 As the Philistine moved closer to attack him, David ran quickly toward the
battle line to meet him. 49 Reaching into
his bag and taking out a stone, he slung it
and struck the Philistine on the forehead.
The stone sank into his forehead, and he
fell facedown on the ground.
50 So David triumphed over the Philistine with a sling and a stone; without
a sword in his hand he struck down the
Philistine and killed him.
51 David ran and stood over him. He
took hold of the Philistine's sword and
drew it from the sheath. After he killed
him, he cut off his head with the sword.
When the Philistines saw that their
hero was dead, they turned and ran.
52 Then the men of Israel and Judah
surged forward with a shout and pursued
the Philistines to the entrance of Gath[a]
and to the gates of Ekron. Their dead
were strewn along the Shaaraim road to
Gath and Ekron. 53 When the Israelites returned from chasing the Philistines, they
plundered their camp.
54 David took the Philistine's head and
brought it to Jerusalem; he put the Philistine's weapons in his own tent.
55 As Saul watched David going out to
meet the Philistine, he said to Abner,
commander of the army, "Abner, whose
son is that young man?"
Abner replied, "As surely as you live,
Your Majesty, I don't know."
56 The king said, "Find out whose son
this young man is."
57 As soon as David returned from killing the Philistine, Abner took him and
brought him before Saul, with David still
holding the Philistine's head.
58 "Whose son are you, young man?"
Saul asked him.
David said, "I am the son of your servant Jesse of Bethlehem."

18 After David had finished talking
with Saul, Jonathan became one in
spirit with David, and he loved him as
himself. 2 From that day Saul kept David
with him and did not let him return home
to his family. 3 And Jonathan made a covenant with David because he loved him
as himself. 4 Jonathan took off the robe he
was wearing and gave it to David, along
with his tunic, and even his sword, his
bow and his belt.
5 Whatever mission Saul sent him on,
David was so successful that Saul gave
him a high rank in the army. This pleased
all the troops, and Saul's officers as well.
6 When the men were returning home
after David had killed the Philistine,
the women came out from all the towns
of Israel to meet King Saul with singing
and dancing, with joyful songs and with
timbrels and lyres. 7 As they danced, they
sang:

"Saul has slain his thousands,
and David his tens of thousands."

8 Saul was very angry; this refrain displeased him greatly. "They have credited David with tens of thousands," he
thought, "but me with only thousands.
What more can he get but the kingdom?"
9 And from that time on Saul kept a close
eye on David.
10 The next day an evil[b] spirit from God
came forcefully on Saul. He was prophesying in his house, while David was playing the lyre, as he usually did. Saul had a
spear in his hand 11 and he hurled it, saying to himself, "I'll pin David to the wall."
But David eluded him twice.
12 Saul was afraid of David, because the
LORD was with David but had departed
from Saul. 13 So he sent David away from
him and gave him command over a thousand men, and David led the troops in
their campaigns. 14 In everything he did

[a] *52* Some Septuagint manuscripts; Hebrew *of a valley*
[b] *10* Or *a harmful*

he had great success, because the LORD was with him. [15]When Saul saw how successful he was, he was afraid of him. [16]But all Israel and Judah loved David, because he led them in their campaigns.

[17]Saul said to David, "Here is my older daughter Merab. I will give her to you in marriage; only serve me bravely and fight the battles of the LORD." For Saul said to himself, "I will not raise a hand against him. Let the Philistines do that!"

[18]But David said to Saul, "Who am I, and what is my family or my clan in Israel, that I should become the king's son-in-law?" [19]So[a] when the time came for Merab, Saul's daughter, to be given to David, she was given in marriage to Adriel of Meholah.

[20]Now Saul's daughter Michal was in love with David, and when they told Saul about it, he was pleased. [21]"I will give her to him," he thought, "so that she may be a snare to him and so that the hand of the Philistines may be against him." So Saul said to David, "Now you have a second opportunity to become my son-in-law."

[22]Then Saul ordered his attendants: "Speak to David privately and say, 'Look, the king likes you, and his attendants all love you; now become his son-in-law.' "

[23]They repeated these words to David. But David said, "Do you think it is a small matter to become the king's son-in-law? I'm only a poor man and little known."

[24]When Saul's servants told him what David had said, [25]Saul replied, "Say to David, 'The king wants no other price for the bride than a hundred Philistine foreskins, to take revenge on his enemies.' " Saul's plan was to have David fall by the hands of the Philistines.

[26]When the attendants told David these things, he was pleased to become the king's son-in-law. So before the allotted time elapsed, [27]David took his men with him and went out and killed two hundred Philistines and brought back their foreskins. They counted out the full number to the king so that David might become the king's son-in-law. Then Saul gave him his daughter Michal in marriage.

[28]When Saul realized that the LORD was with David and that his daughter Michal loved David, [29]Saul became still more afraid of him, and he remained his enemy the rest of his days.

[30]The Philistine commanders continued to go out to battle, and as often as they did, David met with more success than the rest of Saul's officers, and his name became well known.

19 Saul told his son Jonathan and all the attendants to kill David. But Jonathan had taken a great liking to David [2]and warned him, "My father Saul is looking for a chance to kill you. Be on your guard tomorrow morning; go into hiding and stay there. [3]I will go out and stand with my father in the field where you are. I'll speak to him about you and will tell you what I find out."

[4]Jonathan spoke well of David to Saul his father and said to him, "Let not the king do wrong to his servant David; he has not wronged you, and what he has done has benefited you greatly. [5]He took his life in his hands when he killed the Philistine. The LORD won a great victory for all Israel, and you saw it and were glad. Why then would you do wrong to an innocent man like David by killing him for no reason?"

[6]Saul listened to Jonathan and took this oath: "As surely as the LORD lives, David will not be put to death."

[7]So Jonathan called David and told him the whole conversation. He brought him to Saul, and David was with Saul as before.

[8]Once more war broke out, and David went out and fought the Philistines. He struck them with such force that they fled before him.

[9]But an evil[b] spirit from the LORD came on Saul as he was sitting in his house with his spear in his hand. While David was playing the lyre, [10]Saul tried to pin him to the wall with his spear, but David eluded him as Saul drove the spear into the wall. That night David made good his escape.

[11]Saul sent men to David's house to watch it and to kill him in the morning. But Michal, David's wife, warned him, "If you don't run for your life tonight, tomorrow you'll be killed." [12]So Michal let David down through a window, and he fled and escaped. [13]Then Michal took an idol and laid it on the bed, covering it with a garment and putting some goats' hair at the head.

[14]When Saul sent the men to capture David, Michal said, "He is ill."

[a] *19* Or *However,* [b] *9* Or *But a harmful*

15 Then Saul sent the men back to see
David and told them, "Bring him up to
me in his bed so that I may kill him."
16 But when the men entered, there was
the idol in the bed, and at the head was
some goats' hair.
17 Saul said to Michal, "Why did you
deceive me like this and send my enemy
away so that he escaped?"
Michal told him, "He said to me, 'Let
me get away. Why should I kill you?' "
18 When David had fled and made his
escape, he went to Samuel at Ramah and
told him all that Saul had done to him.
Then he and Samuel went to Naioth and
stayed there. 19 Word came to Saul: "David is in Naioth at Ramah"; 20 so he sent
men to capture him. But when they saw
a group of prophets prophesying, with
Samuel standing there as their leader,
the Spirit of God came on Saul's men,
and they also prophesied. 21 Saul was told
about it, and he sent more men, and they
prophesied too. Saul sent men a third
time, and they also prophesied. 22 Finally, he himself left for Ramah and went to
the great cistern at Seku. And he asked,
"Where are Samuel and David?"
"Over in Naioth at Ramah," they said.
23 So Saul went to Naioth at Ramah. But
the Spirit of God came even on him, and
he walked along prophesying until he
came to Naioth. 24 He stripped off his garments, and he too prophesied in Samuel's
presence. He lay naked all that day and
all that night. This is why people say, "Is
Saul also among the prophets?"
20 Then David fled from Naioth at
Ramah and went to Jonathan and
asked, "What have I done? What is my
crime? How have I wronged your father,
that he is trying to kill me?"
2 "Never!" Jonathan replied. "You are
not going to die! Look, my father doesn't
do anything, great or small, without letting me know. Why would he hide this
from me? It isn't so!"
3 But David took an oath and said,
"Your father knows very well that I have
found favor in your eyes, and he has said
to himself, 'Jonathan must not know this
or he will be grieved.' Yet as surely as the
LORD lives and as you live, there is only a
step between me and death."
4 Jonathan said to David, "Whatever
you want me to do, I'll do for you."
5 So David said, "Look, tomorrow is
the New Moon feast, and I am supposed
to dine with the king; but let me go and
hide in the field until the evening of the
day after tomorrow. 6 If your father misses
me at all, tell him, 'David earnestly asked
my permission to hurry to Bethlehem, his
hometown, because an annual sacrifice
is being made there for his whole clan.'
7 If he says, 'Very well,' then your servant
is safe. But if he loses his temper, you can
be sure that he is determined to harm
me. 8 As for you, show kindness to your
servant, for you have brought him into
a covenant with you before the LORD. If
I am guilty, then kill me yourself! Why
hand me over to your father?"
9 "Never!" Jonathan said. "If I had the
least inkling that my father was determined to harm you, wouldn't I tell you?"
10 David asked, "Who will tell me if your
father answers you harshly?"
11 "Come," Jonathan said, "let's go out
into the field." So they went there together.
12 Then Jonathan said to David, "I swear
by the LORD, the God of Israel, that I will
surely sound out my father by this time
the day after tomorrow! If he is favorably
disposed toward you, will I not send you
word and let you know? 13 But if my father
intends to harm you, may the LORD deal
with Jonathan, be it ever so severely, if I
do not let you know and send you away
in peace. May the LORD be with you as he
has been with my father. 14 But show me
unfailing kindness like the LORD's kindness as long as I live, so that I may not be
killed, 15 and do not ever cut off your kindness from my family — not even when the
LORD has cut off every one of David's enemies from the face of the earth."
16 So Jonathan made a covenant with
the house of David, saying, "May the
LORD call David's enemies to account."
17 And Jonathan had David reaffirm his
oath out of love for him, because he loved
him as he loved himself.
18 Then Jonathan said to David, "Tomorrow is the New Moon feast. You will
be missed, because your seat will be
empty. 19 The day after tomorrow, toward
evening, go to the place where you hid
when this trouble began, and wait by the
stone Ezel. 20 I will shoot three arrows to
the side of it, as though I were shooting
at a target. 21 Then I will send a boy and
say, 'Go, find the arrows.' If I say to him,

'Look, the arrows are on this side of you;
bring them here,' then come, because,
as surely as the LORD lives, you are safe;
there is no danger. 22But if I say to the boy,
'Look, the arrows are beyond you,' then
you must go, because the LORD has sent
you away. 23And about the matter you
and I discussed — remember, the LORD is
witness between you and me forever."

24So David hid in the field, and when
the New Moon feast came, the king sat
down to eat. 25He sat in his customary
place by the wall, opposite Jonathan,[a]
and Abner sat next to Saul, but David's
place was empty. 26Saul said nothing
that day, for he thought, "Something
must have happened to David to make
him ceremonially unclean — surely he is
unclean." 27But the next day, the second
day of the month, David's place was empty again. Then Saul said to his son Jonathan, "Why hasn't the son of Jesse come
to the meal, either yesterday or today?"

28Jonathan answered, "David earnestly
asked me for permission to go to Bethlehem. 29He said, 'Let me go, because our
family is observing a sacrifice in the town
and my brother has ordered me to be
there. If I have found favor in your eyes,
let me get away to see my brothers.' That is
why he has not come to the king's table."

30Saul's anger flared up at Jonathan
and he said to him, "You son of a perverse
and rebellious woman! Don't I know that
you have sided with the son of Jesse to
your own shame and to the shame of
the mother who bore you? 31As long as
the son of Jesse lives on this earth, neither you nor your kingdom will be established. Now send someone to bring him
to me, for he must die!"

32"Why should he be put to death?
What has he done?" Jonathan asked his
father. 33But Saul hurled his spear at him
to kill him. Then Jonathan knew that his
father intended to kill David.

34Jonathan got up from the table in
fierce anger; on that second day of the
feast he did not eat, because he was
grieved at his father's shameful treatment of David.

35In the morning Jonathan went out to
the field for his meeting with David. He
had a small boy with him, 36and he said
to the boy, "Run and find the arrows I
shoot." As the boy ran, he shot an arrow
beyond him. 37When the boy came to the
place where Jonathan's arrow had fallen,
Jonathan called out after him, "Isn't the
arrow beyond you?" 38Then he shouted,
"Hurry! Go quickly! Don't stop!" The boy
picked up the arrow and returned to his
master. 39(The boy knew nothing about
all this; only Jonathan and David knew.)
40Then Jonathan gave his weapons to
the boy and said, "Go, carry them back
to town."

41After the boy had gone, David got
up from the south side of the stone and
bowed down before Jonathan three
times, with his face to the ground. Then
they kissed each other and wept together — but David wept the most.

42Jonathan said to David, "Go in peace,
for we have sworn friendship with each
other in the name of the LORD, saying,
'The LORD is witness between you and
me, and between your descendants and
my descendants forever.'" Then David left, and Jonathan went back to the
town.[b]

21 [c] David went to Nob, to Ahimelek the
priest. Ahimelek trembled when he
met him, and asked, "Why are you alone?
Why is no one with you?"

2David answered Ahimelek the priest,
"The king sent me on a mission and said
to me, 'No one is to know anything about
the mission I am sending you on.' As for
my men, I have told them to meet me at
a certain place. 3Now then, what do you
have on hand? Give me five loaves of
bread, or whatever you can find."

4But the priest answered David, "I
don't have any ordinary bread on hand;
however, there is some consecrated
bread here — provided the men have kept
themselves from women."

5David replied, "Indeed women have
been kept from us, as usual whenever[d] I
set out. The men's bodies are holy even
on missions that are not holy. How much
more so today!" 6So the priest gave him
the consecrated bread, since there was no
bread there except the bread of the Presence that had been removed from before
the LORD and replaced by hot bread on
the day it was taken away.

7Now one of Saul's servants was there
that day, detained before the LORD; he

[a] 25 Septuagint; Hebrew *wall. Jonathan arose*
[b] 42 In Hebrew texts this sentence (20:42b) is numbered 21:1.
[c] In Hebrew texts 21:1-15 is numbered 21:2-16.
[d] 5 Or *from us in the past few days since*

was Doeg the Edomite, Saul's chief shepherd.

8David asked Ahimelek, "Don't you have a spear or a sword here? I haven't brought my sword or any other weapon, because the king's mission was urgent."

9The priest replied, "The sword of Goliath the Philistine, whom you killed in the Valley of Elah, is here; it is wrapped in a cloth behind the ephod. If you want it, take it; there is no sword here but that one."

David said, "There is none like it; give it to me."

10That day David fled from Saul and went to Achish king of Gath. 11But the servants of Achish said to him, "Isn't this David, the king of the land? Isn't he the one they sing about in their dances:

"'Saul has slain his thousands,
and David his tens of thousands'?"

12David took these words to heart and was very much afraid of Achish king of Gath. 13So he pretended to be insane in their presence; and while he was in their hands he acted like a madman, making marks on the doors of the gate and letting saliva run down his beard.

14Achish said to his servants, "Look at the man! He is insane! Why bring him to me? 15Am I so short of madmen that you have to bring this fellow here to carry on like this in front of me? Must this man come into my house?"

22 David left Gath and escaped to the cave of Adullam. When his brothers and his father's household heard about it, they went down to him there. 2All those who were in distress or in debt or discontented gathered around him, and he became their commander. About four hundred men were with him.

3From there David went to Mizpah in Moab and said to the king of Moab, "Would you let my father and mother come and stay with you until I learn what God will do for me?" 4So he left them with the king of Moab, and they stayed with him as long as David was in the stronghold.

5But the prophet Gad said to David, "Do not stay in the stronghold. Go into the land of Judah." So David left and went to the forest of Hereth.

6Now Saul heard that David and his men had been discovered. And Saul was seated, spear in hand, under the tamarisk tree on the hill at Gibeah, with all his officials standing at his side. 7He said to them, "Listen, men of Benjamin! Will the son of Jesse give all of you fields and vineyards? Will he make all of you commanders of thousands and commanders of hundreds? 8Is that why you have all conspired against me? No one tells me when my son makes a covenant with the son of Jesse. None of you is concerned about me or tells me that my son has incited my servant to lie in wait for me, as he does today."

9But Doeg the Edomite, who was standing with Saul's officials, said, "I saw the son of Jesse come to Ahimelek son of Ahitub at Nob. 10Ahimelek inquired of the LORD for him; he also gave him provisions and the sword of Goliath the Philistine."

11Then the king sent for the priest Ahimelek son of Ahitub and all the men of his family, who were the priests at Nob, and they all came to the king. 12Saul said, "Listen now, son of Ahitub."

"Yes, my lord," he answered.

13Saul said to him, "Why have you conspired against me, you and the son of Jesse, giving him bread and a sword and inquiring of God for him, so that he has rebelled against me and lies in wait for me, as he does today?"

14Ahimelek answered the king, "Who of all your servants is as loyal as David, the king's son-in-law, captain of your bodyguard and highly respected in your household? 15Was that day the first time I inquired of God for him? Of course not! Let not the king accuse your servant or any of his father's family, for your servant knows nothing at all about this whole affair."

16But the king said, "You will surely die, Ahimelek, you and your whole family."

17Then the king ordered the guards at his side: "Turn and kill the priests of the LORD, because they too have sided with David. They knew he was fleeing, yet they did not tell me."

But the king's officials were unwilling to raise a hand to strike the priests of the LORD.

18The king then ordered Doeg, "You turn and strike down the priests." So Doeg the Edomite turned and struck them down. That day he killed eighty-five men who wore the linen ephod. 19He also put to the sword Nob, the town of the

priests, with its men and women, its children and infants, and its cattle, donkeys
and sheep.
20 But one son of Ahimelek son of Ahitub, named Abiathar, escaped and fled
to join David. 21 He told David that Saul
had killed the priests of the LORD. 22 Then
David said to Abiathar, "That day, when
Doeg the Edomite was there, I knew he
would be sure to tell Saul. I am responsible for the death of your whole family.
23 Stay with me; don't be afraid. The man
who wants to kill you is trying to kill me
too. You will be safe with me."

23 When David was told, "Look, the
Philistines are fighting against Keilah and are looting the threshing floors,"
2 he inquired of the LORD, saying, "Shall I
go and attack these Philistines?"
The LORD answered him, "Go, attack
the Philistines and save Keilah."
3 But David's men said to him, "Here
in Judah we are afraid. How much more,
then, if we go to Keilah against the Philistine forces!"
4 Once again David inquired of the
LORD, and the LORD answered him, "Go
down to Keilah, for I am going to give
the Philistines into your hand." 5 So David and his men went to Keilah, fought
the Philistines and carried off their livestock. He inflicted heavy losses on the
Philistines and saved the people of Keilah. 6 (Now Abiathar son of Ahimelek had
brought the ephod down with him when
he fled to David at Keilah.)
7 Saul was told that David had gone to
Keilah, and he said, "God has delivered
him into my hands, for David has imprisoned himself by entering a town with
gates and bars." 8 And Saul called up all
his forces for battle, to go down to Keilah
to besiege David and his men.
9 When David learned that Saul was
plotting against him, he said to Abiathar
the priest, "Bring the ephod." 10 David
said, "LORD, God of Israel, your servant
has heard definitely that Saul plans to
come to Keilah and destroy the town on
account of me. 11 Will the citizens of Keilah surrender me to him? Will Saul come
down, as your servant has heard? LORD,
God of Israel, tell your servant."
And the LORD said, "He will."
12 Again David asked, "Will the citizens of Keilah surrender me and my men
to Saul?"
And the LORD said, "They will."
13 So David and his men, about six
hundred in number, left Keilah and kept
moving from place to place. When Saul
was told that David had escaped from
Keilah, he did not go there.
14 David stayed in the wilderness
strongholds and in the hills of the Desert of Ziph. Day after day Saul searched
for him, but God did not give David into
his hands.
15 While David was at Horesh in the
Desert of Ziph, he learned that[a] Saul had
come out to take his life. 16 And Saul's
son Jonathan went to David at Horesh
and helped him find strength in God.
17 "Don't be afraid," he said. "My father
Saul will not lay a hand on you. You will
be king over Israel, and I will be second
to you. Even my father Saul knows this."
18 The two of them made a covenant before the LORD. Then Jonathan went home,
but David remained at Horesh.
19 The Ziphites went up to Saul at Gibeah and said, "Is not David hiding among
us in the strongholds at Horesh, on
the hill of Hakilah, south of Jeshimon?
20 Now, Your Majesty, come down whenever it pleases you to do so, and we will
be responsible for giving him into your
hands."
21 Saul replied, "The LORD bless you for
your concern for me. 22 Go and get more
information. Find out where David usually goes and who has seen him there.
They tell me he is very crafty. 23 Find out
about all the hiding places he uses and
come back to me with definite information. Then I will go with you; if he is in the
area, I will track him down among all the
clans of Judah."
24 So they set out and went to Ziph
ahead of Saul. Now David and his men
were in the Desert of Maon, in the Arabah
south of Jeshimon. 25 Saul and his men
began the search, and when David was
told about it, he went down to the rock
and stayed in the Desert of Maon. When
Saul heard this, he went into the Desert of
Maon in pursuit of David.
26 Saul was going along one side of the
mountain, and David and his men were
on the other side, hurrying to get away

[a] 15 Or *he was afraid because*

from Saul. As Saul and his forces were
closing in on David and his men to capture them, 27 a messenger came to Saul,
saying, "Come quickly! The Philistines
are raiding the land." 28 Then Saul broke
off his pursuit of David and went to meet
the Philistines. That is why they call this
place Sela Hammahlekoth.[a] 29 And David went up from there and lived in the
strongholds of En Gedi.[b]

24[c] After Saul returned from pursuing
the Philistines, he was told, "David
is in the Desert of En Gedi." 2 So Saul took
three thousand able young men from all
Israel and set out to look for David and his
men near the Crags of the Wild Goats.
3 He came to the sheep pens along the
way; a cave was there, and Saul went in to
relieve himself. David and his men were
far back in the cave. 4 The men said, "This
is the day the LORD spoke of when he
said[d] to you, 'I will give your enemy into
your hands for you to deal with as you
wish.'" Then David crept up unnoticed
and cut off a corner of Saul's robe.
5 Afterward, David was conscience-
stricken for having cut off a corner of
his robe. 6 He said to his men, "The LORD
forbid that I should do such a thing to my
master, the LORD's anointed, or lay my
hand on him; for he is the anointed of the
LORD." 7 With these words David sharply
rebuked his men and did not allow them
to attack Saul. And Saul left the cave and
went his way.
8 Then David went out of the cave and
called out to Saul, "My lord the king!"
When Saul looked behind him, David
bowed down and prostrated himself with
his face to the ground. 9 He said to Saul,
"Why do you listen when men say, 'David is bent on harming you'? 10 This day
you have seen with your own eyes how
the LORD delivered you into my hands
in the cave. Some urged me to kill you,
but I spared you; I said, 'I will not lay my
hand on my lord, because he is the LORD's
anointed.' 11 See, my father, look at this
piece of your robe in my hand! I cut off
the corner of your robe but did not kill
you. See that there is nothing in my hand
to indicate that I am guilty of wrongdoing
or rebellion. I have not wronged you, but
you are hunting me down to take my life.
12 May the LORD judge between you and
me. And may the LORD avenge the wrongs
you have done to me, but my hand will
not touch you. 13 As the old saying goes,
'From evildoers come evil deeds,' so my
hand will not touch you.
14 "Against whom has the king of Israel
come out? Who are you pursuing? A dead
dog? A flea? 15 May the LORD be our judge
and decide between us. May he consider
my cause and uphold it; may he vindicate
me by delivering me from your hand."
16 When David finished saying this,
Saul asked, "Is that your voice, David my
son?" And he wept aloud. 17 "You are more
righteous than I," he said. "You have
treated me well, but I have treated you
badly. 18 You have just now told me about
the good you did to me; the LORD delivered me into your hands, but you did not
kill me. 19 When a man finds his enemy,
does he let him get away unharmed? May
the LORD reward you well for the way you
treated me today. 20 I know that you will
surely be king and that the kingdom of
Israel will be established in your hands.
21 Now swear to me by the LORD that you
will not kill off my descendants or wipe
out my name from my father's family."
22 So David gave his oath to Saul. Then
Saul returned home, but David and his
men went up to the stronghold.

25 Now Samuel died, and all Israel assembled and mourned for him; and
they buried him at his home in Ramah.
Then David moved down into the Desert
of Paran.[e]
2 A certain man in Maon, who had property there at Carmel, was very wealthy. He
had a thousand goats and three thousand
sheep, which he was shearing in Carmel.
3 His name was Nabal and his wife's name
was Abigail. She was an intelligent and
beautiful woman, but her husband was
surly and mean in his dealings—he was
a Calebite.
4 While David was in the wilderness, he
heard that Nabal was shearing sheep. 5 So
he sent ten young men and said to them,
"Go up to Nabal at Carmel and greet him
in my name. 6 Say to him: 'Long life to you!
Good health to you and your household!
And good health to all that is yours!
7 "'Now I hear that it is sheep-shearing

[a] 28 *Sela Hammahlekoth* means *rock of parting.* [b] 29 In Hebrew texts this verse (23:29) is numbered 24:1.
[c] In Hebrew texts 24:1-22 is numbered 24:2-23. [d] 4 Or *"Today the LORD is saying* [e] 1 Hebrew and some
Septuagint manuscripts; other Septuagint manuscripts *Maon*

time. When your shepherds were with
us, we did not mistreat them, and the
whole time they were at Carmel nothing
of theirs was missing. 8Ask your own servants and they will tell you. Therefore be
favorable toward my men, since we come
at a festive time. Please give your servants and your son David whatever you
can find for them.' "
9When David's men arrived, they gave
Nabal this message in David's name.
Then they waited.
10Nabal answered David's servants,
"Who is this David? Who is this son of
Jesse? Many servants are breaking away
from their masters these days. 11Why
should I take my bread and water, and
the meat I have slaughtered for my shearers, and give it to men coming from who
knows where?"
12David's men turned around and
went back. When they arrived, they reported every word. 13David said to his
men, "Each of you strap on your sword!"
So they did, and David strapped his on as
well. About four hundred men went up
with David, while two hundred stayed
with the supplies.
14One of the servants told Abigail, Nabal's wife, "David sent messengers from
the wilderness to give our master his
greetings, but he hurled insults at them.
15Yet these men were very good to us.
They did not mistreat us, and the whole
time we were out in the fields near them
nothing was missing. 16Night and day
they were a wall around us the whole
time we were herding our sheep near
them. 17Now think it over and see what
you can do, because disaster is hanging
over our master and his whole household. He is such a wicked man that no one
can talk to him."
18Abigail acted quickly. She took two
hundred loaves of bread, two skins of
wine, five dressed sheep, five seahs[a] of
roasted grain, a hundred cakes of raisins
and two hundred cakes of pressed figs,
and loaded them on donkeys. 19Then
she told her servants, "Go on ahead; I'll
follow you." But she did not tell her husband Nabal.
20As she came riding her donkey into
a mountain ravine, there were David
and his men descending toward her, and
she met them. 21David had just said, "It's
been useless—all my watching over this
fellow's property in the wilderness so
that nothing of his was missing. He has
paid me back evil for good. 22May God
deal with David,[b] be it ever so severely,
if by morning I leave alive one male of all
who belong to him!"
23When Abigail saw David, she quickly
got off her donkey and bowed down before David with her face to the ground.
24She fell at his feet and said: "Pardon
your servant, my lord, and let me speak
to you; hear what your servant has to say.
25Please pay no attention, my lord, to
that wicked man Nabal. He is just like his
name—his name means Fool, and folly
goes with him. And as for me, your servant, I did not see the men my lord sent.
26And now, my lord, as surely as the LORD
your God lives and as you live, since the
LORD has kept you from bloodshed and
from avenging yourself with your own
hands, may your enemies and all who are
intent on harming my lord be like Nabal.
27And let this gift, which your servant has
brought to my lord, be given to the men
who follow you.
28"Please forgive your servant's presumption. The LORD your God will certainly make a lasting dynasty for my lord,
because you fight the LORD's battles, and
no wrongdoing will be found in you as
long as you live. 29Even though someone
is pursuing you to take your life, the life
of my lord will be bound securely in the
bundle of the living by the LORD your
God, but the lives of your enemies he will
hurl away as from the pocket of a sling.
30When the LORD has fulfilled for my
lord every good thing he promised concerning him and has appointed him ruler over Israel, 31my lord will not have on
his conscience the staggering burden of
needless bloodshed or of having avenged
himself. And when the LORD your God
has brought my lord success, remember
your servant."
32David said to Abigail, "Praise be
to the LORD, the God of Israel, who has
sent you today to meet me. 33May you
be blessed for your good judgment and
for keeping me from bloodshed this day
and from avenging myself with my own
hands. 34Otherwise, as surely as the

[a] *18* That is, probably about 60 pounds or about 27 kilograms [b] *22* Some Septuagint manuscripts; Hebrew *with David's enemies*

LORD, the God of Israel, lives, who has
kept me from harming you, if you had not
come quickly to meet me, not one male
belonging to Nabal would have been left
alive by daybreak."
35 Then David accepted from her hand
what she had brought him and said, "Go
home in peace. I have heard your words
and granted your request."
36 When Abigail went to Nabal, he was
in the house holding a banquet like that
of a king. He was in high spirits and very
drunk. So she told him nothing at all
until daybreak. 37 Then in the morning,
when Nabal was sober, his wife told him
all these things, and his heart failed him
and he became like a stone. 38 About ten
days later, the LORD struck Nabal and he
died.
39 When David heard that Nabal was
dead, he said, "Praise be to the LORD,
who has upheld my cause against Nabal
for treating me with contempt. He has
kept his servant from doing wrong and
has brought Nabal's wrongdoing down
on his own head."
Then David sent word to Abigail, asking her to become his wife. 40 His servants
went to Carmel and said to Abigail, "David has sent us to you to take you to become his wife."
41 She bowed down with her face to the
ground and said, "I am your servant and
am ready to serve you and wash the feet
of my lord's servants." 42 Abigail quickly got on a donkey and, attended by her
five female servants, went with David's
messengers and became his wife. 43 David had also married Ahinoam of Jezreel,
and they both were his wives. 44 But Saul
had given his daughter Michal, David's
wife, to Paltiel[a] son of Laish, who was
from Gallim.

26 The Ziphites went to Saul at Gibeah
and said, "Is not David hiding on the
hill of Hakilah, which faces Jeshimon?"
2 So Saul went down to the Desert of
Ziph, with his three thousand select Israelite troops, to search there for David.
3 Saul made his camp beside the road on
the hill of Hakilah facing Jeshimon, but
David stayed in the wilderness. When he
saw that Saul had followed him there, 4 he
sent out scouts and learned that Saul had
definitely arrived.
5 Then David set out and went to the
place where Saul had camped. He saw
where Saul and Abner son of Ner, the
commander of the army, had lain down.
Saul was lying inside the camp, with the
army encamped around him.
6 David then asked Ahimelek the Hittite
and Abishai son of Zeruiah, Joab's brother, "Who will go down into the camp with
me to Saul?"
"I'll go with you," said Abishai.
7 So David and Abishai went to the army
by night, and there was Saul, lying asleep
inside the camp with his spear stuck in
the ground near his head. Abner and the
soldiers were lying around him.
8 Abishai said to David, "Today God has
delivered your enemy into your hands.
Now let me pin him to the ground with
one thrust of the spear; I won't strike him
twice."
9 But David said to Abishai, "Don't destroy him! Who can lay a hand on the
LORD's anointed and be guiltless? 10 As
surely as the LORD lives," he said, "the
LORD himself will strike him, or his time
will come and he will die, or he will go
into battle and perish. 11 But the LORD forbid that I should lay a hand on the LORD's
anointed. Now get the spear and water
jug that are near his head, and let's go."
12 So David took the spear and water
jug near Saul's head, and they left. No
one saw or knew about it, nor did anyone wake up. They were all sleeping, because the LORD had put them into a deep
sleep.
13 Then David crossed over to the other
side and stood on top of the hill some distance away; there was a wide space between them. 14 He called out to the army
and to Abner son of Ner, "Aren't you going
to answer me, Abner?"
Abner replied, "Who are you who calls
to the king?"
15 David said, "You're a man, aren't
you? And who is like you in Israel? Why
didn't you guard your lord the king?
Someone came to destroy your lord the
king. 16 What you have done is not good.
As surely as the LORD lives, you and your
men must die, because you did not guard
your master, the LORD's anointed. Look
around you. Where are the king's spear
and water jug that were near his head?"

[a] 44 Hebrew *Palti*, a variant of *Paltiel*

17 Saul recognized David's voice and
said, "Is that your voice, David my son?"
David replied, "Yes it is, my lord the
king." 18 And he added, "Why is my lord
pursuing his servant? What have I done,
and what wrong am I guilty of? 19 Now
let my lord the king listen to his servant's words. If the LORD has incited you
against me, then may he accept an offering. If, however, people have done it, may
they be cursed before the LORD! They
have driven me today from my share in
the LORD's inheritance and have said,
'Go, serve other gods.' 20 Now do not let
my blood fall to the ground far from the
presence of the LORD. The king of Israel
has come out to look for a flea—as one
hunts a partridge in the mountains."
21 Then Saul said, "I have sinned. Come
back, David my son. Because you considered my life precious today, I will not try
to harm you again. Surely I have acted like
a fool and have been terribly wrong."
22 "Here is the king's spear," David answered. "Let one of your young men come
over and get it. 23 The LORD rewards everyone for their righteousness and faithfulness. The LORD delivered you into my
hands today, but I would not lay a hand
on the LORD's anointed. 24 As surely as I
valued your life today, so may the LORD
value my life and deliver me from all
trouble."
25 Then Saul said to David, "May you be
blessed, David my son; you will do great
things and surely triumph."
So David went on his way, and Saul returned home.

27 But David thought to himself, "One
of these days I will be destroyed by
the hand of Saul. The best thing I can do
is to escape to the land of the Philistines.
Then Saul will give up searching for me
anywhere in Israel, and I will slip out of
his hand."
2 So David and the six hundred men
with him left and went over to Achish son
of Maok king of Gath. 3 David and his men
settled in Gath with Achish. Each man
had his family with him, and David had
his two wives: Ahinoam of Jezreel and
Abigail of Carmel, the widow of Nabal.
4 When Saul was told that David had fled
to Gath, he no longer searched for him.
5 Then David said to Achish, "If I have
found favor in your eyes, let a place be assigned to me in one of the country towns,
that I may live there. Why should your
servant live in the royal city with you?"
6 So on that day Achish gave him Ziklag, and it has belonged to the kings of Judah ever since. 7 David lived in Philistine
territory a year and four months.
8 Now David and his men went up and
raided the Geshurites, the Girzites and
the Amalekites. (From ancient times
these peoples had lived in the land extending to Shur and Egypt.) 9 Whenever
David attacked an area, he did not leave a
man or woman alive, but took sheep and
cattle, donkeys and camels, and clothes.
Then he returned to Achish.
10 When Achish asked, "Where did
you go raiding today?" David would say,
"Against the Negev of Judah" or "Against
the Negev of Jerahmeel" or "Against the
Negev of the Kenites." 11 He did not leave
a man or woman alive to be brought to
Gath, for he thought, "They might inform
on us and say, 'This is what David did.'"
And such was his practice as long as he
lived in Philistine territory. 12 Achish
trusted David and said to himself, "He
has become so obnoxious to his people,
the Israelites, that he will be my servant
for life."

28 In those days the Philistines gathered their forces to fight against
Israel. Achish said to David, "You must
understand that you and your men will
accompany me in the army."
2 David said, "Then you will see for
yourself what your servant can do."
Achish replied, "Very well, I will make
you my bodyguard for life."
3 Now Samuel was dead, and all Israel
had mourned for him and buried him
in his own town of Ramah. Saul had expelled the mediums and spiritists from
the land.
4 The Philistines assembled and came
and set up camp at Shunem, while Saul
gathered all Israel and set up camp at Gilboa. 5 When Saul saw the Philistine army,
he was afraid; terror filled his heart. 6 He
inquired of the LORD, but the LORD did
not answer him by dreams or Urim or
prophets. 7 Saul then said to his attendants, "Find me a woman who is a medium, so I may go and inquire of her."
"There is one in Endor," they said.
8 So Saul disguised himself, putting on
other clothes, and at night he and two
men went to the woman. "Consult a spir-

26 When David reached Ziklag, he sent
some of the plunder to the elders of Judah, who were his friends, saying, “Here
is a gift for you from the plunder of the
LORD's enemies.”
27 David sent it to those who were in
Bethel, Ramoth Negev and Jattir; 28 to
those in Aroer, Siphmoth, Eshtemoa
29 and Rakal; to those in the towns of the
Jerahmeelites and the Kenites; 30 to those
in Hormah, Bor Ashan, Athak 31 and Hebron; and to those in all the other places
where he and his men had roamed.

31 Now the Philistines fought against
Israel; the Israelites fled before
them, and many fell dead on Mount Gilboa. 2 The Philistines were in hot pursuit
of Saul and his sons, and they killed his
sons Jonathan, Abinadab and Malki-
Shua. 3 The fighting grew fierce around
Saul, and when the archers overtook him,
they wounded him critically.
4 Saul said to his armor-bearer, “Draw
your sword and run me through, or these
uncircumcised fellows will come and run
me through and abuse me.”
But his armor-bearer was terrified
and would not do it; so Saul took his own
sword and fell on it. 5 When the armor-
bearer saw that Saul was dead, he too fell
on his sword and died with him. 6 So Saul
and his three sons and his armor-bearer
and all his men died together that same
day.
7 When the Israelites along the valley
and those across the Jordan saw that the
Israelite army had fled and that Saul and
his sons had died, they abandoned their
towns and fled. And the Philistines came
and occupied them.
8 The next day, when the Philistines
came to strip the dead, they found Saul
and his three sons fallen on Mount Gilboa.
9 They cut off his head and stripped off his
armor, and they sent messengers throughout the land of the Philistines to proclaim
the news in the temple of their idols and
among their people. 10 They put his armor
in the temple of the Ashtoreths and fastened his body to the wall of Beth Shan.
11 When the people of Jabesh Gilead
heard what the Philistines had done to
Saul, 12 all their valiant men marched
through the night to Beth Shan. They
took down the bodies of Saul and his sons
from the wall of Beth Shan and went to
Jabesh, where they burned them. 13 Then
they took their bones and buried them
under a tamarisk tree at Jabesh, and they
fasted seven days.

2 SAMUEL

See the Invitation to Samuel-Kings on p. 240.

1 After the death of Saul, David returned from striking down the Amalekites and stayed in Ziklag two days. 2 On
the third day a man arrived from Saul's
camp with his clothes torn and dust on
his head. When he came to David, he fell
to the ground to pay him honor.
3 “Where have you come from?” David
asked him.
He answered, “I have escaped from the
Israelite camp.”
4 “What happened?” David asked.
“Tell me.”
“The men fled from the battle,” he replied. “Many of them fell and died. And
Saul and his son Jonathan are dead.”
5 Then David said to the young man
who brought him the report, “How do
you know that Saul and his son Jonathan
are dead?”
6 “I happened to be on Mount Gilboa,”
the young man said, “and there was Saul,
leaning on his spear, with the chariots
and their drivers in hot pursuit. 7 When
he turned around and saw me, he called
out to me, and I said, ‘What can I do?’

8 "He asked me, 'Who are you?'
" 'An Amalekite,' I answered.
9 "Then he said to me, 'Stand here by
me and kill me! I'm in the throes of death,
but I'm still alive.'
10 "So I stood beside him and killed
him, because I knew that after he had
fallen he could not survive. And I took
the crown that was on his head and the
band on his arm and have brought them
here to my lord."
11 Then David and all the men with him
took hold of their clothes and tore them.
12 They mourned and wept and fasted till
evening for Saul and his son Jonathan,
and for the army of the LORD and for the
nation of Israel, because they had fallen
by the sword.
13 David said to the young man who
brought him the report, "Where are you
from?"
"I am the son of a foreigner, an Amalekite," he answered.
14 David asked him, "Why weren't you
afraid to lift your hand to destroy the
LORD's anointed?"
15 Then David called one of his men and
said, "Go, strike him down!" So he struck
him down, and he died. 16 For David had
said to him, "Your blood be on your own
head. Your own mouth testified against
you when you said, 'I killed the LORD's
anointed.' "
17 David took up this lament concerning Saul and his son Jonathan, 18 and
he ordered that the people of Judah be
taught this lament of the bow (it is written in the Book of Jashar):

19 "A gazelle[a] lies slain on your heights,
Israel.
How the mighty have fallen!

20 "Tell it not in Gath,
proclaim it not in the streets of
Ashkelon,
lest the daughters of the Philistines be
glad,
lest the daughters of the
uncircumcised rejoice.

21 "Mountains of Gilboa,
may you have neither dew nor rain,
may no showers fall on your
terraced fields.[b]
For there the shield of the mighty was
despised,
the shield of Saul—no longer
rubbed with oil.

22 "From the blood of the slain,
from the flesh of the mighty,
the bow of Jonathan did not turn back,
the sword of Saul did not return
unsatisfied.
23 Saul and Jonathan—
in life they were loved and admired,
and in death they were not parted.
They were swifter than eagles,
they were stronger than lions.

24 "Daughters of Israel,
weep for Saul,
who clothed you in scarlet and finery,
who adorned your garments with
ornaments of gold.

25 "How the mighty have fallen in battle!
Jonathan lies slain on your heights.
26 I grieve for you, Jonathan my brother;
you were very dear to me.
Your love for me was wonderful,
more wonderful than that of
women.

27 "How the mighty have fallen!
The weapons of war have perished!"

2 In the course of time, David inquired
of the LORD. "Shall I go up to one of the
towns of Judah?" he asked.
The LORD said, "Go up."
David asked, "Where shall I go?"
"To Hebron," the LORD answered.
2 So David went up there with his two
wives, Ahinoam of Jezreel and Abigail,
the widow of Nabal of Carmel. 3 David
also took the men who were with him,
each with his family, and they settled in
Hebron and its towns. 4 Then the men of
Judah came to Hebron, and there they
anointed David king over the tribe of Judah.
When David was told that it was the
men from Jabesh Gilead who had buried
Saul, 5 he sent messengers to them to say
to them, "The LORD bless you for showing this kindness to Saul your master by
burying him. 6 May the LORD now show
you kindness and faithfulness, and I too
will show you the same favor because you
have done this. 7 Now then, be strong and
brave, for Saul your master is dead, and
the people of Judah have anointed me
king over them."

[a] 19 *Gazelle* here symbolizes a human dignitary. [b] 21 Or / *nor fields that yield grain for offerings*

8 Meanwhile, Abner son of Ner, the
commander of Saul's army, had taken
Ish-Bosheth son of Saul and brought him
over to Mahanaim. 9 He made him king
over Gilead, Ashuri and Jezreel, and also
over Ephraim, Benjamin and all Israel.

10 Ish-Bosheth son of Saul was forty
years old when he became king over Israel, and he reigned two years. The tribe
of Judah, however, remained loyal to David. 11 The length of time David was king
in Hebron over Judah was seven years
and six months.

12 Abner son of Ner, together with the
men of Ish-Bosheth son of Saul, left Mahanaim and went to Gibeon. 13 Joab son
of Zeruiah and David's men went out
and met them at the pool of Gibeon. One
group sat down on one side of the pool
and one group on the other side.

14 Then Abner said to Joab, "Let's have
some of the young men get up and fight
hand to hand in front of us."

"All right, let them do it," Joab said.

15 So they stood up and were counted off—twelve men for Benjamin and
Ish-Bosheth son of Saul, and twelve for
David. 16 Then each man grabbed his opponent by the head and thrust his dagger
into his opponent's side, and they fell
down together. So that place in Gibeon
was called Helkath Hazzurim.[a]

17 The battle that day was very fierce,
and Abner and the Israelites were defeated by David's men.

18 The three sons of Zeruiah were there:
Joab, Abishai and Asahel. Now Asahel
was as fleet-footed as a wild gazelle. 19 He
chased Abner, turning neither to the right
nor to the left as he pursued him. 20 Abner
looked behind him and asked, "Is that
you, Asahel?"

"It is," he answered.

21 Then Abner said to him, "Turn aside
to the right or to the left; take on one of
the young men and strip him of his weapons." But Asahel would not stop chasing
him.

22 Again Abner warned Asahel, "Stop
chasing me! Why should I strike you
down? How could I look your brother
Joab in the face?"

23 But Asahel refused to give up the pursuit; so Abner thrust the butt of his spear
into Asahel's stomach, and the spear
came out through his back. He fell there
and died on the spot. And every man
stopped when he came to the place where
Asahel had fallen and died.

24 But Joab and Abishai pursued Abner,
and as the sun was setting, they came to
the hill of Ammah, near Giah on the way
to the wasteland of Gibeon. 25 Then the
men of Benjamin rallied behind Abner.
They formed themselves into a group and
took their stand on top of a hill.

26 Abner called out to Joab, "Must the
sword devour forever? Don't you realize
that this will end in bitterness? How long
before you order your men to stop pursuing their fellow Israelites?"

27 Joab answered, "As surely as God
lives, if you had not spoken, the men
would have continued pursuing them
until morning."

28 So Joab blew the trumpet, and all
the troops came to a halt; they no longer
pursued Israel, nor did they fight anymore.

29 All that night Abner and his men
marched through the Arabah. They
crossed the Jordan, continued through
the morning hours[b] and came to Mahanaim.

30 Then Joab stopped pursuing Abner
and assembled the whole army. Besides
Asahel, nineteen of David's men were
found missing. 31 But David's men had
killed three hundred and sixty Benjamites who were with Abner. 32 They took
Asahel and buried him in his father's
tomb at Bethlehem. Then Joab and his
men marched all night and arrived at
Hebron by daybreak.

3 The war between the house of Saul
and the house of David lasted a long
time. David grew stronger and stronger,
while the house of Saul grew weaker and
weaker.

2 Sons were born to David in Hebron:
His firstborn was Amnon the son of
Ahinoam of Jezreel;
3 his second, Kileab the son of Abigail the widow of Nabal of Carmel;
the third, Absalom the son of Maakah daughter of Talmai king of
Geshur;
4 the fourth, Adonijah the son of
Haggith;

[a] 16 *Helkath Hazzurim* means *field of daggers* or *field of hostilities*. [b] 29 See Septuagint; the meaning of the Hebrew for this phrase is uncertain.

the fifth, Shephatiah the son of
Abital;
5 and the sixth, Ithream the son of
David's wife Eglah.
These were born to David in He-
bron.

6 During the war between the house of
Saul and the house of David, Abner had
been strengthening his own position in
the house of Saul. 7 Now Saul had had a
concubine named Rizpah daughter of
Aiah. And Ish-Bosheth said to Abner,
"Why did you sleep with my father's concubine?"
8 Abner was very angry because of what
Ish-Bosheth said. So he answered, "Am I
a dog's head — on Judah's side? This very
day I am loyal to the house of your father Saul and to his family and friends.
I haven't handed you over to David. Yet
now you accuse me of an offense involving this woman! 9 May God deal with Abner, be it ever so severely, if I do not do
for David what the LORD promised him
on oath 10 and transfer the kingdom from
the house of Saul and establish David's
throne over Israel and Judah from Dan to
Beersheba." 11 Ish-Bosheth did not dare
to say another word to Abner, because he
was afraid of him.
12 Then Abner sent messengers on his
behalf to say to David, "Whose land is it?
Make an agreement with me, and I will
help you bring all Israel over to you."
13 "Good," said David. "I will make an
agreement with you. But I demand one
thing of you: Do not come into my presence unless you bring Michal daughter of
Saul when you come to see me." 14 Then
David sent messengers to Ish-Bosheth
son of Saul, demanding, "Give me my
wife Michal, whom I betrothed to myself for the price of a hundred Philistine
foreskins."
15 So Ish-Bosheth gave orders and had
her taken away from her husband Paltiel son of Laish. 16 Her husband, however,
went with her, weeping behind her all the
way to Bahurim. Then Abner said to him,
"Go back home!" So he went back.
17 Abner conferred with the elders of
Israel and said, "For some time you have
wanted to make David your king. 18 Now
do it! For the LORD promised David, 'By
my servant David I will rescue my people
Israel from the hand of the Philistines
and from the hand of all their enemies.'"
19 Abner also spoke to the Benjamites
in person. Then he went to Hebron to
tell David everything that Israel and the
whole tribe of Benjamin wanted to do.
20 When Abner, who had twenty men with
him, came to David at Hebron, David prepared a feast for him and his men. 21 Then
Abner said to David, "Let me go at once
and assemble all Israel for my lord the
king, so that they may make a covenant
with you, and that you may rule over all
that your heart desires." So David sent
Abner away, and he went in peace.
22 Just then David's men and Joab returned from a raid and brought with
them a great deal of plunder. But Abner
was no longer with David in Hebron, because David had sent him away, and he
had gone in peace. 23 When Joab and all
the soldiers with him arrived, he was told
that Abner son of Ner had come to the
king and that the king had sent him away
and that he had gone in peace.
24 So Joab went to the king and said,
"What have you done? Look, Abner came
to you. Why did you let him go? Now he
is gone! 25 You know Abner son of Ner; he
came to deceive you and observe your
movements and find out everything you
are doing."
26 Joab then left David and sent messengers after Abner, and they brought
him back from the cistern at Sirah. But
David did not know it. 27 Now when Abner
returned to Hebron, Joab took him aside
into an inner chamber, as if to speak with
him privately. And there, to avenge the
blood of his brother Asahel, Joab stabbed
him in the stomach, and he died.
28 Later, when David heard about this,
he said, "I and my kingdom are forever
innocent before the LORD concerning
the blood of Abner son of Ner. 29 May his
blood fall on the head of Joab and on his
whole family! May Joab's family never
be without someone who has a running
sore or leprosy[a] or who leans on a crutch
or who falls by the sword or who lacks
food."
30 (Joab and his brother Abishai murdered Abner because he had killed their
brother Asahel in the battle at Gibeon.)
31 Then David said to Joab and all the

[a] 29 The Hebrew for *leprosy* was used for various diseases affecting the skin.

people with him, "Tear your clothes and
put on sackcloth and walk in mourning
in front of Abner." King David himself
walked behind the bier. 32They buried Abner in Hebron, and the king wept
aloud at Abner's tomb. All the people
wept also.
33The king sang this lament for Abner:

"Should Abner have died as the
lawless die?
34 Your hands were not bound,
your feet were not fettered.
You fell as one falls before the wicked."

And all the people wept over him
again.
35Then they all came and urged David
to eat something while it was still day;
but David took an oath, saying, "May
God deal with me, be it ever so severely,
if I taste bread or anything else before the
sun sets!"
36All the people took note and were
pleased; indeed, everything the king did
pleased them. 37So on that day all the
people there and all Israel knew that the
king had no part in the murder of Abner
son of Ner.
38Then the king said to his men, "Do
you not realize that a commander and a
great man has fallen in Israel this day?
39And today, though I am the anointed
king, I am weak, and these sons of Zeruiah are too strong for me. May the LORD
repay the evildoer according to his evil
deeds!"

4 When Ish-Bosheth son of Saul heard
that Abner had died in Hebron, he lost
courage, and all Israel became alarmed.
2Now Saul's son had two men who were
leaders of raiding bands. One was named
Baanah and the other Rekab; they were
sons of Rimmon the Beerothite from the
tribe of Benjamin—Beeroth is considered part of Benjamin, 3because the people of Beeroth fled to Gittaim and have
resided there as foreigners to this day.
4(Jonathan son of Saul had a son who
was lame in both feet. He was five years
old when the news about Saul and Jonathan came from Jezreel. His nurse picked
him up and fled, but as she hurried to
leave, he fell and became disabled. His
name was Mephibosheth.)
5Now Rekab and Baanah, the sons of
Rimmon the Beerothite, set out for the
house of Ish-Bosheth, and they arrived
there in the heat of the day while he was
taking his noonday rest. 6They went into
the inner part of the house as if to get
some wheat, and they stabbed him in the
stomach. Then Rekab and his brother Baanah slipped away.
7They had gone into the house while he
was lying on the bed in his bedroom. After they stabbed and killed him, they cut
off his head. Taking it with them, they
traveled all night by way of the Arabah.
8They brought the head of Ish-Bosheth
to David at Hebron and said to the king,
"Here is the head of Ish-Bosheth son of
Saul, your enemy, who tried to kill you.
This day the LORD has avenged my lord
the king against Saul and his offspring."
9David answered Rekab and his brother Baanah, the sons of Rimmon the Beerothite, "As surely as the LORD lives, who
has delivered me out of every trouble,
10when someone told me, 'Saul is dead,'
and thought he was bringing good news,
I seized him and put him to death in Ziklag. That was the reward I gave him for his
news! 11How much more—when wicked
men have killed an innocent man in his
own house and on his own bed—should
I not now demand his blood from your
hand and rid the earth of you!"
12So David gave an order to his men,
and they killed them. They cut off their
hands and feet and hung the bodies by
the pool in Hebron. But they took the
head of Ish-Bosheth and buried it in Abner's tomb at Hebron.

5 All the tribes of Israel came to David
at Hebron and said, "We are your own
flesh and blood. 2In the past, while Saul
was king over us, you were the one who
led Israel on their military campaigns.
And the LORD said to you, 'You will shepherd my people Israel, and you will become their ruler.'"
3When all the elders of Israel had come
to King David at Hebron, the king made
a covenant with them at Hebron before
the LORD, and they anointed David king
over Israel.

4David was thirty years old when he
became king, and he reigned forty years.
5In Hebron he reigned over Judah seven
years and six months, and in Jerusalem
he reigned over all Israel and Judah thirty-three years.
6The king and his men marched to Je-

rusalem to attack the Jebusites, who lived
there. The Jebusites said to David, "You
will not get in here; even the blind and
the lame can ward you off." They thought,
"David cannot get in here." 7 Nevertheless, David captured the fortress of
Zion — which is the City of David.
8 On that day David had said, "Anyone
who conquers the Jebusites will have to
use the water shaft to reach those 'lame
and blind' who are David's enemies.[a]"
That is why they say, "The 'blind and
lame' will not enter the palace."
9 David then took up residence in the
fortress and called it the City of David.
He built up the area around it, from the
terraces[b] inward. 10 And he became more
and more powerful, because the LORD
God Almighty was with him.
11 Now Hiram king of Tyre sent envoys
to David, along with cedar logs and carpenters and stonemasons, and they built
a palace for David. 12 Then David knew
that the LORD had established him as
king over Israel and had exalted his kingdom for the sake of his people Israel.
13 After he left Hebron, David took more
concubines and wives in Jerusalem, and
more sons and daughters were born to
him. 14 These are the names of the children born to him there: Shammua, Shobab, Nathan, Solomon, 15 Ibhar, Elishua,
Nepheg, Japhia, 16 Elishama, Eliada and
Eliphelet.
17 When the Philistines heard that David had been anointed king over Israel,
they went up in full force to search for
him, but David heard about it and went
down to the stronghold. 18 Now the Philistines had come and spread out in the
Valley of Rephaim; 19 so David inquired
of the LORD, "Shall I go and attack the
Philistines? Will you deliver them into
my hands?"
The LORD answered him, "Go, for I will
surely deliver the Philistines into your
hands."
20 So David went to Baal Perazim, and
there he defeated them. He said, "As waters break out, the LORD has broken out
against my enemies before me." So that
place was called Baal Perazim.[c] 21 The
Philistines abandoned their idols there,
and David and his men carried them off.
22 Once more the Philistines came up
and spread out in the Valley of Rephaim;
23 so David inquired of the LORD, and he
answered, "Do not go straight up, but circle around behind them and attack them
in front of the poplar trees. 24 As soon as
you hear the sound of marching in the
tops of the poplar trees, move quickly,
because that will mean the LORD has
gone out in front of you to strike the Philistine army." 25 So David did as the LORD
commanded him, and he struck down
the Philistines all the way from Gibeon[d]
to Gezer.

6 David again brought together all the
able young men of Israel — thirty
thousand. 2 He and all his men went to
Baalah[e] in Judah to bring up from there
the ark of God, which is called by the
Name,[f] the name of the LORD Almighty,
who is enthroned between the cherubim
on the ark. 3 They set the ark of God on a
new cart and brought it from the house of
Abinadab, which was on the hill. Uzzah
and Ahio, sons of Abinadab, were guiding
the new cart 4 with the ark of God on it,[g]
and Ahio was walking in front of it. 5 David and all Israel were celebrating with
all their might before the LORD, with cas-
tanets,[h] harps, lyres, timbrels, sistrums
and cymbals.
6 When they came to the threshing floor
of Nakon, Uzzah reached out and took
hold of the ark of God, because the oxen
stumbled. 7 The LORD's anger burned
against Uzzah because of his irreverent
act; therefore God struck him down, and
he died there beside the ark of God.
8 Then David was angry because the
LORD's wrath had broken out against Uzzah, and to this day that place is called
Perez Uzzah.[i]
9 David was afraid of the LORD that day
and said, "How can the ark of the LORD
ever come to me?" 10 He was not willing to
take the ark of the LORD to be with him in
the City of David. Instead, he took it to the
house of Obed-Edom the Gittite. 11 The

[a] 8 Or *are hated by David* [b] 9 Or *the Millo* [c] 20 *Baal Perazim* means *the lord who breaks out.*
[d] 25 Septuagint (see also 1 Chron. 14:16); Hebrew *Geba* [e] 2 That is, Kiriath Jearim (see 1 Chron. 13:6)
[f] 2 Hebrew; Septuagint and Vulgate do not have *the Name.* [g] 3,4 Dead Sea Scrolls and some Septuagint manuscripts; Masoretic Text *cart* [4]*and they brought it with the ark of God from the house of Abinadab, which was on the hill* [h] 5 Masoretic Text; Dead Sea Scrolls and Septuagint (see also 1 Chron. 13:8) *songs*
[i] 8 *Perez Uzzah* means *outbreak against Uzzah.*

ark of the LORD remained in the house of
Obed-Edom the Gittite for three months,
and the LORD blessed him and his entire
household.
12 Now King David was told, "The LORD
has blessed the household of Obed-Edom
and everything he has, because of the ark
of God." So David went to bring up the ark
of God from the house of Obed-Edom to
the City of David with rejoicing. 13 When
those who were carrying the ark of the
LORD had taken six steps, he sacrificed a
bull and a fattened calf. 14 Wearing a lin-
en ephod, David was dancing before the
LORD with all his might, 15 while he and
all Israel were bringing up the ark of the
LORD with shouts and the sound of trumpets.
16 As the ark of the LORD was entering
the City of David, Michal daughter of
Saul watched from a window. And when
she saw King David leaping and dancing
before the LORD, she despised him in her
heart.
17 They brought the ark of the LORD
and set it in its place inside the tent that
David had pitched for it, and David sacrificed burnt offerings and fellowship
offerings before the LORD. 18 After he had
finished sacrificing the burnt offerings
and fellowship offerings, he blessed the
people in the name of the LORD Almighty.
19 Then he gave a loaf of bread, a cake of
dates and a cake of raisins to each person in the whole crowd of Israelites, both
men and women. And all the people went
to their homes.
20 When David returned home to bless
his household, Michal daughter of Saul
came out to meet him and said, "How the
king of Israel has distinguished himself
today, going around half-naked in full
view of the slave girls of his servants as
any vulgar fellow would!"
21 David said to Michal, "It was before
the LORD, who chose me rather than your
father or anyone from his house when he
appointed me ruler over the LORD's people Israel—I will celebrate before the
LORD. 22 I will become even more undig-
nified than this, and I will be humiliated
in my own eyes. But by these slave girls
you spoke of, I will be held in honor."
23 And Michal daughter of Saul had no
children to the day of her death.

7 After the king was settled in his palace
and the LORD had given him rest from
all his enemies around him, 2 he said to
Nathan the prophet, "Here I am, living in
a house of cedar, while the ark of God remains in a tent."
3 Nathan replied to the king, "Whatever
you have in mind, go ahead and do it, for
the LORD is with you."
4 But that night the word of the LORD
came to Nathan, saying:

5 "Go and tell my servant David,
'This is what the LORD says: Are you
the one to build me a house to dwell
in? 6 I have not dwelt in a house from
the day I brought the Israelites up out
of Egypt to this day. I have been moving from place to place with a tent
as my dwelling. 7 Wherever I have
moved with all the Israelites, did I
ever say to any of their rulers whom I
commanded to shepherd my people
Israel, "Why have you not built me a
house of cedar?"'
8 "Now then, tell my servant David, 'This is what the LORD Almighty
says: I took you from the pasture,
from tending the flock, and appointed you ruler over my people Israel. 9 I have been with you wherever
you have gone, and I have cut off all
your enemies from before you. Now I
will make your name great, like the
names of the greatest men on earth.
10 And I will provide a place for my
people Israel and will plant them so
that they can have a home of their
own and no longer be disturbed.
Wicked people will not oppress them
anymore, as they did at the beginning 11 and have done ever since the
time I appointed leaders[a] over my
people Israel. I will also give you rest
from all your enemies.
"'The LORD declares to you that
the LORD himself will establish a
house for you: 12 When your days
are over and you rest with your ancestors, I will raise up your offspring
to succeed you, your own flesh and
blood, and I will establish his kingdom. 13 He is the one who will build
a house for my Name, and I will establish the throne of his kingdom
forever. 14 I will be his father, and he

[a] 11 Traditionally *judges*

will be my son. When he does wrong,
I will punish him with a rod wield-
ed by men, with floggings inflicted by human hands. 15But my love
will never be taken away from him,
as I took it away from Saul, whom I
removed from before you. 16Your
house and your kingdom will endure
forever before me[a]; your throne will
be established forever.' "

17Nathan reported to David all the
words of this entire revelation.

18Then King David went in and sat before the LORD, and he said:

"Who am I, Sovereign LORD, and
what is my family, that you have
brought me this far? 19And as if this
were not enough in your sight, Sovereign LORD, you have also spoken
about the future of the house of your
servant — and this decree, Sovereign
LORD, is for a mere human![b]
20"What more can David say to
you? For you know your servant, Sovereign LORD. 21For the sake of your
word and according to your will, you
have done this great thing and made
it known to your servant.
22"How great you are, Sovereign
LORD! There is no one like you, and
there is no God but you, as we have
heard with our own ears. 23And who
is like your people Israel — the one
nation on earth that God went out to
redeem as a people for himself, and
to make a name for himself, and to
perform great and awesome wonders by driving out nations and their
gods from before your people, whom
you redeemed from Egypt?[c] 24You
have established your people Israel
as your very own forever, and you,
LORD, have become their God.
25"And now, LORD God, keep forever the promise you have made concerning your servant and his house.
Do as you promised, 26so that your
name will be great forever. Then
people will say, 'The LORD Almighty
is God over Israel!' And the house
of your servant David will be established in your sight.
27"LORD Almighty, God of Israel,
you have revealed this to your servant, saying, 'I will build a house
for you.' So your servant has found
courage to pray this prayer to you.
28Sovereign LORD, you are God! Your
covenant is trustworthy, and you
have promised these good things
to your servant. 29Now be pleased
to bless the house of your servant,
that it may continue forever in your
sight; for you, Sovereign LORD, have
spoken, and with your blessing the
house of your servant will be blessed
forever."

8 In the course of time, David defeated
the Philistines and subdued them,
and he took Metheg Ammah from the
control of the Philistines.
2David also defeated the Moabites. He
made them lie down on the ground and
measured them off with a length of cord.
Every two lengths of them were put to
death, and the third length was allowed
to live. So the Moabites became subject to
David and brought him tribute.
3Moreover, David defeated Hadadezer son of Rehob, king of Zobah, when
he went to restore his monument at[d]
the Euphrates River. 4David captured a
thousand of his chariots, seven thousand
charioteers[e] and twenty thousand foot
soldiers. He hamstrung all but a hundred
of the chariot horses.
5When the Arameans of Damascus
came to help Hadadezer king of Zobah,
David struck down twenty-two thousand of them. 6He put garrisons in the
Aramean kingdom of Damascus, and the
Arameans became subject to him and
brought tribute. The LORD gave David
victory wherever he went.
7David took the gold shields that belonged to the officers of Hadadezer and
brought them to Jerusalem. 8From Tebah[f] and Berothai, towns that belonged
to Hadadezer, King David took a great
quantity of bronze.
9When Tou[g] king of Hamath heard

[a] *16* Some Hebrew manuscripts and Septuagint; most Hebrew manuscripts *you* [b] *19* Or *for the human race* [c] *23* See Septuagint and 1 Chron. 17:21; Hebrew *wonders for your land and before your people, whom you redeemed from Egypt, from the nations and their gods.* [d] *3* Or *his control along* [e] *4* Septuagint (see also Dead Sea Scrolls and 1 Chron. 18:4); Masoretic Text *captured seventeen hundred of his charioteers* [f] *8* See some Septuagint manuscripts (see also 1 Chron. 18:8); Hebrew *Betah.* [g] *9* Hebrew *Toi,* a variant of *Tou;* also in verse 10

that David had defeated the entire army
of Hadadezer, 10 he sent his son Joram[a] to
King David to greet him and congratulate
him on his victory in battle over Hadadezer, who had been at war with Tou. Joram
brought with him articles of silver, of gold
and of bronze.
11 King David dedicated these articles
to the LORD, as he had done with the silver and gold from all the nations he had
subdued: 12 Edom[b] and Moab, the Ammonites and the Philistines, and Amalek.
He also dedicated the plunder taken from
Hadadezer son of Rehob, king of Zobah.
13 And David became famous after he
returned from striking down eighteen
thousand Edomites[c] in the Valley of Salt.
14 He put garrisons throughout Edom,
and all the Edomites became subject
to David. The LORD gave David victory
wherever he went.
15 David reigned over all Israel, doing
what was just and right for all his people.
16 Joab son of Zeruiah was over the army;
Jehoshaphat son of Ahilud was recorder; 17 Zadok son of Ahitub and Ahimelek
son of Abiathar were priests; Seraiah was
secretary; 18 Benaiah son of Jehoiada was
over the Kerethites and Pelethites; and
David's sons were priests.[d]

9 David asked, "Is there anyone still
left of the house of Saul to whom I can
show kindness for Jonathan's sake?"
2 Now there was a servant of Saul's
household named Ziba. They summoned
him to appear before David, and the king
said to him, "Are you Ziba?"
"At your service," he replied.
3 The king asked, "Is there no one still
alive from the house of Saul to whom I
can show God's kindness?"
Ziba answered the king, "There is still a
son of Jonathan; he is lame in both feet."
4 "Where is he?" the king asked.
Ziba answered, "He is at the house of
Makir son of Ammiel in Lo Debar."
5 So King David had him brought from
Lo Debar, from the house of Makir son of
Ammiel.
6 When Mephibosheth son of Jonathan,
the son of Saul, came to David, he bowed
down to pay him honor.
David said, "Mephibosheth!"
"At your service," he replied.
7 "Don't be afraid," David said to him,
"for I will surely show you kindness for
the sake of your father Jonathan. I will
restore to you all the land that belonged
to your grandfather Saul, and you will always eat at my table."
8 Mephibosheth bowed down and said,
"What is your servant, that you should
notice a dead dog like me?"
9 Then the king summoned Ziba, Saul's
steward, and said to him, "I have given
your master's grandson everything that
belonged to Saul and his family. 10 You
and your sons and your servants are to
farm the land for him and bring in the
crops, so that your master's grandson
may be provided for. And Mephibosheth,
grandson of your master, will always eat
at my table." (Now Ziba had fifteen sons
and twenty servants.)
11 Then Ziba said to the king, "Your servant will do whatever my lord the king
commands his servant to do." So Mephibosheth ate at David's[e] table like one
of the king's sons.
12 Mephibosheth had a young son
named Mika, and all the members of Ziba's household were servants of Mephibosheth. 13 And Mephibosheth lived in
Jerusalem, because he always ate at the
king's table; he was lame in both feet.

10 In the course of time, the king of
the Ammonites died, and his son
Hanun succeeded him as king. 2 David
thought, "I will show kindness to Hanun
son of Nahash, just as his father showed
kindness to me." So David sent a delegation to express his sympathy to Hanun
concerning his father.
When David's men came to the land
of the Ammonites, 3 the Ammonite commanders said to Hanun their lord, "Do
you think David is honoring your father
by sending envoys to you to express sympathy? Hasn't David sent them to you
only to explore the city and spy it out and
overthrow it?" 4 So Hanun seized David's
envoys, shaved off half of each man's
beard, cut off their garments at the buttocks, and sent them away.
5 When David was told about this, he
sent messengers to meet the men, for

[a] 10 A variant of *Hadoram* [b] 12 Some Hebrew manuscripts, Septuagint and Syriac (see also 1 Chron. 18:11); most Hebrew manuscripts *Aram* [c] 13 A few Hebrew manuscripts, Septuagint and Syriac (see also 1 Chron. 18:12); most Hebrew manuscripts *Aram* (that is, Arameans) [d] 18 Or *were chief officials* (see Septuagint and Targum; see also 1 Chron. 18:17) [e] 11 Septuagint; Hebrew *my*

they were greatly humiliated. The king
said, "Stay at Jericho till your beards have
grown, and then come back."
6When the Ammonites realized that
they had become obnoxious to David,
they hired twenty thousand Aramean
foot soldiers from Beth Rehob and Zobah, as well as the king of Maakah with a
thousand men, and also twelve thousand
men from Tob.
7On hearing this, David sent Joab out
with the entire army of fighting men.
8The Ammonites came out and drew
up in battle formation at the entrance of
their city gate, while the Arameans of Zobah and Rehob and the men of Tob and
Maakah were by themselves in the open
country.
9Joab saw that there were battle lines
in front of him and behind him; so he selected some of the best troops in Israel
and deployed them against the Arameans. 10He put the rest of the men under
the command of Abishai his brother and
deployed them against the Ammonites. 11Joab said, "If the Arameans are
too strong for me, then you are to come
to my rescue; but if the Ammonites are
too strong for you, then I will come to
rescue you. 12Be strong, and let us fight
bravely for our people and the cities of
our God. The LORD will do what is good
in his sight."
13Then Joab and the troops with him
advanced to fight the Arameans, and they
fled before him. 14When the Ammonites
realized that the Arameans were fleeing,
they fled before Abishai and went inside
the city. So Joab returned from fighting
the Ammonites and came to Jerusalem.
15After the Arameans saw that they had
been routed by Israel, they regrouped.
16Hadadezer had Arameans brought from
beyond the Euphrates River; they went to
Helam, with Shobak the commander of
Hadadezer's army leading them.
17When David was told of this, he
gathered all Israel, crossed the Jordan and went to Helam. The Arameans
formed their battle lines to meet David
and fought against him. 18But they fled
before Israel, and David killed seven
hundred of their charioteers and forty
thousand of their foot soldiers.[a] He also
struck down Shobak the commander of
their army, and he died there. 19When all
the kings who were vassals of Hadadezer
saw that they had been routed by Israel,
they made peace with the Israelites and
became subject to them.

So the Arameans were afraid to help
the Ammonites anymore.

11 In the spring, at the time when kings
go off to war, David sent Joab out
with the king's men and the whole Israelite army. They destroyed the Ammonites and besieged Rabbah. But David remained in Jerusalem.
2One evening David got up from his
bed and walked around on the roof of the
palace. From the roof he saw a woman
bathing. The woman was very beautiful, 3and David sent someone to find out
about her. The man said, "She is Bathsheba, the daughter of Eliam and the wife of
Uriah the Hittite." 4Then David sent messengers to get her. She came to him, and
he slept with her. (Now she was purifying
herself from her monthly uncleanness.)
Then she went back home. 5The woman
conceived and sent word to David, saying, "I am pregnant."
6So David sent this word to Joab: "Send
me Uriah the Hittite." And Joab sent him
to David. 7When Uriah came to him, David asked him how Joab was, how the soldiers were and how the war was going.
8Then David said to Uriah, "Go down to
your house and wash your feet." So Uriah left the palace, and a gift from the
king was sent after him. 9But Uriah slept
at the entrance to the palace with all his
master's servants and did not go down to
his house.
10David was told, "Uriah did not go
home." So he asked Uriah, "Haven't you
just come from a military campaign?
Why didn't you go home?"
11Uriah said to David, "The ark and Israel and Judah are staying in tents,[b] and
my commander Joab and my lord's men
are camped in the open country. How
could I go to my house to eat and drink
and make love to my wife? As surely as
you live, I will not do such a thing!"
12Then David said to him, "Stay here
one more day, and tomorrow I will send
you back." So Uriah remained in Jerusalem that day and the next. 13At David's
invitation, he ate and drank with him,

[a] *18* Some Septuagint manuscripts (see also 1 Chron. 19:18); Hebrew *horsemen* [b] *11* Or *staying at Sukkoth*

and David made him drunk. But in the evening Uriah went out to sleep on his mat among his master's servants; he did not go home.

14 In the morning David wrote a letter to Joab and sent it with Uriah. 15 In it he wrote, "Put Uriah out in front where the fighting is fiercest. Then withdraw from him so he will be struck down and die."

16 So while Joab had the city under siege, he put Uriah at a place where he knew the strongest defenders were. 17 When the men of the city came out and fought against Joab, some of the men in David's army fell; moreover, Uriah the Hittite died.

18 Joab sent David a full account of the battle. 19 He instructed the messenger: "When you have finished giving the king this account of the battle, 20 the king's anger may flare up, and he may ask you, 'Why did you get so close to the city to fight? Didn't you know they would shoot arrows from the wall? 21 Who killed Abimelek son of Jerub-Besheth[a]? Didn't a woman drop an upper millstone on him from the wall, so that he died in Thebez? Why did you get so close to the wall?' If he asks you this, then say to him, 'Moreover, your servant Uriah the Hittite is dead.' "

22 The messenger set out, and when he arrived he told David everything Joab had sent him to say. 23 The messenger said to David, "The men overpowered us and came out against us in the open, but we drove them back to the entrance of the city gate. 24 Then the archers shot arrows at your servants from the wall, and some of the king's men died. Moreover, your servant Uriah the Hittite is dead."

25 David told the messenger, "Say this to Joab: 'Don't let this upset you; the sword devours one as well as another. Press the attack against the city and destroy it.' Say this to encourage Joab."

26 When Uriah's wife heard that her husband was dead, she mourned for him. 27 After the time of mourning was over, David had her brought to his house, and she became his wife and bore him a son. But the thing David had done displeased the LORD.

12 The LORD sent Nathan to David. When he came to him, he said, "There were two men in a certain town, one rich and the other poor. 2 The rich man had a very large number of sheep and cattle, 3 but the poor man had nothing except one little ewe lamb he had bought. He raised it, and it grew up with him and his children. It shared his food, drank from his cup and even slept in his arms. It was like a daughter to him.

4 "Now a traveler came to the rich man, but the rich man refrained from taking one of his own sheep or cattle to prepare a meal for the traveler who had come to him. Instead, he took the ewe lamb that belonged to the poor man and prepared it for the one who had come to him."

5 David burned with anger against the man and said to Nathan, "As surely as the LORD lives, the man who did this must die! 6 He must pay for that lamb four times over, because he did such a thing and had no pity."

7 Then Nathan said to David, "You are the man! This is what the LORD, the God of Israel, says: 'I anointed you king over Israel, and I delivered you from the hand of Saul. 8 I gave your master's house to you, and your master's wives into your arms. I gave you all Israel and Judah. And if all this had been too little, I would have given you even more. 9 Why did you despise the word of the LORD by doing what is evil in his eyes? You struck down Uriah the Hittite with the sword and took his wife to be your own. You killed him with the sword of the Ammonites. 10 Now, therefore, the sword will never depart from your house, because you despised me and took the wife of Uriah the Hittite to be your own.'

11 "This is what the LORD says: 'Out of your own household I am going to bring calamity on you. Before your very eyes I will take your wives and give them to one who is close to you, and he will sleep with your wives in broad daylight. 12 You did it in secret, but I will do this thing in broad daylight before all Israel.' "

13 Then David said to Nathan, "I have sinned against the LORD."

Nathan replied, "The LORD has taken away your sin. You are not going to die. 14 But because by doing this you have shown utter contempt for[b] the LORD, the son born to you will die."

15 After Nathan had gone home, the

[a] *21* Also known as *Jerub-Baal* (that is, Gideon)

[b] *14* An ancient Hebrew scribal tradition; Masoretic Text *for the enemies of*

LORD struck the child that Uriah's wife had borne to David, and he became ill. 16 David pleaded with God for the child. He fasted and spent the nights lying in sackcloth[a] on the ground. 17 The elders of his household stood beside him to get him up from the ground, but he refused, and he would not eat any food with them.

18 On the seventh day the child died. David's attendants were afraid to tell him that the child was dead, for they thought, "While the child was still living, he wouldn't listen to us when we spoke to him. How can we now tell him the child is dead? He may do something desperate."

19 David noticed that his attendants were whispering among themselves, and he realized the child was dead. "Is the child dead?" he asked.

"Yes," they replied, "he is dead."

20 Then David got up from the ground. After he had washed, put on lotions and changed his clothes, he went into the house of the LORD and worshiped. Then he went to his own house, and at his request they served him food, and he ate.

21 His attendants asked him, "Why are you acting this way? While the child was alive, you fasted and wept, but now that the child is dead, you get up and eat!"

22 He answered, "While the child was still alive, I fasted and wept. I thought, 'Who knows? The LORD may be gracious to me and let the child live.' 23 But now that he is dead, why should I go on fasting? Can I bring him back again? I will go to him, but he will not return to me."

24 Then David comforted his wife Bathsheba, and he went to her and made love to her. She gave birth to a son, and they named him Solomon. The LORD loved him; 25 and because the LORD loved him, he sent word through Nathan the prophet to name him Jedidiah.[b]

26 Meanwhile Joab fought against Rabbah of the Ammonites and captured the royal citadel. 27 Joab then sent messengers to David, saying, "I have fought against Rabbah and taken its water supply. 28 Now muster the rest of the troops and besiege the city and capture it. Otherwise I will take the city, and it will be named after me."

29 So David mustered the entire army and went to Rabbah, and attacked and captured it. 30 David took the crown from their king's[c] head, and it was placed on his own head. It weighed a talent[d] of gold, and it was set with precious stones. David took a great quantity of plunder from the city 31 and brought out the people who were there, consigning them to labor with saws and with iron picks and axes, and he made them work at brickmaking.[e] David did this to all the Ammonite towns. Then he and his entire army returned to Jerusalem.

13 In the course of time, Amnon son of David fell in love with Tamar, the beautiful sister of Absalom son of David.

2 Amnon became so obsessed with his sister Tamar that he made himself ill. She was a virgin, and it seemed impossible for him to do anything to her.

3 Now Amnon had an adviser named Jonadab son of Shimeah, David's brother. Jonadab was a very shrewd man. 4 He asked Amnon, "Why do you, the king's son, look so haggard morning after morning? Won't you tell me?"

Amnon said to him, "I'm in love with Tamar, my brother Absalom's sister."

5 "Go to bed and pretend to be ill," Jonadab said. "When your father comes to see you, say to him, 'I would like my sister Tamar to come and give me something to eat. Let her prepare the food in my sight so I may watch her and then eat it from her hand.'"

6 So Amnon lay down and pretended to be ill. When the king came to see him, Amnon said to him, "I would like my sister Tamar to come and make some special bread in my sight, so I may eat from her hand."

7 David sent word to Tamar at the palace: "Go to the house of your brother Amnon and prepare some food for him." 8 So Tamar went to the house of her brother Amnon, who was lying down. She took some dough, kneaded it, made the bread in his sight and baked it. 9 Then she took the pan and served him the bread, but he refused to eat.

"Send everyone out of here," Amnon said. So everyone left him. 10 Then Amnon said to Tamar, "Bring the food here

[a] *16* Dead Sea Scrolls and Septuagint; Masoretic Text does not have *in sackcloth.* [b] *25* *Jedidiah* means *loved by the LORD.* [c] *30* Or *from Milkom's* (that is, Molek's) [d] *30* That is, about 75 pounds or about 34 kilograms [e] *31* The meaning of the Hebrew for this clause is uncertain.

into my bedroom so I may eat from your
hand." And Tamar took the bread she had
prepared and brought it to her brother
Amnon in his bedroom. 11 But when she
took it to him to eat, he grabbed her and
said, "Come to bed with me, my sister."
12 "No, my brother!" she said to him.
"Don't force me! Such a thing should not
be done in Israel! Don't do this wicked
thing. 13 What about me? Where could I get
rid of my disgrace? And what about you?
You would be like one of the wicked fools
in Israel. Please speak to the king; he will
not keep me from being married to you."
14 But he refused to listen to her, and since
he was stronger than she, he raped her.
15 Then Amnon hated her with intense
hatred. In fact, he hated her more than he
had loved her. Amnon said to her, "Get up
and get out!"
16 "No!" she said to him. "Sending me
away would be a greater wrong than what
you have already done to me."
But he refused to listen to her. 17 He
called his personal servant and said, "Get
this woman out of my sight and bolt the
door after her." 18 So his servant put her
out and bolted the door after her. She was
wearing an ornate[a] robe, for this was the
kind of garment the virgin daughters of the
king wore. 19 Tamar put ashes on her head
and tore the ornate robe she was wearing.
She put her hands on her head and went
away, weeping aloud as she went.
20 Her brother Absalom said to her,
"Has that Amnon, your brother, been
with you? Be quiet for now, my sister; he
is your brother. Don't take this thing to
heart." And Tamar lived in her brother
Absalom's house, a desolate woman.
21 When King David heard all this, he
was furious. 22 And Absalom never said
a word to Amnon, either good or bad; he
hated Amnon because he had disgraced
his sister Tamar.
23 Two years later, when Absalom's
sheepshearers were at Baal Hazor near
the border of Ephraim, he invited all the
king's sons to come there. 24 Absalom
went to the king and said, "Your servant
has had shearers come. Will the king and
his attendants please join me?"
25 "No, my son," the king replied. "All
of us should not go; we would only be a
burden to you." Although Absalom urged
him, he still refused to go but gave him
his blessing.
26 Then Absalom said, "If not, please let
my brother Amnon come with us."
The king asked him, "Why should he go
with you?" 27 But Absalom urged him, so
he sent with him Amnon and the rest of
the king's sons.
28 Absalom ordered his men, "Listen!
When Amnon is in high spirits from
drinking wine and I say to you, 'Strike
Amnon down,' then kill him. Don't be
afraid. Haven't I given you this order?
Be strong and brave." 29 So Absalom's
men did to Amnon what Absalom had
ordered. Then all the king's sons got up,
mounted their mules and fled.
30 While they were on their way, the
report came to David: "Absalom has
struck down all the king's sons; not one
of them is left." 31 The king stood up, tore
his clothes and lay down on the ground;
and all his attendants stood by with their
clothes torn.
32 But Jonadab son of Shimeah, David's
brother, said, "My lord should not think
that they killed all the princes; only Amnon is dead. This has been Absalom's
express intention ever since the day Amnon raped his sister Tamar. 33 My lord the
king should not be concerned about the
report that all the king's sons are dead.
Only Amnon is dead."
34 Meanwhile, Absalom had fled.
Now the man standing watch looked
up and saw many people on the road west
of him, coming down the side of the hill.
The watchman went and told the king, "I
see men in the direction of Horonaim, on
the side of the hill."[b]
35 Jonadab said to the king, "See, the
king's sons have come; it has happened
just as your servant said."
36 As he finished speaking, the king's
sons came in, wailing loudly. The king,
too, and all his attendants wept very bitterly.
37 Absalom fled and went to Talmai son
of Ammihud, the king of Geshur. But King
David mourned many days for his son.
38 After Absalom fled and went to Geshur, he stayed there three years. 39 And
King David longed to go to Absalom, for
he was consoled concerning Amnon's
death.

[a] *18* The meaning of the Hebrew for this word is uncertain; also in verse 19. [b] *34* Septuagint; Hebrew does not have this sentence.

14 Joab son of Zeruiah knew that the
king's heart longed for Absalom.
2 So Joab sent someone to Tekoa and had
a wise woman brought from there. He
said to her, "Pretend you are in mourning. Dress in mourning clothes, and don't
use any cosmetic lotions. Act like a woman who has spent many days grieving for
the dead. 3 Then go to the king and speak
these words to him." And Joab put the
words in her mouth.
4 When the woman from Tekoa went[a]
to the king, she fell with her face to the
ground to pay him honor, and she said,
"Help me, Your Majesty!"
5 The king asked her, "What is troubling
you?"
She said, "I am a widow; my husband is
dead. 6 I your servant had two sons. They
got into a fight with each other in the
field, and no one was there to separate
them. One struck the other and killed
him. 7 Now the whole clan has risen up
against your servant; they say, 'Hand over
the one who struck his brother down, so
that we may put him to death for the life
of his brother whom he killed; then we
will get rid of the heir as well.' They would
put out the only burning coal I have left,
leaving my husband neither name nor
descendant on the face of the earth."
8 The king said to the woman, "Go
home, and I will issue an order in your
behalf."
9 But the woman from Tekoa said to
him, "Let my lord the king pardon me and
my family, and let the king and his throne
be without guilt."
10 The king replied, "If anyone says anything to you, bring them to me, and they
will not bother you again."
11 She said, "Then let the king invoke
the LORD his God to prevent the avenger
of blood from adding to the destruction,
so that my son will not be destroyed."
"As surely as the LORD lives," he said,
"not one hair of your son's head will fall
to the ground."
12 Then the woman said, "Let your servant speak a word to my lord the king."
"Speak," he replied.
13 The woman said, "Why then have
you devised a thing like this against the
people of God? When the king says this,
does he not convict himself, for the king
has not brought back his banished son?
14 Like water spilled on the ground, which
cannot be recovered, so we must die. But
that is not what God desires; rather, he
devises ways so that a banished person
does not remain banished from him.
15 "And now I have come to say this to
my lord the king because the people have
made me afraid. Your servant thought,
'I will speak to the king; perhaps he will
grant his servant's request. 16 Perhaps
the king will agree to deliver his servant
from the hand of the man who is trying
to cut off both me and my son from God's
inheritance.'
17 "And now your servant says, 'May the
word of my lord the king secure my inheritance, for my lord the king is like an
angel of God in discerning good and evil.
May the LORD your God be with you.' "
18 Then the king said to the woman,
"Don't keep from me the answer to what I
am going to ask you."
"Let my lord the king speak," the woman said.
19 The king asked, "Isn't the hand of
Joab with you in all this?"
The woman answered, "As surely as
you live, my lord the king, no one can
turn to the right or to the left from anything my lord the king says. Yes, it was
your servant Joab who instructed me to
do this and who put all these words into
the mouth of your servant. 20 Your servant
Joab did this to change the present situation. My lord has wisdom like that of an
angel of God — he knows everything that
happens in the land."
21 The king said to Joab, "Very well, I
will do it. Go, bring back the young man
Absalom."
22 Joab fell with his face to the ground to
pay him honor, and he blessed the king.
Joab said, "Today your servant knows
that he has found favor in your eyes, my
lord the king, because the king has granted his servant's request."
23 Then Joab went to Geshur and
brought Absalom back to Jerusalem.
24 But the king said, "He must go to his
own house; he must not see my face." So
Absalom went to his own house and did
not see the face of the king.
25 In all Israel there was not a man so
highly praised for his handsome ap-

[a] 4 Many Hebrew manuscripts, Septuagint, Vulgate and Syriac; most Hebrew manuscripts *spoke*

pearance as Absalom. From the top of
his head to the sole of his foot there was
no blemish in him. 26 Whenever he cut
the hair of his head—he used to cut his
hair once a year because it became too
heavy for him—he would weigh it, and
its weight was two hundred shekels[a] by
the royal standard.

27 Three sons and a daughter were
born to Absalom. His daughter's name
was Tamar, and she became a beautiful
woman.

28 Absalom lived two years in Jerusalem without seeing the king's face.
29 Then Absalom sent for Joab in order to
send him to the king, but Joab refused to
come to him. So he sent a second time,
but he refused to come. 30 Then he said to
his servants, "Look, Joab's field is next to
mine, and he has barley there. Go and set
it on fire." So Absalom's servants set the
field on fire.

31 Then Joab did go to Absalom's house,
and he said to him, "Why have your servants set my field on fire?"

32 Absalom said to Joab, "Look, I sent
word to you and said, 'Come here so I can
send you to the king to ask, "Why have I
come from Geshur? It would be better for
me if I were still there!"' Now then, I want
to see the king's face, and if I am guilty of
anything, let him put me to death."

33 So Joab went to the king and told him
this. Then the king summoned Absalom,
and he came in and bowed down with his
face to the ground before the king. And
the king kissed Absalom.

15 In the course of time, Absalom provided himself with a chariot and
horses and with fifty men to run ahead
of him. 2 He would get up early and stand
by the side of the road leading to the city
gate. Whenever anyone came with a complaint to be placed before the king for a
decision, Absalom would call out to him,
"What town are you from?" He would
answer, "Your servant is from one of the
tribes of Israel." 3 Then Absalom would
say to him, "Look, your claims are valid
and proper, but there is no representative of the king to hear you." 4 And Absalom would add, "If only I were appointed
judge in the land! Then everyone who has
a complaint or case could come to me and
I would see that they receive justice."

5 Also, whenever anyone approached
him to bow down before him, Absalom
would reach out his hand, take hold of
him and kiss him. 6 Absalom behaved
in this way toward all the Israelites who
came to the king asking for justice, and so
he stole the hearts of the people of Israel.

7 At the end of four[b] years, Absalom
said to the king, "Let me go to Hebron and
fulfill a vow I made to the LORD. 8 While
your servant was living at Geshur in
Aram, I made this vow: 'If the LORD takes
me back to Jerusalem, I will worship the
LORD in Hebron.[c]'"

9 The king said to him, "Go in peace." So
he went to Hebron.

10 Then Absalom sent secret messengers throughout the tribes of Israel to
say, "As soon as you hear the sound of
the trumpets, then say, 'Absalom is king
in Hebron.'" 11 Two hundred men from
Jerusalem had accompanied Absalom.
They had been invited as guests and went
quite innocently, knowing nothing about
the matter. 12 While Absalom was offering
sacrifices, he also sent for Ahithophel the
Gilonite, David's counselor, to come from
Giloh, his hometown. And so the conspiracy gained strength, and Absalom's following kept on increasing.

13 A messenger came and told David,
"The hearts of the people of Israel are
with Absalom."

14 Then David said to all his officials
who were with him in Jerusalem, "Come!
We must flee, or none of us will escape
from Absalom. We must leave immediately, or he will move quickly to overtake
us and bring ruin on us and put the city
to the sword."

15 The king's officials answered him,
"Your servants are ready to do whatever
our lord the king chooses."

16 The king set out, with his entire
household following him; but he left ten
concubines to take care of the palace.
17 So the king set out, with all the people following him, and they halted at the
edge of the city. 18 All his men marched
past him, along with all the Kerethites
and Pelethites; and all the six hundred
Gittites who had accompanied him from
Gath marched before the king.

19 The king said to Ittai the Gittite,
"Why should you come along with us? Go

[a] *26* That is, about 5 pounds or about 2.3 kilograms [b] *7* Some Septuagint manuscripts, Syriac and Josephus; Hebrew *forty* [c] *8* Some Septuagint manuscripts; Hebrew does not have *in Hebron.*

back and stay with King Absalom. You
are a foreigner, an exile from your homeland. 20 You came only yesterday. And today shall I make you wander about with
us, when I do not know where I am going?
Go back, and take your people with you.
May the LORD show you kindness and
faithfulness."[a]

21 But Ittai replied to the king, "As surely as the LORD lives, and as my lord the
king lives, wherever my lord the king may
be, whether it means life or death, there
will your servant be."

22 David said to Ittai, "Go ahead, march
on." So Ittai the Gittite marched on with
all his men and the families that were
with him.

23 The whole countryside wept aloud
as all the people passed by. The king also
crossed the Kidron Valley, and all the
people moved on toward the wilderness.

24 Zadok was there, too, and all the Levites who were with him were carrying
the ark of the covenant of God. They set
down the ark of God, and Abiathar offered sacrifices until all the people had
finished leaving the city.

25 Then the king said to Zadok, "Take
the ark of God back into the city. If I find
favor in the LORD's eyes, he will bring me
back and let me see it and his dwelling
place again. 26 But if he says, 'I am not
pleased with you,' then I am ready; let
him do to me whatever seems good to
him."

27 The king also said to Zadok the priest,
"Do you understand? Go back to the city
with my blessing. Take your son Ahimaaz with you, and also Abiathar's son Jonathan. You and Abiathar return with your
two sons. 28 I will wait at the fords in the
wilderness until word comes from you
to inform me." 29 So Zadok and Abiathar
took the ark of God back to Jerusalem and
stayed there.

30 But David continued up the Mount of
Olives, weeping as he went; his head was
covered and he was barefoot. All the people with him covered their heads too and
were weeping as they went up. 31 Now David had been told, "Ahithophel is among
the conspirators with Absalom." So David prayed, "LORD, turn Ahithophel's
counsel into foolishness."

32 When David arrived at the summit,
where people used to worship God, Hushai the Arkite was there to meet him, his
robe torn and dust on his head. 33 David
said to him, "If you go with me, you will
be a burden to me. 34 But if you return to
the city and say to Absalom, 'Your Majesty, I will be your servant; I was your father's servant in the past, but now I will
be your servant,' then you can help me by
frustrating Ahithophel's advice. 35 Won't
the priests Zadok and Abiathar be there
with you? Tell them anything you hear
in the king's palace. 36 Their two sons,
Ahimaaz son of Zadok and Jonathan son
of Abiathar, are there with them. Send
them to me with anything you hear."

37 So Hushai, David's confidant, arrived at Jerusalem as Absalom was entering the city.

16 When David had gone a short distance beyond the summit, there
was Ziba, the steward of Mephibosheth,
waiting to meet him. He had a string of
donkeys saddled and loaded with two
hundred loaves of bread, a hundred
cakes of raisins, a hundred cakes of figs
and a skin of wine.

2 The king asked Ziba, "Why have you
brought these?"

Ziba answered, "The donkeys are for
the king's household to ride on, the bread
and fruit are for the men to eat, and the
wine is to refresh those who become exhausted in the wilderness."

3 The king then asked, "Where is your
master's grandson?"

Ziba said to him, "He is staying in Jerusalem, because he thinks, 'Today the
Israelites will restore to me my grandfather's kingdom.' "

4 Then the king said to Ziba, "All that belonged to Mephibosheth is now yours."

"I humbly bow," Ziba said. "May I find
favor in your eyes, my lord the king."

5 As King David approached Bahurim,
a man from the same clan as Saul's family came out from there. His name was
Shimei son of Gera, and he cursed as he
came out. 6 He pelted David and all the
king's officials with stones, though all the
troops and the special guard were on David's right and left. 7 As he cursed, Shimei
said, "Get out, get out, you murderer, you
scoundrel! 8 The LORD has repaid you for
all the blood you shed in the household

[a] 20 Septuagint; Hebrew *May kindness and faithfulness be with you*

of Saul, in whose place you have reigned.
The LORD has given the kingdom into the
hands of your son Absalom. You have
come to ruin because you are a murderer!"
9 Then Abishai son of Zeruiah said to
the king, "Why should this dead dog
curse my lord the king? Let me go over
and cut off his head."
10 But the king said, "What does this
have to do with you, you sons of Zeruiah?
If he is cursing because the LORD said to
him, 'Curse David,' who can ask, 'Why do
you do this?' "
11 David then said to Abishai and all
his officials, "My son, my own flesh and
blood, is trying to kill me. How much
more, then, this Benjamite! Leave him
alone; let him curse, for the LORD has
told him to. 12 It may be that the LORD
will look upon my misery and restore to
me his covenant blessing instead of his
curse today."
13 So David and his men continued
along the road while Shimei was going
along the hillside opposite him, cursing
as he went and throwing stones at him
and showering him with dirt. 14 The king
and all the people with him arrived at
their destination exhausted. And there
he refreshed himself.
15 Meanwhile, Absalom and all the men
of Israel came to Jerusalem, and Ahithophel was with him. 16 Then Hushai the Arkite, David's confidant, went to Absalom
and said to him, "Long live the king! Long
live the king!"
17 Absalom said to Hushai, "So this is
the love you show your friend? If he's your
friend, why didn't you go with him?"
18 Hushai said to Absalom, "No, the one
chosen by the LORD, by these people, and
by all the men of Israel—his I will be, and
I will remain with him. 19 Furthermore,
whom should I serve? Should I not serve
the son? Just as I served your father, so I
will serve you."
20 Absalom said to Ahithophel, "Give us
your advice. What should we do?"
21 Ahithophel answered, "Sleep with
your father's concubines whom he left
to take care of the palace. Then all Israel
will hear that you have made yourself obnoxious to your father, and the hands of
everyone with you will be more resolute."
22 So they pitched a tent for Absalom on
the roof, and he slept with his father's
concubines in the sight of all Israel.
23 Now in those days the advice Ahithophel gave was like that of one who in-
quires of God. That was how both David
and Absalom regarded all of Ahithophel's
advice.

17 Ahithophel said to Absalom, "I
would[a] choose twelve thousand
men and set out tonight in pursuit of David. 2 I would attack him while he is weary
and weak. I would strike him with terror,
and then all the people with him will
flee. I would strike down only the king
3 and bring all the people back to you.
The death of the man you seek will mean
the return of all; all the people will be unharmed." 4 This plan seemed good to Absalom and to all the elders of Israel.
5 But Absalom said, "Summon also Hushai the Arkite, so we can hear what he
has to say as well." 6 When Hushai came
to him, Absalom said, "Ahithophel has
given this advice. Should we do what he
says? If not, give us your opinion."
7 Hushai replied to Absalom, "The advice Ahithophel has given is not good this
time. 8 You know your father and his men;
they are fighters, and as fierce as a wild
bear robbed of her cubs. Besides, your father is an experienced fighter; he will not
spend the night with the troops. 9 Even
now, he is hidden in a cave or some other place. If he should attack your troops
first,[b] whoever hears about it will say,
'There has been a slaughter among the
troops who follow Absalom.' 10 Then even
the bravest soldier, whose heart is like the
heart of a lion, will melt with fear, for all
Israel knows that your father is a fighter
and that those with him are brave.
11 "So I advise you: Let all Israel, from
Dan to Beersheba—as numerous as the
sand on the seashore—be gathered to
you, with you yourself leading them into
battle. 12 Then we will attack him wherever he may be found, and we will fall on
him as dew settles on the ground. Neither
he nor any of his men will be left alive.
13 If he withdraws into a city, then all Israel will bring ropes to that city, and we
will drag it down to the valley until not so
much as a pebble is left."
14 Absalom and all the men of Israel

[a] *1* Or *Let me* [b] *9* Or *When some of the men fall at the first attack*

said, "The advice of Hushai the Arkite is
better than that of Ahithophel." For the
LORD had determined to frustrate the
good advice of Ahithophel in order to
bring disaster on Absalom.
15 Hushai told Zadok and Abiathar, the
priests, "Ahithophel has advised Absalom and the elders of Israel to do such
and such, but I have advised them to do
so and so. 16 Now send a message at once
and tell David, 'Do not spend the night
at the fords in the wilderness; cross over
without fail, or the king and all the people
with him will be swallowed up.'"
17 Jonathan and Ahimaaz were staying
at En Rogel. A female servant was to go
and inform them, and they were to go
and tell King David, for they could not
risk being seen entering the city. 18 But a
young man saw them and told Absalom.
So the two of them left at once and went
to the house of a man in Bahurim. He had
a well in his courtyard, and they climbed
down into it. 19 His wife took a covering
and spread it out over the opening of the
well and scattered grain over it. No one
knew anything about it.
20 When Absalom's men came to the
woman at the house, they asked, "Where
are Ahimaaz and Jonathan?"
The woman answered them, "They
crossed over the brook."[a] The men
searched but found no one, so they returned to Jerusalem.
21 After they had gone, the two climbed
out of the well and went to inform King
David. They said to him, "Set out and cross
the river at once; Ahithophel has advised
such and such against you." 22 So David
and all the people with him set out and
crossed the Jordan. By daybreak, no one
was left who had not crossed the Jordan.
23 When Ahithophel saw that his advice had not been followed, he saddled
his donkey and set out for his house in
his hometown. He put his house in order
and then hanged himself. So he died and
was buried in his father's tomb.
24 David went to Mahanaim, and Absalom crossed the Jordan with all the men
of Israel. 25 Absalom had appointed Amasa over the army in place of Joab. Amasa was the son of Jether,[b] an Ishmaelite[c]
who had married Abigal, the daughter of
Nahash and sister of Zeruiah the mother of Joab. 26 The Israelites and Absalom
camped in the land of Gilead.
27 When David came to Mahanaim,
Shobi son of Nahash from Rabbah of the
Ammonites, and Makir son of Ammiel
from Lo Debar, and Barzillai the Gileadite from Rogelim 28 brought bedding
and bowls and articles of pottery. They
also brought wheat and barley, flour and
roasted grain, beans and lentils,[d] 29 honey and curds, sheep, and cheese from
cows' milk for David and his people to
eat. For they said, "The people have become exhausted and hungry and thirsty
in the wilderness."

18 David mustered the men who were
with him and appointed over them
commanders of thousands and commanders of hundreds. 2 David sent out
his troops, a third under the command of
Joab, a third under Joab's brother Abishai
son of Zeruiah, and a third under Ittai the
Gittite. The king told the troops, "I myself
will surely march out with you."
3 But the men said, "You must not go
out; if we are forced to flee, they won't
care about us. Even if half of us die, they
won't care; but you are worth ten thousand of us.[e] It would be better now for you
to give us support from the city."
4 The king answered, "I will do whatever seems best to you."
So the king stood beside the gate while
all his men marched out in units of hundreds and of thousands. 5 The king commanded Joab, Abishai and Ittai, "Be gentle with the young man Absalom for my
sake." And all the troops heard the king
giving orders concerning Absalom to
each of the commanders.
6 David's army marched out of the city
to fight Israel, and the battle took place
in the forest of Ephraim. 7 There Israel's
troops were routed by David's men, and
the casualties that day were great—
twenty thousand men. 8 The battle spread
out over the whole countryside, and the
forest swallowed up more men that day
than the sword.

[a] *20* Or *"They passed by the sheep pen toward the water."* [b] *25* Hebrew *Ithra*, a variant of *Jether* [c] *25* Some Septuagint manuscripts (see also 1 Chron. 2:17); Hebrew and other Septuagint manuscripts *Israelite*
[d] *28* Most Septuagint manuscripts and Syriac; Hebrew *lentils, and roasted grain* [e] *3* Two Hebrew manuscripts, some Septuagint manuscripts and Vulgate; most Hebrew manuscripts *care; for now there are ten thousand like us*

9 Now Absalom happened to meet David's men. He was riding his mule, and as
the mule went under the thick branches
of a large oak, Absalom's hair got caught
in the tree. He was left hanging in midair, while the mule he was riding kept on
going.
10 When one of the men saw what had
happened, he told Joab, "I just saw Absalom hanging in an oak tree."
11 Joab said to the man who had told
him this, "What! You saw him? Why didn't
you strike him to the ground right there?
Then I would have had to give you ten
shekels[a] of silver and a warrior's belt."
12 But the man replied, "Even if a thousand shekels[b] were weighed out into my
hands, I would not lay a hand on the king's
son. In our hearing the king commanded
you and Abishai and Ittai, 'Protect the
young man Absalom for my sake.[c]' 13 And
if I had put my life in jeopardy[d]—and
nothing is hidden from the king—you
would have kept your distance from me."
14 Joab said, "I'm not going to wait like
this for you." So he took three javelins in
his hand and plunged them into Absalom's heart while Absalom was still alive
in the oak tree. 15 And ten of Joab's armor-
bearers surrounded Absalom, struck him
and killed him.
16 Then Joab sounded the trumpet, and
the troops stopped pursuing Israel, for
Joab halted them. 17 They took Absalom,
threw him into a big pit in the forest and
piled up a large heap of rocks over him.
Meanwhile, all the Israelites fled to their
homes.
18 During his lifetime Absalom had
taken a pillar and erected it in the King's
Valley as a monument to himself, for he
thought, "I have no son to carry on the
memory of my name." He named the
pillar after himself, and it is called Absalom's Monument to this day.
19 Now Ahimaaz son of Zadok said, "Let
me run and take the news to the king that
the LORD has vindicated him by delivering him from the hand of his enemies."
20 "You are not the one to take the news
today," Joab told him. "You may take the
news another time, but you must not do
so today, because the king's son is dead."
21 Then Joab said to a Cushite, "Go, tell
the king what you have seen." The Cushite bowed down before Joab and ran off.
22 Ahimaaz son of Zadok again said to
Joab, "Come what may, please let me run
behind the Cushite."
But Joab replied, "My son, why do you
want to go? You don't have any news that
will bring you a reward."
23 He said, "Come what may, I want to
run."
So Joab said, "Run!" Then Ahimaaz
ran by way of the plain[e] and outran the
Cushite.
24 While David was sitting between
the inner and outer gates, the watchman
went up to the roof of the gateway by the
wall. As he looked out, he saw a man running alone. 25 The watchman called out to
the king and reported it.
The king said, "If he is alone, he must
have good news." And the runner came
closer and closer.
26 Then the watchman saw another runner, and he called down to the gatekeeper,
"Look, another man running alone!"
The king said, "He must be bringing
good news, too."
27 The watchman said, "It seems to me
that the first one runs like Ahimaaz son
of Zadok."
"He's a good man," the king said. "He
comes with good news."
28 Then Ahimaaz called out to the king,
"All is well!" He bowed down before the
king with his face to the ground and said,
"Praise be to the LORD your God! He has
delivered up those who lifted their hands
against my lord the king."
29 The king asked, "Is the young man
Absalom safe?"
Ahimaaz answered, "I saw great confusion just as Joab was about to send the
king's servant and me, your servant, but I
don't know what it was."
30 The king said, "Stand aside and wait
here." So he stepped aside and stood
there.
31 Then the Cushite arrived and said,
"My lord the king, hear the good news!
The LORD has vindicated you today by
delivering you from the hand of all who
rose up against you."

[a] *11* That is, about 4 ounces or about 115 grams [b] *12* That is, about 25 pounds or about 12 kilograms
[c] *12* A few Hebrew manuscripts, Septuagint, Vulgate and Syriac; most Hebrew manuscripts may be translated *Absalom, whoever you may be.* [d] *13* Or *Otherwise, if I had acted treacherously toward him* [e] *23* That is, the plain of the Jordan

32The king asked the Cushite, "Is the
young man Absalom safe?"
The Cushite replied, "May the enemies
of my lord the king and all who rise up to
harm you be like that young man."
33The king was shaken. He went up to
the room over the gateway and wept. As
he went, he said: "O my son Absalom! My
son, my son Absalom! If only I had died
instead of you — O Absalom, my son, my
son!"[a]
19[b] Joab was told, "The king is weeping and mourning for Absalom."
2And for the whole army the victory that
day was turned into mourning, because
on that day the troops heard it said, "The
king is grieving for his son." 3The men
stole into the city that day as men steal
in who are ashamed when they flee from
battle. 4The king covered his face and
cried aloud, "O my son Absalom! O Absalom, my son, my son!"
5Then Joab went into the house to the
king and said, "Today you have humiliated all your men, who have just saved your
life and the lives of your sons and daughters and the lives of your wives and concubines. 6You love those who hate you
and hate those who love you. You have
made it clear today that the commanders and their men mean nothing to you.
I see that you would be pleased if Absalom were alive today and all of us were
dead. 7Now go out and encourage your
men. I swear by the LORD that if you don't
go out, not a man will be left with you by
nightfall. This will be worse for you than
all the calamities that have come on you
from your youth till now."
8So the king got up and took his seat
in the gateway. When the men were told,
"The king is sitting in the gateway," they
all came before him.
Meanwhile, the Israelites had fled to
their homes.
9Throughout the tribes of Israel, all the
people were arguing among themselves,
saying, "The king delivered us from the
hand of our enemies; he is the one who
rescued us from the hand of the Philistines. But now he has fled the country to
escape from Absalom; 10and Absalom,
whom we anointed to rule over us, has
died in battle. So why do you say nothing
about bringing the king back?"
11King David sent this message to Zadok and Abiathar, the priests: "Ask the
elders of Judah, 'Why should you be the
last to bring the king back to his palace,
since what is being said throughout Israel has reached the king at his quarters?
12You are my relatives, my own flesh and
blood. So why should you be the last to
bring back the king?' 13And say to Amasa, 'Are you not my own flesh and blood?
May God deal with me, be it ever so severely, if you are not the commander of
my army for life in place of Joab.' "
14He won over the hearts of the men of
Judah so that they were all of one mind.
They sent word to the king, "Return, you
and all your men." 15Then the king returned and went as far as the Jordan.
Now the men of Judah had come to Gilgal to go out and meet the king and bring
him across the Jordan. 16Shimei son of
Gera, the Benjamite from Bahurim, hurried down with the men of Judah to meet
King David. 17With him were a thousand
Benjamites, along with Ziba, the steward of Saul's household, and his fifteen
sons and twenty servants. They rushed
to the Jordan, where the king was. 18They
crossed at the ford to take the king's household over and to do whatever he wished.
When Shimei son of Gera crossed the
Jordan, he fell prostrate before the king
19and said to him, "May my lord not hold
me guilty. Do not remember how your
servant did wrong on the day my lord the
king left Jerusalem. May the king put it out
of his mind. 20For I your servant know that
I have sinned, but today I have come here
as the first from the tribes of Joseph to
come down and meet my lord the king."
21Then Abishai son of Zeruiah said,
"Shouldn't Shimei be put to death for
this? He cursed the LORD's anointed."
22David replied, "What does this have
to do with you, you sons of Zeruiah? What
right do you have to interfere? Should
anyone be put to death in Israel today?
Don't I know that today I am king over Israel?" 23So the king said to Shimei, "You
shall not die." And the king promised
him on oath.
24Mephibosheth, Saul's grandson, also
went down to meet the king. He had not
taken care of his feet or trimmed his mustache or washed his clothes from the day

[a] 33 In Hebrew texts this verse (18:33) is numbered 19:1.
[b] In Hebrew texts 19:1-43 is numbered 19:2-44.

the king left until the day he returned
safely. 25When he came from Jerusalem
to meet the king, the king asked him,
"Why didn't you go with me, Mephibosheth?"

26He said, "My lord the king, since I
your servant am lame, I said, 'I will have
my donkey saddled and will ride on it,
so I can go with the king.' But Ziba my
servant betrayed me. 27And he has slandered your servant to my lord the king.
My lord the king is like an angel of God; so
do whatever you wish. 28All my grandfather's descendants deserved nothing but
death from my lord the king, but you gave
your servant a place among those who eat
at your table. So what right do I have to
make any more appeals to the king?"

29The king said to him, "Why say more?
I order you and Ziba to divide the land."

30Mephibosheth said to the king, "Let
him take everything, now that my lord
the king has returned home safely."

31Barzillai the Gileadite also came
down from Rogelim to cross the Jordan
with the king and to send him on his way
from there. 32Now Barzillai was very old,
eighty years of age. He had provided for
the king during his stay in Mahanaim,
for he was a very wealthy man. 33The king
said to Barzillai, "Cross over with me and
stay with me in Jerusalem, and I will provide for you."

34But Barzillai answered the king,
"How many more years will I live, that I
should go up to Jerusalem with the king?
35I am now eighty years old. Can I tell the
difference between what is enjoyable and
what is not? Can your servant taste what
he eats and drinks? Can I still hear the
voices of male and female singers? Why
should your servant be an added burden
to my lord the king? 36Your servant will
cross over the Jordan with the king for a
short distance, but why should the king
reward me in this way? 37Let your servant
return, that I may die in my own town
near the tomb of my father and mother.
But here is your servant Kimham. Let
him cross over with my lord the king. Do
for him whatever you wish."

38The king said, "Kimham shall cross
over with me, and I will do for him whatever you wish. And anything you desire
from me I will do for you."

39So all the people crossed the Jordan,
and then the king crossed over. The king
kissed Barzillai and bid him farewell, and
Barzillai returned to his home.

40When the king crossed over to Gilgal,
Kimham crossed with him. All the troops
of Judah and half the troops of Israel had
taken the king over.

41Soon all the men of Israel were coming to the king and saying to him, "Why
did our brothers, the men of Judah, steal
the king away and bring him and his
household across the Jordan, together
with all his men?"

42All the men of Judah answered the
men of Israel, "We did this because the
king is closely related to us. Why are you
angry about it? Have we eaten any of the
king's provisions? Have we taken anything for ourselves?"

43Then the men of Israel answered the
men of Judah, "We have ten shares in the
king; so we have a greater claim on David than you have. Why then do you treat
us with contempt? Weren't we the first to
speak of bringing back our king?"

But the men of Judah pressed their
claims even more forcefully than the
men of Israel.

20 Now a troublemaker named Sheba
son of Bikri, a Benjamite, happened
to be there. He sounded the trumpet and
shouted,

"We have no share in David,
no part in Jesse's son!
Every man to his tent, Israel!"

2So all the men of Israel deserted David
to follow Sheba son of Bikri. But the men
of Judah stayed by their king all the way
from the Jordan to Jerusalem.

3When David returned to his palace in
Jerusalem, he took the ten concubines he
had left to take care of the palace and put
them in a house under guard. He provided for them but had no sexual relations
with them. They were kept in confine-
ment till the day of their death, living as
widows.

4Then the king said to Amasa, "Summon the men of Judah to come to me
within three days, and be here yourself."
5But when Amasa went to summon Judah, he took longer than the time the
king had set for him.

6David said to Abishai, "Now Sheba son
of Bikri will do us more harm than Absalom did. Take your master's men and
pursue him, or he will find fortified cities

and escape from us."[a] 7So Joab's men and
the Kerethites and Pelethites and all the
mighty warriors went out under the command of Abishai. They marched out from
Jerusalem to pursue Sheba son of Bikri.

8While they were at the great rock
in Gibeon, Amasa came to meet them.
Joab was wearing his military tunic, and
strapped over it at his waist was a belt
with a dagger in its sheath. As he stepped
forward, it dropped out of its sheath.

9Joab said to Amasa, "How are you, my
brother?" Then Joab took Amasa by the
beard with his right hand to kiss him.
10Amasa was not on his guard against
the dagger in Joab's hand, and Joab
plunged it into his belly, and his intestines spilled out on the ground. Without
being stabbed again, Amasa died. Then
Joab and his brother Abishai pursued
Sheba son of Bikri.

11One of Joab's men stood beside Amasa and said, "Whoever favors Joab, and
whoever is for David, let him follow Joab!"
12Amasa lay wallowing in his blood in the
middle of the road, and the man saw that
all the troops came to a halt there. When
he realized that everyone who came up
to Amasa stopped, he dragged him from
the road into a field and threw a garment
over him. 13After Amasa had been removed from the road, everyone went on
with Joab to pursue Sheba son of Bikri.

14Sheba passed through all the tribes of
Israel to Abel Beth Maakah and through
the entire region of the Bikrites,[b] who
gathered together and followed him. 15All
the troops with Joab came and besieged
Sheba in Abel Beth Maakah. They built
a siege ramp up to the city, and it stood
against the outer fortifications. While
they were battering the wall to bring it
down, 16a wise woman called from the
city, "Listen! Listen! Tell Joab to come
here so I can speak to him." 17He went toward her, and she asked, "Are you Joab?"

"I am," he answered.

She said, "Listen to what your servant
has to say."

"I'm listening," he said.

18She continued, "Long ago they used
to say, 'Get your answer at Abel,' and
that settled it. 19We are the peaceful and
faithful in Israel. You are trying to destroy a city that is a mother in Israel. Why
do you want to swallow up the LORD's inheritance?"

20"Far be it from me!" Joab replied, "Far
be it from me to swallow up or destroy!
21That is not the case. A man named Sheba son of Bikri, from the hill country of
Ephraim, has lifted up his hand against
the king, against David. Hand over this
one man, and I'll withdraw from the city."

The woman said to Joab, "His head will
be thrown to you from the wall."

22Then the woman went to all the people with her wise advice, and they cut off
the head of Sheba son of Bikri and threw
it to Joab. So he sounded the trumpet, and
his men dispersed from the city, each returning to his home. And Joab went back
to the king in Jerusalem.

23Joab was over Israel's entire army; Benaiah son of Jehoiada was over the Kerethites and Pelethites; 24Adoniram[c] was
in charge of forced labor; Jehoshaphat son
of Ahilud was recorder; 25Sheva was secretary; Zadok and Abiathar were priests;
26and Ira the Jairite[d] was David's priest.

21 During the reign of David, there was
a famine for three successive years;
so David sought the face of the LORD. The
LORD said, "It is on account of Saul and
his blood-stained house; it is because he
put the Gibeonites to death."

2The king summoned the Gibeonites
and spoke to them. (Now the Gibeonites
were not a part of Israel but were survivors of the Amorites; the Israelites had
sworn to spare them, but Saul in his zeal
for Israel and Judah had tried to annihilate them.) 3David asked the Gibeonites, "What shall I do for you? How shall
I make atonement so that you will bless
the LORD's inheritance?"

4The Gibeonites answered him, "We
have no right to demand silver or gold
from Saul or his family, nor do we have the
right to put anyone in Israel to death."

"What do you want me to do for you?"
David asked.

5They answered the king, "As for
the man who destroyed us and plotted
against us so that we have been decimat-
ed and have no place anywhere in Israel, 6let seven of his male descendants be
given to us to be killed and their bodies

[a] *6* Or *and do us serious injury* [b] *14* See Septuagint and Vulgate; Hebrew *Berites.* [c] *24* Some Septuagint manuscripts (see also 1 Kings 4:6 and 5:14); Hebrew *Adoram* [d] *26* Hebrew; some Septuagint manuscripts and Syriac (see also 23:38) *Ithrite*

exposed before the LORD at Gibeah of
Saul—the LORD's chosen one."

So the king said, "I will give them to
you."

7 The king spared Mephibosheth son of
Jonathan, the son of Saul, because of the
oath before the LORD between David and
Jonathan son of Saul. 8 But the king took
Armoni and Mephibosheth, the two sons
of Aiah's daughter Rizpah, whom she
had borne to Saul, together with the five
sons of Saul's daughter Merab,[a] whom
she had borne to Adriel son of Barzillai
the Meholathite. 9 He handed them over
to the Gibeonites, who killed them and
exposed their bodies on a hill before the
LORD. All seven of them fell together; they
were put to death during the first days of
the harvest, just as the barley harvest was
beginning.

10 Rizpah daughter of Aiah took sackcloth and spread it out for herself on a
rock. From the beginning of the harvest
till the rain poured down from the heavens on the bodies, she did not let the birds
touch them by day or the wild animals by
night. 11 When David was told what Aiah's
daughter Rizpah, Saul's concubine, had
done, 12 he went and took the bones of
Saul and his son Jonathan from the citizens of Jabesh Gilead. (They had stolen
their bodies from the public square at
Beth Shan, where the Philistines had
hung them after they struck Saul down
on Gilboa.) 13 David brought the bones
of Saul and his son Jonathan from there,
and the bones of those who had been
killed and exposed were gathered up.

14 They buried the bones of Saul and
his son Jonathan in the tomb of Saul's
father Kish, at Zela in Benjamin, and did
everything the king commanded. After
that, God answered prayer in behalf of
the land.

15 Once again there was a battle between the Philistines and Israel. David
went down with his men to fight against
the Philistines, and he became exhausted. 16 And Ishbi-Benob, one of the descendants of Rapha, whose bronze spearhead
weighed three hundred shekels[b] and
who was armed with a new sword, said
he would kill David. 17 But Abishai son of
Zeruiah came to David's rescue; he struck
the Philistine down and killed him. Then
David's men swore to him, saying, "Never
again will you go out with us to battle, so
that the lamp of Israel will not be extinguished."

18 In the course of time, there was another battle with the Philistines, at Gob. At
that time Sibbekai the Hushathite killed
Saph, one of the descendants of Rapha.

19 In another battle with the Philistines
at Gob, Elhanan son of Jair[c] the Bethle-
hemite killed the brother of[d] Goliath the
Gittite, who had a spear with a shaft like
a weaver's rod.

20 In still another battle, which took
place at Gath, there was a huge man with
six fingers on each hand and six toes on
each foot—twenty-four in all. He also
was descended from Rapha. 21 When he
taunted Israel, Jonathan son of Shimeah,
David's brother, killed him.

22 These four were descendants of Rapha in Gath, and they fell at the hands of
David and his men.

22 David sang to the LORD the words of
this song when the LORD delivered
him from the hand of all his enemies and
from the hand of Saul. 2 He said:

"The LORD is my rock, my fortress and
my deliverer;
3 my God is my rock, in whom I take
refuge,
my shield[e] and the horn[f] of my
salvation.
He is my stronghold, my refuge and
my savior—
from violent people you save me.
4 "I called to the LORD, who is worthy of
praise,
and have been saved from my
enemies.
5 The waves of death swirled about me;
the torrents of destruction
overwhelmed me.
6 The cords of the grave coiled around
me;
the snares of death confronted me.
7 "In my distress I called to the LORD;
I called out to my God.

[a] *8* Two Hebrew manuscripts, some Septuagint manuscripts and Syriac (see also 1 Samuel 18:19); most Hebrew and Septuagint manuscripts *Michal*
[b] *16* That is, about 7 1/2 pounds or about 3.5 kilograms
[c] *19* See 1 Chron. 20:5; Hebrew *Jaare-Oregim.*
[d] *19* See 1 Chron. 20:5; Hebrew does not have *the brother of.*
[e] *3* Or *sovereign*
[f] *3* *Horn* here symbolizes strength.

From his temple he heard my voice;
my cry came to his ears.
8 The earth trembled and quaked,
the foundations of the heavens[a] shook;
they trembled because he was angry.
9 Smoke rose from his nostrils;
consuming fire came from his mouth,
burning coals blazed out of it.
10 He parted the heavens and came down;
dark clouds were under his feet.
11 He mounted the cherubim and flew;
he soared[b] on the wings of the wind.
12 He made darkness his canopy around him—
the dark[c] rain clouds of the sky.
13 Out of the brightness of his presence
bolts of lightning blazed forth.
14 The LORD thundered from heaven;
the voice of the Most High resounded.
15 He shot his arrows and scattered the enemy,
with great bolts of lightning he routed them.
16 The valleys of the sea were exposed
and the foundations of the earth laid bare
at the rebuke of the LORD,
at the blast of breath from his nostrils.

17 "He reached down from on high and took hold of me;
he drew me out of deep waters.
18 He rescued me from my powerful enemy,
from my foes, who were too strong for me.
19 They confronted me in the day of my disaster,
but the LORD was my support.
20 He brought me out into a spacious place;
he rescued me because he delighted in me.

21 "The LORD has dealt with me according to my righteousness;
according to the cleanness of my hands he has rewarded me.
22 For I have kept the ways of the LORD;
I am not guilty of turning from my God.
23 All his laws are before me;
I have not turned away from his decrees.
24 I have been blameless before him
and have kept myself from sin.
25 The LORD has rewarded me according to my righteousness,
according to my cleanness[d] in his sight.

26 "To the faithful you show yourself faithful,
to the blameless you show yourself blameless,
27 to the pure you show yourself pure,
but to the devious you show yourself shrewd.
28 You save the humble,
but your eyes are on the haughty to bring them low.
29 You, LORD, are my lamp;
the LORD turns my darkness into light.
30 With your help I can advance against a troop[e];
with my God I can scale a wall.

31 "As for God, his way is perfect:
The LORD's word is flawless;
he shields all who take refuge in him.
32 For who is God besides the LORD?
And who is the Rock except our God?
33 It is God who arms me with strength[f]
and keeps my way secure.
34 He makes my feet like the feet of a deer;
he causes me to stand on the heights.
35 He trains my hands for battle;
my arms can bend a bow of bronze.
36 You make your saving help my shield;
your help has made[g] me great.
37 You provide a broad path for my feet,
so that my ankles do not give way.

38 "I pursued my enemies and crushed them;
I did not turn back till they were destroyed.

[a] *8* Hebrew; Vulgate and Syriac (see also Psalm 18:7) *mountains* [b] *11* Many Hebrew manuscripts (see also Psalm 18:10); most Hebrew manuscripts *appeared* [c] *12* Septuagint (see also Psalm 18:11); Hebrew *massed* [d] *25* Hebrew; Septuagint and Vulgate (see also Psalm 18:24) *to the cleanness of my hands* [e] *30* Or *can run through a barricade* [f] *33* Dead Sea Scrolls, some Septuagint manuscripts, Vulgate and Syriac (see also Psalm 18:32); Masoretic Text *who is my strong refuge* [g] *36* Dead Sea Scrolls; Masoretic Text *shield; / you stoop down to make*

39 I crushed them completely, and they could not rise;
they fell beneath my feet.
40 You armed me with strength for battle;
you humbled my adversaries before me.
41 You made my enemies turn their backs in flight,
and I destroyed my foes.
42 They cried for help, but there was no one to save them —
to the LORD, but he did not answer.
43 I beat them as fine as the dust of the earth;
I pounded and trampled them like mud in the streets.

44 "You have delivered me from the attacks of the peoples;
you have preserved me as the head of nations.
People I did not know now serve me,
45 foreigners cower before me;
as soon as they hear of me, they obey me.
46 They all lose heart;
they come trembling[a] from their strongholds.

47 "The LORD lives! Praise be to my Rock!
Exalted be my God, the Rock, my Savior!
48 He is the God who avenges me,
who puts the nations under me,
49 who sets me free from my enemies.
You exalted me above my foes;
from a violent man you rescued me.
50 Therefore I will praise you, LORD, among the nations;
I will sing the praises of your name.

51 "He gives his king great victories;
he shows unfailing kindness to his anointed,
to David and his descendants forever."

23 These are the last words of David:

"The inspired utterance of David son of Jesse,
the utterance of the man exalted by the Most High,
the man anointed by the God of Jacob,
the hero of Israel's songs:

2 "The Spirit of the LORD spoke through me;
his word was on my tongue.
3 The God of Israel spoke,
the Rock of Israel said to me:
'When one rules over people in righteousness,
when he rules in the fear of God,
4 he is like the light of morning at sunrise
on a cloudless morning,
like the brightness after rain
that brings grass from the earth.'
5 "If my house were not right with God,
surely he would not have made with me an everlasting covenant,
arranged and secured in every part;
surely he would not bring to fruition my salvation
and grant me my every desire.
6 But evil men are all to be cast aside like thorns,
which are not gathered with the hand.
7 Whoever touches thorns
uses a tool of iron or the shaft of a spear;
they are burned up where they lie."

8 These are the names of David's mighty warriors:

Josheb-Basshebeth,[b] a Tahkemonite,[c]
was chief of the Three; he raised his
spear against eight hundred men, whom
he killed[d] in one encounter.
9 Next to him was Eleazar son of Dodai
the Ahohite. As one of the three mighty
warriors, he was with David when they
taunted the Philistines gathered at Pas
Dammim[e] for battle. Then the Israelites
retreated, 10 but Eleazar stood his ground
and struck down the Philistines till his
hand grew tired and froze to the sword.
The LORD brought about a great victory
that day. The troops returned to Eleazar,
but only to strip the dead.
11 Next to him was Shammah son of
Agee the Hararite. When the Philistines
banded together at a place where there
was a field full of lentils, Israel's troops

[a] 46 Some Septuagint manuscripts and Vulgate (see also Psalm 18:45); Masoretic Text *they arm themselves* [b] 8 Hebrew; some Septuagint manuscripts suggest *Ish-Bosheth,* that is, *Esh-Baal* (see also 1 Chron. 11:11 *Jashobeam*). [c] 8 Probably a variant of *Hakmonite* (see 1 Chron. 11:11) [d] 8 Some Septuagint manuscripts (see also 1 Chron. 11:11); Hebrew and other Septuagint manuscripts *Three; it was Adino the Eznite who killed eight hundred men* [e] 9 See 1 Chron. 11:13; Hebrew *gathered there.*

fled from them. 12 But Shammah took his stand in the middle of the field. He defended it and struck the Philistines down, and the LORD brought about a great victory.

13 During harvest time, three of the thirty chief warriors came down to David at the cave of Adullam, while a band of Philistines was encamped in the Valley of Rephaim. 14 At that time David was in the stronghold, and the Philistine garrison was at Bethlehem. 15 David longed for water and said, "Oh, that someone would get me a drink of water from the well near the gate of Bethlehem!" 16 So the three mighty warriors broke through the Philistine lines, drew water from the well near the gate of Bethlehem and carried it back to David. But he refused to drink it; instead, he poured it out before the LORD. 17 "Far be it from me, LORD, to do this!" he said. "Is it not the blood of men who went at the risk of their lives?" And David would not drink it.

Such were the exploits of the three mighty warriors.

18 Abishai the brother of Joab son of Zeruiah was chief of the Three.[a] He raised his spear against three hundred men, whom he killed, and so he became as famous as the Three. 19 Was he not held in greater honor than the Three? He became their commander, even though he was not included among them.

20 Benaiah son of Jehoiada, a valiant fighter from Kabzeel, performed great exploits. He struck down Moab's two mightiest warriors. He also went down into a pit on a snowy day and killed a lion. 21 And he struck down a huge Egyptian. Although the Egyptian had a spear in his hand, Benaiah went against him with a club. He snatched the spear from the Egyptian's hand and killed him with his own spear. 22 Such were the exploits of Benaiah son of Jehoiada; he too was as famous as the three mighty warriors. 23 He was held in greater honor than any of the Thirty, but he was not included among the Three. And David put him in charge of his bodyguard.

24 Among the Thirty were:
Asahel the brother of Joab,
Elhanan son of Dodo from Bethlehem,
25 Shammah the Harodite,
Elika the Harodite,
26 Helez the Paltite,
Ira son of Ikkesh from Tekoa,
27 Abiezer from Anathoth,
Sibbekai[b] the Hushathite,
28 Zalmon the Ahohite,
Maharai the Netophathite,
29 Heled[c] son of Baanah the Netophathite,
Ithai son of Ribai from Gibeah in Benjamin,
30 Benaiah the Pirathonite,
Hiddai[d] from the ravines of Gaash,
31 Abi-Albon the Arbathite,
Azmaveth the Barhumite,
32 Eliahba the Shaalbonite,
the sons of Jashen,
Jonathan 33 son of[e] Shammah the Hararite,
Ahiam son of Sharar[f] the Hararite,
34 Eliphelet son of Ahasbai the Maakathite,
Eliam son of Ahithophel the Gilonite,
35 Hezro the Carmelite,
Paarai the Arbite,
36 Igal son of Nathan from Zobah,
the son of Hagri,[g]
37 Zelek the Ammonite,
Naharai the Beerothite, the armor-bearer of Joab son of Zeruiah,
38 Ira the Ithrite,
Gareb the Ithrite
39 and Uriah the Hittite.
There were thirty-seven in all.

24 Again the anger of the LORD burned against Israel, and he incited David against them, saying, "Go and take a census of Israel and Judah."

2 So the king said to Joab and the army commanders[h] with him, "Go throughout the tribes of Israel from Dan to Beersheba and enroll the fighting men, so that I may know how many there are."

[a] *18* Most Hebrew manuscripts (see also 1 Chron. 11:20); two Hebrew manuscripts and Syriac *Thirty* [b] *27* Some Septuagint manuscripts (see also 21:18; 1 Chron. 11:29); Hebrew *Mebunnai* [c] *29* Some Hebrew manuscripts and Vulgate (see also 1 Chron. 11:30); most Hebrew manuscripts *Heleb* [d] *30* Hebrew; some Septuagint manuscripts (see also 1 Chron. 11:32) *Hurai* [e] *33* Some Septuagint manuscripts (see also 1 Chron. 11:34); Hebrew does not have *son of.* [f] *33* Hebrew; some Septuagint manuscripts (see also 1 Chron. 11:35) *Sakar* [g] *36* Some Septuagint manuscripts (see also 1 Chron. 11:38); Hebrew *Haggadi*
[h] *2* Septuagint (see also verse 4 and 1 Chron. 21:2); Hebrew *Joab the army commander*

3 But Joab replied to the king, "May
the LORD your God multiply the troops a
hundred times over, and may the eyes of
my lord the king see it. But why does my
lord the king want to do such a thing?"

4 The king's word, however, overruled
Joab and the army commanders; so they
left the presence of the king to enroll the
fighting men of Israel.

5 After crossing the Jordan, they
camped near Aroer, south of the town
in the gorge, and then went through Gad
and on to Jazer. 6 They went to Gilead
and the region of Tahtim Hodshi, and on
to Dan Jaan and around toward Sidon.
7 Then they went toward the fortress of
Tyre and all the towns of the Hivites and
Canaanites. Finally, they went on to Beersheba in the Negev of Judah.

8 After they had gone through the entire
land, they came back to Jerusalem at the
end of nine months and twenty days.

9 Joab reported the number of the fighting men to the king: In Israel there were
eight hundred thousand able-bodied
men who could handle a sword, and in
Judah five hundred thousand.

10 David was conscience-stricken after
he had counted the fighting men, and he
said to the LORD, "I have sinned greatly in
what I have done. Now, LORD, I beg you,
take away the guilt of your servant. I have
done a very foolish thing."

11 Before David got up the next morning, the word of the LORD had come to
Gad the prophet, David's seer: 12 "Go and
tell David, 'This is what the LORD says: I
am giving you three options. Choose one
of them for me to carry out against you.' "

13 So Gad went to David and said to him,
"Shall there come on you three[a] years of
famine in your land? Or three months
of fleeing from your enemies while they
pursue you? Or three days of plague in
your land? Now then, think it over and
decide how I should answer the one who
sent me."

14 David said to Gad, "I am in deep distress. Let us fall into the hands of the
LORD, for his mercy is great; but do not let
me fall into human hands."

15 So the LORD sent a plague on Israel
from that morning until the end of the
time designated, and seventy thousand
of the people from Dan to Beersheba
died. 16 When the angel stretched out his
hand to destroy Jerusalem, the LORD relented concerning the disaster and said
to the angel who was afflicting the people, "Enough! Withdraw your hand." The
angel of the LORD was then at the threshing floor of Araunah the Jebusite.

17 When David saw the angel who was
striking down the people, he said to the
LORD, "I have sinned; I, the shepherd,[b]
have done wrong. These are but sheep.
What have they done? Let your hand fall
on me and my family."

18 On that day Gad went to David and
said to him, "Go up and build an altar to
the LORD on the threshing floor of Araunah the Jebusite." 19 So David went up,
as the LORD had commanded through
Gad. 20 When Araunah looked and saw
the king and his officials coming toward
him, he went out and bowed down before
the king with his face to the ground.

21 Araunah said, "Why has my lord the
king come to his servant?"

"To buy your threshing floor," David
answered, "so I can build an altar to the
LORD, that the plague on the people may
be stopped."

22 Araunah said to David, "Let my lord
the king take whatever he wishes and
offer it up. Here are oxen for the burnt
offering, and here are threshing sledges
and ox yokes for the wood. 23 Your Majesty, Araunah[c] gives all this to the king."
Araunah also said to him, "May the LORD
your God accept you."

24 But the king replied to Araunah, "No,
I insist on paying you for it. I will not sacrifice to the LORD my God burnt offerings
that cost me nothing."

So David bought the threshing floor
and the oxen and paid fifty shekels[d] of silver for them. 25 David built an altar to the
LORD there and sacrificed burnt offerings
and fellowship offerings. Then the LORD
answered his prayer in behalf of the land,
and the plague on Israel was stopped.

[a] *13* Septuagint (see also 1 Chron. 21:12); Hebrew *seven* [b] *17* Dead Sea Scrolls and Septuagint; Masoretic Text does not have *the shepherd.* [c] *23* Some Hebrew manuscripts and Septuagint; most Hebrew manuscripts *King Araunah* [d] *24* That is, about 1 1/4 pounds or about 575 grams

1 KINGS

See the Invitation to Samuel-Kings on p. 240.

1 When King David was very old, he
could not keep warm even when they
put covers over him. 2So his attendants
said to him, "Let us look for a young virgin to serve the king and take care of him.
She can lie beside him so that our lord the
king may keep warm."
3Then they searched throughout Israel
for a beautiful young woman and found
Abishag, a Shunammite, and brought her
to the king. 4The woman was very beautiful; she took care of the king and waited
on him, but the king had no sexual relations with her.
5Now Adonijah, whose mother was
Haggith, put himself forward and said, "I
will be king." So he got chariots and horses[a] ready, with fifty men to run ahead of
him. 6(His father had never rebuked him
by asking, "Why do you behave as you
do?" He was also very handsome and was
born next after Absalom.)
7Adonijah conferred with Joab son of
Zeruiah and with Abiathar the priest, and
they gave him their support. 8But Zadok
the priest, Benaiah son of Jehoiada, Nathan the prophet, Shimei and Rei and David's special guard did not join Adonijah.
9Adonijah then sacrificed sheep, cattle and fattened calves at the Stone of Zo-
heleth near En Rogel. He invited all his
brothers, the king's sons, and all the royal
officials of Judah, 10but he did not invite
Nathan the prophet or Benaiah or the
special guard or his brother Solomon.
11Then Nathan asked Bathsheba, Solomon's mother, "Have you not heard that
Adonijah, the son of Haggith, has become
king, and our lord David knows nothing
about it? 12Now then, let me advise you
how you can save your own life and the
life of your son Solomon. 13Go in to King
David and say to him, 'My lord the king,
did you not swear to me your servant:
"Surely Solomon your son shall be king
after me, and he will sit on my throne"?
Why then has Adonijah become king?'
14While you are still there talking to the
king, I will come in and add my word to
what you have said."
15So Bathsheba went to see the aged
king in his room, where Abishag the Shunammite was attending him. 16Bathshe-
ba bowed down, prostrating herself before the king.
"What is it you want?" the king asked.
17She said to him, "My lord, you yourself swore to me your servant by the LORD
your God: 'Solomon your son shall be king
after me, and he will sit on my throne.'
18But now Adonijah has become king,
and you, my lord the king, do not know
about it. 19He has sacrificed great numbers of cattle, fattened calves, and sheep,
and has invited all the king's sons, Abiathar the priest and Joab the commander
of the army, but he has not invited Solomon your servant. 20My lord the king, the
eyes of all Israel are on you, to learn from
you who will sit on the throne of my lord
the king after him. 21Otherwise, as soon
as my lord the king is laid to rest with his
ancestors, I and my son Solomon will be
treated as criminals."
22While she was still speaking with the
king, Nathan the prophet arrived. 23And
the king was told, "Nathan the prophet
is here." So he went before the king and
bowed with his face to the ground.
24Nathan said, "Have you, my lord
the king, declared that Adonijah shall
be king after you, and that he will sit on
your throne? 25Today he has gone down
and sacrificed great numbers of cattle,
fattened calves, and sheep. He has invited all the king's sons, the commanders of
the army and Abiathar the priest. Right
now they are eating and drinking with
him and saying, 'Long live King Adonijah!' 26But me your servant, and Zadok
the priest, and Benaiah son of Jehoiada,
and your servant Solomon he did not invite. 27Is this something my lord the king
has done without letting his servants
know who should sit on the throne of my
lord the king after him?"
28Then King David said, "Call in Bathsheba." So she came into the king's presence and stood before him.
29The king then took an oath: "As sure-

[a] 5 Or *charioteers*

father David knowing it he attacked two
men and killed them with the sword. Both
of them — Abner son of Ner, commander
of Israel's army, and Amasa son of Jether,
commander of Judah's army — were better men and more upright than he. 33 May
the guilt of their blood rest on the head
of Joab and his descendants forever. But
on David and his descendants, his house
and his throne, may there be the LORD's
peace forever."

34 So Benaiah son of Jehoiada went up
and struck down Joab and killed him,
and he was buried at his home out in the
country. 35 The king put Benaiah son of
Jehoiada over the army in Joab's position and replaced Abiathar with Zadok
the priest.

36 Then the king sent for Shimei and
said to him, "Build yourself a house in
Jerusalem and live there, but do not go
anywhere else. 37 The day you leave and
cross the Kidron Valley, you can be sure
you will die; your blood will be on your
own head."

38 Shimei answered the king, "What
you say is good. Your servant will do as
my lord the king has said." And Shimei
stayed in Jerusalem for a long time.

39 But three years later, two of Shimei's
slaves ran off to Achish son of Maakah,
king of Gath, and Shimei was told, "Your
slaves are in Gath." 40 At this, he saddled
his donkey and went to Achish at Gath in
search of his slaves. So Shimei went away
and brought the slaves back from Gath.

41 When Solomon was told that Shimei
had gone from Jerusalem to Gath and had
returned, 42 the king summoned Shimei and said to him, "Did I not make you
swear by the LORD and warn you, 'On the
day you leave to go anywhere else, you
can be sure you will die'? At that time you
said to me, 'What you say is good. I will
obey.' 43 Why then did you not keep your
oath to the LORD and obey the command
I gave you?"

44 The king also said to Shimei, "You
know in your heart all the wrong you did
to my father David. Now the LORD will repay you for your wrongdoing. 45 But King
Solomon will be blessed, and David's
throne will remain secure before the
LORD forever."

46 Then the king gave the order to Benа-
iah son of Jehoiada, and he went out and
struck Shimei down and he died.

The kingdom was now established in
Solomon's hands.

3 Solomon made an alliance with Pharaoh king of Egypt and married his
daughter. He brought her to the City of
David until he finished building his palace and the temple of the LORD, and the
wall around Jerusalem. 2 The people,
however, were still sacrificing at the high
places, because a temple had not yet been
built for the Name of the LORD. 3 Solomon
showed his love for the LORD by walking
according to the instructions given him
by his father David, except that he offered sacrifices and burned incense on
the high places.

4 The king went to Gibeon to offer sacrifices, for that was the most important
high place, and Solomon offered a thousand burnt offerings on that altar. 5 At
Gibeon the LORD appeared to Solomon
during the night in a dream, and God
said, "Ask for whatever you want me to
give you."

6 Solomon answered, "You have shown
great kindness to your servant, my father
David, because he was faithful to you and
righteous and upright in heart. You have
continued this great kindness to him and
have given him a son to sit on his throne
this very day.

7 "Now, LORD my God, you have made
your servant king in place of my father
David. But I am only a little child and
do not know how to carry out my duties.
8 Your servant is here among the people
you have chosen, a great people, too numerous to count or number. 9 So give your
servant a discerning heart to govern your
people and to distinguish between right
and wrong. For who is able to govern this
great people of yours?"

10 The Lord was pleased that Solomon
had asked for this. 11 So God said to him,
"Since you have asked for this and not for
long life or wealth for yourself, nor have
asked for the death of your enemies but
for discernment in administering justice,
12 I will do what you have asked. I will give
you a wise and discerning heart, so that
there will never have been anyone like
you, nor will there ever be. 13 Moreover,
I will give you what you have not asked
for — both wealth and honor — so that
in your lifetime you will have no equal
among kings. 14 And if you walk in obedience to me and keep my decrees and

commands as David your father did. I
will give you a long life." 15Then Solomon
awoke—and he realized it had been a
dream.

He returned to Jerusalem, stood before the ark of the Lord's covenant and sacrificed burnt offerings and fellowship offerings. Then he gave a feast for all his court.

16Now two prostitutes came to the king
and stood before him. 17One of them said,
"Pardon me, my lord. This woman and I
live in the same house, and I had a baby
while she was there with me. 18The third
day after my child was born, this woman
also had a baby. We were alone; there was
no one in the house but the two of us.

19"During the night this woman's son
died because she lay on him. 20So she got
up in the middle of the night and took my
son from my side while I your servant was
asleep. She put him by her breast and put
her dead son by my breast. 21The next
morning, I got up to nurse my son—and
he was dead! But when I looked at him
closely in the morning light, I saw that it
wasn't the son I had borne."

22The other woman said, "No! The living one is my son; the dead one is yours."

But the first one insisted, "No! The dead one is yours; the living one is mine." And so they argued before the king.

23The king said, "This one says, 'My son is alive and your son is dead,' while that one says, 'No! Your son is dead and mine is alive.'"

24Then the king said, "Bring me a
sword." So they brought a sword for the
king. 25He then gave an order: "Cut the
living child in two and give half to one
and half to the other."

26The woman whose son was alive was deeply moved out of love for her son and said to the king, "Please, my lord, give her the living baby! Don't kill him!"

But the other said, "Neither I nor you shall have him. Cut him in two!"

27Then the king gave his ruling: "Give the living baby to the first woman. Do not kill him; she is his mother."

28When all Israel heard the verdict the king had given, they held the king in awe, because they saw that he had wisdom from God to administer justice.

4 So King Solomon ruled over all Israel.
2And these were his chief officials:

Azariah son of Zadok—the priest;
3Elihoreph and Ahijah, sons of Shisha—secretaries;
Jehoshaphat son of Ahilud—recorder;
4Benaiah son of Jehoiada—commander in chief;
Zadok and Abiathar—priests;
5Azariah son of Nathan—in charge of the district governors;
Zabud son of Nathan—a priest and adviser to the king;
6Ahishar—palace administrator;
Adoniram son of Abda—in charge of forced labor.

7Solomon had twelve district governors over all Israel, who supplied provisions for the king and the royal household. Each one had to provide supplies for one month in the year. 8These are
their names:

Ben-Hur—in the hill country of Ephraim;
9Ben-Deker—in Makaz, Shaalbim, Beth Shemesh and Elon Bethhanan;
10Ben-Hesed—in Arubboth (Sokoh and all the land of Hepher were his);
11Ben-Abinadab—in Naphoth Dor (he was married to Taphath daughter of Solomon);
12Baana son of Ahilud—in Taanach and Megiddo, and in all of Beth Shan next to Zarethan below Jezreel, from Beth Shan to Abel Meholah across to Jokmeam;
13Ben-Geber—in Ramoth Gilead (the settlements of Jair son of Manasseh in Gilead were his, as well as the region of Argob in Bashan and its sixty large walled cities with bronze gate bars);
14Ahinadab son of Iddo—in Mahanaim;
15Ahimaaz—in Naphtali (he had married Basemath daughter of Solomon);
16Baana son of Hushai—in Asher and in Aloth;
17Jehoshaphat son of Paruah—in Issachar;
18Shimei son of Ela—in Benjamin;
19Geber son of Uri—in Gilead (the country of Sihon king of the Amorites and the country of Og king of Bashan). He was the only governor over the district.

20 The people of Judah and Israel were
as numerous as the sand on the seashore;
they ate, they drank and they were happy.
21 And Solomon ruled over all the kingdoms from the Euphrates River to the
land of the Philistines, as far as the border of Egypt. These countries brought
tribute and were Solomon's subjects all
his life.

22 Solomon's daily provisions were
thirty cors[a] of the finest flour and sixty cors[b] of meal, 23 ten head of stall-fed
cattle, twenty of pasture-fed cattle and
a hundred sheep and goats, as well as
deer, gazelles, roebucks and choice fowl.
24 For he ruled over all the kingdoms west
of the Euphrates River, from Tiphsah to
Gaza, and had peace on all sides. 25 During Solomon's lifetime Judah and Israel,
from Dan to Beersheba, lived in safety,
everyone under their own vine and under their own fig tree.

26 Solomon had four[c] thousand stalls
for chariot horses, and twelve thousand
horses.[d]

27 The district governors, each in his
month, supplied provisions for King Solomon and all who came to the king's table.
They saw to it that nothing was lacking.
28 They also brought to the proper place
their quotas of barley and straw for the
chariot horses and the other horses.

29 God gave Solomon wisdom and very
great insight, and a breadth of understanding as measureless as the sand on
the seashore. 30 Solomon's wisdom was
greater than the wisdom of all the people of the East, and greater than all the
wisdom of Egypt. 31 He was wiser than
anyone else, including Ethan the Ezrahite—wiser than Heman, Kalkol and
Darda, the sons of Mahol. And his fame
spread to all the surrounding nations.
32 He spoke three thousand proverbs and
his songs numbered a thousand and five.
33 He spoke about plant life, from the cedar of Lebanon to the hyssop that grows
out of walls. He also spoke about animals
and birds, reptiles and fish. 34 From all
nations people came to listen to Solomon's wisdom, sent by all the kings of the
world, who had heard of his wisdom.[e]

5[f] When Hiram king of Tyre heard that
Solomon had been anointed king to
succeed his father David, he sent his envoys to Solomon, because he had always
been on friendly terms with David. 2 Solomon sent back this message to Hiram:

3 "You know that because of the
wars waged against my father David
from all sides, he could not build a
temple for the Name of the LORD his
God until the LORD put his enemies
under his feet. 4 But now the LORD my
God has given me rest on every side,
and there is no adversary or disaster.
5 I intend, therefore, to build a temple
for the Name of the LORD my God, as
the LORD told my father David, when
he said, 'Your son whom I will put on
the throne in your place will build
the temple for my Name.'

6 "So give orders that cedars of Lebanon be cut for me. My men will work
with yours, and I will pay you for your
men whatever wages you set. You
know that we have no one so skilled
in felling timber as the Sidonians."

7 When Hiram heard Solomon's message, he was greatly pleased and said,
"Praise be to the LORD today, for he has
given David a wise son to rule over this
great nation."

8 So Hiram sent word to Solomon:

"I have received the message you
sent me and will do all you want in
providing the cedar and juniper
logs. 9 My men will haul them down
from Lebanon to the Mediterranean
Sea, and I will float them as rafts by
sea to the place you specify. There I
will separate them and you can take
them away. And you are to grant my
wish by providing food for my royal
household."

10 In this way Hiram kept Solomon supplied with all the cedar and juniper logs
he wanted, 11 and Solomon gave Hiram
twenty thousand cors[g] of wheat as food
for his household, in addition to twenty
thousand baths[h,i] of pressed olive oil.
Solomon continued to do this for Hiram

[a] *22* That is, probably about 5 1/2 tons or about 5 metric tons [b] *22* That is, probably about 11 tons or about 10 metric tons [c] *26* Some Septuagint manuscripts (see also 2 Chron. 9:25); Hebrew *forty* [d] *26* Or *charioteers* [e] *34* In Hebrew texts 4:21-34 is numbered 5:1-14. [f] In Hebrew texts 5:1-18 is numbered 5:15-32. [g] *11* That is, probably about 3,600 tons or about 3,250 metric tons [h] *11* Septuagint (see also 2 Chron. 2:10); Hebrew *twenty cors* [i] *11* That is, about 120,000 gallons or about 440,000 liters

year after year. 12The LORD gave Solomon
wisdom, just as he had promised him.
There were peaceful relations between
Hiram and Solomon, and the two of them
made a treaty.
13King Solomon conscripted laborers
from all Israel—thirty thousand men.
14He sent them off to Lebanon in shifts of
ten thousand a month, so that they spent
one month in Lebanon and two months
at home. Adoniram was in charge of the
forced labor. 15Solomon had seventy thousand carriers and eighty thousand stonecutters in the hills, 16as well as thirty-
three hundred[a] foremen who supervised
the project and directed the workers. 17At
the king's command they removed from
the quarry large blocks of high-grade
stone to provide a foundation of dressed
stone for the temple. 18The craftsmen of
Solomon and Hiram and workers from
Byblos cut and prepared the timber and
stone for the building of the temple.

6 In the four hundred and eightieth[b]
year after the Israelites came out of
Egypt, in the fourth year of Solomon's
reign over Israel, in the month of Ziv, the
second month, he began to build the temple of the LORD.
2The temple that King Solomon built
for the LORD was sixty cubits long, twenty wide and thirty high.[c] 3The portico at
the front of the main hall of the temple
extended the width of the temple, that is
twenty cubits,[d] and projected ten cubits[e]
from the front of the temple. 4He made
narrow windows high up in the temple
walls. 5Against the walls of the main hall
and inner sanctuary he built a structure
around the building, in which there were
side rooms. 6The lowest floor was five
cubits[f] wide, the middle floor six cubits[g]
and the third floor seven.[h] He made off-
set ledges around the outside of the temple so that nothing would be inserted
into the temple walls.
7In building the temple, only blocks
dressed at the quarry were used, and no
hammer, chisel or any other iron tool was
heard at the temple site while it was being built.
8The entrance to the lowest[i] floor
was on the south side of the temple; a
stairway led up to the middle level and
from there to the third. 9So he built the
temple and completed it, roofing it with
beams and cedar planks. 10And he built
the side rooms all along the temple. The
height of each was five cubits, and they
were attached to the temple by beams
of cedar.
11The word of the LORD came to Solomon: 12"As for this temple you are building, if you follow my decrees, observe
my laws and keep all my commands
and obey them, I will fulfill through you
the promise I gave to David your father.
13And I will live among the Israelites and
will not abandon my people Israel."
14So Solomon built the temple and
completed it. 15He lined its interior
walls with cedar boards, paneling them
from the floor of the temple to the ceiling, and covered the floor of the temple
with planks of juniper. 16He partitioned
off twenty cubits at the rear of the temple
with cedar boards from floor to ceiling
to form within the temple an inner sanctuary, the Most Holy Place. 17The main
hall in front of this room was forty cubits[j]
long. 18The inside of the temple was cedar, carved with gourds and open flowers. Everything was cedar; no stone was
to be seen.
19He prepared the inner sanctuary
within the temple to set the ark of the
covenant of the LORD there. 20The inner
sanctuary was twenty cubits long, twenty
wide and twenty high. He overlaid the inside with pure gold, and he also overlaid
the altar of cedar. 21Solomon covered the
inside of the temple with pure gold, and
he extended gold chains across the front
of the inner sanctuary, which was overlaid with gold. 22So he overlaid the whole
interior with gold. He also overlaid with
gold the altar that belonged to the inner
sanctuary.
23For the inner sanctuary he made a
pair of cherubim out of olive wood, each
ten cubits high. 24One wing of the first
cherub was five cubits long, and the oth-

[a] *16* Hebrew; some Septuagint manuscripts (see also 2 Chron. 2:2,18) *thirty-six hundred* [b] *1* Hebrew; Septuagint *four hundred and fortieth* [c] *2* That is, about 90 feet long, 30 feet wide and 45 feet high or about 27 meters long, 9 meters wide and 14 meters high [d] *3* That is, about 30 feet or about 9 meters; also in verses 16 and 20 [e] *3* That is, about 15 feet or about 4.5 meters; also in verses 23-26 [f] *6* That is, about 7 1/2 feet or about 2.3 meters; also in verses 10 and 24 [g] *6* That is, about 9 feet or about 2.7 meters [h] *6* That is, about 11 feet or about 3.2 meters [i] *8* Septuagint; Hebrew *middle* [j] *17* That is, about 60 feet or about 18 meters

er wing five cubits—ten cubits from wing
tip to wing tip. 25 The second cherub also
measured ten cubits, for the two cherubim were identical in size and shape.
26 The height of each cherub was ten cubits. 27 He placed the cherubim inside the
innermost room of the temple, with their
wings spread out. The wing of one cherub
touched one wall, while the wing of the
other touched the other wall, and their
wings touched each other in the middle
of the room. 28 He overlaid the cherubim
with gold.

29 On the walls all around the temple,
in both the inner and outer rooms, he
carved cherubim, palm trees and open
flowers. 30 He also covered the floors of
both the inner and outer rooms of the
temple with gold.

31 For the entrance to the inner sanctuary he made doors out of olive wood that
were one fifth of the width of the sanctuary. 32 And on the two olive-wood doors
he carved cherubim, palm trees and open
flowers, and overlaid the cherubim and
palm trees with hammered gold. 33 In the
same way, for the entrance to the main
hall he made doorframes out of olive
wood that were one fourth of the width
of the hall. 34 He also made two doors out
of juniper wood, each having two leaves
that turned in sockets. 35 He carved cherubim, palm trees and open flowers on
them and overlaid them with gold hammered evenly over the carvings.

36 And he built the inner courtyard of
three courses of dressed stone and one
course of trimmed cedar beams.

37 The foundation of the temple of the
LORD was laid in the fourth year, in the
month of Ziv. 38 In the eleventh year in the
month of Bul, the eighth month, the temple was finished in all its details according to its specifications. He had spent
seven years building it.

7 It took Solomon thirteen years, however, to complete the construction of
his palace. 2 He built the Palace of the
Forest of Lebanon a hundred cubits long,
fifty wide and thirty high,[a] with four rows
of cedar columns supporting trimmed
cedar beams. 3 It was roofed with cedar
above the beams that rested on the columns—forty-five beams, fifteen to a row.
4 Its windows were placed high in sets of
three, facing each other. 5 All the doorways had rectangular frames; they were
in the front part in sets of three, facing
each other.[b]

6 He made a colonnade fifty cubits long
and thirty wide.[c] In front of it was a portico, and in front of that were pillars and
an overhanging roof.

7 He built the throne hall, the Hall of
Justice, where he was to judge, and he
covered it with cedar from floor to ceiling.[d] 8 And the palace in which he was to
live, set farther back, was similar in design. Solomon also made a palace like
this hall for Pharaoh's daughter, whom
he had married.

9 All these structures, from the outside
to the great courtyard and from foundation to eaves, were made of blocks of high-
grade stone cut to size and smoothed on
their inner and outer faces. 10 The foundations were laid with large stones of good
quality, some measuring ten cubits[e] and
some eight.[f] 11 Above were high-grade
stones, cut to size, and cedar beams.
12 The great courtyard was surrounded by
a wall of three courses of dressed stone
and one course of trimmed cedar beams,
as was the inner courtyard of the temple
of the LORD with its portico.

13 King Solomon sent to Tyre and
brought Huram,[g] 14 whose mother was
a widow from the tribe of Naphtali and
whose father was from Tyre and a skilled
craftsman in bronze. Huram was filled
with wisdom, with understanding and
with knowledge to do all kinds of bronze
work. He came to King Solomon and did
all the work assigned to him.

15 He cast two bronze pillars, each
eighteen cubits high and twelve cubits
in circumference.[h] 16 He also made two
capitals of cast bronze to set on the tops
of the pillars; each capital was five cubits[i]
high. 17 A network of interwoven chains
adorned the capitals on top of the pillars,
seven for each capital. 18 He made pome-

[a] *2* That is, about 150 feet long, 75 feet wide and 45 feet high or about 45 meters long, 23 meters wide and 14 meters high [b] *5* The meaning of the Hebrew for this verse is uncertain. [c] *6* That is, about 75 feet long and 45 feet wide or about 23 meters long and 14 meters wide [d] *7* Vulgate and Syriac; Hebrew *floor* [e] *10* That is, about 15 feet or about 4.5 meters; also in verse 23 [f] *10* That is, about 12 feet or about 3.6 meters [g] *13* Hebrew *Hiram*, a variant of *Huram*; also in verses 40 and 45 [h] *15* That is, about 27 feet high and 18 feet in circumference or about 8.1 meters high and 5.4 meters in circumference [i] *16* That is, about 7 1/2 feet or about 2.3 meters; also in verse 23

granates in two rows[a] encircling each
network to decorate the capitals on top
of the pillars.[b] He did the same for each
capital. 19The capitals on top of the pillars in the portico were in the shape of lilies, four cubits[c] high. 20On the capitals of
both pillars, above the bowl-shaped part
next to the network, were the two hundred pomegranates in rows all around.
21He erected the pillars at the portico
of the temple. The pillar to the south he
named Jakin[d] and the one to the north
Boaz.[e] 22The capitals on top were in the
shape of lilies. And so the work on the pillars was completed.

23He made the Sea of cast metal, circular in shape, measuring ten cubits from
rim to rim and five cubits high. It took a
line of thirty cubits[f] to measure around
it. 24Below the rim, gourds encircled it—
ten to a cubit. The gourds were cast in two
rows in one piece with the Sea.

25The Sea stood on twelve bulls, three
facing north, three facing west, three facing south and three facing east. The Sea
rested on top of them, and their hind-
quarters were toward the center. 26It was
a handbreadth[g] in thickness, and its rim
was like the rim of a cup, like a lily blossom. It held two thousand baths.[h]

27He also made ten movable stands of
bronze; each was four cubits long, four
wide and three high.[i] 28This is how the
stands were made: They had side panels
attached to uprights. 29On the panels between the uprights were lions, bulls and
cherubim—and on the uprights as well.
Above and below the lions and bulls were
wreaths of hammered work. 30Each stand
had four bronze wheels with bronze axles, and each had a basin resting on four
supports, cast with wreaths on each side.
31On the inside of the stand there was an
opening that had a circular frame one cubit[j] deep. This opening was round, and
with its basework it measured a cubit and
a half.[k] Around its opening there was engraving. The panels of the stands were
square, not round. 32The four wheels
were under the panels, and the axles of
the wheels were attached to the stand.
The diameter of each wheel was a cubit
and a half. 33The wheels were made like
chariot wheels; the axles, rims, spokes
and hubs were all of cast metal.

34Each stand had four handles, one on
each corner, projecting from the stand.
35At the top of the stand there was a circular band half a cubit[l] deep. The supports and panels were attached to the top
of the stand. 36He engraved cherubim,
lions and palm trees on the surfaces of
the supports and on the panels, in every
available space, with wreaths all around.
37This is the way he made the ten stands.
They were all cast in the same molds and
were identical in size and shape.

38He then made ten bronze basins,
each holding forty baths[m] and measuring four cubits across, one basin to go on
each of the ten stands. 39He placed five of
the stands on the south side of the temple
and five on the north. He placed the Sea
on the south side, at the southeast corner
of the temple. 40He also made the pots[n]
and shovels and sprinkling bowls.

So Huram finished all the work he had
undertaken for King Solomon in the temple of the LORD:

41the two pillars;
the two bowl-shaped capitals on top of the pillars;
the two sets of network decorating the two bowl-shaped capitals on top of the pillars;
42the four hundred pomegranates for the two sets of network (two rows of pomegranates for each network decorating the bowl-shaped capitals on top of the pillars);
43the ten stands with their ten basins;
44the Sea and the twelve bulls under it;
45the pots, shovels and sprinkling bowls.

[a] *18* Two Hebrew manuscripts and Septuagint; most Hebrew manuscripts *made the pillars, and there were two rows* [b] *18* Many Hebrew manuscripts and Syriac; most Hebrew manuscripts *pomegranates* [c] *19* That is, about 6 feet or about 1.8 meters; also in verse 38 [d] *21* *Jakin* probably means *he establishes.* [e] *21* *Boaz* probably means *in him is strength.* [f] *23* That is, about 45 feet or about 14 meters [g] *26* That is, about 3 inches or about 7.5 centimeters [h] *26* That is, about 12,000 gallons or about 44,000 liters; the Septuagint does not have this sentence. [i] *27* That is, about 6 feet long and wide and about 4 1/2 feet high or about 1.8 meters long and wide and 1.4 meters high [j] *31* That is, about 18 inches or about 45 centimeters [k] *31* That is, about 2 1/4 feet or about 68 centimeters; also in verse 32 [l] *35* That is, about 9 inches or about 23 centimeters [m] *38* That is, about 240 gallons or about 880 liters [n] *40* Many Hebrew manuscripts, Septuagint, Syriac and Vulgate (see also verse 45 and 2 Chron. 4:11); many other Hebrew manuscripts *basins*

All these objects that Huram made
for King Solomon for the temple of the
LORD were of burnished bronze. 46The
king had them cast in clay molds in the
plain of the Jordan between Sukkoth and
Zarethan. 47Solomon left all these things
unweighed, because there were so many;
the weight of the bronze was not determined.

48Solomon also made all the furnishings that were in the LORD's temple:

the golden altar;
the golden table on which was the
bread of the Presence;
49the lampstands of pure gold (five
on the right and five on the left, in
front of the inner sanctuary);
the gold floral work and lamps and
tongs;
50the pure gold basins, wick trimmers,
sprinkling bowls, dishes and censers;
and the gold sockets for the doors of
the innermost room, the Most Holy
Place, and also for the doors of the
main hall of the temple.

51When all the work King Solomon had
done for the temple of the LORD was finished, he brought in the things his father
David had dedicated — the silver and
gold and the furnishings — and he placed
them in the treasuries of the LORD's temple.

8 Then King Solomon summoned into
his presence at Jerusalem the elders of
Israel, all the heads of the tribes and the
chiefs of the Israelite families, to bring up
the ark of the LORD's covenant from Zion,
the City of David. 2All the Israelites came
together to King Solomon at the time of
the festival in the month of Ethanim, the
seventh month.

3When all the elders of Israel had arrived, the priests took up the ark, 4and
they brought up the ark of the LORD and
the tent of meeting and all the sacred
furnishings in it. The priests and Levites
carried them up, 5and King Solomon and
the entire assembly of Israel that had
gathered about him were before the ark,
sacrificing so many sheep and cattle that
they could not be recorded or counted.

6The priests then brought the ark of the
LORD's covenant to its place in the inner
sanctuary of the temple, the Most Holy
Place, and put it beneath the wings of the
cherubim. 7The cherubim spread their
wings over the place of the ark and over-
shadowed the ark and its carrying poles.
8These poles were so long that their ends
could be seen from the Holy Place in
front of the inner sanctuary, but not from
outside the Holy Place; and they are still
there today. 9There was nothing in the
ark except the two stone tablets that Moses had placed in it at Horeb, where the
LORD made a covenant with the Israelites
after they came out of Egypt.

10When the priests withdrew from
the Holy Place, the cloud filled the temple of the LORD. 11And the priests could
not perform their service because of the
cloud, for the glory of the LORD filled his
temple.

12Then Solomon said, "The LORD has
said that he would dwell in a dark cloud;
13I have indeed built a magnificent temple for you, a place for you to dwell forever."

14While the whole assembly of Israel was standing there, the king turned
around and blessed them. 15Then he
said:

"Praise be to the LORD, the God of
Israel, who with his own hand has
fulfilled what he promised with his
own mouth to my father David. For
he said, 16'Since the day I brought my
people Israel out of Egypt, I have not
chosen a city in any tribe of Israel to
have a temple built so that my Name
might be there, but I have chosen David to rule my people Israel.'

17"My father David had it in his
heart to build a temple for the Name
of the LORD, the God of Israel. 18But
the LORD said to my father David,
'You did well to have it in your heart
to build a temple for my Name.
19Nevertheless, you are not the one
to build the temple, but your son,
your own flesh and blood — he is the
one who will build the temple for my
Name.'

20"The LORD has kept the promise he made: I have succeeded David
my father and now I sit on the throne
of Israel, just as the LORD promised,
and I have built the temple for the
Name of the LORD, the God of Israel. 21I have provided a place there for
the ark, in which is the covenant of
the LORD that he made with our an-

cestors when he brought them out of
Egypt."

22 Then Solomon stood before the altar
of the LORD in front of the whole assembly of Israel, spread out his hands toward
heaven 23 and said:

"LORD, the God of Israel, there
is no God like you in heaven above
or on earth below—you who keep
your covenant of love with your servants who continue wholeheartedly
in your way. 24 You have kept your
promise to your servant David my
father; with your mouth you have
promised and with your hand you
have fulfilled it—as it is today.

25 "Now LORD, the God of Israel,
keep for your servant David my father the promises you made to him
when you said, 'You shall never fail
to have a successor to sit before me
on the throne of Israel, if only your
descendants are careful in all they
do to walk before me faithfully as
you have done.' 26 And now, God of
Israel, let your word that you promised your servant David my father
come true.

27 "But will God really dwell on
earth? The heavens, even the highest heaven, cannot contain you. How
much less this temple I have built!
28 Yet give attention to your servant's
prayer and his plea for mercy, LORD
my God. Hear the cry and the prayer
that your servant is praying in your
presence this day. 29 May your eyes
be open toward this temple night and
day, this place of which you said, 'My
Name shall be there,' so that you will
hear the prayer your servant prays
toward this place. 30 Hear the supplication of your servant and of your
people Israel when they pray toward
this place. Hear from heaven, your
dwelling place, and when you hear,
forgive.

31 "When anyone wrongs their
neighbor and is required to take an
oath and they come and swear the
oath before your altar in this temple, 32 then hear from heaven and
act. Judge between your servants,
condemning the guilty by bringing
down on their heads what they have
done, and vindicating the innocent
by treating them in accordance with
their innocence.

33 "When your people Israel have
been defeated by an enemy because
they have sinned against you, and
when they turn back to you and give
praise to your name, praying and
making supplication to you in this
temple, 34 then hear from heaven and
forgive the sin of your people Israel
and bring them back to the land you
gave to their ancestors.

35 "When the heavens are shut up
and there is no rain because your
people have sinned against you, and
when they pray toward this place
and give praise to your name and
turn from their sin because you have
afflicted them, 36 then hear from
heaven and forgive the sin of your
servants, your people Israel. Teach
them the right way to live, and send
rain on the land you gave your people
for an inheritance.

37 "When famine or plague comes
to the land, or blight or mildew, locusts or grasshoppers, or when an
enemy besieges them in any of their
cities, whatever disaster or disease
may come, 38 and when a prayer or
plea is made by anyone among your
people Israel—being aware of the
afflictions of their own hearts, and
spreading out their hands toward
this temple— 39 then hear from heav-
en, your dwelling place. Forgive and
act; deal with everyone according
to all they do, since you know their
hearts (for you alone know every human heart), 40 so that they will fear
you all the time they live in the land
you gave our ancestors.

41 "As for the foreigner who does
not belong to your people Israel but
has come from a distant land because of your name— 42 for they will
hear of your great name and your
mighty hand and your outstretched
arm—when they come and pray toward this temple, 43 then hear from
heaven, your dwelling place. Do
whatever the foreigner asks of you,
so that all the peoples of the earth
may know your name and fear you,
as do your own people Israel, and
may know that this house I have built
bears your Name.

44 "When your people go to war
against their enemies, wherever you
send them, and when they pray to the
LORD toward the city you have chosen and the temple I have built for
your Name, 45 then hear from heaven
their prayer and their plea, and uphold their cause.

46 "When they sin against you—for
there is no one who does not sin—
and you become angry with them
and give them over to their enemies,
who take them captive to their own
lands, far away or near; 47 and if they
have a change of heart in the land
where they are held captive, and repent and plead with you in the land
of their captors and say, 'We have
sinned, we have done wrong, we
have acted wickedly'; 48 and if they
turn back to you with all their heart
and soul in the land of their enemies
who took them captive, and pray to
you toward the land you gave their
ancestors, toward the city you have
chosen and the temple I have built for
your Name; 49 then from heaven, your
dwelling place, hear their prayer and
their plea, and uphold their cause.
50 And forgive your people, who have
sinned against you; forgive all the offenses they have committed against
you, and cause their captors to show
them mercy; 51 for they are your people and your inheritance, whom you
brought out of Egypt, out of that iron-
smelting furnace.

52 "May your eyes be open to your
servant's plea and to the plea of your
people Israel, and may you listen to
them whenever they cry out to you.
53 For you singled them out from all
the nations of the world to be your
own inheritance, just as you declared through your servant Moses
when you, Sovereign LORD, brought
our ancestors out of Egypt."

54 When Solomon had finished all these
prayers and supplications to the LORD,
he rose from before the altar of the LORD,
where he had been kneeling with his
hands spread out toward heaven. 55 He
stood and blessed the whole assembly of
Israel in a loud voice, saying:

56 "Praise be to the LORD, who has
given rest to his people Israel just
as he promised. Not one word has
failed of all the good promises he
gave through his servant Moses.
57 May the LORD our God be with us
as he was with our ancestors; may he
never leave us nor forsake us. 58 May
he turn our hearts to him, to walk in
obedience to him and keep the commands, decrees and laws he gave our
ancestors. 59 And may these words
of mine, which I have prayed before
the LORD, be near to the LORD our
God day and night, that he may uphold the cause of his servant and the
cause of his people Israel according
to each day's need, 60 so that all the
peoples of the earth may know that
the LORD is God and that there is no
other. 61 And may your hearts be fully
committed to the LORD our God, to
live by his decrees and obey his commands, as at this time."

62 Then the king and all Israel with him
offered sacrifices before the LORD. 63 Solomon offered a sacrifice of fellowship
offerings to the LORD: twenty-two thousand cattle and a hundred and twenty
thousand sheep and goats. So the king
and all the Israelites dedicated the temple of the LORD.

64 On that same day the king consecrated the middle part of the courtyard in
front of the temple of the LORD, and there
he offered burnt offerings, grain offerings
and the fat of the fellowship offerings, because the bronze altar that stood before
the LORD was too small to hold the burnt
offerings, the grain offerings and the fat
of the fellowship offerings.

65 So Solomon observed the festival at
that time, and all Israel with him—a vast
assembly, people from Lebo Hamath to
the Wadi of Egypt. They celebrated it before the LORD our God for seven days and
seven days more, fourteen days in all.
66 On the following day he sent the people away. They blessed the king and then
went home, joyful and glad in heart for all
the good things the LORD had done for his
servant David and his people Israel.

9 When Solomon had finished building
the temple of the LORD and the royal
palace, and had achieved all he had desired to do, 2 the LORD appeared to him a
second time, as he had appeared to him
at Gibeon. 3 The LORD said to him:

"I have heard the prayer and plea
you have made before me; I have
consecrated this temple, which you
have built, by putting my Name there
forever. My eyes and my heart will always be there.

4 "As for you, if you walk before
me faithfully with integrity of heart
and uprightness, as David your father did, and do all I command and
observe my decrees and laws, 5 I will
establish your royal throne over Israel forever, as I promised David your
father when I said, 'You shall never
fail to have a successor on the throne
of Israel.'

6 "But if you[a] or your descendants
turn away from me and do not observe the commands and decrees I
have given you[a] and go off to serve
other gods and worship them, 7 then I
will cut off Israel from the land I have
given them and will reject this temple I have consecrated for my Name.
Israel will then become a byword
and an object of ridicule among all
peoples. 8 This temple will become
a heap of rubble. All[b] who pass by
will be appalled and will scoff and
say, 'Why has the LORD done such
a thing to this land and to this temple?' 9 People will answer, 'Because
they have forsaken the LORD their
God, who brought their ancestors
out of Egypt, and have embraced
other gods, worshiping and serving
them — that is why the LORD brought
all this disaster on them.'"

10 At the end of twenty years, during
which Solomon built these two buildings — the temple of the LORD and the
royal palace — 11 King Solomon gave
twenty towns in Galilee to Hiram king of
Tyre, because Hiram had supplied him
with all the cedar and juniper and gold
he wanted. 12 But when Hiram went from
Tyre to see the towns that Solomon had
given him, he was not pleased with them.
13 "What kind of towns are these you have
given me, my brother?" he asked. And he
called them the Land of Kabul,[c] a name
they have to this day. 14 Now Hiram had
sent to the king 120 talents[d] of gold.

15 Here is the account of the forced labor
King Solomon conscripted to build the
LORD's temple, his own palace, the terraces,[e] the wall of Jerusalem, and Hazor, Megiddo and Gezer. 16 (Pharaoh king of Egypt
had attacked and captured Gezer. He had
set it on fire. He killed its Canaanite inhabitants and then gave it as a wedding
gift to his daughter, Solomon's wife. 17 And
Solomon rebuilt Gezer.) He built up Lower Beth Horon, 18 Baalath, and Tadmor[f] in
the desert, within his land, 19 as well as all
his store cities and the towns for his chariots and for his horses[g] — whatever he desired to build in Jerusalem, in Lebanon
and throughout all the territory he ruled.

20 There were still people left from the
Amorites, Hittites, Perizzites, Hivites and
Jebusites (these peoples were not Israelites). 21 Solomon conscripted the descendants of all these peoples remaining in
the land — whom the Israelites could not
exterminate[h] — to serve as slave labor,
as it is to this day. 22 But Solomon did not
make slaves of any of the Israelites; they
were his fighting men, his government officials, his officers, his captains, and the
commanders of his chariots and charioteers. 23 They were also the chief officials
in charge of Solomon's projects — 550 officials supervising those who did the work.

24 After Pharaoh's daughter had come
up from the City of David to the palace
Solomon had built for her, he constructed the terraces.

25 Three times a year Solomon sacrificed burnt offerings and fellowship offerings on the altar he had built for the
LORD, burning incense before the LORD
along with them, and so fulfilled the temple obligations.

26 King Solomon also built ships at Ezion Geber, which is near Elath in Edom,
on the shore of the Red Sea.[i] 27 And Hiram sent his men — sailors who knew the
sea — to serve in the fleet with Solomon's
men. 28 They sailed to Ophir and brought
back 420 talents[j] of gold, which they delivered to King Solomon.

[a] *6* The Hebrew is plural. [b] *8* See some Septuagint manuscripts, Old Latin, Syriac, Arabic and Targum; Hebrew *And though this temple is now imposing, all* [c] *13* *Kabul* sounds like the Hebrew for *good-for-nothing.* [d] *14* That is, about 4 1/2 tons or about 4 metric tons [e] *15* Or *the Millo*; also in verse 24 [f] *18* The Hebrew may also be read *Tamar.* [g] *19* Or *charioteers* [h] *21* The Hebrew term refers to the irrevocable giving over of things or persons to the LORD, often by totally destroying them. [i] *26* Or *the Sea of Reeds* [j] *28* That is, about 16 tons or about 14 metric tons

10 When the queen of Sheba heard about the fame of Solomon and his relationship to the LORD, she came to test Solomon with hard questions. 2Arriving at Jerusalem with a very great caravan — with camels carrying spices, large quantities of gold, and precious stones — she came to Solomon and talked with him about all that she had on her mind. 3Solomon answered all her questions; nothing was too hard for the king to explain to her. 4When the queen of Sheba saw all the wisdom of Solomon and the palace he had built, 5the food on his table, the seating of his officials, the attending servants in their robes, his cupbearers, and the burnt offerings he made at[a] the temple of the LORD, she was overwhelmed.

6She said to the king, "The report I heard in my own country about your achievements and your wisdom is true. 7But I did not believe these things until I came and saw with my own eyes. Indeed, not even half was told me; in wisdom and wealth you have far exceeded the report I heard. 8How happy your people must be! How happy your officials, who continually stand before you and hear your wisdom! 9Praise be to the LORD your God, who has delighted in you and placed you on the throne of Israel. Because of the LORD's eternal love for Israel, he has made you king to maintain justice and righteousness."

10And she gave the king 120 talents[b] of gold, large quantities of spices, and precious stones. Never again were so many spices brought in as those the queen of Sheba gave to King Solomon.

11(Hiram's ships brought gold from Ophir; and from there they brought great cargoes of almugwood[c] and precious stones. 12The king used the almugwood to make supports[d] for the temple of the LORD and for the royal palace, and to make harps and lyres for the musicians. So much almugwood has never been imported or seen since that day.)

13King Solomon gave the queen of Sheba all she desired and asked for, besides what he had given her out of his royal bounty. Then she left and returned with her retinue to her own country.

14The weight of the gold that Solomon received yearly was 666 talents,[e] 15not including the revenues from merchants and traders and from all the Arabian kings and the governors of the territories.

16King Solomon made two hundred large shields of hammered gold; six hundred shekels[f] of gold went into each shield. 17He also made three hundred small shields of hammered gold, with three minas[g] of gold in each shield. The king put them in the Palace of the Forest of Lebanon.

18Then the king made a great throne covered with ivory and overlaid with fine gold. 19The throne had six steps, and its back had a rounded top. On both sides of the seat were armrests, with a lion standing beside each of them. 20Twelve lions stood on the six steps, one at either end of each step. Nothing like it had ever been made for any other kingdom. 21All King Solomon's goblets were gold, and all the household articles in the Palace of the Forest of Lebanon were pure gold. Nothing was made of silver, because silver was considered of little value in Solomon's days. 22The king had a fleet of trading ships[h] at sea along with the ships of Hiram. Once every three years it returned, carrying gold, silver and ivory, and apes and baboons.

23King Solomon was greater in riches and wisdom than all the other kings of the earth. 24The whole world sought audience with Solomon to hear the wisdom God had put in his heart. 25Year after year, everyone who came brought a gift — articles of silver and gold, robes, weapons and spices, and horses and mules.

26Solomon accumulated chariots and horses; he had fourteen hundred chariots and twelve thousand horses,[i] which he kept in the chariot cities and also with him in Jerusalem. 27The king made silver as common in Jerusalem as stones, and cedar as plentiful as sycamore-fig trees in the foothills. 28Solomon's horses were imported from Egypt and from

[a] *5* Or *the ascent by which he went up to* [b] *10* That is, about 4 1/2 tons or about 4 metric tons
[c] *11* Probably a variant of *algumwood*; also in verse 12 [d] *12* The meaning of the Hebrew for this word is uncertain. [e] *14* That is, about 25 tons or about 23 metric tons [f] *16* That is, about 15 pounds or about 6.9 kilograms; also in verse 29 [g] *17* That is, about 3 3/4 pounds or about 1.7 kilograms; or perhaps reference is to double minas, that is, about 7 1/2 pounds or about 3.5 kilograms. [h] *22* Hebrew *of ships of Tarshish*
[i] *26* Or *charioteers*

Kue[a] — the royal merchants purchased
them from Kue at the current price.
29They imported a chariot from Egypt
for six hundred shekels of silver, and a
horse for a hundred and fifty.[b] They also
exported them to all the kings of the Hittites and of the Arameans.

11 King Solomon, however, loved
many foreign women besides Pharaoh's daughter — Moabites, Ammonites,
Edomites, Sidonians and Hittites. 2They
were from nations about which the LORD
had told the Israelites, "You must not intermarry with them, because they will
surely turn your hearts after their gods."
Nevertheless, Solomon held fast to them
in love. 3He had seven hundred wives of
royal birth and three hundred concubines, and his wives led him astray. 4As
Solomon grew old, his wives turned his
heart after other gods, and his heart was
not fully devoted to the LORD his God, as
the heart of David his father had been.
5He followed Ashtoreth the goddess of
the Sidonians, and Molek the detestable
god of the Ammonites. 6So Solomon did
evil in the eyes of the LORD; he did not
follow the LORD completely, as David his
father had done.

7On a hill east of Jerusalem, Solomon
built a high place for Chemosh the detestable god of Moab, and for Molek the
detestable god of the Ammonites. 8He
did the same for all his foreign wives, who
burned incense and offered sacrifices to
their gods.

9The LORD became angry with Solomon because his heart had turned away
from the LORD, the God of Israel, who had
appeared to him twice. 10Although he had
forbidden Solomon to follow other gods,
Solomon did not keep the LORD's command. 11So the LORD said to Solomon,
"Since this is your attitude and you have
not kept my covenant and my decrees,
which I commanded you, I will most certainly tear the kingdom away from you
and give it to one of your subordinates.
12Nevertheless, for the sake of David your
father, I will not do it during your lifetime.
I will tear it out of the hand of your son.
13Yet I will not tear the whole kingdom
from him, but will give him one tribe for
the sake of David my servant and for the
sake of Jerusalem, which I have chosen."

14Then the LORD raised up against Solomon an adversary, Hadad the Edomite,
from the royal line of Edom. 15Earlier
when David was fighting with Edom,
Joab the commander of the army, who
had gone up to bury the dead, had struck
down all the men in Edom. 16Joab and all
the Israelites stayed there for six months,
until they had destroyed all the men in
Edom. 17But Hadad, still only a boy, fled
to Egypt with some Edomite officials who
had served his father. 18They set out from
Midian and went to Paran. Then taking
people from Paran with them, they went
to Egypt, to Pharaoh king of Egypt, who
gave Hadad a house and land and provided him with food.

19Pharaoh was so pleased with Hadad
that he gave him a sister of his own wife,
Queen Tahpenes, in marriage. 20The sister of Tahpenes bore him a son named
Genubath, whom Tahpenes brought up
in the royal palace. There Genubath lived
with Pharaoh's own children.

21While he was in Egypt, Hadad heard
that David rested with his ancestors and
that Joab the commander of the army was
also dead. Then Hadad said to Pharaoh,
"Let me go, that I may return to my own
country."

22"What have you lacked here that you
want to go back to your own country?"
Pharaoh asked.

"Nothing," Hadad replied, "but do let
me go!"

23And God raised up against Solomon
another adversary, Rezon son of Eliada,
who had fled from his master, Hadadezer
king of Zobah. 24When David destroyed
Zobah's army, Rezon gathered a band of
men around him and became their leader; they went to Damascus, where they
settled and took control. 25Rezon was Israel's adversary as long as Solomon lived,
adding to the trouble caused by Hadad.
So Rezon ruled in Aram and was hostile
toward Israel.

26Also, Jeroboam son of Nebat rebelled
against the king. He was one of Solomon's
officials, an Ephraimite from Zeredah,
and his mother was a widow named Ze-
ruah.

27Here is the account of how he rebelled against the king: Solomon had
built the terraces[c] and had filled in the

[a] *28* Probably *Cilicia* [b] *29* That is, about 3 3/4 pounds or about 1.7 kilograms [c] *27* Or *the Millo*

gap in the wall of the city of David his
father. 28 Now Jeroboam was a man of
standing, and when Solomon saw how
well the young man did his work, he put
him in charge of the whole labor force of
the tribes of Joseph.

29 About that time Jeroboam was going
out of Jerusalem, and Ahijah the prophet of Shiloh met him on the way, wearing
a new cloak. The two of them were alone
out in the country, 30 and Ahijah took
hold of the new cloak he was wearing and
tore it into twelve pieces. 31 Then he said
to Jeroboam, "Take ten pieces for yourself, for this is what the LORD, the God of
Israel, says: 'See, I am going to tear the
kingdom out of Solomon's hand and give
you ten tribes. 32 But for the sake of my
servant David and the city of Jerusalem,
which I have chosen out of all the tribes
of Israel, he will have one tribe. 33 I will do
this because they have[a] forsaken me and
worshiped Ashtoreth the goddess of the
Sidonians, Chemosh the god of the Moabites, and Molek the god of the Ammonites, and have not walked in obedience to
me, nor done what is right in my eyes, nor
kept my decrees and laws as David, Solomon's father, did.

34 " 'But I will not take the whole kingdom out of Solomon's hand; I have made
him ruler all the days of his life for the
sake of David my servant, whom I chose
and who obeyed my commands and decrees. 35 I will take the kingdom from his
son's hands and give you ten tribes. 36 I
will give one tribe to his son so that David my servant may always have a lamp
before me in Jerusalem, the city where
I chose to put my Name. 37 However, as
for you, I will take you, and you will rule
over all that your heart desires; you will
be king over Israel. 38 If you do whatever
I command you and walk in obedience
to me and do what is right in my eyes by
obeying my decrees and commands, as
David my servant did, I will be with you.
I will build you a dynasty as enduring as
the one I built for David and will give Israel to you. 39 I will humble David's descendants because of this, but not forever.' "

40 Solomon tried to kill Jeroboam, but
Jeroboam fled to Egypt, to Shishak the
king, and stayed there until Solomon's
death.

41 As for the other events of Solomon's
reign—all he did and the wisdom he displayed—are they not written in the book
of the annals of Solomon? 42 Solomon
reigned in Jerusalem over all Israel forty
years. 43 Then he rested with his ancestors and was buried in the city of David
his father. And Rehoboam his son succeeded him as king.

12 Rehoboam went to Shechem, for
all Israel had gone there to make
him king. 2 When Jeroboam son of Nebat
heard this (he was still in Egypt, where
he had fled from King Solomon), he returned from[b] Egypt. 3 So they sent for Jeroboam, and he and the whole assembly
of Israel went to Rehoboam and said to
him: 4 "Your father put a heavy yoke on
us, but now lighten the harsh labor and
the heavy yoke he put on us, and we will
serve you."

5 Rehoboam answered, "Go away for
three days and then come back to me."
So the people went away.

6 Then King Rehoboam consulted the
elders who had served his father Solomon during his lifetime. "How would
you advise me to answer these people?"
he asked.

7 They replied, "If today you will be a
servant to these people and serve them
and give them a favorable answer, they
will always be your servants."

8 But Rehoboam rejected the advice
the elders gave him and consulted the
young men who had grown up with him
and were serving him. 9 He asked them,
"What is your advice? How should we answer these people who say to me, 'Light-
en the yoke your father put on us'?"

10 The young men who had grown up
with him replied, "These people have
said to you, 'Your father put a heavy yoke
on us, but make our yoke lighter.' Now tell
them, 'My little finger is thicker than my
father's waist. 11 My father laid on you a
heavy yoke; I will make it even heavier.
My father scourged you with whips; I will
scourge you with scorpions.' "

12 Three days later Jeroboam and all
the people returned to Rehoboam, as
the king had said, "Come back to me in
three days." 13 The king answered the
people harshly. Rejecting the advice giv-

[a] 33 Hebrew; Septuagint, Vulgate and Syriac *because he has* [b] 2 Or *he remained in*

en him by the elders, 14 he followed the
advice of the young men and said, "My
father made your yoke heavy; I will make
it even heavier. My father scourged you
with whips; I will scourge you with scorpions." 15 So the king did not listen to the
people, for this turn of events was from
the LORD, to fulfill the word the LORD had
spoken to Jeroboam son of Nebat through
Ahijah the Shilonite.
16 When all Israel saw that the king refused to listen to them, they answered
the king:

"What share do we have in David,
what part in Jesse's son?
To your tents, Israel!
Look after your own house, David!"

So the Israelites went home. 17 But as
for the Israelites who were living in the
towns of Judah, Rehoboam still ruled
over them.
18 King Rehoboam sent out Adoniram,[a]
who was in charge of forced labor, but all
Israel stoned him to death. King Rehoboam, however, managed to get into his
chariot and escape to Jerusalem. 19 So
Israel has been in rebellion against the
house of David to this day.
20 When all the Israelites heard that Jeroboam had returned, they sent and called
him to the assembly and made him king
over all Israel. Only the tribe of Judah remained loyal to the house of David.
21 When Rehoboam arrived in Jerusalem, he mustered all Judah and the tribe
of Benjamin—a hundred and eighty
thousand able young men—to go to war
against Israel and to regain the kingdom
for Rehoboam son of Solomon.
22 But this word of God came to Shemaiah the man of God: 23 "Say to Rehoboam
son of Solomon king of Judah, to all Judah and Benjamin, and to the rest of the
people, 24 'This is what the LORD says: Do
not go up to fight against your brothers,
the Israelites. Go home, every one of you,
for this is my doing.'" So they obeyed the
word of the LORD and went home again,
as the LORD had ordered.
25 Then Jeroboam fortified Shechem
in the hill country of Ephraim and lived
there. From there he went out and built
up Peniel.[b]
26 Jeroboam thought to himself, "The
kingdom will now likely revert to the
house of David. 27 If these people go up to
offer sacrifices at the temple of the LORD
in Jerusalem, they will again give their
allegiance to their lord, Rehoboam king
of Judah. They will kill me and return to
King Rehoboam."
28 After seeking advice, the king made
two golden calves. He said to the people,
"It is too much for you to go up to Jerusalem. Here are your gods, Israel, who
brought you up out of Egypt." 29 One he
set up in Bethel, and the other in Dan.
30 And this thing became a sin; the people came to worship the one at Bethel and
went as far as Dan to worship the other.[c]
31 Jeroboam built shrines on high places and appointed priests from all sorts of
people, even though they were not Levites.
32 He instituted a festival on the fifteenth
day of the eighth month, like the festival
held in Judah, and offered sacrifices on
the altar. This he did in Bethel, sacrificing
to the calves he had made. And at Bethel
he also installed priests at the high places
he had made. 33 On the fifteenth day of the
eighth month, a month of his own choosing, he offered sacrifices on the altar he
had built at Bethel. So he instituted the
festival for the Israelites and went up to
the altar to make offerings.
13 By the word of the LORD a man of
God came from Judah to Bethel,
as Jeroboam was standing by the altar to make an offering. 2 By the word of
the LORD he cried out against the altar:
"Altar, altar! This is what the LORD says:
'A son named Josiah will be born to the
house of David. On you he will sacrifice
the priests of the high places who make
offerings here, and human bones will
be burned on you.'" 3 That same day the
man of God gave a sign: "This is the sign
the LORD has declared: The altar will
be split apart and the ashes on it will be
poured out."
4 When King Jeroboam heard what the
man of God cried out against the altar at
Bethel, he stretched out his hand from
the altar and said, "Seize him!" But the
hand he stretched out toward the man
shriveled up, so that he could not pull it
back. 5 Also, the altar was split apart and

[a] 18 Some Septuagint manuscripts and Syriac (see also 4:6 and 5:14); Hebrew *Adoram* [b] 25 Hebrew *Penuel,* a variant of *Peniel* [c] 30 Probable reading of the original Hebrew text; Masoretic Text *people went to the one as far as Dan*

its ashes poured out according to the sign
given by the man of God by the word of
the LORD.
6Then the king said to the man of God,
"Intercede with the LORD your God and
pray for me that my hand may be restored." So the man of God interceded
with the LORD, and the king's hand was
restored and became as it was before.
7The king said to the man of God,
"Come home with me for a meal, and I
will give you a gift."
8But the man of God answered the
king, "Even if you were to give me half
your possessions, I would not go with
you, nor would I eat bread or drink water
here. 9For I was commanded by the word
of the LORD: 'You must not eat bread or
drink water or return by the way you
came.'" 10So he took another road and
did not return by the way he had come to
Bethel.
11Now there was a certain old prophet
living in Bethel, whose sons came and
told him all that the man of God had done
there that day. They also told their father
what he had said to the king. 12Their father asked them, "Which way did he go?"
And his sons showed him which road the
man of God from Judah had taken. 13So
he said to his sons, "Saddle the donkey for
me." And when they had saddled the donkey for him, he mounted it 14and rode after the man of God. He found him sitting
under an oak tree and asked, "Are you the
man of God who came from Judah?"
"I am," he replied.
15So the prophet said to him, "Come
home with me and eat."
16The man of God said, "I cannot turn
back and go with you, nor can I eat bread
or drink water with you in this place. 17I
have been told by the word of the LORD:
'You must not eat bread or drink water
there or return by the way you came.'"
18The old prophet answered, "I too am
a prophet, as you are. And an angel said
to me by the word of the LORD: 'Bring
him back with you to your house so that
he may eat bread and drink water.'" (But
he was lying to him.) 19So the man of God
returned with him and ate and drank in
his house.
20While they were sitting at the table, the word of the LORD came to the
old prophet who had brought him back.
21He cried out to the man of God who
had come from Judah, "This is what the
LORD says: 'You have defied the word
of the LORD and have not kept the command the LORD your God gave you. 22You
came back and ate bread and drank water
in the place where he told you not to eat
or drink. Therefore your body will not be
buried in the tomb of your ancestors.'"
23When the man of God had finished
eating and drinking, the prophet who
had brought him back saddled his donkey for him. 24As he went on his way, a
lion met him on the road and killed him,
and his body was left lying on the road,
with both the donkey and the lion standing beside it. 25Some people who passed
by saw the body lying there, with the lion
standing beside the body, and they went
and reported it in the city where the old
prophet lived.
26When the prophet who had brought
him back from his journey heard of it, he
said, "It is the man of God who defied the
word of the LORD. The LORD has given
him over to the lion, which has mauled
him and killed him, as the word of the
LORD had warned him."
27The prophet said to his sons, "Saddle the donkey for me," and they did so.
28Then he went out and found the body
lying on the road, with the donkey and
the lion standing beside it. The lion had
neither eaten the body nor mauled the
donkey. 29So the prophet picked up the
body of the man of God, laid it on the donkey, and brought it back to his own city to
mourn for him and bury him. 30Then he
laid the body in his own tomb, and they
mourned over him and said, "Alas, my
brother!"
31After burying him, he said to his sons,
"When I die, bury me in the grave where
the man of God is buried; lay my bones
beside his bones. 32For the message he
declared by the word of the LORD against
the altar in Bethel and against all the
shrines on the high places in the towns
of Samaria will certainly come true."
33Even after this, Jeroboam did not
change his evil ways, but once more appointed priests for the high places from
all sorts of people. Anyone who wanted
to become a priest he consecrated for
the high places. 34This was the sin of the
house of Jeroboam that led to its downfall and to its destruction from the face of
the earth.

14 At that time Abijah son of Jeroboam
became ill, 2and Jeroboam said to
his wife, "Go, disguise yourself, so you
won't be recognized as the wife of Jeroboam. Then go to Shiloh. Ahijah the
prophet is there — the one who told me I
would be king over this people. 3Take ten
loaves of bread with you, some cakes and
a jar of honey, and go to him. He will tell
you what will happen to the boy." 4So Jeroboam's wife did what he said and went
to Ahijah's house in Shiloh.

Now Ahijah could not see; his sight was
gone because of his age. 5But the LORD
had told Ahijah, "Jeroboam's wife is coming to ask you about her son, for he is ill,
and you are to give her such and such an
answer. When she arrives, she will pretend to be someone else."

6So when Ahijah heard the sound of
her footsteps at the door, he said, "Come
in, wife of Jeroboam. Why this pretense?
I have been sent to you with bad news.
7Go, tell Jeroboam that this is what the
LORD, the God of Israel, says: 'I raised
you up from among the people and appointed you ruler over my people Israel.
8I tore the kingdom away from the house
of David and gave it to you, but you have
not been like my servant David, who kept
my commands and followed me with all
his heart, doing only what was right in my
eyes. 9You have done more evil than all
who lived before you. You have made for
yourself other gods, idols made of metal;
you have aroused my anger and turned
your back on me.

10"'Because of this, I am going to bring
disaster on the house of Jeroboam. I will
cut off from Jeroboam every last male in
Israel — slave or free.[a] I will burn up the
house of Jeroboam as one burns dung,
until it is all gone. 11Dogs will eat those
belonging to Jeroboam who die in the city,
and the birds will feed on those who die
in the country. The LORD has spoken!'

12"As for you, go back home. When you
set foot in your city, the boy will die. 13All
Israel will mourn for him and bury him.
He is the only one belonging to Jeroboam
who will be buried, because he is the only
one in the house of Jeroboam in whom
the LORD, the God of Israel, has found
anything good.

14"The LORD will raise up for himself a
king over Israel who will cut off the family
of Jeroboam. Even now this is beginning
to happen.[b] 15And the LORD will strike Israel, so that it will be like a reed swaying
in the water. He will uproot Israel from
this good land that he gave to their ancestors and scatter them beyond the Euphrates River, because they aroused the
LORD's anger by making Asherah poles.[c]
16And he will give Israel up because of
the sins Jeroboam has committed and
has caused Israel to commit."

17Then Jeroboam's wife got up and
left and went to Tirzah. As soon as she
stepped over the threshold of the house,
the boy died. 18They buried him, and
all Israel mourned for him, as the LORD
had said through his servant the prophet Ahijah.

19The other events of Jeroboam's reign,
his wars and how he ruled, are written in
the book of the annals of the kings of Israel. 20He reigned for twenty-two years and
then rested with his ancestors. And Nadab his son succeeded him as king.

21Rehoboam son of Solomon was king
in Judah. He was forty-one years old
when he became king, and he reigned
seventeen years in Jerusalem, the city
the LORD had chosen out of all the tribes
of Israel in which to put his Name. His
mother's name was Naamah; she was an
Ammonite.

22Judah did evil in the eyes of the LORD.
By the sins they committed they stirred
up his jealous anger more than those
who were before them had done. 23They
also set up for themselves high places, sacred stones and Asherah poles on every
high hill and under every spreading tree.
24There were even male shrine prostitutes in the land; the people engaged in all
the detestable practices of the nations the
LORD had driven out before the Israelites.

25In the fifth year of King Rehoboam,
Shishak king of Egypt attacked Jerusalem. 26He carried off the treasures of the
temple of the LORD and the treasures of
the royal palace. He took everything, including all the gold shields Solomon had
made. 27So King Rehoboam made bronze
shields to replace them and assigned
these to the commanders of the guard on
duty at the entrance to the royal palace.

[a] *10* Or *Israel — every ruler or leader* [b] *14* The meaning of the Hebrew for this sentence is uncertain.
[c] *15* That is, wooden symbols of the goddess Asherah; here and elsewhere in 1 Kings

28 Whenever the king went to the LORD's
temple, the guards bore the shields, and
afterward they returned them to the
guardroom.
29 As for the other events of Rehoboam's
reign, and all he did, are they not written
in the book of the annals of the kings
of Judah? 30 There was continual warfare between Rehoboam and Jeroboam.
31 And Rehoboam rested with his ancestors and was buried with them in the City
of David. His mother's name was Naamah; she was an Ammonite. And Abijah[a]
his son succeeded him as king.

15 In the eighteenth year of the reign
of Jeroboam son of Nebat, Abijah[b]
became king of Judah, 2 and he reigned
in Jerusalem three years. His mother's
name was Maakah daughter of Abishalom.[c]
3 He committed all the sins his father
had done before him; his heart was not
fully devoted to the LORD his God, as the
heart of David his forefather had been.
4 Nevertheless, for David's sake the LORD
his God gave him a lamp in Jerusalem
by raising up a son to succeed him and
by making Jerusalem strong. 5 For David
had done what was right in the eyes of
the LORD and had not failed to keep any
of the LORD's commands all the days of
his life—except in the case of Uriah the
Hittite.
6 There was war between Abijah[d] and
Jeroboam throughout Abijah's lifetime.
7 As for the other events of Abijah's reign,
and all he did, are they not written in the
book of the annals of the kings of Judah?
There was war between Abijah and Jeroboam. 8 And Abijah rested with his ancestors and was buried in the City of David.
And Asa his son succeeded him as king.

9 In the twentieth year of Jeroboam
king of Israel, Asa became king of Judah,
10 and he reigned in Jerusalem forty-one
years. His grandmother's name was Maakah daughter of Abishalom.
11 Asa did what was right in the eyes of
the LORD, as his father David had done.
12 He expelled the male shrine prostitutes
from the land and got rid of all the idols his
ancestors had made. 13 He even deposed
his grandmother Maakah from her position as queen mother, because she had
made a repulsive image for the worship of
Asherah. Asa cut it down and burned it in
the Kidron Valley. 14 Although he did not
remove the high places, Asa's heart was
fully committed to the LORD all his life.
15 He brought into the temple of the LORD
the silver and gold and the articles that he
and his father had dedicated.
16 There was war between Asa and Baasha king of Israel throughout their reigns.
17 Baasha king of Israel went up against
Judah and fortified Ramah to prevent
anyone from leaving or entering the territory of Asa king of Judah.
18 Asa then took all the silver and gold
that was left in the treasuries of the
LORD's temple and of his own palace. He
entrusted it to his officials and sent them
to Ben-Hadad son of Tabrimmon, the son
of Hezion, the king of Aram, who was ruling in Damascus. 19 "Let there be a treaty
between me and you," he said, "as there
was between my father and your father.
See, I am sending you a gift of silver and
gold. Now break your treaty with Baasha king of Israel so he will withdraw
from me."
20 Ben-Hadad agreed with King Asa
and sent the commanders of his forces
against the towns of Israel. He conquered
Ijon, Dan, Abel Beth Maakah and all Kinnereth in addition to Naphtali. 21 When
Baasha heard this, he stopped building
Ramah and withdrew to Tirzah. 22 Then
King Asa issued an order to all Judah—
no one was exempt—and they carried
away from Ramah the stones and timber
Baasha had been using there. With them
King Asa built up Geba in Benjamin, and
also Mizpah.
23 As for all the other events of Asa's
reign, all his achievements, all he did
and the cities he built, are they not written in the book of the annals of the kings
of Judah? In his old age, however, his feet
became diseased. 24 Then Asa rested
with his ancestors and was buried with
them in the city of his father David. And
Jehoshaphat his son succeeded him as
king.

[a] *31* Some Hebrew manuscripts and Septuagint (see also 2 Chron. 12:16); most Hebrew manuscripts *Abijam*
[b] *1* Some Hebrew manuscripts and Septuagint (see also 2 Chron. 12:16); most Hebrew manuscripts *Abijam*; also in verses 7 and 8 [c] *2* A variant of *Absalom*; also in verse 10 [d] *6* Some Hebrew manuscripts and Syriac *Abijam* (that is, Abijah); most Hebrew manuscripts *Rehoboam*

25Nadab son of Jeroboam became
king of Israel in the second year of Asa
king of Judah, and he reigned over Israel two years. 26He did evil in the eyes of
the LORD, following the ways of his father
and committing the same sin his father
had caused Israel to commit.
27Baasha son of Ahijah from the tribe
of Issachar plotted against him, and he
struck him down at Gibbethon, a Philistine town, while Nadab and all Israel
were besieging it. 28Baasha killed Nadab
in the third year of Asa king of Judah and
succeeded him as king.
29As soon as he began to reign, he
killed Jeroboam's whole family. He
did not leave Jeroboam anyone that
breathed, but destroyed them all, according to the word of the LORD given
through his servant Ahijah the Shilonite. 30This happened because of the
sins Jeroboam had committed and had
caused Israel to commit, and because he
aroused the anger of the LORD, the God
of Israel.
31As for the other events of Nadab's
reign, and all he did, are they not written
in the book of the annals of the kings of
Israel? 32There was war between Asa and
Baasha king of Israel throughout their
reigns.

33In the third year of Asa king of Judah,
Baasha son of Ahijah became king of all
Israel in Tirzah, and he reigned twenty-
four years. 34He did evil in the eyes of the
LORD, following the ways of Jeroboam
and committing the same sin Jeroboam
had caused Israel to commit.
16 Then the word of the LORD came to
Jehu son of Hanani concerning Baasha: 2"I lifted you up from the dust and
appointed you ruler over my people Israel, but you followed the ways of Jeroboam
and caused my people Israel to sin and to
arouse my anger by their sins. 3So I am
about to wipe out Baasha and his house,
and I will make your house like that of
Jeroboam son of Nebat. 4Dogs will eat
those belonging to Baasha who die in the
city, and birds will feed on those who die
in the country."
5As for the other events of Baasha's
reign, what he did and his achievements,
are they not written in the book of the annals of the kings of Israel? 6Baasha rested with his ancestors and was buried in
Tirzah. And Elah his son succeeded him
as king.
7Moreover, the word of the LORD came
through the prophet Jehu son of Hanani
to Baasha and his house, because of all
the evil he had done in the eyes of the
LORD, arousing his anger by the things he
did, becoming like the house of Jeroboam—and also because he destroyed it.

8In the twenty-sixth year of Asa king of
Judah, Elah son of Baasha became king
of Israel, and he reigned in Tirzah two
years.
9Zimri, one of his officials, who had
command of half his chariots, plotted against him. Elah was in Tirzah at
the time, getting drunk in the home of
Arza, the palace administrator at Tirzah.
10Zimri came in, struck him down and
killed him in the twenty-seventh year
of Asa king of Judah. Then he succeeded
him as king.
11As soon as he began to reign and was
seated on the throne, he killed off Baasha's whole family. He did not spare a
single male, whether relative or friend.
12So Zimri destroyed the whole family of
Baasha, in accordance with the word of
the LORD spoken against Baasha through
the prophet Jehu— 13because of all the
sins Baasha and his son Elah had committed and had caused Israel to commit,
so that they aroused the anger of the
LORD, the God of Israel, by their worthless idols.
14As for the other events of Elah's reign,
and all he did, are they not written in the
book of the annals of the kings of Israel?

15In the twenty-seventh year of Asa king
of Judah, Zimri reigned in Tirzah seven
days. The army was encamped near Gibbethon, a Philistine town. 16When the Israelites in the camp heard that Zimri had
plotted against the king and murdered
him, they proclaimed Omri, the commander of the army, king over Israel that
very day there in the camp. 17Then Omri
and all the Israelites with him withdrew
from Gibbethon and laid siege to Tirzah.
18When Zimri saw that the city was tak-
en, he went into the citadel of the royal
palace and set the palace on fire around
him. So he died, 19because of the sins he
had committed, doing evil in the eyes of
the LORD and following the ways of Jero-

boam and committing the same sin Jeroboam had caused Israel to commit.
20 As for the other events of Zimri's
reign, and the rebellion he carried out,
are they not written in the book of the annals of the kings of Israel?

21 Then the people of Israel were split
into two factions; half supported Tibni
son of Ginath for king, and the other half
supported Omri. 22 But Omri's followers
proved stronger than those of Tibni son
of Ginath. So Tibni died and Omri became king.
23 In the thirty-first year of Asa king of
Judah, Omri became king of Israel, and
he reigned twelve years, six of them in
Tirzah. 24 He bought the hill of Samaria
from Shemer for two talents[a] of silver and
built a city on the hill, calling it Samaria, after Shemer, the name of the former
owner of the hill.
25 But Omri did evil in the eyes of the
LORD and sinned more than all those before him. 26 He followed completely the
ways of Jeroboam son of Nebat, committing the same sin Jeroboam had caused
Israel to commit, so that they aroused the
anger of the LORD, the God of Israel, by
their worthless idols.
27 As for the other events of Omri's
reign, what he did and the things he
achieved, are they not written in the
book of the annals of the kings of Israel?
28 Omri rested with his ancestors and was
buried in Samaria. And Ahab his son succeeded him as king.

29 In the thirty-eighth year of Asa king
of Judah, Ahab son of Omri became king
of Israel, and he reigned in Samaria over
Israel twenty-two years. 30 Ahab son
of Omri did more evil in the eyes of the
LORD than any of those before him. 31 He
not only considered it trivial to commit
the sins of Jeroboam son of Nebat, but he
also married Jezebel daughter of Ethbaal
king of the Sidonians, and began to serve
Baal and worship him. 32 He set up an altar for Baal in the temple of Baal that he
built in Samaria. 33 Ahab also made an
Asherah pole and did more to arouse the
anger of the LORD, the God of Israel, than
did all the kings of Israel before him.
34 In Ahab's time, Hiel of Bethel rebuilt
Jericho. He laid its foundations at the cost
of his firstborn son Abiram, and he set up
its gates at the cost of his youngest son Segub, in accordance with the word of the
LORD spoken by Joshua son of Nun.

17 Now Elijah the Tishbite, from Tish-
be[b] in Gilead, said to Ahab, "As the
LORD, the God of Israel, lives, whom I
serve, there will be neither dew nor rain
in the next few years except at my word."
2 Then the word of the LORD came to
Elijah: 3 "Leave here, turn eastward and
hide in the Kerith Ravine, east of the Jordan. 4 You will drink from the brook, and
I have directed the ravens to supply you
with food there."
5 So he did what the LORD had told
him. He went to the Kerith Ravine, east
of the Jordan, and stayed there. 6 The ravens brought him bread and meat in the
morning and bread and meat in the evening, and he drank from the brook.
7 Some time later the brook dried up
because there had been no rain in the
land. 8 Then the word of the LORD came
to him: 9 "Go at once to Zarephath in the
region of Sidon and stay there. I have directed a widow there to supply you with
food." 10 So he went to Zarephath. When
he came to the town gate, a widow was
there gathering sticks. He called to her
and asked, "Would you bring me a little
water in a jar so I may have a drink?" 11 As
she was going to get it, he called, "And
bring me, please, a piece of bread."
12 "As surely as the LORD your God
lives," she replied, "I don't have any
bread—only a handful of flour in a jar
and a little olive oil in a jug. I am gathering a few sticks to take home and make a
meal for myself and my son, that we may
eat it—and die."
13 Elijah said to her, "Don't be afraid. Go
home and do as you have said. But first
make a small loaf of bread for me from
what you have and bring it to me, and
then make something for yourself and
your son. 14 For this is what the LORD, the
God of Israel, says: 'The jar of flour will
not be used up and the jug of oil will not
run dry until the day the LORD sends rain
on the land.'"
15 She went away and did as Elijah had
told her. So there was food every day for
Elijah and for the woman and her fami-

[a] *24* That is, about 150 pounds or about 68 kilograms
[b] *1* Or *Tishbite, of the settlers*

ly. 16For the jar of flour was not used up and the jug of oil did not run dry, in keeping with the word of the LORD spoken by Elijah.

17Some time later the son of the woman who owned the house became ill. He grew worse and worse, and finally stopped breathing. 18She said to Elijah, "What do you have against me, man of God? Did you come to remind me of my sin and kill my son?"

19"Give me your son," Elijah replied. He took him from her arms, carried him to the upper room where he was staying, and laid him on his bed. 20Then he cried out to the LORD, "LORD my God, have you brought tragedy even on this widow I am staying with, by causing her son to die?" 21Then he stretched himself out on the boy three times and cried out to the LORD, "LORD my God, let this boy's life return to him!"

22The LORD heard Elijah's cry, and the boy's life returned to him, and he lived. 23Elijah picked up the child and carried him down from the room into the house. He gave him to his mother and said, "Look, your son is alive!"

24Then the woman said to Elijah, "Now I know that you are a man of God and that the word of the LORD from your mouth is the truth."

18 After a long time, in the third year, the word of the LORD came to Elijah: "Go and present yourself to Ahab, and I will send rain on the land." 2So Elijah went to present himself to Ahab.

Now the famine was severe in Samaria, 3and Ahab had summoned Obadiah, his palace administrator. (Obadiah was a devout believer in the LORD. 4While Jezebel was killing off the LORD's prophets, Obadiah had taken a hundred prophets and hidden them in two caves, fifty in each, and had supplied them with food and water.) 5Ahab had said to Obadiah, "Go through the land to all the springs and valleys. Maybe we can find some grass to keep the horses and mules alive so we will not have to kill any of our animals." 6So they divided the land they were to cover, Ahab going in one direction and Obadiah in another.

7As Obadiah was walking along, Elijah met him. Obadiah recognized him, bowed down to the ground, and said, "Is it really you, my lord Elijah?"

8"Yes," he replied. "Go tell your master, 'Elijah is here.'"

9"What have I done wrong," asked Obadiah, "that you are handing your servant over to Ahab to be put to death? 10As surely as the LORD your God lives, there is not a nation or kingdom where my master has not sent someone to look for you. And whenever a nation or kingdom claimed you were not there, he made them swear they could not find you. 11But now you tell me to go to my master and say, 'Elijah is here.' 12I don't know where the Spirit of the LORD may carry you when I leave you. If I go and tell Ahab and he doesn't find you, he will kill me. Yet I your servant have worshiped the LORD since my youth. 13Haven't you heard, my lord, what I did while Jezebel was killing the prophets of the LORD? I hid a hundred of the LORD's prophets in two caves, fifty in each, and supplied them with food and water. 14And now you tell me to go to my master and say, 'Elijah is here.' He will kill me!"

15Elijah said, "As the LORD Almighty lives, whom I serve, I will surely present myself to Ahab today."

16So Obadiah went to meet Ahab and told him, and Ahab went to meet Elijah. 17When he saw Elijah, he said to him, "Is that you, you troubler of Israel?"

18"I have not made trouble for Israel," Elijah replied. "But you and your father's family have. You have abandoned the LORD's commands and have followed the Baals. 19Now summon the people from all over Israel to meet me on Mount Carmel. And bring the four hundred and fifty prophets of Baal and the four hundred prophets of Asherah, who eat at Jezebel's table."

20So Ahab sent word throughout all Israel and assembled the prophets on Mount Carmel. 21Elijah went before the people and said, "How long will you waver between two opinions? If the LORD is God, follow him; but if Baal is God, follow him."

But the people said nothing.

22Then Elijah said to them, "I am the only one of the LORD's prophets left, but Baal has four hundred and fifty prophets. 23Get two bulls for us. Let Baal's prophets choose one for themselves, and let them cut it into pieces and put it on the wood but not set fire to it. I will prepare the oth-

er bull and put it on the wood but not set
fire to it. 24 Then you call on the name of
your god, and I will call on the name of
the LORD. The god who answers by fire —
he is God."
Then all the people said, "What you say
is good."
25 Elijah said to the prophets of Baal,
"Choose one of the bulls and prepare it
first, since there are so many of you. Call
on the name of your god, but do not light
the fire." 26 So they took the bull given
them and prepared it.
Then they called on the name of Baal
from morning till noon. "Baal, answer
us!" they shouted. But there was no response; no one answered. And they
danced around the altar they had made.
27 At noon Elijah began to taunt them.
"Shout louder!" he said. "Surely he is a
god! Perhaps he is deep in thought, or
busy, or traveling. Maybe he is sleeping and must be awakened." 28 So they
shouted louder and slashed themselves
with swords and spears, as was their custom, until their blood flowed. 29 Midday
passed, and they continued their frantic
prophesying until the time for the evening sacrifice. But there was no response,
no one answered, no one paid attention.
30 Then Elijah said to all the people,
"Come here to me." They came to him,
and he repaired the altar of the LORD,
which had been torn down. 31 Elijah
took twelve stones, one for each of the
tribes descended from Jacob, to whom
the word of the LORD had come, saying,
"Your name shall be Israel." 32 With the
stones he built an altar in the name of the
LORD, and he dug a trench around it large
enough to hold two seahs[a] of seed. 33 He
arranged the wood, cut the bull into pieces and laid it on the wood. Then he said to
them, "Fill four large jars with water and
pour it on the offering and on the wood."
34 "Do it again," he said, and they did
it again.
"Do it a third time," he ordered, and
they did it the third time. 35 The water ran
down around the altar and even filled
the trench.
36 At the time of sacrifice, the prophet Elijah stepped forward and prayed:
"LORD, the God of Abraham, Isaac and
Israel, let it be known today that you are
God in Israel and that I am your servant
and have done all these things at your
command. 37 Answer me, LORD, answer
me, so these people will know that you,
LORD, are God, and that you are turning
their hearts back again."
38 Then the fire of the LORD fell and
burned up the sacrifice, the wood, the
stones and the soil, and also licked up
the water in the trench.
39 When all the people saw this, they
fell prostrate and cried, "The LORD — he
is God! The LORD — he is God!"
40 Then Elijah commanded them,
"Seize the prophets of Baal. Don't let anyone get away!" They seized them, and Elijah had them brought down to the Kishon
Valley and slaughtered there.
41 And Elijah said to Ahab, "Go, eat and
drink, for there is the sound of a heavy
rain." 42 So Ahab went off to eat and drink,
but Elijah climbed to the top of Carmel,
bent down to the ground and put his face
between his knees.
43 "Go and look toward the sea," he told
his servant. And he went up and looked.
"There is nothing there," he said.
Seven times Elijah said, "Go back."
44 The seventh time the servant reported, "A cloud as small as a man's hand is
rising from the sea."
So Elijah said, "Go and tell Ahab, 'Hitch
up your chariot and go down before the
rain stops you.' "
45 Meanwhile, the sky grew black
with clouds, the wind rose, a heavy rain
started falling and Ahab rode off to Jezreel. 46 The power of the LORD came on Elijah and, tucking his cloak into his belt, he
ran ahead of Ahab all the way to Jezreel.
19 Now Ahab told Jezebel everything
Elijah had done and how he had
killed all the prophets with the sword.
2 So Jezebel sent a messenger to Elijah
to say, "May the gods deal with me, be it
ever so severely, if by this time tomorrow
I do not make your life like that of one of
them."
3 Elijah was afraid[b] and ran for his life.
When he came to Beersheba in Judah, he
left his servant there, 4 while he himself
went a day's journey into the wilderness.
He came to a broom bush, sat down under it and prayed that he might die. "I
have had enough, LORD," he said. "Take

[a] *32* That is, probably about 24 pounds or about 11 kilograms [b] *3* Or *Elijah saw*

my life; I am no better than my ancestors." 5Then he lay down under the bush
and fell asleep.
All at once an angel touched him
and said, "Get up and eat." 6He looked
around, and there by his head was some
bread baked over hot coals, and a jar of
water. He ate and drank and then lay
down again.
7The angel of the LORD came back a
second time and touched him and said,
"Get up and eat, for the journey is too
much for you." 8So he got up and ate and
drank. Strengthened by that food, he
traveled forty days and forty nights until
he reached Horeb, the mountain of God.
9There he went into a cave and spent the
night.
And the word of the LORD came to him:
"What are you doing here, Elijah?"
10He replied, "I have been very zealous
for the LORD God Almighty. The Israelites have rejected your covenant, torn
down your altars, and put your prophets
to death with the sword. I am the only
one left, and now they are trying to kill
me too."
11The LORD said, "Go out and stand
on the mountain in the presence of the
LORD, for the LORD is about to pass by."
Then a great and powerful wind tore
the mountains apart and shattered the
rocks before the LORD, but the LORD was
not in the wind. After the wind there was
an earthquake, but the LORD was not in
the earthquake. 12After the earthquake
came a fire, but the LORD was not in the
fire. And after the fire came a gentle whisper. 13When Elijah heard it, he pulled
his cloak over his face and went out and
stood at the mouth of the cave.
Then a voice said to him, "What are you
doing here, Elijah?"
14He replied, "I have been very zealous
for the LORD God Almighty. The Israelites have rejected your covenant, torn
down your altars, and put your prophets
to death with the sword. I am the only
one left, and now they are trying to kill
me too."
15The LORD said to him, "Go back the
way you came, and go to the Desert of
Damascus. When you get there, anoint
Hazael king over Aram. 16Also, anoint
Jehu son of Nimshi king over Israel, and
anoint Elisha son of Shaphat from Abel
Meholah to succeed you as prophet.
17Jehu will put to death any who escape
the sword of Hazael, and Elisha will put
to death any who escape the sword of
Jehu. 18Yet I reserve seven thousand in
Israel — all whose knees have not bowed
down to Baal and whose mouths have not
kissed him."
19So Elijah went from there and found
Elisha son of Shaphat. He was plowing
with twelve yoke of oxen, and he himself
was driving the twelfth pair. Elijah went
up to him and threw his cloak around
him. 20Elisha then left his oxen and ran
after Elijah. "Let me kiss my father and
mother goodbye," he said, "and then I
will come with you."
"Go back," Elijah replied. "What have
I done to you?"
21So Elisha left him and went back. He
took his yoke of oxen and slaughtered
them. He burned the plowing equipment
to cook the meat and gave it to the people,
and they ate. Then he set out to follow Elijah and became his servant.

20 Now Ben-Hadad king of Aram mustered his entire army. Accompanied
by thirty-two kings with their horses and
chariots, he went up and besieged Samaria and attacked it. 2He sent messengers
into the city to Ahab king of Israel, saying, "This is what Ben-Hadad says: 3'Your
silver and gold are mine, and the best of
your wives and children are mine.'"
4The king of Israel answered, "Just as
you say, my lord the king. I and all I have
are yours."
5The messengers came again and said,
"This is what Ben-Hadad says: 'I sent to
demand your silver and gold, your wives
and your children. 6But about this time
tomorrow I am going to send my officials
to search your palace and the houses of
your officials. They will seize everything
you value and carry it away.'"
7The king of Israel summoned all
the elders of the land and said to them,
"See how this man is looking for trouble! When he sent for my wives and my
children, my silver and my gold, I did not
refuse him."
8The elders and the people all answered, "Don't listen to him or agree to
his demands."
9So he replied to Ben-Hadad's messengers, "Tell my lord the king, 'Your servant
will do all you demanded the first time,
but this demand I cannot meet.'" They

left and took the answer back to Ben-Hadad.

10 Then Ben-Hadad sent another message to Ahab: "May the gods deal with me, be it ever so severely, if enough dust remains in Samaria to give each of my men a handful."

11 The king of Israel answered, "Tell him: 'One who puts on his armor should not boast like one who takes it off.' "

12 Ben-Hadad heard this message while he and the kings were drinking in their tents,[a] and he ordered his men: "Prepare to attack." So they prepared to attack the city.

13 Meanwhile a prophet came to Ahab king of Israel and announced, "This is what the LORD says: 'Do you see this vast army? I will give it into your hand today, and then you will know that I am the LORD.' "

14 "But who will do this?" asked Ahab.

The prophet replied, "This is what the LORD says: 'The junior officers under the provincial commanders will do it.' "

"And who will start the battle?" he asked.

The prophet answered, "You will."

15 So Ahab summoned the 232 junior officers under the provincial commanders. Then he assembled the rest of the Israelites, 7,000 in all. 16 They set out at noon while Ben-Hadad and the 32 kings allied with him were in their tents getting drunk. 17 The junior officers under the provincial commanders went out first.

Now Ben-Hadad had dispatched scouts, who reported, "Men are advancing from Samaria."

18 He said, "If they have come out for peace, take them alive; if they have come out for war, take them alive."

19 The junior officers under the provincial commanders marched out of the city with the army behind them 20 and each one struck down his opponent. At that, the Arameans fled, with the Israelites in pursuit. But Ben-Hadad king of Aram escaped on horseback with some of his horsemen. 21 The king of Israel advanced and overpowered the horses and chariots and inflicted heavy losses on the Arameans.

22 Afterward, the prophet came to the king of Israel and said, "Strengthen your position and see what must be done, because next spring the king of Aram will attack you again."

23 Meanwhile, the officials of the king of Aram advised him, "Their gods are gods of the hills. That is why they were too strong for us. But if we fight them on the plains, surely we will be stronger than they. 24 Do this: Remove all the kings from their commands and replace them with other officers. 25 You must also raise an army like the one you lost — horse for horse and chariot for chariot — so we can fight Israel on the plains. Then surely we will be stronger than they." He agreed with them and acted accordingly.

26 The next spring Ben-Hadad mustered the Arameans and went up to Aphek to fight against Israel. 27 When the Israelites were also mustered and given provisions, they marched out to meet them. The Israelites camped opposite them like two small flocks of goats, while the Arameans covered the countryside.

28 The man of God came up and told the king of Israel, "This is what the LORD says: 'Because the Arameans think the LORD is a god of the hills and not a god of the valleys, I will deliver this vast army into your hands, and you will know that I am the LORD.' "

29 For seven days they camped opposite each other, and on the seventh day the battle was joined. The Israelites inflicted a hundred thousand casualties on the Aramean foot soldiers in one day. 30 The rest of them escaped to the city of Aphek, where the wall collapsed on twenty-seven thousand of them. And Ben-Hadad fled to the city and hid in an inner room.

31 His officials said to him, "Look, we have heard that the kings of Israel are merciful. Let us go to the king of Israel with sackcloth around our waists and ropes around our heads. Perhaps he will spare your life."

32 Wearing sackcloth around their waists and ropes around their heads, they went to the king of Israel and said, "Your servant Ben-Hadad says: 'Please let me live.' "

The king answered, "Is he still alive? He is my brother."

33 The men took this as a good sign and

[a] *12* Or *in Sukkoth*; also in verse 16

were quick to pick up his word. "Yes, your
brother Ben-Hadad!" they said.
"Go and get him," the king said. When
Ben-Hadad came out, Ahab had him
come up into his chariot.
34 "I will return the cities my father
took from your father," Ben-Hadad offered. "You may set up your own market
areas in Damascus, as my father did in
Samaria."
Ahab said, "On the basis of a treaty
I will set you free." So he made a treaty
with him, and let him go.
35 By the word of the LORD one of the
company of the prophets said to his companion, "Strike me with your weapon,"
but he refused.
36 So the prophet said, "Because you
have not obeyed the LORD, as soon as you
leave me a lion will kill you." And after
the man went away, a lion found him and
killed him.
37 The prophet found another man and
said, "Strike me, please." So the man
struck him and wounded him. 38 Then
the prophet went and stood by the road
waiting for the king. He disguised himself with his headband down over his
eyes. 39 As the king passed by, the prophet
called out to him, "Your servant went into
the thick of the battle, and someone came
to me with a captive and said, 'Guard this
man. If he is missing, it will be your life
for his life, or you must pay a talent[a] of silver.' 40 While your servant was busy here
and there, the man disappeared."
"That is your sentence," the king of Israel said. "You have pronounced it yourself."
41 Then the prophet quickly removed
the headband from his eyes, and the king
of Israel recognized him as one of the
prophets. 42 He said to the king, "This is
what the LORD says: 'You have set free
a man I had determined should die.[b]
Therefore it is your life for his life, your
people for his people.'" 43 Sullen and angry, the king of Israel went to his palace
in Samaria.

21 Some time later there was an incident involving a vineyard belonging to Naboth the Jezreelite. The vineyard was in Jezreel, close to the palace of
Ahab king of Samaria. 2 Ahab said to Naboth, "Let me have your vineyard to use
for a vegetable garden, since it is close to
my palace. In exchange I will give you a
better vineyard or, if you prefer, I will pay
you whatever it is worth."
3 But Naboth replied, "The LORD forbid
that I should give you the inheritance of
my ancestors."
4 So Ahab went home, sullen and angry
because Naboth the Jezreelite had said,
"I will not give you the inheritance of my
ancestors." He lay on his bed sulking and
refused to eat.
5 His wife Jezebel came in and asked
him, "Why are you so sullen? Why won't
you eat?"
6 He answered her, "Because I said to
Naboth the Jezreelite, 'Sell me your vineyard; or if you prefer, I will give you another vineyard in its place.' But he said, 'I
will not give you my vineyard.'"
7 Jezebel his wife said, "Is this how you
act as king over Israel? Get up and eat!
Cheer up. I'll get you the vineyard of Naboth the Jezreelite."
8 So she wrote letters in Ahab's name,
placed his seal on them, and sent them
to the elders and nobles who lived in Naboth's city with him. 9 In those letters she
wrote:

> "Proclaim a day of fasting and seat
> Naboth in a prominent place among
> the people. 10 But seat two scoundrels
> opposite him and have them bring
> charges that he has cursed both God
> and the king. Then take him out and
> stone him to death."

11 So the elders and nobles who lived
in Naboth's city did as Jezebel directed
in the letters she had written to them.
12 They proclaimed a fast and seated Naboth in a prominent place among the
people. 13 Then two scoundrels came
and sat opposite him and brought charges against Naboth before the people,
saying, "Naboth has cursed both God
and the king." So they took him outside
the city and stoned him to death. 14 Then
they sent word to Jezebel: "Naboth has
been stoned to death."
15 As soon as Jezebel heard that Naboth had been stoned to death, she said
to Ahab, "Get up and take possession
of the vineyard of Naboth the Jezreelite that he refused to sell you. He is no

[a] *39* That is, about 75 pounds or about 34 kilograms
[b] *42* The Hebrew term refers to the irrevocable giving over of things or persons to the LORD, often by totally destroying them.

longer alive, but dead." 16 When Ahab
heard that Naboth was dead, he got up
and went down to take possession of Naboth's vineyard.

17 Then the word of the LORD came to
Elijah the Tishbite: 18 "Go down to meet
Ahab king of Israel, who rules in Samaria. He is now in Naboth's vineyard, where
he has gone to take possession of it. 19 Say
to him, 'This is what the LORD says: Have
you not murdered a man and seized his
property?' Then say to him, 'This is what
the LORD says: In the place where dogs
licked up Naboth's blood, dogs will lick
up your blood—yes, yours!'"

20 Ahab said to Elijah, "So you have
found me, my enemy!"

"I have found you," he answered, "because you have sold yourself to do evil
in the eyes of the LORD. 21 He says, 'I am
going to bring disaster on you. I will wipe
out your descendants and cut off from
Ahab every last male in Israel—slave or
free.[a] 22 I will make your house like that of
Jeroboam son of Nebat and that of Baasha
son of Ahijah, because you have aroused
my anger and have caused Israel to sin.'

23 "And also concerning Jezebel the
LORD says: 'Dogs will devour Jezebel by
the wall of[b] Jezreel.'

24 "Dogs will eat those belonging to
Ahab who die in the city, and the birds
will feed on those who die in the country."

25 (There was never anyone like Ahab,
who sold himself to do evil in the eyes of
the LORD, urged on by Jezebel his wife.
26 He behaved in the vilest manner by going after idols, like the Amorites the LORD
drove out before Israel.)

27 When Ahab heard these words, he
tore his clothes, put on sackcloth and
fasted. He lay in sackcloth and went
around meekly.

28 Then the word of the LORD came to
Elijah the Tishbite: 29 "Have you noticed
how Ahab has humbled himself before
me? Because he has humbled himself, I
will not bring this disaster in his day, but
I will bring it on his house in the days of
his son."

22 For three years there was no war
between Aram and Israel. 2 But in
the third year Jehoshaphat king of Judah
went down to see the king of Israel. 3 The
king of Israel had said to his officials,
"Don't you know that Ramoth Gilead belongs to us and yet we are doing nothing
to retake it from the king of Aram?"

4 So he asked Jehoshaphat, "Will you
go with me to fight against Ramoth Gilead?"

Jehoshaphat replied to the king of Israel, "I am as you are, my people as your
people, my horses as your horses." 5 But
Jehoshaphat also said to the king of Israel, "First seek the counsel of the LORD."

6 So the king of Israel brought together the prophets—about four hundred
men—and asked them, "Shall I go to
war against Ramoth Gilead, or shall I refrain?"

"Go," they answered, "for the Lord will
give it into the king's hand."

7 But Jehoshaphat asked, "Is there no
longer a prophet of the LORD here whom
we can inquire of?"

8 The king of Israel answered Jehoshaphat, "There is still one prophet through
whom we can inquire of the LORD, but I
hate him because he never prophesies
anything good about me, but always bad.
He is Micaiah son of Imlah."

"The king should not say such a thing,"
Jehoshaphat replied.

9 So the king of Israel called one of his
officials and said, "Bring Micaiah son of
Imlah at once."

10 Dressed in their royal robes, the king
of Israel and Jehoshaphat king of Judah were sitting on their thrones at the
threshing floor by the entrance of the
gate of Samaria, with all the prophets
prophesying before them. 11 Now Zedekiah son of Kenaanah had made iron horns
and he declared, "This is what the LORD
says: 'With these you will gore the Arameans until they are destroyed.'"

12 All the other prophets were prophesying the same thing. "Attack Ramoth
Gilead and be victorious," they said,
"for the LORD will give it into the king's
hand."

13 The messenger who had gone to
summon Micaiah said to him, "Look,
the other prophets without exception are
predicting success for the king. Let your
word agree with theirs, and speak favorably."

14 But Micaiah said, "As surely as the

[a] *21* Or *Israel—every ruler or leader* [b] *23* Most Hebrew manuscripts; a few Hebrew manuscripts, Vulgate and Syriac (see also 2 Kings 9:26) *the plot of ground at*

LORD lives, I can tell him only what the
LORD tells me."
15 When he arrived, the king asked him,
"Micaiah, shall we go to war against Ramoth Gilead, or not?"
"Attack and be victorious," he answered, "for the LORD will give it into the
king's hand."
16 The king said to him, "How many
times must I make you swear to tell me
nothing but the truth in the name of the
LORD?"
17 Then Micaiah answered, "I saw all
Israel scattered on the hills like sheep
without a shepherd, and the LORD said,
'These people have no master. Let each
one go home in peace.'"
18 The king of Israel said to Jehoshaphat, "Didn't I tell you that he never
prophesies anything good about me, but
only bad?"
19 Micaiah continued, "Therefore hear
the word of the LORD: I saw the LORD
sitting on his throne with all the multitudes of heaven standing around him on
his right and on his left. 20 And the LORD
said, 'Who will entice Ahab into attacking Ramoth Gilead and going to his death
there?'
"One suggested this, and another that.
21 Finally, a spirit came forward, stood
before the LORD and said, 'I will entice
him.'
22 "'By what means?' the LORD asked.
"'I will go out and be a deceiving spirit in the mouths of all his prophets,' he
said.
"'You will succeed in enticing him,'
said the LORD. 'Go and do it.'
23 "So now the LORD has put a deceiving
spirit in the mouths of all these prophets
of yours. The LORD has decreed disaster
for you."
24 Then Zedekiah son of Kenaanah
went up and slapped Micaiah in the
face. "Which way did the spirit from[a] the
LORD go when he went from me to speak
to you?" he asked.
25 Micaiah replied, "You will find out on
the day you go to hide in an inner room."
26 The king of Israel then ordered, "Take
Micaiah and send him back to Amon the
ruler of the city and to Joash the king's
son 27 and say, 'This is what the king says:
Put this fellow in prison and give him
nothing but bread and water until I return safely.'"
28 Micaiah declared, "If you ever return
safely, the LORD has not spoken through
me." Then he added, "Mark my words, all
you people!"
29 So the king of Israel and Jehoshaphat
king of Judah went up to Ramoth Gilead.
30 The king of Israel said to Jehoshaphat,
"I will enter the battle in disguise, but
you wear your royal robes." So the king
of Israel disguised himself and went into
battle.
31 Now the king of Aram had ordered
his thirty-two chariot commanders, "Do
not fight with anyone, small or great,
except the king of Israel." 32 When the
chariot commanders saw Jehoshaphat,
they thought, "Surely this is the king of
Israel." So they turned to attack him, but
when Jehoshaphat cried out, 33 the chariot commanders saw that he was not the
king of Israel and stopped pursuing him.
34 But someone drew his bow at random
and hit the king of Israel between the sections of his armor. The king told his chariot driver, "Wheel around and get me out
of the fighting. I've been wounded." 35 All
day long the battle raged, and the king
was propped up in his chariot facing the
Arameans. The blood from his wound ran
onto the floor of the chariot, and that evening he died. 36 As the sun was setting, a
cry spread through the army: "Every man
to his town. Every man to his land!"
37 So the king died and was brought
to Samaria, and they buried him there.
38 They washed the chariot at a pool in
Samaria (where the prostitutes bathed),[b]
and the dogs licked up his blood, as the
word of the LORD had declared.
39 As for the other events of Ahab's
reign, including all he did, the palace he
built and adorned with ivory, and the cities he fortified, are they not written in the
book of the annals of the kings of Israel?
40 Ahab rested with his ancestors. And
Ahaziah his son succeeded him as king.

41 Jehoshaphat son of Asa became king
of Judah in the fourth year of Ahab king
of Israel. 42 Jehoshaphat was thirty-five
years old when he became king, and he
reigned in Jerusalem twenty-five years.
His mother's name was Azubah daughter

[a] 24 Or *Spirit of* [b] 38 Or *Samaria and cleaned the weapons*

of Shilhi. 43 In everything he followed the
ways of his father Asa and did not stray
from them; he did what was right in the
eyes of the LORD. The high places, however, were not removed, and the people
continued to offer sacrifices and burn incense there.[a] 44 Jehoshaphat was also at
peace with the king of Israel.

45 As for the other events of Jehoshaphat's reign, the things he achieved and
his military exploits, are they not written
in the book of the annals of the kings of
Judah? 46 He rid the land of the rest of the
male shrine prostitutes who remained
there even after the reign of his father
Asa. 47 There was then no king in Edom;
a provincial governor ruled.

48 Now Jehoshaphat built a fleet of trading ships[b] to go to Ophir for gold, but they
never set sail—they were wrecked at Ezion Geber. 49 At that time Ahaziah son of
Ahab said to Jehoshaphat, "Let my men
sail with yours," but Jehoshaphat refused.

50 Then Jehoshaphat rested with his ancestors and was buried with them in the
city of David his father. And Jehoram his
son succeeded him as king.

51 Ahaziah son of Ahab became king
of Israel in Samaria in the seventeenth
year of Jehoshaphat king of Judah, and
he reigned over Israel two years. 52 He
did evil in the eyes of the LORD, because
he followed the ways of his father and
mother and of Jeroboam son of Nebat,
who caused Israel to sin. 53 He served and
worshiped Baal and aroused the anger of
the LORD, the God of Israel, just as his father had done.

2 KINGS

See the Invitation to Samuel-Kings on p. 240.

1 After Ahab's death, Moab rebelled
against Israel. 2 Now Ahaziah had fall-
en through the lattice of his upper room
in Samaria and injured himself. So he
sent messengers, saying to them, "Go and
consult Baal-Zebub, the god of Ekron, to
see if I will recover from this injury."

3 But the angel of the LORD said to Elijah
the Tishbite, "Go up and meet the messengers of the king of Samaria and ask
them, 'Is it because there is no God in Israel that you are going off to consult Baal-
Zebub, the god of Ekron?' 4 Therefore this
is what the LORD says: 'You will not leave
the bed you are lying on. You will certainly die!'" So Elijah went.

5 When the messengers returned to
the king, he asked them, "Why have you
come back?"

6 "A man came to meet us," they replied.
"And he said to us, 'Go back to the king
who sent you and tell him, "This is what
the LORD says: Is it because there is no
God in Israel that you are sending messengers to consult Baal-Zebub, the god of
Ekron? Therefore you will not leave the
bed you are lying on. You will certainly
die!"'"

7 The king asked them, "What kind of
man was it who came to meet you and
told you this?"

8 They replied, "He had a garment of
hair[c] and had a leather belt around his
waist."

The king said, "That was Elijah the
Tishbite."

9 Then he sent to Elijah a captain with
his company of fifty men. The captain

[a] *43* In Hebrew texts this sentence (22:43b) is numbered 22:44, and 22:44-53 is numbered 22:45-54.
[b] *48* Hebrew *of ships of Tarshish* [c] *8* Or *He was a hairy man*

went up to Elijah, who was sitting on the
top of a hill, and said to him, "Man of
God, the king says, 'Come down!'"
10 Elijah answered the captain, "If I am
a man of God, may fire come down from
heaven and consume you and your fifty men!" Then fire fell from heaven and
consumed the captain and his men.
11 At this the king sent to Elijah another
captain with his fifty men. The captain
said to him, "Man of God, this is what the
king says, 'Come down at once!'"
12 "If I am a man of God," Elijah replied,
"may fire come down from heaven and
consume you and your fifty men!" Then
the fire of God fell from heaven and consumed him and his fifty men.
13 So the king sent a third captain with
his fifty men. This third captain went up
and fell on his knees before Elijah. "Man
of God," he begged, "please have respect
for my life and the lives of these fifty men,
your servants! 14 See, fire has fallen from
heaven and consumed the first two captains and all their men. But now have respect for my life!"
15 The angel of the LORD said to Elijah,
"Go down with him; do not be afraid of
him." So Elijah got up and went down
with him to the king.
16 He told the king, "This is what the
LORD says: Is it because there is no God
in Israel for you to consult that you have
sent messengers to consult Baal-Zebub,
the god of Ekron? Because you have done
this, you will never leave the bed you are
lying on. You will certainly die!" 17 So he
died, according to the word of the LORD
that Elijah had spoken.
Because Ahaziah had no son, Joram[a]
succeeded him as king in the second year
of Jehoram son of Jehoshaphat king of Judah. 18 As for all the other events of Ahaziah's reign, and what he did, are they not
written in the book of the annals of the
kings of Israel?

2 When the LORD was about to take Elijah up to heaven in a whirlwind, Elijah and Elisha were on their way from
Gilgal. 2 Elijah said to Elisha, "Stay here;
the LORD has sent me to Bethel."
But Elisha said, "As surely as the LORD
lives and as you live, I will not leave you."
So they went down to Bethel.
3 The company of the prophets at Bethel came out to Elisha and asked, "Do you
know that the LORD is going to take your
master from you today?"
"Yes, I know," Elisha replied, "so be
quiet."
4 Then Elijah said to him, "Stay here,
Elisha; the LORD has sent me to Jericho."
And he replied, "As surely as the LORD
lives and as you live, I will not leave you."
So they went to Jericho.
5 The company of the prophets at Jericho went up to Elisha and asked him, "Do
you know that the LORD is going to take
your master from you today?"
"Yes, I know," he replied, "so be quiet."
6 Then Elijah said to him, "Stay here;
the LORD has sent me to the Jordan."
And he replied, "As surely as the LORD
lives and as you live, I will not leave you."
So the two of them walked on.
7 Fifty men from the company of the
prophets went and stood at a distance,
facing the place where Elijah and Elisha
had stopped at the Jordan. 8 Elijah took
his cloak, rolled it up and struck the water
with it. The water divided to the right and
to the left, and the two of them crossed
over on dry ground.
9 When they had crossed, Elijah said to
Elisha, "Tell me, what can I do for you before I am taken from you?"
"Let me inherit a double portion of your
spirit," Elisha replied.
10 "You have asked a difficult thing,"
Elijah said, "yet if you see me when I am
taken from you, it will be yours—otherwise, it will not."
11 As they were walking along and talking together, suddenly a chariot of fire
and horses of fire appeared and separated the two of them, and Elijah went up to
heaven in a whirlwind. 12 Elisha saw this
and cried out, "My father! My father! The
chariots and horsemen of Israel!" And
Elisha saw him no more. Then he took
hold of his garment and tore it in two.
13 Elisha then picked up Elijah's cloak
that had fallen from him and went back
and stood on the bank of the Jordan. 14 He
took the cloak that had fallen from Elijah
and struck the water with it. "Where now
is the LORD, the God of Elijah?" he asked.
When he struck the water, it divided to the
right and to the left, and he crossed over.

[a] 17 Hebrew *Jehoram,* a variant of *Joram*

15The company of the prophets from
Jericho, who were watching, said, "The
spirit of Elijah is resting on Elisha." And
they went to meet him and bowed to the
ground before him. 16"Look," they said,
"we your servants have fifty able men.
Let them go and look for your master.
Perhaps the Spirit of the LORD has picked
him up and set him down on some mountain or in some valley."

"No," Elisha replied, "do not send
them."

17But they persisted until he was too
embarrassed to refuse. So he said, "Send
them." And they sent fifty men, who
searched for three days but did not find
him. 18When they returned to Elisha,
who was staying in Jericho, he said to
them, "Didn't I tell you not to go?"

19The people of the city said to Elisha,
"Look, our lord, this town is well situated,
as you can see, but the water is bad and
the land is unproductive."

20"Bring me a new bowl," he said, "and
put salt in it." So they brought it to him.

21Then he went out to the spring and
threw the salt into it, saying, "This is what
the LORD says: 'I have healed this water.
Never again will it cause death or make
the land unproductive.'" 22And the water
has remained pure to this day, according
to the word Elisha had spoken.

23From there Elisha went up to Bethel.
As he was walking along the road, some
boys came out of the town and jeered at
him. "Get out of here, baldy!" they said.
"Get out of here, baldy!" 24He turned
around, looked at them and called down
a curse on them in the name of the LORD.
Then two bears came out of the woods
and mauled forty-two of the boys. 25And
he went on to Mount Carmel and from
there returned to Samaria.

3 Joram[a] son of Ahab became king of
Israel in Samaria in the eighteenth
year of Jehoshaphat king of Judah, and
he reigned twelve years. 2He did evil in
the eyes of the LORD, but not as his father
and mother had done. He got rid of the
sacred stone of Baal that his father had
made. 3Nevertheless he clung to the sins
of Jeroboam son of Nebat, which he had
caused Israel to commit; he did not turn
away from them.

4Now Mesha king of Moab raised
sheep, and he had to pay the king of Israel a tribute of a hundred thousand lambs
and the wool of a hundred thousand
rams. 5But after Ahab died, the king of
Moab rebelled against the king of Israel.
6So at that time King Joram set out from
Samaria and mobilized all Israel. 7He
also sent this message to Jehoshaphat
king of Judah: "The king of Moab has rebelled against me. Will you go with me to
fight against Moab?"

"I will go with you," he replied. "I am
as you are, my people as your people, my
horses as your horses."

8"By what route shall we attack?" he
asked.

"Through the Desert of Edom," he answered.

9So the king of Israel set out with the
king of Judah and the king of Edom. After
a roundabout march of seven days, the
army had no more water for themselves
or for the animals with them.

10"What!" exclaimed the king of Israel.
"Has the LORD called us three kings together only to deliver us into the hands
of Moab?"

11But Jehoshaphat asked, "Is there no
prophet of the LORD here, through whom
we may inquire of the LORD?"

An officer of the king of Israel an-
swered, "Elisha son of Shaphat is here.
He used to pour water on the hands of
Elijah.[b]"

12Jehoshaphat said, "The word of the
LORD is with him." So the king of Israel
and Jehoshaphat and the king of Edom
went down to him.

13Elisha said to the king of Israel, "Why
do you want to involve me? Go to the
prophets of your father and the prophets
of your mother."

"No," the king of Israel answered,
"because it was the LORD who called us
three kings together to deliver us into the
hands of Moab."

14Elisha said, "As surely as the LORD
Almighty lives, whom I serve, if I did not
have respect for the presence of Jehoshaphat king of Judah, I would not pay any
attention to you. 15But now bring me a
harpist."

While the harpist was playing, the
hand of the LORD came on Elisha 16and

[a] *1* Hebrew *Jehoram,* a variant of *Joram;* also in verse 6

[b] *11* That is, he was Elijah's personal servant.

he said, "This is what the LORD says: I will
fill this valley with pools of water. 17For
this is what the LORD says: You will see
neither wind nor rain, yet this valley will
be filled with water, and you, your cattle and your other animals will drink.
18This is an easy thing in the eyes of the
LORD; he will also deliver Moab into your
hands. 19You will overthrow every fortified city and every major town. You will
cut down every good tree, stop up all the
springs, and ruin every good field with
stones."
20The next morning, about the time for
offering the sacrifice, there it was—water
flowing from the direction of Edom! And
the land was filled with water.
21Now all the Moabites had heard that
the kings had come to fight against them;
so every man, young and old, who could
bear arms was called up and stationed
on the border. 22When they got up early in the morning, the sun was shining
on the water. To the Moabites across the
way, the water looked red—like blood.
23"That's blood!" they said. "Those kings
must have fought and slaughtered each
other. Now to the plunder, Moab!"
24But when the Moabites came to the
camp of Israel, the Israelites rose up and
fought them until they fled. And the Israelites invaded the land and slaughtered the Moabites. 25They destroyed
the towns, and each man threw a stone
on every good field until it was covered.
They stopped up all the springs and cut
down every good tree. Only Kir Hareseth
was left with its stones in place, but men
armed with slings surrounded it and attacked it.
26When the king of Moab saw that the
battle had gone against him, he took with
him seven hundred swordsmen to break
through to the king of Edom, but they
failed. 27Then he took his firstborn son,
who was to succeed him as king, and offered him as a sacrifice on the city wall.
The fury against Israel was great; they
withdrew and returned to their own
land.
4 The wife of a man from the company
of the prophets cried out to Elisha,
"Your servant my husband is dead, and
you know that he revered the LORD. But
now his creditor is coming to take my two
boys as his slaves."
2Elisha replied to her, "How can I help
you? Tell me, what do you have in your
house?"
"Your servant has nothing there at all,"
she said, "except a small jar of olive oil."
3Elisha said, "Go around and ask all
your neighbors for empty jars. Don't ask
for just a few. 4Then go inside and shut
the door behind you and your sons. Pour
oil into all the jars, and as each is filled,
put it to one side."
5She left him and shut the door behind
her and her sons. They brought the jars to
her and she kept pouring. 6When all the
jars were full, she said to her son, "Bring
me another one."
But he replied, "There is not a jar left."
Then the oil stopped flowing.
7She went and told the man of God,
and he said, "Go, sell the oil and pay your
debts. You and your sons can live on what
is left."
8One day Elisha went to Shunem. And a
well-to-do woman was there, who urged
him to stay for a meal. So whenever he
came by, he stopped there to eat. 9She
said to her husband, "I know that this
man who often comes our way is a holy
man of God. 10Let's make a small room
on the roof and put in it a bed and a table,
a chair and a lamp for him. Then he can
stay there whenever he comes to us."
11One day when Elisha came, he went
up to his room and lay down there. 12He
said to his servant Gehazi, "Call the
Shunammite." So he called her, and she
stood before him. 13Elisha said to him,
"Tell her, 'You have gone to all this trouble for us. Now what can be done for you?
Can we speak on your behalf to the king
or the commander of the army?'"
She replied, "I have a home among my
own people."
14"What can be done for her?" Elisha
asked.
Gehazi said, "She has no son, and her
husband is old."
15Then Elisha said, "Call her." So he
called her, and she stood in the doorway.
16"About this time next year," Elisha said,
"you will hold a son in your arms."
"No, my lord!" she objected. "Please,
man of God, don't mislead your servant!"
17But the woman became pregnant,
and the next year about that same time
she gave birth to a son, just as Elisha had
told her.

master, Elisha asked him, "Where have
you been, Gehazi?"
"Your servant didn't go anywhere," Gehazi answered.
26 But Elisha said to him, "Was not my
spirit with you when the man got down
from his chariot to meet you? Is this the
time to take money or to accept clothes—
or olive groves and vineyards, or flocks
and herds, or male and female slaves?
27 Naaman's leprosy will cling to you
and to your descendants forever." Then
Gehazi went from Elisha's presence and
his skin was leprous—it had become as
white as snow.

6 The company of the prophets said
to Elisha, "Look, the place where we
meet with you is too small for us. 2 Let us
go to the Jordan, where each of us can get
a pole; and let us build a place there for
us to meet."
And he said, "Go."
3 Then one of them said, "Won't you
please come with your servants?"
"I will," Elisha replied. 4 And he went
with them.
They went to the Jordan and began to
cut down trees. 5 As one of them was cutting down a tree, the iron axhead fell into
the water. "Oh no, my lord!" he cried out.
"It was borrowed!"
6 The man of God asked, "Where did
it fall?" When he showed him the place,
Elisha cut a stick and threw it there, and
made the iron float. 7 "Lift it out," he said.
Then the man reached out his hand and
took it.
8 Now the king of Aram was at war with
Israel. After conferring with his officers,
he said, "I will set up my camp in such
and such a place."
9 The man of God sent word to the king
of Israel: "Beware of passing that place,
because the Arameans are going down
there." 10 So the king of Israel checked on
the place indicated by the man of God.
Time and again Elisha warned the king, so
that he was on his guard in such places.
11 This enraged the king of Aram. He
summoned his officers and demanded of
them, "Tell me! Which of us is on the side
of the king of Israel?"
12 "None of us, my lord the king," said
one of his officers, "but Elisha, the prophet who is in Israel, tells the king of Israel
the very words you speak in your bedroom."
13 "Go, find out where he is," the king
ordered, "so I can send men and capture
him." The report came back: "He is in Dothan." 14 Then he sent horses and chariots and a strong force there. They went by
night and surrounded the city.
15 When the servant of the man of God
got up and went out early the next morning, an army with horses and chariots
had surrounded the city. "Oh no, my lord!
What shall we do?" the servant asked.
16 "Don't be afraid," the prophet answered. "Those who are with us are more
than those who are with them."
17 And Elisha prayed, "Open his eyes,
LORD, so that he may see." Then the LORD
opened the servant's eyes, and he looked
and saw the hills full of horses and chariots of fire all around Elisha.
18 As the enemy came down toward
him, Elisha prayed to the LORD, "Strike
this army with blindness." So he struck
them with blindness, as Elisha had
asked.
19 Elisha told them, "This is not the road
and this is not the city. Follow me, and I
will lead you to the man you are looking
for." And he led them to Samaria.
20 After they entered the city, Elisha
said, "LORD, open the eyes of these men
so they can see." Then the LORD opened
their eyes and they looked, and there they
were, inside Samaria.
21 When the king of Israel saw them, he
asked Elisha, "Shall I kill them, my father? Shall I kill them?"
22 "Do not kill them," he answered.
"Would you kill those you have captured
with your own sword or bow? Set food
and water before them so that they may
eat and drink and then go back to their
master." 23 So he prepared a great feast
for them, and after they had finished
eating and drinking, he sent them away,
and they returned to their master. So the
bands from Aram stopped raiding Israel's
territory.
24 Some time later, Ben-Hadad king
of Aram mobilized his entire army and
marched up and laid siege to Samaria.
25 There was a great famine in the city;
the siege lasted so long that a donkey's
head sold for eighty shekels[a] of silver,

[a] *25* That is, about 2 pounds or about 920 grams

and a quarter of a cab[a] of seed pods[b] for
five shekels.[c]
26 As the king of Israel was passing by
on the wall, a woman cried to him, "Help
me, my lord the king!"
27 The king replied, "If the LORD does
not help you, where can I get help for you?
From the threshing floor? From the winepress?" 28 Then he asked her, "What's the
matter?"
She answered, "This woman said to
me, 'Give up your son so we may eat him
today, and tomorrow we'll eat my son.'
29 So we cooked my son and ate him. The
next day I said to her, 'Give up your son
so we may eat him,' but she had hidden
him."
30 When the king heard the woman's
words, he tore his robes. As he went along
the wall, the people looked, and they saw
that, under his robes, he had sackcloth
on his body. 31 He said, "May God deal
with me, be it ever so severely, if the head
of Elisha son of Shaphat remains on his
shoulders today!"
32 Now Elisha was sitting in his house,
and the elders were sitting with him.
The king sent a messenger ahead, but
before he arrived, Elisha said to the elders, "Don't you see how this murderer
is sending someone to cut off my head?
Look, when the messenger comes, shut
the door and hold it shut against him. Is
not the sound of his master's footsteps
behind him?" 33 While he was still talking to them, the messenger came down
to him.
The king said, "This disaster is from the
LORD. Why should I wait for the LORD any
longer?"
7 Elisha replied, "Hear the word of the
LORD. This is what the LORD says:
About this time tomorrow, a seah[d] of the
finest flour will sell for a shekel[e] and two
seahs[f] of barley for a shekel at the gate of
Samaria."
2 The officer on whose arm the king
was leaning said to the man of God,
"Look, even if the LORD should open the
floodgates of the heavens, could this happen?"
"You will see it with your own eyes,"
answered Elisha, "but you will not eat
any of it!"
3 Now there were four men with leprosy[g] at the entrance of the city gate. They
said to each other, "Why stay here until we die? 4 If we say, 'We'll go into the
city'—the famine is there, and we will
die. And if we stay here, we will die. So
let's go over to the camp of the Arameans
and surrender. If they spare us, we live; if
they kill us, then we die."
5 At dusk they got up and went to the
camp of the Arameans. When they
reached the edge of the camp, no one was
there, 6 for the Lord had caused the Arameans to hear the sound of chariots and
horses and a great army, so that they said
to one another, "Look, the king of Israel
has hired the Hittite and Egyptian kings
to attack us!" 7 So they got up and fled in
the dusk and abandoned their tents and
their horses and donkeys. They left the
camp as it was and ran for their lives.
8 The men who had leprosy reached the
edge of the camp, entered one of the tents
and ate and drank. Then they took silver,
gold and clothes, and went off and hid
them. They returned and entered another tent and took some things from it and
hid them also.
9 Then they said to each other, "What
we're doing is not right. This is a day of
good news and we are keeping it to ourselves. If we wait until daylight, punishment will overtake us. Let's go at once
and report this to the royal palace."
10 So they went and called out to the
city gatekeepers and told them, "We
went into the Aramean camp and no one
was there—not a sound of anyone—only
tethered horses and donkeys, and the
tents left just as they were." 11 The gatekeepers shouted the news, and it was reported within the palace.
12 The king got up in the night and said
to his officers, "I will tell you what the Arameans have done to us. They know we
are starving; so they have left the camp to
hide in the countryside, thinking, 'They
will surely come out, and then we will
take them alive and get into the city.'"
13 One of his officers answered, "Have

[a] *25* That is, probably about 1/4 pound or about 100 grams [b] *25* Or *of doves' dung* [c] *25* That is, about 2 ounces or about 58 grams [d] *1* That is, probably about 12 pounds or about 5.5 kilograms of flour; also in verses 16 and 18 [e] *1* That is, about 2/5 ounce or about 12 grams; also in verses 16 and 18 [f] *1* That is, probably about 20 pounds or about 9 kilograms of barley; also in verses 16 and 18 [g] *3* The Hebrew for *leprosy* was used for various diseases affecting the skin; also in verse 8.

some men take five of the horses that are
left in the city. Their plight will be like
that of all the Israelites left here—yes,
they will only be like all these Israelites
who are doomed. So let us send them to
find out what happened."
14 So they selected two chariots with
their horses, and the king sent them after the Aramean army. He commanded
the drivers, "Go and find out what has
happened." 15 They followed them as far
as the Jordan, and they found the whole
road strewn with the clothing and equipment the Arameans had thrown away
in their headlong flight. So the messengers returned and reported to the king.
16 Then the people went out and plundered the camp of the Arameans. So a
seah of the finest flour sold for a shekel,
and two seahs of barley sold for a shekel,
as the LORD had said.
17 Now the king had put the officer on
whose arm he leaned in charge of the
gate, and the people trampled him in the
gateway, and he died, just as the man of
God had foretold when the king came
down to his house. 18 It happened as the
man of God had said to the king: "About
this time tomorrow, a seah of the finest
flour will sell for a shekel and two seahs
of barley for a shekel at the gate of Samaria."
19 The officer had said to the man of
God, "Look, even if the LORD should open
the floodgates of the heavens, could this
happen?" The man of God had replied,
"You will see it with your own eyes, but
you will not eat any of it!" 20 And that is
exactly what happened to him, for the
people trampled him in the gateway, and
he died.

8 Now Elisha had said to the woman
whose son he had restored to life, "Go
away with your family and stay for a while
wherever you can, because the LORD has
decreed a famine in the land that will last
seven years." 2 The woman proceeded to
do as the man of God said. She and her
family went away and stayed in the land
of the Philistines seven years.
3 At the end of the seven years she came
back from the land of the Philistines and
went to appeal to the king for her house
and land. 4 The king was talking to Gehazi, the servant of the man of God, and had
said, "Tell me about all the great things
Elisha has done." 5 Just as Gehazi was telling the king how Elisha had restored the
dead to life, the woman whose son Elisha
had brought back to life came to appeal to
the king for her house and land.
Gehazi said, "This is the woman, my
lord the king, and this is her son whom
Elisha restored to life." 6 The king asked
the woman about it, and she told him.
Then he assigned an official to her case
and said to him, "Give back everything
that belonged to her, including all the income from her land from the day she left
the country until now."
7 Elisha went to Damascus, and Ben-
Hadad king of Aram was ill. When the
king was told, "The man of God has come
all the way up here," 8 he said to Hazael,
"Take a gift with you and go to meet the
man of God. Consult the LORD through
him; ask him, 'Will I recover from this
illness?' "
9 Hazael went to meet Elisha, taking
with him as a gift forty camel-loads of all
the finest wares of Damascus. He went
in and stood before him, and said, "Your
son Ben-Hadad king of Aram has sent me
to ask, 'Will I recover from this illness?' "
10 Elisha answered, "Go and say to him,
'You will certainly recover.' Nevertheless,[a] the LORD has revealed to me that he
will in fact die." 11 He stared at him with a
fixed gaze until Hazael was embarrassed.
Then the man of God began to weep.
12 "Why is my lord weeping?" asked
Hazael.
"Because I know the harm you will do
to the Israelites," he answered. "You will
set fire to their fortified places, kill their
young men with the sword, dash their little children to the ground, and rip open
their pregnant women."
13 Hazael said, "How could your servant, a mere dog, accomplish such a
feat?"
"The LORD has shown me that you will
become king of Aram," answered Elisha.
14 Then Hazael left Elisha and returned
to his master. When Ben-Hadad asked,
"What did Elisha say to you?" Hazael replied, "He told me that you would
certainly recover." 15 But the next day
he took a thick cloth, soaked it in water
and spread it over the king's face, so that

[a] 10 The Hebrew may also be read *Go and say, 'You will certainly not recover,' for.*

he died. Then Hazael succeeded him as
king.

16 In the fifth year of Joram son of Ahab
king of Israel, when Jehoshaphat was king
of Judah, Jehoram son of Jehoshaphat began his reign as king of Judah. 17 He was
thirty-two years old when he became
king, and he reigned in Jerusalem eight
years. 18 He followed the ways of the kings
of Israel, as the house of Ahab had done,
for he married a daughter of Ahab. He did
evil in the eyes of the LORD. 19 Nevertheless, for the sake of his servant David, the
LORD was not willing to destroy Judah.
He had promised to maintain a lamp for
David and his descendants forever.
20 In the time of Jehoram, Edom rebelled against Judah and set up its own
king. 21 So Jehoram[a] went to Zair with all
his chariots. The Edomites surrounded
him and his chariot commanders, but he
rose up and broke through by night; his
army, however, fled back home. 22 To this
day Edom has been in rebellion against
Judah. Libnah revolted at the same time.
23 As for the other events of Jehoram's
reign, and all he did, are they not written
in the book of the annals of the kings of
Judah? 24 Jehoram rested with his ancestors and was buried with them in the City
of David. And Ahaziah his son succeeded
him as king.

25 In the twelfth year of Joram son of
Ahab king of Israel, Ahaziah son of Jehoram king of Judah began to reign. 26 Ahaziah was twenty-two years old when he
became king, and he reigned in Jerusalem one year. His mother's name was
Athaliah, a granddaughter of Omri king
of Israel. 27 He followed the ways of the
house of Ahab and did evil in the eyes of
the LORD, as the house of Ahab had done,
for he was related by marriage to Ahab's
family.
28 Ahaziah went with Joram son of Ahab
to war against Hazael king of Aram at Ramoth Gilead. The Arameans wounded Joram; 29 so King Joram returned to Jezreel
to recover from the wounds the Arameans had inflicted on him at Ramoth[b] in
his battle with Hazael king of Aram.
Then Ahaziah son of Jehoram king
of Judah went down to Jezreel to see Joram son of Ahab, because he had been
wounded.

9 The prophet Elisha summoned a man
from the company of the prophets and
said to him, "Tuck your cloak into your
belt, take this flask of olive oil with you
and go to Ramoth Gilead. 2 When you get
there, look for Jehu son of Jehoshaphat,
the son of Nimshi. Go to him, get him
away from his companions and take him
into an inner room. 3 Then take the flask
and pour the oil on his head and declare,
'This is what the LORD says: I anoint you
king over Israel.' Then open the door and
run; don't delay!"
4 So the young prophet went to Ramoth
Gilead. 5 When he arrived, he found the
army officers sitting together. "I have a
message for you, commander," he said.
"For which of us?" asked Jehu.
"For you, commander," he replied.
6 Jehu got up and went into the house.
Then the prophet poured the oil on Jehu's head and declared, "This is what the
LORD, the God of Israel, says: 'I anoint you
king over the LORD's people Israel. 7 You
are to destroy the house of Ahab your
master, and I will avenge the blood of my
servants the prophets and the blood of all
the LORD's servants shed by Jezebel. 8 The
whole house of Ahab will perish. I will cut
off from Ahab every last male in Israel—
slave or free.[c] 9 I will make the house of
Ahab like the house of Jeroboam son of
Nebat and like the house of Baasha son of
Ahijah. 10 As for Jezebel, dogs will devour
her on the plot of ground at Jezreel, and
no one will bury her.'" Then he opened
the door and ran.
11 When Jehu went out to his fellow
officers, one of them asked him, "Is everything all right? Why did this maniac
come to you?"
"You know the man and the sort of
things he says," Jehu replied.
12 "That's not true!" they said. "Tell us."
Jehu said, "Here is what he told me:
'This is what the LORD says: I anoint you
king over Israel.'"
13 They quickly took their cloaks and
spread them under him on the bare steps.
Then they blew the trumpet and shouted,
"Jehu is king!"
14 So Jehu son of Jehoshaphat, the son of
Nimshi, conspired against Joram. (Now

[a] *21* Hebrew *Joram,* a variant of *Jehoram*; also in verses 23 and 24 [b] *29* Hebrew *Ramah,* a variant of *Ramoth*
[c] *8* Or *Israel—every ruler or leader*

Joram and all Israel had been defending Ramoth Gilead against Hazael king of Aram, 15 but King Joram[a] had returned to Jezreel to recover from the wounds the Arameans had inflicted on him in the battle with Hazael king of Aram.) Jehu said, "If you desire to make me king, don't let anyone slip out of the city to go and tell the news in Jezreel." 16 Then he got into his chariot and rode to Jezreel, because Joram was resting there and Ahaziah king of Judah had gone down to see him.

17 When the lookout standing on the tower in Jezreel saw Jehu's troops approaching, he called out, "I see some troops coming."

"Get a horseman," Joram ordered. "Send him to meet them and ask, 'Do you come in peace?' "

18 The horseman rode off to meet Jehu and said, "This is what the king says: 'Do you come in peace?' "

"What do you have to do with peace?" Jehu replied. "Fall in behind me."

The lookout reported, "The messenger has reached them, but he isn't coming back."

19 So the king sent out a second horseman. When he came to them he said, "This is what the king says: 'Do you come in peace?' "

Jehu replied, "What do you have to do with peace? Fall in behind me."

20 The lookout reported, "He has reached them, but he isn't coming back either. The driving is like that of Jehu son of Nimshi—he drives like a maniac."

21 "Hitch up my chariot," Joram ordered. And when it was hitched up, Joram king of Israel and Ahaziah king of Judah rode out, each in his own chariot, to meet Jehu. They met him at the plot of ground that had belonged to Naboth the Jezreelite. 22 When Joram saw Jehu he asked, "Have you come in peace, Jehu?"

"How can there be peace," Jehu replied, "as long as all the idolatry and witchcraft of your mother Jezebel abound?"

23 Joram turned about and fled, calling out to Ahaziah, "Treachery, Ahaziah!"

24 Then Jehu drew his bow and shot Joram between the shoulders. The arrow pierced his heart and he slumped down in his chariot. 25 Jehu said to Bidkar, his chariot officer, "Pick him up and throw him on the field that belonged to Naboth the Jezreelite. Remember how you and I were riding together in chariots behind Ahab his father when the LORD spoke this prophecy against him: 26 'Yesterday I saw the blood of Naboth and the blood of his sons, declares the LORD, and I will surely make you pay for it on this plot of ground, declares the LORD.'[b] Now then, pick him up and throw him on that plot, in accordance with the word of the LORD."

27 When Ahaziah king of Judah saw what had happened, he fled up the road to Beth Haggan.[c] Jehu chased him, shouting, "Kill him too!" They wounded him in his chariot on the way up to Gur near Ibleam, but he escaped to Megiddo and died there. 28 His servants took him by chariot to Jerusalem and buried him with his ancestors in his tomb in the City of David. 29 (In the eleventh year of Joram son of Ahab, Ahaziah had become king of Judah.)

30 Then Jehu went to Jezreel. When Jezebel heard about it, she put on eye makeup, arranged her hair and looked out of a window. 31 As Jehu entered the gate, she asked, "Have you come in peace, you Zimri, you murderer of your master?"[d]

32 He looked up at the window and called out, "Who is on my side? Who?" Two or three eunuchs looked down at him. 33 "Throw her down!" Jehu said. So they threw her down, and some of her blood spattered the wall and the horses as they trampled her underfoot.

34 Jehu went in and ate and drank. "Take care of that cursed woman," he said, "and bury her, for she was a king's daughter." 35 But when they went out to bury her, they found nothing except her skull, her feet and her hands. 36 They went back and told Jehu, who said, "This is the word of the LORD that he spoke through his servant Elijah the Tishbite: On the plot of ground at Jezreel dogs will devour Jezebel's flesh.[e] 37 Jezebel's body will be like dung on the ground in the plot at Jezreel, so that no one will be able to say, 'This is Jezebel.' "

10 Now there were in Samaria seventy sons of the house of Ahab. So Jehu wrote letters and sent them to Samaria: to

[a] 15 Hebrew *Jehoram,* a variant of *Joram;* also in verses 17 and 21-24 [b] 26 See 1 Kings 21:19.
[c] 27 Or *fled by way of the garden house* [d] 31 Or *"Was there peace for Zimri, who murdered his master?"*
[e] 36 See 1 Kings 21:23.

the officials of Jezreel,[a] to the elders and
to the guardians of Ahab's children. He
said, 2"You have your master's sons with
you and you have chariots and horses, a
fortified city and weapons. Now as soon
as this letter reaches you, 3choose the
best and most worthy of your master's
sons and set him on his father's throne.
Then fight for your master's house."
4But they were terrified and said, "If two
kings could not resist him, how can we?"
5So the palace administrator, the city
governor, the elders and the guardians
sent this message to Jehu: "We are your
servants and we will do anything you say.
We will not appoint anyone as king; you
do whatever you think best."
6Then Jehu wrote them a second letter,
saying, "If you are on my side and will
obey me, take the heads of your master's
sons and come to me in Jezreel by this
time tomorrow."

Now the royal princes, seventy of them,
were with the leading men of the city,
who were rearing them. 7When the letter
arrived, these men took the princes and
slaughtered all seventy of them. They put
their heads in baskets and sent them to
Jehu in Jezreel. 8When the messenger arrived, he told Jehu, "They have brought
the heads of the princes."

Then Jehu ordered, "Put them in two
piles at the entrance of the city gate until
morning."
9The next morning Jehu went out. He
stood before all the people and said, "You
are innocent. It was I who conspired
against my master and killed him, but
who killed all these? 10Know, then, that
not a word the LORD has spoken against
the house of Ahab will fail. The LORD has
done what he announced through his
servant Elijah." 11So Jehu killed everyone in Jezreel who remained of the house
of Ahab, as well as all his chief men, his
close friends and his priests, leaving him
no survivor.
12Jehu then set out and went toward
Samaria. At Beth Eked of the Shepherds,
13he met some relatives of Ahaziah king
of Judah and asked, "Who are you?"

They said, "We are relatives of Ahaziah, and we have come down to greet
the families of the king and of the queen
mother."
14"Take them alive!" he ordered. So
they took them alive and slaughtered
them by the well of Beth Eked—forty-two
of them. He left no survivor.
15After he left there, he came upon Jehonadab son of Rekab, who was on his
way to meet him. Jehu greeted him and
said, "Are you in accord with me, as I am
with you?"

"I am," Jehonadab answered.

"If so," said Jehu, "give me your hand."
So he did, and Jehu helped him up into
the chariot. 16Jehu said, "Come with me
and see my zeal for the LORD." Then he
had him ride along in his chariot.
17When Jehu came to Samaria, he
killed all who were left there of Ahab's
family; he destroyed them, according to
the word of the LORD spoken to Elijah.
18Then Jehu brought all the people together and said to them, "Ahab served
Baal a little; Jehu will serve him much.
19Now summon all the prophets of Baal,
all his servants and all his priests. See
that no one is missing, because I am going to hold a great sacrifice for Baal. Anyone who fails to come will no longer live."
But Jehu was acting deceptively in order
to destroy the servants of Baal.
20Jehu said, "Call an assembly in hon-
or of Baal." So they proclaimed it. 21Then
he sent word throughout Israel, and all
the servants of Baal came; not one stayed
away. They crowded into the temple
of Baal until it was full from one end to
the other. 22And Jehu said to the keeper
of the wardrobe, "Bring robes for all the
servants of Baal." So he brought out robes
for them.
23Then Jehu and Jehonadab son of Rekab went into the temple of Baal. Jehu
said to the servants of Baal, "Look around
and see that no one who serves the LORD
is here with you—only servants of Baal."
24So they went in to make sacrifices and
burnt offerings. Now Jehu had posted
eighty men outside with this warning: "If
one of you lets any of the men I am placing in your hands escape, it will be your
life for his life."
25As soon as Jehu had finished making
the burnt offering, he ordered the guards
and officers: "Go in and kill them; let no
one escape." So they cut them down with
the sword. The guards and officers threw

[a] *1* Hebrew; some Septuagint manuscripts and Vulgate *of the city*

the bodies out and then entered the inner shrine of the temple of Baal. 26They
brought the sacred stone out of the temple of Baal and burned it. 27They demolished the sacred stone of Baal and tore
down the temple of Baal, and people have
used it for a latrine to this day.
28So Jehu destroyed Baal worship in
Israel. 29However, he did not turn away
from the sins of Jeroboam son of Nebat,
which he had caused Israel to commit—
the worship of the golden calves at Bethel
and Dan.
30The LORD said to Jehu, "Because you
have done well in accomplishing what
is right in my eyes and have done to the
house of Ahab all I had in mind to do,
your descendants will sit on the throne
of Israel to the fourth generation." 31Yet
Jehu was not careful to keep the law of
the LORD, the God of Israel, with all his
heart. He did not turn away from the sins
of Jeroboam, which he had caused Israel
to commit.
32In those days the LORD began to
reduce the size of Israel. Hazael overpowered the Israelites throughout their
territory 33east of the Jordan in all the
land of Gilead (the region of Gad, Reuben
and Manasseh), from Aroer by the Arnon
Gorge through Gilead to Bashan.
34As for the other events of Jehu's reign,
all he did, and all his achievements, are
they not written in the book of the annals
of the kings of Israel?
35Jehu rested with his ancestors and
was buried in Samaria. And Jehoahaz his
son succeeded him as king. 36The time
that Jehu reigned over Israel in Samaria
was twenty-eight years.

11 When Athaliah the mother of Ahaziah saw that her son was dead, she
proceeded to destroy the whole royal
family. 2But Jehosheba, the daughter
of King Jehoram[a] and sister of Ahaziah,
took Joash son of Ahaziah and stole him
away from among the royal princes, who
were about to be murdered. She put him
and his nurse in a bedroom to hide him
from Athaliah; so he was not killed. 3He
remained hidden with his nurse at the
temple of the LORD for six years while
Athaliah ruled the land.
4In the seventh year Jehoiada sent for
the commanders of units of a hundred,
the Carites and the guards and had them
brought to him at the temple of the LORD.
He made a covenant with them and put
them under oath at the temple of the
LORD. Then he showed them the king's
son. 5He commanded them, saying,
"This is what you are to do: You who are
in the three companies that are going
on duty on the Sabbath—a third of you
guarding the royal palace, 6a third at the
Sur Gate, and a third at the gate behind
the guard, who take turns guarding the
temple— 7and you who are in the other
two companies that normally go off Sabbath duty are all to guard the temple for
the king. 8Station yourselves around the
king, each of you with weapon in hand.
Anyone who approaches your ranks[b] is
to be put to death. Stay close to the king
wherever he goes."
9The commanders of units of a hundred did just as Jehoiada the priest ordered. Each one took his men—those
who were going on duty on the Sabbath
and those who were going off duty—and
came to Jehoiada the priest. 10Then he
gave the commanders the spears and
shields that had belonged to King David and that were in the temple of the
LORD. 11The guards, each with weapon
in hand, stationed themselves around
the king—near the altar and the temple,
from the south side to the north side of
the temple.
12Jehoiada brought out the king's son
and put the crown on him; he presented
him with a copy of the covenant and proclaimed him king. They anointed him,
and the people clapped their hands and
shouted, "Long live the king!"
13When Athaliah heard the noise made
by the guards and the people, she went
to the people at the temple of the LORD.
14She looked and there was the king,
standing by the pillar, as the custom was.
The officers and the trumpeters were beside the king, and all the people of the
land were rejoicing and blowing trumpets. Then Athaliah tore her robes and
called out, "Treason! Treason!"
15Jehoiada the priest ordered the commanders of units of a hundred, who were
in charge of the troops: "Bring her out
between the ranks[c] and put to the sword

[a] 2 Hebrew *Joram,* a variant of *Jehoram* [b] 8 Or *approaches the precincts* [c] 15 Or *out from the precincts*

anyone who follows her." For the priest
had said, "She must not be put to death in
the temple of the LORD." 16So they seized
her as she reached the place where the
horses enter the palace grounds, and
there she was put to death.
17Jehoiada then made a covenant between the LORD and the king and people
that they would be the LORD's people. He
also made a covenant between the king
and the people. 18All the people of the
land went to the temple of Baal and tore it
down. They smashed the altars and idols
to pieces and killed Mattan the priest of
Baal in front of the altars.
Then Jehoiada the priest posted guards
at the temple of the LORD. 19He took with
him the commanders of hundreds, the
Carites, the guards and all the people of
the land, and together they brought the
king down from the temple of the LORD
and went into the palace, entering by
way of the gate of the guards. The king
then took his place on the royal throne.
20All the people of the land rejoiced, and
the city was calm, because Athaliah had
been slain with the sword at the palace.

21Joash[a] was seven years old when he
began to reign.[b]

12[c] In the seventh year of Jehu, Joash[d]
became king, and he reigned in Jerusalem forty years. His mother's name
was Zibiah; she was from Beersheba.
2Joash did what was right in the eyes of
the LORD all the years Jehoiada the priest
instructed him. 3The high places, however, were not removed; the people continued to offer sacrifices and burn incense
there.
4Joash said to the priests, "Collect all
the money that is brought as sacred offerings to the temple of the LORD — the money collected in the census, the money received from personal vows and the money
brought voluntarily to the temple. 5Let every priest receive the money from one of
the treasurers, then use it to repair whatever damage is found in the temple."
6But by the twenty-third year of King
Joash the priests still had not repaired
the temple. 7Therefore King Joash summoned Jehoiada the priest and the other priests and asked them, "Why aren't
you repairing the damage done to the
temple? Take no more money from your
treasurers, but hand it over for repairing
the temple." 8The priests agreed that they
would not collect any more money from
the people and that they would not repair
the temple themselves.
9Jehoiada the priest took a chest and
bored a hole in its lid. He placed it beside
the altar, on the right side as one enters
the temple of the LORD. The priests who
guarded the entrance put into the chest
all the money that was brought to the
temple of the LORD. 10Whenever they saw
that there was a large amount of money
in the chest, the royal secretary and the
high priest came, counted the money
that had been brought into the temple of
the LORD and put it into bags. 11When the
amount had been determined, they gave
the money to the men appointed to supervise the work on the temple. With it they
paid those who worked on the temple of
the LORD — the carpenters and builders,
12the masons and stonecutters. They
purchased timber and blocks of dressed
stone for the repair of the temple of the
LORD, and met all the other expenses of
restoring the temple.
13The money brought into the temple
was not spent for making silver basins,
wick trimmers, sprinkling bowls, trumpets or any other articles of gold or silver
for the temple of the LORD; 14it was paid
to the workers, who used it to repair the
temple. 15They did not require an accounting from those to whom they gave
the money to pay the workers, because
they acted with complete honesty. 16The
money from the guilt offerings and sin offerings[e] was not brought into the temple
of the LORD; it belonged to the priests.
17About this time Hazael king of Aram
went up and attacked Gath and captured
it. Then he turned to attack Jerusalem.
18But Joash king of Judah took all the sacred objects dedicated by his predecessors — Jehoshaphat, Jehoram and Ahaziah, the kings of Judah — and the gifts he
himself had dedicated and all the gold
found in the treasuries of the temple of
the LORD and of the royal palace, and he
sent them to Hazael king of Aram, who
then withdrew from Jerusalem.

[a] *21* Hebrew *Jehoash,* a variant of *Joash* [b] *21* In Hebrew texts this verse (11:21) is numbered 12:1. [c] In Hebrew texts 12:1-21 is numbered 12:2-22. [d] *1* Hebrew *Jehoash,* a variant of *Joash*; also in verses 2, 4, 6, 7 and 18 [e] *16* Or *purification offerings*

19 As for the other events of the reign of
Joash, and all he did, are they not written
in the book of the annals of the kings of
Judah? 20 His officials conspired against
him and assassinated him at Beth Millo,
on the road down to Silla. 21 The officials
who murdered him were Jozabad son of
Shimeath and Jehozabad son of Shomer.
He died and was buried with his ancestors in the City of David. And Amaziah
his son succeeded him as king.

13 In the twenty-third year of Joash son
of Ahaziah king of Judah, Jehoahaz
son of Jehu became king of Israel in Samaria, and he reigned seventeen years.
2 He did evil in the eyes of the LORD by following the sins of Jeroboam son of Nebat,
which he had caused Israel to commit,
and he did not turn away from them. 3 So
the LORD's anger burned against Israel,
and for a long time he kept them under
the power of Hazael king of Aram and
Ben-Hadad his son.

4 Then Jehoahaz sought the LORD's favor, and the LORD listened to him, for he
saw how severely the king of Aram was
oppressing Israel. 5 The LORD provided
a deliverer for Israel, and they escaped
from the power of Aram. So the Israelites lived in their own homes as they had
before. 6 But they did not turn away from
the sins of the house of Jeroboam, which
he had caused Israel to commit; they continued in them. Also, the Asherah pole[a]
remained standing in Samaria.

7 Nothing had been left of the army
of Jehoahaz except fifty horsemen, ten
chariots and ten thousand foot soldiers,
for the king of Aram had destroyed the
rest and made them like the dust at
threshing time.

8 As for the other events of the reign
of Jehoahaz, all he did and his achievements, are they not written in the book of
the annals of the kings of Israel? 9 Jehoahaz rested with his ancestors and was
buried in Samaria. And Jehoash[b] his son
succeeded him as king.

10 In the thirty-seventh year of Joash
king of Judah, Jehoash son of Jehoahaz
became king of Israel in Samaria, and he
reigned sixteen years. 11 He did evil in the
eyes of the LORD and did not turn away
from any of the sins of Jeroboam son of
Nebat, which he had caused Israel to
commit; he continued in them.

12 As for the other events of the reign of
Jehoash, all he did and his achievements,
including his war against Amaziah king
of Judah, are they not written in the book
of the annals of the kings of Israel? 13 Jehoash rested with his ancestors, and Jeroboam succeeded him on the throne.
Jehoash was buried in Samaria with the
kings of Israel.

14 Now Elisha had been suffering from
the illness from which he died. Jehoash
king of Israel went down to see him and
wept over him. "My father! My father!"
he cried. "The chariots and horsemen of
Israel!"

15 Elisha said, "Get a bow and some arrows," and he did so. 16 "Take the bow in
your hands," he said to the king of Israel. When he had taken it, Elisha put his
hands on the king's hands.

17 "Open the east window," he said, and
he opened it. "Shoot!" Elisha said, and he
shot. "The LORD's arrow of victory, the
arrow of victory over Aram!" Elisha declared. "You will completely destroy the
Arameans at Aphek."

18 Then he said, "Take the arrows,"
and the king took them. Elisha told him,
"Strike the ground." He struck it three
times and stopped. 19 The man of God
was angry with him and said, "You should
have struck the ground five or six times;
then you would have defeated Aram and
completely destroyed it. But now you will
defeat it only three times."

20 Elisha died and was buried.

Now Moabite raiders used to enter the
country every spring. 21 Once while some
Israelites were burying a man, suddenly
they saw a band of raiders; so they threw
the man's body into Elisha's tomb. When
the body touched Elisha's bones, the man
came to life and stood up on his feet.

22 Hazael king of Aram oppressed Israel throughout the reign of Jehoahaz.
23 But the LORD was gracious to them and
had compassion and showed concern for
them because of his covenant with Abraham, Isaac and Jacob. To this day he has
been unwilling to destroy them or banish
them from his presence.

24 Hazael king of Aram died, and Ben-

[a] 6 That is, a wooden symbol of the goddess Asherah; here and elsewhere in 2 Kings [b] 9 Hebrew *Joash,* a variant of *Jehoash;* also in verses 12-14 and 25

Hadad his son succeeded him as king.
25Then Jehoash son of Jehoahaz recaptured from Ben-Hadad son of Hazael the towns he had taken in battle from his father Jehoahaz. Three times Jehoash defeated him, and so he recovered the Israelite towns.

14 In the second year of Jehoash[a] son of Jehoahaz king of Israel, Amaziah son of Joash king of Judah began to reign.
2He was twenty-five years old when he became king, and he reigned in Jerusalem twenty-nine years. His mother's name was Jehoaddan; she was from Jerusalem.
3He did what was right in the eyes of the LORD, but not as his father David had done. In everything he followed the example of his father Joash.
4The high places, however, were not removed; the people continued to offer sacrifices and burn incense there.

5After the kingdom was firmly in his grasp, he executed the officials who had murdered his father the king.
6Yet he did not put the children of the assassins to death, in accordance with what is written in the Book of the Law of Moses where the LORD commanded: "Parents are not to be put to death for their children, nor children put to death for their parents; each will die for their own sin."[b]

7He was the one who defeated ten thousand Edomites in the Valley of Salt and captured Sela in battle, calling it Joktheel, the name it has to this day.

8Then Amaziah sent messengers to Jehoash son of Jehoahaz, the son of Jehu, king of Israel, with the challenge: "Come, let us face each other in battle."

9But Jehoash king of Israel replied to Amaziah king of Judah: "A thistle in Lebanon sent a message to a cedar in Lebanon, 'Give your daughter to my son in marriage.' Then a wild beast in Lebanon came along and trampled the thistle underfoot.
10You have indeed defeated Edom and now you are arrogant. Glory in your victory, but stay at home! Why ask for trouble and cause your own downfall and that of Judah also?"

11Amaziah, however, would not listen, so Jehoash king of Israel attacked. He and Amaziah king of Judah faced each other at Beth Shemesh in Judah.
12Judah was routed by Israel, and every man fled to his home.
13Jehoash king of Israel captured Amaziah king of Judah, the son of Joash, the son of Ahaziah, at Beth Shemesh. Then Jehoash went to Jerusalem and broke down the wall of Jerusalem from the Ephraim Gate to the Corner Gate — a section about four hundred cubits long.[c]
14He took all the gold and silver and all the articles found in the temple of the LORD and in the treasuries of the royal palace. He also took hostages and returned to Samaria.

15As for the other events of the reign of Jehoash, what he did and his achievements, including his war against Amaziah king of Judah, are they not written in the book of the annals of the kings of Israel?
16Jehoash rested with his ancestors and was buried in Samaria with the kings of Israel. And Jeroboam his son succeeded him as king.

17Amaziah son of Joash king of Judah lived for fifteen years after the death of Jehoash son of Jehoahaz king of Israel.
18As for the other events of Amaziah's reign, are they not written in the book of the annals of the kings of Judah?

19They conspired against him in Jerusalem, and he fled to Lachish, but they sent men after him to Lachish and killed him there.
20He was brought back by horse and was buried in Jerusalem with his ancestors, in the City of David.

21Then all the people of Judah took Azariah,[d] who was sixteen years old, and made him king in place of his father Amaziah.
22He was the one who rebuilt Elath and restored it to Judah after Amaziah rested with his ancestors.

23In the fifteenth year of Amaziah son of Joash king of Judah, Jeroboam son of Jehoash king of Israel became king in Samaria, and he reigned forty-one years.
24He did evil in the eyes of the LORD and did not turn away from any of the sins of Jeroboam son of Nebat, which he had caused Israel to commit.
25He was the one who restored the boundaries of Israel from Lebo Hamath to the Dead Sea,[e] in accordance with the word of the LORD, the God of Israel, spoken through his servant Jonah son of Amittai, the prophet from Gath Hepher.

[a] *1* Hebrew *Joash,* a variant of *Jehoash;* also in verses 13, 23 and 27 [b] *6* Deut. 24:16 [c] *13* That is, about 600 feet or about 180 meters [d] *21* Also called *Uzziah* [e] *25* Hebrew *the Sea of the Arabah*

26 The LORD had seen how bitterly everyone in Israel, whether slave or free,
was suffering;[a] there was no one to help
them. 27 And since the LORD had not said
he would blot out the name of Israel from
under heaven, he saved them by the hand
of Jeroboam son of Jehoash.
28 As for the other events of Jeroboam's
reign, all he did, and his military achievements, including how he recovered for Israel both Damascus and Hamath, which
had belonged to Judah, are they not written in the book of the annals of the kings
of Israel? 29 Jeroboam rested with his ancestors, the kings of Israel. And Zechariah his son succeeded him as king.

15 In the twenty-seventh year of Jeroboam king of Israel, Azariah[b] son of
Amaziah king of Judah began to reign.
2 He was sixteen years old when he became king, and he reigned in Jerusalem
fifty-two years. His mother's name was
Jekoliah; she was from Jerusalem. 3 He
did what was right in the eyes of the LORD,
just as his father Amaziah had done. 4 The
high places, however, were not removed;
the people continued to offer sacrifices
and burn incense there.
5 The LORD afflicted the king with leprosy[c] until the day he died, and he lived
in a separate house.[d] Jotham the king's
son had charge of the palace and governed the people of the land.
6 As for the other events of Azariah's
reign, and all he did, are they not written
in the book of the annals of the kings of
Judah? 7 Azariah rested with his ancestors and was buried near them in the City
of David. And Jotham his son succeeded
him as king.

8 In the thirty-eighth year of Azariah
king of Judah, Zechariah son of Jeroboam became king of Israel in Samaria, and
he reigned six months. 9 He did evil in the
eyes of the LORD, as his predecessors had
done. He did not turn away from the sins
of Jeroboam son of Nebat, which he had
caused Israel to commit.
10 Shallum son of Jabesh conspired
against Zechariah. He attacked him in
front of the people,[e] assassinated him
and succeeded him as king. 11 The other
events of Zechariah's reign are written
in the book of the annals of the kings of
Israel. 12 So the word of the LORD spoken to Jehu was fulfilled: "Your descendants will sit on the throne of Israel to the
fourth generation."[f]

13 Shallum son of Jabesh became king
in the thirty-ninth year of Uzziah king
of Judah, and he reigned in Samaria one
month. 14 Then Menahem son of Gadi
went from Tirzah up to Samaria. He attacked Shallum son of Jabesh in Samaria, assassinated him and succeeded him
as king.
15 The other events of Shallum's reign,
and the conspiracy he led, are written
in the book of the annals of the kings of
Israel.
16 At that time Menahem, starting out
from Tirzah, attacked Tiphsah and everyone in the city and its vicinity, because they refused to open their gates.
He sacked Tiphsah and ripped open all
the pregnant women.
17 In the thirty-ninth year of Azariah
king of Judah, Menahem son of Gadi became king of Israel, and he reigned in Samaria ten years. 18 He did evil in the eyes
of the LORD. During his entire reign he
did not turn away from the sins of Jeroboam son of Nebat, which he had caused
Israel to commit.
19 Then Pul[g] king of Assyria invaded
the land, and Menahem gave him a thousand talents[h] of silver to gain his support
and strengthen his own hold on the kingdom. 20 Menahem exacted this money
from Israel. Every wealthy person had
to contribute fifty shekels[i] of silver to be
given to the king of Assyria. So the king of
Assyria withdrew and stayed in the land
no longer.
21 As for the other events of Menahem's
reign, and all he did, are they not written
in the book of the annals of the kings of
Israel? 22 Menahem rested with his ancestors. And Pekahiah his son succeeded
him as king.

[a] *26* Or *Israel was suffering. They were without a ruler or leader, and* [b] *1* Also called *Uzziah*; also in verses 6, 7, 8, 17, 23 and 27 [c] *5* The Hebrew for *leprosy* was used for various diseases affecting the skin. [d] *5* Or *in a house where he was relieved of responsibilities* [e] *10* Hebrew; some Septuagint manuscripts *in Ibleam* [f] *12* 2 Kings 10:30 [g] *19* Also called *Tiglath-Pileser* [h] *19* That is, about 38 tons or about 34 metric tons [i] *20* That is, about 1 1/4 pounds or about 575 grams

23 In the fiftieth year of Azariah king
of Judah, Pekahiah son of Menahem became king of Israel in Samaria, and he
reigned two years. 24 Pekahiah did evil
in the eyes of the LORD. He did not turn
away from the sins of Jeroboam son of
Nebat, which he had caused Israel to
commit. 25 One of his chief officers, Pekah son of Remaliah, conspired against
him. Taking fifty men of Gilead with him,
he assassinated Pekahiah, along with Argob and Arieh, in the citadel of the royal
palace at Samaria. So Pekah killed Pekahiah and succeeded him as king.
26 The other events of Pekahiah's reign,
and all he did, are written in the book of
the annals of the kings of Israel.

27 In the fifty-second year of Azariah
king of Judah, Pekah son of Remaliah
became king of Israel in Samaria, and he
reigned twenty years. 28 He did evil in the
eyes of the LORD. He did not turn away
from the sins of Jeroboam son of Nebat,
which he had caused Israel to commit.
29 In the time of Pekah king of Israel,
Tiglath-Pileser king of Assyria came and
took Ijon, Abel Beth Maakah, Janoah,
Kedesh and Hazor. He took Gilead and
Galilee, including all the land of Naphtali, and deported the people to Assyria.
30 Then Hoshea son of Elah conspired
against Pekah son of Remaliah. He attacked and assassinated him, and then
succeeded him as king in the twentieth
year of Jotham son of Uzziah.
31 As for the other events of Pekah's
reign, and all he did, are they not written
in the book of the annals of the kings of
Israel?

32 In the second year of Pekah son of
Remaliah king of Israel, Jotham son of
Uzziah king of Judah began to reign.
33 He was twenty-five years old when he
became king, and he reigned in Jerusalem sixteen years. His mother's name
was Jerusha daughter of Zadok. 34 He did
what was right in the eyes of the LORD,
just as his father Uzziah had done. 35 The
high places, however, were not removed;
the people continued to offer sacrifices and burn incense there. Jotham rebuilt the Upper Gate of the temple of the
LORD.
36 As for the other events of Jotham's
reign, and what he did, are they not written in the book of the annals of the kings
of Judah? 37 (In those days the LORD began to send Rezin king of Aram and Pekah son of Remaliah against Judah.) 38 Jotham rested with his ancestors and was
buried with them in the City of David, the
city of his father. And Ahaz his son succeeded him as king.

16 In the seventeenth year of Pekah son
of Remaliah, Ahaz son of Jotham
king of Judah began to reign. 2 Ahaz was
twenty years old when he became king,
and he reigned in Jerusalem sixteen
years. Unlike David his father, he did
not do what was right in the eyes of the
LORD his God. 3 He followed the ways of
the kings of Israel and even sacrificed his
son in the fire, engaging in the detestable practices of the nations the LORD
had driven out before the Israelites. 4 He
offered sacrifices and burned incense at
the high places, on the hilltops and under
every spreading tree.
5 Then Rezin king of Aram and Pekah
son of Remaliah king of Israel marched
up to fight against Jerusalem and besieged Ahaz, but they could not overpower him. 6 At that time, Rezin king of Aram
recovered Elath for Aram by driving
out the people of Judah. Edomites then
moved into Elath and have lived there to
this day.
7 Ahaz sent messengers to say to Tiglath-Pileser king of Assyria, "I am your
servant and vassal. Come up and save
me out of the hand of the king of Aram
and of the king of Israel, who are attacking me." 8 And Ahaz took the silver and
gold found in the temple of the LORD
and in the treasuries of the royal palace
and sent it as a gift to the king of Assyria. 9 The king of Assyria complied by attacking Damascus and capturing it. He
deported its inhabitants to Kir and put
Rezin to death.
10 Then King Ahaz went to Damascus
to meet Tiglath-Pileser king of Assyria.
He saw an altar in Damascus and sent to
Uriah the priest a sketch of the altar, with
detailed plans for its construction. 11 So
Uriah the priest built an altar in accordance with all the plans that King Ahaz
had sent from Damascus and finished it
before King Ahaz returned. 12 When the
king came back from Damascus and saw
the altar, he approached it and presented

offerings[a] on it. 13 He offered up his burnt
offering and grain offering, poured out his
drink offering, and splashed the blood of
his fellowship offerings against the altar.
14 As for the bronze altar that stood before
the LORD, he brought it from the front of
the temple — from between the new altar
and the temple of the LORD — and put it
on the north side of the new altar.

15 King Ahaz then gave these orders to
Uriah the priest: "On the large new altar,
offer the morning burnt offering and the
evening grain offering, the king's burnt
offering and his grain offering, and the
burnt offering of all the people of the
land, and their grain offering and their
drink offering. Splash against this altar
the blood of all the burnt offerings and
sacrifices. But I will use the bronze altar
for seeking guidance." 16 And Uriah the
priest did just as King Ahaz had ordered.

17 King Ahaz cut off the side panels and
removed the basins from the movable
stands. He removed the Sea from the
bronze bulls that supported it and set it
on a stone base. 18 He took away the Sabbath canopy[b] that had been built at the
temple and removed the royal entryway
outside the temple of the LORD, in defer-
ence to the king of Assyria.

19 As for the other events of the reign of
Ahaz, and what he did, are they not written in the book of the annals of the kings
of Judah? 20 Ahaz rested with his ancestors and was buried with them in the City
of David. And Hezekiah his son succeeded him as king.

17 In the twelfth year of Ahaz king of
Judah, Hoshea son of Elah became
king of Israel in Samaria, and he reigned
nine years. 2 He did evil in the eyes of the
LORD, but not like the kings of Israel who
preceded him.

3 Shalmaneser king of Assyria came
up to attack Hoshea, who had been Shalmaneser's vassal and had paid him tribute. 4 But the king of Assyria discovered
that Hoshea was a traitor, for he had sent
envoys to So[c] king of Egypt, and he no
longer paid tribute to the king of Assyria, as he had done year by year. Therefore
Shalmaneser seized him and put him in
prison. 5 The king of Assyria invaded the
entire land, marched against Samaria
and laid siege to it for three years. 6 In the
ninth year of Hoshea, the king of Assyria captured Samaria and deported the
Israelites to Assyria. He settled them in
Halah, in Gozan on the Habor River and
in the towns of the Medes.

7 All this took place because the Israelites had sinned against the LORD their
God, who had brought them up out of
Egypt from under the power of Pharaoh
king of Egypt. They worshiped other gods
8 and followed the practices of the nations
the LORD had driven out before them, as
well as the practices that the kings of Israel had introduced. 9 The Israelites secretly
did things against the LORD their God that
were not right. From watchtower to fortified city they built themselves high places in all their towns. 10 They set up sacred
stones and Asherah poles on every high
hill and under every spreading tree. 11 At
every high place they burned incense, as
the nations whom the LORD had driven
out before them had done. They did wicked things that aroused the LORD's anger.
12 They worshiped idols, though the LORD
had said, "You shall not do this."[d] 13 The
LORD warned Israel and Judah through
all his prophets and seers: "Turn from
your evil ways. Observe my commands
and decrees, in accordance with the entire Law that I commanded your ancestors to obey and that I delivered to you
through my servants the prophets."

14 But they would not listen and were as
stiff-necked as their ancestors, who did
not trust in the LORD their God. 15 They
rejected his decrees and the covenant
he had made with their ancestors and
the statutes he had warned them to keep.
They followed worthless idols and themselves became worthless. They imitated
the nations around them although the
LORD had ordered them, "Do not do as
they do."

16 They forsook all the commands of the
LORD their God and made for themselves
two idols cast in the shape of calves, and
an Asherah pole. They bowed down to
all the starry hosts, and they worshiped
Baal. 17 They sacrificed their sons and
daughters in the fire. They practiced
divination and sought omens and sold
themselves to do evil in the eyes of the
LORD, arousing his anger.

[a] *12* Or *and went up* [b] *18* Or *the dais of his throne* (see Septuagint) [c] *4* *So* is probably an abbreviation for *Osorkon.* [d] *12* Exodus 20:4,5

18So the LORD was very angry with Israel and removed them from his presence.
Only the tribe of Judah was left, 19and
even Judah did not keep the commands
of the LORD their God. They followed the
practices Israel had introduced. 20There-
fore the LORD rejected all the people of Israel; he afflicted them and gave them into
the hands of plunderers, until he thrust
them from his presence.

21When he tore Israel away from the
house of David, they made Jeroboam son
of Nebat their king. Jeroboam enticed Israel away from following the LORD and
caused them to commit a great sin. 22The
Israelites persisted in all the sins of Jeroboam and did not turn away from them
23until the LORD removed them from his
presence, as he had warned through all
his servants the prophets. So the people
of Israel were taken from their homeland
into exile in Assyria, and they are still
there.

24The king of Assyria brought people
from Babylon, Kuthah, Avva, Hamath
and Sepharvaim and settled them in the
towns of Samaria to replace the Israelites. They took over Samaria and lived in
its towns. 25When they first lived there,
they did not worship the LORD; so he sent
lions among them and they killed some
of the people. 26It was reported to the
king of Assyria: "The people you deported and resettled in the towns of Samaria
do not know what the god of that country
requires. He has sent lions among them,
which are killing them off, because the
people do not know what he requires."

27Then the king of Assyria gave this
order: "Have one of the priests you took
captive from Samaria go back to live there
and teach the people what the god of the
land requires." 28So one of the priests
who had been exiled from Samaria came
to live in Bethel and taught them how to
worship the LORD.

29Nevertheless, each national group
made its own gods in the several towns
where they settled, and set them up in
the shrines the people of Samaria had
made at the high places. 30The people
from Babylon made Sukkoth Benoth,
those from Kuthah made Nergal, and
those from Hamath made Ashima; 31the
Avvites made Nibhaz and Tartak, and
the Sepharvites burned their children in
the fire as sacrifices to Adrammelek and
Anammelek, the gods of Sepharvaim.
32They worshiped the LORD, but they also
appointed all sorts of their own people to
officiate for them as priests in the shrines
at the high places. 33They worshiped the
LORD, but they also served their own gods
in accordance with the customs of the nations from which they had been brought.

34To this day they persist in their former practices. They neither worship the
LORD nor adhere to the decrees and regulations, the laws and commands that
the LORD gave the descendants of Jacob,
whom he named Israel. 35When the LORD
made a covenant with the Israelites, he
commanded them: "Do not worship any
other gods or bow down to them, serve
them or sacrifice to them. 36But the LORD,
who brought you up out of Egypt with
mighty power and outstretched arm, is
the one you must worship. To him you
shall bow down and to him offer sacrifices. 37You must always be careful to keep
the decrees and regulations, the laws and
commands he wrote for you. Do not worship other gods. 38Do not forget the covenant I have made with you, and do not
worship other gods. 39Rather, worship the
LORD your God; it is he who will deliver
you from the hand of all your enemies."

40They would not listen, however,
but persisted in their former practices.
41Even while these people were worshiping the LORD, they were serving
their idols. To this day their children and
grandchildren continue to do as their ancestors did.

18 In the third year of Hoshea son of
Elah king of Israel, Hezekiah son of
Ahaz king of Judah began to reign. 2He
was twenty-five years old when he became king, and he reigned in Jerusalem
twenty-nine years. His mother's name
was Abijah[a] daughter of Zechariah. 3He
did what was right in the eyes of the
LORD, just as his father David had done.
4He removed the high places, smashed
the sacred stones and cut down the
Asherah poles. He broke into pieces the
bronze snake Moses had made, for up to
that time the Israelites had been burning
incense to it. (It was called Nehushtan.[b])

[a] 2 Hebrew *Abi*, a variant of *Abijah* [b] 4 *Nehushtan* sounds like the Hebrew for both *bronze* and *snake*.

5 Hezekiah trusted in the LORD, the
God of Israel. There was no one like him
among all the kings of Judah, either before him or after him. 6 He held fast to the
LORD and did not stop following him; he
kept the commands the LORD had given
Moses. 7 And the LORD was with him; he
was successful in whatever he undertook.
He rebelled against the king of Assyria
and did not serve him. 8 From watchtower to fortified city, he defeated the Philistines, as far as Gaza and its territory.
9 In King Hezekiah's fourth year, which
was the seventh year of Hoshea son of
Elah king of Israel, Shalmaneser king
of Assyria marched against Samaria
and laid siege to it. 10 At the end of three
years the Assyrians took it. So Samaria
was captured in Hezekiah's sixth year,
which was the ninth year of Hoshea king
of Israel. 11 The king of Assyria deported
Israel to Assyria and settled them in Halah, in Gozan on the Habor River and in
towns of the Medes. 12 This happened because they had not obeyed the LORD their
God, but had violated his covenant—all
that Moses the servant of the LORD commanded. They neither listened to the
commands nor carried them out.
13 In the fourteenth year of King Hezekiah's reign, Sennacherib king of Assyria
attacked all the fortified cities of Judah
and captured them. 14 So Hezekiah king
of Judah sent this message to the king of
Assyria at Lachish: "I have done wrong.
Withdraw from me, and I will pay whatever you demand of me." The king of
Assyria exacted from Hezekiah king of
Judah three hundred talents[a] of silver
and thirty talents[b] of gold. 15 So Hezekiah gave him all the silver that was found
in the temple of the LORD and in the treasuries of the royal palace.
16 At this time Hezekiah king of Judah
stripped off the gold with which he had
covered the doors and doorposts of the
temple of the LORD, and gave it to the
king of Assyria.
17 The king of Assyria sent his supreme
commander, his chief officer and his
field commander with a large army, from
Lachish to King Hezekiah at Jerusalem.
They came up to Jerusalem and stopped
at the aqueduct of the Upper Pool, on the
road to the Washerman's Field. 18 They
called for the king; and Eliakim son of
Hilkiah the palace administrator, Shebna the secretary, and Joah son of Asaph
the recorder went out to them.
19 The field commander said to them,
"Tell Hezekiah:

"'This is what the great king, the
king of Assyria, says: On what are
you basing this confidence of yours?
20 You say you have the counsel and
the might for war—but you speak
only empty words. On whom are you
depending, that you rebel against
me? 21 Look, I know you are depending on Egypt, that splintered reed of
a staff, which pierces the hand of anyone who leans on it! Such is Pharaoh
king of Egypt to all who depend on
him. 22 But if you say to me, "We are
depending on the LORD our God"—
isn't he the one whose high places and
altars Hezekiah removed, saying to
Judah and Jerusalem, "You must worship before this altar in Jerusalem"?
23 "'Come now, make a bargain
with my master, the king of Assyria: I
will give you two thousand horses—
if you can put riders on them! 24 How
can you repulse one officer of the
least of my master's officials, even
though you are depending on Egypt
for chariots and horsemen[c]? 25 Furthermore, have I come to attack and
destroy this place without word from
the LORD? The LORD himself told me
to march against this country and
destroy it.'"

26 Then Eliakim son of Hilkiah, and
Shebna and Joah said to the field commander, "Please speak to your servants
in Aramaic, since we understand it. Don't
speak to us in Hebrew in the hearing of
the people on the wall."
27 But the commander replied, "Was it
only to your master and you that my master sent me to say these things, and not to
the people sitting on the wall—who, like
you, will have to eat their own excrement
and drink their own urine?"
28 Then the commander stood and
called out in Hebrew, "Hear the word of
the great king, the king of Assyria! 29 This
is what the king says: Do not let Hezekiah
deceive you. He cannot deliver you from

[a] *14* That is, about 11 tons or about 10 metric tons [b] *14* That is, about 1 ton or about 1 metric ton
[c] *24* Or *charioteers*

my hand. 30Do not let Hezekiah persuade
you to trust in the LORD when he says,
'The LORD will surely deliver us; this city
will not be given into the hand of the king
of Assyria.'

31"Do not listen to Hezekiah. This is
what the king of Assyria says: Make peace
with me and come out to me. Then each
of you will eat fruit from your own vine
and fig tree and drink water from your
own cistern, 32until I come and take you
to a land like your own—a land of grain
and new wine, a land of bread and vineyards, a land of olive trees and honey.
Choose life and not death!

"Do not listen to Hezekiah, for he is
misleading you when he says, 'The LORD
will deliver us.' 33Has the god of any nation ever delivered his land from the
hand of the king of Assyria? 34Where are
the gods of Hamath and Arpad? Where
are the gods of Sepharvaim, Hena and
Ivvah? Have they rescued Samaria from
my hand? 35Who of all the gods of these
countries has been able to save his land
from me? How then can the LORD deliver
Jerusalem from my hand?"

36But the people remained silent and
said nothing in reply, because the king
had commanded, "Do not answer him."

37Then Eliakim son of Hilkiah the palace administrator, Shebna the secretary,
and Joah son of Asaph the recorder went
to Hezekiah, with their clothes torn, and
told him what the field commander had
said.

19 When King Hezekiah heard this, he
tore his clothes and put on sackcloth
and went into the temple of the LORD.
2He sent Eliakim the palace administrator, Shebna the secretary and the leading priests, all wearing sackcloth, to the
prophet Isaiah son of Amoz. 3They told
him, "This is what Hezekiah says: This
day is a day of distress and rebuke and
disgrace, as when children come to the
moment of birth and there is no strength
to deliver them. 4It may be that the LORD
your God will hear all the words of the
field commander, whom his master, the
king of Assyria, has sent to ridicule the
living God, and that he will rebuke him
for the words the LORD your God has
heard. Therefore pray for the remnant
that still survives."

5When King Hezekiah's officials came
to Isaiah, 6Isaiah said to them, "Tell your
master, 'This is what the LORD says: Do
not be afraid of what you have heard—
those words with which the underlings of
the king of Assyria have blasphemed me.
7Listen! When he hears a certain report, I
will make him want to return to his own
country, and there I will have him cut
down with the sword.'"

8When the field commander heard
that the king of Assyria had left Lachish,
he withdrew and found the king fighting
against Libnah.

9Now Sennacherib received a report
that Tirhakah, the king of Cush,[a] was
marching out to fight against him. So he
again sent messengers to Hezekiah with
this word: 10"Say to Hezekiah king of Judah: Do not let the god you depend on
deceive you when he says, 'Jerusalem will
not be given into the hands of the king of
Assyria.' 11Surely you have heard what
the kings of Assyria have done to all the
countries, destroying them completely.
And will you be delivered? 12Did the gods
of the nations that were destroyed by my
predecessors deliver them—the gods of
Gozan, Harran, Rezeph and the people of
Eden who were in Tel Assar? 13Where is
the king of Hamath or the king of Arpad?
Where are the kings of Lair, Sepharvaim,
Hena and Ivvah?"

14Hezekiah received the letter from the
messengers and read it. Then he went up
to the temple of the LORD and spread it
out before the LORD. 15And Hezekiah
prayed to the LORD: "LORD, the God of Israel, enthroned between the cherubim,
you alone are God over all the kingdoms
of the earth. You have made heaven and
earth. 16Give ear, LORD, and hear; open
your eyes, LORD, and see; listen to the
words Sennacherib has sent to ridicule
the living God.

17"It is true, LORD, that the Assyrian
kings have laid waste these nations and
their lands. 18They have thrown their
gods into the fire and destroyed them,
for they were not gods but only wood and
stone, fashioned by human hands. 19Now,
LORD our God, deliver us from his hand,
so that all the kingdoms of the earth may
know that you alone, LORD, are God."

20Then Isaiah son of Amoz sent a mes-

[a] 9 That is, the upper Nile region

sage to Hezekiah: "This is what the LORD, the God of Israel, says: I have heard your prayer concerning Sennacherib king of Assyria.
21 This is the word that the LORD has spoken against him:

"'Virgin Daughter Zion
despises you and mocks you.
Daughter Jerusalem
tosses her head as you flee.
22 Who is it you have ridiculed and
blasphemed?
Against whom have you raised your
voice
and lifted your eyes in pride?
Against the Holy One of Israel!
23 By your messengers
you have ridiculed the Lord.
And you have said,
"With my many chariots
I have ascended the heights of the
mountains,
the utmost heights of Lebanon.
I have cut down its tallest cedars,
the choicest of its junipers.
I have reached its remotest parts,
the finest of its forests.
24 I have dug wells in foreign lands
and drunk the water there.
With the soles of my feet
I have dried up all the streams of
Egypt."

25 "'Have you not heard?
Long ago I ordained it.
In days of old I planned it;
now I have brought it to pass,
that you have turned fortified cities
into piles of stone.
26 Their people, drained of power,
are dismayed and put to shame.
They are like plants in the field,
like tender green shoots,
like grass sprouting on the roof,
scorched before it grows up.

27 "'But I know where you are
and when you come and go
and how you rage against me.
28 Because you rage against me
and because your insolence has
reached my ears,
I will put my hook in your nose
and my bit in your mouth,
and I will make you return
by the way you came.'

29 "This will be the sign for you, Hezekiah:

"This year you will eat what grows by
itself,
and the second year what springs
from that.
But in the third year sow and reap,
plant vineyards and eat their fruit.
30 Once more a remnant of the kingdom
of Judah
will take root below and bear fruit
above.
31 For out of Jerusalem will come a
remnant,
and out of Mount Zion a band of
survivors.

"The zeal of the LORD Almighty will accomplish this.

32 "Therefore this is what the LORD says concerning the king of Assyria:

"'He will not enter this city
or shoot an arrow here.
He will not come before it with shield
or build a siege ramp against it.
33 By the way that he came he will
return;
he will not enter this city,
declares the LORD.
34 I will defend this city and save it,
for my sake and for the sake of David
my servant.'"

35 That night the angel of the LORD
went out and put to death a hundred
and eighty-five thousand in the Assyrian camp. When the people got up the
next morning—there were all the dead
bodies! 36 So Sennacherib king of Assyria
broke camp and withdrew. He returned
to Nineveh and stayed there.
37 One day, while he was worshiping
in the temple of his god Nisrok, his sons
Adrammelek and Sharezer killed him
with the sword, and they escaped to the
land of Ararat. And Esarhaddon his son
succeeded him as king.

20 In those days Hezekiah became ill
and was at the point of death. The
prophet Isaiah son of Amoz went to him
and said, "This is what the LORD says: Put
your house in order, because you are going to die; you will not recover."
2 Hezekiah turned his face to the wall
and prayed to the LORD, 3 "Remember,
LORD, how I have walked before you
faithfully and with wholehearted devotion and have done what is good in your
eyes." And Hezekiah wept bitterly.

4 Before Isaiah had left the middle
court, the word of the LORD came to him:
5 "Go back and tell Hezekiah, the ruler of
my people, 'This is what the LORD, the
God of your father David, says: I have
heard your prayer and seen your tears; I
will heal you. On the third day from now
you will go up to the temple of the LORD.
6 I will add fifteen years to your life. And
I will deliver you and this city from the
hand of the king of Assyria. I will defend
this city for my sake and for the sake of
my servant David.' "

7 Then Isaiah said, "Prepare a poultice
of figs." They did so and applied it to the
boil, and he recovered.

8 Hezekiah had asked Isaiah, "What
will be the sign that the LORD will heal
me and that I will go up to the temple of
the LORD on the third day from now?"

9 Isaiah answered, "This is the LORD's
sign to you that the LORD will do what
he has promised: Shall the shadow go
forward ten steps, or shall it go back ten
steps?"

10 "It is a simple matter for the shadow
to go forward ten steps," said Hezekiah.
"Rather, have it go back ten steps."

11 Then the prophet Isaiah called on the
LORD, and the LORD made the shadow go
back the ten steps it had gone down on
the stairway of Ahaz.

12 At that time Marduk-Baladan son of
Baladan king of Babylon sent Hezekiah
letters and a gift, because he had heard of
Hezekiah's illness. 13 Hezekiah received
the envoys and showed them all that was
in his storehouses—the silver, the gold,
the spices and the fine olive oil—his armory and everything found among his
treasures. There was nothing in his palace or in all his kingdom that Hezekiah
did not show them.

14 Then Isaiah the prophet went to
King Hezekiah and asked, "What did
those men say, and where did they come
from?"

"From a distant land," Hezekiah replied. "They came from Babylon."

15 The prophet asked, "What did they
see in your palace?"

"They saw everything in my palace,"
Hezekiah said. "There is nothing among
my treasures that I did not show them."

16 Then Isaiah said to Hezekiah, "Hear
the word of the LORD: 17 The time will
surely come when everything in your palace, and all that your predecessors have
stored up until this day, will be carried off
to Babylon. Nothing will be left, says the
LORD. 18 And some of your descendants,
your own flesh and blood who will be
born to you, will be taken away, and they
will become eunuchs in the palace of the
king of Babylon."

19 "The word of the LORD you have spoken is good," Hezekiah replied. For he
thought, "Will there not be peace and security in my lifetime?"

20 As for the other events of Hezekiah's
reign, all his achievements and how he
made the pool and the tunnel by which
he brought water into the city, are they
not written in the book of the annals of
the kings of Judah? 21 Hezekiah rested
with his ancestors. And Manasseh his
son succeeded him as king.

21 Manasseh was twelve years old
when he became king, and he
reigned in Jerusalem fifty-five years. His
mother's name was Hephzibah. 2 He did
evil in the eyes of the LORD, following
the detestable practices of the nations
the LORD had driven out before the Israelites. 3 He rebuilt the high places his
father Hezekiah had destroyed; he also
erected altars to Baal and made an Asherah pole, as Ahab king of Israel had done.
He bowed down to all the starry hosts
and worshiped them. 4 He built altars
in the temple of the LORD, of which the
LORD had said, "In Jerusalem I will put
my Name." 5 In the two courts of the temple of the LORD, he built altars to all the
starry hosts. 6 He sacrificed his own son
in the fire, practiced divination, sought
omens, and consulted mediums and
spiritists. He did much evil in the eyes of
the LORD, arousing his anger.

7 He took the carved Asherah pole he
had made and put it in the temple, of
which the LORD had said to David and
to his son Solomon, "In this temple and
in Jerusalem, which I have chosen out of
all the tribes of Israel, I will put my Name
forever. 8 I will not again make the feet
of the Israelites wander from the land I
gave their ancestors, if only they will be
careful to do everything I commanded
them and will keep the whole Law that
my servant Moses gave them." 9 But the
people did not listen. Manasseh led them
astray, so that they did more evil than the

nations the LORD had destroyed before
the Israelites.
10 The LORD said through his servants
the prophets: 11 "Manasseh king of Judah
has committed these detestable sins. He
has done more evil than the Amorites
who preceded him and has led Judah into
sin with his idols. 12 Therefore this is what
the LORD, the God of Israel, says: I am going to bring such disaster on Jerusalem
and Judah that the ears of everyone who
hears of it will tingle. 13 I will stretch out
over Jerusalem the measuring line used
against Samaria and the plumb line used
against the house of Ahab. I will wipe out
Jerusalem as one wipes a dish, wiping it
and turning it upside down. 14 I will forsake the remnant of my inheritance and
give them into the hands of enemies.
They will be looted and plundered by all
their enemies; 15 they have done evil in
my eyes and have aroused my anger from
the day their ancestors came out of Egypt
until this day."
16 Moreover, Manasseh also shed so
much innocent blood that he filled Jerusalem from end to end — besides the sin
that he had caused Judah to commit, so
that they did evil in the eyes of the LORD.
17 As for the other events of Manasseh's
reign, and all he did, including the sin he
committed, are they not written in the
book of the annals of the kings of Judah?
18 Manasseh rested with his ancestors
and was buried in his palace garden, the
garden of Uzza. And Amon his son succeeded him as king.

19 Amon was twenty-two years old
when he became king, and he reigned in
Jerusalem two years. His mother's name
was Meshullemeth daughter of Haruz;
she was from Jotbah. 20 He did evil in the
eyes of the LORD, as his father Manasseh
had done. 21 He followed completely the
ways of his father, worshiping the idols
his father had worshiped, and bowing
down to them. 22 He forsook the LORD, the
God of his ancestors, and did not walk in
obedience to him.
23 Amon's officials conspired against
him and assassinated the king in his palace. 24 Then the people of the land killed
all who had plotted against King Amon,
and they made Josiah his son king in his
place.
25 As for the other events of Amon's
reign, and what he did, are they not written in the book of the annals of the kings
of Judah? 26 He was buried in his tomb in
the garden of Uzza. And Josiah his son
succeeded him as king.

22 Josiah was eight years old when he
became king, and he reigned in Jerusalem thirty-one years. His mother's
name was Jedidah daughter of Adaiah;
she was from Bozkath. 2 He did what was
right in the eyes of the LORD and followed
completely the ways of his father David,
not turning aside to the right or to the
left.
3 In the eighteenth year of his reign,
King Josiah sent the secretary, Shaphan
son of Azaliah, the son of Meshullam,
to the temple of the LORD. He said: 4 "Go
up to Hilkiah the high priest and have
him get ready the money that has been
brought into the temple of the LORD,
which the doorkeepers have collected
from the people. 5 Have them entrust it
to the men appointed to supervise the
work on the temple. And have these men
pay the workers who repair the temple of
the LORD — 6 the carpenters, the builders and the masons. Also have them purchase timber and dressed stone to repair
the temple. 7 But they need not account
for the money entrusted to them, because
they are honest in their dealings."
8 Hilkiah the high priest said to Shaphan the secretary, "I have found the
Book of the Law in the temple of the
LORD." He gave it to Shaphan, who read
it. 9 Then Shaphan the secretary went to
the king and reported to him: "Your officials have paid out the money that was in
the temple of the LORD and have entrusted it to the workers and supervisors at the
temple." 10 Then Shaphan the secretary
informed the king, "Hilkiah the priest
has given me a book." And Shaphan read
from it in the presence of the king.
11 When the king heard the words of the
Book of the Law, he tore his robes. 12 He
gave these orders to Hilkiah the priest,
Ahikam son of Shaphan, Akbor son of Micaiah, Shaphan the secretary and Asaiah
the king's attendant: 13 "Go and inquire
of the LORD for me and for the people
and for all Judah about what is written
in this book that has been found. Great
is the LORD's anger that burns against us
because those who have gone before us

have not obeyed the words of this book;
they have not acted in accordance with
all that is written there concerning us."
14 Hilkiah the priest, Ahikam, Akbor,
Shaphan and Asaiah went to speak to
the prophet Huldah, who was the wife of
Shallum son of Tikvah, the son of Harhas,
keeper of the wardrobe. She lived in Jerusalem, in the New Quarter.
15 She said to them, "This is what the
LORD, the God of Israel, says: Tell the
man who sent you to me, 16 'This is what
the LORD says: I am going to bring disaster on this place and its people, according
to everything written in the book the king
of Judah has read. 17 Because they have
forsaken me and burned incense to other gods and aroused my anger by all the
idols their hands have made,[a] my anger
will burn against this place and will not
be quenched.' 18 Tell the king of Judah,
who sent you to inquire of the LORD, 'This
is what the LORD, the God of Israel, says
concerning the words you heard: 19 Because your heart was responsive and you
humbled yourself before the LORD when
you heard what I have spoken against this
place and its people—that they would
become a curse[b] and be laid waste—and
because you tore your robes and wept in
my presence, I also have heard you, declares the LORD. 20 Therefore I will gather you to your ancestors, and you will be
buried in peace. Your eyes will not see all
the disaster I am going to bring on this
place.'"
So they took her answer back to the
king.

23 Then the king called together all
the elders of Judah and Jerusalem.
2 He went up to the temple of the LORD
with the people of Judah, the inhabitants
of Jerusalem, the priests and the prophets—all the people from the least to the
greatest. He read in their hearing all the
words of the Book of the Covenant, which
had been found in the temple of the
LORD. 3 The king stood by the pillar and
renewed the covenant in the presence of
the LORD—to follow the LORD and keep
his commands, statutes and decrees
with all his heart and all his soul, thus
confirming the words of the covenant
written in this book. Then all the people
pledged themselves to the covenant.
4 The king ordered Hilkiah the high
priest, the priests next in rank and the
doorkeepers to remove from the temple
of the LORD all the articles made for Baal
and Asherah and all the starry hosts. He
burned them outside Jerusalem in the
fields of the Kidron Valley and took the
ashes to Bethel. 5 He did away with the
idolatrous priests appointed by the kings
of Judah to burn incense on the high
places of the towns of Judah and on those
around Jerusalem—those who burned
incense to Baal, to the sun and moon, to
the constellations and to all the starry
hosts. 6 He took the Asherah pole from the
temple of the LORD to the Kidron Valley
outside Jerusalem and burned it there.
He ground it to powder and scattered
the dust over the graves of the common
people. 7 He also tore down the quarters
of the male shrine prostitutes that were
in the temple of the LORD, the quarters
where women did weaving for Asherah.
8 Josiah brought all the priests from the
towns of Judah and desecrated the high
places, from Geba to Beersheba, where
the priests had burned incense. He broke
down the gateway at the entrance of the
Gate of Joshua, the city governor, which
was on the left of the city gate. 9 Although
the priests of the high places did not
serve at the altar of the LORD in Jerusalem, they ate unleavened bread with their
fellow priests.
10 He desecrated Topheth, which was in
the Valley of Ben Hinnom, so no one could
use it to sacrifice their son or daughter in
the fire to Molek. 11 He removed from the
entrance to the temple of the LORD the
horses that the kings of Judah had dedicated to the sun. They were in the court[c]
near the room of an official named Na-
than-Melek. Josiah then burned the
chariots dedicated to the sun.
12 He pulled down the altars the kings
of Judah had erected on the roof near the
upper room of Ahaz, and the altars Manasseh had built in the two courts of the
temple of the LORD. He removed them
from there, smashed them to pieces and
threw the rubble into the Kidron Valley. 13 The king also desecrated the high
places that were east of Jerusalem on the
south of the Hill of Corruption—the ones
Solomon king of Israel had built for Ash-

[a] *17* Or *by everything they have done* [b] *19* That is, their names would be used in cursing (see Jer. 29:22); or, others would see that they are cursed. [c] *11* The meaning of the Hebrew for this word is uncertain.

toreth the vile goddess of the Sidonians, for Chemosh the vile god of Moab, and for Molek the detestable god of the people of Ammon. 14 Josiah smashed the sacred stones and cut down the Asherah poles and covered the sites with human bones.

15 Even the altar at Bethel, the high place made by Jeroboam son of Nebat, who had caused Israel to sin—even that altar and high place he demolished. He burned the high place and ground it to powder, and burned the Asherah pole also. 16 Then Josiah looked around, and when he saw the tombs that were there on the hillside, he had the bones removed from them and burned on the altar to defile it, in accordance with the word of the LORD proclaimed by the man of God who foretold these things.

17 The king asked, "What is that tombstone I see?"

The people of the city said, "It marks the tomb of the man of God who came from Judah and pronounced against the altar of Bethel the very things you have done to it."

18 "Leave it alone," he said. "Don't let anyone disturb his bones." So they spared his bones and those of the prophet who had come from Samaria.

19 Just as he had done at Bethel, Josiah removed all the shrines at the high places that the kings of Israel had built in the towns of Samaria and that had aroused the LORD's anger. 20 Josiah slaughtered all the priests of those high places on the altars and burned human bones on them. Then he went back to Jerusalem.

21 The king gave this order to all the people: "Celebrate the Passover to the LORD your God, as it is written in this Book of the Covenant." 22 Neither in the days of the judges who led Israel nor in the days of the kings of Israel and the kings of Judah had any such Passover been observed. 23 But in the eighteenth year of King Josiah, this Passover was celebrated to the LORD in Jerusalem.

24 Furthermore, Josiah got rid of the mediums and spiritists, the household gods, the idols and all the other detestable things seen in Judah and Jerusalem. This he did to fulfill the requirements of the law written in the book that Hilkiah the priest had discovered in the temple of the LORD. 25 Neither before nor after Josiah was there a king like him who turned to the LORD as he did—with all his heart and with all his soul and with all his strength, in accordance with all the Law of Moses.

26 Nevertheless, the LORD did not turn away from the heat of his fierce anger, which burned against Judah because of all that Manasseh had done to arouse his anger. 27 So the LORD said, "I will remove Judah also from my presence as I removed Israel, and I will reject Jerusalem, the city I chose, and this temple, about which I said, 'My Name shall be there.'[a]"

28 As for the other events of Josiah's reign, and all he did, are they not written in the book of the annals of the kings of Judah?

29 While Josiah was king, Pharaoh Necho king of Egypt went up to the Euphrates River to help the king of Assyria. King Josiah marched out to meet him in battle, but Necho faced him and killed him at Megiddo. 30 Josiah's servants brought his body in a chariot from Megiddo to Jerusalem and buried him in his own tomb. And the people of the land took Jehoahaz son of Josiah and anointed him and made him king in place of his father.

31 Jehoahaz was twenty-three years old when he became king, and he reigned in Jerusalem three months. His mother's name was Hamutal daughter of Jeremiah; she was from Libnah. 32 He did evil in the eyes of the LORD, just as his predecessors had done. 33 Pharaoh Necho put him in chains at Riblah in the land of Hamath so that he might not reign in Jerusalem, and he imposed on Judah a levy of a hundred talents[b] of silver and a talent[c] of gold. 34 Pharaoh Necho made Eliakim son of Josiah king in place of his father Josiah and changed Eliakim's name to Jehoiakim. But he took Jehoahaz and carried him off to Egypt, and there he died. 35 Jehoiakim paid Pharaoh Necho the silver and gold he demanded. In order to do so, he taxed the land and exacted the silver and gold from the people of the land according to their assessments.

36 Jehoiakim was twenty-five years old when he became king, and he reigned

[a] *27* 1 Kings 8:29 [b] *33* That is, about 3 3/4 tons or about 3.4 metric tons [c] *33* That is, about 75 pounds or about 34 kilograms

in Jerusalem eleven years. His mother's
name was Zebidah daughter of Pedaiah;
she was from Rumah. 37 And he did evil in
the eyes of the LORD, just as his predecessors had done.

24 During Jehoiakim's reign, Nebuchadnezzar king of Babylon invaded the land, and Jehoiakim became his
vassal for three years. But then he turned
against Nebuchadnezzar and rebelled.
2 The LORD sent Babylonian,[a] Aramean,
Moabite and Ammonite raiders against
him to destroy Judah, in accordance
with the word of the LORD proclaimed by
his servants the prophets. 3 Surely these
things happened to Judah according to
the LORD's command, in order to remove
them from his presence because of the
sins of Manasseh and all he had done,
4 including the shedding of innocent
blood. For he had filled Jerusalem with
innocent blood, and the LORD was not
willing to forgive.

5 As for the other events of Jehoiakim's
reign, and all he did, are they not written
in the book of the annals of the kings of
Judah? 6 Jehoiakim rested with his ancestors. And Jehoiachin his son succeeded
him as king.

7 The king of Egypt did not march out
from his own country again, because the
king of Babylon had taken all his territory, from the Wadi of Egypt to the Euphrates River.

8 Jehoiachin was eighteen years old
when he became king, and he reigned
in Jerusalem three months. His mother's
name was Nehushta daughter of Elnathan; she was from Jerusalem. 9 He did
evil in the eyes of the LORD, just as his father had done.

10 At that time the officers of Nebuchadnezzar king of Babylon advanced
on Jerusalem and laid siege to it, 11 and
Nebuchadnezzar himself came up to the
city while his officers were besieging it.
12 Jehoiachin king of Judah, his mother,
his attendants, his nobles and his officials all surrendered to him.

In the eighth year of the reign of the
king of Babylon, he took Jehoiachin prisoner. 13 As the LORD had declared, Nebuchadnezzar removed the treasures from
the temple of the LORD and from the royal
palace, and cut up the gold articles that
Solomon king of Israel had made for the
temple of the LORD. 14 He carried all Jerusalem into exile: all the officers and fighting men, and all the skilled workers and
artisans—a total of ten thousand. Only
the poorest people of the land were left.

15 Nebuchadnezzar took Jehoiachin
captive to Babylon. He also took from
Jerusalem to Babylon the king's mother,
his wives, his officials and the prominent
people of the land. 16 The king of Babylon
also deported to Babylon the entire force
of seven thousand fighting men, strong
and fit for war, and a thousand skilled
workers and artisans. 17 He made Mattaniah, Jehoiachin's uncle, king in his place
and changed his name to Zedekiah.

18 Zedekiah was twenty-one years old
when he became king, and he reigned
in Jerusalem eleven years. His mother's
name was Hamutal daughter of Jeremiah; she was from Libnah. 19 He did evil in
the eyes of the LORD, just as Jehoiakim
had done. 20 It was because of the LORD's
anger that all this happened to Jerusalem
and Judah, and in the end he thrust them
from his presence.

Now Zedekiah rebelled against the
king of Babylon.

25 So in the ninth year of Zedekiah's
reign, on the tenth day of the tenth
month, Nebuchadnezzar king of Babylon marched against Jerusalem with his
whole army. He encamped outside the
city and built siege works all around it.
2 The city was kept under siege until the
eleventh year of King Zedekiah.

3 By the ninth day of the fourth[b] month
the famine in the city had become so severe that there was no food for the people to eat. 4 Then the city wall was broken through, and the whole army fled at
night through the gate between the two
walls near the king's garden, though the
Babylonians[c] were surrounding the city.
They fled toward the Arabah,[d] 5 but the
Babylonian[e] army pursued the king and
overtook him in the plains of Jericho. All
his soldiers were separated from him and
scattered, 6 and he was captured.

He was taken to the king of Babylon at

[a] 2 Or *Chaldean* [b] 3 Probable reading of the original Hebrew text (see Jer. 52:6); Masoretic Text does not have *fourth.* [c] 4 Or *Chaldeans*; also in verses 13, 25 and 26 [d] 4 Or *the Jordan Valley* [e] 5 Or *Chaldean*; also in verses 10 and 24

Riblah, where sentence was pronounced
on him. 7 They killed the sons of Zedekiah before his eyes. Then they put out his
eyes, bound him with bronze shackles
and took him to Babylon.
8 On the seventh day of the fifth month,
in the nineteenth year of Nebuchadnezzar king of Babylon, Nebuzaradan commander of the imperial guard, an official
of the king of Babylon, came to Jerusalem.
9 He set fire to the temple of the LORD, the
royal palace and all the houses of Jerusalem. Every important building he burned
down. 10 The whole Babylonian army under the commander of the imperial guard
broke down the walls around Jerusalem.
11 Nebuzaradan the commander of the
guard carried into exile the people who
remained in the city, along with the rest
of the populace and those who had deserted to the king of Babylon. 12 But the
commander left behind some of the
poorest people of the land to work
the vineyards and fields.
13 The Babylonians broke up the
bronze pillars, the movable stands and
the bronze Sea that were at the temple of
the LORD and they carried the bronze to
Babylon. 14 They also took away the pots,
shovels, wick trimmers, dishes and all
the bronze articles used in the temple
service. 15 The commander of the imperial guard took away the censers and sprinkling bowls — all that were made of pure
gold or silver.
16 The bronze from the two pillars, the
Sea and the movable stands, which Solomon had made for the temple of the
LORD, was more than could be weighed.
17 Each pillar was eighteen cubits[a] high.
The bronze capital on top of one pillar
was three cubits[b] high and was decorated with a network and pomegranates of
bronze all around. The other pillar, with
its network, was similar.
18 The commander of the guard took
as prisoners Seraiah the chief priest,
Zephaniah the priest next in rank and
the three doorkeepers. 19 Of those still in
the city, he took the officer in charge of
the fighting men, and five royal advisers.
He also took the secretary who was chief
officer in charge of conscripting the people of the land and sixty of the conscripts
who were found in the city. 20 Nebuzaradan the commander took them all and
brought them to the king of Babylon at
Riblah. 21 There at Riblah, in the land of
Hamath, the king had them executed.
So Judah went into captivity, away from
her land.
22 Nebuchadnezzar king of Babylon
appointed Gedaliah son of Ahikam, the
son of Shaphan, to be over the people he
had left behind in Judah. 23 When all the
army officers and their men heard that
the king of Babylon had appointed Gedaliah as governor, they came to Gedaliah
at Mizpah — Ishmael son of Nethaniah,
Johanan son of Kareah, Seraiah son of
Tanhumeth the Netophathite, Jaazaniah the son of the Maakathite, and their
men. 24 Gedaliah took an oath to reassure them and their men. "Do not be
afraid of the Babylonian officials," he
said. "Settle down in the land and serve
the king of Babylon, and it will go well
with you."
25 In the seventh month, however, Ishmael son of Nethaniah, the son of Elishama, who was of royal blood, came with
ten men and assassinated Gedaliah and
also the men of Judah and the Babylonians who were with him at Mizpah. 26 At
this, all the people from the least to the
greatest, together with the army officers,
fled to Egypt for fear of the Babylonians.

27 In the thirty-seventh year of the exile of Jehoiachin king of Judah, in the year
Awel-Marduk became king of Babylon,
he released Jehoiachin king of Judah
from prison. He did this on the twenty-
seventh day of the twelfth month. 28 He
spoke kindly to him and gave him a seat
of honor higher than those of the other kings who were with him in Babylon.
29 So Jehoiachin put aside his prison
clothes and for the rest of his life ate regularly at the king's table. 30 Day by day the
king gave Jehoiachin a regular allowance
as long as he lived.

[a] *17* That is, about 27 feet or about 8.1 meters [b] *17* That is, about 4 1/2 feet or about 1.4 meters

1 CHRONICLES

In the fifth century BC, many Judeans were returning from exile to the southern part of the land of Israel. They faced great difficulties: their capital city and temple had been destroyed, foreigners had moved in, and they were no longer ruled by their own king. But the books of Chronicles, Ezra and Nehemiah insist that God's people can still fulfill his purpose. They must form a unique society centered on the worship of God in a rebuilt temple in Jerusalem. (These books are really one long book, telling a continuous story; one can see, for example, how the end of 2 Chronicles overlaps with the beginning of Ezra.)

The book presents a sweeping chronicle of Israel's history, beginning with a long genealogy or ancestor list. Going all the way back to Adam, it situates the people of Israel among the nations and reminds them of their calling. Special attention is given to Judah, ancestor of the royal line of David, and to Levi, ancestor of the priests and temple attendants.

The second main part describes the kings who ruled in Jerusalem down to the time of the exile. David receives more attention than others, but many details of his life told elsewhere are left out. The focus is on his military campaigns and his elaborate plans for the temple in Jerusalem. The reason is clear when we see that David was not permitted to build the temple because he was a warrior. God wanted a man of peace to build the place where all nations would come to pray. The honor therefore fell to David's son Solomon. More space is devoted to him than to any king besides David, describing his construction of the temple and the splendors of his reign.

The final part of the book relates the experiences of the returned exiles. The memoirs of Ezra and Nehemiah, leaders of the second generation of returned Judeans, are incorporated into the history. These leaders helped create a distinct community by forbidding intermarriage with the surrounding peoples, and they directed the rebuilding of Jerusalem's walls. Included here is a description of a great covenant renewal ceremony led by Ezra and Nehemiah.

An important theme of the entire history—which can appropriately be called a temple history—is that pure worship is offered on God's terms, not ours. God has chosen Israel to welcome the nations into true worship. Through all the ups and downs of history he is working to bring this purpose to fulfillment.

---

1 Adam, Seth, Enosh, 2 Kenan, Mahalalel, Jared, 3 Enoch, Methuselah, Lamech, Noah.

4 The sons of Noah:[a]
Shem, Ham and Japheth.

5 The sons[b] of Japheth:
Gomer, Magog, Madai, Javan, Tubal, Meshek and Tiras.
6 The sons of Gomer:
Ashkenaz, Riphath[c] and Togarmah.
7 The sons of Javan:
Elishah, Tarshish, the Kittites and the Rodanites.

8 The sons of Ham:
Cush, Egypt, Put and Canaan.
9 The sons of Cush:
Seba, Havilah, Sabta, Raamah and Sabteka.
The sons of Raamah:
Sheba and Dedan.
10 Cush was the father[d] of
Nimrod, who became a mighty warrior on earth.
11 Egypt was the father of
the Ludites, Anamites, Lehabites, Naphtuhites, 12 Pathrusites, Kasluhites (from whom the Philistines came) and Caphtorites.
13 Canaan was the father of
Sidon his firstborn,[e] and of the Hittites, 14 Jebusites, Amorites, Girgashites, 15 Hivites, Arkites, Sinites, 16 Arvadites, Zemarites and Hamathites.

[a] *4* Septuagint; Hebrew does not have this line. [b] *5* *Sons* may mean *descendants* or *successors* or *nations*; also in verses 6-9, 17 and 23. [c] *6* Many Hebrew manuscripts and Vulgate (see also Septuagint and Gen. 10:3); most Hebrew manuscripts *Diphath* [d] *10* *Father* may mean *ancestor* or *predecessor* or *founder*; also in verses 11, 13, 18 and 20. [e] *13* Or *of the Sidonians, the foremost*

17 The sons of Shem:
Elam, Ashur, Arphaxad, Lud and
Aram.
The sons of Aram:[a]
Uz, Hul, Gether and Meshek.
18 Arphaxad was the father of Shelah,
and Shelah the father of Eber.
19 Two sons were born to Eber:
One was named Peleg,[b] because in
his time the earth was divided; his
brother was named Joktan.
20 Joktan was the father of
Almodad, Sheleph, Hazarmaveth,
Jerah, 21 Hadoram, Uzal, Diklah,
22 Obal,[c] Abimael, Sheba, 23 Ophir,
Havilah and Jobab. All these were
sons of Joktan.

24 Shem, Arphaxad,[d] Shelah,
25 Eber, Peleg, Reu,
26 Serug, Nahor, Terah
27 and Abram (that is, Abraham).

28 The sons of Abraham:
Isaac and Ishmael.

29 These were their descendants:
Nebaioth the firstborn of Ishmael,
Kedar, Adbeel, Mibsam, 30 Mish-
ma, Dumah, Massa, Hadad, Tema,
31 Jetur, Naphish and Kedemah.
These were the sons of Ishmael.

32 The sons born to Keturah, Abraham's
concubine:
Zimran, Jokshan, Medan, Midian,
Ishbak and Shuah.
The sons of Jokshan:
Sheba and Dedan.
33 The sons of Midian:
Ephah, Epher, Hanok, Abida and
Eldaah.
All these were descendants of Ketu-
rah.
34 Abraham was the father of Isaac.
The sons of Isaac:
Esau and Israel.

35 The sons of Esau:
Eliphaz, Reuel, Jeush, Jalam and
Korah.
36 The sons of Eliphaz:
Teman, Omar, Zepho,[e] Gatam and
Kenaz;
by Timna: Amalek.[f]
37 The sons of Reuel:
Nahath, Zerah, Shammah and
Mizzah.

38 The sons of Seir:
Lotan, Shobal, Zibeon, Anah, Di-
shon, Ezer and Dishan.
39 The sons of Lotan:
Hori and Homam. Timna was Lo-
tan's sister.
40 The sons of Shobal:
Alvan,[g] Manahath, Ebal, Shepho
and Onam.
The sons of Zibeon:
Aiah and Anah.
41 The son of Anah:
Dishon.
The sons of Dishon:
Hemdan,[h] Eshban, Ithran and Ke-
ran.
42 The sons of Ezer:
Bilhan, Zaavan and Akan.[i]
The sons of Dishan[j]:
Uz and Aran.

43 These were the kings who reigned
in Edom before any Israelite king
reigned:
Bela son of Beor, whose city was
named Dinhabah.
44 When Bela died, Jobab son of Zerah
from Bozrah succeeded him as
king.
45 When Jobab died, Husham from the
land of the Temanites succeeded
him as king.
46 When Husham died, Hadad son of
Bedad, who defeated Midian in the
country of Moab, succeeded him
as king. His city was named Avith.
47 When Hadad died, Samlah from
Masrekah succeeded him as king.
48 When Samlah died, Shaul from Re-

[a] *17* One Hebrew manuscript and some Septuagint manuscripts (see also Gen. 10:23); most Hebrew manuscripts do not have this line. [b] *19* *Peleg* means *division.* [c] *22* Some Hebrew manuscripts and Syriac (see also Gen. 10:28); most Hebrew manuscripts *Ebal* [d] *24* Hebrew; some Septuagint manuscripts *Arphaxad, Cainan* (see also note at Gen. 11:10) [e] *36* Many Hebrew manuscripts, some Septuagint manuscripts and Syriac (see also Gen. 36:11); most Hebrew manuscripts *Zephi* [f] *36* Some Septuagint manuscripts (see also Gen. 36:12); Hebrew *Gatam, Kenaz, Timna and Amalek* [g] *40* Many Hebrew manuscripts and some Septuagint manuscripts (see also Gen. 36:23); most Hebrew manuscripts *Alian* [h] *41* Many Hebrew manuscripts and some Septuagint manuscripts (see also Gen. 36:26); most Hebrew manuscripts *Hamran* [i] *42* Many Hebrew and Septuagint manuscripts (see also Gen. 36:27); most Hebrew manuscripts *Zaavan, Jaakan* [j] *42* See Gen. 36:28; Hebrew *Dishon,* a variant of *Dishan*

hoboth on the river[a] succeeded
him as king.
49 When Shaul died, Baal-Hanan son of
Akbor succeeded him as king.
50 When Baal-Hanan died, Hadad succeeded him as king. His city was
named Pau,[b] and his wife's name
was Mehetabel daughter of Matred, the daughter of Me-Zahab.
51 Hadad also died.

The chiefs of Edom were:
Timna, Alvah, Jetheth, 52 Oholibamah, Elah, Pinon, 53 Kenaz, Teman, Mibzar, 54 Magdiel and Iram.
These were the chiefs of Edom.

2 These were the sons of Israel:
Reuben, Simeon, Levi, Judah, Issachar, Zebulun, 2 Dan, Joseph, Benjamin, Naphtali, Gad and Asher.

3 The sons of Judah:
Er, Onan and Shelah. These three
were born to him by a Canaanite
woman, the daughter of Shua. Er,
Judah's firstborn, was wicked in
the LORD's sight; so the LORD put
him to death. 4 Judah's daughter-
in-law Tamar bore Perez and Zerah to Judah. He had five sons in
all.
5 The sons of Perez:
Hezron and Hamul.
6 The sons of Zerah:
Zimri, Ethan, Heman, Kalkol and
Darda[c]—five in all.
7 The son of Karmi:
Achar,[d] who brought trouble on Israel by violating the ban on taking
devoted things.[e]
8 The son of Ethan:
Azariah.
9 The sons born to Hezron were:
Jerahmeel, Ram and Caleb.[f]
10 Ram was the father of
Amminadab, and Amminadab the
father of Nahshon, the leader of the
people of Judah. 11 Nahshon was
the father of Salmon,[g] Salmon the
father of Boaz, 12 Boaz the father of
Obed and Obed the father of Jesse.
13 Jesse was the father of
Eliab his firstborn; the second son
was Abinadab, the third Shimea,
14 the fourth Nethanel, the fifth
Raddai, 15 the sixth Ozem and the
seventh David. 16 Their sisters were
Zeruiah and Abigail. Zeruiah's
three sons were Abishai, Joab and
Asahel. 17 Abigail was the mother
of Amasa, whose father was Jether
the Ishmaelite.
18 Caleb son of Hezron had children by
his wife Azubah (and by Jerioth).
These were her sons: Jesher, Shobab and Ardon. 19 When Azubah
died, Caleb married Ephrath, who
bore him Hur. 20 Hur was the father
of Uri, and Uri the father of Bezalel.
21 Later, Hezron, when he was sixty
years old, married the daughter
of Makir the father of Gilead. He
made love to her, and she bore him
Segub. 22 Segub was the father of
Jair, who controlled twenty-three
towns in Gilead. 23 (But Geshur and
Aram captured Havvoth Jair,[h] as
well as Kenath with its surrounding settlements—sixty towns.) All
these were descendants of Makir
the father of Gilead.
24 After Hezron died in Caleb Ephrathah, Abijah the wife of Hezron
bore him Ashhur the father[i] of Tekoa.
25 The sons of Jerahmeel the firstborn
of Hezron:
Ram his firstborn, Bunah, Oren,
Ozem and[j] Ahijah. 26 Jerahmeel had another wife, whose name
was Atarah; she was the mother of
Onam.
27 The sons of Ram the firstborn of Jerahmeel:
Maaz, Jamin and Eker.
28 The sons of Onam:
Shammai and Jada.

[a] *48* Possibly the Euphrates [b] *50* Many Hebrew manuscripts, some Septuagint manuscripts, Vulgate and Syriac (see also Gen. 36:39); most Hebrew manuscripts *Pai* [c] *6* Many Hebrew manuscripts, some Septuagint manuscripts and Syriac (see also 1 Kings 4:31); most Hebrew manuscripts *Dara* [d] *7 Achar* means *trouble; Achar* is called *Achan* in Joshua. [e] *7* The Hebrew term refers to the irrevocable giving over of things or persons to the LORD, often by totally destroying them. [f] *9* Hebrew *Kelubai,* a variant of *Caleb* [g] *11* Septuagint (see also Ruth 4:21); Hebrew *Salma* [h] *23* Or *captured the settlements of Jair* [i] *24 Father* may mean *civic leader* or *military leader*; also in verses 42, 45, 49-52 and possibly elsewhere. [j] *25* Or *Oren and Ozem, by*

The sons of Shammai:
Nadab and Abishur.
29 Abishur's wife was named Abihail,
who bore him Ahban and Molid.
30 The sons of Nadab:
Seled and Appaim. Seled died
without children.
31 The son of Appaim:
Ishi, who was the father of Sheshan.
Sheshan was the father of Ahlai.
32 The sons of Jada, Shammai's brother:
Jether and Jonathan. Jether died
without children.
33 The sons of Jonathan:
Peleth and Zaza.
These were the descendants of Jerahmeel.
34 Sheshan had no sons — only daughters.
He had an Egyptian servant named
Jarha. 35 Sheshan gave his daughter
in marriage to his servant Jarha,
and she bore him Attai.
36 Attai was the father of Nathan,
Nathan the father of Zabad,
37 Zabad the father of Ephlal,
Ephlal the father of Obed,
38 Obed the father of Jehu,
Jehu the father of Azariah,
39 Azariah the father of Helez,
Helez the father of Eleasah,
40 Eleasah the father of Sismai,
Sismai the father of Shallum,
41 Shallum the father of Jekamiah,
and Jekamiah the father of Elishama.
42 The sons of Caleb the brother of Jerahmeel:
Mesha his firstborn, who was the
father of Ziph, and his son Mareshah,[a] who was the father of Hebron.
43 The sons of Hebron:
Korah, Tappuah, Rekem and Shema.
44 Shema was the father of Raham,
and Raham the father of Jorkeam.
Rekem was the father of Shammai.
45 The son of Shammai was Maon,
and Maon was the father of Beth
Zur.
46 Caleb's concubine Ephah was the
mother of Haran, Moza and Gazez.
Haran was the father of Gazez.
47 The sons of Jahdai:
Regem, Jotham, Geshan, Pelet,
Ephah and Shaaph.
48 Caleb's concubine Maakah was the
mother of Sheber and Tirhanah.
49 She also gave birth to Shaaph
the father of Madmannah and to
Sheva the father of Makbenah and
Gibea. Caleb's daughter was Aksah. 50 These were the descendants
of Caleb.

The sons of Hur the firstborn of Ephrathah:
Shobal the father of Kiriath Jearim,
51 Salma the father of Bethlehem,
and Hareph the father of Beth Ga-
der.
52 The descendants of Shobal the father
of Kiriath Jearim were:
Haroeh, half the Manahathites,
53 and the clans of Kiriath Jearim:
the Ithrites, Puthites, Shumathites
and Mishraites. From these descended the Zorathites and Eshta-
olites.
54 The descendants of Salma:
Bethlehem, the Netophathites, Atroth Beth Joab, half the Manahathites, the Zorites, 55 and the clans of
scribes[b] who lived at Jabez: the
Tirathites, Shimeathites and Su-
cathites. These are the Kenites
who came from Hammath, the father of the Rekabites.[c]

3 These were the sons of David born to
him in Hebron:
The firstborn was Amnon the son
of Ahinoam of Jezreel;
the second, Daniel the son of Abigail of Carmel;
2 the third, Absalom the son of Maakah daughter of Talmai king of
Geshur;
the fourth, Adonijah the son of
Haggith;
3 the fifth, Shephatiah the son of
Abital;
and the sixth, Ithream, by his wife
Eglah.
4 These six were born to David in
Hebron, where he reigned seven
years and six months.
David reigned in Jerusalem thirty-three

[a] *42* The meaning of the Hebrew for this phrase is uncertain. [b] *55* Or *of the Sopherites* [c] *55* Or *father of Beth Rekab*

years, 5 and these were the children born
to him there:
Shammua,[a] Shobab, Nathan and
Solomon. These four were by
Bathsheba[b] daughter of Ammiel.
6 There were also Ibhar, Elishua,[c]
Eliphelet, 7 Nogah, Nepheg, Japhia,
8 Elishama, Eliada and Eliphelet—
nine in all. 9 All these were the sons
of David, besides his sons by his
concubines. And Tamar was their
sister.

10 Solomon's son was Rehoboam,
Abijah his son,
Asa his son,
Jehoshaphat his son,
11 Jehoram[d] his son,
Ahaziah his son,
Joash his son,
12 Amaziah his son,
Azariah his son,
Jotham his son,
13 Ahaz his son,
Hezekiah his son,
Manasseh his son,
14 Amon his son,
Josiah his son.
15 The sons of Josiah:
Johanan the firstborn,
Jehoiakim the second son,
Zedekiah the third,
Shallum the fourth.
16 The successors of Jehoiakim:
Jehoiachin[e] his son,
and Zedekiah.

17 The descendants of Jehoiachin the
captive:
Shealtiel his son, 18 Malkiram, Pedaiah, Shenazzar, Jekamiah, Hosh-
ama and Nedabiah.
19 The sons of Pedaiah:
Zerubbabel and Shimei.
The sons of Zerubbabel:
Meshullam and Hananiah.
Shelomith was their sister.
20 There were also five others:
Hashubah, Ohel, Berekiah, Hasa-
diah and Jushab-Hesed.
21 The descendants of Hananiah:
Pelatiah and Jeshaiah, and the sons
of Rephaiah, of Arnan, of Obadiah
and of Shekaniah.
22 The descendants of Shekaniah:
Shemaiah and his sons:
Hattush, Igal, Bariah, Neariah and
Shaphat—six in all.
23 The sons of Neariah:
Elioenai, Hizkiah and Azrikam—
three in all.
24 The sons of Elioenai:
Hodaviah, Eliashib, Pelaiah, Akkub, Johanan, Delaiah and Ana-
ni—seven in all.

4 The descendants of Judah:
Perez, Hezron, Karmi, Hur and
Shobal.
2 Reaiah son of Shobal was the father
of Jahath, and Jahath the father of
Ahumai and Lahad. These were
the clans of the Zorathites.
3 These were the sons[f] of Etam:
Jezreel, Ishma and Idbash. Their
sister was named Hazzelelponi.
4 Penuel was the father of Gedor,
and Ezer the father of Hushah.
These were the descendants of Hur,
the firstborn of Ephrathah and father[g] of Bethlehem.
5 Ashhur the father of Tekoa had two
wives, Helah and Naarah.
6 Naarah bore him Ahuzzam, Hepher,
Temeni and Haahashtari. These
were the descendants of Naarah.
7 The sons of Helah:
Zereth, Zohar, Ethnan, 8 and Koz,
who was the father of Anub and
Hazzobebah and of the clans of
Aharhel son of Harum.

9 Jabez was more honorable than his
brothers. His mother had named him
Jabez,[h] saying, "I gave birth to him in
pain." 10 Jabez cried out to the God of Israel, "Oh, that you would bless me and
enlarge my territory! Let your hand be
with me, and keep me from harm so that
I will be free from pain." And God granted his request.

11 Kelub, Shuhah's brother, was the father of Mehir, who was the father
of Eshton. 12 Eshton was the father

[a] *5* Hebrew *Shimea,* a variant of *Shammua* [b] *5* One Hebrew manuscript and Vulgate (see also Septuagint and 2 Samuel 11:3); most Hebrew manuscripts *Bathshua* [c] *6* Two Hebrew manuscripts (see also 2 Samuel 5:15 and 1 Chron. 14:5); most Hebrew manuscripts *Elishama* [d] *11* Hebrew *Joram,* a variant of *Jehoram* [e] *16* Hebrew *Jeconiah,* a variant of *Jehoiachin*; also in verse 17 [f] *3* Some Septuagint manuscripts (see also Vulgate); Hebrew *father* [g] *4* *Father* may mean *civic leader* or *military leader*; also in verses 12, 14, 17, 18 and possibly elsewhere. [h] *9* *Jabez* sounds like the Hebrew for *pain.*

of Beth Rapha, Paseah and Tehinnah the father of Ir Nahash.[a] These were the men of Rekah.

13 The sons of Kenaz:
Othniel and Seraiah.
The sons of Othniel:
Hathath and Meonothai.[b] 14 Meon-
othai was the father of Ophrah.
Seraiah was the father of Joab,
the father of Ge Harashim.[c] It was called this because its people were skilled workers.
15 The sons of Caleb son of Jephunneh:
Iru, Elah and Naam.
The son of Elah:
Kenaz.
16 The sons of Jehallelel:
Ziph, Ziphah, Tiria and Asarel.
17 The sons of Ezrah:
Jether, Mered, Epher and Jalon.
One of Mered's wives gave birth
to Miriam, Shammai and Ishbah
the father of Eshtemoa. 18 (His wife
from the tribe of Judah gave birth
to Jered the father of Gedor, Heber
the father of Soko, and Jekuthiel the
father of Zanoah.) These were the
children of Pharaoh's daughter Bithiah, whom Mered had married.
19 The sons of Hodiah's wife, the sister of Naham:
the father of Keilah the Garmite, and Eshtemoa the Maakathite.
20 The sons of Shimon:
Amnon, Rinnah, Ben-Hanan and Tilon.
The descendants of Ishi:
Zoheth and Ben-Zoheth.
21 The sons of Shelah son of Judah:
Er the father of Lekah, Laadah the
father of Mareshah and the clans of
the linen workers at Beth Ashbea,
22 Jokim, the men of Kozeba, and Joash and Saraph, who ruled in Moab
and Jashubi Lehem. (These records
are from ancient times.) 23 They
were the potters who lived at Netaim and Gederah; they stayed there and worked for the king.

24 The descendants of Simeon:
Nemuel, Jamin, Jarib, Zerah and Shaul;
25 Shallum was Shaul's son, Mibsam his son and Mishma his son.
26 The descendants of Mishma:
Hammuel his son, Zakkur his son and Shimei his son.

27 Shimei had sixteen sons and six
daughters, but his brothers did not have
many children; so their entire clan did
not become as numerous as the people of
Judah. 28 They lived in Beersheba, Moladah, Hazar Shual, 29 Bilhah, Ezem, To-
lad, 30 Bethuel, Hormah, Ziklag, 31 Beth
Markaboth, Hazar Susim, Beth Biri and
Shaaraim. These were their towns until
the reign of David. 32 Their surrounding
villages were Etam, Ain, Rimmon, Token
and Ashan — five towns — 33 and all the
villages around these towns as far as Baalath.[d] These were their settlements. And they kept a genealogical record.

34 Meshobab, Jamlech, Joshah son
of Amaziah, 35 Joel, Jehu son of Josh-
ibiah, the son of Seraiah, the son of
Asiel, 36 also Elioenai, Jaakobah,
Jeshohaiah, Asaiah, Adiel, Jesimiel,
Benaiah, 37 and Ziza son of Shiphi,
the son of Allon, the son of Jedaiah, the son of Shimri, the son of Shemaiah.

38 The men listed above by name were
leaders of their clans. Their families increased greatly, 39 and they went to the
outskirts of Gedor to the east of the valley in search of pasture for their flocks.
40 They found rich, good pasture, and the land was spacious, peaceful and quiet. Some Hamites had lived there formerly.
41 The men whose names were listed came in the days of Hezekiah king of Judah. They attacked the Hamites in their dwellings and also the Meunites who were there and completely destroyed[e] them, as is evident to this day. Then they
settled in their place, because there was
pasture for their flocks. 42 And five hundred of these Simeonites, led by Pelatiah,
Neariah, Rephaiah and Uzziel, the sons
of Ishi, invaded the hill country of Seir.
43 They killed the remaining Amalekites who had escaped, and they have lived there to this day.

[a] *12* Or *of the city of Nahash* [b] *13* Some Septuagint manuscripts and Vulgate; Hebrew does not have *and Meonothai.* [c] *14* *Ge Harashim* means *valley of skilled workers.* [d] *33* Some Septuagint manuscripts (see also Joshua 19:8); Hebrew *Baal* [e] *41* The Hebrew term refers to the irrevocable giving over of things or persons to the LORD, often by totally destroying them.

5 The sons of Reuben the firstborn of Israel (he was the firstborn, but when he defiled his father's marriage bed, his rights as firstborn were given to the sons of Joseph son of Israel; so he could not be listed in the genealogical record in accordance with his birthright, 2 and though Judah was the strongest of his brothers and a ruler came from him, the rights of the firstborn belonged to Joseph)— 3 the sons of Reuben the firstborn of Israel:

Hanok, Pallu, Hezron and Karmi.

4 The descendants of Joel:

Shemaiah his son, Gog his son,
Shimei his son, 5 Micah his son,
Reaiah his son, Baal his son,
6 and Beerah his son, whom Tiglath-Pileser[a] king of Assyria took into exile. Beerah was a leader of the Reubenites.

7 Their relatives by clans, listed according to their genealogical records:

Jeiel the chief, Zechariah, 8 and Bela son of Azaz, the son of Shema, the son of Joel. They settled in the area from Aroer to Nebo and Baal Meon. 9 To the east they occupied the land up to the edge of the desert that extends to the Euphrates River, because their livestock had increased in Gilead.

10 During Saul's reign they waged war against the Hagrites, who were defeated at their hands; they occupied the dwellings of the Hagrites throughout the entire region east of Gilead.

11 The Gadites lived next to them in Bashan, as far as Salekah:

12 Joel was the chief, Shapham the second, then Janai and Shaphat, in Bashan.

13 Their relatives, by families, were:

Michael, Meshullam, Sheba, Jorai, Jakan, Zia and Eber—seven in all.

14 These were the sons of Abihail son of Huri, the son of Jaroah, the son of Gilead, the son of Michael, the son of Jeshishai, the son of Jahdo, the son of Buz.

15 Ahi son of Abdiel, the son of Guni, was head of their family.

16 The Gadites lived in Gilead, in Bashan and its outlying villages, and on all the pasturelands of Sharon as far as they extended.

17 All these were entered in the genealogical records during the reigns of Jotham king of Judah and Jeroboam king of Israel.

18 The Reubenites, the Gadites and the half-tribe of Manasseh had 44,760 men ready for military service—able-bodied men who could handle shield and sword, who could use a bow, and who were trained for battle. 19 They waged war against the Hagrites, Jetur, Naphish and Nodab. 20 They were helped in fighting them, and God delivered the Hagrites and all their allies into their hands, because they cried out to him during the battle. He answered their prayers, because they trusted in him. 21 They seized the livestock of the Hagrites—fifty thousand camels, two hundred fifty thousand sheep and two thousand donkeys. They also took one hundred thousand people captive, 22 and many others fell slain, because the battle was God's. And they occupied the land until the exile.

23 The people of the half-tribe of Manasseh were numerous; they settled in the land from Bashan to Baal Hermon, that is, to Senir (Mount Hermon).

24 These were the heads of their families: Epher, Ishi, Eliel, Azriel, Jeremiah, Hodaviah and Jahdiel. They were brave warriors, famous men, and heads of their families. 25 But they were unfaithful to the God of their ancestors and prostituted themselves to the gods of the peoples of the land, whom God had destroyed before them. 26 So the God of Israel stirred up the spirit of Pul king of Assyria (that is, Tiglath-Pileser king of Assyria), who took the Reubenites, the Gadites and the half-tribe of Manasseh into exile. He took them to Halah, Habor, Hara and the river of Gozan, where they are to this day.

6[b] The sons of Levi:

Gershon, Kohath and Merari.

2 The sons of Kohath:

Amram, Izhar, Hebron and Uzziel.

3 The children of Amram:

Aaron, Moses and Miriam.

The sons of Aaron:

[a] 6 Hebrew *Tilgath-Pilneser,* a variant of *Tiglath-Pileser;* also in verse 26 [b] In Hebrew texts 6:1-15 is numbered 5:27-41, and 6:16-81 is numbered 6:1-66.

Nadab, Abihu, Eleazar and Ithamar.
4 Eleazar was the father of Phinehas,
Phinehas the father of Abishua,
5 Abishua the father of Bukki,
Bukki the father of Uzzi,
6 Uzzi the father of Zerahiah,
Zerahiah the father of Meraioth,
7 Meraioth the father of Amariah,
Amariah the father of Ahitub,
8 Ahitub the father of Zadok,
Zadok the father of Ahimaaz,
9 Ahimaaz the father of Azariah,
Azariah the father of Johanan,
10 Johanan the father of Azariah (it was he who served as priest in the temple Solomon built in Jerusalem),
11 Azariah the father of Amariah,
Amariah the father of Ahitub,
12 Ahitub the father of Zadok,
Zadok the father of Shallum,
13 Shallum the father of Hilkiah,
Hilkiah the father of Azariah,
14 Azariah the father of Seraiah,
and Seraiah the father of Jozadak.[a]
15 Jozadak was deported when the LORD sent Judah and Jerusalem into exile by the hand of Nebuchadnezzar.

16 The sons of Levi:
Gershon,[b] Kohath and Merari.
17 These are the names of the sons of Gershon:
Libni and Shimei.
18 The sons of Kohath:
Amram, Izhar, Hebron and Uzziel.
19 The sons of Merari:
Mahli and Mushi.
These are the clans of the Levites listed according to their fathers:
20 Of Gershon:
Libni his son, Jahath his son,
Zimmah his son, 21 Joah his son,
Iddo his son, Zerah his son
and Jeatherai his son.
22 The descendants of Kohath:
Amminadab his son, Korah his son,
Assir his son, 23 Elkanah his son,
Ebiasaph his son, Assir his son,
24 Tahath his son, Uriel his son,
Uzziah his son and Shaul his son.
25 The descendants of Elkanah:
Amasai, Ahimoth,
26 Elkanah his son,[c] Zophai his son,
Nahath his son, 27 Eliab his son,
Jeroham his son, Elkanah his son
and Samuel his son.[d]
28 The sons of Samuel:
Joel[e] the firstborn
and Abijah the second son.
29 The descendants of Merari:
Mahli, Libni his son,
Shimei his son, Uzzah his son,
30 Shimea his son, Haggiah his son
and Asaiah his son.

31 These are the men David put in
charge of the music in the house of the
LORD after the ark came to rest there.
32 They ministered with music before
the tabernacle, the tent of meeting, until Solomon built the temple of the LORD in Jerusalem. They performed their duties according to the regulations laid down for them.
33 Here are the men who served, together with their sons:
From the Kohathites:
Heman, the musician,
the son of Joel, the son of Samuel,
34 the son of Elkanah, the son of Jeroham,
the son of Eliel, the son of Toah,
35 the son of Zuph, the son of Elkanah,
the son of Mahath, the son of Amasai,
36 the son of Elkanah, the son of Joel,
the son of Azariah, the son of Zephaniah,
37 the son of Tahath, the son of Assir,
the son of Ebiasaph, the son of Korah,
38 the son of Izhar, the son of Kohath,
the son of Levi, the son of Israel;
39 and Heman's associate Asaph, who served at his right hand:
Asaph son of Berekiah, the son of Shimea,
40 the son of Michael, the son of Baaseiah,[f]

[a] *14* Hebrew *Jehozadak*, a variant of *Jozadak*; also in verse 15 [b] *16* Hebrew *Gershom*, a variant of *Gershon*; also in verses 17, 20, 43, 62 and 71 [c] *26* Some Hebrew manuscripts, Septuagint and Syriac; most Hebrew manuscripts *Ahimoth* [26]*and Elkanah. The sons of Elkanah:* [d] *27* Some Septuagint manuscripts (see also 1 Samuel 1:19,20 and 1 Chron. 6:33,34); Hebrew does not have *and Samuel his son.* [e] *28* Some Septuagint manuscripts and Syriac (see also 1 Samuel 8:2 and 1 Chron. 6:33); Hebrew does not have *Joel.* [f] *40* Most Hebrew manuscripts; some Hebrew manuscripts, one Septuagint manuscript and Syriac *Maaseiah*

the son of Malkijah, 41 the son of
Ethni,
the son of Zerah, the son of Adaiah,
42 the son of Ethan, the son of Zimmah,
the son of Shimei, 43 the son of Jahath,
the son of Gershon, the son of
Levi;
44 and from their associates, the Merarites, at his left hand:
Ethan son of Kishi, the son of
Abdi,
the son of Malluk, 45 the son of
Hashabiah,
the son of Amaziah, the son of Hilkiah,
46 the son of Amzi, the son of Bani,
the son of Shemer, 47 the son of
Mahli,
the son of Mushi, the son of Merari,
the son of Levi.

48 Their fellow Levites were assigned
to all the other duties of the tabernacle,
the house of God. 49 But Aaron and his
descendants were the ones who presented offerings on the altar of burnt offering
and on the altar of incense in connection
with all that was done in the Most Holy
Place, making atonement for Israel, in accordance with all that Moses the servant
of God had commanded.

50 These were the descendants of Aaron:
Eleazar his son, Phinehas his son,
Abishua his son, 51 Bukki his son,
Uzzi his son, Zerahiah his son,
52 Meraioth his son, Amariah his
son,
Ahitub his son, 53 Zadok his son
and Ahimaaz his son.

54 These were the locations of their settlements allotted as their territory (they
were assigned to the descendants of Aaron who were from the Kohathite clan, because the first lot was for them):
55 They were given Hebron in Judah with its surrounding pasturelands. 56 But the fields and villages
around the city were given to Caleb
son of Jephunneh.
57 So the descendants of Aaron
were given Hebron (a city of refuge), and Libnah,[a] Jattir, Eshtemoa,
58 Hilen, Debir, 59 Ashan, Juttah[b] and
Beth Shemesh, together with their
pasturelands. 60 And from the tribe
of Benjamin they were given Gibeon,[c] Geba, Alemeth and Anathoth,
together with their pasturelands.
The total number of towns distributed among the Kohathite clans
came to thirteen.
61 The rest of Kohath's descendants
were allotted ten towns from the clans of
half the tribe of Manasseh.
62 The descendants of Gershon, clan by
clan, were allotted thirteen towns from
the tribes of Issachar, Asher and Naphtali, and from the part of the tribe of Manasseh that is in Bashan.
63 The descendants of Merari, clan by
clan, were allotted twelve towns from the
tribes of Reuben, Gad and Zebulun.
64 So the Israelites gave the Levites
these towns and their pasturelands.
65 From the tribes of Judah, Simeon and
Benjamin they allotted the previously
named towns.
66 Some of the Kohathite clans were
given as their territory towns from the
tribe of Ephraim.
67 In the hill country of Ephraim
they were given Shechem (a city of
refuge), and Gezer,[d] 68 Jokmeam,
Beth Horon, 69 Aijalon and Gath
Rimmon, together with their pasturelands.
70 And from half the tribe of Manasseh the Israelites gave Aner and
Bileam, together with their pasturelands, to the rest of the Kohathite
clans.

71 The Gershonites received the following:
From the clan of the half-tribe of Manasseh
they received Golan in Bashan and
also Ashtaroth, together with their
pasturelands;
72 from the tribe of Issachar
they received Kedesh, Daberath,
73 Ramoth and Anem, together
with their pasturelands;

[a] *57* See Joshua 21:13; Hebrew *given the cities of refuge: Hebron, Libnah.* [b] *59* Syriac (see also Septuagint and Joshua 21:16); Hebrew does not have *Juttah.* [c] *60* See Joshua 21:17; Hebrew does not have *Gibeon.* [d] *67* See Joshua 21:21; Hebrew *given the cities of refuge: Shechem, Gezer.*

74 from the tribe of Asher
they received Mashal, Abdon,
75 Hukok and Rehob, together with
their pasturelands;
76 and from the tribe of Naphtali
they received Kedesh in Galilee,
Hammon and Kiriathaim, together with their pasturelands.

77 The Merarites (the rest of the Levites)
received the following:
From the tribe of Zebulun
they received Jokneam, Kartah,[a]
Rimmono and Tabor, together
with their pasturelands;
78 from the tribe of Reuben across the
Jordan east of Jericho
they received Bezer in the wilderness, Jahzah, 79 Kedemoth and
Mephaath, together with their pasturelands;
80 and from the tribe of Gad
they received Ramoth in Gilead,
Mahanaim, 81 Heshbon and Jazer,
together with their pasturelands.

7 The sons of Issachar:
Tola, Puah, Jashub and Shimron—
four in all.
2 The sons of Tola:
Uzzi, Rephaiah, Jeriel, Jahmai, Ib-
sam and Samuel—heads of their
families. During the reign of David, the descendants of Tola listed
as fighting men in their genealogy
numbered 22,600.
3 The son of Uzzi:
Izrahiah.
The sons of Izrahiah:
Michael, Obadiah, Joel and Ishiah.
All five of them were chiefs. 4 According to their family genealogy,
they had 36,000 men ready for battle, for they had many wives and
children.
5 The relatives who were fighting men
belonging to all the clans of Issachar, as listed in their genealogy,
were 87,000 in all.

6 Three sons of Benjamin:
Bela, Beker and Jediael.
7 The sons of Bela:
Ezbon, Uzzi, Uzziel, Jerimoth and
Iri, heads of families—five in all.
Their genealogical record listed
22,034 fighting men.
8 The sons of Beker:
Zemirah, Joash, Eliezer, Elioenai,
Omri, Jeremoth, Abijah, Anathoth
and Alemeth. All these were the
sons of Beker. 9 Their genealogical
record listed the heads of families
and 20,200 fighting men.
10 The son of Jediael:
Bilhan.
The sons of Bilhan:
Jeush, Benjamin, Ehud, Kenaanah, Zethan, Tarshish and Ahish-
ahar. 11 All these sons of Jediael
were heads of families. There were
17,200 fighting men ready to go out
to war.
12 The Shuppites and Huppites were
the descendants of Ir, and the Hu-
shites[b] the descendants of Aher.

13 The sons of Naphtali:
Jahziel, Guni, Jezer and Shillem[c]—
the descendants of Bilhah.

14 The descendants of Manasseh:
Asriel was his descendant through
his Aramean concubine. She gave
birth to Makir the father of Gilead.
15 Makir took a wife from among the
Huppites and Shuppites. His sister's
name was Maakah.
Another descendant was named
Zelophehad, who had only daughters.
16 Makir's wife Maakah gave birth
to a son and named him Peresh. His
brother was named Sheresh, and his
sons were Ulam and Rakem.
17 The son of Ulam:
Bedan.
These were the sons of Gilead son of
Makir, the son of Manasseh. 18 His
sister Hammoleketh gave birth to
Ishhod, Abiezer and Mahlah.
19 The sons of Shemida were:
Ahian, Shechem, Likhi and Ani-
am.

20 The descendants of Ephraim:
Shuthelah, Bered his son,
Tahath his son, Eleadah his son,
Tahath his son, 21 Zabad his son
and Shuthelah his son.

[a] *77* See Septuagint and Joshua 21:34; Hebrew does not have *Jokneam, Kartah.* [b] *12* Or *Ir. The sons of Dan: Hushim,* (see Gen. 46:23); Hebrew does not have *The sons of Dan.* [c] *13* Some Hebrew and Septuagint manuscripts (see also Gen. 46:24 and Num. 26:49); most Hebrew manuscripts *Shallum*

Ezer and Elead were killed by the
native-born men of Gath, when they
went down to seize their livestock.
22Their father Ephraim mourned
for them many days, and his relatives came to comfort him. 23Then
he made love to his wife again, and
she became pregnant and gave birth
to a son. He named him Beriah,[a] because there had been misfortune in
his family. 24His daughter was Sheerah, who built Lower and Upper Beth
Horon as well as Uzzen Sheerah.
25Rephah was his son, Resheph his
son,[b]
Telah his son, Tahan his son,
26Ladan his son, Ammihud his son,
Elishama his son, 27Nun his son
and Joshua his son.
28Their lands and settlements included
Bethel and its surrounding villages, Na-
aran to the east, Gezer and its villages to
the west, and Shechem and its villages all
the way to Ayyah and its villages. 29Along
the borders of Manasseh were Beth Shan,
Taanach, Megiddo and Dor, together with
their villages. The descendants of Joseph
son of Israel lived in these towns.

30The sons of Asher:
Imnah, Ishvah, Ishvi and Beriah.
Their sister was Serah.
31The sons of Beriah:
Heber and Malkiel, who was the father of Birzaith.
32Heber was the father of Japhlet, Shomer and Hotham and of their sister
Shua.
33The sons of Japhlet:
Pasak, Bimhal and Ashvath.
These were Japhlet's sons.
34The sons of Shomer:
Ahi, Rohgah,[c] Hubbah and Aram.
35The sons of his brother Helem:
Zophah, Imna, Shelesh and Amal.
36The sons of Zophah:
Suah, Harnepher, Shual, Beri, Im-
rah, 37Bezer, Hod, Shamma, Shil-
shah, Ithran[d] and Beera.
38The sons of Jether:
Jephunneh, Pispah and Ara.
39The sons of Ulla:
Arah, Hanniel and Rizia.
40All these were descendants of Asher—heads of families, choice men, brave
warriors and outstanding leaders. The
number of men ready for battle, as listed
in their genealogy, was 26,000.

8 Benjamin was the father of Bela his
firstborn,
Ashbel the second son, Aharah the
third,
2Nohah the fourth and Rapha the
fifth.
3The sons of Bela were:
Addar, Gera, Abihud,[e] 4Abishua,
Naaman, Ahoah, 5Gera, Shephu-
phan and Huram.
6These were the descendants of Ehud,
who were heads of families of those
living in Geba and were deported
to Manahath:
7Naaman, Ahijah, and Gera, who
deported them and who was the
father of Uzza and Ahihud.
8Sons were born to Shaharaim in
Moab after he had divorced his
wives Hushim and Baara. 9By his
wife Hodesh he had Jobab, Zib-
ia, Mesha, Malkam, 10Jeuz, Sakia
and Mirmah. These were his sons,
heads of families. 11By Hushim he
had Abitub and Elpaal.
12The sons of Elpaal:
Eber, Misham, Shemed (who built
Ono and Lod with its surrounding
villages), 13and Beriah and Shema,
who were heads of families of those
living in Aijalon and who drove out
the inhabitants of Gath.
14Ahio, Shashak, Jeremoth, 15Zebadi-
ah, Arad, Eder, 16Michael, Ishpah
and Joha were the sons of Beriah.
17Zebadiah, Meshullam, Hizki, Heber,
18Ishmerai, Izliah and Jobab were
the sons of Elpaal.
19Jakim, Zikri, Zabdi, 20Elienai, Zillethai, Eliel, 21Adaiah, Beraiah and
Shimrath were the sons of Shimei.
22Ishpan, Eber, Eliel, 23Abdon, Zikri,
Hanan, 24Hananiah, Elam, An-
thothijah, 25Iphdeiah and Penuel
were the sons of Shashak.
26Shamsherai, Shehariah, Athaliah,
27Jaareshiah, Elijah and Zikri were
the sons of Jeroham.
28All these were heads of families,

[a] 23 *Beriah* sounds like the Hebrew for *misfortune*. [b] 25 Some Septuagint manuscripts; Hebrew does not have *his son*. [c] 34 Or *of his brother Shomer: Rohgah* [d] 37 Possibly a variant of *Jether* [e] 3 Or *Gera the father of Ehud*

chiefs as listed in their genealogy, and
they lived in Jerusalem.

29 Jeiel[a] the father[b] of Gibeon lived in
Gibeon.
His wife's name was Maakah,
30 and his firstborn son was Abdon, followed by Zur, Kish, Baal,
Ner,[c] Nadab, 31 Gedor, Ahio, Zeker
32 and Mikloth, who was the father
of Shimeah. They too lived near
their relatives in Jerusalem.
33 Ner was the father of Kish, Kish the
father of Saul, and Saul the father
of Jonathan, Malki-Shua, Abinadab and Esh-Baal.[d]
34 The son of Jonathan:
Merib-Baal,[e] who was the father of
Micah.
35 The sons of Micah:
Pithon, Melek, Tarea and Ahaz.
36 Ahaz was the father of Jehoaddah, Jehoaddah was the father of
Alemeth, Azmaveth and Zimri,
and Zimri was the father of Moza.
37 Moza was the father of Binea; Ra-
phah was his son, Eleasah his son
and Azel his son.
38 Azel had six sons, and these were
their names:
Azrikam, Bokeru, Ishmael, Sheari-
ah, Obadiah and Hanan. All these
were the sons of Azel.
39 The sons of his brother Eshek:
Ulam his firstborn, Jeush the second son and Eliphelet the third.
40 The sons of Ulam were brave
warriors who could handle the
bow. They had many sons and
grandsons — 150 in all.
All these were the descendants of
Benjamin.

9 All Israel was listed in the genealogies
recorded in the book of the kings of Israel and Judah. They were taken captive to
Babylon because of their unfaithfulness.

2 Now the first to resettle on their own
property in their own towns were some
Israelites, priests, Levites and temple
servants.
3 Those from Judah, from Benjamin,
and from Ephraim and Manasseh who
lived in Jerusalem were:

4 Uthai son of Ammihud, the son of
Omri, the son of Imri, the son of
Bani, a descendant of Perez son of
Judah.
5 Of the Shelanites[f]:
Asaiah the firstborn and his sons.
6 Of the Zerahites:
Jeuel.
The people from Judah numbered
690.
7 Of the Benjamites:
Sallu son of Meshullam, the son of
Hodaviah, the son of Hassenuah;
8 Ibneiah son of Jeroham; Elah son
of Uzzi, the son of Mikri; and Meshullam son of Shephatiah, the son
of Reuel, the son of Ibnijah.
9 The people from Benjamin, as listed in their genealogy, numbered
956. All these men were heads of
their families.
10 Of the priests:
Jedaiah; Jehoiarib; Jakin;
11 Azariah son of Hilkiah, the son of
Meshullam, the son of Zadok, the
son of Meraioth, the son of Ahitub,
the official in charge of the house
of God;
12 Adaiah son of Jeroham, the son of
Pashhur, the son of Malkijah; and
Maasai son of Adiel, the son of Jah-
zerah, the son of Meshullam, the
son of Meshillemith, the son of
Immer.
13 The priests, who were heads of
families, numbered 1,760. They
were able men, responsible for
ministering in the house of God.
14 Of the Levites:
Shemaiah son of Hasshub, the son
of Azrikam, the son of Hashabiah,
a Merarite; 15 Bakbakkar, Heresh,
Galal and Mattaniah son of Mika,
the son of Zikri, the son of Asaph;
16 Obadiah son of Shemaiah, the
son of Galal, the son of Jeduthun;
and Berekiah son of Asa, the son of
Elkanah, who lived in the villages
of the Netophathites.
17 The gatekeepers:
Shallum, Akkub, Talmon, Ahiman
and their fellow Levites, Shallum
their chief 18 being stationed at the
King's Gate on the east, up to the

[a] 29 Some Septuagint manuscripts (see also 9:35); Hebrew does not have *Jeiel.* [b] 29 *Father* may mean *civic leader* or *military leader.* [c] 30 Some Septuagint manuscripts (see also 9:36); Hebrew does not have *Ner.* [d] 33 Also known as *Ish-Bosheth* [e] 34 Also known as *Mephibosheth* [f] 5 See Num. 26:20; Hebrew *Shilonites.*

present time. These were the gatekeepers belonging to the camp
of the Levites. [19]Shallum son of
Kore, the son of Ebiasaph, the son
of Korah, and his fellow gatekeepers from his family (the Korahites)
were responsible for guarding the
thresholds of the tent just as their
ancestors had been responsible
for guarding the entrance to the
dwelling of the LORD. [20]In earlier
times Phinehas son of Eleazar was
the official in charge of the gatekeepers, and the LORD was with
him. [21]Zechariah son of Meshelemiah was the gatekeeper at the
entrance to the tent of meeting.
[22]Altogether, those chosen to be gatekeepers at the thresholds numbered 212.
They were registered by genealogy in
their villages. The gatekeepers had been
assigned to their positions of trust by David and Samuel the seer. [23]They and their
descendants were in charge of guarding
the gates of the house of the LORD—the
house called the tent of meeting. [24]The
gatekeepers were on the four sides: east,
west, north and south. [25]Their fellow Levites in their villages had to come from
time to time and share their duties for
seven-day periods. [26]But the four princi-
pal gatekeepers, who were Levites, were
entrusted with the responsibility for the
rooms and treasuries in the house of
God. [27]They would spend the night stationed around the house of God, because
they had to guard it; and they had charge
of the key for opening it each morning.
[28]Some of them were in charge of the
articles used in the temple service; they
counted them when they were brought
in and when they were taken out. [29]Oth-
ers were assigned to take care of the furnishings and all the other articles of the
sanctuary, as well as the special flour
and wine, and the olive oil, incense and
spices. [30]But some of the priests took care
of mixing the spices. [31]A Levite named
Mattithiah, the firstborn son of Shallum
the Korahite, was entrusted with the responsibility for baking the offering bread.
[32]Some of the Kohathites, their fellow Levites, were in charge of preparing for every
Sabbath the bread set out on the table.
[33]Those who were musicians, heads of
Levite families, stayed in the rooms of the
temple and were exempt from other duties because they were responsible for the
work day and night.
[34]All these were heads of Levite families, chiefs as listed in their genealogy,
and they lived in Jerusalem.

[35]Jeiel the father[a] of Gibeon lived in
Gibeon.
His wife's name was Maakah,
[36]and his firstborn son was Abdon,
followed by Zur, Kish, Baal, Ner,
Nadab, [37]Gedor, Ahio, Zechariah
and Mikloth. [38]Mikloth was the
father of Shimeam. They too lived
near their relatives in Jerusalem.
[39]Ner was the father of Kish, Kish the
father of Saul, and Saul the father
of Jonathan, Malki-Shua, Abinadab and Esh-Baal.[b]
[40]The son of Jonathan:
Merib-Baal,[c] who was the father of
Micah.
[41]The sons of Micah:
Pithon, Melek, Tahrea and Ahaz.[d]
[42]Ahaz was the father of Jadah, Jadah[e]
was the father of Alemeth, Azmaveth and Zimri, and Zimri was the
father of Moza. [43]Moza was the father of Binea; Rephaiah was his son,
Eleasah his son and Azel his son.
[44]Azel had six sons, and these were
their names:
Azrikam, Bokeru, Ishmael, Shea-
riah, Obadiah and Hanan. These
were the sons of Azel.

10 Now the Philistines fought against
Israel; the Israelites fled before
them, and many fell dead on Mount Gilboa. [2]The Philistines were in hot pursuit
of Saul and his sons, and they killed his
sons Jonathan, Abinadab and Malki-
Shua. [3]The fighting grew fierce around
Saul, and when the archers overtook him,
they wounded him.
[4]Saul said to his armor-bearer, "Draw
your sword and run me through, or these
uncircumcised fellows will come and
abuse me."
But his armor-bearer was terrified and
would not do it; so Saul took his own sword

[a] 35 *Father* may mean *civic leader* or *military leader.* [b] 39 Also known as *Ish-Bosheth* [c] 40 Also known as *Mephibosheth* [d] 41 Vulgate and Syriac (see also Septuagint and 8:35); Hebrew does not have *and Ahaz.* [e] 42 Some Hebrew manuscripts and Septuagint (see also 8:36); most Hebrew manuscripts *Jarah, Jarah*

and fell on it. 5 When the armor-bearer saw that Saul was dead, he too fell on his sword and died. 6 So Saul and his three sons died, and all his house died together.

7 When all the Israelites in the valley saw that the army had fled and that Saul and his sons had died, they abandoned their towns and fled. And the Philistines came and occupied them.

8 The next day, when the Philistines came to strip the dead, they found Saul and his sons fallen on Mount Gilboa. 9 They stripped him and took his head and his armor, and sent messengers throughout the land of the Philistines to proclaim the news among their idols and their people. 10 They put his armor in the temple of their gods and hung up his head in the temple of Dagon.

11 When all the inhabitants of Jabesh Gilead heard what the Philistines had done to Saul, 12 all their valiant men went and took the bodies of Saul and his sons and brought them to Jabesh. Then they buried their bones under the great tree in Jabesh, and they fasted seven days.

13 Saul died because he was unfaithful to the LORD; he did not keep the word of the LORD and even consulted a medium for guidance, 14 and did not inquire of the LORD. So the LORD put him to death and turned the kingdom over to David son of Jesse.

11 All Israel came together to David at Hebron and said, "We are your own flesh and blood. 2 In the past, even while Saul was king, you were the one who led Israel on their military campaigns. And the LORD your God said to you, 'You will shepherd my people Israel, and you will become their ruler.'"

3 When all the elders of Israel had come to King David at Hebron, he made a covenant with them at Hebron before the LORD, and they anointed David king over Israel, as the LORD had promised through Samuel.

4 David and all the Israelites marched to Jerusalem (that is, Jebus). The Jebusites who lived there 5 said to David, "You will not get in here." Nevertheless, David captured the fortress of Zion—which is the City of David.

6 David had said, "Whoever leads the attack on the Jebusites will become commander-in-chief." Joab son of Zeruiah went up first, and so he received the command.

7 David then took up residence in the fortress, and so it was called the City of David. 8 He built up the city around it, from the terraces[a] to the surrounding wall, while Joab restored the rest of the city. 9 And David became more and more powerful, because the LORD Almighty was with him.

10 These were the chiefs of David's mighty warriors—they, together with all Israel, gave his kingship strong support to extend it over the whole land, as the LORD had promised— 11 this is the list of David's mighty warriors:

Jashobeam,[b] a Hakmonite, was chief of the officers[c]; he raised his spear against three hundred men, whom he killed in one encounter.

12 Next to him was Eleazar son of Dodai the Ahohite, one of the three mighty warriors. 13 He was with David at Pas Dammim when the Philistines gathered there for battle. At a place where there was a field full of barley, the troops fled from the Philistines. 14 But they took their stand in the middle of the field. They defended it and struck the Philistines down, and the LORD brought about a great victory.

15 Three of the thirty chiefs came down to David to the rock at the cave of Adullam, while a band of Philistines was encamped in the Valley of Rephaim. 16 At that time David was in the stronghold, and the Philistine garrison was at Bethlehem. 17 David longed for water and said, "Oh, that someone would get me a drink of water from the well near the gate of Bethlehem!" 18 So the Three broke through the Philistine lines, drew water from the well near the gate of Bethlehem and carried it back to David. But he refused to drink it; instead, he poured it out to the LORD. 19 "God forbid that I should do this!" he said. "Should I drink the blood of these men who went at the risk of their lives?" Because they risked their lives to bring it back, David would not drink it.

Such were the exploits of the three mighty warriors.

20 Abishai the brother of Joab was chief

[a] 8 Or *the Millo* [b] 11 Possibly a variant of *Jashob-Baal* [c] 11 Or *Thirty*; some Septuagint manuscripts *Three* (see also 2 Samuel 23:8)

of the Three. He raised his spear against
three hundred men, whom he killed, and
so he became as famous as the Three. 21 He
was doubly honored above the Three and
became their commander, even though
he was not included among them.

22 Benaiah son of Jehoiada, a valiant
fighter from Kabzeel, performed great
exploits. He struck down Moab's two
mightiest warriors. He also went down
into a pit on a snowy day and killed a
lion. 23 And he struck down an Egyptian
who was five cubits[a] tall. Although the
Egyptian had a spear like a weaver's rod
in his hand, Benaiah went against him
with a club. He snatched the spear from
the Egyptian's hand and killed him with
his own spear. 24 Such were the exploits of
Benaiah son of Jehoiada; he too was as famous as the three mighty warriors. 25 He
was held in greater honor than any of the
Thirty, but he was not included among
the Three. And David put him in charge
of his bodyguard.

26 The mighty warriors were:
Asahel the brother of Joab,
Elhanan son of Dodo from Bethlehem,
27 Shammoth the Harorite,
Helez the Pelonite,
28 Ira son of Ikkesh from Tekoa,
Abiezer from Anathoth,
29 Sibbekai the Hushathite,
Ilai the Ahohite,
30 Maharai the Netophathite,
Heled son of Baanah the Netophathite,
31 Ithai son of Ribai from Gibeah in
Benjamin,
Benaiah the Pirathonite,
32 Hurai from the ravines of Gaash,
Abiel the Arbathite,
33 Azmaveth the Baharumite,
Eliahba the Shaalbonite,
34 the sons of Hashem the Gizonite,
Jonathan son of Shagee the Hararite,
35 Ahiam son of Sakar the Hararite,
Eliphal son of Ur,
36 Hepher the Mekerathite,
Ahijah the Pelonite,
37 Hezro the Carmelite,
Naarai son of Ezbai,
38 Joel the brother of Nathan,
Mibhar son of Hagri,
39 Zelek the Ammonite,
Naharai the Berothite, the armor-
bearer of Joab son of Zeruiah,
40 Ira the Ithrite,
Gareb the Ithrite,
41 Uriah the Hittite,
Zabad son of Ahlai,
42 Adina son of Shiza the Reubenite,
who was chief of the Reubenites,
and the thirty with him,
43 Hanan son of Maakah,
Joshaphat the Mithnite,
44 Uzzia the Ashterathite,
Shama and Jeiel the sons of Hotham the Aroerite,
45 Jediael son of Shimri,
his brother Joha the Tizite,
46 Eliel the Mahavite,
Jeribai and Joshaviah the sons of
Elnaam,
Ithmah the Moabite,
47 Eliel, Obed and Jaasiel the Mezo-
baite.

12 These were the men who came to
David at Ziklag, while he was banished from the presence of Saul son of
Kish (they were among the warriors who
helped him in battle; 2 they were armed
with bows and were able to shoot arrows
or to sling stones right-handed or left-
handed; they were relatives of Saul from
the tribe of Benjamin):

3 Ahiezer their chief and Joash the
sons of Shemaah the Gibeathite; Je-
ziel and Pelet the sons of Azmaveth;
Berakah, Jehu the Anathothite, 4 and
Ishmaiah the Gibeonite, a mighty
warrior among the Thirty, who was
a leader of the Thirty; Jeremiah, Jahaziel, Johanan, Jozabad the Gederathite,[b] 5 Eluzai, Jerimoth, Bealiah,
Shemariah and Shephatiah the Ha-
ruphite; 6 Elkanah, Ishiah, Azarel,
Joezer and Jashobeam the Korahites;
7 and Joelah and Zebadiah the sons of
Jeroham from Gedor.

8 Some Gadites defected to David at his
stronghold in the wilderness. They were
brave warriors, ready for battle and able
to handle the shield and spear. Their faces were the faces of lions, and they were
as swift as gazelles in the mountains.

[a] *23* That is, about 7 feet 6 inches or about 2.3 meters

[b] *4* In Hebrew texts the second half of this verse (*Jeremiah . . . Gederathite*) is numbered 12:5, and 12:5-40 is numbered 12:6-41.

9 Ezer was the chief,
Obadiah the second in command,
Eliab the third,
10 Mishmannah the fourth, Jeremiah
the fifth,
11 Attai the sixth, Eliel the seventh,
12 Johanan the eighth, Elzabad the
ninth,
13 Jeremiah the tenth and Makbannai
the eleventh.

14 These Gadites were army commanders; the least was a match for a hundred,
and the greatest for a thousand. 15 It was
they who crossed the Jordan in the first
month when it was overflowing all its
banks, and they put to flight everyone
living in the valleys, to the east and to
the west.

16 Other Benjamites and some men
from Judah also came to David in his
stronghold. 17 David went out to meet
them and said to them, "If you have come
to me in peace to help me, I am ready for
you to join me. But if you have come to
betray me to my enemies when my hands
are free from violence, may the God of
our ancestors see it and judge you."

18 Then the Spirit came on Amasai,
chief of the Thirty, and he said:

"We are yours, David!
We are with you, son of Jesse!
Success, success to you,
and success to those who help you,
for your God will help you."

So David received them and made
them leaders of his raiding bands.

19 Some of the tribe of Manasseh defected to David when he went with the
Philistines to fight against Saul. (He and
his men did not help the Philistines because, after consultation, their rulers
sent him away. They said, "It will cost
us our heads if he deserts to his master
Saul.") 20 When David went to Ziklag,
these were the men of Manasseh who
defected to him: Adnah, Jozabad, Jediael, Michael, Jozabad, Elihu and Zillethai,
leaders of units of a thousand in Manasseh. 21 They helped David against raiding
bands, for all of them were brave warriors, and they were commanders in his
army. 22 Day after day men came to help
David, until he had a great army, like the
army of God.[a]

23 These are the numbers of the men
armed for battle who came to David at
Hebron to turn Saul's kingdom over to
him, as the LORD had said:

24 from Judah, carrying shield and
spear — 6,800 armed for battle;
25 from Simeon, warriors ready for battle — 7,100;
26 from Levi — 4,600, 27 including Jehoiada, leader of the family of Aaron,
with 3,700 men, 28 and Zadok, a
brave young warrior, with 22 officers from his family;
29 from Benjamin, Saul's tribe — 3,000,
most of whom had remained loyal
to Saul's house until then;
30 from Ephraim, brave warriors, famous in their own clans — 20,800;
31 from half the tribe of Manasseh,
designated by name to come and
make David king — 18,000;
32 from Issachar, men who understood
the times and knew what Israel
should do — 200 chiefs, with all
their relatives under their command;
33 from Zebulun, experienced soldiers
prepared for battle with every type
of weapon, to help David with undivided loyalty — 50,000;
34 from Naphtali — 1,000 officers, together with 37,000 men carrying
shields and spears;
35 from Dan, ready for battle — 28,600;
36 from Asher, experienced soldiers
prepared for battle — 40,000;
37 and from east of the Jordan, from
Reuben, Gad and the half-tribe of
Manasseh, armed with every type
of weapon — 120,000.

38 All these were fighting men who volunteered to serve in the ranks. They came
to Hebron fully determined to make David king over all Israel. All the rest of the
Israelites were also of one mind to make
David king. 39 The men spent three days
there with David, eating and drinking,
for their families had supplied provisions
for them. 40 Also, their neighbors from as
far away as Issachar, Zebulun and Naphtali came bringing food on donkeys, camels, mules and oxen. There were plentiful
supplies of flour, fig cakes, raisin cakes,
wine, olive oil, cattle and sheep, for there
was joy in Israel.

[a] 22 Or *a great and mighty army*

13 David conferred with each of his
officers, the commanders of thousands and commanders of hundreds.
2 He then said to the whole assembly of
Israel, "If it seems good to you and if it is
the will of the LORD our God, let us send
word far and wide to the rest of our people throughout the territories of Israel,
and also to the priests and Levites who
are with them in their towns and pasturelands, to come and join us. 3 Let us
bring the ark of our God back to us, for
we did not inquire of[a] it[b] during the reign
of Saul." 4 The whole assembly agreed to
do this, because it seemed right to all the
people.
5 So David assembled all Israel, from
the Shihor River in Egypt to Lebo Hamath, to bring the ark of God from Kiriath
Jearim. 6 David and all Israel went to Baalah of Judah (Kiriath Jearim) to bring up
from there the ark of God the LORD, who
is enthroned between the cherubim—
the ark that is called by the Name.
7 They moved the ark of God from Abinadab's house on a new cart, with Uzzah
and Ahio guiding it. 8 David and all the
Israelites were celebrating with all their
might before God, with songs and with
harps, lyres, timbrels, cymbals and
trumpets.
9 When they came to the threshing floor
of Kidon, Uzzah reached out his hand to
steady the ark, because the oxen stumbled. 10 The LORD's anger burned against
Uzzah, and he struck him down because
he had put his hand on the ark. So he died
there before God.
11 Then David was angry because the
LORD's wrath had broken out against Uzzah, and to this day that place is called
Perez Uzzah.[c]
12 David was afraid of God that day and
asked, "How can I ever bring the ark of
God to me?" 13 He did not take the ark to
be with him in the City of David. Instead,
he took it to the house of Obed-Edom the
Gittite. 14 The ark of God remained with
the family of Obed-Edom in his house for
three months, and the LORD blessed his
household and everything he had.

14 Now Hiram king of Tyre sent messengers to David, along with cedar logs, stonemasons and carpenters
to build a palace for him. 2 And David
knew that the LORD had established him
as king over Israel and that his kingdom
had been highly exalted for the sake of
his people Israel.
3 In Jerusalem David took more wives
and became the father of more sons and
daughters. 4 These are the names of the
children born to him there: Shammua,
Shobab, Nathan, Solomon, 5 Ibhar, Elishua, Elpelet, 6 Nogah, Nepheg, Japhia,
7 Elishama, Beeliada[d] and Eliphelet.
8 When the Philistines heard that David had been anointed king over all Israel, they went up in full force to search for
him, but David heard about it and went
out to meet them. 9 Now the Philistines
had come and raided the Valley of Rephaim; 10 so David inquired of God: "Shall
I go and attack the Philistines? Will you
deliver them into my hands?"
The LORD answered him, "Go, I will deliver them into your hands."
11 So David and his men went up to Baal
Perazim, and there he defeated them. He
said, "As waters break out, God has broken out against my enemies by my hand."
So that place was called Baal Perazim.[e]
12 The Philistines had abandoned their
gods there, and David gave orders to burn
them in the fire.
13 Once more the Philistines raided the
valley; 14 so David inquired of God again,
and God answered him, "Do not go directly after them, but circle around them
and attack them in front of the poplar
trees. 15 As soon as you hear the sound of
marching in the tops of the poplar trees,
move out to battle, because that will
mean God has gone out in front of you
to strike the Philistine army." 16 So David
did as God commanded him, and they
struck down the Philistine army, all the
way from Gibeon to Gezer.
17 So David's fame spread throughout
every land, and the LORD made all the nations fear him.

15 After David had constructed buildings for himself in the City of David,
he prepared a place for the ark of God and
pitched a tent for it. 2 Then David said,
"No one but the Levites may carry the ark
of God, because the LORD chose them to
carry the ark of the LORD and to minister
before him forever."
3 David assembled all Israel in Jerusa-

[a] 3 Or *we neglected* [b] 3 Or *him* [c] 11 *Perez Uzzah* means *outbreak against Uzzah.* [d] 7 A variant of *Eliada* [e] 11 *Baal Perazim* means *the lord who breaks out.*

lem to bring up the ark of the LORD to the
place he had prepared for it. 4 He called
together the descendants of Aaron and
the Levites:

5 From the descendants of Kohath,
Uriel the leader and 120 relatives;
6 from the descendants of Merari,
Asaiah the leader and 220 relatives;
7 from the descendants of Gershon,[a]
Joel the leader and 130 relatives;
8 from the descendants of Elizaphan,
Shemaiah the leader and 200 relatives;
9 from the descendants of Hebron,
Eliel the leader and 80 relatives;
10 from the descendants of Uzziel,
Amminadab the leader and 112 relatives.

11 Then David summoned Zadok and
Abiathar the priests, and Uriel, Asaiah,
Joel, Shemaiah, Eliel and Amminadab
the Levites. 12 He said to them, "You are
the heads of the Levitical families; you
and your fellow Levites are to consecrate yourselves and bring up the ark of
the LORD, the God of Israel, to the place
I have prepared for it. 13 It was because
you, the Levites, did not bring it up the
first time that the LORD our God broke
out in anger against us. We did not inquire of him about how to do it in the prescribed way." 14 So the priests and Levites
consecrated themselves in order to bring
up the ark of the LORD, the God of Israel.
15 And the Levites carried the ark of God
with the poles on their shoulders, as Moses had commanded in accordance with
the word of the LORD.

16 David told the leaders of the Levites to
appoint their fellow Levites as musicians
to make a joyful sound with musical instruments: lyres, harps and cymbals.

17 So the Levites appointed Heman son
of Joel; from his relatives, Asaph son of
Berekiah; and from their relatives the
Merarites, Ethan son of Kushaiah; 18 and
with them their relatives next in rank:
Zechariah,[b] Jaaziel, Shemiramoth, Je-
hiel, Unni, Eliab, Benaiah, Maaseiah,
Mattithiah, Eliphelehu, Mikneiah, Obed-
Edom and Jeiel,[c] the gatekeepers.

19 The musicians Heman, Asaph and
Ethan were to sound the bronze cymbals; 20 Zechariah, Jaaziel,[d] Shemiramoth, Jehiel, Unni, Eliab, Maaseiah and
Benaiah were to play the lyres according
to *alamoth*,[e] 21 and Mattithiah, Eliphelehu, Mikneiah, Obed-Edom, Jeiel and
Azaziah were to play the harps, directing
according to *sheminith*.[e] 22 Kenaniah the
head Levite was in charge of the singing;
that was his responsibility because he
was skillful at it.

23 Berekiah and Elkanah were to be
doorkeepers for the ark. 24 Shebaniah,
Joshaphat, Nethanel, Amasai, Zechariah, Benaiah and Eliezer the priests were
to blow trumpets before the ark of God.
Obed-Edom and Jehiah were also to be
doorkeepers for the ark.

25 So David and the elders of Israel and
the commanders of units of a thousand
went to bring up the ark of the covenant of
the LORD from the house of Obed-Edom,
with rejoicing. 26 Because God had helped
the Levites who were carrying the ark of
the covenant of the LORD, seven bulls
and seven rams were sacrificed. 27 Now
David was clothed in a robe of fine linen,
as were all the Levites who were carrying
the ark, and as were the musicians, and
Kenaniah, who was in charge of the singing of the choirs. David also wore a linen
ephod. 28 So all Israel brought up the ark
of the covenant of the LORD with shouts,
with the sounding of rams' horns and
trumpets, and of cymbals, and the playing of lyres and harps.

29 As the ark of the covenant of the
LORD was entering the City of David,
Michal daughter of Saul watched from a
window. And when she saw King David
dancing and celebrating, she despised
him in her heart.

16 They brought the ark of God and
set it inside the tent that David had
pitched for it, and they presented burnt
offerings and fellowship offerings before
God. 2 After David had finished sacrificing the burnt offerings and fellowship
offerings, he blessed the people in the
name of the LORD. 3 Then he gave a loaf
of bread, a cake of dates and a cake of raisins to each Israelite man and woman.

4 He appointed some of the Levites to

[a] 7 Hebrew *Gershom,* a variant of *Gershon* [b] 18 Three Hebrew manuscripts and most Septuagint manuscripts (see also verse 20 and 16:5); most Hebrew manuscripts *Zechariah son and* or *Zechariah, Ben and* [c] 18 Hebrew; Septuagint (see also verse 21) *Jeiel and Azaziah* [d] 20 See verse 18; Hebrew *Aziel,* a variant of *Jaaziel.* [e] 20,21 Probably a musical term

minister before the ark of the LORD, to
extol,[a] thank, and praise the LORD, the
God of Israel: 5 Asaph was the chief, and
next to him in rank were Zechariah, then
Jaaziel,[b] Shemiramoth, Jehiel, Mattithiah, Eliab, Benaiah, Obed-Edom and Jeiel. They were to play the lyres and harps,
Asaph was to sound the cymbals, 6 and
Benaiah and Jahaziel the priests were to
blow the trumpets regularly before the
ark of the covenant of God.

7 That day David first appointed Asaph
and his associates to give praise to the
LORD in this manner:

8 Give praise to the LORD, proclaim his
name;
make known among the nations
what he has done.
9 Sing to him, sing praise to him;
tell of all his wonderful acts.
10 Glory in his holy name;
let the hearts of those who seek the
LORD rejoice.
11 Look to the LORD and his strength;
seek his face always.

12 Remember the wonders he has done,
his miracles, and the judgments he
pronounced,
13 you his servants, the descendants of
Israel,
his chosen ones, the children of
Jacob.
14 He is the LORD our God;
his judgments are in all the earth.

15 He remembers[c] his covenant forever,
the promise he made, for a thousand
generations,
16 the covenant he made with Abraham,
the oath he swore to Isaac.
17 He confirmed it to Jacob as a decree,
to Israel as an everlasting covenant:
18 "To you I will give the land of Canaan
as the portion you will inherit."

19 When they were but few in number,
few indeed, and strangers in it,
20 they[d] wandered from nation to nation,
from one kingdom to another.
21 He allowed no one to oppress them;
for their sake he rebuked kings:
22 "Do not touch my anointed ones;
do my prophets no harm."

23 Sing to the LORD, all the earth;
proclaim his salvation day after day.
24 Declare his glory among the nations,
his marvelous deeds among all
peoples.

25 For great is the LORD and most worthy
of praise;
he is to be feared above all gods.
26 For all the gods of the nations are
idols,
but the LORD made the heavens.
27 Splendor and majesty are before him;
strength and joy are in his dwelling
place.

28 Ascribe to the LORD, all you families of
nations,
ascribe to the LORD glory and
strength.
29 Ascribe to the LORD the glory due his
name;
bring an offering and come before
him.
Worship the LORD in the splendor of
his[e] holiness.
30 Tremble before him, all the earth!
The world is firmly established; it
cannot be moved.

31 Let the heavens rejoice, let the earth
be glad;
let them say among the nations,
"The LORD reigns!"
32 Let the sea resound, and all that is in it;
let the fields be jubilant, and
everything in them!
33 Let the trees of the forest sing,
let them sing for joy before the LORD,
for he comes to judge the earth.

34 Give thanks to the LORD, for he is
good;
his love endures forever.
35 Cry out, "Save us, God our Savior;
gather us and deliver us from the
nations,
that we may give thanks to your holy
name,
and glory in your praise."
36 Praise be to the LORD, the God of
Israel,
from everlasting to everlasting.

Then all the people said "Amen" and
"Praise the LORD."

[a] *4* Or *petition;* or *invoke* [b] *5* See 15:18,20; Hebrew *Jeiel,* possibly another name for *Jaaziel.* [c] *15* Some Septuagint manuscripts (see also Psalm 105:8); Hebrew *Remember* [d] *18-20* One Hebrew manuscript, Septuagint and Vulgate (see also Psalm 105:12); most Hebrew manuscripts *inherit, / 19 though you are but few in number, / few indeed, and strangers in it." / 20 They* [e] *29* Or *LORD with the splendor of*

37 David left Asaph and his associates
before the ark of the covenant of the LORD
to minister there regularly, according to
each day's requirements. 38 He also left
Obed-Edom and his sixty-eight associates to minister with them. Obed-Edom
son of Jeduthun, and also Hosah, were
gatekeepers.

39 David left Zadok the priest and his
fellow priests before the tabernacle of
the LORD at the high place in Gibeon
40 to present burnt offerings to the LORD
on the altar of burnt offering regularly, morning and evening, in accordance
with everything written in the Law of the
LORD, which he had given Israel. 41 With
them were Heman and Jeduthun and
the rest of those chosen and designated
by name to give thanks to the LORD, "for
his love endures forever." 42 Heman and
Jeduthun were responsible for the sounding of the trumpets and cymbals and for
the playing of the other instruments for
sacred song. The sons of Jeduthun were
stationed at the gate.

43 Then all the people left, each for their
own home, and David returned home to
bless his family.

17 After David was settled in his palace, he said to Nathan the prophet,
"Here I am, living in a house of cedar,
while the ark of the covenant of the LORD
is under a tent."

2 Nathan replied to David, "Whatever
you have in mind, do it, for God is with
you."

3 But that night the word of God came to
Nathan, saying:

4 "Go and tell my servant David,
'This is what the LORD says: You
are not the one to build me a house
to dwell in. 5 I have not dwelt in a
house from the day I brought Israel up out of Egypt to this day. I have
moved from one tent site to another,
from one dwelling place to another. 6 Wherever I have moved with all
the Israelites, did I ever say to any of
their leaders[a] whom I commanded to
shepherd my people, "Why have you
not built me a house of cedar?"'

7 "Now then, tell my servant David, 'This is what the LORD Almighty
says: I took you from the pasture,
from tending the flock, and appointed you ruler over my people Israel.
8 I have been with you wherever you
have gone, and I have cut off all your
enemies from before you. Now I will
make your name like the names of
the greatest men on earth. 9 And I
will provide a place for my people Israel and will plant them so that they
can have a home of their own and no
longer be disturbed. Wicked people
will not oppress them anymore, as
they did at the beginning 10 and have
done ever since the time I appointed
leaders over my people Israel. I will
also subdue all your enemies.

"'I declare to you that the LORD
will build a house for you: 11 When
your days are over and you go to be
with your ancestors, I will raise up
your offspring to succeed you, one
of your own sons, and I will establish
his kingdom. 12 He is the one who will
build a house for me, and I will establish his throne forever. 13 I will be his
father, and he will be my son. I will
never take my love away from him, as
I took it away from your predecessor.
14 I will set him over my house and my
kingdom forever; his throne will be
established forever.'"

15 Nathan reported to David all the
words of this entire revelation.

16 Then King David went in and sat before the LORD, and he said:

"Who am I, LORD God, and what
is my family, that you have brought
me this far? 17 And as if this were not
enough in your sight, my God, you
have spoken about the future of the
house of your servant. You, LORD
God, have looked on me as though I
were the most exalted of men.

18 "What more can David say to you
for honoring your servant? For you
know your servant, 19 LORD. For the
sake of your servant and according
to your will, you have done this great
thing and made known all these
great promises.

20 "There is no one like you, LORD,
and there is no God but you, as we
have heard with our own ears. 21 And
who is like your people Israel—the
one nation on earth whose God went

[a] 6 Traditionally *judges*; also in verse 10

out to redeem a people for himself,
and to make a name for yourself,
and to perform great and awesome
wonders by driving out nations from
before your people, whom you redeemed from Egypt? 22You made
your people Israel your very own
forever, and you, LORD, have become
their God.
23"And now, LORD, let the promise you have made concerning your
servant and his house be established
forever. Do as you promised, 24so
that it will be established and that
your name will be great forever. Then
people will say, 'The LORD Almighty,
the God over Israel, is Israel's God!'
And the house of your servant David
will be established before you.
25"You, my God, have revealed to
your servant that you will build a
house for him. So your servant has
found courage to pray to you. 26You,
LORD, are God! You have promised
these good things to your servant.
27Now you have been pleased to
bless the house of your servant, that
it may continue forever in your sight;
for you, LORD, have blessed it, and it
will be blessed forever."

18 In the course of time, David defeated
the Philistines and subdued them,
and he took Gath and its surrounding villages from the control of the Philistines.
2David also defeated the Moabites, and
they became subject to him and brought
him tribute.
3Moreover, David defeated Hadadezer
king of Zobah, in the vicinity of Hamath,
when he went to set up his monument at[a]
the Euphrates River. 4David captured a
thousand of his chariots, seven thousand
charioteers and twenty thousand foot
soldiers. He hamstrung all but a hundred
of the chariot horses.
5When the Arameans of Damascus
came to help Hadadezer king of Zobah,
David struck down twenty-two thousand of them. 6He put garrisons in the
Aramean kingdom of Damascus, and the
Arameans became subject to him and
brought him tribute. The LORD gave David victory wherever he went.
7David took the gold shields carried
by the officers of Hadadezer and brought
them to Jerusalem. 8From Tebah[b] and
Kun, towns that belonged to Hadadezer,
David took a great quantity of bronze,
which Solomon used to make the bronze
Sea, the pillars and various bronze articles.
9When Tou king of Hamath heard that
David had defeated the entire army of
Hadadezer king of Zobah, 10he sent his
son Hadoram to King David to greet him
and congratulate him on his victory in
battle over Hadadezer, who had been at
war with Tou. Hadoram brought all kinds
of articles of gold, of silver and of bronze.
11King David dedicated these articles
to the LORD, as he had done with the silver and gold he had taken from all these
nations: Edom and Moab, the Ammonites
and the Philistines, and Amalek.
12Abishai son of Zeruiah struck down
eighteen thousand Edomites in the Valley of Salt. 13He put garrisons in Edom,
and all the Edomites became subject
to David. The LORD gave David victory
wherever he went.
14David reigned over all Israel, doing
what was just and right for all his people.
15Joab son of Zeruiah was over the army;
Jehoshaphat son of Ahilud was recorder;
16Zadok son of Ahitub and Ahimelek[c]
son of Abiathar were priests; Shavsha
was secretary; 17Benaiah son of Jehoiada
was over the Kerethites and Pelethites;
and David's sons were chief officials at
the king's side.

19 In the course of time, Nahash king
of the Ammonites died, and his son
succeeded him as king. 2David thought,
"I will show kindness to Hanun son of
Nahash, because his father showed kindness to me." So David sent a delegation to
express his sympathy to Hanun concerning his father.
When David's envoys came to Hanun
in the land of the Ammonites to express
sympathy to him, 3the Ammonite commanders said to Hanun, "Do you think
David is honoring your father by sending envoys to you to express sympathy?
Haven't his envoys come to you only to
explore and spy out the country and overthrow it?" 4So Hanun seized David's envoys, shaved them, cut off their garments
at the buttocks, and sent them away.

[a] *3* Or *to restore his control over* [b] *8* Hebrew *Tibhath,* a variant of *Tebah* [c] *16* Some Hebrew manuscripts, Vulgate and Syriac (see also 2 Samuel 8:17); most Hebrew manuscripts *Abimelek*

5 When someone came and told David about the men, he sent messengers to meet them, for they were greatly humiliated. The king said, "Stay at Jericho till your beards have grown, and then come back."

6 When the Ammonites realized that they had become obnoxious to David, Hanun and the Ammonites sent a thousand talents[a] of silver to hire chariots and charioteers from Aram Naharaim,[b] Aram Maakah and Zobah. 7 They hired thirty-two thousand chariots and charioteers, as well as the king of Maakah with his troops, who came and camped near Medeba, while the Ammonites were mustered from their towns and moved out for battle.

8 On hearing this, David sent Joab out with the entire army of fighting men. 9 The Ammonites came out and drew up in battle formation at the entrance to their city, while the kings who had come were by themselves in the open country.

10 Joab saw that there were battle lines in front of him and behind him; so he selected some of the best troops in Israel and deployed them against the Arameans. 11 He put the rest of the men under the command of Abishai his brother, and they were deployed against the Ammonites. 12 Joab said, "If the Arameans are too strong for me, then you are to rescue me; but if the Ammonites are too strong for you, then I will rescue you. 13 Be strong, and let us fight bravely for our people and the cities of our God. The LORD will do what is good in his sight."

14 Then Joab and the troops with him advanced to fight the Arameans, and they fled before him. 15 When the Ammonites realized that the Arameans were fleeing, they too fled before his brother Abishai and went inside the city. So Joab went back to Jerusalem.

16 After the Arameans saw that they had been routed by Israel, they sent messengers and had Arameans brought from beyond the Euphrates River, with Shophak the commander of Hadadezer's army leading them.

17 When David was told of this, he gathered all Israel and crossed the Jordan; he advanced against them and formed his battle lines opposite them. David formed his lines to meet the Arameans in battle, and they fought against him. 18 But they fled before Israel, and David killed seven thousand of their charioteers and forty thousand of their foot soldiers. He also killed Shophak the commander of their army.

19 When the vassals of Hadadezer saw that they had been routed by Israel, they made peace with David and became subject to him.

So the Arameans were not willing to help the Ammonites anymore.

20 In the spring, at the time when kings go off to war, Joab led out the armed forces. He laid waste the land of the Ammonites and went to Rabbah and besieged it, but David remained in Jerusalem. Joab attacked Rabbah and left it in ruins. 2 David took the crown from the head of their king[c]—its weight was found to be a talent[d] of gold, and it was set with precious stones—and it was placed on David's head. He took a great quantity of plunder from the city 3 and brought out the people who were there, consigning them to labor with saws and with iron picks and axes. David did this to all the Ammonite towns. Then David and his entire army returned to Jerusalem.

4 In the course of time, war broke out with the Philistines, at Gezer. At that time Sibbekai the Hushathite killed Sippai, one of the descendants of the Rephaites, and the Philistines were subjugated.

5 In another battle with the Philistines, Elhanan son of Jair killed Lahmi the brother of Goliath the Gittite, who had a spear with a shaft like a weaver's rod.

6 In still another battle, which took place at Gath, there was a huge man with six fingers on each hand and six toes on each foot—twenty-four in all. He also was descended from Rapha. 7 When he taunted Israel, Jonathan son of Shimea, David's brother, killed him.

8 These were descendants of Rapha in Gath, and they fell at the hands of David and his men.

21 Satan rose up against Israel and incited David to take a census of Israel. 2 So David said to Joab and the commanders of the troops, "Go and count the Israelites from Beersheba to Dan. Then

[a] *6* That is, about 38 tons or about 34 metric tons [b] *6* That is, Northwest Mesopotamia [c] *2* Or *of Milkom,* that is, Molek [d] *2* That is, about 75 pounds or about 34 kilograms

report back to me so that I may know how
many there are."
3But Joab replied, "May the LORD multiply his troops a hundred times over. My
lord the king, are they not all my lord's subjects? Why does my lord want to do this?
Why should he bring guilt on Israel?"
4The king's word, however, overruled
Joab; so Joab left and went throughout
Israel and then came back to Jerusalem.
5Joab reported the number of the fighting men to David: In all Israel there were
one million one hundred thousand men
who could handle a sword, including
four hundred and seventy thousand in
Judah.
6But Joab did not include Levi and
Benjamin in the numbering, because the
king's command was repulsive to him.
7This command was also evil in the sight
of God; so he punished Israel.
8Then David said to God, "I have
sinned greatly by doing this. Now, I beg
you, take away the guilt of your servant. I
have done a very foolish thing."
9The LORD said to Gad, David's seer,
10"Go and tell David, 'This is what the
LORD says: I am giving you three options.
Choose one of them for me to carry out
against you.'"
11So Gad went to David and said to him,
"This is what the LORD says: 'Take your
choice: 12three years of famine, three
months of being swept away[a] before your
enemies, with their swords overtaking
you, or three days of the sword of the
LORD—days of plague in the land, with
the angel of the LORD ravaging every part
of Israel.' Now then, decide how I should
answer the one who sent me."
13David said to Gad, "I am in deep distress. Let me fall into the hands of the
LORD, for his mercy is very great; but do
not let me fall into human hands."
14So the LORD sent a plague on Israel,
and seventy thousand men of Israel fell
dead. 15And God sent an angel to destroy
Jerusalem. But as the angel was doing so,
the LORD saw it and relented concerning
the disaster and said to the angel who
was destroying the people, "Enough!
Withdraw your hand." The angel of the
LORD was then standing at the threshing
floor of Araunah[b] the Jebusite.
16David looked up and saw the angel of
the LORD standing between heaven and
earth, with a drawn sword in his hand
extended over Jerusalem. Then David
and the elders, clothed in sackcloth, fell
facedown.
17David said to God, "Was it not I who
ordered the fighting men to be counted?
I, the shepherd,[c] have sinned and done
wrong. These are but sheep. What have
they done? LORD my God, let your hand
fall on me and my family, but do not let
this plague remain on your people."
18Then the angel of the LORD ordered
Gad to tell David to go up and build an
altar to the LORD on the threshing floor
of Araunah the Jebusite. 19So David went
up in obedience to the word that Gad had
spoken in the name of the LORD.
20While Araunah was threshing wheat,
he turned and saw the angel; his four
sons who were with him hid themselves.
21Then David approached, and when
Araunah looked and saw him, he left the
threshing floor and bowed down before
David with his face to the ground.
22David said to him, "Let me have the
site of your threshing floor so I can build
an altar to the LORD, that the plague on
the people may be stopped. Sell it to me
at the full price."
23Araunah said to David, "Take it! Let
my lord the king do whatever pleases
him. Look, I will give the oxen for the
burnt offerings, the threshing sledges for
the wood, and the wheat for the grain offering. I will give all this."
24But King David replied to Araunah,
"No, I insist on paying the full price. I
will not take for the LORD what is yours,
or sacrifice a burnt offering that costs me
nothing."
25So David paid Araunah six hundred
shekels[d] of gold for the site. 26David built
an altar to the LORD there and sacrificed
burnt offerings and fellowship offerings.
He called on the LORD, and the LORD answered him with fire from heaven on the
altar of burnt offering.
27Then the LORD spoke to the angel,
and he put his sword back into its sheath.
28At that time, when David saw that the
LORD had answered him on the threshing
floor of Araunah the Jebusite, he offered

[a] *12* Hebrew; Septuagint and Vulgate (see also 2 Samuel 24:13) *of fleeing* [b] *15* Hebrew *Ornan,* a variant of *Araunah*; also in verses 18-28 [c] *17* Probable reading of the original Hebrew text (see 2 Samuel 24:17 and note); Masoretic Text does not have *the shepherd.* [d] *25* That is, about 15 pounds or about 6.9 kilograms

sacrifices there. 29 The tabernacle of the LORD, which Moses had made in the wilderness, and the altar of burnt offering were at that time on the high place at Gibeon. 30 But David could not go before it to inquire of God, because he was afraid of the sword of the angel of the LORD.

22 Then David said, "The house of the LORD God is to be here, and also the altar of burnt offering for Israel."

2 So David gave orders to assemble the foreigners residing in Israel, and from among them he appointed stonecutters to prepare dressed stone for building the house of God. 3 He provided a large amount of iron to make nails for the doors of the gateways and for the fittings, and more bronze than could be weighed. 4 He also provided more cedar logs than could be counted, for the Sidonians and Tyrians had brought large numbers of them to David.

5 David said, "My son Solomon is young and inexperienced, and the house to be built for the LORD should be of great magnificence and fame and splendor in the sight of all the nations. Therefore I will make preparations for it." So David made extensive preparations before his death.

6 Then he called for his son Solomon and charged him to build a house for the LORD, the God of Israel. 7 David said to Solomon: "My son, I had it in my heart to build a house for the Name of the LORD my God. 8 But this word of the LORD came to me: 'You have shed much blood and have fought many wars. You are not to build a house for my Name, because you have shed much blood on the earth in my sight. 9 But you will have a son who will be a man of peace and rest, and I will give him rest from all his enemies on every side. His name will be Solomon,[a] and I will grant Israel peace and quiet during his reign. 10 He is the one who will build a house for my Name. He will be my son, and I will be his father. And I will establish the throne of his kingdom over Israel forever.'

11 "Now, my son, the LORD be with you, and may you have success and build the house of the LORD your God, as he said you would. 12 May the LORD give you discretion and understanding when he puts you in command over Israel, so that you may keep the law of the LORD your God. 13 Then you will have success if you are careful to observe the decrees and laws that the LORD gave Moses for Israel. Be strong and courageous. Do not be afraid or discouraged.

14 "I have taken great pains to provide for the temple of the LORD a hundred thousand talents[b] of gold, a million talents[c] of silver, quantities of bronze and iron too great to be weighed, and wood and stone. And you may add to them. 15 You have many workers: stonecutters, masons and carpenters, as well as those skilled in every kind of work 16 in gold and silver, bronze and iron—craftsmen beyond number. Now begin the work, and the LORD be with you."

17 Then David ordered all the leaders of Israel to help his son Solomon. 18 He said to them, "Is not the LORD your God with you? And has he not granted you rest on every side? For he has given the inhabitants of the land into my hands, and the land is subject to the LORD and to his people. 19 Now devote your heart and soul to seeking the LORD your God. Begin to build the sanctuary of the LORD God, so that you may bring the ark of the covenant of the LORD and the sacred articles belonging to God into the temple that will be built for the Name of the LORD."

23 When David was old and full of years, he made his son Solomon king over Israel.

2 He also gathered together all the leaders of Israel, as well as the priests and Levites. 3 The Levites thirty years old or more were counted, and the total number of men was thirty-eight thousand. 4 David said, "Of these, twenty-four thousand are to be in charge of the work of the temple of the LORD and six thousand are to be officials and judges. 5 Four thousand are to be gatekeepers and four thousand are to praise the LORD with the musical instruments I have provided for that purpose."

6 David separated the Levites into divisions corresponding to the sons of Levi: Gershon, Kohath and Merari.

7 Belonging to the Gershonites:
  Ladan and Shimei.
8 The sons of Ladan:
  Jehiel the first, Zetham and Joel—
  three in all.

[a] 9 *Solomon* sounds like and may be derived from the Hebrew for *peace*. [b] 14 That is, about 3,750 tons or about 3,400 metric tons [c] 14 That is, about 37,500 tons or about 34,000 metric tons

9 The sons of Shimei:
Shelomoth, Haziel and Haran—three in all.
These were the heads of the families of Ladan.
10 And the sons of Shimei:
Jahath, Ziza,[a] Jeush and Beriah.
These were the sons of Shimei—four in all.
11 Jahath was the first and Ziza the second, but Jeush and Beriah did not have many sons; so they were counted as one family with one assignment.

12 The sons of Kohath:
Amram, Izhar, Hebron and Uzziel—four in all.
13 The sons of Amram:
Aaron and Moses.
Aaron was set apart, he and his descendants forever, to consecrate the most holy things, to offer sacrifices before the LORD, to minister before him and to pronounce blessings in his name forever.
14 The sons of Moses the man of God were counted as part of the tribe of Levi.
15 The sons of Moses:
Gershom and Eliezer.
16 The descendants of Gershom:
Shubael was the first.
17 The descendants of Eliezer:
Rehabiah was the first.
Eliezer had no other sons, but the sons of Rehabiah were very numerous.
18 The sons of Izhar:
Shelomith was the first.
19 The sons of Hebron:
Jeriah the first, Amariah the second, Jahaziel the third and Jekameam the fourth.
20 The sons of Uzziel:
Micah the first and Ishiah the second.

21 The sons of Merari:
Mahli and Mushi.
The sons of Mahli:
Eleazar and Kish.
22 Eleazar died without having sons: he had only daughters. Their cousins, the sons of Kish, married them.
23 The sons of Mushi:
Mahli, Eder and Jerimoth—three in all.

24 These were the descendants of Levi by their families—the heads of families as they were registered under their names and counted individually, that is, the workers twenty years old or more who served in the temple of the LORD.
25 For David had said, "Since the LORD, the God of Israel, has granted rest to his people and has come to dwell in Jerusalem forever, 26 the Levites no longer need to carry the tabernacle or any of the articles used in its service." 27 According to the last instructions of David, the Levites were counted from those twenty years old or more.
28 The duty of the Levites was to help Aaron's descendants in the service of the temple of the LORD: to be in charge of the courtyards, the side rooms, the purification of all sacred things and the performance of other duties at the house of God. 29 They were in charge of the bread set out on the table, the special flour for the grain offerings, the thin loaves made without yeast, the baking and the mixing, and all measurements of quantity and size. 30 They were also to stand every morning to thank and praise the LORD. They were to do the same in the evening
31 and whenever burnt offerings were presented to the LORD on the Sabbaths, at the New Moon feasts and at the appointed festivals. They were to serve before the LORD regularly in the proper number and in the way prescribed for them.
32 And so the Levites carried out their responsibilities for the tent of meeting, for the Holy Place and, under their relatives the descendants of Aaron, for the service of the temple of the LORD.

24 These were the divisions of the descendants of Aaron:
The sons of Aaron were Nadab, Abihu, Eleazar and Ithamar. 2 But Nadab and Abihu died before their father did, and they had no sons; so Eleazar and Ithamar served as the priests. 3 With the help of Zadok a descendant of Eleazar and Ahimelek a descendant of Ithamar, David separated them into divisions for their appointed order of ministering.

[a] *10* One Hebrew manuscript, Septuagint and Vulgate (see also verse 11); most Hebrew manuscripts *Zina*

4 A larger number of leaders were found
among Eleazar's descendants than
among Ithamar's, and they were divided accordingly: sixteen heads of families
from Eleazar's descendants and eight
heads of families from Ithamar's descendants. 5 They divided them impartially
by casting lots, for there were officials of
the sanctuary and officials of God among
the descendants of both Eleazar and Ithamar.

6 The scribe Shemaiah son of Nethanel, a Levite, recorded their names in the
presence of the king and of the officials:
Zadok the priest, Ahimelek son of Abiathar and the heads of families of the
priests and of the Levites—one family
being taken from Eleazar and then one
from Ithamar.

7 The first lot fell to Jehoiarib,
the second to Jedaiah,
8 the third to Harim,
the fourth to Seorim,
9 the fifth to Malkijah,
the sixth to Mijamin,
10 the seventh to Hakkoz,
the eighth to Abijah,
11 the ninth to Jeshua,
the tenth to Shekaniah,
12 the eleventh to Eliashib,
the twelfth to Jakim,
13 the thirteenth to Huppah,
the fourteenth to Jeshebeab,
14 the fifteenth to Bilgah,
the sixteenth to Immer,
15 the seventeenth to Hezir,
the eighteenth to Happizzez,
16 the nineteenth to Pethahiah,
the twentieth to Jehezkel,
17 the twenty-first to Jakin,
the twenty-second to Gamul,
18 the twenty-third to Delaiah
and the twenty-fourth to Maaziah.

19 This was their appointed order of
ministering when they entered the temple of the LORD, according to the regulations prescribed for them by their ancestor Aaron, as the LORD, the God of Israel,
had commanded him.

20 As for the rest of the descendants of
Levi:
from the sons of Amram: Shubael;
from the sons of Shubael: Jehdeiah.
21 As for Rehabiah, from his sons:
Ishiah was the first.
22 From the Izharites: Shelomoth;
from the sons of Shelomoth: Jahath.
23 The sons of Hebron: Jeriah the first,[a]
Amariah the second, Jahaziel the
third and Jekameam the fourth.
24 The son of Uzziel: Micah;
from the sons of Micah: Shamir.
25 The brother of Micah: Ishiah;
from the sons of Ishiah: Zechariah.
26 The sons of Merari: Mahli and Mushi.
The son of Jaaziah: Beno.
27 The sons of Merari:
from Jaaziah: Beno, Shoham, Zakkur and Ibri.
28 From Mahli: Eleazar, who had no
sons.
29 From Kish: the son of Kish:
Jerahmeel.
30 And the sons of Mushi: Mahli, Eder
and Jerimoth.

These were the Levites, according to
their families. 31 They also cast lots, just
as their relatives the descendants of Aaron did, in the presence of King David
and of Zadok, Ahimelek, and the heads
of families of the priests and of the Levites. The families of the oldest brother were treated the same as those of the
youngest.

25 David, together with the commanders of the army, set apart some of the
sons of Asaph, Heman and Jeduthun for
the ministry of prophesying, accompanied by harps, lyres and cymbals. Here
is the list of the men who performed this
service:

2 From the sons of Asaph:
Zakkur, Joseph, Nethaniah and Asarelah. The sons of Asaph were under
the supervision of Asaph, who prophesied under the king's supervision.
3 As for Jeduthun, from his sons:
Gedaliah, Zeri, Jeshaiah, Shimei,[b]
Hashabiah and Mattithiah, six in all,
under the supervision of their father
Jeduthun, who prophesied, using

[a] *23* Two Hebrew manuscripts and some Septuagint manuscripts (see also 23:19); most Hebrew manuscripts *The sons of Jeriah:* [b] *3* One Hebrew manuscript and some Septuagint manuscripts (see also verse 17); most Hebrew manuscripts do not have *Shimei.*

the harp in thanking and praising
the LORD.
4 As for Heman, from his sons:
Bukkiah, Mattaniah, Uzziel, Shubael and Jerimoth; Hananiah, Hanani,
Eliathah, Giddalti and Romamti-
Ezer; Joshbekashah, Mallothi, Hothir and Mahazioth. 5 (All these were
sons of Heman the king's seer. They
were given him through the promises
of God to exalt him. God gave Heman
fourteen sons and three daughters.)

6 All these men were under the supervision of their father for the music of the
temple of the LORD, with cymbals, lyres
and harps, for the ministry at the house
of God.
Asaph, Jeduthun and Heman were under the supervision of the king. 7 Along
with their relatives — all of them trained
and skilled in music for the LORD — they
numbered 288. 8 Young and old alike,
teacher as well as student, cast lots for
their duties.

9 The first lot, which was for Asaph, fell to Joseph, his sons and relatives[a] 12[b]
the second to Gedaliah, him and his relatives and sons 12
10 the third to Zakkur, his sons and relatives 12
11 the fourth to Izri,[c] his sons and relatives 12
12 the fifth to Nethaniah, his sons and relatives 12
13 the sixth to Bukkiah, his sons and relatives 12
14 the seventh to Jesarelah,[d] his sons and relatives 12
15 the eighth to Jeshaiah, his sons and relatives 12
16 the ninth to Mattaniah, his sons and relatives 12
17 the tenth to Shimei, his sons and relatives 12
18 the eleventh to Azarel,[e] his sons and relatives 12
19 the twelfth to Hashabiah, his sons and relatives 12
20 the thirteenth to Shubael, his sons and relatives 12
21 the fourteenth to Mattithiah, his sons and relatives 12
22 the fifteenth to Jerimoth, his sons and relatives 12
23 the sixteenth to Hananiah, his sons and relatives 12
24 the seventeenth to Joshbekashah, his sons and relatives 12
25 the eighteenth to Hanani, his sons and relatives 12
26 the nineteenth to Mallothi, his sons and relatives 12
27 the twentieth to Eliathah, his sons and relatives 12
28 the twenty-first to Hothir, his sons and relatives 12
29 the twenty-second to Giddalti, his sons and relatives 12
30 the twenty-third to Mahazioth, his sons and relatives 12
31 the twenty-fourth to Romamti-Ezer, his sons and relatives 12.

26 The divisions of the gatekeepers:

From the Korahites: Meshelemi-
ah son of Kore, one of the sons of
Asaph.
2 Meshelemiah had sons:
Zechariah the firstborn,
Jediael the second,
Zebadiah the third,
Jathniel the fourth,
3 Elam the fifth,
Jehohanan the sixth
and Eliehoenai the seventh.
4 Obed-Edom also had sons:
Shemaiah the firstborn,
Jehozabad the second,
Joah the third,
Sakar the fourth,
Nethanel the fifth,
5 Ammiel the sixth,
Issachar the seventh
and Peullethai the eighth.
(For God had blessed Obed-
Edom.)

6 Obed-Edom's son Shemaiah also had
sons, who were leaders in their father's family because they were
very capable men. 7 The sons of
Shemaiah: Othni, Rephael, Obed
and Elzabad; his relatives Elihu
and Semakiah were also able men.
8 All these were descendants of
Obed-Edom; they and their sons

[a] 9 See Septuagint; Hebrew does not have *his sons and relatives.* [b] 9 See the total in verse 7; Hebrew does not have *twelve.* [c] *11* A variant of *Zeri* [d] *14* A variant of *Asarelah* [e] *18* A variant of *Uzziel*

and their relatives were capable
men with the strength to do the
work—descendants of Obed-
Edom, 62 in all.
9 Meshelemiah had sons and relatives,
who were able men—18 in all.

10 Hosah the Merarite had sons: Shimri
the first (although he was not the
firstborn, his father had appointed
him the first), 11 Hilkiah the second, Tabaliah the third and Zechariah the fourth. The sons and relatives of Hosah were 13 in all.

12 These divisions of the gatekeepers,
through their leaders, had duties for ministering in the temple of the LORD, just as
their relatives had. 13 Lots were cast for
each gate, according to their families,
young and old alike.

14 The lot for the East Gate fell to Shelemiah.[a] Then lots were cast for his son
Zechariah, a wise counselor, and the lot
for the North Gate fell to him. 15 The lot
for the South Gate fell to Obed-Edom,
and the lot for the storehouse fell to his
sons. 16 The lots for the West Gate and the
Shalleketh Gate on the upper road fell to
Shuppim and Hosah.

Guard was alongside of guard: 17 There
were six Levites a day on the east, four a
day on the north, four a day on the south
and two at a time at the storehouse. 18 As
for the court[b] to the west, there were four
at the road and two at the court[b] itself.

19 These were the divisions of the gatekeepers who were descendants of Korah
and Merari.

20 Their fellow Levites were[c] in charge
of the treasuries of the house of God and
the treasuries for the dedicated things.

21 The descendants of Ladan, who were
Gershonites through Ladan and who
were heads of families belonging to Ladan the Gershonite, were Jehieli, 22 the
sons of Jehieli, Zetham and his brother
Joel. They were in charge of the treasuries of the temple of the LORD.

23 From the Amramites, the Izharites,
the Hebronites and the Uzzielites:

24 Shubael, a descendant of Gershom
son of Moses, was the official in
charge of the treasuries. 25 His relatives through Eliezer: Rehabiah
his son, Jeshaiah his son, Joram
his son, Zikri his son and Shelomith his son. 26 Shelomith and his
relatives were in charge of all the
treasuries for the things dedicated by King David, by the heads of
families who were the commanders of thousands and commanders
of hundreds, and by the other army
commanders. 27 Some of the plunder taken in battle they dedicated
for the repair of the temple of the
LORD. 28 And everything dedicated
by Samuel the seer and by Saul son
of Kish, Abner son of Ner and Joab
son of Zeruiah, and all the other
dedicated things were in the care
of Shelomith and his relatives.
29 From the Izharites: Kenaniah and
his sons were assigned duties away
from the temple, as officials and
judges over Israel.
30 From the Hebronites: Hashabiah and
his relatives—seventeen hundred
able men—were responsible in Israel west of the Jordan for all the
work of the LORD and for the king's
service. 31 As for the Hebronites,
Jeriah was their chief according to
the genealogical records of their
families. In the fortieth year of
David's reign a search was made
in the records, and capable men
among the Hebronites were found
at Jazer in Gilead. 32 Jeriah had
twenty-seven hundred relatives,
who were able men and heads of
families, and King David put them
in charge of the Reubenites, the
Gadites and the half-tribe of Manasseh for every matter pertaining
to God and for the affairs of the
king.

27 This is the list of the Israelites—
heads of families, commanders of
thousands and commanders of hundreds, and their officers, who served the
king in all that concerned the army divisions that were on duty month by month
throughout the year. Each division consisted of 24,000 men.

2 In charge of the first division, for the
first month, was Jashobeam son of

[a] *14* A variant of *Meshelemiah*
[b] *18* The meaning of the Hebrew for this word is uncertain.
[c] *20* Septuagint; Hebrew *As for the Levites, Ahijah was*

Zabdiel. There were 24,000 men in
his division. 3 He was a descendant
of Perez and chief of all the army officers for the first month.
4 In charge of the division for the second
month was Dodai the Ahohite; Mikloth was the leader of his division.
There were 24,000 men in his division.
5 The third army commander, for the
third month, was Benaiah son of Jehoiada the priest. He was chief and
there were 24,000 men in his division. 6 This was the Benaiah who was
a mighty warrior among the Thirty
and was over the Thirty. His son Ammizabad was in charge of his division.
7 The fourth, for the fourth month, was
Asahel the brother of Joab; his son Zebadiah was his successor. There were 24,000 men in his division.
8 The fifth, for the fifth month, was the
commander Shamhuth the Izrahite. There were 24,000 men in his division.
9 The sixth, for the sixth month, was Ira
the son of Ikkesh the Tekoite. There were 24,000 men in his division.
10 The seventh, for the seventh month,
was Helez the Pelonite, an Ephraimite. There were 24,000 men in his division.
11 The eighth, for the eighth month, was
Sibbekai the Hushathite, a Zerahite. There were 24,000 men in his division.
12 The ninth, for the ninth month, was
Abiezer the Anathothite, a Benjamite. There were 24,000 men in his division.
13 The tenth, for the tenth month, was
Maharai the Netophathite, a Zerahite. There were 24,000 men in his division.
14 The eleventh, for the eleventh month,
was Benaiah the Pirathonite, an Ephraimite. There were 24,000 men in his division.
15 The twelfth, for the twelfth month, was
Heldai the Netophathite, from the family of Othniel. There were 24,000 men in his division.
16 The leaders of the tribes of Israel:
over the Reubenites: Eliezer son of Zikri;
over the Simeonites: Shephatiah son of Maakah;
17 over Levi: Hashabiah son of Kemuel;
over Aaron: Zadok;
18 over Judah: Elihu, a brother of David;
over Issachar: Omri son of Michael;
19 over Zebulun: Ishmaiah son of Obadiah;
over Naphtali: Jerimoth son of Azriel;
20 over the Ephraimites: Hoshea son of Azaziah;
over half the tribe of Manasseh: Joel son of Pedaiah;
21 over the half-tribe of Manasseh in Gilead: Iddo son of Zechariah;
over Benjamin: Jaasiel son of Abner;
22 over Dan: Azarel son of Jeroham.
These were the leaders of the tribes of Israel.

23 David did not take the number of the
men twenty years old or less, because the
LORD had promised to make Israel as numerous as the stars in the sky. 24 Joab son
of Zeruiah began to count the men but
did not finish. God's wrath came on Israel on account of this numbering, and the
number was not entered in the book[a] of
the annals of King David.

25 Azmaveth son of Adiel was in charge
of the royal storehouses.

Jonathan son of Uzziah was in charge of the storehouses in the outlying districts, in the towns, the villages and the watchtowers.

26 Ezri son of Kelub was in charge of the
workers who farmed the land.

27 Shimei the Ramathite was in charge
of the vineyards.

Zabdi the Shiphmite was in charge of the produce of the vineyards for the wine vats.

28 Baal-Hanan the Gederite was in
charge of the olive and sycamore-fig trees in the western foothills.

Joash was in charge of the supplies of olive oil.

29 Shitrai the Sharonite was in charge of
the herds grazing in Sharon.

Shaphat son of Adlai was in charge of the herds in the valleys.

[a] *24* Septuagint; Hebrew *number*

30 Obil the Ishmaelite was in charge of
the camels.
Jehdeiah the Meronothite was in
charge of the donkeys.
31 Jaziz the Hagrite was in charge of the
flocks.
All these were the officials in charge of
King David's property.

32 Jonathan, David's uncle, was a counselor, a man of insight and a scribe. Jehiel
son of Hakmoni took care of the king's
sons.
33 Ahithophel was the king's counsel-
or.
Hushai the Arkite was the king's confidant. 34 Ahithophel was succeeded by Jehoiada son of Benaiah and by Abiathar.
Joab was the commander of the royal
army.

28 David summoned all the officials of
Israel to assemble at Jerusalem: the
officers over the tribes, the commanders
of the divisions in the service of the king,
the commanders of thousands and commanders of hundreds, and the officials in
charge of all the property and livestock
belonging to the king and his sons, together with the palace officials, the warriors and all the brave fighting men.
2 King David rose to his feet and said:
"Listen to me, my fellow Israelites, my
people. I had it in my heart to build a
house as a place of rest for the ark of the
covenant of the LORD, for the footstool
of our God, and I made plans to build it.
3 But God said to me, 'You are not to build
a house for my Name, because you are a
warrior and have shed blood.'
4 "Yet the LORD, the God of Israel, chose
me from my whole family to be king over
Israel forever. He chose Judah as leader,
and from the tribe of Judah he chose my
family, and from my father's sons he was
pleased to make me king over all Israel.
5 Of all my sons—and the LORD has given
me many—he has chosen my son Solomon to sit on the throne of the kingdom
of the LORD over Israel. 6 He said to me:
'Solomon your son is the one who will
build my house and my courts, for I have
chosen him to be my son, and I will be his
father. 7 I will establish his kingdom forever if he is unswerving in carrying out
my commands and laws, as is being done
at this time.'
8 "So now I charge you in the sight of all
Israel and of the assembly of the LORD,
and in the hearing of our God: Be careful
to follow all the commands of the LORD
your God, that you may possess this good
land and pass it on as an inheritance to
your descendants forever.
9 "And you, my son Solomon, acknowledge the God of your father, and serve
him with wholehearted devotion and
with a willing mind, for the LORD searches every heart and understands every desire and every thought. If you seek him,
he will be found by you; but if you forsake
him, he will reject you forever. 10 Consider now, for the LORD has chosen you to
build a house as the sanctuary. Be strong
and do the work."
11 Then David gave his son Solomon
the plans for the portico of the temple,
its buildings, its storerooms, its upper
parts, its inner rooms and the place of
atonement. 12 He gave him the plans of
all that the Spirit had put in his mind for
the courts of the temple of the LORD and
all the surrounding rooms, for the treasuries of the temple of God and for the
treasuries for the dedicated things. 13 He
gave him instructions for the divisions
of the priests and Levites, and for all the
work of serving in the temple of the LORD,
as well as for all the articles to be used in
its service. 14 He designated the weight of
gold for all the gold articles to be used in
various kinds of service, and the weight
of silver for all the silver articles to be
used in various kinds of service: 15 the
weight of gold for the gold lampstands
and their lamps, with the weight for each
lampstand and its lamps; and the weight
of silver for each silver lampstand and
its lamps, according to the use of each
lampstand; 16 the weight of gold for each
table for consecrated bread; the weight of
silver for the silver tables; 17 the weight of
pure gold for the forks, sprinkling bowls
and pitchers; the weight of gold for each
gold dish; the weight of silver for each silver dish; 18 and the weight of the refined
gold for the altar of incense. He also gave
him the plan for the chariot, that is, the
cherubim of gold that spread their wings
and overshadow the ark of the covenant
of the LORD.

19 "All this," David said, "I have in writing as a result of the LORD's hand on me,
and he enabled me to understand all the
details of the plan."

20 David also said to Solomon his son,
"Be strong and courageous, and do the
work. Do not be afraid or discouraged,
for the LORD God, my God, is with you.
He will not fail you or forsake you until
all the work for the service of the temple
of the LORD is finished. 21 The divisions
of the priests and Levites are ready for
all the work on the temple of God, and
every willing person skilled in any craft
will help you in all the work. The officials
and all the people will obey your every
command."

29 Then King David said to the whole
assembly: "My son Solomon, the
one whom God has chosen, is young and
inexperienced. The task is great, because
this palatial structure is not for man but
for the LORD God. 2 With all my resources I have provided for the temple of my
God—gold for the gold work, silver for
the silver, bronze for the bronze, iron
for the iron and wood for the wood, as
well as onyx for the settings, turquoise,[a]
stones of various colors, and all kinds of
fine stone and marble—all of these in
large quantities. 3 Besides, in my devotion to the temple of my God I now give
my personal treasures of gold and silver
for the temple of my God, over and above
everything I have provided for this holy
temple: 4 three thousand talents[b] of gold
(gold of Ophir) and seven thousand talents[c] of refined silver, for the overlaying
of the walls of the buildings, 5 for the gold
work and the silver work, and for all the
work to be done by the craftsmen. Now,
who is willing to consecrate themselves
to the LORD today?"

6 Then the leaders of families, the officers of the tribes of Israel, the commanders of thousands and commanders of
hundreds, and the officials in charge of
the king's work gave willingly. 7 They gave
toward the work on the temple of God
five thousand talents[d] and ten thousand
darics[e] of gold, ten thousand talents[f]
of silver, eighteen thousand talents[g] of
bronze and a hundred thousand talents[h]
of iron. 8 Anyone who had precious stones
gave them to the treasury of the temple
of the LORD in the custody of Jehiel the
Gershonite. 9 The people rejoiced at the
willing response of their leaders, for they
had given freely and wholeheartedly to
the LORD. David the king also rejoiced
greatly.

10 David praised the LORD in the presence of the whole assembly, saying,

"Praise be to you, LORD,
the God of our father Israel,
from everlasting to everlasting.
11 Yours, LORD, is the greatness and the
power
and the glory and the majesty and
the splendor,
for everything in heaven and earth
is yours.
Yours, LORD, is the kingdom;
you are exalted as head over all.
12 Wealth and honor come from you;
you are the ruler of all things.
In your hands are strength and power
to exalt and give strength to all.
13 Now, our God, we give you thanks,
and praise your glorious name.

14 "But who am I, and who are my people, that we should be able to give as
generously as this? Everything comes
from you, and we have given you only
what comes from your hand. 15 We are
foreigners and strangers in your sight,
as were all our ancestors. Our days on
earth are like a shadow, without hope.
16 LORD our God, all this abundance
that we have provided for building you a
temple for your Holy Name comes from
your hand, and all of it belongs to you.
17 I know, my God, that you test the heart
and are pleased with integrity. All these
things I have given willingly and with
honest intent. And now I have seen with
joy how willingly your people who are
here have given to you. 18 LORD, the God
of our fathers Abraham, Isaac and Israel,
keep these desires and thoughts in the
hearts of your people forever, and keep
their hearts loyal to you. 19 And give my
son Solomon the wholehearted devotion
to keep your commands, statutes and decrees and to do everything to build the
palatial structure for which I have provided."

[a] 2 The meaning of the Hebrew for this word is uncertain. [b] 4 That is, about 110 tons or about 100 metric tons [c] 4 That is, about 260 tons or about 235 metric tons [d] 7 That is, about 190 tons or about 170 metric tons [e] 7 That is, about 185 pounds or about 84 kilograms [f] 7 That is, about 380 tons or about 340 metric tons [g] 7 That is, about 675 tons or about 610 metric tons [h] 7 That is, about 3,800 tons or about 3,400 metric tons

[20]Then David said to the whole assembly, "Praise the LORD your God." So
they all praised the LORD, the God of
their fathers; they bowed down, prostrating themselves before the LORD and
the king.
[21]The next day they made sacrifices
to the LORD and presented burnt offerings to him: a thousand bulls, a thousand rams and a thousand male lambs,
together with their drink offerings, and
other sacrifices in abundance for all Israel. [22]They ate and drank with great joy
in the presence of the LORD that day.
Then they acknowledged Solomon son
of David as king a second time, anointing him before the LORD to be ruler and
Zadok to be priest. [23]So Solomon sat on
the throne of the LORD as king in place
of his father David. He prospered and all
Israel obeyed him. [24]All the officers and
warriors, as well as all of King David's
sons, pledged their submission to King
Solomon.
[25]The LORD highly exalted Solomon
in the sight of all Israel and bestowed on
him royal splendor such as no king over
Israel ever had before.
[26]David son of Jesse was king over
all Israel. [27]He ruled over Israel forty
years—seven in Hebron and thirty-
three in Jerusalem. [28]He died at a good
old age, having enjoyed long life, wealth
and honor. His son Solomon succeeded
him as king.
[29]As for the events of King David's
reign, from beginning to end, they are
written in the records of Samuel the seer,
the records of Nathan the prophet and
the records of Gad the seer, [30]together
with the details of his reign and power,
and the circumstances that surrounded
him and Israel and the kingdoms of all
the other lands.

2 CHRONICLES

See the Invitation to Chronicles-Ezra-Nehemiah on p. 354.

1 Solomon son of David established
himself firmly over his kingdom, for
the LORD his God was with him and made
him exceedingly great.
[2]Then Solomon spoke to all Israel—to
the commanders of thousands and commanders of hundreds, to the judges and
to all the leaders in Israel, the heads of
families— [3]and Solomon and the whole
assembly went to the high place at Gibeon, for God's tent of meeting was there,
which Moses the LORD's servant had
made in the wilderness. [4]Now David had
brought up the ark of God from Kiriath
Jearim to the place he had prepared for it,
because he had pitched a tent for it in Jerusalem. [5]But the bronze altar that Bezalel son of Uri, the son of Hur, had made
was in Gibeon in front of the tabernacle of
the LORD; so Solomon and the assembly
inquired of him there. [6]Solomon went up
to the bronze altar before the LORD in the
tent of meeting and offered a thousand
burnt offerings on it.
[7]That night God appeared to Solomon
and said to him, "Ask for whatever you
want me to give you."
[8]Solomon answered God, "You have
shown great kindness to David my father and have made me king in his place.
[9]Now, LORD God, let your promise to my
father David be confirmed, for you have

made me king over a people who are as
numerous as the dust of the earth. 10Give
me wisdom and knowledge, that I may
lead this people, for who is able to govern
this great people of yours?"
11God said to Solomon, "Since this
is your heart's desire and you have not
asked for wealth, possessions or honor,
nor for the death of your enemies, and
since you have not asked for a long life
but for wisdom and knowledge to govern
my people over whom I have made you
king, 12therefore wisdom and knowledge
will be given you. And I will also give you
wealth, possessions and honor, such as
no king who was before you ever had and
none after you will have."
13Then Solomon went to Jerusalem
from the high place at Gibeon, from before the tent of meeting. And he reigned
over Israel.
14Solomon accumulated chariots and
horses; he had fourteen hundred chariots and twelve thousand horses,[a] which
he kept in the chariot cities and also with
him in Jerusalem. 15The king made silver and gold as common in Jerusalem
as stones, and cedar as plentiful as sycamore-fig trees in the foothills. 16Solo-
mon's horses were imported from Egypt
and from Kue[b]—the royal merchants
purchased them from Kue at the current
price. 17They imported a chariot from
Egypt for six hundred shekels[c] of silver,
and a horse for a hundred and fifty.[d] They
also exported them to all the kings of the
Hittites and of the Arameans.

2[e] Solomon gave orders to build a temple for the Name of the LORD and a
royal palace for himself. 2He conscripted 70,000 men as carriers and 80,000 as
stonecutters in the hills and 3,600 as foremen over them.
3Solomon sent this message to Hiram[f]
king of Tyre:

"Send me cedar logs as you did
for my father David when you sent
him cedar to build a palace to live
in. 4Now I am about to build a temple for the Name of the LORD my God
and to dedicate it to him for burning
fragrant incense before him, for setting out the consecrated bread regularly, and for making burnt offerings
every morning and evening and on
the Sabbaths, at the New Moons and
at the appointed festivals of the LORD
our God. This is a lasting ordinance
for Israel.
5"The temple I am going to build
will be great, because our God is
greater than all other gods. 6But
who is able to build a temple for him,
since the heavens, even the highest
heavens, cannot contain him? Who
then am I to build a temple for him,
except as a place to burn sacrifices
before him?
7"Send me, therefore, a man skilled
to work in gold and silver, bronze
and iron, and in purple, crimson and
blue yarn, and experienced in the art
of engraving, to work in Judah and
Jerusalem with my skilled workers,
whom my father David provided.
8"Send me also cedar, juniper
and algum[g] logs from Lebanon, for
I know that your servants are skilled
in cutting timber there. My servants
will work with yours 9to provide me
with plenty of lumber, because the
temple I build must be large and
magnificent. 10I will give your servants, the woodsmen who cut the
timber, twenty thousand cors[h] of
ground wheat, twenty thousand cors[i]
of barley, twenty thousand baths[j] of
wine and twenty thousand baths of
olive oil."

11Hiram king of Tyre replied by letter
to Solomon:

"Because the LORD loves his people, he has made you their king."

12And Hiram added:

"Praise be to the LORD, the God of
Israel, who made heaven and earth!
He has given King David a wise son,
endowed with intelligence and discernment, who will build a temple for
the LORD and a palace for himself.

[a] *14* Or *charioteers* [b] *16* Probably Cilicia [c] *17* That is, about 15 pounds or about 6.9 kilograms [d] *17* That is, about 3 3/4 pounds or about 1.7 kilograms [e] In Hebrew texts 2:1 is numbered 1:18, and 2:2-18 is numbered 2:1-17. [f] *3* Hebrew *Huram,* a variant of *Hiram;* also in verses 11 and 12 [g] *8* Probably a variant of *almug* [h] *10* That is, probably about 3,600 tons or about 3,200 metric tons of wheat [i] *10* That is, probably about 3,000 tons or about 2,700 metric tons of barley [j] *10* That is, about 120,000 gallons or about 440,000 liters

13 "I am sending you Huram-Abi,
a man of great skill, 14 whose mother was from Dan and whose father
was from Tyre. He is trained to work
in gold and silver, bronze and iron,
stone and wood, and with purple
and blue and crimson yarn and fine
linen. He is experienced in all kinds
of engraving and can execute any design given to him. He will work with
your skilled workers and with those
of my lord, David your father.
15 "Now let my lord send his servants the wheat and barley and the
olive oil and wine he promised, 16 and
we will cut all the logs from Lebanon
that you need and will float them as
rafts by sea down to Joppa. You can
then take them up to Jerusalem."

17 Solomon took a census of all the foreigners residing in Israel, after the census his father David had taken; and they
were found to be 153,600. 18 He assigned
70,000 of them to be carriers and 80,000
to be stonecutters in the hills, with 3,600
foremen over them to keep the people
working.

3 Then Solomon began to build the temple of the LORD in Jerusalem on Mount
Moriah, where the LORD had appeared to
his father David. It was on the threshing
floor of Araunah[a] the Jebusite, the place
provided by David. 2 He began building
on the second day of the second month
in the fourth year of his reign.
3 The foundation Solomon laid for
building the temple of God was sixty cubits long and twenty cubits wide[b] (using
the cubit of the old standard). 4 The portico at the front of the temple was twenty
cubits[c] long across the width of the building and twenty[d] cubits high.
He overlaid the inside with pure gold.
5 He paneled the main hall with juniper
and covered it with fine gold and decorated it with palm tree and chain designs.
6 He adorned the temple with precious
stones. And the gold he used was gold of
Parvaim. 7 He overlaid the ceiling beams,
doorframes, walls and doors of the temple with gold, and he carved cherubim on
the walls.
8 He built the Most Holy Place, its
length corresponding to the width of the
temple — twenty cubits long and twenty
cubits wide. He overlaid the inside with
six hundred talents[e] of fine gold. 9 The
gold nails weighed fifty shekels.[f] He also
overlaid the upper parts with gold.
10 For the Most Holy Place he made a
pair of sculptured cherubim and overlaid them with gold. 11 The total wing-
span of the cherubim was twenty cubits.
One wing of the first cherub was five cubits[g] long and touched the temple wall,
while its other wing, also five cubits long,
touched the wing of the other cherub.
12 Similarly one wing of the second cherub was five cubits long and touched the
other temple wall, and its other wing, also
five cubits long, touched the wing of the
first cherub. 13 The wings of these cherubim extended twenty cubits. They stood
on their feet, facing the main hall.[h]
14 He made the curtain of blue, purple
and crimson yarn and fine linen, with
cherubim worked into it.
15 For the front of the temple he made
two pillars, which together were thirty-five cubits[i] long, each with a capital
five cubits high. 16 He made interwoven
chains[j] and put them on top of the pillars. He also made a hundred pomegranates and attached them to the chains.
17 He erected the pillars in the front of the
temple, one to the south and one to the
north. The one to the south he named Jakin[k] and the one to the north Boaz.[l]

4 He made a bronze altar twenty cubits
long, twenty cubits wide and ten cubits high.[m] 2 He made the Sea of cast metal, circular in shape, measuring ten cubits from rim to rim and five cubits[n] high.
It took a line of thirty cubits[o] to measure
around it. 3 Below the rim, figures of bulls
encircled it — ten to a cubit.[p] The bulls

[a] *1* Hebrew *Ornan,* a variant of *Araunah* [b] *3* That is, about 90 feet long and 30 feet wide or about 27 meters long and 9 meters wide [c] *4* That is, about 30 feet or about 9 meters; also in verses 8, 11 and 13 [d] *4* Some Septuagint and Syriac manuscripts; Hebrew *and a hundred and twenty* [e] *8* That is, about 23 tons or about 21 metric tons [f] *9* That is, about 1 1/4 pounds or about 575 grams [g] *11* That is, about 7 1/2 feet or about 2.3 meters; also in verse 15 [h] *13* Or *facing inward* [i] *15* That is, about 53 feet or about 16 meters [j] *16* Or possibly *made chains in the inner sanctuary*; the meaning of the Hebrew for this phrase is uncertain. [k] *17* *Jakin* probably means *he establishes.* [l] *17* *Boaz* probably means *in him is strength.* [m] *1* That is, about 30 feet long and wide and 15 feet high or about 9 meters long and wide and 4.5 meters high [n] *2* That is, about 7 1/2 feet or about 2.3 meters [o] *2* That is, about 45 feet or about 14 meters [p] *3* That is, about 18 inches or about 45 centimeters

were cast in two rows in one piece with
the Sea.
4 The Sea stood on twelve bulls, three
facing north, three facing west, three facing south and three facing east. The Sea
rested on top of them, and their hind-
quarters were toward the center. 5 It was
a handbreadth[a] in thickness, and its rim
was like the rim of a cup, like a lily blossom. It held three thousand baths.[b]
6 He then made ten basins for washing
and placed five on the south side and five
on the north. In them the things to be
used for the burnt offerings were rinsed,
but the Sea was to be used by the priests
for washing.
7 He made ten gold lampstands according to the specifications for them and
placed them in the temple, five on the
south side and five on the north.
8 He made ten tables and placed them
in the temple, five on the south side and
five on the north. He also made a hundred gold sprinkling bowls.
9 He made the courtyard of the priests,
and the large court and the doors for
the court, and overlaid the doors with
bronze. 10 He placed the Sea on the south
side, at the southeast corner.
11 And Huram also made the pots and
shovels and sprinkling bowls.
So Huram finished the work he had undertaken for King Solomon in the temple
of God:

12 the two pillars;
the two bowl-shaped capitals on top of the pillars;
the two sets of network decorating the two bowl-shaped capitals on top of the pillars;
13 the four hundred pomegranates for the two sets of network (two rows of pomegranates for each network, decorating the bowl-shaped capitals on top of the pillars);
14 the stands with their basins;
15 the Sea and the twelve bulls under it;
16 the pots, shovels, meat forks and all related articles.

All the objects that Huram-Abi made
for King Solomon for the temple of the
LORD were of polished bronze. 17 The
king had them cast in clay molds in the
plain of the Jordan between Sukkoth and
Zarethan.[c] 18 All these things that Solomon made amounted to so much that the
weight of the bronze could not be calculated.
19 Solomon also made all the furnishings that were in God's temple:

the golden altar;
the tables on which was the bread of the Presence;
20 the lampstands of pure gold with their lamps, to burn in front of the inner sanctuary as prescribed;
21 the gold floral work and lamps and tongs (they were solid gold);
22 the pure gold wick trimmers, sprinkling bowls, dishes and censers; and the gold doors of the temple: the inner doors to the Most Holy Place and the doors of the main hall.

5 When all the work Solomon had done
for the temple of the LORD was finished, he brought in the things his father
David had dedicated—the silver and gold
and all the furnishings—and he placed
them in the treasuries of God's temple.
2 Then Solomon summoned to Jerusalem the elders of Israel, all the heads of
the tribes and the chiefs of the Israelite
families, to bring up the ark of the LORD's
covenant from Zion, the City of David.
3 And all the Israelites came together to
the king at the time of the festival in the
seventh month.
4 When all the elders of Israel had arrived, the Levites took up the ark, 5 and
they brought up the ark and the tent of
meeting and all the sacred furnishings
in it. The Levitical priests carried them
up; 6 and King Solomon and the entire assembly of Israel that had gathered about
him were before the ark, sacrificing so
many sheep and cattle that they could
not be recorded or counted.
7 The priests then brought the ark of
the LORD's covenant to its place in the
inner sanctuary of the temple, the Most
Holy Place, and put it beneath the wings
of the cherubim. 8 The cherubim spread
their wings over the place of the ark and
covered the ark and its carrying poles.
9 These poles were so long that their ends,
extending from the ark, could be seen

[a] 5 That is, about 3 inches or about 7.5 centimeters
[b] 5 That is, about 18,000 gallons or about 66,000 liters
[c] 17 Hebrew *Zeredatha,* a variant of *Zarethan*

from in front of the inner sanctuary, but
not from outside the Holy Place; and they
are still there today. 10There was nothing
in the ark except the two tablets that Moses had placed in it at Horeb, where the
LORD made a covenant with the Israelites
after they came out of Egypt.

11The priests then withdrew from the
Holy Place. All the priests who were there
had consecrated themselves, regardless
of their divisions. 12All the Levites who
were musicians—Asaph, Heman, Jeduthun and their sons and relatives—stood
on the east side of the altar, dressed in
fine linen and playing cymbals, harps
and lyres. They were accompanied by 120
priests sounding trumpets. 13The trumpeters and musicians joined in unison
to give praise and thanks to the LORD.
Accompanied by trumpets, cymbals and
other instruments, the singers raised their
voices in praise to the LORD and sang:

"He is good;
his love endures forever."

Then the temple of the LORD was filled
with the cloud, 14and the priests could
not perform their service because of the
cloud, for the glory of the LORD filled the
temple of God.

6 Then Solomon said, "The LORD has
said that he would dwell in a dark
cloud; 2I have built a magnificent temple
for you, a place for you to dwell forever."

3While the whole assembly of Israel was
standing there, the king turned around
and blessed them. 4Then he said:

"Praise be to the LORD, the God
of Israel, who with his hands has
fulfilled what he promised with his
mouth to my father David. For he
said, 5'Since the day I brought my
people out of Egypt, I have not chosen a city in any tribe of Israel to have
a temple built so that my Name might
be there, nor have I chosen anyone to
be ruler over my people Israel. 6But
now I have chosen Jerusalem for my
Name to be there, and I have chosen
David to rule my people Israel.'

7"My father David had it in his
heart to build a temple for the Name
of the LORD, the God of Israel. 8But
the LORD said to my father David,
'You did well to have it in your heart
to build a temple for my Name. 9Nev-
ertheless, you are not the one to build
the temple, but your son, your own
flesh and blood—he is the one who
will build the temple for my Name.'

10"The LORD has kept the promise
he made. I have succeeded David my
father and now I sit on the throne of
Israel, just as the LORD promised, and
I have built the temple for the Name
of the LORD, the God of Israel. 11There
I have placed the ark, in which is the
covenant of the LORD that he made
with the people of Israel."

12Then Solomon stood before the altar
of the LORD in front of the whole assembly of Israel and spread out his hands.
13Now he had made a bronze platform,
five cubits long, five cubits wide and
three cubits high,[a] and had placed it in
the center of the outer court. He stood on
the platform and then knelt down before
the whole assembly of Israel and spread
out his hands toward heaven. 14He said:

"LORD, the God of Israel, there
is no God like you in heaven or on
earth—you who keep your covenant
of love with your servants who continue wholeheartedly in your way.
15You have kept your promise to your
servant David my father; with your
mouth you have promised and with
your hand you have fulfilled it—as
it is today.

16"Now, LORD, the God of Israel,
keep for your servant David my father the promises you made to him
when you said, 'You shall never fail to
have a successor to sit before me on
the throne of Israel, if only your descendants are careful in all they do to
walk before me according to my law,
as you have done.' 17And now, LORD,
the God of Israel, let your word that
you promised your servant David
come true.

18"But will God really dwell on
earth with humans? The heavens,
even the highest heavens, cannot
contain you. How much less this
temple I have built! 19Yet, LORD my
God, give attention to your servant's
prayer and his plea for mercy. Hear

[a] *13* That is, about 7 1/2 feet long and wide and 4 1/2 feet high or about 2.3 meters long and wide and 1.4 meters high

the cry and the prayer that your servant is praying in your presence.
20 May your eyes be open toward this
temple day and night, this place of
which you said you would put your
Name there. May you hear the prayer
your servant prays toward this place.
21 Hear the supplications of your servant and of your people Israel when
they pray toward this place. Hear
from heaven, your dwelling place;
and when you hear, forgive.
22 "When anyone wrongs their
neighbor and is required to take an
oath and they come and swear the
oath before your altar in this temple, 23 then hear from heaven and
act. Judge between your servants,
condemning the guilty and bringing
down on their heads what they have
done, and vindicating the innocent
by treating them in accordance with
their innocence.
24 "When your people Israel have
been defeated by an enemy because
they have sinned against you and
when they turn back and give praise
to your name, praying and making
supplication before you in this temple, 25 then hear from heaven and forgive the sin of your people Israel and
bring them back to the land you gave
to them and their ancestors.
26 "When the heavens are shut up
and there is no rain because your
people have sinned against you, and
when they pray toward this place
and give praise to your name and
turn from their sin because you have
afflicted them, 27 then hear from
heaven and forgive the sin of your
servants, your people Israel. Teach
them the right way to live, and send
rain on the land you gave your people
for an inheritance.
28 "When famine or plague comes
to the land, or blight or mildew, locusts or grasshoppers, or when enemies besiege them in any of their
cities, whatever disaster or disease
may come, 29 and when a prayer or
plea is made by anyone among your
people Israel — being aware of their
afflictions and pains, and spreading
out their hands toward this temple —
30 then hear from heaven, your dwelling place. Forgive, and deal with everyone according to all they do, since
you know their hearts (for you alone
know the human heart), 31 so that
they will fear you and walk in obedience to you all the time they live in
the land you gave our ancestors.
32 "As for the foreigner who does
not belong to your people Israel but
has come from a distant land because of your great name and your
mighty hand and your outstretched
arm — when they come and pray toward this temple, 33 then hear from
heaven, your dwelling place. Do
whatever the foreigner asks of you,
so that all the peoples of the earth
may know your name and fear you,
as do your own people Israel, and
may know that this house I have built
bears your Name.
34 "When your people go to war
against their enemies, wherever you
send them, and when they pray to
you toward this city you have chosen and the temple I have built for
your Name, 35 then hear from heaven
their prayer and their plea, and uphold their cause.
36 "When they sin against you —
for there is no one who does not
sin — and you become angry with
them and give them over to the enemy, who takes them captive to a land
far away or near; 37 and if they have
a change of heart in the land where
they are held captive, and repent and
plead with you in the land of their
captivity and say, 'We have sinned,
we have done wrong and acted wickedly'; 38 and if they turn back to you
with all their heart and soul in the
land of their captivity where they
were taken, and pray toward the land
you gave their ancestors, toward the
city you have chosen and toward the
temple I have built for your Name;
39 then from heaven, your dwelling
place, hear their prayer and their
pleas, and uphold their cause. And
forgive your people, who have sinned
against you.
40 "Now, my God, may your eyes be
open and your ears attentive to the
prayers offered in this place.

41 "Now arise, LORD God, and come
to your resting place,
you and the ark of your might.

May your priests, LORD God, be
clothed with salvation,
may your faithful people rejoice
in your goodness.
[42] LORD God, do not reject your
anointed one.
Remember the great love
promised to David your
servant."

7 When Solomon finished praying, fire
came down from heaven and consumed the burnt offering and the sacrifices, and the glory of the LORD filled the
temple. [2]The priests could not enter the
temple of the LORD because the glory of
the LORD filled it. [3]When all the Israelites
saw the fire coming down and the glory
of the LORD above the temple, they knelt
on the pavement with their faces to the
ground, and they worshiped and gave
thanks to the LORD, saying,

"He is good;
his love endures forever."

[4]Then the king and all the people offered
sacrifices before the LORD. [5]And King
Solomon offered a sacrifice of twenty-two
thousand head of cattle and a hundred
and twenty thousand sheep and goats.
So the king and all the people dedicated the temple of God. [6]The priests took
their positions, as did the Levites with
the LORD's musical instruments, which
King David had made for praising the
LORD and which were used when he gave
thanks, saying, "His love endures forever." Opposite the Levites, the priests blew
their trumpets, and all the Israelites were
standing.

[7]Solomon consecrated the middle part
of the courtyard in front of the temple
of the LORD, and there he offered burnt
offerings and the fat of the fellowship offerings, because the bronze altar he had
made could not hold the burnt offerings,
the grain offerings and the fat portions.

[8]So Solomon observed the festival at
that time for seven days, and all Israel
with him — a vast assembly, people from
Lebo Hamath to the Wadi of Egypt. [9]On
the eighth day they held an assembly, for
they had celebrated the dedication of the
altar for seven days and the festival for
seven days more. [10]On the twenty-third
day of the seventh month he sent the
people to their homes, joyful and glad in
heart for the good things the LORD had
done for David and Solomon and for his
people Israel.

[11]When Solomon had finished the temple of the LORD and the royal palace, and
had succeeded in carrying out all he had
in mind to do in the temple of the LORD
and in his own palace, [12]the LORD appeared to him at night and said:

"I have heard your prayer and have
chosen this place for myself as a temple for sacrifices.

[13]"When I shut up the heavens so
that there is no rain, or command
locusts to devour the land or send
a plague among my people, [14]if my
people, who are called by my name,
will humble themselves and pray
and seek my face and turn from their
wicked ways, then I will hear from
heaven, and I will forgive their sin
and will heal their land. [15]Now my
eyes will be open and my ears attentive to the prayers offered in this
place. [16]I have chosen and consecrated this temple so that my Name
may be there forever. My eyes and my
heart will always be there.

[17]"As for you, if you walk before
me faithfully as David your father
did, and do all I command, and observe my decrees and laws, [18]I will
establish your royal throne, as I covenanted with David your father when
I said, 'You shall never fail to have a
successor to rule over Israel.'

[19]"But if you[a] turn away and forsake the decrees and commands I
have given you[a] and go off to serve
other gods and worship them, [20]then
I will uproot Israel from my land,
which I have given them, and will
reject this temple I have consecrated
for my Name. I will make it a byword
and an object of ridicule among all
peoples. [21]This temple will become a
heap of rubble. All[b] who pass by will
be appalled and say, 'Why has the
LORD done such a thing to this land
and to this temple?' [22]People will
answer, 'Because they have forsaken
the LORD, the God of their ancestors,

[a] *19* The Hebrew is plural. [b] *21* See some Septuagint manuscripts, Old Latin, Syriac, Arabic and Targum; Hebrew *And though this temple is now so imposing, all*

who brought them out of Egypt, and
have embraced other gods, worshiping and serving them—that is why he
brought all this disaster on them.'"

8 At the end of twenty years, during
which Solomon built the temple of the
LORD and his own palace, 2 Solomon rebuilt the villages that Hiram[a] had given
him, and settled Israelites in them. 3 Solomon then went to Hamath Zobah and
captured it. 4 He also built up Tadmor in
the desert and all the store cities he had
built in Hamath. 5 He rebuilt Upper Beth
Horon and Lower Beth Horon as fortified
cities, with walls and with gates and bars,
6 as well as Baalath and all his store cities, and all the cities for his chariots and
for his horses[b]—whatever he desired
to build in Jerusalem, in Lebanon and
throughout all the territory he ruled.

7 There were still people left from the
Hittites, Amorites, Perizzites, Hivites
and Jebusites (these people were not Israelites). 8 Solomon conscripted the descendants of all these people remaining
in the land—whom the Israelites had
not destroyed—to serve as slave labor,
as it is to this day. 9 But Solomon did not
make slaves of the Israelites for his work;
they were his fighting men, commanders
of his captains, and commanders of his
chariots and charioteers. 10 They were
also King Solomon's chief officials—two
hundred and fifty officials supervising
the men.

11 Solomon brought Pharaoh's daughter
up from the City of David to the palace he
had built for her, for he said, "My wife
must not live in the palace of David king
of Israel, because the places the ark of the
LORD has entered are holy."

12 On the altar of the LORD that he had
built in front of the portico, Solomon
sacrificed burnt offerings to the LORD,
13 according to the daily requirement for
offerings commanded by Moses for the
Sabbaths, the New Moons and the three
annual festivals—the Festival of Unleavened Bread, the Festival of Weeks and the
Festival of Tabernacles. 14 In keeping with
the ordinance of his father David, he appointed the divisions of the priests for
their duties, and the Levites to lead the
praise and to assist the priests according to each day's requirement. He also
appointed the gatekeepers by divisions
for the various gates, because this was
what David the man of God had ordered.
15 They did not deviate from the king's
commands to the priests or to the Levites
in any matter, including that of the treasuries.

16 All Solomon's work was carried out,
from the day the foundation of the temple
of the LORD was laid until its completion.
So the temple of the LORD was finished.

17 Then Solomon went to Ezion Geber
and Elath on the coast of Edom. 18 And
Hiram sent him ships commanded by
his own men, sailors who knew the sea.
These, with Solomon's men, sailed to
Ophir and brought back four hundred
and fifty talents[c] of gold, which they delivered to King Solomon.

9 When the queen of Sheba heard of Solomon's fame, she came to Jerusalem
to test him with hard questions. Arriving
with a very great caravan—with camels
carrying spices, large quantities of gold,
and precious stones—she came to Solomon and talked with him about all she
had on her mind. 2 Solomon answered all
her questions; nothing was too hard for
him to explain to her. 3 When the queen
of Sheba saw the wisdom of Solomon, as
well as the palace he had built, 4 the food
on his table, the seating of his officials,
the attending servants in their robes, the
cupbearers in their robes and the burnt
offerings he made at[d] the temple of the
LORD, she was overwhelmed.

5 She said to the king, "The report I
heard in my own country about your
achievements and your wisdom is true.
6 But I did not believe what they said until I came and saw with my own eyes.
Indeed, not even half the greatness of
your wisdom was told me; you have far
exceeded the report I heard. 7 How happy
your people must be! How happy your officials, who continually stand before you
and hear your wisdom! 8 Praise be to the
LORD your God, who has delighted in you
and placed you on his throne as king to
rule for the LORD your God. Because of
the love of your God for Israel and his desire to uphold them forever, he has made
you king over them, to maintain justice
and righteousness."

[a] 2 Hebrew *Huram,* a variant of *Hiram*; also in verse 18 [b] 6 Or *charioteers* [c] 18 That is, about 17 tons or about 15 metric tons [d] 4 Or *and the ascent by which he went up to*

9 Then she gave the king 120 talents[a] of
gold, large quantities of spices, and precious stones. There had never been such
spices as those the queen of Sheba gave to
King Solomon.
10 (The servants of Hiram and the servants of Solomon brought gold from
Ophir; they also brought algumwood[b]
and precious stones. 11 The king used the
algumwood to make steps for the temple
of the LORD and for the royal palace, and
to make harps and lyres for the musicians. Nothing like them had ever been
seen in Judah.)
12 King Solomon gave the queen of Sheba all she desired and asked for; he gave
her more than she had brought to him.
Then she left and returned with her retinue to her own country.
13 The weight of the gold that Solomon
received yearly was 666 talents,[c] 14 not including the revenues brought in by merchants and traders. Also all the kings of
Arabia and the governors of the territories brought gold and silver to Solomon.
15 King Solomon made two hundred
large shields of hammered gold; six hundred shekels[d] of hammered gold went
into each shield. 16 He also made three
hundred small shields of hammered
gold, with three hundred shekels[e] of gold
in each shield. The king put them in the
Palace of the Forest of Lebanon.
17 Then the king made a great throne
covered with ivory and overlaid with
pure gold. 18 The throne had six steps,
and a footstool of gold was attached to it.
On both sides of the seat were armrests,
with a lion standing beside each of them.
19 Twelve lions stood on the six steps, one
at either end of each step. Nothing like it
had ever been made for any other kingdom. 20 All King Solomon's goblets were
gold, and all the household articles in the
Palace of the Forest of Lebanon were pure
gold. Nothing was made of silver, because silver was considered of little value
in Solomon's day. 21 The king had a fleet of
trading ships[f] manned by Hiram's[g] servants. Once every three years it returned,
carrying gold, silver and ivory, and apes
and baboons.
22 King Solomon was greater in riches and wisdom than all the other kings
of the earth. 23 All the kings of the earth
sought audience with Solomon to hear
the wisdom God had put in his heart.
24 Year after year, everyone who came
brought a gift—articles of silver and
gold, and robes, weapons and spices, and
horses and mules.
25 Solomon had four thousand stalls
for horses and chariots, and twelve thousand horses,[h] which he kept in the chariot cities and also with him in Jerusalem.
26 He ruled over all the kings from the
Euphrates River to the land of the Philistines, as far as the border of Egypt. 27 The
king made silver as common in Jerusalem as stones, and cedar as plentiful as
sycamore-fig trees in the foothills. 28 Solomon's horses were imported from Egypt
and from all other countries.
29 As for the other events of Solomon's
reign, from beginning to end, are they
not written in the records of Nathan the
prophet, in the prophecy of Ahijah the
Shilonite and in the visions of Iddo the
seer concerning Jeroboam son of Nebat?
30 Solomon reigned in Jerusalem over all
Israel forty years. 31 Then he rested with
his ancestors and was buried in the city of
David his father. And Rehoboam his son
succeeded him as king.

10 Rehoboam went to Shechem, for
all Israel had gone there to make
him king. 2 When Jeroboam son of Nebat
heard this (he was in Egypt, where he had
fled from King Solomon), he returned
from Egypt. 3 So they sent for Jeroboam,
and he and all Israel went to Rehoboam
and said to him: 4 "Your father put a heavy
yoke on us, but now lighten the harsh labor and the heavy yoke he put on us, and
we will serve you."
5 Rehoboam answered, "Come back to
me in three days." So the people went
away.
6 Then King Rehoboam consulted the
elders who had served his father Solomon during his lifetime. "How would
you advise me to answer these people?"
he asked.
7 They replied, "If you will be kind to
these people and please them and give

[a] 9 That is, about 4 1/2 tons or about 4 metric tons [b] 10 Probably a variant of *almugwood* [c] 13 That is, about 25 tons or about 23 metric tons [d] 15 That is, about 15 pounds or about 6.9 kilograms [e] 16 That is, about 7 1/2 pounds or about 3.5 kilograms [f] 21 Hebrew *of ships that could go to Tarshish* [g] 21 Hebrew *Huram,* a variant of *Hiram* [h] 25 Or *charioteers*

them a favorable answer, they will always
be your servants."
8But Rehoboam rejected the advice
the elders gave him and consulted the
young men who had grown up with him
and were serving him. 9He asked them,
"What is your advice? How should we answer these people who say to me, 'Light-
en the yoke your father put on us'?"
10The young men who had grown up
with him replied, "The people have said
to you, 'Your father put a heavy yoke on
us, but make our yoke lighter.' Now tell
them, 'My little finger is thicker than my
father's waist. 11My father laid on you a
heavy yoke; I will make it even heavier.
My father scourged you with whips; I will
scourge you with scorpions.'"
12Three days later Jeroboam and all
the people returned to Rehoboam, as the
king had said, "Come back to me in three
days." 13The king answered them harshly. Rejecting the advice of the elders, 14he
followed the advice of the young men and
said, "My father made your yoke heavy;
I will make it even heavier. My father
scourged you with whips; I will scourge
you with scorpions." 15So the king did
not listen to the people, for this turn of
events was from God, to fulfill the word
the LORD had spoken to Jeroboam son of
Nebat through Ahijah the Shilonite.
16When all Israel saw that the king refused to listen to them, they answered
the king:

"What share do we have in David,
what part in Jesse's son?
To your tents, Israel!
Look after your own house, David!"

So all the Israelites went home. 17But as
for the Israelites who were living in the
towns of Judah, Rehoboam still ruled
over them.
18King Rehoboam sent out Adoniram,[a]
who was in charge of forced labor, but the
Israelites stoned him to death. King Rehoboam, however, managed to get into
his chariot and escape to Jerusalem. 19So
Israel has been in rebellion against the
house of David to this day.

11 When Rehoboam arrived in Jerusalem, he mustered Judah and Benjamin—a hundred and eighty thousand
able young men—to go to war against
Israel and to regain the kingdom for Rehoboam.
2But this word of the LORD came to
Shemaiah the man of God: 3"Say to Rehoboam son of Solomon king of Judah
and to all Israel in Judah and Benjamin,
4'This is what the LORD says: Do not go
up to fight against your fellow Israelites.
Go home, every one of you, for this is my
doing.'" So they obeyed the words of the
LORD and turned back from marching
against Jeroboam.
5Rehoboam lived in Jerusalem and
built up towns for defense in Judah:
6Bethlehem, Etam, Tekoa, 7Beth Zur,
Soko, Adullam, 8Gath, Mareshah, Ziph,
9Adoraim, Lachish, Azekah, 10Zorah,
Aijalon and Hebron. These were fortified cities in Judah and Benjamin. 11He
strengthened their defenses and put
commanders in them, with supplies of
food, olive oil and wine. 12He put shields
and spears in all the cities, and made
them very strong. So Judah and Benjamin were his.
13The priests and Levites from all their
districts throughout Israel sided with
him. 14The Levites even abandoned their
pasturelands and property and came to
Judah and Jerusalem, because Jeroboam
and his sons had rejected them as priests
of the LORD 15when he appointed his own
priests for the high places and for the goat
and calf idols he had made. 16Those from
every tribe of Israel who set their hearts
on seeking the LORD, the God of Israel,
followed the Levites to Jerusalem to offer
sacrifices to the LORD, the God of their
ancestors. 17They strengthened the kingdom of Judah and supported Rehoboam
son of Solomon three years, following
the ways of David and Solomon during
this time.
18Rehoboam married Mahalath, who
was the daughter of David's son Jerimoth
and of Abihail, the daughter of Jesse's son
Eliab. 19She bore him sons: Jeush, Shemariah and Zaham. 20Then he married
Maakah daughter of Absalom, who bore
him Abijah, Attai, Ziza and Shelomith.
21Rehoboam loved Maakah daughter of
Absalom more than any of his other wives
and concubines. In all, he had eighteen
wives and sixty concubines, twenty-eight
sons and sixty daughters.

[a] 18 Hebrew *Hadoram,* a variant of *Adoniram*

22 Rehoboam appointed Abijah son
of Maakah as crown prince among his
brothers, in order to make him king. 23 He
acted wisely, dispersing some of his sons
throughout the districts of Judah and
Benjamin, and to all the fortified cities.
He gave them abundant provisions and
took many wives for them.

12 After Rehoboam's position as king
was established and he had become
strong, he and all Israel[a] with him abandoned the law of the LORD. 2 Because
they had been unfaithful to the LORD,
Shishak king of Egypt attacked Jerusalem in the fifth year of King Rehoboam.
3 With twelve hundred chariots and sixty
thousand horsemen and the innumera-
ble troops of Libyans, Sukkites and Cushites[b] that came with him from Egypt, 4 he
captured the fortified cities of Judah and
came as far as Jerusalem.

5 Then the prophet Shemaiah came to
Rehoboam and to the leaders of Judah
who had assembled in Jerusalem for fear
of Shishak, and he said to them, "This
is what the LORD says, 'You have abandoned me; therefore, I now abandon you
to Shishak.'"

6 The leaders of Israel and the king humbled themselves and said, "The LORD is
just."

7 When the LORD saw that they humbled themselves, this word of the LORD
came to Shemaiah: "Since they have
humbled themselves, I will not destroy
them but will soon give them deliverance. My wrath will not be poured out on
Jerusalem through Shishak. 8 They will,
however, become subject to him, so that
they may learn the difference between
serving me and serving the kings of other lands."

9 When Shishak king of Egypt attacked
Jerusalem, he carried off the treasures of
the temple of the LORD and the treasures
of the royal palace. He took everything,
including the gold shields Solomon had
made. 10 So King Rehoboam made bronze
shields to replace them and assigned
these to the commanders of the guard on
duty at the entrance to the royal palace.
11 Whenever the king went to the LORD's
temple, the guards went with him, bearing the shields, and afterward they returned them to the guardroom.

12 Because Rehoboam humbled himself, the LORD's anger turned from him,
and he was not totally destroyed. Indeed,
there was some good in Judah.

13 King Rehoboam established himself
firmly in Jerusalem and continued as
king. He was forty-one years old when he
became king, and he reigned seventeen
years in Jerusalem, the city the LORD
had chosen out of all the tribes of Israel
in which to put his Name. His mother's
name was Naamah; she was an Ammonite. 14 He did evil because he had not set
his heart on seeking the LORD.

15 As for the events of Rehoboam's
reign, from beginning to end, are they
not written in the records of Shemaiah
the prophet and of Iddo the seer that
deal with genealogies? There was continual warfare between Rehoboam and
Jeroboam. 16 Rehoboam rested with his
ancestors and was buried in the City of
David. And Abijah his son succeeded
him as king.

13 In the eighteenth year of the reign of
Jeroboam, Abijah became king of Judah, 2 and he reigned in Jerusalem three
years. His mother's name was Maakah,[c] a
daughter[d] of Uriel of Gibeah.

There was war between Abijah and
Jeroboam. 3 Abijah went into battle with
an army of four hundred thousand able
fighting men, and Jeroboam drew up a
battle line against him with eight hundred thousand able troops.

4 Abijah stood on Mount Zemaraim,
in the hill country of Ephraim, and said,
"Jeroboam and all Israel, listen to me!
5 Don't you know that the LORD, the God
of Israel, has given the kingship of Israel
to David and his descendants forever by
a covenant of salt? 6 Yet Jeroboam son of
Nebat, an official of Solomon son of David, rebelled against his master. 7 Some
worthless scoundrels gathered around
him and opposed Rehoboam son of Solomon when he was young and indecisive
and not strong enough to resist them.

8 "And now you plan to resist the kingdom of the LORD, which is in the hands
of David's descendants. You are indeed
a vast army and have with you the gold-
en calves that Jeroboam made to be your
gods. 9 But didn't you drive out the priests

[a] *1* That is, Judah, as frequently in 2 Chronicles [b] *3* That is, people from the upper Nile region [c] *2* Most Septuagint manuscripts and Syriac (see also 11:20 and 1 Kings 15:2); Hebrew *Micaiah* [d] *2* Or *granddaughter*

of the LORD, the sons of Aaron, and the
Levites, and make priests of your own
as the peoples of other lands do? Whoever comes to consecrate himself with a
young bull and seven rams may become
a priest of what are not gods.

10 "As for us, the LORD is our God, and
we have not forsaken him. The priests
who serve the LORD are sons of Aaron, and the Levites assist them. 11 Every
morning and evening they present burnt
offerings and fragrant incense to the
LORD. They set out the bread on the ceremonially clean table and light the lamps
on the gold lampstand every evening.
We are observing the requirements of
the LORD our God. But you have forsak-
en him. 12 God is with us; he is our leader. His priests with their trumpets will
sound the battle cry against you. People
of Israel, do not fight against the LORD,
the God of your ancestors, for you will
not succeed."

13 Now Jeroboam had sent troops
around to the rear, so that while he was
in front of Judah the ambush was behind
them. 14 Judah turned and saw that they
were being attacked at both front and
rear. Then they cried out to the LORD.
The priests blew their trumpets 15 and
the men of Judah raised the battle cry. At
the sound of their battle cry, God routed Jeroboam and all Israel before Abijah
and Judah. 16 The Israelites fled before
Judah, and God delivered them into their
hands. 17 Abijah and his troops inflicted heavy losses on them, so that there
were five hundred thousand casualties
among Israel's able men. 18 The Israelites
were subdued on that occasion, and the
people of Judah were victorious because
they relied on the LORD, the God of their
ancestors.

19 Abijah pursued Jeroboam and took
from him the towns of Bethel, Jeshanah
and Ephron, with their surrounding villages. 20 Jeroboam did not regain power
during the time of Abijah. And the LORD
struck him down and he died.

21 But Abijah grew in strength. He married fourteen wives and had twenty-two
sons and sixteen daughters.

22 The other events of Abijah's reign,
what he did and what he said, are written
in the annotations of the prophet Iddo.

14[a] And Abijah rested with his ancestors and was buried in the City of
David. Asa his son succeeded him as
king, and in his days the country was at
peace for ten years.

2 Asa did what was good and right in
the eyes of the LORD his God. 3 He removed the foreign altars and the high
places, smashed the sacred stones and
cut down the Asherah poles.[b] 4 He commanded Judah to seek the LORD, the God
of their ancestors, and to obey his laws
and commands. 5 He removed the high
places and incense altars in every town
in Judah, and the kingdom was at peace
under him. 6 He built up the fortified cities of Judah, since the land was at peace.
No one was at war with him during those
years, for the LORD gave him rest.

7 "Let us build up these towns," he said
to Judah, "and put walls around them,
with towers, gates and bars. The land is
still ours, because we have sought the
LORD our God; we sought him and he has
given us rest on every side." So they built
and prospered.

8 Asa had an army of three hundred
thousand men from Judah, equipped with
large shields and with spears, and two
hundred and eighty thousand from Benjamin, armed with small shields and with
bows. All these were brave fighting men.

9 Zerah the Cushite marched out
against them with an army of thousands
upon thousands and three hundred chariots, and came as far as Mareshah. 10 Asa
went out to meet him, and they took up
battle positions in the Valley of Zepha-
thah near Mareshah.

11 Then Asa called to the LORD his God
and said, "LORD, there is no one like you
to help the powerless against the mighty.
Help us, LORD our God, for we rely on you,
and in your name we have come against
this vast army. LORD, you are our God; do
not let mere mortals prevail against you."

12 The LORD struck down the Cushites
before Asa and Judah. The Cushites fled,
13 and Asa and his army pursued them
as far as Gerar. Such a great number of
Cushites fell that they could not recover;
they were crushed before the LORD and
his forces. The men of Judah carried off
a large amount of plunder. 14 They de-

[a] In Hebrew texts 14:1 is numbered 13:23, and 14:2-15 is numbered 14:1-14. [b] 3 That is, wooden symbols of the goddess Asherah; here and elsewhere in 2 Chronicles

stroyed all the villages around Gerar, for
the terror of the LORD had fallen on them.
They looted all these villages, since there
was much plunder there. 15They also
attacked the camps of the herders and
carried off droves of sheep and goats
and camels. Then they returned to Jerusalem.

15 The Spirit of God came on Azariah
son of Oded. 2He went out to meet
Asa and said to him, "Listen to me, Asa
and all Judah and Benjamin. The LORD is
with you when you are with him. If you
seek him, he will be found by you, but if
you forsake him, he will forsake you. 3For
a long time Israel was without the true
God, without a priest to teach and without the law. 4But in their distress they
turned to the LORD, the God of Israel, and
sought him, and he was found by them.
5In those days it was not safe to travel
about, for all the inhabitants of the lands
were in great turmoil. 6One nation was
being crushed by another and one city
by another, because God was troubling
them with every kind of distress. 7But as
for you, be strong and do not give up, for
your work will be rewarded."

8When Asa heard these words and the
prophecy of Azariah son of[a] Oded the
prophet, he took courage. He removed
the detestable idols from the whole
land of Judah and Benjamin and from
the towns he had captured in the hills
of Ephraim. He repaired the altar of the
LORD that was in front of the portico of
the LORD's temple.

9Then he assembled all Judah and
Benjamin and the people from Ephraim, Manasseh and Simeon who had settled among them, for large numbers had
come over to him from Israel when they
saw that the LORD his God was with him.

10They assembled at Jerusalem in the
third month of the fifteenth year of Asa's
reign. 11At that time they sacrificed to the
LORD seven hundred head of cattle and
seven thousand sheep and goats from the
plunder they had brought back. 12They
entered into a covenant to seek the LORD,
the God of their ancestors, with all their
heart and soul. 13All who would not seek
the LORD, the God of Israel, were to be put
to death, whether small or great, man or
woman. 14They took an oath to the LORD
with loud acclamation, with shouting
and with trumpets and horns. 15All Judah rejoiced about the oath because
they had sworn it wholeheartedly. They
sought God eagerly, and he was found by
them. So the LORD gave them rest on every side.

16King Asa also deposed his grandmother Maakah from her position as
queen mother, because she had made
a repulsive image for the worship of
Asherah. Asa cut it down, broke it up
and burned it in the Kidron Valley. 17Al-
though he did not remove the high places
from Israel, Asa's heart was fully committed to the LORD all his life. 18He brought
into the temple of God the silver and gold
and the articles that he and his father had
dedicated.

19There was no more war until the thir-
ty-fifth year of Asa's reign.

16 In the thirty-sixth year of Asa's
reign Baasha king of Israel went up
against Judah and fortified Ramah to
prevent anyone from leaving or entering
the territory of Asa king of Judah.

2Asa then took the silver and gold out of
the treasuries of the LORD's temple and of
his own palace and sent it to Ben-Hadad
king of Aram, who was ruling in Damascus. 3"Let there be a treaty between me
and you," he said, "as there was between
my father and your father. See, I am sending you silver and gold. Now break your
treaty with Baasha king of Israel so he
will withdraw from me."

4Ben-Hadad agreed with King Asa and
sent the commanders of his forces against
the towns of Israel. They conquered Ijon,
Dan, Abel Maim[b] and all the store cities
of Naphtali. 5When Baasha heard this, he
stopped building Ramah and abandoned
his work. 6Then King Asa brought all the
men of Judah, and they carried away from
Ramah the stones and timber Baasha had
been using. With them he built up Geba
and Mizpah.

7At that time Hanani the seer came to
Asa king of Judah and said to him: "Because you relied on the king of Aram and
not on the LORD your God, the army of
the king of Aram has escaped from your
hand. 8Were not the Cushites[c] and Libyans a mighty army with great numbers
of chariots and horsemen[d]? Yet when you

[a] 8 Vulgate and Syriac (see also Septuagint and verse 1); Hebrew does not have *Azariah son of.* [b] 4 Also known as *Abel Beth Maakah* [c] 8 That is, people from the upper Nile region [d] 8 Or *charioteers*

relied on the LORD, he delivered them into your hand. 9 For the eyes of the LORD range throughout the earth to strengthen those whose hearts are fully committed to him. You have done a foolish thing, and from now on you will be at war."

10 Asa was angry with the seer because of this; he was so enraged that he put him in prison. At the same time Asa brutally oppressed some of the people.

11 The events of Asa's reign, from beginning to end, are written in the book of the kings of Judah and Israel. 12 In the thirty-ninth year of his reign Asa was afflicted with a disease in his feet. Though his disease was severe, even in his illness he did not seek help from the LORD, but only from the physicians. 13 Then in the forty-first year of his reign Asa died and rested with his ancestors. 14 They buried him in the tomb that he had cut out for himself in the City of David. They laid him on a bier covered with spices and various blended perfumes, and they made a huge fire in his honor.

17 Jehoshaphat his son succeeded him as king and strengthened himself against Israel. 2 He stationed troops in all the fortified cities of Judah and put garrisons in Judah and in the towns of Ephraim that his father Asa had captured.

3 The LORD was with Jehoshaphat because he followed the ways of his father David before him. He did not consult the Baals 4 but sought the God of his father and followed his commands rather than the practices of Israel. 5 The LORD established the kingdom under his control; and all Judah brought gifts to Jehoshaphat, so that he had great wealth and honor. 6 His heart was devoted to the ways of the LORD; furthermore, he removed the high places and the Asherah poles from Judah.

7 In the third year of his reign he sent his officials Ben-Hail, Obadiah, Zechariah, Nethanel and Micaiah to teach in the towns of Judah. 8 With them were certain Levites—Shemaiah, Nethaniah, Zebadiah, Asahel, Shemiramoth, Jehonathan, Adonijah, Tobijah and Tob-Adonijah—and the priests Elishama and Jehoram. 9 They taught throughout Judah, taking with them the Book of the Law of the LORD; they went around to all the towns of Judah and taught the people.

10 The fear of the LORD fell on all the kingdoms of the lands surrounding Judah, so that they did not go to war against Jehoshaphat. 11 Some Philistines brought Jehoshaphat gifts and silver as tribute, and the Arabs brought him flocks: seven thousand seven hundred rams and seven thousand seven hundred goats.

12 Jehoshaphat became more and more powerful; he built forts and store cities in Judah 13 and had large supplies in the towns of Judah. He also kept experienced fighting men in Jerusalem. 14 Their enrollment by families was as follows:

From Judah, commanders of units of 1,000:
Adnah the commander, with 300,000 fighting men;
15 next, Jehohanan the commander, with 280,000;
16 next, Amasiah son of Zikri, who volunteered himself for the service of the LORD, with 200,000.
17 From Benjamin:
Eliada, a valiant soldier, with 200,000 men armed with bows and shields;
18 next, Jehozabad, with 180,000 men armed for battle.

19 These were the men who served the king, besides those he stationed in the fortified cities throughout Judah.

18 Now Jehoshaphat had great wealth and honor, and he allied himself with Ahab by marriage. 2 Some years later he went down to see Ahab in Samaria. Ahab slaughtered many sheep and cattle for him and the people with him and urged him to attack Ramoth Gilead. 3 Ahab king of Israel asked Jehoshaphat king of Judah, "Will you go with me against Ramoth Gilead?"

Jehoshaphat replied, "I am as you are, and my people as your people; we will join you in the war." 4 But Jehoshaphat also said to the king of Israel, "First seek the counsel of the LORD."

5 So the king of Israel brought together the prophets—four hundred men—and asked them, "Shall we go to war against Ramoth Gilead, or shall I not?"

"Go," they answered, "for God will give it into the king's hand."

6 But Jehoshaphat asked, "Is there no longer a prophet of the LORD here whom we can inquire of?"

7The king of Israel answered Jehoshaphat, "There is still one prophet through
whom we can inquire of the LORD, but I
hate him because he never prophesies
anything good about me, but always bad.
He is Micaiah son of Imlah."
"The king should not say such a thing,"
Jehoshaphat replied.
8So the king of Israel called one of his
officials and said, "Bring Micaiah son of
Imlah at once."
9Dressed in their royal robes, the king
of Israel and Jehoshaphat king of Judah were sitting on their thrones at the
threshing floor by the entrance of the
gate of Samaria, with all the prophets
prophesying before them. 10Now Zedekiah son of Kenaanah had made iron horns,
and he declared, "This is what the LORD
says: 'With these you will gore the Arameans until they are destroyed.' "
11All the other prophets were prophesying the same thing. "Attack Ramoth
Gilead and be victorious," they said,
"for the LORD will give it into the king's
hand."
12The messenger who had gone to
summon Micaiah said to him, "Look,
the other prophets without exception are
predicting success for the king. Let your
word agree with theirs, and speak favorably."
13But Micaiah said, "As surely as the
LORD lives, I can tell him only what my
God says."
14When he arrived, the king asked him,
"Micaiah, shall we go to war against Ramoth Gilead, or shall I not?"
"Attack and be victorious," he answered, "for they will be given into your
hand."
15The king said to him, "How many
times must I make you swear to tell me
nothing but the truth in the name of the
LORD?"
16Then Micaiah answered, "I saw all
Israel scattered on the hills like sheep
without a shepherd, and the LORD said,
'These people have no master. Let each
one go home in peace.' "
17The king of Israel said to Jehoshaphat,
"Didn't I tell you that he never prophesies
anything good about me, but only bad?"
18Micaiah continued, "Therefore hear
the word of the LORD: I saw the LORD sitting on his throne with all the multitudes
of heaven standing on his right and on
his left. 19And the LORD said, 'Who will
entice Ahab king of Israel into attacking
Ramoth Gilead and going to his death
there?'
"One suggested this, and another that.
20Finally, a spirit came forward, stood
before the LORD and said, 'I will entice
him.'
" 'By what means?' the LORD asked.
21" 'I will go and be a deceiving spirit in
the mouths of all his prophets,' he said.
" 'You will succeed in enticing him,'
said the LORD. 'Go and do it.'
22"So now the LORD has put a deceiving spirit in the mouths of these prophets
of yours. The LORD has decreed disaster
for you."
23Then Zedekiah son of Kenaanah
went up and slapped Micaiah in the
face. "Which way did the spirit from[a] the
LORD go when he went from me to speak
to you?" he asked.
24Micaiah replied, "You will find out on
the day you go to hide in an inner room."
25The king of Israel then ordered, "Take
Micaiah and send him back to Amon the
ruler of the city and to Joash the king's
son, 26and say, 'This is what the king
says: Put this fellow in prison and give
him nothing but bread and water until I
return safely.' "
27Micaiah declared, "If you ever return
safely, the LORD has not spoken through
me." Then he added, "Mark my words, all
you people!"
28So the king of Israel and Jehoshaphat
king of Judah went up to Ramoth Gilead.
29The king of Israel said to Jehoshaphat,
"I will enter the battle in disguise, but
you wear your royal robes." So the king
of Israel disguised himself and went into
battle.
30Now the king of Aram had ordered his
chariot commanders, "Do not fight with
anyone, small or great, except the king of
Israel." 31When the chariot commanders
saw Jehoshaphat, they thought, "This is
the king of Israel." So they turned to attack him, but Jehoshaphat cried out, and
the LORD helped him. God drew them
away from him, 32for when the chariot
commanders saw that he was not the king
of Israel, they stopped pursuing him.

[a] 23 Or *Spirit of*

33 But someone drew his bow at random and hit the king of Israel between
the breastplate and the scale armor.
The king told the chariot driver, "Wheel
around and get me out of the fighting. I've
been wounded." 34 All day long the battle
raged, and the king of Israel propped
himself up in his chariot facing the Arameans until evening. Then at sunset he
died.

19 When Jehoshaphat king of Judah
returned safely to his palace in Jerusalem, 2 Jehu the seer, the son of Hanani, went out to meet him and said to the
king, "Should you help the wicked and
love[a] those who hate the LORD? Because
of this, the wrath of the LORD is on you.
3 There is, however, some good in you, for
you have rid the land of the Asherah poles
and have set your heart on seeking God."

4 Jehoshaphat lived in Jerusalem, and
he went out again among the people from
Beersheba to the hill country of Ephraim
and turned them back to the LORD, the
God of their ancestors. 5 He appointed
judges in the land, in each of the fortified
cities of Judah. 6 He told them, "Consider
carefully what you do, because you are
not judging for mere mortals but for the
LORD, who is with you whenever you give
a verdict. 7 Now let the fear of the LORD be
on you. Judge carefully, for with the LORD
our God there is no injustice or partiality
or bribery."

8 In Jerusalem also, Jehoshaphat appointed some of the Levites, priests and
heads of Israelite families to administer
the law of the LORD and to settle disputes. And they lived in Jerusalem. 9 He
gave them these orders: "You must serve
faithfully and wholeheartedly in the fear
of the LORD. 10 In every case that comes
before you from your people who live in
the cities—whether bloodshed or other
concerns of the law, commands, decrees
or regulations—you are to warn them
not to sin against the LORD; otherwise his
wrath will come on you and your people.
Do this, and you will not sin.

11 "Amariah the chief priest will be over
you in any matter concerning the LORD,
and Zebadiah son of Ishmael, the leader
of the tribe of Judah, will be over you in
any matter concerning the king, and the
Levites will serve as officials before you.
Act with courage, and may the LORD be
with those who do well."

20 After this, the Moabites and Ammonites with some of the Meunites[b]
came to wage war against Jehoshaphat.

2 Some people came and told Jehoshaphat, "A vast army is coming against you
from Edom,[c] from the other side of the
Dead Sea. It is already in Hazezon Tamar"
(that is, En Gedi). 3 Alarmed, Jehoshaphat
resolved to inquire of the LORD, and he
proclaimed a fast for all Judah. 4 The people of Judah came together to seek help
from the LORD; indeed, they came from
every town in Judah to seek him.

5 Then Jehoshaphat stood up in the
assembly of Judah and Jerusalem at the
temple of the LORD in the front of the new
courtyard 6 and said:

"LORD, the God of our ancestors,
are you not the God who is in heav-
en? You rule over all the kingdoms of
the nations. Power and might are in
your hand, and no one can withstand
you. 7 Our God, did you not drive out
the inhabitants of this land before
your people Israel and give it forever
to the descendants of Abraham your
friend? 8 They have lived in it and
have built in it a sanctuary for your
Name, saying, 9 'If calamity comes
upon us, whether the sword of judgment, or plague or famine, we will
stand in your presence before this
temple that bears your Name and
will cry out to you in our distress, and
you will hear us and save us.'

10 "But now here are men from Ammon, Moab and Mount Seir, whose
territory you would not allow Israel to
invade when they came from Egypt;
so they turned away from them and
did not destroy them. 11 See how they
are repaying us by coming to drive
us out of the possession you gave us
as an inheritance. 12 Our God, will
you not judge them? For we have no
power to face this vast army that is
attacking us. We do not know what to
do, but our eyes are on you."

13 All the men of Judah, with their wives
and children and little ones, stood there
before the LORD.

14 Then the Spirit of the LORD came on

[a] *2* Or *and make alliances with* [b] *1* Some Septuagint manuscripts; Hebrew *Ammonites* [c] *2* One Hebrew
manuscript; most Hebrew manuscripts, Septuagint and Vulgate *Aram*

Jahaziel son of Zechariah, the son of Benaiah, the son of Jeiel, the son of Mattaniah, a Levite and descendant of Asaph, as
he stood in the assembly.
15 He said: "Listen, King Jehoshaphat
and all who live in Judah and Jerusalem!
This is what the LORD says to you: 'Do not
be afraid or discouraged because of this
vast army. For the battle is not yours, but
God's. 16 Tomorrow march down against
them. They will be climbing up by the
Pass of Ziz, and you will find them at the
end of the gorge in the Desert of Jeruel.
17 You will not have to fight this battle.
Take up your positions; stand firm and
see the deliverance the LORD will give
you, Judah and Jerusalem. Do not be
afraid; do not be discouraged. Go out to
face them tomorrow, and the LORD will
be with you.'"
18 Jehoshaphat bowed down with his
face to the ground, and all the people of
Judah and Jerusalem fell down in worship before the LORD. 19 Then some Levites from the Kohathites and Korahites
stood up and praised the LORD, the God
of Israel, with a very loud voice.
20 Early in the morning they left for the
Desert of Tekoa. As they set out, Jehoshaphat stood and said, "Listen to me, Judah
and people of Jerusalem! Have faith in
the LORD your God and you will be upheld; have faith in his prophets and you
will be successful." 21 After consulting
the people, Jehoshaphat appointed men
to sing to the LORD and to praise him for
the splendor of his[a] holiness as they went
out at the head of the army, saying:

"Give thanks to the LORD,
for his love endures forever."

22 As they began to sing and praise, the
LORD set ambushes against the men of
Ammon and Moab and Mount Seir who
were invading Judah, and they were defeated. 23 The Ammonites and Moabites
rose up against the men from Mount Seir
to destroy and annihilate them. After
they finished slaughtering the men from
Seir, they helped to destroy one another.
24 When the men of Judah came to
the place that overlooks the desert and
looked toward the vast army, they saw
only dead bodies lying on the ground;
no one had escaped. 25 So Jehoshaphat
and his men went to carry off their plunder, and they found among them a great
amount of equipment and clothing[b] and
also articles of value—more than they
could take away. There was so much
plunder that it took three days to collect
it. 26 On the fourth day they assembled in
the Valley of Berakah, where they praised
the LORD. This is why it is called the Valley of Berakah[c] to this day.
27 Then, led by Jehoshaphat, all the men
of Judah and Jerusalem returned joyfully to Jerusalem, for the LORD had given
them cause to rejoice over their enemies.
28 They entered Jerusalem and went to
the temple of the LORD with harps and
lyres and trumpets.
29 The fear of God came on all the surrounding kingdoms when they heard
how the LORD had fought against the enemies of Israel. 30 And the kingdom of Jehoshaphat was at peace, for his God had
given him rest on every side.
31 So Jehoshaphat reigned over Judah.
He was thirty-five years old when he became king of Judah, and he reigned in Jerusalem twenty-five years. His mother's
name was Azubah daughter of Shilhi.
32 He followed the ways of his father Asa
and did not stray from them; he did what
was right in the eyes of the LORD. 33 The
high places, however, were not removed,
and the people still had not set their
hearts on the God of their ancestors.
34 The other events of Jehoshaphat's
reign, from beginning to end, are written in the annals of Jehu son of Hanani,
which are recorded in the book of the
kings of Israel.
35 Later, Jehoshaphat king of Judah
made an alliance with Ahaziah king of
Israel, whose ways were wicked. 36 He
agreed with him to construct a fleet of
trading ships.[d] After these were built at
Ezion Geber, 37 Eliezer son of Dodavahu
of Mareshah prophesied against Jehoshaphat, saying, "Because you have made
an alliance with Ahaziah, the LORD will
destroy what you have made." The ships
were wrecked and were not able to set sail
to trade.[e]

21 Then Jehoshaphat rested with his
ancestors and was buried with them

[a] 21 Or *him with the splendor of* [b] 25 Some Hebrew manuscripts and Vulgate; most Hebrew manuscripts *corpses* [c] 26 *Berakah* means *praise.* [d] 36 Hebrew *of ships that could go to Tarshish* [e] 37 Hebrew *sail for Tarshish*

in the City of David. And Jehoram his son
succeeded him as king. [2]Jehoram's brothers, the sons of Jehoshaphat, were Azariah, Jehiel, Zechariah, Azariahu, Michael
and Shephatiah. All these were sons of
Jehoshaphat king of Israel.[a] [3]Their father
had given them many gifts of silver and
gold and articles of value, as well as fortified cities in Judah, but he had given the
kingdom to Jehoram because he was his
firstborn son.

[4]When Jehoram established himself
firmly over his father's kingdom, he put
all his brothers to the sword along with
some of the officials of Israel. [5]Jehoram
was thirty-two years old when he became
king, and he reigned in Jerusalem eight
years. [6]He followed the ways of the kings
of Israel, as the house of Ahab had done,
for he married a daughter of Ahab. He did
evil in the eyes of the LORD. [7]Neverthe-
less, because of the covenant the LORD
had made with David, the LORD was not
willing to destroy the house of David. He
had promised to maintain a lamp for him
and his descendants forever.

[8]In the time of Jehoram, Edom rebelled
against Judah and set up its own king. [9]So
Jehoram went there with his officers and
all his chariots. The Edomites surrounded him and his chariot commanders, but
he rose up and broke through by night.
[10]To this day Edom has been in rebellion
against Judah.

Libnah revolted at the same time, because Jehoram had forsaken the LORD,
the God of his ancestors. [11]He had also
built high places on the hills of Judah
and had caused the people of Jerusalem
to prostitute themselves and had led Judah astray.

[12]Jehoram received a letter from Elijah
the prophet, which said:

"This is what the LORD, the God of
your father David, says: 'You have
not followed the ways of your father
Jehoshaphat or of Asa king of Judah.
[13]But you have followed the ways of
the kings of Israel, and you have led
Judah and the people of Jerusalem
to prostitute themselves, just as the
house of Ahab did. You have also murdered your own brothers, members of
your own family, men who were better
than you. [14]So now the LORD is about
to strike your people, your sons, your
wives and everything that is yours,
with a heavy blow. [15]You yourself will
be very ill with a lingering disease of
the bowels, until the disease causes
your bowels to come out.'"

[16]The LORD aroused against Jehoram
the hostility of the Philistines and of the
Arabs who lived near the Cushites. [17]They
attacked Judah, invaded it and carried off
all the goods found in the king's palace,
together with his sons and wives. Not a
son was left to him except Ahaziah,[b] the
youngest.

[18]After all this, the LORD afflicted Jehoram with an incurable disease of the
bowels. [19]In the course of time, at the
end of the second year, his bowels came
out because of the disease, and he died
in great pain. His people made no funeral
fire in his honor, as they had for his predecessors.

[20]Jehoram was thirty-two years old
when he became king, and he reigned in
Jerusalem eight years. He passed away,
to no one's regret, and was buried in the
City of David, but not in the tombs of the
kings.

22 The people of Jerusalem made Ahaziah, Jehoram's youngest son, king
in his place, since the raiders, who came
with the Arabs into the camp, had killed
all the older sons. So Ahaziah son of Jehoram king of Judah began to reign.

[2]Ahaziah was twenty-two[c] years old
when he became king, and he reigned in
Jerusalem one year. His mother's name
was Athaliah, a granddaughter of Omri.

[3]He too followed the ways of the house
of Ahab, for his mother encouraged him
to act wickedly. [4]He did evil in the eyes of
the LORD, as the house of Ahab had done,
for after his father's death they became
his advisers, to his undoing. [5]He also followed their counsel when he went with
Joram[d] son of Ahab king of Israel to wage
war against Hazael king of Aram at Ramoth Gilead. The Arameans wounded Joram; [6]so he returned to Jezreel to recover

[a] *2* That is, Judah, as frequently in 2 Chronicles [b] *17* Hebrew *Jehoahaz,* a variant of *Ahaziah* [c] *2* Some Septuagint manuscripts and Syriac (see also 2 Kings 8:26); Hebrew *forty-two* [d] *5* Hebrew *Jehoram,* a variant of *Joram;* also in verses 6 and 7

from the wounds they had inflicted on him at Ramoth[a] in his battle with Hazael king of Aram.

Then Ahaziah[b] son of Jehoram king of Judah went down to Jezreel to see Joram son of Ahab because he had been wounded.

[7]Through Ahaziah's visit to Joram, God brought about Ahaziah's downfall. When Ahaziah arrived, he went out with Joram to meet Jehu son of Nimshi, whom the LORD had anointed to destroy the house of Ahab. [8]While Jehu was executing judgment on the house of Ahab, he found the officials of Judah and the sons of Ahaziah's relatives, who had been attending Ahaziah, and he killed them. [9]He then went in search of Ahaziah, and his men captured him while he was hiding in Samaria. He was brought to Jehu and put to death. They buried him, for they said, "He was a son of Jehoshaphat, who sought the LORD with all his heart." So there was no one in the house of Ahaziah powerful enough to retain the kingdom.

[10]When Athaliah the mother of Ahaziah saw that her son was dead, she proceeded to destroy the whole royal family of the house of Judah. [11]But Jehosheba,[c] the daughter of King Jehoram, took Joash son of Ahaziah and stole him away from among the royal princes who were about to be murdered and put him and his nurse in a bedroom. Because Jehosheba,[c] the daughter of King Jehoram and wife of the priest Jehoiada, was Ahaziah's sister, she hid the child from Athaliah so she could not kill him. [12]He remained hidden with them at the temple of God for six years while Athaliah ruled the land.

23 In the seventh year Jehoiada showed his strength. He made a covenant with the commanders of units of a hundred: Azariah son of Jeroham, Ishmael son of Jehohanan, Azariah son of Obed, Maaseiah son of Adaiah, and Elishaphat son of Zikri. [2]They went throughout Judah and gathered the Levites and the heads of Israelite families from all the towns. When they came to Jerusalem, [3]the whole assembly made a covenant with the king at the temple of God.

Jehoiada said to them, "The king's son shall reign, as the LORD promised concerning the descendants of David. [4]Now this is what you are to do: A third of you priests and Levites who are going on duty on the Sabbath are to keep watch at the doors, [5]a third of you at the royal palace and a third at the Foundation Gate, and all the others are to be in the courtyards of the temple of the LORD. [6]No one is to enter the temple of the LORD except the priests and Levites on duty; they may enter because they are consecrated, but all the others are to observe the LORD's command not to enter.[d] [7]The Levites are to station themselves around the king, each with weapon in hand. Anyone who enters the temple is to be put to death. Stay close to the king wherever he goes."

[8]The Levites and all the men of Judah did just as Jehoiada the priest ordered. Each one took his men—those who were going on duty on the Sabbath and those who were going off duty—for Jehoiada the priest had not released any of the divisions. [9]Then he gave the commanders of units of a hundred the spears and the large and small shields that had belonged to King David and that were in the temple of God. [10]He stationed all the men, each with his weapon in his hand, around the king—near the altar and the temple, from the south side to the north side of the temple.

[11]Jehoiada and his sons brought out the king's son and put the crown on him; they presented him with a copy of the covenant and proclaimed him king. They anointed him and shouted, "Long live the king!"

[12]When Athaliah heard the noise of the people running and cheering the king, she went to them at the temple of the LORD. [13]She looked, and there was the king, standing by his pillar at the entrance. The officers and the trumpeters were beside the king, and all the people of the land were rejoicing and blowing trumpets, and musicians with their instruments were leading the praises. Then Athaliah tore her robes and shouted, "Treason! Treason!"

[14]Jehoiada the priest sent out the commanders of units of a hundred, who were in charge of the troops, and said to them: "Bring her out between the ranks[e] and

[a] 6 Hebrew *Ramah,* a variant of *Ramoth* [b] 6 Some Hebrew manuscripts, Septuagint, Vulgate and Syriac (see also 2 Kings 8:29); most Hebrew manuscripts *Azariah* [c] 11 Hebrew *Jehoshabeath,* a variant of *Jehosheba* [d] 6 Or *are to stand guard where the LORD has assigned them* [e] 14 Or *out from the precincts*

put to the sword anyone who follows
her." For the priest had said, "Do not put
her to death at the temple of the LORD."
15So they seized her as she reached the
entrance of the Horse Gate on the palace
grounds, and there they put her to death.

16Jehoiada then made a covenant that
he, the people and the king[a] would be
the LORD's people. 17All the people went
to the temple of Baal and tore it down.
They smashed the altars and idols and
killed Mattan the priest of Baal in front
of the altars.

18Then Jehoiada placed the oversight
of the temple of the LORD in the hands
of the Levitical priests, to whom David
had made assignments in the temple, to
present the burnt offerings of the LORD
as written in the Law of Moses, with rejoicing and singing, as David had ordered. 19He also stationed gatekeepers at
the gates of the LORD's temple so that no
one who was in any way unclean might
enter.

20He took with him the commanders
of hundreds, the nobles, the rulers of the
people and all the people of the land and
brought the king down from the temple
of the LORD. They went into the palace
through the Upper Gate and seated the
king on the royal throne. 21All the people of the land rejoiced, and the city was
calm, because Athaliah had been slain
with the sword.

24 Joash was seven years old when he
became king, and he reigned in Jerusalem forty years. His mother's name
was Zibiah; she was from Beersheba. 2Jo-
ash did what was right in the eyes of the
LORD all the years of Jehoiada the priest.
3Jehoiada chose two wives for him, and
he had sons and daughters.

4Some time later Joash decided to restore the temple of the LORD. 5He called
together the priests and Levites and said
to them, "Go to the towns of Judah and
collect the money due annually from all
Israel, to repair the temple of your God.
Do it now." But the Levites did not act at
once.

6Therefore the king summoned Jehoiada the chief priest and said to him, "Why
haven't you required the Levites to bring
in from Judah and Jerusalem the tax imposed by Moses the servant of the LORD
and by the assembly of Israel for the tent
of the covenant law?"

7Now the sons of that wicked woman
Athaliah had broken into the temple of
God and had used even its sacred objects
for the Baals.

8At the king's command, a chest was
made and placed outside, at the gate of
the temple of the LORD. 9A proclamation
was then issued in Judah and Jerusalem
that they should bring to the LORD the
tax that Moses the servant of God had
required of Israel in the wilderness. 10All
the officials and all the people brought
their contributions gladly, dropping them
into the chest until it was full. 11When-
ever the chest was brought in by the Levites to the king's officials and they saw
that there was a large amount of money,
the royal secretary and the officer of the
chief priest would come and empty the
chest and carry it back to its place. They
did this regularly and collected a great
amount of money. 12The king and Jehoiada gave it to those who carried out the
work required for the temple of the LORD.
They hired masons and carpenters to restore the LORD's temple, and also workers
in iron and bronze to repair the temple.

13The men in charge of the work were
diligent, and the repairs progressed under them. They rebuilt the temple of God
according to its original design and rein-
forced it. 14When they had finished, they
brought the rest of the money to the king
and Jehoiada, and with it were made articles for the LORD's temple: articles for the
service and for the burnt offerings, and
also dishes and other objects of gold and
silver. As long as Jehoiada lived, burnt offerings were presented continually in the
temple of the LORD.

15Now Jehoiada was old and full of
years, and he died at the age of a hundred and thirty. 16He was buried with the
kings in the City of David, because of the
good he had done in Israel for God and
his temple.

17After the death of Jehoiada, the officials of Judah came and paid homage to
the king, and he listened to them. 18They
abandoned the temple of the LORD, the
God of their ancestors, and worshiped
Asherah poles and idols. Because of their
guilt, God's anger came on Judah and

[a] 16 Or *covenant between the LORD and the people and the king that they* (see 2 Kings 11:17)

Jerusalem. 19 Although the LORD sent prophets to the people to bring them back to him, and though they testified against them, they would not listen.

20 Then the Spirit of God came on Zechariah son of Jehoiada the priest. He stood before the people and said, "This is what God says: 'Why do you disobey the LORD's commands? You will not prosper. Because you have forsaken the LORD, he has forsaken you.' "

21 But they plotted against him, and by order of the king they stoned him to death in the courtyard of the LORD's temple. 22 King Joash did not remember the kindness Zechariah's father Jehoiada had shown him but killed his son, who said as he lay dying, "May the LORD see this and call you to account."

23 At the turn of the year,[a] the army of Aram marched against Joash; it invaded Judah and Jerusalem and killed all the leaders of the people. They sent all the plunder to their king in Damascus. 24 Although the Aramean army had come with only a few men, the LORD delivered into their hands a much larger army. Because Judah had forsaken the LORD, the God of their ancestors, judgment was executed on Joash. 25 When the Arameans withdrew, they left Joash severely wounded. His officials conspired against him for murdering the son of Jehoiada the priest, and they killed him in his bed. So he died and was buried in the City of David, but not in the tombs of the kings.

26 Those who conspired against him were Zabad,[b] son of Shimeath an Ammonite woman, and Jehozabad, son of Shimrith[c] a Moabite woman. 27 The account of his sons, the many prophecies about him, and the record of the restoration of the temple of God are written in the annotations on the book of the kings. And Amaziah his son succeeded him as king.

25 Amaziah was twenty-five years old when he became king, and he reigned in Jerusalem twenty-nine years. His mother's name was Jehoaddan; she was from Jerusalem. 2 He did what was right in the eyes of the LORD, but not wholeheartedly. 3 After the kingdom was firmly in his control, he executed the officials who had murdered his father the king. 4 Yet he did not put their children to death, but acted in accordance with what is written in the Law, in the Book of Moses, where the LORD commanded: "Parents shall not be put to death for their children, nor children be put to death for their parents; each will die for their own sin."[d]

5 Amaziah called the people of Judah together and assigned them according to their families to commanders of thousands and commanders of hundreds for all Judah and Benjamin. He then mustered those twenty years old or more and found that there were three hundred thousand men fit for military service, able to handle the spear and shield. 6 He also hired a hundred thousand fighting men from Israel for a hundred talents[e] of silver.

7 But a man of God came to him and said, "Your Majesty, these troops from Israel must not march with you, for the LORD is not with Israel — not with any of the people of Ephraim. 8 Even if you go and fight courageously in battle, God will overthrow you before the enemy, for God has the power to help or to overthrow."

9 Amaziah asked the man of God, "But what about the hundred talents I paid for these Israelite troops?"

The man of God replied, "The LORD can give you much more than that."

10 So Amaziah dismissed the troops who had come to him from Ephraim and sent them home. They were furious with Judah and left for home in a great rage.

11 Amaziah then marshaled his strength and led his army to the Valley of Salt, where he killed ten thousand men of Seir. 12 The army of Judah also captured ten thousand men alive, took them to the top of a cliff and threw them down so that all were dashed to pieces.

13 Meanwhile the troops that Amaziah had sent back and had not allowed to take part in the war raided towns belonging to Judah from Samaria to Beth Horon. They killed three thousand people and carried off great quantities of plunder.

14 When Amaziah returned from slaughtering the Edomites, he brought back the gods of the people of Seir. He set them up as his own gods, bowed down to them and burned sacrifices to them.

[a] *23* Probably in the spring [b] *26* A variant of *Jozabad* [c] *26* A variant of *Shomer* [d] *4* Deut. 24:16
[e] *6* That is, about 3 3/4 tons or about 3.4 metric tons; also in verse 9

15The anger of the LORD burned against
Amaziah, and he sent a prophet to him,
who said, "Why do you consult this people's gods, which could not save their
own people from your hand?"
16While he was still speaking, the king
said to him, "Have we appointed you an
adviser to the king? Stop! Why be struck
down?"

So the prophet stopped but said, "I
know that God has determined to destroy
you, because you have done this and have
not listened to my counsel."

17After Amaziah king of Judah consulted his advisers, he sent this challenge to
Jehoash[a] son of Jehoahaz, the son of Jehu,
king of Israel: "Come, let us face each other in battle."

18But Jehoash king of Israel replied
to Amaziah king of Judah: "A thistle in
Lebanon sent a message to a cedar in
Lebanon, 'Give your daughter to my son
in marriage.' Then a wild beast in Lebanon came along and trampled the thistle
underfoot. 19You say to yourself that you
have defeated Edom, and now you are
arrogant and proud. But stay at home!
Why ask for trouble and cause your own
downfall and that of Judah also?"

20Amaziah, however, would not listen, for God so worked that he might
deliver them into the hands of Jehoash,
because they sought the gods of Edom.
21So Jehoash king of Israel attacked. He
and Amaziah king of Judah faced each
other at Beth Shemesh in Judah. 22Ju-
dah was routed by Israel, and every man
fled to his home. 23Jehoash king of Israel captured Amaziah king of Judah, the
son of Joash, the son of Ahaziah,[b] at Beth
Shemesh. Then Jehoash brought him to
Jerusalem and broke down the wall of
Jerusalem from the Ephraim Gate to the
Corner Gate — a section about four hundred cubits[c] long. 24He took all the gold
and silver and all the articles found in the
temple of God that had been in the care
of Obed-Edom, together with the palace
treasures and the hostages, and returned
to Samaria.

25Amaziah son of Joash king of Judah
lived for fifteen years after the death of
Jehoash son of Jehoahaz king of Israel.
26As for the other events of Amaziah's
reign, from beginning to end, are they not
written in the book of the kings of Judah
and Israel? 27From the time that Amaziah turned away from following the LORD,
they conspired against him in Jerusalem
and he fled to Lachish, but they sent men
after him to Lachish and killed him there.
28He was brought back by horse and was
buried with his ancestors in the City of
Judah.[d]

26 Then all the people of Judah took
Uzziah,[e] who was sixteen years old,
and made him king in place of his father
Amaziah. 2He was the one who rebuilt
Elath and restored it to Judah after Am-
aziah rested with his ancestors.

3Uzziah was sixteen years old when he
became king, and he reigned in Jerusalem fifty-two years. His mother's name
was Jekoliah; she was from Jerusalem.
4He did what was right in the eyes of the
LORD, just as his father Amaziah had
done. 5He sought God during the days
of Zechariah, who instructed him in the
fear[f] of God. As long as he sought the
LORD, God gave him success.

6He went to war against the Philistines
and broke down the walls of Gath, Jabneh
and Ashdod. He then rebuilt towns near
Ashdod and elsewhere among the Philistines. 7God helped him against the Philistines and against the Arabs who lived
in Gur Baal and against the Meunites.
8The Ammonites brought tribute to Uzziah, and his fame spread as far as the
border of Egypt, because he had become
very powerful.

9Uzziah built towers in Jerusalem at the
Corner Gate, at the Valley Gate and at the
angle of the wall, and he fortified them.
10He also built towers in the wilderness
and dug many cisterns, because he had
much livestock in the foothills and in the
plain. He had people working his fields
and vineyards in the hills and in the fertile lands, for he loved the soil.

11Uzziah had a well-trained army,
ready to go out by divisions according to
their numbers as mustered by Jeiel the
secretary and Maaseiah the officer under
the direction of Hananiah, one of the roy-

[a] *17* Hebrew *Joash,* a variant of *Jehoash;* also in verses 18, 21, 23 and 25 [b] *23* Hebrew *Jehoahaz,* a variant of *Ahaziah* [c] *23* That is, about 600 feet or about 180 meters [d] *28* Most Hebrew manuscripts; some Hebrew manuscripts, Septuagint, Vulgate and Syriac (see also 2 Kings 14:20) *David* [e] *1* Also called *Azariah* [f] *5* Many Hebrew manuscripts, Septuagint and Syriac; other Hebrew manuscripts *vision*

al officials. 12The total number of family leaders over the fighting men was 2,600. 13Under their command was an army of 307,500 men trained for war, a powerful force to support the king against his enemies. 14Uzziah provided shields, spears, helmets, coats of armor, bows and slingstones for the entire army. 15In Jerusalem he made devices invented for use on the towers and on the corner defenses so that soldiers could shoot arrows and hurl large stones from the walls. His fame spread far and wide, for he was greatly helped until he became powerful.

16But after Uzziah became powerful, his pride led to his downfall. He was unfaithful to the LORD his God, and entered the temple of the LORD to burn incense on the altar of incense. 17Azariah the priest with eighty other courageous priests of the LORD followed him in. 18They confronted King Uzziah and said, "It is not right for you, Uzziah, to burn incense to the LORD. That is for the priests, the descendants of Aaron, who have been consecrated to burn incense. Leave the sanctuary, for you have been unfaithful; and you will not be honored by the LORD God."

19Uzziah, who had a censer in his hand ready to burn incense, became angry. While he was raging at the priests in their presence before the incense altar in the LORD's temple, leprosy[a] broke out on his forehead. 20When Azariah the chief priest and all the other priests looked at him, they saw that he had leprosy on his forehead, so they hurried him out. Indeed, he himself was eager to leave, because the LORD had afflicted him.

21King Uzziah had leprosy until the day he died. He lived in a separate house[b]—leprous, and banned from the temple of the LORD. Jotham his son had charge of the palace and governed the people of the land.

22The other events of Uzziah's reign, from beginning to end, are recorded by the prophet Isaiah son of Amoz. 23Uzziah rested with his ancestors and was buried near them in a cemetery that belonged to the kings, for people said, "He had leprosy." And Jotham his son succeeded him as king.

27 Jotham was twenty-five years old when he became king, and he reigned in Jerusalem sixteen years. His mother's name was Jerusha daughter of Zadok. 2He did what was right in the eyes of the LORD, just as his father Uzziah had done, but unlike him he did not enter the temple of the LORD. The people, however, continued their corrupt practices. 3Jotham rebuilt the Upper Gate of the temple of the LORD and did extensive work on the wall at the hill of Ophel. 4He built towns in the hill country of Judah and forts and towers in the wooded areas.

5Jotham waged war against the king of the Ammonites and conquered them. That year the Ammonites paid him a hundred talents[c] of silver, ten thousand cors[d] of wheat and ten thousand cors[e] of barley. The Ammonites brought him the same amount also in the second and third years.

6Jotham grew powerful because he walked steadfastly before the LORD his God.

7The other events in Jotham's reign, including all his wars and the other things he did, are written in the book of the kings of Israel and Judah. 8He was twenty-five years old when he became king, and he reigned in Jerusalem sixteen years. 9Jotham rested with his ancestors and was buried in the City of David. And Ahaz his son succeeded him as king.

28 Ahaz was twenty years old when he became king, and he reigned in Jerusalem sixteen years. Unlike David his father, he did not do what was right in the eyes of the LORD. 2He followed the ways of the kings of Israel and also made idols for worshiping the Baals. 3He burned sacrifices in the Valley of Ben Hinnom and sacrificed his children in the fire, engaging in the detestable practices of the nations the LORD had driven out before the Israelites. 4He offered sacrifices and burned incense at the high places, on the hilltops and under every spreading tree.

5Therefore the LORD his God delivered him into the hands of the king of Aram. The Arameans defeated him and

[a] *19* The Hebrew for *leprosy* was used for various diseases affecting the skin; also in verses 20, 21 and 23.
[b] *21* Or *in a house where he was relieved of responsibilities* [c] *5* That is, about 3 3/4 tons or about 3.4 metric tons [d] *5* That is, probably about 1,800 tons or about 1,600 metric tons of wheat [e] *5* That is, probably about 1,500 tons or about 1,350 metric tons of barley

took many of his people as prisoners and
brought them to Damascus.
He was also given into the hands of the
king of Israel, who inflicted heavy casualties on him. 6 In one day Pekah son of Remaliah killed a hundred and twenty thousand soldiers in Judah—because Judah
had forsaken the LORD, the God of their
ancestors. 7 Zikri, an Ephraimite warrior,
killed Maaseiah the king's son, Azrikam
the officer in charge of the palace, and
Elkanah, second to the king. 8 The men of
Israel took captive from their fellow Israelites who were from Judah two hundred
thousand wives, sons and daughters. They
also took a great deal of plunder, which
they carried back to Samaria.
9 But a prophet of the LORD named
Oded was there, and he went out to meet
the army when it returned to Samaria.
He said to them, "Because the LORD, the
God of your ancestors, was angry with
Judah, he gave them into your hand. But
you have slaughtered them in a rage that
reaches to heaven. 10 And now you intend
to make the men and women of Judah and
Jerusalem your slaves. But aren't you also
guilty of sins against the LORD your God?
11 Now listen to me! Send back your fellow
Israelites you have taken as prisoners, for
the LORD's fierce anger rests on you."
12 Then some of the leaders in Ephraim—Azariah son of Jehohanan, Berekiah son of Meshillemoth, Jehizkiah son of
Shallum, and Amasa son of Hadlai—confronted those who were arriving from the
war. 13 "You must not bring those prisoners here," they said, "or we will be guilty
before the LORD. Do you intend to add to
our sin and guilt? For our guilt is already
great, and his fierce anger rests on Israel."
14 So the soldiers gave up the prisoners
and plunder in the presence of the officials
and all the assembly. 15 The men designated by name took the prisoners, and from
the plunder they clothed all who were
naked. They provided them with clothes
and sandals, food and drink, and healing
balm. All those who were weak they put
on donkeys. So they took them back to
their fellow Israelites at Jericho, the City
of Palms, and returned to Samaria.
16 At that time King Ahaz sent to the
kings[a] of Assyria for help. 17 The Edomites
had again come and attacked Judah and
carried away prisoners, 18 while the Philistines had raided towns in the foothills
and in the Negev of Judah. They captured
and occupied Beth Shemesh, Aijalon and
Gederoth, as well as Soko, Timnah and
Gimzo, with their surrounding villages. 19 The LORD had humbled Judah because of Ahaz king of Israel,[b] for he had
promoted wickedness in Judah and had
been most unfaithful to the LORD. 20 Tiglath-Pileser[c] king of Assyria came to him,
but he gave him trouble instead of help.
21 Ahaz took some of the things from the
temple of the LORD and from the royal
palace and from the officials and presented them to the king of Assyria, but
that did not help him.
22 In his time of trouble King Ahaz became even more unfaithful to the LORD.
23 He offered sacrifices to the gods of Damascus, who had defeated him; for he
thought, "Since the gods of the kings of
Aram have helped them, I will sacrifice
to them so they will help me." But they
were his downfall and the downfall of
all Israel.
24 Ahaz gathered together the furnishings from the temple of God and cut them
in pieces. He shut the doors of the LORD's
temple and set up altars at every street
corner in Jerusalem. 25 In every town in
Judah he built high places to burn sacrifices to other gods and aroused the anger
of the LORD, the God of his ancestors.
26 The other events of his reign and
all his ways, from beginning to end, are
written in the book of the kings of Judah
and Israel. 27 Ahaz rested with his ancestors and was buried in the city of Jerusalem, but he was not placed in the tombs of
the kings of Israel. And Hezekiah his son
succeeded him as king.

29 Hezekiah was twenty-five years
old when he became king, and he
reigned in Jerusalem twenty-nine years.
His mother's name was Abijah daughter
of Zechariah. 2 He did what was right in
the eyes of the LORD, just as his father David had done.
3 In the first month of the first year of
his reign, he opened the doors of the temple of the LORD and repaired them. 4 He
brought in the priests and the Levites, assembled them in the square on the east

[a] *16* Most Hebrew manuscripts; one Hebrew manuscript, Septuagint and Vulgate (see also 2 Kings 16:7) *king*
[b] *19* That is, Judah, as frequently in 2 Chronicles [c] *20* Hebrew *Tilgath-Pilneser,* a variant of *Tiglath-Pileser*

side 5and said: "Listen to me, Levites!
Consecrate yourselves now and consecrate the temple of the LORD, the God of
your ancestors. Remove all defilement
from the sanctuary. 6Our parents were
unfaithful; they did evil in the eyes of
the LORD our God and forsook him. They
turned their faces away from the LORD's
dwelling place and turned their backs
on him. 7They also shut the doors of the
portico and put out the lamps. They did
not burn incense or present any burnt
offerings at the sanctuary to the God of
Israel. 8Therefore, the anger of the LORD
has fallen on Judah and Jerusalem; he has
made them an object of dread and horror and scorn, as you can see with your
own eyes. 9This is why our fathers have
fallen by the sword and why our sons and
daughters and our wives are in captivity. 10Now I intend to make a covenant
with the LORD, the God of Israel, so that
his fierce anger will turn away from us.
11My sons, do not be negligent now, for
the LORD has chosen you to stand before
him and serve him, to minister before
him and to burn incense."

12Then these Levites set to work:
from the Kohathites,
Mahath son of Amasai and Joel son of Azariah;
from the Merarites,
Kish son of Abdi and Azariah son of Jehallelel;
from the Gershonites,
Joah son of Zimmah and Eden son of Joah;
13from the descendants of Elizaphan,
Shimri and Jeiel;
from the descendants of Asaph,
Zechariah and Mattaniah;
14from the descendants of Heman,
Jehiel and Shimei;
from the descendants of Jeduthun,
Shemaiah and Uzziel.

15When they had assembled their fellow Levites and consecrated themselves,
they went in to purify the temple of the
LORD, as the king had ordered, following
the word of the LORD. 16The priests went
into the sanctuary of the LORD to purify
it. They brought out to the courtyard of
the LORD's temple everything unclean
that they found in the temple of the LORD.
The Levites took it and carried it out to the
Kidron Valley. 17They began the consecration on the first day of the first month,
and by the eighth day of the month they
reached the portico of the LORD. For eight
more days they consecrated the temple of
the LORD itself, finishing on the sixteenth
day of the first month.

18Then they went in to King Hezekiah
and reported: "We have purified the entire temple of the LORD, the altar of burnt
offering with all its utensils, and the table for setting out the consecrated bread,
with all its articles. 19We have prepared
and consecrated all the articles that King
Ahaz removed in his unfaithfulness
while he was king. They are now in front
of the LORD's altar."

20Early the next morning King Hezekiah gathered the city officials together and
went up to the temple of the LORD. 21They
brought seven bulls, seven rams, seven
male lambs and seven male goats as a sin
offering[a] for the kingdom, for the sanctuary and for Judah. The king commanded
the priests, the descendants of Aaron, to
offer these on the altar of the LORD. 22So
they slaughtered the bulls, and the priests
took the blood and splashed it against
the altar; next they slaughtered the rams
and splashed their blood against the altar; then they slaughtered the lambs
and splashed their blood against the altar. 23The goats for the sin offering were
brought before the king and the assembly, and they laid their hands on them.
24The priests then slaughtered the goats
and presented their blood on the altar
for a sin offering to atone for all Israel,
because the king had ordered the burnt
offering and the sin offering for all Israel.

25He stationed the Levites in the temple of the LORD with cymbals, harps
and lyres in the way prescribed by David and Gad the king's seer and Nathan
the prophet; this was commanded by
the LORD through his prophets. 26So the
Levites stood ready with David's instruments, and the priests with their trumpets.

27Hezekiah gave the order to sacrifice
the burnt offering on the altar. As the offering began, singing to the LORD began
also, accompanied by trumpets and the
instruments of David king of Israel. 28The
whole assembly bowed in worship, while

[a] *21* Or *purification offering*; also in verses 23 and 24

the musicians played and the trumpets
sounded. All this continued until the
sacrifice of the burnt offering was completed.
29When the offerings were finished,
the king and everyone present with him
knelt down and worshiped. 30King Hezekiah and his officials ordered the Levites
to praise the LORD with the words of David and of Asaph the seer. So they sang
praises with gladness and bowed down
and worshiped.
31Then Hezekiah said, "You have now
dedicated yourselves to the LORD. Come
and bring sacrifices and thank offerings
to the temple of the LORD." So the assembly brought sacrifices and thank offerings, and all whose hearts were willing
brought burnt offerings.
32The number of burnt offerings the
assembly brought was seventy bulls, a
hundred rams and two hundred male
lambs — all of them for burnt offerings to
the LORD. 33The animals consecrated as
sacrifices amounted to six hundred bulls
and three thousand sheep and goats.
34The priests, however, were too few to
skin all the burnt offerings; so their relatives the Levites helped them until the
task was finished and until other priests
had been consecrated, for the Levites had
been more conscientious in consecrating
themselves than the priests had been.
35There were burnt offerings in abundance, together with the fat of the fellowship offerings and the drink offerings
that accompanied the burnt offerings.
So the service of the temple of the LORD
was reestablished. 36Hezekiah and all the
people rejoiced at what God had brought
about for his people, because it was done
so quickly.

30 Hezekiah sent word to all Israel
and Judah and also wrote letters to
Ephraim and Manasseh, inviting them to
come to the temple of the LORD in Jerusalem and celebrate the Passover to the
LORD, the God of Israel. 2The king and his
officials and the whole assembly in Jerusalem decided to celebrate the Passover
in the second month. 3They had not been
able to celebrate it at the regular time
because not enough priests had consecrated themselves and the people had
not assembled in Jerusalem. 4The plan
seemed right both to the king and to the
whole assembly. 5They decided to send
a proclamation throughout Israel, from
Beersheba to Dan, calling the people
to come to Jerusalem and celebrate the
Passover to the LORD, the God of Israel. It
had not been celebrated in large numbers
according to what was written.
6At the king's command, couriers went
throughout Israel and Judah with letters from the king and from his officials,
which read:

"People of Israel, return to the
LORD, the God of Abraham, Isaac
and Israel, that he may return to
you who are left, who have escaped
from the hand of the kings of Assyria. 7Do not be like your parents and
your fellow Israelites, who were unfaithful to the LORD, the God of their
ancestors, so that he made them an
object of horror, as you see. 8Do not
be stiff-necked, as your ancestors
were; submit to the LORD. Come to
his sanctuary, which he has consecrated forever. Serve the LORD your
God, so that his fierce anger will turn
away from you. 9If you return to the
LORD, then your fellow Israelites and
your children will be shown compassion by their captors and will return
to this land, for the LORD your God is
gracious and compassionate. He will
not turn his face from you if you return to him."

10The couriers went from town to town
in Ephraim and Manasseh, as far as Zebulun, but people scorned and ridiculed
them. 11Nevertheless, some from Asher,
Manasseh and Zebulun humbled themselves and went to Jerusalem. 12Also in
Judah the hand of God was on the people
to give them unity of mind to carry out
what the king and his officials had ordered, following the word of the LORD.
13A very large crowd of people assembled in Jerusalem to celebrate the Festival of Unleavened Bread in the second
month. 14They removed the altars in Jerusalem and cleared away the incense
altars and threw them into the Kidron
Valley.
15They slaughtered the Passover
lamb on the fourteenth day of the second month. The priests and the Levites
were ashamed and consecrated themselves and brought burnt offerings to the
temple of the LORD. 16Then they took up

their regular positions as prescribed in
the Law of Moses the man of God. The
priests splashed against the altar the
blood handed to them by the Levites.
17 Since many in the crowd had not consecrated themselves, the Levites had to
kill the Passover lambs for all those who
were not ceremonially clean and could
not consecrate their lambs[a] to the LORD.
18 Although most of the many people who
came from Ephraim, Manasseh, Issachar
and Zebulun had not purified themselves, yet they ate the Passover, contrary to what was written. But Hezekiah
prayed for them, saying, "May the LORD,
who is good, pardon everyone 19 who sets
their heart on seeking God — the LORD,
the God of their ancestors — even if they
are not clean according to the rules of the
sanctuary." 20 And the LORD heard Hezekiah and healed the people.

21 The Israelites who were present in
Jerusalem celebrated the Festival of Unleavened Bread for seven days with great
rejoicing, while the Levites and priests
praised the LORD every day with resounding instruments dedicated to the
LORD.[b]

22 Hezekiah spoke encouragingly to
all the Levites, who showed good understanding of the service of the LORD. For
the seven days they ate their assigned
portion and offered fellowship offerings
and praised[c] the LORD, the God of their
ancestors.

23 The whole assembly then agreed to
celebrate the festival seven more days;
so for another seven days they celebrated
joyfully. 24 Hezekiah king of Judah provided a thousand bulls and seven thousand sheep and goats for the assembly,
and the officials provided them with a
thousand bulls and ten thousand sheep
and goats. A great number of priests
consecrated themselves. 25 The entire
assembly of Judah rejoiced, along with
the priests and Levites and all who had
assembled from Israel, including the foreigners who had come from Israel and
also those who resided in Judah. 26 There
was great joy in Jerusalem, for since the
days of Solomon son of David king of Israel there had been nothing like this in
Jerusalem. 27 The priests and the Levites
stood to bless the people, and God heard
them, for their prayer reached heaven,
his holy dwelling place.

31 When all this had ended, the Israelites who were there went out to
the towns of Judah, smashed the sacred
stones and cut down the Asherah poles.
They destroyed the high places and the
altars throughout Judah and Benjamin
and in Ephraim and Manasseh. After
they had destroyed all of them, the Israelites returned to their own towns and to
their own property.

2 Hezekiah assigned the priests and Levites to divisions — each of them according to their duties as priests or Levites —
to offer burnt offerings and fellowship
offerings, to minister, to give thanks and
to sing praises at the gates of the LORD's
dwelling. 3 The king contributed from
his own possessions for the morning and
evening burnt offerings and for the burnt
offerings on the Sabbaths, at the New
Moons and at the appointed festivals as
written in the Law of the LORD. 4 He ordered the people living in Jerusalem to
give the portion due the priests and Levites so they could devote themselves
to the Law of the LORD. 5 As soon as the
order went out, the Israelites generously gave the firstfruits of their grain, new
wine, olive oil and honey and all that the
fields produced. They brought a great
amount, a tithe of everything. 6 The people of Israel and Judah who lived in the
towns of Judah also brought a tithe of
their herds and flocks and a tithe of the
holy things dedicated to the LORD their
God, and they piled them in heaps. 7 They
began doing this in the third month and
finished in the seventh month. 8 When
Hezekiah and his officials came and saw
the heaps, they praised the LORD and
blessed his people Israel.

9 Hezekiah asked the priests and Levites about the heaps; 10 and Azariah the
chief priest, from the family of Zadok,
answered, "Since the people began to
bring their contributions to the temple of
the LORD, we have had enough to eat and
plenty to spare, because the LORD has
blessed his people, and this great amount
is left over."

11 Hezekiah gave orders to prepare storerooms in the temple of the LORD, and this
was done. 12 Then they faithfully brought

[a] *17* Or *consecrate themselves* [b] *21* Or *priests sang to the LORD every day, accompanied by the LORD's instruments of praise* [c] *22* Or *and confessed their sins to*

in the contributions, tithes and dedicated
gifts. Konaniah, a Levite, was the overseer
in charge of these things, and his brother
Shimei was next in rank. 13Jehiel, Azaziah, Nahath, Asahel, Jerimoth, Jozabad,
Eliel, Ismakiah, Mahath and Benaiah
were assistants of Konaniah and Shimei
his brother. All these served by appoint-
ment of King Hezekiah and Azariah the
official in charge of the temple of God.

14Kore son of Imnah the Levite, keeper of the East Gate, was in charge of the
freewill offerings given to God, distributing the contributions made to the LORD
and also the consecrated gifts. 15Eden,
Miniamin, Jeshua, Shemaiah, Amariah
and Shekaniah assisted him faithfully
in the towns of the priests, distributing
to their fellow priests according to their
divisions, old and young alike.

16In addition, they distributed to the
males three years old or more whose
names were in the genealogical records—all who would enter the temple of
the LORD to perform the daily duties of
their various tasks, according to their responsibilities and their divisions. 17And
they distributed to the priests enrolled
by their families in the genealogical records and likewise to the Levites twenty
years old or more, according to their responsibilities and their divisions. 18They
included all the little ones, the wives,
and the sons and daughters of the whole
community listed in these genealogical
records. For they were faithful in consecrating themselves.

19As for the priests, the descendants
of Aaron, who lived on the farmlands
around their towns or in any other towns,
men were designated by name to distribute portions to every male among them
and to all who were recorded in the genealogies of the Levites.

20This is what Hezekiah did throughout Judah, doing what was good and right
and faithful before the LORD his God.
21In everything that he undertook in the
service of God's temple and in obedience
to the law and the commands, he sought
his God and worked wholeheartedly. And
so he prospered.

32 After all that Hezekiah had so faithfully done, Sennacherib king of Assyria came and invaded Judah. He laid
siege to the fortified cities, thinking to
conquer them for himself. 2When Hezekiah saw that Sennacherib had come and
that he intended to wage war against Jerusalem, 3he consulted with his officials
and military staff about blocking off the
water from the springs outside the city,
and they helped him. 4They gathered
a large group of people who blocked all
the springs and the stream that flowed
through the land. "Why should the
kings[a] of Assyria come and find plenty of
water?" they said. 5Then he worked hard
repairing all the broken sections of the
wall and building towers on it. He built
another wall outside that one and rein-
forced the terraces[b] of the City of David.
He also made large numbers of weapons
and shields.

6He appointed military officers over
the people and assembled them before
him in the square at the city gate and encouraged them with these words: 7"Be
strong and courageous. Do not be afraid
or discouraged because of the king of
Assyria and the vast army with him, for
there is a greater power with us than with
him. 8With him is only the arm of flesh,
but with us is the LORD our God to help us
and to fight our battles." And the people
gained confidence from what Hezekiah
the king of Judah said.

9Later, when Sennacherib king of Assyria and all his forces were laying siege
to Lachish, he sent his officers to Jerusalem with this message for Hezekiah king
of Judah and for all the people of Judah
who were there:

10"This is what Sennacherib king of
Assyria says: On what are you basing
your confidence, that you remain in
Jerusalem under siege? 11When Hezekiah says, 'The LORD our God will
save us from the hand of the king of
Assyria,' he is misleading you, to let
you die of hunger and thirst. 12Did
not Hezekiah himself remove this
god's high places and altars, saying
to Judah and Jerusalem, 'You must
worship before one altar and burn
sacrifices on it'?

13"Do you not know what I and my
predecessors have done to all the
peoples of the other lands? Were the
gods of those nations ever able to de-

[a] 4 Hebrew; Septuagint and Syriac *king* [b] 5 Or *the Millo*

liver their land from my hand? 14Who
of all the gods of these nations that
my predecessors destroyed has been
able to save his people from me? How
then can your god deliver you from
my hand? 15Now do not let Hezekiah deceive you and mislead you like
this. Do not believe him, for no god of
any nation or kingdom has been able
to deliver his people from my hand
or the hand of my predecessors. How
much less will your god deliver you
from my hand!"

16Sennacherib's officers spoke further
against the LORD God and against his
servant Hezekiah. 17The king also wrote
letters ridiculing the LORD, the God of
Israel, and saying this against him: "Just
as the gods of the peoples of the other
lands did not rescue their people from
my hand, so the god of Hezekiah will not
rescue his people from my hand." 18Then
they called out in Hebrew to the people of
Jerusalem who were on the wall, to terrify them and make them afraid in order to
capture the city. 19They spoke about the
God of Jerusalem as they did about the
gods of the other peoples of the world —
the work of human hands.

20King Hezekiah and the prophet Isaiah son of Amoz cried out in prayer to
heaven about this. 21And the LORD sent
an angel, who annihilated all the fighting men and the commanders and officers in the camp of the Assyrian king. So
he withdrew to his own land in disgrace.
And when he went into the temple of his
god, some of his sons, his own flesh and
blood, cut him down with the sword.

22So the LORD saved Hezekiah and the
people of Jerusalem from the hand of
Sennacherib king of Assyria and from the
hand of all others. He took care of them[a]
on every side. 23Many brought offerings to
Jerusalem for the LORD and valuable gifts
for Hezekiah king of Judah. From then on
he was highly regarded by all the nations.

24In those days Hezekiah became ill
and was at the point of death. He prayed
to the LORD, who answered him and gave
him a miraculous sign. 25But Hezekiah's
heart was proud and he did not respond
to the kindness shown him; therefore the
LORD's wrath was on him and on Judah
and Jerusalem. 26Then Hezekiah repented of the pride of his heart, as did the
people of Jerusalem; therefore the LORD's
wrath did not come on them during the
days of Hezekiah.

27Hezekiah had very great wealth and
honor, and he made treasuries for his silver and gold and for his precious stones,
spices, shields and all kinds of valuables.
28He also made buildings to store the
harvest of grain, new wine and olive oil;
and he made stalls for various kinds of
cattle, and pens for the flocks. 29He built
villages and acquired great numbers of
flocks and herds, for God had given him
very great riches.

30It was Hezekiah who blocked the upper outlet of the Gihon spring and chan-
neled the water down to the west side of
the City of David. He succeeded in everything he undertook. 31But when envoys
were sent by the rulers of Babylon to ask
him about the miraculous sign that had
occurred in the land, God left him to test
him and to know everything that was in
his heart.

32The other events of Hezekiah's reign
and his acts of devotion are written in the
vision of the prophet Isaiah son of Amoz
in the book of the kings of Judah and Israel. 33Hezekiah rested with his ancestors and was buried on the hill where the
tombs of David's descendants are. All Judah and the people of Jerusalem honored
him when he died. And Manasseh his son
succeeded him as king.

33 Manasseh was twelve years old
when he became king, and he
reigned in Jerusalem fifty-five years. 2He
did evil in the eyes of the LORD, following the detestable practices of the nations
the LORD had driven out before the Israelites. 3He rebuilt the high places his father
Hezekiah had demolished; he also erected altars to the Baals and made Asherah
poles. He bowed down to all the starry
hosts and worshiped them. 4He built altars in the temple of the LORD, of which
the LORD had said, "My Name will remain
in Jerusalem forever." 5In both courts of
the temple of the LORD, he built altars
to all the starry hosts. 6He sacrificed his
children in the fire in the Valley of Ben
Hinnom, practiced divination and witchcraft, sought omens, and consulted me-

[a] 22 Hebrew; Septuagint and Vulgate *He gave them rest*

diums and spiritists. He did much evil in
the eyes of the LORD, arousing his anger.
7He took the image he had made and
put it in God's temple, of which God had
said to David and to his son Solomon,
"In this temple and in Jerusalem, which
I have chosen out of all the tribes of Israel, I will put my Name forever. 8I will not
again make the feet of the Israelites leave
the land I assigned to your ancestors, if
only they will be careful to do everything I commanded them concerning all
the laws, decrees and regulations given
through Moses." 9But Manasseh led Judah and the people of Jerusalem astray,
so that they did more evil than the nations the LORD had destroyed before the
Israelites.
10The LORD spoke to Manasseh and his
people, but they paid no attention. 11So
the LORD brought against them the army
commanders of the king of Assyria, who
took Manasseh prisoner, put a hook in
his nose, bound him with bronze shackles and took him to Babylon. 12In his distress he sought the favor of the LORD his
God and humbled himself greatly before
the God of his ancestors. 13And when he
prayed to him, the LORD was moved by
his entreaty and listened to his plea; so
he brought him back to Jerusalem and to
his kingdom. Then Manasseh knew that
the LORD is God.
14Afterward he rebuilt the outer wall
of the City of David, west of the Gihon
spring in the valley, as far as the entrance
of the Fish Gate and encircling the hill of
Ophel; he also made it much higher. He
stationed military commanders in all the
fortified cities in Judah.
15He got rid of the foreign gods and
removed the image from the temple of
the LORD, as well as all the altars he had
built on the temple hill and in Jerusalem; and he threw them out of the city.
16Then he restored the altar of the LORD
and sacrificed fellowship offerings and
thank offerings on it, and told Judah to
serve the LORD, the God of Israel. 17The
people, however, continued to sacrifice
at the high places, but only to the LORD
their God.
18The other events of Manasseh's reign,
including his prayer to his God and the
words the seers spoke to him in the name
of the LORD, the God of Israel, are written in the annals of the kings of Israel.[a]
19His prayer and how God was moved by
his entreaty, as well as all his sins and unfaithfulness, and the sites where he built
high places and set up Asherah poles and
idols before he humbled himself—all
these are written in the records of the
seers.[b] 20Manasseh rested with his ancestors and was buried in his palace. And
Amon his son succeeded him as king.

21Amon was twenty-two years old
when he became king, and he reigned in
Jerusalem two years. 22He did evil in the
eyes of the LORD, as his father Manasseh
had done. Amon worshiped and offered
sacrifices to all the idols Manasseh had
made. 23But unlike his father Manasseh,
he did not humble himself before the
LORD; Amon increased his guilt.
24Amon's officials conspired against
him and assassinated him in his palace. 25Then the people of the land killed
all who had plotted against King Amon,
and they made Josiah his son king in his
place.

34 Josiah was eight years old when he
became king, and he reigned in Jerusalem thirty-one years. 2He did what
was right in the eyes of the LORD and followed the ways of his father David, not
turning aside to the right or to the left.
3In the eighth year of his reign, while
he was still young, he began to seek the
God of his father David. In his twelfth
year he began to purge Judah and Jerusalem of high places, Asherah poles and
idols. 4Under his direction the altars of
the Baals were torn down; he cut to pieces the incense altars that were above
them, and smashed the Asherah poles
and the idols. These he broke to pieces
and scattered over the graves of those
who had sacrificed to them. 5He burned
the bones of the priests on their altars,
and so he purged Judah and Jerusalem.
6In the towns of Manasseh, Ephraim and
Simeon, as far as Naphtali, and in the ruins around them, 7he tore down the altars
and the Asherah poles and crushed the
idols to powder and cut to pieces all the
incense altars throughout Israel. Then he
went back to Jerusalem.

[a] *18* That is, Judah, as frequently in 2 Chronicles Hebrew manuscripts *of Hozai*
[b] *19* One Hebrew manuscript and Septuagint; most

8 In the eighteenth year of Josiah's reign, to purify the land and the temple, he sent Shaphan son of Azaliah and Maaseiah the ruler of the city, with Joah son of Joahaz, the recorder, to repair the temple of the LORD his God.

9 They went to Hilkiah the high priest and gave him the money that had been brought into the temple of God, which the Levites who were the gatekeepers had collected from the people of Manasseh, Ephraim and the entire remnant of Israel and from all the people of Judah and Benjamin and the inhabitants of Jerusalem. 10 Then they entrusted it to the men appointed to supervise the work on the LORD's temple. These men paid the workers who repaired and restored the temple. 11 They also gave money to the carpenters and builders to purchase dressed stone, and timber for joists and beams for the buildings that the kings of Judah had allowed to fall into ruin.

12 The workers labored faithfully. Over them to direct them were Jahath and Obadiah, Levites descended from Merari, and Zechariah and Meshullam, descended from Kohath. The Levites—all who were skilled in playing musical instruments— 13 had charge of the laborers and supervised all the workers from job to job. Some of the Levites were secretaries, scribes and gatekeepers.

14 While they were bringing out the money that had been taken into the temple of the LORD, Hilkiah the priest found the Book of the Law of the LORD that had been given through Moses. 15 Hilkiah said to Shaphan the secretary, "I have found the Book of the Law in the temple of the LORD." He gave it to Shaphan.

16 Then Shaphan took the book to the king and reported to him: "Your officials are doing everything that has been committed to them. 17 They have paid out the money that was in the temple of the LORD and have entrusted it to the supervisors and workers." 18 Then Shaphan the secretary informed the king, "Hilkiah the priest has given me a book." And Shaphan read from it in the presence of the king.

19 When the king heard the words of the Law, he tore his robes. 20 He gave these orders to Hilkiah, Ahikam son of Shaphan, Abdon son of Micah,[a] Shaphan the secretary and Asaiah the king's attendant: 21 "Go and inquire of the LORD for me and for the remnant in Israel and Judah about what is written in this book that has been found. Great is the LORD's anger that is poured out on us because those who have gone before us have not kept the word of the LORD; they have not acted in accordance with all that is written in this book."

22 Hilkiah and those the king had sent with him[b] went to speak to the prophet Huldah, who was the wife of Shallum son of Tokhath,[c] the son of Hasrah,[d] keeper of the wardrobe. She lived in Jerusalem, in the New Quarter.

23 She said to them, "This is what the LORD, the God of Israel, says: Tell the man who sent you to me, 24 'This is what the LORD says: I am going to bring disaster on this place and its people—all the curses written in the book that has been read in the presence of the king of Judah. 25 Because they have forsaken me and burned incense to other gods and aroused my anger by all that their hands have made,[e] my anger will be poured out on this place and will not be quenched.' 26 Tell the king of Judah, who sent you to inquire of the LORD, 'This is what the LORD, the God of Israel, says concerning the words you heard: 27 Because your heart was responsive and you humbled yourself before God when you heard what he spoke against this place and its people, and because you humbled yourself before me and tore your robes and wept in my presence, I have heard you, declares the LORD. 28 Now I will gather you to your ancestors, and you will be buried in peace. Your eyes will not see all the disaster I am going to bring on this place and on those who live here.'"

So they took her answer back to the king.

29 Then the king called together all the elders of Judah and Jerusalem. 30 He went up to the temple of the LORD with the people of Judah, the inhabitants of Jerusalem, the priests and the Levites—all the people from the least to the greatest. He read in their hearing all the words of the Book of the Covenant, which had been found in the temple of the LORD. 31 The king stood

[a] 20 Also called *Akbor son of Micaiah* [b] 22 One Hebrew manuscript, Vulgate and Syriac; most Hebrew manuscripts do not have *had sent with him.* [c] 22 Also called *Tikvah* [d] 22 Also called *Harhas*
[e] 25 Or *by everything they have done*

by his pillar and renewed the covenant in
the presence of the LORD — to follow the
LORD and keep his commands, statutes
and decrees with all his heart and all his
soul, and to obey the words of the covenant written in this book.
32Then he had everyone in Jerusalem
and Benjamin pledge themselves to it;
the people of Jerusalem did this in accordance with the covenant of God, the God
of their ancestors.
33Josiah removed all the detestable
idols from all the territory belonging to
the Israelites, and he had all who were
present in Israel serve the LORD their
God. As long as he lived, they did not fail
to follow the LORD, the God of their ancestors.

35 Josiah celebrated the Passover to
the LORD in Jerusalem, and the
Passover lamb was slaughtered on the
fourteenth day of the first month. 2He
appointed the priests to their duties and
encouraged them in the service of the
LORD's temple. 3He said to the Levites,
who instructed all Israel and who had
been consecrated to the LORD: "Put the
sacred ark in the temple that Solomon
son of David king of Israel built. It is not to
be carried about on your shoulders. Now
serve the LORD your God and his people
Israel. 4Prepare yourselves by families in
your divisions, according to the instructions written by David king of Israel and
by his son Solomon.
5"Stand in the holy place with a group
of Levites for each subdivision of the families of your fellow Israelites, the lay people. 6Slaughter the Passover lambs, consecrate yourselves and prepare the lambs
for your fellow Israelites, doing what the
LORD commanded through Moses."
7Josiah provided for all the lay people
who were there a total of thirty thousand
lambs and goats for the Passover offerings, and also three thousand cattle — all
from the king's own possessions.
8His officials also contributed voluntarily to the people and the priests and
Levites. Hilkiah, Zechariah and Jehiel,
the officials in charge of God's temple,
gave the priests twenty-six hundred Passover offerings and three hundred cattle.
9Also Konaniah along with Shemaiah
and Nethanel, his brothers, and Hashabiah, Jeiel and Jozabad, the leaders of the
Levites, provided five thousand Passover
offerings and five hundred head of cattle
for the Levites.
10The service was arranged and the
priests stood in their places with the Levites in their divisions as the king had ordered. 11The Passover lambs were slaughtered, and the priests splashed against
the altar the blood handed to them, while
the Levites skinned the animals. 12They
set aside the burnt offerings to give them
to the subdivisions of the families of the
people to offer to the LORD, as it is written
in the Book of Moses. They did the same
with the cattle. 13They roasted the Passover animals over the fire as prescribed,
and boiled the holy offerings in pots, cal-
drons and pans and served them quickly
to all the people. 14After this, they made
preparations for themselves and for the
priests, because the priests, the descendants of Aaron, were sacrificing the burnt
offerings and the fat portions until nightfall. So the Levites made preparations for
themselves and for the Aaronic priests.
15The musicians, the descendants of
Asaph, were in the places prescribed by
David, Asaph, Heman and Jeduthun the
king's seer. The gatekeepers at each gate
did not need to leave their posts, because
their fellow Levites made the preparations for them.
16So at that time the entire service of
the LORD was carried out for the celebration of the Passover and the offering of
burnt offerings on the altar of the LORD,
as King Josiah had ordered. 17The Israelites who were present celebrated the
Passover at that time and observed the
Festival of Unleavened Bread for seven
days. 18The Passover had not been observed like this in Israel since the days
of the prophet Samuel; and none of the
kings of Israel had ever celebrated such
a Passover as did Josiah, with the priests,
the Levites and all Judah and Israel who
were there with the people of Jerusalem.
19This Passover was celebrated in the
eighteenth year of Josiah's reign.
20After all this, when Josiah had set the
temple in order, Necho king of Egypt went
up to fight at Carchemish on the Euphrates, and Josiah marched out to meet him
in battle. 21But Necho sent messengers to
him, saying, "What quarrel is there, king
of Judah, between you and me? It is not
you I am attacking at this time, but the
house with which I am at war. God has

told me to hurry; so stop opposing God,
who is with me, or he will destroy you."
22 Josiah, however, would not turn away
from him, but disguised himself to engage him in battle. He would not listen to
what Necho had said at God's command
but went to fight him on the plain of Megiddo.
23 Archers shot King Josiah, and he told
his officers, "Take me away; I am badly wounded." 24 So they took him out of
his chariot, put him in his other chariot
and brought him to Jerusalem, where he
died. He was buried in the tombs of his
ancestors, and all Judah and Jerusalem
mourned for him.
25 Jeremiah composed laments for Josiah, and to this day all the male and female singers commemorate Josiah in the
laments. These became a tradition in Israel and are written in the Laments.
26 The other events of Josiah's reign and
his acts of devotion in accordance with
what is written in the Law of the LORD—
27 all the events, from beginning to end,
are written in the book of the kings of
36 Israel and Judah. 1 And the people of
the land took Jehoahaz son of Josiah
and made him king in Jerusalem in place
of his father.

2 Jehoahaz[a] was twenty-three years old
when he became king, and he reigned in
Jerusalem three months. 3 The king of
Egypt dethroned him in Jerusalem and
imposed on Judah a levy of a hundred talents[b] of silver and a talent[c] of gold. 4 The
king of Egypt made Eliakim, a brother of
Jehoahaz, king over Judah and Jerusalem
and changed Eliakim's name to Jehoiakim. But Necho took Eliakim's brother
Jehoahaz and carried him off to Egypt.

5 Jehoiakim was twenty-five years old
when he became king, and he reigned in
Jerusalem eleven years. He did evil in the
eyes of the LORD his God. 6 Nebuchadnezzar king of Babylon attacked him and
bound him with bronze shackles to take
him to Babylon. 7 Nebuchadnezzar also
took to Babylon articles from the temple
of the LORD and put them in his temple[d]
there.
8 The other events of Jehoiakim's reign,
the detestable things he did and all that
was found against him, are written in
the book of the kings of Israel and Judah.
And Jehoiachin his son succeeded him
as king.
9 Jehoiachin was eighteen[e] years old
when he became king, and he reigned in
Jerusalem three months and ten days. He
did evil in the eyes of the LORD. 10 In the
spring, King Nebuchadnezzar sent for
him and brought him to Babylon, together with articles of value from the temple
of the LORD, and he made Jehoiachin's
uncle,[f] Zedekiah, king over Judah and
Jerusalem.

11 Zedekiah was twenty-one years old
when he became king, and he reigned
in Jerusalem eleven years. 12 He did evil
in the eyes of the LORD his God and did
not humble himself before Jeremiah
the prophet, who spoke the word of the
LORD. 13 He also rebelled against King
Nebuchadnezzar, who had made him
take an oath in God's name. He became
stiff-necked and hardened his heart and
would not turn to the LORD, the God of Israel. 14 Furthermore, all the leaders of the
priests and the people became more and
more unfaithful, following all the detestable practices of the nations and defiling
the temple of the LORD, which he had
consecrated in Jerusalem.
15 The LORD, the God of their ancestors, sent word to them through his messengers again and again, because he had
pity on his people and on his dwelling
place. 16 But they mocked God's messengers, despised his words and scoffed at
his prophets until the wrath of the LORD
was aroused against his people and there
was no remedy. 17 He brought up against
them the king of the Babylonians,[g] who
killed their young men with the sword in
the sanctuary, and did not spare young
men or young women, the elderly or the
infirm. God gave them all into the hands
of Nebuchadnezzar. 18 He carried to Babylon all the articles from the temple of
God, both large and small, and the treasures of the LORD's temple and the trea-

[a] 2 Hebrew *Joahaz,* a variant of *Jehoahaz;* also in verse 4 [b] 3 That is, about 3 3/4 tons or about 3.4 metric tons [c] 3 That is, about 75 pounds or about 34 kilograms [d] 7 Or *palace* [e] 9 One Hebrew manuscript, some Septuagint manuscripts and Syriac (see also 2 Kings 24:8); most Hebrew manuscripts *eight* [f] 10 Hebrew *brother,* that is, relative (see 2 Kings 24:17) [g] 17 Or *Chaldeans*

sures of the king and his officials. 19They
set fire to God's temple and broke down
the wall of Jerusalem; they burned all the
palaces and destroyed everything of value there.
20He carried into exile to Babylon the
remnant, who escaped from the sword,
and they became servants to him and
his successors until the kingdom of Persia came to power. 21The land enjoyed
its sabbath rests; all the time of its desolation it rested, until the seventy years
were completed in fulfillment of the word
of the LORD spoken by Jeremiah.
22In the first year of Cyrus king of Persia, in order to fulfill the word of the LORD
spoken by Jeremiah, the LORD moved the
heart of Cyrus king of Persia to make a
proclamation throughout his realm and
also to put it in writing:
23"This is what Cyrus king of Persia
says:

"'The LORD, the God of heaven,
has given me all the kingdoms of the
earth and he has appointed me to
build a temple for him at Jerusalem
in Judah. Any of his people among
you may go up, and may the LORD
their God be with them.'"

EZRA

See the Invitation to Chronicles-Ezra-Nehemiah on p. 354.

1 In the first year of Cyrus king of Persia,
in order to fulfill the word of the LORD
spoken by Jeremiah, the LORD moved the
heart of Cyrus king of Persia to make a
proclamation throughout his realm and
also to put it in writing:
2"This is what Cyrus king of Persia
says:

"'The LORD, the God of heaven,
has given me all the kingdoms of
the earth and he has appointed me
to build a temple for him at Jerusalem in Judah. 3Any of his people
among you may go up to Jerusalem
in Judah and build the temple of the
LORD, the God of Israel, the God who
is in Jerusalem, and may their God
be with them. 4And in any locality
where survivors may now be living,
the people are to provide them with
silver and gold, with goods and livestock, and with freewill offerings for
the temple of God in Jerusalem.'"

5Then the family heads of Judah and
Benjamin, and the priests and Levites—
everyone whose heart God had moved—
prepared to go up and build the house of
the LORD in Jerusalem. 6All their neighbors assisted them with articles of silver
and gold, with goods and livestock, and
with valuable gifts, in addition to all the
freewill offerings.
7Moreover, King Cyrus brought out the
articles belonging to the temple of the
LORD, which Nebuchadnezzar had carried away from Jerusalem and had placed
in the temple of his god.[a] 8Cyrus king of
Persia had them brought by Mithredath
the treasurer, who counted them out to
Sheshbazzar the prince of Judah.
9This was the inventory:

gold dishes	30
silver dishes	1,000
silver pans[b]	29
10 gold bowls	30
matching silver bowls	410
other articles	1,000

11In all, there were 5,400 articles of
gold and of silver. Sheshbazzar brought
all these along with the exiles when they
came up from Babylon to Jerusalem.

2 Now these are the people of the province who came up from the captivity
of the exiles, whom Nebuchadnezzar

a 7 Or *gods* b 9 The meaning of the Hebrew for this word is uncertain.

king of Babylon had taken captive to
Babylon (they returned to Jerusalem and
Judah, each to their own town, 2 in com-
pany with Zerubbabel, Joshua, Nehemi-
ah, Seraiah, Reelaiah, Mordecai, Bilshan,
Mispar, Bigvai, Rehum and Baanah):

The list of the men of the people of Israel:

3 the descendants of Parosh 2,172
4 of Shephatiah 372
5 of Arah 775
6 of Pahath-Moab (through the line of Jeshua and Joab) 2,812
7 of Elam 1,254
8 of Zattu 945
9 of Zakkai 760
10 of Bani 642
11 of Bebai 623
12 of Azgad 1,222
13 of Adonikam 666
14 of Bigvai 2,056
15 of Adin 454
16 of Ater (through Hezekiah) 98
17 of Bezai 323
18 of Jorah 112
19 of Hashum 223
20 of Gibbar 95

21 the men of Bethlehem 123
22 of Netophah 56
23 of Anathoth 128
24 of Azmaveth 42
25 of Kiriath Jearim,[a] Kephirah and Beeroth 743
26 of Ramah and Geba 621
27 of Mikmash 122
28 of Bethel and Ai 223
29 of Nebo 52
30 of Magbish 156
31 of the other Elam 1,254
32 of Harim 320
33 of Lod, Hadid and Ono 725
34 of Jericho 345
35 of Senaah 3,630

36 The priests:

the descendants of Jedaiah (through the family of Jeshua) 973
37 of Immer 1,052
38 of Pashhur 1,247
39 of Harim 1,017

40 The Levites:

the descendants of Jeshua and Kadmiel (of the line of Hodaviah) 74

41 The musicians:

the descendants of Asaph 128

42 The gatekeepers of the temple:

the descendants of Shallum, Ater, Talmon, Akkub, Hatita and Shobai 139

43 The temple servants:

the descendants of
Ziha, Hasupha, Tabbaoth,
44 Keros, Siaha, Padon,
45 Lebanah, Hagabah, Akkub,
46 Hagab, Shalmai, Hanan,
47 Giddel, Gahar, Reaiah,
48 Rezin, Nekoda, Gazzam,
49 Uzza, Paseah, Besai,
50 Asnah, Meunim, Nephusim,
51 Bakbuk, Hakupha, Harhur,
52 Bazluth, Mehida, Harsha,
53 Barkos, Sisera, Temah,
54 Neziah and Hatipha

55 The descendants of the servants of Solomon:

the descendants of
Sotai, Hassophereth, Peruda,
56 Jaala, Darkon, Giddel,
57 Shephatiah, Hattil,
Pokereth-Hazzebaim and Ami

58 The temple servants and the descendants of the servants of Solomon 392

59 The following came up from
the towns of Tel Melah, Tel Harsha,
Kerub, Addon and Immer, but they
could not show that their families
were descended from Israel:

60 The descendants of Delaiah, Tobiah and Nekoda 652

61 And from among the priests:

The descendants of
Hobaiah, Hakkoz and Barzillai (a man who had married a daughter of Barzillai the Gileadite and was called by that name).

62 These searched for their fami-

[a] *25* See Septuagint (see also Neh. 7:29); Hebrew *Kiriath Arim.*

ly records, but they could not find
them and so were excluded from the
priesthood as unclean. 63The governor ordered them not to eat any of
the most sacred food until there was
a priest ministering with the Urim
and Thummim.

64The whole company numbered
42,360, 65besides their 7,337 male
and female slaves; and they also had
200 male and female singers. 66They
had 736 horses, 245 mules, 67435
camels and 6,720 donkeys.

68When they arrived at the house of the
LORD in Jerusalem, some of the heads of
the families gave freewill offerings toward the rebuilding of the house of God
on its site. 69According to their ability
they gave to the treasury for this work
61,000 darics[a] of gold, 5,000 minas[b] of
silver and 100 priestly garments.

70The priests, the Levites, the musicians, the gatekeepers and the temple
servants settled in their own towns,
along with some of the other people, and
the rest of the Israelites settled in their
towns.

3 When the seventh month came and
the Israelites had settled in their
towns, the people assembled together
as one in Jerusalem. 2Then Joshua son
of Jozadak and his fellow priests and Zerubbabel son of Shealtiel and his associates began to build the altar of the God
of Israel to sacrifice burnt offerings on it,
in accordance with what is written in the
Law of Moses the man of God. 3Despite
their fear of the peoples around them,
they built the altar on its foundation and
sacrificed burnt offerings on it to the
LORD, both the morning and evening sacrifices. 4Then in accordance with what is
written, they celebrated the Festival of
Tabernacles with the required number of
burnt offerings prescribed for each day.
5After that, they presented the regular
burnt offerings, the New Moon sacrifices and the sacrifices for all the appointed sacred festivals of the LORD, as well
as those brought as freewill offerings to
the LORD. 6On the first day of the seventh
month they began to offer burnt offerings
to the LORD, though the foundation of the
LORD's temple had not yet been laid.

7Then they gave money to the masons
and carpenters, and gave food and drink
and olive oil to the people of Sidon and
Tyre, so that they would bring cedar logs
by sea from Lebanon to Joppa, as authorized by Cyrus king of Persia.

8In the second month of the second
year after their arrival at the house of
God in Jerusalem, Zerubbabel son of
Shealtiel, Joshua son of Jozadak and the
rest of the people (the priests and the Levites and all who had returned from the
captivity to Jerusalem) began the work.
They appointed Levites twenty years old
and older to supervise the building of
the house of the LORD. 9Joshua and his
sons and brothers and Kadmiel and his
sons (descendants of Hodaviah[c]) and
the sons of Henadad and their sons and
brothers—all Levites—joined together in supervising those working on the
house of God.

10When the builders laid the foundation of the temple of the LORD, the priests
in their vestments and with trumpets,
and the Levites (the sons of Asaph) with
cymbals, took their places to praise the
LORD, as prescribed by David king of Israel. 11With praise and thanksgiving they
sang to the LORD:

"He is good;
his love toward Israel endures
forever."

And all the people gave a great shout of
praise to the LORD, because the foundation of the house of the LORD was laid.
12But many of the older priests and Levites and family heads, who had seen the
former temple, wept aloud when they saw
the foundation of this temple being laid,
while many others shouted for joy. 13No
one could distinguish the sound of the
shouts of joy from the sound of weeping,
because the people made so much noise.
And the sound was heard far away.

4 When the enemies of Judah and Benjamin heard that the exiles were
building a temple for the LORD, the God
of Israel, 2they came to Zerubbabel and
to the heads of the families and said, "Let
us help you build because, like you, we
seek your God and have been sacrificing
to him since the time of Esarhaddon king
of Assyria, who brought us here."

[a] 69 That is, about 1,100 pounds or about 500 kilograms
[b] 69 That is, about 3 tons or about 2.8 metric tons
[c] 9 Hebrew *Yehudah,* a variant of *Hodaviah*

3 But Zerubbabel, Joshua and the rest
of the heads of the families of Israel answered,
"You have no part with us in
building a temple to our God. We alone
will build it for the LORD, the God of Israel,
as King Cyrus, the king of Persia, commanded us."

4 Then the peoples around them set out
to discourage the people of Judah and
make them afraid to go on building.[a]
5 They bribed officials to work against
them and frustrate their plans during
the entire reign of Cyrus king of Persia
and down to the reign of Darius king of
Persia.

6 At the beginning of the reign of Xerxes,[b]
they lodged an accusation against
the people of Judah and Jerusalem.

7 And in the days of Artaxerxes king of
Persia, Bishlam, Mithredath, Tabeel and
the rest of his associates wrote a letter
to Artaxerxes. The letter was written in
Aramaic script and in the Aramaic language.[c,d]

8 Rehum the commanding officer and
Shimshai the secretary wrote a letter
against Jerusalem to Artaxerxes the king
as follows:

9 Rehum the commanding officer
and Shimshai the secretary, together
with the rest of their associates — the
judges, officials and administrators
over the people from Persia, Uruk
and Babylon, the Elamites of Susa,
10 and the other people whom the
great and honorable Ashurbanipal
deported and settled in the city of
Samaria and elsewhere in Trans-Euphrates.

11 (This is a copy of the letter they sent
him.)

To King Artaxerxes,
From your servants in Trans-Euphrates:

12 The king should know that the
people who came up to us from you
have gone to Jerusalem and are rebuilding
that rebellious and wicked
city. They are restoring the walls and
repairing the foundations.
13 Furthermore, the king should
know that if this city is built and
its walls are restored, no more taxes,
tribute or duty will be paid, and
eventually the royal revenues will
suffer.[e] 14 Now since we are under
obligation to the palace and it is not
proper for us to see the king dishonored,
we are sending this message to
inform the king, 15 so that a search
may be made in the archives of your
predecessors. In these records you
will find that this city is a rebellious
city, troublesome to kings and provinces,
a place with a long history of
sedition. That is why this city was
destroyed. 16 We inform the king that
if this city is built and its walls are restored,
you will be left with nothing
in Trans-Euphrates.

17 The king sent this reply:

To Rehum the commanding officer,
Shimshai the secretary and the rest
of their associates living in Samaria
and elsewhere in Trans-Euphrates:

Greetings.

18 The letter you sent us has been
read and translated in my presence.
19 I issued an order and a search was
made, and it was found that this city
has a long history of revolt against
kings and has been a place of rebellion
and sedition. 20 Jerusalem has
had powerful kings ruling over the
whole of Trans-Euphrates, and taxes,
tribute and duty were paid to them.
21 Now issue an order to these men to
stop work, so that this city will not be
rebuilt until I so order. 22 Be careful
not to neglect this matter. Why let
this threat grow, to the detriment of
the royal interests?

23 As soon as the copy of the letter of
King Artaxerxes was read to Rehum and
Shimshai the secretary and their associates,
they went immediately to the Jews
in Jerusalem and compelled them by
force to stop.

24 Thus the work on the house of God in
Jerusalem came to a standstill until the
second year of the reign of Darius king
of Persia.

[a] 4 Or *and troubled them as they built* [b] 6 Hebrew *Ahasuerus* [c] 7 Or *written in Aramaic and translated*
[d] 7 The text of 4:8 - 6:18 is in Aramaic. [e] 13 The meaning of the Aramaic for this clause is uncertain.

5 Now Haggai the prophet and Zechariah the prophet, a descendant of Iddo,
prophesied to the Jews in Judah and Jerusalem in the name of the God of Israel,
who was over them. 2 Then Zerubbabel
son of Shealtiel and Joshua son of Jozadak
set to work to rebuild the house of God in
Jerusalem. And the prophets of God were
with them, supporting them.
3 At that time Tattenai, governor of
Trans-Euphrates, and Shethar-Bozenai
and their associates went to them and
asked, "Who authorized you to rebuild
this temple and to finish it?" 4 They[a] also
asked, "What are the names of those who
are constructing this building?" 5 But
the eye of their God was watching over
the elders of the Jews, and they were not
stopped until a report could go to Darius
and his written reply be received.
6 This is a copy of the letter that Tattenai, governor of Trans-Euphrates, and
Shethar-Bozenai and their associates,
the officials of Trans-Euphrates, sent to
King Darius. 7 The report they sent him
read as follows:

To King Darius:

Cordial greetings.

8 The king should know that we
went to the district of Judah, to the
temple of the great God. The people
are building it with large stones and
placing the timbers in the walls. The
work is being carried on with diligence and is making rapid progress
under their direction.
9 We questioned the elders and
asked them, "Who authorized you
to rebuild this temple and to finish it?" 10 We also asked them their
names, so that we could write down
the names of their leaders for your
information.
11 This is the answer they gave us:
"We are the servants of the God
of heaven and earth, and we are rebuilding the temple that was built
many years ago, one that a great king
of Israel built and finished. 12 But
because our ancestors angered the
God of heaven, he gave them into
the hands of Nebuchadnezzar the
Chaldean, king of Babylon, who destroyed this temple and deported the
people to Babylon.
13 "However, in the first year of Cyrus king of Babylon, King Cyrus issued a decree to rebuild this house
of God. 14 He even removed from
the temple[b] of Babylon the gold and
silver articles of the house of God,
which Nebuchadnezzar had taken
from the temple in Jerusalem and
brought to the temple[b] in Babylon.
Then King Cyrus gave them to a man
named Sheshbazzar, whom he had
appointed governor, 15 and he told
him, 'Take these articles and go and
deposit them in the temple in Jerusalem. And rebuild the house of God
on its site.'
16 "So this Sheshbazzar came and
laid the foundations of the house of
God in Jerusalem. From that day to
the present it has been under construction but is not yet finished."

17 Now if it pleases the king, let a
search be made in the royal archives
of Babylon to see if King Cyrus did
in fact issue a decree to rebuild this
house of God in Jerusalem. Then let
the king send us his decision in this
matter.

6 King Darius then issued an order, and
they searched in the archives stored
in the treasury at Babylon. 2 A scroll was
found in the citadel of Ecbatana in the
province of Media, and this was written
on it:

Memorandum:

3 In the first year of King Cyrus, the
king issued a decree concerning the
temple of God in Jerusalem:

Let the temple be rebuilt as a place
to present sacrifices, and let its foundations be laid. It is to be sixty cubits[c]
high and sixty cubits wide, 4 with
three courses of large stones and
one of timbers. The costs are to be
paid by the royal treasury. 5 Also, the
gold and silver articles of the house
of God, which Nebuchadnezzar took
from the temple in Jerusalem and
brought to Babylon, are to be returned to their places in the temple

[a] 4 See Septuagint; Aramaic *We.* [b] 14 Or *palace* [c] 3 That is, about 90 feet or about 27 meters

in Jerusalem; they are to be deposited in the house of God.

6 Now then, Tattenai, governor of
Trans-Euphrates, and Shethar-Bozenai and you other officials of that
province, stay away from there. 7 Do
not interfere with the work on this
temple of God. Let the governor of
the Jews and the Jewish elders rebuild this house of God on its site.

8 Moreover, I hereby decree what
you are to do for these elders of the
Jews in the construction of this
house of God:

Their expenses are to be fully paid
out of the royal treasury, from the
revenues of Trans-Euphrates, so that
the work will not stop. 9 Whatever is
needed—young bulls, rams, male
lambs for burnt offerings to the God
of heaven, and wheat, salt, wine and
olive oil, as requested by the priests
in Jerusalem—must be given them
daily without fail, 10 so that they may
offer sacrifices pleasing to the God of
heaven and pray for the well-being of
the king and his sons.

11 Furthermore, I decree that if
anyone defies this edict, a beam is
to be pulled from their house and
they are to be impaled on it. And for
this crime their house is to be made
a pile of rubble. 12 May God, who has
caused his Name to dwell there, overthrow any king or people who lifts a
hand to change this decree or to destroy this temple in Jerusalem.

I Darius have decreed it. Let it be
carried out with diligence.

13 Then, because of the decree King
Darius had sent, Tattenai, governor of
Trans-Euphrates, and Shethar-Bozenai
and their associates carried it out with
diligence. 14 So the elders of the Jews
continued to build and prosper under
the preaching of Haggai the prophet and
Zechariah, a descendant of Iddo. They
finished building the temple according
to the command of the God of Israel and
the decrees of Cyrus, Darius and Artaxerxes, kings of Persia. 15 The temple was
completed on the third day of the month
Adar, in the sixth year of the reign of King
Darius.

16 Then the people of Israel—the
priests, the Levites and the rest of the
exiles—celebrated the dedication of the
house of God with joy. 17 For the dedication of this house of God they offered a
hundred bulls, two hundred rams, four
hundred male lambs and, as a sin offering[a] for all Israel, twelve male goats, one
for each of the tribes of Israel. 18 And they
installed the priests in their divisions and
the Levites in their groups for the service
of God at Jerusalem, according to what is
written in the Book of Moses.

19 On the fourteenth day of the first
month, the exiles celebrated the Passover. 20 The priests and Levites had purified themselves and were all ceremonially clean. The Levites slaughtered the
Passover lamb for all the exiles, for their
relatives the priests and for themselves.
21 So the Israelites who had returned from
the exile ate it, together with all who had
separated themselves from the unclean
practices of their Gentile neighbors in
order to seek the LORD, the God of Israel. 22 For seven days they celebrated with
joy the Festival of Unleavened Bread, because the LORD had filled them with joy
by changing the attitude of the king of Assyria so that he assisted them in the work
on the house of God, the God of Israel.

7 After these things, during the reign
of Artaxerxes king of Persia, Ezra son
of Seraiah, the son of Azariah, the son of
Hilkiah, 2 the son of Shallum, the son of
Zadok, the son of Ahitub, 3 the son of Amariah, the son of Azariah, the son of Meraioth, 4 the son of Zerahiah, the son of Uzzi,
the son of Bukki, 5 the son of Abishua, the
son of Phinehas, the son of Eleazar, the
son of Aaron the chief priest— 6 this Ezra
came up from Babylon. He was a teacher well versed in the Law of Moses, which
the LORD, the God of Israel, had given.
The king had granted him everything he
asked, for the hand of the LORD his God
was on him. 7 Some of the Israelites, including priests, Levites, musicians, gatekeepers and temple servants, also came
up to Jerusalem in the seventh year of
King Artaxerxes.

8 Ezra arrived in Jerusalem in the fifth
month of the seventh year of the king.
9 He had begun his journey from Babylon

[a] 17 Or *purification offering*

on the first day of the first month, and he
arrived in Jerusalem on the first day of the
fifth month, for the gracious hand of his
God was on him. 10For Ezra had devoted
himself to the study and observance of
the Law of the LORD, and to teaching its
decrees and laws in Israel.
11This is a copy of the letter King Artaxerxes had given to Ezra the priest,
a teacher of the Law, a man learned in
matters concerning the commands and
decrees of the LORD for Israel:

12Artaxerxes, king of kings,

To Ezra the priest, teacher of the Law of the God of heaven:

Greetings.

13Now I decree that any of the Israelites in my kingdom, including
priests and Levites, who volunteer
to go to Jerusalem with you, may
go. 14You are sent by the king and
his seven advisers to inquire about
Judah and Jerusalem with regard
to the Law of your God, which is in
your hand. 15Moreover, you are to
take with you the silver and gold that
the king and his advisers have freely given to the God of Israel, whose
dwelling is in Jerusalem, 16together
with all the silver and gold you may
obtain from the province of Babylon,
as well as the freewill offerings of the
people and priests for the temple of
their God in Jerusalem. 17With this
money be sure to buy bulls, rams
and male lambs, together with their
grain offerings and drink offerings,
and sacrifice them on the altar of the
temple of your God in Jerusalem.
18You and your fellow Israelites
may then do whatever seems best
with the rest of the silver and gold, in
accordance with the will of your God.
19Deliver to the God of Jerusalem all
the articles entrusted to you for worship in the temple of your God. 20And
anything else needed for the temple
of your God that you are responsible
to supply, you may provide from the
royal treasury.
21Now I, King Artaxerxes, decree
that all the treasurers of Trans-Euphrates are to provide with diligence
whatever Ezra the priest, the teacher of the Law of the God of heaven,
may ask of you — 22up to a hundred
talents[a] of silver, a hundred cors[b] of
wheat, a hundred baths[c] of wine, a
hundred baths[c] of olive oil, and salt
without limit. 23Whatever the God of
heaven has prescribed, let it be done
with diligence for the temple of the
God of heaven. Why should his wrath
fall on the realm of the king and of his
sons? 24You are also to know that you
have no authority to impose taxes,
tribute or duty on any of the priests,
Levites, musicians, gatekeepers,
temple servants or other workers at
this house of God.
25And you, Ezra, in accordance
with the wisdom of your God, which
you possess, appoint magistrates
and judges to administer justice to
all the people of Trans-Euphrates —
all who know the laws of your God.
And you are to teach any who do not
know them. 26Whoever does not
obey the law of your God and the law
of the king must surely be punished
by death, banishment, confiscation
of property, or imprisonment.[d]

27Praise be to the LORD, the God of our
ancestors, who has put it into the king's
heart to bring honor to the house of the
LORD in Jerusalem in this way 28and
who has extended his good favor to me
before the king and his advisers and all
the king's powerful officials. Because the
hand of the LORD my God was on me, I
took courage and gathered leaders from
Israel to go up with me.

8 These are the family heads and those
registered with them who came up
with me from Babylon during the reign
of King Artaxerxes:

2 of the descendants of Phinehas, Gershom;
of the descendants of Ithamar, Daniel;
of the descendants of David, Hattush
3 of the descendants of Shekaniah;
of the descendants of Parosh, Zechariah, and with him were registered 150 men;
4 of the descendants of Pahath-Moab,

[a] 22 That is, about 3 3/4 tons or about 3.4 metric tons [b] 22 That is, probably about 18 tons or about 16 metric tons [c] 22 That is, about 600 gallons or about 2 200 liters [d] 26 The text of 7:12-26 is in Aramaic.

Eliehoenai son of Zerahiah, and
with him 200 men;
5 of the descendants of Zattu,[a] Shekaniah son of Jahaziel, and with him 300 men;
6 of the descendants of Adin, Ebed son of Jonathan, and with him 50 men;
7 of the descendants of Elam, Jeshaiah son of Athaliah, and with him 70 men;
8 of the descendants of Shephatiah, Zebadiah son of Michael, and with him 80 men;
9 of the descendants of Joab, Obadiah son of Jehiel, and with him 218 men;
10 of the descendants of Bani,[b] Shelomith son of Josiphiah, and with him 160 men;
11 of the descendants of Bebai, Zechariah son of Bebai, and with him 28 men;
12 of the descendants of Azgad, Johanan son of Hakkatan, and with him 110 men;
13 of the descendants of Adonikam, the last ones, whose names were Eliphelet, Jeuel and Shemaiah, and with them 60 men;
14 of the descendants of Bigvai, Uthai and Zakkur, and with them 70 men.

15 I assembled them at the canal that
flows toward Ahava, and we camped
there three days. When I checked among
the people and the priests, I found no Levites there. 16 So I summoned Eliezer, Ariel, Shemaiah, Elnathan, Jarib, Elnathan,
Nathan, Zechariah and Meshullam,
who were leaders, and Joiarib and Elnathan, who were men of learning, 17 and
I ordered them to go to Iddo, the leader
in Kasiphia. I told them what to say to
Iddo and his fellow Levites, the temple
servants in Kasiphia, so that they might
bring attendants to us for the house of our
God. 18 Because the gracious hand of our
God was on us, they brought us Sherebiah, a capable man, from the descendants
of Mahli son of Levi, the son of Israel, and
Sherebiah's sons and brothers, 18 in all;
19 and Hashabiah, together with Jeshaiah
from the descendants of Merari, and his
brothers and nephews, 20 in all. 20 They
also brought 220 of the temple servants —
a body that David and the officials had
established to assist the Levites. All were
registered by name.

21 There, by the Ahava Canal, I proclaimed a fast, so that we might humble
ourselves before our God and ask him for
a safe journey for us and our children,
with all our possessions. 22 I was ashamed
to ask the king for soldiers and horsemen
to protect us from enemies on the road,
because we had told the king, "The gracious hand of our God is on everyone who
looks to him, but his great anger is against
all who forsake him." 23 So we fasted and
petitioned our God about this, and he answered our prayer.

24 Then I set apart twelve of the leading
priests, namely, Sherebiah, Hashabiah
and ten of their brothers, 25 and I weighed
out to them the offering of silver and gold
and the articles that the king, his advisers,
his officials and all Israel present there
had donated for the house of our God. 26 I
weighed out to them 650 talents[c] of silver,
silver articles weighing 100 talents,[d] 100
talents[d] of gold, 27 20 bowls of gold valued
at 1,000 darics,[e] and two fine articles of
polished bronze, as precious as gold.

28 I said to them, "You as well as these
articles are consecrated to the LORD. The
silver and gold are a freewill offering
to the LORD, the God of your ancestors.
29 Guard them carefully until you weigh
them out in the chambers of the house of
the LORD in Jerusalem before the leading
priests and the Levites and the family
heads of Israel." 30 Then the priests and
Levites received the silver and gold and
sacred articles that had been weighed
out to be taken to the house of our God
in Jerusalem.

31 On the twelfth day of the first month
we set out from the Ahava Canal to go to
Jerusalem. The hand of our God was on
us, and he protected us from enemies and
bandits along the way. 32 So we arrived in
Jerusalem, where we rested three days.

33 On the fourth day, in the house of our
God, we weighed out the silver and gold
and the sacred articles into the hands of,

[a] 5 Some Septuagint manuscripts (also 1 Esdras 8:32); Hebrew does not have *Zattu.* [b] 10 Some Septuagint manuscripts (also 1 Esdras 8:36); Hebrew does not have *Bani.* [c] 26 That is, about 24 tons or about 22 metric tons [d] 26 That is, about 3 3/4 tons or about 3.4 metric tons [e] 27 That is, about 19 pounds or about 8.4 kilograms

Meremoth son of Uriah, the priest. Eleazar son of Phinehas was with him, and
so were the Levites Jozabad son of Jeshua and Noadiah son of Binnui. 34 Everything was accounted for by number and
weight, and the entire weight was recorded at that time.
35 Then the exiles who had returned
from captivity sacrificed burnt offerings
to the God of Israel: twelve bulls for all Israel, ninety-six rams, seventy-seven male
lambs and, as a sin offering,[a] twelve male
goats. All this was a burnt offering to the
LORD. 36 They also delivered the king's orders to the royal satraps and to the governors of Trans-Euphrates, who then gave
assistance to the people and to the house
of God.

9 After these things had been done, the
leaders came to me and said, "The people of Israel, including the priests and the
Levites, have not kept themselves separate from the neighboring peoples with
their detestable practices, like those of
the Canaanites, Hittites, Perizzites, Jebusites, Ammonites, Moabites, Egyptians
and Amorites. 2 They have taken some of
their daughters as wives for themselves
and their sons, and have mingled the
holy race with the peoples around them.
And the leaders and officials have led the
way in this unfaithfulness."
3 When I heard this, I tore my tunic
and cloak, pulled hair from my head and
beard and sat down appalled. 4 Then everyone who trembled at the words of the
God of Israel gathered around me because of this unfaithfulness of the exiles.
And I sat there appalled until the evening
sacrifice.
5 Then, at the evening sacrifice, I rose
from my self-abasement, with my tunic
and cloak torn, and fell on my knees with
my hands spread out to the LORD my God
6 and prayed:

"I am too ashamed and disgraced,
my God, to lift up my face to you, because our sins are higher than our
heads and our guilt has reached to
the heavens. 7 From the days of our
ancestors until now, our guilt has
been great. Because of our sins, we
and our kings and our priests have
been subjected to the sword and
captivity, to pillage and humiliation
at the hand of foreign kings, as it is
today.
8 "But now, for a brief moment, the
LORD our God has been gracious in
leaving us a remnant and giving us a
firm place[b] in his sanctuary, and so
our God gives light to our eyes and a
little relief in our bondage. 9 Though
we are slaves, our God has not forsak-
en us in our bondage. He has shown
us kindness in the sight of the kings
of Persia: He has granted us new life
to rebuild the house of our God and
repair its ruins, and he has given us
a wall of protection in Judah and Jerusalem.
10 "But now, our God, what can we
say after this? For we have forsaken
the commands 11 you gave through
your servants the prophets when you
said: 'The land you are entering to
possess is a land polluted by the corruption of its peoples. By their detestable practices they have filled it with
their impurity from one end to the
other. 12 Therefore, do not give your
daughters in marriage to their sons
or take their daughters for your sons.
Do not seek a treaty of friendship
with them at any time, that you may
be strong and eat the good things of
the land and leave it to your children
as an everlasting inheritance.'
13 "What has happened to us is a
result of our evil deeds and our great
guilt, and yet, our God, you have
punished us less than our sins deserved and have given us a remnant
like this. 14 Shall we then break your
commands again and intermarry
with the peoples who commit such
detestable practices? Would you not
be angry enough with us to destroy
us, leaving us no remnant or survivor? 15 LORD, the God of Israel, you
are righteous! We are left this day as
a remnant. Here we are before you
in our guilt, though because of it
not one of us can stand in your presence."

10 While Ezra was praying and confessing, weeping and throwing himself down before the house of God, a large
crowd of Israelites — men, women and
children — gathered around him. They

[a] 35 Or *purification offering* [b] 8 Or *a foothold*

too wept bitterly. 2 Then Shekaniah son
of Jehiel, one of the descendants of Elam,
said to Ezra, "We have been unfaithful
to our God by marrying foreign women
from the peoples around us. But in spite
of this, there is still hope for Israel. 3 Now
let us make a covenant before our God
to send away all these women and their
children, in accordance with the counsel
of my lord and of those who fear the commands of our God. Let it be done according to the Law. 4 Rise up; this matter is in
your hands. We will support you, so take
courage and do it."

5 So Ezra rose up and put the leading
priests and Levites and all Israel under
oath to do what had been suggested. And
they took the oath. 6 Then Ezra withdrew
from before the house of God and went to
the room of Jehohanan son of Eliashib.
While he was there, he ate no food and
drank no water, because he continued
to mourn over the unfaithfulness of the
exiles.

7 A proclamation was then issued
throughout Judah and Jerusalem for
all the exiles to assemble in Jerusalem.
8 Anyone who failed to appear within
three days would forfeit all his property,
in accordance with the decision of the officials and elders, and would himself be
expelled from the assembly of the exiles.

9 Within the three days, all the men
of Judah and Benjamin had gathered
in Jerusalem. And on the twentieth day
of the ninth month, all the people were
sitting in the square before the house of
God, greatly distressed by the occasion
and because of the rain. 10 Then Ezra the
priest stood up and said to them, "You
have been unfaithful; you have married
foreign women, adding to Israel's guilt.
11 Now honor[a] the LORD, the God of your
ancestors, and do his will. Separate yourselves from the peoples around you and
from your foreign wives."

12 The whole assembly responded with
a loud voice: "You are right! We must do
as you say. 13 But there are many people
here and it is the rainy season; so we cannot stand outside. Besides, this matter
cannot be taken care of in a day or two,
because we have sinned greatly in this
thing. 14 Let our officials act for the whole
assembly. Then let everyone in our towns
who has married a foreign woman come
at a set time, along with the elders and
judges of each town, until the fierce anger of our God in this matter is turned
away from us." 15 Only Jonathan son of
Asahel and Jahzeiah son of Tikvah, supported by Meshullam and Shabbethai
the Levite, opposed this.

16 So the exiles did as was proposed.
Ezra the priest selected men who were
family heads, one from each family division, and all of them designated by name.
On the first day of the tenth month they
sat down to investigate the cases, 17 and
by the first day of the first month they finished dealing with all the men who had
married foreign women.

18 Among the descendants of the
priests, the following had married
foreign women:

From the descendants of Joshua son
of Jozadak, and his brothers: Maaseiah, Eliezer, Jarib and Gedaliah. 19 (They all gave their hands in
pledge to put away their wives, and
for their guilt they each presented
a ram from the flock as a guilt offering.)

20 From the descendants of Immer:
Hanani and Zebadiah.

21 From the descendants of Harim:
Maaseiah, Elijah, Shemaiah, Jehiel
and Uzziah.

22 From the descendants of Pashhur:
Elioenai, Maaseiah, Ishmael, Nethanel, Jozabad and Elasah.

23 Among the Levites:

Jozabad, Shimei, Kelaiah (that is,
Kelita), Pethahiah, Judah and Eliezer.

24 From the musicians:
Eliashib.

From the gatekeepers:
Shallum, Telem and Uri.

25 And among the other Israelites:

From the descendants of Parosh:
Ramiah, Izziah, Malkijah, Mijamin, Eleazar, Malkijah and Benaiah.

26 From the descendants of Elam:
Mattaniah, Zechariah, Jehiel,
Abdi, Jeremoth and Elijah.

[a] *11* Or *Now make confession to*

27 From the descendants of Zattu:
Elioenai, Eliashib, Mattaniah, Jeremoth, Zabad and Aziza.
28 From the descendants of Bebai:
Jehohanan, Hananiah, Zabbai and
Athlai.
29 From the descendants of Bani:
Meshullam, Malluk, Adaiah, Jashub, Sheal and Jeremoth.
30 From the descendants of Pahath-
Moab:
Adna, Kelal, Benaiah, Maaseiah,
Mattaniah, Bezalel, Binnui and
Manasseh.
31 From the descendants of Harim:
Eliezer, Ishijah, Malkijah, Shemaiah, Shimeon, 32 Benjamin, Malluk
and Shemariah.
33 From the descendants of Hashum:
Mattenai, Mattattah, Zabad, Eliphelet, Jeremai, Manasseh and Shimei.
34 From the descendants of Bani:
Maadai, Amram, Uel, 35 Benaiah,
Bedeiah, Keluhi, 36 Vaniah, Meremoth, Eliashib, 37 Mattaniah, Mattenai and Jaasu.
38 From the descendants of Binnui:[a]
Shimei, 39 Shelemiah, Nathan,
Adaiah, 40 Maknadebai, Sha-
shai, Sharai, 41 Azarel, Shelemiah,
Shemariah, 42 Shallum, Amariah
and Joseph.
43 From the descendants of Nebo:
Jeiel, Mattithiah, Zabad, Zebina,
Jaddai, Joel and Benaiah.

44 All these had married foreign wom-
en, and some of them had children by
these wives.[b]

NEHEMIAH

See the Invitation to Chronicles-Ezra-Nehemiah on p. 354.

---

1 The words of Nehemiah son of Hakaliah:

In the month of Kislev in the twentieth year, while I was in the citadel of
Susa, 2 Hanani, one of my brothers, came
from Judah with some other men, and I
questioned them about the Jewish remnant that had survived the exile, and also
about Jerusalem.

3 They said to me, "Those who survived
the exile and are back in the province are
in great trouble and disgrace. The wall of
Jerusalem is broken down, and its gates
have been burned with fire."

4 When I heard these things, I sat down
and wept. For some days I mourned and
fasted and prayed before the God of heav-
en. 5 Then I said:

"LORD, the God of heaven, the
great and awesome God, who keeps
his covenant of love with those who
love him and keep his commandments, 6 let your ear be attentive and
your eyes open to hear the prayer
your servant is praying before you
day and night for your servants, the
people of Israel. I confess the sins
we Israelites, including myself and
my father's family, have committed
against you. 7 We have acted very
wickedly toward you. We have not
obeyed the commands, decrees and
laws you gave your servant Moses.

8 "Remember the instruction you
gave your servant Moses, saying, 'If
you are unfaithful, I will scatter you
among the nations, 9 but if you return
to me and obey my commands, then
even if your exiled people are at the
farthest horizon, I will gather them
from there and bring them to the
place I have chosen as a dwelling for
my Name.'

10 "They are your servants and
your people, whom you redeemed by
your great strength and your mighty
hand. 11 Lord, let your ear be atten-

[a] 37,38 See Septuagint (also 1 Esdras 9:34); Hebrew *Jaasu* 38*and Bani and Binnui,* [b] 44 Or *and they sent them away with their children*

tive to the prayer of this your servant and to the prayer of your servants who delight in revering your name. Give your servant success today by granting him favor in the presence of this man."

I was cupbearer to the king.

2 In the month of Nisan in the twentieth year of King Artaxerxes, when wine was brought for him, I took the wine and gave it to the king. I had not been sad in his presence before, 2 so the king asked me, "Why does your face look so sad when you are not ill? This can be nothing but sadness of heart."

I was very much afraid, 3 but I said to the king, "May the king live forever! Why should my face not look sad when the city where my ancestors are buried lies in ruins, and its gates have been destroyed by fire?"

4 The king said to me, "What is it you want?"

Then I prayed to the God of heaven, 5 and I answered the king, "If it pleases the king and if your servant has found favor in his sight, let him send me to the city in Judah where my ancestors are buried so that I can rebuild it."

6 Then the king, with the queen sitting beside him, asked me, "How long will your journey take, and when will you get back?" It pleased the king to send me; so I set a time.

7 I also said to him, "If it pleases the king, may I have letters to the governors of Trans-Euphrates, so that they will provide me safe-conduct until I arrive in Judah? 8 And may I have a letter to Asaph, keeper of the royal park, so he will give me timber to make beams for the gates of the citadel by the temple and for the city wall and for the residence I will occupy?" And because the gracious hand of my God was on me, the king granted my requests. 9 So I went to the governors of Trans-Euphrates and gave them the king's letters. The king had also sent army officers and cavalry with me.

10 When Sanballat the Horonite and Tobiah the Ammonite official heard about this, they were very much disturbed that someone had come to promote the welfare of the Israelites.

11 I went to Jerusalem, and after staying there three days 12 I set out during the night with a few others. I had not told anyone what my God had put in my heart to do for Jerusalem. There were no mounts with me except the one I was riding on.

13 By night I went out through the Valley Gate toward the Jackal[a] Well and the Dung Gate, examining the walls of Jerusalem, which had been broken down, and its gates, which had been destroyed by fire. 14 Then I moved on toward the Fountain Gate and the King's Pool, but there was not enough room for my mount to get through; 15 so I went up the valley by night, examining the wall. Finally, I turned back and reentered through the Valley Gate. 16 The officials did not know where I had gone or what I was doing, because as yet I had said nothing to the Jews or the priests or nobles or officials or any others who would be doing the work.

17 Then I said to them, "You see the trouble we are in: Jerusalem lies in ruins, and its gates have been burned with fire. Come, let us rebuild the wall of Jerusalem, and we will no longer be in disgrace." 18 I also told them about the gracious hand of my God on me and what the king had said to me.

They replied, "Let us start rebuilding." So they began this good work.

19 But when Sanballat the Horonite, Tobiah the Ammonite official and Geshem the Arab heard about it, they mocked and ridiculed us. "What is this you are doing?" they asked. "Are you rebelling against the king?"

20 I answered them by saying, "The God of heaven will give us success. We his servants will start rebuilding, but as for you, you have no share in Jerusalem or any claim or historic right to it."

3 Eliashib the high priest and his fellow priests went to work and rebuilt the Sheep Gate. They dedicated it and set its doors in place, building as far as the Tower of the Hundred, which they dedicated, and as far as the Tower of Hananel. 2 The men of Jericho built the adjoining section, and Zakkur son of Imri built next to them.

3 The Fish Gate was rebuilt by the sons of Hassenaah. They laid its beams and put its doors and bolts and bars in place.

[a] *13* Or *Serpent* or *Fig*

4Meremoth son of Uriah, the son of Hakkoz, repaired the next section. Next to
him Meshullam son of Berekiah, the son
of Meshezabel, made repairs, and next
to him Zadok son of Baana also made repairs. 5The next section was repaired by
the men of Tekoa, but their nobles would
not put their shoulders to the work under
their supervisors.[a]

6The Jeshanah[b] Gate was repaired by
Joiada son of Paseah and Meshullam son
of Besodeiah. They laid its beams and
put its doors with their bolts and bars in
place. 7Next to them, repairs were made
by men from Gibeon and Mizpah—Mel-
atiah of Gibeon and Jadon of Meron-
oth—places under the authority of the
governor of Trans-Euphrates. 8Uzziel
son of Harhaiah, one of the goldsmiths,
repaired the next section; and Hananiah,
one of the perfume-makers, made repairs
next to that. They restored Jerusalem as
far as the Broad Wall. 9Rephaiah son of
Hur, ruler of a half-district of Jerusalem,
repaired the next section. 10Adjoining
this, Jedaiah son of Harumaph made
repairs opposite his house, and Hattush
son of Hashabneiah made repairs next
to him. 11Malkijah son of Harim and
Hasshub son of Pahath-Moab repaired
another section and the Tower of the Ovens. 12Shallum son of Hallohesh, ruler of
a half-district of Jerusalem, repaired the
next section with the help of his daughters.

13The Valley Gate was repaired by Hanun and the residents of Zanoah. They
rebuilt it and put its doors with their bolts
and bars in place. They also repaired a
thousand cubits[c] of the wall as far as the
Dung Gate.

14The Dung Gate was repaired by Malkijah son of Rekab, ruler of the district of
Beth Hakkerem. He rebuilt it and put its
doors with their bolts and bars in place.

15The Fountain Gate was repaired by
Shallun son of Kol-Hozeh, ruler of the
district of Mizpah. He rebuilt it, roofing
it over and putting its doors and bolts
and bars in place. He also repaired the
wall of the Pool of Siloam,[d] by the King's
Garden, as far as the steps going down
from the City of David. 16Beyond him,
Nehemiah son of Azbuk, ruler of a half-
district of Beth Zur, made repairs up to
a point opposite the tombs[e] of David, as
far as the artificial pool and the House of
the Heroes.

17Next to him, the repairs were made
by the Levites under Rehum son of Bani.
Beside him, Hashabiah, ruler of half the
district of Keilah, carried out repairs for
his district. 18Next to him, the repairs
were made by their fellow Levites under
Binnui[f] son of Henadad, ruler of the other half-district of Keilah. 19Next to him,
Ezer son of Jeshua, ruler of Mizpah, repaired another section, from a point facing the ascent to the armory as far as the
angle of the wall. 20Next to him, Baruch
son of Zabbai zealously repaired another section, from the angle to the entrance
of the house of Eliashib the high priest.
21Next to him, Meremoth son of Uriah, the son of Hakkoz, repaired another
section, from the entrance of Eliashib's
house to the end of it.

22The repairs next to him were made by
the priests from the surrounding region.
23Beyond them, Benjamin and Hasshub
made repairs in front of their house; and
next to them, Azariah son of Maaseiah,
the son of Ananiah, made repairs beside
his house. 24Next to him, Binnui son of
Henadad repaired another section, from
Azariah's house to the angle and the corner, 25and Palal son of Uzai worked opposite the angle and the tower projecting
from the upper palace near the court of
the guard. Next to him, Pedaiah son of
Parosh 26and the temple servants living
on the hill of Ophel made repairs up to a
point opposite the Water Gate toward the
east and the projecting tower. 27Next to
them, the men of Tekoa repaired another
section, from the great projecting tower
to the wall of Ophel.

28Above the Horse Gate, the priests
made repairs, each in front of his own
house. 29Next to them, Zadok son of Immer made repairs opposite his house.
Next to him, Shemaiah son of Shekaniah,
the guard at the East Gate, made repairs.

[a] *5* Or *their Lord* or *the governor* [b] *6* Or *Ola* [c] *13* That is, about 1,500 feet or about 450 meters
[d] *15* Hebrew *Shelah,* a variant of *Shiloah,* that is, Siloam [e] *16* Hebrew; Septuagint, some Vulgate manuscripts and Syriac *tomb* [f] *18* Two Hebrew manuscripts and Syriac (see also Septuagint and verse 24); most Hebrew manuscripts *Bavvai*

30Next to him, Hananiah son of Shelemiah, and Hanun, the sixth son of Zalaph,
repaired another section. Next to them,
Meshullam son of Berekiah made repairs opposite his living quarters. 31Next
to him, Malkijah, one of the goldsmiths,
made repairs as far as the house of the
temple servants and the merchants, opposite the Inspection Gate, and as far
as the room above the corner; 32and between the room above the corner and
the Sheep Gate the goldsmiths and merchants made repairs.

4[a] When Sanballat heard that we were
rebuilding the wall, he became angry and was greatly incensed. He ridiculed the Jews, 2and in the presence of
his associates and the army of Samaria,
he said, "What are those feeble Jews doing? Will they restore their wall? Will
they offer sacrifices? Will they finish in
a day? Can they bring the stones back to
life from those heaps of rubble—burned
as they are?"

3Tobiah the Ammonite, who was at
his side, said, "What they are building—
even a fox climbing up on it would break
down their wall of stones!"

4Hear us, our God, for we are despised.
Turn their insults back on their own
heads. Give them over as plunder in a
land of captivity. 5Do not cover up their
guilt or blot out their sins from your sight,
for they have thrown insults in the face
of[b] the builders.

6So we rebuilt the wall till all of it
reached half its height, for the people
worked with all their heart.

7But when Sanballat, Tobiah, the
Arabs, the Ammonites and the people of
Ashdod heard that the repairs to Jerusalem's walls had gone ahead and that the
gaps were being closed, they were very
angry. 8They all plotted together to come
and fight against Jerusalem and stir up
trouble against it. 9But we prayed to our
God and posted a guard day and night to
meet this threat.

10Meanwhile, the people in Judah said,
"The strength of the laborers is giving
out, and there is so much rubble that we
cannot rebuild the wall."

11Also our enemies said, "Before they
know it or see us, we will be right there
among them and will kill them and put
an end to the work."

12Then the Jews who lived near them
came and told us ten times over, "Wherever you turn, they will attack us."

13Therefore I stationed some of the
people behind the lowest points of the
wall at the exposed places, posting them
by families, with their swords, spears
and bows. 14After I looked things over, I
stood up and said to the nobles, the officials and the rest of the people, "Don't be
afraid of them. Remember the Lord, who
is great and awesome, and fight for your
families, your sons and your daughters,
your wives and your homes."

15When our enemies heard that we
were aware of their plot and that God had
frustrated it, we all returned to the wall,
each to our own work.

16From that day on, half of my men
did the work, while the other half were
equipped with spears, shields, bows and
armor. The officers posted themselves
behind all the people of Judah 17who were
building the wall. Those who carried ma-
terials did their work with one hand and
held a weapon in the other, 18and each of
the builders wore his sword at his side as
he worked. But the man who sounded the
trumpet stayed with me.

19Then I said to the nobles, the officials
and the rest of the people, "The work is
extensive and spread out, and we are
widely separated from each other along
the wall. 20Wherever you hear the sound
of the trumpet, join us there. Our God
will fight for us!"

21So we continued the work with half
the men holding spears, from the first
light of dawn till the stars came out. 22At
that time I also said to the people, "Have
every man and his helper stay inside Jerusalem at night, so they can serve us
as guards by night and as workers by
day." 23Neither I nor my brothers nor my
men nor the guards with me took off our
clothes; each had his weapon, even when
he went for water.[c]

5 Now the men and their wives raised a
great outcry against their fellow Jews.
2Some were saying, "We and our sons
and daughters are numerous; in order
for us to eat and stay alive, we must get
grain."

[a] In Hebrew texts 4:1-6 is numbered 3:33-38, and 4:7-23 is numbered 4:1-17. [b] *5* Or *have aroused your anger before* [c] *23* The meaning of the Hebrew for this clause is uncertain.

3Others were saying, "We are mort-
gaging our fields, our vineyards and our
homes to get grain during the famine."
4Still others were saying, "We have had
to borrow money to pay the king's tax on
our fields and vineyards. 5Although we
are of the same flesh and blood as our
fellow Jews and though our children are
as good as theirs, yet we have to subject
our sons and daughters to slavery. Some
of our daughters have already been enslaved, but we are powerless, because
our fields and our vineyards belong to
others."
6When I heard their outcry and these
charges, I was very angry. 7I pondered
them in my mind and then accused the
nobles and officials. I told them, "You are
charging your own people interest!" So
I called together a large meeting to deal
with them 8and said: "As far as possible,
we have bought back our fellow Jews who
were sold to the Gentiles. Now you are
selling your own people, only for them to
be sold back to us!" They kept quiet, because they could find nothing to say.
9So I continued, "What you are doing is
not right. Shouldn't you walk in the fear
of our God to avoid the reproach of our
Gentile enemies? 10I and my brothers
and my men are also lending the people
money and grain. But let us stop charging interest! 11Give back to them immediately their fields, vineyards, olive groves
and houses, and also the interest you are
charging them—one percent of the money, grain, new wine and olive oil."
12"We will give it back," they said. "And
we will not demand anything more from
them. We will do as you say."
Then I summoned the priests and
made the nobles and officials take an
oath to do what they had promised. 13I
also shook out the folds of my robe and
said, "In this way may God shake out of
their house and possessions anyone who
does not keep this promise. So may such
a person be shaken out and emptied!"
At this the whole assembly said,
"Amen," and praised the LORD. And the
people did as they had promised.
14Moreover, from the twentieth year of
King Artaxerxes, when I was appointed
to be their governor in the land of Judah,
until his thirty-second year—twelve
years—neither I nor my brothers ate
the food allotted to the governor. 15But
the earlier governors—those preceding
me—placed a heavy burden on the people and took forty shekels[a] of silver from
them in addition to food and wine. Their
assistants also lorded it over the people.
But out of reverence for God I did not act
like that. 16Instead, I devoted myself to
the work on this wall. All my men were
assembled there for the work; we[b] did
not acquire any land.
17Furthermore, a hundred and fifty
Jews and officials ate at my table, as well
as those who came to us from the surrounding nations. 18Each day one ox,
six choice sheep and some poultry were
prepared for me, and every ten days an
abundant supply of wine of all kinds. In
spite of all this, I never demanded the
food allotted to the governor, because the
demands were heavy on these people.
19Remember me with favor, my God,
for all I have done for these people.

6 When word came to Sanballat, Tobiah, Geshem the Arab and the rest of
our enemies that I had rebuilt the wall
and not a gap was left in it—though up
to that time I had not set the doors in the
gates—2Sanballat and Geshem sent me
this message: "Come, let us meet together in one of the villages[c] on the plain of
Ono."
But they were scheming to harm me;
3so I sent messengers to them with this
reply: "I am carrying on a great project
and cannot go down. Why should the
work stop while I leave it and go down to
you?" 4Four times they sent me the same
message, and each time I gave them the
same answer.
5Then, the fifth time, Sanballat sent his
aide to me with the same message, and
in his hand was an unsealed letter 6in
which was written:

"It is reported among the nations—
and Geshem[d] says it is true—that you
and the Jews are plotting to revolt,
and therefore you are building the
wall. Moreover, according to these
reports you are about to become
their king 7and have even appointed
prophets to make this proclamation
about you in Jerusalem: 'There is a

[a] *15* That is, about 1 pound or about 460 grams [b] *16* Most Hebrew manuscripts; some Hebrew manuscripts, Septuagint, Vulgate and Syriac *I* [c] *2* Or *in Kephirim* [d] *6* Hebrew *Gashmu*, a variant of *Geshem*

king in Judah!' Now this report will
get back to the king; so come, let us
meet together."

8I sent him this reply: "Nothing like
what you are saying is happening; you are
just making it up out of your head."

9They were all trying to frighten us,
thinking, "Their hands will get too weak
for the work, and it will not be completed."

But I prayed, "Now strengthen my
hands."

10One day I went to the house of Shemaiah son of Delaiah, the son of Mehetabel, who was shut in at his home. He
said, "Let us meet in the house of God,
inside the temple, and let us close the
temple doors, because men are coming
to kill you—by night they are coming to
kill you."

11But I said, "Should a man like me run
away? Or should someone like me go into
the temple to save his life? I will not go!"
12I realized that God had not sent him,
but that he had prophesied against me
because Tobiah and Sanballat had hired
him. 13He had been hired to intimidate
me so that I would commit a sin by doing
this, and then they would give me a bad
name to discredit me.

14Remember Tobiah and Sanballat, my
God, because of what they have done; remember also the prophet Noadiah and
how she and the rest of the prophets have
been trying to intimidate me. 15So the
wall was completed on the twenty-fifth
of Elul, in fifty-two days.

16When all our enemies heard about
this, all the surrounding nations were
afraid and lost their self-confidence, because they realized that this work had
been done with the help of our God.

17Also, in those days the nobles of Judah were sending many letters to Tobiah,
and replies from Tobiah kept coming to
them. 18For many in Judah were under
oath to him, since he was son-in-law to
Shekaniah son of Arah, and his son Jehohanan had married the daughter of
Meshullam son of Berekiah. 19Moreover,
they kept reporting to me his good deeds
and then telling him what I said. And Tobiah sent letters to intimidate me.

7 After the wall had been rebuilt and I
had set the doors in place, the gatekeepers, the musicians and the Levites
were appointed. 2I put in charge of Jerusalem my brother Hanani, along with
Hananiah the commander of the citadel,
because he was a man of integrity and
feared God more than most people do.
3I said to them, "The gates of Jerusalem
are not to be opened until the sun is hot.
While the gatekeepers are still on duty,
have them shut the doors and bar them.
Also appoint residents of Jerusalem as
guards, some at their posts and some
near their own houses."

4Now the city was large and spacious,
but there were few people in it, and the
houses had not yet been rebuilt. 5So my
God put it into my heart to assemble
the nobles, the officials and the common people for registration by families.
I found the genealogical record of those
who had been the first to return. This is
what I found written there:

6These are the people of the province who came up from the captivity
of the exiles whom Nebuchadnezzar
king of Babylon had taken captive
(they returned to Jerusalem and Judah, each to his own town, 7in company with Zerubbabel, Joshua, Nehemiah, Azariah, Raamiah, Nahamani,
Mordecai, Bilshan, Mispereth, Bigvai, Nehum and Baanah):

The list of the men of Israel:

8the descendants of Parosh 2,172
9of Shephatiah 372
10of Arah 652
11of Pahath-Moab (through
the line of Jeshua and
Joab) 2,818
12of Elam 1,254
13of Zattu 845
14of Zakkai 760
15of Binnui 648
16of Bebai 628
17of Azgad 2,322
18of Adonikam 667
19of Bigvai 2,067
20of Adin 655
21of Ater (through Hezekiah) 98
22of Hashum 328
23of Bezai 324
24of Hariph 112
25of Gibeon 95

26the men of Bethlehem and
Netophah 188
27of Anathoth 128

28 of Beth Azmaveth 42
29 of Kiriath Jearim, Kephirah
and Beeroth 743
30 of Ramah and Geba 621
31 of Mikmash 122
32 of Bethel and Ai 123
33 of the other Nebo 52
34 of the other Elam 1,254
35 of Harim 320
36 of Jericho 345
37 of Lod, Hadid and Ono 721
38 of Senaah 3,930

39 The priests:

the descendants of Jedaiah
(through the family of
Jeshua) 973
40 of Immer 1,052
41 of Pashhur 1,247
42 of Harim 1,017

43 The Levites:

the descendants of Jeshua
(through Kadmiel through
the line of Hodaviah) 74

44 The musicians:

the descendants of Asaph 148

45 The gatekeepers:

the descendants of
Shallum, Ater, Talmon,
Akkub, Hatita and Shobai 138

46 The temple servants:

the descendants of
Ziha, Hasupha, Tabbaoth,
47 Keros, Sia, Padon,
48 Lebana, Hagaba, Shalmai,
49 Hanan, Giddel, Gahar,
50 Reaiah, Rezin, Nekoda,
51 Gazzam, Uzza, Paseah,
52 Besai, Meunim, Nephusim,
53 Bakbuk, Hakupha, Harhur,
54 Bazluth, Mehida, Harsha,
55 Barkos, Sisera, Temah,
56 Neziah and Hatipha

57 The descendants of the servants of Solomon:

the descendants of
Sotai, Sophereth, Perida,
58 Jaala, Darkon, Giddel,
59 Shephatiah, Hattil,
Pokereth-Hazzebaim and Amon

60 The temple servants and the
descendants of the servants
of Solomon 392

61 The following came up from
the towns of Tel Melah, Tel Harsha,
Kerub, Addon and Immer, but they
could not show that their families
were descended from Israel:

62 the descendants of
Delaiah, Tobiah and Nekoda 642

63 And from among the priests:

the descendants of
Hobaiah, Hakkoz and Barzillai
(a man who had married
a daughter of Barzillai the
Gileadite and was called by that
name).

64 These searched for their family records, but they could not find
them and so were excluded from the
priesthood as unclean. 65 The governor, therefore, ordered them not to
eat any of the most sacred food until
there should be a priest ministering
with the Urim and Thummim.

66 The whole company numbered
42,360, 67 besides their 7,337 male
and female slaves; and they also had
245 male and female singers. 68 There
were 736 horses, 245 mules,[a] 69 435
camels and 6,720 donkeys.

70 Some of the heads of the families
contributed to the work. The governor gave to the treasury 1,000 darics[b]
of gold, 50 bowls and 530 garments
for priests. 71 Some of the heads of the
families gave to the treasury for the
work 20,000 darics[c] of gold and 2,200
minas[d] of silver. 72 The total given by
the rest of the people was 20,000 darics of gold, 2,000 minas[e] of silver and
67 garments for priests.

73 The priests, the Levites, the gatekeepers, the musicians and the temple servants, along with certain of
the people and the rest of the Israelites, settled in their own towns.

[a] *68* Some Hebrew manuscripts (see also Ezra 2:66); most Hebrew manuscripts do not have this verse.
[b] *70* That is, about 19 pounds or about 8.4 kilograms [c] *71* That is, about 375 pounds or about 170 kilograms; also in verse 72 [d] *71* That is, about 1 1/3 tons or about 1.2 metric tons [e] *72* That is, about 1 1/4 tons or about 1.1 metric tons

When the seventh month came and the
8 Israelites had settled in their towns,
1 all the people came together as one
in the square before the Water Gate. They
told Ezra the teacher of the Law to bring
out the Book of the Law of Moses, which
the LORD had commanded for Israel.
2 So on the first day of the seventh
month Ezra the priest brought the Law
before the assembly, which was made up
of men and women and all who were able
to understand. 3 He read it aloud from
daybreak till noon as he faced the square
before the Water Gate in the presence of
the men, women and others who could
understand. And all the people listened
attentively to the Book of the Law.
4 Ezra the teacher of the Law stood on a
high wooden platform built for the occasion. Beside him on his right stood Mattithiah, Shema, Anaiah, Uriah, Hilkiah
and Maaseiah; and on his left were Pedaiah, Mishael, Malkijah, Hashum, Hash-
baddanah, Zechariah and Meshullam.
5 Ezra opened the book. All the people
could see him because he was standing
above them; and as he opened it, the
people all stood up. 6 Ezra praised the
LORD, the great God; and all the people
lifted their hands and responded, "Amen!
Amen!" Then they bowed down and worshiped the LORD with their faces to the
ground.
7 The Levites — Jeshua, Bani, Sherebiah, Jamin, Akkub, Shabbethai, Hodiah,
Maaseiah, Kelita, Azariah, Jozabad, Hanan and Pelaiah — instructed the people
in the Law while the people were standing there. 8 They read from the Book of the
Law of God, making it clear[a] and giving
the meaning so that the people understood what was being read.
9 Then Nehemiah the governor, Ezra
the priest and teacher of the Law, and the
Levites who were instructing the people
said to them all, "This day is holy to the
LORD your God. Do not mourn or weep."
For all the people had been weeping as
they listened to the words of the Law.
10 Nehemiah said, "Go and enjoy choice
food and sweet drinks, and send some to
those who have nothing prepared. This
day is holy to our Lord. Do not grieve, for
the joy of the LORD is your strength."
11 The Levites calmed all the people,
saying, "Be still, for this is a holy day. Do
not grieve."
12 Then all the people went away to eat
and drink, to send portions of food and
to celebrate with great joy, because they
now understood the words that had been
made known to them.
13 On the second day of the month, the
heads of all the families, along with the
priests and the Levites, gathered around
Ezra the teacher to give attention to the
words of the Law. 14 They found written in
the Law, which the LORD had commanded through Moses, that the Israelites
were to live in temporary shelters during
the festival of the seventh month 15 and
that they should proclaim this word and
spread it throughout their towns and in
Jerusalem: "Go out into the hill country
and bring back branches from olive and
wild olive trees, and from myrtles, palms
and shade trees, to make temporary shelters" — as it is written.[b]
16 So the people went out and brought
back branches and built themselves
temporary shelters on their own roofs,
in their courtyards, in the courts of the
house of God and in the square by the
Water Gate and the one by the Gate of
Ephraim. 17 The whole company that had
returned from exile built temporary shelters and lived in them. From the days of
Joshua son of Nun until that day, the Israelites had not celebrated it like this. And
their joy was very great.
18 Day after day, from the first day to the
last, Ezra read from the Book of the Law
of God. They celebrated the festival for
seven days, and on the eighth day, in accordance with the regulation, there was
an assembly.
9 On the twenty-fourth day of the same
month, the Israelites gathered together, fasting and wearing sackcloth and
putting dust on their heads. 2 Those of
Israelite descent had separated themselves from all foreigners. They stood
in their places and confessed their sins
and the sins of their ancestors. 3 They
stood where they were and read from the
Book of the Law of the LORD their God
for a quarter of the day, and spent another quarter in confession and in worshiping the LORD their God. 4 Standing
on the stairs of the Levites were Jeshua,

[a] *8* Or *God, translating it* [b] *15* See Lev. 23:37-40.

Bani, Kadmiel, Shebaniah, Bunni, Sherebiah, Bani and Kenani. They cried out
with loud voices to the LORD their God.
5And the Levites—Jeshua, Kadmiel,
Bani, Hashabneiah, Sherebiah, Hodiah,
Shebaniah and Pethahiah—said: "Stand
up and praise the LORD your God, who is
from everlasting to everlasting.[a]"

"Blessed be your glorious name,
and may it be exalted above all blessing and praise. 6You alone are the
LORD. You made the heavens, even
the highest heavens, and all their
starry host, the earth and all that is
on it, the seas and all that is in them.
You give life to everything, and the
multitudes of heaven worship you.

7"You are the LORD God, who chose
Abram and brought him out of Ur of
the Chaldeans and named him Abraham. 8You found his heart faithful to
you, and you made a covenant with
him to give to his descendants the
land of the Canaanites, Hittites, Amorites, Perizzites, Jebusites and Girgashites. You have kept your promise
because you are righteous.

9"You saw the suffering of our ancestors in Egypt; you heard their cry
at the Red Sea.[b] 10You sent signs and
wonders against Pharaoh, against all
his officials and all the people of his
land, for you knew how arrogantly the
Egyptians treated them. You made a
name for yourself, which remains to
this day. 11You divided the sea before
them, so that they passed through it
on dry ground, but you hurled their
pursuers into the depths, like a stone
into mighty waters. 12By day you led
them with a pillar of cloud, and by
night with a pillar of fire to give them
light on the way they were to take.

13"You came down on Mount Sinai; you spoke to them from heaven.
You gave them regulations and laws
that are just and right, and decrees
and commands that are good. 14You
made known to them your holy Sabbath and gave them commands, decrees and laws through your servant
Moses. 15In their hunger you gave
them bread from heaven and in their
thirst you brought them water from
the rock; you told them to go in and
take possession of the land you had
sworn with uplifted hand to give
them.

16"But they, our ancestors, became arrogant and stiff-necked, and
they did not obey your commands.
17They refused to listen and failed
to remember the miracles you performed among them. They became
stiff-necked and in their rebellion appointed a leader in order to return to
their slavery. But you are a forgiving
God, gracious and compassionate,
slow to anger and abounding in love.
Therefore you did not desert them,
18even when they cast for themselves
an image of a calf and said, 'This is
your god, who brought you up out of
Egypt,' or when they committed awful blasphemies.

19"Because of your great compassion you did not abandon them in the
wilderness. By day the pillar of cloud
did not fail to guide them on their
path, nor the pillar of fire by night to
shine on the way they were to take.
20You gave your good Spirit to instruct them. You did not withhold
your manna from their mouths, and
you gave them water for their thirst.
21For forty years you sustained them
in the wilderness; they lacked nothing, their clothes did not wear out nor
did their feet become swollen.

22"You gave them kingdoms and
nations, allotting to them even the
remotest frontiers. They took over
the country of Sihon[c] king of Heshbon and the country of Og king of
Bashan. 23You made their children
as numerous as the stars in the sky,
and you brought them into the land
that you told their parents to enter
and possess. 24Their children went
in and took possession of the land.
You subdued before them the Canaanites, who lived in the land; you
gave the Canaanites into their hands,
along with their kings and the peoples of the land, to deal with them as
they pleased. 25They captured fortified cities and fertile land; they took
possession of houses filled with all
kinds of good things, wells already

[a] 5 Or *God for ever and ever* [b] 9 Or *the Sea of Reeds* [c] 22 One Hebrew manuscript and Septuagint; most Hebrew manuscripts *Sihon, that is, the country of the*

dug, vineyards, olive groves and fruit
trees in abundance. They ate to the
full and were well-nourished; they
reveled in your great goodness.
26 "But they were disobedient and
rebelled against you; they turned
their backs on your law. They killed
your prophets, who had warned
them in order to turn them back to
you; they committed awful blasphemies. 27 So you delivered them into
the hands of their enemies, who oppressed them. But when they were
oppressed they cried out to you.
From heaven you heard them, and
in your great compassion you gave
them deliverers, who rescued them
from the hand of their enemies.
28 "But as soon as they were at rest,
they again did what was evil in your
sight. Then you abandoned them
to the hand of their enemies so that
they ruled over them. And when they
cried out to you again, you heard
from heaven, and in your compassion you delivered them time after
time.
29 "You warned them in order to
turn them back to your law, but they
became arrogant and disobeyed
your commands. They sinned
against your ordinances, of which
you said, 'The person who obeys
them will live by them.' Stubbornly
they turned their backs on you, became stiff-necked and refused to
listen. 30 For many years you were
patient with them. By your Spirit you
warned them through your prophets. Yet they paid no attention, so
you gave them into the hands of the
neighboring peoples. 31 But in your
great mercy you did not put an end to
them or abandon them, for you are a
gracious and merciful God.
32 "Now therefore, our God, the
great God, mighty and awesome,
who keeps his covenant of love, do
not let all this hardship seem trifling
in your eyes — the hardship that has
come on us, on our kings and leaders,
on our priests and prophets, on our
ancestors and all your people, from
the days of the kings of Assyria until
today. 33 In all that has happened to
us, you have remained righteous; you
have acted faithfully, while we acted
wickedly. 34 Our kings, our leaders,
our priests and our ancestors did
not follow your law; they did not pay
attention to your commands or the
statutes you warned them to keep.
35 Even while they were in their kingdom, enjoying your great goodness to
them in the spacious and fertile land
you gave them, they did not serve you
or turn from their evil ways.
36 "But see, we are slaves today,
slaves in the land you gave our ancestors so they could eat its fruit and
the other good things it produces.
37 Because of our sins, its abundant
harvest goes to the kings you have
placed over us. They rule over our
bodies and our cattle as they please.
We are in great distress.

38 "In view of all this, we are making
a binding agreement, putting it in writing, and our leaders, our Levites and our
priests are affixing their seals to it."[a]

10[b] Those who sealed it were:

Nehemiah the governor, the son of Hakaliah.

Zedekiah, 2 Seraiah, Azariah, Jeremiah,
3 Pashhur, Amariah, Malkijah,
4 Hattush, Shebaniah, Malluk,
5 Harim, Meremoth, Obadiah,
6 Daniel, Ginnethon, Baruch,
7 Meshullam, Abijah, Mijamin,
8 Maaziah, Bilgai and Shemaiah.
These were the priests.

9 The Levites:

Jeshua son of Azaniah, Binnui of the sons of Henadad, Kadmiel,
10 and their associates: Shebaniah,
Hodiah, Kelita, Pelaiah, Hanan,
11 Mika, Rehob, Hashabiah,
12 Zakkur, Sherebiah, Shebaniah,
13 Hodiah, Bani and Beninu.

14 The leaders of the people:

Parosh, Pahath-Moab, Elam, Zattu, Bani,
15 Bunni, Azgad, Bebai,
16 Adonijah, Bigvai, Adin,
17 Ater, Hezekiah, Azzur,

[a] *38* In Hebrew texts this verse (9:38) is numbered 10:1.
[b] In Hebrew texts 10:1-39 is numbered 10:2-40.

18 Hodiah, Hashum, Bezai,
19 Hariph, Anathoth, Nebai,
20 Magpiash, Meshullam, Hezir,
21 Meshezabel, Zadok, Jaddua,
22 Pelatiah, Hanan, Anaiah,
23 Hoshea, Hananiah, Hasshub,
24 Hallohesh, Pilha, Shobek,
25 Rehum, Hashabnah, Maaseiah,
26 Ahiah, Hanan, Anan,
27 Malluk, Harim and Baanah.

28 "The rest of the people — priests,
Levites, gatekeepers, musicians,
temple servants and all who separated themselves from the neighboring peoples for the sake of the Law of
God, together with their wives and
all their sons and daughters who are
able to understand — 29 all these now
join their fellow Israelites the nobles,
and bind themselves with a curse
and an oath to follow the Law of God
given through Moses the servant
of God and to obey carefully all the
commands, regulations and decrees
of the LORD our Lord.

30 "We promise not to give our
daughters in marriage to the peoples
around us or take their daughters for
our sons.

31 "When the neighboring peoples
bring merchandise or grain to sell
on the Sabbath, we will not buy from
them on the Sabbath or on any holy
day. Every seventh year we will forgo working the land and will cancel
all debts.

32 "We assume the responsibility
for carrying out the commands to
give a third of a shekel[a] each year for
the service of the house of our God:
33 for the bread set out on the table;
for the regular grain offerings and
burnt offerings; for the offerings
on the Sabbaths, at the New Moon
feasts and at the appointed festivals;
for the holy offerings; for sin offerings[b] to make atonement for Israel;
and for all the duties of the house of
our God.

34 "We — the priests, the Levites
and the people — have cast lots to
determine when each of our families
is to bring to the house of our God at
set times each year a contribution of
wood to burn on the altar of the LORD
our God, as it is written in the Law.

35 "We also assume responsibility
for bringing to the house of the LORD
each year the firstfruits of our crops
and of every fruit tree.

36 "As it is also written in the Law,
we will bring the firstborn of our sons
and of our cattle, of our herds and of
our flocks to the house of our God, to
the priests ministering there.

37 "Moreover, we will bring to the
storerooms of the house of our God,
to the priests, the first of our ground
meal, of our grain offerings, of the
fruit of all our trees and of our new
wine and olive oil. And we will bring
a tithe of our crops to the Levites, for
it is the Levites who collect the tithes
in all the towns where we work. 38 A
priest descended from Aaron is to
accompany the Levites when they
receive the tithes, and the Levites are
to bring a tenth of the tithes up to the
house of our God, to the storerooms
of the treasury. 39 The people of Israel, including the Levites, are to bring
their contributions of grain, new
wine and olive oil to the storerooms,
where the articles for the sanctuary
and for the ministering priests, the
gatekeepers and the musicians are
also kept.

"We will not neglect the house of
our God."

11 Now the leaders of the people settled
in Jerusalem. The rest of the people
cast lots to bring one out of every ten of
them to live in Jerusalem, the holy city,
while the remaining nine were to stay
in their own towns. 2 The people commended all who volunteered to live in
Jerusalem.

3 These are the provincial leaders who
settled in Jerusalem (now some Israelites, priests, Levites, temple servants and
descendants of Solomon's servants lived
in the towns of Judah, each on their own
property in the various towns, 4 while
other people from both Judah and Benjamin lived in Jerusalem):

From the descendants of Judah:

Athaiah son of Uzziah, the son of
Zechariah, the son of Amariah, the

[a] 32 That is, about 1/8 ounce or about 4 grams [b] 33 Or *purification offerings*

son of Shephatiah, the son of Mahalalel, a descendant of Perez; 5 and
Maaseiah son of Baruch, the son of
Kol-Hozeh, the son of Hazaiah, the
son of Adaiah, the son of Joiarib, the
son of Zechariah, a descendant of
Shelah. 6 The descendants of Perez
who lived in Jerusalem totaled 468
men of standing.

7 From the descendants of Benjamin:

Sallu son of Meshullam, the son of
Joed, the son of Pedaiah, the son of
Kolaiah, the son of Maaseiah, the
son of Ithiel, the son of Jeshaiah,
8 and his followers, Gabbai and Sal-
lai — 928 men. 9 Joel son of Zikri was
their chief officer, and Judah son of
Hassenuah was over the New Quarter of the city.

10 From the priests:

Jedaiah; the son of Joiarib; Jakin;
11 Seraiah son of Hilkiah, the son of
Meshullam, the son of Zadok, the
son of Meraioth, the son of Ahitub,
the official in charge of the house
of God, 12 and their associates, who
carried on work for the temple — 822
men; Adaiah son of Jeroham, the son
of Pelaliah, the son of Amzi, the son
of Zechariah, the son of Pashhur, the
son of Malkijah, 13 and his associates,
who were heads of families — 242
men; Amashsai son of Azarel, the son
of Ahzai, the son of Meshillemoth,
the son of Immer, 14 and his[a] associates, who were men of standing —
128. Their chief officer was Zabdiel
son of Haggedolim.

15 From the Levites:

Shemaiah son of Hasshub, the son
of Azrikam, the son of Hashabiah,
the son of Bunni; 16 Shabbethai and
Jozabad, two of the heads of the Levites, who had charge of the outside
work of the house of God; 17 Mattaniah son of Mika, the son of Zabdi, the
son of Asaph, the director who led
in thanksgiving and prayer; Bakbukiah, second among his associates;
and Abda son of Shammua, the son
of Galal, the son of Jeduthun. 18 The
Levites in the holy city totaled 284.

19 The gatekeepers:

Akkub, Talmon and their associates,
who kept watch at the gates — 172
men.

20 The rest of the Israelites, with the
priests and Levites, were in all the towns
of Judah, each on their ancestral property.
21 The temple servants lived on the hill
of Ophel, and Ziha and Gishpa were in
charge of them.
22 The chief officer of the Levites in Jerusalem was Uzzi son of Bani, the son of
Hashabiah, the son of Mattaniah, the son
of Mika. Uzzi was one of Asaph's descendants, who were the musicians responsible for the service of the house of God.
23 The musicians were under the king's
orders, which regulated their daily activity.
24 Pethahiah son of Meshezabel, one of
the descendants of Zerah son of Judah,
was the king's agent in all affairs relating
to the people.
25 As for the villages with their fields,
some of the people of Judah lived in
Kiriath Arba and its surrounding settlements, in Dibon and its settlements, in
Jekabzeel and its villages, 26 in Jeshua, in
Moladah, in Beth Pelet, 27 in Hazar Shual, in Beersheba and its settlements, 28 in
Ziklag, in Mekonah and its settlements,
29 in En Rimmon, in Zorah, in Jarmuth,
30 Zanoah, Adullam and their villages,
in Lachish and its fields, and in Azekah
and its settlements. So they were living
all the way from Beersheba to the Valley
of Hinnom.
31 The descendants of the Benjamites
from Geba lived in Mikmash, Aija, Bethel and its settlements, 32 in Anathoth,
Nob and Ananiah, 33 in Hazor, Ramah
and Gittaim, 34 in Hadid, Zeboim and
Neballat, 35 in Lod and Ono, and in Ge
Harashim.
36 Some of the divisions of the Levites of
Judah settled in Benjamin.

12 These were the priests and Levites
who returned with Zerubbabel son
of Shealtiel and with Joshua:

Seraiah, Jeremiah, Ezra,
2 Amariah, Malluk, Hattush,
3 Shekaniah, Rehum, Meremoth,
4 Iddo, Ginnethon,[b] Abijah,

[a] *14* Most Septuagint manuscripts; Hebrew *their*
[b] *4* Many Hebrew manuscripts and Vulgate (see also verse 16); most Hebrew manuscripts *Ginnethoi*

5 Mijamin,[a] Moadiah, Bilgah,
6 Shemaiah, Joiarib, Jedaiah,
7 Sallu, Amok, Hilkiah and Jedaiah.
These were the leaders of the priests and
their associates in the days of Joshua.
8 The Levites were Jeshua, Binnui, Kadmiel, Sherebiah, Judah, and also Mattaniah, who, together with his associates, was
in charge of the songs of thanksgiving.
9 Bakbukiah and Unni, their associates,
stood opposite them in the services.

10 Joshua was the father of Joiakim,
Joiakim the father of Eliashib, Eliashib
the father of Joiada, 11 Joiada the father
of Jonathan, and Jonathan the father of
Jaddua.

12 In the days of Joiakim, these were the
heads of the priestly families:
of Seraiah's family, Meraiah;
of Jeremiah's, Hananiah;
13 of Ezra's, Meshullam;
of Amariah's, Jehohanan;
14 of Malluk's, Jonathan;
of Shekaniah's,[b] Joseph;
15 of Harim's, Adna;
of Meremoth's,[c] Helkai;
16 of Iddo's, Zechariah;
of Ginnethon's, Meshullam;
17 of Abijah's, Zikri;
of Miniamin's and of Moadiah's, Piltai;
18 of Bilgah's, Shammua;
of Shemaiah's, Jehonathan;
19 of Joiarib's, Mattenai;
of Jedaiah's, Uzzi;
20 of Sallu's, Kallai;
of Amok's, Eber;
21 of Hilkiah's, Hashabiah;
of Jedaiah's, Nethanel.

22 The family heads of the Levites in the
days of Eliashib, Joiada, Johanan and Jaddua, as well as those of the priests, were
recorded in the reign of Darius the Persian. 23 The family heads among the descendants of Levi up to the time of Johanan son of Eliashib were recorded in the
book of the annals. 24 And the leaders of
the Levites were Hashabiah, Sherebiah,
Jeshua son of Kadmiel, and their associates, who stood opposite them to give
praise and thanksgiving, one section re-
sponding to the other, as prescribed by
David the man of God.
25 Mattaniah, Bakbukiah, Obadiah,
Meshullam, Talmon and Akkub were
gatekeepers who guarded the storerooms
at the gates. 26 They served in the days of
Joiakim son of Joshua, the son of Jozadak,
and in the days of Nehemiah the governor and of Ezra the priest, the teacher of
the Law.

27 At the dedication of the wall of Jerusalem, the Levites were sought out from
where they lived and were brought to
Jerusalem to celebrate joyfully the dedication with songs of thanksgiving and
with the music of cymbals, harps and
lyres. 28 The musicians also were brought
together from the region around Jerusalem—from the villages of the Netophathites, 29 from Beth Gilgal, and from the
area of Geba and Azmaveth, for the musicians had built villages for themselves
around Jerusalem. 30 When the priests
and Levites had purified themselves ceremonially, they purified the people, the
gates and the wall.

31 I had the leaders of Judah go up on
top of[d] the wall. I also assigned two large
choirs to give thanks. One was to proceed
on top of[e] the wall to the right, toward
the Dung Gate. 32 Hoshaiah and half the
leaders of Judah followed them, 33 along
with Azariah, Ezra, Meshullam, 34 Judah,
Benjamin, Shemaiah, Jeremiah, 35 as well
as some priests with trumpets, and also
Zechariah son of Jonathan, the son of
Shemaiah, the son of Mattaniah, the son
of Micaiah, the son of Zakkur, the son of
Asaph, 36 and his associates—Shemaiah,
Azarel, Milalai, Gilalai, Maai, Nethanel,
Judah and Hanani—with musical instruments prescribed by David the man
of God. Ezra the teacher of the Law led
the procession. 37 At the Fountain Gate
they continued directly up the steps of
the City of David on the ascent to the wall
and passed above the site of David's palace to the Water Gate on the east.

38 The second choir proceeded in the
opposite direction. I followed them on
top of[f] the wall, together with half the
people—past the Tower of the Ovens to
the Broad Wall, 39 over the Gate of Ephraim, the Jeshanah[g] Gate, the Fish Gate, the

[a] *5* A variant of *Miniamin* [b] *14* Very many Hebrew manuscripts, some Septuagint manuscripts and Syriac (see also verse 3); most Hebrew manuscripts *Shebaniah's* [c] *15* Some Septuagint manuscripts (see also verse 3); Hebrew *Meraioth's* [d] *31* Or *go alongside* [e] *31* Or *proceed alongside* [f] *38* Or *them alongside* [g] *39* Or *Old*

Tower of Hananel and the Tower of the
Hundred, as far as the Sheep Gate. At the
Gate of the Guard they stopped.

40 The two choirs that gave thanks then
took their places in the house of God; so
did I, together with half the officials, 41 as
well as the priests—Eliakim, Maaseiah,
Miniamin, Micaiah, Elioenai, Zechariah and Hananiah with their trumpets—
42 and also Maaseiah, Shemaiah, Eleazar,
Uzzi, Jehohanan, Malkijah, Elam and
Ezer. The choirs sang under the direction of Jezrahiah. 43 And on that day they
offered great sacrifices, rejoicing because
God had given them great joy. The wom-
en and children also rejoiced. The sound
of rejoicing in Jerusalem could be heard
far away.

44 At that time men were appointed to
be in charge of the storerooms for the
contributions, firstfruits and tithes. From
the fields around the towns they were to
bring into the storerooms the portions required by the Law for the priests and the
Levites, for Judah was pleased with the
ministering priests and Levites. 45 They
performed the service of their God and
the service of purification, as did also the
musicians and gatekeepers, according to
the commands of David and his son Solomon. 46 For long ago, in the days of David
and Asaph, there had been directors for
the musicians and for the songs of praise
and thanksgiving to God. 47 So in the days
of Zerubbabel and of Nehemiah, all Israel contributed the daily portions for the
musicians and the gatekeepers. They also
set aside the portion for the other Levites,
and the Levites set aside the portion for
the descendants of Aaron.

13 On that day the Book of Moses was
read aloud in the hearing of the people and there it was found written that no
Ammonite or Moabite should ever be
admitted into the assembly of God, 2 because they had not met the Israelites with
food and water but had hired Balaam to
call a curse down on them. (Our God,
however, turned the curse into a blessing.) 3 When the people heard this law,
they excluded from Israel all who were of
foreign descent.

4 Before this, Eliashib the priest had
been put in charge of the storerooms of
the house of our God. He was closely associated with Tobiah, 5 and he had provided him with a large room formerly
used to store the grain offerings and incense and temple articles, and also the
tithes of grain, new wine and olive oil
prescribed for the Levites, musicians and
gatekeepers, as well as the contributions
for the priests.

6 But while all this was going on, I was
not in Jerusalem, for in the thirty-second
year of Artaxerxes king of Babylon I had
returned to the king. Some time later I
asked his permission 7 and came back to
Jerusalem. Here I learned about the evil
thing Eliashib had done in providing Tobiah a room in the courts of the house of
God. 8 I was greatly displeased and threw
all Tobiah's household goods out of the
room. 9 I gave orders to purify the rooms,
and then I put back into them the equipment of the house of God, with the grain
offerings and the incense.

10 I also learned that the portions assigned to the Levites had not been given
to them, and that all the Levites and musicians responsible for the service had
gone back to their own fields. 11 So I rebuked the officials and asked them, "Why
is the house of God neglected?" Then I
called them together and stationed them
at their posts.

12 All Judah brought the tithes of grain,
new wine and olive oil into the storerooms. 13 I put Shelemiah the priest, Zadok the scribe, and a Levite named Pedaiah in charge of the storerooms and made
Hanan son of Zakkur, the son of Mattaniah, their assistant, because they were
considered trustworthy. They were made
responsible for distributing the supplies
to their fellow Levites.

14 Remember me for this, my God, and
do not blot out what I have so faithfully
done for the house of my God and its services.

15 In those days I saw people in Judah
treading winepresses on the Sabbath
and bringing in grain and loading it on
donkeys, together with wine, grapes, figs
and all other kinds of loads. And they
were bringing all this into Jerusalem on
the Sabbath. Therefore I warned them
against selling food on that day. 16 People
from Tyre who lived in Jerusalem were
bringing in fish and all kinds of merchandise and selling them in Jerusalem
on the Sabbath to the people of Judah.
17 I rebuked the nobles of Judah and said

to them, "What is this wicked thing you
are doing—desecrating the Sabbath
day? 18Didn't your ancestors do the same
things, so that our God brought all this
calamity on us and on this city? Now you
are stirring up more wrath against Israel
by desecrating the Sabbath."

19When evening shadows fell on the
gates of Jerusalem before the Sabbath,
I ordered the doors to be shut and not
opened until the Sabbath was over. I stationed some of my own men at the gates
so that no load could be brought in on the
Sabbath day. 20Once or twice the merchants and sellers of all kinds of goods
spent the night outside Jerusalem. 21But
I warned them and said, "Why do you
spend the night by the wall? If you do this
again, I will arrest you." From that time
on they no longer came on the Sabbath.
22Then I commanded the Levites to purify themselves and go and guard the gates
in order to keep the Sabbath day holy.

Remember me for this also, my God, and show mercy to me according to your great love.

23Moreover, in those days I saw men
of Judah who had married women from
Ashdod, Ammon and Moab. 24Half of
their children spoke the language of Ashdod or the language of one of the other
peoples, and did not know how to speak
the language of Judah. 25I rebuked them
and called curses down on them. I beat
some of the men and pulled out their hair.
I made them take an oath in God's name
and said: "You are not to give your daughters in marriage to their sons, nor are you
to take their daughters in marriage for
your sons or for yourselves. 26Was it not
because of marriages like these that Solomon king of Israel sinned? Among the
many nations there was no king like him.
He was loved by his God, and God made
him king over all Israel, but even he was
led into sin by foreign women. 27Must we
hear now that you too are doing all this
terrible wickedness and are being unfaithful to our God by marrying foreign
women?"

28One of the sons of Joiada son of Eliashib the high priest was son-in-law to
Sanballat the Horonite. And I drove him
away from me.

29Remember them, my God, because
they defiled the priestly office and the
covenant of the priesthood and of the
Levites.

30So I purified the priests and the Levites of everything foreign, and assigned
them duties, each to his own task. 31I
also made provision for contributions
of wood at designated times, and for the
firstfruits.

Remember me with favor, my God.

ESTHER

The book of Esther explains why Jews in the Persian period began celebrating a new festival called Purim. The law of Moses had earlier described how God's mighty acts of deliverance lay behind holidays such as Passover and Tabernacles. The book of Esther shows how God intervened once again to save the Jews, leading to a commemoration of this great rescue in the feast of Purim.

This fast-moving story occurs during the reign of the Persian king Xerxes (most likely Xerxes I, 486–465 BC). It relates the adventures that take place when a Jewish exile named Esther and her cousin and guardian Mordecai work to rescue their people from a plot to destroy them. While the story never mentions God by name, God's hand of protection can be detected in the timing and combination of events as they unfold.

The book features numerous banquets, including two hosted by Xerxes at the beginning, two given by Esther in the middle, and two celebrated by the grateful Jews at the end. Since this story was told to later generations during the feast of Purim itself, the audience is placed right in the middle of the action. Those who read it can not only join in celebrating God's deliverance, they can ask themselves, as Mordecai asked Esther, for what great purpose God may have brought them to their own position in life.

---

1 This is what happened during the time of Xerxes,[a] the Xerxes who ruled over 127 provinces stretching from India to Cush[b]: 2 At that time King Xerxes reigned from his royal throne in the citadel of Susa, 3 and in the third year of his reign he gave a banquet for all his nobles and officials. The military leaders of Persia and Media, the princes, and the nobles of the provinces were present.

4 For a full 180 days he displayed the vast wealth of his kingdom and the splendor and glory of his majesty. 5 When these days were over, the king gave a banquet, lasting seven days, in the enclosed garden of the king's palace, for all the people from the least to the greatest who were in the citadel of Susa. 6 The garden had hangings of white and blue linen, fastened with cords of white linen and purple material to silver rings on marble pillars. There were couches of gold and silver on a mosaic pavement of porphyry, marble, mother-of-pearl and other costly stones. 7 Wine was served in goblets of gold, each one different from the other, and the royal wine was abundant, in keeping with the king's liberality. 8 By the king's command each guest was allowed to drink with no restrictions, for the king instructed all the wine stewards to serve each man what he wished.

9 Queen Vashti also gave a banquet for the women in the royal palace of King Xerxes.

10 On the seventh day, when King Xerxes was in high spirits from wine, he commanded the seven eunuchs who served him—Mehuman, Biztha, Harbona, Bigtha, Abagtha, Zethar and Karkas— 11 to bring before him Queen Vashti, wearing her royal crown, in order to display her beauty to the people and nobles, for she was lovely to look at. 12 But when the attendants delivered the king's command, Queen Vashti refused to come. Then the king became furious and burned with anger.

13 Since it was customary for the king to consult experts in matters of law and justice, he spoke with the wise men who understood the times 14 and were closest to the king—Karshena, Shethar, Admatha, Tarshish, Meres, Marsena and Memukan, the seven nobles of Persia and Media who had special access to the king and were highest in the kingdom.

15 "According to law, what must be done to Queen Vashti?" he asked. "She has not obeyed the command of King Xerxes that the eunuchs have taken to her."

16 Then Memukan replied in the presence of the king and the nobles, "Queen Vashti has done wrong, not only against the king but also against all the nobles and the peoples of all the provinces of King Xerxes. 17 For the queen's conduct will become known to all the women, and so they will despise their husbands and say, 'King Xerxes commanded Queen

[a] *1* Hebrew *Ahasuerus*; here and throughout Esther [b] *1* That is, the upper Nile region

Vashti to be brought before him, but she would not come.' 18 This very day the Persian and Median women of the nobility who have heard about the queen's conduct will respond to all the king's nobles in the same way. There will be no end of disrespect and discord.

19 "Therefore, if it pleases the king, let him issue a royal decree and let it be written in the laws of Persia and Media, which cannot be repealed, that Vashti is never again to enter the presence of King Xerxes. Also let the king give her royal position to someone else who is better than she. 20 Then when the king's edict is proclaimed throughout all his vast realm, all the women will respect their husbands, from the least to the greatest."

21 The king and his nobles were pleased with this advice, so the king did as Memukan proposed. 22 He sent dispatches to all parts of the kingdom, to each province in its own script and to each people in their own language, proclaiming that every man should be ruler over his own household, using his native tongue.

2 Later when King Xerxes' fury had subsided, he remembered Vashti and what she had done and what he had decreed about her. 2 Then the king's personal attendants proposed, "Let a search be made for beautiful young virgins for the king. 3 Let the king appoint commissioners in every province of his realm to bring all these beautiful young women into the harem at the citadel of Susa. Let them be placed under the care of Hegai, the king's eunuch, who is in charge of the women; and let beauty treatments be given to them. 4 Then let the young woman who pleases the king be queen instead of Vashti." This advice appealed to the king, and he followed it.

5 Now there was in the citadel of Susa a Jew of the tribe of Benjamin, named Mordecai son of Jair, the son of Shimei, the son of Kish, 6 who had been carried into exile from Jerusalem by Nebuchadnezzar king of Babylon, among those taken captive with Jehoiachin[a] king of Judah. 7 Mordecai had a cousin named Hadassah, whom he had brought up because she had neither father nor mother. This young woman, who was also known as Esther, had a lovely figure and was beautiful. Mordecai had taken her as his own daughter when her father and mother died.

8 When the king's order and edict had been proclaimed, many young women were brought to the citadel of Susa and put under the care of Hegai. Esther also was taken to the king's palace and entrusted to Hegai, who had charge of the harem. 9 She pleased him and won his favor. Immediately he provided her with her beauty treatments and special food. He assigned to her seven female attendants selected from the king's palace and moved her and her attendants into the best place in the harem.

10 Esther had not revealed her nationality and family background, because Mordecai had forbidden her to do so. 11 Every day he walked back and forth near the courtyard of the harem to find out how Esther was and what was happening to her.

12 Before a young woman's turn came to go in to King Xerxes, she had to complete twelve months of beauty treatments prescribed for the women, six months with oil of myrrh and six with perfumes and cosmetics. 13 And this is how she would go to the king: Anything she wanted was given her to take with her from the harem to the king's palace. 14 In the evening she would go there and in the morning return to another part of the harem to the care of Shaashgaz, the king's eunuch who was in charge of the concubines. She would not return to the king unless he was pleased with her and summoned her by name.

15 When the turn came for Esther (the young woman Mordecai had adopted, the daughter of his uncle Abihail) to go to the king, she asked for nothing other than what Hegai, the king's eunuch who was in charge of the harem, suggested. And Esther won the favor of everyone who saw her. 16 She was taken to King Xerxes in the royal residence in the tenth month, the month of Tebeth, in the seventh year of his reign.

17 Now the king was attracted to Esther more than to any of the other women, and she won his favor and approval more than any of the other virgins. So he set a royal crown on her head and made her queen instead of Vashti. 18 And the king gave a

[a] 6 Hebrew *Jeconiah,* a variant of *Jehoiachin*

great banquet, Esther's banquet, for all
his nobles and officials. He proclaimed
a holiday throughout the provinces and
distributed gifts with royal liberality.
19 When the virgins were assembled a
second time, Mordecai was sitting at the
king's gate. 20 But Esther had kept secret
her family background and nationality
just as Mordecai had told her to do, for
she continued to follow Mordecai's instructions as she had done when he was
bringing her up.
21 During the time Mordecai was sitting
at the king's gate, Bigthana[a] and Teresh,
two of the king's officers who guarded the
doorway, became angry and conspired to
assassinate King Xerxes. 22 But Mordecai
found out about the plot and told Queen
Esther, who in turn reported it to the
king, giving credit to Mordecai. 23 And
when the report was investigated and
found to be true, the two officials were
impaled on poles. All this was recorded
in the book of the annals in the presence
of the king.

3 After these events, King Xerxes honored Haman son of Hammedatha, the
Agagite, elevating him and giving him a
seat of honor higher than that of all the
other nobles. 2 All the royal officials at the
king's gate knelt down and paid honor to
Haman, for the king had commanded this
concerning him. But Mordecai would not
kneel down or pay him honor.
3 Then the royal officials at the king's
gate asked Mordecai, "Why do you disobey the king's command?" 4 Day after
day they spoke to him but he refused
to comply. Therefore they told Haman
about it to see whether Mordecai's behavior would be tolerated, for he had told
them he was a Jew.
5 When Haman saw that Mordecai
would not kneel down or pay him honor,
he was enraged. 6 Yet having learned who
Mordecai's people were, he scorned the
idea of killing only Mordecai. Instead Haman looked for a way to destroy all Mordecai's people, the Jews, throughout the
whole kingdom of Xerxes.
7 In the twelfth year of King Xerxes, in
the first month, the month of Nisan, the
pur (that is, the lot) was cast in the presence of Haman to select a day and month.
And the lot fell on[b] the twelfth month, the
month of Adar.
8 Then Haman said to King Xerxes,
"There is a certain people dispersed
among the peoples in all the provinces of
your kingdom who keep themselves separate. Their customs are different from
those of all other people, and they do not
obey the king's laws; it is not in the king's
best interest to tolerate them. 9 If it pleases the king, let a decree be issued to destroy them, and I will give ten thousand
talents[c] of silver to the king's administrators for the royal treasury."
10 So the king took his signet ring from
his finger and gave it to Haman son of
Hammedatha, the Agagite, the enemy of
the Jews. 11 "Keep the money," the king
said to Haman, "and do with the people
as you please."
12 Then on the thirteenth day of the
first month the royal secretaries were
summoned. They wrote out in the script
of each province and in the language of
each people all Haman's orders to the
king's satraps, the governors of the various provinces and the nobles of the various peoples. These were written in the
name of King Xerxes himself and sealed
with his own ring. 13 Dispatches were
sent by couriers to all the king's provinces with the order to destroy, kill and
annihilate all the Jews — young and old,
women and children — on a single day,
the thirteenth day of the twelfth month,
the month of Adar, and to plunder their
goods. 14 A copy of the text of the edict
was to be issued as law in every province
and made known to the people of every
nationality so they would be ready for
that day.
15 The couriers went out, spurred on by
the king's command, and the edict was
issued in the citadel of Susa. The king and
Haman sat down to drink, but the city of
Susa was bewildered.

4 When Mordecai learned of all that had
been done, he tore his clothes, put on
sackcloth and ashes, and went out into
the city, wailing loudly and bitterly. 2 But
he went only as far as the king's gate, because no one clothed in sackcloth was
allowed to enter it. 3 In every province
to which the edict and order of the king
came, there was great mourning among

[a] 21 Hebrew *Bigthan,* a variant of *Bigthana* [b] 7 Septuagint; Hebrew does not have *And the lot fell on.*
[c] 9 That is, about 375 tons or about 340 metric tons

the Jews, with fasting, weeping and wailing. Many lay in sackcloth and ashes.
4When Esther's eunuchs and female
attendants came and told her about Mordecai, she was in great distress. She sent
clothes for him to put on instead of his
sackcloth, but he would not accept them.
5Then Esther summoned Hathak, one
of the king's eunuchs assigned to attend
her, and ordered him to find out what was
troubling Mordecai and why.
6So Hathak went out to Mordecai in
the open square of the city in front of
the king's gate. 7Mordecai told him everything that had happened to him, including the exact amount of money Haman had promised to pay into the royal
treasury for the destruction of the Jews.
8He also gave him a copy of the text of
the edict for their annihilation, which
had been published in Susa, to show to
Esther and explain it to her, and he told
him to instruct her to go into the king's
presence to beg for mercy and plead with
him for her people.
9Hathak went back and reported to Esther what Mordecai had said. 10Then she
instructed him to say to Mordecai, 11"All
the king's officials and the people of the
royal provinces know that for any man or
woman who approaches the king in the
inner court without being summoned
the king has but one law: that they be put
to death unless the king extends the gold
scepter to them and spares their lives.
But thirty days have passed since I was
called to go to the king."
12When Esther's words were reported
to Mordecai, 13he sent back this answer:
"Do not think that because you are in the
king's house you alone of all the Jews will
escape. 14For if you remain silent at this
time, relief and deliverance for the Jews
will arise from another place, but you and
your father's family will perish. And who
knows but that you have come to your
royal position for such a time as this?"
15Then Esther sent this reply to Mordecai: 16"Go, gather together all the Jews
who are in Susa, and fast for me. Do not
eat or drink for three days, night or day.
I and my attendants will fast as you do.
When this is done, I will go to the king,
even though it is against the law. And if I
perish, I perish."
17So Mordecai went away and carried
out all of Esther's instructions.

5 On the third day Esther put on her royal robes and stood in the inner court of
the palace, in front of the king's hall. The
king was sitting on his royal throne in the
hall, facing the entrance. 2When he saw
Queen Esther standing in the court, he
was pleased with her and held out to her
the gold scepter that was in his hand. So
Esther approached and touched the tip of
the scepter.
3Then the king asked, "What is it,
Queen Esther? What is your request?
Even up to half the kingdom, it will be
given you."
4"If it pleases the king," replied Esther, "let the king, together with Haman,
come today to a banquet I have prepared
for him."
5"Bring Haman at once," the king said,
"so that we may do what Esther asks."
So the king and Haman went to the
banquet Esther had prepared. 6As they
were drinking wine, the king again asked
Esther, "Now what is your petition? It will
be given you. And what is your request?
Even up to half the kingdom, it will be
granted."
7Esther replied, "My petition and my
request is this: 8If the king regards me
with favor and if it pleases the king to
grant my petition and fulfill my request, let the king and Haman come
tomorrow to the banquet I will prepare
for them. Then I will answer the king's
question."
9Haman went out that day happy and
in high spirits. But when he saw Mordecai at the king's gate and observed that he
neither rose nor showed fear in his presence, he was filled with rage against Mordecai. 10Nevertheless, Haman restrained
himself and went home.
Calling together his friends and Zeresh,
his wife, 11Haman boasted to them about
his vast wealth, his many sons, and all
the ways the king had honored him and
how he had elevated him above the other nobles and officials. 12"And that's not
all," Haman added. "I'm the only person
Queen Esther invited to accompany the
king to the banquet she gave. And she has
invited me along with the king tomorrow.
13But all this gives me no satisfaction as
long as I see that Jew Mordecai sitting at
the king's gate."
14His wife Zeresh and all his friends
said to him, "Have a pole set up, reach-

ing to a height of fifty cubits,[a] and ask the king in the morning to have Mordecai impaled on it. Then go with the king to the banquet and enjoy yourself." This suggestion delighted Haman, and he had the pole set up.

6 That night the king could not sleep; so he ordered the book of the chronicles, the record of his reign, to be brought in and read to him. [2]It was found recorded there that Mordecai had exposed Bigthana and Teresh, two of the king's officers who guarded the doorway, who had conspired to assassinate King Xerxes.

[3]"What honor and recognition has Mordecai received for this?" the king asked.

"Nothing has been done for him," his attendants answered.

[4]The king said, "Who is in the court?" Now Haman had just entered the outer court of the palace to speak to the king about impaling Mordecai on the pole he had set up for him.

[5]His attendants answered, "Haman is standing in the court."

"Bring him in," the king ordered.

[6]When Haman entered, the king asked him, "What should be done for the man the king delights to honor?"

Now Haman thought to himself, "Who is there that the king would rather honor than me?" [7]So he answered the king, "For the man the king delights to honor, [8]have them bring a royal robe the king has worn and a horse the king has ridden, one with a royal crest placed on its head. [9]Then let the robe and horse be entrusted to one of the king's most noble princes. Let them robe the man the king delights to honor, and lead him on the horse through the city streets, proclaiming before him, 'This is what is done for the man the king delights to honor!' "

[10]"Go at once," the king commanded Haman. "Get the robe and the horse and do just as you have suggested for Mordecai the Jew, who sits at the king's gate. Do not neglect anything you have recommended."

[11]So Haman got the robe and the horse. He robed Mordecai, and led him on horseback through the city streets, proclaiming before him, "This is what is done for the man the king delights to honor!"

[12]Afterward Mordecai returned to the king's gate. But Haman rushed home, with his head covered in grief, [13]and told Zeresh his wife and all his friends everything that had happened to him.

His advisers and his wife Zeresh said to him, "Since Mordecai, before whom your downfall has started, is of Jewish origin, you cannot stand against him—you will surely come to ruin!" [14]While they were still talking with him, the king's eunuchs arrived and hurried Haman away to the banquet Esther had prepared.

7 So the king and Haman went to Queen Esther's banquet, [2]and as they were drinking wine on the second day, the king again asked, "Queen Esther, what is your petition? It will be given you. What is your request? Even up to half the kingdom, it will be granted."

[3]Then Queen Esther answered, "If I have found favor with you, Your Majesty, and if it pleases you, grant me my life—this is my petition. And spare my people—this is my request. [4]For I and my people have been sold to be destroyed, killed and annihilated. If we had merely been sold as male and female slaves, I would have kept quiet, because no such distress would justify disturbing the king.[b]"

[5]King Xerxes asked Queen Esther, "Who is he? Where is he—the man who has dared to do such a thing?"

[6]Esther said, "An adversary and enemy! This vile Haman!"

Then Haman was terrified before the king and queen. [7]The king got up in a rage, left his wine and went out into the palace garden. But Haman, realizing that the king had already decided his fate, stayed behind to beg Queen Esther for his life.

[8]Just as the king returned from the palace garden to the banquet hall, Haman was falling on the couch where Esther was reclining.

The king exclaimed, "Will he even molest the queen while she is with me in the house?"

As soon as the word left the king's mouth, they covered Haman's face. [9]Then Harbona, one of the eunuchs at-

[a] *14* That is, about 75 feet or about 23 meters [b] *4* Or *quiet, but the compensation our adversary offers cannot be compared with the loss the king would suffer*

tending the king, said, "A pole reaching to a height of fifty cubits[a] stands by Haman's house. He had it set up for Mordecai, who spoke up to help the king."

The king said, "Impale him on it!" 10So they impaled Haman on the pole he had set up for Mordecai. Then the king's fury subsided.

8 That same day King Xerxes gave Queen Esther the estate of Haman, the enemy of the Jews. And Mordecai came into the presence of the king, for Esther had told how he was related to her. 2The king took off his signet ring, which he had reclaimed from Haman, and presented it to Mordecai. And Esther appointed him over Haman's estate.

3Esther again pleaded with the king, falling at his feet and weeping. She begged him to put an end to the evil plan of Haman the Agagite, which he had devised against the Jews. 4Then the king extended the gold scepter to Esther and she arose and stood before him.

5"If it pleases the king," she said, "and if he regards me with favor and thinks it the right thing to do, and if he is pleased with me, let an order be written overruling the dispatches that Haman son of Hammedatha, the Agagite, devised and wrote to destroy the Jews in all the king's provinces. 6For how can I bear to see disaster fall on my people? How can I bear to see the destruction of my family?"

7King Xerxes replied to Queen Esther and to Mordecai the Jew, "Because Haman attacked the Jews, I have given his estate to Esther, and they have impaled him on the pole he set up. 8Now write another decree in the king's name in behalf of the Jews as seems best to you, and seal it with the king's signet ring—for no document written in the king's name and sealed with his ring can be revoked."

9At once the royal secretaries were summoned—on the twenty-third day of the third month, the month of Sivan. They wrote out all Mordecai's orders to the Jews, and to the satraps, governors and nobles of the 127 provinces stretching from India to Cush.[b] These orders were written in the script of each province and the language of each people and also to the Jews in their own script and language. 10Mordecai wrote in the name of King Xerxes, sealed the dispatches with the king's signet ring, and sent them by mounted couriers, who rode fast horses especially bred for the king.

11The king's edict granted the Jews in every city the right to assemble and protect themselves; to destroy, kill and annihilate the armed men of any nationality or province who might attack them and their women and children,[c] and to plunder the property of their enemies. 12The day appointed for the Jews to do this in all the provinces of King Xerxes was the thirteenth day of the twelfth month, the month of Adar. 13A copy of the text of the edict was to be issued as law in every province and made known to the people of every nationality so that the Jews would be ready on that day to avenge themselves on their enemies.

14The couriers, riding the royal horses, went out, spurred on by the king's command, and the edict was issued in the citadel of Susa.

15When Mordecai left the king's presence, he was wearing royal garments of blue and white, a large crown of gold and a purple robe of fine linen. And the city of Susa held a joyous celebration. 16For the Jews it was a time of happiness and joy, gladness and honor. 17In every province and in every city to which the edict of the king came, there was joy and gladness among the Jews, with feasting and celebrating. And many people of other nationalities became Jews because fear of the Jews had seized them.

9 On the thirteenth day of the twelfth month, the month of Adar, the edict commanded by the king was to be carried out. On this day the enemies of the Jews had hoped to overpower them, but now the tables were turned and the Jews got the upper hand over those who hated them. 2The Jews assembled in their cities in all the provinces of King Xerxes to attack those determined to destroy them. No one could stand against them, because the people of all the other nationalities were afraid of them. 3And all the nobles of the provinces, the satraps, the governors and the king's administrators helped the Jews, because fear of Mordecai had seized them. 4Mordecai was

[a] 9 That is, about 75 feet or about 23 meters [b] 9 That is, the upper Nile region [c] 11 Or *province, together with their women and children, who might attack them;*

prominent in the palace; his reputation
spread throughout the provinces, and he
became more and more powerful.

5 The Jews struck down all their enemies with the sword, killing and destroying them, and they did what they pleased
to those who hated them. 6 In the citadel
of Susa, the Jews killed and destroyed five
hundred men. 7 They also killed Parshan-
datha, Dalphon, Aspatha, 8 Poratha, Ada-
lia, Aridatha, 9 Parmashta, Arisai, Aridai
and Vaizatha, 10 the ten sons of Haman
son of Hammedatha, the enemy of the
Jews. But they did not lay their hands on
the plunder.

11 The number of those killed in the citadel of Susa was reported to the king that
same day. 12 The king said to Queen Esther, "The Jews have killed and destroyed
five hundred men and the ten sons of Haman in the citadel of Susa. What have
they done in the rest of the king's provinces? Now what is your petition? It will
be given you. What is your request? It will
also be granted."

13 "If it pleases the king," Esther answered, "give the Jews in Susa permission to carry out this day's edict tomorrow also, and let Haman's ten sons be
impaled on poles."

14 So the king commanded that this be
done. An edict was issued in Susa, and
they impaled the ten sons of Haman.
15 The Jews in Susa came together on the
fourteenth day of the month of Adar, and
they put to death in Susa three hundred
men, but they did not lay their hands on
the plunder.

16 Meanwhile, the remainder of the
Jews who were in the king's provinces
also assembled to protect themselves
and get relief from their enemies. They
killed seventy-five thousand of them but
did not lay their hands on the plunder.
17 This happened on the thirteenth day of
the month of Adar, and on the fourteenth
they rested and made it a day of feasting
and joy.

18 The Jews in Susa, however, had assembled on the thirteenth and fourteenth, and then on the fifteenth they
rested and made it a day of feasting and
joy.

19 That is why rural Jews — those living in villages — observe the fourteenth
of the month of Adar as a day of joy and
feasting, a day for giving presents to each
other.

20 Mordecai recorded these events, and
he sent letters to all the Jews throughout
the provinces of King Xerxes, near and
far, 21 to have them celebrate annually
the fourteenth and fifteenth days of the
month of Adar 22 as the time when the
Jews got relief from their enemies, and as
the month when their sorrow was turned
into joy and their mourning into a day of
celebration. He wrote them to observe
the days as days of feasting and joy and
giving presents of food to one another
and gifts to the poor.

23 So the Jews agreed to continue the
celebration they had begun, doing what
Mordecai had written to them. 24 For Haman son of Hammedatha, the Agagite,
the enemy of all the Jews, had plotted
against the Jews to destroy them and
had cast the *pur* (that is, the lot) for their
ruin and destruction. 25 But when the plot
came to the king's attention,[a] he issued
written orders that the evil scheme Haman had devised against the Jews should
come back onto his own head, and that he
and his sons should be impaled on poles.
26 (Therefore these days were called
Purim, from the word *pur*.) Because of
everything written in this letter and because of what they had seen and what had
happened to them, 27 the Jews took it on
themselves to establish the custom that
they and their descendants and all who
join them should without fail observe
these two days every year, in the way
prescribed and at the time appointed.
28 These days should be remembered and
observed in every generation by every
family, and in every province and in every city. And these days of Purim should
never fail to be celebrated by the Jews —
nor should the memory of these days die
out among their descendants.

29 So Queen Esther, daughter of Abihail, along with Mordecai the Jew, wrote
with full authority to confirm this second
letter concerning Purim. 30 And Mordecai sent letters to all the Jews in the 127
provinces of Xerxes' kingdom — words of
goodwill and assurance — 31 to establish
these days of Purim at their designated
times, as Mordecai the Jew and Queen

[a] 25 Or *when Esther came before the king*

Esther had decreed for them, and as they
had established for themselves and their
descendants in regard to their times of
fasting and lamentation. 32Esther's decree confirmed these regulations about
Purim, and it was written down in the
records.

10 King Xerxes imposed tribute
throughout the empire, to its distant shores. 2And all his acts of power
and might, together with a full account
of the greatness of Mordecai, whom the
king had promoted, are they not written
in the book of the annals of the kings of
Media and Persia? 3Mordecai the Jew
was second in rank to King Xerxes, pre-
eminent among the Jews, and held in
high esteem by his many fellow Jews,
because he worked for the good of his
people and spoke up for the welfare of
all the Jews.

JOB

The wisdom of Proverbs describes how godly character generally leads to success. Ecclesiastes tempers this, warning that rewards are not guaranteed, since a kind of "crookedness" has come into our world. The book of Job goes further, exploring how righteous people sometimes suffer. The book of Job uses a common literary device from the wisdom traditions of the ancient world: an extended conversation based on poetic speeches.

Job is introduced as a good man. But "the adversary" (*satan* in Hebrew) points out an apparent problem in God's moral oversight of the universe. If goodness is always rewarded, how can we know if it's born from love of God or desire for gain? So God allows the adversary to bring suffering into Job's life.

Job doesn't curse God as the adversary predicted but ends up debating with three friends: Eliphaz, Bildad and Zophar. Their overly rigid view of the moral universe convinces them that Job's own wrongdoing has caused his suffering. A young man Elihu joins the conversation later, while Job continues to insist that he has done nothing wrong and deserves a hearing before God.

Finally, God reveals the power and wisdom shown in his oversight of creation. Job then humbly admits his own limited understanding. When God rebukes Job's three friends, we see they are guilty of a far worse assumption than Job. In the end God blesses Job with twice as much as he had before. The book warns us to avoid reducing God's moral rule to easy formulas.

---

1 In the land of Uz there lived a man
whose name was Job. This man was
blameless and upright; he feared God
and shunned evil. 2He had seven sons
and three daughters, 3and he owned
seven thousand sheep, three thousand
camels, five hundred yoke of oxen and
five hundred donkeys, and had a large
number of servants. He was the greatest
man among all the people of the East.
4His sons used to hold feasts in their
homes on their birthdays, and they
would invite their three sisters to eat and
drink with them. 5When a period of feasting had run its course, Job would make
arrangements for them to be purified.
Early in the morning he would sacrifice
a burnt offering for each of them, thinking, "Perhaps my children have sinned
and cursed God in their hearts." This was
Job's regular custom.
6One day the angels[a] came to present
themselves before the LORD, and Satan[b]
also came with them. 7The LORD said to
Satan, "Where have you come from?"
Satan answered the LORD, "From roaming throughout the earth, going back and
forth on it."
8Then the LORD said to Satan, "Have
you considered my servant Job? There is

[a] 6 Hebrew *the sons of God* [b] 6 Hebrew *satan* means *adversary*.

no one on earth like him; he is blameless
and upright, a man who fears God and
shuns evil."
9 "Does Job fear God for nothing?" Satan replied. 10 "Have you not put a hedge
around him and his household and everything he has? You have blessed the
work of his hands, so that his flocks and
herds are spread throughout the land.
11 But now stretch out your hand and
strike everything he has, and he will
surely curse you to your face."
12 The LORD said to Satan, "Very well,
then, everything he has is in your power, but on the man himself do not lay a
finger."
Then Satan went out from the presence
of the LORD.
13 One day when Job's sons and daughters were feasting and drinking wine at
the oldest brother's house, 14 a messenger came to Job and said, "The oxen were
plowing and the donkeys were grazing
nearby, 15 and the Sabeans attacked and
made off with them. They put the servants to the sword, and I am the only one
who has escaped to tell you!"
16 While he was still speaking, another messenger came and said, "The fire of
God fell from the heavens and burned up
the sheep and the servants, and I am the
only one who has escaped to tell you!"
17 While he was still speaking, another
messenger came and said, "The Chaldeans formed three raiding parties and
swept down on your camels and made off
with them. They put the servants to the
sword, and I am the only one who has escaped to tell you!"
18 While he was still speaking, yet another messenger came and said, "Your
sons and daughters were feasting and
drinking wine at the oldest brother's
house, 19 when suddenly a mighty wind
swept in from the desert and struck the
four corners of the house. It collapsed
on them and they are dead, and I am the
only one who has escaped to tell you!"
20 At this, Job got up and tore his robe
and shaved his head. Then he fell to the
ground in worship 21 and said:

"Naked I came from my mother's
womb,
and naked I will depart.[a]
The LORD gave and the LORD has
taken away;
may the name of the LORD be
praised."

22 In all this, Job did not sin by charging
God with wrongdoing.

2 On another day the angels[b] came to
present themselves before the LORD,
and Satan also came with them to present himself before him. 2 And the LORD
said to Satan, "Where have you come
from?"
Satan answered the LORD, "From roaming throughout the earth, going back and
forth on it."
3 Then the LORD said to Satan, "Have
you considered my servant Job? There is
no one on earth like him; he is blameless
and upright, a man who fears God and
shuns evil. And he still maintains his
integrity, though you incited me against
him to ruin him without any reason."
4 "Skin for skin!" Satan replied. "A man
will give all he has for his own life. 5 But
now stretch out your hand and strike his
flesh and bones, and he will surely curse
you to your face."
6 The LORD said to Satan, "Very well,
then, he is in your hands; but you must
spare his life."
7 So Satan went out from the presence
of the LORD and afflicted Job with painful sores from the soles of his feet to the
crown of his head. 8 Then Job took a piece
of broken pottery and scraped himself
with it as he sat among the ashes.
9 His wife said to him, "Are you still
maintaining your integrity? Curse God
and die!"
10 He replied, "You are talking like a
foolish[c] woman. Shall we accept good
from God, and not trouble?"
In all this, Job did not sin in what he
said.

11 When Job's three friends, Eliphaz the
Temanite, Bildad the Shuhite and Zophar
the Naamathite, heard about all the troubles that had come upon him, they set
out from their homes and met together
by agreement to go and sympathize with
him and comfort him. 12 When they saw
him from a distance, they could hardly
recognize him; they began to weep aloud,

[a] *21* Or *will return there* [b] *1* Hebrew *the sons of God* [c] *10* The Hebrew word rendered *foolish* denotes moral deficiency.

and they tore their robes and sprinkled
dust on their heads. 13 Then they sat on
the ground with him for seven days and
seven nights. No one said a word to him,
because they saw how great his suffering
was.

3 After this, Job opened his mouth and
cursed the day of his birth. 2 He said:

3 "May the day of my birth perish,
and the night that said, 'A boy is conceived!'
4 That day — may it turn to darkness;
may God above not care about it;
may no light shine on it.
5 May gloom and utter darkness claim it once more;
may a cloud settle over it;
may blackness overwhelm it.
6 That night — may thick darkness seize it;
may it not be included among the days of the year
nor be entered in any of the months.
7 May that night be barren;
may no shout of joy be heard in it.
8 May those who curse days[a] curse that day,
those who are ready to rouse Leviathan.
9 May its morning stars become dark;
may it wait for daylight in vain
and not see the first rays of dawn,
10 for it did not shut the doors of the womb on me
to hide trouble from my eyes.

11 "Why did I not perish at birth,
and die as I came from the womb?
12 Why were there knees to receive me
and breasts that I might be nursed?
13 For now I would be lying down in peace;
I would be asleep and at rest
14 with kings and rulers of the earth,
who built for themselves places now lying in ruins,
15 with princes who had gold,
who filled their houses with silver.
16 Or why was I not hidden away in the ground like a stillborn child,
like an infant who never saw the light of day?
17 There the wicked cease from turmoil,
and there the weary are at rest.
18 Captives also enjoy their ease;
they no longer hear the slave driver's shout.
19 The small and the great are there,
and the slaves are freed from their owners.

20 "Why is light given to those in misery,
and life to the bitter of soul,
21 to those who long for death that does not come,
who search for it more than for hidden treasure,
22 who are filled with gladness
and rejoice when they reach the grave?
23 Why is life given to a man
whose way is hidden,
whom God has hedged in?
24 For sighing has become my daily food;
my groans pour out like water.
25 What I feared has come upon me;
what I dreaded has happened to me.
26 I have no peace, no quietness;
I have no rest, but only turmoil."

4 Then Eliphaz the Temanite replied:

2 "If someone ventures a word with you,
will you be impatient?
But who can keep from speaking?
3 Think how you have instructed many,
how you have strengthened feeble hands.
4 Your words have supported those who stumbled;
you have strengthened faltering knees.
5 But now trouble comes to you, and you are discouraged;
it strikes you, and you are dismayed.
6 Should not your piety be your confidence
and your blameless ways your hope?

7 "Consider now: Who, being innocent, has ever perished?
Where were the upright ever destroyed?
8 As I have observed, those who plow evil
and those who sow trouble reap it.
9 At the breath of God they perish;
at the blast of his anger they are no more.
10 The lions may roar and growl,

[a] 8 Or *curse the sea*

yet the teeth of the great lions are
broken.
11 The lion perishes for lack of prey,
and the cubs of the lioness are
scattered.

12 "A word was secretly brought to me,
my ears caught a whisper of it.
13 Amid disquieting dreams in the night,
when deep sleep falls on people,
14 fear and trembling seized me
and made all my bones shake.
15 A spirit glided past my face,
and the hair on my body stood on
end.
16 It stopped,
but I could not tell what it was.
A form stood before my eyes,
and I heard a hushed voice:
17 'Can a mortal be more righteous than
God?
Can even a strong man be more pure
than his Maker?
18 If God places no trust in his servants,
if he charges his angels with error,
19 how much more those who live in
houses of clay,
whose foundations are in the dust,
who are crushed more readily than
a moth!
20 Between dawn and dusk they are
broken to pieces;
unnoticed, they perish forever.
21 Are not the cords of their tent pulled
up,
so that they die without wisdom?'

5 "Call if you will, but who will answer
you?
To which of the holy ones will you
turn?
2 Resentment kills a fool,
and envy slays the simple.
3 I myself have seen a fool taking root,
but suddenly his house was cursed.
4 His children are far from safety,
crushed in court without a defender.
5 The hungry consume his harvest,
taking it even from among thorns,
and the thirsty pant after his wealth.
6 For hardship does not spring from the
soil,
nor does trouble sprout from the
ground.
7 Yet man is born to trouble
as surely as sparks fly upward.

8 "But if I were you, I would appeal to
God;
I would lay my cause before him.
9 He performs wonders that cannot be
fathomed,
miracles that cannot be counted.
10 He provides rain for the earth;
he sends water on the countryside.
11 The lowly he sets on high,
and those who mourn are lifted to
safety.
12 He thwarts the plans of the crafty,
so that their hands achieve no
success.
13 He catches the wise in their craftiness,
and the schemes of the wily are
swept away.
14 Darkness comes upon them in the
daytime;
at noon they grope as in the night.
15 He saves the needy from the sword in
their mouth;
he saves them from the clutches of
the powerful.
16 So the poor have hope,
and injustice shuts its mouth.

17 "Blessed is the one whom God
corrects;
so do not despise the discipline of
the Almighty.[a]
18 For he wounds, but he also binds up;
he injures, but his hands also heal.
19 From six calamities he will rescue
you;
in seven no harm will touch you.
20 In famine he will deliver you from
death,
and in battle from the stroke of the
sword.
21 You will be protected from the lash of
the tongue,
and need not fear when destruction
comes.
22 You will laugh at destruction and
famine,
and need not fear the wild animals.
23 For you will have a covenant with the
stones of the field,
and the wild animals will be at
peace with you.
24 You will know that your tent is secure;
you will take stock of your property
and find nothing missing.
25 You will know that your children will
be many,

[a] *17* Hebrew *Shaddai*; here and throughout Job

and your descendants like the grass
of the earth.
26 You will come to the grave in full
vigor,
like sheaves gathered in season.

27 "We have examined this, and it is
true.
So hear it and apply it to yourself."

6 Then Job replied:

2 "If only my anguish could be weighed
and all my misery be placed on the
scales!
3 It would surely outweigh the sand of
the seas —
no wonder my words have been
impetuous.
4 The arrows of the Almighty are in me,
my spirit drinks in their poison;
God's terrors are marshaled against
me.
5 Does a wild donkey bray when it has
grass,
or an ox bellow when it has fodder?
6 Is tasteless food eaten without salt,
or is there flavor in the sap of the
mallow[a]?
7 I refuse to touch it;
such food makes me ill.

8 "Oh, that I might have my request,
that God would grant what I hope
for,
9 that God would be willing to crush
me,
to let loose his hand and cut off my
life!
10 Then I would still have this
consolation —
my joy in unrelenting pain —
that I had not denied the words of
the Holy One.

11 "What strength do I have, that I should
still hope?
What prospects, that I should be
patient?
12 Do I have the strength of stone?
Is my flesh bronze?
13 Do I have any power to help myself,
now that success has been driven
from me?

14 "Anyone who withholds kindness
from a friend
forsakes the fear of the Almighty.
15 But my brothers are as undependable
as intermittent streams,
as the streams that overflow
16 when darkened by thawing ice
and swollen with melting snow,
17 but that stop flowing in the dry
season,
and in the heat vanish from their
channels.
18 Caravans turn aside from their routes;
they go off into the wasteland and
perish.
19 The caravans of Tema look for water,
the traveling merchants of Sheba
look in hope.
20 They are distressed, because they had
been confident;
they arrive there, only to be
disappointed.
21 Now you too have proved to be of no
help;
you see something dreadful and are
afraid.
22 Have I ever said, 'Give something on
my behalf,
pay a ransom for me from your
wealth,
23 deliver me from the hand of the
enemy,
rescue me from the clutches of the
ruthless'?

24 "Teach me, and I will be quiet;
show me where I have been wrong.
25 How painful are honest words!
But what do your arguments prove?
26 Do you mean to correct what I say,
and treat my desperate words as
wind?
27 You would even cast lots for the
fatherless
and barter away your friend.

28 "But now be so kind as to look at me.
Would I lie to your face?
29 Relent, do not be unjust;
reconsider, for my integrity is at
stake.[b]
30 Is there any wickedness on my lips?
Can my mouth not discern malice?

7 "Do not mortals have hard service
on earth?
Are not their days like those of hired
laborers?
2 Like a slave longing for the evening
shadows,

[a] 6 The meaning of the Hebrew for this phrase is uncertain. [b] 29 Or *my righteousness still stands*

or a hired laborer waiting to be paid,
3 so I have been allotted months of
futility,
and nights of misery have been
assigned to me.
4 When I lie down I think, 'How long
before I get up?'
The night drags on, and I toss and
turn until dawn.
5 My body is clothed with worms and
scabs,
my skin is broken and festering.

6 "My days are swifter than a weaver's
shuttle,
and they come to an end without
hope.
7 Remember, O God, that my life is but a
breath;
my eyes will never see happiness
again.
8 The eye that now sees me will see me
no longer;
you will look for me, but I will be no
more.
9 As a cloud vanishes and is gone,
so one who goes down to the grave
does not return.
10 He will never come to his house again;
his place will know him no more.

11 "Therefore I will not keep silent;
I will speak out in the anguish of my
spirit,
I will complain in the bitterness of
my soul.
12 Am I the sea, or the monster of the
deep,
that you put me under guard?
13 When I think my bed will comfort me
and my couch will ease my
complaint,
14 even then you frighten me with dreams
and terrify me with visions,
15 so that I prefer strangling and death,
rather than this body of mine.
16 I despise my life; I would not live
forever.
Let me alone; my days have no
meaning.

17 "What is mankind that you make so
much of them,
that you give them so much
attention,
18 that you examine them every morning
and test them every moment?
19 Will you never look away from me,
or let me alone even for an instant?
20 If I have sinned, what have I done to
you,
you who sees everything we do?
Why have you made me your target?
Have I become a burden to you?[a]
21 Why do you not pardon my offenses
and forgive my sins?
For I will soon lie down in the dust;
you will search for me, but I will be
no more."

8 Then Bildad the Shuhite replied:

2 "How long will you say such things?
Your words are a blustering wind.
3 Does God pervert justice?
Does the Almighty pervert what is
right?
4 When your children sinned against
him,
he gave them over to the penalty of
their sin.
5 But if you will seek God earnestly
and plead with the Almighty,
6 if you are pure and upright,
even now he will rouse himself on
your behalf
and restore you to your prosperous
state.
7 Your beginnings will seem humble,
so prosperous will your future be.

8 "Ask the former generation
and find out what their ancestors
learned,
9 for we were born only yesterday and
know nothing,
and our days on earth are but a
shadow.
10 Will they not instruct you and tell you?
Will they not bring forth words from
their understanding?
11 Can papyrus grow tall where there is
no marsh?
Can reeds thrive without water?
12 While still growing and uncut,
they wither more quickly than grass.
13 Such is the destiny of all who forget
God;
so perishes the hope of the godless.
14 What they trust in is fragile[b];

[a] *20* A few manuscripts of the Masoretic Text, an ancient Hebrew scribal tradition and Septuagint; most manuscripts of the Masoretic Text *I have become a burden to myself.* [b] *14* The meaning of the Hebrew for this word is uncertain.

what they rely on is a spider's web.
15 They lean on the web, but it gives way;
they cling to it, but it does not hold.
16 They are like a well-watered plant in
the sunshine,
spreading its shoots over the
garden;
17 it entwines its roots around a pile of
rocks
and looks for a place among the
stones.
18 But when it is torn from its spot,
that place disowns it and says, 'I
never saw you.'
19 Surely its life withers away,
and[a] from the soil other plants grow.
20 "Surely God does not reject one who is
blameless
or strengthen the hands of
evildoers.
21 He will yet fill your mouth with
laughter
and your lips with shouts of joy.
22 Your enemies will be clothed in
shame,
and the tents of the wicked will be
no more."

9 Then Job replied:

2 "Indeed, I know that this is true.
But how can mere mortals prove
their innocence before God?
3 Though they wished to dispute with
him,
they could not answer him one time
out of a thousand.
4 His wisdom is profound, his power is
vast.
Who has resisted him and come out
unscathed?
5 He moves mountains without their
knowing it
and overturns them in his anger.
6 He shakes the earth from its place
and makes its pillars tremble.
7 He speaks to the sun and it does not
shine;
he seals off the light of the stars.
8 He alone stretches out the heavens
and treads on the waves of the sea.
9 He is the Maker of the Bear[b] and
Orion,
the Pleiades and the constellations
of the south.
10 He performs wonders that cannot be
fathomed,
miracles that cannot be counted.
11 When he passes me, I cannot see him;
when he goes by, I cannot perceive
him.
12 If he snatches away, who can stop
him?
Who can say to him, 'What are you
doing?'
13 God does not restrain his anger;
even the cohorts of Rahab cowered
at his feet.
14 "How then can I dispute with him?
How can I find words to argue with
him?
15 Though I were innocent, I could not
answer him;
I could only plead with my Judge for
mercy.
16 Even if I summoned him and he
responded,
I do not believe he would give me a
hearing.
17 He would crush me with a storm
and multiply my wounds for no
reason.
18 He would not let me catch my breath
but would overwhelm me with
misery.
19 If it is a matter of strength, he is
mighty!
And if it is a matter of justice, who
can challenge him[c]?
20 Even if I were innocent, my mouth
would condemn me;
if I were blameless, it would
pronounce me guilty.
21 "Although I am blameless,
I have no concern for myself;
I despise my own life.
22 It is all the same; that is why I say,
'He destroys both the blameless and
the wicked.'
23 When a scourge brings sudden death,
he mocks the despair of the
innocent.
24 When a land falls into the hands of the
wicked,
he blindfolds its judges.
If it is not he, then who is it?
25 "My days are swifter than a runner;
they fly away without a glimpse of
joy.

[a] 19 Or *Surely all the joy it has / is that* [b] 9 Cr *of Leo* [c] 19 See Septuagint; Hebrew *me.*

26 They skim past like boats of papyrus,
like eagles swooping down on their
prey.
27 If I say, 'I will forget my complaint,
I will change my expression, and
smile,'
28 I still dread all my sufferings,
for I know you will not hold me
innocent.
29 Since I am already found guilty,
why should I struggle in vain?
30 Even if I washed myself with soap
and my hands with cleansing
powder,
31 you would plunge me into a slime pit
so that even my clothes would detest
me.

32 "He is not a mere mortal like me that I
might answer him,
that we might confront each other in
court.
33 If only there were someone to mediate
between us,
someone to bring us together,
34 someone to remove God's rod from
me,
so that his terror would frighten me
no more.
35 Then I would speak up without fear of
him,
but as it now stands with me, I
cannot.

10 "I loathe my very life;
therefore I will give free rein to my
complaint
and speak out in the bitterness of my
soul.
2 I say to God: Do not declare me guilty,
but tell me what charges you have
against me.
3 Does it please you to oppress me,
to spurn the work of your hands,
while you smile on the plans of the
wicked?
4 Do you have eyes of flesh?
Do you see as a mortal sees?
5 Are your days like those of a mortal
or your years like those of a strong
man,
6 that you must search out my faults
and probe after my sin—
7 though you know that I am not guilty
and that no one can rescue me from
your hand?

8 "Your hands shaped me and made me.
Will you now turn and destroy me?
9 Remember that you molded me like
clay.
Will you now turn me to dust again?
10 Did you not pour me out like milk
and curdle me like cheese,
11 clothe me with skin and flesh
and knit me together with bones
and sinews?
12 You gave me life and showed me
kindness,
and in your providence watched
over my spirit.

13 "But this is what you concealed in
your heart,
and I know that this was in your
mind:
14 If I sinned, you would be watching me
and would not let my offense go
unpunished.
15 If I am guilty—woe to me!
Even if I am innocent, I cannot lift
my head,
for I am full of shame
and drowned in[a] my affliction.
16 If I hold my head high, you stalk me
like a lion
and again display your awesome
power against me.
17 You bring new witnesses against me
and increase your anger toward
me;
your forces come against me wave
upon wave.

18 "Why then did you bring me out of the
womb?
I wish I had died before any eye saw
me.
19 If only I had never come into being,
or had been carried straight from
the womb to the grave!
20 Are not my few days almost over?
Turn away from me so I can have a
moment's joy
21 before I go to the place of no return,
to the land of gloom and utter
darkness,
22 to the land of deepest night,
of utter darkness and disorder,
where even the light is like
darkness."

11 Then Zophar the Naamathite replied:

[a] 15 Or *and aware of*

2 "Are all these words to go
unanswered?
Is this talker to be vindicated?
3 Will your idle talk reduce others to
silence?
Will no one rebuke you when you
mock?
4 You say to God, 'My beliefs are
flawless
and I am pure in your sight.'
5 Oh, how I wish that God would speak,
that he would open his lips against
you
6 and disclose to you the secrets of
wisdom,
for true wisdom has two sides.
Know this: God has even forgotten
some of your sin.

7 "Can you fathom the mysteries of
God?
Can you probe the limits of the
Almighty?
8 They are higher than the heavens
above — what can you do?
They are deeper than the depths
below — what can you know?
9 Their measure is longer than the
earth
and wider than the sea.

10 "If he comes along and confines you in
prison
and convenes a court, who can
oppose him?
11 Surely he recognizes deceivers;
and when he sees evil, does he not
take note?
12 But the witless can no more become
wise
than a wild donkey's colt can be
born human.[a]

13 "Yet if you devote your heart to him
and stretch out your hands to him,
14 if you put away the sin that is in your
hand
and allow no evil to dwell in your
tent,
15 then, free of fault, you will lift up your
face;
you will stand firm and without fear.
16 You will surely forget your trouble,
recalling it only as waters gone by.
17 Life will be brighter than noonday,
and darkness will become like
morning.
18 You will be secure, because there is
hope;
you will look about you and take
your rest in safety.
19 You will lie down, with no one to make
you afraid,
and many will court your favor.
20 But the eyes of the wicked will fail,
and escape will elude them;
their hope will become a dying
gasp."

12 Then Job replied:

2 "Doubtless you are the only people
who matter,
and wisdom will die with you!
3 But I have a mind as well as you;
I am not inferior to you.
Who does not know all these things?

4 "I have become a laughingstock to my
friends,
though I called on God and he
answered —
a mere laughingstock, though
righteous and blameless!
5 Those who are at ease have contempt
for misfortune
as the fate of those whose feet are
slipping.
6 The tents of marauders are
undisturbed,
and those who provoke God are
secure —
those God has in his hand.[b]

7 "But ask the animals, and they will
teach you,
or the birds in the sky, and they will
tell you;
8 or speak to the earth, and it will teach
you,
or let the fish in the sea inform you.
9 Which of all these does not know
that the hand of the LORD has done
this?
10 In his hand is the life of every creature
and the breath of all mankind.
11 Does not the ear test words
as the tongue tastes food?
12 Is not wisdom found among the aged?
Does not long life bring
understanding?

13 "To God belong wisdom and power;
counsel and understanding are his.

[a] 12 Or *wild donkey can be born tame* [b] 6 Or *those whose god is in their own hand*

14 What he tears down cannot be rebuilt;
those he imprisons cannot be released.
15 If he holds back the waters, there is drought;
if he lets them loose, they devastate the land.
16 To him belong strength and insight;
both deceived and deceiver are his.
17 He leads rulers away stripped
and makes fools of judges.
18 He takes off the shackles put on by kings
and ties a loincloth[a] around their waist.
19 He leads priests away stripped
and overthrows officials long established.
20 He silences the lips of trusted advisers
and takes away the discernment of elders.
21 He pours contempt on nobles
and disarms the mighty.
22 He reveals the deep things of darkness
and brings utter darkness into the light.
23 He makes nations great, and destroys them;
he enlarges nations, and disperses them.
24 He deprives the leaders of the earth of their reason;
he makes them wander in a trackless waste.
25 They grope in darkness with no light;
he makes them stagger like drunkards.

13 "My eyes have seen all this,
my ears have heard and understood it.
2 What you know, I also know;
I am not inferior to you.
3 But I desire to speak to the Almighty
and to argue my case with God.
4 You, however, smear me with lies;
you are worthless physicians, all of you!
5 If only you would be altogether silent!
For you, that would be wisdom.
6 Hear now my argument;
listen to the pleas of my lips.
7 Will you speak wickedly on God's behalf?
Will you speak deceitfully for him?
8 Will you show him partiality?
Will you argue the case for God?
9 Would it turn out well if he examined you?
Could you deceive him as you might deceive a mortal?
10 He would surely call you to account
if you secretly showed partiality.
11 Would not his splendor terrify you?
Would not the dread of him fall on you?
12 Your maxims are proverbs of ashes;
your defenses are defenses of clay.

13 "Keep silent and let me speak;
then let come to me what may.
14 Why do I put myself in jeopardy
and take my life in my hands?
15 Though he slay me, yet will I hope in him;
I will surely[b] defend my ways to his face.
16 Indeed, this will turn out for my deliverance,
for no godless person would dare come before him!
17 Listen carefully to what I say;
let my words ring in your ears.
18 Now that I have prepared my case,
I know I will be vindicated.
19 Can anyone bring charges against me?
If so, I will be silent and die.

20 "Only grant me these two things, God,
and then I will not hide from you:
21 Withdraw your hand far from me,
and stop frightening me with your terrors.
22 Then summon me and I will answer,
or let me speak, and you reply to me.
23 How many wrongs and sins have I committed?
Show me my offense and my sin.
24 Why do you hide your face
and consider me your enemy?
25 Will you torment a windblown leaf?
Will you chase after dry chaff?
26 For you write down bitter things against me
and make me reap the sins of my youth.
27 You fasten my feet in shackles;
you keep close watch on all my paths
by putting marks on the soles of my feet.

[a] *18* Or *shackles of kings / and ties a belt* [b] *15* Or *He will surely slay me; I have no hope — / yet I will*

28 "So man wastes away like something
rotten,
like a garment eaten by moths.

14 "Mortals, born of woman,
are of few days and full of trouble.
2 They spring up like flowers and wither
away;
like fleeting shadows, they do not
endure.
3 Do you fix your eye on them?
Will you bring them[a] before you for
judgment?
4 Who can bring what is pure from the
impure?
No one!
5 A person's days are determined;
you have decreed the number of his
months
and have set limits he cannot
exceed.
6 So look away from him and let him
alone,
till he has put in his time like a hired
laborer.

7 "At least there is hope for a tree:
If it is cut down, it will sprout again,
and its new shoots will not fail.
8 Its roots may grow old in the ground
and its stump die in the soil,
9 yet at the scent of water it will bud
and put forth shoots like a plant.
10 But a man dies and is laid low;
he breathes his last and is no more.
11 As the water of a lake dries up
or a riverbed becomes parched and
dry,
12 so he lies down and does not rise;
till the heavens are no more, people
will not awake
or be roused from their sleep.

13 "If only you would hide me in the
grave
and conceal me till your anger has
passed!
If only you would set me a time
and then remember me!
14 If someone dies, will they live again?
All the days of my hard service
I will wait for my renewal[b] to come.
15 You will call and I will answer you;
you will long for the creature your
hands have made.
16 Surely then you will count my steps
but not keep track of my sin.
17 My offenses will be sealed up in a bag;
you will cover over my sin.

18 "But as a mountain erodes and
crumbles
and as a rock is moved from its
place,
19 as water wears away stones
and torrents wash away the soil,
so you destroy a person's hope.
20 You overpower them once for all, and
they are gone;
you change their countenance and
send them away.
21 If their children are honored, they do
not know it;
if their offspring are brought low,
they do not see it.
22 They feel but the pain of their own
bodies
and mourn only for themselves."

15 Then Eliphaz the Temanite replied:

2 "Would a wise person answer with
empty notions
or fill their belly with the hot east
wind?
3 Would they argue with useless words,
with speeches that have no value?
4 But you even undermine piety
and hinder devotion to God.
5 Your sin prompts your mouth;
you adopt the tongue of the crafty.
6 Your own mouth condemns you, not
mine;
your own lips testify against you.

7 "Are you the first man ever born?
Were you brought forth before the
hills?
8 Do you listen in on God's council?
Do you have a monopoly on
wisdom?
9 What do you know that we do not
know?
What insights do you have that we
do not have?
10 The gray-haired and the aged are on
our side,
men even older than your father.
11 Are God's consolations not enough for
you,
words spoken gently to you?
12 Why has your heart carried you away,
and why do your eyes flash,
13 so that you vent your rage against God

a 3 Septuagint, Vulgate and Syriac; Hebrew *me* b 14 Or *release*

and pour out such words from your
mouth?
14 "What are mortals, that they could be
pure,
or those born of woman, that they
could be righteous?
15 If God places no trust in his holy ones,
if even the heavens are not pure in
his eyes,
16 how much less mortals, who are vile
and corrupt,
who drink up evil like water!

17 "Listen to me and I will explain to you;
let me tell you what I have seen,
18 what the wise have declared,
hiding nothing received from their
ancestors
19 (to whom alone the land was given
when no foreigners moved among
them):
20 All his days the wicked man suffers
torment,
the ruthless man through all the
years stored up for him.
21 Terrifying sounds fill his ears;
when all seems well, marauders
attack him.
22 He despairs of escaping the realm of
darkness;
he is marked for the sword.
23 He wanders about for food like a
vulture;
he knows the day of darkness is at
hand.
24 Distress and anguish fill him with
terror;
troubles overwhelm him, like a king
poised to attack,
25 because he shakes his fist at God
and vaunts himself against the
Almighty,
26 defiantly charging against him
with a thick, strong shield.

27 "Though his face is covered with fat
and his waist bulges with flesh,
28 he will inhabit ruined towns
and houses where no one lives,
houses crumbling to rubble.
29 He will no longer be rich and his
wealth will not endure,
nor will his possessions spread over
the land.
30 He will not escape the darkness;
a flame will wither his shoots,
and the breath of God's mouth will
carry him away.
31 Let him not deceive himself by
trusting what is worthless,
for he will get nothing in return.
32 Before his time he will wither,
and his branches will not flourish.
33 He will be like a vine stripped of its
unripe grapes,
like an olive tree shedding its
blossoms.
34 For the company of the godless will be
barren,
and fire will consume the tents of
those who love bribes.
35 They conceive trouble and give birth
to evil;
their womb fashions deceit."

16 Then Job replied:

2 "I have heard many things like these;
you are miserable comforters, all of
you!
3 Will your long-winded speeches never
end?
What ails you that you keep on
arguing?
4 I also could speak like you,
if you were in my place;
I could make fine speeches against
you
and shake my head at you.
5 But my mouth would encourage you;
comfort from my lips would bring
you relief.

6 "Yet if I speak, my pain is not
relieved;
and if I refrain, it does not go away.
7 Surely, God, you have worn me out;
you have devastated my entire
household.
8 You have shriveled me up — and it has
become a witness;
my gauntness rises up and testifies
against me.
9 God assails me and tears me in his
anger
and gnashes his teeth at me;
my opponent fastens on me his
piercing eyes.
10 People open their mouths to jeer at
me;
they strike my cheek in scorn
and unite together against me.
11 God has turned me over to the
ungodly
and thrown me into the clutches of
the wicked.

12 All was well with me, but he shattered
me;
he seized me by the neck and
crushed me.
He has made me his target;
13 his archers surround me.
Without pity, he pierces my kidneys
and spills my gall on the ground.
14 Again and again he bursts upon me;
he rushes at me like a warrior.

15 "I have sewed sackcloth over my skin
and buried my brow in the dust.
16 My face is red with weeping,
dark shadows ring my eyes;
17 yet my hands have been free of
violence
and my prayer is pure.

18 "Earth, do not cover my blood;
may my cry never be laid to rest!
19 Even now my witness is in heaven;
my advocate is on high.
20 My intercessor is my friend[a]
as my eyes pour out tears to God;
21 on behalf of a man he pleads with
God
as one pleads for a friend.

22 "Only a few years will pass
before I take the path of no return.

17 1 My spirit is broken,
my days are cut short,
the grave awaits me.
2 Surely mockers surround me;
my eyes must dwell on their
hostility.

3 "Give me, O God, the pledge you
demand.
Who else will put up security for
me?
4 You have closed their minds to
understanding;
therefore you will not let them
triumph.
5 If anyone denounces their friends for
reward,
the eyes of their children will fail.

6 "God has made me a byword to
everyone,
a man in whose face people spit.
7 My eyes have grown dim with grief;
my whole frame is but a shadow.
8 The upright are appalled at this;
the innocent are aroused against
the ungodly.
9 Nevertheless, the righteous will hold
to their ways,
and those with clean hands will
grow stronger.

10 "But come on, all of you, try again!
I will not find a wise man among
you.
11 My days have passed, my plans are
shattered.
Yet the desires of my heart
12 turn night into day;
in the face of the darkness light is
near.
13 If the only home I hope for is the grave,
if I spread out my bed in the realm of
darkness,
14 if I say to corruption, 'You are my
father,'
and to the worm, 'My mother' or 'My
sister,'
15 where then is my hope—
who can see any hope for me?
16 Will it go down to the gates of death?
Will we descend together into the
dust?"

18 Then Bildad the Shuhite replied:

2 "When will you end these speeches?
Be sensible, and then we can talk.
3 Why are we regarded as cattle
and considered stupid in your sight?
4 You who tear yourself to pieces in your
anger,
is the earth to be abandoned for
your sake?
Or must the rocks be moved from
their place?

5 "The lamp of a wicked man is snuffed
out;
the flame of his fire stops burning.
6 The light in his tent becomes dark;
the lamp beside him goes out.
7 The vigor of his step is weakened;
his own schemes throw him down.
8 His feet thrust him into a net;
he wanders into its mesh.
9 A trap seizes him by the heel;
a snare holds him fast.
10 A noose is hidden for him on the
ground;
a trap lies in his path.
11 Terrors startle him on every side
and dog his every step.
12 Calamity is hungry for him;

[a] 20 Or *My friends treat me with scorn*

disaster is ready for him when he
falls.
13 It eats away parts of his skin;
death's firstborn devours his limbs.
14 He is torn from the security of his
tent
and marched off to the king of
terrors.
15 Fire resides[a] in his tent;
burning sulfur is scattered over his
dwelling.
16 His roots dry up below
and his branches wither above.
17 The memory of him perishes from the
earth;
he has no name in the land.
18 He is driven from light into the realm
of darkness
and is banished from the world.
19 He has no offspring or descendants
among his people,
no survivor where once he lived.
20 People of the west are appalled at his
fate;
those of the east are seized with
horror.
21 Surely such is the dwelling of an evil
man;
such is the place of one who does not
know God."

19 Then Job replied:

2 "How long will you torment me
and crush me with words?
3 Ten times now you have reproached
me;
shamelessly you attack me.
4 If it is true that I have gone astray,
my error remains my concern alone.
5 If indeed you would exalt yourselves
above me
and use my humiliation against me,
6 then know that God has wronged me
and drawn his net around me.

7 "Though I cry, 'Violence!' I get no
response;
though I call for help, there is no
justice.
8 He has blocked my way so I cannot
pass;
he has shrouded my paths in
darkness.
9 He has stripped me of my honor
and removed the crown from my
head.
10 He tears me down on every side till I
am gone;
he uproots my hope like a tree.
11 His anger burns against me;
he counts me among his enemies.
12 His troops advance in force;
they build a siege ramp against me
and encamp around my tent.

13 "He has alienated my family from me;
my acquaintances are completely
estranged from me.
14 My relatives have gone away;
my closest friends have forgotten
me.
15 My guests and my female servants
count me a foreigner;
they look on me as on a stranger.
16 I summon my servant, but he does not
answer,
though I beg him with my own
mouth.
17 My breath is offensive to my wife;
I am loathsome to my own family.
18 Even the little boys scorn me;
when I appear, they ridicule me.
19 All my intimate friends detest me;
those I love have turned against me.
20 I am nothing but skin and bones;
I have escaped only by the skin of
my teeth.[b]

21 "Have pity on me, my friends, have
pity,
for the hand of God has struck me.
22 Why do you pursue me as God does?
Will you never get enough of my
flesh?

23 "Oh, that my words were recorded,
that they were written on a scroll,
24 that they were inscribed with an iron
tool on[c] lead,
or engraved in rock forever!
25 I know that my redeemer[d] lives,
and that in the end he will stand on
the earth.[e]
26 And after my skin has been destroyed,
yet[f] in[g] my flesh I will see God;
27 I myself will see him
with my own eyes—I, and not
another.
How my heart yearns within me!

[a] 15 Or *Nothing he had remains* [b] 20 Or *only by my gums* [c] 24 Or *and* [d] 25 Or *vindicator*
[e] 25 Or *on my grave* [f] 26 Or *And after I awake, / though this body has been destroyed, / then*
[g] 26 Or *destroyed, / apart from*

28 "If you say, 'How we will hound him,
since the root of the trouble lies in
him,[a]'
29 you should fear the sword yourselves;
for wrath will bring punishment by
the sword,
and then you will know that there is
judgment.[b]"

20 Then Zophar the Naamathite replied:

2 "My troubled thoughts prompt me to
answer
because I am greatly disturbed.
3 I hear a rebuke that dishonors me,
and my understanding inspires me
to reply.

4 "Surely you know how it has been from
of old,
ever since mankind[c] was placed on
the earth,
5 that the mirth of the wicked is brief,
the joy of the godless lasts but a
moment.
6 Though the pride of the godless
person reaches to the heavens
and his head touches the clouds,
7 he will perish forever, like his own
dung;
those who have seen him will say,
'Where is he?'
8 Like a dream he flies away, no more to
be found,
banished like a vision of the night.
9 The eye that saw him will not see him
again;
his place will look on him no more.
10 His children must make amends to the
poor;
his own hands must give back his
wealth.
11 The youthful vigor that fills his
bones
will lie with him in the dust.

12 "Though evil is sweet in his mouth
and he hides it under his tongue,
13 though he cannot bear to let it go
and lets it linger in his mouth,
14 yet his food will turn sour in his
stomach;
it will become the venom of serpents
within him.
15 He will spit out the riches he
swallowed;
God will make his stomach vomit
them up.
16 He will suck the poison of serpents;
the fangs of an adder will kill him.
17 He will not enjoy the streams,
the rivers flowing with honey and
cream.
18 What he toiled for he must give back
uneaten;
he will not enjoy the profit from his
trading.
19 For he has oppressed the poor and left
them destitute;
he has seized houses he did not
build.

20 "Surely he will have no respite from
his craving;
he cannot save himself by his
treasure.
21 Nothing is left for him to devour;
his prosperity will not endure.
22 In the midst of his plenty, distress will
overtake him;
the full force of misery will come
upon him.
23 When he has filled his belly,
God will vent his burning anger
against him
and rain down his blows on him.
24 Though he flees from an iron weapon,
a bronze-tipped arrow pierces him.
25 He pulls it out of his back,
the gleaming point out of his liver.
Terrors will come over him;
26 total darkness lies in wait for his
treasures.
A fire unfanned will consume him
and devour what is left in his tent.
27 The heavens will expose his guilt;
the earth will rise up against him.
28 A flood will carry off his house,
rushing waters[d] on the day of God's
wrath.
29 Such is the fate God allots the wicked,
the heritage appointed for them by
God."

21 Then Job replied:

2 "Listen carefully to my words;
let this be the consolation you give
me.

[a] 28 Many Hebrew manuscripts, Septuagint and Vulgate; most Hebrew manuscripts *me* [b] 29 Or *sword, / that you may come to know the Almighty* [c] 4 Or *Adam* [d] 28 Or *The possessions in his house will be carried off, / washed away*

3 Bear with me while I speak,
and after I have spoken, mock on.

4 "Is my complaint directed to a human being?
Why should I not be impatient?
5 Look at me and be appalled;
clap your hand over your mouth.
6 When I think about this, I am terrified;
trembling seizes my body.
7 Why do the wicked live on,
growing old and increasing in power?
8 They see their children established around them,
their offspring before their eyes.
9 Their homes are safe and free from fear;
the rod of God is not on them.
10 Their bulls never fail to breed;
their cows calve and do not miscarry.
11 They send forth their children as a flock;
their little ones dance about.
12 They sing to the music of timbrel and lyre;
they make merry to the sound of the pipe.
13 They spend their years in prosperity
and go down to the grave in peace.[a]
14 Yet they say to God, 'Leave us alone!
We have no desire to know your ways.
15 Who is the Almighty, that we should serve him?
What would we gain by praying to him?'
16 But their prosperity is not in their own hands,
so I stand aloof from the plans of the wicked.

17 "Yet how often is the lamp of the wicked snuffed out?
How often does calamity come upon them,
the fate God allots in his anger?
18 How often are they like straw before the wind,
like chaff swept away by a gale?
19 It is said, 'God stores up the punishment of the wicked for their children.'
Let him repay the wicked, so that they themselves will experience it!
20 Let their own eyes see their destruction;
let them drink the cup of the wrath of the Almighty.
21 For what do they care about the families they leave behind
when their allotted months come to an end?

22 "Can anyone teach knowledge to God,
since he judges even the highest?
23 One person dies in full vigor,
completely secure and at ease,
24 well nourished in body,[b]
bones rich with marrow.
25 Another dies in bitterness of soul,
never having enjoyed anything good.
26 Side by side they lie in the dust,
and worms cover them both.

27 "I know full well what you are thinking,
the schemes by which you would wrong me.
28 You say, 'Where now is the house of the great,
the tents where the wicked lived?'
29 Have you never questioned those who travel?
Have you paid no regard to their accounts—
30 that the wicked are spared from the day of calamity,
that they are delivered from[c] the day of wrath?
31 Who denounces their conduct to their face?
Who repays them for what they have done?
32 They are carried to the grave,
and watch is kept over their tombs.
33 The soil in the valley is sweet to them;
everyone follows after them,
and a countless throng goes[d] before them.

34 "So how can you console me with your nonsense?
Nothing is left of your answers but falsehood!"

22 Then Eliphaz the Temanite replied:

2 "Can a man be of benefit to God?
Can even a wise person benefit him?

[a] 13 Or *in an instant* [b] 24 The meaning of the Hebrew for this word is uncertain. [c] 30 Or *wicked are reserved for the day of calamity, / that they are brought forth to* [d] 33 Or *them, / as a countless throng went*

3 What pleasure would it give the
Almighty if you were righteous?
What would he gain if your ways
were blameless?

4 "Is it for your piety that he rebukes
you
and brings charges against you?
5 Is not your wickedness great?
Are not your sins endless?
6 You demanded security from your
relatives for no reason;
you stripped people of their
clothing, leaving them naked.
7 You gave no water to the weary
and you withheld food from the
hungry,
8 though you were a powerful man,
owning land —
an honored man, living on it.
9 And you sent widows away empty-
handed
and broke the strength of the
fatherless.
10 That is why snares are all around you,
why sudden peril terrifies you,
11 why it is so dark you cannot see,
and why a flood of water covers you.

12 "Is not God in the heights of heaven?
And see how lofty are the highest
stars!
13 Yet you say, 'What does God know?
Does he judge through such
darkness?
14 Thick clouds veil him, so he does not
see us
as he goes about in the vaulted
heavens.'
15 Will you keep to the old path
that the wicked have trod?
16 They were carried off before their
time,
their foundations washed away by a
flood.
17 They said to God, 'Leave us alone!
What can the Almighty do to us?'
18 Yet it was he who filled their houses
with good things,
so I stand aloof from the plans of the
wicked.
19 The righteous see their ruin and
rejoice;
the innocent mock them, saying,
20 'Surely our foes are destroyed,
and fire devours their wealth.'

21 "Submit to God and be at peace with
him;
in this way prosperity will come to
you.
22 Accept instruction from his mouth
and lay up his words in your heart.
23 If you return to the Almighty, you will
be restored:
If you remove wickedness far from
your tent
24 and assign your nuggets to the dust,
your gold of Ophir to the rocks in the
ravines,
25 then the Almighty will be your gold,
the choicest silver for you.
26 Surely then you will find delight in the
Almighty
and will lift up your face to God.
27 You will pray to him, and he will hear
you,
and you will fulfill your vows.
28 What you decide on will be done,
and light will shine on your ways.
29 When people are brought low and you
say, 'Lift them up!'
then he will save the downcast.
30 He will deliver even one who is not
innocent,
who will be delivered through the
cleanness of your hands."

23 Then Job replied:

2 "Even today my complaint is bitter;
his hand[a] is heavy in spite of[b] my
groaning.
3 If only I knew where to find him;
if only I could go to his dwelling!
4 I would state my case before him
and fill my mouth with arguments.
5 I would find out what he would answer
me,
and consider what he would say to
me.
6 Would he vigorously oppose me?
No, he would not press charges
against me.
7 There the upright can establish their
innocence before him,
and there I would be delivered
forever from my judge.

8 "But if I go to the east, he is not there;
if I go to the west, I do not find him.
9 When he is at work in the north, I do
not see him;

[a] 2 Septuagint and Syriac; Hebrew / *the hand on me* [b] 2 Or *heavy on me in*

when he turns to the south, I catch
no glimpse of him.
10 But he knows the way that I take;
when he has tested me, I will come
forth as gold.
11 My feet have closely followed his
steps;
I have kept to his way without
turning aside.
12 I have not departed from the
commands of his lips;
I have treasured the words of his
mouth more than my daily
bread.

13 "But he stands alone, and who can
oppose him?
He does whatever he pleases.
14 He carries out his decree against me,
and many such plans he still has in
store.
15 That is why I am terrified before him;
when I think of all this, I fear him.
16 God has made my heart faint;
the Almighty has terrified me.
17 Yet I am not silenced by the darkness,
by the thick darkness that covers my
face.

24 "Why does the Almighty not set
times for judgment?
Why must those who know him look
in vain for such days?
2 There are those who move boundary
stones;
they pasture flocks they have
stolen.
3 They drive away the orphan's donkey
and take the widow's ox in pledge.
4 They thrust the needy from the path
and force all the poor of the land
into hiding.
5 Like wild donkeys in the desert,
the poor go about their labor of
foraging food;
the wasteland provides food for
their children.
6 They gather fodder in the fields
and glean in the vineyards of the
wicked.
7 Lacking clothes, they spend the night
naked;
they have nothing to cover
themselves in the cold.
8 They are drenched by mountain rains
and hug the rocks for lack of shelter.
9 The fatherless child is snatched from
the breast;
the infant of the poor is seized for a
debt.
10 Lacking clothes, they go about naked;
they carry the sheaves, but still go
hungry.
11 They crush olives among the
terraces[a];
they tread the winepresses, yet
suffer thirst.
12 The groans of the dying rise from the
city,
and the souls of the wounded cry
out for help.
But God charges no one with
wrongdoing.

13 "There are those who rebel against the
light,
who do not know its ways
or stay in its paths.
14 When daylight is gone, the murderer
rises up,
kills the poor and needy,
and in the night steals forth like a
thief.
15 The eye of the adulterer watches for
dusk;
he thinks, 'No eye will see me,'
and he keeps his face concealed.
16 In the dark, thieves break into houses,
but by day they shut themselves in;
they want nothing to do with the
light.
17 For all of them, midnight is their
morning;
they make friends with the terrors of
darkness.

18 "Yet they are foam on the surface of
the water;
their portion of the land is cursed,
so that no one goes to the vineyards.
19 As heat and drought snatch away the
melted snow,
so the grave snatches away those
who have sinned.
20 The womb forgets them,
the worm feasts on them;
the wicked are no longer remembered
but are broken like a tree.
21 They prey on the barren and childless
woman,
and to the widow they show no
kindness.

[a] *11* The meaning of the Hebrew for this word is uncertain.

22 But God drags away the mighty by his
power;
though they become established,
they have no assurance of life.
23 He may let them rest in a feeling of
security,
but his eyes are on their ways.
24 For a little while they are exalted, and
then they are gone;
they are brought low and gathered
up like all others;
they are cut off like heads of grain.
25 "If this is not so, who can prove me
false
and reduce my words to nothing?"

25

Then Bildad the Shuhite replied:

2 "Dominion and awe belong to God;
he establishes order in the heights of
heaven.
3 Can his forces be numbered?
On whom does his light not rise?
4 How then can a mortal be righteous
before God?
How can one born of woman be
pure?
5 If even the moon is not bright
and the stars are not pure in his
eyes,
6 how much less a mortal, who is but a
maggot—
a human being, who is only a
worm!"

26

Then Job replied:

2 "How you have helped the
powerless!
How you have saved the arm that is
feeble!
3 What advice you have offered to one
without wisdom!
And what great insight you have
displayed!
4 Who has helped you utter these
words?
And whose spirit spoke from your
mouth?
5 "The dead are in deep anguish,
those beneath the waters and all
that live in them.
6 The realm of the dead is naked before
God;
Destruction[a] lies uncovered.
7 He spreads out the northern skies over
empty space;
he suspends the earth over
nothing.
8 He wraps up the waters in his clouds,
yet the clouds do not burst under
their weight.
9 He covers the face of the full moon,
spreading his clouds over it.
10 He marks out the horizon on the face
of the waters
for a boundary between light and
darkness.
11 The pillars of the heavens quake,
aghast at his rebuke.
12 By his power he churned up the sea;
by his wisdom he cut Rahab to
pieces.
13 By his breath the skies became fair;
his hand pierced the gliding
serpent.
14 And these are but the outer fringe of
his works;
how faint the whisper we hear of
him!
Who then can understand the
thunder of his power?"

27

And Job continued his discourse:

2 "As surely as God lives, who has
denied me justice,
the Almighty, who has made my life
bitter,
3 as long as I have life within me,
the breath of God in my nostrils,
4 my lips will not say anything wicked,
and my tongue will not utter lies.
5 I will never admit you are in the right;
till I die, I will not deny my integrity.
6 I will maintain my innocence and
never let go of it;
my conscience will not reproach me
as long as I live.
7 "May my enemy be like the wicked,
my adversary like the unjust!
8 For what hope have the godless when
they are cut off,
when God takes away their life?
9 Does God listen to their cry
when distress comes upon them?
10 Will they find delight in the Almighty?
Will they call on God at all times?
11 "I will teach you about the power of
God;

[a] 6 Hebrew *Abaddon*

the ways of the Almighty I will not
conceal.
12 You have all seen this yourselves.
Why then this meaningless talk?

13 "Here is the fate God allots to the
wicked,
the heritage a ruthless man receives
from the Almighty:
14 However many his children, their fate
is the sword;
his offspring will never have enough
to eat.
15 The plague will bury those who
survive him,
and their widows will not weep for
them.
16 Though he heaps up silver like dust
and clothes like piles of clay,
17 what he lays up the righteous will
wear,
and the innocent will divide his
silver.
18 The house he builds is like a moth's
cocoon,
like a hut made by a watchman.
19 He lies down wealthy, but will do so no
more;
when he opens his eyes, all is gone.
20 Terrors overtake him like a flood;
a tempest snatches him away in the
night.
21 The east wind carries him off, and he
is gone;
it sweeps him out of his place.
22 It hurls itself against him without
mercy
as he flees headlong from its power.
23 It claps its hands in derision
and hisses him out of his place."

28 There is a mine for silver
and a place where gold is refined.
2 Iron is taken from the earth,
and copper is smelted from ore.
3 Mortals put an end to the darkness;
they search out the farthest recesses
for ore in the blackest darkness.
4 Far from human dwellings they cut a
shaft,
in places untouched by human feet;
far from other people they dangle
and sway.
5 The earth, from which food comes,
is transformed below as by fire;
6 lapis lazuli comes from its rocks,
and its dust contains nuggets of
gold.
7 No bird of prey knows that hidden
path,
no falcon's eye has seen it.
8 Proud beasts do not set foot on it,
and no lion prowls there.
9 People assault the flinty rock with
their hands
and lay bare the roots of the
mountains.
10 They tunnel through the rock;
their eyes see all its treasures.
11 They search[a] the sources of the rivers
and bring hidden things to light.

12 But where can wisdom be found?
Where does understanding dwell?
13 No mortal comprehends its worth;
it cannot be found in the land of the
living.
14 The deep says, "It is not in me";
the sea says, "It is not with me."
15 It cannot be bought with the finest
gold,
nor can its price be weighed out in
silver.
16 It cannot be bought with the gold of
Ophir,
with precious onyx or lapis lazuli.
17 Neither gold nor crystal can compare
with it,
nor can it be had for jewels of gold.
18 Coral and jasper are not worthy of
mention;
the price of wisdom is beyond
rubies.
19 The topaz of Cush cannot compare
with it;
it cannot be bought with pure gold.

20 Where then does wisdom come from?
Where does understanding dwell?
21 It is hidden from the eyes of every
living thing,
concealed even from the birds in the
sky.
22 Destruction[b] and Death say,
"Only a rumor of it has reached our
ears."
23 God understands the way to it
and he alone knows where it
dwells,
24 for he views the ends of the earth
and sees everything under the
heavens.

[a] *11* Septuagint, Aquila and Vulgate; Hebrew *They dam up* [b] *22* Hebrew *Abaddon*

25 When he established the force of the wind
and measured out the waters,
26 when he made a decree for the rain
and a path for the thunderstorm,
27 then he looked at wisdom and appraised it;
he confirmed it and tested it.
28 And he said to the human race,
"The fear of the Lord — that is wisdom,
and to shun evil is understanding."

29

Job continued his discourse:

2 "How I long for the months gone by,
for the days when God watched over me,
3 when his lamp shone on my head
and by his light I walked through darkness!
4 Oh, for the days when I was in my prime,
when God's intimate friendship blessed my house,
5 when the Almighty was still with me
and my children were around me,
6 when my path was drenched with cream
and the rock poured out for me streams of olive oil.

7 "When I went to the gate of the city
and took my seat in the public square,
8 the young men saw me and stepped aside
and the old men rose to their feet;
9 the chief men refrained from speaking
and covered their mouths with their hands;
10 the voices of the nobles were hushed,
and their tongues stuck to the roof of their mouths.
11 Whoever heard me spoke well of me,
and those who saw me commended me,
12 because I rescued the poor who cried for help,
and the fatherless who had none to assist them.
13 The one who was dying blessed me;
I made the widow's heart sing.
14 I put on righteousness as my clothing;
justice was my robe and my turban.
15 I was eyes to the blind
and feet to the lame.
16 I was a father to the needy;
I took up the case of the stranger.
17 I broke the fangs of the wicked
and snatched the victims from their teeth.

18 "I thought, 'I will die in my own house,
my days as numerous as the grains of sand.
19 My roots will reach to the water,
and the dew will lie all night on my branches.
20 My glory will not fade;
the bow will be ever new in my hand.'

21 "People listened to me expectantly,
waiting in silence for my counsel.
22 After I had spoken, they spoke no more;
my words fell gently on their ears.
23 They waited for me as for showers
and drank in my words as the spring rain.
24 When I smiled at them, they scarcely believed it;
the light of my face was precious to them.[a]
25 I chose the way for them and sat as their chief;
I dwelt as a king among his troops;
I was like one who comforts mourners.

30

"But now they mock me,
men younger than I,
whose fathers I would have disdained
to put with my sheep dogs.
2 Of what use was the strength of their hands to me,
since their vigor had gone from them?
3 Haggard from want and hunger,
they roamed[b] the parched land
in desolate wastelands at night.
4 In the brush they gathered salt herbs,
and their food[c] was the root of the broom bush.
5 They were banished from human society,
shouted at as if they were thieves.
6 They were forced to live in the dry stream beds,
among the rocks and in holes in the ground.
7 They brayed among the bushes

[a] *24* The meaning of the Hebrew for this clause is uncertain. [b] *3* Or *gnawed* [c] *4* Or *fuel*

and huddled in the undergrowth.
8 A base and nameless brood,
they were driven out of the land.

9 "And now those young men mock me in song;
I have become a byword among them.
10 They detest me and keep their distance;
they do not hesitate to spit in my face.
11 Now that God has unstrung my bow and afflicted me,
they throw off restraint in my presence.
12 On my right the tribe[a] attacks;
they lay snares for my feet,
they build their siege ramps against me.
13 They break up my road;
they succeed in destroying me.
'No one can help him,' they say.
14 They advance as through a gaping breach;
amid the ruins they come rolling in.
15 Terrors overwhelm me;
my dignity is driven away as by the wind,
my safety vanishes like a cloud.

16 "And now my life ebbs away;
days of suffering grip me.
17 Night pierces my bones;
my gnawing pains never rest.
18 In his great power God becomes like clothing to me[b];
he binds me like the neck of my garment.
19 He throws me into the mud,
and I am reduced to dust and ashes.

20 "I cry out to you, God, but you do not answer;
I stand up, but you merely look at me.
21 You turn on me ruthlessly;
with the might of your hand you attack me.
22 You snatch me up and drive me before the wind;
you toss me about in the storm.
23 I know you will bring me down to death,
to the place appointed for all the living.

24 "Surely no one lays a hand on a broken man
when he cries for help in his distress.
25 Have I not wept for those in trouble?
Has not my soul grieved for the poor?
26 Yet when I hoped for good, evil came;
when I looked for light, then came darkness.
27 The churning inside me never stops;
days of suffering confront me.
28 I go about blackened, but not by the sun;
I stand up in the assembly and cry for help.
29 I have become a brother of jackals,
a companion of owls.
30 My skin grows black and peels;
my body burns with fever.
31 My lyre is tuned to mourning,
and my pipe to the sound of wailing.

31 "I made a covenant with my eyes
not to look lustfully at a young woman.
2 For what is our lot from God above,
our heritage from the Almighty on high?
3 Is it not ruin for the wicked,
disaster for those who do wrong?
4 Does he not see my ways
and count my every step?

5 "If I have walked with falsehood
or my foot has hurried after deceit—
6 let God weigh me in honest scales
and he will know that I am blameless—
7 if my steps have turned from the path,
if my heart has been led by my eyes,
or if my hands have been defiled,
8 then may others eat what I have sown,
and may my crops be uprooted.

9 "If my heart has been enticed by a woman,
or if I have lurked at my neighbor's door,
10 then may my wife grind another man's grain,
and may other men sleep with her.
11 For that would have been wicked,
a sin to be judged.
12 It is a fire that burns to Destruction[c];
it would have uprooted my harvest.

[a] *12* The meaning of the Hebrew for this word is uncertain. [b] *18* Hebrew; Septuagint *power he grasps my clothing* [c] *12* Hebrew *Abaddon*

13 "If I have denied justice to any of my servants,
whether male or female,
when they had a grievance against me,
14 what will I do when God confronts me?
What will I answer when called to account?
15 Did not he who made me in the womb make them?
Did not the same one form us both within our mothers?

16 "If I have denied the desires of the poor
or let the eyes of the widow grow weary,
17 if I have kept my bread to myself,
not sharing it with the fatherless—
18 but from my youth I reared them as a father would,
and from my birth I guided the widow—
19 if I have seen anyone perishing for lack of clothing,
or the needy without garments,
20 and their hearts did not bless me
for warming them with the fleece from my sheep,
21 if I have raised my hand against the fatherless,
knowing that I had influence in court,
22 then let my arm fall from the shoulder,
let it be broken off at the joint.
23 For I dreaded destruction from God,
and for fear of his splendor I could not do such things.

24 "If I have put my trust in gold
or said to pure gold, 'You are my security,'
25 if I have rejoiced over my great wealth,
the fortune my hands had gained,
26 if I have regarded the sun in its radiance
or the moon moving in splendor,
27 so that my heart was secretly enticed
and my hand offered them a kiss of homage,
28 then these also would be sins to be judged,
for I would have been unfaithful to God on high.

29 "If I have rejoiced at my enemy's misfortune
or gloated over the trouble that came to him—
30 I have not allowed my mouth to sin
by invoking a curse against their life—
31 if those of my household have never said,
'Who has not been filled with Job's meat?'—
32 but no stranger had to spend the night in the street,
for my door was always open to the traveler—
33 if I have concealed my sin as people do,[a]
by hiding my guilt in my heart
34 because I so feared the crowd
and so dreaded the contempt of the clans
that I kept silent and would not go outside—

35 ("Oh, that I had someone to hear me!
I sign now my defense—let the Almighty answer me;
let my accuser put his indictment in writing.
36 Surely I would wear it on my shoulder,
I would put it on like a crown.
37 I would give him an account of my every step;
I would present it to him as to a ruler.)—

38 "if my land cries out against me
and all its furrows are wet with tears,
39 if I have devoured its yield without payment
or broken the spirit of its tenants,
40 then let briers come up instead of wheat
and stinkweed instead of barley."
The words of Job are ended.

32 So these three men stopped answering Job, because he was righteous in
his own eyes. 2 But Elihu son of Barakel
the Buzite, of the family of Ram, became
very angry with Job for justifying himself
rather than God. 3 He was also angry with
the three friends, because they had found
no way to refute Job, and yet had con-

a 33 Or *as Adam did*

demned him.[a] 4 Now Elihu had waited
before speaking to Job because they were
older than he. 5 But when he saw that the
three men had nothing more to say, his
anger was aroused.

6 So Elihu son of Barakel the Buzite
said:

"I am young in years,
and you are old;
that is why I was fearful,
not daring to tell you what I know.
7 I thought, 'Age should speak;
advanced years should teach wisdom.'
8 But it is the spirit[b] in a person,
the breath of the Almighty, that gives them understanding.
9 It is not only the old[c] who are wise,
not only the aged who understand what is right.

10 "Therefore I say: Listen to me;
I too will tell you what I know.
11 I waited while you spoke,
I listened to your reasoning;
while you were searching for words,
12 I gave you my full attention.
But not one of you has proved Job wrong;
none of you has answered his arguments.
13 Do not say, 'We have found wisdom;
let God, not a man, refute him.'
14 But Job has not marshaled his words against me,
and I will not answer him with your arguments.

15 "They are dismayed and have no more to say;
words have failed them.
16 Must I wait, now that they are silent,
now that they stand there with no reply?
17 I too will have my say;
I too will tell what I know.
18 For I am full of words,
and the spirit within me compels me;
19 inside I am like bottled-up wine,
like new wineskins ready to burst.
20 I must speak and find relief;
I must open my lips and reply.
21 I will show no partiality,
nor will I flatter anyone;
22 for if I were skilled in flattery,
my Maker would soon take me away.

33 "But now, Job, listen to my words;
pay attention to everything I say.
2 I am about to open my mouth;
my words are on the tip of my tongue.
3 My words come from an upright heart;
my lips sincerely speak what I know.
4 The Spirit of God has made me;
the breath of the Almighty gives me life.
5 Answer me then, if you can;
stand up and argue your case before me.
6 I am the same as you in God's sight;
I too am a piece of clay.
7 No fear of me should alarm you,
nor should my hand be heavy on you.

8 "But you have said in my hearing—
I heard the very words—
9 'I am pure, I have done no wrong;
I am clean and free from sin.
10 Yet God has found fault with me;
he considers me his enemy.
11 He fastens my feet in shackles;
he keeps close watch on all my paths.'

12 "But I tell you, in this you are not right,
for God is greater than any mortal.
13 Why do you complain to him
that he responds to no one's words[d]?
14 For God does speak—now one way,
now another—
though no one perceives it.
15 In a dream, in a vision of the night,
when deep sleep falls on people
as they slumber in their beds,
16 he may speak in their ears
and terrify them with warnings,
17 to turn them from wrongdoing
and keep them from pride,
18 to preserve them from the pit,
their lives from perishing by the sword.[e]

19 "Or someone may be chastened on a bed of pain
with constant distress in their bones,
20 so that their body finds food repulsive

[a] 3 Masoretic Text; an ancient Hebrew scribal tradition *Job, and so had condemned God* [b] 8 Or *Spirit*; also in verse 18 [c] 9 Or *many*; or *great* [d] 13 Or *that he does not answer for any of his actions* [e] 18 Or *from crossing the river*

and their soul loathes the choicest
meal.
21 Their flesh wastes away to nothing,
and their bones, once hidden, now
stick out.
22 They draw near to the pit,
and their life to the messengers of
death.[a]
23 Yet if there is an angel at their side,
a messenger, one out of a thousand,
sent to tell them how to be upright,
24 and he is gracious to that person and
says to God,
'Spare them from going down to the
pit;
I have found a ransom for them —
25 let their flesh be renewed like a
child's;
let them be restored as in the days of
their youth' —
26 then that person can pray to God and
find favor with him,
they will see God's face and shout
for joy;
he will restore them to full well-
being.
27 And they will go to others and say,
'I have sinned, I have perverted
what is right,
but I did not get what I deserved.
28 God has delivered me from going
down to the pit,
and I shall live to enjoy the light of
life.'

29 "God does all these things to a
person —
twice, even three times —
30 to turn them back from the pit,
that the light of life may shine on
them.

31 "Pay attention, Job, and listen to me;
be silent, and I will speak.
32 If you have anything to say, answer
me;
speak up, for I want to vindicate you.
33 But if not, then listen to me;
be silent, and I will teach you
wisdom."

34 Then Elihu said:

2 "Hear my words, you wise men;
listen to me, you men of learning.
3 For the ear tests words
as the tongue tastes food.
4 Let us discern for ourselves what is
right;
let us learn together what is good.

5 "Job says, 'I am innocent,
but God denies me justice.
6 Although I am right,
I am considered a liar;
although I am guiltless,
his arrow inflicts an incurable
wound.'
7 Is there anyone like Job,
who drinks scorn like water?
8 He keeps company with evildoers;
he associates with the wicked.
9 For he says, 'There is no profit
in trying to please God.'

10 "So listen to me, you men of
understanding.
Far be it from God to do evil,
from the Almighty to do wrong.
11 He repays everyone for what they have
done;
he brings on them what their
conduct deserves.
12 It is unthinkable that God would do
wrong,
that the Almighty would pervert
justice.
13 Who appointed him over the earth?
Who put him in charge of the whole
world?
14 If it were his intention
and he withdrew his spirit[b] and
breath,
15 all humanity would perish together
and mankind would return to the
dust.

16 "If you have understanding, hear this;
listen to what I say.
17 Can someone who hates justice
govern?
Will you condemn the just and
mighty One?
18 Is he not the One who says to kings,
'You are worthless,'
and to nobles, 'You are wicked,'
19 who shows no partiality to princes
and does not favor the rich over the
poor,
for they are all the work of his
hands?
20 They die in an instant, in the middle of
the night;

[a] 22 Or *to the place of the dead* [b] 14 Or *Spirit*

the people are shaken and they pass away;
the mighty are removed without human hand.

21 "His eyes are on the ways of mortals;
he sees their every step.
22 There is no deep shadow, no utter darkness,
where evildoers can hide.
23 God has no need to examine people further,
that they should come before him for judgment.
24 Without inquiry he shatters the mighty
and sets up others in their place.
25 Because he takes note of their deeds,
he overthrows them in the night and they are crushed.
26 He punishes them for their wickedness
where everyone can see them,
27 because they turned from following him
and had no regard for any of his ways.
28 They caused the cry of the poor to come before him,
so that he heard the cry of the needy.
29 But if he remains silent, who can condemn him?
If he hides his face, who can see him?
Yet he is over individual and nation alike,
30 to keep the godless from ruling,
from laying snares for the people.

31 "Suppose someone says to God,
'I am guilty but will offend no more.
32 Teach me what I cannot see;
if I have done wrong, I will not do so again.'
33 Should God then reward you on your terms,
when you refuse to repent?
You must decide, not I;
so tell me what you know.

34 "Men of understanding declare,
wise men who hear me say to me,
35 'Job speaks without knowledge;
his words lack insight.'
36 Oh, that Job might be tested to the utmost
for answering like a wicked man!
37 To his sin he adds rebellion;
scornfully he claps his hands among us
and multiplies his words against God."

35 Then Elihu said:

2 "Do you think this is just?
You say, 'I am in the right, not God.'
3 Yet you ask him, 'What profit is it to me,[a]
and what do I gain by not sinning?'

4 "I would like to reply to you
and to your friends with you.
5 Look up at the heavens and see;
gaze at the clouds so high above you.
6 If you sin, how does that affect him?
If your sins are many, what does that do to him?
7 If you are righteous, what do you give to him,
or what does he receive from your hand?
8 Your wickedness only affects humans like yourself,
and your righteousness only other people.

9 "People cry out under a load of oppression;
they plead for relief from the arm of the powerful.
10 But no one says, 'Where is God my Maker,
who gives songs in the night,
11 who teaches us more than he teaches[b] the beasts of the earth
and makes us wiser than[c] the birds in the sky?'
12 He does not answer when people cry out
because of the arrogance of the wicked.
13 Indeed, God does not listen to their empty plea;
the Almighty pays no attention to it.
14 How much less, then, will he listen
when you say that you do not see him,
that your case is before him
and you must wait for him,
15 and further, that his anger never punishes

[a] 3 Or *you* [b] *10,11* Or *night, / [11]who teaches us by* [c] *11* Or *us wise by*

and he does not take the least notice
of wickedness.[a]
16 So Job opens his mouth with empty
talk;
without knowledge he multiplies
words."

36 Elihu continued:

2 "Bear with me a little longer and I will
show you
that there is more to be said in God's
behalf.
3 I get my knowledge from afar;
I will ascribe justice to my Maker.
4 Be assured that my words are not
false;
one who has perfect knowledge is
with you.

5 "God is mighty, but despises no one;
he is mighty, and firm in his
purpose.
6 He does not keep the wicked alive
but gives the afflicted their rights.
7 He does not take his eyes off the
righteous;
he enthrones them with kings
and exalts them forever.
8 But if people are bound in chains,
held fast by cords of affliction,
9 he tells them what they have done —
that they have sinned arrogantly.
10 He makes them listen to correction
and commands them to repent of
their evil.
11 If they obey and serve him,
they will spend the rest of their days
in prosperity
and their years in contentment.
12 But if they do not listen,
they will perish by the sword[b]
and die without knowledge.

13 "The godless in heart harbor
resentment;
even when he fetters them, they do
not cry for help.
14 They die in their youth,
among male prostitutes of the
shrines.
15 But those who suffer he delivers in
their suffering;
he speaks to them in their affliction.

16 "He is wooing you from the jaws of
distress
to a spacious place free from
restriction,
to the comfort of your table laden
with choice food.
17 But now you are laden with the
judgment due the wicked;
judgment and justice have taken
hold of you.
18 Be careful that no one entices you by
riches;
do not let a large bribe turn you
aside.
19 Would your wealth or even all your
mighty efforts
sustain you so you would not be in
distress?
20 Do not long for the night,
to drag people away from their
homes.[c]
21 Beware of turning to evil,
which you seem to prefer to
affliction.

22 "God is exalted in his power.
Who is a teacher like him?
23 Who has prescribed his ways for him,
or said to him, 'You have done
wrong'?
24 Remember to extol his work,
which people have praised in song.
25 All humanity has seen it;
mortals gaze on it from afar.
26 How great is God — beyond our
understanding!
The number of his years is past
finding out.

27 "He draws up the drops of water,
which distill as rain to the streams[d];
28 the clouds pour down their moisture
and abundant showers fall on
mankind.
29 Who can understand how he spreads
out the clouds,
how he thunders from his pavilion?
30 See how he scatters his lightning
about him,
bathing the depths of the sea.
31 This is the way he governs[e] the nations
and provides food in abundance.
32 He fills his hands with lightning
and commands it to strike its mark.

[a] *15* Symmachus, Theodotion and Vulgate; the meaning of the Hebrew for this word is uncertain.
[b] *12* Or *will cross the river*
[c] *20* The meaning of the Hebrew for verses 18-20 is uncertain.
[d] *27* Or *distill from the mist as rain*
[e] *31* Or *nourishes*

33 His thunder announces the coming
storm;
even the cattle make known its
approach.[a]

37 "At this my heart pounds
and leaps from its place.
2 Listen! Listen to the roar of his voice,
to the rumbling that comes from his
mouth.
3 He unleashes his lightning beneath
the whole heaven
and sends it to the ends of the earth.
4 After that comes the sound of his roar;
he thunders with his majestic voice.
When his voice resounds,
he holds nothing back.
5 God's voice thunders in marvelous
ways;
he does great things beyond our
understanding.
6 He says to the snow, 'Fall on the earth,'
and to the rain shower, 'Be a mighty
downpour.'
7 So that everyone he has made may
know his work,
he stops all people from their labor.[b]
8 The animals take cover;
they remain in their dens.
9 The tempest comes out from its
chamber,
the cold from the driving winds.
10 The breath of God produces ice,
and the broad waters become
frozen.
11 He loads the clouds with moisture;
he scatters his lightning through
them.
12 At his direction they swirl around
over the face of the whole earth
to do whatever he commands them.
13 He brings the clouds to punish people,
or to water his earth and show his
love.

14 "Listen to this, Job;
stop and consider God's wonders.
15 Do you know how God controls the
clouds
and makes his lightning flash?
16 Do you know how the clouds hang
poised,
those wonders of him who has
perfect knowledge?
17 You who swelter in your clothes
when the land lies hushed under the
south wind,
18 can you join him in spreading out the
skies,
hard as a mirror of cast bronze?

19 "Tell us what we should say to him;
we cannot draw up our case because
of our darkness.
20 Should he be told that I want to speak?
Would anyone ask to be swallowed
up?
21 Now no one can look at the sun,
bright as it is in the skies
after the wind has swept them
clean.
22 Out of the north he comes in golden
splendor;
God comes in awesome majesty.
23 The Almighty is beyond our reach and
exalted in power;
in his justice and great
righteousness, he does not
oppress.
24 Therefore, people revere him,
for does he not have regard for all
the wise in heart?[c]"

38 Then the LORD spoke to Job out of the storm. He said:

2 "Who is this that obscures my plans
with words without knowledge?
3 Brace yourself like a man;
I will question you,
and you shall answer me.

4 "Where were you when I laid the
earth's foundation?
Tell me, if you understand.
5 Who marked off its dimensions?
Surely you know!
Who stretched a measuring line
across it?
6 On what were its footings set,
or who laid its cornerstone—
7 while the morning stars sang together
and all the angels[d] shouted for joy?

8 "Who shut up the sea behind doors
when it burst forth from the womb,
9 when I made the clouds its garment
and wrapped it in thick darkness,
10 when I fixed limits for it
and set its doors and bars in place,
11 when I said, 'This far you may come
and no farther;

[a] 33 Or *announces his coming— / the One zealous against evil* [b] 7 Or *work, / he fills all people with fear by his power* [c] 24 Or *for he does not have regard for any who think they are wise.* [d] 7 Hebrew *the sons of God*

here is where your proud waves
halt'?
12 "Have you ever given orders to the
morning,
or shown the dawn its place,
13 that it might take the earth by the
edges
and shake the wicked out of it?
14 The earth takes shape like clay under
a seal;
its features stand out like those of a
garment.
15 The wicked are denied their light,
and their upraised arm is broken.

16 "Have you journeyed to the springs of
the sea
or walked in the recesses of the
deep?
17 Have the gates of death been shown to
you?
Have you seen the gates of the
deepest darkness?
18 Have you comprehended the vast
expanses of the earth?
Tell me, if you know all this.

19 "What is the way to the abode of light?
And where does darkness reside?
20 Can you take them to their places?
Do you know the paths to their
dwellings?
21 Surely you know, for you were already
born!
You have lived so many years!

22 "Have you entered the storehouses of
the snow
or seen the storehouses of the hail,
23 which I reserve for times of trouble,
for days of war and battle?
24 What is the way to the place where the
lightning is dispersed,
or the place where the east winds
are scattered over the earth?
25 Who cuts a channel for the torrents of
rain,
and a path for the thunderstorm,
26 to water a land where no one lives,
an uninhabited desert,
27 to satisfy a desolate wasteland
and make it sprout with grass?
28 Does the rain have a father?
Who fathers the drops of dew?
29 From whose womb comes the ice?
Who gives birth to the frost from the
heavens
30 when the waters become hard as
stone,
when the surface of the deep is
frozen?

31 "Can you bind the chains[a] of the
Pleiades?
Can you loosen Orion's belt?
32 Can you bring forth the constellations
in their seasons[b]
or lead out the Bear[c] with its cubs?
33 Do you know the laws of the heavens?
Can you set up God's[d] dominion
over the earth?

34 "Can you raise your voice to the
clouds
and cover yourself with a flood of
water?
35 Do you send the lightning bolts on
their way?
Do they report to you, 'Here we are'?
36 Who gives the ibis wisdom[e]
or gives the rooster understanding?[f]
37 Who has the wisdom to count the
clouds?
Who can tip over the water jars of
the heavens
38 when the dust becomes hard
and the clods of earth stick
together?

39 "Do you hunt the prey for the lioness
and satisfy the hunger of the lions
40 when they crouch in their dens
or lie in wait in a thicket?
41 Who provides food for the raven
when its young cry out to God
and wander about for lack of food?

39 "Do you know when the mountain
goats give birth?
Do you watch when the doe bears
her fawn?
2 Do you count the months till they
bear?
Do you know the time they give
birth?
3 They crouch down and bring forth
their young;
their labor pains are ended.
4 Their young thrive and grow strong in
the wilds;
they leave and do not return.

[a] *31* Septuagint; Hebrew *beauty* [b] *32* Or *the morning star in its season* [c] *32* Or *out Leo* [d] *33* Or *their*
[e] *36* That is, wisdom about the flooding of the Nile [f] *36* That is, understanding of when to crow; the meaning of the Hebrew for this verse is uncertain.

5 "Who let the wild donkey go free?
Who untied its ropes?
6 I gave it the wasteland as its home,
the salt flats as its habitat.
7 It laughs at the commotion in the town;
it does not hear a driver's shout.
8 It ranges the hills for its pasture
and searches for any green thing.

9 "Will the wild ox consent to serve you?
Will it stay by your manger at night?
10 Can you hold it to the furrow with a harness?
Will it till the valleys behind you?
11 Will you rely on it for its great strength?
Will you leave your heavy work to it?
12 Can you trust it to haul in your grain
and bring it to your threshing floor?

13 "The wings of the ostrich flap joyfully,
though they cannot compare
with the wings and feathers of the stork.
14 She lays her eggs on the ground
and lets them warm in the sand,
15 unmindful that a foot may crush them,
that some wild animal may trample them.
16 She treats her young harshly, as if they were not hers;
she cares not that her labor was in vain,
17 for God did not endow her with wisdom
or give her a share of good sense.
18 Yet when she spreads her feathers to run,
she laughs at horse and rider.

19 "Do you give the horse its strength
or clothe its neck with a flowing mane?
20 Do you make it leap like a locust,
striking terror with its proud snorting?
21 It paws fiercely, rejoicing in its strength,
and charges into the fray.
22 It laughs at fear, afraid of nothing;
it does not shy away from the sword.
23 The quiver rattles against its side,
along with the flashing spear and lance.
24 In frenzied excitement it eats up the ground;
it cannot stand still when the trumpet sounds.
25 At the blast of the trumpet it snorts, 'Aha!'
It catches the scent of battle from afar,
the shout of commanders and the battle cry.

26 "Does the hawk take flight by your wisdom
and spread its wings toward the south?
27 Does the eagle soar at your command
and build its nest on high?
28 It dwells on a cliff and stays there at night;
a rocky crag is its stronghold.
29 From there it looks for food;
its eyes detect it from afar.
30 Its young ones feast on blood,
and where the slain are, there it is."

40 The LORD said to Job:

2 "Will the one who contends with the Almighty correct him?
Let him who accuses God answer him!"

3 Then Job answered the LORD:

4 "I am unworthy — how can I reply to you?
I put my hand over my mouth.
5 I spoke once, but I have no answer —
twice, but I will say no more."

6 Then the LORD spoke to Job out of the storm:

7 "Brace yourself like a man;
I will question you,
and you shall answer me.

8 "Would you discredit my justice?
Would you condemn me to justify yourself?
9 Do you have an arm like God's,
and can your voice thunder like his?
10 Then adorn yourself with glory and splendor,
and clothe yourself in honor and majesty.
11 Unleash the fury of your wrath,
look at all who are proud and bring them low,
12 look at all who are proud and humble them,
crush the wicked where they stand.

13 Bury them all in the dust together;
shroud their faces in the grave.
14 Then I myself will admit to you
that your own right hand can save
you.

15 "Look at Behemoth,
which I made along with you
and which feeds on grass like an ox.
16 What strength it has in its loins,
what power in the muscles of its
belly!
17 Its tail sways like a cedar;
the sinews of its thighs are close-
knit.
18 Its bones are tubes of bronze,
its limbs like rods of iron.
19 It ranks first among the works of God,
yet its Maker can approach it with
his sword.
20 The hills bring it their produce,
and all the wild animals play
nearby.
21 Under the lotus plants it lies,
hidden among the reeds in the
marsh.
22 The lotuses conceal it in their shadow;
the poplars by the stream surround
it.
23 A raging river does not alarm it;
it is secure, though the Jordan
should surge against its mouth.
24 Can anyone capture it by the eyes,
or trap it and pierce its nose?

41 [a] "Can you pull in Leviathan with a
fishhook
or tie down its tongue with a rope?
2 Can you put a cord through its nose
or pierce its jaw with a hook?
3 Will it keep begging you for mercy?
Will it speak to you with gentle
words?
4 Will it make an agreement with you
for you to take it as your slave for
life?
5 Can you make a pet of it like a bird
or put it on a leash for the young
women in your house?
6 Will traders barter for it?
Will they divide it up among the
merchants?
7 Can you fill its hide with harpoons
or its head with fishing spears?
8 If you lay a hand on it,
you will remember the struggle and
never do it again!
9 Any hope of subduing it is false;
the mere sight of it is overpowering.
10 No one is fierce enough to rouse it.
Who then is able to stand against
me?
11 Who has a claim against me that I
must pay?
Everything under heaven belongs to
me.

12 "I will not fail to speak of Leviathan's
limbs,
its strength and its graceful form.
13 Who can strip off its outer coat?
Who can penetrate its double coat of
armor[b]?
14 Who dares open the doors of its
mouth,
ringed about with fearsome teeth?
15 Its back has[c] rows of shields
tightly sealed together;
16 each is so close to the next
that no air can pass between.
17 They are joined fast to one another;
they cling together and cannot be
parted.
18 Its snorting throws out flashes of light;
its eyes are like the rays of dawn.
19 Flames stream from its mouth;
sparks of fire shoot out.
20 Smoke pours from its nostrils
as from a boiling pot over burning
reeds.
21 Its breath sets coals ablaze,
and flames dart from its mouth.
22 Strength resides in its neck;
dismay goes before it.
23 The folds of its flesh are tightly joined;
they are firm and immovable.
24 Its chest is hard as rock,
hard as a lower millstone.
25 When it rises up, the mighty are
terrified;
they retreat before its thrashing.
26 The sword that reaches it has no effect,
nor does the spear or the dart or the
javelin.
27 Iron it treats like straw
and bronze like rotten wood.
28 Arrows do not make it flee;
slingstones are like chaff to it.
29 A club seems to it but a piece of straw;
it laughs at the rattling of the lance.

[a] In Hebrew texts 41:1-8 is numbered 40:25-32, and 41:9-34 is numbered 41:1-26. [b] *13* Septuagint; Hebrew *double bridle* [c] *15* Or *Its pride is its*

30 Its undersides are jagged potsherds,
leaving a trail in the mud like a
threshing sledge.
31 It makes the depths churn like a
boiling caldron
and stirs up the sea like a pot of
ointment.
32 It leaves a glistening wake behind it;
one would think the deep had white
hair.
33 Nothing on earth is its equal—
a creature without fear.
34 It looks down on all that are haughty;
it is king over all that are proud."

42 Then Job replied to the LORD:

2 "I know that you can do all things;
no purpose of yours can be
thwarted.
3 You asked, 'Who is this that obscures
my plans without knowledge?'
Surely I spoke of things I did not
understand,
things too wonderful for me to
know.
4 "You said, 'Listen now, and I will
speak;
I will question you,
and you shall answer me.'
5 My ears had heard of you
but now my eyes have seen you.
6 Therefore I despise myself
and repent in dust and ashes."

7 After the LORD had said these things
to Job, he said to Eliphaz the Temanite, "I
am angry with you and your two friends,
because you have not spoken the truth
about me, as my servant Job has.
8 So now
take seven bulls and seven rams and go
to my servant Job and sacrifice a burnt offering for yourselves. My servant Job will
pray for you, and I will accept his prayer
and not deal with you according to your
folly. You have not spoken the truth about
me, as my servant Job has."
9 So Eliphaz
the Temanite, Bildad the Shuhite and Zophar the Naamathite did what the LORD
told them; and the LORD accepted Job's
prayer.

10 After Job had prayed for his friends,
the LORD restored his fortunes and gave
him twice as much as he had before.
11 All
his brothers and sisters and everyone
who had known him before came and
ate with him in his house. They comforted and consoled him over all the trouble
the LORD had brought on him, and each
one gave him a piece of silver[a] and a gold
ring.

12 The LORD blessed the latter part of
Job's life more than the former part. He
had fourteen thousand sheep, six thousand camels, a thousand yoke of oxen
and a thousand donkeys.
13 And he also
had seven sons and three daughters.
14 The first daughter he named Jemimah,
the second Keziah and the third Keren-Happuch.
15 Nowhere in all the land
were there found women as beautiful as
Job's daughters, and their father granted them an inheritance along with their
brothers.

16 After this, Job lived a hundred and
forty years; he saw his children and their
children to the fourth generation.
17 And
so Job died, an old man and full of years.

[a] *11* Hebrew *him a kesitah;* a kesitah was a unit of money of unknown weight and value.

PSALMS

The book of Psalms is a collection of song lyrics. Like many songs, they were first written in response to events in the lives of their authors. Later, the whole community used them in worship. When Israel returned from exile in Babylon many of the songs from over the centuries were collectec in the book of Psalms.

The book is structured into five parts marked off by the phrase, *Praise be to the LORD . . . Amen and Amen!* These five "books" remind the reader of the five books of Moses. Like the law, these song lyrics can be read and studied for instruction. Psalm 1 emphasizes such meditation and seems to have been placed first to make this point.

The five books also tell a three-part story of Israel's redemption: monarchy, exile and return. The psalms of King David dominate books one and two. The beginning and ending of book three highlight Israel's exile. The fourth book ends with a plea that God bring the exiled people home. The fifth book declares that God has done just that. Now the reason for the group of praise psalms at the end of the book is apparent: God has been faithful, judging Israel in exile but then bringing the nation home again.

The book of Psalms thus operates at two levels: individually the songs explore a wide variety of honest spiritual responses to God, while the overall collection tells, and celebrates, the work of God in history to save his people.

BOOK I

Psalms 1–41

Psalm 1

1 Blessed is the one
who does not walk in step with the wicked
or stand in the way that sinners take
or sit in the company of mockers,
2 but whose delight is in the law of the LORD,
and who meditates on his law day and night.
3 That person is like a tree planted by streams of water,
which yields its fruit in season
and whose leaf does not wither—
whatever they do prospers.

4 Not so the wicked!
They are like chaff
that the wind blows away.
5 Therefore the wicked will not stand in the judgment,
nor sinners in the assembly of the righteous.

6 For the LORD watches over the way of the righteous,
but the way of the wicked leads to destruction.

Psalm 2

1 Why do the nations conspire[a]
and the peoples plot in vain?
2 The kings of the earth rise up
and the rulers band together
against the LORD and against his anointed, saying,
3 "Let us break their chains
and throw off their shackles."
4 The One enthroned in heaven laughs;
the Lord scoffs at them.
5 He rebukes them in his anger
and terrifies them in his wrath, saying,
6 "I have installed my king
on Zion, my holy mountain."

7 I will proclaim the LORD's decree:

He said to me, "You are my son;
today I have become your father.
8 Ask me,
and I will make the nations your inheritance,
the ends of the earth your possession.
9 You will break them with a rod of iron[b];
you will dash them to pieces like pottery."

10 Therefore, you kings, be wise;
be warned, you rulers of the earth.
11 Serve the LORD with fear

[a] *1* Hebrew; Septuagint *rage* [b] 9 Or *will rule them with an iron scepter* (see Septuagint and Syriac)

and celebrate his rule with
trembling.
12 Kiss his son, or he will be angry
and your way will lead to your
destruction,
for his wrath can flare up in a
moment.
Blessed are all who take refuge in
him.

Psalm 3[a]

A psalm of David. When he fled from his son Absalom.

1 LORD, how many are my foes!
How many rise up against me!
2 Many are saying of me,
"God will not deliver him."[b]

3 But you, LORD, are a shield around me,
my glory, the One who lifts my head
high.
4 I call out to the LORD,
and he answers me from his holy
mountain.

5 I lie down and sleep;
I wake again, because the LORD
sustains me.
6 I will not fear though tens of
thousands
assail me on every side.

7 Arise, LORD!
Deliver me, my God!
Strike all my enemies on the jaw;
break the teeth of the wicked.

8 From the LORD comes deliverance.
May your blessing be on your
people.

Psalm 4[c]

For the director of music. With stringed instruments. A psalm of David.

1 Answer me when I call to you,
my righteous God.
Give me relief from my distress;
have mercy on me and hear my
prayer.

2 How long will you people turn my
glory into shame?
How long will you love delusions
and seek false gods[d]?[e]
3 Know that the LORD has set apart his
faithful servant for himself;
the LORD hears when I call to him.

4 Tremble and[f] do not sin;
when you are on your beds,
search your hearts and be silent.
5 Offer the sacrifices of the righteous
and trust in the LORD.

6 Many, LORD, are asking, "Who will
bring us prosperity?"
Let the light of your face shine on us.
7 Fill my heart with joy
when their grain and new wine
abound.

8 In peace I will lie down and sleep,
for you alone, LORD,
make me dwell in safety.

Psalm 5[g]

For the director of music. For pipes. A psalm of David.

1 Listen to my words, LORD,
consider my lament.
2 Hear my cry for help,
my King and my God,
for to you I pray.

3 In the morning, LORD, you hear my
voice;
in the morning I lay my requests
before you
and wait expectantly.
4 For you are not a God who is pleased
with wickedness;
with you, evil people are not
welcome.
5 The arrogant cannot stand
in your presence.
You hate all who do wrong;
6 you destroy those who tell lies.
The bloodthirsty and deceitful
you, LORD, detest.
7 But I, by your great love,
can come into your house;
in reverence I bow down
toward your holy temple.

8 Lead me, LORD, in your righteousness
because of my enemies—
make your way straight before me.
9 Not a word from their mouth can be
trusted;

[a] In Hebrew texts 3:1-8 is numbered 3:2-9. [b] *2* The Hebrew has *Selah* (a word of uncertain meaning) here and at the end of verses 4 and 8. [c] In Hebrew texts 4:1-8 is numbered 4:2-9. [d] *2* Or *seek lies* [e] *2* The Hebrew has *Selah* (a word of uncertain meaning) here and at the end of verse 4. [f] *4* Or *In your anger* (see Septuagint) [g] In Hebrew texts 5:1-12 is numbered 5:2-13.

their heart is filled with malice.
Their throat is an open grave;
with their tongues they tell lies.
10 Declare them guilty, O God!
Let their intrigues be their downfall.
Banish them for their many sins,
for they have rebelled against you.
11 But let all who take refuge in you be glad;
let them ever sing for joy.
Spread your protection over them,
that those who love your name may rejoice in you.
12 Surely, LORD, you bless the righteous;
you surround them with your favor
as with a shield.

Psalm 6[a]

For the director of music. With stringed instruments. According to sheminith.[b] *A psalm of David.*

1 LORD, do not rebuke me in your anger
or discipline me in your wrath.
2 Have mercy on me, LORD, for I am faint;
heal me, LORD, for my bones are in agony.
3 My soul is in deep anguish.
How long, LORD, how long?

4 Turn, LORD, and deliver me;
save me because of your unfailing love.
5 Among the dead no one proclaims your name.
Who praises you from the grave?

6 I am worn out from my groaning.

All night long I flood my bed with weeping
and drench my couch with tears.
7 My eyes grow weak with sorrow;
they fail because of all my foes.

8 Away from me, all you who do evil,
for the LORD has heard my weeping.
9 The LORD has heard my cry for mercy;
the LORD accepts my prayer.
10 All my enemies will be overwhelmed
with shame and anguish;
they will turn back and suddenly be put to shame.

Psalm 7[c]

A shiggaion[d] *of David, which he sang to the LORD concerning Cush, a Benjamite.*

1 LORD my God, I take refuge in you;
save and deliver me from all who pursue me,
2 or they will tear me apart like a lion
and rip me to pieces with no one to rescue me.

3 LORD my God, if I have done this
and there is guilt on my hands —
4 if I have repaid my ally with evil
or without cause have robbed my foe —
5 then let my enemy pursue and overtake me;
let him trample my life to the ground
and make me sleep in the dust.[e]

6 Arise, LORD, in your anger;
rise up against the rage of my enemies.
Awake, my God; decree justice.
7 Let the assembled peoples gather around you,
while you sit enthroned over them on high.
8 Let the LORD judge the peoples.
Vindicate me, LORD, according to my righteousness,
according to my integrity, O Most High.
9 Bring to an end the violence of the wicked
and make the righteous secure —
you, the righteous God
who probes minds and hearts.

10 My shield[f] is God Most High,
who saves the upright in heart.
11 God is a righteous judge,
a God who displays his wrath every day.
12 If he does not relent,
he[g] will sharpen his sword;
he will bend and string his bow.
13 He has prepared his deadly weapons;
he makes ready his flaming arrows.

14 Whoever is pregnant with evil
conceives trouble and gives birth to disillusionment.
15 Whoever digs a hole and scoops it out

[a] In Hebrew texts 6:1-10 is numbered 6:2-11. [b] Title: Probably a musical term [c] In Hebrew texts 7:1-17 is numbered 7:2-18. [d] Title: Probably a literary or musical term [e] 5 The Hebrew has *Selah* (a word of uncertain meaning) here. [f] *10* Or *sovereign* [g] *12* Or *If anyone does not repent, / God*

falls into the pit they have made.
16 The trouble they cause recoils on
them;
their violence comes down on their
own heads.

17 I will give thanks to the LORD because
of his righteousness;
I will sing the praises of the name of
the LORD Most High.

Psalm 8[a]

For the director of music. According to gittith.[b] *A psalm of David.*

1 LORD, our Lord,
how majestic is your name in all the
earth!

You have set your glory
in the heavens.
2 Through the praise of children and
infants
you have established a stronghold
against your enemies,
to silence the foe and the avenger.
3 When I consider your heavens,
the work of your fingers,
the moon and the stars,
which you have set in place,
4 what is mankind that you are mindful
of them,
human beings that you care for
them?[c]

5 You have made them[d] a little lower
than the angels[e]
and crowned them[d] with glory and
honor.
6 You made them rulers over the works
of your hands;
you put everything under their[f]
feet:
7 all flocks and herds,
and the animals of the wild,
8 the birds in the sky,
and the fish in the sea,
all that swim the paths of the
seas.

9 LORD, our Lord,
how majestic is your name in all the
earth!

Psalm 9[g,h]

For the director of music. To the tune of "The Death of the Son." A psalm of David.

1 I will give thanks to you, LORD, with
all my heart;
I will tell of all your wonderful deeds.
2 I will be glad and rejoice in you;
I will sing the praises of your name,
O Most High.

3 My enemies turn back;
they stumble and perish before you.
4 For you have upheld my right and my
cause,
sitting enthroned as the righteous
judge.
5 You have rebuked the nations and
destroyed the wicked;
you have blotted out their name for
ever and ever.
6 Endless ruin has overtaken my
enemies,
you have uprooted their cities;
even the memory of them has
perished.

7 The LORD reigns forever;
he has established his throne for
judgment.
8 He rules the world in righteousness
and judges the peoples with equity.
9 The LORD is a refuge for the oppressed,
a stronghold in times of trouble.
10 Those who know your name trust in
you,
for you, LORD, have never forsaken
those who seek you.

11 Sing the praises of the LORD,
enthroned in Zion;
proclaim among the nations what
he has done.
12 For he who avenges blood remembers;
he does not ignore the cries of the
afflicted.

13 LORD, see how my enemies persecute
me!
Have mercy and lift me up from the
gates of death,
14 that I may declare your praises
in the gates of Daughter Zion,
and there rejoice in your salvation.

[a] In Hebrew texts 8:1-9 is numbered 8:2-10. [b] Title: Probably a musical term [c] 4 Or *what is a human being that you are mindful of him, / a son of man that you care for him?* [d] 5 Or *him* [e] 5 Or *than God* [f] 6 Or *made him ruler . . . ; / . . . his* [g] Psalms 9 and 10 may originally have been a single acrostic poem in which alternating lines began with the successive letters of the Hebrew alphabet. In the Septuagint they constitute one psalm. [h] In Hebrew texts 9:1-20 is numbered 9:2-21.

15 The nations have fallen into the pit
they have dug;
their feet are caught in the net they
have hidden.
16 The LORD is known by his acts of
justice;
the wicked are ensnared by the work
of their hands.[a]
17 The wicked go down to the realm of
the dead,
all the nations that forget God.
18 But God will never forget the needy;
the hope of the afflicted will never
perish.

19 Arise, LORD, do not let mortals
triumph;
let the nations be judged in your
presence.
20 Strike them with terror, LORD;
let the nations know they are only
mortal.

Psalm 10[b]

1 Why, LORD, do you stand far off?
Why do you hide yourself in times of
trouble?

2 In his arrogance the wicked man
hunts down the weak,
who are caught in the schemes he
devises.
3 He boasts about the cravings of his
heart;
he blesses the greedy and reviles the
LORD.
4 In his pride the wicked man does not
seek him;
in all his thoughts there is no room
for God.
5 His ways are always prosperous;
your laws are rejected by[c] him;
he sneers at all his enemies.
6 He says to himself, "Nothing will ever
shake me."
He swears, "No one will ever do me
harm."

7 His mouth is full of lies and threats;
trouble and evil are under his
tongue.
8 He lies in wait near the villages;
from ambush he murders the
innocent.
His eyes watch in secret for his
victims;
9 like a lion in cover he lies in wait.
He lies in wait to catch the helpless;
he catches the helpless and drags
them off in his net.
10 His victims are crushed, they
collapse;
they fall under his strength.
11 He says to himself, "God will never
notice;
he covers his face and never sees."

12 Arise, LORD! Lift up your hand, O God.
Do not forget the helpless.
13 Why does the wicked man revile God?
Why does he say to himself,
"He won't call me to account"?
14 But you, God, see the trouble of the
afflicted;
you consider their grief and take it
in hand.
The victims commit themselves to
you;
you are the helper of the fatherless.
15 Break the arm of the wicked man;
call the evildoer to account for his
wickedness
that would not otherwise be found
out.

16 The LORD is King for ever and ever;
the nations will perish from his
land.
17 You, LORD, hear the desire of the
afflicted;
you encourage them, and you listen
to their cry,
18 defending the fatherless and the
oppressed,
so that mere earthly mortals
will never again strike terror.

Psalm 11

For the director of music. Of David.

1 In the LORD I take refuge.
How then can you say to me:
"Flee like a bird to your mountain.
2 For look, the wicked bend their bows;
they set their arrows against the
strings
to shoot from the shadows
at the upright in heart.

[a] *16* The Hebrew has *Higgaion* and *Selah* (words of uncertain meaning) here; *Selah* occurs also at the end of verse 20. [b] Psalms 9 and 10 may originally have been a single acrostic poem in which alternating lines began with the successive letters of the Hebrew alphabet. In the Septuagint they constitute one psalm. [c] *5* See Septuagint; Hebrew / *they are haughty, and your laws are far from*

3 When the foundations are being
destroyed,
what can the righteous do?"

4 The LORD is in his holy temple;
the LORD is on his heavenly throne.
He observes everyone on earth;
his eyes examine them.
5 The LORD examines the righteous,
but the wicked, those who love
violence,
he hates with a passion.
6 On the wicked he will rain
fiery coals and burning sulfur;
a scorching wind will be their lot.

7 For the LORD is righteous,
he loves justice;
the upright will see his face.

Psalm 12[a]

For the director of music. According to sheminith.[b] *A psalm of David.*

1 Help, LORD, for no one is faithful
anymore;
those who are loyal have vanished
from the human race.
2 Everyone lies to their neighbor;
they flatter with their lips
but harbor deception in their
hearts.

3 May the LORD silence all flattering lips
and every boastful tongue—
4 those who say,
"By our tongues we will prevail;
our own lips will defend us—who is
lord over us?"

5 "Because the poor are plundered and
the needy groan,
I will now arise," says the LORD.
"I will protect them from those who
malign them."
6 And the words of the LORD are
flawless,
like silver purified in a crucible,
like gold[c] refined seven times.

7 You, LORD, will keep the needy safe
and will protect us forever from the
wicked,
8 who freely strut about
when what is vile is honored by the
human race.

Psalm 13[d]

For the director of music. A psalm of David.

1 How long, LORD? Will you forget me
forever?
How long will you hide your face
from me?
2 How long must I wrestle with my
thoughts
and day after day have sorrow in my
heart?
How long will my enemy triumph
over me?

3 Look on me and answer, LORD my
God.
Give light to my eyes, or I will sleep
in death,
4 and my enemy will say, "I have
overcome him,"
and my foes will rejoice when I fall.

5 But I trust in your unfailing love;
my heart rejoices in your salvation.
6 I will sing the LORD's praise,
for he has been good to me.

Psalm 14

For the director of music. Of David.

1 The fool[e] says in his heart,
"There is no God."
They are corrupt, their deeds are vile;
there is no one who does good.

2 The LORD looks down from heaven
on all mankind
to see if there are any who understand,
any who seek God.
3 All have turned away, all have become
corrupt;
there is no one who does good,
not even one.

4 Do all these evildoers know nothing?

They devour my people as though
eating bread;
they never call on the LORD.
5 But there they are, overwhelmed with
dread,
for God is present in the company of
the righteous.
6 You evildoers frustrate the plans of the
poor,
but the LORD is their refuge.

[a] In Hebrew texts 12:1-8 is numbered 12:2-9. [b] Title: Probably a musical term [c] *6* Probable reading of the original Hebrew text; Masoretic Text *earth* [d] In Hebrew texts 13:1-6 is numbered 13:2-6. [e] *1* The Hebrew words rendered *fool* in Psalms denote one who is morally deficient.

7 Oh, that salvation for Israel would
come out of Zion!
When the LORD restores his people,
let Jacob rejoice and Israel be glad!

Psalm 15

A psalm of David.

1 LORD, who may dwell in your sacred
tent?
Who may live on your holy
mountain?
2 The one whose walk is blameless,
who does what is righteous,
who speaks the truth from their
heart;
3 whose tongue utters no slander,
who does no wrong to a neighbor,
and casts no slur on others;
4 who despises a vile person
but honors those who fear the LORD;
who keeps an oath even when it
hurts,
and does not change their mind;
5 who lends money to the poor without
interest;
who does not accept a bribe against
the innocent.

Whoever does these things
will never be shaken.

Psalm 16

A miktam[a] *of David.*

1 Keep me safe, my God,
for in you I take refuge.
2 I say to the LORD, "You are my Lord;
apart from you I have no good
thing."
3 I say of the holy people who are in the
land,
"They are the noble ones in whom is
all my delight."
4 Those who run after other gods will
suffer more and more.
I will not pour out libations of blood
to such gods
or take up their names on my lips.
5 LORD, you alone are my portion and
my cup;
you make my lot secure.
6 The boundary lines have fallen for me
in pleasant places;
surely I have a delightful
inheritance.
7 I will praise the LORD, who counsels
me;
even at night my heart instructs me.
8 I keep my eyes always on the LORD.
With him at my right hand, I will not
be shaken.
9 Therefore my heart is glad and my
tongue rejoices;
my body also will rest secure,
10 because you will not abandon me to
the realm of the dead,
nor will you let your faithful[b] one
see decay.
11 You make known to me the path of
life;
you will fill me with joy in your
presence,
with eternal pleasures at your right
hand.

Psalm 17

A prayer of David.

1 Hear me, LORD, my plea is just;
listen to my cry.
Hear my prayer—
it does not rise from deceitful lips.
2 Let my vindication come from you;
may your eyes see what is right.
3 Though you probe my heart,
though you examine me at night
and test me,
you will find that I have planned no
evil;
my mouth has not transgressed.
4 Though people tried to bribe me,
I have kept myself from the ways of
the violent
through what your lips have
commanded.
5 My steps have held to your paths;
my feet have not stumbled.
6 I call on you, my God, for you will
answer me;
turn your ear to me and hear my
prayer.
7 Show me the wonders of your great
love,
you who save by your right hand
those who take refuge in you from
their foes.
8 Keep me as the apple of your eye;

[a] Title: Probably a literary or musical term [b] *10* Or *holy*

hide me in the shadow of your wings
9 from the wicked who are out to
destroy me,
from my mortal enemies who
surround me.

10 They close up their callous hearts,
and their mouths speak with
arrogance.
11 They have tracked me down, they now
surround me,
with eyes alert, to throw me to the
ground.
12 They are like a lion hungry for prey,
like a fierce lion crouching in cover.

13 Rise up, LORD, confront them, bring
them down;
with your sword rescue me from the
wicked.
14 By your hand save me from such
people, LORD,
from those of this world whose
reward is in this life.
May what you have stored up for the
wicked fill their bellies;
may their children gorge themselves
on it,
and may there be leftovers for their
little ones.

15 As for me, I will be vindicated and will
see your face;
when I awake, I will be satisfied
with seeing your likeness.

Psalm 18[a]

For the director of music. Of David the servant of the LORD. He sang to the LORD the words of this song when the LORD delivered him from the hand of all his enemies and from the hand of Saul. He said:

1 I love you, LORD, my strength.

2 The LORD is my rock, my fortress and
my deliverer;
my God is my rock, in whom I take
refuge,
my shield[b] and the horn[c] of my
salvation, my stronghold.

3 I called to the LORD, who is worthy of
praise,
and I have been saved from my
enemies.
4 The cords of death entangled me;
the torrents of destruction
overwhelmed me.
5 The cords of the grave coiled around
me;
the snares of death confronted me.

6 In my distress I called to the LORD;
I cried to my God for help.
From his temple he heard my voice;
my cry came before him, into his
ears.
7 The earth trembled and quaked,
and the foundations of the
mountains shook;
they trembled because he was
angry.
8 Smoke rose from his nostrils;
consuming fire came from his
mouth,
burning coals blazed out of it.
9 He parted the heavens and came
down;
dark clouds were under his feet.
10 He mounted the cherubim and flew;
he soared on the wings of the
wind.
11 He made darkness his covering, his
canopy around him —
the dark rain clouds of the sky.
12 Out of the brightness of his presence
clouds advanced,
with hailstones and bolts of
lightning.
13 The LORD thundered from heaven;
the voice of the Most High
resounded.[d]
14 He shot his arrows and scattered the
enemy,
with great bolts of lightning he
routed them.
15 The valleys of the sea were exposed
and the foundations of the earth
laid bare
at your rebuke, LORD,
at the blast of breath from your
nostrils.

16 He reached down from on high and
took hold of me;
he drew me out of deep waters.
17 He rescued me from my powerful
enemy,
from my foes, who were too strong
for me.

[a] In Hebrew texts 18:1-50 is numbered 18:2-51. [b] *2* Or *sovereign* [c] *2* *Horn* here symbolizes strength.
[d] *13* Some Hebrew manuscripts and Septuagint (see also 2 Samuel 22:14); most Hebrew manuscripts *resounded, / amid hailstones and bolts of lightning*

18 They confronted me in the day of my
disaster,
but the LORD was my support.
19 He brought me out into a spacious
place;
he rescued me because he delighted
in me.

20 The LORD has dealt with me according
to my righteousness;
according to the cleanness of my
hands he has rewarded me.
21 For I have kept the ways of the LORD;
I am not guilty of turning from my
God.
22 All his laws are before me;
I have not turned away from his
decrees.
23 I have been blameless before him
and have kept myself from sin.
24 The LORD has rewarded me according
to my righteousness,
according to the cleanness of my
hands in his sight.

25 To the faithful you show yourself
faithful,
to the blameless you show yourself
blameless,
26 to the pure you show yourself pure,
but to the devious you show yourself
shrewd.
27 You save the humble
but bring low those whose eyes are
haughty.
28 You, LORD, keep my lamp burning;
my God turns my darkness into
light.
29 With your help I can advance against a
troop[a];
with my God I can scale a wall.

30 As for God, his way is perfect:
The LORD's word is flawless;
he shields all who take refuge in
him.
31 For who is God besides the LORD?
And who is the Rock except our
God?
32 It is God who arms me with s
trength
and keeps my way secure.
33 He makes my feet like the feet of a
deer;
he causes me to stand on the
heights.
34 He trains my hands for battle;
my arms can bend a bow of bronze.
35 You make your saving help my shield,
and your right hand sustains me;
your help has made me great.
36 You provide a broad path for my feet,
so that my ankles do not give way.

37 I pursued my enemies and overtook
them;
I did not turn back till they were
destroyed.
38 I crushed them so that they could not
rise;
they fell beneath my feet.
39 You armed me with strength for
battle;
you humbled my adversaries before
me.
40 You made my enemies turn their
backs in flight,
and I destroyed my foes.
41 They cried for help, but there was no
one to save them—
to the LORD, but he did not answer.
42 I beat them as fine as windblown dust;
I trampled them[b] like mud in the
streets.
43 You have delivered me from the
attacks of the people;
you have made me the head of
nations.
People I did not know now serve me,
44 foreigners cower before me;
as soon as they hear of me, they
obey me.
45 They all lose heart;
they come trembling from their
strongholds.

46 The LORD lives! Praise be to my Rock!
Exalted be God my Savior!
47 He is the God who avenges me,
who subdues nations under me,
48 who saves me from my enemies.
You exalted me above my foes;
from a violent man you rescued me.
49 Therefore I will praise you, LORD,
among the nations;
I will sing the praises of your name.

50 He gives his king great victories;
he shows unfailing love to his
anointed,
to David and to his descendants
forever.

[a] 29 Or *can run through a barricade* [b] 42 Many Hebrew manuscripts, Septuagint, Syriac and Targum (see also 2 Samuel 22:43); Masoretic Text *I poured them out*

Psalm 19[a]

For the director of music. A psalm of David.

1 The heavens declare the glory of God;
the skies proclaim the work of his hands.
2 Day after day they pour forth speech;
night after night they reveal knowledge.
3 They have no speech, they use no words;
no sound is heard from them.
4 Yet their voice[b] goes out into all the earth,
their words to the ends of the world.
In the heavens God has pitched a tent for the sun.
5 It is like a bridegroom coming out of his chamber,
like a champion rejoicing to run his course.
6 It rises at one end of the heavens
and makes its circuit to the other;
nothing is deprived of its warmth.

7 The law of the LORD is perfect,
refreshing the soul.
The statutes of the LORD are trustworthy,
making wise the simple.
8 The precepts of the LORD are right,
giving joy to the heart.
The commands of the LORD are radiant,
giving light to the eyes.
9 The fear of the LORD is pure,
enduring forever.
The decrees of the LORD are firm,
and all of them are righteous.

10 They are more precious than gold,
than much pure gold;
they are sweeter than honey,
than honey from the honeycomb.
11 By them your servant is warned;
in keeping them there is great reward.
12 But who can discern their own errors?
Forgive my hidden faults.
13 Keep your servant also from willful sins;
may they not rule over me.
Then I will be blameless,
innocent of great transgression.

14 May these words of my mouth and this meditation of my heart
be pleasing in your sight,
LORD, my Rock and my Redeemer.

Psalm 20[c]

For the director of music. A psalm of David.

1 May the LORD answer you when you are in distress;
may the name of the God of Jacob protect you.
2 May he send you help from the sanctuary
and grant you support from Zion.
3 May he remember all your sacrifices
and accept your burnt offerings.[d]
4 May he give you the desire of your heart
and make all your plans succeed.
5 May we shout for joy over your victory
and lift up our banners in the name of our God.

May the LORD grant all your requests.

6 Now this I know:
The LORD gives victory to his anointed.
He answers him from his heavenly sanctuary
with the victorious power of his right hand.
7 Some trust in chariots and some in horses,
but we trust in the name of the LORD our God.
8 They are brought to their knees and fall,
but we rise up and stand firm.
9 LORD, give victory to the king!
Answer us when we call!

Psalm 21[e]

For the director of music. A psalm of David.

1 The king rejoices in your strength, LORD.
How great is his joy in the victories you give!
2 You have granted him his heart's desire
and have not withheld the request of his lips.[d]

[a] In Hebrew texts 19:1-14 is numbered 19:2-15. [b] *4* Septuagint, Jerome and Syriac; Hebrew *measuring line*
[c] In Hebrew texts 20:1-9 is numbered 20:2-10. [d] *3,2* The Hebrew has *Selah* (a word of uncertain meaning) here. [e] In Hebrew texts 21:1-13 is numbered 21:2-14.

3 You came to greet him with rich
blessings
and placed a crown of pure gold on
his head.
4 He asked you for life, and you gave it to
him —
length of days, for ever and ever.
5 Through the victories you gave, his
glory is great;
you have bestowed on him splendor
and majesty.
6 Surely you have granted him
unending blessings
and made him glad with the joy of
your presence.
7 For the king trusts in the LORD;
through the unfailing love of the
Most High
he will not be shaken.

8 Your hand will lay hold on all your
enemies;
your right hand will seize your
foes.
9 When you appear for battle,
you will burn them up as in a
blazing furnace.
The LORD will swallow them up in his
wrath,
and his fire will consume them.
10 You will destroy their descendants
from the earth,
their posterity from mankind.
11 Though they plot evil against you
and devise wicked schemes, they
cannot succeed.
12 You will make them turn their backs
when you aim at them with drawn
bow.

13 Be exalted in your strength, LORD;
we will sing and praise your might.

Psalm 22[a]

For the director of music. To the tune of "The Doe of the Morning." A psalm of David.

1 My God, my God, why have you
forsaken me?
Why are you so far from saving me,
so far from my cries of anguish?
2 My God, I cry out by day, but you do
not answer,
by night, but I find no rest.[b]
3 Yet you are enthroned as the Holy
One;
you are the one Israel praises.[c]
4 In you our ancestors put their trust;
they trusted and you delivered
them.
5 To you they cried out and were saved;
in you they trusted and were not put
to shame.

6 But I am a worm and not a man,
scorned by everyone, despised by
the people.
7 All who see me mock me;
they hurl insults, shaking their
heads.
8 "He trusts in the LORD," they say,
"let the LORD rescue him.
Let him deliver him,
since he delights in him."

9 Yet you brought me out of the womb;
you made me trust in you, even at
my mother's breast.
10 From birth I was cast on you;
from my mother's womb you have
been my God.

11 Do not be far from me,
for trouble is near
and there is no one to help.

12 Many bulls surround me;
strong bulls of Bashan encircle me.
13 Roaring lions that tear their prey
open their mouths wide against me.
14 I am poured out like water,
and all my bones are out of joint.
My heart has turned to wax;
it has melted within me.
15 My mouth[d] is dried up like a potsherd,
and my tongue sticks to the roof of
my mouth;
you lay me in the dust of death.

16 Dogs surround me,
a pack of villains encircles me;
they pierce[e] my hands and my feet.
17 All my bones are on display;
people stare and gloat over me.
18 They divide my clothes among them
and cast lots for my garment.

19 But you, LORD, do not be far from me.
You are my strength; come quickly
to help me.

[a] In Hebrew texts 22:1-31 is numbered 22:2-32. [b] *2* Or *night, and am not silent* [c] *3* Or *Yet you are holy, / enthroned on the praises of Israel* [d] *15* Probable reading of the original Hebrew text; Masoretic Text *strength* [e] *16* Dead Sea Scrolls and some manuscripts of the Masoretic Text, Septuagint and Syriac; most manuscripts of the Masoretic Text *me, / like a lion*

20 Deliver me from the sword,
my precious life from the power of the dogs.
21 Rescue me from the mouth of the lions;
save me from the horns of the wild oxen.

22 I will declare your name to my people;
in the assembly I will praise you.
23 You who fear the LORD, praise him!
All you descendants of Jacob, honor him!
Revere him, all you descendants of Israel!
24 For he has not despised or scorned
the suffering of the afflicted one;
he has not hidden his face from him
but has listened to his cry for help.

25 From you comes the theme of my praise in the great assembly;
before those who fear you[a] I will fulfill my vows.
26 The poor will eat and be satisfied;
those who seek the LORD will praise him—
may your hearts live forever!

27 All the ends of the earth
will remember and turn to the LORD,
and all the families of the nations
will bow down before him,
28 for dominion belongs to the LORD
and he rules over the nations.

29 All the rich of the earth will feast and worship;
all who go down to the dust will kneel before him—
those who cannot keep themselves alive.
30 Posterity will serve him;
future generations will be told about the Lord.
31 They will proclaim his righteousness,
declaring to a people yet unborn:
He has done it!

Psalm 23

A psalm of David.

1 The LORD is my shepherd, I lack nothing.
2 He makes me lie down in green pastures,
he leads me beside quiet waters,
3 he refreshes my soul.
He guides me along the right paths
for his name's sake.
4 Even though I walk
through the darkest valley,[b]
I will fear no evil,
for you are with me;
your rod and your staff,
they comfort me.

5 You prepare a table before me
in the presence of my enemies.
You anoint my head with oil;
my cup overflows.
6 Surely your goodness and love will follow me
all the days of my life,
and I will dwell in the house of the LORD
forever.

Psalm 24

Of David. A psalm.

1 The earth is the LORD's, and everything in it,
the world, and all who live in it;
2 for he founded it on the seas
and established it on the waters.

3 Who may ascend the mountain of the LORD?
Who may stand in his holy place?
4 The one who has clean hands and a pure heart,
who does not trust in an idol
or swear by a false god.[c]

5 They will receive blessing from the LORD
and vindication from God their Savior.
6 Such is the generation of those who seek him,
who seek your face, God of Jacob.[d,e]

7 Lift up your heads, you gates;
be lifted up, you ancient doors,
that the King of glory may come in.
8 Who is this King of glory?
The LORD strong and mighty,
the LORD mighty in battle.
9 Lift up your heads, you gates;
lift them up, you ancient doors,
that the King of glory may come in.

[a] 25 Hebrew *him* [b] 4 Or *the valley of the shadow of death* [c] 4 Or *swear falsely* [d] 6 Two Hebrew manuscripts and Syriac (see also Septuagint); most Hebrew manuscripts *face, Jacob* [e] 6 The Hebrew has *Selah* (a word of uncertain meaning) here and at the end of verse 10.

10 Who is he, this King of glory?
The LORD Almighty—
he is the King of glory.

Psalm 25[a]

Of David.

1 In you, LORD my God,
I put my trust.

2 I trust in you;
do not let me be put to shame,
nor let my enemies triumph over
me.
3 No one who hopes in you
will ever be put to shame,
but shame will come on those
who are treacherous without cause.

4 Show me your ways, LORD,
teach me your paths.
5 Guide me in your truth and teach me,
for you are God my Savior,
and my hope is in you all day long.
6 Remember, LORD, your great mercy
and love,
for they are from of old.
7 Do not remember the sins of my youth
and my rebellious ways;
according to your love remember me,
for you, LORD, are good.

8 Good and upright is the LORD;
therefore he instructs sinners in his
ways.
9 He guides the humble in what is right
and teaches them his way.
10 All the ways of the LORD are loving
and faithful
toward those who keep the
demands of his covenant.
11 For the sake of your name, LORD,
forgive my iniquity, though it is
great.

12 Who, then, are those who fear the
LORD?
He will instruct them in the ways
they should choose.[b]
13 They will spend their days in
prosperity,
and their descendants will inherit
the land.
14 The LORD confides in those who fear
him;
he makes his covenant known to
them.
15 My eyes are ever on the LORD,
for only he will release my feet from
the snare.

16 Turn to me and be gracious to me,
for I am lonely and afflicted.
17 Relieve the troubles of my heart
and free me from my anguish.
18 Look on my affliction and my distress
and take away all my sins.
19 See how numerous are my enemies
and how fiercely they hate me!

20 Guard my life and rescue me;
do not let me be put to shame,
for I take refuge in you.
21 May integrity and uprightness protect
me,
because my hope, LORD,[c] is in you.

22 Deliver Israel, O God,
from all their troubles!

Psalm 26

Of David.

1 Vindicate me, LORD,
for I have led a blameless life;
I have trusted in the LORD
and have not faltered.
2 Test me, LORD, and try me,
examine my heart and my mind;
3 for I have always been mindful of your
unfailing love
and have lived in reliance on your
faithfulness.

4 I do not sit with the deceitful,
nor do I associate with hypocrites.
5 I abhor the assembly of evildoers
and refuse to sit with the wicked.
6 I wash my hands in innocence,
and go about your altar, LORD,
7 proclaiming aloud your praise
and telling of all your wonderful
deeds.

8 LORD, I love the house where you live,
the place where your glory dwells.
9 Do not take away my soul along with
sinners,
my life with those who are
bloodthirsty,
10 in whose hands are wicked schemes,
whose right hands are full of bribes.
11 I lead a blameless life;
deliver me and be merciful to me.

[a] This psalm is an acrostic poem, the verses of which begin with the successive letters of the Hebrew alphabet.
[b] *12* Or *ways he chooses* [c] *21* Septuagint; Hebrew does not have *LORD*.

12 My feet stand on level ground;
in the great congregation I will praise the LORD.

Psalm 27

Of David.

1 The LORD is my light and my salvation—
whom shall I fear?
The LORD is the stronghold of my life—
of whom shall I be afraid?

2 When the wicked advance against me
to devour[a] me,
it is my enemies and my foes
who will stumble and fall.
3 Though an army besiege me,
my heart will not fear;
though war break out against me,
even then I will be confident.

4 One thing I ask from the LORD,
this only do I seek:
that I may dwell in the house of the LORD
all the days of my life,
to gaze on the beauty of the LORD
and to seek him in his temple.
5 For in the day of trouble
he will keep me safe in his dwelling;
he will hide me in the shelter of his sacred tent
and set me high upon a rock.

6 Then my head will be exalted
above the enemies who surround me;
at his sacred tent I will sacrifice with shouts of joy;
I will sing and make music to the LORD.

7 Hear my voice when I call, LORD;
be merciful to me and answer me.
8 My heart says of you, "Seek his face!"
Your face, LORD, I will seek.
9 Do not hide your face from me,
do not turn your servant away in anger;
you have been my helper.
Do not reject me or forsake me,
God my Savior.
10 Though my father and mother forsake me,
the LORD will receive me.
11 Teach me your way, LORD;
lead me in a straight path
because of my oppressors.
12 Do not turn me over to the desire of my foes,
for false witnesses rise up against me,
spouting malicious accusations.

13 I remain confident of this:
I will see the goodness of the LORD
in the land of the living.
14 Wait for the LORD;
be strong and take heart
and wait for the LORD.

Psalm 28

Of David.

1 To you, LORD, I call;
you are my Rock,
do not turn a deaf ear to me.
For if you remain silent,
I will be like those who go down to the pit.
2 Hear my cry for mercy
as I call to you for help,
as I lift up my hands
toward your Most Holy Place.

3 Do not drag me away with the wicked,
with those who do evil,
who speak cordially with their neighbors
but harbor malice in their hearts.
4 Repay them for their deeds
and for their evil work;
repay them for what their hands have done
and bring back on them what they deserve.

5 Because they have no regard for the deeds of the LORD
and what his hands have done,
he will tear them down
and never build them up again.

6 Praise be to the LORD,
for he has heard my cry for mercy.
7 The LORD is my strength and my shield;
my heart trusts in him, and he helps me.
My heart leaps for joy,
and with my song I praise him.

[a] 2 Or *slander*

8 The LORD is the strength of his people,
a fortress of salvation for his
anointed one.
9 Save your people and bless your
inheritance;
be their shepherd and carry them
forever.

Psalm 29

A psalm of David.

1 Ascribe to the LORD, you heavenly
beings,
ascribe to the LORD glory and
strength.
2 Ascribe to the LORD the glory due his
name;
worship the LORD in the splendor of
his[a] holiness.

3 The voice of the LORD is over the waters;
the God of glory thunders,
the LORD thunders over the mighty
waters.
4 The voice of the LORD is powerful;
the voice of the LORD is majestic.
5 The voice of the LORD breaks the
cedars;
the LORD breaks in pieces the cedars
of Lebanon.
6 He makes Lebanon leap like a calf,
Sirion[b] like a young wild ox.
7 The voice of the LORD strikes
with flashes of lightning.
8 The voice of the LORD shakes the
desert;
the LORD shakes the Desert of
Kadesh.
9 The voice of the LORD twists the oaks[c]
and strips the forests bare.
And in his temple all cry, "Glory!"

10 The LORD sits enthroned over the flood;
the LORD is enthroned as King
forever.
11 The LORD gives strength to his people;
the LORD blesses his people with
peace.

Psalm 30[d]

A psalm. A song. For the dedication of the temple.[e] Of David.

1 I will exalt you, LORD,
for you lifted me out of the depths
and did not let my enemies gloat
over me.
2 LORD my God, I called to you for help,
and you healed me.
3 You, LORD, brought me up from the
realm of the dead;
you spared me from going down to
the pit.

4 Sing the praises of the LORD, you his
faithful people;
praise his holy name.
5 For his anger lasts only a moment,
but his favor lasts a lifetime;
weeping may stay for the night,
but rejoicing comes in the
morning.

6 When I felt secure, I said,
"I will never be shaken."
7 LORD, when you favored me,
you made my royal mountain[f] stand
firm;
but when you hid your face,
I was dismayed.

8 To you, LORD, I called;
to the Lord I cried for mercy:
9 "What is gained if I am silenced,
if I go down to the pit?
Will the dust praise you?
Will it proclaim your faithfulness?
10 Hear, LORD, and be merciful to me;
LORD, be my help."

11 You turned my wailing into dancing;
you removed my sackcloth and
clothed me with joy,
12 that my heart may sing your praises
and not be silent.
LORD my God, I will praise you
forever.

Psalm 31[g]

For the director of music. A psalm of David.

1 In you, LORD, I have taken refuge;
let me never be put to shame;
deliver me in your righteousness.
2 Turn your ear to me,
come quickly to my rescue;
be my rock of refuge,
a strong fortress to save me.
3 Since you are my rock and my fortress,
for the sake of your name lead and
guide me.

[a] 2 Or *LORD with the splendor of* [b] 6 That is, Mount Hermon [c] 9 Or *LORD makes the deer give birth* [d] In Hebrew texts 30:1-12 is numbered 30:2-13. [e] Title: Or *palace* [f] 7 That is, Mount Zion [g] In Hebrew texts 31:1-24 is numbered 31:2-25.

4 Keep me free from the trap that is set
for me,
for you are my refuge.
5 Into your hands I commit my spirit;
deliver me, LORD, my faithful God.

6 I hate those who cling to worthless
idols;
as for me, I trust in the LORD.
7 I will be glad and rejoice in your love,
for you saw my affliction
and knew the anguish of my soul.
8 You have not given me into the hands
of the enemy
but have set my feet in a spacious
place.

9 Be merciful to me, LORD, for I am in
distress;
my eyes grow weak with sorrow,
my soul and body with grief.
10 My life is consumed by anguish
and my years by groaning;
my strength fails because of my
affliction,[a]
and my bones grow weak.
11 Because of all my enemies,
I am the utter contempt of my
neighbors
and an object of dread to my closest
friends—
those who see me on the street flee
from me.
12 I am forgotten as though I were dead;
I have become like broken pottery.
13 For I hear many whispering,
"Terror on every side!"
They conspire against me
and plot to take my life.

14 But I trust in you, LORD;
I say, "You are my God."
15 My times are in your hands;
deliver me from the hands of my
enemies,
from those who pursue me.
16 Let your face shine on your servant;
save me in your unfailing love.
17 Let me not be put to shame, LORD,
for I have cried out to you;
but let the wicked be put to shame
and be silent in the realm of the dead.
18 Let their lying lips be silenced,
for with pride and contempt
they speak arrogantly against the
righteous.

19 How abundant are the good things
that you have stored up for those
who fear you,
that you bestow in the sight of all,
on those who take refuge in you.
20 In the shelter of your presence you
hide them
from all human intrigues;
you keep them safe in your dwelling
from accusing tongues.

21 Praise be to the LORD,
for he showed me the wonders of his
love
when I was in a city under siege.
22 In my alarm I said,
"I am cut off from your sight!"
Yet you heard my cry for mercy
when I called to you for help.

23 Love the LORD, all his faithful people!
The LORD preserves those who are
true to him,
but the proud he pays back in full.
24 Be strong and take heart,
all you who hope in the LORD.

Psalm 32

Of David. A maskil.[b]

1 Blessed is the one
whose transgressions are forgiven,
whose sins are covered.
2 Blessed is the one
whose sin the LORD does not count
against them
and in whose spirit is no deceit.

3 When I kept silent,
my bones wasted away
through my groaning all day long.
4 For day and night
your hand was heavy on me;
my strength was sapped
as in the heat of summer.[c]

5 Then I acknowledged my sin to you
and did not cover up my iniquity.
I said, "I will confess
my transgressions to the LORD."
And you forgave
the guilt of my sin.

6 Therefore let all the faithful pray to
you
while you may be found;
surely the rising of the mighty waters

[a] *10* Or *guilt* [b] Title: Probably a literary or musical term [c] *4* The Hebrew has *Selah* (a word of uncertain meaning) here and at the end of verses 5 and 7.

will not reach them.
7 You are my hiding place;
you will protect me from trouble
and surround me with songs of
deliverance.

8 I will instruct you and teach you in the
way you should go;
I will counsel you with my loving
eye on you.
9 Do not be like the horse or the mule,
which have no understanding
but must be controlled by bit and
bridle
or they will not come to you.
10 Many are the woes of the wicked,
but the LORD's unfailing love
surrounds the one who trusts in
him.

11 Rejoice in the LORD and be glad, you
righteous;
sing, all you who are upright in
heart!

Psalm 33

1 Sing joyfully to the LORD, you
righteous;
it is fitting for the upright to praise
him.
2 Praise the LORD with the harp;
make music to him on the ten-
stringed lyre.
3 Sing to him a new song;
play skillfully, and shout for joy.

4 For the word of the LORD is right and
true;
he is faithful in all he does.
5 The LORD loves righteousness and
justice;
the earth is full of his unfailing
love.

6 By the word of the LORD the heavens
were made,
their starry host by the breath of his
mouth.
7 He gathers the waters of the sea into
jars[a];
he puts the deep into storehouses.
8 Let all the earth fear the LORD;
let all the people of the world revere
him.
9 For he spoke, and it came to be;
he commanded, and it stood firm.
10 The LORD foils the plans of the
nations;
he thwarts the purposes of the
peoples.
11 But the plans of the LORD stand firm
forever,
the purposes of his heart through all
generations.

12 Blessed is the nation whose God is the
LORD,
the people he chose for his
inheritance.
13 From heaven the LORD looks down
and sees all mankind;
14 from his dwelling place he watches
all who live on earth—
15 he who forms the hearts of all,
who considers everything they do.

16 No king is saved by the size of his
army;
no warrior escapes by his great
strength.
17 A horse is a vain hope for deliverance;
despite all its great strength it
cannot save.
18 But the eyes of the LORD are on those
who fear him,
on those whose hope is in his
unfailing love,
19 to deliver them from death
and keep them alive in famine.

20 We wait in hope for the LORD;
he is our help and our shield.
21 In him our hearts rejoice,
for we trust in his holy name.
22 May your unfailing love be with us,
LORD,
even as we put our hope in you.

Psalm 34[b,c]

Of David. When he pretended to be insane before Abimelek, who drove him away, and he left.

1 I will extol the LORD at all times;
his praise will always be on my lips.
2 I will glory in the LORD;
let the afflicted hear and rejoice.
3 Glorify the LORD with me;
let us exalt his name together.

4 I sought the LORD, and he answered
me;
he delivered me from all my fears.

[a] 7 Or *sea as into a heap* [b] This psalm is an acrostic poem, the verses of which begin with the successive letters of the Hebrew alphabet. [c] In Hebrew texts 34:1-22 is numbered 34:2-23.

5 Those who look to him are radiant;
their faces are never covered with shame.
6 This poor man called, and the LORD heard him;
he saved him out of all his troubles.
7 The angel of the LORD encamps around those who fear him,
and he delivers them.

8 Taste and see that the LORD is good;
blessed is the one who takes refuge in him.
9 Fear the LORD, you his holy people,
for those who fear him lack nothing.
10 The lions may grow weak and hungry,
but those who seek the LORD lack no good thing.
11 Come, my children, listen to me;
I will teach you the fear of the LORD.
12 Whoever of you loves life
and desires to see many good days,
13 keep your tongue from evil
and your lips from telling lies.
14 Turn from evil and do good;
seek peace and pursue it.

15 The eyes of the LORD are on the righteous,
and his ears are attentive to their cry;
16 but the face of the LORD is against those who do evil,
to blot out their name from the earth.

17 The righteous cry out, and the LORD hears them;
he delivers them from all their troubles.
18 The LORD is close to the brokenhearted
and saves those who are crushed in spirit.

19 The righteous person may have many troubles,
but the LORD delivers him from them all;
20 he protects all his bones,
not one of them will be broken.

21 Evil will slay the wicked;
the foes of the righteous will be condemned.
22 The LORD will rescue his servants;
no one who takes refuge in him will be condemned.

Psalm 35

Of David.

1 Contend, LORD, with those who contend with me;
fight against those who fight against me.
2 Take up shield and armor;
arise and come to my aid.
3 Brandish spear and javelin[a]
against those who pursue me.
Say to me,
"I am your salvation."

4 May those who seek my life
be disgraced and put to shame;
may those who plot my ruin
be turned back in dismay.
5 May they be like chaff before the wind,
with the angel of the LORD driving them away;
6 may their path be dark and slippery,
with the angel of the LORD pursuing them.

7 Since they hid their net for me without cause
and without cause dug a pit for me,
8 may ruin overtake them by surprise—
may the net they hid entangle them,
may they fall into the pit, to their ruin.
9 Then my soul will rejoice in the LORD
and delight in his salvation.
10 My whole being will exclaim,
"Who is like you, LORD?
You rescue the poor from those too strong for them,
the poor and needy from those who rob them."
11 Ruthless witnesses come forward;
they question me on things I know nothing about.
12 They repay me evil for good
and leave me like one bereaved.
13 Yet when they were ill, I put on sackcloth
and humbled myself with fasting.
When my prayers returned to me unanswered,
14 I went about mourning
as though for my friend or brother.
I bowed my head in grief
as though weeping for my mother.
15 But when I stumbled, they gathered in glee;

[a] 3 Or *and block the way*

assailants gathered against me
without my knowledge.
They slandered me without
ceasing.
16 Like the ungodly they maliciously
mocked;[a]
they gnashed their teeth at me.

17 How long, Lord, will you look on?
Rescue me from their ravages,
my precious life from these lions.
18 I will give you thanks in the great
assembly;
among the throngs I will praise
you.
19 Do not let those gloat over me
who are my enemies without
cause;
do not let those who hate me without
reason
maliciously wink the eye.
20 They do not speak peaceably,
but devise false accusations
against those who live quietly in the
land.
21 They sneer at me and say, "Aha! Aha!
With our own eyes we have seen it."
22 LORD, you have seen this; do not be
silent.
Do not be far from me, Lord.
23 Awake, and rise to my defense!
Contend for me, my God and Lord.
24 Vindicate me in your righteousness,
LORD my God;
do not let them gloat over me.
25 Do not let them think, "Aha, just what
we wanted!"
or say, "We have swallowed him up."

26 May all who gloat over my distress
be put to shame and confusion;
may all who exalt themselves over me
be clothed with shame and
disgrace.
27 May those who delight in my
vindication
shout for joy and gladness;
may they always say, "The LORD be
exalted,
who delights in the well-being of his
servant."
28 My tongue will proclaim your
righteousness,
your praises all day long.

Psalm 36[b]

For the director of music. Of David the servant of the LORD.

1 I have a message from God in my heart
concerning the sinfulness of the
wicked:[c]
There is no fear of God
before their eyes.

2 In their own eyes they flatter
themselves
too much to detect or hate their sin.
3 The words of their mouths are wicked
and deceitful;
they fail to act wisely or do good.
4 Even on their beds they plot evil;
they commit themselves to a sinful
course
and do not reject what is wrong.

5 Your love, LORD, reaches to the
heavens,
your faithfulness to the skies.
6 Your righteousness is like the highest
mountains,
your justice like the great deep.
You, LORD, preserve both people
and animals.
7 How priceless is your unfailing love,
O God!
People take refuge in the shadow of
your wings.
8 They feast on the abundance of your
house;
you give them drink from your river
of delights.
9 For with you is the fountain of life;
in your light we see light.

10 Continue your love to those who know
you,
your righteousness to the upright in
heart.
11 May the foot of the proud not come
against me,
nor the hand of the wicked drive me
away.
12 See how the evildoers lie fallen —
thrown down, not able to rise!

Psalm 37[d]

Of David.

1 Do not fret because of those who are
evil

[a] *16* Septuagint; Hebrew may mean *Like an ungodly circle of mockers,* [b] In Hebrew texts 36:1-12 is numbered 36:2-13. [c] *1* Or *A message from God: The transgression of the wicked / resides in their hearts.* [d] This psalm is an acrostic poem, the stanzas of which begin with the successive letters of the Hebrew alphabet.

or be envious of those who do
wrong;
2 for like the grass they will soon wither,
like green plants they will soon die
away.

3 Trust in the LORD and do good;
dwell in the land and enjoy safe
pasture.
4 Take delight in the LORD,
and he will give you the desires of
your heart.

5 Commit your way to the LORD;
trust in him and he will do this:
6 He will make your righteous reward
shine like the dawn,
your vindication like the noonday
sun.

7 Be still before the LORD
and wait patiently for him;
do not fret when people succeed in
their ways,
when they carry out their wicked
schemes.

8 Refrain from anger and turn from
wrath;
do not fret—it leads only to evil.
9 For those who are evil will be
destroyed,
but those who hope in the LORD will
inherit the land.

10 A little while, and the wicked will be
no more;
though you look for them, they will
not be found.
11 But the meek will inherit the land
and enjoy peace and prosperity.

12 The wicked plot against the righteous
and gnash their teeth at them;
13 but the Lord laughs at the wicked,
for he knows their day is coming.

14 The wicked draw the sword
and bend the bow
to bring down the poor and needy,
to slay those whose ways are upright.
15 But their swords will pierce their own
hearts,
and their bows will be broken.

16 Better the little that the righteous have
than the wealth of many wicked;
17 for the power of the wicked will be
broken,
but the LORD upholds the righteous.

18 The blameless spend their days under
the LORD's care,
and their inheritance will endure
forever.
19 In times of disaster they will not
wither;
in days of famine they will enjoy
plenty.

20 But the wicked will perish:
Though the LORD's enemies are like
the flowers of the field,
they will be consumed, they will go
up in smoke.

21 The wicked borrow and do not repay,
but the righteous give generously;
22 those the LORD blesses will inherit the
land,
but those he curses will be
destroyed.

23 The LORD makes firm the steps
of the one who delights in him;
24 though he may stumble, he will not fall,
for the LORD upholds him with his
hand.

25 I was young and now I am old,
yet I have never seen the righteous
forsaken
or their children begging bread.
26 They are always generous and lend
freely;
their children will be a blessing.[a]

27 Turn from evil and do good;
then you will dwell in the land
forever.
28 For the LORD loves the just
and will not forsake his faithful ones.

Wrongdoers will be completely
destroyed[b];
the offspring of the wicked will
perish.
29 The righteous will inherit the land
and dwell in it forever.

30 The mouths of the righteous utter
wisdom,
and their tongues speak what is just.
31 The law of their God is in their hearts;
their feet do not slip.

32 The wicked lie in wait for the righteous,
intent on putting them to death;

[a] 26 Or *freely; / the names of their children will be used in blessings* (see Gen. 48:20); or *freely; / others will see that their children are blessed* [b] 28 See Septuagint; Hebrew *They will be protected forever*

33 but the LORD will not leave them in the power of the wicked
or let them be condemned when brought to trial.
34 Hope in the LORD
and keep his way.
He will exalt you to inherit the land;
when the wicked are destroyed, you will see it.
35 I have seen a wicked and ruthless man
flourishing like a luxuriant native tree,
36 but he soon passed away and was no more;
though I looked for him, he could not be found.
37 Consider the blameless, observe the upright;
a future awaits those who seek peace.[a]
38 But all sinners will be destroyed;
there will be no future[b] for the wicked.
39 The salvation of the righteous comes from the LORD;
he is their stronghold in time of trouble.
40 The LORD helps them and delivers them;
he delivers them from the wicked and saves them,
because they take refuge in him.

Psalm 38[c]

A psalm of David. A petition.

1 LORD, do not rebuke me in your anger
or discipline me in your wrath.
2 Your arrows have pierced me,
and your hand has come down on me.
3 Because of your wrath there is no health in my body;
there is no soundness in my bones because of my sin.
4 My guilt has overwhelmed me
like a burden too heavy to bear.
5 My wounds fester and are loathsome
because of my sinful folly.
6 I am bowed down and brought very low;
all day long I go about mourning.
7 My back is filled with searing pain;
there is no health in my body.
8 I am feeble and utterly crushed;
I groan in anguish of heart.
9 All my longings lie open before you, Lord;
my sighing is not hidden from you.
10 My heart pounds, my strength fails me;
even the light has gone from my eyes.
11 My friends and companions avoid me because of my wounds;
my neighbors stay far away.
12 Those who want to kill me set their traps,
those who would harm me talk of my ruin;
all day long they scheme and lie.
13 I am like the deaf, who cannot hear,
like the mute, who cannot speak;
14 I have become like one who does not hear,
whose mouth can offer no reply.
15 LORD, I wait for you;
you will answer, Lord my God.
16 For I said, "Do not let them gloat
or exalt themselves over me when my feet slip."
17 For I am about to fall,
and my pain is ever with me.
18 I confess my iniquity;
I am troubled by my sin.
19 Many have become my enemies without cause[d];
those who hate me without reason are numerous.
20 Those who repay my good with evil
lodge accusations against me,
though I seek only to do what is good.
21 LORD, do not forsake me;
do not be far from me, my God.
22 Come quickly to help me,
my Lord and my Savior.

Psalm 39[e]

For the director of music. For Jeduthun. A psalm of David.

1 I said, "I will watch my ways
and keep my tongue from sin;
I will put a muzzle on my mouth

[a] 37 Or *upright; / those who seek peace will have posterity* [b] 38 Or *posterity* [c] In Hebrew texts 38:1-22 is numbered 38:2-23. [d] 19 One Dead Sea Scrolls manuscript; Masoretic Text *my vigorous enemies* [e] In Hebrew texts 39:1-13 is numbered 39:2-14.

while in the presence of the wicked."
2 So I remained utterly silent,
not even saying anything good.
But my anguish increased;
3 my heart grew hot within me.
While I meditated, the fire burned;
then I spoke with my tongue:

4 "Show me, LORD, my life's end
and the number of my days;
let me know how fleeting my life is.
5 You have made my days a mere
handbreadth;
the span of my years is as nothing
before you.
Everyone is but a breath,
even those who seem secure.[a]

6 "Surely everyone goes around like a
mere phantom;
in vain they rush about, heaping up
wealth
without knowing whose it will
finally be.

7 "But now, Lord, what do I look for?
My hope is in you.
8 Save me from all my transgressions;
do not make me the scorn of fools.
9 I was silent; I would not open my
mouth,
for you are the one who has done
this.
10 Remove your scourge from me;
I am overcome by the blow of your
hand.
11 When you rebuke and discipline
anyone for their sin,
you consume their wealth like a
moth —
surely everyone is but a breath.

12 "Hear my prayer, LORD,
listen to my cry for help;
do not be deaf to my weeping.
I dwell with you as a foreigner,
a stranger, as all my ancestors were.
13 Look away from me, that I may enjoy
life again
before I depart and am no more."

Psalm 40[b]

For the director of music. Of David. A psalm.

1 I waited patiently for the LORD;
he turned to me and heard my cry.
2 He lifted me out of the slimy pit,
out of the mud and mire;
he set my feet on a rock
and gave me a firm place to stand.
3 He put a new song in my mouth,
a hymn of praise to our God.
Many will see and fear the LORD
and put their trust in him.

4 Blessed is the one
who trusts in the LORD,
who does not look to the proud,
to those who turn aside to false
gods.[c]
5 Many, LORD my God,
are the wonders you have done,
the things you planned for us.
None can compare with you;
were I to speak and tell of your deeds,
they would be too many to declare.

6 Sacrifice and offering you did not
desire —
but my ears you have opened[d] —
burnt offerings and sin offerings[e]
you did not require.
7 Then I said, "Here I am, I have come —
it is written about me in the scroll.[f]
8 I desire to do your will, my God;
your law is within my heart."

9 I proclaim your saving acts in the
great assembly;
I do not seal my lips, LORD,
as you know.
10 I do not hide your righteousness in my
heart;
I speak of your faithfulness and your
saving help.
I do not conceal your love and your
faithfulness
from the great assembly.

11 Do not withhold your mercy from me,
LORD;
may your love and faithfulness
always protect me.
12 For troubles without number
surround me;
my sins have overtaken me, and I
cannot see.
They are more than the hairs of my
head,
and my heart fails within me.
13 Be pleased to save me, LORD;
come quickly, LORD, to help me.

[a] 5 The Hebrew has *Selah* (a word of uncertain meaning) here and at the end of verse 11. [b] In Hebrew texts 40:1-17 is numbered 40:2-18. [c] 4 Or *to lies* [d] 6 Hebrew; some Septuagint manuscripts *but a body you have prepared for me* [e] 6 Or *purification offerings* [f] 7 Or *come / with the scroll written for me*

14 May all who want to take my life
be put to shame and confusion;
may all who desire my ruin
be turned back in disgrace.
15 May those who say to me, "Aha! Aha!"
be appalled at their own shame.
16 But may all who seek you
rejoice and be glad in you;
may those who long for your saving
help always say,
"The LORD is great!"
17 But as for me, I am poor and needy;
may the Lord think of me.
You are my help and my deliverer;
you are my God, do not delay.

Psalm 41[a]

For the director of music. A psalm of David.

1 Blessed are those who have regard for
the weak;
the LORD delivers them in times of
trouble.
2 The LORD protects and preserves
them —
they are counted among the blessed
in the land —
he does not give them over to the
desire of their foes.
3 The LORD sustains them on their
sickbed
and restores them from their bed of
illness.
4 I said, "Have mercy on me, LORD;
heal me, for I have sinned against
you."
5 My enemies say of me in malice,
"When will he die and his name
perish?"
6 When one of them comes to see me,
he speaks falsely, while his heart
gathers slander;
then he goes out and spreads it
around.
7 All my enemies whisper together
against me;
they imagine the worst for me, saying,
8 "A vile disease has afflicted him;
he will never get up from the place
where he lies."
9 Even my close friend,
someone I trusted,
one who shared my bread,
has turned[b] against me.
10 But may you have mercy on me, LORD;
raise me up, that I may repay them.
11 I know that you are pleased with me,
for my enemy does not triumph over
me.
12 Because of my integrity you uphold me
and set me in your presence forever.
13 Praise be to the LORD, the God of
Israel,
from everlasting to everlasting.
Amen and Amen.

BOOK II

Psalms 42–72

Psalm 42[c,d]

For the director of music. A maskil[e] *of the Sons of Korah.*

1 As the deer pants for streams of water,
so my soul pants for you, my God.
2 My soul thirsts for God, for the living
God.
When can I go and meet with God?
3 My tears have been my food
day and night,
while people say to me all day long,
"Where is your God?"
4 These things I remember
as I pour out my soul:
how I used to go to the house of God
under the protection of the Mighty
One[f]
with shouts of joy and praise
among the festive throng.
5 Why, my soul, are you downcast?
Why so disturbed within me?
Put your hope in God,
for I will yet praise him,
my Savior and my God.
6 My soul is downcast within me;
therefore I will remember you
from the land of the Jordan,
the heights of Hermon — from
Mount Mizar.
7 Deep calls to deep
in the roar of your waterfalls;

[a] In Hebrew texts 41:1-13 is numbered 41:2-14. [b] 9 Hebrew *has lifted up his heel* [c] In many Hebrew manuscripts Psalms 42 and 43 constitute one psalm. [d] In Hebrew texts 42:1-11 is numbered 42:2-12. [e] Title: Probably a literary or musical term [f] 4 See Septuagint and Syriac; the meaning of the Hebrew for this line is uncertain.

all your waves and breakers
have swept over me.

8 By day the LORD directs his love,
at night his song is with me —
a prayer to the God of my life.

9 I say to God my Rock,
"Why have you forgotten me?
Why must I go about mourning,
oppressed by the enemy?"
10 My bones suffer mortal agony
as my foes taunt me,
saying to me all day long,
"Where is your God?"

11 Why, my soul, are you downcast?
Why so disturbed within me?
Put your hope in God,
for I will yet praise him,
my Savior and my God.

Psalm 43[a]

1 Vindicate me, my God,
and plead my cause
against an unfaithful nation.
Rescue me from those who are
deceitful and wicked.
2 You are God my stronghold.
Why have you rejected me?
Why must I go about mourning,
oppressed by the enemy?
3 Send me your light and your faithful
care,
let them lead me;
let them bring me to your holy
mountain,
to the place where you dwell.
4 Then I will go to the altar of God,
to God, my joy and my delight.
I will praise you with the lyre,
O God, my God.

5 Why, my soul, are you downcast?
Why so disturbed within me?
Put your hope in God,
for I will yet praise him,
my Savior and my God.

Psalm 44[b]

For the director of music. Of the Sons of Korah.
A maskil.[c]

1 We have heard it with our ears, O God;
our ancestors have told us
what you did in their days,
in days long ago.
2 With your hand you drove out the
nations
and planted our ancestors;
you crushed the peoples
and made our ancestors flourish.
3 It was not by their sword that they won
the land,
nor did their arm bring them
victory;
it was your right hand, your arm,
and the light of your face, for you
loved them.
4 You are my King and my God,
who decrees[d] victories for Jacob.
5 Through you we push back our
enemies;
through your name we trample our
foes.
6 I put no trust in my bow,
my sword does not bring me victory;
7 but you give us victory over our
enemies,
you put our adversaries to shame.
8 In God we make our boast all day long,
and we will praise your name
forever.[e]

9 But now you have rejected and
humbled us;
you no longer go out with our
armies.
10 You made us retreat before the enemy,
and our adversaries have plundered
us.
11 You gave us up to be devoured like
sheep
and have scattered us among the
nations.
12 You sold your people for a pittance,
gaining nothing from their sale.

13 You have made us a reproach to our
neighbors,
the scorn and derision of those
around us.
14 You have made us a byword among
the nations;
the peoples shake their heads at us.
15 I live in disgrace all day long,
and my face is covered with shame
16 at the taunts of those who reproach
and revile me,

[a] In many Hebrew manuscripts Psalms 42 and 43 constitute one psalm. [b] In Hebrew texts 44:1-26 is numbered 44:2-27. [c] Title: Probably a literary or musical term [d] *4* Septuagint, Aquila and Syriac; Hebrew *King, O God; / command* [e] *8* The Hebrew has *Selah* (a word of uncertain meaning) here.

because of the enemy, who is bent
on revenge.

17 All this came upon us,
though we had not forgotten you;
we had not been false to your
covenant.
18 Our hearts had not turned back;
our feet had not strayed from your
path.
19 But you crushed us and made us a
haunt for jackals;
you covered us over with deep
darkness.

20 If we had forgotten the name of our God
or spread out our hands to a foreign
god,
21 would not God have discovered it,
since he knows the secrets of the
heart?
22 Yet for your sake we face death all day
long;
we are considered as sheep to be
slaughtered.

23 Awake, Lord! Why do you sleep?
Rouse yourself! Do not reject us
forever.
24 Why do you hide your face
and forget our misery and
oppression?

25 We are brought down to the dust;
our bodies cling to the ground.
26 Rise up and help us;
rescue us because of your unfailing
love.

Psalm 45[a]

For the director of music. To the tune of "Lilies." Of the Sons of Korah. A maskil.[b] *A wedding song.*

1 My heart is stirred by a noble theme
as I recite my verses for the king;
my tongue is the pen of a skillful
writer.

2 You are the most excellent of men
and your lips have been anointed
with grace,
since God has blessed you forever.

3 Gird your sword on your side, you
mighty one;
clothe yourself with splendor and
majesty.
4 In your majesty ride forth victoriously
in the cause of truth, humility and
justice;
let your right hand achieve awesome
deeds.
5 Let your sharp arrows pierce the
hearts of the king's enemies;
let the nations fall beneath your
feet.
6 Your throne, O God,[c] will last for ever
and ever;
a scepter of justice will be the
scepter of your kingdom.
7 You love righteousness and hate
wickedness;
therefore God, your God, has set you
above your companions
by anointing you with the oil of joy.
8 All your robes are fragrant with myrrh
and aloes and cassia;
from palaces adorned with ivory
the music of the strings makes you
glad.
9 Daughters of kings are among your
honored women;
at your right hand is the royal bride
in gold of Ophir.

10 Listen, daughter, and pay careful
attention:
Forget your people and your father's
house.
11 Let the king be enthralled by your
beauty;
honor him, for he is your lord.
12 The city of Tyre will come with a gift,[d]
people of wealth will seek your favor.
13 All glorious is the princess within her
chamber;
her gown is interwoven with gold.
14 In embroidered garments she is led to
the king;
her virgin companions follow her —
those brought to be with her.
15 Led in with joy and gladness,
they enter the palace of the king.

16 Your sons will take the place of your
fathers;
you will make them princes
throughout the land.

17 I will perpetuate your memory
through all generations;
therefore the nations will praise you
for ever and ever.

[a] In Hebrew texts 45:1-17 is numbered 45:2-18. [b] Title: Probably a literary or musical term [c] 6 Here the king is addressed as God's representative. [d] 12 Or *A Tyrian robe is among the gifts*

Psalm 46[a]

For the director of music. Of the Sons of Korah. According to alamoth.[b] *A song.*

1 God is our refuge and strength,
an ever-present help in trouble.
2 Therefore we will not fear, though the earth give way
and the mountains fall into the heart of the sea,
3 though its waters roar and foam
and the mountains quake with their surging.[c]
4 There is a river whose streams make glad the city of God,
the holy place where the Most High dwells.
5 God is within her, she will not fall;
God will help her at break of day.
6 Nations are in uproar, kingdoms fall;
he lifts his voice, the earth melts.

7 The LORD Almighty is with us;
the God of Jacob is our fortress.

8 Come and see what the LORD has done,
the desolations he has brought on the earth.
9 He makes wars cease
to the ends of the earth.
He breaks the bow and shatters the spear;
he burns the shields[d] with fire.
10 He says, "Be still, and know that I am God;
I will be exalted among the nations,
I will be exalted in the earth."

11 The LORD Almighty is with us;
the God of Jacob is our fortress.

Psalm 47[e]

For the director of music. Of the Sons of Korah. A psalm.

1 Clap your hands, all you nations;
shout to God with cries of joy.

2 For the LORD Most High is awesome,
the great King over all the earth.
3 He subdued nations under us,
peoples under our feet.
4 He chose our inheritance for us,
the pride of Jacob, whom he loved.[f]

5 God has ascended amid shouts of joy,
the LORD amid the sounding of trumpets.
6 Sing praises to God, sing praises;
sing praises to our King, sing praises.
7 For God is the King of all the earth;
sing to him a psalm of praise.

8 God reigns over the nations;
God is seated on his holy throne.
9 The nobles of the nations assemble
as the people of the God of Abraham,
for the kings[g] of the earth belong to God;
he is greatly exalted.

Psalm 48[h]

A song. A psalm of the Sons of Korah.

1 Great is the LORD, and most worthy of praise,
in the city of our God, his holy mountain.

2 Beautiful in its loftiness,
the joy of the whole earth,
like the heights of Zaphon[i] is Mount Zion,
the city of the Great King.
3 God is in her citadels;
he has shown himself to be her fortress.

4 When the kings joined forces,
when they advanced together,
5 they saw her and were astounded;
they fled in terror.
6 Trembling seized them there,
pain like that of a woman in labor.
7 You destroyed them like ships of Tarshish
shattered by an east wind.

8 As we have heard,
so we have seen
in the city of the LORD Almighty,
in the city of our God:
God makes her secure
forever.[f]

9 Within your temple, O God,
we meditate on your unfailing love.
10 Like your name, O God,

[a] In Hebrew texts 46:1-11 is numbered 46:2-12. [b] Title: Probably a musical term [c] 3 The Hebrew has *Selah* (a word of uncertain meaning) here and at the end of verses 7 and 11. [d] 9 Or *chariots* [e] In Hebrew texts 47:1-9 is numbered 47:2-10. [f] 4 The Hebrew has *Selah* (a word of uncertain meaning) here. [g] 9 Or *shields* [h] In Hebrew texts 48:1-14 is numbered 48:2-15. [i] 2 *Zaphon* was the most sacred mountain of the Canaanites.

your praise reaches to the ends of
the earth;
your right hand is filled with
righteousness.
11 Mount Zion rejoices,
the villages of Judah are glad
because of your judgments.
12 Walk about Zion, go around her,
count her towers,
13 consider well her ramparts,
view her citadels,
that you may tell of them
to the next generation.
14 For this God is our God for ever and
ever;
he will be our guide even to the end.

Psalm 49[a]

For the director of music. Of the Sons of Korah. A psalm.

1 Hear this, all you peoples;
listen, all who live in this world,
2 both low and high,
rich and poor alike:
3 My mouth will speak words of
wisdom;
the meditation of my heart will give
you understanding.
4 I will turn my ear to a proverb;
with the harp I will expound my
riddle:
5 Why should I fear when evil days
come,
when wicked deceivers surround
me—
6 those who trust in their wealth
and boast of their great riches?
7 No one can redeem the life of another
or give to God a ransom for them—
8 the ransom for a life is costly,
no payment is ever enough—
9 so that they should live on forever
and not see decay.
10 For all can see that the wise die,
that the foolish and the senseless
also perish,
leaving their wealth to others.
11 Their tombs will remain their houses[b]
forever,
their dwellings for endless
generations,
though they had[c] named lands after
themselves.
12 People, despite their wealth, do not
endure;
they are like the beasts that perish.
13 This is the fate of those who trust in
themselves,
and of their followers, who approve
their sayings.[d]
14 They are like sheep and are destined
to die;
death will be their shepherd
(but the upright will prevail over
them in the morning).
Their forms will decay in the grave,
far from their princely mansions.
15 But God will redeem me from the
realm of the dead;
he will surely take me to himself.
16 Do not be overawed when others grow
rich,
when the splendor of their houses
increases;
17 for they will take nothing with them
when they die,
their splendor will not descend with
them.
18 Though while they live they count
themselves blessed—
and people praise you when you
prosper—
19 they will join those who have gone
before them,
who will never again see the light of
life.
20 People who have wealth but lack
understanding
are like the beasts that perish.

Psalm 50

A psalm of Asaph.

1 The Mighty One, God, the LORD,
speaks and summons the earth
from the rising of the sun to where it
sets.
2 From Zion, perfect in beauty,
God shines forth.
3 Our God comes
and will not be silent;
a fire devours before him,
and around him a tempest rages.

[a] In Hebrew texts 49:1-20 is numbered 49:2-21. [b] *11* Septuagint and Syriac; Hebrew *In their thoughts their houses will remain* [c] *11* Or *generations, / for they have* [d] *13* The Hebrew has *Selah* (a word of uncertain meaning) here and at the end of verse 15.

4 He summons the heavens above,
and the earth, that he may judge his people:
5 "Gather to me this consecrated people,
who made a covenant with me by sacrifice."
6 And the heavens proclaim his righteousness,
for he is a God of justice.[a,b]

7 "Listen, my people, and I will speak;
I will testify against you, Israel:
I am God, your God.
8 I bring no charges against you
concerning your sacrifices
or concerning your burnt offerings,
which are ever before me.
9 I have no need of a bull from your stall
or of goats from your pens,
10 for every animal of the forest is mine,
and the cattle on a thousand hills.
11 I know every bird in the mountains,
and the insects in the fields are mine.
12 If I were hungry I would not tell you,
for the world is mine, and all that is in it.
13 Do I eat the flesh of bulls
or drink the blood of goats?

14 "Sacrifice thank offerings to God,
fulfill your vows to the Most High,
15 and call on me in the day of trouble;
I will deliver you, and you will honor me."

16 But to the wicked person, God says:

"What right have you to recite my laws
or take my covenant on your lips?
17 You hate my instruction
and cast my words behind you.
18 When you see a thief, you join with him;
you throw in your lot with adulterers.
19 You use your mouth for evil
and harness your tongue to deceit.
20 You sit and testify against your brother
and slander your own mother's son.
21 When you did these things and I kept silent,
you thought I was exactly[c] like you.
But I now arraign you
and set my accusations before you.

22 "Consider this, you who forget God,
or I will tear you to pieces, with no one to rescue you:
23 Those who sacrifice thank offerings honor me,
and to the blameless[d] I will show my salvation."

Psalm 51[e]

For the director of music. A psalm of David. When the prophet Nathan came to him after David had committed adultery with Bathsheba.

1 Have mercy on me, O God,
according to your unfailing love;
according to your great compassion
blot out my transgressions.
2 Wash away all my iniquity
and cleanse me from my sin.

3 For I know my transgressions,
and my sin is always before me.
4 Against you, you only, have I sinned
and done what is evil in your sight;
so you are right in your verdict
and justified when you judge.
5 Surely I was sinful at birth,
sinful from the time my mother conceived me.
6 Yet you desired faithfulness even in the womb;
you taught me wisdom in that secret place.

7 Cleanse me with hyssop, and I will be clean;
wash me, and I will be whiter than snow.
8 Let me hear joy and gladness;
let the bones you have crushed rejoice.
9 Hide your face from my sins
and blot out all my iniquity.

10 Create in me a pure heart, O God,
and renew a steadfast spirit within me.
11 Do not cast me from your presence
or take your Holy Spirit from me.
12 Restore to me the joy of your salvation
and grant me a willing spirit, to sustain me.

[a] 6 With a different word division of the Hebrew; Masoretic Text *for God himself is judge* [b] 6 The Hebrew has *Selah* (a word of uncertain meaning) here. [c] 21 Or *thought the 'I AM' was* [d] 23 Probable reading of the original Hebrew text; the meaning of the Masoretic Text for this phrase is uncertain. [e] In Hebrew texts 51:1-19 is numbered 51:3-21.

13 Then I will teach transgressors your
ways,
so that sinners will turn back to you.
14 Deliver me from the guilt of
bloodshed, O God,
you who are God my Savior,
and my tongue will sing of your
righteousness.
15 Open my lips, Lord,
and my mouth will declare your
praise.
16 You do not delight in sacrifice, or I
would bring it;
you do not take pleasure in burnt
offerings.
17 My sacrifice, O God, is[a] a broken
spirit;
a broken and contrite heart
you, God, will not despise.

18 May it please you to prosper Zion,
to build up the walls of Jerusalem.
19 Then you will delight in the sacrifices
of the righteous,
in burnt offerings offered whole;
then bulls will be offered on your
altar.

Psalm 52[b]

For the director of music. A maskil[c] *of David. When Doeg the Edomite had gone to Saul and told him: "David has gone to the house of Ahimelek."*

1 Why do you boast of evil, you mighty
hero?
Why do you boast all day long,
you who are a disgrace in the eyes of
God?
2 You who practice deceit,
your tongue plots destruction;
it is like a sharpened razor.
3 You love evil rather than good,
falsehood rather than speaking the
truth.[d]
4 You love every harmful word,
you deceitful tongue!

5 Surely God will bring you down to
everlasting ruin:
He will snatch you up and pluck you
from your tent;
he will uproot you from the land of
the living.
6 The righteous will see and fear;
they will laugh at you, saying,
7 "Here now is the man
who did not make God his
stronghold
but trusted in his great wealth
and grew strong by destroying
others!"

8 But I am like an olive tree
flourishing in the house of God;
I trust in God's unfailing love
for ever and ever.
9 For what you have done I will always
praise you
in the presence of your faithful
people.
And I will hope in your name,
for your name is good.

Psalm 53[e]

For the director of music. According to mahalath.[f] *A* maskil[c] *of David.*

1 The fool says in his heart,
"There is no God."
They are corrupt, and their ways are
vile;
there is no one who does good.

2 God looks down from heaven
on all mankind
to see if there are any who
understand,
any who seek God.
3 Everyone has turned away, all have
become corrupt;
there is no one who does good,
not even one.

4 Do all these evildoers know nothing?

They devour my people as though
eating bread;
they never call on God.
5 But there they are, overwhelmed with
dread,
where there was nothing to dread.
God scattered the bones of those who
attacked you;
you put them to shame, for God
despised them.

6 Oh, that salvation for Israel would
come out of Zion!
When God restores his people,
let Jacob rejoice and Israel be glad!

[a] *17* Or *The sacrifices of God are* [b] In Hebrew texts 52:1-9 is numbered 52:3-11. [c] Title: Probably a literary or musical term [d] *3* The Hebrew has *Selah* (a word of uncertain meaning) here and at the end of verse 5. [e] In Hebrew texts 53:1-6 is numbered 53:2-7. [f] Title: Probably a musical term

Psalm 54[a]

For the director of music. With stringed instruments. A maskil[b] *of David. When the Ziphites had gone to Saul and said, "Is not David hiding among us?"*

1 Save me, O God, by your name;
vindicate me by your might.
2 Hear my prayer, O God;
listen to the words of my mouth.

3 Arrogant foes are attacking me;
ruthless people are trying to kill me—
people without regard for God.[c]

4 Surely God is my help;
the Lord is the one who sustains me.
5 Let evil recoil on those who slander me;
in your faithfulness destroy them.

6 I will sacrifice a freewill offering to you;
I will praise your name, LORD, for it is good.
7 You have delivered me from all my troubles,
and my eyes have looked in triumph on my foes.

Psalm 55[d]

For the director of music. With stringed instruments. A maskil[b] *of David.*

1 Listen to my prayer, O God,
do not ignore my plea;
2 hear me and answer me.
My thoughts trouble me and I am distraught
3 because of what my enemy is saying,
because of the threats of the wicked;
for they bring down suffering on me
and assail me in their anger.

4 My heart is in anguish within me;
the terrors of death have fallen on me.
5 Fear and trembling have beset me;
horror has overwhelmed me.
6 I said, "Oh, that I had the wings of a dove!
I would fly away and be at rest.
7 I would flee far away
and stay in the desert;[e]
8 I would hurry to my place of shelter,
far from the tempest and storm."

9 Lord, confuse the wicked, confound their words,
for I see violence and strife in the city.
10 Day and night they prowl about on its walls;
malice and abuse are within it.
11 Destructive forces are at work in the city;
threats and lies never leave its streets.

12 If an enemy were insulting me,
I could endure it;
if a foe were rising against me,
I could hide.
13 But it is you, a man like myself,
my companion, my close friend,
14 with whom I once enjoyed sweet fellowship
at the house of God,
as we walked about
among the worshipers.

15 Let death take my enemies by surprise;
let them go down alive to the realm of the dead,
for evil finds lodging among them.

16 As for me, I call to God,
and the LORD saves me.
17 Evening, morning and noon
I cry out in distress,
and he hears my voice.
18 He rescues me unharmed
from the battle waged against me,
even though many oppose me.
19 God, who is enthroned from of old,
who does not change—
he will hear them and humble them,
because they have no fear of God.

20 My companion attacks his friends;
he violates his covenant.
21 His talk is smooth as butter,
yet war is in his heart;
his words are more soothing than oil,
yet they are drawn swords.

22 Cast your cares on the LORD
and he will sustain you;
he will never let
the righteous be shaken.

[a] In Hebrew texts 54:1-7 is numbered 54:3-9. [b] Title: Probably a literary or musical term [c] *3* The Hebrew has *Selah* (a word of uncertain meaning) here. [d] In Hebrew texts 55:1-23 is numbered 55:2-24. [e] *7* The Hebrew has *Selah* (a word of uncertain meaning) here and in the middle of verse 19.

23 But you, God, will bring down the wicked
into the pit of decay;
the bloodthirsty and deceitful
will not live out half their days.

But as for me, I trust in you.

Psalm 56[a]

For the director of music. To the tune of "A Dove on Distant Oaks." Of David. A miktam.[b] *When the Philistines had seized him in Gath.*

1 Be merciful to me, my God,
for my enemies are in hot pursuit;
all day long they press their attack.
2 My adversaries pursue me all day long;
in their pride many are attacking me.

3 When I am afraid, I put my trust in you.
4 In God, whose word I praise —
in God I trust and am not afraid.
What can mere mortals do to me?

5 All day long they twist my words;
all their schemes are for my ruin.
6 They conspire, they lurk,
they watch my steps,
hoping to take my life.
7 Because of their wickedness do not[c]
let them escape;
in your anger, God, bring the nations down.

8 Record my misery;
list my tears on your scroll[d] —
are they not in your record?
9 Then my enemies will turn back
when I call for help.
By this I will know that God is for me.

10 In God, whose word I praise,
in the LORD, whose word I praise —
11 in God I trust and am not afraid.
What can man do to me?

12 I am under vows to you, my God;
I will present my thank offerings to you.
13 For you have delivered me from death
and my feet from stumbling,
that I may walk before God
in the light of life.

Psalm 57[e]

For the director of music. To the tune of "Do Not Destroy." Of David. A miktam.[b] *When he had fled from Saul into the cave.*

1 Have mercy on me, my God, have mercy on me,
for in you I take refuge.
I will take refuge in the shadow of your wings
until the disaster has passed.

2 I cry out to God Most High,
to God, who vindicates me.
3 He sends from heaven and saves me,
rebuking those who hotly pursue me —[f]
God sends forth his love and his faithfulness.

4 I am in the midst of lions;
I am forced to dwell among ravenous beasts —
men whose teeth are spears and arrows,
whose tongues are sharp swords.

5 Be exalted, O God, above the heavens;
let your glory be over all the earth.

6 They spread a net for my feet —
I was bowed down in distress.
They dug a pit in my path —
but they have fallen into it themselves.

7 My heart, O God, is steadfast,
my heart is steadfast;
I will sing and make music.
8 Awake, my soul!
Awake, harp and lyre!
I will awaken the dawn.

9 I will praise you, Lord, among the nations;
I will sing of you among the peoples.
10 For great is your love, reaching to the heavens;
your faithfulness reaches to the skies.

11 Be exalted, O God, above the heavens;
let your glory be over all the earth.

[a] In Hebrew texts 56:1-13 is numbered 56:2-14. [b] Title: Probably a literary or musical term [c] *7* Probable reading of the original Hebrew text; Masoretic Text does not have *do not.* [d] *8* Or *misery; / put my tears in your wineskin* [e] In Hebrew texts 57:1-11 is numbered 57:2-12. [f] *3* The Hebrew has *Selah* (a word of uncertain meaning) here and at the end of verse 6.

Psalm 58[a]

For the director of music. To the tune of "Do Not Destroy." Of David. A miktam.[b]

1 Do you rulers indeed speak justly?
Do you judge people with equity?
2 No, in your heart you devise injustice,
and your hands mete out violence
on the earth.

3 Even from birth the wicked go astray;
from the womb they are wayward,
spreading lies.
4 Their venom is like the venom of a
snake,
like that of a cobra that has stopped
its ears,
5 that will not heed the tune of the
charmer,
however skillful the enchanter may
be.

6 Break the teeth in their mouths, O God;
LORD, tear out the fangs of those
lions!
7 Let them vanish like water that flows
away;
when they draw the bow, let their
arrows fall short.
8 May they be like a slug that melts away
as it moves along,
like a stillborn child that never sees
the sun.

9 Before your pots can feel the heat of
the thorns —
whether they be green or dry — the
wicked will be swept away.[c]
10 The righteous will be glad when they
are avenged,
when they dip their feet in the blood
of the wicked.
11 Then people will say,
"Surely the righteous still are
rewarded;
surely there is a God who judges the
earth."

Psalm 59[d]

For the director of music. To the tune of "Do Not Destroy." Of David. A miktam.[b] *When Saul had sent men to watch David's house in order to kill him.*

1 Deliver me from my enemies, O God;
be my fortress against those who are
attacking me.
2 Deliver me from evildoers
and save me from those who are
after my blood.

3 See how they lie in wait for me!
Fierce men conspire against me
for no offense or sin of mine, LORD.
4 I have done no wrong, yet they are
ready to attack me.
Arise to help me; look on my plight!
5 You, LORD God Almighty,
you who are the God of Israel,
rouse yourself to punish all the
nations;
show no mercy to wicked traitors.[e]

6 They return at evening,
snarling like dogs,
and prowl about the city.
7 See what they spew from their
mouths —
the words from their lips are sharp
as swords,
and they think, "Who can hear us?"
8 But you laugh at them, LORD;
you scoff at all those nations.

9 You are my strength, I watch for you;
you, God, are my fortress,
10 my God on whom I can rely.

God will go before me
and will let me gloat over those who
slander me.
11 But do not kill them, Lord our shield,[f]
or my people will forget.
In your might uproot them
and bring them down.
12 For the sins of their mouths,
for the words of their lips,
let them be caught in their pride.
For the curses and lies they utter,
13 consume them in your wrath,
consume them till they are no more.
Then it will be known to the ends of
the earth
that God rules over Jacob.

14 They return at evening,
snarling like dogs,
and prowl about the city.
15 They wander about for food
and howl if not satisfied.
16 But I will sing of your strength,

[a] In Hebrew texts 58:1-11 is numbered 58:2-12. [b] Title: Probably a literary or musical term
[c] 9 The meaning of the Hebrew for this verse is uncertain. [d] In Hebrew texts 59:1-17 is numbered 59:2-18.
[e] 5 The Hebrew has *Selah* (a word of uncertain meaning) here and at the end of verse 13. [f] *11* Or *sovereign*

in the morning I will sing of your
love;
for you are my fortress,
my refuge in times of trouble.

17 You are my strength, I sing praise to
you;
you, God, are my fortress,
my God on whom I can rely.

Psalm 60[a]

For the director of music. To the tune of "The Lily of the Covenant." A miktam[b] *of David. For teaching. When he fought Aram Naharaim*[c] *and Aram Zobah,*[d] *and when Joab returned and struck down twelve thousand Edomites in the Valley of Salt.*

1 You have rejected us, God, and burst
upon us;
you have been angry — now restore
us!
2 You have shaken the land and torn it
open;
mend its fractures, for it is quaking.
3 You have shown your people
desperate times;
you have given us wine that makes
us stagger.
4 But for those who fear you, you have
raised a banner
to be unfurled against the bow.[e]

5 Save us and help us with your right
hand,
that those you love may be delivered.
6 God has spoken from his sanctuary:
"In triumph I will parcel out
Shechem
and measure off the Valley of
Sukkoth.
7 Gilead is mine, and Manasseh is mine;
Ephraim is my helmet,
Judah is my scepter.
8 Moab is my washbasin,
on Edom I toss my sandal;
over Philistia I shout in triumph."

9 Who will bring me to the fortified city?
Who will lead me to Edom?
10 Is it not you, God, you who have now
rejected us
and no longer go out with our
armies?
11 Give us aid against the enemy,
for human help is worthless.
12 With God we will gain the victory,
and he will trample down our
enemies.

Psalm 61[f]

For the director of music. With stringed instruments. Of David.

1 Hear my cry, O God;
listen to my prayer.

2 From the ends of the earth I call to
you,
I call as my heart grows faint;
lead me to the rock that is higher
than I.
3 For you have been my refuge,
a strong tower against the foe.

4 I long to dwell in your tent forever
and take refuge in the shelter of your
wings.[e]
5 For you, God, have heard my vows;
you have given me the heritage of
those who fear your name.

6 Increase the days of the king's life,
his years for many generations.
7 May he be enthroned in God's
presence forever;
appoint your love and faithfulness
to protect him.
8 Then I will ever sing in praise of your
name
and fulfill my vows day after day.

Psalm 62[g]

For the director of music. For Jeduthun. A psalm of David.

1 Truly my soul finds rest in God;
my salvation comes from him.
2 Truly he is my rock and my salvation;
he is my fortress, I will never be
shaken.

3 How long will you assault me?
Would all of you throw me down —
this leaning wall, this tottering
fence?
4 Surely they intend to topple me
from my lofty place;

[a] In Hebrew texts 60:1-12 is numbered 60:3-14. [b] Title: Probably a literary or musical term [c] Title: That is, Arameans of Northwest Mesopotamia [d] Title: That is, Arameans of central Syria [e] *4* The Hebrew has *Selah* (a word of uncertain meaning) here. [f] In Hebrew texts 61:1-8 is numbered 61:2-9. [g] In Hebrew texts 62:1-12 is numbered 62:2-13.

they take delight in lies.
With their mouths they bless,
but in their hearts they curse.[a]
5 Yes, my soul, find rest in God;
my hope comes from him.
6 Truly he is my rock and my salvation;
he is my fortress, I will not be shaken.
7 My salvation and my honor depend on God[b];
he is my mighty rock, my refuge.
8 Trust in him at all times, you people;
pour out your hearts to him,
for God is our refuge.
9 Surely the lowborn are but a breath,
the highborn are but a lie.
If weighed on a balance, they are nothing;
together they are only a breath.
10 Do not trust in extortion
or put vain hope in stolen goods;
though your riches increase,
do not set your heart on them.
11 One thing God has spoken,
two things I have heard:
"Power belongs to you, God,
12 and with you, Lord, is unfailing love";
and, "You reward everyone
according to what they have done."

Psalm 63[c]

A psalm of David. When he was in the Desert of Judah.

1 You, God, are my God,
earnestly I seek you;
I thirst for you,
my whole being longs for you,
in a dry and parched land
where there is no water.
2 I have seen you in the sanctuary
and beheld your power and your glory.
3 Because your love is better than life,
my lips will glorify you.
4 I will praise you as long as I live,
and in your name I will lift up my hands.
5 I will be fully satisfied as with the richest of foods;
with singing lips my mouth will praise you.
6 On my bed I remember you;
I think of you through the watches of the night.
7 Because you are my help,
I sing in the shadow of your wings.
8 I cling to you;
your right hand upholds me.
9 Those who want to kill me will be destroyed;
they will go down to the depths of the earth.
10 They will be given over to the sword
and become food for jackals.
11 But the king will rejoice in God;
all who swear by God will glory in him,
while the mouths of liars will be silenced.

Psalm 64[d]

For the director of music. A psalm of David.

1 Hear me, my God, as I voice my complaint;
protect my life from the threat of the enemy.
2 Hide me from the conspiracy of the wicked,
from the plots of evildoers.
3 They sharpen their tongues like swords
and aim cruel words like deadly arrows.
4 They shoot from ambush at the innocent;
they shoot suddenly, without fear.
5 They encourage each other in evil plans,
they talk about hiding their snares;
they say, "Who will see it[e]?"
6 They plot injustice and say,
"We have devised a perfect plan!"
Surely the human mind and heart are cunning.
7 But God will shoot them with his arrows;
they will suddenly be struck down.
8 He will turn their own tongues against them
and bring them to ruin;
all who see them will shake their heads in scorn.

[a] 4 The Hebrew has *Selah* (a word of uncertain meaning) here and at the end of verse 8. [b] 7 Or / *God Most High is my salvation and my honor* [c] In Hebrew texts 63:1-11 is numbered 63:2-12. [d] In Hebrew texts 64:1-10 is numbered 64:2-11. [e] 5 Or *us*

9 All people will fear;
they will proclaim the works of God
and ponder what he has done.

10 The righteous will rejoice in the LORD
and take refuge in him;
all the upright in heart will glory in him!

Psalm 65[a]

For the director of music. A psalm of David. A song.

1 Praise awaits[b] you, our God, in Zion;
to you our vows will be fulfilled.
2 You who answer prayer,
to you all people will come.
3 When we were overwhelmed by sins,
you forgave[c] our transgressions.
4 Blessed are those you choose
and bring near to live in your courts!
We are filled with the good things of your house,
of your holy temple.

5 You answer us with awesome and righteous deeds,
God our Savior,
the hope of all the ends of the earth
and of the farthest seas,
6 who formed the mountains by your power,
having armed yourself with strength,
7 who stilled the roaring of the seas,
the roaring of their waves,
and the turmoil of the nations.
8 The whole earth is filled with awe at your wonders;
where morning dawns, where evening fades,
you call forth songs of joy.

9 You care for the land and water it;
you enrich it abundantly.
The streams of God are filled with water
to provide the people with grain,
for so you have ordained it.[d]
10 You drench its furrows and level its ridges;
you soften it with showers and bless its crops.
11 You crown the year with your bounty,
and your carts overflow with abundance.
12 The grasslands of the wilderness overflow;
the hills are clothed with gladness.
13 The meadows are covered with flocks
and the valleys are mantled with grain;
they shout for joy and sing.

Psalm 66

For the director of music. A song. A psalm.

1 Shout for joy to God, all the earth!
2 Sing the glory of his name;
make his praise glorious.
3 Say to God, "How awesome are your deeds!
So great is your power
that your enemies cringe before you.
4 All the earth bows down to you;
they sing praise to you,
they sing the praises of your name."[e]
5 Come and see what God has done,
his awesome deeds for mankind!
6 He turned the sea into dry land,
they passed through the waters on foot—
come, let us rejoice in him.
7 He rules forever by his power,
his eyes watch the nations—
let not the rebellious rise up against him.

8 Praise our God, all peoples,
let the sound of his praise be heard;
9 he has preserved our lives
and kept our feet from slipping.
10 For you, God, tested us;
you refined us like silver.
11 You brought us into prison
and laid burdens on our backs.
12 You let people ride over our heads;
we went through fire and water,
but you brought us to a place of abundance.

13 I will come to your temple with burnt offerings
and fulfill my vows to you—
14 vows my lips promised and my mouth spoke
when I was in trouble.
15 I will sacrifice fat animals to you
and an offering of rams;
I will offer bulls and goats.

[a] In Hebrew texts 65:1-13 is numbered 65:2-14. [b] *1* Or *befits;* the meaning of the Hebrew for this word is uncertain. [c] *3* Or *made atonement for* [d] *9* Or *for that is how you prepare the land* [e] *4* The Hebrew has *Selah* (a word of uncertain meaning) here and at the end of verses 7 and 15.

16 Come and hear, all you who fear God;
let me tell you what he has done for me.
17 I cried out to him with my mouth;
his praise was on my tongue.
18 If I had cherished sin in my heart,
the Lord would not have listened;
19 but God has surely listened
and has heard my prayer.
20 Praise be to God,
who has not rejected my prayer
or withheld his love from me!

Psalm 67[a]

For the director of music. With stringed instruments. A psalm. A song.

1 May God be gracious to us and bless us
and make his face shine on us —[b]
2 so that your ways may be known on earth,
your salvation among all nations.

3 May the peoples praise you, God;
may all the peoples praise you.
4 May the nations be glad and sing for joy,
for you rule the peoples with equity
and guide the nations of the earth.
5 May the peoples praise you, God;
may all the peoples praise you.

6 The land yields its harvest;
God, our God, blesses us.
7 May God bless us still,
so that all the ends of the earth will fear him.

Psalm 68[c]

For the director of music. Of David. A psalm. A song.

1 May God arise, may his enemies be scattered;
may his foes flee before him.
2 May you blow them away like smoke —
as wax melts before the fire,
may the wicked perish before God.
3 But may the righteous be glad
and rejoice before God;
may they be happy and joyful.

4 Sing to God, sing in praise of his name,
extol him who rides on the clouds[d];
rejoice before him — his name is the Lord.
5 A father to the fatherless, a defender of widows,
is God in his holy dwelling.
6 God sets the lonely in families,[e]
he leads out the prisoners with singing;
but the rebellious live in a sun-scorched land.

7 When you, God, went out before your people,
when you marched through the wilderness,[f]
8 the earth shook, the heavens poured down rain,
before God, the One of Sinai,
before God, the God of Israel.
9 You gave abundant showers, O God;
you refreshed your weary inheritance.
10 Your people settled in it,
and from your bounty, God, you provided for the poor.

11 The Lord announces the word,
and the women who proclaim it are a mighty throng:
12 "Kings and armies flee in haste;
the women at home divide the plunder.
13 Even while you sleep among the sheep pens,[g]
the wings of my dove are sheathed with silver,
its feathers with shining gold."
14 When the Almighty[h] scattered the kings in the land,
it was like snow fallen on Mount Zalmon.

15 Mount Bashan, majestic mountain,
Mount Bashan, rugged mountain,
16 why gaze in envy, you rugged mountain,
at the mountain where God chooses to reign,
where the Lord himself will dwell forever?
17 The chariots of God are tens of thousands
and thousands of thousands;

[a] In Hebrew texts 67:1-7 is numbered 67:2-8. [b] *1* The Hebrew has *Selah* (a word of uncertain meaning) here and at the end of verse 4. [c] In Hebrew texts 68:1-35 is numbered 68:2-36. [d] *4* Or *name, / prepare the way for him who rides through the deserts* [e] *6* Or *the desolate in a homeland* [f] *7* The Hebrew has *Selah* (a word of uncertain meaning) here and at the end of verses 19 and 32. [g] *13* Or *the campfires;* or *the saddlebags* [h] *14* Hebrew *Shaddai*

the Lord has come from Sinai into
his sanctuary.[a]
18 When you ascended on high,
you took many captives;
you received gifts from people,
even from[b] the rebellious —
that you,[c] LORD God, might dwell
there.
19 Praise be to the Lord, to God our
Savior,
who daily bears our burdens.
20 Our God is a God who saves;
from the Sovereign LORD comes
escape from death.
21 Surely God will crush the heads of his
enemies,
the hairy crowns of those who go on
in their sins.
22 The Lord says, "I will bring them from
Bashan;
I will bring them from the depths of
the sea,
23 that your feet may wade in the blood of
your foes,
while the tongues of your dogs have
their share."

24 Your procession, God, has come into
view,
the procession of my God and King
into the sanctuary.
25 In front are the singers, after them the
musicians;
with them are the young women
playing the timbrels.
26 Praise God in the great congregation;
praise the LORD in the assembly of
Israel.
27 There is the little tribe of Benjamin,
leading them,
there the great throng of Judah's
princes,
and there the princes of Zebulun
and of Naphtali.

28 Summon your power, God[d];
show us your strength, our God, as
you have done before.
29 Because of your temple at Jerusalem
kings will bring you gifts.
30 Rebuke the beast among the reeds,
the herd of bulls among the calves of
the nations.
Humbled, may the beast bring bars of
silver.
Scatter the nations who delight in
war.
31 Envoys will come from Egypt;
Cush[e] will submit herself to God.
32 Sing to God, you kingdoms of the
earth,
sing praise to the Lord,
33 to him who rides across the highest
heavens, the ancient heavens,
who thunders with mighty voice.
34 Proclaim the power of God,
whose majesty is over Israel,
whose power is in the heavens.
35 You, God, are awesome in your
sanctuary;
the God of Israel gives power and
strength to his people.

Praise be to God!

Psalm 69[f]

For the director of music. To the tune of "Lilies." Of David.

1 Save me, O God,
for the waters have come up to my
neck.
2 I sink in the miry depths,
where there is no foothold.
I have come into the deep waters;
the floods engulf me.
3 I am worn out calling for help;
my throat is parched.
My eyes fail,
looking for my God.
4 Those who hate me without reason
outnumber the hairs of my head;
many are my enemies without cause,
those who seek to destroy me.
I am forced to restore
what I did not steal.

5 You, God, know my folly;
my guilt is not hidden from you.

6 Lord, the LORD Almighty,
may those who hope in you
not be disgraced because of me;
God of Israel,
may those who seek you
not be put to shame because of me.
7 For I endure scorn for your sake,

[a] *17* Probable reading of the original Hebrew text; Masoretic Text *Lord is among them at Sinai in holiness*
[b] *18* Or *gifts for people, / even* [c] *18* Or *they* [d] *28* Many Hebrew manuscripts, Septuagint and Syriac; most Hebrew manuscripts *Your God has summoned power for you* [e] *31* That is, the upper Nile region
[f] In Hebrew texts 69:1-36 is numbered 69:2-37.

and shame covers my face.
8 I am a foreigner to my own family,
a stranger to my own mother's children;
9 for zeal for your house consumes me,
and the insults of those who insult you fall on me.
10 When I weep and fast,
I must endure scorn;
11 when I put on sackcloth,
people make sport of me.
12 Those who sit at the gate mock me,
and I am the song of the drunkards.

13 But I pray to you, LORD,
in the time of your favor;
in your great love, O God,
answer me with your sure salvation.
14 Rescue me from the mire,
do not let me sink;
deliver me from those who hate me,
from the deep waters.
15 Do not let the floodwaters engulf me
or the depths swallow me up
or the pit close its mouth over me.

16 Answer me, LORD, out of the goodness of your love;
in your great mercy turn to me.
17 Do not hide your face from your servant;
answer me quickly, for I am in trouble.
18 Come near and rescue me;
deliver me because of my foes.

19 You know how I am scorned,
disgraced and shamed;
all my enemies are before you.
20 Scorn has broken my heart
and has left me helpless;
I looked for sympathy, but there was none,
for comforters, but I found none.
21 They put gall in my food
and gave me vinegar for my thirst.

22 May the table set before them become a snare;
may it become retribution and[a] a trap.
23 May their eyes be darkened so they cannot see,
and their backs be bent forever.
24 Pour out your wrath on them;
let your fierce anger overtake them.
25 May their place be deserted;
let there be no one to dwell in their tents.
26 For they persecute those you wound
and talk about the pain of those you hurt.
27 Charge them with crime upon crime;
do not let them share in your salvation.
28 May they be blotted out of the book of life
and not be listed with the righteous.

29 But as for me, afflicted and in pain—
may your salvation, God, protect me.

30 I will praise God's name in song
and glorify him with thanksgiving.
31 This will please the LORD more than an ox,
more than a bull with its horns and hooves.
32 The poor will see and be glad—
you who seek God, may your hearts live!
33 The LORD hears the needy
and does not despise his captive people.

34 Let heaven and earth praise him,
the seas and all that move in them,
35 for God will save Zion
and rebuild the cities of Judah.
Then people will settle there and possess it;
36 the children of his servants will inherit it,
and those who love his name will dwell there.

Psalm 70[b]

For the director of music. Of David. A petition.

1 Hasten, O God, to save me;
come quickly, LORD, to help me.

2 May those who want to take my life
be put to shame and confusion;
may all who desire my ruin
be turned back in disgrace.
3 May those who say to me, "Aha! Aha!"
turn back because of their shame.
4 But may all who seek you
rejoice and be glad in you;
may those who long for your saving help always say,
"The LORD is great!"

[a] 22 Or *snare / and their fellowship become* [b] In Hebrew texts 70:1-5 is numbered 70:2-6.

5 But as for me, I am poor and needy;
come quickly to me, O God.
You are my help and my deliverer;
LORD, do not delay.

Psalm 71

1 In you, LORD, I have taken refuge;
let me never be put to shame.
2 In your righteousness, rescue me and
deliver me;
turn your ear to me and save me.
3 Be my rock of refuge,
to which I can always go;
give the command to save me,
for you are my rock and my
fortress.
4 Deliver me, my God, from the hand of
the wicked,
from the grasp of those who are evil
and cruel.

5 For you have been my hope, Sovereign
LORD,
my confidence since my youth.
6 From birth I have relied on you;
you brought me forth from my
mother's womb.
I will ever praise you.
7 I have become a sign to many;
you are my strong refuge.
8 My mouth is filled with your praise,
declaring your splendor all day
long.

9 Do not cast me away when I am old;
do not forsake me when my strength
is gone.
10 For my enemies speak against me;
those who wait to kill me conspire
together.
11 They say, "God has forsaken him;
pursue him and seize him,
for no one will rescue him."
12 Do not be far from me, my God;
come quickly, God, to help me.
13 May my accusers perish in shame;
may those who want to harm me
be covered with scorn and disgrace.

14 As for me, I will always have hope;
I will praise you more and more.
15 My mouth will tell of your righteous
deeds,
of your saving acts all day long—
though I know not how to relate
them all.
16 I will come and proclaim your mighty
acts, Sovereign LORD;
I will proclaim your righteous
deeds, yours alone.
17 Since my youth, God, you have taught
me,
and to this day I declare your
marvelous deeds.
18 Even when I am old and gray,
do not forsake me, my God,
till I declare your power to the next
generation,
your mighty acts to all who are to
come.

19 Your righteousness, God, reaches to
the heavens,
you who have done great things.
Who is like you, God?
20 Though you have made me see
troubles,
many and bitter,
you will restore my life again;
from the depths of the earth
you will again bring me up.
21 You will increase my honor
and comfort me once more.

22 I will praise you with the harp
for your faithfulness, my God;
I will sing praise to you with the
lyre,
Holy One of Israel.
23 My lips will shout for joy
when I sing praise to you—
I whom you have delivered.
24 My tongue will tell of your righteous
acts
all day long,
for those who wanted to harm me
have been put to shame and
confusion.

Psalm 72

Of Solomon.

1 Endow the king with your justice,
O God,
the royal son with your
righteousness.
2 May he judge your people in
righteousness,
your afflicted ones with justice.
3 May the mountains bring prosperity
to the people,
the hills the fruit of righteousness.
4 May he defend the afflicted among the
people
and save the children of the needy;
may he crush the oppressor.

5 May he endure[a] as long as the sun,
as long as the moon, through all generations.
6 May he be like rain falling on a mown field,
like showers watering the earth.
7 In his days may the righteous flourish
and prosperity abound till the moon is no more.

8 May he rule from sea to sea
and from the River[b] to the ends of the earth.
9 May the desert tribes bow before him
and his enemies lick the dust.
10 May the kings of Tarshish and of distant shores
bring tribute to him.
May the kings of Sheba and Seba
present him gifts.
11 May all kings bow down to him
and all nations serve him.

12 For he will deliver the needy who cry out,
the afflicted who have no one to help.
13 He will take pity on the weak and the needy
and save the needy from death.
14 He will rescue them from oppression and violence,
for precious is their blood in his sight.

15 Long may he live!
May gold from Sheba be given him.
May people ever pray for him
and bless him all day long.
16 May grain abound throughout the land;
on the tops of the hills may it sway.
May the crops flourish like Lebanon
and thrive[c] like the grass of the field.
17 May his name endure forever;
may it continue as long as the sun.

Then all nations will be blessed through him,[d]
and they will call him blessed.

18 Praise be to the LORD God, the God of Israel,
who alone does marvelous deeds.
19 Praise be to his glorious name forever;
may the whole earth be filled with his glory.
Amen and Amen.

20 This concludes the prayers of David son of Jesse.

BOOK III

Psalms 73–89

Psalm 73

A psalm of Asaph.

1 Surely God is good to Israel,
to those who are pure in heart.

2 But as for me, my feet had almost slipped;
I had nearly lost my foothold.
3 For I envied the arrogant
when I saw the prosperity of the wicked.

4 They have no struggles;
their bodies are healthy and strong.[e]
5 They are free from common human burdens;
they are not plagued by human ills.
6 Therefore pride is their necklace;
they clothe themselves with violence.
7 From their callous hearts comes iniquity[f];
their evil imaginations have no limits.
8 They scoff, and speak with malice;
with arrogance they threaten oppression.
9 Their mouths lay claim to heaven,
and their tongues take possession of the earth.
10 Therefore their people turn to them
and drink up waters in abundance.[g]
11 They say, "How would God know?
Does the Most High know anything?"

12 This is what the wicked are like —
always free of care, they go on amassing wealth.

13 Surely in vain I have kept my heart pure

[a] 5 Septuagint; Hebrew *You will be feared* [b] 8 That is, the Euphrates [c] 16 Probable reading of the original Hebrew text; Masoretic Text *Lebanon, / from the city* [d] 17 Or *will use his name in blessings* (see Gen. 48:20) [e] 4 With a different word division of the Hebrew; Masoretic Text *struggles at their death; / their bodies are healthy* [f] 7 Syriac (see also Septuagint); Hebrew *Their eyes bulge with fat* [g] 10 The meaning of the Hebrew for this verse is uncertain.

and have washed my hands in
innocence.
14 All day long I have been afflicted,
and every morning brings new
punishments.

15 If I had spoken out like that,
I would have betrayed your
children.
16 When I tried to understand all this,
it troubled me deeply
17 till I entered the sanctuary of God;
then I understood their final
destiny.

18 Surely you place them on slippery
ground;
you cast them down to ruin.
19 How suddenly are they destroyed,
completely swept away by terrors!
20 They are like a dream when one
awakes;
when you arise, Lord,
you will despise them as fantasies.

21 When my heart was grieved
and my spirit embittered,
22 I was senseless and ignorant;
I was a brute beast before you.

23 Yet I am always with you;
you hold me by my right hand.
24 You guide me with your counsel,
and afterward you will take me into
glory.
25 Whom have I in heaven but you?
And earth has nothing I desire
besides you.
26 My flesh and my heart may fail,
but God is the strength of my heart
and my portion forever.

27 Those who are far from you will perish;
you destroy all who are unfaithful to
you.
28 But as for me, it is good to be near God.
I have made the Sovereign LORD my
refuge;
I will tell of all your deeds.

Psalm 74

A maskil[a] *of Asaph.*

1 O God, why have you rejected us
forever?
Why does your anger smolder
against the sheep of your
pasture?

2 Remember the nation you purchased
long ago,
the people of your inheritance,
whom you redeemed —
Mount Zion, where you dwelt.
3 Turn your steps toward these
everlasting ruins,
all this destruction the enemy has
brought on the sanctuary.

4 Your foes roared in the place where
you met with us;
they set up their standards as signs.
5 They behaved like men wielding axes
to cut through a thicket of trees.
6 They smashed all the carved
paneling
with their axes and hatchets.
7 They burned your sanctuary to the
ground;
they defiled the dwelling place of
your Name.
8 They said in their hearts, "We will
crush them completely!"
They burned every place where God
was worshiped in the land.

9 We are given no signs from God;
no prophets are left,
and none of us knows how long this
will be.
10 How long will the enemy mock you,
God?
Will the foe revile your name
forever?
11 Why do you hold back your hand, your
right hand?
Take it from the folds of your
garment and destroy them!

12 But God is my King from long ago;
he brings salvation on the earth.

13 It was you who split open the sea by
your power;
you broke the heads of the monster
in the waters.
14 It was you who crushed the heads of
Leviathan
and gave it as food to the creatures
of the desert.
15 It was you who opened up springs and
streams;
you dried up the ever-flowing rivers.
16 The day is yours, and yours also the
night;
you established the sun and moon.

[a] Title: Probably a literary or musical term

17 It was you who set all the boundaries
of the earth;
you made both summer and winter.

18 Remember how the enemy has
mocked you, LORD,
how foolish people have reviled
your name.
19 Do not hand over the life of your dove
to wild beasts;
do not forget the lives of your
afflicted people forever.
20 Have regard for your covenant,
because haunts of violence fill the
dark places of the land.
21 Do not let the oppressed retreat in
disgrace;
may the poor and needy praise your
name.
22 Rise up, O God, and defend your
cause;
remember how fools mock you all
day long.
23 Do not ignore the clamor of your
adversaries,
the uproar of your enemies, which
rises continually.

Psalm 75[a]

For the director of music. To the tune of "Do Not Destroy." A psalm of Asaph. A song.

1 We praise you, God,
we praise you, for your Name is
near;
people tell of your wonderful deeds.

2 You say, "I choose the appointed time;
it is I who judge with equity.
3 When the earth and all its people
quake,
it is I who hold its pillars firm.[b]
4 To the arrogant I say, 'Boast no more,'
and to the wicked, 'Do not lift up
your horns.[c]
5 Do not lift your horns against heaven;
do not speak so defiantly.' "

6 No one from the east or the west
or from the desert can exalt
themselves.
7 It is God who judges:
He brings one down, he exalts
another.
8 In the hand of the LORD is a cup
full of foaming wine mixed with
spices;
he pours it out, and all the wicked of
the earth
drink it down to its very dregs.

9 As for me, I will declare this forever;
I will sing praise to the God of Jacob,
10 who says, "I will cut off the horns of all
the wicked,
but the horns of the righteous will
be lifted up."

Psalm 76[d]

For the director of music. With stringed instruments. A psalm of Asaph. A song.

1 God is renowned in Judah;
in Israel his name is great.
2 His tent is in Salem,
his dwelling place in Zion.
3 There he broke the flashing arrows,
the shields and the swords, the
weapons of war.[e]

4 You are radiant with light,
more majestic than mountains rich
with game.
5 The valiant lie plundered,
they sleep their last sleep;
not one of the warriors
can lift his hands.
6 At your rebuke, God of Jacob,
both horse and chariot lie still.

7 It is you alone who are to be feared.
Who can stand before you when you
are angry?
8 From heaven you pronounced
judgment,
and the land feared and was quiet—
9 when you, God, rose up to judge,
to save all the afflicted of the land.
10 Surely your wrath against mankind
brings you praise,
and the survivors of your wrath are
restrained.[f]

11 Make vows to the LORD your God and
fulfill them;
let all the neighboring lands
bring gifts to the One to be feared.
12 He breaks the spirit of rulers;
he is feared by the kings of the earth.

[a] In Hebrew texts 75:1-10 is numbered 75:2-11. [b] *3* The Hebrew has *Selah* (a word of uncertain meaning) here. [c] *4* *Horns* here symbolize strength; also in verses 5 and 10. [d] In Hebrew texts 76:1-12 is numbered 76:2-13. [e] *3* The Hebrew has *Selah* (a word of uncertain meaning) here and at the end of verse 9.
[f] *10* Or *Surely the wrath of mankind brings you praise, / and with the remainder of wrath you arm yourself*

Psalm 77[a]

For the director of music. For Jeduthun. Of Asaph. A psalm.

1 I cried out to God for help;
I cried out to God to hear me.
2 When I was in distress, I sought the Lord;
at night I stretched out untiring hands,
and I would not be comforted.
3 I remembered you, God, and I groaned;
I meditated, and my spirit grew faint.[b]
4 You kept my eyes from closing;
I was too troubled to speak.
5 I thought about the former days,
the years of long ago;
6 I remembered my songs in the night.
My heart meditated and my spirit asked:
7 "Will the Lord reject forever?
Will he never show his favor again?
8 Has his unfailing love vanished forever?
Has his promise failed for all time?
9 Has God forgotten to be merciful?
Has he in anger withheld his compassion?"
10 Then I thought, "To this I will appeal:
the years when the Most High stretched out his right hand.
11 I will remember the deeds of the LORD;
yes, I will remember your miracles of long ago.
12 I will consider all your works
and meditate on all your mighty deeds."
13 Your ways, God, are holy.
What god is as great as our God?
14 You are the God who performs miracles;
you display your power among the peoples.
15 With your mighty arm you redeemed your people,
the descendants of Jacob and Joseph.
16 The waters saw you, God,
the waters saw you and writhed;
the very depths were convulsed.
17 The clouds poured down water,
the heavens resounded with thunder;
your arrows flashed back and forth.
18 Your thunder was heard in the whirlwind,
your lightning lit up the world;
the earth trembled and quaked.
19 Your path led through the sea,
your way through the mighty waters,
though your footprints were not seen.
20 You led your people like a flock
by the hand of Moses and Aaron.

Psalm 78

A maskil[c] of Asaph.

1 My people, hear my teaching;
listen to the words of my mouth.
2 I will open my mouth with a parable;
I will utter hidden things, things from of old —
3 things we have heard and known,
things our ancestors have told us.
4 We will not hide them from their descendants;
we will tell the next generation
the praiseworthy deeds of the LORD,
his power, and the wonders he has done.
5 He decreed statutes for Jacob
and established the law in Israel,
which he commanded our ancestors
to teach their children,
6 so the next generation would know them,
even the children yet to be born,
and they in turn would tell their children.
7 Then they would put their trust in God
and would not forget his deeds
but would keep his commands.
8 They would not be like their ancestors —
a stubborn and rebellious generation,
whose hearts were not loyal to God,
whose spirits were not faithful to him.
9 The men of Ephraim, though armed with bows,
turned back on the day of battle;

[a] In Hebrew texts 77:1-20 is numbered 77:2-21. [b] *3* The Hebrew has *Selah* (a word of uncertain meaning) here and at the end of verses 9 and 15. [c] Title: Probably a literary or musical term

10 they did not keep God's covenant
and refused to live by his law.
11 They forgot what he had done,
the wonders he had shown them.
12 He did miracles in the sight of their ancestors
in the land of Egypt, in the region of Zoan.
13 He divided the sea and led them through;
he made the water stand up like a wall.
14 He guided them with the cloud by day
and with light from the fire all night.
15 He split the rocks in the wilderness
and gave them water as abundant as the seas;
16 he brought streams out of a rocky crag
and made water flow down like rivers.

17 But they continued to sin against him,
rebelling in the wilderness against the Most High.
18 They willfully put God to the test
by demanding the food they craved.
19 They spoke against God;
they said, "Can God really
spread a table in the wilderness?
20 True, he struck the rock,
and water gushed out,
streams flowed abundantly,
but can he also give us bread?
Can he supply meat for his people?"
21 When the LORD heard them, he was furious;
his fire broke out against Jacob,
and his wrath rose against Israel,
22 for they did not believe in God
or trust in his deliverance.
23 Yet he gave a command to the skies above
and opened the doors of the heavens;
24 he rained down manna for the people to eat,
he gave them the grain of heaven.
25 Human beings ate the bread of angels;
he sent them all the food they could eat.
26 He let loose the east wind from the heavens
and by his power made the south wind blow.
27 He rained meat down on them like dust,
birds like sand on the seashore.
28 He made them come down inside their camp,
all around their tents.
29 They ate till they were gorged—
he had given them what they craved.
30 But before they turned from what they craved,
even while the food was still in their mouths,
31 God's anger rose against them;
he put to death the sturdiest among them,
cutting down the young men of Israel.

32 In spite of all this, they kept on sinning;
in spite of his wonders, they did not believe.
33 So he ended their days in futility
and their years in terror.
34 Whenever God slew them, they would seek him;
they eagerly turned to him again.
35 They remembered that God was their Rock,
that God Most High was their Redeemer.
36 But then they would flatter him with their mouths,
lying to him with their tongues;
37 their hearts were not loyal to him,
they were not faithful to his covenant.
38 Yet he was merciful;
he forgave their iniquities
and did not destroy them.
Time after time he restrained his anger
and did not stir up his full wrath.
39 He remembered that they were but flesh,
a passing breeze that does not return.

40 How often they rebelled against him
in the wilderness
and grieved him in the wasteland!
41 Again and again they put God to the test;
they vexed the Holy One of Israel.
42 They did not remember his power—
the day he redeemed them from the oppressor,
43 the day he displayed his signs in Egypt,
his wonders in the region of Zoan.
44 He turned their river into blood;

they could not drink from their
streams.
45 He sent swarms of flies that devoured
them,
and frogs that devastated them.
46 He gave their crops to the
grasshopper,
their produce to the locust.
47 He destroyed their vines with hail
and their sycamore-figs with sleet.
48 He gave over their cattle to the hail,
their livestock to bolts of lightning.
49 He unleashed against them his hot
anger,
his wrath, indignation and
hostility—
a band of destroying angels.
50 He prepared a path for his anger;
he did not spare them from death
but gave them over to the plague.
51 He struck down all the firstborn of
Egypt,
the firstfruits of manhood in the
tents of Ham.
52 But he brought his people out like a
flock;
he led them like sheep through the
wilderness.
53 He guided them safely, so they were
unafraid;
but the sea engulfed their enemies.
54 And so he brought them to the border
of his holy land,
to the hill country his right hand
had taken.
55 He drove out nations before them
and allotted their lands to them as
an inheritance;
he settled the tribes of Israel in their
homes.
56 But they put God to the test
and rebelled against the Most High;
they did not keep his statutes.
57 Like their ancestors they were disloyal
and faithless,
as unreliable as a faulty bow.
58 They angered him with their high
places;
they aroused his jealousy with their
idols.
59 When God heard them, he was
furious;
he rejected Israel completely.
60 He abandoned the tabernacle of
Shiloh,
the tent he had set up among
humans.
61 He sent the ark of his might into
captivity,
his splendor into the hands of the
enemy.
62 He gave his people over to the sword;
he was furious with his inheritance.
63 Fire consumed their young men,
and their young women had no
wedding songs;
64 their priests were put to the sword,
and their widows could not weep.
65 Then the Lord awoke as from sleep,
as a warrior wakes from the stupor
of wine.
66 He beat back his enemies;
he put them to everlasting shame.
67 Then he rejected the tents of Joseph,
he did not choose the tribe of
Ephraim;
68 but he chose the tribe of Judah,
Mount Zion, which he loved.
69 He built his sanctuary like the
heights,
like the earth that he established
forever.
70 He chose David his servant
and took him from the sheep pens;
71 from tending the sheep he brought
him
to be the shepherd of his people
Jacob,
of Israel his inheritance.
72 And David shepherded them with
integrity of heart;
with skillful hands he led them.

Psalm 79

A psalm of Asaph.

1 O God, the nations have invaded your
inheritance;
they have defiled your holy temple,
they have reduced Jerusalem to
rubble.
2 They have left the dead bodies of your
servants
as food for the birds of the sky,
the flesh of your own people for the
animals of the wild.
3 They have poured out blood like water
all around Jerusalem,
and there is no one to bury the
dead.
4 We are objects of contempt to our
neighbors,
of scorn and derision to those
around us.

5 How long, LORD? Will you be angry
forever?
How long will your jealousy burn
like fire?
6 Pour out your wrath on the nations
that do not acknowledge you,
on the kingdoms
that do not call on your name;
7 for they have devoured Jacob
and devastated his homeland.

8 Do not hold against us the sins of past
generations;
may your mercy come quickly to
meet us,
for we are in desperate need.
9 Help us, God our Savior,
for the glory of your name;
deliver us and forgive our sins
for your name's sake.
10 Why should the nations say,
"Where is their God?"

Before our eyes, make known among
the nations
that you avenge the outpoured
blood of your servants.
11 May the groans of the prisoners come
before you;
with your strong arm preserve those
condemned to die.
12 Pay back into the laps of our neighbors
seven times
the contempt they have hurled at
you, Lord.
13 Then we your people, the sheep of
your pasture,
will praise you forever;
from generation to generation
we will proclaim your praise.

Psalm 80[a]

For the director of music. To the tune of "The Lilies of the Covenant." Of Asaph. A psalm.

1 Hear us, Shepherd of Israel,
you who lead Joseph like a flock.
You who sit enthroned between the
cherubim,
shine forth 2 before Ephraim,
Benjamin and Manasseh.
Awaken your might;
come and save us.
3 Restore us, O God;
make your face shine on us,
that we may be saved.
4 How long, LORD God Almighty,
will your anger smolder
against the prayers of your people?
5 You have fed them with the bread of
tears;
you have made them drink tears by
the bowlful.
6 You have made us an object of
derision[b] to our neighbors,
and our enemies mock us.

7 Restore us, God Almighty;
make your face shine on us,
that we may be saved.

8 You transplanted a vine from Egypt;
you drove out the nations and
planted it.
9 You cleared the ground for it,
and it took root and filled the land.
10 The mountains were covered with its
shade,
the mighty cedars with its branches.
11 Its branches reached as far as the Sea,[c]
its shoots as far as the River.[d]

12 Why have you broken down its walls
so that all who pass by pick its
grapes?
13 Boars from the forest ravage it,
and insects from the fields feed
on it.
14 Return to us, God Almighty!
Look down from heaven and see!
Watch over this vine,
15 the root your right hand has
planted,
the son[e] you have raised up for
yourself.

16 Your vine is cut down, it is burned
with fire;
at your rebuke your people perish.
17 Let your hand rest on the man at your
right hand,
the son of man you have raised up
for yourself.
18 Then we will not turn away from you;
revive us, and we will call on your
name.

19 Restore us, LORD God Almighty;
make your face shine on us,
that we may be saved.

[a] In Hebrew texts 80:1-19 is numbered 80:2-20. [b] *6* Probable reading of the original Hebrew text; Masoretic Text *contention* [c] *11* Probably the Mediterranean [d] *11* That is, the Euphrates [e] *15* Or *branch*

Psalm 81[a]

For the director of music. According to gittith.[b] *Of Asaph.*

1 Sing for joy to God our strength;
shout aloud to the God of Jacob!
2 Begin the music, strike the timbrel,
play the melodious harp and lyre.

3 Sound the ram's horn at the New Moon,
and when the moon is full, on the day of our festival;
4 this is a decree for Israel,
an ordinance of the God of Jacob.
5 When God went out against Egypt,
he established it as a statute for Joseph.

I heard an unknown voice say:

6 "I removed the burden from their shoulders;
their hands were set free from the basket.
7 In your distress you called and I rescued you,
I answered you out of a thundercloud;
I tested you at the waters of Meribah.[c]
8 Hear me, my people, and I will warn you—
if you would only listen to me, Israel!
9 You shall have no foreign god among you;
you shall not worship any god other than me.
10 I am the LORD your God,
who brought you up out of Egypt.
Open wide your mouth and I will fill it.

11 "But my people would not listen to me;
Israel would not submit to me.
12 So I gave them over to their stubborn hearts
to follow their own devices.

13 "If my people would only listen to me,
if Israel would only follow my ways,
14 how quickly I would subdue their enemies
and turn my hand against their foes!
15 Those who hate the LORD would cringe before him,
and their punishment would last forever.
16 But you would be fed with the finest of wheat;
with honey from the rock I would satisfy you."

Psalm 82

A psalm of Asaph.

1 God presides in the great assembly;
he renders judgment among the "gods":

2 "How long will you[d] defend the unjust
and show partiality to the wicked?[c]
3 Defend the weak and the fatherless;
uphold the cause of the poor and the oppressed.
4 Rescue the weak and the needy;
deliver them from the hand of the wicked.

5 "The 'gods' know nothing, they understand nothing.
They walk about in darkness;
all the foundations of the earth are shaken.

6 "I said, 'You are "gods";
you are all sons of the Most High.'
7 But you will die like mere mortals;
you will fall like every other ruler."

8 Rise up, O God, judge the earth,
for all the nations are your inheritance.

Psalm 83[e]

A song. A psalm of Asaph.

1 O God, do not remain silent;
do not turn a deaf ear,
do not stand aloof, O God.
2 See how your enemies growl,
how your foes rear their heads.
3 With cunning they conspire against your people;
they plot against those you cherish.
4 "Come," they say, "let us destroy them as a nation,
so that Israel's name is remembered no more."

5 With one mind they plot together;
they form an alliance against you—
6 the tents of Edom and the Ishmaelites,
of Moab and the Hagrites,

[a] In Hebrew texts 81:1-16 is numbered 81:2-17. [b] Title: Probably a musical term [c] *7,2* The Hebrew has *Selah* (a word of uncertain meaning) here. [d] *2* The Hebrew is plural. [e] In Hebrew texts 83:1-18 is numbered 83:2-19.

7 Byblos, Ammon and Amalek,
Philistia, with the people of Tyre.
8 Even Assyria has joined them
to reinforce Lot's descendants.[a]

9 Do to them as you did to Midian,
as you did to Sisera and Jabin at the river Kishon,
10 who perished at Endor
and became like dung on the ground.
11 Make their nobles like Oreb and Zeeb,
all their princes like Zebah and Zalmunna,
12 who said, "Let us take possession
of the pasturelands of God."

13 Make them like tumbleweed, my God,
like chaff before the wind.
14 As fire consumes the forest
or a flame sets the mountains ablaze,
15 so pursue them with your tempest
and terrify them with your storm.
16 Cover their faces with shame, LORD,
so that they will seek your name.

17 May they ever be ashamed and dismayed;
may they perish in disgrace.
18 Let them know that you, whose name is the LORD —
that you alone are the Most High
over all the earth.

Psalm 84[b]

For the director of music. According to gittith.[c] *Of the Sons of Korah. A psalm.*

1 How lovely is your dwelling place,
LORD Almighty!
2 My soul yearns, even faints,
for the courts of the LORD;
my heart and my flesh cry out
for the living God.
3 Even the sparrow has found a home,
and the swallow a nest for herself,
where she may have her young —
a place near your altar,
LORD Almighty, my King and my God.
4 Blessed are those who dwell in your house;
they are ever praising you.[d]

5 Blessed are those whose strength is in you,
whose hearts are set on pilgrimage.
6 As they pass through the Valley of Baka,
they make it a place of springs;
the autumn rains also cover it with pools.[e]
7 They go from strength to strength,
till each appears before God in Zion.

8 Hear my prayer, LORD God Almighty;
listen to me, God of Jacob.
9 Look on our shield,[f] O God;
look with favor on your anointed one.

10 Better is one day in your courts
than a thousand elsewhere;
I would rather be a doorkeeper in the house of my God
than dwell in the tents of the wicked.
11 For the LORD God is a sun and shield;
the LORD bestows favor and honor;
no good thing does he withhold
from those whose walk is blameless.

12 LORD Almighty,
blessed is the one who trusts in you.

Psalm 85[g]

For the director of music. Of the Sons of Korah. A psalm.

1 You, LORD, showed favor to your land;
you restored the fortunes of Jacob.
2 You forgave the iniquity of your people
and covered all their sins.[a]
3 You set aside all your wrath
and turned from your fierce anger.

4 Restore us again, God our Savior,
and put away your displeasure toward us.
5 Will you be angry with us forever?
Will you prolong your anger through all generations?
6 Will you not revive us again,
that your people may rejoice in you?
7 Show us your unfailing love, LORD,
and grant us your salvation.

8 I will listen to what God the LORD says;
he promises peace to his people, his faithful servants —

[a] *8,2* The Hebrew has *Selah* (a word of uncertain meaning) here. [b] In Hebrew texts 84:1-12 is numbered 84:2-13. [c] Title: Probably a musical term [d] *4* The Hebrew has *Selah* (a word of uncertain meaning) here and at the end of verse 8. [e] *6* Or *blessings* [f] *9* Or *sovereign* [g] In Hebrew texts 85:1-13 is numbered 85:2-14.

but let them not turn to folly.
9 Surely his salvation is near those who fear him,
that his glory may dwell in our land.

10 Love and faithfulness meet together;
righteousness and peace kiss each other.
11 Faithfulness springs forth from the earth,
and righteousness looks down from heaven.
12 The LORD will indeed give what is good,
and our land will yield its harvest.
13 Righteousness goes before him
and prepares the way for his steps.

Psalm 86

A prayer of David.

1 Hear me, LORD, and answer me,
for I am poor and needy.
2 Guard my life, for I am faithful to you;
save your servant who trusts in you.
You are my God; 3 have mercy on me, Lord,
for I call to you all day long.
4 Bring joy to your servant, Lord,
for I put my trust in you.

5 You, Lord, are forgiving and good,
abounding in love to all who call to you.
6 Hear my prayer, LORD;
listen to my cry for mercy.
7 When I am in distress, I call to you,
because you answer me.

8 Among the gods there is none like you, Lord;
no deeds can compare with yours.
9 All the nations you have made
will come and worship before you, Lord;
they will bring glory to your name.
10 For you are great and do marvelous deeds;
you alone are God.

11 Teach me your way, LORD,
that I may rely on your faithfulness;
give me an undivided heart,
that I may fear your name.
12 I will praise you, Lord my God, with all my heart;
I will glorify your name forever.
13 For great is your love toward me;
you have delivered me from the depths,
from the realm of the dead.

14 Arrogant foes are attacking me, O God;
ruthless people are trying to kill me—
they have no regard for you.
15 But you, Lord, are a compassionate and gracious God,
slow to anger, abounding in love and faithfulness.
16 Turn to me and have mercy on me;
show your strength in behalf of your servant;
save me, because I serve you
just as my mother did.
17 Give me a sign of your goodness,
that my enemies may see it and be put to shame,
for you, LORD, have helped me and comforted me.

Psalm 87

Of the Sons of Korah. A psalm. A song.

1 He has founded his city on the holy mountain.
2 The LORD loves the gates of Zion
more than all the other dwellings of Jacob.

3 Glorious things are said of you,
city of God:[a]
4 "I will record Rahab[b] and Babylon
among those who acknowledge me—
Philistia too, and Tyre, along with Cush[c]—
and will say, 'This one was born in Zion.' "[d]
5 Indeed, of Zion it will be said,
"This one and that one were born in her,
and the Most High himself will establish her."
6 The LORD will write in the register of the peoples:
"This one was born in Zion."
7 As they make music they will sing,
"All my fountains are in you."

[a] 3 The Hebrew has *Selah* (a word of uncertain meaning) here and at the end of verse 6. [b] 4 A poetic name for Egypt [c] 4 That is, the upper Nile region [d] 4 Or *"I will record concerning those who acknowledge me: / 'This one was born in Zion.' / Hear this, Rahab and Babylon, / and you too, Philistia, Tyre and Cush."*

Psalm 88[a]

A song. A psalm of the Sons of Korah. For the director of music. According to mahalath leannoth.[b] *A* maskil[c] *of Heman the Ezrahite.*

1 LORD, you are the God who saves me;
day and night I cry out to you.
2 May my prayer come before you;
turn your ear to my cry.

3 I am overwhelmed with troubles
and my life draws near to death.
4 I am counted among those who go down to the pit;
I am like one without strength.
5 I am set apart with the dead,
like the slain who lie in the grave,
whom you remember no more,
who are cut off from your care.

6 You have put me in the lowest pit,
in the darkest depths.
7 Your wrath lies heavily on me;
you have overwhelmed me with all your waves.[d]
8 You have taken from me my closest friends
and have made me repulsive to them.
I am confined and cannot escape;
9 my eyes are dim with grief.

I call to you, LORD, every day;
I spread out my hands to you.
10 Do you show your wonders to the dead?
Do their spirits rise up and praise you?
11 Is your love declared in the grave,
your faithfulness in Destruction[e]?
12 Are your wonders known in the place of darkness,
or your righteous deeds in the land of oblivion?

13 But I cry to you for help, LORD;
in the morning my prayer comes before you.
14 Why, LORD, do you reject me
and hide your face from me?

15 From my youth I have suffered and been close to death;
I have borne your terrors and am in despair.
16 Your wrath has swept over me;
your terrors have destroyed me.
17 All day long they surround me like a flood;
they have completely engulfed me.
18 You have taken from me friend and neighbor —
darkness is my closest friend.

Psalm 89[f]

A maskil[c] *of Ethan the Ezrahite.*

1 I will sing of the LORD's great love forever;
with my mouth I will make your faithfulness known
through all generations.
2 I will declare that your love stands firm forever,
that you have established your faithfulness in heaven itself.
3 You said, "I have made a covenant with my chosen one,
I have sworn to David my servant,
4 'I will establish your line forever
and make your throne firm through all generations.' "[g]

5 The heavens praise your wonders, LORD,
your faithfulness too, in the assembly of the holy ones.
6 For who in the skies above can compare with the LORD?
Who is like the LORD among the heavenly beings?
7 In the council of the holy ones God is greatly feared;
he is more awesome than all who surround him.
8 Who is like you, LORD God Almighty?
You, LORD, are mighty, and your faithfulness surrounds you.

9 You rule over the surging sea;
when its waves mount up, you still them.
10 You crushed Rahab like one of the slain;
with your strong arm you scattered your enemies.
11 The heavens are yours, and yours also the earth;
you founded the world and all that is in it.

[a] In Hebrew texts 88:1-18 is numbered 88:2-19. [b] Title: Possibly a tune, "The Suffering of Affliction" [c] Title: Probably a literary or musical term [d] 7 The Hebrew has *Selah* (a word of uncertain meaning) here and at the end of verse 10. [e] 11 Hebrew *Abaddon* [f] In Hebrew texts 89:1-52 is numbered 89:2-53. [g] 4 The Hebrew has *Selah* (a word of uncertain meaning) here and at the end of verses 37, 45 and 48.

12 You created the north and the south;
Tabor and Hermon sing for joy at your name.
13 Your arm is endowed with power;
your hand is strong, your right hand exalted.

14 Righteousness and justice are the foundation of your throne;
love and faithfulness go before you.
15 Blessed are those who have learned to acclaim you,
who walk in the light of your presence, LORD.
16 They rejoice in your name all day long;
they celebrate your righteousness.
17 For you are their glory and strength,
and by your favor you exalt our horn.[a]
18 Indeed, our shield[b] belongs to the LORD,
our king to the Holy One of Israel.

19 Once you spoke in a vision,
to your faithful people you said:
"I have bestowed strength on a warrior;
I have raised up a young man from among the people.
20 I have found David my servant;
with my sacred oil I have anointed him.
21 My hand will sustain him;
surely my arm will strengthen him.
22 The enemy will not get the better of him;
the wicked will not oppress him.
23 I will crush his foes before him
and strike down his adversaries.
24 My faithful love will be with him,
and through my name his horn[c] will be exalted.
25 I will set his hand over the sea,
his right hand over the rivers.
26 He will call out to me, 'You are my Father,
my God, the Rock my Savior.'
27 And I will appoint him to be my firstborn,
the most exalted of the kings of the earth.
28 I will maintain my love to him forever,
and my covenant with him will never fail.
29 I will establish his line forever,
his throne as long as the heavens endure.

30 "If his sons forsake my law
and do not follow my statutes,
31 if they violate my decrees
and fail to keep my commands,
32 I will punish their sin with the rod,
their iniquity with flogging;
33 but I will not take my love from him,
nor will I ever betray my faithfulness.
34 I will not violate my covenant
or alter what my lips have uttered.
35 Once for all, I have sworn by my holiness—
and I will not lie to David—
36 that his line will continue forever
and his throne endure before me like the sun;
37 it will be established forever like the moon,
the faithful witness in the sky."

38 But you have rejected, you have spurned,
you have been very angry with your anointed one.
39 You have renounced the covenant with your servant
and have defiled his crown in the dust.
40 You have broken through all his walls
and reduced his strongholds to ruins.
41 All who pass by have plundered him;
he has become the scorn of his neighbors.
42 You have exalted the right hand of his foes;
you have made all his enemies rejoice.
43 Indeed, you have turned back the edge of his sword
and have not supported him in battle.
44 You have put an end to his splendor
and cast his throne to the ground.
45 You have cut short the days of his youth;
you have covered him with a mantle of shame.

46 How long, LORD? Will you hide yourself forever?
How long will your wrath burn like fire?
47 Remember how fleeting is my life.

[a] 17 *Horn* here symbolizes strong one. [b] 18 Or *sovereign* [c] 24 *Horn* here symbolizes strength.

For what futility you have created all
humanity!
48 Who can live and not see death,
or who can escape the power of the
grave?
49 Lord, where is your former great love,
which in your faithfulness you
swore to David?
50 Remember, Lord, how your servant
has[a] been mocked,
how I bear in my heart the taunts of
all the nations,
51 the taunts with which your enemies,
LORD, have mocked,
with which they have mocked every
step of your anointed one.

52 Praise be to the LORD forever!
Amen and Amen.

BOOK IV

Psalms 90–106

Psalm 90

A prayer of Moses the man of God.

1 Lord, you have been our dwelling
place
throughout all generations.
2 Before the mountains were born
or you brought forth the whole world,
from everlasting to everlasting you
are God.

3 You turn people back to dust,
saying, "Return to dust, you
mortals."
4 A thousand years in your sight
are like a day that has just gone by,
or like a watch in the night.
5 Yet you sweep people away in the
sleep of death—
they are like the new grass of the
morning:
6 In the morning it springs up new,
but by evening it is dry and
withered.

7 We are consumed by your anger
and terrified by your indignation.
8 You have set our iniquities before you,
our secret sins in the light of your
presence.
9 All our days pass away under your
wrath;
we finish our years with a moan.
10 Our days may come to seventy years,
or eighty, if our strength endures;
yet the best of them are but trouble
and sorrow,
for they quickly pass, and we fly
away.
11 If only we knew the power of your
anger!
Your wrath is as great as the fear
that is your due.
12 Teach us to number our days,
that we may gain a heart of
wisdom.

13 Relent, LORD! How long will it be?
Have compassion on your servants.
14 Satisfy us in the morning with your
unfailing love,
that we may sing for joy and be glad
all our days.
15 Make us glad for as many days as you
have afflicted us,
for as many years as we have seen
trouble.
16 May your deeds be shown to your
servants,
your splendor to their children.

17 May the favor[b] of the Lord our God
rest on us;
establish the work of our hands for
us—
yes, establish the work of our hands.

Psalm 91

1 Whoever dwells in the shelter of the
Most High
will rest in the shadow of the
Almighty.[c]
2 I will say of the LORD, "He is my refuge
and my fortress,
my God, in whom I trust."

3 Surely he will save you
from the fowler's snare
and from the deadly pestilence.
4 He will cover you with his feathers,
and under his wings you will find
refuge;
his faithfulness will be your shield
and rampart.
5 You will not fear the terror of night,
nor the arrow that flies by day,
6 nor the pestilence that stalks in the
darkness,

[a] 50 Or *your servants have* [b] 17 Or *beauty* [c] 1 Hebrew *Shaddai*

nor the plague that destroys at
midday.
7 A thousand may fall at your side,
ten thousand at your right hand,
but it will not come near you.
8 You will only observe with your eyes
and see the punishment of the
wicked.

9 If you say, "The LORD is my refuge,"
and you make the Most High your
dwelling,
10 no harm will overtake you,
no disaster will come near your tent.
11 For he will command his angels
concerning you
to guard you in all your ways;
12 they will lift you up in their hands,
so that you will not strike your foot
against a stone.
13 You will tread on the lion and the cobra;
you will trample the great lion and
the serpent.

14 "Because he[a] loves me," says the
LORD, "I will rescue him;
I will protect him, for he
acknowledges my name.
15 He will call on me, and I will answer
him;
I will be with him in trouble,
I will deliver him and honor him.
16 With long life I will satisfy him
and show him my salvation."

Psalm 92[b]

A psalm. A song. For the Sabbath day.

1 It is good to praise the LORD
and make music to your name,
O Most High,
2 proclaiming your love in the morning
and your faithfulness at night,
3 to the music of the ten-stringed lyre
and the melody of the harp.

4 For you make me glad by your deeds,
LORD;
I sing for joy at what your hands
have done.
5 How great are your works, LORD,
how profound your thoughts!
6 Senseless people do not know,
fools do not understand,
7 that though the wicked spring up like
grass
and all evildoers flourish,
they will be destroyed forever.

8 But you, LORD, are forever exalted.
9 For surely your enemies, LORD,
surely your enemies will perish;
all evildoers will be scattered.
10 You have exalted my horn[c] like that of
a wild ox;
fine oils have been poured on me.
11 My eyes have seen the defeat of my
adversaries;
my ears have heard the rout of my
wicked foes.

12 The righteous will flourish like a palm
tree,
they will grow like a cedar of
Lebanon;
13 planted in the house of the LORD,
they will flourish in the courts of
our God.
14 They will still bear fruit in old age,
they will stay fresh and green,
15 proclaiming, "The LORD is upright;
he is my Rock, and there is no
wickedness in him."

Psalm 93

1 The LORD reigns, he is robed in
majesty;
the LORD is robed in majesty and
armed with strength;
indeed, the world is established,
firm and secure.
2 Your throne was established long ago;
you are from all eternity.
3 The seas have lifted up, LORD,
the seas have lifted up their voice;
the seas have lifted up their
pounding waves.
4 Mightier than the thunder of the great
waters,
mightier than the breakers of the
sea—
the LORD on high is mighty.

5 Your statutes, LORD, stand firm;
holiness adorns your house
for endless days.

Psalm 94

1 The LORD is a God who avenges.
O God who avenges, shine forth.

[a] *14* That is, probably the king [b] In Hebrew texts 92:1-15 is numbered 92:2-16. [c] *10* *Horn* here symbolizes strength.

2 Rise up, Judge of the earth;
pay back to the proud what they deserve.
3 How long, LORD, will the wicked,
how long will the wicked be jubilant?

4 They pour out arrogant words;
all the evildoers are full of boasting.
5 They crush your people, LORD;
they oppress your inheritance.
6 They slay the widow and the foreigner;
they murder the fatherless.
7 They say, "The LORD does not see;
the God of Jacob takes no notice."

8 Take notice, you senseless ones among the people;
you fools, when will you become wise?
9 Does he who fashioned the ear not hear?
Does he who formed the eye not see?
10 Does he who disciplines nations not punish?
Does he who teaches mankind lack knowledge?
11 The LORD knows all human plans;
he knows that they are futile.

12 Blessed is the one you discipline, LORD,
the one you teach from your law;
13 you grant them relief from days of trouble,
till a pit is dug for the wicked.
14 For the LORD will not reject his people;
he will never forsake his inheritance.
15 Judgment will again be founded on righteousness,
and all the upright in heart will follow it.

16 Who will rise up for me against the wicked?
Who will take a stand for me against evildoers?
17 Unless the LORD had given me help,
I would soon have dwelt in the silence of death.
18 When I said, "My foot is slipping,"
your unfailing love, LORD, supported me.
19 When anxiety was great within me,
your consolation brought me joy.

20 Can a corrupt throne be allied with you—
a throne that brings on misery by its decrees?
21 The wicked band together against the righteous
and condemn the innocent to death.
22 But the LORD has become my fortress,
and my God the rock in whom I take refuge.
23 He will repay them for their sins
and destroy them for their wickedness;
the LORD our God will destroy them.

Psalm 95

1 Come, let us sing for joy to the LORD;
let us shout aloud to the Rock of our salvation.
2 Let us come before him with thanksgiving
and extol him with music and song.

3 For the LORD is the great God,
the great King above all gods.
4 In his hand are the depths of the earth,
and the mountain peaks belong to him.
5 The sea is his, for he made it,
and his hands formed the dry land.

6 Come, let us bow down in worship,
let us kneel before the LORD our Maker;
7 for he is our God
and we are the people of his pasture,
the flock under his care.

Today, if only you would hear his voice,
8 "Do not harden your hearts as you did at Meribah,[a]
as you did that day at Massah[b] in the wilderness,
9 where your ancestors tested me;
they tried me, though they had seen what I did.
10 For forty years I was angry with that generation;
I said, 'They are a people whose hearts go astray,
and they have not known my ways.'
11 So I declared on oath in my anger,
'They shall never enter my rest.'"

[a] 8 *Meribah* means *quarreling*. [b] 8 *Massah* means *testing*.

Psalm 96

1 Sing to the LORD a new song;
sing to the LORD, all the earth.
2 Sing to the LORD, praise his name;
proclaim his salvation day after day.
3 Declare his glory among the nations,
his marvelous deeds among all peoples.
4 For great is the LORD and most worthy of praise;
he is to be feared above all gods.
5 For all the gods of the nations are idols,
but the LORD made the heavens.
6 Splendor and majesty are before him;
strength and glory are in his sanctuary.
7 Ascribe to the LORD, all you families of nations,
ascribe to the LORD glory and strength.
8 Ascribe to the LORD the glory due his name;
bring an offering and come into his courts.
9 Worship the LORD in the splendor of his[a] holiness;
tremble before him, all the earth.
10 Say among the nations, "The LORD reigns."
The world is firmly established, it cannot be moved;
he will judge the peoples with equity.
11 Let the heavens rejoice, let the earth be glad;
let the sea resound, and all that is in it.
12 Let the fields be jubilant, and everything in them;
let all the trees of the forest sing for joy.
13 Let all creation rejoice before the LORD, for he comes,
he comes to judge the earth.
He will judge the world in righteousness
and the peoples in his faithfulness.

Psalm 97

1 The LORD reigns, let the earth be glad;
let the distant shores rejoice.
2 Clouds and thick darkness surround him;
righteousness and justice are the foundation of his throne.
3 Fire goes before him
and consumes his foes on every side.
4 His lightning lights up the world;
the earth sees and trembles.
5 The mountains melt like wax before the LORD,
before the Lord of all the earth.
6 The heavens proclaim his righteousness,
and all peoples see his glory.
7 All who worship images are put to shame,
those who boast in idols—
worship him, all you gods!
8 Zion hears and rejoices
and the villages of Judah are glad
because of your judgments, LORD.
9 For you, LORD, are the Most High over all the earth;
you are exalted far above all gods.
10 Let those who love the LORD hate evil,
for he guards the lives of his faithful ones
and delivers them from the hand of the wicked.
11 Light shines[b] on the righteous
and joy on the upright in heart.
12 Rejoice in the LORD, you who are righteous,
and praise his holy name.

Psalm 98

A psalm.

1 Sing to the LORD a new song,
for he has done marvelous things;
his right hand and his holy arm
have worked salvation for him.
2 The LORD has made his salvation known
and revealed his righteousness to the nations.
3 He has remembered his love
and his faithfulness to Israel;
all the ends of the earth have seen
the salvation of our God.
4 Shout for joy to the LORD, all the earth,
burst into jubilant song with music;

[a] 9 Or *LORD with the splendor of* [b] 11 One Hebrew manuscript and ancient versions (see also 112:4); most Hebrew manuscripts *Light is sown*

5 make music to the LORD with the harp,
with the harp and the sound of singing,
6 with trumpets and the blast of the ram's horn —
shout for joy before the LORD, the King.

7 Let the sea resound, and everything in it,
the world, and all who live in it.
8 Let the rivers clap their hands,
let the mountains sing together for joy;
9 let them sing before the LORD,
for he comes to judge the earth.
He will judge the world in righteousness
and the peoples with equity.

Psalm 99

1 The LORD reigns,
let the nations tremble;
he sits enthroned between the cherubim,
let the earth shake.
2 Great is the LORD in Zion;
he is exalted over all the nations.
3 Let them praise your great and awesome name —
he is holy.

4 The King is mighty, he loves justice —
you have established equity;
in Jacob you have done
what is just and right.
5 Exalt the LORD our God
and worship at his footstool;
he is holy.

6 Moses and Aaron were among his priests,
Samuel was among those who called on his name;
they called on the LORD
and he answered them.
7 He spoke to them from the pillar of cloud;
they kept his statutes and the decrees he gave them.

8 LORD our God,
you answered them;
you were to Israel a forgiving God,
though you punished their misdeeds.[a]
9 Exalt the LORD our God
and worship at his holy mountain,
for the LORD our God is holy.

Psalm 100

A psalm. For giving grateful praise.

1 Shout for joy to the LORD, all the earth.
2 Worship the LORD with gladness;
come before him with joyful songs.
3 Know that the LORD is God.
It is he who made us, and we are his[b];
we are his people, the sheep of his pasture.
4 Enter his gates with thanksgiving
and his courts with praise;
give thanks to him and praise his name.
5 For the LORD is good and his love endures forever;
his faithfulness continues through all generations.

Psalm 101

Of David. A psalm.

1 I will sing of your love and justice;
to you, LORD, I will sing praise.
2 I will be careful to lead a blameless life —
when will you come to me?

I will conduct the affairs of my house
with a blameless heart.
3 I will not look with approval
on anything that is vile.

I hate what faithless people do;
I will have no part in it.
4 The perverse of heart shall be far from me;
I will have nothing to do with what is evil.

5 Whoever slanders their neighbor in secret,
I will put to silence;
whoever has haughty eyes and a proud heart,
I will not tolerate.

6 My eyes will be on the faithful in the land,
that they may dwell with me;
the one whose walk is blameless
will minister to me.

[a] 8 Or *God, / an avenger of the wrongs done to them*
[b] 3 Or *and not we ourselves*

7 No one who practices deceit
will dwell in my house;
no one who speaks falsely
will stand in my presence.

8 Every morning I will put to silence
all the wicked in the land;
I will cut off every evildoer
from the city of the LORD.

Psalm 102[a]

A prayer of an afflicted person who has grown weak and pours out a lament before the LORD.

1 Hear my prayer, LORD;
let my cry for help come to you.
2 Do not hide your face from me
when I am in distress.
Turn your ear to me;
when I call, answer me quickly.

3 For my days vanish like smoke;
my bones burn like glowing embers.
4 My heart is blighted and withered like grass;
I forget to eat my food.
5 In my distress I groan aloud
and am reduced to skin and bones.
6 I am like a desert owl,
like an owl among the ruins.
7 I lie awake; I have become
like a bird alone on a roof.
8 All day long my enemies taunt me;
those who rail against me use my name as a curse.
9 For I eat ashes as my food
and mingle my drink with tears
10 because of your great wrath,
for you have taken me up and thrown me aside.
11 My days are like the evening shadow;
I wither away like grass.

12 But you, LORD, sit enthroned forever;
your renown endures through all generations.
13 You will arise and have compassion on Zion,
for it is time to show favor to her;
the appointed time has come.
14 For her stones are dear to your servants;
her very dust moves them to pity.
15 The nations will fear the name of the LORD,
all the kings of the earth will revere your glory.
16 For the LORD will rebuild Zion
and appear in his glory.
17 He will respond to the prayer of the destitute;
he will not despise their plea.

18 Let this be written for a future generation,
that a people not yet created may praise the LORD:
19 "The LORD looked down from his sanctuary on high,
from heaven he viewed the earth,
20 to hear the groans of the prisoners
and release those condemned to death."
21 So the name of the LORD will be declared in Zion
and his praise in Jerusalem
22 when the peoples and the kingdoms
assemble to worship the LORD.

23 In the course of my life[b] he broke my strength;
he cut short my days.
24 So I said:
"Do not take me away, my God, in the midst of my days;
your years go on through all generations.
25 In the beginning you laid the foundations of the earth,
and the heavens are the work of your hands.
26 They will perish, but you remain;
they will all wear out like a garment.
Like clothing you will change them
and they will be discarded.
27 But you remain the same,
and your years will never end.
28 The children of your servants will live in your presence;
their descendants will be established before you."

Psalm 103

Of David.

1 Praise the LORD, my soul;
all my inmost being, praise his holy name.
2 Praise the LORD, my soul,
and forget not all his benefits —
3 who forgives all your sins
and heals all your diseases,
4 who redeems your life from the pit

[a] In Hebrew texts 102:1-28 is numbered 102:2-29. [b] 23 Or *By his power*

and crowns you with love and
compassion,
5 who satisfies your desires with good
things
so that your youth is renewed like
the eagle's.

6 The LORD works righteousness
and justice for all the oppressed.

7 He made known his ways to Moses,
his deeds to the people of Israel:
8 The LORD is compassionate and
gracious,
slow to anger, abounding in love.
9 He will not always accuse,
nor will he harbor his anger forever;
10 he does not treat us as our sins deserve
or repay us according to our
iniquities.
11 For as high as the heavens are above
the earth,
so great is his love for those who fear
him;
12 as far as the east is from the west,
so far has he removed our
transgressions from us.

13 As a father has compassion on his
children,
so the LORD has compassion on
those who fear him;
14 for he knows how we are formed,
he remembers that we are dust.
15 The life of mortals is like grass,
they flourish like a flower of the
field;
16 the wind blows over it and it is gone,
and its place remembers it no more.
17 But from everlasting to everlasting
the LORD's love is with those who
fear him,
and his righteousness with their
children's children —
18 with those who keep his covenant
and remember to obey his precepts.

19 The LORD has established his throne
in heaven,
and his kingdom rules over all.

20 Praise the LORD, you his angels,
you mighty ones who do his
bidding,
who obey his word.
21 Praise the LORD, all his heavenly
hosts,
you his servants who do his will.
22 Praise the LORD, all his works
everywhere in his dominion.

Praise the LORD, my soul.

Psalm 104

1 Praise the LORD, my soul.

LORD my God, you are very great;
you are clothed with splendor and
majesty.

2 The LORD wraps himself in light as
with a garment;
he stretches out the heavens like a
tent
3 and lays the beams of his upper
chambers on their waters.
He makes the clouds his chariot
and rides on the wings of the wind.
4 He makes winds his messengers,[a]
flames of fire his servants.

5 He set the earth on its foundations;
it can never be moved.
6 You covered it with the watery depths
as with a garment;
the waters stood above the
mountains.
7 But at your rebuke the waters fled,
at the sound of your thunder they
took to flight;
8 they flowed over the mountains,
they went down into the valleys,
to the place you assigned for them.
9 You set a boundary they cannot cross;
never again will they cover the earth.

10 He makes springs pour water into the
ravines;
it flows between the mountains.
11 They give water to all the beasts of the
field;
the wild donkeys quench their
thirst.
12 The birds of the sky nest by the waters;
they sing among the branches.
13 He waters the mountains from his
upper chambers;
the land is satisfied by the fruit of
his work.
14 He makes grass grow for the cattle,
and plants for people to cultivate —
bringing forth food from the earth:
15 wine that gladdens human hearts,
oil to make their faces shine,
and bread that sustains their hearts.

[a] 4 Or *angels*

16 The trees of the LORD are well
watered,
the cedars of Lebanon that he
planted.
17 There the birds make their nests;
the stork has its home in the
junipers.
18 The high mountains belong to the
wild goats;
the crags are a refuge for the hyrax.

19 He made the moon to mark the
seasons,
and the sun knows when to go
down.
20 You bring darkness, it becomes night,
and all the beasts of the forest prowl.
21 The lions roar for their prey
and seek their food from God.
22 The sun rises, and they steal away;
they return and lie down in their
dens.
23 Then people go out to their work,
to their labor until evening.

24 How many are your works, LORD!
In wisdom you made them all;
the earth is full of your creatures.
25 There is the sea, vast and spacious,
teeming with creatures beyond
number —
living things both large and small.
26 There the ships go to and fro,
and Leviathan, which you formed to
frolic there.

27 All creatures look to you
to give them their food at the proper
time.
28 When you give it to them,
they gather it up;
when you open your hand,
they are satisfied with good things.
29 When you hide your face,
they are terrified;
when you take away their breath,
they die and return to the dust.
30 When you send your Spirit,
they are created,
and you renew the face of the
ground.

31 May the glory of the LORD endure
forever;
may the LORD rejoice in his works —
32 he who looks at the earth, and it
trembles,
who touches the mountains, and
they smoke.

33 I will sing to the LORD all my life;
I will sing praise to my God as long
as I live.
34 May my meditation be pleasing to
him,
as I rejoice in the LORD.
35 But may sinners vanish from the earth
and the wicked be no more.

Praise the LORD, my soul.

Praise the LORD.[a]

Psalm 105

1 Give praise to the LORD, proclaim his
name;
make known among the nations
what he has done.
2 Sing to him, sing praise to him;
tell of all his wonderful acts.
3 Glory in his holy name;
let the hearts of those who seek the
LORD rejoice.
4 Look to the LORD and his strength;
seek his face always.

5 Remember the wonders he has done,
his miracles, and the judgments he
pronounced,
6 you his servants, the descendants of
Abraham,
his chosen ones, the children of
Jacob.
7 He is the LORD our God;
his judgments are in all the earth.

8 He remembers his covenant forever,
the promise he made, for a thousand
generations,
9 the covenant he made with Abraham,
the oath he swore to Isaac.
10 He confirmed it to Jacob as a decree,
to Israel as an everlasting covenant:
11 "To you I will give the land of Canaan
as the portion you will inherit."

12 When they were but few in number,
few indeed, and strangers in it,
13 they wandered from nation to nation,
from one kingdom to another.
14 He allowed no one to oppress them;
for their sake he rebuked kings:
15 "Do not touch my anointed ones;
do my prophets no harm."

[a] *35* Hebrew *Hallelu Yah*; in the Septuagint this line stands at the beginning of Psalm 105.

16 He called down famine on the land
and destroyed all their supplies of food;
17 and he sent a man before them—
Joseph, sold as a slave.
18 They bruised his feet with shackles,
his neck was put in irons,
19 till what he foretold came to pass,
till the word of the LORD proved him true.
20 The king sent and released him,
the ruler of peoples set him free.
21 He made him master of his household,
ruler over all he possessed,
22 to instruct his princes as he pleased
and teach his elders wisdom.

23 Then Israel entered Egypt;
Jacob resided as a foreigner in the land of Ham.
24 The LORD made his people very fruitful;
he made them too numerous for their foes,
25 whose hearts he turned to hate his people,
to conspire against his servants.
26 He sent Moses his servant,
and Aaron, whom he had chosen.
27 They performed his signs among them,
his wonders in the land of Ham.
28 He sent darkness and made the land dark—
for had they not rebelled against his words?
29 He turned their waters into blood,
causing their fish to die.
30 Their land teemed with frogs,
which went up into the bedrooms of their rulers.
31 He spoke, and there came swarms of flies,
and gnats throughout their country.
32 He turned their rain into hail,
with lightning throughout their land;
33 he struck down their vines and fig trees
and shattered the trees of their country.
34 He spoke, and the locusts came,
grasshoppers without number;
35 they ate up every green thing in their land,
ate up the produce of their soil.
36 Then he struck down all the firstborn in their land,
the firstfruits of all their manhood.
37 He brought out Israel, laden with silver and gold,
and from among their tribes no one faltered.
38 Egypt was glad when they left,
because dread of Israel had fallen on them.

39 He spread out a cloud as a covering,
and a fire to give light at night.
40 They asked, and he brought them quail;
he fed them well with the bread of heaven.
41 He opened the rock, and water gushed out;
it flowed like a river in the desert.

42 For he remembered his holy promise
given to his servant Abraham.
43 He brought out his people with rejoicing,
his chosen ones with shouts of joy;
44 he gave them the lands of the nations,
and they fell heir to what others had toiled for—
45 that they might keep his precepts
and observe his laws.

Praise the LORD.[a]

Psalm 106

1 Praise the LORD.[b]

Give thanks to the LORD, for he is good;
his love endures forever.

2 Who can proclaim the mighty acts of the LORD
or fully declare his praise?
3 Blessed are those who act justly,
who always do what is right.

4 Remember me, LORD, when you show favor to your people,
come to my aid when you save them,
5 that I may enjoy the prosperity of your chosen ones,
that I may share in the joy of your nation
and join your inheritance in giving praise.

[a] 45 Hebrew *Hallelu Yah* [b] 1 Hebrew *Hallelu Yah*; also in verse 48

6 We have sinned, even as our ancestors did;
we have done wrong and acted wickedly.
7 When our ancestors were in Egypt,
they gave no thought to your miracles;
they did not remember your many kindnesses,
and they rebelled by the sea, the Red Sea.[a]
8 Yet he saved them for his name's sake,
to make his mighty power known.
9 He rebuked the Red Sea, and it dried up;
he led them through the depths as through a desert.
10 He saved them from the hand of the foe;
from the hand of the enemy he redeemed them.
11 The waters covered their adversaries;
not one of them survived.
12 Then they believed his promises
and sang his praise.

13 But they soon forgot what he had done
and did not wait for his plan to unfold.
14 In the desert they gave in to their craving;
in the wilderness they put God to the test.
15 So he gave them what they asked for,
but sent a wasting disease among them.

16 In the camp they grew envious of Moses
and of Aaron, who was consecrated to the LORD.
17 The earth opened up and swallowed Dathan;
it buried the company of Abiram.
18 Fire blazed among their followers;
a flame consumed the wicked.
19 At Horeb they made a calf
and worshiped an idol cast from metal.
20 They exchanged their glorious God
for an image of a bull, which eats grass.
21 They forgot the God who saved them,
who had done great things in Egypt,
22 miracles in the land of Ham
and awesome deeds by the Red Sea.
23 So he said he would destroy them —
had not Moses, his chosen one,
stood in the breach before him
to keep his wrath from destroying them.

24 Then they despised the pleasant land;
they did not believe his promise.
25 They grumbled in their tents
and did not obey the LORD.
26 So he swore to them with uplifted hand
that he would make them fall in the wilderness,
27 make their descendants fall among the nations
and scatter them throughout the lands.

28 They yoked themselves to the Baal of Peor
and ate sacrifices offered to lifeless gods;
29 they aroused the LORD's anger by their wicked deeds,
and a plague broke out among them.
30 But Phinehas stood up and intervened,
and the plague was checked.
31 This was credited to him as righteousness
for endless generations to come.
32 By the waters of Meribah they angered the LORD,
and trouble came to Moses because of them;
33 for they rebelled against the Spirit of God,
and rash words came from Moses' lips.[b]

34 They did not destroy the peoples
as the LORD had commanded them,
35 but they mingled with the nations
and adopted their customs.
36 They worshiped their idols,
which became a snare to them.
37 They sacrificed their sons
and their daughters to false gods.
38 They shed innocent blood,
the blood of their sons and daughters,
whom they sacrificed to the idols of Canaan,
and the land was desecrated by their blood.

[a] 7 Or *the Sea of Reeds*; also in verses 9 and 22
[b] 33 Or *against his spirit, / and rash words came from his lips*

39 They defiled themselves by what they did;
by their deeds they prostituted themselves.
40 Therefore the LORD was angry with his people
and abhorred his inheritance.
41 He gave them into the hands of the nations,
and their foes ruled over them.
42 Their enemies oppressed them
and subjected them to their power.
43 Many times he delivered them,
but they were bent on rebellion
and they wasted away in their sin.
44 Yet he took note of their distress
when he heard their cry;
45 for their sake he remembered his covenant
and out of his great love he relented.
46 He caused all who held them captive
to show them mercy.

47 Save us, LORD our God,
and gather us from the nations,
that we may give thanks to your holy name
and glory in your praise.

48 Praise be to the LORD, the God of Israel,
from everlasting to everlasting.

Let all the people say, "Amen!"

Praise the LORD.

BOOK V

Psalms 107–150

Psalm 107

1 Give thanks to the LORD, for he is good;
his love endures forever.

2 Let the redeemed of the LORD tell their story—
those he redeemed from the hand of the foe,
3 those he gathered from the lands,
from east and west, from north and south.[a]

4 Some wandered in desert wastelands,
finding no way to a city where they could settle.
5 They were hungry and thirsty,
and their lives ebbed away.
6 Then they cried out to the LORD in their trouble,
and he delivered them from their distress.
7 He led them by a straight way
to a city where they could settle.
8 Let them give thanks to the LORD for his unfailing love
and his wonderful deeds for mankind,
9 for he satisfies the thirsty
and fills the hungry with good things.

10 Some sat in darkness, in utter darkness,
prisoners suffering in iron chains,
11 because they rebelled against God's commands
and despised the plans of the Most High.
12 So he subjected them to bitter labor;
they stumbled, and there was no one to help.
13 Then they cried to the LORD in their trouble,
and he saved them from their distress.
14 He brought them out of darkness, the utter darkness,
and broke away their chains.
15 Let them give thanks to the LORD for his unfailing love
and his wonderful deeds for mankind,
16 for he breaks down gates of bronze
and cuts through bars of iron.

17 Some became fools through their rebellious ways
and suffered affliction because of their iniquities.
18 They loathed all food
and drew near the gates of death.
19 Then they cried to the LORD in their trouble,
and he saved them from their distress.
20 He sent out his word and healed them;
he rescued them from the grave.
21 Let them give thanks to the LORD for his unfailing love
and his wonderful deeds for mankind.

a 3 Hebrew *north and the sea*

22 Let them sacrifice thank offerings
and tell of his works with songs of joy.

23 Some went out on the sea in ships;
they were merchants on the mighty waters.
24 They saw the works of the LORD,
his wonderful deeds in the deep.
25 For he spoke and stirred up a tempest
that lifted high the waves.
26 They mounted up to the heavens and went down to the depths;
in their peril their courage melted away.
27 They reeled and staggered like drunkards;
they were at their wits' end.
28 Then they cried out to the LORD in their trouble,
and he brought them out of their distress.
29 He stilled the storm to a whisper;
the waves of the sea[a] were hushed.
30 They were glad when it grew calm,
and he guided them to their desired haven.
31 Let them give thanks to the LORD for his unfailing love
and his wonderful deeds for mankind.
32 Let them exalt him in the assembly of the people
and praise him in the council of the elders.

33 He turned rivers into a desert,
flowing springs into thirsty ground,
34 and fruitful land into a salt waste,
because of the wickedness of those who lived there.
35 He turned the desert into pools of water
and the parched ground into flowing springs;
36 there he brought the hungry to live,
and they founded a city where they could settle.
37 They sowed fields and planted vineyards
that yielded a fruitful harvest;
38 he blessed them, and their numbers greatly increased,
and he did not let their herds diminish.

39 Then their numbers decreased, and they were humbled
by oppression, calamity and sorrow;
40 he who pours contempt on nobles
made them wander in a trackless waste.
41 But he lifted the needy out of their affliction
and increased their families like flocks.
42 The upright see and rejoice,
but all the wicked shut their mouths.

43 Let the one who is wise heed these things
and ponder the loving deeds of the LORD.

Psalm 108[b]

A song. A psalm of David.

1 My heart, O God, is steadfast;
I will sing and make music with all my soul.
2 Awake, harp and lyre!
I will awaken the dawn.
3 I will praise you, LORD, among the nations;
I will sing of you among the peoples.
4 For great is your love, higher than the heavens;
your faithfulness reaches to the skies.
5 Be exalted, O God, above the heavens;
let your glory be over all the earth.

6 Save us and help us with your right hand,
that those you love may be delivered.
7 God has spoken from his sanctuary:
"In triumph I will parcel out Shechem
and measure off the Valley of Sukkoth.
8 Gilead is mine, Manasseh is mine;
Ephraim is my helmet,
Judah is my scepter.
9 Moab is my washbasin,
on Edom I toss my sandal;
over Philistia I shout in triumph."

10 Who will bring me to the fortified city?
Who will lead me to Edom?
11 Is it not you, God, you who have rejected us
and no longer go out with our armies?
12 Give us aid against the enemy,
for human help is worthless.

[a] *29* Dead Sea Scrolls; Masoretic Text / *their waves*
[b] In Hebrew texts 108:1-13 is numbered 108:2-14.

13 With God we will gain the victory,
and he will trample down our enemies.

Psalm 109

For the director of music. Of David. A psalm.

1 My God, whom I praise,
do not remain silent,
2 for people who are wicked and deceitful
have opened their mouths against me;
they have spoken against me with lying tongues.
3 With words of hatred they surround me;
they attack me without cause.
4 In return for my friendship they accuse me,
but I am a man of prayer.
5 They repay me evil for good,
and hatred for my friendship.

6 Appoint someone evil to oppose my enemy;
let an accuser stand at his right hand.
7 When he is tried, let him be found guilty,
and may his prayers condemn him.
8 May his days be few;
may another take his place of leadership.
9 May his children be fatherless
and his wife a widow.
10 May his children be wandering beggars;
may they be driven[a] from their ruined homes.
11 May a creditor seize all he has;
may strangers plunder the fruits of his labor.
12 May no one extend kindness to him
or take pity on his fatherless children.
13 May his descendants be cut off,
their names blotted out from the next generation.
14 May the iniquity of his fathers be remembered before the LORD;
may the sin of his mother never be blotted out.
15 May their sins always remain before the LORD,
that he may blot out their name from the earth.

16 For he never thought of doing a kindness,
but hounded to death the poor
and the needy and the brokenhearted.
17 He loved to pronounce a curse —
may it come back on him.
He found no pleasure in blessing —
may it be far from him.
18 He wore cursing as his garment;
it entered into his body like water,
into his bones like oil.
19 May it be like a cloak wrapped about him,
like a belt tied forever around him.
20 May this be the LORD's payment to my accusers,
to those who speak evil of me.

21 But you, Sovereign LORD,
help me for your name's sake;
out of the goodness of your love,
deliver me.
22 For I am poor and needy,
and my heart is wounded within me.
23 I fade away like an evening shadow;
I am shaken off like a locust.
24 My knees give way from fasting;
my body is thin and gaunt.
25 I am an object of scorn to my accusers;
when they see me, they shake their heads.

26 Help me, LORD my God;
save me according to your unfailing love.
27 Let them know that it is your hand,
that you, LORD, have done it.
28 While they curse, may you bless;
may those who attack me be put to shame,
but may your servant rejoice.
29 May my accusers be clothed with disgrace
and wrapped in shame as in a cloak.
30 With my mouth I will greatly extol the LORD;
in the great throng of worshipers I will praise him.
31 For he stands at the right hand of the needy,
to save their lives from those who would condemn them.

[a] *10* Septuagint; Hebrew *sought*

Psalm 110

Of David. A psalm.

1 The LORD says to my lord:[a]

"Sit at my right hand
until I make your enemies
a footstool for your feet."

2 The LORD will extend your mighty
scepter from Zion, saying,
"Rule in the midst of your enemies!"
3 Your troops will be willing
on your day of battle.
Arrayed in holy splendor,
your young men will come to you
like dew from the morning's womb.[b]

4 The LORD has sworn
and will not change his mind:
"You are a priest forever,
in the order of Melchizedek."

5 The Lord is at your right hand[c];
he will crush kings on the day of his
wrath.
6 He will judge the nations, heaping up
the dead
and crushing the rulers of the whole
earth.
7 He will drink from a brook along the
way,[d]
and so he will lift his head high.

Psalm 111[e]

1 Praise the LORD.[f]

I will extol the LORD with all my heart
in the council of the upright and in
the assembly.

2 Great are the works of the LORD;
they are pondered by all who delight
in them.
3 Glorious and majestic are his deeds,
and his righteousness endures
forever.
4 He has caused his wonders to be
remembered;
the LORD is gracious and
compassionate.
5 He provides food for those who fear
him;
he remembers his covenant forever.
6 He has shown his people the power of
his works,
giving them the lands of other
nations.
7 The works of his hands are faithful
and just;
all his precepts are trustworthy.
8 They are established for ever and ever,
enacted in faithfulness and
uprightness.
9 He provided redemption for his
people;
he ordained his covenant forever —
holy and awesome is his name.

10 The fear of the LORD is the beginning
of wisdom;
all who follow his precepts have
good understanding.
To him belongs eternal praise.

Psalm 112[e]

1 Praise the LORD.[f]

Blessed are those who fear the LORD,
who find great delight in his
commands.

2 Their children will be mighty in the
land;
the generation of the upright will be
blessed.
3 Wealth and riches are in their houses,
and their righteousness endures
forever.
4 Even in darkness light dawns for the
upright,
for those who are gracious and
compassionate and righteous.
5 Good will come to those who are
generous and lend freely,
who conduct their affairs with
justice.

6 Surely the righteous will never be
shaken;
they will be remembered forever.
7 They will have no fear of bad news;
their hearts are steadfast, trusting
in the LORD.
8 Their hearts are secure, they will have
no fear;
in the end they will look in triumph
on their foes.
9 They have freely scattered their gifts
to the poor,
their righteousness endures forever;

[a] *1* Or *Lord* [b] *3* The meaning of the Hebrew for this sentence is uncertain. [c] *5* Or *My lord is at your right hand, LORD* [d] *7* The meaning of the Hebrew for this clause is uncertain. [e] This psalm is an acrostic poem, the lines of which begin with the successive letters of the Hebrew alphabet. [f] *1* Hebrew *Hallelu Yah*

their horn[a] will be lifted high in
honor.
10 The wicked will see and be vexed,
they will gnash their teeth and
waste away;
the longings of the wicked will come
to nothing.

Psalm 113

1 Praise the LORD.[b]

Praise the LORD, you his servants;
praise the name of the LORD.
2 Let the name of the LORD be praised,
both now and forevermore.
3 From the rising of the sun to the place
where it sets,
the name of the LORD is to be
praised.

4 The LORD is exalted over all the
nations,
his glory above the heavens.
5 Who is like the LORD our God,
the One who sits enthroned on high,
6 who stoops down to look
on the heavens and the earth?

7 He raises the poor from the dust
and lifts the needy from the ash
heap;
8 he seats them with princes,
with the princes of his people.
9 He settles the childless woman in her
home
as a happy mother of children.

Praise the LORD.

Psalm 114

1 When Israel came out of Egypt,
Jacob from a people of foreign
tongue,
2 Judah became God's sanctuary,
Israel his dominion.

3 The sea looked and fled,
the Jordan turned back;
4 the mountains leaped like rams,
the hills like lambs.

5 Why was it, sea, that you fled?
Why, Jordan, did you turn back?
6 Why, mountains, did you leap like
rams,
you hills, like lambs?

7 Tremble, earth, at the presence of the
Lord,
at the presence of the God of Jacob,
8 who turned the rock into a pool,
the hard rock into springs of water.

Psalm 115

1 Not to us, LORD, not to us
but to your name be the glory,
because of your love and
faithfulness.

2 Why do the nations say,
"Where is their God?"
3 Our God is in heaven;
he does whatever pleases him.
4 But their idols are silver and gold,
made by human hands.
5 They have mouths, but cannot speak,
eyes, but cannot see.
6 They have ears, but cannot hear,
noses, but cannot smell.
7 They have hands, but cannot feel,
feet, but cannot walk,
nor can they utter a sound with their
throats.
8 Those who make them will be like
them,
and so will all who trust in them.

9 All you Israelites, trust in the LORD—
he is their help and shield.
10 House of Aaron, trust in the LORD—
he is their help and shield.
11 You who fear him, trust in the LORD—
he is their help and shield.

12 The LORD remembers us and will
bless us:
He will bless his people Israel,
he will bless the house of Aaron,
13 he will bless those who fear the
LORD—
small and great alike.

14 May the LORD cause you to flourish,
both you and your children.
15 May you be blessed by the LORD,
the Maker of heaven and earth.

16 The highest heavens belong to the
LORD,
but the earth he has given to
mankind.
17 It is not the dead who praise the LORD,
those who go down to the place of
silence;

[a] 9 *Horn* here symbolizes dignity. [b] 1 Hebrew *Hallelu Yah*; also in verse 9

18 it is we who extol the LORD,
both now and forevermore.

Praise the LORD.[a]

Psalm 116

1 I love the LORD, for he heard my voice;
he heard my cry for mercy.
2 Because he turned his ear to me,
I will call on him as long as I live.

3 The cords of death entangled me,
the anguish of the grave came over me;
I was overcome by distress and sorrow.
4 Then I called on the name of the LORD:
"LORD, save me!"

5 The LORD is gracious and righteous;
our God is full of compassion.
6 The LORD protects the unwary;
when I was brought low, he saved me.

7 Return to your rest, my soul,
for the LORD has been good to you.

8 For you, LORD, have delivered me from death,
my eyes from tears,
my feet from stumbling,
9 that I may walk before the LORD
in the land of the living.

10 I trusted in the LORD when I said,
"I am greatly afflicted";
11 in my alarm I said,
"Everyone is a liar."

12 What shall I return to the LORD
for all his goodness to me?

13 I will lift up the cup of salvation
and call on the name of the LORD.
14 I will fulfill my vows to the LORD
in the presence of all his people.

15 Precious in the sight of the LORD
is the death of his faithful servants.
16 Truly I am your servant, LORD;
I serve you just as my mother did;
you have freed me from my chains.

17 I will sacrifice a thank offering to you
and call on the name of the LORD.
18 I will fulfill my vows to the LORD
in the presence of all his people,
19 in the courts of the house of the LORD—
in your midst, Jerusalem.

Praise the LORD.[a]

Psalm 117

1 Praise the LORD, all you nations;
extol him, all you peoples.
2 For great is his love toward us,
and the faithfulness of the LORD endures forever.

Praise the LORD.[a]

Psalm 118

1 Give thanks to the LORD, for he is good;
his love endures forever.

2 Let Israel say:
"His love endures forever."
3 Let the house of Aaron say:
"His love endures forever."
4 Let those who fear the LORD say:
"His love endures forever."

5 When hard pressed, I cried to the LORD;
he brought me into a spacious place.
6 The LORD is with me; I will not be afraid.
What can mere mortals do to me?
7 The LORD is with me; he is my helper.
I look in triumph on my enemies.

8 It is better to take refuge in the LORD
than to trust in humans.
9 It is better to take refuge in the LORD
than to trust in princes.
10 All the nations surrounded me,
but in the name of the LORD I cut them down.
11 They surrounded me on every side,
but in the name of the LORD I cut them down.
12 They swarmed around me like bees,
but they were consumed as quickly as burning thorns;
in the name of the LORD I cut them down.
13 I was pushed back and about to fall,
but the LORD helped me.
14 The LORD is my strength and my defense[b];
he has become my salvation.

[a] *18,19,2* Hebrew *Hallelu Yah* [b] *14* Or *song*

15 Shouts of joy and victory
resound in the tents of the righteous:
"The LORD's right hand has done mighty things!
16 The LORD's right hand is lifted high;
the LORD's right hand has done mighty things!"
17 I will not die but live,
and will proclaim what the LORD has done.
18 The LORD has chastened me severely,
but he has not given me over to death.
19 Open for me the gates of the righteous;
I will enter and give thanks to the LORD.
20 This is the gate of the LORD
through which the righteous may enter.
21 I will give you thanks, for you answered me;
you have become my salvation.

22 The stone the builders rejected
has become the cornerstone;
23 the LORD has done this,
and it is marvelous in our eyes.
24 The LORD has done it this very day;
let us rejoice today and be glad.

25 LORD, save us!
LORD, grant us success!
26 Blessed is he who comes in the name of the LORD.
From the house of the LORD we bless you.[a]
27 The LORD is God,
and he has made his light shine on us.
With boughs in hand, join in the festal procession
up[b] to the horns of the altar.

28 You are my God, and I will praise you;
you are my God, and I will exalt you.
29 Give thanks to the LORD, for he is good;
his love endures forever.

Psalm 119[c]

א Aleph

1 Blessed are those whose ways are blameless,
who walk according to the law of the LORD.
2 Blessed are those who keep his statutes
and seek him with all their heart—
3 they do no wrong
but follow his ways.
4 You have laid down precepts
that are to be fully obeyed.
5 Oh, that my ways were steadfast
in obeying your decrees!
6 Then I would not be put to shame
when I consider all your commands.
7 I will praise you with an upright heart
as I learn your righteous laws.
8 I will obey your decrees;
do not utterly forsake me.

ב Beth

9 How can a young person stay on the path of purity?
By living according to your word.
10 I seek you with all my heart;
do not let me stray from your commands.
11 I have hidden your word in my heart
that I might not sin against you.
12 Praise be to you, LORD;
teach me your decrees.
13 With my lips I recount
all the laws that come from your mouth.
14 I rejoice in following your statutes
as one rejoices in great riches.
15 I meditate on your precepts
and consider your ways.
16 I delight in your decrees;
I will not neglect your word.

ג Gimel

17 Be good to your servant while I live,
that I may obey your word.
18 Open my eyes that I may see
wonderful things in your law.
19 I am a stranger on earth;
do not hide your commands from me.
20 My soul is consumed with longing
for your laws at all times.
21 You rebuke the arrogant, who are accursed,
those who stray from your commands.

a 26 The Hebrew is plural. b 27 Or *Bind the festal sacrifice with ropes / and take it* c This psalm is an acrostic poem, the stanzas of which begin with successive letters of the Hebrew alphabet; moreover, the verses of each stanza begin with the same letter of the Hebrew alphabet.

22 Remove from me their scorn and contempt,
for I keep your statutes.
23 Though rulers sit together and slander me,
your servant will meditate on your decrees.
24 Your statutes are my delight;
they are my counselors.

ד Daleth

25 I am laid low in the dust;
preserve my life according to your word.
26 I gave an account of my ways and you answered me;
teach me your decrees.
27 Cause me to understand the way of your precepts,
that I may meditate on your wonderful deeds.
28 My soul is weary with sorrow;
strengthen me according to your word.
29 Keep me from deceitful ways;
be gracious to me and teach me your law.
30 I have chosen the way of faithfulness;
I have set my heart on your laws.
31 I hold fast to your statutes, LORD;
do not let me be put to shame.
32 I run in the path of your commands,
for you have broadened my understanding.

ה He

33 Teach me, LORD, the way of your decrees,
that I may follow it to the end.[a]
34 Give me understanding, so that I may keep your law
and obey it with all my heart.
35 Direct me in the path of your commands,
for there I find delight.
36 Turn my heart toward your statutes
and not toward selfish gain.
37 Turn my eyes away from worthless things;
preserve my life according to your word.[b]
38 Fulfill your promise to your servant,
so that you may be feared.
39 Take away the disgrace I dread,
for your laws are good.
40 How I long for your precepts!
In your righteousness preserve my life.

ו Waw

41 May your unfailing love come to me, LORD,
your salvation, according to your promise;
42 then I can answer anyone who taunts me,
for I trust in your word.
43 Never take your word of truth from my mouth,
for I have put my hope in your laws.
44 I will always obey your law,
for ever and ever.
45 I will walk about in freedom,
for I have sought out your precepts.
46 I will speak of your statutes before kings
and will not be put to shame,
47 for I delight in your commands
because I love them.
48 I reach out for your commands, which I love,
that I may meditate on your decrees.

ז Zayin

49 Remember your word to your servant,
for you have given me hope.
50 My comfort in my suffering is this:
Your promise preserves my life.
51 The arrogant mock me unmercifully,
but I do not turn from your law.
52 I remember, LORD, your ancient laws,
and I find comfort in them.
53 Indignation grips me because of the wicked,
who have forsaken your law.
54 Your decrees are the theme of my song
wherever I lodge.
55 In the night, LORD, I remember your name,
that I may keep your law.
56 This has been my practice:
I obey your precepts.

ח Heth

57 You are my portion, LORD;
I have promised to obey your words.

[a] 33 Or *follow it for its reward* [b] 37 Two manuscripts of the Masoretic Text and Dead Sea Scrolls; most manuscripts of the Masoretic Text *life in your way*

58 I have sought your face with all my
heart;
be gracious to me according to your
promise.
59 I have considered my ways
and have turned my steps to your
statutes.
60 I will hasten and not delay
to obey your commands.
61 Though the wicked bind me with
ropes,
I will not forget your law.
62 At midnight I rise to give you thanks
for your righteous laws.
63 I am a friend to all who fear you,
to all who follow your precepts.
64 The earth is filled with your love,
LORD;
teach me your decrees.

ט Teth

65 Do good to your servant
according to your word, LORD.
66 Teach me knowledge and good
judgment,
for I trust your commands.
67 Before I was afflicted I went astray,
but now I obey your word.
68 You are good, and what you do is
good;
teach me your decrees.
69 Though the arrogant have smeared
me with lies,
I keep your precepts with all my
heart.
70 Their hearts are callous and
unfeeling,
but I delight in your law.
71 It was good for me to be afflicted
so that I might learn your decrees.
72 The law from your mouth is more
precious to me
than thousands of pieces of silver
and gold.

י Yodh

73 Your hands made me and formed me;
give me understanding to learn your
commands.
74 May those who fear you rejoice when
they see me,
for I have put my hope in your word.
75 I know, LORD, that your laws are
righteous,
and that in faithfulness you have
afflicted me.
76 May your unfailing love be my
comfort,
according to your promise to your
servant.
77 Let your compassion come to me that I
may live,
for your law is my delight.
78 May the arrogant be put to shame for
wronging me without cause;
but I will meditate on your precepts.
79 May those who fear you turn to me,
those who understand your statutes.
80 May I wholeheartedly follow your
decrees,
that I may not be put to shame.

כ Kaph

81 My soul faints with longing for your
salvation,
but I have put my hope in your word.
82 My eyes fail, looking for your promise;
I say, "When will you comfort me?"
83 Though I am like a wineskin in the
smoke,
I do not forget your decrees.
84 How long must your servant wait?
When will you punish my
persecutors?
85 The arrogant dig pits to trap me,
contrary to your law.
86 All your commands are trustworthy;
help me, for I am being persecuted
without cause.
87 They almost wiped me from the earth,
but I have not forsaken your
precepts.
88 In your unfailing love preserve my life,
that I may obey the statutes of your
mouth.

ל Lamedh

89 Your word, LORD, is eternal;
it stands firm in the heavens.
90 Your faithfulness continues through
all generations;
you established the earth, and it
endures.
91 Your laws endure to this day,
for all things serve you.
92 If your law had not been my delight,
I would have perished in my
affliction.
93 I will never forget your precepts,
for by them you have preserved my
life.
94 Save me, for I am yours;

I have sought out your precepts.
95 The wicked are waiting to destroy me,
but I will ponder your statutes.
96 To all perfection I see a limit,
but your commands are boundless.

מ Mem

97 Oh, how I love your law!
I meditate on it all day long.
98 Your commands are always with me
and make me wiser than my
enemies.
99 I have more insight than all my
teachers,
for I meditate on your statutes.
100 I have more understanding than the
elders,
for I obey your precepts.
101 I have kept my feet from every evil
path
so that I might obey your word.
102 I have not departed from your laws,
for you yourself have taught me.
103 How sweet are your words to my
taste,
sweeter than honey to my mouth!
104 I gain understanding from your
precepts;
therefore I hate every wrong path.

נ Nun

105 Your word is a lamp for my feet,
a light on my path.
106 I have taken an oath and confirmed it,
that I will follow your righteous
laws.
107 I have suffered much;
preserve my life, LORD, according to
your word.
108 Accept, LORD, the willing praise of my
mouth,
and teach me your laws.
109 Though I constantly take my life in
my hands,
I will not forget your law.
110 The wicked have set a snare for me,
but I have not strayed from your
precepts.
111 Your statutes are my heritage
forever;
they are the joy of my heart.
112 My heart is set on keeping your
decrees
to the very end.[a]

ס Samekh

113 I hate double-minded people,
but I love your law.
114 You are my refuge and my shield;
I have put my hope in your word.
115 Away from me, you evildoers,
that I may keep the commands of
my God!
116 Sustain me, my God, according to
your promise, and I will live;
do not let my hopes be dashed.
117 Uphold me, and I will be delivered;
I will always have regard for your
decrees.
118 You reject all who stray from your
decrees,
for their delusions come to nothing.
119 All the wicked of the earth you
discard like dross;
therefore I love your statutes.
120 My flesh trembles in fear of you;
I stand in awe of your laws.

ע Ayin

121 I have done what is righteous and
just;
do not leave me to my oppressors.
122 Ensure your servant's well-being;
do not let the arrogant oppress me.
123 My eyes fail, looking for your
salvation,
looking for your righteous promise.
124 Deal with your servant according to
your love
and teach me your decrees.
125 I am your servant; give me
discernment
that I may understand your statutes.
126 It is time for you to act, LORD;
your law is being broken.
127 Because I love your commands
more than gold, more than pure
gold,
128 and because I consider all your
precepts right,
I hate every wrong path.

פ Pe

129 Your statutes are wonderful;
therefore I obey them.
130 The unfolding of your words gives
light;
it gives understanding to the simple.
131 I open my mouth and pant,

[a] 112 Or *decrees / for their enduring reward*

longing for your commands.
132 Turn to me and have mercy on me,
as you always do to those who love your name.
133 Direct my footsteps according to your word;
let no sin rule over me.
134 Redeem me from human oppression,
that I may obey your precepts.
135 Make your face shine on your servant
and teach me your decrees.
136 Streams of tears flow from my eyes,
for your law is not obeyed.

צ Tsadhe

137 You are righteous, LORD,
and your laws are right.
138 The statutes you have laid down are righteous;
they are fully trustworthy.
139 My zeal wears me out,
for my enemies ignore your words.
140 Your promises have been thoroughly tested,
and your servant loves them.
141 Though I am lowly and despised,
I do not forget your precepts.
142 Your righteousness is everlasting
and your law is true.
143 Trouble and distress have come upon me,
but your commands give me delight.
144 Your statutes are always righteous;
give me understanding that I may live.

ק Qoph

145 I call with all my heart; answer me, LORD,
and I will obey your decrees.
146 I call out to you; save me
and I will keep your statutes.
147 I rise before dawn and cry for help;
I have put my hope in your word.
148 My eyes stay open through the watches of the night,
that I may meditate on your promises.
149 Hear my voice in accordance with your love;
preserve my life, LORD, according to your laws.
150 Those who devise wicked schemes are near,
but they are far from your law.
151 Yet you are near, LORD,
and all your commands are true.
152 Long ago I learned from your statutes
that you established them to last forever.

ר Resh

153 Look on my suffering and deliver me,
for I have not forgotten your law.
154 Defend my cause and redeem me;
preserve my life according to your promise.
155 Salvation is far from the wicked,
for they do not seek out your decrees.
156 Your compassion, LORD, is great;
preserve my life according to your laws.
157 Many are the foes who persecute me,
but I have not turned from your statutes.
158 I look on the faithless with loathing,
for they do not obey your word.
159 See how I love your precepts;
preserve my life, LORD, in accordance with your love.
160 All your words are true;
all your righteous laws are eternal.

ש Sin and Shin

161 Rulers persecute me without cause,
but my heart trembles at your word.
162 I rejoice in your promise
like one who finds great spoil.
163 I hate and detest falsehood
but I love your law.
164 Seven times a day I praise you
for your righteous laws.
165 Great peace have those who love your law,
and nothing can make them stumble.
166 I wait for your salvation, LORD,
and I follow your commands.
167 I obey your statutes,
for I love them greatly.
168 I obey your precepts and your statutes,
for all my ways are known to you.

ת Taw

169 May my cry come before you, LORD;
give me understanding according to your word.
170 May my supplication come before you;

deliver me according to your
promise.
171 May my lips overflow with praise,
for you teach me your decrees.
172 May my tongue sing of your word,
for all your commands are
righteous.
173 May your hand be ready to help me,
for I have chosen your precepts.
174 I long for your salvation, LORD,
and your law gives me delight.
175 Let me live that I may praise you,
and may your laws sustain me.
176 I have strayed like a lost sheep.
Seek your servant,
for I have not forgotten your
commands.

Psalm 120

A song of ascents.

1 I call on the LORD in my distress,
and he answers me.
2 Save me, LORD,
from lying lips
and from deceitful tongues.

3 What will he do to you,
and what more besides,
you deceitful tongue?
4 He will punish you with a warrior's
sharp arrows,
with burning coals of the broom
bush.

5 Woe to me that I dwell in Meshek,
that I live among the tents of Kedar!
6 Too long have I lived
among those who hate peace.
7 I am for peace;
but when I speak, they are for war.

Psalm 121

A song of ascents.

1 I lift up my eyes to the mountains —
where does my help come from?
2 My help comes from the LORD,
the Maker of heaven and earth.

3 He will not let your foot slip —
he who watches over you will not
slumber;
4 indeed, he who watches over Israel
will neither slumber nor sleep.

5 The LORD watches over you —
the LORD is your shade at your right
hand;
6 the sun will not harm you by day,
nor the moon by night.

7 The LORD will keep you from all
harm —
he will watch over your life;
8 the LORD will watch over your coming
and going
both now and forevermore.

Psalm 122

A song of ascents. Of David.

1 I rejoiced with those who said to me,
"Let us go to the house of the LORD."
2 Our feet are standing
in your gates, Jerusalem.

3 Jerusalem is built like a city
that is closely compacted together.
4 That is where the tribes go up —
the tribes of the LORD —
to praise the name of the LORD
according to the statute given to
Israel.
5 There stand the thrones for judgment,
the thrones of the house of David.

6 Pray for the peace of Jerusalem:
"May those who love you be
secure.
7 May there be peace within your walls
and security within your citadels."
8 For the sake of my family and
friends,
I will say, "Peace be within you."
9 For the sake of the house of the LORD
our God,
I will seek your prosperity.

Psalm 123

A song of ascents.

1 I lift up my eyes to you,
to you who sit enthroned in heaven.
2 As the eyes of slaves look to the hand
of their master,
as the eyes of a female slave look to
the hand of her mistress,
so our eyes look to the LORD our God,
till he shows us his mercy.

3 Have mercy on us, LORD, have mercy
on us,
for we have endured no end of
contempt.
4 We have endured no end
of ridicule from the arrogant,
of contempt from the proud.

Psalm 124

A song of ascents. Of David.

1 If the LORD had not been on our side—
let Israel say—
2 if the LORD had not been on our side
when people attacked us,
3 they would have swallowed us alive
when their anger flared against us;
4 the flood would have engulfed us,
the torrent would have swept over us,
5 the raging waters
would have swept us away.

6 Praise be to the LORD,
who has not let us be torn by their teeth.
7 We have escaped like a bird
from the fowler's snare;
the snare has been broken,
and we have escaped.
8 Our help is in the name of the LORD,
the Maker of heaven and earth.

Psalm 125

A song of ascents.

1 Those who trust in the LORD are like Mount Zion,
which cannot be shaken but endures forever.
2 As the mountains surround Jerusalem,
so the LORD surrounds his people
both now and forevermore.

3 The scepter of the wicked will not remain
over the land allotted to the righteous,
for then the righteous might use
their hands to do evil.

4 LORD, do good to those who are good,
to those who are upright in heart.
5 But those who turn to crooked ways
the LORD will banish with the evildoers.

Peace be on Israel.

Psalm 126

A song of ascents.

1 When the LORD restored the fortunes of[a] Zion,
we were like those who dreamed.[b]
2 Our mouths were filled with laughter,
our tongues with songs of joy.
Then it was said among the nations,
"The LORD has done great things for them."
3 The LORD has done great things for us,
and we are filled with joy.

4 Restore our fortunes,[c] LORD,
like streams in the Negev.
5 Those who sow with tears
will reap with songs of joy.
6 Those who go out weeping,
carrying seed to sow,
will return with songs of joy,
carrying sheaves with them.

Psalm 127

A song of ascents. Of Solomon.

1 Unless the LORD builds the house,
the builders labor in vain.
Unless the LORD watches over the city,
the guards stand watch in vain.
2 In vain you rise early
and stay up late,
toiling for food to eat—
for he grants sleep to[d] those he loves.

3 Children are a heritage from the LORD,
offspring a reward from him.
4 Like arrows in the hands of a warrior
are children born in one's youth.
5 Blessed is the man
whose quiver is full of them.
They will not be put to shame
when they contend with their opponents in court.

Psalm 128

A song of ascents.

1 Blessed are all who fear the LORD,
who walk in obedience to him.
2 You will eat the fruit of your labor;
blessings and prosperity will be yours.
3 Your wife will be like a fruitful vine
within your house;
your children will be like olive shoots
around your table.
4 Yes, this will be the blessing
for the man who fears the LORD.

[a] *1* Or *LORD brought back the captives to* [b] *1* Or *those restored to health* [c] *4* Or *Bring back our captives*
[d] *2* Or *eat— / for while they sleep he provides for*

5 May the LORD bless you from Zion;
may you see the prosperity of Jerusalem
all the days of your life.
6 May you live to see your children's children —
peace be on Israel.

Psalm 129

A song of ascents.

1 "They have greatly oppressed me from my youth,"
let Israel say;
2 "they have greatly oppressed me from my youth,
but they have not gained the victory over me.
3 Plowmen have plowed my back
and made their furrows long.
4 But the LORD is righteous;
he has cut me free from the cords of the wicked."

5 May all who hate Zion
be turned back in shame.
6 May they be like grass on the roof,
which withers before it can grow;
7 a reaper cannot fill his hands with it,
nor one who gathers fill his arms.
8 May those who pass by not say to them,
"The blessing of the LORD be on you;
we bless you in the name of the LORD."

Psalm 130

A song of ascents.

1 Out of the depths I cry to you, LORD;
2 Lord, hear my voice.
Let your ears be attentive
to my cry for mercy.

3 If you, LORD, kept a record of sins,
Lord, who could stand?
4 But with you there is forgiveness,
so that we can, with reverence, serve you.

5 I wait for the LORD, my whole being waits,
and in his word I put my hope.
6 I wait for the Lord
more than watchmen wait for the morning,
more than watchmen wait for the morning.

7 Israel, put your hope in the LORD,
for with the LORD is unfailing love
and with him is full redemption.
8 He himself will redeem Israel
from all their sins.

Psalm 131

A song of ascents. Of David.

1 My heart is not proud, LORD,
my eyes are not haughty;
I do not concern myself with great matters
or things too wonderful for me.
2 But I have calmed and quieted myself,
I am like a weaned child with its mother;
like a weaned child I am content.

3 Israel, put your hope in the LORD
both now and forevermore.

Psalm 132

A song of ascents.

1 LORD, remember David
and all his self-denial.

2 He swore an oath to the LORD,
he made a vow to the Mighty One of Jacob:
3 "I will not enter my house
or go to my bed,
4 I will allow no sleep to my eyes
or slumber to my eyelids,
5 till I find a place for the LORD,
a dwelling for the Mighty One of Jacob."

6 We heard it in Ephrathah,
we came upon it in the fields of Jaar:[a]
7 "Let us go to his dwelling place,
let us worship at his footstool, saying,
8 'Arise, LORD, and come to your resting place,
you and the ark of your might.
9 May your priests be clothed with your righteousness;
may your faithful people sing for joy.' "

10 For the sake of your servant David,
do not reject your anointed one.

[a] 6 Or *heard of it in Ephrathah, / we found it in the fields of Jearim.* (See 1 Chron. 13:5,6) (And no quotation marks around verses 7-9)

11 The LORD swore an oath to David,
a sure oath he will not revoke:
"One of your own descendants
I will place on your throne.
12 If your sons keep my covenant
and the statutes I teach them,
then their sons will sit
on your throne for ever and ever."

13 For the LORD has chosen Zion,
he has desired it for his dwelling,
saying,
14 "This is my resting place for ever and
ever;
here I will sit enthroned, for I have
desired it.
15 I will bless her with abundant
provisions;
her poor I will satisfy with food.
16 I will clothe her priests with
salvation,
and her faithful people will ever
sing for joy.

17 "Here I will make a horn[a] grow for
David
and set up a lamp for my anointed
one.
18 I will clothe his enemies with shame,
but his head will be adorned with a
radiant crown."

Psalm 133

A song of ascents. Of David.

1 How good and pleasant it is
when God's people live together in
unity!

2 It is like precious oil poured on the
head,
running down on the beard,
running down on Aaron's beard,
down on the collar of his robe.
3 It is as if the dew of Hermon
were falling on Mount Zion.
For there the LORD bestows his
blessing,
even life forevermore.

Psalm 134

A song of ascents.

1 Praise the LORD, all you servants of
the LORD
who minister by night in the house
of the LORD.
2 Lift up your hands in the sanctuary
and praise the LORD.

3 May the LORD bless you from Zion,
he who is the Maker of heaven and
earth.

Psalm 135

1 Praise the LORD.[b]

Praise the name of the LORD;
praise him, you servants of the
LORD,
2 you who minister in the house of the
LORD,
in the courts of the house of our
God.

3 Praise the LORD, for the LORD is good;
sing praise to his name, for that is
pleasant.
4 For the LORD has chosen Jacob to be
his own,
Israel to be his treasured
possession.

5 I know that the LORD is great,
that our Lord is greater than all gods.
6 The LORD does whatever pleases him,
in the heavens and on the earth,
in the seas and all their depths.
7 He makes clouds rise from the ends of
the earth;
he sends lightning with the rain
and brings out the wind from his
storehouses.

8 He struck down the firstborn of Egypt,
the firstborn of people and animals.
9 He sent his signs and wonders into
your midst, Egypt,
against Pharaoh and all his
servants.
10 He struck down many nations
and killed mighty kings —
11 Sihon king of the Amorites,
Og king of Bashan,
and all the kings of Canaan —
12 and he gave their land as an
inheritance,
an inheritance to his people Israel.

13 Your name, LORD, endures forever,
your renown, LORD, through all
generations.
14 For the LORD will vindicate his people
and have compassion on his
servants.

[a] *17 Horn* here symbolizes strong one, that is, king.
[b] *1* Hebrew *Hallelu Yah*; also in verses 3 and 21

15 The idols of the nations are silver and
gold,
made by human hands.
16 They have mouths, but cannot speak,
eyes, but cannot see.
17 They have ears, but cannot hear,
nor is there breath in their mouths.
18 Those who make them will be like
them,
and so will all who trust in them.

19 All you Israelites, praise the LORD;
house of Aaron, praise the LORD;
20 house of Levi, praise the LORD;
you who fear him, praise the LORD.
21 Praise be to the LORD from Zion,
to him who dwells in Jerusalem.

Praise the LORD.

Psalm 136

1 Give thanks to the LORD, for he is good.
His love endures forever.
2 Give thanks to the God of gods.
His love endures forever.
3 Give thanks to the Lord of lords:
His love endures forever.
4 to him who alone does great wonders,
His love endures forever.
5 who by his understanding made the
heavens,
His love endures forever.
6 who spread out the earth upon the
waters,
His love endures forever.
7 who made the great lights —
His love endures forever.
8 the sun to govern the day,
His love endures forever.
9 the moon and stars to govern the
night;
His love endures forever.
10 to him who struck down the firstborn
of Egypt
His love endures forever.
11 and brought Israel out from among
them
His love endures forever.
12 with a mighty hand and outstretched
arm;
His love endures forever.
13 to him who divided the Red Sea[a]
asunder
His love endures forever.
14 and brought Israel through the midst
of it,
His love endures forever.
15 but swept Pharaoh and his army into
the Red Sea;
His love endures forever.
16 to him who led his people through the
wilderness;
His love endures forever.
17 to him who struck down great kings,
His love endures forever.
18 and killed mighty kings —
His love endures forever.
19 Sihon king of the Amorites
His love endures forever.
20 and Og king of Bashan —
His love endures forever.
21 and gave their land as an inheritance,
His love endures forever.
22 an inheritance to his servant Israel.
His love endures forever.
23 He remembered us in our low estate
His love endures forever.
24 and freed us from our enemies.
His love endures forever.
25 He gives food to every creature.
His love endures forever.
26 Give thanks to the God of heaven.
His love endures forever.

Psalm 137

1 By the rivers of Babylon we sat and
wept
when we remembered Zion.
2 There on the poplars
we hung our harps,
3 for there our captors asked us for
songs,
our tormentors demanded songs of
joy;
they said, "Sing us one of the songs
of Zion!"
4 How can we sing the songs of the
LORD
while in a foreign land?
5 If I forget you, Jerusalem,
may my right hand forget its skill.
6 May my tongue cling to the roof of my
mouth
if I do not remember you,
if I do not consider Jerusalem
my highest joy.

[a] *13* Or *the Sea of Reeds*; also in verse 15

7 Remember, LORD, what the Edomites did
on the day Jerusalem fell.
"Tear it down," they cried,
"tear it down to its foundations!"
8 Daughter Babylon, doomed to destruction,
happy is the one who repays you
according to what you have done to us.
9 Happy is the one who seizes your infants
and dashes them against the rocks.

Psalm 138

Of David.

1 I will praise you, LORD, with all my heart;
before the "gods" I will sing your praise.
2 I will bow down toward your holy temple
and will praise your name
for your unfailing love and your faithfulness,
for you have so exalted your solemn decree
that it surpasses your fame.
3 When I called, you answered me;
you greatly emboldened me.

4 May all the kings of the earth praise you, LORD,
when they hear what you have decreed.
5 May they sing of the ways of the LORD,
for the glory of the LORD is great.
6 Though the LORD is exalted, he looks kindly on the lowly;
though lofty, he sees them from afar.
7 Though I walk in the midst of trouble,
you preserve my life.
You stretch out your hand against the anger of my foes;
with your right hand you save me.
8 The LORD will vindicate me;
your love, LORD, endures forever—
do not abandon the works of your hands.

Psalm 139

For the director of music. Of David. A psalm.

1 You have searched me, LORD,
and you know me.
2 You know when I sit and when I rise;
you perceive my thoughts from afar.
3 You discern my going out and my lying down;
you are familiar with all my ways.
4 Before a word is on my tongue
you, LORD, know it completely.
5 You hem me in behind and before,
and you lay your hand upon me.
6 Such knowledge is too wonderful for me,
too lofty for me to attain.

7 Where can I go from your Spirit?
Where can I flee from your presence?
8 If I go up to the heavens, you are there;
if I make my bed in the depths, you are there.
9 If I rise on the wings of the dawn,
if I settle on the far side of the sea,
10 even there your hand will guide me,
your right hand will hold me fast.
11 If I say, "Surely the darkness will hide me
and the light become night around me,"
12 even the darkness will not be dark to you;
the night will shine like the day,
for darkness is as light to you.

13 For you created my inmost being;
you knit me together in my mother's womb.
14 I praise you because I am fearfully and wonderfully made;
your works are wonderful,
I know that full well.
15 My frame was not hidden from you
when I was made in the secret place,
when I was woven together in the depths of the earth.
16 Your eyes saw my unformed body;
all the days ordained for me were written in your book
before one of them came to be.
17 How precious to me are your thoughts,[a] God!
How vast is the sum of them!
18 Were I to count them,
they would outnumber the grains of sand—
when I awake, I am still with you.

19 If only you, God, would slay the wicked!
Away from me, you who are bloodthirsty!

[a] 17 Or *How amazing are your thoughts concerning me*

20 They speak of you with evil intent;
your adversaries misuse your name.
21 Do I not hate those who hate you, LORD,
and abhor those who are in rebellion against you?
22 I have nothing but hatred for them;
I count them my enemies.
23 Search me, God, and know my heart;
test me and know my anxious thoughts.
24 See if there is any offensive way in me,
and lead me in the way everlasting.

Psalm 140[a]

For the director of music. A psalm of David.

1 Rescue me, LORD, from evildoers;
protect me from the violent,
2 who devise evil plans in their hearts
and stir up war every day.
3 They make their tongues as sharp as a serpent's;
the poison of vipers is on their lips.[b]

4 Keep me safe, LORD, from the hands of the wicked;
protect me from the violent,
who devise ways to trip my feet.
5 The arrogant have hidden a snare for me;
they have spread out the cords of their net
and have set traps for me along my path.

6 I say to the LORD, "You are my God."
Hear, LORD, my cry for mercy.
7 Sovereign LORD, my strong deliverer,
you shield my head in the day of battle.
8 Do not grant the wicked their desires, LORD;
do not let their plans succeed.

9 Those who surround me proudly rear their heads;
may the mischief of their lips engulf them.
10 May burning coals fall on them;
may they be thrown into the fire,
into miry pits, never to rise.
11 May slanderers not be established in the land;
may disaster hunt down the violent.
12 I know that the LORD secures justice for the poor
and upholds the cause of the needy.
13 Surely the righteous will praise your name,
and the upright will live in your presence.

Psalm 141

A psalm of David.

1 I call to you, LORD, come quickly to me;
hear me when I call to you.
2 May my prayer be set before you like incense;
may the lifting up of my hands be like the evening sacrifice.

3 Set a guard over my mouth, LORD;
keep watch over the door of my lips.
4 Do not let my heart be drawn to what is evil
so that I take part in wicked deeds
along with those who are evildoers;
do not let me eat their delicacies.

5 Let a righteous man strike me — that is a kindness;
let him rebuke me — that is oil on my head.
My head will not refuse it,
for my prayer will still be against the deeds of evildoers.

6 Their rulers will be thrown down from the cliffs,
and the wicked will learn that my words were well spoken.
7 They will say, "As one plows and breaks up the earth,
so our bones have been scattered at the mouth of the grave."

8 But my eyes are fixed on you, Sovereign LORD;
in you I take refuge — do not give me over to death.
9 Keep me safe from the traps set by evildoers,
from the snares they have laid for me.
10 Let the wicked fall into their own nets,
while I pass by in safety.

[a] In Hebrew texts 140:1-13 is numbered 140:2-14. [b] 3 The Hebrew has *Selah* (a word of uncertain meaning) here and at the end of verses 5 and 8.

Psalm 142[a]

A maskil[b] of David. When he was in the cave. A prayer.

1 I cry aloud to the LORD;
I lift up my voice to the LORD for mercy.
2 I pour out before him my complaint;
before him I tell my trouble.

3 When my spirit grows faint within me,
it is you who watch over my way.
In the path where I walk
people have hidden a snare for me.
4 Look and see, there is no one at my right hand;
no one is concerned for me.
I have no refuge;
no one cares for my life.

5 I cry to you, LORD;
I say, "You are my refuge,
my portion in the land of the living."

6 Listen to my cry,
for I am in desperate need;
rescue me from those who pursue me,
for they are too strong for me.
7 Set me free from my prison,
that I may praise your name.
Then the righteous will gather about me
because of your goodness to me.

Psalm 143

A psalm of David.

1 LORD, hear my prayer,
listen to my cry for mercy;
in your faithfulness and righteousness
come to my relief.
2 Do not bring your servant into judgment,
for no one living is righteous before you.
3 The enemy pursues me,
he crushes me to the ground;
he makes me dwell in the darkness
like those long dead.
4 So my spirit grows faint within me;
my heart within me is dismayed.
5 I remember the days of long ago;
I meditate on all your works
and consider what your hands have done.
6 I spread out my hands to you;
I thirst for you like a parched land.[c]

7 Answer me quickly, LORD;
my spirit fails.
Do not hide your face from me
or I will be like those who go down to the pit.
8 Let the morning bring me word of your unfailing love,
for I have put my trust in you.
Show me the way I should go,
for to you I entrust my life.
9 Rescue me from my enemies, LORD,
for I hide myself in you.
10 Teach me to do your will,
for you are my God;
may your good Spirit
lead me on level ground.

11 For your name's sake, LORD, preserve my life;
in your righteousness, bring me out of trouble.
12 In your unfailing love, silence my enemies;
destroy all my foes,
for I am your servant.

Psalm 144

Of David.

1 Praise be to the LORD my Rock,
who trains my hands for war,
my fingers for battle.
2 He is my loving God and my fortress,
my stronghold and my deliverer,
my shield, in whom I take refuge,
who subdues peoples[d] under me.

3 LORD, what are human beings that you care for them,
mere mortals that you think of them?
4 They are like a breath;
their days are like a fleeting shadow.

5 Part your heavens, LORD, and come down;
touch the mountains, so that they smoke.
6 Send forth lightning and scatter the enemy;
shoot your arrows and rout them.
7 Reach down your hand from on high;
deliver me and rescue me

[a] In Hebrew texts 142:1-7 is numbered 142:2-8. [b] Title: Probably a literary or musical term [c] 6 The Hebrew has *Selah* (a word of uncertain meaning) here. [d] 2 Many manuscripts of the Masoretic Text, Dead Sea Scrolls, Aquila, Jerome and Syriac; most manuscripts of the Masoretic Text *subdues my people*

from the mighty waters,
from the hands of foreigners
8 whose mouths are full of lies,
whose right hands are deceitful.

9 I will sing a new song to you, my God;
on the ten-stringed lyre I will make music to you,
10 to the One who gives victory to kings,
who delivers his servant David.

From the deadly sword 11 deliver me;
rescue me from the hands of foreigners
whose mouths are full of lies,
whose right hands are deceitful.

12 Then our sons in their youth
will be like well-nurtured plants,
and our daughters will be like pillars
carved to adorn a palace.
13 Our barns will be filled
with every kind of provision.
Our sheep will increase by thousands,
by tens of thousands in our fields;
14 our oxen will draw heavy loads.[a]
There will be no breaching of walls,
no going into captivity,
no cry of distress in our streets.
15 Blessed is the people of whom this is true;
blessed is the people whose God is the LORD.

Psalm 145[b]

A psalm of praise. Of David.

1 I will exalt you, my God the King;
I will praise your name for ever and ever.
2 Every day I will praise you
and extol your name for ever and ever.

3 Great is the LORD and most worthy of praise;
his greatness no one can fathom.
4 One generation commends your works to another;
they tell of your mighty acts.
5 They speak of the glorious splendor of your majesty—
and I will meditate on your wonderful works.[c]
6 They tell of the power of your awesome works—
and I will proclaim your great deeds.
7 They celebrate your abundant goodness
and joyfully sing of your righteousness.

8 The LORD is gracious and compassionate,
slow to anger and rich in love.

9 The LORD is good to all;
he has compassion on all he has made.
10 All your works praise you, LORD;
your faithful people extol you.
11 They tell of the glory of your kingdom
and speak of your might,
12 so that all people may know of your mighty acts
and the glorious splendor of your kingdom.
13 Your kingdom is an everlasting kingdom,
and your dominion endures through all generations.

The LORD is trustworthy in all he promises
and faithful in all he does.[d]
14 The LORD upholds all who fall
and lifts up all who are bowed down.
15 The eyes of all look to you,
and you give them their food at the proper time.
16 You open your hand
and satisfy the desires of every living thing.

17 The LORD is righteous in all his ways
and faithful in all he does.
18 The LORD is near to all who call on him,
to all who call on him in truth.
19 He fulfills the desires of those who fear him;
he hears their cry and saves them.
20 The LORD watches over all who love him,
but all the wicked he will destroy.

21 My mouth will speak in praise of the LORD.
Let every creature praise his holy name
for ever and ever.

[a] *14* Or *our chieftains will be firmly established* [b] This psalm is an acrostic poem, the verses of which (including verse 13b) begin with the successive letters of the Hebrew alphabet. [c] *5* Dead Sea Scrolls and Syriac (see also Septuagint); Masoretic Text *On the glorious splendor of your majesty / and on your wonderful works I will meditate* [d] *13* One manuscript of the Masoretic Text, Dead Sea Scrolls and Syriac (see also Septuagint); most manuscripts of the Masoretic Text do not have the last two lines of verse 13.

Psalm 146

1 Praise the LORD.[a]

Praise the LORD, my soul.

2 I will praise the LORD all my life;
I will sing praise to my God as long as I live.
3 Do not put your trust in princes,
in human beings, who cannot save.
4 When their spirit departs, they return to the ground;
on that very day their plans come to nothing.
5 Blessed are those whose help is the God of Jacob,
whose hope is in the LORD their God.
6 He is the Maker of heaven and earth,
the sea, and everything in them —
he remains faithful forever.
7 He upholds the cause of the oppressed
and gives food to the hungry.
The LORD sets prisoners free,
8 the LORD gives sight to the blind,
the LORD lifts up those who are bowed down,
the LORD loves the righteous.
9 The LORD watches over the foreigner
and sustains the fatherless and the widow,
but he frustrates the ways of the wicked.
10 The LORD reigns forever,
your God, O Zion, for all generations.

Praise the LORD.

Psalm 147

1 Praise the LORD.[b]

How good it is to sing praises to our God,
how pleasant and fitting to praise him!

2 The LORD builds up Jerusalem;
he gathers the exiles of Israel.
3 He heals the brokenhearted
and binds up their wounds.
4 He determines the number of the stars
and calls them each by name.
5 Great is our Lord and mighty in power;
his understanding has no limit.
6 The LORD sustains the humble
but casts the wicked to the ground.

7 Sing to the LORD with grateful praise;
make music to our God on the harp.

8 He covers the sky with clouds;
he supplies the earth with rain
and makes grass grow on the hills.
9 He provides food for the cattle
and for the young ravens when they call.

10 His pleasure is not in the strength of the horse,
nor his delight in the legs of the warrior;
11 the LORD delights in those who fear him,
who put their hope in his unfailing love.

12 Extol the LORD, Jerusalem;
praise your God, Zion.

13 He strengthens the bars of your gates
and blesses your people within you.
14 He grants peace to your borders
and satisfies you with the finest of wheat.

15 He sends his command to the earth;
his word runs swiftly.
16 He spreads the snow like wool
and scatters the frost like ashes.
17 He hurls down his hail like pebbles.
Who can withstand his icy blast?
18 He sends his word and melts them;
he stirs up his breezes, and the waters flow.

19 He has revealed his word to Jacob,
his laws and decrees to Israel.
20 He has done this for no other nation;
they do not know his laws.[c]

Praise the LORD.

Psalm 148

1 Praise the LORD.[d]

Praise the LORD from the heavens;
praise him in the heights above.
2 Praise him, all his angels;
praise him, all his heavenly hosts.
3 Praise him, sun and moon;
praise him, all you shining stars.

[a] *1* Hebrew *Hallelu Yah*; also in verse 10 [b] *1* Hebrew *Hallelu Yah*; also in verse 20 [c] *20* Masoretic Text; Dead Sea Scrolls and Septuagint *nation; / he has not made his laws known to them* [d] *1* Hebrew *Hallelu Yah*; also in verse 14

4 Praise him, you highest heavens
and you waters above the skies.
5 Let them praise the name of the LORD,
for at his command they were created,
6 and he established them for ever and ever—
he issued a decree that will never pass away.
7 Praise the LORD from the earth,
you great sea creatures and all ocean depths,
8 lightning and hail, snow and clouds,
stormy winds that do his bidding,
9 you mountains and all hills,
fruit trees and all cedars,
10 wild animals and all cattle,
small creatures and flying birds,
11 kings of the earth and all nations,
you princes and all rulers on earth,
12 young men and women,
old men and children.
13 Let them praise the name of the LORD,
for his name alone is exalted;
his splendor is above the earth and the heavens.
14 And he has raised up for his people a horn,[a]
the praise of all his faithful servants,
of Israel, the people close to his heart.

Praise the LORD.

Psalm 149

1 Praise the LORD.[b]

Sing to the LORD a new song,
his praise in the assembly of his faithful people.
2 Let Israel rejoice in their Maker;
let the people of Zion be glad in their King.
3 Let them praise his name with dancing
and make music to him with timbrel and harp.
4 For the LORD takes delight in his people;
he crowns the humble with victory.
5 Let his faithful people rejoice in this honor
and sing for joy on their beds.
6 May the praise of God be in their mouths
and a double-edged sword in their hands,
7 to inflict vengeance on the nations
and punishment on the peoples,
8 to bind their kings with fetters,
their nobles with shackles of iron,
9 to carry out the sentence written against them—
this is the glory of all his faithful people.

Praise the LORD.

Psalm 150

1 Praise the LORD.[c]

Praise God in his sanctuary;
praise him in his mighty heavens.
2 Praise him for his acts of power;
praise him for his surpassing greatness.
3 Praise him with the sounding of the trumpet,
praise him with the harp and lyre,
4 praise him with timbrel and dancing,
praise him with the strings and pipe,
5 praise him with the clash of cymbals,
praise him with resounding cymbals.
6 Let everything that has breath praise the LORD.

Praise the LORD.

[a] *14 Horn* here symbolizes strength. [b] *1* Hebrew *Hallelu Yah*; also in verse 9 [c] *1* Hebrew *Hallelu Yah*; also in verse 6

PROVERBS

Israel understood that the Creator had placed an order in his world that could be discovered. The book of Proverbs captures these lessons in compact, memorable sayings passed down from the wisest among their elders. Many of them are from Solomon, a king renowned for his wisdom (see p. 301). These proverbs are especially designed to help younger people avoid common pitfalls and find the path to prosperity, health and security.

After a short section of teaching, wisdom itself, personified as a woman, calls out to the simple and invites them to grow in knowledge. This section ends by presenting two banquets, one hosted by Wisdom and one by Folly, illustrating the essential choice to be made in life. A collection of 375 proverbs of Solomon follows, reflecting the numerical value of his name in Hebrew. (Hebrew letters were also used as numbers, so words had a value equal to the sum of their letters.) After some "sayings of the wise," next is a collection of Solomon's wisdom compiled by the men of Hezekiah, king of Judah. Here the count is 130, equaling the value of Hezekiah's name. The book closes with sayings from Agur and Lemuel, ending with a poem whose 22 parts begin with consecutive letters of the Hebrew alphabet. The character qualities praised throughout the book are seen in a description of the ideal wife.

This rich book of short, pithy wisdom presents a consistent theme: *the fear of the* LORD *is the beginning of knowledge.*

---

1 The proverbs of Solomon son of David,
king of Israel:

2 for gaining wisdom and instruction;
for understanding words of insight;
3 for receiving instruction in prudent
behavior,
doing what is right and just and fair;
4 for giving prudence to those who are
simple,[a]
knowledge and discretion to the
young—
5 let the wise listen and add to their
learning,
and let the discerning get
guidance—
6 for understanding proverbs and
parables,
the sayings and riddles of the wise.[b]

7 The fear of the LORD is the beginning
of knowledge,
but fools[c] despise wisdom and
instruction.

8 Listen, my son, to your father's
instruction
and do not forsake your mother's
teaching.
9 They are a garland to grace your head
and a chain to adorn your neck.

10 My son, if sinful men entice you,
do not give in to them.
11 If they say, "Come along with us;
let's lie in wait for innocent blood,
let's ambush some harmless soul;
12 let's swallow them alive, like the
grave,
and whole, like those who go down
to the pit;
13 we will get all sorts of valuable things
and fill our houses with plunder;
14 cast lots with us;
we will all share the loot"—
15 my son, do not go along with them,
do not set foot on their paths;
16 for their feet rush into evil,
they are swift to shed blood.
17 How useless to spread a net
where every bird can see it!
18 These men lie in wait for their own
blood;
they ambush only themselves!
19 Such are the paths of all who go after
ill-gotten gain;
it takes away the life of those who
get it.

20 Out in the open wisdom calls aloud,
she raises her voice in the public
square;
21 on top of the wall[d] she cries out,

---

[a] *4* The Hebrew word rendered *simple* in Proverbs denotes a person who is gullible, without moral direction and inclined to evil. [b] *6* Or *understanding a proverb, namely, a parable, / and the sayings of the wise, their riddles* [c] *7* The Hebrew words rendered *fool* in Proverbs, and often elsewhere in the Old Testament, denote a person who is morally deficient. [d] *21* Septuagint; Hebrew / *at noisy street corners*

at the city gate she makes her
speech:

22 "How long will you who are simple
love your simple ways?
How long will mockers delight in
mockery
and fools hate knowledge?
23 Repent at my rebuke!
Then I will pour out my thoughts to
you,
I will make known to you my
teachings.
24 But since you refuse to listen when I
call
and no one pays attention when I
stretch out my hand,
25 since you disregard all my advice
and do not accept my rebuke,
26 I in turn will laugh when disaster
strikes you;
I will mock when calamity overtakes
you—
27 when calamity overtakes you like a
storm,
when disaster sweeps over you like a
whirlwind,
when distress and trouble
overwhelm you.

28 "Then they will call to me but I will not
answer;
they will look for me but will not
find me,
29 since they hated knowledge
and did not choose to fear the LORD.
30 Since they would not accept my advice
and spurned my rebuke,
31 they will eat the fruit of their ways
and be filled with the fruit of their
schemes.
32 For the waywardness of the simple
will kill them,
and the complacency of fools will
destroy them;
33 but whoever listens to me will live in
safety
and be at ease, without fear of
harm."

2 My son, if you accept my words
and store up my commands within
you,
2 turning your ear to wisdom
and applying your heart to
understanding—
3 indeed, if you call out for insight
and cry aloud for understanding,
4 and if you look for it as for silver
and search for it as for hidden
treasure,
5 then you will understand the fear of
the LORD
and find the knowledge of God.
6 For the LORD gives wisdom;
from his mouth come knowledge
and understanding.
7 He holds success in store for the
upright,
he is a shield to those whose walk is
blameless,
8 for he guards the course of the just
and protects the way of his faithful
ones.

9 Then you will understand what is right
and just
and fair—every good path.
10 For wisdom will enter your heart,
and knowledge will be pleasant to
your soul.
11 Discretion will protect you,
and understanding will guard you.
12 Wisdom will save you from the ways of
wicked men,
from men whose words are
perverse,
13 who have left the straight paths
to walk in dark ways,
14 who delight in doing wrong
and rejoice in the perverseness of
evil,
15 whose paths are crooked
and who are devious in their ways.

16 Wisdom will save you also from the
adulterous woman,
from the wayward woman with her
seductive words,
17 who has left the partner of her youth
and ignored the covenant she made
before God.[a]
18 Surely her house leads down to death
and her paths to the spirits of the
dead.
19 None who go to her return
or attain the paths of life.

20 Thus you will walk in the ways of the
good
and keep to the paths of the
righteous.
21 For the upright will live in the land,

[a] 17 Or *covenant of her God*

and the blameless will remain in it;
22 but the wicked will be cut off from the land,
and the unfaithful will be torn from it.

3 My son, do not forget my teaching,
but keep my commands in your heart,
2 for they will prolong your life many years
and bring you peace and prosperity.

3 Let love and faithfulness never leave you;
bind them around your neck,
write them on the tablet of your heart.
4 Then you will win favor and a good name
in the sight of God and man.
5 Trust in the LORD with all your heart
and lean not on your own understanding;
6 in all your ways submit to him,
and he will make your paths straight.[a]

7 Do not be wise in your own eyes;
fear the LORD and shun evil.
8 This will bring health to your body
and nourishment to your bones.

9 Honor the LORD with your wealth,
with the firstfruits of all your crops;
10 then your barns will be filled to overflowing,
and your vats will brim over with new wine.

11 My son, do not despise the LORD's discipline,
and do not resent his rebuke,
12 because the LORD disciplines those he loves,
as a father the son he delights in.[b]

13 Blessed are those who find wisdom,
those who gain understanding,
14 for she is more profitable than silver
and yields better returns than gold.
15 She is more precious than rubies;
nothing you desire can compare with her.
16 Long life is in her right hand;
in her left hand are riches and honor.
17 Her ways are pleasant ways,
and all her paths are peace.
18 She is a tree of life to those who take hold of her;
those who hold her fast will be blessed.

19 By wisdom the LORD laid the earth's foundations,
by understanding he set the heavens in place;
20 by his knowledge the watery depths were divided,
and the clouds let drop the dew.

21 My son, do not let wisdom and understanding out of your sight,
preserve sound judgment and discretion;
22 they will be life for you,
an ornament to grace your neck.
23 Then you will go on your way in safety,
and your foot will not stumble.
24 When you lie down, you will not be afraid;
when you lie down, your sleep will be sweet.
25 Have no fear of sudden disaster
or of the ruin that overtakes the wicked,
26 for the LORD will be at your side
and will keep your foot from being snared.

27 Do not withhold good from those to whom it is due,
when it is in your power to act.
28 Do not say to your neighbor,
"Come back tomorrow and I'll give it to you" —
when you already have it with you.
29 Do not plot harm against your neighbor,
who lives trustfully near you.
30 Do not accuse anyone for no reason —
when they have done you no harm.

31 Do not envy the violent
or choose any of their ways.
32 For the LORD detests the perverse
but takes the upright into his confidence.
33 The LORD's curse is on the house of the wicked,
but he blesses the home of the righteous.
34 He mocks proud mockers
but shows favor to the humble and oppressed.

[a] 6 Or *will direct your paths* [b] 12 Hebrew; Septuagint *loves, / and he chastens everyone he accepts as his child*

35 The wise inherit honor,
but fools get only shame.

4 Listen, my sons, to a father's
instruction;
pay attention and gain
understanding.
2 I give you sound learning,
so do not forsake my teaching.
3 For I too was a son to my father,
still tender, and cherished by my
mother.
4 Then he taught me, and he said to me,
"Take hold of my words with all your
heart;
keep my commands, and you will
live.
5 Get wisdom, get understanding;
do not forget my words or turn away
from them.
6 Do not forsake wisdom, and she will
protect you;
love her, and she will watch over
you.
7 The beginning of wisdom is this: Get[a]
wisdom.
Though it cost all you have,[b] get
understanding.
8 Cherish her, and she will exalt you;
embrace her, and she will honor
you.
9 She will give you a garland to grace
your head
and present you with a glorious
crown."
10 Listen, my son, accept what I say,
and the years of your life will be
many.
11 I instruct you in the way of wisdom
and lead you along straight paths.
12 When you walk, your steps will not be
hampered;
when you run, you will not stumble.
13 Hold on to instruction, do not let it go;
guard it well, for it is your life.
14 Do not set foot on the path of the
wicked
or walk in the way of evildoers.
15 Avoid it, do not travel on it;
turn from it and go on your way.
16 For they cannot rest until they do evil;
they are robbed of sleep till they
make someone stumble.
17 They eat the bread of wickedness
and drink the wine of violence.
18 The path of the righteous is like the
morning sun,
shining ever brighter till the full
light of day.
19 But the way of the wicked is like deep
darkness;
they do not know what makes them
stumble.

20 My son, pay attention to what I say;
turn your ear to my words.
21 Do not let them out of your sight,
keep them within your heart;
22 for they are life to those who find them
and health to one's whole body.
23 Above all else, guard your heart,
for everything you do flows from it.
24 Keep your mouth free of perversity;
keep corrupt talk far from your lips.
25 Let your eyes look straight ahead;
fix your gaze directly before you.
26 Give careful thought to the[c] paths for
your feet
and be steadfast in all your ways.
27 Do not turn to the right or the left;
keep your foot from evil.

5 My son, pay attention to my wisdom,
turn your ear to my words of insight,
2 that you may maintain discretion
and your lips may preserve
knowledge.
3 For the lips of the adulterous woman
drip honey,
and her speech is smoother than oil;
4 but in the end she is bitter as gall,
sharp as a double-edged sword.
5 Her feet go down to death;
her steps lead straight to the grave.
6 She gives no thought to the way of life;
her paths wander aimlessly, but she
does not know it.

7 Now then, my sons, listen to me;
do not turn aside from what I say.
8 Keep to a path far from her,
do not go near the door of her house,
9 lest you lose your honor to others
and your dignity[d] to one who is
cruel,
10 lest strangers feast on your wealth
and your toil enrich the house of
another.
11 At the end of your life you will groan,
when your flesh and body are spent.
12 You will say, "How I hated discipline!

[a] 7 Or *Wisdom is supreme; therefore get* [b] 7 Or *wisdom. / Whatever else you get* [c] 26 Or *Make level*
[d] 9 Or *years*

How my heart spurned correction!
13 I would not obey my teachers
or turn my ear to my instructors.
14 And I was soon in serious trouble
in the assembly of God's people."

15 Drink water from your own cistern,
running water from your own well.
16 Should your springs overflow in the streets,
your streams of water in the public squares?
17 Let them be yours alone,
never to be shared with strangers.
18 May your fountain be blessed,
and may you rejoice in the wife of your youth.
19 A loving doe, a graceful deer—
may her breasts satisfy you always,
may you ever be intoxicated with her love.
20 Why, my son, be intoxicated with another man's wife?
Why embrace the bosom of a wayward woman?

21 For your ways are in full view of the LORD,
and he examines all your paths.
22 The evil deeds of the wicked ensnare them;
the cords of their sins hold them fast.
23 For lack of discipline they will die,
led astray by their own great folly.

6 My son, if you have put up security for your neighbor,
if you have shaken hands in pledge for a stranger,
2 you have been trapped by what you said,
ensnared by the words of your mouth.
3 So do this, my son, to free yourself,
since you have fallen into your neighbor's hands:
Go—to the point of exhaustion—[a]
and give your neighbor no rest!
4 Allow no sleep to your eyes,
no slumber to your eyelids.
5 Free yourself, like a gazelle from the hand of the hunter,
like a bird from the snare of the fowler.

6 Go to the ant, you sluggard;
consider its ways and be wise!
7 It has no commander,
no overseer or ruler,
8 yet it stores its provisions in summer
and gathers its food at harvest.

9 How long will you lie there, you sluggard?
When will you get up from your sleep?
10 A little sleep, a little slumber,
a little folding of the hands to rest—
11 and poverty will come on you like a thief
and scarcity like an armed man.

12 A troublemaker and a villain,
who goes about with a corrupt mouth,
13 who winks maliciously with his eye,
signals with his feet
and motions with his fingers,
14 who plots evil with deceit in his heart—
he always stirs up conflict.
15 Therefore disaster will overtake him in an instant;
he will suddenly be destroyed—
without remedy.

16 There are six things the LORD hates,
seven that are detestable to him:
17 haughty eyes,
a lying tongue,
hands that shed innocent blood,
18 a heart that devises wicked schemes,
feet that are quick to rush into evil,
19 a false witness who pours out lies
and a person who stirs up conflict in the community.

20 My son, keep your father's command
and do not forsake your mother's teaching.
21 Bind them always on your heart;
fasten them around your neck.
22 When you walk, they will guide you;
when you sleep, they will watch over you;
when you awake, they will speak to you.
23 For this command is a lamp,
this teaching is a light,
and correction and instruction
are the way to life,

[a] 3 Or *Go and humble yourself,*

24 keeping you from your neighbor's
wife,
from the smooth talk of a wayward
woman.
25 Do not lust in your heart after her
beauty
or let her captivate you with her
eyes.
26 For a prostitute can be had for a loaf of
bread,
but another man's wife preys on
your very life.
27 Can a man scoop fire into his lap
without his clothes being burned?
28 Can a man walk on hot coals
without his feet being scorched?
29 So is he who sleeps with another
man's wife;
no one who touches her will go
unpunished.
30 People do not despise a thief if he
steals
to satisfy his hunger when he is
starving.
31 Yet if he is caught, he must pay
sevenfold,
though it costs him all the wealth of
his house.
32 But a man who commits adultery has
no sense;
whoever does so destroys himself.
33 Blows and disgrace are his lot,
and his shame will never be wiped
away.
34 For jealousy arouses a husband's fury,
and he will show no mercy when he
takes revenge.
35 He will not accept any compensation;
he will refuse a bribe, however great
it is.

7 My son, keep my words
and store up my commands within
you.
2 Keep my commands and you will live;
guard my teachings as the apple of
your eye.
3 Bind them on your fingers;
write them on the tablet of your
heart.
4 Say to wisdom, "You are my sister,"
and to insight, "You are my relative."
5 They will keep you from the
adulterous woman,
from the wayward woman with her
seductive words.
6 At the window of my house
I looked down through the lattice.
7 I saw among the simple,
I noticed among the young men,
a youth who had no sense.
8 He was going down the street near her
corner,
walking along in the direction of her
house
9 at twilight, as the day was fading,
as the dark of night set in.
10 Then out came a woman to meet him,
dressed like a prostitute and with
crafty intent.
11 (She is unruly and defiant,
her feet never stay at home;
12 now in the street, now in the squares,
at every corner she lurks.)
13 She took hold of him and kissed him
and with a brazen face she said:
14 "Today I fulfilled my vows,
and I have food from my fellowship
offering at home.
15 So I came out to meet you;
I looked for you and have found you!
16 I have covered my bed
with colored linens from Egypt.
17 I have perfumed my bed
with myrrh, aloes and cinnamon.
18 Come, let's drink deeply of love till
morning;
let's enjoy ourselves with love!
19 My husband is not at home;
he has gone on a long journey.
20 He took his purse filled with money
and will not be home till full moon."
21 With persuasive words she led him
astray;
she seduced him with her smooth
talk.
22 All at once he followed her
like an ox going to the slaughter,
like a deer[a] stepping into a noose[b]
23 till an arrow pierces his liver,
like a bird darting into a snare,
little knowing it will cost him his
life.
24 Now then, my sons, listen to me;
pay attention to what I say.
25 Do not let your heart turn to her ways
or stray into her paths.

[a] 22 Syriac (see also Septuagint); Hebrew *fool* [b] 22 The meaning of the Hebrew for this line is uncertain.

26 Many are the victims she has brought
down;
her slain are a mighty throng.
27 Her house is a highway to the grave,
leading down to the chambers of
death.

8 Does not wisdom call out?
Does not understanding raise her
voice?
2 At the highest point along the way,
where the paths meet, she takes her
stand;
3 beside the gate leading into the city,
at the entrance, she cries aloud:
4 "To you, O people, I call out;
I raise my voice to all mankind.
5 You who are simple, gain prudence;
you who are foolish, set your hearts
on it.[a]
6 Listen, for I have trustworthy things to
say;
I open my lips to speak what is right.
7 My mouth speaks what is true,
for my lips detest wickedness.
8 All the words of my mouth are just;
none of them is crooked or perverse.
9 To the discerning all of them are right;
they are upright to those who have
found knowledge.
10 Choose my instruction instead of
silver,
knowledge rather than choice gold,
11 for wisdom is more precious than
rubies,
and nothing you desire can
compare with her.
12 "I, wisdom, dwell together with
prudence;
I possess knowledge and discretion.
13 To fear the LORD is to hate evil;
I hate pride and arrogance,
evil behavior and perverse speech.
14 Counsel and sound judgment are
mine;
I have insight, I have power.
15 By me kings reign
and rulers issue decrees that are
just;
16 by me princes govern,
and nobles — all who rule on earth.[b]
17 I love those who love me,
and those who seek me find me.
18 With me are riches and honor,
enduring wealth and prosperity.
19 My fruit is better than fine gold;
what I yield surpasses choice silver.
20 I walk in the way of righteousness,
along the paths of justice,
21 bestowing a rich inheritance on those
who love me
and making their treasuries full.
22 "The LORD brought me forth as the
first of his works,[c,d]
before his deeds of old;
23 I was formed long ages ago,
at the very beginning, when the
world came to be.
24 When there were no watery depths, I
was given birth,
when there were no springs
overflowing with water;
25 before the mountains were settled in
place,
before the hills, I was given birth,
26 before he made the world or its fields
or any of the dust of the earth.
27 I was there when he set the heavens in
place,
when he marked out the horizon on
the face of the deep,
28 when he established the clouds
above
and fixed securely the fountains of
the deep,
29 when he gave the sea its boundary
so the waters would not overstep his
command,
and when he marked out the
foundations of the earth.
30 Then I was constantly[e] at his side.
I was filled with delight day after day,
rejoicing always in his presence,
31 rejoicing in his whole world
and delighting in mankind.

32 "Now then, my children, listen to me;
blessed are those who keep my
ways.
33 Listen to my instruction and be wise;
do not disregard it.
34 Blessed are those who listen to me,
watching daily at my doors,
waiting at my doorway.
35 For those who find me find life
and receive favor from the LORD.

[a] 5 Septuagint; Hebrew *foolish, instruct your minds* [b] 16 Some Hebrew manuscripts and Septuagint; other Hebrew manuscripts *all righteous rulers* [c] 22 Or *way*; or *dominion* [d] 22 Or *The LORD possessed me at the beginning of his work*; or *The LORD brought me forth at the beginning of his work* [e] 30 Or *was the artisan*; or *was a little child*

36 But those who fail to find me harm
themselves;
all who hate me love death."

9 Wisdom has built her house;
she has set up[a] its seven pillars.
2 She has prepared her meat and mixed
her wine;
she has also set her table.
3 She has sent out her servants, and she
calls
from the highest point of the city,
4 "Let all who are simple come to my
house!"
To those who have no sense she says,
5 "Come, eat my food
and drink the wine I have mixed.
6 Leave your simple ways and you will
live;
walk in the way of insight."

7 Whoever corrects a mocker invites
insults;
whoever rebukes the wicked incurs
abuse.
8 Do not rebuke mockers or they will
hate you;
rebuke the wise and they will love
you.
9 Instruct the wise and they will be
wiser still;
teach the righteous and they will
add to their learning.

10 The fear of the LORD is the beginning
of wisdom,
and knowledge of the Holy One is
understanding.
11 For through wisdom[b] your days will
be many,
and years will be added to your life.
12 If you are wise, your wisdom will
reward you;
if you are a mocker, you alone will
suffer.

13 Folly is an unruly woman;
she is simple and knows nothing.
14 She sits at the door of her house,
on a seat at the highest point of the
city,
15 calling out to those who pass by,
who go straight on their way,
16 "Let all who are simple come to my
house!"
To those who have no sense she says,
17 "Stolen water is sweet;
food eaten in secret is delicious!"
18 But little do they know that the dead
are there,
that her guests are deep in the realm
of the dead.

10 The proverbs of Solomon:

A wise son brings joy to his father,
but a foolish son brings grief to his
mother.

2 Ill-gotten treasures have no lasting
value,
but righteousness delivers from
death.

3 The LORD does not let the righteous go
hungry,
but he thwarts the craving of the
wicked.

4 Lazy hands make for poverty,
but diligent hands bring wealth.

5 He who gathers crops in summer is a
prudent son,
but he who sleeps during harvest is
a disgraceful son.

6 Blessings crown the head of the
righteous,
but violence overwhelms the mouth
of the wicked.[c]

7 The name of the righteous is used in
blessings,[d]
but the name of the wicked will rot.

8 The wise in heart accept commands,
but a chattering fool comes to ruin.

9 Whoever walks in integrity walks
securely,
but whoever takes crooked paths
will be found out.

10 Whoever winks maliciously causes
grief,
and a chattering fool comes to ruin.

11 The mouth of the righteous is a
fountain of life,
but the mouth of the wicked
conceals violence.

12 Hatred stirs up conflict,
but love covers over all wrongs.

13 Wisdom is found on the lips of the
discerning,

[a] *1* Septuagint, Syriac and Targum; Hebrew *has hewn out* [b] *11* Septuagint, Syriac and Targum; Hebrew *me*
[c] *6* Or *righteous, / but the mouth of the wicked conceals violence* [d] *7* See Gen. 48:20.

but a rod is for the back of one who
has no sense.

14 The wise store up knowledge,
but the mouth of a fool invites ruin.

15 The wealth of the rich is their fortified
city,
but poverty is the ruin of the poor.

16 The wages of the righteous is life,
but the earnings of the wicked are
sin and death.

17 Whoever heeds discipline shows the
way to life,
but whoever ignores correction
leads others astray.

18 Whoever conceals hatred with lying
lips
and spreads slander is a fool.

19 Sin is not ended by multiplying words,
but the prudent hold their tongues.

20 The tongue of the righteous is choice
silver,
but the heart of the wicked is of little
value.

21 The lips of the righteous nourish
many,
but fools die for lack of sense.

22 The blessing of the LORD brings
wealth,
without painful toil for it.

23 A fool finds pleasure in wicked
schemes,
but a person of understanding
delights in wisdom.

24 What the wicked dread will overtake
them;
what the righteous desire will be
granted.

25 When the storm has swept by, the
wicked are gone,
but the righteous stand firm forever.

26 As vinegar to the teeth and smoke to
the eyes,
so are sluggards to those who send
them.

27 The fear of the LORD adds length to
life,
but the years of the wicked are cut
short.

28 The prospect of the righteous is joy,
but the hopes of the wicked come to
nothing.

29 The way of the LORD is a refuge for the
blameless,
but it is the ruin of those who do
evil.

30 The righteous will never be
uprooted,
but the wicked will not remain in
the land.

31 From the mouth of the righteous
comes the fruit of wisdom,
but a perverse tongue will be
silenced.

32 The lips of the righteous know what
finds favor,
but the mouth of the wicked only
what is perverse.

11 The LORD detests dishonest scales,
but accurate weights find favor
with him.

2 When pride comes, then comes
disgrace,
but with humility comes wisdom.

3 The integrity of the upright guides
them,
but the unfaithful are destroyed by
their duplicity.

4 Wealth is worthless in the day of
wrath,
but righteousness delivers from
death.

5 The righteousness of the blameless
makes their paths straight,
but the wicked are brought down by
their own wickedness.

6 The righteousness of the upright
delivers them,
but the unfaithful are trapped by
evil desires.

7 Hopes placed in mortals die with
them;
all the promise of[a] their power
comes to nothing.

8 The righteous person is rescued from
trouble,
and it falls on the wicked instead.

[a] 7 Two Hebrew manuscripts; most Hebrew manuscripts, Vulgate, Syriac and Targum *When the wicked die, their hope perishes; / all they expected from*

9 With their mouths the godless destroy
their neighbors,
but through knowledge the
righteous escape.

10 When the righteous prosper, the city
rejoices;
when the wicked perish, there are
shouts of joy.

11 Through the blessing of the upright a
city is exalted,
but by the mouth of the wicked it is
destroyed.

12 Whoever derides their neighbor has
no sense,
but the one who has understanding
holds their tongue.

13 A gossip betrays a confidence,
but a trustworthy person keeps a
secret.

14 For lack of guidance a nation falls,
but victory is won through many
advisers.

15 Whoever puts up security for a
stranger will surely suffer,
but whoever refuses to shake hands
in pledge is safe.

16 A kindhearted woman gains honor,
but ruthless men gain only
wealth.

17 Those who are kind benefit
themselves,
but the cruel bring ruin on
themselves.

18 A wicked person earns deceptive
wages,
but the one who sows righteousness
reaps a sure reward.

19 Truly the righteous attain life,
but whoever pursues evil finds
death.

20 The LORD detests those whose hearts
are perverse,
but he delights in those whose ways
are blameless.

21 Be sure of this: The wicked will not go
unpunished,
but those who are righteous will go
free.

22 Like a gold ring in a pig's snout
is a beautiful woman who shows no
discretion.

23 The desire of the righteous ends only
in good,
but the hope of the wicked only in
wrath.

24 One person gives freely, yet gains even
more;
another withholds unduly, but
comes to poverty.

25 A generous person will prosper;
whoever refreshes others will be
refreshed.

26 People curse the one who hoards
grain,
but they pray God's blessing on the
one who is willing to sell.

27 Whoever seeks good finds favor,
but evil comes to one who searches
for it.

28 Those who trust in their riches will fall,
but the righteous will thrive like a
green leaf.

29 Whoever brings ruin on their family
will inherit only wind,
and the fool will be servant to the
wise.

30 The fruit of the righteous is a tree of
life,
and the one who is wise saves lives.

31 If the righteous receive their due on
earth,
how much more the ungodly and
the sinner!

12 Whoever loves discipline loves
knowledge,
but whoever hates correction is
stupid.

2 Good people obtain favor from the
LORD,
but he condemns those who devise
wicked schemes.

3 No one can be established through
wickedness,
but the righteous cannot be
uprooted.

4 A wife of noble character is her
husband's crown,
but a disgraceful wife is like decay
in his bones.

5 The plans of the righteous are just,
but the advice of the wicked is
deceitful.

6 The words of the wicked lie in wait for blood,
but the speech of the upright rescues them.

7 The wicked are overthrown and are no more,
but the house of the righteous stands firm.

8 A person is praised according to their prudence,
and one with a warped mind is despised.

9 Better to be a nobody and yet have a servant
than pretend to be somebody and have no food.

10 The righteous care for the needs of their animals,
but the kindest acts of the wicked are cruel.

11 Those who work their land will have abundant food,
but those who chase fantasies have no sense.

12 The wicked desire the stronghold of evildoers,
but the root of the righteous endures.

13 Evildoers are trapped by their sinful talk,
and so the innocent escape trouble.

14 From the fruit of their lips people are filled with good things,
and the work of their hands brings them reward.

15 The way of fools seems right to them,
but the wise listen to advice.

16 Fools show their annoyance at once,
but the prudent overlook an insult.

17 An honest witness tells the truth,
but a false witness tells lies.

18 The words of the reckless pierce like swords,
but the tongue of the wise brings healing.

19 Truthful lips endure forever,
but a lying tongue lasts only a moment.

20 Deceit is in the hearts of those who plot evil,
but those who promote peace have joy.

21 No harm overtakes the righteous,
but the wicked have their fill of trouble.

22 The LORD detests lying lips,
but he delights in people who are trustworthy.

23 The prudent keep their knowledge to themselves,
but a fool's heart blurts out folly.

24 Diligent hands will rule,
but laziness ends in forced labor.

25 Anxiety weighs down the heart,
but a kind word cheers it up.

26 The righteous choose their friends carefully,
but the way of the wicked leads them astray.

27 The lazy do not roast[a] any game,
but the diligent feed on the riches of the hunt.

28 In the way of righteousness there is life;
along that path is immortality.

13 A wise son heeds his father's instruction,
but a mocker does not respond to rebukes.

2 From the fruit of their lips people enjoy good things,
but the unfaithful have an appetite for violence.

3 Those who guard their lips preserve their lives,
but those who speak rashly will come to ruin.

4 A sluggard's appetite is never filled,
but the desires of the diligent are fully satisfied.

5 The righteous hate what is false,
but the wicked make themselves a stench
and bring shame on themselves.

6 Righteousness guards the person of integrity,

[a] 27 The meaning of the Hebrew for this word is uncertain.

but wickedness overthrows the sinner.

7 One person pretends to be rich, yet has nothing;
another pretends to be poor, yet has great wealth.

8 A person's riches may ransom their life,
but the poor cannot respond to threatening rebukes.

9 The light of the righteous shines brightly,
but the lamp of the wicked is snuffed out.

10 Where there is strife, there is pride,
but wisdom is found in those who take advice.

11 Dishonest money dwindles away,
but whoever gathers money little by little makes it grow.

12 Hope deferred makes the heart sick,
but a longing fulfilled is a tree of life.

13 Whoever scorns instruction will pay for it,
but whoever respects a command is rewarded.

14 The teaching of the wise is a fountain of life,
turning a person from the snares of death.

15 Good judgment wins favor,
but the way of the unfaithful leads to their destruction.[a]

16 All who are prudent act with[b] knowledge,
but fools expose their folly.

17 A wicked messenger falls into trouble,
but a trustworthy envoy brings healing.

18 Whoever disregards discipline comes to poverty and shame,
but whoever heeds correction is honored.

19 A longing fulfilled is sweet to the soul,
but fools detest turning from evil.

20 Walk with the wise and become wise,
for a companion of fools suffers harm.

21 Trouble pursues the sinner,
but the righteous are rewarded with good things.

22 A good person leaves an inheritance for their children's children,
but a sinner's wealth is stored up for the righteous.

23 An unplowed field produces food for the poor,
but injustice sweeps it away.

24 Whoever spares the rod hates their children,
but the one who loves their children is careful to discipline them.

25 The righteous eat to their hearts' content,
but the stomach of the wicked goes hungry.

14 The wise woman builds her house,
but with her own hands the foolish one tears hers down.

2 Whoever fears the LORD walks uprightly,
but those who despise him are devious in their ways.

3 A fool's mouth lashes out with pride,
but the lips of the wise protect them.

4 Where there are no oxen, the manger is empty,
but from the strength of an ox come abundant harvests.

5 An honest witness does not deceive,
but a false witness pours out lies.

6 The mocker seeks wisdom and finds none,
but knowledge comes easily to the discerning.

7 Stay away from a fool,
for you will not find knowledge on their lips.

8 The wisdom of the prudent is to give thought to their ways,
but the folly of fools is deception.

9 Fools mock at making amends for sin,
but goodwill is found among the upright.

10 Each heart knows its own bitterness,
and no one else can share its joy.

[a] *15* Septuagint and Syriac; the meaning of the Hebrew for this phrase is uncertain. [b] *16* Or *prudent protect themselves through*

11 The house of the wicked will be destroyed,
but the tent of the upright will flourish.

12 There is a way that appears to be right,
but in the end it leads to death.

13 Even in laughter the heart may ache,
and rejoicing may end in grief.

14 The faithless will be fully repaid for their ways,
and the good rewarded for theirs.

15 The simple believe anything,
but the prudent give thought to their steps.

16 The wise fear the LORD and shun evil,
but a fool is hotheaded and yet feels secure.

17 A quick-tempered person does foolish things,
and the one who devises evil schemes is hated.

18 The simple inherit folly,
but the prudent are crowned with knowledge.

19 Evildoers will bow down in the presence of the good,
and the wicked at the gates of the righteous.

20 The poor are shunned even by their neighbors,
but the rich have many friends.

21 It is a sin to despise one's neighbor,
but blessed is the one who is kind to the needy.

22 Do not those who plot evil go astray?
But those who plan what is good find[a] love and faithfulness.

23 All hard work brings a profit,
but mere talk leads only to poverty.

24 The wealth of the wise is their crown,
but the folly of fools yields folly.

25 A truthful witness saves lives,
but a false witness is deceitful.

26 Whoever fears the LORD has a secure fortress,
and for their children it will be a refuge.

27 The fear of the LORD is a fountain of life,
turning a person from the snares of death.

28 A large population is a king's glory,
but without subjects a prince is ruined.

29 Whoever is patient has great understanding,
but one who is quick-tempered displays folly.

30 A heart at peace gives life to the body,
but envy rots the bones.

31 Whoever oppresses the poor shows contempt for their Maker,
but whoever is kind to the needy honors God.

32 When calamity comes, the wicked are brought down,
but even in death the righteous seek refuge in God.

33 Wisdom reposes in the heart of the discerning
and even among fools she lets herself be known.[b]

34 Righteousness exalts a nation,
but sin condemns any people.

35 A king delights in a wise servant,
but a shameful servant arouses his fury.

15 A gentle answer turns away wrath,
but a harsh word stirs up anger.

2 The tongue of the wise adorns knowledge,
but the mouth of the fool gushes folly.

3 The eyes of the LORD are everywhere,
keeping watch on the wicked and the good.

4 The soothing tongue is a tree of life,
but a perverse tongue crushes the spirit.

5 A fool spurns a parent's discipline,
but whoever heeds correction shows prudence.

6 The house of the righteous contains great treasure,

[a] 22 Or *show* [b] 33 Hebrew; Septuagint and Syriac *discerning / but in the heart of fools she is not known*

but the income of the wicked brings
ruin.

7 The lips of the wise spread knowledge,
but the hearts of fools are not
upright.

8 The LORD detests the sacrifice of the
wicked,
but the prayer of the upright pleases
him.

9 The LORD detests the way of the
wicked,
but he loves those who pursue
righteousness.

10 Stern discipline awaits anyone who
leaves the path;
the one who hates correction will
die.

11 Death and Destruction[a] lie open
before the LORD —
how much more do human hearts!

12 Mockers resent correction,
so they avoid the wise.

13 A happy heart makes the face
cheerful,
but heartache crushes the spirit.

14 The discerning heart seeks
knowledge,
but the mouth of a fool feeds on folly.

15 All the days of the oppressed are
wretched,
but the cheerful heart has a
continual feast.

16 Better a little with the fear of the LORD
than great wealth with turmoil.

17 Better a small serving of vegetables
with love
than a fattened calf with hatred.

18 A hot-tempered person stirs up
conflict,
but the one who is patient calms a
quarrel.

19 The way of the sluggard is blocked
with thorns,
but the path of the upright is a
highway.

20 A wise son brings joy to his father,
but a foolish man despises his
mother.

21 Folly brings joy to one who has no
sense,
but whoever has understanding
keeps a straight course.

22 Plans fail for lack of counsel,
but with many advisers they succeed.

23 A person finds joy in giving an apt
reply —
and how good is a timely word!

24 The path of life leads upward for the
prudent
to keep them from going down to
the realm of the dead.

25 The LORD tears down the house of the
proud,
but he sets the widow's boundary
stones in place.

26 The LORD detests the thoughts of the
wicked,
but gracious words are pure in his
sight.

27 The greedy bring ruin to their
households,
but the one who hates bribes will
live.

28 The heart of the righteous weighs its
answers,
but the mouth of the wicked gushes
evil.

29 The LORD is far from the wicked,
but he hears the prayer of the
righteous.

30 Light in a messenger's eyes brings joy
to the heart,
and good news gives health to the
bones.

31 Whoever heeds life-giving correction
will be at home among the wise.

32 Those who disregard discipline
despise themselves,
but the one who heeds correction
gains understanding.

33 Wisdom's instruction is to fear the
LORD,
and humility comes before honor.

16

To humans belong the plans of the
heart,
but from the LORD comes the proper
answer of the tongue.

[a] *11* Hebrew *Abaddon*

2 All a person's ways seem pure to them,
but motives are weighed by the LORD.
3 Commit to the LORD whatever you do,
and he will establish your plans.
4 The LORD works out everything to its proper end —
even the wicked for a day of disaster.
5 The LORD detests all the proud of heart.
Be sure of this: They will not go unpunished.
6 Through love and faithfulness sin is atoned for;
through the fear of the LORD evil is avoided.
7 When the LORD takes pleasure in anyone's way,
he causes their enemies to make peace with them.
8 Better a little with righteousness
than much gain with injustice.
9 In their hearts humans plan their course,
but the LORD establishes their steps.
10 The lips of a king speak as an oracle,
and his mouth does not betray justice.
11 Honest scales and balances belong to the LORD;
all the weights in the bag are of his making.
12 Kings detest wrongdoing,
for a throne is established through righteousness.
13 Kings take pleasure in honest lips;
they value the one who speaks what is right.
14 A king's wrath is a messenger of death,
but the wise will appease it.
15 When a king's face brightens, it means life;
his favor is like a rain cloud in spring.
16 How much better to get wisdom than gold,
to get insight rather than silver!
17 The highway of the upright avoids evil;
those who guard their ways preserve their lives.
18 Pride goes before destruction,
a haughty spirit before a fall.
19 Better to be lowly in spirit along with the oppressed
than to share plunder with the proud.
20 Whoever gives heed to instruction prospers,[a]
and blessed is the one who trusts in the LORD.
21 The wise in heart are called discerning,
and gracious words promote instruction.[b]
22 Prudence is a fountain of life to the prudent,
but folly brings punishment to fools.
23 The hearts of the wise make their mouths prudent,
and their lips promote instruction.[c]
24 Gracious words are a honeycomb,
sweet to the soul and healing to the bones.
25 There is a way that appears to be right,
but in the end it leads to death.
26 The appetite of laborers works for them;
their hunger drives them on.
27 A scoundrel plots evil,
and on their lips it is like a scorching fire.
28 A perverse person stirs up conflict,
and a gossip separates close friends.
29 A violent person entices their neighbor
and leads them down a path that is not good.
30 Whoever winks with their eye is plotting perversity;
whoever purses their lips is bent on evil.
31 Gray hair is a crown of splendor;
it is attained in the way of righteousness.

[a] 20 Or *whoever speaks prudently finds what is good*
[b] 21 Or *words make a person persuasive*
[c] 23 Or *prudent / and make their lips persuasive*

32 Better a patient person than a warrior,
one with self-control than one who takes a city.

33 The lot is cast into the lap,
but its every decision is from the LORD.

17

Better a dry crust with peace and quiet
than a house full of feasting, with strife.

2 A prudent servant will rule over a disgraceful son
and will share the inheritance as one of the family.

3 The crucible for silver and the furnace for gold,
but the LORD tests the heart.

4 A wicked person listens to deceitful lips;
a liar pays attention to a destructive tongue.

5 Whoever mocks the poor shows contempt for their Maker;
whoever gloats over disaster will not go unpunished.

6 Children's children are a crown to the aged,
and parents are the pride of their children.

7 Eloquent lips are unsuited to a godless fool—
how much worse lying lips to a ruler!

8 A bribe is seen as a charm by the one who gives it;
they think success will come at every turn.

9 Whoever would foster love covers over an offense,
but whoever repeats the matter separates close friends.

10 A rebuke impresses a discerning person
more than a hundred lashes a fool.

11 Evildoers foster rebellion against God;
the messenger of death will be sent against them.

12 Better to meet a bear robbed of her cubs
than a fool bent on folly.

13 Evil will never leave the house
of one who pays back evil for good.

14 Starting a quarrel is like breaching a dam;
so drop the matter before a dispute breaks out.

15 Acquitting the guilty and condemning the innocent—
the LORD detests them both.

16 Why should fools have money in hand to buy wisdom,
when they are not able to understand it?

17 A friend loves at all times,
and a brother is born for a time of adversity.

18 One who has no sense shakes hands in pledge
and puts up security for a neighbor.

19 Whoever loves a quarrel loves sin;
whoever builds a high gate invites destruction.

20 One whose heart is corrupt does not prosper;
one whose tongue is perverse falls into trouble.

21 To have a fool for a child brings grief;
there is no joy for the parent of a godless fool.

22 A cheerful heart is good medicine,
but a crushed spirit dries up the bones.

23 The wicked accept bribes in secret
to pervert the course of justice.

24 A discerning person keeps wisdom in view,
but a fool's eyes wander to the ends of the earth.

25 A foolish son brings grief to his father
and bitterness to the mother who bore him.

26 If imposing a fine on the innocent is not good,
surely to flog honest officials is not right.

27 The one who has knowledge uses words with restraint,
and whoever has understanding is even-tempered.

28 Even fools are thought wise if they
keep silent,
and discerning if they hold their
tongues.

18 An unfriendly person pursues
selfish ends
and against all sound judgment
starts quarrels.

2 Fools find no pleasure in
understanding
but delight in airing their own
opinions.

3 When wickedness comes, so does
contempt,
and with shame comes reproach.

4 The words of the mouth are deep
waters,
but the fountain of wisdom is a
rushing stream.

5 It is not good to be partial to the
wicked
and so deprive the innocent of
justice.

6 The lips of fools bring them strife,
and their mouths invite a beating.

7 The mouths of fools are their undoing,
and their lips are a snare to their
very lives.

8 The words of a gossip are like choice
morsels;
they go down to the inmost parts.

9 One who is slack in his work
is brother to one who destroys.

10 The name of the LORD is a fortified
tower;
the righteous run to it and are safe.

11 The wealth of the rich is their fortified
city;
they imagine it a wall too high to
scale.

12 Before a downfall the heart is haughty,
but humility comes before honor.

13 To answer before listening —
that is folly and shame.

14 The human spirit can endure in
sickness,
but a crushed spirit who can bear?

15 The heart of the discerning acquires
knowledge,
for the ears of the wise seek it out.

16 A gift opens the way
and ushers the giver into the
presence of the great.

17 In a lawsuit the first to speak seems
right,
until someone comes forward and
cross-examines.

18 Casting the lot settles disputes
and keeps strong opponents apart.

19 A brother wronged is more unyielding
than a fortified city;
disputes are like the barred gates of
a citadel.

20 From the fruit of their mouth a
person's stomach is filled;
with the harvest of their lips they
are satisfied.

21 The tongue has the power of life and
death,
and those who love it will eat its
fruit.

22 He who finds a wife finds what is good
and receives favor from the LORD.

23 The poor plead for mercy,
but the rich answer harshly.

24 One who has unreliable friends soon
comes to ruin,
but there is a friend who sticks
closer than a brother.

19 Better the poor whose walk is
blameless
than a fool whose lips are perverse.

2 Desire without knowledge is not
good —
how much more will hasty feet miss
the way!

3 A person's own folly leads to their
ruin,
yet their heart rages against the
LORD.

4 Wealth attracts many friends,
but even the closest friend of the
poor person deserts them.

5 A false witness will not go
unpunished,
and whoever pours out lies will not
go free.

6 Many curry favor with a ruler,
and everyone is the friend of one
who gives gifts.

7 The poor are shunned by all their
relatives —
how much more do their friends
avoid them!
Though the poor pursue them with
pleading,
they are nowhere to be found.[a]

8 The one who gets wisdom loves life;
the one who cherishes
understanding will soon
prosper.

9 A false witness will not go
unpunished,
and whoever pours out lies will
perish.

10 It is not fitting for a fool to live in
luxury —
how much worse for a slave to rule
over princes!

11 A person's wisdom yields patience;
it is to one's glory to overlook an
offense.

12 A king's rage is like the roar of a lion,
but his favor is like dew on the grass.

13 A foolish child is a father's ruin,
and a quarrelsome wife is like
the constant dripping of a leaky
roof.

14 Houses and wealth are inherited from
parents,
but a prudent wife is from the LORD.

15 Laziness brings on deep sleep,
and the shiftless go hungry.

16 Whoever keeps commandments keeps
their life,
but whoever shows contempt for
their ways will die.

17 Whoever is kind to the poor lends to
the LORD,
and he will reward them for what
they have done.

18 Discipline your children, for in that
there is hope;
do not be a willing party to their
death.

19 A hot-tempered person must pay the
penalty;
rescue them, and you will have to do
it again.

20 Listen to advice and accept discipline,
and at the end you will be counted
among the wise.

21 Many are the plans in a person's heart,
but it is the LORD's purpose that
prevails.

22 What a person desires is unfailing
love[b];
better to be poor than a liar.

23 The fear of the LORD leads to life;
then one rests content, untouched
by trouble.

24 A sluggard buries his hand in the dish;
he will not even bring it back to his
mouth!

25 Flog a mocker, and the simple will
learn prudence;
rebuke the discerning, and they will
gain knowledge.

26 Whoever robs their father and drives
out their mother
is a child who brings shame and
disgrace.

27 Stop listening to instruction, my son,
and you will stray from the words of
knowledge.

28 A corrupt witness mocks at justice,
and the mouth of the wicked gulps
down evil.

29 Penalties are prepared for mockers,
and beatings for the backs of fools.

20 Wine is a mocker and beer a
brawler;
whoever is led astray by them is not
wise.

2 A king's wrath strikes terror like the
roar of a lion;
those who anger him forfeit their
lives.

3 It is to one's honor to avoid strife,
but every fool is quick to quarrel.

4 Sluggards do not plow in season;
so at harvest time they look but find
nothing.

5 The purposes of a person's heart are
deep waters,
but one who has insight draws them
out.

[a] 7 The meaning of the Hebrew for this sentence is uncertain. [b] 22 Or *Greed is a person's shame*

6 Many claim to have unfailing love,
but a faithful person who can find?

7 The righteous lead blameless lives;
blessed are their children after them.

8 When a king sits on his throne to judge,
he winnows out all evil with his eyes.

9 Who can say, "I have kept my heart pure;
I am clean and without sin"?

10 Differing weights and differing measures—
the LORD detests them both.

11 Even small children are known by their actions,
so is their conduct really pure and upright?

12 Ears that hear and eyes that see—
the LORD has made them both.

13 Do not love sleep or you will grow poor;
stay awake and you will have food to spare.

14 "It's no good, it's no good!" says the buyer—
then goes off and boasts about the purchase.

15 Gold there is, and rubies in abundance,
but lips that speak knowledge are a rare jewel.

16 Take the garment of one who puts up security for a stranger;
hold it in pledge if it is done for an outsider.

17 Food gained by fraud tastes sweet,
but one ends up with a mouth full of gravel.

18 Plans are established by seeking advice;
so if you wage war, obtain guidance.

19 A gossip betrays a confidence;
so avoid anyone who talks too much.

20 If someone curses their father or mother,
their lamp will be snuffed out in pitch darkness.

21 An inheritance claimed too soon
will not be blessed at the end.

22 Do not say, "I'll pay you back for this wrong!"
Wait for the LORD, and he will avenge you.

23 The LORD detests differing weights,
and dishonest scales do not please him.

24 A person's steps are directed by the LORD.
How then can anyone understand their own way?

25 It is a trap to dedicate something rashly
and only later to consider one's vows.

26 A wise king winnows out the wicked;
he drives the threshing wheel over them.

27 The human spirit is[a] the lamp of the LORD
that sheds light on one's inmost being.

28 Love and faithfulness keep a king safe;
through love his throne is made secure.

29 The glory of young men is their strength,
gray hair the splendor of the old.

30 Blows and wounds scrub away evil,
and beatings purge the inmost being.

21 In the LORD's hand the king's heart is a stream of water
that he channels toward all who please him.

2 A person may think their own ways are right,
but the LORD weighs the heart.

3 To do what is right and just
is more acceptable to the LORD than sacrifice.

4 Haughty eyes and a proud heart—
the unplowed field of the wicked—
produce sin.

[a] 27 Or *A person's words are*

5 The plans of the diligent lead to profit
as surely as haste leads to poverty.

6 A fortune made by a lying tongue
is a fleeting vapor and a deadly snare.[a]

7 The violence of the wicked will drag them away,
for they refuse to do what is right.

8 The way of the guilty is devious,
but the conduct of the innocent is upright.

9 Better to live on a corner of the roof
than share a house with a quarrelsome wife.

10 The wicked crave evil;
their neighbors get no mercy from them.

11 When a mocker is punished, the simple gain wisdom;
by paying attention to the wise they get knowledge.

12 The Righteous One[b] takes note of the house of the wicked
and brings the wicked to ruin.

13 Whoever shuts their ears to the cry of the poor
will also cry out and not be answered.

14 A gift given in secret soothes anger,
and a bribe concealed in the cloak pacifies great wrath.

15 When justice is done, it brings joy to the righteous
but terror to evildoers.

16 Whoever strays from the path of prudence
comes to rest in the company of the dead.

17 Whoever loves pleasure will become poor;
whoever loves wine and olive oil will never be rich.

18 The wicked become a ransom for the righteous,
and the unfaithful for the upright.

19 Better to live in a desert
than with a quarrelsome and nagging wife.

20 The wise store up choice food and olive oil,
but fools gulp theirs down.

21 Whoever pursues righteousness and love
finds life, prosperity[c] and honor.

22 One who is wise can go up against the city of the mighty
and pull down the stronghold in which they trust.

23 Those who guard their mouths and their tongues
keep themselves from calamity.

24 The proud and arrogant person — "Mocker" is his name —
behaves with insolent fury.

25 The craving of a sluggard will be the death of him,
because his hands refuse to work.

26 All day long he craves for more,
but the righteous give without sparing.

27 The sacrifice of the wicked is detestable —
how much more so when brought with evil intent!

28 A false witness will perish,
but a careful listener will testify successfully.

29 The wicked put up a bold front,
but the upright give thought to their ways.

30 There is no wisdom, no insight, no plan
that can succeed against the LORD.

31 The horse is made ready for the day of battle,
but victory rests with the LORD.

22 A good name is more desirable than great riches;
to be esteemed is better than silver or gold.

2 Rich and poor have this in common:
The LORD is the Maker of them all.

3 The prudent see danger and take refuge,
but the simple keep going and pay the penalty.

[a] *6* Some Hebrew manuscripts, Septuagint and Vulgate; most Hebrew manuscripts *vapor for those who seek death* [b] *12* Or *The righteous person* [c] *21* Or *righteousness*

4 Humility is the fear of the LORD;
its wages are riches and honor and life.

5 In the paths of the wicked are snares and pitfalls,
but those who would preserve their life stay far from them.

6 Start children off on the way they should go,
and even when they are old they will not turn from it.

7 The rich rule over the poor,
and the borrower is slave to the lender.

8 Whoever sows injustice reaps calamity,
and the rod they wield in fury will be broken.

9 The generous will themselves be blessed,
for they share their food with the poor.

10 Drive out the mocker, and out goes strife;
quarrels and insults are ended.

11 One who loves a pure heart and who speaks with grace
will have the king for a friend.

12 The eyes of the LORD keep watch over knowledge,
but he frustrates the words of the unfaithful.

13 The sluggard says, "There's a lion outside!
I'll be killed in the public square!"

14 The mouth of an adulterous woman is a deep pit;
a man who is under the LORD's wrath falls into it.

15 Folly is bound up in the heart of a child,
but the rod of discipline will drive it far away.

16 One who oppresses the poor to increase his wealth
and one who gives gifts to the rich—
both come to poverty.

17 Pay attention and turn your ear to the sayings of the wise;
apply your heart to what I teach,
18 for it is pleasing when you keep them in your heart
and have all of them ready on your lips.
19 So that your trust may be in the LORD,
I teach you today, even you.
20 Have I not written thirty sayings for you,
sayings of counsel and knowledge,
21 teaching you to be honest and to speak the truth,
so that you bring back truthful reports
to those you serve?

22 Do not exploit the poor because they are poor
and do not crush the needy in court,
23 for the LORD will take up their case
and will exact life for life.

24 Do not make friends with a hot-tempered person,
do not associate with one easily angered,
25 or you may learn their ways
and get yourself ensnared.

26 Do not be one who shakes hands in pledge
or puts up security for debts;
27 if you lack the means to pay,
your very bed will be snatched from under you.

28 Do not move an ancient boundary stone
set up by your ancestors.

29 Do you see someone skilled in their work?
They will serve before kings;
they will not serve before officials of low rank.

23 When you sit to dine with a ruler,
note well what[a] is before you,
2 and put a knife to your throat
if you are given to gluttony.
3 Do not crave his delicacies,
for that food is deceptive.

4 Do not wear yourself out to get rich;
do not trust your own cleverness.
5 Cast but a glance at riches, and they are gone,

[a] *1* Or *who*

for they will surely sprout wings
and fly off to the sky like an eagle.

6 Do not eat the food of a begrudging host,
do not crave his delicacies;
7 for he is the kind of person
who is always thinking about the cost.[a]
"Eat and drink," he says to you,
but his heart is not with you.
8 You will vomit up the little you have eaten
and will have wasted your compliments.

9 Do not speak to fools,
for they will scorn your prudent words.

10 Do not move an ancient boundary stone
or encroach on the fields of the fatherless,
11 for their Defender is strong;
he will take up their case against you.

12 Apply your heart to instruction
and your ears to words of knowledge.

13 Do not withhold discipline from a child;
if you punish them with the rod, they will not die.
14 Punish them with the rod
and save them from death.

15 My son, if your heart is wise,
then my heart will be glad indeed;
16 my inmost being will rejoice
when your lips speak what is right.

17 Do not let your heart envy sinners,
but always be zealous for the fear of the LORD.
18 There is surely a future hope for you,
and your hope will not be cut off.

19 Listen, my son, and be wise,
and set your heart on the right path:
20 Do not join those who drink too much wine
or gorge themselves on meat,
21 for drunkards and gluttons become poor,
and drowsiness clothes them in rags.

22 Listen to your father, who gave you life,
and do not despise your mother when she is old.
23 Buy the truth and do not sell it —
wisdom, instruction and insight as well.
24 The father of a righteous child has great joy;
a man who fathers a wise son rejoices in him.
25 May your father and mother rejoice;
may she who gave you birth be joyful!

26 My son, give me your heart
and let your eyes delight in my ways,
27 for an adulterous woman is a deep pit,
and a wayward wife is a narrow well.
28 Like a bandit she lies in wait
and multiplies the unfaithful among men.

29 Who has woe? Who has sorrow?
Who has strife? Who has complaints?
Who has needless bruises? Who has bloodshot eyes?
30 Those who linger over wine,
who go to sample bowls of mixed wine.
31 Do not gaze at wine when it is red,
when it sparkles in the cup,
when it goes down smoothly!
32 In the end it bites like a snake
and poisons like a viper.
33 Your eyes will see strange sights,
and your mind will imagine confusing things.
34 You will be like one sleeping on the high seas,
lying on top of the rigging.
35 "They hit me," you will say, "but I'm not hurt!
They beat me, but I don't feel it!
When will I wake up
so I can find another drink?"

24 Do not envy the wicked,
do not desire their company;
2 for their hearts plot violence,
and their lips talk about making trouble.

3 By wisdom a house is built,
and through understanding it is established;

[a] 7 Or *for as he thinks within himself, / so he is*; or *for as he puts on a feast, / so he is*

4 through knowledge its rooms are filled
with rare and beautiful treasures.
5 The wise prevail through great power,
and those who have knowledge muster their strength.
6 Surely you need guidance to wage war,
and victory is won through many advisers.

7 Wisdom is too high for fools;
in the assembly at the gate they must not open their mouths.

8 Whoever plots evil
will be known as a schemer.
9 The schemes of folly are sin,
and people detest a mocker.

10 If you falter in a time of trouble,
how small is your strength!
11 Rescue those being led away to death;
hold back those staggering toward slaughter.
12 If you say, "But we knew nothing about this,"
does not he who weighs the heart perceive it?
Does not he who guards your life know it?
Will he not repay everyone according to what they have done?

13 Eat honey, my son, for it is good;
honey from the comb is sweet to your taste.
14 Know also that wisdom is like honey for you:
If you find it, there is a future hope for you,
and your hope will not be cut off.

15 Do not lurk like a thief near the house of the righteous,
do not plunder their dwelling place;
16 for though the righteous fall seven times, they rise again,
but the wicked stumble when calamity strikes.

17 Do not gloat when your enemy falls;
when they stumble, do not let your heart rejoice,
18 or the LORD will see and disapprove
and turn his wrath away from them.

19 Do not fret because of evildoers
or be envious of the wicked,
20 for the evildoer has no future hope,
and the lamp of the wicked will be snuffed out.

21 Fear the LORD and the king, my son,
and do not join with rebellious officials,
22 for those two will send sudden destruction on them,
and who knows what calamities they can bring?

23 These also are sayings of the wise:

To show partiality in judging is not good:
24 Whoever says to the guilty, "You are innocent,"
will be cursed by peoples and denounced by nations.
25 But it will go well with those who convict the guilty,
and rich blessing will come on them.

26 An honest answer
is like a kiss on the lips.

27 Put your outdoor work in order
and get your fields ready;
after that, build your house.

28 Do not testify against your neighbor without cause—
would you use your lips to mislead?
29 Do not say, "I'll do to them as they have done to me;
I'll pay them back for what they did."

30 I went past the field of a sluggard,
past the vineyard of someone who has no sense;
31 thorns had come up everywhere,
the ground was covered with weeds,
and the stone wall was in ruins.
32 I applied my heart to what I observed
and learned a lesson from what I saw:
33 A little sleep, a little slumber,
a little folding of the hands to rest—
34 and poverty will come on you like a thief
and scarcity like an armed man.

25 These are more proverbs of Solomon, compiled by the men of Hezekiah king of Judah:

2 It is the glory of God to conceal a matter;
to search out a matter is the glory of kings.

3 As the heavens are high and the earth
is deep,
so the hearts of kings are
unsearchable.
4 Remove the dross from the silver,
and a silversmith can produce a
vessel;
5 remove wicked officials from the
king's presence,
and his throne will be established
through righteousness.
6 Do not exalt yourself in the king's
presence,
and do not claim a place among his
great men;
7 it is better for him to say to you, "Come
up here,"
than for him to humiliate you before
his nobles.
What you have seen with your eyes
8 do not bring[a] hastily to court,
for what will you do in the end
if your neighbor puts you to shame?
9 If you take your neighbor to court,
do not betray another's confidence,
10 or the one who hears it may shame you
and the charge against you will
stand.
11 Like apples[b] of gold in settings of
silver
is a ruling rightly given.
12 Like an earring of gold or an ornament
of fine gold
is the rebuke of a wise judge to a
listening ear.
13 Like a snow-cooled drink at harvest
time
is a trustworthy messenger to the
one who sends him;
he refreshes the spirit of his master.
14 Like clouds and wind without rain
is one who boasts of gifts never
given.
15 Through patience a ruler can be
persuaded,
and a gentle tongue can break a
bone.
16 If you find honey, eat just enough —
too much of it, and you will vomit.
17 Seldom set foot in your neighbor's
house —
too much of you, and they will hate
you.
18 Like a club or a sword or a sharp arrow
is one who gives false testimony
against a neighbor.
19 Like a broken tooth or a lame foot
is reliance on the unfaithful in a
time of trouble.
20 Like one who takes away a garment on
a cold day,
or like vinegar poured on a wound,
is one who sings songs to a heavy
heart.
21 If your enemy is hungry, give him food
to eat;
if he is thirsty, give him water to
drink.
22 In doing this, you will heap burning
coals on his head,
and the LORD will reward you.
23 Like a north wind that brings
unexpected rain
is a sly tongue — which provokes a
horrified look.
24 Better to live on a corner of the roof
than share a house with a
quarrelsome wife.
25 Like cold water to a weary soul
is good news from a distant land.
26 Like a muddied spring or a polluted
well
are the righteous who give way to
the wicked.
27 It is not good to eat too much honey,
nor is it honorable to search out
matters that are too deep.
28 Like a city whose walls are broken
through
is a person who lacks self-control.

26 Like snow in summer or rain in
harvest,
honor is not fitting for a fool.
2 Like a fluttering sparrow or a darting
swallow,
an undeserved curse does not come
to rest.
3 A whip for the horse, a bridle for the
donkey,
and a rod for the backs of fools!
4 Do not answer a fool according to his
folly,
or you yourself will be just like him.

a 7,8 Or *nobles / on whom you had set your eyes. / 8Do not go*   b 11 Or possibly *apricots*

5 Answer a fool according to his folly,
or he will be wise in his own eyes.
6 Sending a message by the hands of a fool
is like cutting off one's feet or drinking poison.
7 Like the useless legs of one who is lame
is a proverb in the mouth of a fool.
8 Like tying a stone in a sling
is the giving of honor to a fool.
9 Like a thornbush in a drunkard's hand
is a proverb in the mouth of a fool.
10 Like an archer who wounds at random
is one who hires a fool or any passer-by.
11 As a dog returns to its vomit,
so fools repeat their folly.
12 Do you see a person wise in their own eyes?
There is more hope for a fool than for them.

13 A sluggard says, "There's a lion in the road,
a fierce lion roaming the streets!"
14 As a door turns on its hinges,
so a sluggard turns on his bed.
15 A sluggard buries his hand in the dish;
he is too lazy to bring it back to his mouth.
16 A sluggard is wiser in his own eyes
than seven people who answer discreetly.

17 Like one who grabs a stray dog by the ears
is someone who rushes into a quarrel not their own.
18 Like a maniac shooting
flaming arrows of death
19 is one who deceives their neighbor
and says, "I was only joking!"

20 Without wood a fire goes out;
without a gossip a quarrel dies down.
21 As charcoal to embers and as wood to fire,
so is a quarrelsome person for kindling strife.
22 The words of a gossip are like choice morsels;
they go down to the inmost parts.

23 Like a coating of silver dross on earthenware
are fervent[a] lips with an evil heart.
24 Enemies disguise themselves with their lips,
but in their hearts they harbor deceit.
25 Though their speech is charming, do not believe them,
for seven abominations fill their hearts.
26 Their malice may be concealed by deception,
but their wickedness will be exposed in the assembly.
27 Whoever digs a pit will fall into it;
if someone rolls a stone, it will roll back on them.
28 A lying tongue hates those it hurts,
and a flattering mouth works ruin.

27 Do not boast about tomorrow,
for you do not know what a day may bring.

2 Let someone else praise you, and not your own mouth;
an outsider, and not your own lips.

3 Stone is heavy and sand a burden,
but a fool's provocation is heavier than both.

4 Anger is cruel and fury overwhelming,
but who can stand before jealousy?

5 Better is open rebuke
than hidden love.

6 Wounds from a friend can be trusted,
but an enemy multiplies kisses.

7 One who is full loathes honey from the comb,
but to the hungry even what is bitter tastes sweet.

8 Like a bird that flees its nest
is anyone who flees from home.

9 Perfume and incense bring joy to the heart,
and the pleasantness of a friend
springs from their heartfelt advice.

10 Do not forsake your friend or a friend of your family,
and do not go to your relative's house when disaster strikes you—
better a neighbor nearby than a relative far away.

[a] *23* Hebrew; Septuagint *smooth*

11 Be wise, my son, and bring joy to my
heart;
then I can answer anyone who treats
me with contempt.

12 The prudent see danger and take
refuge,
but the simple keep going and pay
the penalty.

13 Take the garment of one who puts up
security for a stranger;
hold it in pledge if it is done for an
outsider.

14 If anyone loudly blesses their neighbor
early in the morning,
it will be taken as a curse.

15 A quarrelsome wife is like the
dripping
of a leaky roof in a rainstorm;
16 restraining her is like restraining the
wind
or grasping oil with the hand.

17 As iron sharpens iron,
so one person sharpens another.

18 The one who guards a fig tree will eat
its fruit,
and whoever protects their master
will be honored.

19 As water reflects the face,
so one's life reflects the heart.[a]

20 Death and Destruction[b] are never
satisfied,
and neither are human eyes.

21 The crucible for silver and the furnace
for gold,
but people are tested by their praise.

22 Though you grind a fool in a mortar,
grinding them like grain with a
pestle,
you will not remove their folly from
them.

23 Be sure you know the condition of
your flocks,
give careful attention to your herds;
24 for riches do not endure forever,
and a crown is not secure for all
generations.
25 When the hay is removed and new
growth appears
and the grass from the hills is
gathered in,
26 the lambs will provide you with
clothing,
and the goats with the price of a
field.
27 You will have plenty of goats' milk to
feed your family
and to nourish your female
servants.

28

1 The wicked flee though no one
pursues,
but the righteous are as bold as a
lion.

2 When a country is rebellious, it has
many rulers,
but a ruler with discernment and
knowledge maintains order.

3 A ruler[c] who oppresses the poor
is like a driving rain that leaves no
crops.

4 Those who forsake instruction praise
the wicked,
but those who heed it resist them.

5 Evildoers do not understand what is
right,
but those who seek the LORD
understand it fully.

6 Better the poor whose walk is
blameless
than the rich whose ways are
perverse.

7 A discerning son heeds instruction,
but a companion of gluttons
disgraces his father.

8 Whoever increases wealth by taking
interest or profit from the
poor
amasses it for another, who will be
kind to the poor.

9 If anyone turns a deaf ear to my
instruction,
even their prayers are detestable.

10 Whoever leads the upright along an
evil path
will fall into their own trap,
but the blameless will receive a
good inheritance.

11 The rich are wise in their own eyes;
one who is poor and discerning sees
how deluded they are.

[a] *19* Or *so others reflect your heart back to you* [b] *20* Hebrew *Abaddon* [c] *3* Or *A poor person*

12 When the righteous triumph, there is great elation;
but when the wicked rise to power, people go into hiding.

13 Whoever conceals their sins does not prosper,
but the one who confesses and renounces them finds mercy.

14 Blessed is the one who always trembles before God,
but whoever hardens their heart falls into trouble.

15 Like a roaring lion or a charging bear
is a wicked ruler over a helpless people.

16 A tyrannical ruler practices extortion,
but one who hates ill-gotten gain will enjoy a long reign.

17 Anyone tormented by the guilt of murder
will seek refuge in the grave;
let no one hold them back.

18 The one whose walk is blameless is kept safe,
but the one whose ways are perverse will fall into the pit.[a]

19 Those who work their land will have abundant food,
but those who chase fantasies will have their fill of poverty.

20 A faithful person will be richly blessed,
but one eager to get rich will not go unpunished.

21 To show partiality is not good—
yet a person will do wrong for a piece of bread.

22 The stingy are eager to get rich
and are unaware that poverty awaits them.

23 Whoever rebukes a person will in the end gain favor
rather than one who has a flattering tongue.

24 Whoever robs their father or mother
and says, "It's not wrong,"
is partner to one who destroys.

25 The greedy stir up conflict,
but those who trust in the LORD will prosper.

26 Those who trust in themselves are fools,
but those who walk in wisdom are kept safe.

27 Those who give to the poor will lack nothing,
but those who close their eyes to them receive many curses.

28 When the wicked rise to power, people go into hiding;
but when the wicked perish, the righteous thrive.

29 Whoever remains stiff-necked after many rebukes
will suddenly be destroyed—without remedy.

2 When the righteous thrive, the people rejoice;
when the wicked rule, the people groan.

3 A man who loves wisdom brings joy to his father,
but a companion of prostitutes squanders his wealth.

4 By justice a king gives a country stability,
but those who are greedy for[b] bribes tear it down.

5 Those who flatter their neighbors
are spreading nets for their feet.

6 Evildoers are snared by their own sin,
but the righteous shout for joy and are glad.

7 The righteous care about justice for the poor,
but the wicked have no such concern.

8 Mockers stir up a city,
but the wise turn away anger.

9 If a wise person goes to court with a fool,
the fool rages and scoffs, and there is no peace.

10 The bloodthirsty hate a person of integrity
and seek to kill the upright.

[a] *18* Syriac (see Septuagint); Hebrew *into one* [b] *4* Or *who give*

11 Fools give full vent to their rage,
but the wise bring calm in the end.

12 If a ruler listens to lies,
all his officials become wicked.

13 The poor and the oppressor have this in common:
The LORD gives sight to the eyes of both.

14 If a king judges the poor with fairness,
his throne will be established forever.

15 A rod and a reprimand impart wisdom,
but a child left undisciplined disgraces its mother.

16 When the wicked thrive, so does sin,
but the righteous will see their downfall.

17 Discipline your children, and they will give you peace;
they will bring you the delights you desire.

18 Where there is no revelation, people cast off restraint;
but blessed is the one who heeds wisdom's instruction.

19 Servants cannot be corrected by mere words;
though they understand, they will not respond.

20 Do you see someone who speaks in haste?
There is more hope for a fool than for them.

21 A servant pampered from youth
will turn out to be insolent.

22 An angry person stirs up conflict,
and a hot-tempered person commits many sins.

23 Pride brings a person low,
but the lowly in spirit gain honor.

24 The accomplices of thieves are their own enemies;
they are put under oath and dare not testify.

25 Fear of man will prove to be a snare,
but whoever trusts in the LORD is kept safe.

26 Many seek an audience with a ruler,
but it is from the LORD that one gets justice.

27 The righteous detest the dishonest;
the wicked detest the upright.

30 The sayings of Agur son of Jakeh — an inspired utterance.

This man's utterance to Ithiel:

"I am weary, God,
but I can prevail.[a]
2 Surely I am only a brute, not a man;
I do not have human understanding.
3 I have not learned wisdom,
nor have I attained to the knowledge of the Holy One.
4 Who has gone up to heaven and come down?
Whose hands have gathered up the wind?
Who has wrapped up the waters in a cloak?
Who has established all the ends of the earth?
What is his name, and what is the name of his son?
Surely you know!

5 "Every word of God is flawless;
he is a shield to those who take refuge in him.
6 Do not add to his words,
or he will rebuke you and prove you a liar.

7 "Two things I ask of you, LORD;
do not refuse me before I die:
8 Keep falsehood and lies far from me;
give me neither poverty nor riches,
but give me only my daily bread.
9 Otherwise, I may have too much and disown you
and say, 'Who is the LORD?'
Or I may become poor and steal,
and so dishonor the name of my God.

10 "Do not slander a servant to their master,
or they will curse you, and you will pay for it.

11 "There are those who curse their fathers
and do not bless their mothers;

[a] *1* With a different word division of the Hebrew; Masoretic Text *utterance to Ithiel, / to Ithiel and Ukal:*

12 those who are pure in their own eyes
and yet are not cleansed of their
filth;
13 those whose eyes are ever so haughty,
whose glances are so disdainful;
14 those whose teeth are swords
and whose jaws are set with knives
to devour the poor from the earth
and the needy from among
mankind.

15 "The leech has two daughters.
'Give! Give!' they cry.

"There are three things that are never
satisfied,
four that never say, 'Enough!':
16 the grave, the barren womb,
land, which is never satisfied with
water,
and fire, which never says, 'Enough!'

17 "The eye that mocks a father,
that scorns an aged mother,
will be pecked out by the ravens of the
valley,
will be eaten by the vultures.

18 "There are three things that are too
amazing for me,
four that I do not understand:
19 the way of an eagle in the sky,
the way of a snake on a rock,
the way of a ship on the high seas,
and the way of a man with a young
woman.

20 "This is the way of an adulterous
woman:
She eats and wipes her mouth
and says, 'I've done nothing wrong.'

21 "Under three things the earth
trembles,
under four it cannot bear up:
22 a servant who becomes king,
a godless fool who gets plenty to eat,
23 a contemptible woman who gets
married,
and a servant who displaces her
mistress.

24 "Four things on earth are small,
yet they are extremely wise:
25 Ants are creatures of little strength,
yet they store up their food in the
summer;
26 hyraxes are creatures of little power,
yet they make their home in the
crags;
27 locusts have no king,
yet they advance together in ranks;
28 a lizard can be caught with the hand,
yet it is found in kings' palaces.

29 "There are three things that are stately
in their stride,
four that move with stately bearing:
30 a lion, mighty among beasts,
who retreats before nothing;
31 a strutting rooster, a he-goat,
and a king secure against revolt.[a]

32 "If you play the fool and exalt yourself,
or if you plan evil,
clap your hand over your mouth!
33 For as churning cream produces
butter,
and as twisting the nose produces
blood,
so stirring up anger produces strife."

31 The sayings of King Lemuel—an inspired utterance his mother taught
him.

2 Listen, my son! Listen, son of my
womb!
Listen, my son, the answer to my
prayers!
3 Do not spend your strength[b] on
women,
your vigor on those who ruin kings.

4 It is not for kings, Lemuel—
it is not for kings to drink wine,
not for rulers to crave beer,
5 lest they drink and forget what has
been decreed,
and deprive all the oppressed of
their rights.
6 Let beer be for those who are
perishing,
wine for those who are in anguish!
7 Let them drink and forget their
poverty
and remember their misery no
more.

8 Speak up for those who cannot speak
for themselves,
for the rights of all who are
destitute.
9 Speak up and judge fairly;
defend the rights of the poor and
needy.

[a] *31* The meaning of the Hebrew for this phrase is uncertain. [b] *3* Or *wealth*

10 [a]A wife of noble character who can find?
She is worth far more than rubies.
11 Her husband has full confidence in her
and lacks nothing of value.
12 She brings him good, not harm,
all the days of her life.
13 She selects wool and flax
and works with eager hands.
14 She is like the merchant ships,
bringing her food from afar.
15 She gets up while it is still night;
she provides food for her family
and portions for her female servants.
16 She considers a field and buys it;
out of her earnings she plants a vineyard.
17 She sets about her work vigorously;
her arms are strong for her tasks.
18 She sees that her trading is profitable,
and her lamp does not go out at night.
19 In her hand she holds the distaff
and grasps the spindle with her fingers.
20 She opens her arms to the poor
and extends her hands to the needy.
21 When it snows, she has no fear for her household;
for all of them are clothed in scarlet.
22 She makes coverings for her bed;
she is clothed in fine linen and purple.
23 Her husband is respected at the city gate,
where he takes his seat among the elders of the land.
24 She makes linen garments and sells them,
and supplies the merchants with sashes.
25 She is clothed with strength and dignity;
she can laugh at the days to come.
26 She speaks with wisdom,
and faithful instruction is on her tongue.
27 She watches over the affairs of her household
and does not eat the bread of idleness.
28 Her children arise and call her blessed;
her husband also, and he praises her:
29 "Many women do noble things,
but you surpass them all."
30 Charm is deceptive, and beauty is fleeting;
but a woman who fears the LORD is to be praised.
31 Honor her for all that her hands have done,
and let her works bring her praise at the city gate.

[a] *10* Verses 10-31 are an acrostic poem, the verses of which begin with the successive letters of the Hebrew alphabet.

ECCLESIASTES

Ecclesiastes is the collected words of a "teacher" or "preacher." The Teacher is described as having been king over Israel in Jerusalem, and as the son of David. Both of these mean that he was in the royal line of Judah. He is not further identified, and while tradition identifies him with Solomon, it is appropriate to leave this cloak of anonymity in place.

The repeated phrase *Meaningless! Meaningless! Everything is meaningless!* warns us that life's rewards are uncertain and ultimately unsatisfying. The Teacher pursues this insight in a long discourse that shifts between prose and poetry, and between autobiography and straightforward teaching. The book makes observations and poses questions, returning to themes like the wind— *round and round it goes, ever returning on its course.*

When the Teacher says *What is crooked cannot be straightened,* he reminds us that something wrong has intruded into our world. This fits the larger Jewish story told in the rest of the Scriptures. Setting things right again is what this bigger drama is about. The Teacher, however, does not tell us about God's attempts at straightening the world. He is content to say that God is sovereign over all things and it is our duty to follow his ways for living, since *God will bring every deed into judgment.*

---

1 The words of the Teacher,[a] son of David, king in Jerusalem:

2 "Meaningless! Meaningless!"
says the Teacher.
"Utterly meaningless!
Everything is meaningless."

3 What do people gain from all their labors
at which they toil under the sun?
4 Generations come and generations go,
but the earth remains forever.
5 The sun rises and the sun sets,
and hurries back to where it rises.
6 The wind blows to the south
and turns to the north;
round and round it goes,
ever returning on its course.
7 All streams flow into the sea,
yet the sea is never full.
To the place the streams come from,
there they return again.
8 All things are wearisome,
more than one can say.
The eye never has enough of seeing,
nor the ear its fill of hearing.
9 What has been will be again,
what has been done will be done again;
there is nothing new under the sun.
10 Is there anything of which one can say,
"Look! This is something new"?
It was here already, long ago;
it was here before our time.
11 No one remembers the former generations,
and even those yet to come
will not be remembered
by those who follow them.

12 I, the Teacher, was king over Israel in
Jerusalem. 13 I applied my mind to study
and to explore by wisdom all that is done
under the heavens. What a heavy burden
God has laid on mankind! 14 I have seen
all the things that are done under the
sun; all of them are meaningless, a chasing after the wind.

15 What is crooked cannot be straightened;
what is lacking cannot be counted.

16 I said to myself, "Look, I have increased in wisdom more than anyone
who has ruled over Jerusalem before me;
I have experienced much of wisdom and
knowledge." 17 Then I applied myself to
the understanding of wisdom, and also
of madness and folly, but I learned that
this, too, is a chasing after the wind.

18 For with much wisdom comes much sorrow;
the more knowledge, the more grief.

2 I said to myself, "Come now, I will test
you with pleasure to find out what is
good." But that also proved to be meaningless. 2 "Laughter," I said, "is madness.

a 1 Or *the leader of the assembly*; also in verses 2 and 12

And what does pleasure accomplish?" 3I
tried cheering myself with wine, and embracing folly — my mind still guiding me
with wisdom. I wanted to see what was
good for people to do under the heavens
during the few days of their lives.
4I undertook great projects: I built
houses for myself and planted vineyards.
5I made gardens and parks and planted
all kinds of fruit trees in them. 6I made
reservoirs to water groves of flourishing
trees. 7I bought male and female slaves
and had other slaves who were born in
my house. I also owned more herds and
flocks than anyone in Jerusalem before
me. 8I amassed silver and gold for myself,
and the treasure of kings and provinces.
I acquired male and female singers, and
a harem[a] as well — the delights of a man's
heart. 9I became greater by far than anyone in Jerusalem before me. In all this my
wisdom stayed with me.

10 I denied myself nothing my eyes
desired;
I refused my heart no pleasure.
My heart took delight in all my labor,
and this was the reward for all my
toil.
11 Yet when I surveyed all that my hands
had done
and what I had toiled to achieve,
everything was meaningless, a
chasing after the wind;
nothing was gained under the sun.

12 Then I turned my thoughts to consider
wisdom,
and also madness and folly.
What more can the king's successor do
than what has already been done?
13 I saw that wisdom is better than folly,
just as light is better than darkness.
14 The wise have eyes in their heads,
while the fool walks in the
darkness;
but I came to realize
that the same fate overtakes them
both.

15 Then I said to myself,
"The fate of the fool will overtake me
also.
What then do I gain by being wise?"
I said to myself,
"This too is meaningless."
16 For the wise, like the fool, will not be
long remembered;
the days have already come when
both have been forgotten.
Like the fool, the wise too must die!

17 So I hated life, because the work that
is done under the sun was grievous to
me. All of it is meaningless, a chasing after the wind. 18 I hated all the things I had
toiled for under the sun, because I must
leave them to the one who comes after
me. 19 And who knows whether that person will be wise or foolish? Yet they will
have control over all the fruit of my toil
into which I have poured my effort and
skill under the sun. This too is meaningless. 20 So my heart began to despair
over all my toilsome labor under the sun.
21 For a person may labor with wisdom,
knowledge and skill, and then they must
leave all they own to another who has not
toiled for it. This too is meaningless and
a great misfortune. 22 What do people get
for all the toil and anxious striving with
which they labor under the sun? 23 All
their days their work is grief and pain;
even at night their minds do not rest. This
too is meaningless.
24 A person can do nothing better than
to eat and drink and find satisfaction
in their own toil. This too, I see, is from
the hand of God, 25 for without him, who
can eat or find enjoyment? 26 To the person who pleases him, God gives wisdom,
knowledge and happiness, but to the
sinner he gives the task of gathering and
storing up wealth to hand it over to the
one who pleases God. This too is meaningless, a chasing after the wind.

3 There is a time for everything,
and a season for every activity under
the heavens:

2 a time to be born and a time to die,
a time to plant and a time to uproot,
3 a time to kill and a time to heal,
a time to tear down and a time to
build,
4 a time to weep and a time to laugh,
a time to mourn and a time to
dance,
5 a time to scatter stones and a time to
gather them,
a time to embrace and a time to
refrain from embracing,

[a] *8* The meaning of the Hebrew for this phrase is uncertain.

6 a time to search and a time to give
up,
a time to keep and a time to throw
away,
7 a time to tear and a time to mend,
a time to be silent and a time to
speak,
8 a time to love and a time to hate,
a time for war and a time for peace.

9 What do workers gain from their toil?
10 I have seen the burden God has laid on
the human race. 11 He has made everything beautiful in its time. He has also
set eternity in the human heart; yet[a] no
one can fathom what God has done from
beginning to end. 12 I know that there is
nothing better for people than to be happy and to do good while they live. 13 That
each of them may eat and drink, and find
satisfaction in all their toil—this is the
gift of God. 14 I know that everything God
does will endure forever; nothing can be
added to it and nothing taken from it.
God does it so that people will fear him.

15 Whatever is has already been,
and what will be has been before;
and God will call the past to
account.[b]

16 And I saw something else under the
sun:

In the place of judgment—wickedness
was there,
in the place of justice—wickedness
was there.

17 I said to myself,

"God will bring into judgment
both the righteous and the wicked,
for there will be a time for every
activity,
a time to judge every deed."

18 I also said to myself, "As for humans,
God tests them so that they may see that
they are like the animals. 19 Surely the
fate of human beings is like that of the
animals; the same fate awaits them both:
As one dies, so dies the other. All have the
same breath[c]; humans have no advantage
over animals. Everything is meaningless.
20 All go to the same place; all come from
dust, and to dust all return. 21 Who knows
if the human spirit rises upward and if
the spirit of the animal goes down into
the earth?"

22 So I saw that there is nothing better
for a person than to enjoy their work,
because that is their lot. For who can
bring them to see what will happen after them?

4 Again I looked and saw all the oppression that was taking place under the
sun:

I saw the tears of the oppressed—
and they have no comforter;
power was on the side of their
oppressors—
and they have no comforter.
2 And I declared that the dead,
who had already died,
are happier than the living,
who are still alive.
3 But better than both
is the one who has never been born,
who has not seen the evil
that is done under the sun.

4 And I saw that all toil and all achieve-
ment spring from one person's envy of
another. This too is meaningless, a chasing after the wind.

5 Fools fold their hands
and ruin themselves.
6 Better one handful with tranquillity
than two handfuls with toil
and chasing after the wind.

7 Again I saw something meaningless
under the sun:

8 There was a man all alone;
he had neither son nor brother.
There was no end to his toil,
yet his eyes were not content with
his wealth.
"For whom am I toiling," he asked,
"and why am I depriving myself of
enjoyment?"
This too is meaningless—
a miserable business!

9 Two are better than one,
because they have a good return for
their labor:
10 If either of them falls down,
one can help the other up.
But pity anyone who falls
and has no one to help them up.

[a] 11 Or *also placed ignorance in the human heart, so that* [b] 15 Or *God calls back the past* [c] 19 Or *spirit*

11 Also, if two lie down together, they
will keep warm.
But how can one keep warm alone?
12 Though one may be overpowered,
two can defend themselves.
A cord of three strands is not quickly
broken.

13 Better a poor but wise youth than an
old but foolish king who no longer knows
how to heed a warning. 14 The youth may
have come from prison to the kingship, or
he may have been born in poverty within his kingdom. 15 I saw that all who lived
and walked under the sun followed the
youth, the king's successor. 16 There was
no end to all the people who were before
them. But those who came later were not
pleased with the successor. This too is
meaningless, a chasing after the wind.

5[a] Guard your steps when you go to the
house of God. Go near to listen rather
than to offer the sacrifice of fools, who do
not know that they do wrong.

2 Do not be quick with your mouth,
do not be hasty in your heart
to utter anything before God.
God is in heaven
and you are on earth,
so let your words be few.
3 A dream comes when there are many
cares,
and many words mark the speech of
a fool.

4 When you make a vow to God, do not
delay to fulfill it. He has no pleasure in
fools; fulfill your vow. 5 It is better not to
make a vow than to make one and not
fulfill it. 6 Do not let your mouth lead you
into sin. And do not protest to the temple
messenger, "My vow was a mistake." Why
should God be angry at what you say and
destroy the work of your hands? 7 Much
dreaming and many words are meaningless. Therefore fear God.

8 If you see the poor oppressed in a district, and justice and rights denied, do
not be surprised at such things; for one
official is eyed by a higher one, and over
them both are others higher still. 9 The
increase from the land is taken by all; the
king himself profits from the fields.

10 Whoever loves money never has
enough;
whoever loves wealth is never
satisfied with their income.
This too is meaningless.

11 As goods increase,
so do those who consume them.
And what benefit are they to the
owners
except to feast their eyes on them?
12 The sleep of a laborer is sweet,
whether they eat little or much,
but as for the rich, their abundance
permits them no sleep.

13 I have seen a grievous evil under the
sun:

wealth hoarded to the harm of its
owners,
14 or wealth lost through some
misfortune,
so that when they have children
there is nothing left for them to
inherit.
15 Everyone comes naked from their
mother's womb,
and as everyone comes, so they
depart.
They take nothing from their toil
that they can carry in their hands.

16 This too is a grievous evil:
As everyone comes, so they depart,
and what do they gain,
since they toil for the wind?
17 All their days they eat in darkness,
with great frustration, affliction and
anger.

18 This is what I have observed to be
good: that it is appropriate for a person
to eat, to drink and to find satisfaction in
their toilsome labor under the sun during
the few days of life God has given them —
for this is their lot. 19 Moreover, when God
gives someone wealth and possessions,
and the ability to enjoy them, to accept
their lot and be happy in their toil — this
is a gift of God. 20 They seldom reflect on
the days of their life, because God keeps
them occupied with gladness of heart.

6 I have seen another evil under the
sun, and it weighs heavily on mankind: 2 God gives some people wealth,
possessions and honor, so that they lack
nothing their hearts desire, but God does
not grant them the ability to enjoy them,

[a] In Hebrew texts 5:1 is numbered 4:17, and 5:2-20 is numbered 5:1-19.

and strangers enjoy them instead. This is
meaningless, a grievous evil.
3 A man may have a hundred children
and live many years; yet no matter how
long he lives, if he cannot enjoy his prosperity and does not receive proper burial, I say that a stillborn child is better
off than he. 4 It comes without meaning,
it departs in darkness, and in darkness
its name is shrouded. 5 Though it never saw the sun or knew anything, it has
more rest than does that man— 6 even if
he lives a thousand years twice over but
fails to enjoy his prosperity. Do not all go
to the same place?

7 Everyone's toil is for their mouth,
yet their appetite is never
satisfied.
8 What advantage have the wise over
fools?
What do the poor gain
by knowing how to conduct
themselves before others?
9 Better what the eye sees
than the roving of the appetite.
This too is meaningless,
a chasing after the wind.

10 Whatever exists has already been
named,
and what humanity is has been
known;
no one can contend
with someone who is stronger.
11 The more the words,
the less the meaning,
and how does that profit anyone?

12 For who knows what is good for a person in life, during the few and meaningless days they pass through like a shadow? Who can tell them what will happen
under the sun after they are gone?

7 A good name is better than fine
perfume,
and the day of death better than the
day of birth.
2 It is better to go to a house of
mourning
than to go to a house of feasting,
for death is the destiny of everyone;
the living should take this to heart.
3 Frustration is better than laughter,
because a sad face is good for the
heart.
4 The heart of the wise is in the house of
mourning,
but the heart of fools is in the house
of pleasure.
5 It is better to heed the rebuke of a wise
person
than to listen to the song of fools.
6 Like the crackling of thorns under the
pot,
so is the laughter of fools.
This too is meaningless.

7 Extortion turns a wise person into a
fool,
and a bribe corrupts the heart.

8 The end of a matter is better than its
beginning,
and patience is better than pride.
9 Do not be quickly provoked in your
spirit,
for anger resides in the lap of fools.

10 Do not say, "Why were the old days
better than these?"
For it is not wise to ask such
questions.

11 Wisdom, like an inheritance, is a good
thing
and benefits those who see the sun.
12 Wisdom is a shelter
as money is a shelter,
but the advantage of knowledge is
this:
Wisdom preserves those who
have it.

13 Consider what God has done:

Who can straighten
what he has made crooked?
14 When times are good, be happy;
but when times are bad, consider
this:
God has made the one
as well as the other.
Therefore, no one can discover
anything about their future.

15 In this meaningless life of mine I
have seen both of these:

the righteous perishing in their
righteousness,
and the wicked living long in their
wickedness.
16 Do not be overrighteous,
neither be overwise—
why destroy yourself?
17 Do not be overwicked,
and do not be a fool—
why die before your time?

18 It is good to grasp the one
and not let go of the other.
Whoever fears God will avoid all
extremes.[a]
19 Wisdom makes one wise person more
powerful
than ten rulers in a city.
20 Indeed, there is no one on earth who is
righteous,
no one who does what is right and
never sins.
21 Do not pay attention to every word
people say,
or you may hear your servant
cursing you —
22 for you know in your heart
that many times you yourself have
cursed others.

23 All this I tested by wisdom and I said,

"I am determined to be wise" —
but this was beyond me.
24 Whatever exists is far off and most
profound —
who can discover it?
25 So I turned my mind to understand,
to investigate and to search out
wisdom and the scheme of
things
and to understand the stupidity of
wickedness
and the madness of folly.
26 I find more bitter than death
the woman who is a snare,
whose heart is a trap
and whose hands are chains.
The man who pleases God will escape
her,
but the sinner she will ensnare.

27 "Look," says the Teacher,[b] "this is
what I have discovered:

"Adding one thing to another to
discover the scheme of things —
28 while I was still searching
but not finding —
I found one upright man among a
thousand,
but not one upright woman among
them all.
29 This only have I found:
God created mankind upright,
but they have gone in search of
many schemes."

8

1 Who is like the wise?
Who knows the explanation of
things?
A person's wisdom brightens their
face
and changes its hard appearance.

2 Obey the king's command, I say, because you took an oath before God. 3 Do
not be in a hurry to leave the king's presence. Do not stand up for a bad cause, for
he will do whatever he pleases. 4 Since a
king's word is supreme, who can say to
him, "What are you doing?"

5 Whoever obeys his command will
come to no harm,
and the wise heart will know the
proper time and procedure.
6 For there is a proper time and
procedure for every matter,
though a person may be weighed
down by misery.
7 Since no one knows the future,
who can tell someone else what is to
come?
8 As no one has power over the wind to
contain it,
so[c] no one has power over the time
of their death.
As no one is discharged in time of war,
so wickedness will not release those
who practice it.

9 All this I saw, as I applied my mind to
everything done under the sun. There is
a time when a man lords it over others to
his own[d] hurt. 10 Then too, I saw the wicked buried — those who used to come and
go from the holy place and receive praise[e]
in the city where they did this. This too is
meaningless.

11 When the sentence for a crime is not
quickly carried out, people's hearts are
filled with schemes to do wrong. 12 Although a wicked person who commits a
hundred crimes may live a long time, I
know that it will go better with those who
fear God, who are reverent before him.
13 Yet because the wicked do not fear God,
it will not go well with them, and their
days will not lengthen like a shadow.

[a] *18* Or *will follow them both* [b] *27* Or *the leader of the assembly* [c] *8* Or *over the human spirit to retain it, / and so* [d] *9* Or *to their* [e] *10* Some Hebrew manuscripts and Septuagint (Aquila); most Hebrew manuscripts *and are forgotten*

14 There is something else meaningless that occurs on earth: the righteous
who get what the wicked deserve, and
the wicked who get what the righteous
deserve. This too, I say, is meaningless.
15 So I commend the enjoyment of life, because there is nothing better for a person
under the sun than to eat and drink and
be glad. Then joy will accompany them
in their toil all the days of the life God has
given them under the sun.

16 When I applied my mind to know
wisdom and to observe the labor that is
done on earth—people getting no sleep
day or night— 17 then I saw all that God
has done. No one can comprehend what
goes on under the sun. Despite all their
efforts to search it out, no one can discover its meaning. Even if the wise claim
they know, they cannot really comprehend it.

9 So I reflected on all this and concluded that the righteous and the wise and
what they do are in God's hands, but no
one knows whether love or hate awaits
them. 2 All share a common destiny—
the righteous and the wicked, the good
and the bad,[a] the clean and the unclean,
those who offer sacrifices and those who
do not.

As it is with the good,
so with the sinful;
as it is with those who take oaths,
so with those who are afraid to take
them.

3 This is the evil in everything that happens under the sun: The same destiny
overtakes all. The hearts of people, moreover, are full of evil and there is madness
in their hearts while they live, and afterward they join the dead. 4 Anyone who is
among the living has hope[b]—even a live
dog is better off than a dead lion!

5 For the living know that they will die,
but the dead know nothing;
they have no further reward,
and even their name is forgotten.
6 Their love, their hate
and their jealousy have long since
vanished;
never again will they have a part
in anything that happens under the
sun.

7 Go, eat your food with gladness, and
drink your wine with a joyful heart, for
God has already approved what you do.
8 Always be clothed in white, and always
anoint your head with oil. 9 Enjoy life with
your wife, whom you love, all the days of
this meaningless life that God has given
you under the sun—all your meaningless days. For this is your lot in life and
in your toilsome labor under the sun.
10 Whatever your hand finds to do, do it
with all your might, for in the realm of
the dead, where you are going, there is
neither working nor planning nor knowledge nor wisdom.

11 I have seen something else under
the sun:

The race is not to the swift
or the battle to the strong,
nor does food come to the wise
or wealth to the brilliant
or favor to the learned;
but time and chance happen to them
all.

12 Moreover, no one knows when their
hour will come:

As fish are caught in a cruel net,
or birds are taken in a snare,
so people are trapped by evil times
that fall unexpectedly upon them.

13 I also saw under the sun this example of wisdom that greatly impressed me:
14 There was once a small city with only
a few people in it. And a powerful king
came against it, surrounded it and built
huge siege works against it. 15 Now there
lived in that city a man poor but wise, and
he saved the city by his wisdom. But nobody remembered that poor man. 16 So I
said, "Wisdom is better than strength."
But the poor man's wisdom is despised,
and his words are no longer heeded.

17 The quiet words of the wise are more
to be heeded
than the shouts of a ruler of fools.
18 Wisdom is better than weapons of war,
but one sinner destroys much good.

10 As dead flies give perfume a bad
smell,
so a little folly outweighs wisdom
and honor.

[a] 2 Septuagint (Aquila), Vulgate and Syriac; Hebrew does not have *and the bad.* [b] 4 Or *What then is to be chosen? With all who live, there is hope*

2 The heart of the wise inclines to the right,
but the heart of the fool to the left.
3 Even as fools walk along the road,
they lack sense
and show everyone how stupid they are.
4 If a ruler's anger rises against you,
do not leave your post;
calmness can lay great offenses to rest.

5 There is an evil I have seen under the sun,
the sort of error that arises from a ruler:
6 Fools are put in many high positions,
while the rich occupy the low ones.
7 I have seen slaves on horseback,
while princes go on foot like slaves.

8 Whoever digs a pit may fall into it;
whoever breaks through a wall may be bitten by a snake.
9 Whoever quarries stones may be injured by them;
whoever splits logs may be endangered by them.

10 If the ax is dull
and its edge unsharpened,
more strength is needed,
but skill will bring success.

11 If a snake bites before it is charmed,
the charmer receives no fee.

12 Words from the mouth of the wise are gracious,
but fools are consumed by their own lips.
13 At the beginning their words are folly;
at the end they are wicked madness—
14 and fools multiply words.

No one knows what is coming—
who can tell someone else what will happen after them?

15 The toil of fools wearies them;
they do not know the way to town.

16 Woe to the land whose king was a servant[a]
and whose princes feast in the morning.
17 Blessed is the land whose king is of noble birth
and whose princes eat at a proper time—
for strength and not for drunkenness.

18 Through laziness, the rafters sag;
because of idle hands, the house leaks.

19 A feast is made for laughter,
wine makes life merry,
and money is the answer for everything.

20 Do not revile the king even in your thoughts,
or curse the rich in your bedroom,
because a bird in the sky may carry your words,
and a bird on the wing may report what you say.

11 Ship your grain across the sea;
after many days you may receive a return.
2 Invest in seven ventures, yes, in eight;
you do not know what disaster may come upon the land.

3 If clouds are full of water,
they pour rain on the earth.
Whether a tree falls to the south or to the north,
in the place where it falls, there it will lie.
4 Whoever watches the wind will not plant;
whoever looks at the clouds will not reap.

5 As you do not know the path of the wind,
or how the body is formed[b] in a mother's womb,
so you cannot understand the work of God,
the Maker of all things.

6 Sow your seed in the morning,
and at evening let your hands not be idle,
for you do not know which will succeed,
whether this or that,
or whether both will do equally well.

7 Light is sweet,
and it pleases the eyes to see the sun.

[a] 16 Or *king is a child* [b] 5 Or *know how life* (or *the spirit*) / *enters the body being formed*

8 However many years anyone may live,
let them enjoy them all.
But let them remember the days of darkness,
for there will be many.
Everything to come is meaningless.

9 You who are young, be happy while you are young,
and let your heart give you joy in the days of your youth.
Follow the ways of your heart
and whatever your eyes see,
but know that for all these things
God will bring you into judgment.
10 So then, banish anxiety from your heart
and cast off the troubles of your body,
for youth and vigor are meaningless.

12 Remember your Creator
in the days of your youth,
before the days of trouble come
and the years approach when you will say,
"I find no pleasure in them"—
2 before the sun and the light
and the moon and the stars grow dark,
and the clouds return after the rain;
3 when the keepers of the house tremble,
and the strong men stoop,
when the grinders cease because they are few,
and those looking through the windows grow dim;
4 when the doors to the street are closed
and the sound of grinding fades;
when people rise up at the sound of birds,
but all their songs grow faint;
5 when people are afraid of heights
and of dangers in the streets;
when the almond tree blossoms
and the grasshopper drags itself along
and desire no longer is stirred.
Then people go to their eternal home
and mourners go about the streets.

6 Remember him—before the silver cord is severed,
and the golden bowl is broken;
before the pitcher is shattered at the spring,
and the wheel broken at the well,
7 and the dust returns to the ground it came from,
and the spirit returns to God who gave it.

8 "Meaningless! Meaningless!" says the Teacher.[a]
"Everything is meaningless!"

9 Not only was the Teacher wise, but he
also imparted knowledge to the people.
He pondered and searched out and set
in order many proverbs. 10 The Teacher
searched to find just the right words, and
what he wrote was upright and true.
11 The words of the wise are like goads,
their collected sayings like firmly em-
bedded nails—given by one shepherd.[b]
12 Be warned, my son, of anything in addition to them.
Of making many books there is no end,
and much study wearies the body.

13 Now all has been heard;
here is the conclusion of the matter:
Fear God and keep his commandments,
for this is the duty of all mankind.
14 For God will bring every deed into judgment,
including every hidden thing,
whether it is good or evil.

a 8 Or *the leader of the assembly*; also in verses 9 and 10 b 11 Or *Shepherd*

SONG OF SONGS

Traditional wedding celebrations in the Middle East cast the bride and groom in the roles of a king and his queen. The festivities include love songs and also special songs that praise the physical beauty of the bride or the handsomeness of the groom. The custom has a long history and is reflected in the anthology of wedding songs we know as the Song of Songs. The individual songs may have been used repeatedly in marriage celebrations and eventually gathered together, just as the psalms were collected after years of use in worship. The title Solomon's Song of Songs can be taken to mean that King Solomon, a renowned composer (see p. 301), was the author of its songs. However, it could also be a reference to Solomon as the kind of glorious king the groom represents.

The songs are arranged to tell the courtship story of a man and woman, of their marriage (described as a royal wedding) and its consummation, and of the beginning of their new life together. After a short introduction the book presents six episodes, each typically ending with a reference to the friends of the man and woman. This may refer to others attending the wedding to join in the celebration. Together the songs celebrate the delights of married love and the beauty of the human body, using vivid imagery from the natural world to show that these things are part of the creation that God declared very good.

---

1 Solomon's Song of Songs.

She[a]

2 Let him kiss me with the kisses of his
mouth —
for your love is more delightful than
wine.
3 Pleasing is the fragrance of your
perfumes;
your name is like perfume poured
out.
No wonder the young women love
you!
4 Take me away with you — let us hurry!
Let the king bring me into his
chambers.

Friends

We rejoice and delight in you[b];
we will praise your love more than
wine.

She

How right they are to adore you!

5 Dark am I, yet lovely,
daughters of Jerusalem,
dark like the tents of Kedar,
like the tent curtains of Solomon.[c]
6 Do not stare at me because I am dark,
because I am darkened by the sun.
My mother's sons were angry with me
and made me take care of the
vineyards;
my own vineyard I had to neglect.
7 Tell me, you whom I love,
where you graze your flock
and where you rest your sheep at
midday.
Why should I be like a veiled woman
beside the flocks of your friends?

Friends

8 If you do not know, most beautiful of
women,
follow the tracks of the sheep
and graze your young goats
by the tents of the shepherds.

He

9 I liken you, my darling, to a mare
among Pharaoh's chariot horses.
10 Your cheeks are beautiful with
earrings,
your neck with strings of jewels.
11 We will make you earrings of gold,
studded with silver.

She

12 While the king was at his table,
my perfume spread its fragrance.
13 My beloved is to me a sachet of myrrh
resting between my breasts.

[a] The main male and female speakers (identified primarily on the basis of the gender of the relevant Hebrew forms) are indicated by the captions *He* and *She* respectively. The words of others are marked *Friends*. In some instances the divisions and their captions are debatable. [b] 4 The Hebrew is masculine singular.
[c] 5 Or *Salma*

14 My beloved is to me a cluster of henna
blossoms
from the vineyards of En Gedi.

He

15 How beautiful you are, my darling!
Oh, how beautiful!
Your eyes are doves.

She

16 How handsome you are, my beloved!
Oh, how charming!
And our bed is verdant.

He

17 The beams of our house are cedars;
our rafters are firs.

She[a]

2 I am a rose[b] of Sharon,
a lily of the valleys.

He

2 Like a lily among thorns
is my darling among the young
women.

She

3 Like an apple[c] tree among the trees of
the forest
is my beloved among the young
men.
I delight to sit in his shade,
and his fruit is sweet to my taste.
4 Let him lead me to the banquet hall,
and let his banner over me be love.
5 Strengthen me with raisins,
refresh me with apples,
for I am faint with love.
6 His left arm is under my head,
and his right arm embraces me.
7 Daughters of Jerusalem, I charge you
by the gazelles and by the does of
the field:
Do not arouse or awaken love
until it so desires.

8 Listen! My beloved!
Look! Here he comes,
leaping across the mountains,
bounding over the hills.
9 My beloved is like a gazelle or a young
stag.
Look! There he stands behind our
wall,
gazing through the windows,
peering through the lattice.
10 My beloved spoke and said to me,
"Arise, my darling,
my beautiful one, come with me.
11 See! The winter is past;
the rains are over and gone.
12 Flowers appear on the earth;
the season of singing has come,
the cooing of doves
is heard in our land.
13 The fig tree forms its early fruit;
the blossoming vines spread their
fragrance.
Arise, come, my darling;
my beautiful one, come with me."

He

14 My dove in the clefts of the rock,
in the hiding places on the
mountainside,
show me your face,
let me hear your voice;
for your voice is sweet,
and your face is lovely.
15 Catch for us the foxes,
the little foxes
that ruin the vineyards,
our vineyards that are in bloom.

She

16 My beloved is mine and I am his;
he browses among the lilies.
17 Until the day breaks
and the shadows flee,
turn, my beloved,
and be like a gazelle
or like a young stag
on the rugged hills.[d]

3 All night long on my bed
I looked for the one my heart loves;
I looked for him but did not find
him.
2 I will get up now and go about the city,
through its streets and squares;
I will search for the one my heart
loves.
So I looked for him but did not find
him.
3 The watchmen found me
as they made their rounds in the
city.
"Have you seen the one my heart
loves?"

[a] Or *He* [b] *1* Probably a member of the crocus family [c] *3* Or possibly *apricot*; here and elsewhere in Song of Songs [d] *17* Or *the hills of Bether*

4 Scarcely had I passed them
when I found the one my heart loves.
I held him and would not let him go
till I had brought him to my mother's house,
to the room of the one who conceived me.
5 Daughters of Jerusalem, I charge you
by the gazelles and by the does of the field:
Do not arouse or awaken love
until it so desires.

6 Who is this coming up from the wilderness
like a column of smoke,
perfumed with myrrh and incense
made from all the spices of the merchant?
7 Look! It is Solomon's carriage,
escorted by sixty warriors,
the noblest of Israel,
8 all of them wearing the sword,
all experienced in battle,
each with his sword at his side,
prepared for the terrors of the night.
9 King Solomon made for himself the carriage;
he made it of wood from Lebanon.
10 Its posts he made of silver,
its base of gold.
Its seat was upholstered with purple,
its interior inlaid with love.
Daughters of Jerusalem, 11 come out,
and look, you daughters of Zion.
Look[a] on King Solomon wearing a crown,
the crown with which his mother crowned him
on the day of his wedding,
the day his heart rejoiced.

He

4 How beautiful you are, my darling!
Oh, how beautiful!
Your eyes behind your veil are doves.
Your hair is like a flock of goats
descending from the hills of Gilead.
2 Your teeth are like a flock of sheep just shorn,
coming up from the washing.
Each has its twin;
not one of them is alone.
3 Your lips are like a scarlet ribbon;
your mouth is lovely.
Your temples behind your veil
are like the halves of a pomegranate.
4 Your neck is like the tower of David,
built with courses of stone[b];
on it hang a thousand shields,
all of them shields of warriors.
5 Your breasts are like two fawns,
like twin fawns of a gazelle
that browse among the lilies.
6 Until the day breaks
and the shadows flee,
I will go to the mountain of myrrh
and to the hill of incense.
7 You are altogether beautiful, my darling;
there is no flaw in you.

8 Come with me from Lebanon, my bride,
come with me from Lebanon.
Descend from the crest of Amana,
from the top of Senir, the summit of Hermon,
from the lions' dens
and the mountain haunts of leopards.
9 You have stolen my heart, my sister, my bride;
you have stolen my heart
with one glance of your eyes,
with one jewel of your necklace.
10 How delightful is your love, my sister, my bride!
How much more pleasing is your love than wine,
and the fragrance of your perfume
more than any spice!
11 Your lips drop sweetness as the honeycomb, my bride;
milk and honey are under your tongue.
The fragrance of your garments
is like the fragrance of Lebanon.
12 You are a garden locked up, my sister, my bride;
you are a spring enclosed, a sealed fountain.
13 Your plants are an orchard of pomegranates
with choice fruits,
with henna and nard,
14 nard and saffron,
calamus and cinnamon,

[a] 10,11 Or *interior lovingly inlaid / by the daughters of Jerusalem. / 11Come out, you daughters of Zion, / and look*
[b] 4 The meaning of the Hebrew for this phrase is uncertain.

with every kind of incense tree,
with myrrh and aloes
and all the finest spices.
15 You are[a] a garden fountain,
a well of flowing water
streaming down from Lebanon.

She

16 Awake, north wind,
and come, south wind!
Blow on my garden,
that its fragrance may spread
everywhere.
Let my beloved come into his garden
and taste its choice fruits.

He

5 I have come into my garden, my
sister, my bride;
I have gathered my myrrh with my
spice.
I have eaten my honeycomb and my
honey;
I have drunk my wine and my milk.

Friends

Eat, friends, and drink;
drink your fill of love.

She

2 I slept but my heart was awake.
Listen! My beloved is knocking:
"Open to me, my sister, my darling,
my dove, my flawless one.
My head is drenched with dew,
my hair with the dampness of the
night."
3 I have taken off my robe —
must I put it on again?
I have washed my feet —
must I soil them again?
4 My beloved thrust his hand through
the latch-opening;
my heart began to pound for him.
5 I arose to open for my beloved,
and my hands dripped with myrrh,
my fingers with flowing myrrh,
on the handles of the bolt.
6 I opened for my beloved,
but my beloved had left; he was
gone.
My heart sank at his departure.[b]
I looked for him but did not find him.
I called him but he did not answer.
7 The watchmen found me
as they made their rounds in the
city.
They beat me, they bruised me;
they took away my cloak,
those watchmen of the walls!
8 Daughters of Jerusalem, I charge
you —
if you find my beloved,
what will you tell him?
Tell him I am faint with love.

Friends

9 How is your beloved better than
others,
most beautiful of women?
How is your beloved better than
others,
that you so charge us?

She

10 My beloved is radiant and ruddy,
outstanding among ten thousand.
11 His head is purest gold;
his hair is wavy
and black as a raven.
12 His eyes are like doves
by the water streams,
washed in milk,
mounted like jewels.
13 His cheeks are like beds of spice
yielding perfume.
His lips are like lilies
dripping with myrrh.
14 His arms are rods of gold
set with topaz.
His body is like polished ivory
decorated with lapis lazuli.
15 His legs are pillars of marble
set on bases of pure gold.
His appearance is like Lebanon,
choice as its cedars.
16 His mouth is sweetness itself;
he is altogether lovely.
This is my beloved, this is my friend,
daughters of Jerusalem.

Friends

6 Where has your beloved gone,
most beautiful of women?
Which way did your beloved turn,
that we may look for him with you?

She

2 My beloved has gone down to his
garden,

[a] 15 Or *I am* (spoken by *She*) [b] 6 Or *heart had gone out to him when he spoke*

to the beds of spices,
to browse in the gardens
and to gather lilies.
3 I am my beloved's and my beloved is mine;
he browses among the lilies.

He

4 You are as beautiful as Tirzah, my darling,
as lovely as Jerusalem,
as majestic as troops with banners.
5 Turn your eyes from me;
they overwhelm me.
Your hair is like a flock of goats
descending from Gilead.
6 Your teeth are like a flock of sheep
coming up from the washing.
Each has its twin,
not one of them is missing.
7 Your temples behind your veil
are like the halves of a pomegranate.
8 Sixty queens there may be,
and eighty concubines,
and virgins beyond number;
9 but my dove, my perfect one, is unique,
the only daughter of her mother,
the favorite of the one who bore her.
The young women saw her and called her blessed;
the queens and concubines praised her.

Friends

10 Who is this that appears like the dawn,
fair as the moon, bright as the sun,
majestic as the stars in procession?

He

11 I went down to the grove of nut trees
to look at the new growth in the valley,
to see if the vines had budded
or the pomegranates were in bloom.
12 Before I realized it,
my desire set me among the royal chariots of my people.[a]

Friends

13 Come back, come back,
O Shulammite;
come back, come back, that we may gaze on you!

He

Why would you gaze on the Shulammite
as on the dance of Mahanaim?[b]

7[c] How beautiful your sandaled feet,
O prince's daughter!
Your graceful legs are like jewels,
the work of an artist's hands.
2 Your navel is a rounded goblet
that never lacks blended wine.
Your waist is a mound of wheat
encircled by lilies.
3 Your breasts are like two fawns,
like twin fawns of a gazelle.
4 Your neck is like an ivory tower.
Your eyes are the pools of Heshbon
by the gate of Bath Rabbim.
Your nose is like the tower of Lebanon
looking toward Damascus.
5 Your head crowns you like Mount Carmel.
Your hair is like royal tapestry;
the king is held captive by its tresses.
6 How beautiful you are and how pleasing,
my love, with your delights!
7 Your stature is like that of the palm,
and your breasts like clusters of fruit.
8 I said, "I will climb the palm tree;
I will take hold of its fruit."
May your breasts be like clusters of grapes on the vine,
the fragrance of your breath like apples,
9 and your mouth like the best wine.

She

May the wine go straight to my beloved,
flowing gently over lips and teeth.[d]
10 I belong to my beloved,
and his desire is for me.
11 Come, my beloved, let us go to the countryside,
let us spend the night in the villages.[e]
12 Let us go early to the vineyards
to see if the vines have budded,
if their blossoms have opened,
and if the pomegranates are in bloom —

[a] *12* Or *among the chariots of Amminadab*; or *among the chariots of the people of the prince* [b] *13* In Hebrew texts this verse (6:13) is numbered 7:1. [c] In Hebrew texts 7:1-13 is numbered 7:2-14. [d] *9* Septuagint, Aquila, Vulgate and Syriac; Hebrew *lips of sleepers* [e] *11* Or *the henna bushes*

there I will give you my love.
13 The mandrakes send out their
fragrance,
and at our door is every delicacy,
both new and old,
that I have stored up for you, my
beloved.

8 If only you were to me like a brother,
who was nursed at my mother's
breasts!
Then, if I found you outside,
I would kiss you,
and no one would despise me.
2 I would lead you
and bring you to my mother's
house —
she who has taught me.
I would give you spiced wine to drink,
the nectar of my pomegranates.
3 His left arm is under my head
and his right arm embraces me.
4 Daughters of Jerusalem, I charge you:
Do not arouse or awaken love
until it so desires.

Friends

5 Who is this coming up from the
wilderness
leaning on her beloved?

She

Under the apple tree I roused you;
there your mother conceived you,
there she who was in labor gave you
birth.
6 Place me like a seal over your heart,
like a seal on your arm;
for love is as strong as death,
its jealousy[a] unyielding as the grave.
It burns like blazing fire,
like a mighty flame.[b]
7 Many waters cannot quench love;
rivers cannot sweep it away.
If one were to give
all the wealth of one's house for love,
it[c] would be utterly scorned.

Friends

8 We have a little sister,
and her breasts are not yet grown.
What shall we do for our sister
on the day she is spoken for?
9 If she is a wall,
we will build towers of silver on her.
If she is a door,
we will enclose her with panels of
cedar.

She

10 I am a wall,
and my breasts are like towers.
Thus I have become in his eyes
like one bringing contentment.
11 Solomon had a vineyard in Baal
Hamon;
he let out his vineyard to tenants.
Each was to bring for its fruit
a thousand shekels[d] of silver.
12 But my own vineyard is mine to give;
the thousand shekels are for you,
Solomon,
and two hundred[e] are for those who
tend its fruit.

He

13 You who dwell in the gardens
with friends in attendance,
let me hear your voice!

She

14 Come away, my beloved,
and be like a gazelle
or like a young stag
on the spice-laden mountains.

[a] 6 Or *ardor* [b] 6 Or *fire, / like the very flame of the LORD* [c] 7 Or *he* [d] 11 That is, about 25 pounds or about 12 kilograms; also in verse 12 [e] 12 That is, about 5 pounds or about 2.3 kilograms

ISAIAH

The prophet Isaiah addressed the kingdom of Judah for forty years, beginning in the year that King Uzziah died (around 740 BC) and continuing at least to the Assyrian siege of Jerusalem in 701 BC. As with all the prophets, Isaiah based his message on the deep covenant bond between God and his people Israel. Prophets typically delivered their messages by composing oracles—poetic speeches they recited in public. Unlike some other prophets, Isaiah had personal access to the kings of his day. He was able to bring godly counsel to kings Ahaz and Hezekiah when the powerful Assyrian Empire threatened the life of the nation. Isaiah maintains an international perspective throughout his book, revealing that Israel's life is bound up with the affairs of the broader world.

Isaiah urges the people to care for the poor and needy, commit to follow God's ways, and pursue social and economic justice. In typical prophetic pattern, he speaks of coming judgment because of Israel's failure, but also of promised restoration, and moving from Israel to the wider world. God's correction is in the service of renewal. Isaiah's later oracles introduce the complex figure of the servant, whose personal sacrifice brings healing. These "servant songs" fit into the bigger picture of Israel's return from exile, the LORD's return to his people, and the nations turning to God. New Testament writers will turn to Isaiah often to explain how Israel's ancient commission to bring blessing to the world was fulfilled.

---

1 The vision concerning Judah and Jerusalem that Isaiah son of Amoz saw during the reigns of Uzziah, Jotham, Ahaz and Hezekiah, kings of Judah.

2 Hear me, you heavens! Listen, earth!
For the LORD has spoken:
"I reared children and brought them up,
but they have rebelled against me.
3 The ox knows its master,
the donkey its owner's manger,
but Israel does not know,
my people do not understand."

4 Woe to the sinful nation,
a people whose guilt is great,
a brood of evildoers,
children given to corruption!
They have forsaken the LORD;
they have spurned the Holy One of Israel
and turned their backs on him.

5 Why should you be beaten anymore?
Why do you persist in rebellion?
Your whole head is injured,
your whole heart afflicted.
6 From the sole of your foot to the top of your head
there is no soundness—
only wounds and welts
and open sores,
not cleansed or bandaged
or soothed with olive oil.

7 Your country is desolate,
your cities burned with fire;
your fields are being stripped by foreigners
right before you,
laid waste as when overthrown by strangers.
8 Daughter Zion is left
like a shelter in a vineyard,
like a hut in a cucumber field,
like a city under siege.
9 Unless the LORD Almighty
had left us some survivors,
we would have become like Sodom,
we would have been like Gomorrah.

10 Hear the word of the LORD,
you rulers of Sodom;
listen to the instruction of our God,
you people of Gomorrah!
11 "The multitude of your sacrifices—
what are they to me?" says the LORD.
"I have more than enough of burnt offerings,
of rams and the fat of fattened animals;
I have no pleasure
in the blood of bulls and lambs and goats.
12 When you come to appear before me,
who has asked this of you,
this trampling of my courts?
13 Stop bringing meaningless offerings!
Your incense is detestable to me.

New Moons, Sabbaths and
convocations —
I cannot bear your worthless
assemblies.
14 Your New Moon feasts and your
appointed festivals
I hate with all my being.
They have become a burden to me;
I am weary of bearing them.
15 When you spread out your hands in
prayer,
I hide my eyes from you;
even when you offer many prayers,
I am not listening.

Your hands are full of blood!

16 Wash and make yourselves clean.
Take your evil deeds out of my
sight;
stop doing wrong.
17 Learn to do right; seek justice.
Defend the oppressed.[a]
Take up the cause of the fatherless;
plead the case of the widow.

18 "Come now, let us settle the matter,"
says the LORD.
"Though your sins are like scarlet,
they shall be as white as snow;
though they are red as crimson,
they shall be like wool.
19 If you are willing and obedient,
you will eat the good things of the
land;
20 but if you resist and rebel,
you will be devoured by the sword."
For the mouth of the LORD
has spoken.

21 See how the faithful city
has become a prostitute!
She once was full of justice;
righteousness used to dwell in
her —
but now murderers!
22 Your silver has become dross,
your choice wine is diluted with
water.
23 Your rulers are rebels,
partners with thieves;
they all love bribes
and chase after gifts.
They do not defend the cause of the
fatherless;
the widow's case does not come
before them.

24 Therefore the Lord, the LORD
Almighty,
the Mighty One of Israel, declares:
"Ah! I will vent my wrath on my foes
and avenge myself on my enemies.
25 I will turn my hand against you;[b]
I will thoroughly purge away your
dross
and remove all your impurities.
26 I will restore your leaders as in days of
old,
your rulers as at the beginning.
Afterward you will be called
the City of Righteousness,
the Faithful City."

27 Zion will be delivered with justice,
her penitent ones with
righteousness.
28 But rebels and sinners will both be
broken,
and those who forsake the LORD
will perish.

29 "You will be ashamed because of the
sacred oaks
in which you have delighted;
you will be disgraced because of the
gardens
that you have chosen.
30 You will be like an oak with fading
leaves,
like a garden without water.
31 The mighty man will become tinder
and his work a spark;
both will burn together,
with no one to quench the fire."

2 This is what Isaiah son of Amoz saw
concerning Judah and Jerusalem:

2 In the last days
the mountain of the LORD's temple
will be established
as the highest of the mountains;
it will be exalted above the hills,
and all nations will stream to it.

3 Many peoples will come and say,

"Come, let us go up to the mountain of
the LORD,
to the temple of the God of Jacob.
He will teach us his ways,
so that we may walk in his paths."
The law will go out from Zion,
the word of the LORD from
Jerusalem.

[a] 17 Or *justice. / Correct the oppressor* [b] 25 That is, against Jerusalem

4 He will judge between the nations
and will settle disputes for many peoples.
They will beat their swords into plowshares
and their spears into pruning hooks.
Nation will not take up sword against nation,
nor will they train for war anymore.

5 Come, descendants of Jacob,
let us walk in the light of the LORD.

6 You, LORD, have abandoned your people,
the descendants of Jacob.
They are full of superstitions from the East;
they practice divination like the Philistines
and embrace pagan customs.
7 Their land is full of silver and gold;
there is no end to their treasures.
Their land is full of horses;
there is no end to their chariots.
8 Their land is full of idols;
they bow down to the work of their hands,
to what their fingers have made.
9 So people will be brought low
and everyone humbled —
do not forgive them.[a]
10 Go into the rocks, hide in the ground
from the fearful presence of the LORD
and the splendor of his majesty!
11 The eyes of the arrogant will be humbled
and human pride brought low;
the LORD alone will be exalted in that day.

12 The LORD Almighty has a day in store
for all the proud and lofty,
for all that is exalted
(and they will be humbled),
13 for all the cedars of Lebanon, tall and lofty,
and all the oaks of Bashan,
14 for all the towering mountains
and all the high hills,
15 for every lofty tower
and every fortified wall,
16 for every trading ship[b]
and every stately vessel.
17 The arrogance of man will be brought low
and human pride humbled;
the LORD alone will be exalted in that day,
18 and the idols will totally disappear.

19 People will flee to caves in the rocks
and to holes in the ground
from the fearful presence of the LORD
and the splendor of his majesty,
when he rises to shake the earth.
20 In that day people will throw away
to the moles and bats
their idols of silver and idols of gold,
which they made to worship.
21 They will flee to caverns in the rocks
and to the overhanging crags
from the fearful presence of the LORD
and the splendor of his majesty,
when he rises to shake the earth.

22 Stop trusting in mere humans,
who have but a breath in their nostrils.
Why hold them in esteem?

3 See now, the Lord,
the LORD Almighty,
is about to take from Jerusalem and Judah
both supply and support:
all supplies of food and all supplies of water,
2 the hero and the warrior,
the judge and the prophet,
the diviner and the elder,
3 the captain of fifty and the man of rank,
the counselor, skilled craftsman
and clever enchanter.

4 "I will make mere youths their officials;
children will rule over them."

5 People will oppress each other —
man against man, neighbor against neighbor.
The young will rise up against the old,
the nobody against the honored.

6 A man will seize one of his brothers
in his father's house, and say,
"You have a cloak, you be our leader;
take charge of this heap of ruins!"
7 But in that day he will cry out,
"I have no remedy.

[a] 9 Or *not raise them up* [b] 16 Hebrew *every ship of Tarshish*

I have no food or clothing in my
house;
do not make me the leader of the
people."

8 Jerusalem staggers,
Judah is falling;
their words and deeds are against the
LORD,
defying his glorious presence.
9 The look on their faces testifies
against them;
they parade their sin like Sodom;
they do not hide it.
Woe to them!
They have brought disaster upon
themselves.

10 Tell the righteous it will be well with
them,
for they will enjoy the fruit of their
deeds.
11 Woe to the wicked!
Disaster is upon them!
They will be paid back
for what their hands have done.

12 Youths oppress my people,
women rule over them.
My people, your guides lead you
astray;
they turn you from the path.

13 The LORD takes his place in court;
he rises to judge the people.
14 The LORD enters into judgment
against the elders and leaders of his
people:
"It is you who have ruined my
vineyard;
the plunder from the poor is in your
houses.
15 What do you mean by crushing my
people
and grinding the faces of the poor?"
declares the Lord,
the LORD Almighty.

16 The LORD says,
"The women of Zion are haughty,
walking along with outstretched
necks,
flirting with their eyes,
strutting along with swaying hips,
with ornaments jingling on their
ankles.
17 Therefore the Lord will bring sores on
the heads of the women of Zion;
the LORD will make their scalps
bald."

18 In that day the Lord will snatch away
their finery: the bangles and headbands
and crescent necklaces, 19 the earrings
and bracelets and veils, 20 the headdress-
es and anklets and sashes, the perfume
bottles and charms, 21 the signet rings
and nose rings, 22 the fine robes and the
capes and cloaks, the purses 23 and mirrors, and the linen garments and tiaras
and shawls.

24 Instead of fragrance there will be a
stench;
instead of a sash, a rope;
instead of well-dressed hair,
baldness;
instead of fine clothing, sackcloth;
instead of beauty, branding.
25 Your men will fall by the sword,
your warriors in battle.
26 The gates of Zion will lament and
mourn;
destitute, she will sit on the ground.

4 1 In that day seven women
will take hold of one man
and say, "We will eat our own food
and provide our own clothes;
only let us be called by your name.
Take away our disgrace!"

2 In that day the Branch of the LORD will
be beautiful and glorious, and the fruit of
the land will be the pride and glory of the
survivors in Israel. 3 Those who are left in
Zion, who remain in Jerusalem, will be
called holy, all who are recorded among
the living in Jerusalem. 4 The Lord will
wash away the filth of the women of Zion;
he will cleanse the bloodstains from Jerusalem by a spirit[a] of judgment and a
spirit[a] of fire. 5 Then the LORD will create over all of Mount Zion and over those
who assemble there a cloud of smoke by
day and a glow of flaming fire by night;
over everything the glory[b] will be a canopy. 6 It will be a shelter and shade from
the heat of the day, and a refuge and hiding place from the storm and rain.

5 I will sing for the one I love
a song about his vineyard:
My loved one had a vineyard
on a fertile hillside.
2 He dug it up and cleared it of stones

[a] 4 Or *the Spirit* [b] 5 Or *over all the glory there*

and planted it with the choicest
vines.
He built a watchtower in it
and cut out a winepress as well.
Then he looked for a crop of good
grapes,
but it yielded only bad fruit.

3 "Now you dwellers in Jerusalem and
people of Judah,
judge between me and my vineyard.
4 What more could have been done for
my vineyard
than I have done for it?
When I looked for good grapes,
why did it yield only bad?
5 Now I will tell you
what I am going to do to my vineyard:
I will take away its hedge,
and it will be destroyed;
I will break down its wall,
and it will be trampled.
6 I will make it a wasteland,
neither pruned nor cultivated,
and briers and thorns will grow
there.
I will command the clouds
not to rain on it."

7 The vineyard of the LORD Almighty
is the nation of Israel,
and the people of Judah
are the vines he delighted in.
And he looked for justice, but saw
bloodshed;
for righteousness, but heard cries of
distress.

8 Woe to you who add house to house
and join field to field
till no space is left
and you live alone in the land.

9 The LORD Almighty has declared in
my hearing:

"Surely the great houses will become
desolate,
the fine mansions left without
occupants.
10 A ten-acre vineyard will produce only
a bath[a] of wine;
a homer[b] of seed will yield only an
ephah[c] of grain."

11 Woe to those who rise early in the
morning
to run after their drinks,
who stay up late at night
till they are inflamed with wine.
12 They have harps and lyres at their
banquets,
pipes and timbrels and wine,
but they have no regard for the deeds
of the LORD,
no respect for the work of his hands.
13 Therefore my people will go into exile
for lack of understanding;
those of high rank will die of hunger
and the common people will be
parched with thirst.
14 Therefore Death expands its jaws,
opening wide its mouth;
into it will descend their nobles and
masses
with all their brawlers and revelers.
15 So people will be brought low
and everyone humbled,
the eyes of the arrogant humbled.
16 But the LORD Almighty will be exalted
by his justice,
and the holy God will be proved
holy by his righteous acts.
17 Then sheep will graze as in their own
pasture;
lambs will feed[d] among the ruins of
the rich.

18 Woe to those who draw sin along with
cords of deceit,
and wickedness as with cart ropes,
19 to those who say, "Let God hurry;
let him hasten his work
so we may see it.
The plan of the Holy One of Israel —
let it approach, let it come into view,
so we may know it."

20 Woe to those who call evil good
and good evil,
who put darkness for light
and light for darkness,
who put bitter for sweet
and sweet for bitter.

21 Woe to those who are wise in their
own eyes
and clever in their own sight.

22 Woe to those who are heroes at
drinking wine
and champions at mixing drinks,
23 who acquit the guilty for a bribe,

[a] *10* That is, about 6 gallons or about 22 liters [b] *10* That is, probably about 360 pounds or about 160 kilograms [c] *10* That is, probably about 36 pounds or about 16 kilograms [d] *17* Septuagint; Hebrew / *strangers will eat*

but deny justice to the innocent.
24 Therefore, as tongues of fire lick up straw
and as dry grass sinks down in the flames,
so their roots will decay
and their flowers blow away like dust;
for they have rejected the law of the LORD Almighty
and spurned the word of the Holy One of Israel.
25 Therefore the LORD's anger burns against his people;
his hand is raised and he strikes them down.
The mountains shake,
and the dead bodies are like refuse in the streets.

Yet for all this, his anger is not turned away,
his hand is still upraised.

26 He lifts up a banner for the distant nations,
he whistles for those at the ends of the earth.
Here they come,
swiftly and speedily!
27 Not one of them grows tired or stumbles,
not one slumbers or sleeps;
not a belt is loosened at the waist,
not a sandal strap is broken.
28 Their arrows are sharp,
all their bows are strung;
their horses' hooves seem like flint,
their chariot wheels like a whirlwind.
29 Their roar is like that of the lion,
they roar like young lions;
they growl as they seize their prey
and carry it off with no one to rescue.
30 In that day they will roar over it
like the roaring of the sea.
And if one looks at the land,
there is only darkness and distress;
even the sun will be darkened by clouds.

6 In the year that King Uzziah died, I
saw the Lord, high and exalted, seated on a throne; and the train of his robe
filled the temple. 2 Above him were seraphim, each with six wings: With two
wings they covered their faces, with two
they covered their feet, and with two
they were flying. 3 And they were calling
to one another:

"Holy, holy, holy is the LORD Almighty;
the whole earth is full of his glory."

4 At the sound of their voices the doorposts and thresholds shook and the temple was filled with smoke.
5 "Woe to me!" I cried. "I am ruined!
For I am a man of unclean lips, and I live
among a people of unclean lips, and my
eyes have seen the King, the LORD Almighty."
6 Then one of the seraphim flew to me
with a live coal in his hand, which he had
taken with tongs from the altar. 7 With it
he touched my mouth and said, "See, this
has touched your lips; your guilt is taken
away and your sin atoned for."
8 Then I heard the voice of the Lord saying, "Whom shall I send? And who will
go for us?"
And I said, "Here am I. Send me!"
9 He said, "Go and tell this people:
"'Be ever hearing, but never understanding;
be ever seeing, but never perceiving.'
10 Make the heart of this people calloused;
make their ears dull
and close their eyes.[a]
Otherwise they might see with their eyes,
hear with their ears,
understand with their hearts,
and turn and be healed."
11 Then I said, "For how long, Lord?"
And he answered:

"Until the cities lie ruined
and without inhabitant,
until the houses are left deserted
and the fields ruined and ravaged,
12 until the LORD has sent everyone far away
and the land is utterly forsaken.
13 And though a tenth remains in the land,

[a] *9,10* Hebrew; Septuagint *'You will be ever hearing, but never understanding; / you will be ever seeing, but never perceiving.' / 10 This people's heart has become calloused; / they hardly hear with their ears, / and they have closed their eyes*

it will again be laid waste.
But as the terebinth and oak
leave stumps when they are cut
down,
so the holy seed will be the stump in
the land."

7 When Ahaz son of Jotham, the son of
Uzziah, was king of Judah, King Rezin of Aram and Pekah son of Remaliah
king of Israel marched up to fight against
Jerusalem, but they could not overpower it.

2 Now the house of David was told,
"Aram has allied itself with[a] Ephraim";
so the hearts of Ahaz and his people
were shaken, as the trees of the forest are
shaken by the wind.

3 Then the LORD said to Isaiah, "Go out,
you and your son Shear-Jashub,[b] to meet
Ahaz at the end of the aqueduct of the
Upper Pool, on the road to the Launderer's Field. 4 Say to him, 'Be careful, keep
calm and don't be afraid. Do not lose
heart because of these two smoldering
stubs of firewood — because of the fierce
anger of Rezin and Aram and of the son
of Remaliah. 5 Aram, Ephraim and Remaliah's son have plotted your ruin, saying, 6 "Let us invade Judah; let us tear it
apart and divide it among ourselves, and
make the son of Tabeel king over it." 7 Yet
this is what the Sovereign LORD says:

" 'It will not take place,
it will not happen,
8 for the head of Aram is Damascus,
and the head of Damascus is only
Rezin.
Within sixty-five years
Ephraim will be too shattered to be
a people.
9 The head of Ephraim is Samaria,
and the head of Samaria is only
Remaliah's son.
If you do not stand firm in your faith,
you will not stand at all.' "

10 Again the LORD spoke to Ahaz, 11 "Ask
the LORD your God for a sign, whether
in the deepest depths or in the highest
heights."

12 But Ahaz said, "I will not ask; I will
not put the LORD to the test."

13 Then Isaiah said, "Hear now, you
house of David! Is it not enough to try
the patience of humans? Will you try the
patience of my God also? 14 Therefore the
Lord himself will give you[c] a sign: The
virgin[d] will conceive and give birth to a
son, and[e] will call him Immanuel.[f] 15 He
will be eating curds and honey when he
knows enough to reject the wrong and
choose the right, 16 for before the boy
knows enough to reject the wrong and
choose the right, the land of the two
kings you dread will be laid waste. 17 The
LORD will bring on you and on your people and on the house of your father a time
unlike any since Ephraim broke away
from Judah — he will bring the king of
Assyria."

18 In that day the LORD will whistle for
flies from the Nile delta in Egypt and for
bees from the land of Assyria. 19 They
will all come and settle in the steep ravines and in the crevices in the rocks, on
all the thornbushes and at all the water
holes. 20 In that day the Lord will use a
razor hired from beyond the Euphrates
River — the king of Assyria — to shave
your head and private parts, and to cut
off your beard also. 21 In that day, a person will keep alive a young cow and two
goats. 22 And because of the abundance
of the milk they give, there will be curds
to eat. All who remain in the land will eat
curds and honey. 23 In that day, in every
place where there were a thousand vines
worth a thousand silver shekels,[g] there
will be only briers and thorns. 24 Hunters will go there with bow and arrow, for
the land will be covered with briers and
thorns. 25 As for all the hills once cultivated by the hoe, you will no longer go
there for fear of the briers and thorns;
they will become places where cattle are
turned loose and where sheep run.

8 The LORD said to me, "Take a large
scroll and write on it with an ordinary
pen: Maher-Shalal-Hash-Baz."[h] 2 So I
called in Uriah the priest and Zechariah
son of Jeberekiah as reliable witnesses
for me. 3 Then I made love to the proph-
etess, and she conceived and gave birth
to a son. And the LORD said to me, "Name
him Maher-Shalal-Hash-Baz. 4 For be-

[a] *2* Or *has set up camp in* [b] *3* *Shear-Jashub* means *a remnant will return.* [c] *14* The Hebrew is plural. [d] *14* Or *young woman* [e] *14* Masoretic Text; Dead Sea Scrolls *son, and he* or *son, and they* [f] *14* *Immanuel* means *God with us.* [g] *23* That is, about 25 pounds or about 12 kilograms [h] *1* *Maher-Shalal-Hash-Baz* means *quick to the plunder, swift to the spoil*; also in verse 3.

fore the boy knows how to say 'My father'
or 'My mother,' the wealth of Damascus
and the plunder of Samaria will be carried off by the king of Assyria."
5 The LORD spoke to me again:

6 "Because this people has rejected
the gently flowing waters of Shiloah
and rejoices over Rezin
and the son of Remaliah,
7 therefore the Lord is about to bring
against them
the mighty floodwaters of the
Euphrates —
the king of Assyria with all his
pomp.
It will overflow all its channels,
run over all its banks
8 and sweep on into Judah, swirling
over it,
passing through it and reaching up
to the neck.
Its outspread wings will cover the
breadth of your land,
Immanuel[a]!"

9 Raise the war cry,[b] you nations, and
be shattered!
Listen, all you distant lands.
Prepare for battle, and be shattered!
Prepare for battle, and be shattered!
10 Devise your strategy, but it will be
thwarted;
propose your plan, but it will not
stand,
for God is with us.[c]

11 This is what the LORD says to me with
his strong hand upon me, warning me
not to follow the way of this people:

12 "Do not call conspiracy
everything this people calls a
conspiracy;
do not fear what they fear,
and do not dread it.
13 The LORD Almighty is the one you are
to regard as holy,
he is the one you are to fear,
he is the one you are to dread.
14 He will be a holy place;
for both Israel and Judah he will be
a stone that causes people to stumble
and a rock that makes them fall.
And for the people of Jerusalem he
will be
a trap and a snare.
15 Many of them will stumble;
they will fall and be broken,
they will be snared and captured."
16 Bind up this testimony of warning
and seal up God's instruction
among my disciples.
17 I will wait for the LORD,
who is hiding his face from the
descendants of Jacob.
I will put my trust in him.

18 Here am I, and the children the LORD
has given me. We are signs and symbols
in Israel from the LORD Almighty, who
dwells on Mount Zion.
19 When someone tells you to consult
mediums and spiritists, who whisper
and mutter, should not a people inquire
of their God? Why consult the dead on
behalf of the living? 20 Consult God's
instruction and the testimony of warning. If anyone does not speak according
to this word, they have no light of dawn.
21 Distressed and hungry, they will roam
through the land; when they are famished, they will become enraged and,
looking upward, will curse their king
and their God. 22 Then they will look toward the earth and see only distress and
darkness and fearful gloom, and they
will be thrust into utter darkness.

9[d] Nevertheless, there will be no more
gloom for those who were in distress. In the past he humbled the land
of Zebulun and the land of Naphtali, but
in the future he will honor Galilee of the
nations, by the Way of the Sea, beyond
the Jordan —

2 The people walking in darkness
have seen a great light;
on those living in the land of deep
darkness
a light has dawned.
3 You have enlarged the nation
and increased their joy;
they rejoice before you
as people rejoice at the harvest,
as warriors rejoice
when dividing the plunder.
4 For as in the day of Midian's defeat,
you have shattered
the yoke that burdens them,
the bar across their shoulders,
the rod of their oppressor.

[a] 8 *Immanuel* means *God with us.* [b] 9 Or *Do your worst* [c] *10* Hebrew *Immanuel* [d] In Hebrew texts 9:1 is numbered 8:23, and 9:2-21 is numbered 9:1-20.

5 Every warrior's boot used in battle
and every garment rolled in blood
will be destined for burning,
will be fuel for the fire.
6 For to us a child is born,
to us a son is given,
and the government will be on his
shoulders.
And he will be called
Wonderful Counselor, Mighty God,
Everlasting Father, Prince of
Peace.
7 Of the greatness of his government
and peace
there will be no end.
He will reign on David's throne
and over his kingdom,
establishing and upholding it
with justice and righteousness
from that time on and forever.
The zeal of the LORD Almighty
will accomplish this.

8 The Lord has sent a message against
Jacob;
it will fall on Israel.
9 All the people will know it—
Ephraim and the inhabitants of
Samaria—
who say with pride
and arrogance of heart,
10 "The bricks have fallen down,
but we will rebuild with dressed
stone;
the fig trees have been felled,
but we will replace them with
cedars."
11 But the LORD has strengthened
Rezin's foes against them
and has spurred their enemies on.
12 Arameans from the east and
Philistines from the west
have devoured Israel with open
mouth.

Yet for all this, his anger is not turned
away,
his hand is still upraised.

13 But the people have not returned to
him who struck them,
nor have they sought the LORD
Almighty.
14 So the LORD will cut off from Israel
both head and tail,
both palm branch and reed in a
single day;
15 the elders and dignitaries are the
head,
the prophets who teach lies are the
tail.
16 Those who guide this people mislead
them,
and those who are guided are led
astray.
17 Therefore the Lord will take no
pleasure in the young men,
nor will he pity the fatherless and
widows,
for everyone is ungodly and wicked,
every mouth speaks folly.

Yet for all this, his anger is not turned
away,
his hand is still upraised.

18 Surely wickedness burns like a fire;
it consumes briers and thorns,
it sets the forest thickets ablaze,
so that it rolls upward in a column
of smoke.
19 By the wrath of the LORD Almighty
the land will be scorched
and the people will be fuel for the fire;
they will not spare one another.
20 On the right they will devour,
but still be hungry;
on the left they will eat,
but not be satisfied.
Each will feed on the flesh of their
own offspring[a]:
21 Manasseh will feed on Ephraim,
and Ephraim on Manasseh;
together they will turn against
Judah.

Yet for all this, his anger is not turned
away,
his hand is still upraised.

10 Woe to those who make unjust
laws,
to those who issue oppressive
decrees,
2 to deprive the poor of their rights
and withhold justice from the
oppressed of my people,
making widows their prey
and robbing the fatherless.
3 What will you do on the day of
reckoning,
when disaster comes from afar?
To whom will you run for help?
Where will you leave your riches?

[a] 20 Or *arm*

4 Nothing will remain but to cringe
among the captives
or fall among the slain.

Yet for all this, his anger is not turned
away,
his hand is still upraised.

5 "Woe to the Assyrian, the rod of my
anger,
in whose hand is the club of my
wrath!
6 I send him against a godless nation,
I dispatch him against a people who
anger me,
to seize loot and snatch plunder,
and to trample them down like mud
in the streets.
7 But this is not what he intends,
this is not what he has in mind;
his purpose is to destroy,
to put an end to many nations.
8 'Are not my commanders all kings?'
he says.
9 'Has not Kalno fared like
Carchemish?
Is not Hamath like Arpad,
and Samaria like Damascus?
10 As my hand seized the kingdoms of
the idols,
kingdoms whose images excelled
those of Jerusalem and
Samaria—
11 shall I not deal with Jerusalem and
her images
as I dealt with Samaria and her
idols?'"

12 When the Lord has finished all his
work against Mount Zion and Jerusalem, he will say, "I will punish the king of
Assyria for the willful pride of his heart
and the haughty look in his eyes. 13 For
he says:

"'By the strength of my hand I have
done this,
and by my wisdom, because I have
understanding.
I removed the boundaries of nations,
I plundered their treasures;
like a mighty one I subdued[a] their
kings.
14 As one reaches into a nest,
so my hand reached for the wealth
of the nations;
as people gather abandoned eggs,
so I gathered all the countries;
not one flapped a wing,
or opened its mouth to chirp.'"

15 Does the ax raise itself above the
person who swings it,
or the saw boast against the one
who uses it?
As if a rod were to wield the person
who lifts it up,
or a club brandish the one who is
not wood!
16 Therefore, the Lord, the LORD
Almighty,
will send a wasting disease upon his
sturdy warriors;
under his pomp a fire will be kindled
like a blazing flame.
17 The Light of Israel will become a fire,
their Holy One a flame;
in a single day it will burn and
consume
his thorns and his briers.
18 The splendor of his forests and fertile
fields
it will completely destroy,
as when a sick person wastes away.
19 And the remaining trees of his forests
will be so few
that a child could write them
down.

20 In that day the remnant of Israel,
the survivors of Jacob,
will no longer rely on him
who struck them down
but will truly rely on the LORD,
the Holy One of Israel.
21 A remnant will return,[b] a remnant of
Jacob
will return to the Mighty God.
22 Though your people be like the sand
by the sea, Israel,
only a remnant will return.
Destruction has been decreed,
overwhelming and righteous.
23 The Lord, the LORD Almighty, will
carry out
the destruction decreed upon the
whole land.

24 Therefore this is what the Lord, the
LORD Almighty, says:

"My people who live in Zion,
do not be afraid of the Assyrians,
who beat you with a rod

[a] 13 Or *treasures; / I subdued the mighty,*
[b] 21 Hebrew *shear-jashub* (see 7:3 and note); also in verse 22

and lift up a club against you, as
Egypt did.
25 Very soon my anger against you will
end
and my wrath will be directed to
their destruction."
26 The LORD Almighty will lash them
with a whip,
as when he struck down Midian at
the rock of Oreb;
and he will raise his staff over the
waters,
as he did in Egypt.
27 In that day their burden will be lifted
from your shoulders,
their yoke from your neck;
the yoke will be broken
because you have grown so fat.[a]

28 They enter Aiath;
they pass through Migron;
they store supplies at Mikmash.
29 They go over the pass, and say,
"We will camp overnight at Geba."
Ramah trembles;
Gibeah of Saul flees.
30 Cry out, Daughter Gallim!
Listen, Laishah!
Poor Anathoth!
31 Madmenah is in flight;
the people of Gebim take cover.
32 This day they will halt at Nob;
they will shake their fist
at the mount of Daughter Zion,
at the hill of Jerusalem.

33 See, the Lord, the LORD Almighty,
will lop off the boughs with great
power.
The lofty trees will be felled,
the tall ones will be brought low.
34 He will cut down the forest thickets
with an ax;
Lebanon will fall before the Mighty
One.

11 A shoot will come up from the
stump of Jesse;
from his roots a Branch will bear
fruit.
2 The Spirit of the LORD will rest on
him —
the Spirit of wisdom and of
understanding,
the Spirit of counsel and of might,
the Spirit of the knowledge and fear
of the LORD —
3 and he will delight in the fear of the
LORD.

He will not judge by what he sees with
his eyes,
or decide by what he hears with his
ears;
4 but with righteousness he will judge
the needy,
with justice he will give decisions
for the poor of the earth.
He will strike the earth with the rod of
his mouth;
with the breath of his lips he will
slay the wicked.
5 Righteousness will be his belt
and faithfulness the sash around
his waist.

6 The wolf will live with the lamb,
the leopard will lie down with the
goat,
the calf and the lion and the yearling[b]
together;
and a little child will lead them.
7 The cow will feed with the bear,
their young will lie down together,
and the lion will eat straw like the
ox.
8 The infant will play near the cobra's
den,
the young child will put its hand
into the viper's nest.
9 They will neither harm nor destroy
on all my holy mountain,
for the earth will be filled with the
knowledge of the LORD
as the waters cover the sea.

10 In that day the Root of Jesse will
stand as a banner for the peoples; the
nations will rally to him, and his resting
place will be glorious. 11 In that day the
Lord will reach out his hand a second
time to reclaim the surviving remnant
of his people from Assyria, from Lower
Egypt, from Upper Egypt, from Cush,[c]
from Elam, from Babylonia,[d] from Hamath and from the islands of the Mediterranean.

12 He will raise a banner for the nations
and gather the exiles of Israel;
he will assemble the scattered people
of Judah

[a] *27* Hebrew; Septuagint *broken / from your shoulders*
[b] *6* Hebrew; Septuagint *lion will feed*
[c] *11* That is, the upper Nile region
[d] *11* Hebrew *Shinar*

from the four quarters of the earth.
13 Ephraim's jealousy will vanish,
and Judah's enemies[a] will be destroyed;
Ephraim will not be jealous of Judah,
nor Judah hostile toward Ephraim.
14 They will swoop down on the slopes of Philistia to the west;
together they will plunder the people to the east.
They will subdue Edom and Moab,
and the Ammonites will be subject to them.
15 The LORD will dry up
the gulf of the Egyptian sea;
with a scorching wind he will sweep his hand
over the Euphrates River.
He will break it up into seven streams
so that anyone can cross over in sandals.
16 There will be a highway for the remnant of his people
that is left from Assyria,
as there was for Israel
when they came up from Egypt.

12 In that day you will say:

"I will praise you, LORD.
Although you were angry with me,
your anger has turned away
and you have comforted me.
2 Surely God is my salvation;
I will trust and not be afraid.
The LORD, the LORD himself, is my strength and my defense[b];
he has become my salvation."
3 With joy you will draw water
from the wells of salvation.

4 In that day you will say:

"Give praise to the LORD, proclaim his name;
make known among the nations what he has done,
and proclaim that his name is exalted.
5 Sing to the LORD, for he has done glorious things;
let this be known to all the world.
6 Shout aloud and sing for joy, people of Zion,
for great is the Holy One of Israel among you."

13 A prophecy against Babylon that Isaiah son of Amoz saw:

2 Raise a banner on a bare hilltop,
shout to them;
beckon to them
to enter the gates of the nobles.
3 I have commanded those I prepared for battle;
I have summoned my warriors to carry out my wrath —
those who rejoice in my triumph.
4 Listen, a noise on the mountains,
like that of a great multitude!
Listen, an uproar among the kingdoms,
like nations massing together!
The LORD Almighty is mustering
an army for war.
5 They come from faraway lands,
from the ends of the heavens —
the LORD and the weapons of his wrath —
to destroy the whole country.
6 Wail, for the day of the LORD is near;
it will come like destruction from the Almighty.[c]
7 Because of this, all hands will go limp,
every heart will melt with fear.
8 Terror will seize them,
pain and anguish will grip them;
they will writhe like a woman in labor.
They will look aghast at each other,
their faces aflame.

9 See, the day of the LORD is coming
— a cruel day, with wrath and fierce anger —
to make the land desolate
and destroy the sinners within it.
10 The stars of heaven and their constellations
will not show their light.
The rising sun will be darkened
and the moon will not give its light.
11 I will punish the world for its evil,
the wicked for their sins.
I will put an end to the arrogance of the haughty
and will humble the pride of the ruthless.
12 I will make people scarcer than pure gold,
more rare than the gold of Ophir.

[a] 13 Or *hostility* [b] 2 Or *song* [c] 6 Hebrew *Shaddai*

13 Therefore I will make the heavens tremble;
and the earth will shake from its place
at the wrath of the LORD Almighty,
in the day of his burning anger.
14 Like a hunted gazelle,
like sheep without a shepherd,
they will all return to their own people,
they will flee to their native land.
15 Whoever is captured will be thrust through;
all who are caught will fall by the sword.
16 Their infants will be dashed to pieces before their eyes;
their houses will be looted and their wives violated.

17 See, I will stir up against them the Medes,
who do not care for silver
and have no delight in gold.
18 Their bows will strike down the young men;
they will have no mercy on infants,
nor will they look with compassion on children.
19 Babylon, the jewel of kingdoms,
the pride and glory of the Babylonians,[a]
will be overthrown by God
like Sodom and Gomorrah.
20 She will never be inhabited
or lived in through all generations;
there no nomads will pitch their tents,
there no shepherds will rest their flocks.
21 But desert creatures will lie there,
jackals will fill her houses;
there the owls will dwell,
and there the wild goats will leap about.
22 Hyenas will inhabit her strongholds,
jackals her luxurious palaces.
Her time is at hand,
and her days will not be prolonged.

14 The LORD will have compassion on Jacob;
once again he will choose Israel
and will settle them in their own land.
Foreigners will join them
and unite with the descendants of Jacob.
2 Nations will take them
and bring them to their own place.
And Israel will take possession of the nations
and make them male and female servants in the LORD's land.
They will make captives of their captors
and rule over their oppressors.

3 On the day the LORD gives you relief from your suffering and turmoil and from the harsh labor forced on you, 4 you will take up this taunt against the king of Babylon:

How the oppressor has come to an end!
How his fury[b] has ended!
5 The LORD has broken the rod of the wicked,
the scepter of the rulers,
6 which in anger struck down peoples
with unceasing blows,
and in fury subdued nations
with relentless aggression.
7 All the lands are at rest and at peace;
they break into singing.
8 Even the junipers and the cedars of Lebanon
gloat over you and say,
"Now that you have been laid low,
no one comes to cut us down."
9 The realm of the dead below is all astir
to meet you at your coming;
it rouses the spirits of the departed to greet you—
all those who were leaders in the world;
it makes them rise from their thrones—
all those who were kings over the nations.
10 They will all respond,
they will say to you,
"You also have become weak, as we are;
you have become like us."
11 All your pomp has been brought down to the grave,
along with the noise of your harps;
maggots are spread out beneath you
and worms cover you.

[a] 19 Or *Chaldeans* [b] 4 Dead Sea Scrolls, Septuagint and Syriac; the meaning of the word in the Masoretic Text is uncertain.

12 How you have fallen from heaven,
morning star, son of the dawn!
You have been cast down to the earth,
you who once laid low the nations!
13 You said in your heart,
"I will ascend to the heavens;
I will raise my throne
above the stars of God;
I will sit enthroned on the mount of
assembly,
on the utmost heights of Mount
Zaphon.[a]
14 I will ascend above the tops of the
clouds;
I will make myself like the Most
High."
15 But you are brought down to the
realm of the dead,
to the depths of the pit.

16 Those who see you stare at you,
they ponder your fate:
"Is this the man who shook the earth
and made kingdoms tremble,
17 the man who made the world a
wilderness,
who overthrew its cities
and would not let his captives go
home?"

18 All the kings of the nations lie in
state,
each in his own tomb.
19 But you are cast out of your tomb
like a rejected branch;
you are covered with the slain,
with those pierced by the sword,
those who descend to the stones of
the pit.
Like a corpse trampled underfoot,
20 you will not join them in burial,
for you have destroyed your land
and killed your people.

Let the offspring of the wicked
never be mentioned again.
21 Prepare a place to slaughter his
children
for the sins of their ancestors;
they are not to rise to inherit the land
and cover the earth with their
cities.
22 "I will rise up against them,"
declares the LORD Almighty.
"I will wipe out Babylon's name and
survivors,
her offspring and descendants,"
declares the LORD.
23 "I will turn her into a place for owls
and into swampland;
I will sweep her with the broom of
destruction,"
declares the LORD Almighty.

24 The LORD Almighty has sworn,

"Surely, as I have planned, so it will be,
and as I have purposed, so it will
happen.
25 I will crush the Assyrian in my land;
on my mountains I will trample him
down.
His yoke will be taken from my
people,
and his burden removed from their
shoulders."

26 This is the plan determined for the
whole world;
this is the hand stretched out over
all nations.
27 For the LORD Almighty has purposed,
and who can thwart him?
His hand is stretched out, and who
can turn it back?

28 This prophecy came in the year King
Ahaz died:

29 Do not rejoice, all you Philistines,
that the rod that struck you is
broken;
from the root of that snake will spring
up a viper,
its fruit will be a darting, venomous
serpent.
30 The poorest of the poor will find
pasture,
and the needy will lie down in
safety.
But your root I will destroy by famine;
it will slay your survivors.

31 Wail, you gate! Howl, you city!
Melt away, all you Philistines!
A cloud of smoke comes from the
north,
and there is not a straggler in its
ranks.
32 What answer shall be given
to the envoys of that nation?
"The LORD has established Zion,
and in her his afflicted people will
find refuge."

[a] 13 Or *of the north*; Zaphon was the most sacred mountain of the Canaanites.

15 A prophecy against Moab:

Ar in Moab is ruined,
destroyed in a night!
Kir in Moab is ruined,
destroyed in a night!
2 Dibon goes up to its temple,
to its high places to weep;
Moab wails over Nebo and Medeba.
Every head is shaved
and every beard cut off.
3 In the streets they wear sackcloth;
on the roofs and in the public squares
they all wail,
prostrate with weeping.
4 Heshbon and Elealeh cry out,
their voices are heard all the way to Jahaz.
Therefore the armed men of Moab cry out,
and their hearts are faint.
5 My heart cries out over Moab;
her fugitives flee as far as Zoar,
as far as Eglath Shelishiyah.
They go up the hill to Luhith,
weeping as they go;
on the road to Horonaim
they lament their destruction.
6 The waters of Nimrim are dried up
and the grass is withered;
the vegetation is gone
and nothing green is left.
7 So the wealth they have acquired and stored up
they carry away over the Ravine of the Poplars.
8 Their outcry echoes along the border of Moab;
their wailing reaches as far as Eglaim,
their lamentation as far as Beer Elim.
9 The waters of Dimon[a] are full of blood,
but I will bring still more upon Dimon[a] —
a lion upon the fugitives of Moab
and upon those who remain in the land.

16 Send lambs as tribute
to the ruler of the land,
from Sela, across the desert,
to the mount of Daughter Zion.
2 Like fluttering birds
pushed from the nest,
so are the women of Moab
at the fords of the Arnon.

3 "Make up your mind," Moab says.
"Render a decision.
Make your shadow like night —
at high noon.
Hide the fugitives,
do not betray the refugees.
4 Let the Moabite fugitives stay with you;
be their shelter from the destroyer."

The oppressor will come to an end,
and destruction will cease;
the aggressor will vanish from the land.
5 In love a throne will be established;
in faithfulness a man will sit on it —
one from the house[b] of David —
one who in judging seeks justice
and speeds the cause of righteousness.

6 We have heard of Moab's pride —
how great is her arrogance! —
of her conceit, her pride and her insolence;
but her boasts are empty.
7 Therefore the Moabites wail,
they wail together for Moab.
Lament and grieve
for the raisin cakes of Kir Hareseth.
8 The fields of Heshbon wither,
the vines of Sibmah also.
The rulers of the nations
have trampled down the choicest vines,
which once reached Jazer
and spread toward the desert.
Their shoots spread out
and went as far as the sea.[c]
9 So I weep, as Jazer weeps,
for the vines of Sibmah.
Heshbon and Elealeh,
I drench you with tears!
The shouts of joy over your ripened fruit
and over your harvests have been stilled.
10 Joy and gladness are taken away from the orchards;
no one sings or shouts in the vineyards;

[a] 9 *Dimon*, a wordplay on *Dibon* (see verse 2), sounds like the Hebrew for *blood*.
[b] 5 Hebrew *tent*
[c] 8 Probably the Dead Sea

no one treads out wine at the presses,
for I have put an end to the
shouting.
11 My heart laments for Moab like a
harp,
my inmost being for Kir Hareseth.
12 When Moab appears at her high place,
she only wears herself out;
when she goes to her shrine to pray,
it is to no avail.

13 This is the word the LORD has already spoken concerning Moab. 14 But
now the LORD says: "Within three years,
as a servant bound by contract would
count them, Moab's splendor and all her
many people will be despised, and her
survivors will be very few and feeble."

17 A prophecy against Damascus:

"See, Damascus will no longer be a
city
but will become a heap of ruins.
2 The cities of Aroer will be deserted
and left to flocks, which will lie
down,
with no one to make them afraid.
3 The fortified city will disappear from
Ephraim,
and royal power from Damascus;
the remnant of Aram will be
like the glory of the Israelites,"
declares the LORD Almighty.

4 "In that day the glory of Jacob will fade;
the fat of his body will waste away.
5 It will be as when reapers harvest the
standing grain,
gathering the grain in their arms —
as when someone gleans heads of
grain
in the Valley of Rephaim.
6 Yet some gleanings will remain,
as when an olive tree is beaten,
leaving two or three olives on the
topmost branches,
four or five on the fruitful boughs,"
declares the LORD, the God
of Israel.

7 In that day people will look to their
Maker
and turn their eyes to the Holy One
of Israel.
8 They will not look to the altars,
the work of their hands,
and they will have no regard for the
Asherah poles[a]
and the incense altars their fingers
have made.

9 In that day their strong cities, which
they left because of the Israelites, will be
like places abandoned to thickets and
undergrowth. And all will be desolation.

10 You have forgotten God your Savior;
you have not remembered the Rock,
your fortress.
Therefore, though you set out the
finest plants
and plant imported vines,
11 though on the day you set them out,
you make them grow,
and on the morning when you plant
them, you bring them to bud,
yet the harvest will be as nothing
in the day of disease and incurable
pain.

12 Woe to the many nations that rage —
they rage like the raging sea!
Woe to the peoples who roar —
they roar like the roaring of great
waters!
13 Although the peoples roar like the
roar of surging waters,
when he rebukes them they flee far
away,
driven before the wind like chaff on
the hills,
like tumbleweed before a gale.
14 In the evening, sudden terror!
Before the morning, they are gone!
This is the portion of those who loot us,
the lot of those who plunder us.

18 Woe to the land of whirring wings[b]
along the rivers of Cush,[c]
2 which sends envoys by sea
in papyrus boats over the water.

Go, swift messengers,
to a people tall and smooth-skinned,
to a people feared far and wide,
an aggressive nation of strange
speech,
whose land is divided by rivers.

3 All you people of the world,
you who live on the earth,
when a banner is raised on the
mountains,
you will see it,

[a] *8* That is, wooden symbols of the goddess Asherah [b] *1* Or *of locusts* [c] *1* That is, the upper Nile region

and when a trumpet sounds,
you will hear it.
4 This is what the LORD says to me:
"I will remain quiet and will look on
from my dwelling place,
like shimmering heat in the sunshine,
like a cloud of dew in the heat of
harvest."
5 For, before the harvest, when the
blossom is gone
and the flower becomes a ripening
grape,
he will cut off the shoots with pruning
knives,
and cut down and take away the
spreading branches.
6 They will all be left to the mountain
birds of prey
and to the wild animals;
the birds will feed on them all
summer,
the wild animals all winter.

7 At that time gifts will be brought to the LORD Almighty

from a people tall and smooth-
skinned,
from a people feared far and wide,
an aggressive nation of strange
speech,
whose land is divided by rivers—

the gifts will be brought to Mount Zion, the place of the Name of the LORD Almighty.

19

A prophecy against Egypt:

See, the LORD rides on a swift cloud
and is coming to Egypt.
The idols of Egypt tremble before him,
and the hearts of the Egyptians melt
with fear.

2 "I will stir up Egyptian against
Egyptian—
brother will fight against brother,
neighbor against neighbor,
city against city,
kingdom against kingdom.
3 The Egyptians will lose heart,
and I will bring their plans to
nothing;
they will consult the idols and the
spirits of the dead,
the mediums and the spiritists.
4 I will hand the Egyptians over
to the power of a cruel master,
and a fierce king will rule over them,"
declares the Lord, the LORD
Almighty.

5 The waters of the river will dry up,
and the riverbed will be parched
and dry.
6 The canals will stink;
the streams of Egypt will dwindle
and dry up.
The reeds and rushes will wither,
7 also the plants along the Nile,
at the mouth of the river.
Every sown field along the Nile
will become parched, will blow
away and be no more.
8 The fishermen will groan and lament,
all who cast hooks into the Nile;
those who throw nets on the water
will pine away.
9 Those who work with combed flax
will despair,
the weavers of fine linen will lose
hope.
10 The workers in cloth will be dejected,
and all the wage earners will be sick
at heart.

11 The officials of Zoan are nothing but
fools;
the wise counselors of Pharaoh give
senseless advice.
How can you say to Pharaoh,
"I am one of the wise men,
a disciple of the ancient kings"?

12 Where are your wise men now?
Let them show you and make
known
what the LORD Almighty
has planned against Egypt.
13 The officials of Zoan have become
fools,
the leaders of Memphis are
deceived;
the cornerstones of her peoples
have led Egypt astray.
14 The LORD has poured into them
a spirit of dizziness;
they make Egypt stagger in all that
she does,
as a drunkard staggers around in
his vomit.
15 There is nothing Egypt can do—
head or tail, palm branch or reed.

16 In that day the Egyptians will become weaklings. They will shudder with fear at the uplifted hand that the LORD Almighty raises against them. 17 And the land of Ju-

dah will bring terror to the Egyptians; everyone to whom Judah is mentioned will
be terrified, because of what the LORD Almighty is planning against them.
18 In that day five cities in Egypt will
speak the language of Canaan and swear
allegiance to the LORD Almighty. One of
them will be called the City of the Sun.[a]
19 In that day there will be an altar to the
LORD in the heart of Egypt, and a monument to the LORD at its border. 20 It will be
a sign and witness to the LORD Almighty
in the land of Egypt. When they cry out to
the LORD because of their oppressors, he
will send them a savior and defender, and
he will rescue them. 21 So the LORD will
make himself known to the Egyptians,
and in that day they will acknowledge
the LORD. They will worship with sacrifices and grain offerings; they will make
vows to the LORD and keep them. 22 The
LORD will strike Egypt with a plague; he
will strike them and heal them. They will
turn to the LORD, and he will respond to
their pleas and heal them.
23 In that day there will be a highway
from Egypt to Assyria. The Assyrians will
go to Egypt and the Egyptians to Assyria.
The Egyptians and Assyrians will worship together. 24 In that day Israel will be
the third, along with Egypt and Assyria,
a blessing[b] on the earth. 25 The LORD Almighty will bless them, saying, "Blessed
be Egypt my people, Assyria my handiwork, and Israel my inheritance."

20 In the year that the supreme commander, sent by Sargon king of
Assyria, came to Ashdod and attacked
and captured it— 2 at that time the LORD
spoke through Isaiah son of Amoz. He
said to him, "Take off the sackcloth
from your body and the sandals from
your feet." And he did so, going around
stripped and barefoot.
3 Then the LORD said, "Just as my servant Isaiah has gone stripped and barefoot for three years, as a sign and portent
against Egypt and Cush,[c] 4 so the king of
Assyria will lead away stripped and barefoot the Egyptian captives and Cushite exiles, young and old, with buttocks
bared—to Egypt's shame. 5 Those who
trusted in Cush and boasted in Egypt
will be dismayed and put to shame. 6 In
that day the people who live on this coast
will say, 'See what has happened to those
we relied on, those we fled to for help and
deliverance from the king of Assyria!
How then can we escape?'"

21 A prophecy against the Desert by
the Sea:

Like whirlwinds sweeping through
the southland,
an invader comes from the desert,
from a land of terror.

2 A dire vision has been shown to me:
The traitor betrays, the looter takes
loot.
Elam, attack! Media, lay siege!
I will bring to an end all the
groaning she caused.

3 At this my body is racked with pain,
pangs seize me, like those of a
woman in labor;
I am staggered by what I hear,
I am bewildered by what I see.
4 My heart falters,
fear makes me tremble;
the twilight I longed for
has become a horror to me.

5 They set the tables,
they spread the rugs,
they eat, they drink!
Get up, you officers,
oil the shields!

6 This is what the Lord says to me:

"Go, post a lookout
and have him report what he sees.
7 When he sees chariots
with teams of horses,
riders on donkeys
or riders on camels,
let him be alert,
fully alert."

8 And the lookout[d] shouted,

"Day after day, my lord, I stand on the
watchtower;
every night I stay at my post.
9 Look, here comes a man in a chariot
with a team of horses.
And he gives back the answer:

[a] *18* Some manuscripts of the Masoretic Text, Dead Sea Scrolls, Symmachus and Vulgate; most manuscripts of the Masoretic Text *City of Destruction* [b] *24* Or *Assyria, whose names will be used in blessings* (see Gen. 48:20); or *Assyria, who will be seen by others as blessed* [c] *3* That is, the upper Nile region; also in verse 5
[d] *8* Dead Sea Scrolls and Syriac; Masoretic Text *A lion*

'Babylon has fallen, has fallen!
All the images of its gods
lie shattered on the ground!'"
10 My people who are crushed on the threshing floor,
I tell you what I have heard
from the LORD Almighty,
from the God of Israel.

11 A prophecy against Dumah[a]:

Someone calls to me from Seir,
"Watchman, what is left of the night?
Watchman, what is left of the night?"
12 The watchman replies,
"Morning is coming, but also the night.
If you would ask, then ask;
and come back yet again."

13 A prophecy against Arabia:

You caravans of Dedanites,
who camp in the thickets of Arabia,
14 bring water for the thirsty;
you who live in Tema,
bring food for the fugitives.
15 They flee from the sword,
from the drawn sword,
from the bent bow
and from the heat of battle.

16 This is what the Lord says to me:
"Within one year, as a servant bound by
contract would count it, all the splendor
of Kedar will come to an end. 17 The survivors of the archers, the warriors of Kedar, will be few." The LORD, the God of
Israel, has spoken.

22 A prophecy against the Valley of Vision:

What troubles you now,
that you have all gone up on the roofs,
2 you town so full of commotion,
you city of tumult and revelry?
Your slain were not killed by the sword,
nor did they die in battle.
3 All your leaders have fled together;
they have been captured without using the bow.
All you who were caught were taken prisoner together,
having fled while the enemy was still far away.
4 Therefore I said, "Turn away from me;
let me weep bitterly.
Do not try to console me
over the destruction of my people."
5 The Lord, the LORD Almighty, has a day
of tumult and trampling and terror
in the Valley of Vision,
a day of battering down walls
and of crying out to the mountains.
6 Elam takes up the quiver,
with her charioteers and horses;
Kir uncovers the shield.
7 Your choicest valleys are full of chariots,
and horsemen are posted at the city gates.
8 The Lord stripped away the defenses of Judah,
and you looked in that day
to the weapons in the Palace of the Forest.
9 You saw that the walls of the City of David
were broken through in many places;
you stored up water
in the Lower Pool.
10 You counted the buildings in Jerusalem
and tore down houses to strengthen the wall.
11 You built a reservoir between the two walls
for the water of the Old Pool,
but you did not look to the One who made it,
or have regard for the One who planned it long ago.
12 The Lord, the LORD Almighty,
called you on that day
to weep and to wail,
to tear out your hair and put on sackcloth.
13 But see, there is joy and revelry,
slaughtering of cattle and killing of sheep,
eating of meat and drinking of wine!
"Let us eat and drink," you say,
"for tomorrow we die!"

14 The LORD Almighty has revealed this
in my hearing: "Till your dying day this

[a] 11 *Dumah*, a wordplay on *Edom*, means *silence* or *stillness*.

sin will not be atoned for," says the Lord, the LORD Almighty.

15 This is what the Lord, the LORD Almighty, says:

"Go, say to this steward,
to Shebna the palace administrator:
16 What are you doing here and who gave you permission
to cut out a grave for yourself here,
hewing your grave on the height
and chiseling your resting place in the rock?
17 "Beware, the LORD is about to take firm hold of you
and hurl you away, you mighty man.
18 He will roll you up tightly like a ball
and throw you into a large country.
There you will die
and there the chariots you were so proud of
will become a disgrace to your master's house.
19 I will depose you from your office,
and you will be ousted from your position.

20 "In that day I will summon my servant, Eliakim son of Hilkiah. 21 I will clothe him with your robe and fasten your sash around him and hand your authority over to him. He will be a father to those who live in Jerusalem and to the people of Judah. 22 I will place on his shoulder the key to the house of David; what he opens no one can shut, and what he shuts no one can open. 23 I will drive him like a peg into a firm place; he will become a seat[a] of honor for the house of his father. 24 All the glory of his family will hang on him: its offspring and offshoots—all its lesser vessels, from the bowls to all the jars.

25 "In that day," declares the LORD Almighty, "the peg driven into the firm place will give way; it will be sheared off and will fall, and the load hanging on it will be cut down." The LORD has spoken.

23 A prophecy against Tyre:

Wail, you ships of Tarshish!
For Tyre is destroyed
and left without house or harbor.
From the land of Cyprus
word has come to them.

2 Be silent, you people of the island
and you merchants of Sidon,
whom the seafarers have enriched.
3 On the great waters
came the grain of the Shihor;
the harvest of the Nile[b] was the revenue of Tyre,
and she became the marketplace of the nations.

4 Be ashamed, Sidon, and you fortress of the sea,
for the sea has spoken:
"I have neither been in labor nor given birth;
I have neither reared sons nor brought up daughters."
5 When word comes to Egypt,
they will be in anguish at the report from Tyre.

6 Cross over to Tarshish;
wail, you people of the island.
7 Is this your city of revelry,
the old, old city,
whose feet have taken her
to settle in far-off lands?
8 Who planned this against Tyre,
the bestower of crowns,
whose merchants are princes,
whose traders are renowned in the earth?
9 The LORD Almighty planned it,
to bring down her pride in all her splendor
and to humble all who are renowned on the earth.

10 Till[c] your land as they do along the Nile,
Daughter Tarshish,
for you no longer have a harbor.
11 The LORD has stretched out his hand over the sea
and made its kingdoms tremble.
He has given an order concerning Phoenicia
that her fortresses be destroyed.
12 He said, "No more of your reveling,
Virgin Daughter Sidon, now crushed!

[a] 23 Or *throne* [b] 2,3 Masoretic Text; Dead Sea Scrolls *Sidon, / who cross over the sea; / your envoys 3are on the great waters. / The grain of the Shihor, / the harvest of the Nile,* [c] 10 Dead Sea Scrolls and some Septuagint manuscripts; Masoretic Text *Go through*

"Up, cross over to Cyprus;
even there you will find no rest."
13 Look at the land of the Babylonians,[a]
this people that is now of no account!
The Assyrians have made it
a place for desert creatures;
they raised up their siege towers,
they stripped its fortresses bare
and turned it into a ruin.

14 Wail, you ships of Tarshish;
your fortress is destroyed!

15 At that time Tyre will be forgotten for seventy years, the span of a king's life. But at the end of these seventy years, it will happen to Tyre as in the song of the prostitute:

16 "Take up a harp, walk through the city,
you forgotten prostitute;
play the harp well, sing many a song,
so that you will be remembered."

17 At the end of seventy years, the LORD will deal with Tyre. She will return to her lucrative prostitution and will ply her trade with all the kingdoms on the face of the earth.
18 Yet her profit and her earnings will be set apart for the LORD; they will not be stored up or hoarded. Her profits will go to those who live before the LORD, for abundant food and fine clothes.

24

See, the LORD is going to lay waste the earth
and devastate it;
he will ruin its face
and scatter its inhabitants—
2 it will be the same
for priest as for people,
for the master as for his servant,
for the mistress as for her servant,
for seller as for buyer,
for borrower as for lender,
for debtor as for creditor.
3 The earth will be completely laid waste
and totally plundered.
The LORD has spoken this word.

4 The earth dries up and withers,
the world languishes and withers,
the heavens languish with the earth.
5 The earth is defiled by its people;
they have disobeyed the laws,
violated the statutes
and broken the everlasting covenant.
6 Therefore a curse consumes the earth;
its people must bear their guilt.
Therefore earth's inhabitants are burned up,
and very few are left.
7 The new wine dries up and the vine withers;
all the merrymakers groan.
8 The joyful timbrels are stilled,
the noise of the revelers has stopped,
the joyful harp is silent.
9 No longer do they drink wine with a song;
the beer is bitter to its drinkers.
10 The ruined city lies desolate;
the entrance to every house is barred.
11 In the streets they cry out for wine;
all joy turns to gloom,
all joyful sounds are banished from the earth.
12 The city is left in ruins,
its gate is battered to pieces.
13 So will it be on the earth
and among the nations,
as when an olive tree is beaten,
or as when gleanings are left after the grape harvest.

14 They raise their voices, they shout for joy;
from the west they acclaim the LORD's majesty.
15 Therefore in the east give glory to the LORD;
exalt the name of the LORD, the God of Israel,
in the islands of the sea.
16 From the ends of the earth we hear singing:
"Glory to the Righteous One."
But I said, "I waste away, I waste away!
Woe to me!
The treacherous betray!
With treachery the treacherous betray!"
17 Terror and pit and snare await you,
people of the earth.
18 Whoever flees at the sound of terror
will fall into a pit;

[a] 13 Or *Chaldeans*

whoever climbs out of the pit
will be caught in a snare.

The floodgates of the heavens are opened,
the foundations of the earth shake.
19 The earth is broken up,
the earth is split asunder,
the earth is violently shaken.
20 The earth reels like a drunkard,
it sways like a hut in the wind;
so heavy upon it is the guilt of its rebellion
that it falls — never to rise again.

21 In that day the LORD will punish
the powers in the heavens above
and the kings on the earth below.
22 They will be herded together
like prisoners bound in a dungeon;
they will be shut up in prison
and be punished[a] after many days.
23 The moon will be dismayed,
the sun ashamed;
for the LORD Almighty will reign
on Mount Zion and in Jerusalem,
and before its elders — with great glory.

25 LORD, you are my God;
I will exalt you and praise your name,
for in perfect faithfulness
you have done wonderful things,
things planned long ago.
2 You have made the city a heap of rubble,
the fortified town a ruin,
the foreigners' stronghold a city no more;
it will never be rebuilt.
3 Therefore strong peoples will honor you;
cities of ruthless nations will revere you.
4 You have been a refuge for the poor,
a refuge for the needy in their distress,
a shelter from the storm
and a shade from the heat.
For the breath of the ruthless
is like a storm driving against a wall
5 and like the heat of the desert.
You silence the uproar of foreigners;
as heat is reduced by the shadow of a cloud,
so the song of the ruthless is stilled.

6 On this mountain the LORD Almighty will prepare
a feast of rich food for all peoples,
a banquet of aged wine —
the best of meats and the finest of wines.
7 On this mountain he will destroy
the shroud that enfolds all peoples,
the sheet that covers all nations;
8 he will swallow up death forever.
The Sovereign LORD will wipe away the tears
from all faces;
he will remove his people's disgrace
from all the earth.
The LORD has spoken.

9 In that day they will say,
"Surely this is our God;
we trusted in him, and he saved us.
This is the LORD, we trusted in him;
let us rejoice and be glad in his salvation."

10 The hand of the LORD will rest on this mountain;
but Moab will be trampled in their land
as straw is trampled down in the manure.
11 They will stretch out their hands in it,
as swimmers stretch out their hands to swim.
God will bring down their pride
despite the cleverness[b] of their hands.
12 He will bring down your high fortified walls
and lay them low;
he will bring them down to the ground,
to the very dust.

26 In that day this song will be sung in the land of Judah:

We have a strong city;
God makes salvation
its walls and ramparts.
2 Open the gates
that the righteous nation may enter,
the nation that keeps faith.
3 You will keep in perfect peace
those whose minds are steadfast,
because they trust in you.
4 Trust in the LORD forever,

[a] 22 Or *released* [b] 11 The meaning of the Hebrew for this word is uncertain.

for the LORD, the LORD himself, is
the Rock eternal.
5 He humbles those who dwell on high,
he lays the lofty city low;
he levels it to the ground
and casts it down to the dust.
6 Feet trample it down—
the feet of the oppressed,
the footsteps of the poor.

7 The path of the righteous is level;
you, the Upright One, make the way
of the righteous smooth.
8 Yes, LORD, walking in the way of your
laws,[a]
we wait for you;
your name and renown
are the desire of our hearts.
9 My soul yearns for you in the night;
in the morning my spirit longs for
you.
When your judgments come upon the
earth,
the people of the world learn
righteousness.
10 But when grace is shown to the wicked,
they do not learn righteousness;
even in a land of uprightness they go
on doing evil
and do not regard the majesty of the
LORD.
11 LORD, your hand is lifted high,
but they do not see it.
Let them see your zeal for your people
and be put to shame;
let the fire reserved for your
enemies consume them.
12 LORD, you establish peace for us;
all that we have accomplished you
have done for us.
13 LORD our God, other lords besides you
have ruled over us,
but your name alone do we honor.
14 They are now dead, they live no more;
their spirits do not rise.
You punished them and brought them
to ruin;
you wiped out all memory of them.
15 You have enlarged the nation, LORD;
you have enlarged the nation.
You have gained glory for yourself;
you have extended all the borders of
the land.

16 LORD, they came to you in their
distress;
when you disciplined them,
they could barely whisper a prayer.[b]
17 As a pregnant woman about to give
birth
writhes and cries out in her pain,
so were we in your presence, LORD.
18 We were with child, we writhed in
labor,
but we gave birth to wind.
We have not brought salvation to the
earth,
and the people of the world have not
come to life.

19 But your dead will live, LORD;
their bodies will rise—
let those who dwell in the dust
wake up and shout for joy—
your dew is like the dew of the
morning;
the earth will give birth to her dead.
20 Go, my people, enter your rooms
and shut the doors behind you;
hide yourselves for a little while
until his wrath has passed by.
21 See, the LORD is coming out of his
dwelling
to punish the people of the earth for
their sins.
The earth will disclose the blood shed
on it;
the earth will conceal its slain no
longer.

27 In that day,

the LORD will punish with his
sword—
his fierce, great and powerful
sword—
Leviathan the gliding serpent,
Leviathan the coiling serpent;
he will slay the monster of the sea.

2 In that day—

"Sing about a fruitful vineyard:
3 I, the LORD, watch over it;
I water it continually.
I guard it day and night
so that no one may harm it.
4 I am not angry.
If only there were briers and thorns
confronting me!
I would march against them in
battle;
I would set them all on fire.

[a] 8 Or *judgments* [b] 16 The meaning of the Hebrew for this clause is uncertain.

5 Or else let them come to me for refuge;
let them make peace with me,
yes, let them make peace with me."

6 In days to come Jacob will take root,
Israel will bud and blossom
and fill all the world with fruit.

7 Has the LORD struck her
as he struck down those who struck her?
Has she been killed
as those were killed who killed her?
8 By warfare[a] and exile you contend with her—
with his fierce blast he drives her out,
as on a day the east wind blows.
9 By this, then, will Jacob's guilt be atoned for,
and this will be the full fruit of the removal of his sin:
When he makes all the altar stones
to be like limestone crushed to pieces,
no Asherah poles[b] or incense altars
will be left standing.
10 The fortified city stands desolate,
an abandoned settlement, forsaken like the wilderness;
there the calves graze,
there they lie down;
they strip its branches bare.
11 When its twigs are dry, they are broken off
and women come and make fires with them.
For this is a people without understanding;
so their Maker has no compassion on them,
and their Creator shows them no favor.

12 In that day the LORD will thresh
from the flowing Euphrates to the Wadi
of Egypt, and you, Israel, will be gathered up one by one. 13 And in that day a
great trumpet will sound. Those who
were perishing in Assyria and those who
were exiled in Egypt will come and worship the LORD on the holy mountain in
Jerusalem.

28 Woe to that wreath, the pride of Ephraim's drunkards,
to the fading flower, his glorious beauty,
set on the head of a fertile valley—
to that city, the pride of those laid low by wine!
2 See, the Lord has one who is powerful and strong.
Like a hailstorm and a destructive wind,
like a driving rain and a flooding downpour,
he will throw it forcefully to the ground.
3 That wreath, the pride of Ephraim's drunkards,
will be trampled underfoot.
4 That fading flower, his glorious beauty,
set on the head of a fertile valley,
will be like figs ripe before harvest—
as soon as people see them and take them in hand,
they swallow them.

5 In that day the LORD Almighty
will be a glorious crown,
a beautiful wreath
for the remnant of his people.
6 He will be a spirit of justice
to the one who sits in judgment,
a source of strength
to those who turn back the battle at the gate.
7 And these also stagger from wine
and reel from beer:
Priests and prophets stagger from beer
and are befuddled with wine;
they reel from beer,
they stagger when seeing visions,
they stumble when rendering decisions.
8 All the tables are covered with vomit
and there is not a spot without filth.

9 "Who is it he is trying to teach?
To whom is he explaining his message?
To children weaned from their milk,
to those just taken from the breast?
10 For it is:
Do this, do that,
a rule for this, a rule for that[c];
a little here, a little there."

[a] *8* See Septuagint; the meaning of the Hebrew for this word is uncertain. [b] *9* That is, wooden symbols of the goddess Asherah [c] *10* Hebrew / *sav lasav sav lasav / kav lakav kav lakav* (probably meaningless sounds mimicking the prophet's words); also in verse 13

11 Very well then, with foreign lips and strange tongues
God will speak to this people,
12 to whom he said,
"This is the resting place, let the weary rest";
and, "This is the place of repose" —
but they would not listen.
13 So then, the word of the LORD to them will become:
Do this, do that,
a rule for this, a rule for that;
a little here, a little there —
so that as they go they will fall backward;
they will be injured and snared and captured.

14 Therefore hear the word of the LORD, you scoffers
who rule this people in Jerusalem.
15 You boast, "We have entered into a covenant with death,
with the realm of the dead we have made an agreement.
When an overwhelming scourge sweeps by,
it cannot touch us,
for we have made a lie our refuge
and falsehood[a] our hiding place."

16 So this is what the Sovereign LORD says:

"See, I lay a stone in Zion, a tested stone,
a precious cornerstone for a sure foundation;
the one who relies on it
will never be stricken with panic.
17 I will make justice the measuring line
and righteousness the plumb line;
hail will sweep away your refuge, the lie,
and water will overflow your hiding place.
18 Your covenant with death will be annulled;
your agreement with the realm of the dead will not stand.
When the overwhelming scourge sweeps by,
you will be beaten down by it.
19 As often as it comes it will carry you away;
morning after morning, by day and by night,
it will sweep through."

The understanding of this message will bring sheer terror.
20 The bed is too short to stretch out on,
the blanket too narrow to wrap around you.
21 The LORD will rise up as he did at Mount Perazim,
he will rouse himself as in the Valley of Gibeon —
to do his work, his strange work,
and perform his task, his alien task.
22 Now stop your mocking,
or your chains will become heavier;
the Lord, the LORD Almighty, has told me
of the destruction decreed against the whole land.

23 Listen and hear my voice;
pay attention and hear what I say.
24 When a farmer plows for planting,
does he plow continually?
Does he keep on breaking up and working the soil?
25 When he has leveled the surface,
does he not sow caraway and scatter cumin?
Does he not plant wheat in its place,[b]
barley in its plot,[b]
and spelt in its field?
26 His God instructs him
and teaches him the right way.

27 Caraway is not threshed with a sledge,
nor is the wheel of a cart rolled over cumin;
caraway is beaten out with a rod,
and cumin with a stick.
28 Grain must be ground to make bread;
so one does not go on threshing it forever.
The wheels of a threshing cart may be rolled over it,
but one does not use horses to grind grain.
29 All this also comes from the LORD Almighty,
whose plan is wonderful,
whose wisdom is magnificent.

29 Woe to you, Ariel, Ariel,
the city where David settled!
Add year to year
and let your cycle of festivals go on.
2 Yet I will besiege Ariel;
she will mourn and lament,

[a] 15 Or *false gods* [b] 25 The meaning of the Hebrew for this word is uncertain.

she will be to me like an altar hearth.[a]
3 I will encamp against you on all sides;
I will encircle you with towers
and set up my siege works against you.
4 Brought low, you will speak from the ground;
your speech will mumble out of the dust.
Your voice will come ghostlike from the earth;
out of the dust your speech will whisper.

5 But your many enemies will become like fine dust,
the ruthless hordes like blown chaff.
Suddenly, in an instant,
6 the LORD Almighty will come
with thunder and earthquake and great noise,
with windstorm and tempest and flames of a devouring fire.
7 Then the hordes of all the nations that fight against Ariel,
that attack her and her fortress and besiege her,
will be as it is with a dream,
with a vision in the night—
8 as when a hungry person dreams of eating,
but awakens hungry still;
as when a thirsty person dreams of drinking,
but awakens faint and thirsty still.
So will it be with the hordes of all the nations
that fight against Mount Zion.

9 Be stunned and amazed,
blind yourselves and be sightless;
be drunk, but not from wine,
stagger, but not from beer.
10 The LORD has brought over you a deep sleep:
He has sealed your eyes (the prophets);
he has covered your heads (the seers).

11 For you this whole vision is nothing
but words sealed in a scroll. And if you
give the scroll to someone who can read,
and say, "Read this, please," they will answer, "I can't; it is sealed."
12 Or if you give
the scroll to someone who cannot read,
and say, "Read this, please," they will answer, "I don't know how to read."

13 The Lord says:

"These people come near to me with their mouth
and honor me with their lips,
but their hearts are far from me.
Their worship of me
is based on merely human rules
they have been taught.[b]
14 Therefore once more I will astound these people
with wonder upon wonder;
the wisdom of the wise will perish,
the intelligence of the intelligent will vanish."
15 Woe to those who go to great depths
to hide their plans from the LORD,
who do their work in darkness and think,
"Who sees us? Who will know?"
16 You turn things upside down,
as if the potter were thought to be like the clay!
Shall what is formed say to the one who formed it,
"You did not make me"?
Can the pot say to the potter,
"You know nothing"?

17 In a very short time, will not Lebanon be turned into a fertile field
and the fertile field seem like a forest?
18 In that day the deaf will hear the words of the scroll,
and out of gloom and darkness
the eyes of the blind will see.
19 Once more the humble will rejoice in the LORD;
the needy will rejoice in the Holy One of Israel.
20 The ruthless will vanish,
the mockers will disappear,
and all who have an eye for evil will be cut down—
21 those who with a word make someone out to be guilty,
who ensnare the defender in court
and with false testimony deprive the innocent of justice.

22 Therefore this is what the LORD, who
redeemed Abraham, says to the descendants of Jacob:

[a] 2 The Hebrew for *altar hearth* sounds like the Hebrew for *Ariel*. [b] 13 Hebrew; Septuagint *They worship me in vain; / their teachings are merely human rules*

"No longer will Jacob be ashamed;
no longer will their faces grow pale.
23 When they see among them their children,
the work of my hands,
they will keep my name holy;
they will acknowledge the holiness of the Holy One of Jacob,
and will stand in awe of the God of Israel.
24 Those who are wayward in spirit will gain understanding;
those who complain will accept instruction."

30 "Woe to the obstinate children,"
declares the LORD,
"to those who carry out plans that are not mine,
forming an alliance, but not by my Spirit,
heaping sin upon sin;
2 who go down to Egypt
without consulting me;
who look for help to Pharaoh's protection,
to Egypt's shade for refuge.
3 But Pharaoh's protection will be to your shame,
Egypt's shade will bring you disgrace.
4 Though they have officials in Zoan
and their envoys have arrived in Hanes,
5 everyone will be put to shame
because of a people useless to them,
who bring neither help nor advantage,
but only shame and disgrace."

6 A prophecy concerning the animals of the Negev:

Through a land of hardship and distress,
of lions and lionesses,
of adders and darting snakes,
the envoys carry their riches on donkeys' backs,
their treasures on the humps of camels,
to that unprofitable nation,
7 to Egypt, whose help is utterly useless.
Therefore I call her
Rahab the Do-Nothing.

8 Go now, write it on a tablet for them,
inscribe it on a scroll,
that for the days to come
it may be an everlasting witness.
9 For these are rebellious people,
deceitful children,
children unwilling to listen to the LORD's instruction.
10 They say to the seers,
"See no more visions!"
and to the prophets,
"Give us no more visions of what is right!
Tell us pleasant things,
prophesy illusions.
11 Leave this way,
get off this path,
and stop confronting us
with the Holy One of Israel!"

12 Therefore this is what the Holy One of Israel says:

"Because you have rejected this message,
relied on oppression
and depended on deceit,
13 this sin will become for you
like a high wall, cracked and bulging,
that collapses suddenly, in an instant.
14 It will break in pieces like pottery,
shattered so mercilessly
that among its pieces not a fragment will be found
for taking coals from a hearth
or scooping water out of a cistern."

15 This is what the Sovereign LORD, the Holy One of Israel, says:

"In repentance and rest is your salvation,
in quietness and trust is your strength,
but you would have none of it.
16 You said, 'No, we will flee on horses.'
Therefore you will flee!
You said, 'We will ride off on swift horses.'
Therefore your pursuers will be swift!
17 A thousand will flee
at the threat of one;
at the threat of five
you will all flee away,
till you are left
like a flagstaff on a mountaintop,
like a banner on a hill."

18 Yet the LORD longs to be gracious to you;

therefore he will rise up to show you
compassion.
For the LORD is a God of justice.
Blessed are all who wait for him!

19 People of Zion, who live in Jerusalem, you will weep no more. How gracious he will be when you cry for help!
As soon as he hears, he will answer you.
20 Although the Lord gives you the bread
of adversity and the water of affliction,
your teachers will be hidden no more;
with your own eyes you will see them.
21 Whether you turn to the right or to the
left, your ears will hear a voice behind
you, saying, "This is the way; walk in
it." 22 Then you will desecrate your idols
overlaid with silver and your images covered with gold; you will throw them away
like a menstrual cloth and say to them,
"Away with you!"

23 He will also send you rain for the
seed you sow in the ground, and the food
that comes from the land will be rich
and plentiful. In that day your cattle will
graze in broad meadows. 24 The oxen and
donkeys that work the soil will eat fodder and mash, spread out with fork and
shovel. 25 In the day of great slaughter,
when the towers fall, streams of water
will flow on every high mountain and every lofty hill. 26 The moon will shine like
the sun, and the sunlight will be seven
times brighter, like the light of seven full
days, when the LORD binds up the bruises of his people and heals the wounds he
inflicted.

27 See, the Name of the LORD comes
from afar,
with burning anger and dense
clouds of smoke;
his lips are full of wrath,
and his tongue is a consuming
fire.
28 His breath is like a rushing torrent,
rising up to the neck.
He shakes the nations in the sieve of
destruction;
he places in the jaws of the peoples
a bit that leads them astray.
29 And you will sing
as on the night you celebrate a holy
festival;
your hearts will rejoice
as when people playing pipes go up
to the mountain of the LORD,
to the Rock of Israel.
30 The LORD will cause people to hear
his majestic voice
and will make them see his arm
coming down
with raging anger and consuming
fire,
with cloudburst, thunderstorm and
hail.
31 The voice of the LORD will shatter
Assyria;
with his rod he will strike them
down.
32 Every stroke the LORD lays on them
with his punishing club
will be to the music of timbrels and
harps,
as he fights them in battle with the
blows of his arm.
33 Topheth has long been prepared;
it has been made ready for the king.
Its fire pit has been made deep and
wide,
with an abundance of fire and
wood;
the breath of the LORD,
like a stream of burning sulfur,
sets it ablaze.

31 Woe to those who go down to Egypt
for help,
who rely on horses,
who trust in the multitude of their
chariots
and in the great strength of their
horsemen,
but do not look to the Holy One of
Israel,
or seek help from the LORD.
2 Yet he too is wise and can bring
disaster;
he does not take back his words.
He will rise up against that wicked
nation,
against those who help evildoers.
3 But the Egyptians are mere mortals
and not God;
their horses are flesh and not spirit.
When the LORD stretches out his
hand,
those who help will stumble,
those who are helped will fall;
all will perish together.

4 This is what the LORD says to me:

"As a lion growls,
a great lion over its prey —
and though a whole band of
shepherds

is called together against it,
it is not frightened by their shouts
or disturbed by their clamor —
so the LORD Almighty will come down
to do battle on Mount Zion and on
its heights.
5 Like birds hovering overhead,
the LORD Almighty will shield
Jerusalem;
he will shield it and deliver it,
he will 'pass over' it and will rescue
it."

6 Return, you Israelites, to the One you
have so greatly revolted against. 7 For in
that day every one of you will reject the
idols of silver and gold your sinful hands
have made.

8 "Assyria will fall by no human sword;
a sword, not of mortals, will devour
them.
They will flee before the sword
and their young men will be put to
forced labor.
9 Their stronghold will fall because of
terror;
at the sight of the battle standard
their commanders will panic,"
declares the LORD,
whose fire is in Zion,
whose furnace is in Jerusalem.

32 See, a king will reign in
righteousness
and rulers will rule with justice.
2 Each one will be like a shelter from
the wind
and a refuge from the storm,
like streams of water in the desert
and the shadow of a great rock in a
thirsty land.
3 Then the eyes of those who see will no
longer be closed,
and the ears of those who hear will
listen.
4 The fearful heart will know and
understand,
and the stammering tongue will be
fluent and clear.
5 No longer will the fool be called noble
nor the scoundrel be highly
respected.
6 For fools speak folly,
their hearts are bent on evil:
They practice ungodliness
and spread error concerning the
LORD;
the hungry they leave empty
and from the thirsty they withhold
water.
7 Scoundrels use wicked methods,
they make up evil schemes
to destroy the poor with lies,
even when the plea of the needy is
just.
8 But the noble make noble plans,
and by noble deeds they stand.

9 You women who are so complacent,
rise up and listen to me;
you daughters who feel secure,
hear what I have to say!
10 In little more than a year
you who feel secure will tremble;
the grape harvest will fail,
and the harvest of fruit will not
come.
11 Tremble, you complacent women;
shudder, you daughters who feel
secure!
Strip off your fine clothes
and wrap yourselves in rags.
12 Beat your breasts for the pleasant
fields,
for the fruitful vines
13 and for the land of my people,
a land overgrown with thorns and
briers —
yes, mourn for all houses of
merriment
and for this city of revelry.
14 The fortress will be abandoned,
the noisy city deserted;
citadel and watchtower will become a
wasteland forever,
the delight of donkeys, a pasture for
flocks,
15 till the Spirit is poured on us from on
high,
and the desert becomes a fertile
field,
and the fertile field seems like a
forest.
16 The LORD's justice will dwell in the
desert,
his righteousness live in the fertile
field.
17 The fruit of that righteousness will be
peace;
its effect will be quietness and
confidence forever.
18 My people will live in peaceful
dwelling places,
in secure homes,
in undisturbed places of rest.

19 Though hail flattens the forest
and the city is leveled completely,
20 how blessed you will be,
sowing your seed by every stream,
and letting your cattle and donkeys
range free.

33 Woe to you, destroyer,
you who have not been destroyed!
Woe to you, betrayer,
you who have not been betrayed!
When you stop destroying,
you will be destroyed;
when you stop betraying,
you will be betrayed.

2 LORD, be gracious to us;
we long for you.
Be our strength every morning,
our salvation in time of distress.
3 At the uproar of your army, the
peoples flee;
when you rise up, the nations
scatter.
4 Your plunder, O nations, is harvested
as by young locusts;
like a swarm of locusts people
pounce on it.
5 The LORD is exalted, for he dwells on
high;
he will fill Zion with his justice and
righteousness.
6 He will be the sure foundation for
your times,
a rich store of salvation and wisdom
and knowledge;
the fear of the LORD is the key to this
treasure.[a]

7 Look, their brave men cry aloud in the
streets;
the envoys of peace weep bitterly.
8 The highways are deserted,
no travelers are on the roads.
The treaty is broken,
its witnesses[b] are despised,
no one is respected.
9 The land dries up and wastes away,
Lebanon is ashamed and withers;
Sharon is like the Arabah,
and Bashan and Carmel drop their
leaves.

10 "Now will I arise," says the LORD.
"Now will I be exalted;
now will I be lifted up.
11 You conceive chaff,
you give birth to straw;
your breath is a fire that consumes
you.
12 The peoples will be burned to ashes;
like cut thornbushes they will be set
ablaze."

13 You who are far away, hear what I
have done;
you who are near, acknowledge my
power!
14 The sinners in Zion are terrified;
trembling grips the godless:
"Who of us can dwell with the
consuming fire?
Who of us can dwell with
everlasting burning?"
15 Those who walk righteously
and speak what is right,
who reject gain from extortion
and keep their hands from
accepting bribes,
who stop their ears against plots of
murder
and shut their eyes against
contemplating evil—
16 they are the ones who will dwell on
the heights,
whose refuge will be the mountain
fortress.
Their bread will be supplied,
and water will not fail them.

17 Your eyes will see the king in his
beauty
and view a land that stretches afar.
18 In your thoughts you will ponder the
former terror:
"Where is that chief officer?
Where is the one who took the
revenue?
Where is the officer in charge of the
towers?"
19 You will see those arrogant people no
more,
people whose speech is obscure,
whose language is strange and
incomprehensible.

20 Look on Zion, the city of our festivals;
your eyes will see Jerusalem,
a peaceful abode, a tent that will not
be moved;
its stakes will never be pulled up,
nor any of its ropes broken.
21 There the LORD will be our Mighty
One.

[a] 6 Or *is a treasure from him* [b] 8 Dead Sea Scrolls; Masoretic Text / *the cities*

It will be like a place of broad rivers
and streams.
No galley with oars will ride them,
no mighty ship will sail them.
22 For the LORD is our judge,
the LORD is our lawgiver,
the LORD is our king;
it is he who will save us.

23 Your rigging hangs loose:
The mast is not held secure,
the sail is not spread.
Then an abundance of spoils will be
divided
and even the lame will carry off
plunder.
24 No one living in Zion will say, "I am
ill";
and the sins of those who dwell
there will be forgiven.

34 Come near, you nations, and
listen;
pay attention, you peoples!
Let the earth hear, and all that is in it,
the world, and all that comes out
of it!
2 The LORD is angry with all nations;
his wrath is on all their armies.
He will totally destroy[a] them,
he will give them over to slaughter.
3 Their slain will be thrown out,
their dead bodies will stink;
the mountains will be soaked with
their blood.
4 All the stars in the sky will be
dissolved
and the heavens rolled up like a
scroll;
all the starry host will fall
like withered leaves from the vine,
like shriveled figs from the fig tree.

5 My sword has drunk its fill in the
heavens;
see, it descends in judgment on
Edom,
the people I have totally destroyed.
6 The sword of the LORD is bathed in
blood,
it is covered with fat—
the blood of lambs and goats,
fat from the kidneys of rams.
For the LORD has a sacrifice in Bozrah
and a great slaughter in the land of
Edom.
7 And the wild oxen will fall with them,
the bull calves and the great bulls.
Their land will be drenched with
blood,
and the dust will be soaked with fat.

8 For the LORD has a day of vengeance,
a year of retribution, to uphold
Zion's cause.
9 Edom's streams will be turned into
pitch,
her dust into burning sulfur;
her land will become blazing pitch!
10 It will not be quenched night or day;
its smoke will rise forever.
From generation to generation it will
lie desolate;
no one will ever pass through it
again.
11 The desert owl[b] and screech owl[b] will
possess it;
the great owl[b] and the raven will
nest there.
God will stretch out over Edom
the measuring line of chaos
and the plumb line of desolation.
12 Her nobles will have nothing there to
be called a kingdom,
all her princes will vanish away.
13 Thorns will overrun her citadels,
nettles and brambles her
strongholds.
She will become a haunt for jackals,
a home for owls.
14 Desert creatures will meet with
hyenas,
and wild goats will bleat to each
other;
there the night creatures will also lie
down
and find for themselves places of
rest.
15 The owl will nest there and lay eggs,
she will hatch them, and care for
her young
under the shadow of her wings;
there also the falcons will gather,
each with its mate.

16 Look in the scroll of the LORD and read:

None of these will be missing,
not one will lack her mate.
For it is his mouth that has given the
order,

[a] 2 The Hebrew term refers to the irrevocable giving over of things or persons to the LORD, often by totally destroying them; also in verse 5. [b] 11 The precise identification of these birds is uncertain.

and his Spirit will gather them
together.
17 He allots their portions;
his hand distributes them by
measure.
They will possess it forever
and dwell there from generation to
generation.

35 The desert and the parched land
will be glad;
the wilderness will rejoice and
blossom.
Like the crocus, 2 it will burst into
bloom;
it will rejoice greatly and shout for
joy.
The glory of Lebanon will be given
to it,
the splendor of Carmel and Sharon;
they will see the glory of the LORD,
the splendor of our God.

3 Strengthen the feeble hands,
steady the knees that give way;
4 say to those with fearful hearts,
"Be strong, do not fear;
your God will come,
he will come with vengeance;
with divine retribution
he will come to save you."

5 Then will the eyes of the blind be
opened
and the ears of the deaf unstopped.
6 Then will the lame leap like a deer,
and the mute tongue shout for joy.
Water will gush forth in the
wilderness
and streams in the desert.
7 The burning sand will become a pool,
the thirsty ground bubbling springs.
In the haunts where jackals once lay,
grass and reeds and papyrus will
grow.

8 And a highway will be there;
it will be called the Way of Holiness;
it will be for those who walk on that
Way.
The unclean will not journey on it;
wicked fools will not go about on it.
9 No lion will be there,
nor any ravenous beast;
they will not be found there.
But only the redeemed will walk
there,
10 and those the LORD has rescued will
return.
They will enter Zion with singing;
everlasting joy will crown their
heads.
Gladness and joy will overtake them,
and sorrow and sighing will flee
away.

36 In the fourteenth year of King Hezekiah's reign, Sennacherib king of
Assyria attacked all the fortified cities
of Judah and captured them. 2 Then the
king of Assyria sent his field commander
with a large army from Lachish to King
Hezekiah at Jerusalem. When the commander stopped at the aqueduct of the
Upper Pool, on the road to the Launderer's Field, 3 Eliakim son of Hilkiah the
palace administrator, Shebna the secretary, and Joah son of Asaph the recorder
went out to him.
4 The field commander said to them,
"Tell Hezekiah:

"'This is what the great king, the
king of Assyria, says: On what are
you basing this confidence of yours?
5 You say you have counsel and
might for war—but you speak only
empty words. On whom are you depending, that you rebel against me?
6 Look, I know you are depending
on Egypt, that splintered reed of a
staff, which pierces the hand of anyone who leans on it! Such is Pharaoh
king of Egypt to all who depend on
him. 7 But if you say to me, "We are
depending on the LORD our God"—
isn't he the one whose high places
and altars Hezekiah removed, saying to Judah and Jerusalem, "You
must worship before this altar"?
8 "'Come now, make a bargain with
my master, the king of Assyria: I will
give you two thousand horses—if
you can put riders on them! 9 How
then can you repulse one officer of
the least of my master's officials,
even though you are depending on
Egypt for chariots and horsemen[a]?
10 Furthermore, have I come to attack and destroy this land without
the LORD? The LORD himself told me
to march against this country and
destroy it.'"

[a] 9 Or *charioteers*

11Then Eliakim, Shebna and Joah said
to the field commander, "Please speak
to your servants in Aramaic, since we
understand it. Don't speak to us in Hebrew in the hearing of the people on the
wall."

12But the commander replied, "Was it
only to your master and you that my master sent me to say these things, and not to
the people sitting on the wall — who, like
you, will have to eat their own excrement
and drink their own urine?"

13Then the commander stood and
called out in Hebrew, "Hear the words
of the great king, the king of Assyria!
14This is what the king says: Do not let
Hezekiah deceive you. He cannot deliver
you! 15Do not let Hezekiah persuade you
to trust in the LORD when he says, 'The
LORD will surely deliver us; this city will
not be given into the hand of the king of
Assyria.'

16"Do not listen to Hezekiah. This
is what the king of Assyria says: Make
peace with me and come out to me. Then
each of you will eat fruit from your own
vine and fig tree and drink water from
your own cistern, 17until I come and
take you to a land like your own — a land
of grain and new wine, a land of bread
and vineyards.

18"Do not let Hezekiah mislead you
when he says, 'The LORD will deliver us.'
Have the gods of any nations ever delivered their lands from the hand of the
king of Assyria? 19Where are the gods of
Hamath and Arpad? Where are the gods
of Sepharvaim? Have they rescued Samaria from my hand? 20Who of all the
gods of these countries have been able
to save their lands from me? How then
can the LORD deliver Jerusalem from my
hand?"

21But the people remained silent and
said nothing in reply, because the king
had commanded, "Do not answer him."

22Then Eliakim son of Hilkiah the palace administrator, Shebna the secretary
and Joah son of Asaph the recorder went
to Hezekiah, with their clothes torn, and
told him what the field commander had
said.

37 When King Hezekiah heard this, he
tore his clothes and put on sackcloth
and went into the temple of the LORD.
2He sent Eliakim the palace administrator, Shebna the secretary, and the leading priests, all wearing sackcloth, to the
prophet Isaiah son of Amoz. 3They told
him, "This is what Hezekiah says: This
day is a day of distress and rebuke and
disgrace, as when children come to the
moment of birth and there is no strength
to deliver them. 4It may be that the LORD
your God will hear the words of the field
commander, whom his master, the king
of Assyria, has sent to ridicule the living God, and that he will rebuke him for
the words the LORD your God has heard.
Therefore pray for the remnant that still
survives."

5When King Hezekiah's officials came
to Isaiah, 6Isaiah said to them, "Tell your
master, 'This is what the LORD says: Do
not be afraid of what you have heard —
those words with which the underlings
of the king of Assyria have blasphemed
me. 7Listen! When he hears a certain report, I will make him want to return to
his own country, and there I will have
him cut down with the sword.'"

8When the field commander heard
that the king of Assyria had left Lachish,
he withdrew and found the king fighting
against Libnah.

9Now Sennacherib received a report
that Tirhakah, the king of Cush,[a] was
marching out to fight against him. When
he heard it, he sent messengers to Hezekiah with this word: 10"Say to Hezekiah king of Judah: Do not let the god you
depend on deceive you when he says,
'Jerusalem will not be given into the
hands of the king of Assyria.' 11Surely
you have heard what the kings of Assyria
have done to all the countries, destroying them completely. And will you be
delivered? 12Did the gods of the nations
that were destroyed by my predecessors
deliver them — the gods of Gozan, Harran, Rezeph and the people of Eden who
were in Tel Assar? 13Where is the king of
Hamath or the king of Arpad? Where are
the kings of Lair, Sepharvaim, Hena and
Ivvah?"

14Hezekiah received the letter from
the messengers and read it. Then he went
up to the temple of the LORD and spread
it out before the LORD. 15And Hezekiah
prayed to the LORD: 16"LORD Almighty,

[a] 9 That is, the upper Nile region

the God of Israel, enthroned between the
cherubim, you alone are God over all the
kingdoms of the earth. You have made
heaven and earth. 17 Give ear, LORD, and
hear; open your eyes, LORD, and see; listen to all the words Sennacherib has sent
to ridicule the living God.
18 "It is true, LORD, that the Assyrian
kings have laid waste all these peoples
and their lands. 19 They have thrown
their gods into the fire and destroyed
them, for they were not gods but only
wood and stone, fashioned by human
hands. 20 Now, LORD our God, deliver us
from his hand, so that all the kingdoms
of the earth may know that you, LORD,
are the only God.[a]"
21 Then Isaiah son of Amoz sent a message to Hezekiah: "This is what the LORD,
the God of Israel, says: Because you have
prayed to me concerning Sennacherib
king of Assyria, 22 this is the word the
LORD has spoken against him:

"Virgin Daughter Zion
despises and mocks you.
Daughter Jerusalem
tosses her head as you flee.
23 Who is it you have ridiculed and
blasphemed?
Against whom have you raised your
voice
and lifted your eyes in pride?
Against the Holy One of Israel!
24 By your messengers
you have ridiculed the Lord.
And you have said,
'With my many chariots
I have ascended the heights of the
mountains,
the utmost heights of Lebanon.
I have cut down its tallest cedars,
the choicest of its junipers.
I have reached its remotest heights,
the finest of its forests.
25 I have dug wells in foreign lands[b]
and drunk the water there.
With the soles of my feet
I have dried up all the streams of
Egypt.'

26 "Have you not heard?
Long ago I ordained it.
In days of old I planned it;
now I have brought it to pass,
that you have turned fortified cities
into piles of stone.
27 Their people, drained of power,
are dismayed and put to shame.
They are like plants in the field,
like tender green shoots,
like grass sprouting on the roof,
scorched[c] before it grows up.

28 "But I know where you are
and when you come and go
and how you rage against me.
29 Because you rage against me
and because your insolence has
reached my ears,
I will put my hook in your nose
and my bit in your mouth,
and I will make you return
by the way you came.

30 "This will be the sign for you, Hezekiah:

"This year you will eat what grows by
itself,
and the second year what springs
from that.
But in the third year sow and reap,
plant vineyards and eat their fruit.
31 Once more a remnant of the kingdom
of Judah
will take root below and bear fruit
above.
32 For out of Jerusalem will come a
remnant,
and out of Mount Zion a band of
survivors.
The zeal of the LORD Almighty
will accomplish this.

33 "Therefore this is what the LORD says
concerning the king of Assyria:

"He will not enter this city
or shoot an arrow here.
He will not come before it with shield
or build a siege ramp against it.
34 By the way that he came he will
return;
he will not enter this city,"
declares the LORD.
35 "I will defend this city and save it,
for my sake and for the sake of
David my servant!"

[a] *20* Dead Sea Scrolls (see also 2 Kings 19:19); Masoretic Text *you alone are the LORD* [b] *25* Dead Sea Scrolls (see also 2 Kings 19:24); Masoretic Text does not have *in foreign lands.* [c] *27* Some manuscripts of the Masoretic Text, Dead Sea Scrolls and some Septuagint manuscripts (see also 2 Kings 19:26); most manuscripts of the Masoretic Text *roof / and terraced fields*

36 Then the angel of the LORD went
out and put to death a hundred and
eighty-five thousand in the Assyrian
camp. When the people got up the next
morning — there were all the dead bodies! 37 So Sennacherib king of Assyria
broke camp and withdrew. He returned
to Nineveh and stayed there.

38 One day, while he was worshiping
in the temple of his god Nisrok, his sons
Adrammelek and Sharezer killed him
with the sword, and they escaped to the
land of Ararat. And Esarhaddon his son
succeeded him as king.

38 In those days Hezekiah became ill
and was at the point of death. The
prophet Isaiah son of Amoz went to him
and said, "This is what the LORD says: Put
your house in order, because you are going to die; you will not recover."

2 Hezekiah turned his face to the wall
and prayed to the LORD, 3 "Remember,
LORD, how I have walked before you
faithfully and with wholehearted devotion and have done what is good in your
eyes." And Hezekiah wept bitterly.

4 Then the word of the LORD came to
Isaiah: 5 "Go and tell Hezekiah, 'This is
what the LORD, the God of your father
David, says: I have heard your prayer and
seen your tears; I will add fifteen years to
your life. 6 And I will deliver you and this
city from the hand of the king of Assyria.
I will defend this city.

7 " 'This is the LORD's sign to you that
the LORD will do what he has promised: 8 I
will make the shadow cast by the sun go
back the ten steps it has gone down on the
stairway of Ahaz.' " So the sunlight went
back the ten steps it had gone down.

9 A writing of Hezekiah king of Judah
after his illness and recovery:

10 I said, "In the prime of my life
must I go through the gates of death
and be robbed of the rest of my
years?"
11 I said, "I will not again see the LORD
himself
in the land of the living;
no longer will I look on my fellow
man,
or be with those who now dwell in
this world.
12 Like a shepherd's tent my house
has been pulled down and taken
from me.
Like a weaver I have rolled up my life,
and he has cut me off from the
loom;
day and night you made an end of
me.
13 I waited patiently till dawn,
but like a lion he broke all my bones;
day and night you made an end of
me.
14 I cried like a swift or thrush,
I moaned like a mourning dove.
My eyes grew weak as I looked to the
heavens.
I am being threatened; Lord, come
to my aid!"

15 But what can I say?
He has spoken to me, and he
himself has done this.
I will walk humbly all my years
because of this anguish of my soul.
16 Lord, by such things people live;
and my spirit finds life in them too.
You restored me to health
and let me live.
17 Surely it was for my benefit
that I suffered such anguish.
In your love you kept me
from the pit of destruction;
you have put all my sins
behind your back.
18 For the grave cannot praise you,
death cannot sing your praise;
those who go down to the pit
cannot hope for your faithfulness.
19 The living, the living — they praise
you,
as I am doing today;
parents tell their children
about your faithfulness.

20 The LORD will save me,
and we will sing with stringed
instruments
all the days of our lives
in the temple of the LORD.

21 Isaiah had said, "Prepare a poultice
of figs and apply it to the boil, and he will
recover."

22 Hezekiah had asked, "What will be
the sign that I will go up to the temple of
the LORD?"

39 At that time Marduk-Baladan son
of Baladan king of Babylon sent
Hezekiah letters and a gift, because he
had heard of his illness and recovery.
2 Hezekiah received the envoys gladly
and showed them what was in his store-

houses — the silver, the gold, the spices,
the fine olive oil — his entire armory and
everything found among his treasures.
There was nothing in his palace or in all
his kingdom that Hezekiah did not show
them.
3 Then Isaiah the prophet went to
King Hezekiah and asked, "What did
those men say, and where did they come
from?"
"From a distant land," Hezekiah replied.
"They came to me from Babylon."
4 The prophet asked, "What did they
see in your palace?"
"They saw everything in my palace,"
Hezekiah said. "There is nothing among
my treasures that I did not show them."
5 Then Isaiah said to Hezekiah, "Hear
the word of the LORD Almighty: 6 The
time will surely come when everything
in your palace, and all that your predecessors
have stored up until this day,
will be carried off to Babylon. Nothing
will be left, says the LORD. 7 And some of
your descendants, your own flesh and
blood who will be born to you, will be
taken away, and they will become eunuchs
in the palace of the king of Babylon."
8 "The word of the LORD you have spoken
is good," Hezekiah replied. For he
thought, "There will be peace and security
in my lifetime."

40 Comfort, comfort my people,
says your God.
2 Speak tenderly to Jerusalem,
and proclaim to her
that her hard service has been
completed,
that her sin has been paid for,
that she has received from the LORD's
hand
double for all her sins.

3 A voice of one calling:
"In the wilderness prepare
the way for the LORD[a];
make straight in the desert
a highway for our God.[b]
4 Every valley shall be raised up,
every mountain and hill made low;
the rough ground shall become level,
the rugged places a plain.
5 And the glory of the LORD will be
revealed,
and all people will see it together.
For the mouth of the LORD
has spoken."
6 A voice says, "Cry out."
And I said, "What shall I cry?"

"All people are like grass,
and all their faithfulness is like the
flowers of the field.
7 The grass withers and the flowers fall,
because the breath of the LORD
blows on them.
Surely the people are grass.
8 The grass withers and the flowers fall,
but the word of our God endures
forever."

9 You who bring good news to Zion,
go up on a high mountain.
You who bring good news to
Jerusalem,[c]
lift up your voice with a shout,
lift it up, do not be afraid;
say to the towns of Judah,
"Here is your God!"
10 See, the Sovereign LORD comes with
power,
and he rules with a mighty arm.
See, his reward is with him,
and his recompense accompanies
him.
11 He tends his flock like a shepherd:
He gathers the lambs in his arms
and carries them close to his heart;
he gently leads those that have
young.

12 Who has measured the waters in the
hollow of his hand,
or with the breadth of his hand
marked off the heavens?
Who has held the dust of the earth in a
basket,
or weighed the mountains on the
scales
and the hills in a balance?
13 Who can fathom the Spirit[d] of the
LORD,
or instruct the LORD as his
counselor?
14 Whom did the LORD consult to
enlighten him,
and who taught him the right way?

[a] 3 Or *A voice of one calling in the wilderness: / "Prepare the way for the LORD* [b] 3 Hebrew; Septuagint *make straight the paths of our God* [c] 9 Or *Zion, bringer of good news, / go up on a high mountain. / Jerusalem, bringer of good news* [d] 13 Or *mind*

Who was it that taught him
knowledge,
or showed him the path of
understanding?
15 Surely the nations are like a drop in a
bucket;
they are regarded as dust on the
scales;
he weighs the islands as though
they were fine dust.
16 Lebanon is not sufficient for altar
fires,
nor its animals enough for burnt
offerings.
17 Before him all the nations are as
nothing;
they are regarded by him as
worthless
and less than nothing.

18 With whom, then, will you compare
God?
To what image will you liken him?
19 As for an idol, a metalworker casts it,
and a goldsmith overlays it with
gold
and fashions silver chains for it.
20 A person too poor to present such an
offering
selects wood that will not rot;
they look for a skilled worker
to set up an idol that will not topple.

21 Do you not know?
Have you not heard?
Has it not been told you from the
beginning?
Have you not understood since the
earth was founded?
22 He sits enthroned above the circle of
the earth,
and its people are like
grasshoppers.
He stretches out the heavens like a
canopy,
and spreads them out like a tent to
live in.
23 He brings princes to naught
and reduces the rulers of this world
to nothing.
24 No sooner are they planted,
no sooner are they sown,
no sooner do they take root in the
ground,
than he blows on them and they
wither,
and a whirlwind sweeps them away
like chaff.

25 "To whom will you compare me?
Or who is my equal?" says the Holy
One.
26 Lift up your eyes and look to the
heavens:
Who created all these?
He who brings out the starry host one
by one
and calls forth each of them by
name.
Because of his great power and
mighty strength,
not one of them is missing.

27 Why do you complain, Jacob?
Why do you say, Israel,
"My way is hidden from the LORD;
my cause is disregarded by my
God"?
28 Do you not know?
Have you not heard?
The LORD is the everlasting God,
the Creator of the ends of the earth.
He will not grow tired or weary,
and his understanding no one can
fathom.
29 He gives strength to the weary
and increases the power of the
weak.
30 Even youths grow tired and weary,
and young men stumble and fall;
31 but those who hope in the LORD
will renew their strength.
They will soar on wings like eagles;
they will run and not grow weary,
they will walk and not be faint.

41 "Be silent before me, you islands!
Let the nations renew their
strength!
Let them come forward and speak;
let us meet together at the place of
judgment.

2 "Who has stirred up one from the
east,
calling him in righteousness to his
service[a]?
He hands nations over to him
and subdues kings before him.
He turns them to dust with his sword,
to windblown chaff with his bow.
3 He pursues them and moves on
unscathed,

[a] 2 Or *east, / whom victory meets at every step*

by a path his feet have not traveled
before.
4 Who has done this and carried it
through,
calling forth the generations from
the beginning?
I, the LORD—with the first of them
and with the last—I am he."

5 The islands have seen it and fear;
the ends of the earth tremble.
They approach and come forward;
6 they help each other
and say to their companions, "Be
strong!"
7 The metalworker encourages the
goldsmith,
and the one who smooths with the
hammer
spurs on the one who strikes the
anvil.
One says of the welding, "It is good."
The other nails down the idol so it
will not topple.

8 "But you, Israel, my servant,
Jacob, whom I have chosen,
you descendants of Abraham my
friend,
9 I took you from the ends of the earth,
from its farthest corners I called
you.
I said, 'You are my servant';
I have chosen you and have not
rejected you.
10 So do not fear, for I am with you;
do not be dismayed, for I am your
God.
I will strengthen you and help you;
I will uphold you with my righteous
right hand.

11 "All who rage against you
will surely be ashamed and
disgraced;
those who oppose you
will be as nothing and perish.
12 Though you search for your enemies,
you will not find them.
Those who wage war against you
will be as nothing at all.
13 For I am the LORD your God
who takes hold of your right hand
and says to you, Do not fear;
I will help you.
14 Do not be afraid, you worm Jacob,
little Israel, do not fear,
for I myself will help you," declares
the LORD,
your Redeemer, the Holy One of
Israel.
15 "See, I will make you into a threshing
sledge,
new and sharp, with many teeth.
You will thresh the mountains and
crush them,
and reduce the hills to chaff.
16 You will winnow them, the wind will
pick them up,
and a gale will blow them away.
But you will rejoice in the LORD
and glory in the Holy One of Israel.

17 "The poor and needy search for water,
but there is none;
their tongues are parched with
thirst.
But I the LORD will answer them;
I, the God of Israel, will not forsake
them.
18 I will make rivers flow on barren
heights,
and springs within the valleys.
I will turn the desert into pools of
water,
and the parched ground into
springs.
19 I will put in the desert
the cedar and the acacia, the myrtle
and the olive.
I will set junipers in the wasteland,
the fir and the cypress together,
20 so that people may see and know,
may consider and understand,
that the hand of the LORD has done
this,
that the Holy One of Israel has
created it.

21 "Present your case," says the LORD.
"Set forth your arguments," says
Jacob's King.
22 "Tell us, you idols,
what is going to happen.
Tell us what the former things were,
so that we may consider them
and know their final outcome.
Or declare to us the things to come,
23 tell us what the future holds,
so we may know that you are gods.
Do something, whether good or bad,
so that we will be dismayed and
filled with fear.
24 But you are less than nothing
and your works are utterly
worthless;
whoever chooses you is detestable.

25 "I have stirred up one from the north,
and he comes —
one from the rising sun who calls on my name.
He treads on rulers as if they were mortar,
as if he were a potter treading the clay.
26 Who told of this from the beginning,
so we could know,
or beforehand, so we could say, 'He was right'?
No one told of this,
no one foretold it,
no one heard any words from you.
27 I was the first to tell Zion, 'Look, here they are!'
I gave to Jerusalem a messenger of good news.
28 I look but there is no one —
no one among the gods to give counsel,
no one to give answer when I ask them.
29 See, they are all false!
Their deeds amount to nothing;
their images are but wind and confusion.

42 "Here is my servant, whom I uphold,
my chosen one in whom I delight;
I will put my Spirit on him,
and he will bring justice to the nations.
2 He will not shout or cry out,
or raise his voice in the streets.
3 A bruised reed he will not break,
and a smoldering wick he will not snuff out.
In faithfulness he will bring forth justice;
4 he will not falter or be discouraged
till he establishes justice on earth.
In his teaching the islands will put their hope."
5 This is what God the LORD says —
the Creator of the heavens, who stretches them out,
who spreads out the earth with all that springs from it,
who gives breath to its people,
and life to those who walk on it:
6 "I, the LORD, have called you in righteousness;
I will take hold of your hand.
I will keep you and will make you
to be a covenant for the people
and a light for the Gentiles,
7 to open eyes that are blind,
to free captives from prison
and to release from the dungeon
those who sit in darkness.
8 "I am the LORD; that is my name!
I will not yield my glory to another
or my praise to idols.
9 See, the former things have taken place,
and new things I declare;
before they spring into being
I announce them to you."
10 Sing to the LORD a new song,
his praise from the ends of the earth,
you who go down to the sea, and all that is in it,
you islands, and all who live in them.
11 Let the wilderness and its towns raise their voices;
let the settlements where Kedar lives rejoice.
Let the people of Sela sing for joy;
let them shout from the mountaintops.
12 Let them give glory to the LORD
and proclaim his praise in the islands.
13 The LORD will march out like a champion,
like a warrior he will stir up his zeal;
with a shout he will raise the battle cry
and will triumph over his enemies.
14 "For a long time I have kept silent,
I have been quiet and held myself back.
But now, like a woman in childbirth,
I cry out, I gasp and pant.
15 I will lay waste the mountains and hills
and dry up all their vegetation;
I will turn rivers into islands
and dry up the pools.
16 I will lead the blind by ways they have not known,
along unfamiliar paths I will guide them;
I will turn the darkness into light before them
and make the rough places smooth.
These are the things I will do;
I will not forsake them.

17 But those who trust in idols,
who say to images, 'You are our gods,'
will be turned back in utter shame.

18 "Hear, you deaf;
look, you blind, and see!
19 Who is blind but my servant,
and deaf like the messenger I send?
Who is blind like the one in covenant with me,
blind like the servant of the LORD?
20 You have seen many things, but you pay no attention;
your ears are open, but you do not listen."
21 It pleased the LORD
for the sake of his righteousness
to make his law great and glorious.
22 But this is a people plundered and looted,
all of them trapped in pits
or hidden away in prisons.
They have become plunder,
with no one to rescue them;
they have been made loot,
with no one to say, "Send them back."
23 Which of you will listen to this
or pay close attention in time to come?
24 Who handed Jacob over to become loot,
and Israel to the plunderers?
Was it not the LORD,
against whom we have sinned?
For they would not follow his ways;
they did not obey his law.
25 So he poured out on them his burning anger,
the violence of war.
It enveloped them in flames, yet they did not understand;
it consumed them, but they did not take it to heart.

43 But now, this is what the LORD says—
he who created you, Jacob,
he who formed you, Israel:
"Do not fear, for I have redeemed you;
I have summoned you by name; you are mine.
2 When you pass through the waters,
I will be with you;
and when you pass through the rivers,
they will not sweep over you.
When you walk through the fire,
you will not be burned;
the flames will not set you ablaze.
3 For I am the LORD your God,
the Holy One of Israel, your Savior;
I give Egypt for your ransom,
Cush[a] and Seba in your stead.
4 Since you are precious and honored in my sight,
and because I love you,
I will give people in exchange for you,
nations in exchange for your life.
5 Do not be afraid, for I am with you;
I will bring your children from the east
and gather you from the west.
6 I will say to the north, 'Give them up!'
and to the south, 'Do not hold them back.'
Bring my sons from afar
and my daughters from the ends of the earth—
7 everyone who is called by my name,
whom I created for my glory,
whom I formed and made."

8 Lead out those who have eyes but are blind,
who have ears but are deaf.
9 All the nations gather together
and the peoples assemble.
Which of their gods foretold this
and proclaimed to us the former things?
Let them bring in their witnesses to prove they were right,
so that others may hear and say, "It is true."
10 "You are my witnesses," declares the LORD,
"and my servant whom I have chosen,
so that you may know and believe me
and understand that I am he.
Before me no god was formed,
nor will there be one after me.
11 I, even I, am the LORD,
and apart from me there is no savior.
12 I have revealed and saved and proclaimed—
I, and not some foreign god among you.
You are my witnesses," declares the LORD, "that I am God.

[a] 3 That is, the upper Nile region

13 Yes, and from ancient days I am he.
No one can deliver out of my hand.
When I act, who can reverse it?"

14 This is what the LORD says—
your Redeemer, the Holy One of Israel:
"For your sake I will send to Babylon
and bring down as fugitives all the Babylonians,[a]
in the ships in which they took pride.
15 I am the LORD, your Holy One,
Israel's Creator, your King."

16 This is what the LORD says—
he who made a way through the sea,
a path through the mighty waters,
17 who drew out the chariots and horses,
the army and reinforcements together,
and they lay there, never to rise again,
extinguished, snuffed out like a wick:
18 "Forget the former things;
do not dwell on the past.
19 See, I am doing a new thing!
Now it springs up; do you not perceive it?
I am making a way in the wilderness
and streams in the wasteland.
20 The wild animals honor me,
the jackals and the owls,
because I provide water in the wilderness
and streams in the wasteland,
to give drink to my people, my chosen,
21 the people I formed for myself
that they may proclaim my praise.

22 "Yet you have not called on me, Jacob,
you have not wearied yourselves for[b] me, Israel.
23 You have not brought me sheep for burnt offerings,
nor honored me with your sacrifices.
I have not burdened you with grain offerings
nor wearied you with demands for incense.
24 You have not bought any fragrant calamus for me,
or lavished on me the fat of your sacrifices.
But you have burdened me with your sins
and wearied me with your offenses.

25 "I, even I, am he who blots out
your transgressions, for my own sake,
and remembers your sins no more.
26 Review the past for me,
let us argue the matter together;
state the case for your innocence.
27 Your first father sinned;
those I sent to teach you rebelled against me.
28 So I disgraced the dignitaries of your temple;
I consigned Jacob to destruction[c]
and Israel to scorn.

44

"But now listen, Jacob, my servant,
Israel, whom I have chosen.
2 This is what the LORD says—
he who made you, who formed you in the womb,
and who will help you:
Do not be afraid, Jacob, my servant,
Jeshurun,[d] whom I have chosen.
3 For I will pour water on the thirsty land,
and streams on the dry ground;
I will pour out my Spirit on your offspring,
and my blessing on your descendants.
4 They will spring up like grass in a meadow,
like poplar trees by flowing streams.
5 Some will say, 'I belong to the LORD';
others will call themselves by the name of Jacob;
still others will write on their hand, 'The LORD's,'
and will take the name Israel.

6 "This is what the LORD says—
Israel's King and Redeemer, the LORD Almighty:
I am the first and I am the last;
apart from me there is no God.
7 Who then is like me? Let him proclaim it.
Let him declare and lay out before me

[a] 14 Or *Chaldeans* [b] 22 Or *Jacob; / surely you have grown weary of* [c] 28 The Hebrew term refers to the irrevocable giving over of things or persons to the LORD, often by totally destroying them. [d] 2 *Jeshurun* means *the upright one*, that is, Israel.

what has happened since I
established my ancient people,
and what is yet to come—
yes, let them foretell what will
come.
8 Do not tremble, do not be afraid.
Did I not proclaim this and foretell
it long ago?
You are my witnesses. Is there any
God besides me?
No, there is no other Rock; I know
not one."

9 All who make idols are nothing,
and the things they treasure are
worthless.
Those who would speak up for them
are blind;
they are ignorant, to their own
shame.
10 Who shapes a god and casts an idol,
which can profit nothing?
11 People who do that will be put to
shame;
such craftsmen are only human
beings.
Let them all come together and take
their stand;
they will be brought down to terror
and shame.
12 The blacksmith takes a tool
and works with it in the coals;
he shapes an idol with hammers,
he forges it with the might of his
arm.
He gets hungry and loses his strength;
he drinks no water and grows faint.
13 The carpenter measures with a line
and makes an outline with a
marker;
he roughs it out with chisels
and marks it with compasses.
He shapes it in human form,
human form in all its glory,
that it may dwell in a shrine.
14 He cut down cedars,
or perhaps took a cypress or oak.
He let it grow among the trees of the
forest,
or planted a pine, and the rain made
it grow.
15 It is used as fuel for burning;
some of it he takes and warms
himself,
he kindles a fire and bakes bread.
But he also fashions a god and
worships it;
he makes an idol and bows down
to it.
16 Half of the wood he burns in the fire;
over it he prepares his meal,
he roasts his meat and eats his fill.
He also warms himself and says,
"Ah! I am warm; I see the fire."
17 From the rest he makes a god, his
idol;
he bows down to it and worships.
He prays to it and says,
"Save me! You are my god!"
18 They know nothing, they understand
nothing;
their eyes are plastered over so they
cannot see,
and their minds closed so they
cannot understand.
19 No one stops to think,
no one has the knowledge or
understanding to say,
"Half of it I used for fuel;
I even baked bread over its coals,
I roasted meat and I ate.
Shall I make a detestable thing from
what is left?
Shall I bow down to a block of
wood?"
20 Such a person feeds on ashes; a
deluded heart misleads him;
he cannot save himself, or say,
"Is not this thing in my right hand a
lie?"

21 "Remember these things, Jacob,
for you, Israel, are my servant.
I have made you, you are my servant;
Israel, I will not forget you.
22 I have swept away your offenses like a
cloud,
your sins like the morning mist.
Return to me,
for I have redeemed you."

23 Sing for joy, you heavens, for the LORD
has done this;
shout aloud, you earth beneath.
Burst into song, you mountains,
you forests and all your trees,
for the LORD has redeemed Jacob,
he displays his glory in Israel.

24 "This is what the LORD says—
your Redeemer, who formed you in
the womb:

I am the LORD,
the Maker of all things,
who stretches out the heavens,

who spreads out the earth by
myself,
25 who foils the signs of false prophets
and makes fools of diviners,
who overthrows the learning of the
wise
and turns it into nonsense,
26 who carries out the words of his
servants
and fulfills the predictions of his
messengers,
who says of Jerusalem, 'It shall be
inhabited,'
of the towns of Judah, 'They shall be
rebuilt,'
and of their ruins, 'I will restore
them,'
27 who says to the watery deep, 'Be dry,
and I will dry up your streams,'
28 who says of Cyrus, 'He is my
shepherd
and will accomplish all that I
please;
he will say of Jerusalem, "Let it be
rebuilt,"
and of the temple, "Let its
foundations be laid." '

45 "This is what the LORD says to his
anointed,
to Cyrus, whose right hand I take
hold of
to subdue nations before him
and to strip kings of their armor,
to open doors before him
so that gates will not be shut:
2 I will go before you
and will level the mountains[a];
I will break down gates of bronze
and cut through bars of iron.
3 I will give you hidden treasures,
riches stored in secret places,
so that you may know that I am the
LORD,
the God of Israel, who summons
you by name.
4 For the sake of Jacob my servant,
of Israel my chosen,
I summon you by name
and bestow on you a title of honor,
though you do not acknowledge me.
5 I am the LORD, and there is no other;
apart from me there is no God.
I will strengthen you,
though you have not acknowledged
me,
6 so that from the rising of the sun
to the place of its setting
people may know there is none
besides me.
I am the LORD, and there is no
other.
7 I form the light and create darkness,
I bring prosperity and create
disaster;
I, the LORD, do all these things.

8 "You heavens above, rain down my
righteousness;
let the clouds shower it down.
Let the earth open wide,
let salvation spring up,
let righteousness flourish with it;
I, the LORD, have created it.

9 "Woe to those who quarrel with their
Maker,
those who are nothing but
potsherds
among the potsherds on the
ground.
Does the clay say to the potter,
'What are you making?'
Does your work say,
'The potter has no hands'?
10 Woe to the one who says to a father,
'What have you begotten?'
or to a mother,
'What have you brought to birth?'

11 "This is what the LORD says—
the Holy One of Israel, and its
Maker:
Concerning things to come,
do you question me about my
children,
or give me orders about the work of
my hands?
12 It is I who made the earth
and created mankind on it.
My own hands stretched out the
heavens;
I marshaled their starry hosts.
13 I will raise up Cyrus[b] in my
righteousness:
I will make all his ways straight.
He will rebuild my city
and set my exiles free,
but not for a price or reward,
says the LORD Almighty."

[a] *2* Dead Sea Scrolls and Septuagint; the meaning of the word in the Masoretic Text is uncertain.
[b] *13* Hebrew *him*

[14]This is what the LORD says:

"The products of Egypt and the
merchandise of Cush,[a]
and those tall Sabeans—
they will come over to you
and will be yours;
they will trudge behind you,
coming over to you in chains.
They will bow down before you
and plead with you, saying,
'Surely God is with you, and there is
no other;
there is no other god.'"

[15]Truly you are a God who has been
hiding himself,
the God and Savior of Israel.
[16]All the makers of idols will be put to
shame and disgraced;
they will go off into disgrace
together.
[17]But Israel will be saved by the LORD
with an everlasting salvation;
you will never be put to shame or
disgraced,
to ages everlasting.

[18]For this is what the LORD says—
he who created the heavens,
he is God;
he who fashioned and made the earth,
he founded it;
he did not create it to be empty,
but formed it to be inhabited—
he says:
"I am the LORD,
and there is no other.
[19]I have not spoken in secret,
from somewhere in a land of
darkness;
I have not said to Jacob's descendants,
'Seek me in vain.'
I, the LORD, speak the truth;
I declare what is right.

[20]"Gather together and come;
assemble, you fugitives from the
nations.
Ignorant are those who carry about
idols of wood,
who pray to gods that cannot save.
[21]Declare what is to be, present it—
let them take counsel together.
Who foretold this long ago,
who declared it from the distant
past?
Was it not I, the LORD?
And there is no God apart from
me,
a righteous God and a Savior;
there is none but me.

[22]"Turn to me and be saved,
all you ends of the earth;
for I am God, and there is no other.
[23]By myself I have sworn,
my mouth has uttered in all
integrity
a word that will not be revoked:
Before me every knee will bow;
by me every tongue will swear.
[24]They will say of me, 'In the LORD
alone
are deliverance and strength.'"
All who have raged against him
will come to him and be put to
shame.
[25]But all the descendants of Israel
will find deliverance in the LORD
and will make their boast in him.

46 Bel bows down, Nebo stoops low;
their idols are borne by beasts of
burden.[b]
The images that are carried about are
burdensome,
a burden for the weary.
[2]They stoop and bow down together;
unable to rescue the burden,
they themselves go off into
captivity.

[3]"Listen to me, you descendants of
Jacob,
all the remnant of the people of
Israel,
you whom I have upheld since your
birth,
and have carried since you were
born.
[4]Even to your old age and gray hairs
I am he, I am he who will sustain
you.
I have made you and I will carry you;
I will sustain you and I will rescue
you.

[5]"With whom will you compare me or
count me equal?
To whom will you liken me that we
may be compared?
[6]Some pour out gold from their bags
and weigh out silver on the scales;

[a] *14* That is, the upper Nile region [b] *1* Or *are but beasts and cattle*

they hire a goldsmith to make it into a
god,
and they bow down and worship it.
7 They lift it to their shoulders and
carry it;
they set it up in its place, and there
it stands.
From that spot it cannot move.
Even though someone cries out to it, it
cannot answer;
it cannot save them from their
troubles.
8 "Remember this, keep it in mind,
take it to heart, you rebels.
9 Remember the former things, those of
long ago;
I am God, and there is no other;
I am God, and there is none like me.
10 I make known the end from the
beginning,
from ancient times, what is still to
come.
I say, 'My purpose will stand,
and I will do all that I please.'
11 From the east I summon a bird of
prey;
from a far-off land, a man to fulfill
my purpose.
What I have said, that I will bring
about;
what I have planned, that I will do.
12 Listen to me, you stubborn-hearted,
you who are now far from my
righteousness.
13 I am bringing my righteousness near,
it is not far away;
and my salvation will not be
delayed.
I will grant salvation to Zion,
my splendor to Israel.

47 "Go down, sit in the dust,
Virgin Daughter Babylon;
sit on the ground without a throne,
queen city of the Babylonians.[a]
No more will you be called
tender or delicate.
2 Take millstones and grind flour;
take off your veil.
Lift up your skirts, bare your legs,
and wade through the streams.
3 Your nakedness will be exposed
and your shame uncovered.
I will take vengeance;
I will spare no one."
4 Our Redeemer — the LORD Almighty
is his name —
is the Holy One of Israel.
5 "Sit in silence, go into darkness,
queen city of the Babylonians;
no more will you be called
queen of kingdoms.
6 I was angry with my people
and desecrated my inheritance;
I gave them into your hand,
and you showed them no mercy.
Even on the aged
you laid a very heavy yoke.
7 You said, 'I am forever —
the eternal queen!'
But you did not consider these things
or reflect on what might happen.
8 "Now then, listen, you lover of
pleasure,
lounging in your security
and saying to yourself,
'I am, and there is none besides me.
I will never be a widow
or suffer the loss of children.'
9 Both of these will overtake you
in a moment, on a single day:
loss of children and widowhood.
They will come upon you in full
measure,
in spite of your many sorceries
and all your potent spells.
10 You have trusted in your wickedness
and have said, 'No one sees me.'
Your wisdom and knowledge mislead
you
when you say to yourself,
'I am, and there is none besides me.'
11 Disaster will come upon you,
and you will not know how to
conjure it away.
A calamity will fall upon you
that you cannot ward off with a
ransom;
a catastrophe you cannot foresee
will suddenly come upon you.
12 "Keep on, then, with your magic
spells
and with your many sorceries,
which you have labored at since
childhood.
Perhaps you will succeed,
perhaps you will cause terror.
13 All the counsel you have received has
only worn you out!

[a] *1* Or *Chaldeans*; also in verse 5

Let your astrologers come forward,
those stargazers who make
predictions month by month,
let them save you from what is
coming upon you.
14 Surely they are like stubble;
the fire will burn them up.
They cannot even save themselves
from the power of the flame.
These are not coals for warmth;
this is not a fire to sit by.
15 That is all they are to you —
these you have dealt with
and labored with since childhood.
All of them go on in their error;
there is not one that can save you.

48 "Listen to this, you descendants
of Jacob,
you who are called by the name of
Israel
and come from the line of Judah,
you who take oaths in the name of the
LORD
and invoke the God of Israel —
but not in truth or righteousness —
2 you who call yourselves citizens of the
holy city
and claim to rely on the God of
Israel —
the LORD Almighty is his name:
3 I foretold the former things long ago,
my mouth announced them and I
made them known;
then suddenly I acted, and they
came to pass.
4 For I knew how stubborn you were;
your neck muscles were iron,
your forehead was bronze.
5 Therefore I told you these things long
ago;
before they happened I announced
them to you
so that you could not say,
'My images brought them about;
my wooden image and metal god
ordained them.'
6 You have heard these things; look at
them all.
Will you not admit them?
"From now on I will tell you of new
things,
of hidden things unknown to you.
7 They are created now, and not long
ago;
you have not heard of them before
today.
So you cannot say,
'Yes, I knew of them.'
8 You have neither heard nor
understood;
from of old your ears have not been
open.
Well do I know how treacherous you
are;
you were called a rebel from birth.
9 For my own name's sake I delay my
wrath;
for the sake of my praise I hold it
back from you,
so as not to destroy you completely.
10 See, I have refined you, though not as
silver;
I have tested you in the furnace of
affliction.
11 For my own sake, for my own sake, I
do this.
How can I let myself be defamed?
I will not yield my glory to another.

12 "Listen to me, Jacob,
Israel, whom I have called:
I am he;
I am the first and I am the last.
13 My own hand laid the foundations of
the earth,
and my right hand spread out the
heavens;
when I summon them,
they all stand up together.
14 "Come together, all of you, and listen:
Which of the idols has foretold
these things?
The LORD's chosen ally
will carry out his purpose against
Babylon;
his arm will be against the
Babylonians.[a]
15 I, even I, have spoken;
yes, I have called him.
I will bring him,
and he will succeed in his mission.
16 "Come near me and listen to this:
"From the first announcement I have
not spoken in secret;
at the time it happens, I am there."
And now the Sovereign LORD has sent
me,
endowed with his Spirit.

[a] *14* Or *Chaldeans*; also in verse 20

17 This is what the LORD says —
your Redeemer, the Holy One of Israel:
"I am the LORD your God,
who teaches you what is best for you,
who directs you in the way you should go.
18 If only you had paid attention to my commands,
your peace would have been like a river,
your well-being like the waves of the sea.
19 Your descendants would have been like the sand,
your children like its numberless grains;
their name would never be blotted out
nor destroyed from before me."

20 Leave Babylon,
flee from the Babylonians!
Announce this with shouts of joy
and proclaim it.
Send it out to the ends of the earth;
say, "The LORD has redeemed his servant Jacob."
21 They did not thirst when he led them through the deserts;
he made water flow for them from the rock;
he split the rock
and water gushed out.

22 "There is no peace," says the LORD,
"for the wicked."

49 Listen to me, you islands;
hear this, you distant nations:
Before I was born the LORD called me;
from my mother's womb he has spoken my name.
2 He made my mouth like a sharpened sword,
in the shadow of his hand he hid me;
he made me into a polished arrow
and concealed me in his quiver.
3 He said to me, "You are my servant,
Israel, in whom I will display my splendor."
4 But I said, "I have labored in vain;
I have spent my strength for nothing at all.
Yet what is due me is in the LORD's hand,
and my reward is with my God."

5 And now the LORD says —
he who formed me in the womb to be his servant
to bring Jacob back to him
and gather Israel to himself,
for I am[a] honored in the eyes of the LORD
and my God has been my strength —
6 he says:
"It is too small a thing for you to be my servant
to restore the tribes of Jacob
and bring back those of Israel I have kept.
I will also make you a light for the Gentiles,
that my salvation may reach to the ends of the earth."

7 This is what the LORD says —
the Redeemer and Holy One of Israel —
to him who was despised and abhorred by the nation,
to the servant of rulers:
"Kings will see you and stand up,
princes will see and bow down,
because of the LORD, who is faithful,
the Holy One of Israel, who has chosen you."
8 This is what the LORD says:

"In the time of my favor I will answer you,
and in the day of salvation I will help you;
I will keep you and will make you
to be a covenant for the people,
to restore the land
and to reassign its desolate inheritances,
9 to say to the captives, 'Come out,'
and to those in darkness, 'Be free!'
"They will feed beside the roads
and find pasture on every barren hill.
10 They will neither hunger nor thirst,
nor will the desert heat or the sun beat down on them.
He who has compassion on them will guide them
and lead them beside springs of water.

[a] 5 Or *him, / but Israel would not be gathered; / yet I will be*

11 I will turn all my mountains into
roads,
and my highways will be raised up.
12 See, they will come from afar—
some from the north, some from the
west,
some from the region of Aswan.[a]"
13 Shout for joy, you heavens;
rejoice, you earth;
burst into song, you mountains!
For the LORD comforts his people
and will have compassion on his
afflicted ones.

14 But Zion said, "The LORD has forsaken
me,
the Lord has forgotten me."

15 "Can a mother forget the baby at her
breast
and have no compassion on the
child she has borne?
Though she may forget,
I will not forget you!
16 See, I have engraved you on the palms
of my hands;
your walls are ever before me.
17 Your children hasten back,
and those who laid you waste
depart from you.
18 Lift up your eyes and look around;
all your children gather and come
to you.
As surely as I live," declares the LORD,
"you will wear them all as
ornaments;
you will put them on, like a bride.

19 "Though you were ruined and made
desolate
and your land laid waste,
now you will be too small for your
people,
and those who devoured you will be
far away.
20 The children born during your
bereavement
will yet say in your hearing,
'This place is too small for us;
give us more space to live in.'
21 Then you will say in your heart,
'Who bore me these?
I was bereaved and barren;
I was exiled and rejected.
Who brought these up?
I was left all alone,
but these—where have they come
from?'"

22 This is what the Sovereign LORD
says:

"See, I will beckon to the nations,
I will lift up my banner to the
peoples;
they will bring your sons in their arms
and carry your daughters on their
hips.
23 Kings will be your foster fathers,
and their queens your nursing
mothers.
They will bow down before you with
their faces to the ground;
they will lick the dust at your feet.
Then you will know that I am the
LORD;
those who hope in me will not be
disappointed."

24 Can plunder be taken from warriors,
or captives be rescued from the
fierce[b]?

25 But this is what the LORD says:

"Yes, captives will be taken from
warriors,
and plunder retrieved from the
fierce;
I will contend with those who contend
with you,
and your children I will save.
26 I will make your oppressors eat their
own flesh;
they will be drunk on their own
blood, as with wine.
Then all mankind will know
that I, the LORD, am your Savior,
your Redeemer, the Mighty One of
Jacob."

50 This is what the LORD says:

"Where is your mother's certificate of
divorce
with which I sent her away?
Or to which of my creditors
did I sell you?
Because of your sins you were sold;
because of your transgressions your
mother was sent away.
2 When I came, why was there no one?

[a] *12* Dead Sea Scrolls; Masoretic Text *Sinim* [b] *24* Dead Sea Scrolls, Vulgate and Syriac (see also Septuagint and verse 25); Masoretic Text *righteous*

When I called, why was there no
one to answer?
Was my arm too short to deliver you?
Do I lack the strength to rescue you?
By a mere rebuke I dry up the sea,
I turn rivers into a desert;
their fish rot for lack of water
and die of thirst.
3 I clothe the heavens with darkness
and make sackcloth its covering."

4 The Sovereign LORD has given me a
well-instructed tongue,
to know the word that sustains the
weary.
He wakens me morning by morning,
wakens my ear to listen like one
being instructed.
5 The Sovereign LORD has opened my
ears;
I have not been rebellious,
I have not turned away.
6 I offered my back to those who beat
me,
my cheeks to those who pulled out
my beard;
I did not hide my face
from mocking and spitting.
7 Because the Sovereign LORD helps
me,
I will not be disgraced.
Therefore have I set my face like flint,
and I know I will not be put to
shame.
8 He who vindicates me is near.
Who then will bring charges against
me?
Let us face each other!
Who is my accuser?
Let him confront me!
9 It is the Sovereign LORD who helps
me.
Who will condemn me?
They will all wear out like a garment;
the moths will eat them up.

10 Who among you fears the LORD
and obeys the word of his servant?
Let the one who walks in the dark,
who has no light,
trust in the name of the LORD
and rely on their God.
11 But now, all you who light fires
and provide yourselves with
flaming torches,
go, walk in the light of your fires
and of the torches you have set
ablaze.
This is what you shall receive from my
hand:
You will lie down in torment.

51 "Listen to me, you who pursue
righteousness
and who seek the LORD:
Look to the rock from which you were
cut
and to the quarry from which you
were hewn;
2 look to Abraham, your father,
and to Sarah, who gave you birth.
When I called him he was only one
man,
and I blessed him and made him
many.
3 The LORD will surely comfort Zion
and will look with compassion on
all her ruins;
he will make her deserts like Eden,
her wastelands like the garden of
the LORD.
Joy and gladness will be found in her,
thanksgiving and the sound of
singing.

4 "Listen to me, my people;
hear me, my nation:
Instruction will go out from me;
my justice will become a light to the
nations.
5 My righteousness draws near
speedily,
my salvation is on the way,
and my arm will bring justice to the
nations.
The islands will look to me
and wait in hope for my arm.
6 Lift up your eyes to the heavens,
look at the earth beneath;
the heavens will vanish like smoke,
the earth will wear out like a
garment
and its inhabitants die like flies.
But my salvation will last forever,
my righteousness will never fail.

7 "Hear me, you who know what is
right,
you people who have taken my
instruction to heart:
Do not fear the reproach of mere
mortals
or be terrified by their insults.
8 For the moth will eat them up like a
garment;
the worm will devour them like
wool.

But my righteousness will last forever,
my salvation through all
generations."

9 Awake, awake, arm of the LORD,
clothe yourself with strength!
Awake, as in days gone by,
as in generations of old.
Was it not you who cut Rahab to
pieces,
who pierced that monster
through?
10 Was it not you who dried up the sea,
the waters of the great deep,
who made a road in the depths of the
sea
so that the redeemed might cross
over?
11 Those the LORD has rescued will
return.
They will enter Zion with singing;
everlasting joy will crown their
heads.
Gladness and joy will overtake them,
and sorrow and sighing will flee
away.

12 "I, even I, am he who comforts you.
Who are you that you fear mere
mortals,
human beings who are but grass,
13 that you forget the LORD your Maker,
who stretches out the heavens
and who lays the foundations of the
earth,
that you live in constant terror every
day
because of the wrath of the
oppressor,
who is bent on destruction?
For where is the wrath of the
oppressor?
14 The cowering prisoners will soon be
set free;
they will not die in their dungeon,
nor will they lack bread.
15 For I am the LORD your God,
who stirs up the sea so that its
waves roar—
the LORD Almighty is his name.
16 I have put my words in your mouth
and covered you with the shadow of
my hand—
I who set the heavens in place,
who laid the foundations of the
earth,
and who say to Zion, 'You are my
people.'"

17 Awake, awake!
Rise up, Jerusalem,
you who have drunk from the hand of
the LORD
the cup of his wrath,
you who have drained to its dregs
the goblet that makes people
stagger.
18 Among all the children she bore
there was none to guide her;
among all the children she reared
there was none to take her by the
hand.
19 These double calamities have come
upon you—
who can comfort you?—
ruin and destruction, famine and
sword—
who can[a] console you?
20 Your children have fainted;
they lie at every street corner,
like antelope caught in a net.
They are filled with the wrath of the
LORD,
with the rebuke of your God.

21 Therefore hear this, you afflicted
one,
made drunk, but not with wine.
22 This is what your Sovereign LORD
says,
your God, who defends his people:
"See, I have taken out of your hand
the cup that made you stagger;
from that cup, the goblet of my wrath,
you will never drink again.
23 I will put it into the hands of your
tormentors,
who said to you,
'Fall prostrate that we may walk on
you.'
And you made your back like the
ground,
like a street to be walked on."

52 Awake, awake, Zion,
clothe yourself with strength!
Put on your garments of splendor,
Jerusalem, the holy city.
The uncircumcised and defiled
will not enter you again.
2 Shake off your dust;
rise up, sit enthroned, Jerusalem.

[a] *19* Dead Sea Scrolls, Septuagint, Vulgate and Syriac; Masoretic Text / *how can I*

Free yourself from the chains on your
neck,
Daughter Zion, now a captive.

3 For this is what the LORD says:

"You were sold for nothing,
and without money you will be
redeemed."

4 For this is what the Sovereign LORD says:

"At first my people went down to
Egypt to live;
lately, Assyria has oppressed them.

5 "And now what do I have here?" declares the LORD.

"For my people have been taken away
for nothing,
and those who rule them mock,[a]"
declares the LORD.
"And all day long
my name is constantly blasphemed.
6 Therefore my people will know my
name;
therefore in that day they will know
that it is I who foretold it.
Yes, it is I."

7 How beautiful on the mountains
are the feet of those who bring good
news,
who proclaim peace,
who bring good tidings,
who proclaim salvation,
who say to Zion,
"Your God reigns!"
8 Listen! Your watchmen lift up their
voices;
together they shout for joy.
When the LORD returns to Zion,
they will see it with their own eyes.
9 Burst into songs of joy together,
you ruins of Jerusalem,
for the LORD has comforted his
people,
he has redeemed Jerusalem.
10 The LORD will lay bare his holy arm
in the sight of all the nations,
and all the ends of the earth will see
the salvation of our God.

11 Depart, depart, go out from there!
Touch no unclean thing!
Come out from it and be pure,
you who carry the articles of the
LORD's house.
12 But you will not leave in haste
or go in flight;
for the LORD will go before you,
the God of Israel will be your rear
guard.

13 See, my servant will act wisely[b];
he will be raised and lifted up and
highly exalted.
14 Just as there were many who were
appalled at him[c]—
his appearance was so disfigured
beyond that of any human
being
and his form marred beyond
human likeness—
15 so he will sprinkle many nations,[d]
and kings will shut their mouths
because of him.
For what they were not told, they will
see,
and what they have not heard, they
will understand.

53 Who has believed our message
and to whom has the arm of the
LORD been revealed?
2 He grew up before him like a tender
shoot,
and like a root out of dry ground.
He had no beauty or majesty to attract
us to him,
nothing in his appearance that we
should desire him.
3 He was despised and rejected by
mankind,
a man of suffering, and familiar
with pain.
Like one from whom people hide their
faces
he was despised, and we held him
in low esteem.

4 Surely he took up our pain
and bore our suffering,
yet we considered him punished by
God,
stricken by him, and afflicted.
5 But he was pierced for our
transgressions,
he was crushed for our iniquities;
the punishment that brought us peace
was on him,
and by his wounds we are healed.

[a] 5 Dead Sea Scrolls and Vulgate; Masoretic Text *wail* [b] 13 Or *will prosper* [c] 14 Hebrew *you* [d] 15 Or *so will many nations be amazed at him* (see also Septuagint)

6 We all, like sheep, have gone astray,
each of us has turned to our own way;
and the LORD has laid on him
the iniquity of us all.

7 He was oppressed and afflicted,
yet he did not open his mouth;
he was led like a lamb to the slaughter,
and as a sheep before its shearers is silent,
so he did not open his mouth.
8 By oppression[a] and judgment he was taken away.
Yet who of his generation protested?
For he was cut off from the land of the living;
for the transgression of my people
he was punished.[b]
9 He was assigned a grave with the wicked,
and with the rich in his death,
though he had done no violence,
nor was any deceit in his mouth.

10 Yet it was the LORD's will to crush him
and cause him to suffer,
and though the LORD makes[c] his life an offering for sin,
he will see his offspring and prolong his days,
and the will of the LORD will
prosper in his hand.
11 After he has suffered,
he will see the light of life[d] and be satisfied[e];
by his knowledge[f] my righteous
servant will justify many,
and he will bear their iniquities.
12 Therefore I will give him a portion among the great,[g]
and he will divide the spoils with the strong,[h]
because he poured out his life unto death,
and was numbered with the transgressors.
For he bore the sin of many,
and made intercession for the transgressors.

54 "Sing, barren woman,
you who never bore a child;
burst into song, shout for joy,
you who were never in labor;
because more are the children of the desolate woman
than of her who has a husband,"
says the LORD.
2 "Enlarge the place of your tent,
stretch your tent curtains wide,
do not hold back;
lengthen your cords,
strengthen your stakes.
3 For you will spread out to the right and to the left;
your descendants will dispossess nations
and settle in their desolate cities.

4 "Do not be afraid; you will not be put to shame.
Do not fear disgrace; you will not be humiliated.
You will forget the shame of your youth
and remember no more the
reproach of your widowhood.
5 For your Maker is your husband—
the LORD Almighty is his name—
the Holy One of Israel is your Redeemer;
he is called the God of all the earth.
6 The LORD will call you back
as if you were a wife deserted and distressed in spirit—
a wife who married young,
only to be rejected," says your God.
7 "For a brief moment I abandoned you,
but with deep compassion I will bring you back.
8 In a surge of anger
I hid my face from you for a moment,
but with everlasting kindness
I will have compassion on you,"
says the LORD your Redeemer.

9 "To me this is like the days of Noah,
when I swore that the waters of
Noah would never again cover the earth.
So now I have sworn not to be angry with you,
never to rebuke you again.
10 Though the mountains be shaken
and the hills be removed,

[a] 8 Or *From arrest* [b] 8 Or *generation considered / that he was cut off from the land of the living, / that he was punished for the transgression of my people?* [c] 10 Hebrew *though you make* [d] 11 Dead Sea Scrolls (see also Septuagint); Masoretic Text does not have *the light of life.* [e] 11 Or (with Masoretic Text) [11]*He will see the fruit of his suffering / and will be satisfied* [f] 11 Or *by knowledge of him* [g] 12 Or *many* [h] 12 Or *numerous*

yet my unfailing love for you will not
be shaken
nor my covenant of peace be
removed,"
says the LORD, who has compassion
on you.

11 "Afflicted city, lashed by storms and
not comforted,
I will rebuild you with stones of
turquoise,[a]
your foundations with lapis lazuli.
12 I will make your battlements of
rubies,
your gates of sparkling jewels,
and all your walls of precious
stones.
13 All your children will be taught by the
LORD,
and great will be their peace.
14 In righteousness you will be
established:
Tyranny will be far from you;
you will have nothing to fear.
Terror will be far removed;
it will not come near you.
15 If anyone does attack you, it will not
be my doing;
whoever attacks you will surrender
to you.

16 "See, it is I who created the
blacksmith
who fans the coals into flame
and forges a weapon fit for its
work.
And it is I who have created the
destroyer to wreak havoc;
17 no weapon forged against you will
prevail,
and you will refute every tongue
that accuses you.
This is the heritage of the servants of
the LORD,
and this is their vindication from
me,"
declares the LORD.

55 "Come, all you who are thirsty,
come to the waters;
and you who have no money,
come, buy and eat!
Come, buy wine and milk
without money and without cost.
2 Why spend money on what is not
bread,
and your labor on what does not
satisfy?
Listen, listen to me, and eat what is
good,
and you will delight in the richest of
fare.
3 Give ear and come to me;
listen, that you may live.
I will make an everlasting covenant
with you,
my faithful love promised to David.
4 See, I have made him a witness to the
peoples,
a ruler and commander of the
peoples.
5 Surely you will summon nations you
know not,
and nations you do not know will
come running to you,
because of the LORD your God,
the Holy One of Israel,
for he has endowed you with
splendor."

6 Seek the LORD while he may be found;
call on him while he is near.
7 Let the wicked forsake their ways
and the unrighteous their thoughts.
Let them turn to the LORD, and he will
have mercy on them,
and to our God, for he will freely
pardon.

8 "For my thoughts are not your
thoughts,
neither are your ways my ways,"
declares the LORD.
9 "As the heavens are higher than the
earth,
so are my ways higher than your
ways
and my thoughts than your
thoughts.
10 As the rain and the snow
come down from heaven,
and do not return to it
without watering the earth
and making it bud and flourish,
so that it yields seed for the sower
and bread for the eater,
11 so is my word that goes out from my
mouth:
It will not return to me empty,
but will accomplish what I desire
and achieve the purpose for which I
sent it.

[a] *11* The meaning of the Hebrew for this word is uncertain.

12 You will go out in joy
and be led forth in peace;
the mountains and hills
will burst into song before you,
and all the trees of the field
will clap their hands.
13 Instead of the thornbush will grow
the juniper,
and instead of briers the myrtle will
grow.
This will be for the LORD's renown,
for an everlasting sign,
that will endure forever."

56 This is what the LORD says:

"Maintain justice
and do what is right,
for my salvation is close at hand
and my righteousness will soon be
revealed.
2 Blessed is the one who does this —
the person who holds it fast,
who keeps the Sabbath without
desecrating it,
and keeps their hands from doing
any evil."
3 Let no foreigner who is bound to the
LORD say,
"The LORD will surely exclude me
from his people."
And let no eunuch complain,
"I am only a dry tree."
4 For this is what the LORD says:

"To the eunuchs who keep my
Sabbaths,
who choose what pleases me
and hold fast to my covenant —
5 to them I will give within my temple
and its walls
a memorial and a name
better than sons and daughters;
I will give them an everlasting name
that will endure forever.
6 And foreigners who bind themselves
to the LORD
to minister to him,
to love the name of the LORD,
and to be his servants,
all who keep the Sabbath without
desecrating it
and who hold fast to my covenant —
7 these I will bring to my holy mountain
and give them joy in my house of
prayer.
Their burnt offerings and sacrifices
will be accepted on my altar;
for my house will be called
a house of prayer for all nations."
8 The Sovereign LORD declares —
he who gathers the exiles of Israel:
"I will gather still others to them
besides those already gathered."

9 Come, all you beasts of the field,
come and devour, all you beasts of
the forest!
10 Israel's watchmen are blind,
they all lack knowledge;
they are all mute dogs,
they cannot bark;
they lie around and dream,
they love to sleep.
11 They are dogs with mighty appetites;
they never have enough.
They are shepherds who lack
understanding;
they all turn to their own way,
they seek their own gain.
12 "Come," each one cries, "let me get
wine!
Let us drink our fill of beer!
And tomorrow will be like today,
or even far better."

57 The righteous perish,
and no one takes it to heart;
the devout are taken away,
and no one understands
that the righteous are taken away
to be spared from evil.
2 Those who walk uprightly
enter into peace;
they find rest as they lie in death.

3 "But you — come here, you children of
a sorceress,
you offspring of adulterers and
prostitutes!
4 Who are you mocking?
At whom do you sneer
and stick out your tongue?
Are you not a brood of rebels,
the offspring of liars?
5 You burn with lust among the oaks
and under every spreading tree;
you sacrifice your children in the
ravines
and under the overhanging crags.
6 The idols among the smooth stones of
the ravines are your portion;
indeed, they are your lot.
Yes, to them you have poured out
drink offerings

and offered grain offerings.
In view of all this, should I relent?
7 You have made your bed on a high and lofty hill;
there you went up to offer your sacrifices.
8 Behind your doors and your doorposts
you have put your pagan symbols.
Forsaking me, you uncovered your bed,
you climbed into it and opened it wide;
you made a pact with those whose beds you love,
and you looked with lust on their naked bodies.
9 You went to Molek[a] with olive oil
and increased your perfumes.
You sent your ambassadors[b] far away;
you descended to the very realm of the dead!
10 You wearied yourself by such going about,
but you would not say, 'It is hopeless.'
You found renewal of your strength,
and so you did not faint.

11 "Whom have you so dreaded and feared
that you have not been true to me,
and have neither remembered me
nor taken this to heart?
Is it not because I have long been silent
that you do not fear me?
12 I will expose your righteousness and your works,
and they will not benefit you.
13 When you cry out for help,
let your collection of idols save you!
The wind will carry all of them off,
a mere breath will blow them away.
But whoever takes refuge in me
will inherit the land
and possess my holy mountain."

14 And it will be said:

"Build up, build up, prepare the road!
Remove the obstacles out of the way of my people."
15 For this is what the high and exalted One says —
he who lives forever, whose name is holy:
"I live in a high and holy place,
but also with the one who is contrite and lowly in spirit,
to revive the spirit of the lowly
and to revive the heart of the contrite.
16 I will not accuse them forever,
nor will I always be angry,
for then they would faint away because of me —
the very people I have created.
17 I was enraged by their sinful greed;
I punished them, and hid my face in anger,
yet they kept on in their willful ways.
18 I have seen their ways, but I will heal them;
I will guide them and restore
comfort to Israel's mourners,
19 creating praise on their lips.
Peace, peace, to those far and near,"
says the LORD. "And I will heal them."
20 But the wicked are like the tossing sea,
which cannot rest,
whose waves cast up mire and mud.
21 "There is no peace," says my God, "for the wicked."

58 "Shout it aloud, do not hold back.
Raise your voice like a trumpet.
Declare to my people their rebellion
and to the descendants of Jacob their sins.
2 For day after day they seek me out;
they seem eager to know my ways,
as if they were a nation that does what is right
and has not forsaken the commands of its God.
They ask me for just decisions
and seem eager for God to come near them.
3 'Why have we fasted,' they say,
'and you have not seen it?
Why have we humbled ourselves,
and you have not noticed?'

"Yet on the day of your fasting, you do as you please
and exploit all your workers.
4 Your fasting ends in quarreling and strife,
and in striking each other with wicked fists.

[a] 9 Or *to the king* [b] 9 Or *idols*

You cannot fast as you do today
and expect your voice to be heard
on high.
5 Is this the kind of fast I have chosen,
only a day for people to humble
themselves?
Is it only for bowing one's head like a
reed
and for lying in sackcloth and
ashes?
Is that what you call a fast,
a day acceptable to the LORD?

6 "Is not this the kind of fasting I have
chosen:
to loose the chains of injustice
and untie the cords of the yoke,
to set the oppressed free
and break every yoke?
7 Is it not to share your food with the
hungry
and to provide the poor wanderer
with shelter—
when you see the naked, to clothe
them,
and not to turn away from your own
flesh and blood?
8 Then your light will break forth like
the dawn,
and your healing will quickly
appear;
then your righteousness[a] will go
before you,
and the glory of the LORD will be
your rear guard.
9 Then you will call, and the LORD will
answer;
you will cry for help, and he will say:
Here am I.

"If you do away with the yoke of
oppression,
with the pointing finger and
malicious talk,
10 and if you spend yourselves in behalf
of the hungry
and satisfy the needs of the
oppressed,
then your light will rise in the
darkness,
and your night will become like the
noonday.
11 The LORD will guide you always;
he will satisfy your needs in a sun-
scorched land
and will strengthen your frame.
You will be like a well-watered
garden,
like a spring whose waters never
fail.
12 Your people will rebuild the ancient
ruins
and will raise up the age-old
foundations;
you will be called Repairer of Broken
Walls,
Restorer of Streets with Dwellings.

13 "If you keep your feet from breaking
the Sabbath
and from doing as you please on my
holy day,
if you call the Sabbath a delight
and the LORD's holy day
honorable,
and if you honor it by not going your
own way
and not doing as you please or
speaking idle words,
14 then you will find your joy in the
LORD,
and I will cause you to ride in
triumph on the heights of the
land
and to feast on the inheritance of
your father Jacob."
For the mouth of the LORD
has spoken.

59 Surely the arm of the LORD is not
too short to save,
nor his ear too dull to hear.
2 But your iniquities have separated
you from your God;
your sins have hidden his face from
you,
so that he will not hear.
3 For your hands are stained with
blood,
your fingers with guilt.
Your lips have spoken falsely,
and your tongue mutters wicked
things.
4 No one calls for justice;
no one pleads a case with integrity.
They rely on empty arguments, they
utter lies;
they conceive trouble and give birth
to evil.
5 They hatch the eggs of vipers
and spin a spider's web.
Whoever eats their eggs will die,

[a] 8 Or *your righteous One*

and when one is broken, an adder is
hatched.
6 Their cobwebs are useless for
clothing;
they cannot cover themselves with
what they make.
Their deeds are evil deeds,
and acts of violence are in their
hands.
7 Their feet rush into sin;
they are swift to shed innocent
blood.
They pursue evil schemes;
acts of violence mark their ways.
8 The way of peace they do not know;
there is no justice in their paths.
They have turned them into crooked
roads;
no one who walks along them will
know peace.

9 So justice is far from us,
and righteousness does not reach
us.
We look for light, but all is darkness;
for brightness, but we walk in deep
shadows.
10 Like the blind we grope along the
wall,
feeling our way like people without
eyes.
At midday we stumble as if it were
twilight;
among the strong, we are like the
dead.
11 We all growl like bears;
we moan mournfully like doves.
We look for justice, but find none;
for deliverance, but it is far away.

12 For our offenses are many in your
sight,
and our sins testify against us.
Our offenses are ever with us,
and we acknowledge our iniquities:
13 rebellion and treachery against the
Lord,
turning our backs on our God,
inciting revolt and oppression,
uttering lies our hearts have
conceived.
14 So justice is driven back,
and righteousness stands at a
distance;
truth has stumbled in the streets,
honesty cannot enter.
15 Truth is nowhere to be found,
and whoever shuns evil becomes a
prey.

The Lord looked and was displeased
that there was no justice.
16 He saw that there was no one,
he was appalled that there was no
one to intervene;
so his own arm achieved salvation for
him,
and his own righteousness
sustained him.
17 He put on righteousness as his
breastplate,
and the helmet of salvation on his
head;
he put on the garments of vengeance
and wrapped himself in zeal as in a
cloak.
18 According to what they have done,
so will he repay
wrath to his enemies
and retribution to his foes;
he will repay the islands their due.
19 From the west, people will fear the
name of the Lord,
and from the rising of the sun, they
will revere his glory.
For he will come like a pent-up flood
that the breath of the Lord drives
along.[a]

20 "The Redeemer will come to Zion,
to those in Jacob who repent of their
sins,"
declares the Lord.

21 "As for me, this is my covenant with
them," says the Lord. "My Spirit, who is
on you, will not depart from you, and my
words that I have put in your mouth will
always be on your lips, on the lips of your
children and on the lips of their descendants — from this time on and forever,"
says the Lord.

60 "Arise, shine, for your light has
come,
and the glory of the Lord rises upon
you.
2 See, darkness covers the earth
and thick darkness is over the
peoples,
but the Lord rises upon you
and his glory appears over you.
3 Nations will come to your light,

[a] 19 Or *When enemies come in like a flood, / the Spirit of the Lord will put them to flight*

and kings to the brightness of your
dawn.
4 "Lift up your eyes and look about you:
All assemble and come to you;
your sons come from afar,
and your daughters are carried on
the hip.
5 Then you will look and be radiant,
your heart will throb and swell with
joy;
the wealth on the seas will be brought
to you,
to you the riches of the nations will
come.
6 Herds of camels will cover your land,
young camels of Midian and Ephah.
And all from Sheba will come,
bearing gold and incense
and proclaiming the praise of the
LORD.
7 All Kedar's flocks will be gathered to
you,
the rams of Nebaioth will serve you;
they will be accepted as offerings on
my altar,
and I will adorn my glorious temple.

8 "Who are these that fly along like
clouds,
like doves to their nests?
9 Surely the islands look to me;
in the lead are the ships of
Tarshish,[a]
bringing your children from afar,
with their silver and gold,
to the honor of the LORD your God,
the Holy One of Israel,
for he has endowed you with
splendor.

10 "Foreigners will rebuild your walls,
and their kings will serve you.
Though in anger I struck you,
in favor I will show you compassion.
11 Your gates will always stand open,
they will never be shut, day or night,
so that people may bring you the
wealth of the nations—
their kings led in triumphal
procession.
12 For the nation or kingdom that will
not serve you will perish;
it will be utterly ruined.

13 "The glory of Lebanon will come to
you,
the juniper, the fir and the cypress
together,
to adorn my sanctuary;
and I will glorify the place for my
feet.
14 The children of your oppressors will
come bowing before you;
all who despise you will bow down
at your feet
and will call you the City of the LORD,
Zion of the Holy One of Israel.

15 "Although you have been forsaken
and hated,
with no one traveling through,
I will make you the everlasting pride
and the joy of all generations.
16 You will drink the milk of nations
and be nursed at royal breasts.
Then you will know that I, the LORD,
am your Savior,
your Redeemer, the Mighty One of
Jacob.
17 Instead of bronze I will bring you
gold,
and silver in place of iron.
Instead of wood I will bring you
bronze,
and iron in place of stones.
I will make peace your governor
and well-being your ruler.
18 No longer will violence be heard in
your land,
nor ruin or destruction within your
borders,
but you will call your walls Salvation
and your gates Praise.
19 The sun will no more be your light by
day,
nor will the brightness of the moon
shine on you,
for the LORD will be your everlasting
light,
and your God will be your glory.
20 Your sun will never set again,
and your moon will wane no more;
the LORD will be your everlasting
light,
and your days of sorrow will end.
21 Then all your people will be righteous
and they will possess the land
forever.
They are the shoot I have planted,
the work of my hands,
for the display of my splendor.

a 9 Or *the trading ships*

22 The least of you will become a
thousand,
the smallest a mighty nation.
I am the LORD;
in its time I will do this swiftly."

61

The Spirit of the Sovereign LORD
is on me,
because the LORD has anointed me
to proclaim good news to the poor.
He has sent me to bind up the
brokenhearted,
to proclaim freedom for the
captives
and release from darkness for the
prisoners,[a]
2 to proclaim the year of the LORD's
favor
and the day of vengeance of our
God,
to comfort all who mourn,
3 and provide for those who grieve in
Zion —
to bestow on them a crown of beauty
instead of ashes,
the oil of joy
instead of mourning,
and a garment of praise
instead of a spirit of despair.
They will be called oaks of
righteousness,
a planting of the LORD
for the display of his splendor.

4 They will rebuild the ancient ruins
and restore the places long
devastated;
they will renew the ruined cities
that have been devastated for
generations.
5 Strangers will shepherd your flocks;
foreigners will work your fields and
vineyards.
6 And you will be called priests of the
LORD,
you will be named ministers of our
God.
You will feed on the wealth of nations,
and in their riches you will boast.

7 Instead of your shame
you will receive a double portion,
and instead of disgrace
you will rejoice in your inheritance.
And so you will inherit a double
portion in your land,
and everlasting joy will be yours.

8 "For I, the LORD, love justice;
I hate robbery and wrongdoing.
In my faithfulness I will reward my
people
and make an everlasting covenant
with them.
9 Their descendants will be known
among the nations
and their offspring among the
peoples.
All who see them will acknowledge
that they are a people the LORD has
blessed."

10 I delight greatly in the LORD;
my soul rejoices in my God.
For he has clothed me with garments
of salvation
and arrayed me in a robe of his
righteousness,
as a bridegroom adorns his head like
a priest,
and as a bride adorns herself with
her jewels.
11 For as the soil makes the sprout come
up
and a garden causes seeds to grow,
so the Sovereign LORD will make
righteousness
and praise spring up before all
nations.

62

For Zion's sake I will not keep
silent,
for Jerusalem's sake I will not
remain quiet,
till her vindication shines out like the
dawn,
her salvation like a blazing torch.
2 The nations will see your vindication,
and all kings your glory;
you will be called by a new name
that the mouth of the LORD will
bestow.
3 You will be a crown of splendor in the
LORD's hand,
a royal diadem in the hand of your
God.
4 No longer will they call you Deserted,
or name your land Desolate.
But you will be called Hephzibah,[b]
and your land Beulah[c];
for the LORD will take delight in you,
and your land will be married.
5 As a young man marries a young
woman,

[a] *1* Hebrew; Septuagint *the blind* [b] *4* *Hephzibah* means *my delight is in her.* [c] *4* *Beulah* means *married.*

so will your Builder marry you;
as a bridegroom rejoices over his bride,
so will your God rejoice over you.

6 I have posted watchmen on your walls, Jerusalem;
they will never be silent day or night.
You who call on the LORD,
give yourselves no rest,
7 and give him no rest till he establishes Jerusalem
and makes her the praise of the earth.

8 The LORD has sworn by his right hand
and by his mighty arm:
"Never again will I give your grain
as food for your enemies,
and never again will foreigners drink the new wine
for which you have toiled;
9 but those who harvest it will eat it
and praise the LORD,
and those who gather the grapes will drink it
in the courts of my sanctuary."

10 Pass through, pass through the gates!
Prepare the way for the people.
Build up, build up the highway!
Remove the stones.
Raise a banner for the nations.

11 The LORD has made proclamation
to the ends of the earth:
"Say to Daughter Zion,
'See, your Savior comes!
See, his reward is with him,
and his recompense accompanies him.'"
12 They will be called the Holy People,
the Redeemed of the LORD;
and you will be called Sought After,
the City No Longer Deserted.

63 Who is this coming from Edom,
from Bozrah, with his garments stained crimson?
Who is this, robed in splendor,
striding forward in the greatness of his strength?
"It is I, proclaiming victory,
mighty to save."

2 Why are your garments red,
like those of one treading the winepress?

3 "I have trodden the winepress alone;
from the nations no one was with me.
I trampled them in my anger
and trod them down in my wrath;
their blood spattered my garments,
and I stained all my clothing.
4 It was for me the day of vengeance;
the year for me to redeem had come.
5 I looked, but there was no one to help,
I was appalled that no one gave support;
so my own arm achieved salvation for me,
and my own wrath sustained me.
6 I trampled the nations in my anger;
in my wrath I made them drunk
and poured their blood on the ground."

7 I will tell of the kindnesses of the LORD,
the deeds for which he is to be praised,
according to all the LORD has done for us—
yes, the many good things
he has done for Israel,
according to his compassion and many kindnesses.
8 He said, "Surely they are my people,
children who will be true to me";
and so he became their Savior.
9 In all their distress he too was distressed,
and the angel of his presence saved them.[a]
In his love and mercy he redeemed them;
he lifted them up and carried them
all the days of old.
10 Yet they rebelled
and grieved his Holy Spirit.
So he turned and became their enemy
and he himself fought against them.

11 Then his people recalled[b] the days of old,
the days of Moses and his people—
where is he who brought them
through the sea,

[a] 9 Or *Savior* [9] *in their distress. / It was no envoy or angel / but his own presence that saved them* [b] 11 Or *But may he recall*

with the shepherd of his flock?
Where is he who set
his Holy Spirit among them,
12 who sent his glorious arm of power
to be at Moses' right hand,
who divided the waters before them,
to gain for himself everlasting
renown,
13 who led them through the depths?
Like a horse in open country,
they did not stumble;
14 like cattle that go down to the plain,
they were given rest by the Spirit of
the LORD.
This is how you guided your people
to make for yourself a glorious name.

15 Look down from heaven and see,
from your lofty throne, holy and
glorious.
Where are your zeal and your might?
Your tenderness and compassion
are withheld from us.
16 But you are our Father,
though Abraham does not know us
or Israel acknowledge us;
you, LORD, are our Father,
our Redeemer from of old is your
name.
17 Why, LORD, do you make us wander
from your ways
and harden our hearts so we do not
revere you?
Return for the sake of your servants,
the tribes that are your inheritance.
18 For a little while your people
possessed your holy place,
but now our enemies have trampled
down your sanctuary.
19 We are yours from of old;
but you have not ruled over them,
they have not been called[a] by your
name.

64[b] Oh, that you would rend the
heavens and come down,
that the mountains would tremble
before you!
2 As when fire sets twigs ablaze
and causes water to boil,
come down to make your name
known to your enemies
and cause the nations to quake
before you!
3 For when you did awesome things
that we did not expect,
you came down, and the mountains
trembled before you.
4 Since ancient times no one has heard,
no ear has perceived,
no eye has seen any God besides you,
who acts on behalf of those who
wait for him.
5 You come to the help of those who
gladly do right,
who remember your ways.
But when we continued to sin against
them,
you were angry.
How then can we be saved?
6 All of us have become like one who is
unclean,
and all our righteous acts are like
filthy rags;
we all shrivel up like a leaf,
and like the wind our sins sweep us
away.
7 No one calls on your name
or strives to lay hold of you;
for you have hidden your face from us
and have given us over to[c] our sins.

8 Yet you, LORD, are our Father.
We are the clay, you are the potter;
we are all the work of your hand.
9 Do not be angry beyond measure,
LORD;
do not remember our sins forever.
Oh, look on us, we pray,
for we are all your people.
10 Your sacred cities have become a
wasteland;
even Zion is a wasteland, Jerusalem
a desolation.
11 Our holy and glorious temple, where
our ancestors praised you,
has been burned with fire,
and all that we treasured lies in
ruins.
12 After all this, LORD, will you hold
yourself back?
Will you keep silent and punish us
beyond measure?

65 "I revealed myself to those who did
not ask for me;
I was found by those who did not
seek me.

[a] 19 Or *We are like those you have never ruled, / like those never called* [b] In Hebrew texts 64:1 is numbered 63:19b, and 64:2-12 is numbered 64:1-11. [c] 7 Septuagint, Syriac and Targum; Hebrew *have made us melt because of*

To a nation that did not call on my
name,
I said, 'Here am I, here am I.'
2 All day long I have held out my hands
to an obstinate people,
who walk in ways not good,
pursuing their own imaginations —
3 a people who continually provoke
me
to my very face,
offering sacrifices in gardens
and burning incense on altars of
brick;
4 who sit among the graves
and spend their nights keeping
secret vigil;
who eat the flesh of pigs,
and whose pots hold broth of
impure meat;
5 who say, 'Keep away; don't come near
me,
for I am too sacred for you!'
Such people are smoke in my nostrils,
a fire that keeps burning all day.

6 "See, it stands written before me:
I will not keep silent but will pay
back in full;
I will pay it back into their laps —
7 both your sins and the sins of your
ancestors,"
says the LORD.
"Because they burned sacrifices on
the mountains
and defied me on the hills,
I will measure into their laps
the full payment for their former
deeds."

8 This is what the LORD says:

"As when juice is still found in a
cluster of grapes
and people say, 'Don't destroy it,
there is still a blessing in it,'
so will I do in behalf of my servants;
I will not destroy them all.
9 I will bring forth descendants from
Jacob,
and from Judah those who will
possess my mountains;
my chosen people will inherit them,
and there will my servants live.
10 Sharon will become a pasture for
flocks,
and the Valley of Achor a resting
place for herds,
for my people who seek me.

11 "But as for you who forsake the LORD
and forget my holy mountain,
who spread a table for Fortune
and fill bowls of mixed wine for
Destiny,
12 I will destine you for the sword,
and all of you will fall in the
slaughter;
for I called but you did not answer,
I spoke but you did not listen.
You did evil in my sight
and chose what displeases me."

13 Therefore this is what the Sovereign
LORD says:

"My servants will eat,
but you will go hungry;
my servants will drink,
but you will go thirsty;
my servants will rejoice,
but you will be put to shame.
14 My servants will sing
out of the joy of their hearts,
but you will cry out
from anguish of heart
and wail in brokenness of spirit.
15 You will leave your name
for my chosen ones to use in their
curses;
the Sovereign LORD will put you to
death,
but to his servants he will give
another name.
16 Whoever invokes a blessing in the
land
will do so by the one true God;
whoever takes an oath in the land
will swear by the one true God.
For the past troubles will be forgotten
and hidden from my eyes.
17 "See, I will create
new heavens and a new earth.
The former things will not be
remembered,
nor will they come to mind.
18 But be glad and rejoice forever
in what I will create,
for I will create Jerusalem to be a
delight
and its people a joy.
19 I will rejoice over Jerusalem
and take delight in my people;
the sound of weeping and of crying
will be heard in it no more.

20 "Never again will there be in it
an infant who lives but a few days,

or an old man who does not live out
his years;
the one who dies at a hundred
will be thought a mere child;
the one who fails to reach[a] a hundred
will be considered accursed.
21 They will build houses and dwell in
them;
they will plant vineyards and eat
their fruit.
22 No longer will they build houses and
others live in them,
or plant and others eat.
For as the days of a tree,
so will be the days of my people;
my chosen ones will long enjoy
the work of their hands.
23 They will not labor in vain,
nor will they bear children doomed
to misfortune;
for they will be a people blessed by
the LORD,
they and their descendants with
them.
24 Before they call I will answer;
while they are still speaking I will
hear.
25 The wolf and the lamb will feed
together,
and the lion will eat straw like the
ox,
and dust will be the serpent's food.
They will neither harm nor destroy
on all my holy mountain,"
says the LORD.

66 This is what the LORD says:

"Heaven is my throne,
and the earth is my footstool.
Where is the house you will build for
me?
Where will my resting place be?
2 Has not my hand made all these
things,
and so they came into being?"
declares the LORD.

"These are the ones I look on with
favor:
those who are humble and contrite
in spirit,
and who tremble at my word.
3 But whoever sacrifices a bull
is like one who kills a person,
and whoever offers a lamb
is like one who breaks a dog's neck;
whoever makes a grain offering
is like one who presents pig's blood,
and whoever burns memorial incense
is like one who worships an idol.
They have chosen their own ways,
and they delight in their
abominations;
4 so I also will choose harsh treatment
for them
and will bring on them what they
dread.
For when I called, no one answered,
when I spoke, no one listened.
They did evil in my sight
and chose what displeases me."

5 Hear the word of the LORD,
you who tremble at his word:
"Your own people who hate you,
and exclude you because of my
name, have said,
'Let the LORD be glorified,
that we may see your joy!'
Yet they will be put to shame.
6 Hear that uproar from the city,
hear that noise from the temple!
It is the sound of the LORD
repaying his enemies all they
deserve.

7 "Before she goes into labor,
she gives birth;
before the pains come upon her,
she delivers a son.
8 Who has ever heard of such things?
Who has ever seen things like this?
Can a country be born in a day
or a nation be brought forth in a
moment?
Yet no sooner is Zion in labor
than she gives birth to her children.
9 Do I bring to the moment of birth
and not give delivery?" says the
LORD.
"Do I close up the womb
when I bring to delivery?" says your
God.
10 "Rejoice with Jerusalem and be glad
for her,
all you who love her;
rejoice greatly with her,
all you who mourn over her.
11 For you will nurse and be satisfied
at her comforting breasts;
you will drink deeply

[a] 20 Or *the sinner who reaches*

and delight in her overflowing
abundance."

12 For this is what the LORD says:

"I will extend peace to her like a river
and the wealth of nations like a
flooding stream;
you will nurse and be carried on her
arm
and dandled on her knees.
13 As a mother comforts her child,
so will I comfort you;
and you will be comforted over
Jerusalem."
14 When you see this, your heart will
rejoice
and you will flourish like grass;
the hand of the LORD will be made
known to his servants,
but his fury will be shown to his
foes.
15 See, the LORD is coming with fire,
and his chariots are like a
whirlwind;
he will bring down his anger with
fury,
and his rebuke with flames of fire.
16 For with fire and with his sword
the LORD will execute judgment on
all people,
and many will be those slain by the
LORD.

17 "Those who consecrate and purify
themselves to go into the gardens, following one who is among those who eat
the flesh of pigs, rats and other unclean
things — they will meet their end together with the one they follow," declares the
LORD.

18 "And I, because of what they have
planned and done, am about to come[a]
and gather the people of all nations and
languages, and they will come and see
my glory.
19 "I will set a sign among them, and I
will send some of those who survive to
the nations — to Tarshish, to the Libyans[b] and Lydians (famous as archers),
to Tubal and Greece, and to the distant
islands that have not heard of my fame
or seen my glory. They will proclaim my
glory among the nations. 20 And they will
bring all your people, from all the nations, to my holy mountain in Jerusalem
as an offering to the LORD — on horses, in
chariots and wagons, and on mules and
camels," says the LORD. "They will bring
them, as the Israelites bring their grain
offerings, to the temple of the LORD in
ceremonially clean vessels. 21 And I will
select some of them also to be priests and
Levites," says the LORD.

22 "As the new heavens and the new
earth that I make will endure before
me," declares the LORD, "so will your
name and descendants endure. 23 From
one New Moon to another and from one
Sabbath to another, all mankind will
come and bow down before me," says the
LORD. 24 "And they will go out and look
on the dead bodies of those who rebelled
against me; the worms that eat them will
not die, the fire that burns them will not
be quenched, and they will be loathsome
to all mankind."

[a] *18* The meaning of the Hebrew for this clause is uncertain. [b] *19* Some Septuagint manuscripts *Put* (Libyans); Hebrew *Pul*

JEREMIAH

The prophet Jeremiah spoke to the kingdom of Judah for forty years—from the end of the Assyrian period until Judah was destroyed by Babylon. The book mixes sermons, prophetic oracles, and biographical narratives of Jeremiah's experiences during the last years of the Judean kingdom. We are given an intimate look into the prophet's own heart as he brings God's message to his fellow Judeans, who reject him and even conspire to kill him.

The book begins and ends with historical references to the event Jeremiah was best known for predicting: the fall of Jerusalem. The four main parts generally consist (in order) of oracles, narratives (two sections), and then oracles. Significantly, each of these four parts ends with a reference to Jeremiah's words being written in a book or scroll. A long poetic oracle is inserted in the middle narrative of the book. So Jeremiah's prophecies appear at the beginning, middle and end of the book, highlighting their importance. The middle oracle, promising a new covenant designed to change the human heart, is shown to be the most important of all. God will do more than simply punish evil—he will overcome it with good.

The book of Jeremiah carries us back and forth in place and time as we turn its pages, yet its themes are consistent. The message of judgment for wrongdoing is followed by the restorative power of forgiveness and new life: *to uproot and tear down, to destroy and overthrow, to build and to plant.*

---

1 The words of Jeremiah son of Hilkiah, one of the priests at Anathoth in
the territory of Benjamin. 2 The word of
the LORD came to him in the thirteenth
year of the reign of Josiah son of Amon
king of Judah, 3 and through the reign of
Jehoiakim son of Josiah king of Judah,
down to the fifth month of the eleventh
year of Zedekiah son of Josiah king of Judah, when the people of Jerusalem went
into exile.

4 The word of the LORD came to me,
saying,

5 "Before I formed you in the womb I
knew[a] you,
before you were born I set you apart;
I appointed you as a prophet to the
nations."

6 "Alas, Sovereign LORD," I said, "I do
not know how to speak; I am too young."
7 But the LORD said to me, "Do not say, 'I
am too young.' You must go to everyone I
send you to and say whatever I command
you. 8 Do not be afraid of them, for I am
with you and will rescue you," declares
the LORD.
9 Then the LORD reached out his hand
and touched my mouth and said to me,
"I have put my words in your mouth.
10 See, today I appoint you over nations
and kingdoms to uproot and tear down,
to destroy and overthrow, to build and
to plant."
11 The word of the LORD came to me:
"What do you see, Jeremiah?"
"I see the branch of an almond tree," I
replied.
12 The LORD said to me, "You have seen
correctly, for I am watching[b] to see that
my word is fulfilled."
13 The word of the LORD came to me
again: "What do you see?"
"I see a pot that is boiling," I answered.
"It is tilting toward us from the north."
14 The LORD said to me, "From the north
disaster will be poured out on all who live
in the land. 15 I am about to summon all
the peoples of the northern kingdoms,"
declares the LORD.

"Their kings will come and set up their
thrones
in the entrance of the gates of
Jerusalem;
they will come against all her
surrounding walls
and against all the towns of Judah.
16 I will pronounce my judgments on my
people
because of their wickedness in
forsaking me,
in burning incense to other gods
and in worshiping what their hands
have made.

[a] 5 Or *chose* [b] 12 The Hebrew for *watching* sounds like the Hebrew for *almond tree.*

You have defiled the land
with your prostitution and
wickedness.
3 Therefore the showers have been
withheld,
and no spring rains have fallen.
Yet you have the brazen look of a
prostitute;
you refuse to blush with shame.
4 Have you not just called to me:
'My Father, my friend from my
youth,
5 will you always be angry?
Will your wrath continue forever?'
This is how you talk,
but you do all the evil you can."

6 During the reign of King Josiah, the
LORD said to me, "Have you seen what
faithless Israel has done? She has gone
up on every high hill and under every
spreading tree and has committed adultery there. 7 I thought that after she had
done all this she would return to me but
she did not, and her unfaithful sister Judah saw it. 8 I gave faithless Israel her certificate of divorce and sent her away because of all her adulteries. Yet I saw that
her unfaithful sister Judah had no fear;
she also went out and committed adultery. 9 Because Israel's immorality mat-
tered so little to her, she defiled the land
and committed adultery with stone and
wood. 10 In spite of all this, her unfaithful
sister Judah did not return to me with all
her heart, but only in pretense," declares
the LORD.

11 The LORD said to me, "Faithless Israel
is more righteous than unfaithful Judah.
12 Go, proclaim this message toward the
north:

"'Return, faithless Israel,' declares the
LORD,
'I will frown on you no longer,
for I am faithful,' declares the LORD,
'I will not be angry forever.
13 Only acknowledge your guilt—
you have rebelled against the LORD
your God,
you have scattered your favors to
foreign gods
under every spreading tree,
and have not obeyed me,'"
declares the LORD.

14 "Return, faithless people," declares
the LORD, "for I am your husband. I will
choose you—one from a town and two
from a clan—and bring you to Zion.
15 Then I will give you shepherds after
my own heart, who will lead you with
knowledge and understanding. 16 In
those days, when your numbers have increased greatly in the land," declares the
LORD, "people will no longer say, 'The ark
of the covenant of the LORD.' It will never enter their minds or be remembered; it
will not be missed, nor will another one
be made. 17 At that time they will call Jerusalem The Throne of the LORD, and all
nations will gather in Jerusalem to hon-
or the name of the LORD. No longer will
they follow the stubbornness of their
evil hearts. 18 In those days the people of
Judah will join the people of Israel, and
together they will come from a northern
land to the land I gave your ancestors as
an inheritance.

19 "I myself said,

"'How gladly would I treat you like my
children
and give you a pleasant land,
the most beautiful inheritance of
any nation.'
I thought you would call me 'Father'
and not turn away from following
me.
20 But like a woman unfaithful to her
husband,
so you, Israel, have been unfaithful
to me,"
declares the LORD.

21 A cry is heard on the barren heights,
the weeping and pleading of the
people of Israel,
because they have perverted their
ways
and have forgotten the LORD their
God.
22 "Return, faithless people;
I will cure you of backsliding."

"Yes, we will come to you,
for you are the LORD our God.
23 Surely the idolatrous commotion on
the hills
and mountains is a deception;
surely in the LORD our God
is the salvation of Israel.
24 From our youth shameful gods have
consumed
the fruits of our ancestors' labor—
their flocks and herds,
their sons and daughters.

25 Let us lie down in our shame,
and let our disgrace cover us.
We have sinned against the LORD our God,
both we and our ancestors;
from our youth till this day
we have not obeyed the LORD our God."

4 "If you, Israel, will return,
then return to me,"
declares the LORD.
"If you put your detestable idols out of my sight
and no longer go astray,
2 and if in a truthful, just and righteous way
you swear, 'As surely as the LORD lives,'
then the nations will invoke blessings by him
and in him they will boast."

3 This is what the LORD says to the people of Judah and to Jerusalem:

"Break up your unplowed ground
and do not sow among thorns.
4 Circumcise yourselves to the LORD,
circumcise your hearts,
you people of Judah and inhabitants of Jerusalem,
or my wrath will flare up and burn like fire
because of the evil you have done—
burn with no one to quench it.

5 "Announce in Judah and proclaim in Jerusalem and say:
'Sound the trumpet throughout the land!'
Cry aloud and say:
'Gather together!
Let us flee to the fortified cities!'
6 Raise the signal to go to Zion!
Flee for safety without delay!
For I am bringing disaster from the north,
even terrible destruction."

7 A lion has come out of his lair;
a destroyer of nations has set out.
He has left his place
to lay waste your land.
Your towns will lie in ruins
without inhabitant.
8 So put on sackcloth,
lament and wail,
for the fierce anger of the LORD
has not turned away from us.

9 "In that day," declares the LORD,
"the king and the officials will lose heart,
the priests will be horrified,
and the prophets will be appalled."

10 Then I said, "Alas, Sovereign LORD!
How completely you have deceived this
people and Jerusalem by saying, 'You
will have peace,' when the sword is at our
throats!"

11 At that time this people and Jerusalem will be told, "A scorching wind from
the barren heights in the desert blows
toward my people, but not to winnow
or cleanse; 12 a wind too strong for that
comes from me. Now I pronounce my
judgments against them."

13 Look! He advances like the clouds,
his chariots come like a whirlwind,
his horses are swifter than eagles.
Woe to us! We are ruined!
14 Jerusalem, wash the evil from your heart and be saved.
How long will you harbor wicked thoughts?
15 A voice is announcing from Dan,
proclaiming disaster from the hills of Ephraim.
16 "Tell this to the nations,
proclaim concerning Jerusalem:
'A besieging army is coming from a distant land,
raising a war cry against the cities of Judah.
17 They surround her like men guarding a field,
because she has rebelled against me,' "
declares the LORD.
18 "Your own conduct and actions
have brought this on you.
This is your punishment.
How bitter it is!
How it pierces to the heart!"

19 Oh, my anguish, my anguish!
I writhe in pain.
Oh, the agony of my heart!
My heart pounds within me,
I cannot keep silent.
For I have heard the sound of the trumpet;
I have heard the battle cry.
20 Disaster follows disaster;
the whole land lies in ruins.
In an instant my tents are destroyed,
my shelter in a moment.

21 How long must I see the battle
standard
and hear the sound of the trumpet?

22 "My people are fools;
they do not know me.
They are senseless children;
they have no understanding.
They are skilled in doing evil;
they know not how to do good."

23 I looked at the earth,
and it was formless and empty;
and at the heavens,
and their light was gone.
24 I looked at the mountains,
and they were quaking;
all the hills were swaying.
25 I looked, and there were no people;
every bird in the sky had flown
away.
26 I looked, and the fruitful land was a
desert;
all its towns lay in ruins
before the LORD, before his fierce
anger.

27 This is what the LORD says:

"The whole land will be ruined,
though I will not destroy it
completely.
28 Therefore the earth will mourn
and the heavens above grow dark,
because I have spoken and will not
relent,
I have decided and will not turn
back."

29 At the sound of horsemen and archers
every town takes to flight.
Some go into the thickets;
some climb up among the rocks.
All the towns are deserted;
no one lives in them.

30 What are you doing, you devastated
one?
Why dress yourself in scarlet
and put on jewels of gold?
Why highlight your eyes with
makeup?
You adorn yourself in vain.
Your lovers despise you;
they want to kill you.

31 I hear a cry as of a woman in labor,
a groan as of one bearing her first
child—
the cry of Daughter Zion gasping for
breath,
stretching out her hands and saying,
"Alas! I am fainting;
my life is given over to murderers."

5 "Go up and down the streets of
Jerusalem,
look around and consider,
search through her squares.
If you can find but one person
who deals honestly and seeks the
truth,
I will forgive this city.
2 Although they say, 'As surely as the
LORD lives,'
still they are swearing falsely."

3 LORD, do not your eyes look for truth?
You struck them, but they felt no
pain;
you crushed them, but they refused
correction.
They made their faces harder than
stone
and refused to repent.
4 I thought, "These are only the poor;
they are foolish,
for they do not know the way of the
LORD,
the requirements of their God.
5 So I will go to the leaders
and speak to them;
surely they know the way of the LORD,
the requirements of their God."
But with one accord they too had
broken off the yoke
and torn off the bonds.
6 Therefore a lion from the forest will
attack them,
a wolf from the desert will ravage
them,
a leopard will lie in wait near their
towns
to tear to pieces any who venture
out,
for their rebellion is great
and their backslidings many.

7 "Why should I forgive you?
Your children have forsaken me
and sworn by gods that are not gods.
I supplied all their needs,
yet they committed adultery
and thronged to the houses of
prostitutes.
8 They are well-fed, lusty stallions,
each neighing for another man's
wife.
9 Should I not punish them for this?"
declares the LORD.

"Should I not avenge myself
on such a nation as this?

10 "Go through her vineyards and ravage
them,
but do not destroy them completely.
Strip off her branches,
for these people do not belong to the
LORD.
11 The people of Israel and the people of
Judah
have been utterly unfaithful to me,"
declares the LORD.

12 They have lied about the LORD;
they said, "He will do nothing!
No harm will come to us;
we will never see sword or famine.
13 The prophets are but wind
and the word is not in them;
so let what they say be done to
them."

14 Therefore this is what the LORD God
Almighty says:

"Because the people have spoken
these words,
I will make my words in your mouth
a fire
and these people the wood it
consumes.
15 People of Israel," declares the LORD,
"I am bringing a distant nation
against you —
an ancient and enduring nation,
a people whose language you do not
know,
whose speech you do not
understand.
16 Their quivers are like an open grave;
all of them are mighty warriors.
17 They will devour your harvests and
food,
devour your sons and daughters;
they will devour your flocks and
herds,
devour your vines and fig trees.
With the sword they will destroy
the fortified cities in which you
trust.

18 "Yet even in those days," declares the
LORD, "I will not destroy you completely. 19 And when the people ask, 'Why has
the LORD our God done all this to us?'
you will tell them, 'As you have forsaken
me and served foreign gods in your own
land, so now you will serve foreigners in
a land not your own.'

20 "Announce this to the descendants of
Jacob
and proclaim it in Judah:
21 Hear this, you foolish and senseless
people,
who have eyes but do not see,
who have ears but do not hear:
22 Should you not fear me?" declares the
LORD.
"Should you not tremble in my
presence?
I made the sand a boundary for the
sea,
an everlasting barrier it cannot
cross.
The waves may roll, but they cannot
prevail;
they may roar, but they cannot
cross it.
23 But these people have stubborn and
rebellious hearts;
they have turned aside and gone
away.
24 They do not say to themselves,
'Let us fear the LORD our God,
who gives autumn and spring rains in
season,
who assures us of the regular weeks
of harvest.'
25 Your wrongdoings have kept these
away;
your sins have deprived you of good.

26 "Among my people are the wicked
who lie in wait like men who snare
birds
and like those who set traps to catch
people.
27 Like cages full of birds,
their houses are full of deceit;
they have become rich and powerful
28 and have grown fat and sleek.
Their evil deeds have no limit;
they do not seek justice.
They do not promote the case of the
fatherless;
they do not defend the just cause of
the poor.
29 Should I not punish them for this?"
declares the LORD.
"Should I not avenge myself
on such a nation as this?

30 "A horrible and shocking thing
has happened in the land:
31 The prophets prophesy lies,
the priests rule by their own
authority,

and my people love it this way.
But what will you do in the end?

6 "Flee for safety, people of Benjamin!
Flee from Jerusalem!
Sound the trumpet in Tekoa!
Raise the signal over Beth Hakkerem!
For disaster looms out of the north,
even terrible destruction.
2 I will destroy Daughter Zion,
so beautiful and delicate.
3 Shepherds with their flocks will come against her;
they will pitch their tents around her,
each tending his own portion."

4 "Prepare for battle against her!
Arise, let us attack at noon!
But, alas, the daylight is fading,
and the shadows of evening grow long.
5 So arise, let us attack at night
and destroy her fortresses!"

6 This is what the LORD Almighty says:

"Cut down the trees
and build siege ramps against Jerusalem.
This city must be punished;
it is filled with oppression.
7 As a well pours out its water,
so she pours out her wickedness.
Violence and destruction resound in her;
her sickness and wounds are ever before me.
8 Take warning, Jerusalem,
or I will turn away from you
and make your land desolate
so no one can live in it."

9 This is what the LORD Almighty says:

"Let them glean the remnant of Israel
as thoroughly as a vine;
pass your hand over the branches again,
like one gathering grapes."

10 To whom can I speak and give warning?
Who will listen to me?
Their ears are closed[a]
so they cannot hear.
The word of the LORD is offensive to them;
they find no pleasure in it.
11 But I am full of the wrath of the LORD,
and I cannot hold it in.

"Pour it out on the children in the street
and on the young men gathered together;
both husband and wife will be caught in it,
and the old, those weighed down with years.
12 Their houses will be turned over to others,
together with their fields and their wives,
when I stretch out my hand
against those who live in the land,"
declares the LORD.
13 "From the least to the greatest,
all are greedy for gain;
prophets and priests alike,
all practice deceit.
14 They dress the wound of my people
as though it were not serious.
'Peace, peace,' they say,
when there is no peace.
15 Are they ashamed of their detestable conduct?
No, they have no shame at all;
they do not even know how to blush.
So they will fall among the fallen;
they will be brought down when I punish them,"
says the LORD.

16 This is what the LORD says:

"Stand at the crossroads and look;
ask for the ancient paths,
ask where the good way is, and walk in it,
and you will find rest for your souls.
But you said, 'We will not walk in it.'
17 I appointed watchmen over you and said,
'Listen to the sound of the trumpet!'
But you said, 'We will not listen.'
18 Therefore hear, you nations;
you who are witnesses,
observe what will happen to them.
19 Hear, you earth:
I am bringing disaster on this people,
the fruit of their schemes,
because they have not listened to my words

[a] *10* Hebrew *uncircumcised*

and have rejected my law.
20 What do I care about incense from Sheba
or sweet calamus from a distant land?
Your burnt offerings are not acceptable;
your sacrifices do not please me."

21 Therefore this is what the LORD says:

"I will put obstacles before this people.
Parents and children alike will stumble over them;
neighbors and friends will perish."

22 This is what the LORD says:

"Look, an army is coming
from the land of the north;
a great nation is being stirred up
from the ends of the earth.
23 They are armed with bow and spear;
they are cruel and show no mercy.
They sound like the roaring sea
as they ride on their horses;
they come like men in battle formation
to attack you, Daughter Zion."

24 We have heard reports about them,
and our hands hang limp.
Anguish has gripped us,
pain like that of a woman in labor.
25 Do not go out to the fields
or walk on the roads,
for the enemy has a sword,
and there is terror on every side.
26 Put on sackcloth, my people,
and roll in ashes;
mourn with bitter wailing
as for an only son,
for suddenly the destroyer
will come upon us.

27 "I have made you a tester of metals
and my people the ore,
that you may observe
and test their ways.
28 They are all hardened rebels,
going about to slander.
They are bronze and iron;
they all act corruptly.
29 The bellows blow fiercely
to burn away the lead with fire,
but the refining goes on in vain;
the wicked are not purged out.
30 They are called rejected silver,
because the LORD has rejected them."

7 This is the word that came to Jeremiah from the LORD: 2 "Stand at the gate
of the LORD's house and there proclaim
this message:

"'Hear the word of the LORD, all you
people of Judah who come through these
gates to worship the LORD. 3 This is what
the LORD Almighty, the God of Israel,
says: Reform your ways and your actions,
and I will let you live in this place. 4 Do not
trust in deceptive words and say, "This is
the temple of the LORD, the temple of the
LORD, the temple of the LORD!" 5 If you
really change your ways and your actions
and deal with each other justly, 6 if you do
not oppress the foreigner, the fatherless
or the widow and do not shed innocent
blood in this place, and if you do not follow other gods to your own harm, 7 then I
will let you live in this place, in the land
I gave your ancestors for ever and ever.
8 But look, you are trusting in deceptive
words that are worthless.

9 "'Will you steal and murder, commit
adultery and perjury,[a] burn incense to
Baal and follow other gods you have not
known, 10 and then come and stand before me in this house, which bears my
Name, and say, "We are safe"—safe to
do all these detestable things? 11 Has this
house, which bears my Name, become
a den of robbers to you? But I have been
watching! declares the LORD.

12 "'Go now to the place in Shiloh where
I first made a dwelling for my Name, and
see what I did to it because of the wickedness of my people Israel. 13 While you
were doing all these things, declares the
LORD, I spoke to you again and again, but
you did not listen; I called you, but you
did not answer. 14 Therefore, what I did
to Shiloh I will now do to the house that
bears my Name, the temple you trust in,
the place I gave to you and your ancestors. 15 I will thrust you from my presence,
just as I did all your fellow Israelites, the
people of Ephraim.'

16 "So do not pray for this people nor offer any plea or petition for them; do not
plead with me, for I will not listen to you.
17 Do you not see what they are doing in
the towns of Judah and in the streets of

[a] 9 Or *and swear by false gods*

Jerusalem? 18The children gather wood,
the fathers light the fire, and the women
knead the dough and make cakes to offer
to the Queen of Heaven. They pour out
drink offerings to other gods to arouse
my anger. 19But am I the one they are
provoking? declares the LORD. Are they
not rather harming themselves, to their
own shame?

20" 'Therefore this is what the Sovereign LORD says: My anger and my wrath
will be poured out on this place—on
man and beast, on the trees of the field
and on the crops of your land—and it will
burn and not be quenched.

21" 'This is what the LORD Almighty, the
God of Israel, says: Go ahead, add your
burnt offerings to your other sacrifices
and eat the meat yourselves! 22For when
I brought your ancestors out of Egypt and
spoke to them, I did not just give them
commands about burnt offerings and
sacrifices, 23but I gave them this command: Obey me, and I will be your God
and you will be my people. Walk in obedience to all I command you, that it may go
well with you. 24But they did not listen or
pay attention; instead, they followed the
stubborn inclinations of their evil hearts.
They went backward and not forward.
25From the time your ancestors left Egypt
until now, day after day, again and again I
sent you my servants the prophets. 26But
they did not listen to me or pay attention.
They were stiff-necked and did more evil
than their ancestors.'

27"When you tell them all this, they
will not listen to you; when you call to
them, they will not answer. 28Therefore
say to them, 'This is the nation that has
not obeyed the LORD its God or responded to correction. Truth has perished; it
has vanished from their lips.

29" 'Cut off your hair and throw it away;
take up a lament on the barren heights,
for the LORD has rejected and abandoned
this generation that is under his wrath

30" 'The people of Judah have done
evil in my eyes, declares the LORD. They
have set up their detestable idols in the
house that bears my Name and have defiled it. 31They have built the high places
of Topheth in the Valley of Ben Hinnom
to burn their sons and daughters in the
fire—something I did not command,
nor did it enter my mind. 32So beware,
the days are coming, declares the LORD,
when people will no longer call it Topheth
or the Valley of Ben Hinnom, but the Valley of Slaughter, for they will bury the
dead in Topheth until there is no more
room. 33Then the carcasses of this people will become food for the birds and the
wild animals, and there will be no one to
frighten them away. 34I will bring an end
to the sounds of joy and gladness and to
the voices of bride and bridegroom in the
towns of Judah and the streets of Jerusalem, for the land will become desolate.

8 " 'At that time, declares the LORD, the
bones of the kings and officials of Judah, the bones of the priests and prophets, and the bones of the people of Jerusalem will be removed from their graves.
2They will be exposed to the sun and the
moon and all the stars of the heavens,
which they have loved and served and
which they have followed and consulted
and worshiped. They will not be gathered
up or buried, but will be like dung lying
on the ground. 3Wherever I banish them,
all the survivors of this evil nation will
prefer death to life, declares the LORD
Almighty.'

4"Say to them, 'This is what the LORD
says:

" 'When people fall down, do they not
get up?
When someone turns away, do they
not return?
5Why then have these people turned
away?
Why does Jerusalem always turn
away?
They cling to deceit;
they refuse to return.
6I have listened attentively,
but they do not say what is right.
None of them repent of their
wickedness,
saying, "What have I done?"
Each pursues their own course
like a horse charging into battle.
7Even the stork in the sky
knows her appointed seasons,
and the dove, the swift and the thrush
observe the time of their migration.
But my people do not know
the requirements of the LORD.

8" 'How can you say, "We are wise,
for we have the law of the LORD,"
when actually the lying pen of the
scribes

has handled it falsely?
9 The wise will be put to shame;
they will be dismayed and trapped.
Since they have rejected the word of the LORD,
what kind of wisdom do they have?
10 Therefore I will give their wives to other men
and their fields to new owners.
From the least to the greatest,
all are greedy for gain;
prophets and priests alike,
all practice deceit.
11 They dress the wound of my people
as though it were not serious.
"Peace, peace," they say,
when there is no peace.
12 Are they ashamed of their detestable conduct?
No, they have no shame at all;
they do not even know how to blush.
So they will fall among the fallen;
they will be brought down when they are punished,
says the LORD.
13 " 'I will take away their harvest,
declares the LORD.
There will be no grapes on the vine.
There will be no figs on the tree,
and their leaves will wither.
What I have given them
will be taken from them.[a] ' "

14 Why are we sitting here?
Gather together!
Let us flee to the fortified cities
and perish there!
For the LORD our God has doomed us to perish
and given us poisoned water to drink,
because we have sinned against him.
15 We hoped for peace
but no good has come,
for a time of healing
but there is only terror.
16 The snorting of the enemy's horses
is heard from Dan;
at the neighing of their stallions
the whole land trembles.
They have come to devour
the land and everything in it,
the city and all who live there.

17 "See, I will send venomous snakes among you,
vipers that cannot be charmed,
and they will bite you,"
declares the LORD.

18 You who are my Comforter[b] in sorrow,
my heart is faint within me.
19 Listen to the cry of my people
from a land far away:
"Is the LORD not in Zion?
Is her King no longer there?"

"Why have they aroused my anger
with their images,
with their worthless foreign idols?"

20 "The harvest is past,
the summer has ended,
and we are not saved."

21 Since my people are crushed, I am crushed;
I mourn, and horror grips me.
22 Is there no balm in Gilead?
Is there no physician there?
Why then is there no healing
for the wound of my people?

9[c] 1 Oh, that my head were a spring of water
and my eyes a fountain of tears!
I would weep day and night
for the slain of my people.
2 Oh, that I had in the desert
a lodging place for travelers,
so that I might leave my people
and go away from them;
for they are all adulterers,
a crowd of unfaithful people.

3 "They make ready their tongue
like a bow, to shoot lies;
it is not by truth
that they triumph[d] in the land.
They go from one sin to another;
they do not acknowledge me,"
declares the LORD.
4 "Beware of your friends;
do not trust anyone in your clan.
For every one of them is a deceiver,[e]
and every friend a slanderer.
5 Friend deceives friend,
and no one speaks the truth.
They have taught their tongues to lie;
they weary themselves with sinning.

[a] *13* The meaning of the Hebrew for this sentence is uncertain. [b] *18* The meaning of the Hebrew for this word is uncertain. [c] In Hebrew texts 9:1 is numbered 8:23, and 9:2-26 is numbered 9:1-25. [d] *3* Or *lies; / they are not valiant for truth* [e] *4* Or *a deceiving Jacob*

6 You[a] live in the midst of deception;
in their deceit they refuse to
acknowledge me,"
declares the LORD.

7 Therefore this is what the LORD Almighty says:

"See, I will refine and test them,
for what else can I do
because of the sin of my people?
8 Their tongue is a deadly arrow;
it speaks deceitfully.
With their mouths they all speak
cordially to their neighbors,
but in their hearts they set traps for
them.
9 Should I not punish them for this?"
declares the LORD.
"Should I not avenge myself
on such a nation as this?"

10 I will weep and wail for the mountains
and take up a lament concerning
the wilderness grasslands.
They are desolate and untraveled,
and the lowing of cattle is not heard.
The birds have all fled
and the animals are gone.

11 "I will make Jerusalem a heap of ruins,
a haunt of jackals;
and I will lay waste the towns of Judah
so no one can live there."

12 Who is wise enough to understand
this? Who has been instructed by the
LORD and can explain it? Why has the
land been ruined and laid waste like a
desert that no one can cross?
13 The LORD said, "It is because they
have forsaken my law, which I set before
them; they have not obeyed me or followed my law. 14 Instead, they have followed the stubbornness of their hearts;
they have followed the Baals, as their ancestors taught them." 15 Therefore this is
what the LORD Almighty, the God of Israel, says: "See, I will make this people eat
bitter food and drink poisoned water. 16 I
will scatter them among nations that neither they nor their ancestors have known,
and I will pursue them with the sword
until I have made an end of them."

17 This is what the LORD Almighty says:

"Consider now! Call for the wailing
women to come;
send for the most skillful of them.
18 Let them come quickly
and wail over us
till our eyes overflow with tears
and water streams from our
eyelids.
19 The sound of wailing is heard from
Zion:
'How ruined we are!
How great is our shame!
We must leave our land
because our houses are in ruins.'"

20 Now, you women, hear the word of the
LORD;
open your ears to the words of his
mouth.
Teach your daughters how to wail;
teach one another a lament.
21 Death has climbed in through our
windows
and has entered our fortresses;
it has removed the children from the
streets
and the young men from the public
squares.

22 Say, "This is what the LORD declares:

"'Dead bodies will lie
like dung on the open field,
like cut grain behind the reaper,
with no one to gather them.'"

23 This is what the LORD says:

"Let not the wise boast of their
wisdom
or the strong boast of their strength
or the rich boast of their riches,
24 but let the one who boasts boast about
this:
that they have the understanding to
know me,
that I am the LORD, who exercises
kindness,
justice and righteousness on earth,
for in these I delight,"
declares the LORD.

25 "The days are coming," declares the
LORD, "when I will punish all who are
circumcised only in the flesh — 26 Egypt,
Judah, Edom, Ammon, Moab and all who
live in the wilderness in distant places.[b]
For all these nations are really uncircumcised, and even the whole house of Israel
is uncircumcised in heart."

[a] 6 That is, Jeremiah (the Hebrew is singular)
[b] 26 Or *wilderness and who clip the hair by their foreheads*

10 Hear what the LORD says to you, people of Israel. 2 This is what the LORD says:

"Do not learn the ways of the nations
or be terrified by signs in the heavens,
though the nations are terrified by them.
3 For the practices of the peoples are worthless;
they cut a tree out of the forest,
and a craftsman shapes it with his chisel.
4 They adorn it with silver and gold;
they fasten it with hammer and nails
so it will not totter.
5 Like a scarecrow in a cucumber field,
their idols cannot speak;
they must be carried
because they cannot walk.
Do not fear them;
they can do no harm
nor can they do any good."

6 No one is like you, LORD;
you are great,
and your name is mighty in power.
7 Who should not fear you,
King of the nations?
This is your due.
Among all the wise leaders of the nations
and in all their kingdoms,
there is no one like you.

8 They are all senseless and foolish;
they are taught by worthless wooden idols.
9 Hammered silver is brought from Tarshish
and gold from Uphaz.
What the craftsman and goldsmith have made
is then dressed in blue and purple—
all made by skilled workers.
10 But the LORD is the true God;
he is the living God, the eternal King.
When he is angry, the earth trembles;
the nations cannot endure his wrath.

11 "Tell them this: 'These gods, who did not make the heavens and the earth, will perish from the earth and from under the heavens.' "[a]

12 But God made the earth by his power;
he founded the world by his wisdom
and stretched out the heavens by his understanding.
13 When he thunders, the waters in the heavens roar;
he makes clouds rise from the ends of the earth.
He sends lightning with the rain
and brings out the wind from his storehouses.

14 Everyone is senseless and without knowledge;
every goldsmith is shamed by his idols.
The images he makes are a fraud;
they have no breath in them.
15 They are worthless, the objects of mockery;
when their judgment comes, they will perish.
16 He who is the Portion of Jacob is not like these,
for he is the Maker of all things,
including Israel, the people of his inheritance—
the LORD Almighty is his name.

17 Gather up your belongings to leave the land,
you who live under siege.
18 For this is what the LORD says:
"At this time I will hurl out
those who live in this land;
I will bring distress on them
so that they may be captured."

19 Woe to me because of my injury!
My wound is incurable!
Yet I said to myself,
"This is my sickness, and I must endure it."
20 My tent is destroyed;
all its ropes are snapped.
My children are gone from me and are no more;
no one is left now to pitch my tent
or to set up my shelter.
21 The shepherds are senseless
and do not inquire of the LORD;
so they do not prosper
and all their flock is scattered.

[a] *11* The text of this verse is in Aramaic.

22 Listen! The report is coming—
a great commotion from the land of
the north!
It will make the towns of Judah
desolate,
a haunt of jackals.

23 LORD, I know that people's lives are
not their own;
it is not for them to direct their
steps.
24 Discipline me, LORD, but only in due
measure—
not in your anger,
or you will reduce me to nothing.
25 Pour out your wrath on the nations
that do not acknowledge you,
on the peoples who do not call on
your name.
For they have devoured Jacob;
they have devoured him completely
and destroyed his homeland.

11 This is the word that came to Jeremiah from the LORD: 2 "Listen to the
terms of this covenant and tell them to
the people of Judah and to those who live
in Jerusalem. 3 Tell them that this is what
the LORD, the God of Israel, says: 'Cursed
is the one who does not obey the terms of
this covenant— 4 the terms I commanded your ancestors when I brought them
out of Egypt, out of the iron-smelting furnace.' I said, 'Obey me and do everything
I command you, and you will be my people, and I will be your God. 5 Then I will
fulfill the oath I swore to your ancestors,
to give them a land flowing with milk and
honey'—the land you possess today."
I answered, "Amen, LORD."
6 The LORD said to me, "Proclaim all
these words in the towns of Judah and
in the streets of Jerusalem: 'Listen to the
terms of this covenant and follow them.
7 From the time I brought your ancestors
up from Egypt until today, I warned them
again and again, saying, "Obey me." 8 But
they did not listen or pay attention; instead, they followed the stubbornness
of their evil hearts. So I brought on them
all the curses of the covenant I had commanded them to follow but that they did
not keep.'"
9 Then the LORD said to me, "There is
a conspiracy among the people of Judah
and those who live in Jerusalem. 10 They
have returned to the sins of their ancestors, who refused to listen to my words.
They have followed other gods to serve
them. Both Israel and Judah have broken
the covenant I made with their ancestors.
11 Therefore this is what the LORD says: 'I
will bring on them a disaster they cannot
escape. Although they cry out to me, I will
not listen to them. 12 The towns of Judah
and the people of Jerusalem will go and
cry out to the gods to whom they burn incense, but they will not help them at all
when disaster strikes. 13 You, Judah, have
as many gods as you have towns; and the
altars you have set up to burn incense to
that shameful god Baal are as many as
the streets of Jerusalem.'
14 "Do not pray for this people or offer
any plea or petition for them, because I
will not listen when they call to me in the
time of their distress.

15 "What is my beloved doing in my
temple
as she, with many others, works out
her evil schemes?
Can consecrated meat avert your
punishment?
When you engage in your wickedness,
then you rejoice.[a]"

16 The LORD called you a thriving olive
tree
with fruit beautiful in form.
But with the roar of a mighty storm
he will set it on fire,
and its branches will be broken.

17 The LORD Almighty, who planted you,
has decreed disaster for you, because
the people of both Israel and Judah have
done evil and aroused my anger by burning incense to Baal.
18 Because the LORD revealed their
plot to me, I knew it, for at that time he
showed me what they were doing. 19 I had
been like a gentle lamb led to the slaughter; I did not realize that they had plotted
against me, saying,

"Let us destroy the tree and its fruit;
let us cut him off from the land of
the living,
that his name be remembered no
more."
20 But you, LORD Almighty, who judge
righteously

[a] 15 Or *Could consecrated meat avert your punishment? / Then you would rejoice*

and test the heart and mind,
let me see your vengeance on them,
for to you I have committed my cause.

21 Therefore this is what the LORD says
about the people of Anathoth who are
threatening to kill you, saying, "Do not
prophesy in the name of the LORD or you
will die by our hands" — 22 therefore this
is what the LORD Almighty says: "I will
punish them. Their young men will die
by the sword, their sons and daughters
by famine. 23 Not even a remnant will be
left to them, because I will bring disaster
on the people of Anathoth in the year of
their punishment."

12 You are always righteous, LORD,
when I bring a case before you.
Yet I would speak with you about your justice:
Why does the way of the wicked prosper?
Why do all the faithless live at ease?
2 You have planted them, and they have taken root;
they grow and bear fruit.
You are always on their lips
but far from their hearts.
3 Yet you know me, LORD;
you see me and test my thoughts about you.
Drag them off like sheep to be butchered!
Set them apart for the day of slaughter!
4 How long will the land lie parched
and the grass in every field be withered?
Because those who live in it are wicked,
the animals and birds have perished.
Moreover, the people are saying,
"He will not see what happens to us."

5 "If you have raced with men on foot
and they have worn you out,
how can you compete with horses?
If you stumble[a] in safe country,
how will you manage in the thickets by[b] the Jordan?
6 Your relatives, members of your own family —
even they have betrayed you;
they have raised a loud cry against you.
Do not trust them,
though they speak well of you.

7 "I will forsake my house,
abandon my inheritance;
I will give the one I love
into the hands of her enemies.
8 My inheritance has become to me
like a lion in the forest.
She roars at me;
therefore I hate her.
9 Has not my inheritance become to me
like a speckled bird of prey
that other birds of prey surround and attack?
Go and gather all the wild beasts;
bring them to devour.
10 Many shepherds will ruin my vineyard
and trample down my field;
they will turn my pleasant field
into a desolate wasteland.
11 It will be made a wasteland,
parched and desolate before me;
the whole land will be laid waste
because there is no one who cares.
12 Over all the barren heights in the desert
destroyers will swarm,
for the sword of the LORD will devour
from one end of the land to the other;
no one will be safe.
13 They will sow wheat but reap thorns;
they will wear themselves out but gain nothing.
They will bear the shame of their harvest
because of the LORD's fierce anger."

14 This is what the LORD says: "As for all
my wicked neighbors who seize the inheritance I gave my people Israel, I will
uproot them from their lands and I will
uproot the people of Judah from among
them. 15 But after I uproot them, I will
again have compassion and will bring
each of them back to their own inheritance and their own country. 16 And if
they learn well the ways of my people
and swear by my name, saying, 'As surely as the LORD lives' — even as they once
taught my people to swear by Baal — then
they will be established among my peo-

[a] 5 Or *you feel secure only* [b] 5 Or *the flooding of*

ple. 17 But if any nation does not listen, I
will completely uproot and destroy it,"
declares the LORD.

13 This is what the LORD said to me:
"Go and buy a linen belt and put it
around your waist, but do not let it touch
water." 2 So I bought a belt, as the LORD
directed, and put it around my waist.
3 Then the word of the LORD came to me
a second time: 4 "Take the belt you bought
and are wearing around your waist, and
go now to Perath[a] and hide it there in a
crevice in the rocks." 5 So I went and hid
it at Perath, as the LORD told me.
6 Many days later the LORD said to me,
"Go now to Perath and get the belt I told
you to hide there." 7 So I went to Perath
and dug up the belt and took it from the
place where I had hidden it, but now it
was ruined and completely useless.
8 Then the word of the LORD came to
me: 9 "This is what the LORD says: 'In the
same way I will ruin the pride of Judah
and the great pride of Jerusalem. 10 These
wicked people, who refuse to listen to
my words, who follow the stubbornness
of their hearts and go after other gods to
serve and worship them, will be like this
belt — completely useless! 11 For as a belt
is bound around the waist, so I bound all
the people of Israel and all the people of
Judah to me,' declares the LORD, 'to be
my people for my renown and praise and
honor. But they have not listened.'
12 "Say to them: 'This is what the LORD,
the God of Israel, says: Every wineskin
should be filled with wine.' And if they
say to you, 'Don't we know that every
wineskin should be filled with wine?'
13 then tell them, 'This is what the LORD
says: I am going to fill with drunkenness all who live in this land, including
the kings who sit on David's throne, the
priests, the prophets and all those living
in Jerusalem. 14 I will smash them one
against the other, parents and children
alike, declares the LORD. I will allow no
pity or mercy or compassion to keep me
from destroying them.'"

15 Hear and pay attention,
do not be arrogant,
for the LORD has spoken.
16 Give glory to the LORD your God
before he brings the darkness,
before your feet stumble
on the darkening hills.
You hope for light,
but he will turn it to utter darkness
and change it to deep gloom.
17 If you do not listen,
I will weep in secret
because of your pride;
my eyes will weep bitterly,
overflowing with tears,
because the LORD's flock will be
taken captive.

18 Say to the king and to the queen
mother,
"Come down from your thrones,
for your glorious crowns
will fall from your heads."
19 The cities in the Negev will be shut
up,
and there will be no one to open
them.
All Judah will be carried into exile,
carried completely away.

20 Look up and see
those who are coming from the
north.
Where is the flock that was entrusted
to you,
the sheep of which you boasted?
21 What will you say when the LORD sets
over you
those you cultivated as your special
allies?
Will not pain grip you
like that of a woman in labor?
22 And if you ask yourself,
"Why has this happened to me?" —
it is because of your many sins
that your skirts have been torn off
and your body mistreated.
23 Can an Ethiopian[b] change his skin
or a leopard its spots?
Neither can you do good
who are accustomed to doing evil.

24 "I will scatter you like chaff
driven by the desert wind.
25 This is your lot,
the portion I have decreed for you,"
declares the LORD,
"because you have forgotten me
and trusted in false gods.
26 I will pull up your skirts over your face
that your shame may be seen —

[a] 4 Or possibly *to the Euphrates*; similarly in verses 5-7
[b] 23 Hebrew *Cushite* (probably a person from the upper Nile region)

27 your adulteries and lustful neighings,
your shameless prostitution!
I have seen your detestable acts
on the hills and in the fields.
Woe to you, Jerusalem!
How long will you be unclean?"

14

This is the word of the LORD that came to Jeremiah concerning the drought:

2 "Judah mourns,
her cities languish;
they wail for the land,
and a cry goes up from Jerusalem.
3 The nobles send their servants for water;
they go to the cisterns
but find no water.
They return with their jars unfilled;
dismayed and despairing,
they cover their heads.
4 The ground is cracked
because there is no rain in the land;
the farmers are dismayed
and cover their heads.
5 Even the doe in the field
deserts her newborn fawn
because there is no grass.
6 Wild donkeys stand on the barren heights
and pant like jackals;
their eyes fail
for lack of food."

7 Although our sins testify against us,
do something, LORD, for the sake of your name.
For we have often rebelled;
we have sinned against you.
8 You who are the hope of Israel,
its Savior in times of distress,
why are you like a stranger in the land,
like a traveler who stays only a night?
9 Why are you like a man taken by surprise,
like a warrior powerless to save?
You are among us, LORD,
and we bear your name;
do not forsake us!

10 This is what the LORD says about this people:

"They greatly love to wander;
they do not restrain their feet.
So the LORD does not accept them;
he will now remember their wickedness
and punish them for their sins."

11 Then the LORD said to me, "Do not
pray for the well-being of this people.
12 Although they fast, I will not listen to
their cry; though they offer burnt offerings and grain offerings, I will not accept
them. Instead, I will destroy them with
the sword, famine and plague."
13 But I said, "Alas, Sovereign LORD!
The prophets keep telling them, 'You
will not see the sword or suffer famine.
Indeed, I will give you lasting peace in
this place.'"
14 Then the LORD said to me, "The
prophets are prophesying lies in my
name. I have not sent them or appointed
them or spoken to them. They are prophesying to you false visions, divinations,
idolatries[a] and the delusions of their
own minds. 15 Therefore this is what the
LORD says about the prophets who are
prophesying in my name: I did not send
them, yet they are saying, 'No sword or
famine will touch this land.' Those same
prophets will perish by sword and famine. 16 And the people they are prophesying to will be thrown out into the streets
of Jerusalem because of the famine and
sword. There will be no one to bury them,
their wives, their sons and their daughters. I will pour out on them the calamity
they deserve.
17 "Speak this word to them:

"'Let my eyes overflow with tears
night and day without ceasing;
for the Virgin Daughter, my people,
has suffered a grievous wound,
a crushing blow.
18 If I go into the country,
I see those slain by the sword;
if I go into the city,
I see the ravages of famine.
Both prophet and priest
have gone to a land they know not.'"

19 Have you rejected Judah completely?
Do you despise Zion?
Why have you afflicted us
so that we cannot be healed?
We hoped for peace
but no good has come,
for a time of healing

[a] 14 Or *visions, worthless divinations*

but there is only terror.
20 We acknowledge our wickedness, LORD,
and the guilt of our ancestors;
we have indeed sinned against you.
21 For the sake of your name do not despise us;
do not dishonor your glorious throne.
Remember your covenant with us
and do not break it.
22 Do any of the worthless idols of the nations bring rain?
Do the skies themselves send down showers?
No, it is you, LORD our God.
Therefore our hope is in you,
for you are the one who does all this.

15 Then the LORD said to me: "Even if
Moses and Samuel were to stand before me, my heart would not go out to this
people. Send them away from my presence! Let them go! 2 And if they ask you,
'Where shall we go?' tell them, 'This is
what the LORD says:

" 'Those destined for death, to death;
those for the sword, to the sword;
those for starvation, to starvation;
those for captivity, to captivity.'

3 "I will send four kinds of destroyers
against them," declares the LORD, "the
sword to kill and the dogs to drag away
and the birds and the wild animals to devour and destroy. 4 I will make them abhorrent to all the kingdoms of the earth
because of what Manasseh son of Hezekiah king of Judah did in Jerusalem.

5 "Who will have pity on you, Jerusalem?
Who will mourn for you?
Who will stop to ask how you are?
6 You have rejected me," declares the LORD.
"You keep on backsliding.
So I will reach out and destroy you;
I am tired of holding back.
7 I will winnow them with a winnowing fork
at the city gates of the land.
I will bring bereavement and destruction on my people,
for they have not changed their ways.
8 I will make their widows more numerous
than the sand of the sea.
At midday I will bring a destroyer
against the mothers of their young men;
suddenly I will bring down on them
anguish and terror.
9 The mother of seven will grow faint
and breathe her last.
Her sun will set while it is still day;
she will be disgraced and humiliated.
I will put the survivors to the sword
before their enemies,"
declares the LORD.

10 Alas, my mother, that you gave me birth,
a man with whom the whole land
strives and contends!
I have neither lent nor borrowed,
yet everyone curses me.

11 The LORD said,

"Surely I will deliver you for a good purpose;
surely I will make your enemies
plead with you
in times of disaster and times of distress.

12 "Can a man break iron—
iron from the north—or bronze?
13 "Your wealth and your treasures
I will give as plunder, without charge,
because of all your sins
throughout your country.
14 I will enslave you to your enemies
in[a] a land you do not know,
for my anger will kindle a fire
that will burn against you."

15 LORD, you understand;
remember me and care for me.
Avenge me on my persecutors.
You are long-suffering—do not take me away;
think of how I suffer reproach for your sake.
16 When your words came, I ate them;
they were my joy and my heart's delight,
for I bear your name,
LORD God Almighty.

[a] 14 Some Hebrew manuscripts, Septuagint and Syriac (see also 17:4); most Hebrew manuscripts *I will cause your enemies to bring you / into*

17 I never sat in the company of revelers,
never made merry with them;
I sat alone because your hand was on me
and you had filled me with indignation.
18 Why is my pain unending
and my wound grievous and incurable?
You are to me like a deceptive brook,
like a spring that fails.

19 Therefore this is what the LORD says:

"If you repent, I will restore you
that you may serve me;
if you utter worthy, not worthless, words,
you will be my spokesman.
Let this people turn to you,
but you must not turn to them.
20 I will make you a wall to this people,
a fortified wall of bronze;
they will fight against you
but will not overcome you,
for I am with you
to rescue and save you,"
declares the LORD.
21 "I will save you from the hands of the wicked
and deliver you from the grasp of the cruel."

16 Then the word of the LORD came to
me: 2 "You must not marry and have
sons or daughters in this place." 3 For this
is what the LORD says about the sons and
daughters born in this land and about the
women who are their mothers and the
men who are their fathers: 4 "They will
die of deadly diseases. They will not be
mourned or buried but will be like dung
lying on the ground. They will perish by
sword and famine, and their dead bodies
will become food for the birds and the
wild animals."
5 For this is what the LORD says: "Do
not enter a house where there is a funeral
meal; do not go to mourn or show sympathy, because I have withdrawn my blessing, my love and my pity from this people," declares the LORD. 6 "Both high and
low will die in this land. They will not be
buried or mourned, and no one will cut
themselves or shave their head for the
dead. 7 No one will offer food to comfort
those who mourn for the dead — not even
for a father or a mother — nor will anyone
give them a drink to console them.
8 "And do not enter a house where there
is feasting and sit down to eat and drink.
9 For this is what the LORD Almighty, the
God of Israel, says: Before your eyes and
in your days I will bring an end to the
sounds of joy and gladness and to the
voices of bride and bridegroom in this
place.
10 "When you tell these people all this
and they ask you, 'Why has the LORD decreed such a great disaster against us?
What wrong have we done? What sin
have we committed against the LORD our
God?' 11 then say to them, 'It is because
your ancestors forsook me,' declares
the LORD, 'and followed other gods and
served and worshiped them. They forsook me and did not keep my law. 12 But
you have behaved more wickedly than
your ancestors. See how all of you are
following the stubbornness of your evil
hearts instead of obeying me. 13 So I will
throw you out of this land into a land neither you nor your ancestors have known,
and there you will serve other gods day
and night, for I will show you no favor.'
14 "However, the days are coming," declares the LORD, "when it will no longer
be said, 'As surely as the LORD lives, who
brought the Israelites up out of Egypt,'
15 but it will be said, 'As surely as the LORD
lives, who brought the Israelites up out of
the land of the north and out of all the
countries where he had banished them.'
For I will restore them to the land I gave
their ancestors.
16 "But now I will send for many fishermen," declares the LORD, "and they
will catch them. After that I will send for
many hunters, and they will hunt them
down on every mountain and hill and
from the crevices of the rocks. 17 My eyes
are on all their ways; they are not hidden
from me, nor is their sin concealed from
my eyes. 18 I will repay them double for
their wickedness and their sin, because
they have defiled my land with the lifeless forms of their vile images and have
filled my inheritance with their detestable idols."

19 LORD, my strength and my fortress,
my refuge in time of distress,
to you the nations will come
from the ends of the earth and say,
"Our ancestors possessed nothing but
false gods,

worthless idols that did them no good.
20 Do people make their own gods?
Yes, but they are not gods!"
21 "Therefore I will teach them—
this time I will teach them
my power and might.
Then they will know
that my name is the LORD.

17 "Judah's sin is engraved with an iron tool,
inscribed with a flint point,
on the tablets of their hearts
and on the horns of their altars.
2 Even their children remember
their altars and Asherah poles[a]
beside the spreading trees
and on the high hills.
3 My mountain in the land
and your[b] wealth and all your treasures
I will give away as plunder,
together with your high places,
because of sin throughout your country.
4 Through your own fault you will lose
the inheritance I gave you.
I will enslave you to your enemies
in a land you do not know,
for you have kindled my anger,
and it will burn forever."

5 This is what the LORD says:

"Cursed is the one who trusts in man,
who draws strength from mere flesh
and whose heart turns away from the LORD.
6 That person will be like a bush in the wastelands;
they will not see prosperity when it comes.
They will dwell in the parched places of the desert,
in a salt land where no one lives.

7 "But blessed is the one who trusts in the LORD,
whose confidence is in him.
8 They will be like a tree planted by the water
that sends out its roots by the stream.
It does not fear when heat comes;
its leaves are always green.
It has no worries in a year of drought
and never fails to bear fruit."
9 The heart is deceitful above all things
and beyond cure.
Who can understand it?
10 "I the LORD search the heart
and examine the mind,
to reward each person according to their conduct,
according to what their deeds deserve."

11 Like a partridge that hatches eggs it did not lay
are those who gain riches by unjust means.
When their lives are half gone, their riches will desert them,
and in the end they will prove to be fools.

12 A glorious throne, exalted from the beginning,
is the place of our sanctuary.
13 LORD, you are the hope of Israel;
all who forsake you will be put to shame.
Those who turn away from you will be written in the dust
because they have forsaken the LORD,
the spring of living water.

14 Heal me, LORD, and I will be healed;
save me and I will be saved,
for you are the one I praise.
15 They keep saying to me,
"Where is the word of the LORD?
Let it now be fulfilled!"
16 I have not run away from being your shepherd;
you know I have not desired the day of despair.
What passes my lips is open before you.
17 Do not be a terror to me;
you are my refuge in the day of disaster.
18 Let my persecutors be put to shame,
but keep me from shame;
let them be terrified,
but keep me from terror.
Bring on them the day of disaster;
destroy them with double destruction.

a 2 That is, wooden symbols of the goddess Asherah

b 2,3 Or *hills / 3and the mountains of the land. / Your*

19This is what the LORD said to me:
"Go and stand at the Gate of the People,[a]
through which the kings of Judah go in
and out; stand also at all the other gates
of Jerusalem. 20Say to them, 'Hear the
word of the LORD, you kings of Judah and
all people of Judah and everyone living in
Jerusalem who come through these gates.
21This is what the LORD says: Be careful
not to carry a load on the Sabbath day or
bring it through the gates of Jerusalem.
22Do not bring a load out of your houses
or do any work on the Sabbath, but keep
the Sabbath day holy, as I commanded
your ancestors. 23Yet they did not listen
or pay attention; they were stiff-necked
and would not listen or respond to discipline.
24But if you are careful to obey
me, declares the LORD, and bring no load
through the gates of this city on the Sabbath,
but keep the Sabbath day holy by not
doing any work on it, 25then kings who
sit on David's throne will come through
the gates of this city with their officials.
They and their officials will come riding
in chariots and on horses, accompanied
by the men of Judah and those living in
Jerusalem, and this city will be inhabited
forever. 26People will come from the
towns of Judah and the villages around
Jerusalem, from the territory of Benjamin
and the western foothills, from the
hill country and the Negev, bringing
burnt offerings and sacrifices, grain offerings
and incense, and bringing thank
offerings to the house of the LORD. 27But
if you do not obey me to keep the Sabbath
day holy by not carrying any load as you
come through the gates of Jerusalem on
the Sabbath day, then I will kindle an unquenchable
fire in the gates of Jerusalem
that will consume her fortresses.'"

18 This is the word that came to Jeremiah
from the LORD: 2"Go down to the
potter's house, and there I will give you
my message." 3So I went down to the potter's
house, and I saw him working at the
wheel. 4But the pot he was shaping from
the clay was marred in his hands; so the
potter formed it into another pot, shaping
it as seemed best to him.

5Then the word of the LORD came to me.
6He said, "Can I not do with you, Israel,
as this potter does?" declares the LORD.
"Like clay in the hand of the potter, so are
you in my hand, Israel. 7If at any time I
announce that a nation or kingdom is to
be uprooted, torn down and destroyed,
8and if that nation I warned repents of
its evil, then I will relent and not inflict
on it the disaster I had planned. 9And if
at another time I announce that a nation
or kingdom is to be built up and planted,
10and if it does evil in my sight and does
not obey me, then I will reconsider the
good I had intended to do for it.

11"Now therefore say to the people
of Judah and those living in Jerusalem,
'This is what the LORD says: Look! I am
preparing a disaster for you and devising
a plan against you. So turn from your evil
ways, each one of you, and reform your
ways and your actions.' 12But they will
reply, 'It's no use. We will continue with
our own plans; we will all follow the stubbornness
of our evil hearts.'"

13Therefore this is what the LORD says:

"Inquire among the nations:
Who has ever heard anything like this?
A most horrible thing has been done
by Virgin Israel.
14Does the snow of Lebanon
ever vanish from its rocky slopes?
Do its cool waters from distant sources
ever stop flowing?[b]
15Yet my people have forgotten me;
they burn incense to worthless idols,
which made them stumble in their ways,
in the ancient paths.
They made them walk in byways,
on roads not built up.
16Their land will be an object of horror
and of lasting scorn;
all who pass by will be appalled
and will shake their heads.
17Like a wind from the east,
I will scatter them before their enemies;
I will show them my back and not my face
in the day of their disaster."

18They said, "Come, let's make plans
against Jeremiah; for the teaching of the
law by the priest will not cease, nor will
counsel from the wise, nor the word from
the prophets. So come, let's attack him

[a] 19 Or *Army* [b] 14 The meaning of the Hebrew for this sentence is uncertain.

with our tongues and pay no attention to
anything he says."

19 Listen to me, LORD;
hear what my accusers are saying!
20 Should good be repaid with evil?
Yet they have dug a pit for me.
Remember that I stood before you
and spoke in their behalf
to turn your wrath away from them.
21 So give their children over to famine;
hand them over to the power of the sword.
Let their wives be made childless and widows;
let their men be put to death,
their young men slain by the sword in battle.
22 Let a cry be heard from their houses
when you suddenly bring invaders against them,
for they have dug a pit to capture me
and have hidden snares for my feet.
23 But you, LORD, know
all their plots to kill me.
Do not forgive their crimes
or blot out their sins from your sight.
Let them be overthrown before you;
deal with them in the time of your anger.

19 This is what the LORD says: "Go and
buy a clay jar from a potter. Take
along some of the elders of the people
and of the priests 2 and go out to the Valley of Ben Hinnom, near the entrance of
the Potsherd Gate. There proclaim the
words I tell you, 3 and say, 'Hear the word
of the LORD, you kings of Judah and people of Jerusalem. This is what the LORD
Almighty, the God of Israel, says: Listen! I
am going to bring a disaster on this place
that will make the ears of everyone who
hears of it tingle. 4 For they have forsaken
me and made this a place of foreign gods;
they have burned incense in it to gods
that neither they nor their ancestors nor
the kings of Judah ever knew, and they
have filled this place with the blood of
the innocent. 5 They have built the high
places of Baal to burn their children in
the fire as offerings to Baal—something
I did not command or mention, nor did it
enter my mind. 6 So beware, the days are
coming, declares the LORD, when people
will no longer call this place Topheth or
the Valley of Ben Hinnom, but the Valley
of Slaughter.
7 "'In this place I will ruin[a] the plans of
Judah and Jerusalem. I will make them
fall by the sword before their enemies,
at the hands of those who want to kill
them, and I will give their carcasses as
food to the birds and the wild animals.
8 I will devastate this city and make it an
object of horror and scorn; all who pass
by will be appalled and will scoff because
of all its wounds. 9 I will make them eat
the flesh of their sons and daughters, and
they will eat one another's flesh because
their enemies will press the siege so hard
against them to destroy them.'
10 "Then break the jar while those who
go with you are watching, 11 and say to
them, 'This is what the LORD Almighty
says: I will smash this nation and this city
just as this potter's jar is smashed and
cannot be repaired. They will bury the
dead in Topheth until there is no more
room. 12 This is what I will do to this place
and to those who live here, declares the
LORD. I will make this city like Topheth.
13 The houses in Jerusalem and those of
the kings of Judah will be defiled like this
place, Topheth—all the houses where
they burned incense on the roofs to all
the starry hosts and poured out drink offerings to other gods.'"
14 Jeremiah then returned from Topheth, where the LORD had sent him to
prophesy, and stood in the court of the
LORD's temple and said to all the people, 15 "This is what the LORD Almighty,
the God of Israel, says: 'Listen! I am
going to bring on this city and all the
villages around it every disaster I pronounced against them, because they
were stiff-necked and would not listen to
my words.'"

20 When the priest Pashhur son of
Immer, the official in charge of
the temple of the LORD, heard Jeremiah
prophesying these things, 2 he had Jeremiah the prophet beaten and put in the
stocks at the Upper Gate of Benjamin at
the LORD's temple. 3 The next day, when
Pashhur released him from the stocks,
Jeremiah said to him, "The LORD's name
for you is not Pashhur, but Terror on Every Side. 4 For this is what the LORD says:
'I will make you a terror to yourself and

[a] 7 The Hebrew for *ruin* sounds like the Hebrew for *jar* (see verses 1 and 10).

to all your friends; with your own eyes you will see them fall by the sword of their enemies. I will give all Judah into the hands of the king of Babylon, who will carry them away to Babylon or put them to the sword.
5 I will deliver all the wealth of this city into the hands of their enemies—all its products, all its valuables and all the treasures of the kings of Judah. They will take it away as plunder and carry it off to Babylon.
6 And you, Pashhur, and all who live in your house will go into exile to Babylon. There you will die and be buried, you and all your friends to whom you have prophesied lies.'"

7 You deceived[a] me, LORD, and I was
deceived[a];
you overpowered me and prevailed.
I am ridiculed all day long;
everyone mocks me.
8 Whenever I speak, I cry out
proclaiming violence and
destruction.
So the word of the LORD has brought
me
insult and reproach all day long.
9 But if I say, "I will not mention his
word
or speak anymore in his name,"
his word is in my heart like a fire,
a fire shut up in my bones.
I am weary of holding it in;
indeed, I cannot.
10 I hear many whispering,
"Terror on every side!
Denounce him! Let's denounce
him!"
All my friends
are waiting for me to slip, saying,
"Perhaps he will be deceived;
then we will prevail over him
and take our revenge on him."

11 But the LORD is with me like a mighty
warrior;
so my persecutors will stumble and
not prevail.
They will fail and be thoroughly
disgraced;
their dishonor will never be
forgotten.
12 LORD Almighty, you who examine the
righteous
and probe the heart and mind,
let me see your vengeance on them,
for to you I have committed my
cause.

13 Sing to the LORD!
Give praise to the LORD!
He rescues the life of the needy
from the hands of the wicked.

14 Cursed be the day I was born!
May the day my mother bore me not
be blessed!
15 Cursed be the man who brought my
father the news,
who made him very glad, saying,
"A child is born to you—a son!"
16 May that man be like the towns
the LORD overthrew without pity.
May he hear wailing in the morning,
a battle cry at noon.
17 For he did not kill me in the womb,
with my mother as my grave,
her womb enlarged forever.
18 Why did I ever come out of the womb
to see trouble and sorrow
and to end my days in shame?

21 The word came to Jeremiah from the LORD when King Zedekiah sent to him Pashhur son of Malkijah and the priest Zephaniah son of Maaseiah. They said:
2 "Inquire now of the LORD for us because Nebuchadnezzar[b] king of Babylon is attacking us. Perhaps the LORD will perform wonders for us as in times past so that he will withdraw from us."
3 But Jeremiah answered them, "Tell Zedekiah,
4 'This is what the LORD, the God of Israel, says: I am about to turn against you the weapons of war that are in your hands, which you are using to fight the king of Babylon and the Babylonians[c] who are outside the wall besieging you. And I will gather them inside this city.
5 I myself will fight against you with an outstretched hand and a mighty arm in furious anger and in great wrath.
6 I will strike down those who live in this city—both man and beast—and they will die of a terrible plague.
7 After that, declares the LORD, I will give Zedekiah king of Judah, his officials and the people in this city who survive the plague, sword and famine, into the hands of Nebuchadnezzar king of Babylon and to their enemies who want to kill them. He will put them

[a] 7 Or *persuaded* [b] 2 Hebrew *Nebuchadrezzar,* of which *Nebuchadnezzar* is a variant; here and often in Jeremiah and Ezekiel [c] 4 Or *Chaldeans;* also in verse 9

to the sword; he will show them no mercy
or pity or compassion.'
8"Furthermore, tell the people, 'This
is what the LORD says: See, I am setting
before you the way of life and the way of
death. 9Whoever stays in this city will die
by the sword, famine or plague. But whoever goes out and surrenders to the Babylonians who are besieging you will live;
they will escape with their lives. 10I have
determined to do this city harm and not
good, declares the LORD. It will be given
into the hands of the king of Babylon, and
he will destroy it with fire.'
11"Moreover, say to the royal house of
Judah, 'Hear the word of the LORD. 12This
is what the LORD says to you, house of David:

"'Administer justice every morning;
rescue from the hand of the
oppressor
the one who has been robbed,
or my wrath will break out and burn
like fire
because of the evil you have done—
burn with no one to quench it.
13I am against you, Jerusalem,
you who live above this valley
on the rocky plateau, declares the
LORD—
you who say, "Who can come against
us?
Who can enter our refuge?"
14I will punish you as your deeds
deserve,
declares the LORD.
I will kindle a fire in your forests
that will consume everything
around you.'"

22 This is what the LORD says: "Go
down to the palace of the king of
Judah and proclaim this message there:
2'Hear the word of the LORD to you, king
of Judah, you who sit on David's throne—
you, your officials and your people who
come through these gates. 3This is what
the LORD says: Do what is just and right.
Rescue from the hand of the oppressor
the one who has been robbed. Do no
wrong or violence to the foreigner, the
fatherless or the widow, and do not shed
innocent blood in this place. 4For if you
are careful to carry out these commands,
then kings who sit on David's throne will
come through the gates of this palace,
riding in chariots and on horses, accompanied by their officials and their people.
5But if you do not obey these commands,
declares the LORD, I swear by myself that
this palace will become a ruin.'"
6For this is what the LORD says about
the palace of the king of Judah:

"Though you are like Gilead to me,
like the summit of Lebanon,
I will surely make you like a
wasteland,
like towns not inhabited.
7I will send destroyers against you,
each man with his weapons,
and they will cut up your fine cedar
beams
and throw them into the fire.

8"People from many nations will pass
by this city and will ask one another,
'Why has the LORD done such a thing
to this great city?' 9And the answer will
be: 'Because they have forsaken the covenant of the LORD their God and have
worshiped and served other gods.'"

10Do not weep for the dead king or
mourn his loss;
rather, weep bitterly for him who is
exiled,
because he will never return
nor see his native land again.

11For this is what the LORD says about
Shallum[a] son of Josiah, who succeeded
his father as king of Judah but has gone
from this place: "He will never return.
12He will die in the place where they have
led him captive; he will not see this land
again."

13"Woe to him who builds his palace by
unrighteousness,
his upper rooms by injustice,
making his own people work for
nothing,
not paying them for their labor.
14He says, 'I will build myself a great
palace
with spacious upper rooms.'
So he makes large windows in it,
panels it with cedar
and decorates it in red.

15"Does it make you a king
to have more and more cedar?

[a] 11 Also called *Jehoahaz*

Did not your father have food and
drink?
He did what was right and just,
so all went well with him.
16 He defended the cause of the poor and
needy,
and so all went well.
Is that not what it means to know me?"
declares the LORD.
17 "But your eyes and your heart
are set only on dishonest gain,
on shedding innocent blood
and on oppression and extortion."

18 Therefore this is what the LORD says
about Jehoiakim son of Josiah king of Judah:

"They will not mourn for him:
'Alas, my brother! Alas, my sister!'
They will not mourn for him:
'Alas, my master! Alas, his splendor!'
19 He will have the burial of a donkey —
dragged away and thrown
outside the gates of Jerusalem."

20 "Go up to Lebanon and cry out,
let your voice be heard in Bashan,
cry out from Abarim,
for all your allies are crushed.
21 I warned you when you felt secure,
but you said, 'I will not listen!'
This has been your way from your
youth;
you have not obeyed me.
22 The wind will drive all your shepherds
away,
and your allies will go into exile.
Then you will be ashamed and
disgraced
because of all your wickedness.
23 You who live in 'Lebanon,[a]'
who are nestled in cedar buildings,
how you will groan when pangs come
upon you,
pain like that of a woman in labor!

24 "As surely as I live," declares the
LORD, "even if you, Jehoiachin[b] son of
Jehoiakim king of Judah, were a signet
ring on my right hand, I would still pull
you off. 25 I will deliver you into the hands
of those who want to kill you, those you
fear — Nebuchadnezzar king of Babylon
and the Babylonians.[c] 26 I will hurl you
and the mother who gave you birth into
another country, where neither of you
was born, and there you both will die.
27 You will never come back to the land
you long to return to."

28 Is this man Jehoiachin a despised,
broken pot,
an object no one wants?
Why will he and his children be
hurled out,
cast into a land they do not know?
29 O land, land, land,
hear the word of the LORD!
30 This is what the LORD says:
"Record this man as if childless,
a man who will not prosper in his
lifetime,
for none of his offspring will prosper,
none will sit on the throne of David
or rule anymore in Judah."

23 "Woe to the shepherds who are destroying and scattering the sheep of
my pasture!" declares the LORD. 2 Therefore this is what the LORD, the God of Israel, says to the shepherds who tend my
people: "Because you have scattered my
flock and driven them away and have
not bestowed care on them, I will bestow
punishment on you for the evil you have
done," declares the LORD. 3 "I myself will
gather the remnant of my flock out of all
the countries where I have driven them
and will bring them back to their pasture,
where they will be fruitful and increase
in number. 4 I will place shepherds over
them who will tend them, and they will
no longer be afraid or terrified, nor will
any be missing," declares the LORD.

5 "The days are coming," declares the
LORD,
"when I will raise up for David[d] a
righteous Branch,
a King who will reign wisely
and do what is just and right in the
land.
6 In his days Judah will be saved
and Israel will live in safety.
This is the name by which he will be
called:
The LORD Our Righteous Savior.

7 "So then, the days are coming," declares
the LORD, "when people will no longer
say, 'As surely as the LORD lives, who
brought the Israelites up out of Egypt,'
8 but they will say, 'As surely as the LORD

[a] *23* That is, the palace in Jerusalem (see 1 Kings 7:2) [b] *24* Hebrew *Koniah,* a variant of *Jehoiachin*; also in verse 28 [c] *25* Or *Chaldeans* [d] *5* Or *up from David's line*

lives, who brought the descendants of Israel up out of the land of the north and out of all the countries where he had banished them.' Then they will live in their own land."

9 Concerning the prophets:

My heart is broken within me;
  all my bones tremble.
I am like a drunken man,
  like a strong man overcome by wine,
because of the LORD
  and his holy words.
10 The land is full of adulterers;
  because of the curse[a] the land lies parched
  and the pastures in the wilderness are withered.
The prophets follow an evil course
  and use their power unjustly.
11 "Both prophet and priest are godless;
  even in my temple I find their wickedness,"
      declares the LORD.
12 "Therefore their path will become slippery;
  they will be banished to darkness
  and there they will fall.
I will bring disaster on them
  in the year they are punished,"
      declares the LORD.
13 "Among the prophets of Samaria
  I saw this repulsive thing:
They prophesied by Baal
  and led my people Israel astray.
14 And among the prophets of Jerusalem
  I have seen something horrible:
  They commit adultery and live a lie.
They strengthen the hands of evildoers,
  so that not one of them turns from their wickedness.
They are all like Sodom to me;
  the people of Jerusalem are like Gomorrah."

15 Therefore this is what the LORD Almighty says concerning the prophets:

"I will make them eat bitter food
  and drink poisoned water,
because from the prophets of Jerusalem
  ungodliness has spread throughout the land."

16 This is what the LORD Almighty says:

"Do not listen to what the prophets are prophesying to you;
  they fill you with false hopes.
They speak visions from their own minds,
  not from the mouth of the LORD.
17 They keep saying to those who despise me,
  'The LORD says: You will have peace.'
And to all who follow the stubbornness of their hearts
  they say, 'No harm will come to you.'
18 But which of them has stood in the council of the LORD
  to see or to hear his word?
  Who has listened and heard his word?
19 See, the storm of the LORD
  will burst out in wrath,
a whirlwind swirling down
  on the heads of the wicked.
20 The anger of the LORD will not turn back
  until he fully accomplishes
  the purposes of his heart.
In days to come
  you will understand it clearly.
21 I did not send these prophets,
  yet they have run with their message;
I did not speak to them,
  yet they have prophesied.
22 But if they had stood in my council,
  they would have proclaimed my words to my people
and would have turned them from their evil ways
  and from their evil deeds.
23 "Am I only a God nearby,"
      declares the LORD,
  "and not a God far away?
24 Who can hide in secret places
  so that I cannot see them?"
      declares the LORD.
  "Do not I fill heaven and earth?"
      declares the LORD.

25 "I have heard what the prophets say
who prophesy lies in my name. They say,
'I had a dream! I had a dream!' 26 How long
will this continue in the hearts of these
lying prophets, who prophesy the delusions of their own minds? 27 They think

[a] 10 Or *because of these things*

the dreams they tell one another will
make my people forget my name, just as
their ancestors forgot my name through
Baal worship. 28 Let the prophet who has
a dream recount the dream, but let the
one who has my word speak it faithfully. For what has straw to do with grain?"
declares the LORD. 29 "Is not my word like
fire," declares the LORD, "and like a hammer that breaks a rock in pieces?
30 "Therefore," declares the LORD, "I
am against the prophets who steal from
one another words supposedly from me.
31 Yes," declares the LORD, "I am against
the prophets who wag their own tongues
and yet declare, 'The LORD declares.'
32 Indeed, I am against those who prophesy false dreams," declares the LORD.
"They tell them and lead my people
astray with their reckless lies, yet I did
not send or appoint them. They do not
benefit these people in the least," declares the LORD.
33 "When these people, or a prophet or a
priest, ask you, 'What is the message from
the LORD?' say to them, 'What message? I
will forsake you, declares the LORD.' 34 If a
prophet or a priest or anyone else claims,
'This is a message from the LORD,' I will
punish them and their household. 35 This
is what each of you keeps saying to your
friends and other Israelites: 'What is the
LORD's answer?' or 'What has the LORD
spoken?' 36 But you must not mention 'a
message from the LORD' again, because
each one's word becomes their own message. So you distort the words of the living God, the LORD Almighty, our God.
37 This is what you keep saying to a prophet: 'What is the LORD's answer to you?' or
'What has the LORD spoken?' 38 Although
you claim, 'This is a message from the
LORD,' this is what the LORD says: You
used the words, 'This is a message from
the LORD,' even though I told you that you
must not claim, 'This is a message from
the LORD.' 39 Therefore, I will surely forget you and cast you out of my presence
along with the city I gave to you and your
ancestors. 40 I will bring on you everlasting disgrace—everlasting shame that
will not be forgotten."

24 After Jehoiachin[a] son of Jehoiakim
king of Judah and the officials, the
skilled workers and the artisans of Judah
were carried into exile from Jerusalem
to Babylon by Nebuchadnezzar king of
Babylon, the LORD showed me two baskets of figs placed in front of the temple
of the LORD. 2 One basket had very good
figs, like those that ripen early; the other basket had very bad figs, so bad they
could not be eaten.
3 Then the LORD asked me, "What do
you see, Jeremiah?"
"Figs," I answered. "The good ones are
very good, but the bad ones are so bad
they cannot be eaten."
4 Then the word of the LORD came to
me: 5 "This is what the LORD, the God of
Israel, says: 'Like these good figs, I regard
as good the exiles from Judah, whom I
sent away from this place to the land of
the Babylonians.[b] 6 My eyes will watch
over them for their good, and I will bring
them back to this land. I will build them
up and not tear them down; I will plant
them and not uproot them. 7 I will give
them a heart to know me, that I am the
LORD. They will be my people, and I will
be their God, for they will return to me
with all their heart.
8 " 'But like the bad figs, which are so
bad they cannot be eaten,' says the LORD,
'so will I deal with Zedekiah king of Judah, his officials and the survivors from
Jerusalem, whether they remain in this
land or live in Egypt. 9 I will make them
abhorrent and an offense to all the kingdoms of the earth, a reproach and a byword, a curse[c] and an object of ridicule,
wherever I banish them. 10 I will send the
sword, famine and plague against them
until they are destroyed from the land I
gave to them and their ancestors.' "

25 The word came to Jeremiah concerning all the people of Judah in
the fourth year of Jehoiakim son of Josiah king of Judah, which was the first year
of Nebuchadnezzar king of Babylon. 2 So
Jeremiah the prophet said to all the people of Judah and to all those living in Jerusalem: 3 For twenty-three years—from
the thirteenth year of Josiah son of Amon
king of Judah until this very day—the
word of the LORD has come to me and I
have spoken to you again and again, but
you have not listened.
4 And though the LORD has sent all his
servants the prophets to you again and

[a] *1* Hebrew *Jeconiah,* a variant of *Jehoiachin* [b] *5* Or *Chaldeans* [c] *9* That is, their names will be used in cursing (see 29:22); or, others will see that they are cursed.

again, you have not listened or paid any
attention. 5They said, "Turn now, each
of you, from your evil ways and your evil
practices, and you can stay in the land
the LORD gave to you and your ancestors
for ever and ever. 6Do not follow other
gods to serve and worship them; do not
arouse my anger with what your hands
have made. Then I will not harm you."
7"But you did not listen to me," declares
the LORD, "and you have aroused my anger with what your hands have made, and
you have brought harm to yourselves."
8Therefore the LORD Almighty says
this: "Because you have not listened to
my words, 9I will summon all the peoples of the north and my servant Nebuchadnezzar king of Babylon," declares
the LORD, "and I will bring them against
this land and its inhabitants and against
all the surrounding nations. I will completely destroy[a] them and make them an
object of horror and scorn, and an everlasting ruin. 10I will banish from them
the sounds of joy and gladness, the voices of bride and bridegroom, the sound
of millstones and the light of the lamp.
11This whole country will become a desolate wasteland, and these nations will
serve the king of Babylon seventy years.
12"But when the seventy years are fulfilled, I will punish the king of Babylon
and his nation, the land of the Babylonians,[b] for their guilt," declares the LORD,
"and will make it desolate forever. 13I will
bring on that land all the things I have
spoken against it, all that are written in
this book and prophesied by Jeremiah
against all the nations. 14They themselves will be enslaved by many nations
and great kings; I will repay them according to their deeds and the work of their
hands."

15This is what the LORD, the God of Israel, said to me: "Take from my hand this
cup filled with the wine of my wrath and
make all the nations to whom I send you
drink it. 16When they drink it, they will
stagger and go mad because of the sword
I will send among them."
17So I took the cup from the LORD's
hand and made all the nations to whom
he sent me drink it: 18Jerusalem and the
towns of Judah, its kings and officials, to
make them a ruin and an object of horror
and scorn, a curse[c]—as they are today;
19Pharaoh king of Egypt, his attendants,
his officials and all his people, 20and all
the foreign people there; all the kings of
Uz; all the kings of the Philistines (those
of Ashkelon, Gaza, Ekron, and the people
left at Ashdod); 21Edom, Moab and Ammon; 22all the kings of Tyre and Sidon;
the kings of the coastlands across the
sea; 23Dedan, Tema, Buz and all who are
in distant places[d]; 24all the kings of Arabia and all the kings of the foreign people
who live in the wilderness; 25all the kings
of Zimri, Elam and Media; 26and all the
kings of the north, near and far, one after
the other—all the kingdoms on the face
of the earth. And after all of them, the
king of Sheshak[e] will drink it too.
27"Then tell them, 'This is what the
LORD Almighty, the God of Israel, says:
Drink, get drunk and vomit, and fall to
rise no more because of the sword I will
send among you.' 28But if they refuse to
take the cup from your hand and drink,
tell them, 'This is what the LORD Almighty says: You must drink it! 29See,
I am beginning to bring disaster on the
city that bears my Name, and will you indeed go unpunished? You will not go unpunished, for I am calling down a sword
on all who live on the earth, declares the
LORD Almighty.'
30"Now prophesy all these words
against them and say to them:

"'The LORD will roar from on high;
he will thunder from his holy
dwelling
and roar mightily against his land.
He will shout like those who tread the
grapes,
shout against all who live on the
earth.
31The tumult will resound to the ends of
the earth,
for the LORD will bring charges
against the nations;
he will bring judgment on all mankind
and put the wicked to the sword,'"
declares the LORD.

[a] 9 The Hebrew term refers to the irrevocable giving over of things or persons to the LORD, often by totally destroying them. [b] 12 Or *Chaldeans* [c] 18 That is, their names to be used in cursing (see 29:22); or, to be seen by others as cursed [d] 23 Or *who clip the hair by their foreheads* [e] 26 *Sheshak* is a cryptogram for Babylon.

32 This is what the LORD Almighty
says:

"Look! Disaster is spreading
from nation to nation;
a mighty storm is rising
from the ends of the earth."

33 At that time those slain by the LORD
will be everywhere—from one end of
the earth to the other. They will not be
mourned or gathered up or buried, but
will be like dung lying on the ground.

34 Weep and wail, you shepherds;
roll in the dust, you leaders of the
flock.
For your time to be slaughtered has
come;
you will fall like the best of the
rams.[a]
35 The shepherds will have nowhere to
flee,
the leaders of the flock no place to
escape.
36 Hear the cry of the shepherds,
the wailing of the leaders of the
flock,
for the LORD is destroying their
pasture.
37 The peaceful meadows will be laid
waste
because of the fierce anger of the
LORD.
38 Like a lion he will leave his lair,
and their land will become desolate
because of the sword[b] of the oppressor
and because of the LORD's fierce
anger.

26 Early in the reign of Jehoiakim son
of Josiah king of Judah, this word
came from the LORD: 2 "This is what the
LORD says: Stand in the courtyard of the
LORD's house and speak to all the people
of the towns of Judah who come to worship in the house of the LORD. Tell them
everything I command you; do not omit
a word. 3 Perhaps they will listen and
each will turn from their evil ways. Then
I will relent and not inflict on them the
disaster I was planning because of the
evil they have done. 4 Say to them, 'This
is what the LORD says: If you do not listen to me and follow my law, which I have
set before you, 5 and if you do not listen
to the words of my servants the prophets,
whom I have sent to you again and again
(though you have not listened), 6 then I
will make this house like Shiloh and this
city a curse[c] among all the nations of the
earth.'"

7 The priests, the prophets and all the
people heard Jeremiah speak these words
in the house of the LORD. 8 But as soon as
Jeremiah finished telling all the people
everything the LORD had commanded
him to say, the priests, the prophets and
all the people seized him and said, "You
must die! 9 Why do you prophesy in the
LORD's name that this house will be like
Shiloh and this city will be desolate and
deserted?" And all the people crowded around Jeremiah in the house of the
LORD.

10 When the officials of Judah heard
about these things, they went up from
the royal palace to the house of the LORD
and took their places at the entrance of
the New Gate of the LORD's house. 11 Then
the priests and the prophets said to the
officials and all the people, "This man
should be sentenced to death because he
has prophesied against this city. You have
heard it with your own ears!"

12 Then Jeremiah said to all the officials
and all the people: "The LORD sent me to
prophesy against this house and this city
all the things you have heard. 13 Now reform your ways and your actions and
obey the LORD your God. Then the LORD
will relent and not bring the disaster he
has pronounced against you. 14 As for me,
I am in your hands; do with me whatever
you think is good and right. 15 Be assured,
however, that if you put me to death, you
will bring the guilt of innocent blood on
yourselves and on this city and on those
who live in it, for in truth the LORD has
sent me to you to speak all these words in
your hearing."

16 Then the officials and all the people
said to the priests and the prophets, "This
man should not be sentenced to death!
He has spoken to us in the name of the
LORD our God."

17 Some of the elders of the land stepped
forward and said to the entire assembly
of people, 18 "Micah of Moresheth prophesied in the days of Hezekiah king of Ju-

[a] *34* Septuagint; Hebrew *fall and be shattered like fine pottery* [b] *38* Some Hebrew manuscripts and Septuagint (see also 46:16 and 50:16); most Hebrew manuscripts *anger* [c] *6* That is, its name will be used in cursing (see 29:22); or, others will see that it is cursed.

dah. He told all the people of Judah, 'This
is what the LORD Almighty says:

"'Zion will be plowed like a field,
Jerusalem will become a heap of
rubble,
the temple hill a mound overgrown
with thickets.'[a]

19 "Did Hezekiah king of Judah or anyone else in Judah put him to death? Did
not Hezekiah fear the LORD and seek his
favor? And did not the LORD relent, so
that he did not bring the disaster he pronounced against them? We are about to
bring a terrible disaster on ourselves!"
20 (Now Uriah son of Shemaiah from
Kiriath Jearim was another man who
prophesied in the name of the LORD;
he prophesied the same things against
this city and this land as Jeremiah did.
21 When King Jehoiakim and all his officers and officials heard his words, the
king was determined to put him to death.
But Uriah heard of it and fled in fear to
Egypt. 22 King Jehoiakim, however, sent
Elnathan son of Akbor to Egypt, along
with some other men. 23 They brought
Uriah out of Egypt and took him to King
Jehoiakim, who had him struck down
with a sword and his body thrown into
the burial place of the common people.)
24 Furthermore, Ahikam son of Shaphan supported Jeremiah, and so he was
not handed over to the people to be put
to death.

27 Early in the reign of Zedekiah[b] son
of Josiah king of Judah, this word
came to Jeremiah from the LORD: 2 This is
what the LORD said to me: "Make a yoke
out of straps and crossbars and put it on
your neck. 3 Then send word to the kings
of Edom, Moab, Ammon, Tyre and Sidon
through the envoys who have come to Jerusalem to Zedekiah king of Judah. 4 Give
them a message for their masters and say,
'This is what the LORD Almighty, the God
of Israel, says: "Tell this to your masters:
5 With my great power and outstretched
arm I made the earth and its people and
the animals that are on it, and I give it to
anyone I please. 6 Now I will give all your
countries into the hands of my servant
Nebuchadnezzar king of Babylon; I will
make even the wild animals subject to
him. 7 All nations will serve him and his
son and his grandson until the time for
his land comes; then many nations and
great kings will subjugate him.
8 "'"If, however, any nation or kingdom
will not serve Nebuchadnezzar king of
Babylon or bow its neck under his yoke,
I will punish that nation with the sword,
famine and plague, declares the LORD,
until I destroy it by his hand. 9 So do not
listen to your prophets, your diviners,
your interpreters of dreams, your mediums or your sorcerers who tell you, 'You
will not serve the king of Babylon.' 10 They
prophesy lies to you that will only serve
to remove you far from your lands; I will
banish you and you will perish. 11 But if
any nation will bow its neck under the
yoke of the king of Babylon and serve
him, I will let that nation remain in its
own land to till it and to live there, declares the LORD."'"
12 I gave the same message to Zedekiah
king of Judah. I said, "Bow your neck under the yoke of the king of Babylon; serve
him and his people, and you will live.
13 Why will you and your people die by the
sword, famine and plague with which the
LORD has threatened any nation that will
not serve the king of Babylon? 14 Do not
listen to the words of the prophets who
say to you, 'You will not serve the king of
Babylon,' for they are prophesying lies to
you. 15 'I have not sent them,' declares the
LORD. 'They are prophesying lies in my
name. Therefore, I will banish you and
you will perish, both you and the prophets who prophesy to you.'"
16 Then I said to the priests and all these
people, "This is what the LORD says: Do
not listen to the prophets who say, 'Very
soon now the articles from the LORD's
house will be brought back from Babylon.' They are prophesying lies to you.
17 Do not listen to them. Serve the king of
Babylon, and you will live. Why should
this city become a ruin? 18 If they are
prophets and have the word of the LORD,
let them plead with the LORD Almighty
that the articles remaining in the house
of the LORD and in the palace of the king
of Judah and in Jerusalem not be taken to
Babylon. 19 For this is what the LORD Almighty says about the pillars, the bronze
Sea, the movable stands and the other
articles that are left in this city, 20 which

[a] *18* Micah 3:12 [b] *1* A few Hebrew manuscripts and Syriac (see also 27:3,12 and 28:1); most Hebrew manuscripts *Jehoiakim* (Most Septuagint manuscripts do not have this verse.)

Nebuchadnezzar king of Babylon did not
take away when he carried Jehoiachin[a]
son of Jehoiakim king of Judah into exile
from Jerusalem to Babylon, along with
all the nobles of Judah and Jerusalem—
21 yes, this is what the LORD Almighty, the
God of Israel, says about the things that
are left in the house of the LORD and in
the palace of the king of Judah and in Jerusalem: 22 'They will be taken to Babylon
and there they will remain until the day I
come for them,' declares the LORD. 'Then
I will bring them back and restore them
to this place.'"

28 In the fifth month of that same year,
the fourth year, early in the reign
of Zedekiah king of Judah, the prophet
Hananiah son of Azzur, who was from
Gibeon, said to me in the house of the
LORD in the presence of the priests and
all the people: 2 "This is what the LORD
Almighty, the God of Israel, says: 'I will
break the yoke of the king of Babylon.
3 Within two years I will bring back to this
place all the articles of the LORD's house
that Nebuchadnezzar king of Babylon removed from here and took to Babylon. 4 I
will also bring back to this place Jehoiachin[a] son of Jehoiakim king of Judah and
all the other exiles from Judah who went
to Babylon,' declares the LORD, 'for I will
break the yoke of the king of Babylon.'"

5 Then the prophet Jeremiah replied to
the prophet Hananiah before the priests
and all the people who were standing in
the house of the LORD. 6 He said, "Amen!
May the LORD do so! May the LORD fulfill
the words you have prophesied by bringing the articles of the LORD's house and
all the exiles back to this place from Babylon. 7 Nevertheless, listen to what I have
to say in your hearing and in the hearing of all the people: 8 From early times
the prophets who preceded you and me
have prophesied war, disaster and plague
against many countries and great kingdoms. 9 But the prophet who prophesies
peace will be recognized as one truly sent
by the LORD only if his prediction comes
true."

10 Then the prophet Hananiah took the
yoke off the neck of the prophet Jeremiah and broke it, 11 and he said before all
the people, "This is what the LORD says:
'In the same way I will break the yoke of
Nebuchadnezzar king of Babylon off the
neck of all the nations within two years.'"
At this, the prophet Jeremiah went on his
way.

12 After the prophet Hananiah had broken the yoke off the neck of the prophet
Jeremiah, the word of the LORD came to
Jeremiah: 13 "Go and tell Hananiah, 'This
is what the LORD says: You have broken a
wooden yoke, but in its place you will get
a yoke of iron. 14 This is what the LORD Almighty, the God of Israel, says: I will put
an iron yoke on the necks of all these nations to make them serve Nebuchadnezzar king of Babylon, and they will serve
him. I will even give him control over the
wild animals.'"

15 Then the prophet Jeremiah said to
Hananiah the prophet, "Listen, Hananiah! The LORD has not sent you, yet
you have persuaded this nation to trust
in lies. 16 Therefore this is what the LORD
says: 'I am about to remove you from the
face of the earth. This very year you are
going to die, because you have preached
rebellion against the LORD.'"

17 In the seventh month of that same
year, Hananiah the prophet died.

29 This is the text of the letter that the
prophet Jeremiah sent from Jerusalem to the surviving elders among the
exiles and to the priests, the prophets
and all the other people Nebuchadnezzar had carried into exile from Jerusalem
to Babylon. 2 (This was after King Jehoiachin[a] and the queen mother, the court
officials and the leaders of Judah and
Jerusalem, the skilled workers and the
artisans had gone into exile from Jerusalem.) 3 He entrusted the letter to Elasah
son of Shaphan and to Gemariah son of
Hilkiah, whom Zedekiah king of Judah
sent to King Nebuchadnezzar in Babylon. It said:

4 This is what the LORD Almighty,
the God of Israel, says to all those I
carried into exile from Jerusalem to
Babylon: 5 "Build houses and settle
down; plant gardens and eat what
they produce. 6 Marry and have sons
and daughters; find wives for your
sons and give your daughters in marriage, so that they too may have sons
and daughters. Increase in number
there; do not decrease. 7 Also, seek

[a] *20,4,2* Hebrew *Jeconiah,* a variant of *Jehoiachin*

the peace and prosperity of the city
to which I have carried you into exile. Pray to the LORD for it, because
if it prospers, you too will prosper."
[8]Yes, this is what the LORD Almighty,
the God of Israel, says: "Do not let
the prophets and diviners among
you deceive you. Do not listen to the
dreams you encourage them to have.
[9]They are prophesying lies to you in
my name. I have not sent them," declares the LORD.

[10]This is what the LORD says:
"When seventy years are completed
for Babylon, I will come to you and
fulfill my good promise to bring you
back to this place. [11]For I know the
plans I have for you," declares the
LORD, "plans to prosper you and not
to harm you, plans to give you hope
and a future. [12]Then you will call on
me and come and pray to me, and I
will listen to you. [13]You will seek me
and find me when you seek me with
all your heart. [14]I will be found by
you," declares the LORD, "and will
bring you back from captivity.[a] I will
gather you from all the nations and
places where I have banished you,"
declares the LORD, "and will bring
you back to the place from which I
carried you into exile."

[15]You may say, "The LORD has
raised up prophets for us in Babylon," [16]but this is what the LORD
says about the king who sits on David's throne and all the people who
remain in this city, your fellow citizens who did not go with you into exile — [17]yes, this is what the LORD Almighty says: "I will send the sword,
famine and plague against them and
I will make them like figs that are so
bad they cannot be eaten. [18]I will
pursue them with the sword, famine and plague and will make them
abhorrent to all the kingdoms of the
earth, a curse[b] and an object of horror, of scorn and reproach, among all
the nations where I drive them. [19]For
they have not listened to my words,"
declares the LORD, "words that I sent
to them again and again by my servants the prophets. And you exiles
have not listened either," declares
the LORD.

[20]Therefore, hear the word of the
LORD, all you exiles whom I have sent
away from Jerusalem to Babylon.
[21]This is what the LORD Almighty, the
God of Israel, says about Ahab son of
Kolaiah and Zedekiah son of Maaseiah, who are prophesying lies to you
in my name: "I will deliver them into
the hands of Nebuchadnezzar king
of Babylon, and he will put them to
death before your very eyes. [22]Be-
cause of them, all the exiles from Judah who are in Babylon will use this
curse: 'May the LORD treat you like
Zedekiah and Ahab, whom the king
of Babylon burned in the fire.' [23]For
they have done outrageous things
in Israel; they have committed adultery with their neighbors' wives, and
in my name they have uttered lies —
which I did not authorize. I know it
and am a witness to it," declares the
LORD.

[24]Tell Shemaiah the Nehelamite,
[25]"This is what the LORD Almighty, the
God of Israel, says: You sent letters in
your own name to all the people in Jerusalem, to the priest Zephaniah son of
Maaseiah, and to all the other priests.
You said to Zephaniah, [26]'The LORD has
appointed you priest in place of Jehoiada
to be in charge of the house of the LORD;
you should put any maniac who acts like
a prophet into the stocks and neck-irons.
[27]So why have you not reprimanded Jeremiah from Anathoth, who poses as a
prophet among you? [28]He has sent this
message to us in Babylon: It will be a long
time. Therefore build houses and settle
down; plant gardens and eat what they
produce.'"

[29]Zephaniah the priest, however, read
the letter to Jeremiah the prophet. [30]Then
the word of the LORD came to Jeremiah:
[31]"Send this message to all the exiles:
'This is what the LORD says about Shemaiah the Nehelamite: Because Shemaiah
has prophesied to you, even though I did
not send him, and has persuaded you to
trust in lies, [32]this is what the LORD says:
I will surely punish Shemaiah the Nehelamite and his descendants. He will have

[a] 14 Or *will restore your fortunes* [b] 18 That is, their names will be used in cursing (see verse 22); or, others will see that they are cursed.

no one left among this people, nor will he
see the good things I will do for my people, declares the LORD, because he has
preached rebellion against me.' "

30 This is the word that came to Jeremiah from the LORD: 2 "This is what
the LORD, the God of Israel, says: 'Write
in a book all the words I have spoken to
you. 3 The days are coming,' declares the
LORD, 'when I will bring my people Israel
and Judah back from captivity[a] and restore them to the land I gave their ancestors to possess,' says the LORD."
4 These are the words the LORD spoke
concerning Israel and Judah: 5 "This is
what the LORD says:

" 'Cries of fear are heard—
terror, not peace.
6 Ask and see:
Can a man bear children?
Then why do I see every strong man
with his hands on his stomach like a woman in labor,
every face turned deathly pale?
7 How awful that day will be!
No other will be like it.
It will be a time of trouble for Jacob,
but he will be saved out of it.

8 " 'In that day,' declares the LORD Almighty,
'I will break the yoke off their necks
and will tear off their bonds;
no longer will foreigners enslave them.
9 Instead, they will serve the LORD their God
and David their king,
whom I will raise up for them.

10 " 'So do not be afraid, Jacob my servant;
do not be dismayed, Israel,'
declares the LORD.
'I will surely save you out of a distant place,
your descendants from the land of their exile.
Jacob will again have peace and security,
and no one will make him afraid.
11 I am with you and will save you,'
declares the LORD.
'Though I completely destroy all the nations
among which I scatter you,
I will not completely destroy you.
I will discipline you but only in due measure;
I will not let you go entirely unpunished.'

12 "This is what the LORD says:
" 'Your wound is incurable,
your injury beyond healing.
13 There is no one to plead your cause,
no remedy for your sore,
no healing for you.
14 All your allies have forgotten you;
they care nothing for you.
I have struck you as an enemy would
and punished you as would the cruel,
because your guilt is so great
and your sins so many.
15 Why do you cry out over your wound,
your pain that has no cure?
Because of your great guilt and many sins
I have done these things to you.

16 " 'But all who devour you will be devoured;
all your enemies will go into exile.
Those who plunder you will be plundered;
all who make spoil of you I will despoil.
17 But I will restore you to health
and heal your wounds,'
declares the LORD,
'because you are called an outcast,
Zion for whom no one cares.'

18 "This is what the LORD says:
" 'I will restore the fortunes of Jacob's tents
and have compassion on his dwellings;
the city will be rebuilt on her ruins,
and the palace will stand in its proper place.
19 From them will come songs of thanksgiving
and the sound of rejoicing.
I will add to their numbers,
and they will not be decreased;
I will bring them honor,
and they will not be disdained.
20 Their children will be as in days of old,
and their community will be established before me;

[a] 3 Or *will restore the fortunes of my people Israel and Judah*

I will punish all who oppress
them.
21 Their leader will be one of their own;
their ruler will arise from among
them.
I will bring him near and he will come
close to me —
for who is he who will devote
himself
to be close to me?'
declares the LORD.
22 "'So you will be my people,
and I will be your God.'"

23 See, the storm of the LORD
will burst out in wrath,
a driving wind swirling down
on the heads of the wicked.
24 The fierce anger of the LORD will not
turn back
until he fully accomplishes
the purposes of his heart.
In days to come
you will understand this.

31 "At that time," declares the LORD, "I
will be the God of all the families of
Israel, and they will be my people."
2 This is what the LORD says:

"The people who survive the sword
will find favor in the wilderness;
I will come to give rest to Israel."

3 The LORD appeared to us in the past,[a]
saying:

"I have loved you with an everlasting
love;
I have drawn you with unfailing
kindness.
4 I will build you up again,
and you, Virgin Israel, will be
rebuilt.
Again you will take up your timbrels
and go out to dance with the
joyful.
5 Again you will plant vineyards
on the hills of Samaria;
the farmers will plant them
and enjoy their fruit.
6 There will be a day when watchmen
cry out
on the hills of Ephraim,
'Come, let us go up to Zion,
to the LORD our God.'"

7 This is what the LORD says:

"Sing with joy for Jacob;
shout for the foremost of the
nations.
Make your praises heard, and say,
'LORD, save your people,
the remnant of Israel.'
8 See, I will bring them from the land of
the north
and gather them from the ends of
the earth.
Among them will be the blind and the
lame,
expectant mothers and women in
labor;
a great throng will return.
9 They will come with weeping;
they will pray as I bring them back.
I will lead them beside streams of
water
on a level path where they will not
stumble,
because I am Israel's father,
and Ephraim is my firstborn son.

10 "Hear the word of the LORD, you
nations;
proclaim it in distant coastlands:
'He who scattered Israel will gather
them
and will watch over his flock like a
shepherd.'
11 For the LORD will deliver Jacob
and redeem them from the hand of
those stronger than they.
12 They will come and shout for joy on
the heights of Zion;
they will rejoice in the bounty of the
LORD —
the grain, the new wine and the olive
oil,
the young of the flocks and herds.
They will be like a well-watered
garden,
and they will sorrow no more.
13 Then young women will dance and be
glad,
young men and old as well.
I will turn their mourning into
gladness;
I will give them comfort and joy
instead of sorrow.
14 I will satisfy the priests with
abundance,
and my people will be filled with my
bounty,"
declares the LORD.

[a] 3 Or *LORD has appeared to us from afar*

15 This is what the LORD says:

"A voice is heard in Ramah,
mourning and great weeping,
Rachel weeping for her children
and refusing to be comforted,
because they are no more."

16 This is what the LORD says:

"Restrain your voice from weeping
and your eyes from tears,
for your work will be rewarded,"
declares the LORD.
"They will return from the land of
the enemy.
17 So there is hope for your descendants,"
declares the LORD.
"Your children will return to their
own land.

18 "I have surely heard Ephraim's
moaning:
'You disciplined me like an unruly
calf,
and I have been disciplined.
Restore me, and I will return,
because you are the LORD my God.
19 After I strayed,
I repented;
after I came to understand,
I beat my breast.
I was ashamed and humiliated
because I bore the disgrace of my
youth.'
20 Is not Ephraim my dear son,
the child in whom I delight?
Though I often speak against him,
I still remember him.
Therefore my heart yearns for him;
I have great compassion for him,"
declares the LORD.

21 "Set up road signs;
put up guideposts.
Take note of the highway,
the road that you take.
Return, Virgin Israel,
return to your towns.
22 How long will you wander,
unfaithful Daughter Israel?
The LORD will create a new thing on
earth —
the woman will return to[a] the
man."

23 This is what the LORD Almighty, the
God of Israel, says: "When I bring them
back from captivity,[b] the people in the
land of Judah and in its towns will once
again use these words: 'The LORD bless
you, you prosperous city, you sacred
mountain.' 24 People will live together
in Judah and all its towns — farmers and
those who move about with their flocks.
25 I will refresh the weary and satisfy the
faint."

26 At this I awoke and looked around.
My sleep had been pleasant to me.

27 "The days are coming," declares the
LORD, "when I will plant the kingdoms
of Israel and Judah with the offspring of
people and of animals. 28 Just as I watched
over them to uproot and tear down, and
to overthrow, destroy and bring disaster,
so I will watch over them to build and to
plant," declares the LORD. 29 "In those
days people will no longer say,

'The parents have eaten sour grapes,
and the children's teeth are set on
edge.'

30 Instead, everyone will die for their own
sin; whoever eats sour grapes — their
own teeth will be set on edge.

31 "The days are coming," declares the
LORD,
"when I will make a new covenant
with the people of Israel
and with the people of Judah.
32 It will not be like the covenant
I made with their ancestors
when I took them by the hand
to lead them out of Egypt,
because they broke my covenant,
though I was a husband to[c] them,[d]"
declares the LORD.
33 "This is the covenant I will make with
the people of Israel
after that time," declares the LORD.
"I will put my law in their minds
and write it on their hearts.
I will be their God,
and they will be my people.
34 No longer will they teach their
neighbor,
or say to one another, 'Know the
LORD,'
because they will all know me,
from the least of them to the
greatest,"
declares the LORD.

[a] 22 Or *will protect* [b] 23 Or *I restore their fortunes away from* [d] 32 Or *was their master* [c] 32 Hebrew; Septuagint and Syriac / *and I turned*

"For I will forgive their wickedness
and will remember their sins no
more."

35 This is what the LORD says,

he who appoints the sun
to shine by day,
who decrees the moon and stars
to shine by night,
who stirs up the sea
so that its waves roar—
the LORD Almighty is his name:
36 "Only if these decrees vanish from my
sight,"
declares the LORD,
"will Israel ever cease
being a nation before me."

37 This is what the LORD says:

"Only if the heavens above can be
measured
and the foundations of the earth
below be searched out
will I reject all the descendants of
Israel
because of all they have done,"
declares the LORD.

38 "The days are coming," declares the
LORD, "when this city will be rebuilt for
me from the Tower of Hananel to the
Corner Gate. 39 The measuring line will
stretch from there straight to the hill
of Gareb and then turn to Goah. 40 The
whole valley where dead bodies and ashes are thrown, and all the terraces out to
the Kidron Valley on the east as far as the
corner of the Horse Gate, will be holy to
the LORD. The city will never again be uprooted or demolished."

32 This is the word that came to Jeremiah from the LORD in the tenth
year of Zedekiah king of Judah, which
was the eighteenth year of Nebuchadnezzar. 2 The army of the king of Babylon
was then besieging Jerusalem, and Jeremiah the prophet was confined in the
courtyard of the guard in the royal palace of Judah.

3 Now Zedekiah king of Judah had imprisoned him there, saying, "Why do you
prophesy as you do? You say, 'This is what
the LORD says: I am about to give this city
into the hands of the king of Babylon,
and he will capture it. 4 Zedekiah king
of Judah will not escape the Babylonians[a] but will certainly be given into the
hands of the king of Babylon, and will
speak with him face to face and see him
with his own eyes. 5 He will take Zedekiah to Babylon, where he will remain until
I deal with him, declares the LORD. If you
fight against the Babylonians, you will
not succeed.'"

6 Jeremiah said, "The word of the LORD
came to me: 7 Hanamel son of Shallum
your uncle is going to come to you and
say, 'Buy my field at Anathoth, because
as nearest relative it is your right and
duty to buy it.'

8 "Then, just as the LORD had said, my
cousin Hanamel came to me in the courtyard of the guard and said, 'Buy my field
at Anathoth in the territory of Benjamin.
Since it is your right to redeem it and possess it, buy it for yourself.'

"I knew that this was the word of the
LORD; 9 so I bought the field at Anathoth
from my cousin Hanamel and weighed
out for him seventeen shekels[b] of silver.
10 I signed and sealed the deed, had it witnessed, and weighed out the silver on the
scales. 11 I took the deed of purchase—
the sealed copy containing the terms
and conditions, as well as the unsealed
copy— 12 and I gave this deed to Baruch
son of Neriah, the son of Mahseiah, in
the presence of my cousin Hanamel and
of the witnesses who had signed the deed
and of all the Jews sitting in the courtyard
of the guard.

13 "In their presence I gave Baruch
these instructions: 14 'This is what the
LORD Almighty, the God of Israel, says:
Take these documents, both the sealed
and unsealed copies of the deed of purchase, and put them in a clay jar so they
will last a long time. 15 For this is what the
LORD Almighty, the God of Israel, says:
Houses, fields and vineyards will again
be bought in this land.'

16 "After I had given the deed of purchase to Baruch son of Neriah, I prayed
to the LORD:

17 "Ah, Sovereign LORD, you have
made the heavens and the earth by
your great power and outstretched
arm. Nothing is too hard for you.
18 You show love to thousands but
bring the punishment for the parents' sins into the laps of their chil-

[a] 4 Or *Chaldeans*; also in verses 5, 24, 25, 28, 29 and 43
[b] 9 That is, about 7 ounces or about 200 grams

dren after them. Great and mighty
God, whose name is the LORD Almighty, 19great are your purposes
and mighty are your deeds. Your eyes
are open to the ways of all mankind;
you reward each person according
to their conduct and as their deeds
deserve. 20You performed signs and
wonders in Egypt and have continued them to this day, in Israel
and among all mankind, and have
gained the renown that is still yours.
21You brought your people Israel out
of Egypt with signs and wonders, by
a mighty hand and an outstretched
arm and with great terror. 22You gave
them this land you had sworn to give
their ancestors, a land flowing with
milk and honey. 23They came in and
took possession of it, but they did not
obey you or follow your law; they did
not do what you commanded them
to do. So you brought all this disaster on them.

24"See how the siege ramps are
built up to take the city. Because of
the sword, famine and plague, the
city will be given into the hands of
the Babylonians who are attacking it.
What you said has happened, as you
now see. 25And though the city will
be given into the hands of the Babylonians, you, Sovereign LORD, say
to me, 'Buy the field with silver and
have the transaction witnessed.'"

26Then the word of the LORD came to
Jeremiah: 27"I am the LORD, the God of
all mankind. Is anything too hard for
me? 28Therefore this is what the LORD
says: I am about to give this city into the
hands of the Babylonians and to Nebuchadnezzar king of Babylon, who will
capture it. 29The Babylonians who are
attacking this city will come in and set it
on fire; they will burn it down, along with
the houses where the people aroused my
anger by burning incense on the roofs to
Baal and by pouring out drink offerings
to other gods.

30"The people of Israel and Judah have
done nothing but evil in my sight from
their youth; indeed, the people of Israel
have done nothing but arouse my anger
with what their hands have made, declares the LORD. 31From the day it was
built until now, this city has so aroused
my anger and wrath that I must remove it
from my sight. 32The people of Israel and
Judah have provoked me by all the evil
they have done—they, their kings and
officials, their priests and prophets, the
people of Judah and those living in Jerusalem. 33They turned their backs to me
and not their faces; though I taught them
again and again, they would not listen or
respond to discipline. 34They set up their
vile images in the house that bears my
Name and defiled it. 35They built high
places for Baal in the Valley of Ben Hinnom to sacrifice their sons and daughters to Molek, though I never commanded—nor did it enter my mind—that they
should do such a detestable thing and so
make Judah sin.

36"You are saying about this city, 'By the
sword, famine and plague it will be given
into the hands of the king of Babylon'; but
this is what the LORD, the God of Israel,
says: 37I will surely gather them from all
the lands where I banish them in my furious anger and great wrath; I will bring
them back to this place and let them live
in safety. 38They will be my people, and I
will be their God. 39I will give them sin-
gleness of heart and action, so that they
will always fear me and that all will then
go well for them and for their children
after them. 40I will make an everlasting
covenant with them: I will never stop doing good to them, and I will inspire them
to fear me, so that they will never turn
away from me. 41I will rejoice in doing
them good and will assuredly plant them
in this land with all my heart and soul.

42"This is what the LORD says: As I
have brought all this great calamity on
this people, so I will give them all the
prosperity I have promised them. 43Once
more fields will be bought in this land
of which you say, 'It is a desolate waste,
without people or animals, for it has
been given into the hands of the Babylonians.' 44Fields will be bought for silver,
and deeds will be signed, sealed and
witnessed in the territory of Benjamin,
in the villages around Jerusalem, in the
towns of Judah and in the towns of the
hill country, of the western foothills and
of the Negev, because I will restore their
fortunes,[a] declares the LORD."

[a] 44 Or *will bring them back from captivity*

33 While Jeremiah was still confined in the courtyard of the guard, the word of the LORD came to him a second time: 2"This is what the LORD says, he who made the earth, the LORD who formed it and established it—the LORD is his name: 3'Call to me and I will answer you and tell you great and unsearchable things you do not know.' 4For this is what the LORD, the God of Israel, says about the houses in this city and the royal palaces of Judah that have been torn down to be used against the siege ramps and the sword 5in the fight with the Babylonians[a]: 'They will be filled with the dead bodies of the people I will slay in my anger and wrath. I will hide my face from this city because of all its wickedness.

6" 'Nevertheless, I will bring health and healing to it; I will heal my people and will let them enjoy abundant peace and security. 7I will bring Judah and Israel back from captivity[b] and will rebuild them as they were before. 8I will cleanse them from all the sin they have committed against me and will forgive all their sins of rebellion against me. 9Then this city will bring me renown, joy, praise and honor before all nations on earth that hear of all the good things I do for it; and they will be in awe and will tremble at the abundant prosperity and peace I provide for it.'

10"This is what the LORD says: 'You say about this place, "It is a desolate waste, without people or animals." Yet in the towns of Judah and the streets of Jerusalem that are deserted, inhabited by neither people nor animals, there will be heard once more 11the sounds of joy and gladness, the voices of bride and bridegroom, and the voices of those who bring thank offerings to the house of the LORD, saying,

"Give thanks to the LORD Almighty,
for the LORD is good;
his love endures forever."

For I will restore the fortunes of the land as they were before,' says the LORD.

12"This is what the LORD Almighty says: 'In this place, desolate and without people or animals—in all its towns there will again be pastures for shepherds to rest their flocks. 13In the towns of the hill country, of the western foothills and of the Negev, in the territory of Benjamin, in the villages around Jerusalem and in the towns of Judah, flocks will again pass under the hand of the one who counts them,' says the LORD.

14" 'The days are coming,' declares the LORD, 'when I will fulfill the good promise I made to the people of Israel and Judah.

15" 'In those days and at that time
I will make a righteous Branch
sprout from David's line;
he will do what is just and right in
the land.
16In those days Judah will be saved
and Jerusalem will live in safety.
This is the name by which it[c] will be
called:
The LORD Our Righteous Savior.'

17For this is what the LORD says: 'David will never fail to have a man to sit on the throne of Israel, 18nor will the Levitical priests ever fail to have a man to stand before me continually to offer burnt offerings, to burn grain offerings and to present sacrifices.' "

19The word of the LORD came to Jeremiah: 20"This is what the LORD says: 'If you can break my covenant with the day and my covenant with the night, so that day and night no longer come at their appointed time, 21then my covenant with David my servant—and my covenant with the Levites who are priests ministering before me—can be broken and David will no longer have a descendant to reign on his throne. 22I will make the descendants of David my servant and the Levites who minister before me as countless as the stars in the sky and as measureless as the sand on the seashore.' "

23The word of the LORD came to Jeremiah: 24"Have you not noticed that these people are saying, 'The LORD has rejected the two kingdoms[d] he chose'? So they despise my people and no longer regard them as a nation. 25This is what the LORD says: 'If I have not made my covenant with day and night and established the laws of heaven and earth, 26then I will reject the descendants of Jacob and David my servant and will not choose one of his sons to rule over the descendants

[a] 5 Or *Chaldeans* [b] 7 Or *will restore the fortunes of Judah and Israel* [c] 16 Or *he* [d] 24 Or *families*

of Abraham, Isaac and Jacob. For I will
restore their fortunes[a] and have compassion on them.' "

34 While Nebuchadnezzar king of
Babylon and all his army and all
the kingdoms and peoples in the empire
he ruled were fighting against Jerusalem and all its surrounding towns, this
word came to Jeremiah from the LORD:
2 "This is what the LORD, the God of Israel, says: Go to Zedekiah king of Judah
and tell him, 'This is what the LORD says:
I am about to give this city into the hands
of the king of Babylon, and he will burn
it down. 3 You will not escape from his
grasp but will surely be captured and giv-
en into his hands. You will see the king of
Babylon with your own eyes, and he will
speak with you face to face. And you will
go to Babylon.

4 " 'Yet hear the LORD's promise to you,
Zedekiah king of Judah. This is what the
LORD says concerning you: You will not
die by the sword; 5 you will die peacefully. As people made a funeral fire in hon-
or of your predecessors, the kings who
ruled before you, so they will make a fire
in your honor and lament, "Alas, master!"
I myself make this promise, declares the
LORD.' "

6 Then Jeremiah the prophet told all
this to Zedekiah king of Judah, in Jerusalem, 7 while the army of the king of
Babylon was fighting against Jerusalem
and the other cities of Judah that were
still holding out—Lachish and Azekah.
These were the only fortified cities left
in Judah.

8 The word came to Jeremiah from the
LORD after King Zedekiah had made a
covenant with all the people in Jerusalem
to proclaim freedom for the slaves. 9 Everyone was to free their Hebrew slaves,
both male and female; no one was to
hold a fellow Hebrew in bondage. 10 So all
the officials and people who entered into
this covenant agreed that they would free
their male and female slaves and no longer hold them in bondage. They agreed,
and set them free. 11 But afterward they
changed their minds and took back the
slaves they had freed and enslaved them
again.

12 Then the word of the LORD came to
Jeremiah: 13 "This is what the LORD, the
God of Israel, says: I made a covenant
with your ancestors when I brought them
out of Egypt, out of the land of slavery. I
said, 14 'Every seventh year each of you
must free any fellow Hebrews who have
sold themselves to you. After they have
served you six years, you must let them
go free.'[b] Your ancestors, however, did
not listen to me or pay attention to me.
15 Recently you repented and did what is
right in my sight: Each of you proclaimed
freedom to your own people. You even
made a covenant before me in the house
that bears my Name. 16 But now you have
turned around and profaned my name;
each of you has taken back the male and
female slaves you had set free to go where
they wished. You have forced them to become your slaves again.

17 "Therefore this is what the LORD says:
You have not obeyed me; you have not
proclaimed freedom to your own people.
So I now proclaim 'freedom' for you, declares the LORD—'freedom' to fall by the
sword, plague and famine. I will make
you abhorrent to all the kingdoms of the
earth. 18 Those who have violated my covenant and have not fulfilled the terms of
the covenant they made before me, I will
treat like the calf they cut in two and then
walked between its pieces. 19 The leaders
of Judah and Jerusalem, the court officials, the priests and all the people of the
land who walked between the pieces of
the calf, 20 I will deliver into the hands
of their enemies who want to kill them.
Their dead bodies will become food for
the birds and the wild animals.

21 "I will deliver Zedekiah king of Judah
and his officials into the hands of their
enemies who want to kill them, to the
army of the king of Babylon, which has
withdrawn from you. 22 I am going to give
the order, declares the LORD, and I will
bring them back to this city. They will
fight against it, take it and burn it down.
And I will lay waste the towns of Judah so
no one can live there."

35 This is the word that came to Jeremiah from the LORD during the
reign of Jehoiakim son of Josiah king of
Judah: 2 "Go to the Rekabite family and
invite them to come to one of the side
rooms of the house of the LORD and give
them wine to drink."

[a] *26* Or *will bring them back from captivity* [b] *14* Deut. 15:12

3 So I went to get Jaazaniah son of Jeremiah, the son of Habazziniah, and his brothers and all his sons—the whole family of the Rekabites. 4 I brought them into the house of the LORD, into the room of the sons of Hanan son of Igdaliah the man of God. It was next to the room of the officials, which was over that of Maaseiah son of Shallum the doorkeeper. 5 Then I set bowls full of wine and some cups before the Rekabites and said to them, "Drink some wine."

6 But they replied, "We do not drink wine, because our forefather Jehonadab[a] son of Rekab gave us this command: 'Neither you nor your descendants must ever drink wine. 7 Also you must never build houses, sow seed or plant vineyards; you must never have any of these things, but must always live in tents. Then you will live a long time in the land where you are nomads.' 8 We have obeyed everything our forefather Jehonadab son of Rekab commanded us. Neither we nor our wives nor our sons and daughters have ever drunk wine 9 or built houses to live in or had vineyards, fields or crops. 10 We have lived in tents and have fully obeyed everything our forefather Jehonadab commanded us. 11 But when Nebuchadnezzar king of Babylon invaded this land, we said, 'Come, we must go to Jerusalem to escape the Babylonian[b] and Aramean armies.' So we have remained in Jerusalem."

12 Then the word of the LORD came to Jeremiah, saying: 13 "This is what the LORD Almighty, the God of Israel, says: Go and tell the people of Judah and those living in Jerusalem, 'Will you not learn a lesson and obey my words?' declares the LORD. 14 'Jehonadab son of Rekab ordered his descendants not to drink wine and this command has been kept. To this day they do not drink wine, because they obey their forefather's command. But I have spoken to you again and again, yet you have not obeyed me. 15 Again and again I sent all my servants the prophets to you. They said, "Each of you must turn from your wicked ways and reform your actions; do not follow other gods to serve them. Then you will live in the land I have given to you and your ancestors." But you have not paid attention or listened to me. 16 The descendants of Jehonadab son of Rekab have carried out the command their forefather gave them, but these people have not obeyed me.'

17 "Therefore this is what the LORD God Almighty, the God of Israel, says: 'Listen! I am going to bring on Judah and on everyone living in Jerusalem every disaster I pronounced against them. I spoke to them, but they did not listen; I called to them, but they did not answer.'"

18 Then Jeremiah said to the family of the Rekabites, "This is what the LORD Almighty, the God of Israel, says: 'You have obeyed the command of your forefather Jehonadab and have followed all his instructions and have done everything he ordered.' 19 Therefore this is what the LORD Almighty, the God of Israel, says: 'Jehonadab son of Rekab will never fail to have a descendant to serve me.'"

36 In the fourth year of Jehoiakim son of Josiah king of Judah, this word came to Jeremiah from the LORD: 2 "Take a scroll and write on it all the words I have spoken to you concerning Israel, Judah and all the other nations from the time I began speaking to you in the reign of Josiah till now. 3 Perhaps when the people of Judah hear about every disaster I plan to inflict on them, they will each turn from their wicked ways; then I will forgive their wickedness and their sin."

4 So Jeremiah called Baruch son of Neriah, and while Jeremiah dictated all the words the LORD had spoken to him, Baruch wrote them on the scroll. 5 Then Jeremiah told Baruch, "I am restricted; I am not allowed to go to the LORD's temple. 6 So you go to the house of the LORD on a day of fasting and read to the people from the scroll the words of the LORD that you wrote as I dictated. Read them to all the people of Judah who come in from their towns. 7 Perhaps they will bring their petition before the LORD and will each turn from their wicked ways, for the anger and wrath pronounced against this people by the LORD are great."

8 Baruch son of Neriah did everything Jeremiah the prophet told him to do; at the LORD's temple he read the words of the LORD from the scroll. 9 In the ninth month of the fifth year of Jehoiakim son of Josiah king of Judah, a time of fast-

[a] 6 Hebrew *Jonadab*, a variant of *Jehonadab*; here and often in this chapter [b] 11 Or *Chaldean*

ing before the LORD was proclaimed for
all the people in Jerusalem and those
who had come from the towns of Judah.
10 From the room of Gemariah son of Shaphan the secretary, which was in the upper courtyard at the entrance of the New
Gate of the temple, Baruch read to all the
people at the LORD's temple the words of
Jeremiah from the scroll.
11 When Micaiah son of Gemariah, the
son of Shaphan, heard all the words of the
LORD from the scroll, 12 he went down to
the secretary's room in the royal palace,
where all the officials were sitting: Elishama the secretary, Delaiah son of Shemaiah, Elnathan son of Akbor, Gemariah
son of Shaphan, Zedekiah son of Hananiah, and all the other officials. 13 After Micaiah told them everything he had heard
Baruch read to the people from the scroll,
14 all the officials sent Jehudi son of Nethaniah, the son of Shelemiah, the son of
Cushi, to say to Baruch, "Bring the scroll
from which you have read to the people and come." So Baruch son of Neriah
went to them with the scroll in his hand.
15 They said to him, "Sit down, please, and
read it to us."
So Baruch read it to them. 16 When they
heard all these words, they looked at each
other in fear and said to Baruch, "We
must report all these words to the king."
17 Then they asked Baruch, "Tell us, how
did you come to write all this? Did Jeremiah dictate it?"
18 "Yes," Baruch replied, "he dictated
all these words to me, and I wrote them
in ink on the scroll."
19 Then the officials said to Baruch,
"You and Jeremiah, go and hide. Don't let
anyone know where you are."
20 After they put the scroll in the room
of Elishama the secretary, they went to
the king in the courtyard and reported
everything to him. 21 The king sent Jehudi to get the scroll, and Jehudi brought it
from the room of Elishama the secretary
and read it to the king and all the officials
standing beside him. 22 It was the ninth
month and the king was sitting in the
winter apartment, with a fire burning in
the firepot in front of him. 23 Whenever
Jehudi had read three or four columns
of the scroll, the king cut them off with
a scribe's knife and threw them into the
firepot, until the entire scroll was burned
in the fire. 24 The king and all his attendants who heard all these words showed
no fear, nor did they tear their clothes.
25 Even though Elnathan, Delaiah and
Gemariah urged the king not to burn the
scroll, he would not listen to them. 26 Instead, the king commanded Jerahmeel, a
son of the king, Seraiah son of Azriel and
Shelemiah son of Abdeel to arrest Baruch
the scribe and Jeremiah the prophet. But
the LORD had hidden them.
27 After the king burned the scroll containing the words that Baruch had written at Jeremiah's dictation, the word of
the LORD came to Jeremiah: 28 "Take another scroll and write on it all the words
that were on the first scroll, which Jehoiakim king of Judah burned up. 29 Also tell
Jehoiakim king of Judah, 'This is what the
LORD says: You burned that scroll and
said, "Why did you write on it that the
king of Babylon would certainly come
and destroy this land and wipe from it
both man and beast?" 30 Therefore this
is what the LORD says about Jehoiakim
king of Judah: He will have no one to sit
on the throne of David; his body will be
thrown out and exposed to the heat by
day and the frost by night. 31 I will punish him and his children and his attendants for their wickedness; I will bring
on them and those living in Jerusalem
and the people of Judah every disaster I
pronounced against them, because they
have not listened.' "
32 So Jeremiah took another scroll and
gave it to the scribe Baruch son of Neriah,
and as Jeremiah dictated, Baruch wrote
on it all the words of the scroll that Jehoiakim king of Judah had burned in the
fire. And many similar words were added
to them.

37 Zedekiah son of Josiah was made
king of Judah by Nebuchadnezzar
king of Babylon; he reigned in place of Jehoiachin[a] son of Jehoiakim. 2 Neither he
nor his attendants nor the people of the
land paid any attention to the words the
LORD had spoken through Jeremiah the
prophet.
3 King Zedekiah, however, sent Jehukal
son of Shelemiah with the priest Zephaniah son of Maaseiah to Jeremiah the

[a] *1* Hebrew *Koniah,* a variant of *Jehoiachin*

prophet with this message: "Please pray
to the LORD our God for us."
4 Now Jeremiah was free to come and
go among the people, for he had not yet
been put in prison. 5 Pharaoh's army had
marched out of Egypt, and when the Babylonians[a] who were besieging Jerusalem
heard the report about them, they withdrew from Jerusalem.
6 Then the word of the LORD came to
Jeremiah the prophet: 7 "This is what the
LORD, the God of Israel, says: Tell the king
of Judah, who sent you to inquire of me,
'Pharaoh's army, which has marched out
to support you, will go back to its own
land, to Egypt. 8 Then the Babylonians
will return and attack this city; they will
capture it and burn it down.'
9 "This is what the LORD says: Do not
deceive yourselves, thinking, 'The Babylonians will surely leave us.' They will
not! 10 Even if you were to defeat the entire
Babylonian[b] army that is attacking you
and only wounded men were left in their
tents, they would come out and burn this
city down."
11 After the Babylonian army had withdrawn from Jerusalem because of Pharaoh's army, 12 Jeremiah started to leave
the city to go to the territory of Benjamin
to get his share of the property among the
people there. 13 But when he reached the
Benjamin Gate, the captain of the guard,
whose name was Irijah son of Shelemiah, the son of Hananiah, arrested him
and said, "You are deserting to the Babylonians!"
14 "That's not true!" Jeremiah said. "I
am not deserting to the Babylonians." But
Irijah would not listen to him; instead, he
arrested Jeremiah and brought him to the
officials. 15 They were angry with Jeremiah and had him beaten and imprisoned
in the house of Jonathan the secretary,
which they had made into a prison.
16 Jeremiah was put into a vaulted cell
in a dungeon, where he remained a long
time. 17 Then King Zedekiah sent for him
and had him brought to the palace, where
he asked him privately, "Is there any word
from the LORD?"
"Yes," Jeremiah replied, "you will be
delivered into the hands of the king of
Babylon."
18 Then Jeremiah said to King Zedekiah, "What crime have I committed
against you or your attendants or this
people, that you have put me in prison?
19 Where are your prophets who prophesied to you, 'The king of Babylon will not
attack you or this land'? 20 But now, my
lord the king, please listen. Let me bring
my petition before you: Do not send me
back to the house of Jonathan the secretary, or I will die there."
21 King Zedekiah then gave orders for
Jeremiah to be placed in the courtyard of
the guard and given a loaf of bread from
the street of the bakers each day until all
the bread in the city was gone. So Jeremiah remained in the courtyard of the
guard.

38 Shephatiah son of Mattan, Gedaliah son of Pashhur, Jehukal[c] son of
Shelemiah, and Pashhur son of Malkijah heard what Jeremiah was telling all
the people when he said, 2 "This is what
the LORD says: 'Whoever stays in this city
will die by the sword, famine or plague,
but whoever goes over to the Babylonians[d] will live. They will escape with their
lives; they will live.' 3 And this is what the
LORD says: 'This city will certainly be giv-
en into the hands of the army of the king
of Babylon, who will capture it.' "
4 Then the officials said to the king,
"This man should be put to death. He is
discouraging the soldiers who are left in
this city, as well as all the people, by the
things he is saying to them. This man is
not seeking the good of these people but
their ruin."
5 "He is in your hands," King Zedekiah
answered. "The king can do nothing to
oppose you."
6 So they took Jeremiah and put him
into the cistern of Malkijah, the king's
son, which was in the courtyard of the
guard. They lowered Jeremiah by ropes
into the cistern; it had no water in it, only
mud, and Jeremiah sank down into the
mud.
7 But Ebed-Melek, a Cushite,[e] an official[f] in the royal palace, heard that they
had put Jeremiah into the cistern. While
the king was sitting in the Benjamin
Gate, 8 Ebed-Melek went out of the palace
and said to him, 9 "My lord the king, these

[a] 5 Or *Chaldeans*; also in verses 8, 9, 13 and 14 [b] 10 Or *Chaldean*; also in verse 11 [c] 1 Hebrew *Jukal*, a variant of *Jehukal* [d] 2 Or *Chaldeans*; also in verses 18, 19 and 23 [e] 7 Probably from the upper Nile region [f] 7 Or *a eunuch*

men have acted wickedly in all they have done to Jeremiah the prophet. They have thrown him into a cistern, where he will starve to death when there is no longer any bread in the city."

10 Then the king commanded Ebed-Melek the Cushite, "Take thirty men from here with you and lift Jeremiah the prophet out of the cistern before he dies."

11 So Ebed-Melek took the men with him and went to a room under the treasury in the palace. He took some old rags and worn-out clothes from there and let them down with ropes to Jeremiah in
the cistern. 12 Ebed-Melek the Cushite said to Jeremiah, "Put these old rags and worn-out clothes under your arms to pad
the ropes." Jeremiah did so, 13 and they pulled him up with the ropes and lifted him out of the cistern. And Jeremiah remained in the courtyard of the guard.

14 Then King Zedekiah sent for Jeremiah the prophet and had him brought to the third entrance to the temple of the LORD. "I am going to ask you something," the king said to Jeremiah. "Do not hide anything from me."

15 Jeremiah said to Zedekiah, "If I give you an answer, will you not kill me? Even if I did give you counsel, you would not listen to me."

16 But King Zedekiah swore this oath secretly to Jeremiah: "As surely as the LORD lives, who has given us breath, I will neither kill you nor hand you over to those who want to kill you."

17 Then Jeremiah said to Zedekiah, "This is what the LORD God Almighty, the God of Israel, says: 'If you surrender to the officers of the king of Babylon, your life will be spared and this city will not be burned down; you and your family will live. 18 But if you will not surrender to the officers of the king of Babylon, this city will be given into the hands of the Babylonians and they will burn it down; you yourself will not escape from them.' "

19 King Zedekiah said to Jeremiah, "I am afraid of the Jews who have gone over to the Babylonians, for the Babylonians may hand me over to them and they will mistreat me."

20 "They will not hand you over," Jeremiah replied. "Obey the LORD by doing what I tell you. Then it will go well with you, and your life will be spared. 21 But if you refuse to surrender, this is what the LORD has revealed to me: 22 All the women left in the palace of the king of Judah will be brought out to the officials of the king of Babylon. Those women will say to you:

" 'They misled you and overcame
you —
those trusted friends of yours.
Your feet are sunk in the mud;
your friends have deserted you.'

23 "All your wives and children will be brought out to the Babylonians. You yourself will not escape from their hands but will be captured by the king of Babylon; and this city will[a] be burned down."

24 Then Zedekiah said to Jeremiah, "Do not let anyone know about this conversation, or you may die. 25 If the officials hear that I talked with you, and they come to you and say, 'Tell us what you said to the king and what the king said to you; do not hide it from us or we will kill you,' 26 then tell them, 'I was pleading with the king not to send me back to Jonathan's house to die there.' "

27 All the officials did come to Jeremiah and question him, and he told them everything the king had ordered him to say. So they said no more to him, for no one had heard his conversation with the king.

28 And Jeremiah remained in the courtyard of the guard until the day Jerusalem was captured.

39 This is how Jerusalem was taken:
1 In the ninth year of Zedekiah king of Judah, in the tenth month, Nebuchadnezzar king of Babylon marched against Jerusalem with his whole army and laid
siege to it. 2 And on the ninth day of the fourth month of Zedekiah's eleventh year, the city wall was broken through.
3 Then all the officials of the king of Babylon came and took seats in the Middle Gate: Nergal-Sharezer of Samgar, Nebo-Sarsekim a chief officer, Nergal-Sharezer a high official and all the other officials of the king of Babylon. 4 When Zedekiah king of Judah and all the soldiers saw them, they fled; they left the city at night by way of the king's garden, through the

[a] 23 Or *and you will cause this city to*

gate between the two walls, and headed
toward the Arabah.[a]
5But the Babylonian[b] army pursued
them and overtook Zedekiah in the
plains of Jericho. They captured him
and took him to Nebuchadnezzar king
of Babylon at Riblah in the land of Hamath, where he pronounced sentence on
him. 6There at Riblah the king of Babylon
slaughtered the sons of Zedekiah before
his eyes and also killed all the nobles of
Judah. 7Then he put out Zedekiah's eyes
and bound him with bronze shackles to
take him to Babylon.
8The Babylonians[c] set fire to the royal
palace and the houses of the people and
broke down the walls of Jerusalem. 9Neb-
uzaradan commander of the imperial
guard carried into exile to Babylon the
people who remained in the city, along
with those who had gone over to him,
and the rest of the people. 10But Nebuzaradan the commander of the guard
left behind in the land of Judah some of
the poor people, who owned nothing;
and at that time he gave them vineyards
and fields.
11Now Nebuchadnezzar king of Babylon had given these orders about Jeremiah through Nebuzaradan commander of
the imperial guard: 12"Take him and look
after him; don't harm him but do for him
whatever he asks." 13So Nebuzaradan the
commander of the guard, Nebushazban
a chief officer, Nergal-Sharezer a high
official and all the other officers of the
king of Babylon 14sent and had Jeremiah
taken out of the courtyard of the guard.
They turned him over to Gedaliah son of
Ahikam, the son of Shaphan, to take him
back to his home. So he remained among
his own people.
15While Jeremiah had been confined
in the courtyard of the guard, the word
of the LORD came to him: 16"Go and tell
Ebed-Melek the Cushite, 'This is what the
LORD Almighty, the God of Israel, says: I
am about to fulfill my words against this
city—words concerning disaster, not
prosperity. At that time they will be fulfilled before your eyes. 17But I will rescue
you on that day, declares the LORD; you
will not be given into the hands of those
you fear. 18I will save you; you will not fall
by the sword but will escape with your
life, because you trust in me, declares
the LORD.'"

40 The word came to Jeremiah from
the LORD after Nebuzaradan commander of the imperial guard had released him at Ramah. He had found
Jeremiah bound in chains among all
the captives from Jerusalem and Judah
who were being carried into exile to
Babylon. 2When the commander of the
guard found Jeremiah, he said to him,
"The LORD your God decreed this disaster for this place. 3And now the LORD has
brought it about; he has done just as he
said he would. All this happened because
you people sinned against the LORD and
did not obey him. 4But today I am freeing
you from the chains on your wrists. Come
with me to Babylon, if you like, and I will
look after you; but if you do not want to,
then don't come. Look, the whole country
lies before you; go wherever you please."
5However, before Jeremiah turned to go,[d]
Nebuzaradan added, "Go back to Gedaliah son of Ahikam, the son of Shaphan,
whom the king of Babylon has appointed over the towns of Judah, and live with
him among the people, or go anywhere
else you please."
Then the commander gave him provisions and a present and let him go.
6So Jeremiah went to Gedaliah son of
Ahikam at Mizpah and stayed with him
among the people who were left behind
in the land.
7When all the army officers and their
men who were still in the open country heard that the king of Babylon had
appointed Gedaliah son of Ahikam as
governor over the land and had put him
in charge of the men, women and children who were the poorest in the land
and who had not been carried into exile
to Babylon, 8they came to Gedaliah at
Mizpah—Ishmael son of Nethaniah, Johanan and Jonathan the sons of Kareah,
Seraiah son of Tanhumeth, the sons of
Ephai the Netophathite, and Jaazaniah[e]
the son of the Maakathite, and their men.
9Gedaliah son of Ahikam, the son of Shaphan, took an oath to reassure them and
their men. "Do not be afraid to serve the
Babylonians,[f]" he said. "Settle down in
the land and serve the king of Babylon,
and it will go well with you. 10I myself

[a] 4 Or *the Jordan Valley* [b] 5 Or *Chaldean* [c] 8 Or *Chaldeans* [d] 5 Or *Jeremiah answered* [e] 8 Hebrew *Jezaniah*, a variant of *Jaazaniah* [f] 9 Or *Chaldeans*; also in verse 10

will stay at Mizpah to represent you before the Babylonians who come to us, but
you are to harvest the wine, summer fruit
and olive oil, and put them in your storage jars, and live in the towns you have
taken over."
11 When all the Jews in Moab, Ammon,
Edom and all the other countries heard
that the king of Babylon had left a remnant in Judah and had appointed Gedaliah son of Ahikam, the son of Shaphan,
as governor over them, 12 they all came
back to the land of Judah, to Gedaliah
at Mizpah, from all the countries where
they had been scattered. And they harvested an abundance of wine and summer fruit.
13 Johanan son of Kareah and all the
army officers still in the open country
came to Gedaliah at Mizpah 14 and said
to him, "Don't you know that Baalis king
of the Ammonites has sent Ishmael son of
Nethaniah to take your life?" But Gedaliah son of Ahikam did not believe them.
15 Then Johanan son of Kareah said privately to Gedaliah in Mizpah, "Let me go
and kill Ishmael son of Nethaniah, and
no one will know it. Why should he take
your life and cause all the Jews who are
gathered around you to be scattered and
the remnant of Judah to perish?"
16 But Gedaliah son of Ahikam said to
Johanan son of Kareah, "Don't do such a
thing! What you are saying about Ishmael
is not true."

41 In the seventh month Ishmael son
of Nethaniah, the son of Elishama,
who was of royal blood and had been one
of the king's officers, came with ten men
to Gedaliah son of Ahikam at Mizpah.
While they were eating together there,
2 Ishmael son of Nethaniah and the ten
men who were with him got up and struck
down Gedaliah son of Ahikam, the son of
Shaphan, with the sword, killing the one
whom the king of Babylon had appointed
as governor over the land. 3 Ishmael also
killed all the men of Judah who were with
Gedaliah at Mizpah, as well as the Babylonian[a] soldiers who were there.
4 The day after Gedaliah's assassi-
nation, before anyone knew about it,
5 eighty men who had shaved off their
beards, torn their clothes and cut themselves came from Shechem, Shiloh and
Samaria, bringing grain offerings and
incense with them to the house of the
Lord. 6 Ishmael son of Nethaniah went
out from Mizpah to meet them, weeping as he went. When he met them, he
said, "Come to Gedaliah son of Ahikam."
7 When they went into the city, Ishmael
son of Nethaniah and the men who were
with him slaughtered them and threw
them into a cistern. 8 But ten of them said
to Ishmael, "Don't kill us! We have wheat
and barley, olive oil and honey, hidden
in a field." So he let them alone and did
not kill them with the others. 9 Now the
cistern where he threw all the bodies of
the men he had killed along with Gedaliah was the one King Asa had made as
part of his defense against Baasha king of
Israel. Ishmael son of Nethaniah filled it
with the dead.
10 Ishmael made captives of all the rest
of the people who were in Mizpah — the
king's daughters along with all the others
who were left there, over whom Nebuzaradan commander of the imperial guard
had appointed Gedaliah son of Ahikam.
Ishmael son of Nethaniah took them captive and set out to cross over to the Ammonites.
11 When Johanan son of Kareah and
all the army officers who were with him
heard about all the crimes Ishmael son
of Nethaniah had committed, 12 they
took all their men and went to fight Ishmael son of Nethaniah. They caught up
with him near the great pool in Gibeon.
13 When all the people Ishmael had with
him saw Johanan son of Kareah and the
army officers who were with him, they
were glad. 14 All the people Ishmael had
taken captive at Mizpah turned and went
over to Johanan son of Kareah. 15 But Ishmael son of Nethaniah and eight of his
men escaped from Johanan and fled to
the Ammonites.
16 Then Johanan son of Kareah and all
the army officers who were with him led
away all the people of Mizpah who had
survived, whom Johanan had recovered
from Ishmael son of Nethaniah after Ishmael had assassinated Gedaliah son of
Ahikam — the soldiers, women, children
and court officials he had recovered from
Gibeon. 17 And they went on, stopping at
Geruth Kimham near Bethlehem on their

[a] 3 Or *Chaldean*

way to Egypt 18 to escape the Babylonians.[a] They were afraid of them because
Ishmael son of Nethaniah had killed
Gedaliah son of Ahikam, whom the king
of Babylon had appointed as governor
over the land.

42 Then all the army officers, including Johanan son of Kareah and Jezaniah[b] son of Hoshaiah, and all the people
from the least to the greatest approached
2 Jeremiah the prophet and said to him,
"Please hear our petition and pray to the
LORD your God for this entire remnant.
For as you now see, though we were once
many, now only a few are left. 3 Pray that
the LORD your God will tell us where we
should go and what we should do."
4 "I have heard you," replied Jeremiah
the prophet. "I will certainly pray to the
LORD your God as you have requested;
I will tell you everything the LORD says
and will keep nothing back from you."
5 Then they said to Jeremiah, "May
the LORD be a true and faithful witness
against us if we do not act in accordance
with everything the LORD your God sends
you to tell us. 6 Whether it is favorable or
unfavorable, we will obey the LORD our
God, to whom we are sending you, so that
it will go well with us, for we will obey the
LORD our God."
7 Ten days later the word of the LORD
came to Jeremiah. 8 So he called together
Johanan son of Kareah and all the army
officers who were with him and all the
people from the least to the greatest. 9 He
said to them, "This is what the LORD, the
God of Israel, to whom you sent me to
present your petition, says: 10 'If you stay
in this land, I will build you up and not
tear you down; I will plant you and not
uproot you, for I have relented concerning the disaster I have inflicted on you.
11 Do not be afraid of the king of Babylon,
whom you now fear. Do not be afraid of
him, declares the LORD, for I am with you
and will save you and deliver you from
his hands. 12 I will show you compassion
so that he will have compassion on you
and restore you to your land.'
13 "However, if you say, 'We will not stay
in this land,' and so disobey the LORD
your God, 14 and if you say, 'No, we will go
and live in Egypt, where we will not see
war or hear the trumpet or be hungry for
bread,' 15 then hear the word of the LORD,
you remnant of Judah. This is what the
LORD Almighty, the God of Israel, says:
'If you are determined to go to Egypt and
you do go to settle there, 16 then the sword
you fear will overtake you there, and the
famine you dread will follow you into
Egypt, and there you will die. 17 Indeed,
all who are determined to go to Egypt to
settle there will die by the sword, famine
and plague; not one of them will survive
or escape the disaster I will bring on
them.' 18 This is what the LORD Almighty,
the God of Israel, says: 'As my anger and
wrath have been poured out on those who
lived in Jerusalem, so will my wrath be
poured out on you when you go to Egypt.
You will be a curse[c] and an object of horror, a curse[c] and an object of reproach;
you will never see this place again.'
19 "Remnant of Judah, the LORD has told
you, 'Do not go to Egypt.' Be sure of this:
I warn you today 20 that you made a fatal
mistake when you sent me to the LORD
your God and said, 'Pray to the LORD our
God for us; tell us everything he says and
we will do it.' 21 I have told you today, but
you still have not obeyed the LORD your
God in all he sent me to tell you. 22 So now,
be sure of this: You will die by the sword,
famine and plague in the place where you
want to go to settle."

43 When Jeremiah had finished telling the people all the words of the
LORD their God—everything the LORD
had sent him to tell them— 2 Azariah son
of Hoshaiah and Johanan son of Kareah
and all the arrogant men said to Jeremiah, "You are lying! The LORD our God has
not sent you to say, 'You must not go to
Egypt to settle there.' 3 But Baruch son of
Neriah is inciting you against us to hand
us over to the Babylonians,[a] so they may
kill us or carry us into exile to Babylon."
4 So Johanan son of Kareah and all
the army officers and all the people disobeyed the LORD's command to stay in
the land of Judah. 5 Instead, Johanan son
of Kareah and all the army officers led
away all the remnant of Judah who had
come back to live in the land of Judah
from all the nations where they had been
scattered. 6 They also led away all those
whom Nebuzaradan commander of the
imperial guard had left with Gedaliah

[a] *18,3* Or *Chaldeans* [b] *1* Hebrew; Septuagint (see also 43:2) *Azariah* [c] *18* That is, your name will be used in cursing (see 29:22); or, others will see that you are cursed.

son of Ahikam, the son of Shaphan—the
men, the women, the children and the
king's daughters. And they took Jeremiah the prophet and Baruch son of Neriah
along with them. 7So they entered Egypt
in disobedience to the LORD and went as
far as Tahpanhes.
8In Tahpanhes the word of the LORD
came to Jeremiah: 9"While the Jews are
watching, take some large stones with
you and bury them in clay in the brick
pavement at the entrance to Pharaoh's
palace in Tahpanhes. 10Then say to them,
'This is what the LORD Almighty, the God
of Israel, says: I will send for my servant
Nebuchadnezzar king of Babylon, and
I will set his throne over these stones I
have buried here; he will spread his royal
canopy above them. 11He will come and
attack Egypt, bringing death to those
destined for death, captivity to those destined for captivity, and the sword to those
destined for the sword. 12He will set fire
to the temples of the gods of Egypt; he will
burn their temples and take their gods
captive. As a shepherd picks his garment
clean of lice, so he will pick Egypt clean
and depart. 13There in the temple of the
sun[a] in Egypt he will demolish the sacred
pillars and will burn down the temples of
the gods of Egypt.'"

44 This word came to Jeremiah concerning all the Jews living in Lower
Egypt—in Migdol, Tahpanhes and Memphis—and in Upper Egypt: 2"This is what
the LORD Almighty, the God of Israel,
says: You saw the great disaster I brought
on Jerusalem and on all the towns of Judah. Today they lie deserted and in ruins 3because of the evil they have done.
They aroused my anger by burning incense to and worshiping other gods that
neither they nor you nor your ancestors
ever knew. 4Again and again I sent my
servants the prophets, who said, 'Do
not do this detestable thing that I hate!'
5But they did not listen or pay attention;
they did not turn from their wickedness
or stop burning incense to other gods.
6Therefore, my fierce anger was poured
out; it raged against the towns of Judah
and the streets of Jerusalem and made
them the desolate ruins they are today.
7"Now this is what the LORD God Almighty, the God of Israel, says: Why
bring such great disaster on yourselves
by cutting off from Judah the men and
women, the children and infants, and
so leave yourselves without a remnant?
8Why arouse my anger with what your
hands have made, burning incense to
other gods in Egypt, where you have
come to live? You will destroy yourselves
and make yourselves a curse[b] and an object of reproach among all the nations on
earth. 9Have you forgotten the wickedness committed by your ancestors and
by the kings and queens of Judah and
the wickedness committed by you and
your wives in the land of Judah and the
streets of Jerusalem? 10To this day they
have not humbled themselves or shown
reverence, nor have they followed my law
and the decrees I set before you and your
ancestors.
11"Therefore this is what the LORD Almighty, the God of Israel, says: I am determined to bring disaster on you and to
destroy all Judah. 12I will take away the
remnant of Judah who were determined
to go to Egypt to settle there. They will
all perish in Egypt; they will fall by the
sword or die from famine. From the least
to the greatest, they will die by sword or
famine. They will become a curse and an
object of horror, a curse and an object of
reproach. 13I will punish those who live
in Egypt with the sword, famine and
plague, as I punished Jerusalem. 14None
of the remnant of Judah who have gone
to live in Egypt will escape or survive to
return to the land of Judah, to which they
long to return and live; none will return
except a few fugitives."
15Then all the men who knew that
their wives were burning incense to other gods, along with all the women who
were present—a large assembly—and
all the people living in Lower and Upper
Egypt, said to Jeremiah, 16"We will not
listen to the message you have spoken to
us in the name of the LORD! 17We will certainly do everything we said we would:
We will burn incense to the Queen of
Heaven and will pour out drink offerings
to her just as we and our ancestors, our
kings and our officials did in the towns of
Judah and in the streets of Jerusalem. At
that time we had plenty of food and were
well off and suffered no harm. 18But ever

[a] *13* Or *in Heliopolis* [b] *8* That is, your name will be used in cursing (see 29:22); or, others will see that you are cursed; also in verse 12; similarly in verse 22.

since we stopped burning incense to the
Queen of Heaven and pouring out drink
offerings to her, we have had nothing
and have been perishing by sword and
famine."
19 The women added, "When we burned
incense to the Queen of Heaven and
poured out drink offerings to her, did not
our husbands know that we were making cakes impressed with her image and
pouring out drink offerings to her?"
20 Then Jeremiah said to all the people,
both men and women, who were answering him, 21 "Did not the LORD remember
and call to mind the incense burned in
the towns of Judah and the streets of Jerusalem by you and your ancestors, your
kings and your officials and the people
of the land? 22 When the LORD could no
longer endure your wicked actions and
the detestable things you did, your land
became a curse and a desolate waste
without inhabitants, as it is today. 23 Because you have burned incense and have
sinned against the LORD and have not
obeyed him or followed his law or his decrees or his stipulations, this disaster has
come upon you, as you now see."
24 Then Jeremiah said to all the people,
including the women, "Hear the word
of the LORD, all you people of Judah in
Egypt. 25 This is what the LORD Almighty,
the God of Israel, says: You and your
wives have done what you said you would
do when you promised, 'We will certainly
carry out the vows we made to burn incense and pour out drink offerings to the
Queen of Heaven.'
"Go ahead then, do what you promised!
Keep your vows! 26 But hear the word of
the LORD, all you Jews living in Egypt: 'I
swear by my great name,' says the LORD,
'that no one from Judah living anywhere
in Egypt will ever again invoke my name
or swear, "As surely as the Sovereign
LORD lives." 27 For I am watching over
them for harm, not for good; the Jews in
Egypt will perish by sword and famine
until they are all destroyed. 28 Those who
escape the sword and return to the land
of Judah from Egypt will be very few.
Then the whole remnant of Judah who
came to live in Egypt will know whose
word will stand — mine or theirs.
29 " 'This will be the sign to you that I
will punish you in this place,' declares
the LORD, 'so that you will know that my
threats of harm against you will surely
stand.' 30 This is what the LORD says: 'I am
going to deliver Pharaoh Hophra king of
Egypt into the hands of his enemies who
want to kill him, just as I gave Zedekiah
king of Judah into the hands of Nebuchadnezzar king of Babylon, the enemy
who wanted to kill him.' "

45 When Baruch son of Neriah wrote
on a scroll the words Jeremiah the
prophet dictated in the fourth year of Jehoiakim son of Josiah king of Judah, Jeremiah said this to Baruch: 2 "This is what
the LORD, the God of Israel, says to you,
Baruch: 3 You said, 'Woe to me! The LORD
has added sorrow to my pain; I am worn
out with groaning and find no rest.' 4 But
the LORD has told me to say to you, 'This
is what the LORD says: I will overthrow
what I have built and uproot what I have
planted, throughout the earth. 5 Should
you then seek great things for yourself?
Do not seek them. For I will bring disaster on all people, declares the LORD, but
wherever you go I will let you escape with
your life.' "

46 This is the word of the LORD that
came to Jeremiah the prophet concerning the nations:

2 Concerning Egypt:

This is the message against the army of
Pharaoh Necho king of Egypt, which was
defeated at Carchemish on the Euphrates
River by Nebuchadnezzar king of Babylon in the fourth year of Jehoiakim son
of Josiah king of Judah:

3 "Prepare your shields, both large and
small,
and march out for battle!
4 Harness the horses,
mount the steeds!
Take your positions
with helmets on!
Polish your spears,
put on your armor!
5 What do I see?
They are terrified,
they are retreating,
their warriors are defeated.
They flee in haste
without looking back,
and there is terror on every side,"
declares the LORD.
6 "The swift cannot flee
nor the strong escape.

In the north by the River Euphrates
they stumble and fall.

7 "Who is this that rises like the Nile,
like rivers of surging waters?
8 Egypt rises like the Nile,
like rivers of surging waters.
She says, 'I will rise and cover the
earth;
I will destroy cities and their
people.'
9 Charge, you horses!
Drive furiously, you charioteers!
March on, you warriors — men of
Cush[a] and Put who carry
shields,
men of Lydia who draw the bow.
10 But that day belongs to the Lord, the
LORD Almighty —
a day of vengeance, for vengeance
on his foes.
The sword will devour till it is
satisfied,
till it has quenched its thirst with
blood.
For the Lord, the LORD Almighty, will
offer sacrifice
in the land of the north by the River
Euphrates.

11 "Go up to Gilead and get balm,
Virgin Daughter Egypt.
But you try many medicines in vain;
there is no healing for you.
12 The nations will hear of your shame;
your cries will fill the earth.
One warrior will stumble over
another;
both will fall down together."

13 This is the message the LORD spoke
to Jeremiah the prophet about the coming of Nebuchadnezzar king of Babylon
to attack Egypt:

14 "Announce this in Egypt, and
proclaim it in Migdol;
proclaim it also in Memphis and
Tahpanhes:
'Take your positions and get ready,
for the sword devours those around
you.'
15 Why will your warriors be laid low?
They cannot stand, for the LORD will
push them down.
16 They will stumble repeatedly;
they will fall over each other.
They will say, 'Get up, let us go back
to our own people and our native
lands,
away from the sword of the
oppressor.'
17 There they will exclaim,
'Pharaoh king of Egypt is only a loud
noise;
he has missed his opportunity.'

18 "As surely as I live," declares the King,
whose name is the LORD Almighty,
"one will come who is like Tabor
among the mountains,
like Carmel by the sea.
19 Pack your belongings for exile,
you who live in Egypt,
for Memphis will be laid waste
and lie in ruins without inhabitant.

20 "Egypt is a beautiful heifer,
but a gadfly is coming
against her from the north.
21 The mercenaries in her ranks
are like fattened calves.
They too will turn and flee together,
they will not stand their ground,
for the day of disaster is coming upon
them,
the time for them to be punished.
22 Egypt will hiss like a fleeing serpent
as the enemy advances in force;
they will come against her with axes,
like men who cut down trees.
23 They will chop down her forest,"
declares the LORD,
"dense though it be.
They are more numerous than
locusts,
they cannot be counted.
24 Daughter Egypt will be put to shame,
given into the hands of the people of
the north."

25 The LORD Almighty, the God of Israel, says: "I am about to bring punishment
on Amon god of Thebes, on Pharaoh, on
Egypt and her gods and her kings, and on
those who rely on Pharaoh.
26 I will give
them into the hands of those who want
to kill them — Nebuchadnezzar king of
Babylon and his officers. Later, however,
Egypt will be inhabited as in times past,"
declares the LORD.

27 "Do not be afraid, Jacob my servant;
do not be dismayed, Israel.

[a] 9 That is, the upper Nile region

I will surely save you out of a distant
place,
your descendants from the land of
their exile.
Jacob will again have peace and
security,
and no one will make him afraid.
28 Do not be afraid, Jacob my servant,
for I am with you," declares the
LORD.
"Though I completely destroy all the
nations
among which I scatter you,
I will not completely destroy you.
I will discipline you but only in due
measure;
I will not let you go entirely
unpunished."

47 This is the word of the LORD that
came to Jeremiah the prophet concerning the Philistines before Pharaoh
attacked Gaza:

2 This is what the LORD says:

"See how the waters are rising in the
north;
they will become an overflowing
torrent.
They will overflow the land and
everything in it,
the towns and those who live in
them.
The people will cry out;
all who dwell in the land will wail
3 at the sound of the hooves of galloping
steeds,
at the noise of enemy chariots
and the rumble of their wheels.
Parents will not turn to help their
children;
their hands will hang limp.
4 For the day has come
to destroy all the Philistines
and to remove all survivors
who could help Tyre and Sidon.
The LORD is about to destroy the
Philistines,
the remnant from the coasts of
Caphtor.[a]
5 Gaza will shave her head in mourning;
Ashkelon will be silenced.
You remnant on the plain,
how long will you cut yourselves?
6 " 'Alas, sword of the LORD,
how long till you rest?
Return to your sheath;
cease and be still.'
7 But how can it rest
when the LORD has commanded it,
when he has ordered it
to attack Ashkelon and the coast?"

48 Concerning Moab:

This is what the LORD Almighty, the
God of Israel, says:

"Woe to Nebo, for it will be ruined.
Kiriathaim will be disgraced and
captured;
the stronghold[b] will be disgraced
and shattered.
2 Moab will be praised no more;
in Heshbon[c] people will plot her
downfall:
'Come, let us put an end to that
nation.'
You, the people of Madmen,[d] will also
be silenced;
the sword will pursue you.
3 Cries of anguish arise from Horonaim,
cries of great havoc and
destruction.
4 Moab will be broken;
her little ones will cry out.[e]
5 They go up the hill to Luhith,
weeping bitterly as they go;
on the road down to Horonaim
anguished cries over the
destruction are heard.
6 Flee! Run for your lives;
become like a bush[f] in the desert.
7 Since you trust in your deeds and
riches,
you too will be taken captive,
and Chemosh will go into exile,
together with his priests and
officials.
8 The destroyer will come against every
town,
and not a town will escape.
The valley will be ruined
and the plateau destroyed,
because the LORD has spoken.
9 Put salt on Moab,
for she will be laid waste[g];
her towns will become desolate,
with no one to live in them.

[a] 4 That is, Crete [b] 1 Or *captured; / Misgab* [c] 2 The Hebrew for *Heshbon* sounds like the Hebrew for *plot.*
[d] 2 The name of the Moabite town Madmen sounds like the Hebrew for *be silenced.* [e] 4 Hebrew; Septuagint
| proclaim it to Zoar [f] 6 Or *like Aroer* [g] 9 Or *Give wings to Moab, / for she will fly away*

10 "A curse on anyone who is lax in doing
the LORD's work!
A curse on anyone who keeps their
sword from bloodshed!

11 "Moab has been at rest from youth,
like wine left on its dregs,
not poured from one jar to another—
she has not gone into exile.
So she tastes as she did,
and her aroma is unchanged.
12 But days are coming,"
declares the LORD,
"when I will send men who pour from
pitchers,
and they will pour her out;
they will empty her pitchers
and smash her jars.
13 Then Moab will be ashamed of
Chemosh,
as Israel was ashamed
when they trusted in Bethel.

14 "How can you say, 'We are warriors,
men valiant in battle'?
15 Moab will be destroyed and her towns
invaded;
her finest young men will go down
in the slaughter,"
declares the King, whose name is
the LORD Almighty.
16 "The fall of Moab is at hand;
her calamity will come quickly.
17 Mourn for her, all who live around her,
all who know her fame;
say, 'How broken is the mighty
scepter,
how broken the glorious staff!'

18 "Come down from your glory
and sit on the parched ground,
you inhabitants of Daughter Dibon,
for the one who destroys Moab
will come up against you
and ruin your fortified cities.
19 Stand by the road and watch,
you who live in Aroer.
Ask the man fleeing and the woman
escaping,
ask them, 'What has happened?'
20 Moab is disgraced, for she is shattered.
Wail and cry out!
Announce by the Arnon
that Moab is destroyed.
21 Judgment has come to the plateau—
to Holon, Jahzah and Mephaath,
22 to Dibon, Nebo and Beth
Diblathaim,
23 to Kiriathaim, Beth Gamul and Beth
Meon,
24 to Kerioth and Bozrah—
to all the towns of Moab, far and
near.
25 Moab's horn[a] is cut off;
her arm is broken,"
declares the LORD.

26 "Make her drunk,
for she has defied the LORD.
Let Moab wallow in her vomit;
let her be an object of ridicule.
27 Was not Israel the object of your
ridicule?
Was she caught among thieves,
that you shake your head in scorn
whenever you speak of her?
28 Abandon your towns and dwell among
the rocks,
you who live in Moab.
Be like a dove that makes its nest
at the mouth of a cave.

29 "We have heard of Moab's pride—
how great is her arrogance!—
of her insolence, her pride, her
conceit
and the haughtiness of her heart.
30 I know her insolence but it is futile,"
declares the LORD,
"and her boasts accomplish
nothing.
31 Therefore I wail over Moab,
for all Moab I cry out,
I moan for the people of Kir
Hareseth.
32 I weep for you, as Jazer weeps,
you vines of Sibmah.
Your branches spread as far as the
sea[b];
they reached as far as[c] Jazer.
The destroyer has fallen
on your ripened fruit and grapes.
33 Joy and gladness are gone
from the orchards and fields of
Moab.
I have stopped the flow of wine from
the presses;
no one treads them with shouts of
joy.
Although there are shouts,
they are not shouts of joy.

a 25 *Horn* here symbolizes strength. b 32 Probably the Dead Sea c 32 Two Hebrew manuscripts and Septuagint; most Hebrew manuscripts *as far as the Sea of*

34 "The sound of their cry rises
from Heshbon to Elealeh and Jahaz,
from Zoar as far as Horonaim and
Eglath Shelishiyah,
for even the waters of Nimrim are
dried up.
35 In Moab I will put an end
to those who make offerings on the
high places
and burn incense to their gods,"
declares the LORD.
36 "So my heart laments for Moab like
the music of a pipe;
it laments like a pipe for the people
of Kir Hareseth.
The wealth they acquired is gone.
37 Every head is shaved
and every beard cut off;
every hand is slashed
and every waist is covered with
sackcloth.
38 On all the roofs in Moab
and in the public squares
there is nothing but mourning,
for I have broken Moab
like a jar that no one wants,"
declares the LORD.
39 "How shattered she is! How they wail!
How Moab turns her back in shame!
Moab has become an object of
ridicule,
an object of horror to all those
around her."

40 This is what the LORD says:

"Look! An eagle is swooping down,
spreading its wings over Moab.
41 Kerioth[a] will be captured
and the strongholds taken.
In that day the hearts of Moab's
warriors
will be like the heart of a woman in
labor.
42 Moab will be destroyed as a nation
because she defied the LORD.
43 Terror and pit and snare await you,
you people of Moab,"
declares the LORD.
44 "Whoever flees from the terror
will fall into a pit,
whoever climbs out of the pit
will be caught in a snare;
for I will bring on Moab
the year of her punishment,"
declares the LORD.
45 "In the shadow of Heshbon
the fugitives stand helpless,
for a fire has gone out from Heshbon,
a blaze from the midst of Sihon;
it burns the foreheads of Moab,
the skulls of the noisy boasters.
46 Woe to you, Moab!
The people of Chemosh are
destroyed;
your sons are taken into exile
and your daughters into captivity.

47 "Yet I will restore the fortunes of Moab
in days to come,"
declares the LORD.

Here ends the judgment on Moab.

49 Concerning the Ammonites:

This is what the LORD says:

"Has Israel no sons?
Has Israel no heir?
Why then has Molek[b] taken
possession of Gad?
Why do his people live in its towns?
2 But the days are coming,"
declares the LORD,
"when I will sound the battle cry
against Rabbah of the Ammonites;
it will become a mound of ruins,
and its surrounding villages will be
set on fire.
Then Israel will drive out
those who drove her out,"
says the LORD.
3 "Wail, Heshbon, for Ai is destroyed!
Cry out, you inhabitants of Rabbah!
Put on sackcloth and mourn;
rush here and there inside the walls,
for Molek will go into exile,
together with his priests and officials.
4 Why do you boast of your valleys,
boast of your valleys so fruitful?
Unfaithful Daughter Ammon,
you trust in your riches and say,
'Who will attack me?'
5 I will bring terror on you
from all those around you,"
declares the Lord,
the LORD Almighty.
"Every one of you will be driven away,
and no one will gather the fugitives.

6 "Yet afterward, I will restore the
fortunes of the Ammonites,"
declares the LORD.

[a] 41 Or *The cities* [b] 1 Or *their king*; also in verse 3

7 Concerning Edom:

This is what the LORD Almighty says:
"Is there no longer wisdom in Teman?
Has counsel perished from the prudent?
Has their wisdom decayed?
8 Turn and flee, hide in deep caves,
you who live in Dedan,
for I will bring disaster on Esau
at the time when I punish him.
9 If grape pickers came to you,
would they not leave a few grapes?
If thieves came during the night,
would they not steal only as much as they wanted?
10 But I will strip Esau bare;
I will uncover his hiding places,
so that he cannot conceal himself.
His armed men are destroyed,
also his allies and neighbors,
so there is no one to say,
11 'Leave your fatherless children; I will keep them alive.
Your widows too can depend on me.'"

12 This is what the LORD says: "If those
who do not deserve to drink the cup must
drink it, why should you go unpunished?
You will not go unpunished, but must
drink it. 13 I swear by myself," declares
the LORD, "that Bozrah will become a
ruin and a curse,[a] an object of horror and
reproach; and all its towns will be in ruins forever."

14 I have heard a message from the LORD;
an envoy was sent to the nations to say,
"Assemble yourselves to attack it!
Rise up for battle!"
15 "Now I will make you small among the nations,
despised by mankind.
16 The terror you inspire
and the pride of your heart have deceived you,
you who live in the clefts of the rocks,
who occupy the heights of the hill.
Though you build your nest as high as the eagle's,
from there I will bring you down,"
declares the LORD.
17 "Edom will become an object of horror;
all who pass by will be appalled and will scoff
because of all its wounds.
18 As Sodom and Gomorrah were overthrown,
along with their neighboring towns,"
says the LORD,
"so no one will live there;
no people will dwell in it.
19 "Like a lion coming up from Jordan's thickets
to a rich pastureland,
I will chase Edom from its land in an instant.
Who is the chosen one I will appoint for this?
Who is like me and who can challenge me?
And what shepherd can stand against me?"
20 Therefore, hear what the LORD has planned against Edom,
what he has purposed against those who live in Teman:
The young of the flock will be dragged away;
their pasture will be appalled at their fate.
21 At the sound of their fall the earth will tremble;
their cry will resound to the Red Sea.[b]
22 Look! An eagle will soar and swoop down,
spreading its wings over Bozrah.
In that day the hearts of Edom's warriors
will be like the heart of a woman in labor.

23 Concerning Damascus:

"Hamath and Arpad are dismayed,
for they have heard bad news.
They are disheartened,
troubled like[c] the restless sea.
24 Damascus has become feeble,
she has turned to flee
and panic has gripped her;
anguish and pain have seized her,
pain like that of a woman in labor.

[a] *13* That is, its name will be used in cursing (see 29:22); or, others will see that it is cursed. [b] *21* Or *the Sea of Reeds* [c] *23* Hebrew *on* or *by*

25 Why has the city of renown not been
abandoned,
the town in which I delight?
26 Surely, her young men will fall in the
streets;
all her soldiers will be silenced in
that day,"
declares the LORD Almighty.
27 "I will set fire to the walls of
Damascus;
it will consume the fortresses of
Ben-Hadad."

28 Concerning Kedar and the kingdoms
of Hazor, which Nebuchadnezzar king of
Babylon attacked:

This is what the LORD says:

"Arise, and attack Kedar
and destroy the people of the East.
29 Their tents and their flocks will be
taken;
their shelters will be carried off
with all their goods and camels.
People will shout to them,
'Terror on every side!'

30 "Flee quickly away!
Stay in deep caves, you who live in
Hazor,"
declares the LORD.
"Nebuchadnezzar king of Babylon has
plotted against you;
he has devised a plan against you.

31 "Arise and attack a nation at ease,
which lives in confidence,"
declares the LORD,
"a nation that has neither gates nor
bars;
its people live far from danger.
32 Their camels will become plunder,
and their large herds will be spoils
of war.
I will scatter to the winds those who
are in distant places[a]
and will bring disaster on them from
every side,"
declares the LORD.
33 "Hazor will become a haunt of jackals,
a desolate place forever.
No one will live there;
no people will dwell in it."

34 This is the word of the LORD that
came to Jeremiah the prophet concerning Elam, early in the reign of Zedekiah
king of Judah:

35 This is what the LORD Almighty
says:

"See, I will break the bow of Elam,
the mainstay of their might.
36 I will bring against Elam the four
winds
from the four quarters of heaven;
I will scatter them to the four winds,
and there will not be a nation
where Elam's exiles do not go.
37 I will shatter Elam before their foes,
before those who want to kill them;
I will bring disaster on them,
even my fierce anger,"
declares the LORD.
"I will pursue them with the sword
until I have made an end of them.
38 I will set my throne in Elam
and destroy her king and officials,"
declares the LORD.

39 "Yet I will restore the fortunes of Elam
in days to come,"
declares the LORD.

50 This is the word the LORD spoke
through Jeremiah the prophet concerning Babylon and the land of the Babylonians[b]:

2 "Announce and proclaim among the
nations,
lift up a banner and proclaim it;
keep nothing back, but say,
'Babylon will be captured;
Bel will be put to shame,
Marduk filled with terror.
Her images will be put to shame
and her idols filled with terror.'
3 A nation from the north will attack her
and lay waste her land.
No one will live in it;
both people and animals will flee
away.

4 "In those days, at that time,"
declares the LORD,
"the people of Israel and the people of
Judah together
will go in tears to seek the LORD
their God.
5 They will ask the way to Zion
and turn their faces toward it.

a 32 Or *who clip the hair by their foreheads* b 1 Or *Chaldeans*; also in verses 8, 25, 35 and 45

They will come and bind themselves
to the Lord
in an everlasting covenant
that will not be forgotten.

6 "My people have been lost sheep;
their shepherds have led them
astray
and caused them to roam on the
mountains.
They wandered over mountain and
hill
and forgot their own resting place.
7 Whoever found them devoured them;
their enemies said, 'We are not
guilty,
for they sinned against the Lord, their
verdant pasture,
the Lord, the hope of their
ancestors.'

8 "Flee out of Babylon;
leave the land of the Babylonians,
and be like the goats that lead the
flock.
9 For I will stir up and bring against
Babylon
an alliance of great nations from the
land of the north.
They will take up their positions
against her,
and from the north she will be
captured.
Their arrows will be like skilled
warriors
who do not return empty-handed.
10 So Babylonia[a] will be plundered;
all who plunder her will have their
fill,"
declares the Lord.

11 "Because you rejoice and are glad,
you who pillage my inheritance,
because you frolic like a heifer
threshing grain
and neigh like stallions,
12 your mother will be greatly ashamed;
she who gave you birth will be
disgraced.
She will be the least of the nations —
a wilderness, a dry land, a desert.
13 Because of the Lord's anger she will
not be inhabited
but will be completely desolate.
All who pass Babylon will be appalled;
they will scoff because of all her
wounds.

14 "Take up your positions around
Babylon,
all you who draw the bow.
Shoot at her! Spare no arrows,
for she has sinned against the Lord.
15 Shout against her on every side!
She surrenders, her towers fall,
her walls are torn down.
Since this is the vengeance of the
Lord,
take vengeance on her;
do to her as she has done to others.
16 Cut off from Babylon the sower,
and the reaper with his sickle at
harvest.
Because of the sword of the oppressor
let everyone return to their own
people,
let everyone flee to their own land.

17 "Israel is a scattered flock
that lions have chased away.
The first to devour them
was the king of Assyria;
the last to crush their bones
was Nebuchadnezzar king of
Babylon."

18 Therefore this is what the Lord Almighty, the God of Israel, says:

"I will punish the king of Babylon and
his land
as I punished the king of Assyria.
19 But I will bring Israel back to their
own pasture,
and they will graze on Carmel and
Bashan;
their appetite will be satisfied
on the hills of Ephraim and Gilead.
20 In those days, at that time,"
declares the Lord,
"search will be made for Israel's guilt,
but there will be none,
and for the sins of Judah,
but none will be found,
for I will forgive the remnant I spare.

21 "Attack the land of Merathaim
and those who live in Pekod.
Pursue, kill and completely destroy[b]
them,"
declares the Lord.

[a] 10 Or *Chaldea* [b] 21 The Hebrew term refers to the irrevocable giving over of things or persons to the Lord, often by totally destroying them; also in verse 26.

"Do everything I have commanded
you.
22 The noise of battle is in the land,
the noise of great destruction!
23 How broken and shattered
is the hammer of the whole earth!
How desolate is Babylon
among the nations!
24 I set a trap for you, Babylon,
and you were caught before you
knew it;
you were found and captured
because you opposed the LORD.
25 The LORD has opened his arsenal
and brought out the weapons of his
wrath,
for the Sovereign LORD Almighty has
work to do
in the land of the Babylonians.
26 Come against her from afar.
Break open her granaries;
pile her up like heaps of grain.
Completely destroy her
and leave her no remnant.
27 Kill all her young bulls;
let them go down to the slaughter!
Woe to them! For their day has come,
the time for them to be punished.
28 Listen to the fugitives and refugees
from Babylon
declaring in Zion
how the LORD our God has taken
vengeance,
vengeance for his temple.

29 "Summon archers against Babylon,
all those who draw the bow.
Encamp all around her;
let no one escape.
Repay her for her deeds;
do to her as she has done.
For she has defied the LORD,
the Holy One of Israel.
30 Therefore, her young men will fall in
the streets;
all her soldiers will be silenced in
that day,"
declares the LORD.
31 "See, I am against you, you arrogant
one,"
declares the Lord, the LORD
Almighty,
"for your day has come,
the time for you to be punished.
32 The arrogant one will stumble and fall
and no one will help her up;
I will kindle a fire in her towns
that will consume all who are
around her."

33 This is what the LORD Almighty
says:

"The people of Israel are oppressed,
and the people of Judah as well.
All their captors hold them fast,
refusing to let them go.
34 Yet their Redeemer is strong;
the LORD Almighty is his name.
He will vigorously defend their cause
so that he may bring rest to their
land,
but unrest to those who live in
Babylon.

35 "A sword against the Babylonians!"
declares the LORD—
"against those who live in Babylon
and against her officials and wise
men!
36 A sword against her false prophets!
They will become fools.
A sword against her warriors!
They will be filled with terror.
37 A sword against her horses and
chariots
and all the foreigners in her ranks!
They will become weaklings.
A sword against her treasures!
They will be plundered.
38 A drought on[a] her waters!
They will dry up.
For it is a land of idols,
idols that will go mad with terror.

39 "So desert creatures and hyenas will
live there,
and there the owl will dwell.
It will never again be inhabited
or lived in from generation to
generation.
40 As I overthrew Sodom and Gomorrah
along with their neighboring
towns,"
declares the LORD,
"so no one will live there;
no people will dwell in it.

41 "Look! An army is coming from the
north;
a great nation and many kings
are being stirred up from the ends of
the earth.
42 They are armed with bows and spears;

[a] 38 Or *A sword against*

they are cruel and without mercy.
They sound like the roaring sea
as they ride on their horses;
they come like men in battle
formation
to attack you, Daughter Babylon.
43 The king of Babylon has heard reports
about them,
and his hands hang limp.
Anguish has gripped him,
pain like that of a woman in labor.
44 Like a lion coming up from Jordan's
thickets
to a rich pastureland,
I will chase Babylon from its land in
an instant.
Who is the chosen one I will appoint
for this?
Who is like me and who can challenge
me?
And what shepherd can stand
against me?"

45 Therefore, hear what the LORD has
planned against Babylon,
what he has purposed against the
land of the Babylonians:
The young of the flock will be dragged
away;
their pasture will be appalled at
their fate.
46 At the sound of Babylon's capture the
earth will tremble;
its cry will resound among the
nations.

51 This is what the LORD says:

"See, I will stir up the spirit of a
destroyer
against Babylon and the people of
Leb Kamai.[a]
2 I will send foreigners to Babylon
to winnow her and to devastate her
land;
they will oppose her on every side
in the day of her disaster.
3 Let not the archer string his bow,
nor let him put on his armor.
Do not spare her young men;
completely destroy[b] her army.
4 They will fall down slain in Babylon,[c]
fatally wounded in her streets.
5 For Israel and Judah have not been
forsaken
by their God, the LORD Almighty,
though their land[d] is full of guilt
before the Holy One of Israel.

6 "Flee from Babylon!
Run for your lives!
Do not be destroyed because of her
sins.
It is time for the LORD's vengeance;
he will repay her what she deserves.
7 Babylon was a gold cup in the LORD's
hand;
she made the whole earth drunk.
The nations drank her wine;
therefore they have now gone mad.
8 Babylon will suddenly fall and be
broken.
Wail over her!
Get balm for her pain;
perhaps she can be healed.

9 " 'We would have healed Babylon,
but she cannot be healed;
let us leave her and each go to our own
land,
for her judgment reaches to the
skies,
it rises as high as the heavens.'

10 " 'The LORD has vindicated us;
come, let us tell in Zion
what the LORD our God has done.'

11 "Sharpen the arrows,
take up the shields!
The LORD has stirred up the kings of
the Medes,
because his purpose is to destroy
Babylon.
The LORD will take vengeance,
vengeance for his temple.
12 Lift up a banner against the walls of
Babylon!
Reinforce the guard,
station the watchmen,
prepare an ambush!
The LORD will carry out his purpose,
his decree against the people of
Babylon.
13 You who live by many waters
and are rich in treasures,
your end has come,
the time for you to be destroyed.
14 The LORD Almighty has sworn by
himself:

[a] *1 Leb Kamai* is a cryptogram for Chaldea, that is, Babylonia. [b] *3* The Hebrew term refers to the irrevocable giving over of things or persons to the LORD, often by totally destroying them. [c] *4* Or *Chaldea*
[d] *5* Or *Almighty, / and the land of the Babylonians*

I will surely fill you with troops, as
with a swarm of locusts,
and they will shout in triumph over
you.
15 "He made the earth by his power;
he founded the world by his wisdom
and stretched out the heavens by his
understanding.
16 When he thunders, the waters in the
heavens roar;
he makes clouds rise from the ends
of the earth.
He sends lightning with the rain
and brings out the wind from his
storehouses.

17 "Everyone is senseless and without
knowledge;
every goldsmith is shamed by his
idols.
The images he makes are a fraud;
they have no breath in them.
18 They are worthless, the objects of
mockery;
when their judgment comes, they
will perish.
19 He who is the Portion of Jacob is not
like these,
for he is the Maker of all things,
including the people of his
inheritance —
the LORD Almighty is his name.

20 "You are my war club,
my weapon for battle —
with you I shatter nations,
with you I destroy kingdoms,
21 with you I shatter horse and rider,
with you I shatter chariot and driver,
22 with you I shatter man and woman,
with you I shatter old man and
youth,
with you I shatter young man and
young woman,
23 with you I shatter shepherd and
flock,
with you I shatter farmer and oxen,
with you I shatter governors and
officials.

24 "Before your eyes I will repay Babylon and all who live in Babylonia[a] for all the wrong they have done in Zion," declares the LORD.

25 "I am against you, you destroying
mountain,
you who destroy the whole earth,"
declares the LORD.
"I will stretch out my hand against
you,
roll you off the cliffs,
and make you a burned-out
mountain.
26 No rock will be taken from you for a
cornerstone,
nor any stone for a foundation,
for you will be desolate forever,"
declares the LORD.

27 "Lift up a banner in the land!
Blow the trumpet among the
nations!
Prepare the nations for battle against
her;
summon against her these
kingdoms:
Ararat, Minni and Ashkenaz.
Appoint a commander against her;
send up horses like a swarm of
locusts.
28 Prepare the nations for battle against
her —
the kings of the Medes,
their governors and all their officials,
and all the countries they rule.
29 The land trembles and writhes,
for the LORD's purposes against
Babylon stand —
to lay waste the land of Babylon
so that no one will live there.
30 Babylon's warriors have stopped
fighting;
they remain in their strongholds.
Their strength is exhausted;
they have become weaklings.
Her dwellings are set on fire;
the bars of her gates are broken.
31 One courier follows another
and messenger follows messenger
to announce to the king of Babylon
that his entire city is captured,
32 the river crossings seized,
the marshes set on fire,
and the soldiers terrified."

33 This is what the LORD Almighty, the God of Israel, says:

"Daughter Babylon is like a threshing
floor
at the time it is trampled;
the time to harvest her will soon
come."

[a] *24* Or *Chaldea*; also in verse 35

34 "Nebuchadnezzar king of Babylon has
devoured us,
he has thrown us into confusion,
he has made us an empty jar.
Like a serpent he has swallowed us
and filled his stomach with our
delicacies,
and then has spewed us out.
35 May the violence done to our flesh[a] be
on Babylon,"
say the inhabitants of Zion.
"May our blood be on those who live
in Babylonia,"
says Jerusalem.

36 Therefore this is what the LORD says:

"See, I will defend your cause
and avenge you;
I will dry up her sea
and make her springs dry.
37 Babylon will be a heap of ruins,
a haunt of jackals,
an object of horror and scorn,
a place where no one lives.
38 Her people all roar like young lions,
they growl like lion cubs.
39 But while they are aroused,
I will set out a feast for them
and make them drunk,
so that they shout with laughter —
then sleep forever and not awake,"
declares the LORD.
40 "I will bring them down
like lambs to the slaughter,
like rams and goats.

41 "How Sheshak[b] will be captured,
the boast of the whole earth seized!
How desolate Babylon will be
among the nations!
42 The sea will rise over Babylon;
its roaring waves will cover her.
43 Her towns will be desolate,
a dry and desert land,
a land where no one lives,
through which no one travels.
44 I will punish Bel in Babylon
and make him spew out what he has
swallowed.
The nations will no longer stream to
him.
And the wall of Babylon will fall.

45 "Come out of her, my people!
Run for your lives!
Run from the fierce anger of the
LORD.
46 Do not lose heart or be afraid
when rumors are heard in the land;
one rumor comes this year, another
the next,
rumors of violence in the land
and of ruler against ruler.
47 For the time will surely come
when I will punish the idols of
Babylon;
her whole land will be disgraced
and her slain will all lie fallen
within her.
48 Then heaven and earth and all that is
in them
will shout for joy over Babylon,
for out of the north
destroyers will attack her,"
declares the LORD.

49 "Babylon must fall because of Israel's
slain,
just as the slain in all the earth
have fallen because of Babylon.
50 You who have escaped the sword,
leave and do not linger!
Remember the LORD in a distant
land,
and call to mind Jerusalem."

51 "We are disgraced,
for we have been insulted
and shame covers our faces,
because foreigners have entered
the holy places of the LORD's house."

52 "But days are coming," declares the
LORD,
"when I will punish her idols,
and throughout her land
the wounded will groan.
53 Even if Babylon ascends to the
heavens
and fortifies her lofty stronghold,
I will send destroyers against her,"
declares the LORD.

54 "The sound of a cry comes from
Babylon,
the sound of great destruction
from the land of the Babylonians.[c]
55 The LORD will destroy Babylon;
he will silence her noisy din.
Waves of enemies will rage like great
waters;
the roar of their voices will resound.

[a] *35* Or *done to us and to our children* [b] *41* *Sheshak* is a cryptogram for Babylon. [c] *54* Or *Chaldeans*

56 A destroyer will come against
Babylon;
her warriors will be captured,
and their bows will be broken.
For the LORD is a God of retribution;
he will repay in full.
57 I will make her officials and wise men
drunk,
her governors, officers and warriors
as well;
they will sleep forever and not awake,"
declares the King, whose name is
the LORD Almighty.

58 This is what the LORD Almighty
says:

"Babylon's thick wall will be leveled
and her high gates set on fire;
the peoples exhaust themselves for
nothing,
the nations' labor is only fuel for the
flames."

59 This is the message Jeremiah the
prophet gave to the staff officer Seraiah
son of Neriah, the son of Mahseiah, when
he went to Babylon with Zedekiah king
of Judah in the fourth year of his reign.
60 Jeremiah had written on a scroll about
all the disasters that would come upon
Babylon—all that had been recorded
concerning Babylon. 61 He said to Seraiah, "When you get to Babylon, see that
you read all these words aloud. 62 Then
say, 'LORD, you have said you will destroy
this place, so that neither people nor
animals will live in it; it will be desolate
forever.' 63 When you finish reading this
scroll, tie a stone to it and throw it into
the Euphrates. 64 Then say, 'So will Babylon sink to rise no more because of the
disaster I will bring on her. And her people will fall.' "

The words of Jeremiah end here.

52 Zedekiah was twenty-one years
old when he became king, and he
reigned in Jerusalem eleven years. His
mother's name was Hamutal daughter
of Jeremiah; she was from Libnah. 2 He
did evil in the eyes of the LORD, just as
Jehoiakim had done. 3 It was because of
the LORD's anger that all this happened
to Jerusalem and Judah, and in the end he
thrust them from his presence.

Now Zedekiah rebelled against the
king of Babylon.
4 So in the ninth year of Zedekiah's
reign, on the tenth day of the tenth
month, Nebuchadnezzar king of Babylon marched against Jerusalem with his
whole army. They encamped outside the
city and built siege works all around it.
5 The city was kept under siege until the
eleventh year of King Zedekiah.
6 By the ninth day of the fourth month
the famine in the city had become so severe that there was no food for the people to eat. 7 Then the city wall was broken
through, and the whole army fled. They
left the city at night through the gate between the two walls near the king's garden, though the Babylonians[a] were surrounding the city. They fled toward the
Arabah,[b] 8 but the Babylonian[c] army pursued King Zedekiah and overtook him in
the plains of Jericho. All his soldiers were
separated from him and scattered, 9 and
he was captured.

He was taken to the king of Babylon at
Riblah in the land of Hamath, where he
pronounced sentence on him. 10 There
at Riblah the king of Babylon killed the
sons of Zedekiah before his eyes; he also
killed all the officials of Judah. 11 Then he
put out Zedekiah's eyes, bound him with
bronze shackles and took him to Babylon, where he put him in prison till the
day of his death.
12 On the tenth day of the fifth month,
in the nineteenth year of Nebuchadnezzar king of Babylon, Nebuzaradan
commander of the imperial guard, who
served the king of Babylon, came to Jerusalem. 13 He set fire to the temple of the
LORD, the royal palace and all the houses
of Jerusalem. Every important building
he burned down. 14 The whole Babylonian army, under the commander of the
imperial guard, broke down all the walls
around Jerusalem. 15 Nebuzaradan the
commander of the guard carried into exile some of the poorest people and those
who remained in the city, along with the
rest of the craftsmen[d] and those who had
deserted to the king of Babylon. 16 But
Nebuzaradan left behind the rest of the
poorest people of the land to work the
vineyards and fields.
17 The Babylonians broke up the

[a] 7 Or *Chaldeans*; also in verse 17 [b] 7 Or *the Jordan Valley* [c] 8 Or *Chaldean*; also in verse 14
[d] 15 Or *the populace*

bronze pillars, the movable stands and the bronze Sea that were at the temple of the LORD and they carried all the bronze to Babylon. [18]They also took away the pots, shovels, wick trimmers, sprinkling bowls, dishes and all the bronze articles used in the temple service. [19]The commander of the imperial guard took away the basins, censers, sprinkling bowls, pots, lampstands, dishes and bowls used for drink offerings — all that were made of pure gold or silver.

[20]The bronze from the two pillars, the Sea and the twelve bronze bulls under it, and the movable stands, which King Solomon had made for the temple of the LORD, was more than could be weighed. [21]Each pillar was eighteen cubits high and twelve cubits in circumference[a]; each was four fingers thick, and hollow. [22]The bronze capital on top of one pillar was five cubits[b] high and was decorated with a network and pomegranates of bronze all around. The other pillar, with its pomegranates, was similar. [23]There were ninety-six pomegranates on the sides; the total number of pomegranates above the surrounding network was a hundred.

[24]The commander of the guard took as prisoners Seraiah the chief priest, Zephaniah the priest next in rank and the three doorkeepers. [25]Of those still in the city, he took the officer in charge of the fighting men, and seven royal advisers. He also took the secretary who was chief officer in charge of conscripting the people of the land, sixty of whom were found in the city. [26]Nebuzaradan the commander took them all and brought them to the king of Babylon at Riblah. [27]There at Riblah, in the land of Hamath, the king had them executed.

So Judah went into captivity, away from her land. [28]This is the number of the people Nebuchadnezzar carried into exile:

in the seventh year, 3,023 Jews;
[29]in Nebuchadnezzar's eighteenth year,
832 people from Jerusalem;
[30]in his twenty-third year,
745 Jews taken into exile by Nebuzaradan the commander of the imperial guard.
There were 4,600 people in all.

[31]In the thirty-seventh year of the exile of Jehoiachin king of Judah, in the year Awel-Marduk became king of Babylon, on the twenty-fifth day of the twelfth month, he released Jehoiachin king of Judah and freed him from prison. [32]He spoke kindly to him and gave him a seat of honor higher than those of the other kings who were with him in Babylon. [33]So Jehoiachin put aside his prison clothes and for the rest of his life ate regularly at the king's table. [34]Day by day the king of Babylon gave Jehoiachin a regular allowance as long as he lived, till the day of his death.

[a] *21* That is, about 27 feet high and 18 feet in circumference or about 8.1 meters high and 5.4 meters in circumference [b] *22* That is, about 7 1/2 feet or about 2.3 meters

LAMENTATIONS

When the Babylonians conquered Jerusalem and deported much of its population, some residents were left behind in terrible conditions in and around the shattered city. To express their deep shame and grief over the destruction of their home, they wrote songs about its desolation and about the sufferings they were witnessing and experiencing. The book of Lamentations does not tell us who wrote these songs, although tradition ascribes them to Jeremiah. Here we witness people of faith putting into words their struggle to understand how God could have allowed the city they loved to be so devastated.

Each of the five songs preserved in the book has 22 stanzas. The first four songs begin with the 22 letters of the Hebrew alphabet in consecutive order. In the third song the letters are repeated at the start of each of the three lines in the stanza. There are few expressions of hope, but they are placed in the center of the book to give them extra prominence in a situation where they are badly needed. Overall, this collection of laments reminds us that expressing anguish over a broken, fallen world is a legitimate part of the biblical drama.

---

1 [a] How deserted lies the city,
once so full of people!
How like a widow is she,
who once was great among the nations!
She who was queen among the provinces
has now become a slave.

2 Bitterly she weeps at night,
tears are on her cheeks.
Among all her lovers
there is no one to comfort her.
All her friends have betrayed her;
they have become her enemies.

3 After affliction and harsh labor,
Judah has gone into exile.
She dwells among the nations;
she finds no resting place.
All who pursue her have overtaken her
in the midst of her distress.

4 The roads to Zion mourn,
for no one comes to her appointed festivals.
All her gateways are desolate,
her priests groan,
her young women grieve,
and she is in bitter anguish.

5 Her foes have become her masters;
her enemies are at ease.
The LORD has brought her grief
because of her many sins.
Her children have gone into exile,
captive before the foe.

6 All the splendor has departed
from Daughter Zion.
Her princes are like deer
that find no pasture;
in weakness they have fled
before the pursuer.

7 In the days of her affliction and wandering
Jerusalem remembers all the treasures
that were hers in days of old.
When her people fell into enemy hands,
there was no one to help her.
Her enemies looked at her
and laughed at her destruction.

8 Jerusalem has sinned greatly
and so has become unclean.
All who honored her despise her,
for they have all seen her naked;
she herself groans
and turns away.

9 Her filthiness clung to her skirts;
she did not consider her future.
Her fall was astounding;
there was none to comfort her.
"Look, LORD, on my affliction,
for the enemy has triumphed."

10 The enemy laid hands
on all her treasures;
she saw pagan nations
enter her sanctuary—
those you had forbidden
to enter your assembly.

[a] This chapter is an acrostic poem, the verses of which begin with the successive letters of the Hebrew alphabet.

11 All her people groan
as they search for bread;
they barter their treasures for food
to keep themselves alive.
"Look, LORD, and consider,
for I am despised."

12 "Is it nothing to you, all you who
pass by?
Look around and see.
Is any suffering like my suffering
that was inflicted on me,
that the LORD brought on me
in the day of his fierce anger?

13 "From on high he sent fire,
sent it down into my bones.
He spread a net for my feet
and turned me back.
He made me desolate,
faint all the day long.

14 "My sins have been bound into a
yoke[a];
by his hands they were woven
together.
They have been hung on my neck,
and the Lord has sapped my
strength.
He has given me into the hands
of those I cannot withstand.

15 "The Lord has rejected
all the warriors in my midst;
he has summoned an army against me
to[b] crush my young men.
In his winepress the Lord has
trampled
Virgin Daughter Judah.

16 "This is why I weep
and my eyes overflow with tears.
No one is near to comfort me,
no one to restore my spirit.
My children are destitute
because the enemy has prevailed."

17 Zion stretches out her hands,
but there is no one to comfort her.
The LORD has decreed for Jacob
that his neighbors become his foes;
Jerusalem has become
an unclean thing among them.

18 "The LORD is righteous,
yet I rebelled against his command.
Listen, all you peoples;
look on my suffering.
My young men and young women
have gone into exile.

19 "I called to my allies
but they betrayed me.
My priests and my elders
perished in the city
while they searched for food
to keep themselves alive.

20 "See, LORD, how distressed I am!
I am in torment within,
and in my heart I am disturbed,
for I have been most rebellious.
Outside, the sword bereaves;
inside, there is only death.

21 "People have heard my groaning,
but there is no one to comfort me.
All my enemies have heard of my
distress;
they rejoice at what you have done.
May you bring the day you have
announced
so they may become like me.

22 "Let all their wickedness come before
you;
deal with them
as you have dealt with me
because of all my sins.
My groans are many
and my heart is faint."

2[c] How the Lord has covered Daughter
Zion
with the cloud of his anger[d]!
He has hurled down the splendor of
Israel
from heaven to earth;
he has not remembered his footstool
in the day of his anger.

2 Without pity the Lord has swallowed
up
all the dwellings of Jacob;
in his wrath he has torn down
the strongholds of Daughter Judah.
He has brought her kingdom and its
princes
down to the ground in dishonor.

3 In fierce anger he has cut off
every horn[e,f] of Israel.

[a] *14* Most Hebrew manuscripts; many Hebrew manuscripts and Septuagint *He kept watch over my sins*
[b] *15* Or *has set a time for me / when he will*
[c] This chapter is an acrostic poem, the verses of which begin with the successive letters of the Hebrew alphabet.
[d] *1* Or *How the Lord in his anger / has treated Daughter Zion with contempt*
[e] *3* Or *off / all the strength*; or *every king*
[f] *3* *Horn* here symbolizes strength.

He has withdrawn his right hand
at the approach of the enemy.
He has burned in Jacob like a flaming fire
that consumes everything around it.

4 Like an enemy he has strung his bow;
his right hand is ready.
Like a foe he has slain
all who were pleasing to the eye;
he has poured out his wrath like fire
on the tent of Daughter Zion.

5 The Lord is like an enemy;
he has swallowed up Israel.
He has swallowed up all her palaces
and destroyed her strongholds.
He has multiplied mourning and lamentation
for Daughter Judah.

6 He has laid waste his dwelling like a garden;
he has destroyed his place of meeting.
The LORD has made Zion forget
her appointed festivals and her Sabbaths;
in his fierce anger he has spurned
both king and priest.

7 The Lord has rejected his altar
and abandoned his sanctuary.
He has given the walls of her palaces
into the hands of the enemy;
they have raised a shout in the house of the LORD
as on the day of an appointed festival.

8 The LORD determined to tear down
the wall around Daughter Zion.
He stretched out a measuring line
and did not withhold his hand from destroying.
He made ramparts and walls lament;
together they wasted away.

9 Her gates have sunk into the ground;
their bars he has broken and destroyed.
Her king and her princes are exiled
among the nations,
the law is no more,
and her prophets no longer find
visions from the LORD.

10 The elders of Daughter Zion
sit on the ground in silence;
they have sprinkled dust on their heads
and put on sackcloth.
The young women of Jerusalem
have bowed their heads to the ground.

11 My eyes fail from weeping,
I am in torment within;
my heart is poured out on the ground
because my people are destroyed,
because children and infants faint
in the streets of the city.

12 They say to their mothers,
"Where is bread and wine?"
as they faint like the wounded
in the streets of the city,
as their lives ebb away
in their mothers' arms.

13 What can I say for you?
With what can I compare you,
Daughter Jerusalem?
To what can I liken you,
that I may comfort you,
Virgin Daughter Zion?
Your wound is as deep as the sea.
Who can heal you?

14 The visions of your prophets
were false and worthless;
they did not expose your sin
to ward off your captivity.
The prophecies they gave you
were false and misleading.

15 All who pass your way
clap their hands at you;
they scoff and shake their heads
at Daughter Jerusalem:
"Is this the city that was called
the perfection of beauty,
the joy of the whole earth?"

16 All your enemies open their mouths
wide against you;
they scoff and gnash their teeth
and say, "We have swallowed her up.
This is the day we have waited for;
we have lived to see it."

17 The LORD has done what he planned;
he has fulfilled his word,
which he decreed long ago.
He has overthrown you without pity,
he has let the enemy gloat over you,

he has exalted the horn[a] of your foes.

18 The hearts of the people
cry out to the Lord.
You walls of Daughter Zion,
let your tears flow like a river
day and night;
give yourself no relief,
your eyes no rest.

19 Arise, cry out in the night,
as the watches of the night begin;
pour out your heart like water
in the presence of the Lord.
Lift up your hands to him
for the lives of your children,
who faint from hunger
at every street corner.

20 "Look, LORD, and consider:
Whom have you ever treated like this?
Should women eat their offspring,
the children they have cared for?
Should priest and prophet be killed
in the sanctuary of the Lord?

21 "Young and old lie together
in the dust of the streets;
my young men and young women
have fallen by the sword.
You have slain them in the day of your anger;
you have slaughtered them without pity.

22 "As you summon to a feast day,
so you summoned against me
terrors on every side.
In the day of the LORD's anger
no one escaped or survived;
those I cared for and reared
my enemy has destroyed."

3[b] I am the man who has seen affliction
by the rod of the LORD's wrath.
2 He has driven me away and made me walk
in darkness rather than light;
3 indeed, he has turned his hand against me
again and again, all day long.

4 He has made my skin and my flesh grow old
and has broken my bones.
5 He has besieged me and surrounded me
with bitterness and hardship.
6 He has made me dwell in darkness
like those long dead.

7 He has walled me in so I cannot escape;
he has weighed me down with chains.
8 Even when I call out or cry for help,
he shuts out my prayer.
9 He has barred my way with blocks of stone;
he has made my paths crooked.

10 Like a bear lying in wait,
like a lion in hiding,
11 he dragged me from the path and mangled me
and left me without help.
12 He drew his bow
and made me the target for his arrows.

13 He pierced my heart
with arrows from his quiver.
14 I became the laughingstock of all my people;
they mock me in song all day long.
15 He has filled me with bitter herbs
and given me gall to drink.

16 He has broken my teeth with gravel;
he has trampled me in the dust.
17 I have been deprived of peace;
I have forgotten what prosperity is.
18 So I say, "My splendor is gone
and all that I had hoped from the LORD."

19 I remember my affliction and my wandering,
the bitterness and the gall.
20 I well remember them,
and my soul is downcast within me.
21 Yet this I call to mind
and therefore I have hope:

22 Because of the LORD's great love we are not consumed,
for his compassions never fail.
23 They are new every morning;
great is your faithfulness.

[a] *17 Horn* here symbolizes strength. [b] This chapter is an acrostic poem; the verses of each stanza begin with the successive letters of the Hebrew alphabet, and the verses within each stanza begin with the same letter.

24 I say to myself, "The LORD is my
portion;
therefore I will wait for him."

25 The LORD is good to those whose hope
is in him,
to the one who seeks him;
26 it is good to wait quietly
for the salvation of the LORD.
27 It is good for a man to bear the yoke
while he is young.

28 Let him sit alone in silence,
for the LORD has laid it on him.
29 Let him bury his face in the dust—
there may yet be hope.
30 Let him offer his cheek to one who
would strike him,
and let him be filled with disgrace.

31 For no one is cast off
by the Lord forever.
32 Though he brings grief, he will show
compassion,
so great is his unfailing love.
33 For he does not willingly bring
affliction
or grief to anyone.

34 To crush underfoot
all prisoners in the land,
35 to deny people their rights
before the Most High,
36 to deprive them of justice—
would not the Lord see such
things?

37 Who can speak and have it happen
if the Lord has not decreed it?
38 Is it not from the mouth of the Most
High
that both calamities and good
things come?
39 Why should the living complain
when punished for their sins?

40 Let us examine our ways and test
them,
and let us return to the LORD.
41 Let us lift up our hearts and our
hands
to God in heaven, and say:
42 "We have sinned and rebelled
and you have not forgiven.

43 "You have covered yourself with
anger and pursued us;
you have slain without pity.
44 You have covered yourself with a
cloud
so that no prayer can get through.
45 You have made us scum and refuse
among the nations.

46 "All our enemies have opened their
mouths
wide against us.
47 We have suffered terror and pitfalls,
ruin and destruction."
48 Streams of tears flow from my eyes
because my people are destroyed.

49 My eyes will flow unceasingly,
without relief,
50 until the LORD looks down
from heaven and sees.
51 What I see brings grief to my soul
because of all the women of my
city.

52 Those who were my enemies without
cause
hunted me like a bird.
53 They tried to end my life in a pit
and threw stones at me;
54 the waters closed over my head,
and I thought I was about to perish.

55 I called on your name, LORD,
from the depths of the pit.
56 You heard my plea: "Do not close your
ears
to my cry for relief."
57 You came near when I called you,
and you said, "Do not fear."

58 You, Lord, took up my case;
you redeemed my life.
59 LORD, you have seen the wrong done
to me.
Uphold my cause!
60 You have seen the depth of their
vengeance,
all their plots against me.

61 LORD, you have heard their insults,
all their plots against me—
62 what my enemies whisper and
mutter
against me all day long.
63 Look at them! Sitting or standing,
they mock me in their songs.

64 Pay them back what they deserve,
LORD,
for what their hands have done.
65 Put a veil over their hearts,
and may your curse be on them!
66 Pursue them in anger and destroy
them
from under the heavens of the
LORD.

4 [a] How the gold has lost its luster,
the fine gold become dull!
The sacred gems are scattered
at every street corner.

2 How the precious children of Zion,
once worth their weight in gold,
are now considered as pots of clay,
the work of a potter's hands!

3 Even jackals offer their breasts
to nurse their young,
but my people have become heartless
like ostriches in the desert.

4 Because of thirst the infant's tongue
sticks to the roof of its mouth;
the children beg for bread,
but no one gives it to them.

5 Those who once ate delicacies
are destitute in the streets.
Those brought up in royal purple
now lie on ash heaps.

6 The punishment of my people
is greater than that of Sodom,
which was overthrown in a moment
without a hand turned to help her.

7 Their princes were brighter than snow
and whiter than milk,
their bodies more ruddy than rubies,
their appearance like lapis lazuli.

8 But now they are blacker than soot;
they are not recognized in the streets.
Their skin has shriveled on their bones;
it has become as dry as a stick.

9 Those killed by the sword are better off
than those who die of famine;
racked with hunger, they waste away
for lack of food from the field.

10 With their own hands compassionate women
have cooked their own children,
who became their food
when my people were destroyed.

11 The LORD has given full vent to his wrath;
he has poured out his fierce anger.
He kindled a fire in Zion
that consumed her foundations.

12 The kings of the earth did not believe,
nor did any of the peoples of the world,
that enemies and foes could enter
the gates of Jerusalem.

13 But it happened because of the sins of her prophets
and the iniquities of her priests,
who shed within her
the blood of the righteous.

14 Now they grope through the streets
as if they were blind.
They are so defiled with blood
that no one dares to touch their garments.

15 "Go away! You are unclean!" people cry to them.
"Away! Away! Don't touch us!"
When they flee and wander about,
people among the nations say,
"They can stay here no longer."

16 The LORD himself has scattered them;
he no longer watches over them.
The priests are shown no honor,
the elders no favor.

17 Moreover, our eyes failed,
looking in vain for help;
from our towers we watched
for a nation that could not save us.

18 People stalked us at every step,
so we could not walk in our streets.
Our end was near, our days were numbered,
for our end had come.

19 Our pursuers were swifter
than eagles in the sky;
they chased us over the mountains
and lay in wait for us in the desert.

20 The LORD's anointed, our very life breath,
was caught in their traps.
We thought that under his shadow
we would live among the nations.

21 Rejoice and be glad, Daughter Edom,
you who live in the land of Uz.
But to you also the cup will be passed;
you will be drunk and stripped naked.

22 Your punishment will end, Daughter Zion;

[a] This chapter is an acrostic poem, the verses of which begin with the successive letters of the Hebrew alphabet.

he will not prolong your exile.
But he will punish your sin, Daughter
Edom,
and expose your wickedness.

5 Remember, LORD, what has
happened to us;
look, and see our disgrace.
2 Our inheritance has been turned over
to strangers,
our homes to foreigners.
3 We have become fatherless,
our mothers are widows.
4 We must buy the water we drink;
our wood can be had only at a price.
5 Those who pursue us are at our heels;
we are weary and find no rest.
6 We submitted to Egypt and Assyria
to get enough bread.
7 Our ancestors sinned and are no
more,
and we bear their punishment.
8 Slaves rule over us,
and there is no one to free us from
their hands.
9 We get our bread at the risk of our
lives
because of the sword in the desert.
10 Our skin is hot as an oven,
feverish from hunger.
11 Women have been violated in Zion,
and virgins in the towns of Judah.
12 Princes have been hung up by their
hands;
elders are shown no respect.
13 Young men toil at the millstones;
boys stagger under loads of wood.
14 The elders are gone from the city gate;
the young men have stopped their
music.
15 Joy is gone from our hearts;
our dancing has turned to
mourning.
16 The crown has fallen from our head.
Woe to us, for we have sinned!
17 Because of this our hearts are faint,
because of these things our eyes
grow dim
18 for Mount Zion, which lies desolate,
with jackals prowling over it.

19 You, LORD, reign forever;
your throne endures from
generation to generation.
20 Why do you always forget us?
Why do you forsake us so long?
21 Restore us to yourself, LORD, that we
may return;
renew our days as of old
22 unless you have utterly rejected us
and are angry with us beyond
measure.

EZEKIEL

The priest Ezekiel was among the Judeans that Nebuchadnezzar brought to Babylon in 597 BC. Five years into this exile, God called Ezekiel to go to Israel (both those in Babylon and those back in Judea) and *speak my words to them*. Ezekiel often brought this message by composing finely polished poetic oracles and speaking (or perhaps singing) them in public. But he also told stories with symbolic meanings, performed symbolic actions, and described extraordinary visions that he had received.

The book of Ezekiel organizes these messages into three main parts: oracles of judgment against Israel, oracles against other nations, and then promises of Israel's restoration. These divisions are marked by references to the prophet losing and then regaining his ability to speak. A key vision near the beginning describes how God removed his presence from the Jerusalem temple because of Israel's evil. The oracles against the nations make it clear that though God's temple was destroyed, no one should conclude that God is not still in control of the world. Those who threaten his people will be defeated in the end. The book's closing promises confirm that God will renew the hearts of his people and refresh all life on the face of the earth. Ezekiel's visions fit the ongoing drama of the Bible: a broken world will be healed when the LORD returns to live with his people in a land that has become like the garden of Eden.

---

1 In my thirtieth year, in the fourth
month on the fifth day, while I was
among the exiles by the Kebar River, the
heavens were opened and I saw visions
of God.
2 On the fifth of the month—it was
the fifth year of the exile of King Jehoiachin— 3 the word of the LORD came to
Ezekiel the priest, the son of Buzi, by the
Kebar River in the land of the Babylonians.[a] There the hand of the LORD was on
him.
4 I looked, and I saw a windstorm coming out of the north—an immense cloud
with flashing lightning and surrounded by brilliant light. The center of the
fire looked like glowing metal, 5 and in
the fire was what looked like four living
creatures. In appearance their form was
human, 6 but each of them had four faces
and four wings. 7 Their legs were straight;
their feet were like those of a calf and
gleamed like burnished bronze. 8 Under their wings on their four sides they
had human hands. All four of them had
faces and wings, 9 and the wings of one
touched the wings of another. Each one
went straight ahead; they did not turn as
they moved.
10 Their faces looked like this: Each
of the four had the face of a human being, and on the right side each had the
face of a lion, and on the left the face of
an ox; each also had the face of an eagle. 11 Such were their faces. They each
had two wings spreading out upward,
each wing touching that of the creature on either side; and each had two
other wings covering its body. 12 Each
one went straight ahead. Wherever the
spirit would go, they would go, without
turning as they went. 13 The appearance
of the living creatures was like burning
coals of fire or like torches. Fire moved
back and forth among the creatures; it
was bright, and lightning flashed out of
it. 14 The creatures sped back and forth
like flashes of lightning.
15 As I looked at the living creatures, I
saw a wheel on the ground beside each
creature with its four faces. 16 This was
the appearance and structure of the
wheels: They sparkled like topaz, and all
four looked alike. Each appeared to be
made like a wheel intersecting a wheel.
17 As they moved, they would go in any
one of the four directions the creatures
faced; the wheels did not change direction as the creatures went. 18 Their rims
were high and awesome, and all four
rims were full of eyes all around.
19 When the living creatures moved,
the wheels beside them moved; and
when the living creatures rose from the
ground, the wheels also rose. 20 Wherever the spirit would go, they would go,
and the wheels would rise along with
them, because the spirit of the living
creatures was in the wheels. 21 When the
creatures moved, they also moved; when

[a] 3 Or *Chaldeans*

the creatures stood still, they also stood
still; and when the creatures rose from
the ground, the wheels rose along with
them, because the spirit of the living
creatures was in the wheels.
22 Spread out above the heads of the
living creatures was what looked something like a vault, sparkling like crystal,
and awesome. 23 Under the vault their
wings were stretched out one toward the
other, and each had two wings covering
its body. 24 When the creatures moved, I
heard the sound of their wings, like the
roar of rushing waters, like the voice
of the Almighty,[a] like the tumult of an
army. When they stood still, they lowered their wings.
25 Then there came a voice from above
the vault over their heads as they stood
with lowered wings. 26 Above the vault
over their heads was what looked like a
throne of lapis lazuli, and high above on
the throne was a figure like that of a man.
27 I saw that from what appeared to be his
waist up he looked like glowing metal, as
if full of fire, and that from there down
he looked like fire; and brilliant light surrounded him. 28 Like the appearance of a
rainbow in the clouds on a rainy day, so
was the radiance around him.
This was the appearance of the likeness of the glory of the LORD. When I saw
it, I fell facedown, and I heard the voice
of one speaking.
2 He said to me, "Son of man,[b] stand up
on your feet and I will speak to you."
2 As he spoke, the Spirit came into me
and raised me to my feet, and I heard him
speaking to me.
3 He said: "Son of man, I am sending
you to the Israelites, to a rebellious nation that has rebelled against me; they
and their ancestors have been in revolt
against me to this very day. 4 The people
to whom I am sending you are obstinate
and stubborn. Say to them, 'This is what
the Sovereign LORD says.' 5 And whether
they listen or fail to listen — for they are
a rebellious people — they will know that
a prophet has been among them. 6 And
you, son of man, do not be afraid of them
or their words. Do not be afraid, though
briers and thorns are all around you and
you live among scorpions. Do not be
afraid of what they say or be terrified by
them, though they are a rebellious people. 7 You must speak my words to them,
whether they listen or fail to listen, for
they are rebellious. 8 But you, son of man,
listen to what I say to you. Do not rebel
like that rebellious people; open your
mouth and eat what I give you."
9 Then I looked, and I saw a hand
stretched out to me. In it was a scroll,
10 which he unrolled before me. On both
sides of it were written words of lament
and mourning and woe.
3 And he said to me, "Son of man, eat
what is before you, eat this scroll; then
go and speak to the people of Israel." 2 So
I opened my mouth, and he gave me the
scroll to eat.
3 Then he said to me, "Son of man, eat
this scroll I am giving you and fill your
stomach with it." So I ate it, and it tasted
as sweet as honey in my mouth.
4 He then said to me: "Son of man, go
now to the people of Israel and speak my
words to them. 5 You are not being sent to
a people of obscure speech and strange
language, but to the people of Israel —
6 not to many peoples of obscure speech
and strange language, whose words you
cannot understand. Surely if I had sent
you to them, they would have listened
to you. 7 But the people of Israel are not
willing to listen to you because they are
not willing to listen to me, for all the Israelites are hardened and obstinate.
8 But I will make you as unyielding and
hardened as they are. 9 I will make your
forehead like the hardest stone, harder
than flint. Do not be afraid of them or
terrified by them, though they are a rebellious people."
10 And he said to me, "Son of man, listen
carefully and take to heart all the words
I speak to you. 11 Go now to your people
in exile and speak to them. Say to them,
'This is what the Sovereign LORD says,'
whether they listen or fail to listen."
12 Then the Spirit lifted me up, and I
heard behind me a loud rumbling sound
as the glory of the LORD rose from the
place where it was standing.[c] 13 It was
the sound of the wings of the living crea-

[a] 24 Hebrew *Shaddai* [b] 1 The Hebrew phrase *ben adam* means *human being*. The phrase *son of man* is retained as a form of address here and throughout Ezekiel because of its possible association with "Son of Man" in the New Testament. [c] 12 Probable reading of the original Hebrew text; Masoretic Text *sound — may the glory of the LORD be praised from his place*

tures brushing against each other and
the sound of the wheels beside them, a
loud rumbling sound. 14The Spirit then
lifted me up and took me away, and I
went in bitterness and in the anger of my
spirit, with the strong hand of the LORD
on me. 15I came to the exiles who lived at
Tel Aviv near the Kebar River. And there,
where they were living, I sat among them
for seven days—deeply distressed.
16At the end of seven days the word of
the LORD came to me: 17"Son of man, I
have made you a watchman for the people of Israel; so hear the word I speak and
give them warning from me. 18When I say
to a wicked person, 'You will surely die,'
and you do not warn them or speak out to
dissuade them from their evil ways in order to save their life, that wicked person
will die for[a] their sin, and I will hold you
accountable for their blood. 19But if you
do warn the wicked person and they do
not turn from their wickedness or from
their evil ways, they will die for their sin;
but you will have saved yourself.
20"Again, when a righteous person
turns from their righteousness and does
evil, and I put a stumbling block before
them, they will die. Since you did not
warn them, they will die for their sin.
The righteous things that person did will
not be remembered, and I will hold you
accountable for their blood. 21But if you
do warn the righteous person not to sin
and they do not sin, they will surely live
because they took warning, and you will
have saved yourself."
22The hand of the LORD was on me
there, and he said to me, "Get up and go
out to the plain, and there I will speak to
you." 23So I got up and went out to the
plain. And the glory of the LORD was
standing there, like the glory I had seen
by the Kebar River, and I fell facedown.
24Then the Spirit came into me and
raised me to my feet. He spoke to me
and said: "Go, shut yourself inside your
house. 25And you, son of man, they will
tie with ropes; you will be bound so that
you cannot go out among the people. 26I
will make your tongue stick to the roof
of your mouth so that you will be silent
and unable to rebuke them, for they are a
rebellious people. 27But when I speak to
you, I will open your mouth and you shall
say to them, 'This is what the Sovereign
LORD says.' Whoever will listen let them
listen, and whoever will refuse let them
refuse; for they are a rebellious people.
4 "Now, son of man, take a block of clay,
put it in front of you and draw the city
of Jerusalem on it. 2Then lay siege to it:
Erect siege works against it, build a ramp
up to it, set up camps against it and put
battering rams around it. 3Then take an
iron pan, place it as an iron wall between
you and the city and turn your face toward it. It will be under siege, and you
shall besiege it. This will be a sign to the
people of Israel.
4"Then lie on your left side and put the
sin of the people of Israel upon yourself.[b]
You are to bear their sin for the number
of days you lie on your side. 5I have assigned you the same number of days as
the years of their sin. So for 390 days you
will bear the sin of the people of Israel.
6"After you have finished this, lie
down again, this time on your right side,
and bear the sin of the people of Judah. I
have assigned you 40 days, a day for each
year. 7Turn your face toward the siege of
Jerusalem and with bared arm prophesy
against her. 8I will tie you up with ropes
so that you cannot turn from one side
to the other until you have finished the
days of your siege.
9"Take wheat and barley, beans and
lentils, millet and spelt; put them in a
storage jar and use them to make bread
for yourself. You are to eat it during the
390 days you lie on your side. 10Weigh out
twenty shekels[c] of food to eat each day
and eat it at set times. 11Also measure out
a sixth of a hin[d] of water and drink it at set
times. 12Eat the food as you would a loaf
of barley bread; bake it in the sight of the
people, using human excrement for fuel."
13The LORD said, "In this way the people
of Israel will eat defiled food among the
nations where I will drive them."
14Then I said, "Not so, Sovereign
LORD! I have never defiled myself. From
my youth until now I have never eaten
anything found dead or torn by wild animals. No impure meat has ever entered
my mouth."
15"Very well," he said, "I will let you
bake your bread over cow dung instead
of human excrement."

[a] *18* Or *in*; also in verses 19 and 20 [b] *4* Or *upon your side* [c] *10* That is, about 8 ounces or about 230 grams
[d] *11* That is, about 2/3 quart or about 0.6 liter

16 He then said to me: "Son of man, I am
about to cut off the food supply in Jerusalem. The people will eat rationed food in
anxiety and drink rationed water in despair, 17 for food and water will be scarce.
They will be appalled at the sight of each
other and will waste away because of[a]
their sin.

5 "Now, son of man, take a sharp sword
and use it as a barber's razor to shave
your head and your beard. Then take
a set of scales and divide up the hair.
2 When the days of your siege come to an
end, burn a third of the hair inside the
city. Take a third and strike it with the
sword all around the city. And scatter a
third to the wind. For I will pursue them
with drawn sword. 3 But take a few hairs
and tuck them away in the folds of your
garment. 4 Again, take a few of these and
throw them into the fire and burn them
up. A fire will spread from there to all Israel.

5 "This is what the Sovereign LORD says:
This is Jerusalem, which I have set in the
center of the nations, with countries all
around her. 6 Yet in her wickedness she
has rebelled against my laws and decrees
more than the nations and countries
around her. She has rejected my laws and
has not followed my decrees.

7 "Therefore this is what the Sovereign
LORD says: You have been more unruly
than the nations around you and have
not followed my decrees or kept my laws.
You have not even[b] conformed to the
standards of the nations around you.

8 "Therefore this is what the Sovereign
LORD says: I myself am against you, Jerusalem, and I will inflict punishment
on you in the sight of the nations. 9 Because of all your detestable idols, I will
do to you what I have never done before
and will never do again. 10 Therefore in
your midst parents will eat their children, and children will eat their parents.
I will inflict punishment on you and will
scatter all your survivors to the winds.
11 Therefore as surely as I live, declares
the Sovereign LORD, because you have
defiled my sanctuary with all your vile
images and detestable practices, I myself will shave you; I will not look on you
with pity or spare you. 12 A third of your
people will die of the plague or perish by
famine inside you; a third will fall by the
sword outside your walls; and a third I
will scatter to the winds and pursue with
drawn sword.

13 "Then my anger will cease and my
wrath against them will subside, and I
will be avenged. And when I have spent
my wrath on them, they will know that I
the LORD have spoken in my zeal.

14 "I will make you a ruin and a reproach among the nations around you,
in the sight of all who pass by. 15 You will
be a reproach and a taunt, a warning and
an object of horror to the nations around
you when I inflict punishment on you in
anger and in wrath and with stinging rebuke. I the LORD have spoken. 16 When
I shoot at you with my deadly and destructive arrows of famine, I will shoot
to destroy you. I will bring more and
more famine upon you and cut off your
supply of food. 17 I will send famine and
wild beasts against you, and they will
leave you childless. Plague and bloodshed will sweep through you, and I will
bring the sword against you. I the LORD
have spoken."

6 The word of the LORD came to me:
2 "Son of man, set your face against
the mountains of Israel; prophesy
against them 3 and say: 'You mountains
of Israel, hear the word of the Sovereign
LORD. This is what the Sovereign LORD
says to the mountains and hills, to the
ravines and valleys: I am about to bring
a sword against you, and I will destroy
your high places. 4 Your altars will be
demolished and your incense altars will
be smashed; and I will slay your people in front of your idols. 5 I will lay the
dead bodies of the Israelites in front of
their idols, and I will scatter your bones
around your altars. 6 Wherever you live,
the towns will be laid waste and the high
places demolished, so that your altars
will be laid waste and devastated, your
idols smashed and ruined, your incense
altars broken down, and what you have
made wiped out. 7 Your people will fall
slain among you, and you will know that
I am the LORD.

8 " 'But I will spare some, for some of
you will escape the sword when you
are scattered among the lands and nations. 9 Then in the nations where they

[a] 17 Or *away in* [b] 7 Most Hebrew manuscripts; some Hebrew manuscripts and Syriac *You have*

have been carried captive, those who
escape will remember me—how I have
been grieved by their adulterous hearts,
which have turned away from me, and
by their eyes, which have lusted after
their idols. They will loathe themselves
for the evil they have done and for all
their detestable practices. 10 And they
will know that I am the LORD; I did not
threaten in vain to bring this calamity
on them.

11 "'This is what the Sovereign LORD
says: Strike your hands together and
stamp your feet and cry out "Alas!" because of all the wicked and detestable
practices of the people of Israel, for
they will fall by the sword, famine and
plague. 12 One who is far away will die
of the plague, and one who is near will
fall by the sword, and anyone who survives and is spared will die of famine. So
will I pour out my wrath on them. 13 And
they will know that I am the LORD, when
their people lie slain among their idols
around their altars, on every high hill
and on all the mountaintops, under
every spreading tree and every leafy
oak—places where they offered fragrant incense to all their idols. 14 And I
will stretch out my hand against them
and make the land a desolate waste
from the desert to Diblah[a]—wherever
they live. Then they will know that I am
the LORD.'"

7 The word of the LORD came to me:
2 "Son of man, this is what the Sovereign LORD says to the land of Israel:

"'The end! The end has come
upon the four corners of the land!
3 The end is now upon you,
and I will unleash my anger against you.
I will judge you according to your conduct
and repay you for all your detestable practices.
4 I will not look on you with pity;
I will not spare you.
I will surely repay you for your conduct
and for the detestable practices among you.

"'Then you will know that I am the LORD.'

5 "This is what the Sovereign LORD says:

"'Disaster! Unheard-of[b] disaster!
See, it comes!
6 The end has come!
The end has come!
It has roused itself against you.
See, it comes!
7 Doom has come upon you,
upon you who dwell in the land.
The time has come! The day is near!
There is panic, not joy, on the mountains.
8 I am about to pour out my wrath on you
and spend my anger against you.
I will judge you according to your conduct
and repay you for all your detestable practices.
9 I will not look on you with pity;
I will not spare you.
I will repay you for your conduct
and for the detestable practices among you.

"'Then you will know that it is I the LORD
who strikes you.

10 "'See, the day!
See, it comes!
Doom has burst forth,
the rod has budded,
arrogance has blossomed!
11 Violence has arisen,[c]
a rod to punish the wicked.
None of the people will be left,
none of that crowd—
none of their wealth,
nothing of value.
12 The time has come!
The day has arrived!
Let not the buyer rejoice
nor the seller grieve,
for my wrath is on the whole crowd.
13 The seller will not recover
the property that was sold—
as long as both buyer and seller live.
For the vision concerning the whole crowd
will not be reversed.
Because of their sins, not one of them
will preserve their life.

14 "'They have blown the trumpet,
they have made all things ready,

[a] *14* Most Hebrew manuscripts; a few Hebrew manuscripts *Riblah* [b] *5* Most Hebrew manuscripts; some Hebrew manuscripts and Syriac *Disaster after* [c] *11* Or *The violent one has become*

but no one will go into battle,
  for my wrath is on the whole crowd.
15 Outside is the sword;
  inside are plague and famine.
Those in the country
  will die by the sword;
those in the city
  will be devoured by famine and
    plague.
16 The fugitives who escape
  will flee to the mountains.
Like doves of the valleys,
  they will all moan,
  each for their own sins.
17 Every hand will go limp;
  every leg will be wet with urine.
18 They will put on sackcloth
  and be clothed with terror.
Every face will be covered with shame,
  and every head will be shaved.

19 " 'They will throw their silver into the
    streets,
  and their gold will be treated as a
    thing unclean.
Their silver and gold
  will not be able to deliver them
  in the day of the LORD's wrath.
It will not satisfy their hunger
  or fill their stomachs,
  for it has caused them to stumble
    into sin.
20 They took pride in their beautiful
    jewelry
  and used it to make their detestable
    idols.
They made it into vile images;
  therefore I will make it a thing
    unclean for them.
21 I will give their wealth as plunder to
    foreigners
  and as loot to the wicked of the
    earth,
  who will defile it.
22 I will turn my face away from the
    people,
  and robbers will desecrate the place
    I treasure.
They will enter it
  and will defile it.

23 " 'Prepare chains!
  For the land is full of bloodshed,
  and the city is full of violence.
24 I will bring the most wicked of nations
  to take possession of their houses.
I will put an end to the pride of the
    mighty,
  and their sanctuaries will be
    desecrated.
25 When terror comes,
  they will seek peace in vain.
26 Calamity upon calamity will come,
  and rumor upon rumor.
They will go searching for a vision
    from the prophet,
  priestly instruction in the law will
    cease,
  the counsel of the elders will come
    to an end.
27 The king will mourn,
  the prince will be clothed with
    despair,
  and the hands of the people of the
    land will tremble.
I will deal with them according to
    their conduct,
  and by their own standards I will
    judge them.

" 'Then they will know that I am the
LORD.' "

8 In the sixth year, in the sixth month on
the fifth day, while I was sitting in my
house and the elders of Judah were sitting before me, the hand of the Sovereign
LORD came on me there. 2 I looked, and
I saw a figure like that of a man.[a] From
what appeared to be his waist down he
was like fire, and from there up his appearance was as bright as glowing metal. 3 He stretched out what looked like a
hand and took me by the hair of my head.
The Spirit lifted me up between earth
and heaven and in visions of God he
took me to Jerusalem, to the entrance of
the north gate of the inner court, where
the idol that provokes to jealousy stood.
4 And there before me was the glory of the
God of Israel, as in the vision I had seen
in the plain.

5 Then he said to me, "Son of man, look
toward the north." So I looked, and in the
entrance north of the gate of the altar I
saw this idol of jealousy.

6 And he said to me, "Son of man, do
you see what they are doing — the utterly
detestable things the Israelites are doing
here, things that will drive me far from
my sanctuary? But you will see things
that are even more detestable."

[a] 2 Or *saw a fiery figure*

7Then he brought me to the entrance
to the court. I looked, and I saw a hole
in the wall. 8He said to me, "Son of man,
now dig into the wall." So I dug into the
wall and saw a doorway there.
9And he said to me, "Go in and see the
wicked and detestable things they are
doing here." 10So I went in and looked,
and I saw portrayed all over the walls
all kinds of crawling things and unclean
animals and all the idols of Israel. 11In
front of them stood seventy elders of Israel, and Jaazaniah son of Shaphan was
standing among them. Each had a censer
in his hand, and a fragrant cloud of incense was rising.
12He said to me, "Son of man, have you
seen what the elders of Israel are doing
in the darkness, each at the shrine of
his own idol? They say, 'The LORD does
not see us; the LORD has forsaken the
land.'" 13Again, he said, "You will see
them doing things that are even more
detestable."
14Then he brought me to the entrance
of the north gate of the house of the
LORD, and I saw women sitting there,
mourning the god Tammuz. 15He said
to me, "Do you see this, son of man? You
will see things that are even more detestable than this."
16He then brought me into the inner
court of the house of the LORD, and there
at the entrance to the temple, between
the portico and the altar, were about
twenty-five men. With their backs toward the temple of the LORD and their
faces toward the east, they were bowing
down to the sun in the east.
17He said to me, "Have you seen this,
son of man? Is it a trivial matter for the
people of Judah to do the detestable
things they are doing here? Must they
also fill the land with violence and continually arouse my anger? Look at them
putting the branch to their nose! 18There-
fore I will deal with them in anger; I will
not look on them with pity or spare them.
Although they shout in my ears, I will not
listen to them."

9 Then I heard him call out in a loud
voice, "Bring near those who are appointed to execute judgment on the city,
each with a weapon in his hand." 2And I
saw six men coming from the direction of
the upper gate, which faces north, each
with a deadly weapon in his hand. With
them was a man clothed in linen who
had a writing kit at his side. They came
in and stood beside the bronze altar.
3Now the glory of the God of Israel
went up from above the cherubim, where
it had been, and moved to the threshold
of the temple. Then the LORD called to
the man clothed in linen who had the
writing kit at his side 4and said to him,
"Go throughout the city of Jerusalem and
put a mark on the foreheads of those who
grieve and lament over all the detestable
things that are done in it."
5As I listened, he said to the others,
"Follow him through the city and kill,
without showing pity or compassion.
6Slaughter the old men, the young men
and women, the mothers and children,
but do not touch anyone who has the
mark. Begin at my sanctuary." So they
began with the old men who were in
front of the temple.
7Then he said to them, "Defile the
temple and fill the courts with the slain.
Go!" So they went out and began killing
throughout the city. 8While they were
killing and I was left alone, I fell facedown, crying out, "Alas, Sovereign LORD!
Are you going to destroy the entire remnant of Israel in this outpouring of your
wrath on Jerusalem?"
9He answered me, "The sin of the people of Israel and Judah is exceedingly
great; the land is full of bloodshed and
the city is full of injustice. They say, 'The
LORD has forsaken the land; the LORD
does not see.' 10So I will not look on them
with pity or spare them, but I will bring
down on their own heads what they have
done."
11Then the man in linen with the writing kit at his side brought back word, saying, "I have done as you commanded."

10 I looked, and I saw the likeness of
a throne of lapis lazuli above the
vault that was over the heads of the cherubim. 2The LORD said to the man clothed
in linen, "Go in among the wheels beneath the cherubim. Fill your hands with
burning coals from among the cherubim
and scatter them over the city." And as I
watched, he went in.
3Now the cherubim were standing on
the south side of the temple when the
man went in, and a cloud filled the inner
court. 4Then the glory of the LORD rose
from above the cherubim and moved to

the threshold of the temple. The cloud
filled the temple, and the court was full
of the radiance of the glory of the LORD.
5The sound of the wings of the cherubim
could be heard as far away as the outer
court, like the voice of God Almighty[a]
when he speaks.
6When the LORD commanded the
man in linen, "Take fire from among the
wheels, from among the cherubim," the
man went in and stood beside a wheel.
7Then one of the cherubim reached out
his hand to the fire that was among them.
He took up some of it and put it into the
hands of the man in linen, who took it
and went out. 8(Under the wings of the
cherubim could be seen what looked like
human hands.)
9I looked, and I saw beside the cherubim four wheels, one beside each of the
cherubim; the wheels sparkled like topaz. 10As for their appearance, the four of
them looked alike; each was like a wheel
intersecting a wheel. 11As they moved,
they would go in any one of the four directions the cherubim faced; the wheels
did not turn about[b] as the cherubim
went. The cherubim went in whatever
direction the head faced, without turning as they went. 12Their entire bodies,
including their backs, their hands and
their wings, were completely full of
eyes, as were their four wheels. 13I heard
the wheels being called "the whirling
wheels." 14Each of the cherubim had
four faces: One face was that of a cherub, the second the face of a human being,
the third the face of a lion, and the fourth
the face of an eagle.
15Then the cherubim rose upward.
These were the living creatures I had
seen by the Kebar River. 16When the
cherubim moved, the wheels beside them
moved; and when the cherubim spread
their wings to rise from the ground, the
wheels did not leave their side. 17When
the cherubim stood still, they also stood
still; and when the cherubim rose, they
rose with them, because the spirit of the
living creatures was in them.
18Then the glory of the LORD departed
from over the threshold of the temple and
stopped above the cherubim. 19While
I watched, the cherubim spread their
wings and rose from the ground, and as
they went, the wheels went with them.
They stopped at the entrance of the east
gate of the LORD's house, and the glory of
the God of Israel was above them.
20These were the living creatures I had
seen beneath the God of Israel by the Kebar River, and I realized that they were
cherubim. 21Each had four faces and
four wings, and under their wings was
what looked like human hands. 22Their
faces had the same appearance as those
I had seen by the Kebar River. Each one
went straight ahead.

11 Then the Spirit lifted me up and
brought me to the gate of the house
of the LORD that faces east. There at the
entrance of the gate were twenty-five
men, and I saw among them Jaazaniah
son of Azzur and Pelatiah son of Benaiah,
leaders of the people. 2The LORD said to
me, "Son of man, these are the men who
are plotting evil and giving wicked advice in this city. 3They say, 'Haven't our
houses been recently rebuilt? This city is
a pot, and we are the meat in it.' 4There-
fore prophesy against them; prophesy,
son of man."
5Then the Spirit of the LORD came on
me, and he told me to say: "This is what
the LORD says: That is what you are saying, you leaders in Israel, but I know what
is going through your mind. 6You have
killed many people in this city and filled
its streets with the dead.
7"Therefore this is what the Sovereign
LORD says: The bodies you have thrown
there are the meat and this city is the pot,
but I will drive you out of it. 8You fear the
sword, and the sword is what I will bring
against you, declares the Sovereign
LORD. 9I will drive you out of the city and
deliver you into the hands of foreigners
and inflict punishment on you. 10You
will fall by the sword, and I will execute
judgment on you at the borders of Israel.
Then you will know that I am the LORD.
11This city will not be a pot for you, nor
will you be the meat in it; I will execute
judgment on you at the borders of Israel.
12And you will know that I am the LORD,
for you have not followed my decrees or
kept my laws but have conformed to the
standards of the nations around you."
13Now as I was prophesying, Pelatiah
son of Benaiah died. Then I fell facedown

[a] 5 Hebrew *El-Shaddai* [b] 11 Or *aside*

and cried out in a loud voice, "Alas, Sovereign LORD! Will you completely destroy
the remnant of Israel?"
14The word of the LORD came to me:
15"Son of man, the people of Jerusalem
have said of your fellow exiles and all the
other Israelites, 'They are far away from
the LORD; this land was given to us as our
possession.'
16"Therefore say: 'This is what the Sovereign LORD says: Although I sent them
far away among the nations and scattered
them among the countries, yet for a little
while I have been a sanctuary for them in
the countries where they have gone.'
17"Therefore say: 'This is what the Sovereign LORD says: I will gather you from
the nations and bring you back from the
countries where you have been scattered, and I will give you back the land
of Israel again.'
18"They will return to it and remove
all its vile images and detestable idols.
19I will give them an undivided heart
and put a new spirit in them; I will remove from them their heart of stone and
give them a heart of flesh. 20Then they
will follow my decrees and be careful to
keep my laws. They will be my people,
and I will be their God. 21But as for those
whose hearts are devoted to their vile
images and detestable idols, I will bring
down on their own heads what they have
done, declares the Sovereign LORD."
22Then the cherubim, with the wheels
beside them, spread their wings, and
the glory of the God of Israel was above
them. 23The glory of the LORD went up
from within the city and stopped above
the mountain east of it. 24The Spirit lifted me up and brought me to the exiles
in Babylonia[a] in the vision given by the
Spirit of God.
Then the vision I had seen went up
from me, 25and I told the exiles everything the LORD had shown me.

12 The word of the LORD came to me:
2"Son of man, you are living among
a rebellious people. They have eyes to see
but do not see and ears to hear but do not
hear, for they are a rebellious people.
3"Therefore, son of man, pack your belongings for exile and in the daytime, as
they watch, set out and go from where
you are to another place. Perhaps they
will understand, though they are a rebellious people. 4During the daytime, while
they watch, bring out your belongings
packed for exile. Then in the evening,
while they are watching, go out like those
who go into exile. 5While they watch, dig
through the wall and take your belongings out through it. 6Put them on your
shoulder as they are watching and carry
them out at dusk. Cover your face so that
you cannot see the land, for I have made
you a sign to the Israelites."
7So I did as I was commanded. During
the day I brought out my things packed
for exile. Then in the evening I dug
through the wall with my hands. I took
my belongings out at dusk, carrying them
on my shoulders while they watched.
8In the morning the word of the LORD
came to me: 9"Son of man, did not the Israelites, that rebellious people, ask you,
'What are you doing?'
10"Say to them, 'This is what the Sovereign LORD says: This prophecy concerns
the prince in Jerusalem and all the Israelites who are there.' 11Say to them, 'I am
a sign to you.'
"As I have done, so it will be done to
them. They will go into exile as captives.
12"The prince among them will put
his things on his shoulder at dusk and
leave, and a hole will be dug in the wall
for him to go through. He will cover his
face so that he cannot see the land. 13I
will spread my net for him, and he will
be caught in my snare; I will bring him to
Babylonia, the land of the Chaldeans, but
he will not see it, and there he will die. 14I
will scatter to the winds all those around
him — his staff and all his troops — and I
will pursue them with drawn sword.
15"They will know that I am the LORD,
when I disperse them among the nations
and scatter them through the countries.
16But I will spare a few of them from the
sword, famine and plague, so that in the
nations where they go they may acknowledge all their detestable practices. Then
they will know that I am the LORD."
17The word of the LORD came to me:
18"Son of man, tremble as you eat your
food, and shudder in fear as you drink
your water. 19Say to the people of the
land: 'This is what the Sovereign LORD
says about those living in Jerusalem and

[a] 24 Or *Chaldea*

in the land of Israel: They will eat their
food in anxiety and drink their water in
despair, for their land will be stripped of
everything in it because of the violence
of all who live there. 20 The inhabited
towns will be laid waste and the land will
be desolate. Then you will know that I am
the LORD.' "

21 The word of the LORD came to me:
22 "Son of man, what is this proverb you
have in the land of Israel: 'The days go
by and every vision comes to nothing'?
23 Say to them, 'This is what the Sovereign LORD says: I am going to put an end
to this proverb, and they will no longer
quote it in Israel.' Say to them, 'The days
are near when every vision will be fulfilled. 24 For there will be no more false
visions or flattering divinations among
the people of Israel. 25 But I the LORD will
speak what I will, and it shall be fulfilled
without delay. For in your days, you rebellious people, I will fulfill whatever I
say, declares the Sovereign LORD.' "

26 The word of the LORD came to me:
27 "Son of man, the Israelites are saying,
'The vision he sees is for many years from
now, and he prophesies about the distant
future.'

28 "Therefore say to them, 'This is what
the Sovereign LORD says: None of my
words will be delayed any longer; whatever I say will be fulfilled, declares the
Sovereign LORD.' "

13 The word of the LORD came to me:
2 "Son of man, prophesy against the
prophets of Israel who are now prophesying. Say to those who prophesy out of
their own imagination: 'Hear the word
of the LORD! 3 This is what the Sovereign
LORD says: Woe to the foolish[a] prophets who follow their own spirit and have
seen nothing! 4 Your prophets, Israel, are
like jackals among ruins. 5 You have not
gone up to the breaches in the wall to
repair it for the people of Israel so that it
will stand firm in the battle on the day
of the LORD. 6 Their visions are false and
their divinations a lie. Even though the
LORD has not sent them, they say, "The
LORD declares," and expect him to fulfill
their words. 7 Have you not seen false visions and uttered lying divinations when
you say, "The LORD declares," though I
have not spoken?

8 " 'Therefore this is what the Sovereign LORD says: Because of your false
words and lying visions, I am against
you, declares the Sovereign LORD. 9 My
hand will be against the prophets who
see false visions and utter lying divinations. They will not belong to the council
of my people or be listed in the records
of Israel, nor will they enter the land of
Israel. Then you will know that I am the
Sovereign LORD.

10 " 'Because they lead my people astray,
saying, "Peace," when there is no peace,
and because, when a flimsy wall is built,
they cover it with whitewash, 11 therefore
tell those who cover it with whitewash
that it is going to fall. Rain will come in
torrents, and I will send hailstones hur-
tling down, and violent winds will burst
forth. 12 When the wall collapses, will
people not ask you, "Where is the whitewash you covered it with?"

13 " 'Therefore this is what the Sovereign LORD says: In my wrath I will unleash a violent wind, and in my anger
hailstones and torrents of rain will fall
with destructive fury. 14 I will tear down
the wall you have covered with whitewash and will level it to the ground so
that its foundation will be laid bare.
When it[b] falls, you will be destroyed in
it; and you will know that I am the LORD.
15 So I will pour out my wrath against the
wall and against those who covered it
with whitewash. I will say to you, "The
wall is gone and so are those who whitewashed it, 16 those prophets of Israel who
prophesied to Jerusalem and saw visions
of peace for her when there was no peace,
declares the Sovereign LORD." '

17 "Now, son of man, set your face
against the daughters of your people
who prophesy out of their own imagination. Prophesy against them 18 and
say, 'This is what the Sovereign LORD
says: Woe to the women who sew magic
charms on all their wrists and make veils
of various lengths for their heads in order to ensnare people. Will you ensnare
the lives of my people but preserve your
own? 19 You have profaned me among my
people for a few handfuls of barley and
scraps of bread. By lying to my people,
who listen to lies, you have killed those

[a] 3 Or *wicked* [b] 14 Or *the city*

who should not have died and have
spared those who should not live.
20"'Therefore this is what the Sovereign LORD says: I am against your magic
charms with which you ensnare people
like birds and I will tear them from your
arms; I will set free the people that you
ensnare like birds. 21I will tear off your
veils and save my people from your
hands, and they will no longer fall prey
to your power. Then you will know that
I am the LORD. 22Because you disheartened the righteous with your lies, when I
had brought them no grief, and because
you encouraged the wicked not to turn
from their evil ways and so save their
lives, 23therefore you will no longer see
false visions or practice divination. I will
save my people from your hands. And
then you will know that I am the LORD.'"
14 Some of the elders of Israel came
to me and sat down in front of me.
2Then the word of the LORD came to
me: 3"Son of man, these men have set
up idols in their hearts and put wicked stumbling blocks before their faces.
Should I let them inquire of me at all?
4Therefore speak to them and tell them,
'This is what the Sovereign LORD says:
When any of the Israelites set up idols in
their hearts and put a wicked stumbling
block before their faces and then go to
a prophet, I the LORD will answer them
myself in keeping with their great idolatry. 5I will do this to recapture the hearts
of the people of Israel, who have all deserted me for their idols.'
6"Therefore say to the people of Israel, 'This is what the Sovereign LORD says:
Repent! Turn from your idols and renounce all your detestable practices!
7"'When any of the Israelites or any
foreigner residing in Israel separate
themselves from me and set up idols in
their hearts and put a wicked stumbling
block before their faces and then go to a
prophet to inquire of me, I the LORD will
answer them myself. 8I will set my face
against them and make them an example and a byword. I will remove them
from my people. Then you will know that
I am the LORD.
9"'And if the prophet is enticed to utter a prophecy, I the LORD have enticed
that prophet, and I will stretch out my
hand against him and destroy him from
among my people Israel. 10They will bear
their guilt—the prophet will be as guilty
as the one who consults him. 11Then the
people of Israel will no longer stray from
me, nor will they defile themselves anymore with all their sins. They will be my
people, and I will be their God, declares
the Sovereign LORD.'"
12The word of the LORD came to me:
13"Son of man, if a country sins against
me by being unfaithful and I stretch out
my hand against it to cut off its food supply and send famine upon it and kill its
people and their animals, 14even if these
three men—Noah, Daniel[a] and Job—
were in it, they could save only themselves by their righteousness, declares
the Sovereign LORD.
15"Or if I send wild beasts through that
country and they leave it childless and
it becomes desolate so that no one can
pass through it because of the beasts,
16as surely as I live, declares the Sovereign LORD, even if these three men were
in it, they could not save their own sons
or daughters. They alone would be saved,
but the land would be desolate.
17"Or if I bring a sword against that
country and say, 'Let the sword pass
throughout the land,' and I kill its people and their animals, 18as surely as I
live, declares the Sovereign LORD, even
if these three men were in it, they could
not save their own sons or daughters.
They alone would be saved.
19"Or if I send a plague into that land
and pour out my wrath on it through
bloodshed, killing its people and their
animals, 20as surely as I live, declares
the Sovereign LORD, even if Noah, Daniel and Job were in it, they could save neither son nor daughter. They would save
only themselves by their righteousness.
21"For this is what the Sovereign LORD
says: How much worse will it be when I
send against Jerusalem my four dreadful
judgments—sword and famine and wild
beasts and plague—to kill its men and
their animals! 22Yet there will be some
survivors—sons and daughters who will
be brought out of it. They will come to you,
and when you see their conduct and their
actions, you will be consoled regarding
the disaster I have brought on Jerusa-

[a] *14* Or *Danel*, a man of renown in ancient literature; also in verse 20

lem — every disaster I have brought on it.
23 You will be consoled when you see their
conduct and their actions, for you will
know that I have done nothing in it without cause, declares the Sovereign LORD."

15 The word of the LORD came to me:
2 "Son of man, how is the wood of a
vine different from that of a branch from
any of the trees in the forest? 3 Is wood
ever taken from it to make anything useful? Do they make pegs from it to hang
things on? 4 And after it is thrown on the
fire as fuel and the fire burns both ends
and chars the middle, is it then useful
for anything? 5 If it was not useful for
anything when it was whole, how much
less can it be made into something useful when the fire has burned it and it is
charred?

6 "Therefore this is what the Sovereign
LORD says: As I have given the wood of
the vine among the trees of the forest as
fuel for the fire, so will I treat the people
living in Jerusalem. 7 I will set my face
against them. Although they have come
out of the fire, the fire will yet consume
them. And when I set my face against
them, you will know that I am the LORD.
8 I will make the land desolate because
they have been unfaithful, declares the
Sovereign LORD."

16 The word of the LORD came to me:
2 "Son of man, confront Jerusalem
with her detestable practices 3 and say,
'This is what the Sovereign LORD says to
Jerusalem: Your ancestry and birth were
in the land of the Canaanites; your father
was an Amorite and your mother a Hittite. 4 On the day you were born your cord
was not cut, nor were you washed with
water to make you clean, nor were you
rubbed with salt or wrapped in cloths.
5 No one looked on you with pity or had
compassion enough to do any of these
things for you. Rather, you were thrown
out into the open field, for on the day you
were born you were despised.

6 " 'Then I passed by and saw you kicking about in your blood, and as you lay
there in your blood I said to you, "Live!"[a]
7 I made you grow like a plant of the field.
You grew and developed and entered
puberty. Your breasts had formed and
your hair had grown, yet you were stark
naked.

8 " 'Later I passed by, and when I looked
at you and saw that you were old enough
for love, I spread the corner of my garment over you and covered your naked
body. I gave you my solemn oath and entered into a covenant with you, declares
the Sovereign LORD, and you became
mine.

9 " 'I bathed you with water and washed
the blood from you and put ointments
on you. 10 I clothed you with an embroidered dress and put sandals of fine leather on you. I dressed you in fine linen and
covered you with costly garments. 11 I
adorned you with jewelry: I put bracelets
on your arms and a necklace around your
neck, 12 and I put a ring on your nose, earrings on your ears and a beautiful crown
on your head. 13 So you were adorned with
gold and silver; your clothes were of fine
linen and costly fabric and embroidered
cloth. Your food was honey, olive oil and
the finest flour. You became very beautiful and rose to be a queen. 14 And your
fame spread among the nations on account of your beauty, because the splendor I had given you made your beauty
perfect, declares the Sovereign LORD.

15 " 'But you trusted in your beauty
and used your fame to become a prostitute. You lavished your favors on anyone
who passed by and your beauty became
his. 16 You took some of your garments
to make gaudy high places, where you
carried on your prostitution. You went
to him, and he possessed your beauty.[b]
17 You also took the fine jewelry I gave
you, the jewelry made of my gold and
silver, and you made for yourself male
idols and engaged in prostitution with
them. 18 And you took your embroidered
clothes to put on them, and you offered
my oil and incense before them. 19 Also
the food I provided for you — the flour,
olive oil and honey I gave you to eat —
you offered as fragrant incense before
them. That is what happened, declares
the Sovereign LORD.

20 " 'And you took your sons and daughters whom you bore to me and sacrificed
them as food to the idols. Was your prostitution not enough? 21 You slaughtered
my children and sacrificed them to the
idols. 22 In all your detestable practices
and your prostitution you did not re-

[a] 6 A few Hebrew manuscripts, Septuagint and Syriac; most Hebrew manuscripts repeat *and as you lay there in your blood I said to you, "Live!"* [b] 16 The meaning of the Hebrew for this sentence is uncertain.

member the days of your youth, when
you were naked and bare, kicking about
in your blood.
23 " 'Woe! Woe to you, declares the Sovereign LORD. In addition to all your other wickedness, 24 you built a mound for
yourself and made a lofty shrine in every
public square. 25 At every street corner
you built your lofty shrines and degraded your beauty, spreading your legs with
increasing promiscuity to anyone who
passed by. 26 You engaged in prostitution
with the Egyptians, your neighbors with
large genitals, and aroused my anger
with your increasing promiscuity. 27 So I
stretched out my hand against you and
reduced your territory; I gave you over
to the greed of your enemies, the daughters of the Philistines, who were shocked
by your lewd conduct. 28 You engaged
in prostitution with the Assyrians too,
because you were insatiable; and even
after that, you still were not satisfied.
29 Then you increased your promiscuity to include Babylonia,[a] a land of merchants, but even with this you were not
satisfied.
30 " 'I am filled with fury against you,[b]
declares the Sovereign LORD, when you
do all these things, acting like a brazen prostitute! 31 When you built your
mounds at every street corner and made
your lofty shrines in every public square,
you were unlike a prostitute, because
you scorned payment.
32 " 'You adulterous wife! You prefer
strangers to your own husband! 33 All
prostitutes receive gifts, but you give
gifts to all your lovers, bribing them to
come to you from everywhere for your il-
licit favors. 34 So in your prostitution you
are the opposite of others; no one runs
after you for your favors. You are the very
opposite, for you give payment and none
is given to you.
35 " 'Therefore, you prostitute, hear the
word of the LORD! 36 This is what the Sovereign LORD says: Because you poured
out your lust and exposed your naked
body in your promiscuity with your lovers, and because of all your detestable
idols, and because you gave them your
children's blood, 37 therefore I am going
to gather all your lovers, with whom you
found pleasure, those you loved as well
as those you hated. I will gather them
against you from all around and will
strip you in front of them, and they will
see you stark naked. 38 I will sentence you
to the punishment of women who commit adultery and who shed blood; I will
bring on you the blood vengeance of my
wrath and jealous anger. 39 Then I will
deliver you into the hands of your lovers,
and they will tear down your mounds
and destroy your lofty shrines. They will
strip you of your clothes and take your
fine jewelry and leave you stark naked.
40 They will bring a mob against you, who
will stone you and hack you to pieces with
their swords. 41 They will burn down your
houses and inflict punishment on you
in the sight of many women. I will put a
stop to your prostitution, and you will no
longer pay your lovers. 42 Then my wrath
against you will subside and my jealous
anger will turn away from you; I will be
calm and no longer angry.
43 " 'Because you did not remember the
days of your youth but enraged me with
all these things, I will surely bring down
on your head what you have done, declares the Sovereign LORD. Did you not
add lewdness to all your other detestable
practices?
44 " 'Everyone who quotes proverbs
will quote this proverb about you: "Like
mother, like daughter." 45 You are a true
daughter of your mother, who despised
her husband and her children; and you
are a true sister of your sisters, who despised their husbands and their children. Your mother was a Hittite and your
father an Amorite. 46 Your older sister
was Samaria, who lived to the north of
you with her daughters; and your younger sister, who lived to the south of you
with her daughters, was Sodom. 47 You
not only followed their ways and copied
their detestable practices, but in all your
ways you soon became more depraved
than they. 48 As surely as I live, declares
the Sovereign LORD, your sister Sodom
and her daughters never did what you
and your daughters have done.
49 " 'Now this was the sin of your sister
Sodom: She and her daughters were arrogant, overfed and unconcerned; they
did not help the poor and needy. 50 They
were haughty and did detestable things

[a] 29 Or *Chaldea* [b] 30 Or *How feverish is your heart,*

before me. Therefore I did away with
them as you have seen. 51 Samaria did
not commit half the sins you did. You
have done more detestable things than
they, and have made your sisters seem
righteous by all these things you have
done. 52 Bear your disgrace, for you have
furnished some justification for your
sisters. Because your sins were more vile
than theirs, they appear more righteous
than you. So then, be ashamed and bear
your disgrace, for you have made your
sisters appear righteous.
53 " 'However, I will restore the fortunes of Sodom and her daughters and
of Samaria and her daughters, and your
fortunes along with them, 54 so that you
may bear your disgrace and be ashamed
of all you have done in giving them comfort. 55 And your sisters, Sodom with her
daughters and Samaria with her daughters, will return to what they were before
and you and your daughters will return
to what you were before. 56 You would
not even mention your sister Sodom in
the day of your pride, 57 before your wickedness was uncovered. Even so, you are
now scorned by the daughters of Edom[a]
and all her neighbors and the daughters
of the Philistines — all those around you
who despise you. 58 You will bear the consequences of your lewdness and your detestable practices, declares the LORD.
59 " 'This is what the Sovereign LORD
says: I will deal with you as you deserve,
because you have despised my oath by
breaking the covenant. 60 Yet I will remember the covenant I made with you in
the days of your youth, and I will establish an everlasting covenant with you.
61 Then you will remember your ways
and be ashamed when you receive your
sisters, both those who are older than
you and those who are younger. I will
give them to you as daughters, but not on
the basis of my covenant with you. 62 So
I will establish my covenant with you,
and you will know that I am the LORD.
63 Then, when I make atonement for you
for all you have done, you will remember
and be ashamed and never again open
your mouth because of your humiliation,
declares the Sovereign LORD.' "

17 The word of the LORD came to me:
2 "Son of man, set forth an allegory
and tell it to the Israelites as a parable.
3 Say to them, 'This is what the Sovereign
LORD says: A great eagle with powerful
wings, long feathers and full plumage of
varied colors came to Lebanon. Taking
hold of the top of a cedar, 4 he broke off
its topmost shoot and carried it away to
a land of merchants, where he planted it
in a city of traders.
5 " 'He took one of the seedlings of the
land and put it in fertile soil. He planted
it like a willow by abundant water, 6 and
it sprouted and became a low, spreading
vine. Its branches turned toward him,
but its roots remained under it. So it became a vine and produced branches and
put out leafy boughs.
7 " 'But there was another great eagle
with powerful wings and full plumage.
The vine now sent out its roots toward
him from the plot where it was planted
and stretched out its branches to him for
water. 8 It had been planted in good soil
by abundant water so that it would produce branches, bear fruit and become a
splendid vine.'
9 "Say to them, 'This is what the Sovereign LORD says: Will it thrive? Will it
not be uprooted and stripped of its fruit
so that it withers? All its new growth will
wither. It will not take a strong arm or
many people to pull it up by the roots.
10 It has been planted, but will it thrive?
Will it not wither completely when the
east wind strikes it — wither away in the
plot where it grew?' "
11 Then the word of the LORD came to
me: 12 "Say to this rebellious people, 'Do
you not know what these things mean?'
Say to them: 'The king of Babylon went
to Jerusalem and carried off her king and
her nobles, bringing them back with him
to Babylon. 13 Then he took a member of
the royal family and made a treaty with
him, putting him under oath. He also
carried away the leading men of the land,
14 so that the kingdom would be brought
low, unable to rise again, surviving only
by keeping his treaty. 15 But the king rebelled against him by sending his envoys
to Egypt to get horses and a large army.
Will he succeed? Will he who does such
things escape? Will he break the treaty
and yet escape?
16 " 'As surely as I live, declares the Sov-

[a] 57 Many Hebrew manuscripts and Syriac; most Hebrew manuscripts, Septuagint and Vulgate *Aram*

ereign LORD, he shall die in Babylon,
in the land of the king who put him on
the throne, whose oath he despised and
whose treaty he broke. 17 Pharaoh with
his mighty army and great horde will be
of no help to him in war, when ramps are
built and siege works erected to destroy
many lives. 18 He despised the oath by
breaking the covenant. Because he had
given his hand in pledge and yet did all
these things, he shall not escape.
19 "'Therefore this is what the Sovereign
LORD says: As surely as I live, I will repay
him for despising my oath and breaking
my covenant. 20 I will spread my net for
him, and he will be caught in my snare.
I will bring him to Babylon and execute
judgment on him there because he was
unfaithful to me. 21 All his choice troops
will fall by the sword, and the survivors
will be scattered to the winds. Then you
will know that I the LORD have spoken.
22 "'This is what the Sovereign LORD
says: I myself will take a shoot from the
very top of a cedar and plant it; I will break
off a tender sprig from its topmost shoots
and plant it on a high and lofty mountain.
23 On the mountain heights of Israel I will
plant it; it will produce branches and bear
fruit and become a splendid cedar. Birds
of every kind will nest in it; they will find
shelter in the shade of its branches. 24 All
the trees of the forest will know that I the
LORD bring down the tall tree and make
the low tree grow tall. I dry up the green
tree and make the dry tree flourish.

"'I the LORD have spoken, and I will do it.'"

18 The word of the LORD came to me:
2 "What do you people mean by
quoting this proverb about the land of
Israel:

"'The parents eat sour grapes,
and the children's teeth are set on edge'?

3 "As surely as I live, declares the Sovereign LORD, you will no longer quote this
proverb in Israel. 4 For everyone belongs
to me, the parent as well as the child—
both alike belong to me. The one who
sins is the one who will die.

5 "Suppose there is a righteous man
who does what is just and right.
6 He does not eat at the mountain shrines
or look to the idols of Israel.
He does not defile his neighbor's wife
or have sexual relations with a woman during her period.
7 He does not oppress anyone,
but returns what he took in pledge for a loan.
He does not commit robbery
but gives his food to the hungry
and provides clothing for the naked.
8 He does not lend to them at interest
or take a profit from them.
He withholds his hand from doing wrong
and judges fairly between two parties.
9 He follows my decrees
and faithfully keeps my laws.
That man is righteous;
he will surely live,
declares the Sovereign LORD.

10 "Suppose he has a violent son, who
sheds blood or does any of these other
things[a] 11 (though the father has done
none of them):

"He eats at the mountain shrines.
He defiles his neighbor's wife.
12 He oppresses the poor and needy.
He commits robbery.
He does not return what he took in pledge.
He looks to the idols.
He does detestable things.
13 He lends at interest and takes a profit.

Will such a man live? He will not! Because he has done all these detestable
things, he is to be put to death; his blood
will be on his own head.
14 "But suppose this son has a son who
sees all the sins his father commits, and
though he sees them, he does not do such
things:

15 "He does not eat at the mountain shrines
or look to the idols of Israel.
He does not defile his neighbor's wife.
16 He does not oppress anyone
or require a pledge for a loan.
He does not commit robbery
but gives his food to the hungry
and provides clothing for the naked.

[a] 10 Or *things to a brother*

17 He withholds his hand from
mistreating the poor
and takes no interest or profit from
them.
He keeps my laws and follows my
decrees.

He will not die for his father's sin; he will
surely live. 18 But his father will die for his
own sin, because he practiced extortion,
robbed his brother and did what was
wrong among his people.
19 "Yet you ask, 'Why does the son not
share the guilt of his father?' Since the
son has done what is just and right and
has been careful to keep all my decrees,
he will surely live. 20 The one who sins is
the one who will die. The child will not
share the guilt of the parent, nor will the
parent share the guilt of the child. The
righteousness of the righteous will be
credited to them, and the wickedness
of the wicked will be charged against
them.
21 "But if a wicked person turns away
from all the sins they have committed
and keeps all my decrees and does what
is just and right, that person will surely
live; they will not die. 22 None of the offenses they have committed will be remembered against them. Because of the
righteous things they have done, they
will live. 23 Do I take any pleasure in the
death of the wicked? declares the Sovereign LORD. Rather, am I not pleased when
they turn from their ways and live?
24 "But if a righteous person turns from
their righteousness and commits sin
and does the same detestable things the
wicked person does, will they live? None
of the righteous things that person has
done will be remembered. Because of
the unfaithfulness they are guilty of and
because of the sins they have committed,
they will die.
25 "Yet you say, 'The way of the Lord is
not just.' Hear, you Israelites: Is my way
unjust? Is it not your ways that are unjust? 26 If a righteous person turns from
their righteousness and commits sin,
they will die for it; because of the sin
they have committed they will die. 27 But
if a wicked person turns away from the
wickedness they have committed and
does what is just and right, they will save
their life. 28 Because they consider all the
offenses they have committed and turn
away from them, that person will surely
live; they will not die. 29 Yet the Israelites
say, 'The way of the Lord is not just.' Are
my ways unjust, people of Israel? Is it not
your ways that are unjust?
30 "Therefore, you Israelites, I will
judge each of you according to your own
ways, declares the Sovereign LORD. Repent! Turn away from all your offenses;
then sin will not be your downfall. 31 Rid
yourselves of all the offenses you have
committed, and get a new heart and a
new spirit. Why will you die, people of Israel? 32 For I take no pleasure in the death
of anyone, declares the Sovereign LORD.
Repent and live!

19 "Take up a lament concerning the
princes of Israel 2 and say:

" 'What a lioness was your mother
among the lions!
She lay down among them
and reared her cubs.
3 She brought up one of her cubs,
and he became a strong lion.
He learned to tear the prey
and he became a man-eater.
4 The nations heard about him,
and he was trapped in their pit.
They led him with hooks
to the land of Egypt.

5 " 'When she saw her hope unfulfilled,
her expectation gone,
she took another of her cubs
and made him a strong lion.
6 He prowled among the lions,
for he was now a strong lion.
He learned to tear the prey
and he became a man-eater.
7 He broke down[a] their strongholds
and devastated their towns.
The land and all who were in it
were terrified by his roaring.
8 Then the nations came against him,
those from regions round about.
They spread their net for him,
and he was trapped in their pit.
9 With hooks they pulled him into a
cage
and brought him to the king of
Babylon.
They put him in prison,
so his roar was heard no longer
on the mountains of Israel.

[a] 7 Targum (see Septuagint); Hebrew *He knew*

10 " 'Your mother was like a vine in your
vineyard[a]
planted by the water;
it was fruitful and full of branches
because of abundant water.
11 Its branches were strong,
fit for a ruler's scepter.
It towered high
above the thick foliage,
conspicuous for its height
and for its many branches.
12 But it was uprooted in fury
and thrown to the ground.
The east wind made it shrivel,
it was stripped of its fruit;
its strong branches withered
and fire consumed them.
13 Now it is planted in the desert,
in a dry and thirsty land.
14 Fire spread from one of its main[b]
branches
and consumed its fruit.
No strong branch is left on it
fit for a ruler's scepter.'

"This is a lament and is to be used as a lament."

20 In the seventh year, in the fifth
month on the tenth day, some of
the elders of Israel came to inquire of the
LORD, and they sat down in front of me.
2 Then the word of the LORD came to
me: 3 "Son of man, speak to the elders of
Israel and say to them, 'This is what the
Sovereign LORD says: Have you come to
inquire of me? As surely as I live, I will
not let you inquire of me, declares the
Sovereign LORD.'
4 "Will you judge them? Will you judge
them, son of man? Then confront them
with the detestable practices of their
ancestors 5 and say to them: 'This is
what the Sovereign LORD says: On the
day I chose Israel, I swore with uplifted
hand to the descendants of Jacob and
revealed myself to them in Egypt. With
uplifted hand I said to them, "I am the
LORD your God." 6 On that day I swore
to them that I would bring them out of
Egypt into a land I had searched out for
them, a land flowing with milk and honey, the most beautiful of all lands. 7 And
I said to them, "Each of you, get rid of
the vile images you have set your eyes
on, and do not defile yourselves with
the idols of Egypt. I am the LORD your
God."
8 " 'But they rebelled against me and
would not listen to me; they did not get
rid of the vile images they had set their
eyes on, nor did they forsake the idols
of Egypt. So I said I would pour out my
wrath on them and spend my anger
against them in Egypt. 9 But for the sake
of my name, I brought them out of Egypt.
I did it to keep my name from being profaned in the eyes of the nations among
whom they lived and in whose sight I
had revealed myself to the Israelites.
10 Therefore I led them out of Egypt and
brought them into the wilderness. 11 I
gave them my decrees and made known
to them my laws, by which the person
who obeys them will live. 12 Also I gave
them my Sabbaths as a sign between us,
so they would know that I the LORD made
them holy.
13 " 'Yet the people of Israel rebelled
against me in the wilderness. They did
not follow my decrees but rejected my
laws—by which the person who obeys
them will live—and they utterly desecrated my Sabbaths. So I said I would
pour out my wrath on them and destroy
them in the wilderness. 14 But for the sake
of my name I did what would keep it from
being profaned in the eyes of the nations
in whose sight I had brought them out.
15 Also with uplifted hand I swore to
them in the wilderness that I would not
bring them into the land I had given
them—a land flowing with milk and
honey, the most beautiful of all lands—
16 because they rejected my laws and did
not follow my decrees and desecrated my
Sabbaths. For their hearts were devoted
to their idols. 17 Yet I looked on them with
pity and did not destroy them or put an
end to them in the wilderness. 18 I said
to their children in the wilderness, "Do
not follow the statutes of your parents or
keep their laws or defile yourselves with
their idols. 19 I am the LORD your God;
follow my decrees and be careful to keep
my laws. 20 Keep my Sabbaths holy, that
they may be a sign between us. Then you
will know that I am the LORD your God."
21 " 'But the children rebelled against
me: They did not follow my decrees,
they were not careful to keep my laws,

[a] *10* Two Hebrew manuscripts; most Hebrew manuscripts *your blood* [b] *14* Or *from under its*

of which I said, "The person who obeys
them will live by them," and they desecrated my Sabbaths. So I said I would
pour out my wrath on them and spend
my anger against them in the wilderness. 22 But I withheld my hand, and for
the sake of my name I did what would
keep it from being profaned in the eyes of
the nations in whose sight I had brought
them out. 23 Also with uplifted hand I
swore to them in the wilderness that I
would disperse them among the nations
and scatter them through the countries,
24 because they had not obeyed my laws
but had rejected my decrees and desecrated my Sabbaths, and their eyes
lusted after their parents' idols. 25 So I
gave them other statutes that were not
good and laws through which they could
not live; 26 I defiled them through their
gifts — the sacrifice of every firstborn —
that I might fill them with horror so they
would know that I am the LORD.'

27 "Therefore, son of man, speak to
the people of Israel and say to them,
'This is what the Sovereign LORD says:
In this also your ancestors blasphemed
me by being unfaithful to me: 28 When I
brought them into the land I had sworn
to give them and they saw any high hill
or any leafy tree, there they offered their
sacrifices, made offerings that aroused
my anger, presented their fragrant incense and poured out their drink offerings. 29 Then I said to them: What is this
high place you go to?' " (It is called Bamah[a] to this day.)

30 "Therefore say to the Israelites: 'This
is what the Sovereign LORD says: Will you
defile yourselves the way your ancestors did and lust after their vile images?
31 When you offer your gifts — the sacrifice of your children in the fire — you
continue to defile yourselves with all
your idols to this day. Am I to let you inquire of me, you Israelites? As surely as I
live, declares the Sovereign LORD, I will
not let you inquire of me.

32 " 'You say, "We want to be like the nations, like the peoples of the world, who
serve wood and stone." But what you have
in mind will never happen. 33 As surely as
I live, declares the Sovereign LORD, I will
reign over you with a mighty hand and
an outstretched arm and with outpoured
wrath. 34 I will bring you from the nations
and gather you from the countries where
you have been scattered — with a mighty
hand and an outstretched arm and with
outpoured wrath. 35 I will bring you into
the wilderness of the nations and there,
face to face, I will execute judgment
upon you. 36 As I judged your ancestors
in the wilderness of the land of Egypt, so
I will judge you, declares the Sovereign
LORD. 37 I will take note of you as you pass
under my rod, and I will bring you into
the bond of the covenant. 38 I will purge
you of those who revolt and rebel against
me. Although I will bring them out of the
land where they are living, yet they will
not enter the land of Israel. Then you will
know that I am the LORD.

39 " 'As for you, people of Israel, this is
what the Sovereign LORD says: Go and
serve your idols, every one of you! But afterward you will surely listen to me and
no longer profane my holy name with
your gifts and idols. 40 For on my holy
mountain, the high mountain of Israel,
declares the Sovereign LORD, there in the
land all the people of Israel will serve me,
and there I will accept them. There I will
require your offerings and your choice
gifts,[b] along with all your holy sacrifices. 41 I will accept you as fragrant incense
when I bring you out from the nations
and gather you from the countries where
you have been scattered, and I will be
proved holy through you in the sight of
the nations. 42 Then you will know that I
am the LORD, when I bring you into the
land of Israel, the land I had sworn with
uplifted hand to give to your ancestors.
43 There you will remember your conduct
and all the actions by which you have
defiled yourselves, and you will loathe
yourselves for all the evil you have done.
44 You will know that I am the LORD,
when I deal with you for my name's sake
and not according to your evil ways and
your corrupt practices, you people of Israel, declares the Sovereign LORD.' "

45 The word of the LORD came to me:
46 "Son of man, set your face toward the
south; preach against the south and
prophesy against the forest of the southland. 47 Say to the southern forest: 'Hear
the word of the LORD. This is what the
Sovereign LORD says: I am about to set fire

[a] 29 *Bamah* means *high place.* [b] 40 Or *and the gifts of your firstfruits*

to you, and it will consume all your trees,
both green and dry. The blazing flame
will not be quenched, and every face
from south to north will be scorched by it.
48Everyone will see that I the LORD have
kindled it; it will not be quenched.'"
49Then I said, "Sovereign LORD, they
are saying of me, 'Isn't he just telling
parables?'"[a]

21[b] The word of the LORD came to me:
2"Son of man, set your face against
Jerusalem and preach against the sanctuary. Prophesy against the land of Israel
3and say to her: 'This is what the LORD
says: I am against you. I will draw my
sword from its sheath and cut off from
you both the righteous and the wicked.
4Because I am going to cut off the righteous and the wicked, my sword will be
unsheathed against everyone from south
to north. 5Then all people will know that
I the LORD have drawn my sword from its
sheath; it will not return again.'
6"Therefore groan, son of man! Groan
before them with broken heart and bitter
grief. 7And when they ask you, 'Why are
you groaning?' you shall say, 'Because of
the news that is coming. Every heart will
melt with fear and every hand go limp;
every spirit will become faint and every
leg will be wet with urine.' It is coming! It
will surely take place, declares the Sovereign LORD."
8The word of the LORD came to me:
9"Son of man, prophesy and say, 'This is
what the Lord says:

"'A sword, a sword,
sharpened and polished—
10sharpened for the slaughter,
polished to flash like lightning!

"'Shall we rejoice in the scepter of my royal son? The sword despises every such stick.

11"'The sword is appointed to be
polished,
to be grasped with the hand;
it is sharpened and polished,
made ready for the hand of the
slayer.
12Cry out and wail, son of man,
for it is against my people;
it is against all the princes of Israel.
They are thrown to the sword
along with my people.
Therefore beat your breast.

13"'Testing will surely come. And what
if even the scepter, which the sword despises, does not continue? declares the
Sovereign LORD.'

14"So then, son of man, prophesy
and strike your hands together.
Let the sword strike twice,
even three times.
It is a sword for slaughter—
a sword for great slaughter,
closing in on them from every side.
15So that hearts may melt with fear
and the fallen be many,
I have stationed the sword for
slaughter[c]
at all their gates.
Look! It is forged to strike like
lightning,
it is grasped for slaughter.
16Slash to the right, you sword,
then to the left,
wherever your blade is turned.
17I too will strike my hands together,
and my wrath will subside.
I the LORD have spoken."

18The word of the LORD came to me:
19"Son of man, mark out two roads for
the sword of the king of Babylon to take,
both starting from the same country.
Make a signpost where the road branches off to the city. 20Mark out one road for
the sword to come against Rabbah of the
Ammonites and another against Judah
and fortified Jerusalem. 21For the king of
Babylon will stop at the fork in the road,
at the junction of the two roads, to seek
an omen: He will cast lots with arrows,
he will consult his idols, he will examine
the liver. 22Into his right hand will come
the lot for Jerusalem, where he is to set up
battering rams, to give the command to
slaughter, to sound the battle cry, to set
battering rams against the gates, to build
a ramp and to erect siege works. 23It will
seem like a false omen to those who have
sworn allegiance to him, but he will remind them of their guilt and take them
captive.
24"Therefore this is what the Sovereign
LORD says: 'Because you people have
brought to mind your guilt by your open

[a] *49* In Hebrew texts 20:45-49 is numbered 21:1-5. [b] In Hebrew texts 21:1-32 is numbered 21:6-37.
[c] *15* Septuagint; the meaning of the Hebrew for this word is uncertain.

rebellion, revealing your sins in all that
you do—because you have done this
you will be taken captive.

25“ ‘You profane and wicked prince of
Israel, whose day has come, whose time
of punishment has reached its climax,
26this is what the Sovereign LORD says:
Take off the turban, remove the crown.
It will not be as it was: The lowly will be
exalted and the exalted will be brought
low. 27A ruin! A ruin! I will make it a ruin!
The crown will not be restored until he to
whom it rightfully belongs shall come; to
him I will give it.’

28“And you, son of man, prophesy and
say, ‘This is what the Sovereign LORD
says about the Ammonites and their insults:

“ ‘A sword, a sword,
drawn for the slaughter,
polished to consume
and to flash like lightning!
29Despite false visions concerning you
and lying divinations about you,
it will be laid on the necks
of the wicked who are to be slain,
whose day has come,
whose time of punishment has
reached its climax.
30“ ‘Let the sword return to its sheath.
In the place where you were
created,
in the land of your ancestry,
I will judge you.
31I will pour out my wrath on you
and breathe out my fiery anger
against you;
I will deliver you into the hands of
brutal men,
men skilled in destruction.
32You will be fuel for the fire,
your blood will be shed in your
land,
you will be remembered no more;
for I the LORD have spoken.’ ”

22

The word of the LORD came to me:
2“Son of man, will you judge her? Will
you judge this city of bloodshed? Then
confront her with all her detestable practices 3and say: ‘This is what the Sovereign
LORD says: You city that brings on herself
doom by shedding blood in her midst
and defiles herself by making idols, 4you
have become guilty because of the blood
you have shed and have become defiled
by the idols you have made. You have
brought your days to a close, and the end
of your years has come. Therefore I will
make you an object of scorn to the nations and a laughingstock to all the countries. 5Those who are near and those who
are far away will mock you, you infamous
city, full of turmoil.

6“ ‘See how each of the princes of Israel who are in you uses his power to shed
blood. 7In you they have treated father
and mother with contempt; in you they
have oppressed the foreigner and mistreated the fatherless and the widow.
8You have despised my holy things and
desecrated my Sabbaths. 9In you are
slanderers who are bent on shedding
blood; in you are those who eat at the
mountain shrines and commit lewd acts.
10In you are those who dishonor their father’s bed; in you are those who violate
women during their period, when they
are ceremonially unclean. 11In you one
man commits a detestable offense with
his neighbor’s wife, another shamefully
defiles his daughter-in-law, and another violates his sister, his own father’s
daughter. 12In you are people who accept bribes to shed blood; you take interest and make a profit from the poor. You
extort unjust gain from your neighbors.
And you have forgotten me, declares the
Sovereign LORD.

13“ ‘I will surely strike my hands together at the unjust gain you have made
and at the blood you have shed in your
midst. 14Will your courage endure or
your hands be strong in the day I deal
with you? I the LORD have spoken, and
I will do it. 15I will disperse you among
the nations and scatter you through the
countries; and I will put an end to your
uncleanness. 16When you have been defiled[a] in the eyes of the nations, you will
know that I am the LORD.’ ”

17Then the word of the LORD came to
me: 18“Son of man, the people of Israel
have become dross to me; all of them are
the copper, tin, iron and lead left inside a
furnace. They are but the dross of silver.
19Therefore this is what the Sovereign
LORD says: ‘Because you have all become
dross, I will gather you into Jerusalem.

a 16 Or *When I have allotted you your inheritance*

20As silver, copper, iron, lead and tin
are gathered into a furnace to be melted
with a fiery blast, so will I gather you in
my anger and my wrath and put you inside the city and melt you. 21I will gather
you and I will blow on you with my fiery
wrath, and you will be melted inside her.
22As silver is melted in a furnace, so you
will be melted inside her, and you will
know that I the LORD have poured out
my wrath on you.'"

23Again the word of the LORD came to
me: 24"Son of man, say to the land, 'You
are a land that has not been cleansed or
rained on in the day of wrath.' 25There is
a conspiracy of her princes[a] within her
like a roaring lion tearing its prey; they
devour people, take treasures and precious things and make many widows
within her. 26Her priests do violence to
my law and profane my holy things; they
do not distinguish between the holy and
the common; they teach that there is no
difference between the unclean and the
clean; and they shut their eyes to the
keeping of my Sabbaths, so that I am profaned among them. 27Her officials within her are like wolves tearing their prey;
they shed blood and kill people to make
unjust gain. 28Her prophets whitewash
these deeds for them by false visions
and lying divinations. They say, 'This is
what the Sovereign LORD says'—when
the LORD has not spoken. 29The people
of the land practice extortion and commit robbery; they oppress the poor and
needy and mistreat the foreigner, denying them justice.

30"I looked for someone among them
who would build up the wall and stand
before me in the gap on behalf of the
land so I would not have to destroy it, but
I found no one. 31So I will pour out my
wrath on them and consume them with
my fiery anger, bringing down on their
own heads all they have done, declares
the Sovereign LORD."

23 The word of the LORD came to me:
2"Son of man, there were two wom-
en, daughters of the same mother. 3They
became prostitutes in Egypt, engaging
in prostitution from their youth. In that
land their breasts were fondled and their
virgin bosoms caressed. 4The older was
named Oholah, and her sister was Oholibah. They were mine and gave birth to
sons and daughters. Oholah is Samaria,
and Oholibah is Jerusalem.

5"Oholah engaged in prostitution
while she was still mine; and she lusted
after her lovers, the Assyrians—warriors
6clothed in blue, governors and commanders, all of them handsome young
men, and mounted horsemen. 7She gave
herself as a prostitute to all the elite of
the Assyrians and defiled herself with
all the idols of everyone she lusted after.
8She did not give up the prostitution she
began in Egypt, when during her youth
men slept with her, caressed her virgin
bosom and poured out their lust on her.

9"Therefore I delivered her into the
hands of her lovers, the Assyrians, for
whom she lusted. 10They stripped her
naked, took away her sons and daughters and killed her with the sword. She
became a byword among women, and
punishment was inflicted on her.

11"Her sister Oholibah saw this, yet in
her lust and prostitution she was more
depraved than her sister. 12She too lusted after the Assyrians—governors and
commanders, warriors in full dress,
mounted horsemen, all handsome young
men. 13I saw that she too defiled herself;
both of them went the same way.

14"But she carried her prostitution
still further. She saw men portrayed on
a wall, figures of Chaldeans[b] portrayed
in red, 15with belts around their waists
and flowing turbans on their heads; all
of them looked like Babylonian chariot
officers, natives of Chaldea.[c] 16As soon
as she saw them, she lusted after them
and sent messengers to them in Chaldea. 17Then the Babylonians came to
her, to the bed of love, and in their lust
they defiled her. After she had been defiled by them, she turned away from
them in disgust. 18When she carried on
her prostitution openly and exposed her
naked body, I turned away from her in
disgust, just as I had turned away from
her sister. 19Yet she became more and
more promiscuous as she recalled the
days of her youth, when she was a prostitute in Egypt. 20There she lusted after her lovers, whose genitals were like
those of donkeys and whose emission
was like that of horses. 21So you longed

[a] *25* Septuagint; Hebrew *prophets* [b] *14* Or *Babylonians* [c] *15* Or *Babylonia*; also in verse 16

for the lewdness of your youth, when in
Egypt your bosom was caressed and your
young breasts fondled.[a]
22 “Therefore, Oholibah, this is what
the Sovereign LORD says: I will stir up
your lovers against you, those you turned
away from in disgust, and I will bring
them against you from every side—
23 the Babylonians and all the Chaldeans, the men of Pekod and Shoa and Koa,
and all the Assyrians with them, handsome young men, all of them governors
and commanders, chariot officers and
men of high rank, all mounted on horses. 24 They will come against you with
weapons,[b] chariots and wagons and with
a throng of people; they will take up positions against you on every side with large
and small shields and with helmets. I will
turn you over to them for punishment,
and they will punish you according to
their standards. 25 I will direct my jealous anger against you, and they will deal
with you in fury. They will cut off your
noses and your ears, and those of you
who are left will fall by the sword. They
will take away your sons and daughters,
and those of you who are left will be consumed by fire. 26 They will also strip you
of your clothes and take your fine jewelry. 27 So I will put a stop to the lewdness
and prostitution you began in Egypt. You
will not look on these things with longing
or remember Egypt anymore.
28 “For this is what the Sovereign LORD
says: I am about to deliver you into the
hands of those you hate, to those you
turned away from in disgust. 29 They
will deal with you in hatred and take
away everything you have worked for.
They will leave you stark naked, and the
shame of your prostitution will be exposed. Your lewdness and promiscuity
30 have brought this on you, because you
lusted after the nations and defiled yourself with their idols. 31 You have gone the
way of your sister; so I will put her cup
into your hand.
32 “This is what the Sovereign LORD
says:

“You will drink your sister’s cup,
a cup large and deep;
it will bring scorn and derision,
for it holds so much.
33 You will be filled with drunkenness
and sorrow,
the cup of ruin and desolation,
the cup of your sister Samaria.
34 You will drink it and drain it dry
and chew on its pieces—
and you will tear your breasts.

I have spoken, declares the Sovereign
LORD.
35 “Therefore this is what the Sovereign
LORD says: Since you have forgotten me
and turned your back on me, you must
bear the consequences of your lewdness
and prostitution.”
36 The LORD said to me: “Son of man,
will you judge Oholah and Oholibah?
Then confront them with their detestable practices, 37 for they have committed
adultery and blood is on their hands. They
committed adultery with their idols; they
even sacrificed their children, whom they
bore to me, as food for them. 38 They have
also done this to me: At that same time
they defiled my sanctuary and desecrated
my Sabbaths. 39 On the very day they sacrificed their children to their idols, they
entered my sanctuary and desecrated it.
That is what they did in my house.
40 “They even sent messengers for men
who came from far away, and when they
arrived you bathed yourself for them, applied eye makeup and put on your jewelry. 41 You sat on an elegant couch, with a
table spread before it on which you had
placed the incense and olive oil that belonged to me.
42 “The noise of a carefree crowd was
around her; drunkards were brought
from the desert along with men from
the rabble, and they put bracelets on the
wrists of the woman and her sister and
beautiful crowns on their heads. 43 Then
I said about the one worn out by adultery,
‘Now let them use her as a prostitute, for
that is all she is.’ 44 And they slept with
her. As men sleep with a prostitute, so
they slept with those lewd women, Oholah and Oholibah. 45 But righteous judges
will sentence them to the punishment of
women who commit adultery and shed
blood, because they are adulterous and
blood is on their hands.
46 “This is what the Sovereign LORD
says: Bring a mob against them and give

[a] *21* Syriac (see also verse 3); Hebrew *caressed because of your young breasts* [b] *24* The meaning of the Hebrew for this word is uncertain.

them over to terror and plunder. 47The
mob will stone them and cut them down
with their swords; they will kill their
sons and daughters and burn down their
houses.

48"So I will put an end to lewdness in
the land, that all women may take warning and not imitate you. 49You will suffer
the penalty for your lewdness and bear
the consequences of your sins of idolatry.
Then you will know that I am the Sovereign LORD."

24 In the ninth year, in the tenth
month on the tenth day, the word
of the LORD came to me: 2"Son of man,
record this date, this very date, because
the king of Babylon has laid siege to Jerusalem this very day. 3Tell this rebellious
people a parable and say to them: 'This is
what the Sovereign LORD says:

"'Put on the cooking pot; put it on
  and pour water into it.
4Put into it the pieces of meat,
  all the choice pieces — the leg and
    the shoulder.
Fill it with the best of these bones;
5 take the pick of the flock.
Pile wood beneath it for the bones;
  bring it to a boil
  and cook the bones in it.

6"'For this is what the Sovereign LORD
says:

"'Woe to the city of bloodshed,
  to the pot now encrusted,
  whose deposit will not go away!
Take the meat out piece by piece
  in whatever order it comes.

7"'For the blood she shed is in her
    midst:
  She poured it on the bare rock;
she did not pour it on the ground,
  where the dust would cover it.
8To stir up wrath and take revenge
  I put her blood on the bare rock,
  so that it would not be covered.

9"'Therefore this is what the Sovereign
LORD says:

"'Woe to the city of bloodshed!
  I, too, will pile the wood high.
10So heap on the wood
  and kindle the fire.
Cook the meat well,
  mixing in the spices;
  and let the bones be charred.
11Then set the empty pot on the coals
  till it becomes hot and its copper
    glows,
so that its impurities may be melted
  and its deposit burned away.
12It has frustrated all efforts;
  its heavy deposit has not been
    removed,
  not even by fire.

13"'Now your impurity is lewdness.
Because I tried to cleanse you but you
would not be cleansed from your impurity, you will not be clean again until my
wrath against you has subsided.

14"'I the LORD have spoken. The time
has come for me to act. I will not hold
back; I will not have pity, nor will I relent. You will be judged according to
your conduct and your actions, declares
the Sovereign LORD.'"

15The word of the LORD came to me:
16"Son of man, with one blow I am about
to take away from you the delight of your
eyes. Yet do not lament or weep or shed
any tears. 17Groan quietly; do not mourn
for the dead. Keep your turban fastened
and your sandals on your feet; do not
cover your mustache and beard or eat the
customary food of mourners."

18So I spoke to the people in the morning, and in the evening my wife died.
The next morning I did as I had been
commanded.

19Then the people asked me, "Won't
you tell us what these things have to do
with us? Why are you acting like this?"

20So I said to them, "The word of the
LORD came to me: 21Say to the people of
Israel, 'This is what the Sovereign LORD
says: I am about to desecrate my sanctuary — the stronghold in which you
take pride, the delight of your eyes, the
object of your affection. The sons and
daughters you left behind will fall by
the sword. 22And you will do as I have
done. You will not cover your mustache
and beard or eat the customary food of
mourners. 23You will keep your turbans
on your heads and your sandals on your
feet. You will not mourn or weep but will
waste away because of[a] your sins and
groan among yourselves. 24Ezekiel will

[a] 23 Or *away in*

be a sign to you; you will do just as he has
done. When this happens, you will know
that I am the Sovereign LORD.'
25 "And you, son of man, on the day
I take away their stronghold, their joy
and glory, the delight of their eyes, their
heart's desire, and their sons and daughters as well — 26 on that day a fugitive will
come to tell you the news. 27 At that time
your mouth will be opened; you will
speak with him and will no longer be silent. So you will be a sign to them, and
they will know that I am the LORD."

25 The word of the LORD came to me:
2 "Son of man, set your face against
the Ammonites and prophesy against
them. 3 Say to them, 'Hear the word of the
Sovereign LORD. This is what the Sovereign LORD says: Because you said "Aha!"
over my sanctuary when it was desecrated and over the land of Israel when it was
laid waste and over the people of Judah
when they went into exile, 4 therefore
I am going to give you to the people of
the East as a possession. They will set up
their camps and pitch their tents among
you; they will eat your fruit and drink
your milk. 5 I will turn Rabbah into a pasture for camels and Ammon into a resting place for sheep. Then you will know
that I am the LORD. 6 For this is what the
Sovereign LORD says: Because you have
clapped your hands and stamped your
feet, rejoicing with all the malice of your
heart against the land of Israel, 7 therefore I will stretch out my hand against
you and give you as plunder to the nations. I will wipe you out from among
the nations and exterminate you from
the countries. I will destroy you, and you
will know that I am the LORD.'"
8 "This is what the Sovereign LORD
says: 'Because Moab and Seir said,
"Look, Judah has become like all the other nations," 9 therefore I will expose the
flank of Moab, beginning at its frontier
towns — Beth Jeshimoth, Baal Meon and
Kiriathaim — the glory of that land. 10 I
will give Moab along with the Ammonites to the people of the East as a possession, so that the Ammonites will not be
remembered among the nations; 11 and
I will inflict punishment on Moab. Then
they will know that I am the LORD.'"
12 "This is what the Sovereign LORD
says: 'Because Edom took revenge on
Judah and became very guilty by doing
so, 13 therefore this is what the Sovereign
LORD says: I will stretch out my hand
against Edom and kill both man and
beast. I will lay it waste, and from Teman
to Dedan they will fall by the sword. 14 I
will take vengeance on Edom by the hand
of my people Israel, and they will deal
with Edom in accordance with my anger
and my wrath; they will know my vengeance, declares the Sovereign LORD.'"
15 "This is what the Sovereign LORD
says: 'Because the Philistines acted in
vengeance and took revenge with malice
in their hearts, and with ancient hostility
sought to destroy Judah, 16 therefore this is
what the Sovereign LORD says: I am about
to stretch out my hand against the Philistines, and I will wipe out the Kerethites
and destroy those remaining along the
coast. 17 I will carry out great vengeance
on them and punish them in my wrath.
Then they will know that I am the LORD,
when I take vengeance on them.'"

26 In the eleventh month of the
twelfth[a] year, on the first day of the
month, the word of the LORD came to me:
2 "Son of man, because Tyre has said of
Jerusalem, 'Aha! The gate to the nations
is broken, and its doors have swung open
to me; now that she lies in ruins I will
prosper,' 3 therefore this is what the Sovereign LORD says: I am against you, Tyre,
and I will bring many nations against
you, like the sea casting up its waves.
4 They will destroy the walls of Tyre and
pull down her towers; I will scrape away
her rubble and make her a bare rock.
5 Out in the sea she will become a place
to spread fishnets, for I have spoken, declares the Sovereign LORD. She will become plunder for the nations, 6 and her
settlements on the mainland will be ravaged by the sword. Then they will know
that I am the LORD.
7 "For this is what the Sovereign LORD
says: From the north I am going to bring
against Tyre Nebuchadnezzar[b] king of
Babylon, king of kings, with horses and
chariots, with horsemen and a great
army. 8 He will ravage your settlements on
the mainland with the sword; he will set
up siege works against you, build a ramp

[a] 1 Probable reading of the original Hebrew text; Masoretic Text does not have *month of the twelfth*.
[b] 7 Hebrew *Nebuchadrezzar,* of which *Nebuchadnezzar* is a variant; here and often in Ezekiel and Jeremiah

up to your walls and raise his shields
against you. 9He will direct the blows of
his battering rams against your walls and
demolish your towers with his weapons.
10His horses will be so many that they will
cover you with dust. Your walls will tremble at the noise of the warhorses, wagons
and chariots when he enters your gates as
men enter a city whose walls have been
broken through.
11The hooves of his
horses will trample all your streets; he
will kill your people with the sword, and
your strong pillars will fall to the ground.
12They will plunder your wealth and loot
your merchandise; they will break down
your walls and demolish your fine houses
and throw your stones, timber and rubble into the sea.
13I will put an end to your
noisy songs, and the music of your harps
will be heard no more.
14I will make you a
bare rock, and you will become a place to
spread fishnets. You will never be rebuilt,
for I the LORD have spoken, declares the
Sovereign LORD.

15"This is what the Sovereign LORD
says to Tyre: Will not the coastlands
tremble at the sound of your fall, when
the wounded groan and the slaughter
takes place in you?
16Then all the princes of the coast will step down from their
thrones and lay aside their robes and
take off their embroidered garments.
Clothed with terror, they will sit on the
ground, trembling every moment, appalled at you.
17Then they will take up a
lament concerning you and say to you:

"'How you are destroyed, city of
renown,
peopled by men of the sea!
You were a power on the seas,
you and your citizens;
you put your terror
on all who lived there.
18Now the coastlands tremble
on the day of your fall;
the islands in the sea
are terrified at your collapse.'

19"This is what the Sovereign LORD
says: When I make you a desolate city,
like cities no longer inhabited, and when
I bring the ocean depths over you and its
vast waters cover you,
20then I will bring
you down with those who go down to the
pit, to the people of long ago. I will make
you dwell in the earth below, as in ancient ruins, with those who go down to
the pit, and you will not return or take
your place[a] in the land of the living.
21I
will bring you to a horrible end and you
will be no more. You will be sought, but
you will never again be found, declares
the Sovereign LORD."

27 The word of the LORD came to me:
2"Son of man, take up a lament concerning Tyre.
3Say to Tyre, situated at the
gateway to the sea, merchant of peoples
on many coasts, 'This is what the Sovereign LORD says:

"'You say, Tyre,
"I am perfect in beauty."
4Your domain was on the high seas;
your builders brought your beauty
to perfection.
5They made all your timbers
of juniper from Senir[b];
they took a cedar from Lebanon
to make a mast for you.
6Of oaks from Bashan
they made your oars;
of cypress wood[c] from the coasts of
Cyprus
they made your deck, adorned with
ivory.
7Fine embroidered linen from Egypt
was your sail
and served as your banner;
your awnings were of blue and purple
from the coasts of Elishah.
8Men of Sidon and Arvad were your
oarsmen;
your skilled men, Tyre, were aboard
as your sailors.
9Veteran craftsmen of Byblos were on
board
as shipwrights to caulk your seams.
All the ships of the sea and their
sailors
came alongside to trade for your
wares.

10"'Men of Persia, Lydia and Put
served as soldiers in your army.
They hung their shields and helmets
on your walls,
bringing you splendor.
11Men of Arvad and Helek
guarded your walls on every side;
men of Gammad
were in your towers.

[a] *20* Septuagint; Hebrew *return, and I will give glory* [b] *5* That is, Mount Hermon [c] *6* Targum; the Masoretic Text has a different division of the consonants.

They hung their shields around your
walls;
they brought your beauty to
perfection.

12 "'Tarshish did business with you because of your great wealth of goods; they exchanged silver, iron, tin and lead for your merchandise.

13 "'Greece, Tubal and Meshek did business with you; they traded human beings and articles of bronze for your wares.

14 "'Men of Beth Togarmah exchanged chariot horses, cavalry horses and mules for your merchandise.

15 "'The men of Rhodes[a] traded with you, and many coastlands were your customers; they paid you with ivory tusks and ebony.

16 "'Aram[b] did business with you because of your many products; they exchanged turquoise, purple fabric, embroidered work, fine linen, coral and rubies for your merchandise.

17 "'Judah and Israel traded with you; they exchanged wheat from Minnith and confections,[c] honey, olive oil and balm for your wares.

18 "'Damascus did business with you because of your many products and great wealth of goods. They offered wine from Helbon, wool from Zahar
19 and casks of wine from Izal in exchange for your wares: wrought iron, cassia and calamus.

20 "'Dedan traded in saddle blankets with you.

21 "'Arabia and all the princes of Kedar were your customers; they did business with you in lambs, rams and goats.

22 "'The merchants of Sheba and Raamah traded with you; for your merchandise they exchanged the finest of all kinds of spices and precious stones, and gold.

23 "'Harran, Kanneh and Eden and merchants of Sheba, Ashur and Kilmad traded with you.
24 In your marketplace they traded with you beautiful garments, blue fabric, embroidered work and multicolored rugs with cords twisted and tightly knotted.

25 "'The ships of Tarshish serve
as carriers for your wares.
You are filled with heavy cargo
as you sail the sea.
26 Your oarsmen take you
out to the high seas.
But the east wind will break you to
pieces
far out at sea.
27 Your wealth, merchandise and wares,
your mariners, sailors and
shipwrights,
your merchants and all your soldiers,
and everyone else on board
will sink into the heart of the sea
on the day of your shipwreck.
28 The shorelands will quake
when your sailors cry out.
29 All who handle the oars
will abandon their ships;
the mariners and all the sailors
will stand on the shore.
30 They will raise their voice
and cry bitterly over you;
they will sprinkle dust on their heads
and roll in ashes.
31 They will shave their heads because
of you
and will put on sackcloth.
They will weep over you with anguish
of soul
and with bitter mourning.
32 As they wail and mourn over you,
they will take up a lament
concerning you:
"Who was ever silenced like Tyre,
surrounded by the sea?"
33 When your merchandise went out on
the seas,
you satisfied many nations;
with your great wealth and your wares
you enriched the kings of the earth.
34 Now you are shattered by the sea
in the depths of the waters;
your wares and all your company
have gone down with you.
35 All who live in the coastlands
are appalled at you;
their kings shudder with horror
and their faces are distorted with
fear.
36 The merchants among the nations
scoff at you;
you have come to a horrible end
and will be no more.'"

28 The word of the LORD came to me:
2 "Son of man, say to the ruler of Tyre,
'This is what the Sovereign LORD says:

[a] *15* Septuagint; Hebrew *Dedan* [b] *16* Most Hebrew manuscripts; some Hebrew manuscripts and Syriac *Edom* [c] *17* The meaning of the Hebrew for this word is uncertain.

"'In the pride of your heart
you say, "I am a god;
I sit on the throne of a god
in the heart of the seas."
But you are a mere mortal and not a god,
though you think you are as wise as a god.
3 Are you wiser than Daniel[a]?
Is no secret hidden from you?
4 By your wisdom and understanding
you have gained wealth for yourself
and amassed gold and silver
in your treasuries.
5 By your great skill in trading
you have increased your wealth,
and because of your wealth
your heart has grown proud.

6 "'Therefore this is what the Sovereign LORD says:

"'Because you think you are wise,
as wise as a god,
7 I am going to bring foreigners against you,
the most ruthless of nations;
they will draw their swords against
your beauty and wisdom
and pierce your shining splendor.
8 They will bring you down to the pit,
and you will die a violent death
in the heart of the seas.
9 Will you then say, "I am a god,"
in the presence of those who kill you?
You will be but a mortal, not a god,
in the hands of those who slay you.
10 You will die the death of the uncircumcised
at the hands of foreigners.

I have spoken, declares the Sovereign LORD.'"

11 The word of the LORD came to me:
12 "Son of man, take up a lament concerning the king of Tyre and say to him:
'This is what the Sovereign LORD says:

"'You were the seal of perfection,
full of wisdom and perfect in beauty.
13 You were in Eden,
the garden of God;
every precious stone adorned you:
carnelian, chrysolite and emerald,
topaz, onyx and jasper,
lapis lazuli, turquoise and beryl.[b]
Your settings and mountings[c] were made of gold;
on the day you were created they were prepared.
14 You were anointed as a guardian cherub,
for so I ordained you.
You were on the holy mount of God;
you walked among the fiery stones.
15 You were blameless in your ways
from the day you were created
till wickedness was found in you.
16 Through your widespread trade
you were filled with violence,
and you sinned.
So I drove you in disgrace from the mount of God,
and I expelled you, guardian cherub,
from among the fiery stones.
17 Your heart became proud
on account of your beauty,
and you corrupted your wisdom
because of your splendor.
So I threw you to the earth;
I made a spectacle of you before kings.
18 By your many sins and dishonest trade
you have desecrated your sanctuaries.
So I made a fire come out from you,
and it consumed you,
and I reduced you to ashes on the ground
in the sight of all who were watching.
19 All the nations who knew you
are appalled at you;
you have come to a horrible end
and will be no more.'"

20 The word of the LORD came to me:
21 "Son of man, set your face against Sidon; prophesy against her
22 and say:
'This is what the Sovereign LORD says:

"'I am against you, Sidon,
and among you I will display my glory.
You will know that I am the LORD,
when I inflict punishment on you
and within you am proved to be holy.

[a] 3 Or *Danel,* a man of renown in ancient literature [b] 13 The precise identification of some of these precious stones is uncertain. [c] 13 The meaning of the Hebrew for this phrase is uncertain.

23 I will send a plague upon you
and make blood flow in your streets.
The slain will fall within you,
with the sword against you on every
side.
Then you will know that I am the LORD.

24 " 'No longer will the people of Israel
have malicious neighbors who are painful briers and sharp thorns. Then they
will know that I am the Sovereign LORD.
25 " 'This is what the Sovereign LORD
says: When I gather the people of Israel
from the nations where they have been
scattered, I will be proved holy through
them in the sight of the nations. Then they
will live in their own land, which I gave to
my servant Jacob. 26 They will live there
in safety and will build houses and plant
vineyards; they will live in safety when I
inflict punishment on all their neighbors
who maligned them. Then they will know
that I am the LORD their God.' "

29 In the tenth year, in the tenth month
on the twelfth day, the word of the
LORD came to me: 2 "Son of man, set your
face against Pharaoh king of Egypt and
prophesy against him and against all
Egypt. 3 Speak to him and say: 'This is
what the Sovereign LORD says:

" 'I am against you, Pharaoh king of
Egypt,
you great monster lying among your
streams.
You say, "The Nile belongs to me;
I made it for myself."
4 But I will put hooks in your jaws
and make the fish of your streams
stick to your scales.
I will pull you out from among your
streams,
with all the fish sticking to your
scales.
5 I will leave you in the desert,
you and all the fish of your streams.
You will fall on the open field
and not be gathered or picked up.
I will give you as food
to the beasts of the earth and the
birds of the sky.

6 Then all who live in Egypt will know
that I am the LORD.

" 'You have been a staff of reed for the
people of Israel. 7 When they grasped
you with their hands, you splintered and
you tore open their shoulders; when they
leaned on you, you broke and their backs
were wrenched.[a]
8 " 'Therefore this is what the Sovereign
LORD says: I will bring a sword against
you and kill both man and beast. 9 Egypt
will become a desolate wasteland. Then
they will know that I am the LORD.
" 'Because you said, "The Nile is mine; I
made it," 10 therefore I am against you and
against your streams, and I will make the
land of Egypt a ruin and a desolate waste
from Migdol to Aswan, as far as the border of Cush.[b] 11 The foot of neither man
nor beast will pass through it; no one will
live there for forty years. 12 I will make the
land of Egypt desolate among devastated
lands, and her cities will lie desolate forty
years among ruined cities. And I will disperse the Egyptians among the nations
and scatter them through the countries.
13 " 'Yet this is what the Sovereign LORD
says: At the end of forty years I will gather the Egyptians from the nations where
they were scattered. 14 I will bring them
back from captivity and return them to
Upper Egypt, the land of their ancestry.
There they will be a lowly kingdom. 15 It
will be the lowliest of kingdoms and will
never again exalt itself above the other nations. I will make it so weak that it
will never again rule over the nations.
16 Egypt will no longer be a source of confidence for the people of Israel but will be
a reminder of their sin in turning to her
for help. Then they will know that I am
the Sovereign LORD.' "
17 In the twenty-seventh year, in the
first month on the first day, the word of
the LORD came to me: 18 "Son of man,
Nebuchadnezzar king of Babylon drove
his army in a hard campaign against
Tyre; every head was rubbed bare and
every shoulder made raw. Yet he and his
army got no reward from the campaign
he led against Tyre. 19 Therefore this is
what the Sovereign LORD says: I am going
to give Egypt to Nebuchadnezzar king of
Babylon, and he will carry off its wealth.
He will loot and plunder the land as pay
for his army. 20 I have given him Egypt as
a reward for his efforts because he and
his army did it for me, declares the Sovereign LORD.

[a] 7 Syriac (see also Septuagint and Vulgate); Hebrew *and you caused their backs to stand* [b] 10 That is, the upper Nile region

21 "On that day I will make a horn[a] grow for the Israelites, and I will open your mouth among them. Then they will know that I am the LORD."

30 The word of the LORD came to me:
2 "Son of man, prophesy and say:
'This is what the Sovereign LORD says:

" 'Wail and say,
"Alas for that day!"
3 For the day is near,
the day of the LORD is near—
a day of clouds,
a time of doom for the nations.
4 A sword will come against Egypt,
and anguish will come upon Cush.[b]
When the slain fall in Egypt,
her wealth will be carried away
and her foundations torn down.

5 Cush and Libya, Lydia and all Arabia, Kub and the people of the covenant land will fall by the sword along with Egypt.

6 " 'This is what the LORD says:

" 'The allies of Egypt will fall
and her proud strength will fail.
From Migdol to Aswan
they will fall by the sword within her,
declares the Sovereign LORD.
7 " 'They will be desolate
among desolate lands,
and their cities will lie
among ruined cities.
8 Then they will know that I am the
LORD,
when I set fire to Egypt
and all her helpers are crushed.

9 " 'On that day messengers will go out
from me in ships to frighten Cush out of
her complacency. Anguish will take hold
of them on the day of Egypt's doom, for it
is sure to come.

10 " 'This is what the Sovereign LORD says:

" 'I will put an end to the hordes of
Egypt
by the hand of Nebuchadnezzar
king of Babylon.
11 He and his army—the most ruthless
of nations—
will be brought in to destroy the
land.
They will draw their swords against
Egypt
and fill the land with the slain.
12 I will dry up the waters of the Nile
and sell the land to an evil nation;
by the hand of foreigners
I will lay waste the land and
everything in it.

I the LORD have spoken.

13 " 'This is what the Sovereign LORD says:

" 'I will destroy the idols
and put an end to the images in
Memphis.
No longer will there be a prince in
Egypt,
and I will spread fear throughout
the land.
14 I will lay waste Upper Egypt,
set fire to Zoan
and inflict punishment on Thebes.
15 I will pour out my wrath on Pelusium,
the stronghold of Egypt,
and wipe out the hordes of Thebes.
16 I will set fire to Egypt;
Pelusium will writhe in agony.
Thebes will be taken by storm;
Memphis will be in constant
distress.
17 The young men of Heliopolis and
Bubastis
will fall by the sword,
and the cities themselves will go
into captivity.
18 Dark will be the day at Tahpanhes
when I break the yoke of Egypt;
there her proud strength will come
to an end.
She will be covered with clouds,
and her villages will go into
captivity.
19 So I will inflict punishment on Egypt,
and they will know that I am the
LORD.' "

20 In the eleventh year, in the first
month on the seventh day, the word of
the LORD came to me: 21 "Son of man, I
have broken the arm of Pharaoh king
of Egypt. It has not been bound up to be
healed or put in a splint so that it may
become strong enough to hold a sword.
22 Therefore this is what the Sovereign
LORD says: I am against Pharaoh king
of Egypt. I will break both his arms, the
good arm as well as the broken one, and

a 21 *Horn* here symbolizes strength.
b 4 That is, the upper Nile region; also in verses 5 and 9

make the sword fall from his hand. 23I
will disperse the Egyptians among the
nations and scatter them through the
countries. 24I will strengthen the arms
of the king of Babylon and put my sword
in his hand, but I will break the arms of
Pharaoh, and he will groan before him
like a mortally wounded man. 25I will
strengthen the arms of the king of Babylon, but the arms of Pharaoh will fall
limp. Then they will know that I am the
LORD, when I put my sword into the hand
of the king of Babylon and he brandish-
es it against Egypt. 26I will disperse the
Egyptians among the nations and scatter
them through the countries. Then they
will know that I am the LORD."

31 In the eleventh year, in the third
month on the first day, the word
of the LORD came to me: 2"Son of man,
say to Pharaoh king of Egypt and to his
hordes:

"'Who can be compared with you in
 majesty?
3Consider Assyria, once a cedar in
 Lebanon,
 with beautiful branches
 overshadowing the forest;
it towered on high,
 its top above the thick foliage.
4The waters nourished it,
 deep springs made it grow tall;
their streams flowed
 all around its base
and sent their channels
 to all the trees of the field.
5So it towered higher
 than all the trees of the field;
its boughs increased
 and its branches grew long,
 spreading because of abundant
 waters.
6All the birds of the sky
 nested in its boughs,
all the animals of the wild
 gave birth under its branches;
all the great nations
 lived in its shade.
7It was majestic in beauty,
 with its spreading boughs,
for its roots went down
 to abundant waters.
8The cedars in the garden of God
 could not rival it,
nor could the junipers
 equal its boughs,
nor could the plane trees
 compare with its branches—
no tree in the garden of God
 could match its beauty.
9I made it beautiful
 with abundant branches,
the envy of all the trees of Eden
 in the garden of God.

10"'Therefore this is what the Sovereign
LORD says: Because the great cedar towered over the thick foliage, and because
it was proud of its height, 11I gave it into
the hands of the ruler of the nations, for
him to deal with according to its wickedness. I cast it aside, 12and the most ruthless of foreign nations cut it down and left
it. Its boughs fell on the mountains and
in all the valleys; its branches lay broken
in all the ravines of the land. All the nations of the earth came out from under its
shade and left it. 13All the birds settled on
the fallen tree, and all the wild animals
lived among its branches. 14Therefore
no other trees by the waters are ever to
tower proudly on high, lifting their tops
above the thick foliage. No other trees
so well-watered are ever to reach such a
height; they are all destined for death, for
the earth below, among mortals who go
down to the realm of the dead.

15"'This is what the Sovereign LORD
says: On the day it was brought down to
the realm of the dead I covered the deep
springs with mourning for it; I held back
its streams, and its abundant waters
were restrained. Because of it I clothed
Lebanon with gloom, and all the trees of
the field withered away. 16I made the nations tremble at the sound of its fall when
I brought it down to the realm of the dead
to be with those who go down to the pit.
Then all the trees of Eden, the choicest
and best of Lebanon, the well-watered
trees, were consoled in the earth below. 17They too, like the great cedar, had
gone down to the realm of the dead, to
those killed by the sword, along with the
armed men who lived in its shade among
the nations.

18"'Which of the trees of Eden can be
compared with you in splendor and majesty? Yet you, too, will be brought down
with the trees of Eden to the earth below;
you will lie among the uncircumcised,
with those killed by the sword.

"'This is Pharaoh and all his hordes,
declares the Sovereign LORD.'"

32 In the twelfth year, in the twelfth
month on the first day, the word of
the LORD came to me: 2 "Son of man, take
up a lament concerning Pharaoh king of
Egypt and say to him:

"'You are like a lion among the
nations;
you are like a monster in the seas
thrashing about in your streams,
churning the water with your feet
and muddying the streams.

3 "'This is what the Sovereign LORD
says:

"'With a great throng of people
I will cast my net over you,
and they will haul you up in my net.
4 I will throw you on the land
and hurl you on the open field.
I will let all the birds of the sky settle
on you
and all the animals of the wild
gorge themselves on you.
5 I will spread your flesh on the
mountains
and fill the valleys with your
remains.
6 I will drench the land with your
flowing blood
all the way to the mountains,
and the ravines will be filled with
your flesh.
7 When I snuff you out, I will cover the
heavens
and darken their stars;
I will cover the sun with a cloud,
and the moon will not give its light.
8 All the shining lights in the heavens
I will darken over you;
I will bring darkness over your land,
declares the Sovereign LORD.
9 I will trouble the hearts of many
peoples
when I bring about your destruction
among the nations,
among[a] lands you have not known.
10 I will cause many peoples to be
appalled at you,
and their kings will shudder with
horror because of you
when I brandish my sword before
them.
On the day of your downfall
each of them will tremble
every moment for his life.

11 "'For this is what the Sovereign LORD
says:

"'The sword of the king of Babylon
will come against you.
12 I will cause your hordes to fall
by the swords of mighty men—
the most ruthless of all nations.
They will shatter the pride of Egypt,
and all her hordes will be
overthrown.
13 I will destroy all her cattle
from beside abundant waters
no longer to be stirred by the foot of
man
or muddied by the hooves of cattle.
14 Then I will let her waters settle
and make her streams flow like oil,
declares the Sovereign LORD.
15 When I make Egypt desolate
and strip the land of everything
in it,
when I strike down all who live there,
then they will know that I am the
LORD.'

16 "This is the lament they will chant
for her. The daughters of the nations
will chant it; for Egypt and all her hordes
they will chant it, declares the Sovereign
LORD."

17 In the twelfth year, on the fifteenth
day of the month, the word of the LORD
came to me: 18 "Son of man, wail for the
hordes of Egypt and consign to the earth
below both her and the daughters of
mighty nations, along with those who
go down to the pit. 19 Say to them, 'Are
you more favored than others? Go down
and be laid among the uncircumcised.'
20 They will fall among those killed by
the sword. The sword is drawn; let her be
dragged off with all her hordes. 21 From
within the realm of the dead the mighty
leaders will say of Egypt and her allies,
'They have come down and they lie with
the uncircumcised, with those killed by
the sword.'

22 "Assyria is there with her whole
army; she is surrounded by the graves of
all her slain, all who have fallen by the
sword. 23 Their graves are in the depths
of the pit and her army lies around her
grave. All who had spread terror in the
land of the living are slain, fallen by the
sword.

[a] 9 Hebrew; Septuagint *bring you into captivity among the nations, / to*

24 “Elam is there, with all her hordes
around her grave. All of them are slain,
fallen by the sword. All who had spread
terror in the land of the living went down
uncircumcised to the earth below. They
bear their shame with those who go down
to the pit. 25 A bed is made for her among
the slain, with all her hordes around her
grave. All of them are uncircumcised,
killed by the sword. Because their terror
had spread in the land of the living, they
bear their shame with those who go down
to the pit; they are laid among the slain.

26 “Meshek and Tubal are there, with
all their hordes around their graves. All
of them are uncircumcised, killed by the
sword because they spread their terror in
the land of the living. 27 But they do not lie
with the fallen warriors of old,[a] who went
down to the realm of the dead with their
weapons of war—their swords placed under
der their heads and their shields[b] resting
on their bones—though these warriors
also had terrorized the land of the living.

28 “You too, Pharaoh, will be broken
and will lie among the uncircumcised,
with those killed by the sword.

29 “Edom is there, her kings and all her
princes; despite their power, they are
laid with those killed by the sword. They
lie with the uncircumcised, with those
who go down to the pit.

30 “All the princes of the north and all
the Sidonians are there; they went down
with the slain in disgrace despite the terror caused by their power. They lie uncircumcised with those killed by the sword
and bear their shame with those who go
down to the pit.

31 “Pharaoh—he and all his army—
will see them and he will be consoled
for all his hordes that were killed by the
sword, declares the Sovereign LORD.
32 Although I had him spread terror in
the land of the living, Pharaoh and all his
hordes will be laid among the uncircumcised, with those killed by the sword, declares the Sovereign LORD.”

33 The word of the LORD came to me:
2 “Son of man, speak to your people
and say to them: ‘When I bring the sword
against a land, and the people of the land
choose one of their men and make him
their watchman, 3 and he sees the sword
coming against the land and blows the
trumpet to warn the people, 4 then if anyone hears the trumpet but does not heed
the warning and the sword comes and
takes their life, their blood will be on their
own head. 5 Since they heard the sound of
the trumpet but did not heed the warning,
their blood will be on their own head. If
they had heeded the warning, they would
have saved themselves. 6 But if the watchman sees the sword coming and does not
blow the trumpet to warn the people and
the sword comes and takes someone’s life,
that person’s life will be taken because of
their sin, but I will hold the watchman accountable for their blood.’

7 “Son of man, I have made you a watchman for the people of Israel; so hear the
word I speak and give them warning
from me. 8 When I say to the wicked, ‘You
wicked person, you will surely die,’ and
you do not speak out to dissuade them
from their ways, that wicked person will
die for[c] their sin, and I will hold you accountable for their blood. 9 But if you do
warn the wicked person to turn from
their ways and they do not do so, they
will die for their sin, though you yourself
will be saved.

10 “Son of man, say to the Israelites, ‘This
is what you are saying: “Our offenses and
sins weigh us down, and we are wasting
away because of[d] them. How then can we
live?” ’ 11 Say to them, ‘As surely as I live,
declares the Sovereign LORD, I take no
pleasure in the death of the wicked, but
rather that they turn from their ways and
live. Turn! Turn from your evil ways! Why
will you die, people of Israel?’

12 “Therefore, son of man, say to your
people, ‘If someone who is righteous
disobeys, that person’s former righteousness will count for nothing. And
if someone who is wicked repents, that
person’s former wickedness will not
bring condemnation. The righteous person who sins will not be allowed to live
even though they were formerly righteous.’ 13 If I tell a righteous person that
they will surely live, but then they trust
in their righteousness and do evil, none
of the righteous things that person has
done will be remembered; they will die
for the evil they have done. 14 And if I say
to a wicked person, ‘You will surely die,’

[a] 27 Septuagint; Hebrew *warriors who were uncircumcised* [b] 27 Probable reading of the original Hebrew text; Masoretic Text *punishment* [c] 8 Or *in*; also in verse 9 [d] 10 Or *away in*

but they then turn away from their sin
and do what is just and right— 15if they
give back what they took in pledge for a
loan, return what they have stolen, follow the decrees that give life, and do no
evil—that person will surely live; they
will not die. 16None of the sins that person has committed will be remembered
against them. They have done what is
just and right; they will surely live.

17"Yet your people say, 'The way of the
Lord is not just.' But it is their way that
is not just. 18If a righteous person turns
from their righteousness and does evil,
they will die for it. 19And if a wicked person turns away from their wickedness
and does what is just and right, they will
live by doing so. 20Yet you Israelites say,
'The way of the Lord is not just.' But I will
judge each of you according to your own
ways."

21In the twelfth year of our exile, in the
tenth month on the fifth day, a man who
had escaped from Jerusalem came to me
and said, "The city has fallen!" 22Now
the evening before the man arrived,
the hand of the LORD was on me, and he
opened my mouth before the man came
to me in the morning. So my mouth was
opened and I was no longer silent.

23Then the word of the LORD came to
me: 24"Son of man, the people living in
those ruins in the land of Israel are saying, 'Abraham was only one man, yet he
possessed the land. But we are many;
surely the land has been given to us
as our possession.' 25Therefore say to
them, 'This is what the Sovereign LORD
says: Since you eat meat with the blood
still in it and look to your idols and shed
blood, should you then possess the land?
26You rely on your sword, you do detestable things, and each of you defiles his
neighbor's wife. Should you then possess
the land?'

27"Say this to them: 'This is what the
Sovereign LORD says: As surely as I live,
those who are left in the ruins will fall by
the sword, those out in the country I will
give to the wild animals to be devoured,
and those in strongholds and caves will
die of a plague. 28I will make the land a
desolate waste, and her proud strength
will come to an end, and the mountains of
Israel will become desolate so that no one
will cross them. 29Then they will know
that I am the LORD, when I have made the
land a desolate waste because of all the
detestable things they have done.'

30"As for you, son of man, your people are talking together about you by
the walls and at the doors of the houses,
saying to each other, 'Come and hear the
message that has come from the LORD.'
31My people come to you, as they usually
do, and sit before you to hear your words,
but they do not put them into practice.
Their mouths speak of love, but their
hearts are greedy for unjust gain. 32In-
deed, to them you are nothing more than
one who sings love songs with a beautiful
voice and plays an instrument well, for
they hear your words but do not put them
into practice.

33"When all this comes true—and it
surely will—then they will know that a
prophet has been among them."

34 The word of the LORD came to me:
2"Son of man, prophesy against the
shepherds of Israel; prophesy and say to
them: 'This is what the Sovereign LORD
says: Woe to you shepherds of Israel who
only take care of yourselves! Should not
shepherds take care of the flock? 3You
eat the curds, clothe yourselves with the
wool and slaughter the choice animals,
but you do not take care of the flock.
4You have not strengthened the weak or
healed the sick or bound up the injured.
You have not brought back the strays
or searched for the lost. You have ruled
them harshly and brutally. 5So they were
scattered because there was no shepherd, and when they were scattered they
became food for all the wild animals.
6My sheep wandered over all the mountains and on every high hill. They were
scattered over the whole earth, and no
one searched or looked for them.

7"'Therefore, you shepherds, hear the
word of the LORD: 8As surely as I live, declares the Sovereign LORD, because my
flock lacks a shepherd and so has been
plundered and has become food for all
the wild animals, and because my shepherds did not search for my flock but
cared for themselves rather than for my
flock, 9therefore, you shepherds, hear the
word of the LORD: 10This is what the Sovereign LORD says: I am against the shepherds and will hold them accountable for
my flock. I will remove them from tending the flock so that the shepherds can
no longer feed themselves. I will rescue

my flock from their mouths, and it will
no longer be food for them.
[11]“‘For this is what the Sovereign LORD
says: I myself will search for my sheep and
look after them. [12]As a shepherd looks after his scattered flock when he is with
them, so will I look after my sheep. I will
rescue them from all the places where
they were scattered on a day of clouds
and darkness. [13]I will bring them out
from the nations and gather them from
the countries, and I will bring them into
their own land. I will pasture them on
the mountains of Israel, in the ravines
and in all the settlements in the land. [14]I
will tend them in a good pasture, and the
mountain heights of Israel will be their
grazing land. There they will lie down
in good grazing land, and there they will
feed in a rich pasture on the mountains of
Israel. [15]I myself will tend my sheep and
have them lie down, declares the Sovereign LORD. [16]I will search for the lost and
bring back the strays. I will bind up the
injured and strengthen the weak, but the
sleek and the strong I will destroy. I will
shepherd the flock with justice.
[17]“‘As for you, my flock, this is what
the Sovereign LORD says: I will judge
between one sheep and another, and between rams and goats. [18]Is it not enough
for you to feed on the good pasture? Must
you also trample the rest of your pasture
with your feet? Is it not enough for you to
drink clear water? Must you also mud-
dy the rest with your feet? [19]Must my
flock feed on what you have trampled
and drink what you have muddied with
your feet?
[20]“‘Therefore this is what the Sovereign LORD says to them: See, I myself will
judge between the fat sheep and the lean
sheep. [21]Because you shove with flank
and shoulder, butting all the weak sheep
with your horns until you have driven
them away, [22]I will save my flock, and
they will no longer be plundered. I will
judge between one sheep and another.
[23]I will place over them one shepherd,
my servant David, and he will tend them;
he will tend them and be their shepherd.
[24]I the LORD will be their God, and my
servant David will be prince among
them. I the LORD have spoken.
[25]“‘I will make a covenant of peace
with them and rid the land of savage
beasts so that they may live in the wilderness and sleep in the forests in safety. [26]I will make them and the places
surrounding my hill a blessing.[a] I will
send down showers in season; there
will be showers of blessing. [27]The trees
will yield their fruit and the ground will
yield its crops; the people will be secure
in their land. They will know that I am
the LORD, when I break the bars of their
yoke and rescue them from the hands of
those who enslaved them. [28]They will no
longer be plundered by the nations, nor
will wild animals devour them. They will
live in safety, and no one will make them
afraid. [29]I will provide for them a land
renowned for its crops, and they will no
longer be victims of famine in the land
or bear the scorn of the nations. [30]Then
they will know that I, the LORD their
God, am with them and that they, the
Israelites, are my people, declares the
Sovereign LORD. [31]You are my sheep, the
sheep of my pasture, and I am your God,
declares the Sovereign LORD.’ ”

35 The word of the LORD came to me:
[2]“Son of man, set your face against
Mount Seir; prophesy against it [3]and say:
‘This is what the Sovereign LORD says: I
am against you, Mount Seir, and I will
stretch out my hand against you and
make you a desolate waste. [4]I will turn
your towns into ruins and you will be
desolate. Then you will know that I am
the LORD.
[5]“‘Because you harbored an ancient
hostility and delivered the Israelites over
to the sword at the time of their calamity, the time their punishment reached
its climax, [6]therefore as surely as I live,
declares the Sovereign LORD, I will give
you over to bloodshed and it will pursue
you. Since you did not hate bloodshed,
bloodshed will pursue you. [7]I will make
Mount Seir a desolate waste and cut off
from it all who come and go. [8]I will fill
your mountains with the slain; those
killed by the sword will fall on your hills
and in your valleys and in all your ravines. [9]I will make you desolate forever;
your towns will not be inhabited. Then
you will know that I am the LORD.
[10]“‘Because you have said, “These two

[a] 26 Or *I will cause them and the places surrounding my hill to be named in blessings* (see Gen. 48:20); or *I will cause them and the places surrounding my hill to be seen as blessed*

nations and countries will be ours and
we will take possession of them," even
though I the LORD was there, [11]therefore
as surely as I live, declares the Sovereign LORD, I will treat you in accordance
with the anger and jealousy you showed
in your hatred of them and I will make
myself known among them when I judge
you. [12]Then you will know that I the
LORD have heard all the contemptible
things you have said against the mountains of Israel. You said, "They have been
laid waste and have been given over to us
to devour." [13]You boasted against me and
spoke against me without restraint, and
I heard it. [14]This is what the Sovereign
LORD says: While the whole earth rejoices, I will make you desolate. [15]Because
you rejoiced when the inheritance of Israel became desolate, that is how I will
treat you. You will be desolate, Mount
Seir, you and all of Edom. Then they will
know that I am the LORD.' "

36 "Son of man, prophesy to the mountains of Israel and say, 'Mountains
of Israel, hear the word of the LORD.
[2]This is what the Sovereign LORD says:
The enemy said of you, "Aha! The ancient heights have become our possession." ' [3]Therefore prophesy and say,
'This is what the Sovereign LORD says:
Because they ravaged and crushed you
from every side so that you became the
possession of the rest of the nations and
the object of people's malicious talk and
slander, [4]therefore, mountains of Israel, hear the word of the Sovereign LORD:
This is what the Sovereign LORD says
to the mountains and hills, to the ravines and valleys, to the desolate ruins
and the deserted towns that have been
plundered and ridiculed by the rest of
the nations around you — [5]this is what
the Sovereign LORD says: In my burning zeal I have spoken against the rest
of the nations, and against all Edom,
for with glee and with malice in their
hearts they made my land their own
possession so that they might plunder
its pastureland.' [6]Therefore prophesy
concerning the land of Israel and say to
the mountains and hills, to the ravines
and valleys: 'This is what the Sovereign
LORD says: I speak in my jealous wrath
because you have suffered the scorn of
the nations. [7]Therefore this is what the
Sovereign LORD says: I swear with uplifted hand that the nations around you will
also suffer scorn.

[8]" 'But you, mountains of Israel, will
produce branches and fruit for my people Israel, for they will soon come home.
[9]I am concerned for you and will look on
you with favor; you will be plowed and
sown, [10]and I will cause many people to
live on you — yes, all of Israel. The towns
will be inhabited and the ruins rebuilt.
[11]I will increase the number of people
and animals living on you, and they will
be fruitful and become numerous. I will
settle people on you as in the past and will
make you prosper more than before. Then
you will know that I am the LORD. [12]I will
cause people, my people Israel, to live on
you. They will possess you, and you will
be their inheritance; you will never again
deprive them of their children.

[13]" 'This is what the Sovereign LORD
says: Because some say to you, "You
devour people and deprive your nation
of its children," [14]therefore you will no
longer devour people or make your nation childless, declares the Sovereign
LORD. [15]No longer will I make you hear
the taunts of the nations, and no longer
will you suffer the scorn of the peoples
or cause your nation to fall, declares the
Sovereign LORD.' "

[16]Again the word of the LORD came to
me: [17]"Son of man, when the people of
Israel were living in their own land, they
defiled it by their conduct and their actions. Their conduct was like a woman's
monthly uncleanness in my sight. [18]So I
poured out my wrath on them because
they had shed blood in the land and because they had defiled it with their idols.
[19]I dispersed them among the nations,
and they were scattered through the
countries; I judged them according to
their conduct and their actions. [20]And
wherever they went among the nations
they profaned my holy name, for it was
said of them, 'These are the LORD's people, and yet they had to leave his land.'
[21]I had concern for my holy name, which
the people of Israel profaned among the
nations where they had gone.

[22]"Therefore say to the Israelites, 'This
is what the Sovereign LORD says: It is
not for your sake, people of Israel, that I
am going to do these things, but for the
sake of my holy name, which you have
profaned among the nations where you

have gone. 23I will show the holiness of my great name, which has been profaned among the nations, the name you have profaned among them. Then the nations will know that I am the LORD, declares the Sovereign LORD, when I am proved holy through you before their eyes.

24"'For I will take you out of the nations; I will gather you from all the countries and bring you back into your own land. 25I will sprinkle clean water on you, and you will be clean; I will cleanse you from all your impurities and from all your idols. 26I will give you a new heart and put a new spirit in you; I will remove from you your heart of stone and give you a heart of flesh. 27And I will put my Spirit in you and move you to follow my decrees and be careful to keep my laws. 28Then you will live in the land I gave your ancestors; you will be my people, and I will be your God. 29I will save you from all your uncleanness. I will call for the grain and make it plentiful and will not bring famine upon you. 30I will increase the fruit of the trees and the crops of the field, so that you will no longer suffer disgrace among the nations because of famine. 31Then you will remember your evil ways and wicked deeds, and you will loathe yourselves for your sins and detestable practices. 32I want you to know that I am not doing this for your sake, declares the Sovereign LORD. Be ashamed and disgraced for your conduct, people of Israel!

33"'This is what the Sovereign LORD says: On the day I cleanse you from all your sins, I will resettle your towns, and the ruins will be rebuilt. 34The desolate land will be cultivated instead of lying desolate in the sight of all who pass through it. 35They will say, "This land that was laid waste has become like the garden of Eden; the cities that were lying in ruins, desolate and destroyed, are now fortified and inhabited." 36Then the nations around you that remain will know that I the LORD have rebuilt what was destroyed and have replanted what was desolate. I the LORD have spoken, and I will do it.'

37"This is what the Sovereign LORD says: Once again I will yield to Israel's plea and do this for them: I will make their people as numerous as sheep, 38as numerous as the flocks for offerings at Jerusalem during her appointed festivals. So will the ruined cities be filled with flocks of people. Then they will know that I am the LORD."

37 The hand of the LORD was on me, and he brought me out by the Spirit of the LORD and set me in the middle of a valley; it was full of bones. 2He led me back and forth among them, and I saw a great many bones on the floor of the valley, bones that were very dry. 3He asked me, "Son of man, can these bones live?"

I said, "Sovereign LORD, you alone know."

4Then he said to me, "Prophesy to these bones and say to them, 'Dry bones, hear the word of the LORD! 5This is what the Sovereign LORD says to these bones: I will make breath[a] enter you, and you will come to life. 6I will attach tendons to you and make flesh come upon you and cover you with skin; I will put breath in you, and you will come to life. Then you will know that I am the LORD.'"

7So I prophesied as I was commanded. And as I was prophesying, there was a noise, a rattling sound, and the bones came together, bone to bone. 8I looked, and tendons and flesh appeared on them and skin covered them, but there was no breath in them.

9Then he said to me, "Prophesy to the breath; prophesy, son of man, and say to it, 'This is what the Sovereign LORD says: Come, breath, from the four winds and breathe into these slain, that they may live.'" 10So I prophesied as he commanded me, and breath entered them; they came to life and stood up on their feet—a vast army.

11Then he said to me: "Son of man, these bones are the people of Israel. They say, 'Our bones are dried up and our hope is gone; we are cut off.' 12Therefore prophesy and say to them: 'This is what the Sovereign LORD says: My people, I am going to open your graves and bring you up from them; I will bring you back to the land of Israel. 13Then you, my people, will know that I am the LORD, when I open your graves and bring you up from them. 14I will put my Spirit in you and you will live, and I will settle you in your

[a] 5 The Hebrew for this word can also mean *wind* or *spirit* (see verses 6-14).

own land. Then you will know that I the
LORD have spoken, and I have done it,
declares the LORD.' "
15The word of the LORD came to me:
16"Son of man, take a stick of wood and
write on it, 'Belonging to Judah and the
Israelites associated with him.' Then take
another stick of wood, and write on it,
'Belonging to Joseph (that is, to Ephraim)
and all the Israelites associated with him.'
17Join them together into one stick so that
they will become one in your hand.
18"When your people ask you, 'Won't
you tell us what you mean by this?'
19say to them, 'This is what the Sovereign LORD says: I am going to take the
stick of Joseph—which is in Ephraim's
hand—and of the Israelite tribes associated with him, and join it to Judah's
stick. I will make them into a single stick
of wood, and they will become one in my
hand.' 20Hold before their eyes the sticks
you have written on 21and say to them,
'This is what the Sovereign LORD says: I
will take the Israelites out of the nations
where they have gone. I will gather them
from all around and bring them back
into their own land. 22I will make them
one nation in the land, on the mountains
of Israel. There will be one king over all
of them and they will never again be two
nations or be divided into two kingdoms.
23They will no longer defile themselves
with their idols and vile images or with
any of their offenses, for I will save them
from all their sinful backsliding,[a] and I
will cleanse them. They will be my people, and I will be their God.
24" 'My servant David will be king over
them, and they will all have one shepherd. They will follow my laws and be
careful to keep my decrees. 25They will
live in the land I gave to my servant Jacob, the land where your ancestors
lived. They and their children and their
children's children will live there forever, and David my servant will be their
prince forever. 26I will make a covenant
of peace with them; it will be an everlasting covenant. I will establish them and
increase their numbers, and I will put
my sanctuary among them forever. 27My
dwelling place will be with them; I will
be their God, and they will be my people.
28Then the nations will know that I the
LORD make Israel holy, when my sanctuary is among them forever.' "

38 The word of the LORD came to me:
2"Son of man, set your face against
Gog, of the land of Magog, the chief
prince of[b] Meshek and Tubal; prophesy
against him 3and say: 'This is what the
Sovereign LORD says: I am against you,
Gog, chief prince of[c] Meshek and Tubal. 4I will turn you around, put hooks
in your jaws and bring you out with your
whole army—your horses, your horsemen fully armed, and a great horde with
large and small shields, all of them bran-
dishing their swords. 5Persia, Cush[d] and
Put will be with them, all with shields
and helmets, 6also Gomer with all its
troops, and Beth Togarmah from the far
north with all its troops—the many nations with you.
7" 'Get ready; be prepared, you and all
the hordes gathered about you, and take
command of them. 8After many days you
will be called to arms. In future years
you will invade a land that has recovered
from war, whose people were gathered
from many nations to the mountains of
Israel, which had long been desolate.
They had been brought out from the nations, and now all of them live in safety.
9You and all your troops and the many
nations with you will go up, advancing
like a storm; you will be like a cloud covering the land.
10" 'This is what the Sovereign LORD
says: On that day thoughts will come
into your mind and you will devise an
evil scheme. 11You will say, "I will invade a land of unwalled villages; I will
attack a peaceful and unsuspecting people—all of them living without walls and
without gates and bars. 12I will plunder
and loot and turn my hand against the
resettled ruins and the people gathered
from the nations, rich in livestock and
goods, living at the center of the land.[e]"
13Sheba and Dedan and the merchants
of Tarshish and all her villages[f] will say
to you, "Have you come to plunder? Have
you gathered your hordes to loot, to carry
off silver and gold, to take away livestock
and goods and to seize much plunder?" '

[a] *23* Many Hebrew manuscripts (see also Septuagint); most Hebrew manuscripts *all their dwelling places where they sinned* [b] *2* Or *the prince of Rosh,* [c] *3* Or *Gog, prince of Rosh,* [d] *5* That is, the upper Nile region [e] *12* The Hebrew for this phrase means *the navel of the earth.* [f] *13* Or *her strong lions*

14 "Therefore, son of man, prophesy
and say to Gog: 'This is what the Sovereign LORD says: In that day, when my
people Israel are living in safety, will
you not take notice of it? 15 You will come
from your place in the far north, you and
many nations with you, all of them riding
on horses, a great horde, a mighty army.
16 You will advance against my people
Israel like a cloud that covers the land.
In days to come, Gog, I will bring you
against my land, so that the nations may
know me when I am proved holy through
you before their eyes.
17 " 'This is what the Sovereign LORD
says: You are the one I spoke of in former days by my servants the prophets
of Israel. At that time they prophesied
for years that I would bring you against
them. 18 This is what will happen in that
day: When Gog attacks the land of Israel,
my hot anger will be aroused, declares
the Sovereign LORD. 19 In my zeal and fiery wrath I declare that at that time there
shall be a great earthquake in the land
of Israel. 20 The fish in the sea, the birds
in the sky, the beasts of the field, every
creature that moves along the ground,
and all the people on the face of the
earth will tremble at my presence. The
mountains will be overturned, the cliffs
will crumble and every wall will fall to
the ground. 21 I will summon a sword
against Gog on all my mountains, declares the Sovereign LORD. Every man's
sword will be against his brother. 22 I will
execute judgment on him with plague
and bloodshed; I will pour down torrents
of rain, hailstones and burning sulfur on
him and on his troops and on the many
nations with him. 23 And so I will show
my greatness and my holiness, and I will
make myself known in the sight of many
nations. Then they will know that I am
the LORD.'

39 "Son of man, prophesy against Gog
and say: 'This is what the Sovereign
LORD says: I am against you, Gog, chief
prince of[a] Meshek and Tubal. 2 I will turn
you around and drag you along. I will
bring you from the far north and send
you against the mountains of Israel.
3 Then I will strike your bow from your
left hand and make your arrows drop
from your right hand. 4 On the mountains of Israel you will fall, you and all
your troops and the nations with you. I
will give you as food to all kinds of car-
rion birds and to the wild animals. 5 You
will fall in the open field, for I have spoken, declares the Sovereign LORD. 6 I will
send fire on Magog and on those who live
in safety in the coastlands, and they will
know that I am the LORD.
7 " 'I will make known my holy name
among my people Israel. I will no longer
let my holy name be profaned, and the
nations will know that I the LORD am the
Holy One in Israel. 8 It is coming! It will
surely take place, declares the Sovereign
LORD. This is the day I have spoken of.
9 " 'Then those who live in the towns of
Israel will go out and use the weapons for
fuel and burn them up—the small and
large shields, the bows and arrows, the
war clubs and spears. For seven years
they will use them for fuel. 10 They will
not need to gather wood from the fields
or cut it from the forests, because they
will use the weapons for fuel. And they
will plunder those who plundered them
and loot those who looted them, declares
the Sovereign LORD.
11 " 'On that day I will give Gog a burial
place in Israel, in the valley of those who
travel east of the Sea. It will block the
way of travelers, because Gog and all his
hordes will be buried there. So it will be
called the Valley of Hamon Gog.[b]
12 " 'For seven months the Israelites
will be burying them in order to cleanse
the land. 13 All the people of the land will
bury them, and the day I display my glory will be a memorable day for them, declares the Sovereign LORD. 14 People will
be continually employed in cleansing the
land. They will spread out across the land
and, along with others, they will bury any
bodies that are lying on the ground.
" 'After the seven months they will carry out a more detailed search. 15 As they
go through the land, anyone who sees a
human bone will leave a marker beside it
until the gravediggers bury it in the Valley of Hamon Gog, 16 near a town called
Hamonah.[c] And so they will cleanse the
land.'
17 "Son of man, this is what the Sovereign LORD says: Call out to every kind of
bird and all the wild animals: 'Assemble

[a] 1 Or *Gog, prince of Rosh,* [b] 11 *Hamon Gog* means *hordes of Gog.* [c] 16 *Hamonah* means *horde.*

and come together from all around to
the sacrifice I am preparing for you, the
great sacrifice on the mountains of Israel. There you will eat flesh and drink
blood. 18You will eat the flesh of mighty
men and drink the blood of the princes of
the earth as if they were rams and lambs,
goats and bulls—all of them fattened
animals from Bashan. 19At the sacrifice
I am preparing for you, you will eat fat till
you are glutted and drink blood till you
are drunk. 20At my table you will eat your
fill of horses and riders, mighty men and
soldiers of every kind,' declares the Sovereign LORD.

21"I will display my glory among the
nations, and all the nations will see the
punishment I inflict and the hand I lay
on them. 22From that day forward the
people of Israel will know that I am the
LORD their God. 23And the nations will
know that the people of Israel went into
exile for their sin, because they were unfaithful to me. So I hid my face from them
and handed them over to their enemies,
and they all fell by the sword. 24I dealt
with them according to their uncleanness and their offenses, and I hid my face
from them.

25"Therefore this is what the Sovereign LORD says: I will now restore the
fortunes of Jacob[a] and will have compassion on all the people of Israel, and I will
be zealous for my holy name. 26They will
forget their shame and all the unfaithfulness they showed toward me when
they lived in safety in their land with no
one to make them afraid. 27When I have
brought them back from the nations and
have gathered them from the countries
of their enemies, I will be proved holy
through them in the sight of many nations. 28Then they will know that I am
the LORD their God, for though I sent
them into exile among the nations, I will
gather them to their own land, not leaving any behind. 29I will no longer hide
my face from them, for I will pour out my
Spirit on the people of Israel, declares the
Sovereign LORD."

40 In the twenty-fifth year of our exile, at the beginning of the year, on
the tenth of the month, in the fourteenth
year after the fall of the city—on that
very day the hand of the LORD was on me
and he took me there. 2In visions of God
he took me to the land of Israel and set
me on a very high mountain, on whose
south side were some buildings that
looked like a city. 3He took me there, and
I saw a man whose appearance was like
bronze; he was standing in the gateway
with a linen cord and a measuring rod
in his hand. 4The man said to me, "Son
of man, look carefully and listen closely
and pay attention to everything I am going to show you, for that is why you have
been brought here. Tell the people of Israel everything you see."

5I saw a wall completely surrounding
the temple area. The length of the measuring rod in the man's hand was six long
cubits,[b] each of which was a cubit and a
handbreadth. He measured the wall; it
was one measuring rod thick and one
rod high.

6Then he went to the east gate. He
climbed its steps and measured the
threshold of the gate; it was one rod deep.
7The alcoves for the guards were one rod
long and one rod wide, and the projecting walls between the alcoves were five
cubits[c] thick. And the threshold of the
gate next to the portico facing the temple was one rod deep.

8Then he measured the portico of the
gateway; 9it[d] was eight cubits[e] deep and
its jambs were two cubits[f] thick. The portico of the gateway faced the temple.

10Inside the east gate were three alcoves on each side; the three had the
same measurements, and the faces of
the projecting walls on each side had the
same measurements. 11Then he measured the width of the entrance of the
gateway; it was ten cubits and its length
was thirteen cubits.[g] 12In front of each
alcove was a wall one cubit high, and the
alcoves were six cubits square. 13Then
he measured the gateway from the top of
the rear wall of one alcove to the top of

[a] *25* Or *now bring Jacob back from captivity* [b] *5* That is, about 11 feet or about 3.2 meters; also in verse 12. The long cubit of about 21 inches or about 53 centimeters is the basic unit of measurement of length throughout chapters 40–48. [c] *7* That is, about 8 3/4 feet or about 2.7 meters; also in verse 48 [d] *8,9* Many Hebrew manuscripts, Septuagint, Vulgate and Syriac; most Hebrew manuscripts *gateway facing the temple; it was one rod deep. 9Then he measured the portico of the gateway; it* [e] *9* That is, about 14 feet or about 4.2 meters [f] *9* That is, about 3 1/2 feet or about 1 meter [g] *11* That is, about 18 feet wide and 23 feet long or about 5.3 meters wide and 6.9 meters long

the opposite one; the distance was twenty-five cubits[a] from one parapet opening to the opposite one. 14He measured
along the faces of the projecting walls all
around the inside of the gateway—sixty
cubits.[b] The measurement was up to the
portico[c] facing the courtyard.[d] 15The distance from the entrance of the gateway to
the far end of its portico was fifty cubits.[e]
16The alcoves and the projecting walls
inside the gateway were surmounted by
narrow parapet openings all around, as
was the portico; the openings all around
faced inward. The faces of the projecting
walls were decorated with palm trees.

17Then he brought me into the outer court. There I saw some rooms and
a pavement that had been constructed
all around the court; there were thirty
rooms along the pavement. 18It abut-
ted the sides of the gateways and was
as wide as they were long; this was the
lower pavement. 19Then he measured
the distance from the inside of the lower
gateway to the outside of the inner court;
it was a hundred cubits[f] on the east side
as well as on the north.

20Then he measured the length and
width of the north gate, leading into the
outer court. 21Its alcoves—three on each
side—its projecting walls and its portico
had the same measurements as those of
the first gateway. It was fifty cubits long
and twenty-five cubits wide. 22Its openings, its portico and its palm tree decorations had the same measurements as
those of the gate facing east. Seven steps
led up to it, with its portico opposite them.
23There was a gate to the inner court facing the north gate, just as there was on the
east. He measured from one gate to the
opposite one; it was a hundred cubits.

24Then he led me to the south side
and I saw the south gate. He measured
its jambs and its portico, and they had
the same measurements as the others.
25The gateway and its portico had narrow openings all around, like the openings of the others. It was fifty cubits long
and twenty-five cubits wide. 26Seven
steps led up to it, with its portico opposite them; it had palm tree decorations
on the faces of the projecting walls on
each side. 27The inner court also had a
gate facing south, and he measured from
this gate to the outer gate on the south
side; it was a hundred cubits.

28Then he brought me into the inner court through the south gate, and
he measured the south gate; it had the
same measurements as the others. 29Its
alcoves, its projecting walls and its portico had the same measurements as the
others. The gateway and its portico had
openings all around. It was fifty cubits
long and twenty-five cubits wide. 30(The
porticoes of the gateways around the inner court were twenty-five cubits wide
and five cubits deep.) 31Its portico faced
the outer court; palm trees decorated its
jambs, and eight steps led up to it.

32Then he brought me to the inner
court on the east side, and he measured
the gateway; it had the same measurements as the others. 33Its alcoves, its projecting walls and its portico had the same
measurements as the others. The gateway
and its portico had openings all around.
It was fifty cubits long and twenty-five
cubits wide. 34Its portico faced the outer
court; palm trees decorated the jambs on
either side, and eight steps led up to it.

35Then he brought me to the north
gate and measured it. It had the same
measurements as the others, 36as did its
alcoves, its projecting walls and its portico, and it had openings all around. It was
fifty cubits long and twenty-five cubits
wide. 37Its portico[g] faced the outer court;
palm trees decorated the jambs on either
side, and eight steps led up to it.

38A room with a doorway was by the
portico in each of the inner gateways,
where the burnt offerings were washed.
39In the portico of the gateway were two
tables on each side, on which the burnt
offerings, sin offerings[h] and guilt offerings were slaughtered. 40By the outside
wall of the portico of the gateway, near
the steps at the entrance of the north
gateway were two tables, and on the other side of the steps were two tables. 41So
there were four tables on one side of the
gateway and four on the other—eight ta-

[a] *13* That is, about 44 feet or about 13 meters; also in verses 21, 25, 29, 30, 33 and 36 [b] *14* That is, about 105 feet or about 32 meters [c] *14* Septuagint; Hebrew *projecting wall* [d] *14* The meaning of the Hebrew for this verse is uncertain. [e] *15* That is, about 88 feet or about 27 meters; also in verses 21, 25, 29, 33 and 36 [f] *19* That is, about 175 feet or about 53 meters; also in verses 23, 27 and 47 [g] *37* Septuagint (see also verses 31 and 34); Hebrew *jambs* [h] *39* Or *purification offerings*

bles in all—on which the sacrifices were slaughtered. 42 There were also four tables of dressed stone for the burnt offerings, each a cubit and a half long, a cubit and a half wide and a cubit high.[a] On them were placed the utensils for slaughtering the burnt offerings and the other sacrifices. 43 And double-pronged hooks, each a handbreadth[b] long, were attached to the wall all around. The tables were for the flesh of the offerings.

44 Outside the inner gate, within the inner court, were two rooms, one[c] at the side of the north gate and facing south, and another at the side of the south[d] gate and facing north. 45 He said to me, "The room facing south is for the priests who guard the temple, 46 and the room facing north is for the priests who guard the altar. These are the sons of Zadok, who are the only Levites who may draw near to the LORD to minister before him."

47 Then he measured the court: It was square—a hundred cubits long and a hundred cubits wide. And the altar was in front of the temple.

48 He brought me to the portico of the temple and measured the jambs of the portico; they were five cubits wide on either side. The width of the entrance was fourteen cubits[e] and its projecting walls were[f] three cubits[g] wide on either side. 49 The portico was twenty cubits[h] wide, and twelve[i] cubits[j] from front to back. It was reached by a flight of stairs,[k] and there were pillars on each side of the jambs.

41 Then the man brought me to the main hall and measured the jambs; the width of the jambs was six cubits[l] on each side.[m] 2 The entrance was ten cubits[n] wide, and the projecting walls on each side of it were five cubits[o] wide. He also measured the main hall; it was forty cubits long and twenty cubits wide.[p]

3 Then he went into the inner sanctuary and measured the jambs of the entrance; each was two cubits[q] wide. The entrance was six cubits wide, and the projecting walls on each side of it were seven cubits[r] wide. 4 And he measured the length of the inner sanctuary; it was twenty cubits, and its width was twenty cubits across the end of the main hall. He said to me, "This is the Most Holy Place."

5 Then he measured the wall of the temple; it was six cubits thick, and each side room around the temple was four cubits[s] wide. 6 The side rooms were on three levels, one above another, thirty on each level. There were ledges all around the wall of the temple to serve as supports for the side rooms, so that the supports were not inserted into the wall of the temple. 7 The side rooms all around the temple were wider at each successive level. The structure surrounding the temple was built in ascending stages, so that the rooms widened as one went upward. A stairway went up from the lowest floor to the top floor through the middle floor.

8 I saw that the temple had a raised base all around it, forming the foundation of the side rooms. It was the length of the rod, six long cubits. 9 The outer wall of the side rooms was five cubits thick. The open area between the side rooms of the temple 10 and the priests' rooms was twenty cubits wide all around the temple. 11 There were entrances to the side rooms from the open area, one on the north and another on the south; and the base adjoining the open area was five cubits wide all around.

12 The building facing the temple courtyard on the west side was seventy cubits[t] wide. The wall of the building was five cubits thick all around, and its length was ninety cubits.[u]

13 Then he measured the temple; it was a hundred cubits[v] long, and the temple courtyard and the building with its walls

[a] *42* That is, about 2 2/3 feet long and wide and 21 inches high or about 80 centimeters long and wide and 53 centimeters high [b] *43* That is, about 3 1/2 inches or about 9 centimeters [c] *44* Septuagint; Hebrew *were rooms for singers, which were* [d] *44* Septuagint; Hebrew *east* [e] *48* That is, about 25 feet or about 7.4 meters [f] *48* Septuagint; Hebrew *entrance was* [g] *48* That is, about 5 1/4 feet or about 1.6 meters [h] *49* That is, about 35 feet or about 11 meters [i] *49* Septuagint; Hebrew *eleven* [j] *49* That is, about 21 feet or about 6.4 meters [k] *49* Hebrew; Septuagint *Ten steps led up to it* [l] *1* That is, about 11 feet or about 3.2 meters; also in verses 3, 5 and 8 [m] *1* One Hebrew manuscript and Septuagint; most Hebrew manuscripts *side, the width of the tent* [n] *2* That is, about 18 feet or about 5.3 meters [o] *2* That is, about 8 3/4 feet or about 2.7 meters; also in verses 9, 11 and 12 [p] *2* That is, about 70 feet long and 35 feet wide or about 21 meters long and 11 meters wide [q] *3* That is, about 3 1/2 feet or about 1.1 meters; also in verse 22 [r] *3* That is, about 12 feet or about 3.7 meters [s] *5* That is, about 7 feet or about 2.1 meters [t] *12* That is, about 123 feet or about 37 meters [u] *12* That is, about 158 feet or about 48 meters [v] *13* That is, about 175 feet or about 53 meters; also in verses 14 and 15

were also a hundred cubits long. 14The
width of the temple courtyard on the
east, including the front of the temple,
was a hundred cubits.
15Then he measured the length of the
building facing the courtyard at the rear
of the temple, including its galleries on
each side; it was a hundred cubits.
The main hall, the inner sanctuary and
the portico facing the court, 16as well as
the thresholds and the narrow windows
and galleries around the three of them—
everything beyond and including the
threshold was covered with wood. The
floor, the wall up to the windows, and
the windows were covered. 17In the
space above the outside of the entrance
to the inner sanctuary and on the walls
at regular intervals all around the inner and outer sanctuary 18were carved
cherubim and palm trees. Palm trees
alternated with cherubim. Each cherub
had two faces: 19the face of a human being toward the palm tree on one side and
the face of a lion toward the palm tree on
the other. They were carved all around
the whole temple. 20From the floor to the
area above the entrance, cherubim and
palm trees were carved on the wall of the
main hall.
21The main hall had a rectangular
doorframe, and the one at the front of
the Most Holy Place was similar. 22There
was a wooden altar three cubits[a] high
and two cubits square[b]; its corners, its
base[c] and its sides were of wood. The
man said to me, "This is the table that
is before the LORD." 23Both the main
hall and the Most Holy Place had double
doors. 24Each door had two leaves—two
hinged leaves for each door. 25And on the
doors of the main hall were carved cherubim and palm trees like those carved on
the walls, and there was a wooden over-
hang on the front of the portico. 26On
the sidewalls of the portico were narrow
windows with palm trees carved on each
side. The side rooms of the temple also
had overhangs.

42 Then the man led me northward
into the outer court and brought me
to the rooms opposite the temple courtyard and opposite the outer wall on the
north side. 2The building whose door
faced north was a hundred cubits long
and fifty cubits wide.[d] 3Both in the section twenty cubits[e] from the inner court
and in the section opposite the pavement
of the outer court, gallery faced gallery
at the three levels. 4In front of the rooms
was an inner passageway ten cubits
wide and a hundred cubits[f] long.[g] Their
doors were on the north. 5Now the upper
rooms were narrower, for the galleries
took more space from them than from
the rooms on the lower and middle floors
of the building. 6The rooms on the top
floor had no pillars, as the courts had;
so they were smaller in floor space than
those on the lower and middle floors.
7There was an outer wall parallel to the
rooms and the outer court; it extended in
front of the rooms for fifty cubits. 8While
the row of rooms on the side next to the
outer court was fifty cubits long, the row
on the side nearest the sanctuary was a
hundred cubits long. 9The lower rooms
had an entrance on the east side as one
enters them from the outer court.
10On the south side[h] along the length
of the wall of the outer court, adjoining
the temple courtyard and opposite the
outer wall, were rooms 11with a passageway in front of them. These were like the
rooms on the north; they had the same
length and width, with similar exits and
dimensions. Similar to the doorways on
the north 12were the doorways of the
rooms on the south. There was a doorway at the beginning of the passageway
that was parallel to the corresponding
wall extending eastward, by which one
enters the rooms.
13Then he said to me, "The north and
south rooms facing the temple courtyard
are the priests' rooms, where the priests
who approach the LORD will eat the most
holy offerings. There they will put the
most holy offerings—the grain offerings, the sin offerings[i] and the guilt offerings—for the place is holy. 14Once the
priests enter the holy precincts, they are
not to go into the outer court until they
leave behind the garments in which they

[a] 22 That is, about 5 1/4 feet or about 1.5 meters [b] 22 Septuagint; Hebrew *long* [c] 22 Septuagint; Hebrew *length* [d] 2 That is, about 175 feet long and 88 feet wide or about 53 meters long and 27 meters wide [e] 3 That is, about 35 feet or about 11 meters [f] 4 Septuagint and Syriac; Hebrew *and one cubit* [g] 4 That is, about 18 feet wide and 175 feet long or about 5.3 meters wide and 53 meters long [h] 10 Septuagint; Hebrew *Eastward* [i] 13 Or *purification offerings*

minister, for these are holy. They are to
put on other clothes before they go near
the places that are for the people."
15 When he had finished measuring
what was inside the temple area, he led
me out by the east gate and measured the
area all around: 16 He measured the east
side with the measuring rod; it was five
hundred cubits.[a,b] 17 He measured the
north side; it was five hundred cubits[c] by
the measuring rod. 18 He measured the
south side; it was five hundred cubits by
the measuring rod. 19 Then he turned to
the west side and measured; it was five
hundred cubits by the measuring rod.
20 So he measured the area on all four
sides. It had a wall around it, five hundred cubits long and five hundred cubits wide, to separate the holy from the
common.

43 Then the man brought me to the
gate facing east, 2 and I saw the glory of the God of Israel coming from the
east. His voice was like the roar of rushing waters, and the land was radiant with
his glory. 3 The vision I saw was like the
vision I had seen when he[d] came to destroy the city and like the visions I had
seen by the Kebar River, and I fell facedown. 4 The glory of the LORD entered
the temple through the gate facing east.
5 Then the Spirit lifted me up and brought
me into the inner court, and the glory of
the LORD filled the temple.
6 While the man was standing beside
me, I heard someone speaking to me
from inside the temple. 7 He said: "Son of
man, this is the place of my throne and
the place for the soles of my feet. This is
where I will live among the Israelites forever. The people of Israel will never again
defile my holy name—neither they nor
their kings—by their prostitution and the
funeral offerings[e] for their kings at their
death.[f] 8 When they placed their threshold
next to my threshold and their doorposts
beside my doorposts, with only a wall between me and them, they defiled my holy
name by their detestable practices. So
I destroyed them in my anger. 9 Now let
them put away from me their prostitution
and the funeral offerings for their kings,
and I will live among them forever.
10 "Son of man, describe the temple
to the people of Israel, that they may be
ashamed of their sins. Let them consider
its perfection, 11 and if they are ashamed
of all they have done, make known to
them the design of the temple—its ar-
rangement, its exits and entrances—its
whole design and all its regulations[g] and
laws. Write these down before them so
that they may be faithful to its design and
follow all its regulations.
12 "This is the law of the temple: All the
surrounding area on top of the mountain
will be most holy. Such is the law of the
temple.
13 "These are the measurements of the
altar in long cubits,[h] that cubit being a
cubit and a handbreadth: Its gutter is a
cubit deep and a cubit wide, with a rim
of one span[i] around the edge. And this
is the height of the altar: 14 From the gutter on the ground up to the lower ledge
that goes around the altar it is two cubits high, and the ledge is a cubit wide.[j]
From this lower ledge to the upper ledge
that goes around the altar it is four cubits
high, and that ledge is also a cubit wide.[k]
15 Above that, the altar hearth is four cubits high, and four horns project upward
from the hearth. 16 The altar hearth is
square, twelve cubits[l] long and twelve
cubits wide. 17 The upper ledge also is
square, fourteen cubits[m] long and fourteen cubits wide. All around the altar is
a gutter of one cubit with a rim of half a
cubit.[i] The steps of the altar face east."
18 Then he said to me, "Son of man, this
is what the Sovereign LORD says: These
will be the regulations for sacrificing
burnt offerings and splashing blood
against the altar when it is built: 19 You
are to give a young bull as a sin offering[n]
to the Levitical priests of the family of

[a] *16* See Septuagint of verse 17; Hebrew *rods*; also in verses 18 and 19. [b] *16* Five hundred cubits equal about 875 feet or about 265 meters; also in verses 17, 18 and 19. [c] *17* Septuagint; Hebrew *rods* [d] *3* Some Hebrew manuscripts and Vulgate; most Hebrew manuscripts *I* [e] *7* Or *the memorial monuments*; also in verse 9 [f] *7* Or *their high places* [g] *11* Some Hebrew manuscripts and Septuagint; most Hebrew manuscripts *regulations and its whole design* [h] *13* That is, about 21 inches or about 53 centimeters; also in verses 14 and 17. The long cubit is the basic unit for linear measurement throughout Ezekiel 40–48. [i] *13,17* That is, about 11 inches or about 27 centimeters [j] *14* That is, about 3 1/2 feet high and 1 3/4 feet wide or about 105 centimeters high and 53 centimeters wide [k] *14* That is, about 7 feet high and 1 3/4 feet wide or about 2.1 meters high and 53 centimeters wide [l] *16* That is, about 21 feet or about 6.4 meters [m] *17* That is, about 25 feet or about 7.4 meters [n] *19* Or *purification offering*; also in verses 21, 22 and 25

Zadok, who come near to minister before me, declares the Sovereign LORD.
20 You are to take some of its blood and
put it on the four horns of the altar and on
the four corners of the upper ledge and
all around the rim, and so purify the altar and make atonement for it. 21 You are
to take the bull for the sin offering and
burn it in the designated part of the temple area outside the sanctuary.
22 "On the second day you are to offer
a male goat without defect for a sin offering, and the altar is to be purified as
it was purified with the bull. 23 When you
have finished purifying it, you are to offer a young bull and a ram from the flock,
both without defect. 24 You are to offer
them before the LORD, and the priests
are to sprinkle salt on them and sacrifice
them as a burnt offering to the LORD.
25 "For seven days you are to provide a
male goat daily for a sin offering; you are
also to provide a young bull and a ram
from the flock, both without defect. 26 For
seven days they are to make atonement
for the altar and cleanse it; thus they will
dedicate it. 27 At the end of these days,
from the eighth day on, the priests are to
present your burnt offerings and fellowship offerings on the altar. Then I will accept you, declares the Sovereign LORD."
44 Then the man brought me back to
the outer gate of the sanctuary, the
one facing east, and it was shut. 2 The
LORD said to me, "This gate is to remain
shut. It must not be opened; no one may
enter through it. It is to remain shut because the LORD, the God of Israel, has entered through it. 3 The prince himself is
the only one who may sit inside the gateway to eat in the presence of the LORD.
He is to enter by way of the portico of the
gateway and go out the same way."
4 Then the man brought me by way of
the north gate to the front of the temple.
I looked and saw the glory of the LORD
filling the temple of the LORD, and I fell
facedown.
5 The LORD said to me, "Son of man,
look carefully, listen closely and give attention to everything I tell you concerning all the regulations and instructions
regarding the temple of the LORD. Give
attention to the entrance to the temple
and all the exits of the sanctuary. 6 Say to
rebellious Israel, 'This is what the Sovereign LORD says: Enough of your detestable practices, people of Israel! 7 In addition to all your other detestable practices,
you brought foreigners uncircumcised in
heart and flesh into my sanctuary, desecrating my temple while you offered me
food, fat and blood, and you broke my
covenant. 8 Instead of carrying out your
duty in regard to my holy things, you put
others in charge of my sanctuary. 9 This
is what the Sovereign LORD says: No foreigner uncircumcised in heart and flesh
is to enter my sanctuary, not even the foreigners who live among the Israelites.
10 " 'The Levites who went far from me
when Israel went astray and who wandered from me after their idols must bear
the consequences of their sin. 11 They may
serve in my sanctuary, having charge of
the gates of the temple and serving in it;
they may slaughter the burnt offerings
and sacrifices for the people and stand
before the people and serve them. 12 But
because they served them in the presence of their idols and made the people of
Israel fall into sin, therefore I have sworn
with uplifted hand that they must bear
the consequences of their sin, declares
the Sovereign LORD. 13 They are not to
come near to serve me as priests or come
near any of my holy things or my most
holy offerings; they must bear the shame
of their detestable practices. 14 And I will
appoint them to guard the temple for all
the work that is to be done in it.
15 " 'But the Levitical priests, who are
descendants of Zadok and who guarded
my sanctuary when the Israelites went
astray from me, are to come near to minister before me; they are to stand before
me to offer sacrifices of fat and blood, declares the Sovereign LORD. 16 They alone
are to enter my sanctuary; they alone are
to come near my table to minister before
me and serve me as guards.
17 " 'When they enter the gates of the inner court, they are to wear linen clothes;
they must not wear any woolen garment
while ministering at the gates of the inner court or inside the temple. 18 They
are to wear linen turbans on their heads
and linen undergarments around their
waists. They must not wear anything
that makes them perspire. 19 When they
go out into the outer court where the
people are, they are to take off the clothes
they have been ministering in and are to
leave them in the sacred rooms, and put

on other clothes, so that the people are
not consecrated through contact with
their garments.
20 "'They must not shave their heads
or let their hair grow long, but they are
to keep the hair of their heads trimmed.
21 No priest is to drink wine when he enters the inner court. 22 They must not
marry widows or divorced women; they
may marry only virgins of Israelite descent or widows of priests. 23 They are to
teach my people the difference between
the holy and the common and show them
how to distinguish between the unclean
and the clean.
24 "'In any dispute, the priests are to
serve as judges and decide it according
to my ordinances. They are to keep my
laws and my decrees for all my appointed festivals, and they are to keep my Sabbaths holy.
25 "'A priest must not defile himself by
going near a dead person; however, if the
dead person was his father or mother, son
or daughter, brother or unmarried sister,
then he may defile himself. 26 After he is
cleansed, he must wait seven days. 27 On
the day he goes into the inner court of the
sanctuary to minister in the sanctuary,
he is to offer a sin offering[a] for himself,
declares the Sovereign LORD.
28 "'I am to be the only inheritance the
priests have. You are to give them no possession in Israel; I will be their possession. 29 They will eat the grain offerings,
the sin offerings and the guilt offerings;
and everything in Israel devoted[b] to the
LORD will belong to them. 30 The best of
all the firstfruits and of all your special
gifts will belong to the priests. You are to
give them the first portion of your ground
meal so that a blessing may rest on your
household. 31 The priests must not eat
anything, whether bird or animal, found
dead or torn by wild animals.

45 "'When you allot the land as an inheritance, you are to present to the
LORD a portion of the land as a sacred
district, 25,000 cubits[c] long and 20,000[d]
cubits[e] wide; the entire area will be holy.
2 Of this, a section 500 cubits[f] square is
to be for the sanctuary, with 50 cubits[g]
around it for open land. 3 In the sacred
district, measure off a section 25,000
cubits long and 10,000 cubits[h] wide. In
it will be the sanctuary, the Most Holy
Place. 4 It will be the sacred portion of the
land for the priests, who minister in the
sanctuary and who draw near to minister before the LORD. It will be a place for
their houses as well as a holy place for the
sanctuary. 5 An area 25,000 cubits long
and 10,000 cubits wide will belong to the
Levites, who serve in the temple, as their
possession for towns to live in.[i]
6 "'You are to give the city as its property an area 5,000 cubits[j] wide and 25,000
cubits long, adjoining the sacred portion;
it will belong to all Israel.
7 "'The prince will have the land bordering each side of the area formed by
the sacred district and the property of
the city. It will extend westward from
the west side and eastward from the east
side, running lengthwise from the western to the eastern border parallel to one
of the tribal portions. 8 This land will be
his possession in Israel. And my princes
will no longer oppress my people but will
allow the people of Israel to possess the
land according to their tribes.
9 "'This is what the Sovereign LORD
says: You have gone far enough, princes
of Israel! Give up your violence and oppression and do what is just and right.
Stop dispossessing my people, declares
the Sovereign LORD. 10 You are to use accurate scales, an accurate ephah[k] and an
accurate bath.[l] 11 The ephah and the bath
are to be the same size, the bath containing a tenth of a homer and the ephah a
tenth of a homer; the homer is to be the
standard measure for both. 12 The shekel[m] is to consist of twenty gerahs. Twenty
shekels plus twenty-five shekels plus fifteen shekels equal one mina.[n]

[a] *27* Or *purification offering*; also in verse 29 [b] *29* The Hebrew term refers to the irrevocable giving over of things or persons to the LORD. [c] *1* That is, about 8 miles or about 13 kilometers; also in verses 3, 5 and 6 [d] *1* Septuagint (see also verses 3 and 5 and 48:9); Hebrew *10,000* [e] *1* That is, about 6 1/2 miles or about 11 kilometers [f] *2* That is, about 875 feet or about 265 meters [g] *2* That is, about 88 feet or about 27 meters [h] *3* That is, about 3 1/3 miles or about 5.3 kilometers; also in verse 5 [i] *5* Septuagint; Hebrew *temple; they will have as their possession 20 rooms* [j] *6* That is, about 1 2/3 miles or about 2.7 kilometers [k] *10* An ephah was a dry measure having the capacity of about 3/5 bushel or about 22 liters. [l] *10* A bath was a liquid measure equaling about 6 gallons or about 22 liters. [m] *12* A shekel weighed about 2/5 ounce or about 12 grams. [n] *12* That is, 60 shekels; the common mina was 50 shekels. Sixty shekels were about 1 1/2 pounds or about 690 grams.

13“‘This is the special gift you are to
offer: a sixth of an ephah[a] from each homer of wheat and a sixth of an ephah[b]
from each homer of barley. 14The prescribed portion of olive oil, measured
by the bath, is a tenth of a bath[c] from
each cor (which consists of ten baths or
one homer, for ten baths are equivalent
to a homer). 15Also one sheep is to be
taken from every flock of two hundred
from the well-watered pastures of Israel. These will be used for the grain offerings, burnt offerings and fellowship
offerings to make atonement for the
people, declares the Sovereign LORD.
16All the people of the land will be required to give this special offering to the
prince in Israel. 17It will be the duty of
the prince to provide the burnt offerings,
grain offerings and drink offerings at the
festivals, the New Moons and the Sabbaths—at all the appointed festivals of
Israel. He will provide the sin offerings,[d]
grain offerings, burnt offerings and fellowship offerings to make atonement for
the Israelites.

18“‘This is what the Sovereign LORD
says: In the first month on the first day
you are to take a young bull without
defect and purify the sanctuary. 19The
priest is to take some of the blood of the
sin offering and put it on the doorposts
of the temple, on the four corners of the
upper ledge of the altar and on the gate-
posts of the inner court. 20You are to
do the same on the seventh day of the
month for anyone who sins unintentionally or through ignorance; so you are to
make atonement for the temple.

21“‘In the first month on the fourteenth
day you are to observe the Passover, a
festival lasting seven days, during which
you shall eat bread made without yeast.
22On that day the prince is to provide a
bull as a sin offering for himself and for
all the people of the land. 23Every day
during the seven days of the festival he
is to provide seven bulls and seven rams
without defect as a burnt offering to the
LORD, and a male goat for a sin offering.
24He is to provide as a grain offering an
ephah for each bull and an ephah for
each ram, along with a hin[e] of olive oil
for each ephah.

25“‘During the seven days of the festival, which begins in the seventh month
on the fifteenth day, he is to make the
same provision for sin offerings, burnt
offerings, grain offerings and oil.

46 “‘This is what the Sovereign LORD
says: The gate of the inner court facing east is to be shut on the six working
days, but on the Sabbath day and on the
day of the New Moon it is to be opened.
2The prince is to enter from the outside
through the portico of the gateway and
stand by the gatepost. The priests are to
sacrifice his burnt offering and his fellowship offerings. He is to bow down in
worship at the threshold of the gateway
and then go out, but the gate will not be
shut until evening. 3On the Sabbaths and
New Moons the people of the land are to
worship in the presence of the LORD at
the entrance of that gateway. 4The burnt
offering the prince brings to the LORD on
the Sabbath day is to be six male lambs
and a ram, all without defect. 5The grain
offering given with the ram is to be an
ephah,[f] and the grain offering with the
lambs is to be as much as he pleases,
along with a hin[g] of olive oil for each
ephah. 6On the day of the New Moon he
is to offer a young bull, six lambs and a
ram, all without defect. 7He is to provide
as a grain offering one ephah with the
bull, one ephah with the ram, and with
the lambs as much as he wants to give,
along with a hin of oil for each ephah.
8When the prince enters, he is to go in
through the portico of the gateway, and
he is to come out the same way.

9“‘When the people of the land come
before the LORD at the appointed festivals, whoever enters by the north gate
to worship is to go out the south gate;
and whoever enters by the south gate is
to go out the north gate. No one is to return through the gate by which they entered, but each is to go out the opposite
gate. 10The prince is to be among them,
going in when they go in and going out
when they go out. 11At the feasts and the
appointed festivals, the grain offering

[a] 13 That is, probably about 6 pounds or about 2.7 kilograms [b] 13 That is, probably about 5 pounds or about 2.3 kilograms [c] 14 That is, about 2 1/2 quarts or about 2.2 liters [d] 17 Or *purification offerings*; also in verses 19, 22, 23 and 25 [e] 24 That is, about 1 gallon or about 3.8 liters [f] 5 That is, probably about 35 pounds or about 16 kilograms; also in verses 7 and 11 [g] 5 That is, about 1 gallon or about 3.8 liters; also in verses 7 and 11

is to be an ephah with a bull, an ephah with a ram, and with the lambs as much as he pleases, along with a hin of oil for each ephah.

12"'When the prince provides a freewill offering to the LORD—whether a burnt offering or fellowship offerings—the gate facing east is to be opened for him. He shall offer his burnt offering or his fellowship offerings as he does on the Sabbath day. Then he shall go out, and after he has gone out, the gate will be shut.

13"'Every day you are to provide a year-old lamb without defect for a burnt offering to the LORD; morning by morning you shall provide it. 14You are also to provide with it morning by morning a grain offering, consisting of a sixth of an ephah[a] with a third of a hin[b] of oil to moisten the flour. The presenting of this grain offering to the LORD is a lasting ordinance. 15So the lamb and the grain offering and the oil shall be provided morning by morning for a regular burnt offering.

16"'This is what the Sovereign LORD says: If the prince makes a gift from his inheritance to one of his sons, it will also belong to his descendants; it is to be their property by inheritance. 17If, however, he makes a gift from his inheritance to one of his servants, the servant may keep it until the year of freedom; then it will revert to the prince. His inheritance belongs to his sons only; it is theirs. 18The prince must not take any of the inheritance of the people, driving them off their property. He is to give his sons their inheritance out of his own property, so that not one of my people will be separated from their property.'"

19Then the man brought me through the entrance at the side of the gate to the sacred rooms facing north, which belonged to the priests, and showed me a place at the western end. 20He said to me, "This is the place where the priests are to cook the guilt offering and the sin offering[c] and bake the grain offering, to avoid bringing them into the outer court and consecrating the people."

21He then brought me to the outer court and led me around to its four corners, and I saw in each corner another court. 22In the four corners of the outer court were enclosed[d] courts, forty cubits long and thirty cubits wide;[e] each of the courts in the four corners was the same size. 23Around the inside of each of the four courts was a ledge of stone, with places for fire built all around under the ledge. 24He said to me, "These are the kitchens where those who minister at the temple are to cook the sacrifices of the people."

47 The man brought me back to the entrance to the temple, and I saw water coming out from under the threshold of the temple toward the east (for the temple faced east). The water was coming down from under the south side of the temple, south of the altar. 2He then brought me out through the north gate and led me around the outside to the outer gate facing east, and the water was trickling from the south side.

3As the man went eastward with a measuring line in his hand, he measured off a thousand cubits[f] and then led me through water that was ankle-deep. 4He measured off another thousand cubits and led me through water that was knee-deep. He measured off another thousand and led me through water that was up to the waist. 5He measured off another thousand, but now it was a river that I could not cross, because the water had risen and was deep enough to swim in—a river that no one could cross. 6He asked me, "Son of man, do you see this?"

Then he led me back to the bank of the river. 7When I arrived there, I saw a great number of trees on each side of the river. 8He said to me, "This water flows toward the eastern region and goes down into the Arabah,[g] where it enters the Dead Sea. When it empties into the sea, the salty water there becomes fresh. 9Swarms of living creatures will live wherever the river flows. There will be large numbers of fish, because this water flows there and makes the salt water fresh; so where the river flows everything will live. 10Fishermen will stand along the shore; from En Gedi to En Eglaim there will be places for spreading nets. The fish will be of many

[a] *14* That is, probably about 6 pounds or about 2.7 kilograms [b] *14* That is, about 1 1/2 quarts or about 1.3 liters [c] *20* Or *purification offering* [d] *22* The meaning of the Hebrew for this word is uncertain. [e] *22* That is, about 70 feet long and 53 feet wide or about 21 meters long and 16 meters wide [f] *3* That is, about 1,700 feet or about 530 meters [g] *8* Or *the Jordan Valley*

kinds—like the fish of the Mediterranean Sea. 11But the swamps and marshes
will not become fresh; they will be left for
salt. 12Fruit trees of all kinds will grow on
both banks of the river. Their leaves will
not wither, nor will their fruit fail. Every
month they will bear fruit, because the
water from the sanctuary flows to them.
Their fruit will serve for food and their
leaves for healing."

13This is what the Sovereign LORD says:
"These are the boundaries of the land
that you will divide among the twelve
tribes of Israel as their inheritance, with
two portions for Joseph. 14You are to divide it equally among them. Because
I swore with uplifted hand to give it to
your ancestors, this land will become
your inheritance.

15"This is to be the boundary of the
land:

"On the north side it will run from the
Mediterranean Sea by the Hethlon
road past Lebo Hamath to Zedad,
16Berothah[a] and Sibraim (which
lies on the border between Damascus and Hamath), as far as Hazer
Hattikon, which is on the border of
Hauran. 17The boundary will extend
from the sea to Hazar Enan,[b] along
the northern border of Damascus,
with the border of Hamath to the
north. This will be the northern
boundary.

18"On the east side the boundary will
run between Hauran and Damascus, along the Jordan between Gilead and the land of Israel, to the Dead
Sea and as far as Tamar.[c] This will be
the eastern boundary.

19"On the south side it will run from
Tamar as far as the waters of Meribah Kadesh, then along the Wadi
of Egypt to the Mediterranean Sea.
This will be the southern boundary.

20"On the west side, the Mediterranean
Sea will be the boundary to a point
opposite Lebo Hamath. This will be
the western boundary.

21"You are to distribute this land
among yourselves according to the
tribes of Israel. 22You are to allot it as an
inheritance for yourselves and for the
foreigners residing among you and who
have children. You are to consider them
as native-born Israelites; along with you
they are to be allotted an inheritance
among the tribes of Israel. 23In whatever tribe a foreigner resides, there you are
to give them their inheritance," declares
the Sovereign LORD.

48 "These are the tribes, listed by
name: At the northern frontier,
Dan will have one portion; it will follow
the Hethlon road to Lebo Hamath; Hazar
Enan and the northern border of Damascus next to Hamath will be part of its border from the east side to the west side.

2"Asher will have one portion; it will
border the territory of Dan from east to
west.

3"Naphtali will have one portion; it
will border the territory of Asher from
east to west.

4"Manasseh will have one portion; it
will border the territory of Naphtali from
east to west.

5"Ephraim will have one portion; it
will border the territory of Manasseh
from east to west.

6"Reuben will have one portion; it will
border the territory of Ephraim from east
to west.

7"Judah will have one portion; it will
border the territory of Reuben from east
to west.

8"Bordering the territory of Judah from
east to west will be the portion you are to
present as a special gift. It will be 25,000
cubits[d] wide, and its length from east to
west will equal one of the tribal portions;
the sanctuary will be in the center of it.

9"The special portion you are to offer
to the LORD will be 25,000 cubits long
and 10,000 cubits[e] wide. 10This will be
the sacred portion for the priests. It will
be 25,000 cubits long on the north side,
10,000 cubits wide on the west side,
10,000 cubits wide on the east side and
25,000 cubits long on the south side. In
the center of it will be the sanctuary of
the LORD. 11This will be for the consecrated priests, the Zadokites, who were

[a] *15,16* See Septuagint and 48:1; Hebrew *road to go into Zedad, 16Hamath, Berothah.* [b] *17* Hebrew *Enon,* a variant of *Enan* [c] *18* See Syriac; Hebrew *Israel. You will measure to the Dead Sea.* [d] *8* That is, about 8 miles or about 13 kilometers; also in verses 9, 10, 13, 15, 20 and 21 [e] *9* That is, about 3 1/3 miles or about 5.3 kilometers; also in verses 10, 13 and 18

faithful in serving me and did not go
astray as the Levites did when the Israelites went astray. 12 It will be a special gift
to them from the sacred portion of the
land, a most holy portion, bordering the
territory of the Levites.
13 "Alongside the territory of the priests,
the Levites will have an allotment 25,000
cubits long and 10,000 cubits wide. Its
total length will be 25,000 cubits and its
width 10,000 cubits. 14 They must not sell
or exchange any of it. This is the best of
the land and must not pass into other
hands, because it is holy to the LORD.
15 "The remaining area, 5,000 cubits[a]
wide and 25,000 cubits long, will be for
the common use of the city, for houses and for pastureland. The city will be
in the center of it 16 and will have these
measurements: the north side 4,500 cubits,[b] the south side 4,500 cubits, the east
side 4,500 cubits, and the west side 4,500
cubits. 17 The pastureland for the city will
be 250 cubits[c] on the north, 250 cubits on
the south, 250 cubits on the east, and 250
cubits on the west. 18 What remains of
the area, bordering on the sacred portion and running the length of it, will be
10,000 cubits on the east side and 10,000
cubits on the west side. Its produce will
supply food for the workers of the city.
19 The workers from the city who farm
it will come from all the tribes of Israel.
20 The entire portion will be a square,
25,000 cubits on each side. As a special
gift you will set aside the sacred portion,
along with the property of the city.
21 "What remains on both sides of the
area formed by the sacred portion and
the property of the city will belong to the
prince. It will extend eastward from the
25,000 cubits of the sacred portion to
the eastern border, and westward from
the 25,000 cubits to the western border.
Both these areas running the length
of the tribal portions will belong to the
prince, and the sacred portion with the
temple sanctuary will be in the center
of them. 22 So the property of the Levites
and the property of the city will lie in
the center of the area that belongs to the
prince. The area belonging to the prince
will lie between the border of Judah and
the border of Benjamin.
23 "As for the rest of the tribes: Benjamin will have one portion; it will extend
from the east side to the west side.
24 "Simeon will have one portion; it will
border the territory of Benjamin from
east to west.
25 "Issachar will have one portion; it
will border the territory of Simeon from
east to west.
26 "Zebulun will have one portion; it
will border the territory of Issachar from
east to west.
27 "Gad will have one portion; it will
border the territory of Zebulun from east
to west.
28 "The southern boundary of Gad will
run south from Tamar to the waters of
Meribah Kadesh, then along the Wadi of
Egypt to the Mediterranean Sea.
29 "This is the land you are to allot as
an inheritance to the tribes of Israel, and
these will be their portions," declares the
Sovereign LORD.

30 "These will be the exits of the city:
Beginning on the north side, which is
4,500 cubits long, 31 the gates of the city
will be named after the tribes of Israel.
The three gates on the north side will be
the gate of Reuben, the gate of Judah and
the gate of Levi.
32 "On the east side, which is 4,500 cubits long, will be three gates: the gate of
Joseph, the gate of Benjamin and the gate
of Dan.
33 "On the south side, which measures
4,500 cubits, will be three gates: the gate
of Simeon, the gate of Issachar and the
gate of Zebulun.
34 "On the west side, which is 4,500
cubits long, will be three gates: the gate
of Gad, the gate of Asher and the gate of
Naphtali.
35 "The distance all around will be
18,000 cubits.[d]
"And the name of the city from that
time on will be:

THE LORD IS THERE."

[a] *15* That is, about 1 2/3 miles or about 2.7 kilometers; also in verses 30, 32, 33 and 34 [b] *16* That is, about 1 1/2 miles or about 2.4 kilometers; [c] *17* That is, about 440 feet or about 135 meters [d] *35* That is, about 6 miles or about 9.5 kilometers

DANIEL

The book of Daniel combines two types of literature: court narrative and apocalypse. The opening narrative section presents six stories of how God protected and promoted four young men who were taken into exile in Babylon. When Daniel and his friends Shadrach, Meshach and Abednego demonstrate their faithfulness to God, they are delivered from deadly perils by God's mighty acts. Daniel was given the ability to interpret dreams, earning him a valued place in the royal court of Babylon, and later in the Persian Empire.

The second part of the book describes visions and messages Daniel received from God through angelic messengers. These visions are presented in the cryptic language and symbolic terms typical of apocalyptic literature. Within them we see the outlines of Near Eastern history: the empires of Babylon and Persia; the conquests of Alexander the Great; and the ongoing strife between the Ptolemies in Egypt and the Seleucids in Syria. The visions anticipate an arrogant ruler, the Seleucid emperor Antiochus IV Epiphanes, who desecrated the Jerusalem temple in 167 BC. This led to the Maccabean revolt, which restored the nation's independence and preserved the worship of Israel's God.

The visions in Daniel can also be understood to reveal the conditions at the end of the present age, showing it to be a time of definitive conflict between God's people and their enemies. The people of God will be sustained through their persecutions knowing they will receive the kingdom.

---

1 In the third year of the reign of Jehoiakim king of Judah, Nebuchadnezzar
king of Babylon came to Jerusalem and
besieged it. 2 And the Lord delivered Jehoiakim king of Judah into his hand,
along with some of the articles from the
temple of God. These he carried off to the
temple of his god in Babylonia[a] and put in
the treasure house of his god.
3 Then the king ordered Ashpenaz,
chief of his court officials, to bring into
the king's service some of the Israelites
from the royal family and the nobility—
4 young men without any physical defect,
handsome, showing aptitude for every
kind of learning, well informed, quick to
understand, and qualified to serve in the
king's palace. He was to teach them the
language and literature of the Babylonians.[b] 5 The king assigned them a daily
amount of food and wine from the king's
table. They were to be trained for three
years, and after that they were to enter
the king's service.
6 Among those who were chosen were
some from Judah: Daniel, Hananiah,
Mishael and Azariah. 7 The chief official
gave them new names: to Daniel, the
name Belteshazzar; to Hananiah, Shadrach; to Mishael, Meshach; and to Azariah, Abednego.
8 But Daniel resolved not to defile himself with the royal food and wine, and he
asked the chief official for permission
not to defile himself this way. 9 Now God
had caused the official to show favor and
compassion to Daniel, 10 but the official
told Daniel, "I am afraid of my lord the
king, who has assigned your[c] food and
drink. Why should he see you looking
worse than the other young men your
age? The king would then have my head
because of you."
11 Daniel then said to the guard whom
the chief official had appointed over
Daniel, Hananiah, Mishael and Azariah,
12 "Please test your servants for ten days:
Give us nothing but vegetables to eat and
water to drink. 13 Then compare our appearance with that of the young men who
eat the royal food, and treat your servants
in accordance with what you see." 14 So
he agreed to this and tested them for ten
days.
15 At the end of the ten days they looked
healthier and better nourished than any
of the young men who ate the royal food.
16 So the guard took away their choice
food and the wine they were to drink and
gave them vegetables instead.
17 To these four young men God gave
knowledge and understanding of all
kinds of literature and learning. And

[a] 2 Hebrew *Shinar* [b] 4 Or *Chaldeans* [c] 10 The Hebrew for *your* and *you* in this verse is plural.

Daniel could understand visions and
dreams of all kinds.
18 At the end of the time set by the king
to bring them into his service, the chief
official presented them to Nebuchadnezzar. 19 The king talked with them, and he
found none equal to Daniel, Hananiah,
Mishael and Azariah; so they entered the
king's service. 20 In every matter of wisdom and understanding about which the
king questioned them, he found them ten
times better than all the magicians and
enchanters in his whole kingdom.
21 And Daniel remained there until the
first year of King Cyrus.

2 In the second year of his reign, Nebuchadnezzar had dreams; his mind was
troubled and he could not sleep. 2 So the
king summoned the magicians, enchanters, sorcerers and astrologers[a] to tell him
what he had dreamed. When they came
in and stood before the king, 3 he said to
them, "I have had a dream that troubles
me and I want to know what it means.[b]"
4 Then the astrologers answered the
king,[c] "May the king live forever! Tell
your servants the dream, and we will interpret it."
5 The king replied to the astrologers,
"This is what I have firmly decided: If
you do not tell me what my dream was
and interpret it, I will have you cut into
pieces and your houses turned into piles
of rubble. 6 But if you tell me the dream
and explain it, you will receive from me
gifts and rewards and great honor. So tell
me the dream and interpret it for me."
7 Once more they replied, "Let the king
tell his servants the dream, and we will
interpret it."
8 Then the king answered, "I am certain that you are trying to gain time, because you realize that this is what I have
firmly decided: 9 If you do not tell me the
dream, there is only one penalty for you.
You have conspired to tell me misleading
and wicked things, hoping the situation
will change. So then, tell me the dream,
and I will know that you can interpret it
for me."
10 The astrologers answered the king,
"There is no one on earth who can do
what the king asks! No king, however
great and mighty, has ever asked such a
thing of any magician or enchanter or as-
trologer. 11 What the king asks is too difficult. No one can reveal it to the king except the gods, and they do not live among
humans."
12 This made the king so angry and furious that he ordered the execution of all
the wise men of Babylon. 13 So the decree
was issued to put the wise men to death,
and men were sent to look for Daniel and
his friends to put them to death.
14 When Arioch, the commander of the
king's guard, had gone out to put to death
the wise men of Babylon, Daniel spoke to
him with wisdom and tact. 15 He asked the
king's officer, "Why did the king issue such
a harsh decree?" Arioch then explained
the matter to Daniel. 16 At this, Daniel went
in to the king and asked for time, so that he
might interpret the dream for him.
17 Then Daniel returned to his house
and explained the matter to his friends
Hananiah, Mishael and Azariah. 18 He
urged them to plead for mercy from the
God of heaven concerning this mystery, so
that he and his friends might not be executed with the rest of the wise men of Babylon. 19 During the night the mystery was
revealed to Daniel in a vision. Then Daniel
praised the God of heaven 20 and said:

"Praise be to the name of God for ever
and ever;
wisdom and power are his.
21 He changes times and seasons;
he deposes kings and raises up
others.
He gives wisdom to the wise
and knowledge to the discerning.
22 He reveals deep and hidden things;
he knows what lies in darkness,
and light dwells with him.
23 I thank and praise you, God of my
ancestors:
You have given me wisdom and
power,
you have made known to me what we
asked of you,
you have made known to us the
dream of the king."

24 Then Daniel went to Arioch, whom
the king had appointed to execute the
wise men of Babylon, and said to him,
"Do not execute the wise men of Babylon.
Take me to the king, and I will interpret
his dream for him."

[a] 2 Or *Chaldeans*; also in verses 4, 5 and 10 [b] 3 Or *was* [c] 4 At this point the Hebrew text has *in Aramaic*, indicating that the text from here through the end of chapter 7 is in Aramaic.

25 Arioch took Daniel to the king at once
and said, "I have found a man among the
exiles from Judah who can tell the king
what his dream means."

26 The king asked Daniel (also called
Belteshazzar), "Are you able to tell
me what I saw in my dream and interpret it?"

27 Daniel replied, "No wise man, enchanter, magician or diviner can explain
to the king the mystery he has asked
about, 28 but there is a God in heaven
who reveals mysteries. He has shown
King Nebuchadnezzar what will happen
in days to come. Your dream and the visions that passed through your mind as
you were lying in bed are these:

29 "As Your Majesty was lying there,
your mind turned to things to come,
and the revealer of mysteries showed
you what is going to happen. 30 As for me,
this mystery has been revealed to me,
not because I have greater wisdom than
anyone else alive, but so that Your Majesty may know the interpretation and that
you may understand what went through
your mind.

31 "Your Majesty looked, and there before you stood a large statue—an enormous, dazzling statue, awesome in appearance. 32 The head of the statue was
made of pure gold, its chest and arms of
silver, its belly and thighs of bronze, 33 its
legs of iron, its feet partly of iron and partly of baked clay. 34 While you were watching, a rock was cut out, but not by human
hands. It struck the statue on its feet of
iron and clay and smashed them. 35 Then
the iron, the clay, the bronze, the silver
and the gold were all broken to pieces and
became like chaff on a threshing floor in
the summer. The wind swept them away
without leaving a trace. But the rock that
struck the statue became a huge mountain and filled the whole earth.

36 "This was the dream, and now we
will interpret it to the king. 37 Your Majesty, you are the king of kings. The God of
heaven has given you dominion and power and might and glory; 38 in your hands
he has placed all mankind and the beasts
of the field and the birds in the sky. Wherever they live, he has made you ruler over
them all. You are that head of gold.

39 "After you, another kingdom will
arise, inferior to yours. Next, a third
kingdom, one of bronze, will rule over
the whole earth. 40 Finally, there will be a
fourth kingdom, strong as iron—for iron
breaks and smashes everything—and
as iron breaks things to pieces, so it will
crush and break all the others. 41 Just as
you saw that the feet and toes were partly
of baked clay and partly of iron, so this
will be a divided kingdom; yet it will have
some of the strength of iron in it, even as
you saw iron mixed with clay. 42 As the
toes were partly iron and partly clay, so
this kingdom will be partly strong and
partly brittle. 43 And just as you saw the
iron mixed with baked clay, so the people will be a mixture and will not remain
united, any more than iron mixes with
clay.

44 "In the time of those kings, the God
of heaven will set up a kingdom that will
never be destroyed, nor will it be left to
another people. It will crush all those
kingdoms and bring them to an end, but
it will itself endure forever. 45 This is the
meaning of the vision of the rock cut out
of a mountain, but not by human hands—
a rock that broke the iron, the bronze, the
clay, the silver and the gold to pieces.

"The great God has shown the king
what will take place in the future. The
dream is true and its interpretation is
trustworthy."

46 Then King Nebuchadnezzar fell prostrate before Daniel and paid him honor
and ordered that an offering and incense
be presented to him. 47 The king said to
Daniel, "Surely your God is the God of
gods and the Lord of kings and a revealer
of mysteries, for you were able to reveal
this mystery."

48 Then the king placed Daniel in a
high position and lavished many gifts on
him. He made him ruler over the entire
province of Babylon and placed him in
charge of all its wise men. 49 Moreover,
at Daniel's request the king appointed
Shadrach, Meshach and Abednego administrators over the province of Babylon, while Daniel himself remained at
the royal court.

3 King Nebuchadnezzar made an image
of gold, sixty cubits high and six cubits
wide,[a] and set it up on the plain of Dura in
the province of Babylon. 2 He then sum-

[a] *1* That is, about 90 feet high and 9 feet wide or about 27 meters high and 2.7 meters wide

moned the satraps, prefects, governors,
advisers, treasurers, judges, magistrates
and all the other provincial officials to
come to the dedication of the image he
had set up. 3 So the satraps, prefects, governors, advisers, treasurers, judges, magistrates and all the other provincial officials assembled for the dedication of the
image that King Nebuchadnezzar had set
up, and they stood before it.
4 Then the herald loudly proclaimed,
"Nations and peoples of every language,
this is what you are commanded to do:
5 As soon as you hear the sound of the
horn, flute, zither, lyre, harp, pipe and all
kinds of music, you must fall down and
worship the image of gold that King Nebuchadnezzar has set up. 6 Whoever does
not fall down and worship will immediately be thrown into a blazing furnace."
7 Therefore, as soon as they heard the
sound of the horn, flute, zither, lyre, harp
and all kinds of music, all the nations and
peoples of every language fell down and
worshiped the image of gold that King
Nebuchadnezzar had set up.
8 At this time some astrologers[a] came
forward and denounced the Jews. 9 They
said to King Nebuchadnezzar, "May the
king live forever! 10 Your Majesty has issued a decree that everyone who hears
the sound of the horn, flute, zither, lyre,
harp, pipe and all kinds of music must
fall down and worship the image of gold,
11 and that whoever does not fall down
and worship will be thrown into a blazing
furnace. 12 But there are some Jews whom
you have set over the affairs of the province of Babylon—Shadrach, Meshach
and Abednego—who pay no attention
to you, Your Majesty. They neither serve
your gods nor worship the image of gold
you have set up."
13 Furious with rage, Nebuchadnezzar summoned Shadrach, Meshach and
Abednego. So these men were brought
before the king, 14 and Nebuchadnezzar
said to them, "Is it true, Shadrach, Meshach and Abednego, that you do not
serve my gods or worship the image of
gold I have set up? 15 Now when you hear
the sound of the horn, flute, zither, lyre,
harp, pipe and all kinds of music, if you
are ready to fall down and worship the
image I made, very good. But if you do
not worship it, you will be thrown immediately into a blazing furnace. Then
what god will be able to rescue you from
my hand?"
16 Shadrach, Meshach and Abednego
replied to him, "King Nebuchadnezzar,
we do not need to defend ourselves before
you in this matter. 17 If we are thrown into
the blazing furnace, the God we serve is
able to deliver us from it, and he will deliver us[b] from Your Majesty's hand. 18 But
even if he does not, we want you to know,
Your Majesty, that we will not serve your
gods or worship the image of gold you
have set up."
19 Then Nebuchadnezzar was furious
with Shadrach, Meshach and Abednego,
and his attitude toward them changed.
He ordered the furnace heated seven
times hotter than usual 20 and commanded some of the strongest soldiers
in his army to tie up Shadrach, Meshach
and Abednego and throw them into the
blazing furnace. 21 So these men, wearing
their robes, trousers, turbans and other
clothes, were bound and thrown into the
blazing furnace. 22 The king's command
was so urgent and the furnace so hot that
the flames of the fire killed the soldiers
who took up Shadrach, Meshach and
Abednego, 23 and these three men, firmly tied, fell into the blazing furnace.
24 Then King Nebuchadnezzar leaped
to his feet in amazement and asked his
advisers, "Weren't there three men that
we tied up and threw into the fire?"
They replied, "Certainly, Your Majesty."
25 He said, "Look! I see four men walking around in the fire, unbound and unharmed, and the fourth looks like a son
of the gods."
26 Nebuchadnezzar then approached
the opening of the blazing furnace and
shouted, "Shadrach, Meshach and Abednego, servants of the Most High God,
come out! Come here!"
So Shadrach, Meshach and Abednego
came out of the fire, 27 and the satraps,
prefects, governors and royal advisers
crowded around them. They saw that the
fire had not harmed their bodies, nor was
a hair of their heads singed; their robes
were not scorched, and there was no
smell of fire on them.

[a] 8 Or *Chaldeans* [b] 17 Or *If the God we serve is able to deliver us, then he will deliver us from the blazing furnace and*

28 Then Nebuchadnezzar said, "Praise
be to the God of Shadrach, Meshach and
Abednego, who has sent his angel and
rescued his servants! They trusted in him
and defied the king's command and were
willing to give up their lives rather than
serve or worship any god except their
own God. 29 Therefore I decree that the
people of any nation or language who say
anything against the God of Shadrach,
Meshach and Abednego be cut into pieces and their houses be turned into piles
of rubble, for no other god can save in
this way."
30 Then the king promoted Shadrach,
Meshach and Abednego in the province
of Babylon.

4 [a] King Nebuchadnezzar,

To the nations and peoples of every
language, who live in all the earth:

May you prosper greatly!

2 It is my pleasure to tell you about
the miraculous signs and wonders
that the Most High God has performed for me.

3 How great are his signs,
how mighty his wonders!
His kingdom is an eternal
kingdom;
his dominion endures from
generation to generation.

4 I, Nebuchadnezzar, was at home
in my palace, contented and prosperous. 5 I had a dream that made
me afraid. As I was lying in bed,
the images and visions that passed
through my mind terrified me. 6 So I
commanded that all the wise men of
Babylon be brought before me to interpret the dream for me. 7 When the
magicians, enchanters, astrologers[b]
and diviners came, I told them the
dream, but they could not interpret it
for me. 8 Finally, Daniel came into my
presence and I told him the dream.
(He is called Belteshazzar, after the
name of my god, and the spirit of the
holy gods is in him.)
9 I said, "Belteshazzar, chief of the
magicians, I know that the spirit of
the holy gods is in you, and no mystery is too difficult for you. Here is my
dream; interpret it for me. 10 These
are the visions I saw while lying in
bed: I looked, and there before me
stood a tree in the middle of the
land. Its height was enormous. 11 The
tree grew large and strong and its top
touched the sky; it was visible to the
ends of the earth. 12 Its leaves were
beautiful, its fruit abundant, and on
it was food for all. Under it the wild
animals found shelter, and the birds
lived in its branches; from it every
creature was fed.
13 "In the visions I saw while lying
in bed, I looked, and there before me
was a holy one, a messenger,[c] coming down from heaven. 14 He called
in a loud voice: 'Cut down the tree
and trim off its branches; strip off
its leaves and scatter its fruit. Let the
animals flee from under it and the
birds from its branches. 15 But let the
stump and its roots, bound with iron
and bronze, remain in the ground, in
the grass of the field.

"'Let him be drenched with the
dew of heaven, and let him live with
the animals among the plants of the
earth. 16 Let his mind be changed
from that of a man and let him be giv-
en the mind of an animal, till seven
times[d] pass by for him.
17 "'The decision is announced by
messengers, the holy ones declare
the verdict, so that the living may
know that the Most High is sovereign
over all kingdoms on earth and gives
them to anyone he wishes and sets
over them the lowliest of people.'
18 "This is the dream that I, King
Nebuchadnezzar, had. Now, Belteshazzar, tell me what it means, for
none of the wise men in my kingdom
can interpret it for me. But you can,
because the spirit of the holy gods is
in you."

19 Then Daniel (also called Belteshazzar) was greatly perplexed for
a time, and his thoughts terrified
him. So the king said, "Belteshazzar,
do not let the dream or its meaning
alarm you."
Belteshazzar answered, "My lord,

[a] In Aramaic texts 4:1-3 is numbered 3:31-33, and 4:4-37 is numbered 4:1-34. [b] *7* Or *Chaldeans*
[c] *13* Or *watchman*; also in verses 17 and 23 [d] *16* Or *years*; also in verses 23, 25 and 32

if only the dream applied to your
enemies and its meaning to your
adversaries! 20The tree you saw,
which grew large and strong, with
its top touching the sky, visible to the
whole earth, 21with beautiful leaves
and abundant fruit, providing food
for all, giving shelter to the wild animals, and having nesting places in
its branches for the birds — 22Your
Majesty, you are that tree! You have
become great and strong; your greatness has grown until it reaches the
sky, and your dominion extends to
distant parts of the earth.
23"Your Majesty saw a holy one,
a messenger, coming down from
heaven and saying, 'Cut down the
tree and destroy it, but leave the
stump, bound with iron and bronze,
in the grass of the field, while its
roots remain in the ground. Let
him be drenched with the dew of
heaven; let him live with the wild
animals, until seven times pass by
for him.'
24"This is the interpretation, Your
Majesty, and this is the decree the
Most High has issued against my
lord the king: 25You will be driven
away from people and will live with
the wild animals; you will eat grass
like the ox and be drenched with the
dew of heaven. Seven times will pass
by for you until you acknowledge
that the Most High is sovereign over
all kingdoms on earth and gives
them to anyone he wishes. 26The
command to leave the stump of the
tree with its roots means that your
kingdom will be restored to you
when you acknowledge that Heav-
en rules. 27Therefore, Your Majesty, be pleased to accept my advice:
Renounce your sins by doing what
is right, and your wickedness by being kind to the oppressed. It may be
that then your prosperity will continue."

28All this happened to King Nebuchadnezzar. 29Twelve months later,
as the king was walking on the roof
of the royal palace of Babylon, 30he
said, "Is not this the great Babylon I
have built as the royal residence, by
my mighty power and for the glory of
my majesty?"

31Even as the words were on his
lips, a voice came from heaven,
"This is what is decreed for you,
King Nebuchadnezzar: Your royal
authority has been taken from you.
32You will be driven away from people and will live with the wild animals; you will eat grass like the ox.
Seven times will pass by for you until you acknowledge that the Most
High is sovereign over all kingdoms
on earth and gives them to anyone
he wishes."
33Immediately what had been said
about Nebuchadnezzar was fulfilled.
He was driven away from people and
ate grass like the ox. His body was
drenched with the dew of heaven
until his hair grew like the feathers of
an eagle and his nails like the claws
of a bird.

34At the end of that time, I, Nebuchadnezzar, raised my eyes toward
heaven, and my sanity was restored.
Then I praised the Most High; I honored and glorified him who lives forever.

His dominion is an eternal dominion;
his kingdom endures from
generation to generation.
35All the peoples of the earth
are regarded as nothing.
He does as he pleases
with the powers of heaven
and the peoples of the earth.
No one can hold back his hand
or say to him: "What have you
done?"

36At the same time that my sanity
was restored, my honor and splendor
were returned to me for the glory of
my kingdom. My advisers and nobles
sought me out, and I was restored to
my throne and became even greater
than before. 37Now I, Nebuchadnezzar, praise and exalt and glorify the
King of heaven, because everything
he does is right and all his ways are
just. And those who walk in pride he
is able to humble.

5 King Belshazzar gave a great banquet
for a thousand of his nobles and drank
wine with them. 2While Belshazzar was
drinking his wine, he gave orders to
bring in the gold and silver goblets that

Nebuchadnezzar his father[a] had taken
from the temple in Jerusalem, so that
the king and his nobles, his wives and
his concubines might drink from them.
3 So they brought in the gold goblets that
had been taken from the temple of God
in Jerusalem, and the king and his nobles, his wives and his concubines drank
from them. 4 As they drank the wine, they
praised the gods of gold and silver, of
bronze, iron, wood and stone.

5 Suddenly the fingers of a human hand
appeared and wrote on the plaster of the
wall, near the lampstand in the royal
palace. The king watched the hand as it
wrote. 6 His face turned pale and he was
so frightened that his legs became weak
and his knees were knocking.

7 The king summoned the enchanters,
astrologers[b] and diviners. Then he said
to these wise men of Babylon, "Whoever reads this writing and tells me what it
means will be clothed in purple and have
a gold chain placed around his neck, and
he will be made the third highest ruler in
the kingdom."

8 Then all the king's wise men came
in, but they could not read the writing or
tell the king what it meant. 9 So King Belshazzar became even more terrified and
his face grew more pale. His nobles were
baffled.

10 The queen,[c] hearing the voices of the
king and his nobles, came into the banquet hall. "May the king live forever!" she
said. "Don't be alarmed! Don't look so
pale! 11 There is a man in your kingdom
who has the spirit of the holy gods in him.
In the time of your father he was found to
have insight and intelligence and wisdom
like that of the gods. Your father, King
Nebuchadnezzar, appointed him chief
of the magicians, enchanters, astrologers and diviners. 12 He did this because
Daniel, whom the king called Belteshazzar, was found to have a keen mind and
knowledge and understanding, and also
the ability to interpret dreams, explain
riddles and solve difficult problems. Call
for Daniel, and he will tell you what the
writing means."

13 So Daniel was brought before the
king, and the king said to him, "Are you
Daniel, one of the exiles my father the
king brought from Judah? 14 I have heard
that the spirit of the gods is in you and
that you have insight, intelligence and
outstanding wisdom. 15 The wise men
and enchanters were brought before me
to read this writing and tell me what it
means, but they could not explain it.
16 Now I have heard that you are able to
give interpretations and to solve difficult
problems. If you can read this writing
and tell me what it means, you will be
clothed in purple and have a gold chain
placed around your neck, and you will
be made the third highest ruler in the
kingdom."

17 Then Daniel answered the king, "You
may keep your gifts for yourself and give
your rewards to someone else. Nevertheless, I will read the writing for the king
and tell him what it means.

18 "Your Majesty, the Most High God
gave your father Nebuchadnezzar sovereignty and greatness and glory and
splendor. 19 Because of the high position
he gave him, all the nations and peoples
of every language dreaded and feared
him. Those the king wanted to put to
death, he put to death; those he wanted to
spare, he spared; those he wanted to promote, he promoted; and those he wanted
to humble, he humbled. 20 But when his
heart became arrogant and hardened
with pride, he was deposed from his royal throne and stripped of his glory. 21 He
was driven away from people and given
the mind of an animal; he lived with the
wild donkeys and ate grass like the ox;
and his body was drenched with the dew
of heaven, until he acknowledged that
the Most High God is sovereign over all
kingdoms on earth and sets over them
anyone he wishes.

22 "But you, Belshazzar, his son,[d] have
not humbled yourself, though you knew
all this. 23 Instead, you have set yourself
up against the Lord of heaven. You had
the goblets from his temple brought to
you, and you and your nobles, your wives
and your concubines drank wine from
them. You praised the gods of silver and
gold, of bronze, iron, wood and stone,
which cannot see or hear or understand.
But you did not honor the God who holds
in his hand your life and all your ways.
24 Therefore he sent the hand that wrote
the inscription.

[a] *2* Or *ancestor*; or *predecessor*; also in verses 11, 13 and 18 [b] *7* Or *Chaldeans*; also in verse 11
[c] *10* Or *queen mother* [d] *22* Or *descendant*; or *successor*

25 "This is the inscription that was written:

MENE, MENE, TEKEL, PARSIN

26 "Here is what these words mean:

Mene[a]: God has numbered
the days of your reign and
brought it to an end.
27 *Tekel*[b]: You have been weighed
on the scales and found
wanting.
28 *Peres*[c]: Your kingdom is divided and given to the Medes
and Persians."

29 Then at Belshazzar's command,
Daniel was clothed in purple, a gold
chain was placed around his neck, and
he was proclaimed the third highest ruler in the kingdom.
30 That very night Belshazzar, king of
the Babylonians,[d] was slain, 31 and Darius the Mede took over the kingdom, at the
age of sixty-two.[e]

6[f] It pleased Darius to appoint 120 satraps to rule throughout the kingdom, 2 with three administrators over
them, one of whom was Daniel. The satraps were made accountable to them so
that the king might not suffer loss. 3 Now
Daniel so distinguished himself among
the administrators and the satraps by
his exceptional qualities that the king
planned to set him over the whole kingdom. 4 At this, the administrators and the
satraps tried to find grounds for charges
against Daniel in his conduct of government affairs, but they were unable to do
so. They could find no corruption in him,
because he was trustworthy and neither
corrupt nor negligent. 5 Finally these
men said, "We will never find any basis
for charges against this man Daniel unless it has something to do with the law
of his God."
6 So these administrators and satraps
went as a group to the king and said:
"May King Darius live forever! 7 The royal
administrators, prefects, satraps, advisers and governors have all agreed that
the king should issue an edict and en-
force the decree that anyone who prays to
any god or human being during the next
thirty days, except to you, Your Majesty,
shall be thrown into the lions' den. 8 Now,
Your Majesty, issue the decree and put it
in writing so that it cannot be altered—in
accordance with the law of the Medes and
Persians, which cannot be repealed." 9 So
King Darius put the decree in writing.
10 Now when Daniel learned that the decree had been published, he went home
to his upstairs room where the windows
opened toward Jerusalem. Three times a
day he got down on his knees and prayed,
giving thanks to his God, just as he had
done before. 11 Then these men went as
a group and found Daniel praying and
asking God for help. 12 So they went to the
king and spoke to him about his royal decree: "Did you not publish a decree that
during the next thirty days anyone who
prays to any god or human being except
to you, Your Majesty, would be thrown
into the lions' den?"
The king answered, "The decree
stands—in accordance with the law of
the Medes and Persians, which cannot
be repealed."
13 Then they said to the king, "Daniel,
who is one of the exiles from Judah, pays
no attention to you, Your Majesty, or to the
decree you put in writing. He still prays
three times a day." 14 When the king heard
this, he was greatly distressed; he was determined to rescue Daniel and made every effort until sundown to save him.
15 Then the men went as a group to King
Darius and said to him, "Remember, Your
Majesty, that according to the law of the
Medes and Persians no decree or edict
that the king issues can be changed."
16 So the king gave the order, and they
brought Daniel and threw him into the
lions' den. The king said to Daniel, "May
your God, whom you serve continually,
rescue you!"
17 A stone was brought and placed over
the mouth of the den, and the king sealed
it with his own signet ring and with the
rings of his nobles, so that Daniel's situation might not be changed. 18 Then the
king returned to his palace and spent the
night without eating and without any en-
tertainment being brought to him. And
he could not sleep.

[a] 26 *Mene* can mean *numbered* or *mina* (a unit of money). [b] 27 *Tekel* can mean *weighed* or *shekel.* [c] 28 *Peres* (the singular of *Parsin*) can mean *divided* or *Persia* or *a half mina* or *a half shekel.* [d] 30 Or *Chaldeans* [e] 31 In Aramaic texts this verse (5:31) is numbered 6:1. [f] In Aramaic texts 6:1-28 is numbered 6:2-29.

19 At the first light of dawn, the king got
up and hurried to the lions' den. 20 When
he came near the den, he called to Daniel
in an anguished voice, "Daniel, servant
of the living God, has your God, whom
you serve continually, been able to rescue you from the lions?"

21 Daniel answered, "May the king live
forever! 22 My God sent his angel, and he
shut the mouths of the lions. They have
not hurt me, because I was found innocent in his sight. Nor have I ever done any
wrong before you, Your Majesty."

23 The king was overjoyed and gave
orders to lift Daniel out of the den. And
when Daniel was lifted from the den, no
wound was found on him, because he
had trusted in his God.

24 At the king's command, the men who
had falsely accused Daniel were brought
in and thrown into the lions' den, along
with their wives and children. And before they reached the floor of the den, the
lions overpowered them and crushed all
their bones.

25 Then King Darius wrote to all the nations and peoples of every language in all
the earth:

"May you prosper greatly!

26 "I issue a decree that in every
part of my kingdom people must fear
and reverence the God of Daniel.

"For he is the living God
  and he endures forever;
his kingdom will not be destroyed,
  his dominion will never end.
27 He rescues and he saves;
  he performs signs and wonders
  in the heavens and on the earth.
He has rescued Daniel
  from the power of the lions."

28 So Daniel prospered during the reign
of Darius and the reign of Cyrus[a] the Persian.

7 In the first year of Belshazzar king
of Babylon, Daniel had a dream, and
visions passed through his mind as he
was lying in bed. He wrote down the substance of his dream.

2 Daniel said: "In my vision at night I
looked, and there before me were the four
winds of heaven churning up the great
sea. 3 Four great beasts, each different
from the others, came up out of the sea.

4 "The first was like a lion, and it had
the wings of an eagle. I watched until its
wings were torn off and it was lifted from
the ground so that it stood on two feet like
a human being, and the mind of a human
was given to it.

5 "And there before me was a second
beast, which looked like a bear. It was
raised up on one of its sides, and it had
three ribs in its mouth between its teeth. It
was told, 'Get up and eat your fill of flesh!'

6 "After that, I looked, and there before
me was another beast, one that looked
like a leopard. And on its back it had four
wings like those of a bird. This beast had
four heads, and it was given authority to
rule.

7 "After that, in my vision at night I
looked, and there before me was a fourth
beast—terrifying and frightening and
very powerful. It had large iron teeth; it
crushed and devoured its victims and
trampled underfoot whatever was left. It
was different from all the former beasts,
and it had ten horns.

8 "While I was thinking about the
horns, there before me was another horn,
a little one, which came up among them;
and three of the first horns were uprooted
before it. This horn had eyes like the eyes
of a human being and a mouth that spoke
boastfully.

9 "As I looked,

"thrones were set in place,
  and the Ancient of Days took his
    seat.
His clothing was as white as snow;
  the hair of his head was white like
    wool.
His throne was flaming with fire,
  and its wheels were all ablaze.
10 A river of fire was flowing,
  coming out from before him.
Thousands upon thousands attended
    him;
  ten thousand times ten thousand
    stood before him.
The court was seated,
  and the books were opened.

11 "Then I continued to watch because
of the boastful words the horn was speaking. I kept looking until the beast was

[a] 28 Or *Darius, that is, the reign of Cyrus*

slain and its body destroyed and thrown
into the blazing fire. 12(The other beasts
had been stripped of their authority, but
were allowed to live for a period of time.)
13"In my vision at night I looked, and
there before me was one like a son of
man,[a] coming with the clouds of heaven.
He approached the Ancient of Days and
was led into his presence. 14He was giv-
en authority, glory and sovereign power;
all nations and peoples of every language
worshiped him. His dominion is an everlasting dominion that will not pass away,
and his kingdom is one that will never be
destroyed.
15"I, Daniel, was troubled in spirit, and
the visions that passed through my mind
disturbed me. 16I approached one of
those standing there and asked him the
meaning of all this.
"So he told me and gave me the interpretation of these things: 17'The four
great beasts are four kings that will rise
from the earth. 18But the holy people of
the Most High will receive the kingdom
and will possess it forever—yes, for ever
and ever.'
19"Then I wanted to know the meaning
of the fourth beast, which was different
from all the others and most terrifying,
with its iron teeth and bronze claws—the
beast that crushed and devoured its victims and trampled underfoot whatever
was left. 20I also wanted to know about the
ten horns on its head and about the other horn that came up, before which three
of them fell—the horn that looked more
imposing than the others and that had
eyes and a mouth that spoke boastfully. 21As I watched, this horn was waging
war against the holy people and defeating
them, 22until the Ancient of Days came
and pronounced judgment in favor of the
holy people of the Most High, and the time
came when they possessed the kingdom.
23"He gave me this explanation: 'The
fourth beast is a fourth kingdom that
will appear on earth. It will be different
from all the other kingdoms and will devour the whole earth, trampling it down
and crushing it. 24The ten horns are ten
kings who will come from this kingdom.
After them another king will arise, different from the earlier ones; he will subdue
three kings. 25He will speak against the
Most High and oppress his holy people
and try to change the set times and the
laws. The holy people will be delivered
into his hands for a time, times and half
a time.[b]
26"'But the court will sit, and his power will be taken away and completely destroyed forever. 27Then the sovereignty,
power and greatness of all the kingdoms
under heaven will be handed over to the
holy people of the Most High. His kingdom will be an everlasting kingdom, and
all rulers will worship and obey him.'
28"This is the end of the matter. I, Daniel, was deeply troubled by my thoughts,
and my face turned pale, but I kept the
matter to myself."

8 In the third year of King Belshazzar's
reign, I, Daniel, had a vision, after the
one that had already appeared to me. 2In
my vision I saw myself in the citadel of
Susa in the province of Elam; in the vision
I was beside the Ulai Canal. 3I looked up,
and there before me was a ram with two
horns, standing beside the canal, and the
horns were long. One of the horns was
longer than the other but grew up later.
4I watched the ram as it charged toward
the west and the north and the south. No
animal could stand against it, and none
could rescue from its power. It did as it
pleased and became great.
5As I was thinking about this, suddenly a goat with a prominent horn between
its eyes came from the west, crossing
the whole earth without touching the
ground. 6It came toward the two-horned
ram I had seen standing beside the canal
and charged at it in great rage. 7I saw it
attack the ram furiously, striking the ram
and shattering its two horns. The ram
was powerless to stand against it; the goat
knocked it to the ground and trampled on
it, and none could rescue the ram from
its power. 8The goat became very great,
but at the height of its power the large
horn was broken off, and in its place four
prominent horns grew up toward the four
winds of heaven.
9Out of one of them came another horn,
which started small but grew in power to
the south and to the east and toward the

[a] *13* The Aramaic phrase *bar enash* means *human being.* The phrase *son of man* is retained here because of its use in the New Testament as a title of Jesus, probably based largely on this verse. [b] *25* Or *for a year, two years and half a year*

Beautiful Land. 10 It grew until it reached
the host of the heavens, and it threw some
of the starry host down to the earth and
trampled on them. 11 It set itself up to be
as great as the commander of the army of
the LORD; it took away the daily sacrifice
from the LORD, and his sanctuary was
thrown down. 12 Because of rebellion,
the LORD's people[a] and the daily sacrifice were given over to it. It prospered in
everything it did, and truth was thrown
to the ground.

13 Then I heard a holy one speaking, and
another holy one said to him, "How long
will it take for the vision to be fulfilled —
the vision concerning the daily sacrifice,
the rebellion that causes desolation, the
surrender of the sanctuary and the trampling underfoot of the LORD's people?"

14 He said to me, "It will take 2,300 evenings and mornings; then the sanctuary
will be reconsecrated."

15 While I, Daniel, was watching the
vision and trying to understand it, there
before me stood one who looked like a
man. 16 And I heard a man's voice from
the Ulai calling, "Gabriel, tell this man
the meaning of the vision."

17 As he came near the place where
I was standing, I was terrified and fell
prostrate. "Son of man,"[b] he said to me,
"understand that the vision concerns the
time of the end."

18 While he was speaking to me, I was in
a deep sleep, with my face to the ground.
Then he touched me and raised me to my
feet.

19 He said: "I am going to tell you what
will happen later in the time of wrath, because the vision concerns the appointed
time of the end.[c] 20 The two-horned ram
that you saw represents the kings of Media and Persia. 21 The shaggy goat is the
king of Greece, and the large horn between its eyes is the first king. 22 The four
horns that replaced the one that was broken off represent four kingdoms that will
emerge from his nation but will not have
the same power.

23 "In the latter part of their reign, when
rebels have become completely wicked, a
fierce-looking king, a master of intrigue,
will arise. 24 He will become very strong,
but not by his own power. He will cause
astounding devastation and will succeed in whatever he does. He will destroy
those who are mighty, the holy people.
25 He will cause deceit to prosper, and
he will consider himself superior. When
they feel secure, he will destroy many
and take his stand against the Prince of
princes. Yet he will be destroyed, but not
by human power.

26 "The vision of the evenings and
mornings that has been given you is true,
but seal up the vision, for it concerns the
distant future."

27 I, Daniel, was worn out. I lay exhausted for several days. Then I got up
and went about the king's business. I was
appalled by the vision; it was beyond understanding.

9 In the first year of Darius son of Xerxes[d] (a Mede by descent), who was
made ruler over the Babylonian[e] kingdom — 2 in the first year of his reign, I,
Daniel, understood from the Scriptures,
according to the word of the LORD given
to Jeremiah the prophet, that the desolation of Jerusalem would last seventy
years. 3 So I turned to the Lord God and
pleaded with him in prayer and petition,
in fasting, and in sackcloth and ashes.

4 I prayed to the LORD my God and confessed:

"Lord, the great and awesome God,
who keeps his covenant of love with
those who love him and keep his
commandments, 5 we have sinned
and done wrong. We have been wicked and have rebelled; we have turned
away from your commands and laws.
6 We have not listened to your servants the prophets, who spoke in
your name to our kings, our princes
and our ancestors, and to all the people of the land.

7 "Lord, you are righteous, but this
day we are covered with shame — the
people of Judah and the inhabitants
of Jerusalem and all Israel, both near
and far, in all the countries where
you have scattered us because of our
unfaithfulness to you. 8 We and our
kings, our princes and our ances-

[a] 12 Or *rebellion, the armies* [b] 17 The Hebrew phrase *ben adam* means *human being.* The phrase *son of man* is retained as a form of address here because of its possible association with "Son of Man" in the New Testament. [c] 19 Or *because the end will be at the appointed time* [d] 1 Hebrew *Ahasuerus* [e] 1 Or *Chaldean*

tors are covered with shame, LORD,
because we have sinned against you.
9The Lord our God is merciful and
forgiving, even though we have rebelled against him; 10we have not
obeyed the LORD our God or kept the
laws he gave us through his servants
the prophets. 11All Israel has transgressed your law and turned away,
refusing to obey you.

"Therefore the curses and sworn
judgments written in the Law of Moses, the servant of God, have been
poured out on us, because we have
sinned against you. 12You have fulfilled the words spoken against us
and against our rulers by bringing
on us great disaster. Under the whole
heaven nothing has ever been done
like what has been done to Jerusalem. 13Just as it is written in the Law
of Moses, all this disaster has come
on us, yet we have not sought the favor of the LORD our God by turning
from our sins and giving attention
to your truth. 14The LORD did not
hesitate to bring the disaster on us,
for the LORD our God is righteous in
everything he does; yet we have not
obeyed him.

15"Now, Lord our God, who
brought your people out of Egypt
with a mighty hand and who made
for yourself a name that endures to
this day, we have sinned, we have
done wrong. 16Lord, in keeping with
all your righteous acts, turn away
your anger and your wrath from Jerusalem, your city, your holy hill.
Our sins and the iniquities of our
ancestors have made Jerusalem and
your people an object of scorn to all
those around us.

17"Now, our God, hear the prayers
and petitions of your servant. For
your sake, Lord, look with favor on
your desolate sanctuary. 18Give ear,
our God, and hear; open your eyes
and see the desolation of the city that
bears your Name. We do not make
requests of you because we are righteous, but because of your great mercy. 19Lord, listen! Lord, forgive! Lord,
hear and act! For your sake, my God,
do not delay, because your city and
your people bear your Name."

20While I was speaking and praying,
confessing my sin and the sin of my people Israel and making my request to the
LORD my God for his holy hill — 21while I
was still in prayer, Gabriel, the man I had
seen in the earlier vision, came to me in
swift flight about the time of the evening
sacrifice. 22He instructed me and said to
me, "Daniel, I have now come to give you
insight and understanding. 23As soon as
you began to pray, a word went out, which
I have come to tell you, for you are highly
esteemed. Therefore, consider the word
and understand the vision:

24"Seventy 'sevens'[a] are decreed for
your people and your holy city to finish[b] transgression, to put an end to sin,
to atone for wickedness, to bring in everlasting righteousness, to seal up vision
and prophecy and to anoint the Most
Holy Place.[c]

25"Know and understand this: From
the time the word goes out to restore
and rebuild Jerusalem until the Anointed One,[d] the ruler, comes, there will be
seven 'sevens,' and sixty-two 'sevens.' It
will be rebuilt with streets and a trench,
but in times of trouble. 26After the sixty-
two 'sevens,' the Anointed One will be
put to death and will have nothing.[e] The
people of the ruler who will come will destroy the city and the sanctuary. The end
will come like a flood: War will continue
until the end, and desolations have been
decreed. 27He will confirm a covenant
with many for one 'seven.'[f] In the middle
of the 'seven'[f] he will put an end to sacrifice and offering. And at the temple[g] he
will set up an abomination that causes
desolation, until the end that is decreed
is poured out on him.[h]"[i]

10 In the third year of Cyrus king of
Persia, a revelation was given to
Daniel (who was called Belteshazzar).
Its message was true and it concerned
a great war.[j] The understanding of the
message came to him in a vision.

2At that time I, Daniel, mourned for

[a] 24 Or *'weeks'*; also in verses 25 and 26 [b] 24 Or *restrain* [c] 24 Or *the most holy One* [d] 25 Or *an anointed one*; also in verse 26 [e] 26 Or *death and will have no one*; or *death, but not for himself* [f] 27 Or *'week'* [g] 27 Septuagint and Theodotion; Hebrew *wing* [h] 27 Or *it* [i] 27 Or *And one who causes desolation will come upon the wing of the abominable temple, until the end that is decreed is poured out on the desolated city* [j] 1 Or *true and burdensome*

three weeks. 3I ate no choice food; no
meat or wine touched my lips; and I used
no lotions at all until the three weeks
were over.
4On the twenty-fourth day of the first
month, as I was standing on the bank of
the great river, the Tigris, 5I looked up
and there before me was a man dressed in
linen, with a belt of fine gold from Uphaz
around his waist. 6His body was like topaz, his face like lightning, his eyes like
flaming torches, his arms and legs like
the gleam of burnished bronze, and his
voice like the sound of a multitude.
7I, Daniel, was the only one who saw
the vision; those who were with me did
not see it, but such terror overwhelmed
them that they fled and hid themselves.
8So I was left alone, gazing at this great
vision; I had no strength left, my face
turned deathly pale and I was helpless.
9Then I heard him speaking, and as I listened to him, I fell into a deep sleep, my
face to the ground.
10A hand touched me and set me trembling on my hands and knees. 11He said,
"Daniel, you who are highly esteemed,
consider carefully the words I am about
to speak to you, and stand up, for I have
now been sent to you." And when he said
this to me, I stood up trembling.
12Then he continued, "Do not be
afraid, Daniel. Since the first day that
you set your mind to gain understanding
and to humble yourself before your God,
your words were heard, and I have come
in response to them. 13But the prince of
the Persian kingdom resisted me twenty-one days. Then Michael, one of the
chief princes, came to help me, because
I was detained there with the king of Persia. 14Now I have come to explain to you
what will happen to your people in the
future, for the vision concerns a time yet
to come."
15While he was saying this to me, I
bowed with my face toward the ground
and was speechless. 16Then one who
looked like a man[a] touched my lips, and
I opened my mouth and began to speak.
I said to the one standing before me, "I
am overcome with anguish because of
the vision, my lord, and I feel very weak.
17How can I, your servant, talk with you,
my lord? My strength is gone and I can
hardly breathe."
18Again the one who looked like a man
touched me and gave me strength. 19"Do
not be afraid, you who are highly esteemed," he said. "Peace! Be strong now;
be strong."
When he spoke to me, I was strengthened and said, "Speak, my lord, since you
have given me strength."
20So he said, "Do you know why I have
come to you? Soon I will return to fight
against the prince of Persia, and when
I go, the prince of Greece will come;
21but first I will tell you what is written
in the Book of Truth. (No one supports
me against them except Michael, your
11 prince. 1And in the first year of Darius the Mede, I took my stand to support and protect him.)
2"Now then, I tell you the truth: Three
more kings will arise in Persia, and then a
fourth, who will be far richer than all the
others. When he has gained power by his
wealth, he will stir up everyone against
the kingdom of Greece. 3Then a mighty
king will arise, who will rule with great
power and do as he pleases. 4After he has
arisen, his empire will be broken up and
parceled out toward the four winds of
heaven. It will not go to his descendants,
nor will it have the power he exercised,
because his empire will be uprooted and
given to others.
5"The king of the South will become
strong, but one of his commanders will
become even stronger than he and will
rule his own kingdom with great power.
6After some years, they will become allies. The daughter of the king of the South
will go to the king of the North to make an
alliance, but she will not retain her power, and he and his power[b] will not last. In
those days she will be betrayed, together
with her royal escort and her father[c] and
the one who supported her.
7"One from her family line will arise to
take her place. He will attack the forces
of the king of the North and enter his fortress; he will fight against them and be
victorious. 8He will also seize their gods,
their metal images and their valuable articles of silver and gold and carry them off
to Egypt. For some years he will leave the

[a] 16 Most manuscripts of the Masoretic Text; one manuscript of the Masoretic Text, Dead Sea Scrolls and Septuagint *Then something that looked like a human hand* [b] 6 Or *offspring* [c] 6 Or *child* (see Vulgate and Syriac)

king of the North alone. 9Then the king
of the North will invade the realm of the
king of the South but will retreat to his
own country. 10His sons will prepare for
war and assemble a great army, which
will sweep on like an irresistible flood
and carry the battle as far as his fortress.
11"Then the king of the South will
march out in a rage and fight against the
king of the North, who will raise a large
army, but it will be defeated. 12When the
army is carried off, the king of the South
will be filled with pride and will slaughter
many thousands, yet he will not remain
triumphant. 13For the king of the North
will muster another army, larger than the
first; and after several years, he will advance with a huge army fully equipped.
14"In those times many will rise
against the king of the South. Those
who are violent among your own people will rebel in fulfillment of the vision,
but without success. 15Then the king of
the North will come and build up siege
ramps and will capture a fortified city.
The forces of the South will be powerless
to resist; even their best troops will not
have the strength to stand. 16The invader will do as he pleases; no one will be
able to stand against him. He will establish himself in the Beautiful Land and
will have the power to destroy it. 17He
will determine to come with the might
of his entire kingdom and will make an
alliance with the king of the South. And
he will give him a daughter in marriage
in order to overthrow the kingdom, but
his plans[a] will not succeed or help him.
18Then he will turn his attention to the
coastlands and will take many of them,
but a commander will put an end to his
insolence and will turn his insolence
back on him. 19After this, he will turn
back toward the fortresses of his own
country but will stumble and fall, to be
seen no more.
20"His successor will send out a tax collector to maintain the royal splendor. In a
few years, however, he will be destroyed,
yet not in anger or in battle.
21"He will be succeeded by a contemptible person who has not been given the
honor of royalty. He will invade the kingdom when its people feel secure, and he
will seize it through intrigue. 22Then an
overwhelming army will be swept away
before him; both it and a prince of the
covenant will be destroyed. 23After coming to an agreement with him, he will act
deceitfully, and with only a few people
he will rise to power. 24When the richest
provinces feel secure, he will invade them
and will achieve what neither his fathers
nor his forefathers did. He will distribute
plunder, loot and wealth among his followers. He will plot the overthrow of fortresses — but only for a time.
25"With a large army he will stir up his
strength and courage against the king of
the South. The king of the South will wage
war with a large and very powerful army,
but he will not be able to stand because
of the plots devised against him. 26Those
who eat from the king's provisions will
try to destroy him; his army will be swept
away, and many will fall in battle. 27The
two kings, with their hearts bent on evil,
will sit at the same table and lie to each
other, but to no avail, because an end will
still come at the appointed time. 28The
king of the North will return to his own
country with great wealth, but his heart
will be set against the holy covenant. He
will take action against it and then return
to his own country.
29"At the appointed time he will invade
the South again, but this time the outcome will be different from what it was
before. 30Ships of the western coastlands
will oppose him, and he will lose heart.
Then he will turn back and vent his fury
against the holy covenant. He will return
and show favor to those who forsake the
holy covenant.
31"His armed forces will rise up to desecrate the temple fortress and will abolish the daily sacrifice. Then they will set
up the abomination that causes desolation. 32With flattery he will corrupt those
who have violated the covenant, but the
people who know their God will firmly
resist him.
33"Those who are wise will instruct
many, though for a time they will fall by
the sword or be burned or captured or
plundered. 34When they fall, they will receive a little help, and many who are not
sincere will join them. 35Some of the wise
will stumble, so that they may be refined,
purified and made spotless until the time

[a] *17* Or *but she*

of the end, for it will still come at the appointed time.
36 "The king will do as he pleases. He
will exalt and magnify himself above every god and will say unheard-of things
against the God of gods. He will be successful until the time of wrath is completed, for what has been determined must
take place. 37 He will show no regard for
the gods of his ancestors or for the one
desired by women, nor will he regard any
god, but will exalt himself above them
all. 38 Instead of them, he will honor a
god of fortresses; a god unknown to his
ancestors he will honor with gold and
silver, with precious stones and costly
gifts. 39 He will attack the mightiest fortresses with the help of a foreign god and
will greatly honor those who acknowledge him. He will make them rulers over
many people and will distribute the land
at a price.[a]
40 "At the time of the end the king of the
South will engage him in battle, and the
king of the North will storm out against
him with chariots and cavalry and a
great fleet of ships. He will invade many
countries and sweep through them like
a flood. 41 He will also invade the Beautiful Land. Many countries will fall, but
Edom, Moab and the leaders of Ammon
will be delivered from his hand. 42 He will
extend his power over many countries;
Egypt will not escape. 43 He will gain
control of the treasures of gold and silver
and all the riches of Egypt, with the Libyans and Cushites[b] in submission. 44 But
reports from the east and the north will
alarm him, and he will set out in a great
rage to destroy and annihilate many.
45 He will pitch his royal tents between
the seas at[c] the beautiful holy mountain.
Yet he will come to his end, and no one
will help him.

12 "At that time Michael, the great
prince who protects your people,
will arise. There will be a time of distress such as has not happened from the
beginning of nations until then. But at
that time your people—everyone whose
name is found written in the book—will
be delivered. 2 Multitudes who sleep in
the dust of the earth will awake: some
to everlasting life, others to shame and
everlasting contempt. 3 Those who are
wise[d] will shine like the brightness of
the heavens, and those who lead many to
righteousness, like the stars for ever and
ever. 4 But you, Daniel, roll up and seal
the words of the scroll until the time of
the end. Many will go here and there to
increase knowledge."

5 Then I, Daniel, looked, and there before me stood two others, one on this bank
of the river and one on the opposite bank.
6 One of them said to the man clothed in
linen, who was above the waters of the
river, "How long will it be before these
astonishing things are fulfilled?"
7 The man clothed in linen, who was
above the waters of the river, lifted his
right hand and his left hand toward heav-
en, and I heard him swear by him who
lives forever, saying, "It will be for a time,
times and half a time.[e] When the power
of the holy people has been finally broken, all these things will be completed."
8 I heard, but I did not understand. So
I asked, "My lord, what will the outcome
of all this be?"
9 He replied, "Go your way, Daniel, because the words are rolled up and sealed
until the time of the end. 10 Many will be
purified, made spotless and refined, but
the wicked will continue to be wicked.
None of the wicked will understand, but
those who are wise will understand.
11 "From the time that the daily sacrifice is abolished and the abomination
that causes desolation is set up, there
will be 1,290 days. 12 Blessed is the one
who waits for and reaches the end of the
1,335 days.
13 "As for you, go your way till the end.
You will rest, and then at the end of the
days you will rise to receive your allotted
inheritance."

[a] 39 Or *land for a reward* [b] 43 That is, people from the upper Nile region [c] 45 Or *the sea and*
[d] 3 Or *who impart wisdom* [e] 7 Or *a year, two years and half a year*

HOSEA

The prophet Hosea spoke to the northern kingdom of Israel in the turbulent period of the 8th century BC. Following the death of Jeroboam II, Israel had six different kings in just over twenty years; four were assassinated and the last was forcibly removed from the throne. The rising empire of Assyria invaded Israel, and by 722 BC had completely conquered the nation and carried off much of its population into exile.

Israel had made the mistake of identifying the Lord with Baal, a Canaanite nature god. This identification may have begun innocently enough, since *baal* simply means "master." But by the time of Hosea, the people were visiting shrine prostitutes, and had adopted the magical practices of fertility cults. Hosea repeatedly denounces this corrupted worship as spiritual prostitution. He also condemns the nation's foolish foreign intrigues, its rejection of the moral law, and its callous greed. The people dismissed Hosea's warnings, however, and simply mocked him.

The book is structured into two main parts. The shorter first part tells how God commanded Hosea to marry the unfaithful woman Gomer. She is symbolic of Israel's wavering faithfulness to the LORD. The prophet's own life thus provided a picture of God's intentions toward wayward Israel. The longer second part contains oracles delivered during the decline after King Jeroboam, alternating hope and doom as Hosea both threatens and pleads with the kingdom of Israel in the last years before its exile.

---

1 The word of the LORD that came to
Hosea son of Beeri during the reigns
of Uzziah, Jotham, Ahaz and Hezekiah,
kings of Judah, and during the reign of
Jeroboam son of Jehoash[a] king of Israel:

2 When the LORD began to speak
through Hosea, the LORD said to him,
"Go, marry a promiscuous woman and
have children with her, for like an adulterous wife this land is guilty of unfaithfulness to the LORD." 3 So he married
Gomer daughter of Diblaim, and she
conceived and bore him a son.
4 Then the LORD said to Hosea, "Call
him Jezreel, because I will soon punish
the house of Jehu for the massacre at Jezreel, and I will put an end to the kingdom
of Israel. 5 In that day I will break Israel's
bow in the Valley of Jezreel."
6 Gomer conceived again and gave
birth to a daughter. Then the LORD said
to Hosea, "Call her Lo-Ruhamah (which
means "not loved"), for I will no longer
show love to Israel, that I should at all forgive them. 7 Yet I will show love to Judah;
and I will save them — not by bow, sword
or battle, or by horses and horsemen, but
I, the LORD their God, will save them."
8 After she had weaned Lo-Ruhamah,
Gomer had another son. 9 Then the LORD
said, "Call him Lo-Ammi (which means
"not my people"), for you are not my people, and I am not your God.[b]
10 "Yet the Israelites will be like the
sand on the seashore, which cannot be
measured or counted. In the place where
it was said to them, 'You are not my people,' they will be called 'children of the
living God.' 11 The people of Judah and
the people of Israel will come together; they will appoint one leader and will
come up out of the land, for great will be
the day of Jezreel.[c]

2[d] "Say of your brothers, 'My people,'
and of your sisters, 'My loved one.'

2 "Rebuke your mother, rebuke her,
for she is not my wife,
and I am not her husband.
Let her remove the adulterous look
from her face
and the unfaithfulness from
between her breasts.
3 Otherwise I will strip her naked
and make her as bare as on the day
she was born;
I will make her like a desert,
turn her into a parched land,
and slay her with thirst.
4 I will not show my love to her children,
because they are the children of
adultery.
5 Their mother has been unfaithful
and has conceived them in disgrace.

[a] *1* Hebrew *Joash,* a variant of *Jehoash* [b] *9* Or *your I AM* [c] *11* In Hebrew texts 1:10,11 is numbered 2:1,2.
[d] In Hebrew texts 2:1-23 is numbered 2:3-25.

She said, 'I will go after my lovers,
who give me my food and my water,
my wool and my linen, my olive oil
and my drink.'
6 Therefore I will block her path with
thornbushes;
I will wall her in so that she cannot
find her way.
7 She will chase after her lovers but not
catch them;
she will look for them but not find
them.
Then she will say,
'I will go back to my husband as at
first,
for then I was better off than now.'
8 She has not acknowledged that I was
the one
who gave her the grain, the new
wine and oil,
who lavished on her the silver and
gold—
which they used for Baal.

9 "Therefore I will take away my grain
when it ripens,
and my new wine when it is ready.
I will take back my wool and my linen,
intended to cover her naked body.
10 So now I will expose her lewdness
before the eyes of her lovers;
no one will take her out of my hands.
11 I will stop all her celebrations:
her yearly festivals, her New Moons,
her Sabbath days—all her
appointed festivals.
12 I will ruin her vines and her fig trees,
which she said were her pay from
her lovers;
I will make them a thicket,
and wild animals will devour them.
13 I will punish her for the days
she burned incense to the Baals;
she decked herself with rings and
jewelry,
and went after her lovers,
but me she forgot,"
declares the LORD.

14 "Therefore I am now going to allure
her;
I will lead her into the wilderness
and speak tenderly to her.
15 There I will give her back her
vineyards,
and will make the Valley of Achor[a] a
door of hope.
There she will respond[b] as in the days
of her youth,
as in the day she came up out of
Egypt.

16 "In that day," declares the LORD,
"you will call me 'my husband';
you will no longer call me 'my
master.[c]'
17 I will remove the names of the Baals
from her lips;
no longer will their names be
invoked.
18 In that day I will make a covenant for
them
with the beasts of the field, the birds
in the sky
and the creatures that move along
the ground.
Bow and sword and battle
I will abolish from the land,
so that all may lie down in safety.
19 I will betroth you to me forever;
I will betroth you in[d] righteousness
and justice,
in[d] love and compassion.
20 I will betroth you in[d] faithfulness,
and you will acknowledge the LORD.

21 "In that day I will respond,"
declares the LORD—
"I will respond to the skies,
and they will respond to the earth;
22 and the earth will respond to the
grain,
the new wine and the olive oil,
and they will respond to Jezreel.[e]
23 I will plant her for myself in the land;
I will show my love to the one I
called 'Not my loved one.[f]'
I will say to those called 'Not my
people,[g]' 'You are my people';
and they will say, 'You are my God.'"

3 The LORD said to me, "Go, show your
love to your wife again, though she is
loved by another man and is an adulteress. Love her as the LORD loves the Israelites, though they turn to other gods and
love the sacred raisin cakes."
2 So I bought her for fifteen shekels[h] of
silver and about a homer and a lethek[i] of
barley. 3 Then I told her, "You are to live

[a] 15 *Achor* means *trouble.* [b] 15 Or *sing* [c] 16 Hebrew *baal* [d] 19,20 Or *with* [e] 22 *Jezreel* means *God plants.* [f] 23 Hebrew *Lo-Ruhamah* (see 1:6) [g] 23 Hebrew *Lo-Ammi* (see 1:9) [h] 2 That is, about 6 ounces or about 170 grams [i] 2 A homer and a lethek possibly weighed about 430 pounds or about 195 kilograms.

with me many days; you must not be a
prostitute or be intimate with any man,
and I will behave the same way toward
you."
4 For the Israelites will live many days
without king or prince, without sacrifice
or sacred stones, without ephod or household gods. 5 Afterward the Israelites will
return and seek the LORD their God and
David their king. They will come trembling to the LORD and to his blessings in
the last days.

4 Hear the word of the LORD, you
Israelites,
because the LORD has a charge to
bring
against you who live in the land:
"There is no faithfulness, no love,
no acknowledgment of God in the
land.
2 There is only cursing,[a] lying and
murder,
stealing and adultery;
they break all bounds,
and bloodshed follows bloodshed.
3 Because of this the land dries up,
and all who live in it waste away;
the beasts of the field, the birds in the
sky
and the fish in the sea are swept
away.

4 "But let no one bring a charge,
let no one accuse another,
for your people are like those
who bring charges against a priest.
5 You stumble day and night,
and the prophets stumble with you.
So I will destroy your mother —
6 my people are destroyed from lack
of knowledge.

"Because you have rejected
knowledge,
I also reject you as my priests;
because you have ignored the law of
your God,
I also will ignore your children.
7 The more priests there were,
the more they sinned against me;
they exchanged their glorious God[b]
for something disgraceful.
8 They feed on the sins of my people
and relish their wickedness.
9 And it will be: Like people, like priests.
I will punish both of them for their
ways
and repay them for their deeds.

10 "They will eat but not have enough;
they will engage in prostitution but
not flourish,
because they have deserted the LORD
to give themselves 11 to prostitution;
old wine and new wine
take away their understanding.
12 My people consult a wooden idol,
and a diviner's rod speaks to them.
A spirit of prostitution leads them
astray;
they are unfaithful to their God.
13 They sacrifice on the mountaintops
and burn offerings on the hills,
under oak, poplar and terebinth,
where the shade is pleasant.
Therefore your daughters turn to
prostitution
and your daughters-in-law to
adultery.

14 "I will not punish your daughters
when they turn to prostitution,
nor your daughters-in-law
when they commit adultery,
because the men themselves consort
with harlots
and sacrifice with shrine
prostitutes —
a people without understanding will
come to ruin!

15 "Though you, Israel, commit
adultery,
do not let Judah become guilty.

"Do not go to Gilgal;
do not go up to Beth Aven.[c]
And do not swear, 'As surely as the
LORD lives!'
16 The Israelites are stubborn,
like a stubborn heifer.
How then can the LORD pasture them
like lambs in a meadow?
17 Ephraim is joined to idols;
leave him alone!
18 Even when their drinks are gone,
they continue their prostitution;
their rulers dearly love shameful
ways.
19 A whirlwind will sweep them away,

[a] *2* That is, to pronounce a curse on
[b] *7* Syriac (see also an ancient Hebrew scribal tradition); Masoretic Text *me; / I will exchange their glory*
[c] *15* *Beth Aven* means *house of wickedness* (a derogatory name for Bethel, which means *house of God*).

and their sacrifices will bring them
shame.

5 "Hear this, you priests!
Pay attention, you Israelites!
Listen, royal house!
This judgment is against you:
You have been a snare at Mizpah,
a net spread out on Tabor.
2 The rebels are knee-deep in slaughter.
I will discipline all of them.
3 I know all about Ephraim;
Israel is not hidden from me.
Ephraim, you have now turned to
prostitution;
Israel is corrupt.

4 "Their deeds do not permit them
to return to their God.
A spirit of prostitution is in their heart;
they do not acknowledge the LORD.
5 Israel's arrogance testifies against
them;
the Israelites, even Ephraim,
stumble in their sin;
Judah also stumbles with them.
6 When they go with their flocks and
herds
to seek the LORD,
they will not find him;
he has withdrawn himself from
them.
7 They are unfaithful to the LORD;
they give birth to illegitimate
children.
When they celebrate their New Moon
feasts,
he will devour[a] their fields.

8 "Sound the trumpet in Gibeah,
the horn in Ramah.
Raise the battle cry in Beth Aven[b];
lead on, Benjamin.
9 Ephraim will be laid waste
on the day of reckoning.
Among the tribes of Israel
I proclaim what is certain.
10 Judah's leaders are like those
who move boundary stones.
I will pour out my wrath on them
like a flood of water.
11 Ephraim is oppressed,
trampled in judgment,
intent on pursuing idols.[c]
12 I am like a moth to Ephraim,
like rot to the people of Judah.

13 "When Ephraim saw his sickness,
and Judah his sores,
then Ephraim turned to Assyria,
and sent to the great king for help.
But he is not able to cure you,
not able to heal your sores.
14 For I will be like a lion to Ephraim,
like a great lion to Judah.
I will tear them to pieces and go away;
I will carry them off, with no one to
rescue them.
15 Then I will return to my lair
until they have borne their guilt
and seek my face—
in their misery
they will earnestly seek me."

6 "Come, let us return to the LORD.
He has torn us to pieces
but he will heal us;
he has injured us
but he will bind up our wounds.
2 After two days he will revive us;
on the third day he will restore us,
that we may live in his presence.
3 Let us acknowledge the LORD;
let us press on to acknowledge him.
As surely as the sun rises,
he will appear;
he will come to us like the winter
rains,
like the spring rains that water the
earth."

4 "What can I do with you, Ephraim?
What can I do with you, Judah?
Your love is like the morning mist,
like the early dew that disappears.
5 Therefore I cut you in pieces with my
prophets,
I killed you with the words of my
mouth—
then my judgments go forth like the
sun.[d]
6 For I desire mercy, not sacrifice,
and acknowledgment of God rather
than burnt offerings.
7 As at Adam,[e] they have broken the
covenant;
they were unfaithful to me there.
8 Gilead is a city of evildoers,

[a] 7 Or *Now their New Moon feasts / will devour them and* [b] 8 *Beth Aven* means *house of wickedness* (a derogatory name for Bethel, which means *house of God*). [c] 11 The meaning of the Hebrew for this word is uncertain. [d] 5 The meaning of the Hebrew for this line is uncertain. [e] 7 Or *Like Adam*; or *Like human beings*

stained with footprints of blood.
9 As marauders lie in ambush for a victim,
so do bands of priests;
they murder on the road to Shechem,
carrying out their wicked schemes.
10 I have seen a horrible thing in Israel:
There Ephraim is given to prostitution,
Israel is defiled.

11 "Also for you, Judah,
a harvest is appointed.

"Whenever I would restore the fortunes of my people,

7
1 whenever I would heal Israel,
the sins of Ephraim are exposed
and the crimes of Samaria revealed.
They practice deceit,
thieves break into houses,
bandits rob in the streets;
2 but they do not realize
that I remember all their evil deeds.
Their sins engulf them;
they are always before me.

3 "They delight the king with their wickedness,
the princes with their lies.
4 They are all adulterers,
burning like an oven
whose fire the baker need not stir
from the kneading of the dough till it rises.
5 On the day of the festival of our king
the princes become inflamed with wine,
and he joins hands with the mockers.
6 Their hearts are like an oven;
they approach him with intrigue.
Their passion smolders all night;
in the morning it blazes like a flaming fire.
7 All of them are hot as an oven;
they devour their rulers.
All their kings fall,
and none of them calls on me.

8 "Ephraim mixes with the nations;
Ephraim is a flat loaf not turned over.
9 Foreigners sap his strength,
but he does not realize it.
His hair is sprinkled with gray,
but he does not notice.
10 Israel's arrogance testifies against him,
but despite all this
he does not return to the LORD his God
or search for him.

11 "Ephraim is like a dove,
easily deceived and senseless —
now calling to Egypt,
now turning to Assyria.
12 When they go, I will throw my net over them;
I will pull them down like the birds in the sky.
When I hear them flocking together,
I will catch them.
13 Woe to them,
because they have strayed from me!
Destruction to them,
because they have rebelled against me!
I long to redeem them
but they speak about me falsely.
14 They do not cry out to me from their hearts
but wail on their beds.
They slash themselves,[a] appealing to their gods
for grain and new wine,
but they turn away from me.
15 I trained them and strengthened their arms,
but they plot evil against me.
16 They do not turn to the Most High;
they are like a faulty bow.
Their leaders will fall by the sword
because of their insolent words.
For this they will be ridiculed
in the land of Egypt.

8
"Put the trumpet to your lips!
An eagle is over the house of the LORD
because the people have broken my covenant
and rebelled against my law.
2 Israel cries out to me,
'Our God, we acknowledge you!'
3 But Israel has rejected what is good;
an enemy will pursue him.
4 They set up kings without my consent;
they choose princes without my approval.
With their silver and gold
they make idols for themselves
to their own destruction.

[a] *14* Some Hebrew manuscripts and Septuagint; most Hebrew manuscripts *They gather together*

5 Samaria, throw out your calf-idol!
My anger burns against them.
How long will they be incapable of
purity?
6 They are from Israel!
This calf—a metalworker has made it;
it is not God.
It will be broken in pieces,
that calf of Samaria.

7 "They sow the wind
and reap the whirlwind.
The stalk has no head;
it will produce no flour.
Were it to yield grain,
foreigners would swallow it up.
8 Israel is swallowed up;
now she is among the nations
like something no one wants.
9 For they have gone up to Assyria
like a wild donkey wandering alone.
Ephraim has sold herself to lovers.
10 Although they have sold themselves
among the nations,
I will now gather them together.
They will begin to waste away
under the oppression of the mighty
king.

11 "Though Ephraim built many altars
for sin offerings,
these have become altars for
sinning.
12 I wrote for them the many things of my
law,
but they regarded them as
something foreign.
13 Though they offer sacrifices as gifts to
me,
and though they eat the meat,
the LORD is not pleased with them.
Now he will remember their
wickedness
and punish their sins:
They will return to Egypt.
14 Israel has forgotten their Maker
and built palaces;
Judah has fortified many towns.
But I will send fire on their cities
that will consume their fortresses.

9 Do not rejoice, Israel;
do not be jubilant like the other
nations.
For you have been unfaithful to your
God;
you love the wages of a prostitute
at every threshing floor.
2 Threshing floors and winepresses will
not feed the people;
the new wine will fail them.
3 They will not remain in the LORD's
land;
Ephraim will return to Egypt
and eat unclean food in Assyria.
4 They will not pour out wine offerings
to the LORD,
nor will their sacrifices please him.
Such sacrifices will be to them like the
bread of mourners;
all who eat them will be unclean.
This food will be for themselves;
it will not come into the temple of
the LORD.

5 What will you do on the day of your
appointed festivals,
on the feast days of the LORD?
6 Even if they escape from destruction,
Egypt will gather them,
and Memphis will bury them.
Their treasures of silver will be taken
over by briers,
and thorns will overrun their tents.
7 The days of punishment are coming,
the days of reckoning are at hand.
Let Israel know this.
Because your sins are so many
and your hostility so great,
the prophet is considered a fool,
the inspired person a maniac.
8 The prophet, along with my God,
is the watchman over Ephraim,[a]
yet snares await him on all his paths,
and hostility in the house of his God.
9 They have sunk deep into corruption,
as in the days of Gibeah.
God will remember their wickedness
and punish them for their sins.

10 "When I found Israel,
it was like finding grapes in the
desert;
when I saw your ancestors,
it was like seeing the early fruit on
the fig tree.
But when they came to Baal Peor,
they consecrated themselves to that
shameful idol
and became as vile as the thing they
loved.
11 Ephraim's glory will fly away like a
bird—

[a] 8 Or *The prophet is the watchman over Ephraim, / the people of my God*

no birth, no pregnancy, no
conception.
12 Even if they rear children,
I will bereave them of every one.
Woe to them
when I turn away from them!
13 I have seen Ephraim, like Tyre,
planted in a pleasant place.
But Ephraim will bring out
their children to the slayer."

14 Give them, LORD—
what will you give them?
Give them wombs that miscarry
and breasts that are dry.

15 "Because of all their wickedness in
Gilgal,
I hated them there.
Because of their sinful deeds,
I will drive them out of my house.
I will no longer love them;
all their leaders are rebellious.
16 Ephraim is blighted,
their root is withered,
they yield no fruit.
Even if they bear children,
I will slay their cherished offspring."

17 My God will reject them
because they have not obeyed him;
they will be wanderers among the
nations.

10 Israel was a spreading vine;
he brought forth fruit for himself.
As his fruit increased,
he built more altars;
as his land prospered,
he adorned his sacred stones.
2 Their heart is deceitful,
and now they must bear their guilt.
The LORD will demolish their altars
and destroy their sacred stones.

3 Then they will say, "We have no king
because we did not revere the LORD.
But even if we had a king,
what could he do for us?"
4 They make many promises,
take false oaths
and make agreements;
therefore lawsuits spring up
like poisonous weeds in a plowed
field.
5 The people who live in Samaria fear
for the calf-idol of Beth Aven.[a]
Its people will mourn over it,
and so will its idolatrous priests,
those who had rejoiced over its
splendor,
because it is taken from them into
exile.
6 It will be carried to Assyria
as tribute for the great king.
Ephraim will be disgraced;
Israel will be ashamed of its foreign
alliances.
7 Samaria's king will be destroyed,
swept away like a twig on the
surface of the waters.
8 The high places of wickedness[b] will be
destroyed—
it is the sin of Israel.
Thorns and thistles will grow up
and cover their altars.
Then they will say to the mountains,
"Cover us!"
and to the hills, "Fall on us!"

9 "Since the days of Gibeah, you have
sinned, Israel,
and there you have remained.[c]
Will not war again overtake
the evildoers in Gibeah?
10 When I please, I will punish them;
nations will be gathered against
them
to put them in bonds for their
double sin.
11 Ephraim is a trained heifer
that loves to thresh;
so I will put a yoke
on her fair neck.
I will drive Ephraim,
Judah must plow,
and Jacob must break up the ground.
12 Sow righteousness for yourselves,
reap the fruit of unfailing love,
and break up your unplowed ground;
for it is time to seek the LORD,
until he comes
and showers his righteousness on
you.
13 But you have planted wickedness,
you have reaped evil,
you have eaten the fruit of
deception.
Because you have depended on your
own strength

[a] 5 *Beth Aven* means *house of wickedness* (a derogatory name for Bethel, which means *house of God*).
[b] 8 Hebrew *aven,* a reference to Beth Aven (a derogatory name for Bethel); see verse 5. [c] 9 Or *there a stand was taken*

and on your many warriors,
14 the roar of battle will rise against your people,
so that all your fortresses will be devastated —
as Shalman devastated Beth Arbel on the day of battle,
when mothers were dashed to the ground with their children.
15 So will it happen to you, Bethel,
because your wickedness is great.
When that day dawns,
the king of Israel will be completely destroyed.

11 "When Israel was a child, I loved him,
and out of Egypt I called my son.
2 But the more they were called,
the more they went away from me.[a]
They sacrificed to the Baals
and they burned incense to images
3 It was I who taught Ephraim to walk,
taking them by the arms;
but they did not realize
it was I who healed them.
4 I led them with cords of human kindness,
with ties of love.
To them I was like one who lifts
a little child to the cheek,
and I bent down to feed them.

5 "Will they not return to Egypt
and will not Assyria rule over them
because they refuse to repent?
6 A sword will flash in their cities;
it will devour their false prophets
and put an end to their plans.
7 My people are determined to turn from me.
Even though they call me God Most High,
I will by no means exalt them.

8 "How can I give you up, Ephraim?
How can I hand you over, Israel?
How can I treat you like Admah?
How can I make you like Zeboyim
My heart is changed within me;
all my compassion is aroused.
9 I will not carry out my fierce anger,
nor will I devastate Ephraim again.
For I am God, and not a man —
the Holy One among you.
I will not come against their cities.
10 They will follow the LORD;
he will roar like a lion.
When he roars,
his children will come trembling from the west.
11 They will come from Egypt,
trembling like sparrows,
from Assyria, fluttering like doves.
I will settle them in their homes,"
declares the LORD.

12 Ephraim has surrounded me with lies,
Israel with deceit.
And Judah is unruly against God,
even against the faithful Holy One.[b]

12[c] 1 Ephraim feeds on the wind;
he pursues the east wind all day
and multiplies lies and violence.
He makes a treaty with Assyria
and sends olive oil to Egypt.
2 The LORD has a charge to bring against Judah;
he will punish Jacob[d] according to his ways
and repay him according to his deeds.
3 In the womb he grasped his brother's heel;
as a man he struggled with God.
4 He struggled with the angel and overcame him;
he wept and begged for his favor.
He found him at Bethel
and talked with him there —
5 the LORD God Almighty,
the LORD is his name!
6 But you must return to your God;
maintain love and justice,
and wait for your God always.

7 The merchant uses dishonest scales
and loves to defraud.
8 Ephraim boasts,
"I am very rich; I have become wealthy.
With all my wealth they will not find in me
any iniquity or sin."

9 "I have been the LORD your God
ever since you came out of Egypt;
I will make you live in tents again,
as in the days of your appointed festivals.

[a] 2 Septuagint; Hebrew *them* [b] 12 In Hebrew texts this verse (11:12) is numbered 12:1. [c] In Hebrew texts 12:1-14 is numbered 12:2-15. [d] 2 *Jacob* means *he grasps the heel,* a Hebrew idiom for *he takes advantage of* or *he deceives.*

10 I spoke to the prophets,
gave them many visions
and told parables through them."
11 Is Gilead wicked?
Its people are worthless!
Do they sacrifice bulls in Gilgal?
Their altars will be like piles of stones
on a plowed field.
12 Jacob fled to the country of Aram[a];
Israel served to get a wife,
and to pay for her he tended sheep.
13 The LORD used a prophet to bring
Israel up from Egypt,
by a prophet he cared for him.
14 But Ephraim has aroused his bitter anger;
his Lord will leave on him the guilt
of his bloodshed
and will repay him for his contempt.

13 When Ephraim spoke, people trembled;
he was exalted in Israel.
But he became guilty of Baal
worship and died.
2 Now they sin more and more;
they make idols for themselves from
their silver,
cleverly fashioned images,
all of them the work of craftsmen.
It is said of these people,
"They offer human sacrifices!
They kiss[b] calf-idols!"
3 Therefore they will be like the
morning mist,
like the early dew that disappears,
like chaff swirling from a threshing
floor,
like smoke escaping through a
window.
4 "But I have been the LORD your God
ever since you came out of Egypt.
You shall acknowledge no God but me,
no Savior except me.
5 I cared for you in the wilderness,
in the land of burning heat.
6 When I fed them, they were satisfied;
when they were satisfied, they
became proud;
then they forgot me.
7 So I will be like a lion to them,
like a leopard I will lurk by the path.
8 Like a bear robbed of her cubs,
I will attack them and rip them open;
like a lion I will devour them —
a wild animal will tear them apart.
9 "You are destroyed, Israel,
because you are against me, against
your helper.
10 Where is your king, that he may save
you?
Where are your rulers in all your
towns,
of whom you said,
'Give me a king and princes'?
11 So in my anger I gave you a king,
and in my wrath I took him away.
12 The guilt of Ephraim is stored up,
his sins are kept on record.
13 Pains as of a woman in childbirth
come to him,
but he is a child without wisdom;
when the time arrives,
he doesn't have the sense to come
out of the womb.
14 "I will deliver this people from the
power of the grave;
I will redeem them from death.
Where, O death, are your plagues?
Where, O grave, is your destruction?

"I will have no compassion,
15 even though he thrives among his
brothers.
An east wind from the LORD will
come,
blowing in from the desert;
his spring will fail
and his well dry up.
His storehouse will be plundered
of all its treasures.
16 The people of Samaria must bear their
guilt,
because they have rebelled against
their God.
They will fall by the sword;
their little ones will be dashed to the
ground,
their pregnant women ripped
open."[c]

14[d] Return, Israel, to the LORD your
God.
Your sins have been your downfall!
2 Take words with you
and return to the LORD.
Say to him:
"Forgive all our sins

[a] *12* That is, Northwest Mesopotamia [b] *2* Or *"Men who sacrifice / kiss* [c] *16* In Hebrew texts this verse (13:16) is numbered 14:1. [d] In Hebrew texts 14:1-9 is numbered 14:2-10.

and receive us graciously,
that we may offer the fruit of our lips.[a]
3 Assyria cannot save us;
we will not mount warhorses.
We will never again say 'Our gods'
to what our own hands have made,
for in you the fatherless find compassion."

4 "I will heal their waywardness
and love them freely,
for my anger has turned away from them.
5 I will be like the dew to Israel;
he will blossom like a lily.
Like a cedar of Lebanon
he will send down his roots;
6 his young shoots will grow.
His splendor will be like an olive tree,
his fragrance like a cedar of Lebanon.
7 People will dwell again in his shade;
they will flourish like the grain,
they will blossom like the vine—
Israel's fame will be like the wine of Lebanon.
8 Ephraim, what more have I[b] to do with idols?
I will answer him and care for him.
I am like a flourishing juniper;
your fruitfulness comes from me."

9 Who is wise? Let them realize these things.
Who is discerning? Let them understand.
The ways of the LORD are right;
the righteous walk in them,
but the rebellious stumble in them.

JOEL

The exact date of the book of Joel is difficult to know, since it does not refer to the reign of any particular king. The specific occasion of the book, however, is very clear and Joel uses this occasion to deliver a powerful spiritual message.

The book begins by graphically describing how a swarm of locusts has overrun the land of Judah and eaten everything in sight. After calling for the people to repent in response to this disaster, the book offers a detailed description of the locust swarm itself. The locusts are like an invading army, with God at their head. Joel asserts that the day of the LORD—a day of judgment—has come. He renews his call for repentance through fasting, community prayer and heartfelt contrition. In response, he promises that God will not only drive the locusts away, but restore more than they have devoured. He foretells God's defeat of all the nations that oppose his people, and how God will pour out his Spirit on the survivors in Judah. If the people return to the LORD with all of their hearts, they will see the return of their prosperity when the day of the LORD arrives.

---

1 The word of the LORD that came to Joel son of Pethuel.

2 Hear this, you elders;
listen, all who live in the land.
Has anything like this ever happened in your days
or in the days of your ancestors?
3 Tell it to your children,
and let your children tell it to their children,
and their children to the next generation.
4 What the locust swarm has left
the great locusts have eaten;
what the great locusts have left
the young locusts have eaten;
what the young locusts have left
other locusts[c] have eaten.

5 Wake up, you drunkards, and weep!
Wail, all you drinkers of wine;

[a] 2 Or *offer our lips as sacrifices of bulls* [b] 8 Or Hebrew; Septuagint *What more has Ephraim* [c] 4 The precise meaning of the four Hebrew words used here for locusts is uncertain.

wail because of the new wine,
for it has been snatched from your lips.
6 A nation has invaded my land,
a mighty army without number;
it has the teeth of a lion,
the fangs of a lioness.
7 It has laid waste my vines
and ruined my fig trees.
It has stripped off their bark
and thrown it away,
leaving their branches white.

8 Mourn like a virgin in sackcloth
grieving for the betrothed of her youth.
9 Grain offerings and drink offerings
are cut off from the house of the LORD.
The priests are in mourning,
those who minister before the LORD.
10 The fields are ruined,
the ground is dried up;
the grain is destroyed,
the new wine is dried up,
the olive oil fails.

11 Despair, you farmers,
wail, you vine growers;
grieve for the wheat and the barley,
because the harvest of the field is destroyed.
12 The vine is dried up
and the fig tree is withered;
the pomegranate, the palm and the apple[a] tree—
all the trees of the field—are dried up.
Surely the people's joy
is withered away.

13 Put on sackcloth, you priests, and mourn;
wail, you who minister before the altar.
Come, spend the night in sackcloth,
you who minister before my God;
for the grain offerings and drink offerings
are withheld from the house of your God.
14 Declare a holy fast;
call a sacred assembly.
Summon the elders
and all who live in the land
to the house of the LORD your God,
and cry out to the LORD.

15 Alas for that day!
For the day of the LORD is near;
it will come like destruction from the Almighty.[b]
16 Has not the food been cut off
before our very eyes—
joy and gladness
from the house of our God?
17 The seeds are shriveled
beneath the clods.[c]
The storehouses are in ruins,
the granaries have been broken down,
for the grain has dried up.
18 How the cattle moan!
The herds mill about
because they have no pasture;
even the flocks of sheep are suffering.

19 To you, LORD, I call,
for fire has devoured the pastures in the wilderness
and flames have burned up all the trees of the field.
20 Even the wild animals pant for you;
the streams of water have dried up
and fire has devoured the pastures
in the wilderness.

2 Blow the trumpet in Zion;
sound the alarm on my holy hill.

Let all who live in the land tremble,
for the day of the LORD is coming.
It is close at hand—
2 a day of darkness and gloom,
a day of clouds and blackness.
Like dawn spreading across the mountains
a large and mighty army comes,
such as never was in ancient times
nor ever will be in ages to come.

3 Before them fire devours,
behind them a flame blazes.
Before them the land is like the garden of Eden,
behind them, a desert waste—
nothing escapes them.
4 They have the appearance of horses;
they gallop along like cavalry.
5 With a noise like that of chariots
they leap over the mountaintops,

[a] *12* Or possibly *apricot* [b] *15* Hebrew *Shaddai* [c] *17* The meaning of the Hebrew for this word is uncertain.

like a crackling fire consuming
stubble,
like a mighty army drawn up for
battle.
6 At the sight of them, nations are in
anguish;
every face turns pale.
7 They charge like warriors;
they scale walls like soldiers.
They all march in line,
not swerving from their course.
8 They do not jostle each other;
each marches straight ahead.
They plunge through defenses
without breaking ranks.
9 They rush upon the city;
they run along the wall.
They climb into the houses;
like thieves they enter through the
windows.

10 Before them the earth shakes,
the heavens tremble,
the sun and moon are darkened,
and the stars no longer shine.
11 The LORD thunders
at the head of his army;
his forces are beyond number,
and mighty is the army that obeys
his command.
The day of the LORD is great;
it is dreadful.
Who can endure it?

12 "Even now," declares the LORD,
"return to me with all your heart,
with fasting and weeping and
mourning."

13 Rend your heart
and not your garments.
Return to the LORD your God,
for he is gracious and
compassionate,
slow to anger and abounding in love
and he relents from sending
calamity.
14 Who knows? He may turn and relent
and leave behind a blessing—
grain offerings and drink offerings
for the LORD your God.

15 Blow the trumpet in Zion,
declare a holy fast,
call a sacred assembly.
16 Gather the people,
consecrate the assembly;
bring together the elders,
gather the children,
those nursing at the breast.
Let the bridegroom leave his room
and the bride her chamber.
17 Let the priests, who minister before
the LORD,
weep between the portico and the
altar.
Let them say, "Spare your people,
LORD.
Do not make your inheritance an
object of scorn,
a byword among the nations.
Why should they say among the
peoples,
'Where is their God?'"

18 Then the LORD was jealous for his land
and took pity on his people.

19 The LORD replied[a] to them:
"I am sending you grain, new wine
and olive oil,
enough to satisfy you fully;
never again will I make you
an object of scorn to the nations.

20 "I will drive the northern horde far
from you,
pushing it into a parched and barren
land;
its eastern ranks will drown in the
Dead Sea
and its western ranks in the
Mediterranean Sea.
And its stench will go up;
its smell will rise."

Surely he has done great things!
21 Do not be afraid, land of Judah;
be glad and rejoice.
Surely the LORD has done great
things!
22 Do not be afraid, you wild animals,
for the pastures in the wilderness
are becoming green.
The trees are bearing their fruit;
the fig tree and the vine yield their
riches.
23 Be glad, people of Zion,
rejoice in the LORD your God,
for he has given you the autumn rains
because he is faithful.
He sends you abundant showers,
both autumn and spring rains, as
before.

a 18,19 Or LORD will be jealous . . . / and take pity . . . / 19The LORD will reply

24 The threshing floors will be filled with grain;
the vats will overflow with new wine and oil.

25 "I will repay you for the years the locusts have eaten—
the great locust and the young locust,
the other locusts and the locust swarm[a]—
my great army that I sent among you.
26 You will have plenty to eat, until you are full,
and you will praise the name of the LORD your God,
who has worked wonders for you;
never again will my people be shamed.
27 Then you will know that I am in Israel,
that I am the LORD your God,
and that there is no other;
never again will my people be shamed.

28 "And afterward,
I will pour out my Spirit on all people.
Your sons and daughters will prophesy,
your old men will dream dreams,
your young men will see visions.
29 Even on my servants, both men and women,
I will pour out my Spirit in those days.
30 I will show wonders in the heavens
and on the earth,
blood and fire and billows of smoke.
31 The sun will be turned to darkness
and the moon to blood
before the coming of the great and dreadful day of the LORD.
32 And everyone who calls
on the name of the LORD will be saved;
for on Mount Zion and in Jerusalem
there will be deliverance,
as the LORD has said,
even among the survivors
whom the LORD calls.[b]

3[c] "In those days and at that time,
when I restore the fortunes of Judah and Jerusalem,
2 I will gather all nations
and bring them down to the Valley of Jehoshaphat.[d]
There I will put them on trial
for what they did to my inheritance,
my people Israel,
because they scattered my people
among the nations
and divided up my land.
3 They cast lots for my people
and traded boys for prostitutes;
they sold girls for wine to drink.

4 "Now what have you against me, Tyre
and Sidon and all you regions of Philistia? Are you repaying me for something
I have done? If you are paying me back, I
will swiftly and speedily return on your
own heads what you have done. 5 For you
took my silver and my gold and carried
off my finest treasures to your temples.[e]
6 You sold the people of Judah and Jerusalem to the Greeks, that you might send
them far from their homeland.
7 "See, I am going to rouse them out of
the places to which you sold them, and
I will return on your own heads what
you have done. 8 I will sell your sons and
daughters to the people of Judah, and
they will sell them to the Sabeans, a nation far away." The LORD has spoken.

9 Proclaim this among the nations:
Prepare for war!
Rouse the warriors!
Let all the fighting men draw near and attack.
10 Beat your plowshares into swords
and your pruning hooks into spears.
Let the weakling say,
"I am strong!"
11 Come quickly, all you nations from every side,
and assemble there.

Bring down your warriors, LORD!

12 "Let the nations be roused;
let them advance into the Valley of Jehoshaphat,
for there I will sit
to judge all the nations on every side.
13 Swing the sickle,
for the harvest is ripe.
Come, trample the grapes,
for the winepress is full

[a] *25* The precise meaning of the four Hebrew words used here for locusts is uncertain. [b] *32* In Hebrew texts 2:28-32 is numbered 3:1-5. [c] In Hebrew texts 3:1-21 is numbered 4:1-21. [d] *2* *Jehoshaphat* means *the LORD judges*; also in verse 12. [e] *5* Or *palaces*

and the vats overflow —
so great is their wickedness!"

14 Multitudes, multitudes
in the valley of decision!
For the day of the LORD is near
in the valley of decision.
15 The sun and moon will be darkened,
and the stars no longer shine.
16 The LORD will roar from Zion
and thunder from Jerusalem;
the earth and the heavens will
tremble.
But the LORD will be a refuge for his
people,
a stronghold for the people of Israel.
17 "Then you will know that I, the LORD
your God,
dwell in Zion, my holy hill.
Jerusalem will be holy;
never again will foreigners invade
her.

18 "In that day the mountains will drip
new wine,
and the hills will flow with milk;
all the ravines of Judah will run with
water.
A fountain will flow out of the LORD's
house
and will water the valley of acacias.[a]
19 But Egypt will be desolate,
Edom a desert waste,
because of violence done to the people
of Judah,
in whose land they shed innocent
blood.
20 Judah will be inhabited forever
and Jerusalem through all
generations.
21 Shall I leave their innocent blood
unavenged?
No, I will not."

The LORD dwells in Zion!

AMOS

The northern kingdom of Israel reached its greatest heights in the first half of the 8th century BC (p. 340), during the forty-one-year reign of the powerful Jeroboam II. Confident in their nation's victories, their worship, and their heritage, the people adopted the motto, "God is with us!" They were anticipating *the day of the LORD,* when God would strike down all their enemies and establish Israel as the undisputed ruler of the region.

Into this atmosphere of overconfident nationalism steps Amos, a shepherd from the southern kingdom of Judah. He stands in the great royal temple at Bethel and announces that God is stirring up a nation to conquer Israel. *The day of the LORD,* he insisted, *will be darkness, not light.* God isn't impressed with Israel's wealth, military might, or self-indulgent way of life. He is looking for justice, while the rich and powerful are taking advantage of the poor. God is calling Israel to repentance as the only way to avoid destruction.

The message causes an uproar. Amaziah, the high priest at Bethel, accuses Amos of treason. Amos is banished from the kingdom, but his oracles are recorded, creating one of the earliest collections we have from any Hebrew prophet. The book consists of roughly three dozen separate oracles, plus the story of his expulsion. Most of the book is loosely assembled, but it conveys one strong and consistent message: *Let justice roll on like a river, righteousness like a never-failing stream!*

---

1 The words of Amos, one of the shepherds of Tekoa — the vision he saw concerning Israel two years before the earthquake, when Uzziah was king of Judah and Jeroboam son of Jehoash[b] was king of Israel.

2 He said:

"The LORD roars from Zion
and thunders from Jerusalem;
the pastures of the shepherds dry up,
and the top of Carmel withers."

[a] *18* Or *Valley of Shittim* [b] *1* Hebrew *Joash,* a variant of *Jehoash*

3 This is what the LORD says:

"For three sins of Damascus,
even for four, I will not relent.
Because she threshed Gilead
with sledges having iron teeth,
4 I will send fire on the house of Hazael
that will consume the fortresses of Ben-Hadad.
5 I will break down the gate of Damascus;
I will destroy the king who is in[a] the Valley of Aven[b]
and the one who holds the scepter in Beth Eden.
The people of Aram will go into exile to Kir,"
says the LORD.

6 This is what the LORD says:

"For three sins of Gaza,
even for four, I will not relent.
Because she took captive whole communities
and sold them to Edom,
7 I will send fire on the walls of Gaza
that will consume her fortresses.
8 I will destroy the king[c] of Ashdod
and the one who holds the scepter in Ashkelon.
I will turn my hand against Ekron,
till the last of the Philistines are dead,"
says the Sovereign LORD.

9 This is what the LORD says:

"For three sins of Tyre,
even for four, I will not relent.
Because she sold whole communities of captives to Edom,
disregarding a treaty of brotherhood,
10 I will send fire on the walls of Tyre
that will consume her fortresses."

11 This is what the LORD says:

"For three sins of Edom,
even for four, I will not relent.
Because he pursued his brother with a sword
and slaughtered the women of the land,
because his anger raged continually
and his fury flamed unchecked,
12 I will send fire on Teman
that will consume the fortresses of Bozrah."

13 This is what the LORD says:

"For three sins of Ammon,
even for four, I will not relent.
Because he ripped open the pregnant women of Gilead
in order to extend his borders,
14 I will set fire to the walls of Rabbah
that will consume her fortresses
amid war cries on the day of battle,
amid violent winds on a stormy day.
15 Her king[d] will go into exile,
he and his officials together,"
says the LORD.

2 This is what the LORD says:

"For three sins of Moab,
even for four, I will not relent.
Because he burned to ashes
the bones of Edom's king,
2 I will send fire on Moab
that will consume the fortresses of Kerioth.[e]
Moab will go down in great tumult
amid war cries and the blast of the trumpet.
3 I will destroy her ruler
and kill all her officials with him,"
says the LORD.

4 This is what the LORD says:

"For three sins of Judah,
even for four, I will not relent.
Because they have rejected the law of the LORD
and have not kept his decrees,
because they have been led astray by false gods,[f]
the gods[g] their ancestors followed,
5 I will send fire on Judah
that will consume the fortresses of Jerusalem."

6 This is what the LORD says:

"For three sins of Israel,
even for four, I will not relent.
They sell the innocent for silver,
and the needy for a pair of sandals.
7 They trample on the heads of the poor
as on the dust of the ground
and deny justice to the oppressed.
Father and son use the same girl

[a] 5 Or *the inhabitants of her cities* [b] 5 *Aven* means *wickedness.* [c] 8 Or *inhabitants* [d] 15 Or / *Molek* [e] 2 Or *of* [f] 4 Or *by lies* [g] 4 Or *lies*

and so profane my holy name.
8 They lie down beside every altar
on garments taken in pledge.
In the house of their god
they drink wine taken as fines.

9 "Yet I destroyed the Amorites before them,
though they were tall as the cedars
and strong as the oaks.
I destroyed their fruit above
and their roots below.
10 I brought you up out of Egypt
and led you forty years in the wilderness
to give you the land of the Amorites.

11 "I also raised up prophets from among your children
and Nazirites from among your youths.
Is this not true, people of Israel?"
declares the LORD.
12 "But you made the Nazirites drink wine
and commanded the prophets not to prophesy.

13 "Now then, I will crush you
as a cart crushes when loaded with grain.
14 The swift will not escape,
the strong will not muster their strength,
and the warrior will not save his life.
15 The archer will not stand his ground,
the fleet-footed soldier will not get away,
and the horseman will not save his life.
16 Even the bravest warriors
will flee naked on that day,"
declares the LORD.

3 Hear this word, people of Israel, the
word the LORD has spoken against
you — against the whole family I brought
up out of Egypt:

2 "You only have I chosen
of all the families of the earth;
therefore I will punish you
for all your sins."

3 Do two walk together
unless they have agreed to do so?
4 Does a lion roar in the thicket
when it has no prey?
Does it growl in its den
when it has caught nothing?
5 Does a bird swoop down to a trap on the ground
when no bait is there?
Does a trap spring up from the ground
if it has not caught anything?
6 When a trumpet sounds in a city,
do not the people tremble?
When disaster comes to a city,
has not the LORD caused it?

7 Surely the Sovereign LORD does nothing
without revealing his plan
to his servants the prophets.

8 The lion has roared —
who will not fear?
The Sovereign LORD has spoken —
who can but prophesy?

9 Proclaim to the fortresses of Ashdod
and to the fortresses of Egypt:
"Assemble yourselves on the mountains of Samaria;
see the great unrest within her
and the oppression among her people."

10 "They do not know how to do right,"
declares the LORD,
"who store up in their fortresses
what they have plundered and looted."

11 Therefore this is what the Sovereign
LORD says:

"An enemy will overrun your land,
pull down your strongholds
and plunder your fortresses."

12 This is what the LORD says:

"As a shepherd rescues from the lion's mouth
only two leg bones or a piece of an ear,
so will the Israelites living in Samaria be rescued,
with only the head of a bed
and a piece of fabric[a] from a couch.[b]"

13 "Hear this and testify against the descendants of Jacob," declares the Lord,
the LORD God Almighty.

[a] 12 The meaning of the Hebrew for this phrase is uncertain. [b] 12 Or *Israelites be rescued, / those who sit in Samaria / on the edge of their beds / and in Damascus on their couches.*

14 "On the day I punish Israel for her sins,
I will destroy the altars of Bethel;
the horns of the altar will be cut off
and fall to the ground.
15 I will tear down the winter house
along with the summer house;
the houses adorned with ivory will be destroyed
and the mansions will be demolished,"
declares the LORD.

4 Hear this word, you cows of Bashan
on Mount Samaria,
you women who oppress the poor
and crush the needy
and say to your husbands, "Bring us some drinks!"
2 The Sovereign LORD has sworn by his holiness:
"The time will surely come
when you will be taken away with hooks,
the last of you with fishhooks.[a]
3 You will each go straight out
through breaches in the wall,
and you will be cast out toward Harmon,[b]"
declares the LORD.

4 "Go to Bethel and sin;
go to Gilgal and sin yet more.
Bring your sacrifices every morning,
your tithes every three years.[c]
5 Burn leavened bread as a thank offering
and brag about your freewill offerings—
boast about them, you Israelites,
for this is what you love to do,"
declares the Sovereign LORD.

6 "I gave you empty stomachs in every city
and lack of bread in every town,
yet you have not returned to me,"
declares the LORD.

7 "I also withheld rain from you
when the harvest was still three months away.
I sent rain on one town,
but withheld it from another.
One field had rain;
another had none and dried up.
8 People staggered from town to town for water
but did not get enough to drink,
yet you have not returned to me,"
declares the LORD.

9 "Many times I struck your gardens
and vineyards,
destroying them with blight and mildew.
Locusts devoured your fig and olive trees,
yet you have not returned to me,"
declares the LORD.

10 "I sent plagues among you
as I did to Egypt.
I killed your young men with the sword,
along with your captured horses.
I filled your nostrils with the stench of your camps,
yet you have not returned to me,"
declares the LORD.

11 "I overthrew some of you
as I overthrew Sodom and Gomorrah.
You were like a burning stick snatched from the fire,
yet you have not returned to me,"
declares the LORD.

12 "Therefore this is what I will do to you, Israel,
and because I will do this to you, Israel,
prepare to meet your God."

13 He who forms the mountains,
who creates the wind,
and who reveals his thoughts to mankind,
who turns dawn to darkness,
and treads on the heights of the earth—
the LORD God Almighty is his name.

5 Hear this word, Israel, this lament I take up concerning you:

2 "Fallen is Virgin Israel,
never to rise again,
deserted in her own land,
with no one to lift her up."

3 This is what the Sovereign LORD says to Israel:

"Your city that marches out a thousand strong

[a] 2 Or *away in baskets, / the last of you in fish baskets* [b] 3 Masoretic Text; with a different word division of the Hebrew (see Septuagint) *out, you mountain of oppression* [c] 4 Or *days*

will have only a hundred left;
your town that marches out a hundred
strong
will have only ten left."

4 This is what the LORD says to Israel:

"Seek me and live;
5 do not seek Bethel,
do not go to Gilgal,
do not journey to Beersheba.
For Gilgal will surely go into exile,
and Bethel will be reduced to
nothing.[a]"
6 Seek the LORD and live,
or he will sweep through the tribes
of Joseph like a fire;
it will devour them,
and Bethel will have no one to
quench it.

7 There are those who turn justice into
bitterness
and cast righteousness to the
ground.

8 He who made the Pleiades and
Orion,
who turns midnight into dawn
and darkens day into night,
who calls for the waters of the sea
and pours them out over the face of
the land—
the LORD is his name.
9 With a blinding flash he destroys the
stronghold
and brings the fortified city to ruin.
10 There are those who hate the one who
upholds justice in court
and detest the one who tells the
truth.

11 You levy a straw tax on the poor
and impose a tax on their grain.
Therefore, though you have built stone
mansions,
you will not live in them;
though you have planted lush
vineyards,
you will not drink their wine.
12 For I know how many are your
offenses
and how great your sins.

There are those who oppress the
innocent and take bribes
and deprive the poor of justice in
the courts.
13 Therefore the prudent keep quiet in
such times,
for the times are evil.

14 Seek good, not evil,
that you may live.
Then the LORD God Almighty will be
with you,
just as you say he is.
15 Hate evil, love good;
maintain justice in the courts.
Perhaps the LORD God Almighty will
have mercy
on the remnant of Joseph.

16 Therefore this is what the Lord, the
LORD God Almighty, says:

"There will be wailing in all the streets
and cries of anguish in every public
square.
The farmers will be summoned to
weep
and the mourners to wail.
17 There will be wailing in all the
vineyards,
for I will pass through your midst,"
says the LORD.

18 Woe to you who long
for the day of the LORD!
Why do you long for the day of the
LORD?
That day will be darkness, not light.
19 It will be as though a man fled from a
lion
only to meet a bear,
as though he entered his house
and rested his hand on the wall
only to have a snake bite him.
20 Will not the day of the LORD be
darkness, not light—
pitch-dark, without a ray of
brightness?

21 "I hate, I despise your religious
festivals;
your assemblies are a stench to me.
22 Even though you bring me burnt
offerings and grain offerings,
I will not accept them.
Though you bring choice fellowship
offerings,
I will have no regard for them.
23 Away with the noise of your songs!
I will not listen to the music of your
harps.
24 But let justice roll on like a river,

[a] 5 Hebrew *aven,* a reference to Beth Aven (a derogatory name for Bethel); see Hosea 4:15.

righteousness like a never-failing
stream!

25 "Did you bring me sacrifices and
offerings
forty years in the wilderness, people
of Israel?
26 You have lifted up the shrine of your
king,
the pedestal of your idols,
the star of your god[a] —
which you made for yourselves.
27 Therefore I will send you into exile
beyond Damascus,"
says the LORD, whose name is God
Almighty.

6 Woe to you who are complacent in
Zion,
and to you who feel secure on
Mount Samaria,
you notable men of the foremost nation,
to whom the people of Israel come!
2 Go to Kalneh and look at it;
go from there to great Hamath,
and then go down to Gath in
Philistia.
Are they better off than your two
kingdoms?
Is their land larger than yours?
3 You put off the day of disaster
and bring near a reign of terror.
4 You lie on beds adorned with ivory
and lounge on your couches.
You dine on choice lambs
and fattened calves.
5 You strum away on your harps like
David
and improvise on musical
instruments.
6 You drink wine by the bowlful
and use the finest lotions,
but you do not grieve over the ruin
of Joseph.
7 Therefore you will be among the first
to go into exile;
your feasting and lounging will end.

8 The Sovereign LORD has sworn by himself — the LORD God Almighty declares:

"I abhor the pride of Jacob
and detest his fortresses;
I will deliver up the city
and everything in it."

9 If ten people are left in one house,
they too will die. 10 And if the relative
who comes to carry the bodies out of the
house to burn them[b] asks anyone who
might be hiding there, "Is anyone else
with you?" and he says, "No," then he will
go on to say, "Hush! We must not mention
the name of the LORD."

11 For the LORD has given the command,
and he will smash the great house
into pieces
and the small house into bits.

12 Do horses run on the rocky crags?
Does one plow the sea[c] with oxen?
But you have turned justice into
poison
and the fruit of righteousness into
bitterness —
13 you who rejoice in the conquest of Lo
Debar[d]
and say, "Did we not take Karnaim[e]
by our own strength?"

14 For the LORD God Almighty declares,
"I will stir up a nation against you,
Israel,
that will oppress you all the way
from Lebo Hamath to the valley of
the Arabah."

7 This is what the Sovereign LORD
showed me: He was preparing swarms
of locusts after the king's share had been
harvested and just as the late crops were
coming up. 2 When they had stripped the
land clean, I cried out, "Sovereign LORD,
forgive! How can Jacob survive? He is so
small!"
3 So the LORD relented.
"This will not happen," the LORD said.
4 This is what the Sovereign LORD
showed me: The Sovereign LORD was
calling for judgment by fire; it dried up
the great deep and devoured the land.
5 Then I cried out, "Sovereign LORD, I beg
you, stop! How can Jacob survive? He is
so small!"
6 So the LORD relented.
"This will not happen either," the Sovereign LORD said.

7 This is what he showed me: The Lord
was standing by a wall that had been built

[a] 26 Or *lifted up Sakkuth your king / and Kaiwan your idols, / your star-gods*; Septuagint *lifted up the shrine of Molek / and the star of your god Rephan, / their idols* [b] 10 Or *to make a funeral fire in honor of the dead* [c] 12 With a different word division of the Hebrew; Masoretic Text *plow there* [d] 13 *Lo Debar* means *nothing.* [e] 13 *Karnaim* means *horns; horn* here symbolizes strength.

true to plumb,[a] with a plumb line[b] in his
hand. 8 And the LORD asked me, "What do
you see, Amos?"

"A plumb line," I replied.

Then the Lord said, "Look, I am setting
a plumb line among my people Israel; I
will spare them no longer.

9 "The high places of Isaac will be
destroyed
and the sanctuaries of Israel will be
ruined;
with my sword I will rise against the
house of Jeroboam."

10 Then Amaziah the priest of Bethel
sent a message to Jeroboam king of Israel:
"Amos is raising a conspiracy against you
in the very heart of Israel. The land cannot bear all his words. 11 For this is what
Amos is saying:

" 'Jeroboam will die by the sword,
and Israel will surely go into exile,
away from their native land.' "

12 Then Amaziah said to Amos, "Get out,
you seer! Go back to the land of Judah.
Earn your bread there and do your prophesying there. 13 Don't prophesy anymore
at Bethel, because this is the king's sanctuary and the temple of the kingdom."

14 Amos answered Amaziah, "I was neither a prophet nor the son of a prophet,
but I was a shepherd, and I also took care
of sycamore-fig trees. 15 But the LORD
took me from tending the flock and said
to me, 'Go, prophesy to my people Israel.'
16 Now then, hear the word of the LORD.
You say,

" 'Do not prophesy against Israel,
and stop preaching against the
descendants of Isaac.'

17 "Therefore this is what the LORD
says:

" 'Your wife will become a prostitute in
the city,
and your sons and daughters will
fall by the sword.
Your land will be measured and
divided up,
and you yourself will die in a pagan[c]
country.
And Israel will surely go into exile,
away from their native land.' "

8 This is what the Sovereign LORD
showed me: a basket of ripe fruit.
2 "What do you see, Amos?" he asked.

"A basket of ripe fruit," I answered.

Then the LORD said to me, "The time
is ripe for my people Israel; I will spare
them no longer.

3 "In that day," declares the Sovereign
LORD, "the songs in the temple will turn
to wailing.[d] Many, many bodies—flung
everywhere! Silence!"

4 Hear this, you who trample the needy
and do away with the poor of the
land,

5 saying,

"When will the New Moon be over
that we may sell grain,
and the Sabbath be ended
that we may market wheat?"—
skimping on the measure,
boosting the price
and cheating with dishonest
scales,
6 buying the poor with silver
and the needy for a pair of sandals,
selling even the sweepings with the
wheat.

7 The LORD has sworn by himself, the
Pride of Jacob: "I will never forget anything they have done.

8 "Will not the land tremble for this,
and all who live in it mourn?
The whole land will rise like the Nile;
it will be stirred up and then sink
like the river of Egypt.

9 "In that day," declares the Sovereign
LORD,

"I will make the sun go down at noon
and darken the earth in broad
daylight.
10 I will turn your religious festivals into
mourning
and all your singing into weeping.
I will make all of you wear sackcloth
and shave your heads.
I will make that time like mourning
for an only son
and the end of it like a bitter day.

11 "The days are coming," declares the
Sovereign LORD,

[a] 7 The meaning of the Hebrew for this phrase is uncertain. [b] 7 The meaning of the Hebrew for this phrase is uncertain; also in verse 8. [c] 17 Hebrew *an unclean* [d] 3 Or *"the temple singers will wail*

"when I will send a famine through
the land—
not a famine of food or a thirst for
water,
but a famine of hearing the words of
the LORD.
12 People will stagger from sea to sea
and wander from north to east,
searching for the word of the LORD,
but they will not find it.

13 "In that day

"the lovely young women and strong
young men
will faint because of thirst.
14 Those who swear by the sin of
Samaria—
who say, 'As surely as your god lives,
Dan,'
or, 'As surely as the god[a] of
Beersheba lives'—
they will fall, never to rise
again."

9 I saw the Lord standing by the altar,
and he said:

"Strike the tops of the pillars
so that the thresholds shake.
Bring them down on the heads of all
the people;
those who are left I will kill with the
sword.
Not one will get away,
none will escape.
2 Though they dig down to the depths
below,
from there my hand will take
them.
Though they climb up to the heavens
above,
from there I will bring them
down.
3 Though they hide themselves on the
top of Carmel,
there I will hunt them down and
seize them.
Though they hide from my eyes at the
bottom of the sea,
there I will command the serpent to
bite them.
4 Though they are driven into exile by
their enemies,
there I will command the sword to
slay them.

"I will keep my eye on them
for harm and not for good."

5 The Lord, the LORD Almighty—
he touches the earth and it melts,
and all who live in it mourn;
the whole land rises like the Nile,
then sinks like the river of Egypt;
6 he builds his lofty palace[b] in the
heavens
and sets its foundation[c] on the
earth;
he calls for the waters of the sea
and pours them out over the face of
the land—
the LORD is his name.

7 "Are not you Israelites
the same to me as the Cushites[d]?"
declares the LORD.
"Did I not bring Israel up from Egypt,
the Philistines from Caphtor[e]
and the Arameans from Kir?

8 "Surely the eyes of the Sovereign
LORD
are on the sinful kingdom.
I will destroy it
from the face of the earth.
Yet I will not totally destroy
the descendants of Jacob,"
declares the LORD.
9 "For I will give the command,
and I will shake the people of Israel
among all the nations
as grain is shaken in a sieve,
and not a pebble will reach the
ground.
10 All the sinners among my people
will die by the sword,
all those who say,
'Disaster will not overtake or meet
us.'

11 "In that day

"I will restore David's fallen shelter—
I will repair its broken walls
and restore its ruins—
and will rebuild it as it used to be,
12 so that they may possess the remnant
of Edom
and all the nations that bear my
name,[f]"
declares the LORD,
who will do these things.

[a] 14 Hebrew *the way* [b] 6 The meaning of the Hebrew for this phrase is uncertain. [c] 6 The meaning of the Hebrew for this word is uncertain. [d] 7 That is, people from the upper Nile region [e] 7 That is, Crete [f] 12 Hebrew; Septuagint *so that the remnant of people / and all the nations that bear my name may seek me*

13 "The days are coming," declares the LORD,
"when the reaper will be overtaken by the plowman
and the planter by the one treading grapes.
New wine will drip from the mountains
and flow from all the hills,
14 and I will bring my people Israel back from exile.[a]
"They will rebuild the ruined cities and live in them.
They will plant vineyards and drink their wine;
they will make gardens and eat their fruit.
15 I will plant Israel in their own land,
never again to be uprooted
from the land I have given them,"
says the LORD your God.

OBADIAH

When Judah's capital city of Jerusalem fell to the Babylonian army in 587/6 BC, those in the neighboring kingdom of Edom joined in looting the city. They intercepted fleeing Judeans and turned them over to the Babylonians to be executed or enslaved. They showed no compassion even though they were related to the Judeans. Edom was descended from Esau, the brother of Jacob, who was the ancestor of the Israelites.

The prophet Obadiah seems to have been among those who remained behind when the Judeans were taken into exile. His oracle first rebukes the Edomites for their ruthless treatment of their helpless neighbors and foretells their destruction. He then assures the people of his community that God would restore their fortunes. He assures Judah that in the end, the kingdom will be the LORD's.

---

1 The vision of Obadiah.

This is what the Sovereign LORD says about Edom—

We have heard a message from the LORD:
An envoy was sent to the nations to say,
"Rise, let us go against her for battle"—

2 "See, I will make you small among the nations;
you will be utterly despised.
3 The pride of your heart has deceived you,
you who live in the clefts of the rocks[b]
and make your home on the heights,
you who say to yourself,
'Who can bring me down to the ground?'
4 Though you soar like the eagle
and make your nest among the stars,
from there I will bring you down,"
declares the LORD.

5 "If thieves came to you,
if robbers in the night—
oh, what a disaster awaits you!—
would they not steal only as much as they wanted?
If grape pickers came to you,
would they not leave a few grapes?
6 But how Esau will be ransacked,
his hidden treasures pillaged!
7 All your allies will force you to the border;
your friends will deceive and overpower you;

[a] 14 Or *will restore the fortunes of my people Israel* [b] 3 Or *of Sela*

those who eat your bread will set a
trap for you,[a]
but you will not detect it.

8 "In that day," declares the LORD,
"will I not destroy the wise men of
Edom,
those of understanding in the
mountains of Esau?
9 Your warriors, Teman, will be
terrified,
and everyone in Esau's mountains
will be cut down in the slaughter.
10 Because of the violence against your
brother Jacob,
you will be covered with shame;
you will be destroyed forever.
11 On the day you stood aloof
while strangers carried off his
wealth
and foreigners entered his gates
and cast lots for Jerusalem,
you were like one of them.
12 You should not gloat over your brother
in the day of his misfortune,
nor rejoice over the people of Judah
in the day of their destruction,
nor boast so much
in the day of their trouble.
13 You should not march through the
gates of my people
in the day of their disaster,
nor gloat over them in their calamity
in the day of their disaster,
nor seize their wealth
in the day of their disaster.
14 You should not wait at the crossroads
to cut down their fugitives,
nor hand over their survivors
in the day of their trouble.

15 "The day of the LORD is near
for all nations.
As you have done, it will be done to
you;
your deeds will return upon your
own head.
16 Just as you drank on my holy hill,
so all the nations will drink
continually;
they will drink and drink
and be as if they had never been.
17 But on Mount Zion will be
deliverance;
it will be holy,
and Jacob will possess his
inheritance.
18 Jacob will be a fire
and Joseph a flame;
Esau will be stubble,
and they will set him on fire and
destroy him.
There will be no survivors
from Esau."
The LORD has spoken.

19 People from the Negev will occupy
the mountains of Esau,
and people from the foothills will
possess
the land of the Philistines.
They will occupy the fields of Ephraim
and Samaria,
and Benjamin will possess Gilead.
20 This company of Israelite exiles who
are in Canaan
will possess the land as far as
Zarephath;
the exiles from Jerusalem who are in
Sepharad
will possess the towns of the
Negev.
21 Deliverers will go up on[b] Mount Zion
to govern the mountains of Esau.
And the kingdom will be the LORD's.

[a] 7 The meaning of the Hebrew for this clause is uncertain. [b] 21 Or *from*

JONAH

The book relates how the word of the LORD came to Jonah, a prophet during the reign of Jeroboam II in the 8th century BC. It is unique among prophetic books in focusing on a story about a prophet rather than a collection of oracles. The book contains only a single sentence of prophecy.

The story concerns God's call to Jonah to warn the people of Nineveh of its coming destruction. The book is structured into two main acts with two scenes each. The repetition of God's command to *Go to the great city of Nineveh* marks the beginning of each act. The first scene is set on a ship as Jonah tries to avoid his mission. The second scene takes place in the belly of a huge fish which has swallowed Jonah. In the second act both scenes are associated with Nineveh itself, the first within the city as Jonah preaches and Nineveh repents, the second just outside the city as Jonah struggles with God's mercy.

Jonah's role in the book is to represent the attitude of many in Israel toward other nations. Instead of accepting their own calling to help these nations come to know the true God, they considered them enemies and expected God to destroy them. The book teaches that God's love extends beyond Israel to other nations, indeed, to the whole creation. God's final question to Jonah is intended for all the book's readers.

---

1 The word of the LORD came to Jonah
son of Amittai: 2 "Go to the great city
of Nineveh and preach against it, because
its wickedness has come up before me."
3 But Jonah ran away from the LORD
and headed for Tarshish. He went down
to Joppa, where he found a ship bound for
that port. After paying the fare, he went
aboard and sailed for Tarshish to flee
from the LORD.
4 Then the LORD sent a great wind on
the sea, and such a violent storm arose
that the ship threatened to break up. 5 All
the sailors were afraid and each cried out
to his own god. And they threw the cargo
into the sea to lighten the ship.
But Jonah had gone below deck, where
he lay down and fell into a deep sleep.
6 The captain went to him and said, "How
can you sleep? Get up and call on your
god! Maybe he will take notice of us so
that we will not perish."
7 Then the sailors said to each other,
"Come, let us cast lots to find out who is
responsible for this calamity." They cast
lots and the lot fell on Jonah. 8 So they
asked him, "Tell us, who is responsible
for making all this trouble for us? What
kind of work do you do? Where do you
come from? What is your country? From
what people are you?"
9 He answered, "I am a Hebrew and I
worship the LORD, the God of heaven,
who made the sea and the dry land."
10 This terrified them and they asked,
"What have you done?" (They knew he
was running away from the LORD, because he had already told them so.)
11 The sea was getting rougher and
rougher. So they asked him, "What
should we do to you to make the sea calm
down for us?"
12 "Pick me up and throw me into the
sea," he replied, "and it will become
calm. I know that it is my fault that this
great storm has come upon you."
13 Instead, the men did their best to row
back to land. But they could not, for the
sea grew even wilder than before. 14 Then
they cried out to the LORD, "Please, LORD,
do not let us die for taking this man's life.
Do not hold us accountable for killing an
innocent man, for you, LORD, have done
as you pleased." 15 Then they took Jonah
and threw him overboard, and the raging
sea grew calm. 16 At this the men greatly
feared the LORD, and they offered a sacrifice to the LORD and made vows to him.
17 Now the LORD provided a huge fish to
swallow Jonah, and Jonah was in the belly of the fish three days and three nights.
2 [a] 1 From inside the fish Jonah prayed to
the LORD his God. 2 He said:

"In my distress I called to the LORD,
 and he answered me.
From deep in the realm of the dead I
 called for help,
 and you listened to my cry.
3 You hurled me into the depths,

[a] In Hebrew texts 2:1 is numbered 1:17, and 2:1-10 is numbered 2:2-11.

into the very heart of the seas,
and the currents swirled about me;
all your waves and breakers
swept over me.
4 I said, 'I have been banished
from your sight;
yet I will look again
toward your holy temple.'
5 The engulfing waters threatened me,[a]
the deep surrounded me;
seaweed was wrapped around my
head.
6 To the roots of the mountains I sank
down;
the earth beneath barred me in
forever.
But you, LORD my God,
brought my life up from the pit.

7 "When my life was ebbing away,
I remembered you, LORD,
and my prayer rose to you,
to your holy temple.

8 "Those who cling to worthless idols
turn away from God's love for them.
9 But I, with shouts of grateful praise,
will sacrifice to you.
What I have vowed I will make good.
I will say, 'Salvation comes from the
LORD.'"

10 And the LORD commanded the fish,
and it vomited Jonah onto dry land.

3 Then the word of the LORD came to Jonah a second time: 2 "Go to the great
city of Nineveh and proclaim to it the
message I give you."
3 Jonah obeyed the word of the LORD
and went to Nineveh. Now Nineveh was
a very large city; it took three days to go
through it. 4 Jonah began by going a day's
journey into the city, proclaiming, "Forty more days and Nineveh will be overthrown." 5 The Ninevites believed God. A
fast was proclaimed, and all of them, from
the greatest to the least, put on sackcloth.
6 When Jonah's warning reached the
king of Nineveh, he rose from his throne,
took off his royal robes, covered himself
with sackcloth and sat down in the dust.
7 This is the proclamation he issued in
Nineveh:

"By the decree of the king and his
nobles:

Do not let people or animals, herds
or flocks, taste anything; do not let
them eat or drink. 8 But let people
and animals be covered with sackcloth. Let everyone call urgently on
God. Let them give up their evil ways
and their violence. 9 Who knows?
God may yet relent and with compassion turn from his fierce anger so
that we will not perish."

10 When God saw what they did and
how they turned from their evil ways, he
relented and did not bring on them the
destruction he had threatened.

4 But to Jonah this seemed very wrong,
and he became angry. 2 He prayed to
the LORD, "Isn't this what I said, LORD,
when I was still at home? That is what I
tried to forestall by fleeing to Tarshish. I
knew that you are a gracious and compassionate God, slow to anger and abounding
in love, a God who relents from sending
calamity. 3 Now, LORD, take away my life,
for it is better for me to die than to live."
4 But the LORD replied, "Is it right for
you to be angry?"
5 Jonah had gone out and sat down at a
place east of the city. There he made himself a shelter, sat in its shade and waited to
see what would happen to the city. 6 Then
the LORD God provided a leafy plant[b] and
made it grow up over Jonah to give shade
for his head to ease his discomfort, and
Jonah was very happy about the plant.
7 But at dawn the next day God provided
a worm, which chewed the plant so that it
withered. 8 When the sun rose, God provided a scorching east wind, and the sun
blazed on Jonah's head so that he grew
faint. He wanted to die, and said, "It would
be better for me to die than to live."
9 But God said to Jonah, "Is it right for
you to be angry about the plant?"
"It is," he said. "And I'm so angry I wish
I were dead."
10 But the LORD said, "You have been
concerned about this plant, though you
did not tend it or make it grow. It sprang
up overnight and died overnight. 11 And
should I not have concern for the great city
of Nineveh, in which there are more than
a hundred and twenty thousand people
who cannot tell their right hand from
their left—and also many animals?"

[a] 5 Or *waters were at my throat* [b] 6 The precise identification of this plant is uncertain; also in verses 7, 9 and 10.

MICAH

The prophet Micah speaks to the southern kingdom of Judah during the reigns of Jotham, Ahaz and Hezekiah (late 8th century BC). He foresees that Samaria and Jerusalem, the capital cities of Israel and Judah, will be destroyed because of their injustice and corrupt religion. The people have abandoned the covenant God made with them, taking up the pagan religious practices of the Canaanites. The rich and powerful are ruthlessly exploiting the poor, ignoring the law of Moses. Micah warns that in punishment for their unfaithfulness and injustice, both kingdoms will be invaded, conquered and exiled. As he predicts, Samaria falls to the Assyrians in 722 BC and Jerusalem falls to the Babylonians in 587/6 BC.

Micah's prophecies alternate between warnings of destruction and promises of restoration. Each of Micah's three groups of oracles begins with a series of judgments, and then concludes with promises of restoration. Micah proclaims that in compassion and covenant faithfulness God will save a remnant of the people and bring them back to their own land. There they will be ruled by a righteous king and become a light to the whole world, pointing all nations to the ways of the LORD. God will help Israel find its place in the biblical drama.

---

1 The word of the LORD that came to Micah of Moresheth during the reigns of Jotham, Ahaz and Hezekiah, kings of Judah — the vision he saw concerning Samaria and Jerusalem.

2 Hear, you peoples, all of you,
listen, earth and all who live in it,
that the Sovereign LORD may bear witness against you,
the Lord from his holy temple.

3 Look! The LORD is coming from his dwelling place;
he comes down and treads on the heights of the earth.
4 The mountains melt beneath him
and the valleys split apart,
like wax before the fire,
like water rushing down a slope.
5 All this is because of Jacob's transgression,
because of the sins of the people of Israel.
What is Jacob's transgression?
Is it not Samaria?
What is Judah's high place?
Is it not Jerusalem?

6 "Therefore I will make Samaria a heap of rubble,
a place for planting vineyards.
I will pour her stones into the valley
and lay bare her foundations.
7 All her idols will be broken to pieces;
all her temple gifts will be burned with fire;
I will destroy all her images.
Since she gathered her gifts from the wages of prostitutes,
as the wages of prostitutes they will again be used."

8 Because of this I will weep and wail;
I will go about barefoot and naked.
I will howl like a jackal
and moan like an owl.
9 For Samaria's plague is incurable;
it has spread to Judah.
It has reached the very gate of my people,
even to Jerusalem itself.
10 Tell it not in Gath[a];
weep not at all.
In Beth Ophrah[b]
roll in the dust.
11 Pass by naked and in shame,
you who live in Shaphir.[c]
Those who live in Zaanan[d]
will not come out.
Beth Ezel is in mourning;
it no longer protects you.
12 Those who live in Maroth[e] writhe in pain,
waiting for relief,
because disaster has come from the LORD,
even to the gate of Jerusalem.
13 You who live in Lachish,
harness fast horses to the chariot.

[a] 10 *Gath* sounds like the Hebrew for *tell.* [b] 10 *Beth Ophrah* means *house of dust.* [c] 11 *Shaphir* means *pleasant.* [d] 11 *Zaanan* sounds like the Hebrew for *come out.* [e] 12 *Maroth* sounds like the Hebrew for *bitter.*

You are where the sin of Daughter
Zion began,
for the transgressions of Israel were
found in you.
14 Therefore you will give parting gifts
to Moresheth Gath.
The town of Akzib[a] will prove
deceptive
to the kings of Israel.
15 I will bring a conqueror against you
who live in Mareshah.[b]
The nobles of Israel
will flee to Adullam.
16 Shave your head in mourning
for the children in whom you
delight;
make yourself as bald as the vulture,
for they will go from you into exile.

2 Woe to those who plan iniquity,
to those who plot evil on their beds!
At morning's light they carry it out
because it is in their power to do it.
2 They covet fields and seize them,
and houses, and take them.
They defraud people of their homes,
they rob them of their inheritance.

3 Therefore, the LORD says:

"I am planning disaster against this
people,
from which you cannot save
yourselves.
You will no longer walk proudly,
for it will be a time of calamity.
4 In that day people will ridicule you;
they will taunt you with this
mournful song:
'We are utterly ruined;
my people's possession is divided
up.
He takes it from me!
He assigns our fields to traitors.' "
5 Therefore you will have no one in the
assembly of the LORD
to divide the land by lot.

6 "Do not prophesy," their prophets say.
"Do not prophesy about these
things;
disgrace will not overtake us."
7 You descendants of Jacob, should it be
said,
"Does the LORD become[c]
impatient?
Does he do such things?"

"Do not my words do good
to the one whose ways are upright?
8 Lately my people have risen up
like an enemy.
You strip off the rich robe
from those who pass by without a
care,
like men returning from battle.
9 You drive the women of my people
from their pleasant homes.
You take away my blessing
from their children forever.
10 Get up, go away!
For this is not your resting place,
because it is defiled,
it is ruined, beyond all remedy.
11 If a liar and deceiver comes and says,
'I will prophesy for you plenty of
wine and beer,'
that would be just the prophet for
this people!

12 "I will surely gather all of you, Jacob;
I will surely bring together the
remnant of Israel.
I will bring them together like sheep
in a pen,
like a flock in its pasture;
the place will throng with people.
13 The One who breaks open the way
will go up before them;
they will break through the gate
and go out.
Their King will pass through before
them,
the LORD at their head."

3 Then I said,

"Listen, you leaders of Jacob,
you rulers of Israel.
Should you not embrace justice,
2 you who hate good and love evil;
who tear the skin from my people
and the flesh from their bones;
3 who eat my people's flesh,
strip off their skin
and break their bones in pieces;
who chop them up like meat for the
pan,
like flesh for the pot?"

4 Then they will cry out to the LORD,
but he will not answer them.

[a] *14 Akzib* means *deception.* [b] *15 Mareshah* sounds like the Hebrew for *conqueror.* [c] *7* Or *Is the Spirit of the LORD*

At that time he will hide his face from
them
because of the evil they have done.

5 This is what the LORD says:

"As for the prophets
who lead my people astray,
they proclaim 'peace'
if they have something to eat,
but prepare to wage war against
anyone
who refuses to feed them.
6 Therefore night will come over you,
without visions,
and darkness, without divination.
The sun will set for the prophets,
and the day will go dark for them.
7 The seers will be ashamed
and the diviners disgraced.
They will all cover their faces
because there is no answer from
God."
8 But as for me, I am filled with power,
with the Spirit of the LORD,
and with justice and might,
to declare to Jacob his transgression,
to Israel his sin.

9 Hear this, you leaders of Jacob,
you rulers of Israel,
who despise justice
and distort all that is right;
10 who build Zion with bloodshed,
and Jerusalem with wickedness.
11 Her leaders judge for a bribe,
her priests teach for a price,
and her prophets tell fortunes for
money.
Yet they look for the LORD's support
and say,
"Is not the LORD among us?
No disaster will come upon us."
12 Therefore because of you,
Zion will be plowed like a field,
Jerusalem will become a heap of
rubble,
the temple hill a mound overgrown
with thickets.

4 In the last days

the mountain of the LORD's temple
will be established
as the highest of the mountains;
it will be exalted above the hills,
and peoples will stream to it.

2 Many nations will come and say,

"Come, let us go up to the mountain of
the LORD,
to the temple of the God of Jacob.
He will teach us his ways,
so that we may walk in his paths."
The law will go out from Zion,
the word of the LORD from
Jerusalem.
3 He will judge between many peoples
and will settle disputes for strong
nations far and wide.
They will beat their swords into
plowshares
and their spears into pruning
hooks.
Nation will not take up sword against
nation,
nor will they train for war anymore.
4 Everyone will sit under their own vine
and under their own fig tree,
and no one will make them afraid,
for the LORD Almighty has spoken.
5 All the nations may walk
in the name of their gods,
but we will walk in the name of the
LORD
our God for ever and ever.

6 "In that day," declares the LORD,

"I will gather the lame;
I will assemble the exiles
and those I have brought to grief.
7 I will make the lame my remnant,
those driven away a strong nation.
The LORD will rule over them in
Mount Zion
from that day and forever.
8 As for you, watchtower of the flock,
stronghold[a] of Daughter Zion,
the former dominion will be restored
to you;
kingship will come to Daughter
Jerusalem."

9 Why do you now cry aloud—
have you no king[b]?
Has your ruler[c] perished,
that pain seizes you like that of a
woman in labor?
10 Writhe in agony, Daughter Zion,
like a woman in labor,
for now you must leave the city
to camp in the open field.
You will go to Babylon;

[a] 8 Or *hill* [b] 9 Or *King* [c] 9 Or *Ruler*

there you will be rescued.
There the LORD will redeem you
out of the hand of your enemies.

11 But now many nations
are gathered against you.
They say, "Let her be defiled,
let our eyes gloat over Zion!"
12 But they do not know
the thoughts of the LORD;
they do not understand his plan,
that he has gathered them like
sheaves to the threshing floor.
13 "Rise and thresh, Daughter Zion,
for I will give you horns of iron;
I will give you hooves of bronze,
and you will break to pieces many
nations."
You will devote their ill-gotten gains
to the LORD,
their wealth to the Lord of all the
earth.

5[a] Marshal your troops now, city of
troops,
for a siege is laid against us.
They will strike Israel's ruler
on the cheek with a rod.

2 "But you, Bethlehem Ephrathah,
though you are small among the
clans[b] of Judah,
out of you will come for me
one who will be ruler over Israel,
whose origins are from of old,
from ancient times."

3 Therefore Israel will be abandoned
until the time when she who is in
labor bears a son,
and the rest of his brothers return
to join the Israelites.

4 He will stand and shepherd his flock
in the strength of the LORD,
in the majesty of the name of the
LORD his God.
And they will live securely, for then
his greatness
will reach to the ends of the earth.

5 And he will be our peace
when the Assyrians invade our land
and march through our fortresses.
We will raise against them seven
shepherds,
even eight commanders,
6 who will rule[c] the land of Assyria with
the sword,
the land of Nimrod with drawn
sword.[d]
He will deliver us from the Assyrians
when they invade our land
and march across our borders.

7 The remnant of Jacob will be
in the midst of many peoples
like dew from the LORD,
like showers on the grass,
which do not wait for anyone
or depend on man.
8 The remnant of Jacob will be among
the nations,
in the midst of many peoples,
like a lion among the beasts of the
forest,
like a young lion among flocks of
sheep,
which mauls and mangles as it goes,
and no one can rescue.
9 Your hand will be lifted up in triumph
over your enemies,
and all your foes will be destroyed.
10 "In that day," declares the LORD,

"I will destroy your horses from
among you
and demolish your chariots.
11 I will destroy the cities of your land
and tear down all your
strongholds.
12 I will destroy your witchcraft
and you will no longer cast spells.
13 I will destroy your idols
and your sacred stones from among
you;
you will no longer bow down
to the work of your hands.
14 I will uproot from among you your
Asherah poles[e]
when I demolish your cities.
15 I will take vengeance in anger and
wrath
on the nations that have not obeyed
me."

6 Listen to what the LORD says:

"Stand up, plead my case before the
mountains;
let the hills hear what you have to
say.

[a] In Hebrew texts 5:1 is numbered 4:14, and 5:2-15 is numbered 5:1-14. [b] 2 Or *rulers* [c] 6 Or *crush*
[d] 6 Or *Nimrod in its gates* [e] 14 That is, wooden symbols of the goddess Asherah

NAHUM

In 612 BC the Assyrian Empire was nearing collapse. Its capital Nineveh was about to fall before a combined invasion of Babylonian, Medean and Scythian forces. But those living in the nations that Assyria had cruelly oppressed felt little pity. In their view, the Assyrians were simply getting a long-overdue taste of their own medicine. The prophet Nahum echoes these thoughts on behalf of the people of Judah. He situates this event within the context of God's rule over all kingdoms on earth. God will judge the Assyrians, even though he had used them as his own instrument, because they were excessively destructive and proud.

Nahum's oracle describes God's character and power, announcing God's purpose to judge Assyria. Words of comfort to Judah alternate with words of doom to Nineveh. The defense of the Assyrian capital will prove futile and the city will be plundered, confirming God's judgment.

---

1 A prophecy concerning Nineveh. The book of the vision of Nahum the Elkoshite.

2 The LORD is a jealous and avenging God;
the LORD takes vengeance and is filled with wrath.
The LORD takes vengeance on his foes
and vents his wrath against his enemies.
3 The LORD is slow to anger but great in power;
the LORD will not leave the guilty unpunished.
His way is in the whirlwind and the storm,
and clouds are the dust of his feet.
4 He rebukes the sea and dries it up;
he makes all the rivers run dry.
Bashan and Carmel wither
and the blossoms of Lebanon fade.
5 The mountains quake before him
and the hills melt away.
The earth trembles at his presence,
the world and all who live in it.
6 Who can withstand his indignation?
Who can endure his fierce anger?
His wrath is poured out like fire;
the rocks are shattered before him.

7 The LORD is good,
a refuge in times of trouble.
He cares for those who trust in him,
8 but with an overwhelming flood
he will make an end of Nineveh;
he will pursue his foes into the realm of darkness.

9 Whatever they plot against the LORD
he will bring[a] to an end;
trouble will not come a second time.
10 They will be entangled among thorns
and drunk from their wine;
they will be consumed like dry stubble.[b]
11 From you, Nineveh, has one come forth
who plots evil against the LORD
and devises wicked plans.
12 This is what the LORD says:

"Although they have allies and are numerous,
they will be destroyed and pass away.
Although I have afflicted you, Judah,
I will afflict you no more.
13 Now I will break their yoke from your neck
and tear your shackles away."
14 The LORD has given a command
concerning you, Nineveh:
"You will have no descendants to bear your name.
I will destroy the images and idols
that are in the temple of your gods.
I will prepare your grave,
for you are vile."

15 Look, there on the mountains,
the feet of one who brings good news,
who proclaims peace!
Celebrate your festivals, Judah,
and fulfill your vows.
No more will the wicked invade you;
they will be completely destroyed.[c]

a 9 Or *What do you foes plot against the LORD? / He will bring it* b 10 The meaning of the Hebrew for this verse is uncertain. c 15 In Hebrew texts this verse (1:15) is numbered 2:1.

2 [a] An attacker advances against you,
Nineveh.
Guard the fortress,
watch the road,
brace yourselves,
marshal all your strength!

2 The LORD will restore the splendor of
Jacob
like the splendor of Israel,
though destroyers have laid them
waste
and have ruined their vines.

3 The shields of the soldiers are red;
the warriors are clad in scarlet.
The metal on the chariots flashes
on the day they are made ready;
the spears of juniper are
brandished.[b]
4 The chariots storm through the
streets,
rushing back and forth through the
squares.
They look like flaming torches;
they dart about like lightning.

5 Nineveh summons her picked troops,
yet they stumble on their way.
They dash to the city wall;
the protective shield is put in place.
6 The river gates are thrown open
and the palace collapses.
7 It is decreed[c] that Nineveh
be exiled and carried away.
Her female slaves moan like doves
and beat on their breasts.
8 Nineveh is like a pool
whose water is draining away.
"Stop! Stop!" they cry,
but no one turns back.
9 Plunder the silver!
Plunder the gold!
The supply is endless,
the wealth from all its treasures!
10 She is pillaged, plundered, stripped!
Hearts melt, knees give way,
bodies tremble, every face grows
pale.

11 Where now is the lions' den,
the place where they fed their
young,
where the lion and lioness went,
and the cubs, with nothing to fear?
12 The lion killed enough for his cubs
and strangled the prey for his mate,
filling his lairs with the kill
and his dens with the prey.

13 "I am against you,"
declares the LORD Almighty.
"I will burn up your chariots in
smoke,
and the sword will devour your
young lions.
I will leave you no prey on the
earth.
The voices of your messengers
will no longer be heard."

3 Woe to the city of blood,
full of lies,
full of plunder,
never without victims!
2 The crack of whips,
the clatter of wheels,
galloping horses
and jolting chariots!
3 Charging cavalry,
flashing swords
and glittering spears!
Many casualties,
piles of dead,
bodies without number,
people stumbling over the
corpses—
4 all because of the wanton lust of a
prostitute,
alluring, the mistress of sorceries,
who enslaved nations by her
prostitution
and peoples by her witchcraft.

5 "I am against you," declares the LORD
Almighty.
"I will lift your skirts over your
face.
I will show the nations your
nakedness
and the kingdoms your shame.
6 I will pelt you with filth,
I will treat you with contempt
and make you a spectacle.
7 All who see you will flee from you and
say,
'Nineveh is in ruins—who will
mourn for her?'
Where can I find anyone to comfort
you?"

8 Are you better than Thebes,
situated on the Nile,
with water around her?

[a] In Hebrew texts 2:1-13 is numbered 2:2-14. [b] 3 Hebrew; Septuagint and Syriac *ready; / the horsemen rush to and fro.* [c] 7 The meaning of the Hebrew for this word is uncertain.

The river was her defense,
the waters her wall.
9 Cush[a] and Egypt were her boundless strength;
Put and Libya were among her allies.
10 Yet she was taken captive
and went into exile.
Her infants were dashed to pieces
at every street corner.
Lots were cast for her nobles,
and all her great men were put in chains.
11 You too will become drunk;
you will go into hiding
and seek refuge from the enemy.

12 All your fortresses are like fig trees
with their first ripe fruit;
when they are shaken,
the figs fall into the mouth of the eater.
13 Look at your troops —
they are all weaklings.
The gates of your land
are wide open to your enemies;
fire has consumed the bars of your gates.

14 Draw water for the siege,
strengthen your defenses!
Work the clay,
tread the mortar,
repair the brickwork!
15 There the fire will consume you;
the sword will cut you down —
they will devour you like a swarm of locusts.
Multiply like grasshoppers,
multiply like locusts!
16 You have increased the number of your merchants
till they are more numerous than the stars in the sky,
but like locusts they strip the land
and then fly away.
17 Your guards are like locusts,
your officials like swarms of locusts
that settle in the walls on a cold day —
but when the sun appears they fly away,
and no one knows where.

18 King of Assyria, your shepherds[b] slumber;
your nobles lie down to rest.
Your people are scattered on the mountains
with no one to gather them.
19 Nothing can heal you;
your wound is fatal.
All who hear the news about you
clap their hands at your fall,
for who has not felt
your endless cruelty?

a 9 That is, the upper Nile region b 18 That is, rulers

HABAKKUK

Near the time of the transition from the Assyrian to the Babylonian empires (late 7th century BC), the prophet Habakkuk engaged in a profound dialogue with Israel's God. The form of his book is a short series of complaints, or laments, followed by the divine responses. When Habakkuk's cries are answered, he closes with a hymn of confidence in God's expected victory.

The prophet begins by asking how long God will allow evil to triumph. The divine reply is that God is raising up the Babylonians as his tool of correction. This leads to Habakkuk's second question: Why do you allow the wicked to *swallow up those more righteous than themselves*? God replies again, explaining that the Babylonians will be judged just like the Assyrians, and that the righteous must await this in faith and patience. The inevitability of Babylon's doom is emphasized when God pronounces a series of five woes against it.

When Habakkuk's dialogue with God concludes, the book moves to what is called *A prayer of Habakkuk*. But its musical notations reveal that it is clearly meant to be sung. Habakkuk celebrates God's dramatic intervention for Israel in the past and prays that God will do it again. The prophet resolves in the meantime to wait patiently for God's coming.

---

1 The prophecy that Habakkuk the prophet received.

2 How long, LORD, must I call for help,
but you do not listen?
Or cry out to you, "Violence!"
but you do not save?
3 Why do you make me look at injustice?
Why do you tolerate wrongdoing?
Destruction and violence are before me;
there is strife, and conflict abounds.
4 Therefore the law is paralyzed,
and justice never prevails.
The wicked hem in the righteous,
so that justice is perverted.

5 "Look at the nations and watch —
and be utterly amazed.
For I am going to do something in your days
that you would not believe,
even if you were told.
6 I am raising up the Babylonians,[a]
that ruthless and impetuous people,
who sweep across the whole earth
to seize dwellings not their own.
7 They are a feared and dreaded people;
they are a law to themselves
and promote their own honor.
8 Their horses are swifter than leopards,
fiercer than wolves at dusk.
Their cavalry gallops headlong;
their horsemen come from afar.
They fly like an eagle swooping to devour;
9 they all come intent on violence.
Their hordes[b] advance like a desert wind
and gather prisoners like sand.
10 They mock kings
and scoff at rulers.
They laugh at all fortified cities;
by building earthen ramps they capture them.
11 Then they sweep past like the wind and go on —
guilty people, whose own strength is their god."

12 LORD, are you not from everlasting?
My God, my Holy One, you[c] will never die.
You, LORD, have appointed them to execute judgment;
you, my Rock, have ordained them to punish.
13 Your eyes are too pure to look on evil;
you cannot tolerate wrongdoing.
Why then do you tolerate the treacherous?
Why are you silent while the wicked
swallow up those more righteous than themselves?
14 You have made people like the fish in the sea,
like the sea creatures that have no ruler.

[a] 6 Or *Chaldeans* [b] 9 The meaning of the Hebrew for this word is uncertain. [c] *12* An ancient Hebrew scribal tradition; Masoretic Text *we*

15 The wicked foe pulls all of them up
with hooks,
he catches them in his net,
he gathers them up in his dragnet;
and so he rejoices and is glad.
16 Therefore he sacrifices to his net
and burns incense to his dragnet,
for by his net he lives in luxury
and enjoys the choicest food.
17 Is he to keep on emptying his net,
destroying nations without mercy?

2 I will stand at my watch
and station myself on the ramparts;
I will look to see what he will say to
me,
and what answer I am to give to this
complaint.[a]

2 Then the LORD replied:

"Write down the revelation
and make it plain on tablets
so that a herald[b] may run with it.
3 For the revelation awaits an appointed
time;
it speaks of the end
and will not prove false.
Though it linger, wait for it;
it[c] will certainly come
and will not delay.

4 "See, the enemy is puffed up;
his desires are not upright —
but the righteous person will live by
his faithfulness[d] —
5 indeed, wine betrays him;
he is arrogant and never at rest.
Because he is as greedy as the grave
and like death is never satisfied,
he gathers to himself all the nations
and takes captive all the peoples.

6 "Will not all of them taunt him with
ridicule and scorn, saying,

" 'Woe to him who piles up stolen
goods
and makes himself wealthy by
extortion!
How long must this go on?'
7 Will not your creditors suddenly
arise?
Will they not wake up and make you
tremble?
Then you will become their prey.
8 Because you have plundered many
nations,
the peoples who are left will plunder
you.
For you have shed human blood;
you have destroyed lands and cities
and everyone in them.

9 "Woe to him who builds his house by
unjust gain,
setting his nest on high
to escape the clutches of ruin!
10 You have plotted the ruin of many
peoples,
shaming your own house and
forfeiting your life.
11 The stones of the wall will cry out,
and the beams of the woodwork will
echo it.

12 "Woe to him who builds a city with
bloodshed
and establishes a town by injustice!
13 Has not the LORD Almighty
determined
that the people's labor is only fuel
for the fire,
that the nations exhaust themselves
for nothing?
14 For the earth will be filled with the
knowledge of the glory of the
LORD
as the waters cover the sea.

15 "Woe to him who gives drink to his
neighbors,
pouring it from the wineskin till
they are drunk,
so that he can gaze on their naked
bodies!
16 You will be filled with shame instead
of glory.
Now it is your turn! Drink and let
your nakedness be exposed[e]!
The cup from the LORD's right hand is
coming around to you,
and disgrace will cover your
glory.
17 The violence you have done to
Lebanon will overwhelm you,
and your destruction of animals will
terrify you.
For you have shed human blood;
you have destroyed lands and cities
and everyone in them.

[a] 1 Or *and what to answer when I am rebuked* [b] 2 Or *so that whoever reads it* [c] 3 Or *Though he linger, wait for him; / he* [d] 4 Or *faith* [e] 16 Masoretic Text; Dead Sea Scrolls, Aquila, Vulgate and Syriac (see also Septuagint) *and stagger*

18 "Of what value is an idol carved by a craftsman?
Or an image that teaches lies?
For the one who makes it trusts in his own creation;
he makes idols that cannot speak.
19 Woe to him who says to wood, 'Come to life!'
Or to lifeless stone, 'Wake up!'
Can it give guidance?
It is covered with gold and silver;
there is no breath in it."
20 The LORD is in his holy temple;
let all the earth be silent before him.

3

A prayer of Habakkuk the prophet. On *shigionoth*.[a]

2 LORD, I have heard of your fame;
I stand in awe of your deeds, LORD.
Repeat them in our day,
in our time make them known;
in wrath remember mercy.

3 God came from Teman,
the Holy One from Mount Paran.[b]
His glory covered the heavens
and his praise filled the earth.
4 His splendor was like the sunrise;
rays flashed from his hand,
where his power was hidden.
5 Plague went before him;
pestilence followed his steps.
6 He stood, and shook the earth;
he looked, and made the nations tremble.
The ancient mountains crumbled
and the age-old hills collapsed —
but he marches on forever.
7 I saw the tents of Cushan in distress,
the dwellings of Midian in anguish.

8 Were you angry with the rivers, LORD?
Was your wrath against the streams?
Did you rage against the sea
when you rode your horses
and your chariots to victory?
9 You uncovered your bow,
you called for many arrows.
You split the earth with rivers;
10 the mountains saw you and writhed.
Torrents of water swept by;
the deep roared
and lifted its waves on high.

11 Sun and moon stood still in the heavens
at the glint of your flying arrows,
at the lightning of your flashing spear.
12 In wrath you strode through the earth
and in anger you threshed the nations.
13 You came out to deliver your people,
to save your anointed one.
You crushed the leader of the land of wickedness,
you stripped him from head to foot.
14 With his own spear you pierced his head
when his warriors stormed out to scatter us,
gloating as though about to devour
the wretched who were in hiding.
15 You trampled the sea with your horses,
churning the great waters.

16 I heard and my heart pounded,
my lips quivered at the sound;
decay crept into my bones,
and my legs trembled.
Yet I will wait patiently for the day of calamity
to come on the nation invading us.
17 Though the fig tree does not bud
and there are no grapes on the vines,
though the olive crop fails
and the fields produce no food,
though there are no sheep in the pen
and no cattle in the stalls,
18 yet I will rejoice in the LORD,
I will be joyful in God my Savior.

19 The Sovereign LORD is my strength;
he makes my feet like the feet of a deer,
he enables me to tread on the heights.

For the director of music. On my stringed instruments.

[a] *1* Probably a literary or musical term [b] *3* The Hebrew has *Selah* (a word of uncertain meaning) here and at the middle of verse 9 and at the end of verse 13

ZEPHANIAH

The reign of King Manasseh of Judah was the time of greatest corruption, injustice and paganism in Judah's history. But Manasseh's grandson King Josiah reasserted the nation's faith and obedience to God and its independence from foreign empires. One reason for this seems to be that a member of his court stood up and warned that Judah's breaking of the covenant had led it to the brink of destruction. The person who offered this warning was the prophet Zephaniah.

The book's prologue identifies Zephaniah as the great-great-grandson of Hezekiah. No other prophet's ancestry is traced back four generations, so this seems intended to associate Zephaniah with the great reforming king of Judah. It is likely that Zephaniah was of royal blood, since he was familiar with particular districts in Jerusalem and with specific activities in the capital.

This collection of prophecies has three main parts. First is a description of *the day of the LORD* that is coming against Judah and Jerusalem. Next is a call for national repentance, along with oracles of destruction against the Philistines, Moabites, Cushites (Ethiopians), Assyrians and Jerusalem itself. In the final section, Zephaniah promises that God will restore a humble remnant when he returns as a Mighty Warrior among his people.

---

1 The word of the LORD that came to Zephaniah son of Cushi, the son of Gedaliah, the son of Amariah, the son of Hezekiah, during the reign of Josiah son of Amon king of Judah:

2 "I will sweep away everything
from the face of the earth,"
declares the LORD.
3 "I will sweep away both man and beast;
I will sweep away the birds in the sky
and the fish in the sea—
and the idols that cause the wicked to stumble."[a]

"When I destroy all mankind
on the face of the earth,"
declares the LORD,
4 "I will stretch out my hand against Judah
and against all who live in Jerusalem.
I will destroy every remnant of Baal worship in this place,
the very names of the idolatrous priests—
5 those who bow down on the roofs
to worship the starry host,
those who bow down and swear by the LORD
and who also swear by Molek,[b]
6 those who turn back from following the LORD
and neither seek the LORD nor inquire of him."

7 Be silent before the Sovereign LORD,
for the day of the LORD is near.
The LORD has prepared a sacrifice;
he has consecrated those he has invited.
8 "On the day of the LORD's sacrifice
I will punish the officials
and the king's sons
and all those clad
in foreign clothes.
9 On that day I will punish
all who avoid stepping on the threshold,[c]
who fill the temple of their gods
with violence and deceit.

10 "On that day,"
declares the LORD,
"a cry will go up from the Fish Gate,
wailing from the New Quarter,
and a loud crash from the hills.
11 Wail, you who live in the market district[d];
all your merchants will be wiped out,
all who trade with[e] silver will be destroyed.
12 At that time I will search Jerusalem with lamps
and punish those who are complacent,

[a] 3 The meaning of the Hebrew for this line is uncertain. [b] 5 Hebrew *Malkam* [c] 9 See 1 Samuel 5:5.
[d] 11 Or *the Mortar* [e] 11 Or *in*

who are like wine left on its dregs,
who think, 'The LORD will do nothing,
either good or bad.'
13 Their wealth will be plundered,
their houses demolished.
Though they build houses,
they will not live in them;
though they plant vineyards,
they will not drink the wine."

14 The great day of the LORD is near—
near and coming quickly.
The cry on the day of the LORD is
bitter;
the Mighty Warrior shouts his battle
cry.
15 That day will be a day of wrath—
a day of distress and anguish,
a day of trouble and ruin,
a day of darkness and gloom,
a day of clouds and blackness—
16 a day of trumpet and battle cry
against the fortified cities
and against the corner towers.

17 "I will bring such distress on all
people
that they will grope about like those
who are blind,
because they have sinned against
the LORD.
Their blood will be poured out like
dust
and their entrails like dung.
18 Neither their silver nor their gold
will be able to save them
on the day of the LORD's wrath."

In the fire of his jealousy
the whole earth will be consumed,
for he will make a sudden end
of all who live on the earth.

2 Gather together, gather yourselves
together,
you shameful nation,
2 before the decree takes effect
and that day passes like windblown
chaff,
before the LORD's fierce anger
comes upon you,
before the day of the LORD's wrath
comes upon you.
3 Seek the LORD, all you humble of the
land,
you who do what he commands.
Seek righteousness, seek humility;
perhaps you will be sheltered
on the day of the LORD's anger.

4 Gaza will be abandoned
and Ashkelon left in ruins.
At midday Ashdod will be emptied
and Ekron uprooted.
5 Woe to you who live by the sea,
you Kerethite people;
the word of the LORD is against you,
Canaan, land of the Philistines.
He says, "I will destroy you,
and none will be left."
6 The land by the sea will become
pastures
having wells for shepherds
and pens for flocks.
7 That land will belong
to the remnant of the people of
Judah;
there they will find pasture.
In the evening they will lie down
in the houses of Ashkelon.
The LORD their God will care for them;
he will restore their fortunes.[a]

8 "I have heard the insults of Moab
and the taunts of the Ammonites,
who insulted my people
and made threats against their land.
9 Therefore, as surely as I live,"
declares the LORD Almighty,
the God of Israel,
"surely Moab will become like Sodom,
the Ammonites like Gomorrah—
a place of weeds and salt pits,
a wasteland forever.
The remnant of my people will
plunder them;
the survivors of my nation will
inherit their land."

10 This is what they will get in return for
their pride,
for insulting and mocking
the people of the LORD Almighty.
11 The LORD will be awesome to them
when he destroys all the gods of the
earth.
Distant nations will bow down to him,
all of them in their own lands.

12 "You Cushites,[b] too,
will be slain by my sword."

13 He will stretch out his hand against
the north
and destroy Assyria,

[a] 7 Or *will bring back their captives* [b] 12 That is, people from the upper Nile region

leaving Nineveh utterly desolate
and dry as the desert.
14 Flocks and herds will lie down there,
creatures of every kind.
The desert owl and the screech owl
will roost on her columns.
Their hooting will echo through the
windows,
rubble will fill the doorways,
the beams of cedar will be exposed.
15 This is the city of revelry
that lived in safety.
She said to herself,
"I am the one! And there is none
besides me."
What a ruin she has become,
a lair for wild beasts!
All who pass by her scoff
and shake their fists.

3 Woe to the city of oppressors,
rebellious and defiled!
2 She obeys no one,
she accepts no correction.
She does not trust in the LORD,
she does not draw near to her God.
3 Her officials within her
are roaring lions;
her rulers are evening wolves,
who leave nothing for the morning.
4 Her prophets are unprincipled;
they are treacherous people.
Her priests profane the sanctuary
and do violence to the law.
5 The LORD within her is righteous;
he does no wrong.
Morning by morning he dispenses his
justice,
and every new day he does not fail,
yet the unrighteous know no shame.

6 "I have destroyed nations;
their strongholds are demolished.
I have left their streets deserted,
with no one passing through.
Their cities are laid waste;
they are deserted and empty.
7 Of Jerusalem I thought,
'Surely you will fear me
and accept correction!'
Then her place of refuge[a] would not be
destroyed,
nor all my punishments come upon[b]
her.
But they were still eager
to act corruptly in all they did.

8 Therefore wait for me,"
declares the LORD,
"for the day I will stand up to
testify.[c]
I have decided to assemble the
nations,
to gather the kingdoms
and to pour out my wrath on them —
all my fierce anger.
The whole world will be consumed
by the fire of my jealous anger.

9 "Then I will purify the lips of the
peoples,
that all of them may call on the
name of the LORD
and serve him shoulder to shoulder.
10 From beyond the rivers of Cush[d]
my worshipers, my scattered people,
will bring me offerings.
11 On that day you, Jerusalem, will not be
put to shame
for all the wrongs you have done to
me,
because I will remove from you
your arrogant boasters.
Never again will you be haughty
on my holy hill.
12 But I will leave within you
the meek and humble.
The remnant of Israel
will trust in the name of the LORD.
13 They will do no wrong;
they will tell no lies.
A deceitful tongue
will not be found in their mouths.
They will eat and lie down
and no one will make them afraid."
14 Sing, Daughter Zion;
shout aloud, Israel!
Be glad and rejoice with all your heart,
Daughter Jerusalem!
15 The LORD has taken away your
punishment,
he has turned back your enemy.
The LORD, the King of Israel, is with
you;
never again will you fear any harm.
16 On that day
they will say to Jerusalem,
"Do not fear, Zion;
do not let your hands hang limp.
17 The LORD your God is with you,
the Mighty Warrior who saves.

[a] 7 Or *her sanctuary* [b] 7 Or *all those I appointed over plunder* [c] 8 Septuagint and Syriac; Hebrew *will rise up to* [d] 10 That is, the upper Nile region

He will take great delight in you;
in his love he will no longer rebuke you,
but will rejoice over you with singing."

18 "I will remove from you
all who mourn over the loss of your appointed festivals,
which is a burden and reproach for you.
19 At that time I will deal
with all who oppressed you.
I will rescue the lame;
I will gather the exiles.
I will give them praise and honor
in every land where they have suffered shame.
20 At that time I will gather you;
at that time I will bring you home.
I will give you honor and praise
among all the peoples of the earth
when I restore your fortunes[a]
before your very eyes,"
says the LORD.

HAGGAI

When Cyrus, king of Persia, conquered Babylon in 539 BC, he allowed the exiled Jews to return home and rebuild the temple in Jerusalem. One group returned the next year, completing and dedicating the temple foundation within two more years. But they were stopped by suspicious and resentful neighbors who had influence in the Persian court (see pp. 421-424). Sixteen years later, when King Darius takes the throne, the prophet Haggai urges the people to restart their work. He calls specifically on Zerubbabel, the appointed governor, and Joshua the high priest, to lead the project. Within four years the reconstruction was completed and worship in the temple resumed.

Haggai delivers his four messages during a strategic four-month period at the beginning of Darius' reign. The first message explains that Israel's crops aren't being blessed because God's house has been left in ruins. The second message gives encouragement to those who found the new temple disappointing compared to Solomon's original temple. God promises that its glory will outshine the first temple. The third message assures the people that from now on their crops will be blessed. The final message is a personal encouragement to Zerubbabel himself, the heir to the throne of David. The people are back in their land, and so is God's blessing.

---

1 In the second year of King Darius,
on the first day of the sixth month,
the word of the LORD came through the
prophet Haggai to Zerubbabel son of Shealtiel, governor of Judah, and to Joshua[b]
son of Jozadak,[c] the high priest:
2This is what the LORD Almighty says:
"These people say, 'The time has not yet
come to rebuild the LORD's house.'"
3Then the word of the LORD came
through the prophet Haggai:
4"Is it a
time for you yourselves to be living in
your paneled houses, while this house
remains a ruin?"
5Now this is what the LORD Almighty
says: "Give careful thought to your ways.
6You have planted much, but harvested
little. You eat, but never have enough.
You drink, but never have your fill. You
put on clothes, but are not warm. You
earn wages, only to put them in a purse
with holes in it."
7This is what the LORD Almighty says:
"Give careful thought to your ways.
8Go
up into the mountains and bring down
timber and build my house, so that I may
take pleasure in it and be honored," says
the LORD.
9"You expected much, but

[a] 20 Or *I bring back your captives* [b] *1* A variant of *Jeshua*; here and elsewhere in Haggai [c] *1* Hebrew *Jehozadak*, a variant of *Jozadak*; also in verses 12 and 14

see, it turned out to be little. What you
brought home, I blew away. Why?" declares the LORD Almighty. "Because of
my house, which remains a ruin, while
each of you is busy with your own house.
10 Therefore, because of you the heavens
have withheld their dew and the earth
its crops. 11 I called for a drought on the
fields and the mountains, on the grain,
the new wine, the olive oil and everything else the ground produces, on people and livestock, and on all the labor of
your hands."

12 Then Zerubbabel son of Shealtiel,
Joshua son of Jozadak, the high priest,
and the whole remnant of the people
obeyed the voice of the LORD their God
and the message of the prophet Haggai,
because the LORD their God had sent
him. And the people feared the LORD.
13 Then Haggai, the LORD's messenger, gave this message of the LORD to
the people: "I am with you," declares the
LORD. 14 So the LORD stirred up the spirit
of Zerubbabel son of Shealtiel, governor
of Judah, and the spirit of Joshua son of
Jozadak, the high priest, and the spirit of
the whole remnant of the people. They
came and began to work on the house of
the LORD Almighty, their God, 15 on the
twenty-fourth day of the sixth month.

2 In the second year of King Darius,
1 on the twenty-first day of the seventh month, the word of the LORD came
through the prophet Haggai: 2 "Speak to
Zerubbabel son of Shealtiel, governor of
Judah, to Joshua son of Jozadak,[a] the high
priest, and to the remnant of the people.
Ask them, 3 'Who of you is left who saw
this house in its former glory? How does
it look to you now? Does it not seem to you
like nothing? 4 But now be strong, Zerubbabel,' declares the LORD. 'Be strong,
Joshua son of Jozadak, the high priest.
Be strong, all you people of the land,' declares the LORD, 'and work. For I am with
you,' declares the LORD Almighty. 5 'This
is what I covenanted with you when you
came out of Egypt. And my Spirit remains
among you. Do not fear.'
6 "This is what the LORD Almighty says:
'In a little while I will once more shake
the heavens and the earth, the sea and
the dry land. 7 I will shake all nations,
and what is desired by all nations will
come, and I will fill this house with glory,' says the LORD Almighty. 8 'The silver
is mine and the gold is mine,' declares
the LORD Almighty. 9 'The glory of this
present house will be greater than the
glory of the former house,' says the LORD
Almighty. 'And in this place I will grant
peace,' declares the LORD Almighty."

10 On the twenty-fourth day of the
ninth month, in the second year of Darius, the word of the LORD came to the
prophet Haggai: 11 "This is what the LORD
Almighty says: 'Ask the priests what the
law says: 12 If someone carries consecrated meat in the fold of their garment,
and that fold touches some bread or stew,
some wine, olive oil or other food, does it
become consecrated?'"
The priests answered, "No."
13 Then Haggai said, "If a person defiled
by contact with a dead body touches one
of these things, does it become defiled?"
"Yes," the priests replied, "it becomes
defiled."
14 Then Haggai said, "'So it is with this
people and this nation in my sight,' declares the LORD. 'Whatever they do and
whatever they offer there is defiled.
15 "'Now give careful thought to this
from this day on[b]—consider how things
were before one stone was laid on another in the LORD's temple. 16 When anyone
came to a heap of twenty measures, there
were only ten. When anyone went to a
wine vat to draw fifty measures, there
were only twenty. 17 I struck all the work of
your hands with blight, mildew and hail,
yet you did not return to me,' declares
the LORD. 18 'From this day on, from this
twenty-fourth day of the ninth month,
give careful thought to the day when the
foundation of the LORD's temple was laid.
Give careful thought: 19 Is there yet any
seed left in the barn? Until now, the vine
and the fig tree, the pomegranate and the
olive tree have not borne fruit.
"'From this day on I will bless you.'"

20 The word of the LORD came to Haggai
a second time on the twenty-fourth day
of the month: 21 "Tell Zerubbabel governor of Judah that I am going to shake the

[a] 2 Hebrew *Jehozadak*, a variant of *Jozadak*; also in verse 4 [b] 15 Or *to the days past*

heavens and the earth. 22I will overturn
royal thrones and shatter the power of
the foreign kingdoms. I will overthrow
chariots and their drivers; horses and
their riders will fall, each by the sword of
his brother.

23"'On that day,' declares the LORD Almighty, 'I will take you, my servant Zerubbabel son of Shealtiel,' declares the
LORD, 'and I will make you like my signet
ring, for I have chosen you,' declares the
LORD Almighty."

ZECHARIAH

The prophet Zechariah brought his messages to the returned exiles of Judah beginning in the second year of King Darius of Persia (520 BC). The book has two main parts. The first contains two sequences of prophecies, primarily in the form of symbolic vision reports. The second main part is made up mostly of poetic oracles concerned with the nation's leaders.

After a general call to repentance, Zechariah records a series of eight visions to encourage the people in rebuilding the temple. The first and last describe four differently colored horses and their riders sent over the earth. The second and third visions show that hostile foreign powers no longer threaten the country. The sixth and seventh visions report the removal of the people's sins. The two central visions depict God establishing Joshua the high priest and Zerubbabel the governor. The overall message is that God has everything in place for the rebuilding project.

The second sequence of prophecies has six parts. Ever since the disaster of the exile and the temple's destruction, the people had been fasting at certain times of the year. The messages here urge the people to practice justice as the true form of fasting and to focus on rebuilding. Then Zechariah announces that all their fasts will become joyful celebrations.

The book's final section predicts that after the people suffer under bad shepherds, God will send a righteous king from David's line. The LORD will triumph over every enemy and be king over the whole earth.

---

1 In the eighth month of the second
year of Darius, the word of the LORD
came to the prophet Zechariah son of
Berekiah, the son of Iddo:
2"The LORD was very angry with your
ancestors. 3Therefore tell the people:
This is what the LORD Almighty says: 'Return to me,' declares the LORD Almighty,
'and I will return to you,' says the LORD
Almighty. 4Do not be like your ancestors, to whom the earlier prophets proclaimed: This is what the LORD Almighty
says: 'Turn from your evil ways and your
evil practices.' But they would not listen or pay attention to me, declares the
LORD. 5Where are your ancestors now?
And the prophets, do they live forever?
6But did not my words and my decrees,
which I commanded my servants the
prophets, overtake your ancestors?
"Then they repented and said, 'The
LORD Almighty has done to us what our
ways and practices deserve, just as he determined to do.'"
7On the twenty-fourth day of the eleventh month, the month of Shebat, in the
second year of Darius, the word of the
LORD came to the prophet Zechariah son
of Berekiah, the son of Iddo.
8During the night I had a vision, and
there before me was a man mounted
on a red horse. He was standing among
the myrtle trees in a ravine. Behind him
were red, brown and white horses.
9I asked, "What are these, my lord?"
The angel who was talking with me answered, "I will show you what they are."
10Then the man standing among the
myrtle trees explained, "They are the
ones the LORD has sent to go throughout
the earth."
11And they reported to the angel of the

LORD who was standing among the myrtle trees, "We have gone throughout the
earth and found the whole world at rest
and in peace."
12 Then the angel of the LORD said,
"LORD Almighty, how long will you withhold mercy from Jerusalem and from the
towns of Judah, which you have been angry with these seventy years?" 13 So the
LORD spoke kind and comforting words
to the angel who talked with me.
14 Then the angel who was speaking
to me said, "Proclaim this word: This is
what the LORD Almighty says: 'I am very
jealous for Jerusalem and Zion, 15 and I
am very angry with the nations that feel
secure. I was only a little angry, but they
went too far with the punishment.'
16 "Therefore this is what the LORD
says: 'I will return to Jerusalem with
mercy, and there my house will be rebuilt. And the measuring line will be
stretched out over Jerusalem,' declares
the LORD Almighty.
17 "Proclaim further: This is what the
LORD Almighty says: 'My towns will
again overflow with prosperity, and the
LORD will again comfort Zion and choose
Jerusalem.'"
18 Then I looked up, and there before
me were four horns. 19 I asked the angel who was speaking to me, "What are
these?"
He answered me, "These are the horns
that scattered Judah, Israel and Jerusalem."
20 Then the LORD showed me four
craftsmen. 21 I asked, "What are these
coming to do?"
He answered, "These are the horns
that scattered Judah so that no one could
raise their head, but the craftsmen have
come to terrify them and throw down
these horns of the nations who lifted up
their horns against the land of Judah to
scatter its people."[a]

2 [b] Then I looked up, and there before
me was a man with a measuring line
in his hand. 2 I asked, "Where are you going?"
He answered me, "To measure Jerusalem, to find out how wide and how long
it is."
3 While the angel who was speaking
to me was leaving, another angel came
to meet him 4 and said to him: "Run, tell
that young man, 'Jerusalem will be a city
without walls because of the great number of people and animals in it. 5 And I
myself will be a wall of fire around it,'
declares the LORD, 'and I will be its glory within.'
6 "Come! Come! Flee from the land of
the north," declares the LORD, "for I have
scattered you to the four winds of heav-
en," declares the LORD.
7 "Come, Zion! Escape, you who live in
Daughter Babylon!" 8 For this is what the
LORD Almighty says: "After the Glorious
One has sent me against the nations that
have plundered you—for whoever touches you touches the apple of his eye— 9 I
will surely raise my hand against them
so that their slaves will plunder them.[c]
Then you will know that the LORD Almighty has sent me.
10 "Shout and be glad, Daughter Zion.
For I am coming, and I will live among
you," declares the LORD. 11 "Many nations
will be joined with the LORD in that day
and will become my people. I will live
among you and you will know that the
LORD Almighty has sent me to you. 12 The
LORD will inherit Judah as his portion in
the holy land and will again choose Jerusalem. 13 Be still before the LORD, all
mankind, because he has roused himself
from his holy dwelling."

3 Then he showed me Joshua[d] the high
priest standing before the angel of the
LORD, and Satan[e] standing at his right
side to accuse him. 2 The LORD said to
Satan, "The LORD rebuke you, Satan!
The LORD, who has chosen Jerusalem,
rebuke you! Is not this man a burning
stick snatched from the fire?"
3 Now Joshua was dressed in filthy
clothes as he stood before the angel. 4 The
angel said to those who were standing
before him, "Take off his filthy clothes."
Then he said to Joshua, "See, I have
taken away your sin, and I will put fine
garments on you."
5 Then I said, "Put a clean turban on his
head." So they put a clean turban on his
head and clothed him, while the angel of
the LORD stood by.
6 The angel of the LORD gave this

[a] *21* In Hebrew texts 1:18-21 is numbered 2:1-4. [b] In Hebrew texts 2:1-13 is numbered 2:5-17. [c] *8,9* Or *says after . . . eye: 9"I . . . plunder them."* [d] *1* A variant of *Jeshua*; here and elsewhere in Zechariah [e] *1* Hebrew *satan* means *adversary.*

charge to Joshua: 7 "This is what the LORD
Almighty says: 'If you will walk in obedience to me and keep my requirements,
then you will govern my house and have
charge of my courts, and I will give you a
place among these standing here.
8 " 'Listen, High Priest Joshua, you and
your associates seated before you, who
are men symbolic of things to come:
I am going to bring my servant, the
Branch. 9 See, the stone I have set in front
of Joshua! There are seven eyes[a] on that
one stone, and I will engrave an inscription on it,' says the LORD Almighty, 'and
I will remove the sin of this land in a single day.
10 " 'In that day each of you will invite
your neighbor to sit under your vine and
fig tree,' declares the LORD Almighty."

4 Then the angel who talked with me
returned and woke me up, like someone awakened from sleep. 2 He asked me,
"What do you see?"
I answered, "I see a solid gold lampstand with a bowl at the top and seven
lamps on it, with seven channels to the
lamps. 3 Also there are two olive trees by
it, one on the right of the bowl and the
other on its left."
4 I asked the angel who talked with me,
"What are these, my lord?"
5 He answered, "Do you not know what
these are?"
"No, my lord," I replied.
6 So he said to me, "This is the word of
the LORD to Zerubbabel: 'Not by might
nor by power, but by my Spirit,' says the
LORD Almighty.
7 "What are you, mighty mountain?
Before Zerubbabel you will become level ground. Then he will bring out the
capstone to shouts of 'God bless it! God
bless it!' "
8 Then the word of the LORD came to
me: 9 "The hands of Zerubbabel have
laid the foundation of this temple; his
hands will also complete it. Then you
will know that the LORD Almighty has
sent me to you.
10 "Who dares despise the day of small
things, since the seven eyes of the LORD
that range throughout the earth will rejoice when they see the chosen capstone[b]
in the hand of Zerubbabel?"
11 Then I asked the angel, "What are
these two olive trees on the right and the
left of the lampstand?"
12 Again I asked him, "What are these
two olive branches beside the two gold
pipes that pour out golden oil?"
13 He replied, "Do you not know what
these are?"
"No, my lord," I said.
14 So he said, "These are the two who
are anointed to[c] serve the Lord of all the
earth."

5 I looked again, and there before me
was a flying scroll.
2 He asked me, "What do you see?"
I answered, "I see a flying scroll, twenty cubits long and ten cubits wide.[d]"
3 And he said to me, "This is the curse
that is going out over the whole land; for
according to what it says on one side, every thief will be banished, and according to what it says on the other, everyone
who swears falsely will be banished.
4 The LORD Almighty declares, 'I will
send it out, and it will enter the house of
the thief and the house of anyone who
swears falsely by my name. It will remain
in that house and destroy it completely,
both its timbers and its stones.' "
5 Then the angel who was speaking to
me came forward and said to me, "Look
up and see what is appearing."
6 I asked, "What is it?"
He replied, "It is a basket." And he added, "This is the iniquity[e] of the people
throughout the land."
7 Then the cover of lead was raised, and
there in the basket sat a woman! 8 He said,
"This is wickedness," and he pushed her
back into the basket and pushed its lead
cover down on it.
9 Then I looked up—and there before
me were two women, with the wind in
their wings! They had wings like those
of a stork, and they lifted up the basket
between heaven and earth.
10 "Where are they taking the basket?"
I asked the angel who was speaking
to me.
11 He replied, "To the country of Babylonia[f] to build a house for it. When the
house is ready, the basket will be set
there in its place."

6 I looked up again, and there before me
were four chariots coming out from
between two mountains—mountains of

[a] 9 Or *facets* [b] 10 Or *the plumb line* [c] 14 Or *two who bring oil and* [d] 2 That is, about 30 feet long and 15 feet wide or about 9 meters long and 4.5 meters wide [e] 6 Or *appearance* [f] 11 Hebrew *Shinar*

bronze. 2The first chariot had red horses,
the second black, 3the third white, and
the fourth dappled — all of them powerful. 4I asked the angel who was speaking
to me, "What are these, my lord?"
5The angel answered me, "These are
the four spirits[a] of heaven, going out from
standing in the presence of the Lord of
the whole world. 6The one with the black
horses is going toward the north country, the one with the white horses toward
the west,[b] and the one with the dappled
horses toward the south."
7When the powerful horses went out,
they were straining to go throughout
the earth. And he said, "Go throughout
the earth!" So they went throughout the
earth.
8Then he called to me, "Look, those going toward the north country have given
my Spirit[c] rest in the land of the north."
9The word of the LORD came to me:
10"Take silver and gold from the exiles
Heldai, Tobijah and Jedaiah, who have
arrived from Babylon. Go the same day
to the house of Josiah son of Zephaniah.
11Take the silver and gold and make a
crown, and set it on the head of the high
priest, Joshua son of Jozadak.[d] 12Tell
him this is what the LORD Almighty
says: 'Here is the man whose name is the
Branch, and he will branch out from his
place and build the temple of the LORD.
13It is he who will build the temple of the
LORD, and he will be clothed with majesty and will sit and rule on his throne.
And he[e] will be a priest on his throne.
And there will be harmony between the
two.' 14The crown will be given to Heldai,[f] Tobijah, Jedaiah and Hen[g] son of
Zephaniah as a memorial in the temple
of the LORD. 15Those who are far away
will come and help to build the temple
of the LORD, and you will know that the
LORD Almighty has sent me to you. This
will happen if you diligently obey the
LORD your God."

7 In the fourth year of King Darius,
the word of the LORD came to Zechariah on the fourth day of the ninth
month, the month of Kislev. 2The people of Bethel had sent Sharezer and Re-
gem-Melek, together with their men, to
entreat the LORD 3by asking the priests
of the house of the LORD Almighty and
the prophets, "Should I mourn and fast
in the fifth month, as I have done for so
many years?"
4Then the word of the LORD Almighty
came to me: 5"Ask all the people of the
land and the priests, 'When you fasted
and mourned in the fifth and seventh
months for the past seventy years, was it
really for me that you fasted? 6And when
you were eating and drinking, were you
not just feasting for yourselves? 7Are
these not the words the LORD proclaimed
through the earlier prophets when Jerusalem and its surrounding towns were at
rest and prosperous, and the Negev and
the western foothills were settled?' "
8And the word of the LORD came again
to Zechariah: 9"This is what the LORD
Almighty said: 'Administer true justice;
show mercy and compassion to one another. 10Do not oppress the widow or the
fatherless, the foreigner or the poor. Do
not plot evil against each other.'
11"But they refused to pay attention;
stubbornly they turned their backs and
covered their ears. 12They made their
hearts as hard as flint and would not
listen to the law or to the words that the
LORD Almighty had sent by his Spirit through the earlier prophets. So the
LORD Almighty was very angry.
13" 'When I called, they did not listen;
so when they called, I would not listen,'
says the LORD Almighty. 14'I scattered
them with a whirlwind among all the
nations, where they were strangers. The
land they left behind them was so desolate that no one traveled through it. This
is how they made the pleasant land desolate.' "

8 The word of the LORD Almighty came
to me.
2This is what the LORD Almighty says:
"I am very jealous for Zion; I am burning
with jealousy for her."
3This is what the LORD says: "I will
return to Zion and dwell in Jerusalem.
Then Jerusalem will be called the Faithful City, and the mountain of the LORD
Almighty will be called the Holy Mountain."
4This is what the LORD Almighty says:
"Once again men and women of ripe old
age will sit in the streets of Jerusalem,
each of them with cane in hand because

[a] 5 Or *winds* [b] 6 Or *horses after them* [c] 8 Or *spirit* [d] 11 Hebrew *Jehozadak*, a variant of *Jozadak*
[e] 13 Or *there* [f] 14 Syriac; Hebrew *Helem* [g] 14 Or *and the gracious one, the*

of their age. 5 The city streets will be filled
with boys and girls playing there."
6 This is what the LORD Almighty says:
"It may seem marvelous to the remnant
of this people at that time, but will it
seem marvelous to me?" declares the
LORD Almighty.
7 This is what the LORD Almighty says:
"I will save my people from the countries
of the east and the west. 8 I will bring
them back to live in Jerusalem; they will
be my people, and I will be faithful and
righteous to them as their God."
9 This is what the LORD Almighty says:
"Now hear these words, 'Let your hands
be strong so that the temple may be
built.' This is also what the prophets said
who were present when the foundation
was laid for the house of the LORD Almighty.
10 Before that time there were no
wages for people or hire for animals. No
one could go about their business safely
because of their enemies, since I had
turned everyone against their neighbor.
11 But now I will not deal with the remnant
of this people as I did in the past,"
declares the LORD Almighty.
12 "The seed will grow well, the vine
will yield its fruit, the ground will produce
its crops, and the heavens will drop
their dew. I will give all these things as
an inheritance to the remnant of this
people. 13 Just as you, Judah and Israel,
have been a curse[a] among the nations,
so I will save you, and you will be a blessing.[b]
Do not be afraid, but let your hands
be strong."
14 This is what the LORD Almighty says:
"Just as I had determined to bring disaster
on you and showed no pity when your
ancestors angered me," says the LORD
Almighty, 15 "so now I have determined
to do good again to Jerusalem and Judah.
Do not be afraid. 16 These are the
things you are to do: Speak the truth to
each other, and render true and sound
judgment in your courts; 17 do not plot
evil against each other, and do not love
to swear falsely. I hate all this," declares
the LORD.
18 The word of the LORD Almighty came
to me.
19 This is what the LORD Almighty says:
"The fasts of the fourth, fifth, seventh
and tenth months will become joyful and
glad occasions and happy festivals for Judah.
Therefore love truth and peace."
20 This is what the LORD Almighty
says: "Many peoples and the inhabitants
of many cities will yet come, 21 and the
inhabitants of one city will go to another
and say, 'Let us go at once to entreat
the LORD and seek the LORD Almighty. I
myself am going.' 22 And many peoples
and powerful nations will come to Jerusalem
to seek the LORD Almighty and to
entreat him."
23 This is what the LORD Almighty says:
"In those days ten people from all languages
and nations will take firm hold
of one Jew by the hem of his robe and
say, 'Let us go with you, because we have
heard that God is with you.'"

9 A prophecy:

The word of the LORD is against the
land of Hadrak
and will come to rest on
Damascus—
for the eyes of all people and all the
tribes of Israel
are on the LORD—[c]
2 and on Hamath too, which borders
on it,
and on Tyre and Sidon, though they
are very skillful.
3 Tyre has built herself a stronghold;
she has heaped up silver like dust,
and gold like the dirt of the streets.
4 But the Lord will take away her
possessions
and destroy her power on the sea,
and she will be consumed by fire.
5 Ashkelon will see it and fear;
Gaza will writhe in agony,
and Ekron too, for her hope will
wither.
Gaza will lose her king
and Ashkelon will be deserted.
6 A mongrel people will occupy
Ashdod,
and I will put an end to the pride of
the Philistines.
7 I will take the blood from their
mouths,
the forbidden food from between
their teeth.

[a] *13* That is, your name has been used in cursing (see Jer. 29:22); or, you have been regarded as under a curse. [b] *13* Or *and your name will be used in blessings* (see Gen. 48:20); or *and you will be seen as blessed*
[c] *1* Or *Damascus. / For the eye of the LORD is on all people, / as well as on the tribes of Israel,*

Those who are left will belong to our
God
and become a clan in Judah,
and Ekron will be like the Jebusites.
8 But I will encamp at my temple
to guard it against marauding
forces.
Never again will an oppressor
overrun my people,
for now I am keeping watch.

9 Rejoice greatly, Daughter Zion!
Shout, Daughter Jerusalem!
See, your king comes to you,
righteous and victorious,
lowly and riding on a donkey,
on a colt, the foal of a donkey.
10 I will take away the chariots from
Ephraim
and the warhorses from Jerusalem,
and the battle bow will be broken.
He will proclaim peace to the nations.
His rule will extend from sea to sea
and from the River[a] to the ends of
the earth.
11 As for you, because of the blood of my
covenant with you,
I will free your prisoners from the
waterless pit.
12 Return to your fortress, you prisoners
of hope;
even now I announce that I will
restore twice as much to you.
13 I will bend Judah as I bend my bow
and fill it with Ephraim.
I will rouse your sons, Zion,
against your sons, Greece,
and make you like a warrior's
sword.

14 Then the LORD will appear over them;
his arrow will flash like lightning.
The Sovereign LORD will sound the
trumpet;
he will march in the storms of the
south,
15 and the LORD Almighty will shield
them.
They will destroy
and overcome with slingstones.
They will drink and roar as with wine;
they will be full like a bowl
used for sprinkling[b] the corners of
the altar.
16 The LORD their God will save his
people on that day
as a shepherd saves his flock.
They will sparkle in his land
like jewels in a crown.
17 How attractive and beautiful they will
be!
Grain will make the young men
thrive,
and new wine the young women.

10 Ask the LORD for rain in the
springtime;
it is the LORD who sends the
thunderstorms.
He gives showers of rain to all people,
and plants of the field to everyone.
2 The idols speak deceitfully,
diviners see visions that lie;
they tell dreams that are false,
they give comfort in vain.
Therefore the people wander like
sheep
oppressed for lack of a shepherd.

3 "My anger burns against the
shepherds,
and I will punish the leaders;
for the LORD Almighty will care
for his flock, the people of Judah,
and make them like a proud horse
in battle.
4 From Judah will come the
cornerstone,
from him the tent peg,
from him the battle bow,
from him every ruler.
5 Together they[c] will be like warriors in
battle
trampling their enemy into the mud
of the streets.
They will fight because the LORD is
with them,
and they will put the enemy
horsemen to shame.

6 "I will strengthen Judah
and save the tribes of Joseph.
I will restore them
because I have compassion on
them.
They will be as though
I had not rejected them,
for I am the LORD their God
and I will answer them.
7 The Ephraimites will become like
warriors,
and their hearts will be glad as with
wine.

[a] *10* That is, the Euphrates [b] *15* Or *bowl, / like* [c] *4,5* Or *ruler, all of them together. / [5]They*

Their children will see it and be
joyful;
their hearts will rejoice in the LORD.
8 I will signal for them
and gather them in.
Surely I will redeem them;
they will be as numerous as before.
9 Though I scatter them among the
peoples,
yet in distant lands they will
remember me.
They and their children will survive,
and they will return.
10 I will bring them back from Egypt
and gather them from Assyria.
I will bring them to Gilead and
Lebanon,
and there will not be room enough
for them.
11 They will pass through the sea of
trouble;
the surging sea will be subdued
and all the depths of the Nile will
dry up.
Assyria's pride will be brought down
and Egypt's scepter will pass away.
12 I will strengthen them in the LORD
and in his name they will live
securely,"
declares the LORD.

11 Open your doors, Lebanon,
so that fire may devour your
cedars!
2 Wail, you juniper, for the cedar has
fallen;
the stately trees are ruined!
Wail, oaks of Bashan;
the dense forest has been cut down!
3 Listen to the wail of the shepherds;
their rich pastures are destroyed!
Listen to the roar of the lions;
the lush thicket of the Jordan is
ruined!

4 This is what the LORD my God says:
"Shepherd the flock marked for slaughter. 5 Their buyers slaughter them and go
unpunished. Those who sell them say,
'Praise the LORD, I am rich!' Their own
shepherds do not spare them. 6 For I will
no longer have pity on the people of the
land," declares the LORD. "I will give everyone into the hands of their neighbors
and their king. They will devastate the
land, and I will not rescue anyone from
their hands."

7 So I shepherded the flock marked for
slaughter, particularly the oppressed
of the flock. Then I took two staffs and
called one Favor and the other Union,
and I shepherded the flock. 8 In one
month I got rid of the three shepherds.

The flock detested me, and I grew
weary of them 9 and said, "I will not be
your shepherd. Let the dying die, and
the perishing perish. Let those who are
left eat one another's flesh."

10 Then I took my staff called Favor and
broke it, revoking the covenant I had
made with all the nations. 11 It was revoked on that day, and so the oppressed
of the flock who were watching me knew
it was the word of the LORD.

12 I told them, "If you think it best, give
me my pay; but if not, keep it." So they
paid me thirty pieces of silver.

13 And the LORD said to me, "Throw it
to the potter"—the handsome price at
which they valued me! So I took the thirty pieces of silver and threw them to the
potter at the house of the LORD.

14 Then I broke my second staff called
Union, breaking the family bond between Judah and Israel.

15 Then the LORD said to me, "Take
again the equipment of a foolish shepherd. 16 For I am going to raise up a shepherd over the land who will not care for
the lost, or seek the young, or heal the
injured, or feed the healthy, but will eat
the meat of the choice sheep, tearing off
their hooves.

17 "Woe to the worthless shepherd,
who deserts the flock!
May the sword strike his arm and his
right eye!
May his arm be completely
withered,
his right eye totally blinded!"

12 A prophecy: The word of the LORD
concerning Israel.

The LORD, who stretches out the heavens, who lays the foundation of the earth,
and who forms the human spirit within
a person, declares: 2 "I am going to make
Jerusalem a cup that sends all the surrounding peoples reeling. Judah will be
besieged as well as Jerusalem. 3 On that
day, when all the nations of the earth are
gathered against her, I will make Jerusalem an immovable rock for all the nations. All who try to move it will injure
themselves. 4 On that day I will strike

every horse with panic and its rider with
madness," declares the LORD. "I will
keep a watchful eye over Judah, but I will
blind all the horses of the nations. 5 Then
the clans of Judah will say in their hearts,
'The people of Jerusalem are strong, because the LORD Almighty is their God.'

6 "On that day I will make the clans of
Judah like a firepot in a woodpile, like a
flaming torch among sheaves. They will
consume all the surrounding peoples
right and left, but Jerusalem will remain
intact in her place.

7 "The LORD will save the dwellings of
Judah first, so that the honor of the house
of David and of Jerusalem's inhabitants
may not be greater than that of Judah.
8 On that day the LORD will shield those
who live in Jerusalem, so that the fee-
blest among them will be like David, and
the house of David will be like God, like
the angel of the LORD going before them.
9 On that day I will set out to destroy all
the nations that attack Jerusalem.

10 "And I will pour out on the house
of David and the inhabitants of Jerusalem a spirit[a] of grace and supplication.
They will look on[b] me, the one they have
pierced, and they will mourn for him as
one mourns for an only child, and grieve
bitterly for him as one grieves for a firstborn son. 11 On that day the weeping in
Jerusalem will be as great as the weeping of Hadad Rimmon in the plain of Megiddo. 12 The land will mourn, each clan
by itself, with their wives by themselves:
the clan of the house of David and their
wives, the clan of the house of Nathan
and their wives, 13 the clan of the house
of Levi and their wives, the clan of Shimei and their wives, 14 and all the rest of the
clans and their wives.

13 "On that day a fountain will be
opened to the house of David and
the inhabitants of Jerusalem, to cleanse
them from sin and impurity.

2 "On that day, I will banish the names
of the idols from the land, and they will
be remembered no more," declares the
LORD Almighty. "I will remove both the
prophets and the spirit of impurity from
the land. 3 And if anyone still prophesies,
their father and mother, to whom they
were born, will say to them, 'You must
die, because you have told lies in the
LORD's name.' Then their own parents
will stab the one who prophesies.

4 "On that day every prophet will be
ashamed of their prophetic vision. They
will not put on a prophet's garment of
hair in order to deceive. 5 Each will say,
'I am not a prophet. I am a farmer; the
land has been my livelihood since my
youth.[c]' 6 If someone asks, 'What are
these wounds on your body[d]?' they will
answer, 'The wounds I was given at the
house of my friends.'

7 "Awake, sword, against my shepherd,
against the man who is close to me!"
declares the LORD Almighty.
"Strike the shepherd,
and the sheep will be scattered,
and I will turn my hand against the
little ones.
8 In the whole land," declares the LORD,
"two-thirds will be struck down and
perish;
yet one-third will be left in it.
9 This third I will put into the fire;
I will refine them like silver
and test them like gold.
They will call on my name
and I will answer them;
I will say, 'They are my people,'
and they will say, 'The LORD is our
God.'"

14 A day of the LORD is coming, Jerusalem, when your possessions will
be plundered and divided up within your
very walls.

2 I will gather all the nations to Jerusalem to fight against it; the city will be
captured, the houses ransacked, and the
women raped. Half of the city will go into
exile, but the rest of the people will not be
taken from the city. 3 Then the LORD will
go out and fight against those nations, as
he fights on a day of battle. 4 On that day
his feet will stand on the Mount of Olives,
east of Jerusalem, and the Mount of Olives will be split in two from east to west,
forming a great valley, with half of the
mountain moving north and half moving south. 5 You will flee by my mountain
valley, for it will extend to Azel. You will
flee as you fled from the earthquake[e] in
the days of Uzziah king of Judah. Then

[a] 10 Or *the Spirit* [b] 10 Or *to* [c] 5 Or *farmer; a man sold me in my youth* [d] 6 Or *wounds between your hands* [e] 5 Or *My mountain valley will be blocked and will extend to Azel. It will be blocked as it was blocked because of the earthquake*

the LORD my God will come, and all the
holy ones with him.
6 On that day there will be neither sunlight nor cold, frosty darkness. 7 It will be
a unique day — a day known only to the
LORD — with no distinction between day
and night. When evening comes, there
will be light.
8 On that day living water will flow out
from Jerusalem, half of it east to the Dead
Sea and half of it west to the Mediterranean Sea, in summer and in winter.
9 The LORD will be king over the whole
earth. On that day there will be one
LORD, and his name the only name.
10 The whole land, from Geba to Rimmon, south of Jerusalem, will become
like the Arabah. But Jerusalem will be
raised up high from the Benjamin Gate
to the site of the First Gate, to the Corner
Gate, and from the Tower of Hananel to
the royal winepresses, and will remain
in its place. 11 It will be inhabited; never
again will it be destroyed. Jerusalem will
be secure.
12 This is the plague with which the
LORD will strike all the nations that
fought against Jerusalem: Their flesh
will rot while they are still standing
on their feet, their eyes will rot in their
sockets, and their tongues will rot in
their mouths. 13 On that day people will
be stricken by the LORD with great panic. They will seize each other by the hand
and attack one another. 14 Judah too will
fight at Jerusalem. The wealth of all the
surrounding nations will be collected —
great quantities of gold and silver and
clothing. 15 A similar plague will strike
the horses and mules, the camels and
donkeys, and all the animals in those
camps.
16 Then the survivors from all the nations that have attacked Jerusalem will go
up year after year to worship the King, the
LORD Almighty, and to celebrate the Festival of Tabernacles. 17 If any of the peoples of the earth do not go up to Jerusalem
to worship the King, the LORD Almighty,
they will have no rain. 18 If the Egyptian
people do not go up and take part, they
will have no rain. The LORD[a] will bring on
them the plague he inflicts on the nations
that do not go up to celebrate the Festival
of Tabernacles. 19 This will be the punishment of Egypt and the punishment of all
the nations that do not go up to celebrate
the Festival of Tabernacles.
20 On that day HOLY TO THE LORD will be
inscribed on the bells of the horses, and
the cooking pots in the LORD's house will
be like the sacred bowls in front of the altar. 21 Every pot in Jerusalem and Judah
will be holy to the LORD Almighty, and all
who come to sacrifice will take some of
the pots and cook in them. And on that
day there will no longer be a Canaanite[b]
in the house of the LORD Almighty.

[a] 18 Or *part, then the LORD* [b] 21 Or *merchant*

MALACHI

The rebuilding of the temple under Zerubbabel and Joshua, inspired by the prophecies of Haggai and Zechariah, was completed in 516 BC. The new temple was meant to be the centerpiece of a community in which there was true justice and genuine worship. In this way Israel could fulfill its calling and be a light, revealing God to the nations.

Unfortunately, as the years went by, the people fell further and further away from this ideal. By the middle of the next century, their worship had become corrupt, and their society was plagued with injustice. Malachi ("my messenger") challenges the people to honor God properly in their worship and in their dealings with one another. The world could then come to know the LORD as the great king.

Malachi brings his challenges in a distinctive style. He first offers an abrupt charge, voices the anticipated objections, and finally answers those objections. The book records that some of the people repent in response to these challenges, and that God says he will spare them when he comes to judge the earth. The book ends with God's promise to send the prophet Elijah back *before that great and dreadful day of the* LORD.

---

1 A prophecy: The word of the LORD to
Israel through Malachi.[a]

2 "I have loved you," says the LORD.
"But you ask, 'How have you loved us?'
"Was not Esau Jacob's brother?" declares the LORD. "Yet I have loved Jacob,
3 but Esau I have hated, and I have turned
his hill country into a wasteland and left
his inheritance to the desert jackals."
4 Edom may say, "Though we have been
crushed, we will rebuild the ruins."
But this is what the LORD Almighty
says: "They may build, but I will demolish. They will be called the Wicked Land,
a people always under the wrath of the
LORD. 5 You will see it with your own eyes
and say, 'Great is the LORD—even beyond the borders of Israel!'
6 "A son honors his father, and a slave
his master. If I am a father, where is the
honor due me? If I am a master, where is
the respect due me?" says the LORD Almighty.
"It is you priests who show contempt
for my name.
"But you ask, 'How have we shown
contempt for your name?'
7 "By offering defiled food on my altar.
"But you ask, 'How have we defiled
you?'
"By saying that the LORD's table is
contemptible. 8 When you offer blind
animals for sacrifice, is that not wrong?
When you sacrifice lame or diseased
animals, is that not wrong? Try offering them to your governor! Would he be
pleased with you? Would he accept you?"
says the LORD Almighty.
9 "Now plead with God to be gracious
to us. With such offerings from your
hands, will he accept you?"—says the
LORD Almighty.
10 "Oh, that one of you would shut the
temple doors, so that you would not
light useless fires on my altar! I am not
pleased with you," says the LORD Almighty, "and I will accept no offering
from your hands. 11 My name will be
great among the nations, from where
the sun rises to where it sets. In every
place incense and pure offerings will be
brought to me, because my name will be
great among the nations," says the LORD
Almighty.
12 "But you profane it by saying, 'The
Lord's table is defiled,' and, 'Its food is
contemptible.' 13 And you say, 'What a
burden!' and you sniff at it contemptuously," says the LORD Almighty.
"When you bring injured, lame or diseased animals and offer them as sacrifices, should I accept them from your
hands?" says the LORD. 14 "Cursed is the
cheat who has an acceptable male in his
flock and vows to give it, but then sacrifices a blemished animal to the Lord.
For I am a great king," says the LORD
Almighty, "and my name is to be feared
among the nations.

[a] 1 *Malachi* means *my messenger.*

2 "And now, you priests, this warning is
for you. 2 If you do not listen, and if you
do not resolve to honor my name," says
the LORD Almighty, "I will send a curse
on you, and I will curse your blessings.
Yes, I have already cursed them, because
you have not resolved to honor me.
3 "Because of you I will rebuke your
descendants[a]; I will smear on your faces the dung from your festival sacrifices,
and you will be carried off with it. 4 And
you will know that I have sent you this
warning so that my covenant with Levi
may continue," says the LORD Almighty.
5 "My covenant was with him, a covenant
of life and peace, and I gave them to him;
this called for reverence and he revered
me and stood in awe of my name. 6 True
instruction was in his mouth and nothing false was found on his lips. He walked
with me in peace and uprightness, and
turned many from sin.
7 "For the lips of a priest ought to preserve knowledge, because he is the
messenger of the LORD Almighty and
people seek instruction from his mouth.
8 But you have turned from the way and
by your teaching have caused many to
stumble; you have violated the covenant
with Levi," says the LORD Almighty. 9 "So
I have caused you to be despised and humiliated before all the people, because
you have not followed my ways but have
shown partiality in matters of the law."
10 Do we not all have one Father[b]? Did
not one God create us? Why do we profane the covenant of our ancestors by being unfaithful to one another?
11 Judah has been unfaithful. A detestable thing has been committed in Israel
and in Jerusalem: Judah has desecrated
the sanctuary the LORD loves by marrying women who worship a foreign god.
12 As for the man who does this, whoever he may be, may the LORD remove him
from the tents of Jacob[c]—even though
he brings an offering to the LORD Almighty.
13 Another thing you do: You flood the
LORD's altar with tears. You weep and
wail because he no longer looks with
favor on your offerings or accepts them
with pleasure from your hands. 14 You
ask, "Why?" It is because the LORD is the
witness between you and the wife of your
youth. You have been unfaithful to her,
though she is your partner, the wife of
your marriage covenant.
15 Has not the one God made you? You
belong to him in body and spirit. And
what does the one God seek? Godly offspring.[d] So be on your guard, and do not
be unfaithful to the wife of your youth.
16 "The man who hates and divorces
his wife," says the LORD, the God of Israel, "does violence to the one he should
protect,"[e] says the LORD Almighty.
So be on your guard, and do not be unfaithful.
17 You have wearied the LORD with
your words.
"How have we wearied him?" you ask.
By saying, "All who do evil are good in
the eyes of the LORD, and he is pleased
with them" or "Where is the God of justice?"

3 "I will send my messenger, who will
prepare the way before me. Then suddenly the Lord you are seeking will come
to his temple; the messenger of the covenant, whom you desire, will come," says
the LORD Almighty.
2 But who can endure the day of his
coming? Who can stand when he appears? For he will be like a refiner's fire
or a launderer's soap. 3 He will sit as a refiner and purifier of silver; he will purify
the Levites and refine them like gold and
silver. Then the LORD will have men who
will bring offerings in righteousness,
4 and the offerings of Judah and Jerusalem will be acceptable to the LORD, as in
days gone by, as in former years.
5 "So I will come to put you on trial. I
will be quick to testify against sorcerers,
adulterers and perjurers, against those
who defraud laborers of their wages,
who oppress the widows and the fatherless, and deprive the foreigners among
you of justice, but do not fear me," says
the LORD Almighty.
6 "I the LORD do not change. So you, the
descendants of Jacob, are not destroyed.
7 Ever since the time of your ancestors
you have turned away from my decrees
and have not kept them. Return to me,

[a] 3 Or *will blight your grain* [b] 10 Or *father* [c] 12 Or *12 May the LORD remove from the tents of Jacob anyone who gives testimony in behalf of the man who does this* [d] 15 The meaning of the Hebrew for the first part of this verse is uncertain. [e] 16 Or *"I hate divorce," says the LORD, the God of Israel, "because the man who divorces his wife covers his garment with violence,"*

and I will return to you," says the LORD
Almighty.
"But you ask, 'How are we to return?'
[8]"Will a mere mortal rob God? Yet you
rob me.
"But you ask, 'How are we robbing
you?'
"In tithes and offerings. [9]You are under
a curse—your whole nation—because
you are robbing me. [10]Bring the whole
tithe into the storehouse, that there may
be food in my house. Test me in this,"
says the LORD Almighty, "and see if I will
not throw open the floodgates of heav-
en and pour out so much blessing that
there will not be room enough to store
it. [11]I will prevent pests from devouring
your crops, and the vines in your fields
will not drop their fruit before it is ripe,"
says the LORD Almighty. [12]"Then all the
nations will call you blessed, for yours
will be a delightful land," says the LORD
Almighty.
[13]"You have spoken arrogantly against
me," says the LORD.
"Yet you ask, 'What have we said
against you?'
[14]"You have said, 'It is futile to serve
God. What do we gain by carrying out
his requirements and going about like
mourners before the LORD Almighty?
[15]But now we call the arrogant blessed.
Certainly evildoers prosper, and even
when they put God to the test, they get
away with it.'"
[16]Then those who feared the LORD
talked with each other, and the LORD
listened and heard. A scroll of remembrance was written in his presence concerning those who feared the LORD and
honored his name.
[17]"On the day when I act," says the
LORD Almighty, "they will be my treasured possession. I will spare them, just
as a father has compassion and spares
his son who serves him. [18]And you will
again see the distinction between the
righteous and the wicked, between those
who serve God and those who do not.
4[a] "Surely the day is coming; it will
burn like a furnace. All the arrogant and every evildoer will be stubble,
and the day that is coming will set them
on fire," says the LORD Almighty. "Not a
root or a branch will be left to them. [2]But
for you who revere my name, the sun of
righteousness will rise with healing in its
rays. And you will go out and frolic like
well-fed calves. [3]Then you will trample
on the wicked; they will be ashes under
the soles of your feet on the day when I
act," says the LORD Almighty.
[4]"Remember the law of my servant
Moses, the decrees and laws I gave him
at Horeb for all Israel.
[5]"See, I will send the prophet Elijah to
you before that great and dreadful day of
the LORD comes. [6]He will turn the hearts
of the parents to their children, and the
hearts of the children to their parents; or
else I will come and strike the land with
total destruction."

[a] In Hebrew texts 4:1-6 is numbered 3:19-24.

Israel's continuing story and its climax in

THE LIFE, DEATH
AND RESURRECTION OF
JESUS THE MESSIAH,

the announcement of

GOD'S VICTORY OVER HUMANITY'S
ENEMIES SIN AND DEATH,

and the invitation for

ALL PEOPLES TO BE
RECONCILED TO GOD

and to share in his

RESTORATION OF ALL THINGS,

PRESENTED
IN THE BOOKS OF THE

NEW TESTAMENT

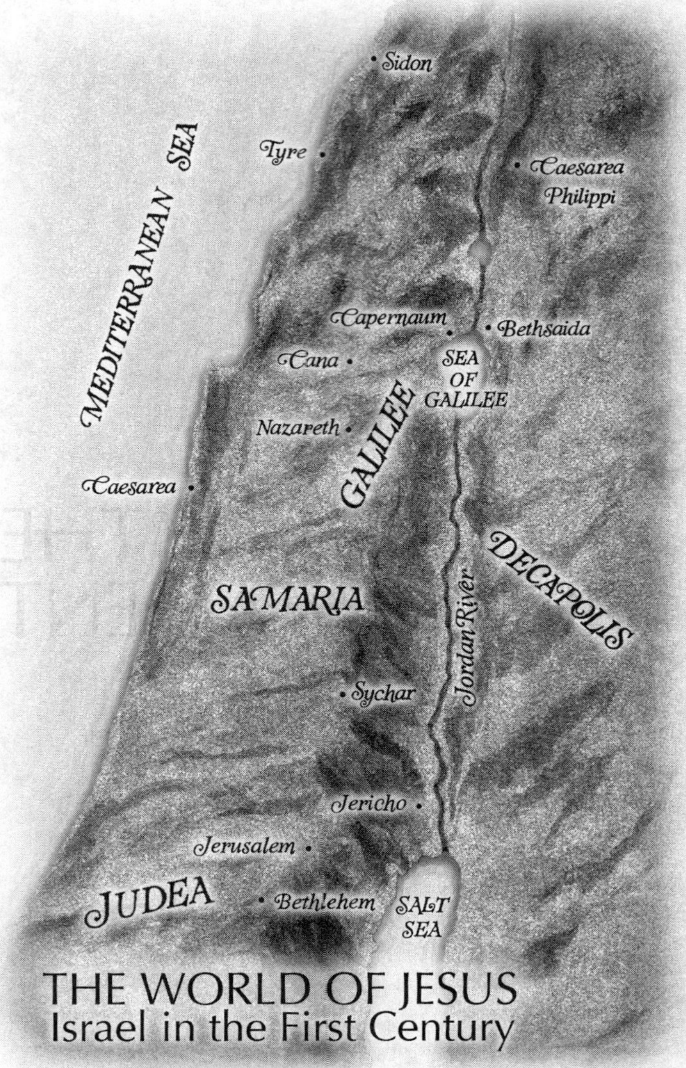

THE WORLD OF JESUS
Israel in the First Century

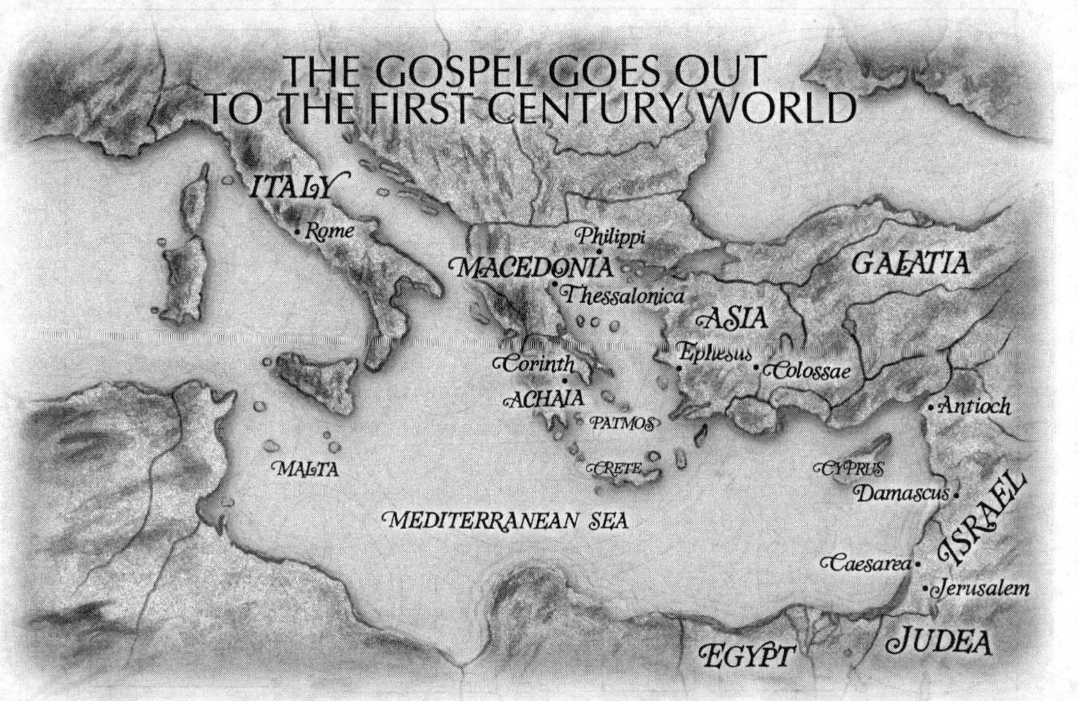
THE GOSPEL GOES OUT
TO THE FIRST CENTURY WORLD
ITALY
Rome
MACEDONIA
Philippi
Thessalonica
GALATIA
ASIA
Ephesus
Colossae
Corinth
ACHAIA
PATMOS
CRETE
MALTA
MEDITERRANEAN SEA
Antioch
CYPRUS
Damascus
ISRAEL
Caesarea
Jerusalem
JUDEA
EGYPT

David Thomason 2010

MATTHEW

Matthew's purpose is to show that God has kept his ancient promises to Israel through the life, death and resurrection of Jesus the Messiah. The long-expected reign of heaven is now coming to earth, bringing the Jewish story to its climax. Matthew begins by highlighting that Jesus was the son of David, Israel's most famous king, and the son of Abraham, Israel's founding patriarch. Jesus is the true Israelite and God's promised Messiah.

The Messiah is shown as reliving the story of Israel—going down into the Jordan River, facing temptation in the wilderness, gathering twelve disciples as twelve new tribes, ascending a mountain to deliver a new Torah, etc. The author highlights the idea of Jesus as a new Moses by collecting his teachings into five long speeches. These are marked off by some variation of the phrase *When Jesus had finished saying these things*. Just as the Torah had five books, Matthew presents five major sections.

The book concludes by telling how Jesus brought about the great new act of redemption for his people. As in the story of Israel's Exodus, a Passover meal is celebrated and then deliverance comes. Jesus gives his life for the sake of the world and is then raised from the dead. At the beginning of the book, Jesus is given the name *Immanuel*, meaning "God with us." At the end, Jesus sends his followers into the world with the promise that *surely I am with you always*.

---

1 This is the genealogy[a] of Jesus the Messiah[b] the son of David, the son of Abraham:

2 Abraham was the father of Isaac,
Isaac the father of Jacob,
Jacob the father of Judah and his
brothers,
3 Judah the father of Perez and Zerah, whose mother was Tamar,
Perez the father of Hezron,
Hezron the father of Ram,
4 Ram the father of Amminadab,
Amminadab the father of Nahshon,
Nahshon the father of Salmon,
5 Salmon the father of Boaz, whose
mother was Rahab,
Boaz the father of Obed, whose
mother was Ruth,
Obed the father of Jesse,
6 and Jesse the father of King
David.

David was the father of Solomon,
whose mother had been Uriah's
wife,
7 Solomon the father of Rehoboam,
Rehoboam the father of Abijah,
Abijah the father of Asa,
8 Asa the father of Jehoshaphat,
Jehoshaphat the father of Jehoram,
Jehoram the father of Uzziah,
9 Uzziah the father of Jotham,
Jotham the father of Ahaz,
Ahaz the father of Hezekiah,
10 Hezekiah the father of Manasseh,
Manasseh the father of Amon,
Amon the father of Josiah,
11 and Josiah the father of Jeconiah[c]
and his brothers at the time of
the exile to Babylon.

12 After the exile to Babylon:
Jeconiah was the father of Shealtiel,
Shealtiel the father of Zerubbabel,
13 Zerubbabel the father of Abihud,
Abihud the father of Eliakim,
Eliakim the father of Azor,
14 Azor the father of Zadok,
Zadok the father of Akim,
Akim the father of Elihud,
15 Elihud the father of Eleazar,
Eleazar the father of Matthan,
Matthan the father of Jacob,
16 and Jacob the father of Joseph, the
husband of Mary, and Mary was
the mother of Jesus who is called
the Messiah.

17 Thus there were fourteen generations in all from Abraham to David, fourteen from David to the exile to Babylon, and fourteen from the exile to the Messiah.

[a] *1* Or *is an account of the origin*
[b] *1* Or *Jesus Christ. Messiah* (Hebrew) and *Christ* (Greek) both mean *Anointed One*; also in verse 18.
[c] *11* That is, Jehoiachin; also in verse 12

18This is how the birth of Jesus the
Messiah came about[a]: His mother Mary
was pledged to be married to Joseph, but
before they came together, she was found
to be pregnant through the Holy Spirit.
19Because Joseph her husband was faithful to the law, and yet[b] did not want to
expose her to public disgrace, he had in
mind to divorce her quietly.

20But after he had considered this, an
angel of the Lord appeared to him in a
dream and said, "Joseph son of David, do
not be afraid to take Mary home as your
wife, because what is conceived in her is
from the Holy Spirit. 21She will give birth
to a son, and you are to give him the name
Jesus,[c] because he will save his people
from their sins."

22All this took place to fulfill what
the Lord had said through the prophet:
23"The virgin will conceive and give birth
to a son, and they will call him Immanuel"[d] (which means "God with us").

24When Joseph woke up, he did what
the angel of the Lord had commanded
him and took Mary home as his wife.
25But he did not consummate their marriage until she gave birth to a son. And he
gave him the name Jesus.

2 After Jesus was born in Bethlehem in
Judea, during the time of King Herod,
Magi[e] from the east came to Jerusalem
2and asked, "Where is the one who has
been born king of the Jews? We saw his
star when it rose and have come to worship him."

3When King Herod heard this he was
disturbed, and all Jerusalem with him.
4When he had called together all the people's chief priests and teachers of the law,
he asked them where the Messiah was to
be born. 5"In Bethlehem in Judea," they
replied, "for this is what the prophet has
written:

6"'But you, Bethlehem, in the land of
Judah,
are by no means least among the
rulers of Judah;
for out of you will come a ruler
who will shepherd my people
Israel.'[f]"

7Then Herod called the Magi secretly
and found out from them the exact time
the star had appeared. 8He sent them
to Bethlehem and said, "Go and search
carefully for the child. As soon as you
find him, report to me, so that I too may
go and worship him."

9After they had heard the king, they
went on their way, and the star they had
seen when it rose went ahead of them
until it stopped over the place where
the child was. 10When they saw the star,
they were overjoyed. 11On coming to
the house, they saw the child with his
mother Mary, and they bowed down and
worshiped him. Then they opened their
treasures and presented him with gifts
of gold, frankincense and myrrh. 12And
having been warned in a dream not to
go back to Herod, they returned to their
country by another route.

13When they had gone, an angel of the
Lord appeared to Joseph in a dream. "Get
up," he said, "take the child and his mother and escape to Egypt. Stay there until I
tell you, for Herod is going to search for
the child to kill him."

14So he got up, took the child and his
mother during the night and left for
Egypt, 15where he stayed until the death
of Herod. And so was fulfilled what the
Lord had said through the prophet: "Out
of Egypt I called my son."[g]

16When Herod realized that he had
been outwitted by the Magi, he was furious, and he gave orders to kill all the
boys in Bethlehem and its vicinity who
were two years old and under, in accordance with the time he had learned from
the Magi. 17Then what was said through
the prophet Jeremiah was fulfilled:

18"A voice is heard in Ramah,
weeping and great mourning,
Rachel weeping for her children
and refusing to be comforted,
because they are no more."[h]

19After Herod died, an angel of the
Lord appeared in a dream to Joseph in
Egypt 20and said, "Get up, take the child
and his mother and go to the land of Israel, for those who were trying to take the
child's life are dead."

21So he got up, took the child and his
mother and went to the land of Israel.
22But when he heard that Archelaus was

[a] *18* Or *The origin of Jesus the Messiah was like this* [b] *19* Or *was a righteous man and* [c] *21* *Jesus* is the Greek form of *Joshua,* which means *the LORD saves.* [d] *23* Isaiah 7:14 [e] *1* Traditionally *wise men* [f] *6* Micah 5:2,4 [g] *15* Hosea 11:1 [h] *18* Jer. 31:15

reigning in Judea in place of his father Herod, he was afraid to go there. Having been warned in a dream, he withdrew to the district of Galilee, 23and he went and lived in a town called Nazareth. So was fulfilled what was said through the prophets, that he would be called a Nazarene.

3 In those days John the Baptist came, preaching in the wilderness of Judea 2and saying, "Repent, for the kingdom of heaven has come near." 3This is he who was spoken of through the prophet Isaiah:

"A voice of one calling in the
wilderness,
'Prepare the way for the Lord,
make straight paths for him.' "[a]

4John's clothes were made of camel's hair, and he had a leather belt around his waist. His food was locusts and wild honey. 5People went out to him from Jerusalem and all Judea and the whole region of the Jordan. 6Confessing their sins, they were baptized by him in the Jordan River.

7But when he saw many of the Pharisees and Sadducees coming to where he was baptizing, he said to them: "You brood of vipers! Who warned you to flee from the coming wrath? 8Produce fruit in keeping with repentance. 9And do not think you can say to yourselves, 'We have Abraham as our father.' I tell you that out of these stones God can raise up children for Abraham. 10The ax is already at the root of the trees, and every tree that does not produce good fruit will be cut down and thrown into the fire.

11"I baptize you with[b] water for repentance. But after me comes one who is more powerful than I, whose sandals I am not worthy to carry. He will baptize you with[b] the Holy Spirit and fire. 12His winnowing fork is in his hand, and he will clear his threshing floor, gathering his wheat into the barn and burning up the chaff with unquenchable fire."

13Then Jesus came from Galilee to the Jordan to be baptized by John. 14But John tried to deter him, saying, "I need to be baptized by you, and do you come to me?"

15Jesus replied, "Let it be so now; it is proper for us to do this to fulfill all righteousness." Then John consented.

16As soon as Jesus was baptized, he went up out of the water. At that moment heaven was opened, and he saw the Spirit of God descending like a dove and alighting on him. 17And a voice from heaven said, "This is my Son, whom I love; with him I am well pleased."

4 Then Jesus was led by the Spirit into the wilderness to be tempted[c] by the devil. 2After fasting forty days and forty nights, he was hungry. 3The tempter came to him and said, "If you are the Son of God, tell these stones to become bread."

4Jesus answered, "It is written: 'Man shall not live on bread alone, but on every word that comes from the mouth of God.'[d]"

5Then the devil took him to the holy city and had him stand on the highest point of the temple. 6"If you are the Son of God," he said, "throw yourself down. For it is written:

" 'He will command his angels
concerning you,
and they will lift you up in their
hands,
so that you will not strike your foot
against a stone.'[e]"

7Jesus answered him, "It is also written: 'Do not put the Lord your God to the test.'[f]"

8Again, the devil took him to a very high mountain and showed him all the kingdoms of the world and their splendor. 9"All this I will give you," he said, "if you will bow down and worship me."

10Jesus said to him, "Away from me, Satan! For it is written: 'Worship the Lord your God, and serve him only.'[g]"

11Then the devil left him, and angels came and attended him.

12When Jesus heard that John had been put in prison, he withdrew to Galilee. 13Leaving Nazareth, he went and lived in Capernaum, which was by the lake in the area of Zebulun and Naphtali— 14to fulfill what was said through the prophet Isaiah:

15"Land of Zebulun and land of Naphtali,
the Way of the Sea, beyond the
Jordan,

[a] 3 Isaiah 40:3 [b] 11 Or *in* [c] 1 The Greek for *tempted* can also mean *tested.* [d] 4 Deut. 8:3
[e] 6 Psalm 91:11,12 [f] 7 Deut. 6:16 [g] 10 Deut. 6:13

Galilee of the Gentiles —
16 the people living in darkness
have seen a great light;
on those living in the land of the
shadow of death
a light has dawned."[a]

17 From that time on Jesus began to
preach, "Repent, for the kingdom of heav-
en has come near."

18 As Jesus was walking beside the Sea
of Galilee, he saw two brothers, Simon
called Peter and his brother Andrew.
They were casting a net into the lake, for
they were fishermen. 19 "Come, follow
me," Jesus said, "and I will send you out to
fish for people." 20 At once they left their
nets and followed him.

21 Going on from there, he saw two other brothers, James son of Zebedee and his
brother John. They were in a boat with
their father Zebedee, preparing their
nets. Jesus called them, 22 and immediately they left the boat and their father
and followed him.

23 Jesus went throughout Galilee, teaching in their synagogues, proclaiming the
good news of the kingdom, and healing
every disease and sickness among the
people. 24 News about him spread all over
Syria, and people brought to him all who
were ill with various diseases, those suffering severe pain, the demon-possessed,
those having seizures, and the paralyzed;
and he healed them. 25 Large crowds from
Galilee, the Decapolis,[b] Jerusalem, Judea
and the region across the Jordan followed
him.

5 Now when Jesus saw the crowds, he
went up on a mountainside and sat
down. His disciples came to him, 2 and
he began to teach them.
He said:

3 "Blessed are the poor in spirit,
for theirs is the kingdom of heaven.
4 Blessed are those who mourn,
for they will be comforted.
5 Blessed are the meek,
for they will inherit the earth.
6 Blessed are those who hunger and
thirst for righteousness,
for they will be filled.
7 Blessed are the merciful,
for they will be shown mercy.
8 Blessed are the pure in heart,
for they will see God.
9 Blessed are the peacemakers,
for they will be called children of
God.
10 Blessed are those who are persecuted
because of righteousness,
for theirs is the kingdom of heaven.

11 "Blessed are you when people insult
you, persecute you and falsely say all
kinds of evil against you because of me.
12 Rejoice and be glad, because great is
your reward in heaven, for in the same
way they persecuted the prophets who
were before you.

13 "You are the salt of the earth. But if
the salt loses its saltiness, how can it be
made salty again? It is no longer good for
anything, except to be thrown out and
trampled underfoot.

14 "You are the light of the world. A town
built on a hill cannot be hidden. 15 Neither
do people light a lamp and put it under a
bowl. Instead they put it on its stand, and
it gives light to everyone in the house. 16 In
the same way, let your light shine before
others, that they may see your good deeds
and glorify your Father in heaven.

17 "Do not think that I have come to
abolish the Law or the Prophets; I have
not come to abolish them but to fulfill
them. 18 For truly I tell you, until heaven
and earth disappear, not the smallest letter, not the least stroke of a pen, will by
any means disappear from the Law until
everything is accomplished. 19 Therefore
anyone who sets aside one of the least
of these commands and teaches others
accordingly will be called least in the
kingdom of heaven, but whoever practices and teaches these commands will
be called great in the kingdom of heaven.
20 For I tell you that unless your righteousness surpasses that of the Pharisees and
the teachers of the law, you will certainly
not enter the kingdom of heaven.

21 "You have heard that it was said to
the people long ago, 'You shall not murder,[c] and anyone who murders will be
subject to judgment.' 22 But I tell you that
anyone who is angry with a brother or sister[d,e] will be subject to judgment. Again,
anyone who says to a brother or sister,

[a] *16* Isaiah 9:1,2 [b] *25* That is, the Ten Cities [c] *21* Exodus 20:13 [d] *22* The Greek word for *brother or sister* (*adelphos*) refers here to a fellow disciple, whether man or woman; also in verse 23. [e] *22* Some manuscripts *brother or sister without cause*

'Raca,'[a] is answerable to the court. And
anyone who says, 'You fool!' will be in
danger of the fire of hell.

23 "Therefore, if you are offering your
gift at the altar and there remember that
your brother or sister has something
against you, 24 leave your gift there in
front of the altar. First go and be reconciled to them; then come and offer your
gift.

25 "Settle matters quickly with your adversary who is taking you to court. Do it
while you are still together on the way, or
your adversary may hand you over to the
judge, and the judge may hand you over
to the officer, and you may be thrown into
prison. 26 Truly I tell you, you will not get
out until you have paid the last penny.

27 "You have heard that it was said, 'You
shall not commit adultery.'[b] 28 But I tell
you that anyone who looks at a woman
lustfully has already committed adultery
with her in his heart. 29 If your right eye
causes you to stumble, gouge it out and
throw it away. It is better for you to lose
one part of your body than for your whole
body to be thrown into hell. 30 And if your
right hand causes you to stumble, cut it
off and throw it away. It is better for you
to lose one part of your body than for your
whole body to go into hell.

31 "It has been said, 'Anyone who divorces his wife must give her a certificate
of divorce.'[c] 32 But I tell you that anyone
who divorces his wife, except for sexual
immorality, makes her the victim of adultery, and anyone who marries a divorced
woman commits adultery.

33 "Again, you have heard that it was
said to the people long ago, 'Do not break
your oath, but fulfill to the Lord the vows
you have made.' 34 But I tell you, do not
swear an oath at all: either by heaven, for
it is God's throne; 35 or by the earth, for it is
his footstool; or by Jerusalem, for it is the
city of the Great King. 36 And do not swear
by your head, for you cannot make even
one hair white or black. 37 All you need to
say is simply 'Yes' or 'No'; anything beyond this comes from the evil one.[d]

38 "You have heard that it was said, 'Eye
for eye, and tooth for tooth.'[e] 39 But I tell
you, do not resist an evil person. If anyone slaps you on the right cheek, turn to
them the other cheek also. 40 And if anyone wants to sue you and take your shirt,
hand over your coat as well. 41 If anyone
forces you to go one mile, go with them
two miles. 42 Give to the one who asks
you, and do not turn away from the one
who wants to borrow from you.

43 "You have heard that it was said,
'Love your neighbor[f] and hate your enemy.' 44 But I tell you, love your enemies
and pray for those who persecute you,
45 that you may be children of your Father in heaven. He causes his sun to rise
on the evil and the good, and sends rain
on the righteous and the unrighteous.
46 If you love those who love you, what
reward will you get? Are not even the tax
collectors doing that? 47 And if you greet
only your own people, what are you doing
more than others? Do not even pagans
do that? 48 Be perfect, therefore, as your
heavenly Father is perfect.

6 "Be careful not to practice your righteousness in front of others to be seen
by them. If you do, you will have no reward from your Father in heaven.

2 "So when you give to the needy, do not
announce it with trumpets, as the hypocrites do in the synagogues and on the
streets, to be honored by others. Truly I
tell you, they have received their reward
in full. 3 But when you give to the needy,
do not let your left hand know what your
right hand is doing, 4 so that your giving
may be in secret. Then your Father, who
sees what is done in secret, will reward
you.

5 "And when you pray, do not be like the
hypocrites, for they love to pray standing
in the synagogues and on the street corners to be seen by others. Truly I tell you,
they have received their reward in full.
6 But when you pray, go into your room,
close the door and pray to your Father,
who is unseen. Then your Father, who
sees what is done in secret, will reward
you. 7 And when you pray, do not keep
on babbling like pagans, for they think
they will be heard because of their many
words. 8 Do not be like them, for your Father knows what you need before you ask
him.

9 "This, then, is how you should pray:

"'Our Father in heaven,
hallowed be your name,

[a] *22* An Aramaic term of contempt [b] *27* Exodus 20:14 [c] *31* Deut. 24:1 [d] *37* Or *from evil*
[e] *38* Exodus 21:24; Lev. 24:20; Deut. 19:21 [f] *43* Lev. 19:18

10 your kingdom come,
your will be done,
on earth as it is in heaven.
11 Give us today our daily bread.
12 And forgive us our debts,
as we also have forgiven our
debtors.
13 And lead us not into temptation,[a]
but deliver us from the evil one.[b]'

14 For if you forgive other people when
they sin against you, your heavenly Father will also forgive you. 15 But if you do
not forgive others their sins, your Father
will not forgive your sins.
16 "When you fast, do not look somber
as the hypocrites do, for they disfigure
their faces to show others they are fasting. Truly I tell you, they have received
their reward in full. 17 But when you fast,
put oil on your head and wash your face,
18 so that it will not be obvious to others
that you are fasting, but only to your Father, who is unseen; and your Father,
who sees what is done in secret, will reward you.
19 "Do not store up for yourselves treasures on earth, where moths and vermin
destroy, and where thieves break in and
steal. 20 But store up for yourselves treasures in heaven, where moths and vermin do not destroy, and where thieves do
not break in and steal. 21 For where your
treasure is, there your heart will be also.
22 "The eye is the lamp of the body. If
your eyes are healthy,[c] your whole body
will be full of light. 23 But if your eyes are
unhealthy,[d] your whole body will be full
of darkness. If then the light within you is
darkness, how great is that darkness!
24 "No one can serve two masters. Either you will hate the one and love the
other, or you will be devoted to the one
and despise the other. You cannot serve
both God and money.
25 "Therefore I tell you, do not worry about your life, what you will eat or
drink; or about your body, what you will
wear. Is not life more than food, and the
body more than clothes? 26 Look at the
birds of the air; they do not sow or reap or
store away in barns, and yet your heavenly Father feeds them. Are you not much
more valuable than they? 27 Can any one
of you by worrying add a single hour to
your life[e]?
28 "And why do you worry about clothes?
See how the flowers of the field grow.
They do not labor or spin. 29 Yet I tell you
that not even Solomon in all his splendor was dressed like one of these. 30 If
that is how God clothes the grass of the
field, which is here today and tomorrow
is thrown into the fire, will he not much
more clothe you—you of little faith? 31 So
do not worry, saying, 'What shall we eat?'
or 'What shall we drink?' or 'What shall
we wear?' 32 For the pagans run after all
these things, and your heavenly Father
knows that you need them. 33 But seek
first his kingdom and his righteousness,
and all these things will be given to you
as well. 34 Therefore do not worry about
tomorrow, for tomorrow will worry about
itself. Each day has enough trouble of its
own.

7 "Do not judge, or you too will be
judged. 2 For in the same way you
judge others, you will be judged, and with
the measure you use, it will be measured
to you.
3 "Why do you look at the speck of sawdust in your brother's eye and pay no
attention to the plank in your own eye?
4 How can you say to your brother, 'Let
me take the speck out of your eye,' when
all the time there is a plank in your own
eye? 5 You hypocrite, first take the plank
out of your own eye, and then you will
see clearly to remove the speck from your
brother's eye.
6 "Do not give dogs what is sacred; do
not throw your pearls to pigs. If you do,
they may trample them under their feet,
and turn and tear you to pieces.
7 "Ask and it will be given to you; seek
and you will find; knock and the door
will be opened to you. 8 For everyone who
asks receives; the one who seeks finds;
and to the one who knocks, the door will
be opened.
9 "Which of you, if your son asks for
bread, will give him a stone? 10 Or if he
asks for a fish, will give him a snake? 11 If
you, then, though you are evil, know how
to give good gifts to your children, how
much more will your Father in heaven
give good gifts to those who ask him!

[a] *13* The Greek for *temptation* can also mean *testing.* [b] *13* Or *from evil*; some late manuscripts *one, / for yours is the kingdom and the power and the glory forever. Amen.* [c] *22* The Greek for *healthy* here implies *generous.* [d] *23* The Greek for *unhealthy* here implies *stingy.* [e] *27* Or *single cubit to your height*

12 So in everything, do to others what you
would have them do to you, for this sums
up the Law and the Prophets.
13 "Enter through the narrow gate. For
wide is the gate and broad is the road
that leads to destruction, and many enter through it. 14 But small is the gate and
narrow the road that leads to life, and
only a few find it.
15 "Watch out for false prophets. They
come to you in sheep's clothing, but inwardly they are ferocious wolves. 16 By
their fruit you will recognize them. Do
people pick grapes from thornbushes, or
figs from thistles? 17 Likewise, every good
tree bears good fruit, but a bad tree bears
bad fruit. 18 A good tree cannot bear bad
fruit, and a bad tree cannot bear good
fruit. 19 Every tree that does not bear good
fruit is cut down and thrown into the fire.
20 Thus, by their fruit you will recognize
them.
21 "Not everyone who says to me, 'Lord,
Lord,' will enter the kingdom of heaven,
but only the one who does the will of my
Father who is in heaven. 22 Many will say
to me on that day, 'Lord, Lord, did we not
prophesy in your name and in your name
drive out demons and in your name perform many miracles?' 23 Then I will tell
them plainly, 'I never knew you. Away
from me, you evildoers!'
24 "Therefore everyone who hears these
words of mine and puts them into practice is like a wise man who built his house
on the rock. 25 The rain came down, the
streams rose, and the winds blew and
beat against that house; yet it did not fall,
because it had its foundation on the rock.
26 But everyone who hears these words of
mine and does not put them into practice
is like a foolish man who built his house
on sand. 27 The rain came down, the
streams rose, and the winds blew and
beat against that house, and it fell with a
great crash."

28 When Jesus had finished saying
these things, the crowds were amazed at
his teaching, 29 because he taught as one
who had authority, and not as their teachers of the law.

8 When Jesus came down from the
mountainside, large crowds followed
him. 2 A man with leprosy[a] came and
knelt before him and said, "Lord, if you
are willing, you can make me clean."
3 Jesus reached out his hand and
touched the man. "I am willing," he said.
"Be clean!" Immediately he was cleansed
of his leprosy. 4 Then Jesus said to him,
"See that you don't tell anyone. But go,
show yourself to the priest and offer the
gift Moses commanded, as a testimony
to them."
5 When Jesus had entered Capernaum,
a centurion came to him, asking for help.
6 "Lord," he said, "my servant lies at home
paralyzed, suffering terribly."
7 Jesus said to him, "Shall I come and
heal him?"
8 The centurion replied, "Lord, I do not
deserve to have you come under my roof.
But just say the word, and my servant will
be healed. 9 For I myself am a man under
authority, with soldiers under me. I tell
this one, 'Go,' and he goes; and that one,
'Come,' and he comes. I say to my servant, 'Do this,' and he does it."
10 When Jesus heard this, he was
amazed and said to those following him,
"Truly I tell you, I have not found anyone
in Israel with such great faith. 11 I say to
you that many will come from the east
and the west, and will take their places at
the feast with Abraham, Isaac and Jacob
in the kingdom of heaven. 12 But the subjects of the kingdom will be thrown outside, into the darkness, where there will
be weeping and gnashing of teeth."
13 Then Jesus said to the centurion,
"Go! Let it be done just as you believed
it would." And his servant was healed at
that moment.
14 When Jesus came into Peter's house,
he saw Peter's mother-in-law lying in bed
with a fever. 15 He touched her hand and
the fever left her, and she got up and began to wait on him.
16 When evening came, many who were
demon-possessed were brought to him,
and he drove out the spirits with a word
and healed all the sick. 17 This was to fulfill what was spoken through the prophet
Isaiah:

> "He took up our infirmities
> and bore our diseases."[b]

18 When Jesus saw the crowd around
him, he gave orders to cross to the other

[a] 2 The Greek word traditionally translated *leprosy* was used for various diseases affecting the skin.
[b] 17 Isaiah 53:4 (see Septuagint)

side of the lake. 19Then a teacher of the law came to him and said, "Teacher, I will follow you wherever you go."

20Jesus replied, "Foxes have dens and birds have nests, but the Son of Man has no place to lay his head."

21Another disciple said to him, "Lord, first let me go and bury my father."

22But Jesus told him, "Follow me, and let the dead bury their own dead."

23Then he got into the boat and his disciples followed him. 24Suddenly a furious storm came up on the lake, so that the waves swept over the boat. But Jesus was sleeping. 25The disciples went and woke him, saying, "Lord, save us! We're going to drown!"

26He replied, "You of little faith, why are you so afraid?" Then he got up and rebuked the winds and the waves, and it was completely calm.

27The men were amazed and asked, "What kind of man is this? Even the winds and the waves obey him!"

28When he arrived at the other side in the region of the Gadarenes,[a] two demon-possessed men coming from the tombs met him. They were so violent that no one could pass that way. 29"What do you want with us, Son of God?" they shouted. "Have you come here to torture us before the appointed time?"

30Some distance from them a large herd of pigs was feeding. 31The demons begged Jesus, "If you drive us out, send us into the herd of pigs."

32He said to them, "Go!" So they came out and went into the pigs, and the whole herd rushed down the steep bank into the lake and died in the water. 33Those tending the pigs ran off, went into the town and reported all this, including what had happened to the demon-possessed men. 34Then the whole town went out to meet Jesus. And when they saw him, they pleaded with him to leave their region.

9 Jesus stepped into a boat, crossed over and came to his own town. 2Some men brought to him a paralyzed man, lying on a mat. When Jesus saw their faith, he said to the man, "Take heart, son; your sins are forgiven."

3At this, some of the teachers of the law said to themselves, "This fellow is blaspheming!"

4Knowing their thoughts, Jesus said, "Why do you entertain evil thoughts in your hearts? 5Which is easier: to say, 'Your sins are forgiven,' or to say, 'Get up and walk'? 6But I want you to know that the Son of Man has authority on earth to forgive sins." So he said to the paralyzed man, "Get up, take your mat and go home." 7Then the man got up and went home. 8When the crowd saw this, they were filled with awe; and they praised God, who had given such authority to man.

9As Jesus went on from there, he saw a man named Matthew sitting at the tax collector's booth. "Follow me," he told him, and Matthew got up and followed him.

10While Jesus was having dinner at Matthew's house, many tax collectors and sinners came and ate with him and his disciples. 11When the Pharisees saw this, they asked his disciples, "Why does your teacher eat with tax collectors and sinners?"

12On hearing this, Jesus said, "It is not the healthy who need a doctor, but the sick. 13But go and learn what this means: 'I desire mercy, not sacrifice.'[b] For I have not come to call the righteous, but sinners."

14Then John's disciples came and asked him, "How is it that we and the Pharisees fast often, but your disciples do not fast?"

15Jesus answered, "How can the guests of the bridegroom mourn while he is with them? The time will come when the bridegroom will be taken from them; then they will fast.

16"No one sews a patch of unshrunk cloth on an old garment, for the patch will pull away from the garment, making the tear worse. 17Neither do people pour new wine into old wineskins. If they do, the skins will burst; the wine will run out and the wineskins will be ruined. No, they pour new wine into new wineskins, and both are preserved."

18While he was saying this, a synagogue leader came and knelt before him and said, "My daughter has just died. But come and put your hand on her, and she will live." 19Jesus got up and went with him, and so did his disciples.

[a] *28* Some manuscripts *Gergesenes*; other manuscripts *Gerasenes* [b] *13* Hosea 6:6

20 Just then a woman who had been
subject to bleeding for twelve years came
up behind him and touched the edge of
his cloak. 21 She said to herself, "If I only
touch his cloak, I will be healed."

22 Jesus turned and saw her. "Take
heart, daughter," he said, "your faith has
healed you." And the woman was healed
at that moment.

23 When Jesus entered the synagogue
leader's house and saw the noisy crowd
and people playing pipes, 24 he said, "Go
away. The girl is not dead but asleep." But
they laughed at him. 25 After the crowd
had been put outside, he went in and
took the girl by the hand, and she got up.
26 News of this spread through all that
region.

27 As Jesus went on from there, two
blind men followed him, calling out,
"Have mercy on us, Son of David!"

28 When he had gone indoors, the
blind men came to him, and he asked
them, "Do you believe that I am able to
do this?"

"Yes, Lord," they replied.

29 Then he touched their eyes and said,
"According to your faith let it be done to
you"; 30 and their sight was restored. Jesus
warned them sternly, "See that no one
knows about this." 31 But they went out
and spread the news about him all over
that region.

32 While they were going out, a man
who was demon-possessed and could not
talk was brought to Jesus. 33 And when the
demon was driven out, the man who had
been mute spoke. The crowd was amazed
and said, "Nothing like this has ever been
seen in Israel."

34 But the Pharisees said, "It is by the
prince of demons that he drives out demons."

35 Jesus went through all the towns and
villages, teaching in their synagogues,
proclaiming the good news of the kingdom and healing every disease and sickness. 36 When he saw the crowds, he had
compassion on them, because they were
harassed and helpless, like sheep without a shepherd. 37 Then he said to his
disciples, "The harvest is plentiful but
the workers are few. 38 Ask the Lord of the
harvest, therefore, to send out workers
into his harvest field."

10 Jesus called his twelve disciples
to him and gave them authority to
drive out impure spirits and to heal every
disease and sickness.

2 These are the names of the twelve
apostles: first, Simon (who is called Peter) and his brother Andrew; James son
of Zebedee, and his brother John; 3 Philip
and Bartholomew; Thomas and Matthew
the tax collector; James son of Alphaeus,
and Thaddaeus; 4 Simon the Zealot and
Judas Iscariot, who betrayed him.

5 These twelve Jesus sent out with the
following instructions: "Do not go among
the Gentiles or enter any town of the Samaritans. 6 Go rather to the lost sheep of
Israel. 7 As you go, proclaim this message:
'The kingdom of heaven has come near.'
8 Heal the sick, raise the dead, cleanse
those who have leprosy,[a] drive out demons. Freely you have received; freely
give.

9 "Do not get any gold or silver or copper
to take with you in your belts — 10 no bag
for the journey or extra shirt or sandals
or a staff, for the worker is worth his keep.
11 Whatever town or village you enter,
search there for some worthy person and
stay at their house until you leave. 12 As
you enter the home, give it your greeting.
13 If the home is deserving, let your peace
rest on it; if it is not, let your peace return
to you. 14 If anyone will not welcome you
or listen to your words, leave that home
or town and shake the dust off your feet.
15 Truly I tell you, it will be more bearable
for Sodom and Gomorrah on the day of
judgment than for that town.

16 "I am sending you out like sheep
among wolves. Therefore be as shrewd
as snakes and as innocent as doves. 17 Be
on your guard; you will be handed over to
the local councils and be flogged in the
synagogues. 18 On my account you will
be brought before governors and kings
as witnesses to them and to the Gentiles.
19 But when they arrest you, do not worry
about what to say or how to say it. At that
time you will be given what to say, 20 for it
will not be you speaking, but the Spirit of
your Father speaking through you.

21 "Brother will betray brother to death,
and a father his child; children will rebel
against their parents and have them put
to death. 22 You will be hated by everyone

[a] *8* The Greek word traditionally translated *leprosy* was used for various diseases affecting the skin.

because of me, but the one who stands
firm to the end will be saved. 23When
you are persecuted in one place, flee to
another. Truly I tell you, you will not finish going through the towns of Israel before the Son of Man comes.
24"The student is not above the teacher, nor a servant above his master. 25It is
enough for students to be like their teachers, and servants like their masters. If the
head of the house has been called Beelzebul, how much more the members of his
household!
26"So do not be afraid of them, for there
is nothing concealed that will not be disclosed, or hidden that will not be made
known. 27What I tell you in the dark,
speak in the daylight; what is whispered
in your ear, proclaim from the roofs. 28Do
not be afraid of those who kill the body
but cannot kill the soul. Rather, be afraid
of the One who can destroy both soul and
body in hell. 29Are not two sparrows sold
for a penny? Yet not one of them will fall
to the ground outside your Father's care.[a]
30And even the very hairs of your head are
all numbered. 31So don't be afraid; you
are worth more than many sparrows.
32"Whoever acknowledges me before
others, I will also acknowledge before my
Father in heaven. 33But whoever disowns
me before others, I will disown before my
Father in heaven.
34"Do not suppose that I have come to
bring peace to the earth. I did not come
to bring peace, but a sword. 35For I have
come to turn

"'a man against his father,
a daughter against her mother,
a daughter-in-law against her mother-
in-law—
36 a man's enemies will be the
members of his own
household.'[b]

37"Anyone who loves their father or
mother more than me is not worthy
of me; anyone who loves their son or
daughter more than me is not worthy of
me. 38Whoever does not take up their
cross and follow me is not worthy of me.
39Whoever finds their life will lose it, and
whoever loses their life for my sake will
find it.
40"Anyone who welcomes you welcomes me, and anyone who welcomes me
welcomes the one who sent me. 41Who-
ever welcomes a prophet as a prophet will
receive a prophet's reward, and whoever
welcomes a righteous person as a righteous person will receive a righteous
person's reward. 42And if anyone gives
even a cup of cold water to one of these
little ones who is my disciple, truly I tell
you, that person will certainly not lose
their reward."

11 After Jesus had finished instructing
his twelve disciples, he went on from
there to teach and preach in the towns of
Galilee.[c]
2When John, who was in prison, heard
about the deeds of the Messiah, he sent
his disciples 3to ask him, "Are you the
one who is to come, or should we expect
someone else?"
4Jesus replied, "Go back and report to
John what you hear and see: 5The blind
receive sight, the lame walk, those who
have leprosy[d] are cleansed, the deaf hear,
the dead are raised, and the good news is
proclaimed to the poor. 6Blessed is anyone who does not stumble on account
of me."
7As John's disciples were leaving, Jesus
began to speak to the crowd about John:
"What did you go out into the wilderness
to see? A reed swayed by the wind? 8If not,
what did you go out to see? A man dressed
in fine clothes? No, those who wear fine
clothes are in kings' palaces. 9Then what
did you go out to see? A prophet? Yes, I tell
you, and more than a prophet. 10This is
the one about whom it is written:

"'I will send my messenger ahead of
you,
who will prepare your way before
you.'[e]

11Truly I tell you, among those born of
women there has not risen anyone greater than John the Baptist; yet whoever is
least in the kingdom of heaven is greater
than he. 12From the days of John the Baptist until now, the kingdom of heaven has
been subjected to violence,[f] and violent
people have been raiding it. 13For all the
Prophets and the Law prophesied until

[a] 29 Or *will*; or *knowledge* [b] 36 Micah 7:6 [c] 1 Greek *in their towns* [d] 5 The Greek word traditionally translated *leprosy* was used for various diseases affecting the skin. [e] 10 Mal. 3:1 [f] 12 Or *been forcefully advancing*

John. 14And if you are willing to accept it,
he is the Elijah who was to come. 15Who-
ever has ears, let them hear.
16"To what can I compare this generation? They are like children sitting in the
marketplaces and calling out to others:

17"'We played the pipe for you,
and you did not dance;
we sang a dirge,
and you did not mourn.'

18For John came neither eating nor
drinking, and they say, 'He has a demon.'
19The Son of Man came eating and drinking, and they say, 'Here is a glutton and a
drunkard, a friend of tax collectors and
sinners.' But wisdom is proved right by
her deeds."
20Then Jesus began to denounce the
towns in which most of his miracles had
been performed, because they did not
repent. 21"Woe to you, Chorazin! Woe to
you, Bethsaida! For if the miracles that
were performed in you had been performed in Tyre and Sidon, they would
have repented long ago in sackcloth and
ashes. 22But I tell you, it will be more
bearable for Tyre and Sidon on the day of
judgment than for you. 23And you, Capernaum, will you be lifted to the heavens?
No, you will go down to Hades.[a] For if the
miracles that were performed in you had
been performed in Sodom, it would have
remained to this day. 24But I tell you that
it will be more bearable for Sodom on the
day of judgment than for you."
25At that time Jesus said, "I praise you,
Father, Lord of heaven and earth, because you have hidden these things from
the wise and learned, and revealed them
to little children. 26Yes, Father, for this is
what you were pleased to do.
27"All things have been committed to
me by my Father. No one knows the Son
except the Father, and no one knows the
Father except the Son and those to whom
the Son chooses to reveal him.
28"Come to me, all you who are weary
and burdened, and I will give you rest.
29Take my yoke upon you and learn from
me, for I am gentle and humble in heart,
and you will find rest for your souls. 30For
my yoke is easy and my burden is light."

12 At that time Jesus went through
the grainfields on the Sabbath. His
disciples were hungry and began to pick
some heads of grain and eat them. 2When
the Pharisees saw this, they said to him,
"Look! Your disciples are doing what is
unlawful on the Sabbath."
3He answered, "Haven't you read what
David did when he and his companions
were hungry? 4He entered the house of
God, and he and his companions ate the
consecrated bread — which was not lawful for them to do, but only for the priests.
5Or haven't you read in the Law that the
priests on Sabbath duty in the temple
desecrate the Sabbath and yet are innocent? 6I tell you that something greater than the temple is here. 7If you had
known what these words mean, 'I desire
mercy, not sacrifice,'[b] you would not have
condemned the innocent. 8For the Son of
Man is Lord of the Sabbath."
9Going on from that place, he went
into their synagogue, 10and a man with
a shriveled hand was there. Looking for
a reason to bring charges against Jesus,
they asked him, "Is it lawful to heal on the
Sabbath?"
11He said to them, "If any of you has a
sheep and it falls into a pit on the Sabbath, will you not take hold of it and lift it
out? 12How much more valuable is a person than a sheep! Therefore it is lawful to
do good on the Sabbath."
13Then he said to the man, "Stretch out
your hand." So he stretched it out and it
was completely restored, just as sound as
the other. 14But the Pharisees went out
and plotted how they might kill Jesus.
15Aware of this, Jesus withdrew from
that place. A large crowd followed him,
and he healed all who were ill. 16He
warned them not to tell others about
him. 17This was to fulfill what was spoken through the prophet Isaiah:

18"Here is my servant whom I have
chosen,
the one I love, in whom I delight;
I will put my Spirit on him,
and he will proclaim justice to the
nations.
19He will not quarrel or cry out;
no one will hear his voice in the
streets.
20A bruised reed he will not break,
and a smoldering wick he will not
snuff out,

[a] 23 That is, the realm of the dead [b] 7 Hosea 6:6

till he has brought justice through to
victory.
21 In his name the nations will put
their hope."[a]

22Then they brought him a demon-
possessed man who was blind and mute,
and Jesus healed him, so that he could
both talk and see. 23All the people were
astonished and said, "Could this be the
Son of David?"
24But when the Pharisees heard this,
they said, "It is only by Beelzebul, the
prince of demons, that this fellow drives
out demons."
25Jesus knew their thoughts and said
to them, "Every kingdom divided against
itself will be ruined, and every city or
household divided against itself will not
stand. 26If Satan drives out Satan, he is
divided against himself. How then can
his kingdom stand? 27And if I drive out
demons by Beelzebul, by whom do your
people drive them out? So then, they will
be your judges. 28But if it is by the Spirit
of God that I drive out demons, then the
kingdom of God has come upon you.
29"Or again, how can anyone enter a
strong man's house and carry off his possessions unless he first ties up the strong
man? Then he can plunder his house.
30"Whoever is not with me is against
me, and whoever does not gather with
me scatters. 31And so I tell you, every
kind of sin and slander can be forgiven,
but blasphemy against the Spirit will not
be forgiven. 32Anyone who speaks a word
against the Son of Man will be forgiven,
but anyone who speaks against the Holy
Spirit will not be forgiven, either in this
age or in the age to come.
33"Make a tree good and its fruit will
be good, or make a tree bad and its fruit
will be bad, for a tree is recognized by its
fruit. 34You brood of vipers, how can you
who are evil say anything good? For the
mouth speaks what the heart is full of. 35A
good man brings good things out of the
good stored up in him, and an evil man
brings evil things out of the evil stored up
in him. 36But I tell you that everyone will
have to give account on the day of judgment for every empty word they have
spoken. 37For by your words you will be
acquitted, and by your words you will be
condemned."
38Then some of the Pharisees and
teachers of the law said to him, "Teacher,
we want to see a sign from you."
39He answered, "A wicked and adulterous generation asks for a sign! But none
will be given it except the sign of the
prophet Jonah. 40For as Jonah was three
days and three nights in the belly of a
huge fish, so the Son of Man will be three
days and three nights in the heart of the
earth. 41The men of Nineveh will stand
up at the judgment with this generation
and condemn it; for they repented at the
preaching of Jonah, and now something
greater than Jonah is here. 42The Queen
of the South will rise at the judgment with
this generation and condemn it; for she
came from the ends of the earth to listen
to Solomon's wisdom, and now something greater than Solomon is here.
43"When an impure spirit comes out
of a person, it goes through arid places
seeking rest and does not find it. 44Then
it says, 'I will return to the house I left.'
When it arrives, it finds the house un-
occupied, swept clean and put in order.
45Then it goes and takes with it seven
other spirits more wicked than itself, and
they go in and live there. And the final
condition of that person is worse than
the first. That is how it will be with this
wicked generation."
46While Jesus was still talking to
the crowd, his mother and brothers
stood outside, wanting to speak to him.
47Someone told him, "Your mother and
brothers are standing outside, wanting
to speak to you."
48He replied to him, "Who is my mother, and who are my brothers?" 49Pointing
to his disciples, he said, "Here are my
mother and my brothers. 50For whoever
does the will of my Father in heaven is my
brother and sister and mother."
13 That same day Jesus went out of the
house and sat by the lake. 2Such
large crowds gathered around him that
he got into a boat and sat in it, while all
the people stood on the shore. 3Then he
told them many things in parables, saying: "A farmer went out to sow his seed.
4As he was scattering the seed, some
fell along the path, and the birds came
and ate it up. 5Some fell on rocky places, where it did not have much soil. It

[a] *21* Isaiah 42:1-4

sprang up quickly, because the soil was
shallow. 6But when the sun came up, the
plants were scorched, and they withered because they had no root. 7Other
seed fell among thorns, which grew up
and choked the plants. 8Still other seed
fell on good soil, where it produced a
crop—a hundred, sixty or thirty times
what was sown. 9Whoever has ears, let
them hear."

10The disciples came to him and asked,
"Why do you speak to the people in parables?"

11He replied, "Because the knowledge
of the secrets of the kingdom of heaven
has been given to you, but not to them.
12Whoever has will be given more, and
they will have an abundance. Whoever
does not have, even what they have will
be taken from them. 13This is why I speak
to them in parables:

"Though seeing, they do not see;
    though hearing, they do not hear or
        understand.

14In them is fulfilled the prophecy of Isaiah:

" 'You will be ever hearing but never
        understanding;
    you will be ever seeing but never
        perceiving.
15For this people's heart has become
        calloused;
    they hardly hear with their ears,
    and they have closed their eyes.
Otherwise they might see with their
        eyes,
    hear with their ears,
    understand with their hearts
and turn, and I would heal them.'[a]

16But blessed are your eyes because they
see, and your ears because they hear.
17For truly I tell you, many prophets and
righteous people longed to see what you
see but did not see it, and to hear what
you hear but did not hear it.

18"Listen then to what the parable of
the sower means: 19When anyone hears
the message about the kingdom and does
not understand it, the evil one comes and
snatches away what was sown in their
heart. This is the seed sown along the
path. 20The seed falling on rocky ground
refers to someone who hears the word
and at once receives it with joy. 21But
since they have no root, they last only a
short time. When trouble or persecution
comes because of the word, they quickly
fall away. 22The seed falling among the
thorns refers to someone who hears the
word, but the worries of this life and the
deceitfulness of wealth choke the word,
making it unfruitful. 23But the seed falling on good soil refers to someone who
hears the word and understands it. This
is the one who produces a crop, yielding
a hundred, sixty or thirty times what was
sown."

24Jesus told them another parable:
"The kingdom of heaven is like a man
who sowed good seed in his field. 25But
while everyone was sleeping, his enemy came and sowed weeds among the
wheat, and went away. 26When the wheat
sprouted and formed heads, then the
weeds also appeared.

27"The owner's servants came to him
and said, 'Sir, didn't you sow good seed
in your field? Where then did the weeds
come from?'

28" 'An enemy did this,' he replied.

"The servants asked him, 'Do you want
us to go and pull them up?'

29" 'No,' he answered, 'because while
you are pulling the weeds, you may uproot the wheat with them. 30Let both
grow together until the harvest. At that
time I will tell the harvesters: First collect
the weeds and tie them in bundles to be
burned; then gather the wheat and bring
it into my barn.' "

31He told them another parable: "The
kingdom of heaven is like a mustard
seed, which a man took and planted in
his field. 32Though it is the smallest of
all seeds, yet when it grows, it is the largest of garden plants and becomes a tree,
so that the birds come and perch in its
branches."

33He told them still another parable:
"The kingdom of heaven is like yeast
that a woman took and mixed into about
sixty pounds[b] of flour until it worked all
through the dough."

34Jesus spoke all these things to the
crowd in parables; he did not say anything to them without using a parable. 35So was fulfilled what was spoken
through the prophet:

[a] *15* Isaiah 6:9,10 (see Septuagint) [b] *33* Or about 27 kilograms

"I will open my mouth in parables,
I will utter things hidden since the
creation of the world."[a]

36Then he left the crowd and went into
the house. His disciples came to him and
said, "Explain to us the parable of the
weeds in the field."
37He answered, "The one who sowed
the good seed is the Son of Man. 38The
field is the world, and the good seed
stands for the people of the kingdom.
The weeds are the people of the evil one,
39and the enemy who sows them is the
devil. The harvest is the end of the age,
and the harvesters are angels.
40"As the weeds are pulled up and
burned in the fire, so it will be at the end
of the age. 41The Son of Man will send out
his angels, and they will weed out of his
kingdom everything that causes sin and
all who do evil. 42They will throw them
into the blazing furnace, where there
will be weeping and gnashing of teeth.
43Then the righteous will shine like the
sun in the kingdom of their Father. Whoever has ears, let them hear.
44"The kingdom of heaven is like treasure hidden in a field. When a man found
it, he hid it again, and then in his joy went
and sold all he had and bought that field.
45"Again, the kingdom of heaven is
like a merchant looking for fine pearls.
46When he found one of great value, he
went away and sold everything he had
and bought it.
47"Once again, the kingdom of heav-
en is like a net that was let down into the
lake and caught all kinds of fish. 48When
it was full, the fishermen pulled it up on
the shore. Then they sat down and collected the good fish in baskets, but threw
the bad away. 49This is how it will be at
the end of the age. The angels will come
and separate the wicked from the righteous 50and throw them into the blazing
furnace, where there will be weeping and
gnashing of teeth.
51"Have you understood all these
things?" Jesus asked.
"Yes," they replied.
52He said to them, "Therefore every
teacher of the law who has become a disciple in the kingdom of heaven is like the
owner of a house who brings out of his
storeroom new treasures as well as old."
53When Jesus had finished these parables, he moved on from there. 54Coming
to his hometown, he began teaching the
people in their synagogue, and they were
amazed. "Where did this man get this
wisdom and these miraculous powers?"
they asked. 55"Isn't this the carpenter's
son? Isn't his mother's name Mary, and
aren't his brothers James, Joseph, Simon
and Judas? 56Aren't all his sisters with
us? Where then did this man get all these
things?" 57And they took offense at him.
But Jesus said to them, "A prophet is
not without honor except in his own town
and in his own home."
58And he did not do many miracles
there because of their lack of faith.

14 At that time Herod the tetrarch
heard the reports about Jesus, 2and
he said to his attendants, "This is John
the Baptist; he has risen from the dead!
That is why miraculous powers are at
work in him."
3Now Herod had arrested John and
bound him and put him in prison because of Herodias, his brother Philip's
wife, 4for John had been saying to him:
"It is not lawful for you to have her." 5Her-
od wanted to kill John, but he was afraid
of the people, because they considered
John a prophet.
6On Herod's birthday the daughter
of Herodias danced for the guests and
pleased Herod so much 7that he promised with an oath to give her whatever
she asked. 8Prompted by her mother,
she said, "Give me here on a platter the
head of John the Baptist." 9The king was
distressed, but because of his oaths and
his dinner guests, he ordered that her request be granted 10and had John beheaded in the prison. 11His head was brought
in on a platter and given to the girl, who
carried it to her mother. 12John's disciples came and took his body and buried
it. Then they went and told Jesus.
13When Jesus heard what had happened, he withdrew by boat privately
to a solitary place. Hearing of this, the
crowds followed him on foot from the
towns. 14When Jesus landed and saw a
large crowd, he had compassion on them
and healed their sick.
15As evening approached, the disciples
came to him and said, "This is a remote

[a] 35 Psalm 78:2

son of Jonah, for this was not revealed to
you by flesh and blood, but by my Father
in heaven. 18And I tell you that you are
Peter,[a] and on this rock I will build my
church, and the gates of Hades[b] will not
overcome it. 19I will give you the keys of
the kingdom of heaven; whatever you
bind on earth will be[c] bound in heaven,
and whatever you loose on earth will be[c]
loosed in heaven." 20Then he ordered his
disciples not to tell anyone that he was
the Messiah.

21From that time on Jesus began to explain to his disciples that he must go to
Jerusalem and suffer many things at the
hands of the elders, the chief priests and
the teachers of the law, and that he must
be killed and on the third day be raised
to life.

22Peter took him aside and began to rebuke him. "Never, Lord!" he said. "This
shall never happen to you!"

23Jesus turned and said to Peter, "Get
behind me, Satan! You are a stumbling
block to me; you do not have in mind the
concerns of God, but merely human concerns."

24Then Jesus said to his disciples,
"Whoever wants to be my disciple must
deny themselves and take up their cross
and follow me. 25For whoever wants to
save their life[d] will lose it, but whoever
loses their life for me will find it. 26What
good will it be for someone to gain the
whole world, yet forfeit their soul? Or
what can anyone give in exchange for
their soul? 27For the Son of Man is going
to come in his Father's glory with his angels, and then he will reward each person
according to what they have done.

28"Truly I tell you, some who are standing here will not taste death before they
see the Son of Man coming in his kingdom."

17 After six days Jesus took with him
Peter, James and John the brother of
James, and led them up a high mountain
by themselves. 2There he was transfigured before them. His face shone like the
sun, and his clothes became as white as
the light. 3Just then there appeared before them Moses and Elijah, talking with
Jesus.

4Peter said to Jesus, "Lord, it is good
for us to be here. If you wish, I will put up
three shelters — one for you, one for Moses and one for Elijah."

5While he was still speaking, a bright
cloud covered them, and a voice from
the cloud said, "This is my Son, whom I
love; with him I am well pleased. Listen
to him!"

6When the disciples heard this, they
fell facedown to the ground, terrified.
7But Jesus came and touched them. "Get
up," he said. "Don't be afraid." 8When
they looked up, they saw no one except
Jesus.

9As they were coming down the mountain, Jesus instructed them, "Don't tell
anyone what you have seen, until the Son
of Man has been raised from the dead."

10The disciples asked him, "Why then
do the teachers of the law say that Elijah
must come first?"

11Jesus replied, "To be sure, Elijah
comes and will restore all things. 12But
I tell you, Elijah has already come, and
they did not recognize him, but have
done to him everything they wished. In
the same way the Son of Man is going to
suffer at their hands." 13Then the disciples understood that he was talking to
them about John the Baptist.

14When they came to the crowd, a man
approached Jesus and knelt before him.
15"Lord, have mercy on my son," he said.
"He has seizures and is suffering greatly.
He often falls into the fire or into the water. 16I brought him to your disciples, but
they could not heal him."

17"You unbelieving and perverse generation," Jesus replied, "how long shall
I stay with you? How long shall I put up
with you? Bring the boy here to me."
18Jesus rebuked the demon, and it came
out of the boy, and he was healed at that
moment.

19Then the disciples came to Jesus in
private and asked, "Why couldn't we
drive it out?"

20He replied, "Because you have so little faith. Truly I tell you, if you have faith
as small as a mustard seed, you can say to
this mountain, 'Move from here to there,'
and it will move. Nothing will be impossible for you." [21][e]

22When they came together in Galilee,

[a] *18* The Greek word for *Peter* means *rock*. [b] *18* That is, the realm of the dead [c] *19* Or *will have been*
[d] *25* The Greek word means either *life* or *soul*; also in verse 26. [e] *21* Some manuscripts include here words similar to Mark 9:29.

he said to them, "The Son of Man is going to be delivered into the hands of men.
23 They will kill him, and on the third day
he will be raised to life." And the disciples
were filled with grief.
24 After Jesus and his disciples arrived
in Capernaum, the collectors of the two-
drachma temple tax came to Peter and
asked, "Doesn't your teacher pay the
temple tax?"
25 "Yes, he does," he replied.
When Peter came into the house, Jesus
was the first to speak. "What do you
think, Simon?" he asked. "From whom
do the kings of the earth collect duty and
taxes — from their own children or from
others?"
26 "From others," Peter answered.
"Then the children are exempt," Jesus
said to him. 27 "But so that we may not
cause offense, go to the lake and throw
out your line. Take the first fish you catch;
open its mouth and you will find a four-
drachma coin. Take it and give it to them
for my tax and yours."
18 At that time the disciples came to
Jesus and asked, "Who, then, is the
greatest in the kingdom of heaven?"
2 He called a little child to him, and
placed the child among them. 3 And he
said: "Truly I tell you, unless you change
and become like little children, you
will never enter the kingdom of heaven.
4 Therefore, whoever takes the lowly position of this child is the greatest in the
kingdom of heaven. 5 And whoever welcomes one such child in my name welcomes me.
6 "If anyone causes one of these little ones — those who believe in me — to
stumble, it would be better for them to
have a large millstone hung around their
neck and to be drowned in the depths of
the sea. 7 Woe to the world because of the
things that cause people to stumble! Such
things must come, but woe to the person
through whom they come! 8 If your hand
or your foot causes you to stumble, cut it
off and throw it away. It is better for you
to enter life maimed or crippled than to
have two hands or two feet and be thrown
into eternal fire. 9 And if your eye causes
you to stumble, gouge it out and throw it
away. It is better for you to enter life with
one eye than to have two eyes and be
thrown into the fire of hell.
10 "See that you do not despise one of
these little ones. For I tell you that their
angels in heaven always see the face of
my Father in heaven. [11][a]
12 "What do you think? If a man owns a
hundred sheep, and one of them wanders
away, will he not leave the ninety-nine on
the hills and go to look for the one that
wandered off? 13 And if he finds it, truly
I tell you, he is happier about that one
sheep than about the ninety-nine that
did not wander off. 14 In the same way
your Father in heaven is not willing that
any of these little ones should perish.
15 "If your brother or sister[b] sins,[c] go
and point out their fault, just between
the two of you. If they listen to you, you
have won them over. 16 But if they will not
listen, take one or two others along, so
that 'every matter may be established by
the testimony of two or three witnesses.'[d]
17 If they still refuse to listen, tell it to the
church; and if they refuse to listen even
to the church, treat them as you would a
pagan or a tax collector.
18 "Truly I tell you, whatever you bind
on earth will be[e] bound in heaven, and
whatever you loose on earth will be[e]
loosed in heaven.
19 "Again, truly I tell you that if two of
you on earth agree about anything they
ask for, it will be done for them by my
Father in heaven. 20 For where two or
three gather in my name, there am I with
them."
21 Then Peter came to Jesus and asked,
"Lord, how many times shall I forgive my
brother or sister who sins against me? Up
to seven times?"
22 Jesus answered, "I tell you, not seven
times, but seventy-seven times.[f]
23 "Therefore, the kingdom of heaven
is like a king who wanted to settle accounts with his servants. 24 As he began
the settlement, a man who owed him ten
thousand bags of gold[g] was brought to
him. 25 Since he was not able to pay, the
master ordered that he and his wife and
his children and all that he had be sold to
repay the debt.

[a] *11* Some manuscripts include here the words of Luke 19:10. [b] *15* The Greek word for *brother or sister* (*adelphos*) refers here to a fellow disciple, whether man or woman; also in verses 21 and 35. [c] *15* Some manuscripts *sins against you* [d] *16* Deut. 19:15 [e] *18* Or *will have been* [f] *22* Or *seventy times seven* [g] *24* Greek *ten thousand talents*; a talent was worth about 20 years of a day laborer's wages.

26 “At this the servant fell on his knees
before him. ‘Be patient with me,’ he
begged, ‘and I will pay back everything.’
27 The servant’s master took pity on him,
canceled the debt and let him go.
28 “But when that servant went out, he
found one of his fellow servants who owed
him a hundred silver coins.[a] He grabbed
him and began to choke him. ‘Pay back
what you owe me!’ he demanded.
29 “His fellow servant fell to his knees
and begged him, ‘Be patient with me, and
I will pay it back.’
30 “But he refused. Instead, he went off
and had the man thrown into prison until
he could pay the debt.
31 When the other
servants saw what had happened, they
were outraged and went and told their
master everything that had happened.
32 “Then the master called the servant
in. ‘You wicked servant,’ he said, ‘I canceled all that debt of yours because you
begged me to.
33 Shouldn’t you have had
mercy on your fellow servant just as I had
on you?’
34 In anger his master handed
him over to the jailers to be tortured, until he should pay back all he owed.
35 “This is how my heavenly Father will
treat each of you unless you forgive your
brother or sister from your heart.”

19 When Jesus had finished saying
these things, he left Galilee and
went into the region of Judea to the other side of the Jordan.
2 Large crowds fol-
lowed him, and he healed them there.
3 Some Pharisees came to him to test
him. They asked, “Is it lawful for a man
to divorce his wife for any and every reason?”
4 “Haven’t you read,” he replied, “that
at the beginning the Creator ‘made them
male and female,’[b]
5 and said, ‘For this
reason a man will leave his father and
mother and be united to his wife, and the
two will become one flesh’[c]?
6 So they are
no longer two, but one flesh. Therefore
what God has joined together, let no one
separate.”
7 “Why then,” they asked, “did Moses
command that a man give his wife a certificate of divorce and send her away?”
8 Jesus replied, “Moses permitted you to
divorce your wives because your hearts
were hard. But it was not this way from
the beginning.
9 I tell you that anyone
who divorces his wife, except for sexual
immorality, and marries another woman
commits adultery.”
10 The disciples said to him, “If this is
the situation between a husband and
wife, it is better not to marry.”
11 Jesus replied, “Not everyone can accept this word, but only those to whom it
has been given.
12 For there are eunuchs
who were born that way, and there are
eunuchs who have been made eunuchs
by others—and there are those who
choose to live like eunuchs for the sake of
the kingdom of heaven. The one who can
accept this should accept it.”
13 Then people brought little children
to Jesus for him to place his hands on
them and pray for them. But the disciples
rebuked them.
14 Jesus said, “Let the little children
come to me, and do not hinder them, for
the kingdom of heaven belongs to such as
these.”
15 When he had placed his hands
on them, he went on from there.
16 Just then a man came up to Jesus and
asked, “Teacher, what good thing must I
do to get eternal life?”
17 “Why do you ask me about what is
good?” Jesus replied. “There is only One
who is good. If you want to enter life, keep
the commandments.”
18 “Which ones?” he inquired.
Jesus replied, “ ‘You shall not murder,
you shall not commit adultery, you shall
not steal, you shall not give false testimony,
19 honor your father and mother,’[d] and
‘love your neighbor as yourself.’[e]”
20 “All these I have kept,” the young
man said. “What do I still lack?”
21 Jesus answered, “If you want to be
perfect, go, sell your possessions and give
to the poor, and you will have treasure in
heaven. Then come, follow me.”
22 When the young man heard this,
he went away sad, because he had great
wealth.
23 Then Jesus said to his disciples, “Truly I tell you, it is hard for someone who
is rich to enter the kingdom of heaven.
24 Again I tell you, it is easier for a camel
to go through the eye of a needle than for
someone who is rich to enter the kingdom of God.”
25 When the disciples heard this, they

[a] *28* Greek *a hundred denarii;* a denarius was the usual daily wage of a day laborer (see 20:2). [b] *4* Gen. 1:27
[c] *5* Gen. 2:24 [d] *19* Exodus 20:12-16; Deut. 5:16-20 [e] *19* Lev. 19:18

were greatly astonished and asked, "Who
then can be saved?"
26 Jesus looked at them and said, "With
man this is impossible, but with God all
things are possible."
27 Peter answered him, "We have left
everything to follow you! What then will
there be for us?"
28 Jesus said to them, "Truly I tell you, at
the renewal of all things, when the Son of
Man sits on his glorious throne, you who
have followed me will also sit on twelve
thrones, judging the twelve tribes of Israel. 29 And everyone who has left houses
or brothers or sisters or father or mother
or wife[a] or children or fields for my sake
will receive a hundred times as much and
will inherit eternal life. 30 But many who
are first will be last, and many who are
last will be first.

20 "For the kingdom of heaven is like a
landowner who went out early in the
morning to hire workers for his vineyard.
2 He agreed to pay them a denarius[b] for
the day and sent them into his vineyard.
3 "About nine in the morning he went
out and saw others standing in the marketplace doing nothing. 4 He told them,
'You also go and work in my vineyard,
and I will pay you whatever is right.' 5 So
they went.
"He went out again about noon and
about three in the afternoon and did the
same thing. 6 About five in the afternoon
he went out and found still others standing around. He asked them, 'Why have
you been standing here all day long doing nothing?'
7 "'Because no one has hired us,' they
answered.
"He said to them, 'You also go and work
in my vineyard.'
8 "When evening came, the owner of
the vineyard said to his foreman, 'Call
the workers and pay them their wages,
beginning with the last ones hired and
going on to the first.'
9 "The workers who were hired about
five in the afternoon came and each received a denarius. 10 So when those came
who were hired first, they expected to
receive more. But each one of them also
received a denarius. 11 When they received it, they began to grumble against
the landowner. 12 'These who were hired
last worked only one hour,' they said,
'and you have made them equal to us
who have borne the burden of the work
and the heat of the day.'
13 "But he answered one of them, 'I am
not being unfair to you, friend. Didn't you
agree to work for a denarius? 14 Take your
pay and go. I want to give the one who was
hired last the same as I gave you. 15 Don't I
have the right to do what I want with my
own money? Or are you envious because
I am generous?'
16 "So the last will be first, and the first
will be last."
17 Now Jesus was going up to Jerusalem. On the way, he took the Twelve aside
and said to them, 18 "We are going up to
Jerusalem, and the Son of Man will be
delivered over to the chief priests and the
teachers of the law. They will condemn
him to death 19 and will hand him over
to the Gentiles to be mocked and flogged
and crucified. On the third day he will be
raised to life!"
20 Then the mother of Zebedee's sons
came to Jesus with her sons and, kneeling down, asked a favor of him.
21 "What is it you want?" he asked.
She said, "Grant that one of these two
sons of mine may sit at your right and the
other at your left in your kingdom."
22 "You don't know what you are asking," Jesus said to them. "Can you drink
the cup I am going to drink?"
"We can," they answered.
23 Jesus said to them, "You will indeed
drink from my cup, but to sit at my right
or left is not for me to grant. These places
belong to those for whom they have been
prepared by my Father."
24 When the ten heard about this, they
were indignant with the two brothers.
25 Jesus called them together and said,
"You know that the rulers of the Gentiles
lord it over them, and their high officials
exercise authority over them. 26 Not so
with you. Instead, whoever wants to
become great among you must be your
servant, 27 and whoever wants to be first
must be your slave— 28 just as the Son
of Man did not come to be served, but to
serve, and to give his life as a ransom for
many."
29 As Jesus and his disciples were leaving Jericho, a large crowd followed him.

[a] 29 Some manuscripts do not have *or wife*. [b] 2 A denarius was the usual daily wage of a day laborer.

30Two blind men were sitting by the roadside, and when they heard that Jesus was
going by, they shouted, "Lord, Son of David, have mercy on us!"
31The crowd rebuked them and told
them to be quiet, but they shouted all the
louder, "Lord, Son of David, have mercy
on us!"
32Jesus stopped and called them.
"What do you want me to do for you?" he
asked.
33"Lord," they answered, "we want our
sight."
34Jesus had compassion on them and
touched their eyes. Immediately they received their sight and followed him.

21 As they approached Jerusalem and
came to Bethphage on the Mount of
Olives, Jesus sent two disciples, 2saying to
them, "Go to the village ahead of you, and
at once you will find a donkey tied there,
with her colt by her. Untie them and bring
them to me. 3If anyone says anything to
you, say that the Lord needs them, and he
will send them right away."
4This took place to fulfill what was spoken through the prophet:

5"Say to Daughter Zion,
'See, your king comes to you,
gentle and riding on a donkey,
and on a colt, the foal of a donkey.'"[a]

6The disciples went and did as Jesus
had instructed them. 7They brought the
donkey and the colt and placed their
cloaks on them for Jesus to sit on. 8A very
large crowd spread their cloaks on the
road, while others cut branches from the
trees and spread them on the road. 9The
crowds that went ahead of him and those
that followed shouted,

"Hosanna[b] to the Son of David!"

"Blessed is he who comes in the name
of the Lord!"[c]

"Hosanna[b] in the highest heaven!"

10When Jesus entered Jerusalem, the
whole city was stirred and asked, "Who
is this?"
11The crowds answered, "This is Jesus,
the prophet from Nazareth in Galilee."
12Jesus entered the temple courts and
drove out all who were buying and selling there. He overturned the tables of
the money changers and the benches of
those selling doves. 13"It is written," he
said to them, " 'My house will be called a
house of prayer,'[d] but you are making it 'a
den of robbers.'[e]"
14The blind and the lame came to him
at the temple, and he healed them. 15But
when the chief priests and the teachers of
the law saw the wonderful things he did
and the children shouting in the temple
courts, "Hosanna to the Son of David,"
they were indignant.
16"Do you hear what these children are
saying?" they asked him.
"Yes," replied Jesus, "have you never
read,

" 'From the lips of children and infants
you, Lord, have called forth your
praise'[f]?"

17And he left them and went out of
the city to Bethany, where he spent the
night.
18Early in the morning, as Jesus was on
his way back to the city, he was hungry.
19Seeing a fig tree by the road, he went up
to it but found nothing on it except leaves.
Then he said to it, "May you never bear
fruit again!" Immediately the tree withered.
20When the disciples saw this, they
were amazed. "How did the fig tree wither so quickly?" they asked.
21Jesus replied, "Truly I tell you, if you
have faith and do not doubt, not only can
you do what was done to the fig tree, but
also you can say to this mountain, 'Go,
throw yourself into the sea,' and it will
be done. 22If you believe, you will receive
whatever you ask for in prayer."
23Jesus entered the temple courts, and,
while he was teaching, the chief priests
and the elders of the people came to him.
"By what authority are you doing these
things?" they asked. "And who gave you
this authority?"
24Jesus replied, "I will also ask you one
question. If you answer me, I will tell
you by what authority I am doing these
things. 25John's baptism—where did it
come from? Was it from heaven, or of human origin?"
They discussed it among themselves
and said, "If we say, 'From heaven,' he will
ask, 'Then why didn't you believe him?'

[a] 5 Zech. 9:9 [b] 9 A Hebrew expression meaning "Save!" which became an exclamation of praise; also in verse 15 [c] 9 Psalm 118:25,26 [d] 13 Isaiah 56:7 [e] 13 Jer. 7:11 [f] 16 Psalm 8:2 (see Septuagint)

26 But if we say, 'Of human origin'—we
are afraid of the people, for they all hold
that John was a prophet."
27 So they answered Jesus, "We don't
know."
Then he said, "Neither will I tell you by
what authority I am doing these things.
28 "What do you think? There was a
man who had two sons. He went to the
first and said, 'Son, go and work today in
the vineyard.'
29 " 'I will not,' he answered, but later he
changed his mind and went.
30 "Then the father went to the other son
and said the same thing. He answered, 'I
will, sir,' but he did not go.
31 "Which of the two did what his father
wanted?"
"The first," they answered.
Jesus said to them, "Truly I tell you, the
tax collectors and the prostitutes are entering the kingdom of God ahead of you.
32 For John came to you to show you the
way of righteousness, and you did not believe him, but the tax collectors and the
prostitutes did. And even after you saw
this, you did not repent and believe him.
33 "Listen to another parable: There was
a landowner who planted a vineyard. He
put a wall around it, dug a winepress in it
and built a watchtower. Then he rented
the vineyard to some farmers and moved
to another place. 34 When the harvest
time approached, he sent his servants to
the tenants to collect his fruit.
35 "The tenants seized his servants;
they beat one, killed another, and stoned
a third. 36 Then he sent other servants
to them, more than the first time, and
the tenants treated them the same way.
37 Last of all, he sent his son to them.
'They will respect my son,' he said.
38 "But when the tenants saw the son,
they said to each other, 'This is the heir.
Come, let's kill him and take his inheritance.' 39 So they took him and threw him
out of the vineyard and killed him.
40 "Therefore, when the owner of the
vineyard comes, what will he do to those
tenants?"
41 "He will bring those wretches to a
wretched end," they replied, "and he will
rent the vineyard to other tenants, who
will give him his share of the crop at harvest time."
42 Jesus said to them, "Have you never
read in the Scriptures:

" 'The stone the builders rejected
has become the cornerstone;
the Lord has done this,
and it is marvelous in our eyes'[a]?

43 "Therefore I tell you that the kingdom of God will be taken away from you
and given to a people who will produce
its fruit. 44 Anyone who falls on this stone
will be broken to pieces; anyone on whom
it falls will be crushed."[b]
45 When the chief priests and the Pharisees heard Jesus' parables, they knew he
was talking about them. 46 They looked
for a way to arrest him, but they were
afraid of the crowd because the people
held that he was a prophet.
22 Jesus spoke to them again in parables, saying: 2 "The kingdom of
heaven is like a king who prepared a
wedding banquet for his son. 3 He sent his
servants to those who had been invited to
the banquet to tell them to come, but they
refused to come.
4 "Then he sent some more servants and
said, 'Tell those who have been invited
that I have prepared my dinner: My oxen
and fattened cattle have been butchered,
and everything is ready. Come to the
wedding banquet.'
5 "But they paid no attention and went
off—one to his field, another to his
business. 6 The rest seized his servants,
mistreated them and killed them. 7 The
king was enraged. He sent his army and
destroyed those murderers and burned
their city.
8 "Then he said to his servants, 'The
wedding banquet is ready, but those I invited did not deserve to come. 9 So go to
the street corners and invite to the banquet anyone you find.' 10 So the servants
went out into the streets and gathered
all the people they could find, the bad as
well as the good, and the wedding hall
was filled with guests.
11 "But when the king came in to see
the guests, he noticed a man there who
was not wearing wedding clothes. 12 He
asked, 'How did you get in here without
wedding clothes, friend?' The man was
speechless.
13 "Then the king told the attendants,

[a] *42* Psalm 118:22,23 [b] *44* Some manuscripts do not have verse 44.

'Tie him hand and foot, and throw him
outside, into the darkness, where there
will be weeping and gnashing of teeth.'
14"For many are invited, but few are
chosen."
15Then the Pharisees went out and laid
plans to trap him in his words. 16They
sent their disciples to him along with
the Herodians. "Teacher," they said, "we
know that you are a man of integrity and
that you teach the way of God in accordance with the truth. You aren't swayed
by others, because you pay no attention
to who they are. 17Tell us then, what is
your opinion? Is it right to pay the imperial tax[a] to Caesar or not?"
18But Jesus, knowing their evil intent,
said, "You hypocrites, why are you trying
to trap me? 19Show me the coin used for
paying the tax." They brought him a denarius, 20and he asked them, "Whose image is this? And whose inscription?"
21"Caesar's," they replied.
Then he said to them, "So give back to
Caesar what is Caesar's, and to God what
is God's."
22When they heard this, they were
amazed. So they left him and went away.
23That same day the Sadducees, who
say there is no resurrection, came to him
with a question. 24"Teacher," they said,
"Moses told us that if a man dies without
having children, his brother must marry
the widow and raise up offspring for him.
25Now there were seven brothers among
us. The first one married and died, and
since he had no children, he left his wife
to his brother. 26The same thing happened to the second and third brother,
right on down to the seventh. 27Finally,
the woman died. 28Now then, at the resurrection, whose wife will she be of the
seven, since all of them were married to
her?"
29Jesus replied, "You are in error because you do not know the Scriptures or
the power of God. 30At the resurrection
people will neither marry nor be given in
marriage; they will be like the angels in
heaven. 31But about the resurrection of
the dead—have you not read what God
said to you, 32'I am the God of Abraham,
the God of Isaac, and the God of Jacob'[b]?
He is not the God of the dead but of the
living."
33When the crowds heard this, they
were astonished at his teaching.
34Hearing that Jesus had silenced the
Sadducees, the Pharisees got together.
35One of them, an expert in the law, tested him with this question: 36"Teacher,
which is the greatest commandment in
the Law?"
37Jesus replied: "'Love the Lord your
God with all your heart and with all your
soul and with all your mind.'[c] 38This is
the first and greatest commandment.
39And the second is like it: 'Love your
neighbor as yourself.'[d] 40All the Law and
the Prophets hang on these two commandments."
41While the Pharisees were gathered
together, Jesus asked them, 42"What do
you think about the Messiah? Whose son
is he?"
"The son of David," they replied.
43He said to them, "How is it then that
David, speaking by the Spirit, calls him
'Lord'? For he says,

44"'The Lord said to my Lord:
"Sit at my right hand
until I put your enemies
under your feet."'[e]

45If then David calls him 'Lord,' how can
he be his son?" 46No one could say a word
in reply, and from that day on no one
dared to ask him any more questions.

23 Then Jesus said to the crowds and to
his disciples: 2"The teachers of the
law and the Pharisees sit in Moses' seat.
3So you must be careful to do everything
they tell you. But do not do what they do,
for they do not practice what they preach.
4They tie up heavy, cumbersome loads
and put them on other people's shoulders, but they themselves are not willing
to lift a finger to move them.
5"Everything they do is done for people to see: They make their phylacteries[f]
wide and the tassels on their garments
long; 6they love the place of honor at
banquets and the most important seats
in the synagogues; 7they love to be greeted with respect in the marketplaces and
to be called 'Rabbi' by others.
8"But you are not to be called 'Rabbi,'
for you have one Teacher, and you are
all brothers. 9And do not call anyone on
earth 'father,' for you have one Father,

[a] 17 A special tax levied on subject peoples, not on Roman citizens [b] 32 Exodus 3:6 [c] 37 Deut. 6:5
[d] 39 Lev. 19:18 [e] 44 Psalm 110:1 [f] 5 That is, boxes containing Scripture verses, worn on forehead and arm

and he is in heaven. [10]Nor are you to be called instructors, for you have one Instructor, the Messiah. [11]The greatest among you will be your servant. [12]For those who exalt themselves will be humbled, and those who humble themselves will be exalted.

[13]"Woe to you, teachers of the law and Pharisees, you hypocrites! You shut the door of the kingdom of heaven in people's faces. You yourselves do not enter, nor will you let those enter who are trying to. [14][a]

[15]"Woe to you, teachers of the law and Pharisees, you hypocrites! You travel over land and sea to win a single convert, and when you have succeeded, you make them twice as much a child of hell as you are.

[16]"Woe to you, blind guides! You say, 'If anyone swears by the temple, it means nothing; but anyone who swears by the gold of the temple is bound by that oath.' [17]You blind fools! Which is greater: the gold, or the temple that makes the gold sacred? [18]You also say, 'If anyone swears by the altar, it means nothing; but anyone who swears by the gift on the altar is bound by that oath.' [19]You blind men! Which is greater: the gift, or the altar that makes the gift sacred? [20]Therefore, anyone who swears by the altar swears by it and by everything on it. [21]And anyone who swears by the temple swears by it and by the one who dwells in it. [22]And anyone who swears by heaven swears by God's throne and by the one who sits on it.

[23]"Woe to you, teachers of the law and Pharisees, you hypocrites! You give a tenth of your spices—mint, dill and cumin. But you have neglected the more important matters of the law—justice, mercy and faithfulness. You should have practiced the latter, without neglecting the former. [24]You blind guides! You strain out a gnat but swallow a camel.

[25]"Woe to you, teachers of the law and Pharisees, you hypocrites! You clean the outside of the cup and dish, but inside they are full of greed and self-indulgence. [26]Blind Pharisee! First clean the inside of the cup and dish, and then the outside also will be clean.

[27]"Woe to you, teachers of the law and Pharisees, you hypocrites! You are like whitewashed tombs, which look beautiful on the outside but on the inside are full of the bones of the dead and everything unclean. [28]In the same way, on the outside you appear to people as righteous but on the inside you are full of hypocrisy and wickedness.

[29]"Woe to you, teachers of the law and Pharisees, you hypocrites! You build tombs for the prophets and decorate the graves of the righteous. [30]And you say, 'If we had lived in the days of our ancestors, we would not have taken part with them in shedding the blood of the prophets.' [31]So you testify against yourselves that you are the descendants of those who murdered the prophets. [32]Go ahead, then, and complete what your ancestors started!

[33]"You snakes! You brood of vipers! How will you escape being condemned to hell? [34]Therefore I am sending you prophets and sages and teachers. Some of them you will kill and crucify; others you will flog in your synagogues and pursue from town to town. [35]And so upon you will come all the righteous blood that has been shed on earth, from the blood of righteous Abel to the blood of Zechariah son of Berekiah, whom you murdered between the temple and the altar. [36]Truly I tell you, all this will come on this generation.

[37]"Jerusalem, Jerusalem, you who kill the prophets and stone those sent to you, how often I have longed to gather your children together, as a hen gathers her chicks under her wings, and you were not willing. [38]Look, your house is left to you desolate. [39]For I tell you, you will not see me again until you say, 'Blessed is he who comes in the name of the Lord.'[b]"

24 Jesus left the temple and was walking away when his disciples came up to him to call his attention to its buildings. [2]"Do you see all these things?" he asked. "Truly I tell you, not one stone here will be left on another; every one will be thrown down."

[3]As Jesus was sitting on the Mount of Olives, the disciples came to him privately. "Tell us," they said, "when will this happen, and what will be the sign of your coming and of the end of the age?"

[a] *14* Some manuscripts include here words similar to Mark 12:40 and Luke 20:47. [b] *39* Psalm 118:26

4Jesus answered: "Watch out that no one deceives you. 5For many will come in my name, claiming, 'I am the Messiah,' and will deceive many. 6You will hear of wars and rumors of wars, but see to it that you are not alarmed. Such things must happen, but the end is still to come. 7Nation will rise against nation, and kingdom against kingdom. There will be famines and earthquakes in various places. 8All these are the beginning of birth pains.

9"Then you will be handed over to be persecuted and put to death, and you will be hated by all nations because of me. 10At that time many will turn away from the faith and will betray and hate each other, 11and many false prophets will appear and deceive many people. 12Because of the increase of wickedness, the love of most will grow cold, 13but the one who stands firm to the end will be saved. 14And this gospel of the kingdom will be preached in the whole world as a testimony to all nations, and then the end will come.

15"So when you see standing in the holy place 'the abomination that causes desolation,'[a] spoken of through the prophet Daniel—let the reader understand— 16then let those who are in Judea flee to the mountains. 17Let no one on the housetop go down to take anything out of the house. 18Let no one in the field go back to get their cloak. 19How dreadful it will be in those days for pregnant women and nursing mothers! 20Pray that your flight will not take place in winter or on the Sabbath. 21For then there will be great distress, unequaled from the beginning of the world until now—and never to be equaled again.

22"If those days had not been cut short, no one would survive, but for the sake of the elect those days will be shortened. 23At that time if anyone says to you, 'Look, here is the Messiah!' or, 'There he is!' do not believe it. 24For false messiahs and false prophets will appear and perform great signs and wonders to deceive, if possible, even the elect. 25See, I have told you ahead of time.

26"So if anyone tells you, 'There he is, out in the wilderness,' do not go out; or, 'Here he is, in the inner rooms,' do not believe it. 27For as lightning that comes from the east is visible even in the west, so will be the coming of the Son of Man. 28Wherever there is a carcass, there the vultures will gather.

29"Immediately after the distress of those days

"'the sun will be darkened,
and the moon will not give its light;
the stars will fall from the sky,
and the heavenly bodies will be shaken.'[b]

30"Then will appear the sign of the Son of Man in heaven. And then all the peoples of the earth[c] will mourn when they see the Son of Man coming on the clouds of heaven, with power and great glory.[d] 31And he will send his angels with a loud trumpet call, and they will gather his elect from the four winds, from one end of the heavens to the other.

32"Now learn this lesson from the fig tree: As soon as its twigs get tender and its leaves come out, you know that summer is near. 33Even so, when you see all these things, you know that it[e] is near, right at the door. 34Truly I tell you, this generation will certainly not pass away until all these things have happened. 35Heaven and earth will pass away, but my words will never pass away.

36"But about that day or hour no one knows, not even the angels in heaven, nor the Son,[f] but only the Father. 37As it was in the days of Noah, so it will be at the coming of the Son of Man. 38For in the days before the flood, people were eating and drinking, marrying and giving in marriage, up to the day Noah entered the ark; 39and they knew nothing about what would happen until the flood came and took them all away. That is how it will be at the coming of the Son of Man. 40Two men will be in the field; one will be taken and the other left. 41Two women will be grinding with a hand mill; one will be taken and the other left.

42"Therefore keep watch, because you do not know on what day your Lord will come. 43But understand this: If the owner of the house had known at what time of night the thief was coming, he would have kept watch and would not have let his house be broken into. 44So you also

[a] *15* Daniel 9:27; 11:31; 12:11 [b] *29* Isaiah 13:10; 34:4 [c] *30* Or *the tribes of the land* [d] *30* See Daniel 7:13-14. [e] *33* Or *he* [f] *36* Some manuscripts do not have *nor the Son.*

must be ready, because the Son of Man
will come at an hour when you do not expect him.
45 "Who then is the faithful and wise
servant, whom the master has put in
charge of the servants in his household to
give them their food at the proper time?
46 It will be good for that servant whose
master finds him doing so when he returns. 47 Truly I tell you, he will put him
in charge of all his possessions. 48 But
suppose that servant is wicked and says
to himself, 'My master is staying away a
long time,' 49 and he then begins to beat
his fellow servants and to eat and drink
with drunkards. 50 The master of that
servant will come on a day when he does
not expect him and at an hour he is not
aware of. 51 He will cut him to pieces and
assign him a place with the hypocrites,
where there will be weeping and gnashing of teeth.

25 "At that time the kingdom of heav-
en will be like ten virgins who took
their lamps and went out to meet the
bridegroom. 2 Five of them were foolish
and five were wise. 3 The foolish ones
took their lamps but did not take any
oil with them. 4 The wise ones, however,
took oil in jars along with their lamps.
5 The bridegroom was a long time in coming, and they all became drowsy and fell
asleep.
6 "At midnight the cry rang out: 'Here's
the bridegroom! Come out to meet him!'
7 "Then all the virgins woke up and
trimmed their lamps. 8 The foolish ones
said to the wise, 'Give us some of your oil;
our lamps are going out.'
9 "'No,' they replied, 'there may not be
enough for both us and you. Instead, go
to those who sell oil and buy some for
yourselves.'
10 "But while they were on their way to
buy the oil, the bridegroom arrived. The
virgins who were ready went in with him
to the wedding banquet. And the door
was shut.
11 "Later the others also came. 'Lord,
Lord,' they said, 'open the door for us!'
12 "But he replied, 'Truly I tell you, I
don't know you.'
13 "Therefore keep watch, because you
do not know the day or the hour.
14 "Again, it will be like a man going on
a journey, who called his servants and
entrusted his wealth to them. 15 To one
he gave five bags of gold, to another two
bags, and to another one bag,[a] each according to his ability. Then he went on
his journey. 16 The man who had received
five bags of gold went at once and put
his money to work and gained five bags
more. 17 So also, the one with two bags
of gold gained two more. 18 But the man
who had received one bag went off, dug
a hole in the ground and hid his master's
money.
19 "After a long time the master of those
servants returned and settled accounts
with them. 20 The man who had received
five bags of gold brought the other five.
'Master,' he said, 'you entrusted me with
five bags of gold. See, I have gained five
more.'
21 "His master replied, 'Well done,
good and faithful servant! You have been
faithful with a few things; I will put you in
charge of many things. Come and share
your master's happiness!'
22 "The man with two bags of gold also
came. 'Master,' he said, 'you entrusted me with two bags of gold; see, I have
gained two more.'
23 "His master replied, 'Well done,
good and faithful servant! You have been
faithful with a few things; I will put you in
charge of many things. Come and share
your master's happiness!'
24 "Then the man who had received
one bag of gold came. 'Master,' he said, 'I
knew that you are a hard man, harvesting
where you have not sown and gathering
where you have not scattered seed. 25 So
I was afraid and went out and hid your
gold in the ground. See, here is what belongs to you.'
26 "His master replied, 'You wicked,
lazy servant! So you knew that I harvest where I have not sown and gather
where I have not scattered seed? 27 Well
then, you should have put my money on
deposit with the bankers, so that when
I returned I would have received it back
with interest.
28 "'So take the bag of gold from him
and give it to the one who has ten bags.
29 For whoever has will be given more,
and they will have an abundance. Whoever does not have, even what they have

[a] *15* Greek *five talents . . . two talents . . . one talent*; also throughout this parable; a talent was worth about 20 years of a day laborer's wage.

will be taken from them. 30 And throw that worthless servant outside, into the darkness, where there will be weeping and gnashing of teeth.'

31 "When the Son of Man comes in his glory, and all the angels with him, he will sit on his glorious throne. 32 All the nations will be gathered before him, and he will separate the people one from another as a shepherd separates the sheep from the goats. 33 He will put the sheep on his right and the goats on his left.

34 "Then the King will say to those on his right, 'Come, you who are blessed by my Father; take your inheritance, the kingdom prepared for you since the creation of the world. 35 For I was hungry and you gave me something to eat, I was thirsty and you gave me something to drink, I was a stranger and you invited me in, 36 I needed clothes and you clothed me, I was sick and you looked after me, I was in prison and you came to visit me.'

37 "Then the righteous will answer him, 'Lord, when did we see you hungry and feed you, or thirsty and give you something to drink? 38 When did we see you a stranger and invite you in, or needing clothes and clothe you? 39 When did we see you sick or in prison and go to visit you?'

40 "The King will reply, 'Truly I tell you, whatever you did for one of the least of these brothers and sisters of mine, you did for me.'

41 "Then he will say to those on his left, 'Depart from me, you who are cursed, into the eternal fire prepared for the devil and his angels. 42 For I was hungry and you gave me nothing to eat, I was thirsty and you gave me nothing to drink, 43 I was a stranger and you did not invite me in, I needed clothes and you did not clothe me, I was sick and in prison and you did not look after me.'

44 "They also will answer, 'Lord, when did we see you hungry or thirsty or a stranger or needing clothes or sick or in prison, and did not help you?'

45 "He will reply, 'Truly I tell you, whatever you did not do for one of the least of these, you did not do for me.'

46 "Then they will go away to eternal punishment, but the righteous to eternal life."

26 When Jesus had finished saying all these things, he said to his disciples, 2 "As you know, the Passover is two days away—and the Son of Man will be handed over to be crucified."

3 Then the chief priests and the elders of the people assembled in the palace of the high priest, whose name was Caiaphas, 4 and they schemed to arrest Jesus secretly and kill him. 5 "But not during the festival," they said, "or there may be a riot among the people."

6 While Jesus was in Bethany in the home of Simon the Leper, 7 a woman came to him with an alabaster jar of very expensive perfume, which she poured on his head as he was reclining at the table.

8 When the disciples saw this, they were indignant. "Why this waste?" they asked. 9 "This perfume could have been sold at a high price and the money given to the poor."

10 Aware of this, Jesus said to them, "Why are you bothering this woman? She has done a beautiful thing to me. 11 The poor you will always have with you,[a] but you will not always have me. 12 When she poured this perfume on my body, she did it to prepare me for burial. 13 Truly I tell you, wherever this gospel is preached throughout the world, what she has done will also be told, in memory of her."

14 Then one of the Twelve—the one called Judas Iscariot—went to the chief priests 15 and asked, "What are you willing to give me if I deliver him over to you?" So they counted out for him thirty pieces of silver. 16 From then on Judas watched for an opportunity to hand him over.

17 On the first day of the Festival of Unleavened Bread, the disciples came to Jesus and asked, "Where do you want us to make preparations for you to eat the Passover?"

18 He replied, "Go into the city to a certain man and tell him, 'The Teacher says: My appointed time is near. I am going to celebrate the Passover with my disciples at your house.'" 19 So the disciples did as Jesus had directed them and prepared the Passover.

20 When evening came, Jesus was reclining at the table with the Twelve. 21 And while they were eating, he said, "Truly I tell you, one of you will betray me."

[a] 11 See Deut. 15:11.

22They were very sad and began to say
to him one after the other, "Surely you
don't mean me, Lord?"
23Jesus replied, "The one who has
dipped his hand into the bowl with me
will betray me. 24The Son of Man will go
just as it is written about him. But woe to
that man who betrays the Son of Man! It
would be better for him if he had not been
born."
25Then Judas, the one who would betray him, said, "Surely you don't mean
me, Rabbi?"
Jesus answered, "You have said so."
26While they were eating, Jesus took
bread, and when he had given thanks, he
broke it and gave it to his disciples, saying, "Take and eat; this is my body."
27Then he took a cup, and when he had
given thanks, he gave it to them, saying,
"Drink from it, all of you. 28This is my
blood of the[a] covenant, which is poured
out for many for the forgiveness of sins.
29I tell you, I will not drink from this fruit
of the vine from now on until that day
when I drink it new with you in my Father's kingdom."
30When they had sung a hymn, they
went out to the Mount of Olives.
31Then Jesus told them, "This very
night you will all fall away on account of
me, for it is written:

"'I will strike the shepherd,
and the sheep of the flock will be
scattered.'[b]

32But after I have risen, I will go ahead of
you into Galilee."
33Peter replied, "Even if all fall away on
account of you, I never will."
34"Truly I tell you," Jesus answered,
"this very night, before the rooster crows,
you will disown me three times."
35But Peter declared, "Even if I have to
die with you, I will never disown you."
And all the other disciples said the same.
36Then Jesus went with his disciples to
a place called Gethsemane, and he said to
them, "Sit here while I go over there and
pray." 37He took Peter and the two sons
of Zebedee along with him, and he began
to be sorrowful and troubled. 38Then he
said to them, "My soul is overwhelmed
with sorrow to the point of death. Stay
here and keep watch with me."
39Going a little farther, he fell with his
face to the ground and prayed, "My Father, if it is possible, may this cup be tak-
en from me. Yet not as I will, but as you
will."
40Then he returned to his disciples
and found them sleeping. "Couldn't you
men keep watch with me for one hour?"
he asked Peter. 41"Watch and pray so that
you will not fall into temptation. The spirit is willing, but the flesh is weak."
42He went away a second time and
prayed, "My Father, if it is not possible for
this cup to be taken away unless I drink it,
may your will be done."
43When he came back, he again found
them sleeping, because their eyes were
heavy. 44So he left them and went away
once more and prayed the third time,
saying the same thing.
45Then he returned to the disciples
and said to them, "Are you still sleeping
and resting? Look, the hour has come,
and the Son of Man is delivered into the
hands of sinners. 46Rise! Let us go! Here
comes my betrayer!"
47While he was still speaking, Judas,
one of the Twelve, arrived. With him was
a large crowd armed with swords and
clubs, sent from the chief priests and the
elders of the people. 48Now the betrayer
had arranged a signal with them: "The
one I kiss is the man; arrest him." 49Go-
ing at once to Jesus, Judas said, "Greetings, Rabbi!" and kissed him.
50Jesus replied, "Do what you came for,
friend."[c]
Then the men stepped forward, seized
Jesus and arrested him. 51With that, one
of Jesus' companions reached for his
sword, drew it out and struck the servant
of the high priest, cutting off his ear.
52"Put your sword back in its place,"
Jesus said to him, "for all who draw the
sword will die by the sword. 53Do you
think I cannot call on my Father, and he
will at once put at my disposal more than
twelve legions of angels? 54But how then
would the Scriptures be fulfilled that say
it must happen in this way?"
55In that hour Jesus said to the crowd,
"Am I leading a rebellion, that you have
come out with swords and clubs to capture me? Every day I sat in the temple
courts teaching, and you did not arrest

[a] *28* Some manuscripts *the new* [b] *31* Zech. 13:7 [c] *50* Or *"Why have you come, friend?"*

me. 56 But this has all taken place that
the writings of the prophets might be
fulfilled." Then all the disciples deserted
him and fled.

57 Those who had arrested Jesus took
him to Caiaphas the high priest, where
the teachers of the law and the elders had
assembled. 58 But Peter followed him at a
distance, right up to the courtyard of the
high priest. He entered and sat down with
the guards to see the outcome.

59 The chief priests and the whole Sanhedrin were looking for false evidence
against Jesus so that they could put him
to death. 60 But they did not find any,
though many false witnesses came forward.

Finally two came forward 61 and declared, "This fellow said, 'I am able to destroy the temple of God and rebuild it in
three days.'"

62 Then the high priest stood up and
said to Jesus, "Are you not going to answer? What is this testimony that these
men are bringing against you?" 63 But
Jesus remained silent.

The high priest said to him, "I charge
you under oath by the living God: Tell us
if you are the Messiah, the Son of God."

64 "You have said so," Jesus replied.
"But I say to all of you: From now on you
will see the Son of Man sitting at the right
hand of the Mighty One and coming on
the clouds of heaven."[a]

65 Then the high priest tore his clothes
and said, "He has spoken blasphemy!
Why do we need any more witnesses?
Look, now you have heard the blasphemy. 66 What do you think?"

"He is worthy of death," they answered.

67 Then they spit in his face and struck
him with their fists. Others slapped him
68 and said, "Prophesy to us, Messiah.
Who hit you?"

69 Now Peter was sitting out in the
courtyard, and a servant girl came to
him. "You also were with Jesus of Galilee," she said.

70 But he denied it before them all. "I
don't know what you're talking about,"
he said.

71 Then he went out to the gateway,
where another servant girl saw him and
said to the people there, "This fellow was
with Jesus of Nazareth."

72 He denied it again, with an oath: "I
don't know the man!"

73 After a little while, those standing
there went up to Peter and said, "Surely
you are one of them; your accent gives
you away."

74 Then he began to call down curses,
and he swore to them, "I don't know the
man!"

Immediately a rooster crowed. 75 Then
Peter remembered the word Jesus had
spoken: "Before the rooster crows, you
will disown me three times." And he went
outside and wept bitterly.

27 Early in the morning, all the chief
priests and the elders of the people made their plans how to have Jesus
executed. 2 So they bound him, led him
away and handed him over to Pilate the
governor.

3 When Judas, who had betrayed him,
saw that Jesus was condemned, he was
seized with remorse and returned the
thirty pieces of silver to the chief priests
and the elders. 4 "I have sinned," he said,
"for I have betrayed innocent blood."

"What is that to us?" they replied.
"That's your responsibility."

5 So Judas threw the money into the
temple and left. Then he went away and
hanged himself.

6 The chief priests picked up the coins
and said, "It is against the law to put this
into the treasury, since it is blood money." 7 So they decided to use the money to
buy the potter's field as a burial place for
foreigners. 8 That is why it has been called
the Field of Blood to this day. 9 Then what
was spoken by Jeremiah the prophet was
fulfilled: "They took the thirty pieces of
silver, the price set on him by the people
of Israel, 10 and they used them to buy the
potter's field, as the Lord commanded
me."[b]

11 Meanwhile Jesus stood before the
governor, and the governor asked him,
"Are you the king of the Jews?"

"You have said so," Jesus replied.

12 When he was accused by the chief
priests and the elders, he gave no answer.
13 Then Pilate asked him, "Don't you hear
the testimony they are bringing against
you?" 14 But Jesus made no reply, not even
to a single charge—to the great amazement of the governor.

[a] *64* See Psalm 110:1; Daniel 7:13. [b] *10* See Zech. 11:12,13; Jer. 19:1-13; 32:6-9.

15 Now it was the governor's custom at
the festival to release a prisoner chosen
by the crowd. 16 At that time they had a
well-known prisoner whose name was
Jesus[a] Barabbas. 17 So when the crowd
had gathered, Pilate asked them, "Which
one do you want me to release to you:
Jesus Barabbas, or Jesus who is called
the Messiah?" 18 For he knew it was out of
self-interest that they had handed Jesus
over to him.
19 While Pilate was sitting on the judge's
seat, his wife sent him this message:
"Don't have anything to do with that innocent man, for I have suffered a great
deal today in a dream because of him."
20 But the chief priests and the elders
persuaded the crowd to ask for Barabbas
and to have Jesus executed.
21 "Which of the two do you want me to
release to you?" asked the governor.
"Barabbas," they answered.
22 "What shall I do, then, with Jesus who
is called the Messiah?" Pilate asked.
They all answered, "Crucify him!"
23 "Why? What crime has he committed?" asked Pilate.
But they shouted all the louder, "Crucify him!"
24 When Pilate saw that he was getting
nowhere, but that instead an uproar was
starting, he took water and washed his
hands in front of the crowd. "I am innocent of this man's blood," he said. "It is
your responsibility!"
25 All the people answered, "His blood
is on us and on our children!"
26 Then he released Barabbas to them.
But he had Jesus flogged, and handed
him over to be crucified.
27 Then the governor's soldiers took
Jesus into the Praetorium and gathered
the whole company of soldiers around
him. 28 They stripped him and put a
scarlet robe on him, 29 and then twisted together a crown of thorns and set it
on his head. They put a staff in his right
hand. Then they knelt in front of him and
mocked him. "Hail, king of the Jews!"
they said. 30 They spit on him, and took
the staff and struck him on the head again
and again. 31 After they had mocked him,
they took off the robe and put his own
clothes on him. Then they led him away
to crucify him.
32 As they were going out, they met a
man from Cyrene, named Simon, and
they forced him to carry the cross. 33 They
came to a place called Golgotha (which
means "the place of the skull"). 34 There
they offered Jesus wine to drink, mixed
with gall; but after tasting it, he refused to
drink it. 35 When they had crucified him,
they divided up his clothes by casting
lots. 36 And sitting down, they kept watch
over him there. 37 Above his head they
placed the written charge against him:
THIS IS JESUS, THE KING OF THE JEWS.
38 Two rebels were crucified with him,
one on his right and one on his left.
39 Those who passed by hurled insults at
him, shaking their heads 40 and saying,
"You who are going to destroy the temple
and build it in three days, save yourself!
Come down from the cross, if you are the
Son of God!" 41 In the same way the chief
priests, the teachers of the law and the
elders mocked him. 42 "He saved others,"
they said, "but he can't save himself! He's
the king of Israel! Let him come down
now from the cross, and we will believe
in him. 43 He trusts in God. Let God rescue him now if he wants him, for he said,
'I am the Son of God.'" 44 In the same way
the rebels who were crucified with him
also heaped insults on him.
45 From noon until three in the afternoon darkness came over all the land.
46 About three in the afternoon Jesus
cried out in a loud voice, *"Eli, Eli,*[b] *lema
sabachthani?"* (which means "My God,
my God, why have you forsaken me?").[c]
47 When some of those standing there
heard this, they said, "He's calling Elijah."
48 Immediately one of them ran and got
a sponge. He filled it with wine vinegar,
put it on a staff, and offered it to Jesus to
drink. 49 The rest said, "Now leave him
alone. Let's see if Elijah comes to save
him."
50 And when Jesus had cried out again
in a loud voice, he gave up his spirit.
51 At that moment the curtain of the
temple was torn in two from top to bottom. The earth shook, the rocks split
52 and the tombs broke open. The bodies of many holy people who had died
were raised to life. 53 They came out of
the tombs after Jesus' resurrection and[d]

[a] *16* Many manuscripts do not have *Jesus*; also in verse 17. [b] *46* Some manuscripts *Eloi, Eloi*
[c] *46* Psalm 22:1 [d] *53* Or *tombs, and after Jesus' resurrection they*

went into the holy city and appeared to
many people.
54 When the centurion and those with
him who were guarding Jesus saw the
earthquake and all that had happened,
they were terrified, and exclaimed,
"Surely he was the Son of God!"
55 Many women were there, watching from a distance. They had followed
Jesus from Galilee to care for his needs.
56 Among them were Mary Magdalene,
Mary the mother of James and Joseph,[a]
and the mother of Zebedee's sons.
57 As evening approached, there came
a rich man from Arimathea, named Joseph, who had himself become a disciple of Jesus. 58 Going to Pilate, he asked
for Jesus' body, and Pilate ordered that it
be given to him. 59 Joseph took the body,
wrapped it in a clean linen cloth, 60 and
placed it in his own new tomb that he had
cut out of the rock. He rolled a big stone
in front of the entrance to the tomb and
went away. 61 Mary Magdalene and the
other Mary were sitting there opposite
the tomb.
62 The next day, the one after Preparation Day, the chief priests and the Pharisees went to Pilate. 63 "Sir," they said, "we
remember that while he was still alive
that deceiver said, 'After three days I will
rise again.' 64 So give the order for the
tomb to be made secure until the third
day. Otherwise, his disciples may come
and steal the body and tell the people
that he has been raised from the dead.
This last deception will be worse than
the first."
65 "Take a guard," Pilate answered. "Go,
make the tomb as secure as you know
how." 66 So they went and made the tomb
secure by putting a seal on the stone and
posting the guard.
28 After the Sabbath, at dawn on the
first day of the week, Mary Magdalene and the other Mary went to look at
the tomb.
2 There was a violent earthquake, for an
angel of the Lord came down from heav-
en and, going to the tomb, rolled back the
stone and sat on it. 3 His appearance was
like lightning, and his clothes were white
as snow. 4 The guards were so afraid of
him that they shook and became like
dead men.
5 The angel said to the women, "Do not
be afraid, for I know that you are looking
for Jesus, who was crucified. 6 He is not
here; he has risen, just as he said. Come
and see the place where he lay. 7 Then go
quickly and tell his disciples: 'He has ris-
en from the dead and is going ahead of
you into Galilee. There you will see him.'
Now I have told you."
8 So the women hurried away from the
tomb, afraid yet filled with joy, and ran
to tell his disciples. 9 Suddenly Jesus met
them. "Greetings," he said. They came
to him, clasped his feet and worshiped
him. 10 Then Jesus said to them, "Do not
be afraid. Go and tell my brothers to go to
Galilee; there they will see me."
11 While the women were on their way,
some of the guards went into the city
and reported to the chief priests everything that had happened. 12 When the
chief priests had met with the elders and
devised a plan, they gave the soldiers a
large sum of money, 13 telling them, "You
are to say, 'His disciples came during the
night and stole him away while we were
asleep.' 14 If this report gets to the governor, we will satisfy him and keep you
out of trouble." 15 So the soldiers took the
money and did as they were instructed.
And this story has been widely circulated
among the Jews to this very day.
16 Then the eleven disciples went to
Galilee, to the mountain where Jesus had
told them to go. 17 When they saw him,
they worshiped him; but some doubt-
ed. 18 Then Jesus came to them and said,
"All authority in heaven and on earth has
been given to me. 19 Therefore go and
make disciples of all nations, baptizing
them in the name of the Father and of the
Son and of the Holy Spirit, 20 and teaching them to obey everything I have commanded you. And surely I am with you
always, to the very end of the age."

[a] 56 Greek *Joses*, a variant of *Joseph*

MARK

Mark appears to be written for an audience in Rome. A Roman centurion's declaration near the end of the book—*Surely this man was the Son of God!*—models the witness to Jesus this gospel calls for.

The opening half of this fast-moving drama keys on the question: *Who do you say I am?* An episode at the end of the first half shows Jesus healing a blind man in two stages, so that he slowly comes to see. In the same way the disciples have only gradually come to recognize who Jesus is. Then in a key moment in the story, between its two halves, Peter confesses that Jesus is the Messiah.

Now the conflict moves out into the open. Jesus has come to introduce a radical new way of life that will undercut existing power relationships. The second half of the drama depicts this in three acts:

: First, Jesus and his disciples travel to Jerusalem.
: Next, Jesus teaches in the temple and clashes with the established leadership.
: In the final act, that leadership executes its plan and has Jesus arrested and crucified, seemingly overturning all he has done. But then God overturns their deed and raises Jesus to life. So Mark's readers are called to be faithful to Jesus, even in suffering, because this is how God continues to overturn the existing order and establish the way of life that Jesus taught.

---

1 The beginning of the good news about
Jesus the Messiah,[a] the Son of God,[b]
2 as it is written in Isaiah the prophet:

"I will send my messenger ahead of
you,
who will prepare your way"[c]—
3 "a voice of one calling in the
wilderness,
'Prepare the way for the Lord,
make straight paths for him.'"[d]

4 And so John the Baptist appeared in
the wilderness, preaching a baptism of
repentance for the forgiveness of sins.
5 The whole Judean countryside and all
the people of Jerusalem went out to him.
Confessing their sins, they were baptized
by him in the Jordan River. 6 John wore
clothing made of camel's hair, with a
leather belt around his waist, and he ate
locusts and wild honey. 7 And this was his
message: "After me comes the one more
powerful than I, the straps of whose sandals I am not worthy to stoop down and
untie. 8 I baptize you with[e] water, but he
will baptize you with[e] the Holy Spirit."

9 At that time Jesus came from Nazareth in Galilee and was baptized by John
in the Jordan. 10 Just as Jesus was coming
up out of the water, he saw heaven being
torn open and the Spirit descending on
him like a dove. 11 And a voice came from
heaven: "You are my Son, whom I love;
with you I am well pleased."

12 At once the Spirit sent him out into
the wilderness, 13 and he was in the wilderness forty days, being tempted[f] by Satan. He was with the wild animals, and
angels attended him.

14 After John was put in prison, Jesus
went into Galilee, proclaiming the good
news of God. 15 "The time has come," he
said. "The kingdom of God has come
near. Repent and believe the good
news!"

16 As Jesus walked beside the Sea of
Galilee, he saw Simon and his brother
Andrew casting a net into the lake, for
they were fishermen. 17 "Come, follow
me," Jesus said, "and I will send you out
to fish for people." 18 At once they left
their nets and followed him.

19 When he had gone a little farther, he
saw James son of Zebedee and his brother John in a boat, preparing their nets.
20 Without delay he called them, and they
left their father Zebedee in the boat with
the hired men and followed him.

21 They went to Capernaum, and when
the Sabbath came, Jesus went into the
synagogue and began to teach. 22 The

[a] *1* Or *Jesus Christ. Messiah* (Hebrew) and *Christ* (Greek) both mean *Anointed One.* [b] *1* Some manuscripts do not have *the Son of God.* [c] *2* Mal. 3:1 [d] *3* Isaiah 40:3 [e] *8* Or *in* [f] *13* The Greek for *tempted* can also mean *tested.*

people were amazed at his teaching,
because he taught them as one who had
authority, not as the teachers of the law.
23 Just then a man in their synagogue
who was possessed by an impure spirit
cried out, 24 "What do you want with us,
Jesus of Nazareth? Have you come to destroy us? I know who you are—the Holy
One of God!"
25 "Be quiet!" said Jesus sternly. "Come
out of him!" 26 The impure spirit shook
the man violently and came out of him
with a shriek.
27 The people were all so amazed that
they asked each other, "What is this?
A new teaching—and with authority!
He even gives orders to impure spirits
and they obey him." 28 News about him
spread quickly over the whole region of
Galilee.
29 As soon as they left the synagogue,
they went with James and John to the
home of Simon and Andrew. 30 Simon's
mother-in-law was in bed with a fever,
and they immediately told Jesus about
her. 31 So he went to her, took her hand
and helped her up. The fever left her and
she began to wait on them.
32 That evening after sunset the people
brought to Jesus all the sick and demon-
possessed. 33 The whole town gathered at
the door, 34 and Jesus healed many who
had various diseases. He also drove out
many demons, but he would not let the
demons speak because they knew who
he was.
35 Very early in the morning, while it
was still dark, Jesus got up, left the house
and went off to a solitary place, where he
prayed. 36 Simon and his companions
went to look for him, 37 and when they
found him, they exclaimed: "Everyone is
looking for you!"
38 Jesus replied, "Let us go somewhere
else—to the nearby villages—so I can
preach there also. That is why I have
come." 39 So he traveled throughout Galilee, preaching in their synagogues and
driving out demons.
40 A man with leprosy[a] came to him
and begged him on his knees, "If you are
willing, you can make me clean."
41 Jesus was indignant.[b] He reached
out his hand and touched the man. "I am
willing," he said. "Be clean!" 42 Immediately the leprosy left him and he was
cleansed.
43 Jesus sent him away at once with a
strong warning: 44 "See that you don't
tell this to anyone. But go, show yourself
to the priest and offer the sacrifices that
Moses commanded for your cleansing,
as a testimony to them." 45 Instead he
went out and began to talk freely, spreading the news. As a result, Jesus could no
longer enter a town openly but stayed
outside in lonely places. Yet the people
still came to him from everywhere.

2 A few days later, when Jesus again entered Capernaum, the people heard
that he had come home. 2 They gathered
in such large numbers that there was no
room left, not even outside the door, and
he preached the word to them. 3 Some
men came, bringing to him a paralyzed
man, carried by four of them. 4 Since they
could not get him to Jesus because of the
crowd, they made an opening in the roof
above Jesus by digging through it and
then lowered the mat the man was lying
on. 5 When Jesus saw their faith, he said
to the paralyzed man, "Son, your sins are
forgiven."
6 Now some teachers of the law were
sitting there, thinking to themselves,
7 "Why does this fellow talk like that?
He's blaspheming! Who can forgive sins
but God alone?"
8 Immediately Jesus knew in his spirit
that this was what they were thinking in
their hearts, and he said to them, "Why
are you thinking these things? 9 Which is
easier: to say to this paralyzed man, 'Your
sins are forgiven,' or to say, 'Get up, take
your mat and walk'? 10 But I want you to
know that the Son of Man has authority
on earth to forgive sins." So he said to the
man, 11 "I tell you, get up, take your mat
and go home." 12 He got up, took his mat
and walked out in full view of them all.
This amazed everyone and they praised
God, saying, "We have never seen anything like this!"
13 Once again Jesus went out beside
the lake. A large crowd came to him, and
he began to teach them. 14 As he walked
along, he saw Levi son of Alphaeus sitting at the tax collector's booth. "Follow
me," Jesus told him, and Levi got up and
followed him.

[a] 40 The Greek word traditionally translated *leprosy* was used for various diseases affecting the skin.
[b] 41 Many manuscripts *Jesus was filled with compassion*

[15]While Jesus was having dinner at Levi's house, many tax collectors and sinners were eating with him and his disciples, for there were many who followed him. [16]When the teachers of the law who were Pharisees saw him eating with the sinners and tax collectors, they asked his disciples: "Why does he eat with tax collectors and sinners?"

[17]On hearing this, Jesus said to them, "It is not the healthy who need a doctor, but the sick. I have not come to call the righteous, but sinners."

[18]Now John's disciples and the Pharisees were fasting. Some people came and asked Jesus, "How is it that John's disciples and the disciples of the Pharisees are fasting, but yours are not?"

[19]Jesus answered, "How can the guests of the bridegroom fast while he is with them? They cannot, so long as they have him with them. [20]But the time will come when the bridegroom will be taken from them, and on that day they will fast.

[21]"No one sews a patch of unshrunk cloth on an old garment. Otherwise, the new piece will pull away from the old, making the tear worse. [22]And no one pours new wine into old wineskins. Otherwise, the wine will burst the skins, and both the wine and the wineskins will be ruined. No, they pour new wine into new wineskins."

[23]One Sabbath Jesus was going through the grainfields, and as his disciples walked along, they began to pick some heads of grain. [24]The Pharisees said to him, "Look, why are they doing what is unlawful on the Sabbath?"

[25]He answered, "Have you never read what David did when he and his companions were hungry and in need? [26]In the days of Abiathar the high priest, he entered the house of God and ate the consecrated bread, which is lawful only for priests to eat. And he also gave some to his companions."

[27]Then he said to them, "The Sabbath was made for man, not man for the Sabbath. [28]So the Son of Man is Lord even of the Sabbath."

3 Another time Jesus went into the synagogue, and a man with a shriveled hand was there. [2]Some of them were looking for a reason to accuse Jesus, so they watched him closely to see if he would heal him on the Sabbath. [3]Jesus said to the man with the shriveled hand, "Stand up in front of everyone."

[4]Then Jesus asked them, "Which is lawful on the Sabbath: to do good or to do evil, to save life or to kill?" But they remained silent.

[5]He looked around at them in anger and, deeply distressed at their stubborn hearts, said to the man, "Stretch out your hand." He stretched it out, and his hand was completely restored. [6]Then the Pharisees went out and began to plot with the Herodians how they might kill Jesus.

[7]Jesus withdrew with his disciples to the lake, and a large crowd from Galilee followed. [8]When they heard about all he was doing, many people came to him from Judea, Jerusalem, Idumea, and the regions across the Jordan and around Tyre and Sidon. [9]Because of the crowd he told his disciples to have a small boat ready for him, to keep the people from crowding him. [10]For he had healed many, so that those with diseases were pushing forward to touch him. [11]Whenever the impure spirits saw him, they fell down before him and cried out, "You are the Son of God." [12]But he gave them strict orders not to tell others about him.

[13]Jesus went up on a mountainside and called to him those he wanted, and they came to him. [14]He appointed twelve[a] that they might be with him and that he might send them out to preach [15]and to have authority to drive out demons. [16]These are the twelve he appointed: Simon (to whom he gave the name Peter), [17]James son of Zebedee and his brother John (to them he gave the name Boanerges, which means "sons of thunder"), [18]Andrew, Philip, Bartholomew, Matthew, Thomas, James son of Alphaeus, Thaddaeus, Simon the Zealot [19]and Judas Iscariot, who betrayed him.

[20]Then Jesus entered a house, and again a crowd gathered, so that he and his disciples were not even able to eat. [21]When his family[b] heard about this, they went to take charge of him, for they said, "He is out of his mind."

[22]And the teachers of the law who

[a] *14* Some manuscripts *twelve—designating them apostles—* [b] *21* Or *his associates*

came down from Jerusalem said, "He is
possessed by Beelzebul! By the prince of
demons he is driving out demons."
23 So Jesus called them over to him
and began to speak to them in parables:
"How can Satan drive out Satan? 24 If a
kingdom is divided against itself, that
kingdom cannot stand. 25 If a house is
divided against itself, that house cannot stand. 26 And if Satan opposes himself and is divided, he cannot stand;
his end has come. 27 In fact, no one can
enter a strong man's house without first
tying him up. Then he can plunder the
strong man's house. 28 Truly I tell you,
people can be forgiven all their sins and
every slander they utter, 29 but whoever
blasphemes against the Holy Spirit will
never be forgiven; they are guilty of an
eternal sin."
30 He said this because they were saying, "He has an impure spirit."
31 Then Jesus' mother and brothers arrived. Standing outside, they sent someone in to call him. 32 A crowd was sitting
around him, and they told him, "Your
mother and brothers are outside looking
for you."
33 "Who are my mother and my brothers?" he asked.
34 Then he looked at those seated in a
circle around him and said, "Here are
my mother and my brothers! 35 Whoever
does God's will is my brother and sister
and mother."

4 Again Jesus began to teach by the
lake. The crowd that gathered around
him was so large that he got into a boat
and sat in it out on the lake, while all
the people were along the shore at the
water's edge. 2 He taught them many
things by parables, and in his teaching
said: 3 "Listen! A farmer went out to sow
his seed. 4 As he was scattering the seed,
some fell along the path, and the birds
came and ate it up. 5 Some fell on rocky
places, where it did not have much soil.
It sprang up quickly, because the soil was
shallow. 6 But when the sun came up, the
plants were scorched, and they withered
because they had no root. 7 Other seed
fell among thorns, which grew up and
choked the plants, so that they did not
bear grain. 8 Still other seed fell on good
soil. It came up, grew and produced a
crop, some multiplying thirty, some sixty, some a hundred times."
9 Then Jesus said, "Whoever has ears to
hear, let them hear."
10 When he was alone, the Twelve and
the others around him asked him about
the parables. 11 He told them, "The secret
of the kingdom of God has been given to
you. But to those on the outside everything is said in parables 12 so that,

" 'they may be ever seeing but never
perceiving,
and ever hearing but never
understanding;
otherwise they might turn and be
forgiven!'[a]"

13 Then Jesus said to them, "Don't you
understand this parable? How then
will you understand any parable? 14 The
farmer sows the word. 15 Some people are
like seed along the path, where the word
is sown. As soon as they hear it, Satan
comes and takes away the word that was
sown in them. 16 Others, like seed sown
on rocky places, hear the word and at
once receive it with joy. 17 But since they
have no root, they last only a short time.
When trouble or persecution comes because of the word, they quickly fall away.
18 Still others, like seed sown among
thorns, hear the word; 19 but the worries
of this life, the deceitfulness of wealth
and the desires for other things come in
and choke the word, making it unfruitful. 20 Others, like seed sown on good
soil, hear the word, accept it, and produce a crop—some thirty, some sixty,
some a hundred times what was sown."
21 He said to them, "Do you bring in
a lamp to put it under a bowl or a bed?
Instead, don't you put it on its stand?
22 For whatever is hidden is meant to be
disclosed, and whatever is concealed is
meant to be brought out into the open.
23 If anyone has ears to hear, let them
hear."
24 "Consider carefully what you hear,"
he continued. "With the measure you
use, it will be measured to you—and
even more. 25 Whoever has will be given
more; whoever does not have, even what
they have will be taken from them."
26 He also said, "This is what the kingdom of God is like. A man scatters seed

[a] *12* Isaiah 6:9,10

on the ground. 27Night and day, whether
he sleeps or gets up, the seed sprouts and
grows, though he does not know how.
28All by itself the soil produces grain—
first the stalk, then the head, then the
full kernel in the head. 29As soon as the
grain is ripe, he puts the sickle to it, because the harvest has come."
30Again he said, "What shall we say the
kingdom of God is like, or what parable
shall we use to describe it? 31It is like a
mustard seed, which is the smallest of
all seeds on earth. 32Yet when planted, it
grows and becomes the largest of all garden plants, with such big branches that
the birds can perch in its shade."
33With many similar parables Jesus
spoke the word to them, as much as they
could understand. 34He did not say anything to them without using a parable.
But when he was alone with his own disciples, he explained everything.
35That day when evening came, he
said to his disciples, "Let us go over to the
other side." 36Leaving the crowd behind,
they took him along, just as he was, in the
boat. There were also other boats with
him. 37A furious squall came up, and
the waves broke over the boat, so that it
was nearly swamped. 38Jesus was in the
stern, sleeping on a cushion. The disciples woke him and said to him, "Teacher,
don't you care if we drown?"
39He got up, rebuked the wind and said
to the waves, "Quiet! Be still!" Then the
wind died down and it was completely
calm.
40He said to his disciples, "Why are you
so afraid? Do you still have no faith?"
41They were terrified and asked each
other, "Who is this? Even the wind and
the waves obey him!"
5 They went across the lake to the region of the Gerasenes.[a] 2When Jesus
got out of the boat, a man with an impure
spirit came from the tombs to meet him.
3This man lived in the tombs, and no one
could bind him anymore, not even with
a chain. 4For he had often been chained
hand and foot, but he tore the chains
apart and broke the irons on his feet. No
one was strong enough to subdue him.
5Night and day among the tombs and in
the hills he would cry out and cut himself
with stones.
6When he saw Jesus from a distance,
he ran and fell on his knees in front of
him. 7He shouted at the top of his voice,
"What do you want with me, Jesus, Son
of the Most High God? In God's name
don't torture me!" 8For Jesus had said to
him, "Come out of this man, you impure
spirit!"
9Then Jesus asked him, "What is your
name?"
"My name is Legion," he replied, "for
we are many." 10And he begged Jesus
again and again not to send them out of
the area.
11A large herd of pigs was feeding
on the nearby hillside. 12The demons
begged Jesus, "Send us among the pigs;
allow us to go into them." 13He gave them
permission, and the impure spirits came
out and went into the pigs. The herd,
about two thousand in number, rushed
down the steep bank into the lake and
were drowned.
14Those tending the pigs ran off and reported this in the town and countryside,
and the people went out to see what had
happened. 15When they came to Jesus,
they saw the man who had been possessed by the legion of demons, sitting
there, dressed and in his right mind; and
they were afraid. 16Those who had seen
it told the people what had happened to
the demon-possessed man—and told
about the pigs as well. 17Then the people
began to plead with Jesus to leave their
region.
18As Jesus was getting into the boat,
the man who had been demon-possessed begged to go with him. 19Jesus did
not let him, but said, "Go home to your
own people and tell them how much the
Lord has done for you, and how he has
had mercy on you." 20So the man went
away and began to tell in the Decapolis[b]
how much Jesus had done for him. And
all the people were amazed.
21When Jesus had again crossed over
by boat to the other side of the lake, a
large crowd gathered around him while
he was by the lake. 22Then one of the
synagogue leaders, named Jairus, came,
and when he saw Jesus, he fell at his feet.
23He pleaded earnestly with him, "My
little daughter is dying. Please come and
put your hands on her so that she will be

[a] *1* Some manuscripts *Gadarenes*; other manuscripts *Gergesenes* [b] *20* That is, the Ten Cities

healed and live." 24 So Jesus went with him.

A large crowd followed and pressed around him. 25 And a woman was there who had been subject to bleeding for twelve years. 26 She had suffered a great deal under the care of many doctors and had spent all she had, yet instead of getting better she grew worse. 27 When she heard about Jesus, she came up behind him in the crowd and touched his cloak, 28 because she thought, "If I just touch his clothes, I will be healed." 29 Immediately her bleeding stopped and she felt in her body that she was freed from her suffering.

30 At once Jesus realized that power had gone out from him. He turned around in the crowd and asked, "Who touched my clothes?"

31 "You see the people crowding against you," his disciples answered, "and yet you can ask, 'Who touched me?'"

32 But Jesus kept looking around to see who had done it. 33 Then the woman, knowing what had happened to her, came and fell at his feet and, trembling with fear, told him the whole truth. 34 He said to her, "Daughter, your faith has healed you. Go in peace and be freed from your suffering."

35 While Jesus was still speaking, some people came from the house of Jairus, the synagogue leader. "Your daughter is dead," they said. "Why bother the teacher anymore?"

36 Overhearing[a] what they said, Jesus told him, "Don't be afraid; just believe."

37 He did not let anyone follow him except Peter, James and John the brother of James. 38 When they came to the home of the synagogue leader, Jesus saw a commotion, with people crying and wailing loudly. 39 He went in and said to them, "Why all this commotion and wailing? The child is not dead but asleep." 40 But they laughed at him.

After he put them all out, he took the child's father and mother and the disciples who were with him, and went in where the child was. 41 He took her by the hand and said to her, *"Talitha koum!"* (which means "Little girl, I say to you, get up!"). 42 Immediately the girl stood up and began to walk around (she was twelve years old). At this they were completely astonished. 43 He gave strict orders not to let anyone know about this, and told them to give her something to eat.

6 Jesus left there and went to his hometown, accompanied by his disciples. 2 When the Sabbath came, he began to teach in the synagogue, and many who heard him were amazed.

"Where did this man get these things?" they asked. "What's this wisdom that has been given him? What are these remarkable miracles he is performing? 3 Isn't this the carpenter? Isn't this Mary's son and the brother of James, Joseph,[b] Judas and Simon? Aren't his sisters here with us?" And they took offense at him.

4 Jesus said to them, "A prophet is not without honor except in his own town, among his relatives and in his own home." 5 He could not do any miracles there, except lay his hands on a few sick people and heal them. 6 He was amazed at their lack of faith.

Then Jesus went around teaching from village to village. 7 Calling the Twelve to him, he began to send them out two by two and gave them authority over impure spirits.

8 These were his instructions: "Take nothing for the journey except a staff—no bread, no bag, no money in your belts. 9 Wear sandals but not an extra shirt. 10 Whenever you enter a house, stay there until you leave that town. 11 And if any place will not welcome you or listen to you, leave that place and shake the dust off your feet as a testimony against them."

12 They went out and preached that people should repent. 13 They drove out many demons and anointed many sick people with oil and healed them.

14 King Herod heard about this, for Jesus' name had become well known. Some were saying,[c] "John the Baptist has been raised from the dead, and that is why miraculous powers are at work in him."

15 Others said, "He is Elijah."

And still others claimed, "He is a prophet, like one of the prophets of long ago."

[a] 36 Or *Ignoring* [b] 3 Greek *Joses,* a variant of *Joseph* [c] 14 Some early manuscripts *He was saying*

16But when Herod heard this, he said,
"John, whom I beheaded, has been raised
from the dead!"
17For Herod himself had given orders
to have John arrested, and he had him
bound and put in prison. He did this because of Herodias, his brother Philip's
wife, whom he had married. 18For John
had been saying to Herod, "It is not lawful for you to have your brother's wife."
19So Herodias nursed a grudge against
John and wanted to kill him. But she was
not able to, 20because Herod feared John
and protected him, knowing him to be
a righteous and holy man. When Herod
heard John, he was greatly puzzled[a]; yet
he liked to listen to him.
21Finally the opportune time came. On
his birthday Herod gave a banquet for his
high officials and military commanders
and the leading men of Galilee. 22When
the daughter of[b] Herodias came in and
danced, she pleased Herod and his dinner guests.

The king said to the girl, "Ask me for
anything you want, and I'll give it to
you." 23And he promised her with an
oath, "Whatever you ask I will give you,
up to half my kingdom."
24She went out and said to her mother,
"What shall I ask for?"

"The head of John the Baptist," she answered.
25At once the girl hurried in to the king
with the request: "I want you to give me
right now the head of John the Baptist on
a platter."
26The king was greatly distressed,
but because of his oaths and his dinner
guests, he did not want to refuse her.
27So he immediately sent an execution-
er with orders to bring John's head. The
man went, beheaded John in the prison,
28and brought back his head on a platter.
He presented it to the girl, and she gave
it to her mother. 29On hearing of this,
John's disciples came and took his body
and laid it in a tomb.
30The apostles gathered around Jesus
and reported to him all they had done
and taught. 31Then, because so many
people were coming and going that they
did not even have a chance to eat, he said
to them, "Come with me by yourselves to
a quiet place and get some rest."
32So they went away by themselves in a
boat to a solitary place. 33But many who
saw them leaving recognized them and
ran on foot from all the towns and got
there ahead of them. 34When Jesus landed and saw a large crowd, he had compassion on them, because they were like
sheep without a shepherd. So he began
teaching them many things.
35By this time it was late in the day, so
his disciples came to him. "This is a remote place," they said, "and it's already
very late. 36Send the people away so that
they can go to the surrounding countryside and villages and buy themselves
something to eat."
37But he answered, "You give them
something to eat."

They said to him, "That would take
more than half a year's wages[c]! Are we
to go and spend that much on bread and
give it to them to eat?"
38"How many loaves do you have?" he
asked. "Go and see."

When they found out, they said,
"Five—and two fish."
39Then Jesus directed them to have
all the people sit down in groups on the
green grass. 40So they sat down in groups
of hundreds and fifties. 41Taking the five
loaves and the two fish and looking up
to heaven, he gave thanks and broke the
loaves. Then he gave them to his disciples to distribute to the people. He also
divided the two fish among them all.
42They all ate and were satisfied, 43and
the disciples picked up twelve basketfuls
of broken pieces of bread and fish. 44The
number of the men who had eaten was
five thousand.
45Immediately Jesus made his disciples get into the boat and go on ahead of
him to Bethsaida, while he dismissed the
crowd. 46After leaving them, he went up
on a mountainside to pray.
47Later that night, the boat was in the
middle of the lake, and he was alone on
land. 48He saw the disciples straining at
the oars, because the wind was against
them. Shortly before dawn he went out to
them, walking on the lake. He was about
to pass by them, 49but when they saw him
walking on the lake, they thought he was
a ghost. They cried out, 50because they
all saw him and were terrified.

[a] 20 Some early manuscripts *he did many things*
[b] 22 Some early manuscripts *When his daughter*
[c] 37 Greek *take two hundred denarii*

Immediately he spoke to them and
said, "Take courage! It is I. Don't be
afraid." 51 Then he climbed into the boat
with them, and the wind died down.
They were completely amazed, 52 for they
had not understood about the loaves;
their hearts were hardened.

53 When they had crossed over, they
landed at Gennesaret and anchored
there. 54 As soon as they got out of the
boat, people recognized Jesus. 55 They
ran throughout that whole region and
carried the sick on mats to wherever
they heard he was. 56 And wherever he
went—into villages, towns or countryside—they placed the sick in the marketplaces. They begged him to let them
touch even the edge of his cloak, and all
who touched it were healed.

7 The Pharisees and some of the teachers of the law who had come from
Jerusalem gathered around Jesus 2 and
saw some of his disciples eating food
with hands that were defiled, that is, un-
washed. 3 (The Pharisees and all the Jews
do not eat unless they give their hands a
ceremonial washing, holding to the tradition of the elders. 4 When they come
from the marketplace they do not eat unless they wash. And they observe many
other traditions, such as the washing of
cups, pitchers and kettles.[a])

5 So the Pharisees and teachers of the
law asked Jesus, "Why don't your disciples live according to the tradition of the
elders instead of eating their food with
defiled hands?"

6 He replied, "Isaiah was right when he
prophesied about you hypocrites; as it is
written:

" 'These people honor me with their
lips,
but their hearts are far from me.
7 They worship me in vain;
their teachings are merely human
rules.'[b]

8 You have let go of the commands of
God and are holding on to human traditions."

9 And he continued, "You have a fine
way of setting aside the commands of
God in order to observe[c] your own traditions! 10 For Moses said, 'Honor your
father and mother,'[d] and, 'Anyone who
curses their father or mother is to be put
to death.'[e] 11 But you say that if anyone
declares that what might have been used
to help their father or mother is Corban
(that is, devoted to God)— 12 then you
no longer let them do anything for their
father or mother. 13 Thus you nullify the
word of God by your tradition that you
have handed down. And you do many
things like that."

14 Again Jesus called the crowd to him
and said, "Listen to me, everyone, and
understand this. 15 Nothing outside a
person can defile them by going into
them. Rather, it is what comes out of a
person that defiles them." [16][f]

17 After he had left the crowd and entered the house, his disciples asked him
about this parable. 18 "Are you so dull?"
he asked. "Don't you see that nothing
that enters a person from the outside can
defile them? 19 For it doesn't go into their
heart but into their stomach, and then
out of the body." (In saying this, Jesus
declared all foods clean.)

20 He went on: "What comes out of a
person is what defiles them. 21 For it is
from within, out of a person's heart, that
evil thoughts come—sexual immorality,
theft, murder, 22 adultery, greed, malice,
deceit, lewdness, envy, slander, arrogance and folly. 23 All these evils come
from inside and defile a person."

24 Jesus left that place and went to the
vicinity of Tyre.[g] He entered a house
and did not want anyone to know it; yet
he could not keep his presence secret.
25 In fact, as soon as she heard about
him, a woman whose little daughter
was possessed by an impure spirit came
and fell at his feet. 26 The woman was a
Greek, born in Syrian Phoenicia. She
begged Jesus to drive the demon out of
her daughter.

27 "First let the children eat all they
want," he told her, "for it is not right to
take the children's bread and toss it to
the dogs."

28 "Lord," she replied, "even the dogs under the table eat the children's crumbs."

29 Then he told her, "For such a reply,
you may go; the demon has left your
daughter."

[a] *4* Some early manuscripts *pitchers, kettles and dining couches* [b] *6,7* Isaiah 29:13 [c] *9* Some manuscripts *set up* [d] *10* Exodus 20:12; Deut. 5:16 [e] *10* Exodus 21:17; Lev. 20:9 [f] *16* Some manuscripts include here the words of 4:23. [g] *24* Many early manuscripts *Tyre and Sidon*

30She went home and found her child
lying on the bed, and the demon gone.
31Then Jesus left the vicinity of Tyre
and went through Sidon, down to the Sea
of Galilee and into the region of the Decapolis.[a] 32There some people brought to
him a man who was deaf and could hardly talk, and they begged Jesus to place his
hand on him.
33After he took him aside, away from
the crowd, Jesus put his fingers into the
man's ears. Then he spit and touched the
man's tongue. 34He looked up to heaven
and with a deep sigh said to him, *"Eph-
phatha!"* (which means "Be opened!").
35At this, the man's ears were opened,
his tongue was loosened and he began to
speak plainly.
36Jesus commanded them not to tell
anyone. But the more he did so, the more
they kept talking about it. 37People were
overwhelmed with amazement. "He has
done everything well," they said. "He
even makes the deaf hear and the mute
speak."

8 During those days another large
crowd gathered. Since they had nothing to eat, Jesus called his disciples to
him and said, 2"I have compassion for
these people; they have already been
with me three days and have nothing to
eat. 3If I send them home hungry, they
will collapse on the way, because some
of them have come a long distance."
4His disciples answered, "But where in
this remote place can anyone get enough
bread to feed them?"
5"How many loaves do you have?"
Jesus asked.
"Seven," they replied.
6He told the crowd to sit down on the
ground. When he had taken the seven
loaves and given thanks, he broke them
and gave them to his disciples to distribute to the people, and they did so.
7They had a few small fish as well; he
gave thanks for them also and told the
disciples to distribute them. 8The people ate and were satisfied. Afterward the
disciples picked up seven basketfuls of
broken pieces that were left over. 9About
four thousand were present. After he had
sent them away, 10he got into the boat
with his disciples and went to the region
of Dalmanutha.
11The Pharisees came and began to
question Jesus. To test him, they asked
him for a sign from heaven. 12He sighed
deeply and said, "Why does this generation ask for a sign? Truly I tell you, no sign
will be given to it." 13Then he left them,
got back into the boat and crossed to the
other side.
14The disciples had forgotten to bring
bread, except for one loaf they had with
them in the boat. 15"Be careful," Jesus
warned them. "Watch out for the yeast of
the Pharisees and that of Herod."
16They discussed this with one another and said, "It is because we have no
bread."
17Aware of their discussion, Jesus
asked them: "Why are you talking about
having no bread? Do you still not see or
understand? Are your hearts hardened?
18Do you have eyes but fail to see, and
ears but fail to hear? And don't you remember? 19When I broke the five loaves
for the five thousand, how many basketfuls of pieces did you pick up?"
"Twelve," they replied.
20"And when I broke the seven loaves
for the four thousand, how many basketfuls of pieces did you pick up?"
They answered, "Seven."
21He said to them, "Do you still not understand?"
22They came to Bethsaida, and some
people brought a blind man and begged
Jesus to touch him. 23He took the blind
man by the hand and led him outside the
village. When he had spit on the man's
eyes and put his hands on him, Jesus
asked, "Do you see anything?"
24He looked up and said, "I see people;
they look like trees walking around."
25Once more Jesus put his hands on the
man's eyes. Then his eyes were opened,
his sight was restored, and he saw everything clearly. 26Jesus sent him home,
saying, "Don't even go into[b] the village."
27Jesus and his disciples went on to the
villages around Caesarea Philippi. On
the way he asked them, "Who do people
say I am?"
28They replied, "Some say John the
Baptist; others say Elijah; and still others, one of the prophets."
29"But what about you?" he asked.
"Who do you say I am?"

[a] *31* That is, the Ten Cities [b] *26* Some manuscripts *go and tell anyone in*

Peter answered, "You are the Messiah."
30 Jesus warned them not to tell anyone
about him.

31 He then began to teach them that the
Son of Man must suffer many things and
be rejected by the elders, the chief priests
and the teachers of the law, and that he
must be killed and after three days rise
again. 32 He spoke plainly about this,
and Peter took him aside and began to
rebuke him.
33 But when Jesus turned and looked
at his disciples, he rebuked Peter. "Get
behind me, Satan!" he said. "You do not
have in mind the concerns of God, but
merely human concerns."
34 Then he called the crowd to him
along with his disciples and said: "Whoever wants to be my disciple must deny
themselves and take up their cross and
follow me. 35 For whoever wants to save
their life[a] will lose it, but whoever loses their life for me and for the gospel
will save it. 36 What good is it for someone to gain the whole world, yet forfeit
their soul? 37 Or what can anyone give
in exchange for their soul? 38 If anyone
is ashamed of me and my words in this
adulterous and sinful generation, the
Son of Man will be ashamed of them
when he comes in his Father's glory with
the holy angels."
9 And he said to them, "Truly I tell you,
some who are standing here will not
taste death before they see that the kingdom of God has come with power."
2 After six days Jesus took Peter, James
and John with him and led them up a
high mountain, where they were all
alone. There he was transfigured before them. 3 His clothes became dazzling
white, whiter than anyone in the world
could bleach them. 4 And there appeared
before them Elijah and Moses, who were
talking with Jesus.
5 Peter said to Jesus, "Rabbi, it is good
for us to be here. Let us put up three shelters — one for you, one for Moses and one
for Elijah." 6 (He did not know what to say,
they were so frightened.)
7 Then a cloud appeared and covered
them, and a voice came from the cloud:
"This is my Son, whom I love. Listen to
him!"
8 Suddenly, when they looked around,
they no longer saw anyone with them except Jesus.
9 As they were coming down the mountain, Jesus gave them orders not to tell
anyone what they had seen until the Son
of Man had risen from the dead. 10 They
kept the matter to themselves, discuss-
ing what "rising from the dead" meant.
11 And they asked him, "Why do the
teachers of the law say that Elijah must
come first?"
12 Jesus replied, "To be sure, Elijah
does come first, and restores all things.
Why then is it written that the Son of Man
must suffer much and be rejected? 13 But
I tell you, Elijah has come, and they have
done to him everything they wished, just
as it is written about him."
14 When they came to the other disciples, they saw a large crowd around them
and the teachers of the law arguing with
them. 15 As soon as all the people saw
Jesus, they were overwhelmed with wonder and ran to greet him.
16 "What are you arguing with them
about?" he asked.
17 A man in the crowd answered,
"Teacher, I brought you my son, who is
possessed by a spirit that has robbed
him of speech. 18 Whenever it seizes him,
it throws him to the ground. He foams at
the mouth, gnashes his teeth and becomes rigid. I asked your disciples to
drive out the spirit, but they could not."
19 "You unbelieving generation," Jesus
replied, "how long shall I stay with you?
How long shall I put up with you? Bring
the boy to me."
20 So they brought him. When the
spirit saw Jesus, it immediately threw
the boy into a convulsion. He fell to the
ground and rolled around, foaming at
the mouth.
21 Jesus asked the boy's father, "How
long has he been like this?"
"From childhood," he answered. 22 "It
has often thrown him into fire or water to
kill him. But if you can do anything, take
pity on us and help us."
23 "'If you can'?" said Jesus. "Everything is possible for one who believes."
24 Immediately the boy's father exclaimed, "I do believe; help me overcome
my unbelief!"

[a] 35 The Greek word means either *life* or *soul*; also in verses 36 and 37.

25When Jesus saw that a crowd was
running to the scene, he rebuked the
impure spirit. "You deaf and mute spirit," he said, "I command you, come out of
him and never enter him again."

26The spirit shrieked, convulsed him
violently and came out. The boy looked
so much like a corpse that many said,
"He's dead." 27But Jesus took him by the
hand and lifted him to his feet, and he
stood up.

28After Jesus had gone indoors, his disciples asked him privately, "Why couldn't
we drive it out?"

29He replied, "This kind can come out
only by prayer.[a]"

30They left that place and passed
through Galilee. Jesus did not want
anyone to know where they were, 31be-
cause he was teaching his disciples. He
said to them, "The Son of Man is going
to be delivered into the hands of men.
They will kill him, and after three days
he will rise." 32But they did not understand what he meant and were afraid to
ask him about it.

33They came to Capernaum. When he
was in the house, he asked them, "What
were you arguing about on the road?"
34But they kept quiet because on the
way they had argued about who was the
greatest.

35Sitting down, Jesus called the Twelve
and said, "Anyone who wants to be first
must be the very last, and the servant of
all."

36He took a little child whom he placed
among them. Taking the child in his
arms, he said to them, 37"Whoever welcomes one of these little children in my
name welcomes me; and whoever welcomes me does not welcome me but the
one who sent me."

38"Teacher," said John, "we saw someone driving out demons in your name
and we told him to stop, because he was
not one of us."

39"Do not stop him," Jesus said. "For
no one who does a miracle in my name
can in the next moment say anything
bad about me, 40for whoever is not
against us is for us. 41Truly I tell you,
anyone who gives you a cup of water
in my name because you belong to the
Messiah will certainly not lose their reward.

42"If anyone causes one of these little ones — those who believe in me — to
stumble, it would be better for them if a
large millstone were hung around their
neck and they were thrown into the sea.
43If your hand causes you to stumble,
cut it off. It is better for you to enter life
maimed than with two hands to go into
hell, where the fire never goes out. [44][b]
45And if your foot causes you to stumble,
cut it off. It is better for you to enter life
crippled than to have two feet and be
thrown into hell. [46][b] 47And if your eye
causes you to stumble, pluck it out. It is
better for you to enter the kingdom of
God with one eye than to have two eyes
and be thrown into hell, 48where

"'the worms that eat them do not die,
and the fire is not quenched.'[c]

49Everyone will be salted with fire.

50"Salt is good, but if it loses its saltiness, how can you make it salty again?
Have salt among yourselves, and be at
peace with each other."

10 Jesus then left that place and went
into the region of Judea and across
the Jordan. Again crowds of people came
to him, and as was his custom, he taught
them.

2Some Pharisees came and tested him
by asking, "Is it lawful for a man to divorce his wife?"

3"What did Moses command you?" he
replied.

4They said, "Moses permitted a man
to write a certificate of divorce and send
her away."

5"It was because your hearts were hard
that Moses wrote you this law," Jesus replied. 6"But at the beginning of creation
God 'made them male and female.'[d]
7'For this reason a man will leave his
father and mother and be united to his
wife,[e] 8and the two will become one
flesh.'[f] So they are no longer two, but one
flesh. 9Therefore what God has joined together, let no one separate."

10When they were in the house again,
the disciples asked Jesus about this. 11He
answered, "Anyone who divorces his
wife and marries another woman com-

[a] *29* Some manuscripts *prayer and fasting* [b] *44,46* Some manuscripts include here the words of verse 48.
[c] *48* Isaiah 66:24 [d] *6* Gen. 1:27 [e] *7* Some early manuscripts do not have *and be united to his wife.*
[f] *8* Gen. 2:24

mits adultery against her. 12And if she divorces her husband and marries another
man, she commits adultery."
13People were bringing little children
to Jesus for him to place his hands on
them, but the disciples rebuked them.
14When Jesus saw this, he was indignant.
He said to them, "Let the little children
come to me, and do not hinder them,
for the kingdom of God belongs to such
as these. 15Truly I tell you, anyone who
will not receive the kingdom of God like
a little child will never enter it." 16And he
took the children in his arms, placed his
hands on them and blessed them.
17As Jesus started on his way, a man
ran up to him and fell on his knees before
him. "Good teacher," he asked, "what
must I do to inherit eternal life?"
18"Why do you call me good?" Jesus
answered. "No one is good—except God
alone. 19You know the commandments:
'You shall not murder, you shall not commit adultery, you shall not steal, you shall
not give false testimony, you shall not defraud, honor your father and mother.'[a]"
20"Teacher," he declared, "all these I
have kept since I was a boy."
21Jesus looked at him and loved him.
"One thing you lack," he said. "Go, sell
everything you have and give to the poor,
and you will have treasure in heaven.
Then come, follow me."
22At this the man's face fell. He went
away sad, because he had great wealth.
23Jesus looked around and said to his
disciples, "How hard it is for the rich to
enter the kingdom of God!"
24The disciples were amazed at his
words. But Jesus said again, "Children, how hard it is[b] to enter the kingdom of God! 25It is easier for a camel to
go through the eye of a needle than for
someone who is rich to enter the kingdom of God."
26The disciples were even more
amazed, and said to each other, "Who
then can be saved?"
27Jesus looked at them and said, "With
man this is impossible, but not with God;
all things are possible with God."
28Then Peter spoke up, "We have left
everything to follow you!"
29"Truly I tell you," Jesus replied, "no
one who has left home or brothers or sisters or mother or father or children or
fields for me and the gospel 30will fail to
receive a hundred times as much in this
present age: homes, brothers, sisters,
mothers, children and fields—along
with persecutions—and in the age to
come eternal life. 31But many who are
first will be last, and the last first."
32They were on their way up to Jerusalem, with Jesus leading the way, and the
disciples were astonished, while those
who followed were afraid. Again he took
the Twelve aside and told them what was
going to happen to him. 33"We are going up to Jerusalem," he said, "and the
Son of Man will be delivered over to the
chief priests and the teachers of the law.
They will condemn him to death and will
hand him over to the Gentiles, 34who will
mock him and spit on him, flog him and
kill him. Three days later he will rise."
35Then James and John, the sons of
Zebedee, came to him. "Teacher," they
said, "we want you to do for us whatever we ask."
36"What do you want me to do for you?"
he asked.
37They replied, "Let one of us sit at
your right and the other at your left in
your glory."
38"You don't know what you are asking," Jesus said. "Can you drink the cup
I drink or be baptized with the baptism I
am baptized with?"
39"We can," they answered.
Jesus said to them, "You will drink the
cup I drink and be baptized with the
baptism I am baptized with, 40but to sit
at my right or left is not for me to grant.
These places belong to those for whom
they have been prepared."
41When the ten heard about this, they
became indignant with James and John.
42Jesus called them together and said,
"You know that those who are regarded
as rulers of the Gentiles lord it over them,
and their high officials exercise authority over them. 43Not so with you. Instead,
whoever wants to become great among
you must be your servant, 44and whoever wants to be first must be slave of all.
45For even the Son of Man did not come
to be served, but to serve, and to give his
life as a ransom for many."
46Then they came to Jericho. As Jesus

[a] *19* Exodus 20:12-16; Deut. 5:16-20 [b] *24* Some manuscripts *is for those who trust in riches*

and his disciples, together with a large
crowd, were leaving the city, a blind man,
Bartimaeus (which means "son of Ti-
maeus"), was sitting by the roadside begging. 47 When he heard that it was Jesus of
Nazareth, he began to shout, "Jesus, Son
of David, have mercy on me!"
48 Many rebuked him and told him to
be quiet, but he shouted all the more,
"Son of David, have mercy on me!"
49 Jesus stopped and said, "Call him."
So they called to the blind man, "Cheer
up! On your feet! He's calling you."
50 Throwing his cloak aside, he jumped
to his feet and came to Jesus.
51 "What do you want me to do for you?"
Jesus asked him.
The blind man said, "Rabbi, I want to
see."
52 "Go," said Jesus, "your faith has
healed you." Immediately he received his
sight and followed Jesus along the road.

11 As they approached Jerusalem and
came to Bethphage and Bethany at
the Mount of Olives, Jesus sent two of his
disciples, 2 saying to them, "Go to the village ahead of you, and just as you enter it,
you will find a colt tied there, which no
one has ever ridden. Untie it and bring it
here. 3 If anyone asks you, 'Why are you
doing this?' say, 'The Lord needs it and
will send it back here shortly.'"
4 They went and found a colt outside
in the street, tied at a doorway. As they
untied it, 5 some people standing there
asked, "What are you doing, untying
that colt?" 6 They answered as Jesus had
told them to, and the people let them go.
7 When they brought the colt to Jesus and
threw their cloaks over it, he sat on it.
8 Many people spread their cloaks on the
road, while others spread branches they
had cut in the fields. 9 Those who went
ahead and those who followed shouted,

"Hosanna![a]"

"Blessed is he who comes in the name
of the Lord!"[b]

10 "Blessed is the coming kingdom of
our father David!"

"Hosanna in the highest heaven!"

11 Jesus entered Jerusalem and went
into the temple courts. He looked around
at everything, but since it was already
late, he went out to Bethany with the
Twelve.
12 The next day as they were leaving
Bethany, Jesus was hungry. 13 Seeing in
the distance a fig tree in leaf, he went
to find out if it had any fruit. When he
reached it, he found nothing but leaves,
because it was not the season for figs.
14 Then he said to the tree, "May no one
ever eat fruit from you again." And his
disciples heard him say it.
15 On reaching Jerusalem, Jesus entered the temple courts and began
driving out those who were buying and
selling there. He overturned the tables
of the money changers and the benches of those selling doves, 16 and would
not allow anyone to carry merchandise
through the temple courts. 17 And as he
taught them, he said, "Is it not written:
'My house will be called a house of prayer
for all nations'[c]? But you have made it 'a
den of robbers.'[d]"
18 The chief priests and the teachers
of the law heard this and began looking
for a way to kill him, for they feared him,
because the whole crowd was amazed at
his teaching.
19 When evening came, Jesus and his
disciples[e] went out of the city.
20 In the morning, as they went along,
they saw the fig tree withered from the
roots. 21 Peter remembered and said
to Jesus, "Rabbi, look! The fig tree you
cursed has withered!"
22 "Have faith in God," Jesus answered.
23 "Truly[f] I tell you, if anyone says to this
mountain, 'Go, throw yourself into the
sea,' and does not doubt in their heart but
believes that what they say will happen,
it will be done for them. 24 Therefore I tell
you, whatever you ask for in prayer, believe that you have received it, and it will
be yours. 25 And when you stand praying,
if you hold anything against anyone, forgive them, so that your Father in heaven
may forgive you your sins." [26][g]
27 They arrived again in Jerusalem,
and while Jesus was walking in the temple courts, the chief priests, the teachers

[a] 9 A Hebrew expression meaning "Save!" which became an exclamation of praise; also in verse 10
[b] 9 Psalm 118:25,26 [c] *17* Isaiah 56:7 [d] *17* Jer. 7:11 [e] *19* Some early manuscripts *came, Jesus*
[f] *22,23* Some early manuscripts *"If you have faith in God," Jesus answered, 23"truly* [g] *26* Some manuscripts include here words similar to Matt. 6:15.

of the law and the elders came to him.
28 "By what authority are you doing these
things?" they asked. "And who gave you
authority to do this?"
29 Jesus replied, "I will ask you one
question. Answer me, and I will tell
you by what authority I am doing these
things. 30 John's baptism—was it from
heaven, or of human origin? Tell me!"
31 They discussed it among themselves and said, "If we say, 'From heav-
en,' he will ask, 'Then why didn't you
believe him?' 32 But if we say, 'Of human
origin' . . ." (They feared the people, for
everyone held that John really was a
prophet.)
33 So they answered Jesus, "We don't
know."
Jesus said, "Neither will I tell you by
what authority I am doing these things."

12 Jesus then began to speak to them
in parables: "A man planted a vineyard. He put a wall around it, dug a pit
for the winepress and built a watchtower. Then he rented the vineyard to some
farmers and moved to another place.
2 At harvest time he sent a servant to the
tenants to collect from them some of the
fruit of the vineyard. 3 But they seized
him, beat him and sent him away empty-handed. 4 Then he sent another servant to them; they struck this man on
the head and treated him shamefully.
5 He sent still another, and that one they
killed. He sent many others; some of
them they beat, others they killed.
6 "He had one left to send, a son, whom
he loved. He sent him last of all, saying,
'They will respect my son.'
7 "But the tenants said to one another,
'This is the heir. Come, let's kill him, and
the inheritance will be ours.' 8 So they
took him and killed him, and threw him
out of the vineyard.
9 "What then will the owner of the
vineyard do? He will come and kill those
tenants and give the vineyard to others.
10 Haven't you read this passage of Scripture:

" 'The stone the builders rejected
has become the cornerstone;
11 the Lord has done this,
and it is marvelous in our eyes'[a]?"

12 Then the chief priests, the teachers
of the law and the elders looked for a way
to arrest him because they knew he had
spoken the parable against them. But
they were afraid of the crowd; so they left
him and went away.
13 Later they sent some of the Pharisees
and Herodians to Jesus to catch him in
his words. 14 They came to him and said,
"Teacher, we know that you are a man
of integrity. You aren't swayed by others, because you pay no attention to who
they are; but you teach the way of God in
accordance with the truth. Is it right to
pay the imperial tax[b] to Caesar or not?
15 Should we pay or shouldn't we?"
But Jesus knew their hypocrisy. "Why
are you trying to trap me?" he asked.
"Bring me a denarius and let me look
at it." 16 They brought the coin, and he
asked them, "Whose image is this? And
whose inscription?"
"Caesar's," they replied.
17 Then Jesus said to them, "Give back
to Caesar what is Caesar's and to God
what is God's."
And they were amazed at him.
18 Then the Sadducees, who say there
is no resurrection, came to him with a
question. 19 "Teacher," they said, "Moses wrote for us that if a man's brother
dies and leaves a wife but no children,
the man must marry the widow and
raise up offspring for his brother. 20 Now
there were seven brothers. The first one
married and died without leaving any
children. 21 The second one married the
widow, but he also died, leaving no child.
It was the same with the third. 22 In fact,
none of the seven left any children. Last
of all, the woman died too. 23 At the resurrection[c] whose wife will she be, since
the seven were married to her?"
24 Jesus replied, "Are you not in error
because you do not know the Scriptures
or the power of God? 25 When the dead
rise, they will neither marry nor be giv-
en in marriage; they will be like the angels in heaven. 26 Now about the dead
rising—have you not read in the Book
of Moses, in the account of the burning
bush, how God said to him, 'I am the
God of Abraham, the God of Isaac, and
the God of Jacob'[d]? 27 He is not the God of
the dead, but of the living. You are badly
mistaken!"

[a] *11* Psalm 118:22,23 [b] *14* A special tax levied on subject peoples, not on Roman citizens [c] *23* Some manuscripts *resurrection, when people rise from the dead,* [d] *26* Exodus 3:6

28 One of the teachers of the law came
and heard them debating. Noticing that
Jesus had given them a good answer, he
asked him, "Of all the commandments,
which is the most important?"
29 "The most important one," answered
Jesus, "is this: 'Hear, O Israel: The Lord
our God, the Lord is one.[a] 30 Love the
Lord your God with all your heart and
with all your soul and with all your mind
and with all your strength.'[b] 31 The second is this: 'Love your neighbor as yourself.'[c] There is no commandment greater
than these."
32 "Well said, teacher," the man replied.
"You are right in saying that God is one
and there is no other but him. 33 To love
him with all your heart, with all your understanding and with all your strength,
and to love your neighbor as yourself is
more important than all burnt offerings
and sacrifices."
34 When Jesus saw that he had answered wisely, he said to him, "You are
not far from the kingdom of God." And
from then on no one dared ask him any
more questions.
35 While Jesus was teaching in the temple courts, he asked, "Why do the teachers of the law say that the Messiah is the
son of David? 36 David himself, speaking
by the Holy Spirit, declared:

"'The Lord said to my Lord:
"Sit at my right hand
until I put your enemies
under your feet."'[d]

37 David himself calls him 'Lord.' How
then can he be his son?"
The large crowd listened to him with
delight.
38 As he taught, Jesus said, "Watch out
for the teachers of the law. They like to
walk around in flowing robes and be
greeted with respect in the marketplaces, 39 and have the most important seats
in the synagogues and the places of hon-
or at banquets. 40 They devour widows'
houses and for a show make lengthy
prayers. These men will be punished
most severely."
41 Jesus sat down opposite the place
where the offerings were put and
watched the crowd putting their money
into the temple treasury. Many rich people threw in large amounts. 42 But a poor
widow came and put in two very small
copper coins, worth only a few cents.
43 Calling his disciples to him, Jesus
said, "Truly I tell you, this poor widow
has put more into the treasury than all
the others. 44 They all gave out of their
wealth; but she, out of her poverty, put in
everything—all she had to live on."

13 As Jesus was leaving the temple, one
of his disciples said to him, "Look,
Teacher! What massive stones! What
magnificent buildings!"
2 "Do you see all these great buildings?" replied Jesus. "Not one stone here
will be left on another; every one will be
thrown down."
3 As Jesus was sitting on the Mount of
Olives opposite the temple, Peter, James,
John and Andrew asked him privately,
4 "Tell us, when will these things happen?
And what will be the sign that they are all
about to be fulfilled?"
5 Jesus said to them: "Watch out that no
one deceives you. 6 Many will come in my
name, claiming, 'I am he,' and will deceive many. 7 When you hear of wars and
rumors of wars, do not be alarmed. Such
things must happen, but the end is still
to come. 8 Nation will rise against nation,
and kingdom against kingdom. There
will be earthquakes in various places,
and famines. These are the beginning of
birth pains.
9 "You must be on your guard. You will
be handed over to the local councils and
flogged in the synagogues. On account of
me you will stand before governors and
kings as witnesses to them. 10 And the
gospel must first be preached to all nations. 11 Whenever you are arrested and
brought to trial, do not worry beforehand about what to say. Just say whatever is given you at the time, for it is not you
speaking, but the Holy Spirit.
12 "Brother will betray brother to death,
and a father his child. Children will rebel
against their parents and have them put
to death. 13 Everyone will hate you because of me, but the one who stands firm
to the end will be saved.
14 "When you see 'the abomination
that causes desolation'[e] standing where
it[f] does not belong—let the reader understand—then let those who are in

[a] *29* Or *The Lord our God is one Lord* [b] *30* Deut. 6:4,5 [c] *31* Lev. 19:18 [d] *36* Psalm 110:1 [e] *14* Daniel 9:27; 11:31; 12:11 [f] *14* Or *he*

Judea flee to the mountains. [15]Let no
one on the housetop go down or enter
the house to take anything out. [16]Let no
one in the field go back to get their cloak.
[17]How dreadful it will be in those days
for pregnant women and nursing mothers! [18]Pray that this will not take place in
winter, [19]because those will be days of
distress unequaled from the beginning,
when God created the world, until now—
and never to be equaled again.

[20]"If the Lord had not cut short those
days, no one would survive. But for the
sake of the elect, whom he has chosen,
he has shortened them. [21]At that time
if anyone says to you, 'Look, here is the
Messiah!' or, 'Look, there he is!' do not
believe it. [22]For false messiahs and false
prophets will appear and perform signs
and wonders to deceive, if possible, even
the elect. [23]So be on your guard; I have
told you everything ahead of time.

[24]"But in those days, following that
distress,

" 'the sun will be darkened,
and the moon will not give its
light;
[25]the stars will fall from the sky,
and the heavenly bodies will be
shaken.'[a]

[26]"At that time people will see the
Son of Man coming in clouds with great
power and glory. [27]And he will send his
angels and gather his elect from the four
winds, from the ends of the earth to the
ends of the heavens.

[28]"Now learn this lesson from the
fig tree: As soon as its twigs get tender
and its leaves come out, you know that
summer is near. [29]Even so, when you
see these things happening, you know
that it[b] is near, right at the door. [30]Truly
I tell you, this generation will certainly not pass away until all these things
have happened. [31]Heaven and earth will
pass away, but my words will never pass
away.

[32]"But about that day or hour no one
knows, not even the angels in heaven,
nor the Son, but only the Father. [33]Be on
guard! Be alert[c]! You do not know when
that time will come. [34]It's like a man going away: He leaves his house and puts
his servants in charge, each with their
assigned task, and tells the one at the
door to keep watch.

[35]"Therefore keep watch because
you do not know when the owner of the
house will come back—whether in the
evening, or at midnight, or when the
rooster crows, or at dawn. [36]If he comes
suddenly, do not let him find you sleeping. [37]What I say to you, I say to everyone:
'Watch!' "

14 Now the Passover and the Festival
of Unleavened Bread were only two
days away, and the chief priests and the
teachers of the law were scheming to arrest Jesus secretly and kill him. [2]"But not
during the festival," they said, "or the
people may riot."

[3]While he was in Bethany, reclining at
the table in the home of Simon the Leper, a woman came with an alabaster jar
of very expensive perfume, made of pure
nard. She broke the jar and poured the
perfume on his head.

[4]Some of those present were saying
indignantly to one another, "Why this
waste of perfume? [5]It could have been
sold for more than a year's wages[d] and
the money given to the poor." And they
rebuked her harshly.

[6]"Leave her alone," said Jesus. "Why
are you bothering her? She has done a
beautiful thing to me. [7]The poor you will
always have with you,[e] and you can help
them any time you want. But you will not
always have me. [8]She did what she could.
She poured perfume on my body beforehand to prepare for my burial. [9]Truly I
tell you, wherever the gospel is preached
throughout the world, what she has done
will also be told, in memory of her."

[10]Then Judas Iscariot, one of the
Twelve, went to the chief priests to betray
Jesus to them. [11]They were delighted to
hear this and promised to give him money. So he watched for an opportunity to
hand him over.

[12]On the first day of the Festival of Unleavened Bread, when it was customary
to sacrifice the Passover lamb, Jesus' disciples asked him, "Where do you want us
to go and make preparations for you to
eat the Passover?"

[13]So he sent two of his disciples, telling them, "Go into the city, and a man

[a] *25* Isaiah 13:10; 34:4 [b] *29* Or *he* [c] *33* Some manuscripts *alert and pray* [d] *5* Greek *than three hundred denarii* [e] *7* See Deut. 15:11.

carrying a jar of water will meet you.
Follow him. 14 Say to the owner of the
house he enters, 'The Teacher asks:
Where is my guest room, where I may eat
the Passover with my disciples?' 15 He
will show you a large room upstairs,
furnished and ready. Make preparations
for us there."

16 The disciples left, went into the city
and found things just as Jesus had told
them. So they prepared the Passover.

17 When evening came, Jesus arrived
with the Twelve. 18 While they were reclining at the table eating, he said, "Truly
I tell you, one of you will betray me — one
who is eating with me."

19 They were saddened, and one by one
they said to him, "Surely you don't mean
me?"

20 "It is one of the Twelve," he replied,
"one who dips bread into the bowl with
me. 21 The Son of Man will go just as it is
written about him. But woe to that man
who betrays the Son of Man! It would be
better for him if he had not been born."

22 While they were eating, Jesus took
bread, and when he had given thanks,
he broke it and gave it to his disciples,
saying, "Take it; this is my body."

23 Then he took a cup, and when he had
given thanks, he gave it to them, and they
all drank from it.

24 "This is my blood of the[a] covenant,
which is poured out for many," he said to
them. 25 "Truly I tell you, I will not drink
again from the fruit of the vine until that
day when I drink it new in the kingdom
of God."

26 When they had sung a hymn, they
went out to the Mount of Olives.

27 "You will all fall away," Jesus told
them, "for it is written:

"'I will strike the shepherd,
and the sheep will be scattered.'[b]

28 But after I have risen, I will go ahead of
you into Galilee."

29 Peter declared, "Even if all fall away,
I will not."

30 "Truly I tell you," Jesus answered,
"today — yes, tonight — before the rooster crows twice[c] you yourself will disown
me three times."

31 But Peter insisted emphatically,
"Even if I have to die with you, I will never disown you." And all the others said
the same.

32 They went to a place called Gethsemane, and Jesus said to his disciples,
"Sit here while I pray." 33 He took Peter,
James and John along with him, and he
began to be deeply distressed and troubled. 34 "My soul is overwhelmed with
sorrow to the point of death," he said to
them. "Stay here and keep watch."

35 Going a little farther, he fell to the
ground and prayed that if possible the
hour might pass from him. 36 "*Abba*,[d] Father," he said, "everything is possible for
you. Take this cup from me. Yet not what
I will, but what you will."

37 Then he returned to his disciples and
found them sleeping. "Simon," he said to
Peter, "are you asleep? Couldn't you keep
watch for one hour? 38 Watch and pray so
that you will not fall into temptation. The
spirit is willing, but the flesh is weak."

39 Once more he went away and prayed
the same thing. 40 When he came back,
he again found them sleeping, because
their eyes were heavy. They did not know
what to say to him.

41 Returning the third time, he said to
them, "Are you still sleeping and resting?
Enough! The hour has come. Look, the
Son of Man is delivered into the hands
of sinners. 42 Rise! Let us go! Here comes
my betrayer!"

43 Just as he was speaking, Judas, one
of the Twelve, appeared. With him was
a crowd armed with swords and clubs,
sent from the chief priests, the teachers
of the law, and the elders.

44 Now the betrayer had arranged a
signal with them: "The one I kiss is the
man; arrest him and lead him away under guard." 45 Going at once to Jesus, Judas said, "Rabbi!" and kissed him. 46 The
men seized Jesus and arrested him.
47 Then one of those standing near drew
his sword and struck the servant of the
high priest, cutting off his ear.

48 "Am I leading a rebellion," said Jesus,
"that you have come out with swords and
clubs to capture me? 49 Every day I was
with you, teaching in the temple courts,
and you did not arrest me. But the Scriptures must be fulfilled." 50 Then everyone
deserted him and fled.

51 A young man, wearing nothing but

[a] 24 Some manuscripts *the new* [b] 27 Zech. 13:7 [c] 30 Some early manuscripts do not have *twice*.
[d] 36 Aramaic for *father*

a linen garment, was following Jesus. When they seized him, 52 he fled naked, leaving his garment behind.

53 They took Jesus to the high priest, and all the chief priests, the elders and the teachers of the law came together. 54 Peter followed him at a distance, right into the courtyard of the high priest. There he sat with the guards and warmed himself at the fire.

55 The chief priests and the whole Sanhedrin were looking for evidence against Jesus so that they could put him to death, but they did not find any. 56 Many testified falsely against him, but their statements did not agree.

57 Then some stood up and gave this false testimony against him: 58 "We heard him say, 'I will destroy this temple made with human hands and in three days will build another, not made with hands.' " 59 Yet even then their testimony did not agree.

60 Then the high priest stood up before them and asked Jesus, "Are you not going to answer? What is this testimony that these men are bringing against you?" 61 But Jesus remained silent and gave no answer.

Again the high priest asked him, "Are you the Messiah, the Son of the Blessed One?"

62 "I am," said Jesus. "And you will see the Son of Man sitting at the right hand of the Mighty One and coming on the clouds of heaven."

63 The high priest tore his clothes. "Why do we need any more witnesses?" he asked. 64 "You have heard the blasphemy. What do you think?"

They all condemned him as worthy of death. 65 Then some began to spit at him; they blindfolded him, struck him with their fists, and said, "Prophesy!" And the guards took him and beat him.

66 While Peter was below in the courtyard, one of the servant girls of the high priest came by. 67 When she saw Peter warming himself, she looked closely at him.

"You also were with that Nazarene, Jesus," she said.

68 But he denied it. "I don't know or understand what you're talking about," he said, and went out into the entryway.[a]

69 When the servant girl saw him there, she said again to those standing around, "This fellow is one of them." 70 Again he denied it.

After a little while, those standing near said to Peter, "Surely you are one of them, for you are a Galilean."

71 He began to call down curses, and he swore to them, "I don't know this man you're talking about."

72 Immediately the rooster crowed the second time.[b] Then Peter remembered the word Jesus had spoken to him: "Before the rooster crows twice[c] you will disown me three times." And he broke down and wept.

15 Very early in the morning, the chief priests, with the elders, the teachers of the law and the whole Sanhedrin, made their plans. So they bound Jesus, led him away and handed him over to Pilate.

2 "Are you the king of the Jews?" asked Pilate.

"You have said so," Jesus replied.

3 The chief priests accused him of many things. 4 So again Pilate asked him, "Aren't you going to answer? See how many things they are accusing you of."

5 But Jesus still made no reply, and Pilate was amazed.

6 Now it was the custom at the festival to release a prisoner whom the people requested. 7 A man called Barabbas was in prison with the insurrectionists who had committed murder in the uprising. 8 The crowd came up and asked Pilate to do for them what he usually did.

9 "Do you want me to release to you the king of the Jews?" asked Pilate, 10 knowing it was out of self-interest that the chief priests had handed Jesus over to him. 11 But the chief priests stirred up the crowd to have Pilate release Barabbas instead.

12 "What shall I do, then, with the one you call the king of the Jews?" Pilate asked them.

13 "Crucify him!" they shouted.

14 "Why? What crime has he committed?" asked Pilate.

But they shouted all the louder, "Crucify him!"

15 Wanting to satisfy the crowd, Pilate released Barabbas to them. He had Jesus

[a] 68 Some early manuscripts *entryway and the rooster crowed* [b] 72 Some early manuscripts do not have *the second time.* [c] 72 Some early manuscripts do not have *twice.*

flogged, and handed him over to be crucified.

16The soldiers led Jesus away into the palace (that is, the Praetorium) and called together the whole company of soldiers. 17They put a purple robe on him, then twisted together a crown of thorns and set it on him. 18And they began to call out to him, "Hail, king of the Jews!" 19Again and again they struck him on the head with a staff and spit on him. Falling on their knees, they paid homage to him. 20And when they had mocked him, they took off the purple robe and put his own clothes on him. Then they led him out to crucify him.

21A certain man from Cyrene, Simon, the father of Alexander and Rufus, was passing by on his way in from the country, and they forced him to carry the cross. 22They brought Jesus to the place called Golgotha (which means "the place of the skull"). 23Then they offered him wine mixed with myrrh, but he did not take it. 24And they crucified him. Dividing up his clothes, they cast lots to see what each would get.

25It was nine in the morning when they crucified him. 26The written notice of the charge against him read: THE KING OF THE JEWS.

27They crucified two rebels with him, one on his right and one on his left. [28][a] 29Those who passed by hurled insults at him, shaking their heads and saying, "So! You who are going to destroy the temple and build it in three days, 30come down from the cross and save yourself!" 31In the same way the chief priests and the teachers of the law mocked him among themselves. "He saved others," they said, "but he can't save himself! 32Let this Messiah, this king of Israel, come down now from the cross, that we may see and believe." Those crucified with him also heaped insults on him.

33At noon, darkness came over the whole land until three in the afternoon. 34And at three in the afternoon Jesus cried out in a loud voice, *"Eloi, Eloi, lema sabachthani?"* (which means "My God, my God, why have you forsaken me?").[b]

35When some of those standing near heard this, they said, "Listen, he's calling Elijah."

36Someone ran, filled a sponge with wine vinegar, put it on a staff, and offered it to Jesus to drink. "Now leave him alone. Let's see if Elijah comes to take him down," he said.

37With a loud cry, Jesus breathed his last.

38The curtain of the temple was torn in two from top to bottom. 39And when the centurion, who stood there in front of Jesus, saw how he died,[c] he said, "Surely this man was the Son of God!"

40Some women were watching from a distance. Among them were Mary Magdalene, Mary the mother of James the younger and of Joseph,[d] and Salome. 41In Galilee these women had followed him and cared for his needs. Many other women who had come up with him to Jerusalem were also there.

42It was Preparation Day (that is, the day before the Sabbath). So as evening approached, 43Joseph of Arimathea, a prominent member of the Council, who was himself waiting for the kingdom of God, went boldly to Pilate and asked for Jesus' body. 44Pilate was surprised to hear that he was already dead. Summoning the centurion, he asked him if Jesus had already died. 45When he learned from the centurion that it was so, he gave the body to Joseph. 46So Joseph bought some linen cloth, took down the body, wrapped it in the linen, and placed it in a tomb cut out of rock. Then he rolled a stone against the entrance of the tomb. 47Mary Magdalene and Mary the mother of Joseph saw where he was laid.

16 When the Sabbath was over, Mary Magdalene, Mary the mother of James, and Salome bought spices so that they might go to anoint Jesus' body. 2Very early on the first day of the week, just after sunrise, they were on their way to the tomb 3and they asked each other, "Who will roll the stone away from the entrance of the tomb?"

4But when they looked up, they saw that the stone, which was very large, had been rolled away. 5As they entered the tomb, they saw a young man dressed in a white robe sitting on the right side, and they were alarmed.

6"Don't be alarmed," he said. "You are looking for Jesus the Nazarene, who was

[a] *28* Some manuscripts include here words similar to Luke 22:37. [b] *34* Psalm 22:1 [c] *39* Some manuscripts *saw that he died with such a cry* [d] *40* Greek *Joses,* a variant of *Joseph;* also in verse 47

crucified. He has risen! He is not here.
See the place where they laid him. 7 But
go, tell his disciples and Peter, 'He is going ahead of you into Galilee. There you
will see him, just as he told you.' "
8 Trembling and bewildered, the wom-
en went out and fled from the tomb. They
said nothing to anyone, because they
were afraid.[a]

[The earliest manuscripts and some other ancient witnesses do not have verses 9–20.]

9 When Jesus rose early on the first day of the
week, he appeared first to Mary Magdalene, out
of whom he had driven seven demons. 10 She
went and told those who had been with him and
who were mourning and weeping. 11 When they
heard that Jesus was alive and that she had seen
him, they did not believe it.
12 Afterward Jesus appeared in a different
form to two of them while they were walking in
the country. 13 These returned and reported it to
the rest; but they did not believe them either.
14 Later Jesus appeared to the Eleven as they
were eating; he rebuked them for their lack of
faith and their stubborn refusal to believe those
who had seen him after he had risen.
15 He said to them, "Go into all the world and
preach the gospel to all creation. 16 Whoever be-
lieves and is baptized will be saved, but whoever
does not believe will be condemned. 17 And these
signs will accompany those who believe: In my
name they will drive out demons; they will speak
in new tongues; 18 they will pick up snakes with
their hands; and when they drink deadly poison,
it will not hurt them at all; they will place their
hands on sick people, and they will get well."
19 After the Lord Jesus had spoken to them, he
was taken up into heaven and he sat at the right
hand of God. 20 Then the disciples went out and
preached everywhere, and the Lord worked with
them and confirmed his word by the signs that
accompanied it.

[a] 8 Some manuscripts have the following ending between verses 8 and 9, and one manuscript has it after verse 8 (omitting verses 9-20): *Then they quickly reported all these instructions to those around Peter. After this, Jesus himself also sent out through them from east to west the sacred and imperishable proclamation of eternal salvation. Amen.*

LUKE

The books of Luke and Acts are two volumes of a single work (see p. 974 for a more detailed introduction to Acts). Together they tell the story of how God first invited the people of Israel, and then all nations, to follow Jesus. In the first volume, the movement is toward Jerusalem, the center of Jewish national life. In the second, the movement is from Jerusalem to other nations, closing with Paul proclaiming the kingdom of God in Rome, the capital of the empire.

Luke addresses his history to *most excellent Theophilus*, most likely a Roman official. His volumes are stocked with details from sources Luke had available: letters, speeches, songs, travel accounts, trial transcripts and biographical anecdotes. Luke's purpose is to show the fulfillment of God's plan to bring his light to the world through Israel. The earliest Jesus-followers take up this calling by announcing Jesus' victory over sin and death to all the nations.

The first volume, Luke's telling of the story of Jesus, has three main sections:

: First, Jesus ministers in Galilee, the northern area of the land of Israel.
: Next, he takes a long journey to Jerusalem, during which he welcomes people into the way of God's reign and challenges Israel's current understanding of the kingdom.
: Third, Luke tells how Jesus gives his life in Jerusalem and then rises from the dead to be revealed as Israel's King and the world's true Lord.

---

1 Many have undertaken to draw up an
account of the things that have been
fulfilled[a] among us, 2just as they were
handed down to us by those who from
the first were eyewitnesses and servants
of the word. 3With this in mind, since I
myself have carefully investigated everything from the beginning, I too decided
to write an orderly account for you, most
excellent Theophilus, 4so that you may
know the certainty of the things you have
been taught.

5In the time of Herod king of Judea
there was a priest named Zechariah,
who belonged to the priestly division of
Abijah; his wife Elizabeth was also a descendant of Aaron. 6Both of them were
righteous in the sight of God, observing
all the Lord's commands and decrees
blamelessly. 7But they were childless because Elizabeth was not able to conceive,
and they were both very old.

8Once when Zechariah's division was
on duty and he was serving as priest before God, 9he was chosen by lot, according to the custom of the priesthood, to go
into the temple of the Lord and burn incense. 10And when the time for the burning of incense came, all the assembled
worshipers were praying outside.

11Then an angel of the Lord appeared
to him, standing at the right side of the
altar of incense. 12When Zechariah saw
him, he was startled and was gripped
with fear. 13But the angel said to him:
"Do not be afraid, Zechariah; your prayer
has been heard. Your wife Elizabeth will
bear you a son, and you are to call him
John. 14He will be a joy and delight to
you, and many will rejoice because of his
birth, 15for he will be great in the sight
of the Lord. He is never to take wine or
other fermented drink, and he will be
filled with the Holy Spirit even before
he is born. 16He will bring back many
of the people of Israel to the Lord their
God. 17And he will go on before the Lord,
in the spirit and power of Elijah, to turn
the hearts of the parents to their children
and the disobedient to the wisdom of the
righteous — to make ready a people prepared for the Lord."

18Zechariah asked the angel, "How can
I be sure of this? I am an old man and my
wife is well along in years."

19The angel said to him, "I am Gabriel.
I stand in the presence of God, and I have
been sent to speak to you and to tell you
this good news. 20And now you will be
silent and not able to speak until the day
this happens, because you did not believe

[a] *1* Or *been surely believed*

my words, which will come true at their
appointed time."
21 Meanwhile, the people were waiting for Zechariah and wondering why
he stayed so long in the temple. 22 When
he came out, he could not speak to them.
They realized he had seen a vision in the
temple, for he kept making signs to them
but remained unable to speak.
23 When his time of service was completed, he returned home. 24 After this
his wife Elizabeth became pregnant and
for five months remained in seclusion.
25 "The Lord has done this for me," she
said. "In these days he has shown his favor and taken away my disgrace among
the people."
26 In the sixth month of Elizabeth's
pregnancy, God sent the angel Gabriel to
Nazareth, a town in Galilee, 27 to a virgin
pledged to be married to a man named
Joseph, a descendant of David. The virgin's name was Mary. 28 The angel went
to her and said, "Greetings, you who are
highly favored! The Lord is with you."
29 Mary was greatly troubled at his
words and wondered what kind of greeting this might be. 30 But the angel said to
her, "Do not be afraid, Mary; you have
found favor with God. 31 You will conceive and give birth to a son, and you are
to call him Jesus. 32 He will be great and
will be called the Son of the Most High.
The Lord God will give him the throne of
his father David, 33 and he will reign over
Jacob's descendants forever; his kingdom
will never end."
34 "How will this be," Mary asked the
angel, "since I am a virgin?"
35 The angel answered, "The Holy Spirit will come on you, and the power of the
Most High will overshadow you. So the
holy one to be born will be called[a] the
Son of God. 36 Even Elizabeth your relative is going to have a child in her old age,
and she who was said to be unable to conceive is in her sixth month. 37 For no word
from God will ever fail."
38 "I am the Lord's servant," Mary answered. "May your word to me be fulfilled." Then the angel left her.
39 At that time Mary got ready and hurried to a town in the hill country of Judea,
40 where she entered Zechariah's home
and greeted Elizabeth. 41 When Elizabeth
heard Mary's greeting, the baby leaped in
her womb, and Elizabeth was filled with
the Holy Spirit. 42 In a loud voice she exclaimed: "Blessed are you among wom-
en, and blessed is the child you will bear!
43 But why am I so favored, that the mother
of my Lord should come to me? 44 As soon
as the sound of your greeting reached my
ears, the baby in my womb leaped for joy.
45 Blessed is she who has believed that the
Lord would fulfill his promises to her!"
46 And Mary said:

"My soul glorifies the Lord
47 and my spirit rejoices in God my
Savior,
48 for he has been mindful
of the humble state of his servant.
From now on all generations will call
me blessed,
49 for the Mighty One has done great
things for me —
holy is his name.
50 His mercy extends to those who fear
him,
from generation to generation.
51 He has performed mighty deeds with
his arm;
he has scattered those who are
proud in their inmost thoughts.
52 He has brought down rulers from their
thrones
but has lifted up the humble.
53 He has filled the hungry with good
things
but has sent the rich away empty.
54 He has helped his servant Israel,
remembering to be merciful
55 to Abraham and his descendants
forever,
just as he promised our ancestors."

56 Mary stayed with Elizabeth for about
three months and then returned home.
57 When it was time for Elizabeth to
have her baby, she gave birth to a son.
58 Her neighbors and relatives heard that
the Lord had shown her great mercy, and
they shared her joy.
59 On the eighth day they came to circumcise the child, and they were going
to name him after his father Zechariah,
60 but his mother spoke up and said, "No!
He is to be called John."
61 They said to her, "There is no one
among your relatives who has that name."

[a] 35 Or *So the child to be born will be called holy,*

62 Then they made signs to his father,
to find out what he would like to name
the child. 63 He asked for a writing tablet, and to everyone's astonishment he
wrote, "His name is John." 64 Immediately his mouth was opened and his tongue
set free, and he began to speak, praising
God. 65 All the neighbors were filled with
awe, and throughout the hill country of
Judea people were talking about all these
things. 66 Everyone who heard this wondered about it, asking, "What then is this
child going to be?" For the Lord's hand
was with him.
67 His father Zechariah was filled with
the Holy Spirit and prophesied:

68 "Praise be to the Lord, the God of
Israel,
because he has come to his people
and redeemed them.
69 He has raised up a horn[a] of salvation
for us
in the house of his servant David
70 (as he said through his holy prophets
of long ago),
71 salvation from our enemies
and from the hand of all who hate
us—
72 to show mercy to our ancestors
and to remember his holy covenant,
73 the oath he swore to our father
Abraham:
74 to rescue us from the hand of our
enemies,
and to enable us to serve him
without fear
75 in holiness and righteousness
before him all our days.

76 And you, my child, will be called a
prophet of the Most High;
for you will go on before the Lord to
prepare the way for him,
77 to give his people the knowledge of
salvation
through the forgiveness of their
sins,
78 because of the tender mercy of our
God,
by which the rising sun will come to
us from heaven
79 to shine on those living in darkness
and in the shadow of death,
to guide our feet into the path of
peace."

80 And the child grew and became
strong in spirit[b]; and he lived in the wilderness until he appeared publicly to
Israel.

2 In those days Caesar Augustus issued
a decree that a census should be taken
of the entire Roman world. 2 (This was the
first census that took place while[c] Quirin-
ius was governor of Syria.) 3 And everyone
went to their own town to register.
4 So Joseph also went up from the town
of Nazareth in Galilee to Judea, to Bethlehem the town of David, because he belonged to the house and line of David.
5 He went there to register with Mary,
who was pledged to be married to him
and was expecting a child. 6 While they
were there, the time came for the baby to
be born, 7 and she gave birth to her firstborn, a son. She wrapped him in cloths
and placed him in a manger, because
there was no guest room available for
them.
8 And there were shepherds living out
in the fields nearby, keeping watch over
their flocks at night. 9 An angel of the Lord
appeared to them, and the glory of the
Lord shone around them, and they were
terrified. 10 But the angel said to them,
"Do not be afraid. I bring you good news
that will cause great joy for all the people.
11 Today in the town of David a Savior has
been born to you; he is the Messiah, the
Lord. 12 This will be a sign to you: You will
find a baby wrapped in cloths and lying
in a manger."
13 Suddenly a great company of the
heavenly host appeared with the angel,
praising God and saying,

14 "Glory to God in the highest heaven,
and on earth peace to those on
whom his favor rests."

15 When the angels had left them and
gone into heaven, the shepherds said to
one another, "Let's go to Bethlehem and
see this thing that has happened, which
the Lord has told us about."
16 So they hurried off and found Mary
and Joseph, and the baby, who was lying in the manger. 17 When they had
seen him, they spread the word concerning what had been told them about this
child, 18 and all who heard it were amazed
at what the shepherds said to them. 19 But

[a] *69 Horn* here symbolizes a strong king. [b] *80* Or *in the Spirit* [c] *2* Or *This census took place before*

Mary treasured up all these things and
pondered them in her heart. 20The shepherds returned, glorifying and praising
God for all the things they had heard and
seen, which were just as they had been
told.

21On the eighth day, when it was time
to circumcise the child, he was named
Jesus, the name the angel had given him
before he was conceived.

22When the time came for the purification rites required by the Law of Moses,
Joseph and Mary took him to Jerusalem to
present him to the Lord 23(as it is written
in the Law of the Lord, "Every firstborn
male is to be consecrated to the Lord"[a])
24and to offer a sacrifice in keeping with
what is said in the Law of the Lord: "a pair
of doves or two young pigeons."[b]

25Now there was a man in Jerusalem
called Simeon, who was righteous and
devout. He was waiting for the consolation of Israel, and the Holy Spirit was on
him. 26It had been revealed to him by the
Holy Spirit that he would not die before
he had seen the Lord's Messiah. 27Moved
by the Spirit, he went into the temple
courts. When the parents brought in the
child Jesus to do for him what the custom
of the Law required, 28Simeon took him
in his arms and praised God, saying:

29 "Sovereign Lord, as you have
promised,
you may now dismiss[c] your servant
in peace.
30 For my eyes have seen your salvation,
31 which you have prepared in the
sight of all nations:
32 a light for revelation to the Gentiles,
and the glory of your people Israel."

33The child's father and mother marveled at what was said about him. 34Then
Simeon blessed them and said to Mary,
his mother: "This child is destined to
cause the falling and rising of many in Israel, and to be a sign that will be spoken
against, 35so that the thoughts of many
hearts will be revealed. And a sword will
pierce your own soul too."

36There was also a prophet, Anna, the
daughter of Penuel, of the tribe of Asher. She was very old; she had lived with
her husband seven years after her marriage, 37and then was a widow until she
was eighty-four.[d] She never left the temple but worshiped night and day, fasting and praying. 38Coming up to them
at that very moment, she gave thanks to
God and spoke about the child to all who
were looking forward to the redemption
of Jerusalem.

39When Joseph and Mary had done
everything required by the Law of the
Lord, they returned to Galilee to their
own town of Nazareth. 40And the child
grew and became strong; he was filled
with wisdom, and the grace of God was
on him.

41Every year Jesus' parents went to Jerusalem for the Festival of the Passover.
42When he was twelve years old, they
went up to the festival, according to the
custom. 43After the festival was over,
while his parents were returning home,
the boy Jesus stayed behind in Jerusalem,
but they were unaware of it. 44Thinking
he was in their company, they traveled
on for a day. Then they began looking for
him among their relatives and friends.
45When they did not find him, they went
back to Jerusalem to look for him. 46After
three days they found him in the temple
courts, sitting among the teachers, listening to them and asking them questions.
47Everyone who heard him was amazed
at his understanding and his answers.
48When his parents saw him, they were
astonished. His mother said to him, "Son,
why have you treated us like this? Your father and I have been anxiously searching
for you."

49"Why were you searching for me?" he
asked. "Didn't you know I had to be in my
Father's house?"[e] 50But they did not understand what he was saying to them.

51Then he went down to Nazareth with
them and was obedient to them. But his
mother treasured all these things in her
heart. 52And Jesus grew in wisdom and
stature, and in favor with God and man.

3 In the fifteenth year of the reign of Ti-
berius Caesar—when Pontius Pilate
was governor of Judea, Herod tetrarch of
Galilee, his brother Philip tetrarch of Itu-
rea and Traconitis, and Lysanias tetrarch
of Abilene— 2during the high-priest-
hood of Annas and Caiaphas, the word of
God came to John son of Zechariah in the
wilderness. 3He went into all the country

[a] 23 Exodus 13:2,12 [b] 24 Lev. 12:8 [c] 29 Or *promised, / now dismiss* [d] 37 Or *then had been a widow for eighty-four years.* [e] 49 Or *be about my Father's business*

around the Jordan, preaching a baptism
of repentance for the forgiveness of sins.
4 As it is written in the book of the words
of Isaiah the prophet:

"A voice of one calling in the
wilderness,
'Prepare the way for the Lord,
make straight paths for him.
5 Every valley shall be filled in,
every mountain and hill made low.
The crooked roads shall become
straight,
the rough ways smooth.
6 And all people will see God's
salvation.' "[a]

7 John said to the crowds coming out to
be baptized by him, "You brood of vipers!
Who warned you to flee from the coming
wrath? 8 Produce fruit in keeping with
repentance. And do not begin to say to
yourselves, 'We have Abraham as our father.' For I tell you that out of these stones
God can raise up children for Abraham.
9 The ax is already at the root of the trees,
and every tree that does not produce
good fruit will be cut down and thrown
into the fire."

10 "What should we do then?" the crowd
asked.

11 John answered, "Anyone who has two
shirts should share with the one who has
none, and anyone who has food should
do the same."

12 Even tax collectors came to be baptized. "Teacher," they asked, "what
should we do?"

13 "Don't collect any more than you are
required to," he told them.

14 Then some soldiers asked him, "And
what should we do?"

He replied, "Don't extort money and don't accuse people falsely—be content with your pay."

15 The people were waiting expectantly and were all wondering in their hearts
if John might possibly be the Messiah.
16 John answered them all, "I baptize you
with[b] water. But one who is more powerful than I will come, the straps of whose
sandals I am not worthy to untie. He will
baptize you with[b] the Holy Spirit and
fire. 17 His winnowing fork is in his hand
to clear his threshing floor and to gather
the wheat into his barn, but he will burn
up the chaff with unquenchable fire."
18 And with many other words John ex-
horted the people and proclaimed the
good news to them.

19 But when John rebuked Herod the tetrarch because of his marriage to Herodias, his brother's wife, and all the other
evil things he had done, 20 Herod added
this to them all: He locked John up in
prison.

21 When all the people were being baptized, Jesus was baptized too. And as he
was praying, heaven was opened 22 and
the Holy Spirit descended on him in
bodily form like a dove. And a voice came
from heaven: "You are my Son, whom I
love; with you I am well pleased."

23 Now Jesus himself was about thirty
years old when he began his ministry. He
was the son, so it was thought, of Joseph,

the son of Heli, 24 the son of Matthat,
the son of Levi, the son of Melki,
the son of Jannai, the son of Joseph,
25 the son of Mattathias, the son of
Amos,
the son of Nahum, the son of Esli,
the son of Naggai, 26 the son of Ma-
ath,
the son of Mattathias, the son of Sem-
ein,
the son of Josek, the son of Joda,
27 the son of Joanan, the son of Rhesa,
the son of Zerubbabel, the son of
Shealtiel,
the son of Neri, 28 the son of Melki,
the son of Addi, the son of Cosam,
the son of Elmadam, the son of Er,
29 the son of Joshua, the son of Eliezer,
the son of Jorim, the son of Matthat,
the son of Levi, 30 the son of Simeon,
the son of Judah, the son of Joseph,
the son of Jonam, the son of Eliakim,
31 the son of Melea, the son of Menna,
the son of Mattatha, the son of Nathan,
the son of David, 32 the son of Jesse,
the son of Obed, the son of Boaz,
the son of Salmon,[c] the son of Nahshon,
33 the son of Amminadab, the son of
Ram,[d]
the son of Hezron, the son of Perez,
the son of Judah, 34 the son of Jacob,
the son of Isaac, the son of Abraham,

[a] *6* Isaiah 40:3-5 [b] *16* Or *in* [c] *32* Some early manuscripts *Sala* [d] *33* Some manuscripts *Amminadab, the son of Admin, the son of Arni*; other manuscripts vary widely.

the son of Terah, the son of Nahor,
35 the son of Serug, the son of Reu,
the son of Peleg, the son of Eber,
the son of Shelah, 36 the son of Cainan,
the son of Arphaxad, the son of Shem,
the son of Noah, the son of Lamech,
37 the son of Methuselah, the son of Enoch,
the son of Jared, the son of Mahalalel,
the son of Kenan, 38 the son of Enosh,
the son of Seth, the son of Adam,
the son of God.

4 Jesus, full of the Holy Spirit, left the
Jordan and was led by the Spirit into
the wilderness, 2 where for forty days he
was tempted[a] by the devil. He ate nothing
during those days, and at the end of them
he was hungry.
3 The devil said to him, "If you are the
Son of God, tell this stone to become
bread."
4 Jesus answered, "It is written: 'Man
shall not live on bread alone.'[b]"
5 The devil led him up to a high place
and showed him in an instant all the
kingdoms of the world. 6 And he said to
him, "I will give you all their authority
and splendor; it has been given to me,
and I can give it to anyone I want to. 7 If
you worship me, it will all be yours."
8 Jesus answered, "It is written: 'Worship
the Lord your God and serve him
only.'[c]"
9 The devil led him to Jerusalem and
had him stand on the highest point of
the temple. "If you are the Son of God,"
he said, "throw yourself down from here.
10 For it is written:

"'He will command his angels
concerning you
to guard you carefully;
11 they will lift you up in their hands,
so that you will not strike your foot
against a stone.'[d]"

12 Jesus answered, "It is said: 'Do not
put the Lord your God to the test.'[e]"
13 When the devil had finished all this
tempting, he left him until an opportune
time.
14 Jesus returned to Galilee in the power
of the Spirit, and news about him spread
through the whole countryside. 15 He was
teaching in their synagogues, and everyone
praised him.
16 He went to Nazareth, where he had
been brought up, and on the Sabbath day
he went into the synagogue, as was his
custom. He stood up to read, 17 and the
scroll of the prophet Isaiah was handed
to him. Unrolling it, he found the place
where it is written:

18 "The Spirit of the Lord is on me,
because he has anointed me
to proclaim good news to the poor.
He has sent me to proclaim freedom
for the prisoners
and recovery of sight for the blind,
to set the oppressed free,
19 to proclaim the year of the Lord's
favor."[f]

20 Then he rolled up the scroll, gave it
back to the attendant and sat down. The
eyes of everyone in the synagogue were
fastened on him. 21 He began by saying to
them, "Today this scripture is fulfilled in
your hearing."
22 All spoke well of him and were
amazed at the gracious words that came
from his lips. "Isn't this Joseph's son?"
they asked.
23 Jesus said to them, "Surely you will
quote this proverb to me: 'Physician, heal
yourself!' And you will tell me, 'Do here
in your hometown what we have heard
that you did in Capernaum.'"
24 "Truly I tell you," he continued, "no
prophet is accepted in his hometown. 25 I
assure you that there were many widows
in Israel in Elijah's time, when the sky
was shut for three and a half years and
there was a severe famine throughout the
land. 26 Yet Elijah was not sent to any of
them, but to a widow in Zarephath in the
region of Sidon. 27 And there were many
in Israel with leprosy[g] in the time of Elisha
the prophet, yet not one of them was
cleansed — only Naaman the Syrian."
28 All the people in the synagogue were
furious when they heard this. 29 They got
up, drove him out of the town, and took
him to the brow of the hill on which the
town was built, in order to throw him off

a 2 The Greek for *tempted* can also mean *tested*. b 4 Deut. 8:3 c 8 Deut. 6:13 d 11 Psalm 91:11,12
e 12 Deut. 6:16 f 19 Isaiah 61:1,2 (see Septuagint); Isaiah 58:6 g 27 The Greek word traditionally
translated *leprosy* was used for various diseases affecting the skin.

the cliff. [30]But he walked right through
the crowd and went on his way.
[31]Then he went down to Capernaum,
a town in Galilee, and on the Sabbath he
taught the people. [32]They were amazed
at his teaching, because his words had
authority.
[33]In the synagogue there was a man
possessed by a demon, an impure spirit.
He cried out at the top of his voice, [34]"Go
away! What do you want with us, Jesus
of Nazareth? Have you come to destroy
us? I know who you are — the Holy One
of God!"
[35]"Be quiet!" Jesus said sternly. "Come
out of him!" Then the demon threw the
man down before them all and came out
without injuring him.
[36]All the people were amazed and
said to each other, "What words these
are! With authority and power he gives
orders to impure spirits and they come
out!" [37]And the news about him spread
throughout the surrounding area.
[38]Jesus left the synagogue and went to
the home of Simon. Now Simon's mother-in-law was suffering from a high fever,
and they asked Jesus to help her. [39]So he
bent over her and rebuked the fever, and
it left her. She got up at once and began to
wait on them.
[40]At sunset, the people brought to Jesus
all who had various kinds of sickness, and
laying his hands on each one, he healed
them. [41]Moreover, demons came out of
many people, shouting, "You are the Son
of God!" But he rebuked them and would
not allow them to speak, because they
knew he was the Messiah.
[42]At daybreak, Jesus went out to a solitary place. The people were looking for
him and when they came to where he
was, they tried to keep him from leaving
them. [43]But he said, "I must proclaim the
good news of the kingdom of God to the
other towns also, because that is why I
was sent." [44]And he kept on preaching in
the synagogues of Judea.

5 One day as Jesus was standing by the
Lake of Gennesaret,[a] the people were
crowding around him and listening to
the word of God. [2]He saw at the water's
edge two boats, left there by the fishermen, who were washing their nets. [3]He
got into one of the boats, the one belonging to Simon, and asked him to put out a
little from shore. Then he sat down and
taught the people from the boat.
[4]When he had finished speaking, he
said to Simon, "Put out into deep water,
and let down the nets for a catch."
[5]Simon answered, "Master, we've
worked hard all night and haven't caught
anything. But because you say so, I will
let down the nets."
[6]When they had done so, they caught
such a large number of fish that their nets
began to break. [7]So they signaled their
partners in the other boat to come and
help them, and they came and filled both
boats so full that they began to sink.
[8]When Simon Peter saw this, he fell at
Jesus' knees and said, "Go away from me,
Lord; I am a sinful man!" [9]For he and all
his companions were astonished at the
catch of fish they had taken, [10]and so
were James and John, the sons of Zebedee, Simon's partners.
Then Jesus said to Simon, "Don't be
afraid; from now on you will fish for people." [11]So they pulled their boats up on
shore, left everything and followed him.
[12]While Jesus was in one of the towns,
a man came along who was covered with
leprosy.[b] When he saw Jesus, he fell with
his face to the ground and begged him,
"Lord, if you are willing, you can make
me clean."
[13]Jesus reached out his hand and
touched the man. "I am willing," he said.
"Be clean!" And immediately the leprosy
left him.
[14]Then Jesus ordered him, "Don't tell
anyone, but go, show yourself to the
priest and offer the sacrifices that Moses
commanded for your cleansing, as a testimony to them."
[15]Yet the news about him spread all
the more, so that crowds of people came
to hear him and to be healed of their
sicknesses. [16]But Jesus often withdrew to
lonely places and prayed.
[17]One day Jesus was teaching, and
Pharisees and teachers of the law were
sitting there. They had come from every
village of Galilee and from Judea and Jerusalem. And the power of the Lord was
with Jesus to heal the sick. [18]Some men
came carrying a paralyzed man on a mat
and tried to take him into the house to

[a] *1* That is, the Sea of Galilee [b] *12* The Greek word traditionally translated *leprosy* was used for various diseases affecting the skin.

lay him before Jesus. 19When they could not find a way to do this because of the crowd, they went up on the roof and lowered him on his mat through the tiles into the middle of the crowd, right in front of Jesus.

20When Jesus saw their faith, he said, "Friend, your sins are forgiven."

21The Pharisees and the teachers of the law began thinking to themselves, "Who is this fellow who speaks blasphemy? Who can forgive sins but God alone?"

22Jesus knew what they were thinking and asked, "Why are you thinking these things in your hearts? 23Which is easier: to say, 'Your sins are forgiven,' or to say, 'Get up and walk'? 24But I want you to know that the Son of Man has authority on earth to forgive sins." So he said to the paralyzed man, "I tell you, get up, take your mat and go home." 25Immediately he stood up in front of them, took what he had been lying on and went home praising God. 26Everyone was amazed and gave praise to God. They were filled with awe and said, "We have seen remarkable things today."

27After this, Jesus went out and saw a tax collector by the name of Levi sitting at his tax booth. "Follow me," Jesus said to him, 28and Levi got up, left everything and followed him.

29Then Levi held a great banquet for Jesus at his house, and a large crowd of tax collectors and others were eating with them. 30But the Pharisees and the teachers of the law who belonged to their sect complained to his disciples, "Why do you eat and drink with tax collectors and sinners?"

31Jesus answered them, "It is not the healthy who need a doctor, but the sick. 32I have not come to call the righteous, but sinners to repentance."

33They said to him, "John's disciples often fast and pray, and so do the disciples of the Pharisees, but yours go on eating and drinking."

34Jesus answered, "Can you make the friends of the bridegroom fast while he is with them? 35But the time will come when the bridegroom will be taken from them; in those days they will fast."

36He told them this parable: "No one tears a piece out of a new garment to patch an old one. Otherwise, they will have torn the new garment, and the patch from the new will not match the old. 37And no one pours new wine into old wineskins. Otherwise, the new wine will burst the skins; the wine will run out and the wineskins will be ruined. 38No, new wine must be poured into new wineskins. 39And no one after drinking old wine wants the new, for they say, 'The old is better.'"

6 One Sabbath Jesus was going through the grainfields, and his disciples began to pick some heads of grain, rub them in their hands and eat the kernels. 2Some of the Pharisees asked, "Why are you doing what is unlawful on the Sabbath?"

3Jesus answered them, "Have you never read what David did when he and his companions were hungry? 4He entered the house of God, and taking the consecrated bread, he ate what is lawful only for priests to eat. And he also gave some to his companions." 5Then Jesus said to them, "The Son of Man is Lord of the Sabbath."

6On another Sabbath he went into the synagogue and was teaching, and a man was there whose right hand was shriveled. 7The Pharisees and the teachers of the law were looking for a reason to accuse Jesus, so they watched him closely to see if he would heal on the Sabbath. 8But Jesus knew what they were thinking and said to the man with the shriveled hand, "Get up and stand in front of everyone." So he got up and stood there.

9Then Jesus said to them, "I ask you, which is lawful on the Sabbath: to do good or to do evil, to save life or to destroy it?"

10He looked around at them all, and then said to the man, "Stretch out your hand." He did so, and his hand was completely restored. 11But the Pharisees and the teachers of the law were furious and began to discuss with one another what they might do to Jesus.

12One of those days Jesus went out to a mountainside to pray, and spent the night praying to God. 13When morning came, he called his disciples to him and chose twelve of them, whom he also designated apostles: 14Simon (whom he named Peter), his brother Andrew, James, John, Philip, Bartholomew, 15Matthew, Thomas, James son of Alphaeus, Simon who was called the Zealot, 16Judas son of James, and Judas Iscariot, who became a traitor.

17 He went down with them and stood
on a level place. A large crowd of his disciples was there and a great number of
people from all over Judea, from Jerusalem, and from the coastal region around
Tyre and Sidon, 18 who had come to hear
him and to be healed of their diseases.
Those troubled by impure spirits were
cured, 19 and the people all tried to touch
him, because power was coming from
him and healing them all.

20 Looking at his disciples, he said:

"Blessed are you who are poor,
for yours is the kingdom of God.
21 Blessed are you who hunger now,
for you will be satisfied.
Blessed are you who weep now,
for you will laugh.
22 Blessed are you when people hate you,
when they exclude you and insult you
and reject your name as evil,
because of the Son of Man.

23 "Rejoice in that day and leap for joy,
because great is your reward in heaven.
For that is how their ancestors treated the
prophets.

24 "But woe to you who are rich,
for you have already received your comfort.
25 Woe to you who are well fed now,
for you will go hungry.
Woe to you who laugh now,
for you will mourn and weep.
26 Woe to you when everyone speaks well of you,
for that is how their ancestors
treated the false prophets.

27 "But to you who are listening I say:
Love your enemies, do good to those
who hate you, 28 bless those who curse
you, pray for those who mistreat you. 29 If
someone slaps you on one cheek, turn
to them the other also. If someone takes
your coat, do not withhold your shirt
from them. 30 Give to everyone who asks
you, and if anyone takes what belongs to
you, do not demand it back. 31 Do to others as you would have them do to you.

32 "If you love those who love you,
what credit is that to you? Even sinners
love those who love them. 33 And if you
do good to those who are good to you,
what credit is that to you? Even sinners
do that. 34 And if you lend to those from
whom you expect repayment, what credit
is that to you? Even sinners lend to sinners, expecting to be repaid in full. 35 But
love your enemies, do good to them, and
lend to them without expecting to get
anything back. Then your reward will
be great, and you will be children of the
Most High, because he is kind to the ungrateful and wicked. 36 Be merciful, just
as your Father is merciful.

37 "Do not judge, and you will not be
judged. Do not condemn, and you will
not be condemned. Forgive, and you will
be forgiven. 38 Give, and it will be given
to you. A good measure, pressed down,
shaken together and running over, will
be poured into your lap. For with the
measure you use, it will be measured to
you."

39 He also told them this parable: "Can
the blind lead the blind? Will they not
both fall into a pit? 40 The student is not
above the teacher, but everyone who is
fully trained will be like their teacher.

41 "Why do you look at the speck of
sawdust in your brother's eye and pay
no attention to the plank in your own
eye? 42 How can you say to your brother,
'Brother, let me take the speck out of your
eye,' when you yourself fail to see the
plank in your own eye? You hypocrite,
first take the plank out of your eye, and
then you will see clearly to remove the
speck from your brother's eye.

43 "No good tree bears bad fruit, nor
does a bad tree bear good fruit. 44 Each
tree is recognized by its own fruit. People do not pick figs from thornbushes, or
grapes from briers. 45 A good man brings
good things out of the good stored up in
his heart, and an evil man brings evil
things out of the evil stored up in his
heart. For the mouth speaks what the
heart is full of.

46 "Why do you call me, 'Lord, Lord,'
and do not do what I say? 47 As for everyone who comes to me and hears my
words and puts them into practice, I will
show you what they are like. 48 They are
like a man building a house, who dug
down deep and laid the foundation on
rock. When a flood came, the torrent
struck that house but could not shake it,
because it was well built. 49 But the one
who hears my words and does not put
them into practice is like a man who built
a house on the ground without a founda-

tion. The moment the torrent struck that
house, it collapsed and its destruction
was complete."

7 When Jesus had finished saying all
this to the people who were listening,
he entered Capernaum. 2There a centurion's servant, whom his master valued
highly, was sick and about to die. 3The
centurion heard of Jesus and sent some
elders of the Jews to him, asking him to
come and heal his servant. 4When they
came to Jesus, they pleaded earnestly
with him, "This man deserves to have
you do this, 5because he loves our nation
and has built our synagogue." 6So Jesus
went with them.

He was not far from the house when
the centurion sent friends to say to him:
"Lord, don't trouble yourself, for I do not
deserve to have you come under my roof.
7That is why I did not even consider myself worthy to come to you. But say the
word, and my servant will be healed. 8For
I myself am a man under authority, with
soldiers under me. I tell this one, 'Go,'
and he goes; and that one, 'Come,' and he
comes. I say to my servant, 'Do this,' and
he does it."

9When Jesus heard this, he was amazed
at him, and turning to the crowd following him, he said, "I tell you, I have not
found such great faith even in Israel."
10Then the men who had been sent returned to the house and found the servant well.

11Soon afterward, Jesus went to a town
called Nain, and his disciples and a large
crowd went along with him. 12As he approached the town gate, a dead person
was being carried out—the only son of
his mother, and she was a widow. And a
large crowd from the town was with her.
13When the Lord saw her, his heart went
out to her and he said, "Don't cry."

14Then he went up and touched the
bier they were carrying him on, and the
bearers stood still. He said, "Young man,
I say to you, get up!" 15The dead man sat
up and began to talk, and Jesus gave him
back to his mother.

16They were all filled with awe and
praised God. "A great prophet has appeared among us," they said. "God has
come to help his people." 17This news
about Jesus spread throughout Judea and
the surrounding country.

18John's disciples told him about all
these things. Calling two of them, 19he
sent them to the Lord to ask, "Are you the
one who is to come, or should we expect
someone else?"

20When the men came to Jesus, they
said, "John the Baptist sent us to you to
ask, 'Are you the one who is to come, or
should we expect someone else?'"

21At that very time Jesus cured many
who had diseases, sicknesses and evil
spirits, and gave sight to many who were
blind. 22So he replied to the messengers,
"Go back and report to John what you
have seen and heard: The blind receive
sight, the lame walk, those who have
leprosy[a] are cleansed, the deaf hear, the
dead are raised, and the good news is
proclaimed to the poor. 23Blessed is anyone who does not stumble on account
of me."

24After John's messengers left, Jesus
began to speak to the crowd about John:
"What did you go out into the wilderness
to see? A reed swayed by the wind? 25If
not, what did you go out to see? A man
dressed in fine clothes? No, those who
wear expensive clothes and indulge in
luxury are in palaces. 26But what did you
go out to see? A prophet? Yes, I tell you,
and more than a prophet. 27This is the
one about whom it is written:

"'I will send my messenger ahead of
you,
who will prepare your way before
you.'[b]

28I tell you, among those born of women
there is no one greater than John; yet the
one who is least in the kingdom of God is
greater than he."

29(All the people, even the tax collectors, when they heard Jesus' words, acknowledged that God's way was right,
because they had been baptized by John.
30But the Pharisees and the experts in
the law rejected God's purpose for themselves, because they had not been baptized by John.)

31Jesus went on to say, "To what, then,
can I compare the people of this generation? What are they like? 32They are like

[a] 22 The Greek word traditionally translated *leprosy* was used for various diseases affecting the skin.
[b] 27 Mal. 3:1

children sitting in the marketplace and
calling out to each other:

"'We played the pipe for you,
and you did not dance;
we sang a dirge,
and you did not cry.'

33For John the Baptist came neither eating bread nor drinking wine, and you say,
'He has a demon.' 34The Son of Man came
eating and drinking, and you say, 'Here is
a glutton and a drunkard, a friend of tax
collectors and sinners.' 35But wisdom is
proved right by all her children."

36When one of the Pharisees invited
Jesus to have dinner with him, he went to
the Pharisee's house and reclined at the
table. 37A woman in that town who lived
a sinful life learned that Jesus was eating
at the Pharisee's house, so she came there
with an alabaster jar of perfume. 38As she
stood behind him at his feet weeping, she
began to wet his feet with her tears. Then
she wiped them with her hair, kissed
them and poured perfume on them.

39When the Pharisee who had invited
him saw this, he said to himself, "If this
man were a prophet, he would know who
is touching him and what kind of woman
she is — that she is a sinner."

40Jesus answered him, "Simon, I have
something to tell you."

"Tell me, teacher," he said.

41"Two people owed money to a certain
moneylender. One owed him five hundred denarii,[a] and the other fifty. 42Nei-
ther of them had the money to pay him
back, so he forgave the debts of both. Now
which of them will love him more?"

43Simon replied, "I suppose the one
who had the bigger debt forgiven."

"You have judged correctly," Jesus
said.

44Then he turned toward the woman and said to Simon, "Do you see this
woman? I came into your house. You did
not give me any water for my feet, but
she wet my feet with her tears and wiped
them with her hair. 45You did not give me
a kiss, but this woman, from the time I
entered, has not stopped kissing my feet.
46You did not put oil on my head, but she
has poured perfume on my feet. 47There-
fore, I tell you, her many sins have been
forgiven — as her great love has shown.
But whoever has been forgiven little loves
little."

48Then Jesus said to her, "Your sins are
forgiven."

49The other guests began to say among
themselves, "Who is this who even forgives sins?"

50Jesus said to the woman, "Your faith
has saved you; go in peace."

8 After this, Jesus traveled about from
one town and village to another, proclaiming the good news of the kingdom
of God. The Twelve were with him, 2and
also some women who had been cured
of evil spirits and diseases: Mary (called
Magdalene) from whom seven demons
had come out; 3Joanna the wife of Chu-
za, the manager of Herod's household;
Susanna; and many others. These wom-
en were helping to support them out of
their own means.

4While a large crowd was gathering
and people were coming to Jesus from
town after town, he told this parable: 5"A
farmer went out to sow his seed. As he was
scattering the seed, some fell along the
path; it was trampled on, and the birds
ate it up. 6Some fell on rocky ground, and
when it came up, the plants withered because they had no moisture. 7Other seed
fell among thorns, which grew up with it
and choked the plants. 8Still other seed
fell on good soil. It came up and yielded
a crop, a hundred times more than was
sown."

When he said this, he called out, "Whoever has ears to hear, let them hear."

9His disciples asked him what this parable meant. 10He said, "The knowledge
of the secrets of the kingdom of God has
been given to you, but to others I speak in
parables, so that,

"'though seeing, they may not see;
though hearing, they may not
understand.'[b]

11"This is the meaning of the parable:
The seed is the word of God. 12Those
along the path are the ones who hear,
and then the devil comes and takes away
the word from their hearts, so that they
may not believe and be saved. 13Those
on the rocky ground are the ones who receive the word with joy when they hear it,
but they have no root. They believe for a

[a] *41* A denarius was the usual daily wage of a day laborer (see Matt. 20:2). [b] *10* Isaiah 6:9

while, but in the time of testing they fall
away. 14 The seed that fell among thorns
stands for those who hear, but as they
go on their way they are choked by life's
worries, riches and pleasures, and they
do not mature. 15 But the seed on good
soil stands for those with a noble and
good heart, who hear the word, retain it,
and by persevering produce a crop.

16 "No one lights a lamp and hides it in
a clay jar or puts it under a bed. Instead,
they put it on a stand, so that those who
come in can see the light. 17 For there
is nothing hidden that will not be disclosed, and nothing concealed that will
not be known or brought out into the
open. 18 Therefore consider carefully
how you listen. Whoever has will be giv-
en more; whoever does not have, even
what they think they have will be taken
from them."

19 Now Jesus' mother and brothers
came to see him, but they were not able
to get near him because of the crowd.
20 Someone told him, "Your mother and
brothers are standing outside, wanting
to see you."

21 He replied, "My mother and brothers
are those who hear God's word and put it
into practice."

22 One day Jesus said to his disciples,
"Let us go over to the other side of the
lake." So they got into a boat and set out.
23 As they sailed, he fell asleep. A squall
came down on the lake, so that the boat
was being swamped, and they were in
great danger.

24 The disciples went and woke him,
saying, "Master, Master, we're going to
drown!"

He got up and rebuked the wind and
the raging waters; the storm subsided,
and all was calm. 25 "Where is your faith?"
he asked his disciples.

In fear and amazement they asked one
another, "Who is this? He commands
even the winds and the water, and they
obey him."

26 They sailed to the region of the Gerasenes,[a] which is across the lake from Galilee. 27 When Jesus stepped ashore, he was
met by a demon-possessed man from the
town. For a long time this man had no
worn clothes or lived in a house, but had
lived in the tombs. 28 When he saw Jesus
he cried out and fell at his feet, shouting at the top of his voice, "What do you
want with me, Jesus, Son of the Most High
God? I beg you, don't torture me!" 29 For
Jesus had commanded the impure spirit
to come out of the man. Many times it had
seized him, and though he was chained
hand and foot and kept under guard, he
had broken his chains and had been driv-
en by the demon into solitary places.

30 Jesus asked him, "What is your
name?"

"Legion," he replied, because many
demons had gone into him. 31 And they
begged Jesus repeatedly not to order
them to go into the Abyss.

32 A large herd of pigs was feeding there
on the hillside. The demons begged Jesus
to let them go into the pigs, and he gave
them permission. 33 When the demons
came out of the man, they went into the
pigs, and the herd rushed down the steep
bank into the lake and was drowned.

34 When those tending the pigs saw
what had happened, they ran off and reported this in the town and countryside,
35 and the people went out to see what
had happened. When they came to Jesus,
they found the man from whom the demons had gone out, sitting at Jesus' feet,
dressed and in his right mind; and they
were afraid. 36 Those who had seen it told
the people how the demon-possessed
man had been cured. 37 Then all the people of the region of the Gerasenes asked
Jesus to leave them, because they were
overcome with fear. So he got into the
boat and left.

38 The man from whom the demons had
gone out begged to go with him, but Jesus
sent him away, saying, 39 "Return home
and tell how much God has done for you."
So the man went away and told all over
town how much Jesus had done for him.

40 Now when Jesus returned, a crowd
welcomed him, for they were all expecting him. 41 Then a man named Jairus, a
synagogue leader, came and fell at Jesus'
feet, pleading with him to come to his
house 42 because his only daughter, a girl
of about twelve, was dying.

As Jesus was on his way, the crowds almost crushed him. 43 And a woman was
there who had been subject to bleeding
for twelve years,[b] but no one could heal

[a] 26 Some manuscripts *Gadarenes*; other manuscripts *Gergesenes*; also in verse 37 [b] 43 Many manuscripts *years, and she had spent all she had on doctors*

her. 44She came up behind him and
touched the edge of his cloak, and immediately her bleeding stopped.
45"Who touched me?" Jesus asked.
When they all denied it, Peter said,
"Master, the people are crowding and
pressing against you."
46But Jesus said, "Someone touched
me; I know that power has gone out
from me."
47Then the woman, seeing that she
could not go unnoticed, came trembling
and fell at his feet. In the presence of all
the people, she told why she had touched
him and how she had been instantly
healed. 48Then he said to her, "Daughter,
your faith has healed you. Go in peace."
49While Jesus was still speaking,
someone came from the house of Jairus,
the synagogue leader. "Your daughter is
dead," he said. "Don't bother the teacher
anymore."
50Hearing this, Jesus said to Jairus,
"Don't be afraid; just believe, and she
will be healed."
51When he arrived at the house of Jairus, he did not let anyone go in with him
except Peter, John and James, and the
child's father and mother. 52Meanwhile,
all the people were wailing and mourning for her. "Stop wailing," Jesus said.
"She is not dead but asleep."
53They laughed at him, knowing that
she was dead. 54But he took her by the
hand and said, "My child, get up!" 55Her
spirit returned, and at once she stood up.
Then Jesus told them to give her something to eat. 56Her parents were astonished, but he ordered them not to tell
anyone what had happened.
9 When Jesus had called the Twelve
together, he gave them power and
authority to drive out all demons and to
cure diseases, 2and he sent them out to
proclaim the kingdom of God and to heal
the sick. 3He told them: "Take nothing for
the journey — no staff, no bag, no bread,
no money, no extra shirt. 4Whatever
house you enter, stay there until you leave
that town. 5If people do not welcome you,
leave their town and shake the dust off
your feet as a testimony against them."
6So they set out and went from village to
village, proclaiming the good news and
healing people everywhere.
7Now Herod the tetrarch heard about
all that was going on. And he was perplexed because some were saying that
John had been raised from the dead,
8others that Elijah had appeared, and
still others that one of the prophets of
long ago had come back to life. 9But Herod said, "I beheaded John. Who, then, is
this I hear such things about?" And he
tried to see him.
10When the apostles returned, they reported to Jesus what they had done. Then
he took them with him and they withdrew
by themselves to a town called Bethsaida, 11but the crowds learned about it and
followed him. He welcomed them and
spoke to them about the kingdom of God,
and healed those who needed healing.
12Late in the afternoon the Twelve
came to him and said, "Send the crowd
away so they can go to the surrounding
villages and countryside and find food
and lodging, because we are in a remote
place here."
13He replied, "You give them something to eat."
They answered, "We have only five
loaves of bread and two fish — unless
we go and buy food for all this crowd."
14(About five thousand men were there.)
But he said to his disciples, "Have them
sit down in groups of about fifty each."
15The disciples did so, and everyone sat
down. 16Taking the five loaves and the
two fish and looking up to heaven, he
gave thanks and broke them. Then he
gave them to the disciples to distribute to
the people. 17They all ate and were satisfied, and the disciples picked up twelve
basketfuls of broken pieces that were left
over.
18Once when Jesus was praying in private and his disciples were with him,
he asked them, "Who do the crowds say
I am?"
19They replied, "Some say John the
Baptist; others say Elijah; and still others, that one of the prophets of long ago
has come back to life."
20"But what about you?" he asked.
"Who do you say I am?"
Peter answered, "God's Messiah."
21Jesus strictly warned them not to tell
this to anyone. 22And he said, "The Son
of Man must suffer many things and be
rejected by the elders, the chief priests
and the teachers of the law, and he must
be killed and on the third day be raised
to life."

23 Then he said to them all: "Whoever
wants to be my disciple must deny themselves and take up their cross daily and
follow me. 24 For whoever wants to save
their life will lose it, but whoever loses
their life for me will save it. 25 What good
is it for someone to gain the whole world,
and yet lose or forfeit their very self?
26 Whoever is ashamed of me and my
words, the Son of Man will be ashamed
of them when he comes in his glory and
in the glory of the Father and of the holy
angels.

27 "Truly I tell you, some who are standing here will not taste death before they
see the kingdom of God."

28 About eight days after Jesus said this,
he took Peter, John and James with him
and went up onto a mountain to pray.
29 As he was praying, the appearance
of his face changed, and his clothes became as bright as a flash of lightning.
30 Two men, Moses and Elijah, appeared
in glorious splendor, talking with Jesus.
31 They spoke about his departure,[a]
which he was about to bring to fulfillment at Jerusalem. 32 Peter and his companions were very sleepy, but when they
became fully awake, they saw his glory
and the two men standing with him. 33 As
the men were leaving Jesus, Peter said to
him, "Master, it is good for us to be here.
Let us put up three shelters — one for you,
one for Moses and one for Elijah." (He did
not know what he was saying.)

34 While he was speaking, a cloud
appeared and covered them, and they
were afraid as they entered the cloud.
35 A voice came from the cloud, saying,
"This is my Son, whom I have chosen;
listen to him." 36 When the voice had
spoken, they found that Jesus was alone.
The disciples kept this to themselves
and did not tell anyone at that time what
they had seen.

37 The next day, when they came down
from the mountain, a large crowd met
him. 38 A man in the crowd called out,
"Teacher, I beg you to look at my son, for
he is my only child. 39 A spirit seizes him
and he suddenly screams; it throws him
into convulsions so that he foams at the
mouth. It scarcely ever leaves him and is
destroying him. 40 I begged your disciples
to drive it out, but they could not."

41 "You unbelieving and perverse generation," Jesus replied, "how long shall I
stay with you and put up with you? Bring
your son here."

42 Even while the boy was coming, the
demon threw him to the ground in a convulsion. But Jesus rebuked the impure
spirit, healed the boy and gave him back
to his father. 43 And they were all amazed
at the greatness of God.

While everyone was marveling at all
that Jesus did, he said to his disciples,
44 "Listen carefully to what I am about to
tell you: The Son of Man is going to be delivered into the hands of men." 45 But they
did not understand what this meant. It
was hidden from them, so that they did
not grasp it, and they were afraid to ask
him about it.

46 An argument started among the disciples as to which of them would be the
greatest. 47 Jesus, knowing their thoughts,
took a little child and had him stand beside him. 48 Then he said to them, "Whoever welcomes this little child in my name
welcomes me; and whoever welcomes me
welcomes the one who sent me. For it is
the one who is least among you all who
is the greatest."

49 "Master," said John, "we saw someone driving out demons in your name
and we tried to stop him, because he is
not one of us."

50 "Do not stop him," Jesus said, "for
whoever is not against you is for you."

51 As the time approached for him to be
taken up to heaven, Jesus resolutely set
out for Jerusalem. 52 And he sent messengers on ahead, who went into a Samaritan
village to get things ready for him; 53 but
the people there did not welcome him,
because he was heading for Jerusalem.
54 When the disciples James and John saw
this, they asked, "Lord, do you want us to
call fire down from heaven to destroy
them[b]?" 55 But Jesus turned and rebuked
them. 56 Then he and his disciples went to
another village.

57 As they were walking along the road,
a man said to him, "I will follow you
wherever you go."

58 Jesus replied, "Foxes have dens and
birds have nests, but the Son of Man has
no place to lay his head."

[a] *31* Greek *exodus* [b] *54* Some manuscripts *them, just as Elijah did*

59He said to another man, "Follow
me."
But he replied, "Lord, first let me go and
bury my father."
60Jesus said to him, "Let the dead bury
their own dead, but you go and proclaim
the kingdom of God."
61Still another said, "I will follow you,
Lord; but first let me go back and say
goodbye to my family."
62Jesus replied, "No one who puts a
hand to the plow and looks back is fit for
service in the kingdom of God."

10 After this the Lord appointed seventy-two[a] others and sent them two by
two ahead of him to every town and place
where he was about to go. 2He told them,
"The harvest is plentiful, but the workers are few. Ask the Lord of the harvest,
therefore, to send out workers into his
harvest field. 3Go! I am sending you out
like lambs among wolves. 4Do not take a
purse or bag or sandals; and do not greet
anyone on the road.
5"When you enter a house, first say,
'Peace to this house.' 6If someone who
promotes peace is there, your peace will
rest on them; if not, it will return to you.
7Stay there, eating and drinking whatever they give you, for the worker deserves
his wages. Do not move around from
house to house.
8"When you enter a town and are welcomed, eat what is offered to you. 9Heal
the sick who are there and tell them, 'The
kingdom of God has come near to you.'
10But when you enter a town and are not
welcomed, go into its streets and say,
11'Even the dust of your town we wipe
from our feet as a warning to you. Yet
be sure of this: The kingdom of God has
come near.' 12I tell you, it will be more
bearable on that day for Sodom than for
that town.
13"Woe to you, Chorazin! Woe to you,
Bethsaida! For if the miracles that were
performed in you had been performed in
Tyre and Sidon, they would have repented long ago, sitting in sackcloth and ashes. 14But it will be more bearable for Tyre
and Sidon at the judgment than for you.
15And you, Capernaum, will you be lifted to the heavens? No, you will go down
to Hades.[b]
16"Whoever listens to you listens to
me; whoever rejects you rejects me; but
whoever rejects me rejects him who
sent me."
17The seventy-two returned with joy
and said, "Lord, even the demons submit
to us in your name."
18He replied, "I saw Satan fall like lightning from heaven. 19I have given you authority to trample on snakes and scorpions and to overcome all the power of the
enemy; nothing will harm you. 20Howev-
er, do not rejoice that the spirits submit
to you, but rejoice that your names are
written in heaven."
21At that time Jesus, full of joy through
the Holy Spirit, said, "I praise you, Father,
Lord of heaven and earth, because you
have hidden these things from the wise
and learned, and revealed them to little
children. Yes, Father, for this is what you
were pleased to do.
22"All things have been committed
to me by my Father. No one knows who
the Son is except the Father, and no one
knows who the Father is except the Son
and those to whom the Son chooses to
reveal him."
23Then he turned to his disciples and
said privately, "Blessed are the eyes that
see what you see. 24For I tell you that
many prophets and kings wanted to see
what you see but did not see it, and to
hear what you hear but did not hear it."
25On one occasion an expert in the
law stood up to test Jesus. "Teacher," he
asked, "what must I do to inherit eternal
life?"
26"What is written in the Law?" he replied. "How do you read it?"
27He answered, " 'Love the Lord your
God with all your heart and with all your
soul and with all your strength and with
all your mind'[c]; and, 'Love your neighbor
as yourself.'[d]"
28"You have answered correctly," Jesus
replied. "Do this and you will live."
29But he wanted to justify himself, so
he asked Jesus, "And who is my neighbor?"
30In reply Jesus said: "A man was going down from Jerusalem to Jericho,
when he was attacked by robbers. They
stripped him of his clothes, beat him and
went away, leaving him half dead. 31A
priest happened to be going down the

[a] *1* Some manuscripts *seventy*; also in verse 17 [b] *15* That is, the realm of the dead [c] *27* Deut. 6:5
[d] *27* Lev. 19:18

same road, and when he saw the man,
he passed by on the other side. 32 So too,
a Levite, when he came to the place and
saw him, passed by on the other side.
33 But a Samaritan, as he traveled, came
where the man was; and when he saw
him, he took pity on him. 34 He went to
him and bandaged his wounds, pouring
on oil and wine. Then he put the man on
his own donkey, brought him to an inn
and took care of him. 35 The next day he
took out two denarii[a] and gave them to
the innkeeper. 'Look after him,' he said,
'and when I return, I will reimburse you
for any extra expense you may have.'

36 "Which of these three do you think
was a neighbor to the man who fell into
the hands of robbers?"

37 The expert in the law replied, "The
one who had mercy on him."

Jesus told him, "Go and do likewise."

38 As Jesus and his disciples were on
their way, he came to a village where
a woman named Martha opened her
home to him. 39 She had a sister called
Mary, who sat at the Lord's feet listening
to what he said. 40 But Martha was dis-
tracted by all the preparations that had
to be made. She came to him and asked,
"Lord, don't you care that my sister has
left me to do the work by myself? Tell her
to help me!"

41 "Martha, Martha," the Lord answered, "you are worried and upset about
many things, 42 but few things are needed — or indeed only one.[b] Mary has chosen what is better, and it will not be taken
away from her."

11 One day Jesus was praying in a certain place. When he finished, one of
his disciples said to him, "Lord, teach us
to pray, just as John taught his disciples."

2 He said to them, "When you pray, say:

"'Father,[c]
hallowed be your name,
your kingdom come.[d]
3 Give us each day our daily bread.
4 Forgive us our sins,
for we also forgive everyone who
sins against us.[e]
And lead us not into temptation.[f]'"

5 Then Jesus said to them, "Suppose
you have a friend, and you go to him at
midnight and say, 'Friend, lend me three
loaves of bread; 6 a friend of mine on a
journey has come to me, and I have no
food to offer him.' 7 And suppose the one
inside answers, 'Don't bother me. The
door is already locked, and my children
and I are in bed. I can't get up and give
you anything.' 8 I tell you, even though he
will not get up and give you the bread because of friendship, yet because of your
shameless audacity[g] he will surely get up
and give you as much as you need.

9 "So I say to you: Ask and it will be giv-
en to you; seek and you will find; knock
and the door will be opened to you. 10 For
everyone who asks receives; the one who
seeks finds; and to the one who knocks,
the door will be opened.

11 "Which of you fathers, if your son
asks for[h] a fish, will give him a snake instead? 12 Or if he asks for an egg, will give
him a scorpion? 13 If you then, though you
are evil, know how to give good gifts to
your children, how much more will your
Father in heaven give the Holy Spirit to
those who ask him!"

14 Jesus was driving out a demon that
was mute. When the demon left, the man
who had been mute spoke, and the crowd
was amazed. 15 But some of them said,
"By Beelzebul, the prince of demons, he
is driving out demons." 16 Others tested
him by asking for a sign from heaven.

17 Jesus knew their thoughts and said
to them: "Any kingdom divided against
itself will be ruined, and a house divided
against itself will fall. 18 If Satan is divided against himself, how can his kingdom
stand? I say this because you claim that
I drive out demons by Beelzebul. 19 Now
if I drive out demons by Beelzebul, by
whom do your followers drive them out?
So then, they will be your judges. 20 But if
I drive out demons by the finger of God,
then the kingdom of God has come upon
you.

21 "When a strong man, fully armed,
guards his own house, his possessions
are safe. 22 But when someone stronger
attacks and overpowers him, he takes

[a] 35 A denarius was the usual daily wage of a day laborer (see Matt. 20:2). [b] 42 Some manuscripts *but only one thing is needed* [c] 2 Some manuscripts *Our Father in heaven* [d] 2 Some manuscripts *come. May your will be done on earth as it is in heaven.* [e] 4 Greek *everyone who is indebted to us* [f] 4 Some manuscripts *temptation, but deliver us from the evil one* [g] 8 Or *yet to preserve his good name* [h] 11 Some manuscripts *for bread, will give him a stone? Or if he asks for*

away the armor in which the man trusted and divides up his plunder.
23 "Whoever is not with me is against
me, and whoever does not gather with
me scatters.
24 "When an impure spirit comes out of
a person, it goes through arid places seeking rest and does not find it. Then it says,
'I will return to the house I left.' 25 When
it arrives, it finds the house swept clean
and put in order. 26 Then it goes and takes
seven other spirits more wicked than itself, and they go in and live there. And
the final condition of that person is worse
than the first."
27 As Jesus was saying these things, a
woman in the crowd called out, "Blessed
is the mother who gave you birth and
nursed you."
28 He replied, "Blessed rather are those
who hear the word of God and obey it."
29 As the crowds increased, Jesus said,
"This is a wicked generation. It asks for a
sign, but none will be given it except the
sign of Jonah. 30 For as Jonah was a sign to
the Ninevites, so also will the Son of Man
be to this generation. 31 The Queen of the
South will rise at the judgment with the
people of this generation and condemn
them, for she came from the ends of the
earth to listen to Solomon's wisdom; and
now something greater than Solomon is
here. 32 The men of Nineveh will stand
up at the judgment with this generation
and condemn it, for they repented at the
preaching of Jonah; and now something
greater than Jonah is here.
33 "No one lights a lamp and puts it
in a place where it will be hidden, or
under a bowl. Instead they put it on its
stand, so that those who come in may
see the light. 34 Your eye is the lamp of
your body. When your eyes are healthy,[a]
your whole body also is full of light. But
when they are unhealthy,[b] your body
also is full of darkness. 35 See to it, then,
that the light within you is not darkness.
36 Therefore, if your whole body is full of
light, and no part of it dark, it will be just
as full of light as when a lamp shines its
light on you."
37 When Jesus had finished speaking, a
Pharisee invited him to eat with him; so
he went in and reclined at the table. 38 But
the Pharisee was surprised when he noticed that Jesus did not first wash before
the meal.
39 Then the Lord said to him, "Now
then, you Pharisees clean the outside of
the cup and dish, but inside you are full
of greed and wickedness. 40 You foolish
people! Did not the one who made the
outside make the inside also? 41 But now
as for what is inside you—be generous
to the poor, and everything will be clean
for you.
42 "Woe to you Pharisees, because you
give God a tenth of your mint, rue and
all other kinds of garden herbs, but you
neglect justice and the love of God. You
should have practiced the latter without
leaving the former undone.
43 "Woe to you Pharisees, because you
love the most important seats in the synagogues and respectful greetings in the
marketplaces.
44 "Woe to you, because you are like un-
marked graves, which people walk over
without knowing it."
45 One of the experts in the law answered him, "Teacher, when you say
these things, you insult us also."
46 Jesus replied, "And you experts in the
law, woe to you, because you load people
down with burdens they can hardly carry, and you yourselves will not lift one
finger to help them.
47 "Woe to you, because you build
tombs for the prophets, and it was your
ancestors who killed them. 48 So you testify that you approve of what your ancestors did; they killed the prophets, and
you build their tombs. 49 Because of this,
God in his wisdom said, 'I will send them
prophets and apostles, some of whom
they will kill and others they will persecute.' 50 Therefore this generation will be
held responsible for the blood of all the
prophets that has been shed since the beginning of the world, 51 from the blood of
Abel to the blood of Zechariah, who was
killed between the altar and the sanctuary. Yes, I tell you, this generation will be
held responsible for it all.
52 "Woe to you experts in the law, because you have taken away the key to
knowledge. You yourselves have not entered, and you have hindered those who
were entering."
53 When Jesus went outside, the Phari-

[a] *34* The Greek for *healthy* here implies *generous*. [b] *34* The Greek for *unhealthy* here implies *stingy*.

sees and the teachers of the law began to
oppose him fiercely and to besiege him
with questions, 54waiting to catch him in
something he might say.

12 Meanwhile, when a crowd of many
thousands had gathered, so that
they were trampling on one another,
Jesus began to speak first to his disciples,
saying: "Be[a] on your guard against the
yeast of the Pharisees, which is hypocrisy. 2There is nothing concealed that will
not be disclosed, or hidden that will not
be made known. 3What you have said in
the dark will be heard in the daylight, and
what you have whispered in the ear in the
inner rooms will be proclaimed from the
roofs.

4"I tell you, my friends, do not be afraid
of those who kill the body and after that
can do no more. 5But I will show you
whom you should fear: Fear him who,
after your body has been killed, has authority to throw you into hell. Yes, I tell
you, fear him. 6Are not five sparrows sold
for two pennies? Yet not one of them is
forgotten by God. 7Indeed, the very hairs
of your head are all numbered. Don't be
afraid; you are worth more than many
sparrows.

8"I tell you, whoever publicly acknowledges me before others, the Son of Man
will also acknowledge before the angels
of God. 9But whoever disowns me before
others will be disowned before the angels of God. 10And everyone who speaks
a word against the Son of Man will be
forgiven, but anyone who blasphemes
against the Holy Spirit will not be forgiven.

11"When you are brought before synagogues, rulers and authorities, do not
worry about how you will defend yourselves or what you will say, 12for the Holy
Spirit will teach you at that time what you
should say."

13Someone in the crowd said to him,
"Teacher, tell my brother to divide the inheritance with me."

14Jesus replied, "Man, who appointed
me a judge or an arbiter between you?"
15Then he said to them, "Watch out! Be
on your guard against all kinds of greed;
life does not consist in an abundance of
possessions."

16And he told them this parable: "The
ground of a certain rich man yielded an
abundant harvest. 17He thought to himself, 'What shall I do? I have no place to
store my crops.'

18"Then he said, 'This is what I'll do. I
will tear down my barns and build bigger ones, and there I will store my surplus
grain. 19And I'll say to myself, "You have
plenty of grain laid up for many years.
Take life easy; eat, drink and be merry." '

20"But God said to him, 'You fool! This
very night your life will be demanded
from you. Then who will get what you
have prepared for yourself?'

21"This is how it will be with whoever
stores up things for themselves but is not
rich toward God."

22Then Jesus said to his disciples:
"Therefore I tell you, do not worry about
your life, what you will eat; or about your
body, what you will wear. 23For life is
more than food, and the body more than
clothes. 24Consider the ravens: They do
not sow or reap, they have no storeroom
or barn; yet God feeds them. And how
much more valuable you are than birds!
25Who of you by worrying can add a single hour to your life[b]? 26Since you cannot
do this very little thing, why do you worry
about the rest?

27"Consider how the wild flowers grow.
They do not labor or spin. Yet I tell you,
not even Solomon in all his splendor was
dressed like one of these. 28If that is how
God clothes the grass of the field, which is
here today, and tomorrow is thrown into
the fire, how much more will he clothe
you — you of little faith! 29And do not set
your heart on what you will eat or drink;
do not worry about it. 30For the pagan
world runs after all such things, and your
Father knows that you need them. 31But
seek his kingdom, and these things will
be given to you as well.

32"Do not be afraid, little flock, for your
Father has been pleased to give you the
kingdom. 33Sell your possessions and
give to the poor. Provide purses for yourselves that will not wear out, a treasure in
heaven that will never fail, where no thief
comes near and no moth destroys. 34For
where your treasure is, there your heart
will be also.

35"Be dressed ready for service and
keep your lamps burning, 36like servants

[a] 1 Or *speak to his disciples, saying: "First of all, be*
[b] 25 Or *single cubit to your height*

waiting for their master to return from a
wedding banquet, so that when he comes
and knocks they can immediately open
the door for him. 37 It will be good for
those servants whose master finds them
watching when he comes. Truly I tell you,
he will dress himself to serve, will have
them recline at the table and will come
and wait on them. 38 It will be good for
those servants whose master finds them
ready, even if he comes in the middle of
the night or toward daybreak. 39 But understand this: If the owner of the house
had known at what hour the thief was
coming, he would not have let his house
be broken into. 40 You also must be ready,
because the Son of Man will come at an
hour when you do not expect him."

41 Peter asked, "Lord, are you telling
this parable to us, or to everyone?"

42 The Lord answered, "Who then is
the faithful and wise manager, whom
the master puts in charge of his servants
to give them their food allowance at the
proper time? 43 It will be good for that
servant whom the master finds doing so
when he returns. 44 Truly I tell you, he will
put him in charge of all his possessions.
45 But suppose the servant says to himself, 'My master is taking a long time in
coming,' and he then begins to beat the
other servants, both men and women,
and to eat and drink and get drunk. 46 The
master of that servant will come on a day
when he does not expect him and at an
hour he is not aware of. He will cut him
to pieces and assign him a place with the
unbelievers.

47 "The servant who knows the master's will and does not get ready or does
not do what the master wants will be
beaten with many blows. 48 But the one
who does not know and does things deserving punishment will be beaten with
few blows. From everyone who has been
given much, much will be demanded;
and from the one who has been entrusted
with much, much more will be asked.

49 "I have come to bring fire on the
earth, and how I wish it were already
kindled! 50 But I have a baptism to undergo, and what constraint I am under until
it is completed! 51 Do you think I came to
bring peace on earth? No, I tell you, but
division. 52 From now on there will be five
in one family divided against each other,
three against two and two against three.
53 They will be divided, father against son
and son against father, mother against
daughter and daughter against mother,
mother-in-law against daughter-in-law
and daughter-in-law against mother-in-
law."

54 He said to the crowd: "When you see
a cloud rising in the west, immediately
you say, 'It's going to rain,' and it does.
55 And when the south wind blows, you
say, 'It's going to be hot,' and it is. 56 Hypocrites! You know how to interpret the appearance of the earth and the sky. How
is it that you don't know how to interpret
this present time?

57 "Why don't you judge for yourselves
what is right? 58 As you are going with
your adversary to the magistrate, try hard
to be reconciled on the way, or your adversary may drag you off to the judge, and
the judge turn you over to the officer, and
the officer throw you into prison. 59 I tell
you, you will not get out until you have
paid the last penny."

13 Now there were some present at
that time who told Jesus about the
Galileans whose blood Pilate had mixed
with their sacrifices. 2 Jesus answered,
"Do you think that these Galileans were
worse sinners than all the other Galileans because they suffered this way? 3 I
tell you, no! But unless you repent, you
too will all perish. 4 Or those eighteen
who died when the tower in Siloam fell
on them — do you think they were more
guilty than all the others living in Jerusalem? 5 I tell you, no! But unless you repent,
you too will all perish."

6 Then he told this parable: "A man had
a fig tree growing in his vineyard, and he
went to look for fruit on it but did not find
any. 7 So he said to the man who took care
of the vineyard, 'For three years now I've
been coming to look for fruit on this fig
tree and haven't found any. Cut it down!
Why should it use up the soil?'

8 " 'Sir,' the man replied, 'leave it alone
for one more year, and I'll dig around it
and fertilize it. 9 If it bears fruit next year,
fine! If not, then cut it down.' "

10 On a Sabbath Jesus was teaching in
one of the synagogues, 11 and a woman was there who had been crippled by
a spirit for eighteen years. She was bent
over and could not straighten up at all.
12 When Jesus saw her, he called her forward and said to her, "Woman, you are

set free from your infirmity." 13 Then he
put his hands on her, and immediately
she straightened up and praised God.
14 Indignant because Jesus had healed
on the Sabbath, the synagogue leader
said to the people, "There are six days for
work. So come and be healed on those
days, not on the Sabbath."
15 The Lord answered him, "You hypocrites! Doesn't each of you on the Sabbath
untie your ox or donkey from the stall and
lead it out to give it water? 16 Then should
not this woman, a daughter of Abraham,
whom Satan has kept bound for eighteen
long years, be set free on the Sabbath day
from what bound her?"
17 When he said this, all his opponents
were humiliated, but the people were delighted with all the wonderful things he
was doing.
18 Then Jesus asked, "What is the kingdom of God like? What shall I compare
it to? 19 It is like a mustard seed, which a
man took and planted in his garden. It
grew and became a tree, and the birds
perched in its branches."
20 Again he asked, "What shall I compare the kingdom of God to? 21 It is like
yeast that a woman took and mixed
into about sixty pounds[a] of flour until it
worked all through the dough."
22 Then Jesus went through the towns
and villages, teaching as he made his
way to Jerusalem. 23 Someone asked him,
"Lord, are only a few people going to be
saved?"
He said to them, 24 "Make every effort to
enter through the narrow door, because
many, I tell you, will try to enter and will
not be able to. 25 Once the owner of the
house gets up and closes the door, you
will stand outside knocking and pleading, 'Sir, open the door for us.'
"But he will answer, 'I don't know you
or where you come from.'
26 "Then you will say, 'We ate and drank
with you, and you taught in our streets.'
27 "But he will reply, 'I don't know you or
where you come from. Away from me, all
you evildoers!'
28 "There will be weeping there, and
gnashing of teeth, when you see Abraham, Isaac and Jacob and all the prophets in the kingdom of God, but you yourselves thrown out. 29 People will come
from east and west and north and south,
and will take their places at the feast in
the kingdom of God. 30 Indeed there are
those who are last who will be first, and
first who will be last."
31 At that time some Pharisees came to
Jesus and said to him, "Leave this place
and go somewhere else. Herod wants to
kill you."
32 He replied, "Go tell that fox, 'I will
keep on driving out demons and healing
people today and tomorrow, and on the
third day I will reach my goal.' 33 In any
case, I must press on today and tomorrow
and the next day — for surely no prophet
can die outside Jerusalem!
34 "Jerusalem, Jerusalem, you who kill
the prophets and stone those sent to you,
how often I have longed to gather your
children together, as a hen gathers her
chicks under her wings, and you were
not willing. 35 Look, your house is left to
you desolate. I tell you, you will not see
me again until you say, 'Blessed is he who
comes in the name of the Lord.'[b]"

14 One Sabbath, when Jesus went to eat
in the house of a prominent Pharisee, he was being carefully watched.
2 There in front of him was a man suffering from abnormal swelling of his body.
3 Jesus asked the Pharisees and experts in
the law, "Is it lawful to heal on the Sabbath or not?" 4 But they remained silent.
So taking hold of the man, he healed him
and sent him on his way.
5 Then he asked them, "If one of you has
a child[c] or an ox that falls into a well on
the Sabbath day, will you not immediately pull it out?" 6 And they had nothing
to say.
7 When he noticed how the guests
picked the places of honor at the table,
he told them this parable: 8 "When someone invites you to a wedding feast, do not
take the place of honor, for a person more
distinguished than you may have been
invited. 9 If so, the host who invited both
of you will come and say to you, 'Give
this person your seat.' Then, humiliated,
you will have to take the least important
place. 10 But when you are invited, take
the lowest place, so that when your host
comes, he will say to you, 'Friend, move
up to a better place.' Then you will be
honored in the presence of all the other

[a] *21* Or about 27 kilograms [b] *35* Psalm 118:26 [c] *5* Some manuscripts *donkey*

guests. 11For all those who exalt themselves will be humbled, and those who humble themselves will be exalted."

12Then Jesus said to his host, "When you give a luncheon or dinner, do not invite your friends, your brothers or sisters, your relatives, or your rich neighbors; if you do, they may invite you back and so you will be repaid. 13But when you give a banquet, invite the poor, the crippled, the lame, the blind, 14and you will be blessed. Although they cannot repay you, you will be repaid at the resurrection of the righteous."

15When one of those at the table with him heard this, he said to Jesus, "Blessed is the one who will eat at the feast in the kingdom of God."

16Jesus replied: "A certain man was preparing a great banquet and invited many guests. 17At the time of the banquet he sent his servant to tell those who had been invited, 'Come, for everything is now ready.'

18"But they all alike began to make excuses. The first said, 'I have just bought a field, and I must go and see it. Please excuse me.'

19"Another said, 'I have just bought five yoke of oxen, and I'm on my way to try them out. Please excuse me.'

20"Still another said, 'I just got married, so I can't come.'

21"The servant came back and reported this to his master. Then the owner of the house became angry and ordered his servant, 'Go out quickly into the streets and alleys of the town and bring in the poor, the crippled, the blind and the lame.'

22"'Sir,' the servant said, 'what you ordered has been done, but there is still room.'

23"Then the master told his servant, 'Go out to the roads and country lanes and compel them to come in, so that my house will be full. 24I tell you, not one of those who were invited will get a taste of my banquet.'"

25Large crowds were traveling with Jesus, and turning to them he said: 26"If anyone comes to me and does not hate father and mother, wife and children, brothers and sisters—yes, even their own life—such a person cannot be my disciple. 27And whoever does not carry their cross and follow me cannot be my disciple.

28"Suppose one of you wants to build a tower. Won't you first sit down and estimate the cost to see if you have enough money to complete it? 29For if you lay the foundation and are not able to finish it, everyone who sees it will ridicule you, 30saying, 'This person began to build and wasn't able to finish.'

31"Or suppose a king is about to go to war against another king. Won't he first sit down and consider whether he is able with ten thousand men to oppose the one coming against him with twenty thousand? 32If he is not able, he will send a delegation while the other is still a long way off and will ask for terms of peace. 33In the same way, those of you who do not give up everything you have cannot be my disciples.

34"Salt is good, but if it loses its saltiness, how can it be made salty again? 35It is fit neither for the soil nor for the manure pile; it is thrown out.

"Whoever has ears to hear, let them hear."

15 Now the tax collectors and sinners were all gathering around to hear Jesus. 2But the Pharisees and the teachers of the law muttered, "This man welcomes sinners and eats with them."

3Then Jesus told them this parable: 4"Suppose one of you has a hundred sheep and loses one of them. Doesn't he leave the ninety-nine in the open country and go after the lost sheep until he finds it? 5And when he finds it, he joyfully puts it on his shoulders 6and goes home. Then he calls his friends and neighbors together and says, 'Rejoice with me; I have found my lost sheep.' 7I tell you that in the same way there will be more rejoicing in heaven over one sinner who repents than over ninety-nine righteous persons who do not need to repent.

8"Or suppose a woman has ten silver coins[a] and loses one. Doesn't she light a lamp, sweep the house and search carefully until she finds it? 9And when she finds it, she calls her friends and neighbors together and says, 'Rejoice with me; I have found my lost coin.' 10In the same way, I tell you, there is rejoicing in the

[a] 8 Greek *ten drachmas,* each worth about a day's wages

presence of the angels of God over one sinner who repents."

11 Jesus continued: "There was a man who had two sons. 12 The younger one said to his father, 'Father, give me my share of the estate.' So he divided his property between them.

13 "Not long after that, the younger son got together all he had, set off for a distant country and there squandered his wealth in wild living. 14 After he had spent everything, there was a severe famine in that whole country, and he began to be in need. 15 So he went and hired himself out to a citizen of that country, who sent him to his fields to feed pigs. 16 He longed to fill his stomach with the pods that the pigs were eating, but no one gave him anything.

17 "When he came to his senses, he said, 'How many of my father's hired servants have food to spare, and here I am starving to death! 18 I will set out and go back to my father and say to him: Father, I have sinned against heaven and against you. 19 I am no longer worthy to be called your son; make me like one of your hired servants.' 20 So he got up and went to his father.

"But while he was still a long way off, his father saw him and was filled with compassion for him; he ran to his son, threw his arms around him and kissed him.

21 "The son said to him, 'Father, I have sinned against heaven and against you. I am no longer worthy to be called your son.'

22 "But the father said to his servants, 'Quick! Bring the best robe and put it on him. Put a ring on his finger and sandals on his feet. 23 Bring the fattened calf and kill it. Let's have a feast and celebrate. 24 For this son of mine was dead and is alive again; he was lost and is found.' So they began to celebrate.

25 "Meanwhile, the older son was in the field. When he came near the house, he heard music and dancing. 26 So he called one of the servants and asked him what was going on. 27 'Your brother has come,' he replied, 'and your father has killed the fattened calf because he has him back safe and sound.'

28 "The older brother became angry and refused to go in. So his father went out and pleaded with him. 29 But he answered his father, 'Look! All these years I've been slaving for you and never disobeyed your orders. Yet you never gave me even a young goat so I could celebrate with my friends. 30 But when this son of yours who has squandered your property with prostitutes comes home, you kill the fattened calf for him!'

31 " 'My son,' the father said, 'you are always with me, and everything I have is yours. 32 But we had to celebrate and be glad, because this brother of yours was dead and is alive again; he was lost and is found.' "

16 Jesus told his disciples: "There was a rich man whose manager was accused of wasting his possessions. 2 So he called him in and asked him, 'What is this I hear about you? Give an account of your management, because you cannot be manager any longer.'

3 "The manager said to himself, 'What shall I do now? My master is taking away my job. I'm not strong enough to dig, and I'm ashamed to beg— 4 I know what I'll do so that, when I lose my job here, people will welcome me into their houses.'

5 "So he called in each one of his master's debtors. He asked the first, 'How much do you owe my master?'

6 " 'Nine hundred gallons[a] of olive oil,' he replied.

"The manager told him, 'Take your bill, sit down quickly, and make it four hundred and fifty.'

7 "Then he asked the second, 'And how much do you owe?'

" 'A thousand bushels[b] of wheat,' he replied.

"He told him, 'Take your bill and make it eight hundred.'

8 "The master commended the dishonest manager because he had acted shrewdly. For the people of this world are more shrewd in dealing with their own kind than are the people of the light. 9 I tell you, use worldly wealth to gain friends for yourselves, so that when it is gone, you will be welcomed into eternal dwellings.

10 "Whoever can be trusted with very little can also be trusted with much, and whoever is dishonest with very little will

[a] 6 Or about 3,000 liters [b] 7 Or about 30 tons

also be dishonest with much. 11 So if you
have not been trustworthy in handling
worldly wealth, who will trust you with
true riches? 12 And if you have not been
trustworthy with someone else's property, who will give you property of your
own?

13 "No one can serve two masters. Either you will hate the one and love the
other, or you will be devoted to the one
and despise the other. You cannot serve
both God and money."

14 The Pharisees, who loved money,
heard all this and were sneering at Jesus.
15 He said to them, "You are the ones who
justify yourselves in the eyes of others,
but God knows your hearts. What people
value highly is detestable in God's sight.

16 "The Law and the Prophets were
proclaimed until John. Since that time,
the good news of the kingdom of God is
being preached, and everyone is forcing
their way into it. 17 It is easier for heaven
and earth to disappear than for the least
stroke of a pen to drop out of the Law.

18 "Anyone who divorces his wife and
marries another woman commits adultery, and the man who marries a divorced
woman commits adultery.

19 "There was a rich man who was
dressed in purple and fine linen and lived
in luxury every day. 20 At his gate was laid
a beggar named Lazarus, covered with
sores 21 and longing to eat what fell from
the rich man's table. Even the dogs came
and licked his sores.

22 "The time came when the beggar
died and the angels carried him to Abraham's side. The rich man also died and
was buried. 23 In Hades, where he was in
torment, he looked up and saw Abraham
far away, with Lazarus by his side. 24 So
he called to him, 'Father Abraham, have
pity on me and send Lazarus to dip the tip
of his finger in water and cool my tongue,
because I am in agony in this fire.'

25 "But Abraham replied, 'Son, remember that in your lifetime you received
your good things, while Lazarus received
bad things, but now he is comforted here
and you are in agony. 26 And besides all
this, between us and you a great chasm
has been set in place, so that those who
want to go from here to you cannot, nor
can anyone cross over from there to us.'

27 "He answered, 'Then I beg you, father, send Lazarus to my family, 28 for I
have five brothers. Let him warn them, so
that they will not also come to this place
of torment.'

29 "Abraham replied, 'They have Moses and the Prophets; let them listen to
them.'

30 " 'No, father Abraham,' he said, 'but
if someone from the dead goes to them,
they will repent.'

31 "He said to him, 'If they do not listen
to Moses and the Prophets, they will not
be convinced even if someone rises from
the dead.' "

17 Jesus said to his disciples: "Things
that cause people to stumble are
bound to come, but woe to anyone
through whom they come. 2 It would be
better for them to be thrown into the sea
with a millstone tied around their neck
than to cause one of these little ones to
stumble. 3 So watch yourselves.

"If your brother or sister[a] sins against
you, rebuke them; and if they repent, forgive them. 4 Even if they sin against you
seven times in a day and seven times
come back to you saying 'I repent,' you
must forgive them."

5 The apostles said to the Lord, "Increase our faith!"

6 He replied, "If you have faith as small
as a mustard seed, you can say to this
mulberry tree, 'Be uprooted and planted
in the sea,' and it will obey you.

7 "Suppose one of you has a servant
plowing or looking after the sheep. Will
he say to the servant when he comes in
from the field, 'Come along now and sit
down to eat'? 8 Won't he rather say, 'Prepare my supper, get yourself ready and
wait on me while I eat and drink; after
that you may eat and drink'? 9 Will he
thank the servant because he did what
he was told to do? 10 So you also, when
you have done everything you were told
to do, should say, 'We are unworthy servants; we have only done our duty.' "

11 Now on his way to Jerusalem, Jesus
traveled along the border between Samaria and Galilee. 12 As he was going
into a village, ten men who had leprosy[b]
met him. They stood at a distance 13 and
called out in a loud voice, "Jesus, Master,
have pity on us!"

[a] *3* The Greek word for *brother or sister* (*adelphos*) refers here to a fellow disciple, whether man or woman.
[b] *12* The Greek word traditionally translated *leprosy* was used for various diseases affecting the skin.

14 When he saw them, he said, "Go,
show yourselves to the priests." And as
they went, they were cleansed.
15 One of them, when he saw he was
healed, came back, praising God in a
loud voice. 16 He threw himself at Jesus'
feet and thanked him — and he was a Samaritan.
17 Jesus asked, "Were not all ten
cleansed? Where are the other nine?
18 Has no one returned to give praise to
God except this foreigner?" 19 Then he
said to him, "Rise and go; your faith has
made you well."
20 Once, on being asked by the Pharisees when the kingdom of God would
come, Jesus replied, "The coming of the
kingdom of God is not something that
can be observed, 21 nor will people say,
'Here it is,' or 'There it is,' because the
kingdom of God is in your midst."[a]
22 Then he said to his disciples, "The
time is coming when you will long to
see one of the days of the Son of Man,
but you will not see it. 23 People will tell
you, 'There he is!' or 'Here he is!' Do not
go running off after them. 24 For the Son
of Man in his day[b] will be like the lightning, which flashes and lights up the sky
from one end to the other. 25 But first he
must suffer many things and be rejected
by this generation.
26 "Just as it was in the days of Noah,
so also will it be in the days of the Son
of Man. 27 People were eating, drinking,
marrying and being given in marriage up
to the day Noah entered the ark. Then the
flood came and destroyed them all.
28 "It was the same in the days of Lot.
People were eating and drinking, buying
and selling, planting and building. 29 But
the day Lot left Sodom, fire and sulfur
rained down from heaven and destroyed
them all.
30 "It will be just like this on the day the
Son of Man is revealed. 31 On that day no
one who is on the housetop, with possessions inside, should go down to get them.
Likewise, no one in the field should go
back for anything. 32 Remember Lot's
wife! 33 Whoever tries to keep their life
will lose it, and whoever loses their life
will preserve it. 34 I tell you, on that night
two people will be in one bed; one will be
taken and the other left. 35 Two women
will be grinding grain together; one will
be taken and the other left." [36][c]
37 "Where, Lord?" they asked.
He replied, "Where there is a dead
body, there the vultures will gather."

18 Then Jesus told his disciples a parable to show them that they should
always pray and not give up. 2 He said:
"In a certain town there was a judge who
neither feared God nor cared what people thought. 3 And there was a widow in
that town who kept coming to him with
the plea, 'Grant me justice against my
adversary.'
4 "For some time he refused. But finally he said to himself, 'Even though I don't
fear God or care what people think, 5 yet
because this widow keeps bothering me,
I will see that she gets justice, so that she
won't eventually come and attack me!'"
6 And the Lord said, "Listen to what
the unjust judge says. 7 And will not God
bring about justice for his chosen ones,
who cry out to him day and night? Will
he keep putting them off? 8 I tell you, he
will see that they get justice, and quickly. However, when the Son of Man comes,
will he find faith on the earth?"
9 To some who were confident of their
own righteousness and looked down on
everyone else, Jesus told this parable:
10 "Two men went up to the temple to
pray, one a Pharisee and the other a tax
collector. 11 The Pharisee stood by himself and prayed: 'God, I thank you that I
am not like other people — robbers, evildoers, adulterers — or even like this tax
collector. 12 I fast twice a week and give a
tenth of all I get.'
13 "But the tax collector stood at a distance. He would not even look up to heav-
en, but beat his breast and said, 'God,
have mercy on me, a sinner.'
14 "I tell you that this man, rather than
the other, went home justified before
God. For all those who exalt themselves
will be humbled, and those who humble
themselves will be exalted."
15 People were also bringing babies
to Jesus for him to place his hands on
them. When the disciples saw this, they
rebuked them. 16 But Jesus called the
children to him and said, "Let the little
children come to me, and do not hinder
them, for the kingdom of God belongs to

[a] 21 Or *is within you* [b] 24 Some manuscripts do not have *in his day.* [c] 36 Some manuscripts include here words similar to Matt. 24:40.

such as these. 17Truly I tell you, anyone
who will not receive the kingdom of God
like a little child will never enter it."
18A certain ruler asked him, "Good
teacher, what must I do to inherit eternal life?"
19"Why do you call me good?" Jesus
answered. "No one is good — except God
alone. 20You know the commandments:
'You shall not commit adultery, you shall
not murder, you shall not steal, you shall
not give false testimony, honor your father and mother.'[a]"
21"All these I have kept since I was a
boy," he said.
22When Jesus heard this, he said to
him, "You still lack one thing. Sell everything you have and give to the poor, and
you will have treasure in heaven. Then
come, follow me."
23When he heard this, he became very
sad, because he was very wealthy. 24Jesus
looked at him and said, "How hard it is for
the rich to enter the kingdom of God! 25In-
deed, it is easier for a camel to go through
the eye of a needle than for someone who
is rich to enter the kingdom of God."
26Those who heard this asked, "Who
then can be saved?"
27Jesus replied, "What is impossible
with man is possible with God."
28Peter said to him, "We have left all we
had to follow you!"
29"Truly I tell you," Jesus said to them,
"no one who has left home or wife or
brothers or sisters or parents or children for the sake of the kingdom of God
30will fail to receive many times as much
in this age, and in the age to come eternal life."
31Jesus took the Twelve aside and told
them, "We are going up to Jerusalem, and
everything that is written by the prophets about the Son of Man will be fulfilled.
32He will be delivered over to the Gentiles. They will mock him, insult him and
spit on him; 33they will flog him and kill
him. On the third day he will rise again."
34The disciples did not understand
any of this. Its meaning was hidden from
them, and they did not know what he was
talking about.
35As Jesus approached Jericho, a blind
man was sitting by the roadside begging.
36When he heard the crowd going by, he
asked what was happening. 37They told
him, "Jesus of Nazareth is passing by."
38He called out, "Jesus, Son of David,
have mercy on me!"
39Those who led the way rebuked him
and told him to be quiet, but he shouted
all the more, "Son of David, have mercy
on me!"
40Jesus stopped and ordered the man
to be brought to him. When he came
near, Jesus asked him, 41"What do you
want me to do for you?"
"Lord, I want to see," he replied.
42Jesus said to him, "Receive your sight;
your faith has healed you." 43Immedi-
ately he received his sight and followed
Jesus, praising God. When all the people
saw it, they also praised God.

19 Jesus entered Jericho and was passing through. 2A man was there by
the name of Zacchaeus; he was a chief tax
collector and was wealthy. 3He wanted
to see who Jesus was, but because he was
short he could not see over the crowd. 4So
he ran ahead and climbed a sycamore-fig
tree to see him, since Jesus was coming
that way.
5When Jesus reached the spot, he
looked up and said to him, "Zacchaeus,
come down immediately. I must stay at
your house today." 6So he came down at
once and welcomed him gladly.
7All the people saw this and began to
mutter, "He has gone to be the guest of a
sinner."
8But Zacchaeus stood up and said to
the Lord, "Look, Lord! Here and now I
give half of my possessions to the poor,
and if I have cheated anybody out of
anything, I will pay back four times the
amount."
9Jesus said to him, "Today salvation
has come to this house, because this
man, too, is a son of Abraham. 10For the
Son of Man came to seek and to save the
lost."
11While they were listening to this,
he went on to tell them a parable, because he was near Jerusalem and the
people thought that the kingdom of God
was going to appear at once. 12He said:
"A man of noble birth went to a distant
country to have himself appointed king
and then to return. 13So he called ten of
his servants and gave them ten minas.[b]

[a] 20 Exodus 20:12-16; Deut. 5:16-20 [b] 13 A mina was about three months' wages.

'Put this money to work,' he said, 'until
I come back.'
14 "But his subjects hated him and sent
a delegation after him to say, 'We don't
want this man to be our king.'
15 "He was made king, however, and
returned home. Then he sent for the servants to whom he had given the money,
in order to find out what they had gained
with it.
16 "The first one came and said, 'Sir,
your mina has earned ten more.'
17 " 'Well done, my good servant!' his
master replied. 'Because you have been
trustworthy in a very small matter, take
charge of ten cities.'
18 "The second came and said, 'Sir, your
mina has earned five more.'
19 "His master answered, 'You take
charge of five cities.'
20 "Then another servant came and
said, 'Sir, here is your mina; I have kept it
laid away in a piece of cloth. 21 I was afraid
of you, because you are a hard man. You
take out what you did not put in and reap
what you did not sow.'
22 "His master replied, 'I will judge you
by your own words, you wicked servant!
You knew, did you, that I am a hard man,
taking out what I did not put in, and reaping what I did not sow? 23 Why then didn't
you put my money on deposit, so that
when I came back, I could have collected
it with interest?'
24 "Then he said to those standing by,
'Take his mina away from him and give it
to the one who has ten minas.'
25 " 'Sir,' they said, 'he already has ten!'
26 "He replied, 'I tell you that to everyone who has, more will be given, but as
for the one who has nothing, even what
they have will be taken away. 27 But those
enemies of mine who did not want me to
be king over them—bring them here and
kill them in front of me.' "

28 After Jesus had said this, he went
on ahead, going up to Jerusalem. 29 As
he approached Bethphage and Bethany
at the hill called the Mount of Olives, he
sent two of his disciples, saying to them,
30 "Go to the village ahead of you, and as
you enter it, you will find a colt tied there,
which no one has ever ridden. Untie it
and bring it here. 31 If anyone asks you,
'Why are you untying it?' say, 'The Lord
needs it.' "
32 Those who were sent ahead went and
found it just as he had told them. 33 As
they were untying the colt, its owners
asked them, "Why are you untying the
colt?"
34 They replied, "The Lord needs it."
35 They brought it to Jesus, threw their
cloaks on the colt and put Jesus on it. 36 As
he went along, people spread their cloaks
on the road.
37 When he came near the place where
the road goes down the Mount of Olives,
the whole crowd of disciples began joyfully to praise God in loud voices for all
the miracles they had seen:

38 "Blessed is the king who comes in the
name of the Lord!"[a]
"Peace in heaven and glory in the
highest!"

39 Some of the Pharisees in the crowd
said to Jesus, "Teacher, rebuke your disciples!"
40 "I tell you," he replied, "if they keep
quiet, the stones will cry out."
41 As he approached Jerusalem and saw
the city, he wept over it 42 and said, "If you,
even you, had only known on this day
what would bring you peace—but now it
is hidden from your eyes. 43 The days will
come upon you when your enemies will
build an embankment against you and
encircle you and hem you in on every
side. 44 They will dash you to the ground,
you and the children within your walls.
They will not leave one stone on another,
because you did not recognize the time of
God's coming to you."
45 When Jesus entered the temple
courts, he began to drive out those who
were selling. 46 "It is written," he said
to them, " 'My house will be a house of
prayer'[b]; but you have made it 'a den of
robbers.'[c]"
47 Every day he was teaching at the temple. But the chief priests, the teachers of
the law and the leaders among the people
were trying to kill him. 48 Yet they could
not find any way to do it, because all the
people hung on his words.

20 One day as Jesus was teaching the
people in the temple courts and
proclaiming the good news, the chief

[a] *38* Psalm 118:26 [b] *46* Isaiah 56:7 [c] *46* Jer. 7:11

priests and the teachers of the law, together with the elders, came up to him.
2 "Tell us by what authority you are doing
these things," they said. "Who gave you
this authority?"
3 He replied, "I will also ask you a question. Tell me: 4 John's baptism—was it
from heaven, or of human origin?"
5 They discussed it among themselves
and said, "If we say, 'From heaven,' he
will ask, 'Why didn't you believe him?'
6 But if we say, 'Of human origin,' all the
people will stone us, because they are
persuaded that John was a prophet."
7 So they answered, "We don't know
where it was from."
8 Jesus said, "Neither will I tell you by
what authority I am doing these things."
9 He went on to tell the people this parable: "A man planted a vineyard, rented
it to some farmers and went away for a
long time. 10 At harvest time he sent a
servant to the tenants so they would give
him some of the fruit of the vineyard.
But the tenants beat him and sent him
away empty-handed. 11 He sent another
servant, but that one also they beat and
treated shamefully and sent away empty-
handed. 12 He sent still a third, and they
wounded him and threw him out.
13 "Then the owner of the vineyard said,
'What shall I do? I will send my son, whom
I love; perhaps they will respect him.'
14 "But when the tenants saw him, they
talked the matter over. 'This is the heir,'
they said. 'Let's kill him, and the inheritance will be ours.' 15 So they threw him
out of the vineyard and killed him.
"What then will the owner of the vineyard do to them? 16 He will come and kill
those tenants and give the vineyard to
others."
When the people heard this, they said,
"God forbid!"
17 Jesus looked directly at them and
asked, "Then what is the meaning of that
which is written:

"'The stone the builders rejected
has become the cornerstone'[a]?

18 Everyone who falls on that stone will be
broken to pieces; anyone on whom it falls
will be crushed."
19 The teachers of the law and the chief
priests looked for a way to arrest him
immediately, because they knew he had
spoken this parable against them. But
they were afraid of the people.
20 Keeping a close watch on him, they
sent spies, who pretended to be sincere.
They hoped to catch Jesus in something
he said, so that they might hand him over
to the power and authority of the governor. 21 So the spies questioned him:
"Teacher, we know that you speak and
teach what is right, and that you do not
show partiality but teach the way of God
in accordance with the truth. 22 Is it right
for us to pay taxes to Caesar or not?"
23 He saw through their duplicity and
said to them, 24 "Show me a denarius.
Whose image and inscription are on it?"
"Caesar's," they replied.
25 He said to them, "Then give back to
Caesar what is Caesar's, and to God what
is God's."
26 They were unable to trap him in what
he had said there in public. And astonished by his answer, they became silent.
27 Some of the Sadducees, who say
there is no resurrection, came to Jesus
with a question. 28 "Teacher," they said,
"Moses wrote for us that if a man's brother dies and leaves a wife but no children,
the man must marry the widow and raise
up offspring for his brother. 29 Now there
were seven brothers. The first one married a woman and died childless. 30 The
second 31 and then the third married her,
and in the same way the seven died, leaving no children. 32 Finally, the woman
died too. 33 Now then, at the resurrection
whose wife will she be, since the seven
were married to her?"
34 Jesus replied, "The people of this age
marry and are given in marriage. 35 But
those who are considered worthy of taking part in the age to come and in the resurrection from the dead will neither marry nor be given in marriage, 36 and they
can no longer die; for they are like the angels. They are God's children, since they
are children of the resurrection. 37 But in
the account of the burning bush, even
Moses showed that the dead rise, for he
calls the Lord 'the God of Abraham, and
the God of Isaac, and the God of Jacob.'[b]
38 He is not the God of the dead, but of the
living, for to him all are alive."
39 Some of the teachers of the law re-

[a] *17* Psalm 118:22 [b] *37* Exodus 3:6

sponded, "Well said, teacher!" [40]And no
one dared to ask him any more questions.
[41]Then Jesus said to them, "Why is it
said that the Messiah is the son of David?
[42]David himself declares in the Book of
Psalms:

"'The Lord said to my Lord:
"Sit at my right hand
[43]until I make your enemies
a footstool for your feet."'[a]

[44]David calls him 'Lord.' How then can
he be his son?"
[45]While all the people were listening,
Jesus said to his disciples, [46]"Beware of
the teachers of the law. They like to walk
around in flowing robes and love to be
greeted with respect in the marketplaces and have the most important seats in
the synagogues and the places of honor at
banquets. [47]They devour widows' houses and for a show make lengthy prayers.
These men will be punished most severely."

21

As Jesus looked up, he saw the rich
putting their gifts into the temple
treasury. [2]He also saw a poor widow put
in two very small copper coins. [3]"Truly I
tell you," he said, "this poor widow has
put in more than all the others. [4]All these
people gave their gifts out of their wealth;
but she out of her poverty put in all she
had to live on."
[5]Some of his disciples were remarking
about how the temple was adorned with
beautiful stones and with gifts dedicated
to God. But Jesus said, [6]"As for what you
see here, the time will come when not one
stone will be left on another; every one of
them will be thrown down."
[7]"Teacher," they asked, "when will
these things happen? And what will
be the sign that they are about to take
place?"
[8]He replied: "Watch out that you are
not deceived. For many will come in
my name, claiming, 'I am he,' and, 'The
time is near.' Do not follow them. [9]When
you hear of wars and uprisings, do not
be frightened. These things must happen first, but the end will not come right
away."
[10]Then he said to them: "Nation will
rise against nation, and kingdom against
kingdom. [11]There will be great earthquakes, famines and pestilences in various places, and fearful events and great
signs from heaven.
[12]"But before all this, they will seize
you and persecute you. They will hand
you over to synagogues and put you in
prison, and you will be brought before
kings and governors, and all on account
of my name. [13]And so you will bear testimony to me. [14]But make up your mind
not to worry beforehand how you will
defend yourselves. [15]For I will give you
words and wisdom that none of your
adversaries will be able to resist or contradict. [16]You will be betrayed even by
parents, brothers and sisters, relatives
and friends, and they will put some of
you to death. [17]Everyone will hate you
because of me. [18]But not a hair of your
head will perish. [19]Stand firm, and you
will win life.
[20]"When you see Jerusalem being surrounded by armies, you will know that its
desolation is near. [21]Then let those who
are in Judea flee to the mountains, let
those in the city get out, and let those in
the country not enter the city. [22]For this is
the time of punishment in fulfillment of
all that has been written. [23]How dreadful it will be in those days for pregnant
women and nursing mothers! There will
be great distress in the land and wrath
against this people. [24]They will fall by the
sword and will be taken as prisoners to all
the nations. Jerusalem will be trampled
on by the Gentiles until the times of the
Gentiles are fulfilled.
[25]"There will be signs in the sun, moon
and stars. On the earth, nations will be in
anguish and perplexity at the roaring and
tossing of the sea. [26]People will faint from
terror, apprehensive of what is coming on
the world, for the heavenly bodies will be
shaken. [27]At that time they will see the
Son of Man coming in a cloud with power and great glory. [28]When these things
begin to take place, stand up and lift up
your heads, because your redemption is
drawing near."
[29]He told them this parable: "Look at
the fig tree and all the trees. [30]When they
sprout leaves, you can see for yourselves
and know that summer is near. [31]Even
so, when you see these things happen-

[a] *43* Psalm 110:1

ing, you know that the kingdom of God
is near.
32"Truly I tell you, this generation will
certainly not pass away until all these
things have happened. 33Heaven and
earth will pass away, but my words will
never pass away.
34"Be careful, or your hearts will be
weighed down with carousing, drunkenness and the anxieties of life, and that
day will close on you suddenly like a trap.
35For it will come on all those who live on
the face of the whole earth. 36Be always
on the watch, and pray that you may be
able to escape all that is about to happen,
and that you may be able to stand before
the Son of Man."
37Each day Jesus was teaching at the
temple, and each evening he went out
to spend the night on the hill called the
Mount of Olives, 38and all the people
came early in the morning to hear him at
the temple.

22 Now the Festival of Unleavened
Bread, called the Passover, was
approaching, 2and the chief priests and
the teachers of the law were looking for
some way to get rid of Jesus, for they were
afraid of the people. 3Then Satan entered
Judas, called Iscariot, one of the Twelve.
4And Judas went to the chief priests and
the officers of the temple guard and discussed with them how he might betray
Jesus. 5They were delighted and agreed
to give him money. 6He consented, and
watched for an opportunity to hand
Jesus over to them when no crowd was
present.
7Then came the day of Unleavened
Bread on which the Passover lamb had to
be sacrificed. 8Jesus sent Peter and John,
saying, "Go and make preparations for us
to eat the Passover."
9"Where do you want us to prepare for
it?" they asked.
10He replied, "As you enter the city,
a man carrying a jar of water will meet
you. Follow him to the house that he enters, 11and say to the owner of the house,
'The Teacher asks: Where is the guest
room, where I may eat the Passover with
my disciples?' 12He will show you a large
room upstairs, all furnished. Make preparations there."
13They left and found things just as
Jesus had told them. So they prepared
the Passover.
14When the hour came, Jesus and his
apostles reclined at the table. 15And he
said to them, "I have eagerly desired to
eat this Passover with you before I suffer. 16For I tell you, I will not eat it again
until it finds fulfillment in the kingdom
of God."
17After taking the cup, he gave thanks
and said, "Take this and divide it among
you. 18For I tell you I will not drink again
from the fruit of the vine until the kingdom of God comes."
19And he took bread, gave thanks and
broke it, and gave it to them, saying, "This
is my body given for you; do this in remembrance of me."
20In the same way, after the supper he
took the cup, saying, "This cup is the new
covenant in my blood, which is poured
out for you.[a] 21But the hand of him who
is going to betray me is with mine on the
table. 22The Son of Man will go as it has
been decreed. But woe to that man who
betrays him!" 23They began to question among themselves which of them it
might be who would do this.
24A dispute also arose among them as
to which of them was considered to be
greatest. 25Jesus said to them, "The kings
of the Gentiles lord it over them; and
those who exercise authority over them
call themselves Benefactors. 26But you
are not to be like that. Instead, the greatest among you should be like the youngest, and the one who rules like the one
who serves. 27For who is greater, the one
who is at the table or the one who serves?
Is it not the one who is at the table? But I
am among you as one who serves. 28You
are those who have stood by me in my trials. 29And I confer on you a kingdom, just
as my Father conferred one on me, 30so
that you may eat and drink at my table in
my kingdom and sit on thrones, judging
the twelve tribes of Israel.
31"Simon, Simon, Satan has asked
to sift all of you as wheat. 32But I have
prayed for you, Simon, that your faith
may not fail. And when you have turned
back, strengthen your brothers."
33But he replied, "Lord, I am ready to go
with you to prison and to death."
34Jesus answered, "I tell you, Peter,

[a] *19,20* Some manuscripts do not have *given for you . . . poured out for you.*

before the rooster crows today, you will
deny three times that you know me."
35 Then Jesus asked them, "When I sent
you without purse, bag or sandals, did
you lack anything?"
"Nothing," they answered.
36 He said to them, "But now if you have
a purse, take it, and also a bag; and if you
don't have a sword, sell your cloak and
buy one. 37 It is written: 'And he was numbered with the transgressors'[a]; and I tell
you that this must be fulfilled in me. Yes,
what is written about me is reaching its
fulfillment."
38 The disciples said, "See, Lord, here
are two swords."
"That's enough!" he replied.
39 Jesus went out as usual to the Mount
of Olives, and his disciples followed him.
40 On reaching the place, he said to them,
"Pray that you will not fall into temptation." 41 He withdrew about a stone's
throw beyond them, knelt down and
prayed, 42 "Father, if you are willing, take
this cup from me; yet not my will, but
yours be done." 43 An angel from heaven
appeared to him and strengthened him.
44 And being in anguish, he prayed more
earnestly, and his sweat was like drops of
blood falling to the ground.[b]
45 When he rose from prayer and went
back to the disciples, he found them
asleep, exhausted from sorrow. 46 "Why
are you sleeping?" he asked them. "Get
up and pray so that you will not fall into
temptation."
47 While he was still speaking a crowd
came up, and the man who was called Judas, one of the Twelve, was leading them.
He approached Jesus to kiss him, 48 but
Jesus asked him, "Judas, are you betraying the Son of Man with a kiss?"
49 When Jesus' followers saw what was
going to happen, they said, "Lord, should
we strike with our swords?" 50 And one of
them struck the servant of the high priest,
cutting off his right ear.
51 But Jesus answered, "No more of
this!" And he touched the man's ear and
healed him.
52 Then Jesus said to the chief priests,
the officers of the temple guard, and the
elders, who had come for him, "Am I leading a rebellion, that you have come with
swords and clubs? 53 Every day I was with
you in the temple courts, and you did not
lay a hand on me. But this is your hour —
when darkness reigns."
54 Then seizing him, they led him away
and took him into the house of the high
priest. Peter followed at a distance. 55 And
when some there had kindled a fire in
the middle of the courtyard and had sat
down together, Peter sat down with them.
56 A servant girl saw him seated there in
the firelight. She looked closely at him
and said, "This man was with him."
57 But he denied it. "Woman, I don't
know him," he said.
58 A little later someone else saw him
and said, "You also are one of them."
"Man, I am not!" Peter replied.
59 About an hour later another asserted,
"Certainly this fellow was with him, for
he is a Galilean."
60 Peter replied, "Man, I don't know
what you're talking about!" Just as he was
speaking, the rooster crowed. 61 The Lord
turned and looked straight at Peter. Then
Peter remembered the word the Lord had
spoken to him: "Before the rooster crows
today, you will disown me three times."
62 And he went outside and wept bitterly.
63 The men who were guarding Jesus
began mocking and beating him. 64 They
blindfolded him and demanded, "Prophesy! Who hit you?" 65 And they said many
other insulting things to him.
66 At daybreak the council of the elders
of the people, both the chief priests and
the teachers of the law, met together, and
Jesus was led before them. 67 "If you are
the Messiah," they said, "tell us."
Jesus answered, "If I tell you, you will
not believe me, 68 and if I asked you, you
would not answer. 69 But from now on,
the Son of Man will be seated at the right
hand of the mighty God."
70 They all asked, "Are you then the Son
of God?"
He replied, "You say that I am."
71 Then they said, "Why do we need any
more testimony? We have heard it from
his own lips."

23 Then the whole assembly rose and
led him off to Pilate. 2 And they began to accuse him, saying, "We have
found this man subverting our nation. He
opposes payment of taxes to Caesar and
claims to be Messiah, a king."

[a] *37* Isaiah 53:12 [b] *43,44* Many early manuscripts do not have verses 43 and 44.

[3]So Pilate asked Jesus, "Are you the king of the Jews?"

"You have said so," Jesus replied.

[4]Then Pilate announced to the chief priests and the crowd, "I find no basis for a charge against this man."

[5]But they insisted, "He stirs up the people all over Judea by his teaching. He started in Galilee and has come all the way here."

[6]On hearing this, Pilate asked if the man was a Galilean. [7]When he learned that Jesus was under Herod's jurisdiction, he sent him to Herod, who was also in Jerusalem at that time.

[8]When Herod saw Jesus, he was greatly pleased, because for a long time he had been wanting to see him. From what he had heard about him, he hoped to see him perform a sign of some sort.
[9]He plied him with many questions, but Jesus gave him no answer. [10]The chief priests and the teachers of the law were standing there, vehemently accusing him. [11]Then Herod and his soldiers ridiculed and mocked him. Dressing him in an elegant robe, they sent him back to Pilate. [12]That day Herod and Pilate became friends—before this they had been enemies.

[13]Pilate called together the chief priests, the rulers and the people, [14]and said to them, "You brought me this man as one who was inciting the people to rebellion. I have examined him in your presence and have found no basis for your charges against him. [15]Neither has Herod, for he sent him back to us; as you can see, he has done nothing to deserve death. [16]Therefore, I will punish him and then release him." [17][a]

[18]But the whole crowd shouted, "Away with this man! Release Barabbas to us!"
[19](Barabbas had been thrown into prison for an insurrection in the city, and for murder.)

[20]Wanting to release Jesus, Pilate appealed to them again. [21]But they kept shouting, "Crucify him! Crucify him!"

[22]For the third time he spoke to them: "Why? What crime has this man committed? I have found in him no grounds for the death penalty. Therefore I will have him punished and then release him."

[23]But with loud shouts they insistently demanded that he be crucified, and their shouts prevailed. [24]So Pilate decided to grant their demand. [25]He released the man who had been thrown into prison for insurrection and murder, the one they asked for, and surrendered Jesus to their will.

[26]As the soldiers led him away, they seized Simon from Cyrene, who was on his way in from the country, and put the cross on him and made him carry it behind Jesus. [27]A large number of people followed him, including women who mourned and wailed for him. [28]Jesus turned and said to them, "Daughters of Jerusalem, do not weep for me; weep for yourselves and for your children. [29]For the time will come when you will say, 'Blessed are the childless women, the wombs that never bore and the breasts that never nursed!' [30]Then

"'they will say to the mountains, "Fall on us!"
and to the hills, "Cover us!"'[b]

[31]For if people do these things when the tree is green, what will happen when it is dry?"

[32]Two other men, both criminals, were also led out with him to be executed.
[33]When they came to the place called the Skull, they crucified him there, along with the criminals—one on his right, the other on his left. [34]Jesus said, "Father, forgive them, for they do not know what they are doing."[c] And they divided up his clothes by casting lots.

[35]The people stood watching, and the rulers even sneered at him. They said, "He saved others; let him save himself if he is God's Messiah, the Chosen One."

[36]The soldiers also came up and mocked him. They offered him wine vinegar [37]and said, "If you are the king of the Jews, save yourself."

[38]There was a written notice above him, which read: THIS IS THE KING OF THE JEWS.

[39]One of the criminals who hung there hurled insults at him: "Aren't you the Messiah? Save yourself and us!"

[40]But the other criminal rebuked him. "Don't you fear God," he said, "since you are under the same sentence? [41]We are punished justly, for we are getting what

[a] *17* Some manuscripts include here words similar to Matt. 27:15 and Mark 15:6. [b] *30* Hosea 10:8
[c] *34* Some early manuscripts do not have this sentence.

our deeds deserve. But this man has done
nothing wrong."
42 Then he said, "Jesus, remember me
when you come into your kingdom.[a]"
43 Jesus answered him, "Truly I tell you,
today you will be with me in paradise."
44 It was now about noon, and darkness
came over the whole land until three
in the afternoon, 45 for the sun stopped
shining. And the curtain of the temple
was torn in two. 46 Jesus called out with
a loud voice, "Father, into your hands I
commit my spirit."[b] When he had said
this, he breathed his last.
47 The centurion, seeing what had happened, praised God and said, "Surely this
was a righteous man." 48 When all the
people who had gathered to witness this
sight saw what took place, they beat their
breasts and went away. 49 But all those
who knew him, including the women who
had followed him from Galilee, stood at a
distance, watching these things.
50 Now there was a man named Joseph,
a member of the Council, a good and upright man, 51 who had not consented to
their decision and action. He came from
the Judean town of Arimathea, and he
himself was waiting for the kingdom of
God. 52 Going to Pilate, he asked for Jesus'
body. 53 Then he took it down, wrapped it
in linen cloth and placed it in a tomb cut
in the rock, one in which no one had yet
been laid. 54 It was Preparation Day, and
the Sabbath was about to begin.
55 The women who had come with Jesus
from Galilee followed Joseph and saw
the tomb and how his body was laid in
it. 56 Then they went home and prepared
spices and perfumes. But they rested on
the Sabbath in obedience to the commandment.
24 On the first day of the week, very early in the morning, the women took
the spices they had prepared and went to
the tomb. 2 They found the stone rolled
away from the tomb, 3 but when they entered, they did not find the body of the
Lord Jesus. 4 While they were wondering
about this, suddenly two men in clothes
that gleamed like lightning stood beside
them. 5 In their fright the women bowed
down with their faces to the ground, but
the men said to them, "Why do you look
for the living among the dead? 6 He is not
here; he has risen! Remember how he told
you, while he was still with you in Galilee:
7 'The Son of Man must be delivered over
to the hands of sinners, be crucified and
on the third day be raised again.' " 8 Then
they remembered his words.
9 When they came back from the tomb,
they told all these things to the Eleven and
to all the others. 10 It was Mary Magdalene, Joanna, Mary the mother of James,
and the others with them who told this to
the apostles. 11 But they did not believe
the women, because their words seemed
to them like nonsense. 12 Peter, however,
got up and ran to the tomb. Bending over,
he saw the strips of linen lying by themselves, and he went away, wondering to
himself what had happened.
13 Now that same day two of them were
going to a village called Emmaus, about
seven miles[c] from Jerusalem. 14 They
were talking with each other about everything that had happened. 15 As they
talked and discussed these things with
each other, Jesus himself came up and
walked along with them; 16 but they were
kept from recognizing him.
17 He asked them, "What are you dis-
cussing together as you walk along?"
They stood still, their faces downcast.
18 One of them, named Cleopas, asked
him, "Are you the only one visiting Jerusalem who does not know the things that
have happened there in these days?"
19 "What things?" he asked.
"About Jesus of Nazareth," they replied.
"He was a prophet, powerful in word and
deed before God and all the people.
20 The chief priests and our rulers handed him over to be sentenced to death, and
they crucified him; 21 but we had hoped
that he was the one who was going to redeem Israel. And what is more, it is the
third day since all this took place. 22 In
addition, some of our women amazed us.
They went to the tomb early this morning
23 but didn't find his body. They came and
told us that they had seen a vision of angels, who said he was alive. 24 Then some
of our companions went to the tomb and
found it just as the women had said, but
they did not see Jesus."
25 He said to them, "How foolish you
are, and how slow to believe all that the
prophets have spoken! 26 Did not the Mes-

[a] *42* Some manuscripts *come with your kingly power* [b] *46* Psalm 31:5 [c] *13* Or about 11 kilometers

siah have to suffer these things and then
enter his glory?" 27And beginning with
Moses and all the Prophets, he explained
to them what was said in all the Scriptures concerning himself.

28As they approached the village to
which they were going, Jesus continued
on as if he were going farther. 29But they
urged him strongly, "Stay with us, for it
is nearly evening; the day is almost over."
So he went in to stay with them.

30When he was at the table with them,
he took bread, gave thanks, broke it and
began to give it to them. 31Then their eyes
were opened and they recognized him,
and he disappeared from their sight.
32They asked each other, "Were not our
hearts burning within us while he talked
with us on the road and opened the Scriptures to us?"

33They got up and returned at once to
Jerusalem. There they found the Eleven
and those with them, assembled together
34and saying, "It is true! The Lord has ris-
en and has appeared to Simon." 35Then
the two told what had happened on the
way, and how Jesus was recognized by
them when he broke the bread.

36While they were still talking about
this, Jesus himself stood among them
and said to them, "Peace be with you."

37They were startled and frightened,
thinking they saw a ghost. 38He said to
them, "Why are you troubled, and why do
doubts rise in your minds? 39Look at my
hands and my feet. It is I myself! Touch
me and see; a ghost does not have flesh
and bones, as you see I have."

40When he had said this, he showed
them his hands and feet. 41And while
they still did not believe it because of joy
and amazement, he asked them, "Do you
have anything here to eat?" 42They gave
him a piece of broiled fish, 43and he took
it and ate it in their presence.

44He said to them, "This is what I told
you while I was still with you: Everything
must be fulfilled that is written about me
in the Law of Moses, the Prophets and the
Psalms."

45Then he opened their minds so they
could understand the Scriptures. 46He
told them, "This is what is written: The
Messiah will suffer and rise from the dead
on the third day, 47and repentance for the
forgiveness of sins will be preached in his
name to all nations, beginning at Jerusalem. 48You are witnesses of these things.
49I am going to send you what my Father
has promised; but stay in the city until
you have been clothed with power from
on high."

50When he had led them out to the vicinity of Bethany, he lifted up his hands
and blessed them. 51While he was blessing them, he left them and was taken up
into heaven. 52Then they worshiped him
and returned to Jerusalem with great joy.
53And they stayed continually at the temple, praising God.

JOHN

John closes his book by revealing his purpose in writing Jesus' story: *These are written that you may believe that Jesus is the Messiah, the Son of God, and that by believing you may have life in his name.*

John begins his book by echoing words from the Bible's creation story—*In the beginning*—showing his readers that this is a story of a new creation. Just as the first creation was completed in seven days, John uses the number seven to structure his book. For the Jews the number seven represented completeness and wholeness, a finished work of God revealing his purpose for the world.

The story is told in two main parts. The first describes Jesus' public ministry and has seven sections. Each section closes with a report on how people respond to Jesus, either in faith or unbelief. The second part is devoted to the Passover weekend, when Jesus gave his life for the world.

John records seven instances in which Jesus revealed his identity by using the phrase *I am,* the name by which God had revealed himself earlier. Similarly, John records seven miraculous signs that Jesus performed. John's narrative mentions twice that the resurrection of Jesus took place on the *first day of the week.* In this way he confirms that the power of a new creation has broken into our world.

---

1 In the beginning was the Word, and the Word was with God, and the Word was God. 2He was with God in the beginning. 3Through him all things were made; without him nothing was made that has been made. 4In him was life, and that life was the light of all mankind. 5The light shines in the darkness, and the darkness has not overcome[a] it.

6There was a man sent from God whose name was John. 7He came as a witness to testify concerning that light, so that through him all might believe. 8He himself was not the light; he came only as a witness to the light.

9The true light that gives light to everyone was coming into the world. 10He was in the world, and though the world was made through him, the world did not recognize him. 11He came to that which was his own, but his own did not receive him. 12Yet to all who did receive him, to those who believed in his name, he gave the right to become children of God—13children born not of natural descent, nor of human decision or a husband's will, but born of God.

14The Word became flesh and made his dwelling among us. We have seen his glory, the glory of the one and only Son, who came from the Father, full of grace and truth.

15(John testified concerning him. He cried out, saying, "This is the one I spoke about when I said, 'He who comes after me has surpassed me because he was before me.'") 16Out of his fullness we have all received grace in place of grace already given. 17For the law was given through Moses; grace and truth came through Jesus Christ. 18No one has ever seen God, but the one and only Son, who is himself God and[b] is in closest relationship with the Father, has made him known.

19Now this was John's testimony when the Jewish leaders[c] in Jerusalem sent priests and Levites to ask him who he was. 20He did not fail to confess, but confessed freely, "I am not the Messiah."

21They asked him, "Then who are you? Are you Elijah?"

He said, "I am not."

"Are you the Prophet?"

He answered, "No."

22Finally they said, "Who are you? Give us an answer to take back to those who sent us. What do you say about yourself?"

23John replied in the words of Isaiah the prophet, "I am the voice of one calling in the wilderness, 'Make straight the way for the Lord.'"[d]

24Now the Pharisees who had been sent 25questioned him, "Why then do

---

[a] 5 Or *understood* [b] 18 Some manuscripts *but the only Son, who* [c] 19 The Greek term traditionally translated *the Jews* (*hoi Ioudaioi*) refers here and elsewhere in John's Gospel to those Jewish leaders who opposed Jesus; also in 5:10, 15, 16; 7:1, 11, 13; 9:22; 18:12, 28, 36; 19:7, 12, 31, 38; 20:19. [d] 23 Isaiah 40:3

you baptize if you are not the Messiah,
nor Elijah, nor the Prophet?"
26 "I baptize with[a] water," John replied,
"but among you stands one you do not
know. 27 He is the one who comes after
me, the straps of whose sandals I am not
worthy to untie."
28 This all happened at Bethany on the
other side of the Jordan, where John was
baptizing.
29 The next day John saw Jesus coming
toward him and said, "Look, the Lamb of
God, who takes away the sin of the world!
30 This is the one I meant when I said, 'A
man who comes after me has surpassed
me because he was before me.' 31 I myself
did not know him, but the reason I came
baptizing with water was that he might
be revealed to Israel."
32 Then John gave this testimony: "I
saw the Spirit come down from heav-
en as a dove and remain on him. 33 And
I myself did not know him, but the one
who sent me to baptize with water told
me, 'The man on whom you see the Spirit come down and remain is the one who
will baptize with the Holy Spirit.' 34 I
have seen and I testify that this is God's
Chosen One."[b]
35 The next day John was there again
with two of his disciples. 36 When he
saw Jesus passing by, he said, "Look, the
Lamb of God!"
37 When the two disciples heard him
say this, they followed Jesus. 38 Turning
around, Jesus saw them following and
asked, "What do you want?"
They said, "Rabbi" (which means
"Teacher"), "where are you staying?"
39 "Come," he replied, "and you will
see."
So they went and saw where he was
staying, and they spent that day with
him. It was about four in the afternoon.
40 Andrew, Simon Peter's brother, was
one of the two who heard what John had
said and who had followed Jesus. 41 The
first thing Andrew did was to find his
brother Simon and tell him, "We have
found the Messiah" (that is, the Christ).
42 And he brought him to Jesus.
Jesus looked at him and said, "You are
Simon son of John. You will be called
Cephas" (which, when translated, is Peter[c]).
43 The next day Jesus decided to leave
for Galilee. Finding Philip, he said to
him, "Follow me."
44 Philip, like Andrew and Peter, was
from the town of Bethsaida. 45 Philip
found Nathanael and told him, "We have
found the one Moses wrote about in the
Law, and about whom the prophets also
wrote — Jesus of Nazareth, the son of Joseph."
46 "Nazareth! Can anything good come
from there?" Nathanael asked.
"Come and see," said Philip.
47 When Jesus saw Nathanael approaching, he said of him, "Here truly is
an Israelite in whom there is no deceit."
48 "How do you know me?" Nathanael
asked.
Jesus answered, "I saw you while you
were still under the fig tree before Philip
called you."
49 Then Nathanael declared, "Rabbi,
you are the Son of God; you are the king
of Israel."
50 Jesus said, "You believe[d] because I
told you I saw you under the fig tree. You
will see greater things than that." 51 He
then added, "Very truly I tell you,[e] you[e]
will see 'heaven open, and the angels of
God ascending and descending on'[f] the
Son of Man."

2 On the third day a wedding took
place at Cana in Galilee. Jesus' mother was there, 2 and Jesus and his disciples had also been invited to the wedding. 3 When the wine was gone, Jesus'
mother said to him, "They have no more
wine."
4 "Woman,[g] why do you involve me?"
Jesus replied. "My hour has not yet
come."
5 His mother said to the servants, "Do
whatever he tells you."
6 Nearby stood six stone water jars, the
kind used by the Jews for ceremonial
washing, each holding from twenty to
thirty gallons.[h]
7 Jesus said to the servants, "Fill the
jars with water"; so they filled them to
the brim.
8 Then he told them, "Now draw some

[a] *26* Or *in*; also in verses 31 and 33 (twice) [b] *34* See Isaiah 42:1; many manuscripts *is the Son of God.*
[c] *42* *Cephas* (Aramaic) and *Peter* (Greek) both mean *rock.* [d] *50* Or *Do you believe . . . ?* [e] *51* The Greek is plural. [f] *51* Gen. 28:12 [g] *4* The Greek for *Woman* does not denote any disrespect. [h] *6* Or from about 75 to about 115 liters

out and take it to the master of the banquet."
They did so, 9 and the master of the
banquet tasted the water that had been
turned into wine. He did not realize
where it had come from, though the servants who had drawn the water knew.
Then he called the bridegroom aside
10 and said, "Everyone brings out the
choice wine first and then the cheaper
wine after the guests have had too much
to drink; but you have saved the best till
now."
11 What Jesus did here in Cana of Galilee was the first of the signs through
which he revealed his glory; and his disciples believed in him.
12 After this he went down to Capernaum with his mother and brothers and
his disciples. There they stayed for a few
days.

13 When it was almost time for the Jewish Passover, Jesus went up to Jerusalem.
14 In the temple courts he found people
selling cattle, sheep and doves, and others sitting at tables exchanging money.
15 So he made a whip out of cords, and
drove all from the temple courts, both
sheep and cattle; he scattered the coins
of the money changers and overturned
their tables. 16 To those who sold doves he
said, "Get these out of here! Stop turning
my Father's house into a market!" 17 His
disciples remembered that it is written:
"Zeal for your house will consume me."[a]
18 The Jews then responded to him,
"What sign can you show us to prove
your authority to do all this?"
19 Jesus answered them, "Destroy this
temple, and I will raise it again in three
days."
20 They replied, "It has taken forty-six
years to build this temple, and you are
going to raise it in three days?" 21 But the
temple he had spoken of was his body.
22 After he was raised from the dead,
his disciples recalled what he had said.
Then they believed the scripture and the
words that Jesus had spoken.
23 Now while he was in Jerusalem at the
Passover Festival, many people saw the
signs he was performing and believed in
his name.[b] 24 But Jesus would not entrust
himself to them, for he knew all people.
25 He did not need any testimony about
mankind, for he knew what was in each
person.
3 Now there was a Pharisee, a man
named Nicodemus who was a member of the Jewish ruling council. 2 He
came to Jesus at night and said, "Rabbi,
we know that you are a teacher who has
come from God. For no one could perform the signs you are doing if God were
not with him."
3 Jesus replied, "Very truly I tell you, no
one can see the kingdom of God unless
they are born again.[c]"
4 "How can someone be born when
they are old?" Nicodemus asked. "Surely they cannot enter a second time into
their mother's womb to be born!"
5 Jesus answered, "Very truly I tell you,
no one can enter the kingdom of God unless they are born of water and the Spirit.
6 Flesh gives birth to flesh, but the Spirit[d] gives birth to spirit. 7 You should not
be surprised at my saying, 'You[e] must be
born again.' 8 The wind blows wherever
it pleases. You hear its sound, but you
cannot tell where it comes from or where
it is going. So it is with everyone born of
the Spirit."[f]
9 "How can this be?" Nicodemus
asked.
10 "You are Israel's teacher," said
Jesus, "and do you not understand these
things? 11 Very truly I tell you, we speak
of what we know, and we testify to what
we have seen, but still you people do not
accept our testimony. 12 I have spoken to
you of earthly things and you do not believe; how then will you believe if I speak
of heavenly things? 13 No one has ever
gone into heaven except the one who
came from heaven—the Son of Man.[g]
14 Just as Moses lifted up the snake in the
wilderness, so the Son of Man must be
lifted up,[h] 15 that everyone who believes
may have eternal life in him."[i]
16 For God so loved the world that he
gave his one and only Son, that whoever believes in him shall not perish but
have eternal life. 17 For God did not send
his Son into the world to condemn the

[a] 17 Psalm 69:9 [b] 23 Or *in him* [c] 3 The Greek for *again* also means *from above*; also in verse 7.
[d] 6 Or *but spirit* [e] 7 The Greek is plural. [f] 8 The Greek for *Spirit* is the same as that for *wind*.
[g] 13 Some manuscripts *Man, who is in heaven* [h] 14 The Greek for *lifted up* also means *exalted*.
[i] 15 Some interpreters end the quotation with verse 21.

world, but to save the world through him.
18Whoever believes in him is not condemned, but whoever does not believe
stands condemned already because they
have not believed in the name of God's
one and only Son. 19This is the verdict:
Light has come into the world, but people loved darkness instead of light because their deeds were evil. 20Everyone
who does evil hates the light, and will
not come into the light for fear that their
deeds will be exposed. 21But whoever
lives by the truth comes into the light, so
that it may be seen plainly that what they
have done has been done in the sight of
God.
22After this, Jesus and his disciples
went out into the Judean countryside,
where he spent some time with them, and
baptized. 23Now John also was baptizing
at Aenon near Salim, because there was
plenty of water, and people were coming
and being baptized. 24(This was before
John was put in prison.) 25An argument
developed between some of John's disciples and a certain Jew over the matter
of ceremonial washing. 26They came to
John and said to him, "Rabbi, that man
who was with you on the other side of the
Jordan—the one you testified about—
look, he is baptizing, and everyone is
going to him."
27To this John replied, "A person can
receive only what is given them from
heaven. 28You yourselves can testify that
I said, 'I am not the Messiah but am sent
ahead of him.' 29The bride belongs to the
bridegroom. The friend who attends the
bridegroom waits and listens for him,
and is full of joy when he hears the bridegroom's voice. That joy is mine, and it is
now complete. 30He must become greater; I must become less."[a]
31The one who comes from above is
above all; the one who is from the earth
belongs to the earth, and speaks as one
from the earth. The one who comes
from heaven is above all. 32He testifies
to what he has seen and heard, but no
one accepts his testimony. 33Whoever
has accepted it has certified that God is
truthful. 34For the one whom God has
sent speaks the words of God, for God[b]
gives the Spirit without limit. 35The Father loves the Son and has placed everything in his hands. 36Whoever believes
in the Son has eternal life, but whoever
rejects the Son will not see life, for God's
wrath remains on them.

4 Now Jesus learned that the Pharisees
had heard that he was gaining and
baptizing more disciples than John—
2although in fact it was not Jesus who
baptized, but his disciples. 3So he left Judea and went back once more to Galilee.
4Now he had to go through Samaria.
5So he came to a town in Samaria called
Sychar, near the plot of ground Jacob had
given to his son Joseph. 6Jacob's well was
there, and Jesus, tired as he was from
the journey, sat down by the well. It was
about noon.
7When a Samaritan woman came to
draw water, Jesus said to her, "Will you
give me a drink?" 8(His disciples had
gone into the town to buy food.)
9The Samaritan woman said to
him, "You are a Jew and I am a Samaritan woman. How can you ask me for a
drink?" (For Jews do not associate with
Samaritans.[c])
10Jesus answered her, "If you knew the
gift of God and who it is that asks you for
a drink, you would have asked him and
he would have given you living water."
11"Sir," the woman said, "you have
nothing to draw with and the well is
deep. Where can you get this living water? 12Are you greater than our father
Jacob, who gave us the well and drank
from it himself, as did also his sons and
his livestock?"
13Jesus answered, "Everyone who
drinks this water will be thirsty again,
14but whoever drinks the water I give
them will never thirst. Indeed, the water
I give them will become in them a spring
of water welling up to eternal life."
15The woman said to him, "Sir, give
me this water so that I won't get thirsty
and have to keep coming here to draw
water."
16He told her, "Go, call your husband
and come back."
17"I have no husband," she replied.
Jesus said to her, "You are right when
you say you have no husband. 18The fact
is, you have had five husbands, and the
man you now have is not your husband.
What you have just said is quite true."

[a] *30* Some interpreters end the quotation with verse 36. [b] *34* Greek *he* [c] *9* Or *do not use dishes Samaritans have used*

19 "Sir," the woman said, "I can see that you are a prophet. 20 Our ancestors worshiped on this mountain, but you Jews claim that the place where we must worship is in Jerusalem."

21 "Woman," Jesus replied, "believe me, a time is coming when you will worship the Father neither on this mountain nor in Jerusalem. 22 You Samaritans worship what you do not know; we worship what we do know, for salvation is from the Jews. 23 Yet a time is coming and has now come when the true worshipers will worship the Father in the Spirit and in truth, for they are the kind of worshipers the Father seeks. 24 God is spirit, and his worshipers must worship in the Spirit and in truth."

25 The woman said, "I know that Messiah" (called Christ) "is coming. When he comes, he will explain everything to us."

26 Then Jesus declared, "I, the one speaking to you—I am he."

27 Just then his disciples returned and were surprised to find him talking with a woman. But no one asked, "What do you want?" or "Why are you talking with her?"

28 Then, leaving her water jar, the woman went back to the town and said to the people, 29 "Come, see a man who told me everything I ever did. Could this be the Messiah?" 30 They came out of the town and made their way toward him.

31 Meanwhile his disciples urged him, "Rabbi, eat something."

32 But he said to them, "I have food to eat that you know nothing about."

33 Then his disciples said to each other, "Could someone have brought him food?"

34 "My food," said Jesus, "is to do the will of him who sent me and to finish his work. 35 Don't you have a saying, 'It's still four months until harvest'? I tell you, open your eyes and look at the fields! They are ripe for harvest. 36 Even now the one who reaps draws a wage and harvests a crop for eternal life, so that the sower and the reaper may be glad together. 37 Thus the saying 'One sows and another reaps' is true. 38 I sent you to reap what you have not worked for. Others have done the hard work, and you have reaped the benefits of their labor."

39 Many of the Samaritans from that town believed in him because of the woman's testimony, "He told me everything I ever did." 40 So when the Samaritans came to him, they urged him to stay with them, and he stayed two days. 41 And because of his words many more became believers.

42 They said to the woman, "We no longer believe just because of what you said; now we have heard for ourselves, and we know that this man really is the Savior of the world."

43 After the two days he left for Galilee. 44 (Now Jesus himself had pointed out that a prophet has no honor in his own country.) 45 When he arrived in Galilee, the Galileans welcomed him. They had seen all that he had done in Jerusalem at the Passover Festival, for they also had been there.

46 Once more he visited Cana in Galilee, where he had turned the water into wine. And there was a certain royal official whose son lay sick at Capernaum. 47 When this man heard that Jesus had arrived in Galilee from Judea, he went to him and begged him to come and heal his son, who was close to death.

48 "Unless you people see signs and wonders," Jesus told him, "you will never believe."

49 The royal official said, "Sir, come down before my child dies."

50 "Go," Jesus replied, "your son will live."

The man took Jesus at his word and departed. 51 While he was still on the way, his servants met him with the news that his boy was living. 52 When he inquired as to the time when his son got better, they said to him, "Yesterday, at one in the afternoon, the fever left him."

53 Then the father realized that this was the exact time at which Jesus had said to him, "Your son will live." So he and his whole household believed.

54 This was the second sign Jesus performed after coming from Judea to Galilee.

5 Some time later, Jesus went up to Jerusalem for one of the Jewish festivals. 2 Now there is in Jerusalem near the Sheep Gate a pool, which in Aramaic is called Bethesda[a] and which is surround-

[a] 2 Some manuscripts *Bethzatha*; other manuscripts *Bethsaida*

ed by five covered colonnades. 3Here a
great number of disabled people used
to lie—the blind, the lame, the paralyzed. [4][a] 5One who was there had been
an invalid for thirty-eight years. 6When
Jesus saw him lying there and learned
that he had been in this condition for a
long time, he asked him, "Do you want
to get well?"

7"Sir," the invalid replied, "I have no
one to help me into the pool when the
water is stirred. While I am trying to
get in, someone else goes down ahead
of me."

8Then Jesus said to him, "Get up! Pick
up your mat and walk." 9At once the
man was cured; he picked up his mat
and walked.

The day on which this took place was
a Sabbath, 10and so the Jewish leaders
said to the man who had been healed, "It
is the Sabbath; the law forbids you to carry your mat."

11But he replied, "The man who made
me well said to me, 'Pick up your mat and
walk.'"

12So they asked him, "Who is this fellow who told you to pick it up and walk?"

13The man who was healed had no idea
who it was, for Jesus had slipped away
into the crowd that was there.

14Later Jesus found him at the temple
and said to him, "See, you are well again.
Stop sinning or something worse may
happen to you." 15The man went away
and told the Jewish leaders that it was
Jesus who had made him well.

16So, because Jesus was doing these
things on the Sabbath, the Jewish leaders began to persecute him. 17In his defense Jesus said to them, "My Father is
always at his work to this very day, and
I too am working." 18For this reason they
tried all the more to kill him; not only
was he breaking the Sabbath, but he was
even calling God his own Father, making
himself equal with God.

19Jesus gave them this answer: "Very
truly I tell you, the Son can do nothing
by himself; he can do only what he sees
his Father doing, because whatever the
Father does the Son also does. 20For the
Father loves the Son and shows him all
he does. Yes, and he will show him even
greater works than these, so that you will
be amazed. 21For just as the Father raises the dead and gives them life, even so
the Son gives life to whom he is pleased
to give it. 22Moreover, the Father judges
no one, but has entrusted all judgment to
the Son, 23that all may honor the Son just
as they honor the Father. Whoever does
not honor the Son does not honor the Father, who sent him.

24"Very truly I tell you, whoever hears
my word and believes him who sent me
has eternal life and will not be judged
but has crossed over from death to life.
25Very truly I tell you, a time is coming
and has now come when the dead will
hear the voice of the Son of God and
those who hear will live. 26For as the Father has life in himself, so he has granted
the Son also to have life in himself. 27And
he has given him authority to judge because he is the Son of Man.

28"Do not be amazed at this, for a
time is coming when all who are in their
graves will hear his voice 29and come
out—those who have done what is good
will rise to live, and those who have done
what is evil will rise to be condemned.
30By myself I can do nothing; I judge
only as I hear, and my judgment is just,
for I seek not to please myself but him
who sent me.

31"If I testify about myself, my testimony is not true. 32There is another who
testifies in my favor, and I know that his
testimony about me is true.

33"You have sent to John and he has
testified to the truth. 34Not that I accept
human testimony; but I mention it that
you may be saved. 35John was a lamp that
burned and gave light, and you chose for
a time to enjoy his light.

36"I have testimony weightier than that
of John. For the works that the Father has
given me to finish—the very works that
I am doing—testify that the Father has
sent me. 37And the Father who sent me
has himself testified concerning me. You
have never heard his voice nor seen his
form, 38nor does his word dwell in you,
for you do not believe the one he sent.
39You study[b] the Scriptures diligently
because you think that in them you have
eternal life. These are the very Scriptures

[a] 3,4 Some manuscripts include here, wholly or in part, *paralyzed—and they waited for the moving of the waters. 4From time to time an angel of the Lord would come down and stir up the waters. The first one into the pool after each such disturbance would be cured of whatever disease they had.* [b] 39 Or *39Study*

that testify about me, [40]yet you refuse to
come to me to have life.
[41]"I do not accept glory from human
beings, [42]but I know you. I know that
you do not have the love of God in your
hearts. [43]I have come in my Father's
name, and you do not accept me; but if
someone else comes in his own name,
you will accept him. [44]How can you believe since you accept glory from one
another but do not seek the glory that
comes from the only God[a]?
[45]"But do not think I will accuse you
before the Father. Your accuser is Moses,
on whom your hopes are set. [46]If you believed Moses, you would believe me, for
he wrote about me. [47]But since you do
not believe what he wrote, how are you
going to believe what I say?"

6 Some time after this, Jesus crossed
to the far shore of the Sea of Galilee
(that is, the Sea of Tiberias), [2]and a great
crowd of people followed him because
they saw the signs he had performed by
healing the sick. [3]Then Jesus went up on
a mountainside and sat down with his
disciples. [4]The Jewish Passover Festival
was near.
[5]When Jesus looked up and saw a
great crowd coming toward him, he said
to Philip, "Where shall we buy bread for
these people to eat?" [6]He asked this only
to test him, for he already had in mind
what he was going to do.
[7]Philip answered him, "It would take
more than half a year's wages[b] to buy
enough bread for each one to have a
bite!"
[8]Another of his disciples, Andrew, Simon Peter's brother, spoke up, [9]"Here is
a boy with five small barley loaves and
two small fish, but how far will they go
among so many?"
[10]Jesus said, "Have the people sit
down." There was plenty of grass in
that place, and they sat down (about
five thousand men were there). [11]Jesus
then took the loaves, gave thanks, and
distributed to those who were seated as
much as they wanted. He did the same
with the fish.
[12]When they had all had enough to
eat, he said to his disciples, "Gather the
pieces that are left over. Let nothing be
wasted." [13]So they gathered them and
filled twelve baskets with the pieces of
the five barley loaves left over by those
who had eaten.
[14]After the people saw the sign Jesus
performed, they began to say, "Surely
this is the Prophet who is to come into
the world." [15]Jesus, knowing that they
intended to come and make him king by
force, withdrew again to a mountain by
himself.
[16]When evening came, his disciples
went down to the lake, [17]where they got
into a boat and set off across the lake for
Capernaum. By now it was dark, and
Jesus had not yet joined them. [18]A strong
wind was blowing and the waters grew
rough. [19]When they had rowed about
three or four miles,[c] they saw Jesus approaching the boat, walking on the water;
and they were frightened. [20]But he said
to them, "It is I; don't be afraid." [21]Then
they were willing to take him into the
boat, and immediately the boat reached
the shore where they were heading.
[22]The next day the crowd that had
stayed on the opposite shore of the lake
realized that only one boat had been
there, and that Jesus had not entered it
with his disciples, but that they had gone
away alone. [23]Then some boats from Tiberias landed near the place where the
people had eaten the bread after the Lord
had given thanks. [24]Once the crowd realized that neither Jesus nor his disciples
were there, they got into the boats and
went to Capernaum in search of Jesus.
[25]When they found him on the other
side of the lake, they asked him, "Rabbi,
when did you get here?"
[26]Jesus answered, "Very truly I tell you,
you are looking for me, not because you
saw the signs I performed but because
you ate the loaves and had your fill. [27]Do
not work for food that spoils, but for food
that endures to eternal life, which the
Son of Man will give you. For on him
God the Father has placed his seal of approval."
[28]Then they asked him, "What must
we do to do the works God requires?"
[29]Jesus answered, "The work of God is
this: to believe in the one he has sent."
[30]So they asked him, "What sign then
will you give that we may see it and be-

[a] *44* Some early manuscripts *the Only One* [b] *7* Greek *take two hundred denarii* [c] *19* Or about 5 or 6 kilometers

lieve you? What will you do? 31 Our ancestors ate the manna in the wilderness;
as it is written: 'He gave them bread from
heaven to eat.'[a]"
32 Jesus said to them, "Very truly I tell
you, it is not Moses who has given you
the bread from heaven, but it is my Father who gives you the true bread from
heaven. 33 For the bread of God is the
bread that comes down from heaven and
gives life to the world."
34 "Sir," they said, "always give us this
bread."
35 Then Jesus declared, "I am the bread
of life. Whoever comes to me will never
go hungry, and whoever believes in me
will never be thirsty. 36 But as I told you,
you have seen me and still you do not believe. 37 All those the Father gives me will
come to me, and whoever comes to me I
will never drive away. 38 For I have come
down from heaven not to do my will but
to do the will of him who sent me. 39 And
this is the will of him who sent me, that
I shall lose none of all those he has giv-
en me, but raise them up at the last day.
40 For my Father's will is that everyone
who looks to the Son and believes in him
shall have eternal life, and I will raise
them up at the last day."
41 At this the Jews there began to grumble about him because he said, "I am
the bread that came down from heav-
en." 42 They said, "Is this not Jesus, the
son of Joseph, whose father and mother
we know? How can he now say, 'I came
down from heaven'?"
43 "Stop grumbling among yourselves,"
Jesus answered. 44 "No one can come to
me unless the Father who sent me draws
them, and I will raise them up at the last
day. 45 It is written in the Prophets: 'They
will all be taught by God.'[b] Everyone who
has heard the Father and learned from
him comes to me. 46 No one has seen the
Father except the one who is from God;
only he has seen the Father. 47 Very truly I
tell you, the one who believes has eternal
life. 48 I am the bread of life. 49 Your ancestors ate the manna in the wilderness,
yet they died. 50 But here is the bread that
comes down from heaven, which anyone may eat and not die. 51 I am the living bread that came down from heaven.
Whoever eats this bread will live forever.
This bread is my flesh, which I will give
for the life of the world."
52 Then the Jews began to argue sharply among themselves, "How can this man
give us his flesh to eat?"
53 Jesus said to them, "Very truly I tell
you, unless you eat the flesh of the Son
of Man and drink his blood, you have no
life in you. 54 Whoever eats my flesh and
drinks my blood has eternal life, and I
will raise them up at the last day. 55 For
my flesh is real food and my blood is
real drink. 56 Whoever eats my flesh and
drinks my blood remains in me, and I in
them. 57 Just as the living Father sent me
and I live because of the Father, so the
one who feeds on me will live because of
me. 58 This is the bread that came down
from heaven. Your ancestors ate manna and died, but whoever feeds on this
bread will live forever." 59 He said this
while teaching in the synagogue in Capernaum.
60 On hearing it, many of his disciples
said, "This is a hard teaching. Who can
accept it?"
61 Aware that his disciples were grumbling about this, Jesus said to them,
"Does this offend you? 62 Then what if
you see the Son of Man ascend to where
he was before! 63 The Spirit gives life;
the flesh counts for nothing. The words
I have spoken to you—they are full of
the Spirit[c] and life. 64 Yet there are some
of you who do not believe." For Jesus
had known from the beginning which
of them did not believe and who would
betray him. 65 He went on to say, "This is
why I told you that no one can come to me
unless the Father has enabled them."
66 From this time many of his disciples turned back and no longer followed
him.
67 "You do not want to leave too, do
you?" Jesus asked the Twelve.
68 Simon Peter answered him, "Lord, to
whom shall we go? You have the words
of eternal life. 69 We have come to believe
and to know that you are the Holy One
of God."
70 Then Jesus replied, "Have I not chosen you, the Twelve? Yet one of you is a
devil!" 71 (He meant Judas, the son of
Simon Iscariot, who, though one of the
Twelve, was later to betray him.)

[a] *31* Exodus 16:4; Neh. 9:15; Psalm 78:24,25 [b] *45* Isaiah 54:13 [c] *63* Or *are Spirit*; or *are spirit*

7 After this, Jesus went around in Galilee. He did not want[a] to go about in
Judea because the Jewish leaders there
were looking for a way to kill him. 2 But
when the Jewish Festival of Tabernacles
was near, 3 Jesus' brothers said to him,
"Leave Galilee and go to Judea, so that
your disciples there may see the works
you do. 4 No one who wants to become a
public figure acts in secret. Since you are
doing these things, show yourself to the
world." 5 For even his own brothers did
not believe in him.

6 Therefore Jesus told them, "My time
is not yet here; for you any time will do.
7 The world cannot hate you, but it hates
me because I testify that its works are
evil. 8 You go to the festival. I am not[b] going up to this festival, because my time
has not yet fully come." 9 After he had
said this, he stayed in Galilee.

10 However, after his brothers had left
for the festival, he went also, not publicly, but in secret. 11 Now at the festival the
Jewish leaders were watching for Jesus
and asking, "Where is he?"

12 Among the crowds there was widespread whispering about him. Some
said, "He is a good man."

Others replied, "No, he deceives the
people." 13 But no one would say anything
publicly about him for fear of the leaders.

14 Not until halfway through the festival did Jesus go up to the temple courts
and begin to teach. 15 The Jews there
were amazed and asked, "How did this
man get such learning without having
been taught?"

16 Jesus answered, "My teaching is not
my own. It comes from the one who sent
me. 17 Anyone who chooses to do the will
of God will find out whether my teaching
comes from God or whether I speak on
my own. 18 Whoever speaks on their own
does so to gain personal glory, but he
who seeks the glory of the one who sent
him is a man of truth; there is nothing
false about him. 19 Has not Moses given
you the law? Yet not one of you keeps the
law. Why are you trying to kill me?"

20 "You are demon-possessed," the
crowd answered. "Who is trying to kill
you?"

21 Jesus said to them, "I did one miracle, and you are all amazed. 22 Yet
because Moses gave you circumcision
(though actually it did not come from
Moses, but from the patriarchs), you circumcise a boy on the Sabbath. 23 Now if a
boy can be circumcised on the Sabbath
so that the law of Moses may not be broken, why are you angry with me for healing a man's whole body on the Sabbath?
24 Stop judging by mere appearances, but
instead judge correctly."

25 At that point some of the people of
Jerusalem began to ask, "Isn't this the
man they are trying to kill? 26 Here he is,
speaking publicly, and they are not saying a word to him. Have the authorities
really concluded that he is the Messiah?
27 But we know where this man is from;
when the Messiah comes, no one will
know where he is from."

28 Then Jesus, still teaching in the temple courts, cried out, "Yes, you know me,
and you know where I am from. I am not
here on my own authority, but he who
sent me is true. You do not know him,
29 but I know him because I am from him
and he sent me."

30 At this they tried to seize him, but
no one laid a hand on him, because his
hour had not yet come. 31 Still, many in
the crowd believed in him. They said,
"When the Messiah comes, will he perform more signs than this man?"

32 The Pharisees heard the crowd whispering such things about him. Then the
chief priests and the Pharisees sent temple guards to arrest him.

33 Jesus said, "I am with you for only
a short time, and then I am going to the
one who sent me. 34 You will look for me,
but you will not find me; and where I am,
you cannot come."

35 The Jews said to one another, "Where
does this man intend to go that we cannot find him? Will he go where our people live scattered among the Greeks, and
teach the Greeks? 36 What did he mean
when he said, 'You will look for me, but
you will not find me,' and 'Where I am,
you cannot come'?"

37 On the last and greatest day of the
festival, Jesus stood and said in a loud
voice, "Let anyone who is thirsty come
to me and drink. 38 Whoever believes in
me, as Scripture has said, rivers of living
water will flow from within them."[c] 39 By

[a] *1* Some manuscripts *not have authority* [b] *8* Some manuscripts *not yet* [c] *37,38* Or *me. And let anyone drink* [38] *who believes in me." As Scripture has said, "Out of him* (or *them*) *will flow rivers of living water."*

this he meant the Spirit, whom those who
believed in him were later to receive. Up
to that time the Spirit had not been given,
since Jesus had not yet been glorified.
40On hearing his words, some of the
people said, "Surely this man is the
Prophet."
41Others said, "He is the Messiah."
Still others asked, "How can the Messiah come from Galilee? 42Does not Scripture say that the Messiah will come from
David's descendants and from Bethlehem, the town where David lived?"
43Thus the people were divided because
of Jesus. 44Some wanted to seize him, but
no one laid a hand on him.
45Finally the temple guards went back
to the chief priests and the Pharisees,
who asked them, "Why didn't you bring
him in?"
46"No one ever spoke the way this man
does," the guards replied.
47"You mean he has deceived you
also?" the Pharisees retorted. 48"Have
any of the rulers or of the Pharisees believed in him? 49No! But this mob that
knows nothing of the law—there is a
curse on them."
50Nicodemus, who had gone to Jesus
earlier and who was one of their own
number, asked, 51"Does our law condemn a man without first hearing him to
find out what he has been doing?"
52They replied, "Are you from Galilee,
too? Look into it, and you will find that a
prophet does not come out of Galilee."

[The earliest manuscripts and many other ancient witnesses do not have John 7:53—8:11. A few manuscripts include these verses, wholly or in part, after John 7:36, John 21:25, Luke 21:38 or Luke 24:53.]

8 *53Then they all went home, 1but Jesus went*
to the Mount of Olives.
2At dawn he appeared again in the temple
courts, where all the people gathered around
him, and he sat down to teach them. 3The
teachers of the law and the Pharisees brought
in a woman caught in adultery. They made
her stand before the group 4and said to Jesus,
"Teacher, this woman was caught in the act of
adultery. 5In the Law Moses commanded us
to stone such women. Now what do you say?"
6They were using this question as a trap, in or-
der to have a basis for accusing him.
But Jesus bent down and started to write on
the ground with his finger. 7When they kept on
questioning him, he straightened up and said
to them, "Let any one of you who is without sin
be the first to throw a stone at her." 8Again he
stooped down and wrote on the ground.
9At this, those who heard began to go away
one at a time, the older ones first, until only
Jesus was left, with the woman still standing
there. 10Jesus straightened up and asked her,
"Woman, where are they? Has no one con-
demned you?"
11"No one, sir," she said.
"Then neither do I condemn you," Jesus de-
clared. "Go now and leave your life of sin."

12When Jesus spoke again to the people, he said, "I am the light of the world.
Whoever follows me will never walk in
darkness, but will have the light of life."
13The Pharisees challenged him, "Here
you are, appearing as your own witness;
your testimony is not valid."
14Jesus answered, "Even if I testify on
my own behalf, my testimony is valid,
for I know where I came from and where
I am going. But you have no idea where
I come from or where I am going. 15You
judge by human standards; I pass judgment on no one. 16But if I do judge, my
decisions are true, because I am not
alone. I stand with the Father, who sent
me. 17In your own Law it is written that
the testimony of two witnesses is true. 18I
am one who testifies for myself; my other
witness is the Father, who sent me."
19Then they asked him, "Where is your
father?"
"You do not know me or my Father,"
Jesus replied. "If you knew me, you
would know my Father also." 20He spoke
these words while teaching in the temple
courts near the place where the offerings
were put. Yet no one seized him, because
his hour had not yet come.
21Once more Jesus said to them, "I am
going away, and you will look for me, and
you will die in your sin. Where I go, you
cannot come."
22This made the Jews ask, "Will he kill
himself? Is that why he says, 'Where I go,
you cannot come'?"
23But he continued, "You are from
below; I am from above. You are of this
world; I am not of this world. 24I told you
that you would die in your sins; if you do
not believe that I am he, you will indeed
die in your sins."

25 “Who are you?” they asked.
“Just what I have been telling you from
the beginning,” Jesus replied. 26 “I have
much to say in judgment of you. But he
who sent me is trustworthy, and what I
have heard from him I tell the world.”
27 They did not understand that he was
telling them about his Father. 28 So Jesus
said, “When you have lifted up[a] the Son
of Man, then you will know that I am he
and that I do nothing on my own but
speak just what the Father has taught
me. 29 The one who sent me is with me;
he has not left me alone, for I always do
what pleases him.” 30 Even as he spoke,
many believed in him.
31 To the Jews who had believed him,
Jesus said, “If you hold to my teaching,
you are really my disciples. 32 Then you
will know the truth, and the truth will
set you free.”
33 They answered him, “We are Abraham’s descendants and have never been
slaves of anyone. How can you say that
we shall be set free?”
34 Jesus replied, “Very truly I tell you,
everyone who sins is a slave to sin. 35 Now
a slave has no permanent place in the
family, but a son belongs to it forever.
36 So if the Son sets you free, you will be
free indeed. 37 I know that you are Abraham’s descendants. Yet you are looking
for a way to kill me, because you have
no room for my word. 38 I am telling you
what I have seen in the Father’s presence, and you are doing what you have
heard from your father.[b]”
39 “Abraham is our father,” they answered.
“If you were Abraham’s children,” said
Jesus, “then you would[c] do what Abra
ham did. 40 As it is, you are looking for a
way to kill me, a man who has told you
the truth that I heard from God. Abra
ham did not do such things. 41 You are
doing the works of your own father.”
“We are not illegitimate children,”
they protested. “The only Father we have
is God himself.”
42 Jesus said to them, “If God were your
Father, you would love me, for I have
come here from God. I have not come on
my own; God sent me. 43 Why is my language not clear to you? Because you are
unable to hear what I say. 44 You belong
to your father, the devil, and you want to
carry out your father’s desires. He was a
murderer from the beginning, not holding to the truth, for there is no truth in
him. When he lies, he speaks his native
language, for he is a liar and the father of
lies. 45 Yet because I tell the truth, you do
not believe me! 46 Can any of you prove
me guilty of sin? If I am telling the truth,
why don’t you believe me? 47 Whoever
belongs to God hears what God says. The
reason you do not hear is that you do not
belong to God.”
48 The Jews answered him, “Aren’t we
right in saying that you are a Samaritan
and demon-possessed?”
49 “I am not possessed by a demon,”
said Jesus, “but I honor my Father and
you dishonor me. 50 I am not seeking glory for myself; but there is one who seeks
it, and he is the judge. 51 Very truly I tell
you, whoever obeys my word will never
see death.”
52 At this they exclaimed, “Now we
know that you are demon-possessed!
Abraham died and so did the prophets,
yet you say that whoever obeys your word
will never taste death. 53 Are you greater
than our father Abraham? He died, and
so did the prophets. Who do you think
you are?”
54 Jesus replied, “If I glorify myself,
my glory means nothing. My Father,
whom you claim as your God, is the one
who glorifies me. 55 Though you do not
know him, I know him. If I said I did not,
I would be a liar like you, but I do know
him and obey his word. 56 Your father
Abraham rejoiced at the thought of seeing my day; he saw it and was glad.”
57 “You are not yet fifty years old,” they
said to him, “and you have seen Abraham!”
58 “Very truly I tell you,” Jesus answered, “before Abraham was born, I
am!” 59 At this, they picked up stones to
stone him, but Jesus hid himself, slipping
away from the temple grounds.
9 As he went along, he saw a man blind
from birth. 2 His disciples asked him,
“Rabbi, who sinned, this man or his parents, that he was born blind?”
3 “Neither this man nor his parents
sinned,” said Jesus, “but this happened
so that the works of God might be dis-

[a] 28 The Greek for *lifted up* also means *exalted.* [b] 38 Or *presence. Therefore do what you have heard from the Father.* [c] 39 Some early manuscripts *“If you are Abraham’s children,” said Jesus, “then*

played in him. 4As long as it is day, we
must do the works of him who sent me.
Night is coming, when no one can work.
5While I am in the world, I am the light
of the world."
6After saying this, he spit on the
ground, made some mud with the saliva, and put it on the man's eyes. 7"Go,"
he told him, "wash in the Pool of Siloam"
(this word means "Sent"). So the man
went and washed, and came home seeing.
8His neighbors and those who had formerly seen him begging asked, "Isn't this
the same man who used to sit and beg?"
9Some claimed that he was.
Others said, "No, he only looks like
him."
But he himself insisted, "I am the
man."
10"How then were your eyes opened?"
they asked.
11He replied, "The man they call Jesus
made some mud and put it on my eyes.
He told me to go to Siloam and wash. So I
went and washed, and then I could see."
12"Where is this man?" they asked
him.
"I don't know," he said.
13They brought to the Pharisees the
man who had been blind. 14Now the day
on which Jesus had made the mud and
opened the man's eyes was a Sabbath.
15Therefore the Pharisees also asked
him how he had received his sight. "He
put mud on my eyes," the man replied,
"and I washed, and now I see."
16Some of the Pharisees said, "This
man is not from God, for he does not keep
the Sabbath."
But others asked, "How can a sinner
perform such signs?" So they were divided.
17Then they turned again to the blind
man, "What have you to say about him?
It was your eyes he opened."
The man replied, "He is a prophet."
18They still did not believe that he had
been blind and had received his sight
until they sent for the man's parents.
19"Is this your son?" they asked. "Is this
the one you say was born blind? How is it
that now he can see?"
20"We know he is our son," the parents
answered, "and we know he was born
blind. 21But how he can see now, or who
opened his eyes, we don't know. Ask him.
He is of age; he will speak for himself."
22His parents said this because they
were afraid of the Jewish leaders, who
already had decided that anyone who
acknowledged that Jesus was the Messiah would be put out of the synagogue.
23That was why his parents said, "He is of
age; ask him."
24A second time they summoned the
man who had been blind. "Give glory to
God by telling the truth," they said. "We
know this man is a sinner."
25He replied, "Whether he is a sinner
or not, I don't know. One thing I do know.
I was blind but now I see!"
26Then they asked him, "What did he
do to you? How did he open your eyes?"
27He answered, "I have told you already and you did not listen. Why do you
want to hear it again? Do you want to become his disciples too?"
28Then they hurled insults at him and
said, "You are this fellow's disciple! We
are disciples of Moses! 29We know that
God spoke to Moses, but as for this fellow, we don't even know where he comes
from."
30The man answered, "Now that is
remarkable! You don't know where he
comes from, yet he opened my eyes.
31We know that God does not listen to
sinners. He listens to the godly person
who does his will. 32Nobody has ever
heard of opening the eyes of a man born
blind. 33If this man were not from God,
he could do nothing."
34To this they replied, "You were
steeped in sin at birth; how dare you lecture us!" And they threw him out.
35Jesus heard that they had thrown
him out, and when he found him, he said,
"Do you believe in the Son of Man?"
36"Who is he, sir?" the man asked. "Tell
me so that I may believe in him."
37Jesus said, "You have now seen him;
in fact, he is the one speaking with you."
38Then the man said, "Lord, I believe,"
and he worshiped him.
39Jesus said,[a] "For judgment I have
come into this world, so that the blind
will see and those who see will become
blind."
40Some Pharisees who were with him

[a] *38,39* Some early manuscripts do not have *Then the man said . . . 39Jesus said.*

heard him say this and asked, "What?
Are we blind too?"
41 Jesus said, "If you were blind, you
would not be guilty of sin; but now that
you claim you can see, your guilt remains.
10 "Very truly I tell you Pharisees,
anyone who does not enter the
sheep pen by the gate, but climbs in by
some other way, is a thief and a robber.
2 The one who enters by the gate is the
shepherd of the sheep. 3 The gatekeeper
opens the gate for him, and the sheep listen to his voice. He calls his own sheep
by name and leads them out. 4 When he
has brought out all his own, he goes on
ahead of them, and his sheep follow him
because they know his voice. 5 But they
will never follow a stranger; in fact, they
will run away from him because they do
not recognize a stranger's voice." 6 Jesus
used this figure of speech, but the Pharisees did not understand what he was
telling them.
7 Therefore Jesus said again, "Very truly
I tell you, I am the gate for the sheep. 8 All
who have come before me are thieves
and robbers, but the sheep have not listened to them. 9 I am the gate; whoever
enters through me will be saved.[a] They
will come in and go out, and find pasture. 10 The thief comes only to steal and
kill and destroy; I have come that they
may have life, and have it to the full.
11 "I am the good shepherd. The good
shepherd lays down his life for the sheep.
12 The hired hand is not the shepherd and
does not own the sheep. So when he sees
the wolf coming, he abandons the sheep
and runs away. Then the wolf attacks
the flock and scatters it. 13 The man runs
away because he is a hired hand and
cares nothing for the sheep.
14 "I am the good shepherd; I know my
sheep and my sheep know me— 15 just
as the Father knows me and I know the
Father—and I lay down my life for the
sheep. 16 I have other sheep that are not
of this sheep pen. I must bring them
also. They too will listen to my voice, and
there shall be one flock and one shepherd. 17 The reason my Father loves me is
that I lay down my life—only to take it up
again. 18 No one takes it from me, but I lay
it down of my own accord. I have authority to lay it down and authority to take it
up again. This command I received from
my Father."
19 The Jews who heard these words
were again divided. 20 Many of them said,
"He is demon-possessed and raving mad.
Why listen to him?"
21 But others said, "These are not the
sayings of a man possessed by a demon. Can a demon open the eyes of the
blind?"

22 Then came the Festival of Dedication[b] at Jerusalem. It was winter, 23 and
Jesus was in the temple courts walking
in Solomon's Colonnade. 24 The Jews
who were there gathered around him,
saying, "How long will you keep us in
suspense? If you are the Messiah, tell us
plainly."
25 Jesus answered, "I did tell you, but
you do not believe. The works I do in my
Father's name testify about me, 26 but
you do not believe because you are not
my sheep. 27 My sheep listen to my voice;
I know them, and they follow me. 28 I give
them eternal life, and they shall never
perish; no one will snatch them out of
my hand. 29 My Father, who has given
them to me, is greater than all[c]; no one
can snatch them out of my Father's hand.
30 I and the Father are one."
31 Again his Jewish opponents picked
up stones to stone him, 32 but Jesus said
to them, "I have shown you many good
works from the Father. For which of these
do you stone me?"
33 "We are not stoning you for any good
work," they replied, "but for blasphemy,
because you, a mere man, claim to be
God."
34 Jesus answered them, "Is it not
written in your Law, 'I have said you
are "gods" '[d]? 35 If he called them 'gods,'
to whom the word of God came—and
Scripture cannot be set aside— 36 what
about the one whom the Father set apart
as his very own and sent into the world?
Why then do you accuse me of blasphemy
because I said, 'I am God's Son'? 37 Do not
believe me unless I do the works of my
Father. 38 But if I do them, even though
you do not believe me, believe the works,
that you may know and understand that
the Father is in me, and I in the Father."

[a] 9 Or *kept safe* [b] 22 That is, Hanukkah [c] 29 Many early manuscripts *What my Father has given me is greater than all* [d] 34 Psalm 82:6

39 Again they tried to seize him, but he
escaped their grasp.
40 Then Jesus went back across the Jordan to the place where John had been
baptizing in the early days. There he
stayed, 41 and many people came to him.
They said, "Though John never performed a sign, all that John said about
this man was true." 42 And in that place
many believed in Jesus.

11 Now a man named Lazarus was sick.
He was from Bethany, the village of
Mary and her sister Martha. 2 (This Mary,
whose brother Lazarus now lay sick, was
the same one who poured perfume on
the Lord and wiped his feet with her
hair.) 3 So the sisters sent word to Jesus,
"Lord, the one you love is sick."
4 When he heard this, Jesus said, "This
sickness will not end in death. No, it is for
God's glory so that God's Son may be glorified through it." 5 Now Jesus loved Martha and her sister and Lazarus. 6 So when
he heard that Lazarus was sick, he stayed
where he was two more days, 7 and then
he said to his disciples, "Let us go back
to Judea."
8 "But Rabbi," they said, "a short while
ago the Jews there tried to stone you, and
yet you are going back?"
9 Jesus answered, "Are there not twelve
hours of daylight? Anyone who walks in
the daytime will not stumble, for they see
by this world's light. 10 It is when a person
walks at night that they stumble, for they
have no light."
11 After he had said this, he went on to
tell them, "Our friend Lazarus has fall-
en asleep; but I am going there to wake
him up."
12 His disciples replied, "Lord, if he
sleeps, he will get better." 13 Jesus had
been speaking of his death, but his disciples thought he meant natural sleep.
14 So then he told them plainly, "Lazarus is dead, 15 and for your sake I am glad
I was not there, so that you may believe.
But let us go to him."
16 Then Thomas (also known as Didymus[a]) said to the rest of the disciples,
"Let us also go, that we may die with
him."
17 On his arrival, Jesus found that Lazarus had already been in the tomb for
four days. 18 Now Bethany was less than
two miles[b] from Jerusalem, 19 and many
Jews had come to Martha and Mary to
comfort them in the loss of their brother. 20 When Martha heard that Jesus was
coming, she went out to meet him, but
Mary stayed at home.
21 "Lord," Martha said to Jesus, "if you
had been here, my brother would not
have died. 22 But I know that even now
God will give you whatever you ask."
23 Jesus said to her, "Your brother will
rise again."
24 Martha answered, "I know he will rise
again in the resurrection at the last day."
25 Jesus said to her, "I am the resurrection and the life. The one who believes in
me will live, even though they die; 26 and
whoever lives by believing in me will
never die. Do you believe this?"
27 "Yes, Lord," she replied, "I believe
that you are the Messiah, the Son of God,
who is to come into the world."
28 After she had said this, she went back
and called her sister Mary aside. "The
Teacher is here," she said, "and is asking
for you." 29 When Mary heard this, she
got up quickly and went to him. 30 Now
Jesus had not yet entered the village, but
was still at the place where Martha had
met him. 31 When the Jews who had been
with Mary in the house, comforting her,
noticed how quickly she got up and went
out, they followed her, supposing she was
going to the tomb to mourn there.
32 When Mary reached the place where
Jesus was and saw him, she fell at his feet
and said, "Lord, if you had been here, my
brother would not have died."
33 When Jesus saw her weeping, and
the Jews who had come along with her
also weeping, he was deeply moved in
spirit and troubled. 34 "Where have you
laid him?" he asked.
"Come and see, Lord," they replied.
35 Jesus wept.
36 Then the Jews said, "See how he
loved him!"
37 But some of them said, "Could not
he who opened the eyes of the blind man
have kept this man from dying?"
38 Jesus, once more deeply moved,
came to the tomb. It was a cave with a
stone laid across the entrance. 39 "Take
away the stone," he said.

[a] *16 Thomas* (Aramaic) and *Didymus* (Greek) both mean *twin.* [b] *18* Or about 3 kilometers

"But, Lord," said Martha, the sister of the dead man, "by this time there is a bad odor, for he has been there four days."

40 Then Jesus said, "Did I not tell you that if you believe, you will see the glory of God?"

41 So they took away the stone. Then Jesus looked up and said, "Father, I thank you that you have heard me. 42 I knew that you always hear me, but I said this for the benefit of the people standing here, that they may believe that you sent me."

43 When he had said this, Jesus called in a loud voice, "Lazarus, come out!" 44 The dead man came out, his hands and feet wrapped with strips of linen, and a cloth around his face.

Jesus said to them, "Take off the grave clothes and let him go."

45 Therefore many of the Jews who had come to visit Mary, and had seen what Jesus did, believed in him. 46 But some of them went to the Pharisees and told them what Jesus had done. 47 Then the chief priests and the Pharisees called a meeting of the Sanhedrin.

"What are we accomplishing?" they asked. "Here is this man performing many signs. 48 If we let him go on like this, everyone will believe in him, and then the Romans will come and take away both our temple and our nation."

49 Then one of them, named Caiaphas, who was high priest that year, spoke up, "You know nothing at all! 50 You do not realize that it is better for you that one man die for the people than that the whole nation perish."

51 He did not say this on his own, but as high priest that year he prophesied that Jesus would die for the Jewish nation, 52 and not only for that nation but also for the scattered children of God, to bring them together and make them one. 53 So from that day on they plotted to take his life.

54 Therefore Jesus no longer moved about publicly among the people of Judea. Instead he withdrew to a region near the wilderness, to a village called Ephraim, where he stayed with his disciples.

55 When it was almost time for the Jewish Passover, many went up from the country to Jerusalem for their ceremonial cleansing before the Passover. 56 They kept looking for Jesus, and as they stood in the temple courts they asked one another, "What do you think? Isn't he coming to the festival at all?" 57 But the chief priests and the Pharisees had given orders that anyone who found out where Jesus was should report it so that they might arrest him.

12 Six days before the Passover, Jesus came to Bethany, where Lazarus lived, whom Jesus had raised from the dead. 2 Here a dinner was given in Jesus' honor. Martha served, while Lazarus was among those reclining at the table with him. 3 Then Mary took about a pint[a] of pure nard, an expensive perfume; she poured it on Jesus' feet and wiped his feet with her hair. And the house was filled with the fragrance of the perfume.

4 But one of his disciples, Judas Iscariot, who was later to betray him, objected, 5 "Why wasn't this perfume sold and the money given to the poor? It was worth a year's wages.[b]" 6 He did not say this because he cared about the poor but because he was a thief; as keeper of the money bag, he used to help himself to what was put into it.

7 "Leave her alone," Jesus replied. "It was intended that she should save this perfume for the day of my burial. 8 You will always have the poor among you,[c] but you will not always have me."

9 Meanwhile a large crowd of Jews found out that Jesus was there and came, not only because of him but also to see Lazarus, whom he had raised from the dead. 10 So the chief priests made plans to kill Lazarus as well, 11 for on account of him many of the Jews were going over to Jesus and believing in him.

12 The next day the great crowd that had come for the festival heard that Jesus was on his way to Jerusalem. 13 They took palm branches and went out to meet him, shouting,

"Hosanna![d]"

"Blessed is he who comes in the name
of the Lord!"[e]

"Blessed is the king of Israel!"

14 Jesus found a young donkey and sat on it, as it is written:

[a] 3 Or about 0.5 liter [b] 5 Greek *three hundred denarii* [c] 8 See Deut. 15:11. [d] 13 A Hebrew expression meaning "Save!" which became an exclamation of praise [e] 13 Psalm 118:25,26

15 "Do not be afraid, Daughter Zion;
see, your king is coming,
seated on a donkey's colt."[a]

16 At first his disciples did not understand all this. Only after Jesus was glorified did they realize that these things
had been written about him and that
these things had been done to him.
17 Now the crowd that was with him
when he called Lazarus from the tomb
and raised him from the dead continued to spread the word. 18 Many people, because they had heard that he had
performed this sign, went out to meet
him. 19 So the Pharisees said to one another, "See, this is getting us nowhere.
Look how the whole world has gone after him!"
20 Now there were some Greeks among
those who went up to worship at the festival. 21 They came to Philip, who was
from Bethsaida in Galilee, with a request. "Sir," they said, "we would like to
see Jesus." 22 Philip went to tell Andrew;
Andrew and Philip in turn told Jesus.
23 Jesus replied, "The hour has come
for the Son of Man to be glorified. 24 Very
truly I tell you, unless a kernel of wheat
falls to the ground and dies, it remains
only a single seed. But if it dies, it produces many seeds. 25 Anyone who loves their
life will lose it, while anyone who hates
their life in this world will keep it for
eternal life. 26 Whoever serves me must
follow me; and where I am, my servant
also will be. My Father will honor the one
who serves me.
27 "Now my soul is troubled, and what
shall I say? 'Father, save me from this
hour'? No, it was for this very reason I
came to this hour. 28 Father, glorify your
name!"
Then a voice came from heaven, "I
have glorified it, and will glorify it again."
29 The crowd that was there and heard it
said it had thundered; others said an angel had spoken to him.
30 Jesus said, "This voice was for your
benefit, not mine. 31 Now is the time for
judgment on this world; now the prince
of this world will be driven out. 32 And I,
when I am lifted up[b] from the earth, will
draw all people to myself." 33 He said this
to show the kind of death he was going
to die.
34 The crowd spoke up, "We have heard
from the Law that the Messiah will remain forever, so how can you say, 'The
Son of Man must be lifted up'? Who is
this 'Son of Man'?"
35 Then Jesus told them, "You are going
to have the light just a little while longer.
Walk while you have the light, before
darkness overtakes you. Whoever walks
in the dark does not know where they are
going. 36 Believe in the light while you
have the light, so that you may become
children of light." When he had finished
speaking, Jesus left and hid himself from
them.
37 Even after Jesus had performed so
many signs in their presence, they still
would not believe in him. 38 This was to
fulfill the word of Isaiah the prophet:

"Lord, who has believed our message
and to whom has the arm of the
Lord been revealed?"[c]

39 For this reason they could not believe, because, as Isaiah says elsewhere:

40 "He has blinded their eyes
and hardened their hearts,
so they can neither see with their
eyes,
nor understand with their hearts,
nor turn — and I would heal them."[d]

41 Isaiah said this because he saw Jesus'
glory and spoke about him.
42 Yet at the same time many even
among the leaders believed in him. But
because of the Pharisees they would not
openly acknowledge their faith for fear
they would be put out of the synagogue;
43 for they loved human praise more than
praise from God.
44 Then Jesus cried out, "Whoever believes in me does not believe in me only,
but in the one who sent me. 45 The one
who looks at me is seeing the one who
sent me. 46 I have come into the world as
a light, so that no one who believes in me
should stay in darkness.
47 "If anyone hears my words but
does not keep them, I do not judge that
person. For I did not come to judge the
world, but to save the world. 48 There is
a judge for the one who rejects me and
does not accept my words; the very words
I have spoken will condemn them at the

[a] *15* Zech. 9:9 [b] *32* The Greek for *lifted up* also means *exalted.* [c] *38* Isaiah 53:1 [d] *40* Isaiah 6:10

last day. 49 For I did not speak on my own, but the Father who sent me commanded me to say all that I have spoken. 50 I know that his command leads to eternal life. So whatever I say is just what the Father has told me to say."

13 It was just before the Passover Festival. Jesus knew that the hour had come for him to leave this world and go to the Father. Having loved his own who were in the world, he loved them to the end.

2 The evening meal was in progress, and the devil had already prompted Judas, the son of Simon Iscariot, to betray Jesus. 3 Jesus knew that the Father had put all things under his power, and that he had come from God and was returning to God; 4 so he got up from the meal, took off his outer clothing, and wrapped a towel around his waist. 5 After that, he poured water into a basin and began to wash his disciples' feet, drying them with the towel that was wrapped around him.

6 He came to Simon Peter, who said to him, "Lord, are you going to wash my feet?"

7 Jesus replied, "You do not realize now what I am doing, but later you will understand."

8 "No," said Peter, "you shall never wash my feet."

Jesus answered, "Unless I wash you, you have no part with me."

9 "Then, Lord," Simon Peter replied, "not just my feet but my hands and my head as well!"

10 Jesus answered, "Those who have had a bath need only to wash their feet; their whole body is clean. And you are clean, though not every one of you." 11 For he knew who was going to betray him, and that was why he said not every one was clean.

12 When he had finished washing their feet, he put on his clothes and returned to his place. "Do you understand what I have done for you?" he asked them. 13 "You call me 'Teacher' and 'Lord,' and rightly so, for that is what I am. 14 Now that I, your Lord and Teacher, have washed your feet, you also should wash one another's feet. 15 I have set you an example that you should do as I have done for you. 16 Very truly I tell you, no servant is greater than his master, nor is a messenger greater than the one who sent him. 17 Now that you know these things, you will be blessed if you do them.

18 "I am not referring to all of you; I know those I have chosen. But this is to fulfill this passage of Scripture: 'He who shared my bread has turned[a] against me.'[b]

19 "I am telling you now before it happens, so that when it does happen you will believe that I am who I am. 20 Very truly I tell you, whoever accepts anyone I send accepts me; and whoever accepts me accepts the one who sent me."

21 After he had said this, Jesus was troubled in spirit and testified, "Very truly I tell you, one of you is going to betray me."

22 His disciples stared at one another, at a loss to know which of them he meant. 23 One of them, the disciple whom Jesus loved, was reclining next to him. 24 Simon Peter motioned to this disciple and said, "Ask him which one he means."

25 Leaning back against Jesus, he asked him, "Lord, who is it?"

26 Jesus answered, "It is the one to whom I will give this piece of bread when I have dipped it in the dish." Then, dipping the piece of bread, he gave it to Judas, the son of Simon Iscariot. 27 As soon as Judas took the bread, Satan entered into him.

So Jesus told him, "What you are about to do, do quickly." 28 But no one at the meal understood why Jesus said this to him. 29 Since Judas had charge of the money, some thought Jesus was telling him to buy what was needed for the festival, or to give something to the poor. 30 As soon as Judas had taken the bread, he went out. And it was night.

31 When he was gone, Jesus said, "Now the Son of Man is glorified and God is glorified in him. 32 If God is glorified in him,[c] God will glorify the Son in himself, and will glorify him at once.

33 "My children, I will be with you only a little longer. You will look for me, and just as I told the Jews, so I tell you now: Where I am going, you cannot come.

34 "A new command I give you: Love

[a] 18 Greek *has lifted up his heel* [b] 18 Psalm 41:9 [c] 32 Many early manuscripts do not have *If God is glorified in him.*

one another. As I have loved you, so you
must love one another. 35By this everyone will know that you are my disciples,
if you love one another."
36Simon Peter asked him, "Lord, where
are you going?"
Jesus replied, "Where I am going, you
cannot follow now, but you will follow
later."
37Peter asked, "Lord, why can't I follow you now? I will lay down my life for
you."
38Then Jesus answered, "Will you really lay down your life for me? Very truly
I tell you, before the rooster crows, you
will disown me three times!
14 "Do not let your hearts be troubled.
You believe in God[a]; believe also in
me. 2My Father's house has many rooms;
if that were not so, would I have told you
that I am going there to prepare a place
for you? 3And if I go and prepare a place
for you, I will come back and take you to
be with me that you also may be where
I am. 4You know the way to the place
where I am going."
5Thomas said to him, "Lord, we don't
know where you are going, so how can
we know the way?"
6Jesus answered, "I am the way and
the truth and the life. No one comes to
the Father except through me. 7If you
really know me, you will know[b] my Father as well. From now on, you do know
him and have seen him."
8Philip said, "Lord, show us the Father
and that will be enough for us."
9Jesus answered: "Don't you know me,
Philip, even after I have been among you
such a long time? Anyone who has seen
me has seen the Father. How can you say,
'Show us the Father'? 10Don't you believe
that I am in the Father, and that the Father is in me? The words I say to you I do
not speak on my own authority. Rather,
it is the Father, living in me, who is doing
his work. 11Believe me when I say that I
am in the Father and the Father is in me;
or at least believe on the evidence of the
works themselves. 12Very truly I tell you,
whoever believes in me will do the works
I have been doing, and they will do even
greater things than these, because I am
going to the Father. 13And I will do whatever you ask in my name, so that the Father may be glorified in the Son. 14You
may ask me for anything in my name,
and I will do it.
15"If you love me, keep my commands.
16And I will ask the Father, and he will
give you another advocate to help you
and be with you forever— 17the Spirit
of truth. The world cannot accept him,
because it neither sees him nor knows
him. But you know him, for he lives
with you and will be[c] in you. 18I will not
leave you as orphans; I will come to you.
19Before long, the world will not see me
anymore, but you will see me. Because I
live, you also will live. 20On that day you
will realize that I am in my Father, and
you are in me, and I am in you. 21Who-
ever has my commands and keeps them
is the one who loves me. The one who
loves me will be loved by my Father, and
I too will love them and show myself to
them."
22Then Judas (not Judas Iscariot) said,
"But, Lord, why do you intend to show
yourself to us and not to the world?"
23Jesus replied, "Anyone who loves me
will obey my teaching. My Father will
love them, and we will come to them and
make our home with them. 24Anyone
who does not love me will not obey my
teaching. These words you hear are not
my own; they belong to the Father who
sent me.
25"All this I have spoken while still
with you. 26But the Advocate, the Holy
Spirit, whom the Father will send in my
name, will teach you all things and will
remind you of everything I have said to
you. 27Peace I leave with you; my peace I
give you. I do not give to you as the world
gives. Do not let your hearts be troubled
and do not be afraid.
28"You heard me say, 'I am going away
and I am coming back to you.' If you loved
me, you would be glad that I am going to
the Father, for the Father is greater than
I. 29I have told you now before it happens,
so that when it does happen you will believe. 30I will not say much more to you,
for the prince of this world is coming. He
has no hold over me, 31but he comes so
that the world may learn that I love the
Father and do exactly what my Father
has commanded me.
"Come now; let us leave.

[a] *1* Or *Believe in God* [b] *7* Some manuscripts *If you really knew me, you would know* [c] *17* Some early manuscripts *and is*

15 "I am the true vine, and my Father
is the gardener. 2He cuts off every
branch in me that bears no fruit, while
every branch that does bear fruit he
prunes[a] so that it will be even more fruitful. 3You are already clean because of the
word I have spoken to you. 4Remain in
me, as I also remain in you. No branch
can bear fruit by itself; it must remain in
the vine. Neither can you bear fruit unless you remain in me.

5"I am the vine; you are the branches.
If you remain in me and I in you, you will
bear much fruit; apart from me you can
do nothing. 6If you do not remain in me,
you are like a branch that is thrown away
and withers; such branches are picked
up, thrown into the fire and burned. 7If
you remain in me and my words remain
in you, ask whatever you wish, and it will
be done for you. 8This is to my Father's
glory, that you bear much fruit, showing
yourselves to be my disciples.

9"As the Father has loved me, so have
I loved you. Now remain in my love. 10If
you keep my commands, you will remain in my love, just as I have kept my
Father's commands and remain in his
love. 11I have told you this so that my joy
may be in you and that your joy may be
complete. 12My command is this: Love
each other as I have loved you. 13Great-
er love has no one than this: to lay down
one's life for one's friends. 14You are my
friends if you do what I command. 15I
no longer call you servants, because a
servant does not know his master's business. Instead, I have called you friends,
for everything that I learned from my
Father I have made known to you. 16You
did not choose me, but I chose you and
appointed you so that you might go and
bear fruit—fruit that will last—and so
that whatever you ask in my name the
Father will give you. 17This is my command: Love each other.

18"If the world hates you, keep in mind
that it hated me first. 19If you belonged
to the world, it would love you as its own.
As it is, you do not belong to the world,
but I have chosen you out of the world.
That is why the world hates you. 20Re-
member what I told you: 'A servant is not
greater than his master.'[b] If they persecuted me, they will persecute you also. If
they obeyed my teaching, they will obey
yours also. 21They will treat you this
way because of my name, for they do not
know the one who sent me. 22If I had not
come and spoken to them, they would
not be guilty of sin; but now they have
no excuse for their sin. 23Whoever hates
me hates my Father as well. 24If I had not
done among them the works no one else
did, they would not be guilty of sin. As it
is, they have seen, and yet they have hated both me and my Father. 25But this is to
fulfill what is written in their Law: 'They
hated me without reason.'[c]

26"When the Advocate comes, whom
I will send to you from the Father—the
Spirit of truth who goes out from the Father—he will testify about me. 27And
you also must testify, for you have been
with me from the beginning.

16 "All this I have told you so that you
will not fall away. 2They will put you
out of the synagogue; in fact, the time is
coming when anyone who kills you will
think they are offering a service to God.
3They will do such things because they
have not known the Father or me. 4I have
told you this, so that when their time
comes you will remember that I warned
you about them. I did not tell you this
from the beginning because I was with
you, 5but now I am going to him who sent
me. None of you asks me, 'Where are you
going?' 6Rather, you are filled with grief
because I have said these things. 7But
very truly I tell you, it is for your good that
I am going away. Unless I go away, the
Advocate will not come to you; but if I go,
I will send him to you. 8When he comes,
he will prove the world to be in the wrong
about sin and righteousness and judgment: 9about sin, because people do not
believe in me; 10about righteousness, because I am going to the Father, where you
can see me no longer; 11and about judgment, because the prince of this world
now stands condemned.

12"I have much more to say to you,
more than you can now bear. 13But
when he, the Spirit of truth, comes, he
will guide you into all the truth. He will
not speak on his own; he will speak only
what he hears, and he will tell you what is
yet to come. 14He will glorify me because
it is from me that he will receive what he

[a] 2 The Greek for *he prunes* also means *he cleans.* [b] 20 John 13:16 [c] 25 Psalms 35:19; 69:4

will make known to you. 15All that belongs to the Father is mine. That is why I
said the Spirit will receive from me what
he will make known to you."
16Jesus went on to say, "In a little while
you will see me no more, and then after a
little while you will see me."
17At this, some of his disciples said
to one another, "What does he mean by
saying, 'In a little while you will see me
no more, and then after a little while you
will see me,' and 'Because I am going to
the Father'?" 18They kept asking, "What
does he mean by 'a little while'? We don't
understand what he is saying."
19Jesus saw that they wanted to ask
him about this, so he said to them, "Are
you asking one another what I meant
when I said, 'In a little while you will
see me no more, and then after a little
while you will see me'? 20Very truly I
tell you, you will weep and mourn while
the world rejoices. You will grieve, but
your grief will turn to joy. 21A woman
giving birth to a child has pain because
her time has come; but when her baby
is born she forgets the anguish because
of her joy that a child is born into the
world. 22So with you: Now is your time
of grief, but I will see you again and you
will rejoice, and no one will take away
your joy. 23In that day you will no longer
ask me anything. Very truly I tell you,
my Father will give you whatever you
ask in my name. 24Until now you have
not asked for anything in my name. Ask
and you will receive, and your joy will be
complete.
25"Though I have been speaking figuratively, a time is coming when I will
no longer use this kind of language but
will tell you plainly about my Father.
26In that day you will ask in my name. I
am not saying that I will ask the Father
on your behalf. 27No, the Father himself
loves you because you have loved me and
have believed that I came from God. 28I
came from the Father and entered the
world; now I am leaving the world and
going back to the Father."
29Then Jesus' disciples said, "Now you
are speaking clearly and without figures
of speech. 30Now we can see that you
know all things and that you do not even
need to have anyone ask you questions.
This makes us believe that you came
from God."
31"Do you now believe?" Jesus replied. 32"A time is coming and in fact has
come when you will be scattered, each
to your own home. You will leave me all
alone. Yet I am not alone, for my Father
is with me.
33"I have told you these things, so that
in me you may have peace. In this world
you will have trouble. But take heart! I
have overcome the world."

17 After Jesus said this, he looked toward heaven and prayed:

"Father, the hour has come. Glorify
your Son, that your Son may glorify
you. 2For you granted him authority over all people that he might give
eternal life to all those you have giv-
en him. 3Now this is eternal life: that
they know you, the only true God, and
Jesus Christ, whom you have sent. 4I
have brought you glory on earth by
finishing the work you gave me to do.
5And now, Father, glorify me in your
presence with the glory I had with
you before the world began.
6"I have revealed you[a] to those
whom you gave me out of the world.
They were yours; you gave them to
me and they have obeyed your word.
7Now they know that everything you
have given me comes from you. 8For
I gave them the words you gave me
and they accepted them. They knew
with certainty that I came from you,
and they believed that you sent me.
9I pray for them. I am not praying for
the world, but for those you have giv-
en me, for they are yours. 10All I have
is yours, and all you have is mine.
And glory has come to me through
them. 11I will remain in the world no
longer, but they are still in the world,
and I am coming to you. Holy Father, protect them by the power of[b]
your name, the name you gave me,
so that they may be one as we are
one. 12While I was with them, I protected them and kept them safe by[c]
that name you gave me. None has
been lost except the one doomed to
destruction so that Scripture would
be fulfilled.

[a] 6 Greek *your name*   [b] 11 Or *Father, keep them faithful to*   [c] 12 Or *kept them faithful to*

13 "I am coming to you now, but I
say these things while I am still in
the world, so that they may have the
full measure of my joy within them.
14 I have given them your word and
the world has hated them, for they
are not of the world any more than
I am of the world. 15 My prayer is not
that you take them out of the world
but that you protect them from the
evil one. 16 They are not of the world,
even as I am not of it. 17 Sanctify them
by[a] the truth; your word is truth.
18 As you sent me into the world, I
have sent them into the world. 19 For
them I sanctify myself, that they too
may be truly sanctified.

20 "My prayer is not for them alone.
I pray also for those who will believe
in me through their message, 21 that
all of them may be one, Father, just
as you are in me and I am in you. May
they also be in us so that the world
may believe that you have sent me.
22 I have given them the glory that
you gave me, that they may be one
as we are one — 23 I in them and you
in me — so that they may be brought
to complete unity. Then the world
will know that you sent me and
have loved them even as you have
loved me.

24 "Father, I want those you have
given me to be with me where I am,
and to see my glory, the glory you
have given me because you loved me
before the creation of the world.

25 "Righteous Father, though the
world does not know you, I know
you, and they know that you have
sent me. 26 I have made you[b] known
to them, and will continue to make
you known in order that the love you
have for me may be in them and that
I myself may be in them."

18 When he had finished praying,
Jesus left with his disciples and
crossed the Kidron Valley. On the other
side there was a garden, and he and his
disciples went into it.

2 Now Judas, who betrayed him, knew
the place, because Jesus had often met
there with his disciples. 3 So Judas came
to the garden, guiding a detachment of
soldiers and some officials from the chief
priests and the Pharisees. They were carrying torches, lanterns and weapons.

4 Jesus, knowing all that was going to
happen to him, went out and asked them,
"Who is it you want?"

5 "Jesus of Nazareth," they replied.

"I am he," Jesus said. (And Judas the
traitor was standing there with them.)
6 When Jesus said, "I am he," they drew
back and fell to the ground.

7 Again he asked them, "Who is it you
want?"

"Jesus of Nazareth," they said.

8 Jesus answered, "I told you that I am
he. If you are looking for me, then let
these men go." 9 This happened so that
the words he had spoken would be fulfilled: "I have not lost one of those you
gave me."[c]

10 Then Simon Peter, who had a sword,
drew it and struck the high priest's servant, cutting off his right ear. (The servant's name was Malchus.)

11 Jesus commanded Peter, "Put your
sword away! Shall I not drink the cup the
Father has given me?"

12 Then the detachment of soldiers
with its commander and the Jewish officials arrested Jesus. They bound him
13 and brought him first to Annas, who
was the father-in-law of Caiaphas, the
high priest that year. 14 Caiaphas was the
one who had advised the Jewish leaders
that it would be good if one man died for
the people.

15 Simon Peter and another disciple
were following Jesus. Because this disciple was known to the high priest, he
went with Jesus into the high priest's
courtyard, 16 but Peter had to wait outside at the door. The other disciple, who
was known to the high priest, came back,
spoke to the servant girl on duty there
and brought Peter in.

17 "You aren't one of this man's disciples too, are you?" she asked Peter.

He replied, "I am not."

18 It was cold, and the servants and officials stood around a fire they had made
to keep warm. Peter also was standing
with them, warming himself.

19 Meanwhile, the high priest questioned Jesus about his disciples and his
teaching.

20 "I have spoken openly to the world,"

[a] 17 Or *them to live in accordance with* [b] 26 Greek *your name* [c] 9 John 6:39

Jesus replied. "I always taught in synagogues or at the temple, where all the Jews come together. I said nothing in secret. 21Why question me? Ask those who heard me. Surely they know what I said."

22When Jesus said this, one of the officials nearby slapped him in the face. "Is this the way you answer the high priest?" he demanded.

23"If I said something wrong," Jesus replied, "testify as to what is wrong. But if I spoke the truth, why did you strike me?" 24Then Annas sent him bound to Caiaphas the high priest.

25Meanwhile, Simon Peter was still standing there warming himself. So they asked him, "You aren't one of his disciples too, are you?"

He denied it, saying, "I am not."

26One of the high priest's servants, a relative of the man whose ear Peter had cut off, challenged him, "Didn't I see you with him in the garden?" 27Again Peter denied it, and at that moment a rooster began to crow.

28Then the Jewish leaders took Jesus from Caiaphas to the palace of the Roman governor. By now it was early morning, and to avoid ceremonial uncleanness they did not enter the palace, because they wanted to be able to eat the Passover. 29So Pilate came out to them and asked, "What charges are you bringing against this man?"

30"If he were not a criminal," they replied, "we would not have handed him over to you."

31Pilate said, "Take him yourselves and judge him by your own law."

"But we have no right to execute anyone," they objected. 32This took place to fulfill what Jesus had said about the kind of death he was going to die.

33Pilate then went back inside the palace, summoned Jesus and asked him, "Are you the king of the Jews?"

34"Is that your own idea," Jesus asked, "or did others talk to you about me?"

35"Am I a Jew?" Pilate replied. "Your own people and chief priests handed you over to me. What is it you have done?"

36Jesus said, "My kingdom is not of this world. If it were, my servants would fight to prevent my arrest by the Jewish leaders. But now my kingdom is from another place."

37"You are a king, then!" said Pilate.

Jesus answered, "You say that I am a king. In fact, the reason I was born and came into the world is to testify to the truth. Everyone on the side of truth listens to me."

38"What is truth?" retorted Pilate. With this he went out again to the Jews gathered there and said, "I find no basis for a charge against him. 39But it is your custom for me to release to you one prisoner at the time of the Passover. Do you want me to release 'the king of the Jews'?"

40They shouted back, "No, not him! Give us Barabbas!" Now Barabbas had taken part in an uprising.

19 Then Pilate took Jesus and had him flogged. 2The soldiers twisted together a crown of thorns and put it on his head. They clothed him in a purple robe 3and went up to him again and again, saying, "Hail, king of the Jews!" And they slapped him in the face.

4Once more Pilate came out and said to the Jews gathered there, "Look, I am bringing him out to you to let you know that I find no basis for a charge against him." 5When Jesus came out wearing the crown of thorns and the purple robe, Pilate said to them, "Here is the man!"

6As soon as the chief priests and their officials saw him, they shouted, "Crucify! Crucify!"

But Pilate answered, "You take him and crucify him. As for me, I find no basis for a charge against him."

7The Jewish leaders insisted, "We have a law, and according to that law he must die, because he claimed to be the Son of God."

8When Pilate heard this, he was even more afraid, 9and he went back inside the palace. "Where do you come from?" he asked Jesus, but Jesus gave him no answer. 10"Do you refuse to speak to me?" Pilate said. "Don't you realize I have power either to free you or to crucify you?"

11Jesus answered, "You would have no power over me if it were not given to you from above. Therefore the one who handed me over to you is guilty of a greater sin."

12From then on, Pilate tried to set Jesus free, but the Jewish leaders kept shouting, "If you let this man go, you are no friend of Caesar. Anyone who claims to be a king opposes Caesar."

13 When Pilate heard this, he brought Jesus out and sat down on the judge's seat at a place known as the Stone Pavement (which in Aramaic is Gabbatha). 14 It was the day of Preparation of the Passover; it was about noon.

"Here is your king," Pilate said to the Jews.

15 But they shouted, "Take him away! Take him away! Crucify him!"

"Shall I crucify your king?" Pilate asked.

"We have no king but Caesar," the chief priests answered.

16 Finally Pilate handed him over to them to be crucified.

So the soldiers took charge of Jesus. 17 Carrying his own cross, he went out to the place of the Skull (which in Aramaic is called Golgotha). 18 There they crucified him, and with him two others—one on each side and Jesus in the middle.

19 Pilate had a notice prepared and fastened to the cross. It read: JESUS OF NAZARETH, THE KING OF THE JEWS. 20 Many of the Jews read this sign, for the place where Jesus was crucified was near the city, and the sign was written in Aramaic, Latin and Greek. 21 The chief priests of the Jews protested to Pilate, "Do not write 'The King of the Jews,' but that this man claimed to be king of the Jews."

22 Pilate answered, "What I have written, I have written."

23 When the soldiers crucified Jesus, they took his clothes, dividing them into four shares, one for each of them, with the undergarment remaining. This garment was seamless, woven in one piece from top to bottom.

24 "Let's not tear it," they said to one another. "Let's decide by lot who will get it."

This happened that the scripture might be fulfilled that said,

"They divided my clothes among
 them
and cast lots for my garment."[a]

So this is what the soldiers did.

25 Near the cross of Jesus stood his mother, his mother's sister, Mary the wife of Clopas, and Mary Magdalene. 26 When Jesus saw his mother there, and the disciple whom he loved standing nearby, he said to her, "Woman,[b] here is your son," 27 and to the disciple, "Here is your mother." From that time on, this disciple took her into his home.

28 Later, knowing that everything had now been finished, and so that Scripture would be fulfilled, Jesus said, "I am thirsty." 29 A jar of wine vinegar was there, so they soaked a sponge in it, put the sponge on a stalk of the hyssop plant, and lifted it to Jesus' lips. 30 When he had received the drink, Jesus said, "It is finished." With that, he bowed his head and gave up his spirit.

31 Now it was the day of Preparation, and the next day was to be a special Sabbath. Because the Jewish leaders did not want the bodies left on the crosses during the Sabbath, they asked Pilate to have the legs broken and the bodies taken down. 32 The soldiers therefore came and broke the legs of the first man who had been crucified with Jesus, and then those of the other. 33 But when they came to Jesus and found that he was already dead, they did not break his legs. 34 Instead, one of the soldiers pierced Jesus' side with a spear, bringing a sudden flow of blood and water. 35 The man who saw it has given testimony, and his testimony is true. He knows that he tells the truth, and he testifies so that you also may believe. 36 These things happened so that the scripture would be fulfilled: "Not one of his bones will be broken,"[c] 37 and, as another scripture says, "They will look on the one they have pierced."[d]

38 Later, Joseph of Arimathea asked Pilate for the body of Jesus. Now Joseph was a disciple of Jesus, but secretly because he feared the Jewish leaders. With Pilate's permission, he came and took the body away. 39 He was accompanied by Nicodemus, the man who earlier had visited Jesus at night. Nicodemus brought a mixture of myrrh and aloes, about seventy-five pounds.[e] 40 Taking Jesus' body, the two of them wrapped it, with the spices, in strips of linen. This was in accordance with Jewish burial customs. 41 At the place where Jesus was crucified, there was a garden, and in the garden a new tomb, in which no one had

[a] *24* Psalm 22:18 [b] *26* The Greek for *Woman* does not denote any disrespect. [c] *36* Exodus 12:46; Num. 9:12; Psalm 34:20 [d] *37* Zech. 12:10 [e] *39* Or about 34 kilograms

ever been laid. 42 Because it was the Jewish day of Preparation and since the tomb was nearby, they laid Jesus there.

20 Early on the first day of the week, while it was still dark, Mary Magdalene went to the tomb and saw that the stone had been removed from the entrance. 2 So she came running to Simon Peter and the other disciple, the one Jesus loved, and said, "They have taken the Lord out of the tomb, and we don't know where they have put him!"

3 So Peter and the other disciple started for the tomb. 4 Both were running, but the other disciple outran Peter and reached the tomb first. 5 He bent over and looked in at the strips of linen lying there but did not go in. 6 Then Simon Peter came along behind him and went straight into the tomb. He saw the strips of linen lying there, 7 as well as the cloth that had been wrapped around Jesus' head. The cloth was still lying in its place, separate from the linen. 8 Finally the other disciple, who had reached the tomb first, also went inside. He saw and believed. 9 (They still did not understand from Scripture that Jesus had to rise from the dead.) 10 Then the disciples went back to where they were staying.

11 Now Mary stood outside the tomb crying. As she wept, she bent over to look into the tomb 12 and saw two angels in white, seated where Jesus' body had been, one at the head and the other at the foot.

13 They asked her, "Woman, why are you crying?"

"They have taken my Lord away," she said, "and I don't know where they have put him." 14 At this, she turned around and saw Jesus standing there, but she did not realize that it was Jesus.

15 He asked her, "Woman, why are you crying? Who is it you are looking for?"

Thinking he was the gardener, she said, "Sir, if you have carried him away, tell me where you have put him, and I will get him."

16 Jesus said to her, "Mary."

She turned toward him and cried out in Aramaic, "Rabboni!" (which means "Teacher").

17 Jesus said, "Do not hold on to me, for I have not yet ascended to the Father. Go instead to my brothers and tell them, 'I am ascending to my Father and your Father, to my God and your God.'"

18 Mary Magdalene went to the disciples with the news: "I have seen the Lord!" And she told them that he had said these things to her.

19 On the evening of that first day of the week, when the disciples were together, with the doors locked for fear of the Jewish leaders, Jesus came and stood among them and said, "Peace be with you!" 20 After he said this, he showed them his hands and side. The disciples were overjoyed when they saw the Lord.

21 Again Jesus said, "Peace be with you! As the Father has sent me, I am sending you." 22 And with that he breathed on them and said, "Receive the Holy Spirit. 23 If you forgive anyone's sins, their sins are forgiven; if you do not forgive them, they are not forgiven."

24 Now Thomas (also known as Didymus[a]), one of the Twelve, was not with the disciples when Jesus came. 25 So the other disciples told him, "We have seen the Lord!"

But he said to them, "Unless I see the nail marks in his hands and put my finger where the nails were, and put my hand into his side, I will not believe."

26 A week later his disciples were in the house again, and Thomas was with them. Though the doors were locked, Jesus came and stood among them and said, "Peace be with you!" 27 Then he said to Thomas, "Put your finger here; see my hands. Reach out your hand and put it into my side. Stop doubting and believe."

28 Thomas said to him, "My Lord and my God!"

29 Then Jesus told him, "Because you have seen me, you have believed; blessed are those who have not seen and yet have believed."

30 Jesus performed many other signs in the presence of his disciples, which are not recorded in this book. 31 But these are written that you may believe[b] that Jesus is the Messiah, the Son of God, and that by believing you may have life in his name.

[a] 24 *Thomas* (Aramaic) and *Didymus* (Greek) both mean *twin.* [b] 31 Or *may continue to believe*

21 Afterward Jesus appeared again
to his disciples, by the Sea of Galilee.[a] It happened this way: 2 Simon Peter,
Thomas (also known as Didymus[b]), Nathanael from Cana in Galilee, the sons of
Zebedee, and two other disciples were
together. 3 "I'm going out to fish," Simon
Peter told them, and they said, "We'll
go with you." So they went out and got
into the boat, but that night they caught
nothing.

4 Early in the morning, Jesus stood on
the shore, but the disciples did not realize that it was Jesus.

5 He called out to them, "Friends
haven't you any fish?"

"No," they answered.

6 He said, "Throw your net on the right
side of the boat and you will find some."
When they did, they were unable to haul
the net in because of the large number
of fish.

7 Then the disciple whom Jesus loved
said to Peter, "It is the Lord!" As soon
as Simon Peter heard him say, "It is the
Lord," he wrapped his outer garment
around him (for he had taken it off) and
jumped into the water. 8 The other disciples followed in the boat, towing the
net full of fish, for they were not far from
shore, about a hundred yards.[c] 9 When
they landed, they saw a fire of burning
coals there with fish on it, and some
bread.

10 Jesus said to them, "Bring some of
the fish you have just caught." 11 So Simon Peter climbed back into the boat
and dragged the net ashore. It was full
of large fish, 153, but even with so many
the net was not torn. 12 Jesus said to them,
"Come and have breakfast." None of the
disciples dared ask him, "Who are you?"
They knew it was the Lord. 13 Jesus came,
took the bread and gave it to them, and
did the same with the fish. 14 This was
now the third time Jesus appeared to
his disciples after he was raised from
the dead.

15 When they had finished eating, Jesus
said to Simon Peter, "Simon son of John,
do you love me more than these?"

"Yes, Lord," he said, "you know that I
love you."

Jesus said, "Feed my lambs."

16 Again Jesus said, "Simon son of John,
do you love me?"

He answered, "Yes, Lord, you know
that I love you."

Jesus said, "Take care of my sheep."

17 The third time he said to him, "Simon son of John, do you love me?"

Peter was hurt because Jesus asked
him the third time, "Do you love me?"
He said, "Lord, you know all things; you
know that I love you."

Jesus said, "Feed my sheep. 18 Very truly I tell you, when you were younger you
dressed yourself and went where you
wanted; but when you are old you will
stretch out your hands, and someone
else will dress you and lead you where
you do not want to go." 19 Jesus said this
to indicate the kind of death by which
Peter would glorify God. Then he said to
him, "Follow me!"

20 Peter turned and saw that the disciple whom Jesus loved was following
them. (This was the one who had leaned
back against Jesus at the supper and had
said, "Lord, who is going to betray you?")
21 When Peter saw him, he asked, "Lord,
what about him?"

22 Jesus answered, "If I want him to remain alive until I return, what is that to
you? You must follow me." 23 Because of
this, the rumor spread among the believers that this disciple would not die. But
Jesus did not say that he would not die;
he only said, "If I want him to remain
alive until I return, what is that to you?"

24 This is the disciple who testifies to
these things and who wrote them down.
We know that his testimony is true.

25 Jesus did many other things as well.
If every one of them were written down,
I suppose that even the whole world
would not have room for the books that
would be written.

[a] *1* Greek *Tiberias* [b] *2* *Thomas* (Aramaic) and *Didymus* (Greek) both mean *twin.* [c] *8* Or about 90 meters

ACTS

Luke's second volume is known as the book of Acts (see p. 916 for the Invitation to Luke-Acts, and for more detailed information on the Gospel of Luke). The six parts of the book of Acts each describe a new phase in the expansion of the Messiah-following movement outward from Jerusalem. These sections are all marked by variations on the phrase *the word of God continued to spread and flourish*:

: First, the church is established in Jerusalem and becomes Greek-speaking, allowing it to spread its message throughout the empire.
: Next, the movement expands into the rest of Palestine.
: Third, Gentiles are included in the gathering of Jesus-followers alongside Jews.
: Fourth, messengers are sent west into the Roman province of Asia.
: Fifth, these messengers enter Europe.
: In the sixth and final phase, the movement reaches the capital city of Rome and into the highest levels of society; God's kingdom is thus announced to all nations.

---

1 In my former book, Theophilus, I
wrote about all that Jesus began to do
and to teach 2until the day he was taken
up to heaven, after giving instructions
through the Holy Spirit to the apostles
he had chosen. 3After his suffering, he
presented himself to them and gave
many convincing proofs that he was
alive. He appeared to them over a period
of forty days and spoke about the kingdom of God. 4On one occasion, while
he was eating with them, he gave them
this command: "Do not leave Jerusalem,
but wait for the gift my Father promised,
which you have heard me speak about.
5For John baptized with[a] water, but in a
few days you will be baptized with[a] the
Holy Spirit."
6Then they gathered around him and
asked him, "Lord, are you at this time going to restore the kingdom to Israel?"
7He said to them: "It is not for you to
know the times or dates the Father has
set by his own authority. 8But you will receive power when the Holy Spirit comes
on you; and you will be my witnesses in
Jerusalem, and in all Judea and Samaria,
and to the ends of the earth."
9After he said this, he was taken up before their very eyes, and a cloud hid him
from their sight.
10They were looking intently up into
the sky as he was going, when suddenly
two men dressed in white stood beside
them. 11"Men of Galilee," they said, "why
do you stand here looking into the sky?
This same Jesus, who has been taken
from you into heaven, will come back in
the same way you have seen him go into
heaven."
12Then the apostles returned to Jerusalem from the hill called the Mount of
Olives, a Sabbath day's walk[b] from the
city. 13When they arrived, they went
upstairs to the room where they were
staying. Those present were Peter, John,
James and Andrew; Philip and Thomas,
Bartholomew and Matthew; James son
of Alphaeus and Simon the Zealot, and
Judas son of James. 14They all joined together constantly in prayer, along with
the women and Mary the mother of
Jesus, and with his brothers.
15In those days Peter stood up among
the believers (a group numbering about a
hundred and twenty) 16and said, "Brothers and sisters,[c] the Scripture had to be
fulfilled in which the Holy Spirit spoke
long ago through David concerning Judas, who served as guide for those who
arrested Jesus. 17He was one of our number and shared in our ministry."
18(With the payment he received for
his wickedness, Judas bought a field;
there he fell headlong, his body burst
open and all his intestines spilled out.
19Everyone in Jerusalem heard about
this, so they called that field in their
language Akeldama, that is, Field of
Blood.)
20"For," said Peter, "it is written in the
Book of Psalms:

[a] *5* Or *in* [b] *12* That is, about 5/8 mile or about 1 kilometer [c] *16* The Greek word for *brothers and sisters* (*adelphoi*) refers here to believers, both men and women, as part of God's family; also in 6:3; 11:29; 12:17; 16:40; 18:18, 27; 21:7, 17; 28:14, 15.

" 'May his place be deserted;
let there be no one to dwell in it,'[a]

and,

" 'May another take his place of
leadership.'[b]

21 Therefore it is necessary to choose
one of the men who have been with us
the whole time the Lord Jesus was living
among us, 22 beginning from John's baptism to the time when Jesus was taken up
from us. For one of these must become a
witness with us of his resurrection."
23 So they nominated two men: Joseph
called Barsabbas (also known as Justus) and Matthias. 24 Then they prayed,
"Lord, you know everyone's heart. Show
us which of these two you have chosen
25 to take over this apostolic ministry,
which Judas left to go where he belongs."
26 Then they cast lots, and the lot fell to
Matthias; so he was added to the eleven
apostles.

2 When the day of Pentecost came, they
were all together in one place. 2 Suddenly a sound like the blowing of a violent wind came from heaven and filled
the whole house where they were sitting.
3 They saw what seemed to be tongues of
fire that separated and came to rest on
each of them. 4 All of them were filled
with the Holy Spirit and began to speak
in other tongues[c] as the Spirit enabled
them.
5 Now there were staying in Jerusalem God-fearing Jews from every nation
under heaven. 6 When they heard this
sound, a crowd came together in bewil-
derment, because each one heard their
own language being spoken. 7 Utterly
amazed, they asked: "Aren't all these
who are speaking Galileans? 8 Then how
is it that each of us hears them in our native language? 9 Parthians, Medes and
Elamites; residents of Mesopotamia, Judea and Cappadocia, Pontus and Asia,[d]
10 Phrygia and Pamphylia, Egypt and
the parts of Libya near Cyrene; visitors
from Rome 11 (both Jews and converts to
Judaism); Cretans and Arabs — we hear
them declaring the wonders of God in
our own tongues!" 12 Amazed and perplexed, they asked one another, "What
does this mean?"
13 Some, however, made fun of them
and said, "They have had too much
wine."
14 Then Peter stood up with the Elev-
en, raised his voice and addressed the
crowd: "Fellow Jews and all of you who
live in Jerusalem, let me explain this to
you; listen carefully to what I say. 15 These
people are not drunk, as you suppose. It's
only nine in the morning! 16 No, this is
what was spoken by the prophet Joel:

17 " 'In the last days, God says,
I will pour out my Spirit on all
people.
Your sons and daughters will
prophesy,
your young men will see visions,
your old men will dream dreams.
18 Even on my servants, both men and
women,
I will pour out my Spirit in those
days,
and they will prophesy.
19 I will show wonders in the heavens
above
and signs on the earth below,
blood and fire and billows of smoke.
20 The sun will be turned to darkness
and the moon to blood
before the coming of the great and
glorious day of the Lord.
21 And everyone who calls
on the name of the Lord will be
saved.'[e]

22 "Fellow Israelites, listen to this:
Jesus of Nazareth was a man accredited
by God to you by miracles, wonders and
signs, which God did among you through
him, as you yourselves know. 23 This man
was handed over to you by God's deliberate plan and foreknowledge; and you,
with the help of wicked men,[f] put him to
death by nailing him to the cross. 24 But
God raised him from the dead, freeing
him from the agony of death, because it
was impossible for death to keep its hold
on him. 25 David said about him:

" 'I saw the Lord always before me.
Because he is at my right hand,
I will not be shaken.
26 Therefore my heart is glad and my
tongue rejoices;
my body also will rest in hope,

[a] *20* Psalm 69:25 [b] *20* Psalm 109:8 [c] *4* Or *languages*; also in verse 11 [d] *9* That is, the Roman province by that name [e] *21* Joel 2:28-32 [f] *23* Or *of those not having the law* (that is, Gentiles)

27 because you will not abandon me to
the realm of the dead,
you will not let your holy one see
decay.
28 You have made known to me the
paths of life;
you will fill me with joy in your
presence.'[a]

29 "Fellow Israelites, I can tell you confidently that the patriarch David died
and was buried, and his tomb is here to
this day. 30 But he was a prophet and knew
that God had promised him on oath that
he would place one of his descendants on
his throne. 31 Seeing what was to come,
he spoke of the resurrection of the Messiah, that he was not abandoned to the
realm of the dead, nor did his body see
decay. 32 God has raised this Jesus to life,
and we are all witnesses of it. 33 Exalted
to the right hand of God, he has received
from the Father the promised Holy Spirit and has poured out what you now see
and hear. 34 For David did not ascend to
heaven, and yet he said,

" 'The Lord said to my Lord:
"Sit at my right hand
35 until I make your enemies
a footstool for your feet." '[b]

36 "Therefore let all Israel be assured of
this: God has made this Jesus, whom you
crucified, both Lord and Messiah."

37 When the people heard this, they
were cut to the heart and said to Peter
and the other apostles, "Brothers, what
shall we do?"

38 Peter replied, "Repent and be baptized, every one of you, in the name of
Jesus Christ for the forgiveness of your
sins. And you will receive the gift of the
Holy Spirit. 39 The promise is for you
and your children and for all who are
far off—for all whom the Lord our God
will call."

40 With many other words he warned
them; and he pleaded with them, "Save
yourselves from this corrupt generation."
41 Those who accepted his message were
baptized, and about three thousand were
added to their number that day.

42 They devoted themselves to the
apostles' teaching and to fellowship,
to the breaking of bread and to prayer.
43 Everyone was filled with awe at the
many wonders and signs performed by
the apostles. 44 All the believers were together and had everything in common.
45 They sold property and possessions to
give to anyone who had need. 46 Every
day they continued to meet together in
the temple courts. They broke bread in
their homes and ate together with glad
and sincere hearts, 47 praising God and
enjoying the favor of all the people. And
the Lord added to their number daily
those who were being saved.

3 One day Peter and John were going up
to the temple at the time of prayer—at
three in the afternoon. 2 Now a man who
was lame from birth was being carried to
the temple gate called Beautiful, where
he was put every day to beg from those
going into the temple courts. 3 When he
saw Peter and John about to enter, he
asked them for money. 4 Peter looked
straight at him, as did John. Then Peter
said, "Look at us!" 5 So the man gave them
his attention, expecting to get something
from them.

6 Then Peter said, "Silver or gold I do not
have, but what I do have I give you. In the
name of Jesus Christ of Nazareth, walk."
7 Taking him by the right hand, he helped
him up, and instantly the man's feet and
ankles became strong. 8 He jumped
to his feet and began to walk. Then he
went with them into the temple courts,
walking and jumping, and praising God.
9 When all the people saw him walking
and praising God, 10 they recognized him
as the same man who used to sit begging
at the temple gate called Beautiful, and
they were filled with wonder and amazement at what had happened to him.

11 While the man held on to Peter and
John, all the people were astonished and
came running to them in the place called
Solomon's Colonnade. 12 When Peter saw
this, he said to them: "Fellow Israelites,
why does this surprise you? Why do
you stare at us as if by our own power or
godliness we had made this man walk?
13 The God of Abraham, Isaac and Jacob,
the God of our fathers, has glorified his
servant Jesus. You handed him over to
be killed, and you disowned him before
Pilate, though he had decided to let him
go. 14 You disowned the Holy and Righteous One and asked that a murderer be

[a] *28* Psalm 16:8-11 (see Septuagint) [b] *35* Psalm 110:1

released to you. 15You killed the author of life, but God raised him from the dead. We are witnesses of this. 16By faith in the name of Jesus, this man whom you see and know was made strong. It is Jesus' name and the faith that comes through him that has completely healed him, as you can all see.

17"Now, fellow Israelites, I know that you acted in ignorance, as did your leaders. 18But this is how God fulfilled what he had foretold through all the prophets, saying that his Messiah would suffer. 19Repent, then, and turn to God, so that your sins may be wiped out, that times of refreshing may come from the Lord, 20and that he may send the Messiah, who has been appointed for you—even Jesus. 21Heaven must receive him until the time comes for God to restore everything, as he promised long ago through his holy prophets. 22For Moses said, 'The Lord your God will raise up for you a prophet like me from among your own people; you must listen to everything he tells you. 23Anyone who does not listen to him will be completely cut off from their people.'[a]

24"Indeed, beginning with Samuel, all the prophets who have spoken have foretold these days. 25And you are heirs of the prophets and of the covenant God made with your fathers. He said to Abraham, 'Through your offspring all peoples on earth will be blessed.'[b] 26When God raised up his servant, he sent him first to you to bless you by turning each of you from your wicked ways."

4 The priests and the captain of the temple guard and the Sadducees came up to Peter and John while they were speaking to the people. 2They were greatly disturbed because the apostles were teaching the people, proclaiming in Jesus the resurrection of the dead. 3They seized Peter and John and, because it was evening, they put them in jail until the next day. 4But many who heard the message believed; so the number of men who believed grew to about five thousand.

5The next day the rulers, the elders and the teachers of the law met in Jerusalem. 6Annas the high priest was there, and so were Caiaphas, John, Alexander and others of the high priest's family. 7They had Peter and John brought before them and began to question them: "By what power or what name did you do this?"

8Then Peter, filled with the Holy Spirit, said to them: "Rulers and elders of the people! 9If we are being called to account today for an act of kindness shown to a man who was lame and are being asked how he was healed, 10then know this, you and all the people of Israel: It is by the name of Jesus Christ of Nazareth, whom you crucified but whom God raised from the dead, that this man stands before you healed. 11Jesus is

"'the stone you builders rejected,
which has become the
cornerstone.'[c]

12Salvation is found in no one else, for there is no other name under heaven given to mankind by which we must be saved."

13When they saw the courage of Peter and John and realized that they were unschooled, ordinary men, they were astonished and they took note that these men had been with Jesus. 14But since they could see the man who had been healed standing there with them, there was nothing they could say. 15So they ordered them to withdraw from the Sanhedrin and then conferred together. 16"What are we going to do with these men?" they asked. "Everyone living in Jerusalem knows they have performed a notable sign, and we cannot deny it. 17But to stop this thing from spreading any further among the people, we must warn them to speak no longer to anyone in this name."

18Then they called them in again and commanded them not to speak or teach at all in the name of Jesus. 19But Peter and John replied, "Which is right in God's eyes: to listen to you, or to him? You be the judges! 20As for us, we cannot help speaking about what we have seen and heard."

21After further threats they let them go. They could not decide how to punish them, because all the people were praising God for what had happened. 22For the man who was miraculously healed was over forty years old.

23On their release, Peter and John went

[a] *23* Deut. 18:15,18,19 [b] *25* Gen. 22:18; 26:4 [c] *11* Psalm 118:22

back to their own people and reported all
that the chief priests and the elders had
said to them. 24When they heard this,
they raised their voices together in prayer
to God. "Sovereign Lord," they said, "you
made the heavens and the earth and the
sea, and everything in them. 25You spoke
by the Holy Spirit through the mouth of
your servant, our father David:

"'Why do the nations rage
    and the peoples plot in vain?
26The kings of the earth rise up
    and the rulers band together
against the Lord
    and against his anointed one.[a,b]

27Indeed Herod and Pontius Pilate
met together with the Gentiles and the
people of Israel in this city to conspire
against your holy servant Jesus, whom
you anointed. 28They did what your
power and will had decided beforehand
should happen. 29Now, Lord, consider
their threats and enable your servants
to speak your word with great boldness.
30Stretch out your hand to heal and perform signs and wonders through the
name of your holy servant Jesus."

31After they prayed, the place where
they were meeting was shaken. And they
were all filled with the Holy Spirit and
spoke the word of God boldly.

32All the believers were one in heart
and mind. No one claimed that any of
their possessions was their own, but
they shared everything they had. 33With
great power the apostles continued to
testify to the resurrection of the Lord
Jesus. And God's grace was so powerfully at work in them all 34that there were
no needy persons among them. For from
time to time those who owned land or
houses sold them, brought the money
from the sales 35and put it at the apostles' feet, and it was distributed to anyone who had need.

36Joseph, a Levite from Cyprus, whom
the apostles called Barnabas (which
means "son of encouragement"), 37sold
a field he owned and brought the money
and put it at the apostles' feet.

5 Now a man named Ananias, together with his wife Sapphira, also sold
a piece of property. 2With his wife's full
knowledge he kept back part of the money for himself, but brought the rest and
put it at the apostles' feet.

3Then Peter said, "Ananias, how is it
that Satan has so filled your heart that
you have lied to the Holy Spirit and have
kept for yourself some of the money you
received for the land? 4Didn't it belong to
you before it was sold? And after it was
sold, wasn't the money at your disposal? What made you think of doing such
a thing? You have not lied just to human
beings but to God."

5When Ananias heard this, he fell
down and died. And great fear seized
all who heard what had happened.
6Then some young men came forward,
wrapped up his body, and carried him
out and buried him.

7About three hours later his wife came
in, not knowing what had happened. 8Pe-
ter asked her, "Tell me, is this the price
you and Ananias got for the land?"

"Yes," she said, "that is the price."

9Peter said to her, "How could you conspire to test the Spirit of the Lord? Listen!
The feet of the men who buried your husband are at the door, and they will carry
you out also."

10At that moment she fell down at his
feet and died. Then the young men came
in and, finding her dead, carried her
out and buried her beside her husband.
11Great fear seized the whole church and
all who heard about these events.

12The apostles performed many signs
and wonders among the people. And
all the believers used to meet together
in Solomon's Colonnade. 13No one else
dared join them, even though they were
highly regarded by the people. 14Never-
theless, more and more men and wom-
en believed in the Lord and were added
to their number. 15As a result, people
brought the sick into the streets and laid
them on beds and mats so that at least
Peter's shadow might fall on some of
them as he passed by. 16Crowds gathered
also from the towns around Jerusalem,
bringing their sick and those tormented
by impure spirits, and all of them were
healed.

17Then the high priest and all his associates, who were members of the party
of the Sadducees, were filled with jealousy. 18They arrested the apostles and

[a] *26* That is, Messiah or Christ [b] *26* Psalm 2:1,2

put them in the public jail. 19But during
the night an angel of the Lord opened
the doors of the jail and brought them
out. 20"Go, stand in the temple courts,"
he said, "and tell the people all about this
new life."

21At daybreak they entered the temple
courts, as they had been told, and began
to teach the people.

When the high priest and his associates arrived, they called together the
Sanhedrin—the full assembly of the
elders of Israel—and sent to the jail for
the apostles. 22But on arriving at the
jail, the officers did not find them there.
So they went back and reported, 23"We
found the jail securely locked, with the
guards standing at the doors; but when
we opened them, we found no one inside." 24On hearing this report, the captain of the temple guard and the chief
priests were at a loss, wondering what
this might lead to.

25Then someone came and said, "Look!
The men you put in jail are standing in
the temple courts teaching the people."
26At that, the captain went with his officers and brought the apostles. They did
not use force, because they feared that
the people would stone them.

27The apostles were brought in and
made to appear before the Sanhedrin to
be questioned by the high priest. 28"We
gave you strict orders not to teach in this
name," he said. "Yet you have filled Jerusalem with your teaching and are determined to make us guilty of this man's
blood."

29Peter and the other apostles replied:
"We must obey God rather than human
beings! 30The God of our ancestors raised
Jesus from the dead—whom you killed
by hanging him on a cross. 31God exalted him to his own right hand as Prince
and Savior that he might bring Israel to
repentance and forgive their sins. 32We
are witnesses of these things, and so is
the Holy Spirit, whom God has given to
those who obey him."

33When they heard this, they were furious and wanted to put them to death.
34But a Pharisee named Gamaliel, a
teacher of the law, who was honored by
all the people, stood up in the Sanhedrin and ordered that the men be put
outside for a little while. 35Then he addressed the Sanhedrin: "Men of Israel,
consider carefully what you intend to do
to these men. 36Some time ago Theudas
appeared, claiming to be somebody, and
about four hundred men rallied to him.
He was killed, all his followers were dispersed, and it all came to nothing. 37Af-
ter him, Judas the Galilean appeared in
the days of the census and led a band of
people in revolt. He too was killed, and
all his followers were scattered. 38There-
fore, in the present case I advise you:
Leave these men alone! Let them go! For
if their purpose or activity is of human
origin, it will fail. 39But if it is from God,
you will not be able to stop these men;
you will only find yourselves fighting
against God."

40His speech persuaded them. They
called the apostles in and had them
flogged. Then they ordered them not
to speak in the name of Jesus, and let
them go.

41The apostles left the Sanhedrin, rejoicing because they had been counted worthy of suffering disgrace for the
Name. 42Day after day, in the temple
courts and from house to house, they
never stopped teaching and proclaiming
the good news that Jesus is the Messiah.

6 In those days when the number of disciples was increasing, the Hellenistic
Jews[a] among them complained against
the Hebraic Jews because their widows
were being overlooked in the daily dis-
tribution of food. 2So the Twelve gathered all the disciples together and said,
"It would not be right for us to neglect
the ministry of the word of God in order
to wait on tables. 3Brothers and sisters,
choose seven men from among you who
are known to be full of the Spirit and
wisdom. We will turn this responsibility
over to them 4and will give our attention
to prayer and the ministry of the word."

5This proposal pleased the whole
group. They chose Stephen, a man full of
faith and of the Holy Spirit; also Philip,
Procorus, Nicanor, Timon, Parmenas,
and Nicolas from Antioch, a convert to
Judaism. 6They presented these men to
the apostles, who prayed and laid their
hands on them.

7So the word of God spread. The num-

[a] 1 That is, Jews who had adopted the Greek language and culture

ber of disciples in Jerusalem increased
rapidly, and a large number of priests
became obedient to the faith.

[8]Now Stephen, a man full of God's
grace and power, performed great wonders and signs among the people. [9]Op-
position arose, however, from members
of the Synagogue of the Freedmen (as it
was called)—Jews of Cyrene and Alexandria as well as the provinces of Cilicia and Asia—who began to argue with
Stephen. [10]But they could not stand up
against the wisdom the Spirit gave him
as he spoke.

[11]Then they secretly persuaded some
men to say, "We have heard Stephen
speak blasphemous words against Moses and against God."

[12]So they stirred up the people and the
elders and the teachers of the law. They
seized Stephen and brought him before
the Sanhedrin. [13]They produced false
witnesses, who testified, "This fellow
never stops speaking against this holy
place and against the law. [14]For we have
heard him say that this Jesus of Nazareth
will destroy this place and change the
customs Moses handed down to us."

[15]All who were sitting in the Sanhedrin looked intently at Stephen, and
they saw that his face was like the face
of an angel.

7 Then the high priest asked Stephen,
"Are these charges true?"

[2]To this he replied: "Brothers and fathers, listen to me! The God of glory
appeared to our father Abraham while
he was still in Mesopotamia, before he
lived in Harran. [3]'Leave your country
and your people,' God said, 'and go to
the land I will show you.'[a]

[4]"So he left the land of the Chaldeans
and settled in Harran. After the death
of his father, God sent him to this land
where you are now living. [5]He gave him
no inheritance here, not even enough
ground to set his foot on. But God promised him that he and his descendants
after him would possess the land, even
though at that time Abraham had no
child. [6]God spoke to him in this way:
'For four hundred years your descendants will be strangers in a country not
their own, and they will be enslaved and
mistreated. [7]But I will punish the nation
they serve as slaves,' God said, 'and afterward they will come out of that country
and worship me in this place.'[b] [8]Then he
gave Abraham the covenant of circumcision. And Abraham became the father
of Isaac and circumcised him eight days
after his birth. Later Isaac became the
father of Jacob, and Jacob became the father of the twelve patriarchs.

[9]"Because the patriarchs were jealous
of Joseph, they sold him as a slave into
Egypt. But God was with him [10]and rescued him from all his troubles. He gave
Joseph wisdom and enabled him to gain
the goodwill of Pharaoh king of Egypt. So
Pharaoh made him ruler over Egypt and
all his palace.

[11]"Then a famine struck all Egypt
and Canaan, bringing great suffering,
and our ancestors could not find food.
[12]When Jacob heard that there was grain
in Egypt, he sent our forefathers on their
first visit. [13]On their second visit, Joseph
told his brothers who he was, and Pharaoh learned about Joseph's family. [14]Af-
ter this, Joseph sent for his father Jacob
and his whole family, seventy-five in all.
[15]Then Jacob went down to Egypt, where
he and our ancestors died. [16]Their bodies were brought back to Shechem and
placed in the tomb that Abraham had
bought from the sons of Hamor at Shechem for a certain sum of money.

[17]"As the time drew near for God to fulfill his promise to Abraham, the number
of our people in Egypt had greatly increased. [18]Then 'a new king, to whom
Joseph meant nothing, came to power
in Egypt.'[c] [19]He dealt treacherously with
our people and oppressed our ancestors
by forcing them to throw out their newborn babies so that they would die.

[20]"At that time Moses was born, and he
was no ordinary child.[d] For three months
he was cared for by his family. [21]When he
was placed outside, Pharaoh's daughter
took him and brought him up as her own
son. [22]Moses was educated in all the wisdom of the Egyptians and was powerful
in speech and action.

[23]"When Moses was forty years old, he
decided to visit his own people, the Israelites. [24]He saw one of them being mistreated by an Egyptian, so he went to his

[a] *3* Gen. 12:1 [b] *7* Gen. 15:13,14 [c] *18* Exodus 1:8 [d] *20* Or *was fair in the sight of God*

defense and avenged him by killing the
Egyptian. 25 Moses thought that his own
people would realize that God was using him to rescue them, but they did not.
26 The next day Moses came upon two
Israelites who were fighting. He tried to
reconcile them by saying, 'Men, you are
brothers; why do you want to hurt each
other?'

27 "But the man who was mistreating
the other pushed Moses aside and said,
'Who made you ruler and judge over us?
28 Are you thinking of killing me as you
killed the Egyptian yesterday?'[a] 29 When
Moses heard this, he fled to Midian,
where he settled as a foreigner and had
two sons.

30 "After forty years had passed, an
angel appeared to Moses in the flames
of a burning bush in the desert near
Mount Sinai. 31 When he saw this, he was
amazed at the sight. As he went over to
get a closer look, he heard the Lord say:
32 'I am the God of your fathers, the God
of Abraham, Isaac and Jacob.'[b] Moses
trembled with fear and did not dare to
look.

33 "Then the Lord said to him, 'Take
off your sandals, for the place where you
are standing is holy ground. 34 I have indeed seen the oppression of my people in
Egypt. I have heard their groaning and
have come down to set them free. Now
come, I will send you back to Egypt.'[c]

35 "This is the same Moses they had
rejected with the words, 'Who made
you ruler and judge?' He was sent to be
their ruler and deliverer by God himself,
through the angel who appeared to him
in the bush. 36 He led them out of Egypt
and performed wonders and signs in
Egypt, at the Red Sea and for forty years
in the wilderness.

37 "This is the Moses who told the Israelites, 'God will raise up for you a prophet
like me from your own people.'[d] 38 He was
in the assembly in the wilderness, with
the angel who spoke to him on Mount
Sinai, and with our ancestors; and he received living words to pass on to us.

39 "But our ancestors refused to obey
him. Instead, they rejected him and in
their hearts turned back to Egypt. 40 They
told Aaron, 'Make us gods who will go before us. As for this fellow Moses who led
us out of Egypt — we don't know what has
happened to him!'[e] 41 That was the time
they made an idol in the form of a calf.
They brought sacrifices to it and reveled in what their own hands had made.
42 But God turned away from them and
gave them over to the worship of the sun,
moon and stars. This agrees with what is
written in the book of the prophets:

"'Did you bring me sacrifices and
offerings
forty years in the wilderness, people
of Israel?
43 You have taken up the tabernacle of
Molek
and the star of your god Rephan,
the idols you made to worship.
Therefore I will send you into exile'[f]
beyond Babylon.

44 "Our ancestors had the tabernacle
of the covenant law with them in the
wilderness. It had been made as God
directed Moses, according to the pattern he had seen. 45 After receiving the
tabernacle, our ancestors under Joshua
brought it with them when they took the
land from the nations God drove out before them. It remained in the land until
the time of David, 46 who enjoyed God's
favor and asked that he might provide
a dwelling place for the God of Jacob.[g]
47 But it was Solomon who built a house
for him.

48 "However, the Most High does not
live in houses made by human hands. As
the prophet says:

49 "'Heaven is my throne,
and the earth is my footstool.
What kind of house will you build
for me?
says the Lord.
Or where will my resting place be?
50 Has not my hand made all these
things?'[h]

51 "You stiff-necked people! Your hearts
and ears are still uncircumcised. You are
just like your ancestors: You always resist
the Holy Spirit! 52 Was there ever a prophet your ancestors did not persecute?
They even killed those who predicted
the coming of the Righteous One. And
now you have betrayed and murdered
him — 53 you who have received the law

[a] *28* Exodus 2:14 [b] *32* Exodus 3:6 [c] *34* Exodus 3:5,7,8,10 [d] *37* Deut. 18:15 [e] *40* Exodus 32:1
[f] *43* Amos 5:25-27 (see Septuagint) [g] *46* Some early manuscripts *the house of Jacob* [h] *50* Isaiah 66:1,2

that was given through angels but have
not obeyed it."
54When the members of the Sanhedrin heard this, they were furious and
gnashed their teeth at him. 55But Stephen, full of the Holy Spirit, looked up
to heaven and saw the glory of God, and
Jesus standing at the right hand of God.
56"Look," he said, "I see heaven open
and the Son of Man standing at the right
hand of God."
57At this they covered their ears and,
yelling at the top of their voices, they all
rushed at him, 58dragged him out of the
city and began to stone him. Meanwhile,
the witnesses laid their coats at the feet
of a young man named Saul.
59While they were stoning him, Stephen prayed, "Lord Jesus, receive my
spirit." 60Then he fell on his knees and
cried out, "Lord, do not hold this sin
against them." When he had said this, he
fell asleep.

8 And Saul approved of their killing
him.

On that day a great persecution broke
out against the church in Jerusalem, and
all except the apostles were scattered
throughout Judea and Samaria. 2Godly
men buried Stephen and mourned deeply for him. 3But Saul began to destroy the
church. Going from house to house, he
dragged off both men and women and
put them in prison.
4Those who had been scattered
preached the word wherever they went.
5Philip went down to a city in Samaria and proclaimed the Messiah there.
6When the crowds heard Philip and saw
the signs he performed, they all paid
close attention to what he said. 7For
with shrieks, impure spirits came out of
many, and many who were paralyzed or
lame were healed. 8So there was great joy
in that city.
9Now for some time a man named Simon had practiced sorcery in the city
and amazed all the people of Samaria.
He boasted that he was someone great,
10and all the people, both high and low,
gave him their attention and exclaimed,
"This man is rightly called the Great
Power of God." 11They followed him because he had amazed them for a long
time with his sorcery. 12But when they
believed Philip as he proclaimed the
good news of the kingdom of God and
the name of Jesus Christ, they were baptized, both men and women. 13Simon
himself believed and was baptized. And
he followed Philip everywhere, astonished by the great signs and miracles he
saw.
14When the apostles in Jerusalem
heard that Samaria had accepted the
word of God, they sent Peter and John
to Samaria. 15When they arrived, they
prayed for the new believers there that
they might receive the Holy Spirit, 16be-
cause the Holy Spirit had not yet come
on any of them; they had simply been
baptized in the name of the Lord Jesus.
17Then Peter and John placed their
hands on them, and they received the
Holy Spirit.
18When Simon saw that the Spirit was
given at the laying on of the apostles'
hands, he offered them money 19and
said, "Give me also this ability so that
everyone on whom I lay my hands may
receive the Holy Spirit."
20Peter answered: "May your money
perish with you, because you thought
you could buy the gift of God with money!
21You have no part or share in this ministry, because your heart is not right before
God. 22Repent of this wickedness and
pray to the Lord in the hope that he may
forgive you for having such a thought in
your heart. 23For I see that you are full of
bitterness and captive to sin."
24Then Simon answered, "Pray to the
Lord for me so that nothing you have said
may happen to me."
25After they had further proclaimed
the word of the Lord and testified about
Jesus, Peter and John returned to Jerusalem, preaching the gospel in many Samaritan villages.
26Now an angel of the Lord said to
Philip, "Go south to the road — the desert
road — that goes down from Jerusalem to
Gaza." 27So he started out, and on his way
he met an Ethiopian[a] eunuch, an important official in charge of all the treasury
of the Kandake (which means "queen of
the Ethiopians"). This man had gone to
Jerusalem to worship, 28and on his way
home was sitting in his chariot reading
the Book of Isaiah the prophet. 29The

[a] *27* That is, from the southern Nile region

Spirit told Philip, "Go to that chariot and
stay near it."
30 Then Philip ran up to the chariot
and heard the man reading Isaiah the
prophet. "Do you understand what you
are reading?" Philip asked.
31 "How can I," he said, "unless someone explains it to me?" So he invited
Philip to come up and sit with him.
32 This is the passage of Scripture the
eunuch was reading:

"He was led like a sheep to the
slaughter,
and as a lamb before its shearer is
silent,
so he did not open his mouth.
33 In his humiliation he was deprived of
justice.
Who can speak of his descendants?
For his life was taken from the
earth."[a]

34 The eunuch asked Philip, "Tell me,
please, who is the prophet talking about,
himself or someone else?" 35 Then Philip
began with that very passage of Scripture
and told him the good news about Jesus.
36 As they traveled along the road, they
came to some water and the eunuch said,
"Look, here is water. What can stand in
the way of my being baptized?" [37 [b]]
38 And he gave orders to stop the chariot.
Then both Philip and the eunuch went
down into the water and Philip baptized
him. 39 When they came up out of the water, the Spirit of the Lord suddenly took
Philip away, and the eunuch did not see
him again, but went on his way rejoicing. 40 Philip, however, appeared at Azo-
tus and traveled about, preaching the
gospel in all the towns until he reached
Caesarea.

9 Meanwhile, Saul was still breathing
out murderous threats against the
Lord's disciples. He went to the high
priest 2 and asked him for letters to the
synagogues in Damascus, so that if he
found any there who belonged to the
Way, whether men or women, he might
take them as prisoners to Jerusalem. 3 As
he neared Damascus on his journey, suddenly a light from heaven flashed around
him. 4 He fell to the ground and heard a
voice say to him, "Saul, Saul, why do you
persecute me?"
5 "Who are you, Lord?" Saul asked.
"I am Jesus, whom you are persecuting," he replied. 6 "Now get up and go
into the city, and you will be told what
you must do."
7 The men traveling with Saul stood
there speechless; they heard the sound
but did not see anyone. 8 Saul got up from
the ground, but when he opened his eyes
he could see nothing. So they led him by
the hand into Damascus. 9 For three days
he was blind, and did not eat or drink
anything.
10 In Damascus there was a disciple
named Ananias. The Lord called to him
in a vision, "Ananias!"
"Yes, Lord," he answered.
11 The Lord told him, "Go to the house
of Judas on Straight Street and ask for
a man from Tarsus named Saul, for he
is praying. 12 In a vision he has seen a
man named Ananias come and place his
hands on him to restore his sight."
13 "Lord," Ananias answered, "I have
heard many reports about this man and
all the harm he has done to your holy
people in Jerusalem. 14 And he has come
here with authority from the chief priests
to arrest all who call on your name."
15 But the Lord said to Ananias, "Go!
This man is my chosen instrument to
proclaim my name to the Gentiles and
their kings and to the people of Israel. 16 I
will show him how much he must suffer
for my name."
17 Then Ananias went to the house and
entered it. Placing his hands on Saul, he
said, "Brother Saul, the Lord—Jesus,
who appeared to you on the road as you
were coming here—has sent me so that
you may see again and be filled with the
Holy Spirit." 18 Immediately, something
like scales fell from Saul's eyes, and he
could see again. He got up and was baptized, 19 and after taking some food, he
regained his strength.
Saul spent several days with the disciples in Damascus. 20 At once he began
to preach in the synagogues that Jesus
is the Son of God. 21 All those who heard
him were astonished and asked, "Isn't
he the man who raised havoc in Jerusalem among those who call on this name?
And hasn't he come here to take them
as prisoners to the chief priests?" 22 Yet

[a] 33 Isaiah 53:7,8 (see Septuagint) [b] 37 Some manuscripts include here *Philip said, "If you believe with all your heart, you may." The eunuch answered, "I believe that Jesus Christ is the Son of God."*

Saul grew more and more powerful and
baffled the Jews living in Damascus by
proving that Jesus is the Messiah.
23 After many days had gone by, there
was a conspiracy among the Jews to kill
him, 24 but Saul learned of their plan.
Day and night they kept close watch on
the city gates in order to kill him. 25 But
his followers took him by night and lowered him in a basket through an opening
in the wall.
26 When he came to Jerusalem, he tried
to join the disciples, but they were all
afraid of him, not believing that he really was a disciple. 27 But Barnabas took
him and brought him to the apostles.
He told them how Saul on his journey
had seen the Lord and that the Lord had
spoken to him, and how in Damascus
he had preached fearlessly in the name
of Jesus. 28 So Saul stayed with them and
moved about freely in Jerusalem, speaking boldly in the name of the Lord. 29 He
talked and debated with the Hellenistic
Jews,[a] but they tried to kill him. 30 When
the believers learned of this, they took
him down to Caesarea and sent him off
to Tarsus.
31 Then the church throughout Judea,
Galilee and Samaria enjoyed a time of
peace and was strengthened. Living in
the fear of the Lord and encouraged by
the Holy Spirit, it increased in numbers.

32 As Peter traveled about the country, he went to visit the Lord's people
who lived in Lydda. 33 There he found a
man named Aeneas, who was paralyzed
and had been bedridden for eight years.
34 "Aeneas," Peter said to him, "Jesus
Christ heals you. Get up and roll up your
mat." Immediately Aeneas got up. 35 All
those who lived in Lydda and Sharon saw
him and turned to the Lord.
36 In Joppa there was a disciple named
Tabitha (in Greek her name is Dorcas);
she was always doing good and helping
the poor. 37 About that time she became
sick and died, and her body was washed
and placed in an upstairs room. 38 Lydda
was near Joppa; so when the disciples
heard that Peter was in Lydda, they sent
two men to him and urged him, "Please
come at once!"
39 Peter went with them, and when
he arrived he was taken upstairs to the
room. All the widows stood around him,
crying and showing him the robes and
other clothing that Dorcas had made
while she was still with them.
40 Peter sent them all out of the room;
then he got down on his knees and
prayed. Turning toward the dead woman, he said, "Tabitha, get up." She opened
her eyes, and seeing Peter she sat up.
41 He took her by the hand and helped
her to her feet. Then he called for the believers, especially the widows, and presented her to them alive. 42 This became
known all over Joppa, and many people
believed in the Lord. 43 Peter stayed in
Joppa for some time with a tanner named
Simon.

10 At Caesarea there was a man named
Cornelius, a centurion in what was
known as the Italian Regiment. 2 He and
all his family were devout and God-fearing; he gave generously to those in need
and prayed to God regularly. 3 One day at
about three in the afternoon he had a vision. He distinctly saw an angel of God,
who came to him and said, "Cornelius!"
4 Cornelius stared at him in fear. "What
is it, Lord?" he asked.
The angel answered, "Your prayers
and gifts to the poor have come up as
a memorial offering before God. 5 Now
send men to Joppa to bring back a man
named Simon who is called Peter. 6 He
is staying with Simon the tanner, whose
house is by the sea."
7 When the angel who spoke to him had
gone, Cornelius called two of his servants and a devout soldier who was one
of his attendants. 8 He told them everything that had happened and sent them
to Joppa.
9 About noon the following day as they
were on their journey and approaching
the city, Peter went up on the roof to pray.
10 He became hungry and wanted something to eat, and while the meal was being prepared, he fell into a trance. 11 He
saw heaven opened and something like
a large sheet being let down to earth by
its four corners. 12 It contained all kinds
of four-footed animals, as well as reptiles
and birds. 13 Then a voice told him, "Get
up, Peter. Kill and eat."
14 "Surely not, Lord!" Peter replied. "I

[a] 29 That is, Jews who had adopted the Greek language and culture

have never eaten anything impure or
unclean."
15 The voice spoke to him a second
time, "Do not call anything impure that
God has made clean."
16 This happened three times, and immediately the sheet was taken back to
heaven.
17 While Peter was wondering about
the meaning of the vision, the men sent
by Cornelius found out where Simon's
house was and stopped at the gate.
18 They called out, asking if Simon who
was known as Peter was staying there.
19 While Peter was still thinking about
the vision, the Spirit said to him, "Simon,
three[a] men are looking for you. 20 So get
up and go downstairs. Do not hesitate to
go with them, for I have sent them."
21 Peter went down and said to the men,
"I'm the one you're looking for. Why have
you come?"
22 The men replied, "We have come
from Cornelius the centurion. He is a
righteous and God-fearing man, who
is respected by all the Jewish people. A
holy angel told him to ask you to come
to his house so that he could hear what
you have to say." 23 Then Peter invited the
men into the house to be his guests.
The next day Peter started out with
them, and some of the believers from
Joppa went along. 24 The following day
he arrived in Caesarea. Cornelius was
expecting them and had called together
his relatives and close friends. 25 As Peter entered the house, Cornelius met him
and fell at his feet in reverence. 26 But Peter made him get up. "Stand up," he said,
"I am only a man myself."
27 While talking with him, Peter went
inside and found a large gathering of
people. 28 He said to them: "You are well
aware that it is against our law for a Jew to
associate with or visit a Gentile. But God
has shown me that I should not call anyone impure or unclean. 29 So when I was
sent for, I came without raising any ob-
jection. May I ask why you sent for me?"
30 Cornelius answered: "Three days
ago I was in my house praying at this
hour, at three in the afternoon. Suddenly a man in shining clothes stood before
me 31 and said, 'Cornelius, God has heard
your prayer and remembered your gifts
to the poor. 32 Send to Joppa for Simon
who is called Peter. He is a guest in the
home of Simon the tanner, who lives by
the sea.' 33 So I sent for you immediately, and it was good of you to come. Now
we are all here in the presence of God to
listen to everything the Lord has commanded you to tell us."
34 Then Peter began to speak: "I now
realize how true it is that God does not
show favoritism 35 but accepts from every nation the one who fears him and
does what is right. 36 You know the
message God sent to the people of Israel, announcing the good news of peace
through Jesus Christ, who is Lord of all.
37 You know what has happened throughout the province of Judea, beginning
in Galilee after the baptism that John
preached — 38 how God anointed Jesus of
Nazareth with the Holy Spirit and power,
and how he went around doing good and
healing all who were under the power of
the devil, because God was with him.
39 "We are witnesses of everything
he did in the country of the Jews and in
Jerusalem. They killed him by hanging him on a cross, 40 but God raised
him from the dead on the third day and
caused him to be seen. 41 He was not seen
by all the people, but by witnesses whom
God had already chosen — by us who ate
and drank with him after he rose from
the dead. 42 He commanded us to preach
to the people and to testify that he is the
one whom God appointed as judge of the
living and the dead. 43 All the prophets
testify about him that everyone who believes in him receives forgiveness of sins
through his name."
44 While Peter was still speaking these
words, the Holy Spirit came on all who
heard the message. 45 The circumcised
believers who had come with Peter were
astonished that the gift of the Holy Spirit had been poured out even on Gentiles. 46 For they heard them speaking in
tongues[b] and praising God.
Then Peter said, 47 "Surely no one can
stand in the way of their being baptized
with water. They have received the Holy
Spirit just as we have." 48 So he ordered
that they be baptized in the name of
Jesus Christ. Then they asked Peter to
stay with them for a few days.

[a] *19* One early manuscript *two*; other manuscripts do not have the number. [b] *46* Or *other languages*

11 The apostles and the believers
throughout Judea heard that the
Gentiles also had received the word of
God. 2So when Peter went up to Jerusalem, the circumcised believers criti-
cized him 3and said, "You went into the
house of uncircumcised men and ate
with them."

4Starting from the beginning, Peter
told them the whole story: 5"I was in the
city of Joppa praying, and in a trance I
saw a vision. I saw something like a large
sheet being let down from heaven by its
four corners, and it came down to where
I was. 6I looked into it and saw four-footed animals of the earth, wild beasts, reptiles and birds. 7Then I heard a voice telling me, 'Get up, Peter. Kill and eat.'

8"I replied, 'Surely not, Lord! Nothing
impure or unclean has ever entered my
mouth.'

9"The voice spoke from heaven a second time, 'Do not call anything impure
that God has made clean.' 10This happened three times, and then it was all
pulled up to heaven again.

11"Right then three men who had been
sent to me from Caesarea stopped at the
house where I was staying. 12The Spirit
told me to have no hesitation about going with them. These six brothers also
went with me, and we entered the man's
house. 13He told us how he had seen an
angel appear in his house and say, 'Send
to Joppa for Simon who is called Peter.
14He will bring you a message through
which you and all your household will
be saved.'

15"As I began to speak, the Holy Spirit
came on them as he had come on us at the
beginning. 16Then I remembered what
the Lord had said: 'John baptized with[a]
water, but you will be baptized with[a] the
Holy Spirit.' 17So if God gave them the
same gift he gave us who believed in the
Lord Jesus Christ, who was I to think that
I could stand in God's way?"

18When they heard this, they had no
further objections and praised God, saying, "So then, even to Gentiles God has
granted repentance that leads to life."

19Now those who had been scattered
by the persecution that broke out when
Stephen was killed traveled as far as
Phoenicia, Cyprus and Antioch, spreading the word only among Jews. 20Some
of them, however, men from Cyprus and
Cyrene, went to Antioch and began to
speak to Greeks also, telling them the
good news about the Lord Jesus. 21The
Lord's hand was with them, and a great
number of people believed and turned
to the Lord.

22News of this reached the church in
Jerusalem, and they sent Barnabas to
Antioch. 23When he arrived and saw
what the grace of God had done, he was
glad and encouraged them all to remain
true to the Lord with all their hearts.
24He was a good man, full of the Holy
Spirit and faith, and a great number of
people were brought to the Lord.

25Then Barnabas went to Tarsus to
look for Saul, 26and when he found him,
he brought him to Antioch. So for a
whole year Barnabas and Saul met with
the church and taught great numbers of
people. The disciples were called Christians first at Antioch.

27During this time some prophets
came down from Jerusalem to Antioch.
28One of them, named Agabus, stood up
and through the Spirit predicted that
a severe famine would spread over the
entire Roman world. (This happened
during the reign of Claudius.) 29The disciples, as each one was able, decided to
provide help for the brothers and sisters
living in Judea. 30This they did, sending
their gift to the elders by Barnabas and
Saul.

12 It was about this time that King Herod arrested some who belonged to
the church, intending to persecute them.
2He had James, the brother of John, put
to death with the sword. 3When he saw
that this met with approval among the
Jews, he proceeded to seize Peter also.
This happened during the Festival of
Unleavened Bread. 4After arresting him,
he put him in prison, handing him over
to be guarded by four squads of four soldiers each. Herod intended to bring him
out for public trial after the Passover.

5So Peter was kept in prison, but the
church was earnestly praying to God for
him.

6The night before Herod was to bring
him to trial, Peter was sleeping between
two soldiers, bound with two chains,

[a] *16* Or *in*

and sentries stood guard at the entrance.
7 Suddenly an angel of the Lord appeared
and a light shone in the cell. He struck
Peter on the side and woke him up.
"Quick, get up!" he said, and the chains
fell off Peter's wrists.
8 Then the angel said to him, "Put on
your clothes and sandals." And Peter
did so. "Wrap your cloak around you
and follow me," the angel told him. 9 Peter followed him out of the prison, but
he had no idea that what the angel was
doing was really happening; he thought
he was seeing a vision. 10 They passed the
first and second guards and came to the
iron gate leading to the city. It opened for
them by itself, and they went through it.
When they had walked the length of one
street, suddenly the angel left him.
11 Then Peter came to himself and
said, "Now I know without a doubt that
the Lord has sent his angel and rescued
me from Herod's clutches and from everything the Jewish people were hoping
would happen."
12 When this had dawned on him, he
went to the house of Mary the mother of
John, also called Mark, where many people had gathered and were praying. 13 Peter knocked at the outer entrance, and a
servant named Rhoda came to answer
the door. 14 When she recognized Peter's
voice, she was so overjoyed she ran back
without opening it and exclaimed, "Peter
is at the door!"
15 "You're out of your mind," they told
her. When she kept insisting that it was
so, they said, "It must be his angel."
16 But Peter kept on knocking, and
when they opened the door and saw him,
they were astonished. 17 Peter motioned
with his hand for them to be quiet and
described how the Lord had brought him
out of prison. "Tell James and the other
brothers and sisters about this," he said,
and then he left for another place.
18 In the morning, there was no small
commotion among the soldiers as to
what had become of Peter. 19 After Herod had a thorough search made for him
and did not find him, he cross-examined
the guards and ordered that they be executed.
Then Herod went from Judea to Caesarea and stayed there. 20 He had been
quarreling with the people of Tyre and
Sidon; they now joined together and
sought an audience with him. After se-
curing the support of Blastus, a trusted
personal servant of the king, they asked
for peace, because they depended on the
king's country for their food supply.
21 On the appointed day Herod, wearing his royal robes, sat on his throne and
delivered a public address to the people.
22 They shouted, "This is the voice of a
god, not of a man." 23 Immediately, because Herod did not give praise to God,
an angel of the Lord struck him down,
and he was eaten by worms and died.
24 But the word of God continued to
spread and flourish.

25 When Barnabas and Saul had finished their mission, they returned from[a]
Jerusalem, taking with them John, also
13 called Mark. 1 Now in the church
at Antioch there were prophets
and teachers: Barnabas, Simeon called
Niger, Lucius of Cyrene, Manaen (who
had been brought up with Herod the tetrarch) and Saul. 2 While they were worshiping the Lord and fasting, the Holy
Spirit said, "Set apart for me Barnabas
and Saul for the work to which I have
called them." 3 So after they had fasted
and prayed, they placed their hands on
them and sent them off.
4 The two of them, sent on their way
by the Holy Spirit, went down to Seleu-
cia and sailed from there to Cyprus.
5 When they arrived at Salamis, they
proclaimed the word of God in the Jewish synagogues. John was with them as
their helper.
6 They traveled through the whole island until they came to Paphos. There
they met a Jewish sorcerer and false
prophet named Bar-Jesus, 7 who was an
attendant of the proconsul, Sergius Pau-
lus. The proconsul, an intelligent man,
sent for Barnabas and Saul because he
wanted to hear the word of God. 8 But
Elymas the sorcerer (for that is what his
name means) opposed them and tried to
turn the proconsul from the faith. 9 Then
Saul, who was also called Paul, filled
with the Holy Spirit, looked straight at
Elymas and said, 10 "You are a child of the
devil and an enemy of everything that is

a *25* Some manuscripts *to*

right! You are full of all kinds of deceit
and trickery. Will you never stop pervert-
ing the right ways of the Lord? 11 Now the
hand of the Lord is against you. You are
going to be blind for a time, not even able
to see the light of the sun."

Immediately mist and darkness came
over him, and he groped about, seeking someone to lead him by the hand.
12 When the proconsul saw what had happened, he believed, for he was amazed at
the teaching about the Lord.

13 From Paphos, Paul and his companions sailed to Perga in Pamphylia, where
John left them to return to Jerusalem.
14 From Perga they went on to Pisidian
Antioch. On the Sabbath they entered
the synagogue and sat down. 15 After the
reading from the Law and the Prophets,
the leaders of the synagogue sent word
to them, saying, "Brothers, if you have
a word of exhortation for the people,
please speak."

16 Standing up, Paul motioned with
his hand and said: "Fellow Israelites and
you Gentiles who worship God, listen
to me! 17 The God of the people of Israel
chose our ancestors; he made the people
prosper during their stay in Egypt; with
mighty power he led them out of that
country; 18 for about forty years he endured their conduct[a] in the wilderness;
19 and he overthrew seven nations in Canaan, giving their land to his people as
their inheritance. 20 All this took about
450 years.

"After this, God gave them judges until
the time of Samuel the prophet. 21 Then
the people asked for a king, and he gave
them Saul son of Kish, of the tribe of Benjamin, who ruled forty years. 22 After removing Saul, he made David their king.
God testified concerning him: 'I have
found David son of Jesse, a man after my
own heart; he will do everything I want
him to do.'

23 "From this man's descendants God
has brought to Israel the Savior Jesus,
as he promised. 24 Before the coming of
Jesus, John preached repentance and
baptism to all the people of Israel. 25 As
John was completing his work, he said:
'Who do you suppose I am? I am not the
one you are looking for. But there is one
coming after me whose sandals I am not
worthy to untie.'

26 "Fellow children of Abraham and
you God-fearing Gentiles, it is to us that
this message of salvation has been sent.
27 The people of Jerusalem and their rulers did not recognize Jesus, yet in condemning him they fulfilled the words
of the prophets that are read every Sabbath. 28 Though they found no proper
ground for a death sentence, they asked
Pilate to have him executed. 29 When
they had carried out all that was written about him, they took him down from
the cross and laid him in a tomb. 30 But
God raised him from the dead, 31 and for
many days he was seen by those who had
traveled with him from Galilee to Jerusalem. They are now his witnesses to our
people.

32 "We tell you the good news: What
God promised our ancestors 33 he has
fulfilled for us, their children, by raising
up Jesus. As it is written in the second
Psalm:

"'You are my son;
today I have become your father.'[b]

34 God raised him from the dead so that
he will never be subject to decay. As God
has said,

"'I will give you the holy and sure
blessings promised to David.'[c]

35 So it is also stated elsewhere:

"'You will not let your holy one see
decay.'[d]

36 "Now when David had served God's
purpose in his own generation, he fell
asleep; he was buried with his ancestors and his body decayed. 37 But the one
whom God raised from the dead did not
see decay.

38 "Therefore, my friends, I want you to
know that through Jesus the forgiveness
of sins is proclaimed to you. 39 Through
him everyone who believes is set free
from every sin, a justification you were
not able to obtain under the law of Moses. 40 Take care that what the prophets
have said does not happen to you:

41 "'Look, you scoffers,
wonder and perish,

[a] *18* Some manuscripts *he cared for them* [b] *33* Psalm 2:7 [c] *34* Isaiah 55:3 [d] *35* Psalm 16:10 (see Septuagint)

for I am going to do something in your
days
that you would never believe,
even if someone told you.'[a]"

42As Paul and Barnabas were leaving
the synagogue, the people invited them
to speak further about these things on
the next Sabbath. 43When the congregation was dismissed, many of the Jews
and devout converts to Judaism followed
Paul and Barnabas, who talked with
them and urged them to continue in the
grace of God.
44On the next Sabbath almost the
whole city gathered to hear the word
of the Lord. 45When the Jews saw the
crowds, they were filled with jealousy.
They began to contradict what Paul was
saying and heaped abuse on him.
46Then Paul and Barnabas answered
them boldly: "We had to speak the word
of God to you first. Since you reject it
and do not consider yourselves worthy
of eternal life, we now turn to the Gentiles. 47For this is what the Lord has com
manded us:

"'I have made you[b] a light for the
Gentiles,
that you[b] may bring salvation to the
ends of the earth.'[c]"

48When the Gentiles heard this, they
were glad and honored the word of the
Lord; and all who were appointed for
eternal life believed.
49The word of the Lord spread through
the whole region. 50But the Jewish leaders incited the God-fearing women of
high standing and the leading men of the
city. They stirred up persecution against
Paul and Barnabas, and expelled them
from their region. 51So they shook the
dust off their feet as a warning to them
and went to Iconium. 52And the disciples were filled with joy and with the
Holy Spirit.

14 At Iconium Paul and Barnabas
went as usual into the Jewish synagogue. There they spoke so effectively
that a great number of Jews and Greeks
believed. 2But the Jews who refused to
believe stirred up the other Gentiles and
poisoned their minds against the brothers. 3So Paul and Barnabas spent con-
siderable time there, speaking boldly for
the Lord, who confirmed the message of
his grace by enabling them to perform
signs and wonders. 4The people of the
city were divided; some sided with the
Jews, others with the apostles. 5There
was a plot afoot among both Gentiles
and Jews, together with their leaders, to
mistreat them and stone them. 6But they
found out about it and fled to the Lycaonian cities of Lystra and Derbe and to
the surrounding country, 7where they
continued to preach the gospel.
8In Lystra there sat a man who was
lame. He had been that way from birth
and had never walked. 9He listened to
Paul as he was speaking. Paul looked
directly at him, saw that he had faith to
be healed 10and called out, "Stand up on
your feet!" At that, the man jumped up
and began to walk.
11When the crowd saw what Paul had
done, they shouted in the Lycaonian
language, "The gods have come down
to us in human form!" 12Barnabas they
called Zeus, and Paul they called Hermes because he was the chief speaker.
13The priest of Zeus, whose temple was
just outside the city, brought bulls and
wreaths to the city gates because he and
the crowd wanted to offer sacrifices to
them.
14But when the apostles Barnabas and
Paul heard of this, they tore their clothes
and rushed out into the crowd, shouting: 15"Friends, why are you doing this?
We too are only human, like you. We are
bringing you good news, telling you to
turn from these worthless things to the
living God, who made the heavens and
the earth and the sea and everything in
them. 16In the past, he let all nations go
their own way. 17Yet he has not left himself without testimony: He has shown
kindness by giving you rain from heav-
en and crops in their seasons; he provides you with plenty of food and fills
your hearts with joy." 18Even with these
words, they had difficulty keeping the
crowd from sacrificing to them.
19Then some Jews came from Antioch
and Iconium and won the crowd over.
They stoned Paul and dragged him outside the city, thinking he was dead. 20But
after the disciples had gathered around
him, he got up and went back into the

[a] 41 Hab. 1:5 [b] 47 The Greek is singular. [c] 47 Isaiah 49:6

city. The next day he and Barnabas left for Derbe.

21They preached the gospel in that
city and won a large number of disciples.
Then they returned to Lystra, Iconium
and Antioch, 22strengthening the disciples and encouraging them to remain
true to the faith. "We must go through
many hardships to enter the kingdom of
God," they said. 23Paul and Barnabas appointed elders[a] for them in each church
and, with prayer and fasting, committed
them to the Lord, in whom they had put
their trust. 24After going through Pisidia,
they came into Pamphylia, 25and when
they had preached the word in Perga,
they went down to Attalia.

26From Attalia they sailed back to Antioch, where they had been committed
to the grace of God for the work they had
now completed. 27On arriving there,
they gathered the church together and
reported all that God had done through
them and how he had opened a door of
faith to the Gentiles. 28And they stayed
there a long time with the disciples.

15 Certain people came down from Judea to Antioch and were teaching
the believers: "Unless you are circumcised, according to the custom taught
by Moses, you cannot be saved." 2This
brought Paul and Barnabas into sharp
dispute and debate with them. So Paul
and Barnabas were appointed, along
with some other believers, to go up to
Jerusalem to see the apostles and elders
about this question. 3The church sent
them on their way, and as they traveled
through Phoenicia and Samaria, they
told how the Gentiles had been converted. This news made all the believers
very glad. 4When they came to Jerusalem, they were welcomed by the church
and the apostles and elders, to whom
they reported everything God had done
through them.

5Then some of the believers who belonged to the party of the Pharisees
stood up and said, "The Gentiles must
be circumcised and required to keep the
law of Moses."

6The apostles and elders met to consider this question. 7After much discussion, Peter got up and addressed them:
"Brothers, you know that some time ago
God made a choice among you that the
Gentiles might hear from my lips the
message of the gospel and believe. 8God,
who knows the heart, showed that he
accepted them by giving the Holy Spirit to them, just as he did to us. 9He did
not discriminate between us and them,
for he purified their hearts by faith.
10Now then, why do you try to test God
by putting on the necks of Gentiles a yoke
that neither we nor our ancestors have
been able to bear? 11No! We believe it is
through the grace of our Lord Jesus that
we are saved, just as they are."

12The whole assembly became silent as
they listened to Barnabas and Paul telling about the signs and wonders God had
done among the Gentiles through them.
13When they finished, James spoke up.
"Brothers," he said, "listen to me. 14Si-
mon[b] has described to us how God first
intervened to choose a people for his
name from the Gentiles. 15The words of
the prophets are in agreement with this,
as it is written:

16 "'After this I will return
and rebuild David's fallen tent.
Its ruins I will rebuild,
and I will restore it,
17 that the rest of mankind may seek the
Lord,
even all the Gentiles who bear my
name,
says the Lord, who does these
things'[c]—
18 things known from long ago.[d]

19"It is my judgment, therefore, that
we should not make it difficult for the
Gentiles who are turning to God. 20In-
stead we should write to them, telling
them to abstain from food polluted by
idols, from sexual immorality, from the
meat of strangled animals and from
blood. 21For the law of Moses has been
preached in every city from the earliest
times and is read in the synagogues on
every Sabbath."

22Then the apostles and elders, with
the whole church, decided to choose
some of their own men and send them to
Antioch with Paul and Barnabas. They
chose Judas (called Barsabbas) and Si-

[a] *23* Or *Barnabas ordained elders;* or *Barnabas had elders elected* [b] *14* Greek *Simeon,* a variant of *Simon;* that is, Peter [c] *17* Amos 9:11,12 (see Septuagint) [d] *17,18* Some manuscripts *things'— / 18the Lord's work is known to him from long ago*

las, men who were leaders among the
believers. 23 With them they sent the following letter:

The apostles and elders, your brothers,

To the Gentile believers in Antioch,
Syria and Cilicia:

Greetings.

24 We have heard that some went
out from us without our authoriza-
tion and disturbed you, troubling
your minds by what they said. 25 So
we all agreed to choose some men
and send them to you with our dear
friends Barnabas and Paul— 26 men
who have risked their lives for the
name of our Lord Jesus Christ.
27 Therefore we are sending Judas and Silas to confirm by word
of mouth what we are writing. 28 It
seemed good to the Holy Spirit and to
us not to burden you with anything
beyond the following requirements:
29 You are to abstain from food sacrificed to idols, from blood, from the
meat of strangled animals and from
sexual immorality. You will do well
to avoid these things.

Farewell.

30 So the men were sent off and went
down to Antioch, where they gathered
the church together and delivered the letter. 31 The people read it and were glad for
its encouraging message. 32 Judas and Silas, who themselves were prophets, said
much to encourage and strengthen the
believers. 33 After spending some time
there, they were sent off by the believers with the blessing of peace to return
to those who had sent them. [34][a] 35 But
Paul and Barnabas remained in Antioch,
where they and many others taught and
preached the word of the Lord.

36 Some time later Paul said to Barnabas, "Let us go back and visit the believers in all the towns where we preached
the word of the Lord and see how they
are doing." 37 Barnabas wanted to take
John, also called Mark, with them, 38 but
Paul did not think it wise to take him,
because he had deserted them in Pamphylia and had not continued with them
in the work. 39 They had such a sharp
disagreement that they parted company. Barnabas took Mark and sailed for
Cyprus, 40 but Paul chose Silas and left,
commended by the believers to the grace
of the Lord. 41 He went through Syria and
Cilicia, strengthening the churches.

16 Paul came to Derbe and then to Lystra, where a disciple named Timothy lived, whose mother was Jewish and
a believer but whose father was a Greek.
2 The believers at Lystra and Iconium
spoke well of him. 3 Paul wanted to take
him along on the journey, so he circumcised him because of the Jews who lived
in that area, for they all knew that his father was a Greek. 4 As they traveled from
town to town, they delivered the decisions reached by the apostles and elders
in Jerusalem for the people to obey. 5 So
the churches were strengthened in the
faith and grew daily in numbers.

6 Paul and his companions traveled
throughout the region of Phrygia and Galatia, having been kept by the Holy Spirit
from preaching the word in the province
of Asia. 7 When they came to the border
of Mysia, they tried to enter Bithynia,
but the Spirit of Jesus would not allow
them to. 8 So they passed by Mysia and
went down to Troas. 9 During the night
Paul had a vision of a man of Macedonia
standing and begging him, "Come over
to Macedonia and help us." 10 After Paul
had seen the vision, we got ready at once
to leave for Macedonia, concluding that
God had called us to preach the gospel
to them.

11 From Troas we put out to sea and
sailed straight for Samothrace, and the
next day we went on to Neapolis. 12 From
there we traveled to Philippi, a Roman
colony and the leading city of that district[b] of Macedonia. And we stayed there
several days.

13 On the Sabbath we went outside the
city gate to the river, where we expected
to find a place of prayer. We sat down and
began to speak to the women who had
gathered there. 14 One of those listening
was a woman from the city of Thyatira
named Lydia, a dealer in purple cloth.
She was a worshiper of God. The Lord

[a] 34 Some manuscripts include here *But Silas decided to remain there.* [b] 12 The text and meaning of the Greek for *the leading city of that district* are uncertain.

opened her heart to respond to Paul's
message. 15 When she and the members
of her household were baptized, she invited us to her home. "If you consider me a
believer in the Lord," she said, "come and
stay at my house." And she persuaded us.
16 Once when we were going to the
place of prayer, we were met by a female
slave who had a spirit by which she predicted the future. She earned a great deal
of money for her owners by fortune-tell-
ing. 17 She followed Paul and the rest of
us, shouting, "These men are servants of
the Most High God, who are telling you
the way to be saved." 18 She kept this up
for many days. Finally Paul became so
annoyed that he turned around and said
to the spirit, "In the name of Jesus Christ
I command you to come out of her!" At
that moment the spirit left her.
19 When her owners realized that their
hope of making money was gone, they
seized Paul and Silas and dragged them
into the marketplace to face the authorities. 20 They brought them before the
magistrates and said, "These men are
Jews, and are throwing our city into an
uproar 21 by advocating customs unlawful for us Romans to accept or practice."
22 The crowd joined in the attack against
Paul and Silas, and the magistrates ordered them to be stripped and beaten
with rods. 23 After they had been severely flogged, they were thrown into prison,
and the jailer was commanded to guard
them carefully. 24 When he received these
orders, he put them in the inner cell and
fastened their feet in the stocks.
25 About midnight Paul and Silas were
praying and singing hymns to God, and
the other prisoners were listening to
them. 26 Suddenly there was such a violent earthquake that the foundations of
the prison were shaken. At once all the
prison doors flew open, and everyone's
chains came loose. 27 The jailer woke up,
and when he saw the prison doors open,
he drew his sword and was about to kill
himself because he thought the prisoners had escaped. 28 But Paul shouted,
"Don't harm yourself! We are all here!"
29 The jailer called for lights, rushed in
and fell trembling before Paul and Silas.
30 He then brought them out and asked,
"Sirs, what must I do to be saved?"
31 They replied, "Believe in the Lord
Jesus, and you will be saved—you and
your household." 32 Then they spoke the
word of the Lord to him and to all the
others in his house. 33 At that hour of the
night the jailer took them and washed
their wounds; then immediately he and
all his household were baptized. 34 The
jailer brought them into his house and
set a meal before them; he was filled
with joy because he had come to believe
in God—he and his whole household.
35 When it was daylight, the magistrates sent their officers to the jailer with
the order: "Release those men." 36 The
jailer told Paul, "The magistrates have
ordered that you and Silas be released.
Now you can leave. Go in peace."
37 But Paul said to the officers: "They
beat us publicly without a trial, even
though we are Roman citizens, and
threw us into prison. And now do they
want to get rid of us quietly? No! Let them
come themselves and escort us out."
38 The officers reported this to the
magistrates, and when they heard that
Paul and Silas were Roman citizens, they
were alarmed. 39 They came to appease
them and escorted them from the prison,
requesting them to leave the city. 40 After Paul and Silas came out of the prison,
they went to Lydia's house, where they
met with the brothers and sisters and
encouraged them. Then they left.

17 When Paul and his companions
had passed through Amphipolis
and Apollonia, they came to Thessalonica, where there was a Jewish synagogue.
2 As was his custom, Paul went into the
synagogue, and on three Sabbath days
he reasoned with them from the Scriptures, 3 explaining and proving that the
Messiah had to suffer and rise from the
dead. "This Jesus I am proclaiming to
you is the Messiah," he said. 4 Some of
the Jews were persuaded and joined Paul
and Silas, as did a large number of God-
fearing Greeks and quite a few prominent women.
5 But other Jews were jealous; so they
rounded up some bad characters from
the marketplace, formed a mob and
started a riot in the city. They rushed to
Jason's house in search of Paul and Silas
in order to bring them out to the crowd.[a]

[a] 5 Or *the assembly of the people*

6 But when they did not find them, they dragged Jason and some other believers before the city officials, shouting: "These men who have caused trouble all over the world have now come here, 7 and Jason has welcomed them into his house. They are all defying Caesar's decrees, saying that there is another king, one called Jesus." 8 When they heard this, the crowd and the city officials were thrown into turmoil. 9 Then they made Jason and the others post bond and let them go.

10 As soon as it was night, the believers sent Paul and Silas away to Berea. On arriving there, they went to the Jewish synagogue. 11 Now the Berean Jews were of more noble character than those in Thessalonica, for they received the message with great eagerness and examined the Scriptures every day to see if what Paul said was true. 12 As a result, many of them believed, as did also a number of prominent Greek women and many Greek men.

13 But when the Jews in Thessalonica learned that Paul was preaching the word of God at Berea, some of them went there too, agitating the crowds and stirring them up. 14 The believers immediately sent Paul to the coast, but Silas and Timothy stayed at Berea. 15 Those who escorted Paul brought him to Athens and then left with instructions for Silas and Timothy to join him as soon as possible.

16 While Paul was waiting for them in Athens, he was greatly distressed to see that the city was full of idols. 17 So he reasoned in the synagogue with both Jews and God-fearing Greeks, as well as in the marketplace day by day with those who happened to be there. 18 A group of Epicurean and Stoic philosophers began to debate with him. Some of them asked, "What is this babbler trying to say?" Others remarked, "He seems to be advocating foreign gods." They said this because Paul was preaching the good news about Jesus and the resurrection. 19 Then they took him and brought him to a meeting of the Areopagus, where they said to him, "May we know what this new teaching is that you are presenting? 20 You are bringing some strange ideas to our ears, and we would like to know what they mean." 21 (All the Athenians and the foreigners who lived there spent their time doing nothing but talking about and listening to the latest ideas.)

22 Paul then stood up in the meeting of the Areopagus and said: "People of Athens! I see that in every way you are very religious. 23 For as I walked around and looked carefully at your objects of worship, I even found an altar with this inscription: TO AN UNKNOWN GOD. So you are ignorant of the very thing you worship—and this is what I am going to proclaim to you.

24 "The God who made the world and everything in it is the Lord of heaven and earth and does not live in temples built by human hands. 25 And he is not served by human hands, as if he needed anything. Rather, he himself gives everyone life and breath and everything else. 26 From one man he made all the nations, that they should inhabit the whole earth; and he marked out their appointed times in history and the boundaries of their lands. 27 God did this so that they would seek him and perhaps reach out for him and find him, though he is not far from any one of us. 28 'For in him we live and move and have our being.'[a] As some of your own poets have said, 'We are his offspring.'[b]

29 "Therefore since we are God's offspring, we should not think that the divine being is like gold or silver or stone—an image made by human design and skill. 30 In the past God overlooked such ignorance, but now he commands all people everywhere to repent. 31 For he has set a day when he will judge the world with justice by the man he has appointed. He has given proof of this to everyone by raising him from the dead."

32 When they heard about the resurrection of the dead, some of them sneered, but others said, "We want to hear you again on this subject." 33 At that, Paul left the Council. 34 Some of the people became followers of Paul and believed. Among them was Dionysius, a member of the Areopagus, also a woman named Damaris, and a number of others.

18 After this, Paul left Athens and went to Corinth. 2 There he met a Jew named Aquila, a native of Pontus, who had recently come from Italy

[a] 28 From the Cretan philosopher Epimenides [b] 28 From the Cilician Stoic philosopher Aratus

with his wife Priscilla, because Claudius had ordered all Jews to leave Rome.
Paul went to see them, 3and because he
was a tentmaker as they were, he stayed
and worked with them. 4Every Sabbath
he reasoned in the synagogue, trying to
persuade Jews and Greeks.
5When Silas and Timothy came from
Macedonia, Paul devoted himself exclu-
sively to preaching, testifying to the Jews
that Jesus was the Messiah. 6But when
they opposed Paul and became abusive,
he shook out his clothes in protest and
said to them, "Your blood be on your own
heads! I am innocent of it. From now on I
will go to the Gentiles."
7Then Paul left the synagogue and
went next door to the house of Titius Justus, a worshiper of God. 8Crispus, the
synagogue leader, and his entire household believed in the Lord; and many of
the Corinthians who heard Paul believed
and were baptized.
9One night the Lord spoke to Paul in a
vision: "Do not be afraid; keep on speaking, do not be silent. 10For I am with you,
and no one is going to attack and harm
you, because I have many people in this
city." 11So Paul stayed in Corinth for a
year and a half, teaching them the word
of God.
12While Gallio was proconsul of Achaia, the Jews of Corinth made a united attack on Paul and brought him to the place
of judgment. 13"This man," they charged,
"is persuading the people to worship God
in ways contrary to the law."
14Just as Paul was about to speak, Gallio said to them, "If you Jews were making
a complaint about some misdemeanor
or serious crime, it would be reasonable
for me to listen to you. 15But since it in-
volves questions about words and names
and your own law—settle the matter
yourselves. I will not be a judge of such
things." 16So he drove them off. 17Then
the crowd there turned on Sosthenes the
synagogue leader and beat him in front
of the proconsul; and Gallio showed no
concern whatever.
18Paul stayed on in Corinth for some
time. Then he left the brothers and sisters and sailed for Syria, accompanied
by Priscilla and Aquila. Before he sailed,
he had his hair cut off at Cenchreae because of a vow he had taken. 19They arrived at Ephesus, where Paul left Priscilla and Aquila. He himself went into the
synagogue and reasoned with the Jews.
20When they asked him to spend more
time with them, he declined. 21But as
he left, he promised, "I will come back
if it is God's will." Then he set sail from
Ephesus. 22When he landed at Caesarea,
he went up to Jerusalem and greeted the
church and then went down to Antioch.
23After spending some time in Antioch, Paul set out from there and traveled
from place to place throughout the region of Galatia and Phrygia, strengthening all the disciples.
24Meanwhile a Jew named Apollos, a
native of Alexandria, came to Ephesus.
He was a learned man, with a thorough
knowledge of the Scriptures. 25He had
been instructed in the way of the Lord,
and he spoke with great fervor[a] and
taught about Jesus accurately, though
he knew only the baptism of John. 26He
began to speak boldly in the synagogue.
When Priscilla and Aquila heard him,
they invited him to their home and explained to him the way of God more ad-
equately.
27When Apollos wanted to go to Achaia, the brothers and sisters encouraged
him and wrote to the disciples there to
welcome him. When he arrived, he was
a great help to those who by grace had
believed. 28For he vigorously refuted
his Jewish opponents in public debate,
proving from the Scriptures that Jesus
was the Messiah.
19 While Apollos was at Corinth, Paul
took the road through the interior
and arrived at Ephesus. There he found
some disciples 2and asked them, "Did
you receive the Holy Spirit when[b] you
believed?"
They answered, "No, we have not even
heard that there is a Holy Spirit."
3So Paul asked, "Then what baptism
did you receive?"
"John's baptism," they replied.
4Paul said, "John's baptism was a baptism of repentance. He told the people
to believe in the one coming after him,
that is, in Jesus." 5On hearing this, they
were baptized in the name of the Lord
Jesus. 6When Paul placed his hands on

[a] 25 Or *with fervor in the Spirit* [b] 2 Or *after*

them, the Holy Spirit came on them, and they spoke in tongues[a] and prophesied. 7 There were about twelve men in all.

8 Paul entered the synagogue and spoke boldly there for three months, arguing persuasively about the kingdom of God. 9 But some of them became obstinate; they refused to believe and publicly maligned the Way. So Paul left them. He took the disciples with him and had discussions daily in the lecture hall of Tyrannus. 10 This went on for two years, so that all the Jews and Greeks who lived in the province of Asia heard the word of the Lord.

11 God did extraordinary miracles through Paul, 12 so that even handkerchiefs and aprons that had touched him were taken to the sick, and their illnesses were cured and the evil spirits left them.

13 Some Jews who went around driving out evil spirits tried to invoke the name of the Lord Jesus over those who were demon-possessed. They would say, "In the name of the Jesus whom Paul preaches, I command you to come out." 14 Seven sons of Sceva, a Jewish chief priest, were doing this. 15 One day the evil spirit answered them, "Jesus I know, and Paul I know about, but who are you?" 16 Then the man who had the evil spirit jumped on them and overpowered them all. He gave them such a beating that they ran out of the house naked and bleeding.

17 When this became known to the Jews and Greeks living in Ephesus, they were all seized with fear, and the name of the Lord Jesus was held in high honor. 18 Many of those who believed now came and openly confessed what they had done. 19 A number who had practiced sorcery brought their scrolls together and burned them publicly. When they calculated the value of the scrolls, the total came to fifty thousand drachmas.[b] 20 In this way the word of the Lord spread widely and grew in power.

21 After all this had happened, Paul decided[c] to go to Jerusalem, passing through Macedonia and Achaia. "After I have been there," he said, "I must visit Rome also." 22 He sent two of his helpers, Timothy and Erastus, to Macedonia, while he stayed in the province of Asia a little longer.

23 About that time there arose a great disturbance about the Way. 24 A silversmith named Demetrius, who made silver shrines of Artemis, brought in a lot of business for the craftsmen there. 25 He called them together, along with the workers in related trades, and said: "You know, my friends, that we receive a good income from this business. 26 And you see and hear how this fellow Paul has convinced and led astray large numbers of people here in Ephesus and in practically the whole province of Asia. He says that gods made by human hands are no gods at all. 27 There is danger not only that our trade will lose its good name, but also that the temple of the great goddess Artemis will be discredited; and the goddess herself, who is worshiped throughout the province of Asia and the world, will be robbed of her divine majesty."

28 When they heard this, they were furious and began shouting: "Great is Artemis of the Ephesians!" 29 Soon the whole city was in an uproar. The people seized Gaius and Aristarchus, Paul's traveling companions from Macedonia, and all of them rushed into the theater together. 30 Paul wanted to appear before the crowd, but the disciples would not let him. 31 Even some of the officials of the province, friends of Paul, sent him a message begging him not to venture into the theater.

32 The assembly was in confusion: Some were shouting one thing, some another. Most of the people did not even know why they were there. 33 The Jews in the crowd pushed Alexander to the front, and they shouted instructions to him. He motioned for silence in order to make a defense before the people. 34 But when they realized he was a Jew, they all shouted in unison for about two hours: "Great is Artemis of the Ephesians!"

35 The city clerk quieted the crowd and said: "Fellow Ephesians, doesn't all the world know that the city of Ephesus is the guardian of the temple of the great Artemis and of her image, which fell from heaven? 36 Therefore, since these facts are undeniable, you ought to calm down and not do anything rash. 37 You

[a] 6 Or *other languages* [b] 19 A drachma was a silver coin worth about a day's wages. [c] 21 Or *decided in the Spirit*

have brought these men here, though
they have neither robbed temples nor
blasphemed our goddess. 38If, then, Demetrius and his fellow craftsmen have a
grievance against anybody, the courts
are open and there are proconsuls. They
can press charges. 39If there is anything
further you want to bring up, it must be
settled in a legal assembly. 40As it is, we
are in danger of being charged with ri-
oting because of what happened today.
In that case we would not be able to account for this commotion, since there is
no reason for it." 41After he had said this,
he dismissed the assembly.

20 When the uproar had ended, Paul
sent for the disciples and, after encouraging them, said goodbye
and set out for Macedonia. 2He traveled through that area, speaking many
words of encouragement to the people,
and finally arrived in Greece, 3where
he stayed three months. Because some
Jews had plotted against him just as he
was about to sail for Syria, he decided
to go back through Macedonia. 4He was
accompanied by Sopater son of Pyrrhus
from Berea, Aristarchus and Secundus
from Thessalonica, Gaius from Derbe,
Timothy also, and Tychicus and Trophimus from the province of Asia. 5These
men went on ahead and waited for us at
Troas. 6But we sailed from Philippi after
the Festival of Unleavened Bread, and
five days later joined the others at Troas,
where we stayed seven days.

7On the first day of the week we came
together to break bread. Paul spoke to
the people and, because he intended to
leave the next day, kept on talking until
midnight. 8There were many lamps in
the upstairs room where we were meeting. 9Seated in a window was a young
man named Eutychus, who was sinking
into a deep sleep as Paul talked on and
on. When he was sound asleep, he fell to
the ground from the third story and was
picked up dead. 10Paul went down, threw
himself on the young man and put his
arms around him. "Don't be alarmed,"
he said. "He's alive!" 11Then he went upstairs again and broke bread and ate. After talking until daylight, he left. 12The
people took the young man home alive
and were greatly comforted.

13We went on ahead to the ship and
sailed for Assos, where we were going to
take Paul aboard. He had made this ar-
rangement because he was going there
on foot. 14When he met us at Assos, we
took him aboard and went on to Mityle-
ne. 15The next day we set sail from there
and arrived off Chios. The day after that
we crossed over to Samos, and on the
following day arrived at Miletus. 16Paul
had decided to sail past Ephesus to avoid
spending time in the province of Asia, for
he was in a hurry to reach Jerusalem, if
possible, by the day of Pentecost.

17From Miletus, Paul sent to Ephesus
for the elders of the church. 18When they
arrived, he said to them: "You know how I
lived the whole time I was with you, from
the first day I came into the province of
Asia. 19I served the Lord with great humility and with tears and in the midst of
severe testing by the plots of my Jewish
opponents. 20You know that I have not
hesitated to preach anything that would
be helpful to you but have taught you
publicly and from house to house. 21I
have declared to both Jews and Greeks
that they must turn to God in repentance
and have faith in our Lord Jesus.

22"And now, compelled by the Spirit,
I am going to Jerusalem, not knowing
what will happen to me there. 23I only
know that in every city the Holy Spirit
warns me that prison and hardships are
facing me. 24However, I consider my life
worth nothing to me; my only aim is to
finish the race and complete the task the
Lord Jesus has given me—the task of testifying to the good news of God's grace.

25"Now I know that none of you among
whom I have gone about preaching the
kingdom will ever see me again. 26There-
fore, I declare to you today that I am innocent of the blood of any of you. 27For
I have not hesitated to proclaim to you
the whole will of God. 28Keep watch over
yourselves and all the flock of which the
Holy Spirit has made you overseers. Be
shepherds of the church of God,[a] which
he bought with his own blood.[b] 29I know
that after I leave, savage wolves will
come in among you and will not spare
the flock. 30Even from your own number
men will arise and distort the truth in
order to draw away disciples after them.

[a] 28 Many manuscripts *of the Lord* [b] 28 Or *with the blood of his own Son.*

31So be on your guard! Remember that
for three years I never stopped warning
each of you night and day with tears.
32"Now I commit you to God and to
the word of his grace, which can build
you up and give you an inheritance
among all those who are sanctified. 33I
have not coveted anyone's silver or gold
or clothing. 34You yourselves know that
these hands of mine have supplied my
own needs and the needs of my companions. 35In everything I did, I showed you
that by this kind of hard work we must
help the weak, remembering the words
the Lord Jesus himself said: 'It is more
blessed to give than to receive.'"
36When Paul had finished speaking, he
knelt down with all of them and prayed.
37They all wept as they embraced him
and kissed him. 38What grieved them
most was his statement that they would
never see his face again. Then they accompanied him to the ship.

21 After we had torn ourselves away
from them, we put out to sea and
sailed straight to Kos. The next day we
went to Rhodes and from there to Pat-
ara. 2We found a ship crossing over to
Phoenicia, went on board and set sail.
3After sighting Cyprus and passing to
the south of it, we sailed on to Syria. We
landed at Tyre, where our ship was to
unload its cargo. 4We sought out the disciples there and stayed with them seven
days. Through the Spirit they urged Paul
not to go on to Jerusalem. 5When it was
time to leave, we left and continued on
our way. All of them, including wives and
children, accompanied us out of the city,
and there on the beach we knelt to pray.
6After saying goodbye to each other, we
went aboard the ship, and they returned
home.
7We continued our voyage from Tyre
and landed at Ptolemais, where we greeted the brothers and sisters and stayed
with them for a day. 8Leaving the next
day, we reached Caesarea and stayed at
the house of Philip the evangelist, one
of the Seven. 9He had four unmarried
daughters who prophesied.
10After we had been there a number
of days, a prophet named Agabus came
down from Judea. 11Coming over to us,
he took Paul's belt, tied his own hands
and feet with it and said, "The Holy Spirit says, 'In this way the Jewish leaders
in Jerusalem will bind the owner of this
belt and will hand him over to the Gentiles.'"
12When we heard this, we and the people there pleaded with Paul not to go up
to Jerusalem. 13Then Paul answered,
"Why are you weeping and breaking my
heart? I am ready not only to be bound,
but also to die in Jerusalem for the name
of the Lord Jesus." 14When he would not
be dissuaded, we gave up and said, "The
Lord's will be done."
15After this, we started on our way up to
Jerusalem. 16Some of the disciples from
Caesarea accompanied us and brought
us to the home of Mnason, where we
were to stay. He was a man from Cyprus
and one of the early disciples.
17When we arrived at Jerusalem, the
brothers and sisters received us warmly. 18The next day Paul and the rest of us
went to see James, and all the elders were
present. 19Paul greeted them and reported in detail what God had done among
the Gentiles through his ministry.
20When they heard this, they praised
God. Then they said to Paul: "You see,
brother, how many thousands of Jews
have believed, and all of them are zealous for the law. 21They have been informed that you teach all the Jews who
live among the Gentiles to turn away
from Moses, telling them not to circumcise their children or live according to
our customs. 22What shall we do? They
will certainly hear that you have come,
23so do what we tell you. There are four
men with us who have made a vow.
24Take these men, join in their purification rites and pay their expenses, so that
they can have their heads shaved. Then
everyone will know there is no truth in
these reports about you, but that you
yourself are living in obedience to the
law. 25As for the Gentile believers, we
have written to them our decision that
they should abstain from food sacrificed
to idols, from blood, from the meat of
strangled animals and from sexual immorality."
26The next day Paul took the men and
purified himself along with them. Then
he went to the temple to give notice of the
date when the days of purification would
end and the offering would be made for
each of them.
27When the seven days were near-

ly over, some Jews from the province of
Asia saw Paul at the temple. They stirred
up the whole crowd and seized him,
28shouting, "Fellow Israelites, help us!
This is the man who teaches everyone
everywhere against our people and our
law and this place. And besides, he has
brought Greeks into the temple and defiled this holy place." 29(They had previously seen Trophimus the Ephesian in
the city with Paul and assumed that Paul
had brought him into the temple.)
30The whole city was aroused, and the
people came running from all directions.
Seizing Paul, they dragged him from the
temple, and immediately the gates were
shut. 31While they were trying to kill
him, news reached the commander of
the Roman troops that the whole city of
Jerusalem was in an uproar. 32He at once
took some officers and soldiers and ran
down to the crowd. When the rioters saw
the commander and his soldiers, they
stopped beating Paul.
33The commander came up and arrested him and ordered him to be bound
with two chains. Then he asked who he
was and what he had done. 34Some in the
crowd shouted one thing and some another, and since the commander could
not get at the truth because of the uproar, he ordered that Paul be taken into
the barracks. 35When Paul reached the
steps, the violence of the mob was so
great he had to be carried by the soldiers.
36The crowd that followed kept shouting,
"Get rid of him!"
37As the soldiers were about to take
Paul into the barracks, he asked the commander, "May I say something to you?"
"Do you speak Greek?" he replied.
38"Aren't you the Egyptian who started
a revolt and led four thousand terrorists
out into the wilderness some time ago?"
39Paul answered, "I am a Jew, from
Tarsus in Cilicia, a citizen of no ordinary
city. Please let me speak to the people."
40After receiving the commander's
permission, Paul stood on the steps and
motioned to the crowd. When they were
all silent, he said to them in Aramaic[a]:

22 1"Brothers and fathers, listen now
to my defense."
2When they heard him speak to them
in Aramaic, they became very quiet.

Then Paul said: 3"I am a Jew, born in
Tarsus of Cilicia, but brought up in this
city. I studied under Gamaliel and was
thoroughly trained in the law of our ancestors. I was just as zealous for God as
any of you are today. 4I persecuted the
followers of this Way to their death, arresting both men and women and throwing them into prison, 5as the high priest
and all the Council can themselves testify. I even obtained letters from them to
their associates in Damascus, and went
there to bring these people as prisoners
to Jerusalem to be punished.
6"About noon as I came near Damascus, suddenly a bright light from heaven
flashed around me. 7I fell to the ground
and heard a voice say to me, 'Saul! Saul!
Why do you persecute me?'
8"'Who are you, Lord?' I asked.
"'I am Jesus of Nazareth, whom you
are persecuting,' he replied. 9My companions saw the light, but they did not
understand the voice of him who was
speaking to me.
10"'What shall I do, Lord?' I asked.
"'Get up,' the Lord said, 'and go into
Damascus. There you will be told all
that you have been assigned to do.' 11My
companions led me by the hand into Damascus, because the brilliance of the
light had blinded me.
12"A man named Ananias came to see
me. He was a devout observer of the law
and highly respected by all the Jews living there. 13He stood beside me and said,
'Brother Saul, receive your sight!' And at
that very moment I was able to see him.
14"Then he said: 'The God of our ancestors has chosen you to know his will
and to see the Righteous One and to
hear words from his mouth. 15You will
be his witness to all people of what you
have seen and heard. 16And now what
are you waiting for? Get up, be baptized
and wash your sins away, calling on his
name.'
17"When I returned to Jerusalem and
was praying at the temple, I fell into a
trance 18and saw the Lord speaking
to me. 'Quick!' he said. 'Leave Jerusalem immediately, because the people
here will not accept your testimony
about me.'
19"'Lord,' I replied, 'these people know

[a] *40* Or possibly *Hebrew*; also in 22:2

that I went from one synagogue to another to imprison and beat those who
believe in you. 20And when the blood of
your martyr[a] Stephen was shed, I stood
there giving my approval and guarding
the clothes of those who were killing
him.'
21"Then the Lord said to me, 'Go; I will
send you far away to the Gentiles.'"
22The crowd listened to Paul until he
said this. Then they raised their voices
and shouted, "Rid the earth of him! He's
not fit to live!"
23As they were shouting and throwing off their cloaks and flinging dust
into the air, 24the commander ordered
that Paul be taken into the barracks. He
directed that he be flogged and interro-
gated in order to find out why the people
were shouting at him like this. 25As they
stretched him out to flog him, Paul said
to the centurion standing there, "Is it legal for you to flog a Roman citizen who
hasn't even been found guilty?"
26When the centurion heard this, he
went to the commander and reported
it. "What are you going to do?" he asked.
"This man is a Roman citizen."
27The commander went to Paul and
asked, "Tell me, are you a Roman citizen?"
"Yes, I am," he answered.
28Then the commander said, "I had to
pay a lot of money for my citizenship."
"But I was born a citizen," Paul replied.
29Those who were about to interrogate
him withdrew immediately. The commander himself was alarmed when he
realized that he had put Paul, a Roman
citizen, in chains.
30The commander wanted to find out
exactly why Paul was being accused by
the Jews. So the next day he released him
and ordered the chief priests and all the
members of the Sanhedrin to assemble.
Then he brought Paul and had him stand
before them.
23 Paul looked straight at the Sanhedrin and said, "My brothers, I have
fulfilled my duty to God in all good conscience to this day." 2At this the high
priest Ananias ordered those standing
near Paul to strike him on the mouth.
3Then Paul said to him, "God will strike
you, you whitewashed wall! You sit there
to judge me according to the law, yet you
yourself violate the law by commanding
that I be struck!"
4Those who were standing near Paul
said, "How dare you insult God's high
priest!"
5Paul replied, "Brothers, I did not realize that he was the high priest; for it is
written: 'Do not speak evil about the ruler of your people.'[b]"
6Then Paul, knowing that some of
them were Sadducees and the others
Pharisees, called out in the Sanhedrin,
"My brothers, I am a Pharisee, descended from Pharisees. I stand on trial because of the hope of the resurrection of
the dead." 7When he said this, a dispute
broke out between the Pharisees and the
Sadducees, and the assembly was divided. 8(The Sadducees say that there is no
resurrection, and that there are neither
angels nor spirits, but the Pharisees believe all these things.)
9There was a great uproar, and some of
the teachers of the law who were Pharisees stood up and argued vigorously.
"We find nothing wrong with this man,"
they said. "What if a spirit or an angel has
spoken to him?" 10The dispute became so
violent that the commander was afraid
Paul would be torn to pieces by them. He
ordered the troops to go down and take
him away from them by force and bring
him into the barracks.
11The following night the Lord stood
near Paul and said, "Take courage! As
you have testified about me in Jerusalem, so you must also testify in Rome."
12The next morning some Jews formed
a conspiracy and bound themselves with
an oath not to eat or drink until they had
killed Paul. 13More than forty men were
involved in this plot. 14They went to the
chief priests and the elders and said, "We
have taken a solemn oath not to eat anything until we have killed Paul. 15Now
then, you and the Sanhedrin petition
the commander to bring him before you
on the pretext of wanting more accurate
information about his case. We are ready
to kill him before he gets here."
16But when the son of Paul's sister
heard of this plot, he went into the barracks and told Paul.

[a] 20 Or *witness* [b] 5 Exodus 22:28

[17]Then Paul called one of the centurions and said, "Take this young man
to the commander; he has something to
tell him." [18]So he took him to the commander.

The centurion said, "Paul, the prisoner, sent for me and asked me to bring this
young man to you because he has something to tell you."

[19]The commander took the young man
by the hand, drew him aside and asked,
"What is it you want to tell me?"

[20]He said: "Some Jews have agreed to
ask you to bring Paul before the Sanhedrin tomorrow on the pretext of wanting
more accurate information about him.
[21]Don't give in to them, because more
than forty of them are waiting in ambush
for him. They have taken an oath not to
eat or drink until they have killed him.
They are ready now, waiting for your
consent to their request."

[22]The commander dismissed the
young man with this warning: "Don't
tell anyone that you have reported this
to me."

[23]Then he called two of his centurions
and ordered them, "Get ready a detachment of two hundred soldiers, seventy
horsemen and two hundred spearmen[a]
to go to Caesarea at nine tonight. [24]Pro-
vide horses for Paul so that he may be
taken safely to Governor Felix."

[25]He wrote a letter as follows:

[26]Claudius Lysias,

To His Excellency, Governor Felix:

Greetings.

[27]This man was seized by the Jews
and they were about to kill him, but
I came with my troops and rescued
him, for I had learned that he is a
Roman citizen. [28]I wanted to know
why they were accusing him, so I
brought him to their Sanhedrin. [29]I
found that the accusation had to do
with questions about their law, but
there was no charge against him that
deserved death or imprisonment.
[30]When I was informed of a plot to
be carried out against the man, I sent
him to you at once. I also ordered his
accusers to present to you their case
against him.

[31]So the soldiers, carrying out their
orders, took Paul with them during the
night and brought him as far as Antipa-
tris. [32]The next day they let the cavalry
go on with him, while they returned to
the barracks. [33]When the cavalry arrived
in Caesarea, they delivered the letter to
the governor and handed Paul over to
him. [34]The governor read the letter and
asked what province he was from. Learning that he was from Cilicia, [35]he said, "I
will hear your case when your accusers
get here." Then he ordered that Paul be
kept under guard in Herod's palace.

24 Five days later the high priest Ananias went down to Caesarea with
some of the elders and a lawyer named
Tertullus, and they brought their charges
against Paul before the governor. [2]When
Paul was called in, Tertullus presented
his case before Felix: "We have enjoyed a
long period of peace under you, and your
foresight has brought about reforms in
this nation. [3]Everywhere and in every
way, most excellent Felix, we acknowledge this with profound gratitude. [4]But
in order not to weary you further, I would
request that you be kind enough to hear
us briefly.

[5]"We have found this man to be a troublemaker, stirring up riots among the
Jews all over the world. He is a ringlead-
er of the Nazarene sect [6]and even tried to
desecrate the temple; so we seized him.
[7][b] [8]By examining him yourself you will
be able to learn the truth about all these
charges we are bringing against him."

[9]The other Jews joined in the accusation, asserting that these things were
true.

[10]When the governor motioned for
him to speak, Paul replied: "I know that
for a number of years you have been a
judge over this nation; so I gladly make
my defense. [11]You can easily verify that
no more than twelve days ago I went up
to Jerusalem to worship. [12]My accusers
did not find me arguing with anyone
at the temple, or stirring up a crowd in
the synagogues or anywhere else in the
city. [13]And they cannot prove to you the

[a] *23* The meaning of the Greek for this word is uncertain. [b] *6-8* Some manuscripts include here *him, and we would have judged him in accordance with our law. [7]But the commander Lysias came and took him from us with much violence, [8]ordering his accusers to come before you.*

charges they are now making against
me. 14However, I admit that I worship
the God of our ancestors as a follower
of the Way, which they call a sect. I believe everything that is in accordance
with the Law and that is written in the
Prophets, 15and I have the same hope in
God as these men themselves have, that
there will be a resurrection of both the
righteous and the wicked. 16So I strive always to keep my conscience clear before
God and man.

17"After an absence of several years,
I came to Jerusalem to bring my people
gifts for the poor and to present offerings. 18I was ceremonially clean when
they found me in the temple courts doing
this. There was no crowd with me, nor
was I involved in any disturbance. 19But
there are some Jews from the province
of Asia, who ought to be here before you
and bring charges if they have anything
against me. 20Or these who are here
should state what crime they found in
me when I stood before the Sanhedrin—
21unless it was this one thing I shouted as
I stood in their presence: 'It is concerning the resurrection of the dead that I am
on trial before you today.'"

22Then Felix, who was well acquainted with the Way, adjourned the pro-
ceedings. "When Lysias the commander
comes," he said, "I will decide your case."
23He ordered the centurion to keep Paul
under guard but to give him some freedom and permit his friends to take care
of his needs.

24Several days later Felix came with his
wife Drusilla, who was Jewish. He sent
for Paul and listened to him as he spoke
about faith in Christ Jesus. 25As Paul
talked about righteousness, self-control and the judgment to come, Felix was
afraid and said, "That's enough for now!
You may leave. When I find it convenient,
I will send for you." 26At the same time he
was hoping that Paul would offer him a
bribe, so he sent for him frequently and
talked with him.

27When two years had passed, Felix
was succeeded by Porcius Festus, but
because Felix wanted to grant a favor to
the Jews, he left Paul in prison.

25 Three days after arriving in the
province, Festus went up from
Caesarea to Jerusalem, 2where the chief
priests and the Jewish leaders appeared
before him and presented the charges
against Paul. 3They requested Festus,
as a favor to them, to have Paul trans-
ferred to Jerusalem, for they were preparing an ambush to kill him along the
way. 4Festus answered, "Paul is being
held at Caesarea, and I myself am going
there soon. 5Let some of your leaders
come with me, and if the man has done
anything wrong, they can press charges
against him there."

6After spending eight or ten days with
them, Festus went down to Caesarea.
The next day he convened the court
and ordered that Paul be brought before
him. 7When Paul came in, the Jews who
had come down from Jerusalem stood
around him. They brought many serious
charges against him, but they could not
prove them.

8Then Paul made his defense: "I have
done nothing wrong against the Jewish
law or against the temple or against Caesar."

9Festus, wishing to do the Jews a favor,
said to Paul, "Are you willing to go up
to Jerusalem and stand trial before me
there on these charges?"

10Paul answered: "I am now standing
before Caesar's court, where I ought to
be tried. I have not done any wrong to
the Jews, as you yourself know very well.
11If, however, I am guilty of doing anything deserving death, I do not refuse to
die. But if the charges brought against
me by these Jews are not true, no one has
the right to hand me over to them. I appeal to Caesar!"

12After Festus had conferred with his
council, he declared: "You have appealed
to Caesar. To Caesar you will go!"

13A few days later King Agrippa and
Bernice arrived at Caesarea to pay their
respects to Festus. 14Since they were
spending many days there, Festus discussed Paul's case with the king. He said:
"There is a man here whom Felix left as
a prisoner. 15When I went to Jerusalem,
the chief priests and the elders of the
Jews brought charges against him and
asked that he be condemned.

16"I told them that it is not the Roman
custom to hand over anyone before they
have faced their accusers and have had
an opportunity to defend themselves
against the charges. 17When they came
here with me, I did not delay the case, but

convened the court the next day and ordered the man to be brought in. 18When
his accusers got up to speak, they did
not charge him with any of the crimes I
had expected. 19Instead, they had some
points of dispute with him about their
own religion and about a dead man
named Jesus who Paul claimed was
alive. 20I was at a loss how to investigate
such matters; so I asked if he would be
willing to go to Jerusalem and stand trial
there on these charges. 21But when Paul
made his appeal to be held over for the
Emperor's decision, I ordered him held
until I could send him to Caesar."
22Then Agrippa said to Festus, "I would
like to hear this man myself."

He replied, "Tomorrow you will hear
him."
23The next day Agrippa and Bernice
came with great pomp and entered the
audience room with the high-ranking
military officers and the prominent men
of the city. At the command of Festus,
Paul was brought in. 24Festus said: "King
Agrippa, and all who are present with us,
you see this man! The whole Jewish community has petitioned me about him in
Jerusalem and here in Caesarea, shouting that he ought not to live any longer.
25I found he had done nothing deserving of death, but because he made his
appeal to the Emperor I decided to send
him to Rome. 26But I have nothing definite to write to His Majesty about him.
Therefore I have brought him before all
of you, and especially before you, King
Agrippa, so that as a result of this investigation I may have something to write.
27For I think it is unreasonable to send a
prisoner on to Rome without specifying
the charges against him."

26 Then Agrippa said to Paul, "You
have permission to speak for yourself."

So Paul motioned with his hand and
began his defense: 2"King Agrippa, I
consider myself fortunate to stand before you today as I make my defense
against all the accusations of the Jews,
3and especially so because you are well
acquainted with all the Jewish customs
and controversies. Therefore, I beg you
to listen to me patiently.
4"The Jewish people all know the way
I have lived ever since I was a child, from
the beginning of my life in my own country, and also in Jerusalem. 5They have
known me for a long time and can testify, if they are willing, that I conformed
to the strictest sect of our religion, living
as a Pharisee. 6And now it is because of
my hope in what God has promised our
ancestors that I am on trial today. 7This
is the promise our twelve tribes are
hoping to see fulfilled as they earnestly
serve God day and night. King Agrippa,
it is because of this hope that these Jews
are accusing me. 8Why should any of you
consider it incredible that God raises the
dead?
9"I too was convinced that I ought to
do all that was possible to oppose the
name of Jesus of Nazareth. 10And that is
just what I did in Jerusalem. On the authority of the chief priests I put many of
the Lord's people in prison, and when
they were put to death, I cast my vote
against them. 11Many a time I went from
one synagogue to another to have them
punished, and I tried to force them to
blaspheme. I was so obsessed with persecuting them that I even hunted them
down in foreign cities.
12"On one of these journeys I was going to Damascus with the authority and
commission of the chief priests. 13About
noon, King Agrippa, as I was on the road,
I saw a light from heaven, brighter than
the sun, blazing around me and my companions. 14We all fell to the ground, and
I heard a voice saying to me in Aramaic,[a]
'Saul, Saul, why do you persecute me? It
is hard for you to kick against the goads.'
15"Then I asked, 'Who are you, Lord?'
"'I am Jesus, whom you are persecuting,' the Lord replied. 16'Now get up and
stand on your feet. I have appeared to
you to appoint you as a servant and as a
witness of what you have seen and will
see of me. 17I will rescue you from your
own people and from the Gentiles. I am
sending you to them 18to open their eyes
and turn them from darkness to light,
and from the power of Satan to God, so
that they may receive forgiveness of sins
and a place among those who are sanctified by faith in me.'
19"So then, King Agrippa, I was not
disobedient to the vision from heaven.

[a] 14 Or *Hebrew*

20First to those in Damascus, then to
those in Jerusalem and in all Judea, and
then to the Gentiles, I preached that they
should repent and turn to God and demonstrate their repentance by their deeds.
21That is why some Jews seized me in the
temple courts and tried to kill me. 22But
God has helped me to this very day; so I
stand here and testify to small and great
alike. I am saying nothing beyond what
the prophets and Moses said would happen— 23that the Messiah would suffer
and, as the first to rise from the dead,
would bring the message of light to his
own people and to the Gentiles."

24At this point Festus interrupted
Paul's defense. "You are out of your mind,
Paul!" he shouted. "Your great learning is
driving you insane."

25"I am not insane, most excellent Festus," Paul replied. "What I am saying is
true and reasonable. 26The king is familiar with these things, and I can speak
freely to him. I am convinced that none
of this has escaped his notice, because it
was not done in a corner. 27King Agrippa, do you believe the prophets? I know
you do."

28Then Agrippa said to Paul, "Do you
think that in such a short time you can
persuade me to be a Christian?"

29Paul replied, "Short time or long—I
pray to God that not only you but all who
are listening to me today may become
what I am, except for these chains."

30The king rose, and with him the governor and Bernice and those sitting with
them. 31After they left the room, they began saying to one another, "This man is
not doing anything that deserves death
or imprisonment."

32Agrippa said to Festus, "This man
could have been set free if he had not appealed to Caesar."

27 When it was decided that we would
sail for Italy, Paul and some other
prisoners were handed over to a centurion named Julius, who belonged to
the Imperial Regiment. 2We boarded a
ship from Adramyttium about to sail for
ports along the coast of the province of
Asia, and we put out to sea. Aristarchus,
a Macedonian from Thessalonica, was
with us.

3The next day we landed at Sidon; and
Julius, in kindness to Paul, allowed him
to go to his friends so they might provide
for his needs. 4From there we put out to
sea again and passed to the lee of Cyprus because the winds were against us.
5When we had sailed across the open sea
off the coast of Cilicia and Pamphylia, we
landed at Myra in Lycia. 6There the centurion found an Alexandrian ship sailing
for Italy and put us on board. 7We made
slow headway for many days and had
difficulty arriving off Cnidus. When the
wind did not allow us to hold our course,
we sailed to the lee of Crete, opposite Sal-
mone. 8We moved along the coast with
difficulty and came to a place called Fair
Havens, near the town of Lasea.

9Much time had been lost, and sailing
had already become dangerous because
by now it was after the Day of Atonement.[a] So Paul warned them, 10"Men, I
can see that our voyage is going to be di-
sastrous and bring great loss to ship and
cargo, and to our own lives also." 11But
the centurion, instead of listening to
what Paul said, followed the advice of the
pilot and of the owner of the ship. 12Since
the harbor was unsuitable to winter in,
the majority decided that we should sail
on, hoping to reach Phoenix and winter
there. This was a harbor in Crete, facing
both southwest and northwest.

13When a gentle south wind began to
blow, they saw their opportunity; so they
weighed anchor and sailed along the
shore of Crete. 14Before very long, a wind
of hurricane force, called the Northeast-
er, swept down from the island. 15The
ship was caught by the storm and could
not head into the wind; so we gave way to
it and were driven along. 16As we passed
to the lee of a small island called Cauda,
we were hardly able to make the lifeboat
secure, 17so the men hoisted it aboard.
Then they passed ropes under the ship
itself to hold it together. Because they
were afraid they would run aground on
the sandbars of Syrtis, they lowered the
sea anchor[b] and let the ship be driven
along. 18We took such a violent battering
from the storm that the next day they began to throw the cargo overboard. 19On
the third day, they threw the ship's tackle
overboard with their own hands. 20When
neither sun nor stars appeared for many

[a] 9 That is, Yom Kippur [b] 17 Or *the sails*

days and the storm continued raging, we
finally gave up all hope of being saved.
21 After they had gone a long time without food, Paul stood up before them and
said: "Men, you should have taken my
advice not to sail from Crete; then you
would have spared yourselves this damage and loss. 22 But now I urge you to keep
up your courage, because not one of you
will be lost; only the ship will be destroyed. 23 Last night an angel of the God
to whom I belong and whom I serve stood
beside me 24 and said, 'Do not be afraid,
Paul. You must stand trial before Caesar;
and God has graciously given you the
lives of all who sail with you.' 25 So keep
up your courage, men, for I have faith in
God that it will happen just as he told me.
26 Nevertheless, we must run aground on
some island."
27 On the fourteenth night we were still
being driven across the Adriatic[a] Sea,
when about midnight the sailors sensed
they were approaching land. 28 They took
soundings and found that the water was
a hundred and twenty feet[b] deep. A short
time later they took soundings again and
found it was ninety feet[c] deep. 29 Fearing
that we would be dashed against the
rocks, they dropped four anchors from
the stern and prayed for daylight. 30 In
an attempt to escape from the ship, the
sailors let the lifeboat down into the
sea, pretending they were going to lower
some anchors from the bow. 31 Then Paul
said to the centurion and the soldiers,
"Unless these men stay with the ship,
you cannot be saved." 32 So the soldiers
cut the ropes that held the lifeboat and
let it drift away.
33 Just before dawn Paul urged them
all to eat. "For the last fourteen days,"
he said, "you have been in constant suspense and have gone without food—
you haven't eaten anything. 34 Now I
urge you to take some food. You need
it to survive. Not one of you will lose a
single hair from his head." 35 After he
said this, he took some bread and gave
thanks to God in front of them all. Then
he broke it and began to eat. 36 They
were all encouraged and ate some food
themselves. 37 Altogether there were 276
of us on board. 38 When they had eaten
as much as they wanted, they lightened
the ship by throwing the grain into the
sea.
39 When daylight came, they did not
recognize the land, but they saw a bay
with a sandy beach, where they decided to run the ship aground if they could.
40 Cutting loose the anchors, they left
them in the sea and at the same time
untied the ropes that held the rudders.
Then they hoisted the foresail to the
wind and made for the beach. 41 But the
ship struck a sandbar and ran aground.
The bow stuck fast and would not move,
and the stern was broken to pieces by the
pounding of the surf.
42 The soldiers planned to kill the
prisoners to prevent any of them from
swimming away and escaping. 43 But
the centurion wanted to spare Paul's life
and kept them from carrying out their
plan. He ordered those who could swim
to jump overboard first and get to land.
44 The rest were to get there on planks or
on other pieces of the ship. In this way
everyone reached land safely.
28 Once safely on shore, we found out
that the island was called Malta.
2 The islanders showed us unusual kindness. They built a fire and welcomed us
all because it was raining and cold. 3 Paul
gathered a pile of brushwood and, as he
put it on the fire, a viper, driven out by
the heat, fastened itself on his hand.
4 When the islanders saw the snake
hanging from his hand, they said to each
other, "This man must be a murderer; for
though he escaped from the sea, the goddess Justice has not allowed him to live."
5 But Paul shook the snake off into the
fire and suffered no ill effects. 6 The people expected him to swell up or suddenly
fall dead; but after waiting a long time
and seeing nothing unusual happen to
him, they changed their minds and said
he was a god.
7 There was an estate nearby that belonged to Publius, the chief official of the
island. He welcomed us to his home and
showed us generous hospitality for three
days. 8 His father was sick in bed, suffering from fever and dysentery. Paul went
in to see him and, after prayer, placed his
hands on him and healed him. 9 When
this had happened, the rest of the sick on
the island came and were cured. 10 They

[a] 27 In ancient times the name referred to an area extending well south of Italy. [b] 28 Or about 37 meters
[c] 28 Or about 27 meters

honored us in many ways; and when we
were ready to sail, they furnished us with
the supplies we needed.
11 After three months we put out to
sea in a ship that had wintered in the island—it was an Alexandrian ship with
the figurehead of the twin gods Castor
and Pollux. 12 We put in at Syracuse and
stayed there three days. 13 From there
we set sail and arrived at Rhegium. The
next day the south wind came up, and
on the following day we reached Puteoli.
14 There we found some brothers and sisters who invited us to spend a week with
them. And so we came to Rome. 15 The
brothers and sisters there had heard that
we were coming, and they traveled as far
as the Forum of Appius and the Three
Taverns to meet us. At the sight of these
people Paul thanked God and was encouraged. 16 When we got to Rome, Paul
was allowed to live by himself, with a soldier to guard him.
17 Three days later he called together the local Jewish leaders. When they
had assembled, Paul said to them: "My
brothers, although I have done nothing
against our people or against the customs of our ancestors, I was arrested in
Jerusalem and handed over to the Romans. 18 They examined me and wanted
to release me, because I was not guilty of
any crime deserving death. 19 The Jews
objected, so I was compelled to make an
appeal to Caesar. I certainly did not intend to bring any charge against my own
people. 20 For this reason I have asked to
see you and talk with you. It is because of
the hope of Israel that I am bound with
this chain."
21 They replied, "We have not received
any letters from Judea concerning you,
and none of our people who have come
from there has reported or said anything
bad about you. 22 But we want to hear
what your views are, for we know that
people everywhere are talking against
this sect."
23 They arranged to meet Paul on a certain day, and came in even larger numbers to the place where he was staying.
He witnessed to them from morning till
evening, explaining about the kingdom
of God, and from the Law of Moses and
from the Prophets he tried to persuade
them about Jesus. 24 Some were convinced by what he said, but others would
not believe. 25 They disagreed among
themselves and began to leave after Paul
had made this final statement: "The Holy
Spirit spoke the truth to your ancestors
when he said through Isaiah the prophet:

26 " 'Go to this people and say,
"You will be ever hearing but never
understanding;
you will be ever seeing but never
perceiving."
27 For this people's heart has become
calloused;
they hardly hear with their ears,
and they have closed their eyes.
Otherwise they might see with their
eyes,
hear with their ears,
understand with their hearts
and turn, and I would heal them.'[a]

28 "Therefore I want you to know that
God's salvation has been sent to the Gentiles, and they will listen!" [29][b]
30 For two whole years Paul stayed
there in his own rented house and welcomed all who came to see him. 31 He
proclaimed the kingdom of God and
taught about the Lord Jesus Christ—
with all boldness and without hin-
drance!

[a] 27 Isaiah 6:9,10 (see Septuagint) [b] 29 Some manuscripts include here *After he said this, the Jews left, arguing vigorously among themselves.*

ROMANS

Addressing the believers in Rome, Paul writes what is most likely the meatiest missionary fundraising letter ever written. To Jesus-followers living directly under the shadow of Caesar, he is appealing for help to bring the gospel to the western part of the empire. As an apostle, Paul has been set apart to make the royal announcement about the Lordship of Jesus. God's plan for the world has been revealed through a descendant of king David—Jesus the Messiah. This message demonstrates that God has been faithful to his covenant with Israel.

The flow of the letter follows the pattern of the ancient Jewish story of slavery and rescue. Humanity is in exile due to the entrance of sin and death into the world. Even the Jewish law could not defeat death and bring life. But God has come to rescue both Jews and Gentiles through the death and resurrection of Jesus. A new worldwide family is being created. Baptism into Jesus breaks the power of evil and brings freedom. The Holy Spirit leads the way into this new life that will be complete in a new inheritance—a redeemed creation.

Although many in Israel had failed to believe in the Messiah, this ended up bringing life to the rest of the world. The offer of life through Jesus remains for all, however, and in the end God's mercy will triumph over judgment. The closing emphasis is on the practical shape of a redeemed humanity's new way of life.

---

1 Paul, a servant of Christ Jesus, called
to be an apostle and set apart for the
gospel of God— 2the gospel he promised beforehand through his prophets
in the Holy Scriptures 3regarding his
Son, who as to his earthly life[a] was a descendant of David, 4and who through
the Spirit of holiness was appointed the
Son of God in power[b] by his resurrection
from the dead: Jesus Christ our Lord.
5Through him we received grace and
apostleship to call all the Gentiles to the
obedience that comes from[c] faith for his
name's sake. 6And you also are among
those Gentiles who are called to belong
to Jesus Christ.

7To all in Rome who are loved by God
and called to be his holy people:

Grace and peace to you from God our Father and from the Lord Jesus Christ.

8First, I thank my God through Jesus
Christ for all of you, because your faith is
being reported all over the world. 9God,
whom I serve in my spirit in preaching the gospel of his Son, is my witness
how constantly I remember you 10in
my prayers at all times; and I pray that now at last by God's will the way may be opened for me to come to you.

11I long to see you so that I may impart to you some spiritual gift to make
you strong— 12that is, that you and I
may be mutually encouraged by each
other's faith. 13I do not want you to be
unaware, brothers and sisters,[d] that I planned many times to come to you (but have been prevented from doing so until now) in order that I might have a harvest among you, just as I have had among the other Gentiles.

14I am obligated both to Greeks and
non-Greeks, both to the wise and the
foolish. 15That is why I am so eager to
preach the gospel also to you who are
in Rome.

16For I am not ashamed of the gospel,
because it is the power of God that brings
salvation to everyone who believes: first
to the Jew, then to the Gentile. 17For in
the gospel the righteousness of God is revealed—a righteousness that is by faith from first to last,[e] just as it is written: "The righteous will live by faith."[f]

18The wrath of God is being revealed
from heaven against all the godlessness
and wickedness of people, who suppress
the truth by their wickedness, 19since
what may be known about God is plain to them, because God has made it plain

[a] 3 Or *who according to the flesh* [b] 4 Or *was declared with power to be the Son of God* [c] 5 Or *that is*
[d] 13 The Greek word for *brothers and sisters* (*adelphoi*) refers here to believers, both men and women, as part of God's family; also in 7:1, 4; 8:12, 29; 10:1; 11:25; 12:1; 15:14, 30; 16:14, 17. [e] 17 Or *is from faith to faith*
[f] 17 Hab. 2:4

to them. [20]For since the creation of the
world God's invisible qualities—his
eternal power and divine nature—have
been clearly seen, being understood
from what has been made, so that people are without excuse.

[21]For although they knew God, they
neither glorified him as God nor gave
thanks to him, but their thinking became futile and their foolish hearts were
darkened. [22]Although they claimed to
be wise, they became fools [23]and exchanged the glory of the immortal God
for images made to look like a mortal
human being and birds and animals
and reptiles.

[24]Therefore God gave them over in the
sinful desires of their hearts to sexual
impurity for the degrading of their bodies with one another. [25]They exchanged
the truth about God for a lie, and worshiped and served created things rather than the Creator—who is forever
praised. Amen.

[26]Because of this, God gave them over
to shameful lusts. Even their women
exchanged natural sexual relations for
unnatural ones. [27]In the same way the
men also abandoned natural relations
with women and were inflamed with
lust for one another. Men committed
shameful acts with other men, and received in themselves the due penalty for
their error.

[28]Furthermore, just as they did not
think it worthwhile to retain the knowledge of God, so God gave them over to
a depraved mind, so that they do what
ought not to be done. [29]They have become filled with every kind of wickedness, evil, greed and depravity. They
are full of envy, murder, strife, deceit
and malice. They are gossips, [30]slander-
ers, God-haters, insolent, arrogant and
boastful; they invent ways of doing evil;
they disobey their parents; [31]they have
no understanding, no fidelity, no love,
no mercy. [32]Although they know God's
righteous decree that those who do such
things deserve death, they not only continue to do these very things but also approve of those who practice them.

2 You, therefore, have no excuse, you
who pass judgment on someone else,
for at whatever point you judge another,
you are condemning yourself, because
you who pass judgment do the same
things. [2]Now we know that God's judgment against those who do such things
is based on truth. [3]So when you, a mere
human being, pass judgment on them
and yet do the same things, do you think
you will escape God's judgment? [4]Or do
you show contempt for the riches of his
kindness, forbearance and patience, not
realizing that God's kindness is intended to lead you to repentance?

[5]But because of your stubbornness and
your unrepentant heart, you are storing
up wrath against yourself for the day of
God's wrath, when his righteous judgment will be revealed. [6]God "will repay
each person according to what they have
done."[a] [7]To those who by persistence in
doing good seek glory, honor and immortality, he will give eternal life. [8]But
for those who are self-seeking and who
reject the truth and follow evil, there will
be wrath and anger. [9]There will be trouble and distress for every human being
who does evil: first for the Jew, then for
the Gentile; [10]but glory, honor and peace
for everyone who does good: first for the
Jew, then for the Gentile. [11]For God does
not show favoritism.

[12]All who sin apart from the law will
also perish apart from the law, and all
who sin under the law will be judged by
the law. [13]For it is not those who hear
the law who are righteous in God's sight,
but it is those who obey the law who will
be declared righteous. [14](Indeed, when
Gentiles, who do not have the law, do by
nature things required by the law, they
are a law for themselves, even though
they do not have the law. [15]They show
that the requirements of the law are written on their hearts, their consciences
also bearing witness, and their thoughts
sometimes accusing them and at other
times even defending them.) [16]This will
take place on the day when God judges
people's secrets through Jesus Christ, as
my gospel declares.

[17]Now you, if you call yourself a Jew; if
you rely on the law and boast in God; [18]if
you know his will and approve of what is
superior because you are instructed by
the law; [19]if you are convinced that you
are a guide for the blind, a light for those

[a] 6 Psalm 62:12; Prov. 24:12

who are in the dark, 20an instructor of
the foolish, a teacher of little children,
because you have in the law the embodi-
ment of knowledge and truth— 21you,
then, who teach others, do you not teach
yourself? You who preach against stealing, do you steal? 22You who say that
people should not commit adultery, do
you commit adultery? You who abhor
idols, do you rob temples? 23You who
boast in the law, do you dishonor God
by breaking the law? 24As it is written:
"God's name is blasphemed among the
Gentiles because of you."[a]
25Circumcision has value if you observe the law, but if you break the law,
you have become as though you had not
been circumcised. 26So then, if those
who are not circumcised keep the law's
requirements, will they not be regarded
as though they were circumcised? 27The
one who is not circumcised physically
and yet obeys the law will condemn you
who, even though you have the[b] written
code and circumcision, are a lawbreaker.
28A person is not a Jew who is one only
outwardly, nor is circumcision merely
outward and physical. 29No, a person is
a Jew who is one inwardly; and circumcision is circumcision of the heart, by
the Spirit, not by the written code. Such
a person's praise is not from other people, but from God.

3 What advantage, then, is there in being a Jew, or what value is there in circumcision? 2Much in every way! First of
all, the Jews have been entrusted with
the very words of God.
3What if some were unfaithful? Will
their unfaithfulness nullify God's faithfulness? 4Not at all! Let God be true, and
every human being a liar. As it is written:

"So that you may be proved right
when you speak
and prevail when you judge."[c]

5But if our unrighteousness brings
out God's righteousness more clearly,
what shall we say? That God is unjust
in bringing his wrath on us? (I am using
a human argument.) 6Certainly not! If
that were so, how could God judge the
world? 7Someone might argue, "If my
falsehood enhances God's truthfulness
and so increases his glory, why am I
still condemned as a sinner?" 8Why not
say—as some slanderously claim that
we say—"Let us do evil that good may
result"? Their condemnation is just!
9What shall we conclude then? Do we
have any advantage? Not at all! For we
have already made the charge that Jews
and Gentiles alike are all under the power of sin. 10As it is written:

"There is no one righteous, not even
one;
11 there is no one who understands;
there is no one who seeks God.
12All have turned away,
they have together become
worthless;
there is no one who does good,
not even one."[d]
13"Their throats are open graves;
their tongues practice deceit."[e]
"The poison of vipers is on their lips."[f]
14 "Their mouths are full of cursing
and bitterness."[g]
15"Their feet are swift to shed blood;
16 ruin and misery mark their ways,
17and the way of peace they do not
know."[h]
18 "There is no fear of God before their
eyes."[i]

19Now we know that whatever the law
says, it says to those who are under the
law, so that every mouth may be silenced
and the whole world held accountable to
God. 20Therefore no one will be declared
righteous in God's sight by the works of
the law; rather, through the law we become conscious of our sin.
21But now apart from the law the righteousness of God has been made known,
to which the Law and the Prophets testify. 22This righteousness is given through
faith in[j] Jesus Christ to all who believe.
There is no difference between Jew and
Gentile, 23for all have sinned and fall
short of the glory of God, 24and all are
justified freely by his grace through the
redemption that came by Christ Jesus.
25God presented Christ as a sacrifice of
atonement,[k] through the shedding of his

[a] *24* Isaiah 52:5 (see Septuagint); Ezek. 36:20,22 [b] *27* Or *who, by means of a* [c] *4* Psalm 51:4 [d] *12* Psalms 14:1-3; 53:1-3; Eccles. 7:20 [e] *13* Psalm 5:9 [f] *13* Psalm 140:3 [g] *14* Psalm 10:7 (see Septuagint) [h] *17* Isaiah 59:7,8 [i] *18* Psalm 36:1 [j] *22* Or *through the faithfulness of* [k] *25* The Greek for *sacrifice of atonement* refers to the atonement cover on the ark of the covenant (see Lev. 16:15,16).

blood—to be received by faith. He did this to demonstrate his righteousness, because in his forbearance he had left the sins committed beforehand unpunished— 26 he did it to demonstrate his righteousness at the present time, so as to be just and the one who justifies those who have faith in Jesus.

27 Where, then, is boasting? It is excluded. Because of what law? The law that requires works? No, because of the law that requires faith. 28 For we maintain that a person is justified by faith apart from the works of the law. 29 Or is God the God of Jews only? Is he not the God of Gentiles too? Yes, of Gentiles too, 30 since there is only one God, who will justify the circumcised by faith and the uncircumcised through that same faith. 31 Do we, then, nullify the law by this faith? Not at all! Rather, we uphold the law.

4 What then shall we say that Abraham, our forefather according to the flesh, discovered in this matter? 2 If, in fact, Abraham was justified by works, he had something to boast about—but not before God. 3 What does Scripture say? "Abraham believed God, and it was credited to him as righteousness."[a]

4 Now to the one who works, wages are not credited as a gift but as an obligation. 5 However, to the one who does not work but trusts God who justifies the ungodly, their faith is credited as righteousness. 6 David says the same thing when he speaks of the blessedness of the one to whom God credits righteousness apart from works:

7 "Blessed are those
whose transgressions are forgiven,
whose sins are covered.
8 Blessed is the one
whose sin the Lord will never count
against them."[b]

9 Is this blessedness only for the circumcised, or also for the uncircumcised? We have been saying that Abraham's faith was credited to him as righteousness. 10 Under what circumstances was it credited? Was it after he was circumcised, or before? It was not after, but before! 11 And he received circumcision as a sign, a seal of the righteousness that he had by faith while he was still uncircumcised. So then, he is the father of all who believe but have not been circumcised, in order that righteousness might be credited to them. 12 And he is then also the father of the circumcised who not only are circumcised but who also follow in the footsteps of the faith that our father Abraham had before he was circumcised.

13 It was not through the law that Abraham and his offspring received the promise that he would be heir of the world, but through the righteousness that comes by faith. 14 For if those who depend on the law are heirs, faith means nothing and the promise is worthless, 15 because the law brings wrath. And where there is no law there is no transgression.

16 Therefore, the promise comes by faith, so that it may be by grace and may be guaranteed to all Abraham's offspring—not only to those who are of the law but also to those who have the faith of Abraham. He is the father of us all. 17 As it is written: "I have made you a father of many nations."[c] He is our father in the sight of God, in whom he believed—the God who gives life to the dead and calls into being things that were not.

18 Against all hope, Abraham in hope believed and so became the father of many nations, just as it had been said to him, "So shall your offspring be."[d] 19 Without weakening in his faith, he faced the fact that his body was as good as dead—since he was about a hundred years old—and that Sarah's womb was also dead. 20 Yet he did not waver through unbelief regarding the promise of God, but was strengthened in his faith and gave glory to God, 21 being fully persuaded that God had power to do what he had promised. 22 This is why "it was credited to him as righteousness." 23 The words "it was credited to him" were written not for him alone, 24 but also for us, to whom God will credit righteousness—for us who believe in him who raised Jesus our Lord from the dead. 25 He was delivered over to death for our sins and was raised to life for our justification.

[a] 3 Gen. 15:6; also in verse 22 [b] 8 Psalm 32:1,2 [c] 17 Gen. 17:5 [d] 18 Gen. 15:5

5 Therefore, since we have been justified through faith, we[a] have peace
with God through our Lord Jesus Christ,
2 through whom we have gained access
by faith into this grace in which we now
stand. And we[b] boast in the hope of the
glory of God. 3 Not only so, but we[b] also
glory in our sufferings, because we know
that suffering produces perseverance;
4 perseverance, character; and character, hope. 5 And hope does not put us
to shame, because God's love has been
poured out into our hearts through the
Holy Spirit, who has been given to us.

6 You see, at just the right time, when
we were still powerless, Christ died for
the ungodly. 7 Very rarely will anyone die
for a righteous person, though for a good
person someone might possibly dare to
die. 8 But God demonstrates his own love
for us in this: While we were still sinners,
Christ died for us.

9 Since we have now been justified by
his blood, how much more shall we be
saved from God's wrath through him!
10 For if, while we were God's enemies,
we were reconciled to him through the
death of his Son, how much more, having been reconciled, shall we be saved
through his life! 11 Not only is this so, but
we also boast in God through our Lord
Jesus Christ, through whom we have
now received reconciliation.

12 Therefore, just as sin entered the
world through one man, and death
through sin, and in this way death came
to all people, because all sinned—

13 To be sure, sin was in the world
before the law was given, but sin is
not charged against anyone's account
where there is no law. 14 Nevertheless,
death reigned from the time of Adam to
the time of Moses, even over those who
did not sin by breaking a command, as
did Adam, who is a pattern of the one to
come.

15 But the gift is not like the trespass.
For if the many died by the trespass of
the one man, how much more did God's
grace and the gift that came by the grace
of the one man, Jesus Christ, overflow to
the many! 16 Nor can the gift of God be
compared with the result of one man's
sin: The judgment followed one sin and
brought condemnation, but the gift followed many trespasses and brought justification. 17 For if, by the trespass of the
one man, death reigned through that
one man, how much more will those
who receive God's abundant provision
of grace and of the gift of righteousness
reign in life through the one man, Jesus
Christ!

18 Consequently, just as one trespass
resulted in condemnation for all people, so also one righteous act resulted in
justification and life for all people. 19 For
just as through the disobedience of the
one man the many were made sinners,
so also through the obedience of the one
man the many will be made righteous.

20 The law was brought in so that the
trespass might increase. But where sin
increased, grace increased all the more,
21 so that, just as sin reigned in death,
so also grace might reign through righteousness to bring eternal life through
Jesus Christ our Lord.

6 What shall we say, then? Shall we
go on sinning so that grace may increase? 2 By no means! We are those
who have died to sin; how can we live in
it any longer? 3 Or don't you know that
all of us who were baptized into Christ
Jesus were baptized into his death? 4 We
were therefore buried with him through
baptism into death in order that, just as
Christ was raised from the dead through
the glory of the Father, we too may live
a new life.

5 For if we have been united with him
in a death like his, we will certainly also
be united with him in a resurrection
like his. 6 For we know that our old self
was crucified with him so that the body
ruled by sin might be done away with,[c]
that we should no longer be slaves to
sin— 7 because anyone who has died
has been set free from sin.

8 Now if we died with Christ, we believe
that we will also live with him. 9 For we
know that since Christ was raised from
the dead, he cannot die again; death
no longer has mastery over him. 10 The
death he died, he died to sin once for all;
but the life he lives, he lives to God.

11 In the same way, count yourselves
dead to sin but alive to God in Christ
Jesus. 12 Therefore do not let sin reign
in your mortal body so that you obey

[a] *1* Many manuscripts *let us* [b] *2,3* Or *let us* [c] *6* Or *be rendered powerless*

its evil desires. 13 Do not offer any part of yourself to sin as an instrument of wickedness, but rather offer yourselves to God as those who have been brought from death to life; and offer every part of yourself to him as an instrument of righteousness. 14 For sin shall no longer be your master, because you are not under the law, but under grace.

15 What then? Shall we sin because we are not under the law but under grace? By no means! 16 Don't you know that when you offer yourselves to someone as obedient slaves, you are slaves of the one you obey—whether you are slaves to sin, which leads to death, or to obedience, which leads to righteousness? 17 But thanks be to God that, though you used to be slaves to sin, you have come to obey from your heart the pattern of teaching that has now claimed your allegiance. 18 You have been set free from sin and have become slaves to righteousness.

19 I am using an example from everyday life because of your human limitations. Just as you used to offer yourselves as slaves to impurity and to ever-increasing wickedness, so now offer yourselves as slaves to righteousness leading to holiness. 20 When you were slaves to sin, you were free from the control of righteousness. 21 What benefit did you reap at that time from the things you are now ashamed of? Those things result in death! 22 But now that you have been set free from sin and have become slaves of God, the benefit you reap leads to holiness, and the result is eternal life. 23 For the wages of sin is death, but the gift of God is eternal life in[a] Christ Jesus our Lord.

7 Do you not know, brothers and sisters—for I am speaking to those who know the law—that the law has authority over someone only as long as that person lives? 2 For example, by law a married woman is bound to her husband as long as he is alive, but if her husband dies, she is released from the law that binds her to him. 3 So then, if she has sexual relations with another man while her husband is still alive, she is called an adulteress. But if her husband dies, she is released from that law and is not an adulteress if she marries another man.

4 So, my brothers and sisters, you also died to the law through the body of Christ, that you might belong to another, to him who was raised from the dead, in order that we might bear fruit for God. 5 For when we were in the realm of the flesh,[b] the sinful passions aroused by the law were at work in us, so that we bore fruit for death. 6 But now, by dying to what once bound us, we have been released from the law so that we serve in the new way of the Spirit, and not in the old way of the written code.

7 What shall we say, then? Is the law sinful? Certainly not! Nevertheless, I would not have known what sin was had it not been for the law. For I would not have known what coveting really was if the law had not said, "You shall not covet."[c] 8 But sin, seizing the opportunity afforded by the commandment, produced in me every kind of coveting. For apart from the law, sin was dead. 9 Once I was alive apart from the law; but when the commandment came, sin sprang to life and I died. 10 I found that the very commandment that was intended to bring life actually brought death. 11 For sin, seizing the opportunity afforded by the commandment, deceived me, and through the commandment put me to death. 12 So then, the law is holy, and the commandment is holy, righteous and good.

13 Did that which is good, then, become death to me? By no means! Nevertheless, in order that sin might be recognized as sin, it used what is good to bring about my death, so that through the commandment sin might become utterly sinful.

14 We know that the law is spiritual; but I am unspiritual, sold as a slave to sin. 15 I do not understand what I do. For what I want to do I do not do, but what I hate I do. 16 And if I do what I do not want to do, I agree that the law is good. 17 As it is, it is no longer I myself who do it, but it is sin living in me. 18 For I know that good itself does not dwell in me, that is, in my sinful nature.[d] For I have the desire to do what is good, but I cannot carry it out. 19 For I do not do the good I want to do, but the

[a] *23* Or *through* [b] *5* In contexts like this, the Greek word for *flesh* (*sarx*) refers to the sinful state of human beings, often presented as a power in opposition to the Spirit. [c] *7* Exodus 20:17; Deut. 5:21 [d] *18* Or *my flesh*

evil I do not want to do — this I keep on
doing. 20 Now if I do what I do not want to
do, it is no longer I who do it, but it is sin
living in me that does it.
21 So I find this law at work: Although I
want to do good, evil is right there with
me. 22 For in my inner being I delight in
God's law; 23 but I see another law at work
in me, waging war against the law of my
mind and making me a prisoner of the
law of sin at work within me. 24 What a
wretched man I am! Who will rescue me
from this body that is subject to death?
25 Thanks be to God, who delivers me
through Jesus Christ our Lord!
So then, I myself in my mind am a
slave to God's law, but in my sinful nature[a] a slave to the law of sin.
8 Therefore, there is now no condemnation for those who are in Christ Jesus,
2 because through Christ Jesus the law of
the Spirit who gives life has set you[b] free
from the law of sin and death. 3 For what
the law was powerless to do because it
was weakened by the flesh,[c] God did by
sending his own Son in the likeness of
sinful flesh to be a sin offering.[d] And so
he condemned sin in the flesh, 4 in order
that the righteous requirement of the
law might be fully met in us, who do not
live according to the flesh but according
to the Spirit.
5 Those who live according to the flesh
have their minds set on what the flesh
desires; but those who live in accordance with the Spirit have their minds
set on what the Spirit desires. 6 The
mind governed by the flesh is death, but
the mind governed by the Spirit is life
and peace. 7 The mind governed by the
flesh is hostile to God; it does not submit to God's law, nor can it do so. 8 Those
who are in the realm of the flesh cannot
please God.
9 You, however, are not in the realm of
the flesh but are in the realm of the Spirit, if indeed the Spirit of God lives in you.
And if anyone does not have the Spirit
of Christ, they do not belong to Christ.
10 But if Christ is in you, then even though
your body is subject to death because of
sin, the Spirit gives life[e] because of righteousness. 11 And if the Spirit of him who
raised Jesus from the dead is living in
you, he who raised Christ from the dead
will also give life to your mortal bodies
because of[f] his Spirit who lives in you.
12 Therefore, brothers and sisters, we
have an obligation — but it is not to the
flesh, to live according to it. 13 For if you
live according to the flesh, you will die;
but if by the Spirit you put to death the
misdeeds of the body, you will live.
14 For those who are led by the Spirit of
God are the children of God. 15 The Spirit
you received does not make you slaves,
so that you live in fear again; rather, the
Spirit you received brought about your
adoption to sonship.[g] And by him we
cry, *"Abba,*[h] Father." 16 The Spirit himself testifies with our spirit that we are
God's children. 17 Now if we are children,
then we are heirs — heirs of God and co-
heirs with Christ, if indeed we share in
his sufferings in order that we may also
share in his glory.
18 I consider that our present sufferings
are not worth comparing with the glory
that will be revealed in us. 19 For the creation waits in eager expectation for the
children of God to be revealed. 20 For the
creation was subjected to frustration,
not by its own choice, but by the will of
the one who subjected it, in hope 21 that[i]
the creation itself will be liberated from
its bondage to decay and brought into
the freedom and glory of the children
of God.
22 We know that the whole creation has
been groaning as in the pains of childbirth right up to the present time. 23 Not
only so, but we ourselves, who have the
firstfruits of the Spirit, groan inwardly
as we wait eagerly for our adoption to
sonship, the redemption of our bodies.
24 For in this hope we were saved. But
hope that is seen is no hope at all. Who
hopes for what they already have? 25 But
if we hope for what we do not yet have,
we wait for it patiently.
26 In the same way, the Spirit helps us
in our weakness. We do not know what

[a] *25* Or *in the flesh* [b] *2* The Greek is singular; some manuscripts *me* [c] *3* In contexts like this, the Greek word for *flesh* (*sarx*) refers to the sinful state of human beings, often presented as a power in opposition to the Spirit; also in verses 4-13. [d] *3* Or *flesh, for sin* [e] *10* Or *you, your body is dead because of sin, yet your spirit is alive* [f] *11* Some manuscripts *bodies through* [g] *15* The Greek word for *adoption to sonship* is a term referring to the full legal standing of an adopted male heir in Roman culture; also in verse 23. [h] *15* Aramaic for *father* [i] *20,21* Or *subjected it in hope.* [21]*For*

we ought to pray for, but the Spirit himself intercedes for us through wordless
groans. 27 And he who searches our
hearts knows the mind of the Spirit, because the Spirit intercedes for God's people in accordance with the will of God.
28 And we know that in all things God
works for the good of those who love
him, who[a] have been called according to
his purpose. 29 For those God foreknew
he also predestined to be conformed to
the image of his Son, that he might be the
firstborn among many brothers and sisters. 30 And those he predestined, he also
called; those he called, he also justified;
those he justified, he also glorified.
31 What, then, shall we say in response
to these things? If God is for us, who can
be against us? 32 He who did not spare his
own Son, but gave him up for us all—how
will he not also, along with him, graciously give us all things? 33 Who will bring any
charge against those whom God has chosen? It is God who justifies. 34 Who then is
the one who condemns? No one. Christ
Jesus who died—more than that, who
was raised to life—is at the right hand of
God and is also interceding for us. 35 Who
shall separate us from the love of Christ?
Shall trouble or hardship or persecution
or famine or nakedness or danger or
sword? 36 As it is written:

"For your sake we face death all day
long;
we are considered as sheep to be
slaughtered."[b]

37 No, in all these things we are more than
conquerors through him who loved us.
38 For I am convinced that neither death
nor life, neither angels nor demons,[c] neither the present nor the future, nor any
powers, 39 neither height nor depth, nor
anything else in all creation, will be able
to separate us from the love of God that
is in Christ Jesus our Lord.

9 I speak the truth in Christ—I am
not lying, my conscience confirms it
through the Holy Spirit— 2 I have great
sorrow and unceasing anguish in my
heart. 3 For I could wish that I myself
were cursed and cut off from Christ for
the sake of my people, those of my own
race, 4 the people of Israel. Theirs is the
adoption to sonship; theirs the divine
glory, the covenants, the receiving of the
law, the temple worship and the promises. 5 Theirs are the patriarchs, and from
them is traced the human ancestry of
the Messiah, who is God over all, forever
praised![d] Amen.
6 It is not as though God's word had
failed. For not all who are descended
from Israel are Israel. 7 Nor because they
are his descendants are they all Abraham's children. On the contrary, "It is
through Isaac that your offspring will
be reckoned."[e] 8 In other words, it is not
the children by physical descent who are
God's children, but it is the children of the
promise who are regarded as Abraham's
offspring. 9 For this was how the promise
was stated: "At the appointed time I will
return, and Sarah will have a son."[f]
10 Not only that, but Rebekah's children
were conceived at the same time by our
father Isaac. 11 Yet, before the twins were
born or had done anything good or bad—
in order that God's purpose in election
might stand: 12 not by works but by him
who calls—she was told, "The older will
serve the younger."[g] 13 Just as it is written:
"Jacob I loved, but Esau I hated."[h]
14 What then shall we say? Is God unjust? Not at all! 15 For he says to Moses,

"I will have mercy on whom I have
mercy,
and I will have compassion on
whom I have compassion."[i]

16 It does not, therefore, depend on human desire or effort, but on God's mercy. 17 For Scripture says to Pharaoh: "I
raised you up for this very purpose, that
I might display my power in you and that
my name might be proclaimed in all the
earth."[j] 18 Therefore God has mercy on
whom he wants to have mercy, and he
hardens whom he wants to harden.
19 One of you will say to me: "Then
why does God still blame us? For who
is able to resist his will?" 20 But who are
you, a human being, to talk back to God?

[a] 28 Or *that all things work together for good to those who love God, who*; or *that in all things God works together with those who love him to bring about what is good—with those who* [b] 36 Psalm 44:22 [c] 38 Or *nor heavenly rulers* [d] 5 Or *Messiah, who is over all. God be forever praised!* Or *Messiah. God who is over all be forever praised!* [e] 7 Gen. 21:12 [f] 9 Gen. 18:10,14 [g] 12 Gen. 25:23 [h] 13 Mal. 1:2,3 [i] 15 Exodus 33:19 [j] 17 Exodus 9:16

"Shall what is formed say to the one who
formed it, 'Why did you make me like
this?' "[a] 21 Does not the potter have the
right to make out of the same lump of
clay some pottery for special purposes
and some for common use?
22 What if God, although choosing
to show his wrath and make his power
known, bore with great patience the
objects of his wrath—prepared for destruction?
23 What if he did this to make
the riches of his glory known to the objects
of his mercy, whom he prepared in
advance for glory— 24 even us, whom he
also called, not only from the Jews but
also from the Gentiles? 25 As he says in
Hosea:

"I will call them 'my people' who are
not my people;
and I will call her 'my loved one'
who is not my loved one,"[b]

26 and,

"In the very place where it was said to
them,
'You are not my people,'
there they will be called 'children
of the living God.' "[c]

27 Isaiah cries out concerning Israel:

"Though the number of the Israelites
be like the sand by the sea,
only the remnant will be saved.
28 For the Lord will carry out
his sentence on earth with speed
and finality."[d]

29 It is just as Isaiah said previously:

"Unless the Lord Almighty
had left us descendants,
we would have become like Sodom,
we would have been like
Gomorrah."[e]

30 What then shall we say? That the
Gentiles, who did not pursue righteousness,
have obtained it, a righteousness
that is by faith; 31 but the people of Israel,
who pursued the law as the way of righteousness,
have not attained their goal.
32 Why not? Because they pursued it not
by faith but as if it were by works. They
stumbled over the stumbling stone. 33 As
it is written:

"See, I lay in Zion a stone that causes
people to stumble
and a rock that makes them fall,
and the one who believes in him
will never be put to shame."[f]

10 Brothers and sisters, my heart's
desire and prayer to God for the Israelites
is that they may be saved. 2 For I
can testify about them that they are zealous
for God, but their zeal is not based
on knowledge. 3 Since they did not know
the righteousness of God and sought to
establish their own, they did not submit
to God's righteousness. 4 Christ is
the culmination of the law so that there
may be righteousness for everyone who
believes.
5 Moses writes this about the righteousness
that is by the law: "The person who
does these things will live by them."[g]
6 But the righteousness that is by faith
says: "Do not say in your heart, 'Who will
ascend into heaven?' "[h] (that is, to bring
Christ down) 7 "or 'Who will descend
into the deep?' "[i] (that is, to bring Christ
up from the dead). 8 But what does it say?
"The word is near you; it is in your mouth
and in your heart,"[j] that is, the message
concerning faith that we proclaim: 9 If you
declare with your mouth, "Jesus is Lord,"
and believe in your heart that God raised
him from the dead, you will be saved.
10 For it is with your heart that you believe
and are justified, and it is with your
mouth that you profess your faith and
are saved. 11 As Scripture says, "Anyone
who believes in him will never be put to
shame."[k] 12 For there is no difference between
Jew and Gentile—the same Lord is
Lord of all and richly blesses all who call
on him, 13 for, "Everyone who calls on the
name of the Lord will be saved."[l]
14 How, then, can they call on the one
they have not believed in? And how can
they believe in the one of whom they
have not heard? And how can they hear
without someone preaching to them?
15 And how can anyone preach unless
they are sent? As it is written: "How
beautiful are the feet of those who bring
good news!"[m]
16 But not all the Israelites accepted the
good news. For Isaiah says, "Lord, who has

[a] *20* Isaiah 29:16; 45:9 [b] *25* Hosea 2:23 [c] *26* Hosea 1:10 [d] *28* Isaiah 10:22,23 (see Septuagint)
[e] *29* Isaiah 1:9 [f] *33* Isaiah 8:14; 28:16 [g] *5* Lev. 18:5 [h] *6* Deut. 30:12 [i] *7* Deut. 30:13
[j] *8* Deut. 30:14 [k] *11* Isaiah 28:16 (see Septuagint) [l] *13* Joel 2:32 [m] *15* Isaiah 52:7

believed our message?"[a] 17 Consequently, faith comes from hearing the message, and the message is heard through the word about Christ. 18 But I ask: Did they not hear? Of course they did:

"Their voice has gone out into all the
earth,
their words to the ends of the
world."[b]

19 Again I ask: Did Israel not understand? First, Moses says,

"I will make you envious by those
who are not a nation;
I will make you angry by a nation
that has no understanding."[c]

20 And Isaiah boldly says,

"I was found by those who did not
seek me;
I revealed myself to those who did
not ask for me."[d]

21 But concerning Israel he says,

"All day long I have held out my hands
to a disobedient and obstinate
people."[e]

11 I ask then: Did God reject his people? By no means! I am an Israelite myself, a descendant of Abraham, from the tribe of Benjamin. 2 God did not reject his people, whom he foreknew. Don't you know what Scripture says in the passage about Elijah—how he appealed to God against Israel: 3 "Lord, they have killed your prophets and torn down your altars; I am the only one left, and they are trying to kill me"[f]? 4 And what was God's answer to him? "I have reserved for myself seven thousand who have not bowed the knee to Baal."[g] 5 So too, at the present time there is a remnant chosen by grace. 6 And if by grace, then it cannot be based on works; if it were, grace would no longer be grace.

7 What then? What the people of Israel sought so earnestly they did not obtain. The elect among them did, but the others were hardened, 8 as it is written:

"God gave them a spirit of stupor,
eyes that could not see
and ears that could not hear,
to this very day."[h]

9 And David says:

"May their table become a snare and
a trap,
a stumbling block and a retribution
for them.
10 May their eyes be darkened so they
cannot see,
and their backs be bent forever."[i]

11 Again I ask: Did they stumble so as to fall beyond recovery? Not at all! Rather, because of their transgression, salvation has come to the Gentiles to make Israel envious. 12 But if their transgression means riches for the world, and their loss means riches for the Gentiles, how much greater riches will their full inclusion bring!

13 I am talking to you Gentiles. Inasmuch as I am the apostle to the Gentiles, I take pride in my ministry 14 in the hope that I may somehow arouse my own people to envy and save some of them. 15 For if their rejection brought reconciliation to the world, what will their acceptance be but life from the dead? 16 If the part of the dough offered as firstfruits is holy, then the whole batch is holy; if the root is holy, so are the branches.

17 If some of the branches have been broken off, and you, though a wild olive shoot, have been grafted in among the others and now share in the nourishing sap from the olive root, 18 do not consider yourself to be superior to those other branches. If you do, consider this: You do not support the root, but the root supports you. 19 You will say then, "Branches were broken off so that I could be grafted in." 20 Granted. But they were broken off because of unbelief, and you stand by faith. Do not be arrogant, but tremble. 21 For if God did not spare the natural branches, he will not spare you either.

22 Consider therefore the kindness and sternness of God: sternness to those who fell, but kindness to you, provided that you continue in his kindness. Otherwise, you also will be cut off. 23 And if they do not persist in unbelief, they will be grafted in, for God is able to graft them in again. 24 After all, if you were cut out of an olive tree that is wild by nature, and contrary to nature were grafted into a cultivated olive tree, how much more

[a] *16* Isaiah 53:1 [b] *18* Psalm 19:4 [c] *19* Deut. 32:21 [d] *20* Isaiah 65:1 [e] *21* Isaiah 65:2
[f] *3* 1 Kings 19:10,14 [g] *4* 1 Kings 19:18 [h] *8* Deut. 29:4; Isaiah 29:10 [i] *10* Psalm 69:22,23

readily will these, the natural branches,
be grafted into their own olive tree!
25 I do not want you to be ignorant of
this mystery, brothers and sisters, so
that you may not be conceited: Israel has experienced a hardening in part
until the full number of the Gentiles has
come in, 26 and in this way[a] all Israel will
be saved. As it is written:

"The deliverer will come from Zion;
he will turn godlessness away from
Jacob.
27 And this is[b] my covenant with them
when I take away their sins."[c]

28 As far as the gospel is concerned,
they are enemies for your sake; but as far
as election is concerned, they are loved
on account of the patriarchs, 29 for God's
gifts and his call are irrevocable. 30 Just
as you who were at one time disobedient
to God have now received mercy as a result of their disobedience, 31 so they too
have now become disobedient in order
that they too may now[d] receive mercy
as a result of God's mercy to you. 32 For
God has bound everyone over to disobedience so that he may have mercy
on them all.

33 Oh, the depth of the riches of the
wisdom and[e] knowledge of
God!
How unsearchable his judgments,
and his paths beyond tracing out!
34 "Who has known the mind of the
Lord?
Or who has been his counselor?"[f]
35 "Who has ever given to God,
that God should repay them?"[g]
36 For from him and through him and
for him are all things.
To him be the glory forever! Amen.

12 Therefore, I urge you, brothers and
sisters, in view of God's mercy, to
offer your bodies as a living sacrifice,
holy and pleasing to God—this is your
true and proper worship. 2 Do not conform to the pattern of this world, but be
transformed by the renewing of your
mind. Then you will be able to test and
approve what God's will is—his good,
pleasing and perfect will.

3 For by the grace given me I say to every one of you: Do not think of yourself
more highly than you ought, but rather
think of yourself with sober judgment, in
accordance with the faith God has distributed to each of you. 4 For just as each
of us has one body with many members,
and these members do not all have the
same function, 5 so in Christ we, though
many, form one body, and each member
belongs to all the others. 6 We have different gifts, according to the grace given
to each of us. If your gift is prophesying,
then prophesy in accordance with your[h]
faith; 7 if it is serving, then serve; if it is
teaching, then teach; 8 if it is to encourage, then give encouragement; if it is giving, then give generously; if it is to lead,[i]
do it diligently; if it is to show mercy, do
it cheerfully.

9 Love must be sincere. Hate what is
evil; cling to what is good. 10 Be devoted
to one another in love. Honor one another above yourselves. 11 Never be lacking
in zeal, but keep your spiritual fervor,
serving the Lord. 12 Be joyful in hope,
patient in affliction, faithful in prayer.
13 Share with the Lord's people who are
in need. Practice hospitality.
14 Bless those who persecute you;
bless and do not curse. 15 Rejoice with
those who rejoice; mourn with those
who mourn. 16 Live in harmony with one
another. Do not be proud, but be willing
to associate with people of low position.[j]
Do not be conceited.
17 Do not repay anyone evil for evil. Be
careful to do what is right in the eyes of
everyone. 18 If it is possible, as far as it
depends on you, live at peace with everyone. 19 Do not take revenge, my dear
friends, but leave room for God's wrath,
for it is written: "It is mine to avenge; I
will repay,"[k] says the Lord. 20 On the contrary:

"If your enemy is hungry, feed him;
if he is thirsty, give him something
to drink.
In doing this, you will heap burning
coals on his head."[l]

21 Do not be overcome by evil, but overcome evil with good.

[a] 26 Or *and so* [b] 27 Or *will be* [c] 27 Isaiah 59:20,21; 27:9 (see Septuagint); Jer. 31:33,34
[d] 31 Some manuscripts do not have *now.* [e] 33 Or *riches and the wisdom and the* [f] 34 Isaiah 40:13
[g] 35 Job 41:11 [h] 6 Or *the* [i] 8 Or *to provide for others* [j] 16 Or *willing to do menial work*
[k] 19 Deut. 32:35 [l] 20 Prov. 25:21,22

13 Let everyone be subject to the governing authorities, for there is no
authority except that which God has
established. The authorities that exist
have been established by God. 2Con-
sequently, whoever rebels against the
authority is rebelling against what God
has instituted, and those who do so will
bring judgment on themselves. 3For rulers hold no terror for those who do right,
but for those who do wrong. Do you want
to be free from fear of the one in authority? Then do what is right and you will
be commended. 4For the one in authority is God's servant for your good. But if
you do wrong, be afraid, for rulers do
not bear the sword for no reason. They
are God's servants, agents of wrath to
bring punishment on the wrongdoer.
5Therefore, it is necessary to submit to
the authorities, not only because of possible punishment but also as a matter of
conscience.
6This is also why you pay taxes, for the
authorities are God's servants, who give
their full time to governing. 7Give to everyone what you owe them: If you owe
taxes, pay taxes; if revenue, then revenue; if respect, then respect; if honor,
then honor.
8Let no debt remain outstanding, except the continuing debt to love one
another, for whoever loves others has
fulfilled the law. 9The commandments,
"You shall not commit adultery," "You
shall not murder," "You shall not steal,"
"You shall not covet,"[a] and whatever other command there may be, are
summed up in this one command: "Love
your neighbor as yourself."[b] 10Love does
no harm to a neighbor. Therefore love is
the fulfillment of the law.
11And do this, understanding the present time: The hour has already come for
you to wake up from your slumber, because our salvation is nearer now than
when we first believed. 12The night is
nearly over; the day is almost here. So let
us put aside the deeds of darkness and
put on the armor of light. 13Let us behave
decently, as in the daytime, not in carousing and drunkenness, not in sexual
immorality and debauchery, not in dissension and jealousy. 14Rather, clothe
yourselves with the Lord Jesus Christ,
and do not think about how to gratify
the desires of the flesh.[c]

14 Accept the one whose faith is weak,
without quarreling over disputable
matters. 2One person's faith allows them
to eat anything, but another, whose faith
is weak, eats only vegetables. 3The one
who eats everything must not treat with
contempt the one who does not, and the
one who does not eat everything must
not judge the one who does, for God has
accepted them. 4Who are you to judge
someone else's servant? To their own
master, servants stand or fall. And they
will stand, for the Lord is able to make
them stand.
5One person considers one day more
sacred than another; another considers every day alike. Each of them should
be fully convinced in their own mind.
6Whoever regards one day as special
does so to the Lord. Whoever eats meat
does so to the Lord, for they give thanks
to God; and whoever abstains does so to
the Lord and gives thanks to God. 7For
none of us lives for ourselves alone, and
none of us dies for ourselves alone. 8If we
live, we live for the Lord; and if we die,
we die for the Lord. So, whether we live
or die, we belong to the Lord. 9For this
very reason, Christ died and returned to
life so that he might be the Lord of both
the dead and the living.
10You, then, why do you judge your
brother or sister[d]? Or why do you treat
them with contempt? For we will all
stand before God's judgment seat. 11It
is written:

"'As surely as I live,' says the Lord,
'every knee will bow before me;
every tongue will acknowledge
God.'"[e]

12So then, each of us will give an account
of ourselves to God.
13Therefore let us stop passing judgment on one another. Instead, make
up your mind not to put any stumbling
block or obstacle in the way of a brother
or sister. 14I am convinced, being fully
persuaded in the Lord Jesus, that noth-

[a] *9* Exodus 20:13-15,17; Deut. 5:17-19,21 [b] *9* Lev. 19:18 [c] *14* In contexts like this, the Greek word for *flesh* (*sarx*) refers to the sinful state of human beings, often presented as a power in opposition to the Spirit. [d] *10* The Greek word for *brother or sister* (*adelphos*) refers here to a believer, whether man or woman, as part of God's family; also in verses 13, 15 and 21. [e] *11* Isaiah 45:23

ing is unclean in itself. But if anyone
regards something as unclean, then
for that person it is unclean. [15]If your
brother or sister is distressed because
of what you eat, you are no longer acting in love. Do not by your eating destroy someone for whom Christ died.
[16]Therefore do not let what you know
is good be spoken of as evil. [17]For the
kingdom of God is not a matter of eating and drinking, but of righteousness,
peace and joy in the Holy Spirit, [18]be-
cause anyone who serves Christ in this
way is pleasing to God and receives human approval.

[19]Let us therefore make every effort
to do what leads to peace and to mutual edification. [20]Do not destroy the work
of God for the sake of food. All food is
clean, but it is wrong for a person to eat
anything that causes someone else to
stumble. [21]It is better not to eat meat or
drink wine or to do anything else that
will cause your brother or sister to fall.

[22]So whatever you believe about these
things keep between yourself and God.
Blessed is the one who does not condemn himself by what he approves.
[23]But whoever has doubts is condemned
if they eat, because their eating is not
from faith; and everything that does not
come from faith is sin.[a]

15 We who are strong ought to bear
with the failings of the weak and
not to please ourselves. [2]Each of us
should please our neighbors for their
good, to build them up. [3]For even Christ
did not please himself but, as it is written: "The insults of those who insult you
have fallen on me."[b] [4]For everything
that was written in the past was written
to teach us, so that through the endurance taught in the Scriptures and the
encouragement they provide we might
have hope.

[5]May the God who gives endurance
and encouragement give you the same
attitude of mind toward each other that
Christ Jesus had, [6]so that with one mind
and one voice you may glorify the God
and Father of our Lord Jesus Christ.

[7]Accept one another, then, just as
Christ accepted you, in order to bring
praise to God. [8]For I tell you that Christ
has become a servant of the Jews[c] on behalf of God's truth, so that the promises
made to the patriarchs might be confirmed [9]and, moreover, that the Gentiles might glorify God for his mercy. As
it is written:

"Therefore I will praise you among
the Gentiles;
I will sing the praises of your
name."[d]

[10]Again, it says,

"Rejoice, you Gentiles, with his
people."[e]

[11]And again,

"Praise the Lord, all you Gentiles;
let all the peoples extol him."[f]

[12]And again, Isaiah says,

"The Root of Jesse will spring up,
one who will arise to rule over the
nations;
in him the Gentiles will hope."[g]

[13]May the God of hope fill you with all
joy and peace as you trust in him, so that
you may overflow with hope by the power of the Holy Spirit.

[14]I myself am convinced, my brothers and sisters, that you yourselves are
full of goodness, filled with knowledge
and competent to instruct one another. [15]Yet I have written you quite boldly
on some points to remind you of them
again, because of the grace God gave me
[16]to be a minister of Christ Jesus to the
Gentiles. He gave me the priestly duty of
proclaiming the gospel of God, so that
the Gentiles might become an offering
acceptable to God, sanctified by the
Holy Spirit.

[17]Therefore I glory in Christ Jesus in
my service to God. [18]I will not venture
to speak of anything except what Christ
has accomplished through me in leading the Gentiles to obey God by what I
have said and done — [19]by the power of
signs and wonders, through the power of
the Spirit of God. So from Jerusalem all
the way around to Illyricum, I have fully
proclaimed the gospel of Christ. [20]It has
always been my ambition to preach the
gospel where Christ was not known, so
that I would not be building on some-

[a] *23* Some manuscripts place 16:25-27 here; others after 15:33. [b] *3* Psalm 69:9 [c] *8* Greek *circumcision*
[d] *9* 2 Samuel 22:50; Psalm 18:49 [e] *10* Deut. 32:43 [f] *11* Psalm 117:1 [g] *12* Isaiah 11:10 (see Septuagint)

one else's foundation. 21 Rather, as it is
written:

> "Those who were not told about him
> will see,
> and those who have not heard will
> understand."[a]

22 This is why I have often been hindered
from coming to you.

23 But now that there is no more place
for me to work in these regions, and
since I have been longing for many years
to visit you, 24 I plan to do so when I go
to Spain. I hope to see you while passing
through and to have you assist me on my
journey there, after I have enjoyed your
company for a while. 25 Now, however, I
am on my way to Jerusalem in the service of the Lord's people there. 26 For
Macedonia and Achaia were pleased to
make a contribution for the poor among
the Lord's people in Jerusalem. 27 They
were pleased to do it, and indeed they
owe it to them. For if the Gentiles have
shared in the Jews' spiritual blessings,
they owe it to the Jews to share with
them their material blessings. 28 So after I have completed this task and have
made sure that they have received this
contribution, I will go to Spain and visit you on the way. 29 I know that when I
come to you, I will come in the full measure of the blessing of Christ.

30 I urge you, brothers and sisters, by
our Lord Jesus Christ and by the love of
the Spirit, to join me in my struggle by
praying to God for me. 31 Pray that I may
be kept safe from the unbelievers in Judea and that the contribution I take to
Jerusalem may be favorably received by
the Lord's people there, 32 so that I may
come to you with joy, by God's will, and
in your company be refreshed. 33 The
God of peace be with you all. Amen.

16 I commend to you our sister Phoe-
be, a deacon[b,c] of the church in
Cenchreae. 2 I ask you to receive her in
the Lord in a way worthy of his people
and to give her any help she may need
from you, for she has been the benefac-
tor of many people, including me.

3 Greet Priscilla[d] and Aquila, my co-
workers in Christ Jesus. 4 They
risked their lives for me. Not only I
but all the churches of the Gentiles
are grateful to them.

5 Greet also the church that meets at
their house.

Greet my dear friend Epenetus, who
was the first convert to Christ in the
province of Asia.

6 Greet Mary, who worked very hard for
you.

7 Greet Andronicus and Junia, my fellow Jews who have been in prison with me. They are outstanding
among[e] the apostles, and they were
in Christ before I was.

8 Greet Ampliatus, my dear friend in the
Lord.

9 Greet Urbanus, our co-worker in
Christ, and my dear friend Stachys.

10 Greet Apelles, whose fidelity to Christ
has stood the test.

Greet those who belong to the household of Aristobulus.

11 Greet Herodion, my fellow Jew.

Greet those in the household of Nar-
cissus who are in the Lord.

12 Greet Tryphena and Tryphosa, those
women who work hard in the Lord.

Greet my dear friend Persis, another
woman who has worked very hard
in the Lord.

13 Greet Rufus, chosen in the Lord, and
his mother, who has been a mother
to me, too.

14 Greet Asyncritus, Phlegon, Hermes,
Patrobas, Hermas and the other
brothers and sisters with them.

15 Greet Philologus, Julia, Nereus and
his sister, and Olympas and all the
Lord's people who are with them.

16 Greet one another with a holy kiss.

All the churches of Christ send greetings.

17 I urge you, brothers and sisters,
to watch out for those who cause divisions and put obstacles in your way
that are contrary to the teaching you
have learned. Keep away from them.
18 For such people are not serving our
Lord Christ, but their own appetites. By
smooth talk and flattery they deceive
the minds of naive people. 19 Everyone
has heard about your obedience, so I re-

[a] *21* Isaiah 52:15 (see Septuagint) [b] *1* Or *servant* [c] *1* The word *deacon* refers here to a Christian designated to serve with the overseers/elders of the church in a variety of ways; similarly in Phil. 1:1 and 1 Tim. 3:8,12. [d] *3* Greek *Prisca*, a variant of *Priscilla* [e] *7* Or *are esteemed by*

joice because of you; but I want you to be
wise about what is good, and innocent
about what is evil.
20 The God of peace will soon crush Satan under your feet.

The grace of our Lord Jesus be with you.
21 Timothy, my co-worker, sends his
greetings to you, as do Lucius, Jason and
Sosipater, my fellow Jews.
22 I, Tertius, who wrote down this letter, greet you in the Lord.
23 Gaius, whose hospitality I and the
whole church here enjoy, sends you his
greetings.

Erastus, who is the city's director of
public works, and our brother Quartus
send you their greetings. [24][a]

25 Now to him who is able to establish
you in accordance with my gospel, the
message I proclaim about Jesus Christ,
in keeping with the revelation of the
mystery hidden for long ages past,
26 but
now revealed and made known through
the prophetic writings by the command
of the eternal God, so that all the Gentiles might come to the obedience that
comes from[b] faith—
27 to the only wise
God be glory forever through Jesus
Christ! Amen.

[a] 24 Some manuscripts include here *May the grace of our Lord Jesus Christ be with all of you. Amen.*
[b] 26 Or *that is*

1 CORINTHIANS

The book of Acts describes how Paul brought the royal news about Jesus the Messiah to Macedonia (northern Greece), but then had to flee to Achaia (southern Greece) for his own safety. He visited the city of Corinth there, a wealthy and cosmopolitan commercial center. Many people became believers, so he stayed for a year and a half to teach them.

After he left, the Corinthians wrote to Paul (in a letter we no longer have) with some key questions. The Corinthians had adopted the common Greek idea that physical things are bad, so they wanted to free the human spirit from the body. This affected the way they saw such things as marriage, attendance at ceremonial meals for pagan gods, and even the resurrection of Jesus. In the letter we know as 1 Corinthians Paul addresses all of these concerns as well as questions about worship.

Paul writes that *this world in its present form is passing away*, but the Corinthians can give themselves *fully to the work of the Lord* since their *labor in the Lord is not in vain*. The coming resurrection of the dead and the new world that will accompany it, will show the value of all their current efforts. Paul's practical advice for how to consistently embody the new life of God's kingdom during a particular scene in the biblical drama gives us great insight as we seek to take up our roles today.

---

1 Paul, called to be an apostle of Christ
Jesus by the will of God, and our
brother Sosthenes,

2 To the church of God in Corinth,
to those sanctified in Christ Jesus and
called to be his holy people, together
with all those everywhere who call on
the name of our Lord Jesus Christ—
their Lord and ours:

3 Grace and peace to you from God our
Father and the Lord Jesus Christ.

4 I always thank my God for you because of his grace given you in Christ
Jesus. 5 For in him you have been enriched in every way—with all kinds of
speech and with all knowledge— 6 God
thus confirming our testimony about
Christ among you. 7 Therefore you do not
lack any spiritual gift as you eagerly wait
for our Lord Jesus Christ to be revealed.
8 He will also keep you firm to the end, so
that you will be blameless on the day of
our Lord Jesus Christ. 9 God is faithful,
who has called you into fellowship with
his Son, Jesus Christ our Lord.

10 I appeal to you, brothers and sisters,[a]
in the name of our Lord Jesus Christ,
that all of you agree with one another
in what you say and that there be no divisions among you, but that you be perfectly united in mind and thought. 11 My
brothers and sisters, some from Chloe's
household have informed me that there
are quarrels among you. 12 What I mean
is this: One of you says, "I follow Paul";
another, "I follow Apollos"; another, "I
follow Cephas[b]"; still another, "I follow
Christ."

13 Is Christ divided? Was Paul crucified
for you? Were you baptized in the name
of Paul? 14 I thank God that I did not baptize any of you except Crispus and Gaius,
15 so no one can say that you were baptized in my name. 16 (Yes, I also baptized
the household of Stephanas; beyond
that, I don't remember if I baptized anyone else.) 17 For Christ did not send me
to baptize, but to preach the gospel—
not with wisdom and eloquence, lest the
cross of Christ be emptied of its power.

18 For the message of the cross is foolishness to those who are perishing, but
to us who are being saved it is the power
of God. 19 For it is written:

"I will destroy the wisdom of the wise;
the intelligence of the intelligent I
will frustrate."[c]

20 Where is the wise person? Where is
the teacher of the law? Where is the philosopher of this age? Has not God made
foolish the wisdom of the world? 21 For
since in the wisdom of God the world

[a] *10* The Greek word for *brothers and sisters* (*adelphoi*) refers here to believers, both men and women, as part of God's family; also in verses 11 and 26; and in 2:1; 3:1; 4:6; 6:8; 7:24, 29; 10:1; 11:33; 12:1; 14:6, 20, 26, 39; 15:1, 6, 50, 58; 16:15, 20. [b] *12* That is, Peter [c] *19* Isaiah 29:14

through its wisdom did not know him,
God was pleased through the foolishness of what was preached to save those
who believe. 22 Jews demand signs and
Greeks look for wisdom, 23 but we preach
Christ crucified: a stumbling block to
Jews and foolishness to Gentiles, 24 but
to those whom God has called, both Jews
and Greeks, Christ the power of God and
the wisdom of God. 25 For the foolishness
of God is wiser than human wisdom, and
the weakness of God is stronger than human strength.

26 Brothers and sisters, think of what
you were when you were called. Not
many of you were wise by human standards; not many were influential; not
many were of noble birth. 27 But God
chose the foolish things of the world to
shame the wise; God chose the weak
things of the world to shame the strong.
28 God chose the lowly things of this
world and the despised things—and the
things that are not—to nullify the things
that are, 29 so that no one may boast before him. 30 It is because of him that you
are in Christ Jesus, who has become for
us wisdom from God—that is, our righteousness, holiness and redemption.
31 Therefore, as it is written: "Let the one
who boasts boast in the Lord."[a]

2 And so it was with me, brothers and
sisters. When I came to you, I did not
come with eloquence or human wisdom as I proclaimed to you the testimony about God.[b] 2 For I resolved to know
nothing while I was with you except
Jesus Christ and him crucified. 3 I came
to you in weakness with great fear and
trembling. 4 My message and my preaching were not with wise and persuasive
words, but with a demonstration of the
Spirit's power, 5 so that your faith might
not rest on human wisdom, but on God's
power.

6 We do, however, speak a message of
wisdom among the mature, but not the
wisdom of this age or of the rulers of this
age, who are coming to nothing. 7 No, we
declare God's wisdom, a mystery that
has been hidden and that God destined
for our glory before time began. 8 None
of the rulers of this age understood it, for
if they had, they would not have crucified the Lord of glory. 9 However, as it is
written:

"What no eye has seen,
what no ear has heard,
and what no human mind has
conceived"[c]—
the things God has prepared for
those who love him—

10 these are the things God has revealed
to us by his Spirit.

The Spirit searches all things, even the
deep things of God. 11 For who knows a
person's thoughts except their own spirit within them? In the same way no one
knows the thoughts of God except the
Spirit of God. 12 What we have received
is not the spirit of the world, but the
Spirit who is from God, so that we may
understand what God has freely giv-
en us. 13 This is what we speak, not in
words taught us by human wisdom but
in words taught by the Spirit, explaining spiritual realities with Spirit-taught
words.[d] 14 The person without the Spirit does not accept the things that come
from the Spirit of God but considers
them foolishness, and cannot understand them because they are discerned
only through the Spirit. 15 The person
with the Spirit makes judgments about
all things, but such a person is not subject to merely human judgments, 16 for,

"Who has known the mind of the
Lord
so as to instruct him?"[e]

But we have the mind of Christ.

3 Brothers and sisters, I could not address you as people who live by the
Spirit but as people who are still worldly—mere infants in Christ. 2 I gave you
milk, not solid food, for you were not
yet ready for it. Indeed, you are still not
ready. 3 You are still worldly. For since
there is jealousy and quarreling among
you, are you not worldly? Are you not
acting like mere humans? 4 For when
one says, "I follow Paul," and another,
"I follow Apollos," are you not mere human beings?

5 What, after all, is Apollos? And what
is Paul? Only servants, through whom
you came to believe—as the Lord has
assigned to each his task. 6 I planted the

[a] *31* Jer. 9:24 [b] *1* Some manuscripts *proclaimed to you God's mystery* [c] *9* Isaiah 64:4 [d] *13* Or *Spirit, interpreting spiritual truths to those who are spiritual* [e] *16* Isaiah 40:13

seed, Apollos watered it, but God has been making it grow. 7 So neither the one who plants nor the one who waters is anything, but only God, who makes things grow. 8 The one who plants and the one who waters have one purpose, and they will each be rewarded according to their own labor. 9 For we are co-workers in God's service; you are God's field, God's building.

10 By the grace God has given me, I laid a foundation as a wise builder, and someone else is building on it. But each one should build with care. 11 For no one can lay any foundation other than the one already laid, which is Jesus Christ. 12 If anyone builds on this foundation using gold, silver, costly stones, wood, hay or straw, 13 their work will be shown for what it is, because the Day will bring it to light. It will be revealed with fire, and the fire will test the quality of each person's work. 14 If what has been built survives, the builder will receive a reward. 15 If it is burned up, the builder will suffer loss but yet will be saved—even though only as one escaping through the flames.

16 Don't you know that you yourselves are God's temple and that God's Spirit dwells in your midst? 17 If anyone destroys God's temple, God will destroy that person; for God's temple is sacred, and you together are that temple.

18 Do not deceive yourselves. If any of you think you are wise by the standards of this age, you should become "fools" so that you may become wise. 19 For the wisdom of this world is foolishness in God's sight. As it is written: "He catches the wise in their craftiness"; 20 and again, "The Lord knows that the thoughts of the wise are futile."[b] 21 So then, no more boasting about human leaders! All things are yours, 22 whether Paul or Apollos or Cephas[c] or the world or life or death or the present or the future—all are yours, 23 and you are of Christ, and Christ is of God.

4 This, then, is how you ought to regard us: as servants of Christ and as those entrusted with the mysteries God has revealed. 2 Now it is required that those who have been given a trust must prove faithful. 3 I care very little if I am judged by you or by any human court; indeed, I do not even judge myself. 4 My conscience is clear, but that does not make me innocent. It is the Lord who judges me. 5 Therefore judge nothing before the appointed time; wait until the Lord comes. He will bring to light what is hidden in darkness and will expose the motives of the heart. At that time each will receive their praise from God.

6 Now, brothers and sisters, I have applied these things to myself and Apollos for your benefit, so that you may learn from us the meaning of the saying, "Do not go beyond what is written." Then you will not be puffed up in being a follower of one of us over against the other. 7 For who makes you different from anyone else? What do you have that you did not receive? And if you did receive it, why do you boast as though you did not?

8 Already you have all you want! Already you have become rich! You have begun to reign—and that without us! How I wish that you really had begun to reign so that we also might reign with you! 9 For it seems to me that God has put us apostles on display at the end of the procession, like those condemned to die in the arena. We have been made a spectacle to the whole universe, to angels as well as to human beings. 10 We are fools for Christ, but you are so wise in Christ! We are weak, but you are strong! You are honored, we are dishonored! 11 To this very hour we go hungry and thirsty, we are in rags, we are brutally treated, we are homeless. 12 We work hard with our own hands. When we are cursed, we bless; when we are persecuted, we endure it; 13 when we are slandered, we answer kindly. We have become the scum of the earth, the garbage of the world—right up to this moment.

14 I am writing this not to shame you but to warn you as my dear children. 15 Even if you had ten thousand guardians in Christ, you do not have many fathers, for in Christ Jesus I became your father through the gospel. 16 Therefore I urge you to imitate me. 17 For this reason I have sent to you Timothy, my son whom I love, who is faithful in the Lord. He will remind you of my way of life in Christ Jesus, which agrees with what I teach everywhere in every church.

a *19* Job 5:13 b *20* Psalm 94:11 c *22* That is, Peter

18 Some of you have become arrogant, as if I were not coming to you. 19 But I will come to you very soon, if the Lord is willing, and then I will find out not only how these arrogant people are talking, but what power they have. 20 For the kingdom of God is not a matter of talk but of power. 21 What do you prefer? Shall I come to you with a rod of discipline, or shall I come in love and with a gentle spirit?

5 It is actually reported that there is sexual immorality among you, and of a kind that even pagans do not tolerate: A man is sleeping with his father's wife. 2 And you are proud! Shouldn't you rather have gone into mourning and have put out of your fellowship the man who has been doing this? 3 For my part, even though I am not physically present, I am with you in spirit. As one who is present with you in this way, I have already passed judgment in the name of our Lord Jesus on the one who has been doing this. 4 So when you are assembled and I am with you in spirit, and the power of our Lord Jesus is present, 5 hand this man over to Satan for the destruction of the flesh,[a,b] so that his spirit may be saved on the day of the Lord.

6 Your boasting is not good. Don't you know that a little yeast leavens the whole batch of dough? 7 Get rid of the old yeast, so that you may be a new unleavened batch—as you really are. For Christ, our Passover lamb, has been sacrificed. 8 Therefore let us keep the Festival, not with the old bread leavened with malice and wickedness, but with the unleavened bread of sincerity and truth.

9 I wrote to you in my letter not to associate with sexually immoral people—10 not at all meaning the people of this world who are immoral, or the greedy and swindlers, or idolaters. In that case you would have to leave this world. 11 But now I am writing to you that you must not associate with anyone who claims to be a brother or sister[c] but is sexually immoral or greedy, an idolater or slanderer, a drunkard or swindler. Do not even eat with such people.

12 What business is it of mine to judge those outside the church? Are you not to judge those inside? 13 God will judge those outside. "Expel the wicked person from among you."[d]

6 If any of you has a dispute with another, do you dare to take it before the ungodly for judgment instead of before the Lord's people? 2 Or do you not know that the Lord's people will judge the world? And if you are to judge the world, are you not competent to judge trivial cases? 3 Do you not know that we will judge angels? How much more the things of this life! 4 Therefore, if you have disputes about such matters, do you ask for a ruling from those whose way of life is scorned in the church? 5 I say this to shame you. Is it possible that there is nobody among you wise enough to judge a dispute between believers? 6 But instead, one brother takes another to court—and this in front of unbelievers!

7 The very fact that you have lawsuits among you means you have been completely defeated already. Why not rather be wronged? Why not rather be cheated? 8 Instead, you yourselves cheat and do wrong, and you do this to your brothers and sisters. 9 Or do you not know that wrongdoers will not inherit the kingdom of God? Do not be deceived: Neither the sexually immoral nor idolaters nor adulterers nor men who have sex with men[e] 10 nor thieves nor the greedy nor drunkards nor slanderers nor swindlers will inherit the kingdom of God. 11 And that is what some of you were. But you were washed, you were sanctified, you were justified in the name of the Lord Jesus Christ and by the Spirit of our God.

12 "I have the right to do anything," you say—but not everything is beneficial. "I have the right to do anything"—but I will not be mastered by anything. 13 You say, "Food for the stomach and the stomach for food, and God will destroy them both." The body, however, is not meant

[a] *5* In contexts like this, the Greek word for *flesh* (*sarx*) refers to the sinful state of human beings, often presented as a power in opposition to the Spirit. [b] *5* Or *of his body* [c] *11* The Greek word for *brother or sister* (*adelphos*) refers here to a believer, whether man or woman, as part of God's family; also in 8:11, 13. [d] *13* Deut. 13:5; 17:7; 19:19; 21:21; 22:21,24; 24:7 [e] *9* The words *men who have sex with men* translate two Greek words that refer to the passive and active participants in homosexual acts.

for sexual immorality but for the Lord, and the Lord for the body. [14]By his power God raised the Lord from the dead, and he will raise us also. [15]Do you not know that your bodies are members of Christ himself? Shall I then take the members of Christ and unite them with a prostitute? Never! [16]Do you not know that he who unites himself with a prostitute is one with her in body? For it is said, "The two will become one flesh."[a] [17]But whoever is united with the Lord is one with him in spirit.[b]

[18]Flee from sexual immorality. All other sins a person commits are outside the body, but whoever sins sexually, sins against their own body. [19]Do you not know that your bodies are temples of the Holy Spirit, who is in you, whom you have received from God? You are not your own; [20]you were bought at a price. Therefore honor God with your bodies.

7 Now for the matters you wrote about: "It is good for a man not to have sexual relations with a woman." [2]But since sexual immorality is occurring, each man should have sexual relations with his own wife, and each woman with her own husband. [3]The husband should fulfill his marital duty to his wife, and likewise the wife to her husband. [4]The wife does not have authority over her own body but yields it to her husband. In the same way, the husband does not have authority over his own body but yields it to his wife. [5]Do not deprive each other except perhaps by mutual consent and for a time, so that you may devote yourselves to prayer. Then come together again so that Satan will not tempt you because of your lack of self-control. [6]I say this as a concession, not as a command. [7]I wish that all of you were as I am. But each of you has your own gift from God; one has this gift, another has that.

[8]Now to the unmarried[c] and the widows I say: It is good for them to stay unmarried, as I do. [9]But if they cannot control themselves, they should marry, for it is better to marry than to burn with passion.

[10]To the married I give this command (not I, but the Lord): A wife must not separate from her husband. [11]But if she does, she must remain unmarried or else be reconciled to her husband. And a husband must not divorce his wife.

[12]To the rest I say this (I, not the Lord): If any brother has a wife who is not a believer and she is willing to live with him, he must not divorce her. [13]And if a woman has a husband who is not a believer and he is willing to live with her, she must not divorce him. [14]For the unbelieving husband has been sanctified through his wife, and the unbelieving wife has been sanctified through her believing husband. Otherwise your children would be unclean, but as it is, they are holy.

[15]But if the unbeliever leaves, let it be so. The brother or the sister is not bound in such circumstances; God has called us to live in peace. [16]How do you know, wife, whether you will save your husband? Or, how do you know, husband, whether you will save your wife?

[17]Nevertheless, each person should live as a believer in whatever situation the Lord has assigned to them, just as God has called them. This is the rule I lay down in all the churches. [18]Was a man already circumcised when he was called? He should not become uncircumcised. Was a man uncircumcised when he was called? He should not be circumcised. [19]Circumcision is nothing and uncircumcision is nothing. Keeping God's commands is what counts. [20]Each person should remain in the situation they were in when God called them.

[21]Were you a slave when you were called? Don't let it trouble you—although if you can gain your freedom, do so. [22]For the one who was a slave when called to faith in the Lord is the Lord's freed person; similarly, the one who was free when called is Christ's slave. [23]You were bought at a price; do not become slaves of human beings. [24]Brothers and sisters, each person, as responsible to God, should remain in the situation they were in when God called them.

[25]Now about virgins: I have no command from the Lord, but I give a judgment as one who by the Lord's mercy is trustworthy. [26]Because of the present crisis, I think that it is good for a man to

[a] *16* Gen. 2:24 [b] *17* Or *in the Spirit* [c] *8* Or *widowers*

remain as he is. 27Are you pledged to a
woman? Do not seek to be released. Are
you free from such a commitment? Do
not look for a wife. 28But if you do marry,
you have not sinned; and if a virgin marries, she has not sinned. But those who
marry will face many troubles in this
life, and I want to spare you this.

29What I mean, brothers and sisters, is
that the time is short. From now on those
who have wives should live as if they
do not; 30those who mourn, as if they
did not; those who are happy, as if they
were not; those who buy something, as
if it were not theirs to keep; 31those who
use the things of the world, as if not en-
grossed in them. For this world in its
present form is passing away.

32I would like you to be free from concern. An unmarried man is concerned
about the Lord's affairs—how he can
please the Lord. 33But a married man
is concerned about the affairs of this
world—how he can please his wife—
34and his interests are divided. An unmarried woman or virgin is concerned
about the Lord's affairs: Her aim is to
be devoted to the Lord in both body
and spirit. But a married woman is concerned about the affairs of this world—
how she can please her husband. 35I am
saying this for your own good, not to re-
strict you, but that you may live in a right
way in undivided devotion to the Lord.

36If anyone is worried that he might
not be acting honorably toward the virgin he is engaged to, and if his passions
are too strong[a] and he feels he ought to
marry, he should do as he wants. He is
not sinning. They should get married.
37But the man who has settled the matter in his own mind, who is under no
compulsion but has control over his own
will, and who has made up his mind not
to marry the virgin—this man also does
the right thing. 38So then, he who marries the virgin does right, but he who
does not marry her does better.[b]

39A woman is bound to her husband as
long as he lives. But if her husband dies,
she is free to marry anyone she wishes,
but he must belong to the Lord. 40In my
judgment, she is happier if she stays as
she is—and I think that I too have the
Spirit of God.

8 Now about food sacrificed to idols:
We know that "We all possess knowledge." But knowledge puffs up while
love builds up. 2Those who think they
know something do not yet know as they
ought to know. 3But whoever loves God
is known by God.[c]

4So then, about eating food sacrificed
to idols: We know that "An idol is nothing at all in the world" and that "There
is no God but one." 5For even if there are
so-called gods, whether in heaven or on
earth (as indeed there are many "gods"
and many "lords"), 6yet for us there is
but one God, the Father, from whom
all things came and for whom we live;
and there is but one Lord, Jesus Christ,
through whom all things came and
through whom we live.

7But not everyone possesses this
knowledge. Some people are still so
accustomed to idols that when they eat
sacrificial food they think of it as having
been sacrificed to a god, and since their
conscience is weak, it is defiled. 8But
food does not bring us near to God; we
are no worse if we do not eat, and no better if we do.

9Be careful, however, that the exercise
of your rights does not become a stumbling block to the weak. 10For if someone
with a weak conscience sees you, with all
your knowledge, eating in an idol's temple, won't that person be emboldened to
eat what is sacrificed to idols? 11So this
weak brother or sister, for whom Christ
died, is destroyed by your knowledge.
12When you sin against them in this way
and wound their weak conscience, you
sin against Christ. 13Therefore, if what I
eat causes my brother or sister to fall into
sin, I will never eat meat again, so that I
will not cause them to fall.

[a] 36 Or *if she is getting beyond the usual age for marriage* [b] 36-38 Or *36If anyone thinks he is not treating his daughter properly, and if she is getting along in years* (or *if her passions are too strong*), *and he feels she ought to marry, he should do as he wants. He is not sinning. He should let her get married. 37But the man who has settled the matter in his own mind, who is under no compulsion but has control over his own will, and who has made up his mind to keep the virgin unmarried—this man also does the right thing. 38So then, he who gives his virgin in marriage does right, but he who does not give her in marriage does better.* [c] 2,3 An early manuscript and another ancient witness *think they have knowledge do not yet know as they ought to know. 3But whoever loves truly knows.*

9 Am I not free? Am I not an apostle? Have I not seen Jesus our Lord? Are you not the result of my work in the Lord? 2 Even though I may not be an apostle to others, surely I am to you! For you are the seal of my apostleship in the Lord.

3 This is my defense to those who sit in judgment on me. 4 Don't we have the right to food and drink? 5 Don't we have the right to take a believing wife along with us, as do the other apostles and the Lord's brothers and Cephas[a]? 6 Or is it only I and Barnabas who lack the right to not work for a living?

7 Who serves as a soldier at his own expense? Who plants a vineyard and does not eat its grapes? Who tends a flock and does not drink the milk? 8 Do I say this merely on human authority? Doesn't the Law say the same thing? 9 For it is written in the Law of Moses: "Do not muzzle an ox while it is treading out the grain."[b] Is it about oxen that God is concerned? 10 Surely he says this for us, doesn't he? Yes, this was written for us, because whoever plows and threshes should be able to do so in the hope of sharing in the harvest. 11 If we have sown spiritual seed among you, is it too much if we reap a material harvest from you? 12 If others have this right of support from you, shouldn't we have it all the more?

But we did not use this right. On the contrary, we put up with anything rather than hinder the gospel of Christ.

13 Don't you know that those who serve in the temple get their food from the temple, and that those who serve at the altar share in what is offered on the altar? 14 In the same way, the Lord has commanded that those who preach the gospel should receive their living from the gospel.

15 But I have not used any of these rights. And I am not writing this in the hope that you will do such things for me, for I would rather die than allow anyone to deprive me of this boast. 16 For when I preach the gospel, I cannot boast, since I am compelled to preach. Woe to me if I do not preach the gospel! 17 If I preach voluntarily, I have a reward; if not voluntarily, I am simply discharging the trust committed to me. 18 What then is my reward? Just this: that in preaching the gospel I may offer it free of charge, and so not make full use of my rights as a preacher of the gospel.

19 Though I am free and belong to no one, I have made myself a slave to everyone, to win as many as possible. 20 To the Jews I became like a Jew, to win the Jews. To those under the law I became like one under the law (though I myself am not under the law), so as to win those under the law. 21 To those not having the law I became like one not having the law (though I am not free from God's law but am under Christ's law), so as to win those not having the law. 22 To the weak I became weak, to win the weak. I have become all things to all people so that by all possible means I might save some. 23 I do all this for the sake of the gospel, that I may share in its blessings.

24 Do you not know that in a race all the runners run, but only one gets the prize? Run in such a way as to get the prize. 25 Everyone who competes in the games goes into strict training. They do it to get a crown that will not last, but we do it to get a crown that will last forever. 26 Therefore I do not run like someone running aimlessly; I do not fight like a boxer beating the air. 27 No, I strike a blow to my body and make it my slave so that after I have preached to others, I myself will not be disqualified for the prize.

10 For I do not want you to be ignorant of the fact, brothers and sisters, that our ancestors were all under the cloud and that they all passed through the sea. 2 They were all baptized into Moses in the cloud and in the sea. 3 They all ate the same spiritual food 4 and drank the same spiritual drink; for they drank from the spiritual rock that accompanied them, and that rock was Christ. 5 Nevertheless, God was not pleased with most of them; their bodies were scattered in the wilderness.

6 Now these things occurred as examples to keep us from setting our hearts on evil things as they did. 7 Do not be idolaters, as some of them were; as it is written: "The people sat down to eat and drink and got up to indulge in revelry."[c] 8 We should not commit sexual immorality, as some of them did—and in one day twenty-three thousand of

[a] 5 That is, Peter [b] 9 Deut. 25:4 [c] 7 Exodus 32:6

them died. 9We should not test Christ,[a]
as some of them did—and were killed by
snakes. 10And do not grumble, as some
of them did—and were killed by the destroying angel.
11These things happened to them as
examples and were written down as
warnings for us, on whom the culmination of the ages has come. 12So, if you
think you are standing firm, be careful
that you don't fall! 13No temptation[b] has
overtaken you except what is common
to mankind. And God is faithful; he will
not let you be tempted[b] beyond what you
can bear. But when you are tempted,[b] he
will also provide a way out so that you
can endure it.
14Therefore, my dear friends, flee
from idolatry. 15I speak to sensible people; judge for yourselves what I say. 16Is
not the cup of thanksgiving for which we
give thanks a participation in the blood
of Christ? And is not the bread that we
break a participation in the body of
Christ? 17Because there is one loaf, we,
who are many, are one body, for we all
share the one loaf.
18Consider the people of Israel: Do not
those who eat the sacrifices participate
in the altar? 19Do I mean then that food
sacrificed to an idol is anything, or that
an idol is anything? 20No, but the sacrifices of pagans are offered to demons,
not to God, and I do not want you to be
participants with demons. 21You cannot drink the cup of the Lord and the
cup of demons too; you cannot have a
part in both the Lord's table and the table of demons. 22Are we trying to arouse
the Lord's jealousy? Are we stronger
than he?
23"I have the right to do anything,"
you say—but not everything is beneficial. "I have the right to do anything"—
but not everything is constructive. 24No
one should seek their own good, but the
good of others.
25Eat anything sold in the meat market
without raising questions of conscience,
26for, "The earth is the Lord's, and everything in it."[c]
27If an unbeliever invites you to a meal
and you want to go, eat whatever is put
before you without raising questions
of conscience. 28But if someone says to
you, "This has been offered in sacrifice,"
then do not eat it, both for the sake of
the one who told you and for the sake of
conscience. 29I am referring to the other
person's conscience, not yours. For why
is my freedom being judged by another's
conscience? 30If I take part in the meal
with thankfulness, why am I denounced
because of something I thank God for?
31So whether you eat or drink or whatever you do, do it all for the glory of
God. 32Do not cause anyone to stumble,
whether Jews, Greeks or the church of
God—33even as I try to please everyone
in every way. For I am not seeking my
own good but the good of many, so that
11 they may be saved. 1Follow my example, as I follow the example of
Christ.

2I praise you for remembering me in
everything and for holding to the traditions just as I passed them on to you.
3But I want you to realize that the head
of every man is Christ, and the head of
the woman is man,[d] and the head of
Christ is God. 4Every man who prays
or prophesies with his head covered
dishonors his head. 5But every woman
who prays or prophesies with her head
uncovered dishonors her head—it is the
same as having her head shaved. 6For if
a woman does not cover her head, she
might as well have her hair cut off; but
if it is a disgrace for a woman to have her
hair cut off or her head shaved, then she
should cover her head.
7A man ought not to cover his head,[e]
since he is the image and glory of God;
but woman is the glory of man. 8For man
did not come from woman, but woman
from man; 9neither was man created for
woman, but woman for man. 10It is for
this reason that a woman ought to have
authority over her own[f] head, because of
the angels. 11Nevertheless, in the Lord
woman is not independent of man, nor

[a] 9 Some manuscripts *test the Lord* [b] 13 The Greek for *temptation* and *tempted* can also mean *testing* and *tested.* [c] 26 Psalm 24:1 [d] 3 Or *of the wife is her husband* [e] 4-7 Or *4Every man who prays or prophesies with long hair dishonors his head. 5But every woman who prays or prophesies with no covering of hair dishonors her head—she is just like one of the "shorn women." 6If a woman has no covering, let her be for now with short hair; but since it is a disgrace for a woman to have her hair shorn or shaved, she should grow it again. 7A man ought not to have long hair* [f] 10 Or *have a sign of authority on her*

is man independent of woman. 12 For as woman came from man, so also man is born of woman. But everything comes from God.

13 Judge for yourselves: Is it proper for a woman to pray to God with her head uncovered? 14 Does not the very nature of things teach you that if a man has long hair, it is a disgrace to him, 15 but that if a woman has long hair, it is her glory? For long hair is given to her as a covering. 16 If anyone wants to be contentious about this, we have no other practice—nor do the churches of God.

17 In the following directives I have no praise for you, for your meetings do more harm than good. 18 In the first place, I hear that when you come together as a church, there are divisions among you, and to some extent I believe it. 19 No doubt there have to be differences among you to show which of you have God's approval. 20 So then, when you come together, it is not the Lord's Supper you eat, 21 for when you are eating, some of you go ahead with your own private suppers. As a result, one person remains hungry and another gets drunk. 22 Don't you have homes to eat and drink in? Or do you despise the church of God by humiliating those who have nothing? What shall I say to you? Shall I praise you? Certainly not in this matter!

23 For I received from the Lord what I also passed on to you: The Lord Jesus, on the night he was betrayed, took bread, 24 and when he had given thanks, he broke it and said, "This is my body, which is for you; do this in remembrance of me." 25 In the same way, after supper he took the cup, saying, "This cup is the new covenant in my blood; do this, whenever you drink it, in remembrance of me." 26 For whenever you eat this bread and drink this cup, you proclaim the Lord's death until he comes.

27 So then, whoever eats the bread or drinks the cup of the Lord in an unworthy manner will be guilty of sinning against the body and blood of the Lord. 28 Everyone ought to examine themselves before they eat of the bread and drink from the cup. 29 For those who eat and drink without discerning the body of Christ eat and drink judgment on themselves. 30 That is why many among you are weak and sick, and a number of you have fallen asleep. 31 But if we were more discerning with regard to ourselves, we would not come under such judgment. 32 Nevertheless, when we are judged in this way by the Lord, we are being disciplined so that we will not be finally condemned with the world.

33 So then, my brothers and sisters, when you gather to eat, you should all eat together. 34 Anyone who is hungry should eat something at home, so that when you meet together it may not result in judgment.

And when I come I will give further directions.

12 Now about the gifts of the Spirit, brothers and sisters, I do not want you to be uninformed. 2 You know that when you were pagans, somehow or other you were influenced and led astray to mute idols. 3 Therefore I want you to know that no one who is speaking by the Spirit of God says, "Jesus be cursed," and no one can say, "Jesus is Lord," except by the Holy Spirit.

4 There are different kinds of gifts, but the same Spirit distributes them. 5 There are different kinds of service, but the same Lord. 6 There are different kinds of working, but in all of them and in everyone it is the same God at work.

7 Now to each one the manifestation of the Spirit is given for the common good. 8 To one there is given through the Spirit a message of wisdom, to another a message of knowledge by means of the same Spirit, 9 to another faith by the same Spirit, to another gifts of healing by that one Spirit, 10 to another miraculous powers, to another prophecy, to another distinguishing between spirits, to another speaking in different kinds of tongues,[a] and to still another the interpretation of tongues.[a] 11 All these are the work of one and the same Spirit, and he distributes them to each one, just as he determines.

12 Just as a body, though one, has many parts, but all its many parts form one body, so it is with Christ. 13 For we were all baptized by[b] one Spirit so as to form one body—whether Jews or Gentiles,

[a] *10* Or *languages*; also in verse 28 [b] *13* Or *with*; or *in*

slave or free — and we were all given the
one Spirit to drink. 14 Even so the body is
not made up of one part but of many.
15 Now if the foot should say, "Because
I am not a hand, I do not belong to the
body," it would not for that reason stop
being part of the body. 16 And if the ear
should say, "Because I am not an eye, I
do not belong to the body," it would not
for that reason stop being part of the
body. 17 If the whole body were an eye,
where would the sense of hearing be?
If the whole body were an ear, where
would the sense of smell be? 18 But in fact
God has placed the parts in the body, every one of them, just as he wanted them
to be. 19 If they were all one part, where
would the body be? 20 As it is, there are
many parts, but one body.
21 The eye cannot say to the hand, "I
don't need you!" And the head cannot
say to the feet, "I don't need you!" 22 On
the contrary, those parts of the body that
seem to be weaker are indispensable,
23 and the parts that we think are less
honorable we treat with special honor.
And the parts that are unpresentable are
treated with special modesty, 24 while
our presentable parts need no special
treatment. But God has put the body together, giving greater honor to the parts
that lacked it, 25 so that there should be
no division in the body, but that its parts
should have equal concern for each other. 26 If one part suffers, every part suffers with it; if one part is honored, every
part rejoices with it.
27 Now you are the body of Christ,
and each one of you is a part of it. 28 And
God has placed in the church first of all
apostles, second prophets, third teachers, then miracles, then gifts of healing,
of helping, of guidance, and of different
kinds of tongues. 29 Are all apostles?
Are all prophets? Are all teachers? Do
all work miracles? 30 Do all have gifts of
healing? Do all speak in tongues[a]? Do
all interpret? 31 Now eagerly desire the
greater gifts.

And yet I will show you the most excellent way.

13 If I speak in the tongues[b] of men
or of angels, but do not have love, I
am only a resounding gong or a clang-
ing cymbal. 2 If I have the gift of prophecy and can fathom all mysteries and all
knowledge, and if I have a faith that can
move mountains, but do not have love, I
am nothing. 3 If I give all I possess to the
poor and give over my body to hardship
that I may boast,[c] but do not have love, I
gain nothing.
4 Love is patient, love is kind. It does
not envy, it does not boast, it is not
proud. 5 It does not dishonor others, it is
not self-seeking, it is not easily angered,
it keeps no record of wrongs. 6 Love does
not delight in evil but rejoices with the
truth. 7 It always protects, always trusts,
always hopes, always perseveres.
8 Love never fails. But where there are
prophecies, they will cease; where there
are tongues, they will be stilled; where
there is knowledge, it will pass away.
9 For we know in part and we prophesy in
part, 10 but when completeness comes,
what is in part disappears. 11 When I was
a child, I talked like a child, I thought
like a child, I reasoned like a child.
When I became a man, I put the ways
of childhood behind me. 12 For now we
see only a reflection as in a mirror; then
we shall see face to face. Now I know in
part; then I shall know fully, even as I am
fully known.
13 And now these three remain: faith,
hope and love. But the greatest of these
is love.

14 Follow the way of love and eagerly
desire gifts of the Spirit, especially
prophecy. 2 For anyone who speaks in a
tongue[d] does not speak to people but to
God. Indeed, no one understands them;
they utter mysteries by the Spirit. 3 But
the one who prophesies speaks to people for their strengthening, encouraging and comfort. 4 Anyone who speaks
in a tongue edifies themselves, but the
one who prophesies edifies the church.
5 I would like every one of you to speak
in tongues,[e] but I would rather have
you prophesy. The one who prophesies
is greater than the one who speaks in
tongues,[e] unless someone interprets, so
that the church may be edified.
6 Now, brothers and sisters, if I come
to you and speak in tongues, what good
will I be to you, unless I bring you some

[a] *30* Or *other languages* [b] *1* Or *languages* [c] *3* Some manuscripts *body to the flames* [d] *2* Or *in another language*; also in verses 4, 13, 14, 19, 26 and 27 [e] *5* Or *in other languages*; also in verses 6, 18, 22, 23 and 39

revelation or knowledge or prophecy or word of instruction? 7 Even in the case of lifeless things that make sounds, such as the pipe or harp, how will anyone know what tune is being played unless there is a distinction in the notes? 8 Again, if the trumpet does not sound a clear call, who will get ready for battle? 9 So it is with you. Unless you speak intelligible words with your tongue, how will anyone know what you are saying? You will just be speaking into the air. 10 Undoubtedly there are all sorts of languages in the world, yet none of them is without meaning. 11 If then I do not grasp the meaning of what someone is saying, I am a foreigner to the speaker, and the speaker is a foreigner to me. 12 So it is with you. Since you are eager for gifts of the Spirit, try to excel in those that build up the church.

13 For this reason the one who speaks in a tongue should pray that they may interpret what they say. 14 For if I pray in a tongue, my spirit prays, but my mind is unfruitful. 15 So what shall I do? I will pray with my spirit, but I will also pray with my understanding; I will sing with my spirit, but I will also sing with my understanding. 16 Otherwise when you are praising God in the Spirit, how can someone else, who is now put in the position of an inquirer,[a] say "Amen" to your thanksgiving, since they do not know what you are saying? 17 You are giving thanks well enough, but no one else is edified.

18 I thank God that I speak in tongues more than all of you. 19 But in the church I would rather speak five intelligible words to instruct others than ten thousand words in a tongue.

20 Brothers and sisters, stop thinking like children. In regard to evil be infants, but in your thinking be adults. 21 In the Law it is written:

"With other tongues
 and through the lips of foreigners
I will speak to this people,
 but even then they will not listen
 to me,
 says the Lord."[b]

22 Tongues, then, are a sign, not for believers but for unbelievers; prophecy, however, is not for unbelievers but for believers. 23 So if the whole church comes together and everyone speaks in tongues, and inquirers or unbelievers come in, will they not say that you are out of your mind? 24 But if an unbeliever or an inquirer comes in while everyone is prophesying, they are convicted of sin and are brought under judgment by all, 25 as the secrets of their hearts are laid bare. So they will fall down and worship God, exclaiming, "God is really among you!"

26 What then shall we say, brothers and sisters? When you come together, each of you has a hymn, or a word of instruction, a revelation, a tongue or an interpretation. Everything must be done so that the church may be built up. 27 If anyone speaks in a tongue, two—or at the most three—should speak, one at a time, and someone must interpret. 28 If there is no interpreter, the speaker should keep quiet in the church and speak to himself and to God.

29 Two or three prophets should speak, and the others should weigh carefully what is said. 30 And if a revelation comes to someone who is sitting down, the first speaker should stop. 31 For you can all prophesy in turn so that everyone may be instructed and encouraged. 32 The spirits of prophets are subject to the control of prophets. 33 For God is not a God of disorder but of peace—as in all the congregations of the Lord's people.

34 Women[c] should remain silent in the churches. They are not allowed to speak, but must be in submission, as the law says. 35 If they want to inquire about something, they should ask their own husbands at home; for it is disgraceful for a woman to speak in the church.[d]

36 Or did the word of God originate with you? Or are you the only people it has reached? 37 If anyone thinks they are a prophet or otherwise gifted by the Spirit, let them acknowledge that what I am writing to you is the Lord's command. 38 But if anyone ignores this, they will themselves be ignored.[e]

[a] *16* The Greek word for *inquirer* is a technical term for someone not fully initiated into a religion; also in verses 23 and 24. [b] *21* Isaiah 28:11,12 [c] *33,34* Or *peace. As in all the congregations of the Lord's people, 34women* [d] *34,35* In a few manuscripts these verses come after verse 40. [e] *38* Some manuscripts *But anyone who is ignorant of this will be ignored*

[39]Therefore, my brothers and sisters, be eager to prophesy, and do not forbid speaking in tongues. [40]But everything should be done in a fitting and orderly way.

15 Now, brothers and sisters, I want to remind you of the gospel I preached to you, which you received and on which you have taken your stand. [2]By this gospel you are saved, if you hold firmly to the word I preached to you. Otherwise, you have believed in vain.

[3]For what I received I passed on to you as of first importance[a]: that Christ died for our sins according to the Scriptures, [4]that he was buried, that he was raised on the third day according to the Scriptures, [5]and that he appeared to Cephas,[b] and then to the Twelve. [6]After that, he appeared to more than five hundred of the brothers and sisters at the same time, most of whom are still living, though some have fallen asleep. [7]Then he appeared to James, then to all the apostles, [8]and last of all he appeared to me also, as to one abnormally born.

[9]For I am the least of the apostles and do not even deserve to be called an apostle, because I persecuted the church of God. [10]But by the grace of God I am what I am, and his grace to me was not without effect. No, I worked harder than all of them—yet not I, but the grace of God that was with me. [11]Whether, then, it is I or they, this is what we preach, and this is what you believed.

[12]But if it is preached that Christ has been raised from the dead, how can some of you say that there is no resurrection of the dead? [13]If there is no resurrection of the dead, then not even Christ has been raised. [14]And if Christ has not been raised, our preaching is useless and so is your faith. [15]More than that, we are then found to be false witnesses about God, for we have testified about God that he raised Christ from the dead. But he did not raise him if in fact the dead are not raised. [16]For if the dead are not raised, then Christ has not been raised either. [17]And if Christ has not been raised, your faith is futile; you are still in your sins. [18]Then those also who have fallen asleep in Christ are lost. [19]If only for this life we have hope in Christ, we are of all people most to be pitied.

[20]But Christ has indeed been raised from the dead, the firstfruits of those who have fallen asleep. [21]For since death came through a man, the resurrection of the dead comes also through a man. [22]For as in Adam all die, so in Christ all will be made alive. [23]But each in turn: Christ, the firstfruits; then, when he comes, those who belong to him. [24]Then the end will come, when he hands over the kingdom to God the Father after he has destroyed all dominion, authority and power. [25]For he must reign until he has put all his enemies under his feet. [26]The last enemy to be destroyed is death. [27]For he "has put everything under his feet."[c] Now when it says that "everything" has been put under him, it is clear that this does not include God himself, who put everything under Christ. [28]When he has done this, then the Son himself will be made subject to him who put everything under him, so that God may be all in all.

[29]Now if there is no resurrection, what will those do who are baptized for the dead? If the dead are not raised at all, why are people baptized for them? [30]And as for us, why do we endanger ourselves every hour? [31]I face death every day—yes, just as surely as I boast about you in Christ Jesus our Lord. [32]If I fought wild beasts in Ephesus with no more than human hopes, what have I gained? If the dead are not raised,

"Let us eat and drink,
for tomorrow we die."[d]

[33]Do not be misled: "Bad company corrupts good character."[e] [34]Come back to your senses as you ought, and stop sinning; for there are some who are ignorant of God—I say this to your shame.

[35]But someone will ask, "How are the dead raised? With what kind of body will they come?" [36]How foolish! What you sow does not come to life unless it dies. [37]When you sow, you do not plant the body that will be, but just a seed, perhaps of wheat or of something else. [38]But God gives it a body as he has determined, and to each kind of seed he gives its own body. [39]Not all flesh is the

[a] *3* Or *you at the first* [b] *5* That is, Peter [c] *27* Psalm 8:6 [d] *32* Isaiah 22:13 [e] *33* From the Greek poet Menander

same: People have one kind of flesh, animals have another, birds another and fish another. 40There are also heavenly bodies and there are earthly bodies; but the splendor of the heavenly bodies is one kind, and the splendor of the earthly bodies is another. 41The sun has one kind of splendor, the moon another and the stars another; and star differs from star in splendor.

42So will it be with the resurrection of the dead. The body that is sown is perishable, it is raised imperishable; 43it is sown in dishonor, it is raised in glory; it is sown in weakness, it is raised in power; 44it is sown a natural body, it is raised a spiritual body.

If there is a natural body, there is also a spiritual body. 45So it is written: "The first man Adam became a living being"[a]; the last Adam, a life-giving spirit. 46The spiritual did not come first, but the natural, and after that the spiritual. 47The first man was of the dust of the earth; the second man is of heaven. 48As was the earthly man, so are those who are of the earth; and as is the heavenly man, so also are those who are of heaven. 49And just as we have borne the image of the earthly man, so shall we[b] bear the image of the heavenly man.

50I declare to you, brothers and sisters, that flesh and blood cannot inherit the kingdom of God, nor does the perishable inherit the imperishable. 51Listen, I tell you a mystery: We will not all sleep, but we will all be changed— 52in a flash, in the twinkling of an eye, at the last trumpet. For the trumpet will sound, the dead will be raised imperishable, and we will be changed. 53For the perishable must clothe itself with the imperishable, and the mortal with immortality. 54When the perishable has been clothed with the imperishable, and the mortal with immortality, then the saying that is written will come true: "Death has been swallowed up in victory."[c]

55"Where, O death, is your victory?
Where, O death, is your sting?"[d]

56The sting of death is sin, and the power of sin is the law. 57But thanks be to God! He gives us the victory through our Lord Jesus Christ.

58Therefore, my dear brothers and sisters, stand firm. Let nothing move you. Always give yourselves fully to the work of the Lord, because you know that your labor in the Lord is not in vain.

16 Now about the collection for the Lord's people: Do what I told the Galatian churches to do. 2On the first day of every week, each one of you should set aside a sum of money in keeping with your income, saving it up, so that when I come no collections will have to be made. 3Then, when I arrive, I will give letters of introduction to the men you approve and send them with your gift to Jerusalem. 4If it seems advisable for me to go also, they will accompany me.

5After I go through Macedonia, I will come to you—for I will be going through Macedonia. 6Perhaps I will stay with you for a while, or even spend the winter, so that you can help me on my journey, wherever I go. 7For I do not want to see you now and make only a passing visit; I hope to spend some time with you, if the Lord permits. 8But I will stay on at Ephesus until Pentecost, 9because a great door for effective work has opened to me, and there are many who oppose me.

10When Timothy comes, see to it that he has nothing to fear while he is with you, for he is carrying on the work of the Lord, just as I am. 11No one, then, should treat him with contempt. Send him on his way in peace so that he may return to me. I am expecting him along with the brothers.

12Now about our brother Apollos: I strongly urged him to go to you with the brothers. He was quite unwilling to go now, but he will go when he has the opportunity.

13Be on your guard; stand firm in the faith; be courageous; be strong. 14Do everything in love.

15You know that the household of Stephanas were the first converts in Achaia, and they have devoted themselves to the service of the Lord's people. I urge you, brothers and sisters, 16to submit to such people and to everyone who joins in the work and labors at it. 17I was

[a] *45* Gen. 2:7 [b] *49* Some early manuscripts *so let us* [c] *54* Isaiah 25:8 [d] *55* Hosea 13:14

glad when Stephanas, Fortunatus and
Achaicus arrived, because they have
supplied what was lacking from you.
18 For they refreshed my spirit and yours
also. Such men deserve recognition.
19 The churches in the province of Asia
send you greetings. Aquila and Priscilla[a] greet you warmly in the Lord, and
so does the church that meets at their
house. 20 All the brothers and sisters
here send you greetings. Greet one another with a holy kiss.
21 I, Paul, write this greeting in my own
hand.
22 If anyone does not love the Lord, let
that person be cursed! Come, Lord[b]!
23 The grace of the Lord Jesus be with
you.
24 My love to all of you in Christ Jesus.
Amen.[c]

[a] *19* Greek *Prisca,* a variant of *Priscilla*
[b] *22* The Greek for *Come, Lord* reproduces an Aramaic expression (*Marana tha*) used by early Christians.
[c] *24* Some manuscripts do not have *Amen.*

2 CORINTHIANS

Paul's first letter to the believers in Corinth gives us a glimpse into his deeply personal and tumultuous relationship with this gathering of Jesus-followers. The letter we know as 2 Corinthians further reveals the triumphs and struggles that result when life in the present age meets up with the in-breaking reality of God's kingdom. Here we see Paul working to repair relationships, explain various changes in travel plans, make practical arrangements for collecting a gift for the struggling believers in Jerusalem, and directly confront challenges to his own leadership by the self-proclaimed "super-apostles."

In the four main parts of the letter, each introduced by a reference to a place, Paul envisions himself in different locations, recalling or anticipating his relationship with the Corinthians. The single theme running through these sections is that God will comfort us in all our troubles, and we will offer this comfort to each other. This models the life of Jesus himself, who suffered first and then was comforted. Like the crucified Messiah, we are weak, yet we live in God's power.

In the final section, however, Paul feels he has no choice but to make the Corinthians uncomfortable, to help them face their present condition. But he ends the letter hopefully, calling on them to rejoice in God's grace, love and fellowship.

---

1 Paul, an apostle of Christ Jesus by
the will of God, and Timothy our
brother,

To the church of God in Corinth, together with all his holy people throughout Achaia:

2Grace and peace to you from God our
Father and the Lord Jesus Christ.

3Praise be to the God and Father of our
Lord Jesus Christ, the Father of compassion and the God of all comfort, 4who
comforts us in all our troubles, so that
we can comfort those in any trouble
with the comfort we ourselves receive
from God. 5For just as we share abundantly in the sufferings of Christ, so also
our comfort abounds through Christ. 6If
we are distressed, it is for your comfort
and salvation; if we are comforted, it is
for your comfort, which produces in you
patient endurance of the same sufferings we suffer. 7And our hope for you is
firm, because we know that just as you
share in our sufferings, so also you share
in our comfort.

8We do not want you to be uninformed, brothers and sisters,[a] about the
troubles we experienced in the province
of Asia. We were under great pressure,
far beyond our ability to endure, so
that we despaired of life itself. 9Indeed,
we felt we had received the sentence of
death. But this happened that we might
not rely on ourselves but on God, who
raises the dead. 10He has delivered us
from such a deadly peril, and he will deliver us again. On him we have set our
hope that he will continue to deliver us,
11as you help us by your prayers. Then
many will give thanks on our behalf for
the gracious favor granted us in answer
to the prayers of many.

12Now this is our boast: Our conscience testifies that we have conducted
ourselves in the world, and especially
in our relations with you, with integrity[b] and godly sincerity. We have done
so, relying not on worldly wisdom but
on God's grace. 13For we do not write
you anything you cannot read or understand. And I hope that, 14as you have
understood us in part, you will come to
understand fully that you can boast of us
just as we will boast of you in the day of
the Lord Jesus.

15Because I was confident of this, I
wanted to visit you first so that you might
benefit twice. 16I wanted to visit you on
my way to Macedonia and to come back
to you from Macedonia, and then to have
you send me on my way to Judea. 17Was
I fickle when I intended to do this? Or do
I make my plans in a worldly manner so
that in the same breath I say both "Yes,
yes" and "No, no"?

[a] *8* The Greek word for *brothers and sisters* (*adelphoi*) refers here to believers, both men and women, as part of God's family; also in 8:1; 13:11. [b] *12* Many manuscripts *holiness*

18But as surely as God is faithful, our
message to you is not "Yes" and "No."
19For the Son of God, Jesus Christ, who
was preached among you by us — by me
and Silas[a] and Timothy — was not "Yes"
and "No," but in him it has always been
"Yes." 20For no matter how many promises God has made, they are "Yes" in
Christ. And so through him the "Amen"
is spoken by us to the glory of God.
21Now it is God who makes both us and
you stand firm in Christ. He anointed
us, 22set his seal of ownership on us, and
put his Spirit in our hearts as a deposit,
guaranteeing what is to come.

23I call God as my witness — and I
stake my life on it — that it was in order to spare you that I did not return to
Corinth. 24Not that we lord it over your
faith, but we work with you for your joy,
because it is by faith you stand firm.

2 1So I made up my mind that I would
not make another painful visit to you.
2For if I grieve you, who is left to make
me glad but you whom I have grieved?
3I wrote as I did, so that when I came I
would not be distressed by those who should have made me rejoice. I had confidence in all of you, that you would
all share my joy. 4For I wrote you out of
great distress and anguish of heart and with many tears, not to grieve you but to let you know the depth of my love for you.

5If anyone has caused grief, he has not
so much grieved me as he has grieved all of you to some extent — not to put it too severely. 6The punishment inflicted on him by the majority is sufficient.
7Now instead, you ought to forgive and
comfort him, so that he will not be overwhelmed by excessive sorrow. 8I urge
you, therefore, to reaffirm your love for
him. 9Another reason I wrote you was
to see if you would stand the test and be obedient in everything. 10Anyone
you forgive, I also forgive. And what I have forgiven — if there was anything to forgive — I have forgiven in the sight of
Christ for your sake, 11in order that Sa-
tan might not outwit us. For we are not unaware of his schemes.

12Now when I went to Troas to preach
the gospel of Christ and found that the Lord had opened a door for me, 13I still
had no peace of mind, because I did not find my brother Titus there. So I said goodbye to them and went on to Macedonia.

14But thanks be to God, who always
leads us as captives in Christ's triumphal procession and uses us to spread the aroma of the knowledge of him everywhere. 15For we are to God the
pleasing aroma of Christ among those who are being saved and those who are perishing. 16To the one we are an aroma
that brings death; to the other, an aroma that brings life. And who is equal to such a task? 17Unlike so many, we do not
peddle the word of God for profit. On the contrary, in Christ we speak before God with sincerity, as those sent from God.

3 Are we beginning to commend ourselves again? Or do we need, like some people, letters of recommendation to you or from you? 2You yourselves are
our letter, written on our hearts, known and read by everyone. 3You show that
you are a letter from Christ, the result of our ministry, written not with ink but with the Spirit of the living God, not on tablets of stone but on tablets of human hearts.

4Such confidence we have through
Christ before God. 5Not that we are com-
petent in ourselves to claim anything for ourselves, but our competence comes from God. 6He has made us competent
as ministers of a new covenant — not of the letter but of the Spirit; for the letter kills, but the Spirit gives life.

7Now if the ministry that brought
death, which was engraved in letters on stone, came with glory, so that the Israelites could not look steadily at the face of Moses because of its glory, transitory though it was, 8will not the ministry of
the Spirit be even more glorious? 9If the
ministry that brought condemnation was glorious, how much more glorious is the ministry that brings righteousness!
10For what was glorious has no glory
now in comparison with the surpassing glory. 11And if what was transitory came
with glory, how much greater is the glory of that which lasts!

12Therefore, since we have such a
hope, we are very bold. 13We are not like

[a] *19* Greek *Silvanus,* a variant of *Silas*

Moses, who would put a veil over his
face to prevent the Israelites from seeing the end of what was passing away.
14But their minds were made dull, for
to this day the same veil remains when
the old covenant is read. It has not been
removed, because only in Christ is it tak-
en away. 15Even to this day when Moses
is read, a veil covers their hearts. 16But
whenever anyone turns to the Lord, the
veil is taken away. 17Now the Lord is the
Spirit, and where the Spirit of the Lord is,
there is freedom. 18And we all, who with
unveiled faces contemplate[a] the Lord's
glory, are being transformed into his
image with ever-increasing glory, which
comes from the Lord, who is the Spirit.

4 Therefore, since through God's mercy we have this ministry, we do not
lose heart. 2Rather, we have renounced
secret and shameful ways; we do not use
deception, nor do we distort the word of
God. On the contrary, by setting forth
the truth plainly we commend ourselves to everyone's conscience in the
sight of God. 3And even if our gospel is
veiled, it is veiled to those who are perishing. 4The god of this age has blinded
the minds of unbelievers, so that they
cannot see the light of the gospel that
displays the glory of Christ, who is the
image of God. 5For what we preach is
not ourselves, but Jesus Christ as Lord,
and ourselves as your servants for Jesus'
sake. 6For God, who said, "Let light
shine out of darkness,"[b] made his light
shine in our hearts to give us the light of
the knowledge of God's glory displayed
in the face of Christ.

7But we have this treasure in jars of
clay to show that this all-surpassing
power is from God and not from us. 8We
are hard pressed on every side, but not
crushed; perplexed, but not in despair;
9persecuted, but not abandoned; struck
down, but not destroyed. 10We always
carry around in our body the death of
Jesus, so that the life of Jesus may also
be revealed in our body. 11For we who
are alive are always being given over to
death for Jesus' sake, so that his life may
also be revealed in our mortal body. 12So
then, death is at work in us, but life is at
work in you.

13It is written: "I believed; therefore
I have spoken."[c] Since we have that
same spirit of[d] faith, we also believe and
therefore speak, 14because we know that
the one who raised the Lord Jesus from
the dead will also raise us with Jesus and
present us with you to himself. 15All this
is for your benefit, so that the grace that
is reaching more and more people may
cause thanksgiving to overflow to the
glory of God.

16Therefore we do not lose heart.
Though outwardly we are wasting away,
yet inwardly we are being renewed day
by day. 17For our light and momentary
troubles are achieving for us an eternal
glory that far outweighs them all. 18So
we fix our eyes not on what is seen, but
on what is unseen, since what is seen is
temporary, but what is unseen is eternal.

5 For we know that if the earthly tent we
live in is destroyed, we have a building from God, an eternal house in heav-
en, not built by human hands. 2Mean-
while we groan, longing to be clothed
instead with our heavenly dwelling,
3because when we are clothed, we will
not be found naked. 4For while we are
in this tent, we groan and are burdened,
because we do not wish to be unclothed
but to be clothed instead with our heavenly dwelling, so that what is mortal
may be swallowed up by life. 5Now the
one who has fashioned us for this very
purpose is God, who has given us the
Spirit as a deposit, guaranteeing what
is to come.

6Therefore we are always confident
and know that as long as we are at home
in the body we are away from the Lord.
7For we live by faith, not by sight. 8We
are confident, I say, and would prefer
to be away from the body and at home
with the Lord. 9So we make it our goal to
please him, whether we are at home in
the body or away from it. 10For we must
all appear before the judgment seat of
Christ, so that each of us may receive
what is due us for the things done while
in the body, whether good or bad.

11Since, then, we know what it is to
fear the Lord, we try to persuade others.
What we are is plain to God, and I hope
it is also plain to your conscience. 12We
are not trying to commend ourselves to

a 18 Or *reflect* b 6 Gen. 1:3 c 13 Psalm 116:10 (see Septuagint) d 13 Or *Spirit-given*

you again, but are giving you an opportunity to take pride in us, so that you can
answer those who take pride in what is
seen rather than in what is in the heart.
13If we are "out of our mind," as some
say, it is for God; if we are in our right
mind, it is for you. 14For Christ's love
compels us, because we are convinced
that one died for all, and therefore all
died. 15And he died for all, that those
who live should no longer live for themselves but for him who died for them and
was raised again.
16So from now on we regard no one
from a worldly point of view. Though we
once regarded Christ in this way, we do
so no longer. 17Therefore, if anyone is in
Christ, the new creation has come:[a] The
old has gone, the new is here! 18All this is
from God, who reconciled us to himself
through Christ and gave us the ministry
of reconciliation: 19that God was reconciling the world to himself in Christ,
not counting people's sins against them.
And he has committed to us the message of reconciliation. 20We are therefore Christ's ambassadors, as though
God were making his appeal through
us. We implore you on Christ's behalf:
Be reconciled to God. 21God made him
who had no sin to be sin[b] for us, so that
in him we might become the righteousness of God.

6 As God's co-workers we urge you not
to receive God's grace in vain. 2For
he says,

"In the time of my favor I heard you,
and in the day of salvation I helped
you."[c]

I tell you, now is the time of God's favor,
now is the day of salvation.
3We put no stumbling block in anyone's path, so that our ministry will not
be discredited. 4Rather, as servants of
God we commend ourselves in every
way: in great endurance; in troubles,
hardships and distresses; 5in beatings,
imprisonments and riots; in hard work,
sleepless nights and hunger; 6in purity,
understanding, patience and kindness;
in the Holy Spirit and in sincere love;
7in truthful speech and in the power of
God; with weapons of righteousness in
the right hand and in the left; 8through
glory and dishonor, bad report and good
report; genuine, yet regarded as impos-
tors; 9known, yet regarded as unknown;
dying, and yet we live on; beaten, and yet
not killed; 10sorrowful, yet always rejoicing; poor, yet making many rich; having
nothing, and yet possessing everything.
11We have spoken freely to you, Corinthians, and opened wide our hearts to
you. 12We are not withholding our affection from you, but you are withholding
yours from us. 13As a fair exchange—I
speak as to my children—open wide
your hearts also.
14Do not be yoked together with unbelievers. For what do righteousness and
wickedness have in common? Or what
fellowship can light have with darkness?
15What harmony is there between Christ
and Belial[d]? Or what does a believer have
in common with an unbeliever? 16What
agreement is there between the temple
of God and idols? For we are the temple
of the living God. As God has said:

"I will live with them
and walk among them,
and I will be their God,
and they will be my people."[e]

17Therefore,

"Come out from them
and be separate,
says the Lord.
Touch no unclean thing,
and I will receive you."[f]

18And,

"I will be a Father to you,
and you will be my sons and
daughters,
says the Lord Almighty."[g]

7 Therefore, since we have these
promises, dear friends, let us purify
ourselves from everything that contam-
inates body and spirit, perfecting holiness out of reverence for God.
2Make room for us in your hearts. We
have wronged no one, we have corrupted no one, we have exploited no one. 3I
do not say this to condemn you; I have
said before that you have such a place in
our hearts that we would live or die with

[a] *17* Or *Christ, that person is a new creation.* [b] *21* Or *be a sin offering* [c] *2* Isaiah 49:8 [d] *15* Greek *Beliar,* a variant of *Belial* [e] *16* Lev. 26:12; Jer. 32:38; Ezek. 37:27 [f] *17* Isaiah 52:11; Ezek. 20:34,41 [g] *18* 2 Samuel 7:14; 7:8

you. [4]I have spoken to you with great
frankness; I take great pride in you. I am
greatly encouraged; in all our troubles
my joy knows no bounds.

[5]For when we came into Macedonia,
we had no rest, but we were harassed
at every turn — conflicts on the outside,
fears within. [6]But God, who comforts
the downcast, comforted us by the coming of Titus, [7]and not only by his coming
but also by the comfort you had given
him. He told us about your longing for
me, your deep sorrow, your ardent concern for me, so that my joy was greater
than ever.
[8]Even if I caused you sorrow by my letter, I do not regret it. Though I did regret
it — I see that my letter hurt you, but only
for a little while — [9]yet now I am happy,
not because you were made sorry, but
because your sorrow led you to repentance. For you became sorrowful as God
intended and so were not harmed in any
way by us. [10]Godly sorrow brings repentance that leads to salvation and leaves
no regret, but worldly sorrow brings
death. [11]See what this godly sorrow
has produced in you: what earnestness,
what eagerness to clear yourselves, what
indignation, what alarm, what longing,
what concern, what readiness to see
justice done. At every point you have
proved yourselves to be innocent in this
matter. [12]So even though I wrote to you,
it was neither on account of the one who
did the wrong nor on account of the injured party, but rather that before God
you could see for yourselves how devoted to us you are. [13]By all this we are encouraged.
In addition to our own encouragement, we were especially delighted to
see how happy Titus was, because his
spirit has been refreshed by all of you.
[14]I had boasted to him about you, and
you have not embarrassed me. But just
as everything we said to you was true
so our boasting about you to Titus has
proved to be true as well. [15]And his affection for you is all the greater when he
remembers that you were all obedient
receiving him with fear and trembling.
[16]I am glad I can have complete confidence in you.

8 And now, brothers and sisters, we
want you to know about the grace
that God has given the Macedonian
churches. [2]In the midst of a very severe
trial, their overflowing joy and their extreme poverty welled up in rich generosity. [3]For I testify that they gave as much
as they were able, and even beyond their
ability. Entirely on their own, [4]they urgently pleaded with us for the privilege
of sharing in this service to the Lord's
people. [5]And they exceeded our expec-
tations: They gave themselves first of all
to the Lord, and then by the will of God
also to us. [6]So we urged Titus, just as he
had earlier made a beginning, to bring
also to completion this act of grace on
your part. [7]But since you excel in everything — in faith, in speech, in knowledge, in complete earnestness and in the
love we have kindled in you[a] — see that
you also excel in this grace of giving.
[8]I am not commanding you, but I
want to test the sincerity of your love
by comparing it with the earnestness of
others. [9]For you know the grace of our
Lord Jesus Christ, that though he was
rich, yet for your sake he became poor,
so that you through his poverty might
become rich.
[10]And here is my judgment about what
is best for you in this matter. Last year
you were the first not only to give but
also to have the desire to do so. [11]Now
finish the work, so that your eager willingness to do it may be matched by
your completion of it, according to your
means. [12]For if the willingness is there,
the gift is acceptable according to what
one has, not according to what one does
not have.
[13]Our desire is not that others might
be relieved while you are hard pressed,
but that there might be equality. [14]At
the present time your plenty will supply what they need, so that in turn their
plenty will supply what you need. The
goal is equality, [15]as it is written: "The
one who gathered much did not have
too much, and the one who gathered little did not have too little."[b]
[16]Thanks be to God, who put into the
heart of Titus the same concern I have
for you. [17]For Titus not only welcomed
our appeal, but he is coming to you with

[a] 7 Some manuscripts *and in your love for us* [b] 15 Exodus 16:18

much enthusiasm and on his own initiative. [18]And we are sending along with him the brother who is praised by all the churches for his service to the gospel. [19]What is more, he was chosen by the churches to accompany us as we carry the offering, which we administer in order to honor the Lord himself and to show our eagerness to help. [20]We want to avoid any criticism of the way we administer this liberal gift. [21]For we are taking pains to do what is right, not only in the eyes of the Lord but also in the eyes of man.

[22]In addition, we are sending with them our brother who has often proved to us in many ways that he is zealous, and now even more so because of his great confidence in you. [23]As for Titus, he is my partner and co-worker among you; as for our brothers, they are representatives of the churches and an honor to Christ. [24]Therefore show these men the proof of your love and the reason for our pride in you, so that the churches can see it.

9 There is no need for me to write to you about this service to the Lord's people. [2]For I know your eagerness to help, and I have been boasting about it to the Macedonians, telling them that since last year you in Achaia were ready to give; and your enthusiasm has stirred most of them to action. [3]But I am sending the brothers in order that our boasting about you in this matter should not prove hollow, but that you may be ready, as I said you would be. [4]For if any Macedonians come with me and find you unprepared, we—not to say anything about you—would be ashamed of having been so confident. [5]So I thought it necessary to urge the brothers to visit you in advance and finish the arrangements for the generous gift you had promised. Then it will be ready as a generous gift, not as one grudgingly given.

[6]Remember this: Whoever sows sparingly will also reap sparingly, and whoever sows generously will also reap generously. [7]Each of you should give what you have decided in your heart to give, not reluctantly or under compulsion, for God loves a cheerful giver. [8]And God is able to bless you abundantly, so that in all things at all times, having all that you need, you will abound in every good work. [9]As it is written:

"They have freely scattered their gifts
to the poor;
their righteousness endures
forever."[a]

[10]Now he who supplies seed to the sower and bread for food will also supply and increase your store of seed and will enlarge the harvest of your righteousness. [11]You will be enriched in every way so that you can be generous on every occasion, and through us your generosity will result in thanksgiving to God.

[12]This service that you perform is not only supplying the needs of the Lord's people but is also overflowing in many expressions of thanks to God. [13]Because of the service by which you have proved yourselves, others will praise God for the obedience that accompanies your confession of the gospel of Christ, and for your generosity in sharing with them and with everyone else. [14]And in their prayers for you their hearts will go out to you, because of the surpassing grace God has given you. [15]Thanks be to God for his indescribable gift!

10 By the humility and gentleness of Christ, I appeal to you—I, Paul, who am "timid" when face to face with you, but "bold" toward you when away! [2]I beg you that when I come I may not have to be as bold as I expect to be toward some people who think that we live by the standards of this world. [3]For though we live in the world, we do not wage war as the world does. [4]The weapons we fight with are not the weapons of the world. On the contrary, they have divine power to demolish strongholds. [5]We demolish arguments and every pretension that sets itself up against the knowledge of God, and we take captive every thought to make it obedient to Christ. [6]And we will be ready to punish every act of disobedience, once your obedience is complete.

[7]You are judging by appearances.[b] If anyone is confident that they belong to Christ, they should consider again that we belong to Christ just as much as they

[a] 9 Psalm 112:9 [b] 7 Or *Look at the obvious facts*

do. 8So even if I boast somewhat freely about the authority the Lord gave us for building you up rather than tearing you down, I will not be ashamed of it. 9I do not want to seem to be trying to frighten you with my letters. 10For some say, "His letters are weighty and forceful, but in person he is unimpressive and his speaking amounts to nothing." 11Such people should realize that what we are in our letters when we are absent, we will be in our actions when we are present.

12We do not dare to classify or compare ourselves with some who commend themselves. When they measure themselves by themselves and compare themselves with themselves, they are not wise. 13We, however, will not boast beyond proper limits, but will confine our boasting to the sphere of service God himself has assigned to us, a sphere that also includes you. 14We are not going too far in our boasting, as would be the case if we had not come to you, for we did get as far as you with the gospel of Christ. 15Neither do we go beyond our limits by boasting of work done by others. Our hope is that, as your faith continues to grow, our sphere of activity among you will greatly expand, 16so that we can preach the gospel in the regions beyond you. For we do not want to boast about work already done in someone else's territory. 17But, "Let the one who boasts boast in the Lord."[a] 18For it is not the one who commends himself who is approved, but the one whom the Lord commends.

11 I hope you will put up with me in a little foolishness. Yes, please put up with me! 2I am jealous for you with a godly jealousy. I promised you to one husband, to Christ, so that I might present you as a pure virgin to him. 3But I am afraid that just as Eve was deceived by the serpent's cunning, your minds may somehow be led astray from your sincere and pure devotion to Christ. 4For if someone comes to you and preaches a Jesus other than the Jesus we preached, or if you receive a different spirit from the Spirit you received, or a different gospel from the one you accepted, you put up with it easily enough.

5I do not think I am in the least inferior to those "super-apostles."[b] 6I may indeed be untrained as a speaker, but I do have knowledge. We have made this perfectly clear to you in every way. 7Was it a sin for me to lower myself in order to elevate you by preaching the gospel of God to you free of charge? 8I robbed other churches by receiving support from them so as to serve you. 9And when I was with you and needed something, I was not a burden to anyone, for the brothers who came from Macedonia supplied what I needed. I have kept myself from being a burden to you in any way, and will continue to do so. 10As surely as the truth of Christ is in me, nobody in the regions of Achaia will stop this boasting of mine. 11Why? Because I do not love you? God knows I do!

12And I will keep on doing what I am doing in order to cut the ground from under those who want an opportunity to be considered equal with us in the things they boast about. 13For such people are false apostles, deceitful workers, masquerading as apostles of Christ. 14And no wonder, for Satan himself masquerades as an angel of light. 15It is not surprising, then, if his servants also masquerade as servants of righteousness. Their end will be what their actions deserve.

16I repeat: Let no one take me for a fool. But if you do, then tolerate me just as you would a fool, so that I may do a little boasting. 17In this self-confident boasting I am not talking as the Lord would, but as a fool. 18Since many are boasting in the way the world does, I too will boast. 19You gladly put up with fools since you are so wise! 20In fact, you even put up with anyone who enslaves you or exploits you or takes advantage of you or puts on airs or slaps you in the face. 21To my shame I admit that we were too weak for that!

Whatever anyone else dares to boast about—I am speaking as a fool—I also dare to boast about. 22Are they Hebrews? So am I. Are they Israelites? So am I. Are they Abraham's descendants? So am I. 23Are they servants of Christ? (I am out of my mind to talk like this.) I am more. I have worked much harder, been in prison more frequently, been flogged more severely, and been exposed to

[a] 17 Jer. 9:24 [b] 5 Or *to the most eminent apostles*

death again and again. 24Five times I received from the Jews the forty lashes mi-
nus one. 25Three times I was beaten with
rods, once I was pelted with stones, three
times I was shipwrecked, I spent a night
and a day in the open sea, 26I have been
constantly on the move. I have been in
danger from rivers, in danger from bandits, in danger from my fellow Jews, in
danger from Gentiles; in danger in the
city, in danger in the country, in danger
at sea; and in danger from false believers. 27I have labored and toiled and have
often gone without sleep; I have known
hunger and thirst and have often gone
without food; I have been cold and naked. 28Besides everything else, I face
daily the pressure of my concern for all
the churches. 29Who is weak, and I do
not feel weak? Who is led into sin, and I
do not inwardly burn?

30If I must boast, I will boast of the
things that show my weakness. 31The
God and Father of the Lord Jesus, who
is to be praised forever, knows that I
am not lying. 32In Damascus the governor under King Aretas had the city of
the Damascenes guarded in order to arrest me. 33But I was lowered in a basket
from a window in the wall and slipped
through his hands.

12 I must go on boasting. Although
there is nothing to be gained, I will
go on to visions and revelations from the
Lord. 2I know a man in Christ who fourteen years ago was caught up to the third
heaven. Whether it was in the body or out
of the body I do not know — God knows.
3And I know that this man — whether in
the body or apart from the body I do not
know, but God knows — 4was caught
up to paradise and heard inexpressible
things, things that no one is permitted to
tell. 5I will boast about a man like that,
but I will not boast about myself, except
about my weaknesses. 6Even if I should
choose to boast, I would not be a fool,
because I would be speaking the truth.
But I refrain, so no one will think more
of me than is warranted by what I do or
say, 7or because of these surpassingly
great revelations. Therefore, in order
to keep me from becoming conceited,
I was given a thorn in my flesh, a messenger of Satan, to torment me. 8Three
times I pleaded with the Lord to take it
away from me. 9But he said to me, "My
grace is sufficient for you, for my power
is made perfect in weakness." Therefore
I will boast all the more gladly about my
weaknesses, so that Christ's power may
rest on me. 10That is why, for Christ's
sake, I delight in weaknesses, in insults,
in hardships, in persecutions, in difficulties. For when I am weak, then I am
strong.

11I have made a fool of myself, but you
drove me to it. I ought to have been commended by you, for I am not in the least
inferior to the "super-apostles,"[a] even
though I am nothing. 12I persevered in
demonstrating among you the marks of
a true apostle, including signs, wonders
and miracles. 13How were you inferior
to the other churches, except that I was
never a burden to you? Forgive me this
wrong!

14Now I am ready to visit you for the
third time, and I will not be a burden
to you, because what I want is not your
possessions but you. After all, children
should not have to save up for their parents, but parents for their children. 15So
I will very gladly spend for you everything I have and expend myself as well.
If I love you more, will you love me less?
16Be that as it may, I have not been a burden to you. Yet, crafty fellow that I am,
I caught you by trickery! 17Did I exploit
you through any of the men I sent to you?
18I urged Titus to go to you and I sent our
brother with him. Titus did not exploit
you, did he? Did we not walk in the same
footsteps by the same Spirit?

19Have you been thinking all along
that we have been defending ourselves
to you? We have been speaking in the
sight of God as those in Christ; and everything we do, dear friends, is for your
strengthening. 20For I am afraid that
when I come I may not find you as I want
you to be, and you may not find me as
you want me to be. I fear that there may
be discord, jealousy, fits of rage, selfish
ambition, slander, gossip, arrogance
and disorder. 21I am afraid that when
I come again my God will humble me
before you, and I will be grieved over
many who have sinned earlier and have
not repented of the impurity, sexual sin

[a] *11* Or *the most eminent apostles*

and debauchery in which they have in-
dulged.

13 This will be my third visit to you.
"Every matter must be established
by the testimony of two or three witnesses."[a] 2I already gave you a warning when
I was with you the second time. I now repeat it while absent: On my return I will
not spare those who sinned earlier or any
of the others, 3since you are demanding
proof that Christ is speaking through
me. He is not weak in dealing with you,
but is powerful among you. 4For to be
sure, he was crucified in weakness, yet
he lives by God's power. Likewise, we are
weak in him, yet by God's power we will
live with him in our dealing with you.

5Examine yourselves to see whether you are in the faith; test yourselves.
Do you not realize that Christ Jesus is
in you—unless, of course, you fail the
test? 6And I trust that you will discover
that we have not failed the test. 7Now we
pray to God that you will not do anything
wrong—not so that people will see that
we have stood the test but so that you
will do what is right even though we may
seem to have failed. 8For we cannot do
anything against the truth, but only for
the truth. 9We are glad whenever we are
weak but you are strong; and our prayer
is that you may be fully restored. 10This
is why I write these things when I am absent, that when I come I may not have
to be harsh in my use of authority—the
authority the Lord gave me for building
you up, not for tearing you down.

11Finally, brothers and sisters, rejoice!
Strive for full restoration, encourage one
another, be of one mind, live in peace.
And the God of love and peace will be
with you.

12Greet one another with a holy kiss.
13All God's people here send their greetings.

14May the grace of the Lord Jesus
Christ, and the love of God, and the fellowship of the Holy Spirit be with you
all.

[a] *1* Deut. 19:15

GALATIANS

Galatia was a Roman province in central Asia Minor. Paul traveled here on each of the three journeys he made to spread the message about Jesus. The Galatians received both Paul and his gospel announcement warmly. But later some people Paul calls *agitators* came and challenged Paul's leadership as well as the foundation of his teaching. So Paul wrote to answer the threat to his status as an apostle and to reaffirm the core message that faith in the Messiah is the basis of membership in God's new community.

Paul doesn't open his letter by appealing to the apostles in Jerusalem. Instead, he insists that *the gospel I preached is not of human origin . . . rather, I received it by revelation from Jesus Christ*. Paul is compelled to share this revelation, and he notes that the other apostles support him.

Paul then proceeds to his main argument, which is that Gentiles who have become followers of Jesus do not need to be circumcised. The new worldwide family which had been promised to Abraham is created by faith in Messiah Jesus, not by keeping the Jewish law (Torah). The biblical story had been pointing to this all along.

But if following Torah is not the basis of the gospel, won't there be anarchy? Paul answers by describing what Spirit-empowered life looks like in the community of Messiah-followers. Paul closes by emphasizing the main theme of his letter once more: *Neither circumcision nor uncircumcision means anything; what counts is the new creation.*

---

1 Paul, an apostle — sent not from men
nor by a man, but by Jesus Christ and
God the Father, who raised him from
the dead — 2and all the brothers and
sisters[a] with me,

To the churches in Galatia:

3Grace and peace to you from God our
Father and the Lord Jesus Christ, 4who
gave himself for our sins to rescue us
from the present evil age, according to
the will of our God and Father, 5to whom
be glory for ever and ever. Amen.

6I am astonished that you are so
quickly deserting the one who called
you to live in the grace of Christ and are
turning to a different gospel — 7which
is really no gospel at all. Evidently some
people are throwing you into confusion
and are trying to pervert the gospel of
Christ. 8But even if we or an angel from
heaven should preach a gospel other than the one we preached to you, let
them be under God's curse! 9As we have
already said, so now I say again: If anybody is preaching to you a gospel other
than what you accepted, let them be under God's curse!
10Am I now trying to win the approval
of human beings, or of God? Or am I trying to please people? If I were still trying
to please people, I would not be a servant
of Christ.

11I want you to know, brothers and
sisters, that the gospel I preached is not
of human origin. 12I did not receive it
from any man, nor was I taught it; rather, I received it by revelation from Jesus
Christ.

13For you have heard of my previous
way of life in Judaism, how intensely I
persecuted the church of God and tried
to destroy it. 14I was advancing in Judaism beyond many of my own age among
my people and was extremely zealous for
the traditions of my fathers. 15But when
God, who set me apart from my mother's
womb and called me by his grace, was
pleased 16to reveal his Son in me so that
I might preach him among the Gentiles,
my immediate response was not to consult any human being. 17I did not go up
to Jerusalem to see those who were apostles before I was, but I went into Arabia.
Later I returned to Damascus.

18Then after three years, I went up to
Jerusalem to get acquainted with Cephas[b] and stayed with him fifteen days.
19I saw none of the other apostles — only

[a] *2* The Greek word for *brothers and sisters* (*adelphoi*) refers here to believers, both men and women, as part of God's family; also in verse 11; and in 3:15; 4:12, 28, 31; 5:11, 13; 6:1, 18. [b] *18* That is, Peter

James, the Lord's brother. 20 I assure you
before God that what I am writing you is
no lie.
21 Then I went to Syria and Cilicia. 22 I
was personally unknown to the churches of Judea that are in Christ. 23 They
only heard the report: "The man who
formerly persecuted us is now preaching
the faith he once tried to destroy." 24 And
they praised God because of me.

2 Then after fourteen years, I went up
again to Jerusalem, this time with
Barnabas. I took Titus along also. 2 I
went in response to a revelation and,
meeting privately with those esteemed
as leaders, I presented to them the gospel that I preach among the Gentiles. I
wanted to be sure I was not running and
had not been running my race in vain.
3 Yet not even Titus, who was with me,
was compelled to be circumcised, even
though he was a Greek. 4 This matter
arose because some false believers had
infiltrated our ranks to spy on the freedom we have in Christ Jesus and to make
us slaves. 5 We did not give in to them for
a moment, so that the truth of the gospel
might be preserved for you.
6 As for those who were held in high
esteem — whatever they were makes
no difference to me; God does not show
favoritism — they added nothing to my
message. 7 On the contrary, they recognized that I had been entrusted with the
task of preaching the gospel to the uncircumcised,[a] just as Peter had been to
the circumcised.[b] 8 For God, who was
at work in Peter as an apostle to the circumcised, was also at work in me as an
apostle to the Gentiles. 9 James, Cephas[c]
and John, those esteemed as pillars,
gave me and Barnabas the right hand
of fellowship when they recognized the
grace given to me. They agreed that we
should go to the Gentiles, and they to
the circumcised. 10 All they asked was
that we should continue to remember
the poor, the very thing I had been eager
to do all along.
11 When Cephas came to Antioch, I opposed him to his face, because he stood
condemned. 12 For before certain men
came from James, he used to eat with the
Gentiles. But when they arrived, he began to draw back and separate himself
from the Gentiles because he was afraid
of those who belonged to the circumcision group. 13 The other Jews joined him
in his hypocrisy, so that by their hypocrisy even Barnabas was led astray.
14 When I saw that they were not acting
in line with the truth of the gospel, I said
to Cephas in front of them all, "You are
a Jew, yet you live like a Gentile and not
like a Jew. How is it, then, that you force
Gentiles to follow Jewish customs?
15 "We who are Jews by birth and not
sinful Gentiles 16 know that a person
is not justified by the works of the law,
but by faith in Jesus Christ. So we, too,
have put our faith in Christ Jesus that
we may be justified by faith in[d] Christ
and not by the works of the law, because
by the works of the law no one will be
justified.
17 "But if, in seeking to be justified
in Christ, we Jews find ourselves also
among the sinners, doesn't that mean
that Christ promotes sin? Absolutely
not! 18 If I rebuild what I destroyed, then
I really would be a lawbreaker.
19 "For through the law I died to the
law so that I might live for God. 20 I have
been crucified with Christ and I no longer live, but Christ lives in me. The life
I now live in the body, I live by faith in
the Son of God, who loved me and gave
himself for me. 21 I do not set aside the
grace of God, for if righteousness could
be gained through the law, Christ died
for nothing!"[e]

3 You foolish Galatians! Who has be-
witched you? Before your very eyes
Jesus Christ was clearly portrayed as
crucified. 2 I would like to learn just one
thing from you: Did you receive the Spirit by the works of the law, or by believing what you heard? 3 Are you so foolish?
After beginning by means of the Spirit,
are you now trying to finish by means
of the flesh?[f] 4 Have you experienced[g] so
much in vain — if it really was in vain?
5 So again I ask, does God give you his
Spirit and work miracles among you by
the works of the law, or by your believing
what you heard? 6 So also Abraham "be-

[a] 7 That is, Gentiles [b] 7 That is, Jews; also in verses 8 and 9 [c] 9 That is, Peter; also in verses 11 and 14 [d] 16 Or *but through the faithfulness of . . . justified on the basis of the faithfulness of* [e] 21 Some interpreters end the quotation after verse 14. [f] 3 In contexts like this, the Greek word for *flesh* (*sarx*) refers to the sinful state of human beings, often presented as a power in opposition to the Spirit. [g] 4 Or *suffered*

lieved God, and it was credited to him as
righteousness."[a]
7Understand, then, that those who
have faith are children of Abraham.
8Scripture foresaw that God would justify the Gentiles by faith, and announced
the gospel in advance to Abraham: "All
nations will be blessed through you."[b]
9So those who rely on faith are blessed
along with Abraham, the man of faith.

10For all who rely on the works of
the law are under a curse, as it is written: "Cursed is everyone who does not
continue to do everything written in
the Book of the Law."[c] 11Clearly no one
who relies on the law is justified before
God, because "the righteous will live by
faith."[d] 12The law is not based on faith;
on the contrary, it says, "The person who
does these things will live by them."[e]
13Christ redeemed us from the curse of
the law by becoming a curse for us, for
it is written: "Cursed is everyone who is
hung on a pole."[f] 14He redeemed us in
order that the blessing given to Abraham might come to the Gentiles through
Christ Jesus, so that by faith we might receive the promise of the Spirit.

15Brothers and sisters, let me take an
example from everyday life. Just as no one
can set aside or add to a human covenant
that has been duly established, so it is in
this case. 16The promises were spoken to
Abraham and to his seed. Scripture does
not say "and to seeds," meaning many
people, but "and to your seed,"[g] meaning
one person, who is Christ. 17What I mean
is this: The law, introduced 430 years later, does not set aside the covenant previously established by God and thus do
away with the promise. 18For if the inheritance depends on the law, then it no
longer depends on the promise; but God
in his grace gave it to Abraham through
a promise.

19Why, then, was the law given at all?
It was added because of transgressions
until the Seed to whom the promise
referred had come. The law was given
through angels and entrusted to a mediator. 20A mediator, however, implies
more than one party; but God is one.

21Is the law, therefore, opposed to the
promises of God? Absolutely not! For if
a law had been given that could impart
life, then righteousness would certainly have come by the law. 22But Scripture
has locked up everything under the
control of sin, so that what was promised, being given through faith in Jesus
Christ, might be given to those who believe.

23Before the coming of this faith,[h]
we were held in custody under the law,
locked up until the faith that was to
come would be revealed. 24So the law
was our guardian until Christ came that
we might be justified by faith. 25Now
that this faith has come, we are no longer under a guardian.

26So in Christ Jesus you are all children of God through faith, 27for all of
you who were baptized into Christ have
clothed yourselves with Christ. 28There
is neither Jew nor Gentile, neither slave
nor free, nor is there male and female,
for you are all one in Christ Jesus. 29If
you belong to Christ, then you are Abraham's seed, and heirs according to the
promise.

4 What I am saying is that as long as
an heir is underage, he is no different from a slave, although he owns the
whole estate. 2The heir is subject to
guardians and trustees until the time
set by his father. 3So also, when we were
underage, we were in slavery under the
elemental spiritual forces[i] of the world.
4But when the set time had fully come,
God sent his Son, born of a woman, born
under the law, 5to redeem those under
the law, that we might receive adoption
to sonship.[j] 6Because you are his sons,
God sent the Spirit of his Son into our
hearts, the Spirit who calls out, *"Abba,*[k]
Father." 7So you are no longer a slave,
but God's child; and since you are his
child, God has made you also an heir.

8Formerly, when you did not know
God, you were slaves to those who by
nature are not gods. 9But now that you
know God—or rather are known by
God—how is it that you are turning back
to those weak and miserable forces[l]? Do

[a] *6* Gen. 15:6 [b] *8* Gen. 12:3; 18:18; 22:18 [c] *10* Deut. 27:26 [d] *11* Hab. 2:4 [e] *12* Lev. 18:5
[f] *13* Deut. 21:23 [g] *16* Gen. 12:7; 13:15; 24:7 [h] *22,23* Or *through the faithfulness of Jesus . . . 23Before faith came* [i] *3* Or *under the basic principles* [j] *5* The Greek word for *adoption to sonship* is a legal term referring to the full legal standing of an adopted male heir in Roman culture. [k] *6* Aramaic for *Father*
[l] *9* Or *principles*

you wish to be enslaved by them all over
again? 10 You are observing special days
and months and seasons and years! 11 I
fear for you, that somehow I have wasted
my efforts on you.

12 I plead with you, brothers and sisters, become like me, for I became like
you. You did me no wrong. 13 As you
know, it was because of an illness that
I first preached the gospel to you, 14 and
even though my illness was a trial to
you, you did not treat me with contempt
or scorn. Instead, you welcomed me as if
I were an angel of God, as if I were Christ
Jesus himself. 15 Where, then, is your
blessing of me now? I can testify that, if
you could have done so, you would have
torn out your eyes and given them to
me. 16 Have I now become your enemy
by telling you the truth?

17 Those people are zealous to win you
over, but for no good. What they want is
to alienate you from us, so that you may
have zeal for them. 18 It is fine to be zealous, provided the purpose is good, and
to be so always, not just when I am with
you. 19 My dear children, for whom I am
again in the pains of childbirth until
Christ is formed in you, 20 how I wish I
could be with you now and change my
tone, because I am perplexed about
you!

21 Tell me, you who want to be under
the law, are you not aware of what the
law says? 22 For it is written that Abraham had two sons, one by the slave
woman and the other by the free woman. 23 His son by the slave woman was
born according to the flesh, but his son
by the free woman was born as the result
of a divine promise.

24 These things are being taken figuratively: The women represent two
covenants. One covenant is from Mount
Sinai and bears children who are to
be slaves: This is Hagar. 25 Now Hagar
stands for Mount Sinai in Arabia and
corresponds to the present city of Jerusalem, because she is in slavery with
her children. 26 But the Jerusalem that
is above is free, and she is our mother.
27 For it is written:

"Be glad, barren woman,
you who never bore a child;
shout for joy and cry aloud,
you who were never in labor;
because more are the children of the
desolate woman
than of her who has a husband."[a]

28 Now you, brothers and sisters, like
Isaac, are children of promise. 29 At that
time the son born according to the flesh
persecuted the son born by the power
of the Spirit. It is the same now. 30 But
what does Scripture say? "Get rid of the
slave woman and her son, for the slave
woman's son will never share in the inheritance with the free woman's son."[b]
31 Therefore, brothers and sisters, we are
not children of the slave woman, but of
the free woman.

5 It is for freedom that Christ has set us
free. Stand firm, then, and do not let
yourselves be burdened again by a yoke
of slavery.

2 Mark my words! I, Paul, tell you that
if you let yourselves be circumcised,
Christ will be of no value to you at all.
3 Again I declare to every man who lets
himself be circumcised that he is obligated to obey the whole law. 4 You who
are trying to be justified by the law have
been alienated from Christ; you have
fallen away from grace. 5 For through
the Spirit we eagerly await by faith the
righteousness for which we hope. 6 For
in Christ Jesus neither circumcision nor
uncircumcision has any value. The only
thing that counts is faith expressing itself through love.

7 You were running a good race. Who
cut in on you to keep you from obeying
the truth? 8 That kind of persuasion does
not come from the one who calls you.
9 "A little yeast works through the whole
batch of dough." 10 I am confident in the
Lord that you will take no other view.
The one who is throwing you into confusion, whoever that may be, will have to
pay the penalty. 11 Brothers and sisters,
if I am still preaching circumcision, why
am I still being persecuted? In that case
the offense of the cross has been abolished. 12 As for those agitators, I wish
they would go the whole way and emas-
culate themselves!

13 You, my brothers and sisters, were
called to be free. But do not use your

a 27 Isaiah 54:1 b 30 Gen. 21:10

freedom to indulge the flesh[a]; rather,
serve one another humbly in love. 14For
the entire law is fulfilled in keeping this
one command: "Love your neighbor as
yourself."[b] 15If you bite and devour each
other, watch out or you will be destroyed
by each other.

16So I say, walk by the Spirit, and you
will not gratify the desires of the flesh.
17For the flesh desires what is contrary
to the Spirit, and the Spirit what is contrary to the flesh. They are in conflict
with each other, so that you are not to do
whatever[c] you want. 18But if you are led
by the Spirit, you are not under the law.

19The acts of the flesh are obvious:
sexual immorality, impurity and debauchery; 20idolatry and witchcraft;
hatred, discord, jealousy, fits of rage,
selfish ambition, dissensions, factions
21and envy; drunkenness, orgies, and
the like. I warn you, as I did before, that
those who live like this will not inherit
the kingdom of God.

22But the fruit of the Spirit is love, joy,
peace, forbearance, kindness, goodness,
faithfulness, 23gentleness and self-control. Against such things there is no law.
24Those who belong to Christ Jesus have
crucified the flesh with its passions and
desires. 25Since we live by the Spirit, let
us keep in step with the Spirit. 26Let us
not become conceited, provoking and
envying each other.

6 Brothers and sisters, if someone is
caught in a sin, you who live by the
Spirit should restore that person gently.
But watch yourselves, or you also may be
tempted. 2Carry each other's burdens,
and in this way you will fulfill the law of
Christ. 3If anyone thinks they are something when they are not, they deceive
themselves. 4Each one should test their
own actions. Then they can take pride in
themselves alone, without comparing
themselves to someone else, 5for each
one should carry their own load. 6Nev-
ertheless, the one who receives instruction in the word should share all good
things with their instructor.

7Do not be deceived: God cannot be
mocked. A man reaps what he sows.
8Whoever sows to please their flesh,
from the flesh will reap destruction;
whoever sows to please the Spirit, from
the Spirit will reap eternal life. 9Let us
not become weary in doing good, for at
the proper time we will reap a harvest
if we do not give up. 10Therefore, as we
have opportunity, let us do good to all
people, especially to those who belong
to the family of believers.

11See what large letters I use as I write
to you with my own hand!

12Those who want to impress people by means of the flesh are trying to
compel you to be circumcised. The
only reason they do this is to avoid being persecuted for the cross of Christ.
13Not even those who are circumcised
keep the law, yet they want you to be
circumcised that they may boast about
your circumcision in the flesh. 14May
I never boast except in the cross of our
Lord Jesus Christ, through which[d] the
world has been crucified to me, and I to
the world. 15Neither circumcision nor
uncircumcision means anything; what
counts is the new creation. 16Peace and
mercy to all who follow this rule—to[e]
the Israel of God.

17From now on, let no one cause me
trouble, for I bear on my body the marks
of Jesus.

18The grace of our Lord Jesus Christ
be with your spirit, brothers and sisters.
Amen.

[a] *13* In contexts like this, the Greek word for *flesh* (*sarx*) refers to the sinful state of human beings, often presented as a power in opposition to the Spirit; also in verses 16, 17, 19 and 24; and in 6:8. [b] *14* Lev. 19:18
[c] *17* Or *you do not do what* [d] *14* Or *whom* [e] *16* Or *rule and to*

EPHESIANS

Traditionally named Ephesians, this letter may not actually have been written to the believers in Ephesus. Some of the best early copies of the letter don't include the phrase *in Ephesus* in the greeting. While Paul spent two years in Ephesus, this letter appears to address people Paul has never met.

Paul here presents a two-fold pattern, first explaining the new identity believers have in Christ and then bringing out the implications for their new way of life. God has brought everything together under the rule of the Messiah, exalting Jesus above all things. Paul echoes a phrase from Psalm 8—*God placed all things under his feet*—to show that Jesus is the truly human one. Jesus fulfills the original human calling to rule over the creation properly. Jews and Gentiles have been brought together into one body, with Jesus at the head. God is now creating *one new humanity* from all over the world through the reconciling work of the Messiah.

This means Jesus-followers must give up their former way of life and practice purity in daily living and integrity in their relationships. The reciprocal responsibilities of those in and under authority are used as key examples of the new kinds of relationships God is expecting. Paul cautions his readers that they are entering a spiritual battle. They must arm themselves with all the resources God has provided, until the Messiah brings *unity to all things in heaven and on earth.*

---

1 Paul, an apostle of Christ Jesus by the will of God,

To God's holy people in Ephesus,[a] the faithful in Christ Jesus:

2 Grace and peace to you from God our Father and the Lord Jesus Christ.

3 Praise be to the God and Father of our
Lord Jesus Christ, who has blessed us in
the heavenly realms with every spiritual blessing in Christ. 4 For he chose us
in him before the creation of the world
to be holy and blameless in his sight. In
love 5 he[b] predestined us for adoption to
sonship[c] through Jesus Christ, in accordance with his pleasure and will— 6 to
the praise of his glorious grace, which he
has freely given us in the One he loves.
7 In him we have redemption through
his blood, the forgiveness of sins, in accordance with the riches of God's grace
8 that he lavished on us. With all wisdom
and understanding, 9 he[d] made known
to us the mystery of his will according to
his good pleasure, which he purposed
in Christ, 10 to be put into effect when
the times reach their fulfillment—to
bring unity to all things in heaven and
on earth under Christ.
11 In him we were also chosen,[e] having been predestined according to the
plan of him who works out everything
in conformity with the purpose of his
will, 12 in order that we, who were the
first to put our hope in Christ, might
be for the praise of his glory. 13 And you
also were included in Christ when you
heard the message of truth, the gospel
of your salvation. When you believed,
you were marked in him with a seal, the
promised Holy Spirit, 14 who is a deposit
guaranteeing our inheritance until the
redemption of those who are God's possession—to the praise of his glory.
15 For this reason, ever since I heard
about your faith in the Lord Jesus and
your love for all God's people, 16 I have
not stopped giving thanks for you, remembering you in my prayers. 17 I keep
asking that the God of our Lord Jesus
Christ, the glorious Father, may give you
the Spirit[f] of wisdom and revelation, so
that you may know him better. 18 I pray
that the eyes of your heart may be enlightened in order that you may know
the hope to which he has called you,
the riches of his glorious inheritance
in his holy people, 19 and his incompa-
rably great power for us who believe.
That power is the same as the mighty
strength 20 he exerted when he raised

[a] *1* Some early manuscripts do not have *in Ephesus.* [b] *4,5* Or *sight in love.* [5]*He* [c] *5* The Greek word for *adoption to sonship* is a legal term referring to the full legal standing of an adopted male heir in Roman culture. [d] *8,9* Or *us with all wisdom and understanding.* [9]*And he* [e] *11* Or *were made heirs* [f] *17* Or *a spirit*

Christ from the dead and seated him at
his right hand in the heavenly realms,
21far above all rule and authority, power and dominion, and every name that
is invoked, not only in the present age
but also in the one to come. 22And God
placed all things under his feet and appointed him to be head over everything
for the church, 23which is his body, the
fullness of him who fills everything in
every way.

2 As for you, you were dead in your
transgressions and sins, 2in which
you used to live when you followed the
ways of this world and of the ruler of
the kingdom of the air, the spirit who
is now at work in those who are disobedient. 3All of us also lived among them
at one time, gratifying the cravings of
our flesh[a] and following its desires and
thoughts. Like the rest, we were by nature deserving of wrath. 4But because of
his great love for us, God, who is rich in
mercy, 5made us alive with Christ even
when we were dead in transgressions—
it is by grace you have been saved. 6And
God raised us up with Christ and seated
us with him in the heavenly realms in
Christ Jesus, 7in order that in the coming ages he might show the incompara-
ble riches of his grace, expressed in his
kindness to us in Christ Jesus. 8For it is
by grace you have been saved, through
faith—and this is not from yourselves,
it is the gift of God— 9not by works, so
that no one can boast. 10For we are God's
handiwork, created in Christ Jesus to do
good works, which God prepared in advance for us to do.

11Therefore, remember that formerly
you who are Gentiles by birth and called
"uncircumcised" by those who call
themselves "the circumcision" (which
is done in the body by human hands)—
12remember that at that time you were
separate from Christ, excluded from citizenship in Israel and foreigners to the
covenants of the promise, without hope
and without God in the world. 13But
now in Christ Jesus you who once were
far away have been brought near by the
blood of Christ.

14For he himself is our peace, who has
made the two groups one and has destroyed the barrier, the dividing wall of
hostility, 15by setting aside in his flesh
the law with its commands and regulations. His purpose was to create in himself one new humanity out of the two,
thus making peace, 16and in one body to
reconcile both of them to God through
the cross, by which he put to death their
hostility. 17He came and preached peace
to you who were far away and peace to
those who were near. 18For through him
we both have access to the Father by one
Spirit.

19Consequently, you are no longer foreigners and strangers, but fellow citizens
with God's people and also members of
his household, 20built on the foundation
of the apostles and prophets, with Christ
Jesus himself as the chief cornerstone.
21In him the whole building is joined together and rises to become a holy temple
in the Lord. 22And in him you too are being built together to become a dwelling
in which God lives by his Spirit.

3 For this reason I, Paul, the prisoner of Christ Jesus for the sake of you
Gentiles—

2Surely you have heard about the administration of God's grace that was
given to me for you, 3that is, the mystery
made known to me by revelation, as I
have already written briefly. 4In reading
this, then, you will be able to understand
my insight into the mystery of Christ,
5which was not made known to people
in other generations as it has now been
revealed by the Spirit to God's holy apostles and prophets. 6This mystery is that
through the gospel the Gentiles are heirs
together with Israel, members together
of one body, and sharers together in the
promise in Christ Jesus.

7I became a servant of this gospel by
the gift of God's grace given me through
the working of his power. 8Although I am
less than the least of all the Lord's people, this grace was given me: to preach
to the Gentiles the boundless riches
of Christ, 9and to make plain to everyone the administration of this mystery,
which for ages past was kept hidden in
God, who created all things. 10His intent was that now, through the church,
the manifold wisdom of God should be
made known to the rulers and authorities in the heavenly realms, 11according

[a] 3 In contexts like this, the Greek word for *flesh* (*sarx*) refers to the sinful state of human beings, often presented as a power in opposition to the Spirit.

to his eternal purpose that he accomplished in Christ Jesus our Lord. 12In
him and through faith in him we may
approach God with freedom and confidence. 13I ask you, therefore, not to be
discouraged because of my sufferings
for you, which are your glory.

14For this reason I kneel before the
Father, 15from whom every family[a] in
heaven and on earth derives its name.
16I pray that out of his glorious riches he
may strengthen you with power through
his Spirit in your inner being, 17so that
Christ may dwell in your hearts through
faith. And I pray that you, being rooted and established in love, 18may have
power, together with all the Lord's holy
people, to grasp how wide and long and
high and deep is the love of Christ, 19and
to know this love that surpasses knowledge—that you may be filled to the measure of all the fullness of God.

20Now to him who is able to do im-
measurably more than all we ask or
imagine, according to his power that is
at work within us, 21to him be glory in
the church and in Christ Jesus throughout all generations, for ever and ever!
Amen.

4 As a prisoner for the Lord, then, I urge
you to live a life worthy of the calling
you have received. 2Be completely humble and gentle; be patient, bearing with
one another in love. 3Make every effort
to keep the unity of the Spirit through
the bond of peace. 4There is one body
and one Spirit, just as you were called
to one hope when you were called; 5one
Lord, one faith, one baptism; 6one God
and Father of all, who is over all and
through all and in all.

7But to each one of us grace has been
given as Christ apportioned it. 8This is
why it[b] says:

"When he ascended on high,
he took many captives
and gave gifts to his people."[c]

9(What does "he ascended" mean except that he also descended to the lower,
earthly regions[d]? 10He who descended is
the very one who ascended higher than
all the heavens, in order to fill the whole
universe.) 11So Christ himself gave the
apostles, the prophets, the evangelists,
the pastors and teachers, 12to equip his
people for works of service, so that the
body of Christ may be built up 13until
we all reach unity in the faith and in
the knowledge of the Son of God and
become mature, attaining to the whole
measure of the fullness of Christ.

14Then we will no longer be infants,
tossed back and forth by the waves, and
blown here and there by every wind of
teaching and by the cunning and craftiness of people in their deceitful scheming. 15Instead, speaking the truth in
love, we will grow to become in every
respect the mature body of him who is
the head, that is, Christ. 16From him the
whole body, joined and held together by
every supporting ligament, grows and
builds itself up in love, as each part does
its work.

17So I tell you this, and insist on it in
the Lord, that you must no longer live
as the Gentiles do, in the futility of their
thinking. 18They are darkened in their
understanding and separated from the
life of God because of the ignorance that
is in them due to the hardening of their
hearts. 19Having lost all sensitivity, they
have given themselves over to sensuality
so as to indulge in every kind of impurity, and they are full of greed.

20That, however, is not the way of life
you learned 21when you heard about
Christ and were taught in him in accordance with the truth that is in Jesus.
22You were taught, with regard to your
former way of life, to put off your old self,
which is being corrupted by its deceitful
desires; 23to be made new in the attitude
of your minds; 24and to put on the new
self, created to be like God in true righteousness and holiness.

25Therefore each of you must put off
falsehood and speak truthfully to your
neighbor, for we are all members of one
body. 26"In your anger do not sin"[e]: Do
not let the sun go down while you are
still angry, 27and do not give the devil a
foothold. 28Anyone who has been stealing must steal no longer, but must work,
doing something useful with their own
hands, that they may have something to
share with those in need.

29Do not let any unwholesome talk

[a] *15* The Greek for *family* (*patria*) is derived from the Greek for *father* (*pater*). [b] *8* Or *God*
[c] *8* Psalm 68:18 [d] *9* Or *the depths of the earth* [e] *26* Psalm 4:4 (see Septuagint)

come out of your mouths, but only what
is helpful for building others up according to their needs, that it may benefit
those who listen. 30 And do not grieve the
Holy Spirit of God, with whom you were
sealed for the day of redemption. 31 Get
rid of all bitterness, rage and anger,
brawling and slander, along with every
form of malice. 32 Be kind and compassionate to one another, forgiving each
other, just as in Christ God forgave you.

5 1 Follow God's example, therefore, as
dearly loved children 2 and walk in
the way of love, just as Christ loved us
and gave himself up for us as a fragrant
offering and sacrifice to God.

3 But among you there must not be
even a hint of sexual immorality, or of
any kind of impurity, or of greed, because these are improper for God's holy
people. 4 Nor should there be obscenity,
foolish talk or coarse joking, which are
out of place, but rather thanksgiving.
5 For of this you can be sure: No immoral, impure or greedy person—such a
person is an idolater—has any inheritance in the kingdom of Christ and
of God.[a] 6 Let no one deceive you with
empty words, for because of such things
God's wrath comes on those who are disobedient. 7 Therefore do not be partners
with them.

8 For you were once darkness, but now
you are light in the Lord. Live as children of light 9 (for the fruit of the light
consists in all goodness, righteousness
and truth) 10 and find out what pleases
the Lord. 11 Have nothing to do with the
fruitless deeds of darkness, but rather
expose them. 12 It is shameful even to
mention what the disobedient do in secret. 13 But everything exposed by the
light becomes visible—and everything
that is illuminated becomes a light.
14 This is why it is said:

"Wake up, sleeper,
rise from the dead,
and Christ will shine on you."

15 Be very careful, then, how you live—
not as unwise but as wise, 16 making the
most of every opportunity, because the
days are evil. 17 Therefore do not be foolish, but understand what the Lord's will
is. 18 Do not get drunk on wine, which
leads to debauchery. Instead, be filled
with the Spirit, 19 speaking to one another with psalms, hymns, and songs from
the Spirit. Sing and make music from
your heart to the Lord, 20 always giving
thanks to God the Father for everything,
in the name of our Lord Jesus Christ.

21 Submit to one another out of reverence for Christ.

22 Wives, submit yourselves to your
own husbands as you do to the Lord.
23 For the husband is the head of the wife
as Christ is the head of the church, his
body, of which he is the Savior. 24 Now
as the church submits to Christ, so also
wives should submit to their husbands
in everything.

25 Husbands, love your wives, just
as Christ loved the church and gave
himself up for her 26 to make her holy,
cleansing[b] her by the washing with
water through the word, 27 and to present her to himself as a radiant church,
without stain or wrinkle or any other
blemish, but holy and blameless. 28 In
this same way, husbands ought to love
their wives as their own bodies. He who
loves his wife loves himself. 29 After all,
no one ever hated their own body, but
they feed and care for their body, just as
Christ does the church— 30 for we are
members of his body. 31 "For this reason
a man will leave his father and mother
and be united to his wife, and the two
will become one flesh."[c] 32 This is a profound mystery—but I am talking about
Christ and the church. 33 However, each
one of you also must love his wife as he
loves himself, and the wife must respect
her husband.

6 Children, obey your parents in the
Lord, for this is right. 2 "Honor your
father and mother"—which is the first
commandment with a promise— 3 "so
that it may go well with you and that you
may enjoy long life on the earth."[d]

4 Fathers,[e] do not exasperate your
children; instead, bring them up in the
training and instruction of the Lord.

5 Slaves, obey your earthly masters
with respect and fear, and with sincerity
of heart, just as you would obey Christ.
6 Obey them not only to win their favor
when their eye is on you, but as slaves of
Christ, doing the will of God from your

[a] 5 Or *kingdom of the Messiah and God* [b] 26 Or *having cleansed* [c] 31 Gen. 2:24 [d] 3 Deut. 5:16
[e] 4 Or *Parents*

heart. 7Serve wholeheartedly, as if you
were serving the Lord, not people, 8be-
cause you know that the Lord will reward each one for whatever good they
do, whether they are slave or free.
9And masters, treat your slaves in the
same way. Do not threaten them, since
you know that he who is both their Master and yours is in heaven, and there is
no favoritism with him.
10Finally, be strong in the Lord and in
his mighty power. 11Put on the full armor
of God, so that you can take your stand
against the devil's schemes. 12For our
struggle is not against flesh and blood,
but against the rulers, against the authorities, against the powers of this dark
world and against the spiritual forces
of evil in the heavenly realms. 13There-
fore put on the full armor of God, so that
when the day of evil comes, you may be
able to stand your ground, and after you
have done everything, to stand. 14Stand
firm then, with the belt of truth buckled
around your waist, with the breastplate
of righteousness in place, 15and with
your feet fitted with the readiness that
comes from the gospel of peace. 16In
addition to all this, take up the shield of
faith, with which you can extinguish all
the flaming arrows of the evil one. 17Take
the helmet of salvation and the sword of
the Spirit, which is the word of God.
18And pray in the Spirit on all occasions with all kinds of prayers and requests. With this in mind, be alert and
always keep on praying for all the Lord's
people. 19Pray also for me, that whenever I speak, words may be given me so
that I will fearlessly make known the
mystery of the gospel, 20for which I am
an ambassador in chains. Pray that I
may declare it fearlessly, as I should.

21Tychicus, the dear brother and faithful servant in the Lord, will tell you everything, so that you also may know how
I am and what I am doing. 22I am sending him to you for this very purpose, that
you may know how we are, and that he
may encourage you.
23Peace to the brothers and sisters,[a]
and love with faith from God the Father
and the Lord Jesus Christ. 24Grace to all
who love our Lord Jesus Christ with an
undying love.[b]

[a] 23 The Greek word for *brothers and sisters* (*adelphoi*) refers here to believers, both men and women, as part of God's family. [b] 24 Or *Grace and immortality to all who love our Lord Jesus Christ.*

PHILIPPIANS

On his second journey to bring the gospel to the Gentile world, the apostle Paul helped start a church in the city of Philippi (see pp. 991-992), a colony of retired Roman soldiers. The Philippians became Paul's friends and supporters for the rest of his life. When they heard that he was in Rome as a prisoner, they collected money to assist him and sent it with one of their members, a man named Epaphroditus. Later Paul sent him back with a letter to thank the Philippians for their friendship and support.

Paul knows the Philippians were experiencing a lot of opposition, so he appeals to his own life as an example of how to respond to hardship with joy. *Throughout the whole palace guard*—that is, right in the center of Caesar's realm—Paul is boldly making the royal announcement that Jesus is Lord. Paul's desire is that the Philippians will gain the same confidence and *dare all the more to proclaim the gospel without fear.*

In an amazing hymn, Paul urges the Philippians to have the servant attitude that Jesus had. He did not grasp his high position but humbled himself even to the point of death—all for the sake of others. This is the new way to be human that is revealed in God's kingdom. Our citizenship is in God's realm and so we eagerly await the Savior's return to us. Then he will transform our lowly bodies to become like his glorious resurrected body.

---

1 Paul and Timothy, servants of Christ
Jesus,

To all God's holy people in Christ Jesus
at Philippi, together with the overseers
and deacons[a]:

[2]Grace and peace to you from God our
Father and the Lord Jesus Christ.

[3]I thank my God every time I remember you. [4]In all my prayers for all of you,
I always pray with joy [5]because of your
partnership in the gospel from the first
day until now, [6]being confident of this,
that he who began a good work in you
will carry it on to completion until the
day of Christ Jesus.

[7]It is right for me to feel this way about
all of you, since I have you in my heart
and, whether I am in chains or defending and confirming the gospel, all of you
share in God's grace with me. [8]God can
testify how I long for all of you with the
affection of Christ Jesus.

[9]And this is my prayer: that your love
may abound more and more in knowledge and depth of insight, [10]so that you
may be able to discern what is best and
may be pure and blameless for the day
of Christ, [11]filled with the fruit of righteousness that comes through Jesus
Christ—to the glory and praise of God.

[12]Now I want you to know, brothers
and sisters,[b] that what has happened to
me has actually served to advance the
gospel. [13]As a result, it has become clear
throughout the whole palace guard[c]
and to everyone else that I am in chains
for Christ. [14]And because of my chains,
most of the brothers and sisters have become confident in the Lord and dare all
the more to proclaim the gospel without
fear.

[15]It is true that some preach Christ
out of envy and rivalry, but others out of
goodwill. [16]The latter do so out of love,
knowing that I am put here for the defense of the gospel. [17]The former preach
Christ out of selfish ambition, not sincerely, supposing that they can stir up
trouble for me while I am in chains.
[18]But what does it matter? The important
thing is that in every way, whether from
false motives or true, Christ is preached.
And because of this I rejoice.

Yes, and I will continue to rejoice,
[19]for I know that through your prayers
and God's provision of the Spirit of Jesus
Christ what has happened to me will
turn out for my deliverance.[d] [20]I eagerly

[a] *1* The word *deacons* refers here to Christians designated to serve with the overseers/elders of the church in a variety of ways; similarly in Romans 16:1 and 1 Tim. 3:8,12. [b] *12* The Greek word for *brothers and sisters* (*adelphoi*) refers here to believers, both men and women, as part of God's family; also in verse 14; and in 3:1, 13, 17; 4:1, 8, 21. [c] *13* Or *whole palace* [d] *19* Or *vindication*; or *salvation*

expect and hope that I will in no way be
ashamed, but will have sufficient courage so that now as always Christ will be
exalted in my body, whether by life or by
death. 21 For to me, to live is Christ and
to die is gain. 22 If I am to go on living
in the body, this will mean fruitful labor for me. Yet what shall I choose? I do
not know! 23 I am torn between the two:
I desire to depart and be with Christ,
which is better by far; 24 but it is more
necessary for you that I remain in the
body. 25 Convinced of this, I know that I
will remain, and I will continue with all
of you for your progress and joy in the
faith, 26 so that through my being with
you again your boasting in Christ Jesus
will abound on account of me.

27 Whatever happens, conduct yourselves in a manner worthy of the gospel
of Christ. Then, whether I come and see
you or only hear about you in my absence, I will know that you stand firm in
the one Spirit,[a] striving together as one
for the faith of the gospel 28 without being frightened in any way by those who
oppose you. This is a sign to them that
they will be destroyed, but that you will
be saved—and that by God. 29 For it has
been granted to you on behalf of Christ
not only to believe in him, but also to
suffer for him, 30 since you are going
through the same struggle you saw I
had, and now hear that I still have.

2 Therefore if you have any encouragement from being united with Christ,
if any comfort from his love, if any common sharing in the Spirit, if any tenderness and compassion, 2 then make
my joy complete by being like-minded,
having the same love, being one in spirit and of one mind. 3 Do nothing out of
selfish ambition or vain conceit. Rather,
in humility value others above yourselves, 4 not looking to your own interests but each of you to the interests of
the others.

5 In your relationships with one another, have the same mindset as Christ
Jesus:

6 Who, being in very nature[b] God,
did not consider equality with God
something to be used to his
own advantage;
7 rather, he made himself nothing
by taking the very nature[c] of a
servant,
being made in human likeness.
8 And being found in appearance as a
man,
he humbled himself
by becoming obedient to death—
even death on a cross!

9 Therefore God exalted him to the
highest place
and gave him the name that is
above every name,
10 that at the name of Jesus every knee
should bow,
in heaven and on earth and under
the earth,
11 and every tongue acknowledge that
Jesus Christ is Lord,
to the glory of God the Father.

12 Therefore, my dear friends, as you
have always obeyed—not only in my
presence, but now much more in my absence—continue to work out your salvation with fear and trembling, 13 for it is
God who works in you to will and to act
in order to fulfill his good purpose.

14 Do everything without grumbling
or arguing, 15 so that you may become
blameless and pure, "children of God
without fault in a warped and crooked generation."[d] Then you will shine
among them like stars in the sky 16 as
you hold firmly to the word of life. And
then I will be able to boast on the day of
Christ that I did not run or labor in vain.
17 But even if I am being poured out like
a drink offering on the sacrifice and service coming from your faith, I am glad
and rejoice with all of you. 18 So you too
should be glad and rejoice with me.

19 I hope in the Lord Jesus to send
Timothy to you soon, that I also may
be cheered when I receive news about
you. 20 I have no one else like him, who
will show genuine concern for your welfare. 21 For everyone looks out for their
own interests, not those of Jesus Christ.
22 But you know that Timothy has proved
himself, because as a son with his father
he has served with me in the work of the
gospel. 23 I hope, therefore, to send him
as soon as I see how things go with me.
24 And I am confident in the Lord that I
myself will come soon.

[a] *27* Or *in one spirit* [b] *6* Or *in the form of* [c] *7* O *the form* [d] *15* Deut. 32:5

25 But I think it is necessary to send
back to you Epaphroditus, my brother, co-worker and fellow soldier, who is
also your messenger, whom you sent to
take care of my needs. 26 For he longs for
all of you and is distressed because you
heard he was ill. 27 Indeed he was ill, and
almost died. But God had mercy on him,
and not on him only but also on me, to
spare me sorrow upon sorrow. 28 Therefore I am all the more eager to send him,
so that when you see him again you may
be glad and I may have less anxiety. 29 So
then, welcome him in the Lord with
great joy, and honor people like him,
30 because he almost died for the work
of Christ. He risked his life to make up
for the help you yourselves could not
give me.

3 Further, my brothers and sisters, rejoice in the Lord! It is no trouble for
me to write the same things to you again,
and it is a safeguard for you. 2 Watch out
for those dogs, those evildoers, those
mutilators of the flesh. 3 For it is we who
are the circumcision, we who serve
God by his Spirit, who boast in Christ
Jesus, and who put no confidence in the
flesh — 4 though I myself have reasons
for such confidence.

If someone else thinks they have reasons to put confidence in the flesh, I
have more: 5 circumcised on the eighth
day, of the people of Israel, of the tribe of
Benjamin, a Hebrew of Hebrews; in regard to the law, a Pharisee; 6 as for zeal,
persecuting the church; as for righteousness based on the law, faultless.

7 But whatever were gains to me I
now consider loss for the sake of Christ.
8 What is more, I consider everything a
loss because of the surpassing worth
of knowing Christ Jesus my Lord, for
whose sake I have lost all things. I consider them garbage, that I may gain
Christ 9 and be found in him, not having
a righteousness of my own that comes
from the law, but that which is through
faith in[a] Christ — the righteousness that
comes from God on the basis of faith. 10 I
want to know Christ — yes, to know the
power of his resurrection and participation in his sufferings, becoming like him
in his death, 11 and so, somehow, attaining to the resurrection from the dead.

12 Not that I have already obtained
all this, or have already arrived at my
goal, but I press on to take hold of that
for which Christ Jesus took hold of me.
13 Brothers and sisters, I do not consider myself yet to have taken hold of it. But
one thing I do: Forgetting what is behind
and straining toward what is ahead, 14 I
press on toward the goal to win the prize
for which God has called me heaven-
ward in Christ Jesus.

15 All of us, then, who are mature should
take such a view of things. And if on some
point you think differently, that too God
will make clear to you. 16 Only let us live
up to what we have already attained.

17 Join together in following my example, brothers and sisters, and just as you
have us as a model, keep your eyes on
those who live as we do. 18 For, as I have
often told you before and now tell you
again even with tears, many live as enemies of the cross of Christ. 19 Their destiny is destruction, their god is their stomach, and their glory is in their shame.
Their mind is set on earthly things.
20 But our citizenship is in heaven. And
we eagerly await a Savior from there, the
Lord Jesus Christ, 21 who, by the power
that enables him to bring everything under his control, will transform our lowly
bodies so that they will be like his glorious body.

4 Therefore, my brothers and sisters,
you whom I love and long for, my joy
and crown, stand firm in the Lord in this
way, dear friends!

2 I plead with Euodia and I plead with
Syntyche to be of the same mind in the
Lord. 3 Yes, and I ask you, my true companion, help these women since they
have contended at my side in the cause
of the gospel, along with Clement and
the rest of my co-workers, whose names
are in the book of life.

4 Rejoice in the Lord always. I will say
it again: Rejoice! 5 Let your gentleness
be evident to all. The Lord is near. 6 Do
not be anxious about anything, but in
every situation, by prayer and petition,
with thanksgiving, present your requests to God. 7 And the peace of God,
which transcends all understanding,
will guard your hearts and your minds
in Christ Jesus.

a 9 Or *through the faithfulness of*

8 Finally, brothers and sisters, whatever is true, whatever is noble, whatever is
right, whatever is pure, whatever is lovely, whatever is admirable—if anything
is excellent or praiseworthy—think
about such things. 9 Whatever you have
learned or received or heard from me, or
seen in me—put it into practice. And the
God of peace will be with you.

10 I rejoiced greatly in the Lord that at
last you renewed your concern for me.
Indeed, you were concerned, but you
had no opportunity to show it. 11 I am
not saying this because I am in need,
for I have learned to be content whatever the circumstances. 12 I know what
it is to be in need, and I know what it is
to have plenty. I have learned the secret of being content in any and every
situation, whether well fed or hungry,
whether living in plenty or in want. 13 I
can do all this through him who gives
me strength.

14 Yet it was good of you to share in my
troubles. 15 Moreover, as you Philippians know, in the early days of your ac-
quaintance with the gospel, when I set
out from Macedonia, not one church
shared with me in the matter of giving
and receiving, except you only; 16 for
even when I was in Thessalonica, you
sent me aid more than once when I was
in need. 17 Not that I desire your gifts;
what I desire is that more be credited
to your account. 18 I have received full
payment and have more than enough. I
am amply supplied, now that I have received from Epaphroditus the gifts you
sent. They are a fragrant offering, an
acceptable sacrifice, pleasing to God.
19 And my God will meet all your needs
according to the riches of his glory in
Christ Jesus.

20 To our God and Father be glory for
ever and ever. Amen.

21 Greet all God's people in Christ
Jesus. The brothers and sisters who are
with me send greetings. 22 All God's people here send you greetings, especially
those who belong to Caesar's household.

23 The grace of the Lord Jesus Christ be
with your spirit. Amen.[a]

[a] 23 Some manuscripts do not have *Amen.*

COLOSSIANS

While Paul was in prison in Rome, awaiting his upcoming trial before Caesar, one of the letters he wrote was to the gathering of believers in the city of Colossae. Paul had never met them, but they knew who he was and respected his leadership. Paul had worked with a man named Epaphras when he was in Ephesus. Epaphras was originally from Colossae, about 100 miles to the east. Paul sent him to bring the good news about Jesus to his city and to two other nearby cities, Laodicea and Hierapolis. Epaphras was later arrested and brought to Rome as a prisoner himself. Paul learned from him what was happening in those cities.

The Colossians were mostly Gentiles, but like the Galatians they were being pressured to follow the Jewish law and were adding extra rules and false teachings to the faith. Some of them were priding themselves on having visions and getting secret spiritual knowledge. So Paul wrote them a letter to say, "When you've got Jesus the Messiah, you've got it all!"

Paul emphasizes that all things in heaven and earth were created by the Son and were reconciled to God by the Son's death on the cross. Christ possesses the fullness of God's being. Since the Colossians have been brought into the new kingdom of light, they can live their faith to the fullest. They are to *put on the new self,* awaiting the time the Messiah will appear openly, revealing his glory.

---

1 Paul, an apostle of Christ Jesus by
the will of God, and Timothy our
brother,

2 To God's holy people in Colossae, the
faithful brothers and sisters[a] in Christ:

Grace and peace to you from God our
Father.[b]

3 We always thank God, the Father of
our Lord Jesus Christ, when we pray for
you, 4 because we have heard of your
faith in Christ Jesus and of the love you
have for all God's people— 5 the faith
and love that spring from the hope
stored up for you in heaven and about
which you have already heard in the true
message of the gospel 6 that has come to
you. In the same way, the gospel is bearing fruit and growing throughout the
whole world—just as it has been doing
among you since the day you heard it
and truly understood God's grace. 7 You
learned it from Epaphras, our dear fellow servant,[c] who is a faithful minister
of Christ on our[d] behalf, 8 and who also
told us of your love in the Spirit.
9 For this reason, since the day we
heard about you, we have not stopped
praying for you. We continually ask
God to fill you with the knowledge of his
will through all the wisdom and understanding that the Spirit gives,[e] 10 so that
you may live a life worthy of the Lord and
please him in every way: bearing fruit in
every good work, growing in the knowledge of God, 11 being strengthened with
all power according to his glorious might
so that you may have great endurance
and patience, 12 and giving joyful thanks
to the Father, who has qualified you[f] to
share in the inheritance of his holy people in the kingdom of light. 13 For he has
rescued us from the dominion of darkness and brought us into the kingdom of
the Son he loves, 14 in whom we have redemption, the forgiveness of sins.
15 The Son is the image of the invisible God, the firstborn over all creation.
16 For in him all things were created:
things in heaven and on earth, visible
and invisible, whether thrones or powers or rulers or authorities; all things
have been created through him and for
him. 17 He is before all things, and in
him all things hold together. 18 And he
is the head of the body, the church; he
is the beginning and the firstborn from
among the dead, so that in everything
he might have the supremacy. 19 For God
was pleased to have all his fullness dwell
in him, 20 and through him to reconcile
to himself all things, whether things on
earth or things in heaven, by making

[a] 2 The Greek word for *brothers and sisters* (*adelphoi*) refers here to believers, both men and women, as part of God's family; also in 4:15. [b] 2 Some manuscripts *Father and the Lord Jesus Christ* [c] 7 Or *slave* [d] 7 Some manuscripts *your* [e] 9 Or *all spiritual wisdom and understanding* [f] 12 Some manuscripts *us*

peace through his blood, shed on the
cross.
21 Once you were alienated from God
and were enemies in your minds because of[a] your evil behavior. 22 But now
he has reconciled you by Christ's physical body through death to present you
holy in his sight, without blemish and
free from accusation— 23 if you continue in your faith, established and firm,
and do not move from the hope held out
in the gospel. This is the gospel that you
heard and that has been proclaimed
to every creature under heaven, and of
which I, Paul, have become a servant.
24 Now I rejoice in what I am suffering
for you, and I fill up in my flesh what is
still lacking in regard to Christ's afflictions, for the sake of his body, which is
the church. 25 I have become its servant
by the commission God gave me to present to you the word of God in its fullness— 26 the mystery that has been kept
hidden for ages and generations, but is
now disclosed to the Lord's people. 27 To
them God has chosen to make known
among the Gentiles the glorious riches
of this mystery, which is Christ in you,
the hope of glory.
28 He is the one we proclaim, admon-
ishing and teaching everyone with all
wisdom, so that we may present everyone fully mature in Christ. 29 To this end
I strenuously contend with all the ener-
gy Christ so powerfully works in me.
2 I want you to know how hard I am
contending for you and for those at
Laodicea, and for all who have not met
me personally. 2 My goal is that they may
be encouraged in heart and united in
love, so that they may have the full riches of complete understanding, in order
that they may know the mystery of God,
namely, Christ, 3 in whom are hidden all
the treasures of wisdom and knowledge.
4 I tell you this so that no one may deceive
you by fine-sounding arguments. 5 For
though I am absent from you in body, I
am present with you in spirit and delight
to see how disciplined you are and how
firm your faith in Christ is.
6 So then, just as you received Christ
Jesus as Lord, continue to live your lives
in him, 7 rooted and built up in him,
strengthened in the faith as you were
taught, and overflowing with thankfulness.
8 See to it that no one takes you captive
through hollow and deceptive philoso-
phy, which depends on human tradition
and the elemental spiritual forces[b] of
this world rather than on Christ.
9 For in Christ all the fullness of the De-
ity lives in bodily form, 10 and in Christ
you have been brought to fullness. He is
the head over every power and authority. 11 In him you were also circumcised
with a circumcision not performed by
human hands. Your whole self ruled
by the flesh[c] was put off when you were
circumcised by[d] Christ, 12 having been
buried with him in baptism, in which
you were also raised with him through
your faith in the working of God, who
raised him from the dead.
13 When you were dead in your sins and
in the uncircumcision of your flesh, God
made you[e] alive with Christ. He forgave
us all our sins, 14 having canceled the
charge of our legal indebtedness, which
stood against us and condemned us; he
has taken it away, nailing it to the cross.
15 And having disarmed the powers and
authorities, he made a public spectacle
of them, triumphing over them by the
cross.[f]
16 Therefore do not let anyone judge
you by what you eat or drink, or with regard to a religious festival, a New Moon
celebration or a Sabbath day. 17 These are
a shadow of the things that were to come;
the reality, however, is found in Christ.
18 Do not let anyone who delights in false
humility and the worship of angels dis-
qualify you. Such a person also goes into
great detail about what they have seen;
they are puffed up with idle notions by
their unspiritual mind. 19 They have lost
connection with the head, from whom
the whole body, supported and held
together by its ligaments and sinews,
grows as God causes it to grow.
20 Since you died with Christ to the
elemental spiritual forces of this world,
why, as though you still belonged to the
world, do you submit to its rules: 21 "Do

[a] *21* Or *minds, as shown by* [b] *8* Or *the basic principles*; also in verse 20 [c] *11* In contexts like this, the Greek word for *flesh* (*sarx*) refers to the sinful state of human beings, often presented as a power in opposition to the Spirit; also in verse 13. [d] *11* Or *put off in the circumcision of* [e] *13* Some manuscripts *us* [f] *15* Or *them in him*

not handle! Do not taste! Do not touch!"?
22 These rules, which have to do with
things that are all destined to perish
with use, are based on merely human
commands and teachings. 23 Such regulations indeed have an appearance
of wisdom, with their self-imposed
worship, their false humility and their
harsh treatment of the body, but they
lack any value in restraining sensual in-
dulgence.

3 Since, then, you have been raised
with Christ, set your hearts on things
above, where Christ is, seated at the
right hand of God. 2 Set your minds on
things above, not on earthly things.
3 For you died, and your life is now hidden with Christ in God. 4 When Christ,
who is your[a] life, appears, then you also
will appear with him in glory.

5 Put to death, therefore, whatever
belongs to your earthly nature: sexual
immorality, impurity, lust, evil desires
and greed, which is idolatry. 6 Because
of these, the wrath of God is coming.[b]
7 You used to walk in these ways, in the
life you once lived. 8 But now you must
also rid yourselves of all such things as
these: anger, rage, malice, slander, and
filthy language from your lips. 9 Do not
lie to each other, since you have taken
off your old self with its practices 10 and
have put on the new self, which is being
renewed in knowledge in the image of
its Creator. 11 Here there is no Gentile
or Jew, circumcised or uncircumcised,
barbarian, Scythian, slave or free, but
Christ is all, and is in all.

12 Therefore, as God's chosen people,
holy and dearly loved, clothe yourselves
with compassion, kindness, humility,
gentleness and patience. 13 Bear with
each other and forgive one another if any
of you has a grievance against someone.
Forgive as the Lord forgave you. 14 And
over all these virtues put on love, which
binds them all together in perfect unity.

15 Let the peace of Christ rule in your
hearts, since as members of one body
you were called to peace. And be thankful. 16 Let the message of Christ dwell
among you richly as you teach and admonish one another with all wisdom
through psalms, hymns, and songs from
the Spirit, singing to God with gratitude
in your hearts. 17 And whatever you do,
whether in word or deed, do it all in the
name of the Lord Jesus, giving thanks to
God the Father through him.

18 Wives, submit yourselves to your
husbands, as is fitting in the Lord.

19 Husbands, love your wives and do
not be harsh with them.

20 Children, obey your parents in everything, for this pleases the Lord.

21 Fathers,[c] do not embitter your children, or they will become discouraged.

22 Slaves, obey your earthly masters
in everything; and do it, not only when
their eye is on you and to curry their favor, but with sincerity of heart and reverence for the Lord. 23 Whatever you do,
work at it with all your heart, as working
for the Lord, not for human masters,
24 since you know that you will receive
an inheritance from the Lord as a reward. It is the Lord Christ you are serving. 25 Anyone who does wrong will be
repaid for their wrongs, and there is no
favoritism.

4 Masters, provide your slaves with
what is right and fair, because you
know that you also have a Master in
heaven.

2 Devote yourselves to prayer, being
watchful and thankful. 3 And pray for
us, too, that God may open a door for
our message, so that we may proclaim
the mystery of Christ, for which I am
in chains. 4 Pray that I may proclaim it
clearly, as I should. 5 Be wise in the way
you act toward outsiders; make the most
of every opportunity. 6 Let your conversation be always full of grace, seasoned
with salt, so that you may know how to
answer everyone.

7 Tychicus will tell you all the news
about me. He is a dear brother, a faithful
minister and fellow servant[d] in the Lord.
8 I am sending him to you for the express
purpose that you may know about our[e]
circumstances and that he may encourage your hearts. 9 He is coming with
Onesimus, our faithful and dear brother, who is one of you. They will tell you
everything that is happening here.

10 My fellow prisoner Aristarchus
sends you his greetings, as does Mark,
the cousin of Barnabas. (You have re-

[a] *4* Some manuscripts *our* [b] *6* Some early manuscripts *coming on those who are disobedient*
[c] *21* Or *Parents* [d] *7* Or *slave*; also in verse 12 [e] *8* Some manuscripts *that he may know about your*

ceived instructions about him; if he
comes to you, welcome him.) 11 Jesus,
who is called Justus, also sends greetings. These are the only Jews[a] among
my co-workers for the kingdom of God,
and they have proved a comfort to me.
12 Epaphras, who is one of you and a servant of Christ Jesus, sends greetings. He
is always wrestling in prayer for you, that
you may stand firm in all the will of God,
mature and fully assured. 13 I vouch for
him that he is working hard for you and
for those at Laodicea and Hierapolis.
14 Our dear friend Luke, the doctor, and
Demas send greetings. 15 Give my greetings to the brothers and sisters at Laodicea, and to Nympha and the church in
her house.

16 After this letter has been read to you,
see that it is also read in the church of
the Laodiceans and that you in turn read
the letter from Laodicea.

17 Tell Archippus: "See to it that you
complete the ministry you have received
in the Lord."

18 I, Paul, write this greeting in my own
hand. Remember my chains. Grace be
with you.

a 11 Greek *only ones of the circumcision group*

1 THESSALONIANS

Around AD 51, Paul, Silas and Timothy brought the message about Jesus the Messiah to the city of Thessalonica. Many people became believers, but there was a riot when Paul and Silas were accused of *defying Caesar's decrees, saying that there is another king, one called Jesus* (see p. 992-993). They narrowly escaped with their lives and had to flee.

A little later Paul became concerned that the believers in Thessalonica might fall away from the faith due to the opposition they were facing. So he sent Timothy to encourage them (as a Greek he could make the trip more safely). When Timothy returned to Achaia with the welcome news that the Thessalonians had remained faithful, Paul wrote to express his joy.

In this short letter, Paul first recalls his time in Thessalonica and gives thanks for their continuing faith, despite trials and challenges. He teaches them to avoid sexual immorality, to love one another sincerely, and to work hard to earn their own living.

Paul then addresses a key pastoral question: What is the Christian hope for those who have died? He explains that believers who die before the royal appearance of the Messiah are not lost, but will surely be raised from the dead when he comes. He reminds the Thessalonians that Jesus will appear suddenly and unexpectedly. They should therefore live in such a way that they would be unashamed to greet him. Throughout the letter Paul's basic message is, "Keep up the good work!"

---

1 Paul, Silas[a] and Timothy,

To the church of the Thessalonians in God the Father and the Lord Jesus Christ:

Grace and peace to you.

2We always thank God for all of you
and continually mention you in our
prayers. 3We remember before our God
and Father your work produced by faith,
your labor prompted by love, and your
endurance inspired by hope in our Lord
Jesus Christ.
4For we know, brothers and sisters[b]
loved by God, that he has chosen you,
5because our gospel came to you not
simply with words but also with power,
with the Holy Spirit and deep conviction. You know how we lived among you
for your sake. 6You became imitators of
us and of the Lord, for you welcomed the
message in the midst of severe suffering with the joy given by the Holy Spirit.
7And so you became a model to all the
believers in Macedonia and Achaia.
8The Lord's message rang out from you
not only in Macedonia and Achaia—
your faith in God has become known
everywhere. Therefore we do not need
to say anything about it, 9for they themselves report what kind of reception
you gave us. They tell how you turned
to God from idols to serve the living
and true God, 10and to wait for his Son
from heaven, whom he raised from the
dead—Jesus, who rescues us from the
coming wrath.

2 You know, brothers and sisters, that our visit to you was not without results. 2We had previously suffered and
been treated outrageously in Philippi,
as you know, but with the help of our
God we dared to tell you his gospel in
the face of strong opposition. 3For the
appeal we make does not spring from error or impure motives, nor are we trying
to trick you. 4On the contrary, we speak
as those approved by God to be entrusted with the gospel. We are not trying to
please people but God, who tests our
hearts. 5You know we never used flattery, nor did we put on a mask to cover
up greed—God is our witness. 6We were
not looking for praise from people, not
from you or anyone else, even though as
apostles of Christ we could have asserted our authority. 7Instead, we were like
young children[c] among you.
Just as a nursing mother cares for her

[a] *1* Greek *Silvanus*, a variant of *Silas* [b] *4* The Greek word for *brothers and sisters* (*adelphoi*) refers here to believers, both men and women, as part of God's family; also in 2:1, 9, 14, 17; 3:7; 4:1, 10, 13; 5:1, 4, 12, 14, 25, 27. [c] *7* Some manuscripts *were gentle*

children, [8]so we cared for you. Because
we loved you so much, we were delighted to share with you not only the gospel
of God but our lives as well. [9]Surely you
remember, brothers and sisters, our toil
and hardship; we worked night and day
in order not to be a burden to anyone
while we preached the gospel of God to
you. [10]You are witnesses, and so is God,
of how holy, righteous and blameless
we were among you who believed. [11]For
you know that we dealt with each of you
as a father deals with his own children,
[12]encouraging, comforting and urging
you to live lives worthy of God, who calls
you into his kingdom and glory.

[13]And we also thank God continually
because, when you received the word of
God, which you heard from us, you accepted it not as a human word, but as it
actually is, the word of God, which is indeed at work in you who believe. [14]For
you, brothers and sisters, became imitators of God's churches in Judea, which
are in Christ Jesus: You suffered from
your own people the same things those
churches suffered from the Jews [15]who
killed the Lord Jesus and the prophets
and also drove us out. They displease
God and are hostile to everyone [16]in
their effort to keep us from speaking to
the Gentiles so that they may be saved.
In this way they always heap up their
sins to the limit. The wrath of God has
come upon them at last.[a]

[17]But, brothers and sisters, when we
were orphaned by being separated from
you for a short time (in person, not in
thought), out of our intense longing we
made every effort to see you. [18]For we
wanted to come to you—certainly I,
Paul, did, again and again—but Satan
blocked our way. [19]For what is our hope,
our joy, or the crown in which we will
glory in the presence of our Lord Jesus
when he comes? Is it not you? [20]Indeed,
you are our glory and joy.

3 So when we could stand it no longer,
we thought it best to be left by ourselves in Athens. [2]We sent Timothy, who
is our brother and co-worker in God's
service in spreading the gospel of Christ,
to strengthen and encourage you in your
faith, [3]so that no one would be unsettled
by these trials. For you know quite well
that we are destined for them. [4]In fact,
when we were with you, we kept telling
you that we would be persecuted. And it
turned out that way, as you well know.
[5]For this reason, when I could stand it
no longer, I sent to find out about your
faith. I was afraid that in some way the
tempter had tempted you and that our
labors might have been in vain.

[6]But Timothy has just now come to
us from you and has brought good news
about your faith and love. He has told us
that you always have pleasant memo-
ries of us and that you long to see us, just
as we also long to see you. [7]Therefore,
brothers and sisters, in all our distress
and persecution we were encouraged
about you because of your faith. [8]For
now we really live, since you are standing firm in the Lord. [9]How can we thank
God enough for you in return for all the
joy we have in the presence of our God
because of you? [10]Night and day we
pray most earnestly that we may see you
again and supply what is lacking in your
faith.

[11]Now may our God and Father himself and our Lord Jesus clear the way for
us to come to you. [12]May the Lord make
your love increase and overflow for each
other and for everyone else, just as ours
does for you. [13]May he strengthen your
hearts so that you will be blameless and
holy in the presence of our God and Father when our Lord Jesus comes with all
his holy ones.

4 As for other matters, brothers and
sisters, we instructed you how to live
in order to please God, as in fact you are
living. Now we ask you and urge you in
the Lord Jesus to do this more and more.
[2]For you know what instructions we gave
you by the authority of the Lord Jesus.

[3]It is God's will that you should be
sanctified: that you should avoid sexual immorality; [4]that each of you should
learn to control your own body[b] in a way
that is holy and honorable, [5]not in passionate lust like the pagans, who do not
know God; [6]and that in this matter no
one should wrong or take advantage of
a brother or sister.[c] The Lord will punish all those who commit such sins, as
we told you and warned you before. [7]For
God did not call us to be impure, but to

[a] 16 Or *them fully* [b] 4 Or *learn to live with your own wife*; or *learn to acquire a wife* [c] 6 The Greek word for *brother or sister* (*adelphos*) refers here to a believer, whether man or woman, as part of God's family.

live a holy life. 8Therefore, anyone who
rejects this instruction does not reject a
human being but God, the very God who
gives you his Holy Spirit.
9Now about your love for one another
we do not need to write to you, for you
yourselves have been taught by God to
love each other. 10And in fact, you do
love all of God's family throughout Macedonia. Yet we urge you, brothers and
sisters, to do so more and more, 11and to
make it your ambition to lead a quiet life:
You should mind your own business and
work with your hands, just as we told
you, 12so that your daily life may win the
respect of outsiders and so that you will
not be dependent on anybody.
13Brothers and sisters, we do not want
you to be uninformed about those who
sleep in death, so that you do not grieve
like the rest of mankind, who have no
hope. 14For we believe that Jesus died
and rose again, and so we believe that
God will bring with Jesus those who
have fallen asleep in him. 15According
to the Lord's word, we tell you that we
who are still alive, who are left until the
coming of the Lord, will certainly not
precede those who have fallen asleep.
16For the Lord himself will come down
from heaven, with a loud command,
with the voice of the archangel and with
the trumpet call of God, and the dead in
Christ will rise first. 17After that, we who
are still alive and are left will be caught
up together with them in the clouds to
meet the Lord in the air. And so we will
be with the Lord forever. 18Therefore encourage one another with these words.

5 Now, brothers and sisters, about
times and dates we do not need to
write to you, 2for you know very well
that the day of the Lord will come like a
thief in the night. 3While people are saying, "Peace and safety," destruction will
come on them suddenly, as labor pains
on a pregnant woman, and they will not
escape.
4But you, brothers and sisters, are not
in darkness so that this day should surprise you like a thief. 5You are all children of the light and children of the day.
We do not belong to the night or to the
darkness. 6So then, let us not be like others, who are asleep, but let us be awake
and sober. 7For those who sleep, sleep
at night, and those who get drunk, get
drunk at night. 8But since we belong to
the day, let us be sober, putting on faith
and love as a breastplate, and the hope of
salvation as a helmet. 9For God did not
appoint us to suffer wrath but to receive
salvation through our Lord Jesus Christ.
10He died for us so that, whether we are
awake or asleep, we may live together
with him. 11Therefore encourage one
another and build each other up, just as
in fact you are doing.
12Now we ask you, brothers and sisters, to acknowledge those who work
hard among you, who care for you in
the Lord and who admonish you. 13Hold
them in the highest regard in love because of their work. Live in peace with
each other. 14And we urge you, brothers
and sisters, warn those who are idle and
disruptive, encourage the disheartened,
help the weak, be patient with everyone.
15Make sure that nobody pays back
wrong for wrong, but always strive to do
what is good for each other and for everyone else.
16Rejoice always, 17pray continually,
18give thanks in all circumstances; for
this is God's will for you in Christ Jesus.
19Do not quench the Spirit. 20Do not
treat prophecies with contempt 21but
test them all; hold on to what is good,
22reject every kind of evil.
23May God himself, the God of peace,
sanctify you through and through. May
your whole spirit, soul and body be kept
blameless at the coming of our Lord
Jesus Christ. 24The one who calls you is
faithful, and he will do it.

25Brothers and sisters, pray for us.
26Greet all God's people with a holy kiss.
27I charge you before the Lord to have
this letter read to all the brothers and
sisters.
28The grace of our Lord Jesus Christ
be with you.

2 THESSALONIANS

Apparently only shortly after writing his first letter to the Thessalonians, Paul had to write again to correct a false report that he had said the day of the Lord had already come. The *day of the Lord* was a phrase from the Hebrew prophets to describe God's key victory over every opponent, when his faithful ones would be rewarded. The Thessalonians' concern seems to have been not that the day had come and gone and they had missed it, but that it was now present. That would mean nothing more was to be expected from God in terms of setting things right. Since they continued to suffer persecutions, this was a depressing prospect.

Even before he contradicts this false report, Paul reassures the Thessalonians that God will indeed pay back all those who were troubling them. He reminds them of the details he had discussed with them in person of how the day of the Lord would arrive. He then repeats some instruction from his earlier letter, urging them not to be idle but to work hard and earn their own livings.

At the end of the letter, most of which would have been written by a scribe, Paul adds a greeting in his own handwriting. He wants them to know for sure this teaching is really coming from him!

---

1 Paul, Silas[a] and Timothy,

To the church of the Thessalonians
in God our Father and the Lord Jesus
Christ:

2Grace and peace to you from God the
Father and the Lord Jesus Christ.

3We ought always to thank God for
you, brothers and sisters,[b] and rightly
so, because your faith is growing more
and more, and the love all of you have
for one another is increasing. 4There-
fore, among God's churches we boast
about your perseverance and faith in all
the persecutions and trials you are enduring.
5All this is evidence that God's judgment is right, and as a result you will be
counted worthy of the kingdom of God,
for which you are suffering. 6God is just:
He will pay back trouble to those who
trouble you 7and give relief to you who
are troubled, and to us as well. This will
happen when the Lord Jesus is revealed
from heaven in blazing fire with his
powerful angels. 8He will punish those
who do not know God and do not obey
the gospel of our Lord Jesus. 9They will
be punished with everlasting destruction and shut out from the presence of
the Lord and from the glory of his might
10on the day he comes to be glorified in
his holy people and to be marveled at
among all those who have believed. This
includes you, because you believed our
testimony to you.
11With this in mind, we constantly
pray for you, that our God may make
you worthy of his calling, and that by his
power he may bring to fruition your every desire for goodness and your every
deed prompted by faith. 12We pray this
so that the name of our Lord Jesus may
be glorified in you, and you in him, according to the grace of our God and the
Lord Jesus Christ.[c]
2 Concerning the coming of our Lord
Jesus Christ and our being gathered
to him, we ask you, brothers and sisters, 2not to become easily unsettled or
alarmed by the teaching allegedly from
us — whether by a prophecy or by word
of mouth or by letter — asserting that the
day of the Lord has already come. 3Don't
let anyone deceive you in any way, for
that day will not come until the rebellion occurs and the man of lawlessness[d]
is revealed, the man doomed to destruction. 4He will oppose and will exalt himself over everything that is called God or
is worshiped, so that he sets himself up
in God's temple, proclaiming himself to
be God.
5Don't you remember that when I was
with you I used to tell you these things?
6And now you know what is holding him

[a] 1 Greek *Silvanus*, a variant of *Silas* [b] 3 The Greek word for *brothers and sisters* (*adelphoi*) refers here to believers, both men and women, as part of God's family; also in 2:1, 13, 15; 3:1, 6, 13. [c] 12 Or *God and Lord, Jesus Christ* [d] 3 Some manuscripts *sin*

back, so that he may be revealed at the
proper time. 7For the secret power of
lawlessness is already at work; but the
one who now holds it back will continue to do so till he is taken out of the
way. 8And then the lawless one will be
revealed, whom the Lord Jesus will overthrow with the breath of his mouth and
destroy by the splendor of his coming.
9The coming of the lawless one will be
in accordance with how Satan works.
He will use all sorts of displays of power through signs and wonders that serve
the lie, 10and all the ways that wickedness deceives those who are perishing.
They perish because they refused to love
the truth and so be saved. 11For this reason God sends them a powerful delusion
so that they will believe the lie 12and so
that all will be condemned who have not
believed the truth but have delighted in
wickedness.

13But we ought always to thank God
for you, brothers and sisters loved by the
Lord, because God chose you as firstfruits[a] to be saved through the sanctifying work of the Spirit and through be-
lief in the truth. 14He called you to this
through our gospel, that you might share
in the glory of our Lord Jesus Christ.

15So then, brothers and sisters, stand
firm and hold fast to the teachings[b] we
passed on to you, whether by word of
mouth or by letter.

16May our Lord Jesus Christ himself
and God our Father, who loved us and
by his grace gave us eternal encouragement and good hope, 17encourage your
hearts and strengthen you in every good
deed and word.

3 As for other matters, brothers and
sisters, pray for us that the message
of the Lord may spread rapidly and be
honored, just as it was with you. 2And
pray that we may be delivered from
wicked and evil people, for not everyone
has faith. 3But the Lord is faithful, and
he will strengthen you and protect you
from the evil one. 4We have confidence
in the Lord that you are doing and will
continue to do the things we command.
5May the Lord direct your hearts into
God's love and Christ's perseverance.

6In the name of the Lord Jesus Christ,
we command you, brothers and sisters,
to keep away from every believer who
is idle and disruptive and does not live
according to the teaching[c] you received
from us. 7For you yourselves know how
you ought to follow our example. We
were not idle when we were with you,
8nor did we eat anyone's food without
paying for it. On the contrary, we worked
night and day, laboring and toiling so
that we would not be a burden to any of
you. 9We did this, not because we do not
have the right to such help, but in order
to offer ourselves as a model for you to
imitate. 10For even when we were with
you, we gave you this rule: "The one who
is unwilling to work shall not eat."

11We hear that some among you are
idle and disruptive. They are not busy;
they are busybodies. 12Such people we
command and urge in the Lord Jesus
Christ to settle down and earn the food
they eat. 13And as for you, brothers and
sisters, never tire of doing what is good.

14Take special note of anyone who
does not obey our instruction in this letter. Do not associate with them, in order
that they may feel ashamed. 15Yet do not
regard them as an enemy, but warn them
as you would a fellow believer.

16Now may the Lord of peace himself
give you peace at all times and in every
way. The Lord be with all of you.

17I, Paul, write this greeting in my own
hand, which is the distinguishing mark
in all my letters. This is how I write.

18The grace of our Lord Jesus Christ be
with you all.

[a] *13* Some manuscripts *because from the beginning God chose you* [b] *15* Or *traditions* [c] *6* Or *tradition*

1 TIMOTHY

After Paul was released from prison in Rome, he discovered that leaders in the Ephesian church had distorted the genuine message they had first heard from Paul himself. They had misapplied certain Jewish practices and borrowed some others from the philosophies of the day. They restricted certain foods, forbade marriage and stressed controversial speculations as the path to spiritual progress. At the same time, they tolerated immoral behavior. So Paul sent his co-worker Timothy to Ephesus and wrote him a letter, which he was expected to share with the church. He hoped it would give Timothy the power and influence to set things in order until Paul could get to Ephesus himself.

Paul's focus is on what true leadership in the church looks like. This would help the Ephesians reject those who weren't qualified and replace them with those who were. Paul includes a special warning toward the end of his letter about the dangers of greed, which seemed to be at the root of their problems.

Throughout the letter Paul uses the phrase *Christ Jesus*—that is, Messiah Jesus—which emphasizes the kingly rule of Jesus. This helped remind the church that Jesus is their real leader and is the clearest model of authentic leadership.

---

1 Paul, an apostle of Christ Jesus by the
command of God our Savior and of
Christ Jesus our hope,

2 To Timothy my true son in the faith:

Grace, mercy and peace from God the
Father and Christ Jesus our Lord.

3 As I urged you when I went into Macedonia, stay there in Ephesus so that
you may command certain people not
to teach false doctrines any longer 4 or to
devote themselves to myths and endless
genealogies. Such things promote controversial speculations rather than advancing God's work — which is by faith.
5 The goal of this command is love, which
comes from a pure heart and a good conscience and a sincere faith. 6 Some have
departed from these and have turned
to meaningless talk. 7 They want to be
teachers of the law, but they do not know
what they are talking about or what they
so confidently affirm.

8 We know that the law is good if one
uses it properly. 9 We also know that the
law is made not for the righteous but for
lawbreakers and rebels, the ungodly and
sinful, the unholy and irreligious, for
those who kill their fathers or mothers,
for murderers, 10 for the sexually immoral, for those practicing homosexuality,
for slave traders and liars and perjurers — and for whatever else is contrary
to the sound doctrine 11 that conforms
to the gospel concerning the glory of the
blessed God, which he entrusted to me.

12 I thank Christ Jesus our Lord, who
has given me strength, that he considered me trustworthy, appointing me to
his service. 13 Even though I was once a
blasphemer and a persecutor and a violent man, I was shown mercy because I
acted in ignorance and unbelief. 14 The
grace of our Lord was poured out on me
abundantly, along with the faith and
love that are in Christ Jesus.

15 Here is a trustworthy saying that
deserves full acceptance: Christ Jesus
came into the world to save sinners — of
whom I am the worst. 16 But for that very
reason I was shown mercy so that in me,
the worst of sinners, Christ Jesus might
display his immense patience as an example for those who would believe in
him and receive eternal life. 17 Now to
the King eternal, immortal, invisible,
the only God, be honor and glory for ever
and ever. Amen.

18 Timothy, my son, I am giving you
this command in keeping with the
prophecies once made about you, so
that by recalling them you may fight the
battle well, 19 holding on to faith and a
good conscience, which some have rejected and so have suffered shipwreck
with regard to the faith. 20 Among them
are Hymenaeus and Alexander, whom I
have handed over to Satan to be taught
not to blaspheme.

2 I urge, then, first of all, that petitions,
prayers, intercession and thanksgiving be made for all people — 2 for kings
and all those in authority, that we may

live peaceful and quiet lives in all godliness and holiness. 3This is good, and
pleases God our Savior, 4who wants
all people to be saved and to come to a
knowledge of the truth. 5For there is one
God and one mediator between God and
mankind, the man Christ Jesus, 6who
gave himself as a ransom for all people. This has now been witnessed to at
the proper time. 7And for this purpose
I was appointed a herald and an apostle—I am telling the truth, I am not lying—and a true and faithful teacher of
the Gentiles.

8Therefore I want the men everywhere
to pray, lifting up holy hands without
anger or disputing. 9I also want the
women to dress modestly, with decen-
cy and propriety, adorning themselves,
not with elaborate hairstyles or gold or
pearls or expensive clothes, 10but with
good deeds, appropriate for women who
profess to worship God.

11A woman[a] should learn in quietness
and full submission. 12I do not permit a
woman to teach or to assume authority
over a man;[b] she must be quiet. 13For
Adam was formed first, then Eve. 14And
Adam was not the one deceived; it was
the woman who was deceived and became a sinner. 15But women[c] will be
saved through childbearing—if they
continue in faith, love and holiness with
propriety.

3 Here is a trustworthy saying: Whoever aspires to be an overseer desires
a noble task. 2Now the overseer is to
be above reproach, faithful to his wife,
temperate, self-controlled, respectable,
hospitable, able to teach, 3not given to
drunkenness, not violent but gentle, not
quarrelsome, not a lover of money. 4He
must manage his own family well and
see that his children obey him, and he
must do so in a manner worthy of full[d]
respect. 5(If anyone does not know how
to manage his own family, how can he
take care of God's church?) 6He must not
be a recent convert, or he may become
conceited and fall under the same judgment as the devil. 7He must also have a
good reputation with outsiders, so that
he will not fall into disgrace and into the
devil's trap.

8In the same way, deacons[e] are to be
worthy of respect, sincere, not indulging
in much wine, and not pursuing dishonest gain. 9They must keep hold of the
deep truths of the faith with a clear conscience. 10They must first be tested; and
then if there is nothing against them, let
them serve as deacons.

11In the same way, the women[f] are to
be worthy of respect, not malicious talk-
ers but temperate and trustworthy in
everything.

12A deacon must be faithful to his wife
and must manage his children and his
household well. 13Those who have served
well gain an excellent standing and great
assurance in their faith in Christ Jesus.

14Although I hope to come to you soon,
I am writing you these instructions so
that, 15if I am delayed, you will know
how people ought to conduct themselves
in God's household, which is the church
of the living God, the pillar and foundation of the truth. 16Beyond all question,
the mystery from which true godliness
springs is great:

He appeared in the flesh,
 was vindicated by the Spirit,[g]
was seen by angels,
 was preached among the nations,
was believed on in the world,
 was taken up in glory.

4 The Spirit clearly says that in later
times some will abandon the faith
and follow deceiving spirits and things
taught by demons. 2Such teachings
come through hypocritical liars, whose
consciences have been seared as with a
hot iron. 3They forbid people to marry
and order them to abstain from certain
foods, which God created to be received
with thanksgiving by those who believe
and who know the truth. 4For everything God created is good, and nothing is to be rejected if it is received with
thanksgiving, 5because it is consecrated
by the word of God and prayer.

6If you point these things out to the
brothers and sisters,[h] you will be a good

[a] *11* Or *wife*; also in verse 12 [b] *12* Or *over her husband* [c] *15* Greek *she* [d] *4* Or *him with proper*
[e] *8* The word *deacons* refers here to Christians designated to serve with the overseers/elders of the church in a variety of ways; similarly in verse 12; and in Romans 16:1 and Phil. 1:1. [f] *11* Possibly deacons' wives or women who are deacons [g] *16* Or *vindicated in spirit* [h] *6* The Greek word for *brothers and sisters* (*adelphoi*) refers here to believers, both men and women, as part of God's family.

minister of Christ Jesus, nourished on the truths of the faith and of the good teaching that you have followed. [7]Have nothing to do with godless myths and old wives' tales; rather, train yourself to be godly. [8]For physical training is of some value, but godliness has value for all things, holding promise for both the present life and the life to come. [9]This is a trustworthy saying that deserves full acceptance. [10]That is why we labor and strive, because we have put our hope in the living God, who is the Savior of all people, and especially of those who believe.

[11]Command and teach these things. [12]Don't let anyone look down on you because you are young, but set an example for the believers in speech, in conduct, in love, in faith and in purity. [13]Until I come, devote yourself to the public reading of Scripture, to preaching and to teaching. [14]Do not neglect your gift, which was given you through prophecy when the body of elders laid their hands on you.

[15]Be diligent in these matters; give yourself wholly to them, so that everyone may see your progress. [16]Watch your life and doctrine closely. Persevere in them, because if you do, you will save both yourself and your hearers.

5 Do not rebuke an older man harshly, but exhort him as if he were your father. Treat younger men as brothers, [2]older women as mothers, and younger women as sisters, with absolute purity.

[3]Give proper recognition to those widows who are really in need. [4]But if a widow has children or grandchildren, these should learn first of all to put their religion into practice by caring for their own family and so repaying their parents and grandparents, for this is pleasing to God. [5]The widow who is really in need and left all alone puts her hope in God and continues night and day to pray and to ask God for help. [6]But the widow who lives for pleasure is dead even while she lives. [7]Give the people these instructions, so that no one may be open to blame. [8]Anyone who does not provide for their relatives, and especially for their own household, has denied the faith and is worse than an unbeliever.

[9]No widow may be put on the list of widows unless she is over sixty, has been faithful to her husband, [10]and is well known for her good deeds, such as bringing up children, showing hospitality, washing the feet of the Lord's people, helping those in trouble and devoting herself to all kinds of good deeds.

[11]As for younger widows, do not put them on such a list. For when their sensual desires overcome their dedication to Christ, they want to marry. [12]Thus they bring judgment on themselves, because they have broken their first pledge. [13]Besides, they get into the habit of being idle and going about from house to house. And not only do they become idlers, but also busybodies who talk nonsense, saying things they ought not to. [14]So I counsel younger widows to marry, to have children, to manage their homes and to give the enemy no opportunity for slander. [15]Some have in fact already turned away to follow Satan.

[16]If any woman who is a believer has widows in her care, she should continue to help them and not let the church be burdened with them, so that the church can help those widows who are really in need.

[17]The elders who direct the affairs of the church well are worthy of double honor, especially those whose work is preaching and teaching. [18]For Scripture says, "Do not muzzle an ox while it is treading out the grain,"[a] and "The worker deserves his wages."[b] [19]Do not entertain an accusation against an elder unless it is brought by two or three witnesses. [20]But those elders who are sinning you are to reprove before everyone, so that the others may take warning. [21]I charge you, in the sight of God and Christ Jesus and the elect angels, to keep these instructions without partiality, and to do nothing out of favoritism.

[22]Do not be hasty in the laying on of hands, and do not share in the sins of others. Keep yourself pure.

[23]Stop drinking only water, and use a little wine because of your stomach and your frequent illnesses.

[24]The sins of some are obvious, reaching the place of judgment ahead of them; the sins of others trail behind them. [25]In

[a] *18* Deut. 25:4 [b] *18* Luke 10:7

the same way, good deeds are obvious,
and even those that are not obvious cannot remain hidden forever.

6 All who are under the yoke of slavery
should consider their masters worthy of full respect, so that God's name
and our teaching may not be slandered.
2Those who have believing masters
should not show them disrespect just because they are fellow believers. Instead,
they should serve them even better because their masters are dear to them as
fellow believers and are devoted to the
welfare[a] of their slaves.

These are the things you are to teach
and insist on. 3If anyone teaches otherwise and does not agree to the sound
instruction of our Lord Jesus Christ and
to godly teaching, 4they are conceited
and understand nothing. They have an
unhealthy interest in controversies and
quarrels about words that result in envy,
strife, malicious talk, evil suspicions
5and constant friction between people
of corrupt mind, who have been robbed
of the truth and who think that godliness is a means to financial gain.

6But godliness with contentment is
great gain. 7For we brought nothing into
the world, and we can take nothing out
of it. 8But if we have food and clothing,
we will be content with that. 9Those who
want to get rich fall into temptation and
a trap and into many foolish and harmful desires that plunge people into ruin
and destruction. 10For the love of money
is a root of all kinds of evil. Some people,
eager for money, have wandered from
the faith and pierced themselves with
many griefs.

11But you, man of God, flee from all
this, and pursue righteousness, godliness, faith, love, endurance and gentleness. 12Fight the good fight of the faith.
Take hold of the eternal life to which you
were called when you made your good
confession in the presence of many witnesses. 13In the sight of God, who gives
life to everything, and of Christ Jesus,
who while testifying before Pontius Pilate made the good confession, I charge
you 14to keep this command without
spot or blame until the appearing of
our Lord Jesus Christ, 15which God
will bring about in his own time—God,
the blessed and only Ruler, the King of
kings and Lord of lords, 16who alone is
immortal and who lives in unapproach-
able light, whom no one has seen or can
see. To him be honor and might forever.
Amen.

17Command those who are rich in
this present world not to be arrogant nor
to put their hope in wealth, which is so
uncertain, but to put their hope in God,
who richly provides us with everything
for our enjoyment. 18Command them to
do good, to be rich in good deeds, and
to be generous and willing to share. 19In
this way they will lay up treasure for
themselves as a firm foundation for the
coming age, so that they may take hold
of the life that is truly life.

20Timothy, guard what has been entrusted to your care. Turn away from
godless chatter and the opposing ideas
of what is falsely called knowledge,
21which some have professed and in so
doing have departed from the faith.

Grace be with you all.

[a] 2 Or *and benefit from the service*

2 TIMOTHY

Paul left his co-worker Timothy in the city of Ephesus to deal with some renegade leaders in the church there. When Timothy struggled, however, Paul went back to Ephesus. Once there, Paul suffered *a great deal of harm* from Alexander, one of these leaders, and he was once again imprisoned and taken to Rome. He expected that this time he would be tried and executed. Paul wrote to Timothy to ask him to come to Rome quickly.

Things in Ephesus had not gone as Paul or Timothy expected. Paul had ordered both Alexander and Hymenaeus to step down from leadership, but they were continuing to oppose Paul. Others had joined them, and they were still misdirecting people into a corrupted version of the faith that stressed debate and dissension rather than purity and obedience. Timothy was discouraged and intimidated. Paul's letter includes challenges to stay faithful to the true message—even if this meant suffering or death. Paul reminds Timothy that in the days before the open appearance of Jesus as king, there will be lots of trouble. False teachers, treacherous and insincere people, persecutions and more will all challenge the faithfulness of God's people.

Paul urges Timothy to remember the gospel message: *Jesus Christ, raised from the dead, descended from David*. He points out that the sacred writings Timothy has known since he was a child are God-breathed, and will help him continue in doing good work.

---

1 Paul, an apostle of Christ Jesus by
the will of God, in keeping with the
promise of life that is in Christ Jesus,

2 To Timothy, my dear son:

Grace, mercy and peace from God the
Father and Christ Jesus our Lord.

3 I thank God, whom I serve, as my
ancestors did, with a clear conscience,
as night and day I constantly remember you in my prayers. 4 Recalling your
tears, I long to see you, so that I may be
filled with joy. 5 I am reminded of your
sincere faith, which first lived in your
grandmother Lois and in your mother
Eunice and, I am persuaded, now lives
in you also.
6 For this reason I remind you to fan
into flame the gift of God, which is in you
through the laying on of my hands. 7 For
the Spirit God gave us does not make
us timid, but gives us power, love and
self-discipline. 8 So do not be ashamed
of the testimony about our Lord or of
me his prisoner. Rather, join with me in
suffering for the gospel, by the power of
God. 9 He has saved us and called us to
a holy life—not because of anything we
have done but because of his own purpose and grace. This grace was given
us in Christ Jesus before the beginning
of time, 10 but it has now been revealed
through the appearing of our Savior,
Christ Jesus, who has destroyed death
and has brought life and immortality to
light through the gospel. 11 And of this
gospel I was appointed a herald and an
apostle and a teacher. 12 That is why I am
suffering as I am. Yet this is no cause for
shame, because I know whom I have believed, and am convinced that he is able
to guard what I have entrusted to him
until that day.
13 What you heard from me, keep as
the pattern of sound teaching, with
faith and love in Christ Jesus. 14 Guard
the good deposit that was entrusted to
you—guard it with the help of the Holy
Spirit who lives in us.
15 You know that everyone in the province of Asia has deserted me, including
Phygelus and Hermogenes.
16 May the Lord show mercy to the
household of Onesiphorus, because he
often refreshed me and was not ashamed
of my chains. 17 On the contrary, when he
was in Rome, he searched hard for me
until he found me. 18 May the Lord grant
that he will find mercy from the Lord
on that day! You know very well in how
many ways he helped me in Ephesus.

2 You then, my son, be strong in the
grace that is in Christ Jesus. 2 And
the things you have heard me say in the
presence of many witnesses entrust to

reliable people who will also be qualified to teach others. 3 Join with me in
suffering, like a good soldier of Christ
Jesus. 4 No one serving as a soldier gets
entangled in civilian affairs, but rather
tries to please his commanding officer.
5 Similarly, anyone who competes as
an athlete does not receive the victor's
crown except by competing according
to the rules. 6 The hardworking farmer
should be the first to receive a share of
the crops. 7 Reflect on what I am saying,
for the Lord will give you insight into all
this.

8 Remember Jesus Christ, raised from
the dead, descended from David. This
is my gospel, 9 for which I am suffering
even to the point of being chained like a
criminal. But God's word is not chained.
10 Therefore I endure everything for the
sake of the elect, that they too may obtain the salvation that is in Christ Jesus,
with eternal glory.

11 Here is a trustworthy saying:

If we died with him,
we will also live with him;
12 if we endure,
we will also reign with him.
If we disown him,
he will also disown us;
13 if we are faithless,
he remains faithful,
for he cannot disown himself.

14 Keep reminding God's people of
these things. Warn them before God
against quarreling about words; it is of no
value, and only ruins those who listen.
15 Do your best to present yourself to God
as one approved, a worker who does not
need to be ashamed and who correctly
handles the word of truth. 16 Avoid godless chatter, because those who indulge
in it will become more and more ungodly. 17 Their teaching will spread like gan-
grene. Among them are Hymenaeus and
Philetus, 18 who have departed from the
truth. They say that the resurrection has
already taken place, and they destroy
the faith of some. 19 Nevertheless, God's
solid foundation stands firm, sealed
with this inscription: "The Lord knows
those who are his," and, "Everyone who
confesses the name of the Lord must
turn away from wickedness."

20 In a large house there are articles not
only of gold and silver, but also of wood
and clay; some are for special purposes
and some for common use. 21 Those who
cleanse themselves from the latter will
be instruments for special purposes,
made holy, useful to the Master and prepared to do any good work.

22 Flee the evil desires of youth and
pursue righteousness, faith, love and
peace, along with those who call on the
Lord out of a pure heart. 23 Don't have
anything to do with foolish and stupid arguments, because you know they
produce quarrels. 24 And the Lord's servant must not be quarrelsome but must
be kind to everyone, able to teach, not
resentful. 25 Opponents must be gently instructed, in the hope that God will
grant them repentance leading them to
a knowledge of the truth, 26 and that they
will come to their senses and escape
from the trap of the devil, who has taken
them captive to do his will.

3 But mark this: There will be terrible
times in the last days. 2 People will
be lovers of themselves, lovers of money, boastful, proud, abusive, disobedient to their parents, ungrateful, unholy,
3 without love, unforgiving, slanderous,
without self-control, brutal, not lovers of
the good, 4 treacherous, rash, conceited,
lovers of pleasure rather than lovers of
God— 5 having a form of godliness but
denying its power. Have nothing to do
with such people.

6 They are the kind who worm their
way into homes and gain control over
gullible women, who are loaded down
with sins and are swayed by all kinds of
evil desires, 7 always learning but never
able to come to a knowledge of the truth.
8 Just as Jannes and Jambres opposed
Moses, so also these teachers oppose the
truth. They are men of depraved minds,
who, as far as the faith is concerned, are
rejected. 9 But they will not get very far
because, as in the case of those men,
their folly will be clear to everyone.

10 You, however, know all about my
teaching, my way of life, my purpose,
faith, patience, love, endurance, 11 persecutions, sufferings—what kinds of
things happened to me in Antioch, Iconium and Lystra, the persecutions I endured. Yet the Lord rescued me from all
of them. 12 In fact, everyone who wants
to live a godly life in Christ Jesus will be
persecuted, 13 while evildoers and im-

postors will go from bad to worse, deceiving and being deceived. [14]But as for
you, continue in what you have learned
and have become convinced of, because you know those from whom you
learned it, [15]and how from infancy you
have known the Holy Scriptures, which
are able to make you wise for salvation through faith in Christ Jesus. [16]All
Scripture is God-breathed and is useful for teaching, rebuking, correcting
and training in righteousness, [17]so that
the servant of God[a] may be thoroughly
equipped for every good work.

4 In the presence of God and of Christ
Jesus, who will judge the living and
the dead, and in view of his appearing
and his kingdom, I give you this charge:
[2]Preach the word; be prepared in season
and out of season; correct, rebuke and
encourage—with great patience and
careful instruction. [3]For the time will
come when people will not put up with
sound doctrine. Instead, to suit their
own desires, they will gather around
them a great number of teachers to say
what their itching ears want to hear.
[4]They will turn their ears away from the
truth and turn aside to myths. [5]But you,
keep your head in all situations, endure
hardship, do the work of an evangelist,
discharge all the duties of your minis
try.

[6]For I am already being poured out
like a drink offering, and the time for
my departure is near. [7]I have fought
the good fight, I have finished the race,
I have kept the faith. [8]Now there is in
store for me the crown of righteousness,
which the Lord, the righteous Judge, will
award to me on that day—and not only
to me, but also to all who have longed for
his appearing.

[9]Do your best to come to me quickly, [10]for Demas, because he loved this
world, has deserted me and has gone to
Thessalonica. Crescens has gone to Galatia, and Titus to Dalmatia. [11]Only Luke
is with me. Get Mark and bring him with
you, because he is helpful to me in my
ministry. [12]I sent Tychicus to Ephesus.
[13]When you come, bring the cloak that I
left with Carpus at Troas, and my scrolls,
especially the parchments.

[14]Alexander the metalworker did me
a great deal of harm. The Lord will repay him for what he has done. [15]You too
should be on your guard against him,
because he strongly opposed our message.

[16]At my first defense, no one came to
my support, but everyone deserted me.
May it not be held against them. [17]But
the Lord stood at my side and gave me
strength, so that through me the message might be fully proclaimed and all
the Gentiles might hear it. And I was
delivered from the lion's mouth. [18]The
Lord will rescue me from every evil attack and will bring me safely to his heavenly kingdom. To him be glory for ever
and ever. Amen.

[19]Greet Priscilla[b] and Aquila and the
household of Onesiphorus. [20]Erastus
stayed in Corinth, and I left Trophimus
sick in Miletus. [21]Do your best to get
here before winter. Eubulus greets you,
and so do Pudens, Linus, Claudia and all
the brothers and sisters.[c]

[22]The Lord be with your spirit. Grace
be with you all.

[a] 17 Or *that you, a man of God,* [b] 19 Greek *Prisca,* a variant of *Priscilla* [c] 21 The Greek word for *brothers and sisters* (*adelphoi*) refers here to believers, both men and women, as part of God's family.

TITUS

After the apostle Paul was released from prison in Rome, he discovered that renegade leaders were preying on the people of the church he had founded in Ephesus. He therefore left his long-time co-worker Timothy in that city with a letter authorizing him to replace these leaders and restore order. A similar situation on the island of Crete required Paul to commission another long-time co-worker, Titus, to act as his representative there.

Paul's letter is addressed to Titus, but it is meant for the larger church as well. He confers his own authority on Titus and instructs him to appoint godly leaders. Paul's description of the false teaching matches that in Ephesus: a combination of selective Jewish observances (such as being circumcised and abstaining from certain foods) and the pursuit of controversial speculations. However, the teaching didn't help people live purer lives. Paul tells the community that *the grace of God has appeared that offers salvation to all people*. It is the true message about Jesus that helps God's people live a new kind of life.

Paul reveals his plan to spend the winter in Nicopolis, a city on the west coast of Macedonia. It would provide an excellent jumping-off point for bringing the gospel to the western part of the empire. He trusts that Titus will help restore order in Crete so he can accompany Paul on this new venture.

---

1 Paul, a servant of God and an apostle
of Jesus Christ to further the faith of
God's elect and their knowledge of the
truth that leads to godliness— 2 in the
hope of eternal life, which God, who
does not lie, promised before the beginning of time, 3 and which now at his
appointed season he has brought to light
through the preaching entrusted to me
by the command of God our Savior,

4 To Titus, my true son in our common
faith:

Grace and peace from God the Father
and Christ Jesus our Savior.

5 The reason I left you in Crete was
that you might put in order what was
left unfinished and appoint[a] elders in
every town, as I directed you. 6 An elder must be blameless, faithful to his
wife, a man whose children believe[b]
and are not open to the charge of being
wild and disobedient. 7 Since an overseer manages God's household, he must
be blameless—not overbearing, not
quick-tempered, not given to drunkenness, not violent, not pursuing dishonest
gain. 8 Rather, he must be hospitable, one
who loves what is good, who is self-controlled, upright, holy and disciplined.
9 He must hold firmly to the trustworthy
message as it has been taught, so that he
can encourage others by sound doctrine
and refute those who oppose it.

10 For there are many rebellious people, full of meaningless talk and deception, especially those of the circumcision
group. 11 They must be silenced, because
they are disrupting whole households
by teaching things they ought not to
teach—and that for the sake of dishonest gain. 12 One of Crete's own prophets
has said it: "Cretans are always liars, evil
brutes, lazy gluttons."[c] 13 This saying is
true. Therefore rebuke them sharply, so
that they will be sound in the faith 14 and
will pay no attention to Jewish myths
or to the merely human commands of
those who reject the truth. 15 To the pure,
all things are pure, but to those who are
corrupted and do not believe, nothing is
pure. In fact, both their minds and consciences are corrupted. 16 They claim to
know God, but by their actions they deny
him. They are detestable, disobedient
and unfit for doing anything good.

2 You, however, must teach what is appropriate to sound doctrine. 2 Teach
the older men to be temperate, worthy
of respect, self-controlled, and sound in
faith, in love and in endurance.

3 Likewise, teach the older women
to be reverent in the way they live, not
to be slanderers or addicted to much
wine, but to teach what is good. 4 Then
they can urge the younger women to

[a] 5 Or *ordain* [b] 6 Or *children are trustworthy* [c] *12* From the Cretan philosopher Epimenides

love their husbands and children, 5to
be self-controlled and pure, to be busy
at home, to be kind, and to be subject to
their husbands, so that no one will malign the word of God.

6Similarly, encourage the young men
to be self-controlled. 7In everything set
them an example by doing what is good.
In your teaching show integrity, serious-
ness 8and soundness of speech that cannot be condemned, so that those who
oppose you may be ashamed because
they have nothing bad to say about us.

9Teach slaves to be subject to their
masters in everything, to try to please
them, not to talk back to them, 10and not
to steal from them, but to show that they
can be fully trusted, so that in every way
they will make the teaching about God
our Savior attractive.

11For the grace of God has appeared
that offers salvation to all people. 12It
teaches us to say "No" to ungodliness
and worldly passions, and to live self-
controlled, upright and godly lives in
this present age, 13while we wait for the
blessed hope—the appearing of the
glory of our great God and Savior, Jesus
Christ, 14who gave himself for us to redeem us from all wickedness and to purify for himself a people that are his very
own, eager to do what is good.

15These, then, are the things you
should teach. Encourage and rebuke
with all authority. Do not let anyone despise you.

3 Remind the people to be subject to
rulers and authorities, to be obedient, to be ready to do whatever is good,
2to slander no one, to be peaceable and
considerate, and always to be gentle toward everyone.

3At one time we too were foolish, disobedient, deceived and enslaved by all
kinds of passions and pleasures. We
lived in malice and envy, being hated
and hating one another. 4But when the
kindness and love of God our Savior
appeared, 5he saved us, not because of
righteous things we had done, but because of his mercy. He saved us through
the washing of rebirth and renewal by
the Holy Spirit, 6whom he poured out on
us generously through Jesus Christ our
Savior, 7so that, having been justified by
his grace, we might become heirs having
the hope of eternal life. 8This is a trustworthy saying. And I want you to stress
these things, so that those who have
trusted in God may be careful to devote
themselves to doing what is good. These
things are excellent and profitable for
everyone.

9But avoid foolish controversies and
genealogies and arguments and quarrels about the law, because these are unprofitable and useless. 10Warn a divisive
person once, and then warn them a second time. After that, have nothing to do
with them. 11You may be sure that such
people are warped and sinful; they are
self-condemned.

12As soon as I send Artemas or Tychicus to you, do your best to come to me
at Nicopolis, because I have decided to
winter there. 13Do everything you can
to help Zenas the lawyer and Apollos
on their way and see that they have everything they need. 14Our people must
learn to devote themselves to doing what
is good, in order to provide for urgent
needs and not live unproductive lives.

15Everyone with me sends you greetings. Greet those who love us in the
faith.

Grace be with you all.

PHILEMON

One of the people Paul chose to deliver the letters we know as Colossians and Ephesians was a man named Onesimus. Onesimus was originally from Colossae, and would have been known to the people there. But Paul was compelled to write a separate letter for him. This was because Onesimus had been the slave of a wealthy Colossian named Philemon, in whose home the church met. Onesimus had run away, probably robbing Philemon in the process. In Rome he had become a follower of Jesus. He'd been helping Paul in prison, but now Paul needed him to return to Colossae. Paul's hope was that Philemon would not only forgive Onesimus, but welcome him as a brother and no longer a slave.

Paul's brief letter to Philemon stresses the change in Onesimus's life. His name meant *useful* in Greek, and Paul tells Philemon that while he had formerly been *useless* (a servant Philemon couldn't count on), now he could be useful to both of them. Paul doesn't put Philemon under any obligation. His appeal is on the basis of love, and he promises to honor the demands of justice by making restitution himself if necessary.

Most likely Paul's appeal was successful, or this letter would not have been preserved. In the life of Onesimus we have a clear example of the kind of transformation that occurred in thousands of lives as the gospel message spread throughout the Roman Empire.

---

1 Paul, a prisoner of Christ Jesus, and
Timothy our brother,

To Philemon our dear friend and fellow worker— 2 also to Apphia our sister
and Archippus our fellow soldier—and
to the church that meets in your home:

3 Grace and peace to you[a] from God
our Father and the Lord Jesus Christ.

4 I always thank my God as I remember
you in my prayers, 5 because I hear about
your love for all his holy people and your
faith in the Lord Jesus. 6 I pray that your
partnership with us in the faith may be
effective in deepening your understanding of every good thing we share for the
sake of Christ. 7 Your love has given me
great joy and encouragement, because
you, brother, have refreshed the hearts
of the Lord's people.
8 Therefore, although in Christ I could
be bold and order you to do what you
ought to do, 9 yet I prefer to appeal to you
on the basis of love. It is as none other
than Paul—an old man and now also a
prisoner of Christ Jesus— 10 that I appeal to you for my son Onesimus,[b] who
became my son while I was in chains.
11 Formerly he was useless to you, but
now he has become useful both to you
and to me.
12 I am sending him—who is my very
heart—back to you. 13 I would have liked
to keep him with me so that he could
take your place in helping me while I
am in chains for the gospel. 14 But I did
not want to do anything without your
consent, so that any favor you do would
not seem forced but would be voluntary.
15 Perhaps the reason he was separated
from you for a little while was that you
might have him back forever— 16 no longer as a slave, but better than a slave, as
a dear brother. He is very dear to me but
even dearer to you, both as a fellow man
and as a brother in the Lord.
17 So if you consider me a partner, welcome him as you would welcome me. 18 If
he has done you any wrong or owes you
anything, charge it to me. 19 I, Paul, am
writing this with my own hand. I will pay
it back—not to mention that you owe me
your very self. 20 I do wish, brother, that
I may have some benefit from you in the
Lord; refresh my heart in Christ. 21 Confident of your obedience, I write to you,
knowing that you will do even more than
I ask.
22 And one thing more: Prepare a

[a] *3* The Greek is plural; also in verses 22 and 25; elsewhere in this letter "you" is singular. [b] *10 Onesimus* means *useful.*

guest room for me, because I hope to
be restored to you in answer to your
prayers.

23 Epaphras, my fellow prisoner in
Christ Jesus, sends you greetings. 24 And
so do Mark, Aristarchus, Demas and
Luke, my fellow workers.

25 The grace of the Lord Jesus Christ be
with your spirit.

HEBREWS

Neither the author nor the audience of this book is specifically named, but the book itself reveals its nature and purpose. The recipients are Jesus-believing Jews who are in danger of falling away from the faith. They are likely in Italy, since the author passes on greetings to them from those who are from Italy—probably their friends who are traveling elsewhere. The goal of the whole book is to show the superiority of the final realities God has revealed in the new covenant to the temporary ones of the first covenant. Its readers are encouraged to respond to the threat of persecution by recommitting to the new reality brought by Jesus.

The book alternates between teachings—reviews of Israel's history or the temple worship arrangements—and challenges based on these teachings. There are four teaching-challenge pairs:

: Jesus and the salvation he brings are greater than the angels and the salvation they announced (the law of Moses).

: Jesus is our "apostle" (someone sent by God on a specific mission), and he brings us into a greater rest and promised land than Moses and Joshua brought Israel into.

: Jesus is a more effective high priest than the priests appointed by the law of Moses.

: As God's faithful people have done throughout the ages, we must continue living in light of God's unseen heavenly realities and stepping out in faith. Through the Messiah *we are receiving a kingdom that cannot be shaken.*

---

1 In the past God spoke to our ancestors through the prophets at many
times and in various ways, 2 but in these
last days he has spoken to us by his Son,
whom he appointed heir of all things,
and through whom also he made the
universe. 3 The Son is the radiance of
God's glory and the exact representation
of his being, sustaining all things by his
powerful word. After he had provided
purification for sins, he sat down at the
right hand of the Majesty in heaven. 4 So
he became as much superior to the angels as the name he has inherited is superior to theirs.
5 For to which of the angels did God
ever say,

"You are my Son;
today I have become your
Father"[a]?

Or again,

"I will be his Father,
and he will be my Son"[b]?

6 And again, when God brings his firstborn into the world, he says,

"Let all God's angels worship him."[c]

7 In speaking of the angels he says,

"He makes his angels spirits,
and his servants flames of fire."[d]

8 But about the Son he says,

"Your throne, O God, will last for ever
and ever;
a scepter of justice will be the
scepter of your kingdom.
9 You have loved righteousness and
hated wickedness;
therefore God, your God, has set
you above your companions
by anointing you with the oil of
joy."[e]

10 He also says,

"In the beginning, Lord, you laid the
foundations of the earth,
and the heavens are the work of
your hands.
11 They will perish, but you remain;
they will all wear out like a
garment.
12 You will roll them up like a robe;
like a garment they will be changed.
But you remain the same,
and your years will never end."[f]

[a] *5* Psalm 2:7 [b] *5* 2 Samuel 7:14; 1 Chron. 17:13 [c] *6* Deut. 32:43 (see Dead Sea Scrolls and Septuagint)
[d] *7* Psalm 104:4 [e] *9* Psalm 45:6,7 [f] *12* Psalm 102:25-27

13 To which of the angels did God ever
say,

"Sit at my right hand
until I make your enemies
a footstool for your feet"[a]?

14 Are not all angels ministering spirits
sent to serve those who will inherit salvation?

2 We must pay the most careful attention, therefore, to what we have
heard, so that we do not drift away. 2 For
since the message spoken through angels was binding, and every violation
and disobedience received its just punishment, 3 how shall we escape if we ignore so great a salvation? This salvation,
which was first announced by the Lord,
was confirmed to us by those who heard
him. 4 God also testified to it by signs,
wonders and various miracles, and by
gifts of the Holy Spirit distributed according to his will.

5 It is not to angels that he has subjected the world to come, about which we
are speaking. 6 But there is a place where
someone has testified:

"What is mankind that you are
mindful of them,
a son of man that you care for him?
7 You made them a little[b] lower than
the angels;
you crowned them with glory and
honor
8 and put everything under their
feet."[c,d]

In putting everything under them,[e] God
left nothing that is not subject to them.[e]
Yet at present we do not see everything
subject to them.[e] 9 But we do see Jesus,
who was made lower than the angels for
a little while, now crowned with glory
and honor because he suffered death, so
that by the grace of God he might taste
death for everyone.

10 In bringing many sons and daughters to glory, it was fitting that God, for
whom and through whom everything
exists, should make the pioneer of their
salvation perfect through what he suffered. 11 Both the one who makes people
holy and those who are made holy are of
the same family. So Jesus is not ashamed
to call them brothers and sisters.[f] 12 He
says,

"I will declare your name to my
brothers and sisters;
in the assembly I will sing your
praises."[g]

13 And again,

"I will put my trust in him."[h]

And again he says,

"Here am I, and the children God has
given me."[i]

14 Since the children have flesh and
blood, he too shared in their humanity so that by his death he might break
the power of him who holds the power
of death—that is, the devil— 15 and
free those who all their lives were held
in slavery by their fear of death. 16 For
surely it is not angels he helps, but Abraham's descendants. 17 For this reason he
had to be made like them,[j] fully human
in every way, in order that he might become a merciful and faithful high priest
in service to God, and that he might
make atonement for the sins of the people. 18 Because he himself suffered when
he was tempted, he is able to help those
who are being tempted.

3 Therefore, holy brothers and sisters,
who share in the heavenly calling,
fix your thoughts on Jesus, whom we
acknowledge as our apostle and high
priest. 2 He was faithful to the one who
appointed him, just as Moses was faithful in all God's house. 3 Jesus has been
found worthy of greater honor than Moses, just as the builder of a house has
greater honor than the house itself. 4 For
every house is built by someone, but God
is the builder of everything. 5 "Moses was
faithful as a servant in all God's house,"[k]
bearing witness to what would be spoken by God in the future. 6 But Christ
is faithful as the Son over God's house.
And we are his house, if indeed we hold

[a] *13* Psalm 110:1 [b] *7* Or *them for a little while* [c] *6-8* Psalm 8:4-6 [d] *7,8* Or *7You made him a little lower than the angels;/ you crowned him with glory and honor/ 8and put everything under his feet."* [e] *8* Or *him* [f] *11* The Greek word for *brothers and sisters* (*adelphoi*) refers here to believers, both men and women, as part of God's family; also in verse 12; and in 3:1, 12; 10:19; 13:22. [g] *12* Psalm 22:22 [h] *13* Isaiah 8:17 [i] *13* Isaiah 8:18 [j] *17* Or *like his brothers* [k] *5* Num. 12:7

firmly to our confidence and the hope in
which we glory.
7So, as the Holy Spirit says:

"Today, if you hear his voice,
8 do not harden your hearts
as you did in the rebellion,
during the time of testing in the
wilderness,
9where your ancestors tested and tried
me,
though for forty years they saw
what I did.
10That is why I was angry with that
generation;
I said, 'Their hearts are always
going astray,
and they have not known my ways.'
11So I declared on oath in my anger,
'They shall never enter my rest.' "[a]

12See to it, brothers and sisters, that
none of you has a sinful, unbelieving
heart that turns away from the living
God. 13But encourage one another daily, as long as it is called "Today," so that
none of you may be hardened by sin's
deceitfulness. 14We have come to share
in Christ, if indeed we hold our original
conviction firmly to the very end. 15As
has just been said:

"Today, if you hear his voice,
do not harden your hearts
as you did in the rebellion."[b]

16Who were they who heard and rebelled? Were they not all those Moses
led out of Egypt? 17And with whom was
he angry for forty years? Was it not with
those who sinned, whose bodies perished in the wilderness? 18And to whom
did God swear that they would never enter his rest if not to those who disobeyed?
19So we see that they were not able to enter, because of their unbelief.

4 Therefore, since the promise of entering his rest still stands, let us be
careful that none of you be found to have
fallen short of it. 2For we also have had
the good news proclaimed to us, just as
they did; but the message they heard was
of no value to them, because they did not
share the faith of those who obeyed.[c]
3Now we who have believed enter that
rest, just as God has said,

"So I declared on oath in my anger,
'They shall never enter my rest.' "[d]

And yet his works have been finished
since the creation of the world. 4For
somewhere he has spoken about the
seventh day in these words: "On the seventh day God rested from all his works."[e]
5And again in the passage above he says,
"They shall never enter my rest."

6Therefore since it still remains for
some to enter that rest, and since those
who formerly had the good news proclaimed to them did not go in because
of their disobedience, 7God again set
a certain day, calling it "Today." This
he did when a long time later he spoke
through David, as in the passage already
quoted:

"Today, if you hear his voice,
do not harden your hearts."[b]

8For if Joshua had given them rest, God
would not have spoken later about another day. 9There remains, then, a Sab-
bath-rest for the people of God; 10for
anyone who enters God's rest also rests
from their works,[f] just as God did from
his. 11Let us, therefore, make every effort to enter that rest, so that no one will
perish by following their example of disobedience.

12For the word of God is alive and active. Sharper than any double-edged
sword, it penetrates even to dividing
soul and spirit, joints and marrow; it
judges the thoughts and attitudes of the
heart. 13Nothing in all creation is hidden
from God's sight. Everything is uncovered and laid bare before the eyes of him
to whom we must give account.

14Therefore, since we have a great
high priest who has ascended into heav-
en,[g] Jesus the Son of God, let us hold
firmly to the faith we profess. 15For we
do not have a high priest who is unable
to empathize with our weaknesses, but
we have one who has been tempted in
every way, just as we are — yet he did not
sin. 16Let us then approach God's throne
of grace with confidence, so that we may
receive mercy and find grace to help us
in our time of need.

[a] *11* Psalm 95:7-11 [b] *15,7* Psalm 95:7,8 [c] *2* Some manuscripts *because those who heard did not combine it with faith* [d] *3* Psalm 95:11; also in verse 5 [e] *4* Gen. 2:2 [f] *10* Or *labor* [g] *14* Greek *has gone through the heavens*

5 Every high priest is selected from
among the people and is appointed
to represent the people in matters related to God, to offer gifts and sacrifices for
sins. 2He is able to deal gently with those
who are ignorant and are going astray,
since he himself is subject to weakness.
3This is why he has to offer sacrifices for
his own sins, as well as for the sins of the
people. 4And no one takes this honor on
himself, but he receives it when called
by God, just as Aaron was.
5In the same way, Christ did not take
on himself the glory of becoming a high
priest. But God said to him,

"You are my Son;
today I have become your Father."[a]

6And he says in another place,

"You are a priest forever,
in the order of Melchizedek."[b]

7During the days of Jesus' life on
earth, he offered up prayers and petitions with fervent cries and tears to the
one who could save him from death,
and he was heard because of his reverent submission. 8Son though he was, he
learned obedience from what he suffered 9and, once made perfect, he became the source of eternal salvation for
all who obey him 10and was designated
by God to be high priest in the order of
Melchizedek.
11We have much to say about this, but
it is hard to make it clear to you because
you no longer try to understand. 12In
fact, though by this time you ought to
be teachers, you need someone to teach
you the elementary truths of God's word
all over again. You need milk, not solid
food! 13Anyone who lives on milk, being
still an infant, is not acquainted with
the teaching about righteousness. 14But
solid food is for the mature, who by constant use have trained themselves to distinguish good from evil.

6 Therefore let us move beyond the elementary teachings about Christ and
be taken forward to maturity, not laying
again the foundation of repentance from
acts that lead to death,[c] and of faith in
God, 2instruction about cleansing rites,[d]
the laying on of hands, the resurrection
of the dead, and eternal judgment. 3And
God permitting, we will do so.
4It is impossible for those who have
once been enlightened, who have tasted
the heavenly gift, who have shared in the
Holy Spirit, 5who have tasted the goodness of the word of God and the powers
of the coming age 6and who have fallen[e]
away, to be brought back to repentance.
To their loss they are crucifying the Son
of God all over again and subjecting him
to public disgrace. 7Land that drinks in
the rain often falling on it and that produces a crop useful to those for whom it
is farmed receives the blessing of God.
8But land that produces thorns and thistles is worthless and is in danger of being
cursed. In the end it will be burned.
9Even though we speak like this,
dear friends, we are convinced of better things in your case — the things that
have to do with salvation. 10God is not
unjust; he will not forget your work and
the love you have shown him as you have
helped his people and continue to help
them. 11We want each of you to show
this same diligence to the very end, so
that what you hope for may be fully realized. 12We do not want you to become
lazy, but to imitate those who through
faith and patience inherit what has been
promised.
13When God made his promise to
Abraham, since there was no one greater
for him to swear by, he swore by himself,
14saying, "I will surely bless you and give
you many descendants."[f] 15And so after
waiting patiently, Abraham received
what was promised.
16People swear by someone greater
than themselves, and the oath confirms what is said and puts an end to
all argument. 17Because God wanted to
make the unchanging nature of his purpose very clear to the heirs of what was
promised, he confirmed it with an oath.
18God did this so that, by two unchange-
able things in which it is impossible for
God to lie, we who have fled to take hold
of the hope set before us may be greatly
encouraged. 19We have this hope as an
anchor for the soul, firm and secure. It
enters the inner sanctuary behind the
curtain, 20where our forerunner, Jesus,

[a] 5 Psalm 2:7 [b] 6 Psalm 110:4 [c] 1 Or *from useless rituals* [d] 2 Or *about baptisms* [e] 6 Or *age*, [6]*if they fall* [f] 14 Gen. 22:17

has entered on our behalf. He has become a high priest forever, in the order
of Melchizedek.

7 This Melchizedek was king of Salem
and priest of God Most High. He met
Abraham returning from the defeat of
the kings and blessed him, 2 and Abraham gave him a tenth of everything.
First, the name Melchizedek means
"king of righteousness"; then also, "king
of Salem" means "king of peace." 3 Without father or mother, without genealogy,
without beginning of days or end of life,
resembling the Son of God, he remains a
priest forever.

4 Just think how great he was: Even the
patriarch Abraham gave him a tenth of
the plunder! 5 Now the law requires the
descendants of Levi who become priests
to collect a tenth from the people — that
is, from their fellow Israelites — even
though they also are descended from
Abraham. 6 This man, however, did
not trace his descent from Levi, yet he
collected a tenth from Abraham and
blessed him who had the promises.
7 And without doubt the lesser is blessed
by the greater. 8 In the one case, the tenth
is collected by people who die; but in the
other case, by him who is declared to be
living. 9 One might even say that Levi,
who collects the tenth, paid the tenth
through Abraham, 10 because when Melchizedek met Abraham, Levi was still in
the body of his ancestor.

11 If perfection could have been attained through the Levitical priesthood — and indeed the law given to the
people established that priesthood —
why was there still need for another
priest to come, one in the order of Melchizedek, not in the order of Aaron?
12 For when the priesthood is changed,
the law must be changed also. 13 He of
whom these things are said belonged to
a different tribe, and no one from that
tribe has ever served at the altar. 14 For
it is clear that our Lord descended from
Judah, and in regard to that tribe Moses
said nothing about priests. 15 And what
we have said is even more clear if another priest like Melchizedek appears, 16 one
who has become a priest not on the basis
of a regulation as to his ancestry but on
the basis of the power of an indestructible life. 17 For it is declared:

"You are a priest forever,
in the order of Melchizedek."[a]

18 The former regulation is set aside
because it was weak and useless 19 (for
the law made nothing perfect), and a
better hope is introduced, by which we
draw near to God.

20 And it was not without an oath! Others became priests without any oath,
21 but he became a priest with an oath
when God said to him:

"The Lord has sworn
and will not change his mind:
'You are a priest forever.'"[a]

22 Because of this oath, Jesus has become
the guarantor of a better covenant.

23 Now there have been many of those
priests, since death prevented them
from continuing in office; 24 but because
Jesus lives forever, he has a permanent
priesthood. 25 Therefore he is able to
save completely[b] those who come to
God through him, because he always
lives to intercede for them.

26 Such a high priest truly meets our
need — one who is holy, blameless, pure,
set apart from sinners, exalted above the
heavens. 27 Unlike the other high priests,
he does not need to offer sacrifices day
after day, first for his own sins, and then
for the sins of the people. He sacrificed
for their sins once for all when he offered himself. 28 For the law appoints as
high priests men in all their weakness;
but the oath, which came after the law,
appointed the Son, who has been made
perfect forever.

8 Now the main point of what we are
saying is this: We do have such a high
priest, who sat down at the right hand
of the throne of the Majesty in heaven,
2 and who serves in the sanctuary, the
true tabernacle set up by the Lord, not
by a mere human being.

3 Every high priest is appointed to offer both gifts and sacrifices, and so it
was necessary for this one also to have
something to offer. 4 If he were on earth,
he would not be a priest, for there are
already priests who offer the gifts prescribed by the law. 5 They serve at a

[a] *17,21* Psalm 110:4 [b] *25* Or *forever*

sanctuary that is a copy and shadow of
what is in heaven. This is why Moses was
warned when he was about to build the
tabernacle: "See to it that you make everything according to the pattern shown
you on the mountain."[a] [6]But in fact the
ministry Jesus has received is as superi-
or to theirs as the covenant of which he is
mediator is superior to the old one, since
the new covenant is established on better promises.

[7]For if there had been nothing wrong
with that first covenant, no place would
have been sought for another. [8]But God
found fault with the people and said[b]:

"The days are coming, declares the
Lord,
when I will make a new covenant
with the people of Israel
and with the people of Judah.
[9]It will not be like the covenant
I made with their ancestors
when I took them by the hand
to lead them out of Egypt,
because they did not remain faithful
to my covenant,
and I turned away from them,
declares the Lord.
[10]This is the covenant I will establish
with the people of Israel
after that time, declares the Lord.
I will put my laws in their minds
and write them on their hearts.
I will be their God,
and they will be my people.
[11]No longer will they teach their
neighbor,
or say to one another, 'Know the
Lord,'
because they will all know me,
from the least of them to the
greatest.
[12]For I will forgive their wickedness
and will remember their sins no
more."[c]

[13]By calling this covenant "new," he
has made the first one obsolete; and
what is obsolete and outdated will soon
disappear.

9 Now the first covenant had regulations for worship and also an earthly
sanctuary. [2]A tabernacle was set up. In
its first room were the lampstand and
the table with its consecrated bread; this
was called the Holy Place. [3]Behind the
second curtain was a room called the
Most Holy Place, [4]which had the gold-
en altar of incense and the gold-covered
ark of the covenant. This ark contained
the gold jar of manna, Aaron's staff that
had budded, and the stone tablets of the
covenant. [5]Above the ark were the cherubim of the Glory, overshadowing the
atonement cover. But we cannot discuss
these things in detail now.

[6]When everything had been arranged
like this, the priests entered regularly into the outer room to carry on their
ministry. [7]But only the high priest entered the inner room, and that only once
a year, and never without blood, which
he offered for himself and for the sins
the people had committed in ignorance.
[8]The Holy Spirit was showing by this
that the way into the Most Holy Place
had not yet been disclosed as long as the
first tabernacle was still functioning.
[9]This is an illustration for the present
time, indicating that the gifts and sacrifices being offered were not able to clear
the conscience of the worshiper. [10]They
are only a matter of food and drink and
various ceremonial washings—exter-
nal regulations applying until the time
of the new order.

[11]But when Christ came as high priest
of the good things that are now already
here,[d] he went through the greater and
more perfect tabernacle that is not made
with human hands, that is to say, is not
a part of this creation. [12]He did not enter by means of the blood of goats and
calves; but he entered the Most Holy
Place once for all by his own blood,
thus obtaining[e] eternal redemption.
[13]The blood of goats and bulls and the
ashes of a heifer sprinkled on those
who are ceremonially unclean sanctify
them so that they are outwardly clean.
[14]How much more, then, will the blood
of Christ, who through the eternal Spirit offered himself unblemished to God,
cleanse our consciences from acts that
lead to death,[f] so that we may serve the
living God!

[15]For this reason Christ is the mediator of a new covenant, that those who are

[a] 5 Exodus 25:40 [b] *8* Some manuscripts may be translated *fault and said to the people.* [c] *12* Jer. 31:31-34 [d] *11* Some early manuscripts *are to come* [e] *12* Or *blood, having obtained* [f] *14* Or *from useless rituals*

called may receive the promised eternal
inheritance—now that he has died as
a ransom to set them free from the sins
committed under the first covenant.
16 In the case of a will,[a] it is necessary
to prove the death of the one who made
it, 17 because a will is in force only when
somebody has died; it never takes effect while the one who made it is living.
18 This is why even the first covenant
was not put into effect without blood.
19 When Moses had proclaimed every
command of the law to all the people, he
took the blood of calves, together with
water, scarlet wool and branches of hyssop, and sprinkled the scroll and all the
people. 20 He said, "This is the blood of
the covenant, which God has commanded you to keep."[b] 21 In the same way, he
sprinkled with the blood both the tabernacle and everything used in its cer-
emonies. 22 In fact, the law requires that
nearly everything be cleansed with
blood, and without the shedding of
blood there is no forgiveness.
23 It was necessary, then, for the copies of the heavenly things to be purified
with these sacrifices, but the heavenly
things themselves with better sacrifices than these. 24 For Christ did not enter
a sanctuary made with human hands
that was only a copy of the true one; he
entered heaven itself, now to appear for
us in God's presence. 25 Nor did he enter
heaven to offer himself again and again,
the way the high priest enters the Most
Holy Place every year with blood that is
not his own. 26 Otherwise Christ would
have had to suffer many times since
the creation of the world. But he has
appeared once for all at the culmination of the ages to do away with sin by
the sacrifice of himself. 27 Just as people
are destined to die once, and after that
to face judgment, 28 so Christ was sacrificed once to take away the sins of many;
and he will appear a second time, not to
bear sin, but to bring salvation to those
who are waiting for him.

10 The law is only a shadow of the good
things that are coming—not the realities themselves. For this reason it can
never, by the same sacrifices repeated
endlessly year after year, make perfect
those who draw near to worship. 2 Otherwise, would they not have stopped being
offered? For the worshipers would have
been cleansed once for all, and would no
longer have felt guilty for their sins. 3 But
those sacrifices are an annual reminder
of sins. 4 It is impossible for the blood of
bulls and goats to take away sins.
5 Therefore, when Christ came into the
world, he said:

"Sacrifice and offering you did not
desire,
but a body you prepared for me;
6 with burnt offerings and sin offerings
you were not pleased.
7 Then I said, 'Here I am—it is written
about me in the scroll—
I have come to do your will, my
God.'"[c]

8 First he said, "Sacrifices and offerings,
burnt offerings and sin offerings you
did not desire, nor were you pleased
with them"—though they were offered
in accordance with the law. 9 Then he
said, "Here I am, I have come to do your
will." He sets aside the first to establish
the second. 10 And by that will, we have
been made holy through the sacrifice of
the body of Jesus Christ once for all.
11 Day after day every priest stands
and performs his religious duties; again
and again he offers the same sacrifices,
which can never take away sins. 12 But
when this priest had offered for all time
one sacrifice for sins, he sat down at the
right hand of God, 13 and since that time
he waits for his enemies to be made his
footstool. 14 For by one sacrifice he has
made perfect forever those who are being made holy.
15 The Holy Spirit also testifies to us
about this. First he says:

16 "This is the covenant I will make with
them
after that time, says the Lord.
I will put my laws in their hearts,
and I will write them on their
minds."[d]

17 Then he adds:

"Their sins and lawless acts
I will remember no more."[e]

18 And where these have been forgiven,
sacrifice for sin is no longer necessary.

[a] *16* Same Greek word as *covenant*; also in verse 17 [b] *20* Exodus 24:8 [c] *7* Psalm 40:6-8 (see Septuagint)
[d] *16* Jer. 31:33 [e] *17* Jer. 31:34

19 Therefore, brothers and sisters,
since we have confidence to enter the
Most Holy Place by the blood of Jesus,
20 by a new and living way opened for us
through the curtain, that is, his body,
21 and since we have a great priest over
the house of God, 22 let us draw near to
God with a sincere heart and with the
full assurance that faith brings, having
our hearts sprinkled to cleanse us from a
guilty conscience and having our bodies
washed with pure water. 23 Let us hold
unswervingly to the hope we profess, for
he who promised is faithful. 24 And let us
consider how we may spur one another
on toward love and good deeds, 25 not
giving up meeting together, as some are
in the habit of doing, but encouraging
one another—and all the more as you
see the Day approaching.

26 If we deliberately keep on sinning
after we have received the knowledge
of the truth, no sacrifice for sins is left,
27 but only a fearful expectation of judgment and of raging fire that will consume the enemies of God. 28 Anyone who
rejected the law of Moses died without
mercy on the testimony of two or three
witnesses. 29 How much more severely
do you think someone deserves to be
punished who has trampled the Son of
God underfoot, who has treated as an
unholy thing the blood of the covenant
that sanctified them, and who has insulted the Spirit of grace? 30 For we know
him who said, "It is mine to avenge; I will
repay,"[a] and again, "The Lord will judge
his people."[b] 31 It is a dreadful thing to
fall into the hands of the living God.

32 Remember those earlier days after
you had received the light, when you endured in a great conflict full of suffering.
33 Sometimes you were publicly exposed
to insult and persecution; at other times
you stood side by side with those who
were so treated. 34 You suffered along
with those in prison and joyfully accepted the confiscation of your property because you knew that you yourselves had
better and lasting possessions. 35 So do
not throw away your confidence; it will
be richly rewarded.

36 You need to persevere so that when
you have done the will of God, you will
receive what he has promised. 37 For,

"In just a little while,
he who is coming will come
and will not delay."[c]

38 And,

"But my righteous[d] one will live by
faith.
And I take no pleasure
in the one who shrinks back."[e]

39 But we do not belong to those who
shrink back and are destroyed, but to
those who have faith and are saved.

11 Now faith is confidence in what we
hope for and assurance about what
we do not see. 2 This is what the ancients
were commended for.

3 By faith we understand that the universe was formed at God's command,
so that what is seen was not made out of
what was visible.

4 By faith Abel brought God a better offering than Cain did. By faith he
was commended as righteous, when
God spoke well of his offerings. And by
faith Abel still speaks, even though he
is dead.

5 By faith Enoch was taken from this
life, so that he did not experience death:
"He could not be found, because God
had taken him away."[f] For before he was
taken, he was commended as one who
pleased God. 6 And without faith it is impossible to please God, because anyone
who comes to him must believe that he
exists and that he rewards those who
earnestly seek him.

7 By faith Noah, when warned about
things not yet seen, in holy fear built
an ark to save his family. By his faith he
condemned the world and became heir
of the righteousness that is in keeping
with faith.

8 By faith Abraham, when called to go
to a place he would later receive as his
inheritance, obeyed and went, even
though he did not know where he was
going. 9 By faith he made his home in
the promised land like a stranger in a
foreign country; he lived in tents, as did
Isaac and Jacob, who were heirs with
him of the same promise. 10 For he was
looking forward to the city with foundations, whose architect and builder is

[a] *30* Deut. 32:35 [b] *30* Deut. 32:36; Psalm 135:14 [c] *37* Isaiah 26:20; Hab. 2:3 [d] *38* Some early manuscripts *But the righteous* [e] *38* Hab. 2:4 (see Septuagint) [f] *5* Gen. 5:24

God. 11 And by faith even Sarah, who was
past childbearing age, was enabled to
bear children because she[a] considered
him faithful who had made the promise. 12 And so from this one man, and he
as good as dead, came descendants as
numerous as the stars in the sky and as
countless as the sand on the seashore.
13 All these people were still living by
faith when they died. They did not receive the things promised; they only
saw them and welcomed them from a
distance, admitting that they were foreigners and strangers on earth. 14 People
who say such things show that they are
looking for a country of their own. 15 If
they had been thinking of the country
they had left, they would have had opportunity to return. 16 Instead, they were
longing for a better country—a heavenly one. Therefore God is not ashamed to
be called their God, for he has prepared
a city for them.
17 By faith Abraham, when God tested him, offered Isaac as a sacrifice. He
who had embraced the promises was
about to sacrifice his one and only son,
18 even though God had said to him, "It is
through Isaac that your offspring will be
reckoned."[b] 19 Abraham reasoned that
God could even raise the dead, and so
in a manner of speaking he did receive
Isaac back from death.
20 By faith Isaac blessed Jacob and
Esau in regard to their future.
21 By faith Jacob, when he was dying,
blessed each of Joseph's sons, and worshiped as he leaned on the top of his
staff.
22 By faith Joseph, when his end was
near, spoke about the exodus of the Israelites from Egypt and gave instructions
concerning the burial of his bones.
23 By faith Moses' parents hid him for
three months after he was born, because
they saw he was no ordinary child, and
they were not afraid of the king's edict.
24 By faith Moses, when he had grown
up, refused to be known as the son of
Pharaoh's daughter. 25 He chose to be
mistreated along with the people of God
rather than to enjoy the fleeting pleasures of sin. 26 He regarded disgrace for
the sake of Christ as of greater value than
the treasures of Egypt, because he was
looking ahead to his reward. 27 By faith
he left Egypt, not fearing the king's anger; he persevered because he saw him
who is invisible. 28 By faith he kept the
Passover and the application of blood, so
that the destroyer of the firstborn would
not touch the firstborn of Israel.
29 By faith the people passed through
the Red Sea as on dry land; but when
the Egyptians tried to do so, they were
drowned.
30 By faith the walls of Jericho fell, after
the army had marched around them for
seven days.
31 By faith the prostitute Rahab, because she welcomed the spies, was not
killed with those who were disobedient.[c]
32 And what more shall I say? I do not
have time to tell about Gideon, Barak, Samson and Jephthah, about David
and Samuel and the prophets, 33 who
through faith conquered kingdoms, ad-
ministered justice, and gained what was
promised; who shut the mouths of lions,
34 quenched the fury of the flames, and
escaped the edge of the sword; whose
weakness was turned to strength; and
who became powerful in battle and
routed foreign armies. 35 Women received back their dead, raised to life
again. There were others who were tortured, refusing to be released so that they
might gain an even better resurrection.
36 Some faced jeers and flogging, and
even chains and imprisonment. 37 They
were put to death by stoning;[d] they were
sawed in two; they were killed by the
sword. They went about in sheepskins
and goatskins, destitute, persecuted and
mistreated— 38 the world was not worthy of them. They wandered in deserts
and mountains, living in caves and in
holes in the ground.
39 These were all commended for
their faith, yet none of them received
what had been promised, 40 since God
had planned something better for us so
that only together with us would they be
made perfect.

12 Therefore, since we are surrounded
by such a great cloud of witnesses,
let us throw off everything that hinders

[a] *11* Or *By faith Abraham, even though he was too old to have children—and Sarah herself was not able to conceive—was enabled to become a father because he* [b] *18* Gen. 21:12 [c] *31* Or *unbelieving*
[d] *37* Some early manuscripts *stoning; they were put to the test;*

and the sin that so easily entangles. And
let us run with perseverance the race
marked out for us, 2 fixing our eyes on
Jesus, the pioneer and perfecter of faith.
For the joy set before him he endured the
cross, scorning its shame, and sat down
at the right hand of the throne of God.
3 Consider him who endured such opposition from sinners, so that you will not
grow weary and lose heart.

4 In your struggle against sin, you have
not yet resisted to the point of shedding
your blood. 5 And have you completely
forgotten this word of encouragement
that addresses you as a father addresses
his son? It says,

"My son, do not make light of the
    Lord's discipline,
  and do not lose heart when he
    rebukes you,
6 because the Lord disciplines the one
    he loves,
  and he chastens everyone he
    accepts as his son."[a]

7 Endure hardship as discipline; God
is treating you as his children. For what
children are not disciplined by their father? 8 If you are not disciplined — and
everyone undergoes discipline — then
you are not legitimate, not true sons and
daughters at all. 9 Moreover, we have all
had human fathers who disciplined us
and we respected them for it. How much
more should we submit to the Father of
spirits and live! 10 They disciplined us
for a little while as they thought best;
but God disciplines us for our good, in
order that we may share in his holiness.
11 No discipline seems pleasant at the
time, but painful. Later on, however, it
produces a harvest of righteousness and
peace for those who have been trained
by it.

12 Therefore, strengthen your feeble
arms and weak knees. 13 "Make level
paths for your feet,"[b] so that the lame
may not be disabled, but rather healed.

14 Make every effort to live in peace
with everyone and to be holy; without
holiness no one will see the Lord. 15 See
to it that no one falls short of the grace
of God and that no bitter root grows up
to cause trouble and defile many. 16 See
that no one is sexually immoral, or is
godless like Esau, who for a single meal
sold his inheritance rights as the oldest
son. 17 Afterward, as you know, when he
wanted to inherit this blessing, he was
rejected. Even though he sought the
blessing with tears, he could not change
what he had done.

18 You have not come to a mountain
that can be touched and that is burning
with fire; to darkness, gloom and storm;
19 to a trumpet blast or to such a voice
speaking words that those who heard it
begged that no further word be spoken
to them, 20 because they could not bear
what was commanded: "If even an animal touches the mountain, it must be
stoned to death."[c] 21 The sight was so
terrifying that Moses said, "I am trembling with fear."[d]

22 But you have come to Mount Zion, to
the city of the living God, the heavenly
Jerusalem. You have come to thousands
upon thousands of angels in joyful assembly, 23 to the church of the firstborn,
whose names are written in heaven. You
have come to God, the Judge of all, to the
spirits of the righteous made perfect,
24 to Jesus the mediator of a new covenant, and to the sprinkled blood that
speaks a better word than the blood of
Abel.

25 See to it that you do not refuse him
who speaks. If they did not escape when
they refused him who warned them on
earth, how much less will we, if we turn
away from him who warns us from heav-
en? 26 At that time his voice shook the
earth, but now he has promised, "Once
more I will shake not only the earth
but also the heavens."[e] 27 The words
"once more" indicate the removing of
what can be shaken — that is, created
things — so that what cannot be shaken
may remain.

28 Therefore, since we are receiving a
kingdom that cannot be shaken, let us
be thankful, and so worship God ac-
ceptably with reverence and awe, 29 for
our "God is a consuming fire."[f]

13 Keep on loving one another as
brothers and sisters. 2 Do not forget to show hospitality to strangers, for
by so doing some people have shown

[a] *5,6* Prov. 3:11,12 (see Septuagint) [b] *13* Prov. 4:26 [c] *20* Exodus 19:12,13 [d] *21* See Deut. 9:19.
[e] *26* Haggai 2:6 [f] *29* Deut. 4:24

hospitality to angels without knowing
it. 3 Continue to remember those in prison as if you were together with them in
prison, and those who are mistreated as
if you yourselves were suffering.
4 Marriage should be honored by all,
and the marriage bed kept pure, for God
will judge the adulterer and all the sexually immoral. 5 Keep your lives free from
the love of money and be content with
what you have, because God has said,

"Never will I leave you;
never will I forsake you."[a]

6 So we say with confidence,

"The Lord is my helper; I will not be
afraid.
What can mere mortals do to me?"[b]

7 Remember your leaders, who spoke
the word of God to you. Consider the
outcome of their way of life and imitate
their faith. 8 Jesus Christ is the same yesterday and today and forever.
9 Do not be carried away by all kinds
of strange teachings. It is good for our
hearts to be strengthened by grace, not
by eating ceremonial foods, which is of
no benefit to those who do so. 10 We have
an altar from which those who minister
at the tabernacle have no right to eat.
11 The high priest carries the blood of
animals into the Most Holy Place as a
sin offering, but the bodies are burned
outside the camp. 12 And so Jesus also
suffered outside the city gate to make
the people holy through his own blood.
13 Let us, then, go to him outside the
camp, bearing the disgrace he bore.
14 For here we do not have an enduring
city, but we are looking for the city that
is to come.
15 Through Jesus, therefore, let us
continually offer to God a sacrifice of
praise—the fruit of lips that openly profess his name. 16 And do not forget to do
good and to share with others, for with
such sacrifices God is pleased.
17 Have confidence in your leaders and
submit to their authority, because they
keep watch over you as those who must
give an account. Do this so that their
work will be a joy, not a burden, for that
would be of no benefit to you.
18 Pray for us. We are sure that we have
a clear conscience and desire to live
honorably in every way. 19 I particularly
urge you to pray so that I may be restored
to you soon.
20 Now may the God of peace, who
through the blood of the eternal covenant brought back from the dead our
Lord Jesus, that great Shepherd of the
sheep, 21 equip you with everything
good for doing his will, and may he work
in us what is pleasing to him, through
Jesus Christ, to whom be glory for ever
and ever. Amen.

22 Brothers and sisters, I urge you to
bear with my word of exhortation, for in
fact I have written to you quite briefly.
23 I want you to know that our brother
Timothy has been released. If he arrives
soon, I will come with him to see you.
24 Greet all your leaders and all the
Lord's people. Those from Italy send you
their greetings.
25 Grace be with you all.

[a] 5 Deut. 31:6 [b] 6 Psalm 118:6,7

JAMES

James, one of the brothers of Jesus, became a leader of the church in Jerusalem after Jesus' death and resurrection. He was respected for the advice he gave and for the wise decisions he helped the community of believers make (see p. 990). At one point he decided to write down some of his best teachings and advice and send them to other Jewish believers in Jesus who were scattered throughout the Roman Empire. What he wrote to them has become known as the book of James.

This book begins like a letter because it's being sent to people at a distance. But it is actually not very much like other letters of the time. It is a collection of short sayings and slightly longer discussions of practical topics. The conversational style, the short, pithy sayings and the interweaving of themes all make this book similar to the wisdom writing found in Proverbs and Ecclesiastes.

Like those wisdom books, James concentrates on questions of daily living in God's good creation. He considers such practical issues as concern for the poor, the responsible use of wealth, control of the tongue, purity of life, unity in the community of Christ-followers, and above all patience and endurance during times of trial. The godly wisdom here remains as valuable a guide to living fully human lives as when James first shared it centuries ago.

---

1 James, a servant of God and of the Lord Jesus Christ,

To the twelve tribes scattered among the nations:

Greetings.

2 Consider it pure joy, my brothers and sisters,[a] whenever you face trials of many kinds, 3 because you know that the testing of your faith produces perseverance. 4 Let perseverance finish its work so that you may be mature and complete, not lacking anything. 5 If any of you lacks wisdom, you should ask God, who gives generously to all without finding fault, and it will be given to you. 6 But when you ask, you must believe and not doubt, because the one who doubts is like a wave of the sea, blown and tossed by the wind. 7 That person should not expect to receive anything from the Lord. 8 Such a person is double-minded and unstable in all they do.

9 Believers in humble circumstances ought to take pride in their high position. 10 But the rich should take pride in their humiliation—since they will pass away like a wild flower. 11 For the sun rises with scorching heat and withers the plant; its blossom falls and its beauty is destroyed. In the same way, the rich will fade away even while they go about their business.

12 Blessed is the one who perseveres under trial because, having stood the test, that person will receive the crown of life that the Lord has promised to those who love him.

13 When tempted, no one should say, "God is tempting me." For God cannot be tempted by evil, nor does he tempt anyone; 14 but each person is tempted when they are dragged away by their own evil desire and enticed. 15 Then, after desire has conceived, it gives birth to sin; and sin, when it is full-grown, gives birth to death.

16 Don't be deceived, my dear brothers and sisters. 17 Every good and perfect gift is from above, coming down from the Father of the heavenly lights, who does not change like shifting shadows. 18 He chose to give us birth through the word of truth, that we might be a kind of firstfruits of all he created.

19 My dear brothers and sisters, take note of this: Everyone should be quick to listen, slow to speak and slow to become angry, 20 because human anger does not produce the righteousness that God desires. 21 Therefore, get rid of all moral filth and the evil that is so prevalent and humbly accept the word planted in you, which can save you.

22 Do not merely listen to the word, and so deceive yourselves. Do what it says. 23 Anyone who listens to the word but

[a] 2 The Greek word for *brothers and sisters* (*adelphoi*) refers here to believers, both men and women, as part of God's family; also in verses 16 and 19; and in 2:1, 5, 14; 3:10, 12; 4:11; 5:7, 9, 10, 12, 19.

does not do what it says is like someone
who looks at his face in a mirror 24and,
after looking at himself, goes away and
immediately forgets what he looks like.
25But whoever looks intently into the
perfect law that gives freedom, and continues in it—not forgetting what they
have heard, but doing it—they will be
blessed in what they do.
26Those who consider themselves religious and yet do not keep a tight rein on
their tongues deceive themselves, and
their religion is worthless. 27Religion
that God our Father accepts as pure and
faultless is this: to look after orphans and
widows in their distress and to keep one-
self from being polluted by the world.

2 My brothers and sisters, believers in
our glorious Lord Jesus Christ must
not show favoritism. 2Suppose a man
comes into your meeting wearing a gold
ring and fine clothes, and a poor man in
filthy old clothes also comes in. 3If you
show special attention to the man wearing fine clothes and say, "Here's a good
seat for you," but say to the poor man,
"You stand there" or "Sit on the floor by
my feet," 4have you not discriminated
among yourselves and become judges
with evil thoughts?
5Listen, my dear brothers and sisters:
Has not God chosen those who are poor
in the eyes of the world to be rich in faith
and to inherit the kingdom he promised
those who love him? 6But you have dishonored the poor. Is it not the rich who
are exploiting you? Are they not the ones
who are dragging you into court? 7Are
they not the ones who are blaspheming
the noble name of him to whom you belong?
8If you really keep the royal law found
in Scripture, "Love your neighbor as
yourself,"[a] you are doing right. 9But if
you show favoritism, you sin and are
convicted by the law as lawbreakers.
10For whoever keeps the whole law and
yet stumbles at just one point is guilty of
breaking all of it. 11For he who said, "You
shall not commit adultery,"[b] also said,
"You shall not murder."[c] If you do not
commit adultery but do commit murder,
you have become a lawbreaker.
12Speak and act as those who are going to be judged by the law that gives
freedom, 13because judgment without
mercy will be shown to anyone who has
not been merciful. Mercy triumphs over
judgment.
14What good is it, my brothers and
sisters, if someone claims to have faith
but has no deeds? Can such faith save
them? 15Suppose a brother or a sister is
without clothes and daily food. 16If one
of you says to them, "Go in peace; keep
warm and well fed," but does nothing
about their physical needs, what good is
it? 17In the same way, faith by itself, if it is
not accompanied by action, is dead.
18But someone will say, "You have
faith; I have deeds."
Show me your faith without deeds,
and I will show you my faith by my
deeds. 19You believe that there is one
God. Good! Even the demons believe
that—and shudder.
20You foolish person, do you want evidence that faith without deeds is useless[d]? 21Was not our father Abraham
considered righteous for what he did
when he offered his son Isaac on the
altar? 22You see that his faith and his
actions were working together, and his
faith was made complete by what he did.
23And the scripture was fulfilled that
says, "Abraham believed God, and it was
credited to him as righteousness,"[e] and
he was called God's friend. 24You see
that a person is considered righteous by
what they do and not by faith alone.
25In the same way, was not even Rahab the prostitute considered righteous
for what she did when she gave lodging
to the spies and sent them off in a different direction? 26As the body without the
spirit is dead, so faith without deeds is
dead.

3 Not many of you should become
teachers, my fellow believers, because you know that we who teach will
be judged more strictly. 2We all stumble
in many ways. Anyone who is never at
fault in what they say is perfect, able to
keep their whole body in check.
3When we put bits into the mouths of
horses to make them obey us, we can
turn the whole animal. 4Or take ships as
an example. Although they are so large
and are driven by strong winds, they are
steered by a very small rudder wherev-

[a] *8* Lev. 19:18 [b] *11* Exodus 20:14; Deut. 5:18 [c] *11* Exodus 20:13; Deut. 5:17 [d] *20* Some early manuscripts *dead* [e] *23* Gen. 15:6

er the pilot wants to go. 5 Likewise, the
tongue is a small part of the body, but
it makes great boasts. Consider what a
great forest is set on fire by a small spark.
6 The tongue also is a fire, a world of evil
among the parts of the body. It corrupts
the whole body, sets the whole course of
one's life on fire, and is itself set on fire
by hell.
7 All kinds of animals, birds, reptiles
and sea creatures are being tamed and
have been tamed by mankind, 8 but no
human being can tame the tongue. It is
a restless evil, full of deadly poison.
9 With the tongue we praise our Lord
and Father, and with it we curse human
beings, who have been made in God's
likeness. 10 Out of the same mouth come
praise and cursing. My brothers and sisters, this should not be. 11 Can both fresh
water and salt water flow from the same
spring? 12 My brothers and sisters, can a
fig tree bear olives, or a grapevine bear
figs? Neither can a salt spring produce
fresh water.
13 Who is wise and understanding
among you? Let them show it by their
good life, by deeds done in the humility that comes from wisdom. 14 But if you
harbor bitter envy and selfish ambition in your hearts, do not boast about
it or deny the truth. 15 Such "wisdom"
does not come down from heaven but
is earthly, unspiritual, demonic. 16 For
where you have envy and selfish ambition, there you find disorder and every
evil practice.
17 But the wisdom that comes from
heaven is first of all pure; then peace-
loving, considerate, submissive, full of
mercy and good fruit, impartial and sincere. 18 Peacemakers who sow in peace
reap a harvest of righteousness.

4 What causes fights and quarrels
among you? Don't they come from
your desires that battle within you? 2 You
desire but do not have, so you kill. You
covet but you cannot get what you want,
so you quarrel and fight. You do not have
because you do not ask God. 3 When you
ask, you do not receive, because you ask
with wrong motives, that you may spend
what you get on your pleasures.
4 You adulterous people,[a] don't you
know that friendship with the world
means enmity against God? Therefore,
anyone who chooses to be a friend of the
world becomes an enemy of God. 5 Or do
you think Scripture says without reason that he jealously longs for the spirit
he has caused to dwell in us[b]? 6 But he
gives us more grace. That is why Scripture says:

"God opposes the proud
but shows favor to the humble."[c]

7 Submit yourselves, then, to God. Resist the devil, and he will flee from you.
8 Come near to God and he will come
near to you. Wash your hands, you sinners, and purify your hearts, you double-minded. 9 Grieve, mourn and wail.
Change your laughter to mourning and
your joy to gloom. 10 Humble yourselves
before the Lord, and he will lift you up.
11 Brothers and sisters, do not slander one another. Anyone who speaks
against a brother or sister[d] or judges
them speaks against the law and judges
it. When you judge the law, you are not
keeping it, but sitting in judgment on it.
12 There is only one Lawgiver and Judge,
the one who is able to save and destroy.
But you—who are you to judge your
neighbor?
13 Now listen, you who say, "Today or
tomorrow we will go to this or that city,
spend a year there, carry on business
and make money." 14 Why, you do not
even know what will happen tomorrow. What is your life? You are a mist
that appears for a little while and then
vanishes. 15 Instead, you ought to say, "If
it is the Lord's will, we will live and do
this or that." 16 As it is, you boast in your
arrogant schemes. All such boasting is
evil. 17 If anyone, then, knows the good
they ought to do and doesn't do it, it is
sin for them.

5 Now listen, you rich people, weep
and wail because of the misery that
is coming on you. 2 Your wealth has rot-
ted, and moths have eaten your clothes.
3 Your gold and silver are corroded.
Their corrosion will testify against you
and eat your flesh like fire. You have
hoarded wealth in the last days. 4 Look!
The wages you failed to pay the workers

[a] *4* An allusion to covenant unfaithfulness; see Hosea 3:1. [b] *5* Or *that the spirit he caused to dwell in us envies intensely;* or *that the Spirit he caused to dwell in us longs jealously* [c] *6* Prov. 3:34 [d] *11* The Greek word for *brother or sister* (*adelphos*) refers here to a believer, whether man or woman, as part of God's family.

who mowed your fields are crying out
against you. The cries of the harvesters have reached the ears of the Lord
Almighty. 5You have lived on earth in
luxury and self-indulgence. You have
fattened yourselves in the day of slaughter.[a] 6You have condemned and murdered the innocent one, who was not
opposing you.

7Be patient, then, brothers and sisters, until the Lord's coming. See how
the farmer waits for the land to yield
its valuable crop, patiently waiting for
the autumn and spring rains. 8You too,
be patient and stand firm, because the
Lord's coming is near. 9Don't grumble
against one another, brothers and sisters, or you will be judged. The Judge is
standing at the door!

10Brothers and sisters, as an example
of patience in the face of suffering, take
the prophets who spoke in the name of
the Lord. 11As you know, we count as
blessed those who have persevered. You
have heard of Job's perseverance and
have seen what the Lord finally brought
about. The Lord is full of compassion
and mercy.

12Above all, my brothers and sisters,
do not swear — not by heaven or by earth
or by anything else. All you need to say
is a simple "Yes" or "No." Otherwise you
will be condemned.

13Is anyone among you in trouble? Let
them pray. Is anyone happy? Let them
sing songs of praise. 14Is anyone among
you sick? Let them call the elders of the
church to pray over them and anoint
them with oil in the name of the Lord.
15And the prayer offered in faith will
make the sick person well; the Lord will
raise them up. If they have sinned, they
will be forgiven. 16Therefore confess
your sins to each other and pray for each
other so that you may be healed. The
prayer of a righteous person is powerful
and effective.

17Elijah was a human being, even as
we are. He prayed earnestly that it would
not rain, and it did not rain on the land
for three and a half years. 18Again he
prayed, and the heavens gave rain, and
the earth produced its crops.

19My brothers and sisters, if one of
you should wander from the truth and
someone should bring that person back,
20remember this: Whoever turns a sinner from the error of their way will save
them from death and cover over a multitude of sins.

[a] 5 Or *yourselves as in a day of feasting*

1 PETER

The apostle Peter was one of the twelve disciples Jesus appointed and taught during his time on earth. Peter spent the final years of his life and ministry—in the early 60s AD—as a leader of the church in Rome. When he learned that churches in other Roman provinces (all located in what is now Turkey) were experiencing persecution, he wrote to urge them to remain faithful to Jesus. Peter's letter was delivered by Silas, a man who also worked with the apostle Paul (see pp. 990-993). Peter introduces Silas and explains that he helped to compose the letter.

After the opening, the letter has three main sections:

- Peter first tells his readers to *be holy in all you do.* As Gentiles they once lived in ignorance (they did not know the ways of God). But they are now a holy nation, part of God's own people, and are called to a new way of life.
- Peter then explains how this way of life will impress those who might accuse and persecute them without just cause.
- Finally, Peter acknowledges that his readers are suffering for their faith, but he explains that this is only to be expected. The Messiah himself suffered, and believers all over the world are facing the same challenge. The followers of Jesus are waiting for the day God will visit them, and even in their suffering they can show they belong to God.

---

1 Peter, an apostle of Jesus Christ,

To God's elect, exiles scattered
throughout the provinces of Pontus,
Galatia, Cappadocia, Asia and Bithynia, [2]who have been chosen according
to the foreknowledge of God the Father,
through the sanctifying work of the
Spirit, to be obedient to Jesus Christ and
sprinkled with his blood:

Grace and peace be yours in abundance.

[3]Praise be to the God and Father of
our Lord Jesus Christ! In his great mercy he has given us new birth into a living
hope through the resurrection of Jesus
Christ from the dead, [4]and into an inheritance that can never perish, spoil or
fade. This inheritance is kept in heaven
for you, [5]who through faith are shielded
by God's power until the coming of the
salvation that is ready to be revealed in
the last time. [6]In all this you greatly rejoice, though now for a little while you
may have had to suffer grief in all kinds
of trials. [7]These have come so that the
proven genuineness of your faith—of
greater worth than gold, which perishes even though refined by fire—may
result in praise, glory and honor when
Jesus Christ is revealed. [8]Though you
have not seen him, you love him; and
even though you do not see him now,
you believe in him and are filled with an
inexpressible and glorious joy, [9]for you
are receiving the end result of your faith,
the salvation of your souls.

[10]Concerning this salvation, the
prophets, who spoke of the grace that
was to come to you, searched intently
and with the greatest care, [11]trying to
find out the time and circumstances to
which the Spirit of Christ in them was
pointing when he predicted the sufferings of the Messiah and the glories that
would follow. [12]It was revealed to them
that they were not serving themselves
but you, when they spoke of the things
that have now been told you by those
who have preached the gospel to you by
the Holy Spirit sent from heaven. Even
angels long to look into these things.

[13]Therefore, with minds that are alert
and fully sober, set your hope on the
grace to be brought to you when Jesus
Christ is revealed at his coming. [14]As
obedient children, do not conform to
the evil desires you had when you lived
in ignorance. [15]But just as he who called
you is holy, so be holy in all you do; [16]for
it is written: "Be holy, because I am
holy."[a]

[17]Since you call on a Father who judg-

[a] *16* Lev. 11:44,45; 19:2

es each person's work impartially, live
out your time as foreigners here in reverent fear. 18 For you know that it was not
with perishable things such as silver or
gold that you were redeemed from the
empty way of life handed down to you
from your ancestors, 19 but with the
precious blood of Christ, a lamb without blemish or defect. 20 He was chosen before the creation of the world,
but was revealed in these last times for
your sake. 21 Through him you believe
in God, who raised him from the dead
and glorified him, and so your faith and
hope are in God.

22 Now that you have purified yourselves by obeying the truth so that you
have sincere love for each other, love
one another deeply, from the heart.[a]
23 For you have been born again, not of
perishable seed, but of imperishable,
through the living and enduring word
of God. 24 For,

"All people are like grass,
and all their glory is like the flowers
of the field;
the grass withers and the flowers fall,
25 but the word of the Lord endures
forever."[b]

And this is the word that was preached
to you.

2 Therefore, rid yourselves of all malice
and all deceit, hypocrisy, envy, and
slander of every kind. 2 Like newborn
babies, crave pure spiritual milk, so that
by it you may grow up in your salvation,
3 now that you have tasted that the Lord
is good.

4 As you come to him, the living
Stone — rejected by humans but chosen
by God and precious to him — 5 you also,
like living stones, are being built into a
spiritual house[c] to be a holy priesthood,
offering spiritual sacrifices acceptable
to God through Jesus Christ. 6 For in
Scripture it says:

"See, I lay a stone in Zion,
a chosen and precious cornerstone,
and the one who trusts in him
will never be put to shame."[d]

7 Now to you who believe, this stone is
precious. But to those who do not believe,

"The stone the builders rejected
has become the cornerstone,"[e]

8 and,

"A stone that causes people to
stumble
and a rock that makes them fall."[f]

They stumble because they disobey the
message — which is also what they were
destined for.

9 But you are a chosen people, a royal
priesthood, a holy nation, God's special possession, that you may declare
the praises of him who called you out
of darkness into his wonderful light.
10 Once you were not a people, but now
you are the people of God; once you had
not received mercy, but now you have received mercy.

11 Dear friends, I urge you, as foreigners and exiles, to abstain from sinful desires, which wage war against your soul.
12 Live such good lives among the pagans
that, though they accuse you of doing
wrong, they may see your good deeds
and glorify God on the day he visits us.

13 Submit yourselves for the Lord's
sake to every human authority: whether
to the emperor, as the supreme authority, 14 or to governors, who are sent by him
to punish those who do wrong and to
commend those who do right. 15 For it is
God's will that by doing good you should
silence the ignorant talk of foolish people. 16 Live as free people, but do not use
your freedom as a cover-up for evil; live
as God's slaves. 17 Show proper respect
to everyone, love the family of believers,
fear God, honor the emperor.

18 Slaves, in reverent fear of God submit yourselves to your masters, not only
to those who are good and considerate,
but also to those who are harsh. 19 For
it is commendable if someone bears up
under the pain of unjust suffering because they are conscious of God. 20 But
how is it to your credit if you receive a
beating for doing wrong and endure it?
But if you suffer for doing good and you
endure it, this is commendable before
God. 21 To this you were called, because
Christ suffered for you, leaving you an
example, that you should follow in his
steps.

[a] *22* Some early manuscripts *from a pure heart of the Spirit* [b] *25* Isaiah 40:6-8 (see Septuagint) [c] *5* Or *into a temple* [d] *6* Isaiah 28:16 [e] *7* Psalm 118:22 [f] *8* Isaiah 8:14

22 “He committed no sin,
and no deceit was found in his
mouth.”[a]

23 When they hurled their insults at him,
he did not retaliate; when he suffered, he
made no threats. Instead, he entrusted
himself to him who judges justly. 24 “He
himself bore our sins” in his body on the
cross, so that we might die to sins and
live for righteousness; “by his wounds
you have been healed.” 25 For “you were
like sheep going astray,”[b] but now you
have returned to the Shepherd and
Overseer of your souls.

3 Wives, in the same way submit yourselves to your own husbands so that,
if any of them do not believe the word,
they may be won over without words
by the behavior of their wives, 2 when
they see the purity and reverence of
your lives. 3 Your beauty should not
come from outward adornment, such
as elaborate hairstyles and the wearing
of gold jewelry or fine clothes. 4 Rather,
it should be that of your inner self, the
unfading beauty of a gentle and quiet
spirit, which is of great worth in God’s
sight. 5 For this is the way the holy wom-
en of the past who put their hope in God
used to adorn themselves. They submitted themselves to their own husbands,
6 like Sarah, who obeyed Abraham and
called him her lord. You are her daughters if you do what is right and do not
give way to fear.

7 Husbands, in the same way be considerate as you live with your wives, and
treat them with respect as the weaker
partner and as heirs with you of the gracious gift of life, so that nothing will hinder your prayers.

8 Finally, all of you, be like-minded, be
sympathetic, love one another, be compassionate and humble. 9 Do not repay
evil with evil or insult with insult. On
the contrary, repay evil with blessing,
because to this you were called so that
you may inherit a blessing. 10 For,

“Whoever would love life
and see good days
must keep their tongue from evil
and their lips from deceitful
speech.
11 They must turn from evil and do
good;
they must seek peace and pursue it.
12 For the eyes of the Lord are on the
righteous
and his ears are attentive to their
prayer,
but the face of the Lord is against
those who do evil.”[c]

13 Who is going to harm you if you
are eager to do good? 14 But even if you
should suffer for what is right, you are
blessed. “Do not fear their threats[d]; do
not be frightened.”[e] 15 But in your hearts
revere Christ as Lord. Always be prepared to give an answer to everyone
who asks you to give the reason for the
hope that you have. But do this with gentleness and respect, 16 keeping a clear
conscience, so that those who speak
maliciously against your good behavior
in Christ may be ashamed of their slander. 17 For it is better, if it is God’s will,
to suffer for doing good than for doing
evil. 18 For Christ also suffered once for
sins, the righteous for the unrighteous,
to bring you to God. He was put to death
in the body but made alive in the Spirit.
19 After being made alive,[f] he went and
made proclamation to the imprisoned
spirits— 20 to those who were disobedient long ago when God waited patiently
in the days of Noah while the ark was
being built. In it only a few people, eight
in all, were saved through water, 21 and
this water symbolizes baptism that now
saves you also—not the removal of dirt
from the body but the pledge of a clear
conscience toward God.[g] It saves you by
the resurrection of Jesus Christ, 22 who
has gone into heaven and is at God’s
right hand—with angels, authorities
and powers in submission to him.

4 Therefore, since Christ suffered in his
body, arm yourselves also with the
same attitude, because whoever suffers
in the body is done with sin. 2 As a result,
they do not live the rest of their earthly
lives for evil human desires, but rather
for the will of God. 3 For you have spent
enough time in the past doing what pagans choose to do—living in debauchery, lust, drunkenness, orgies, carous-

[a] *22* Isaiah 53:9 [b] *24,25* Isaiah 53:4,5,6 (see Septuagint) [c] *12* Psalm 34:12-16 [d] *14* Or *fear what they fear* [e] *14* Isaiah 8:12 [f] *18,19* Or *but made alive in the spirit,* [19] *in which also* [g] *21* Or *but an appeal to God for a clear conscience*

ing and detestable idolatry. 4They are
surprised that you do not join them in
their reckless, wild living, and they heap
abuse on you. 5But they will have to give
account to him who is ready to judge
the living and the dead. 6For this is the
reason the gospel was preached even
to those who are now dead, so that they
might be judged according to human
standards in regard to the body, but live
according to God in regard to the spirit.
7The end of all things is near. Therefore be alert and of sober mind so that
you may pray. 8Above all, love each other deeply, because love covers over a
multitude of sins. 9Offer hospitality to
one another without grumbling. 10Each
of you should use whatever gift you have
received to serve others, as faithful stewards of God's grace in its various forms.
11If anyone speaks, they should do so as
one who speaks the very words of God.
If anyone serves, they should do so with
the strength God provides, so that in
all things God may be praised through
Jesus Christ. To him be the glory and the
power for ever and ever. Amen.
12Dear friends, do not be surprised at
the fiery ordeal that has come on you to
test you, as though something strange
were happening to you. 13But rejoice
inasmuch as you participate in the sufferings of Christ, so that you may be
overjoyed when his glory is revealed.
14If you are insulted because of the
name of Christ, you are blessed, for the
Spirit of glory and of God rests on you.
15If you suffer, it should not be as a murderer or thief or any other kind of criminal, or even as a meddler. 16However,
if you suffer as a Christian, do not be
ashamed, but praise God that you bear
that name. 17For it is time for judgment
to begin with God's household; and if it
begins with us, what will the outcome be
for those who do not obey the gospel of
God? 18And,

"If it is hard for the righteous to be
saved,
what will become of the ungodly
and the sinner?"[a]

19So then, those who suffer according
to God's will should commit themselves
to their faithful Creator and continue to
do good.

5 To the elders among you, I appeal as a
fellow elder and a witness of Christ's
sufferings who also will share in the glory to be revealed: 2Be shepherds of God's
flock that is under your care, watching
over them — not because you must, but
because you are willing, as God wants
you to be; not pursuing dishonest gain,
but eager to serve; 3not lording it over
those entrusted to you, but being examples to the flock. 4And when the Chief
Shepherd appears, you will receive the
crown of glory that will never fade away.
5In the same way, you who are younger, submit yourselves to your elders. All
of you, clothe yourselves with humility
toward one another, because,

"God opposes the proud
but shows favor to the humble."[b]

6Humble yourselves, therefore, under
God's mighty hand, that he may lift you
up in due time. 7Cast all your anxiety on
him because he cares for you.
8Be alert and of sober mind. Your enemy the devil prowls around like a roaring lion looking for someone to devour.
9Resist him, standing firm in the faith,
because you know that the family of believers throughout the world is undergo-
ing the same kind of sufferings.
10And the God of all grace, who called
you to his eternal glory in Christ, after
you have suffered a little while, will himself restore you and make you strong,
firm and steadfast. 11To him be the power for ever and ever. Amen.

12With the help of Silas,[c] whom I regard as a faithful brother, I have written
to you briefly, encouraging you and testifying that this is the true grace of God.
Stand fast in it.
13She who is in Babylon, chosen together with you, sends you her greetings, and so does my son Mark. 14Greet
one another with a kiss of love.
Peace to all of you who are in Christ.

[a] *18* Prov. 11:31 (see Septuagint) [b] *5* Prov. 3:34 [c] *12* Greek *Silvanus*, a variant of *Silas*

2 PETER

Around AD 65 the apostle Peter was imprisoned in Rome by the emperor Nero, and he realized that he would soon be executed. Since he was an eyewitness of the ministry of Jesus, he decided to write another letter to the believers he had written to before, confirming what they had been taught about Jesus. False teachers were proposing that, since Jesus hadn't returned already, his return couldn't be expected at all. Because they didn't expect any future judgment, they were living immoral lives. (Peter likely learned about the threat of these teachers from a letter sent by Jude, a brother of Jesus, to warn believers against them. Peter's letter echoes Jude's, but in shorter form. See p. 1106.)

Peter answers the false teachers by stressing that he personally saw the glory and majesty of Jesus *on the sacred mountain* (see p. 905). Everyone will see this glory when Jesus returns. In powerful imagery Peter describes the false teachers' destructive effect on the community and the judgment that awaits them. In the final section of his letter, Peter explains that the Messiah's return has been delayed because God wants everyone to repent. Our proper response is to live good lives filled with hope, since *we are looking forward to a new heaven and a new earth, where righteousness dwells.*

---

1 Simon Peter, a servant and apostle of Jesus Christ,

To those who through the righteousness of our God and Savior Jesus Christ have received a faith as precious as ours:

2 Grace and peace be yours in abundance through the knowledge of God and of Jesus our Lord.

3 His divine power has given us everything we need for a godly life through our knowledge of him who called us by his own glory and goodness. 4 Through these he has given us his very great and precious promises, so that through them you may participate in the divine nature, having escaped the corruption in the world caused by evil desires.

5 For this very reason, make every effort to add to your faith goodness; and to goodness, knowledge; 6 and to knowledge, self-control; and to self-control, perseverance; and to perseverance, godliness; 7 and to godliness, mutual affection; and to mutual affection, love. 8 For if you possess these qualities in increasing measure, they will keep you from being ineffective and unproductive in your knowledge of our Lord Jesus Christ. 9 But whoever does not have them is nearsighted and blind, forgetting that they have been cleansed from their past sins.

10 Therefore, my brothers and sisters,[a] make every effort to confirm your calling and election. For if you do these things, you will never stumble, 11 and you will receive a rich welcome into the eternal kingdom of our Lord and Savior Jesus Christ.

12 So I will always remind you of these things, even though you know them and are firmly established in the truth you now have. 13 I think it is right to refresh your memory as long as I live in the tent of this body, 14 because I know that I will soon put it aside, as our Lord Jesus Christ has made clear to me. 15 And I will make every effort to see that after my departure you will always be able to remember these things.

16 For we did not follow cleverly devised stories when we told you about the coming of our Lord Jesus Christ in power, but we were eyewitnesses of his majesty. 17 He received honor and glory from God the Father when the voice came to him from the Majestic Glory, saying, "This is my Son, whom I love; with him I am well pleased."[b] 18 We ourselves heard this voice that came from heaven when we were with him on the sacred mountain.

19 We also have the prophetic message as something completely reliable, and you will do well to pay attention to it, as to a light shining in a dark place, until

[a] *10* The Greek word for *brothers and sisters* (*adelphoi*) refers here to believers, both men and women, as part of God's family. [b] *17* Matt. 17:5; Mark 9:7; Luke 9:35

the day dawns and the morning star rises in your hearts. 20Above all, you must
understand that no prophecy of Scripture came about by the prophet's own
interpretation of things. 21For prophecy
never had its origin in the human will,
but prophets, though human, spoke
from God as they were carried along by
the Holy Spirit.

2 But there were also false prophets
among the people, just as there will
be false teachers among you. They will
secretly introduce destructive here-
sies, even denying the sovereign Lord
who bought them—bringing swift destruction on themselves. 2Many will
follow their depraved conduct and will
bring the way of truth into disrepute.
3In their greed these teachers will exploit you with fabricated stories. Their
condemnation has long been hanging
over them, and their destruction has not
been sleeping.

4For if God did not spare angels when
they sinned, but sent them to hell,[a] putting them in chains of darkness[b] to be
held for judgment; 5if he did not spare
the ancient world when he brought the
flood on its ungodly people, but protected Noah, a preacher of righteousness,
and seven others; 6if he condemned
the cities of Sodom and Gomorrah by
burning them to ashes, and made them
an example of what is going to happen
to the ungodly; 7and if he rescued Lot,
a righteous man, who was distressed by
the depraved conduct of the lawless 8(for
that righteous man, living among them
day after day, was tormented in his righteous soul by the lawless deeds he saw
and heard)— 9if this is so, then the Lord
knows how to rescue the godly from trials and to hold the unrighteous for punishment on the day of judgment. 10This
is especially true of those who follow the
corrupt desire of the flesh[c] and despise
authority.

Bold and arrogant, they are not afraid
to heap abuse on celestial beings; 11yet
even angels, although they are stronger
and more powerful, do not heap abuse
on such beings when bringing judgment
on them from[d] the Lord. 12But these
people blaspheme in matters they do not
understand. They are like unreasoning
animals, creatures of instinct, born only
to be caught and destroyed, and like animals they too will perish.

13They will be paid back with harm for
the harm they have done. Their idea of
pleasure is to carouse in broad daylight.
They are blots and blemishes, reveling
in their pleasures while they feast with
you.[e] 14With eyes full of adultery, they
never stop sinning; they seduce the unstable; they are experts in greed—an
accursed brood! 15They have left the
straight way and wandered off to follow
the way of Balaam son of Bezer,[f] who
loved the wages of wickedness. 16But
he was rebuked for his wrongdoing by a
donkey—an animal without speech—
who spoke with a human voice and restrained the prophet's madness.

17These people are springs without water and mists driven by a storm.
Blackest darkness is reserved for them.
18For they mouth empty, boastful words
and, by appealing to the lustful desires
of the flesh, they entice people who are
just escaping from those who live in
error. 19They promise them freedom,
while they themselves are slaves of depravity—for "people are slaves to whatever has mastered them." 20If they have
escaped the corruption of the world
by knowing our Lord and Savior Jesus
Christ and are again entangled in it and
are overcome, they are worse off at the
end than they were at the beginning. 21It
would have been better for them not to
have known the way of righteousness,
than to have known it and then to turn
their backs on the sacred command that
was passed on to them. 22Of them the
proverbs are true: "A dog returns to its
vomit,"[g] and, "A sow that is washed returns to her wallowing in the mud."

3 Dear friends, this is now my second
letter to you. I have written both of
them as reminders to stimulate you to
wholesome thinking. 2I want you to recall the words spoken in the past by the
holy prophets and the command given
by our Lord and Savior through your
apostles.

[a] 4 Greek *Tartarus* [b] 4 Some manuscripts *in gloomy dungeons* [c] 10 In contexts like this, the Greek word for *flesh* (*sarx*) refers to the sinful state of human beings, often presented as a power in opposition to the Spirit; also in verse 18. [d] 11 Many manuscripts *beings in the presence of* [e] 13 Some manuscripts *in their love feasts* [f] 15 Greek *Bosor* [g] 22 Prov. 26:11

3Above all, you must understand that
in the last days scoffers will come, scoff-
ing and following their own evil desires.
4They will say, "Where is this 'coming'
he promised? Ever since our ancestors died, everything goes on as it has
since the beginning of creation." 5But
they deliberately forget that long ago by
God's word the heavens came into being
and the earth was formed out of water
and by water. 6By these waters also the
world of that time was deluged and destroyed. 7By the same word the present
heavens and earth are reserved for fire,
being kept for the day of judgment and
destruction of the ungodly.

8But do not forget this one thing, dear
friends: With the Lord a day is like a
thousand years, and a thousand years
are like a day. 9The Lord is not slow in
keeping his promise, as some understand slowness. Instead he is patient
with you, not wanting anyone to perish,
but everyone to come to repentance.

10But the day of the Lord will come like
a thief. The heavens will disappear with
a roar; the elements will be destroyed by
fire, and the earth and everything done
in it will be laid bare.[a]

11Since everything will be destroyed
in this way, what kind of people ought
you to be? You ought to live holy and
godly lives 12as you look forward to the
day of God and speed its coming.[b] That
day will bring about the destruction of
the heavens by fire, and the elements
will melt in the heat. 13But in keeping
with his promise we are looking forward
to a new heaven and a new earth, where
righteousness dwells.

14So then, dear friends, since you are
looking forward to this, make every effort to be found spotless, blameless and
at peace with him. 15Bear in mind that
our Lord's patience means salvation,
just as our dear brother Paul also wrote
you with the wisdom that God gave him.
16He writes the same way in all his letters, speaking in them of these matters.
His letters contain some things that are
hard to understand, which ignorant and
unstable people distort, as they do the
other Scriptures, to their own destruction.

17Therefore, dear friends, since you
have been forewarned, be on your guard
so that you may not be carried away by
the error of the lawless and fall from
your secure position. 18But grow in the
grace and knowledge of our Lord and
Savior Jesus Christ. To him be glory both
now and forever! Amen.

[a] *10* Some manuscripts *be burned up*

[b] *12* Or *as you wait eagerly for the day of God to come*

1 JOHN

The letter known as 1 John was sent to a group of believers who were in the midst of an unsettling situation. Some of them had abandoned faith in Jesus the Messiah as it had first been taught to them. They found the proclamation that God had come in a human body impossible to reconcile with the common Greek idea that the flesh is evil and only spirit is good. But despite their denial of the Messiah, their immoral lives and their lack of practical love, they claimed to know God and belong to God. They asserted that their spiritual insight put them above the rest of the group, which they demonstrated by deserting the fellowship. Those left behind were deeply shaken, uncertain about everything they had been taught.

Someone who was close to this community and who had been an eyewitness of Jesus wrote to reassure them of what they had heard *from the beginning*. The author doesn't identify himself, but very likely he was the apostle John. Much of the language is similar to the Gospel of John. The letter testifies to the reality of the Messiah's coming in the flesh, reassuring the believers that they have full access to the truth. It emphasizes godly living and practical caring as the signs of those who genuinely know God.

---

1 That which was from the beginning,
which we have heard, which we have
seen with our eyes, which we have looked
at and our hands have touched — this we
proclaim concerning the Word of life.
2 The life appeared; we have seen it and
testify to it, and we proclaim to you the
eternal life, which was with the Father
and has appeared to us. 3 We proclaim
to you what we have seen and heard, so
that you also may have fellowship with
us. And our fellowship is with the Father
and with his Son, Jesus Christ. 4 We write
this to make our[a] joy complete.
5 This is the message we have heard
from him and declare to you: God is
light; in him there is no darkness at all.
6 If we claim to have fellowship with him
and yet walk in the darkness, we lie and
do not live out the truth. 7 But if we walk
in the light, as he is in the light, we have
fellowship with one another, and the
blood of Jesus, his Son, purifies us from
all[b] sin.
8 If we claim to be without sin, we deceive ourselves and the truth is not in us.
9 If we confess our sins, he is faithful and
just and will forgive us our sins and purify us from all unrighteousness. 10 If we
claim we have not sinned, we make him
out to be a liar and his word is not in us.
2 My dear children, I write this to you
so that you will not sin. But if anybody does sin, we have an advocate with
the Father — Jesus Christ, the Righteous
One. 2 He is the atoning sacrifice for our
sins, and not only for ours but also for
the sins of the whole world.
3 We know that we have come to know
him if we keep his commands. 4 Whoever says, "I know him," but does not
do what he commands is a liar, and the
truth is not in that person. 5 But if anyone obeys his word, love for God[c] is truly
made complete in them. This is how we
know we are in him: 6 Whoever claims to
live in him must live as Jesus did.
7 Dear friends, I am not writing you
a new command but an old one, which
you have had since the beginning. This
old command is the message you have
heard. 8 Yet I am writing you a new command; its truth is seen in him and in you,
because the darkness is passing and the
true light is already shining.
9 Anyone who claims to be in the light
but hates a brother or sister[d] is still in
the darkness. 10 Anyone who loves their
brother and sister[e] lives in the light,
and there is nothing in them to make
them stumble. 11 But anyone who hates
a brother or sister is in the darkness and
walks around in the darkness. They do
not know where they are going, because
the darkness has blinded them.

[a] *4* Some manuscripts *your* [b] *7* Or *every* [c] *5* Or *word, God's love* [d] *9* The Greek word for *brother or sister* (*adelphos*) refers here to a believer, whether man or woman, as part of God's family; also in verse 11; and in 3:15, 17; 4:20; 5:16. [e] *10* The Greek word for *brother and sister* (*adelphos*) refers here to a believer, whether man or woman, as part of God's family; also in 3:10; 4:20, 21.

12 I am writing to you, dear children,
because your sins have been
forgiven on account of his
name.
13 I am writing to you, fathers,
because you know him who is from
the beginning.
I am writing to you, young men,
because you have overcome the
evil one.

14 I write to you, dear children,
because you know the Father.
I write to you, fathers,
because you know him who is from
the beginning.
I write to you, young men,
because you are strong,
and the word of God lives in you,
and you have overcome the evil
one.

15 Do not love the world or anything
in the world. If anyone loves the world,
love for the Father[a] is not in them. 16 For
everything in the world—the lust of the
flesh, the lust of the eyes, and the pride
of life—comes not from the Father but
from the world. 17 The world and its desires pass away, but whoever does the
will of God lives forever.

18 Dear children, this is the last hour;
and as you have heard that the antichrist
is coming, even now many antichrists
have come. This is how we know it is
the last hour. 19 They went out from us,
but they did not really belong to us. For
if they had belonged to us, they would
have remained with us; but their going
showed that none of them belonged
to us.

20 But you have an anointing from
the Holy One, and all of you know the
truth.[b] 21 I do not write to you because
you do not know the truth, but because
you do know it and because no lie comes
from the truth. 22 Who is the liar? It is
whoever denies that Jesus is the Christ.
Such a person is the antichrist—denying the Father and the Son. 23 No one
who denies the Son has the Father;
whoever acknowledges the Son has the
Father also.

24 As for you, see that what you have
heard from the beginning remains in
you. If it does, you also will remain in the
Son and in the Father. 25 And this is what
he promised us—eternal life.

26 I am writing these things to you
about those who are trying to lead you
astray. 27 As for you, the anointing you
received from him remains in you, and
you do not need anyone to teach you.
But as his anointing teaches you about
all things and as that anointing is real,
not counterfeit—just as it has taught
you, remain in him.

28 And now, dear children, continue in
him, so that when he appears we may be
confident and unashamed before him at
his coming.

29 If you know that he is righteous, you
know that everyone who does what is
right has been born of him.

3 See what great love the Father has lavished on us, that we should be called
children of God! And that is what we are!
The reason the world does not know us is
that it did not know him. 2 Dear friends,
now we are children of God, and what
we will be has not yet been made known.
But we know that when Christ appears,[c]
we shall be like him, for we shall see him
as he is. 3 All who have this hope in him
purify themselves, just as he is pure.

4 Everyone who sins breaks the law; in
fact, sin is lawlessness. 5 But you know
that he appeared so that he might take
away our sins. And in him is no sin. 6 No
one who lives in him keeps on sinning.
No one who continues to sin has either
seen him or known him.

7 Dear children, do not let anyone lead
you astray. The one who does what is
right is righteous, just as he is righteous.
8 The one who does what is sinful is of
the devil, because the devil has been
sinning from the beginning. The reason
the Son of God appeared was to destroy
the devil's work. 9 No one who is born of
God will continue to sin, because God's
seed remains in them; they cannot go on
sinning, because they have been born
of God. 10 This is how we know who the
children of God are and who the children of the devil are: Anyone who does
not do what is right is not God's child,
nor is anyone who does not love their
brother and sister.

11 For this is the message you heard
from the beginning: We should love one

[a] 15 Or *world, the Father's love* [b] 20 Some manuscripts *and you know all things* [c] 2 Or *when it is made known*

another. [12]Do not be like Cain, who belonged to the evil one and murdered his
brother. And why did he murder him?
Because his own actions were evil and
his brother's were righteous. [13]Do not
be surprised, my brothers and sisters,[a] if
the world hates you. [14]We know that we
have passed from death to life, because
we love each other. Anyone who does not
love remains in death. [15]Anyone who
hates a brother or sister is a murderer,
and you know that no murderer has eternal life residing in him.

[16]This is how we know what love is:
Jesus Christ laid down his life for us.
And we ought to lay down our lives for
our brothers and sisters. [17]If anyone has
material possessions and sees a brother
or sister in need but has no pity on them,
how can the love of God be in that person? [18]Dear children, let us not love with
words or speech but with actions and in
truth.

[19]This is how we know that we belong
to the truth and how we set our hearts at
rest in his presence: [20]If our hearts condemn us, we know that God is greater
than our hearts, and he knows everything. [21]Dear friends, if our hearts do
not condemn us, we have confidence
before God [22]and receive from him anything we ask, because we keep his commands and do what pleases him. [23]And
this is his command: to believe in the
name of his Son, Jesus Christ, and to love
one another as he commanded us. [24]The
one who keeps God's commands lives in
him, and he in them. And this is how we
know that he lives in us: We know it by
the Spirit he gave us.

4 Dear friends, do not believe every
spirit, but test the spirits to see whether they are from God, because many false
prophets have gone out into the world.
[2]This is how you can recognize the Spirit of God: Every spirit that acknowledges
that Jesus Christ has come in the flesh
is from God, [3]but every spirit that does
not acknowledge Jesus is not from God.
This is the spirit of the antichrist, which
you have heard is coming and even now
is already in the world.

[4]You, dear children, are from God and
have overcome them, because the one
who is in you is greater than the one who
is in the world. [5]They are from the world
and therefore speak from the viewpoint
of the world, and the world listens to
them. [6]We are from God, and whoever
knows God listens to us; but whoever is
not from God does not listen to us. This
is how we recognize the Spirit[b] of truth
and the spirit of falsehood.

[7]Dear friends, let us love one another,
for love comes from God. Everyone who
loves has been born of God and knows
God. [8]Whoever does not love does not
know God, because God is love. [9]This
is how God showed his love among us:
He sent his one and only Son into the
world that we might live through him.
[10]This is love: not that we loved God,
but that he loved us and sent his Son as
an atoning sacrifice for our sins. [11]Dear
friends, since God so loved us, we also
ought to love one another. [12]No one has
ever seen God; but if we love one another, God lives in us and his love is made
complete in us.

[13]This is how we know that we live in
him and he in us: He has given us of his
Spirit. [14]And we have seen and testify
that the Father has sent his Son to be the
Savior of the world. [15]If anyone acknowledges that Jesus is the Son of God, God
lives in them and they in God. [16]And so
we know and rely on the love God has
for us.

God is love. Whoever lives in love
lives in God, and God in them. [17]This
is how love is made complete among us
so that we will have confidence on the
day of judgment: In this world we are
like Jesus. [18]There is no fear in love. But
perfect love drives out fear, because fear
has to do with punishment. The one who
fears is not made perfect in love.

[19]We love because he first loved us.
[20]Whoever claims to love God yet hates
a brother or sister is a liar. For whoever
does not love their brother and sister,
whom they have seen, cannot love God,
whom they have not seen. [21]And he has
given us this command: Anyone who
loves God must also love their brother
and sister.

5 Everyone who believes that Jesus
is the Christ is born of God, and everyone who loves the father loves his
child as well. [2]This is how we know that

[a] *13* The Greek word for *brothers and sisters* (*adelphoi*) refers here to believers, both men and women, as part of God's family; also in verse 16. [b] *6* Or *spirit*

we love the children of God: by loving
God and carrying out his commands.
[3]In fact, this is love for God: to keep his
commands. And his commands are not
burdensome, [4]for everyone born of God
overcomes the world. This is the victory that has overcome the world, even
our faith. [5]Who is it that overcomes the
world? Only the one who believes that
Jesus is the Son of God.

[6]This is the one who came by water and blood—Jesus Christ. He did
not come by water only, but by water
and blood. And it is the Spirit who testifies, because the Spirit is the truth.
[7]For there are three that testify: [8]the
Spirit, the water and the blood; and the
three are in agreement. [9]We accept human testimony, but God's testimony is
greater because it is the testimony of
God, which he has given about his Son.
[10]Whoever believes in the Son of God
accepts this testimony. Whoever does
not believe God has made him out to be
a liar, because they have not believed
the testimony God has given about his
Son. [11]And this is the testimony: God
has given us eternal life, and this life is
in his Son. [12]Whoever has the Son has
life; whoever does not have the Son of
God does not have life.

[13]I write these things to you who believe in the name of the Son of God so
that you may know that you have eternal life. [14]This is the confidence we
have in approaching God: that if we ask
anything according to his will, he hears
us. [15]And if we know that he hears us—
whatever we ask—we know that we have
what we asked of him.

[16]If you see any brother or sister commit a sin that does not lead to death, you
should pray and God will give them life.
I refer to those whose sin does not lead to
death. There is a sin that leads to death. I
am not saying that you should pray about
that. [17]All wrongdoing is sin, and there is
sin that does not lead to death.

[18]We know that anyone born of God
does not continue to sin; the One who
was born of God keeps them safe, and
the evil one cannot harm them. [19]We
know that we are children of God, and
that the whole world is under the control of the evil one. [20]We know also that
the Son of God has come and has given
us understanding, so that we may know
him who is true. And we are in him who
is true by being in his Son Jesus Christ.
He is the true God and eternal life.

[21]Dear children, keep yourselves from
idols.

[a] 7,8 Late manuscripts of the Vulgate *testify in heaven: the Father, the Word and the Holy Spirit, and these three are one.* [8]*And there are three that testify on earth: the* (not found in any Greek manuscript before the fourteenth century)

2 JOHN

The same person who wrote 1 John to encourage believers also found it necessary to write to other churches where the false teachers might go to spread their ideas and practices. The letter of 2 John addresses one such gathering, referring to the church as a *lady* and its members as her *children*. The author describes the members of his own community as *the children of your sister*. (This was apparently typical of early followers of Jesus; there is a similar greeting at the end of 1 Peter.) He identifies himself as a church leader by using the title *elder*.

Apparently some people from this church had just come to visit him and he was pleased to learn that they were walking in the truth. He warns the church not to support the false teachers in any way. Despite its brevity, this letter expresses all of the themes that receive deeper development in 1 John.

---

1 The elder,

To the lady chosen by God and to her children, whom I love in the truth—and not I only, but also all who know the
truth— 2 because of the truth, which
lives in us and will be with us forever:

3 Grace, mercy and peace from God the Father and from Jesus Christ, the Father's Son, will be with us in truth and love.

4 It has given me great joy to find some of your children walking in the truth,
just as the Father commanded us. 5 And
now, dear lady, I am not writing you a new command but one we have had from the beginning. I ask that we love
one another. 6 And this is love: that we
walk in obedience to his commands. As you have heard from the beginning, his command is that you walk in love.
7 I say this because many deceivers, who do not acknowledge Jesus Christ as coming in the flesh, have gone out into the world. Any such person is the deceiver and the antichrist. 8 Watch out that
you do not lose what we[a] have worked for, but that you may be rewarded ful-
ly. 9 Anyone who runs ahead and does not continue in the teaching of Christ does not have God; whoever continues in the teaching has both the Father and
the Son. 10 If anyone comes to you and
does not bring this teaching, do not take them into your house or welcome them.
11 Anyone who welcomes them shares in their wicked work.

12 I have much to write to you, but I do not want to use paper and ink. Instead, I hope to visit you and talk with you face to face, so that our joy may be complete.

13 The children of your sister, who is chosen by God, send their greetings.

[a] 8 Some manuscripts *you*

3 JOHN

This letter is a note of thanks and encouragement to an individual named Gaius. John had sent a letter to the church of which Gaius was a member, introducing and commending certain individuals, but a leader named Diotrephes refused to accommodate them. He opposed John's authority to the point of actually expelling anyone who supported the people he had sent. Gaius, however, put these preachers up in his own home, enabling them to carry out their mission. John's gratitude makes it clear that the church should provide a base of operations for traveling preachers who were walking in the truth. John also promises to come soon to set matters right.

---

1 The elder,

To my dear friend Gaius, whom I love
in the truth.

2 Dear friend, I pray that you may enjoy good health and that all may go well
with you, even as your soul is getting
along well. 3 It gave me great joy when
some believers came and testified about
your faithfulness to the truth, telling
how you continue to walk in it. 4 I have
no greater joy than to hear that my children are walking in the truth.
5 Dear friend, you are faithful in what
you are doing for the brothers and sisters,[a] even though they are strangers to
you. 6 They have told the church about
your love. Please send them on their way
in a manner that honors God. 7 It was for
the sake of the Name that they went out,
receiving no help from the pagans. 8 We
ought therefore to show hospitality to
such people so that we may work together for the truth.
9 I wrote to the church, but Diotrephes,
who loves to be first, will not welcome
us. 10 So when I come, I will call attention to what he is doing, spreading malicious nonsense about us. Not satisfied
with that, he even refuses to welcome
other believers. He also stops those who
want to do so and puts them out of the
church.
11 Dear friend, do not imitate what
is evil but what is good. Anyone who
does what is good is from God. Anyone
who does what is evil has not seen God.
12 Demetrius is well spoken of by everyone—and even by the truth itself. We
also speak well of him, and you know
that our testimony is true.

13 I have much to write you, but I do
not want to do so with pen and ink. 14 I
hope to see you soon, and we will talk
face to face.

Peace to you. The friends here send their greetings. Greet the friends there by name.

[a] 5 The Greek word for *brothers and sisters* (*adelphoi*) refers here to believers, both men and women, as part of God's family.

JUDE

Jesus had several brothers, two of whom were James and Jude. Much less is known about Jude than James (see p. 1089), but he was clearly a church leader, since he wrote to believers with authority in this letter that bears his name. It cannot be determined exactly who was meant to receive the letter, although the references to angels, to Israel's history and to specific writings indicate that Jewish Christians were in view.

Jude addresses the problem of false teachers who have come and are now threatening *the faith that was once for all entrusted to God's holy people*. On the basis of supposedly inspired dreams, they reject authority and pollute their own bodies. Even though they claim to be bringing God's message, they really *follow mere natural instincts and do not have the Spirit*. The believers must actively resist them and cleanse their community by rejecting both the teaching and the example of these ungodly men.

It seems that the apostle Peter received a copy of Jude's letter and wrote a similar one of his own to show that it faithfully presented the teaching of the apostles of the Lord Jesus Christ (see p. 1097).

1Jude, a servant of Jesus Christ and a
brother of James,

To those who have been called, who
are loved in God the Father and kept for[a]
Jesus Christ:

2Mercy, peace and love be yours in
abundance.

3Dear friends, although I was very eager to write to you about the salvation
we share, I felt compelled to write and
urge you to contend for the faith that
was once for all entrusted to God's holy
people. 4For certain individuals whose
condemnation was written about[b] long
ago have secretly slipped in among you.
They are ungodly people, who pervert
the grace of our God into a license for
immorality and deny Jesus Christ our
only Sovereign and Lord.
5Though you already know all this, I
want to remind you that the Lord[c] at one
time delivered his people out of Egypt,
but later destroyed those who did not believe. 6And the angels who did not keep
their positions of authority but abandoned their proper dwelling — these he
has kept in darkness, bound with everlasting chains for judgment on the great
Day. 7In a similar way, Sodom and Gomorrah and the surrounding towns gave
themselves up to sexual immorality and
perversion. They serve as an example
of those who suffer the punishment of
eternal fire.
8In the very same way, on the strength
of their dreams these ungodly people
pollute their own bodies, reject authority and heap abuse on celestial beings.
9But even the archangel Michael, when
he was disputing with the devil about
the body of Moses, did not himself dare
to condemn him for slander but said,
"The Lord rebuke you!"[d] 10Yet these
people slander whatever they do not understand, and the very things they do
understand by instinct — as irrational
animals do — will destroy them.
11Woe to them! They have taken the
way of Cain; they have rushed for profit
into Balaam's error; they have been destroyed in Korah's rebellion.
12These people are blemishes at your
love feasts, eating with you without
the slightest qualm — shepherds who
feed only themselves. They are clouds
without rain, blown along by the wind;
autumn trees, without fruit and uprooted — twice dead. 13They are wild waves
of the sea, foaming up their shame; wandering stars, for whom blackest darkness
has been reserved forever.
14Enoch, the seventh from Adam,
prophesied about them: "See, the Lord
is coming with thousands upon thousands of his holy ones 15to judge everyone, and to convict all of them of all

[a] *1* Or *by*; or *in* [b] *4* Or *individuals who were marked out for condemnation* [c] *5* Some early manuscripts *Jesus* [d] *9* Jude is alluding to the Jewish *Testament of Moses* (approximately the first century A.D.).

the ungodly acts they have committed
in their ungodliness, and of all the defiant words ungodly sinners have spoken against him."[a] 16 These people are
grumblers and faultfinders; they follow
their own evil desires; they boast about
themselves and flatter others for their
own advantage.

17 But, dear friends, remember what
the apostles of our Lord Jesus Christ
foretold. 18 They said to you, "In the last
times there will be scoffers who will follow their own ungodly desires." 19 These
are the people who divide you, who follow mere natural instincts and do not
have the Spirit.

20 But you, dear friends, by building
yourselves up in your most holy faith
and praying in the Holy Spirit, 21 keep
yourselves in God's love as you wait for
the mercy of our Lord Jesus Christ to
bring you to eternal life.

22 Be merciful to those who doubt;
23 save others by snatching them from
the fire; to others show mercy, mixed
with fear—hating even the clothing
stained by corrupted flesh.[b]

24 To him who is able to keep you from
stumbling and to present you before
his glorious presence without fault and
with great joy— 25 to the only God our
Savior be glory, majesty, power and authority, through Jesus Christ our Lord,
before all ages, now and forevermore!
Amen.

[a] *14,15* From the Jewish *First Book of Enoch* (approximately the first century B.C.) [b] *22,23* The Greek manuscripts of these verses vary at several points.

REVELATION

The ancient Roman Empire defended its economic and political control in spiritual terms, calling its gospel the *Pax Romana*, or Roman Peace. While in exile on the island of Patmos, a Jewish Christian prophet named John received a vision showing that the cult of emperor worship would soon become deadly to followers of the Messiah. The book of Revelation (or Apocalypse, meaning *unveiling*) is a warning, circulated to seven cities in the Roman province of Asia Minor. John's main point is to challenge and encourage the believers in the midst of their opposition and persecution.

Revelation is an apocalypse, a literary form well known in John's day. In an apocalypse a visitor from heaven reveals the secrets of the unseen world and the future through vivid symbols. While the symbols may appear strange at first, they become more clear when seen in their first-century setting and in light of other Bible imagery.

John's vision has four main parts, each marked by the phrase *in the Spirit*. After words of warning and encouragement to each of the seven churches, John's visions then center on Jesus—his role in redemption and the judgments he brings to the world. The immoral political and economic forces that rebel against God will be destroyed, and the Messiah will triumph over all his enemies. The vision closes with the promise that God's faithful servants will reign over the new creation.

Revelation also functions as the appropriate conclusion to the entire drama of the Bible. John concludes with images from the garden of Eden, the first story in the Bible. The world will experience a fresh beginning: *He who was seated on the throne said, "I am making everything new!"*

---

1 The revelation from Jesus Christ,
which God gave him to show his servants what must soon take place. He
made it known by sending his angel to
his servant John, 2who testifies to everything he saw—that is, the word of
God and the testimony of Jesus Christ.
3Blessed is the one who reads aloud the
words of this prophecy, and blessed are
those who hear it and take to heart what
is written in it, because the time is near.

4John,

To the seven churches in the province of Asia:

Grace and peace to you from him who
is, and who was, and who is to come, and
from the seven spirits[a] before his throne,
5and from Jesus Christ, who is the faithful witness, the firstborn from the dead,
and the ruler of the kings of the earth.

To him who loves us and has freed
us from our sins by his blood, 6and has
made us to be a kingdom and priests
to serve his God and Father—to him
be glory and power for ever and ever!
Amen.

7"Look, he is coming with the
clouds,"[b]
and "every eye will see him,
even those who pierced him";
and all peoples on earth "will
mourn because of him."[c]
So shall it be! Amen.

8"I am the Alpha and the Omega," says
the Lord God, "who is, and who was, and
who is to come, the Almighty."

9I, John, your brother and companion
in the suffering and kingdom and patient
endurance that are ours in Jesus, was
on the island of Patmos because of the
word of God and the testimony of Jesus.
10On the Lord's Day I was in the Spirit, and I heard behind me a loud voice
like a trumpet, 11which said: "Write on
a scroll what you see and send it to the
seven churches: to Ephesus, Smyrna,
Pergamum, Thyatira, Sardis, Philadel-
phia and Laodicea."
12I turned around to see the voice that
was speaking to me. And when I turned
I saw seven golden lampstands, 13and
among the lampstands was someone
like a son of man,[d] dressed in a robe

[a] *4* That is, the sevenfold Spirit [b] *7* Daniel 7:13 [c] *7* Zech. 12:10 [d] *13* See Daniel 7:13.

reaching down to his feet and with a
golden sash around his chest. 14 The hair
on his head was white like wool, as white
as snow, and his eyes were like blazing
fire. 15 His feet were like bronze glowing
in a furnace, and his voice was like the
sound of rushing waters. 16 In his right
hand he held seven stars, and coming
out of his mouth was a sharp, double-
edged sword. His face was like the sun
shining in all its brilliance.

17 When I saw him, I fell at his feet as
though dead. Then he placed his right
hand on me and said: "Do not be afraid.
I am the First and the Last. 18 I am the
Living One; I was dead, and now look,
am alive for ever and ever! And I hold the
keys of death and Hades.

19 "Write, therefore, what you have
seen, what is now and what will take
place later. 20 The mystery of the seven
stars that you saw in my right hand and
of the seven golden lampstands is this:
The seven stars are the angels[a] of the
seven churches, and the seven lampstands are the seven churches.

2 "To the angel[b] of the church in Ephesus write:

These are the words of him who
holds the seven stars in his right
hand and walks among the seven
golden lampstands. 2 I know your
deeds, your hard work and your
perseverance. I know that you cannot tolerate wicked people, that
you have tested those who claim
to be apostles but are not, and have
found them false. 3 You have persevered and have endured hardships
for my name, and have not grown
weary.

4 Yet I hold this against you: You
have forsaken the love you had at
first. 5 Consider how far you have
fallen! Repent and do the things
you did at first. If you do not repent,
I will come to you and remove your
lampstand from its place. 6 But you
have this in your favor: You hate the
practices of the Nicolaitans, which I
also hate.

7 Whoever has ears, let them hear
what the Spirit says to the churches. To the one who is victorious, I
will give the right to eat from the
tree of life, which is in the paradise
of God.

8 "To the angel of the church in Smyrna
write:

These are the words of him who is
the First and the Last, who died and
came to life again. 9 I know your afflictions and your poverty—yet you
are rich! I know about the slander of
those who say they are Jews and are
not, but are a synagogue of Satan.
10 Do not be afraid of what you are
about to suffer. I tell you, the devil
will put some of you in prison to test
you, and you will suffer persecution
for ten days. Be faithful, even to the
point of death, and I will give you life
as your victor's crown.

11 Whoever has ears, let them hear
what the Spirit says to the churches.
The one who is victorious will not be
hurt at all by the second death.

12 "To the angel of the church in Pergamum write:

These are the words of him who
has the sharp, double-edged sword.
13 I know where you live—where Satan has his throne. Yet you remain
true to my name. You did not renounce your faith in me, not even in
the days of Antipas, my faithful witness, who was put to death in your
city—where Satan lives.

14 Nevertheless, I have a few things
against you: There are some among
you who hold to the teaching of Balaam, who taught Balak to entice
the Israelites to sin so that they ate
food sacrificed to idols and committed sexual immorality. 15 Likewise, you also have those who hold
to the teaching of the Nicolaitans.
16 Repent therefore! Otherwise, I
will soon come to you and will fight
against them with the sword of my
mouth.

17 Whoever has ears, let them hear
what the Spirit says to the churches.
To the one who is victorious, I will
give some of the hidden manna. I
will also give that person a white
stone with a new name written on

[a] 20 Or *messengers* [b] 1 Or *messenger;* also in verses 8, 12 and 18

it, known only to the one who receives it.

[18]"To the angel of the church in Thyatira write:

These are the words of the Son of
God, whose eyes are like blazing fire
and whose feet are like burnished
bronze. [19]I know your deeds, your
love and faith, your service and perseverance, and that you are now doing more than you did at first.
[20]Nevertheless, I have this against
you: You tolerate that woman Jezebel, who calls herself a prophet. By
her teaching she misleads my servants into sexual immorality and
the eating of food sacrificed to idols.
[21]I have given her time to repent of
her immorality, but she is unwilling.
[22]So I will cast her on a bed of suffering, and I will make those who commit adultery with her suffer intensely, unless they repent of her ways. [23]I
will strike her children dead. Then
all the churches will know that I am
he who searches hearts and minds,
and I will repay each of you according to your deeds.
[24]Now I say to the rest of you in
Thyatira, to you who do not hold to
her teaching and have not learned
Satan's so-called deep secrets, 'I
will not impose any other burden
on you, [25]except to hold on to what
you have until I come.'
[26]To the one who is victorious and
does my will to the end, I will give
authority over the nations— [27]that
one 'will rule them with an iron
scepter and will dash them to pieces like pottery'[a]—just as I have received authority from my Father. [28]I
will also give that one the morning
star. [29]Whoever has ears, let them
hear what the Spirit says to the
churches.

3 "To the angel[b] of the church in Sardis write:

These are the words of him who
holds the seven spirits[c] of God and
the seven stars. I know your deeds;
you have a reputation of being
alive, but you are dead. [2]Wake up!
Strengthen what remains and is
about to die, for I have found your
deeds unfinished in the sight of my
God. [3]Remember, therefore, what
you have received and heard; hold
it fast, and repent. But if you do not
wake up, I will come like a thief, and
you will not know at what time I will
come to you.
[4]Yet you have a few people in Sardis who have not soiled their clothes.
They will walk with me, dressed in
white, for they are worthy. [5]The one
who is victorious will, like them, be
dressed in white. I will never blot
out the name of that person from
the book of life, but will acknowledge that name before my Father
and his angels. [6]Whoever has ears,
let them hear what the Spirit says to
the churches.

[7]"To the angel of the church in Philadel-
phia write:

These are the words of him who
is holy and true, who holds the key
of David. What he opens no one can
shut, and what he shuts no one can
open. [8]I know your deeds. See, I
have placed before you an open door
that no one can shut. I know that you
have little strength, yet you have
kept my word and have not denied
my name. [9]I will make those who
are of the synagogue of Satan, who
claim to be Jews though they are
not, but are liars—I will make them
come and fall down at your feet and
acknowledge that I have loved you.
[10]Since you have kept my command
to endure patiently, I will also keep
you from the hour of trial that is going to come on the whole world to
test the inhabitants of the earth.
[11]I am coming soon. Hold on to
what you have, so that no one will
take your crown. [12]The one who is
victorious I will make a pillar in the
temple of my God. Never again will
they leave it. I will write on them the
name of my God and the name of the
city of my God, the new Jerusalem,
which is coming down out of heav-
en from my God; and I will also write
on them my new name. [13]Whoever

[a] *27* Psalm 2:9 [b] *1* Or *messenger*; also in verses 7 and 14 [c] *1* That is, the sevenfold Spirit

has ears, let them hear what the
Spirit says to the churches.

14"To the angel of the church in Laodicea write:

These are the words of the Amen,
the faithful and true witness, the
ruler of God's creation. 15I know
your deeds, that you are neither
cold nor hot. I wish you were either
one or the other! 16So, because you
are lukewarm—neither hot nor
cold—I am about to spit you out of
my mouth. 17You say, 'I am rich; I
have acquired wealth and do not
need a thing.' But you do not realize
that you are wretched, pitiful, poor,
blind and naked. 18I counsel you to
buy from me gold refined in the fire,
so you can become rich; and white
clothes to wear, so you can cover
your shameful nakedness; and salve
to put on your eyes, so you can see.
19Those whom I love I rebuke and
discipline. So be earnest and repent.
20Here I am! I stand at the door and
knock. If anyone hears my voice
and opens the door, I will come in
and eat with that person, and they
with me.
21To the one who is victorious, I
will give the right to sit with me on
my throne, just as I was victorious
and sat down with my Father on
his throne. 22Whoever has ears, let
them hear what the Spirit says to the
churches."

4 After this I looked, and there before
me was a door standing open in heav-
en. And the voice I had first heard speaking to me like a trumpet said, "Come up
here, and I will show you what must take
place after this." 2At once I was in the
Spirit, and there before me was a throne
in heaven with someone sitting on it.
3And the one who sat there had the appearance of jasper and ruby. A rainbow
that shone like an emerald encircled the
throne. 4Surrounding the throne were
twenty-four other thrones, and seated
on them were twenty-four elders. They
were dressed in white and had crowns
of gold on their heads. 5From the throne
came flashes of lightning, rumblings and
peals of thunder. In front of the throne,
seven lamps were blazing. These are the
seven spirits[a] of God. 6Also in front of
the throne there was what looked like a
sea of glass, clear as crystal.
In the center, around the throne, were
four living creatures, and they were
covered with eyes, in front and in back.
7The first living creature was like a lion,
the second was like an ox, the third had
a face like a man, the fourth was like a
flying eagle. 8Each of the four living
creatures had six wings and was covered with eyes all around, even under
its wings. Day and night they never stop
saying:

"'Holy, holy, holy
is the Lord God Almighty,'[b]
who was, and is, and is to come."

9Whenever the living creatures give glory, honor and thanks to him who sits on
the throne and who lives for ever and
ever, 10the twenty-four elders fall down
before him who sits on the throne and
worship him who lives for ever and ever.
They lay their crowns before the throne
and say:

11"You are worthy, our Lord and God,
to receive glory and honor and
power,
for you created all things,
and by your will they were created
and have their being."

5 Then I saw in the right hand of him
who sat on the throne a scroll with
writing on both sides and sealed with
seven seals. 2And I saw a mighty angel proclaiming in a loud voice, "Who
is worthy to break the seals and open
the scroll?" 3But no one in heaven or on
earth or under the earth could open the
scroll or even look inside it. 4I wept and
wept because no one was found who was
worthy to open the scroll or look inside.
5Then one of the elders said to me, "Do
not weep! See, the Lion of the tribe of Judah, the Root of David, has triumphed.
He is able to open the scroll and its sev-
en seals."
6Then I saw a Lamb, looking as if it
had been slain, standing at the center
of the throne, encircled by the four liv-

[a] 5 That is, the sevenfold Spirit [b] 8 Isaiah 6:3

ing creatures and the elders. The Lamb
had seven horns and seven eyes, which
are the seven spirits[a] of God sent out
into all the earth. 7He went and took
the scroll from the right hand of him
who sat on the throne. 8And when he
had taken it, the four living creatures
and the twenty-four elders fell down
before the Lamb. Each one had a harp
and they were holding golden bowls
full of incense, which are the prayers
of God's people. 9And they sang a new
song, saying:

"You are worthy to take the scroll
and to open its seals,
because you were slain,
and with your blood you purchased
for God
persons from every tribe and
language and people and
nation.
10You have made them to be a kingdom
and priests to serve our God,
and they will reign[b] on the earth."

11Then I looked and heard the voice
of many angels, numbering thousands
upon thousands, and ten thousand times
ten thousand. They encircled the throne
and the living creatures and the elders.
12In a loud voice they were saying:

"Worthy is the Lamb, who was slain,
to receive power and wealth and
wisdom and strength
and honor and glory and praise!"

13Then I heard every creature in heav-
en and on earth and under the earth
and on the sea, and all that is in them,
saying:

"To him who sits on the throne and to
the Lamb
be praise and honor and glory and
power,
for ever and ever!"

14The four living creatures said, "Amen,"
and the elders fell down and worshiped.

6 I watched as the Lamb opened the
first of the seven seals. Then I heard
one of the four living creatures say in a
voice like thunder, "Come!" 2I looked,
and there before me was a white horse!
Its rider held a bow, and he was given a
crown, and he rode out as a conqueror
bent on conquest.

3When the Lamb opened the second
seal, I heard the second living creature
say, "Come!" 4Then another horse came
out, a fiery red one. Its rider was given
power to take peace from the earth and
to make people kill each other. To him
was given a large sword.

5When the Lamb opened the third
seal, I heard the third living creature
say, "Come!" I looked, and there before
me was a black horse! Its rider was holding a pair of scales in his hand. 6Then I
heard what sounded like a voice among
the four living creatures, saying, "Two
pounds[c] of wheat for a day's wages,[d]
and six pounds[e] of barley for a day's
wages,[d] and do not damage the oil and
the wine!"

7When the Lamb opened the fourth
seal, I heard the voice of the fourth living creature say, "Come!" 8I looked, and
there before me was a pale horse! Its
rider was named Death, and Hades was
following close behind him. They were
given power over a fourth of the earth to
kill by sword, famine and plague, and by
the wild beasts of the earth.

9When he opened the fifth seal, I saw
under the altar the souls of those who
had been slain because of the word of
God and the testimony they had main-
tained. 10They called out in a loud voice,
"How long, Sovereign Lord, holy and
true, until you judge the inhabitants of
the earth and avenge our blood?" 11Then
each of them was given a white robe, and
they were told to wait a little longer, until
the full number of their fellow servants,
their brothers and sisters,[f] were killed
just as they had been.

12I watched as he opened the sixth
seal. There was a great earthquake. The
sun turned black like sackcloth made of
goat hair, the whole moon turned blood
red, 13and the stars in the sky fell to
earth, as figs drop from a fig tree when
shaken by a strong wind. 14The heavens
receded like a scroll being rolled up, and
every mountain and island was removed
from its place.

15Then the kings of the earth, the
princes, the generals, the rich, the

[a] *6* That is, the sevenfold Spirit [b] *10* Some manuscripts *they reign* [c] *6* Or about 1 kilogram
[d] *6* Greek *a denarius* [e] *6* Or about 3 kilograms [f] *11* The Greek word for *brothers and sisters* (*adelphoi*)
refers here to believers, both men and women, as part of God's family; also in 12:10; 19:10.

mighty, and everyone else, both slave
and free, hid in caves and among the
rocks of the mountains. 16 They called to
the mountains and the rocks, "Fall on us
and hide us[a] from the face of him who
sits on the throne and from the wrath of
the Lamb! 17 For the great day of their[b]
wrath has come, and who can withstand it?"

7 After this I saw four angels standing
at the four corners of the earth, holding back the four winds of the earth to
prevent any wind from blowing on the
land or on the sea or on any tree. 2 Then
I saw another angel coming up from the
east, having the seal of the living God. He
called out in a loud voice to the four angels who had been given power to harm
the land and the sea: 3 "Do not harm the
land or the sea or the trees until we put
a seal on the foreheads of the servants of
our God." 4 Then I heard the number of
those who were sealed: 144,000 from all
the tribes of Israel.

5 From the tribe of Judah 12,000 were
sealed,
from the tribe of Reuben 12,000,
from the tribe of Gad 12,000,
6 from the tribe of Asher 12,000,
from the tribe of Naphtali 12,000,
from the tribe of Manasseh 12,000,
7 from the tribe of Simeon 12,000,
from the tribe of Levi 12,000,
from the tribe of Issachar 12,000,
8 from the tribe of Zebulun 12,000,
from the tribe of Joseph 12,000,
from the tribe of Benjamin 12,000.

9 After this I looked, and there before
me was a great multitude that no one
could count, from every nation, tribe,
people and language, standing before
the throne and before the Lamb. They
were wearing white robes and were
holding palm branches in their hands.
10 And they cried out in a loud voice:

"Salvation belongs to our God,
who sits on the throne,
and to the Lamb."

11 All the angels were standing around
the throne and around the elders and
the four living creatures. They fell down
on their faces before the throne and worshiped God, 12 saying:

"Amen!
Praise and glory
and wisdom and thanks and honor
and power and strength
be to our God for ever and ever.
Amen!"

13 Then one of the elders asked me,
"These in white robes—who are they,
and where did they come from?"
14 I answered, "Sir, you know."
And he said, "These are they who
have come out of the great tribulation;
they have washed their robes and made
them white in the blood of the Lamb.
15 Therefore,

"they are before the throne of God
and serve him day and night in his
temple;
and he who sits on the throne
will shelter them with his presence.
16 'Never again will they hunger;
never again will they thirst.
The sun will not beat down on them,'[c]
nor any scorching heat.
17 For the Lamb at the center of the
throne
will be their shepherd;
'he will lead them to springs of living
water.'[c]
'And God will wipe away every tear
from their eyes.'[d]"

8 When he opened the seventh seal,
there was silence in heaven for about
half an hour.
2 And I saw the seven angels who stand
before God, and seven trumpets were
given to them.
3 Another angel, who had a golden
censer, came and stood at the altar. He
was given much incense to offer, with
the prayers of all God's people, on the
golden altar in front of the throne. 4 The
smoke of the incense, together with the
prayers of God's people, went up before God from the angel's hand. 5 Then
the angel took the censer, filled it with
fire from the altar, and hurled it on the
earth; and there came peals of thunder,
rumblings, flashes of lightning and an
earthquake.
6 Then the seven angels who had the
seven trumpets prepared to sound
them.
7 The first angel sounded his trumpet,

[a] *16* See Hosea 10:8. [b] *17* Some manuscripts *his* [c] *16,17* Isaiah 49:10 [d] *17* Isaiah 25:8

and there came hail and fire mixed with
blood, and it was hurled down on the
earth. A third of the earth was burned
up, a third of the trees were burned up,
and all the green grass was burned up.
8 The second angel sounded his trumpet, and something like a huge mountain, all ablaze, was thrown into the sea.
A third of the sea turned into blood, 9 a
third of the living creatures in the sea
died, and a third of the ships were destroyed.
10 The third angel sounded his trumpet, and a great star, blazing like a torch,
fell from the sky on a third of the rivers and on the springs of water — 11 the
name of the star is Wormwood.[a] A third
of the waters turned bitter, and many
people died from the waters that had
become bitter.
12 The fourth angel sounded his trumpet, and a third of the sun was struck,
a third of the moon, and a third of the
stars, so that a third of them turned dark.
A third of the day was without light, and
also a third of the night.
13 As I watched, I heard an eagle that
was flying in midair call out in a loud
voice: "Woe! Woe! Woe to the inhabitants of the earth, because of the trumpet blasts about to be sounded by the
other three angels!"

9 The fifth angel sounded his trumpet,
and I saw a star that had fallen from
the sky to the earth. The star was given
the key to the shaft of the Abyss. 2 When
he opened the Abyss, smoke rose from it
like the smoke from a gigantic furnace.
The sun and sky were darkened by the
smoke from the Abyss. 3 And out of the
smoke locusts came down on the earth
and were given power like that of scorpions of the earth. 4 They were told not to
harm the grass of the earth or any plant
or tree, but only those people who did
not have the seal of God on their foreheads. 5 They were not allowed to kill
them but only to torture them for five
months. And the agony they suffered
was like that of the sting of a scorpion
when it strikes. 6 During those days people will seek death but will not find it;
they will long to die, but death will elude
them.
7 The locusts looked like horses prepared for battle. On their heads they
wore something like crowns of gold,
and their faces resembled human faces.
8 Their hair was like women's hair, and
their teeth were like lions' teeth. 9 They
had breastplates like breastplates of
iron, and the sound of their wings was
like the thundering of many horses and
chariots rushing into battle. 10 They had
tails with stingers, like scorpions, and
in their tails they had power to torment
people for five months. 11 They had as
king over them the angel of the Abyss,
whose name in Hebrew is Abaddon and
in Greek is Apollyon (that is, Destroyer).
12 The first woe is past; two other woes
are yet to come.
13 The sixth angel sounded his trumpet, and I heard a voice coming from the
four horns of the golden altar that is before God. 14 It said to the sixth angel who
had the trumpet, "Release the four angels who are bound at the great river Euphrates." 15 And the four angels who had
been kept ready for this very hour and
day and month and year were released
to kill a third of mankind. 16 The number of the mounted troops was twice ten
thousand times ten thousand. I heard
their number.
17 The horses and riders I saw in my vision looked like this: Their breastplates
were fiery red, dark blue, and yellow as
sulfur. The heads of the horses resembled the heads of lions, and out of their
mouths came fire, smoke and sulfur.
18 A third of mankind was killed by the
three plagues of fire, smoke and sulfur
that came out of their mouths. 19 The
power of the horses was in their mouths
and in their tails; for their tails were like
snakes, having heads with which they
inflict injury.
20 The rest of mankind who were not
killed by these plagues still did not repent of the work of their hands; they did
not stop worshiping demons, and idols
of gold, silver, bronze, stone and wood —
idols that cannot see or hear or walk.
21 Nor did they repent of their murders,
their magic arts, their sexual immorality
or their thefts.

10 Then I saw another mighty angel
coming down from heaven. He was
robed in a cloud, with a rainbow above

[a] *11* Wormwood is a bitter substance.

his head; his face was like the sun, and
his legs were like fiery pillars. 2 He was
holding a little scroll, which lay open in
his hand. He planted his right foot on the
sea and his left foot on the land, 3 and he
gave a loud shout like the roar of a lion.
When he shouted, the voices of the sev-
en thunders spoke. 4 And when the seven
thunders spoke, I was about to write; but
I heard a voice from heaven say, "Seal up
what the seven thunders have said and
do not write it down."

5 Then the angel I had seen standing
on the sea and on the land raised his
right hand to heaven. 6 And he swore by
him who lives for ever and ever, who created the heavens and all that is in them,
the earth and all that is in it, and the sea
and all that is in it, and said, "There will
be no more delay! 7 But in the days when
the seventh angel is about to sound his
trumpet, the mystery of God will be accomplished, just as he announced to his
servants the prophets."

8 Then the voice that I had heard from
heaven spoke to me once more: "Go, take
the scroll that lies open in the hand of
the angel who is standing on the sea and
on the land."

9 So I went to the angel and asked him
to give me the little scroll. He said to me,
"Take it and eat it. It will turn your stomach sour, but 'in your mouth it will be as
sweet as honey.'[a]" 10 I took the little scroll
from the angel's hand and ate it. It tasted
as sweet as honey in my mouth, but when
I had eaten it, my stomach turned sour.
11 Then I was told, "You must prophesy
again about many peoples, nations, languages and kings."

11 I was given a reed like a measuring
rod and was told, "Go and measure
the temple of God and the altar, with its
worshipers. 2 But exclude the outer court;
do not measure it, because it has been
given to the Gentiles. They will trample
on the holy city for 42 months. 3 And I will
appoint my two witnesses, and they will
prophesy for 1,260 days, clothed in sackcloth." 4 They are "the two olive trees"
and the two lampstands, and "they stand
before the Lord of the earth."[b] 5 If anyone
tries to harm them, fire comes from their
mouths and devours their enemies. This
is how anyone who wants to harm them
must die. 6 They have power to shut up
the heavens so that it will not rain during the time they are prophesying; and
they have power to turn the waters into
blood and to strike the earth with every
kind of plague as often as they want.

7 Now when they have finished their
testimony, the beast that comes up
from the Abyss will attack them, and
overpower and kill them. 8 Their bodies
will lie in the public square of the great
city—which is figuratively called Sodom and Egypt—where also their Lord
was crucified. 9 For three and a half days
some from every people, tribe, language
and nation will gaze on their bodies and
refuse them burial. 10 The inhabitants of
the earth will gloat over them and will
celebrate by sending each other gifts,
because these two prophets had tormented those who live on the earth.

11 But after the three and a half days the
breath[c] of life from God entered them,
and they stood on their feet, and terror
struck those who saw them. 12 Then they
heard a loud voice from heaven saying to
them, "Come up here." And they went up
to heaven in a cloud, while their enemies
looked on.

13 At that very hour there was a severe
earthquake and a tenth of the city collapsed. Seven thousand people were
killed in the earthquake, and the survivors were terrified and gave glory to the
God of heaven.

14 The second woe has passed; the
third woe is coming soon.

15 The seventh angel sounded his
trumpet, and there were loud voices in
heaven, which said:

"The kingdom of the world has
become
the kingdom of our Lord and of his
Messiah,
and he will reign for ever and ever."

16 And the twenty-four elders, who were
seated on their thrones before God, fell
on their faces and worshiped God, 17 saying:

"We give thanks to you, Lord God
Almighty,
the One who is and who was,
because you have taken your great
power

[a] 9 Ezek. 3:3 [b] 4 See Zech. 4:3,11,14. [c] 11 Or *Spirit* (see Ezek. 37:5,14)

and have begun to reign.
18 The nations were angry,
and your wrath has come.
The time has come for judging the dead,
and for rewarding your servants the prophets
and your people who revere your name,
both great and small—
and for destroying those who destroy the earth."

19 Then God's temple in heaven was
opened, and within his temple was seen
the ark of his covenant. And there came
flashes of lightning, rumblings, peals
of thunder, an earthquake and a severe
hailstorm.

12 A great sign appeared in heaven: a
woman clothed with the sun, with
the moon under her feet and a crown of
twelve stars on her head. 2 She was pregnant and cried out in pain as she was
about to give birth. 3 Then another sign
appeared in heaven: an enormous red
dragon with seven heads and ten horns
and seven crowns on its heads. 4 Its tail
swept a third of the stars out of the sky
and flung them to the earth. The dragon stood in front of the woman who was
about to give birth, so that it might devour her child the moment he was born.
5 She gave birth to a son, a male child,
who "will rule all the nations with an iron
scepter."[a] And her child was snatched up
to God and to his throne. 6 The woman
fled into the wilderness to a place prepared for her by God, where she might
be taken care of for 1,260 days.

7 Then war broke out in heaven. Michael and his angels fought against the
dragon, and the dragon and his angels
fought back. 8 But he was not strong
enough, and they lost their place in
heaven. 9 The great dragon was hurled
down—that ancient serpent called the
devil, or Satan, who leads the whole
world astray. He was hurled to the earth,
and his angels with him.

10 Then I heard a loud voice in heav-
en say:

"Now have come the salvation and the power
and the kingdom of our God,
and the authority of his Messiah.
For the accuser of our brothers and sisters,
who accuses them before our God day and night,
has been hurled down.
11 They triumphed over him
by the blood of the Lamb
and by the word of their testimony;
they did not love their lives so much
as to shrink from death.
12 Therefore rejoice, you heavens
and you who dwell in them!
But woe to the earth and the sea,
because the devil has gone down to you!
He is filled with fury,
because he knows that his time is short."

13 When the dragon saw that he had
been hurled to the earth, he pursued the
woman who had given birth to the male
child. 14 The woman was given the two
wings of a great eagle, so that she might
fly to the place prepared for her in the
wilderness, where she would be taken
care of for a time, times and half a time,
out of the serpent's reach. 15 Then from
his mouth the serpent spewed water
like a river, to overtake the woman and
sweep her away with the torrent. 16 But
the earth helped the woman by opening its mouth and swallowing the river
that the dragon had spewed out of his
mouth. 17 Then the dragon was enraged
at the woman and went off to wage war
against the rest of her offspring—those
who keep God's commands and hold fast
their testimony about Jesus.

13 The dragon[b] stood on the shore of
the sea. And I saw a beast coming
out of the sea. It had ten horns and sev-
en heads, with ten crowns on its horns,
and on each head a blasphemous name.
2 The beast I saw resembled a leopard,
but had feet like those of a bear and a
mouth like that of a lion. The dragon
gave the beast his power and his throne
and great authority. 3 One of the heads
of the beast seemed to have had a fatal
wound, but the fatal wound had been
healed. The whole world was filled with
wonder and followed the beast. 4 People
worshiped the dragon because he had
given authority to the beast, and they

[a] 5 Psalm 2:9 [b] 1 Some manuscripts *And I*

also worshiped the beast and asked,
"Who is like the beast? Who can wage
war against it?"
5The beast was given a mouth to utter
proud words and blasphemies and to exercise its authority for forty-two months.
6It opened its mouth to blaspheme God,
and to slander his name and his dwelling place and those who live in heaven.
7It was given power to wage war against
God's holy people and to conquer them.
And it was given authority over every
tribe, people, language and nation. 8All
inhabitants of the earth will worship the
beast—all whose names have not been
written in the Lamb's book of life, the
Lamb who was slain from the creation
of the world.[a]
9Whoever has ears, let them hear.

10 "If anyone is to go into captivity,
into captivity they will go.
If anyone is to be killed[b] with the
sword,
with the sword they will be killed."[c]

This calls for patient endurance and
faithfulness on the part of God's people.
11Then I saw a second beast, coming
out of the earth. It had two horns like a
lamb, but it spoke like a dragon. 12It exercised all the authority of the first beast
on its behalf, and made the earth and
its inhabitants worship the first beast,
whose fatal wound had been healed.
13And it performed great signs, even
causing fire to come down from heaven
to the earth in full view of the people.
14Because of the signs it was given power
to perform on behalf of the first beast, it
deceived the inhabitants of the earth. It
ordered them to set up an image in hon-
or of the beast who was wounded by the
sword and yet lived. 15The second beast
was given power to give breath to the image of the first beast, so that the image
could speak and cause all who refused
to worship the image to be killed. 16It
also forced all people, great and small,
rich and poor, free and slave, to receive
a mark on their right hands or on their
foreheads, 17so that they could not buy
or sell unless they had the mark, which
is the name of the beast or the number
of its name.
18This calls for wisdom. Let the person
who has insight calculate the number of
the beast, for it is the number of a man.[d]
That number is 666.

14 Then I looked, and there before me
was the Lamb, standing on Mount
Zion, and with him 144,000 who had his
name and his Father's name written on
their foreheads. 2And I heard a sound
from heaven like the roar of rushing waters and like a loud peal of thunder. The
sound I heard was like that of harpists
playing their harps. 3And they sang a
new song before the throne and before
the four living creatures and the elders.
No one could learn the song except the
144,000 who had been redeemed from
the earth. 4These are those who did not
defile themselves with women, for they
remained virgins. They follow the Lamb
wherever he goes. They were purchased
from among mankind and offered as
firstfruits to God and the Lamb. 5No
lie was found in their mouths; they are
blameless.
6Then I saw another angel flying in
midair, and he had the eternal gospel
to proclaim to those who live on the
earth—to every nation, tribe, language
and people. 7He said in a loud voice,
"Fear God and give him glory, because
the hour of his judgment has come. Worship him who made the heavens, the
earth, the sea and the springs of water."
8A second angel followed and said,
"'Fallen! Fallen is Babylon the Great,'[e]
which made all the nations drink the
maddening wine of her adulteries."
9A third angel followed them and said
in a loud voice: "If anyone worships
the beast and its image and receives
its mark on their forehead or on their
hand, 10they, too, will drink the wine of
God's fury, which has been poured full
strength into the cup of his wrath. They
will be tormented with burning sulfur
in the presence of the holy angels and of
the Lamb. 11And the smoke of their torment will rise for ever and ever. There
will be no rest day or night for those
who worship the beast and its image, or
for anyone who receives the mark of its
name." 12This calls for patient endurance on the part of the people of God
who keep his commands and remain
faithful to Jesus.

[a] 8 Or *written from the creation of the world in the book of life belonging to the Lamb who was slain*
[b] 10 Some manuscripts *anyone kills* [c] 10 Jer. 15:2 [d] 18 Or *is humanity's number* [e] 8 Isaiah 21:9

[13]Then I heard a voice from heaven
ay, "Write this: Blessed are the dead
who die in the Lord from now on."

"Yes," says the Spirit, "they will rest from their labor, for their deeds will follow them."

[14]I looked, and there before me was a
white cloud, and seated on the cloud was
one like a son of man[a] with a crown of
gold on his head and a sharp sickle in his
hand. [15]Then another angel came out of
the temple and called in a loud voice to
him who was sitting on the cloud, "Take
your sickle and reap, because the time
to reap has come, for the harvest of the
earth is ripe." [16]So he who was seated
on the cloud swung his sickle over the
earth, and the earth was harvested.

[17]Another angel came out of the temple in heaven, and he too had a sharp
sickle. [18]Still another angel, who had
charge of the fire, came from the altar
and called in a loud voice to him who
had the sharp sickle, "Take your sharp
sickle and gather the clusters of grapes
from the earth's vine, because its grapes
are ripe." [19]The angel swung his sickle
on the earth, gathered its grapes and
threw them into the great winepress
of God's wrath. [20]They were trampled
in the winepress outside the city, and
blood flowed out of the press, rising as
high as the horses' bridles for a distance
of 1,600 stadia.[b]

15 I saw in heaven another great and
marvelous sign: seven angels with
the seven last plagues—last, because
with them God's wrath is completed.
[2]And I saw what looked like a sea of glass
glowing with fire and, standing beside
the sea, those who had been victorious
over the beast and its image and over
the number of its name. They held harps
given them by God [3]and sang the song of
God's servant Moses and of the Lamb:

"Great and marvelous are your deeds,
  Lord God Almighty.
Just and true are your ways,
  King of the nations.[c]
[4]Who will not fear you, Lord,
  and bring glory to your name?
For you alone are holy.
All nations will come
  and worship before you,
for your righteous acts have been
  revealed."[d]

[5]After this I looked, and I saw in heaven the temple—that is, the tabernacle of
the covenant law—and it was opened.
[6]Out of the temple came the seven angels with the seven plagues. They were
dressed in clean, shining linen and
wore golden sashes around their chests.
[7]Then one of the four living creatures
gave to the seven angels seven golden
bowls filled with the wrath of God, who
lives for ever and ever. [8]And the temple
was filled with smoke from the glory of
God and from his power, and no one
could enter the temple until the seven
plagues of the seven angels were completed.

16 Then I heard a loud voice from the
temple saying to the seven angels,
"Go, pour out the seven bowls of God's
wrath on the earth."

[2]The first angel went and poured out
his bowl on the land, and ugly, festering
sores broke out on the people who had
the mark of the beast and worshiped its
image.

[3]The second angel poured out his
bowl on the sea, and it turned into blood
like that of a dead person, and every living thing in the sea died.

[4]The third angel poured out his bowl
on the rivers and springs of water, and
they became blood. [5]Then I heard the
angel in charge of the waters say:

"You are just in these judgments,
  O Holy One,
  you who are and who were;
[6]for they have shed the blood of your
  holy people and your prophets,
  and you have given them blood to
  drink as they deserve."

[7]And I heard the altar respond:

"Yes, Lord God Almighty,
  true and just are your judgments."

[8]The fourth angel poured out his bowl
on the sun, and the sun was allowed
to scorch people with fire. [9]They were
seared by the intense heat and they
cursed the name of God, who had control over these plagues, but they refused
to repent and glorify him.

[a] *14* See Daniel 7:13. [b] *20* That is, about 180 miles or about 300 kilometers [c] *3* Some manuscripts *ages*
[d] *3,4* Phrases in this song are drawn from Psalm 111:2,3; Deut. 32:4; Jer. 10:7; Psalms 86:9; 98:2.

10 The fifth angel poured out his bowl
on the throne of the beast, and its kingdom was plunged into darkness. People
gnawed their tongues in agony 11 and
cursed the God of heaven because of
their pains and their sores, but they refused to repent of what they had done.

12 The sixth angel poured out his bowl
on the great river Euphrates, and its water was dried up to prepare the way for
the kings from the East. 13 Then I saw
three impure spirits that looked like
frogs; they came out of the mouth of the
dragon, out of the mouth of the beast
and out of the mouth of the false prophet. 14 They are demonic spirits that perform signs, and they go out to the kings
of the whole world, to gather them for
the battle on the great day of God Almighty.

> 15 "Look, I come like a thief! Blessed
> is the one who stays awake and re-
> mains clothed, so as not to go naked
> and be shamefully exposed."

16 Then they gathered the kings together to the place that in Hebrew is called
Armageddon.

17 The seventh angel poured out his
bowl into the air, and out of the temple came a loud voice from the throne,
saying, "It is done!" 18 Then there came
flashes of lightning, rumblings, peals
of thunder and a severe earthquake.
No earthquake like it has ever occurred
since mankind has been on earth, so
tremendous was the quake. 19 The great
city split into three parts, and the cities
of the nations collapsed. God remembered Babylon the Great and gave her
the cup filled with the wine of the fury
of his wrath. 20 Every island fled away
and the mountains could not be found.
21 From the sky huge hailstones, each
weighing about a hundred pounds,[a] fell
on people. And they cursed God on account of the plague of hail, because the
plague was so terrible.

17 One of the seven angels who had
the seven bowls came and said to
me, "Come, I will show you the punishment of the great prostitute, who sits by
many waters. 2 With her the kings of the
earth committed adultery, and the inhabitants of the earth were intoxicated
with the wine of her adulteries."

3 Then the angel carried me away in
the Spirit into a wilderness. There I saw
a woman sitting on a scarlet beast that
was covered with blasphemous names
and had seven heads and ten horns.
4 The woman was dressed in purple and
scarlet, and was glittering with gold, precious stones and pearls. She held a gold-
en cup in her hand, filled with abominable things and the filth of her adulteries.
5 The name written on her forehead was
a mystery:

BABYLON THE GREAT
THE MOTHER OF PROSTITUTES
AND OF THE ABOMINATIONS
OF THE EARTH.

6 I saw that the woman was drunk with
the blood of God's holy people, the blood
of those who bore testimony to Jesus.

When I saw her, I was greatly astonished. 7 Then the angel said to me: "Why
are you astonished? I will explain to
you the mystery of the woman and of
the beast she rides, which has the seven
heads and ten horns. 8 The beast, which
you saw, once was, now is not, and yet
will come up out of the Abyss and go to
its destruction. The inhabitants of the
earth whose names have not been written in the book of life from the creation
of the world will be astonished when
they see the beast, because it once was,
now is not, and yet will come.

9 "This calls for a mind with wisdom.
The seven heads are seven hills on
which the woman sits. 10 They are also
seven kings. Five have fallen, one is,
the other has not yet come; but when he
does come, he must remain for only a
little while. 11 The beast who once was,
and now is not, is an eighth king. He
belongs to the seven and is going to his
destruction.

12 "The ten horns you saw are ten
kings who have not yet received a kingdom, but who for one hour will receive
authority as kings along with the beast.
13 They have one purpose and will give
their power and authority to the beast.
14 They will wage war against the Lamb,
but the Lamb will triumph over them
because he is Lord of lords and King of

[a] *21* Or about 45 kilograms

gs — and with him will be his called,
osen and faithful followers."
15 Then the angel said to me, "The
waters you saw, where the prostitute
sits, are peoples, multitudes, nations
and languages. 16 The beast and the ten
horns you saw will hate the prostitute.
They will bring her to ruin and leave her
naked; they will eat her flesh and burn
her with fire. 17 For God has put it into
their hearts to accomplish his purpose
by agreeing to hand over to the beast
their royal authority, until God's words
are fulfilled. 18 The woman you saw is
the great city that rules over the kings of
the earth."

18 After this I saw another angel coming down from heaven. He had great authority, and the earth was illuminated by his splendor. 2 With a mighty voice he shouted:

"'Fallen! Fallen is Babylon the
Great!'[a]
She has become a dwelling for
demons
and a haunt for every impure spirit,
a haunt for every unclean bird,
a haunt for every unclean and
detestable animal.
3 For all the nations have drunk
the maddening wine of her
adulteries.
The kings of the earth committed
adultery with her,
and the merchants of the earth
grew rich from her excessive
luxuries."

4 Then I heard another voice from heaven say:

"'Come out of her, my people,'[b]
so that you will not share in her
sins,
so that you will not receive any of
her plagues;
5 for her sins are piled up to heaven,
and God has remembered her
crimes.
6 Give back to her as she has given;
pay her back double for what she
has done.
Pour her a double portion from her
own cup.
7 Give her as much torment and grief
as the glory and luxury she gave
herself.
In her heart she boasts,
'I sit enthroned as queen.
I am not a widow;[c]
I will never mourn.'
8 Therefore in one day her plagues will
overtake her:
death, mourning and famine.
She will be consumed by fire,
for mighty is the Lord God who
judges her.

9 "When the kings of the earth who
committed adultery with her and
shared her luxury see the smoke of her
burning, they will weep and mourn over
her. 10 Terrified at her torment, they will
stand far off and cry:

"'Woe! Woe to you, great city,
you mighty city of Babylon!
In one hour your doom has come!'

11 "The merchants of the earth will
weep and mourn over her because no
one buys their cargoes anymore —
12 cargoes of gold, silver, precious stones
and pearls; fine linen, purple, silk and
scarlet cloth; every sort of citron wood,
and articles of every kind made of ivory,
costly wood, bronze, iron and marble;
13 cargoes of cinnamon and spice, of incense, myrrh and frankincense, of wine
and olive oil, of fine flour and wheat; cattle and sheep; horses and carriages; and
human beings sold as slaves.
14 "They will say, 'The fruit you longed
for is gone from you. All your luxury and
splendor have vanished, never to be recovered.' 15 The merchants who sold
these things and gained their wealth
from her will stand far off, terrified at
her torment. They will weep and mourn
16 and cry out:

"'Woe! Woe to you, great city,
dressed in fine linen, purple and
scarlet,
and glittering with gold, precious
stones and pearls!
17 In one hour such great wealth has
been brought to ruin!'

"Every sea captain, and all who travel by ship, the sailors, and all who earn
their living from the sea, will stand far
off. 18 When they see the smoke of her

[a] 2 Isaiah 21:9 [b] 4 Jer. 51:45 [c] 7 See Isaiah 47:7,8.

burning, they will exclaim, 'Was there ever a city like this great city?' [19]They will throw dust on their heads, and with weeping and mourning cry out:

"'Woe! Woe to you, great city,
where all who had ships on the sea
became rich through her wealth!
In one hour she has been brought to ruin!'

20 "Rejoice over her, you heavens!
Rejoice, you people of God!
Rejoice, apostles and prophets!
For God has judged her
with the judgment she imposed on you."

[21]Then a mighty angel picked up a boulder the size of a large millstone and threw it into the sea, and said:

"With such violence
the great city of Babylon will be thrown down,
never to be found again.
22 The music of harpists and musicians,
pipers and trumpeters,
will never be heard in you again.
No worker of any trade
will ever be found in you again.
The sound of a millstone
will never be heard in you again.
23 The light of a lamp
will never shine in you again.
The voice of bridegroom and bride
will never be heard in you again.
Your merchants were the world's important people.
By your magic spell all the nations were led astray.
24 In her was found the blood of prophets
and of God's holy people,
of all who have been slaughtered on the earth."

19 After this I heard what sounded like the roar of a great multitude in heaven shouting:

"Hallelujah!
Salvation and glory and power belong to our God,
2 for true and just are his judgments.
He has condemned the great prostitute
who corrupted the earth by her adulteries.
He has avenged on her the blood of his servants."

[3]And again they shouted:

"Hallelujah!
The smoke from her goes up for ever and ever."

[4]The twenty-four elders and the four living creatures fell down and worshiped God, who was seated on the throne. And they cried:

"Amen, Hallelujah!"

[5]Then a voice came from the throne, saying:

"Praise our God,
all you his servants,
you who fear him,
both great and small!"

[6]Then I heard what sounded like a great multitude, like the roar of rushing waters and like loud peals of thunder, shouting:

"Hallelujah!
For our Lord God Almighty reigns.
7 Let us rejoice and be glad
and give him glory!
For the wedding of the Lamb has come,
and his bride has made herself ready.
8 Fine linen, bright and clean,
was given her to wear."
(Fine linen stands for the righteous acts of God's holy people.)

[9]Then the angel said to me, "Write this: Blessed are those who are invited to the wedding supper of the Lamb!" And he added, "These are the true words of God."

[10]At this I fell at his feet to worship him. But he said to me, "Don't do that! I am a fellow servant with you and with your brothers and sisters who hold to the testimony of Jesus. Worship God! For it is the Spirit of prophecy who bears testimony to Jesus."

[11]I saw heaven standing open and there before me was a white horse, whose rider is called Faithful and True. With justice he judges and wages war. [12]His eyes are like blazing fire, and on his head are many crowns. He has a name written on him that no one knows but he himself. [13]He is dressed in a robe dipped in blood, and his name is the

Word of God. 14The armies of heaven
were following him, riding on white
horses and dressed in fine linen, white
and clean. 15Coming out of his mouth is
a sharp sword with which to strike down
the nations. "He will rule them with an
iron scepter."[a] He treads the winepress
of the fury of the wrath of God Almighty.
16On his robe and on his thigh he has
this name written:

KING OF KINGS AND LORD OF LORDS.

17And I saw an angel standing in the
sun, who cried in a loud voice to all the
birds flying in midair, "Come, gather together for the great supper of God, 18so
that you may eat the flesh of kings, generals, and the mighty, of horses and their
riders, and the flesh of all people, free
and slave, great and small."
19Then I saw the beast and the kings
of the earth and their armies gathered
together to wage war against the rider on the horse and his army. 20But the
beast was captured, and with it the false
prophet who had performed the signs on
its behalf. With these signs he had deluded those who had received the mark of
the beast and worshiped its image. The
two of them were thrown alive into the
fiery lake of burning sulfur. 21The rest
were killed with the sword coming out
of the mouth of the rider on the horse,
and all the birds gorged themselves on
their flesh.

20 And I saw an angel coming down
out of heaven, having the key to the
Abyss and holding in his hand a great
chain. 2He seized the dragon, that ancient serpent, who is the devil, or Satan,
and bound him for a thousand years. 3He
threw him into the Abyss, and locked
and sealed it over him, to keep him from
deceiving the nations anymore until the
thousand years were ended. After that,
he must be set free for a short time.

4I saw thrones on which were seated
those who had been given authority to
judge. And I saw the souls of those who
had been beheaded because of their
testimony about Jesus and because of
the word of God. They[b] had not worshiped the beast or its image and had
not received its mark on their foreheads
or their hands. They came to life and
reigned with Christ a thousand years.
5(The rest of the dead did not come to life
until the thousand years were ended.)
This is the first resurrection. 6Blessed
and holy are those who share in the first
resurrection. The second death has no
power over them, but they will be priests
of God and of Christ and will reign with
him for a thousand years.

7When the thousand years are over,
Satan will be released from his prison
8and will go out to deceive the nations
in the four corners of the earth—Gog
and Magog—and to gather them for
battle. In number they are like the sand
on the seashore. 9They marched across
the breadth of the earth and surrounded the camp of God's people, the city he
loves. But fire came down from heaven
and devoured them. 10And the devil,
who deceived them, was thrown into the
lake of burning sulfur, where the beast
and the false prophet had been thrown.
They will be tormented day and night for
ever and ever.

11Then I saw a great white throne and
him who was seated on it. The earth and
the heavens fled from his presence, and
there was no place for them. 12And I saw
the dead, great and small, standing before the throne, and books were opened.
Another book was opened, which is
the book of life. The dead were judged
according to what they had done as recorded in the books. 13The sea gave up
the dead that were in it, and death and
Hades gave up the dead that were in
them, and each person was judged according to what they had done. 14Then
death and Hades were thrown into the
lake of fire. The lake of fire is the second death. 15Anyone whose name was
not found written in the book of life was
thrown into the lake of fire.

21 Then I saw "a new heaven and a
new earth,"[c] for the first heaven
and the first earth had passed away, and
there was no longer any sea. 2I saw the
Holy City, the new Jerusalem, coming
down out of heaven from God, prepared
as a bride beautifully dressed for her
husband. 3And I heard a loud voice from
the throne saying, "Look! God's dwelling
place is now among the people, and he
will dwell with them. They will be his

[a] *15* Psalm 2:9 [b] *4* Or *God; I also saw those who* [c] *1* Isaiah 65:17

people, and God himself will be with
them and be their God. 4'He will wipe
every tear from their eyes. There will be
no more death'[a] or mourning or crying
or pain, for the old order of things has
passed away."

5He who was seated on the throne
said, "I am making everything new!"
Then he said, "Write this down, for these
words are trustworthy and true."

6He said to me: "It is done. I am the Alpha and the Omega, the Beginning and
the End. To the thirsty I will give water
without cost from the spring of the water of life. 7Those who are victorious will
inherit all this, and I will be their God
and they will be my children. 8But the
cowardly, the unbelieving, the vile, the
murderers, the sexually immoral, those
who practice magic arts, the idolaters
and all liars — they will be consigned to
the fiery lake of burning sulfur. This is
the second death."

9One of the seven angels who had
the seven bowls full of the seven last
plagues came and said to me, "Come, I
will show you the bride, the wife of the
Lamb." 10And he carried me away in the
Spirit to a mountain great and high, and
showed me the Holy City, Jerusalem,
coming down out of heaven from God.
11It shone with the glory of God, and its
brilliance was like that of a very precious
jewel, like a jasper, clear as crystal. 12It
had a great, high wall with twelve gates,
and with twelve angels at the gates.
On the gates were written the names
of the twelve tribes of Israel. 13There
were three gates on the east, three on
the north, three on the south and three
on the west. 14The wall of the city had
twelve foundations, and on them were
the names of the twelve apostles of the
Lamb.

15The angel who talked with me had
a measuring rod of gold to measure the
city, its gates and its walls. 16The city
was laid out like a square, as long as it
was wide. He measured the city with
the rod and found it to be 12,000 stadia[b]
in length, and as wide and high as it is
long. 17The angel measured the wall using human measurement, and it was 144
cubits[c] thick.[d] 18The wall was made of
jasper, and the city of pure gold, as pure
as glass. 19The foundations of the city
walls were decorated with every kind of
precious stone. The first foundation was
jasper, the second sapphire, the third agate, the fourth emerald, 20the fifth onyx,
the sixth ruby, the seventh chrysolite,
the eighth beryl, the ninth topaz, the
tenth turquoise, the eleventh jacinth,
and the twelfth amethyst.[e] 21The twelve
gates were twelve pearls, each gate made
of a single pearl. The great street of the
city was of gold, as pure as transparent
glass.

22I did not see a temple in the city, because the Lord God Almighty and the
Lamb are its temple. 23The city does
not need the sun or the moon to shine
on it, for the glory of God gives it light,
and the Lamb is its lamp. 24The nations
will walk by its light, and the kings of
the earth will bring their splendor into
it. 25On no day will its gates ever be shut,
for there will be no night there. 26The
glory and honor of the nations will be
brought into it. 27Nothing impure will
ever enter it, nor will anyone who does
what is shameful or deceitful, but only
those whose names are written in the
Lamb's book of life.

22 Then the angel showed me the river
of the water of life, as clear as crystal, flowing from the throne of God and
of the Lamb 2down the middle of the
great street of the city. On each side of
the river stood the tree of life, bearing
twelve crops of fruit, yielding its fruit every month. And the leaves of the tree are
for the healing of the nations. 3No longer will there be any curse. The throne of
God and of the Lamb will be in the city,
and his servants will serve him. 4They
will see his face, and his name will be on
their foreheads. 5There will be no more
night. They will not need the light of a
lamp or the light of the sun, for the Lord
God will give them light. And they will
reign for ever and ever.

6The angel said to me, "These words
are trustworthy and true. The Lord, the
God who inspires the prophets, sent his
angel to show his servants the things
that must soon take place."

[a] *4* Isaiah 25:8 [b] *16* That is, about 1,400 miles or about 2,200 kilometers [c] *17* That is, about 200 feet or about 65 meters [d] *17* Or *high* [e] *20* The precise identification of some of these precious stones is uncertain.

7"Look, I am coming soon! Blessed
is the one who keeps the words of the
prophecy written in this scroll."

8I, John, am the one who heard and
saw these things. And when I had heard
and seen them, I fell down to worship
at the feet of the angel who had been
showing them to me. 9But he said to
me, "Don't do that! I am a fellow servant
with you and with your fellow prophets
and with all who keep the words of this
scroll. Worship God!"
10Then he told me, "Do not seal up
the words of the prophecy of this scroll,
because the time is near. 11Let the one
who does wrong continue to do wrong;
let the vile person continue to be vile; let
the one who does right continue to do
right; and let the holy person continue
to be holy."
12"Look, I am coming soon! My reward
is with me, and I will give to each person
according to what they have done. 13I am
the Alpha and the Omega, the First and
the Last, the Beginning and the End.
14"Blessed are those who wash their
robes, that they may have the right to
the tree of life and may go through the
gates into the city. 15Outside are the
dogs, those who practice magic arts, the
sexually immoral, the murderers, the
idolaters and everyone who loves and
practices falsehood.
16"I, Jesus, have sent my angel to give
you[a] this testimony for the churches. I
am the Root and the Offspring of David,
and the bright Morning Star."

17The Spirit and the bride say, "Come!"
And let the one who hears say, "Come!"
Let the one who is thirsty come; and let
the one who wishes take the free gift of
the water of life.

18I warn everyone who hears the words
of the prophecy of this scroll: If anyone
adds anything to them, God will add to
that person the plagues described in this
scroll. 19And if anyone takes words away
from this scroll of prophecy, God will
take away from that person any share
in the tree of life and in the Holy City,
which are described in this scroll.
20He who testifies to these things says,
"Yes, I am coming soon."
Amen. Come, Lord Jesus.
21The grace of the Lord Jesus be with
God's people. Amen.

[a] *16* The Greek is plural.

Table of Weights and Measures

	Biblical Unit	Approximate American Equivalent	Approximate Metric Equivalent
Weights	talent (60 minas)	75 pounds	34 kilograms
	mina (50 shekels)	1 1/4 pounds	560 grams
	shekel (2 bekas)	2/5 ounce	11.5 grams
	pim (2/3 shekel)	1/4 ounce	7.8 grams
	beka (10 gerahs)	1/5 ounce	5.7 grams
	gerah	1/50 ounce	0.6 gram
	daric	1/3 ounce	8.4 grams
Length	cubit	18 inches	45 centimeters
	span	9 inches	23 centimeters
	handbreadth	3 inches	7.5 centimeters
	stadion (pl. stadia)	600 feet	183 meters
Capacity			
Dry Measure	cor [homer] (10 ephahs)	6 bushels	220 liters
	lethek (5 ephahs)	3 bushels	110 liters
	ephah (10 omers)	3/5 bushel	22 liters
	seah (1/3 ephah)	7 quarts	7.5 liters
	omer (1/10 ephah)	2 quarts	2 liters
	cab (1/18 ephah)	1 quart	1 liter
Liquid Measure	bath (1 ephah)	6 gallons	22 liters
	hin (1/6 bath)	1 gallon	3.8 liters
	log (1/72 bath)	1/3 quart	0.3 liter

The figures of the table are calculated on the basis of a shekel equaling 11.5 grams, a cubit equaling 18 inches and an ephah equaling 22 liters. The quart referred to is either a dry quart (slightly larger than a liter) or a liquid quart (slightly smaller than a liter), whichever is applicable. The ton referred to in the footnotes is the American ton of 2,000 pounds. These weights are calculated relative to the particular commodity involved. Accordingly, the same measure of capacity in the text may be converted into different weights in the footnotes.

This table is based upon the best available information, but it is not intended to be mathematically precise; like the measurement equivalents in the footnotes, it merely gives approximate amounts and distances. Weights and measures differed somewhat at various times and places in the ancient world. There is uncertainty particularly about the ephah and the bath; further discoveries may shed more light on these units of capacity.

A WORD ABOUT THE NIV

The goal of the New International Version (NIV) is to enable English-speaking people from around the world to read and hear God's eternal Word in their own language. Our work as translators is motivated by our conviction that the Bible is God's Word in written form. We believe that the Bible contains the divine answer to the deepest needs of humanity, sheds unique light on our path in a dark world and sets forth the way to our eternal well-being. Out of these deep convictions, we have sought to recreate as far as possible the experience of the original audience—blending transparency to the original text with accessibility for the millions of English speakers around the world. We have prioritized accuracy, clarity and literary quality with the goal of creating a translation suitable for public and private reading, evangelism, teaching, preaching, memorizing and liturgical use. We have also sought to preserve a measure of continuity with the long tradition of translating the Scriptures into English.

The complete NIV Bible was first published in 1978. It was a completely new translation made by over a hundred scholars working directly from the best available Hebrew, Aramaic and Greek texts. The translators came from the United States, Great Britain, Canada, Australia and New Zealand, giving the translation an international scope. They were from many denominations and churches—including Anglican, Assemblies of God, Baptist, Brethren, Christian Reformed, Church of Christ, Evangelical Covenant, Evangelical Free, Lutheran, Mennonite, Methodist, Nazarene, Presbyterian, Wesleyan and others. This breadth of denominational and theological perspective helped to safeguard the translation from sectarian bias. For these reasons, and by the grace of God, the NIV has gained a wide readership in all parts of the English-speaking world.

The work of translating the Bible is never finished. As good as they are, English translations must be regularly updated so that they will continue to communicate accurately the meaning of God's Word. Updates are needed in order to reflect the latest developments in our understanding of the biblical world and its languages and to keep pace with changes in English usage. Recognizing, then, that the NIV would retain its ability to communicate God's Word accurately only if it were regularly updated, the original translators established the Committee on Bible Translation (CBT). The Committee is a self-perpetuating group of biblical scholars charged with keeping abreast of advances in biblical scholarship and changes in English and issuing periodic updates to the NIV. The CBT is an independent, self-governing body and has sole responsibility for the NIV text. The Committee mirrors the original group of translators in its diverse international and denominational makeup and in its unifying commitment to the Bible as God's inspired Word.

In obedience to its mandate, the Committee has issued periodic updates to the NIV. An initial revision was released in 1984. A more thorough revision process was completed in 2005, resulting in the separately published TNIV. The updated NIV you now have in your hands builds on both the original NIV and the TNIV and represents the latest effort of the Committee to articulate God's unchanging Word in the way the original authors might have said it had they been speaking in English to the global English-speaking audience today.

Translation Philosophy

The Committee's translating work has been governed by three widely accepted principles about the way people use words and about the way we understand them.

First, the meaning of words is determined by the way that users of the language actually use them at any given time. For the biblical languages, therefore, the Committee utilizes the best and most recent scholarship on the way Hebrew, Aramaic and Greek words were being used in biblical times. At the same time, the Committee carefully studies the state of modern English. Good translation is like good communication: one must know the target audience so that the appropriate choices can be made about which English words to use to represent the original words of Scripture. From its inception, the NIV has had as its target the general English-speaking population all over the world, the "International" in its title reflecting this concern. The aim of the Committee is to put the Scriptures into natural English that will communicate effectively with the broadest possible audience of English speakers.

Modern technology has enhanced the Committee's ability to choose the right English words to convey the meaning of the original text. The field of computational linguistics harnesses the power of computers to provide broadly applicable and current data about the state of the language. Translators can now access huge databases of modern English to better understand the current meaning and usage of key words. The Committee utilized this resource in preparing the 2011 edition of the NIV. An area of especially rapid and significant change in English is the way certain nouns and pronouns are used to refer to human beings. The Committee therefore requested experts in computational linguistics at Collins Dictionaries to pose some key questions about this usage to its database of English—the largest in the world, with over 4.4 billion words, gathered from several English-speaking countries and including both spoken and written English. (The Collins Study, called "The Development and Use of Gender Language in Contemporary English," can be accessed at *http://www.thenivbible.com/about-the-niv/about-the-2011-edition/*.) The study revealed that the most popular words to describe the human race in modern U.S. English were "humanity," "man" and "mankind." The Committee then used this data in the updated NIV, choosing from among these three words (and occasionally others also) depending on the context.

A related issue creates a larger problem for modern translations: the move away from using the third-person masculine singular pronouns—"he/him/his"—to refer to men and women equally. This usage does persist in some forms of English, and this revision therefore occasionally uses these pronouns in a generic sense. But the tendency, recognized in day-to-day usage and confirmed by the Collins study, is away from the generic use of "he," "him" and "his." In recognition of this shift in language and in an effort to translate into the natural English that people are actually using, this revision of the NIV generally uses other constructions when the biblical text is plainly addressed to men and women equally. The reader will encounter especially frequently a "they," "their" or "them" to express a generic singular idea. Thus, for instance, Mark 8:36 reads: "What good is it for someone to gain the whole world, yet forfeit their soul?" This generic use of the "distributive" or "singular" "they/them/their" has been used for many centuries by respected writers of English and has now become established as standard English, spoken and written, all over the world.

A second linguistic principle that feeds into the Committee's translation work is that meaning is found not in individual words, as vital as they are, but in larger clusters: phrases, clauses, sentences, discourses. Translation is not, as many people think, a matter of word substitution: English word *x* in place of Hebrew word *y*. Translators must first determine the meaning of the words of the biblical languages in the context of the passage and then select English words that accurately communicate that meaning to modern listeners and readers. This means that accurate translation will not always reflect the exact structure of the original language. To be sure, there is debate over the degree to which translators should try to preserve the "form" of the original text in English. From the beginning, the NIV has taken a mediating position on this issue. The manual produced when the translation that became the NIV was first being planned states: "If the Greek or Hebrew syntax has a good parallel in modern English, it should be used. But if there is no good parallel, the English syntax appropriate to the meaning of the original is to be chosen." It is fine, in other words, to carry over the form of the biblical languages into English—but not at the expense of natural expression. The principle that meaning resides in larger clusters of words means that the Committee has not insisted on a "word-for-word" approach to translation. We certainly believe that every word of Scripture is inspired by God and therefore to be carefully studied to determine what God is saying to us. It is for this reason that the Committee labors over every single word of the original texts, working hard to determine how each of those words contributes to what the text is saying. Ultimately, however, it is how these individual words function in combination with other words that determines meaning.

A third linguistic principle guiding the Committee in its translation work is the recognition that words have a spectrum of meaning. It is popular to define a word by using another word, or "gloss," to substitute for it. This substitute word is then sometimes called the "literal" meaning of a word. In fact, however, words have a range of possible meanings. Those meanings will vary depending on the context, and words in one language will usually not occupy the same semantic range as words in another language. The Committee therefore studies each original word of Scripture in its context to identify its meaning in a particular verse and then chooses an appropriate English word (or phrase) to represent it. It is impossible, then, to translate any given Hebrew, Aramaic or Greek word with the same English word all the time. The Committee does try to translate related occurrences of a word in the original languages with the same English word in order to preserve the connection for the English reader. But the Committee generally privileges clear natural meaning over a concern with consistency in rendering particular words.

Textual Basis

For the Old Testament the standard Hebrew text, the Masoretic Text as published in the latest edition of *Biblia Hebraica*, has been used throughout. The Masoretic Text tradition contains marginal notations that offer variant readings. These have sometimes been followed instead of the text itself. Because such instances involve variants within the Masoretic tradition, they have not been indicated in the textual notes. In a few cases, words in the basic consonantal text have been divided differently than in the Masoretic Text. Such cases are usually indicated in the textual footnotes. The Dead Sea Scrolls contain biblical texts that represent an earlier stage of the transmission of the Hebrew text. They have been consulted, as have been the Samaritan Pentateuch and the ancient scribal traditions concerning deliberate textual changes. The translators also consulted the more important early versions. Readings from these versions, the Dead Sea Scrolls and the scribal traditions were occasionally followed where the Masoretic Text seemed doubtful and where accepted principles of textual criticism showed that one or more of these textual witnesses appeared to provide the correct reading. In rare cases, the translators have emended the Hebrew text where it appears to have become corrupted at an even earlier stage of its transmission. These departures from the Masoretic Text are also indicated in the textual footnotes. Sometimes the vowel indicators (which are later additions to the basic consonantal text) found in the Masoretic Text did not, in the judgment of the translators, represent the correct vowels for the original text. Accordingly, some words have been read with a different set of vowels. These instances are usually not indicated in the footnotes.

The Greek text used in translating the New Testament has been an eclectic one, based on the latest editions of the Nestle-Aland/United Bible Societies' Greek New Testament. The translators have made their choices among the variant readings in accordance with widely accepted principles of New Testament textual criticism. Footnotes call attention to places where uncertainty remains.

The New Testament authors, writing in Greek, often quote the Old Testament from its ancient Greek version, the Septuagint. This is one reason why some of the Old Testament quotations in the NIV New Testament are not identical to the corresponding passages in the NIV Old Testament. Such quotations in the New Testament are indicated with the footnote "(see Septuagint)."

Footnotes and Formatting

Footnotes in this version are of several kinds, most of which need no explanation. Those giving alternative translations begin with "Or" and generally introduce the alternative with the last word preceding it in the text, except when it is a single-word alternative. When poetry is quoted in a footnote a slash mark indicates a line division.

It should be noted that references to diseases, minerals, flora and fauna, architectural details, clothing, jewelry, musical instruments and other articles cannot always be identified with precision. Also, linear measurements and measures of capacity can only be approximated (see the Table of Weights and Measures). Although *Selah*, used mainly in the Psalms, is probably a musical term, its meaning is uncertain. Since it may interrupt reading and distract the reader, this word has not been kept in the English text, but every occurrence has been signaled by a footnote.

As an aid to the reader, sectional headings have been inserted. They are not to be regarded as part of the biblical text and are not intended for oral reading. It is the Committee's hope that these headings may prove more helpful to the reader than the traditional chapter divisions, which were introduced long after the Bible was written.

Sometimes the chapter and/or verse numbering in English translations of the Old Testament differs from that found in published Hebrew texts. This is particularly the case in the Psalms, where the traditional titles are included in the Hebrew verse numbering. Such differences are indicated in the footnotes at the bottom of the page. In the New Testament, verse numbers that marked off portions of the traditional English text not supported by the best Greek manuscripts now appear in brackets, with a footnote indicating the text that has been omitted (see, for example, Matthew 17:[21]).

Mark 16:9–20 and John 7:53—8:11, although long accorded virtually equal status with the rest of the Gospels in which they stand, have a questionable standing in the textual history of the New Testament, as noted in the bracketed annotations with which they are set off. A different typeface has been chosen for these passages to indicate their uncertain status.

Basic formatting of the text, such as lining the poetry, paragraphing (both prose and poetry), setting up of (administrative-like) lists, indenting letters and lengthy prayers within narratives and the insertion of sectional headings, has been the work of the Committee. However, the choice between single-column and double-column formats has been left to the publishers. Also the issuing of "red-letter" editions is a publisher's choice—one that the Committee does not endorse.

The Committee has again been reminded that every human effort is flawed—including this revision of the NIV. We trust, however, that many will find in it an improved representation of the Word of God, through which they hear his call to faith in our Lord Jesus Christ and to service in his kingdom. We offer this version of the Bible to him in whose name and for whose glory it has been made.

The Committee on Bible Translation